The Hebrew Bible
Volume 1B

Textual History of the Bible

Editor in Chief

Armin Lange

Volume Editors for Volume 1

Armin Lange and Emanuel Tov

For more information please visit the Brill website *brill.com/thb* or
for the online edition *brill.com/thbo*

The Hebrew Bible

Volume 1B
Pentateuch, Former and Latter Prophets

Edited by

Armin Lange
Emanuel Tov

Area Editors

Alessandro Maria Bruni (Georgian Translations, Old Church Slavonic Traditions)
Ignacio Carbajosa Pérez (Syriac Translations [Peshitta, Syro-Hexapla, Jacob of Edessa, Syro-Lucianic])
Claude Cox (Armenian Translations)
Sidnie White Crawford (Samaritan Pentateuch)
Steve Delamarter (Ethiopic Translations)
Beate Ego (Targumim)
Frank Feder (Coptic Translations)
Peter J. Gentry (Pre-Hexaplaric, Post-Hexaplaric Translations and the Hexapla)
Michael Graves (Vulgate)
Armin Lange (Ancient Hebrew/Aramaic Texts)
Meira Polliack (Arabic Translations)
Michael Segal (The Biblical Text as Attested in Ancient Literature)
Pablo Antonio Torijano Morales (Vetus Latina)
Emanuel Tov (Septuagint)
Julio Trebolle Barrera (Vetus Latina)

BRILL

LEIDEN | BOSTON

Originally published in hardback in 2016.

 THB logo design: Lika Tov, Jerusalem

Cover design: Celine van Hoek Leiden, the Netherlands.

The Library of Congress has cataloged the hardcover edition as follows:

Names: Lange, Armin, 1961- editor.
Title: The Hebrew Bible / edited by Armin Lange, Emanuel Tov.
Description: Leiden ; Boston : Brill, 2016- | Series: Textual history of the Bible,
   ISSN 2468-3027 | Includes bibliographical references and index.
Contents: Textual History of the Bible Vol. 1B.
Identifiers: LCCN 2016013903 | ISBN 9789004337107 (v. 1B : hardback : alk. paper)
Subjects: LCSH: Bible. Old Testament–Criticism, Textual.
Classification: LCC BS1136 .H43 2016 | DDC 221.6/7–DC23 LC record available at
   https://lccn.loc.gov/2016013903

Typeface for the Latin, Greek, and Cyrillic scripts: "Brill". See and download: brill.com/brill-typeface.

ISSN 2468-3027
ISBN 978-90-04-73611-5 (paperback, 2025)
e-ISSN 2452-4107 (THB online)
ISBN 978-90-04-33710-7 (hardback)

Copyright 2017 by Koninklijke Brill NV, Leiden, The Netherlands.
Koninklijke Brill NV incorporates the imprints Brill, Brill Hes & De Graaf, Brill Nijhoff, Brill Rodopi and Hotei Publishing.
All rights reserved. No part of this publication may be reproduced, translated, stored in a retrieval system, or transmitted in any form or by any means, electronic, mechanical, photocopying, recording or otherwise, without prior written permission from the publisher.
Authorization to photocopy items for internal or personal use is granted by Koninklijke Brill NV provided that the appropriate fees are paid directly to The Copyright Clearance Center, 222 Rosewood Drive, Suite 910, Danvers, MA 01923, USA. Fees are subject to change.

This book is printed on acid-free paper and produced in a sustainable manner.

Contents of THB Volume 1

VOLUME 1A

Preface
Introduction to the Textual History of the Bible
Introduction to Textual History of the Bible, Vol. 1: The Hebrew Bible
Area Editors
Authors
Notes to the Reader / Abbreviations
Collective Bibliography

1   Overview Articles

VOLUME 1B

2	Pentateuch
3–5	Former Prophets
3	Joshua
4	Judges
5	Samuel–Kings
6–9	Latter Prophets
6	Isaiah
7	Jeremiah
8	Ezekiel
9	Minor Prophets

VOLUME 1C

10–20	Ketuvim (Writings)
10	Psalms
11	Job
12	Proverbs
13–17	Five Scrolls
13	Ruth
14	Canticles
15	Qohelet
16	Lamentations
17	Esther
18	Daniel
19	Ezra–Nehemiah
20	1–2 Chronicles
21	The Biblical Text as Attested in Ancient Literature

Contents of THB Volume 1B

Area Editors		XII
Authors		XIII
Notes to the Reader / Abbreviations		XIV
Collective Bibliography		XIX

2 *Pentateuch*

2.1	Textual History of the Pentateuch (Emanuel Tov)		3
2.2	Ancient Hebrew Texts		22
	2.2.1	Ancient, Late Ancient, and Early Medieval Manuscript Evidence (Armin Lange)	22
	2.2.2	Masoretic Texts and Ancient Texts Close to MT (Ronald Hendel)	59
	2.2.3	Other Texts (Ronald Hendel)	72
	2.2.4	SP and Ancient Texts Close to SP	84
		2.2.4.1 Genesis (Ronald Hendel)	84
		2.2.4.2 Exodus (Magnar Kartveit)	86
		2.2.4.3 Leviticus (Sarianna Metso)	93
		2.2.4.4 Numbers (Nathan Jastram)	98
		2.2.4.5 Deuteronomy (Sidnie White Crawford)	101
	2.2.5	Other Sources (Nathan Jastram)	105
		2.2.5.1 Tefillin and Mezuzot	105
		2.2.5.2 Nash Papyrus	111
		2.2.5.3 Silver Scrolls from Ketef Hinnom	115
		2.2.5.4 Severus Scroll	119
2.3	Medieval Text of MT (Elvira Martín Contreras)		126
2.4	Primary Translations		131
	2.4.1	Septuagint	131
		2.4.1.1 Genesis (Martin Rösel)	131
		2.4.1.2 Exodus (Larry Perkins)	135
		2.4.1.3 Leviticus (Moshe A. Zipor)	142
		2.4.1.4 Numbers (Martin Rösel)	145
		2.4.1.5 Deuteronomy (Sidnie White Crawford)	148
	2.4.2	Pre-Hexaplaric Greek Translations (Andrew McClurg)	152
	2.4.3	Targumim (Avigdor Shinan)	152
		2.4.3.1 4QtgLev	152
		2.4.3.2 Targumim - General	153
		2.4.3.3 Targum Onqelos	158
		2.4.3.4 Palestinian Targumim	161
	2.4.4	Samaritan Targum (Abraham Tal)	167
	2.4.5	Peshitta (Jerome Lund)	173
	2.4.6	Hexaplaric Greek Translations and Hexapla of the Octateuch (Andrew McClurg)	180

	2.4.7	Post-Hexaplaric Greek Translations (Matthew M. Dickie)	188
	2.4.8	Vulgate (Matthew Kraus)	189
	2.4.9	Arabic Translations (Ronny Vollandt)	195
2.5	**Secondary Translations**	207
	2.5.1	Vetus Latina (Julio Trebolle Barrera)	207
	2.5.2	Coptic Translations (P. Nagel)	211
	2.5.3	Ethiopic Translation(s) of Octateuch (Steve Delamarter and Curt Niccum)	215
	2.5.4	Late Syriac Translations (Alison Salvesen)	219
	2.5.5	Armenian Translations (Claude Cox)	225
	2.5.6	Georgian Translations (Bernard Outtier)	227
	2.5.7	Old Church Slavonic Translations (Alessandro Maria Bruni)	230
	2.5.8	Arabic Translations (Ronny Vollandt)	239

3–5 *Former Prophets*

3 *Joshua*

3.1 **Textual History of Joshua (Michaël van der Meer)** 251

3.2 **Ancient Hebrew Texts** 257
    3.2.1 Ancient Manuscript Evidence (Armin Lange) 257
    3.2.2 Masoretic Text and Ancient Texts Close to MT (Karin Finsterbusch) 259
    3.2.3 Other Texts (Karin Finsterbusch) 265

3.3 **Septuagint (Michaël van der Meer)** 269

4 *Judges*

4.1 **Textual History of Judges (H. Ausloos)** 277

4.2 **Ancient Hebrew Texts** 281
    4.2.1 Ancient Manuscript Evidence (Armin Lange) 281
    4.2.2 Masoretic Texts and Ancient Texts Close to MT (Julio Trebolle Barrera) 284
    4.2.3 Other Texts (Julio Trebolle Barrera) 289

4.3 **Septuagint (Cécile Dogniez)** 294

5 *Samuel–Kings*

5.1 **Textual History of Samuel (Eugene Ulrich)** 301

5.2 **Textual History of Kings (Philippe Hugo and Adrian Schenker)** 310

5.3	**Ancient Hebrew Texts**		319
	5.3.1	Ancient and Late Ancient Manuscript Evidence (Armin Lange)	319
	5.3.2	Masoretic Texts and Ancient Texts Close to MT (Philippe Hugo & Adrian Schenker)	332
	5.3.3	Other Texts (Philippe Hugo & Adrian Schenker)	339
5.4	**Septuagint (Samuel) (Siegfried Kreuzer)**		349
5.5	**Septuagint (Kings) (Siegfried Kreuzer)**		362
3–5.1	**Primary Translations**		367
	3–5.1.1	Septuagint (Emanuel Tov)	367
	3–5.1.2	Pre-Hexaplaric Greek Translations (Andrew McClurg)	367
		3–5.1.2.1 Joshua-Judges	367
		3–5.1.2.2 Samuel-Kings	367
	3–5.1.3	Targum (Willem Smelik)	367
	3–5.1.4	Peshitta (Craig E. Morrison)	375
	3–5.1.5	Hexapla (Andrew McClurg)	383
		3–5.1.5.1 Joshua-Judges	383
		3–5.1.5.2 Hexaplaric Greek Translations and the Hexapla: Samuel-Kings	383
	3–5.1.6	Post-Hexaplaric Greek Translations (Matthew M. Dickie)	387
		3–5.1.6.1 Joshua-Judges	387
		3–5.1.6.2 Samuel-Kings	389
	3–5.1.7	Vulgate (David Everson)	391
	3–5.1.8	Arabic Translations (Meira Polliack & Meirav Nadler-Akirav)	396
3–5.2	**Secondary Translations**		397
	3–5.2.1	Vetus Latina	397
		3–5.2.1.1 Joshua-Judges (Andrés Piquer Otero)	397
		3–5.2.1.2 Samuel-Kings (Pablo Torijano Morales)	400
	3–5.2.2	Coptic Translations (Alin Suciu)	403
	3–5.2.3	Ethiopic Translations	409
		3–5.2.3.1 Joshua (Steve Delamarter)	409
		3–5.2.3.2 Judges (Michael G. Wechsler)	410
		3–5.2.3.3 1-4 Kingdoms (Curt Niccum & James Prather)	412
		3–5.2.3.4 1-2 Kings (Curt Niccum)	415
	3–5.2.4	Late Syriac Translations (Ignacio Carbajosa)	415
	3–5.2.5	Armenian Translations	420
		3–5.2.5.1 Joshua (Peter Cowe)	420
		3–5.2.5.2 Judges (Peter Cowe)	422
		3–5.2.5.3 1-2 Samuel (1-2 Reigns) (Peter Cowe)	424
		3–5.2.5.4 1-2 Kings (3-4 Kgdms) (Peter Cowe)	427
	3–5.2.6	Georgian Translations (Alessandro Maria Bruni)	429
	3–5.2.7	Old Church Slavonic Translations (Alessandro Maria Bruni)	436
	3–5.2.8	Arabic Translations (Ronny Vollandt)	445
3–5.3	**Medieval text of MT (Elvira Martín Contreras)**		447

6–9 Latter Prophets

6 Isaiah

6.1	Textual History of Isaiah (Arie van der Kooij)	459
6.2	Ancient Hebrew Texts	470
	6.2.1 Ancient Manuscript Evidence (Russell Fuller)	470
	6.2.2 Masoretic Texts and Ancient Texts Close to MT (Russell Fuller & Peter Flint)	476
	6.2.3 Other Texts (Russell Fuller & Peter Flint)	482
6.3	Septuagint (Arie van der Kooij)	489

7 Jeremiah

7.1	Textual History of Jeremiah (Richard D. Weis)	495
7.2	Ancient Hebrew-Aramaic Texts	514
	7.2.1 Ancient Manuscript Evidence (Armin Lange)	514
	7.2.2 Masoretic Texts and Ancient Texts Close to MT (Armin Lange)	518
	7.2.3 Other Texts (Armin Lange)	536
7.3	Septuagint (Georg Fischer)	543

8 Ezekiel

8.1	Textual History of Ezekiel (William A. Tooman)	559
8.2	Ancient Hebrew Texts	570
	8.2.1 Ancient Manuscript Evidence (Armin Lange)	570
	8.2.2 Masoretic Texts and Ancient Texts Close to MT (William A. Tooman)	572
	8.2.3 Other Texts (Armin Lange)	579
8.3	Septuagint (Johan Lust)	581

9 Minor Prophets

9.1	Textual History of the Minor Prophets (Christopher J. Fresch)	589
9.2	Ancient Hebrew Texts	601
	9.2.1 Ancient Manuscript Evidence (Russel Fuller)	601
	9.2.2 Masoretic Texts and Ancient Texts Close to MT (Russel Fuller)	606
	9.2.3 Other Texts (Russel Fuller)	611
9.3	Septuagint (W. Edward Glenny)	614

6–9.1	**Primary Translations**		623
	6–9.1.1	Septuagint (Emanuel Tov)	623
	6–9.1.2	Pre-Hexaplaric Greek Translations (John D. Meade)	623
	6–9.1.3	Targum (Gudrun Elisabeth Lier)	623
	6–9.1.4	Peshitta (Arie van der Kooij)	630
	6–9.1.5	Hexaplaric Greek Translations (John D. Meade)	637
	6–9.1.6	Post-Hexaplaric Greek Translations (Matthew M. Dickie)	643
	6–9.1.7	Vulgate (Michael Graves)	645
	6–9.1.8	Arabic Translations (Meira Polliack and Meirav Nadler-Akirav)	652
6–9.2	**Secondary Translations**		660
	6–9.2.1	Vetus Latina (Julio Trebolle Barrera)	660
	6–9.2.2	Coptic Translations	665
		6–9.2.2.1 Isaiah, Jeremiah, Ezekiel (Frank Feder)	665
		6–9.2.2.2 Minor Prophets (Nathalie Bosson)	671
	6–9.2.3	Ethiopic Translation(s)	677
		6–9.2.3.1 Isaiah (Curt Niccum)	677
		6–9.2.3.2 Jeremiah (Martin Heide)	679
		6–9.2.3.3 Ezekiel (Michael Knibb)	681
		6–9.2.3.4 Minor Prophets (Jeremy Brown, Steve Delamarter, Anke Dorman, Curt Niccum, and Kipp Swinney)	684
	6–9.2.4	Late Syriac Translations (Stephen Ryan)	689
	6–9.2.5	Armenian Translations (Alessandro M. Bruni)	695
		6–9.2.5.1 Isaiah	695
		6–9.2.5.2 Jeremiah	699
		6–9.2.5.3 Ezekiel	702
		6–9.2.5.4 Minor Prophets	703
	6–9.2.6	Georgian Translations (Alessandro Maria Bruni)	707
	6–9.2.7	Old Church Slavonic Translations (Alessandro Maria Bruni)	714
	6–9.2.8	Arabic Translations (Miriam Lindgren Hjälm)	723
6–9.3	**Medieval text of MT (Elvira Martín Contreras)**		731

Area Editors

Alessandro Maria Bruni (Ca' Foscari University of Venice): Georgian and Old Church Slavonic Translations

Ignacio Carbajosa Pérez (Universidad Eclesiástica San Dámaso): Syriac Translations (Peshitta, Syro-Lucianic Translation, Syro-Hexapla, Jacob of Edessa)

Claude Cox (McMaster Divinity College): Armenian Translations

Sidnie White Crawford (University of Nebraska-Lincoln): Samaritan Pentateuch

Steve Delamarter (George Fox Evangelical Seminary): Ethiopic Translations

Beate Ego (Ruhr-Universität Bochum): Targumim

Frank Feder (Akademie der Wissenschaften zu Göttingen): Coptic

Peter J. Gentry (Southern Baptist Theological Seminary): Pre-Hexaplaric Translations, Hexapla, Post-Hexaplaric Translations

Michael Graves (Wheaton College): Vulgate

Armin Lange (University of Vienna): Hebrew/Aramaic Texts

Meira Polliack (Tel Aviv University): Arabic Translations

Michael Segal (Hebrew University of Jerusalem): The Biblical Text as Attested in Ancient Literature

Emanuel Tov (Hebrew University of Jerusalem): Greek Texts

Julio Trebolle Barrerra and Pablo Antonio Torijano Morales (Universidad Complutense, Madrid): Vetus Latina

Authors

Althann, Robert
Amara, Dalia
Ausloos, Hans
Bachmann, Veronika
Balzaretti, Claudio
Bosson, Nathalie
Boud'hors, Anne
Brady, Christian
Brown, Jeremy
Bruni, Alessandro Maria
Cañas Reíllo, José Manuel
Carbajosa, Ignacio
Ceulemans, Reinhart
Cook, Johann
Cowe, Peter
Cox, Claude
Crawford, Sidnie White
De Troyer, Kristin
Delamarter, Steve
Dickie, Matthew M.
Díez Merino, Luis
Dogniez, Cécile
Dorman, Anke
Ego, Beate
Everson, David
Feder, Frank
Finsterbusch, Karin
Fischer, Georg
Flint, Peter
Forti, Tova
Fox, Michael V.
Fresch, Christopher J.
Fried, Lisbeth
Fuller, Russell T.
Gallagher, Edmon L.
Gentry, Peter J.
Gesche, Bonifatia
Glenny, W. Edward
Goldberg, Maya
Gottlieb, Leeor
Graves, Michael
Haelewyck, Jean-Claude
Heide, Martin
Hendel, Ronald
Hiebert, Robert
Hugo, Philippe
Jacobson, Howard
Jassen, Alex P.
Jastram, Nathan
Joosten, Jan
Kartveit, Magnar
Knibb, Michael A.
Knoppers, Gary N.
Köhlmoos, Melanie
Kooij, Arie van der
Kotzé, Gideon
Kraus, Matthew
Kreuzer, Siegfried
Lange, Armin
Lee, Ralph
Lemmelijn, Bénédicte
Lier, Gudrun Elisabeth
Lindgren Hjälm, Miriam
Lund, Jerome A.
Lust, Johan
Marcus, David A.
Martín Contreras, Elvira
McClurg, Andrew
Meade, John D.
Meer, Michaël van der
Meiser, Martin
Metso, Sarianna
Monferrer Sala, Juan Pedro
Monnickendam, Yifat
Morrison, Craig
Müller-Kessler, Christa
Mulugetta, Meley
Nadler-Akirav, Meirav
Nagel, Peter
Niccum, Curt
Olariu, Daniel
Outtier, Bernard
Pajunen, Mika
Parry, Jason T.
Perkins, Larry J.
Phillips, David
Piquer Otero, Andrés
Polliack, Meira
Prather, James
Rodgers, Peter R.
Rogers, Justin M.
Rösel, Martin
Rosen-Zvi, Assaf
Royse, James R.
Ryan, Stephen D.
Salvesen, Alison G.
Sasson, Ilana
Schäfer, Rolf
Schenker, Adrian
Segal, Michael
Shepherd, David
Shinan, Avigdor
Sigismund, Marcus
Skemp, Vincent T.M.
Smelik, Willem
Smith, Jannes
Soenksen, Jason
Spilsbury, Paul
Stec, David M.
Strawn, Brent A.
Suciu, Alin
Swinney, J. Kipp
Tal, Abraham
Talshir, Zipora
Taylor, Richard A.
Terefe, Melaku
Tooman, William A.
Torallas Tovar, Sofía
Torijano Morales, Pablo
Tov, Emanuel
Trebolle Barrera, Julio
Ulrich, Eugene C.
Vollandt, Ronny
Wechsler, Michael G.
Weis, Richard D.
Zahn, Molly
Zewi, Tamar
Zipor, Moshe A.
Zoran, Yair

Notes to the Reader / Abbreviations

In its stylesheet, *THB* follows the first edition of *The SBL Handbook of Style: For Ancient Near Eastern, Biblical, and Early Christian Studies* (eds. P.H. Alexander et al.; Peabody: Hendrickson Publishers, 1999). Publications that are quoted often in the articles of *THB* 1 are collected in a → Collective Bibliography. When quoted, they are indicated with an asterisk and a short title; thus, Lieberman, **Hellenism* refers to S. Lieberman, *Hellenism in Jewish Palestine: Studies in the Literary Transmission, Beliefs and Manners of Palestine in the I Century B.C.E.–IV Century C.E.* (2nd ed.; New York: Jewish Theological Seminary, 1962). Biblical books, deuterocanonical books, and textual witnesses are abbreviated and quoted as follows:

1 **Abbreviations**

Hebrew Bible

Gen	Genesis
Exod	Exodus
Lev	Leviticus
Num	Numbers
Deut	Deuteronomy
Josh	Joshua
Judg	Judges
Ruth	Ruth
1–2 Sam	1–2 Samuel
1–2 Kgdms	1–2 Kingdoms (LXX)
1–2 Kgs	1–2 Kings
3–4 Kgdms	3–4 Kingdoms (LXX)
Isa	Isaiah
Jer	Jeremiah
Ezek	Ezekiel
MinP	Minor Prophets/Dodekapropheton
Hos	Hosea
Joel	Joel
Amos	Amos
Obad	Obadiah
Jonah	Jonah
Mic	Micah
Nah	Nahum
Hab	Habakkuk
Zeph	Zephaniah
Hag	Haggai
Zech	Zechariah
Mal	Malachi
Ps/Pss	Psalm(s)

NOTES TO THE READER / ABBREVIATIONS

Job	Job
Prov	Proverbs
Ruth	Ruth
Cant	Canticles/Song of Songs
Qoh	Qohelet/Ecclesiastes
Lam	Lamentations
Esth	Esther
Dan	Daniel
Ezra	Ezra
Neh	Nehemiah
1–2 Chron	1–2 Chronicles

Deuterocanonical Scriptures

Add Dan	Additions to Daniel
Pr Azar	Prayer of Azariah
Bel	Bel and the Dragon
Sg Three	Song of the Three Young Men
Sus	Susanna
Add Esth	Additions to Esther
Bar	Baruch
2–4 Bar	2–4 Baruch
1–3 En	1–3 Enoch
Ep Jer	Epistle/Letter of Jeremiah
3 Ezra	3 Ezra (1 Esdras)
4–6 Ezra	4–6 Ezra
Jdt	Judith
Jub	Jubilees
1–4 Macc	1–4 Maccabees
Odes Sol	Odes of Solomon
Pss Sol	Psalms of Solomon
Pss 151–155	Psalms 151–155
Ps 151, etc.	Psalm 151, etc.
Sir	Sirach/Ben Sira/Ecclesiasticus
Tob	Tobit
Wis	Wisdom of Solomon

New Testament

Matt	Matthew
Mark	Mark
Luke	Luke
John	John
Acts	Acts
Rom	Romans
1–2 Cor	1–2 Corinthians

Gal	Galatians
Eph	Ephesians
Phil	Philippians
Col	Colossians
1–2 Thess	1–2 Thessalonians
1–2 Tim	1–2 Timothy
Titus	Titus
Phlm	Philemon
Heb	Hebrews
Jas	James
1–2 Pet	1–2 Peter
1–3 John	1–3 John
Jude	Jude
Rev	Revelation

Textual Witnesses

Manuscripts are indicated by numbers and characters in superscript. Versions of biblical books are identified as follows MT-Ezek, LXX-Ezek, VL-Ezek, V-Ezek, Arm-Ezek, LXX-MinP, etc. The Dead Sea Scrolls are abbreviated according to Tov, *Revised Lists*.

anon	anonymous
Aq	Aquila
Arab	Arabic Translation
Arm	Armenian
Arm 1	Armenian Translation 1
Arm 2	Revision of Armenian Translation 1
Cop	Coptic
Cop^{Akh}	Coptic: Akhmimic
Cop^{Boh}	Coptic: Bohairic
Cop^{Sa}	Coptic: Sahidic
Cop^{Fa}	Coptic: Fayyumic
Cop^{Mes}	Coptic: Mesokemic
Cop^{palBoh}	Coptic: paleo-Bohairic
	Manuscript numbers of Coptic manuscripts are given in superscript according to Schüssler, *Biblia Coptica*, e.g., Cop$^{Sa\ 10}$
CPA	Christian Palestinian Aramaic
Eth	Ethiopic
	Designations and numbers of Ethiopic manuscripts are given in superscript as detailed in →, e.g., Eth$^{Ber\ Or\ Fl\ 3067}$. The abbreviations EMIP and EMML refer to the Ethiopic Manuscript Imaging Project and to the *Catalogue of Ethiopian Manuscripts* respectively.
Georg	Georgian
	Designations and numbers of Georgian manuscripts are given in superscript as detailed in →, e.g., Georg^Y.
Hex	Hexapla
kaige-Th	*kaige*-Theodotion
LXX	Septuagint

NOTES TO THE READER / ABBREVIATIONS

	Designations of Greek manuscripts and recensions are quoted in superscript following the abbreviation LXX according to the system of the *Septuaginta Unternehmen*, in particular Rahlfs–Fraenkel, *Verzeichnis. E.g., LXX^A, LXX^{967}, LXX^O.
ms	manuscript
mss	manuscripts
MasF	Masorah Finalis
MasM	Masorah Magna
MasP	Masorah Parva
MT	Masoretic Text
MT+	MT group: MT together with T, (S), V, *kaige*-Th, Aq, Sym
MT^A	MT, Codex Aleppo
MT^B	British Library, Oriental Ms. 4445
MT^{Bl}	British Library Add. 15251
MT^C	Cairo Codex of the Prophets
MT^{C3}	Cairo Pentateuch Codex (Ms Gottheil 18).[1]
MT^{DeRossi}	Masoretic manuscript according to De Rossi, *1784–1788. Manuscript numbers are indicated in superscript, e.g., MT^{DeRossi12}
MT^{Kenn}	Masoretic manuscript according to Kennicott, *1776–1780. Manuscript numbers are indicated in superscript, e.g., MT^{Kenn12}
MT^L	Codex Leningradensis, Codex EBP. I B 19a of the National Library of Russia in St. Petersburg
MT^{L10}	Codex EBP. II B 10 of the National Library of Russia in St. Petersburg
MT^{L17}	Codex EBP. II B 17 of the National Library of Russia in St. Petersburg
MT^{L34}	Codex EBP. II B 34 of the National Library of Russia in St. Petersburg
MT^{L94}	Codex EBP. II B 94 of the National Library of Russia in St. Petersburg
MT^{M1}	Codex M1 in the Complutensian Library of Madrid
MT^{ms}	a single Masoretic manuscript
MT^{mss}	several Masoretic manuscripts
MT^N	Codex New York (E.N. Adler 246 = JTS 232)
MT^P	Codex Babylonicus Petropolitanus
MT^R	Codex Reuchlinianus 3; Badische Landesbibliothek. Karlsruhe
MT^{S1}	Manuscript Sassoon 1053
MT^{S5}	Codex ms Heb 5702 in the National Library of Israel, also named Damascus Pentateuch. Formerly part of the Sassoon Collection (ms 507)
MT^V	Manuscript Vatican ebr. 448
MT^Y	Codex Cambridge University Add. Ms. 1753
OG	Old Greek
OTPh	Philoxenian translation of the Old Testament
proto-MT	proto-Masoretic text
S	Peshitta
	Manuscript designations are given in superscript following the siglum S according to the *List of Old Testament Peshiṭta Manuscripts (Preliminary Issue)* (ed. Peshiṭta Institute, Leiden University; Leiden: Brill, 1961), e.g., S^{7a1}.

---

1 R. Gottheil, "Some Hebrew Manuscripts in Cairo," *JQR* 17 (1905): 608–55 (631–34); J.S. Penkower, "A Tenth-Century Pentateuchal MS from Jerusalem (MS C3), Corrected by Mishael Ben Uzziel," *Tarbiz* 58 (1988): 49–74 (Hebr. with Eng. summary).

semi-MT	semi-Masoretic text
SP	Samaritan Pentateuch
OSC	Old Church Slavonic
Syh	Syro-Hexapla
Syl	Syro-Lucianic
Sym	Symmachus
Th	Theodotion
T	Targum(im)
T^{Frag}	Fragment Targum
T$^{Frag(P)}$	Fragment Targum, Manuscript Paris
T$^{Frag(V)}$	Fragment Targum, Manuscript Venice
T^{Gen}	Targum Fragments from the Genizah
T^J	Targum Jonathan
T^N	Targum Neofiti
T^{Ps-J}	Targum Pseudo-Jonathan
T^O	Targum Onqelos
V	Vulgate
VL	Vetus Latina
	Designations and numbers of Old Latin manuscripts are given in superscript following the abbreviation VL according to Gryson, *Altlateinische Handschriften* 1–2; Gryson, *Répertoire general*, e.g., VL^{109}.
Vrs	Versions

Other Abbreviations

All other abbreviations of ancient literature as well as scholarly journals, book series, and reference works are according to the first edition of *The SBL Handbook of Style: For Ancient Near Eastern, Biblical, and Early Christian Studies* (eds. P.H. Alexander et al.; Peabody: Hendrickson Publishers, 1999). In addition, *THB* uses the following abbreviation:

TAD	B. Porten and A. Yardeni, *Textbook of Aramaic Documents from Ancient Egypt: Newly Copied, Edited and Translated into Hebrew and English* (4 vols. Winona Lake: Eisenbrauns, 1986–1999).

2   Further Information

In all articles, the Hebrew and Aramaic text is quoted with vocalization only when it is taken from MT or when required by the context. Accents are only indicated when necessary for the analysis.

The articles on the biblical Dead Sea Scrolls are updated summaries of Lange, *Handbuch*, except for → 6.2.1 (Isaiah) and → 9.2.1 (Minor Prophets).

Cross references to articles within the same *THB* volume are indicated with Arabic numerals. Thus, in *THB* 1, the cross reference → 6.3 refers the reader to the entry on the Septuagint of Isaiah. In *THB* 2, a cross-reference to the same article would appear as → 1.6.3.

Collective Bibliography

*Accordance
   Accordance computer program.
Aejmelaeus, *Trail
   A. Aejmelaeus, *On the Trail of the Septuagint Translators: Collected Essays* (rev. and expanded ed.; SBET 50; Leuven: Peeters, 2007).
Albrektson, *Text
   B. Albrektson, *Text, Translation, Theology: Selected Essays on the Hebrew Bible* (SOTSMS; Farnham: Ashgate, 2010).
Albright, *"New Light"
   W.F. Albright, "New Light on the Early Recensions of the Hebrew Bible," *BASOR* 140 (1955): 27–33.
Andersen–Forbes, *Spelling
   F.I. Andersen and A.D. Forbes, *Spelling in the Hebrew Bible* (BibOr 41; Rome: Biblical Institute Press, 1986).
Ap-Thomas, *Primer
   D.R. Ap-Thomas, *A Primer of Old Testament Text Criticism* (2nd ed.; FBBS 14; Philadelphia: Fortress Press, 1966).
Barr, *Literalism
   J. Barr, *The Typology of Literalism in Ancient Biblical Translations* (MSU 15; Göttingen: Vandenhoeck & Ruprecht, 1979).
Barr, *Variable Spellings
   J. Barr, *The Variable Spellings of the Hebrew Bible* (The Schweich Lectures of the British Academy; Oxford: Oxford University Press, 1989).
Barthélemy, *Devanciers
   D. Barthélemy, *Les devanciers d'Aquila* (VTSup 10; Leiden: Brill, 1963).
Barthélemy, *Études
   D. Barthélemy, *Études d'histoire du texte de l'Ancien Testament* (OBO 21; Fribourg: Éditions Universitaires, 1978).
Barthélemy, *Interim Report
   D. Barthélemy et al., *Preliminary and Interim Report on the Hebrew Old Testament Text Project* (5 vols.; New York: United Bible Societies, 1974; 2nd ed. 1979–1980).
Barthélemy, *Critique textuelle 1982
   D. Barthélemy, *Critique textuelle de l'Ancien Testament*, Vol. 1: *Josué–Esther* (OBO 50.1; Göttingen: Vandenhoeck & Ruprecht, 1982).
Barthélemy, *Critique textuelle 1986
   D. Barthélemy, *Critique textuelle de l'Ancien Testament*, Vol. 2: *Isaïe, Jérémie, Lamentations* (OBO 50.2; Göttingen: Vandenhoeck & Ruprecht, 1986).
Barthélemy, *Critique textuelle 1992
   D. Barthélemy, *Critique textuelle de l'Ancien Testament*, Vol. 3: *Ézéchiel, Daniel et les 12 Prophètes* (OBO 50.3; Göttingen: Vandenhoeck & Ruprecht, 1992).
Barthélemy, *Critique textuelle 2005
   D. Barthélemy, *Critique textuelle de l'Ancien Testament*, Vol. 4: *Psaumes* (OBO 50.4; Göttingen: Vandenhoeck & Ruprecht, 2005).
Barthélemy, *Studies
   D. Barthélemy, *Studies in the Text of the Old Testament: An Introduction to the Hebrew Old Testament Text Project* (Textual Criticism and the Translator 3; Winona Lake: Eisenbrauns, 2012).
Bassano, *Beluy Kidan
   F. da Bassano, *Beluy Kidan* (4 vols.; Asmarā: ba-Māḥtama Ferānčeskān, 1915–1918).
*BDSS
   J.H. Charlesworth (ed.), *The Bible and the Dead Sea Scrolls: The Second Princeton Symposium on Judaism and Christian Origins* (3 vols.; Waco: Baylor University Press, 2006).
Ben-Hayyim, *LOT
   Z. Ben-Hayyim, *The Literary and Oral Tradition of Hebrew and Aramaic amongst the Samaritans* (5 vols.; Jerusalem: Bialik Institute, 1957–1977) [Hebr.].
Ben-Hayyim, *Grammar of Samaritan Hebrew
   Z. Ben-Hayyim, *A Grammar of Samaritan Hebrew: Based on the Recitation of the Law in Comparison with the Tiberian and Other Jewish Traditions* (Jerusalem: Magnes Press, 2000).
Benoit et al., *"Editing"
   P. Benoit et al., "Editing the Manuscript Fragments from Qumran," *BA* 19 (1956): 75–96.
Benoit et al., *"Travail"
   P. Benoit et al., "Le travail d'edition des fragments manuscrits de Qumrân," *RB* 63 (1956): 49–67.
*BH
   Biblia Hebraica (ed. R. Kittel; Leipzig: Hinrichs, 1905–1906. 2nd ed. 1909–1913. 3rd ed.; eds. R. Kittel and P. Kahle; Stuttgart: Württembergische Bibelanstalt, 1929–1937).
*BHQ
   Biblia Hebraica Quinta (eds. A. Schenker et al.; Stuttgart: Deutsche Bibelgesellschaft, 2004–): Part 5: *Deuteronomium* (ed. C. McCarthy, 2007); Part 7: *Judges* (ed. N. Fernández Marcos, 2011); Part 13: The

Twelve Minor Prophets (ed. A. Gelston, 2010); Part 17: Proverbs (ed. J. de Waard, 2008); Part 18: *General Introduction and Megilloth* (ed. P.B. Dirksen et al., 2004); Part 20: *Ezra and Nehemiah* (ed. D. Marcus, 2006).

*BHS
Biblia Hebraica Stuttgartensia (eds. W. Rudolph and K. Elliger; Stuttgart: Deutsche Bibelgesellschaft, 1967–1977).

*Bible d'Alexandrie
La Bible d'Alexandrie (Paris: Cerf, 1986–).

*BibleWorks
BibleWorks computer program.

*Biblia Coptica
See Schüssler, *Biblia Coptica.

*Biblia Qumranica
Biblia Qumranica, Vol. 3B: *Minor Prophets* (eds. B. Ego et al.; Leiden: Brill, 2004).

*Biblia Sacra Arabica
Biblia Sacra Arabica: Sacrae Congregationis De Propaganda Fide Iussu Edita: Ad usum Ecclesiarum Orientalium: Additis e regione Bibliis Latinis Vulgatis: al-Kitāb al-muqaddas bi-'l-lisān al-'arabī (eds. S. Risius, F. Guadagnoli, and A. Ecchellenis; Rome: Sacrae Congregatio de Propaganda Fide, 1671–1673).

Bickerman, *"Septuagint"
E. Bickerman, "The Septuagint as a Translation," in *Studies in Jewish and Christian History* 1 (AGJU 9; Leiden: Brill, 1976), 167–200 (published first in *PAAJR* 28 [1959]: 1–39).

Bickerman, *"Notes"
E. Bickerman, "Notes on the Greek Book of Esther," *Studies in Jewish and Christian History: A New Edition in English including The God of the Maccabees*, Vol. 1 (AGJU 9; Leiden: Brill, 1976), 246–74.

Blau, *Studien
L. Blau, *Studien zum althebräischen Buchwesen und zur biblischen Literatur- und Textgeschichte* (Strasbourg i.E.: Adolf Alkalay, 1902).

Blau, *Grammar
J. Blau, *A Grammar of Christian Arabic: Based Mainly on South-Palestinian Texts from the First Millennium* (3 vols.; Louvain: Secrétariat Du Corpus SCO, 1966–1967).

Bogaert, *"Septante"
P.-M. Bogaert, "Septante et versions grecques," *DBSup* 12:536–692.

*Border Line
On the Border Line: Textual Meets Literary Criticism: Proceedings of a Conference in Honor of Alexander Rofé on the Occasion of his Seventieth Birthday (eds. Z. Talshir and D. Amara; Beer-Sheva Studies by the Department of Bible and Ancient Near East 18; Beer Sheva: Ben-Gurion University of the Negev Press, 2005) [Hebr.].

Brekelmans, *Questions
Questions disputées d'Ancien Testament: Méthode et théologie (ed. C. Brekelmans; rev. ed.; BETL 33; Leuven: Peeters, 1989).

*Brennpunkt, Vol. 1
Im Brennpunkt: Die Septuaginta, Vol. 1: *Studien zur Entstehung und Bedeutung der griechischen Bibel* (eds. H.-J. Fabry and U. Offerhaus; BWANT 153; Stuttgart: Kohlhammer, 2001).

*Brennpunkt, Vol. 2
Im Brennpunkt: Die Septuaginta, Vol. 2: *Studien zur Entstehung und Bedeutung der Griechischen Bibel* (eds. S. Kreuzer and J.P. Lesch; BWANT 161; Stuttgart: Kohlhammer, 2004).

*Brennpunkt, Vol. 3
Im Brennpunkt: Die Septuaginta, Vol. 3: *Studien zur Theologie, Anthropologie, Ekklesiologie, Eschatologie und Liturgie der Griechischen Bibel* (eds. H.-J. Fabry and D. Böhler; BWANT 174; Stuttgart: Kohlhammer, 2007).

Brock, *"Phenomenon"
S.P. Brock, "The Phenomenon of the Septuagint," *OTS* 17 (1972): 11–36.

Brock, *Bibliography
S.P. Brock et al., *A Classified Bibliography of the Septuagint* (Leiden: Brill, 1973).

Brock, *"Aspects"
S.P. Brock, "Aspects of Translation Technique in Antiquity," *GRBS* 20 (1979): 69–87.

Brooke–McLean, *The Old Testament in Greek
A.E. Brooke and N. McLean, *The Old Testament in Greek according to the Text of Codex Vaticanus: Supplemented from Other Uncial Manuscripts: With a Critical Apparatus Containing the Variants of the Chief Ancient Authorities of the Text of the Septuagint*, Vol. 1: *The Octateuch* (4 parts; Cambridge: Cambridge University Press, 1906–1917).

Brooke–McLean–Thackeray, *The Old Testament in Greek
A.E. Brooke, N. McLean, and H.St.J. Thackeray, *The Old Testament in Greek according to the Text of Codex Vaticanus: Supplemented from Other Uncial Manuscripts: With a Critical Apparatus Containing the Variants of the Chief Ancient Authorities of the Text of the Septuagint*, Vol. 2: *The Later Historical Books* (4 parts; Cambridge: Cambridge University Press, 1906–1935).

*CAL
The Comprehensive Aramaic Lexicon (Bar-Ilan Project, Miqra'ot Gedoloth). Online: http://cal1.cn.huc.edu.

Cappellus, *Critica Sacra
L. Cappellus, *Critica Sacra sive de variis quae in sacris Veteris Testamenti libris occurrunt lectionibus libri sex* (Paris: Cramoisy, 1650; repr. Halle: Hendel, 1775–[1786]).

Carr, *Formation
D.M. Carr, *The Formation of the Bible: A New Reconstruction* (New York: Oxford University Press, 2011).

*Catalogue of Ethiopian Manuscripts
A Catalogue of Ethiopian Manuscripts: Microfilmed for the Ethiopian Manuscript Microfilm Library, Addis Ababa, and for the Hill Monastic Manuscript Microfilm Library, Collegeville (eds. F.W. Macomber and G. Haile; 10 vols.; Collegeville: Monastic Microfilm Library St. John's Abbey, 1979–1993).

*CATSS
Computer-Assisted Tools for Septuagint Studies (directed by R.A. Kraft and E. Tov; Philadelphia and Jerusalem, 1999. http://ccat.sas.upenn.edu/rak/catss.html).

Ciasca, *Fragmenta Copto-Sahidica
A. Ciasca, *Sacrorum Bibliorum Fragmenta Copto-Sahidica Musei Borgiani* (2 vols.; Rome: Typis Eiusdem S. Congregationis, 1885–1889).

Ciasca, *Sacrorum Bibliorum fragmenta I
See Ciasca, *Fragmenta Copto-Sahidica.

Ciasca, *Sacrorum Bibliorum fragmenta II
See Ciasca, *Fragmenta Copto-Sahidica.

Clines, *Dictionary
D.J.A. Clines, *The Dictionary of Classical Hebrew* (9 vols.; Sheffield: Sheffield Academic Press and Sheffield Phoenix Press, 1993–2016).

Cohen, *"Masoretic Text"
M. Cohen, "The 'Masoretic Text' and the Extent of Its Influence on the Transmission of the Biblical Text in the Middle Ages," in *Studies in Bible and Exegesis 2: Presented to Yehuda Elitzur* (ed. U. Simon; Ramat Gan: Bar-Ilan University Press, 1986), 2.229–56 [Hebr.].

Cohen, *Miqra'ot Gedolot "Haketer"
M. Cohen (ed.), *Miqra'ot Gedolot "Haketer": A Revised and Augmented Scientific Edition of 'Miqra'ot Gedolot' Based on the Aleppo Codex and Early Medieval mss* (8 vols.; Ramat Gan: Bar-Ilan University Press, 1992–2007) [Hebr.].

Cohen, *"Introduction"
M. Cohen, *Miqra'ot Gedolot "Haketer": Joshua–Judges* (1992) 16*–99* (Introduction to the *Miqra'ot Gedolot "Haketer"* edition) [Hebr.].

*Complutensian Polyglot
Biblia Sacra Polyglotta, complectentia Vetus Testamentum ... (6 vols.; eds. A. de Lebrixa et al.; Madrid: Complutenti Universitate, 1514–1517).

Cowe, *"The Bible in Armenian"
S.P. Cowe, "The Bible in Armenian," in *The New Cambridge History of the Bible*, Vol. 2: *From 600–1450* (eds. R. Marsden and E.A. Matter; Cambridge: Cambridge University Press, 2012), 143–61.

Cowley, *Ethiopian Biblical Interpretation
R.W. Cowley, *Ethiopian Biblical Interpretation: A Study in Exegetical Tradition and Hermeneutics* (University of Cambridge Oriental Publications 38; Cambridge: Cambridge University Press, 1988).

Cross, *"Development"
F.M. Cross, "The Development of Jewish Scripts," in *The Bible and the Ancient Near East: Essays in Honor of William Foxwell Albright* (ed. G.E. Wright; Garden City: Doubleday, 1961), 133–202.

Cross, *"History"
F.M. Cross, "The History of the Biblical Text in Light of the Discoveries in the Judaean Desert," *HTR* 57 (1964): 281–99 (repr. in Cross–Talmon, *QHBT, 177–95).

Cross, *"Evolution"
F.M. Cross, "The Evolution of a Theory of Local Texts," in Cross–Talmon, *QHBT, 306–20.

Cross, *ALQ1,2,3
F.M. Cross, *The Ancient Library of Qumrân and Modern Biblical Studies* (1st ed.; London: Duckworth, 1958); *The Ancient Library of Qumran and Modern Biblical Studies* (2nd ed.; Grand Rapids: Baker, 1961); *The Ancient Library of Qumran* (3rd ed.; Sheffield: Sheffield Academic Press, 1995).

Cross, *"Fixation"
F.M. Cross, "The Fixation of the Text and Canon of the Hebrew Bible," in F.M. Cross, *From Epic to Canaan: History and Literature in Ancient Israel* (Baltimore: The Johns Hopkins University Press, 1998), 205–18.

Cross *"Paleography"
F.M. Cross, "Palaeography and the Dead Sea Scrolls," in Flint–VanderKam, *DSS, 1.379–402; pls. 8–14.

Cross–Talmon, *QHBT
Qumran and the History of the Biblical Text (eds. F.M. Cross and S. Talmon; Cambridge: Harvard University Press, 1975).

Crown, *The Samaritans
The Samaritans (ed. A.D. Crown; Tübingen: Mohr Siebeck, 1989).

Crown, *Samaritan Scribes
  A.D. Crown, *Samaritan Scribes and Manuscripts* (TSAJ 80; Tübingen: Mohr Siebeck, 2001).
Daniel, *Vocabulaire du Cult
  S. Daniel, *Recherches sur le vocabulaire du culte dans la Septante* (Paris: Libraire C. Klincksieck, 1966).
Debel, *"Variant Literary Editions"
  H. Debel, "Greek 'Variant Literary Editions' to the Hebrew Bible?" *JSJ* 41 (2010): 161–69.
Delitzsch, *Lese- und Schreibfehler
  F. Delitzsch, *Die Lese- und Schreibfehler im Alten Testament nebst den dem Schrifttexte einverleibten Randnoten klassifiziert* (Berlin: Vereinigung Wissenschaftlicher Verleger, 1920).
Díez Merino, *Biblia babilónica
  L. Díez Merino, *La Biblia babilónica* (Madrid: Consejo Superior de Investigaciones Cientificas, 1975).
Dillmann, *Biblia
  A. Dillmann, *Biblia Veteris Testamenti Aethiopica* (2 vols.; Leipzig: F.C.G. Vogel, 1853–1861).
*DJD
  Discoveries in the Judaean Desert (of Jordan) (40 vols.; Oxford: Clarendon Press, 1955–2010).
*DJD I
  D. Barthélemy and J.T. Milik, *Qumran Cave 1* (DJD I; Oxford: Clarendon Press, 1955).
*DJD II
  P. Benoit, J.T. Milik, and R. de Vaux, *Les grottes de Murabba'ât* (DJD II; Oxford: Clarendon Press, 1961).
*DJD III
  M. Baillet et al., *Les 'petites grottes' de Qumrân* (DJD III; Oxford: Clarendon Press, 1962).
*DJD IV
  J.A. Sanders, *The Psalms Scroll of Qumrân Cave 11 (11QPsª)* (DJD IV; Oxford: Clarendon Press, 1965).
*DJD V
  J.M. Allegro, *Qumran Cave 4.I* (with the collaboration of A.A. Anderson; DJD V; Oxford: Clarendon Press, 1968).
*DJD VI
  R. de Vaux and J.T. Milik, *Qumrân grotte 4.II: I. Archéologie, II. Tefillin, Mezuzot et Targums (4Q128–4Q157)* (DJD VI; Oxford: Clarendon Press, 1977).
*DJD VII
  M. Baillet, *Qumrân grotte 4.III (4Q482–4Q520)* (DJD VII; Oxford: Clarendon Press, 1982).
*DJD VIII
  E. Tov with the collaboration of R.A. Kraft, *The Greek Minor Prophets Scroll from Naḥal Ḥever (8ḤevXIIgr) (The Seiyal Collection I)* (DJD VIII; Oxford: Clarendon Press, 1990).
*DJD IX
  P.W. Skehan, E. Ulrich, and J.E. Sanderson, *Qumran Cave 4.IV: Palaeo-Hebrew and Greek Biblical Manuscripts* (DJD IX; Oxford: Clarendon Press, 1992).
*DJD XI
  E. Eshel et al., in consultation with J. VanderKam and M. Brady, *Qumran Cave 4.VI: Poetical and Liturgical Texts*, Part 1 (DJD XI; Oxford: Clarendon Press, 1998).
*DJD XII
  E. Ulrich et al., *Qumran Cave 4.VII: Genesis to Numbers* (DJD XII; Oxford: Clarendon Press, 1994).
*DJD XIII
  H. Attridge et al., *Qumran Cave 4.VIII: Parabiblical Texts*, Part 1 (DJD XIII; Oxford: Clarendon Press, 1994).
*DJD XIV
  E. Ulrich et al., *Qumran Cave 4.IX: Deuteronomy, Joshua, Judges, Kings* (DJD XIV; Oxford: Clarendon Press, 1995).
*DJD XV
  E. Ulrich et al., *Qumran Cave 4.X: The Prophets* (DJD XV; Oxford: Clarendon Press, 1997).
*DJD XVI
  E. Ulrich et al., *Qumran Cave 4.XI: Psalms to Chronicles* (DJD XVI; Oxford: Clarendon Press, 2000).
*DJD XVII
  F.M. Cross et al., *Qumran Cave 4.XII: 1–2 Samuel* (DJD XVII; Oxford: Clarendon Press, 2005).
*DJD XXIII
  F. García Martínez, E.J.C. Tigchelaar, and A.S. van der Woude, *Qumran Cave 11.II: 11Q2–18, 11Q20–30* (DJD XXIII; Oxford: Clarendon Press, 1998).
*DJD XXVIII
  M. Bernstein et al., *Qumran Cave 4.XXVIII: Miscellanea*, Part 2 (DJD XXVIII; Oxford: Clarendon Press, 2001).
*DJD XXX
  D. Dimant, *Qumran Cave 4.XXI: Parabiblical Texts*, Part 4: *Pseudo-Prophetic Texts* (DJD XXX; Oxford: Clarendon Press, 2001).
*DJD XXXII
  E. Ulrich and P.W. Flint, *Qumran Cave 1.II, Parts 1–2: The Isaiah Scrolls* (2 vols; DJD XXXII; Oxford: Clarendon Press, 2010).
*DJD XXXVI
  S. Pfann, P. Alexander, et al., *Qumran Cave 4.XXVI: Cryptic Texts and Miscellanea*, Part 1 (DJD XXXVI; Oxford: Clarendon Press, 2000).

*DJD XXXVIII
: J. Charlesworth et al., in consultation with J. VanderKam and M. Brady, *Miscellaneous Texts from the Judaean Desert* (DJD XXXVIII; Oxford: Clarendon Press, 2000).

*DJD XXXIX
: E. Tov et al., *The Texts from the Judaean Desert: Indices and an Introduction to the Discoveries in the Judaean Desert Series* (DJD XXXIX; Oxford: Clarendon Press, 2002).

Dogniez, *Bibliography
: C. Dogniez, *Bibliography of the Septuagint = Bibliographie de la Septante 1970–1993* (VTSup 60; Leiden: Brill, 1995).

Dorival–Harl–Munnich, *Septante
: G. Dorival, M. Harl, and O. Munnich, *La Bible grecque des Septante: Du judaïsme hellénistique au christianisme ancien* (Paris: Cerf, 1988).

Driver, *Introduction
: S.R. Driver, *An Introduction to the Literature of the Old Testament* (8th ed.; Edinburgh: T & T Clark, 1898; repr. New York: Meridian Books, 1956).

Driver, *Samuel
: S.R. Driver, *Notes on the Hebrew Text and the Topography of the Books of Samuel: With an Introduction on Hebrew Palaeography and the Ancient Versions* (2nd ed.; Oxford: Clarendon, 1913).

*DSI
: *De Septuaginta Investigationes*

*DSSB
: M. Abegg, P. Flint, and E. Ulrich, *The Dead Sea Scrolls Bible* (Edinburgh: T & T Clark, 1999).

*EAE
: *Encyclopaedia Aethiopica* (ed. S. Uhlig; Wiesbaden: Harrassowitz, 2003–).

*EBR
: *Encyclopedia of the Bible and its Reception* (eds. D.C. Allison et al.; Berlin: De Gruyter, 2009–).

Eichhorn, *Einleitung
: J.G. Eichhorn, *Einleitung in das Alte Testament* (3 vols.; Göttingen: Carl Eduard Rosenbusch, ⁴1823).

*EDSS 1–2
: *Encyclopedia of the Dead Sea Scrolls* (eds. L.H. Schiffman and J.C. VanderKam; New York: Oxford University Press, 2000).

Feder, *Biblia Sahidica
: F. Feder, *Biblia Sahidica: Ieremias, Lamentationes (Threni), epistula Ieremiae et Baruch: Die koptisch-sahidische Textgestalt der Bücher Jeremias, Lamentationes, Epistula Ieremiae und Baruch als Übersetzung der Septuaginta* (TUGAL 147; Berlin: De Gruyter, 2002).

Fernandez Marcos, *Introduction
: N. Fernandez Marcos, *The Septuagint in Context: Introduction to the Greek Version of the Bible* (Leiden: Brill, 2000).

Field, *Hexapla
: F. Field, *Origenis Hexaplorum quae supersunt sive veterum interpretum graecorum in totum Vetus Testamentum fragmenta* (Oxford: Clarendon Press, 1875).

Fischer, *Text
: A.A. Fischer, *Der Text des Alten Testaments: Neubearbeitung der Einführung in die Biblia Hebraica von Ernst Würthwein* (Stuttgart: Deutsche Bibelgesellschaft, 2009).

Fischer, *Vulgata
: *Biblia Sacra iuxta vulgatam versionem* (eds. B. Fischer et al.; 2nd ed.; Stuttgart: Deutsche Bibelgesellschaft, 1975).

Fishbane, *Biblical Interpretation
: M. Fishbane, *Biblical Interpretation in Ancient Israel* (Oxford: Clarendon Press, 1985).

Flesher–Chilton, *The Targums
: P.V.M. Flesher and B. Chilton, *The Targums: A Critical Introduction* (Waco: Baylor University Press, 2011).

Flint–VanderKam, *DSS
: *The Dead Sea Scrolls after Fifty Years: A Comprehensive Assessment* (2 vols.; eds. P.W. Flint and J.C. VanderKam; Leiden: Brill, 1998–1999).

Fraenkel, *Studien zur Septuaginta
: *Studien zur Septuaginta: Robert Hanhart zu Ehren* (eds. D. Fraenkel et al.; MSU 20; Göttingen: Vandenhoeck & Ruprecht, 1990).

Frankel, *Vorstudien
: Z. Frankel, *Vorstudien zu der Septuaginta* (Leipzig: Vogel, 1841; repr. Westmead: Gregg, 1972).

Frankel, *Einfluss
: Z. Frankel, *Über den Einfluss der palästinischen Exegese auf die alexandrinische Hermeneutik* (Leipzig: J.A. Barth, 1851).

Geiger, *Urschrift
: A. Geiger, *Urschrift und Übersetzungen der Bibel in ihrer Abhängigkeit von der innern Entwickelung des Judentums* (2nd ed.; Breslau: Heinauer, 1857; repr. Frankfurt a.M.: Madda, 1928).

Gentry, *"Text"
: P.J. Gentry, "The Text of the Old Testament," *JETS* 52 (2009): 19–45.

Gesenius, *Pent. Sam.
: F.H.W. Gesenius, *De Pentateuchi Samaritani origine*

indole et auctoritate commentatio philologico-critica (Halle: Bibliotheca Rengeriana, 1815).

Ginsburg, **Massorah*
C.D. Ginsburg, *The Massorah Compiled from Manuscripts: Alphabetically and Lexically Arranged* (4 vols.; London: Brög, 1880–1905; repr. Jerusalem: Makor, 1971).

Ginsburg, **Introduction*
C.D. Ginsburg, *Introduction to the Massoretico-Critical Edition of the Hebrew Bible* (London: Trinitarian Bible Society, 1897; repr. New York: Ktav, 1966).

Glassius, **Philologia*
Salomonis Glassii Philologia Sacra his temporibus accomodata post primum volume Dathii opera in lucem emissum sunc continuata et in novi plane operis formam redacta, Vol. 2.1: *Critica Sacra* (ed. G.L. Bauer; Leipzig: Sumptibus Weygandianis, 1795).

*Gleanings
Gleanings from the Caves: Dead Sea Scrolls and Artifacts from the Schøyen Collection (ed. T. Elgvin; Library of Second Temple Studies; London: T & T Clark, forthcoming).

Gordis, **Biblical Text*
R. Gordis, *The Biblical Text in the Making: A Study of the Kethib–Qere* (Philadelphia: Dropsie College for Hebrew and Cognate Learning, 1937; repr. New York: Ktav, 1971).

Goshen-Gottstein, **"History"*
M.H. Goshen-Gottstein, "The History of the Bible-Text and Comparative Semitics," *VT* 7 (1957): 195–201.

Goshen-Gottstein, **Sample Edition*
M.H. Goshen-Gottstein, *The Book of Isaiah: Sample Edition with Introduction* (Jerusalem: Magnes Press, 1965).

Goshen-Gottstein, **"Biblical Manuscripts"*
M.H. Goshen-Gottstein, "Hebrew Biblical Manuscripts: Their History and Their Place in the HUBP Edition," *Bib* 48 (1967): 243–90.

Goshen-Gottstein, **HUB, Isaiah*
M.H. Goshen-Gottstein, *The Hebrew University Bible: The Book of Isaiah* (Jerusalem: Magnes Press, 1995).

Goshen-Gottstein–Talmon, **HUB, Ezekiel*
M.H. Goshen-Gottstein and S. Talmon, *The Hebrew University Bible: The Book of Ezekiel* (Jerusalem: Magnes Press, 2004).

Graf, **GCAL 1*
G. Graf, *Geschichte der christlichen Arabischen Literatur*, Vol. 1: *Die Übersetzungen* (Studi e Testi 118; Vatican City: Bibliotheca Apostolica Vaticana, 1944).

Greenberg, **"Stabilization"*
M. Greenberg, "The Stabilization of the Text of the Hebrew Bible Reviewed in the Light of the Biblical Materials from the Judean Desert," *JAOS* 76 (1956): 157–67.

Griffith, **The Bible in Arabic*
S.H. Griffith, *The Bible in Arabic: The Scriptures of the "People of the Book" in the Language of Islam* (Princeton: Princeton University Press, 2013).

Gryson, **Altlateinische Handschriften 1*
R. Gryson, *Altlateinische Handschriften/Manuscrits vieux latins: Répertoire descriptif*, Part 1: *Mss 1–275 (d'après un manuscrit inachevé de Hermann Josef Frede †)* (VL 1.2a; Freiburg i.B.: Herder, 1999).

Gryson, **Altlateinische Handschriften 2*
R. Gryson, *Altlateinische Handschriften/Manuscrits vieux latins: Répertoire descriptif*, part 2: *Mss 300–485 (Manuscrits du psautier)* (VL 1.2b; Freiburg i.B.: Herder, 2004).

Gryson, **Répertoire général*
R. Gryson, *Répertoire général des auteurs ecclésiastiques latins de l'antiquité et du haut moyen-âge* (2 vols.; 5th ed.; VL 1.1–2; Freiburg i.B.: Herder, 2007).

Gryson (ed.), **Vetus Latina Database*
See **Vetus Latina Database*

Habermann, **Ketav*
A.M. Habermann, *Ketav, Lashon Wa-Sefer: Reflections on Books, Dead Sea Scrolls, Language and Folklore* (Jerusalem: R. Mas, 1973) [Hebr.].

Hall, **Companion*
F.W. Hall, *A Companion to Classical Texts* (Oxford: Clarendon Press, 1913; repr. Chicago: Argonaut, 1970).

*HALOT
L. Koehler and W. Baumgartner, *The Hebrew and Aramaic Lexicon of the Old Testament* (trans. M.E.J. Richardson et al.; Leiden: Brill, 1994–2000; based on earlier German editions: 1953; 2nd ed. 1958; 3rd ed. 1967–1996).

Harl–Dorival–Munnich, **Bible grecque*
M. Harl, G. Dorival, and O. Munnich, *La Bible grecque des Septante: Du judaïsme hellénistique au christianisme ancien* (Paris: Cerf, 1988).

Hatch–Redpath, **Concordance*
E. Hatch and H.A. Redpath, *A Concordance to the Septuagint and the Other Greek Versions of the Old Testament* (Oxford: Clarendon Press, 1897–1906; repr. Graz: Akademische Druck- u. Verlagsanstalt, 1954; repr. eds. R.A. Kraft and E. Tov; 2nd ed.; Grand Rapids: Baker, 1998).

Haupt, *Critical Edition*
A Critical Edition of the Hebrew Text, Printed in Colors, Exhibiting the Composite Structure of the Book (ed. P. Haupt; Leipzig: Hinrichs et al., 1893–1904, incomplete).

Haupt, *Polychrome Bible*
The Polychrome Bible: The Sacred Books of the Old and New Testaments: A New English Translation, Printed in Colors, Exhibiting the Composite Structure of the Book (ed. P. Haupt; London: Clark et al., 1897–1899, incomplete).

HBCE
The Hebrew Bible: A Critical Edition (ed. R.S. Hendel; Atlanta: SBL, 2015–).

Hendel, *Genesis 1–11*
R.S. Hendel, The Text of Genesis 1–11: Textual Studies and Critical Edition (New York: Oxford University Press, 1998).

Hendel, *"Prologue"*
R.S. Hendel, "The Oxford Hebrew Bible; Prologue to a New Critical Edition," VT 58 (2008): 324–51.

HOTTP
Hebrew Old Testament Text Project. See Barthélemy, *Interim Report*

Houbigant, *Notae criticae*
A.F. Houbigant, Notae criticae in universos Veteris Testamenti libros: cum Hebraice, tum Graece scriptos (2 vols.; Frankfurt: Varrentrapp Filium & Wenner, 1777).

HUB
The Hebrew University Bible (Jerusalem: Magnes Press, 1995–); The Book of Isaiah (ed. M. Goshen-Gottstein, 1995); The Book of Jeremiah (eds. C. Rabin, S. Talmon, and E. Tov, 1997); The Book of Ezekiel (eds. M.H. Goshen-Gottstein and S. Talmon, 2004).

Jastrow, *Dictionary*
M. Jastrow, A Dictionary of the Targumim, the Talmud Babli and Yerushalmi, and the Midrashic Literature (2nd ed.; New York: Pardes, 1903).

JB
The Jerusalem Bible (Garden City: Doubleday, 1970).

Jellicoe, *SMS*
S. Jellicoe, The Septuagint and Modern Study (Oxford: Clarendon Press, 1968).

Jepsen, *"Aufgaben"*
A. Jepsen, "Von den Aufgaben der alttestamentlichen Textkritik," in Congress Volume: Bonn 1962 (eds. G.W. Anderson et al.; VTSup 9; Leiden: Brill, 1962), 332–41.

Kahle, *"Untersuchungen"*
P. Kahle, "Untersuchungen zur Geschichte des Pentateuchtextes," TSK 88 (1915): 399–439 (repr. in P. Kahle, *Opera Minora* [Leiden: Brill, 1956], 3–37).

Kahle, *Cairo Geniza*
P. Kahle, The Cairo Geniza (2nd ed.; Oxford: Blackwell, 1959).

Karrer–Kraus, *Septuaginta 2008*
Die Septuaginta: Texte, Kontexte, Lebenswelten: Internationale Fachtagung veranstaltet von Septuaginta Deutsch (LXX.D), Wuppertal 20.–23. Juli 2006 (eds. M. Karrer and W. Kraus; WUNT 219; Tübingen: Mohr Siebeck, 2008).

Karrer–Kraus, *Septuaginta 2010*
Die Septuaginta: Texte, Theologien, Einflüsse: 2. Internationale Fachtagung veranstaltet von Septuaginta Deutsch (LXX.D), Wuppertal 23.–27.7.2008 (eds. W. Kraus and M. Karrer; WUNT 252; Tübingen: Mohr Siebeck, 2010).

Kennicott, *Dissertation*
B. Kennicott, The State of the Printed Text of the Old Testament Considered: A Dissertation in Two Parts (Oxford: The Theatre, 1753–1759; = idem, Dissertatio secunda super ratione textus hebraici Veteris Testamenti [trans. G.A. Teller; Leipzig: Dyck, 1765]).

Kennicott, *1776–1780*
B. Kennicott, Vetus Testamentum hebraicum, cum variis lectionibus (2 vols.; Oxford: Clarendon Press, 1776–1780).

Kennicott, *Dissertatio generalis*
B. Kennicott, Appendix to Vol. 2 of Kennicott, *1776–1780: Dissertatio generalis in Vetus Testamentum Hebraicum, cum variis lectionibus ex codicibus manuscriptis et impressis*. Also published separately (Brunovici: Orphanotrophei, 1783).

KJV
King James Version (London: Robert Barker, 1611).

Klein, *Textual Criticism*
R.W. Klein, Textual Criticism of the Old Testament: The Septuagint after Qumran (GBS Old Testament Series 4; Philadelphia: Fortress Press, 1974).

Knibb, *Translating the Bible*
M. Knibb, Translating the Bible: The Ethiopic Version of the Old Testament (Oxford: Oxford University Press, 1999).

Koenig, *"L'activité herméneutique"*
J. Koenig, "L'activité herméneutique des scribes dans la transmission du texte de l'Ancien Testament," RHR 161 (1962): 141–74; 162 (1962): 1–43.

Koenig, *L'herméneutique analogique*
J. Koenig, L'herméneutique analogique du judaïsme

antique d' après les témoins textuels d' Isaïe (VTSup 33; Leiden: Brill, 1982).

Kraft, *Septuagintal Lexicography
Septuagintal Lexicography (ed. R.A. Kraft; SBLSCS 1; Missoula: SBL, 1972).

Kraus–Kreuzer, *Septuaginta 2014
Die Septuaginta: Text, Wirkung, Rezeption: 4. Internationale Fachtagung veranstaltet von Septuaginta Deutsch (LXX.D), Wuppertal 19.–22. Juli 2012 (eds. W. Kraus and S. Kreuzer; WUNT 325; Tübingen: Mohr Siebeck, 2014).

Kreuzer–Meiser–Sigismund, *Septuaginta 2012
Die Septuaginta: Entstehung, Sprache, Geschichte: 3. Internationale Fachtagung veranstaltet von Septuaginta Deutsch (LXX.D), Wuppertal 22.–25. Juli 2010 (eds. S. Kreuzer, M. Meiser, and M. Sigismund; WUNT 286; Tübingen: Mohr Siebeck 2012).

Kutscher, *Language
E.Y. Kutscher, *The Language and Linguistic Background of the Isaiah Scroll (1 Q Isa)* (STDJ 6; Leiden: Brill, 1974).

de Lagarde, *Anmerkungen
P. de Lagarde, *Anmerkungen zur griechischen Übersetzung der Proverbien* (Leipzig: Brockhaus, 1863).

Lamsa, *Holy Bible
G.M. Lamsa, *The Holy Bible from Ancient Eastern Manuscripts Containing the Old and New Testaments: Translated from the Peshitta: The Authorized Bible of the Church of the East* (Nashville: Holman Bible Publishers, 1957).

Lange, *Handbuch
A. Lange, *Handbuch der Textfunde vom Toten Meer*, Vol. 1: *Die Handschriften biblischer Bücher von Qumran und den anderen Fundorten* (Tübingen: Mohr Siebeck, 2009).

Lange et al., *From Qumran to Aleppo
From Qumran to Aleppo: A Discussion with Emanuel Tov about the Textual History of Jewish Scriptures in Honor of his 65th Birthday (eds. A. Lange et al.; FRLANT 230; Göttingen: Vandenhoeck & Ruprecht, 2009).

Leaney, *"Greek Manuscripts"
R.C. Leaney, "Greek Manuscripts from the Judaean Desert," in *Studies in New Testament Language and Text: Essays in Honour of George D. Kilpatrick on the Occasion of His Sixty-Fifth Birthday* (ed. J.K. Elliott; NTSup 44; Leiden: Brill, 1976), 283–300.

Le Jay, *Biblia
G.M. Le Jay, *Biblia: 1. Hebraica, 2. Samaritana, 3. Chaldaica, 4. Græca, 5. Syriaca, 6. Latina, 7. Arabica: quibus textus originales totius scripturae, quorum pars in editione Complutensi, deinde in Antverpiensi regiis sumptibus extat, nunc integri, ex mauscripti toto fere orbe quaesitis exemplaribus, exhibentur* (Paris: Vitré, 1645).

Levita, *Massoreth Ha-Massoreth
E. Levita, *Massoreth Ha-Massoreth* (Venice: D. Bomberg, 1538; repr. ed. C.D. Ginsburg; London: Longmans, Green, Reader & Dyer, 1867; repr. New York: Ktav, 1968).

Lieberman, *Hellenism
S. Lieberman, *Hellenism in Jewish Palestine: Studies in the Literary Transmission, Beliefs and Manners of Palestine in the I Century B.C.E.–IV Century C.E.* (2nd ed.; New York: Jewish Theological Seminary, 1962).

*Logos
Logos computer program

Loveless and Loveless, *Dead Sea Scrolls and the Bible
G. Loveless and S. Loveless, *Dead Sea Scrolls and the Bible: Ancient Artifacts, Timeless Treasures* (Fort Worth: Seminary Hill Press, 2012).

Lust, *Lexicon of the Septuagint
Greek-English Lexicon of the Septuagint (eds. J. Lust et al.; rev. ed.; Stuttgart: Deutsche Bibelgesellschaft, 2003).

Maas, *Textual Criticism
P. Maas, *Textual Criticism* (trans. B. Flower; Oxford: Clarendon Press, 1958 = "Textkritik," in A. Gercke and E. Norden, *Einleitung in die Altertumswissenschaft*, Vol. 1.2 [3rd ed.; Leipzig: Teubner, 1957]).

*Madrid Qumran Congress
The Madrid Qumran Congress: Proceedings of the International Congress on the Dead Sea Scrolls: Madrid, 18–21 March, 1991 (eds. J. Trebolle Barrera and L. Vegas Montaner; 2 vols.; STDJ 11.1–2; Leiden: Brill, 1992).

*Manchester Symposium
Septuagint, Scrolls and Cognate Writings: Papers Presented to the International Symposium on the Septuagint and Its Relations to the Dead Sea Scrolls and Other Writings, Manchester, 1990 (eds. G.J. Brooke and B. Lindars; SBLSCS 33; Atlanta: Scholars Press, 1992).

Margolis, *"Scope"
M.L. Margolis, "The Scope and Methodology of Biblical Philology," *JQR* 1 (1910–1911): 5–41.

Martin, *Scribal Character
M. Martin, *The Scribal Character of the Dead Sea Scrolls* (2 vols.; Bibliothèque du Muséon 44–45; Louvain: Publications Universitaires, 1958).

*Masada I–VIII
*Masada: The Yigael Yadin Excavations 1963–1965: Final

Reports (8 vols.; Jerusalem: Israel Exploration Society, 1989–2007).

Maspero, *"Fragments de la version thébaine de l' Ancien Testament"
G. Maspero, "Fragments de la version thébaine de l' Ancien Testament," *Mémoires publiés par les membres de la Mission archéologique française au Caire* 6.1 (1892): 1–150; 6.3 (1892): 161–296.

McCarter, *Textual Criticism*
P.K. McCarter, *Textual Criticism: Recovering the Text of the Hebrew Bible* (GBS Old Testament Series 11; Philadelphia: Fortress Press, 1986).

McCarthy, *Tiqqune Sopherim*
C. McCarthy, *The Tiqqune Sopherim and Other Theological Corrections in the Masoretic Text of the Old Testament* (OBO 36; Göttingen: Vandenhoeck & Ruprecht, 1981).

Mélanges Barthélemy
Mélanges Dominique Barthélemy: Études bibliques offertes à l'occasion de son 60e anniversaire (eds. P. Casetti et al.; OBO 38; Göttingen: Vandenhoeck & Ruprecht, 1981).

Mikra
Mikra computer program, Bar-Ilan University.

Milik, *Ten Years*
J.T. Milik, *Ten Years of Discovery in the Wilderness of Judaea* (SBT 26; London: SCM Press, 1959).

Morinus, *Exerc.*
J. Morinus, *Exercitationum biblicarum de hebraei graecique textus sinceritate libri duo* (2nd ed.; Paris: G. Meturas, 1660).

Mulder, *Mikra*
Mikra: Text, Translation, Reading and Interpretation of the Hebrew Bible in Ancient Judaism and Early Christianity (ed. M.J. Mulder; CRINT 2.1; Assen: Van Gorcum, 1988).

NEB
The New English Bible with the Apocrypha (Oxford: Oxford University Press, 1970).

NETS
A New English Translation of the Septuagint and the Other Greek Translations Traditionally Included Under That Title (eds. A. Pietersma and B.G. Wright; Oxford: Clarendon Press, 2007).

NIV
Holy Bible: New International Version (Grand Rapids: Zondervan, 1984).

NJPS
Tanakh—The Holy Scriptures: The New JPS Translation According to the Traditional Hebrew Text (Philadelphia: Jewish Publication Society, 1988; 2nd ed. 1999).

NRSV
The Holy Bible Containing the Old and New Testaments with the Apocryphal/Deuterocanonical Books: New Revised Standard Version (Glasgow: Collins, 1989).

Nyberg, *"Problem"*
H.S. Nyberg, "Das textkritische Problem des Alten Testaments am Hoseabuche demonstriert," *ZAW* 52 (1934): 241–54.

Oesch, *Petucha*
J.M. Oesch, *Petucha und Setuma: Untersuchungen zu einer überlieferten Gliederung im hebräischen Text des Alten Testaments* (OBO 27; Göttingen: Vandenhoeck & Ruprecht, 1979).

Okhlah we-Okhlah
Sefer Oklah we-Oklah (ed. F. Díaz Esteban; Madrid: Consejo Superior de Investigaciones Cientificas, 1975).

Olofsson, *Essays*
S. Olofsson, *Translation Technique and Theological Exegesis: Collected Essays on the Septuagint Version* (ConBOT 57; Winona Lake: Eisenbrauns, 2009).

OTP
J.H. Charlesworth, *The Old Testament Pseudepigrapha* (2 vols.; NewYork: Doubleday, 1983–1985).

Pérez Castro, *Profetas de el Cairo*
F. Pérez Castro, *El codice de profetas de el Cairo* (9 vols.; Madrid: Consejo Superior de Investigaciones Cientificas, 1979–1992).

Perles, *Analekten*
F. Perles, *Analekten zur Textkritik des Alten Testaments*, Vol. 1 (Munich: Ackermann, 1895); Vol. 2 (Leipzig: Engel, 1922).

PEUDSS
B.Z. Wacholder and M. Abegg, *A Preliminary Edition of the Unpublished Dead Sea Scrolls: The Hebrew and Aramaic Texts from Cave Four* (4 vols.; Washington: Biblical Archaeology Society, 1991–1996).

Prijs, *Jüdische Tradition*
L. Prijs, *Jüdische Tradition in der Septuaginta* (Leiden: Brill, 1948; repr. Hildesheim: Olms, 1987).

PTSDSSP
The Princeton Theological Seminary Dead Sea Scrolls Project (ed. J.H. Charlesworth; Tübingen: Mohr Siebeck, 1991–).

Qimron, *DSS*
E. Qimron, *The Hebrew of the Dead Sea Scrolls* (HSS 29; Atlanta: Scholars Press, 1986).

Rabin–Talmov–Tov, *HUB, Jeremiah*
C. Rabin, S. Talmon, and E. Tov, *The Hebrew University Bible: The Book of Jeremiah* (Jerusalem: Magnes Press, 1997).

Rahlfs, *Septuaginta*
A. Rahlfs (ed.), *Septuaginta: Id est Vetus Testamentum graece iuxta LXX interpretes* (Stuttgart: Württemberger Bibelanstalt, 1935).

Rahlfs–Fraenkel, *Verzeichnis*
A. Rahlfs and D. Fraenkel, *Verzeichnis der griechischen Handschriften des Alten Testaments: Die Überlieferung bis zum VIII. Jahrhundert* (Septuaginta Vetus Testamentum Graecum Supplement I.1; Göttingen: Vandenhoeck & Ruprecht, 2004).

Rahlfs–Hanhart, *Septuaginta*
A. Rahlfs and R. Hanhart (eds.), *Septuaginta: Id est Vetus Testamentum graece iuxta LXX interpretes* (2nd ed.; Stuttgart: Deutsche Bibelgesellschaft, 2006).

*RB1
F. Pratensis (ed.), *Biblia Rabbinica Miqra'ot Gedolot* (Venice: Daniel Bomberg, 1516–1517).

*RB2
J. ben Hayyim ben Isaac ibn Adonija et al., *Biblia Rabbinica Miqra'ot Gedolot* (4 vols.; 2nd ed.; Venice: Daniel Bomberg, 1524–1525).

*REB
The Revised English Bible with the Apocrypha (Oxford: Oxford University Press, 1989).

Reynolds–Wilson, *Scribes and Scholars*
L.D. Reynolds and N.G. Wilson, *Scribes and Scholars: A Guide to the Transmission of Greek and Latin Literature* (3rd ed.; Oxford: Clarendon Press, 1991).

Roberts, *OTTV*
B.J. Roberts, *The Old Testament Text and Versions: The Hebrew Text in Transmission and the History of the Ancient Versions* (Cardiff: University of Wales Press, 1951).

Rofé, *"Historical Significance"*
A. Rofé, "The Historical Significance of Secondary Readings," in *Quest for Context and Meaning: Studies in Biblical Intertextuality in Honor of James A. Sanders* (eds. C.A. Evans and S. Talmon; Biblical Interpretation Series 28; Leiden: Brill, 1997), 393–402.

Rofé, *Deuteronomy*
A. Rofé, *Deuteronomy: Issues and Interpretation* (OTS; London: T & T Clark, 2002).

De Rossi, *1784–1788*
J.B. De Rossi, *Variae lectiones Veteris Testamenti* (5 vols.; Parma: Regio, 1784–1788; repr. Amsterdam: Philo, 1969).

*RSV
The Bible Containing the Old and New Testaments: Revised Standard Version (2nd ed.; New York: Collins, 1971).

Sabatier, *Bibliorum*
P. Sabatier (ed.), *Bibliorum sacrorum latinae versions antiquae seu vetus Italica, et caeterae quaecunque in codicibus Ms. et antquorum libris reperiri potuerunt: Quae cum Vulgata Latina et cum Textu Graeco comparantur: Accedunt praefationes, observations, ac notae indexque novus advulagatam e regione editam idemque locupletissimus: Opera et studio* (3 vols.; Reims: Florentain, 1743–1749).

Sadaqa, *Jewish and Samaritan Version*
A. and R. Sadaqa, *Jewish and Samaritan Version of the Pentateuch: With Particular Stress on the Differences between Both Texts* (Tel Aviv: R. Mass, 1961–1965).

Salvesen, *Hexapla*
Origen's Hexapla and Fragments: Papers Presented at the Rich Seminar on the Hexapla, Oxford Centre for Hebrew and Jewish Studies, 25th July–3rd August 1994 (ed. A. Salvesen; TSAJ 58; Tübingen: Mohr Siebeck, 1998).

Sanderson, *Exodus Scroll*
J.E. Sanderson, *An Exodus Scroll from Qumran: 4QpaleoExod^m and the Samaritan Tradition* (HSS 30; Atlanta: Scholars Press, 1986).

Schenker, *Septante*
A. Schenker, *Septante et texte Massorétique dans l'histoire la plus ancienne du texte de 1 Rois 2–14* (CahRB 48; Paris: Gabalda, 2000).

Schenker, *Earliest Text*
The Earliest Text of the Hebrew Bible: The Relationship between the Masoretic Text and the Hebrew Base of the Septuagint Reconsidered (ed. A. Schenker; SBLSCS 52; Atlanta: Scholars Press, 2003).

Schenker, *"General Introduction"*
A. Schenker et al., "General Introduction," in *BHQ 18: General Introduction and Megilloth*, vii–xxxvi.

Schenker, *"Ursprung"*
A. Schenker, "Der Ursprung des massoretischen Textes im Licht der literarischen Varianten im Bibeltext," *Text* 23 (2007): 51–67.

Schiffman, Tov, and VanderKam, *Fifty Years*
The Dead Sea Scrolls Fifty Years after their Discovery: Proceedings of the Jerusalem Congress, July 10–25, 1997 (eds. L.H. Schiffman, E. Tov, and J.C. VanderKam; Jerusalem: Israel Exploration Society, 2000).

Schorch, *Euphemismen*
S. Schorch, *Euphemismen in der Hebräischen Bibel*

(Orientalia Biblica et Christiana 12; Wiesbaden: Harrassowitz, 2000).

Schorch, *Vokale
S. Schorch, *Die Vokale des Gesetzes: Die samaritanische Lesetradition als Textzeugin der Tora*, Vol. 1: *Das Buch Genesis* (BZAW 339; Berlin: De Gruyter, 2004).

Schüssler, *Biblia Coptica
K. Schüssler, *Biblia Coptica: Die koptischen Bibeltexte: Das Sahidische Alte und Neue Testament: Vollständiges Verzeichnis mit Standorten*, Vol. 1.1–4 (Wiesbaden: Harrassowitz, 1995–2000, sa 1–120); Vol. 2.1–2 (Wiesbaden: Harrassowitz, 2012–2015, sa 121–260).

*Scrolls and Cognate Writings
See *Manchester Symposium

*Septuaginta Deutsch
M. Karrer and W. Kraus (eds.), *Septuaginta Deutsch: Das griechische Alte Testament in deutscher Übersetzung* (Stuttgart: Deutsche Bibelgesellschaft, 2009).

*Septuaginta Deutsch, Erläuterungen
Septuaginta Deutsch: Erläuterungen und Kommentare zum griechischen Alten Testament (eds. M. Karrer and W. Kraus; Stuttgart: Deutsche Bibelgesellschaft, 2011).

*SESB
Stuttgart Electronic Study Bible computer program.

Sirat, *Papyrus
C. Sirat, *Les papyrus en caractères hébraïques trouvés en Egypte* (with contributions by M. Beit-Arié et al.; calligraphy and illustrations by A. Yardeni; Paris: Centre national de recherche scientifique, 1985).

Skehan, *"Qumran Manuscripts"
P.W. Skehan, "The Qumran Manuscripts and Textual Criticism," in *Volume du Congrès International pour l'étude de l'Ancien Testament, Strabourg 1956* (eds. G.W. Anderson et al.; VTSup 4; Leiden: Brill, 1957), 148–60.

Skehan, *"Qumran, Littérature de Qumran"
P.W. Skehan, "Qumran, Littérature de Qumran, A. Textes bibliques," *DBSup* 9: 805–22.

Sperber, *Bible in Aramaic
A. Sperber, *The Bible in Aramaic Based on Old Manuscripts and Printed Texts* (4 vols.; Leiden: Brill, 1959–1968).

Sperber, *Grammar
A. Sperber, *A Historical Grammar of Biblical Hebrew: A Presentation of Problems with Suggestions to Their Solution* (Leiden: Brill, 1966).

Stipp, *"Textkritik"
H.J. Stipp, "Das Verhältnis von Textkritik und Literarkritik in neueren alttestamentlichen Veröffentlichungen," *BZ* 34 (1990): 16–37.

Strugnell, *"Notes en marge"
J. Strugnell, "Notes en marge du volume v des Discoveries in the Judaean Desert of Jordan," *RevQ* 7 (1969–1971): 163–276.

Sundberg, *Old Testament
A. Sundberg, *The Old Testament of the Early Church* (HTS 20; Cambridge: Harvard University Press, 1964).

Swete, *Introduction
H.B. Swete, *An Introduction to the Old Testament in Greek* (2nd ed.; Cambridge: Cambridge University Press, 1914).

Tal, *Shekhem
A. Tal, *The Samaritan Pentateuch: Edited According to MS 6 (C) of the Shekhem Synagogue* (Texts and Studies in the Hebrew Language and Related Subjects 8; Tel Aviv: Tel Aviv University, 1994).

Tal–Florentin, *Samaritan Version
A. Tal and M. Florentin, *The Pentateuch: The Samaritan Version and the Masoretic Version* (Tel Aviv: Haim Rubin Tel Aviv University Press, 2010).

Talmon, *"Old Testament Text"
S. Talmon, "The Old Testament Text," in *The Cambridge History of the Bible*, Vol. 1: *From the Beginnings to Jerome* (eds. R.P. Ackroyd and C.F. Evans; Cambridge: Cambridge University Press, 1970), 159–99; repr. in Cross–Talmon, *QHBT* (1975): 1–41.

Talmon, *Qumran
S. Talmon, *The World of Qumran from Within: Collected Studies* (Jerusalem: Magnes Press, 1989).

Talmon, *Masada VI
S. Talmon and Y. Yadin, *Masada VI: The Yigael Yadin Excavations 1963–1965, Final Reports, Hebrew Fragments from Masada* (Jerusalem: Israel Exploration Society, 1999).

Talmon, *Text
S. Talmon, *Text and Canon of the Hebrew Bible: Collected Studies* (Winona Lake: Eisenbrauns, 2010).

Talmon, *"New Outlook"
S. Talmon, "The Textual Study of the Bible: A New Outlook," in idem, *Text, 19–84.

Talmon, *"Synonymous Readings"
S. Talmon, "Synonymous Readings in the Masoretic Text," in idem, *Text, 171–216.

Talmon, *"Double Readings"
S. Talmon, "Double Readings in the Masoretic Text," in idem, *Text, 217–67.

Talmon, *"Ancient Versions"
S. Talmon, "Textual Criticism: The Ancient Versions," in idem, *Text, 383–418.

Thackeray, *Grammar
: H.St.J. Thackeray, *A Grammar of the Old Testament in Greek according to the Septuagint* (Cambridge: Cambridge University Press, 1909).

Thackeray, *The Septuagint and Jewish Worship*
: H.St.J. Thackeray, *The Septuagint and Jewish Worship* (Schweich Lectures 1920; London: Milford, 1921).

The Bible as Book
: *The Bible as Book: The Hebrew Bible and the Judaean Desert Discoveries* (eds. E.D. Herbert and E. Tov; London: British Library, 2002).

Theory and Practice
: *Theory and Practice of Translation: Nobel Symposium 39, Stockholm 1976* (ed. L. Grähs et al.; Bern: P. Lang, 1978).

Tigay, *Models*
: *Empirical Models for Biblical Criticism* (ed. J.H. Tigay; Philadelphia: University of Philadelphia Press, 1985).

Van der Toorn, *Scribal Culture*
: K. van der Toorn, *Scribal Culture and the Making of the Hebrew Bible* (Cambridge: Harvard University Press, 2007).

Tov, *Jeremiah–Baruch*
: E. Tov, *The Septuagint Translation of Jeremiah and Baruch: A Discussion of an Early Revision of Jeremiah 29–52 and Baruch 1:1–3:8* (HSM 8; Missoula: Scholars Press, 1976).

Tov, *"Socio-Religious Background"*
: E. Tov, "The Socio-Religious Background of the Paleo-Hebrew Biblical Texts Found at Qumran," in *Geschichte–Tradition–Reflexion: Festschrift für Martin Hengel zum 70. Geburtstag* (eds. H. Cancik et al.; 3 vols.; Tübingen: Mohr Siebeck, 1996), 1.353–74.

Tov, *TCU*
: E. Tov, *The Text-Critical Use of the Septuagint in Biblical Research* (2nd ed.; Jerusalem Biblical Studies 8; Jerusalem: Simor, 1997).

Tov, *Greek-Hebrew Bible*
: E. Tov, *The Greek and Hebrew Bible: Collected Essays on the Septuagint* (VTSup 72; Leiden: Brill, 1999).

Tov, *"Septuagint Translators"*
: E. Tov, "Did the Septuagint Translators Always Understand Their Hebrew Text?" in idem, *Greek-Hebrew Bible*, 203–18.

Tov, *"Synthese"*
: E. Tov, "Die biblischen Handscriften aus der Wüste Juda—Eine neue Synthese," in *Die Textfunde vom Toten Meer und der Text der Hebräischen Bibel* (eds. U. Dahmen, A. Lange, and H. Lichtenberger; Neukirchen-Vluyn: Neukirchener Verlag, 2000), 1–34.

Tov, *TCHB^{1,2}*
: E. Tov, *Textual Criticism of the Hebrew Bible* (Minneapolis: Fortress Press, 1992. 2nd revised ed.; Minneapolis: Fortress Press, 2001).

Tov, *"Biblical Texts"*
: E. Tov, "The Biblical Texts from the Judaean Desert: An Overview and Analysis of the Published Texts," in *The Bible as Book: The Hebrew Bible and the Judaean Desert Discoveries* (eds. E.D. Herbert and E. Tov; London: British Library, 2002), 139–66.

Tov, *"List"*
: E. Tov, "List of the Texts from the Judaean Desert," *DJD* XXXIX, 27–114.

Tov, *"Place of Masoretic Text"*
: E. Tov, "The Place of the Masoretic Text in Modern Text Editions of the Hebrew Bible: The Relevance of Canon," in *The Canon Debate* (eds. L. McDonald and J.A. Sanders; Peabody: Hendrickson, 2002), 234–51.

Tov, *Scribal Practices*
: E. Tov, *Scribal Practices and Approaches Reflected in the Texts Found in the Judean Desert* (STDJ 54; Leiden: Brill, 2004).

Tov, *HB, GB, and Qumran*
: E. Tov, *Hebrew Bible, Greek Bible, and Qumran: Collected Essays* (TSAJ 121; Tübingen: Mohr Siebeck, 2008).

Tov, *"Coincidental Textual Nature"*
: E. Tov, "The Coincidental Textual Nature of the Collections of Ancient Scriptures," in *Congress Volume Ljubljana 2007* (ed. A. Lemaire; VTSup 133; Leiden: Brill, 2010), 153–69.

Tov, *Revised Lists*
: E. Tov, *Revised Lists of the Texts from the Judaean Desert* (Leiden: Brill, 2010).

Tov, *TCHB*
: E. Tov, *Textual Criticism of the Hebrew Bible* (revised and expanded 3rd ed.; Minneapolis: Fortress Press, 2012).

Tov, *Collected Writings 3*
: E. Tov, *Textual Criticism of the Hebrew Bible, Qumran, Septuagint: Collected Writings*, Vol. 3 (VTSup 167; Leiden: Brill, 2015).

Tov, *"Source Criticism"*
: E. Tov, "The Source of Source Criticism: The Relevance of Non-Masoretic Textual Witnesses," in *Text—Textgeschichte—Textwirkung: Festschrift zum 65. Geburtstag von Siegfried Kreuzer* (eds. T. Wagner et al.; AOAT 419; Münster: Ugarit-Verlag, 2015), 283–301.

Trebolle Barrera, *Jewish Bible*
: J. Trebolle Barrera, *The Jewish Bible and the Christian*

Bible: An Introduction to the History of the Bible (trans. W.G.E. Watson; Leiden: Brill, 1998).

Turner, *Greek Manuscripts
E.G. Turner, Greek Manuscripts of the Ancient World (rev. and enlarged by P.J. Parsons; 2nd ed.; Institute of Classical Studies Bulletin Supplement 46; London: University of London, 1987).

Ullendorff, *Ethiopia and the Bible
E. Ullendorff, Ethiopia and the Bible: The Schweich Lectures of the British Academy, 1967 (Oxford: Oxford University Press, 1967).

Ulrich, *DSS
E. Ulrich, The Dead Sea Scrolls and the Origins of the Bible (Grand Rapids/Leiden: Eerdmans/Brill, 1999).

Ulrich, *BQS
E. Ulrich, The Biblical Qumran Scrolls: Transcriptions and Textual Variants (VTSup 134; Leiden: Brill, 2010).

Ulrich, *DSSDCB
E. Ulrich, The Dead Sea Scrolls and the Developmental Composition of the Bible (VTSup 169; Leiden: Brill, 2015).

Van Seters, *Edited Bible
J. Van Seters, The Edited Bible: The Curious History of the "Editor" in Biblical Criticism (Winona Lake: Eisenbrauns, 2006).

Veltri, *Eine Torah
G. Veltri, Eine Tora für den König Talmai: Untersuchungen zum Übersetzungsverständnis in der jüdisch-hellenistischen und rabbinischen Literatur (TSAJ 41; Tübingen: Mohr Siebeck, 1994).

Veltri, *Gegenwart
G. Veltri, Gegenwart der Tradition: Studien zur jüdischen Literatur und Kulturgeschichte (JSJSup 69; Leiden: Brill, 2002).

*Vetus Latina Database
R. Gryson (ed.), Vetus Latina Database: Bible Versions of the Latin Fathers: The Comprehensive Patristic Records of the Vetus Latina Institut in Beuron (CD-ROM; Turnhout, Brepols Publishers, 2002).

Walters, *Text
P. Walters, The Text of the Septuagint: Its Corruptions and Their Emendation (Cambridge: Cambridge University Press, 1973).

Walton, *Polyglotta
B. Walton, Biblia Sacra Polyglotta complectentia textus originales, Hebraicum, cum Pentateucho Samaritano, Chaldaicum, Graecum, versionumque antiquarum, Samaritanae, Graecae LXXII Interpretum, Chaldaicae, Syriacae, Arabicae, Aethiopicae, Persicae, Vulg. Lat. etc. (London: Roycroft, 1653–1657; repr. Graz: Akademische Druck und Verlagsanstalt, 1965).

Walton, *Prolegomena
B. Walton, Briani Waltoni in Biblia Polyglotta Prolegomena (Leipzig: Weygand, 1777).

Weber and Gryson, *Vulgata
Biblia Sacra iuxta vulgatam versionem (eds. R. Weber and R. Gryson; 5th ed.; Stuttgart: Deutsche Bibelgesellschaft, 2007).

Weil, *Massorah Gedolah ... Léningrad
G.E. Weil, Massorah Gedolah manuscrit B.19a de Léningrad, Vol. 1 (Rome: Pontificium Institutum Biblicum, 1971).

Wellhausen, *Bücher Samuelis
J. Wellhausen, Der Text der Bücher Samuelis (Göttingen: Vandenhoeck & Ruprecht, 1871).

Van der Woude, *"Pluriformity and Uniformity"
A.S. van der Woude, "Pluriformity and Uniformity: Reflections on the Transmission of the Text of the Old Testament," in Sacred History and Sacred Texts in Early Judaism: A Symposium in Honour of A.S. van der Woude (eds. J.N. Brenner and F. García Martínez; CBET 5; Kampen: Kok Pharos, 1992), 151–69.

Würthwein, *Text
E. Würthwein, Der Text des Alten Testaments: Eine Einführung in die Biblia Hebraica (5th ed.; Stuttgart: Deutsche Bibelgesellschaft, 1988).

Würthwein, *Text (English)
E. Würthwein, The Text of the Old Testament: An Introduction to the Biblia Hebraica (trans. E.F. Rhodes; 2nd ed.; Grand Rapids: Eerdmans, 1995).

Yardeni, *Hebrew Script
A. Yardeni, The Book of the Hebrew Script: History, Paleography, Script Styles, Calligraphy and Design (Jerusalem: Carta: 1997).

Yeivin, *Introduction
I. Yeivin, Introduction to the Tiberian Masorah (trans. and ed. E.J. Revell; SBLMasS 5; Missoula: Scholars Press, 1980).

Yeivin, *Masorah
I. Yeivin, The Biblical Masorah (Studies in Language 3; Jerusalem: Academy of the Hebrew Language, 2003) [Hebr.].

Young, *"Stabilization"
I. Young, "The Stabilization of the Biblical Text in the Light of Qumran and Masada: A Challenge for Conventional Qumran Chronology?" DSD 9 (2002): 364–90.

Zohrapian, *Scriptures
H. Zohrapian (ed.), Astuatsashunch' Matean ew Nor Ktakaranats' (Scriptures of the Old and New Testa-

ments; Venice, 1805; repr., with introduction by C. Cox [Classical Armenian Text Reprint Series; Delmar: Caravan Books, 1984]).

2
Pentateuch

2.1 Textual History of the Pentateuch

2.1.1 Torah as a Unit

The description of the textual history of the five books of the Torah as one unit is justified because they were joined together and considered a single unit by the biblical authors and subsequent generations.

As a result, the phrases סֵפֶר הַתּוֹרָה "book of the Law," סֵפֶר תּוֹרַת מֹשֶׁה "book of the Law of Moses," and תּוֹרַת מֹשֶׁה "Law of Moses" are used frequently in Scripture, both in Deuteronomy and in the later books. The fact that most Torah scrolls found in the Judean Desert contain single books and not the complete Torah derives from the technical limitations determined by the maximum size of these scrolls (each of the five books of the Torah is sizeable and together they encompass twenty-two percent of the Hebrew canon in MT). At the same time, four Qumran scrolls contain two books, and the 4QRP scrolls contain between two and five books (4QGen-Exod[a] [→ 2.2.1.1.1], 4QpaleoGen-Exod[l] [→ 2.2.1.1.2]; 4QRP[a] [Genesis–Exodus]; 4QRP[b] [Genesis, Exodus, Numbers, Deuteronomy; → 2.2.1.7.1]; 4QRP[c] [Genesis–Deuteronomy; → 2.2.1.7.2]; 4QExod-Lev[c]; 4QRP[d] [Exodus, Numbers, Deuteronomy; → 2.2.1.7.3]; 4QLev-Num[a]; → 2.2.1.7.10). Mur1 (→ 2.2.1.2.6) probably contained Genesis–Numbers as well as Deuteronomy. In later centuries, scrolls containing the complete Torah became the norm, as may be learned from the references to such scrolls in rabbinic literature.

The unity of the Torah is also visible at the scribal-textual level since the individual books of the Torah underwent several similar textual developments: 1) The orthography of the five Torah books in MT is more conservative than that of most other books, especially in Exodus and Leviticus (see below, → 2.1.3); 2) The character of the Hebrew and Greek manuscripts of the Torah differs from that of other books (see below, → 2.1.5); 3) The Samaritan sacred writings are limited to the Torah, although a Samaritan version of Joshua is also known (→ 1.2.3); 4) By far the largest number of textual branches is known for the Torah, deriving from its special popularity (see below, → 2.1.5); 5) Within the careful transmission of the Scripture books in MT, the Torah may have been given special care, as suggested by a relatively large number of cancellation dots (*puncta extraordinaria* [→ 1.5]; ten out of fifteen in the whole Bible) and the relatively small number of *Qere* readings in the Torah (→ 1.5).

2.1.2 Extant Witnesses (→ 2.2; → 2.4)

2.1.2.1 Earliest Textual Evidence

The earliest textual evidence for the Torah, dating to the mid-third century B.C.E., is among the oldest for Scripture as a whole. It is probably no coincidence that five of the eight oldest paleographically dated scrolls contain segments of the Torah (4QExod-Lev[f] dated to 250 B.C.E. [→ 2.2.1.7.9], 4QpaleoDeut[s] dated to 250–200 B.C.E. [→ 2.2.1.10], 4QExod[d] dated to 225–175 B.C.E. [→ 2.2.1.8], and 6QpaleoGen and 6QpaleoLev, both dated to 250–150 B.C.E. [→ 2.2.1.8; → 2.2.1.10]).

The earliest remnants of the Old Greek version, usually dated to 285 B.C.E. (→ 1.3.1.1.5), are a century later: Greek scrolls and codices dating from the second century B.C.E. onwards were discovered in the Judean Desert and Egypt (→ 1.3.1.1.6).

There is no older evidence for the Torah, with the exception of the silver rolls from Ketef Hinnom dating to the seventh or sixth century B.C.E. (see Tov, *TCHB*, 111; → 2.2.5.3), which may be disregarded in the present context since they do not contain a proper biblical text.

Close connections between Torah texts and later books reflect different types of literary links, but little solid evidence is available about possible variants in the later books that quote from the Torah. This pertains to the relation between Ezekiel and Leviticus and that between Jeremiah and Deuteronomy. On the other hand, the Chronicler reflects many textual variants as well as original readings when compared with the Torah, for example in the genealogical lists in the first chapters of 1 Chronicles. However, the date of the variants in Chronicles cannot be determined as they may derive from any period in the transmission of that book, either from the time of the Chronicler himself or from a later period. In another area, the so-called paleo-Hebrew Torah fragments from Qumran do not precede the time of the fragments written in the square script, as they are dated to the Hasmonean period or later (→ 2.2.1).

2.1.3 Textual Features Common to the Torah Books

The five books of the Torah share various textual features. Some of them reflect the stage of the combined Torah scrolls, while others preceded that stage.

– The orthography of MT cannot be presented as consistent or uniform, neither in the Torah nor in the other books. Nevertheless, the five books of the Torah share certain spelling features that set them apart from the other books. It has been suggested that the Torah and Kings reflect a more conservative (defective) orthography than the rest of the biblical books and that they also contain the highest degree of internal consistency; in the Torah, this description applies especially to Exodus and Leviticus.[1]
– Harmonization is a major feature characterizing most Torah texts, especially the Hebrew source of LXX (→ 1.3.1.1.12), SP (→ 1.2.3), and the pre-Samaritan Qumran scrolls. Though harmonization occurs to some degree in all Scripture books, noticeable for example in LXX-Cant, the various texts of Samuel–Kings//Chronicles and the parallel chapters in such books as Psalms, Jeremiah 52//2 Kgs 24:18–25:30, it features as a major phenomenon in the Torah in the non-legal sections and in the phraseology of the legal sections, probably due to its popularity (see below, → 2.1.5).
– Larger number of textual branches than in other books (see below, → 2.1.5).

Special Textual Features in Leviticus

The book of Leviticus differs textually from the other Torah books. Only in this book are there no frequent differences between the textual sources such as evidenced for the other four Torah books (see below, → 2.1.4). If we link this situation to the fact that the orthography of this book is among the most conservative in Scripture (see above in this paragraph), we note that this book was changed very little in the period for which we have textual evidence. This situation derives from the fact that Leviticus contains only legal sections that were not submitted to major rewriting. This is not to say that scribes did not rewrite laws, but in the period for which we have textual sources, only scant textual evidence has been preserved for such rewriting. Some legal rewriting is recognizable in the 4QRP texts (→ 2.2.1.7) and the Hebrew *Vorlage* of LXX-Exod 35–40 (→ 1.3.1.1.12), both probably reflecting exegetical rewriting based on a text like MT.

2.1.4 Literary Variants

Some of the groups of differences between the textual sources (usually blocks of variants) reflect different literary stages of the biblical books, and hence pertain to the literary development of Scripture books. Two groups of such variants may shed light on the Documentary Hypothesis (see below, → 2.1.4.2).

2.1.4.1 Literary Variants in the Torah

Literary differences between MT and the other textual sources are recognized in several concentrations. The first two groups received much attention in scholarship, and the others less so:

---

[1] Thus F.I. Andersen and A.D. Forbes, *Spelling in the Hebrew Bible* (BibOr 41; Rome: Biblical Institute Press, 1986), 312–18. A. Murtonen, "The Fixation in Writing of Various Parts of the Pentateuch," *VT* 3 (1953): 46–53 notes that the Decalogue and the book of the covenant (Exodus 20:22–23:33) are more defective (and hence earlier) than the other segments of the Torah and, by the same token, he found differences between the various Pentateuchal sources.

1) Editorial innovations of the SP group as compared with MT and LXX (→ 1.2.3);
2) Literary and exegetical innovations of three manuscripts of the 4QRP cluster (4QRP^{c,d,e});[2]
3) Differences between MT, LXX, and SP in *Genesis 5 and 11* in genealogies, in which three possible tendencies are recognized. It seems that MT is not recensional in Genesis 11, but may be so in Genesis 5. On the other hand, the *Vorlage* of LXX and SP probably revised MT or a similar text in both chapters in a certain direction, in similar, yet different ways. I posit two recensions (SP, LXX) and one text (MT) in Genesis 11, and possibly three recensions in Genesis 5. The analysis of these chronological systems pertains to the primacy of MT, LXX, SP, or another system in these chapters, and is irrelevant for the source-critical analysis;[3]
4) *Gen 31:46–48* appear in LXX in the sequence 46, 48a, 47. In vv. 45–46, Jacob and his relatives erect a pillar and make a mound. According to LXX, Laban announces that this mound will be a witness between the two (v. 48a), and afterwards they name the place "Mound of Witness" (v. 47). MT+[4] places the Aramaic and Hebrew names (v. 47) before Laban's statements (v. 48a), probably representing a later addition located in different places in MT+ and LXX;
5) *Num 10:34–36*. In LXX, the order of these verses differs from MT+ (35, 36, 34). The sequence of LXX, in which v. 35, referring to *the* Ark, comes immediately after v. 33, where the Ark is also mentioned, is possibly more natural, while in MT+ v. 34 comes between the two. The differing sequences were created by the late addition in different places of the "Song of the Ark" (vv. 35–36), which originally was not included in its present position;
6) *Different Literary Editions of Numbers in LXX and MT+ Visible in Small Details?* In LXX-Num, small pluses appear in Num 2:7, 14, 20, 22, 29 (same plus in all verses); 3:10; 7:88; 10:6a; 14:23 = Deut 1:39; 23:3 (= 4QNum^b); 23:7 = 24:2, 23; 32:30 = context; 36:1 = 27:1. In Num 9:22–23, LXX has a shorter text (MT+ adds details from vv. 21–22; 13:33; 15:35).

The two traditions differ twice in important sequence details. In the census in Numbers 1, in the *Vorlage* of LXX, Gad (MT+ vv. 24–26) follows Manasseh (vv. 34–35). The position of Gad in MT+ is less appropriate, after Reuben (vv. 20–21) and Simeon (vv. 22–23), probably influenced by the sequence in Num 2:10–16 (Reuben, Simeon, Gad). The same change also took place in LXX-Num 26, where Gad was moved from the triad Reuben-Simeon-Gad (vv. 5–18) to vv. 24–27, following Issachar.

7) LXX-Exod 35–40 possibly reflects a Hebrew version that is very different from MT, but further research needs to be carried out on these difficult chapters (see below, → 2.1.4.2).

2.1.4.2 The Documentary Hypothesis

Within the analysis of the relevance of textual sources to the literary history of the Torah, a discussion of their relation to the so-called Documentary Hypothesis is in order. When examining the textual sources on which the Documentary Hypothesis is based, we found only one, the Masoretic Text. In the historical-critical analysis, non-Masoretic sources are taken into consideration all the time, while the theory of the Documentary Hypothesis is based exclusively on MT, with one possible exception, LXX-Exod 35–40. This being the case, we may also formulate our conclusion in a positive way, noting that the Documentary Hypothesis is based on the combined evidence of all the textual sources, including MT.[5] This situation is not

---

[2] The other two manuscripts of 4QRP, 4QRP^{a,b}, belong to the SP group (→ 1.2.3).

[3] See my study "The Genealogical Lists in Genesis 5 and 11 in Three Different Versions," in Tov, *Collected Writings 3*, 221–38 and the bibliography mentioned there. Elaborating on his earlier work, *Genesis 1–11*, R. Hendel repeated in a later study that three different recensions were at work in ch. 5: "A Hasmonean Edition of MT Genesis?: The Implications of the Editions of the Chronology in Genesis 5," *Hebrew Bible and Ancient Israel* 1 (2012): 1–17.

[4] The symbol MT+ refers to the evidence of the MT group (MT, T, S, V).

[5] Actually, MT provides the base for almost all literary theories. The Dtr revisions of Joshua–2 Kings and Jeremiah

the result of coincidence. It implies that all the textual sources reflect the assumed combination of the Pentateuchal documents to the same extent. It also implies that this literary activity took place before the textual sources branched off in different directions. Such an assumption necessarily has implications for our view of the original status of the Scripture text.

If this assumption is correct, the conclusions are intriguing from a textual point of view since we found virtually no additional evidence in the non-MT sources relevant to the Documentary Hypothesis. However, we could also claim that we should not even expect significant ancient variants in the non-Masoretic texts because, as a rule, MT is the most original witness in the Torah, and the other sources are secondary (see below, → 2.1.5). Harmonization is the major driving force behind all these non-Masoretic texts (→ 1.3.1.1.12; → 1.2.3).

By way of exception to this assumption, the following two sets of data could be relevant to the Documentary Hypothesis, although my study reached negative conclusions in this regard (see Tov, "Source Criticism"):

1) The main challenge to the Documentary Hypothesis from textual sources lies in the realm of the *divine names*. In my view, the few known variants in Hebrew sources are negligible. Equally insignificant are the variations in SP. On the other hand, the divine names in LXX do deserve attention. They have often been discussed in the literature, especially since the appearance of Baudissin's monumental monograph on *Kyrios*, which contains a wealth of data.[6] Most of these variations pertain to deviations from the standard LXX equivalents, יהוה/κύριος "Lord" and אלהים/θεός "God." Some of the non-standard renderings (θεός "God" for יהוה "Lord" and κύριος "Lord" for אלהים "God") could have been created by the translators, who might have lacked a fixed translation vocabulary at the beginning of their work. In such a scenario, the LXX evidence would be irrelevant. On the other hand, if LXX were based on differing Hebrew readings, this evidence should be taken into consideration.

However, in my view, this is not the case, with the possible exception of Genesis 1–11, in which LXX appears to differ frequently from the other sources. The equivalents in LXX could be relevant to the Documentary Hypothesis, and this issue was debated much at the beginning of the twentieth century (see below).

It has often been suggested that the unusual equivalents of LXX in these chapters reflect Hebrew variants, possibly shedding light on the Documentary Hypothesis. In Gen 2:4b–3:24, in particular, this suggestion is intriguing. MT of this unit (source J) uses mainly (20×) יְהוָה אֱלֹהִים "Lord God" and also features אֱלֹהִים "God" in 3:1b–5 (5×). If LXX reflects a different Hebrew text, this chapter in LXX would present a different grouping of יְהוָה אֱלֹהִים "Lord God" (13×) and יְהוָה "Lord" (7× + 5×). This evidence would somewhat alter the analysis of the divine names, but in my view it is irrelevant to the Documentary Hypothesis.

The LXX renderings of the divine names in Genesis were brought to bear on the Documentary Hypothesis, especially at the beginning of the twentieth century,[7] and in 2011 by Carr,[8] but no firm suggestions have been made. One argument against the relevance of LXX for the Documentary Hypothesis was presented by Dahse, who claimed that scores of inner-Greek variants uproot the validity

---

seemingly reflect earlier pre-Dtr layers, but this is not the case. See Tov, "Source Criticism."

[6] W.W. Graf von Baudissin, *Kyrios als Gottesname im Judentum und seine Stelle in der Religionsgeschichte* (2 vols.; Giessen: Töpelmann, 1926–1929).

[7] See H.M. Wiener, *Pentateuchal Studies* (London: Elliot Stock, 1912); H.M. Wiener, *Essays in Pentateuchal Criticism* (London: Elliot Stock, 1913), 13–41; J. Skinner, *The Divine Names in Genesis* (London: Hodder and Stoughton, 1914); H.M. Wiener, *The Pentateuchal Text: A Reply to Dr. Skinner* (London: Elliot Stock, 1914) [reprinted from *BSac* 71 (1914): 218–68]; J.B. Harford, *Since Wellhausen: A Brief Survey of Recent Pentateuchal Criticism* (London: Hunter & Longhurst, 1926) [reprinted from *Expositor*, 1925]; Hendel, **Genesis 1–11*, 35–39 likewise assumes that the LXX representation of the divine names reflects Hebrew variants, but he did not connect the evidence to the Documentary Hypothesis.

[8] Carr, **Formation*, 106–10.

of the evidence of LXX for the Documentary Hypothesis.[9] However, most of these variants actually adapt the Old Greek to MT in manuscripts of LXX revisions and therefore are irrelevant to the issue under investigation.[10] In my view, LXX reflects harmonizing renderings that were carried out inconsistently.[11] The most cogent argument against the relevance of LXX for any literary analysis is that there is no visible pattern that could be used for any source-critical analysis.[12] Furthermore, the choice of equivalents for the divine names in LXX is not determined by any context considerations,[13] and the Documentary Hypothesis depends only partially on the distinctive use of the divine names.

2) LXX-Exod 35–40 probably reflects a Hebrew text very different from MT+, but the nature of that text is unclear. The widely divergent LXX text may reflect original elements as in the case of the Greek texts of Jeremiah and Ezekiel, or it may display a rewritten Hebrew text like LXX-1 Kgs, LXX-Esth, and LXX-Dan. The possibility of a rewritten text is suggested by a midrashic element in LXX-Exod 38:22,[14] parallel to MT-Exod 38:1–2. This Greek text contains a midrash-like explanation for the origin of the bronze of the altar (MT v. 1) and the laver (v. 8) created from the censers of the followers of Korah. LXX uses a word καταστασιάσασιν ("to the men who rebelled," למרדים) not found in the story in Num 16:36–40 or anywhere else in LXX. Since the story of Korah appears only in Numbers 16, the Greek text of Exodus probably reflects an exegetical addition based on a Hebrew source.

On the other hand, it is also possible that LXX reflects an earlier or later stage than MT in the development of the Hebrew text.[15] A central difference between the LXX and MT+ versions concerns the garments of the priesthood (MT-Exod 39:1b–31), which in LXX precede the other items (Exod 36:8a–40).[16] The position of the court differs in these texts (MT-Exod 38:9–20; LXX-Exod 37:7–18). In addition,

---

[9] J. Dahse, *Textkritische Materialen zur Hexateuchfrage* (Giessen: Alfred Töpelmann, 1912), 104–21; see also J. Dahse, "Textkritische Bedenken gegen den Ausgangspunkt der heutigen Pentateuchkritik," *AR* 6 (1903): 305–19.

[10] Thus already Skinner, *Divine Names*, 253–61 reacting to Dahse. See the data in J.W. Wevers, *Genesis* (Septuaginta Vetus Testamentum Graecum 1; Göttingen: Vandenhoeck & Ruprecht, 1974).

[11] For a detailed analysis, see Tov, "Source Criticism."

[12] Most of the unusual renderings are in the J section, as expected, since the Greek rendering of אֱלֹהִים "God" is rather stable. The breakdown of the renderings does not add new information, since the rearrangement of the chapters in J and P according to LXX makes little sense from the point of view of content. Thus, in the long J section 2:4b–4:24, if the renderings of יְהוָה אֱלֹהִים "Lord God" and יְהוָה "Lord" with θεός "God" would point to אֱלֹהִים "God," possibly reflecting the P source, these chapters would be composed of patches of J and P without any discernible logic.

[13] For example: Gen 4:26 אָז הוּחַל לִקְרֹא בְּשֵׁם יְהוָה "at that time it was begun to invoke the name of the Lord"/οὗτος ἤλπισεν ἐπικαλεῖσθαι τὸ ὄνομα κυρίου τοῦ θεοῦ "He hoped to invoke the name of the Lord God" (*NETS*). According to MT, God's personal name יְהוָה "Lord" was being used from that point onwards, and it would have been appropriate had LXX used κύριος "Lord." The use of the double name in LXX does not seem to reflect any logic or a specific context in Gen 7:16 כַּאֲשֶׁר צִוָּה אֹתוֹ אֱלֹהִים וַיִּסְגֹּר יְהוָה בַּעֲדוֹ "as God had commanded him. And the Lord shut him in"/καθὰ ἐνετείλατο ὁ θεὸς τῷ Νωε. Καὶ ἔκλεισεν κύριος ὁ θεὸς ἔξωθεν αὐτοῦ τὴν κιβωτόν "as God had commanded Noe. And the Lord God closed the ark apart from him" (*NETS*). The use of two different divine names does not seem to be logical, neither in LXX nor in MT. The translator or his *Vorlage* probably harmonized the two parts of the sentence. The same θεός "God" acted in both parts, but in the second one he is also named κύριος "Lord."

[14] "This one made the bronze altar from the bronze firepans that belonged to the men who rebelled together with the gathering of Kore."

[15] It is less likely that the present LXX text resulted from the Greek translator's manipulations. Finn and Gooding suggested that the translator or a later reviser rearranged the Greek text without regard to the Hebrew: A.H. Finn, "The Tabernacle Chapters," *JTS* 16 (1914–1915): 449–82; D.W. Gooding, *The Account of the Tabernacle* (TS, NS VI; Cambridge: Cambridge University Press, 1959). See further D.W. Gooding, "On the Use of the LXX for Dating Midrashic Elements in the Targums," *JTS* 25 (1974): 1–11 and Jellicoe, **SMS*, 273–76 for a convenient summary. R.D. Nelson, "Studies in the Development of the Text of the Tabernacle Account" (PhD diss., Harvard University, 1986) appears to reflect a mediating position between the assumption of a Hebrew or a Greek source for the different Greek text.

[16] For details, see the tables and lists in A. Kuenen, *An Historico-Critical Inquiry into the Origin and Composition of the Hexateuch* (London: MacMillan, 1886), 76–77; Swete, **Introduction*, 231–32, 234–36; **BHS ad* Exod 36:8. I follow the numbering of the verses of LXX in J.W. Wevers, *Exodus* (Septuaginta

LXX lacks and adds sections. Knohl stresses the fact that LXX lacks the incense altar (MT-Exod 35:15; 37:25–28), although that translation does mention incense in Exod 38:25 = MT-Exod 37:29. According to Knohl, LXX reflects a first compositional layer that mentioned only the *olah* altar, while the later MT refers to two altars.[17] Likewise, according to Kuenen, Aejmelaeus, Schenker, and Carr,[18] the Hebrew text underlying LXX preceded the more developed MT. LXX-Exod 35–40 differs more from the instructions in Exodus 25–31 than those of MT-Exod 35–40, and for Aejmelaeus this is reason enough to consider LXX earlier than the somewhat harmonized version of MT.[19] Therefore, I delay a decision regarding this LXX text; the mentioned midrashic elements in this translation may point to its secondary nature.

2.1.5 Textual Development of the Torah

By its very nature, textual criticism deals with the written stage of the development of a composition. This description therefore focuses on the textual history of that composition starting with the earliest textual evidence, disregarding oral development. Thus, by definition, this analysis does not refer to the comparison or recording of different parallel stories in the Torah.

Our description takes the textual evidence as its point of departure, and not any of the textual theories on the history of the Scripture text, such as de Lagarde's theory of the original text, Kahle's theory of early parallel texts, or the local texts theory (→ 1.1.1.2; → 1.2.1). All these abstract theories derived from general ideas and not the evidence itself. In contrast, the following description attempts to be text-based, but is not necessarily more objective than any of the others.

No solid facts are known about the textual condition of the Torah prior to 250 B.C.E., that is, the period of the first Qumran fragments (→ 2.1.2.1 above; → 2.2.1.7.9), and therefore whatever happened before the third pre-Christian century is mere speculation. For example, scholars speculate on the original text(s) of the biblical books and on the number of copies that circulated in ancient Israel in early times. Large-scale differences between texts, such as in Genesis 5 and 11 (see above, → 2.1.4.1) may have been created in these early centuries, but it is hard to date these and similar developments.

Written documents must have existed from a very early period although the date of the beginning of the textual transmission is unknown. It is natural to assume that the textual transmission began when the compositions contained in the biblical books had been completed. However, limited copying had already begun at an earlier stage when segments of the Scripture books existed in written form prior to the completion of the composition process. A description of the transmission of the biblical text thus begins with the completion of the literary compositions and, to a certain extent, even beforehand.

It seems that each of the literary genres developed differently during the course of their textual transmission. Major differences between textual witnesses are probably found in all types of literature. On the whole, scribes who allowed themselves the liberty of changing the content did so more frequently in prose than in poetry segments because prose texts can be rewritten more easily than poetry. However, by way of exception, some poetic texts were nevertheless rewritten.[20] On the other hand, in the final stages of the literary development of the Torah such as reflected in the textual witnesses, little rewriting activity is evidenced in the reworking of legal sections. Thus, there are hardly any cases where a law has been

---

Vetus Testamentum Graecum 2.1; Göttingen: Vandenhoeck & Ruprecht, 1991).

[17] Conversation 27.5.2013.

[18] Kuenen, *Historico-Critical Inquiry*, 73; A. Aejmelaeus, "Septuagintal Translation Techniques: A Solution to the Problem of the Tabernacle Account," in A. Aejmelaeus, *Trail*, 116–30 (121); A. Schenker, "Der Ursprung des massoretischen Textes im Licht der literarischen Varianten im Bibeltext," *Textus* 23 (2007): 51–67 (59–60); Carr, *Formation*, 104.

[19] Aejmelaeus, "Tabernacle Account," 128–30.

[20] See the rewritten Song of Miriam in 4QRP^c (4Q365) 6aii and c.

added or omitted in one of the textual witnesses. There are also almost no instances in which the core of a law has been harmonized to another one when they differed. For example, it would have been easy to adapt a law in Deuteronomy to a parallel one in Exodus, Leviticus, or Numbers or vice versa but, with very few exceptions, changes of this kind simply were not made. The editors/scribes knew the limitations of their activities, and had they inserted such changes in legal material, they would have been changing divine utterances and would have obliterated the differences between the Pentateuchal law codes. One major exception to this description is found in the small harmonizing additions (less frequently: changes) in LXX, and less so in the SP group and other sources based on the formulation of parallel laws, but as a rule they do not alter the content of the laws themselves.[21]

The textual development of the five books of the Torah differed from that of the other Scripture books, but this fact has escaped the attention of scholars[22] with the exception of an important study made by Kahle on the basis of the limited evidence that was available to him in 1915.[23] The central position of the Torah becomes clear when the following three criteria are reviewed:

1) The percentage of copies of the individual books of the Torah found at Qumran (43 %) is twice as high as its relative position among the Bible books (22.5 %), and three times as high (62.5 %) as the figures at the other Judean Desert sites.[24] Genesis and Deuteronomy were especially popular, not only among the Torah books, but also among the combined Scripture books, along with Isaiah and Psalms. The popularity of the Torah is also shown by the large number of its Targumim (Onqelos and three different Palestinian Targumim: Pseudo-Jonathan, the Fragment Targum, and the Targum included in Codex Neofiti [→ 2.4.3.3]). These manifold translations reflect the importance of the Aramaic versions of the Torah for rabbinic Judaism. For all other books, only a single Targum is known apart from the two Targumim of Esther (→ 13–17.1.3);

2) The Torah is unique in that its textual branches are much more numerous than those of the other Scripture books. In the other Scripture books, one finds attestations of a single textual branch (Judges, Job, Ruth, Qohelet, Lamentations, Psalms, and probably also Isaiah) and rarely of three branches (Joshua and Samuel), but usually of two different branches (MT and LXX), as in 1–2 Kings, Jeremiah, Ezekiel, Proverbs, Esther, Canticles, Daniel, Ezra–Nehemiah, and Chronicles. The large number of text branches in the Torah text indicates the wide exegetical activity displayed in the copies of the Torah, including completely rewritten segments. Such activity took place in spite of its special sacred character and, more likely, because of it. Paradoxically, because of its popularity, the text of the Torah was altered more than that of the other books;

---

[21] See the many examples adduced by Teeter, *Scribal Laws*, 118–74.

[22] For example, this aspect was not mentioned by G.J. Brooke, "Torah in the Qumran Scrolls," in *Bibel in jüdischer und christlicher Tradition: Festschrift für Johann Maier zum 60. Geburtstag* (eds. H. Merklein et al.; Bonn: Anton Hain, 1993), 97–120; S. White Crawford, "The Qumran Pentateuch Scrolls: Their Literary Growth and Textual Tradition," in *The Qumran Legal Texts between the Hebrew Bible and Its Interpretation* (eds. K. De Troyer and A. Lange; Leuven: Peeters, 2011), 3–16.

[23] P. Kahle, "Untersuchungen zur Geschichte des Pentateuchtextes," *TSK* 88 (1915): 399–439; repr. in P. Kahle, *Opera Minora* (Leiden: Brill, 1956), 3–37. This study is quoted according to the page numbers of the latter publication. When Kahle wrote his study in 1915, he was familiar with less than half of the Torah texts known today but, even within the triad of witnesses of MT, LXX, and SP, he sensed that they reflected a special reality that differed from that of the other Scripture books. Some of the major conclusions of that study may not be acceptable, but Kahle opened up the area of the Torah for wide investigation and he had important insights into the nature of SP and LXX.

[24] For the figures, see Tov, *TCHB*, 96–98 and E. Tov, "Some Thoughts about the Diffusion of Biblical Manuscripts in Antiquity," in *Transmission of Traditions and Production of Texts* (eds. S. Metso et al.; STDJ 92; Leiden: Brill, 2010), 151–72.

3) The Torah is unique in that it is the only Scripture book in which *textual* features are recognizable, namely harmonizations and variants replacing problematic readings, all of which reflect a free approach to the text.

Thanks to the Qumran discoveries, we are now aware of many textual branches[25] of the Torah contained in groups of texts and individual texts, together constituting between ten and twelve branches.[26] In my view, all these texts, with the exception of the liturgical texts, enjoyed the status of authoritative Scripture texts. In the current state of knowledge (2016), the MT group may be considered as reflecting the oldest tradition of the Torah text, or the "trunk," from which the other textual groups branched off, while the status of items 9–12 is unclear. A second scenario would be that all known texts would have branched off from a common trunk, but in my view the multitude of secondary readings in the non-MT texts precludes such an option. A third possibility would be the assumption of three parallel stems, à la Paul Kahle, but this assumption has never been substantiated. Therefore I resort to the view of a single trunk, that of MT (block I), from which block II (all other textual traditions) branched off. The following list of the ancient Torah texts includes all presumed textual branches of the Torah, listed in their presumed historical sequence.

1) MT (proto-Masoretic texts; → 2.2.2): all the texts found at the Judean Desert sites except for Qumran are virtually identical to the medieval text of MT (→ 1.2.2). Further, at Qumran we find many scrolls that are *close* to MT and are often named "MT-like" or "semi-Masoretic." In my view (→ 2.1.6 below), the proto-Masoretic texts hold a central place in the development of the Torah text, while the great majority of the other texts represent later developments. The proto-MT group is reflected by Scripture texts from the Judean Desert, *tefillin* (MurPhyl, 34SePhyl, 8QPhyl I), most ancient translations and quotations in rabbinic literature. The MT-like group is reflected by Scripture texts from Qumran and *tefillin* (XHevSePhyl).

The following sources (2–12? = block II) probably derived from the proto-MT group (= block I), as most of them contain many secondary readings in comparison with MT although they contain primary readings as well. These sources probably branched off from MT as one large LXX-SP Palestinian group (2–4), from which again further branches and twigs developed. It seems now clear (2016) that the history of the text of the Torah should be understood in terms of two large text blocks, the group of MT and its congeners (1 = block I) on the one hand, and the LXX-SP group (2–4) and its congeners (5–8) on the other (= block II). Virtually all rewritten compositions are based on the second textual block, while the MT text is quoted only in rabbinic literature.[27] The status of texts 9–12 is unclear.

---

[25] The nature of these "branches" in relation to the "tree" or the "trunk" is unclear because it is not known which part of the texts extant in the last centuries B.C.E. and the first century C.E. has been preserved until today. As a result, the distance between the various witnesses and their number cannot be assessed well. The term "branch" may in some cases seem exaggerated, and for some witnesses the term "twig" may be more appropriate (suggested by S. White Crawford, personal communication, 2015). For example, in the case of the SP group, I characterize the ancient pre-Samaritan scrolls together with the medieval sources as representing two twigs coming from a common branch. I consider the related pre-Samaritan text 4QNum^b a separate branch because of its idiosyncratic nature (see the remark below), but others may consider this a twig in the SP group. Likewise, the nature and number of the Reworked Pentateuch texts and liturgical texts needs to be further defined.

[26] All of these are "texts" with the exception of the SP group (SP and the pre-Samaritan texts), which reflects a recension. The most characteristic readings of the SP group were created by editorial changes inserted in the earlier text. For an analysis of these editorial changes, see M. Segal, "The Text of the Hebrew Bible in Light of the Dead Sea Scrolls," in *Materia giudaica* 12 (2007): 5–20; Tov, **HB, GB, and Qumran*, 57–70; M. Kartveit, *The Origin of the Samaritans* (VTSup 128; Leiden: Brill, 2009), 259–312; M.M. Zahn, *Rethinking Rewritten Scripture: Composition and Exegesis in the 4QReworked Pentateuch Manuscripts* (STDJ 95; Leiden: Brill, 2011).

[27] See my study "The Textual Base of the Biblical Quotations in Second Temple Compositions," forthcoming.

2) The first textual tradition that branched off from the LXX–SP base (→ 2.2.3)[28] was the *Vorlage* of LXX (→ 2.4.1), reflecting early as well as late elements. LXX remained closer to the common LXX-SP base than the SP group.

3–4) At a later stage, the SP (→ 2.2.4) group branched off from the common LXX–SP source. The SP group consists of three layers, in historical sequence: a single pre-Samaritan text 4QNum[b] (3), reflecting a transition stage between LXX and the SP group, the other pre-Samaritan texts (4), and the medieval texts continuing the pre-Samaritan texts (4a).

5) Two additional texts (group 5) reflect a further development of the SP group, viz., 4QRP[a] (4Q158)[29] and 4QRP[b] (4Q364), but they differ substantially from SP since that group almost never inserts elements not found elsewhere in MT. On the other hand, group 5 inserts exegetical elements that are not found in any of the other witnesses (→ 2.2.1.7; → 2.2.3.4).

6–7) The next sources to depart from the SP group are two exegetical Torah scrolls, 4QReworkedPentateuch[c–d], each of them carrying individual features (→ 2.2.1.7; → 2.2.3.4). They contain running biblical texts intertwined with large and small exegetical additions such as an expanded Song of Miriam in 4QRP[c] 6aii and 6c, not equaled by any other source. The two texts are clearly closer to LXX-SP than to MT.

8) Several liturgical texts display more agreements with LXX-SP than with MT: 4QDeut[j, kl, n] → (2.2.1.7.17, → 2.2.1.7.18) that carried the same passages as the *tefillin*[30] and two groups of *tefillin* from Qumran.[31] They probably were based on the LXX-SP group. In these texts, harmonization, including the addition of small pericopes, is the main textual-editorial feature. These texts probably carried authority as liturgical texts, but not as Scripture texts.[32]

9–12) Appendix: Four texts are not exclusively close to any of the mentioned texts:[33] 4Q[Gen-]Exod[b] (→ 2.2.1.7.7), 11QpaleoLev[a] (→ 2.2.1.7.12),[34] 4QDeut[c, h] (→ 2.2.1.7.15; → 2.2.1.7.16). Because many or most of the scrolls from antiquity have been lost, the impression is created as if these four frag-

---

[28] In all five books of the Pentateuch these two sources agree frequently in secondary readings, especially in harmonizing pluses. This agreement is extended to the so-called pre-Samaritan Qumran texts. Compared with MT, the two texts also have in common a revision of the genealogical lists in Genesis 5 and 11, in which clear revisional and hence secondary traits are recognizable. This understanding was initiated by Gesenius, *Pent. Sam.*, 24 who named the common text of the SP and LXX an "Alexandrino-Samaritan edition," and was continued in my own studies such as of Deuteronomy in Tov, *HB, GB, and Qumran*, 271–82.

[29] The 2011 study of M.M. Zahn, "Building Textual Bridges: Towards an Understanding of 4Q158 (4QReworked Pentateuch A)," in *The Mermaid and the Partridge, Essays from the Copenhagen Conference on Revising Texts from Cave Four* (eds. G.J. Brooke and J. Høgenhaven; Leiden: Brill, 2011), 13–32 stressed the independent nature of that text.

[30] 4QDeut[j] contains sections from Deuteronomy 5, 8, 10, 11, 32 and Exodus 12, 13; 4QDeut[kl] contains sections from Deuteronomy 5, 11, 32; 4QDeut[n] contains passages from Deuteronomy 8 and 5.

[31] See my forthcoming study "The *Tefillin* from the Judean Desert and the Textual Criticism of the Hebrew Bible." Two groups of *tefillin* are closely related to the LXX-SP text base as opposed to MT, one written in a conservative spelling pattern, often close to MT (4QPhyl C, D-E-F, R, S; 4QPhyl 4; 8QPhyl II; XQPhyl1–3), while another one is written in the pattern of the Qumran Scribal Practice (4QPhyl A, B, G-H-I, J-K, L-N, O, P, Q).

[32] The liturgical character of 4QDeut[j] is the more likely because of its small size. See Tov, *HB, GB, and Qumran*, 37. Note further that both 4QDeut[j] and 4QDeut[n] start with Deut 5:1 and continue until the beginning of ch. 6. Both texts also contain a fragment that covers Deut 8:5–10. See Eshel, "4QDeut[n]," 151.

[33] Because of their fragmentary condition, not all the Qumran texts that are probably non-aligned are included in this list. Probable candidates are: 4QGen[k]; 4QExod[d], covering Exod 13:15–16 and 15:1, and thus omitting the narrative sections Exod 13:17–22 and Exodus 14, possibly containing an abbreviated Exodus text; 4QDeut[q], in some ways close to LXX (→ 2.2.1.6.3); 5QDeut (→ 2.2.1.5).

[34] See my study "The Textual Character of the Leviticus Scroll from Qumran Cave 11," *Shnaton* 3 (1978): 238–44 [Hebr. with Eng. summ.].

mentary scrolls deserve a special place in the stemma, but due to the loss of data the situation remains unclear.

This classification does not include texts whose major deviation from the others is in their orthographic character. Thus, many texts copied according to the so-called Qumran Scribal Practice reflect an orthography and morphology that diverge widely from the other texts. This practice is best known from 1QIsa[a], but is reflected also in several Torah scrolls and liturgical texts. A substantial group of *tefillin* is connected with the LXX-SP group (see n. 31). The status of 1QDeut[a] and 4QDeut[k2, m] is unclear. In any event, none of the texts written in the Qumran Scribal Practice is close to MT.

Owing to several uncertainties,[35] no precise number can be given for the textual branches in the Torah, but it is probably between ten and twelve, and much larger than the one to three branches in the other biblical books. In any event, the special sacred nature of the Torah, accepted by all, did not prevent its exegetical-literary and textual development as reflected in its widely divergent textual branches from the third century B.C.E. onwards. From our modern perspective, the opposite may have been expected, namely that the special sanctity of the Torah would have created a conservative approach of not allowing any changes in the text, as expressed by *b. Qidd.* 30a: "The ancients were called *soferim* because they counted every letter in the Torah." However, this statement reflects a time much later than that of the Qumran scrolls and it pertains only to the proto-Masoretic manuscripts.[36] This talmudic dictum shows that our modern thinking is often wrongly influenced by the character of only one segment of the transmission history of the Pentateuchal text, namely the proto-Masoretic tradition (see below, → 2.1.6).

All these data lead to the central question as to why so many textual branches were created in the Torah and not in the other books. In my view, this situation was due to the popularity[37] the Torah enjoyed because of its special sanctity.[38] The very act of inserting changes into each new copy of a Torah scroll, often creating a new textual branch, was acceptable in early times. In a way, each scribe created a new version of the composition that was equally as authoritative as its predecessors. Among the known textual sources, only MT disallowed such changes, at least after the mid-third century B.C.E., from which time the oldest scrolls are known (for the dichotomy and the other texts, see below, → 2.1.6).

The popularity of the Torah also brought about the creation of many new literary works, the so-called rewritten Bible compositions that reworked the stories and legal segments of the Torah: *Jubilees, Enoch,* 4–11QTemple, 4QApocryphon of Moses, and many additional Qumran compositions. These new compositions created additional textual branches in addition to those of the direct text witnesses. The biblical quotations in these texts were not based on MT, but on the popularizing pre-Samaritan text tradition and the Hebrew source of LXX, as is visible in 4QTest,[39] 4QComm Gen A (4Q252), 4–11QTemple,[40] *Jubi-*

---

[35] The following uncertainties should be taken into consideration: 1) the SP group is counted as three units, see above, and not as two or one unit(s); 2) the exact number of the liturgical texts is unknown; 3) four "non-aligned" texts were singled out (9–12), but their number could have been larger.

[36] Jeremiah and Ezekiel also display recognizable features, namely a short text tradition (LXX and two Qumran scrolls) as opposed to a long one (MT and two Qumran scrolls), but these features were probably created at the literary-development stage of the books.

[37] See Tov, "The Scribal and Textual Transmission of the Torah Analyzed in Light of Its Sanctity," in *Pentateuchal Traditions in the Late Second Temple Period. Proceedings of the International Workshop in Tokyo, August 28–31, 2007* (eds. A. Moriya and G. Hata; JSJSup 158; Leiden: Brill, 2012), 57–72.

[38] In light of this, it is noteworthy that the copying procedures of the Torah were virtually identical to those of the other biblical books and all the non-biblical books. See Tov, **Scribal Practices,* 99–103, 108–18.

[39] In this sectarian text, each of the biblical sections reflects a different textual pattern: Exod 20:21 (a pre-Samaritan text combining MT-Deut 5:28–29 and 18:18–19 as in SP), Num 24:15–17 (undetermined character), and Deut 33:8–11 (very close to the non-aligned scroll 4QDeut[h]).

[40] See E. Tov, "The Temple Scroll and Old Testament Textual Criticism," *ErIsr* 16 (Harry M. Orlinsky Volume; eds. B.A. Levine

2.1.5 TEXTUAL DEVELOPMENT OF THE TORAH

lees,[41] the Genesis Apocryphon (probably),[42] CD, and the Cave 4 scrolls of the *Damascus Document*.[43] The Qumran textual evidence relating to the scrolls that were brought to Qumran does not show a preponderance of these pre-Samaritan texts since the textual tradition that was close to the MT-like texts was more central for the Qumranites.

It is noteworthy that the popularity and frequent use of Isaiah and Psalms, representing different literary genres, did not create deviating text branches. Probably the scribes of these books did not feel at ease rewriting Isaiah's prophecies or the psalmic literature, while other scribes felt at ease reworking the stories of the Torah.

A description of the features of the textual branches of the Torah allows us to better understand the relation between them and to compose a genealogical tree (*stemma*) that displays these relations graphically. After all, we often try to express an opinion on the relation between all ancient texts as background material for the exegetical and textual comparison of these texts. This stemma pertains only to the Torah. At the top of the stemma[44] stand the sources that do not display secondary features, namely proto-MT (1) continued by the medieval text. From this text branched off the "MT-like" texts, several *tefillin*, and several ancient versions (T, V, kaige-Th, Aquila, and Symmachus). Rather unexpectedly, contextual harmonization becomes the main criterion for characterizing the texts.[45] These harmonizations appear more in the Torah than in the other books, not because these books provide fewer occasions for harmonization, but because the scribes of the Torah scrolls endeavored to create what they considered to be near-perfect copies of the most sacred book of all.

The major group that branched off from MT was the common LXX–SP text. From it branched off in historical sequence: the Hebrew source of LXX (2) the SP group (3–4) and all other texts such as described above.

In this way, we are able to describe in broad strokes the development of the textual witnesses of the Torah. In my view, these proto-MT texts derived from a single copy or a very closely knit tradition. Most other texts branched off from that text or tradition, and their secondary features are often visible in their harmonizing character. Eshel had a premonition of the importance of this development when naming a group of Hebrew texts "harmonis-

---

and A. Malamat; Jerusalem: Israel Exploration Society/Hebrew Union College-Jewish Institute of Religion, 1982), 100–11 [Hebr. with Eng. summ.]; L.H. Schiffman, "The Septuagint and the Temple Scroll: Shared 'Halakhic' Variants," in *Septuagint, Scrolls and Cognate Writings: Papers Presented to the International Symposium on the Septuagint and Its Relations to the Dead Sea Scrolls and Other Writings* (Manchester, 1990) (eds. G.J. Brooke and B. Lindars; SBLSCS 33; Atlanta: Scholars Press, 1992), 277–97. I consider the *Vorlage* of this scroll "non-aligned," while Schiffman emphasizes the links between LXX and the Temple Scroll.

[41] According to J.C. VanderKam, *Textual and Historical Studies in the Book of Jubilees* (HSM 14; Missoula: Scholars Press, 1977), 137, *Jubilees* especially reflects readings of SP and LXX, texts that were "at home in Palestine." Similarly, Lange, **Handbuch*, 165.

[42] See J.C. VanderKam, "The Textual Affinities of the Biblical Citations in the Genesis Apocryphon," *JBL* 97 (1978): 45–55.

[43] See the data provided by Lange, **Handbuch*, 158–64.

[44] A different type of *stemma* is presented by Lange, **Handbuch*, 173. Among the leading ideas of that *stemma* that differ from our own reconstruction are: 1) LXX preceded MT; 2) SP preceded MT; 3) 4QDeut^q ought to be positioned closer to LXX. In determining proximity between textual sources, common mistakes ("Leitfehler") are often taken into consideration. However, in my view, in the case of Hebrew Scripture too few sources have been preserved in order to make this argument a sound principle. Another type of stemma is presented in the exemplification of Kahle's ideas presented best in a chart in E. Sellin and G. Fohrer, *Einleitung in das Alte Testament* (10th ed.; Heidelberg: Quelle & Meyer, 1965), 567 in which the development of the text of the Torah is described as a three-branched tree (MT, LXX, and SP), presenting three text types. This chart illustrates the classical view of both the tripartite division and the character of the textual witnesses that remained standard in the research until the importance of the Dead Sea Scrolls became truly felt. A further type of stemma of the text of Exodus is offered by R.S. Hendel, "Assessing the Text-Critical Theories of the Hebrew Bible after Qumran," in *The Oxford Handbook of the Dead Sea Scrolls* (eds. T.H. Lim and J.J. Collins; Oxford: Oxford University Press, 2010), 281–302.

[45] Thus already E. Eshel, "4QDeut^n." The importance of this textual and literary criterion is also stressed much by Carr, **Formation*, 90–98.

tic."⁴⁶ I go one step further in recognizing harmonizing tendencies in all texts in block II.

Needless to say, this description sketches the development of the texts only in general lines. With regard to individual readings, we are reminded of the famous dictum of de Lagarde: "ich glaube ... das keine hds der LXX so gut ist, dass sie nicht oft genug schlechte lesarten, keine so schlecht dass sie nicht mitunter ein gutes körnchen böte." [I believe ... that no manuscript of the LXX is so good that it contains no bad readings, and that not one is so bad that it does not contain an occasional pearl.]⁴⁷

2.1.6 Two Different Scribal Approaches toward the Sacred Status of the Torah

The Torah had a distinctive, sacred status that could have influenced all of its scribes to approach that book with special care and a lower level of scribal intervention than the other Scripture books. However, the evidence does not support such an assumption across the board. When examining the approach of scribes towards the Torah, a clear distinction can be made between two types of scribes (→ 1.2.2.3): 1) scribes of all the ancient Torah scrolls except for those of the proto-Masoretic tradition; and 2) scribes copying the proto-MT scrolls and subsequently MT. The Torah was greatly hallowed by all the scribes, more so than the other books. However, the adoption of this sanctity had different implications for different groups of scribes. In the period for which we have textual evidence (from 250 B.C.E. onwards), for the scribes of group 2 this sanctity implied an approach of not changing the content. On the other hand, all other scribes (group 1) approached that text like any other text, Scripture or otherwise, freely changing its content, language, small details, and orthography, thus multiplying textual variation. The two groups are unequally distributed among the known scrolls because group 1 contains many more different *types* of witnesses. On the other hand, among the Judean Desert texts, the proto-Masoretic texts are the most frequent.⁴⁸

With regard to both groups, it should be emphasized that in most technical areas, scribes did not distinguish between biblical and non-biblical scrolls.⁴⁹ This conclusion pertains to the following parameters: writing materials; technical aspects of the writing (length of scrolls, sheets, and columns; number of columns per sheet; height of columns, margins, horizontal and vertical ruling; repair-stitching; patching; initial and final handle sheets; use of guide dots/strokes); writing practices, such as divisions between words, small sense units (stichs and verses), and larger sense units; the special layout of poetical units, scribal marks, correction procedures, and scripts.⁵⁰

2.1.6.1 Scribes of All the Texts Except for MT

The scribes of the many different Torah texts found in the Judean Desert together with the SP group and the *Vorlage* of LXX did not interpret the concept of sanctity in the same way as the scribes of the proto-MT texts. They display a free approach at all levels as is visible in the comparison of these sources with

---

⁴⁸ For a different opinion on the number of proto-Masoretic Torah scrolls that once existed, see → 1.2.2.2.3.

⁴⁹ Under these circumstances, it would not be unusual to find scribes who copied both a Torah scroll and other scrolls. Such a scribe has not been found, but relevant evidence has been found beyond the Torah in the scribe who copied the non-biblical texts 1QS, 1QSa, 1QSb, and the biblical 4QSamᶜ. The hand of this scribe is also visible in several corrections in 1QIsaᵃ. For further details regarding Qumran scribes who wrote more than one manuscript, see Tov, *Scribal Practices*, 23–24.

⁵⁰ The rules for the writing of sacred texts recorded in *Massekhet Soferim* and in earlier rabbinic sources create the impression that they were devised especially for the writing of sacred books. However, most details recorded there pertain to writing practices employed in an identical way in non-sacred texts during the Second Temple period. For example, *Sop.* 1.15 states that texts that deviate from the norm regarding the indication of open and closed sections cannot be used as sacred writings. However, this practice, which is basically a paragraphing system, was followed in most compositions written in the Qumran period, biblical and non-biblical. Thus, the practice itself was not limited to the copying of Scripture, and hence was not sacred, but the tradition of indicating a specific type of paragraphing in a given instance in MT carried authority.

---

⁴⁶ Eshel, "4QDeutⁿ," 117–54.

⁴⁷ De Lagarde, *Anmerkungen*, 3 n. 1.

the proto-MT texts and any of the sources of the other Scripture books:

– *Editorial intervention*. The various witnesses of the Torah (SP, many Qumran scrolls listed above in → 2.1.5, the *Vorlage* of LXX) reflect the same degree of editorial intervention as in the other books.
– *Orthography and morphology*. The scribal practice of applying a special, very full orthography and a special morphological system to a number of Qumran scrolls was used for Torah scrolls as well. This idiosyncratic orthography and morphology, best known from 1QIsa^a (→ 6.2.1.1), is found also in 1QDeut^a, 2QExod^b?, 2QNum^b?, 2QDeut^c?, 4Q[Gen]Exod^b, 4QExod^j?, 4QNum^b, 4QDeut^j V–XII, 4QDeut^{k1}, 4QDeut^{k2}, and 4QDeut^m. Most of these scrolls are also copied inconsistently and in careless handwriting.
– *Harmonizations*. The manuscripts of the Torah contain many harmonizing additions and changes in small details. Contrary to the majority view in the scholarly literature, this phenomenon actually prevails more in LXX than in the SP group (→ 1.3.1.1.12). Although there are no comparative statistics regarding the level of harmonization in the various Scripture books, we cannot avoid the impression that there are more such phenomena in the Torah than in the other books. There are many occasions for harmonization in the prose books from Joshua to 2 Kings and in Chronicles that have remained unharmonized. The absence of major harmonizing in the post-Pentateuchal books must be ascribed to a lack of interest in making the details in these books match one another. Presumably there was a constant interest in improving the divine message of the Torah; from a textual point of view, these improvements involved a great amount of freedom.
– *Scribal intervention*. A calculation of the average number of corrections in each scroll[51] shows that the approach towards biblical texts including the Torah is not more careful than that towards non-biblical texts. At the same time, many biblical scrolls display a low level of scribal intervention, especially texts written in the paleo-Hebrew script[52] as well as several other texts. Most other Torah texts hold an intermediate position regarding the amount of scribal intervention.

As a result, paradoxically, many scrolls of the Torah were rewritten and changed more extensively than the texts of other biblical books in the Second Temple period, due to the Torah's popularity resulting from its sanctity, thus causing increased textual variation (see above, → 2.1.5).

2.1.6.2 Scribes of the Proto-Masoretic Tradition

The major feature of the proto-Masoretic texts as compared with the other texts is their precision in matters of content and scribal conventions. This precision is also visible in the Torah pericopes included in the *tefillin* of the MT type (especially Mur-Phyl, 34SePhyl, and 8QPhyl I; see p. 10 above). These pericopes are written in the orthography of MT and reflect the pericopes prescribed in rabbinic literature, differing from the *tefillin* that contain different pericopes and are written in the Qumran Scribal Practice. Accordingly, the concept of sacredness adopted by the circle that perpetuated the proto-Masoretic text was that of not changing the Torah text, at least as it is known to us from the period of the mid-third century B.C.E. onwards.

Reflecting this approach, the proto-Masoretic texts found at the various sites in the Judean Desert other than Qumran were copied with great care.

---

[51] The level of scribal intervention can be measured by dividing the number of lines preserved (in full or in part) by the number of instances of scribal intervention (linear or supralinear corrections, deletions, erasures, reshaping of letters). A high level of scribal intervention (an average of one correction in less than ten lines) is visible in 1QIsa^a and several other biblical scrolls, including two Torah scrolls: 4QDeut^m (Qumran scribal practice), 5QDeut, 4QJosh^b, 4QJudg^b, 4QIsa^a, 4QJer^a, 4QXII^c, 4QXII^e, 11QPs^a, 4QCant^b, 4QQoh^a. See the tabulations in Tov, *Scribal Practices*, 279–88, 332–35.

[52] 4QpaleoGen-Exod^l (MT), 4QpaleoExod^m (SP), 4QpaleoDeut^r (MT), 11QpaleoLev^a (independent). See below.

They were internally identical, and virtually agree with the medieval MT. These texts differ as much from codex MT[L] as the medieval manuscripts of MT differ from one another (Tov, *TCHB*, 29–31). The MT-like manuscripts from Qumran are slightly more distant from the medieval manuscripts (Tov, *TCHB*, 31–33). It seems to us that this identity could have been achieved only if all the manuscripts from the Judean Desert were copied from a single source, a master copy located in a central place, probably the temple until 70 C.E., and subsequently in another central location (Jamnia?).[53]

Two features reflect the scribal care of the proto-Masoretic tradition:

– *Deluxe format.* A remarkably large percentage of the proto-Masoretic Judean Desert scrolls display a *deluxe* format,[54] reflecting scribal care. From 50 B.C.E. onwards, large *deluxe* scroll editions were prepared especially for proto-Masoretic biblical scrolls, and within that group, mainly for the Torah.[55] In fact, *all* the scrolls from Naḥal Ḥever, Murabbaʿat, and Masada for which the margins are known are of this type, while MasLev[a] (2.8 cm), MasLev[b] (2.7 cm), and 5/6HevPs (2.5–2.7 cm) come very close (all the biblical scrolls found at these sites attest an unpointed text that is almost completely identical to the medieval consonantal text of MT).

– *Paleo-Hebrew Torah Scrolls.* The preserved Bible texts written in the paleo-Hebrew script contain only texts of the Torah and Job.[56] These ancient books were thus singled out for writing in the paleo-Hebrew script. Texts written in that script were copied more carefully than most texts written in the square script. Most of these paleo-Hebrew texts reflect the proto-Masoretic text, but since 4QpaleoExod[m] (close to SP) reflects a different tradition, the very minimal scribal intervention should not be connected to the proto-Masoretic character of these scrolls, but rather to the milieu in which scribes wrote in this special script (Sadducees?).[57]

2.1.7 Authoritative Status (→ 11.2.1)

The oldest part of Hebrew Scripture, the Torah, perceived as God's word, carried authority for all later generations, as is visible in the later Scripture books. The Torah influenced the prophets, exemplified by the influence of Leviticus on Ezekiel and that of Deuteronomy on Jeremiah. Likewise, the earlier historical books carried authority in the eyes of the Chronicler, who reworked them.

Before the time of the earliest textual witnesses from Qumran, that is, before the middle of the third century B.C.E., authoritative scrolls were circulating that contained different textual forms. It is necessary to make this assumption if LXX of the Torah was indeed prepared at the beginning of the third

---

[53] This identity is evident from the discussion in *b. B. Bat.* 14b and from the names of the three scrolls found in the temple court relating to passages in the Torah. See *m. Kelim* 15.6; *m. Moʿed Qaṭ.* 3.4; *b. B. Bat.* 14b; *b. Yoma* 69a–b; *y. Sanh.* 2.20c. This master copy is known from rabbinic sources as the *sefer ha-ʿazara* probably referring only to the Torah, but it stands to reason that the other Scripture books were also found in the temple. In rabbinic literature, a scroll copied from this master copy was named a "corrected scroll," *sefer muggah*. For this purpose, the temple employed professional *maggihim*, "correctors" or "revisers," whose task it was to safeguard precision in the copying of the text. For example, "*maggihim* of books in Jerusalem received their fees from the temple funds" (*b. Ketub.* 106a). Tov, *TCHB*, 29–31 suggested that some of these "corrected copies" were found in the Judean Desert at sites other than Qumran (the first circle), and that the MT-like copies found at Qumran (the second circle), which are more distant from MT, were copied from them.

[54] The assumption of *deluxe* editions is based on the following parameters: 1) Large margins usually accompany texts with a large format; 2) The great majority of the scrolls written in *deluxe* format reflect the medieval text of MT. Since the *deluxe* format was used mainly for scrolls of the Masoretic family, we assume that these scrolls followed the rules of the spiritual center of Judaism in Jerusalem, the same center that subsequently formulated the writing instructions that were transmitted in the Talmud and *Massekhet Soferim*; 3) As a rule, *deluxe* rolls had fewer mistakes that needed correction and are therefore characterized by a low level of scribal intervention.

[55] For a list, see Tov, *Scribal Practices*, 125–29. The Torah scrolls are: 2QNum[a], 4QGen[b], 4QExod[c], 4QpaleoGen-Exod[l], 4QpaleoExod[m], 4QDeut[g] 11, 4QDeut[kl], MurGen 1, MurNum 6, XHev/SeNum[b], 34SeNum, MasDeut. Among the thirty Judean Desert luxury scrolls, twelve (40%) are of the Torah.

[56] Note that the latter is traditionally ascribed to Moses.

[57] Thus Tov, *Scribal Practices*, 248.

century B.C.E. (→ 1.3.1.1.5), since its *Vorlage* differed from MT, which probably already existed at that time. However, we have no further tangible evidence for textual plurality in earlier periods.

In the discussion of the status of Scripture scrolls before the first century C.E., we limit ourselves to the known evidence, thus necessarily focusing on the Judean Desert scrolls. The main question is, were *all* the copies of Scripture scrolls found there considered authoritative? There is no unequivocal answer to this question, since there is no consensus among scholars regarding the nature of many "biblical" scrolls.

Authoritative scrolls are scrolls that were considered to contain "Scripture," which one could study, from which one could quote, which one could read in religious gatherings or in one's personal meditation, and which formed the basis for religious practice, especially Halakha. I distinguish between such authoritative Scripture scrolls and scrolls with scriptural content, that is Scripture-like scrolls that were not considered to be Scripture, viz., partial Scripture scrolls, and liturgical scrolls. However, for many scholars, these liturgical and partial scrolls are also considered Scripture, thus complicating the analysis. We distinguish between three types of scrolls found at Qumran. This discussion pertains to Scripture as a whole, with a special application to the Torah.

1) *Authoritative Scripture Scrolls*. In the Qumran corpus, scholars count between 210 and 212 fragmentary Scripture scrolls found in eleven Qumran caves. This number also includes the following two groups, which in my thinking need to be removed from the main group, reducing the overall number of Scripture scrolls by some forty.
2) *Partial Scripture Scrolls*. A small number of Torah scrolls covering only parts of books were probably meant for personal use:
   4QExod^d, covering Exod 13:15–16 and 15:1, thus omitting the narrative sections Exod 13:17–22 and Exodus 14;
   4QDeut^q: This scroll probably covered only the Song of Moses.
3) *Liturgical Scrolls (or Personal Copies)*. The liturgical character of scrolls is presumed for several scrolls of the Torah and Psalms. The assumption of such a use for these scrolls is more commonly accepted for the Torah scrolls than for the Psalms scrolls. In the Torah, we can also easily posit an opposition between liturgical and other scrolls, while in the Qumran Psalms there is no visible opposition between the presumed liturgical scrolls and an MT Psalter since unmistakable copies of an MT Psalter were not found at Qumran (→ 10.2.1.1; → 10.2.2). In other words, the Qumran community did accept the Psalter as authoritative, but its Masoretic character, as in the Masada Psalters, cannot be established. Since the assumption of liturgical scrolls is not without doubt, it is also possible that these scrolls were prepared for personal use.

In the case of the Torah, a number of "Scripture" texts from the Judean Desert only contain segments of chapters that are also included in the *tefillin* and *mezuzot*,[58] as well as Deuteronomy 8,[59] and are therefore often described as liturgical.[60] The argument for their liturgical use is supported by the small size of several scrolls,[61] precluding the possibility that they would have contained a complete biblical book. The liturgical use of these

---

[58] The *tefillin* and *mezuzot* are not regular biblical texts, although they consist of Torah passages, separated by a *vacat* in the middle of the line or a blank line. The range of textual variation in these texts reflects the known variants between biblical manuscripts, and is not specific to these excerpted texts. At the same time, the juxtaposition of different texts is not referred to in literary or text-critical analyses. The Scripture chapters from which excerpts are included in the Qumran copies of these *tefillin* and *mezuzot* are: Exodus 12, 13; Deuteronomy 5, 6, 10, 11, 32. See Tov, "Excerpted and Abbreviated Biblical Texts," in *HB, GB, and Qumran*, 30–32.
[59] The assumption of liturgical use is based on an argument from silence, as other fragments of these scrolls may have been lost. Furthermore, in no case has a join between chapters been preserved in the scrolls mentioned below.
[60] For references to the liturgical use of some texts, see J.A. Duncan, *DJD* XIV: 79 and M. Weinfeld, "Grace after Meals," *JBL* 111 (1992): 427–40.
[61] 4QDeut^j: 14 lines; 4QDeut^n: 12–14 lines; 4QDeut^q: 11 lines; 4QPs^g: 8 lines.

scrolls would have included devotional reading from these chapters, privately or in religious gatherings.[62]

While the mentioned liturgical and abbreviated scrolls probably were not considered authoritative Scripture texts, all others were. However, how can we prove this point? One person's Scripture-like scroll is another's Scripture. I suggest that the default assumption should be that most Qumran scrolls were authoritative.

This assumption implies that the individual scrolls carried authority before the complete Scripture canon existed. We suggest that all the Scripture scrolls found at Qumran were considered authoritative by the Qumran community, as well as by all persons and communities in ancient Israel, although in the latter case it is unclear which source other than tradition granted that authority. The assumption of the acceptance of scrolls as authoritative outside Qumran is necessary since probably most Qumran scrolls were brought there from outside. The concept of "Scripture" refers to all the books of the Hebrew Bible contained in MT, and possibly more. This view on the granting of authority at Qumran and in the Judean Desert in general is based on several arguments that are discussed in detail elsewhere.[63] Typical for this period is the mixture of texts in the sectarian composition 4QTestimonia (4Q175), which quoted from three scrolls of a differing textual nature (together with a quotation from a non-biblical composition, 4QapocrJosh[b] [4Q379] 22), all of them considered authoritative. The first biblical quotation reflects SP in combining two Scripture verses that are remote in MT,[64] while the third one, from Deut 33:8–11, may have been based on 4QDeut[h], a textually independent scroll.[65] The second quotation, Num 24:15–17, is of undetermined character. The different nature of these scrolls shows that the author of 4QTestimonia used different types of scrolls without being aware of their mixture.

The textual plurality of the Qumran corpus comes to light in these data:

a) *Pluralistic collection.* The Qumran corpus is pluralistic,[66] due among other things to the different origin and nature of the scrolls that were imported into the community and copied locally.
b) *Lack of preference for a specific biblical text in the biblical quotations included in the* sectarian *Qumran compositions.* No specific text or text group is preferred in these quotations, as analyzed in detail by Lange, *Handbuch, 158–68.

The further back we go in time, the less the concept of the sanctity of the Torah influenced the textual transmission and, at an earlier stage, the final stage of editing. In the last centuries before the Common Era, the transmission of the Torah manuscripts as reflected in the Judean Desert texts was no more precise than that of the other books, except for the two features recognized (the use of *deluxe* Torah scrolls and of the paleo-Hebrew script; → 2.1.6.2) and they probably pertained only to certain groups within Judaism. This approach is also visible in the development of textual variety everywhere except for the Masoretic family.[67] Because of the great

---

[62] 4QDeut[j], containing sections from Deuteronomy 5, 8, 10, 11, 32, and Exodus 12, 13; 4QDeut[kl], containing sections from Deuteronomy 5, 11, 32; 4QDeut[n], covering Deuteronomy 8, 5 (in that sequence). On the liturgical Psalms scrolls, see → 2.1.5 above.

[63] E. Tov, "Were Early Hebrew Scripture Texts Authoritative?" forthcoming.

[64] The two pericopes that are remote in MT (Deut 5:28–29, 18:18–19) are combined in SP (Exod 20:21). 4QRP[a] (4Q158) frg. 6 likewise juxtaposes the two texts.

[65] See E. Tov, "The Contribution of the Qumran Scrolls to the Understanding of the LXX," in *Septuagint, Scrolls and Cognate Writings: Papers Presented to the International Symposium on the Septuagint and Its Relations to the Dead Sea Scrolls and Other Writings, Manchester, 1990* (eds. G.J. Brooke and B. Lindars; SBLSCS 33; Atlanta: Scholars Press, 1992), 11–47 (31–35); J.A. Duncan, "New Readings for the 'Blessing of Moses' from Qumran," *JBL* 114 (1995): 273–90; Lange, *Handbuch, 163–64.

[66] See Tov, *TCHB, 107–10; E. Ulrich, "Pluriformity in the Biblical Text, Text Groups, and Questions of Canon," in *Madrid Qumran Congress, 1.23–41; A. Lange, "The Textual Plurality of Jewish Scriptures in the Second Temple Period in Light of the Dead Sea Scrolls," in *Qumran and the Bible: Studying the Jewish and Christian Scriptures in Light of the Dead Sea Scrolls* (eds. N. David and A. Lange; CBET 57; Leuven: Peeters, 2010), 43–96.

[67] Only a limited amount of textual variety was created *within* the Masoretic family.

interest in the Torah, a sizeable number of manuscripts and new compositions were circulating, which ultimately gave rise to greater textual variation in the Five Books of Moses than in the other books.

2.1.8 History of Research

The history of research of the Torah parallels that of the complete Bible, but some theories were developed specifically for the Torah. Surprisingly little has been written about the textual development of the Torah with the exception of Kahle's epoch-making study of 1915 (*"Untersuchungen") and the studies recorded below.

Until 1947, when the first Qumran scrolls were discovered, the biblical text was known from many textual witnesses, both Hebrew and translated, early and late. These texts were generally described according to a certain internal hierarchy. From the beginning of the seventeenth century, when SP became known in Europe, scholars presupposed the central status of MT, SP, and the Hebrew *Vorlage* of LXX, and placed the remaining textual witnesses in a subordinate relation to one or the other of them, usually described as recensions or text types. At the same time, the term *recension* is also used with the general meaning of textual tradition or simply text.

As a rule, the text of the Torah has been represented as an entity subdivided into three *recensions* or *text types*: MT (→ 2.2.2), SP (→ 2.2.4), and LXX (→ 2.4.1). Moreover, scholars regarded these three texts as central axes around which other texts formed three distinct groups. The text of the Prophets and Hagiographa was similarly presented as consisting of two recensions (there is no Samaritan text in these books), although nevertheless it was sometimes described as consisting of three groups as well. The theories, descriptions, and terminology changed from one generation to the next, but the assumption of a tripartite division of the texts of the Torah and also, occasionally, of the rest of the biblical books remained constant throughout. Likewise, the understanding that these three texts (or two of them) constitute the central pillars of the biblical text remained constant, and far-reaching theories on the development of the biblical text, such as those of de Lagarde and Kahle, were based upon this belief.

The two conceptions described above developed as self-evident facts, although they have yet to be proven. From the seventeenth century until 1947, relatively few studies were written on the relation between the textual witnesses and the assumed development process of the biblical text. The first thorough description of its development is contained in Kahle, *"Untersuchungen," 1915. Before this time, scholars referred to the character of each textual witness separately, sometimes in connection with its relationship to MT.

Even though few comprehensive descriptions of the history of the biblical text were written in the period reviewed, the assumed relation between the textual witnesses was always reflected in the terminology used for these witnesses. This terminology is subject to passing tendencies and reflects the approach of scholars to the textual witnesses. Until the beginning of the twentieth century, the three main texts were usually described as "the Egyptian ⟨or: Alexandrian⟩ recension" (the reconstructed Hebrew *Vorlage* of LXX), "the Babylonian recension" (MT), and the "Samaritan recension" (SP).

A change in the terminology began to occur with the appearance of Kahle's influential study on the text of the Torah. Kahle called the three main witnesses of the Torah "drei Haupttypen des Pentateuchtextes."[68] In his view, "the three main types of the text of the Pentateuch" differed from one another recensionally, that is, each of them had undergone different recensional activity. Thus, in Kahle's opinion, MT did not always exist in its present form, but was created as the result of a process of revision of earlier texts in approximately 100 C.E. In fact, Kahle's innovation ("Texttypen," text types) was one of terminology rather than of the concept underlying it. The new terminology slowly penetrated the scholarly literature. The clearest exemplification of Kahle's ideas is to be

---

[68] Kahle, *"Untersuchungen," 436.

found in a chart presented by Sellin and Fohrer.[69] It should be noted that in the past (as in the present), no uniform terminology was applied to the textual witnesses. Various scholars used, and continue to use, different terms when referring to the same entity. For example, de Lagarde used the terms *recension* and *family* interchangeably, and this also applies to the mixed terminology used by those who adhere to the "theory of local texts."

The studies undertaken and conclusions drawn are instructive for understanding scholarly opinion on the relation between the textual witnesses. These studies show the self-imposed limitations of the scholars' approach, since they confined themselves to a comparison of the three so-called central texts mentioned above. Likewise, upon its discovery, each new source was immediately integrated into the existing framework of a bipartite or tripartite division. This approach can be illustrated by considering the evaluation of MT at a time when scholars still adhered to the view of there being two central recensions of the Torah (MT and LXX): When SP emerged as a new source in the seventeenth century, it was realized that 1,900 of the assumed 6,000 differences between SP and MT involved readings common to SP and LXX. Subsequently, an endless number of theories appeared concerning the special relation between SP and LXX. Such theories derived from the restricted view that the biblical text was current in a small number of recensions and that all textual witnesses necessarily belonged to one of them. In this case, it was suggested that LXX was translated from SP, or that SP was revised according to LXX, or, conversely, that LXX was revised according to SP. These and other theories show the limitations of an approach that was bound by the assumption of a tripartite or bipartite division of the textual witnesses of the Bible.

When the Qumran scrolls were found in 1947, scholars already had well-developed views concerning the transmission of the biblical texts. With the discovery of the first Qumran scrolls, these views, including the depiction of the relation between the textual witnesses, were not altered because it always takes time for the ramifications of new discoveries to be absorbed. Scholars continued to determine the place of the newly found scrolls within the framework of the tripartite division of the textual witnesses of the Torah that had been developed earlier. Scholars also continued the approach of previous generations in characterizing many Qumran scrolls as recensions or text types.

The assigning of individual Qumran texts to a particular text type is reflected in the literature from the appearance of the first volumes of the *DJD* series onwards, when most of the new scrolls were described as belonging to the MT "type," while some scrolls were assigned to the LXX or SP "type."

As an alternative to the generally accepted theory of a tripartite division of the textual witnesses, it was suggested by Tov in 1982 that the three above-mentioned textual witnesses constitute three of a larger number of *texts*.[70] This suggestion follows an assumption of a multiplicity of texts, rather than that of a tripartite division. However, not all the texts are unrelated to one another, since one can recognize among them two or more clusters. When analyzing those texts that include a few clusters, we should remember that only a few of a larger number of early texts have been preserved, thus complicating an exhaustive view of the relation between the known early texts.

Brooke, G.J., "Torah in the Qumran Scrolls," in *Bibel in jüdischer und christlicher Tradition: Festschrift für Johann Maier zum 60. Geburtstag* (eds. H. Merklein et al.; Bonn: Anton Hain, 1993), 97–120.

Carr, *Formation.

Eshel, E., "4QDeutⁿ: A Text That Has Undergone Harmonistic Editing," *HUCA* 62 (1991): 117–54.

Kahle, *"Untersuchungen"; repr. in P. Kahle, *Opera Minora* (Leiden: Brill, 1956), 3–37.

Lange, *Handbuch.

Lee, K.-J., *The Authority and Authorization of the Torah in the Persian Period* (Leuven: Peeters, 2011).

Skinner, J., *The Divine Names in Genesis* (London: Hodder and Stoughton, 1914).

---

[69] See n. 44.

[70] "A Modern Textual Outlook Based on the Qumran Scrolls," *HUCA* 53 (1982): 11–27.

Teeter, D.A., *Scribal Laws: Exegetical Variation in the Textual Transmission of Biblical Law in the Late Second Temple Period* (FAT 92; Tübingen: Mohr Siebeck, 2014).

Tov, E., "A Modern Textual Outlook Based on the Qumran Scrolls," *HUCA* 53 (1982): 11–27.

Tov, E., "The Scribal and Textual Transmission of the Torah Analyzed in Light of Its Sanctity," in *Pentateuchal Traditions in the Late Second Temple Period: Proceedings of the International Workshop in Tokyo, August 28–31, 2007* (eds. A. Moriya and G. Hata; JSJSup 158; Leiden: Brill, 2012), 57–72.

Tov, E., "Textual Harmonization in the Stories of the Patriarchs," in Tov, *Collected Writings 3*, 166–88.

Tov, E., "The Samaritan Pentateuch and the Dead Sea Scrolls: The Proximity of the Pre-Samaritan Qumran Scrolls to the SP," in Tov, *Collected Writings 3*, 387–410.

Tov, E., "Textual Developments in the Torah," in Tov, *Collected Writings 3*, 239–49.

Tov, E., "The Source of Source Criticism: The Relevance of Non-Masoretic Textual Witnesses," in *Text–Textgeschichte–Textwirkung, Festschrift zum 65. Geburtstag von Siegfried Kreuzer* (eds. Th. Wagner et al.; AOAT 419; Münster: Ugarit-Verlag, 2015), 283–301.

White Crawford, S., "The Qumran Pentateuch Scrolls: Their Literary Growth and Textual Tradition," in *The Qumran Legal Texts between the Hebrew Bible and Its Interpretation* (eds. K. De Troyer and A. Lange; Leuven: Peeters, 2011), 3–16.

Emanuel Tov

2.2 Ancient Hebrew Texts

2.2.1 Ancient, Late Ancient, and Early Medieval Manuscript Evidence

In this article[1] only the Pentateuch manuscripts from the Dead Sea as well as late ancient and early medieval Pentateuch manuscripts are discussed. Other textual evidence from antiquity, such as the Silver Scrolls from Ketef Hinnom, ancient *tefillin* and *mezuzot*, the Nash Papyrus, the Severus Scroll Variant List, and Rabbi Meir's Tora are addressed in → 2.2.5. A total of 106 manuscripts from the various sites around the Dead Sea that attest to the text of the Pentateuch have been published. Of these 106 manuscripts, only thirty-seven can still be classified in their textual typology. Twelve unpublished Dead Sea scrolls attesting to passages of the Pentateuch are held in four collections. Azusa Pacific University owns three fragments attesting to Lev 10:4–7 (Azusa 2); Deut 27:4–6 (Azusa 3; XDeut?); Deut 8:2–5 (Azusa 4) of which Azusa 3 was published by Charlesworth (→ 2.2.1.3.3).[2] The Green Collection includes four fragments attesting to Gen 31:23–25?; 32:3–7 (MOTB.SCR000124 = DSS F.Gen2); Exod 17:4–7 (MOTB.SCR000120 = DSS F.Exod6); Lev 23:4 (MOTB.SCR000122 = DSS F.Lev5); and Num 8:3–5 (MOTB.SCR003173 = DSS F.Num2).[3] Southwestern Baptist Theological Seminary acquired four fragments attesting to Exod 23:8–10 (DSS F.161 = DSS F.Exod2); Lev 20:24→18:28–30 (DSS F.162 = DSS F.Lev2); Deut 9:25–10:1 (DSS F.163 = DSS F.Deut3); Deut 12:11–14 (DSS F.164 = DSS F.Deut4).[4] A Genesis fragment with remnants of Gen 37:14–39:5 is still in the possession of the Kando family.[5] Given their small amount of preserved text, most of these fragments could easily attest to biblical quotations in a non-biblical context. All unpublished fragments are so small that a text-typological classification is difficult if not impossible. The only exception is the large Genesis fragment of the Kando family. The unpublished Pentateuch fragments therefore have little impact on our understanding of the textual history of the Hebrew text of the Pentateuch.

The Pentateuch is among the very few texts for which several late ancient and early medieval manuscripts survive: T-S NS 4.3 + T-S NS 3.21; ms Heb. d. 89 (P) i; P 10598; ms London + ms Ashkar-Gilson; and the Leviticus scroll from En Gedi. These manuscripts are all proto-Masoretic in character. The only other books for which late ancient or early medieval manuscript evidence is extant are 1–2 Kings (→ 5.3.1.13) and Job (→ 11.2.1.6).

In general, the ancient, late ancient, and early medieval Pentateuch manuscripts can be divided into semi- and proto-Masoretic, pre-Samaritan, and non-aligned witnesses as well as manuscripts that are close to the Hebrew parent text of the Septuagint. These classifications are discussed in → 1.2.2. They are based on statistics for which, with few exceptions, reconstructed variants were not recognized. The Masoretic and Samaritan manuscripts are discussed in → 2.2.4 and → 2.3.

4QGen-Exod[a] and 4QpaleoGen-Exod[l] can be characterized as semi-Masoretic and MurGen-Exod.Num[a], 4QGen[b], SdeirGen, MasLev[a], MasLev[b], Mur/ḤevLev, XḤev/SeNum[b], 4QDeut[e], 4QDeut[g], and MasDeut as well as T-S NS 4.3+T-S NS 3.21,

---

[1] I wrote a significant part of this article during my stay at the Israel Institute of Advanced Studies in Jerusalem. I am much obliged to this institution for the ideal research environment they made available to me.

[2] For photographs of the fragments of Azusa Pacific University, see http://cdm16657.contentdm.oclc.org/cdm/landingpage/collection/p16657coll7 (last accessed April 10, 2015).

[3] I am obliged to David Trobisch and Emanuel Tov for this information. The latter also guided me to the list of the holdings of Azusa Pacific University. The biblical fragments of the Green collection will be published in the volume *Dead Sea Scrolls Fragments in the Museum Collection* (eds. E. Tov, K. Davis, and R. Duke; Publications of Museum of Bible 1; Leiden: Brill, 2016), forthcoming.

[4] I am indebted to Sidnie White Crawford for this information. For first photographs of the Southwestern Baptist Theological Seminary fragments, see Loveless and Loveless, *Dead Sea Scrolls and the Bible*, 83–89.

[5] See Loveless and Loveless, *Dead Sea Scrolls and the Bible*, 103 and Elgvin and Davis, "MS 4612/4," note 4, forthcoming.

ms Heb. d. 89 (P) i, P 10598, ms London + ms Ashkar-Gilson, and the Leviticus Scroll from En-Gedi as proto-Masoretic. Only 4QpaleoExod^m and 4QNum^b read a pre-Samaritan text and 4QLev^d, 4QDeut^q, as well as the Nash Papyrus (→ 2.2.5.2) are close to the Hebrew parent text of the Septuagint. Furthermore, 4QRP^b, 4QRP^c, 4QRP^d, 4QRP^e, 4QGen^f, 2QExod^a, 4QExod^b, 4QExod^c, 4QExod-Lev^f, 4QLev-Num^a, 4QLev^b, 11QpaleoLev^a, 1QDeut^b, 4QDeut^b, 4QDeut^c, 4QDeut^h, 4QDeut^j, 4QDeut^k1, 4QDeut^k2, 4QDeut^n, and 4QpaleoDeut^r attest to various non-aligned texts of the Torah. The textual damage to 4QGen^c, 4QGen^e, 4QGen^g, 4QGen^j, 4QLev^c, 4QLev^e, 4QDeut^d, 4QDeut^f, 4QDeut^i, 4QDeut^o, and 5QDeut does not allow for a more precise text-typological classification other than that they are equally close to MT and SP. Extensive textual damage makes impossible the text-typological classification of 1QGen, 2QGen, 4QGen^d, 4QGen^h-title, 4QGen^k, 4QpaleoGen^m, 4QpapGen^o, 6QpaleoGen, 8QGen, MasGen, Mur(?)Gen^b, 1QExod, 2QExod^b, 4QExod^d, 4QExod^e, 4QExod^g, 4QExod^h, 4QExod^j, 1QpaleoLev-Num^a, 2QpaleoLev, 4QLev^g, 11QLev^b, ArugLev, 2QNum^a, 2QNum^b, 5/6ḤevNum^a, 34SeNum, ms Schøyen 4612/5, 1QDeut^a, 2QDeut^b, 2QDeut^c, 4QDeut^a, 4QDeut^l, 4QDeut^m, 4QDeut^p, 4QDeut^t, 4QDeut^u, 11QDeut, MurDeut, XḤevSeDeut, and ms Schøyen 5214/2; in the cases of 4QGen^h1, 4QGen^h2, 4QGen^h-para, 4QGen^n, 4QGen^p, ms Schøyen 4612/4, 2QExod^c, 4QExod^k, 1QpaleoLev^b?, 4Qpap cryptA Lev^h?, 6QpaleoLev, 2QNum^c, 2QNum^d?, 2QDeut^a, 4QDeut^k3, 4QpaleoDeut^s, 6QpapDeut?, and ms Schøyen 5214/1, the damage does not even allow for us to distinguish between a biblical manuscript and a biblical quotation in a non-biblical text. The manuscript XDeut? is likely a forgery. Among the Dead Sea Scrolls there are also excerpted manuscripts attesting to books or passages of the Pentateuch. These excerpted manuscripts attest to different Pentateuchal texts and were used for various purposes: 4QGen^d, 4QGen^f, 4QExod^e, 4QDeut^j, 4QDeut^n, 4QDeut^q, 5QDeut, and the Nash Papyrus. At most, eleven manuscripts with Pentateuch text where copied in paleo-Hebrew characters. The only other biblical book for which this is the case is Job (→ 11.2.1.4). These paleo-Hebrew copies attest to semi-Masoretic (4QpaleoGen-Exod^l), pre-Samaritan (4QpaleoExod^m), and non-aligned (11QpaleoLev^a, 4QpaleoDeut^r) Pentateuch texts or their text typology can no longer be determined (4QpaleoGen^m, 6QpaleoGen, 1QpaleoLev-Num^a, 2QpaleoLev, 1QpaleoLev^b?, 6QpaleoLev, 4QpaleoDeut^s).

Although copies of individual books of the Pentateuch exist among the biblical scrolls from Qumran, the Pentateuch is treated here as a whole because several manuscripts include two or more books of the Pentateuch (1QpaleoLev-Num^a, 4QGen-Exod^a, 4QpaleoGen-Exod^l, 4QExod-Lev^f, 4QLev-Num^a) and because it is likely that other manuscripts attested originally to the whole Torah (4QRP^b, 4QRP^c, 4QRP^d, MurGen-Exod.Num, and maybe 4QExod^b). The Pentateuch was therefore perceived already in antiquity as one textual unit. This textual unity of the Torah is also evident in the phrases "through Moses" (ביד מושה CD A 5:21; 4QD^a 1c–f 2; 4QD^e 7 i 17; 1QS I:3; VIII:15; 4QS^a 1 3; 4QS^e III:6; 1QM X:6; 1QH^a IV:24; 4Qpaleo para-Josh 2 1; 4QapocrJosh 22 i 3; 4Qpap paraKings et al. 104 7; 4QMLM^d 184 1; 4QMLM^g 11 2; 4QInstruction-like Composition A 1 2; 4QDibHam^a V:8; XVIII:15; 11QMelch II:3), "Torah of Moses" (תורת מושה CD A 15:2, 9, 12; 16:2, 5; 4QD^a 8 i 3; 11 6; 4QD^f 4 ii 1; 1QS V:8; VIII:22; 4QS^b IX:7; 4QS^d I:6; 4QOrdinances^b 3–4 5) and "Book of Moses" (ספר מושה 4QJuridical Text 1 3; MMT C 17, 21; 4QMSM 1 verso 1). Nevertheless, the books of the Pentateuch were also copied individually, which led to a limited textual and orthographic division between the five books of the Torah even within the proto-Masoretic text.

2.2.1.1 Semi-Masoretic Manuscripts
2.2.1.1.1 4QGen-Exod^a (4Q1)
The text of thirty-eight of the sixty-two surviving fragments of 4QGen-Exod^a can still be identified. These thirty-eight fragments preserve 933 complete and partial words from Gen 22:14; 27:38–39, 42–43; 34:17–21; 35:17–29; 36:2–10, 12, 19, 21–22, 24–27; 37:5–6, 8, 22–27; 39:11–23; 40:1; 45:23; 47:13–14; 48:2–4, 15–22; 49:1–5; Exod 1:3, 5–17, 22; 2:1–5; 3:8–16, 18–21; 4:4–9, 26–31; 5:1, 3–17; 6:4–21, 25; 7:5–13,

15–20; 8:20–22; 9:8?.[6] The manuscript is executed in an early Hasmonean bookhand from the years 125–100 B.C.E.[7] The supralinear as well as all other corrections in 4QGen-Exod[a] were inserted by the original scribe of the scroll.[8] The orthography of the manuscript is conservative with individual differences toward 𝔐.[9] 4QGen-Exod[a] reads seventy-six times with and nineteen times against 𝔐, fifty-seven times with and thirty-eight times against SP, seventeen times with and sixty-nine time against LXX, as well as eleven times non-aligned. The text of 4QGen-Exod[a] is thus semi-Masoretic in character.[10]

2.2.1.1.2 4QpaleoGen-Exod[l] (4Q11)

Sixty-four fragments survive of 4QpaleoGen-Exod[l]. The text of frgs. 1–38 can be identified and attests to 804 complete and partial words from Gen 50:26; Exod 1:1–2, 4–5; 2:10, 22–25; 3:1–4, 17–21; 8:13–15, 19–21; 9:25–29, 33–35; 10:1–5; 11:4–10; 12:1–12, 42–44, 46; 14:15–24; 16:2–7, 13–14, 18–20, 23–31, 33–35; 17:1–3, 5–11; 18:17–24; 19:24–25; 20:1–2; 22:23–24; 23:5–13, 15–16; 25:7–9, 11–16, 18–20; 26:29–37; 27:1, 6–14; 28:33–35, 40–42; 36:34–36. The paleo-Hebrew script of 4QpaleoGen-Exod[l] is dated paleographically to the years 100–50 or 100–25 B.C.E.[11] The two corrections in Exod 14:16 and 26:20 are not from the original scribe of the scroll.[12] The orthography of 4QpaleoGen-Exod[l] is mixed but lacks the characteristic morphology of the baroque orthographic approach: "The evidence indicates that the scribe had no intention to achieve a systematic approach to orthography. Gen–Exod[l] shares with 𝔖𝔪 a tendency toward a moderate balance between conservative and slightly full orthography, although often they disagree on particular forms. On the other hand, 𝔐 in Exodus tends to be somewhat more conservative."[13] 4QpaleoGen-Exod[l] reads twenty-five times with and twenty-five times against 𝔐, twelve times with and thirty-eight times against SP, fifteen times with and twenty-four times against LXX, as well as twelve times non-aligned. Although the variant statistics seem to be inconclusive, the material reconstruction of the scroll demonstrates that 4QpaleoGen-Exod[l] did not know the characteristic long texts of the pre-Samaritan text tradition.[14]

To describe the text more positively, Gen–Exod[l] belongs to the general textual tradition of the book of Exodus which is represented also by both 𝔐 and the text-base of 𝔖𝔪. Within that larger tradition there are two specific traditions, represented by 𝔐 on the one hand and by Exod[m] and 𝔖𝔪 on the other, the latter tradition being distinguished by sixteen major expansions and two major differences in order of text. In only one instance of a major feature of the Exod[m] 𝔖𝔪 tradition is the witness of Gen–Exod[l] unambigious …; there it agrees with 𝔐 against 𝔖𝔪, but the unusual nature of the variant renders it impossible to generalize about the type of text that Gen–Exod[l] had elsewhere. That instance involves a difference in order of text. While 𝔐 places the instructions for the incense al-

---

[6] After the publication of the *editio princeps*, Puech identified another fragment of 4QGen-Exod[a] with four words from Gen 37:8, which he counts as frg. 7a ("Fragment 7a," 103–06). This fragment is now part of the Schøyen Collection and is catalogued there as MS 5439/1. Identifications of further fragments of 4QGen-Exod[a] suggested by Puech in the above publication are possible but need to remain speculative because only very few characters are preserved of each of these fragments. Elgvin ("MS 5439/1") argues that ms Schøyen 5439/1 belongs more likely to 4Q364 (= 4QRP[b]) than to 4QGen-Exod[a]. I am indebted to Torleif Elgvin for making a preprint copy of his edition available to me.

[7] Davila, "1. 4QGen-Exod[a]," 8; cf. Davila, "Unpublished Pentateuchal Manuscripts," 17–19; Davila, "Name of God," 577; Davila, "Joseph Story," 167–68; Davila, "Text-Type," 10.

[8] Davila, "Unpublished Pentateuchal Manuscripts," 20; Davila, "1. 4QGen-Exod[a]," 10.

[9] Davila, "1. 4QGen-Exod[a]," 9–10; cf. Brooke, "Torah," 99, 102. For a list of orthographic variants, see Davila, "1. 4QGen-Exod[a]," 9, and Davila, "Unpublished Pentateuchal Manuscripts," 12–17.

[10] Cf. Davila, "Unpublished Pentateuchal Manuscripts," 181–83, 190–91; Davila, "Text-Type," 14, 35; Tov, *"Biblical Texts," 154; Lange, *Handbuch*, 44.

---

[11] McLean, "Development," 66–71; cf. Skehan, Ulrich, and Sanderson, "Palaeo-Hebrew Manuscripts," 21; Ulrich, "Palaeo-Hebrew Biblical Manuscripts," 108–09.

[12] Cf. Skehan, Ulrich, and Sanderson, "Palaeo-Hebrew Manuscripts," 25, 35, 44.

[13] Skehan, Ulrich, and Sanderson, "Palaeo-Hebrew Manuscripts," 21.

[14] Cf. Skehan, Ulrich, and Sanderson, "Palaeo-Hebrew Manuscripts," 24.

tar at 30:1–10, Exod^m 𝔪 place that paragraph between 26:35 and 36. Gen–Exod^l clearly agrees with 𝔐 in placing 26:36 after 26:35, but there is no indication as to where 30:1–10 was in Gen–Exod^l, if it was present.[15]

Against earlier classifications of 4QpaleoGen-Exod^l as "quite near to the received text,"[16] the manuscript is best classified as semi-Masoretic.[17]

2.2.1.2 Proto-Masoretic Manuscripts

2.2.1.2.1 4QDeut^e (4Q32)

Eight fragments are preserved of 4QDeut^e. Frgs. 2–5 belong to three subsequent columns of the original scroll. Frgs. 1–5 attest to 126 complete and partial words from Deut 3:24; 7:12–16, 21–26; 8:1–7, 10–11, 15–16. The manuscript was copied in a late Hasmonean bookhand from the years 50–25 B.C.E., which exhibits some semi-cursive influence. Orthographic variants toward MT are rare. 4QDeut^e spells once more defective than MT.[18] 4QDeut^e reads six times with and once against MT, four times with and three times against SP, three times with and four times against LXX, and never non-aligned. Because the text of 4QDeut^e agrees almost completely with MT in both its orthography and text, it can be classified as proto-Masoretic.[19]

2.2.1.2.2 4QDeut^g (4Q34)

The twelve fragments of 4QDeut^g preserve 151 complete and partial words from Deut 9:12–14; 23:18–20; 24:16–22; 25:1–3, 5, 14–19; 26:1–5; 28:21–25, 27–29.[20] The manuscript was copied in a middle Herodian bookhand from the years 1–25 C.E.[21] "The orthographic practice of 4QDeut^g never varies from that of the Massoretic text."[22] The manuscript reads fifteen times with and never against MT, ten times with and five times against SP, three times with and eleven times against LXX and never non-aligned. The total agreement of 4QDeut^g with MT in text and orthography identifies the manuscript as a witness to a proto-Masoretic text.[23]

2.2.1.2.3 MasLev^a (Mas1a)

The single surviving fragment of MasLev^a attests to sixty-three complete and partial words from Lev 4:3–9. The manuscript was copied in an early Herodian bookhand from the last quarter of the first century B.C.E.[24] Except for one plene spelling, the orthography of MasLev^a agrees completely with MT.[25] MasLev^a reads four times with MT against LXX, three times with MT against SP, and once with MT and SP against LXX. Although only little text is preserved, the complete textual and almost complete orthographic agreement with MT identifies the text of MasLev^a as proto-Masoretic.[26]

2.2.1.2.4 MasLev^b (Mas 1b)

More than forty fragments survive of MasLev^b. They derive from two subsequent columns and preserve 457 complete and partial words from Lev

---

[15] Skehan, Ulrich, and Sanderson, "Palaeo-Hebrew Manuscripts," 23.

[16] Skehan, "Biblical Scrolls," 99.

[17] Cf. Ulrich, "Palaeo-Hebrew Biblical Manuscripts," 110–11; Tov, *"Biblical Texts," 154; Lange, *Handbuch, 52.

[18] For the orthography of 4QDeut^e, see Duncan, "32. 4QDeut^e," 39–40; Duncan, "Critical Edition," 42–43.

[19] Cf. Lange, *Handbuch, 89. Against Tov, *"Biblical Texts," 155, who regards 4QDeut^e as equally close to MT and SP.

[20] Beyond the *editio princeps*, Tigchelaar, "Minuscula Qumranica I," 646, succeeded in identifying a further fragment of 4QDeut^g that attests to part of Deut 26:3.

[21] Cf. White Crawford, "34. 4QDeut^g," 55; White Crawford, "Critical Edition," 215–18; White Crawford, "Special Features," 165; White Crawford, "Deuteronomy Manuscripts," 35.

[22] Cf. White Crawford, "34. 4QDeut^g," 55; White Crawford, "Critical Edition," 218; White Crawford, "Special Features," 165; White Crawford, "Deuteronomy Manuscripts," 35–36.

[23] Cf. White Crawford, "34. 4QDeut^g," 56; White Crawford, "Critical Edition," 239; White Crawford, "Special Features," 165–66; "Deuteronomy Manuscripts," 23, 36; Lange, *Handbuch, 91. Against Tov, *"Biblical Texts," 155, who regards 4QDeut^g as equally close to MT and SP.

[24] Y. Yadin, "The Excavation of Masada – 1963/64: Preliminary Report," *IEJ* 15 (1965): 1–120; Talmon, "Two Leviticus Scrolls," 29; Talmon, "Hebrew Fragments," 37.

[25] Talmon, "Two Leviticus Scrolls," 30; Talmon, "Hebrew Fragments," 38; Yadin, "Excavation," 104.

[26] Yadin, "Excavation," 104; Talmon, "Two Leviticus Scrolls," 30; Talmon, "Hebrew Fragments," 37–38; Flint, "Book of Leviticus," 328; Lange, *Handbuch, 78; cf. Ulrich, "Perspectives," 458–59 who opposes the category of proto-Masoretic texts for principal reasons.

8:31, 33–34; 9:1–10, 12–13, 24; 10:1, 9–20; 11:1–13, 15–22, 23–40. The manuscript was copied in a Herodian bookhand from the late first century B.C.E.[27] Its three supralinear corrections were inserted by the original scribe of the scroll.[28] The orthography of MasLev[b] agrees even in orthographic inconsistencies with MT.[29] MasLev[b] reads thirteen times with and never against MT, six times with and seven times against SP, never with and eleven times against LXX, and never non-aligned. The complete orthographic and textual agreement of MasLev[b] with MT characterizes it as a proto-Masoretic manuscript.[30]

2.2.1.2.5 MasDeut (Mas1c)

The four surviving fragments of MasDeut come from two subsequent columns of the original scroll. Of col. I, only two unidentifiable words are preserved. Col. II attests to sixty-eight complete and partial words from Deut 32:46–47; 33:17–24; 34:2–6. MasDeut was copied in an early Herodian bookhand from the years 30–1 B.C.E.[31] Except for one more defective spelling in Deut 33:19, MasDeut agrees in text and orthography with MT. This very close agreement with MT identifies MasDeut as a proto-Masoretic manuscript.[32]

2.2.1.2.6 MurGen-Exod.Num[a] (Mur1)

Seven fragments survive of MurGen-Exod.Num[a] preserving 260 complete and partial words from Gen 32:4–5, 30, 33; 33:1; 34:5–7, 30–31; 35:1, 4–7; Exod 4:28–31; 5:3; 6:5–9, 11; Num 34:10; 36:7–11. Although the current manuscript catalogues of the Dead Sea Scrolls regard Mur1 as three separate manuscripts (MurGen[a], MurExod, MurNum),[33] based on paleographic observations, Milik understands the fragments of Mur1 in his *editio princeps* as belonging to one manuscript deriving from a scroll that once might have included the whole Pentateuch. He calls the manuscript "Genèse, Exode, Nombres."[34] The exceptional height of Mur1 (46.5 cm)[35] confirms Milik's paleographic arguments, because it is unlikely that a scribe would have used such a big scroll to copy anything smaller than the whole Torah.[36] I designate Mur1 hence as MurGen-Exod.Num[a]. The manuscript was copied in a post-Herodian bookhand from the beginning of the second century C.E.[37] The supralinear correction in Gen 34:31 was inserted by the original scribe of the scroll. In the extant text of MurGen-Exod.Num[a], neither a single orthographic nor a single textual variant toward MT[38] can be found. Thus, MurGen-Exod.Num[a] needs to be classified as a proto-Masoretic manuscript.[39]

2.2.1.2.7 SdeirGen (Sdeir1)

The three surviving fragments derive from two subsequent columns of the original scroll and attest to 117 complete and partial words from Gen 35:6–10, 26–29; 36:1–2, 5–17. Where SdeirGen was found is unclear. The manuscript was originally named ḤevGen.[40] However, the Bedouin who sold the manuscript identified its find-site as Wadi Sdeir.[41] The manuscript is written in a late or post-Herodian hand from the years 50–100 C.E.[42] No orthographic deviations from the text of MT[L]

---

[27] Cf. Talmon, "Two Leviticus Scrolls," 32; Talmon, "Hebrew Fragments," 40.
[28] Talmon, "Hebrew Fragments," 47.
[29] Talmon, "Hebrew Fragments," 46; Talmon, "Two Leviticus Scrolls," 33–34.
[30] Cf. Y. Yadin, *Masada: Herod's Fortress and the Zealot's Last Stand* (New York: Random House, 1966), 179. Talmon, "Two Leviticus Scrolls," 34–35; Talmon, "Hebrew Fragments," 42, 47; Flint, "Book of Leviticus," 328.
[31] Talmon, "Deuteronomy Scroll," 154–55; Talmon, "Hebrew Fragments," 53.
[32] Cf. Talmon, "Hebrew Fragments," 55.
[33] Cf., e.g., Tov, *"List,"* 97. But in *Revised Lists*, Tov designates this manuscript as MurGen-Num.
[34] Milik, "2. Deutéronome," 75.
[35] For the measurements of Mur1, see Milik, "2. Deutéronome," 75.
[36] Cf. Lange, *Handbuch*, 55.
[37] Milik, "1. Genèse, Exode, Nombres," 75.
[38] In Gen 34:31, the original scribe even corrected a more defective spelling to the plene spelling of MT.
[39] For the proto-Masoretic character of MurGen-Exod.Num[a], cf. also R. deVaux, "Quelques textes hébreux de Murabba'at," *RB* 60 (1953): 268–75, 268; Milik, "2. Deutéronome," 75; Lange, *Handbuch*, 55.
[40] Cf. Murphy, "1. SdeirGenesis," 117.
[41] See Murphy, "1. SdeirGenesis," 118.
[42] See Murphy, "1. SdeirGenesis," 118.

are attested in SdeirGen.⁴³ The manuscript reads five times with and never against MT, five times against and never with SP, two times with and three times against LXX, and never non-aligned. The complete orthographic and textual agreement with MT identifies SdeirGen as a proto-Masoretic text.⁴⁴

2.2.1.2.8 4QGenᵇ (4Q2)

Four fragments survive of 4QGenᵇ. Frgs. 1–3 attest to 358 complete and partial words from Gen 1:1–28; 2:14–19; 4:2–11. The manuscript was copied in a late or post-Herodian bookhand from the second half of the first century C.E.⁴⁵ Only one orthographic disagreement with MT is attested in 4QGenᵇ (לְמֹארֹת instead of לִמְאוֹרֹת "as lights" in Gen 1:15).⁴⁶ 4QGenᵇ reads twenty-seven times with and never against MT, nineteen times with and eight times against SP, never with and twenty-six times against LXX, and never non-aligned. The almost complete orthographic and complete textual agreement with MT identify 4QGenᵇ without doubt as a proto-Masoretic text.⁴⁷ The paleographic date and its orthographic and textual agreements with MT make it likely that 4QGenᵇ derives from Wadi Murabbaʿat and was only identified as Qumranic in origin by the Bedouin who sold it.⁴⁸

2.2.1.2.9 Mur/ḤevLev (MS Schøyen 4611)

Mur/ḤevLev is part of the Schøyen Collection and was published first by Puech in 2003.⁴⁹ The official edition by Elgvin is forthcoming.⁵⁰ Depending on whose edition is used, either three or five fragments are preserved from two consecutive columns, attesting to either ninety-nine or 107 complete and partial words from Lev 26:3–9, 33–37. The manuscript was written in a late Herodian bookhand probably from the second half the first century C.E.⁵¹ According to Puech, the extant text displays no orthographic differences towards MT.⁵² Elgvin mentions two reconstructed variants toward MT (one of them orthographic) and disagrees in Lev 26:6 with Puech regarding the transcription of the word והשבתי "and I will remove." Elgvin wants to read instead והשמדתי "and I will exterminate." In his opinion, the reading might agree with LXX-Lev (καὶ ἀπολῶ "and I will destroy").⁵³ Depending on Elgvin's transcription, the manuscript reads in its preserved text five times with and never against MT, once with and four times against SP, two times with and three times against LXX, and never non-aligned. That the preserved text of Mur/ḤevLev agrees almost completely with the consonantal text of MTᴸ characterizes the manuscript as a proto-Masoretic witness.⁵⁴

2.2.1.2.10 XḤev/SeNumᵇ (XḤev/Se2)

One fragment with remnants of two columns is preserved of XḤev/SeNumᵇ. It attests to ninety-

---

⁴³ Cf. Murphy, "1. SdeirGenesis," 118.

⁴⁴ Cf. C. Burchard, "Gen 35₆₋₁₀ und 36₅₋₁₂ aus der Wüste Juda (Naḥal Ḥever, Cave of Letters?)," ZAW 78 (1966): 71–75 (75); Lange, *Handbuch, 56.

⁴⁵ Thus Davila, "Unpublished Pentateuch Manuscripts," 66–68; Davila, "Genesis One," 4; Davila, "Text-Type," 14; Davila, "2. 4QGenᵇ," 31.

⁴⁶ Cf. Davila, "2. 4QGenᵇ," 32; Davila, "Unpublished Pentateuchal Manuscripts," 63–66; Davila, "Text-Type," 14.

⁴⁷ For the textual character of 4QGenᵇ, see Davila, "Unpublished Pentateuchal Manuscripts," 191–92, 212; Davila, "Genesis One," 4; Davila, "Text-Type," 14, 16; Brooke, "Torah," 100; Hendel, *Genesis 1–11, 101; Tov, *"Synthese," 17 n. 58; Tov, *"Biblical Texts," 154; Lange, *Handbuch, 45.

⁴⁸ Davila, "2. 4QGenᵇ," 31; cf. Davila, "Unpublished Pentateuchal Manuscripts," 62–63; Davila, "Genesis One," 4–5; Davila, "Text-Type," 14; Brooke, "Torah," 100.

⁴⁹ Puech, "Un autre manuscrit de Lévitique," 311–13.

⁵⁰ Elgvin, "MS 4611," forthcoming. I am obliged to Torleif Elgvin for making a preprint copy of his edition of XLevᶜ available to me.

⁵¹ Puech, "Un autre manuscrit de Lévitique," 311. Alternative paleographic classifications are "elegant, developed late Herodian hand with few parallels, more easily dated after AD 70 than before" (thus Ada Yardeni according to Elgvin, "MS 4611") and "late Herodian formal script with some signs of transition from Herodian to post-Herodian scripts" from the second half of the second century C.E. (thus M. Langlois, "Palaeographical Analysis of the Dead Sea Scrolls," in *Gleanings, forthcoming).

⁵² Puech, "Un autre manuscrit de Lévitique," 313.

⁵³ Elgvin, "MS 4611," forthcoming.

⁵⁴ Cf. Puech, "Un autre manuscrit de Lévitique," 313; Lange, *Handbuch, 77; against Elgvin, "MS 4611," forthcoming, who speaks of an "𝔐-like text."

five complete and partial words from Num 27:2–13; 28:11–12. The manuscript was copied in a late Herodian bookhand from the second half of the first century C.E.[55] In the preserved text of XḤev/SeNum[b], neither orthographic[56] nor textual variants towards MT can be found. The manuscript should thus be classified as proto-Masoretic. "XḤev/Se 2 contains no variant readings against other Judaean scrolls or 𝔐, but sides with 𝔐 against 𝔰𝔪 4QNum[b] once, and with 𝔐 against 𝔰𝔪 five times ... The absence of both textual and orthographic variants against 𝔐 shows that this scroll preserves a text of Numbers very much like that found in the received text."[57]

2.2.1.3 Pre-Samaritan Manuscripts
2.2.1.3.1 4QpaleoExod[m] (4Q22)

The fragments of 4QpaleoExod[m] whose text can still be identified combine to forty-five consecutive columns of the original scroll. Only cols. XIV and XLIII have no preserved text. The forty-five columns attest to 2,050 complete and partial words from Exod 6:25–30; 7:1–19, 29; 8:1, 12–22; 9:5–16, 19–21, 35; 10:1–12, 19–28; 11:8–10; 12:1–2, 6–8, 13–15, 17–22, 31–32, 34–39; 13:3–7, 12–13; 14:3–5, 8–9, 25; 15:23–27; 16:1, 4–5, 7, 31–35; 17:1–16; 18:1–18, 20–27; 19:1, 7–17, 23–25; 20:1, 18–19; 21:5–6, 13–14, 22, 24–32; 22:3–4, 11–13, 16, 18–30; 23:15–16, 29–31; 24:1–4, 6–11; 25:11–12, 20–29, 31–35; 26:8–15, 21–30; 27:1–3, 9–14, 18–19; 28:3–4, 8–12, 22–24, 26–28, 30–36, 38–43; 29:1–5, 20, 22–25, 31–41; 30:10, 12–18, 29–31; 31:1–8, 13–15; 32:2–19, 25–30; 33:12–23; 34:1–3, 10–13, 15–18, 20–24, 27–28; 35:1; 36:21–24. In addition to these forty-five columns, 439 unidentified and untranscribed fragments of 4QpaleoExod[m] exist. Despite earlier suggestions to date 4QpaleoExod[m] to the years 225–175 B.C.E.,[58] 200–175 B.C.E.,[59] and 175–125 B.C.E.[60] respectively, McLean's careful comparative study of paleo-Hebrew scripts left no doubt that the scroll needs to be dated to the years 100–25 B.C.E.[61] The two supralinear corrections to Exod 17:13, 15 are from the original scribe of 4QpaleoExod[m].[62] The repair patch in col. VIII was inscribed by a second hand.[63] Although in its orthography 4QpaleoExod[m] is characterized by the conservative approach, fuller and more defective readings than in MT also occur and in some case even baroque morphological forms are employed.[64]

The textual classification of 4QpaleoExod[m] is complicated. The manuscript reads eighty-two times with and ninety-five times against MT, 104 times with and seventy-three times against SP, thirty-one times with and 129 times against LXX, as well as forty-one times non-aligned. Although the statistics indicate no clear alignment of 4QpaleoExod[m], agreements with SP in major variants from MT do so. 4QpaleoExod[m] attests in Exod 7:18b, 29b; 8:19b; 9:5b, 19b; 10:2b; 18:25; 20:19a; 24:1, 9; 27:19b; 32:10 the longer text of SP. The material reconstruc-

---

[55] Cf. Flint, "2. XḤev/SeNumbers[b],"174; Flint and Alvarez, "Two Biblical Scrolls," 534 ("late Herodian [c. 50–68 CE]"); different A. Yardeni according to J.C. Greenfield, "The Texts from Naḥal Ṣe'elim (Wadi Seiyal)," in *Madrid Qumran Conference, 2.661–65 (663): "early 1st cent."

[56] For the orthography of XḤev/SeNum[b], see Flint, "2. XḤev/SeNumbers[b],"174; Flint and Alvarez, "Two Biblical Scrolls," 534.

[57] Flint, "2. XḤev/SeNumbers[b],"174; cf. Flint and Alvarez, "Two Biblical Scrolls," 535; Lange, *Handbuch, 83.

[58] R.S. Hanson, "Paleo-Hebrew Scripts in the Hasmonean Age," BASOR 175 (1964): 26–42 (34–37). Hanson corrected this early date later on to "around 100 B.C.E." ("Paleography," in Freedman and Mathews, Leviticus Scroll, 15–23 [23]).

[59] P.W. Skehan, "Fragments of Another Exodus Scroll," in Scrolls from the Wilderness of the Dead Sea: A Guide to the Exhibition, The Dead Sea Scrolls of Jordan and the Palestine Archeological Museum (London: Trustees of the British Museum, 1965), 26 note regarding plate 9.

[60] J.D. Purvis, The Samaritan Pentateuch and the Origin of the Samaritan Sect (HSM 2; Cambridge: Harvard University Press, 1968), 37–52.

[61] McLean, "Development," 73–78, esp. 78; cf. Sanderson, "Contributions," 549; Skehan, Ulrich, and Sanderson, "Palaeo-Hebrew Manuscripts," 53, 62; Ulrich, "Palaeo-Hebrew Biblical Manuscripts," 116.

[62] Cf. Sanderson, "Contributions," 550; Skehan, Ulrich, and Sanderson, "Palaeo-Hebrew Manuscripts," 83, 64–65.

[63] Cf. Sanderson, "Contributions," 550; Skehan, Ulrich, and Sanderson, "Palaeo-Hebrew Manuscripts," 65, 85.

[64] See Sanderson, "Contributions," 549. For a detailed description of the orthography of 4QpaleoExod[m] and a list of orthographic variants, see Skehan, Ulrich, and Sanderson, "Palaeo-Hebrew Manuscripts," 62–64; cf. also Ulrich, "Palaeo-Hebrew Biblical Manuscripts," 116–17. Against Skehan, "Exodus," 183: "mild form of that fuller orthography of which examples from Qumran Cave 1 are by now so well known."

tion of 4QpaleoExod^m points to similar agreements in long texts with SP against MT in Exod 8:1b; 11:3b; and 20:21b. In its text sequence, 4QpaleoExod^m also agrees with SP against MT: Exod 30:1–10 follows Exod 26:35 and the material construction makes it likely that Exod 29:21 followed Exod 29:28.[65] But the material reconstruction of 4QpaleoExod^m indicates also a disagreement with SP in at least one macro-variant: "Reconstruction of cols. XX–XXII demonstrates that there is one typological feature of 𝕊𝕞 that the scroll did not contain: Exod 20:17b, the major expansion which constitutes the tenth commandment in 𝕊𝕞 and is composed from Deut 11:29–30 and 27:2–7, commanding the Israelites to build an altar on Mount Gerizim." Therefore, 4QpaleoExod^m cannot be classified as a Samaritan manuscript.[66] That 4QpaleoExod^m neither aligns statistically with SP nor shares its key ideological variant readings on the one hand, but does on the other hand agree in many macro-variants with SP, is best explained if SP and 4QpaleoExod^m share a common textual ancestor or if SP reworked the text of 4QpaleoExod^m ideologically.[67]

2.2.1.3.2 4QNum^b (4Q27)

There are 105 extant fragments of 4QNum^b. Frgs. 1–84 derive from several columns of the original scroll, which the *editio princeps* counts as cols. I–II, VI, VIII, X–XXXII.[68] They attest to 1,517 complete and partial words from Num 11:31–35; 12:1–11; 13:7, 10–13, 15–24; 15:41; 16:1–11, 14–16; 17:12–17; 18:25–32; 19:1–6; 20:12–13, 17, 19–29; 21:1–2, 12–13, 21–22; 22:5–21, 31–34, 37–38, 41; 23:1–4, 6, 13–15, 21–22, 27–30; 24:1–10; 25:4–8, 17–18; 26:1–5, 7–10, 12, 14–34, 63–65; 27:1–5, 7–8, 10, 18–19, 21–23; 28:13–17, 28, 30–31; 29:10–13, 16–18, 26–30; 30:1–3, 5–9, 15–17; 31:2–6, 21–25, 30–33, 35–36, 38, 44, 46–54; 32:1, 4–5, 7–10, 13–17, 19, 21–30, 35, 37–39, 41; 33:1–4, 23, 25, 28, 31, 45, 47–48, 50–52; 34:4–9, 19–21, 23; 35:3–5, 11–12, 14–15, 18–25, 27–28, 33–34; 36:1–2, 4–7.[69] The manuscript is written in an early Herodian semi-formal hand from the years 30 B.C.E.–20 C.E.,[70] most likely from the first decades of that period.[71] The orthography of 4QNum^b is baroque but employs in exceptional cases also the shorter morphology of the conservative orthography known from MT.[72] In the early stages of Qumran research, the text was characterized as being close to LXX.[73] After the complete publication of 4QNum^b, a different understanding emerged. The manuscript reads sixty-eight times with and 129 times against MT, seventy-six times with and 121 times against SP, seventy-three times with and 135 times against LXX, as well as sixty-two times non-aligned. Jastram describes the situation as follows:

> If the variants are counted rather than weighed, 4QNum^b appears to be equidistant from each of the other traditions. For the preserved variants, according to one method of counting the correlations between the witnesses, 4QNum^b agrees with 𝕊𝕞 in c. 42%, with 𝔐 in c. 37%, with 𝔊 in c. 31%, with

---

[65] Cf. Skehan, Ulrich, and Sanderson, "Palaeo-Hebrew Manuscripts," 66–67.

[66] Thus, e.g., Skehan, "Exodus," 182–83, 187; cf. also already Skehan's reports in Benoit et al., *"Editing," 86, and in Benoit et al., *"Travail," 58.

[67] Cf. P.W. Skehan, "Qumran and the Present State of the Old Testament Text Studies: The Masoretic Text," *JBL* 78 (1959): 22–23 ("the type of text the Samaritans have preserved," 23); Sanderson, *Exodus Scroll*, esp. 10–14, 189, 257, 307–08; Sanderson, "Contributions," 550, 559–60; Sanderson, "Old Greek," 88–89; Brooke, "Torah," 103–04; Skehan, Ulrich, and Sanderson, "Palaeo-Hebrew Manuscripts," 53, 65–66, 68–69; Davila, "Text-Type," 35; Ulrich, "Palaeo-Hebrew Biblical Manuscripts," 117–18; Ulrich, "Dead Sea Scrolls," 81–83; Tov, "Proto-Samaritan Texts," 405; Tov, *TCHB, 91–93, 108; Tov, *"Synthese," 18; Tov, *"Biblical Texts," 155; Lange, *Handbuch, 65–66.

[68] Jastram, "27. 4QNum^b," 206–07. Col. I was preceded by several more columns of text in the original scroll.

[69] Puech, "4QNb^b 18a," identified a possible further fragment of 4QNum^b on museum plate PAM 43.610, which he counts as frg. 18a. With two complete and two partial characters out of two lines, the identification must remain speculative although paleographic similarities argue for it. The four extant characters are attested in both CD A 6:2–5 and in Num 21:18.

[70] Cross, *"Development," 138, 173–81; Cross, *"Paleography," plate 10; Jastram, "Book of Numbers," 20–31; Jastram, "27. 4QNum^b," 211.

[71] Thus Cross in an oral communication to Jastram ("Book of Numbers," 31; "27. 4QNum^b," 211); cf. Jastram, "Text," 178 (ca. 30 B.C.E.).

[72] For the orthography of 4QNum^b, see Jastram, "Book of Numbers," 99–114; Jastram, "27. 4QNum^b," 212–13.

[73] Cf., e.g., Milik, *Ten Years, 24–25.

no other witness *c.* 23 %. The percentages total more than 100 % because in many cases 4QNum[b] agrees with more than one other witness, and the agreements with *each* witness were counted. If variants are weighed, however, rather than merely counted, it becomes clearer that 4QNum[b] 𝔐 𝔊 share more significant secondary readings than 4QNum[b] 𝔐, and thus are more closely related. Of the secondary readings in 4QNum[b], the most significant are the major interpolations shared with 𝔐. 4QNum[b] preserves the interpolations in five places (20:13b; 21:12a, 13a, 21a; 31:21a). The remaining five major interpolations of 𝔐 occur in sections too far removed from the preserved fragments for certain conclusions, but there is no reason to suppose their absence. The variants next in significance are the expansions unique to 4QNum[b] (note especially the expansion between 36:2–5 in the last column of the manuscript). Third in significance are the divergent readings and expansions shared with 𝔊. But 4QNum[b] is not merely a conflated text combining the expansions of the other witnesses; it has a significant number of unique readings, and often has shorter readings than 𝔊.[74]

4QNum[b] attests thus to a pre-Samaritan text that is also close to LXX and has non-aligned tendencies.[75] This pre-Samaritan text shares more likely either a common ancestor with SP or was reworked by SP.

2.2.1.3.3 XDeut?

This fragment is part of the collection of the Azusa Pacific University[76] and was published by J.H. Charlesworth first online and later in print.[77]

The fragment includes eighteen complete and partial words from Deut 27:4–6. In Deut 27:4, XDeut? reads with SP בהרגרזים "on Mount Garizim," written not as two words but as one, instead of MT's בְּהַר עֵיבָל "on Mount Ebal" (cf. LXX).[78] Based on this reading, Charlesworth originally regarded the fragment as a remnant of an ancient Samaritan copy of the Pentateuch.[79] Now Charlesworth understands בהרגרזים "on MountGarizim" as an original reading.[80] Lange argues that XDeut? is a forgery[81] because XDeut? writes the word בהרגרזים "on Mount Garizim" not in paleo-Hebrew characters as in the Samaritan fragment from Masada (Mas1o) but in the square script. Another suggestion that this manuscript1 is a forgery lies in the fact that XDeut? uses word dividers in some places but lacks them in others, which is not typical for ancient Hebrew manuscripts written in the square script. Furthermore, the extant characters of XDeut? represent a mixture of various ancient Jewish scripts.[82] Charlesworth wants to explain this mixture though as the work of an old scribe who used archaic forms shortly after the middle of the first century B.C.E.[83]

---

[74] Jastram, "27. 4QNum[b]," 213, 215.

[75] Cf. Cross, *ALQ*[1], 138–39; Cross, *ALQ*[3], 136–37; Jastram, "Text," 197; Jastram, "27. 4QNum[b]," 224–34, 233–34; Brooke, "Torah," 106–07; Tov, "Proto-Samaritan Texts," 406; Tov, "Contribution," 36; Tov, **TCHB*, 92–93, 108; Tov, **"Synthese," 18–19; Tov, **"Biblical Texts," 155; Pike, "Numbers," 173; Ulrich, "Dead Sea Scrolls," 83–84; Lange, **Handbuch*, 81–82.

[76] Cf. http://cdm16657.contentdm.oclc.org/cdm/compoundobject/collection/p16657coll7/id/8 (last accessed April 10, 2015).

[77] The original web address was http://www.ijco.org/?categoryId=28682 (last accessed July 23, 2008). Now, an online edition is available at http://foundationjudaismchristianorigins.org/ftp/pages/dead-sea-scrolls/unpub/DSS-deuteronomy.pdf (last accessed April 6, 2015). For the printed publication, see Charlesworth, "What Is a Variant?"

[78] Further variants towards MT include one textual and three orthographic differences. In Deut 27:5, XDeut? reads עליהן "over them" (feminine) instead of MT's עליהם "over them" (masculine). The reading עליהן is also attested in medieval Masoretic and Samaritan manuscripts. The orthographic variants of XDeut can be found in Deut 27:4, 6: In Deut 27:4, XDeut reads בעברכמ]ה "when you cross" instead of MT's בְּעָבְרְכֶם (cf. SP). In Deut 27:6, XDeut reads אלוהיכ]ה "your God" instead of MT's אֱלֹהֶיךָ (cf. SP) and עולות "burnt-offerings" instead of MT's עֹלֹת (SP has עלות).

[79] http://www.ijco.org/?categoryId=28682 (last accessed July 23, 2008).

[80] Charlesworth, "What Is a Variant?" 207–12.

[81] Lange, *Handbuch*, 106. In his printed edition ("What Is a Variant?" 205), Charlesworth wants to refute Lange, whose publication he does not even mention, by way of reference to the Kando family as the sellers of the fragment. Charlesworth also claims that the patina of the fragment would sparkle "in the ink and in the leather."

[82] For this mixture of various ancient Jewish scripts, see now also Charlesworth, "What Is a Variant?" 202–04.

[83] Charlesworth, "What is a Variant?" 204.

2.2.1.4 Manuscripts That Are Equally Close to MT and SP[84]

Although sometimes preserving even larger amounts of text, the extant text of some Pentateuch manuscripts does not preserve the characteristic textual differences between MT and SP. Despite the fact that these manuscripts align with either MT or SP, a more precise text-typological classification is not possible. These manuscripts are therefore described below only in the form of a list.

4QGen[c] (4Q3): One fragment with portions of two columns; 103 complete and partial words are preseved from Gen 40:12–13, 18–20, 23; 41:1–11; Herodian bookhand from the years 20–68 C.E.; the supralinear addition in Gen 40:9–10 is from the original scribe; conservative orthography; the manuscript reads six times with and three times against MT, four times with and five times against SP, once with and six times against LXX.

4QGen[e] (4Q5): Ten fragments; frgs. 1–9 preserve 177 complete and partial words from Gen 36:43; 37:1–2, 27–30; 40:18–22; 41:1–8, 35–44; 42:17–19; 43:8–14; 49:6–8; bookhand in transition between the late Hasmonean and early Herodian scripts from the third quarter of the first century C.E.; conservative orthography; the manuscript reads twelve times with and five times against MT, ten times with and seven times against SP, once with and thirteen times against LXX, as well as four times non-aligned.

4QGen[g] (4Q7): Three fragments with 143 complete and partial words from Gen 1:1–2, 4–11, 13–22; and 2:6–7 (or 2:18–19); late Hasmonean bookhand from the middle of the first century B.C.E.; the scribe of this scroll also copied 4QGen[f]; conservative orthography; the manuscript reads three times with and five times against MT, four times with and three times against SP, never with and five times against LXX, as well as three times non-aligned.

4QGen[j] (4Q9): Fourteen fragments; frgs. 1–10 and 14 attest to 256 complete and partial words from Gen 41:15–18, 23–27, 29–35, 38–43; 42:15–22, 38; 43:1–2, 5–8; 45:14–22, 26–28; bookhand in transition between the Hasmonean and Herodian scripts from the third quarter of the first century C.E.; the manuscript reads nineteen times with and eight times against MT, thirteen times with and fourteen times against SP, seven times with and fifteen times against LXX, as well as four times non-aligned; the scribe responsible for the two supralinear corrections remains unclear; they read twice with LXX against MT, and once with SP.

4QLev[c] (4Q25): Nine fragments; frgs. 1–6 preserve 115 complete and partial words from Lev 1:1–5, 7; 3:16–17; 4:1–6, 12–14, 23–28; 5:12–13; 8:26–28; late Herodian bookhand from the years 50–68 C.E.; conservative orthography; the manuscript reads six times with and three times against MT, five times with and four times against SP, never with and six times against LXX, as well as twice non-aligned.

4QLev[e] (4Q26a): Ten fragments with 108 complete and partial words from Lev 3:2–8; 19:34–37; 20:1–3, 27; 21:1–4,[85] 9–12, 21–24; 22:4–6,[86] 11–17; early Herodian bookhand from the years 30–1 C.E.; conservative orthography that does not deviate from MT; the manuscript reads four times with and six times against MT, five times with and five times against SP, once with and eight times against LXX, as well as three times non-aligned.

4QDeut[d] (4Q31): Four fragments from two consecutive columns with 258 complete and partial

---

[84] For the paleographic, orthographic, and textual data listed below, see Lange, *Handbuch*, 374–406, and the literature discussed there. If orthographic and textual characterizations are not mentioned, the amount of preserved text does not allow for such classifications.

[85] Tigchelaar, "Partial Reedition," 236–37, identifies frg. 5 of PAM 43.692 as frg. 5a of 4QLev[e], adding thus five more complete and partial words from Lev 20:27; 21:1–2 to the 103 complete and partial words of Tov's edition ("26a. 4QLev[e]").

[86] Tigchelaar, "Partial Reedition," 235–36, identifies frg. 8 not as Lev 22:4–6 but rather as Lev 20:2–4.

words from Deut 2:24–36; 3:14, 16–29; 4:1;[87] middle Hasmonean bookhand from the years 125–75 C.E.; conservative orthography that is more defective than MT; the manuscript reads fourteen times with and ten times against MT, fourteen times with and ten times against SP, three times with and fourteen times against LXX, as well as three times non-aligned.

4QDeut^f (4Q33): Forty-one fragments; frgs. 1–35 preserve 404 complete and partial words from twelve columns of the original scroll from Deut 4:24–26; 7:22–25; 8:2–14; 9:6–7; 17:17–18; 18:6–10, 18–22; 19:14–15, 17–21; 20:1–6; 21:4–12; 22:12, 14–19; 23:21–26; 24:2–7; 25:3, 5–9; 26:18–19; 27:1–10; late Hasomean bookhand from the years 75–50 B.C.E.; the six supralinear corrections were inserted by the original scribe of the scroll; conservative orthography that is sometimes fuller than MT; the manuscript reads thirty-two times with and thirteen against MT; thirty-three times with and twelve times with SP; seventeen times with and thirty-four times against LXX.

4QDeut^i (4Q36): Eight fragments; frgs. 1–6, 8 preserve 107 complete and partial words from Deut 4:49; 5:1; 20:9–13; 21:23; 22:1–9; 23:6–7, 9, 12–16, 23–26; late Hasmonean bookhand from the years 100–50 B.C.E.; the origin of the supralinear correction in Deut 22:4 is unclear; conservative orthography; the manuscript reads nine times with and once against MT, five times with and five times against SP, twice with and six times against LXX.

4QDeut^o (4Q42): Fifteen fragments with ninety-one complete and partial words from Deut 2:8; 4:30–34; 5:1–3, 5, 8–9; 28:15, 18, 33, 35–36, 47–49, 51–52, 58–59, 61–62; 29:22–25; late Hasmonean bookhand from the years 75–50 B.C.E.; conservative orthography that is fuller than MT; the manuscript reads eight times with and twice against MT, six times with and four times against SP, once with and six times against LXX, as well as twice non-aligned.

2.2.1.5 Excerpted Manuscript That is Equally Close to MT and SP[88]

5QDeut (5Q1): Five fragments; frg. 1 preserves 124 complete and partial words from Deut 7:15–24; 8:5, 7–20; 9:1–2; excerpted manuscript because the short height of 13 cm makes it unlikely that 5Q1 included all of Deuteronomy; archaic script from the first half of the second century B.C.E; conservative orthography that is more defective than MT; the manuscript reads four times with and four times against MT, three times with and five times against SP, never with and five times against LXX, as well as twice non-aligned; the four supralinear corrections in Deut 7:15; 8:2, 19; 9:2 are from a later scribe (early Herodian bookhand) who corrected 5QDeut towards the Hebrew *Vorlage* of LXX-Deut.

2.2.1.6 Manuscripts That Are Close to LXX

No manuscript has survived from antiquity that documents the Hebrew *Vorlage* of the Old Greek translations of the books of the Torah without deviation. Nevertheless, three manuscripts from Egypt and Qumran are close in their text to the Old Greek translations of Leviticus and Deuteronomy.

2.2.1.6.1 Nash Papyrus

The Nash Papyrus (→ 2.2.5.2) is a papyrus fragment from Egypt that includes a harmonized version of the Decalogue (Exod 20:2–17 with Deut 5:6–18) as well as the Shema Israel (Deut 6:4–5). In its textual affiliation, the manuscript is close to the text of LXX^B.

2.2.1.6.2 4QLev^d (4Q26)

Eleven fragments survive of 4QLev^d of which frgs. 1–4 attest to 114 complete and partial words from Lev 14:27–29, 33–36; 15:20–24; 17:2–11. The manuscript was copied in a Herodian bookhand from

---

[87] In addition to the text published by White Crawford ("31. 4QDeut^d"), Aadland ("A Forgotten Deuteronomy [4Q31] Fragment") identified a further fragment with five complete and partial words from Deut 2:31–33 on museum plate PAM 41.585, which is now lost.

[88] For the paleographic, orthographic, and textual data listed below, see Lange, *Handbuch*, 374–406, and the literature discussed there. If orthographic and textual characterizations are not mentioned, the amount of preserved text does not allow for such classifications.

the years 30 B.C.E. – 20 C.E.[89] The orthography of 4QLev[d] is conservative but the manuscript reads in eight cases fuller than MT. 4QLev[d] reads three times with and eight times against MT, five times with and six times against SP, six times with and three times against LXX, as well as four times non-aligned. Variant statistics argue thus that the text of 4QLev[d] is close to the Hebrew *Vorlage* of LXX-Lev. The proximity of 4QLev[d] to LXX is confirmed by two long texts that 4QLev[d] shares with LXX-Lev in Lev 17:3 and with LXX-Lev and SP-Lev in Lev 17:4.[90]

2.2.1.6.3 4QDeut[q] (4Q44) – An Excerpted Manuscript Close to the Hebrew Parent Text of LXX

Of 4QDeut[q], five fragments survive preserving fifty-six complete and partial words from Deut 32:9–10, x, 37–43. Frgs. 2–5 derive from two columns of the original scroll. Frg. 2 is followed by a small handlesheet; therefore, 4QDeut[q] ended with Deut 32:43. That 4QDeut[q] ended before the final chapter of Deuteronomy as well as the short height of eleven lines per column, or 11.4 cm, identifies 4QDeut[q] as an excerpted manuscript that probably included only the Song of Moses from Deut 32:1–43.[91] The manuscript was copied in an early Herodian bookhand from the second half of the first century B.C.E.[92] The orthography of 4QDeut[q] is conservative. The manuscript reads once with and twelve times against MT, twice with and eleven times against SP, seven times with and six times against LXX, as well as twice non-aligned. Skehan and Ulrich describe the textual affiliation of 4QDeut[q] as follows:

4QDeut[q] and the Massoretic *textus receptus* display distinctly variant forms of the text – more than one variant for every pair of the scroll's short lines. 4QDeut[q], or its *Vorlage*, however, should not be naïvely dismissed as a so-called 'vulgar text' for a number of reasons. Virtually all of its readings are documented in other biblical manuscripts; some readings (שמים 32:43) are more ancient than those preserved in 𝔐, which revised polytheistic terms secondarily for theological purposes; and other readings (אדמת 32:43) appear superior to unusual forms in 𝔐. Though not identical to 𝔊, 4QDeut[q] shares several unique readings with the Septuagint version of Deuteronomy and bears witness to the existence of the variant Hebrew *Vorlage* used by the Septuagint translator, at least for this section of Deuteronomy ... 4QDeut[q] and 𝔊 agree in seven readings against 𝔐, including all of the significant readings.[93]

Although only little text is preserved of 4QDeut[q], the unequivocal evidence described by Skehan and Ulrich argues that the text attested by 4QDeut[q] was close to the Hebrew *Vorlage* of LXX-Deut but also had non-aligned tendencies.

2.2.1.7 Non-Aligned Manuscripts

A special group among the non-aligned Pentateuch manuscripts from Qumran are 4Q364–367. Tov and White Crawford regarded the manuscripts 4Q158 and 4Q364–367 as five copies of a reworked version of the Pentateuch,[94] which they attributed to the literary genre of rewritten Bible.[95] This supposedly

---

[89] Eshel, "4QLev[d]," 1.

[90] For the textual affiliation of 4QLev[d], cf. Tov, "Contribution," 35–36; Tov, *TCHB, 109; Tov, *"Synthèse," 18–19; Tov, "Biblical Texts," 155; Flint, "Book of Leviticus," 326–27; Lange, *Handbuch, 70–72.

[91] Cf. Stegemann, "Weitere Stücke," 220; Brooke, "Torah," 108–09; Skehan and Ulrich, "44. 4QDeut[q]," 137–38; Duncan, "Excerpted Texts," 44–45.

[92] Cf. Skehan and Ulrich, "44. 4QDeut[q]," 138. Against W.F. Albright, "Some Remarks on the Song of Moses in Deuteronomy XXXII," *VT* 9 (1959): 338–46 (338–39): "from about the Christian era or a little earlier."

[93] Skehan and Ulrich, "44. 4QDeut[q]," 138; cf. also Skehan, "Fragment," 12, 14–15; Skehan, "Qumran Manuscripts," 149–50 and 150 n. 1; Cross, *ALQ¹, 135–36; Lange, *Handbuch, 99–100.

[94] For a synopsis of 4Q158 and 4Q364–367, see Tov, "4QReworked Pentateuch: A Synopsis of Its Content," *RevQ* 16 (1993–1995): 647–53, esp. 650–53.

[95] Tov and White, "Reworked Pentateuch," 187–96; cf. Tov, "Textual Status," 45–48; E. Tov, "Biblical Texts as Reworked in Some Qumran Manuscripts with Special Attention to 4QRP and 4QParaGen–Exod," in *The Community of the Renewed Covenant: The Notre Dame Symposium on the Dead Sea Scrolls* (eds. E. Ulrich and J.C. VanderKam; Christianity and Judaism in Antiquity 10; Notre Dame: University of Notre Dame Press, 1994), 111–34 (123–33); White Crawford, "Preliminary Report," 218, 228; S. White Crawford, "The Rewritten Bible at Qumran," in *The Bible and the Dead Sea Scrolls: The Princeton Symposium on the Dead Sea Scrolls* (3 vols.; ed. J.H. Charlesworth; Waco: Baylor University Press, 2006), 1:131–47 (140–45); S. White

extended version of the Pentateuch was originally named "Pentateuchal Paraphrase" (PP)[96] but in their *editio princeps* Tov and White Crawford used the name "Reworked Pentateuch" (RP).[97] Against Tov and White Crawford, Segal has demonstrated that the manuscripts 4Q158 and 4Q364–367 display different characteristics and that they need to be classified differently. He showed that 4Q364–367 attest to different texts of the Torah while 4Q158 preserves remnants of a rewritten Bible composition.[98] 4Q364–367 are therefore described individually below, while the biblical text that is rewritten in 4Q158 needs to be discussed in entry → 21.2.2.

2.2.1.7.1 4QRP[b] (4Q364)

Sixty-seven fragments survive of 4QRP[b].[99] Frgs. 1–32 attest to 792 complete and partial words from Gen 25:18–21; 26:7–8; 28:x, 6; 29:32, 33?; 30:8–9, 11–14, 26–33, 35–36, x; 31:47–53; 32:18–20, 26–31; 34:2?; 35:28; 37:7–8; 38:14, 16–21; 44:30–34; 45:1, 21–27; 48:14–15?; Exod 19:17?; 21:14–15, 19–22; 24:12–14, 18, x; 25:1–2; 26:1, 33–35; Num 14:16–20, x; 20:17–18; 33:31–33, 38–39, 41–42, 44–49; Deut 1:1, 2, 4–6, 17–21, 23–28, 33, 45–46; 2:8–9, 12–14, 30–37; 3:1–2, 18, 20–23; 9:6–7, 12–18, 21?, 22–24, 25?, 27–29; 10:1–4, x, 6–7?, 10–13, 22; 11:1–2, 6–9, 23–24; 14:24–26.[100] What survives of frg. 3 i attests to either Gen 27:39 or Gen 27:41. Although no Leviticus text survives of 4QRP[b], the manuscript included most likely originally the

---

Crawford, *Rewriting Scripture in Second Temple Times* (Studies in the Dead Sea Scrolls and Related Literature; Grand Rapids: Eerdmans, 2008), 39–59; S. White Crawford, "Genesis in the Dead Sea Scrolls," in *The Book of Genesis: Composition, Reception, and Interpretation* (eds. C.A. Evans; J.N. Lohr, and D.L. Petersen; VTSup 152; Leiden: Brill, 2012), 353–73 (354–57); Brooke, "Torah," 113–14; Fabry, "Levitikus," 318; D. Falk, *The Parabiblical Texts: Strategies for Extending the Scriptures in the Dead Sea Scrolls* (Library of Second Temple Studies 63: London: T & T Clark, 2007), 107–19; I. Knohl, "The Bible Reworked at Qumran: The Temple and 4QReworked Pentateuch," in *The Qumran Scrolls and their World* (ed. M. Kister; Jerusalem: Yad Izhak Ben-Zvi, 2009), 157–68 [Hebr.]; Perrin "Variants,"*passim*. Unlike in his earlier publication ("Torah," 113–14), Brooke suggested in response to Segal's ideas (see n. 97 below) that 4Q158 and 4Q364–367 attest to five different texts that share a literary genre ("4Q158: Reworked Pentateuch or Reworked Pentateuch A?" *DSD* 8 [2001]: 219–41).

[96] Cf., e.g., Tov, "Textual Status," 43; White, "Preliminary Report," 217. The name "Pentateuchal Paraphrase" was suggested by John Strugnell (see Tov, "4QPentateuch," 74).

[97] Tov and White, "Reworked Pentateuch."

[98] Segal, "Reworked Pentateuch," *passim*; cf. also M. Segal, "Biblical Exegesis in 4Q158: Techniques and Genre," *Textus* 19 (1998): 45–62. Like Segal, Ulrich ("The Qumran Scrolls and the Biblical Text," in Schiffman, Tov, and VanderKam, *Fifty Years*, 51–59 [57]; "Dead Sea Scrolls," 88) understands the manuscripts 4Q158 and 4Q364–367 as textual witnesses to the Pentateuch. He describes RP as a "variant literary edition" of the Pentateuch. But unlike Segal, Ulrich understands 4Q158 and 4Q364–367 as several copies of the same literary edition of the Pentateuch. J.C. VanderKam's position ("Questions of Canon Viewed through the Dead Sea Scrolls," in *The Canon Debate* [eds. L.M. McDonald and J.A. Sanders; Peabody: Hendrikson Publishers, 2002], 91–109, 96–100) marks a middle ground between the ideas of Tov and White on the one hand and Segal and Ulrich on the other hand. VanderKam describes the RP manuscripts as belonging to a twilight zone between biblical manuscripts and rewritten Bible. The diverse nature of 4Q158 and 4Q364–367 is also emphasized by M.M. Zahn ("The Problem of Characterizing the 4QReworked Pentateuch Manuscripts: Bible, Rewritten Bible, or None of the Above?" *DSD* 15 [2008]: 315–39; *Rethinking Scripture, passim*). Like VanderKam, she treats the texts of 4Q158 and 4Q364–367 as falling between Pentateuchal manuscripts and rewritten Scripture (*Rewritten Scripture, passim*). Zahn thinks that without further study it cannot be decided whether 4Q158 and 4Q364–367 are Pentateuchal or represent various rewritten Bible compositions ("Problem," *passim*). Influenced by Segal, Tov has revised his understanding of 4Q158 and 4Q364–367. He regards these manuscripts now as five different copies of the Pentateuch that each attest to a different Pentateuchal text ("4QPentateuch," 78–82). Despite her recent publications to the contrary (see above, n. 94), White Crawford also describes 4Q364 and 4Q365 in her book *Rewriting Scripture in Second Temple Times* (Studies in the Dead Sea Scrolls and Related Literature; Grand Rapids: Eerdmans, 2008) as "regular pentateuchal texts" (56).

[99] Tov ("Textual Status," 45; cf. Tov and White, "Reworked Pentateuch," 188–89) speculated whether the four fragments of 4QRP[e] in fact belong to 4QRP[b], because the former includes only remnants of Leviticus while the latter does not. Several points argue against allocating the fragments of 4QRP[e] to 4QRP[b]: The two manuscripts employ different orthographic systems (4QRP[b] is baroque while 4QRP[e] is conservative). In 4QRP[b], every tetragrammaton is preceded by a colon while in 4QRP[e] it is not. The manuscripts were copied by different hands although they employ middle to late Hasmonean and late Hasmonean bookhands respectively.

[100] Elgvin ("MS 5439/1") thinks that frg. 7a of 4QGen-Exod[a] belongs to 4Q364 (= 4QRP[b]), while Puech ("Fragment 7a,") regards it as part of 4QGen-Exod[a]. The fragment preserves four words from Gen 37:8. For more details, see n. 6.

whole Torah. This might be confirmed by the large column height of 4QRP^b (39–41 lines or 31.2–32.8 cm).[101] The manuscript was copied in a "late Hasmonean or transitional formal script" from the years 75–50 B.C.E.[102] The orthography of 4QRP^b is baroque.[103] 4QRP^b reads thirty-four times with and eighty-one times against MT, thirty-nine times with and seventy-six times against SP, seventeen times with and eighty-two times against LXX as well as fifty-eight times non-aligned. The above statistics include nine macrovariants in which 4QRP^b reads never with and nine times against MT, three times with and seven times against SP, never with and nine times against LXX as well as six times non-aligned. Examples for these macrovariants include variant textual sequences as listed above and non-aligned additional text before Gen 28:6, after Exod 24:18, after Num 14:30, and before Deut 10:6. 4QRP^b reads with SP additional text after Gen 30:36 and before Deut 2:8 (= Num 20:17–18). 4QRP^b never included the text of Num 33:40. The manuscript attests to a non-aligned text of the Pentateuch that reworks a pre-Samaritan text.[104]

2.2.1.7.2 4QRP^c + 4QT? (4Q365 + 4Q365a)

An added obstacle to the text-critical study of 4QRP^c are the five fragments that Tov and White designated as 4Q365a (4QT?).[105] These five fragments were copied by the same scribe as the rest of 4QRP^c and employ the same orthography,[106] but they include only non-biblical text. "Frg. 1 contains material concerning the Festival of Unleavened Bread. Frg. 2 I discusses the Day of Firstfruits and other sacrificial ordinances, and then contains the beginning of the description of the middle court of the temple. Col. II give the names of the gates of the outer court. Finally, frgs. 3, 4 and 5 I contain the specifications of certain buildings and objects probably associated with the temple."[107] Furthermore, 4Q365a 2 resembles the text of 11QT^a XXXVIII and XLI–XLII. Therefore, the five fragments of 4Q365a could be:

1) a further copy of the *Temple Scroll*;[108]
2) a copy of a literary source of the *Temple Scroll*;[109]
3) a modified version of the *Temple Scroll*;[110]
4) five further fragments of 4QRP^c.[111]

---

[101] For the measurements of 4QRP^b, cf. Tov and White, "Reworked Pentateuch," 198.

[102] Cf. Tov and White, "Reworked Pentateuch," 201–02, and White Crawford, "Preliminary Report," 217.

[103] Cf. Tov, "Textual Status," 45–46; Tov and White, "Reworked Pentateuch," 202–03; Brooke, "Torah," 113.

[104] Cf. Tov, "Proto-Samaritan Texts," 406; Tov, "Textual Status," 57–64; Tov and White, "Reworked Pentateuch," 193; Tov, *TCHB*², 99. Against Fabry, "Levitikus," 317.

[105] Tov and White, "Reworked Pentateuch."

[106] Cf. Tov and White, "Reworked Pentateuch," 319–20.

[107] Tov and White, "Reworked Pentateuch," 319.

[108] Thus Y. Yadin, *The Temple Scroll* (3. vols.; Bd. 1: Jerusalem: Israel Exploration Society, 1977–1983), 8–9; cf. É. Puech, "Fragments du plus ancient exemplaire du *Rouleau du Temple* (4Q524)," in *Legal Texts and Legal Issues: Proceedings of the Second Meeting of the International Organization for Qumran Studies, Cambridge 1995: Published in Honour of Joseph M. Baumgarten* (eds. M. Bernstein, F. García Martínez, and J. Kampen; STDJ 23; Leiden: Brill, 1997), 18–64 (49–50, 55–57).

[109] Cf. M. Wise, *A Critical Study of the Temple Scroll from Qumran Cave 11* (SAOC 49; Chicago: University of Chicago Press, 1990), 44–59, esp. 58–59; similar Tov, "Textual Status," 48–49; Tov and White, "Reworked Pentateuch," 320; S. White Crawford, "Three Fragments from Qumran Cave 4 and Their Relationship to the Temple Scroll," *JQR* 85 (1994): 259–73 (260–61, 271); S. White Crawford, *The Temple Scroll and Related Texts* (Companion to the Qumran Scrolls 2; Sheffield: Sheffield Academic Press, 2000), 14–15; B.A. Levine, "The Temple Scroll," *BASOR* 232 (1978): 5–23 (5–6).

[110] Thus, e.g., B.Z. Wacholder, "The Fragmentary Remains of the 11QTorah (Temple Scroll): 11QTorah^b and 11QTorah^c plus 4QparaTorah Integrated with 11QTorah^a," *HUCA* 62 (1991): 1–116 (4): either a reworked version of the text of 11QT^a or a divergent source.

[111] Cf. J. Strugnell (letter to B.Z. Wacholder; quoted in B.Z. Wacholder, *The Dawn of Qumran: The Sectarian Torah and the Teacher of Righteousness* [HUCM 8; Cincinnati: Hebrew Union College Press, 1983], 205–06); H. Stegemann, "The Origins of the Temple Scroll," in *Congress Volume: Jerusalem 1986* (ed. J.A. Emerton; VTSup 40; Leiden: Brill, 1988), 235–56 (237); H. Stegemann, "The Literary Composition of the Temple Scroll and Its Status at Qumran," in *Temple Scroll Studies: Papers Presented at the International Symposium on the Temple Scroll, Manchester, December 1987* (ed. G.J. Brooke; JSPSup 7; Sheffield: JSOT Press, 1989), 123–48 (125–26, 135); F. García Martínez, "New Perspectives on the Study of the Dead Sea Scrolls," in *Perspectives on the Study of the Old Testament and Early Judaism: A Symposium in Honour of Adam S. van der Woude on the Occasion of his 70th Birthday* (eds. F. García Martínez and E. Noort; VTSup 73; Leiden: Brill, 1998), 230–48 (237–39); F. García Martínez, "The Temple Scroll and the

In the fourth case, the text attested by 4QRP^c would still be a source of the *Temple Scroll*. An observation by Hartmut Stegemann is decisive.[112] Stegemann argues that the damage patterns of fragments 4Q365a 2 and 4QRP^c 6 resemble each other so clearly that they must have been part of the same scroll. If 4Q365a 2 and 4QRP^c 6 come from the same scroll, then all other fragments of 4Q365a also need to belong to 4QRP^c. This, in turn, means that the text of 4QRP^c preserves one of the sources of the *Temple Scroll*.

Including the fragments designated incorrectly as 4Q365a, sixty-seven fragments survive of 4QRP^c. Frgs. 1–38 attest to 1,204 complete and partial words from Gen 21:9–10; Exod 8:13–19; 9:9–12; 10:19?, 20; 14:10, 12–17, 19–21; 15:16–20, x, 22–26; 17:3–5; 18:13–15; 26:34–36; 28:16–17, 19–20; 29:20–22; 30:37–38; 31:1–3; 35:3–5; 36:32–38; 37:29; 38:1–7; 39:1–5, 8–19; Lev 11:1–2, 17, 21–24, 32, 40–42, 44–45; 13:6–8, 15, 17–18, 51–52; 16:11–12?; 18:26–28; 23:42–44; 24:1–2, x; 25:7–9; 26:17–28, 30–32; 27:34?; Num 1:1–5; 3:26–30; 4:47–49; 7:1, 78–80; 8:11–12; 9:15, 17–19, 22–23; 10:2–3; 13:12, 13, 14–15, 16–25, 29–30; 15:26–28; 17:20–24; 27:11; 36:1–2; Deut 19:20–21; 20:1. Frg. 37 attests to remnants of either Deut 2:24 or 2:36.[113] As passages from all five books of the Torah are extant in 4QRP^c, the scroll included originally the whole Pentateuch. This hypothesis is confirmed by the large column height of 4QRP^c (43–47 lines or 30.1–32.25 cm).[114] Stegemann estimated the original length of 4QRP^c as approximately twenty-five meters.[115]

Tov and White date 4QRP^c paleographically to the years 75–50 B.C.E. and describe its script as "transitional between the late Hasmonean and early Herodian periods."[116] The orthography of 4QRP^c is baroque and somewhat fuller than that of 4QRP^b.[117]

4QRP^c reads fifty-eight times with and 146 times against MT, sixty-nine times with and 135 times against SP, thirty-six times with and 146 times against LXX, as well as ninety-eight times non-aligned.[118] Among these variant readings are seven macro-variants in which 4QRP^c reads once with and six times against MT, never with and seven times against SP, once with and six times against LXX. The seven macro-variants include, on the one hand, additional text preceding Exod 15:22 (remnants of an extensive Song of Miriam)[119] and following Lev 24:2 (detailed regulations for a wood sacrifice that are reminiscent of 11QT^a XXII–XXIV par 11QT^b VI).[120] On the other hand, 4QRP^c never included the text of Exod 39:6–7 and attests to a

---

New Jerusalem," in Flint–VanderKam, *DSS, 2.431–60 (435); E. Qimron, *The Temple Scroll: A Critical Edition with Extensive Reconstructions* (JDS; Jerusalem: Israel Exploration Society, 1996), 4; S. White Crawford, "4QTemple? (4Q365a) Revisited," in *Prayer and Poetry in the Dead Sea Scrolls and Related Literature: Essays in Honor of Eileen Schuller on the Occasion of Her 65th Birthday* (eds. J. Penner, K.M. Penner, and C. Wassen; STDJ 98; Leiden: Brill, 2012), 87–95; M.M. Zahn, "4QReworked Pentateuch C and the Literary Sources of the Temple Scroll: A New (Old) Proposal," *DSD* 19 (2012): 133–58.

[112] Oral communication to the author; cf. Lange, *Handbuch, 40.

[113] E.J.C. Tigchelaar, "Gleanings from the Plates of Unidentified Fragments: Two PAM 43.674 Identifications (4Q365 and 4Q416)," in *'Go Out and Study the Land' (Judges 18:2): Archaeological, Historical and Textual Studies in Honor of Hanan Eshel* (eds. A.M. Maeir, J. Magness, and L.H. Schiffman; JSJSup 148; Leiden: Brill, 2011), 317–22 (318–19), identifies PAM 43.691 frg. 11 as a further fragment of 4Q365, which would attest to four complete and partial words from Exod 22:5–6. Although Tigchelaar's identification seems plausible, it must remain speculative given that only eleven characters are preserved of this fragment.

[114] For the measurements of 4Q365, see Tov and White, "Reworked Pentateuch," 256–57.

[115] Stegemann's work is unpublished but summarized in Tov, "Textual Status," 53, and in Tov and White, "Reworked Pentateuch," 192.

[116] White Crawford, "Preliminary Report," 271; cf. Tov and White, "Reworked Pentateuch," 260–61. The paleographic date to the years 125–75 B.C.E. (White Crawford, "Temple Scroll," 15) [see n. 107] is due to a typographic error (email correspondence of White Crawford with the author from February 20, 2006).

[117] Cf. Brooke, "Torah," 113; Tov, "Textual Status," 45–46; Tov and White, "Reworked Pentateuch," 261.

[118] The above statistics include neither the text of 4QRP^c 37 nor the five fragments of 4Q365a.

[119] For the Song of Miriam in 4Q365, see A. Feldman, "The Song of Mirjam (4Q365 6a ii + 6c 1–7) Revisited," *JBL* 132 (2013): 905–11; and H. Tervanotko, *Denying Her Voice: The Figure of Miriam in Ancient Jewish Literature* (Jyväskylä: Bookwell Oy, 2013), 140–57.

[120] Cf. Tov and White, "Reworked Pentateuch," 293–95.

divergent textual sequence: Num 4:49→7:1; Num 13:15→13:13; Num 27:11→36:1–2. To these macro-variants, the non-biblical passages of the five fragments of 4Q365a need to be added. Given the agreements with SP, there can be no doubt that 4QRP^c attests to a non-aligned text that developed from a pre-Samaritan text.[121] Tov describes the relationship between 4QRP^c and SP as follows:

> 1. In minutiae, 4Q365 is closer to 𝔐 than to the other sources. 2. No evidence, positive or negative, has been preserved with regard to harmonizing additions. 3. In the layout of the Song at the Sea, the spacing resembles that of 𝔐, and not that of 𝔐. 4. 4Q365 does not reflect two cases of editorial manipulation of 𝔐 (sequence: Exod 26:35; 30:1–10; 26,36 ff. [frg. 8a–b]; transposition of Exod 29:21 after v 28 [frg. 9b II]). 5. 4Q365 often differs from 𝔐 in 'non-aligned readings' which should be ascribed to 4QRP's rewriting of the biblical text. Among these are omissions of 4Q365 of the following verses: Exod 14:18; 39:6–7; Lev 11:19; and the different internal sequence of Num 13:12–16.[122]

That the text of 4QRP^c grew from a pre-Samaritan text is for Tov also underlined by its agreements with 4QNum^b: "4QNum^b is closely related to 4Q365, even though no major variants are involved."[123]

2.2.1.7.3 4QRP^d (4Q366)

The five surviving fragments of 4QRP^d preserve 123 complete and partial words from Exod 21:35–37; 22:1–4; Lev 24:20, 22; 25:39–43; Num 29:14, 16–24, 32–39; 30:1; Deut 16:13–14; 14:14–16, 18, 20–21. The scroll most likely once included the whole Pentateuch but at least the books Exodus–Deuteronomy. 4QRP^d was copied in a late Hasmonean bookhand from the years 75–50 B.C.E.[124] The orthography of the manuscript is conservative.[125] Tov and White regard the textual classification of 4QRP^d as impossible due to its extensive damage.[126] Fabry regards it as a pre-Samaritan witness.[127] In the case of smaller textual differences, 4QRP^d reads eleven times with and fifteen times against MT, nine times with and seventeen times against SP, six times with and fourteen times against LXX, as well as six times non-aligned. 4QRP^d further reads three times with 4QRP^a, twice with 4QpaleoExod^m, and once with 4QNum^b. As the text of 4QRP^d is equidistant from MT, SP, and LXX, it can best be classified as non-aligned.[128] This classification is supported by two differences in textual sequence between 4QRP^d on the one hand and MT, SP, and LXX on the other hand: Lev 24:22→25:39 ff.; Num 30:1→Deut 16:13 ff.

2.2.1.7.4 4QRP^e (4Q367)

Four fragments survive of 4QRP^e. Frgs. 1–3 attest to 144 complete and partial words from Lev 11:47; 12:1–8; 13:1; 15:14–15; 19:1–4, 9–15; 20:13; 27:30–34. As only passages from the book of Leviticus are preserved, it remains uncertain whether or not 4QRP^e originally contained the whole Pentateuch. 4QRP^e was copied in a middle or late Hasmonean bookhand (with semi-cursive elements) from the years 100–60(25) B.C.E.[129] The supralinear correction in Lev 12:2 was inserted by the original scribe of the scroll. The orthography of 4QRP^e is conservative.[130] Tov and White regard the textual classification of 4QRP^e as impossible due to its extensive damage.[131] Fabry regards it as a pre-Samaritan witness.[132] In smaller cases of textual variation, 4QRP^e reads twelve times with and twice against MT, twelve times with and twice against SP, as well

---

[121] Cf. Tov, "Textual Status," 65–73; Tov and White, "Reworked Pentateuch," 194–95. Against Fabry, "Levitikus," 317 (4QRP^c is pre-Samaritan) and A.Y. Kim, "The Textual Alignment of the Tabernacle Section of 4Q365 (Fragments 8a–b, 9a–b i, 9b ii, 12a i, 12b iii)," Textus 21 (2002): 45–69 (53–68).

[122] Tov and White, "Reworked Pentateuch," 194.

[123] Tov and White, "Reworked Pentateuch," 194.

[124] Similarly also Tov and White, "Reworked Pentateuch," 336–37.

[125] Cf. Brooke, "Torah," 113; Tov and White, "Reworked Pentateuch," 337.

[126] Tov and White, "Reworked Pentateuch," 195; cf. Tov, "Textual Status," 76.

[127] Fabry, "Levitikus," 317.

[128] Cf. Lange, *Handbuch, 42.

[129] Cf. Tov and White, "Reworked Pentateuch," 346.

[130] Cf. Brooke, "Torah," 113; Tov and White, "Reworked Pentateuch," 346.

[131] Tov and White, "Reworked Pentateuch," 195; cf. Tov, "Textual Status," 77.

[132] Fabry, "Levitikus," 317.

as three times with and nine times against LXX. The extant macro-variants of 4QRP[e] include a textual sequence divergent from MT, SP, and LXX (Lev 15:15→19:1 ff.; Lev 20:13→27:30 ff.), the lack of vv. 5–8 in Leviticus 19, and additional text in Lev 12:5 and before Lev 20:13.[133] Both the macro-variants of 4QRP[e], and the equidistance of the text of this manuscript from MT, SP, and LXX argue for its classification as non-aligned.[134]

2.2.1.7.5 4QGen[f] (4Q6) as an Excerpted Non-Aligned Manuscript

Four fragments survive of 4QGen[f], attesting to 133 complete and partial words from Gen 33:19–20; 34:1–2; 48:1–11.[135] The small height of the scroll of 13.8 cm[136] makes it impossible that 4QGen[f] included the whole book of Genesis. Therefore, the fragments of 4QGen[f] represent the remains of an excerpted manuscript. 4QGen[f] was copied in a late Hasmonean formal hand from the middle of the first century B.C.E.[137] As 4QGen[f] was written in an inexperienced hand, Tov identifies the manuscript as a scribal exercise.[138] As frg. 1a, published by Eshel and Eshel, shows that 4QGen[f] included not only Gen 48:1–11 but also other parts of the book of Genesis, and as scribal exercises were done mostly on single scrap pieces of leather or an ostracon, it is more likely that 4QGen[f] is an excerpted manuscript of Genesis copied by a beginner in the scribal craft. The orthography of 4QGen[f] is conservative but fuller than that of MT.[139] In the little text that is preserved of 4QGen[f], the manuscript reads twelve times with and eight times against MT, ten times with and ten times against SP, never with and fifteen times against LXX, as well as six times non-aligned. Although 4QGen[f] is statistically closest to MT, its text is best characterized as non-aligned[140] because of its six-percent deviation from MT.

2.2.1.7.6 2QExod[a] (2Q2)

Of 2QExod[a], thirteen fragments are extant. Frgs. 1–10 attest to 142 complete and partial words from Exod 1:11–14; 7:1–4; 9:27–29; 11:3–7; 12:32–41; 21:18–19, 20?; 26:11–13; 30:21, 23–25; 32:32–34. 2QExod[a] was copied in a late Herodian bookhand from the years 50–68 C.E.[141] The manuscript's orthography is conservative but baroque morphological forms such as וחברתה "and you shall couple" in Exod 26:11 do occur.[142] 2QExod[a] reads twice with and ten times against MT, three times with and nine times against SP, five times with and seven times against LXX, as well as four times non-aligned. 2QExod[a] is hence equally removed from MT, SP, and LXX. The manuscript is thus best classified as non-aligned,[143] although Baillet emphasizes that it attests to "un certain nombre de variantes de la LXX."[144]

2.2.1.7.7 4QExod[b] (4Q13)

Of 4QExod[b], six fragments survive, attesting to 389 complete and partial words from Exod 1:1, 3–6, 10–11, 16–21; 2:2–18; 3:13–21; 4:1, 3–8; 5:3–14.[145] With a height of 51 cm, the scroll is among the largest from Qumran and might have contained once the whole Pentateuch.[146] The material reconstruction

---

[133] Cf. Tov and White, "Reworked Pentateuch," 348, 351.

[134] Cf. Lange, *Handbuch*, 43.

[135] After the manuscript's *editio princeps* was published (Davila, "6. 4QGen[f]," 53–55), Eshel and Eshel identified a further fragment of 4QGen[f] that is in private ownership, which they count as frg. 1a ("New Fragments," 135–37).

[136] Cf. Davila, "6. 4QGen[f]," 53.

[137] Davila, "6. 4QGen[f]," 53; cf. Davila, "Unpublished Pentateuchal Manuscripts," 119–20; Davila, "Joseph Story," 174; Davila, "Text-Type," 21; Eshel and Eshel, "New Fragments," 135–36.

[138] Tov, *Scribal Practices*, 14; cf. D.M. Carr, *Writing on the Tablet of the Heart: Origins of Scripture and Literature* (Oxford: Oxford University Press, 2005), 230.

[139] Cf. Davila, "6. 4QGen[f]," 52. For lists of orthographic variants, see ibid. and Davila, "Unpublished Pentateuchal Manuscripts," 117–19.

---

[140] Cf. Davila, "Unpublished Pentateuchal Manuscripts," 200–01; Davila, "Text-Type," 22–23; Tov, *"Biblical Texts," 155.

[141] Similarly also Baillet, "2. Exode," 49 ("calligraphie hérodienne soignée").

[142] Cf. Baillet, "2. Exode," 49; Brooke, "Torah," 102. Against Tov, *"Synthese," 17, and *"Biblical Texts," 154 who allocates the manuscript to the so-called Qumran orthography.

[143] Tov, *"Synthese," 17, 20; Tov, *"Biblical Texts," 154, 156.

[144] Baillet, "2. Exode," 49; cf. Brooke, "Torah," 102.

[145] One of the six fragments is not mentioned in the *editio princeps* (Cross, "13. 4QExod[b]") but was identified by Tigchelaar among the unidentified fragments from DJD XXXIII ("Unidentified Fragments," 483).

[146] For the measurements of 4QExod[b], see Cross, "13. 4QExod[b]," 80.

makes it likely that the book of Genesis preceded the book of Exodus in 4QExod^b.¹⁴⁷ The manuscript was copied in an early Herodian semi-cursive hand from the years 30 B.C.E. to 20 C.E.¹⁴⁸ The morphology of 4QExod^b is almost exclusively conservative but the manuscript reads fuller than MT with few exceptions: "The orthography of the manuscript actually stands typologically between the orthography of 𝔐 and the full orthography (coupled with archaic and pseudo-archaic forms) we have labeled 'the baroque style'."¹⁴⁹ Early studies regarded 4QExod^b as a witness of the Hebrew parent text of LXX-Exod.¹⁵⁰ Cross still argues for a certain closeness of this manuscript to LXX-Exod in his text-typological description in his *editio princeps*:

> We can summarize the relationship of 4QExod^b to the textual family standing behind the Old Greek translation as follows: In 23 variants 4QExod^b stands with 𝔊. In 14 cases these are secondary readings, the most important variants for determining filiation. In 13 variants, 4QExod^b agrees with 𝔐, 11 of the 13 in superior readings – the least important readings in determining filiation, since superior (or original) readings may survive independently in different textual families. In 18 variants 4QExod^b agrees with 𝔪, 11 of those 18 in superior readings, 5 of the 18 in secondary readings. We must conclude that 4QExod^b is a collateral witness to the textual family which provided the *Vorlage* of the Old Greek translation.¹⁵¹

Despite this closeness to LXX-Exod, its twenty-four non-aligned readings characterize the text of 4QExod^b as non-aligned.¹⁵²

2.2.1.7.8 4QExod^c (4Q14)

Of the forty-seven surviving fragments of 4QExod^c, only the text of frgs. 1–36 can still be identified. They attest to 802 complete and partial words from Exod 3:13–15; 5:9–14; 7:17–23, 26–28; 8:1, 5–6, 8–9, 11–14, 16–18, 22; 9:11, 15–16, 18–20, 22–25, 27–35; 10:1–5, 7–9, 12–19, 23–24; 11:9–10, 12–16; 12:31–48; 13:18–22; 14:2–5, 7–13; 15:9, 11–21; 17:1–16; 18:1–12.¹⁵³ The manuscript was copied in a late Hasmonean or early Herodian bookhand from the years 50–25 B.C.E.¹⁵⁴ The six supralinear additions were all inserted by the original scribe of the scroll.¹⁵⁵ The orthography of 4QExod^c is conservative but somewhat fuller than that of MT.¹⁵⁶ Variant statistics characterize the text of 4QExod^c as non-aligned:¹⁵⁷ The manuscript reads seventeen times with and forty-one times against MT, seventeen times with and forty-one times against SP, seventeen times with and twenty-five times against LXX, as well as twenty-six times non-aligned. Both the preserved text and the material reconstruction demonstrate that 4QExod^c included neither the characteristic long texts of the pre-Samaritan text nor those of SP.¹⁵⁸

---

¹⁴⁷ Thus Cross, "13. 4QExod^b," 79–80.

¹⁴⁸ Thus Cross, "13. 4QExod^b," 79.

¹⁴⁹ Cross, "13. 4QExod^b," 80, 82.

¹⁵⁰ Cf., e.g., F.M. Cross in Benoit et al., *"Editing," 83, and in Benoit et al., *"Travail," 56; Cross, *ALQ¹, 137–38 with n. 31; Cross, *ALQ³, 134–36 (esp. n. 1); Milik, *Ten Years, 24; Brooke, "Torah," 103.

¹⁵¹ Cross, "13. 4QExod^b," 84; cf. Tov, *TCHB², 115; Tov, *"Synthese," 19–20; Tov, *"Biblical Texts," 155–56.

¹⁵² Cf. Lange, *Handbuch, 59. Tigchelaar's newly identified fragment ("Unidentified Fragments, 483") adds one more non-aligned reading to the statistics of Cross.

¹⁵³ Eshel and Eshel ("Preliminary Report," 272–73) identified two further fragments of this manuscript after the publication of its *editio princeps* that they designate as frgs. 1a–b. Frgs. 1a–b are in private ownership. Photographs are published in L. Biondi, *From the Dead Sea Scrolls to the Forbidden Book: A History of the Bible Told through Ancient Manuscripts and Early Printed Bibles* (2004; place of publication not identified), iv (frg. 1a) and in L. Biondi, *From the Dead Sea Scrolls to the Bible in America: A Brief History of the Bible from Antiquity to Modern America Told through Ancient Manuscripts and Early European and American Printed Bibles* (Chicago: Bible League, 2004), 17 (frg. 1b).

¹⁵⁴ Cf. Sanderson, "14. 4QExod^c," 100.

¹⁵⁵ Cf. Sanderson, "14. 4QExod^c," 97.

¹⁵⁶ For the orthography of 4QExod^c, see Sanderson, "14. 4QExod^c," 100–02; for a list of orthographic variants, see op. cit., 101.

¹⁵⁷ Cf. I. Young, "The 'Archaic' Poetry of the Pentateuch in the MT, Samaritan Pentateuch and 4QExod^c," *AbrN* 35 (1998): 74–83; Eshel and Eshel, "Preliminary Report," 272–73; Lange, *Handbuch, 60; against Tov, *"Biblical Texts," 154.

¹⁵⁸ Thus Sanderson, "14. 4QExod^c," 103.

2.2.1.7.9 4QExod-Lev^f (4Q17)

4QExod-Lev^f survives in five fragments. Frgs. 1–4 preserve 259 complete and partial words from Exod 38:18–22; 39:4–7, 9–11, 13–24; 40:8–27; Lev 1:13–15, 17; 2:1. The unusual column height of sixty lines[159] allows for speculation as to whether 4QExod-Lev^f once included the whole Pentateuch. The paleographic date is set in the middle of the third century B.C.E. 4QExod-Lev^f is thus one of the earliest manuscripts from the Qumran library: "The script is not the formal script of the third century represented by 4QSam^b and 4QJer^a, but belongs to a less formal script tradition which I have called 'protocursive.'"[160] The orthography of 4QExod-Lev^f is conservative but fuller than MT.[161] The manuscript reads twice with and twenty-seven times against MT, six times with and twenty-three times against SP, five times with and thirteen times against LXX, as well as twenty-one times non-aligned. "The order of the text of 4QExod-Lev^f is significant in determining its textual affiliations. Chap. 39:3–24 preserved in this manuscript immediately precedes chap. 40 in agreement with the order of the Massoretic and the Samaritan traditions. On the contrary, in the Septuagint, chap. 39:10–32 is found at 36:10–32 in a radically different ordering of the tradition."[162] Despite these structural agreements with MT, SP, and six further readings with SP, 4QExod-Lev^f cannot be viewed as a pre-Samaritan text.[163] The disproportionally high number of non-aligned readings characterizes the text of 4QExod-Lev^f instead as non-aligned.[164]

---

[159] Cf. Cross, "17. 4QExod-Lev^f," 134.

[160] Cross, "17. 4QExod-Lev^f," 134; cf. Cross, *"Development," 153–58.

[161] Cf. Cross, "17. 4QExod-Lev^f," 135–36. For a list of orthographic variants, see op.cit. 135. For the orthography of 4QExod-Lev^f, see also D.N. Freedman, "The Massoretic Text and the Qumran Scrolls: A Study in Orthography," *Textus* 2 (1962): 87–102 (96, 98–100). Against Freedman and Mathews, *Leviticus Scroll*, 59–60, who list 4QExod-Lev^f under the category of "Proto-Samaritan Spelling"; cf. Brooke, "Torah," 103.

[162] Cross, "17. 4QExod-Lev^f," 135–36.

[163] Against Cross, "17. 4QExod-Lev^f," 136; Tov, *TCHB*, 108; Tov, *"Synthese," 18; Tov, *"Biblical Texts," 155; Fabry, "Leviticus," 315; Flint, "Book of Leviticus," 325.

[164] Cf. Tov, *"Synthese," 20; Tov, *"Biblical Texts," 156; Lange, *Handbuch*, 62.

2.2.1.7.10 4QLev-Num^a (4Q23)

There are 104 extant fragments of 4QLev-Num^a. Frgs. 1–66 and 68–74 preserve 1,073 complete and partial words from Lev 12:32–33; 14:23, 25–34, 40–54; 15:10–11, 19–24; 16:15–29; 18:16–18, 20–21; 19:3–8; 24:11–12; 26:26, 28–33; 27:5–22; Num 1:1–5, 21–22, 36–40; 2:18, 20, 31–32; 3:3–16, 18–19, 51; 4:1–12, 40–49; 5:1–9; 8:7–12, 21–22; 9:3–8, 10, 19–20; 10:13–19, 21–23; 11:4–5, 16–22; 12:3–11; 13:21; 22:5–6, 22–24; 26:5–7; 30:3?; 32:8–15, 23–25, 27–39, 41–42; 33:5–9, 22, 25, 28, 31, 33–34, 52–54; 35:4–5. Frg. 67 attests to one word from Num 30:7, 30:9, or 30:13. A material reconstruction of the manuscript showed that 4QLev-Num^a was originally only six meters or fifty-one columns long and therefore included only the books of Leviticus and Numbers.[165] 4QLev-Num^a was copied in an early Hasmonean bookhand from the middle of the second century B.C.E. or later.[166] "On at least two occasions the scribe omitted apparently an entire verse: at Lev 14:24 and 45 ... At 14:45 the missing verse was supralineally supplied, seemingly by a later hand. On a third occasion, at Lev 14:43, the fragment is not sufficiently extensive to be certain whether the scribe had an original short reading (against all other witnesses) or omitted a phrase through parablepsis." Four further corrections in Lev 14:31, 53; 16:28; and Num 9:10 were all inserted by the original scribe.[167] The orthography of 4QLev-Num^a is conservative but in some cases fuller than MT.[168] 4QLev-Num^a reads thirty times with and eighteen times against MT, thirteen times with and thirty-five against SP, eighteen times with and sixteen times against LXX, as well eleven times non-aligned. Statistically, 4QLev-Num^a is equally close to MT and LXX but somewhat more distant from SP.[169] 4QLev-Num^a does not

---

[165] For the measurements and material reconstruction, see Ulrich, "23. 4QLev–Num^a," 153–54.

[166] Cf. Ulrich, "23. 4QLev–Num^a," 154.

[167] For the corrections and the quote, see Ulrich, "23. 4QLev-Num^a," 154.

[168] Cf. Ulrich, "23. 4QLev–Num^a," 154–55. For a list of orthographic variants, see op.cit., 155.

[169] Against Pike, "Numbers," 172 ("proto-Masoretic"), and Tov, *"Biblical Texts," 155 ("equally close to the medieval texts of MT and to SP"); Flint, "Book of Leviticus," 326 ("*mixed*").

align with any of the three main medieval textual traditions of the Torah. Due, also, to its sixteen non-aligned readings, the text of 4QLev-Num^a should thus be classified as non-aligned and equally close to MT and LXX.[170] The most interesting variant is the lack of Lev 14:14 in 4QLev-Num^a due to *parablepsis* (cf. LXX[528]).

2.2.1.7.11 4QLev^b (4Q24)

Thirty fragments survive of 4QLev^b. Frgs. 1–28 attest to 622 complete and partial words from Lev 1:11–17; 2:1–3, 5–16; 3:1, 8–14; 21:17–18, 20, 24; 22:2–6, 8–26, 28, 30–33; 23:1, 2–5, 8, 10–22, 24–25, 40; 24:2–14, 16–17, 19–21, 23; 25:28–29, 45–49, 51–52. With a column height of on average forty-one lines or 30.75 cm,[171] 4QLev^b could have included the text of the whole Pentateuch. The manuscript was copied in a late Hasmonean bookhand from the middle of the first century B.C.E.[172] The orthography of 4QLev^b is conservative but sometimes fuller than that of MT.[173] In the Leviticus text that is still preserved in the fragments of 4QLev^b, the extant versions vary only to a limited degree from one another. This makes the textual classification of the manuscript difficult. 4QLev^b reads eight times with and twenty-three times against MT, six times with and twenty-five times against SP, sixteen times with and nine times against LXX, as well as twelve times non-aligned. "The manuscript … seems not to have contained the full text of Lev 3:1–11, suggesting either that the *Vorlage* had an abbreviated text or that the scribe may have skipped some text … The manuscript also displays a small plus against 𝔐𝔚𝔊 in Lev 22:22."[174] With the necessary caution, the text of 4QLev^b can be classified as non-aligned with a certain closeness to LXX.[175]

---

[170] See Lange, *Handbuch*, 69; cf. Fabry, "Levitikus," 315.

[171] For the measurements of the scroll, see Ulrich, "24. 4QLev^b," 177.

[172] Ulrich, "24. 4QLev^b," 177.

[173] Cf. Ulrich, "24. 4QLev^b," 177. For a list of orthographic variants, see op.cit., 178.

[174] Ulrich, "24. 4QLev^b," 177.

[175] Cf. Fabry, "Levitikus," 315. Against Ulrich, "24. 4QLev^b," 177, and Tov, *"Biblical Texts," 155, who describe 4QLev^b as equally close to MT and SP. Flint, "Book of Leviticus," 326, classifies the manuscript as "*mixed*."

2.2.1.7.12 11QpaleoLev^a (11Q1)

11QpaleoLev^a is among the best-preserved scrolls from Qumran. In addition to fifteen fragments (frgs. A–M),[176] the remnant of a rolled-up scroll that is 100.5 cm or seven columns long was found in Qumran Cave 11.[177] Col. VII is uninscribed and represents a handlesheet. Frg. L is in private ownership.[178] Nine additional fragments were published by Tigchelaar[179] and additional verses of text were identified by Puech.[180] On the whole, 11QpaleoLev^a attests to remnants of Lev 4:23–24, 31, 33–35?; 6:12–13; 8:10–11; 10:4–7, 9 (or 14?), 15?; 11:27–32; 13:3–9, 33–34?, 39–40, 42–43; 14:16–21, 53–55, 57; 15:2–5; 16:1–6, 34; 17:1–5; 18:27–30; 19:1–4; 20:1–6; 21:6–12; 22:20–27; 23:22–29; 24:8–14; 25:28–36; 26:17–26; 27:11–19.[181] The paleographic date of 11QpaleoLev^a is debated. All studies agree that 11QpaleoLev^a needs to be dated later than 4QpaleoExod^m.[182] Freedman proposed originally a date in the late second or early first century B.C.E.,[183] which Hanson narrowed down to "around 100 B.C.E."[184] As McLean dates 4QpaleoExod^m later than other paleographers, he places 11QpaleoLev^a "between 1 and

---

[176] Frg. L is now part of the Dead Sea Scrolls collection of Southwestern Baptist Theological Seminary (DSS F.169 = DSS F.Lev3) and previously was owned by a private individual from Paris. I am obliged to Sidnie White Crawford for this information.

[177] For the measurements of 11QpaleoLev^a, see Mathews, "Leviticus Scroll," 7; Freedman and Mathews, *Leviticus Scroll*, 5.

[178] The fragment was acquired by the French professor, Georges Roux, in 1967 (cf. Freedman and Mathews, *Leviticus Scroll*, 3).

[179] Tigchelaar, "*11Q1* Fragments," *passim*.

[180] Puech, "Notes en marge," 161–83.

[181] For the different contents identified by Freedman and Mathews on the one hand (*Leviticus Scroll*) and Puech on the other hand ("Notes en marge"), see the table in Lange, *Handbuch*, 74 n. 284.

[182] For the various paleographic dates of 4QpaleoExod^m, see → 2.2.1.3.1.

[183] Freedman, "Variant Readings," 525.

[184] R.S. Hanson, "Paleography," in Freedman and Mathews, *Leviticus Scroll*, 15–23 (23); cf. also op. cit., *passim*, and Mathews, "Leviticus Scroll," 24–27; Mathews, "The Leviticus Scroll (11QpaleoLev) and the Text of the Hebrew Bible," 173; Mathews, "The Paleo-Hebrew Leviticus Scroll from Qumran," 49–50; Puech, "Notes en marges," 167; Brooke, "Torah," 105.

50 AD."[185] The few corrections in this manuscripts were inserted by its original scribe.[186] For the division of paragraphs, 11QpaleoLev[a] employs a *vacat* with a paleo-Hebrew *waw* in its middle. This *waw* is, at the same time, the first character of the following verse.[187] The orthography of 11QpaleoLev[a] is conservative.[188]

The text of 11QpaleoLev[a] was characterized by Freedman as a "mixed text" that represents an earlier stage of pre-SP.[189] Mathews argues similarly: "It (scil. 11QpaleoLev[a]) does not mirror one tradition, it has a mixture of readings and a high number of unique variants as well. It is, therefore, an inferior witness, the kind of text one would expect of a sectarian manuscript antedating the stabilization of the Hebrew Bible."[190] "Q's text evidences a mixture of readings – having no clear dependence on any one source. Its number of unique, but corrupt, readings suggest an inferior witness without strong attachments to any one tradition."[191] However, Tov demonstrated that 11QpaleoLev[a] is not an inferior witness but a text that does not align with MT, SP, and LXX. Tov characterizes it therefore as "independent"[192] or "non-aligned."[193]

2.2.1.7.13 1QDeut[b] (1Q5)

Fifty fragments of 1QDeut[b] are extant. Frgs. 1–22 attest to 237 complete and partial words from Deut 1:9, 11, 13; 8:8–9; 9:10; 11:30–31; 15:14–15; 17:16; 21:8–9; 24:10–11, 14–16; 25:13, 15–16, 18; 28:44–48; 29:9–20; 30:19–20; 31:1–10, 12–13; 32:17, 19–23, 24–27, 29; 33:12–14, 16–19, 21–23.[194] A recent paleographic study by Stökl Ben Ezra dates the manuscript to the years 50 B.C.E. – 30 C.E. or 30–1 B.C.E.[195] Its orthography is conservative.[196] 1QDeut[b] reads fourteen times with and eighteen times against MT, nine times with and twenty-three times against SP, eight times with and eleven times against LXX, as well as six times non-aligned. 1QDeut[b] is hence equally close to MT and LXX[197] and can best be described as non-aligned.[198] Variants of special interest are אֲדֹ[נִי "the L]ord" instead of MT's יְהוָה "Yahweh" in Deut 15:14 and that Deut 33:15 is missing in 1QDeut[b] 20 4 due to scribal corruption.[199]

2.2.1.7.14 4QDeut[b] (4Q29)

The ten surviving fragments of 4QDeut[b] preserve 177 complete and partial words from Deut 29:24–

---

[185] McLean, "Development," 87; cf. op. cit., 83–87.
[186] Cf. Mathews, "Leviticus Scroll," 21–24; Mathews, "The Paleo-Hebrew Leviticus Scroll from Qumran," 48–49; Freedman and Mathews, *Leviticus Scroll*, 12–13.
[187] For this structural marker, cf. Mathews, "Leviticus Scroll," 15–21; Mathews, "The Paleo-Hebrew Leviticus Scroll from Qumran," 47–48; Freedman and Mathews, *Leviticus Scroll*, 10–11.
[188] Cf. Mathews, "Leviticus Scroll," 121–49, esp. 141; Mathews, "The Paleo-Hebrew Leviticus Scroll from Qumran," 50–51; Freedman and Mathews, *Leviticus Scroll*, 69–82; Brooke, "Torah," 105.
[189] Freedman, "Variant Readings," 533–34. The quote is on page 533. Freedman speaks of an earlier stage of the Palestinian text.
[190] Mathews, "The Paleo-Hebrew Leviticus Scroll from Qumran," 51.
[191] Mathews, "The Leviticus Scroll (11QpaleoLev) and the Text of the Hebrew Bible," 198; cf. Mathews, "Leviticus Scroll," 166–207, 249.
[192] Tov, "Textual Character," xxiii and *passim*.
[193] E. Tov, "A Modern Textual Outlook Based on the Qumran Scrolls," *HUCA* 53 (1982): 11–27 (19–21); Tov, *TCHB*[2], 116; Tov, *"Synthese," 20; Tov, *"Biblical Texts," 156; cf. Brooke, "Torah," 105; Fabry, "Levitikus," 317; Flint, "Book of Leviticus," 325.

[194] Barthélemy, "5. Deutéronome," 61, wants to find in frg. 23 one partial word from Deut 33:24, but the characters]רגלו[are attested also in Deut 25:4. Dahmen ("Fragmente," 575; cf. Barthélemy, "5. Deutéronome," 61) wants to identify further text of Deuteronomy in frgs. 28 and 36. Dahmen's identifications are problematic because he is at best able to identify one word of text. Given the many textual variants towards MT in 1QDeut[b], Dahmen's identifications remains thus speculative. Stökl Ben Ezra claimed recently ("Paleographic Observations," 249–55) that frg. 1 (Deut 1:9, 11, 13) and frg. 2 (Deut 8:8–9) were penned by one or even two different scribes than frgs. 3–50. While Stökl Ben Ezra might very well be right in observing various scribal hands in 1Q5, the poor state of preservation of frgs. 1–2 prohibits final paleographic conclusions based on the seven characters of text in frg. 1 and the eight characters of text in frg. 2. Only a complete material reconstruction of the manuscript would allow for more definite conclusions.
[195] Stökl Ben Ezra, "Paleographic Observations," 256–57.
[196] For the orthography of 1QDeut[b], cf. Barthélemy, "5. Deutéronome," 57; Brooke, "Torah," 107.
[197] Against Brooke, "Torah, 108;" Tov, *"Biblical Texts," 155 ("equally close to the medieval texts of MT and to SP").
[198] Cf. Lange, *Handbuch*, 85.
[199] Cf. Barthélemy, "5. Deutéronome," 61.

25, 27; 30:3–14; 31:10–17, 24–30; 32:1–3; 33:29.²⁰⁰ The manuscript was copied in an early Hasmonean bookhand from the years 150–100 B.C.E.²⁰¹ The orthography of 4QDeutᵇ is conservative but somewhat fuller than that of MT.²⁰² The manuscript reads seven times with and ten times against MT, seven times with and seven times against SP, seven times with and six times against LXX, as well as twice non-aligned. As 4QDeutᵇ is equally close to MT, SP, and LXX, Tov classifies this manuscript therefore as non-aligned.²⁰³ That 4QDeutᵇ goes in Deut 30:11, 14; 31:28 with the longer text of LXX-Deut points to a certain closeness to its *Vorlage*.²⁰⁴

2.2.1.7.15 4QDeutᶜ (4Q30)

Sixty-six fragments of 4QDeutᶜ are extant. Frgs. 1–55 preserve 562 complete and partial words from Deut 3:25–26; 4:1,²⁰⁵ 13–17, 31–32; 7:3–4; 8:1–5; 9:12–13, 17–19, 29; 10:1–2, 5–8; 11:9–13, 18; 12:18–19, 26, 31; 13:5, 7, 11–12, 16; 15:1–4, 15–16; 16:2–3, 6–11, 21–22; 17:1–5, 7, 15–20; 18:1; 26:19; 27:1–2, 24–26; 28:1–14, 20, 22–25, 29–30, 48–50, 61; 29:17–19; 31:16–19; 32:3.²⁰⁶ The manuscript was copied in an early Hasmonean bookhand from the years 150–100 B.C.E.²⁰⁷ The orthography of 4QDeutᶜ is more plene than that of MT but employs the morphology of the conservative orthographic system.²⁰⁸ 4QDeutᶜ reads forty-three times with and thirty-eight times against MT, thirty-five times with and forty-six times against SP, nineteen times with and fifty-five times against LXX, as well as twenty-three times non-aligned. "It can be said with assurance that 4QDeutᶜ is not a manuscript of the Samaritan tradition, since, in the one instance in the chapters represented by this manuscript where 𝔐 purposefully revises its text to agree with the parallel text of Numbers (chap. 10), 4QDeutᶜ does not agree with 𝔐, but follows the text of 𝔐 and 𝔊."²⁰⁹ The high number of readings against LXX-Deut excludes a relation with its Hebrew parent text.²¹⁰ As 4QDeutᶜ reads as often with MT as against it and includes twenty-three non-aligned variants, the manuscript is best classified as non-aligned.²¹¹

2.2.1.7.16 4QDeutʰ (4Q35)

The fifteen extant fragments of 4QDeutʰ attest to 376 complete and partial words from Deut 1:1–17, 22–24, 29, 31–39, 41, 43–46; 2:1–6, 28–30; 4:31–34; 19:21?; 31:9–11; 33:8–22. The manuscript is executed in a bookhand in transition between the Hasmonean and Herodian scripts from the years 50–1 B.C.E.²¹² The three supralinear corrections in Deut 1:1; 2:3; and 4:34 were inserted by the original scribe of the scroll.²¹³ The orthography of 4QDeutʰ is conservative but somewhat fuller than that of MT. "Archaic spelling practices are evident, particularly in the poetic material of Deuteronomy 33, although it should be noted that the practices of the

---

²⁰⁰ After the *editio princeps* was published, Tigchelaar identified two further fragments with remnants of Deut 31:13–14; 33:29 ("Minuscula," 646).

²⁰¹ Cf. Duncan, "29. 4QDeutᵇ," 9; Duncan, "Critical Edition," 15–18.

²⁰² For the orthography of 4QDeutᵇ, see Duncan, "29. 4QDeutᵇ," 9–10; Duncan, "Critical Edition," 18–19.

²⁰³ Tov, *TCHB*², 116; Tov, *"Synthese," 20; Tov, *"Biblical Texts," 156.

²⁰⁴ Cf. Brooke, "Torah," 108; Duncan, "Critical Edition", 30–31; Tov, "Contribution," 33–35.

²⁰⁵ For the identification of the text of frg. 63 as Deut 4:1, see Dahmen, "Fragmente," 576.

²⁰⁶ Dahmen ("Fragmente," 576) wants to identify further text from Deuteronomy in frgs. 59 and 65. Dahmen's identifications are problematic as he is only able to identify five or six letters of text. Given the many textual variants towards MT in 4QDeutᶜ, Dahmen's identifications are at best speculative.

²⁰⁷ Cf. White Crawford, "30. 4QDeutᶜ," 15; White Crawford, "Special Features," 161 (ca. 125 B.C.E.).

²⁰⁸ For the orthography of 4QDeutᶜ and a list of orthographic variants, see White Crawford, "30. 4QDeutᶜ," 16; White Crawford, "Critical Edition," 22–23; cf. Brooke, "Torah," 108.

²⁰⁹ White Crawford, "30. 4QDeutᶜ," 17.

²¹⁰ Against White Crawford, "Critical Edition," 121–23; White Crawford, "Special Features," 162 ("related to the tradition of the Old Greek of Deuteronomy"); Brooke, "Torah," 108–09.

²¹¹ Cf. Tov, "Contribution," 33; Tov, *TCHB*², 116; Tov, *"Biblical Texts," 156; Lange, *Handbuch*, 88.

²¹² Thus Duncan, "35. 4QDeutʰ," 61; Duncan, "Critical Edition," 58–61; Duncan, "New Readings," 275; cf. Eshel and Stone, "New Fragment," 487.

²¹³ Duncan, "35. 4QDeutʰ," 62; Duncan, "Critical Edition," 64.

scribe are not consistent."[214] 4QDeut[h] goes twenty times with and twenty-four times against MT, thirteen times with and thirty-one times against SP, thirteen times with and twenty-five times against LXX, as well as eleven times non-aligned. The manuscript is equally close to MT, SP, and LXX and provides a good example of the intermingling of different textual traditions in the Second Temple period. As 4QDeut[h] aligns with none of the major textual traditions of the Pentateuch, Tov characterizes it as non-aligned.[215]

2.2.1.7.17 4QDeut[j] (4Q37) as a Non-Aligned Excerpted Manuscript

Forty-seven fragments survive of 4QDeut[j]. Frgs. 1–35 belong to eight columns of the original scroll, which are counted in the *editio princeps* as cols. I–VII and XI. There are 304 complete and partial words extant from Deut 5:1–11, 13–15, 22–33; 6:1–3; 8:5–10; 11:6–13, 41?; Exod 12:43, 46, 48–51; 13:1–5; Deut 32:7–8 in the listed sequence.[216] The manuscript was copied in a late Herodian bookhand from ca. 50 C.E.[217] The original scribe of 4QDeut[j] is also responsible for one erasure (Exod 12:49) by way of two dots above and below one character (Deut 11:10), and one supralinear correction (Deut 5:25).[218] The orthography of 4QDeut[j] is fuller than that of MT but aligns with the conservative approach. Nevertheless, isolated cases of baroque morphology occur such as the suffix -כה and the affix -תה.[219] Although 4QDeut[j] includes passages from both Exodus and Deuteronomy, its small height of fourteen lines makes it impossible that the scroll once contained both books. 4QDeut[j] is thus a collection of selected references from the Pentateuch.[220] The Decalogue (Deut 5:1–6:3), Deuteronomy 11, and Exod 12:43–13:5 are known from phylacteries from Qumran caves in this textual sequence (cf., e.g., 4QPhyl A and 4QPhyl I), while Deut 8:5–10 and Deuteronomy 32[221] are part of the excerpted manuscripts 4QDeut[n] and 4QDeut[q]. "Although the survival of these passages could arguably be due to chance, the more plausible explanation of this configuration is that the fragments collectively designated as 4QDeut[j] all derive from a single manuscript of biblical excerpts, in the order of the Nash Papyrus … 4QDeut[n], and 4QDeut[q]."[222] 4QDeut[j] reads twelve times with and twenty-three times against MT, fifteen times with and twenty times against SP, eight times with and sixteen times against LXX, as well as twelve times non-aligned. Three of these non-aligned variants pertain to the textual sequence Deut 5:1–6:3; […] 8:5–10; […] 11; Exod 12:43–13:5; […] Deut 32. 4QDeut[j] is thus equally removed from MT, SP, and LXX. As it also includes twelve non-aligned readings, it should be classified as non-aligned.[223]

2.2.1.7.18 4QDeut[k1] (4Q38)

The five extant fragments of 4QDeut[k1] preserve 120 complete and partial words from Deut 5:29–32; 11:6–13; 32:17–18, 22–23, 25–27. The manuscript was copied in an early Herodian bookhand from the years 30–1 B.C.E. The scribe of 4QDeut[k1] also produced 4QDeut[k2]. The two manuscripts differ though in the size of their characters and how the

---

[214] For the orthography of 4QDeut[h] and a list of orthographic variants, see Duncan, "35. 4QDeut[h]," 61–62 (the quote is on p. 61); Duncan, "Critical Edition," 61–63; Duncan, "New Readings," 278.

[215] Tov, *TCHB*[2], 116; Tov, *"Synthese," 20; Tov, *"Biblical Texts," 156. Against Duncan, "Critical Edition," 75–77; and Duncan, "New Readings," 258, who considers a relationship with LXX.

[216] For frg. 35 as a part of Exod 13:3–5, cf. Dahmen, "Fragmente," 580. Dahmen also speculates ibid. on whether frgs. 41 and 47 preserve further text of Exod 13:9, 15. The latter identifications are problematic as Dahmen is only able to identify six letters from each fragment. Given the many textual variants towards MT in 4QDeut[j], the latter two identifications are at best speculative.

[217] Cross, *"Development," 139; Duncan, "37. 4QDeut[j]," 77; Duncan, "Critical Edition," 90–92.

[218] Cf. Duncan, "37. 4QDeut[j]," 79.

[219] For the orthography of 4QDeut[j] and a list of orthographic variants, see Duncan, "37. 4QDeut[j]," 77–78; Duncan, "Critical Edition," 93–94.

[220] Cf. Duncan, "37. 4QDeut[j]," 75–76.

[221] For Deuteronomy 32, cf. also 4QPhyl N.

[222] Duncan, "37. 4QDeut[j]," 79; cf. Duncan, "Critical Edition," 112–14; Duncan, "Considerations," 199–205; Duncan, "Excerpted Texts," 46–47; Brooke, "Torah," 108–09.

[223] Cf. Tov, *TCHB*[2], 116; Tov, *"Synthese," 17, 20; Tov, *"Biblical Texts," 154, 156; Lange, *Handbuch*, 93; against Duncan, "Critical Edition," 110–12, who speaks of a closeness to LXX.

tetragrammaton is written.²²⁴ The original scribe of 4QDeutᵏ¹ is also responsible for the two supralinear corrections in Deut 11:7, 12.²²⁵ The orthography of 4QDeutᵏ¹ is baroque but employs the shorter forms of the pronominal suffixes in the plural, typical of the conservative orthography of MT.²²⁶ 4QDeutᵏ¹ reads ten times with and nine times against MT, seven times with and twelve times against SP, eight times with and eight times against LXX, as well as three times non-aligned. As 4QDeutᵏ¹ does not align with MT, SP, or LXX and as it includes three non-aligned readings, its text can best be described as non-aligned.²²⁷

Duncan regards 4QDeutᵏ¹ as an excerpted manuscript because Deuteronomy 5 and 11 are used often in the Qumran phylacteries and because Deuteronomy 32 can be found in 4QPhyl N as well as in the excerpted manuscripts 4QDtnʲ and 4QDeutᑫ.²²⁸ Because the extant fragments of 4QDeutᵏ¹ do not allow for a material reconstruction of the manuscript, Duncan's characterization of 4QDeutᵏ¹ as an excerpted manuscript must remain speculative.

2.2.1.7.19 4QDeutᵏ² (4Q38a)

Thirteen fragments are preserved from 4QDeutᵏ². Frgs. 1–8 attest to 120 complete and partial words from Deut 19:8–11, 13–16; 20:6–19; 23:22–26; 24:1–3; 25:19; 26:1–5, 18–19; 27:1?.²²⁹ Before the complete publication of the Dead Sea Scrolls, Brooke was doubtful that 4QDeutᵏ² is a copy of Deuteronomy, because the Tetragrammaton is written in Deut 26:3 in paleo-Hebrew script and this scribal habit was known from biblical quotations in the pesharim.²³⁰ Now, manuscripts such as 2QExoxᵇ, 4QExodʲ, 4QLevᵍ, 11QLevᵇ, 4QIsaᶜ, 1QPsᵇ, 11QPsᵃ, and 3QLam show that biblical manuscripts written in square script also executed the Tetragrammaton in paleo-Hebrew.²³¹ 4QDeutᵏ² was copied by the same scribe as 4QDeutᵏ¹ (→ 2.2.1.7.18) in an early Herodian bookhand from the years 30–1 B.C.E.²³² This scribe is also responsible for the supralinear correction in Deut 20:19.²³³ The orthography of 4QDeutᵏ² is baroque.²³⁴ The manuscript reads four times with and eight times against MT, five times with and seven times against SP, once with and seven times against LXX, as well as six times non-aligned. Hence, 4QDeutᵏ² does not align with MT, SP, and LXX and is best described as non-aligned in textual character.²³⁵

2.2.1.7.20 4QDeutⁿ (4Q41) as an Excerpted Non-Aligned Witness

4QDeutⁿ is one of the best-preserved manuscripts from Qumran. Of its six extant columns, col. V is slightly damaged and col. VI is only partly preserved. Col. I is written on a separate sheet that was attached to the scroll already in antiquity as part of a repair.²³⁶ There are 519 extant complete and partial words from Deut 8:5–10; 5:1–29, 31–33; 6:1. The small height (7.1 cm) and length (six columns) of 4QDeutⁿ²³⁷ demonstrates that it never contained the whole text of Deuteronomy

---

[224] For this point and for the paleographic date of 4QDeutᵏ¹, see Duncan, "38. 4QDeutᵏ¹," 93–94.

[225] For the scribal corrections, see Duncan, "38. 4QDeutᵏ¹," 95.

[226] For the orthography of 4QDeutᵏ¹ and a list of orthographic variants, see Duncan, "38. 4QDeutᵏ¹," 94–95; Duncan, "Critical Edition," 137–38.

[227] Cf. Tov, *TCHB, 109; Tov, *"Synthese," 17, 20; Tov, *"Biblical Texts," 154, 156.

[228] Duncan, "38. 4QDeutᵏ¹," 95; Duncan, "Considerations," 205; Duncan, "Excerpted Texts," 47; Brooke, "Torah," 108–09.

[229] Dahmen ("Fragmente," 580) wants to find further text from Deuteronomy in frgs. 8 and 13. Dahmen's identifications are problematic because he is only able to identify four and three letters of each fragment respectively. Given the many textual variants towards MT in 4QDeutᵏ², Dahmen's identifications are at best speculative.

[230] Brooke, "Torah," 108–09.

[231] For the use of the Tetragrammaton in biblical Dead Sea scrolls, see Tov, *Scribal Practices, 238–46.

[232] Duncan, "38a. 4QDeutᵏ²," 99; Duncan, "Critical Edition," 134–37.

[233] Duncan, "38a. 4QDeutᵏ²," 100.

[234] For the orthography of 4QDeutᵏ² and a list of orthographic variants, see Duncan, "38a. 4QDeutᵏ²," 99–100; Duncan, "Critical Edition," 137–38.

[235] Cf. Tov, *TCHB², 116; Tov, *"Synthese," 17, 20; Tov, *"Biblical Texts," 154, 156.

[236] Cf. White Crawford, "41. 4QDeutⁿ," 117.

[237] For the measurements of 4QDeutⁿ, see White Crawford, "41. 4QDeutⁿ," 117.

and therefore is an excerpted text.[238] Cross understands it as a liturgical text due to the small size of the manuscript and the passages from Deuteronomy that it contains.[239] 4QDeut[n] was copied in an early Herodian bookhand from the years 30–1 B.C.E.[240] Col. I can be attributed to the same paleographic epoch, although it is part of a repair sheet.[241]

The orthography of 4QDeut[n] is conservative but fuller than that of MT and employs on rare occasions the longer affixes and suffixes of the baroque orthographic approach, such as -תה and המה-.[242] 4QDeut[n] reads twenty-six times with and twenty-five times against MT, thirty times with and twenty-one times against SP, ten times with and thirty-three times against LXX, as well as thirteen times non-aligned. 4QDeut[n] can therefore be classified as a non-aligned witness.[243] Detailed studies of the variants of 4QDeut[n] demonstrated that the manuscript attests to a harmonizing text.[244] The fact that Deut 8:5–10 precedes Deut 5:1–29 in 4QDeut[n] might be due to the liturgical nature of this manuscript. The version of the Decalogue attested by 4QDeut[n] is regarded as especially important for the textual history of this manuscript: "What finally must be said is that the All Souls Deuteronomy (scil. 4QDeut[n]) bears witness to a text of the Deuteronomic Decalogue, which is, with one important exception, almost free from error and very close to what may be presumed to be the original text of the Deuteronomic Decalogue."[245]

2.2.1.7.21 4QpaleoDeut[r] (4Q45)

Sixty-five fragments survive of 4QpaleoDeut[r]. Frgs. 1–44 attest to 380 complete and partial words from Deut 1:8?; 7:2–7, 16–25; 10:11–12; 11:28, 30–32; 12:1–5, 11–12, 22; 13:19; 14:1–2, 4, 19, 21–22, 26–29; 15:5–6, 8–10; 19:2–3; 22:3–6; 23:7, 12–15; 28:15–18, 20; 31:29; 32:6–8, 10–11, 13–14, 33, 35; 33:3, 5–8, 29; 34:1.[246] The manuscript was executed in a paleo-Hebrew script from the first half or the first three-quarters of the first century B.C.E.[247] The orthography of 4QpaleoDeut[r] resembles that of 4QpaleoGen-Ex[l]. The morphology of 4QpaleoDeut[r] aligns with the conservative orthography, but otherwise 4QpaleoDeut[r] reads sometimes fuller than MT and sometimes more defective.[248] The text of 4QpaleoDeut[r] is non-aligned.

"There are 23 variants preserved of this scroll. One (28:13) involves an entire verse, but the other 22 involve only one word or less. Of the 23, in 3 variants Deut[r] agrees with 𝔐 against 𝔰𝔪 ... In 8 variants Deut[r]

---

[238] Stegemann was the first to recognize that 4QDeut[n] attests to an excerpted text ("Weitere Stücke," 217–27). His view was later confirmed by White Crawford, "41. 4QDeut[n]," 117; White Crawford, "Critical Edition," 295–96; White Crawford, "4QDt[n]," 14–17; Eshel, "4QDeut[n]," 149–51; Duncan, "Considerations," 202–03; Duncan, "Excerpted Texts," 45–46; Brooke, "Torah," 108, 110; Owen, "4QDeut[n]," 164.

[239] F.M. Cross, *Scrolls from the Wilderness of the Dead Sea: A Guide to the Exhibition, the Dead Sea Scrolls of Jordan* (London: Trustees of the British Museum, 1965), 31.

[240] Thus Cross, *Scrolls from the Wilderness*, 31, and White Crawford, "41. 4QDeut[n]," 117–18; cf. White Crawford, "Critical Edition," 263–66; White Crawford, "All Souls Deuteronomy," 193; White Crawford, "4QDt[n]," 14.

[241] Cf. Stegemann, "Weitere Stücke," 221.

[242] For the orthography of 4QDeut[n] and a list of orthographic variants, see White Crawford, "41. 4QDeut[n]," 118–20; cf. White Crawford, "Critical Edition," 266–68; White Crawford, "4QDt[n]," 14) and Eshel, "4QDeut[n]," 132–38.

[243] Cf. Owen, "4QDeut[n]," 162, 176–77; S. White Crawford, "A Response to Elizabeth Owen's '4QDeut[n]: A Pre-Samaritan Text?'" *DSD* 5 (1998): 92–94; Tov, *TCHB*[2], 116; Tov, *"Synthese,"* 20; against White Crawford, "Critical Edition," 295 ("4QDt[n] is a manuscript in the shared tradition of 𝔐 and Sam, but with a great deal of mixing from other traditions"); Tov, "Proto-Samaritan Texts," 406 ("like the Samaritan Pentateuch"; cf. Tov, *"Biblical Texts,"* 155).

[244] J.H. Tigay, "Conflation as a Redactional Technique," in *Empirical Models for Biblical Criticism* (ed. J.H. Tigay; Philadelphia: University of Pennsylvania Press, 1985), 53–95 (55–57);

Eshel, "4QDeut[n]," 141, 147–48; White Crawford, "41. 4QDeut[n]," 120–21; White Crawford, "4QDt[n]," 15.

[245] White Crawford, "All Souls Deuteronomy," 206.

[246] Dahmen ("Fragmente," 581) wants to identify further text from Deuteronomy in frgs. 47, 54, 56, and 65. Dahmen's identifications are problematic because he is only able to identify remnants of two words of text. Given the many textual variants towards MT in 4QpaleoDeut[r], Dahmen's identifications are at best speculative.

[247] Skehan, Ulrich, and Sanderson, "Palaeo-Hebrew Manuscripts," 131.

[248] For the orthography of 4QpaleoDeut[r] and for a list of orthographic variants, see Skehan, Ulrich, and Sanderson, "Palaeo-Hebrew Manuscripts," 132–34; cf. Ulrich, "Palaeo-Hebrew Biblical Manuscripts," 119.

agrees with 𝕾 against 𝔐 ... In 10 variants Deut^r disagrees with both 𝔐 𝕾. In the final 2 variants Deut^r disagrees with 𝔐 and 𝕾, which also disagree with each other." "4QpaleoDeut^r appears to have agreed with 𝔐 𝔊 in lacking the typological features of the Samaritan Deuteronomy. In minor variants the manuscript most often presents a unique reading, less often agrees with 𝕾, and least often agrees with 𝔐."[249]

The material reconstruction of 4QpaleoDeut^r furthermore makes it likely that the manuscript did not have the SP reading מול שכם "opposite Shechem" in Deut 11:30.[250] Due to the high number of non-aligned readings in 4QpaleoDeut^r, the manuscript should be classified as non-aligned.[251]

2.2.1.8 Manuscripts That Cannot be Classified Textually[252]

1QGen (1Q1): Nineteen fragments; frgs. 1–5 preserve forty-eight complete and partial words from Gen 1:18, 20–21; 3:11–14; 22:13–15; 23:17–19; 24:22, 24; early Herodian bookhand from the years 30–1 B.C.E.; conservative orthography.

2QGen (2Q1): Two fragments with twelve complete and partial words from Gen 19:27–28; 36:6, 35–37; late Herodian bookhand from the years 50–68 C.E.

4QGen^h-title (4Q8): One fragment with one word on the recto side: ברשית "in the beginning"; preserves the title of Genesis on the backside of a handlesheet of a scroll; Herodian cursive script from the years 1–68 C.E.

4QGen^k (4Q10): Five fragments with forty-six complete and partial words from Gen 1:9, 14–16, 27–28; 2:1–3; 3:1–2; Herodian bookhand from the years 1–30 C.E.; conservative orthography that is slightly fuller than MT; reads in Gen 1:9 the longer text of LXX-Gen.

4QpaleoGen^m (4Q12): One fragment with eighteen complete and partial words from Gen 26:21–28; paleo-Hebrew script from the middle of the second century B.C.E.; conservative orthography that is slightly fuller than MT.

4QpapGen^o (4Q483): Two fragments of a papyrus scroll with eight complete and partial words from Gen 1:9–10, 28–29;[253] Herodian hand from the end of the first century B.C.E. or the beginning of the first century C.E.

6QpaleoGen (6Q1): One fragment with nineteen complete and partial words from Gen 6:12–21; paleo-Hebrew script from the second half of the second century B.C.E.; the same scribe also copied 1QpaleoLev-Num^a;[254] in what is preserved, the orthography is conservative.

8QGen (8Q1): Five fragments with twenty-two complete and partial words from Gen 13:1–3; 17:12–13, 15–16, 18; 18:20–22, 24–25; Hasmonean or early Herodian bookhand from the years 50–25 B.C.E.; conservative orthography in what is preserved.

MasGen (Mas 1): One fragment with parts of two subsequent columns (no text is preserved from col. ii); eleven complete and partial words from Gen 46:7–11; Hasmonean semi-cursive hand from the beginning of the first century B.C.E.

Mur(?)Gen^b (Mur[?]): One fragment with thirteen complete and partial words from Gen 33:18–20; 34:1–3; post-Herodian bookhand from the beginning of the second century C.E.

---

[249] Skehan, Ulrich, and Sanderson, "Palaeo-Hebrew Manuscripts," 134; cf. Ulrich, "Palaeo-Hebrew Biblical Manuscripts," 119–20.
[250] Cf. Skehan, Ulrich, and Sanderson, "Palaeo-Hebrew Manuscripts," 134, 138.
[251] Cf. Lange, *Handbuch, 101; against Tov, *"Biblical Texts," 155, who characterizes the manuscript as equally close to MT and SP.
[252] For the paleographic, orthographic, and textual data listed below, see Lange, *Handbuch, 374–406, and the literature discussed there. If orthographic and textual characterizations are not mentioned, the amount of preserved text does not allow for such classifications.

[253] For the identification of this manuscript and an edition, see Puech, "Nouveau manuscrit," 259–60.
[254] Cf. McLean, "Development," 60.

1QExod (1Q2): Thirteen fragments; frgs. 1–7 preserve sixty-one complete and partial words from Exod 16:12–16; 19:24–25; 20:1, 5–6, 25–26; 21:1–2, 4–5; Herodian bookhand from the first half of the first century C.E.; conservative orthography; the manuscript reads twice with and once against MT, never with and three times against SP, twice with and never against LXX.

2QExod^b (2Q3): Thirteen fragments; frgs. 1–8 attest to fifty-six complete and partial words from Exod 4:31; 12:26–27, x; 18:21–22; 21:37; 22:1–2, 15–17, 19; 27:17–19; 31:16–17; 19:4; 34:10; Herodian bookhand from the years 1–68 C.E.; the Tetragrammaton is written in paleo-Hebrew characters; the orthography is fuller than that of MT and sometimes employs baroque morphological features; the manuscript reads never with and four times against MT, never with and four times against SP, twice with and once against LXX, as well as twice non-aligned; Exod 34:10 directly follows Exod 19:9.

4QExod^d (4Q15): One fragment with twenty-five complete and partial words from Exod 13:15–16; 15:1; Hasmonean bookhand from the late second or early first century B.C.E.; conservative orthography; Exod 15:1 immediately follows Exod 13:16; either an excerpted manuscript or attesting to a different textual sequence than MT.

4QExod^g (4Q18): One fragment with sixteen complete and partial words from Exod 14:21–27; late Hasmonean hand from the middle of the first century C.E.

4QExod^h (4Q19): One fragment with thirteen complete and partial words from Exod 6:3–6; late Hasmonean or early Herodian semi-cursive hand from the middle or the second half of the first century B.C.E.; more likely a biblical manuscript but as only very little text is preserved a quotation in a non-biblical text cannot be excluded.

4QExod^j (4Q20): Seven fragments; frgs. 1–2 preserve twelve complete and partial words from Exod 7:28–29 and 8:1–2; middle-Herodian bookhand from the early first century C.E.; the Tetragrammaton is written in paleo-Hebrew.

1QpaleoLev-Num^a (1Q3 1–11, 12?, 15?): Thirteen fragments; frgs. 1–9 preserve 108 complete and partial words from Lev 11:10–11; 19:30–34; 20:20–24; 21:24; 22:2–6; 23:4–8; Num 1:48–50; 36:7–8; paleo-Hebrew script from the second half of the second century B.C.E.; the scribe of this manuscript also copied 6QpaleoGen;[255] conservative orthography; the manuscript reads three times against 4QLev^e, four times with and twice against MT, twice with MT^mss, three times with and three times against SP, twice with and three times against LXX, as well as once non-aligned (with MT^mss).

2QpaleoLev (2Q5): One fragment with fifteen complete and partial words from Lev 11:22, 24–29; paleo-Hebrew script from the years 150–75 B.C.E.; the preserved text is orthographically conservative but a little fuller than that of MT.

4QLev^g (4Q26b): One fragment with forty-two complete and partial words from Lev 7:19–21, 23–26; late Hasmonean or early Herodian bookhand from the years 50–1 B.C.E.; the Tetragrammaton and prepositions attached to it are written in paleo-Hebrew; conservative orthography, a little fuller than MT.

11QLev^b (11Q2): Nine fragments; frgs. 1–7 preserve sixty-two complete and partial words from Lev 7:34–35; 8:8? or 8:9?; 9:23–24; 10:1–2; 13:58–59; 14:16–17; 15:18–19; 25:31–33; late Herodian bookhand from the middle of the first century C.E.; the Tetragrammaton is written in paleo-Hebrew; mixed orthography with baroque plene spellings but without baroque morphology; the manuscript reads four times with and nine times against MT, twice with and eleven times against SP, seven times with and four times against LXX, as well as four times non-aligned.

---

[255] Cf. McLean, "Development," 60.

ArugLev: Four fragments; frgs. A–C attest to thirty complete and partial words from Lev 23:38–44; 24:16–28; post-Herodian bookhand from the first third of the second century C.E.; only one orthographic variant against MT.

2QNumᵃ (2Q6): Two fragments with twenty-four complete and partial words from Num 3:38–41, 51; 4:1–3; late Herodian bookhand from the middle of the first century C.E.; conservative orthography.

2QNumᵇ (2Q7): One fragment with nineteen complete and partial words from Num 33:47, 49, 51–53; early Herodian hand from the years 30–1 B.C.E.; baroque orthography?; 2Q9 could be a second fragment of this manuscript.[256]

5/6ḤevNumᵃ (5/6Ḥev1a): Four fragments; frgs. 1–3 preserve sixteen complete and partial words from Num 19:2–4; 20:7–8; late Herodian bookhand from the years 50–68 C.E.

34SeNum (34Se2): Two fragments with four complete and partial words from Num 18:21; 19:11; developed Herodian bookhand.

MS Schøyen 4612/5:[257] One small fragment with ten complete and partial words from Num 16:2–3, 5; Herodian hand from the second half of the first century B.C.E. Elgvin finds one reconstructed orthographic variant toward MT.[258] Although it is more likely a Numbers manuscript, it cannot be excluded that ms Schøyen 4612/5 preserves the remnants of a Numbers quotation in another literary work or the remains of a rewriting.

1QDeutᵃ (1Q4): Fifty-eight fragments; frgs. 1–14 preserve eighty-four complete and partial words from Deut 1:22–25; 4:47, 49; 8:18–19; 9:27–28; 11:27–30; 13:1–6, 14–15; 14:21, 24–25; 16:1, 6–7;[259] early Herodian bookhand from the years 30–1 B.C.E.; baroque orthography; the manuscript reads twice with and nine times against MT, three times with and eight times against SP, three times with and five times against LXX, as well as four times nonaligned.

2QDeutᵇ (2Q11): One fragment with eight complete and partial words from Deut 17:12, 14–15; Herodian bookhand.

2QDeutᶜ (2Q12): One fragment with twelve complete and partial words from Deut 10:8–12; late Herodian bookhand from the first century C.E.; baroque orthography?

4QDeutᵃ (4Q28): One fragment with ninety-seven complete and partial words from Deut 23:26; 24:1–8; bookhand from the transitional period between archaic and Hasmonean scripts (175–150 B.C.E.); conservative orthography, which in three cases is even more defective than MT; the manuscript reads three times with and twice against MT, once with and four times against SP, twice with and three times against LXX.

---

[256] E.J.C. Tigchelaar ("A Qumran Fragment Preserving Part of Numbers 23:5–7[8] (2Q29 1)," in *The Prestige of the Pagan Prophet Balaam in Judaism, Early Christianity and Islam* [eds. G.H. van Kooten and J. van Ruiten; Themes in Biblical Narrative 11; Leiden: Brill, 2008], 83–86) views 2Q29 1 as a further fragment of 2QNumᵇ. In this case, it would attest to five complete and partials words from Num 23:5–7. Tigchelaar speculates further whether 2Q29 3 belongs to 2QNumᵇ. Two complete and partial words could attest to either Num 32:4–5, 13:22–23, or 15:25–26. Given the very small amount of text preserved of 2Q29 frgs. 1 and 3, Tigchelaar's identifications must remain speculative.

[257] I am indebted to Torleif Elgvin who made a preprint copy of his edition of this manuscript ("MS 4612/5") available to me. The paleographic classification relies on M. Langlois, "Palaeographical Analysis of the Dead Sea Scrolls," in *Gleanings*, forthcoming. All other information is summarized according to Elgvin's edition.

[258] In Num 16:2, ms Schøyen 4612/5 reads שׁי שם[וא̊נ] "]and me[n of reputation" (cf. 4QNumᵇ and LXX) instead of MT's אַנְשֵׁי־שֵׁם "men of reputation" (cf. SP). In Num 16:5, ms Schøyen 4612/5 spells the name "Korah" as ק̊ר̊[ו]ח instead of MT's קֹרַח (cf. SP).

[259] Dahmen ("Fragmente," 573–75) wants to identify further text from Deuteronomy in frgs. 15–17, 20, 25–26, 28, 31–32, and 48. Dahmen's identifications are problematic as he is at best able to identify ten characters of text. Given the many textual variants towards MT in 1QDeutᵃ, Dahmen's identifications are at best speculative.

4QDeutˡ (4Q39): Eleven fragments; frgs. 1–10 preserve thirty-nine complete and partial words from Deut 10:12, 14–15; 28:67–68; 29:2–5; 31:12; 33:1–2; 34:4–6; late Hasmonean semi-cursive hand from ca. 50 B.C.E.; conservative orthography; the manuscript reads three times with and three times against MT, once with and five times against SP, as well as once with and three times against LXX.

4QDeutᵐ (4Q40): Five fragments with seventy complete and partial words from Deut 3:18–22; 4:32–33; and 7:18–22; bookhand in transition between the Hasmonean and Herodian scripts from the years 50–1 B.C.E.; two supralinear corrections by the original scribe; baroque orthography; the manuscript reads twice with and six times against MT, twice with and six times against SP, twice with and three times against LXX, as well as four times non-aligned.

4QDeutᵖ (4Q43): Three fragments with seventeen complete and partial words from Deut 6:4–11; late Hasmonean bookhand from the years 75–50 B.C.E.; in the preserved text, conservative orthography.

4QDeutᵗ (4Q38c):[260] Two fragments with remnants of Deut 12:31; 13:1, 3; 14:28–29; Herodian bookhand from the first century C.E.

4QDeutᵘ (4Q38d):[261] One fragment with fourteen complete and partial words from Deut 24:20–22; early Hasmonean bookhand from the middle of the second century B.C.E.;[262] no variant reading towards SP and MT, but 4QDeutᵘ does read the long text of LXX^(A, B, C) in Deut 24:20. As only text from Deut 24:20–22 is preserved, it is possible that 4QDeutᵘ preserves only a Deuteronomy quotation in a non-biblical text, but a biblical manuscript seems more likely as the fragment attests to remnants of three verses.

11QDeut (11Q3): Three fragments; frgs. 1–2 preserve seventeen complete and partial words from Deut 1:4–5; 2:28–30; late Herodian bookhand from ca. 50 C.E.

MurDeut (Mur2): Three fragments; frgs. 1–2 attest to thirty-one complete and partial words from Deut 10:1–3; 11:2–3; 12:25–26; late Herodian bookhand from the time preceding the First Jewish War; no variant readings towards MT preserved.

XḤevSeDeut (XḤevSe3): One fragment with fifteen complete and partial words from Deut 9:4–7, 21–23; late Herodian bookhand from the years 50–75 C.E.; in the preserved text, conservative orthography that is slightly more defective than MT.

MS Schøyen 5214/2:[263] One small fragment with fifteen complete and partial words from Deut 32:5–9; the script is a late Herodian or early post-Herodian formal hand;[264] although one textual and two orthographic variants towards MT are extant in the preserved text,[265] fifteen words of text are in-

---

[260] 4QDeutᵗ was identified by Puech ("Identification," 123). Puech designates the manuscript as 4QDeutéronomeʳ and counts it as 4Q38c. As this designation was assigned previously to 4QpaleoDeutʳ, the manuscript is listed here as 4QDeutᵗ.

[261] This fragment was identified by Tigchelaar, "Forgotten Qumran Cave 4 *Deuteronomy* Fragment." It is not included in any DJD edition of biblical Qumran scrolls. Tigchelaar found it on photograph PAM 43.011.

[262] Cf. Tigchelaar, "Forgotten Qumran Cave 4 *Deuteronomy* Fragment," 526–27.

[263] I am indebted to Torleif Elgvin who made a preprint copy of his edition of ms Schøyen 5214/2 available to me ("5214/2"). All information given about this manuscript is based on Elgvin's publication.

[264] According to Elgvin ("5214/2," forthcoming), Ada Yardeni speaks of a late Herodian formal hand from the year 30–100 C.E. M. Langlois thinks of a late Herodian or early post-Herodian formal hand from the second half of the first century C.E. (M. Langlois, "Palaeographical Analysis of the Dead Sea Scrolls," in *Gleanings*, forthcoming).

[265] The two orthographic variants are קנאך instead of MT's קָנֶךָ "who created you" (cf. SP) in Deut 32:6 and בהנחיל (cf. SP) instead of MT's בְּהַנְחֵל "when he gave an inheritance" in Deut 32:8. In Deut 32:9, ms Schøyen 5214/2 reads תבל נחלת ישראל "the world is the inheritance of Israel" instead of חֶבֶל נַחֲלָתוֹ "the allotment of his inheritance" in MT, חבל נחלתו ישראל "the allotment of his inheritance is Israel" in SP, and σχοίνισμα κληρονομίας αὐτοῦ Ισραηλ "the measured part of his inheritance is Israel" in LXX.

sufficient for the orthographic and textual characterization of ms Schøyen 5214/2.²⁶⁶

2.2.1.9 Excerpted Manuscripts That Cannot be Classified Textually²⁶⁷

4QGenᵈ (4Q4): One fragment with seventy-three words from Gen 1:18–27; late Hasmonean bookhand ca. 50 B.C.E.; conservative orthography, somewhat fuller than MT; one reading with MT and SP against LXX; excerpted manuscript whose height of 11 cm makes it impossible that the original scroll included even the whole book of Genesis.²⁶⁸

4QExodᵉ (4Q16): One fragment with forty complete and partial words from Exod 13:3–5; early Hasmonean semi-cursive hand from the middle or late second century B.C.E.; conservative orthography but fuller than MT; the manuscript reads twice with and five times against MT, once with MTᵐˢˢ; twice with and five times against SP, twice with and four times against LXX, as well as twice non-aligned; the scroll was only 8.2 cm high and the columns were 5.5 cm high with only eight lines per column; excerpted manuscript that attested only to a part of the book of Exodus: "The very small size of the column raises the question of whether this scroll originally contained the entire book of Exodus. Since the column begins at the beginning of one section of instructions for the observance of the feast of unleavened bread, it may be that this was a manuscript for liturgical purposes consisting of selections from the Torah."²⁶⁹

2.2.1.10 Manuscripts for Which It Is Uncertain if They Preserve a Manuscript of a Book of the Pentateuch, a Quotation of Such a Book, or Are Para-Scriptural²⁷⁰

In many cases, only a few words from the Pentateuch are preserved in supposedly biblical manuscripts. In these cases, it cannot be excluded that they attest to what is left of a quotation from or an allusion to a passage from the Torah in a non-biblical context. Even if remnants of two passages are extant it often cannot be excluded that the manuscript in question attests to a rewriting or expansion of a book of the Torah. In other cases, a given manuscript could be the remnant of a *testimonium*, i.e., a collection of quotations, or that it might be a note made by a scribe in preparation for the composition of another literary work such as a pesher. These manuscripts are not discussed below in detail but only listed as they are of little help as textual witnesses to the Torah.

4QGenʰ¹ (4Q8): Remnants of four words from Gen 1:8–10; late Hasmonean or early Herodian bookhand from the years 50–25 B.C.E.

4QGenʰ² (4Q8): Remnants of three words from Gen 2:17–18; middle or late Hasmonean bookhand from the first half of the first century B.C.E.

4QGenʰ⁻ᵖᵃʳᵃ (4Q8): Remnants of three words from Gen 12:4–5; early Hasmonean bookhand from the years 125–100 B.C.E.

4QGenⁿ (4Q576): Remnants of six words from Gen 34:7, 9–10; 50:3?; Hasmonean semi-cursive hand from the second half of the second century B.C.E.

4QGenᵖ (4Q12a): Remnants of five words from Gen 50:15; late Herodian bookhand.

---

²⁶⁶ Against Elgvin who speaks of an "independent text" ("5214/2," forthcoming).

²⁶⁷ For the paleographic, orthographic, and textual data listed below, see Lange, *Handbuch*, 374–406, and the literature discussed there. If orthographic and textual characterizations are not mentioned, the amount of preserved text does not allow for such classifications.

²⁶⁸ Cf. recently G.J. Brooke, "4QGenesisᵈ Reconsidered," in *Textual Criticism and the Dead Sea Scrolls: Studies in Honour of Julio Trebolle Barrera* (JSJSup 157; Leiden: Brill, 2012), 51–70.

²⁶⁹ Sanderson, "16. 4QExodᵉ," 130; cf. Duncan, "Excerpted Texts," 61–62.

²⁷⁰ For the paleographic, orthographic, and textual data listed below, see Lange, *Handbuch*, 374–406, and the literature discussed there. If orthographic and textual characterizations are not mentioned, the amount of preserved text does not allow for such classifications.

MS Schøyen 4612/4:[271] One fragment with thirty complete and partial words from Gen 36:7, 9–16; Hasmonean semi-cursive hand with some Herodian features from the second half of the first century B.C.E.; the characters are very small with an average letter-height of 1.5 millimeters; not a copy of Genesis but either a mantic artefact[272] or maybe a textual note for the preparation of a pesher; textual differences toward MT are due to the special character of the fragment and are of limited text-critical value.

2QExod^c (2Q4): Remnants of three words from Exod 5:3, 5; late Hasmonean or early Herodian hand from the second half of the first century B.C.E.

4QExod^k (4Q21): Remnants of eight words from Exod 36:9–10; late Herodian or post-Herodian hand from the second half of the first century C.E.

1QpaleoLev^b? (1Q3 16–19, 22–23, 12?, 15?, 20?): Only remnants of three words from Lev 27:30–31 can be identified; either a very damaged Leviticus manuscript or a manuscript of a para-Scriptural work; paleo-Hebrew script from the second half of the second century B.C.E.

4Qpap cryptA Lev^h? (4Q249j): Remnants of nine words from Lev 26:14–16. Written in Cryptic A script, which was not used for biblical manuscripts; 4Q249j preserves a quotation of Lev 26:14–16 in another text.[273]

6QpaleoLev (6Q2): Remnants of ten words from Lev 8:12–13; paleo-Hebrew script from the second half of the second century B.C.E.

2QNum^c (2Q8): One fragment with four complete and partial words from Num 7:88; Herodian hand.

2QNum^d? (2Q9): One fragment with three complete and partial words from Num 18:8–9; maybe second fragment of 2Q7.

2QDeut^a (2Q10): Remnants of eight words from Deut 1:7–9; late Hasmonean or early Herodian hand from the years 50–25 B.C.E.

4QDeut^{k3} (4Q38b): Remnants of eleven words from Deut 30:16–18; late Herodian bookhand from ca. 50 C.E.

4QpaleoDeut^s (4Q46): Remnants of ten words from Deut 26:14–15; paleo-Hebrew script from the second half of the third century B.C.E.

6QpapDeut? (6Q3): Remnants of three words from Deut 26:19.

MS Schøyen 5214/1:[274] One small fragment with seven complete and partial words from Deut 6:1–2; Herodian hand;[275] one variant toward MT that is both orthographic and textual is extant in the preserved text of Deut 6:1: והחוקים "and the commandments" instead of MT's הַחֻקִּים "the commandments" (cf. SP).

2.2.1.11 Late Ancient and Early Medieval Pentateuch Manuscripts

Four Pentateuch manuscripts are preserved from late antiquity and early medieval times (see also → 2.2.2). A first list of such manuscripts was published by Gentry.[276] None of the manuscripts in question is properly published and photographs

---

[271] All information given here is based on Elgvin and Davis, "MS 4612/4." I am indebted to the authors for making a pre-print copy of their edition available to me. For the paleographic classification see M. Langlois, "Palaeographical Analysis of the Dead Sea Scrolls," in *Gleanings*, forthcoming.

[272] Thus Elgvin and Davis "MS 4612/4," forthcoming.

[273] Cf. Lange, *Handbuch*, 72–73.

[274] I am obliged to Torleif Elgvin, who gave me access to a pre-print version of his edition of this manuscript ("MS 5214/1"). All information about ms Schøyen 5214/1 given here is based on Elgvin's edition.

[275] According to Elgvin ("MS 5214/1," forthcoming), Ada Yardeni considers this an early or middle Herodian script while M. Langlois characterizes the script as "a somewhat developed Herodian semiformal hand" from the early first century C.E. (Langlois, "Palaeographical Analysis of the Dead Sea Scrolls," in *Gleanings*, forthcoming).

[276] P.J. Gentry, "The Text of the Old Testament," *JETS* 52 (2009): 19–45 (22).

are often not available. As far as they can still be classified, all four are proto-Masoretic in nature.

2.2.1.11.1 T-S NS 4.3 and T-S NS 3.21 (Cambridge, Genizah Collection)

T-S N 4.3 and NS 3.21 designate two fragments from a parchment scroll and are part of the Taylor-Schechter Genizah Collection at Cambridge University Library. The fragments belong to a single scroll[277] that contained either only the book of Genesis or less likely the whole Torah. They preserve remnants of eight columns of unvocalized text from Gen 4:14–17; 5:10–18; 5:32–6:7 (T-S NS 4.3) and Gen 13:10; 14:9–22; 15:5–21; 16:5–17:2; 17:9–20 (T-S NS 3.21). For both fragments, only preliminary studies exist.[278] The paleographic date of this manuscript is debated. For T-S NS 3.21, Sirat suggests a date in the fifth or sixth century C.E.,[279] while Yardeni proposes the eighth or ninth century C.E.[280] The consonantal text of T-S N 4.3 and NS 3.21 is virtually identical to MT[L].

> The Hebrew is almost completely identical to the Masoretic Text, except in 17:1, where the scroll has *shanah* for *shanim* at the end of the verse. There are also two corrections. The first is in 14:9, where the *waw* missing from the beginning of the name Aryokh has been placed above the line by the scribe ... In the second correction, in 16:13, the scribe wrote the Hebrew for 'and he called' instead of 'and she called'

and corrected this by writing a *taw* over the *yod*. Since the *yod* is a narrow letter, the resulting *taw* differs from others in the scroll.[281]

The photograph published in the catalogue of M.P. Brown[282] shows a supralinear correction in Gen 5:12 that adds with a different ink the missing word שנה "year" above ויולד "and he begot." The only other differences from the text of MT[L] concern paragraph divisions.[283] The text of T-S N 4.3 and NS 3.21 should therefore be classified as proto-Masoretic.

2.2.1.11.2 MS Heb. d. 89 (P) i (Oxford, Bodleian Library)

The label ms Heb. d. 89 (P) designates thirteen different fragments from Oxford's Bodleian library, of which not all are written in Hebrew.[284] Sirat counts a small papyrus fragment with nine unvocalized complete and partial words from Exod 2:23–25 as frg. I of this group.[285] Yardeni dates this fragment on paleographic grounds to the second or third century C.E.[286] No differences from MT[L] occur but the small amount of text allows for neither orthographic nor textual classification. Although less likely, it cannot be excluded that ms Heb. d. 89 (P) i preserves the remnants of an Exodus quotation in a non-biblical text.

2.2.1.11.3 P 10598 (Berlin Staatliche Museen)

Sirat lists this manuscript together with other late ancient and early medieval biblical manuscripts without providing a paleographic date.[287] The Trismegistos database mentions a date between 700

---

[277] Cf. Sirat, "Genesis Discovery," 2; B. Outhwaite, "2. Fragment of a Genesis Scroll," in *In the Beginning: Bibles Before the Year 1000* (ed. M.P. Brown; New York: Smithsonian Institutions, 2006), 247, and B. Outhwaite, "4. Fragment of a Genesis Scroll," in op. cit., 248–49 (248). Color photographs of this manuscript can be found in Brown's catalogue on pp. 107 and 110–11.

[278] See Sirat, "Genesis Discovery," 2 and Sirat, "Earliest Known Sefer Torah," 3. A brief report can also be found at http://www.lib.cam.ac.uk/Taylor-Schechter/fotm/november-2010/index.html (last accessed March 3, 2015).

[279] Sirat, "Genesis Discovery," 2; C. Sirat, "Rouleaux de la Tora antérieurs à l'an mille," *Comptes Rendus de séances de L'Academie des Inscriptions et Belles Lettres* (1994): 861–87 (861–62) (with the collaboration of M. Dukan and A. Yardeni); C. Sirat, *Hebrew Manuscripts of the Middle Ages* (Cambridge: Cambridge University Press, 2002), 27 (with plate 11 on p. 28).

[280] Yardeni, "ספר בראשית מן הגניזה," 173–77; Yardeni, *Hebrew Script*, 80.

[281] Sirat, "Genesis Discovery," 2. Cf. also Outhwaite, "4. Fragment of a Genesis Scroll," 249 (see n. 275).

[282] M.P. Brown, *In the Beginning*, 107 (see n. 275).

[283] Yardeni, "ספר בראשית מן הגניזה," 173–77.

[284] Cf. Sirat, *Papyrus*, 123. At least one fragment is not even Hebrew but Nabatean. See J.F. Healey, "A Nabatean Papyrus Fragment (Bodleian MS Heb. d. 89)," *ZPE* 146 (2004), 183–88.

[285] Sirat, *Papyrus*, 32, 123. Drawings of the fragment can be found in Sirat, *Papyrus*, 32; in Sirat, *Hebrew Manuscripts*, 29 plate 12 (see n. 277); and in Yardeni, *Hebrew Script*, 73.

[286] Yardeni, *Hebrew Script*, 73 fig. 90.

[287] Sirat, *Papyrus*, 34–35. For a drawing and photograph, see op. cit., 34 and plate ix respectively.

and 899 C.E.²⁸⁸ Sirat discusses the manuscript together with ms Heb. d. 89 (P) i from the Bodleian Library and two other early medieval manuscripts.²⁸⁹ The identification of the biblical text is debated. Sirat speaks erroneously of Numbers 3–4²⁹⁰ while Hendel identifies the text correctly as Exod 3:13–4:9.²⁹¹ There are extant remnants of two columns from a parchment scroll with 109 unvocalized complete and partial words from Exod 3:13–16, 18–22; 4:1–9. Except for one textual variant in Exod 3:14 (אל בני "to the sons of" instead of לִבְנֵי "to the sons of" in MTᴸ) and one abbreviation in Exod 3:16 (יש instead of יִשְׂרָאֵל "Israel" in MTᴸ), only four orthographic variants towards MTᴸ are extant in P 10598. The manuscript reads three times fuller and one time more defective than MTᴸ. This strong agreement with MTᴸ qualifies P 10598 as proto-Masoretic in character.

2.2.1.11.4 MS London + MS Ashkar-Gilson²⁹²

This manuscript, which originated most likely in Egypt²⁹³ and was found in the Cairo Genizah, is preserved in two parts that are held today in two different libraries.²⁹⁴ The two parts of this scroll attest to the complete text of Exod 9:18–13:2 (manuscript London) and parts of Exod 9:18–16:1 (manuscript Ashkar-Gilson) on two consecutive sheets. That the two parts belong together was first established by Engel and Mishor²⁹⁵ who also published an edition with high-quality photographs and enhanced readings²⁹⁶ following restoration work carried out at the Israel Museum.²⁹⁷ Carbon-14 analysis of the Ashkar-Gilson fragment dates the manuscript to the seventh or eighth century C.E.²⁹⁸ Before this C-14 dating, Birnbaum argued for a date around 700 C.E. based on a paleographic model that has meanwhile been questioned.²⁹⁹ The detailed paleographic analysis of Engel also argues for a date in the seventh or eighth century³⁰⁰ and places manuscript London/Ashkar-Gilson within the "Egyptian School of writing."³⁰¹

A comparison of manuscript London/Askhar-Gilson with later Masoretic manuscripts by Sanders demonstrates that "the consonantal text of AS appears to conform to the Tiberian textual tradition. There are only some minute orthographic differences and they concern only the use or non-use of *matres lectiones*."³⁰² Manuscript London/Ashkar-Gilson reads in all cases of orthographic variation between MTᴬ, MTᴮ, MTᴸ, and MTˢ⁵, recorded by Sanders with the reconstructed text of MTᴬ and the so-called Damascus Pentateuch (MTˢ⁵). In five orthographic disagreements with MTᴸ, manuscript London/Askhar-Gilson reads twice more plene and three times more defective than MTᴸ.³⁰³ Given these minute orthographic variations, manuscript London/Ashkar-Gilson needs to be classified as a proto-Masoretic witness. Based on scribal features and the layout of the Song of the Sea (Exod 15:1–19), Sanders argues that manuscript London/Ashkar-Gilson was consulted by the Tiberian Masoretes when they produced the

---

²⁸⁸ http://www.trismegistos.org/ldab/text.php?tm=113848; last accessed March 24, 2015.

²⁸⁹ Sirat, *Papyrus*, 32–35.

²⁹⁰ Sirat, *Papyrus*, 34. Cf. Gentry, "Text," 22.

²⁹¹ See → 2.2.2.

²⁹² Cf. also → 2.2.2.

²⁹³ See Charlesworth, "Ashkar Manuscript," 66; Engel and Mishor, "Ancient Scroll," 25.

²⁹⁴ Exod 9:18–13:2 was originally held by the Jews' College in London but is now part of the private collection of S. Loewentheil in New York. Exod 13:19–16:1 is in the David M. Ruben Rare Book and Manuscript Library at Duke University (Ashkar-Gilson Hebrew Manuscript #2). Photographs of the manuscript can be found in אנציקלופדיה מקראית *Encyclopaedia Biblica*, Vol. 5 (Jerusalem: Bialik, 1968), plate 14 following pp. 847–48 (manuscript London [Exod 9.18–12:6]); Sirat, *Papyrus*, plate x (manuscript London); and in Sanders, "Ashkar-Gilson Manuscript," 24 plate 2 (manuscript Ashkar-Gilson).

²⁹⁵ M. Mishor and E. Engel, "Two Rare Ancient Scroll Fragments Reunited," *ilMuseums*, June 3, 2010: http://ilmuseums.com/exhibitions/english_article.asp?article_id=3991. (last accessed March 28, 2015); Engel and Mishor, "Ancient Scroll."

²⁹⁶ Engel and Mishor, "Ancient Scroll."

²⁹⁷ See Maggen, "Conservation."

²⁹⁸ Cf. Sanders, "Ashkar-Gilson Manuscript," 2, and esp. Charlesworth, "Ashkar Manuscript," 67–68.

²⁹⁹ S.A. Birnbaum, "A Sheet of an Eighth Century Synagogue Scroll," *VT* 9 (1959): 122–29.

³⁰⁰ See Engel and Mishor, "Ancient Scroll," 51.

³⁰¹ See Engel and Mishor, "Ancient Scroll," 35.

³⁰² Sanders, "Ashkar-Gilson Manuscript," 20. For manuscript London, Birnbaum states: "The text is identical with MT" ("Sheet," 123).

consonantal text of their famous master copies, such as MT^L and MT^A.³⁰⁴ Similarly, Engel and Mishor emphasize that the text of manuscript London/Ashkar-Gilson "corresponds fully to A."³⁰⁵

2.2.1.11.5 The En-Gedi Scroll³⁰⁶

The En-Gedi Scroll was found in the 1970s by a team of archeologists in the ark of the synagogue of En-Gedi. What remains of the scroll are tens of chunks of charred material. These chunks could not be read until a new imaging technology and a micro-CT scanner were used on them.³⁰⁷ So far, computer-generated images of two consecutive columns have been produced that contain text from Leviticus 1–2. At the moment, it remains unclear if the En-Gedi Scroll included originally only Leviticus or also Numbers and Deuteronomy. Carbon-14 dating points to the third or fourth century as the time when the En-Gedi Scroll was produced.³⁰⁸ Therefore, the scroll provides key evidence for the biblical text from the dark period of the Bible's Hebrew textual history between the Dead Sea Scrolls and the early medieval Masoretic codices. Very few biblical manuscripts exist from this time (see the list in → 1.2.2.2.2). All of them attest to a proto-Masoretic text. Along with ms Heb. d. 89 (P) i of Oxford's Bodleian Library (→ 2.2.1.11.2), the En-Gedi Scroll is among the earliest of these late ancient Hebrew biblical manuscripts. Given the size of its remains, its importance for the reconstruction of the late ancient Hebrew textual history of the Bible cannot be overemphasized. As far as the En-Gedi Scroll is deciphered, its text is in total textual agreement with the consonantal text of MT^L. Therefore, the En-Gedi Scroll needs to be classified as proto-Masoretic in character.³⁰⁹

---

[304] Sanders, "Ashkar-Gilson Manuscript," *passim*.

[305] Engel and Mishor, "Ancient Scroll," 35.

[306] I am much obliged to Emanuel Tov and Michael Segal who made an early version of their edition of the En-Gedi Scroll available to me ("The En-Gedi Leviticus[?] Scroll," forthcoming). The description below of the En-Gedi Scroll relies on this early version and their generosity.

[307] W. Harder, "Seales' Research Team Reveals Biblical Text from Damaged Scroll," University of Kentucky News (http://uknow.uky.edu/content/seales-research-team-reveals-biblical-text-damaged-scroll). For further press releases, see "The Most Ancient Hebrew Scroll since the Dead Sea Scrolls has been Deciphered" (http://www.antiquities.org.il/Article_eng.aspx?sec_id=25&subj_id=240&id=4134&hist=1); "Rare Ancient Hebrew Scroll Deciphered" (http://mfa.gov.il/MFA/IsraelExperience/History/Pages/Rare-ancient-Hebrew-scroll-deciphered-20-July-2015.aspx); and "1,500-Year-Old Text Has Been Digitally Resurrected from a Hebrew Scroll" (http://www.smithsonianmag.com/science-nature/1500-year-old-text-has-been-digitally-resurrected-burned-hebrew-scroll-180956031/?no-ist). All press releases last accessed January 5, 2016.

[308] See Tov and Segal, "The En-Gedi Leviticus(?) Scroll." The radiocarbon date of the En-Gedi Scroll was established by way of accelerator mass spectrometry by Dr. Elisabetta Boaretto at the Weizmann Institute D-REAMS Radiocarbon Laboratory (25).

Aadland, I., "A Forgotten Deuteronomy (4Q31) Fragment," *RevQ* 26 (2013–2014): 425–29.

Baillet, M., "1. Genèse," *DJD III.1: 48–49.

Baillet, M., "2. Exode (premiere examplaire)," *DJD III.1: 49–52.

Baillet, M., "3. Exode (deuxième exemplaire)," *DJD III.1: 52–55.

Baillet, M., "4. Exode (troisième exemplaire)," *DJD III.1: 56.

Baillet, M., "5. Lévitique en écriture paléo-hébraïque," *DJD III.1: 56–57.

Baillet, M., "6. Nombres (premiere exemplaire)," *DJD III.1: 57–58.

Baillet, M., "7. Nombres (deuxième exemplaire)," *DJD III.1: 58–59.

Baillet, M., "8. Nombres (troisième exemplaire)," *DJD III.1: 59.

Baillet, M., "9. Nombres (quatrième exemplaire)," *DJD III.1: 59–60.

Baillet, M., "1. Genèse en écriture paléo-hébraïque," *DJD III.1: 105–06.

Baillet, M., "2. Lévitique en écriture paléo-hébraïque," *DJD III.1: 106.

Baillet, M., "3. Deutéronome (?)," *DJD III.1: 106–07.

Baillet, M., "20. Texte en rapport avec le Deutéronome," *DJD III.1: 136–37.

Baillet, M., "1. Genèse," *DJD III.1 (1962): 147–48.

Baillet, M., "483. Genèse ou Livre des Jubilés," *DJD VII: 2.

Barthélemy, D., "1. Genèse," *DJD I: 49–50.

Barthélemy, D., "2. Exode," *DJD I: 50–51.

Barthélemy, D., "2. Lévitique et autres fragments en écriture 'phénicienne'," *DJD I: 51–54.

---

[309] Thus also Tov and Segal, "The En-Gedi Leviticus(?) Scroll."

Barthélemy, D., "4. Deutéronome (premier exemplaire)," *DJD* I: 54–57.

Barthélemy, D., "5. Deutéronome (second exemplaire)," *DJD* I: 57–62.

Birnbaum, S.A., "The Leviticus Fragments from the Cave," *BASOR* 118 (1950): 20–27.

Birnbaum, S.A., "A Sheet of an Eighth Century Synagogue Scroll," *VT* 9 (1959): 122–29.

Brooke, G.J., "Torah in the Qumran Scrolls," in *Bibel in jüdischer und christlicher Tradition: Festschrift für Johann Maier zum 60. Geburtstag* (eds. H. Merklein, K. Müller, and G. Stemberger; BBB 88; Frankfurt a.M.: Athäneum, 1993), 97–120.

Charlesworth, J.H., "What is a Variant? Announcing a Dead Sea Scrolls Fragment of Deuteronomy," *Maarav* 16/2 (2009): 201–12.

Charlesworth, J.H., "Ashkar Manuscript 2: Introducing a Phenomenal New Witness to the Bible," *Israel Museum Studies in Archaeology* 7 (2015): 66–69.

Cross, F.M., "13. 4QExod^b," *DJD* XII: 79–95.

Cross, F.M., "17. 4QExod-Lev^f," *DJD* XII: 133–44.

Dahmen, U., "Neu identifizierte Fragmente in den *Deuteronomium*-Handschriften vom Toten Meer," *RevQ* 20 (2001–2002): 571–81.

Dahmen, U., "Das Deuteronomium in Qumran als ungeschriebene Bibel," in *Das Deuteronomium* (ed. G. Braulik; ÖBS 23; Frankfurt a.M.: Peter Lang, 2003), 269–309.

Davila, J.R., "Unpublished Pentateuchal Manuscripts from Cave IV, Qumran: 4QGenEx^a, 4QGen$^{b-h, j-k}$" (PhD diss., Harvard University, 1988).

Davila, J.R., "New Qumran Readings for Genesis One," in *Of Scribes and Scrolls: Studies on the Hebrew Bible, Intertestamental Judaism, and Christian Origins Presented to John Strugnell on the Occasion of his Sixtieth Birthday* (eds. H.W. Attridge, J.J. Collins, and T.H. Tobin; College Theology Society Resources in Religion 5; Lanham: University Press of America, 1990), 3–11.

Davila, J.R., "The Name of God at Moriah: An Unpublished Fragment from 4QGenExod^a," *JBL* 110 (1991): 577–82.

Davila, J.R., "New Qumran Readings for the Joseph Story (Gen 37–50)," in *Madrid Qumran Congress*, 1.167–75.

Davila, J.R., "Text-Type and Terminology: Genesis and Exodus as Test Cases," *RevQ* 16 (1993–1994): 3–37.

Davila, J.R., "1. 4QGen-Exod^a," *DJD* XII: 7–30.

Davila, J.R., "2. 4QGen^b," *DJD* XII: 31–38.

Davila, J.R., "3. 4QGen^c," *DJD* XII 39–42.

Davila, J.R., "4. 4QGen^d," *DJD* XII: 43–45.

Davila, J.R., "5. 4QGen^e," *DJD* XII: 47–52.

Davila, J.R., "6. 4QGen^f," *DJD* XII: 53–55.

Davila, J.R., "7. 4QGen^g," *DJD* XII: 57–60.

Davila, J.R., "8. 4QGen^h," *DJD* XII: 61–64.

Davila, J.R., "9. 4QGen^j," *DJD* XII: 65–73.

Davila, J.R., "10. 4QGen^k," *DJD* XII: 75–78.

Duncan, J.A., "A Critical Edition of Deuteronomy Manuscripts from Qumran, Cave IV: 4QDt^b, 4QDt^e, 4QDt^h, 4QDt^j, 4QDt^k, 4QDt^l" (PhD diss., Harvard University, 1989).

Duncan, J.A., "Considerations of 4QDt^j in Light of the 'All Souls Deuteronomy' and Cave 4 Phylactery Texts," in *Madrid Qumran Congress*, 199–215.

Duncan, J.A., "29. 4QDeut^b," *DJD* XIV: 9–14.

Duncan, J.A., "32. 4QDeut^e," *DJD* XIV: 39–44.

Duncan, J.A., "35. 4QDeut^h," *DJD* XIV: 61–70.

Duncan, J.A., "37. 4QDeut^j," *DJD* XIV: 75–92.

Duncan, J.A., "38. 4QDeut^{k1}," *DJD* XIV: 93–98.

Duncan, J.A., "38a. 4QDeut^{k2}," *DJD* XIV: 99–105.

Duncan, J.A., "38b. 4QDeut^{k3}," *DJD* XIV: 107.

Duncan, J.A., "39. 4QDeut^l," *DJD* XIV: 109–12.

Duncan, J.A., "40. 4QDeut^m," *DJD* XIV: 113–16.

Duncan, J.A., "New Readings for the 'Blessing of Moses' from Qumran," *JBL* 114 (1995): 273–90.

Duncan, J.A., "Excerpted Texts of *Deuteronomy* at Qumran," *RevQ* 18 (1997–1998): 43–62.

Elgvin, T., "MS 5439/1. 4QReworked Pentateuch^b (4Q364) frg. 8a (Gen. 37.8)," in *Gleanings*, forthcoming.

Elgvin, T., "MS 4611: Mur/HevLev (Lev. 26.3–9, 33–37)," in *Gleanings*, forthcoming.

Elgvin, T., "MS 4612/5: 4Q(?)Num (Num. 16.2–5)," in *Gleanings*, forthcoming.

Elgvin, T., "MS 5214/1: 4Q(?)Deut1 (Deut. 6.1–2)," in *Gleanings*, forthcoming.

Elgvin, T., "MS 5214/2: 4Q(?)Deut2 (Deut. 32.5–9)," in *Gleanings*, forthcoming.

Elgvin, T. and K. Davis, "MS 4612/4: 4Q(?)GenMiniature (Gen. 36.7–16)," in *Gleanings*, forthcoming.

Engel, E. and M. Mishor, "An Ancient Scroll: The Reunion of Two Separate Fragments," *Israel Museum Studies in Archaeology* 7 (2015): 24–60.

Eshel, E., "4QDeut^n – A Text That Has Undergone Harmonistic Editing," *HUCA* 62 (1991): 117–54.

Eshel, E., "4QLev^d: A Possible Source for the Temple Scroll and *Miqṣat Ma'aśe Ha-Torah*," *DSD* 2 (1995): 1–13.

Eshel, E. and H. Eshel, "New Fragments from Qumran: 4QGen^f, 4QIsa^b, 4Q226, 8QGen, and XpapEnoch," *DSD* 12 (2005): 134–57.

Eshel, E. and H. Eshel, "A Preliminary Report on Seven New Fragments from Qumran," *Meghillot* 5–6 (2007): 271–78 [Hebr.].

Eshel, E. and M.E. Stone, "A New Fragment of 4QDeut^h," *JBL* 112 (1993): 487–89.

Eshel, H., Y. Baruchi, and R. Porat, "Fragments of a Biblical Scroll from the Judean Desert," *Meghillot* 3 (2005): 259–60 [Hebr.].

Eshel, H., Y. Baruchi, and R. Porat, "Fragments of a Leviticus Scroll (Arug-Lev) Found in the Judean Desert in 2004," *DSD* 13 (2006): 55–60.

Fabry, H.-J., "Das Buch Levitikus in den Qumrantexten," in *Levitikus als Buch: Tagung der Arbeitsgemeinschaft der Deutschsprachigen Alttestamentlerinnen und Alttestamentler vom 1. bis 5. September 1997 in Trier* (eds. H.-J. Fabry and H.W. Jüngling; BBB 119; Bodenheim: Philo, 1999), 309–41.

Finsterbuch, K., "Identität in der Differenz: Anmerkungen zur Textüberlieferung der Deuteronomium-Handschriften vom Toten Meer," in *Juda und Jerusalem in der Seleukidenzeit: Herrschaft – Widerstand – Identität: Festschrift für Heinz-Josef Fabry* (eds. U. Dahmen and J. Schnocks; BBB 159; Göttingen: V & R unipress, 2010), 339–62.

Flint, P., "1a. 5/6ḤevNumbers^a," *DJD* XXXVIII: 137–40.

Flint, P., "2. XḤev/SeNumbers^b," *DJD* XXXVIII: 173–77.

Flint, P., "3. XḤev/SeDtn," *DJD* XXXVIII: 179–82.

Flint, P., "The Book of Leviticus in the Dead Sea Scrolls," in *The Book of Leviticus: Composition and Reception* (eds. R. Rendtorff and R.A. Kugler; VTSup 93; Leiden: Brill, 2003), 323–41.

Flint, P. and A.E. Alvarez, "Two Biblical Scrolls from Naḥal Ḥever (*XḤev/SeNum^b* and *XḤev/SeDeut*) (Once Claimed to be 'Wadi Seiyal')," *RevQ* 18 (1997–1998): 531–40.

Flint, P. and A.E. Alvarez, "The Preliminary Edition of the First Numbers Scroll from Naḥal Ḥever," *BBR* 9 (1999): 137–43.

Freedman, D.N., "Variant Readings in the Leviticus Scroll from Qumran Cave 11," *CBQ* 36 (1974): 525–34.

Freedman, D.N. and K.A. Mathews, *The Paleo-Hebrew Leviticus Scroll (11QpaleoLev)* (Winona Lake: Eisenbrauns, 1985).

García Martínez, F., "Les manuscrits du désert de Juda et le Deutéronome," in *Studies in Deuteronomy: In Honour of C.J. Labuschagne on the Occasion of his 65th Birthday* (eds. F. García Martínez et al.; VTSup 53; Leiden: Brill, 1994), 63–82.

García Martínez, F., E.J.C. Tigchelaar, and A.S. van der Woude, "2. 11QLeviticus^b," *DJD* XXIII: 1–9.

García Martínez, F., E.J.C. Tigchelaar, and A.S. van der Woude, "3. 11QDeuteronomy," *DJD* XXIII: 11–14.

Jastram, N., "The Book of Numbers from Qumrân, Cave IV (4QNum^b)" (PhD diss., Harvard University, 1990).

Jastram, N., "The Text of 4QNum^b," in *Madrid Qumran Conference*, 1:177–98.

Jastram, N., "27. 4QNum^b," *DJD* XII: 205–67.

Jastram, N., "A Comparison of Two 'Proto-Samaritan' Texts from Qumran: 4QPaleoExod^m and 4QNum^b," *DSD* 5 (1998): 264–89.

Lange, *Handbuch*, 35–183.

Mathews, K.A., "The Paleo-Hebrew Leviticus Scroll from Qumran" (PhD diss., University of Michigan, 1980).

Maggen, M., "Appendix 1: The Conservation of MS Askhar," *Israel Museum Studies in Archaeology* 7 (2015): 62–65.

Mathews, K.A., "The Leviticus Scroll (11QpaleoLev) and the Text of the Hebrew Bible," *CBQ* 48 (1986): 173–207.

Mathews, K.A., "The Paleo-Hebrew Leviticus Scroll from Qumran," *BA* 50 (1987): 45–54.

McLean, M.D., "The Use and Development of Palaeo-Hebrew in the Hellenistic and Roman Periods" (PhD diss., Harvard University, 1982).

Milik, J.T., "1. Genèse, Exode, Nombres," *DJD* II.1: 75–78.

Milik, J.T., "2. Deutéronome," *DJD* II.1: 78–79.

Milik, J.T., "10. Deutéronome (premier exemplaire)," *DJD* III.1: 60.

Milik, J.T., "11. Deutéronome (deuxième exemplaire)," *DJD* III.1: 60–61.

Milik, J.T., 12. Deutéronome (troisième exemplaire), *DJD* III.1: 61–62.

Milik, J.T., "1. Deutéronome," *DJD* III.1: 169–71.

Morgenstern, M., "2. 34SeNumbers," *DJD* XXXVIII: 209.

Murphy, C., "1. SdeirGenesis," *DJD* XXXVIII: 117–24.

Owen, E., "4QDeut^n: A Pre-Samaritan Text," *DSD* 4 (1997): 162–78.

Perrin, A.B., "The Variants of 4Q(Reworked)Pentateuch: A Comprehensive List of the Textual Variants in 4Q158, 4Q364–367 in Biblical Sequence," *JJS* 63 (2012): 127–57.

Pfann, S.J., "249j. 4Qpap cryptA Leviticus^h?," *DJD* XXXVI: 575–77.

Pike, D.M., "The Book of Numbers at Qumran: Text and Context," in *Current Research and Technological Developments on the Dead Sea Scrolls: Conference on the Texts from the Judean Desert, Jerusalem, 30 April, 1995* (eds. D.W. Parry and S.D. Ricks; STDJ 20; Leiden: Brill, 1996), 166–93.

Puech, É., "Fragment d'un rouleau de la Genèse provenant du désert de Juda," *RevQ* 10 (1979–1981): 163–66.

Puech, É., "Notes en marge de 11QpaléoLévitique: Le fragment L, des fragments inédits et une jarre à manuscrits de la grotte 11," *RB* 96 (1989): 161–83.

Puech, É., "576. 4QGenése^n," *DJD* XXV: 191–93.

Puech, É., "Un nouveau manuscrit de la *Gènese* de la grotte 4: *4Q483 = pap4QGenèse^o*," *RevQ* 19 (1999): 259–60.

Puech, É., "Un autre manuscrit de la Genèse récemment identifié dans les fragments de la grotte 4 (*4QGn^n*)," *RevQ* 19 (1999–2000): 637–40.

Puech, É., "Identification de nouveaux manuscrits bibliques: *Deutéronome* et *Proverbes* dans les débris de la grotte 4," *RevQ* 20 (2001–2002): 121–27.

Puech, É., "Un autre manuscrit de Lévitique," *RevQ* 21 (2003–2004): 311–13.

Puech, É., "Un nouveau fragment 7a de 4QGn-Ex^a = 4QGen-Ex 1 et quelques nouvelles lectures et identifications du manuscrit 4Q1," *RevQ* 25 (2011–2012): 103–11.

Puech, É., "Un nouveau fragment du manuscrit 4Q27 – 4QNb^b 18a," *RevQ* 26 (2013–2014): 435–37.

Sanders, P., "The Askar-Gilson Manuscript: Remnant of a Proto-Masoretic Model Scroll of the Torah," *Journal of Hebrew Scriptures* 14 (2014): 1–25 (DOI:10.5508/jhs.2014.v14.a7; last accessed March 3, 2015).

Sanderson, J.E., *An Exodus Scroll from Qumran: 4Qpaleo-Exod^m and the Samaritan Tradition* (HSS 30; Atlanta: Scholars Press, 1986).

Sanderson, J.E., "The Contributions of *4QPaleoExod^m* to Textual Criticism," *RevQ* 13 (1988): 547–60.

Sanderson, J.E., "The Old Greek of Exodus in the Light of 4QpaleoExod^m," *Textus* 14 (1988): 87–104.

Sanderson, J.E., "14. 4QExod^c," *DJD* XII: 97–125.

Sanderson, J.E., "15. 4QExod^d," *DJD* XII: 127–28.

Sanderson, J.E., "16. 4QExod^e," *DJD* XII: 129–31.

Sanderson, J.E., "18. 4QExod^g," *DJD* XII: 145–46.

Sanderson, J.E., "19. 4QExod^h," *DJD* XII: 147.

Sanderson, J.E., "20. 4QExod^j," *DJD* XII: 149–50.

Sanderson, J.E., "21. 4QExod^k," *DJD* XII: 151.

Segal, M., "4QReworked Pentateuch or 4QPentateuch?" in Schiffman, Tov, and VanderKam, *Fifty Years*, 391–99.

Sirat, C., "Genesis Discovery," *Genizah Fragments* 23 (1992): 2.

Sirat, C., "Earliest Known Sefer Torah," *Genizah Fragments* 24 (1992): 3.

Skehan, P.W., "A Fragment of the 'Song of Moses' (Deut. 32) from Qumran," *BASOR* 136 (1954): 12–15.

Skehan, P.W., "Exodus in the Samaritan Recension from Qumran," *JBL* 74 (1955): 182–87.

Skehan, P.W., "The Qumran Manuscripts and Textual Criticism," in *Volume du congrès Strasbourg 1956* (VTSup 4; Leiden: Brill, 1957), 148–60.

Skehan, P.W., "The Biblical Scrolls from Qumran and the Text of the Old Testament," *BA* 28 (1965): 87–100.

Skehan, P.W. and E. Ulrich, "44. 4QDeut^q," *DJD* XIV: 137–42.

Skehan, P.W., E. Ulrich, and J.E. Sanderson, "Palaeo-Hebrew Manuscripts," *DJD* IX: 17–157 (17–154).

Stegemann, H., "Weitere Stücke von 4Qp Psalm 37, von 4QPatriarchal Blessings und Hinweis auf eine unedierte Handschrift von Höhle 4Q mit Exzerpten aus dem Deuteronomium," *RevQ* 6 (1967–1969): 193–227.

Stökl Ben Ezra, D., "Paleographical Observations Regarding 1Q5: One or Several Scrolls?" in *Qumran Cave 1 Revisited: Texts from Cave 1 Sixty Years after Their Discovery: Proceedings of the Sixth Meeting of the IOQS in Ljubljana* (eds. D. Falk et. al.; STDJ 91; Leiden: Brill, 2010), 247–57.

Talmon, S., "Fragments of a Deuteronomy Scroll from Masada: Deuteronomy 33.17–34.6 (1043/A–D)," in *Boundaries of the Ancient Near Eastern World: A Tribute to Cyrus H. Gordon* (eds. M. Lubetski, C. Gottlieb, and S. Keller; JSOTSup 273; Sheffield: Sheffield Academic Press, 1998), 150–61.

Talmon, S., "Fragments of Two Leviticus Scrolls from Masada," *Textus* 19 (1998): 27–44.

Talmon, S., "Hebrew Fragments from Masada," in S. Talmon and Y. Yadin, *Masada VI* (1999), 1–149, esp. 31–35.

Tigchelaar, E.J.C., "Some More Small 11Q1 Fragments," *RevQ* 18 (1997–1998): 325–29.

Tigchelaar, E.J.C., "On the Unidentified Fragments of *DJD* XXXIII and PAM 43.680: A New Manuscript of *4QNarrative and Poetic Composition*, and Fragments of *4Q13, 4Q269, 4Q525* and *4QSb(?)*," *RevQ* 21 (2003–2004): 477–85.

Tigchelaar, E.J.C., "Minuscula Qumranica I," *RevQ* 21 (2003–2004): 643–48.

Tigchelaar, E.J.C., "Publication of PAM 43.398 (IAA #202) Including New Fragments of 4Q269," in *From 4QMMT to Resurrection: mélanges qumraniens en hommage à Émile Puech* (eds. F. García Martínez, A. Steudel, and E. Tigchelaar; STDJ 61; Leiden: Brill, 2006), 265–80 (271–72).

Tigchelaar, E.J.C., "A Forgotten Qumran Cave 4 *Deuteronomy* Fragment (4Q38d = 4QDeut^u)," *RevQ* 23 (2008–2009): 525–28.

Tigchelaar, E.J.C., "A Partial Reedition of 4Q26a

(4QLeviticus^e): A New Fragment and a Reinterpretation," *DSD* 21 (2014): 234–39.

Tov, E., "The Textual Character of the Leviticus Scroll from Qumran Cave 11," *Shnaton* 3 (1978–1979): 238–44, xxiii [Hebr.].

Tov, E., "Proto-Samaritan Texts and the Samaritan Pentateuch," in *The Samaritans* (ed. A.D. Crown; Tübingen: J.C.B. Mohr [Paul Siebeck], 1989), 396–407.

Tov, E., "The Contribution of the Qumran Scrolls to the Understanding of the LXX," in *Manchester Symposium*, 11–47.

Tov, E., "The Textual Status of 4Q364–367 (4QRP)," in *Madrid Qumran Congress*, 1.43–82.

Tov, E., "25. 4QLev^c," *DJD* XII: 189–92.

Tov, E., "26. 4QLev^d," *DJD* XII: 193–95.

Tov, E., "26a. 4QLev^e," *DJD* XII: 197–201.

Tov, E., "26b. 4QLev^g," *DJD* XII: 203–04.

Tov, E., "From 4QReworked Pentateuch to 4QPentateuch (?)," in *Authoritative Scriptures in Ancient Judaism* (ed. M. Popović; JSJSup 141; Leiden: Brill, 2010), 73–91.

Tov, E., M. Segal, et al., "The En-Gedi Leviticus(?) Scroll," *Text*, forthcoming.

Tov, E. and S. White, "Reworked Pentateuch," *DJD* XIII: 187–351.

Ulrich, E., "23. 4QLev–Num^a," *DJD* XII: 153–76.

Ulrich, E., "24. 4QLev^b," *DJD* XII: 177–87.

Ulrich, E., "The Palaeo-Hebrew Biblical Manuscripts from Qumran Cave 4," in *Time to Prepare the Way in the Wilderness: Papers on the Qumran Scrolls by Fellows of the Institute of Advanced Studies of the Hebrew University, Jerusalem, 1989–1990* (eds. D. Dimant and L.H. Schiffman; STDJ 16; Leiden: Brill, 1995), 103–29.

Ulrich, E., "Two Perspectives on Two Pentateuchal Manuscripts from Masada," in *Emanuel: Studies in the Hebrew Bible, Septuagint and Dead Sea Scrolls in Honor of Emanuel Tov* (eds. S.M. Paul et al.; VTSup 94; Leiden: Brill, 2003), 453–64.

Ulrich, E., "A Revised Edition of the 1QpaleoLev–Num^a and 1QpaleoLev^b? Fragments," *RevQ* 22 (2005–2006): 341–47.

Ulrich, E., "The Dead Sea Scrolls and the Hebrew Scriptural Texts," in *The Bible and the Dead Sea Scrolls: The Princeton Symposium on the Dead Sea Scrolls* (3 vols.; ed. J.H. Charlesworth; Waco: Baylor University Press, 2006), 1.77–99.

Ulrich, *BQS*, 1–246.

White, S. see S. White Crawford.

White Crawford, S., "A Critical Edition of Seven Manuscripts of Deuteronomy: 4QDt^a, 4QDt^c, 4QDt^d, 4QDt^f, 4QDt^g, 4QDtⁱ, and 4QDtⁿ" (PhD diss., Harvard University, 1988).

White Crawford, S., "4QDtⁿ, Biblical Manuscript or Excerpted Text?" in *Of Scribes and Scrolls: Studies on the Hebrew Bible, Intertestamental Judaism, and Christian Origins Presented to John Strugnell on the Occasion of his Sixtieth Birthday* (eds. H.W. Attridge, J.J. Collins, and T.H. Tobin; College Theology Society Resources in Religion 5; Lanham: University Press of America, 1990), 13–20.

White Crawford, S., "The All Souls Deuteronomy and the Decalogue," *JBL* 109 (1990): 193–206.

White Crawford, S., "Special Features of Four Biblical Manuscripts from Cave IV, Qumran: *4QDt^a, 4QDt^c, 4QDt^d*, and *4QDt^g*," *RevQ* 15 (1991–1992) 157–67.

White Crawford, S., "4Q364 & 365: A Preliminary Report," in *Madrid Qumran Congress*, 1.217–28.

White Crawford, S., "Three Deuteronomy Manuscripts from Cave 4, Qumran," *JBL* 112 (1993): 23–42.

White Crawford, S., "28. 4QDeut^a," *DJD* XIV: 7–8.

White Crawford, S., "30. 4QDeut^c," *DJD* XIV: 15–34.

White Crawford, S., "31. 4QDeut^d," *DJD* XIV: 35–38.

White Crawford, S., "33. 4QDeut^f," *DJD* XIV: 45–54.

White Crawford, S., "34. 4QDeut^g," *DJD* XIV: 55–59.

White Crawford, S., "36. 4QDeutⁱ," *DJD* XIV: 71–74.

White Crawford, S., "41. 4QDeutⁿ," *DJD* XIV: 117–28.

White Crawford, S., "42. 4QDeut^o," *DJD* XIV: 129–33.

White Crawford, S., "43. 4QDeut^p," *DJD* XIV: 135–36.

Yardeni, A., "שעטנ״ז ג״ץ ופרשות פתוחות וסתומות בקטע חדש של ספר בראשית מן הגניזה," in *Proceedings of the Tenth World Congress of Jewish Studies*, Div. D., vol. 1: *The Hebrew Language, Jewish Languages* (Jerusalem: World Union of Jewish Studies, 1990), 173–80.

Zahn, M.M., *Rethinking Scripture: Composition and Exegesis in the 4QReworked Pentateuch Manuscripts* (STDJ 95; Leiden: Brill, 2011).

Armin Lange

2.2.2 Masoretic Texts and Ancient Texts Close to MT

2.2.2.1 General and Typological Features

The term Masoretic Text (MT) conventionally refers to the vocalized, accented, and annotated biblical codices produced by late medieval Hebrew scribes and their modern heirs. There are three sub-branches of MT (Tiberian, Babylonian, and Palestinian), which differ according to their vocalization systems.¹ The consonantal text does not differ in major details among these sub-branches.² Nonetheless, the consonantal text of each medieval MT manuscript differs in minor details, due to the fluidity of spelling and common types of scribal error. By scholarly convention, the pre-medieval scrolls belonging to the MT textual family are designated proto-MT. The proto-MT textual family can be further subdivided into an inner circle and an outer circle (see below). The oldest complete or nearly complete codices of MT-Pentateuch are from the tenth or early eleventh century C.E.:³

- St. Petersburg Pentateuch Codex EPB. II B 17 (MT^{L17} = National Library of Russia II Firkovitch B 17)⁴
- St. Petersburg Pentateuch Codex EPB. II B 10 (MT^{L10} = National Library of Russia II Firkovitch B10)⁵
- Cairo Pentateuch Codex (MT^{C3} = Gottheil 18)⁶
- Damascus Pentateuch Codex (MT^{S5} = National Library of Israel ms Heb. 4° 5702; formerly ms 507 of the Sassoon Collection)⁷
- London Pentateuch Codex (MT^B = British Library Or. 4445)⁸
- St. Petersburg Bible Codex I B 19a (MT^L = National Library of Russia I Firkovitch B 19a)⁹

MT^L is the oldest complete Pentateuch codex. Most of the Pentateuch is lacking in the Aleppo Codex (MT^A), ca. 930, which is the most accurate MT codex from the Tiberian Ben Asher family with respect to vocalization, accentuation, and Masorah.¹⁰ Another important early Pentateuch codex is Vatican ebr. 448 (MT^V), ca. eleventh through twelfth century.¹¹

The codex format was adopted in the eighth or ninth century for scholarly study. Prior to the late ninth century, all known texts of the Hebrew Bible were written in scroll format.¹² Medieval Torah scrolls, written on leather (parchment), contain the consonantal text of MT with the inevitable small variants. The oldest complete Torah scroll is the Bologna Torah Scroll, dated to the twelfth or early thirteenth century C.E.¹³ The oldest fragments of medieval Torah scrolls, dated inexactly to the fifth

---

¹ Khan, *Introduction*, 43–65.

² See the variants (all minor) in the Cairo Genizah Pentateuch fragments with Palestinian vocalization listed in B. Chiesa, *L'Antico Testamento ebraico secundo la tradizione palestinense* (Turin: Erasmo, 1978), 125–42.

³ See the list of early Bible codices in M. Beit-Arié, "The Damascus Pentateuch: MS Jerusalem, Jewish National and University Library Heb. 4° 5702; Orient, Ca. 1000," in M. Beit-Arié, *The Makings of the Medieval Hebrew Book: Studies in Palaeography and Codicology* (Jerusalem: Magnes Press, 1993), 111–27 (111, 125).

⁴ Dated in colophon to 929 C.E.; extant from Gen 2:6 with many lacunae. The scribe, Solomon ben Buya'a, was also the scribe of MT^A; the *naqdan* was his brother Ephraim. See M. Beit-Arié, C. Sirat, and M. Glatzer, *Codices hebraicis litteris exarati quo tempore scripti fuerint exhibentes*, Vol. 1: *usque ad annum 1020* (Turnhout: Brepols, 1997), 53–64.

⁵ Tenth century; Yeivin, *Introduction*, 23.

⁶ Tenth century; J.S. Penkower, "A Tenth-Century Pentateuchal MS from Jerusalem (MS C3): Corrected by Mishael Ben Uzziel," *Tarbiz* 58 (1988): 49–74 [Hebr.].

⁷ Ca. 1000 C.E.; extant from Gen 9:26, lacking Exod 18:1–23; Beit-Arié, "Damascus Pentateuch"; facsimile edition, *The Damascus Pentateuch* (eds. D.S. Loewinger and M. Beit-Arié; 2 vols.; Copenhagen: Rosenkilde and Bagger, 1978–1982); digitized manuscript at http://jnul.huji.ac.il/dl/mss/heb5702/.

⁸ Mid-tenth century: extant from Gen 39:20 to Deut 1:33, lacking Num 7:46–73; 9:12–10:18; A. Dotan, "Reflections Towards a Critical Edition of Pentateuch Codex Or. 4445," in *Estudios Masoréticos (X Congreso de la IOMS): En memoria de Harry M. Orlinsky* (eds. E. Fernández Tejero and M.T. Ortega Monsterio; Textos y estudios "Cardenal Cisneros" 55; Madrid: Instituto de Filología del CSIC, 1993), 39–50. A digitized version is available at http://www.bl.uk/manuscripts/FullDisplay.aspx?ref=Or_4445, last accessed September, 10th 2015.

⁹ Dated in colophon to 1008 C.E.; *The Leningrad Codex: A Facsimile Edition* (eds. D.N. Freedman et al.; Grand Rapids: Eerdmans, 1998); Beit-Arié, *Codices*, 114–31.

¹⁰ Extant from Deut 28:17; Beit-Arié, *Codices*, 65–72. The Pentateuch text in Cohen, *Miqra'ot Gedolot "Haketer"* is based on Yemenite codices that are elsewhere very close to MT^A.

¹¹ Extant from Gen 7:11; facsimile edition, *The Pentateuch with the Masorah Parva and the Masorah Magna and with Targum Onkelos, MS. Vat. Heb. 448* (ed. A. Díez Macho; Jerusalem: Makor, 1977); digitized manuscript at http://bav.bodleian.ox.ac.uk/vat-ebr-448/.

¹² The earliest dated biblical codex is the Ben Asher Codex of the Prophets (MT^C), dated in the colophon to 894/5; Beit-Arié, "Damascus Pentateuch," 111.

¹³ M. Perani, "Il più antico rotolo del Pentateuco ebraico integro: una scoperta alla Biblioteca Universitaria di Bologna," *TECA: Testimonianze Editoria, Cultura, Arte* 4 (2013): 87–97.

to eighth centuries C.E., are the following. They contain the consonantal text of MT, with minor variants.[14]

- Cairo Genizah, T-S NS 4.3 and 3.21, portions of Gen 4:14–6:5 and 13:10–17:9[15]
- Oxford, Bodleian Library ms Heb. d. 89 (P) (i), portions of Exod 2:23–25[16]
- Berlin, Staatliche Museen P. 10598, portions of Exod 3:13–4:9[17]
- Ms London + ms Ashkar-Gilson, portions of Exod 9:18–16:1[18]

The Oxford scroll, written in small characters and format, was presumably used for study.[19] The others are scrolls with larger formats, which were suitable for synagogue use.

The earliest Pentateuchal texts, all fragmentary, are from the Judean Desert, dating from the mid-third century B.C.E. to the early second century C.E.[20] The earliest proto-MT fragment, 4QLev-Num^a (→ 2.2.17.10), is from the early Hasmonean period (ca. 150–100 B.C.E.; see below). It is unclear whether complete Torah scrolls existed in the Second Temple period, but the multi-book scrolls from the Judean Desert – notably MurGen-Exod-Num^a (see below) – indicates that this is a possibility.[21]

The (proto-)MT-Pentateuch has certain typological features that distinguish it from the other identifiable textual families in the Pentateuch (proto-SP and proto-LXX).[22] These features include several substantive editorial revisions by scribes in the proto-MT tradition. These revisions contrast with the earlier editions or parallel revisions preserved by proto-SP and/or proto-LXX:

1. A revised edition of the chronologies of Genesis 5 and 11. MT, SP, and LXX have three different editions of these chronologies. All three are responses to exegetical problems in the priestly text.[23]
2. An expanded edition of the tabernacle text of Exodus 35–40. LXX has a shorter account of the construction of the tabernacle. The MT edition is expanded, harmonized, and reordered to correspond more closely with God's instructions to Moses in Exodus 25–30.[24]
3. Sequence differences at Gen 47:5–6 and Num 10:34–36. MT-Gen 47:5–11 is reordered and truncated due to problems in the narrative (see below). LXX preserves the earlier edition. MT and LXX have slightly different locations for the "Song of the Ark" in Num 10:34–36. It is unclear whether one placement is secondary or whether the song was a late editorial insertion in both textual traditions.[25]

---

[14] For an earlier inventory, see P.J. Gentry, "The Text of the Old Testament," *JETS* 52 (2009): 19–45 (21–22), → 1.2.2.2 and → 2.2.1.11. My thanks to Armin Lange and Yosef Ofer for advice and bibliography on these manuscripts.

[15] Dated to ca. eighth century C.E. by A. Yardeni, *The Book of Hebrew Scripts: History, Palaeography, Script Styles, Calligraphy and Design* (London: British Library, 2002), 79 and fig. 97; C. Sirat, M. Dukan, and A. Yardeni, "Rouleaux de la Tora antérieurs à l' an mille," *CRAI* 138 (1994): 861–64; C. Sirat, *Hebrew Manuscripts of the Middle Ages* (Cambridge: Cambridge University Press, 2002), 27–28 and pl. 11; digitized images in B. Outhwaite, "The Oldest Hebrew Fragment in the Collection? T-S NS 3.21," *Fragment of the Month: November 2010*: http://www.lib.cam.ac.uk/Taylor-Schechter/fotm/november-2010/. There is a variant at Gen 17:1, where this manuscript has שנה "year" versus the plural שנים "years" in other MT (and SP) manuscripts.

[16] Dated to ca. third century C.E. by A. Yardeni, *Hebrew Scripts*, 73 and fig. 90; C. Sirat, *Les papyrus en caractères hébraïques trouvés en Égypte* (Paris: Centre National de la Recherche Scientifique, 1985), 31–32, 123, and pl. 83; Sirat, *Hebrew Manuscripts*, 29.

[17] Sirat, *Papyrus*, 34–35 and pl. 9; the text is mistakenly identified as Numbers 3–4, but it is Exodus 3–4.

[18] P. Sanders, "The Ashkar-Gilson Manuscript: Remnant of a Proto-Masoretic Model Scroll of the Torah," *JHS* 14 (2014) article 7: DOI:10.5508/jhs.2014.v14.a7.

[19] Sirat, *Papyrus*, 32.

[20] The earliest Pentateuchal text, 4QExod-Lev^f (mid-third century B.C.E.; → 2.2.1.7.9) has affinities with the proto-SP family.

[21] Tov, *Scribal Practices*, 75–77.

[22] On discerning textual families in the Pentateuch, see Hendel, "Assessing," 281–302.

[23] Hendel, *Genesis 1–11*, 61–80; Hendel, "A Hasmonean Edition of MT Genesis? The Implications of the Editions of the Chronology in Genesis 5," *Hebrew Bible and Ancient Israel* 1 (2012): 1–17.

[24] A. Aejmelaeus, "Septuagintal Translation Techniques: A Solution to the Problem of the Tabernacle Account?" in Aejmelaeus, *Trail*, 107–21.

[25] E. Tov, "Some Sequence Differences between the Ma-

4. Theologically motivated revisions at Deut 27:4, 32:8, and 32:43. An anti-Samaritan revision occurs at Deut 27:4, where MT reads "Ebal," replacing "Gerizim" in SP and LXX (restored from the Old Latin; → 2.2.4.5). An anti-polytheistic revision occurs at Deut 32:8, where proto-MT reads "sons of Israel," replacing the original "sons of God," preserved in 4QDeut^j and LXX. Another anti-polytheistic revision occurs in Deut 32:43, where proto-MT deleted a poetic line referring to the "sons of God" and in the parallel line replaced "heaven" with "nations." The original readings are preserved, with variants and expansions, in 4QDeut^q and LXX.[26]

These revisions are sufficiently distinctive to count as typological features of the proto-MT textual family in the Pentateuch. They provide a contrast with the respective typological features of the other Pentateuchal textual families. Aside from these typological features, there are many other smaller-scale scribal revisions in the proto-MT textual family, including harmonizations and explicating glosses.[27] In general, the proto-MT-Pentateuch is a less revised textual family than proto-SP and proto-LXX.

Besides these typological features and smaller revisions, there are many small scribal errors in the (proto-)MT-Pentateuch. These are the inevitable product of scribal transmission of texts. The following is a small sample of the kinds of scribal errors in MT-Pentateuch. These errors are found in all the early MT codices. Additional scribal errors occur in the MT codices and printed editions of the early modern period, as demonstrated in the collations of Benjamin Kennicott (1776–1780) and Giovanni de Rossi (1788).[28] The correct readings below are supplied by non-MT Pentateuchal texts and versions or by conjectural emendation.

Graphic Error

וְדֹדָנִים "*D*odians" MT-Gen 10:4

ורדנים "*R*hodians" SP and LXX, cf. 1 Chr 1:7

Metathesis

וַיֵּלֶךְ מֹשֶׁה וַיְדַבֵּר "Moses *went* to speak" MT-Deut 31:1

ויכל משה לדבר "Moses *finished* speaking" 1QDeut^b and LXX

Dittography

וְאִישׁ אֲשֶׁר יִנְאַף אֶת־אֵשֶׁת אִישׁ אֲשֶׁר יִנְאַף אֶת־אֵשֶׁת רֵעֵהוּ "And a man who commits adultery with the wife of *a man who commits adultery with the wife of* his neighbor" MT-Lev 20:10

ואיש אשר ינאף את אשת רעהו "And a man who commits adultery with the wife of his neighbor" emendation

Haplography

הַגֵּר בְּיִשְׂרָאֵל "*the sojourner* in Israel" MT-Lev 22:18

הגר הגר בישראל "*the sojourner who sojourns* in Israel" 4QLev^b, SP, and LXX

Homoioteleuton

רָר בְּשָׂרוֹ אֶת־זוֹבוֹ אוֹ־הֶחְתִּים בְּשָׂרוֹ מִזּוֹבוֹ "if his flesh runs with his flow *or his flesh is blocked by his flow*" MT-Lev 15:3

רד בשרו את זובו או החתים בשרו מזובו טמא הוא כל ימי זוב בשרו או החתים בשרו מזובו "if his flesh runs with his flow *or his flesh is blocked by his flow*, he is impure all the days that his flesh flows *or his flesh is blocked by his flow*" 11QpaleoLev (partially), SP, and LXX[29]

---

soretic Text and the Septuagint and Their Ramifications for Literary Criticism," in Tov, *Greek-Hebrew Bible*, 414–15.

[26] E. Ulrich, "The Old Latin, Mount Gerizim, and 4QJosh^a," in *Textual Criticism and Dead Sea Scroll Studies in Honour of Julio Trebolle Barrera: Florilegium Complutense* (eds. A. Piquer Otero and P.A. Torijano Morales; JSJSup 157; Leiden: Brill, 2012), 361–75; S. Schorch, "The Samaritan Version of Deuteronomy and the Origin of Deuteronomy," in *Samaria, Samarians, Samaritans: Studies on Bible, History and Linguistics* (ed. J. Zsengellér; SJ 66; Berlin: De Gruyter, 2011), 23–37; G. Knoppers, *Jews and Samaritans: The Origins and History of their Early Relations* (New York: Oxford University Press, 2013), 184–87, 201–12; A. Rofé, "The End of the Song of Moses (Deuteronomy 32:43)," in Rofé, *Deuteronomy*, 47–54.

[27] E.g., Hendel, *Genesis 1–11*, 40–60.

[28] See Goshen-Gottstein, *"Biblical Manuscripts."

[29] SP reads חתום "sealed" instead of the initial החתים "blocked."

2.2.2 Masoretic Texts and Ancient Texts Close to MT

Word Misdivision

עָקֵב מֵאָשֵׁר "heel. *From* Asher" MT-Gen 49:19–20

עקבם אשר "*their* heels. Asher" SP and LXX[30]

Reminiscence

פְּרוּ וּרְבוּ שִׁרְצוּ בָאָרֶץ וּרְבוּ־בָהּ "Be fruitful and multiply, spread on the earth, and *multiply* on it" MT-Gen 9:7 (reminiscence of ורבו "multiply" three words previously)

פרו ורבו שרצו בארץ ורדו בה "Be fruitful and multiply, spread on the earth, and *rule* it" emendation (cf. Gen 1:28)

Eyeskip

וַיֹּאמֶר קַיִן אֶל־הֶבֶל אָחִיו וַיְהִי בִּהְיוֹתָם בַּשָּׂדֶה "Cain said to Abel his brother, and when they were in the field" MT-Gen 4:8

ויאמר קין אל הבל אחיו נלכה השדה ויהי בהיותם בשדה "Cain said to Abel his brother, '*Let us go to the field*,' and when they were in the field" SP and LXX

The orthography of (proto-)MT-Pentateuch reflects roughly the practices of the earliest Qumran biblical scrolls, which date to the third century B.C.E.[31] The distribution of *matres lectionis* in MT-Pentateuch is slightly fuller than in 4QSam[b], but not as full as in 4QExod-Lev[f] or 4QJer[a] (all third-century scrolls). For instance, the use of *waw* to mark word-internal long $\bar{o}$ is infrequent in 4QSam[b], more frequent in MT-Pentateuch, and regular in 4QExod-Lev[f] and later scrolls. Compare the distribution of full and defective spelling of '*ēpōd* ("ephod"): 4QSam[b]: אפד; MT-Pentateuch: אֵפֹד and אֵפוֹד; 4QExod-Lev[f] and later texts (4QSam[a]): אפוד.

MT-Pentateuch also preserves an unusual number of pre-exilic spellings, such as occasionally marking final $\bar{o}$ with *he* (rather than the post-exilic extension of *waw* to this position); e.g. אָהֳלֹה "his tent" in the *Ketiv* of Gen 9:21, 12:8, 13:3, and 35:21. There are also a smattering of late spellings in MT-Pentateuch, e.g., the occasional final *he* in the second masculine singular pronominal suffix: יָדְכָה "your hand" (Exod 13:16); כָּמֹכָה "like you" (Exod 15:11); לְכָה "to you" (Gen 27:37).[32] Generally, in orthography as well as substantive readings, the inner circle (see below) of proto-MT-Pentateuch is less expansionistic than the outer circle or the non-MT Pentateuchal texts. It is also less expansionistic, both in orthography and substantive readings, than the other sections of MT.

2.2.2.2 History of (Proto-)MT-Pentateuch

There are three general models of the history of (proto-)MT-Pentateuch.[33] The first, formulated by Eichhorn, and refined by de Lagarde, holds that MT derives from a particular textual family (Eichhorn) or a particular text (Lagarde; see below), which in turn descends from the textual original (*Urtext*).[34] The original text of the Pentateuch is loosely identified with Ezra's סֵפֶר תּוֹרַת מֹשֶׁה "scroll of the Torah of Moses" in Neh 8:1, which portrays events of the mid-fifth century B.C.E. The second model, formulated by Kahle, holds that MT derives from editorial efforts in the first century C.E. to create a standard version out of the plethora of "vulgar" texts in circulation at the time. A Pentateuchal *Urtext* of the fifth century B.C.E. is not excluded. Kahle argued that MT is itself a "kritischen Reduktion des Vulgärtextes,"[35] that is, a work of ancient textual criticism. A third model, which derives from Kahle's,

---

[30] This error occurred prior to the consistent use of final letters in the post-Herodian era.

[31] D.N. Freedman, "The Massoretic Text and the Qumran Scrolls: A Study in Orthography," in Cross–Talmon, *QHBT, 196–211.

[32] On regularities and irregularities in MT spelling practices, see Barr, *Variable Spellings*; and A. Lange, "The Question of the So-Called Qumran Orthography, the Severus Scroll, and the Masoretic Text," *Hebrew Bible and Ancient Israel* 3 (2014): 424–75.

[33] Cf. the overviews in Lange, "Textual Standardization," 31–45; Tov, "History," 49–66; and B. Chiesa, *Filologia storica della Bibbia ebraica*, Vol. 2: *Dall'età moderna ai giorni nostri* (Brescia: Paideia, 2002), 420–26. Cf. also → 2.1.8; → 1.2.1. For another reconstruction of the textual history of the Pentateuch, see → 2.1.5.

[34] J.G. Eichhorn, *Einleitung in das Alte Testament*, Vol. 2 (2nd improved and enlarged ed.; Leipzig: Weidmanns Erben und Reich, 1787), 203 (cf. pp. 111 and 113); De Lagarde, *Anmerkungen*, 1–2.

[35] Kahle, *"Untersuchungen," 35–36.

was formulated by Talmon, who holds that MT is a written crystallization of one of many oral versions of the Pentateuch in circulation during the Persian period. In his view, "the process culminating in the practically total substitution of written transmission for oral tradition [occurred] toward the end of the Persian age."[36] He holds that the variants in the ancient biblical texts stem from independent oral versions, and that there was no *Urtext* behind these textual crystallizations.

While each of these models is theoretically possible, and others are imaginable, the genealogical textual model of Eichhorn and Lagarde has gained currency in light of the data from the Qumran biblical texts. Against Kahle, there is no reason to regard MT-Pentateuch as the product of systematic editing.[37] Against Talmon, the variants among MT, the biblical Dead Sea scrolls, SP, and LXX are consistently analyzable as scribal errors or revisions, which are made while copying texts (as in the instances above), and are unlikely to stem from independent oral variants. There is no evidence in favor of Talmon's theory of "multiple pristine texts."[38]

Lagarde, following the historical text-critical method of Karl Lachmann and others, observed that MT-Pentateuch has certain para-textual elements that allow us to trace its textual history into pre-medieval times. These features include the *puncta extraordinaria* (dotted letters and words) that are written in scrolls and codices. There are ten cases of dotted words in the Pentateuch and five in later books. Lagarde argued that such distinctive secondary features must ultimately derive from a single manuscript, since such a complex cluster of scribal features cannot have arisen independently in unrelated texts. He inferred that all exemplars of MT descend from a manuscript that he designated (after Lachmann's usage) the "archetype of the Masoretic Text" ("archetypus des masoretischen textes").[39] Noting that the scribal dots are correction marks that mean "delete," he wrote:

> our Hebrew manuscripts of the Old Testament go back to one single exemplar, and have even reproduced as true corrections the correction [marks] of its scribal errors and taken over its random imperfections.[40]

Lagarde maintained that the archetype of MT, viz., the first manuscript with this cluster of secondary features, existed in the first century C.E., primarily since these features are already known in rabbinic literature.

Another set of secondary features that can arguably be used to elucidate the history of MT-Pentateuch is the *qere perpetuum* in the Pentateuch in which הוא (third person masculine singular pronoun) is the *Ketiv* and היא (third person feminine singular pronoun) is the *Qere*. This textual feature occurs around 120 times in the Pentateuch, versus eleven instances where היא is written correctly. This textual phenomenon is either: 1) a retention of a dialectal feature in which the old feminine singular independent pronoun was replaced by an epicene pronoun, הוא;[41] or 2) a systematic graphic confusion of *yod* and *waw* in a proto-MT Torah scroll or scrolls.[42] Since the oldest proto-MT scroll, 4QLev-Num[a] (early Hasmonean period; see below), twice correctly reads היא "she" where MT *Ketiv* is הוא "he" (at Lev 14:44 and Num 5:6), it appears that a systematic graphic error subsequent to the Early Hasmonean period is the more likely solution. Cross has argued that this systematic graphic error stems from the script of the early Herodian period:

---

[36] Talmon, *"Ancient Versions," 393.

[37] Albrektson, "Reflections," 47–62; Tov, *TCHB, 174–80.

[38] See the critiques by Tov, *TCHB, 163–67; Hendel, *"Prologue," 340–42; and Hendel, "Assessing," 289–91.

[39] De Lagarde, *Anmerkungen, 2.

[40] De Lagarde, *Anmerkungen, 2: "unsere hebräischen handschriften des alten testaments auf ein einziges exemplar zurückgehn, dem sie sogar die korrektur seiner schreibfehler als korrektur treu nachgeahmt und dessen zufällige unvollkommenheiten sie herübergenommen haben."

[41] Recently advocated by S.E. Fassberg, "The Kethiv/Qere הוא: Diachrony, and Dialectology," in *Diachrony in Biblical Hebrew* (eds. C.L. Miller-Naudé and Z. Zevit; Winona Lake: Eisenbrauns, 2012), 171–80.

[42] So J.A. Emerton, "Was There an Epicene Pronoun *Hū'* in Early Hebrew?" *JSS* 45 (2000): 267–76.

TABLE 1   *Inner-Circle Proto-MT texts*

MasLev^a	Early Herodian formal script (30–1 B.C.E.)	63 complete or partial words
MasDeut	Early Herodian formal script (30–1 B.C.E.)	68 complete or partial words
MasLev^b	Middle Herodian formal script (1–30 C.E.)	457 complete or partial words
4QDeut^g	Middle Herodian formal script (1–30 C.E.)	151 complete or partial words
XLev^c	Late Herodian formal script (30–75 C.E.)	107 complete or partial words
XḤev/SeNum^b	Late Herodian formal script (30–75 C.E.)	95 complete or partial words
4QGen^b	Late or post-Herodian formal script (50–100 C.E.)	358 complete or partial words
SdeirGen	Late or post-Herodian formal script (50–100 C.E.)	117 complete or partial words
MurGen-Exod-Num^a	Post-Herodian formal script (75–125 C.E.)	260 complete or partial words

The most plausible explanation of this is that the manuscript or manuscripts copied for the Pentateuchal Recension was a manuscript in which *waw* and *yod* were not distinguished in the Jewish script. This occurs at only one time in the development of the Jewish scripts: in the Early Herodian Period (30–1 B.C.E.).[43]

These two genealogical arguments, based on widespread innovations or *Leitfehler* (indicative errors, *errores significativi*) in the proto-MT-Pentateuch converge on the period that is illuminated by the Dead Sea Scrolls.

2.2.2.3 Proto-MT-Pentateuch: The Inner Circle

Tov has usefully distinguished between two categories of proto-MT texts in the Dead Sea Scrolls, an inner and an outer circle:

> We should posit two types of Masoretic scrolls, an inner circle of proto-rabbinic scrolls that agree precisely with codex L and a second circle of scrolls that are very similar to it … Most scrolls found at Qumran belong to this second circle, with only a few texts belonging to the first group. On the other hand, all the scrolls found at sites in the Judean Desert other than Qumran belong to the inner circle of proto-rabbinic scrolls.[44]

Tov's distinction between the inner circle and outer circle of proto-MT texts corresponds to Lange's distinction between proto-Masoretic and semi-Masoretic texts.[45] Since proto-MT conventionally refers to all of the pre-medieval scrolls in this textual family, I will adopt Tov's terminology. I will, however, criticize Tov's use of the term "proto-rabbinic" (following Cross's usage) to designate the proto-MT family.[46]

The criterion for determining the "inner circle" scrolls is relatively simple: they are scrolls that "differ from the medieval manuscripts no more than the latter differ among themselves."[47] The list in Table 1 includes only scrolls with more than fifty words.[48] These proto-MT Pentateuchal texts from the "inner circle" were written in Herodian or post-Herodian script, dating from ca. 30 B.C.E. to 125 C.E. The earliest are from Qumran and Masada. The later scrolls are from the Bar Kokhba caves at Murabbaʿat, Naḥal Ḥever, and Wadi Sdeir (probably including 4QGen^b and XLev^c).[49]

---

[43] F.M. Cross, "The Stabilization of the Canon of the Hebrew Bible," in F.M. Cross, *From Epic to Canon: History and Literature in Ancient Israel* (Baltimore: Johns Hopkins University Press, 1998), 219–29 (223).

[44] E. Tov, "The Text of the Hebrew/Aramaic and Greek Bibles Used in the Ancient Synagogues," in Tov, *HB, GB, and Qumran*, 171–88 (176). On the distinctive character of the Pentateuchal scrolls from Masada and the Bar Kokhba caves, see Young, *"Stabilization," 370–76.

[45] Lange, "Textual Standardization," 47; Lange, *Handbuch*, 16 and → 1.2.2.

[46] E.g., E. Tov, "The Biblical Texts from the Judean Desert: An Overview and Analysis," in Tov, *HB, GB, and Qumran*, 128–54 (146–47); Cross, *"Fixation."

[47] Tov, "Text of the Bible in Ancient Synagogues," 173.

[48] Word-counts are from Lange, *Handbuch*; other details are from the *editiones principes* in DJD. Lange agrees on the assignment of these scrolls to the inner circle/proto-MT (*Handbuch*, 16).

[49] According to Cross, the coarse and poorly prepared

The extant differences between the inner circle scrolls and our early MT codices are purely orthographic, with no substantive variants. The variants from the early MT codices MT^A, MT^L, MT^C3, MT^S5, and MT^V are as follows:

- Gen 1:15 למארת 4QGen^b] לִמְאוֹרֹת (both meaning "as lights") MT^L
- Lev 4:7 ישפוך MasLev^a] יִשְׁפֹּךְ (both meaning "he shall pour out") MT^L, MT^S5, MT^V
- Lev 11:28 הסה MasLev^b] הֵמָה (both meaning "they") MT^L, MT^S5, MT^V
- Deut 33:19 ושפני MasDeut, MT^A, MT^S5, MT^V] וּשְׂפֻנֵי (both meaning "covered") MT^L

The differences in Gen 1:15, Lev 4:7, and Deut 33:19 are cases of plene versus *defectiva* spelling. The difference in Lev 11:28 is a different kind of orthographic variant: a final *mem* in medial position. This phenomenon occurs once in MT (לְמַרְבֵּה "abundant," Isa 9:6), but it is relatively frequent (ca. forty times) in the biblical Dead Sea scrolls.[50]

Of these inner-circle proto-MT scrolls, only the longest, MasLev^b, has text that corresponds to the indicative errors that Lagarde or Cross adduce to approximate the date of the archetype of MT-Pentateuch. MasLev^b has two readings that overlap MT perpetual *Qere* of הוא/היא "he/she." At Lev 10:17 and possibly 11:6, MasLev^b reads הוא "he," agreeing with MT *Ketiv*.[51] And at Lev 11:39, it agrees with MT *Ketiv* in reading היא "she," one of the eleven correct readings of the third person feminine singular pronoun in the Pentateuch. The implications are notable. As Cross notes, the early Herodian script is the likely source for the *yod*/*waw* confusion in the third person feminine singular pronoun. MasLev^b, written in the middle Herodian script, is from the era when a scribe would have had to disambiguate the script of an Early Herodian *Vorlage*. This scroll may be closely related to the MT archetype, but it is not identical to it; note the final *mem* in medial position at Lev 11:28 (above). MasLev^b may provide a partial view of the scribal origins of the MT archetype.

There are two other scrolls that Tov or Lange assign to the inner circle of proto-MT. Tov assigns MasGen (→ 2.2.1.8) to this group.[52] MasGen is written in a Hasmonean semicursive script (ca. 150–50 B.C.E.) and preserves eleven complete or partial words. It is the oldest biblical scroll from Masada. If Tov's assignment is correct, then MasGen would be to the earliest Pentateuchal scroll of this type. However, as Ulrich has observed, the variants argue against Tov's (and previously Talmon's) categorization.[53] In Gen 46:7–8, MasGen twice reads מצרים "Egypt" against MT's מִצְרָיְמָה (with *he*-locale). The second of these agrees with a variant in the (lost) Severus Scroll, whose unusual readings are listed in some medieval texts (→ 2.2.5).[54] In Gen 46:8, MasGen reads את "with" preceding יעקוב "Jacob" against MT. Talmon reconstructs this phrase as את יעקוב [אביהם] "with Jacob [their father]," a reading reflected in Jub 44:11–12.[55] I note that this phrase, את יעקוב אביהם, occurs in 4QExod^b and LXX-Exod 1:1, where it is a scribal expansion of MT's אֶת יַעֲקֹב. The reading in MasGen is arguably a harmonizing plus. In view of these substantive variants and their affinities, MasGen should probably be cat-

---

leather of 4QGen^b suggests that it did not come from Qumran Cave 4 but from one of the other Judean Desert caves "and was inadvertently mixed with the Cave 4 manuscripts by the Bedouin," apud J.R. Davila, "4QGen^b," *DJD* XII: 31–38, 31. XLev^c, from the Schøyen Collection, may come from one of the Bar Kokhba caves; Lange, *Handbuch*, 77.

[50] Tov, *Scribal Practices*, 232–34.

[51] At Lev 10:17, הוא is a supralinear insertion.

[52] Tov, "Biblical Texts from the Judean Desert," 135.

[53] E. Ulrich, "Two Perspectives on Two Pentateuchal Manuscripts from Masada," in *Emanuel: Studies in Hebrew Bible, Septuagint, and Dead Sea Scrolls in Honor of Emanuel Tov* (eds. S.M. Paul et al.; VTSup 94; Leiden: Brill, 2003), 453–64 (454–58).

[54] Talmon, *Masada VI*, 32, misstates the data; J.P. Siegel, *The Severus Scroll and 1QIsa^a* (Missoula: Scholars Press, 1975), 31; A. Lange, "The Severus Scroll Variant List in Light of the Dead Sea Scrolls," in *Tradition, Transmission, and Transformation from Second Temple Literature through Judaism and Christianity in Late Antiquity: Proceedings of the Thirteenth International Symposium of the Orion Center for the Study of the Dead Sea Scrolls and Associated Literture Jointly Sponsored by the Hebrew University Center for the Study of Christianity, 22–24 February, 2011* (eds. M. Kister et al.; STDJ 113; Leiden: Brill, 2015), 179–207.

[55] Talmon, *Masada VI*, 33–34.

egorized as either an "outer circle" or a non-MT-type text.⁵⁶ In sum, this is the only Masada biblical scroll that probably does *not* belong to the inner circle of proto-MT. It is an outlier, which highlights the predominance of the inner circle of proto-MT-Pentateuch scrolls at Masada.

Lange assigns 4QDeutᵉ (→ 2.2.1.2.1) to this inner circle.⁵⁷ 4QDeutᵉ is another relatively early text, written in late Hasmonean formal script (ca. 50–25 B.C.E.), and it preserves 126 complete or partial words. However, it has a notable agreement with LXX in a secondary reading: בידך "into your hand" vs. לְפָנֶיךָ "before you" (MT) in Deut 7:23, probably a harmonization with בידך in the following verse. This is not a large percentage of variation from MT, and hence it falls within Lange's threshold of 2 percent variation from MT for inner-circle/proto-MT texts. However, it is a larger variation than exists among the early MT codices. This shared secondary reading with proto-LXX may be sufficiently weighty to exclude this text from the inner circle of proto-MT scrolls.

Another notable feature is the format of the inner-circle proto-MT scrolls. Tov observes that many scrolls belonging to the inner circle are what he calls "deluxe" scrolls, characterized by ample top and bottom margins (more than 3 cm) and long columns of text.⁵⁸ The inner-circle scrolls do not all feature fine workmanship and materials.⁵⁹ They do, however, conform to the later requirements in rabbinic literature for the vertical margins of single books of the Pentateuch: "in the Five Books, (the margin) below is three fingerbreadths, above is two fingerbreadths" (*b. Menaḥ.* 30a).⁶⁰ It is possible that all of the inner-circle MT-Pentateuch scrolls listed above conform to this standard. The only uncertain cases are MasLevᵃ and MasLevᵇ, whose extant margins are slightly less than 3 cm, but they are broken; and SdeirGen, which has no preserved top or bottom margins.

While there is a tendency for inner-circle scrolls to be deluxe scrolls, there is not a fixed correlation between format and text type. 4QpaleoExodᵐ and 4QSamᵃ also share this format, and they belong, respectively, to the proto-SP and the proto-LXX family. The oldest deluxe Pentateuchal scroll is an outer-circle proto-MT scroll, 4QpaleoGen-Exodˡ (see below). Although ample vertical margins are only one indicator of textual status, the distribution of this format arguably indicates a high status for the inner-circle proto-MT scrolls from at least the early Herodian period.

2.2.2.4 Proto-MT-Pentateuch: The Outer Circle

The criteria for determining the outer circle of the proto-MT-Pentateuch (what Lange calls "semi-Masoretic") are not well defined. Tov regards roughly half of the Qumran Pentateuchal scrolls as belonging to this category.⁶¹ However, as several scholars have noted, Tov's method for determining textual affiliation is biased in favor of proto-MT.⁶² Moreover, his statistics rely predominantly on minor variants, which are not indicative of textual affinity. The only sure criteria to determine textual affinities are shared indicative errors or innovations. As Timpanero emphasizes, "only coincidence in error can indicate the kinship between two manuscripts."⁶³ In textual transmission, there are many categories of error that are non-indicative, viz., those that scribes continually

---

⁵⁶ MurGen also has two orthographic variants: plene spelling of יעקוב (MT יַעֲקֹב) and a medial *kap* in final position (חנוכ).

⁵⁷ Lange, *Handbuch, 154.

⁵⁸ Tov, "Text of the Bible in Synagogues," 176; Tov, *Scribal Practices*, 125–29.

⁵⁹ Compare the well-prepared leather of 4QDeutᵍ with the coarse and poorly prepared leather of 4QGenᵇ. On the characteristics of deluxe Greek papyrus scrolls, see W.A. Johnson, *Bookrolls and Scribes in Oxyrhynchus* (Toronto: University of Toronto Press, 2004), 155–56.

⁶⁰ בחומשין מלמטה שלש אצבעות מלמעלה שתי אצבעות; cited in Talmon, *Masada VI*, 21–22.

⁶¹ Tov, "Biblical Texts from the Judean Desert," 145.

⁶² J.C. VanderKam and P. Flint, *The Meaning of the Dead Sea Scrolls* (San Francisco: Harper, 2002), 146; Lange, *Handbuch*, 15; Debel, *"Variant Literary Editions," 170; S. White Crawford, "Understanding the Textual History of the Hebrew Bible: A New Proposal," in *The Hebrew Bible in Light of the Dead Sea Scrolls* (eds. N. Dávid et al.; FRLANT 239; Göttingen: Vandenhoeck & Ruprecht, 2012), 60–69, 68.

⁶³ S. Timpanero, *The Genesis of Lachmann's Method* (Chicago: University of Chicago Press, 2005), 89; see also Hendel, "Assessing," 283–84.

TABLE 2   *Outer-Circle Proto-MT texts*

4QLev-Num^a	Early Hasmonean formal script (150–100 B.C.E.)	1173 words/parts
4QGen-Exod^a	Early Hasmonean formal script (125–100 B.C.E.)	929 words/parts
4QpaleoGen-Exod^l	Hasmonean paleo-Hebrew script (100–30 B.C.E.)	804 words/parts

commit in all periods (graphic error, dittography, haplography, addition of conjunctive *waw*, etc.). Hence, only distinctive changes are reliable indicators of textual affinity.

The distinctive changes that characterize the proto-MT family in the Pentateuch against the other discernible textual families are (as listed above) the edition of the chronologies in Genesis 5 and 11; the expanded tabernacle text in Exodus 35–40; sequence changes in Gen 47:5–6 and Num 10:34–36; and theological revisions in Deut 27:4, 32:8, and 32:43. Unfortunately, there are no plausibly proto-MT texts (including the inner circle) that overlap with these innovations. We are left with the less exact criterion of non-agreement with distinctive features and indicative errors of the other textual families, proto-SP and proto-LXX.

Using this criterion, we can identify the scrolls listed in Table 2 with substantial text as belonging to the outer circle of the proto-MT-Pentateuch:[64]

The evidence for affiliation is circumstantial: non-agreement with indicative errors in proto-SP and proto-LXX makes it likely – but not demonstrable – that they belong to the outer circle of the proto-MT-Pentateuch.

4QLev-Num^a (→ 2.2.1.7.10), as Jastram observes, has forty distinguishable variants, of which three are helpful for determining affiliation.[65] In Num 3:12 and Num 32:29–33 it lacks distinctive harmonizations shared by LXX and SP, and in Num 4:3 it lacks a distinctive harmonization with LXX. There are sufficient disagreements with MT to indicate that it does not belong to the inner circle of the proto-MT-Pentateuch. Among the disagreements, it twice correctly reads היא "she" where MT has הוא "he" (at Lev 14:44 and Num 5:6). This is an interesting feature, since the distinctive *qere perpetuum* of MT may derive from the period after this scroll (see above).

4QGen-Exod^a (→ 2.2.1.1.1) lacks the distinctive proto-SP harmonizing pluses at Exod 6:9 and 7:18 (based on the reconstructed space) and it lacks several distinctive harmonizing pluses in LXX.[66] There are, again, numerous small disagreements with MT, placing it in the outer circle of proto-MT.

4QpaleoGen-Exod^l (→ 2.2.1.1.2) lacks the distinctive pluses of proto-SP at Exod 8:19; 10:2; and 26:35, and lacks three distinctive LXX readings in the tabernacle text at Exod 27:11.[67] It also has numerous small disagreements with MT, hence it does not belong to the inner circle of proto-MT-Pentateuch. There are two notable features of this early proto-MT scroll. As Tov observes, it is a deluxe scroll, indicated by ample vertical margins (see above). It is the earliest extant proto-MT Pentateuchal scroll in this format. Second, it is also the only identifiable proto-MT Pentateuchal scroll written in paleo-Hebrew. At some point, scribes transmitting proto-MT scrolls eschewed this script, perhaps as a counterpoint to the exclusive use of this script in SP.[68]

The more fragmentary Qumran scrolls (viz., the vast majority) lack sufficient distinctive readings to identify them as outer circle proto-MT scrolls. For example, aside from 4QGen^b (addressed above), the fragmentary Genesis texts from Qumran Cave 4 that contain portions of Genesis 1 (viz., 4QGen^{d,g,h,k}) sometimes lack the distinctive

---

[64] Lange, *Handbuch, 16, lists only 4QGen-Exod^a and 4QpaleoGen-Exod^l as semi-Masoretic Pentateuchal scrolls. As above, word-counts are from Lange, *Handbuch.

[65] N. Jastram, "Numbers, Book of," in *EDSS 2:615–19 (616).

[66] J.R. Davila, "Text-Type and Terminology: Genesis and Exodus as Test Cases," *RevQ* 16 (1993): 2–37 (10–12, 30–33).

[67] P. Skehan, E. Ulrich, and J.E. Sanderson, "11. 4QpaleoGen-Exod^l," *DJD IX: 17–50 (23–25).

[68] See Cross, *"Fixation," 215.

features of the highly harmonized text of Genesis 1 in proto-LXX, but there is insufficient evidence to determine whether they belong to the proto-MT or proto-SP textual family. As a default position, Tov characterizes such texts as proto-MT.[69] But this decision masks our inability to make such determinations. Where we cannot ascertain the textual affinities of a scroll due to its fragmentary state, we should acknowledge the limits of our knowledge and describe it as "affiliation unknown."

2.2.2.5 Who Promulgated the Inner Circle of the Proto-MT-Pentateuch?

Most textual critics have attributed the rise of the inner circle of proto-MT texts to the influence of the early rabbinic or Pharisaic sages. For instance, Tov writes, "the text that was carefully transmitted through the centuries was previously embraced by rabbinic circles."[70] He therefore refers to the proto-MT family as "proto-rabbinic." However, as Lange has recently argued, "whether the Pharisees played an important role in the development of the proto-Masoretic standard text during the early first century C.E. – maybe due to the influence of Hillel – remains doubtful."[71] As Lange correctly emphasizes, both Josephus and rabbinic texts indicate that "the Jerusalem temple played a key role in the process of textual standardization."[72] He concludes "that the standard text was created by priests in the Jerusalem temple."[73] I would emphasize the agency of a particular scribal guild in promulgating the proto-MT-Pentateuch; but it is inferable that this guild was institutionally allied at some point with the Jerusalem temple and its priests.[74]

Lange argues that "the Jerusalem priests employed the principle of majority readings to create a standard text."[75] This is a variant of Kahle's model of the recensional origins of MT. However, Albrektson and Tov have cogently argued against the idea that the "standard text" was created by deliberate editorial activity.[76] The rabbinic narratives of Second Temple sages selecting among variant readings are probably etiologies for particular variants or unusual readings (including the eleven exceptions to the perpetual *Qere* of היא/הוא) rather than reminiscences of ancient textual activity. Talmon aptly describes these tales as reflecting rabbinic discussions that are, in a sense, "a very early case of Masoretic-type notation ... [and] do not relate to the creation of a *textus receptus*."[77] These tales serve to anchor rabbinic authority in the prestigious past of temple and Torah (see below).

In the Second Temple period, the high priest was generally the ruling authority, and the Jerusalem temple was the locus of priestly authority. This authority extended to sacred texts. Josephus, who proudly asserted his priestly lineage, held that, as Gray observes, "the physical care and transmission of sacred texts was a specifically priestly responsibility."[78] According to Josephus, Moses handed over the books of the Torah to the priests, who ensured their accurate transmission (*Ant.* 4.304; *Ag. Ap.* 1.28–29). Moreover, according to Philo, the priestly authority over sacred texts extended to the synagogue. He writes: "Some priest who is present or one of the elders reads the Holy Law to them and expounds them point by point" (*Hypoth.* 7.13). It is plausible, as Goodblatt comments, that "Philo may indicate here a preference for a priestly reader while allowing a lay elder to teach if no priest is available."[79] The Mishnah recalls a similar proce-

---

[69] Tov, "Biblical Texts from the Judean Desert," 144.

[70] Tov, "Text of the Bible in Synagogues," 175, 177.

[71] Lange, "Textual Standardization," 80.

[72] Lange, "Textual Standardization," 76. See also → 1.2.2.4.2.

[73] Lange, "Textual Standardization," 79.

[74] The situation is more complicated for biblical books outside the Pentateuch, whose transmission history is more complex; see White Crawford, "Textual History," 67; J. Trebolle-Barrera, "Qumran Evidence for a Biblical Standard Text and for Non-Standard and Parabiblical Texts," in *The Dead Sea Scrolls in their Historical Context* (ed. T.H. Lim: London: Clark, 2000), 89–106 (89–100); E. Ulrich, "The Canonical Process, Textual Criticism, and Latter Stages in the Composition of the Bible," in Ulrich, *DSS, 51–78 (56–61).

[75] Lange, "Textual Standardization," 79.

[76] See above, n. 21.

[77] S. Talmon, "The Three Scrolls of the Law that were Found in the Temple Court," in Talmon, *Text*, 329–46 (336, 346).

[78] R. Gray, *Prophetic Figures in Late Second Temple Jewish Palestine: The Evidence from Josephus* (New York: Oxford University Press, 1993), 54.

[79] D. Goodblatt, *Elements of Ancient Jewish Nationalism* (Cambridge: Cambridge University Press, 2006), 81.

dure: "A priest reads [the Torah] first, and after him a Levite, and after him an Israelite" (*m. Giṭ.* 5.8). The priests had textual authority in the Jerusalem temple and, so it seems, also in the synagogue, in theory if not always in practice. It may be relevant to note that in an early synagogue inscription, from the Theodotos synagogue of pre-70 C.E. Jerusalem, the benefactor identifies himself as a priest and the head of the synagogue, as were his father and grandfather before him.[80]

It is plausible that the priests also exercised authority over the copyists of sacred books, whom Josephus calls ἱερογραμματεῖς, "sacred scribes." If there were Torah scrolls at the Jerusalem temple, as Josephus and rabbinic texts indicate, then the copying of these scrolls was certainly under priestly authority.[81] According to the Talmud, the "correctors" (מגהים) of Torah scrolls in Jerusalem were paid by "Temple funds" (תרומת הלשכה) (*b. Ketub.* 106a; *y. Šeqal.* 4.48a). Tov observes that "most of the *soferim* whose genealogy is known were priests,"[82] and Daniel Schwartz plausibly argues that many or most of the scribes were Levites or Sadducees.[83] These details and inferences indicate a link between the priests' textual authority and the scribes' textual activity.

However, the Jerusalem priests did not have textual power at Qumran, which defined itself as a breakaway sacred enclave, in contrast to the defiled Jerusalem priesthood. This split arguably accounts for the different profile of the biblical texts at Qumran versus the texts at Masada and the Bar Kokhba caves. Since Qumran and Masada were both destroyed in the First Jewish Revolt, their comparison is salient. The occupants of Masada were originally the *Sicarii* ("dagger-men") from Jerusalem, who were later joined by other refugees. The *Sicarii* were not priests, although one of their founders, Zadok, may have been a scion of a priestly family. These refugees carried their biblical scrolls to Masada, predominantly scrolls from the inner circle of proto-MT. The Qumran library, in contrast, has few inner-circle proto-MT texts, and probably only one from the Pentateuch. The Qumran community had a wide range of texts outside of this circle, including proto-SP and proto-LXX Pentateuchal scrolls. This textual contrast corresponds to a sociological contrast in the locus of textual authority. The Qumran enclave was outside of the textual authority of the Jerusalem priests, whereas the Masada group was, at least originally, within it.

Note that the Pharisees or proto-rabbis have no role in this historical model. Their religious authority was located elsewhere, perhaps as popular interpreters of law in the public domain, including matters of purity, marriage laws, calendar, and tithes.[84] But there is no warrant for assuming their authority in the production, dissemination, or public reading of Torah scrolls in the period from the Maccabees to the Mishnah. According to rabbinic texts, some rabbinic sages were scribes (e.g., R. Meir), but this does not argue for proto-rabbinic authority over scribes. The earliest rabbinic text about the Torah scrolls in the temple court says that the "sages" (חכמים) made the textual decisions (*Sifre* 2.356), but this is what Albrektson calls "rabbinic embroidery" and cannot be relied on as historical evidence.[85] Torah scrolls in the temple court would have been textual icons of priestly authority. It is to be expected that the classical rabbinic texts would assert a memory of the sages' ancient tex-

---

[80] L.I. Levine, *The Ancient Synagogue: The First Thousand Years* (New Haven: Yale University Press, 2005), 57–59.

[81] See A. van der Kooij, "Preservation and Promulgation: The Dead Sea Scrolls and the Textual History of the Hebrew Bible," in *Hebrew Bible in Light of the Dead Sea Scrolls* (eds. N. David et al.; FRLANT 239; Göttingen: Vandenhoeck & Ruprecht, 2012), 29–40.

[82] Tov, *Scribal Practices*, 12.

[83] D.R. Schwartz, "'Scribes and Pharisees, Hypocrites': Who are the 'Scribes' in the New Testament?" in D.R. Schwartz, *Studies in the Jewish Background of Christianity* (WUNT 60; Tübingen: Mohr Siebeck, 1992), 89–101; cf. M. Goodman, "Texts, Scribes and Power in Roman Judaea," in M. Goodman, *Judaism in the Roman World: Collected Essays* (AGJU 66; Leiden: Brill, 2007), 79–90.

[84] S.J.D. Cohen, "The Place of the Rabbi in the Jewish Society of the Second Century," in S.J.D. Cohen, *The Significance of Yavneh and Other Essays in Jewish Hellenism* (TSAJ 136; Tübingen: Mohr Siebeck, 2010), 282–96. Note that these include the areas of Jesus' arguments with the Pharisees in the New Testament.

[85] Albrektson, "Reflections," 54; and see above, n. 73.

tual authority, a historiographic *Tendenz* that Jacob Neusner and Shaye Cohen aptly call the "rabbinization of Jewish history."[86]

Who were the scribes who transmitted and promulgated the inner circle of the proto-MT-Pentateuch? We do not know. All we can say is that this was a relatively conservative group, whose scribal philosophy at some point narrowed to minimal intervention in the text. As noted above, the orthography of MT-Pentateuch preserves spelling practices of the third century B.C.E.; this may be the era when other kinds of textual change were curtailed in this scribal lineage. Another possibility is that a later scribal group used third-century Pentateuchal scrolls as model scrolls. Under either scenario, the third century B.C.E. may have been the *terminus ad quem* for substantive changes in the inner circle of the proto-MT-Pentateuch. (The only likely exception is the change of Gerizim to Ebal in MT-Deut 27:4, which, as noted above, is likely a sectarian revision from the Hasmonean era.[87]) The correct readings in MT-Pentateuch, of course, stem from an earlier period, when the Pentateuch was compiled and made public, which returns us to the portrait of Ezra reading the Torah in Jerusalem in the fifth century B.C.E.

2.2.2.6 Value for Literary (Source) Criticism

Some text-critical features of MT-Pentateuch are valuable for discerning the earlier compositional history of the Pentateuch, particularly where proto-MT scribes found contradictions in the narrative. For example, two of the typological features noted above – the revision of chronologies in Genesis 5 and 11, and the sequence revision at Gen 47:5–11 – are exegetical responses to source-critical problems. The chronological revision in Genesis 5 was motivated by a contradiction between the date of the flood in P and the lifespans of three of Noah's ancestors (Lamech, Methuselah, and Jared) in the סֵפֶר תּוֹלְדֹת אָדָם "Book of the Generations of Adam"

(Gen 5:1), which was a source document of P.[88] The chronological revisions in proto-MT, proto-SP, and proto-LXX are independent attempts to solve what is, in origin, a source-critical problem within P: the overlap between the lifespans of three patriarchs and the onset of the flood.

The revision at Gen 47:5–6 in proto-MT is an attempt to overcome a problem of narrative continuity caused by the combination of J and P. The proto-LXX reading is arguably the superior text.[89] The following quote begins in verse 4, with Joseph's brothers speaking. Pharaoh's two speeches are marked by regular and bold italics.

LXX

(J) And the brothers said to Pharaoh ... "Now let your servants dwell in the land of Goshen." And Pharaoh said to Joseph, *"Let them dwell in the land of Goshen, and if you know that there are capable men among them, appoint them as overseers of my livestock."* (P) And Jacob and his sons came into Egypt to Joseph, and Pharaoh, king of Egypt, heard. And Pharaoh spoke to Joseph, saying, **"Your father and your brothers have come to you. See, the land of Egypt is before you; settle your father and your brothers in the best land."**[90]

MT

And the brothers said to Pharaoh ... "Now let your servants dwell in the land of Goshen." And Pharaoh said to Joseph, saying, **"Your father and your brothers have come to you. The land of Egypt is before you; in the best land settle your father and your brothers.** *Let them dwell in the land of Goshen, and if you know that there are capable men among them, appoint them as rulers of my livestock."*

The revision in MT eliminates the problem of discontinuity by two revisions: a) erasing the second coming of Jacob and his sons, which comes from the P source (ויבאו יעקב ובניו מצרימה אל יעקב וישמע פרעה "And Jacob and his sons came into Egypt to Jacob, and Pharaoh, king of Egypt, heard"); and b)

---

[86] S.J.D. Cohen, "Parallel Historical Tradition in Josephus and Rabbinic Literature," in Cohen, *Significance of Yavneh*, 154–61 (158–59).

[87] See above, n. 23.

[88] See above, n. 21.

[89] See, e.g., J. Skinner, *A Critical and Exegetical Commentary on Genesis* (2nd ed.; ICC; Edinburgh: Clark, 1930), 497–98.

[90] Translation adapted from R.J.V. Hiebert, "Genesis," in *NETS, 1–42 (39).

combining into one Pharaonic speech what were originally two speeches, one from J and the other from P. A corroborating clue for the secondary recombination of sources in MT is the Pentateuchal doublet, אֶרֶץ גֹּשֶׁן "the land of Goshen" (J) and אֶרֶץ רַעְמְסֵס "the land of Rameses" (P; see Gen 47:11), which is consistent in the LXX reading but not in MT. The restructured text in MT is an exegetical response to a problematic source-critical "seam" in the Pentateuch.

As these examples show, the textual history of MT-Pentateuch is in some measure a consequence and continuation of the Pentateuch's literary history. These late literary interventions – after the separation of the proto-LXX and proto-MT textual families – show that the proto-MT scribes were, in Talmon's sense, "minor partner[s] in the variegated aspects of the literary process."[91]

Albrektson, B., "Reflections on the Emergence of a Standard Text of the Hebrew Bible," in Albrektson, *Text, 47–62.
Barthélemy, D., "The Different Forms of the Hebrew Text," in Barthélemy, *Studies, 237–409.
Hendel, R., "Assessing the Text-Critical Theories of the Hebrew Bible after Qumran," in *The Oxford Handbook of the Dead Sea Scrolls* (eds. T.H. Lim and J.J. Collins; Oxford: Oxford University Press, 2010), 281–302.
Khan, G., *A Short Introduction to the Masoretic Hebrew Bible and its Reading Tradition* (Piscataway: Gorgias, 2012).
Lange, A., "'They Confirmed the Reading' (y. Ta'an. 4.68a): The Textual Standardization of Jewish Scriptures in the Second Temple Period," in Lange et al., *From Qumran to Aleppo, 29–80.
Tov, E., "The History and Significance of a Standard Text of the Hebrew Bible," in *Hebrew Bible/Old Testament: The History of Its Interpretation*, Vol. 1: *From the Beginnings to the Middle Ages (Until 1300)*: Part 1: *Antiquity* (ed. M. Sæbø; Göttingen: Vandenhoeck & Ruprecht, 1996), 49–66.
Tov, E., "The Text of the Hebrew/Aramaic and Greek Bibles Used in the Ancient Synagogues," in Tov, *HB, GB, and Qumran, 171–88.
Ulrich, E., "The Old Testament Text and Its Transmission," in *The New Cambridge History of the Bible: From the Beginnings to 600* (eds. J.C. Paget and J. Schaper; Cambridge: Cambridge University Press, 2013), 83–104.
White Crawford, S., "Scribal Traditions in the Pentateuch and the History of the Early Second Temple Period," in *Congress Volume Helsinki 2010* (ed. M. Nissinen; VTSup 148; Leiden: Brill, 2012), 167–84.

Ronald Hendel

2.2.3 Other Texts

This article approaches those ancient Pentateuchal manuscripts that do not align with MT from a genealogical perspective. For a description of the individual Pentateuch scrolls, see Lange, *Handbuch, and entry → 2.2.1.

2.2.3.1 Problems of Classification

There are many possible ways to classify ancient Hebrew manuscripts of the Pentateuch. For instance, one could use the following criteria, which would generate a series of intersecting classifications:

> paleo-Hebrew script vs. square script; iron-based vs. carbon-based ink; papyrus vs. parchment scroll; Qumran orthography vs. conventional orthography; excerpted or abbreviated book; contains more than one book; has unique readings; has affinities with the Samaritan Pentateuch or Septuagint; has top and bottom margin of more than three centimeters; includes interlinear corrections; copied by the same scribe as 4QTestimonia; is unpublished

Each of these criteria has been used to good purpose in scholarly studies.[1]

For any particular classificatory task, one must identify the relevant criteria for classification and eliminate the irrelevant ones; otherwise the results

---

[91] Talmon, *"New Outlook," 84.

[1] For many of these criteria, see Tov, *Scribal Practices*; A. Yardeni, *The Book of Hebrew Script: History, Palaeography, Script Styles, Calligraphy & Design* (London: British Library, 2002); E. Tigchelaar, "In Search of the Scribe of 1QS," in *Emanuel: Studies in the Hebrew Bible, Septuagint, and the Dead Sea Scrolls in Honor of Emanuel Tov* (eds. S.M. Paul et al.; VTSup 94; Leiden: Brill, 2003), 439–52.

are likely to be misleading or meaningless. To ascertain the textual history of the Pentateuch – in contrast to, for example, the history of its scribal production, sometimes called "bibliography" – one must first abstract the "text" from its material manifestations. This requires a series of reductions. First, one must bracket the physical features of a manuscript and focus on its purely semiotic features. Second, one must distinguish between the substantive (or base) semiotic features – viz. the words (lexemes) – and the "accidental" (or presentational) features, such as spelling or script, which vary according to local scribal practice. The primary evidence for textual history consists of the substantive features – the sequence of words – irrespective of their physical manifestations. These features are abstract (viz. non-material), but in a way that linguistically competent readers tacitly recognize.

A further reduction is required for textual history. As textual critics have long established, one must distinguish between substantive features that descend from a common ancestor (monogenetic features) and those that are likely to be independently produced (polygenetic features).[2] Only monogenetic features are useful for classifying manuscripts according to their textual history. A precise designation for such monogenetic features is *shared derived innovations*. This term, borrowed from biology and linguistics, requires some unpacking to clarify its implications. "Shared" means that the relevant traits exist among two or more manuscripts. Traits that exist in only one manuscript are irrelevant for genealogical classification. For instance, nearly all of our Pentateuchal manuscripts contain unique innovations. But these features, since they are unique, have no implications for their genealogical relationships. "Derived" means that the trait descends from a common ancestor. Like unique innovations, traits that are likely to be polygenetic are unreliable or irrelevant for establishing genealogical relationships. Independently generated traits have no implications for genealogy. (However, shared scribal hermeneutics may be relevant for distinguishing among scribal/textual groups; see below.) "Innovation" refers to any type of substantive textual change, including both accidental error and deliberate revision. Since innovations are not limited to errors, the usual text-critical terms for shared derived innovation – *Leitfehler, errores significativi*, indicative error – are somewhat misleading. The term "innovation" is more felicitous than "error" for this designation, as textual critics have noted.[3]

The procedure for ascertaining historical relationships among texts by means of shared derived innovations (often called the Lachmann, genealogical, or common-error method) is aptly characterized by Reeve:

> When copies share an innovation absent from the rest, they are related (more closely, that is, than by being copies of the same work); if none of those that share the innovation can plausibly be regarded as the one where it originated, it must have originated in a lost ancestor common to them all. With luck, the extant copies and their postulated ancestors can be arranged in a family tree.[4]

A degree of luck is necessary for this task because we often lack sufficient evidence to discern the historical patterns of shared derived innovations. For ancient texts, the extant manuscripts are only a small portion of the once-existing evidence; hence the patterns we can discern are only partial glimpses of the full textual history. The genealogy (stemma) that we can discern is, as Trovato observes, "the genealogy of the surviving tradition."[5] It is a reduced and piecemeal version of the whole family tree.

A further complicating factor is that some shared innovations may be the result of copying or correcting parts of a book from manuscripts that

---

[2] See Trovato, *Everything*; and, in our discipline, B. Chiesa, "Textual History and Textual Criticism of the Hebrew Old Testament," in *Madrid Qumran Congress, 256–72.

[3] M.D. Reeve, "Shared Innovations, Dichotomies, and Evolution," in M.D. Reeve, *Manuscripts and Methods: Essays on Editing and Transmission* (Rome: Edizioni di storia e letteratura, 2011), 55–58; Trovato, *Everything*, 54.

[4] M.D. Reeve, "Foreword," in Trovato, *Everything*, 9–12 (9–10).

[5] Trovato, *Everything*, 232.

belong to different branches of the stemma. This is called horizontal transmission, contamination, or conflation, in contrast to the conventional process of vertical transmission, where one manuscript is wholly copied from another.[6] (In linguistics the parallel to horizontal transmission is innovation due to language contact.) The possibility of horizontal transmission complicates the task of textual history, since such innovations indicate a real contact rather than common descent. In the extant Pentateuchal manuscripts, there are no clear indications of horizontal transmission, but this possibility cannot be eliminated.

The character of polygenetic innovations – traits that are similar but independently generated – requires further clarification. In textual criticism, many kinds of scribal change are characteristically polygenetic, and therefore are unreliable – or useless – for ascertaining genealogical affinity. Goshen-Gottstein aptly ascribed polygenetic innovations to "the ever active and repeated force of the 'law of scribes' that creates the illusion of a genetic connection."[7] The "law of scribes" causes such textual changes as haplography, dittography, word misdivision, graphic confusion, and the addition or subtraction of simple particles (e.g., conjunctive *waw*). The effects of this "law" are richly documented in the medieval and early modern manuscripts of the Hebrew Bible, all of which belong to the same (Masoretic) textual family.[8] To ascertain genealogical relationships, one must exclude the background noise of the "law of scribes." Most of the small variants in the ancient and medieval Pentateuchal scrolls belong to this category and are therefore not useful for classification.

The genealogical method of ascertaining textual genealogy assumes that all the manuscripts of a given book belong to a single multi-branched community of descent. Each manuscript, for example of Genesis, belongs to the genealogy of that book, and not to independent genealogies that generated more-or-less identical books of Genesis. This assumption seems self-evident, but it has been contested by some scholars. Talmon has influentially argued for the existence of "divergent pristine textual traditions" that descend from independent oral traditions.[9] In this view, a particular manuscript of Genesis may be textually unrelated to other manuscripts of Genesis. Analogies for such textual phenomena, based on divergent oral traditions, arguably exist for some medieval compositions, for example, the *Song of Roland*. However, as Tov and others have pointed out, there is no evidence for such phenomena in biblical books. The manuscripts are simply too similar to warrant this hypothesis.[10] Most or all variants in the extant manuscripts are accountable by the normal mechanisms of scribal change. They do not correspond to the types and degree of variation characteristic of oral transmission or manuscripts derived from oral formulaic composition.[11] As I have argued elsewhere, the idea of "divergent pristine textual traditions" for the books of the Hebrew Bible is a scholarly chimera.[12]

Each textual family within the genealogy is distinguished by a shared cluster of derived innovations. These are "conjunctive" innovations. Yet it is important to note that there are no objective boundaries between families or sub-units, just as there are no objective boundaries between languages and dialects, or between species and subspecies. As with linguistic and biological distinctions, the analytical boundaries are based on the important innovations or clusters of innovations within the broader field of derived traits. As Huehnergard states, "the most useful criteria for establishing genetic relatedness are shared features that are

---

[6] Trovato, *Everything*, 128–38.

[7] Goshen-Gottstein, *"Biblical Manuscripts,"* 275.

[8] Although one cannot exclude the possibility of the occasional transmission of some extra- or non-MT readings; see Goshen-Gottstein, *"Biblical Manuscripts,"* 85.

[9] Talmon, *"Ancient Versions,"* 406–07, 413–18.

[10] Tov, *TCHB*, 163–65.

[11] For an analogous argument in classical studies on the textual history of the Iliad, see M. Finkelberg, "The *Cypria*, the *Iliad*, and the Problem of Multiformity in Oral and Written Traditions," *CP* 95 (2000): 1–11.

[12] R. Hendel, "The Oxford Hebrew Bible: Its Aims and a Response to Criticisms," *Hebrew Bible and Ancient Israel* 2 (2013): 63–99 (80–83); see further M.V. Fox, *Proverbs: An Eclectic Edition with Introduction and Textual Commentary* (HBCE 1; Atlanta: SBL Press, 2015), 80–81.

2.2.3.2 Editions, Harmonizations, and Textual Families

In recent years, scholars have focused on two clusters of innovations that are prominent in ancient Pentateuch manuscripts: editions and harmonizations. Both of these features allow for the elucidation of textual families and textual history. Editions and harmonizations are complementary and cross-cutting features in the Pentateuch, illuminating multiple dimensions of its textual genealogy.

Ulrich has argued that the distinctions of literary edition should be the first criterion in ascertaining textual affinity. He maintains that "the main lines in the picture of the history of the biblical text were formed by the deliberate activity of a series of creative scribes who produced the new or multiple literary editions of the books of the Bible."[14] It seems reasonable to assert that the creation of new editions – meaning systematic revisions on a large scale – constitutes the most distinctive clusters of innovations, and therefore the most salient criteria for classifying biblical texts. Many Pentateuchal manuscripts are also characterized by varying degrees of harmonization, by which we mean a transfer of textual details or blocks of text between two parallel texts.[15] Clusters of harmonizations, even if they are not sufficiently systematic to constitute a new edition, are useful criteria for classification.

Multiple editions and harmonizations are intersecting phenomena. Two out of the three discernible new editions of Pentateuchal books were created by systematic large-scale harmonizations. But small harmonizations exist in each edition of the Pentateuchal books. A general tendency toward harmonization characterizes some scribal traditions and may be defined as a particular hermeneutical approach to textual transmission. To differing degrees, this tendency is evident in the proto-SP family (→ 1.2.3) and the proto-Old Greek family (→ 1.3.1.1).

A distinctive cluster of large-scale harmonizations characterizes a closely related family of manuscripts designated the proto- or pre-SP family (→ 1.2.3).[16] There are roughly forty large-scale harmonizations, in which significant blocks of textual details have been transferred between parallel texts (viz. from one pericope to another or within a single pericope).[17] Notable clusters of large harmonizations were made in the correspondence between the divine commands and executions in the plague stories (Exodus 7–11), and the correspondence between events recalled by Moses in Deuteronomy 1–3 and the description of those events in Exodus and Numbers.

4QpaleoExod^m (→ 2.2.1.3.1) and 4QNum^b (→ 2.2.1.3.2) share these clusters of innovations and clearly belong to the proto-SP family. Two perspicuous examples of these shared expansions are at Exod 7:18b and Num 27:23b. The Exodus plus is a harmonization of command and execution in the first plague (blood), where the implied execution is here provided explicitly. The Numbers plus is a harmonization of Moses' recollection of his charge to Joshua in Deut 3:21–22 with the commissioning of Joshua in Numbers 27. In both expansions, the source-text provides the exact wording of the harmonizing plus in the target text.

---

[13] J. Huehnergard, "What is Aramaic?" *Aram* 7 (1995): 261–82 (263).

[14] E. Ulrich, "Multiple Literary Editions: Reflections Toward a Theory of the History of the Biblical Text," in Ulrich, *DSS, 99–120 (107).

[15] See E. Tov, "The Nature and Background of Harmonizations in Biblical Manuscripts," *JSOT* 31 (1985): 3–29; E. Eshel, "4QDeut^n – A Text That Has Undergone Harmonistic Editing," *HUCA* 62 (1991): 117–54 (120–23); Crawford, "Scribal Traditions," 167–84.

[16] Eshel ("4QDeut^n," 121) and Eshel and Eshel ("Dating," 228–29) call these "the harmonistic text group," or "harmonistic texts." In my view, this is an infelicitous designation since there are also harmonistic tendencies in the proto-OG family (see below). As the Eshels note, large-scale harmonizations continued to be created in manuscripts of this family after the promulgation of SP, hence the designation "pre-SP group" is also infelicitous.

[17] M. Kartveit, *The Origin of the Samaritans* (VTSup 128; Leiden: Brill, 2009), 276–88, 310–12; E. Tov, "Rewritten Bible Compositions and Biblical Manuscripts, with Special Atten-

4QpaleoExod^m reads at Exod 7:18b:[18]

וי[א]מר אליו יה[וה ...] שלח את עמי ויעבד[ני ...] כה אמר
[...] מ[כ]ה במטה אשר [...] ו[הד]גה אשר בת[וך היאר ...]
מ[צ]רים לש[תות]

And he said to him, "Yah[weh ...] 'Let my people go that they may serve [me ...] 'Thus says [...] am going to strike with the rod that is [...] and the fish that are in the mid[st of the Nile ...] E[g]yptians to dr[ink ...]."

Aside from some small variants, this is the same plus as in SP (→ 2.2.4.2).[19] This plus consists of a verbatim repetition of the words of Yahweh's command to Moses in Exod 7:16–18, with the simple change in the initial verb from command to execution: ואמרת "And say" is changed to ויאמר "And he said." This hermeneutical technique of near-verbatim repetition to fill a perceived gap – here in the relationship of the divine command and its execution – is characteristic of the major pluses in the proto-SP family. The extant text of 4QpaleoExod^m has twelve major expansions in common with SP, and the reconstructed text has a further five. Notably, the reconstructed text of 4QpaleoExod^m lacks only the sectarian expansion at SP-Exod 20:17b, which commands the Israelites to build an altar at Mt. Gerizim. The Gerizim expansion (the Samaritan Tenth Commandment) was an innovation in SP, but follows the general style of proto-SP harmonizing expansions.[20]

4QNum^b (→ 2.2.1.3.2) reads at Num 27:23b:[21]

[ויאמר מוש]ה אליו עיניכה הרואות את אשר עשה יהוה לשני
המ[לכים]

And Mo[ses said] to him, "Your own eyes have seen what Yahweh did to the two ki[ngs]."

This plus is the same as in SP (→ 2.2.4.4), with one variant: מושה "Moses" is lacking in SP. The plus is a near-verbatim harmonization with Deut 3:21–22, where Moses recalls this speech to Joshua. As in the expansions in the plague narrative, this plus fills a perceived gap in the text, making the event and its recollection conform exactly. The extant text of 4QNum^b has five major expansions in common with SP, and the reconstructed text has a further four. 4QNum^b has a further large harmonizing expansion (at Num 36:2–5) that is not shared with SP. This plus indicates that the practice of inserting large harmonizations continued in the proto-SP textual tradition after the genealogical separation of SP.

Similarly, 4QDeut^n (→ 2.2.1.7.20; → 1.2.2.3), an excerpted text that is based on a proto-SP text (as indicated by shared small harmonizations), has an additional large harmonization at Deut 5:15b, imported from Exod 20:11:[22]

לקדשו כי ששת ימים עשה יהוה את השמים ואת הארץ את
הים ואת כול אשר בם וינוח ביום השביעי על כן ברך יהוה את יום
השבת לקדשו

to sanctify it, for in six days Yahweh made the heavens and the earth, the sea and all that is in it, and He rested on the seventh day. Therefore Yahweh blessed the seventh day to sanctify it.

This plus, which is lacking in SP (→ 2.2.4.5), shows that the practice of adding large harmonizations continued after SP's final layer of sectarian revisions. This practice probably persisted into the first century C.E. Similar tendencies are found in some *tefillin* and *mezuzah* (→ 2.2.5.1) texts and in a number of "Rewritten Bible" texts (→ 21.1.1; → 21.2.2).[23]

4QExod-Lev^f (→ 2.2.1.7.9) also arguably belongs to the proto-SP family. It shares a medium length (one-verse long) but significant harmonization with SP at Exod 39:21:[24]

---

tion Paid to the Samaritan Pentateuch," in Tov, *HB, GB, and Qumran*, 57–70 (60–68).

[18] P. Skehan, E. Ulrich, and J.E. Sanderson, "22. 4QpaleoExodus^m," *DJD* IX: 52–130 (67).

[19] The variants are: singular ויאמר "and he said" versus SP plural; and the fuller בתוך היאר "in the midst of the Nile" versus SP ביאר "in the Nile."

[20] Kartveit, *Origin*, 290–94; J.E. Sanderson, *An Exodus Scroll from Qumran: 4QpaleoExod^m and the Samaritan Tradition* (Atlanta: Scholars Press, 1986), 235–37.

[21] N. Jastram, "27. 4QNum^b," *DJD* XII: 205–67 (262–64).

[22] S. White Crawford, "41. 4QDeut^n," *DJD* XIV: 117–28 (125–26); Eshel, "4QDeut^n," 142–47.

[23] Eshel, "4QDeut^n," 122–23; S. White Crawford, *Rewriting Scripture in Second Temple Times* (Grand Rapids: Eerdmans, 2008), 30–56.

[24] On the secondary nature of this expansion, I agree with the analyses of W.H.C. Propp, *Exodus 19–40* (AB 2A; New York:

2.2.3 OTHER TEXTS

TABLE 1 *Variant Editions and Textual Families*

	Base Edition	*New Edition(s)*
Genesis 5; 11	[not extant]	proto-MT, proto-SP, proto-OG
Exodus 35–39	proto-OG	proto-MT ≈ proto-SP
± Large harmonizations	proto-MT ≈ proto-OG	proto-SP

ויעש את האורים ו[את התמים ...] משה

And he made the Urim and [the Thummim ...] Moses.

This plus, shared with SP (with a variation in the verb, plural in SP; → 2.2.4.2), is a harmonization with a matching plus at Exod 28:30 (SP): ועשית את האורם ואת התמים "And you shall make the Urim and the Thummim." In this case, both the command and its execution are lacking in the earlier text (Exod 28:30, MT = LXX) where the Urim and Thummim are mentioned ("You shall place in the breastplate of judgment the Urim and the Thummim.") The absence of a command to make the Urim and the Thummim motivated a proto-SP harmonizing scribe to fill the gap by inserting a command and its execution. This two-fold plus is a perspicuous instance of the hermeneutics of the proto-SP scribal tradition.

Interestingly, since the harmonization technique of the proto-SP scribes consists of near-verbatim transfer of text, some of these harmonizations result in a literarily discordant text, viz. an illogical sequence. Tov describes the harmonization at SP-Num 13:33b, which duplicates the content of the following chapter by importing Deut 1:27–33, as "a rather 'impossible' text."[25] As Segal observes, "there is no attempt ... to alter one of the two passages so that they agree. Rather, the copying of the passage was performed in a mechanical fashion, leaving the contradictory information in each of the (now juxtaposed) passages."[26] In many such cases, the harmonized text is disharmonious.

The cluster of large-scale harmonizations in the proto-SP family, since it is a systematic revision, constitutes a new edition of the Pentateuch. A comparable cluster of harmonizations occurs in the expanded edition of the tabernacle text in Exodus 35–39, where the execution is harmonized with the divine commands in Exodus 25–30.[27] In this case, the first (or base) edition is preserved in LXX (→ 2.4.1.2), and the expanded edition in MT (→ 2.2.2) and SP (→ 2.2.4.2). None of the Qumran Exodus scrolls contain sufficient material in Exodus 35–39 to place them relative to this edition.

In these cases, extensive large harmonizations produced new editions. A third case of new editions in the Pentateuch is in the genealogies of Genesis 5 and 11, where the desire to solve implicit problems in the genealogy (including the apparent survival of three antediluvian patriarchs after the flood) resulted in three different systematic revisions, preserved in MT (→ 2.2.2), SP (→ 2.2.4.1), and LXX (→ 2.4.1.1), respectively.[28] Jubilees (→ 21.1.1) has affinities with SP genealogy in Genesis 5, indicating that this innovation was wider than SP alone.

Accordingly, we can classify the following manuscripts of Pentateuchal books according to the criteria of editions and textual families; see Table 1.

Note that there is no fixed correlation between the editions and the extant textual families: proto-MT (→ 2.2.2), proto-SP (→ 1.2.3), and proto-

---

Doubleday, 2006), 346–47; and Ulrich, "Evolutionary Growth," 42–43; *pace* F.M. Cross, "17. 4QExod-Lev^f," *DJD* XII: 133–44 (139), who argues for the originality of the proto-SP reading.

[25] Tov, "Rewritten," 66.

[26] M. Segal, "The Text of the Hebrew Bible in Light of the Dead Sea Scrolls," *Materia Giudaica* 12 (2007): 5–20 (12–13).

[27] A. Aejmelaeus, "Septuagintal Translation Techniques: A Solution to the Problem of the Tabernacle Account?" in Aejmelaeus, *Trail*, 107–21 (116–20).

[28] Hendel, *Genesis 1–11*, 61–80.

OG (→ 1.3.1.1). In Genesis, all three textual families have secondary editions; in Exodus, proto-OG differs from proto-MT/proto-SP; and in the large harmonization edition, proto-SP differs from proto-MT/proto-OG. Only proto-SP has the later edition in all three cases. This variability supports Ulrich's proposal that editions should have priority in classification.

The distinctive profile of the proto-Old Greek family brings in the issue of harmonization at another level. While LXX (and related manuscripts) lacks the large-scale harmonizations of the proto-SP family and preserves the earlier (unharmonized) edition of the tabernacle text (→ 2.4.1.2), it has an extensive number of small-scale harmonizations from Genesis through Deuteronomy. As Tov observes:

> LXX reflects more contextual harmonizations than SP, often twice as many. In Numbers, these features are shared with 4QNum[b] against all other witnesses, and in Deuteronomy they are often shared with either MT or SP, but are more frequently exclusive to LXX.[29]

The many small harmonizations shared with the proto-SP family (particularly with SP and 4QNum[b]) indicate that the proto-Old Greek and proto-SP branches descend from a common ancestor (hyparchetype), after which the proto-OG texts accumulated further small harmonizations, and the proto-SP texts acquired an extensive cluster of large-scale harmonizations. According to Kim's study of the relationship between LXX and SP, there are 1,441 harmonizations in LXX-Pent, of which 348 are shared with SP.[30] The small harmonizations in LXX constitute a consistent pattern across all the Pentateuchal books.[31]

The Qumran scrolls that are likely members or close affines of the proto-OG family are 4QExod[b] and 4QDeut[q] (an excerpted text). Other Qumran Pentateuchal texts that share some small harmonizing pluses with LXX are 4QDeut[b] and 4QDeut[h], but it is difficult to be confident about their affinity based on relatively small details.

4QExod[b] (→ 2.2.1.7.7) shares a significant harmonizing and exegetical plus with LXX at Exod 1:5.[32] It reads חמש ושבעים "seventy-five" for the descendants of Jacob in Egypt, in contrast to שבעים "seventy" in MT and SP. This is a recalculated number by a proto-Old Greek scribe, who inserted Joseph's five grandsons and great-grandsons from LXX-Num 26:33–39 into LXX-Gen 46:20: Machir, Gilead, Shuthelah, Tahan, and Eran/Edan.[33] This harmonizing expansion may be motivated by the inclusion of Judah's grandsons and great-grandsons in Gen 46:12. By analogy, this genealogical depth was extended to Joseph's line.[34] The new total, "seventy-five," was inserted in LXX at Gen 46:27, Exod 1:5, and Deut 10:22. 4QExod[b] at Exod 1:5 provides valuable testimony that this innovation existed in Hebrew manuscripts belonging to (or with close affinity to) the proto-Old Greek family.

4QDeut[q] (an excerpted text; → 2.2.1.6.3) is also a close affine to the proto-Old Greek family. At Deut 32:43 it reads:[35]

---

[29] E. Tov, "The Qumran Hebrew Texts and the Septuagint: An Overview," in Kreuzer–Meiser–Sigismund, *Septuaginta 2012*, 3–17 (12–13 note 47). See further Tov, "Textual Harmonizations in the Ancient Texts of Deuteronomy," in Tov, *HB, GB, and Qumran*, 271–82; Tov, "Textual Harmonization in the Stories of the Patriarchs," in Tov, *Collected Writings 3*, 166–88.

[30] K.R. Kim, "Studies in the Relationship between the Samaritan Pentateuch and the Septuagint" (PhD diss., Hebrew University of Jerusalem, 1994), according to Tov, "Septuagint," 13 note 47.

[31] A striking example is the harmonization of command and execution in Genesis 1, which parallels the proto-SP tendency but with smaller harmonizing units; see Hendel, *Genesis 1–11*, 20–35.

[32] F.M. Cross, "13. 4QExod[b]," *DJD* XII: 79–95 (84–85).

[33] The variants of the latter name have a reš/dalet confusion: עֵרָן "Eran" (MT/SP in Num 26:36) vs. Εδεν/Εδεμ "Eden" (LXX). MT/SP has an additional grandson, בֶּכֶר "Becher" (Num 26:35) who is lacking in LXX.

[34] LXX-Gen 46:27 counts Joseph's descendants as nine, whereas there are only seven in LXX-Gen 46:20. The enhanced number, added to the sixty-six descendants of Jacob in Gen 46:26, yields seventy-five. This seems to be an alternative strategy for reaching this total, but it creates dissonance in the genealogy. As elsewhere, a scribal harmonization generates disharmony.

[35] S. White Crawford, "44. 4QDeut[q]," *DJD* XIV: 137–42 (141–

2.2.3 OTHER TEXTS

הרנינו שמים עמו והשתחוו לו כל אלהים כי דם בניו יקום ונקם
ישיב לצריו ולמשנאיו ישלם וכפר אדמתו עמו

Rejoice, O heavens, with Him, // and let all the gods bow to Him;
For He will avenge the blood of His sons, // and turn back vengeance on His foes;
And He will repay His enemies, // and cleanse His people's land.

LXX has the same reading, with the following variant: "sons of God" instead of "gods," the insertion of Yahweh in the last clause, and an additional couplet after the first couplet: "Gladden, O nations, His people and let all the sons of God prevail for him." This additional LXX couplet may be a conflate text or a double translation. In any case, LXX is an expanded version of the reading in 4QDeut^q, which contrasts with the shorter version of only two couplets in MT/SP. In this verse, none of the witnesses arguably preserves the ancestral reading, which was arguably approximately the following:

Rejoice, O heavens, with Him, // and let the sons of God exult;
For He will avenge the blood of His servants, // and cleanse His people's land.[36]

The proto-Old Greek reading preserved in 4QDeut^q has a harmonizing expansion, with two clauses imported from Deut 32:41 and changed from first person to third person. This expansion creates an effect comparable to command/execution, but in this case it is divine intention/poetic proclamation:

אשיב נקם לצרי ולמשנאי אשלם ←
ונקם ישיב לצריו ולמשנאיו ישלם

I will turn back vengeance on My foes, // and repay My enemies (v. 41) →
He will turn back vengeance on His foes, // and repay His enemies (v. 43)

The proto-Old Greek reading includes thus a secondary harmonizing expansion, which counts as a shared derived innovation. 4QDeut^q is therefore testimony to a relatively early stage of the proto-OG family.

4QDeut^b (→ 2.2.1.7.14) shares an expansion with LXX at Deut 31:28 in a list of Israelite leaders, adding [זקניכם] ושפטיכם, "[and your elders] and your judges."[37] This duplicates the expansion in a similar list at LXX-Deut 29:9. Although this is a small plus, it has the same character as harmonizing expansions elsewhere in proto-OG. This fragment arguably provides another witness to the proto-OG family.

There are several other Qumran fragments that share readings with LXX against MT/SP, but in the following cases these readings are arguably earlier (archetypal) readings, and as such do not have implications for textual affinity. Original readings can be preserved at multiple locations in the genealogy. If more of these texts had been preserved, we would be able to ascertain their relationship with the proto-OG family, or to other hitherto undiscovered textual families and genealogical sub-units:

– 4QGen^{h1} (→ 2.2.1.8) at 1:9: מקוה "gathering" vs. MT/SP מקום "place"[38]
– 4QGen^k (→ 2.2.1.8) at 1:9: [שה]ותרא היב "and the dry land appeared" > MT/SP[39]
– 4QDeut^j (→ 2.2.1.7.17) at 32:8: בני אלוהים "sons of God" vs. MT/SP בני ישראל "sons of Israel"[40]
– 4QDeut^h (→ 2.2.1.7.16) at 33:8: [י]הבו ללו "Give to Levi" > MT/SP[41]

The many shared small harmonizations in the proto-Old Greek and proto-SP families allow us to infer a more general distinction between these families and the proto-MT family in the Pentateuch.

---

42); A. Rofé, "The End of the Song of Moses (Deuteronomy 32:43)," in Rofé, *Deuteronomy*, 47–54.

[36] Thus Rofé, "Song of Moses," 54.

[37] J.A. Duncan, "29. 4QDeut^b," *DJD* XIV: 9–14 (13–14).

[38] J.R. Davila, "8. 4QGen^h," *DJD* XII: 61–64 (61–62); Hendel, *Genesis 1–11*, 24–25.

[39] J.R. Davila, "10. 4QGen^k," *DJD* XII: 75–78 (76); Hendel, *Genesis 1–11*, 25–27.

[40] J.A. Duncan, "37. 4QDeut^j," *DJD* XIV: 75–91 (90) (an excerpted text); Duncan, "Deuteronomy, Book of," in *EDSS* 1:198–202 (200).

[41] J.A. Duncan, "35. 4QDeut^h," *DJD* XIV: 61–70 (68–69); Duncan, "New Readings for the 'Blessing of Moses' from Qumran," *JBL* 114 (1995): 273–90 (280).

The proto-MT Pentateuch has some harmonizations, but far fewer. This distinction of scribal tendencies has been characterized in different ways, but indicates a general typological distinction. As Crawford emphasizes, "there were two scribal traditions or approaches to Scripture at work in Second Temple period Palestine, transmitting the books that became the Hebrew Bible." The two approaches have been characterized by various binary terms: "pristine" vs. "expansionistic,"[42] "careful approach" vs. "free approach,"[43] non-harmonistic vs. "harmonistic,"[44] "exact/conservative" vs. "creative/free,"[45] and "exact" vs. "facilitating."[46]

Two distinctive scribal traditions or hermeneutical tendencies can be discerned *grosso modo*, one that was antiquarian and conservative, and one that allowed for inner-textual explication by various means, including large- and small-scale harmonization and linguistic modernization. As scholars have cogently argued, the expansionist tradition has rigorous procedures, and hence should not be characterized as "vulgar" or "free."[47] The distinction is one of tacit scribal knowledge of what constitutes right transmission, which varies along a gradient between verbatim copying and actively enhancing intelligibility and formal perfection. The procedures of the latter tendency constitute, as Teeter emphasizes, "an accepted *exegetical method* of sorts within textual transmission."[48] Different scribal schools adopted distinctive exegetical approaches to textual transmission during the Second Temple period.

It remains unclear whether there are social, geographical, or functional distinctions that correspond to these different scribal approaches. An interesting point of comparison is two leather *tefillin* cases from Qumran (→ 2.2.5.1), one containing proto-MT excerpted texts (4QPhyl D, E, F), and the other containing harmonistic excerpted texts (XQPhyl 1, 2, 3).[49] This contrast may reflect different geographical or sociological origins, but it may also indicate that there was no functional distinction between these two kinds of Pentateuchal text at Qumran.

2.2.3.3 Independent (Non-Aligned) Texts?[50]

Tov has argued that many of the Qumran Pentateuchal texts should be classified as "independent" or "non-aligned." By this he means texts that "follow an inconsistent pattern of agreements and disagreements with MT, LXX, and SP and … also contain readings not known from other sources."[51] He cites as a perspicuous example 11QpaleoLev[a] (→ 2.2.1.7.12), which is a sizeable manuscript that has many small variants and one large unique reading (see below), but has no consistent pattern of affinity with MT, LXX, or SP. Therefore, Tov maintains, it "must be regarded as a *fourth* source of the book, previously unknown."[52] Including this substantial scroll, Tov lists seventeen Pentateuchal manuscripts as independent (some with question marks).[53] Lange lists twenty-one Pentateuchal manuscripts as independent (including four manuscripts of 4QRP; see below).[54] Only ten manuscripts are on both lists: 4QExod[b], 4QExod-Lev[f], 11QpaleoLev[a], 4QDeut[b],

---

[42] F.M. Cross, "The Contribution of the Qumran Discoveries to the Study of the Biblical Text," in Cross-Talmon, *QHBT*, 278–92 (283).

[43] Tov, *TCHB*, 184.

[44] Eshel and Eshel, "Dating," 228–30.

[45] Crawford, "Scribal Traditions," 175–77.

[46] D.A. Teeter, *Scribal Laws: Exegetical Variation in the Textual Transmission of Biblical Law in the Late Second Temple Period* (FAT 92; Tübingen: Mohr Siebeck, 2014), 254–60.

[47] Teeter, *Scribal Laws*, 265–67; J. Ben-Dov, "Early Texts of the Torah: Revisiting the Greek Scholarly Context," *Journal of Ancient Judaism* 4 (2013): 210–34 (224–26).

[48] Teeter, *Scribal Laws*, 178.

[49] *Contra* the characterization of XQPhyl 1 and 2 as proto-MT texts in Eshel and Eshel, "Dating," 238; see Y. Adler, "Identifying Sectarian Characteristics in the Phylacteries from Qumran," *RevQ* 23 (2007–2008): 79–92 (88–89).

[50] For non-aligned texts, see → 1.2.2.

[51] Tov, *TCHB*, 109.

[52] E. Tov, "A Modern Textual Outlook Based on the Qumran Scrolls," *HUCA* 53 (1982): 11–27 (20); Tov, "The Textual Character of 11QpaleoLev," *Shnaton* 3 (1978–1979): 238–44 [Hebr.]; Tov, *TCHB*, 159–60.

[53] Tov, *Scribal Practices*, 332–33: 4QGen[k], 2QExod[b]?, 4QExod[b], 4QExod[d], 4QExod[e]?, 4QExod-Lev[f], 11QpaleoLev[a], 11QLev[b]?, 4QDeut[b], 4QDeut[c], 4QDeut[h], 4QDeut[j], 4QDeut[k1], 4QDeut[k2], 4QDeut[m], 4QDeut[n], 5QDeut.

[54] Lange, *Handbuch*, 155: 4QGen[f], 2QExod[a], 4QExod[b], 4QExod[c], 4QExod-Lev[f], 4QLev-Num[a], 4QLev[b], 11QpaleoLev[a],

4QDeut[c], 4QDeut[h], 4QDeut[j], 4QDeut[k1], 4QDeut[k2], 4QDeut[m], and 4QDeut[n].

However, as we have noted above, several of these manuscripts have affinities with one or another textual family. 4QExod-Lev[f] and 4QDeut[n] (an excerpted text) have affinities with the proto-SP family, and 4QExod[b] and 4QDeut[b] have affinities with the proto-Old Greek family. Eshel has argued that 4QDeut[j] and 4QDeut[kl] (both excerpted texts) should also be grouped with the "harmonistic text group" (viz. the proto-SP family).[55]

Aside from these differences in identifying the affiliation of these texts, there are two general problems regarding the cogency of Tov's category of "independent/non-aligned texts."[56] First, to say that a text is "non-aligned" with respect to MT, SP, and LXX privileges these three texts in a manner that Tov elsewhere criticizes.[57] This problem illustrates the advantage of giving primacy in textual history to the criteria of multiple editions and scribal traditions rather than affinity to one of the three major witnesses.

Second, and more problematic, is the purely statistical method of counting *all* variants, no matter how minor, as equally valid in diagnosing textual affinity. As Chiesa observes, "in textual criticism what matters is not the *number* of agreements and disagreements between the various witnesses, but the *nature* of their variant readings and/or errors."[58] The nature of most of the variants in the putative "independent/non-aligned" texts is clearly within the range of the "law of scribes." Other variants may be original or archetypal readings, in which case they have no value for establishing affinity. Independent readings, as noted above, are also of no value for establishing affinity (or, in this case, non-affinity). In sum, the logical structure of the category of "independent/non-aligned texts" is problematic. All biblical manuscripts are "aligned" with respect to the genealogy. Even a manuscript that is "mixed," that is, copied and/or corrected from two or more manuscripts from different places in the stemma, is still "aligned," albeit complexly so. For many of the manuscripts placed by Tov in this category, there is simply insufficient evidence to determine their genealogical affinities.

11QpaleoLev[a] (→ 2.2.1.7.12), Tov's initial exemplar of this category, is one of the better-preserved Pentateuchal scrolls.[59] Since Leviticus has a relatively stable textual history, with few major expansions, one does not expect significant textual drama.[60] In 11QpaleoLev[a], there are only two shared derived innovations that clearly rise above the level of the "law of scribes." At Lev 15:3, the scroll shares a medium-size harmonizing/explicating plus with SP and LXX, which is lacking in MT:[61]

[טמאתו היא] בו כל ימי ז[ב בשרו]

[this is his impurity] in him all the days that [his member] dischar[ges]

There is one variant: SP reads טמא הוא "he is impure" where LXX/11QpaleoLev[a] read either טמאתו היא בו or היא טמאתו בו/αὕτη ἡ ἀκαθαρσία αὐτοῦ ἐν αὐτῷ "this is his impurity in him."

Teeter has recently argued that this plus is "an explanatory gloss on the difficult formulation of the original verse."[62] The original verse, which exists in all the witnesses, begins: וְזֹאת תִּהְיֶה טֻמְאָתוֹ

1QDeut[b], 4QDeut[b], 4QDeut[c], 4QDeut[h], 4QDeut[i,] 4QDeut[kl], 4QDeut[k2], 4QDeut[n], 4QpaleoDeut[r]; see also Lange → 2.2.1.7.

55 Eshel, "4QDeut[n]," 122. On the text-critical complications of the excerpted texts, see B.A. Strawn, "Excerpted Manuscripts at Qumran: Their Significance for the Textual History of the Hebrew Bible and the Socio-Religious History of the Qumran Community and its Literature," in *The Bible and the Dead Sea Scrolls*: Vol. 2: *The Dead Sea Scrolls and the Qumran Community* (ed. J.H. Charlesworth; Waco: Baylor University Press, 2006), 107–67 (130–47).

56 Hendel, "Assessing," 291–95.

57 Tov, *TCHB*, 158–60.

58 Chiesa, "Textual History," 267. For a different opinion, see → 1.2.2.3.

59 Tov, "11QpaleoLev"; D.N. Freedman and K.A. Matthews, *The Paleo-Hebrew Leviticus Scroll (11QpaleoLev)* (Winona Lake: ASOR, 1985).

60 S. Metso, "Evidence from the Qumran Scrolls for the Scribal Transmission of Leviticus," in *Editing the Bible: Assessing the Task Past and Present* (eds. J.S. Kloppenborg and J.H. Newman; SBLRBS 69; Atlanta: SBL, 2012), 67–79.

61 See Teeter, *Scribal Laws*, 94–99.

62 Teeter, *Scribal Laws*, 98. Cf. Tov, "11QpaleoLev," 244, who regards this as a homoioteleuton in MT/SP; so also D.N. Freed-

בְּזוֹ בוֹ דָר בְּשָׂרוֹ אֶת־זוֹבוֹ "And this shall be his impurity in his discharge, [whether] his member runs with his discharge ..." The latter clause is a parenthetical aside. As Teeter observes, a harmonizing/exegetical scribe imported wording from the parallel text of female genital discharge in Lev 15:25, כָּל־יְמֵי זוֹב "all the days that [it] discharges" in order to explicate the duration of the male discharge impurity. As elsewhere in the scribal tradition of the proto-SP and proto-OG families, the strategy is near-verbatim repetition of language from a parallel passage to build the harmonizing/exegetical plus. This shared innovation indicates the affinity of 11QpaleoLev^a with the common substrate (or hyparchetype) of the proto-SP and proto-OG families.

11QpaleoLev^a shares a small harmonizing plus with LXX at Lev 26:24, reading חמת קרי "angry hostility" versus MT/SP קֶרִי "hostility." This is a harmonization with the parallel passage in Lev 26:28, which reads חֲמַת־קֶרִי.[63] This harmonization – and the identical harmonization in LXX-Lev 26:41 – creates a verbally consistent divine discourse. (Notably, SP is not harmonistic in these passages.) In these two shared innovations, at Lev 15:3 and 26:24, 11QpaleoLev^a has affinities with the harmonistic substrate of proto-SP/proto-OG and with the proto-OG family, respectively. In sum, 11QpaleoLev^a is not an independent or non-aligned text, but has notable affinities when examined by the genealogical method.

Most of the putatively independent scrolls lack sufficient diagnostic features to place in a particular textual genealogy. If we had the scrolls in their entirety, their affinities would be more apparent. For instance, the affinities of the Genesis scrolls would be clarified if they contained Genesis 5 and 11; the Exodus scrolls if they contained Exodus 35–40; and so on. For many of the scrolls in their present condition, we cannot infer their affiliation because of the paucity of diagnostic data. This is a condition of our fragmentary evidence, and does not warrant an extra category of "independent/non-aligned" texts. The fragmentary manuscripts whose affinities we cannot detect are best designated texts of unknown affiliation or, in some cases, of mixed affiliation.

2.2.3.4 Is 4QRP a Pentateuchal Text?

The five fragmentary scrolls called 4QReworked Pentateuch (4QRP^a = 4Q158; 4QRP^{b–e} = 4Q364–367) have been characterized by modern scholars as either "rewritten Bible" texts, that is, exegetical compositions that retell portions of the Pentateuch, or as new edition(s) of the Pentateuch.[64] This dichotomy was already expressed by the original editor, John Strugnell. He described 4Q365 as a "copy of a wildly aberrant text of the whole Pentateuch containing several non-biblical additions, some identical with the Samaritan Pentateuch pluses, others unattested elsewhere."[65] But he gave these texts the name 4QPentateuchal Paraphrase, indicating that they are not Pentateuchal texts, but exegetical works. This question – are they Pentateuchal texts or a "Reworked Pentateuch" – continues to perplex. The final editors, Tov and Crawford, have changed their minds at least once on this issue, both recently concluding that the scribes who wrote them meant them to be Pentateuchal texts.[66] Ulrich characterizes it as a "variant literary edition of the Pentateuch."[67] Segal maintains that the manuscripts represent different compositions, one of which is a "rewritten Bible" text (4Q158), another possibly an excerpted Leviticus text (4Q367), and the others texts of the Pentateuch.[68] But these questions are probably undecidable, due to the fragmentary nature of the scrolls and the lack of

---

man, "Variant Readings in the Leviticus Scroll from Qumran Cave 11," *CBQ* 36 (1974): 525–34 (528–29).

63 Freedman and Matthews, *Leviticus Scroll*, 47.

64 See → 2.2.1.7 and → 2.2.1.1–4.

65 Quoted in S. White Crawford, "4QTemple? (4Q365A) Revisited," in *Prayer and Poetry in the Dead Sea Scrolls and Related Literature: Essays in Honor of Eileen Schuller* (eds. J. Penner, K.M. Penner, and C. Wassen; STDJ 98; Leiden: Brill, 2012), 87–95 (88 note 6).

66 Crawford, *Rewriting*, 56; E. Tov, "From 4QReworked Pentateuch to 4QPentateuch (?)," in Tov, **Collected Writings 3*, 45–59.

67 E. Ulrich, "The Qumran Scrolls and the Biblical Text," in Schiffman, Tov, and VanderKam, **Fifty Years*, 51–59 (57).

68 M. Segal, "4QReworked Pentateuch or 4QPentateuch?" in Schiffman, Tov, and VanderKam, **Fifty Years*, 391–99.

2.2.3 OTHER TEXTS

any contextual information (e.g., citations in other sources). Zahn aptly questions whether "in the current state of the texts we are able to decide with any confidence whether the 4QRP texts represent copies of the Pentateuch or compositions belonging to the rewritten Bible genre."[69]

The 4QRP scrolls, some of which may be independent works, have the following characteristics: a) extensive reproduction of Pentateuchal texts; b) large harmonizations; c) rearrangement or linkage of non-contiguous Pentateuchal texts; and d) new compositions. The collocation of features a) and b) are characteristic of many Pentateuchal texts (see above), but features c) and d) are not. Feature c) is characteristic of excerpted Pentateuchal texts. Feature d) is characteristic of "rewritten Bible" texts such as *Jubilees* and the *Temple Scroll*. Some of the new compositions in the 4QRP scrolls are closely related to portions of *Jubilees* and the *Temple Scroll* (see 4Q364 3 with *Jubilees* 27; 4Q365 23 with 11QT^a XXIII–XXIV).[70]

Two of the 4QRP scrolls (4Q158 and 4Q364) have affinities with the proto-SP family, sharing three large harmonizations with this family (4Q158 at Exod 20:19–21; 4Q364 at Gen 30:36 and Deut 2:7). However, another scroll (4Q365) lacks this affinity (no harmonization at Exod 26:35, and no sequence difference at Exod 29:21). The 4QRP compositions seem to have varying textual affinities.[71]

The arrangement of non-contiguous Pentateuchal texts in 4QRP is often motivated by thematic triggers, such as the dangerous encounters with God in Genesis 32 and Exodus 4 (4Q158), the care of the tabernacle in Numbers 4 and 7 (4Q365), and the story of Zelophehad's daughters in Numbers 27 and 36 (4Q365). The harmonistic expansion of the Decalogue (4Q158) is a well-known phenomenon from the proto-SP family and the other harmonistic Pentateuchal texts (see above).

The fragmentary state of these scrolls leaves undecidable the question of whether the omitted texts in these sections were reinserted elsewhere. If they were not, then it is difficult to imagine that any ancient Jew – Essene or not – would have regarded them as Pentateuchal scrolls. As Bernstein observes, "the phenomenon of large-scale deletion (as opposed to rearrangement) of legal material is totally anomalous and unexpected in a biblical text."[72] Falk plausibly comments, "it seems likely there were significant omissions in the presentation of the Pentateuch – thus possibly a sort of excerpted Pentateuch."[73] In Strugnell's terms, it could have been regarded as a "wild" Pentateuch.

Whether the 4QRP scrolls were viewed as innovative editions of the Pentateuch or an exegetically rewritten Pentateuch – or some serial combination of these genres – these texts could have been regarded as authoritative, as were the various instances of rewritten Pentateuch (e.g., *Jubilees*, *Temple Scroll*). 4QRP may best be characterized, in Najman's term, as a Mosaic discourse, an interpretation of the revelation at Sinai that responds to new circumstances and to exegetical imperatives within the Pentateuch.[74] It is a liminal discourse, in a gray area bridging textual transmission and new composition. Perhaps due to its hybridity, it soon became extinct. As Crawford observes, "We may have in the Reworked Pentateuch group the end of a very long tradition of inner-scriptural scribal exegesis, soon to be replaced by another tradition of separating the authoritative text from its commentary."[75]

---

[69] M.M. Zahn, "The Problem of Characterizing the 4QReworked Pentateuch Manuscripts: Bible, Rewritten Bible, or None of the Above?" *DSD* 15 (2008): 315–39 (333).

[70] Crawford, *Rewriting*, 47, 50–51; Crawford, "4QTemple"; M.M. Zahn, *Rethinking Rewritten Scripture: Composition and Exegesis in the 4QReworked Pentateuch Manuscripts* (STDJ 95; Leiden: Brill, 2011), 77–81, 102–07.

[71] E. Tov and S. White, "Reworked Pentateuch," *DJD* XIII: 185–351 (194).

[72] M.J. Bernstein, "What Has Happened to the Laws? The Treatment of Legal Material in 4QReworked Pentateuch," *DSD* 15 (2008): 24–49 (49).

[73] D.K. Falk, *The Parabiblical Texts: Strategies for Extending the Scriptures in the Dead Sea Scrolls* (Library of Second Temple Studies 63; London: T & T Clark, 2007), 111.

[74] H. Najman, *Seconding Sinai: The Development of Mosaic Discourse in Second Temple Judaism* (JSJSup 77; Leiden: Brill, 2003).

[75] Crawford, *Rewriting*, 57.

Eshel, E. and H. Eshel, "Dating the Samaritan Pentateuch's Compilation in Light of the Qumran Biblical Scrolls," in *Emanuel: Studies in the Hebrew Bible, the Septuagint, and the Dead Sea Scrolls in Honor of Emanuel Tov* (eds. S.M. Paul et al.; VTSup 94; Leiden: Brill, 2003), 215–40.

Hendel, R., "Assessing the Text-Critical Theories of the Hebrew Bible after Qumran," in *The Oxford Handbook of the Dead Sea Scrolls* (eds. T.H. Lim and J.J. Collins; Oxford: Oxford University Press, 2010), 281–302.

Tov, E., "Textual Developments in the Torah," in E. Tov, *Textual Criticism of the Hebrew Bible, Qumran, Septuagint: Collected Essays, Volume 3* (VTSup 167; Leiden: Brill, 2015), 239–49.

Trovato, P., *Everything You Always Wanted to Know about Lachmann's Method: A Non-Standard Handbook of Genealogical Textual Criticism in the Age of Post-Structuralism, Cladistics, and Copy-Text* (Padua: Libreria universitaria, 2014).

Ulrich, E., "The Evolutionary Growth of the Pentateuch in the Second Temple Period," in *Pentateuchal Traditions in the Late Second Temple Period: Proceedings of the International Workshop in Tokyo, August 28–31, 2007* (eds. A. Moriya and G. Hata; JSJSup 158; Leiden: Brill, 2012), 39–56.

White Crawford, S., "Scribal Traditions in the Pentateuch and the History of the Early Second Temple Period," in *Congress Volume Helsinki 2010* (ed. M. Nissinen; VTSup 148; Leiden: Brill, 2012), 167–84.

Ronald Hendel

2.2.4 SP and Ancient Texts Close to SP

2.2.4.1 Genesis
2.2.4.1.1 Nature of the Text

The textual family or group to which SP belongs is characterized by the following secondary features (viz. diagnostic errors): 1) a large number of short harmonizations, focused on words and phrases, many of which are shared with the proto-LXX family; 2) a tendency to modernize linguistic and orthographic features; and 3) a limited number of larger-scale revisions, mostly harmonizing pluses, which are distinctive to this family.[1] SP itself has an additional small layer of sectarian revisions (esp. at Exod 20:17; Deut 5:18) that assert the primacy of the cultic site at Mt. Gerizim. Aside from this layer, SP is indistinguishable from the other pre- or proto-SP texts. In Genesis, the proto-SP family is represented directly by SP-Gen and indirectly by *Jubilees* (→ 21.1.1) and a manuscript of the 4QReworked Pentateuch group (4Q364; → 2.2.1.7.1).

In Genesis, there are four large-scale revisions of the type distinctive of the proto-SP family. Two of these are shared with other witnesses of the proto-SP family. Two others are attested only in SP-Gen, due to the paucity of the proto-SP witnesses to Genesis. Each of these revisions was motivated by a local exegetical problem.

1) A revised chronology in Genesis 5 and 11, found in SP-Gen and *Jubilees* (→ 2.1.4.1).[2] The revision of lifespans and the age of "begetting" in Genesis 5 responds to the problem of three patriarchs (Jared, Methuselah, and Lamech) outliving the flood. In the revision, each dies in the year of the flood. The revision in Genesis 11 prevents all of Abraham's postdiluvian ancestors from being alive during Abraham's lifetime. In the revision, only Abraham's father is alive when Abraham is born. The revision of this chapter also fills out the formula of the patriarchs' lifespan and death to harmonize with Genesis 5.

2) A verse-long harmonization at Gen 10:19, found only in SP-Gen. The list of the borders of the land of Canaan is replaced with a concatenation of the borders of the promised land in Gen 15:18 and Deut 11:24 (= Deut 34:2). This harmonization resolves ambiguity in the equation of the land of Canaan with the (future) promised land.

3) A long harmonizing plus at Gen 30:36, found in SP-Gen and 4Q364 (→ 2.2.1.7.1). This addition harmonizes the narrative with Gen 31:11–13, where Jacob recounts a previous dream revelation. The revision inserts a narration of the dream revelation into a prior point in the narrative. This solves the exegetical problem of Jacob's reminiscence of an event that was not narrated. The origin of this problem is source-critical: the reminiscence in Genesis 31 is from the E source,

---

[1] Kartveit, *Origins of the Samaritans*, 276–88.

[2] Hendel, *The Text of Genesis 1–11*, 61–80.

whereas the story in Genesis 30 is from the J source. The harmonizing plus overcomes the difference between these stories.

4) A verse-long harmonizing plus at Gen 42:16, found only in SP-Gen. This addition has the same characteristic of smoothing out a narrative difficulty between two episodes. In Gen 44:22, Judah recalls what the brothers had said to the Egyptian, but this speech is not previously narrated. The plus in Gen 42:16 supplies this prior speech. The origin of this problem is also source-critical: the reminiscence in Genesis 44 is from the J source, whereas the dialogue in Genesis 42 is from the E source.

2.2.4.1.2 Editions and Tools

The most recent and important editions of SP-Gen are by Girón Blanc[3] and Tal and Florentin,[4] which improve on the choice of manuscripts by von Gall and his methods.[5] Girón Blanc's is a diplomatic edition that collates readings from fifteen SP manuscripts dating to the twelfth–fourteenth centuries C.E. The base manuscript is the Codex Zurbil (ms Add. 1846), ca. 1100 C.E. The Tal–Florentin edition is a parallel edition of MT and SP, reproducing one SP manuscript, Shechem 6 (1204 C.E.) and indicating most of the important non-orthographic differences between the two texts. This edition includes a lengthy appendix that records significant differences of vocalization between MT and SP, basing the latter on the Samaritan oral tradition transcribed by Ben-Ḥayyim.[6] A fuller analysis of differences of vocalization between MT-Gen and SP-Gen is presented by Schorch.[7]

2.2.4.1.3 Text-Critical Value

SP-Gen is a major textual version of Genesis, along with MT-Gen (→ 2.2.2), LXX-Gen (→ 2.4.1.1), and the Dead Sea scroll manuscripts (→ 2.2.1). Despite its distinctive secondary features, in many cases it preserves a better (older) reading than MT-Gen.

---

[3] Girón Blanc, *Pentateuco Hebreo-Samaritano*.
[4] Tal–Florentin, **Samaritan Version*.
[5] Von Gall, *Der hebräische Pentateuch der Samaritaner*.
[6] Ben-Hayyim, *LOT.
[7] Schorch, *Die Vokale des Gesetzes*.

Instances in Genesis include Gen 4:7, where SP-Gen (= LXX-Gen) reads נלכה השדה "let us go into the plain," which is lacking in MT-Gen due to scribal error. In Gen 10:4, SP-Gen (= LXX-Gen) correctly reads רודנים "Rhodians," where MT-Gen has דדנים "Dodians," the result of a *reš/dalet* confusion (the addition of *waw* in SP-Gen is a secondary orthographic feature). In Gen 2:2, SP-Gen (= LXX-Gen and Jub 2:16) arguably has the better reading, הששׁ "the sixth" versus MT-Gen's הַשְּׁבִיעִי "the seventh," which probably results from an anticipation of the form in the second half of the verse. As these examples demonstrate, SP-Gen and other proto-SP witnesses also serve to corroborate readings in LXX-Gen, providing evidence for its Hebrew *Vorlage*.

The witnesses of the proto-SP family – including SP-Gen – allow us to reconstruct aspects of the textual genealogy of Genesis prior to the Jewish revolts against Rome. There are clear affinities between the proto-LXX family and the proto-SP family in the many small harmonizations in Genesis, which are particularly numerous in the creation account in Genesis 1 and the flood narrative in Genesis 6–9. On the basis of these distinctive secondary features, we must presume either a common hyparchetype for these two textual families (vertical transmission) or a period of intensive textual contact (horizontal transmission). The distinctive editions of the chronologies of Genesis 5 and 11 in proto-MT, proto-SP, and proto-LXX allow us to classify their respective textual families as involving different editions, in these chapters and in the other large-scale revisions in proto-SP. The differences among these families therefore include several layers of revision, some of which rise to the level of different editions of Genesis.

2.2.4.1.4 Value for Literary Criticism

Many of the major and minor harmonizations in the proto-SP family respond to exegetical difficulties that are caused by the different sources of Genesis. The long harmonizing pluses at Gen 30:36 and 42:16 respond to narrative inconcinnities caused by the combination of J and E texts. Similarly, many small harmonizations smooth over frictions resulting from the combination of sources. For example, in Gen 2:4, SP-Gen (≈ LXX-Gen) harmonizes the order of "heaven" and "earth" in both halves of the verse, yielding the order (ה)שמים ו(ה)ארץ "heaven and earth" in the P and J versets. Similarly, in Gen 7:2, SP-Gen (= LXX-Gen) twice revises the phrase "male and female" from אִישׁ וְאִשְׁתּוֹ "a man and his wife" to זכר ונקבה "male and female," thereby eliminating this difference of J and P diction in the flood story. These and other examples show how the differences in the sources generated a scribal-exegetical desire to harmonize the language of Genesis.

Anderson, R.T. and T. Giles, *The Samaritan Pentateuch: An Introduction to Its Origin, History, and Significance for Biblical Studies* (Atlanta: SBL, 2012).
von Gall, A., *Der hebräische Pentateuch der Samaritaner* (5 vols.; Giessen: Töpelmann, 1914–1918; reprint, Berlin: De Gruyter, 1993).
Girón Blanc, L.-F., *Pentateuco Hebreo-Samaritano: Genesis: Editio critica sobre la base de manuscritos ineditos* (Textos y Estudios "Cardenal Cisneros" 15; Madrid: CSIC, 1976).
Hendel, R., *The Text of Genesis 1–11: Textual Studies and Critical Edition* (New York: Oxford University Press, 1998).
Kartveit, M., *The Origin of the Samaritans* (Leiden: Brill, 2009).
Schorch, S., *Die Vokale des Gesetzes: Die samaritanische Lesetradition als Textzeugin der Tora*: Vol. 1: *Das Buch Genesis* (BZAW 339; Berlin: De Gruyter, 2004).
Tal–Florentin, **Samaritan Version*.

Ronald Hendel

2.2.4.2 Exodus
2.2.4.2.1 Nature of the Text

SP-Exod has the same overall character as SP in general (regarding orthography, vocabulary, short explanations, etc.; → 1.2.3), but is exceptional because of a high number of larger pluses, three of them in Exodus 20 alone, including the important Samaritan tenth commandment. This commandment's reference to Mount Gerizim is supposed to be the major distinguishing mark of the early Samaritans.

2.2.4.2.2 Original Form and Text-Critical Character

A pre-Samaritan version of the book is known from the Dead Sea Scrolls: 4Q22 (4QpaleoExod^m; → 2.2.1.3.1) contains fragments from Exodus 6–37. This manuscript evinces many small variations compared to MT (→ 2.2.2), variations that witness to a tendency to modernize grammar, vocabulary, and orthography, but it also contains the major pluses that are typical of the pre-Samaritan texts and make them a special group. 4Q22 has been dated on paleographical grounds to 100–25 B.C.E. It also has been subjected to radiocarbon dating, the "1-s 1997 Decadel Calibration," at the Tucson facility, with the result "164–144 B.C.E. or 116 B.C.E. – 48 C.E." A special feature of the scroll is a repair patch in col. VIII, that has been dated paleographically to 100–25 B.C.E., while the Tucson facility dated it "51 B.C.E. – 47 C.E." by help of the radiocarbon method.[1]

4Q17 (4QExod-Lev^f; → 2.2.1.7.9) contains text from Exod 28:30, preceded by Exod 39:20–21 and followed by Exod 39:22–23. This textual sequence corresponds to SP-Exod 39:21a, where Exod 28:30 is quoted as an addition to the verse, and it therefore is another pre-Samaritan text. This is one of the oldest Dead Sea scrolls, dated on paleographical grounds to the mid-third century B.C.E.[2]

4Q158 frgs. 7–8 contains text from Exod 20:12–17 in lines 1–2, from Deut 5:30–31 in lines 3–4, introduced by "And Yahweh said to Moses," and followed in line 5 by "And the people returned, each man to his own tent, but Moses remained before [Yahweh]." Lines 6–9 correspond to Exod 20:22–26. SP-Exod 20:21a (last part)–22 is therefore present here, and it follows that also this manuscript displays a pre-Samaritan text. It is written in "a late Hasmonean or transitional formal script," meaning that its date is 75–25 B.C.E.[3]

---

[1] McLean *apud* P.W. Skehan, E. Ulrich, J.E. Sanderson, "4QpaleoParaJoshua," **DJD* IX: 62; B. Webster, "Chronological Index of the Texts from the Judaean Desert," **DJD* XXXIX: 366.
[2] Cross, "4QExod-Lev^f," 133–44.
[3] E. Tov and S. White Crawford, "Reworked Pentateuch," **DJD* XIII: 187–351 (201).

2.2.4 SP AND ANCIENT TEXTS CLOSE TO SP

SP-Exod 7:18a	MT-Exod 7:15–18
וילך משה ואהרן אל פרעה ויאמרו אליו יהוה אלהי העברים שלחנו אליך לאמר שלח את עמי ויעבדני במדבר והנה לא שמעת עד כה כה אמר יהוה בזאת תדע כי אני יהוה הנה אנכי מכה במטה אשר בידי על המים אשר ביאר ונהפכו לדם והדגה אשר ביאר תמות ובאש היאר ונלאו מצרים לשתות מים מן היאר	לֵךְ אֶל־פַּרְעֹה בַּבֹּקֶר הִנֵּה יֹצֵא הַמַּיְמָה וְנִצַּבְתָּ לִקְרָאתוֹ עַל־שְׂפַת הַיְאֹר וְהַמַּטֶּה אֲשֶׁר־נֶהְפַּךְ לְנָחָשׁ תִּקַּח בְּיָדֶךָ: וְאָמַרְתָּ אֵלָיו יְהוָה אֱלֹהֵי הָעִבְרִים שְׁלָחַנִי אֵלֶיךָ לֵאמֹר שַׁלַּח אֶת־עַמִּי וְיַעַבְדֻנִי בַּמִּדְבָּר וְהִנֵּה לֹא־שָׁמַעְתָּ עַד־כֹּה: כֹּה אָמַר יְהוָה בְּזֹאת תֵּדַע כִּי אֲנִי יְהוָה הִנֵּה אָנֹכִי מַכֶּה בַּמַּטֶּה אֲשֶׁר־בְּיָדִי עַל־הַמַּיִם אֲשֶׁר בַּיְאֹר וְנֶהֶפְכוּ לְדָם: וְהַדָּגָה אֲשֶׁר־בַּיְאֹר תָּמוּת וּבָאַשׁ הַיְאֹר וְנִלְאוּ מִצְרַיִם לִשְׁתּוֹת מַיִם מִן־הַיְאֹר:
Moses and Aaron went to Pharaoh and said to him, 'The Lord, the God of the Hebrews, sent us to you to say, "Let my people go, so that they may worship me in the wilderness." But until now you have not listened. Thus says the Lord, "By this you shall know that I am the Lord." See, with the staff that is in my hand I will strike the water that is in the Nile, and it shall be turned to blood. The fish in the river shall die, the river itself shall stink, and the Egyptians shall be unable to drink water from the Nile.'	Go to Pharaoh in the morning, as he is going out to the water; stand by at the riverbank to meet him, and take in your hand the staff that was turned into a snake. Say to him, 'The Lord, the God of the Hebrews, sent me to you to say, "Let my people go, so that they may worship me in the wilderness." But until now you have not listened. Thus says the Lord, "By this you shall know that I am the Lord." See, with the staff that is in my hand I will strike the water that is in the Nile, and it shall be turned to blood. The fish in the river shall die, the river itself shall stink, and the Egyptians shall be unable to drink water from the Nile.'

4Q175 lines 1–8 contain Deut 5:28–29 followed by Deut 18:18–19, which corresponds to SP–Exod 20:21a, and the introduction "And .... [= Yahweh] spoke to Moses, saying," is the same as in SP-Exod 20:21a, whereas MT, LXX, and SP have a different wording as an introduction in Deut 5:28. This text is also a witness to the pre-Samaritan tradition, and it is dated to around 100 B.C.E.[4]

These four Qumran texts prove that the pre-Samaritan text type existed from the middle of the third century B.C.E., predating the Qumran community or being simultaneous with it, and that it was in use until the turn of the era.

When compared to MT, SP-Exod displays many small differences, seventeen larger pluses, and two transpositions. In the main, we are dealing with four sets of larger expansions and transpositions in SP: in the plague narrative, in the theophany at Sinai, in the tabernacle construction, and in the narrative where counterparts are found in the historical survey in Deuteronomy 1–3.

The plague narrative, SP-Exod 6–11, contains ten pluses against MT. SP-Exod 20 has received three long insertions, together covering twenty-one verses. Four expansions and two transpositions are in the large section dealing with the construction of the tabernacle, Exod 25–40. In addition, the narrative has received expansions in chapters 18 and 32. All these cases are found in the pre-Samaritan texts mentioned above, and in SP, except SP-Exod 6:9, where there is no extant pre-Samaritan text, and the Samaritan tenth commandment, which is not found in any pre-Samaritan text.

To illustrate the situation in the plague narrative, SP-Exod 7:18 serves as an example of a large plus against MT, here presented with MT-Exod 7:16–18 in the right column for comparison.

The addition in SP-Exod 7:18a is evidently copied from the preceding verses and adapted to the situation where Moses and Aaron speak to Pharaoh. In MT, there is no report of Moses addressing Pharaoh, and this is remedied in SP. Similar cases are found

---

[4] A. Steudel, "Testimonia," in *Encyclopedia of the Dead Sea Scrolls* (2 vols.; eds. L.C. Schiffman and J.C. VanderKam; Oxford: Oxford University Press, 2000), 2:936.

SP-Exod 11:4a	MT-Exod 4:22–23
ויאמר משה אל פרעה כה אמר יהוה בני ישראל בכורי ואמר אליך שלח את בני ויעבדני ותמאן לשלחו הנה יהוה הרג את בנך בכורך	וְאָמַרְתָּ אֶל־פַּרְעֹה כֹּה אָמַר יְהוָה בְּנִי בְכֹרִי יִשְׂרָאֵל: וָאֹמַר אֵלֶיךָ שַׁלַּח אֶת־בְּנִי וְיַעַבְדֵנִי וַתְּמָאֵן לְשַׁלְּחוֹ הִנֵּה אָנֹכִי הֹרֵג אֶת־בִּנְךָ בְּכֹרֶךָ:
Then Moses said to Pharaoh, 'Thus says the Lord: Israel is my firstborn son, and he is saying to you, "Let my son go that he may worship me." But you refused to let him go; Behold, the Lord will kill your firstborn son.'	Then you shall say to Pharaoh, 'Thus says the Lord: Israel is my firstborn son. I said to you, "Let my son go that he may worship me." But you refused to let him go; now I will kill your firstborn son.'

in SP-Exod 7:29a; 8:19a; 9:5a, 19a. In a reverse situation, in Exod 10:3, 11:4, Moses speaks to Pharaoh without any divine command to do so, but this command is found in SP in the form of text copied from the messages to Pharaoh into the preceding verses. In Exod 8:1, God commands Moses to tell Aaron to stretch out his hand with the stick, and Aaron does so. A report that Moses transmits the command to Aaron is missing in MT, but is found in SP, also as text copied from the preceding divine command and adapted. Finally, SP-Exod 11:4a copies and adapts text from Exod 4:22–23; this adapted text fits well with the context in ch. 11, where the last plague is announced. The two texts are presented here in the Samaritan (11:4a) and MT (4:22–23) versions.

SP-Exod also copies and adapts text from the relevant parts of Deuteronomy in 18:25a (cf. Deut 1:9b–18); 20:19a (Deut 5:24–27); 20:21a (Deut 5:28b–29; 18:18–22; 5:30 f.); and 32:10a (Deut 9:20). To exemplify this phenomenon, the prophecy about a prophet like Moses may serve; see the table on p. 89. It makes use of a "quotation within a quotation" technique (MT-Deut 5:28b–29; 18:18–22; 5:30–31 in the right column).

Two transpositions in SP-Exod, 26:35a and 29:28a, locate the texts in a more logical context: the incense altar belongs more naturally with the interior equipment of the temple in ch. 26, and the sprinkling of blood and oil on the garments of Aaron and his sons reads even better in 29:28a than in MT's 29:21.

The expansions and transpositions share the same formal characteristic: They are all insertions into the text from another Pentateuchal text. Formally, these expansions are exemplified by Exod 32:9, a verse that is present in MT, SP, and 4Q22, but not in LXX. It is copied from Deut 9:13 and adapted to the new context.

ויאמר יהוה אל משה ראיתי את העם הזה והנה עם־קשה ערף הוא

"And the Lord said to Moses, 'I have seen that this people is indeed a stubborn people.'"

4QpaleoExod^m XXXVII:31 contains letters from two of the words in this verse, אל משה "to Moses," and the editor of this Qumran text in DJD, Sanderson, adds the comment that line 32 "was required for the text of the end of v. 9 and for v. 10 through ואעשה; the next word is extant on the top right margin of the following column."[5] In other words, Exod 32:9 is present in 4Q22. The verse is also present in SP, but is not found in LXX.[6] LXX reads

---

[5] Sanderson, "4QpaleoExodus^m," 123.

[6] παρέβησαν ταχὺ ἐκ τῆς ὁδοῦ, ἧς ἐνετείλω αὐτοῖς, ἐποίησαν ἑαυτοῖς μόσχον καὶ προσκεκυνήκασιν αὐτῷ καὶ τεθύκασιν αὐτῷ καὶ εἶπαν Οὗτοι οἱ θεοί σου, Ισραηλ, οἵτινες ἀνεβίβασάν σε ἐκ γῆς Αἰγύπτου. καὶ νῦν ἔασόν με καὶ θυμωθεὶς ὀργῇ εἰς αὐτοὺς ἐκτρίψω αὐτοὺς καὶ ποιήσω σὲ εἰς ἔθνος μέγα "They have deviated quickly from the way that you commanded them. They made for themselves a calf and did obeisance to it and offered sacrifices to it, and they said, 'These are your gods, Israel, who brought you up from the land of Egypt.' And now allow me, and, enraged with Anger against them, I will destroy them and make you into a great nation" (LXX-Exod 32:8–10 = MT-Exod 32:8, 10; *NETS).

[7] Manuscript no. 6 of the Samaritan synagogue in Shekhem presents תמלדם, which is a scribal error for תלמדם "you shall teach them."

2.2.4 SP AND ANCIENT TEXTS CLOSE TO SP

SP-Exod 20:21a | MT-Deut 5:28b–29; 18:18–22; 5:30–31

וידבר יהוה אל משה לאמר שמעתי את קול דברי העם הזה אשר דברו אליך היטיבו כל אשר דברו מי יתן והיה לבבם זה להם ליראה אתי ולשמר את מצותי כל הימים למען ייטב להם ולבניהם לעולם נביא אקים להם מקרב אחיהם כמוך ונתתי דברי בפיו ודבר אליהם את כל אשר אצונו והיה האיש אשר לא ישמע אל דבריו אשר ידבר בשמי אנכי אדרש מעמו אך הנביא אשר יזיד לדבר דבר בשמי את אשר לא צויתיו לדבר ואשר ידבר בשם אלהים אחרים ומת הנביא ההוא וכי תאמר בלבבך איך נדע את הדבר אשר לא דברו יהוה אשר ידבר הנביא בשם יהוה לא יהיה הדבר ולא יבוא הוא הדבר אשר לא דברו יהוה בזידון דברו הנביא לא תגור ממנו

לך אמר להם שובו לכם לאהליכם ואתה פה עמד עמדי ואדברה אליך את כל המצוה החקים והמשפטים אשר (תלמדם)[7] ועשו בארץ אשר אנכי נתן להם לרשתה:

| וַיֹּאמֶר יְהוָה אֵלַי שָׁמַעְתִּי אֶת־קוֹל דִּבְרֵי הָעָם הַזֶּה אֲשֶׁר דִּבְּרוּ אֵלֶיךָ הֵיטִיבוּ כָּל־אֲשֶׁר דִּבֵּרוּ: מִי־יִתֵּן וְהָיָה לְבָבָם זֶה לָהֶם לְיִרְאָה אֹתִי וְלִשְׁמֹר אֶת־כָּל־מִצְוֺתַי כָּל־הַיָּמִים לְמַעַן יִיטַב לָהֶם וְלִבְנֵיהֶם לְעֹלָם נָבִיא אָקִים לָהֶם מִקֶּרֶב אֲחֵיהֶם כָּמוֹךָ וְנָתַתִּי דְבָרַי בְּפִיו וְדִבֶּר אֲלֵיהֶם אֵת כָּל־אֲשֶׁר אֲצַוֶּנּוּ: וְהָיָה הָאִישׁ אֲשֶׁר לֹא־יִשְׁמַע אֶל־דְּבָרַי אֲשֶׁר יְדַבֵּר בִּשְׁמִי אָנֹכִי אֶדְרֹשׁ מֵעִמּוֹ: אַךְ הַנָּבִיא אֲשֶׁר יָזִיד לְדַבֵּר דָּבָר בִּשְׁמִי אֵת אֲשֶׁר לֹא־צִוִּיתִיו לְדַבֵּר וַאֲשֶׁר יְדַבֵּר בְּשֵׁם אֱלֹהִים אֲחֵרִים וּמֵת הַנָּבִיא הַהוּא: וְכִי תֹאמַר בִּלְבָבֶךָ אֵיכָה נֵדַע אֶת־הַדָּבָר אֲשֶׁר לֹא־דִבְּרוֹ יְהוָה: אֲשֶׁר יְדַבֵּר הַנָּבִיא בְּשֵׁם יְהוָה וְלֹא־יִהְיֶה הַדָּבָר וְלֹא יָבוֹא הוּא הַדָּבָר אֲשֶׁר לֹא־דִבְּרוֹ יְהוָה בְּזָדוֹן דִּבְּרוֹ הַנָּבִיא לֹא תָגוּר מִמֶּנּוּ:

לֵךְ אֱמֹר לָהֶם שׁוּבוּ לָכֶם לְאָהֳלֵיכֶם: וְאַתָּה פֹּה עֲמֹד עִמָּדִי וַאֲדַבְּרָה אֵלֶיךָ אֵת כָּל־הַמִּצְוָה וְהַחֻקִּים וְהַמִּשְׁפָּטִים אֲשֶׁר תְּלַמְּדֵם וְעָשׂוּ בָאָרֶץ אֲשֶׁר אָנֹכִי נֹתֵן לָהֶם לְרִשְׁתָּהּ:

The Lord spoke to Moses and said: "I have heard the words of this people, which they have spoken to you; they are right in all that they have spoken. If only they had such a mind as this, to fear me and to keep all my commandments always, so that it might go well with them and with their children forever!
I will raise up for them a prophet like you from among their own people; I will put my words in the mouth of the prophet, who shall speak to them everything that I command. Anyone who does not heed his words, that the prophet shall speak in my name, I myself will hold accountable. But any prophet who speaks in the name of other gods, or who presumes to speak in my name a word that I have not commanded the prophet to speak – that prophet shall die. You may say to yourself, 'How can the word be recognized that the Lord has not spoken?' If a prophet speaks in the name of the Lord but the thing does not take place or prove true, it is a word that the Lord has not spoken. The prophet has spoken it presumptuously; do not be frightened by it.
Go say to them, 'Return to your tents.' But you, stand here by me, and I will tell you all the commandments, the statutes and the ordinances, that you shall teach them, so that they may do them in the land that I am giving them to possess." | The Lord said to me: "I have heard the words of this people, which they have spoken to you; they are right in all that they have spoken. If only they had such a mind as this, to fear me and to keep all my commandments always, so that it might go well with them and with their children forever!"
"I will raise up for them a prophet like you from among their own people; I will put my words in the mouth of the prophet, who shall speak to them everything that I command. Anyone who does not heed my words, that the prophet shall speak in my name, I myself will hold accountable. But any prophet who speaks in the name of other gods, or who presumes to speak in my name a word that I have not commanded the prophet to speak – that prophet shall die. You may say to yourself, 'How can we recognize a word that the Lord has not spoken?' If a prophet speaks in the name of the Lord but the thing does not take place or prove true, it is a word that the Lord has not spoken. The prophet has spoken it presumptuously; do not be frightened by it."
"Go say to them, 'Return to your tents.' But you, stand here by me, and I will tell you all the commandments, the statutes and the ordinances, that you shall teach them, so that they may do them in the land that I am giving them to possess."

smoothly without the verse, even better than MT, as the introductory formula "The Lord said to Moses" in v. 9 sounds awkward inside a divine speech that starts in v. 7 by "And the Lord spoke to Moses," and ends in v. 10. This case shows that the process of expansion was not restricted to non-MT texts only. As it is also found in MT, it seems to be an earlier phenomenon than the pre-Samaritan texts.

The cases treated above are found in pre-Samaritan texts and in SP (except SP-Exod 6:9a), and thus represent a shared tradition. This is different for the Samaritan tenth commandment in SP-Exod 20:17a (and also in SP-Deut 5:18a): it is unique to SP. Accordingly, it is a specific Samaritan phenomenon. It was created by the same literary technique as the one seen in 4Q22, 4Q17, 4Q158, 4Q175, and the pre-Samaritan layer of SP: creating a new theological position by quoting and inserting Pentateuchal text into another context. At the same time, it is a "quotation within a quotation," just like the prophecy for a new prophet in SP-Exod 20:21a. The commandment is composed of parts of Deut 27:2b–7, enclosed in – or framed by – parts of Deut 11:29–30.

The commandment starts with Deut 11:29a. This verse is similar to Deut 27:2a and this explains both the association of these two texts and why Deut 27:2a is not quoted in addition to Deut 11:29a. The commandment quotes Deut 27:4, but with "Gerizim" as the place for the altar, against MT's "Ebal." The Greek text of the Giessen papyrus 19 (LXX[884]) and the Old Latin Lyon manuscript both witness to "Gerizim," and a Hebrew fragment with Deut 27:4–7 presents *Hargerizim*, "Mount Gerizim" (→ 2.2.1.3.3). This fragment has been published by J.H. Charlesworth.[8] If genuine, the Samaritan reading would have here an ancient Hebrew counterpart (for discussion, see → 2.2.4.5). The text of the commandment is presented here with its probable source texts, in the MT version.

2.2.4.2.3 Manuscripts, Editions, and Translations

According to the comprehensive survey presented by Crown in 2001, there are some 750 known Samaritan manuscripts of SP.[9] The most famous is *Sefer Abisha*, presented by the Samaritans to tourists as written by Abishua, the great-grandson of Aaron (1 Chr 6:50), thirteen years after the conquest, but in fact it dates to the twelfth century C.E.

Von Gall's Edition[10] of SP is the most comprehensive, based on some eighty manuscripts and fragments. It is eclectic, prefers *scriptio defectiva*, follows the rules of MT Hebrew grammar, and prefers older to younger forms. Von Gall reconstructed the whole text with three apparatuses, but his principles are contested, and the use of the edition requires some effort if one wishes to reach the genuine Samaritan text. Tal, *Shechem* is a diplomatic editon, where ms no. 6 of the Shechem synagogue is printed in square characters, supplemented with other old manuscripts at the beginning and end, and in lacunae of ms no. 6. Tal–Florentin, *Samaritan Version* presents this text together with the MT version. The same system is used by Shoulson.[11] An English translation of SP compared to the NJPS translation of MT was published by Tsedaka and Sullivan in 2013.[12]

For the pre-Samaritan texts of Exodus, Skehan's article from 1955 on 4Q22 was the first announcement, and Sanderson's *Exodus Scroll* and her article in *RevQ* are fundamental for understanding this text. 4Q22 is published in *DJD* IX. 4Q17 is published by Cross in *DJD* XII; 4Q158 and 4Q175 were first published by Allegro in *DJD* V: with supplementary comments by Strugnell, *"Notes en marge."* The texts are also published in Ulrich, *BQS*.

2.2.4.2.4 Text-Critical Value

Generally speaking, SP-Exod is a witness to the literary development of the Hebrew Bible, and thus reflects efforts to update the language, facil-

---

[8] J.H. Charlesworth, "What is a Variant? Announcing a New Dead Sea Scrolls Fragment of Deuteronomy," *Maarav* 16 (2009): 201–12, 273–74.

[9] Crown, *Samaritan Scribes and Manuscripts*.
[10] Von Gall, *Der hebräische Pentateuch der Samaritaner*.
[11] Shoulson, *The Torah*.
[12] Tsedaka and Sullivan, *The Israelite Samaritan Version of the Torah*.

2.2.4 SP AND ANCIENT TEXTS CLOSE TO SP

SP-Exod 20:17a	MT-Deut 11:29a; 27:2b–7; 11:30
והיה כי יביאך יהוה אלהיך אל ארץ הכנעני אשר אתה בא שמה לרשתה והקמת לך אבנים גדלות ושדת אתם בשיד וכתבת על האבנים את כל דברי התורה הזאת והיה בעברכם את הירדן תקימו את האבנים האלה אשר אנכי מצוה אתכם היום בהר גריזים ובנית שם מזבח ליהוה אלהיך מזבח אבנים לא תניף עליהם ברזל אבנים שלמות תבנה את מזבח יהוה אלהיך והעלית עליו עלות ליהוה אלהיך וזבחת שלמים ואכלת שם ושמחת לפני יהוה אלהיך ההר ההוא בעבר הירדן אחרי דרך מבוא השמש בארץ הכנעני הישב בערבה מול הגלגל אצל אלון מורא מול שכם:	וְהָיָה כִּי יְבִיאֲךָ יְהוָה אֱלֹהֶיךָ אֶל־הָאָרֶץ אֲשֶׁר־אַתָּה בָא־שָׁמָּה לְרִשְׁתָּהּ וַהֲקֵמֹתָ לְךָ אֲבָנִים גְּדֹלוֹת וְשַׂדְתָּ אֹתָם בַּשִּׂיד: וְכָתַבְתָּ עֲלֵיהֶן אֶת־כָּל־דִּבְרֵי הַתּוֹרָה הַזֹּאת בְּעָבְרֶךָ לְמַעַן אֲשֶׁר תָּבֹא אֶל־הָאָרֶץ אֲשֶׁר־יְהוָה אֱלֹהֶיךָ נֹתֵן לְךָ אֶרֶץ זָבַת חָלָב וּדְבַשׁ כַּאֲשֶׁר דִּבֶּר יְהוָה אֱלֹהֵי־אֲבֹתֶיךָ לָךְ: וְהָיָה בְּעָבְרְכֶם אֶת־הַיַּרְדֵּן תָּקִימוּ אֶת־הָאֲבָנִים הָאֵלֶּה אֲשֶׁר אָנֹכִי מְצַוֶּה אֶתְכֶם הַיּוֹם בְּהַר עֵיבָל וְשַׂדְתָּ אוֹתָם בַּשִּׂיד: וּבָנִיתָ שָּׁם מִזְבֵּחַ לַיהוָה אֱלֹהֶיךָ מִזְבַּח אֲבָנִים לֹא־תָנִיף עֲלֵיהֶם בַּרְזֶל: אֲבָנִים שְׁלֵמוֹת תִּבְנֶה אֶת־מִזְבַּח יְהוָה אֱלֹהֶיךָ וְהַעֲלִיתָ עָלָיו עוֹלֹת לַיהוָה אֱלֹהֶיךָ: וְזָבַחְתָּ שְׁלָמִים וְאָכַלְתָּ שָּׁם וְשָׂמַחְתָּ לִפְנֵי יְהוָה אֱלֹהֶיךָ: הֲלֹא־הֵמָּה בְּעֵבֶר הַיַּרְדֵּן אַחֲרֵי דֶּרֶךְ מְבוֹא הַשֶּׁמֶשׁ בְּאֶרֶץ הַכְּנַעֲנִי הַיֹּשֵׁב בָּעֲרָבָה מוּל הַגִּלְגָּל אֵצֶל אֵלוֹנֵי מֹרֶה:
When the Lord your God has brought you into the land of the Canaanites that you are entering to occupy, you shall set up large stones and cover them with plaster. You shall write on the stones all the words of this law. So when you have crossed over the Jordan, you shall set up these stones, about which I am commanding you today, on Mount Gerizim. And you shall build an altar there to the Lord your God, an altar of stones on which you have not used an iron tool. You must build the altar of the Lord your God of unhewn stones. Then offer up burnt offerings on it to the Lord your God, make sacrifices of well-being, and eat them there, rejoicing before the Lord your God. This mountain is beyond the Jordan, some distance to the west, in the land of the Canaanites who live in the Arabah, opposite Gilgal, beside the oak of Moreh, opposite Shekhem.	When the Lord your God has brought you into the land that you are entering to occupy, you shall set up large stones and cover them with plaster. You shall write on them all the words of this law when you have crossed over, to enter the land that the Lord your God is giving you, a land flowing with milk and honey, as the Lord, the God of your ancestors, promised you. So when you have crossed over the Jordan, you shall set up these stones, about which I am commanding you today, on Mount Ebal, and you shall cover them with plaster. And you shall build an altar there to the Lord your God, an altar of stones on which you have not used an iron tool. You must build the altar of the Lord your God of unhewn stones. Then offer up burnt offerings on it to the Lord your God, make sacrifices of well-being, and eat them there, rejoicing before the Lord your God. As you know, they are beyond the Jordan, some distance to the west, in the land of the Canaanites who live in the Arabah, opposite Gilgal, beside the oak of Moreh.

itatereading and understanding, and remove obstacles to understanding Scripture. More specifically, it witnesses to early Samaritan theology in its commandment to build an altar on Mount Gerizim and the changes necessitated by this theologoumenon. It constitutes an early example of exegesis.

The Samaritans chose the text type that had a clear pro-Moses tendency,[13] and after the turn of the era they supplied this text with the tenth commandment and made other changes that were related to the altar on Mount Gerizim. In later Samaritan literature, the status of Moses as prophet

---
[13] Kartveit, *The Origin of the Samaritans*, 240–49.

ויהי בדרך במלון ויפגשהו יהוה ויבקש המיתו: ותקח צפורה צר ותכרת את ערלת בנה ותגע לרגליו ותאמר כי חתן דמים אתה לי: וירף ממנה אז אמרה חתן דמים למלות	וַיְהִ֣י בַדֶּ֔רֶךְ בַּמָּל֑וֹן וַֽיִּפְגְּשֵׁ֣הוּ יְהוָ֔ה וַיְבַקֵּ֖שׁ הֲמִיתֽוֹ׃ וַתִּקַּ֨ח צִפֹּרָ֜ה צֹ֗ר וַתִּכְרֹת֙ אֶת־עָרְלַ֣ת בְּנָ֔הּ וַתַּגַּ֖ע לְרַגְלָ֑יו וַתֹּ֕אמֶר כִּ֧י חֲתַן־דָּמִ֛ים אַתָּ֖ה לִֽי׃ וַיִּ֖רֶף מִמֶּ֑נּוּ אָ֚ז אָֽמְרָ֔ה חֲתַ֥ן דָּמִ֖ים לַמּוּלֹֽת׃
And it came about at the inn on the way that Shemaa met him and sought to stun him (pronounced *aamitoo*). And Seebbooraa took a flint and she circumcised her blocked heart (*binnah*), and she brought herself to his feet. And she said, You are indeed a bridegroom of blood to me. And he let her (SP: ממנה) go. Then she said, A bridegroom of blood, to be circumcised.[14]	On the way, at a place where they spent the night, the Lord met him and tried to kill him. But Zipporah took a flint and cut off her son's foreskin, and touched Moses' feet with it, and said, "Truly you are a bridegroom of blood to me!" So he let him alone. It was then she said, "A bridegroom of blood by circumcision." (NRSV)

and sole mediator was in focus. SP-Exod shows how the biblical text grew through changes and additions. It also bears witness to the reverence for the biblical text: the changes were made by the use of existing text.

According to Sanderson, there are no variants where SP-Exod uniquely preserves a preferable reading.[15] There are, however, two preferable readings preserved by 4Q22 and SP alone, Exod 16:34: את משה "Moses," MT: אֶל־מֹשֶׁה "for Moses"; and 18:23: אל מקומו "to their place," MT: עַל־מְקֹמוֹ "above their place."[16] In other instances, SP presents preferable readings also found in MT and/or LXX.

For a full evaluation of SP-Exod, one should take into account the Samaritan reading tradition. This has been presented by Ben-Hayyim in *LOT III,1 in the form of a phonetic transcription of the reading of SP with extensive footnotes, where pp. 37–55 present relevant text from Exodus 15; 25–29. An edition with vowels was produced by Tsedaka in 2000.[17] Even though the reading of the Torah reflects Samaritan theology and ethics from the centuries subsequent to its creation, it "makes possible a better knowledge of the last stage of living Hebrew in Palestine."[18] According to Ben-Hayyim and Tal, SP reflects a later stage of Hebrew than MT, but still a Second Temple stage.[19]

An example of Samaritan exegesis is SP-Exod 4:24–26. SP here has a different consonantal text only in one place, but two instances where pronunciation reveals a different understanding.

2.2.4.2.5 Value for Literary Criticism

The pre-Samaritan texts show that this text type was still used in Palestine at a time when the Samaritans had become a separate community. The excavations on Mount Gerizim and the inscriptions found there prove that there was a holy site on the mountain around 200 B.C.E., and probably one to two-and-a-half centuries before that period.[20] The Samaritans who worshiped there chose the text type that had an expansionist character, carrying on the tradition that is witnessed to by

---

[14] Translation quoted from Tsedaka and Sullivan, *The Israelite Samaritan Version of the Torah*, 132 f.
[15] Sanderson, *Exodus Scroll*, 85.
[16] Sanderson, *Exodus Scroll*, 58–59.
[17] Tsedaka, *Ha-Torah Ha-Qedosha*.

[18] A. Tal, "Samaritan Literature," in *The Samaritans* (ed. A.D. Crown; Tubingen: Mohr, 1989), 413–67 (443) *apud* Schorch, *Vokale*, 31 n. 86.
[19] Z. Ben-Hayyim and A. Tal, *A Grammar of Samaritan Hebrew: Based on the Recitation of the Law in Comparison with the Tiberian and Other Jewish Traditions* (Jerusalem: Magnes Press, 2000), 4.
[20] M. Kartveit, "Samaritan Self-Consciousness in the First Half of the Second Century B.C.E. in Light of the Inscriptions from Mount Gerizim and Delos," *JSJ* 45 (2014): 1–22.

pre-Samaritan texts starting from the middle of the third century B.C.E.

After the turn of the eras, the Samaritans supplied this text with the tenth commandment and made other changes that were related to the altar on Mount Gerizim. The Samaritan tenth commandment is not found in any of the pre-Samaritan manuscripts. 4Q22 is deemed not to have had sufficient room for this insertion, and it is assumed that this commandment belongs to a stage of development later than that witnessed to by the Dead Sea Scrolls.[21] This commandment was created in the same manner as the major additions in the pre-Samaritan texts, in particular the promise of a prophet like Moses. In a similar vein, the altar law in Exod 20:21 was modified. Instead of MT's בְּכָל־הַמָּקוֹם אֲשֶׁר אַזְכִּיר אֶת־שְׁמִי "in every place where I cause my name to be remembered," SP reads במקום אשר אזכרתי את שמי "in the place where I have mentioned my name," creating a hybrid between the perfect and imperfect forms of the verb.

Tigay has shown the importance of SP for literary criticism in the sense of source criticism.[22]

Allegro, J., "158. Biblical Paraphrase: Genesis, Exodus," *DJD V: 1–5.
Allegro, J., "175. Testimonia," *DJD V: 57–60.
Cross, F.M., "4QExod-Lev^f," *DJD XII: 133–44.
Crown, A.D., Samaritan Scribes and Manuscripts (TSAJ 80; Tübingen: Mohr Siebeck, 2001).
von Gall, A., Der hebräische Pentateuch der Samaritaner (Gießen: Töpelmann, 1914–1918).
Kartveit, M., The Origin of the Samaritans (VTSup 128; Leiden: Brill, 2009).
Sanderson, *Exodus Scroll.
Sanderson, J.E., "The Contributions of 4QPaleoExodus^m to Textual Criticism," RevQ 13 (1988): 547–60.
Sanderson, J.E., "4QpaleoExodus^m," *DJD IX: 53–113.
Shoulson, M., The Torah: Jewish and Samaritan Versions Compared: A Side-by-Side Comparison of the Two Versions with the Differences Highlighted (n.p: Evertype, 2008).

Skehan, P.W., "Exodus in the Samaritan Recension from Qumran," JBL 74 (1955): 182–87.
Strugnell, *"Notes en marge."
Tal, *Shekhem.
Tal–Florentin, *Samaritan Version.
Tigay, J. (ed.), Empirical Models for Biblical Criticism (Philadelphia: University of Pennsylvania Press, 1985).
Tsedaka, B. and S.J. Sullivan, The Israelite Samaritan Version of the Torah: First English Translation Compared with the Masoretic Version (Grand Rapids: Eerdmans, 2013).
Tsedaka, I., Ha-Torah Ha-Qedosha (Holon: A.B. Institute of Samaritan Studies, 1998/2000).
Ulrich, *BQS.

Magnar Kartveit

2.2.4.3 Leviticus
2.2.4.3.1 Nature of the Text

The manuscripts from Qumran (→ 2.2.1.3) have shown that the text of SP has as its base a non-sectarian version circulating in the wider circles of Palestine during the late Second Temple period. This version is often called pre-Samaritan or proto-Samaritan,[1] and its principal characteristic is the insertion of large additions into the earlier text as seen in MT.[2] Although several books of SP underwent editing of this type before the distinctly Samaritan features were added to the text, the textual history of SP-Lev appears somewhat different. All of the known text forms of Leviticus (the Qumran manuscripts, MasLev^{a,b}, MT, SP, and LXX), while containing numerous minor variants, attest a relatively uniform text, displaying only a single textual edition.

---

[21] Sanderson, *Exodus Scroll*; Sanderson, "4Qpaleo-Exodus^m," 68–70.

[22] Tigay, Empirical Models, esp. 68–95.

---

[1] The following manuscripts are commonly considered as belonging to the "pre-Samaritan" group: 4QExod-Lev^f (4Q17); 4QpaleoExod^m (4Q22); 4QLev^d (4Q26); 4QNum^b (4Q27); 4QRP^a (4Q158); 4QRP^b (4Q364); 4QRP^c (4Q365). Sometimes 4QRP^d (4Q366) and 4QRP^e (4Q367) are included as well. 4QDeut^n, too, contains changes similar to those of the pre-SP group, but is not a manuscript of the book of Deuteronomy, but rather excerpts from that book. For editions, see *DJD XII, XIII: and XIV.

[2] A convenient list of these major insertions can be found in Kartveit, Origin, 310–12.

In order to understand the textual character of SP-Lev and its differences from other books, it is helpful to contrast the variants occurring in SP-Lev with the broader spectrum of textual modifications attested in SP: sectarian changes, large editorial insertions, and minor textual variants.

Sectarian changes are secondary readings that are made intentionally to favor one specific group in clear opposition to another, and that are made repeatedly when the opportunity presents itself. Examples of sectarian changes are Mount Gerizim vs. Mount Ebal in Deut 27:4 (as opposed to Deut 11:29; 27:12–13, which are common readings) and other references to Mount Gerizim as the place that God "has chosen" as opposed to MT's reading of the place God "will choose." None of these types of sectarian changes, typical in other books of SP, is attested in Leviticus.

Large editorial insertions, such as those in 4QpaleoExod[m] and 4QNum[b], either narrate explicitly the performance of the Lord's commands (whereas the earlier edition had implicitly assumed that Moses had done what the Lord had commanded) or repeat details mentioned in Deuteronomy but not included in the Exodus or Numbers narrative. These additions do not alter the meaning of the earlier text but rather supplement it, and they do not show any sectarian motivation. Essentially, these changes are insertions of biblical text into biblical text, often described as editorial or harmonizing.[3] It should be noted that harmonizing features were by no means limited to pre-Samaritan texts but occurred relatively often in manuscripts stemming from this period.[4] Interestingly, however, the manuscripts of Leviticus give no evidence of this type of large-scale editing either in the pre-Samaritan or other text groups.[5]

Minor textual variants are small linguistic modifications, clarifying glosses (often borrowed from passages nearby), synonymous words, errors and such, which are frequent in all books of SP, including Leviticus.[6] An example of this type of variant can be seen in Lev 22:31: אתם "them" 4QLev[b] SP OG] + אֲנִי יְהוָה "I am the Lord" MT LXX[mss]. Seldom can one detect systematic patterns of this type of scribal activity in SP-Lev, but grammatical changes regarding verb-number show an interesting tendency in sections describing sacrifices. For example, in Leviticus 1 and 3, SP, often in agreement with LXX-Lev, tends to maintain in verbs the number of the last subject mentioned, whether singular (the priest) or plural (the sons of Aaron), whereas MT-Lev fluctuates. See, e.g., Lev 3:3, והקריב "and he shall offer" 4QLev[e] MT SP] καὶ προσάξουσιν "and they will offer" LXX. These smaller variants could also be called harmonizing, but this type of harmonizing happens at the linguistic rather than content level. Though SP-Lev and LXX-Lev agree frequently in these variants, there is also a sufficient number of disagreements to preclude direct affiliation between the two.

The relative editorial restraint displayed by scribes in regard to Leviticus calls for an explanation. After all, the Pentateuchal legal sections are replete with repetitions and, as such, one would expect them to provide prime material for large-scale harmonization. Two explanations have been offered. On the one hand, the sanctity of legal material may have prevented major editorial interven-

---

[3] The term "harmonizing" is used, e.g., by Eshel and Eshel, "Dating," 215–40 (217–21), and Anderson and Giles, *The Samaritan Pentateuch*, 60–69. E. Tov remarks in his recent work, however, that "these changes should be considered editorial rather than harmonizing" and prefers to reserve the term "harmonizing" for smaller changes in the text ("small harmonizing alterations"); see his *TCHB*, 80, 82–83. But cf. his earlier article ("The Nature and Background of Harmonizations in Biblical Manuscripts," *JSOT* 31 (1985): 3–29 [7]) where he, too, considers the command and fulfillment pattern of 4QpaleoExod[m] as a type of harmonization. For a discussion of the terms editorial and harmonizing, see also → 1.2.2.3.

[4] The point has been made, e.g., by Tov, "Harmonizations,"

3, and M. Segal, "4QReworked Pentateuch or 4QPentateuch?" 392.

[5] Eshel and Eshel state in "Dating," 228: "... we now have fifteen Second Temple period texts with harmonistic editing, similar in character to the harmonistic editing in SP," but "[n]o evidence of Second Temple period text types of the Book of Leviticus with harmonistic editing have yet been found."

[6] For discussions pertaining to classification, see, e.g., Ben-Hayyim, *Grammar*; Eshel and Eshel, "Dating," 216–18; Tov, "Review," 385–91; Anderson and Giles, *The Samaritan Pentateuch*, 71–79.

tion.[7] On the other hand, and perhaps more likely, the dissimilar narrative frames of Pentateuchal legal codes may have led the scribes to view their individual laws as not directly equivalent or conflicting and thus not in need of editorial harmonization.[8] Contrary to the manuscripts of 4QRP (4Q364–367; → 2.2.1.7), for example, the editors of the pre-Samaritan text show little concern for topical rearrangements. In this respect, its editorial reworking is more conservative than that of 4QRP. In minor-level variants, however, 4QRP is very similar to SP and shows the same concerns.[9]

2.2.4.3.2 Original Form, Date, and Milieu

The original form of SP would have been five separate scrolls, one for each of the five books. The text was very close to the "pre-Samaritan" scrolls found at Qumran – 4QpaleoExod^m, 4QExod-Lev^f, and 4QNum^b – but with a thin layer of sectarian emphasis focusing on Mount Gerizim as the place that God had chosen for the dwelling of the divine name. All the forms of the texts were circulating generally in Palestine, although SP was probably soon restricted to northern regions. The textual form of Leviticus, however, would show little variance in manuscripts, whether they were copied in the North or in the South.

As Cross noted, the Qumran scrolls have provided crucial evidence concerning the textual emergence of SP within the historical development of the Hebrew Pentateuch.[10] The earliest preserved Pentateuchal text editions, witnessed generally in MT, were revised and expanded to produce the editions seen in 4QpaleoExod^m, 4QExod-Lev^f, and 4QNum^b, which were in turn expanded in the 4QRP manuscripts. The text type of 4QpaleoExod^m, 4QExod-Lev^f, and 4QNum^b pre-dates the text type of SP,[11] but that of 4QRP post-dates that of SP. Therefore, typologically, SP was produced between the pre-Samaritan and 4QRP traditions. All we have, however, are *copies* of these new editions, not the original editions themselves, so the actual historical emergence of SP must be deduced. Since 4QExod-Lev^f "dates to the mid-third century BCE,"[12] whereas the 4QPentateuch manuscripts (which move beyond the edition seen in SP) date to the early first century B.C.E., the first SP edition could have been as early as the late third century B.C.E. or any time in the ensuing couple of centuries, but presumably there was not a lengthy time between the split of the Samaritans from the Judeans (in the late second century) and the production of the original SP.[13]

The oldest extant Leviticus manuscript representing the pre-Samaritan text group is 4QExod-Lev^f (→ 2.2.1.7.9), dated to ca. 250 B.C.E. Most of the preserved text in the scroll, however, is from Exodus; the small amount of text from Leviticus is from Lev 1:13–15 (col. III, frg. 3), Lev 1:17–2:1 (col. III, frg. 4), and possibly from Lev 2:8 (frg. 5). Only thirteen words in total from the text of Leviticus are preserved in these fragments, and most of them only partially. A small variant that agrees with SP is preserved in Lev 2:1:

לבנה מנחה [היא] "incense, it is a grain offering" 4QExod-Lev^f SP LXX^{BAL} (λίβανον θυσία ἐστίν "incense, it is an offering")] לבנה "incense" MT LXX^O.

The text in SP and 4QExod-Lev^f, which agrees with the Old Greek against MT, is secondary and

---

[7] M.J. Bernstein, "What Has Happened to the Laws? The Treatment of Legal Material," *DSD* 15 (2008): 24–49 (47).

[8] Zahn, *Rethinking Rewritten Scripture*, 175 n. 74: "The clearest explanation for SP's relative disengagement with legal texts is that they do not directly purport to be equivalent. The priestly legislation in Leviticus and Numbers has as its narrative setting God's speech to Moses from the tent of meeting (Lev 1:1; Num 1:1). The Covenant Code (Exodus 21–23), on the other hand, is situated at Mt. Sinai, while Deuteronomy's law code is spoken by Moses on the plains of Moab. Though it is explicitly noted that Moses decrees the laws in accordance with God's instructions (Deut 1:3; 6:1), there is no identification of the law code itself with God's earlier revelation on Sinai. Thus, there is no sense that any of the law codes is, in narrative sense, a repetition of any other, and therefore no need to make them conform to one another."

[9] Bernstein, "What has Happened," 32–33; Zahn, *Rethinking Rewritten Scripture*, 173–75.

[10] Cross, *DJD* XII: 136.

[11] Even though the manuscript 4QNum^b may post-date the SP, the text type it transmits pre-dates it.

[12] Cross, *DJD* XII: 134.

[13] See also Eshel and Eshel, "Dating," 215–40.

anticipates לבנה מחנה היא "incense, it is a grain offering" in Lev 2:15, as noted by Cross.[14]

Another Qumran manuscript of Leviticus showing agreement with SP is 4QLev^d (→ 2.2.1.6.2), which has preserved portions of Lev 14:27–29, 33–36; 15:20–24; and 17:2–11. The text of 4QLev^d is barely legible, however, and no dating has been provided for the script. An interesting variant is preserved in Lev 17:4:

[(הביאו] לעשות אתו עלה [אֹוֹ שלמים ליהוה לרצֹוֹנְבֹּם לֹ]ריח ניחח וישחטהו בחוץ ואל פתח מו[עֵד לוא יביאנו (הביאו SP)

"[(he has brought it) so as to sacrifice it as a burnt offering] or an offering of well-being to the Lord to be acceptable as [a pleasing odor, and has slaughtered it outside and] does not bring it [to the door of the tent of me]eting" 4QLev^d SP LXX] > 11QpaleoLev^a MT.

Again, the text in 4QLev^d and SP agrees with the Old Greek against MT. The 11QpaleoLev^a MT reading is probably a simple parablepsis between הביאו "he has brought it" and הביאו "he has brought it," although the reading of 4QLev^d, SP, and LXX could be an addition to make the law clearer.[15]

2.2.4.3.3 Editions and Tools

The earliest printed editions of SP-Lev are based on a complete fourteenth century copy (Codex B) of SP obtained by Pietro della Valle in 1616. An edited version of this manuscript is included in Le Jay's Paris Polyglot (1645)[16] and in Walton's London Polyglot (1657),[17] and it also forms the basis for Blayney's edition of SP published separately (1790).[18] The critical text of von Gall's edition (1915)[19] is based mostly on Codex B as well, although his edition includes readings from other manuscripts with the goal of reconstructing the original text. In doing so, the edition often corrects the text in the direction of MT. The Sadaqa edition of SP-Lev (1964) is based on two Nablus (Shechem) synagogue manuscripts dated to 1199 and 1210,[20] and the Samaritan text and MT are given in parallel columns. The edition by Tal (1994)[21] presents a diplomatic text of Shechem synagogue ms 6, dated to 1204. An improved edition of this same manuscript was published by Tal and Florentin (2010)[22] with MT on facing pages and significant variants marked. An English translation of SP, based largely on the same manuscripts as those in the Sadaqa Hebrew edition, was published by Tsedaka and Sharon Sullivan in 2013.[23] The two Qumran manuscripts of Leviticus associated with the Samaritan tradition, 4QExod-Lev^f and 4QLev^d, as well as 4QRP, are published in *DJD XII and XIII. A convenient discussion of these and other available editions of SP is available in the 2012 monograph by Anderson and Giles.[24]

2.2.4.3.4 Literary and Exegetical Value

It appears that by the second half of the Second Temple period there was only one principal edition of Leviticus in circulation.[25] It is likely that there were earlier forms of the book, and it is possible that parallel editions existed during this period, but no earlier or contemporary variant edition has been preserved. Thus, most of the textual variants in the preserved manuscripts of Leviticus are minor, grammatical, or otherwise rather pre-

---

[14] Cross, *DJD XII: 144.

[15] J. Milgrom, *Leviticus 17–22* (AB 3A; New York: Doubleday, 2000), 1456; Metso, "Evidence," 69.

[16] Le Jay, *Biblia*.

[17] Walton, *Polyglotta*.

[18] Blayney, *Pentateuchus hebreao-samaritanus*.

[19] Von Gall, *Der hebräische Pentateuch der Samaritaner*, Vol. 3.

[20] A. and R. Sadaqa, *Jewish and Samaritan Version of the Pentateuch*. Although parts of Sadaqa's SP edition also use readings from the Abisha scroll, no text from Leviticus is preserved in the scroll. The text included in the Abisha scroll comprises Numbers 35–Deuteronomy 34. The Abisha scroll is highly esteemed by the Samaritan community, but scholars have determined it was "composed of fragments from several scrolls written between the twelfth and fourteenth century C.E." (Eshel and Eshel, "Dating," 215).

[21] Tal, *Shekhem*.

[22] Tal–Florentin, *Samaritan Version*.

[23] Tsedaka and Sullivan, *The Israelite Samaritan Version of the Torah*.

[24] Anderson and Giles, *The Samaritan Pentateuch*.

[25] See K.A. Mathews, "The Leviticus Scrolls (11QPaleoLev) and the Text of the Hebrew Bible," *CBQ* 48 (1986): 171–207; E. Ulrich, "4QLev-Num^a," "4QLev^b," in *DJD XII: 153–87; E. Tov, "4QLev^c," "4QLev^d," "4QLev^e," "4QLev^g," in *DJD XII: 189–204; Eshel, "Book of Leviticus," 488–93.

dictable. Many of the variants in SP-Lev agree with those long since attested in LXX-Lev or MT-Lev.[26] Remarkably, however, the Qumran manuscripts (11QpaleoLev[a] in particular) also offer a number of independent readings that were unknown from other textual witnesses.

Though there are many individual variants in SP-Lev that agree occasionally with a Qumran scroll, MT, or LXX, most are random, and only rarely does a manuscript align consistently with one tradition or another. An exception perhaps is 4QExod-Lev[f] (→ 2.2.1.7.9); though having some unique readings, it regularly aligns with the pre-Samaritan tradition.[27] It should be stressed, however, that the great majority of its text is from Exodus, with very little text from Leviticus. Thus, there is little significance for SP-Lev.

In the case of Leviticus, it is difficult to consider the textual forms of MT, SP, and LXX as clearly differentiated "standards" in the Second Temple period based on which other textual forms are to be judged. They are simply varying copies of one relatively uniform tradition, and thus SP-Lev has limited relevance for literary or exegetical analysis.

Anderson, R.T. and T. Giles, *The Samaritan Pentateuch: An Introduction to Its Origin, History, and Significance for Biblical Studies* (SBLRBS 72; Atlanta: SBL, 2012).

Ben-Hayyim, Z., *The Literary and Oral Tradition of Hebrew and Aramaic among the Samaritans*, vol. 4 (Jerusalem: Hebrew University Press, 1977).

Ben-Hayyim, Z., *A Grammar of Samaritan Hebrew* (Jerusalem: Magnes Press, 2000).

Bernstein, M.J., "What Has Happened to the Laws? The Treatment of Legal Material," *DSD* 15 (2008): 24–49.

Blayney, B., *Pentateuchus hebreao-samaritanus, charactere hebraeo-chaldaico* (Oxford: Clarendon, 1790).

*DJD XII.

*DJD XIII.

*DJD XIV.

Eshel, E., "Book of Leviticus," *EDSS 1:488–93.

---

[26] A convenient overview of how each of the preserved manuscripts of Leviticus from Qumran and Masada relate to MT, SP, and LXX is available in P. Flint's article "The Book of Leviticus," 323–36.

[27] For detailed discussion of the variants and affiliation of 4QExod-Lev[f], see Cross, *DJD XII: 136.

Eshel, E. and H. Eshel, "Dating the Samaritan Pentateuch Compilation in Light of the Qumran Biblical Scrolls," in *Emanuel: Studies in Hebew Bible, Septuagint, and Dead Sea Scrolls in Honor of Emanuel Tov* (eds. S.M. Paul et al.; VTSup 94; Leiden: Brill, 2003), 215–40.

Flint, P.W., "The Book of Leviticus in the Dead Sea Scrolls," in *The Book of Leviticus: Composition and Reception* (eds. R. Rendtdorff and R. Kugler; VTSup 93; Leiden: Brill, 2003), 323–36.

von Gall, A., *Der hebräische Pentateuch der Samaritaner*, Vols. 1–5 (Giessen: Töpelmann, 1914–1918; repr. Berlin: De Gruyter, 2011).

Kartveit, M., *The Origin of the Samaritans* (VTSup 128; Leiden: Brill, 2009).

Mathews, K.A., "The Leviticus Scrolls (11QPaleoLev) and the Text of the Hebrew Bible," *CBQ* 48 (1986): 171–207.

Metso, S., "Evidence from the Qumran Scrolls for the Scribal Transmission of Leviticus," in *Editing the Bible: Assessing the Task Past and Present* (eds. J.S. Kloppenborg and J.H. Newman; Atlanta: SBL, 2012), 67–80.

Metso, S., "The Character of Leviticus Traditions at Qumran," in *In the Footsteps of Sherlock Holmes: Studies in the Biblical Text in Honour of Anneli Aejmelaeus* (eds. K. de Troyer, T.M. Law, and M. Liljeström; CBET 72; Leuven: Peeters, 2014), 645–57.

Sadaqa, A. and R., *Jewish and Samaritan Version of the Pentateuch with Particular Stress on the Differences between Both Texts: Leviticus* (Jerusalem: Rubin Mass, 1964).

Segal, M., "4QReworked Pentateuch or 4QPentateuch?" in Schiffman, Tov, and VanderKam, *Fifty Years*, 391–99.

Segal, M., "Text of the Hebrew Bible in Light of the Dead Sea Scrolls," *Materia Giudaica* 12 (2007): 5–20.

Tal, *Shekhem.

Tal–Florentin, *Samaritan Version.

Tov, E., "The Nature and Background of Harmonizations in Biblical Manuscripts," *JSOT* 31 (1985): 3–29.

Tov, E., "Rewritten Bible Compositions and Biblical Manuscripts: With Special Attention to the Samaritan Pentateuch," *DSD* 5 (1998): 334–54.

Tov, E., "Review of A. Tal and M. Florentin, *The Pentateuch: The Samaritan and Masoretic Version*," *DSD* 18 (2011): 385–91.

Tov, *TCHB.

Tsedaka, B. and S. Sullivan, *The Israelite Samaritan Version of the Torah: First English Translation Compared with the Masoretic Version* (Grand Rapids: Eerdmans, 2013).

Zahn, M.M., *Rethinking Rewritten Scripture: Composition and Exegesis in the 4QReworked Pentateuch Manuscripts* (STDJ 95; Leiden: Brill, 2011).

Sarianna Metso

2.2.4.4 Numbers
2.2.4.4.1 Nature of the Text

The Samaritan Pentateuch (SP) and the Masoretic Text (MT) are valuable witnesses to the text of the book of Numbers, two separate streams transmitted by communities antagonistic to each other. Though they are two streams, at some time in the past they both must have derived from the same source. The question has been: When did the two streams begin to flow separately? One Dead Sea scroll in particular, dating from around 30 B.C.E., has helped to clarify when the proto-SP textual tradition of Numbers may have begun to be transmitted separately from the proto-Masoretic textual tradition. 4QNumbers[b] (4Q27; → 2.2.1.3.2) shares major expansions of the text associated with SP, but 4QNum[b] has a slightly later form, suggesting that the proto-SP textual tradition may have been transmitted separately from proto-MT since the first century B.C.E.

2.2.4.4.2 Editions and Tools

SP-Num became available to the Western world after 1616 when Pietro della Valle bought a manuscript that was used as the basis of polyglot editions in Paris (1645)[1] and London (1657),[2] and for von Gall's later critical edition (1916).[3] For a detailed discussion of the various editions of SP, see the treatment by Anderson and Giles in their *The Samaritan Pentateuch*. The following comments compare the text of Numbers as it is found in von Gall's text with that found in Tal, **Shekhem*.

Von Gall's text is an eclectic text with variants from many manuscripts listed in the notes, while Tal's text is diplomatic, following the readings of one manuscript. The differences between von Gall and Tal in SP-Num run to 235 variant readings. Von Gall's principles for editing his eclectic text account for the majority of variants. In general, von Gall's principle of "following the rules of Hebrew grammar," as defined by MT, results in agreements with MT against Tal 169 times. In contrast, Tal agrees with MT against von Gall only 28 times. Specifically, von Gall's principle of preferring the *defectiva* form accounts for nearly all of the 135 variants from Tal having to do with *matres lectionis*.

Although one of von Gall's principles is to prefer the earlier grammatical form to the later, in particular always selecting the imperative form צוי "command" and never the form צוה "command," he actually has the imperative form צוה twice in Numbers, at 5:2 (= Tal), and at 28:2 (צוי Tal). In the four variants of grammatical number, Tal has plural forms three times and a singular form once. The remaining variants for the most part are morphological or phonological, including variations in guttural letters, of which some representative samples follow, in the form Tal/von Gall: פדויהם/פדוייהם "their redemption" Num 3:12; המרים/המארים "bitter" Num 5:18; היקרד/היקראך "whether it will happen to you" Num 11:23; חורי/אורי "Hori" Num 13:5; השתרר/אשתרר "to make oneself ruler" Num 16:13; יברא/יברי "he creates" Num 16:30; ותשת/ותשתה "and it drank" Num 20:11; אל/על "upon" Num 23:30. In summary, von Gall's eclectic text is more likely to conceal authentic Samaritan variants while Tal's diplomatic text is more likely to preserve them. Tal's superior text has now been further improved in his updated *The Pentateuch: The Samaritan Version and the Masoretic Version*. The updated text includes discussions of Samaritan textual characteristics and lists of differences, and presents SP and MT in parallel format on facing pages for convenience of comparison.

2.2.4.4.3 Text-Critical Character

SP-Num as a textual witness occupies the middle ground between a biblical Hebrew manuscript and a translated document. The consonantal text often looks like a biblical Hebrew manuscript, but the vocalized text reveals hidden differences in grammar. In the book of Numbers alone, SP has over 2,000 variants from MT (the precise number depends on

---

[1] Le Jay, **Biblia*.
[2] Walton, **Polyglotta*.
[3] Von Gall, *Der hebräische Pentateuch der Samaritaner*, Vol. 4.

how one counts individual variants), but the vast majority of them are more significant for the study of the development of language or of the external characteristics of textual transmission than for textual criticism. For instance, there are 621 variants of *matres lectionis*, 233 variants stemming from morphological or phonological developments, 117 variants concerning paragraph divisions, 41 variants of nominal or adjectival patterns, and 24 variants associated with *qere perpetuum*.

In addition to mistakes made to roots of words because of the weakening of gutturals and of the graphic similarity between some letters, SP-Num has some other variants of roots (e.g., ידו/דגלו "his standard/his part" Num 1:52; וקמץ/והרים "and he should take/and he should raise" Num 5:26; תימנה/צפונה "toward the south/toward the north" Num 10:6; ישיבו/יאשימו "they bring back/they are guilty" Num 18:9; נטה/נסור "we will turn/we will turn aside" Num 20:17; העליתנו/הוצאתנו "he brought us up/he brought us out" Num 21:5; בארץ/בערי "in the land/in the cities" Num 21:31; אלהים/יהוה "God/Yahweh" Num 22:22; הרגתי/הכיתי "I killed/I struck" Num 22:33; פעמים/רגלים "times" (both) Num 24:10; הרצח/המכה "the killer/the striker" Num 35:25).

The most significant of the variants in the book are the ten major longer readings found in SP-Num but not in MT-Num. One of these longer readings includes instructions on how to transport the sacred washbasin [italics mark the longer readings]:

> ... and they shall insert its poles. *And they shall take purple cloth and cover the washbasin and its stand, and they shall place them upon the covering of dugong skin, and they shall place it upon the carrying frame* (Num 4:14; cf. 4:8–12).

Another longer reading of SP fills out an account by creating and inserting a command corresponding to the record of its fulfillment:

> *And Moses said to Eleazar the priest, "Say to the men of the host who have gone to battle, 'This is the statute of the law that Yahweh commanded. Surely the gold and the silver and the bronze and the iron and the tin and the lead, whatever can pass through fire, you shall pass through fire and it will be clean. But also with the water for impurity it shall be purified. And whatever cannot pass through fire, you shall pass through water. And you shall wash your clothes on the seventh day and you will be clean, and afterward you may come into the camp.'"* And Eleazar the priest said to the men of the host who had gone to battle, "This is the statute of the law ..." (Num 31:21–24).

The other major longer readings of SP-Num are quotations of speeches from the first three chapters of Deuteronomy, inserted at the appropriate places in Numbers where the events described in the speeches are first recorded. For instance, before the start of the journey from Mt. Sinai (Num 10:11), SP-Num inserts the command from God to set out from the mountain found in Deut 1:6–8. Before God commands Moses to send spies to explore Canaan (Num 13:1–2), SP-Num inserts Moses' command that the Israelites go to possess Canaan, and the corresponding request from the Israelites that spies be sent to search out the best route of attack (Deut 1:20–23). Before the assembly complains with weeping (Num 14:1), SP-Num inserts the grumbling of the assembly when they heard the report of the spies and Moses' failed attempt to encourage them (Deut 1:27–33). Before Moses tells the Israelites not to attempt to conquer the Amalekites and Canaanites in the hill country (Num 14:41), SP-Num inserts Yahweh's command for Moses to make that speech (Deut 1:42). After the account of Moses' striking the rock at Meribah (Num 20:1–13), SP-Num inserts Moses' plea that he be allowed to enter the promised land and Yahweh's denial of that plea (Deut 3:24–28). A second portion of the insertion at this location adds Yahweh's command that the Israelites turn toward Edom but without provoking them to war (Deut 2:2–6), in preparation for the account of Moses sending peaceful messengers to the king of Edom in the following verse (Num 20:14). After the Israelites arrive at the border of Moab (Num 21:11), SP-Num inserts Yahweh's command that they not harass Moab (Deut 2:9), and, after they arrive at the border of Ammon (Num 21:13), SP-Num inserts Yahweh's command that they not harass the Ammonites (Deut 2:17–19). Injected into the account of Israel sending messengers to Sihon and his refusal to let them pass through his land

and fighting against them (Num 21:21–23), SP-Num inserts Yahweh's command that they attack Sihon and take his land (Deut 2:24–25), the content of the message that the messengers took to Sihon (Deut 2:27–29), and Yahweh's promise that he has begun to give Sihon and his land to them (Deut 2:31). And finally, in Deut 3:28, Yahweh tells Moses to "commission Joshua and to encourage and strengthen him," so after the account of Moses commissioning Joshua (Num 27:23), SP-Num inserts the encouraging speech that Moses made to Joshua as he faced the task of conquering Canaan (Deut 3:21–22).

The Dead Sea Scrolls have shown that these major longer readings of SP are not due to the Samaritans themselves, but to a harmonizing textual tradition in Palestine (→ 1.2.3.1). The major manuscript of Numbers found among the Dead Sea Scrolls, 4QNum[b] (→ 2.2.1.3.2), shares these longer readings with SP-Num wherever it is preserved, and a reconstruction of the missing portions of the manuscript either demands the longer readings or can accommodate them in the available space. Moreover, 4QNum[b] takes the process one step further by adding a significant longer reading to the last chapter, most likely a recap of the previous account of Zelophehad's daughters and the inheritance they were to receive (Num 27:2–11). A similar but not identical merging of these two accounts of Zelophehad's daughters is also seen in 4QRP[c] (4Q365; → 2.2.1.7.2).

While the majority of SP variant readings are secondary, some may preserve original readings lost in MT, particularly where Qumran manuscripts, SP, and LXX share a reading against MT (cf. "The oracle of Balaam the son of Beor, and the oracle of the man whose eye is open" Num 24:3, where the second phrase is omitted in 4QNum[b], SP, and LXX; "God *led him out* of Egypt" Num 24:8 [MT has מוֹצִיאוֹ "he led him out," SP has נחהו "he led him," 4QNum[b] is better reconstructed with the shorter word, LXX has ὡδήγησεν αὐτόν "he led him out," commonly associated with the root נחה]).

2.2.4.4.4 Exegetical Value
Through the process of harmonization, SP-Num reveals how it understands the chronology of events that are described both in Deuteronomy and in Numbers. In all cases, the resulting chronology is logical; commands or prohibitions to act come before the actions (Num 10:11; 13:1; 14:41; 20:14; 21:11, 13, 21; 27:23; 31:21); grumbling comes before weeping (Num 14:1); consequences come after actions (Num 20:13).

Because SP-Num occupies the middle ground between a biblical Hebrew manuscript and a translated document, with the vocalized text sometimes revealing hidden differences in grammar, it serves also as an early exegetical commentary. Most of the differences in grammar make very little difference in interpretation (cf. MT צֻוָּה *pual* "he was commanded," vs. SP צוהו *ṣåbē'u*, *piel*, "[Yahweh] commanded him" with 3rd masc. sg. suf. in Num 3:16). On the other hand, SP-Num helps reveal the history of interpretation of Num 16:5. The verse may refer to a past event: Yahweh had sought out and known Aaron as the one who was his, and had brought him near as the one who was holy and whom he had chosen (cf. 4QNum[b], LXX[ACO]; Num 16:9–11). The other possibility is that the words refer to a future event: in the morning Yahweh would make Aaron known as the one who is his, and would bring him near as the one who is holy and whom he would chose (cf. MT, SP-Num; Num 16:6–7, 16–40). MT and SP-Num exhibit the same sense of the passage, albeit with slightly different verbal forms, suggesting that two independent traditions modified the original meaning from a past occurrence to a future one.

Anderson, R.T. and T. Giles, *The Samaritan Pentateuch: An Introduction to Its Origin, History, and Significance for Biblical Studies* (SBLRBS 72; Atlanta: SBL, 2012).

Ben-Ḥayyim, Z., *The Words of the Pentateuch* (vol. 4 of *The Literary and Oral Tradition of Hebrew and Aramaic amongst the Samaritans*; Jerusalem: Academy of the Hebrew Language, 1957–1977) [Hebr.].

Ben-Ḥayyim, Z., *A Grammar of Samaritan Hebrew: Based on the Recitation of the Law in Comparison with the Tiberian and Other Jewish Traditions* (Eng. rev. ed. with assistance from A. Tal; Winona Lake: Eisenbrauns, 2000).

von Gall, A., *Der Hebräische Pentateuch der Samaritaner*, Vols. 1–5 (Giessen: Töpelmann, 1914–1918; repr. Berlin: De Gruyter, 2011).

Jastram, N.R., "The Text of 4QNum^b," in *Madrid Qumran Congress*, 1:177–98.

Jastram, N.R., "4QNum^b," in *DJD* XII: 205–67.

Jastram, N.R., "A Comparison of Two 'Proto-Samaritan' Texts from Qumran: 4QpaleoExod^m and 4QNum^b," *DSD* 5 (1998): 264–89.

Tal, *Shekhem*.

Tal and Florentin, *Samaritan Version*.

Nathan Jastram

2.2.4.5 Deuteronomy

2.2.4.5.1 Nature of the Text

The SP version of Deuteronomy, first made available to Western scholars in its publication by J. Morinus in the Paris Polyglot of 1635[1] and in Walton's London Polyglot of 1655–1657,[2] has the same basic character as the other books of SP (→ 2.2.4.1; → 2.2.4.2; → 2.2.4.3; → 2.2.4.4), viz. a text marked by scribal alterations such as glosses, interpolations, expansions, and editorial interventions. In addition, SP-Deut is characterized by the variant בחר ("has chosen," as opposed to MT-Deut's יִבְחַר "will choose") in the formula המקום אשר בחר יהוה אלהיכם לשים את שמו שם "the place where the Lord your God has chosen to place his name," Deut 12:5 et al.; and the addition, at Deut 5:18, of the Samaritan tenth commandment, mandating the construction of an altar on Mt. Gerizim.

2.2.4.5.2 Editions and Tools

For the pre-Samaritan manuscript 4Q364, see E. Tov and S. White (Crawford), "4QReworked Pentateuch^b," in *DJD* XIII: 197–254, and E. Ulrich, *BQS*.

The modern critical editions of SP are listed below in chronological order.

von Gall, A., *Der hebräische Pentateuch der Samaritaner* (vols. I–V; Giessen: Töpelmann, 1914–1918; repr. Berlin, 1966).

Sadaqa, A. and R., *Jewish Version, Samaritan Version of the Pentateuch: With Particular Stress on the Differences between Both Texts* (Tel Aviv: Reuven Mas, 1961–1965).

---

[1] Le Jay, *Biblia*.
[2] Walton, *Polyglotta*.

Tal, *Shekhem*.

Tsedaka, I., *ha-Torah ha-Qedosha* (Holon: A.B. Institute of Samaritan Studies, 1998/2000).

Tal–Florentin, *Samaritan Version*.

Tsedaka, B. and S. Sullivan, *The Israelite Samaritan Version of the Torah: First English Translation Compared with the Masoretic Version* (Grand Rapids: Eerdmans, 2013).

2.2.4.5.3 Text-Critical Character

SP-Deut is a descendant of a pre-Samaritan form of Deuteronomy, for which indirect evidence is found in the Qumran manuscript 4Q364 (4QReworked Pentateuch^b; → 2.2.1.7.1). This manuscript is not a direct ancestor of SP-Deut, since it contains readings not found in SP-Deut, but it does share with SP-Deut two major variants not shared with MT- or LXX-Deut. Before Deut 2:8, SP-Deut and 4Q364 (frg. 23a–b, col. i, lines 1–4) share an interpolation from Num 20:14, 17–18:

ואשלחה מלאכים אל מלך אדום לאמר
אעברה בארצך לא אטה בשדה ובכרם ולא נשתה מי בור דרך המלך
נלך לא נסור ימין ושמאל עד אשר נעבר גבולך
ויאמר לא תעבר בי פן בחרב אצא לקראתך

"And I sent messengers to the king of Edom, saying, 'Let me cross over your land. I will not turn aside into the field or the vineyard, and we will not drink water from a well. We will walk the King's Highway, not turning to the right or the left, until we cross your boundary.' But he said, 'You will not cross my [land], lest I come forth to meet you with the sword'."

A scribe has appropriated the Numbers text, altering the person of the verb so that Moses is speaking.

At Deut 10:6, 4Q364 and SP-Deut insert text from Num 33:31–37a, outlining the itinerary of the Israelites in the wilderness prior to the death of Aaron. 4Q364 and SP-Deut have similar, but not identical texts, pointing to a degree of scribal freedom in the transmission of this expansive text tradition.

Thus we can see that, as for the other Pentateuchal books, a version of Deuteronomy from which SP-Deut descends was in general circulation in Palestine in the late Second Temple period.

An important variant in SP-Deut occurs at Deut 27:4:

תקימו את האבנים האלה אשר אנכי מצוה אתכם היום **בהרגריזים**

"You will take these stones which I am commanding you today *on Mount Gerizim* ..."

MT-Deut, supported by most of the versions, reads בְּהַר עֵיבָל "on Mount Ebal." Until recently, this variant was considered a polemical change on the part of SP-Deut, emphasizing the choice of Mt. Gerizim as the proper place for God's sanctuary. This argument was first made by Gesenius, although Kennicott argued to the contrary that the Gerizim reading was original.[3] However, fresh consideration of the evidence has led to a reevaluation of the variant. In addition to SP, two independent witnesses, a VL manuscript (Codex Lugdunensis) and a Greek manuscript, Papyrus Giessen 19, preserve the Gerizim reading.[4] Thus, it can be argued that the reading בהרגרזים "on Mt. Gerizim" is an ancient reading, one that in fact accords better with its context, in which blessings are to be pronounced on Mt. Gerizim and curses on Mt. Ebal (Deut 11:29 and 27:12–13).[5]

In 2009, a small fragment of Deuteronomy, presented as deriving from Qumran Cave 4, was published by Charlesworth.[6] This fragment reads:

(2) [היום בהרגרזים ושדת]

"] today, on Mt. Gerizim, and you will plaster ["

If this fragment is authentic, it would support the argument that the reading "Mount Gerizim" is early, while MT-Deut's "Mount Ebal" is a late, possibly polemical, change.

SP-Deut contains other variants that are most likely from the pre-Samaritan text tradition and are not specifically Samaritan. An example is the variants in the formula לשום/לשכן את שמו שם "to put/place his name there"; Deut 12:5, 11, 21; 14:23, 24: 16:2, 6, 11; 26:2.[7] At Deut 12:5, SP and MT have שום; in all other instances SP has שכן "to place," while MT reads לָשׂוּם "to put" at Deut 12:21 and 14:24, with שכן "to place" in the other instances.[8] SP has the direct object marker את in every iteration of the formula, while MT only reads אֶת at Deut 12:5.

More controversial is the variant יבחר/בחר "he will choose/has chosen" in the formula המקום אשר יבחר/בחר יהוה אלהיכם לשים את שמו שם "the place where the Lord your God will choose/has chosen to place his name," referring to the sanctuary. This formula appears in Deuteronomy twenty-two times, first at Deut 12:5.[9] SP-Deut has בחר "has chosen" throughout, while MT-Deut has יִבְחַר "will choose."[10] Each formulation reflects an election theology; in SP, God has chosen Mt. Gerizim, which is hinted at in Deut 11:29 and fulfilled in

---

[3] Schenker, "Textgeschichtliches," 106.

[4] The Giessen Papyri were first published by P. Glaue and A. Rahlfs, "Fragmente einer griechischen Übersetzung des samaritanischen Pentateuchs," in *Nachrichten der Akademie der Wissenschaften in Göttingen* (1911), 167–200. The fragments have since disappeared, so one must rely on the photographs and transcriptions supplied by Glaue and Rahlfs. The reading at Deut 27:4 appears on col. 1, recto right, lines 3–4, εν αρ(?)γαρ[ι]ζιμ "on Mt. Gerizim." According to Tov, it cannot be determined from the photograph and transcription whether or not αρ(?)γαρ[ι]ζιμ was written as one word or two. Tov suggests that this could be "an ancient not yet sectarian reading." E. Tov, "Pap. Giessen 13, 19, 22, 26: A Revision of the Septuagint?" in Tov, *Greek-Hebrew Bible*, 462, 472. Codex Lugdunenesis was first published by U. Robert, *Pentateuchi versio Latina antiquissima e Codice Lugdunensi: version Latine du Pentateuque antérieure a Saint Jérome. Publie d'après le manuscrit de Lyon. Avec des facsimilés, des observations paléographiques, philologiques et littéraires sur l'origine et la valuer de ce texte* (Paris: Librairie de Fermin-Didot et Cie, Imprimeurs de l'Institut de France, 1881). The Latin reading is *in Monte Garizin*.

[5] See now Tov, *TCHB*, 88 n. 140; Schorch, "The Samaritan Version of Deuteronomy," 26–28; Knoppers, *Jews and Samaritans*, 202.

[6] Charlesworth, "What is a Variant?" 201–12, 273–74. Lange, *Handbuch*, 106, argues on the basis of paleography that the fragment is a forgery.

[7] LXX reads ἐκλέξηται throughout, although there are variants in the manuscript tradition. It can be used to translate either Hebrew verb.

[8] 4QDeut^c agrees with SP and MT at 16:6, reading שכן "to place."

[9] Deut 12:5, 11, 14, 18, 21, 26; 14:23, 24, 25; 15:20, 16:2, 6, 7, 11, 15, 16; 17:8, 10, 15; 18:6; 26:2; and 31:11.

[10] The majority of LXX readings agree with MT. There are no Qumran manuscripts in which the complete reading is extant.

2.2.4 SP AND ANCIENT TEXTS CLOSE TO SP

the Mt. Gerizim reading at Deut 27:4. According to the MT tradition, the place has not yet been chosen; the formula is not fulfilled until 1 Kgs 8:16, with the choice of Jerusalem (and the house of David).[11] Until recently, most scholars argued that the Samaritan reading reflected a late and polemical change, to emphasize the sanctity of Gerizim over Jerusalem.[12] However, Schenker has collected twelve cases in the LXX manuscript tradition where the variant בחר is preserved: Deut 12:5, 11, 14, 21, 26; 14:23, 24, 25; 16:2, 7; and 17:8, 10.[13] These Greek witnesses appear to be independent of SP. Schenker and Schorch have argued, based on this evidence, that בחר is the original reading, and יבחר is a Judean, anti-Samaritan change.[14] However, their arguments for the priority of בחר are not convincing; it is better to conclude from the available evidence that the textual tradition here was more fluid than previously thought, and that the Samaritan and Judean communities each chose the reading that reflected their own ideological position.[15]

As in the other books of SP, SP-Deut has its share of minor substitutions, glosses, expansions, and omissions, many shared with LXX (thus indicating their presence in the text prior to its translation into Greek).[16] Examples of expansions include Deut 2:12 (referring to Deut 2:21), 14:8 (referring to Lev 11:7, shared with LXX), and 24:1 (referring to Deut 22:13). Typical word substitutions occur at Deut 16:8 (substitution of the common word חג "festival" for עצרת "assembly") and 32:10 (where SP, through deliberate metathesis, changes MT's יְמְצָאֵהוּ "he found him" to יאמצהו "he strengthened him").[17] There are also cases where SP's text is shorter than MT/LXX, e.g., at Deut 1:30 and 34:1b–3. All of these minor variants may have been part of the pre-SP layer of SP-Deut.

Finally, SP-Deut contains one major variant that does not belong to the pre-SP layer, but is a deliberate addition by the Samaritan community, the Samaritan tenth commandment following Deut 5:18. This commandment consists of verses woven from Deut 11:29, 27:2–7, and 11:30, with alterations.[18]

והיה כי יביאך יהוה אלהיך אל ארץ הכנעני אשר אתה בא שמה לרשתה
והקמת לך אבנים גדלות ושדת אתם בשיד
וכתבת על האבנים את כל דברי התורה הזאת
והיה בעברכם את הירדן תקימו את האבנים האלה אשר אנכי מצוה
היום בהרגריזים ובנית שם מזבח ליהוה אלהיך מזבח אבנים
לא תניף עליהם ברזל
אבנים שלמות תבנה את מזבח יהוה אלהיך והעלית עליו
עלות ליהוה אלהיך
וזבחת שלמים ואכלת שם ושמחת לפני יהוה אלהיך
ההר ההוא בעבר הירדן אחרי דרך מבוא השמש בארץ הכנעני
היושב בערבה מול הגלגל אצל אלון מורא מול שכם

"And when the Lord your God brings you to the land *of the Canaanites*[19] that you are entering to possess, you shall set up large stones for yourself and cover them with plaster. And you shall write on the stones all the words of this law. And when you have crossed the Jordan, set up these stones on Mount Gerizim as I command you today. Build there an altar to the

---

[11] Knoppers, *Jews and Samaritans*, 186–87.

[12] For reflections of this position, see McCarthy, *BHQ Part 5: Deuteronomy*, 84*–85*, and Tov, *TCHB*, 88.

[13] The manuscripts that contain the reading ἐξελέξατο "has chosen" (aorist) are LXX⁷² (Deut 12:5, 14:23, 14:24, 14:25) and LXX¹⁶ (Deut 16:2). The Bohairic tradition preserves the perfect at Deut 12:5, 12:11, 12:26, 14:24, 14:25, and 17:8, while individual Bohairic manuscripts preserve the perfect at Deut 12:14 (ms F), 14:23 (mss A, C, D, and F), and 16:7 (mss G and H; the sigla for the Bohairic manuscripts are taken from the edition of Peters [see below]). At Deut 12:21, the past tense appears in two Sahidic manuscripts, i.e. Museo Borgiano (Cop^Sa 17) and British Museum Oriental 7594 (Cop^Sa 15). The VL preserves two examples of *elegit* (perfect): at Deut 16:2 in Codex Lugdunensis, and at Deut 17:10 in a citation by Lucifer Calaritanus (this reading also appears in Cop^Sa 15). Schenker, "Le Seigneur," 342–45; M.K.H. Peters, *A Critical Edition of the Coptic (Bohairic) Pentateuch*, Vol. 5: *Deuteronomy* (SBLSCS 15; Chico: Scholars Press, 1983).

[14] Schenker, "Le Seigneur"; Schorch, "The Samaritan Version of Deuteronomy," 32–34. Dušek, *Aramaic and Hebrew Inscriptions*, 90, agrees with Schenker and Schorch but advances no new arguments.

[15] See also Knoppers, *Jews and Samaritans*, 185 n. 43.

[16] For a more comprehensive list, see McCarthy, "Samaritan Readings," 122–28.

[17] LXX has αὐτάρκησεν "he made self-sufficient," a neologism that may reflect the Hebrew of SP. McCarthy, "Samaritan Readings," 126.

[18] M. Kartveit, *The Origin of the Samaritans*, 290–99.

[19] "Of the Canaanites" is a plus in SP-Deut.

Lord your God, an altar of stones. Do not use any iron tool on them. Build the altar of the Lord your God with unhewn stones and offer burnt offerings on it to the Lord your God. Sacrifice whole offerings and eat them there and rejoice in the presence of the Lord your God. *That mountain* is across the Jordan, westwards toward the setting sun, in the territory of the Canaanites who dwell in the Arabah facing Gilgal, near the *oak* of Moreh, *facing Shechem*."[20]

This commandment was added in SP-Deut (as well as in SP-Exod 20) only after an exemplar of the pre-SP tradition of Deuteronomy was chosen as the canonical Samaritan text, at the end of the second century B.C.E.

From the data given above, at least four phases can be discerned for the textual history of SP-Deut. In its first phase, the ancestor of pre-SP-Deut and proto-MT-Deut were very close to one another; that is, pre-SP-Deut descended from a text similar, if not identical, to proto-MT-Deut (→ 2.2.2). In its second phase, an ancestor of pre-SP-Deut (along with an ancestor of the Hebrew *Vorlage* of LXX-Deut; → 2.4.1.5) underwent scribal editing, which resulted in a text altered by minor glosses and harmonizations, word substitutions, and even omissions.[21] In its third phase, pre-SP-Deut was subjected to major content editing by a scribe or group of scribes, done in the same period as the major content editing that took place in SP-Gen, SP-Exod, and SP-Num. During all of these phases, pre-SP-Deut was in general circulation in Palestine.[22] In its fourth phase, after its adoption by the Samaritan community as their canonical text in the late second/early first century B.C.E., it underwent specifically Samaritan editing, characterized in particular by the addition of the Samaritan tenth commandment in Deuteronomy 5, thus arriving at the form in which it is found today.

2.2.4.5.4 Text-Critical Value

SP-Deut is of immense value to the textual critic wishing to determine the relationships among the various versions of Deuteronomy, as well as to recover, as far as possible, earlier readings in the text of Deuteronomy. Because of its shared readings with LXX-Deut (→ 2.4.1.5), all of them in the form of minor variants, SP-Deut provides evidence for a period in the history of the text of Deuteronomy when an ancestor(s) of LXX and SP-Deut had been expanded in sundry minor ways, but before LXX-Deut was translated into Greek. The major alterations in SP-Deut that are not shared with LXX-Deut but are not specifically Samaritan in character point to a period in the history of the text after the separation from LXX-Deut but before the Samaritan community chose one specific exemplar from the pre-SP textual tradition for its canonical text. Finally, the specifically Samaritan changes in SP-Deut (the addition of the Samaritan tenth commandment) indicate the history of the text after it became canonical in the Samaritan community.

2.2.4.5.5 Value for Literary Criticism

SP-Deut is an important resource for understanding the growth of the text of Deuteronomy, and the ways in which scribes felt free to intervene in the text when passing it on to the next generation. Further, SP-Deut is useful in the reconstruction of the history of the Samaritan community. Its first three textual phases (outlined above) indicate that the pre-SP form of Deuteronomy was a text in general circulation in Judea and Samaria before the definitive break between the Jews and the Samaritans, and was freely used by both com-

---

[20] "That mountain" and "facing Shechem" are glosses to make the identity of the mountain as Gerizim quite clear.

[21] As Tov ("Textual Development," 249) notes, the pre-Samaritan texts and the Hebrew source text of LXX are remarkably closely related, probably sharing a common ancestor, although LXX contains more minor glosses and expansions than pre-SP, indicating that they separated at some point in their respective histories.

[22] This sketch is only an overview of the *general* relationship of the various witnesses to one another, and is based on the complete witnesses SP, MT, and LXX. As Tov (*TCHB*, 159) rightly points out, "The preserved early texts relate to each other in an intricate web of agreement and difference, while each text also contains unique readings, that is, readings found only in that source." Tov presents a slightly different stemma from my own (placing proto-MT at the top of the stemma), as does Lange. Tov, "Textual Development," 249–50; Lange, *Handbuch*, 173. Both of these stemmata are for the Pentateuch as a whole, not just Deuteronomy.

munities. Following the destruction of the sanctuary on Mt. Gerizim by John Hyrcanus, which caused the final rupture between Samaritans and Jews, the Samaritans chose a pre-SP exemplar of Deuteronomy that contained the important readings הרגרזים "Mount Gerizim" at Deut 27:4 and בחר "has chosen" (which they had most likely already been using) and made it uniquely and polemically their own by adding the Samaritan tenth commandment.[23] Thus, although SP-Deut as a whole is not specifically Samaritan (that is, it does not alter the basic theology of the book of Deuteronomy), the addition of the Samaritan tenth commandment gives to SP-Deut a Samaritan character.

Charlesworth, J.H., "What is a Variant? Announcing a New Dead Sea Scrolls Fragment of Deuteronomy," *Maarav* 16 (2009): 201–12, 273–74.
Dušek, J., *Aramaic and Hebrew Inscriptions from Mt. Gerizim and Samaria between Antiochus III and Antiochus IV Epiphanes* (Culture and History of the Ancient Near East 54; Leiden: Brill, 2012).
Kartveit, M., *The Origin of the Samaritans* (VTSup 128; Leiden: Brill, 2009).
Knoppers, G., *Jews and Samaritans: The Origins and History of their Early Relations* (New York: Oxford University Press, 2013).
Lange, *Handbuch.
McCarthy, C., *BHQ 5: Deuteronomy (2007).
McCarthy, C., "Samaritan Pentateuch Readings in Deuteronomy," in *Biblical and Near Eastern Essays: Studies in Honour of Kevin J. Cathcart* (eds. J. Healey and C. McCarthy; JSOTSup 375; Sheffield: Sheffield Academic Press, 2004), 118–30.
Schenker, A., "Le Seigneur choisira-t-il le lieu de son nom ou l'a-t-il choisi? L'apport de la Bible grecque ancienne à l'histoire du texte samaritain et massorétique," in *Scripture in Transition: Essays on Septuagint, Hebrew Bible, and Dead Sea Scrolls in Honour of Raija Sollamo* (eds. A. Voitila and J. Jokiranta; JSJSup 126; Leiden: Brill, 2008), 339–52.
Schenker, A., "Textgeschichtliches zum Samaritanischen Pentateuch und Samareitikon," in *Samaritans: Past and Present* (eds. M. Mor and F. Reiterer; Studia Samaritana 5; Berlin: De Gruyter, 2010), 105–22.

[23] Knoppers, *Jews and Samaritans*, 212–16.

Schorch, S., "The Samaritan Version of Deuteronomy and the Origin of Deuteronomy," in *Samaria, Samarians, Samaritans* (ed. J. Zsengellér; Studia Samaritana 6; Berlin: De Gruyter, 2011), 23–38.
Tov, E., "The Samaritan Pentateuch and the Dead Sea Scrolls: The Proximity of the Pre-Samaritan Qumran Scrolls to the SP," in *Keter Shem Tov: Essays on the Dead Sea Scrolls in Memory of Alan Crown* (eds. S. Tzoref and I. Young; Perspectives on Hebrew Scriptures and Its Contexts 20; Piscataway: Gorgias Press, 2013), 59–88. Rev. ed.: Tov, *Collected Writings 3.
Tov, E., "The Textual Development of the Torah," in Tov, *Collected Writings 3, 239–50.
Tov, *TCHB.

Sidnie White Crawford

2.2.5 Other Sources

2.2.5.1 Tefillin and Mezuzot
2.2.5.1.1 History of Research

The study of *tefillin* and *mezuzot* changed dramatically with the discovery and publication of the Dead Sea Scrolls. Controversies in previous years included questions of when *tefillin* should be worn, how *mezuzot* should be affixed to doorways, what materials should be used in their construction, and in what order the passages should be laid out. The Dead Sea Scrolls contributed evidence concerning such questions but also opened new areas of controversy, including questions of the precise passages that were included, the possibility of sectarian differences being reflected in these texts, and the value of the texts for the textual criticism of the Hebrew Bible.[1]

Two broad approaches to the material can be discerned. One approach takes the Halakhic requirements found in the Talmud as representative of mainstream Jewish practice already at the time of the earliest *tefillin* and *mezuzot*, and evaluates the documents as either conforming to that prac-

---

[1] Lange concludes that the documents are not very helpful for textual criticism ("für die textkritische Analyse nur von begrenztem Wert"), ascribing most variants to memory problems of individual scribes; see *Handbuch, 120–22 (the quote is on p. 120), and the literature cited there. For further discussion, see → 2.2.5.1.3 below.

tice or as being sectarian.² In this context, *sectarian* generally is used to mean more than that the *tefillin* and *mezuzot* were produced by members of a sect; the implication is that the content and form of the texts exhibit, either deliberately or inadvertently, attitudes, doctrines, and practices at variance with the mainstream.³

A contrasting and more convincing approach takes the Halakhic requirements as later developments, with the Dead Sea Scrolls providing evidence that at the earliest stage there was considerable freedom in the production and use of *tefillin* and *mezuzot*. This approach can be extended to the biblical texts themselves if the *tefillin* and *mezuzot* are taken as evidence of a somewhat fluid base text rather than as a fluid use of a fixed base text.⁴

2.2.5.1.2 Manuscripts and Editions

Before the Dead Sea Scrolls were discovered, the earliest evidence for the use of *tefillin* and *mezuzot* came second hand through the *Letter of Aristeas*, Philo, Josephus, and the New Testament.⁵ The discovery of the Dead Sea Scrolls furnished first-hand evidence from the artifacts themselves, which were published in the following editions arranged by the date of publication: Barthélemy and Milik, *DJD I (1955; 1Q13); Kuhn, *Phylakterien aus Höhle 4 von Qumran* (1957; 4Q128–129, 4Q135, 4Q137); Milik, *DJD II (1961; Mur4–5); Aharoni, "Expedition B" (1961; 34Ṣe1); Baillet and Milik, *DJD III (1962; 8Q3–4; 5Q8); Yadin, *Tefillin from Qumran* (1969; XQ1–4); Milik, *DJD VI (1977; 4Q128–155); Morgenstern and Segal, *DJD XXXVIII (2000; XḤev/Ṣe5). One has

only to examine the photographs of the fragments to appreciate the enormous contribution of these pioneering scholars. Working with fragments that are often very deteriorated, with minuscule letters that are often only 1 mm or less in height, with texts that often diverge from the standard biblical texts, and with occasional writing on the verso bleeding through to the recto, they were nevertheless able to join the fragments and produce meaningful transcriptions of their contents in most instances. These editions are for the most part reliable, though Kuhn's work had to be updated and improved in many of its readings by Milik in the *DJD* series, and some misprints appear even in the *DJD* series.⁶

2.2.5.1.3 Nature and Text-Critical Character

The many textual variants make the use of the *tefillin* and *mezuzot* for textual criticism challenging. Yet they contain valuable information about the development of the biblical text at a very early date. Attempts to align the *tefillin* and *mezuzot* to the main textual sources (MT, SP, LXX) have not been entirely satisfactory since they rely, in part, on a selective use of the data.⁷ For instance, it is difficult to support aligning 4QPhyl A (4Q128) with MT,⁸ since it varies more often from MT than from SP, and the combined weight of its disagreements with MT is greater than the combined weight of its agreements with MT against either SP or LXX. Yet to classify 4QPhyl A as "unaligned" could give the

---

² "Therefore, of the phylacteries of Cave 4, Group 1 (Qumran practice, not in accord with rabbinic teachings) are sectarian in nature. Group 2, those which do not reflect Qumran practice and conform to rabbinic contents, probably derived from Pharisaic circles" (Schiffman, "Phylacteries and *Mezuzot*," 677).

³ Cf. the related idea developed by W.M. Schniedewind that Qumran Hebrew was "created by conscious linguistic choices intended to set the speakers and their language apart from others" ("Qumran Hebrew as an Antilanguage," *JBL* 118 [1999]: 235–52).

⁴ Cf. the approach of Lange and Weigold, "The Text of the Shema Yisrael," 170–77.

⁵ For a convenient presentation of this evidence, see Lange and Weigold, "The Text of the Shema Yisrael," 159–65.

⁶ Cf. the following misprints in the Milik material: 4QPhyl H (4Q135) עי[נוך for עי[ניך "your eyes" Exod 13:16 (*DJD VI: 62); 4QPhyl H לאהליהם for לאהליכם "to your tents" Deut 5:30 (*DJD VI: 61); 4QPhyl I (4Q136) ובלכתן for ובלכתך "when you walk" Deut 11:19 (*DJD VI: 63); 4QPhyl K (4Q138) מערים for מצרים "Egypt" Deut 11:4 (*DJD VI: 68); 4QPhyl K אחריהמה for אחריכמה "after you" Deut 11:4 (*DJD VI: 68); 4QPhyl K שלה for שמה "thither" Deut 11:11 (*DJD VI: 69). Milik also misidentified, in my opinion, 4QMez A (4Q149) as coming from Exodus rather than from Deuteronomy (*DJD VI: 80). It is also likely that the plural form תאכלו "you [pl.] will eat" that Aharoni transcribed from 34Ṣe Phyl (34Ṣe1) should have been read as the singular תאכל "you [sg.] will eat" Exod 13:6 ("Expedition B," 22).

⁷ See Lange, *Handbuch, 121, for a brief summary of key alignments that have been proposed.

⁸ As does Lange, *Handbuch, 121.

2.2.5 OTHER SOURCES

TABLE 1   *Tefillin and Mezuzot with Problematic Alignments*

Tefillin and *Mezuzot*	Orthography and Morpho-phonology	Pericope	Textual Variants from MT
1QPhyl (1Q13)	Moderately plene orthography, no distinctive "Qumranic" elements	Non-standard	Few minor differences
4QPhyl C (4Q130)	Mixed orthography	Standard	Many minor differences
4QPhyl D (4Q131)	Moderately plene orthography (לוחות, "tablets")	Standard	No differences
4QPhyl F (4Q133)	Moderately plene orthography (יביאכה, "he brings you", חמור, "donkey")	Standard	One minor difference
4QPhyl R (4Q145)	Moderately plene orthography	Standard	Some minor differences
4QMez B (4Q150)	Standard orthography	Non-standard	Two minor differences
4QMez C (4Q151)	Standard orthography	Non-standard	One minor difference
4QMez F (4Q154)	Standard orthography	Non-standard	No differences
8QPhyl Groups I–IV (8Q3)[10]	Moderately plene orthography	Non-standard	Major differences
XḤev/Se Phyl (XḤev/Se5)	Mixed orthography	Standard	Moderate differences

wrong impression that its readings do not normally agree with other witnesses, when, in fact, they normally do agree with at least one other witness.

In a similar way, attempts are often made to link variations in orthography and morpho-phonology to the choice of pericopes and the inclusion of lexical variants. Milik described two types of *tefillin*, Pharisaic and Essene.[9] According to him, the Pharisaic *tefillin* had standard orthography and pericopes while the Essene *tefillin* included plene orthography, modernized morpho-phonology, and non-standard pericopes. It must be said, however, that these traits are linked convincingly only in some *tefillin* and *mezuzot*, not others.

Table 1 shows the "problematic" *tefillin* and *mezuzot*, those that show little or no linking of the traits mentioned above. In the table, the "standard" for orthography and morpho-phonology is taken as MT, and the "standard" for pericopes is taken as the following four sections for *tefillin* (only the last two for *mezuzot*): Exod 13:1–10, 11–16; Deut 6:4–9; 11:13–21. The non-standard pericopes may include portions of Exod 12:43–51; Deut 5:1–6:3; 10:12–11:12; 32:1–43.

The lack of consistent correlation between different categories of variants has also been shown by Martin in those portions of the Dead Sea Scrolls that contain the Decalogue. He uses a statistical analysis of variants to show that "there is no general correlation across all the manuscripts" between orthographic and non-orthographic variants.[11]

Space restrictions do not permit a discussion of all the variant readings preserved in the *tefillin* and *mezuzot*. The following list is restricted to the major variants in which readings differ by ten words or more.

Major omissions:

- Exod 12:48 וְעָשָׂה פֶסַח לַיהוָה הִמּוֹל לוֹ כָל־זָכָר וְאָז יִקְרַב לַעֲשֹׂתוֹ וְהָיָה כְּאֶזְרַח הָאָרֶץ [MT] > 8QPhyl (8Q3) (vid.; abbreviation?)[12]

---

[9] Milik, *DJD* VI: 34–37.
[10] If Group I were considered by itself, however, it would be classified as having standard orthography and standard pericopes.

[11] Martin, *Multiple Originals*, 229; cf. the similar conclusion of Brooke, "Deuteronomy 5–6," 66.
[12] "And would keep the Passover to Yahweh, every male of his must be circumcised, and then he may approach to keep

- Deut 5:11 כִּי לֹא יְנַקֶּה יְהוָה אֵת אֲשֶׁר־יִשָּׂא אֶת־שְׁמוֹ לַשָּׁוְא [MT] > 8QPhyl (8Q3) (vid.; homoioteleuton)[13]
- Deut 5:32–6:2 יָמִין וּשְׂמֹאול בְּכָל־הַדֶּרֶךְ אֲשֶׁר צִוָּה יְהוָה אֱלֹהֵיכֶם אֶתְכֶם תֵּלֵכוּ לְמַעַן תִּחְיוּן וְטוֹב לָכֶם וְהַאֲרַכְתֶּם יָמִים בָּאָרֶץ אֲשֶׁר תִּירָשׁוּן וְזֹאת הַמִּצְוָה הַחֻקִּים וְהַמִּשְׁפָּטִים אֲשֶׁר צִוָּה יְהוָה אֱלֹהֵיכֶם לְלַמֵּד אֶתְכֶם לַעֲשׂוֹת בָּאָרֶץ אֲשֶׁר אַתֶּם עֹבְרִים שָׁמָּה לְרִשְׁתָּהּ לְמַעַן תִּירָא אֶת־יְהוָה אֱלֹהֶיךָ לִשְׁמֹר אֶת־כָּל־חֻקֹּתָיו וּמִצְוֹתָיו [MT] > 4QPhyl J (4Q137) (vid.; abbreviation?)[14]
- Deut 11:10–11 אֲשֶׁר יְצָאתֶם מִשָּׁם אֲשֶׁר תִּזְרַע אֶת־זַרְעֲךָ וְהִשְׁקִיתָ בְרַגְלְךָ כְּגַן הַיָּרָק וְהָאָרֶץ אֲשֶׁר אַתֶּם עֹבְרִים שָׁמָּה לְרִשְׁתָּהּ [MT] > 8QPhyl (8Q3) (abbreviation?)[15]

Major additions:

- Deut 5:1 וּלְמַדְתֶּם כִּי אֶל יהוה [MT] ושמרתם לעשותם אלהי֯[שמ]ע֯ים א֯תם בהר מתוך האש ואנכ֯י֯ [אג]י֯ד דב֯ר֯י ברי[תו היו]ם הזה ולמדתם 4QPhyl G (4Q134) (interpolation)[16]
- Deut 10:22 init. MT] + [בשבעים נפש ירדו אבתיך] מצרימה ועתה] שמכה יהוה [אלוהיכה ככוכבי השמים לרוב ואהבתה את יהוה אלהיך ושמרת משמרתו וחקתיו

---

it; and he shall be as a native of the land." This omission is reconstructed based on the available space. It fits a pattern of abbreviations in this section.

[13] "For Yahweh will not hold innocent the one who takes his name in vain." This omission is reconstructed based on the available space.

[14] "To the right or to the left. In all the way that Yahweh your God commanded you, you should walk, in order that you shall live and it shall go well with you and you will lengthen the days in the land that you shall inherit. And this is the commandment, the statutes, and the judgments that Yahweh your God commanded me to teach you to do in the land over to which you are crossing to inherit, in order that you should fear Yahweh your God to keep all his statutes and his commandments." Cf. 4QPhyl B (4Q129) (vid.) for the first portion of this omission up to the words "to teach you."

[15] "From where you came out, where you would sow your seed and then water it with your foot as a vegetable garden. But the land over to which you are crossing to inherit ..."

[16] "And you shall be careful to keep them, for you must be listening to Yahweh God from the midst of the fire on the mountain, from the midst of the fire, and I am announcing the words of his covenant this day, and you shall learn them." The long reading for the most part is a compilation of other passages: ושמרתם לעשותם "and you shall be careful to keep them" is transposed from the end of the verse; the next section uses words from Deut 4:12 אַתֶּם שֹׁמְעִים ... מִתּוֹךְ הָאֵשׁ ... יְהוָה "Yahweh ... from the midst of the fire ... you must be listening";

- 4QPhyl P וּמִצְוֹתָיו וּמִשְׁפָּטָיו כו]ל הימים וידעתמה היום כי לוא [את בניכמה אשר לוא ידעו ואשר לוא ראו] (4Q143) (dittography of verses)[17]

Major difference other than length:

- Deut 5:14–15 אֲשֶׁר בִּשְׁעָרֶיךָ לְמַעַן יָנוּחַ עַבְדְּךָ וַאֲמָתְךָ כָּמוֹךָ וְזָכַרְתָּ כִּי־עֶבֶד הָיִיתָ בְּאֶרֶץ מִצְרַיִם וַיֹּצִאֲךָ יְהוָה אֱלֹהֶיךָ מִשָּׁם בְּיָד חֲזָקָה וּבִזְרֹעַ נְטוּיָה עַל־כֵּן צִוְּךָ יְהוָה אֱלֹהֶיךָ לַעֲשׂוֹת אֶת־יוֹם הַשַּׁבָּת [MT][18]
- אשר בשעריך כי ששת [ימים עשה] יהוה את ה[ש]מ[ים ואת ה]א֯רץ את הי֯ם ואת כול אשר בם וינח ביום השביע]י֯ על כן ב[ר]ר֯[ד יהוה את [יום הש]ב֯ת ו[י]ק֯דשהו 4QPhyl G (4Q134) (harmonization);[19]
- אשר בשעריך למען ינוח עבדך ואמתך כמוך כי ששת ימים עשה יהוה א[ת השמי]ם ו[את האר]ץ את ה֯ימים [ואת כל אשר בם וינח ביום השביעי על כן ברך יהוה את יום השבת ויקדשהו 4QMez A (4Q149) (harmonization);[20]
- אשר בש[ע]ריך כי ששת ימים] עשה יהוה את [ה]ש֯[מ]ים ואת הארץ ואת הים ואת כל אשר בם וינח ביום הש[ב]י֯[ע]י֯ על כן ב[רך ... 8QPhyl (8Q3) (harmonization)[21]

---

the next section from Deut 5:22 בָּהָר מִתּוֹךְ הָאֵשׁ "On the mountain ... from the midst of the fire"; the last section is very uncertain, perhaps drawing on Deut 4:13 and 5:5.

[17] "As seventy people your fathers went down to Egypt and now Yahweh your God has made you as numerous as the stars in the sky. You shall love Yahweh your God and keep his requirements and his statutes and his commandments and his judgments always. And you know today that [I am speaking] not with your sons who did not know and who did not see ..." Cf. 4QPhyl A (4Q128) for the first portion of this dittography, up to the words "stars in the sky."

[18] "Who are in your gates, in order that your manservant and maidservant might rest as you do. And you shall remember that you used to be servants in the land of Egypt, and that Yahweh your God brought you out of there with a strong hand and an outstretched arm, on account of which Yahweh your God has commanded you to celebrate the Sabbath day."

[19] "Who are in your gates, for in six days Yahweh made the heavens and the earth, the sea and all that is in them, and he rested on the seventh day, on account of which Yahweh blessed the seventh day and sanctified it."

[20] "Who are in your gates, in order that your manservant and maidservant might rest as you do, for in six days Yahweh made the heavens and the earth, the seas and all that is in them, and he rested on the seventh day, on account of which Yahweh blessed the seventh day and sanctified it."

[21] "Who are in your gates, for in six days Yahweh made the

These major variants of omission by abbreviation or homoioteleuton, of additions by interpolation or dittography, and of harmonization illustrate that *tefillin* and *mezuzot* themselves were not considered authoritative texts, but were appropriations of authoritative texts for personal use.

2.2.5.1.4 Date and Milieu

The paleographic dating of the *tefillin* and *mezuzot* is rendered more difficult by their miniscule script, which often remains quite stable for many years. Many of the manuscripts are dated rather broadly to the "Hellenistic–Roman" period, while some are dated more precisely to a period of fifty to a hundred years.[22] See the chart at the end of this article for more detail.

2.2.5.1.5 Relevance for Exegesis and Literary Analysis

These early *tefillin* and *mezuzot* are valuable records of the early history of personal piety. While other excerpted texts such as 4QDeut^j (4Q37), 4QDeut^kl (4Q38), and 4QDeut^n (4Q41) may have been intended for reading in public settings, such was clearly not the case with these texts written in miniscule script, which had been folded and sewn into cases. As personal objects of piety that were not intended to be read in public, there was less need to be as careful when copying the text, so there are cases of major dittographies, omissions, and substitutions of text. Such variants may indicate that the scribes wrote from memory rather than copying from a master text.[23] On the other hand, the texts bear witness to variant biblical exemplars and cannot be ignored in modern textual criticism. Especially where several *tefillin* and *mezuzot* share divergent readings, such as the substitution of Exod 20:11 for Deut 5:15 in the Decalogue, one must acknowledge that such a variant is not merely an idiosyncratic mistake of one scribe, but a characteristic of a family of texts.[24] See further the analysis of the *tefillin* and *mezuzot* in → 2.1.5.

Abegg, M., "The Linguistic Analysis of the Dead Sea Scrolls: More Than (Initially) Meets the Eye," in *Rediscovering the Dead Sea Scrolls: An Assessment of Old and New Approaches and Methods* (ed. M. Grossman; Grand Rapids: Eerdmans, 2010), 48–68.

Adler, Y., "Identifying Sectarian Characteristics in the Phylacteries from Qumran," *RevQ* 23 (2007–2008): 79–92.

Aharoni, Y., "Expedition B," *IEJ* 11 (1961): 11–24.

Baillet, M., "3. Phylactère," *DJD* III.1 (1962): 149–57.

Baillet, M., "4. Mezouza," *DJD* III.1 (1962): 158–61.

Barthélemy, D. and J.T. Milik, "13. Phylactère," *DJD* I (1955): 72–76.

Brooke, G., "Deuteronomy 5–6 in the Phylacteries from Cave 4," in *Emanuel: Studies in Hebrew Bible, Septuagint, and Dead Sea Scrolls in Honor of Emanuel Tov* (eds. S.M. Paul et al.; VTSup 94; Leiden: Brill, 2003), 57–70.

Cohn, Y.B., *Tangled Up in Text: Tefillin in the Ancient World* (BJS 351; Providence: Brown Judaic Studies, 2008).

Kuhn, K.G., *Phylakterien aus Höhle 4 von Qumran* (Heidelberg: Carl Winter Universitätsverlag, 1957).

Lange, *Handbuch*, 116–22.

Lange, A. and M. Weigold, "The Text of the Shema Yisrael in Qumran Literature and Elsewhere," in *Textual Criticism and Dead Sea Scrolls Studies in Honour of Julio Trebolle Barrera: Florilegium Complutense* (eds. A. Piquer Otero and P. Torijano Morales; JSJSup 157; Leiden: Brill, 2012), 147–77.

Lim, T., "Deuteronomy in the Judaism of the Second Temple Period," in *Deuteronomy in the New Testament: The New Testament and the Scriptures of Israel* (eds. M. Menken and S. Moyise; Library of New Testament Studies 358; New York: T & T Clark, 2007), 6–26.

---

heavens and the earth, and the sea and all that is in them, and he rested on the seventh day, on account of which Yahweh blessed …"

[22] The following list omits a *tefillah* of unknown provenance described briefly by Milik in his discussion of MurPhyl (Mur4), as follows: "Les mêmes péricopes, mais mises dans l'ordre de la Bible, se retrouvent dans un autre phylactère, datant de la même époque, mais provenant d'une grotte de localisation incertaine. Elles sont également réparties sur deux morceaux, bien que d'une façon arbitraire puisque le passage d'une pièce à l'autre se fait au milieu de Deut 11:17: את/השמים" (*DJD* II.1: 81).

[23] See the brief discussion and notes in Lange, *Handbuch*, 121.

[24] The substitution is made in the following manuscripts: 4QPhyl G (4Q134); 4QMez A (4Q149); 8QPhyl (8Q3). Cf. the same substitution in the Nash Papyrus, and a conflated reading of both verses in 4QDeut^n (4Q41) and LXX^B.

TABLE 2   *The Dead Sea Scrolls Tefillin and Mezuzot*

Tefillin and *Mezuzot*	Date	Slips	Contents Summary
1QPhyl (1Q13)[25]	Hellenistic–Roman	Group I	Deut 5:1–27
		Group II	Deut 10:[12]17–11:12[21]
		Group III	Exod 13:[1]2–9
		Group IV	Unidentified other passages
4QPhyl A (4Q128)	Hellenistic–Roman		Deut 5:1–14; 5:27–6:3; 10:12–11:21; Exod 12:43–13:7
4QPhyl B (4Q129)	Hellenistic–Roman		Deut 5:1–6:5; Exod 13:9–15
4QPhyl C (4Q130)	Hellenistic–Roman		Exod 13:1–16; Deut 6:4–9; 11:13–21
4QPhyl D–F (4Q131–133)[26]	Hellenistic–Roman	4QPhyl D (4Q131)	Deut 11:13–21
		4QPhyl E (4Q132)	Exod 13:1–9[10]
		4QPhyl F (4Q133)	Exod 13:11–16
4QPhyl G–I (4Q134–136)	Hellenistic–Roman	4QPhyl G (4Q134)	Deut 5:1–21; Exod 13:11–12
		4QPhyl H (4Q135)	Deut 5:22–6:5; Exod 13:14b–16
		4QPhyl I (4Q136)	Deut 11:13–21; Exod 12:[43]44–13:10; Deut 6:6–7
4QPhyl J–K (4Q137–138)	Hellenistic–Roman	4QPhyl J (4Q137)	Deut 5:1–6:3
		4QPhyl K (4Q138)	Deut 10:12–11:12
4QPhyl L–N (4Q139–141)	Hellenistic–Roman	4QPhyl L (4Q139)	Deut 5:[1]7–24[33]
		4QPhyl M (4Q140)	Exod 12:[43[27]]44–13:10; Deut 5:33–6:5
		4QPhyl N (4Q141)	Deut 32:[1]14–20 [probably all intervening verses and] 32–33
4QPhyl O (4Q142)	Hellenistic–Roman		Deut 5:1–16; 6:7–9
4QPhyl P (4Q143)	Hellenistic–Roman		Deut 10:21[28]–11:3, 18–20
4QPhyl Q (4Q144)	Hellenistic–Roman		Deut 11:4–18; Exod 13:4–9
4QPhyl R (4Q145)	Hellenistic–Roman		Exod 13:1–10
4QPhyl S (4Q146)	Hellenistic–Roman		Deut 11:19–21
4QPhyl T (4Q147)	Hellenistic–Roman		Undeciphered
4QPhyl U (4Q148)	Hellenistic–Roman		Undeciphered
4QMez A (4Q149)	2nd–1st cent. B.C.E.		Deut 5:[7,] 11–16[29]
4QMez B (4Q150)	Herodian		Deut 6:5–6; 10:14–11:2
4QMez C (4Q151)	50–1 B.C.E.?		Deut 5:27–6:9; 10:12–20
4QMez D (4Q152)	1st cent. B.C.E.?		Deut 6:5–7
4QMez E (4Q153)	Hellenistic–Roman		Deut 11:17–18
4QMez F (4Q154)	100–50 B.C.E.		Exod 13:1–4
4QMez G (4Q155)	Hellenistic–Roman		Exod 13:11–16
5QPhyl (5Q8)	Hellenistic–Roman		Unopened
8QPhyl (8Q3)	1st cent. C.E.	Group I	Exod 13:1-16; Deut 11:13–21; 6:4–9
		Group II	??; Deut 6:1–3; 10:20–22
		Group III	Deut 10:12–19; Exod 12:43–51; Deut 5:1–15[30]
		Group IV	Deut 10:13; 11:2–3; 10:21–22; 11:1, 6–12
8QMez (8Q4)	Herodian		Deut 10:12–11:21
XQPhyl (XQ1–4)	1–50 C.E.	Slip 1	Exod 12:43–13:10; Deut 10:12–19
		Slip 2	Deut 5:22–6:9
		Slip 3	Deut 5:1–21; Exod 13:11–16
		Slip 4	Undeciphered,[31] not originally with this set
Mur Phyl (Mur4)	Hellenistic–Roman		Exod 13:1-16; Deut 11:13–21; 6:4–9
Mur Mez (Mur5)	Hellenistic–Roman		Undeciphered
XḤev/Se Phyl (XḤev/Se5)	n.d.		Exod 13:1–16; Deut 6:4–9; 11:13–21
34Ṣe Phyl (34Ṣe1)	c. 135 C.E.		Exod 13:2–16

Martin, G.D., *Multiple Originals: New Approaches to Hebrew Bible Textual Criticism* (SBLTCS 7; Atlanta: SBL, 2010).
Milik, J.T., "4. Phylactère," *DJD II.1 (1961): 80–85.
Milik, J.T., "5. Mezouza (?)," *DJD II.1 (1961): 85–86.
Milik, J.T., "8. Phylactère," *DJD III.1 (1962): 178.
Milik, J.T., *DJD VI: 48–85.
Morgenstern, M. and M. Segal, "5. XḤev/SePhylactery," *DJD XXXVIII: 183–91.
Schiffman, L., "Phylacteries and *Mezuzot*," *EDSS 2, 675–77.
Tigay, J., "תפילין," *EncBib* 8 (Jerusalem: Bialik Institute, 1982): 883–95.
Yadin, Y., *Tefillin from Qumran: XQPhyl 1–4* (Jerusalem: The Israel Exploration Society and the Shrine of the Book, 1969).

2.2.5.2 Nash Papyrus
2.2.5.2.1 History of Research, Manuscript and Editions

The papyrus was purchased in either 1898 or 1902 by Walter Nash from an Egyptian antiquities dealer who claimed that it came from the Faiyum.[1] It was first published by Cook in 1903.[2] He concluded that the papyrus was the oldest manuscript of the Hebrew Bible yet found, exhibiting a text from the pre-masoretic era. His discussion of textual variants provided a firm foundation for later scholars, but his transcription of the text was improved by Burkitt in 1903.[3] The following year, Burkitt published a further improved photograph and transcription.[4] Albright later published a seminal paleographical analysis of the papyrus in which he showed that it was considerably older than Cook had thought.[5] Since then, the papyrus has played a major role in dating the Dead Sea Scrolls and in discussions about excerpted texts and the earliest forms of the text of the Hebrew Bible.

The purpose of the Nash Papyrus (NP) has been disputed, with the major question being whether it was an early *tefillah* (*tefillin*). Peters says that it is impossible for the papyrus to be a *tefillah* (*tefillin*) or *mezuzah* unless one supposes that the standard texts were not used in Egypt.[6] With the discovery of the Dead Sea Scrolls, his argument has lost all force. Many early *tefillin* and *mezuzot* (→ 2.2.5.1) contain the Decalogue (1QPhyl Group I, 4QPhyl A, 4QPhyl B, 4QPhyl G, 4QPhyl J, 4QPhyl L, 4QPhyl O, 4QMez A, 8QPhyl Group III, XQPhyl), and others contain portions of Deuteronomy 5–6 that are not included in the standard texts (4QPhyl H, 4QPhyl M, 4QMez C, 8QPhyl Group II, XQPhyl).

Cook discounts the possibility that the NP could be a *tefillah* on the grounds of its physical appearance.[7] It is true that *tefillin* are normally writ-

---

[25] Barthélemy describes the fragments as being folded together when found (*DJD I: 72). Milik says that 1QPhyl (1Q13), along with MurPhyl (Mur4) and a *tefillah* of unknown provenance, are arm *tefillin*, with the pericopes written on one or two pieces of skin that are folded together and placed in a single compartment (*DJD II.1, 81).

[26] These slips were found in separate compartments of one container.

[27] Milik suggests a probable beginning at v. 42, but this could be a misprint since he does not include v. 42 in his reconstruction (*DJD VI: 71).

[28] Spatial considerations favor placing the first illegible letter in v. 21; Milik placed it in v. 22 (*DJD VI: 75).

[29] Milik's identification of the main portion of this fragment is "Ex 20:7–12; cf. Deut 5:11–26," with the added comment that there was probably room for only Exod 20:3 [= Deut 5:7] preceding these verses on the slip (*DJD VI: 80). In view of the other published tefillin, however, it is more likely that also here the Decalogue is based on Deuteronomy with harmonizations toward Exodus.

[30] Baillet identified the last verse as Exod 20:11 ("* DJD III:" 154), but it should probably be considered the alternate form of Deut 5:15, harmonized toward Exod 20:11, as seen also in 4QPhyl G (4Q134), 4QMez A (4Q149), and the Nash Papyrus, with corroboration from 4QDeut^n (4Q41) and G^B.

[31] "Isolated readings can be suggested here and there, but I must admit that I was unable to identify the scriptural portion in a satisfactory manner" (Yadin, *Tefillin*, 31).

---

[1] The earlier date is asserted by the following: "The most prized possession is the *Nash Papyrus*, one of the greatest relics of antiquity. It was acquired in 1898 by W.L. Nash, Secretary of the Society of Biblical Archaeology" (H. Rabinowicz, "Review: Cambridge University Library," *JQR* New Series 53 [1962], 69); the later date is asserted by B. Outhwaite, "Nash Papyrus," Cambridge Digital Library, http://cudl.lib.cam.ac.uk/view/MS-OR-00233 (accessed 3/30/2013).

[2] Cook, "Pre-Massoretic Biblical Papyrus," 34–57.

[3] Burkitt, "Hebrew Papyrus of the Ten Commandments," 392–408.

[4] Burkitt, "Nash Papyrus," 559–61.

[5] Albright, "Biblical Fragment," 145–76.

[6] Peters, *Älteste Abschrift*, 8–9.

[7] Cook, "Pre-Massoretic Biblical Papyrus," 54–55.

ten with minuscule script on animal skin rather than on papyrus, and that the slips are folded into small wads, tied, and placed in a container to be worn on the arm or head. On the other hand, the material of construction in Egypt would be more likely to be papyrus than animal skin. Also the Dead Sea Scrolls show that early *tefillin* and *mezuzot* varied widely in the form of the script, with letter height ranging from 0.5 mm (MurPhyl) to 2.5 mm (XḤev/SePhyl), so the 2 mm height of the letters of the NP fits into that range. The papyrus must have been folded where the pieces later separated, into a wad roughly 30 × 50 mm. By comparison, Cave 4 *tefillin* cases are 10 × 20–30 mm, 5QPhyl (5Q8) is 23 × 13 mm, and XQPhyl (xQ1–4) is 13 × 20 mm.

Eshel's note on this question appears sound: "The similarity between the form in which the Decalogue was written in the NP and the various *tefillin* and *mezuzot* found at Qumran apparently indicates that the NP served as a *tefillin* or *mezuzah* in a period before the ritual laws governing the writing of *tefillin* and *mezuzah* on leather were established."[8] Burkitt further speculates, "I think it not at all unlikely that it was folded up and buried with its former owner as a kind of charm."[9] Burkitt's reasonable speculation has some indirect support from the two silver amulets found at Ketef Hinnom (→ 2.2.5.3).

2.2.5.2.2 Nature and Text-Critical Character

Cook characterizes the text as including important original readings, often agreeing with LXX. His description of the text comes from the time before the Dead Sea Scrolls were discovered, and he conveys the excitement of finding a witness with significant variant readings:

> It contains the Decalogue and the Shemaʿ, but with remarkable divergences from the Massoretic Text; indeed, not only may it be asserted that no one MS. is known to contain so many variants in so short a space, but the majority of them are absolutely unique, and are to be found neither in the collations of a Kennicott or a De Rossi, nor in traditional notices of long-lost manuscripts.[10]

Burkitt agrees with Cook's earlier characterization of the text, saying, "It is a papyrus containing the Decalogue in Hebrew followed by the Shema, the text differing in many notable particulars from the Massoretic standard, and agreeing with that which underlies the Septuagint version."[11] He is inclined, however, to see MT as preserving the more original text while calling the NP "a monument of popular religion, giving a text of the Commandments with the grammatical difficulties smoothed down."[12]

Cook's initial publication discusses the textual variants in detail. A short list of the major variants includes the following: the reason given for the Sabbath command agrees with the Exodus version referring to creation rather than with the Deuteronomy version referring to the period of slavery in Egypt; the commandments concerning murder, adultery, and stealing are arranged as adultery, murder, stealing; the Shema is preceded by a lengthy introduction found also in Codex Vaticanus ("These are the statutes and the judgments that Moses commanded the sons of Israel in the wilderness when they came out of the land of Egypt …"). Now that the Dead Sea Scrolls show that early *tefillin* and *mezuzot* that included the Ten Commandments cited them from Deuteronomy and yet sometimes substituted the Exodus reason for the Sabbath commandment for that in Deuteronomy, there is even more evidence to support that the NP is based upon Deuteronomy with influence from Exodus rather than vice versa.[13]

---

[8] Eshel, "4QDeutⁿ – A Text That Has Undergone Harmonistic Editing," 123 n. 36.

[9] Burkitt, "Hebrew Papyrus of the Ten Commandments," 407.

[10] Cook, "Pre-Massoretic Biblical Papyrus," 36.

[11] Burkitt, "Hebrew Papyrus of the Ten Commandments," 392.

[12] Burkitt, "Hebrew Papyrus of the Ten Commandments," 402.

[13] Cf. 4QPhyl G, 4QMez A, 8QPhyl; both Cook ("Pre-Massoretic Biblical Papyrus," 53) and Albright ("Biblical Fragment," 175) reached the same conclusion apart from the Dead Sea Scroll evidence.

The previously noted agreements with LXX illustrate the antiquity of those readings, but do not establish a clear textual affiliation. The pattern of agreements and disagreements is rather complex. Most of the agreements between the NP and LXX over against MT are minor elements such as the presence or absence of conjunctions (six times) or prepositions (twice), or a change in the person of a pronominal suffix (once). The more significant agreements are the location of the phrase יִיטַב לָךְ "that it may go well with you" (Deut 5:16), the order of the commandments *adultery, murder, steal* (Deut 5:17–19), and the additional introduction to the Shema ("and these are the statutes and the judgments that Moses/Yahweh commanded the sons of Israel in the wilderness when they left the land of Egypt" [cf. Deut 4:45; 5:1, 31; 6:1; 12:1]). On the other hand, NP agrees with MT against LXX on the presence or absence of conjunctions (three times), the verbal root connected with coveting the neighbor's house (ἐπιθυμήσεις = תַחְמֹד [Deut 5:21]; cf. Exod 20:17), and the shorter reading omitting the italicized words "and all *his beasts and all* that is your neighbor's" (Deut 5:21). NP also disagrees with LXX in omitting מִבֵּית עֲבָדִים ("from the house of slavery" [Deut 5:6], vid.; cf. 4QExod^e [Exod 13:3] and XḤev/SePhyl [Exod 13:14]), the verbal root associated with the Sabbath (φύλαξαι = שָׁמוֹר "keep" [Deut 5:12]; cf. Exod 20:8), the presence of the phrase כַּאֲשֶׁר צִוְּךָ יְהוָה אֱלֹהֶיךָ ("as Yahweh your God commanded you" [Deut 5:12, 16]; cf. 4QPhyl G and Exod 20:8, 12), and the reason given for the Sabbath command (creation vs. slavery in Egypt; cf. 4QPhyl G, 4QMez A, 8QPhyl, and Exod 20:11). The tendency of this text to harmonize Deuteronomy and Exodus is a striking feature.

2.2.5.2.3 Date and Milieu

Cook concluded from his initial paleographical analysis that the manuscript should be dated to 100–125 C.E.[14] Burkitt suggested an earlier date, 55 C.E.[15] Albright brought a much broader array of inscriptional evidence to bear on the question, and first proposed that it should be dated to 150–100 B.C.E., but then revised his opinion to the late Maccabaean period, close to 50 B.C.E.[16] With the even broader array of evidence available to him, Cross dated the script back to the earlier range, about 150 B.C.E.[17]

The Egyptian provenance of the papyrus is not disputed, but the claim that it came from Faiyum cannot be corroborated.[18] If the papyrus were a liturgical document, it would support the claim that the Decalogue and the Shema were recited regularly in worship, in Hebrew, by Egyptian Jews at about 150 B.C.E. If it is an early *tefillah* (*tefillin*) or *mezuzah*, as seems more likely, then it says more about which passages were selected to be reproduced as objects of piety or as amulets for protection. In such a case, the papyrus would contribute little toward a discussion of the language that was commonly being spoken by Jews at that time, or about their regular worship practices.

2.2.5.2.4 Relevance for Exegesis and Literary Analysis

In addition to its tendency to harmonize Deuteronomy toward Exodus, the NP contributes to the debate about the intended meaning of the Shema. A monotheistic rendering is "[As for] Yahweh our God, Yahweh is one," while a monolatric rendering is "Yahweh is our God, Yahweh alone." Of crucial importance is whether the second clause is independent, "Yahweh is one," or dependent, "Yahweh alone." Variant texts can be quite helpful here, since the variant readings clarify how the second clause was understood. NP, along with all the other earliest variant texts to which we have access, shows that the second clause was understood as an independent clause. This is indicated either by omitting the first clause or by adding a copula to the second clause; see Table 1.[19]

---

[14] Cook, "Pre-Massoretic Biblical Papyrus," 51.

[15] Burkitt, "Hebrew Papyrus of the Ten Commandments," 400–01.

[16] Albright, "Biblical Fragment," 149; quotations from Albright in Trever, "Paleographic Study," 18 n. 46, 23 n. 65a.

[17] Cross, "Oldest Manuscripts from Qumran," 148 n. 3; see also Cross, *"Development," 148.

[18] Albright, "Biblical Fragment," 145.

[19] In addition to the listed texts, two other phylacteries

TABLE 1 *Ancient Forms of the Shema*

Second Clause	First Clause	Witness
יְהוָה אֶחָד "Yahweh is one"	יְהוָה אֱלֹהֵינוּ "[As for] Yahweh our God"	MT
יהוה אחד "Yahweh is one"		XḤev/SePhyl
יהוה אחד הוא "Yahweh is one"	יהוה אלהינו "[As for] Yahweh our God"	NP
κύριος εἷς ἐστιν "the Lord is one" = (הוא ?) יהוה אחד	κύριος ὁ θεὸς ἡμῶν "[As for] the Lord our God" = יהוה אלהינו	LXX (cf. also Mark 12:29)[20]
יהוה אחד "Yahweh is one" ΕΙΣ ΘΕΟΣ "God is one"		Samaritan inscriptions, magic bowls[21]

Despite the evidence showing a uniformly monotheistic understanding of Deut 6:4 from at least the third century B.C.E. to the Middle Ages, Eshel, Eshel, and Lange affirm the majority position today that the original meaning of the passage was monolatric rather than monotheistic: "In our opinion, Deut 6:4 should be translated as 'Hear, O Israel! The Lord is our God, the Lord alone.'"[22] In their view, the originally monolatric meaning of the passage was altered already in ancient times for apologetic reasons into a monotheistic meaning, which became normative in later Judaism.[23]

It is not certain, however, that the original meaning of the Shema was monolatric rather than monotheistic. The following considerations support an originally monotheistic meaning:

1) The word אֶחָד means "one," not "alone."[24] If the author had intended to teach that Yahweh *alone* was to be acknowledged as God, he could have used the phrase יְהוָה לְבַדּוֹ "Yahweh alone" (see Exod 22:19; 1 Sam 7:4; Isa 2:11, 17; cf. Neh 9:6; Ps 83:19; Isa 37:20).

2) The combination יְהוָה אֱלֹהֵי־ ("Yahweh God" with or without a suffix) occurs 316 times in Deuteronomy alone, always as a composite

---

may have originally had readings that favor a monotheistic understanding. To reconstruct 4QPhyl B (4Q129) with the shorter reading of XḤev/Se Phyl (XḤev/Se5) helps to relieve the spatial constraints in that line of the fragment, and to reconstruct 4QPhyl M (4Q140) with the longer reading of NP fits its available space better.

[20] Whether the Hebrew text underlying LXX here had the personal pronoun is uncertain. The Greek copula may have been inserted by a translator who understood the original shorter phrase as a verbless clause, just as some Hebrew scribes added a personal pronoun as a copula for the same reason.

[21] See a discussion of these inscriptions and further references in Eshel, Eshel, and Lange, "'Hear, O Israel' in Gold," 46, 56.

[22] Eshel, Eshel, and Lange, "'Hear, O Israel' in Gold," 45.

[23] Eshel, Eshel, and Lange, "'Hear, O Israel' in Gold," 50–54.

[24] Even in 1 Kgs 4:19, ונציב אחד אשר בארץ means "and there was *one* ruler who was in the land," and in 1 Chr 29:1, שלמה בני אחד בחר בו אלהים means "Solomon my son, the *one* whom God has chosen …"

personal name of Yahweh ("Yahweh [your/our] God") rather than as an independent clause ("Yahweh *is* [your/our] God"). In the most immediate context, the combination יְהוָה אֱלֹהֵי־ occurs in each verse of Deut 6:1–5, and it should be understood uniformly as the composite name of Yahweh.

3) Understanding יְהוָה אֱלֹהֵי as the composite name of Yahweh favors the monotheistic understanding of the Shema. While an independent clause in the first portion of Deut 6:4 would be *optional* for a monotheistic understanding ("Yahweh *is* our God; Yahweh is one," or "[As for] Yahweh our God, Yahweh is one"), it would be *required* for a monolatric understanding in which the second portion merely qualifies the subject of the first portion ("Yahweh *is* our God, Yahweh alone").

4) There is a pattern in Deuteronomy of using the composite name of Yahweh and then predicating some identifying characteristic of his (Deut 3:22; 4:24; 7:9; 9:3; 10:17; 31:3, 6). To understand the Shema as "[As for] Yahweh our God, Yahweh is one" follows the pattern, but "Yahweh is our God, Yahweh alone" breaks the pattern.

5) That the last two words of the Shema are a nonverbal *independent* clause is supported by the closest linguistic parallel being a verbal *independent* clause asserting the oneness of Yahweh: בַּיּוֹם הַהוּא יִהְיֶה יְהוָה אֶחָד וּשְׁמוֹ אֶחָד "in that day Yahweh will be one and his name one" (Zech 14:9).

The evidence of the NP, combined with the preceding considerations, renders the supposedly original monolatric meaning of the Shema more difficult to support. If the original meaning was actually monotheistic, then the addition of the personal pronoun in the NP does not signal a change in meaning for apologetic reasons, but merely confirms that the scribe understood the original meaning correctly.

Albright, W.F., "A Biblical Fragment from the Maccabaean Age: The Nash Papyrus," *JBL* 56 (1937): 145–76.

Albright, W.F., "On the Date of the Scrolls from 'Ain Feshkha and the Nash Papyrus," *BASOR* 115 (1949): 10–19.

Burkitt, F.C., "The Hebrew Papyrus of the Ten Commandments," *JQR* 15 (1903): 392–408.

Burkitt, F.C., "The Nash Papyrus: A New Photograph," *JQR* 16 (1904): 559–61.

Charles, R.H., *The Decalogue* (New York: Charles Scribner's Sons, 1923).

Cook, S.A., "A Pre-Massoretic Biblical Papyrus," *Proceedings of the Society of Biblical Archaeology* 25 (1903): 34–57.

Crawford, S.W., *Rewriting Scripture in Second Temple Times* (Grand Rapids: Eerdmans, 2008).

Cross, F.M., "The Oldest Manuscripts from Qumran," *JBL* 74 (1955): 147–72.

Eshel, E., "4QDeut^n – A Text That Has Undergone Harmonistic Editing," *HUCA* 62 (1991): 117–54.

Eshel, E., H. Eshel, and A. Lange, "'Hear, O Israel' in Gold: An Ancient Amulet from Halbturn in Austria," *Journal of Ancient Judaism* 1 (2010): 43–64.

Foster, P., "Why Did Matthew Get the Shema Wrong? A Study of Matthew 22:37," *JBL* 122 (2003): 309–33.

von Gall, A., "Ein neuer hebräischer Texte der Zehn Gebote und des Schema," *ZAW* 23 (1903): 347–51.

Himbaza, I., "La Décalogue de Papyrus Nash, Philon, 4QPhyl G, 8QPhyl 3 et 4QMez A," *RevQ* 20 (2001–2002): 411–28.

Martin, G.D., *Multiple Originals: New Approaches to Hebrew Bible Textual Criticism* (SBLTCS 7; Atlanta: SBL, 2010).

Peters, N., *Die älteste Abschrift der zehn Gebote, der Papyrus Nash* (Freiburg i.B.: Herder, 1905).

Trever, J.C., "A Paleographic Study of the Jerusalem Scrolls," *BASOR* 113 (1949): 6–23.

Trever, J.C., "Studies in the Problem of Dating the Dead Sea Scrolls," *Proceedings of the American Philosophical Society* 97 (1953): 184–93.

2.2.5.3 Silver Scrolls from Ketef Hinnom
2.2.5.3.1 History of Research, Manuscripts, and Editions

Two tiny silver scrolls (Ketef Hinnom I [KH I] and Ketef Hinnom II [KH II]) were discovered in the 1979 excavations conducted by Gabriel Barkay southwest of the Old City of Jerusalem, on the western shoulder of the Hinnom Valley. He first published the scrolls in 1989.¹ Because of their small size and deteriorated condition, it was extremely difficult to read them with confidence. As a later article put it, "The text could not be read fully because it could barely be seen."² Two years later, Yardeni published an edition with several different readings and paleographical observations.³ A major advance was made when a team of scholars used new technologies to decipher and record disputed letters and paleographic details and produced a new edition.⁴ The transcriptions and translations below for the most part follow the new edition.⁵

KH I

[...] יֹהוּ [...] הֹ[גֹּדֹ]ל שמר] הֹברית וֹ[הֹ]חסד לאהֹבֹ[וֹ] וֹשמרי [מצותו ...]ת העלֹם o ...] הֹ[ברכה מכל [פֹ]ח ומהרע כי בו גאלה כי יהוה [מֹ]שיבנו [וֹ]צֹור יברך יהוה [וֹיֹ]שמרך [יאֹ]ר יהוה פֹּנֹ[יו ...]

[...] YHW [... the] grea[t ... who keeps] the covenant and [g]raciousness toward those who love [him] and those who keep [his commandments ...] the Eternal? [... the?] blessing more than any [sna]re and more than Evil. For redemption is in him. For Yahweh is our restorer [and] rock. May Yahweh bles[s] you and [may he] keep you. [May] Yahweh make [his face] shine ...

KH II

[...הֹ]וֹ בֹּרֹךְ הֹ[א] ליהוֹ[ה] הֹעֹזֹר והֹגֹער בֹּ[רֹ]עֹ יברֹךְ יהוה ישמרך יאר יה[ו]הֹ פניוֹ [אל]יך ויֹשׂם לך שֹׁ[לֹ]ם

[For PN, (the son/daughter of) xxxx]h/hu. May h[e]/sh[e] be blessed by Yahweh, the warrior [or helper] and the rebuker of [E]vil: May Yahweh bless you, keep you. May Yahweh make his face shine upon you and grant you p[ea]ce.

---

¹ Barkay, "ברכת הכוהנים," 37–76.
² Barkay et al., "Challenges," 164.
³ Yardeni, "Remarks," 176–85.
⁴ Barkay et al., "Amulets from Ketef Hinnom," 41–71.
⁵ The changes from the "summary readings" in Barkay et al., "Amulets from Ketef Hinnom," are as follows: where two alternative readings are presented, the first alternative is followed; the rendering of the Tetragrammaton has been standardized; the typographical error of omitting the ע in the word העלם "the Eternal" from KH I has been fixed.

2.2.5.3.2 Nature and Text-Critical Character

The scrolls generated high interest because of their early date and because of the textual parallels with the Hebrew Bible. The closest textual parallels are laid out in tabular form in Table 1 and 2 on pp. 117–18.

While KH I is too poorly preserved to show whether it included the words וִיחֻנֶּךָּ יִשָּׂא יְהוָה פָּנָיו אֵלֶיךָ "and be gracious to you; may Yahweh lift up his face to you" in the blessing formula, KH II clearly did not include those words. On purely mechanical grounds, an accidental omission of the words by homoioteleuton is quite understandable, with the scribe's eyes jumping from one יְהוָה פָּנָיו אֵלֶיךָ "Yahweh his face to you" to the next, skipping the words between. Such a mechanical accident could correlate with the somewhat casual nature in which the letters were scratched into the surface: "In all likelihood, this is because the inscriptions were never meant to be seen again; that is, like the inscriptions in *mezuzot* and *tefillin*, once written and rolled up, they no longer really act as the components of documents intended to be read."⁶

Waaler creates an eclectic text from Barkay's and Yardeni's early reconstructions to assert that there is "full correspondence" of all the letters of the preserved portion of the priestly blessing on both amulets and in the book of Numbers, and concludes therefore that "the common archetype was available at the time of the inscription."⁷ The newer transcriptions weaken the force of his argument by confirming the following textual differences: both KH I and KH II have only one *kaph* for the MT יְבָרֶכְךָ "may he bless you"; KH II lacks the initial *waw* of וְיִשְׁמְרֶךָ "and may he keep you"; KH II omits the words וִיחֻנֶּךָּ יִשָּׂא יְהוָה פָּנָיו אֵלֶיךָ "and be gracious to you; may Yahweh lift up his face to you"; KH II has too little room for the plene spelling of שָׁלוֹם "peace."

---

⁶ Barkay et al., "Amulets from Ketef Hinnom," 46.
⁷ Waaler, "Revised Date for Pentateuchal Texts?" 47.

2.2.5 OTHER SOURCES

TABLE 1 *The Divine Identification Formula*

KH I	לְ[גָּדֹ]ל [...]	[ה]חסד וֹ[ה]בְּרִית [שמר]	[מצותו] וֹשמרי [לאהב[ו]
Deut 7:9	הָאֵל הַנֶּאֱמָן	שֹׁמֵר הַבְּרִית וְהַחֶסֶד	לְאֹהֲבָיו וּלְשֹׁמְרֵי מִצְוֹתוֹ
Dan 9:4	הָאֵל הַגָּדוֹל וְהַנּוֹרָא	שֹׁמֵר הַבְּרִית וְהַחֶסֶד	לְאֹהֲבָיו וּלְשֹׁמְרֵי מִצְוֹתָיו
Neh 1:5	הָאֵל הַגָּדוֹל וְהַנּוֹרָא	שֹׁמֵר הַבְּרִית וָחֶסֶד	לְאֹהֲבָיו וּלְשֹׁמְרֵי מִצְוֹתָיו
Neh 9:32	הָאֵל הַגָּדוֹל הַגִּבּוֹר וְהַנּוֹרָא	שׁוֹמֵר הַבְּרִית וְהַחֶסֶד	

KH I	[... the] grea[t	[who keeps] the covenant and [the] graciousness	toward those who love [him] and those who keep [his commandments]
Deut 7:9	the faithful God	who keeps the covenant and the graciousness	toward those who love him and toward those who keep his commandments
Dan 9:4	the great and awesome God	who keeps the covenant and the graciousness	toward those who love him and toward those who keep his commandments
Neh 1:5	the great and awesome God	who keeps the covenant and graciousness	toward those who love him and those who keep his commandments
Neh 9:32	the great, mighty, and awesome God	who keeps the covenant and the graciousness	

2.2.5.3.3 Date and Milieu

KH I and KH II are the earliest artifacts of any language to quote texts that are also found in the Hebrew Bible, but published studies have proposed widely different dates for their composition. The recent study by Barkay et al. provides evidence from archaeological stratigraphy, paleography, and orthography to support the following statement: "Our conclusion is that they date from the horizon of the end of the Judaean monarchy – or a palaeographic date of the late seventh century B.C.E. to early sixth century B.C.E."[8] In his proposal for an earlier date, Waaler speculates, "When the amulets were put into the grave, they had been in use for a generation. If this was the case, the amulets could have been made in the first half of the seventh century (700–650 BC)."[9] Pressing for a much later date, Renz proposes a Hellenistic setting.[10] The dating in the new edition by Barkay et al. appears to make the best use of the evidence.

2.2.5.3.4 Relevance for Exegesis and Literary Analysis

The early date of the silver scrolls and the inclusion of texts also found in the Hebrew Bible make them important evidence for the development of the text of the Hebrew Bible. Their small size, deteriorated state, and function as amulets, however, reduce their value for textual criticism of the Hebrew Bible. These two aspects explain the quite different evaluations that scholars have of their significance. For instance, Zevit concludes from his study of the amulets that "the first Amulet can be used to argue for the contemporaneity of P and D (or of incipient P and incipient D) in Jerusalem during the seventh century," whereas Tov concludes that "since these documents contain no running biblical texts, their contribution to textual criticism is limited."[11]

---

[8] Barkay et al., "Amulets from Ketef Hinnom," 42.

[9] Waaler, "Revised Date for Pentateuchal Texts?" 32.

[10] Renz and Röllig, *Die Althebräischen Inschriften*, 450; for a discussion of the various dates proposed for the amulets on the basis of archaeology, paleography, and orthography, see Berlejung, "Ein Programm fürs Leben," 208–12; her own preference is for a date later than that defended in the new edition: "So verdichten sich also m.E. die Zeichen dafür, dass die Amulette frühestens an das Ende des 6. Jh. (mit F.M. Cross) oder mit der frühesten Ansetzung der Stücke durch J. Renz/W. Röllig in das 5. Jh. v.Chr. zu datieren sind."

[11] Tov, *TCHB*, 111; cf. Zevit, "Scratched Silver," 32 (similarly Waaler, "Revised Date for Pentateuchal Texts?" 53).

TABLE 2 *The Priestly Blessing Formula*

		[יא]ר יהוה פנ[י]ו אליך	[וי]שמרך	יהוה	יברך	KH I
וישם לד ש[ל]ם		יאר יה[ו]ה פניו [אל]יך	ישמרך	יהוה	יברך	KH II
וְיָשֵׂם לְךָ שָׁלוֹם	וִיחֻנֶּךָּ יִשָּׂא יְהוָה פָּנָיו אֵלֶיךָ	יָאֵר יְהוָה פָּנָיו אֵלֶיךָ	וְיִשְׁמְרֶךָ	יְהוָה	יְבָרֶכְךָ	Num 6:24–26

KH I	May bless you	Yahweh	[and may he] keep you	[may] Yahweh [make shi]ne [his fa]ce [upon you]		
KH II	May bless you	Yahweh	may he keep you	may Yah[we]h make shine his face [upon] you		and grant you p[ea]ce
Num 6:24–26	May bless you	Yahweh	and may he keep you	may Yahweh make shine his face upon you	and be gracious to you, may Yahweh lift his face to you	and grant you peace

While the contribution of the scrolls to the state of the biblical text at the time is indirect since they were not composed as biblical texts, their contribution to the study of early excerpted texts such as *tefillin* and *mezuzot* is more direct. As Yardeni notes, "There may also be a relation between amulets and the *Tefillin* which are bound on the forehead and on the hand. It is possible that in early times the *Tefillin* were similar in form to amulets as they were also in a later period. A *Tefilla* of silver – *tplh zy ksp* – is mentioned in a papyrus from Edfu from the 3rd century B.C.E."[12] The combination of the priestly blessing with words invoking protection against evil shows that "their function is apotropaic and/or sanctifying; the inscriptions in these plaques exist as amulets to give their wearers protection against evil in the presence of holiness."[13]

Other excerpted texts functioned in a similar way, despite the omission of any specific words invoking protection against evil. Simply invoking the name of God provided protection. This can be seen in the magic bowls, magical papyri, and amulets that include the name of God, particularly in the form of the Shema (Deut 6:4). The gold amulet from Halbturn is a third century C.E. example of this practice, and the Samaritan and Jewish inscriptions of the Shema from Roman times perhaps should be included in the same category.[14] Thus, the first portion of KH I, giving a long form of the name of God, and the repetition of the Tetragrammaton in the priestly blessing in KH I and KH II, may have been considered as important for protection against evil as the specific verbs of protection in the blessing.

Barkay, G., "News from the Field: The Divine Name Found in Jerusalem," *BAR* 9 (1983): 14–19.

Barkay, G., "חפירות כתף־הינום בירושלים," *Qad* 68 (1984): 94–108 [Hebr.].

Barkay, G., "ברכת הכוהנים על לוחיות כסף מכתף הינום בירושלים," *Cathedra* 52 (1989): 37–76 [Hebr.].

Barkay, G. et al., "The Challenges of Ketef Hinnom: Using Advanced Technologies to Reclaim the Earliest Biblical Texts and Their Context," *Near Eastern Archaeology* 66 (2003): 162–71.

Barkay, G. et al., "The Amulets from Ketef Hinnom: A New Edition and Evaluation," *BASOR* 334 (2004): 41–71.

Berlejung, A., "Ein Programm fürs Leben: Theologisches

---

[12] Yardeni, "Two Ancient Amulets," 185.
[13] Barkay et al., "Amulets from Ketef Hinnom," 46.

[14] E. Eshel, H. Eshel, and A. Lange, "'Hear, O Israel' in

Wort und anthropologischer Ort der Silberamulette von Ketef Hinnom," *ZAW* 120 (2008): 204–30.

Eshel, E., "Apotropaic Prayers in the Second Temple Period," in *Liturgical Perspectives: Prayer and Poetry in Light of the Dead Sea Scrolls: Proceedings of the Fifth International Symposium of the Orion Center for the Study of the Dead Sea Scrolls and Associated Literature, 19–23 January 2000* (eds. E.G. Chazon et al.; STDJ 48; Leiden: Brill, 2003), 69–88.

Renz, J. and W. Röllig, *Die Althebräischen Inschriften*, Part 1: *Text und Kommentar* (Handbuch der Althebräischen Epigraphik 1/1; Darmstadt: Wissenschaftlich Buchgesellschaft, 1995).

Waaler, E., "A Revised Date for Pentateuchal Texts? Evidence from Ketef Hinnom," *TynBul* 53 (2002): 29–55.

Yamauchi, E.M., "Scripture as Talisman, Specimen, and Dragoman," *JETS* 50 (2007): 3–30.

Yardeni, A., "Remarks on the Priestly Blessing on Two Ancient Amulets from Jerusalem," *VT* 41 (1991): 176–85.

Zevit, Z., "Scratched Silver and Painted Walls: Can We Date Biblical Texts Archaeologically?" *HS* 48 (2007): 23–37.

2.2.5.4 Severus Scroll
2.2.5.4.1 History of Research

The earliest reference to the Severus Scroll (Sev) may have been by Flavius Josephus, who, as a contemporary of Titus, spoke of a scroll that Titus took as spoils from the temple of Jerusalem to Rome in 70 C.E.[1] Moses ha-Darshan (eleventh century) may have been speaking of the same scroll when he spoke of a scroll "that was removed from Jerusalem in the captivity and taken to Rome. It was stored away in the synagogue of Severus."[2] David Kimhi (ca. 1160–1235) mentioned that a scroll "which was in the Synagogue of Severus" in Rome contained the reading "and lo death is good" instead of the expected "and lo it was very good" (Gen 1:31).[3] Epstein identified the scrolls described by Josephus and ha-Darshan as the same scroll and concluded that the scroll must have been the oldest and most revered scroll of the Jews.[4]

The discovery that this ancient scroll contained a text that differed from the later MT was of immense interest, since the list of variants was the first glimpse into the Hebrew form of a non-sectarian biblical text in the pre-Masoretic era, not dependent on inferences from translations. Epstein concluded that the list of variants might well shake one's faith in the accuracy of MT, but it also provides assurance that the textual changes that had taken place over the years are limited to only a few places.[5] Subsequent discoveries of the Nash Papyrus and the Dead Sea Scrolls have dramatically increased the number of textual changes known to have taken place in the Hebrew text.

Christian Ginsburg included an extensive analysis of Sev variants and the differences between Sev^{MBR} and Sev^P in his monumental *Introduction to the Massoretico-Critical Edition of the Hebrew Bible*.[6] His comparison of the two lists allowed him to make numerous corrections to Epstein's earlier analysis of Sev^{MBR}, and to grasp for the first time that the *textus receptus* against which the Sev variants had been compiled was not the same as MT in every case.[7] Ginsburg also noted with interest that "the registration of anomalous forms," such as the Masoretes famously preserved in lists in their later manuscripts, "began during the period of the second Temple."[8] He agreed with Epstein that the text

---

Gold: An Ancient Amulet from Halbturn in Austria," *Journal of Ancient Judaism* 1 (2010): 43–64.

[1] Josephus, *J.W.*, 7.5.5.

[2] Albeck, *Midrash Bereshit Rabbati*, 209.

[3] Kimhi, פרוש רד״ק על התורה (eds. A. Ginzburg, R.L. Kirchheim, and A. Kohn; Pressburg: A. Edlen von Schmid, 1842), 9b.

[4] "Wenn Titus einen Codex der Mitnahme nach Rom für würdig erachtete, so muß dieser wohl der älteste und ehrwürdigste unter allen gewesen sein, und wir können uns, da seine Entführung nach Rom 70 n. Chr. stattgefunden hat, leicht einen Begriff von seinem hohen Alter machen" (Epstein, "Titus," 337–38).

[5] "Wenn der Glaube an die Richtigkeit unserer Texte dadurch erschüttert wird, so gewinnen wir andererseits die Zuversicht, daß die im Laufe der Zeit vorgenommenen Änderungen sich bloß auf einige wenige Stellen beschränken" (Epstein, "Titus," 350–51).

[6] Ginsburg, *Introduction*, 410–22; see the following section for an explanation of the abbreviations.

[7] See Ginsburg's discussion of מצרימה "to Egypt" (Gen 43:15) and כל עדת "all the congregation" (Num 31:12) in his *Introduction*, 414, 419.

[8] Ginsburg, *Introduction*, 421.

of the Pentateuch "was as a whole substantially the same during the period of the second Temple as it is now."[9]

Later discussions of Sev have commonly categorized it as a vulgar text, following the evaluation of Lieberman.[10] Leeven, Kutscher, Siegel, and Tov have compared the Sev variants with those of the Dead Sea Scrolls and have found many similarities.[11] Against such characterizations of Sev, Lange has argued recently that the Severus Scroll was rather close to the proto-Masoretic text.[12]

2.2.5.4.2 Manuscripts and Editions

Three medieval manuscripts provide four lists of variants from the lost Sev. The oldest witness is *Midrash Bereshit Rabbati* (Sev[MBR]), a compilation of comments by the eleventh-century Moses ha-Darshan. Lange explains the history of that manuscript: "The only known manuscript of MBR from Prague was lost during World War II but formed the basis of a masterly edition by Albeck who preserved this precious work for posterity."[13] Among the comments concerning Gen 45:8 are included the variant readings found in Sev. Although this manuscript is the oldest containing the list of variants, it is also the most difficult to use. In some cases, it cites the location of the variant without citing the variant itself, while in others it cites the variant but in a form differing from that in other lists of Sev variants. In some cases, it is not clear whether it cites a variant or a version of a *textus receptus* that is not the same as the Leningrad Codex (MT[L]). It is not clear how much of this difficulty should be attributed to ha-Darshan himself and how much to the later compiler of his work.

An illuminated manuscript of the Hebrew Bible owned by the Farḥi family in Damascus was produced in the latter part of the fourteenth century and contained folios that preserved two of the lists. Folio 146 contains the list in the body of the text, while folio 403 weaves a micrographic version of the list into a pattern in the margin of the page. Where the two lists agree, the abbreviation Sev[D] is used below, while Sev[D146] and Sev[D403] are used for distinction when they disagree. According to Lange, "In folio 146, the text of the Severus Scroll variant list is carefully written and only few scribal errors occur," while in folio 403, "the scribe copied the Severus Scroll variant list in the micrography ... with amazing accuracy and readability," but "the textual quality of Sev[D403] is mixed," because it displays omissions of letters or words, and various scribal corruptions.[14]

The youngest of the manuscripts containing a list of Sev variants is the illuminated ms Hebreu 31 of the Bibliothèque Nationale in Paris (Sev[P]), produced in 1414. According to Lange, "The textual quality of the variant list in Sev[P] is high. It is less abbreviated than other copies and displays only few scribal errors. In some cases Sev[P] needs nevertheless to be corrected in comparison with Sev[D146] and Sev[D403]."[15]

Epstein produced the first scholarly edition of the Sev variants when he transcribed Sev[MBR] in 1885.[16] In the same year, Sev[D146] was published by Harkavy.[17] Two years later, Sev[P] was published by Neubauer.[18] Some eighty years later, Loewinger published his important study of Sev, including full transcriptions of Sev[MBR] and Sev[P], with notes on Sev[D146] and Sev[D403] where they differ from Sev[P], and with facsimiles of Sev[D146], Sev[D403], and Sev[P].[19] Siegel analyzed the variants and used them to draw historical, text-critical, orthographical, and sociological conclusions, but his monograph suffers from typographical errors and speculative conclusions.[20] All four lists of variants are retranscribed, com-

---

[9] Ginsburg, *Introduction*, 422.
[10] Lieberman, *Hellenism*, esp. 23–26; cf. Greenberg, "Stabilization of the Text," 161.
[11] Leeven, "Orthography," 2.577–83; Kutscher, *Isaiah Scroll*, esp. 87–89; Siegel, *Severus Scroll*; Tov, *TCHB*², 112–13.
[12] Lange, "Severus Scroll Variant List."
[13] Lange, *Severus Scroll Variant List* (pre-publication draft kindly made available by the author for this study).

[14] Lange, *Severus Scroll Variant List*.
[15] Lange, *Severus Scroll Variant List*.
[16] Epstein, "Titus," 337–51.
[17] Harkavy, חדשים גם ישנים, 102–03.
[18] Neubauer, "Pentateuch," 508–09.
[19] Loewinger, ספר תורה, 237–63 with facsimiles of the lists on plates 1–3 between 260–61.
[20] Siegel, *Severus Scroll*.

2.2.5.4.3 Nature and Text-Critical Character

Lists of Sev variants are deceptive in their simplicity, giving the impression that there are between thirty-one and thirty-three variants, one for each entry in the four witnesses. Each of the three different source documents has a different number of variants: Sev^MBR has thirty-three; Sev^P has thirty-two, omitting Exod 31:13; Sev^D has thirty-one, omitting also Lev 15:8. The discrepancy in recording the thirty-some variants adds to the uncertainty about the comprehensiveness of the list of variants.[22]

The lists also arrange the variants in two different orders, neither of which agrees with the standard order in which the passages are found in the Hebrew Bible. For example, the following divergent orders are followed for the latter part of Genesis:

Sev^MBR	36:5	36:10	36:14	43:15	48:7	45:8	46:8
Sev^D Sev^P	36:5	36:14	43:15	36:10	45:8	48:7	46:8

The reason for the divergent orders is not clear. Sev^D and Sev^P group together the two variants concerning the orthography of יעוש "Jeush" (Gen 36:5, 14), but none of the witnesses group together the two variants concerning the locative ending on מצרים "Egypt" (Gen 43:15; 46:8), the use of medial letters in final position (Gen 48:7; Lev 4:34; Deut 1:26; 3:20), or word divisions (Gen 27:2; 36:10; Deut 32:26).

Any complete list of Sev variants must be, to some extent, artificial, a critical reconstruction based on the four divergent witnesses. The critical reconstruction requires frequent filling out of entries in Sev^MBR to supply the *text* of the variant rather than the *location* of the variant cited according to the then-current *textus receptus*, and frequent correcting of the variant readings toward the forms in the other witnesses. A similar difficulty presents itself to one who attempts to reconstruct MT from the *Masorah parva* and *Masorah magna* rather than simply following the reading of MT^L. The great Masoretic manuscripts are not consistent with each other or even with themselves. Sometimes the notations indicate a *textus receptus* that is different from MT^L.[23]

While a critical reconstruction of the original list of Sev variants remains a desideratum, the new approach followed here makes maximum use of the textual data contained in the preserved lists even when they disagree with one another. This approach notes every variant included in each list, whether it is the variant targeted by one of the lists or it is an inadvertent variant accompanying the targeted variant. Such an approach yields many more variants than the standard thirty-three, with many of the accompanying variants being of the same kind as the targeted variants. Both kinds of variants have been categorized in Table 1, omitting details of their source for the sake of simplicity, and otherwise omitting only deliberate changes made when paraphrasing the *location* of variants.[24] Due to the form of the Sev variant lists, whether to categorize a variant as *targeted* or *accompanying* is often a matter of judgment.

This arrangement of data suggests that the scribes who created the Sev variant lists were not concerned about additions of *matres lectionis* or conjunctions, since they made such alterations as accompanying variants but did not target them. On the other hand, they were concerned about every

---

[21] Lange, *Severus Scroll Variant List*.

[22] Contrast the following statements: "Everything else [outside the list of Severus variants] we possess in the same form as the scribe of the Severus text found it – otherwise the reporter would not have refrained from communicating it" (Epstein, "Titus," 351); "We may suppose that this list, like similar other lists in rabbinic literature, is not exhaustive" (Segal, "Promulgation," 47).

[23] Cf. Gérard Weil's summary comments in the prolegomena to *BHS, xiv, where the MasP notes that על־מות is written as two words in two locations (ב׳ כת׳ תרי מילין), but MT^L has only one word in the first location (Ps 9:1 עלמות MT^L] על־מות MT^mlt mss; Ps 48:15 על־מות MT^L] עלמות MT^mlt mss).

[24] The data for this comprehensive list of variants are drawn from the as-yet unpublished new transcriptions of the lists by Lange.

TABLE 1   Comprehensive List of Severus Variants

Category	Targeted Variant	Accompanying Variant
Omission/addition of word(s)	אב "father" (Gen 24:7); מולדת "birth" (Gen 24:7); בריחם 2×? "bars" (Exod 26:27); החטאה "sin offering" (Lev 4:34); חיים "flowing" (Lev 15:8); כל "all" (Num 31:12); אלהים "God" (Deut 29:22)	בני ישראל "sons of Israel" (Gen 46:8);[25] מפר "from a steer" (Lev 4:34);[26] שנתה "her year" (Lev 14:10); ואל אלעזר הכהן "and to Eleazar the priest" (Num 31:12);[27] את direct object marker (Deut 29:22)
Omission/addition of locative	מצרימה "to Egypt" (Gen 43:15; 46:8)	
Omission/addition of final yod	בני "sons of" (Num 36:1)	יוממתי "day of my death" (Gen 27:2); לקרשי 2× "boards of" (Exod 26:27); ראשי "heads of" (Num 36:1); האמרי "the Amorites" (Deut 1:27)
Omission/addition of conjunction		ומארצי "and from my land" (Gen 24:7); וחמשה "and five" (Exod 26:27); ולא "and not" (Deut 22:6)
Omission/addition of other letter	מרעמסס "from Rameses" (Exod 12:37); הבא "the coming one" (Num 4:3)	ואהליבמה "and Oholibamah" (Gen 36:5); לפרעה "to Pharaoh" (Gen 45:8); חמשה "five" (Exod 26:27); מדמה "from its blood" (Lev 4:34); אביתם "you were willing" (Deut 1:26); כמהפכת "like the destruction of" (Deut 29:22)
Changed root	וישני/וישימני "and he placed me/and he lent me" (Gen 45:8);[28] לבני/לבית 2× "to the sons of/to the house of" (Exod 19:3); אחר/אשר "so that/afterwards" (Num 31:2); בני/בית "house of/sons of" (Num 36:1); הבנים/האבנים "the birthing place/the offspring" (Deut 22:6)	ענה/עדה "Adah/Anah" (Gen 36:10); ירק/יטהר "he is made clean/he spits" (Lev 15:8)

other category mentioned above, even when the changes made no difference in meaning, such as medial letters used in final positions, or biforms of certain words. Despite their concern over such changes as shown in the *targeted* variants, they often made similar changes as *accompanying* variants, which should alert textual critics to treat these lists with caution. As a case in point, how much weight should be placed on the change from a plural noun to a singular as a targeted variant of Num

---

[25] Although there is no other witness that omits the words בני ישראל "sons of Israel" here, it is rather frequently omitted in various witnesses at other locations (e.g., Num 1:46; 2:2, 33; 7:84; 8:19, 22; 9:18; 14:7, 10; 15:33; 31:9; 36:13, etc.). Epstein understands this as an omission rather than as an abbreviation and thinks that it is the intended variant here ("Titus," 347).

[26] The final two letters of the word are partially erased in Sev^D146.

[27] Though the omission of this phrase may be a simple abbreviation of the location of the variant, Epstein thinks that the omission is the targeted variant here ("Titus," 349). Cf. a similar variant at Num 36:1, where MT has לפני משה "before Moses" while 4QNum^b (4Q27) has לפני מושה ולפני אל[עזר הכהן "before Moses and before Eleazar the priest"; cf. Num 27:2 לפני משה ולפני אלעזר הכהן (before Moses and before Eleazar the priest).

[28] This change of root is shared by Rabbi Meir's Torah. Segal thinks that the difference is an accidental omission of the מ ("Promulgation," 46), but actually *two* letters would have had to have been omitted, and such an accident is unlikely to have happened to two scribes independently. In addition, Sev^MBR includes a commentary on this change of root, deriving the variant from נשה "lend." Other possibilities are that it should be derived from שנה "Change," or from עשה "make" with the loss of the guttural (see Jastram, "The Severus Scroll and Rabbi Meir's Torah," 140–41 n. 32).

2.2.5 OTHER SOURCES

TABLE 1 *(cont.)*

Category	Targeted Variant	Accompanying Variant
Biform and Aramaizing form	ומארע "and from the land" (Gen 24:7); שרפת/שרפה "a burning" (Deut 29:22)[29]	
Aural confusion	ת/ד *d/t* (Gen 1:31; 3:21); ש/ס *ś/s* (Gen 27:27)	ק/כ *q/k* (Gen 18:21)
Graphic confusion	ב/מ *m/b* (Gen 25:33); י/ו *y/w* (Gen 36:5,14; Exod 31:13)	ד/ר *d/r* (Gen 36:10)
Pronominal suffix change	הכצעקתה/הכצעקתם "whether like their outcry/whether like its outcry" (Gen 18:21)	
Number and/or gender change	תמימה/תמימים "without defect [pl./sg.]" (Lev 14:10); לדרתיכם/לדריכם "to your generations [masc./fem.]" (Num 15:21)	האמורים/האמור "the Amorite/the Amorites" (Deut 1:27)
Word division	יוממתי "the day of my death" (Gen 27:2); בנעדה "the son of Adah" (Gen 36:10); אפאיהם[2×] "I will cut them in pieces/[I said in] anger, where are they?" (Deut 32:26)	
Medial/final letters	שמ "there" (Gen 48:7); מדמ "from the blood" (Lev 4:34); אביתמ "you were willing" (Deut 1:26); המ "they" (Deut 3:20)	
Mater lectionis		מאֹד/מוֹת "death/much" (Gen 1:31); מכירתו "his birthright? his sword? his valuable thing?" (Gen 25:33); וימכור "and he sold" (Gen 25:33); בכורתו "his birthright" (Gen 25:33); מוֹתי "my death" (Gen 27:2); ויקוּמו "and they rose" (Gen 43:15); ותגיד "and you should tell" (Exod 19:3); בריחים "bars" (Exod 26:27); לדרוּתיכם "to your generations" (Num 15:21); עריסוֹתיכם "your coarse meal" (Num 15:21); נקוֹם "take vengeance" (Num 31:2); ויביאו "and they brought" (Num 31:12); לעוֹלת "to go up" (Deut 1:26); האמוֹרים "the Amorites" (Deut 1:27); אוֹתנו "us" (Deut 1:27); סדוֹם "Sodom" (Deut 29:22); ועמוֹרה "and Gomorrah" (Deut 29:22)

36:1 when there are five examples of the loss of a final *yod* in accompanying variants, three of which have the effect of making a plural noun singular?

Previous discussions about the status of Sev, whether it was from the temple in Jerusalem and the most revered of all scrolls or whether it was a vulgar text, have lost some urgency now with the discovery of the Dead Sea Scrolls with their hoard of ancient textual variants. For text-critical purposes, the *status* of the textual witness does not determine the originality of the reading; each variant must be considered on its own merit. The evidence suggests that Sev agreed with MT almost completely,[30] and that the few variants it contained were of the common types that later scribes would

---

[29] Cf. similar biforms בושה/בשת "shame" and תולעה/תולעת "worm."

[30] Thus Lange, "Severus Scroll Variant List."

make as they were copying from the *textus receptus* of their day.

2.2.5.4.4 Date and Milieu

Because Sev is lost and only lists of its variant readings are preserved, the scroll cannot be dated by standard methods. Yet the Aramaic introduction to Sev[MBR] includes the historical detail that "the Law was removed from Jerusalem in the captivity and was taken to Rome. It was stored away in the synagogue of Severus."[31] This corresponds to the statement by Flavius Josephus: "As the last of all the spoils [taken from the temple of Jerusalem by Titus in 70 C.E.] was carried the Law of the Jews" (Josephus, *J.W.*, 7.5.5). Whatever one may think of the character of variant readings of Sev, Epstein's conclusion that these references both speak of Sev appears to be fundamentally sound and establishes the ancient date of Sev as well as strongly suggesting that it held a high status among the Jews first in Jerusalem and then in Rome.[32]

2.2.5.4.5 Relevance for Exegesis and Literary Analysis

The primary value of the lists of Sev variants is to illustrate the kinds of variants that existed even in carefully copied scrolls from the Second Temple period. This serves as a cautionary restraint on proposing far-reaching implications of textual variants in other ancient manuscripts. For instance, there have been attempts to locate the production and use of scrolls by their orthography and by the "free" or "careful" attitude of the scribes who copied the texts. The supposition is that scrolls produced within mainstream Judaism would have an orthography very close to MT[L] and would have few lexical variants. Whatever one thinks of Sev itself, whether it was one of the oldest and most authoritative scrolls at the end of the Second Temple period (cf. Epstein) or a vulgar text (cf. Lieberman), the four lists of its variants were certainly composed and transmitted within mainstream Judaism. That those four lists included many unintentional accompanying variants of orthography and lexicography shows that such variants are not certain indicators of sectarian origin or use.

Albeck, C., *Midrash Bereshit Rabbati ex libro R. Mosis Haddaršan collectus e codice Pragensi cum adnotationibus et introductione* (Jerusalem: Mekize Nirdamim, 1940).

Epstein, A., "Ein von Titus nach Rom gebrachter Pentateuch-Codex und seine Varianten," *MGWJ* 34 (1885): 337–51.

Epstein, A., "Biblische Textkritik bei den Rabbinen," in *Recueil des travaux rédigés en mémoire du Jubilée Scientifique de M. Daniel Chwolson, Professeur émérite à l'Université de St. Pétersbourg, 1846–1896* (ed. D. Gunzburg; Berlin: S. Calvary & Co., 1899), 42–56, esp. 49–55.

Ginsburg, **Introduction*.

Greenberg, M., "The Stabilization of the Text of the Hebrew Bible, Reviewed in the Light of the Biblical Materials from the Judean Desert," *JAOS* 76 (1956): 157–67.

Habermann, A.M., "ספר אורייתא דאשתכחה ברומא," *Sinai* 32 (1953): 161–67 (reprinted in *Ketav Lashon Wa-Sefer: Reflections on Books, Dead Sea Scrolls, Language and Folklore* כתב לשון וספר: פרקי עיון [Jerusalem: Rubin Mass, 1973], 166–75) [Hebr.].

Harkavy, A.A., חדשים גם ישנים: מקורות ומחקרים בתולדות ישראל ובספרותו (Jerusalem: Karmiel, 1969–1970) [reprint of the 1885 ed.].

Jastram, N., "The Severus Scroll and Rabbi Meir's Torah," in *The Text of the Hebrew Bible: From the Rabbis to the Masoretes* (eds. L. Miralles-Maciá and E. Martín Contreras; Journal of Ancient Judaism Supplements 13; Göttingen: Vandenhoeck & Ruprecht, 2014), 137–45.

Kutscher, E.Y., *The Language and Background of the Isaiah Scroll (1QIsaᵃ)* (STDJ 6; Leiden: E.J. Brill, 1974).

Lange, A., *The Severus Scroll Variant List and the Dead Sea Scrolls* (forthcoming monograph).

Lange, A., "The Severus Scroll Variant List in Light of the Dead Sea Scrolls," in *Tradition, Transmission, and Transformation from Second Temple Literature through Judaism and Christianity in Late Antiquity: Proceedings of the Thirteenth International Symposium of the Orion Center for the Study of the Dead Sea Scrolls and Associated Literature Jointly Sponsored by the Hebrew University Center for the Study of Christianity, 22–24 February, 2011* (eds. M. Kister et al.; STDJ 113, Leiden: Brill, 2015), 179–207.

---

[31] *Midrash Bereshit Rabbati*, 209.
[32] Epstein, "Titus," 338.

2.2.5 OTHER SOURCES

Leeven, J., "The Orthography of the Hebrew Scroll of Isaiah A," in *Proceedings of the Twenty-Second Congress of Orientalists Held in Istanbul, September 15th to 22nd, 1951* (2 vols.: ed. Z.V. Togan; Leiden: Brill, 1953–1957), 2.577–83.

Lieberman, **Hellenism*.

Loewinger, D.S., "ספר תורה שהיה גנוז בבית כנסת סוירוס׳ מרומא – יחסו אל בגילות ישעיהו ממדבר יהודה ואל תורתו של רבי מאיר," *Beth Mikra* 42 (1970): 237–63.

Loewinger, D.S., "Prolegomenon," in Victor Aptowitzer, *Das Schriftwort in der rabbinischen Literatur* (ed. S. Loewinger; reprint of Vienna edition, 1906; New York: Ktav Publishing House, 1970), vii–xlv, esp. xxv–xxxviii.

Neubauer, A., "Der Pentateuch der sogenannten Severus-Synagoge," *MGWJ* 36 (1887): 508–09.

Segal, M., "The Promulgation of the Authoritative Text of the Hebrew Bible," *JBL* 73 (1953): 35–47.

Siegel, J.P., *The Severus Scroll and 1QIs^a* (Missoula: Scholars Press, 1975).

Nathan Jastram

2.3 Medieval Text of MT

2.3.1 Original Form, Editions and Auxiliary Tools[1]

Three of the four manuscripts attributed to Ben Asher that form the so-called "medieval Masoretic text" contain all or part of the text of the Pentateuch. The Leningrad Codex B19a (MT^L) has the whole Pentateuch; of the Pentateuch codex of the British Library Or. 4445 (MT^B) text from Gen 39:20 to Deut 1:33 remains, except for the pages corresponding to Num 7:46–73 and 9:12–10,18; and of the Aleppo Codex (MT^A) for the Pentateuch only text from the last word of Deut 28:17 until the end of the book is preserved.

Diplomatic Editions: In 2013 and 2016, in the new edition of MT^L, *BHQ, only the books of Genesis (Tal, *Genesis*) and Deuteronomy (McCarthy, *Deuteronomy*) have been published.

Even though only a few chapters of the book of Deuteronomy remain from MT^A, in the *Miqra'ot Gedolot ha-Keter* project the books of Genesis, Exodus, Numbers, and Deuteronomy have been published (Cohen, *Miqra'ot Gedolot "Haketer"*) in line with the reconstruction made based on new evidence found by Penkower, *New Evidence*.

Auxiliary Tools: The edition and explanation of the MasP and MasM of MT^L to the book of Genesis was done by Dotan (*Thesaurus*). As MT^B remains unpublished, Cassuto's work ("Qeré/ketiv dans le manuscript") on the *Qere-Ketiv* cases marked in this manuscript is a very useful work.

2.3.2 Text-Critical Character

The manuscripts that form the medieval MT contain certain differences in terms of form, consonantal text, vocalization, and Masorot (→ 1.5.4).

The way in which biblical text must be written is specified down to the smallest detail in the *Halakha* and also forms part of the Masorah. Thus, MT^L has a Masorah Finalis (MasF) after each of the books in the Pentateuch in which it gives the total number of verses that each one contains. Furthermore, at the end of Deuteronomy and after its total number of verses, it lists: the number of verses (5,845), words (79,856), and letters (400,945) in the Torah, as well as a list of the *sedarim* (167) of the Pentateuch for each book and a list of the occurrences of the *paseq* in the Pentateuch, ninety-five times in total. MT^A also presents the MasF after Deuteronomy including only the number of verses in the book.

Despite These halakhic requirements, medieval MT manuscripts are not identical in form. There are differences in the way in which MT^L and MT^A present the Song of Moses (Deut 32:1–43). Thus, in accordance with the instructions for the copying in *Maseket Soferim*, the Song of Moses must be in a seventy-line stichographic format, preceded and followed by a prose introduction (Deut 31:28b–31) and epilogue (Deut 32:44–47b) of six lines each, and one empty line (*petuha*) before and after the song. MT^L exhibits striking originality of form vis-à-vis the *Maseket Soferim*' regulations. It has only five full lines before and after the Song (and one word beginning a sixth line in the epilogue), together with two *petuhot*, while the song itself, written stichographically, covers only thirty-seven lines. Neither does MT^A, without going to the extremes of MT^L, fully comply with the rules given in *Maseket Soferim*. The Song of Moses in MT^A is contained in sixty-seven lines, following Maimonides, and the epilogue in five lines.[2]

As regards the different divisions of the biblical text, there are certain discrepancies between MT^A and MT^L in terms of the sections, particularly as regards their types, (תוחה)פ "open section" and (תומה)ס "closed section." For example, Deut 30:10–11 is marked in MT^L as פ and in MT^A as ס; Deut 30:14–

---

[1] Cf. "Medieval Masoretic Text", sections → 1.5.2–1.5.3, and → 1.2.2.2.1 for more detailed information.

[2] C. McCarthy, "A Diplomatic Dilemma in Deuteronomy 32," in *Proceedings of the Irish Biblical Association* 27 (2005): 22–32.

15 appears in MT^L as ס and in MT^A as פ; Deut 31:6–7 in MT^L as פ and in MT^A as ס; Deut 31:15–16 in MT^L as ס and in MT^A it is not marked; Deut 33:7–8 appears in MT^L as ס and in MT^A as פ.

There are also slight differences in the division for the three-year cycle. In MT^L, 168 *sedarim* are marked in the Pentateuch text. However, in the list of the *sedarim* found in its MasF, a total of 167 are listed. According to this list, Deut 20:1 should not be marked.

The Ben Asher manuscripts differ little from one another in their consonantal text, but some differences involve more than the presence or absence of the *matres lectionis*. However, the fragmentary character of the main biblical manuscripts for the Pentateuch makes it impossible to evaluate these differences.

2.3.2.1 Orthographic Irregularities: Extraordinary Points

Ten of the fifteen passages that in the biblical text contain one or several words with points on one or more letters are located in the Pentateuch (→ 1.5.4.1).

In MT^L, in the biblical text, all the letters of one or more words are punctuated in Gen 18:9 (אֵלָיו "to him"), Gen 33:4 (וַיִּשָּׁקֵהוּ "and kissed him"), Gen 37:12 (אֶת), Num 3:39 (וְאַהֲרֹן "and Aaron") and Deut 29:28 (לָנוּ וּלְבָנֵינוּ "to us and to our sons"). In all other cases, only one or some of the letters of the word are punctuated: the second *yod* of וּבֵינֶיךָ "between you" in Gen 16:5; the letters *qop*, *waw*, *mem* of וּבְקוּמָהּ "when she arose" in Gen 19:33; the *he* of רְחֹקָה "a distant" in Num 9:10; the *reš* of אֲשֶׁר "which" in Num 21:30 and the second *waw* of וְעֶשְׂרוֹן "and a tenth" in Num 29:15. Except for Deut 29:28, all the cases have MasP notes. The information contained in the MasP note is: "ten cases dotted in the Torah" in Gen 15:5, 18:9, 19:33, 33:4, Num 3:39, 29:15; in Gen 37:12, Num 9:10, and 21:30, the MasP notes only say "dotted."

In MT^A, due to the lost parts, only the case of Deut 29:28 is present. All the letters of the word are punctuated and there is no MasP note.

2.3.2.2 Orthographic Irregularities: Large Letters

All the letters written in larger than normal size occur in the Pentateuch.

Three letters occur in MT^L. In Num 27:5, the *nun* of מִשְׁפָּטָן "their cause" is large (MasP: "unique *nun* large"). The other two cases are found in Deut 6:4 where the *ayin* of שְׁמַע "hear" and the *dalet* of אֶחָד "one" are larger than usual. There is no MasP note in this case.

The only large letter present in MT^A is found in Deut 32:6. In this passage, the *he* of הליהוה "The Lord?" is large and separate from ליהוה (in MT^L, it is joined by *maqqef*).

2.3.2.3 Orthographic Irregularities: Inverted Nun

Before Num 10:35 and after 10:36, MT^L includes a symbol resembling an inverted *nun*. There is no Masoretic note in the marked passages. According to the explanation found in *Sifre Numbers* on Num 10:35, this sign would serve to indicate that a verse is misplaced. This explanation tallies with that given by modern scholars to these passages.[3]

2.3.2.4 Qere-Ketiv

The main manuscripts disagree on the number and location of *Qere-Ketiv* cases and on how to represent them.[4]

Fifty-two cases of *Qere-Ketiv* are marked in MT^L: sixteen in Genesis, twelve in Exodus, five in Leviticus, nine in Numbers, and ten in Deuteronomy.[5] The most common way of indicating this phenomenon in MT^L is the abbreviation ק׳, followed by קר׳ (nine times), and the full form (seven times). In one case, Deut 32:13, the term *yatir* "superfluous," is also used to indicate this phenomenon. Normally, the whole word is given in the *Qere*, but sometimes it only indicates the letter or letters that are affected (e.g., MasP of שִׁילֹה "Shiloh" in Gen 49:10 לו ק׳ "read שי[לו] 'Shilo' "; MasP of תַּלֻּנֹּת "murmur" in Exod 16:7:

---

[3] Lieberman, *Hellenism*, 38–43.
[4] The calculation of the *Qere-Ketiv* cases refers only to those explicitly indicated as such and not to cases of *yatir*.
[5] Cassuto, *Qeré-Ketib*.

קרי י "it should be read with yod"; etc.). The vowels of the *Qere* tend to appear in the biblical text below the *Ketiv*, although in Gen 30:11, they are also attached to the *Qere*. Six cases have two MasP notes, one on how the word is written and another that gives the *Qere*: e.g., MasP of כְּסוּתֹה "his covering" in Exod 22:26: כסותו ק'; ל' כת' ה' "unique written with *he*; read כסותו ['his covering']." Finally, four cases also have a MasM note which lists the cases which share the same *Qere* reading: e. g. MasM of יִקְרְחָה "they shall make bald" in Lev 21:5, ה' כתיב ה' וקרי' ו' "fifteen [words] are written with *he* [at the end of the word] and it should be read with *waw*."

MT^B lists twenty-three cases of *Qere-Ketiv* (vs. the thirty present in MT^L in the passages shared with MT^B), of which twenty-two are common with MT^L.[6] The word וְנִסְכֹּה "its libation" in Lev 23:13 is marked as *Qere-Ketiv* (MasP: ונסכו קרי, "it should be read ונסכו ['its libation']") but not in MT^L. One case, מִיָּדוֹ "his hands" in Exod 32:19, has no indication of *Qere-Ketiv* in the MasP but in the MasM note it clearly indicates that it is indeed a case of *Qere-Ketiv*: ה' כת' ידו וקריין ידי "five times is written ידו ['of his hand'] but is read וידיו ['of his hands']." MT^B shows a tendency to give as much information as possible about the *Qere-Ketiv*. Thus, eight cases are also accompanied by MasM note, which lists the cases sharing the same *Qere* reading: Exod 4:2, 16:2, 21:8, 27:8, 32:19; Lev 21:5; Num 1:16, 16:7. The MasP of three cases also describes what the readings proposed by the *Qere* consist of and the number of cases: מַזֶּה "what is that" in Exod 4:2, הי מלה דכת' חדה וקר' תרין מלה "fifteen words written as one word, read as two"; לֹא in Lev 11:21, הי' כת לא וקרי לו, "fifteen [times] is written לא 'no' but is read לו 'according to him' "; יִקְרְחָה "they shall make bald" in Lev 21:5, יד מלין דכת' ה' בסוף תיבות וקריין וא "fourteen words written with final *he* but read with *waw*." In addition, four cases have two MasP notes: in three of them, one note relates to the spelling and the other to the *Qere*; and in the fourth, one note gives the *Qere* and the other records the phenomenon.

In the few remaining chapters of Deuteronomy from MT^A, there are four cases of *Qere-Ketiv*, all of

---

[6] Cassuto, "*Qeré/ketiv* dans le manuscript."

them also present in MT^L: Deut 28:27; 28:30; 33:2 and 33:9. The trend in MT^A is that its information is more explicit than in MT^L. Thus, the full form, קרי, is used three times and in the MasP of אֶשְׁדָּת "fire, a law" in Deut 33:2 the phenomenon is explained in detail: כת מלה חדה וקרי תרת מלין "written as one word, read as two," while in the MasP of MT^L the short form is used: אש דת ק' "read [as two words] אש דת," " 'fire,' 'law'."

There are also cases of *qere perpetuum* – frequent words that must be read differently from their written form, no *circellus* or consonantal text is indicated in the margin, while the *Ketiv* is vocalized – that only occur in the Pentateuch. Thus, for instance, the third person singular feminine personal pronoun היא "she" that is always written as the third person singular masculine personal pronoun הוא "he" in the Pentateuch (except for eleven cases, as recorded by the MasP); or נַעֲרָה "maiden" written without the final *he* in the Pentateuch. The latter, however does have a *Qere-Ketiv* annotation between Deut 22:14 and 22:29 in the MasP of MT^L.

2.3.2.5 Sebirin

In MT^L, there are two cases of *sebir* in the Pentateuch, both in Numbers. The MasP to וַיָּבֹא "he came" in Num 13:22 remarks: ח' סבר לשון רבים "eight times the plural is suggested." The MasP to וַיֹּאמֶר "he spoke" in Num 32:25 notes: יב' סיבר "twelve [times] have been suggested [the plural form]." In this case, the information is less explicit and the alternative reading is not given although, from the context of the verse, one concludes that a plural verb would be expected. None of the cases has a MasM note listing the other passages.

2.3.3 Relevance for Exegesis

The Masorah of MT^L to the Pentateuch contains some notes that are directly relevant for the interpretation of the text. Of particular relevance are the semantic content notes that can be divided into two types: 1) those that confirm an unusual meaning of a form; and 2) those that indicate that a word has several meanings. Examples of the first kind are

2.3.3 RELEVANCE FOR EXEGESIS

to be found in: the MasP to הֲדַר "Hadar" in Gen 36:39: ל׳ שם אנש "unique as a man's name"; the word appears nine times in the Bible but only in this case is it a proper noun, and in the rest it is a common noun, "ornament, splendor." The MasP to הָאֵל "these" in Gen 26:4: ח׳ לשון חול "eight times has the meaning of profane," indicates that the word does not mean "God" but that it equals the demonstrative pronoun. Other cases in MT^L: MasP to תַּחַשׁ, "Thahash" in Gen 22:24; MasP to שִׁבְעָה, "Shebah" in Gen 26:33; etc.

The second type of notes indicates homonyms, emphasizing those that have different meanings. For example, the MasP to וָרֹאשׁ in Gen 46:21: ב׳ בתר׳ ליש׳ "twice and in two different meanings"; the Genesis passage has a proper noun, "and Rosh" (a son of Benjamin), in the other case, Lam 3:19, וראש is a noun with the prefixed *waw*, "and gall, and poison." Other cases in MT^L: MasP to מָשְׁחָתָם "their anointing" in Exod 40:15; MasP to נַחְלָה "brook" in Num 34:5; MasM to מָרִים "bitter" in Exod 15:23; MasM to הַצְּפוֹנִי "the Zephonites" in Num 26:15. See further the MasM in MT^A to חִלָּה "has afflicted" in Deut 29:21.

There is another group of notes in MT^L that are useful for intertextual exegesis, i.e. the MasP doublet notes with attached catchwords referring to the other occurrence. These catchwords specify the verse in which the parallel doublet occurs. For example, the MasP to בִּבְנוֹת "the daughters" in Gen 34:1 says: ב׳ האין בבנות אחיך "twice and (the other occurrence is) 'among the daughters of your relatives' [Judg 14:3]." The connection between these two passages would enable the exegete to conclude that the act of Dina, related in Genesis, is disapproved of just as Samson's behavior is explicitly disapproved of in the Judges passage.[7] These notes are very numerous in the Pentateuch (303), distributed as follows: 122 in Genesis; sixty-two in Exodus; thirty-four in Leviticus; forty-two in Numbers, and forty-three in Deuteronomy.

An analysis of the accents and Masorah of Deut 32:5 in MT^L illustrates its role and importance in interpretating the biblical text. The accentuation of the first part of the verse is: מוּמָם שִׁחֵת לוֹ לֹא בָּנָיו. According to the accents, it should be read together: "they behaved corruptly towards him not." In general, exegetes disregard this unusual accentuation, following the more "logical" reading proposed by the consonantal text: "They have acted corruptly toward Him, they are not His children" (NASB). However, the reading proposed by the accents is supported by the Targumim and the MasP of MT^L to לוֹ לֹא: "six times in the Torah." The exegete's first inclination would be to think that it refers to the number of times that these two words appear together, in that order, but the clue to understanding this note lies in the MasM to Gen 38:9: "לֹא לוֹ five times: Gen 38:9; Hab 1:6; 2:6; Prov 26:17; Dan 11:17; and [one with the order] reversed, Deut 35:2." Therefore, Deut 32:5 and its MasP must be understood as referring to the number of times these two words appear together, in any order, and should be read together.[8]

Butin, R., *The Ten Nequdoth of the Torah or the Meaning and Purpose of the Extraordinary Points of the Pentateuch (Massoretic Text): A Contribution to the History of Textual Criticism among the Ancient Jews* (Baltimore: J.H. Furst Company, 1906; repr. New York: Ktav, 1969).

Cassuto, P., *Qeré-Ketib

Cassuto, P., "Qeré/ketiv dans le manuscrit Londres Or. 4445," in *Proceedings of the Eleventh Congress of the International Organization for Masoretic Studies* (ed. A. Dotan; Jerusalem: World Union of Jewish Studies, 1994), 15–24.

Dotan, A., *Thesaurus of the Tiberian Masora: A Comprehensive Alphabetical Collection of Masoretic Notes to the Tiberian Bible Text of the Aaron ben Asher School*, Sample Volume: *The Masora to the Book of Genesis* (Tel Aviv: Tel Aviv University Press, 1977) [Hebr.].

Lieberman, *Hellenism.

---

[7] For the development of this and other cases cf. D. Marcus, "Double Catchwords in the Leningrad Codex," *TC* 12 (2007) (http://rosetta.reltech.org/TC/v12/Marcus2007.pdf).

[8] For a different understanding of the Masoretic notes and of the verse cf. C. McCarthy, "Masoretic Undertones in the Song of Moses," in *Proceedings of the Irish Biblical Association* 25 (2002): 4245.

McCarthy, C. (ed.), *Deuteronomy* (*BHQ 5; Stuttgart: Deutsche Bibelgesellschaft, 2007).

Mynatt, D.S., *The Sub Loco Notes in the Torah of Biblia Hebraica Stuttgartensia* (Fort Worth: Bibal Press, 1994).

Penkower, J.S., *New Evidence for the Pentateuch Text in the Aleppo Codex* (Ramat Gan: Bar-Ilan University Press, 1992) [Hebr.].

Tal, A. (ed.), *Genesis* (*BHQ 1; Stuttgart: Deutsche Bibelgesellschaft, 2016).

Yeivin, **Introduction*.

Elvira Martín Contreras

2.4 Primary Translations

2.4.1 Septuagint

2.4.1.1 Genesis
2.4.1.1.1 Nature

It is generally assumed that the Greek book of Genesis is the oldest of the translations of the Septuagint. It is possible that parts of the Bible were translated earlier (*Let. Aris.*, §§ 314–16) or that there were word lists or vocabularies called *"pinakes,"* because the translation of Genesis is relatively consistent. Moreover, several calques such as διαθήκη for בְּרִית "covenant," and εὐλογέω for ברך (*pi'el*) "to bless," were used, pointing to their preceding use in the community of the translator. Therefore, it is also possible that exegetical and hermeneutical traditions influenced the translation. One striking example is the use from Gen 2:8 onwards of κύριος "Lord" to render the tetragram יהוה and its characteristic use in distinction to θεός for אֱלֹהִים "God."[1] Contrary to the depiction in the *Letter of Aristeas* and subsequent traditions, the Greek Pentateuch was not translated as a single unit, but in separate steps carried out by different translators with differing abilities and approaches. Some characteristics of LXX-Gen prove that it was translated as an individual unit, as seen, for example, in the chronology of the patriarchs, in which the numbers are in agreement with those in the Hebrew book of Exodus rather than with those in the Greek version.[2] Another striking feature relates to the terminology used for sacrifice in Gen 8:20 and for law in Gen 26:5, where different equivalents were used than those found from Exodus onwards.

2.4.1.1.2 Background, Date, Milieu

In general, it is supposed that the translation of Genesis was carried out in Alexandria, because several features of the Greek version point to an urban Hellenistic milieu in Egypt. Thus, in Gen 8:22 the seasons were translated according to the Egyptian calendar, the extensive chronologies in Genesis 5 and 10 are in accordance with the Pharaonic chronology, and especially in the narrative of Joseph in Egypt (Genesis 37–50) many details betray that the translator was familiar with Egyptian customs. He also had knowledge of Hellenistic philosophical traditions, as seen in the account of creation in Genesis 1–2, which is influenced by the Platonic dialogue, *Timaeus*.[3] In addition, the use of κατακλυσμός "deluge" for מַבּוּל "flood" (Gen 6:17) reflects Hellenistic ideas. It is likely that the translation stems from the educated milieu of the *Museion* in Alexandria; LXX-Gen can easily be understood as a kind of foundation narrative of Hellenistic Egyptian Judaism, because it reports on the benevolent deeds of their ancestor.[4]

According to the *Letter of Aristeas*, the translation was carried out during the reign of Ptolemy II (285–246 B.C.E.). Scholars generally agree on a date in this period due to the development level of the Greek *Koine* language, which is in accordance with the linguistic developments in the third century and the vocabulary attested in the papyri.[5] Moreover, in the work of Demetrius the Chronographer one can find references to the Greek books of Genesis and Exodus; therefore, these books must have been translated before the late third century B.C.E.

2.4.1.1.3 Original Form, Editions, Tools

The textual transmission of LXX-Gen is somewhat difficult because its text is not preserved in Codex Sinaiticus (LXX^S), and Codex Vaticanus (LXX^B) has been preserved only from Gen 46:28 onwards. Moreover, Codex Alexandrinus (LXX^A) has a number of peculiar readings and corrections towards

---

[1] See M. Rösel, "The Reading and Translation of the Divine Name in the Masoretic Tradition and the Greek Pentateuch," *JSOT* 31 (2007): 411–28.

[2] Rösel, *Übersetzung*, 135–44.

[3] Rösel, *Übersetzung*, 72–87.

[4] S. Kreuzer, "Die Septuaginta im Kontext alexandrinischer Kultur und Bildung," *Brennpunkt*, Vol. 3, 28–56; Rösel, *Übersetzung*, 254–60.

[5] J.A.L. Lee, *A Lexical Study of the Septuagint Version of the Pentateuch* (SBLSCS 14; Chico: Scholars Press, 1983).

MT. Papyrus LXX911 (third/fourth century C.E.), in which Gen 1:16–35:8 is preserved, is more reliable. The editions of Rahlfs and the Göttingen Septuagint, edited by Wevers,[6] present a reconstructed text based on LXX^A with corrections from other manuscripts. Later manuscripts display traces of the Hexaplaric recension, while the existence of a Lucianic recension (→ 2.4.7) is uncertain.[7] In most cases, the differences between the editions of Rahlfs and Wevers are not relevant to the meaning and textual criticism of the text.[8] In a number of instances, Wevers has proposed changes to his critical text in his *Notes* (pp. 855–56); they are also recorded in **Septuaginta Deutsch, Erläuterungen*, 151–52.

Among the modern translations of LXX-Gen are those in English,[9] French,[10] and German.[11] Helpful explanations and commentaries can be found in the extensive *Notes* by Wevers; also useful is Hendel's reconstruction of the text of Genesis 1–11.[12] The commentary on the Greek Genesis (LXX^A) in the *Septuagint Commentary Series* by Brayford is of limited help due to its serious methodological flaws.[13]

2.4.1.1.4 Translation Character

The *Vorlage* of LXX-Gen was close to the tradition of MT. In some instances, deviating readings are supported by SP (→ 2.2.4.1.3), such as the well-known problems of the sixth (LXX, SP) or seventh (MT) day in Gen 2:2 and the plus נֵלְכָה הַשָּׂדֶה/διέλθωμεν εἰς τὸ πεδίον "let us go into the plain" in Gen 4:8. There are also cases in which LXX readings are supported by fragments found at Qumran.[14] However, it is disputed whether 4QGen^h1 (→ 2.2.1.10) and 4QGen^k (→ 2.2.1.8) support deviating readings of the LXX in Gen 1:9.[15] Harl[16] and especially Prestel and Schorch[17] assume more differences than Wevers and Rösel[18] between the MT tradition and the *Vorlage* of LXX-Gen, which they see as being closer to the Samaritan textual and vocalization traditions. They characterize this *Vorlage* based on its tendency towards harmonization of parallel passages. Unfortunately, the same phenomenon is typical of the work of the translator (see below); therefore, it is difficult to determine whether such a deviation results from the *Vorlage* or the translation technique.

In some cases, the text divisions in MT and LXX were inserted in different ways, visible even in the late chapter division. Thus the same text may appear in what is now a different chapter in MT and LXX. MT-Gen 2:25 equals LXX-Gen 3:1a, and thus the nakedness of the first humans is part of the story of the initial sin. MT-Gen 5:32 equals LXX-Gen 6:1, thus placing Noah at the beginning of a new era; Laban's departure in MT-Gen 32:1 appears in the final v. 55 of Genesis 31 in LXX and SP, thereby reducing the number of verses in Genesis 32. In some cases, there are differences in the division of the verses; in Gen 19:3–4, טֶרֶם יִשְׁכָּבוּ "before they lay down" opens v. 4 in MT, whereas its equivalent πρὸ τοῦ κοιμηθῆναι "before laying down" stands at the end of v. 3 in LXX; cf. also Gen 27:44–45; 30:38–39; 31:53–54; 35:22; 44:4–5; 49:24–25. In a few cases, there are also transpositions of short passages; cf. Gen 31:26 + 27; 35:16 + 21; 47:5 + 6.

2.4.1.1.5 Translation Technique and Inner-Translational Features

The Greek text follows its *Vorlage* closely and often imitates the syntax and idiomatic constructions of the Hebrew, for example, in the dating υἱὸς ἑκατὸν ἐτῶν "son of a hundred years" in Gen 11:10, and in

---

[6] Rahlfs, *Septuaginta; Wevers, *Genesis*.
[7] Wevers, *Text History*; cf. his summary, pp. 228–30.
[8] The differences are recorded in **Septuaginta Deutsch*.
[9] R. Hiebert, *Genesis*, *NETS, 1–42.
[10] M. Harl, *La Genèse*, who pays special attention to the reception history of the Greek text.
[11] P. Prestel and S. Schorch, "Genesis: Das erste Buch Mose," in **Septuaginta Deutsch*, 3–55. The latest commentary on LXX-Gen can be found in Prestel and Schorch, *Genesis*.
[12] Hendel, *Text*.
[13] See Jan Joosten, review of Susan Brayford, *Genesis*, Review of Biblical Literature [http://www.bookreviews.org] (2008).

[14] Cf. Gen 1:14; 6:20; 8:13; 41:6, 7, 24.
[15] Rösel, *Übersetzung*, 38–40; Hendel, *Text*, 120.
[16] Harl, *La Genèse*, 24–26.
[17] Prestel and Schorch, "Genesis," 146–47.
[18] Wevers, *Notes*, xiii–xiv; Rösel, *Übersetzung*, 14–16.

infinitive constructions such as προστίθημι "to add something," which renders יָסַף "to add something"; cf. Gen 4:12. It is interesting to note that the translation is less literal in several passages, especially in the Joseph narrative. Prestel and Schorch suggested that the translator kept closely to his text when he was less familiar with its contents but rendered freely when he knew the stories well.[19]

In most cases, stereotyped renderings were avoided, while in some instances fixed equivalents were accepted.[20] The translator varied his use of equivalents for stylistic reasons, but it is also possible that he was in the process of developing his translation technique.[21] Therefore, in specific cases it is difficult to decide whether his *Vorlage* read the same lexeme as MT. The translator's aim to produce a coherent, readable text also becomes clear from those cases in which he inserted subjects or objects, thus making explicit what was merely implicit in the Hebrew text in order to aid the reader's understanding.[22]

The same idea of aiding the reader may lie behind the attempts to actualize the text, for example, when geographical terms were translated; cf. Ἰδουμαία "Idumea" for Edom in Gen 36:16 and Μεσοποταμία "Mesopotamia" for Paddan Aram in Gen 31:18. Detailed knowledge of the geography of Egypt can be seen in the translation Ἡλίου πόλις "sun city" for אוֹן "On" in Gen 41:45. Moreover, Αἴγυπτος "Egypt" was used when the country was being referred to (Gen 12:10; 13:1), but the same name was transcribed in Gen 10:6 as Μεσραιμ "Mesraim," in order to differentiate between prehistoric and historical dates.[23] Also striking is the use of ᾅδης "Hades" for שְׁאוֹל "underworld" (e.g. Gen 37:25; 42:38), because the lexeme refers to the Greek mythology of the netherworld. This equivalent was also used by later translators; cf. Num 16:30, 33; Deut 32:22.

Even the use of particles betrays the translator's wish to accentuate his text, as can be seen in the use of the adversative δέ "but" for the Hebrew conjunction "and" in Genesis 4.[24] In the same passage, it is interesting to note that the Greek text offers an explanation of why God did not accept the offering of Cain: it was not divided correctly (Gen 4:7). This is a striking example of the translator's exposition of a difficult text.[25]

At the beginning of this section it was mentioned that there are several cases of substantial additions to the text that serve to harmonize parallel passages, thereby producing a more coherent text. This becomes obvious already in Genesis 1, in which the formulaic pattern of the text was improved by pluses in vv. 6, 8, 9, 11, 12, 14, and 20, but also by omissions in vv. 26–28. The same phenomenon can be seen in Genesis 3 and 6–9 and also, to a lesser extent, in the rest of the book. Moreover, the tendency to harmonize texts is also shown by the use of equivalents (cf. Gen 7:2–3, where ἄρσεν καὶ θῆλυ "male and female" is rendering different Hebrew phrases: אִישׁ וְאִשְׁתּוֹ "a man and his wife" and זָכָר וּנְקֵבָה "male and female"). These harmonizations show that the translator was embedding his contextual exegesis in the translation; variants

---

[19] Prestel and Schorch, "Genesis," 148 and cf. the notes to Genesis 24 and 37.

[20] Some examples are listed by Hiebert, "Genesis," 3.

[21] E. Tov, "The Septuagint Translation of Genesis as the First Scripture Translation," in *In the Footsteps of Sherlock Holmes: Studies in the Biblical Text in Honour of Anneli Aejmelaeus* (eds. K. De Troyer, T.M. Law, and M. Liljeström; CBET 72; Leuven: Peeters, 2014), 47–64 (49): "Genesis displays a curious mixture of translation styles."

[22] Thus, in Gen 3:1, the subject ὁ ὄφις "the snake" was repeated for the sake of clarity; cf. also Gen 4:10; 29:25; 31:1. In Gen 26:21, even a movement of Isaac was made explicit; the unusual use of a participle shows that this insertion is not based on a Hebrew text.

[23] The translation of כּוּשׁ "Kush" as Χους "Choos" in Gen 10:6 and as Αἰθιοπία "Ethiopia" in Gen 2:13, where it is a geographical term, is similar.

[24] On the use of δέ, cf. F.H. Polak, "Context Sensitive Translation and Parataxis in Biblical Narrative" in *Emanuel: Studies in Hebrew Bible, Septuagint, and Dead Sea Scrolls in Honor of Emanuel Tov* (eds. S.M. Paul et al.; VTSup 94; Leiden: Brill 2003), 525–39, esp. 537 on Gen 4:3–4.

[25] For an exegesis of LXX-Gen 4, see Rösel, *Übersetzung*, 100–14, and K.H. Jobes and M. Silva, *Invitation to the Septuagint* (Grand Rapids: Baker Academic, 2000), 206–14. Cf. also T.A.W. van der Louw, *Transformations in the Septuagint: Towards an Interaction of Septuagint Studies and Translation Studies* (CBET 47; Leuven: Peeters, 2007), 93–154 for an in-depth analysis of Genesis 2.

like these cannot be used profitably in the textual criticism of the Hebrew Bible.[26]

A special problem is posed by the genealogical lists in Genesis 5 and 11, because the major witnesses, MT (→ 2.2.2), SP (→ 2.2.4.1), and LXX, differ considerably and change the ages of the patriarchs based on their own chronological concepts. It is highly disputed whether these changes should be seen as recensional[27] or scribal[28] activities and whether the underlying chronologies can be reconstructed using data from other biblical books.[29]

2.4.1.1.6 Text-Critical Value

From the discussion of → 2.4.1.1.4–5, it is clear that variant readings in LXX-Gen often do not witness to a different *Vorlage* but rather to the way in which the translator carried out his task (→ 1.3.1.1.12).[30] However, it should be noted that in his critical edition of Genesis 1–11, Hendel[31] replaced many MT readings with variants retroverted from LXX (e.g. Gen 1:9; 2:2; 4:8; 8:10), even an obvious harmonization in Gen 9:7 (cf 1:28). In his view, the Greek version closely follows a Hebrew *Vorlage*, which is not attested to elsewhere. Therefore Hendel assumes that the tendency towards harmonization comes from the Vorlage, not from the translator. Thus the result of Hendel's view is similar in the case of harmonizations: LXX-Gen cannot be seen as a very reliable witness to an older Hebrew text. Therefore, one should follow a reading of LXX-Gen only in cases in which it is supported by other witnesses or when none of the tendencies mentioned above can be assumed.

2.4.1.1.7 Relevance for Exegesis

The Greek book of Genesis is of great importance with regard to the early reception history of the Hebrew Bible and the development of several theological ideas in the Second Temple period, of which only a few can be listed here. Worth mentioning is the influence of Platonic ideas on the creation account, which subsequently impacted the ideas of Philo.[32] A theological concept is displayed in the use of the renderings for the deity, κύριος "Lord" and θεός "God," which emphasize different aspects of God's character, as can be seen clearly in Gen 38:7: κύριος is used for the friendly aspects of God's actions, while θεός depicts his chastising deeds; this differentiation became important in Judaism and Christianity.[33] In Gen 49:9–10, an intertextual connection to Isa 11:1 has been made, thus introducing messianic ideas into the Greek text. These were expanded in the Balaam oracles in LXX-Num 24, as Num 23:24 refers back explicitly to Gen 49:9. Also of interest is the free translation of Gen 5:24 in which Enoch "was well-pleasing to God … because God transferred him"; this is in accordance with the developing Enoch literature and the Enochic tradition that Enoch was taken to heaven and God's secrets were shown to him. Finally, the Joseph story gave rise to the elaborated narrative regarding Joseph and Asenath. Based on the Greek text of Gen 41:45, it narrates that Asenath, the daughter of the heathen priest of Heliopolis, converts and worships the God of Israel after meeting Joseph. Therefore, it is obvious that the Greek Genesis does not serve only as an important, yet complicated, witness of

---

[26] Cf. two articles by E. Tov on the problem of harmonization in Genesis, which conclude that the Greek Genesis is not a good textual source: "Textual Harmonization in the Stories of the Patriarchs," in *Rewriting and Interpreting the Hebrew Bible: The Biblical Patriarchs in the Light of the Dead Sea Scrolls* (eds. D. Dimant and R.G. Kratz; BZAW 439; Berlin: de Gruyter, 2013), 19–50; "The Harmonizing Character of the Septuagint of Genesis 1–11," in Kraus–Kreuzer, *Septuaginta 2014*, 315–32.

[27] E. Tov, "The Genealogical Lists in Genesis 5 and 11 in Three Different Versions," in *From Author to Copyist: Essays on the Composition, Redaction, and Transmission of the Hebrew Bible in Honor of Zipi Talshir* (ed. C. Werman; Winona Lake: Eisenbrauns, 2015), 37–52.

[28] R. Hendel, "A Hasmonean Edition of MT Genesis? The Implications of the Editions of the Chronology in Genesis 5," *Hebrew Bible and Ancient Israel* 1 (2012): 448–64.

[29] Thus Rösel, *Übersetzung*, 129–44: MT calculates the year 4000 *anno mundi* for the inauguration of the temple after the Maccabean Revolt, SP calculates the year 2800 *a.m.* for the inauguration of the temple on Mt. Gerizim; LXX aims at 5000 *a.m.* for the inauguration of the Second Temple in Jerusalem.

[30] Cf. M. Rösel, "The Text-Critical Value of the Genesis-Septuagint," *BIOSCS* 32 (1999): 62–70. But see also the responses by R.S. Hendel and W.P. Brown in *BIOSCS* 33 (2000): 31–39.

[31] Hendel, *Text*.

[32] Rösel, *Übersetzung*, 81–88.

[33] See n. 1.

the biblical text but that it can also be read and understood as an "exegetical document."[34]

Brayford, S., *Genesis* (Septuagint Commentary Series; Leiden: Brill, 2007).
Cook, J., "The Translator of the Greek Genesis," in *La septuaginta en la investigacion contemporanea* (ed. N. Fernández Marcos; Textos y Estudios "Cardenal Cisneros" 34; Madrid: CSIC, 1985), 169–82.
Cook, J., "The Septuagint of Genesis: Text and/or Interpretation?" in *Studies in the Book of Genesis: Literature, Redaction and History* (ed. A. Wénin; BETL 155; Leuven: Peeters, 2001), 315–29.
Harl, M., *La Genèse* (2nd ed.; *Bible d'Alexandrie*; Paris: Cerf, 1994).
Rösel, M., *Übersetzung als Vollendung der Auslegung: Studien zur Genesis-Septuaginta* (BZAW 223; Berlin: de Gruyter, 1994).
Prestel, P. and S. Schorch, "Genesis: Das erste Buch Mose," in *Septuaginta Deutsch, Erläuterungen*, 145–257.
Wevers, J.W., *Text History of the Greek Genesis* (MSU 11; Göttingen: Vandenhoeck & Ruprecht, 1974).
Wevers, J.W., *Genesis* (Septuaginta Vetus Testamentum Graece 1; Göttingen: Vandenhoeck & Ruprecht, 1974).
Wevers, J.W., *Notes on the Greek Text of Genesis* (SBLSCS 35; Atlanta: Scholars Press, 1993).

Martin Rösel

2.4.1.2 Exodus
2.4.1.2.1 Background

Ancient sources indicate that the Greek translation of Exodus was prepared in conjunction with translations of the other Pentateuch books and this formed the first stage in what has come to be known as the "Septuagint." Accounts of this initial work are offered in Let. Aris. 301–21[1] (essentially repeated in Philo, Mos. 2, 25–44 and Josephus, A.J. 11, 118). Although much of these accounts constitutes legend, they consistently locate the translation of LXX-Exod in the first half of the third century B.C.E., associated with the reign of Ptolemy Philadelphus and located in Alexandria. Fragments of Aristobulus' writings (quoted in Eusebius, *Prep. Ev.* 12.1–2)[2] also place the initial translation work during Philadelphus' reign.

Other evidence within the text itself supports this location in time and place. Evans cautiously concludes that verbal syntax in the Greek Pentateuch "is consistent with an early date."[3] Lee in his evaluation of lexical data used in the Greek Pentateuch argues that "our text of the Pentateuch is older than about the middle of the second century B.C."[4] The orientation of the tabernacle (LXX-Exod 26–27) suggests an Egyptian perspective.[5]

The grandson of Ben Sira in the preface to his translation of the book of Ben Sira, probably dated to the reign of Euergetes II (c. 132 B.C.E.), indicates that the Pentateuch was already available in Greek. Caird argues that terminology found in Sir 44:16–45:25 demonstrates that Ben Sira had access to LXX-Exod.[6]

One fragment of LXX-Exod (28:4–6,7), found in Qumran Cave 7 (7Q1) and dated c. 100 B.C.E.,[7] shows that LXX-Exod was known and used in Palestine at that time.

We should also note that translators of later portions of the Jewish Scriptures, particularly LXX-Isa,[8] knew and incorporated material from LXX-Exod into their translations.

All of these various data support the hypothesis that LXX-Exod was completed in the third century B.C.E. within Egypt and that an established text did exist, transmitted with relative faithfulness, but subject to the usual scribal activities of omission, addition, word order variance, and morphological variations.

---

[34] Wevers, *Notes*, xx.
[1] Dorival-Harl-Munnich, *Septante*, 36–44.
[2] Aristobulus may include material from LXX-Exod 9:3; 13:9 (cf. Swete, *Introduction*, 370–71).
[3] Evans, *Verbal Syntax*, 9. "The identification of potential optative function" (263) forms some of the strongest evidence.
[4] Lee, *Lexical Study*, 143.
[5] P.M. Bogaert, "L' orientation du parvis"; Wevers, *Text History*, 123, 146; Fraenkel, "Übersetzungsnorm"; Wade, *Consistency of Translation Techniques*, 98–100.
[6] Caird, "Ben Sira and the Dating of the Septuagint," 97.
[7] Baillet, "Exode," (Ex 28:4–6, 7).
[8] Perkins, "Greek Exodus and Greek Isaiah."

2.4.1.2.2 Original Form, Editions, Tools

The earliest, almost complete text of LXX-Exod is that of Codex Vaticanus (LXX^B; fourth century), complemented by Codex Alexandrinus (LXX^A).[9] In 2006 and 2007 several extensive fragments from a fourth century papyrus codex were published.[10] In addition to 7Q1 mentioned above, little pre-Origen papyri evidence has emerged for LXX-Exod.

Wevers' *Exodus*[11] in the Göttingen edition provides the most useful critical edition. The publication of the Rahlfs-Hanhart, *Septuaginta* incorporates a number of changes to the previous Rahlfs' edition and is an adequate text for general reference.[12]

Wevers' research identified no Lucianic recension (→ 2.4.7) for LXX-Exod. The Syro-Hexapla (→ 2.4.4.2) is one of the primary witnesses for the LXX^O group[13] and preserves a substantial number of hexaplaric signs, as do some manuscripts in the Armenian Version (→ 2.5.5). Wevers also discerned that "no trace whatsoever was found of the kind of revision identified by Barthélemy as belonging to revisers of the *kaige*-Th group."[14] Wevers does indicate that 7Q1 (= LXX^805 in his edition) "shows traces of some recensional activity based on the Hebrew."[15]

Modern translations of LXX-Exod (usually based upon Wevers' edition) exist in English,[16] French,[17] German,[18] and Spanish.[19] Included with these translations or associated with them are notes and commentary that assist in the study of LXX-Exod.

2.4.1.2.3 Translation Character

Exodus contains narrative, poetic (Exodus 15) and legal material (including instructions for constructing the tabernacle). The translator generally rendered his Hebrew text with serial fidelity. However, in the narrative portions (Exodus 1–20; 24; 32–34) he exercised considerable creativity within the boundaries of this strategy, sometimes moving away from his Hebrew text. In comparison, the legal segments (Exodus 21–31; with the exception of Exodus 35–40) tend (apart from short narrative sections such as Exod 23:20–24:18) to follow the Hebrew text more closely. The translation of the final section (Exodus 35–40) which recounts the preparation of the priests' vestments, the construction of the tabernacle and its cultic furniture, has a different order from MT (→ 2.2.2) and is somewhat shorter.[20] The study by Gooding[21] discerned a similar translation character throughout LXX-Exod, even in these chapters, apart perhaps from Exodus 38. Wevers,[22] however, notes several features in Exodus 35–40 which indicate "there is clearly an attempt made to be different …" Wade[23] tentatively concludes that a second translator was involved.

---

[9] Wevers, *Text History*, 81. "Unfortunately Exodus papyri remains older than the text of B are merely bits and pieces; no complete verse obtains among them … This situation makes our oldest mss, B and A from the 4th and 5th Centuries, resp., particularly important for the restoration of the text of Exod, …"

[10] DeSilva and Adams, "Seven Papyrus Fragments" and deSilva, "Five Papyrus Fragment."

[11] Wevers, *Exodus*. His *Text History of the Greek Exodus* provides extensive commentary on the inter-relationships and character of various elements of the LXX-Exod textual tradition. Brooke – Mclean, *The Old Testament in Greek* has been superseded by Wevers' edition.

[12] Rahlfs-Hanhart, *Septuaginta*.

[13] Wevers, *Exodus*, 38.

[14] Wevers, *Text History*, 40.

[15] Wevers, *Text History*, 40. He expands on this topic in his study "PreOrigen Recensional Activity."

[16] Perkins, "Exodus."

[17] Boulluec and Sandevoir, *L'Exode*.

[18] J. Roloff and E. Weber in cooperation with J. Schaper, "Exodos: Das zweite Buch Mose," in Karrer-Kraus, *Septuaginta Deutsch*, 56–98.

[19] Marcos, Spottorno Díaz-Caro, and Reíllo (eds.), *La Biblia griega*.

[20] This is discussed in greater detail in section → 2.4.5.

[21] Gooding, *The Account of the Tabernacle*, 99–101. In his summation Gooding concludes that "there were striking similarities of translation that made it evident that both sections were by the same translator."

[22] Wevers, *Text History*, 117–46 and specifically 143–46.

[23] Wade, *Consistency of Translation Techniques*, 242. She proposes that "the cumulative weight of the minute differences between accounts and the similar nature of the minuses could all be explained by the theory that the second tabernacle account was produced by a second translator who used the translation of the first tabernacle account as his point of reference."

After his exhaustive study of LXX-Exod, Wevers' concluded that "Exod is on the whole written in good Greek, often rendering Hebraic idioms into corresponding Greek idioms."[24] Wifstrand's study of the placement of pronominal enclitics revealed the Exodus translator's tendency to use normal Greek construction.[25] Aejmelaeus' investigation of the translation of clause connectors and other features of the Greek text leads her to conclude that "the translator of Ex may thus be characterized as a competent translator, mindful of genuine Greek expressions, free in his relationship to the original, but still exact in reproducing his original relatively faithfully."[26]

Wevers characterized the translation generally as expansionist in character.[27] However, even when additions occur (e.g. Exod 2:16 and the addition[28] of ποιμαίνουσαι τὰ πρόβατα τοῦ πατρὸς αὐτῶν "who were tending their father's sheep" (*NETS) to characterize Jethro's daughters) the translator before and after follows his translation strategy of isomorphism with his Hebrew text. These additions tend to make explicit what is in the Hebrew text, removing potential ambiguity. The translator, at least in the narrative sections, seems to give attention to the literary aspects of the various stories. He used particles such as δέ "and/then/but" to indicate specific transitions; displacement of pronouns at times give prominence in the Greek text to certain elements; examples of μεταβολή "elegant variation" occur;[29] alliteration also seems to be present (e.g. ἐὰν δέ τις προσέλθῃ πρὸς ὑμᾶς προσήλυτος ποιῆσαι τὸ πάσχα κυρίῳ, περιτεμεῖς αὐτοῦ πᾶν ἀρσενικόν, καὶ τότε προσελεύσεται ποιῆσαι αὐτό ... "But if any guest should draw near to you to keep the Pascha of the Lord, you shall circumcise every male of his, and then he shall draw near to you ..." Exod 12:48).

2.4.1.2.4 Translation Technique and Inner-Translational Features

Once he determined the rendering for a specific Hebrew lexeme or syntactical structure, the translator tended to replicate it. However, he was not slavish or mechanical in this process, because variation occurs frequently. For example, the translator tends to use καί "and" as his equivalent for conjunctive *waw*, but will not hesitate to employ other particles such as δέ "and/then/but" if he thinks this rendering communicates more adequately how the narrative should flow. He regularly omits the apodictic *waw*.[30] He distinguishes carefully when כי "that/because" is introducing an object clause (ὅτι "that") or an explanatory clause (γάρ "because").[31] In the case of pronouns he frequently chooses a word order that reflects Greek idiom, communicating thereby nuances of meaning.[32]

In terms of lexical variation the translator shows both consistency and creativity in his rendering of Hebrew lexemes. For example, he usually rendered דבר by forms of λαλεῖν (both meaning "to speak") but in seventeen cases he chose a form of λέγειν "to say." In contrast forms of λέγειν normally translate אמר (both meaning "to say") with the exception of Exod 31:12 where a form of λαλεῖν "to speak" occurs. When it comes to verbs such as בא "to come" which have more general meanings the variations in renderings multiply (e.g. Qal: δεῦτε "come [now]," εἰσιέναι "enter, go into," εἰσπορεύεσθαι "go into, enter," εἰσέρχεσθαι "go into, enter," ἐπάγειν "bring in," ἔρχεσθαι "go, come," ἥκειν "come into," παραγίνεσθαι "come to, arrive"; Hiphil: ἄγειν "bring," ἀναφέρειν "bring up or back," εἰσάγειν "bring in," εἰσέρχεσθαι "go into, enter," εἰσφέρειν "bring in," ἐπάγειν "bring upon or to," προσάγειν "bring to," προσδέχεσθαι "receive, accept," προσφέρειν "bring to or upon," συνάγειν "bring together, gather"). Stereotypical renderings often

---

[24] Wevers, *Text History*, 147.
[25] Wifstrand, "Die Stellung der enklitischen Personalpronomina."
[26] Aejmelaeus, "What Can We Know about the *Vorlage*?" 100.
[27] Wevers, *Text History*, 148.
[28] This presumes that the translator did not have an equivalent phrase in his Hebrew text.
[29] Lee, "Translations of the Old Testament I: Greek", 777. Exod 21:15–17.

[30] Aejmelaeus, "The Significance of Clause Connectors," 57.
[31] Aejmelaeus, "The Significance of Clause Connectors," 59–60.
[32] Perkins, "The Order of Pronominal Clitics."

occur, such as the rendering of ברית as διαθήκη (both meaning "covenant"). Occasionally the translator chose transliterated forms, some of which may already have had currency among the Greek-speaking Jewish population of Alexandria (e.g. σάββατα "Sabbata," πάσχα "Pascha," μάν "Manna," χερουβίμ "Cherubim," γόμορ "gomor," ἵν "hin"). Sometimes the equivalents seem chosen for their rhetorical effect (e.g. the series of κατα- compound imperfect verbs used in Exod 1:13–14 [κατεδυνάστευον ... κατωδύνων ... κατεδουλοῦντο "were oppressing ... were grieviously afflicting ... were enslaving"]).

Theological perspectives also receive expression through translation choices. For example, θυσιαστήριον regularly renders מזבח when it defines an "altar" used in the Israelite cult, but the translator chose βωμός when it describes a pagan "altar" (Exod 34:13).[33] How then should we interpret 32:5 when Aaron constructs a מזבח "altar" before the golden calf and the translator renders it as θυσιαστήριον "(Israelite) altar"? Daniel argues that the translator was seeking to minimize the fault assigned to Aaron for this episode, a trend apparent in subsequent Jewish sources such as the Targumim.[34] Significantly the translator expresses a theological perspective in his treatment of theophanies, by avoiding any impression that human beings "see" God. People experience phenomena associated with God's presence, but he remains unseen in the Greek text, despite assertions in the Hebrew text (cf. Exod 24:9–11). This seems to be the motivation behind his frequent rendering of the root יעד "to appoint/meet" by the future passive verbal phrase γνωσθήσομαί "I will be known" (Exod 25:22[21]; 29:42; 30:6, 36; cf. Exod 29:43).[35] Another unusual interpretation of the Hebrew text occurs in Exod 22:27(28) which generally is understood to mean "do not blaspheme God (אלהים)." The Greek text in contrast reads θεοὺς οὐ κακολογήσεις "you shall not revile gods" (*NETS), interpreting אלהים as a plural form.[36] The translation of Exod 19:5–6 emphasizes Israel's special status among the nations, explicitly using the term λαός "people" modified by the neologism περιούσιος "special,"[37] which seems to express the idea of uniqueness, as God establishes his covenant with this people. It is also probable that in legal materials the translator sometimes "sought to adapt the text in translation to the concrete legal situation."[38]

Whether the Exodus translator worked phrase by phrase, with little attention paid to the larger literary context, or developed his translation giving attention to creating a coherent narrative in the target language has generated considerable debate. Within the legal materials (Exodus 21–23), including the plans for the tabernacle (Exodus 25–31), the translator seems to pay more attention to the smaller units, given the nature of the material in his Hebrew text. However, several features in the narrative segments indicate that the translator shaped his text with awareness of the larger discourse, e.g. his use of clause connectors such as δέ "and/then/but" (see → 2.4.4). He carefully used tense-forms to show the internal relationship of activities, developing the story or providing background information. He occasionally shapes his translation to express specific theological motifs (see previous paragraph). He makes details explicit in the narrative so that the reader does not lose the thread of the story. In sum, this translator produces a translation that is faithful to his Hebrew text, but accommodative to the target language.

2.4.1.2.5 Text-Critical Value

The general, isomorphic character of the Exodus translation (apart from Exodus 35–40) makes it a significant witness to the state of its Hebrew *Vorlage* in the first half of the third century B.C.E. However, it is not easy at times to discern whether per-

---

[33] These translation choices are consistent in the Greek Pentateuch.

[34] Daniel, *Vocabulaire du Culte*, 17. She indicates that in the Greek Pentateuch the equivalence מזבח/βωμός (both meaning "altar") carries a "pejorative significance" (→ 2.4.1.4.3).

[35] Perkins, "The Greek Translator of Exodus – Interpres."

[36] Josephus (*A.J.* 4,207) and Philo (*Mos.* 2,205) understood that this statement forbids Jewish people from despising other gods.

[37] C. Dogniez and M. Harl, *Le Deutéronome* (*Bible D'Alexandrie* 5; Paris: Cerf, 2007), 65.

[38] Buchner, "*Mekilta De Rabbi Ishmael* and Septuagint Exodus 12–23," 420.

ceived differences between the Greek text formulated by the translator and MT (→ 2.2.2) are due to his desire to accommodate the target language or reflect a Hebrew text distinctive from the MT or another early Hebrew text (→ 1.3.1.1.12). Aejmelaeus[39] argues that when a Greek text longer than the MT reflects Greek idiom, it probably stems from the translator's initiative. If conversely the Greek text differing from MT reflects Hebraisms, then it most likely evidences a different Hebrew text.

Different positions are taken with respect to the value of LXX-Exod for textual criticism of the Hebrew Exodus. Sanderson's evaluation of 4QpaleoExod^m (→ 2.2.1.3.1) led her to conclude that LXX-Exod "gives evidence of being a faithful translation of its Hebrew *Vorlage*" and "preserves uniquely preferable shorter readings as well as uniquely secondary longer readings" which may reflect Hebrew variations from MT.[40] Wevers' assessment that the translation is expansionist suggests caution in using the additions in the Greek text to argue for his use of a different Hebrew *Vorlage*. However, in some cases it seems clear that the translator had a Hebrew text different from MT. In Exod 1:5 the number of Jacob's progeny is πέντε καὶ ἑβδομήκοντα "seventy-five," a figure attested by 4QExod^b (→ 2.2.1.7.7) and probably 4QGen-Exod^a 17–18 (→ 2.2.1.1.1), but not by MT.[41]

Occasionally we cannot determine whether the translator has misread his Hebrew text or had a reading different from the MT. At Exod 4:31 καὶ ἐπίστευσεν ὁ λαὸς καὶ ἐχάρη "and the people believed and were glad" (*NETS) renders ויאמן העם וישמעו "and the people believed and heard." This is the only context in LXX-Exod where a form of שמע is not rendered by some form cognate with ἀκούω (both meaning "to hear"). Did the translator read a form of שמח "to be happy/glad" in his Hebrew text, did he misread the Hebrew, or has he deliberately paraphrased the meaning of the Hebrew text? Wevers argues that the translator had a form of the verb שמח in his text, as he did in Exod 4:14.[42] Given the character of this translation, I would agree with Wevers' conclusion.

An additional example of textual divergence between MT and LXX-Exod occurs in the sequence of the prohibitions of murder (Exod 20:13), adultery (Exod 20:14) and stealing (Exod 20:15). LXX-Exod follows the sequence Exod 20:14, 15, 13, differing from other pre-Christian Jewish traditions expressed in Philo (*Dec.* 12), the Nash Papyrus (→ 2.2.5.2), and MT-Exod (→ 2.2.2), SP-Exod (→ 2.2.4.2), 4QDeut^n (→ 2.2.1.7.20), and LXX-Deut 5 (→ 2.4.1.5). It is difficult to discern whether LXX-Exod is following a different Hebrew text or is altering the order based upon some other principle.

Likewise, renderings of the tetragrammaton, using κύριος "Lord" or θεός "God," cannot normally be used as a sure indicator of what the translator read in his Hebrew text. For example, I have proposed that in Exodus 19 the translator used the generic term for deity (θεός "God") to translate יהוה "Yahweh" when God communicates to Israel as a people. However, when God has a personal instruction for Moses, the translator chooses κύριος "Lord," perhaps in this way emphasizing the special relationship that Moses has with God.[43]

The major textual differences between MT and the LXX-Exod occur in Exodus 35–40 which narrate the tabernacle's construction. The Greek text is reordered and shortened in comparison to MT. It places the preparation of the priestly vestments before preparation of the tabernacle materials, omits the incense altar (MT-Exod 37:25–28), compresses the details about constructing the tabernacle (MT-Exod 36:8–34) into one brief note (LXX-Exod 37:1–2), and abbreviates considerably the construction of the table of presence (MT-Exod 37:10–16) and the lamp stand (MT-Exod 37:17–24).

---

[39] Aejmelaeus, "What Can We Know about the Hebrew *Vorlage* of the Septuagint?" She concludes that "the extensive plusses, it seems, depend on the *Vorlage*, which in some cases undoubtedly represents the original text" (111).
[40] Sanderson, *An Exodus Scroll from Qumran*, 255–57.
[41] C. Martone, "Qumran Readings in Agreement with the Septuagint Against the Masoretic Text: Part One: The Pentateuch," *Henoch* 27 (2005): 53–113 (56).

[42] Wevers, *Notes on the Greek Text of Exodus*, 58.
[43] Perkins, "Literary and Narrative Dimensions." Rösel, "The Reading and Translation of the Divine Name," proposes a different rational, but also agrees that the renderings of the tetragrammaton are due to the translator's work and are not normally textually based.

Tov has demonstrated that SP-Exod and LXX-Exod share many similar examples of harmonization, particularly pluses, (e.g. more occurrences and omissions of καί and ו [both meaning "and"]) over against MT, but the LXX has even more. The analysis of 4QpaleoExod^m (→ 2.2.1.3.1), identified as a pre-Samaritan text, "has shown that the pre-Samaritan scrolls resemble SP and the LXX in the frequency of harmonization and hence could belong to the same group or tradition."[44] Whether LXX-Exod worked with an exemplar that was more in line with the Samaritan Pentateuch (→ 2.2.4.2) stemmata or not remains unclear. The textual value of the LXX and the SP needs to be evaluated on a case by case basis. Tov notes that the *Vorlagen* of the various Septuagint translations reflect texts and not a specific recension.[45]

LXX-Exod shows none of the theological *Tendenz* expressed in SP. For example, the text at Exod 20:24 within SP (→ 2.2.4.2) requires Israel to offer sacrifices "at the place where I have caused my name to be memorialized" (במקום אשר אזכירתי את־שמי). However, MT keeps the location general and Yahweh's designations as future revelations (בכל־המקום אשר אזכיר את־שמי "in every place where I cause my name to be remembered" [NRSV]). This dependent relative clause forms part of a compound sentence "in every place ... I will come to you and bless you." The Greek translator rendered his *Vorlage* as ἐν παντὶ τόπῳ, οὗ ἂν ἐπονομάσω τὸ ὄνομά μου ἐκεῖ "in every place, there where I pronounce my name" (*NETS*), but incorporates into this relative clause two additional relative clauses to form one single complex clause. The translator reflects a text closer to MT and unaffected by what some interpret as the influence of later Samaritan *Tendenz* regarding Mt. Gerizim.

2.4.1.2.6 Value for Literary Criticism

Some scholars contend that most of the differences discerned between LXX-Exod and MT (→ 2.2.2) are due to the translator's work. In their view LXX-Exod does not contribute significantly to our understanding of the literary development of the Hebrew textual tradition. With respect to the reordering and shortening of the Greek text of Exodus 35–40, Wevers concluded that "the difference in order for Part 2 [35–40] need not be textually determined; in fact there are numerous indications that it was Exodus (scil. LXX-Exod) who was responsible for the reordering."[46] The previous study by Gooding reached a similar conclusion and he hypothesized that "changes in chapter 38 [Greek text] are due to a later editor."[47]

Other scholars such as Aejmelaeus argue that these chapters "represent an earlier phase in the development of the [Hebrew] text."[48] She differentiates between the activities of a translator and the work of scribes who edited the Hebrew text. Likewise Lemmelijn applied Aejmelaeus' principles[49] to the plague narratives (Exod 7:14–11:10). She concludes that MT provides the best foundation for the text of Exodus and subsequent literary analysis, with LXX providing preferable readings in a minority of cases.[50]

Research has shown that the LXX-Exod text is expansionist and harmonizing in its tendencies. The translator(s) expresses theological tendencies in the final product and is attentive to the demands of Greek language. Where we draw the line between the translator's work and the form of his *Vorlage* reflected in his translation must be determined on

---

[44] E.Tov, "The Samaritan Pentateuch and the Dead Sea Scrolls: The Proximity of the PreSamaritan Qumran Scrolls to the SP," in *Keter Shem Tov: Essays on the Dead Sea Scrolls in Memory of Alan Crown* (eds. S. Tzoref and I. Young; Perspectives on Hebrew Scriptures and Its Contexts 20; Piscataway: Gorgias Press, 2013), 59–88. Revised Version in Tov *Collected Writings 3, 387–410.

[45] Tov, *TCU 199.

[46] Wevers, *Textual History*, 145.

[47] Gooding, *The Account of the Tabernacle*, 99.

[48] Aejmelaeus, "The Problem of the Tabernacle Account," 129.

[49] Cf. section → 2.4.1.2.5.

[50] Lemmelijn, *A Plague of Texts?* She evaluates the various pluses and minuses in the plague narrative and concludes (209–18) that in some instances they reflect a different Hebrew *Vorlage*, whose literary form shows an alternative text to the MT. Although MT may form the "practical working text for the literary study" of the plague narrative, the Greek text "provided the 'preferable reading' in contrast to M" in seven cases.

a text by text basis and with full consideration of what we can determine about his translation strategy and process, as well as evidence of literary development provided by existent Hebrew texts. The sequence of the Ten Commandments in LXX-Exod 20 probably provides evidence contributing to our understanding of literary development within the Hebrew textual tradition. There seems to be no discernible reason for the translator to change the order that he found in his *Vorlage* and so the order in LXX-Exod should be used as evidence for reconstructing the literary development of the Hebrew text in this instance (→ 1.3.1.1.12).

Aejmelaeus, *Trail.
Baillet, M., "1. Exode," *DJD III: 142–43.
Bogaert, P.M., "L'orientation du parvis du sanctuaire dans la version grecque de l'*Exode* (*Ex.*, 27, 9–13 LXX)," *L'Antiquité classique* 50 (1981): 79–85.
Le Boulluec, A. and P. Sandevoir, *L'Exode* (*Bible d'Alexandrie* 2; Paris: Cerf, 1989).
Brooke–McLean, *The Old Testament in Greek.
Büchner, D., "On the Relationship between *Mekhilta De Rabbi Ishmael* and Septuagint Exodus 12–23," in *IX Congress of the International Organization for Septuagint and Cognate Studies, Cambridge, 1995* (ed. B.A. Taylor; SBLSCS 45; Atlanta: Scholars Press, 1997), 403–20.
Caird, G.B., "Ben Sira and the Dating of the Septuagint," *SE* VII (1982): 95–100.
Daniel, *Vocabulaire du Culte.
deSilva, D.A., and M.P. Adams, "Seven Papyrus Fragments of a Greek Manuscript of Exodus," *VT* 56 (2006): 143–70.
deSilva, D.A., "Five Papyrus Fragments of Greek Exodus," *BIOSCS* 40 (2007): 1–29.
Dorival–Harl–Munnich, *Septante.
Evans, T.V., *Verbal Syntax in the Greek Pentateuch* (Oxford: Oxford University Press, 2001).
Fernández Marcos, N., M.V. Spottorno Díaz-Caro, and J.M.C. Reíllo (eds.), *La Biblia griega – Septuaginta I. Pentateuco* (Salamanca: Ediciones Sígueme of Salamanca, 2008).
Fraenkel, D., "Übersetzungsnorm und literarische Gestaltung – Spuren individueller Übersetzungstechnik in Exodus 25 ff. + 35 ff.," in *VIII Congress of the International Organization for Septuagint and Cognate Studies, 1992* (eds. L. Greenspoon and O. Munnich; SBLSCS 41; Atlanta: Scholars Press, 1995), 72–87.

Frankel, Z., *Einfluss.
Gooding, D.W., *The Account of the Tabernacle: Translation and Textual Problems of the Greek Exodus* (ed. C.H. Dodd; TS 6; Cambridge: Cambridge University Press, 1959).
Gooding, D.W., "Two Possible Examples of Midrashic Interpretation in the Septuagint Exodus," in *Wort, Lied und Gottesspruch: Beiträge zur Septuaginta: Festschrift für Joseph Ziegler* (ed. J. Schreiner; FB 1; Würzburg: Echter Verlag Katholisches Bibelwerk, 1972), 39–49.
Lee, J.A.L., *A Lexical Study of the Septuagint Version of the Pentateuch* (ed. H.M. Orlinsky; SBLSCS 14; Chico: Scholars Press, 1983).
Lee, J.A.L., "Translations of the Old Testament, I: Greek," in *Handbook of Classical Rhetoric in the Hellenistic Period 330 B.C. – A.D. 400* (ed. S. Porter; Leiden: Brill, 1997), 775–83.
Lemmelijn, B., "Free and yet Faithful: On the Translation Technique of LXX Exod 7:14–11:10," *JNSL* 33 (2007): 1–32.
Lemmelijn, B., *A Plague of Texts? A Text-Critical Study of the So-called 'Plagues Narrative' in Exodus 7:14–11:10* (OTS 56; Leiden: Brill, 2009).
Perkins, L., "Exodus," in *NETS, 43–81.
Perkins, L., "Greek Exodus and Greek Isaiah: Detection and Implications of Interdependence in Translation," *BIOSCS* 42 (2009): 18–33.
Perkins, L., "What's in a Name: Proper Names in Greek Exodus," *JSJ* 41 (2010): 447–71.
Perkins, L., "Literary and Narrative Dimensions of Translation in Greek Exodus 19 – A Brief Sortie," Paper presented at the Annual Meeting of the SBL, November 2010.
Perkins, L., "The Greek Translator of Exodus – Interpres (translator) and Expositor (interpretor) – His Treatment of Theophanies," *JSJ* 44 (2013): 16–56.
Rahlfs--Hanhart, *Septuaginta.
Rösel, M., "The Reading and Translation of the Divine Name in the Masoretic Tradition and the Greek Pentateuch," *JSOT* 31 (2007): 411–28.
Sanderson, J.E., *An Exodus Scroll from Qumran: 4QpaleoExod^m and the Samaritan Tradition* (HSS 30; Atlanta: Scholars Press, 1986).
Swete, *Introduction.
Tov, E., *TCU.
Tov, E., "Some Sequence Differences between the Masoretic Text and the Septuagint and their Ramifications for Literary Criticism," in Tov, *Greek--Hebrew Bible, 411–18.

Wade, M., *Consistency of Translation Techniques in the Tabernacle Accounts of Exodus in the Old Greek* (SBLSCS 49; Atlanta: Scholars Press, 2003).

Wevers, J.W., "PreOrigen Recensional Activity in the Greek Exodus," in *Studien zur Septuagint – Robert Hanhart zu Ehren* (eds. D. Fraenkel, U. Quast, and J.W. Wevers; MSU XX; Göttingen: Vandenhoeck & Ruprecht, 1990), 121–39.

Wevers, J.W., *Notes on the Greek Text of Exodus* (ed. C. Cox; SBLSCS 30; Atlanta: Scholars Press, 1990).

Wevers, J.W., *Exodus* (Septuaginta Vetus Testamentum Graecum 2.1; Göttingen: Vandenhoeck & Ruprecht, 1991).

Wevers, J.W., *Text History of the Greek Exodus* (MSU 21; Göttingen: Vandenhoeck & Ruprecht, 1992).

Wifstrand, A., "Die Stellung der enklitischen Personalpronomina bei den Septuaginta," in *K. Humanistiska Vetenskapssamfundetsi Lund Årsberättelse 1949–50*, Vol. 2 (Lund: Gleerup, 1950), 44–70.

Larry Perkins

2.4.1.3 Leviticus

2.4.1.3.1 Name and Editions

Most manuscripts use the name Λευιτικόν "Levitical," although Βιβλίον Λευιτικόν "Levitical Book" is also used. LXX[B] is considered the best manuscript, but needs to be emended occasionally. The best editions of LXX-Lev are Rahlfs, *Septuaginta* and the Göttingen edition, Wevers, *Leviticus*.[1]

2.4.1.3.2 Background

2.4.1.3.2.1 Tradition

The translator of Leviticus would have had at his disposal the translation tradition of other works, the synagogal tradition of oral reading, and probably a written translation of parts of the Pentateuch.

2.4.1.3.2.2 Language

LXX-Lev contains the same type of Greek as the other Torah translations. The translation is moderately literal, seeking to retain the sentence structure, word order, and word choice of the Hebrew text in a fashion usually described as Hebraistic, as would have been acceptable to those living in the cultural milieu in which the translation was produced (→ 2.4.1.3.2.3).

Certain standard equivalents developed, such as κύριος "Lord, master" for the Tetragrammaton followed by V *dominus* and S מריא (both meaning "lord"), reflecting its pronunciation in daily life in Jewish circles as אדני "lord" (see *b. Pesaḥ* 50a); it is the only divine name occurring in Leviticus. אלהים "God" is naturally rendered ὁ θεός "the God." Similarly, תורה is νόμος (both meaning "law"). LXX-Lev uses the Aramaic equivalents σάββατα "Sabbata" and πάσχα "Pascha" for שבת "Sabbat" and פסח "Passover." Several stereotyped equivalents are also used in the other books of the Pentateuch: ברית/διαθήκη (both meaning "covenant, alliance"); גר "sojourner"/προσήλυτος "he who approaches" (the sole equivalent in LXX-Lev).[2] LXX-Lev is strict in using πάροικος "he who dwells with" only for תושב "sojourner" in its entire semantic range.

2.4.1.3.2.3 Hebraisms

In the Septuagint, אדם "human being, person" is normally rendered ἄνθρωπος "human being" (and similarly איש "person," unless it refers to a male, when it is rendered ἀνήρ "man"), even when used as "someone," while איש איש "anyone" is rendered ἄνθρωπος ἄνθρωπος (Lev 17:3, 8).[3] נפש "life, soul, being, creature" is translated stereotypically as ψυχή "life, Soul, being, creature" even when used as "someone" (Lev 2:1; 4:2 etc.) and as "a dead body" (e.g. Lev 21:1; 22:4). זרע "semen" is rendered customarily as σπέρμα "seed," also when used as "offspring" (Lev 20:2; 22:4 etc.). Κοίτη "bed" is the equivalent of משכב "bed," e.g. Lev 15:4, 5 (the root שכב denotes "to lie down," with its wide semantic range); in Lev 20:13 (in pl.), it denotes sexual intercourse (also in non-biblical Greek). Hebrew שכבת זרע "ejaculation of semen" in Lev 15:17 and in 19:20 ("sexual intercourse") is rendered as κοίτη σπέρματος "bed of semen."

---

[1] For Wever's edition see also Wevers, *Text History*, and Wevers, *Notes*.

[2] In other Pentateuch books, πάροικος "he who dwells with" is also used, probably in line with the context. It is also sometimes used for תושב "sojourner."

[3] However, in Lev 19:3, 11, the translation is functional: ἕκαστος "any individual."

2.4.1.3.3 Translation Technique

LXX-Lev usually presents a literal translation (→ 2.4.1.3.2.3), but there are exceptions. For example, בית אביה "house of her father" in Lev 22:13 is idiomatically translated as τὸν οἶκον τὸν πατρικόν "her paternal home."

2.4.1.3.3.1 Cultic Terms

Some of the Hebrew words have a standard or almost standard equivalent in the LXX, including LXX-Lev. Thus, קרבן "offering, sacrifice" is rendered by δῶρον "gift" (not connected with the verb קרב, הקריב "to come near, to bring near, offer," which is rendered προσφέρω "to bring"). δῶρον is also used for לחם "food" (only when referring to God, Lev 21:6) and שלמים "peace offerings." The word אשה "fire offering" is rendered as σωτήριον "thank offering." מנחה as an "offering" (as distinct from a secular donation) is κάρπωμα "fruit-offering." חטאת is ἁμαρτία (both meaning "sin"), and the offering for expiation of the sin is περὶ τῆς ἁμαρτίας "(offer) for the sin."[4] Similarly, אשם as both "guilt" and the "guilt offering" is translated indiscriminately by πλημμέλεια "error" or περὶ τῆς ἁμαρτίας "(offer) for the sin," e.g. Lev 7:1 [6:25]. עלה is ὁλοκάρπωσις and ὁλοκαύτωμα (all meaning "burnt-offering").[5]

2.4.1.3.3.2 Contextual Renderings

Several words are rendered differently in accord with their contexts. Thus, the phrase ראש + פרע, "uncover" + "head"[6] in the context of the priests' mourning customs is translated in Lev 10:6 and 21:10 as ἀποκιδαρόω (removal of the κίδαρις "head covering" of the priests). However, in Lev 13:45, in connection with the leper, it is rendered as ἀκάλυπτος "uncovered."[7] The latter translation may reflect customs practiced in the translator's environment.

Of particular interest is the treatment of פאה "edge," appearing six times in Leviticus. Unlike LXX-Exod, which always uses κλίτος "edge, border," LXX-Lev uses different and unusual equivalents: Lev 19:9 פאת שדך "*the edge* of your field"/τὸν θερισμὸν ὑμῶν τοῦ ἀγροῦ "*the harvest* of your field." The translator does not reflect the meaning "edge, border" for פאה; note the translation in the parallel passage Lev 23:22: τὸ λοιπὸν τοῦ θερισμοῦ τοῦ ἀγροῦ σου "the *remainder* of the harvest of your field."[8] In Lev 19:27a, it is rendered by an enigmatic noun, σισόη,[9] and in v. 27b as well as in Lev 21:5 it is rendered contextually: "the *appearance* (of your beard)" (τὴν ὄψιν τοῦ πώγωνος ὑμῶν).

Each of the three occurrences of כִּלְאַיִם "two kinds" in Lev 19:19 is rendered differently: a) ἑτεροζύγῳ "with a different species" with reference to the breeding of one's cattle; b) διάφορον "different, mixed" with reference to a vineyard (MT: "your field") = MT and LXX in Deut 22:9 (with the same rendering of כִּלְאַיִם "two kinds");[10] c) as ἐκ δύο ὑφασμένον κίβδηλον "woven-of-two false (materials)" referring to a garment of כִּלְאַיִם שַׁעַטְנֵז "two kinds of material,"[11] undoubtedly under the influence of Deut 22:11 (שַׁעַטְנֵז/κίβδηλον).

2.4.1.3.3.3 Unique Expressions

In the translation of rare expressions, LXX-Lev was probably guided either by an exegetical tradition or by context. Thus, אֱלִילִם "idols," found only twice in the Pentateuch, is contextually rendered by χειροποίητα "artifices" in Lev 26:1 and by εἴδωλα "silhouettes" in Lev 19:4 (see also Philo, *Spec. Laws* 1:25–26).[12] On the other hand, there are words with more than one Greek equivalent that are translated indiscriminately, e.g. עַם "people" is usually

---

[4] See D. Büchner, "A Cultic Term (ἁμαρτία) in the Septuagint: Its Meaning and Use from the Third Century B.C.E. until the New Testament," *BIOSCS* 42 (2009): 1–17.

[5] See Daniel, *Vocabulaire du culte*, 239–58; Harlé and Pralon, 32–40; Wevers, *Notes*, 484–87.

[6] The exact significance of the root פרע, especially in connection with "the head," is disputed.

[7] Similarly in Num 5:18, referring to the deviant woman.

[8] Some scholars contend that the LXX interpretation reflects rabbinic Halakha: Frankel, *Einfluss*, 153; Prijs, *Jüdische Tradition*, 105–06. However, it seems that the translator avoided the exact rendering of פאה.

[9] A *hapax* with unknown meaning. See LSJ *sub voce*; Frankel, *Einfluss*, 151–52; Wevers, *Notes*, 306–07.

[10] Similarly in Deut 22:9; → 2.4.1.3.4.1 below.

[11] The exact meaning and etymology of שעטנז is unclear.

[12] גלולים "idols" (Lev 26:30) and תרפים "household gods" (Gen 31:19) are translated by the same equivalent.

rendered as λαός "people," but also as ἔθνος "nation."

2.4.1.3.3.4 Alternative Structure of Phrase

In several references, the Hebrew phrase is probably reconstructed in LXX-Lev. In Lev 20:25, ובכל אשר תרמש האדמה "with anything that crawls the earth" ("the earth" is the subject and the predicate is תרמש) is rendered as ἐν πᾶσι τοῖς ἑρπετοῖς τῆς γῆς "with any creeping things of the earth," possibly reflecting a different *Vorlage* (cf. Gen 1:25).

2.4.1.3.4 Text-Critical Value: Variants and Non-Variants

LXX-Lev reflects numerous readings (variants) that deviate in minor details from MT (→ 2.2.2): a) pluses and minuses; b) different word order; c) different words. Some of these involve an adaptation to parallel passages. It is no easy task to determine whether a deviation from MT in the LXX reflects a Hebrew variant or the translator's style or exegesis, for example, in the case of differences in grammatical categories such as singular/plural and different pronominal forms. However, some such variants are supported by other ancient witnesses, including Hebrew texts such as SP (→ 2.2.4.3) and biblical and non-biblical Dead Sea Scrolls; see, for example, Lev 20:17 MT "he shall bear his iniquity"; LXX-Lev v s "*they* shall bear *their* iniquity," applying to "a man and his sister." In cases of harmonization, scholars differ as to whether they should be attributed to the Greek translator or to his *Vorlage*. When the harmonization refers to a remote location, it is more likely that it was already present in the Hebrew *Vorlage*.

2.4.1.3.4.1 Examples

LXX-Lev 19:19 "your vineyard" (in contrast to MT "your field") certainly reflects a Hebrew *Vorlage* rather than a Halakhic interpretation;[13] see כַּרְמְךָ "your vineyard" in the parallel passage, Deut 22:9;[14] also cf. 4QMMT[c] (4Q396) IV:6–7, where both words appear in this law on prohibited combinations.

2.4.1.3.4.2 Different Vocalization

Sometimes LXX-Lev reflects a different vocalization. Thus, in Lev 20:6, MT אֹתוֹ מִקֶּרֶב עַמּוֹ "him off from the midst of his people"/αὐτήν ἐκ τοῦ λαοῦ αὐτῆς "her off from her people" (probably = אֹתָהּ מקרב עמה) was originally spelled in a different orthography (→ 1.2.2.4.1.2; אתה, עמה) and was transformed to the customary spellings אֹתוֹ, עַמּוֹ. A similar case appears in Lev 22:28 אֹתוֹ וְאֶת־בְּנוֹ "him and his son," referring to the prohibition against slaughtering a bull or sheep together with its offspring on the same day; LXX-Lev αὐτήν καὶ τὰ παιδία αὐτῆς "her and her child" refers to the female animal, a cow or a ewe (compatible with the Halakha),[15] rather than to the male. Here again, an ancient reading אתה ואת בנה was vocalized by LXX-Lev using feminine suffixes, whereas the pre-MT vocalization אתה ואת בנה was later written as אֹתוֹ, בְּנוֹ.

2.4.1.3.4.3 Harmonization

LXX-Lev often reflects harmonizing readings also found in SP (→ 2.2.4.3) or the Qumran scrolls (→ 2.2.1). See the frequent alternation in MT (→ 2.2.2), SP, the Qumran scrolls, and LXX-Lev between "who sanctifies *you*" (= the congregation) and "... *them*" (= the priests) in Leviticus 20–22. An example is Lev 21:8: MT מְקַדִּשְׁכֶם, SP, 11QpaleoLev[a] (→ 2.2.1.7.12) (similarly LXX-Lev) מקדשם.[16]

2.4.1.3.4.4 Pluses and Minuses

LXX-Lev has numerous, mainly minor, pluses. E.g. it frequently adds the epithet ὁ θεός "the God" where MT has the Tetragrammaton only, especially in the formula אֲנִי יְהוָה "I am the Lord." Further, in Lev 21:9, MT has "(she profanes) her father" but LXX-Lev read τὸ ὄνομα τοῦ πατρὸς αὐτῆς "the name of her farther."[17] This plus is seemingly an interpretation.[18] In some cases, a small addition may have Halakhic ramifications. An example is Lev 21:31: MT "And he shall take a woman in her virginity"; LXX-Lev + "*from his people*." This plus

---

[13] Thus Frankel, *Einfluss*, 156.
[14] The functionally parallel words שדה "field" and כרם "vineyard" are often interchangeable.
[15] *Sifra, Emor* 8 e.a.l.
[16] Matthews, "Leviticus Scroll," 182.
[17] Cf. 4QLev[e] (→ 2.2.1.4; *DJD* XII: 199): "the house [of her father she profanes]"; MT-Lev 18:21; 21:6.
[18] See Prijs, *Jüdische Tradition*, 15.

could indicate that a priest may only take a wife from his own stock, the daughter of a priestly family, as understood by Philo, *Spec. Laws* 1:110.¹⁹

LXX-Lev attests to a few minuses; e.g., Lev 21:7, in which the second occurrence of "they shall not take" is absent. In Lev 22:31, "I am the Lord" is absent, as in 4QLev^b (→ 2.2.1.7.11; *DJD* XII: 182).

2.4.1.3.4.5 Variants: Word Order

Some word pairs are reversed in LXX-Lev. For example, the usual MT order of "father ... mother" is reversed on four occasions, but LXX-Lev maintains the usual order by way of harmonization: Lev 19:3 (supported by 4QRP^e [4Q367; → 2.2.1.7.4; *DJD* XIII: 348], V T^N S), 21:2, and 21:9 (as well as Ezek 16:45). Another example is seen in 21:19: רגל ... יד/χειρός ... ποδός (both meaning "hand ... foot"). Also when there is no fixed order, as in Lev 21:18, LXX-Lev (and S) reverses MT עִוֵּר אוֹ פִסֵּחַ "blind or lame."

Büchner, D.L., "Leuitikon," in *NETS, 82–106.
Büchner, D.L., "Some Reflections on Writing a Commentary on the Septuagint of Leviticus," in *Translation is Required: The Septuagint in Retrospect and Prospect* (ed. R.J.V. Hiebert; SBLSCS 56; Atlanta: SBL, 2010), 107–17.
Daniel, S., *Vocabulaire du culte.
Harlé, P. and D. Pralon, *Le Lévitique* (*Bible d'Alexandrie 3; Paris: Cerf, 1988).
Mathews, K.A., "The Leviticus Scroll (11QpaleoLev) and the Text of the Hebrew," *CBQ* 48 (1986): 171–207.
Tov, E., *Greek–Hebrew Bible.
Wevers, J.W., *Leviticus* (Septuaginta Vetus Testamentum Graecum 2.2; Göttingen: Vandenhoeck & Ruprecht, 1986).
Wevers, J.W., *Text History of the Greek Leviticus* (MSU 19; Gottingen: Vandenhoeck & Ruprecht, 1986).
Wevers, J.W., *Notes on the Greek Text of Leviticus* (SBLSCS 44; Atlanta: Scholars Press, 1997).
Zipor, M.A., "The Greek Version of Leviticus," *Bib* 79 (1998): 551–62.
Zipor, M.A., "Notes sur les chapitres xix à xxii du Lévitique dans la Bible d'Alexandrie," *ETL* 57 (1991): 328–37.

Moshe A. Zipor

---

¹⁹ For the pluses in LXX-Lev, see Wevers, *Notes*, 260–61; Büchner, "Some Reflections," 155–61.

2.4.1.4 Numbers
2.4.1.4.1 Nature

Among the translations of the Greek Pentateuch, Numbers poses some specific problems. The translator did not use a homogeneous technique when rendering his *Vorlage*; moreover, at times, one has to judge that he was working carelessly or lacking competence.¹ In other instances, he found good solutions for difficult problems. In some cases he introduced his own interpretations or *ad sensum* translations, e.g., in Num 24:7. Thus, the use of this version for the textual criticism of the Hebrew Bible cannot follow simple rules; each case must be seen in the larger context of how the translator worked in that specific section.

2.4.1.4.2 Background, Date, Milieu

It is generally assumed that the translation of Numbers was carried out in Alexandria, because several features of the Greek version point to an urban, Hellenistic milieu, e.g., the general use of δῆμος "people" for משפחה "clan/family" and σύγκλητοι βουλῆς "chosen councilors" for נשיאי עדה "leaders of the congregation" in Num 16:2. Because LXX-Num accepted equivalents from the earlier books, it is obvious that the book was translated after Genesis and Exodus, presumably in the second half of the third century B.C.E. There are no indications that allow for a more precise dating.

In 2004, a discussion about the relative chronology of the books of the Greek *nomos* was initiated by den Hertog. In his view, Deuteronomy was not the last book of the Greek Pentateuch to be translated, as one would have expected.² The argument is based on several instances in which the translation of Leviticus seems to depend on texts from Deuteronomy; *inter alia* he names the use of ψώρα ἀγρία "malignant itch" in Lev 21:20, which is dependent on Deut 28:27, and the rarely used verb ἐπανατρυγάω "to glean after the vintage" in Lev 19:10, coming from Deut 24:21. According to den Her-

---

¹ See Wevers, *Notes*, ix–xviii for some examples.
² C.G. den Hertog, "Erwägungen zur relativen Chronologie der Bücher Levitikus und Deuteronomium innerhalb der Pentateuchübersetzung," in *Brennpunkt, Vol. 2, 216–28.

tog, Deuteronomy was rendered earlier, because the cultic regulations in Leviticus and Numbers were not so important in the diaspora. On the other hand, Dorival discovered a network of intertextual relations between Numbers, Genesis, Exodus, and Leviticus, but not with Deuteronomy.[3] Moreover, since the fifth book of the Greek Pentateuch displays several neologisms such as ἀπαδικέω "to withhold wrongfully" (Deut 24:14) and ἐμπιστεύω "to trust in" (Deut 1:32),[4] which are absent in Numbers and Leviticus, it is more likely that Deuteronomy was translated last.

2.4.1.4.3 Original Form, Editions, Tools

The textual transmission of LXX-Num is relatively uniform. There are only a few differences between the critical text compiled by Wevers for the Göttingen Septuagint[5] and the edition by Rahlfs,[6] which is based on LXX^A and LXX^B. In some instances, Rahlfs adopted a longer text than Wevers, e.g., in Num 4:29–34; here, the shorter Göttingen edition is usually closer to MT than Rahlfs' edition. In most cases, the differences between the editions pertain only to minutiae and have no impact on the meaning of the text.[7] In a number of instances, Wevers proposed changes to his critical text in his *Notes* (pp. 608–09), and these are also recorded in *Septuaginta Deutsch, Erläuterungen*, 436–37.

The oldest witness for the Greek text of Numbers is 4QLXXNum (first century B.C.E.), containing some verses from Numbers 3 and 4. Its differences from Codex LXX^A and the critical text of the Göttingen LXX (Num 3:40; 4:7) reflect an early revision towards MT (→ 2.2.2), and not original readings.[8] Some important witnesses for the original Greek text belong to the tradition of the Byzantine Text and the Hexaplaric recension.[9] In Num 3:10, a late gloss without Hebrew equivalent has been inserted in the main tradition of the LXX^A and LXX^B text, which can be recognized by the isolated use of βωμός "(heathen) altar," instead of the usual θυσιαστήριον "place of offering."[10]

LXX-Num has been translated into English,[11] French,[12] and German.[13]

2.4.1.4.4 Translation Character

The *Vorlage* of LXX-Num was very close to the tradition of MT (→ 2.2.2). Some of the deviations from MT in the LXX version have parallels in SP (→ 2.2.4.4; e.g., Num 22:4, 32) and the pre-Samaritan tradition attested in 4QNum^b (→ 2.2.1.3.2), e.g., the plus in Num 23:3, which is presumably the oldest reading.[14] However, since SP and LXX have different characteristics, one cannot say that the LXX version was rendered from the Samaritan textual tradition.

A few differences in the numbering of chapters and verses have to be noted: LXX-Num 13:1 corresponds to MT-Num 12:16. Because it is the first verse of the new story, LXX-Num 26:1 has incorporated the fragmentary verse MT-Num 25:19. Of more sig-

---

[3] G. Dorival, "Les phénomènes d'intertextualité dans le livre grec des Nombres," in *Selon les Septante: Trente études sur la Bible grecque des Septante en hommage à Marguerite Harl* (eds. G. Dorival, O. Munnich; Paris: Cerf, 1995), 261–85.

[4] C. Dogniez and M. Harl, *Le Deutéronome: traduction du text grec de la Septante, introduction et notes* (*Bible d'Alexandrie* 5; Paris: Cerf, 1992), 64–68.

[5] J.W. Wevers, *Numeri* (Septuaginta Vetus Testamentum Graecum 3.1; Göttingen: Vandenhoeck & Ruprecht, 1982).

[6] Rahlfs, *Septuaginta*.

[7] See Dorival, *Les Nombres*, 36–37 for a useful list of the differences between the editions; they are also recorded in *Septuaginta Deutsch*.

[8] Dorival, *Les Nombres*, 37–39 and Wevers, *Notes*, ad loc. E. Ulrich, "The Greek Manuscripts of the Pentateuch from Qumran Including Newly-Identified Fragments of Deuteronomy (4QLXXDeut)," in *De Septuaginta: Studies in Honour of John William Wevers* (eds. A. Pietersma, C. Cox; Mississauga: Benben, 1984), 71–82, judges that the text of 4QLXXNum is more original.

[9] See Wevers, *Text History*, 7–65 for details.

[10] A. van der Kooij, "On the Use of βωμός in the Septuagint," in *Hamlet on a Hill: Festschrift T. Muraoka* (eds. M.F.J. Baasten, W.T. van Peursen; OLA 118; Leuven: Peeters, 2003), 601–07.

[11] P. Flint, "Numbers," *NETS*, 107–40.

[12] Dorival, *Les Nombres*.

[13] M. Rösel and C. Schlund, "Arithmoi: Das vierte Buch Mose," in *Septuaginta Deutsch*, 133–75. Helpful explanations and commentaries can be found in the extensive *Notes* by Wevers; Dorival, *Les Nombres*; and in M. Rösel and C. Schlund, "Arithmoi: Numeri/Das vierte Buch Mose," in *Septuaginta Deutsch, Erläuterungen*, 1:431–522. It can be noted that Dorival inclines to assume a different *Vorlage* while Wevers as well as Rösel and Schlund more often opt for changes introduced by the translator.

[14] Cf. Rösel, "Textüberlieferung," 216–17.

nificance is the difference in Numbers 16 and 17: LXX-Num 16:36–50 corresponds to MT-Num 17:1–15, which leads to the problem that LXX-Num 17:1–13 has its parallel in MT-Num 17:16–28.

Some transpositions of verses show traces of a specific exposition: thus, the sequence of the mustered tribes in Num 1:20–37 has been changed in LXX-Num according to the sequence in Gen 35:22–26.[15] A similar phenomenon can be seen in Num 26:15–47, where the altered sequence of the tribes corresponds with the enumeration in Genesis 46. In the Greek version of the priestly Blessing, MT-Num 6:27 has been moved before the actual blessing in vv. 24–26,[16] thus stressing that the blessing is God's act. MT-Num 10:34 is transposed in LXX-Num to 10:36, thus emphasizing God's protection (→ 2.1.4.1).[17]

In general, the translation follows the Hebrew text very closely, but there are some exceptions to this rule: in a number of instances, elements of the Hebrew text were not translated, e.g. in Num 9:5, 21–22, where a deviating *Vorlage* cannot be ruled out.[18] Also pluses as compared to MT-Num can be found in a few cases: Num 3:10 (obviously a later gloss); 4:14 (shared with SP); 7:87 (a harmonization with the context); 9:18 (explication of the subject); 14:12 (inner-biblical harmonization of a formula).

2.4.1.4.5 Translation Technique and Inner-Translational Features

Some of the aforementioned pluses display the translator's willingness to modify the text of his *Vorlage* and to insert words and phrases for the sake of clarification or harmonization. In general, one can see that he was following the Hebrew text very closely in passages with legal content. He rendered formulaic patterns very faithfully and even harmonized the texts where the *Vorlage* had variations, as in Numbers 1; 4; and 7. In narrative contexts, his translation style was less literal, but he still adopted the paratactic syntax of the Hebrew text. In the Balaam story (Numbers 22–24), he switched to a relatively free style in both the prose and poetic sections, even using hypotactic constructions and introducing an eschatological exposition into the text of the oracles.[19]

In comparison with the other translations of the Pentateuch, LXX-Num was less consistent in the use of equivalents, e.g., for particles or prepositions, as more attention was paid to the demands of the target language. For stylistic reasons, the translator also used different equivalents for the same Hebrew word, e.g., חֻקָּה "statute" was translated as νόμος "law" (Num 9:14), δικαίωμα "regulation" (Num 31:21), and διαστολή "constitution" (Num 19:2). On the other hand, the translator used one Greek word for different Hebrew lexemes, e.g., φυλή "tribe" for מַטֶּה "tribe" (Num 34:14), שֵׁבֶט "tribe" (Num 4:18), and מִשְׁפָּחָה "clan, family" (Num 27:11).[20]

The translator obviously wanted to produce a coherent text without inconsistencies. Thus, in a number of cases the differences from the Hebrew text can be explained as harmonizations: the age of the Levites in Num 4:23 is given as twenty-five years (MT: thirty years), obviously to avoid a contradiction with Num 8:24. In Num 4:41, ἐν χειρὶ Μωυσῆ "by the hand of Moses" was added to bring the text in line with v. 37. Harmonizations like these have extended beyond the boundaries of the book, thus, the difference in Num 10:12 refers back to Exod 40:30.[21] The net of intertextual connections between Numbers and Genesis, Exodus, and Leviticus has already been pointed out;[22] this is another characteristic of the specific translation technique of LXX-Num.

Another important aspect are the clear cases of theological exposition: in a number of instances, the roles of Moses and Aaron are strengthened (Num 3:16; 12:6–11; 16:15, 18), while the position of the Levites is minimized (Num 3:9; 8:19). Especially interesting is the specific approach in the Balaam

---

[15] Cf., among others, Dorival, *Les Nombres*, 66; but see also Tov, *TCHB*, 322, who ascribes the change to the *Vorlage* of LXX.

[16] Wevers, *Notes*, 105–06.

[17] But see Tov, *TCHB*, 309, who argues that the sequence in MT is secondary.

[18] Cf. similar minuses in Num 5:27; 6:21; 7:86; 26:1, 29; 36:13.

[19] Wevers, "Balaam"; Rösel, "Textüberlieferung."

[20] See Wevers, *Text History*, 94–103 for these features.

[21] See Dorival, *Les Nombres*, 42–43.

[22] See the literature quoted in n. 3.

pericope: Balaam is judged completely negatively as a heathen prophet, which can be seen *inter alia* in the use of βωμός "heathen altar" in Num 23:1 for Balaam's altar and in the avoidance of κύριος "Lord" and the use of θεός "God" instead, even where the Hebrew text uses the Tetragram.

2.4.1.4.6 Text-Critical Value

The Greek book of Numbers can be seen as an important witness for the Hebrew text of the book (→ 1.3.1.1.12; → 2.2.2). If a Greek reading was not created by one of the translator's idiosyncrasies mentioned above, it probably reflects a Hebrew variant. Such variants are sometimes supported by other witnesses. However, the frequent harmonizations and variations, in particular, make it difficult at times to reach a clear conclusion. Special attention should be given to readings in which LXX and 4QNum^b (→ 2.2.1.3.2) are in agreement. 4QNum^b is often secondary to MT and shares some readings with LXX, e.g., a stylistic improvement in Num 23:3 and the addition of [והואה יושב/καὶ οὗτος ἐγκάθηται ἐχόμενος (both meaning "it is lying in waiting" [*NETS*]) in Num 22:11, which is taken from v. 5. However, there are also cases in which the text of these fragments is shorter than LXX (cf. Num 11:35; 12:1; 20:25). In general, 4QNum^b is closer to SP (→ 2.2.4.4), while it also contains some independent readings.[23] As it "appears to be roughly equidistant from each of the other traditions,"[24] every case has to be examined on its own merits and no overall rule concerning its relation to the Greek version can be formulated.

2.4.1.4.7 Relevance for Exegesis

LXX-Num is especially important for the reception history of the Hebrew Bible and the development of several theological ideas in the Second Temple period. Particularly worth mentioning is the tendency towards a more transcendent theology. A striking example of this can be seen in Num 23:19, where ὡς is inserted in LXX: "God is not *like* a man," while the Hebrew text has "God is not a man." One should also point to the growth of messianic interpretations in the last centuries B.C.E. In Num 24:7, 17, the idea of a coming Messiah has been introduced into Balaam's third and fourth oracles, obviously an intertextual connection with the Greek version of Genesis 49, because LXX-Num 23:24 refers back to the Greek text of Gen 49:9.[25]

Dorival, G., *Les Nombres* (*Bible d'Alexandrie 4*; Paris: Cerf, 1994).

Rösel, M., "Die Textüberlieferung des Buches Numeri am Beispiel der Bileamerzählung," in *Sôfer Mahîr: Essays in Honour of Adrian Schenker Offered by Editors of Biblia Hebraica Quinta* (eds. Y.A.P. Goldman, A. van der Kooij, R.D. Weis; VTSup 110; Leiden: Brill, 2006), 207–26.

Rösel, M. and C. Schlund, *Arithmoi: Das vierte Buch Mose*, in *Septuaginta Deutsch, Erläuterungen*, 431–522.

Voitila, A., "The Translator of Greek Numbers," in *IX Congress of the International Organization for Septuagint and Cognate Studies, Cambridge, 1995* (ed. B.A. Taylor; SBLSCS 45; Atlanta: Scholars Press, 1997), 109–21.

Wevers, J.W., *Text History of the Greek Numbers* (MSU 16; Göttingen: Vandenhoeck & Ruprecht, 1982).

Wevers, J.W., *Notes on the Greek Text of Numbers* (SBLSCS 46; Atlanta: Scholars Press, 1998).

Wevers, J.W., "The Balaam Narrative according to the Septuagint," in *Lectures et Relectures de la Bible: Festschrift P.-M. Bogaert* (eds. J.-M. Auwers, A. Wénin; BETL 144, Leuven: Peeters, 1999), 133–44.

Martin Rösel

2.4.1.5 Deuteronomy
2.4.1.5.1 Background

It is generally accepted that Deuteronomy, along with the other books of the Pentateuch, was translated into Greek in Alexandria in the first half of

---

[23] N. Jastram, "The Text of 4QNum^b," in *Madrid Qumran Congress*, 2.177–98, esp. 184; cf. N. Jastram, "4QNum^b," *DJD* XII: 205–67.

[24] Jastram, "4QNum^b," 213.

[25] M. Rösel, "Jakob, Bileam und der Messias: Messianische Erwartungen in Gen 49 und Num 22–24," in *The Septuagint and Messianism* (ed. M.A. Knibb; BETL 195; Leuven: Peeters, 2006), 151–75, esp. 167. Interestingly enough, it can be seen that the Hebrew text of 4QNum^b also was influenced by Genesis 49, as the variant in Num 24:9 shows (Rösel, "Textüberlieferung," 218).

the third century B.C.E.,[1] although it is likely that Deuteronomy was translated after Genesis and Exodus.[2] The main source for this date is the *Letter of Aristeas*, a second-century B.C.E. pseudepigraphical work (repeated with some minor changes in Philo, *Mos.* 2, 25–44 and Josephus, *A.J.* 11, 118). While the *Letter of Aristeas* gives a highly romanticized account of the translation, it does seem to preserve a relatively accurate witness to the actual date of the translation: in the reign of Ptolemy II Philadelphus (285–264 B.C.E.). According to Lee, the vocabulary of LXX-Deut also suits a date in the third century B.C.E. For example, the word κάρταλλος, used to translate טֶנֶא "basket" is not attested before the third century B.C.E.[3] Evans agrees on syntactical grounds.[4] A third-century date is corroborated by the discovery of 4QLXXDeut, which dates to the mid-second century B.C.E.,[5] as well as the existence of two papyrus manuscripts of Deuteronomy from the second century (Rylands Papyrus 458, which is LXX⁹⁵⁷ in the Göttingen system) and the first century B.C.E. (Pap. Fouad 266; LXX⁸⁴⁸ in the Göttingen system) respectively.[6]

2.4.1.5.2 Original Form, Editions, Tools

The oldest complete text of LXX-Deut is found in Codex Vaticanus (LXX^B), from the fourth century C.E., followed by Codex Alexandrinus (LXX^A), from the fifth century. The critical edition in the Göttingen Septuagint series was produced by Wevers in 1977,[7] and is based on all the extant witnesses at the time of publication. However, Wevers admits that he favors readings that reflect MT-Deut;[8] thus, the user should exercise a degree of caution when consulting Wevers' edition. The Larger Cambridge Septuagint presents a diplomatic edition based on LXX^B. The most recent English translation is that of *NETS*, prepared by Peters.[9]

2.4.1.5.3 Translation Technique and Inner-Translational Features

LXX-Deut typically maintains a very close relationship to its Hebrew source text, translating at the isomorphic level of the word or small phrase, maintaining the typical pleonastic Hebrew style of Deuteronomy. As Aejmelaeus notes, LXX-Deut takes a less free approach to its *Vorlage* than Genesis or Exodus, not deviating from the Hebrew, "even when Greek grammar and style would seem to demand it."[10] As an example, take the typical Deuteronomistic phrase הארץ אשר אתם עברים את הירדן שמה לרשתה "the land that you are crossing the Jordan into to occupy" (Deut 4:26). This is translated τῆς γῆς εἰς ἣν ὑμεῖς διαβαίνετε τὸν Ἰορδάνην ἐκεῖ κληρονομῆσαι "the land that you are crossing the Jordan to inherit there" (*NETS*), exhibiting an almost slavish adherence to the Hebrew word order and syntax. Overall, compared to LXX-Gen and LXX-Exod, LXX-Deut contains a larger number of Hebraisms (often favoring transliteration rather than translation of place names), and uses a more literal approach to the parent text.[11] For example, Deuteronomy exhibits a difference in its translation of the *waw* conjunctive compared to Genesis and Exodus, showing a marked preference for καί "and" (1,068 times) as opposed to postpositive δέ "also" (ninety-seven times), thus reproducing the Hebrew word order in the translation.[12]

LXX-Deut tends to use fixed lexical equivalents for Hebrew words, for example (ἐν τῷ) πέραν "(in the) wilderness" for בעבר "wilderness" (Deut 1:1 et al.). While most of its translations are straightforward formal correspondences, it will also use dynamic equivalence, which can entail a certain

---

[1] Tov, *TCHB*, 131.
[2] Aejmelaeus, *Trail*, 77–78, 165; see also Evans, *Verbal Syntax*, 264.
[3] Lee, *Lexical Study*, 115.
[4] Evans, *Verbal Syntax*, 263.
[5] Skehan, Ulrich, and Sanderson, "4QLXXDeuteronomy," 195.
[6] Wevers, "The LXX Translator," 14–15, 64–85.
[7] Wevers, *Deuteronomy*.
[8] Wevers, *Notes on the Greek Text*, xi–xii, xxii.

[9] Peters, "Deuteronomium." The French translation is that of C. Dogniez and M. Harl, *Le Deutéronome: traduction du text grec de la Septante, introduction et notes* (*Bible d'Alexandrie* 5; Paris: Cerf, 1992). The German translation is found in *Septuaginta Deutsch*.
[10] Aejmelaeus, *Trail*, 165.
[11] Wevers, "The LXX Translator," 58.
[12] Wevers, "The LXX Translator," 58.

amount of interpretation. In 1:31, נשאך "he carried you," referring to God's care for the Israelites in the desert, is translated as ἐτροφοφόρησέν σε "he sustained you." LXX-Deut will also carry through one Greek word for several Hebrew lexemes, e.g. ἐξολεθρεύω "to destroy utterly" for the roots ירש "to dispossess" (Deut 4:38, 47; 9:4, 5; 18:12), חרם "to destroy utterly" (Deut 2:34, 3:6 [2×]), אבד "to destroy" (Deut 7:10; 28:63), שחת "to wipe out" (Deut 9:26; 10:10; 20:19, 20), כרת "to cut off" (Deut 12:29), and שמד "to exterminate" (Deut 1:27; 6:15; 7:4, 23, 24; 9:3, 8, 14, 19, 20, 25; 12:30; 28:20, 45, 48, 61, 63; 31:3, 4). The translator also attempts to resolve ambiguity in his *Vorlage*. For example, הרע means "the evil," but does it refer to a person ("the evil one") or to the abstract concept? LXX-Deut makes it clearly concrete, ὁ πονηρός "the evil one" (Deut 13:5; 17:7, 12; 19:19; 21:21; 22:21, 22, 24; 24:7).

LXX-Deut also coins neologisms for certain Hebrew terms, the most well known being the title given to the book itself, δευτερονόμιον "second law," which renders the phrase משנה התורה "copy of the law" in Deut 17:18.[13] Another example of a neologism is γραμματοεισαγωγεύς "recorders" (*NETS*) for שטרים "magistrates" in Deut 1:15, 16:18, 29:10, and 31:28.

Other prominent translational characteristics of LXX-Deut include a preference for ὅτι over postpositive γάρ when translating כי (all meaning "because") in expressions of indirect causality, thus faithfully following the word order of the Hebrew parent text rather than creating a smoother Greek translation.[14] As in the other books of the Pentateuch, LXX-Deut uses a participial construction in the following cases: λέγων regularly for לאמר (both meaning "saying"); in a temporal expression where Hebrew uses the infinitive construct plus ב (e.g. Deut 6:7); and in a coordinate clause, when Hebrew connects two clauses containing finite verbs with the simple copulative ו "and," LXX-Deut translates the first finite verb as a participle subordinated to the second finite verb (e.g. Deut 29:26).

When encountering the Tetragrammaton, LXX-Deut employs κύριος "Lord" without the definite article, the common practice in the Pentateuch.[15] However, the two early papyri cited above may give evidence for the approach to the Divine Name in the last centuries before the Common Era. At Deut 31:27, pap Fouad 266 (= LXX[848]) renders the Divine Name in Aramaic square script. Rylands Papyrus 458 (= LXX[957]) has a blank in the manuscript where the Divine Name should occur. Perhaps the scribe left a space to fill in the Divine Name, although whether that would have been in Aramaic square script, Greek transliteration, or simple Greek κύριος "Lord" is unresolved.[16]

2.4.1.5.4 Textual and Translation Character

Given its translation technique, which adheres very closely to the Hebrew source texts, LXX-Deut is a useful tool for the textual critic seeking to evaluate the Hebrew text. The most obvious characteristic of the text of Deuteronomy is its repetitive style.[17] MT-Deut contains many phrases and clauses that repeat over and over again, and that feature is even more apparent in LXX-Deut. Wevers lists fifty-six repetitive formulae, including:

– "which I (he) swore to give" – 27 times
– "which the Lord God is giving to you" – 37 times
– "hear the voice" – 29 times
– "ordinances and judgments/commandments" – 26 times
– "guard the commandments/ordinances" – 28 times.[18]

Because of this repetitive character, the text tradition of LXX-Deut was often even further amplified by glossing or the influence of parallel passages, making it difficult to recover the original Greek text.[19] Tov notes that this textual harmonization

---

[13] Peters, "Deuteronomium," 143.
[14] Aejmelaeus, *Trail*, 18–19, who notes that LXX-Deut uses ὅτι 102 times vs. γάρ, thirty-five times.
[15] Rösel, "The Reading and Translation of the Divine Name," 419.
[16] Rösel, "The Reading and Translation of the Divine Name," 415.
[17] Wevers, *Text History*, 86.
[18] Wevers, *Text History*, 86–99.
[19] Wevers, *Text History*, 118.

characterizes LXX-Deut more than any other feature.[20] For example, MT-Deut 6:21, 7:8, and 9:6 contain the phrase בְּיָד חֲזָקָה "with a strong hand." LXX-Deut adds the parallel phrase καὶ ἐν βραχίονι ὑψηλῷ "and a high arm" (see also Deut 3:24; 4:34; 5:15; 7:19; 11:2).

However, LXX-Deut also preserves readings that exhibit a different Hebrew *Vorlage* than the parallel reading in MT. Two parade examples occur in Deuteronomy 32, where the LXX readings are supported by Qumran manuscripts:

4QDeutʲ (→ 2.2.1.7.17) and LXX-Deut agree on the reading "sons (angels) of God," against "sons of Israel" in MT-Deut.

Deut 32:8

MT: בְּהַנְחֵל עֶלְיוֹן גּוֹיִם בְּהַפְרִידוֹ בְּנֵי אָדָם יַצֵּב גְּבֻלֹת עַמִּים לְמִסְפַּר בְּנֵי יִשְׂרָאֵל׃ "When the Most High apportioned the nations, when he divided humankind, he fixed the boundaries of the peoples according to the number of the sons of Israel."

LXX: ὅτε διεμέριζεν ὁ ὕψιστος ἔθνη, ὡς διέσπειρεν υἱοὺς Αδαμ, ἔστησεν ὅρια ἐθνῶν κατὰ ἀριθμὸν υἱῶν θεοῦ "When the Most High was apportioning nations, as he scattered Adam's sons, he fixed boundaries of nations according to the number of divine sons."

4QDeutʲ: בהנחי[ל] עליון גוים בהפרידו בני אדם יצב גבלת עמים למספר] בני אלוהים "When [the Most High] apportion[ed the nations, when he divided humankind, he fixed the boundaries of the peoples according to the number of] the sons of God."

In Deut 32:43, the expansive tendency of LXX-Deut, which knew two Hebrew forms of the text and harmonized them, is evident; the first part of the verse agrees with 4QDeutq (→ 2.2.1.6.3); the second partially agrees with MT-Deut.[21]

Deut 32:43

MT: הַרְנִינוּ גוֹיִם עַמּוֹ כִּי דַם־עֲבָדָיו יִקּוֹם וְנָקָם יָשִׁיב לְצָרָיו וְכִפֶּר אַדְמָתוֹ עַמּוֹ׃ "Praise, O nations, his people, for he will avenge the blood of his servants, and take vengeance on his adversaries, and cleanse his land, his people."

LXX: εὐφράνθητε, οὐρανοί, ἅμα αὐτῷ καὶ προσκυνησάτωσαν αὐτῷ πάντες υἱοὶ θεοῦ

εὐφράνθητε, ἔθνη, μετὰ τοῦ λαοῦ αὐτοῦ, καὶ ἐνισχυσάτωσαν αὐτῷ πάντες ἄγγελοι θεοῦ

ὅτι τὸ αἷμα τῶν υἱῶν αὐτοῦ ἐκδιδᾶται, καὶ ἐκδικήσει καὶ ἀνταποδώσει δίκην τοῖς ἐχθροῖς

καὶ τοῖς μισοῦσιν ἀνταποδώσει καὶ ἐκκαθαριεῖ κύριος τὴν γῆν τοῦ λαοῦ αὐτοῦ "Be glad, O skies, with him, and let all the divine sons do obeisance to him. Be glad, O nations, with his people, and let all the angels of God prevail for him. For he will avenge the blood of his sons and take revenge and repay the enemies with a sentence, and he will repay those who hate, and the Lord shall cleanse the land of his people."

4QDeutq: הרנינו שמים עמו והשתחוו לו כל אלהים כי דם בניו יקום ונקם ישיב לצריו ולמשנאיו ישלם "Praise, O heavens, his people, and worship him, all gods! For he will avenge the blood of his children, and take vengeance on his adversaries, and repay those who hate him."

A final example of a probable difference in the underlying Hebrew text comes from the Decalogue (Deut 5:6–21), where the order of the sixth, seventh, and eighth commandments differs from MT-Deut. LXX-Deut preserves the order of the injunctions against adultery, murder, and theft, while MT has the sequence murder, adultery, and theft.[22]

Finally, on the vexing question of the alternation between 2nd masc. sg. and 2nd masc. pl. suffixes throughout the book, LXX-Deut usually represents the pronominal suffixes of its *Vorlage* faithfully, although it occasionally uses exclusively the 2nd masc. sg. or the 2nd masc. pl. in a given pericope.[23]

2.4.1.5.5 Text-Critical Value

LXX-Deut is useful to the textual critic on the micro level of words and phrases, since the basic shape and chapter order of Deuteronomy remains the same in Hebrew, Greek, and the daughter versions. It often shares minor expansions with SP-Deut (→ 2.2.4.5), although there is no pattern to the

---

[20] Tov, *TCHB*, 136.
[21] Skehan and Ulrich, "4QDeutq," 141.

[22] SP agrees with MT.
[23] Wevers, *Text History*, 103, 107.

agreements, indicating that the expansions most likely took place individually and not as part of an overall editing approach. LXX-Deut does not share any major expansions, including harmonizations, with SP-Deut. Because of the repetitive nature of the language of Deuteronomy, each variant must be studied carefully, taking into consideration all the evidence, including that of the daughter versions. Even then, a definitive decision concerning the preferable reading is often elusive.

Aejmelaeus, *Trail.
Crawford, S.W., J. Joosten, and E. Ulrich, "Sample Editions of the Oxford Hebrew Bible: Deuteronomy 32:1–9, 1 Kings 11:1–8, and Jeremiah 27:1–10 (34 G)," VT 58 (2008): 1–15.
Duncan, J.A., "4QDeutʲ," *DJD XIV: 75–92.
Evans, T.V., *Verbal Syntax in the Greek Pentateuch* (Oxford: Oxford University Press, 2001).
Lee, J.A.L., *A Lexical Study of the Septuagint Version of the Pentateuch* (SBLSCS 14; Chico: Scholars Press, 1983).
Peters, M.K.H., "Deuteronomium," in *NETS, 141–73.
Rösel, M., "The Reading and Translation of the Divine Name in the Masoretic Tradition and the Greek Pentateuch," *JSOT* 31 (2007): 411–28.
Skehan, P.W., "A Fragment of the 'Song of Moses' (Deut. 32) from Qumran," *BASOR* 136 (1954): 12–15.
Skehan, P.W. and E. Ulrich, "4QDeutᑫ," *DJD XIV: 137–42.
Skehan, P.W., E. Ulrich, and J. Sanderson, "4QLXXDeuteronomy," *DJD IX: 195–200.
Wevers, J.W., *Deuteronomium* (Septuaginta, Vetus Testamentum Graecum III.2; Göttingen: Vandenhoeck & Ruprecht, 1977).
Wevers, J.W., "The LXX Translator of Deuteronomy," in *IX Congress of the International Organization for Septuagint and Cognate Studies, Cambridge, 1995* (ed. B. Taylor; Atlanta: Scholars Press, 1997), 57–89.
Wevers, J.W., *Notes on the Greek Text of Deuteronomy* (SBLSCS 39; Atlanta: Scholars Press, 1995).
Wevers, J.W., *Text History of the Greek Deuteronomy* (Philologisch-Historische Klasse Dritte Folge 106; Göttingen: Vandenhoeck & Ruprecht, 1978).

Sidnie White Crawford

2.4.2 Pre-Hexaplaric Greek Translations

See section → 2.4.6 (Hexaplaric Greek Translations and the Hexapla: Octateuch) also for Joshua, Judges and, Ruth, and section → 3–5.1.5.2 (Hexaplaric Greek Translations and the Hexapla: Samuel–Kings).

Andrew McClurg

2.4.3 Targumim

2.4.3.1 4QtgLev

The origins of the Aramaic rendering (Targumim) of the Hebrew Scriptures may be evidenced already in the Bible itself (Neh 8:1–8), but the first physical evidence we have of the existence of an Aramaic Targum dates only to the finds in Qumran Cave 4. This discovery, known in the scholarly literature as 4QtgLev or 4QarLev (4Q156), includes two short passages on parchment containing a partial and quite fragmentary translation of a few verses from Leviticus 16 (more precisely: little more than a few words from vv. 12–15, 18–21).[1] The text reflects a type of word-for-word translation of the words of Leviticus, but because of its fragmentary state – and the need to fill in many missing pieces in order to achieve even a partial reconstruction of the original – it is difficult to say much about it. In any event, it is not identical to any of the Targumim now extant.[2] The text is also too short to say anything about its text-critical value. Its importance lies in that it constitutes proof that written Targumic texts were in circulation as far back as before the Common Era (the manuscript has been dated to the last two centuries B.C.E.). It may be that the members of the Qumran sect did not obey the rabbinic dictum that "the words [of the Torah] that are written you are not at liberty to say by heart, and the words transmitted orally you are not at liberty to recite from writing" (*b. Giṭ.* 10b), so they committed the Targum (one of those things "transmitted orally") to writing, while Targum was transmitted only orally in other sections of Jewish society at that time. Alternatively, it may be merely

---

[1] For further information, see Stuckenbruck and Freedman, "The Fragments"; Safrai, "The Targums," 263; Tov, *TCHB, 149; Flesher and Chilton, *The Targums*, 351.

[2] For the view that this and other Aramaic versions from Qumran differ fundamentally from the rabbinic Targumim, → 11.3.3.2.

happenstance that this Targum reached us among the writings of the Qumran sect – due to the dry atmosphere of the northern Judean Desert and the fact that the texts were hidden in caves that were very difficult to access – and in fact there were many other Targum texts that have not survived to our time.

Milik, J.T., "Targum du Lévitique," *DJD* VI: 86–89.
Flesher, P.V.M. and B. Chilton, *The Targums: A Critical Introduction* (Waco: Baylor University Press, 2011).
Safrai, Z., "The Targums as Part of the Rabbinic Literature," in *The Literature of the Sages* (eds. S. Safrai et al.; CRINT 2.3b; Assen: Van Gorcum, 2006), 243–78.
Stuckenbruck, L.T. and D.N. Freedman, "The Fragments of a Targum to Leviticus in Qumran Cave 4 (4Q156): A Linguistic Comparison and Assessment," in *Targum and Scripture: Studies in Aramaic Translations and Interpretation in Memory of Ernst G. Clarke* (ed. P.V.M. Flesher; Leiden: Brill, 2000), 79–95.
Tov, *TCHB*.

2.4.3.2 Targumim – General
2.4.3.2.1 Introduction[1]

There are a few Pentateuchal Targum texts in our possession whose basis is in the first centuries of the Common Era, the period of the Mishnah and the Talmud and beyond: Targum Onqelos, the Targum attributed to Jonathan ben Uziel (called also: Pseudo-Jonathan), the Targum found in manuscript Neofiti 1 from the Vatican, the Targum known in scholarly literature as the Fragment Targum (which is known mainly from two different versions: Fragment Targum, ms Vatican and Fragment Targum, ms Paris), and Targum fragments from the Cairo Genizah, all of which will be discussed below (→ 2.4.3.3 and → 2.4.3.4).

First, however, we must draw a clear distinction between Targum Onqelos and all the other Aramaic Targumim to the Pentateuch mentioned above. Those latter Targumim, known as "the Palestinian Targumim," present us with a group of texts written mainly in Western Aramaic, unlike Targum Onqelos, whose Aramaic is quite different. (For more on this point, see below.) Another difference between Targum Onqelos and the other Targumim is the status traditionally accorded to them by the Jewish tradition; their respective literary types constitute yet another difference. During the Geonic period (beginning in the sixth to seventh century), Targum Onqelos was accorded a status of unique honor as the Pentateuchal text's official, authorized partner, while the Palestinian Targumim remained at the margins, with no particular distinction attributed to them. Furthermore, Targum Onqelos tends to present a word-for-word Targum – that is, a translation that attempts to adhere closely to the words of the Pentateuch, one after the other, providing the Aramaic equivalent of each one (with the exception of poetic passages, which are difficult to understand and translate) – while the other Targumim quite frequently insert many additions, both haggadic and legal (*Halakhic*), between sections of a translation that tends toward the literal. In most of the topics we will take up as we continue, we will have to distinguish between Targum Onqelos and the other Targumim rather than subjecting them to the same treatment. For the interrelation between the different Pentateuch Targumim, see → 1.3.3.4.4 and → 2.4.3.4; for the text-critical value, see → 1.3.3.7 (especially for Onqelos → 2.4.3.3.3).

The Aramaic Targumim to the Pentateuch circulated and flourished mostly in the cultural and religious milieu of the Sages who gave shape to rabbinic Judaism in the first five or six centuries C.E., until the use of Aramaic came to an end in the wake of the Arab conquest of the Levant. The Targumim were employed in schools (meant for youngsters who had only just begun their studies), in *batei midrash* (houses of learning; the academies where the sages and their disciples sat), and especially in synagogues (attended by people of every social stratum at fixed times). In all these locations, the Targum was an accompaniment to the study of the Hebrew Bible and its exegesis. Since our sources

---
[1] The most helpful and modern introductions to the Targumim are: Levine, *Aramaic Version*; Alexander, "Aramaic Translations"; Safrai, "The Targums"; Flesher and Chilton, *The Targums*. All of them include vast (and sometimes even annotated) bibliographies. I did not find it necessary to duplicate these lists.

teach us that the use of Targum in the synagogues was especially widespread, we will turn our attention from now on to this usage.²

With regard to Targum Onqelos, there remains a tradition (*b. Ber.* 8a) according to which "Rav Huna bar Yehudah says in the name of Rabbi Ammi: A man should always complete his *parashoth* [= portion of the Torah] together with the congregation, twice the Hebrew text and once the Targum." The intention seems to be that each person should read the portion in the Torah that will soon be read (in part or in full) in the synagogue each week, twice in the Hebrew original and once from a Targum, at home or together with the community. From this, we may infer that enough copies of Targum were circulating for people to read them on their own.

With the exception, though, of this one piece of evidence, rabbinic literature presents a clear picture according to which the Targum had to be read aloud by a rabbi, a teacher, or (in the synagogue) a person who specialized in such recitation, known as the *meturgeman*, the translator. The *meturgeman* was an established institution in the synagogues. He would stand beside the person reading from the Scriptures, and the two would alternate in the performance of their respective tasks, verse by verse. Even if Targum texts were available, the public recitation of Targum was performed orally. That the Targumim (especially the group known as "the Palestinian Targumim" [→ 2.4.3.4]) were works recited from memory in the synagogue, in connection with the Torah reading, explains many of their characteristics: they were directed first and foremost to the varied audience of synagogue attendees, which included people from all strata of society, the erudite and the unschooled, men and women, young people and mature adults, and often non-Jews as well. They placed demands on the *meturgeman* to develop varied techniques for memorizing, to adopt a variety of rhetorical techniques that would capture his listeners' attention, and to know how to improvise as well, to face the unexpected, such as any instance in which he forgot the accepted form of translation or if the unit read from the Torah was different from what he had anticipated (a common event in the land of Israel, where there was no fixed lectionary cycle of the Torah in the synagogues). These two important points – the oral character of the public presentation of Targumim and their popular character given the nature of the audience – exercise a decisive influence, as we shall see, on both their contents and the possibility of discovering the precise wording of the Torah text that underlies them.

2.4.3.2.2 Methods of Translation³

Verses of the Torah could, in principle, be translated in any of three basic ways:

1) A translation tending toward literalism, meaning one that shadows the biblical verse word for word and provides an Aramaic equivalent for each one, according to the translator's own understanding of it, of course.
2) A translation tending toward literalism that includes, at the beginning, middle, or end of a given verse, additions of either a legal or non-legal nature that expand upon what is said in the verse.
3) A paraphrastic translation, giving a general equivalent of what is said in the verse without being tied closely in any way to its specific words.

As an example of the first type, we shall cite the Targumim to the opening verse of the Torah, Gen 1:1: בְּרֵאשִׁית בָּרָא אֱלֹהִים אֵת הַשָּׁמַיִם וְאֵת הָאָרֶץ "in the beginning God created the heaven and the earth."⁴

T⁰: בקדמין ברא ה' ית שמיא וית ארעא "In antiquity God created the heaven and the earth"

T^{Ps-J}: מן אולא ברא ה' ית שמיא וית ארעא "From the beginning God created the heaven and the earth"

---

² See York, "Targum"; Kasher, "Sitz im Leben"; Alexander, "Aramaic Translations," 238–41; Shinan, "Late Midrashic."

³ For different modes of categorization, see Alexander, "Aramaic Translations," 225–37; Safrai, "The Targums," 257–59; Flesher and Chilton, *The Targums*, 19–36.

⁴ Translation of biblical texts according to: *Tanakh: A New Translation of the Holy Scriptures – According to the Masoretic Text* (vols. 2–3; Philadelphia: JPS, 1978–1982).

2.4.3 TARGUMIM

T^Frag(v): בחוכמא ברא ה' ית שמיא וית ארעא "With wisdom God created the heaven and the earth"

In spite of the differences between Targum Onqelos and Targum Pseudo-Jonathan (בקדמין "in antiquity" versus מן אולא "from the beginning"), it is clear that these two Targumim are attempting to understand the term בְּרֵאשִׁית "in the beginning" as something related to time, but Fragment Targum (v) does not hesitate to understand it in a completely different way, on the basis of a verse about creation: "The Lord founded the earth by wisdom (בְּחָכְמָה); He established the heavens by understanding" (Prov 3:19, with "by" in both instances representing the same prepositional -ב as in בְּרֵאשִׁית "in the beginning") and on the basis of the phrase "the beginning of wisdom" (רֵאשִׁית חָכְמָה, Ps 111:10), with the two words of this phrase taken by the *meturgeman* to be interchangeable. All three of these translations should be regarded as among those tending toward literalism, even though we must admit that Fragment Targum (v) makes loose and supple use of that definition, and it should be emphasized that the term "literal translation" cannot be identified with what biblical scholarship regards as the simple contextual meaning (*peshat*) of Scriptures.

As stated above, Targum Onqelos tends toward a word-for-word treatment of the biblical text (but does not do so consistently, as we shall see), while the Palestinian Targumim display, alongside verses translated in that manner, many others translated in one of the other two fashions that we shall now explore.

As an example of the second type, we will begin with the Targumim to Gen 27:25b: וַיַּגֶּשׁ־לוֹ וַיֹּאכַל וַיָּבֵא לוֹ יַיִן וַיֵּשְׁתְּ "So he [Jacob] served him [Isaac] and he ate and he brought him wine and he drank."

T^O: וקריב ליה ואכל ואיתי ליה חמרא ושתי "and he served him and he ate and he brought him wine and he drank"

T^N: וקרב ליה ואכל ואייתי ליה חמר ושתי "and he served him and he ate and he brought him wine and he drank"

T^Ps-J: וקרב ליה ואכל ולא הוה חמרא גביה ואזדמן ליה מלאכא ואייתי מן חמרא דאיצטנע בעינבוי מן יומי שירוי עלמא ויהביה ביד יעקב ויעקב אמטי ליה לאבוי ושתי "and he served him and he ate. Since he had no wine with him, an angel provided for him and brought of the wine that had been stored up in its grapes since the days of the beginning of the world and he gave it into Jacob's hand, and Jacob handed it to his father and he drank"

It is easy to see that Targum Onqelos and Targum Neofiti track precisely the words of the verse (while changing, because of the limitations of the Aramaic language, the "conversive *vav*" forms [וַיַּגֶּשׁ – *vayaggesh*, etc.] to the simple past tense), while Targum Pseudo-Jonathan integrates into the flow of translation a long passage (ולא הוה חמרא ... ויעקב) due to which it is forced to translate the end of the verse, which reads "and he brought him wine and he drank," as "and Jacob handed it to his father and he drank," so the reader will not gain the impression that it was the angel who brought the wine to Isaac. This haggadic addition serves to explain, of course, from where Jacob obtained wine to give to his father, since his mother had given him only bread and meat (Gen 27:17). Furthermore, it adds to the story a heavenly angel, a messenger of God, who stands at Jacob's side, indicating divine approbation of his actions, which blunts the negative effect of the theft of the blessing. A partial parallel to this tradition is found in the midrash (*Tanḥuma* [ed. Buber], *Toledot* 16).

Sometimes the addition comes at the head of the verse, before the onset of its actual translation, and sometimes (additionally or solely) at the end of the verse, such as in the following additions, which come at the beginning or end of a verse.

Gen 27:31a: וַיַּעַשׂ גַּם־הוּא מַטְעַמִּים וַיָּבֵא לְאָבִיו "He [Esau] too prepared a dish and brought it to his father."

T^O: ועבד אף הוא תבשילין ועייל לאבוהי "and he also made dishes and brought to his father"

T^N: ועבד אף הוא תבשילין ואייתי לאבוי "and he also made dishes and brought to his father"

T^Ps-J: ועכיב מימרא דה' מיניה צידא דכיא ואשכח כלבא חדא וקטליה ועבד אף הוא מיניה תבשילין ואייתי לאבוי "The Memra of the Lord withheld clean game from him but he found a dog and killed it and he also made dishes of it and brought to his father"

This Targum Pseudo-Jonathan tradition – which has no clear parallel in rabbinic literature – magnifies the evil and vulgar side of Esau's character. The addition of מיניה "he also made dishes of it" serves to emphasize that the food brought to Isaac was made from dog meat, and it is not based on a reading of the biblical verse different from that with which we are familiar.

Gen 33:4b: וַיִּשָּׁקֵהוּ וַיִּבְכּוּ "and he [Esau] kissed him [Jacob] and they wept"

T^O: ונשקיה ובכו "and he kissed him and they wept"

T^N: ונשק יתיה ובכו "and he kissed him and they wept"

T^{Ps-J}: ונשיך ליה ובכון עשו בכא על צערא דשינוי דאתמזמזיו ויעקב בכא על צערא דצואריה "and he bit him and they wept, Esau wept because of the pain of his teeth that were loosened and Jacob wept because of the pain of his neck"

T^{Frag(P)}: ונשיק יתיה ובכון תריהון עשו היה בכי על דקהיין שינוי ויעקב היה בכי על שעיעות צואריה "and he kissed him and they both wept; Esau wept because his teeth were dulled and Jacob wept over the smoothness of his neck"

The addition in the Targum has a parallel in rabbinic literature (*Gen. Rab.* 78, 9), aiming again at a harsh description of Esau.

This type of expansive addition is nearly absent from Targum Onqelos, but many are found in Targum Neofiti and the Fragment Targum, and especially so in Targum Pseudo-Jonathan. In the latter, not infrequently we find three and even five or six expansions woven into a single verse.

The third type of translation is paraphrastic:

Deut 1:1: אֵלֶּה הַדְּבָרִים אֲשֶׁר דִּבֶּר מֹשֶׁה אֶל־כָּל־יִשְׂרָאֵל בְּעֵבֶר הַיַּרְדֵּן בַּמִּדְבָּר בָּעֲרָבָה מוֹל סוּף בֵּין־פָּארָן וּבֵין־תֹּפֶל וְלָבָן וַחֲצֵרֹת וְדִי זָהָב "These are the words that Moses addressed to all Israel on the other side of the Jordan; Through the wilderness, in the Arabah near Suph, between Paran and Tophel, Laban, Hazeroth and Di Zahab."

T^{Frag(P)}: "These are the words that Moses spoke to all of Israel in Trans-Jordan: Moses began by saying to them: Behold in the wilderness, at Mount Sinai the Torah was given to you and in the plain of Moab it was explained to you. How many miracles and mighty acts did the Memra of the Lord perform for you! While you were standing at the shore of the Sea of Reeds [= *suf*] the sea was split before you and it was transformed into twelve streets, each street for each tribe. You brought about anger before Him at the sea and because you rebelled in the matter of the spies who were sent from the wilderness of Paran, He decreed upon you that you shall not enter the land of Israel ..."

Only with difficulty can one discern among the many words of this Targum the impression of the various words of this verse, which, on the face of it, seem merely to report geographic details. The verse as a whole becomes the basis for Moses' statement of rebuke, its words having been made into references to the events that befell the Israelites in the desert, in particular their stiff-necked behavior as expressed in incidents at the places mentioned in the verse (the Sea of Reeds and Paran). The word "gold," in Hebrew זהב (in the place name די־זהב), for example, is alluded to at the end of the Targum (which was not cited here) in mentioning the stories of the golden calf and the gold-plated ark of the covenant.

This sort of Targum of whole verses, or parts thereof, can be found here and there in the Fragment Targum, the Genizah Targumim, and Targum Neofiti, but appears much more frequently in Targum Pseudo-Jonathan, and needless to say it is impossible to make use of Targumim such as these for reconstructing any biblical textual variant that might have been in the translator's hands.

2.4.3.2.3 Beliefs and Concepts[5]

By means of the Targum tending toward word-for-word rendition, the targumic additions to the verse (at its beginning, somewhere in the middle, or at the end), and paraphrastic expansions large and small, the *meturgemanim* succeed in getting across to their audience the words of the Torah accom-

---

[5] Safrai, "The Targums," 259–62; Flesher and Chilton, *The Targums*, 325–38. For a few examples of studies of certain motifs in the Targumim, see Shinan, "Angelology"; Flesher, "Afterlife," and Syren, *Blessings*. A special note should be made in this context of the discussions of the relationship between the Targumim and ancient Christian literature; see McNamara, *New Testament*; Flesher and Chilton, *The Targums*, 383–436.

panied not only by explanations of those words and their intent, added narrative gap-fillers, and the elimination of what might appear to be contradictions, but also by sermonizing or encouraging, added legal instruction, comments on contemporary problems, and much more.

In particular instances, the *meturgemanim* would even refrain from translating a problematic verse (or part thereof), so as not to present their listeners – especially if they did not understand the Hebrew original – with an unpleasant picture of a biblical figure or event. Thus, for example, the Mishnah (*m. Meg.* 4:10 and elsewhere) states that "The story of Reuben is read out but not translated," meaning that the verse relating the incident of Reuben lying with Bilhah, his father's concubine (Gen 35:22), would indeed be read aloud by the person reading from the Torah, but the Aramaic translator would translate it only in part or perhaps not at all. The educational intent of the Targumim thus finds in this case a salient expression.[6]

A similar trend is also expressed in the Targumim in the many areas of beliefs and concepts that the *meturgemanim* sought to inculcate in their listeners' consciousness through their explanation of or additions to the words of Torah. They assigned a major role to emphasizing religious principles such as Torah study, the importance of prayer, and the observance of the commandments. The Targumim also devoted space to dealing with the belief in reward and punishment in this world and that to come (mainly in paradise), forgiveness and repentance, inherited merit (from the patriarchs) serving as protection for the people of Israel, and primarily the image of God, a topic that took up much attention in the Targumim. First and foremost, this refers to the Targumim's way of dealing with what appear to be anthropomorphic descriptions of the image of God (a topic we will take up further when we examine Targum Onqelos; → 2.4.3.3).

Alongside this trend, we can point to another tendency that is characteristic of the Targumim as texts directed toward the common people, namely their desire to present the nation's patriarchs and their life stories in a more positive light than that cast upon them by the biblical text itself. This is expressed not only, as we have seen, in refraining from translating embarrassing verses – such as the story of Reuben and Bilhah or parts of the golden calf incident – but also by attempting to improve their portrayal, such as having Jacob approach Isaac not "with guile" in order to steal his blessings but rather "with wisdom" (Gen 27:35, Targum Onqelos, etc.), having a heavenly voice announce that Judah had not sinned at all in his relationship with Tamar (Gen 38:25, Targum Neofiti, etc.), along with many other examples.

In matters of law as well, the *meturgemanim* tend to depart from what appears to be the Bible's simple contextual meaning in order to conform to the understanding of the law in classical rabbinic literature, such as the translation of "You shall not boil a kid in its mother's milk" (Exod 34:26) as a prohibition against consuming meat and milk together (לא תיכלון בסר בחלב "you shall not eat meat with milk," Targum Onqelos and similarly in other Targumim) or seeing "an eye for an eye" (Lev 24:20) as speaking about financial restitution: דמי עינא חולף עינא "the price of an eye for an eye" (Targum Pseudo-Jonathan, following *b. Ketub.* 32b and elsewhere).

From what has been said here in general about the Targumim – that is, their tendency to distance themselves from the biblical text in places where they saw it necessary to protect the honor of God or of the nation and its forebears, the sharp pedagogic tendency that characterizes their formulations, the desire to update biblical law in order to bring it into line with Jewish law that had developed over time, and especially the popular nature of the intended audience – together with the oral mode of delivery, the need to memorize long passages of Targum, and the need to improvise in unforeseen circumstances severely hinder our ability to identify the wording of the biblical *Vorlage* that the translators had before them. This is certainly the case for any passage for which they did not attempt to offer a word-for-word translation. It must be recalled as well that the Targum texts that are extant, even if they took shape during the

---

[6] Alexander, "Lists"; Klein, "Public."

first few centuries of the Common Era, come to us only from manuscripts originating from centuries later than that, and one cannot know what changes were introduced into them by copyists and redactors, who sometimes even sought to bring the Targum back closer to the text of the Torah as they knew it. Generally, one can draw from the Targumim only corroborating evidence of a given version of a biblical text of which we have independent evidence from another more reliable source. One famous example is the addition to Gen 4:8: After "And Cain said to his brother Abel," the Samaritan Pentateuch, the Septuagint, and the Peshitta add, "Let us go out to the field," which is also reflected in Targum Pseudo-Jonathan and Fragment Targum. The possibility of reconstructing a Hebrew version of the Torah underlying the many and complex strata that have settled upon it in the Targumim (where there is no other evidence for such a reading) is especially limited, and some might say impossible.[7]

Alexander, P.S., "Jewish Aramaic Translations of Hebrew Scriputres," in Mulder, *Mikra*, 217–54.
Alexander, P.S., "The Rabbinic Lists of Forbidden Targumim," *JJS* 27 (1976): 177–91.
Flesher, P.V.M., "The Theology of the Afterlife In the Palestinian Targums to the Pentateuch," in *New Perspectives on Ancient Judaism*, vol. 3 (eds. J. Neusner and E.S. Frerichs; Lanham: University Press of America, 1987), 1–48.
Flesher, P.V.M. and B. Chilton, *The Targums: A Critical Introduction* (Waco: Baylor University Press, 2011).
Kasher, R., "The Aramaic Targumim and their Sitz im Leben," in *Proceedings of the Ninth World Congress of Jewish Studies, Jerusalem, August 4–12, 1985; Panel Sessions: Bible Studies and Ancient Near East* (ed. M. Goshen-Gottstein; Jerusalem: World Union of Jewish Studies, 1988), 75–85.
Klein, M.L., "Not to be Translated in Public," *JJS* 39 (1988): 80–91.
Levine, E., *The Aramaic Version of the Bible: Contents and Context* (BZAW 174; Berlin: De Gruyter, 1988).
McNamara, M.J., *The New Testament and the Palestinian Targums to the Pentateuch* (AnBib 27; Rome: Pontifical Biblical Institute, 1966).

Safrai, Z., "The Targums as Part of the Rabbinic Literature," in *The Literature of the Sages* (eds. S. Safrai et al.; CRINT 2.3b; Assen: Van Gorcum, 2006): 243–78.
Shinan, A., "The Late Midrashic, Paytanic, and Targumic Literature," in *The Cambridge History of Judaism*, Vol. 4: *The Late Roman-Rabbinic Period* (ed. S.T. Katz; Cambridge: Cambrige University Press, 2006), 678–98.
Shinan, A., "The Angelology of the Palestinian Targums to the Pentateuch," *Sef* 43 (1983): 181–98.
Syren, R., *The Blessings In the Targums: A study of the Targumic Interpretation of Genesis 49 and Deuteronomy 32* (Abo: Abo Akademi, 1986).
Tov, *TCHB*.
York, A.D., "The Targum in the Synagogue and the School," *JSJ* 10 (1979): 74–86.

2.4.3.3 Targum Onqelos[1]

2.4.3.3.1 Background and Milieu

Against the backdrop of all that has been said above (→ 2.4.3.2), we will now specify, one by one, the Targum texts we have at our disposal, beginning with the one that earned a special, elevated status: Targum Onqelos. (For the rest of the Targumim, known as the Palestinian Targumim, see → 2.4.3.4.) This Targum, which according to tradition was made by a convert named Onqelos, who was a student of sages at the end of the first century C.E. and the beginning of the second century C.E. (*b. Meg.* 3a), apparently got its name from a misperception of the name Aquila, the Greek translation of the Pentateuch made in the second century. In time, Targum Onqelos achieved a special status in the literature of the Babylonian sages (who referred to it as "our Targum" [*b. Qidd.* 29a]) and the gaonim who followed them, and it was taken to be the official, most important, and best of the Targumim. Since 1482 (when it was published by Avraham ben Hayyim alongside the Torah and Rashi's commentary), it has been printed in every traditional Jewish edition of the Pentateuch and it is widely cited by medieval commentators (such as Rashi), lexi-

---

[7] See Tov, *TCHB*, 121–34.

[1] Useful introductions to Targum Onqelos (which include vast and sometimes annotated bibliographies) are: Alexander, "Aramaic Translations," 217–18, 250–51; Safrai, "The Targums," 263–66; Flesher and Chilton, *The Targums*, 83–87.

cographers, and thinkers as the authoritative Targum to the Torah. The number of manuscripts of Targum Onqelos is high, reaching into the hundreds, but they share a quite unified textual tradition, and a textual apparatus – resembling the biblical Masorah – has even been developed that seeks to achieve precision in wording and an authoritative text.[2] Many are the scholars who have written commentaries to Targum Onqelos and even super-commentaries. The scholarly literature, too, on Targum Onqelos is more extensive than what has been written about all the other Targumim combined.

2.4.3.3.2 Translation Character and Technique

Targum Onqelos is a complete Targum to the entire Pentateuch that tends toward word-for-word translation. It is a very consistent text when it comes to its modes of translation and choice of Aramaic words to represent the Hebrew. Nonetheless, one can find in it – even in non-poetic passages – many hundreds of expansions and additions, explanations and changes, that flow from its desire to clarify and explain the words of the biblical text (e.g., אֲשֶׁר יֵצֵא מִמֵּעֶיךָ "the one that will be issued from your own body" [Gen 15:4] translates as בר דתוליד "the son that you will give birth to"), to introduce changes that result from the passage from one language to another (such as replacing the "conversive vav" forms with a simple past tense, or to translate a place name that ends with a locative he using a different form: וַיֵּלֶךְ חָרָנָה [Gen 28:10] – ואזל לחרן [both meaning "and he went to Haran"]), or to make the text conform to the beliefs and concepts of rabbinic literature (בְּחַרְבִּי וּבְקַשְׁתִּי "with the help of my sword and my bow" [Gen 48:22] – בצלותי ובבעותי "by my prayer and supplication" [cf. b. B. Batra 123a]), or to update place names (חַצְצֹן תָּמָר "Hazzazon Tamar" [Gen 14:7] – עין גדי "Ein Gedi"), to integrate Jewish legal traditions into their textual sources (לֹא תִּרְצָח "you shall not murder" [Exod 20:13] – לא תקטול נפש "you shall not kill a human being" [cf. b. Sanh. 86a]), or to do the same for haggadic traditions (וְהָיוּ יָמָיו מֵאָה וְעֶשְׂרִים שָׁנָה "let his days be a hundred and twenty years" [Gen 6:3] – ארכא יהיב להון מאה ועסרין "they have been granted a hundred and twenty years for repentence" [cf. 'Abot R. Nat., A, 32]), or especially to safeguard the honor of God, the people of Israel, and the Patriarchs.

To that end, Targum Onqelos grapples with biblical expressions that describe God in terms drawn from human physical actions, such as walking, going down (אֵרֲדָה-נָּא "let me go down" [Gen 18:21] – אתגלי כען "let me now reveal myself"), or smelling (וַיָּרַח ה׳) "and God smelled" [Gen 8:21] – וקביל ה׳ ברעוא "and God accepted with favour") or as having human body parts, such as feet (רַגְלָיו "His feet" [Exod 24:10] – כורסי יקריה "His seat of honor"), a hand, or a finger (אֶצְבַּע אֱלֹהִים God's finger [Exod 8:15] – מחא מן קדם ה׳ "a stroke from God"), or human feelings, such as anger, regret (וַיִּנָּחֶם ה׳ "and God regreted" [Gen 6:6] – ותב ה׳ במימריה "and God changed his word") and the like. Targum Onqelos adds an especially large number of superhuman entities that mediate between human beings and God, such as "Presence" (שכינתא), "Glory" (יקרא), and especially "Word" (מימרא), in order to portray a God who is so exalted that no human being can approach Him (e.g., הֲיֵשׁ ה׳ בְּקִרְבֵּנוּ "is God among us" [Exod 17:7] – האית שכינתא דה׳ ביננא "is the Shechinah [= Presence] among us," וַיַּעַל מֵעָלָיו אֱלֹהִים "and God parted from him" [Gen 35:13] – ואסתלק מעלוהי יקרא דה׳ "and the Glory of God parted from him," or וַיְהִי אֱלֹהִים אֶת-הַנַּעַר "and God was with the boy" [Gen 21:20] – והוה מימרא דה׳ בסעדיה דרביא "and the Word of God was with the boy"). This is characteristic of the other Aramaic Targumim as well, but its appearance in a Targum such as Targum Onqelos that tends toward word-for-word translation is particularly striking and has thus attracted a lot of scholarly attention.[3] The same is true of Targum Onqelos' tendency to protect the good name of the patriarchs (e.g., וְעֵינֵי לֵאָה רַכּוֹת "and Leah's eyes were weak" [Gen 29:17] – יאין "beautiful" or בָּא אָחִיךָ בְּמִרְמָה "your brother came with guile" [Gen 27:35] – בחוכמא "with wisdom").

---

[2] M.L. Klein, *The Massorah to Targum Onqelos: Critical Edition with Comments and Introduction* (Binghamton: Global, 2000).

[3] See, e.g., Klein, *Anthropomorphisms*; Chester, *Divine Revelation*.

In other places, however, in certain verses and especially in passages of poetry (Genesis 49 or Deuteronomy 32–33), Targum Onqelos departs from its word-for-word approach and offers expansions and even paraphrases of biblical verses whose language is not infrequently complex and difficult. Take, for example, Gen 49:11:

Gen 49:11: אֹסְרִי לַגֶּפֶן עִירֹה וְלַשֹּׂרֵקָה בְּנִי אֲתֹנוֹ כִּבֵּס בַּיַּיִן לְבֻשׁוֹ וּבְדַם־עֲנָבִים "He tethers his ass to a vine, his ass's foal to a choice vine, he washed his garment in wine, his robe in blood of grapes."

T°: יסחר ישראל לקרתיה עמא יבנון היכליה, יהון צדיקיא סחור סחור ליה ועבדי אוריתא באולפן עמיה, יהי ארגוון טב לבושוהי וכסותיה מילא צבע זהורי וצבענין "He shall lead Israel around his city, the people shall build his temple; the righteous shall be round about him and they that carry out the law shall be with him in study. Let his raiment be of fine purple and his garments all woolen, crimson and of sparkling color."

The commentators on this specific Targum have all found it difficult to understand the connection between the Targum's statements, which mention the Jewish people's return to the city of the Messiah (mentioned in the Targum to the previous verse), the rebuilding of the temple, the study of the Torah, the righteous people accompanying the Messiah, and his splendid clothing on one hand and the biblical verse on the other. Only a few words in the verse, such as עיר (which in Genesis refers to a "young ass" [עַיִר] rather than a "city" [עִיר]) or the wine and blood that bring to mind the color red, make it possible to try to understand that connection.

The question of the source and date of Targum Onqelos and the question of its relationship with the other Targumim to the Pentateuch are the subject of debate among scholars. Most researchers think that Targum Onqelos, even though it took on its final form in Babylonia, is at base a Palestinian Targum, perhaps even from the first or second century C.E., that made its way eastward during the third or fourth century C.E. and there underwent painstaking redaction that gave it its final shape. Its Aramaic is not identical to the Eastern Aramaic of the Babylonian Talmud, but neither is it identical to the Western Aramaic of the Palestinian Talmud, the midrashim, and the Targumim of the land of Israel. Instead, it is what is customarily referred to as "Middle Aramaic," but it is spiced with forms from later Aramaic, sometimes Western and sometimes Eastern, the work of copyists and redactors.

Comparing the manner in which many words are translated, noticing tendencies expressed in the translation, examining the toponyms that appear in it, and comparing the haggadic and legal traditions to which reference is made with what happens in the Palestinian Targumim – all these led researchers to conclude that at the basis of Targum Onqelos lies an ancient Targum (called by some "Proto-Onqelos"), from which the Targum we know descended, parallel to the Palestinian Targumim, which also developed, although at a later date, from that ancient Targum. Over time, ancient copyists and editors of the Palestinian Targumim did not hesitate to change what they had before them to make it accord with the Targum that was accepted and familiar, Targum Onqelos. Thus was formed an exceedingly complex picture of the relations among all the Targumim to the Pentateuch, a question that has not been fully clarified.[4]

2.4.3.3.3 Text-Critical Value

As for the text of the Torah upon which Targum Onqelos is based, it is in many cases identical to what is reflected in other ancient translations or in various manuscripts of the Masoretic Tradition (→ 2.2.2). Thus, for example, it renders וַיָּמָת אַבְרָהָם ... זָקֵן וְשָׂבֵעַ "and Abraham died ... at a good ripe age" (Gen 25:8) as שבע ימים "at a good ripe Age having enjoyed his life," just as in SP (→ 1.2.3), LXX (→ 2.4.1), the Peshitta, (→ 2.4.5) and many Hebrew manuscripts. In Exod 7:19 it adds the object marker "את" to the clause קַח מַטְּךָ "take your rod," as do Hebrew manuscripts and SP. We seem unable to point to a single reading of a biblical passage unique to Targum Onqelos (i.e., for which we have no support from another source) that undoubtedly reflects a

---

[4] See, especially, Alexander, "Aramaic Translations," 244; Flesher and Chilton, *The Targums*, 109–29.

different version of the Bible. It seems that this Targum – important as it is for understanding the ancient Jewish interpretation of the Pentateuch – has no such importance when dealing with its text-critical value.

2.4.3.3.4 Editions

Scholars[5] still make use of the edition of Targum Onqelos published by Alexander Sperber (according to a manuscript in the British Museum, Or. 2363, with a critical apparatus citing many other manuscripts), or of the electronic version found at the CAL website, which offers tools for searching, linguistic analysis, and constructing a concordance. A new English translation was prepared by Grossfeld,[6] and the preferred dictionary is that of Cook,[7] although Jastrow's dictionary[8] is still a useful tool for studying Targum Onqelos, as well as the concordance of Kasovsky.[9]

Alexander, P.S., "Jewish Aramaic Translations of Hebrew Scriputres," in Mulder, *Mikra*, 217–54.
CAL. Online: http://cal1.cn.huc.edu.
Chester, A., *Divine Revelation and Divine Titles in the Pentateuch Targumim* (TSAJ 14; Tübingen: Mohr Siebeck, 1986).
Cook, E.M., *A Glossary of Targum Onkelos* (Studies in the Aramaic Interpretation of Scripture 6; Leiden: Brill, 2008).
Flesher, P.V.M. and B. Chilton, *The Targums: A Critical Introduction* (Waco: Baylor University Press, 2011).
Grossfeld, B., *The Targum Onqelos [Genesis-Deuteronomy]: Translated with a Critical Introduction, Apparatus and Notes* (Wilmington: Michael Glazier, 1988).
Jastrow, M., *A Dictionary of the Targumim, the Talmud Babli and Yerushalmi and the Midrashic Literature* (New York: Pardes Publishing House, 1950).
Kasovsky, H.J., *Ozar Leshon Targum Onkelos: Concordance* (Jerusalem: Magnes Press, 1986).
Klein, M.L., *Anthropomorphisms and Anthropopathisms in the Targumim of the Pentateuch* (Jerusalem: Makor, 1982) [Hebr.].

Safrai, Z., "The Targums as Part of the Rabbinic Literature," in *The Literature of the Sages* (eds. S. Safrai et al.; CRINT 2.3b; Assen: Van Gorcum, 2006), 243–78.
Sperber, A., *The Pentateuch According to Targum Onkelos* (vol. 1 of Sperber, *Bible in Aramaic*; 1959).

2.4.3.4 Palestinian Targumim

Before we turn to the so-called "Palestinian" Targumim[1] to the Pentateuch, it should be pointed out that at base they share a common translation tradition. Indeed, each of the texts that we will now examine displays unique identifying characteristics, but in the end they can all be brought together in one synoptic edition showing that their source is in a single world of thought and literature. This is especially evident in the haggadic additions woven into them, and most especially in the places where the Targumim add a particularly long expansion to one or another verse. These expansions often come in verses that can be seen as peaks in the biblical narrative (such as "And Abraham picked up the knife to slay his son" [Gen 22:10: T^O, T^N, T^{Frag}]) or as verses that played a special role in the Pentateuchal lectionary cycle in the ancient rite of the land of Israel. There – unlike what is customary in most Jewish communities today, where the Pentateuchal reading is completed in a single year of up to fifty-four weekly units – the reading proceeded at a slower pace, known imprecisely in the scholarly literature as the "triennial cycle." In fact, this refers to a division of the Pentateuch into smaller lectionary units about which, as far as we can tell, there were a variety of customs, with the number of units varying between 137 and 175. The verses with which the weekly units began naturally attracted the attention of the *meturgemanim* and were frequently expanded (e.g., Gen 15:1 [T^O, T^N, T^{Gen}, T^{Frag}] or Lev 22:27 [T^{Ps-J}, T^N, T^{Gen}, T^{Frag}] at the beginning of a lectionary unit, and Gen 34:31 [T^{Ps-J}, T^N, T^{Frag}] or Num 12:16 [T^{Ps-J}, T^N, T^{Frag}] at the end of one). In

---

[5] For details, see the bibliography at the end of this section.
[6] Grossfeld, *Targum Onqelos*.
[7] Cook, *Glossary*.
[8] Jastrow, *Dictionary*.
[9] Kasovsky, *Ozar*.

[1] By the term "Palestinian," scholars usually refer to the Aramaic translations of the Pentateuch that are different from Targum Onqelos, which is believed to have acquired its final form in Babylon; → 2.4.3.3.

all these instances, the Targumim have a single tradition, albeit with slight differences, the result of discrete performances by different *meturgemanim* before different audiences in different contexts and of copyists and redactors working with written versions. Aside from that, as we shall see, each one of the Palestinian Targum texts has additions and changes unique to it. We cannot outline a clear connection between the different texts of the extant Palestinian Targumim, but their common origin – in the oral representation of Targum in the synagogues and schools – cannot be disputed. They differ from each other in many ways but still testify to a common basic tradition, the tradition of the *meturgemanim*, which is represented in them in such variegated ways that it is impossible for us to pinpoint any internal consistency in individual texts or in the whole group.

2.4.3.4.1 Targum Pseudo-Jonathan[2]

From many perspectives, Targum Pseudo-Jonathan can be seen as the opposite of Targum Onqelos (as discussed in the previous section, → 2.4.3.3). It too is a translation of the entire Pentateuch, but interspersed in it are many hundreds – if not several thousands – of additions and expansions, both haggadic and legal, and translations of verses that expand into long and detailed sermons (even more so than in the other Palestinian Targumim). This Targum, which was first printed in a Pentateuch published in Venice in 1590–1591, apparently received its name on the basis of a misunderstanding of an abbreviation. It appears that ת״י, which stood for Targum Yerushalmi (i.e., Palestinian Targum), was misunderstood by someone as Targum Yonatan [Jonathan], under the influence of the fact that for the books of the Prophets we do indeed have a Targum attributed to the early rabbinic sage Yonatan ben Uziel. At the end of the nineteenth century, a manuscript of Targum Pseudo-Jonathan was discovered in the British Museum (Add. 27031). It had been copied in 1593 or 1598 in Italy, and it is apparently the only extant manuscript of this composition. Its form is quite close (although not entirely identical) to the printed edition mentioned above. Only a few scattered quotations from Targum Pseudo-Jonathan have been found in medieval literature, and it appears not to have been widely known until the appearance of the Venice edition.

Targum Pseudo-Jonathan incorporates additions preserving many haggadic and legal traditions regarding the translated verse. Removing these additions and expansions often leaves us with a translated text that tends toward a word-for-word rendering, not infrequently similar in character (and even in language) to Targum Onqelos or Targum Neofiti. It should be emphasized that what was stated above about the unlikelihood of discovering the exact Hebrew text that underlies any targumic text is all the more true when we are dealing with Targum Pseudo-Jonathan, which makes no pretense of giving a precise reflection of the biblical text.

In Targum Pseudo-Jonathan, and only there, do we find verses in which there are as many as five or six additions interspersed within one verse (as, for example, in Exod 18:20 and Num 27:17). Also in Targum Pseudo-Jonathan alone do we find that a given haggadic tradition is disassembled, appearing piece by piece in the translation of several verses, even verses that are found at a considerable distance from one another (such as the division of functions among the angels who came to Abraham and continued on from there to Sodom [Genesis 18–19]: see Targum Pseudo-Jonathan to the opening of the story [Gen 18:2] and its treatment of Gen 18:10, 16, 22; 19:1). Targum Pseudo-Jonathan is unique, too, from the perspective of the topics it works into the biblical narrative, above and beyond what is found in the tradition common to all Palestinian Targumim. Thus, for example, it is the only Targum that does not hesitate to add expressions of criticism and opprobrium regarding the patriarchs (such as the statement that Abraham's descendants were punished with Egyptian exile be-

---

[2] Useful introductions to Targum Pseudo-Jonathan (including vast and sometimes annotated bibliographies) are: Alexander, "Aramaic Translations," 219–20, 251; Safrai, "The Targums," 266–68; Flesher and Chilton, *The Targums*, 87–89. Cf. a Hebrew monograph dedicated to the haggadic parts of this targum: Shinan, *Embroidered Targum*.

cause of a lack of faith demonstrated by their ancient forebear [Gen 15:13, with a parallel in *b. Ned.* 32a]), and it is the only Targum that introduces into the biblical story not only heavenly angels (as do other Targumim) but "satan" and other evil powers as well (e.g., Gen 3:6 [with a partial parallel in *Pirqe R. El.* 11] or Exod 31:1 [with a parallel in *b. Šabb.* 89a]). It should also be noted that in this Targum there are many traditions that have no parallel at all, neither in the world of Targum nor outside it (such as the name of the angel who appeared to Moses in the burning bush, Zagnazgael [Exod 3:2], or regarding Eldad and Medad as Moses' brothers [Num 11:25]). The uniqueness of Targum Pseudo-Jonathan among the Palestinian Targumim to the Pentateuch is recognizable, then, from both the literary and thematic perspectives.

A great deal of scholarly effort has been expended on the question of the date of this Targum, and the answers given range from the fourth to the eighth or even the ninth century, all of them focused on the question of how to evaluate the traditions in this Targum that have parallels in compositions whose dates are certainly from the Islamic period (such as references to the names of Mohammed's wife and daughter [Gen 21:21]). If these are to be regarded as an integral part of the Targum, they obviously testify to a late origin, but if they are to be regarded as late additions, they cannot be used to establish a date much later than the other Palestinian Targumim to the Pentateuch. Added to this, the fact that the language in this Targum also points to a late date (as well as to considerable influence from Targum Onqelos) and the absence of any mention of it in the medieval traditional literature combine to point to a preference for a late date for this text.

Targum Pseudo-Jonathan is best cited from the edition of Clarke[3] that was published along with a concordance and is available also through the *CAL project. There is a translation into English by Maher,[4] accompanied by very valuable notes, but we are still without a systematic dictionary (other than the antiquated dictionary of Jastrow[5] and the treatment of words identical to those in Targum Onqelos that have been discussed in works on that Targum) or grammar.[6]

2.4.3.4.2 The Targum in Ms Neofiti 1 and its Marginal Notes[7]

In the 1950s, research into Aramaic Targum was stimulated by the announcement from a Spanish scholar, Alexander Diez-Macho, of the discovery of a continuous text of a Palestinian Targum to the Pentateuch written in Western Aramaic within Codex Neofiti 1 in the library of the Collegium Neophytorum in the Vatican. Until then, as mentioned previously, scholars had only two complete Targumim to the Pentateuch, Targum Onqelos and Targum Pseudo-Jonathan, which are very different from one another, and a partial Targum, the Fragment Targum, discussed below. Diez-Macho's discovery opened up new horizons of research when it became clear that the newly discovered text occupied an intermediate position between the two previously known texts. Targum Neofiti tends in many parts toward word-for-word literalism, like Targum Onqelos, but it is enriched with haggadic and legal expansions and additions similar to those of Targum Pseudo-Jonathan, although in much smaller dimensions.

The manuscript was apparently copied by three scribes, and its colophon dates its copying to Rome in the year 1499 or 1504. Nonetheless, there is no doubt that the Targumic text itself is much earlier. Diez-Macho dated it to the first century C.E. – since he found in it laws at odds with rabbinic law, which he considered to have been possible only before the composition of the Mishnah – but such an early date has not been accepted in the scholarly literature, and it appears that the text should be ascribed to the fourth or fifth century C.E., when Aramaic was still a common language among Jews.

---

[3] Clarke, *Targum Pseudo-Jonathan.*

[4] Maher, *Targum Pseudo-Jonathan.*

[5] Jastrow, *Dictionary.*

[6] For details, see the bibliography at the end of this section.

[7] Useful introductions to Targum ms Neofiti (including vast and sometimes annotated bibliographies) are: Alexander, "Aramaic Translations," 218–19, 251; Safrai, "The Targums," 269–70; Flesher and Chilton, *The Targums*, 74–75.

The existence of Targumim that do not accord with the Mishnaic law is easily explained by the existence of a variety of halakhic outlooks, some mutually contradictory, within the world of the rabbinic sages.

We have Diez-Macho's edition of this Targum (with translations into English and Spanish)[8] and an annotated English translation by McNamara[9] and other scholars. The text of the Targum is included also in the *CAL database. A linguistic treatment of its words can be found in Sokoloff's dictionary, and a concordance has been published by Kaufman and Sokoloff.[10]

In marginal and interlinear notes to Targum Neofiti there are many hundreds of textual variants that were recorded by about ten different copyists. These variants are generally very short (sometimes only a single word) and most of them are known from the other Palestinian Targumim or even from Targum Onqelos. Why did many copyists bother to gather so many variant readings in the margins of Targum Neofiti? We can only surmise that this was part of an effort to publish the manuscript accompanied by textual variants (during the sixteenth century?), but we have no evidence for this suggestion. In any case, these variants do enrich our knowledge of Targum readings that have not survived other than in these marginalia.

2.4.3.4.3 The Fragment Targum[11]

Different and unique in quality is the Targum known in the scholarly literature as "the Fragment Targum," found in various printed editions of the Pentateuch under the name "Targum Yerushalmi." We have at our disposal at least four manuscripts of this Targum: 1) ms Paris, Bibliotheque nationale Heb. 110; 2) ms Vatican, Ebr. 440; 3) ms Nuremburg, Stadtbibliothek Solgar 2, 2; 4) ms Leipzig, Universität B.H. 1. These manuscripts have been dated to the eleventh to thirteenth centuries in Germany and northern France. Ms Nuremburg served as the basis for the first printed edition of Fragment Targum, in the *Biblia Rabbinica* that was published in Venice in 1517–1518, and the other manuscripts were published in various editions in the following centuries, until Klein published all four of them in a complete and precise edition,[12] which indicated that ms Paris, Bibliotheque nationale Heb. 110 represents a separate branch of tradition from the other three manuscripts. Partial fragments of other manuscripts of this Targum have also been published over the years, and they belong to the branch of transmission emanating from ms Paris, Bibliotheque nationale Heb. 110 or ms Vatican, Ebr. 440, while some of them are merely copied from the printed edition.

The Fragment Targum is a fragmentary Targum text that gathers, alongside a continuous translation of individual chapters (such as the Creation Story [Genesis 1] and the Song at the Sea [Exodus 15]), translations of selected verses, sometimes very distant from one another, and of individual words in other verses. In the various manuscripts of this Targum there are somewhere between 300 and 900 verses translated in whole or in part. Thus, for example, in Genesis 11 it translates (in ms Paris, Bibliotheque nationale Heb. 110) vv. 2 and 4 in full and then one word from v. 30, and again isolated words from Gen 12:5, 15, and Gen 13:6, followed by a full translation of v. 7 of chapter 13. In most cases in which a full Targum is given for a verse, it is supplemented by additions and expansions like those we have encountered in the other Palestinian Targumim to the Pentateuch, sometimes clearly resembling them.

Those researching the Targum have wrestled with trying to understand the *Sitz im Leben* of these texts. Since insufficient basis has been found for the views that regarded them as collections of se-

---

[8] Diez Macho, *Neophyti 1*.

[9] McNamara, *Targum Neofiti 1: Translated with Apparatus, Introduction and Notes* [*Genesis, Exodus and Deuteronomy*]; McNamara and Clarke, *Targum Neofiti 1: Translated with Apparatus, Introduction and Notes* [*Numbers*]; McNamara and Hayward, *Targum Neofiti 1: Translated with Apparatus, Introduction and Notes* [*Leviticus*].

[10] For details, see the bibliography at the end of this section.

[11] Useful introductions to the Fragment Targum (including vast and sometimes annotated bibliographies) are Alexander, "Aramaic Translations," 220–21, 251; Safrai, "The Targums," 268–69; Flesher and Chilton, *The Targums*, 77–79.

[12] Klein, *Fragment Targums*.

lected translations chosen from some complete and continuous translation (Targum Onqelos, Targum Pseudo-Jonathan, or even Targum Neofiti), it is necessary to see the Fragment Targum as a composition constructed *ab initio* as it is. An examination of the material found in the Fragment Targum reveals that, in not a few cases, this Targum offers renditions of complete chapters or verses that are known to have played a particular role in the life of the synagogue, such as holiday lectionary selections (e.g., the reading on Shavuot of the story of revelation at Sinai [Exodus 19]) or those that formed the beginning or end of one of the units in the lectionary cycle for Sabbaths during the year (e.g., Gen 30:22 at the beginning of such a unit, or Gen 34:31 at the conclusion). The manuscripts of this Targum also include translations of verses that have been greatly expanded, venturing far from the verse (e.g., Gen 3:9 ["The Lord God called out to the man and said to him, 'Where are you?'"] or Gen 22:10 [discussed above]). This forms the basis for the supposition that the Fragment Targum was composed as a collection of Targumim to chapters and verses of particular importance, assembled to serve as reference and study material for *meturgemanim*, who fulfilled their public function by rote and had to learn and rehearse their words before performing them. As time passed, Targum to individual words was added to these collections, often words that demanded explanation (such as קְשִׂיטָה [refering to a monetary unit] [Gen 33:19] – מרגלין "pearls," or כְּתֹנֶת פַּסִּים "ornamented tunic" [Gen 37:3] – פרגוד מצויר "painted bordered garment").

In any case, the Fragment Targum manuscripts obviously belong to the group of Palestinian Targumim to the Pentateuch, both in terms of their language (Western Aramaic) and their literary characteristics, and in the vast majority of cases they are even essentially identical to them. Their importance lies not in the realm of the biblical text but in their repeated indication of the use made of Targum in the life of the synagogue, and here and there in the helpful exegesis of a particular word.

Additional evidence of the use of these texts in the synagogue emerges from Aramaic *piyyutim* (liturgical poems) that appear in them, *piyyutim* that were incorporated by the *meturgemanim* at high points in the biblical narrative (e.g., a dispute over the question of which month was worthy of being the first month of each new year [Exod 12:2], or a long dispute between Moses and the Sea of Reeds before it was parted [Exod 14:30 in T^Frag(v)]). The age of the Fragment Targum (as distinct from the dates of the extant manuscripts) has not been clarified, with scholars suggesting dates that range from the second to the eighth century C.E., with no way of arriving at a conclusive determination.

The aforementioned Klein edition (accompanied by an English translation) is the best we have at hand, along with Sokoloff's dictionary and the *CAL database.

2.4.3.4.4 Targumim from the Cairo Genizah[13]

The famous Cairo Genizah (discovered at the end of the nineteenth century) also yielded a large number of Targum texts, the Genizah Targumim, seven of which were published first by Kahle.[14] Later, at length and with exacting care, Klein published around forty.[15] The earliest of these fragments has been dated to the eighth century C.E., and this seems to be the oldest extant Targum manuscript (other than the fragments from the Dead Sea Scrolls mentioned above, → 2.4.3.1). The fragments discovered in the Genizah, a single page or a few pages each, combine to form evidence of at least seven continuous Targumim to the Pentateuch, or at least to several of its five books, along with fragments of Targumim that deal with special holiday readings (such as Passover or the beginning of a new year) or special Sabbaths. Much space in

---

[13] Useful introductions to the Targumim found in the Cairo Genizah (including vast and sometimes annotated bibliographies) are Alexander, "Aramaic Translations," 220, 251; Safrai, "The Targums," 270; Flesher and Chilton, *The Targums*, 75–77.

[14] P. Kahle, *Masoreten des Westens*, Vol. 2: *Das Palästinische Pentateuchtargum, die Palästinische Punktation, der Bibeltext des Ben Naftali* (Texte und Untersuchungen zu vormasoretischen Grammtik des Hebräischen 4; Stuttgart: W. Kohlhammer, 1930).

[15] Klein, *Genizah Manuscripts*.

the Genizah Targum fragments is devoted to Aramaic *piyyutim* that were integrated into the recitation of the Targum, as also found in the Fragment Targum (as mentioned above). In many places, the Genizah Targumim share their contents and literary character with the group of Palestinian Targumim.

The aforementioned edition of Klein, the *CAL materials, and Sokoloff's dictionary are all appropriate tools for dealing with these Targumic texts.

2.4.3.4.5 Citations of Targumim in Medieval Literature[16]

Alongside everything previously stated, we should also mention that here and there in various works of classical rabbinic literature or medieval writings there are quotes from passages of Targum that are unknown to us from the Targum compositions listed above. These works include, for example, the *Arukh* – the lexicon compiled by R. Nathan ben Yehiel of Rome (early eleventh century) – and the composition known as *Bereshit Zuta*, the work of R. Shmuel ben Nissim Masnut (twelfth century). These citations too indicate the wide dissemination of Targumim, some of which are no longer extant. As an example, we can cite the Targumim to Gen 14:17 ("which is the Valley of the King"). In T^O, T^N, T^Ps-J, and T^Gen, the word מֶלֶךְ "king" is translated by its Aramaic equivalent, מלכא, as one would expect, but in a Targum preserved in R. Shmuel ben Nissim's book it is rendered as שם רבה "the great Shem," a tradition for which no parallel has been found elsewhere, but whose basis is in identifying the king of Shalem, mentioned in the following verse, with Noah's son Shem (as is also the case in Targum Pseudo-Jonathan and some midrashim).

2.4.3.4.6 Conclusion

The world of Targum is very diverse, and it has much to teach us about the Jewish people in antiquity and the way in which it was exposed to the Hebrew Scriptures. Its contribution to the study of the Pentateuchal text is decidedly minor (for its text-critical value, → 1.3.3.7; → 2.4.3.3.3), but on the other hand its contribution to our understanding of biblical exegesis and the way in which it was presented to its audience is very great.

Alexander, P.S., "Jewish Aramaic Translations of Hebrew Scriputres," in Mulder, *Mikra*, 217–54.

*CAL. Online: http://cal1.cn.huc.edu.

Clarke, E.G. (with collaboration by W.E. Aufrecht, J.C. Hurd, and F.Spitzer), *Targum Pseudo-Jonathan of the Pentatuech: Text and Concordance* (Hoboken: Ktav Publishing House, 1984).

Diez Macho, A., *Neophyti 1: Targum Palestinense Ms de La Biblioteca Vaticana* (6 vols.; Textos y estudios Cardenal Cisneros 7, 8, 9, 10, 11, 20; Madrid: Consejo Superior de Investigaciones Cientificas, 1968–1979).

Flesher, P.V.M. and B. Chilton, *The Targums: A Critical Introduction* (Waco: Baylor University Press, 2011).

Goshen-Gottstein, M., *Fragments of Lost Targumim* (2 vols.; Ramat Gan: Bar Ilan University Press, 1989) [Hebr.].

Jastrow, M., *A Dictionary of the Targumim, the Talmud Babli and Yerushalmi and the Midrashic Literature* (New York: Pardes Publishing House, 1950).

Kaufman, S.A. and M. Sokoloff (with the assistance of E.M. Cook), *A Key-Word-In-Context Concordance of Targum Neofiti* (Baltimore: The Johns Hopkins University Press, 1993).

Klein, M.L., *Genizah Manuscripts of Palestinian Targum to the Pentateuch* (2 vols.; Cincinnati: Hebrew Union College, 1986).

Klein, M.L., "New Fragments of Palestinian Targum from the Cairo Genizah," *Sef* 38 (1988): 123–33.

Klein, M.L., *The Fragment Targums of the Pentateuch: According to their Extant Sources* (AnBib 76; Rome: Biblical Institute Press, 1980).

Maher, M., *Targum Pseudo-Jonathan [Genesis–Deuteronomy]: Translated with Introduction and Notes* (Collegeville: The Liturgical Press, 1992–1997).

McNamara, M.J., *Targum Neofiti 1: Translated with Apparatus, Introduction and Notes [Genesis, Exodus and Deuteronomy]* (Collegeville: The Liturgical Press, 1992–1997).

McNamara, M.J. and E.G. Clarke, *Targum Neofiti 1: Translated with Apparatus, Introduction and Notes [Numbers]* (Collegeville: The Liturgical Press, 1995).

McNamara, M.J. and R. Hayward, *Targum Neofiti 1: Translated with Apparatus, Introduction and Notes [Leviticus]* (Collegeville: The Liturgical Press, 1994).

---

[16] For a discussion of many other lost Targumim, see Goshen-Gottstein, *Fragments*.

Safrai, Z., "The Targums as Part of the Rabbinic Literature," in *The Literature of the Sages* (eds. S. Safrai et al.; CRINT 2.3b; Assen: Van Gorcum, 2006), 243–78.

Shinan, A., *The Embroidered Targum: The Aggadah in Targum Pseudo-Jonathan of the Pentateuch* (Jerusalem: Magnes Press, 1992).

Shinan, A., "The Late Midrashic, Paytanic, and Targumic Literature," in *The Cambridge History of Judaism*, Vol. 4: *The Late Roman-Rabbinic Period* (ed. S.T. Katz; Cambridge: Cambridge University Press, 2006), 678–98.

Sokoloff, M., *A Dictionary of Jewish Palestinian Aramaic* (Ramat Gan: Bar Ilan University Press, 2002).

Avigdor Shinan

2.4.4 Samaritan Targum

2.4.4.1 Background

The Samaritan Targum (ST) of the Pentateuch arose, much like other Targumim, as a response to the linguistic changes that took place in Palestine in late antiquity and that ended up with Aramaic prevailing over Hebrew. By the end of the third century C.E., the process of language shift in Palestine was almost complete and the dominant Aramaic became the principal language spoken and written in the entire area. It was natural that such circumstances should give rise to a variety of Aramaic translations of the Scriptures amidst the various communities in Palestine. Jews, Samaritans, and Christians produced Aramaic translations, each following their scriptural model: MT (→ 1.2.2),[1] SP (→ 1.2.3), and LXX (→ 1.3.1.1), respectively. Naturally, each such translation bears intrinsic dialectal characteristics by which they differ from each other. However, as a translation of the Hebrew Pentateuch, the Samaritan word-for-word Targum distances itself from the contemporary Jewish so-called Jerusalem Targumim (→ 1.3.3), which are replete with homiletic expansions and interpretative digressions. Both communities handed down their Targumim in a relatively great variety, but the present state of study does not provide sufficient criteria on which to establish a clear relationship between their various Targumim of the Pentateuch (→ 2.4.3). It is therefore hard to decide whether the extant manuscripts of the Samaritan Targum are variants of one basic recension, although many clear indications of filiation between certain manuscripts exist. However, there are sufficient reasons to determine that the diversity of the manuscripts of the Samaritan Targum is a result of a process of adaptation to the changing external conditions, in both the linguistic and literary-theologic areas.

Only a few manuscripts of the Samaritan Targum have survived due to several factors, the major one being the gradual extinction of the centers in Damascus, Ashkelon, Gaza, Cairo, etc.[2] Another factor is the loss of relevance of the Targum with the replacement of Aramaic by Arabic as the community's vernacular. In fact, Samaritan scribes did copy targumic manuscripts many centuries later as a traditional activity, but with no intention of meeting any spiritual needs. Consequently, the number of extant manuscripts of the Samaritan Targum is less than a dozen, the oldest one being copied at the turn of the twelfth century, as far as explicit evidence has been preserved. No manuscript copied during the lifetime of Samaritan Aramaic exists. Only one manuscript is complete; the others are, to a larger or smaller extent, in fragmentary state.

At least some of the manuscripts descend from a time when Aramaic was still known by learned members of the community and used in the liturgical service. Belonging to the learned circles, their scribes were reliable agents of transmission and therefore their work constitutes clear evidence of the character of the Samaritan Targum. The prototypes of their copies originated at various periods, so that the products of their labor reflect the stages of development of Aramaic in Palestine. The remainder of the manuscripts were copied in the period when Aramaic was no longer properly understood. On the one hand, their scribes were

---

[1] Onqelos is excluded as, in the present author's opinion, it belongs to another layer of Aramaic Targumim. See A. Tal, "Is There a Raison d' Etre for an Aramaic Targum in a Hebrew-Speaking Society?" *REJ* 160 (2001): 357–78.

[2] A.D. Crown, "The Samaritan Diaspora," in *The Samaritans* (ed. A.D. Crown; Tübingen: J.C.B. Mohr [Paul Siebeck], 1989), 195–217.

strongly influenced by Arabic, their spoken language, and on the other by Hebrew, the language of the Scriptures. Both penetrated deeply into their copies, along with a plethora of errors that largely distorted the Targum.[3]

2.4.4.2 Editions

The first edition of the entire Samaritan Targum ever made is that of Jean Morin in the Paris Polyglott (1645),[4] which reproduces a sixteenth-century Vatican manuscript (Vat. Sam. 2). This very manuscript was reprinted by Edmund Castell with variants taken from another Vatican Manuscript in Walton, *Polyglotta* (1657). The same manuscript was published in square characters by Brüll (1873–1876).[5] Unfortunately, this manuscript is less than representative of the Samaritan Targum, being corrupted by unskilled scribes.[6] The first critical edition based on four manuscripts was done by Petermann and Vollers (1872–1891).[7] A recent critical edition is Tal, *Samaritan Targum* (1980–1983).[8]

2.4.4.3 Useful Resources

The most important studies concerning the Samaritan Targum composed in modern times are the essays of Samuel Kohn.

- *Samaritanische Studien.*
- *Zur Sprache, Literatur und Dogmatik der Samaritaner.*
- "Die samaritanische Pentateuchübersetzung nach der Ausgabe von Petermann und Vollers."

Further important publications include

- Kahle, *Textkritische und lexikalische Bemerkungen zum samaritanischen Pentateuchtargum.*
- Kahle, "Zu den in Nablus befindlichen Handschriften des Samaritanischen Penteuchtargums."
- Goldberg, *Das samaritanische Pentateuchtargum.*

Very instructive for the lexicography of the Targum are the rich notes of Ben-Hayyim in his edition of the medieval Samaritan glossary *Hammeliṣ*.[9] A modern grammar of Samaritan Aramaic based largely on the material of the Targum was prepard by Macuch[10] and a lexicographic description is provided by Tal.[11]

2.4.4.4 Translation Character

The literal character of the Samaritan Targum, expressed by a strict correspondence in length to the Hebrew original as displayed in SP (→ 2.2.4), is rarely abandoned. On the whole, the Samaritan Targum is based on the rule of word-for-word translation, i.e., the Targum has only one Aramaic word for each Hebrew word in the Pentateuch. Only rarely does a manuscript deviate from this rule by adding a word in order to express an exegetic idea. An example can be found in Exod 15:27: ובאילים שתים עשרה עינות מים ושבעים תמרים "at

---

[3] For a detailed description, see the introduction to Tal, *Samaritan Targum*.

[4] Le Jay, *Biblia*.

[5] A. Brüll, *Das samaritanische Targum zum Pentateuch: Zum ersten Male in hebraeischer Quadratschrift: Nebst einem Anhange textkritischen Inhalts* (Frankfurt a.M.: W. Erras, 1873–1876).

[6] See Tal, *Samaritan Targum*, 3:39–43.

[7] J.H. Petermann and K. Vollers, *Pentateuchus Samaritanus ad fidem librorum manuscriptorum Nablusianos repertorum: ed. et varias lectiones adscripsit* (5 vols.; Berlin: Moeser, 1872–1891).

[8] Several fragments of diverse dimensions have been published at various times. See M. Heidenheim's survey in his *Bibliotheca Samaritana* (3 vols.; Leipzig: Otto Schulze, 1884), 1:xxiii–xxv, where he published Genesis according to Vat. Cod. Barberini Or. 1 (with many aberrations). J.W. Nutt published fragments located in the Bodleian and St. Petersburg libraries in *Fragments of a Samaritan Targum* (London: Trübner and Co., 1874), 1–84. The latter fragments were edited by A. Garkavi, *Opisanie Samaritjanskich Rukopisej, Chranjaščichsja v Imperatorskoj Publičnoj Bibliotekě: Opisanie Pergamentnych Rukopisej Samaritjanskago Pjatikniži̇ja i Perevodov Ego; Varianty k Samaritjanskomu Targumu* (St. Petersburg: Tipografija Imperatorskoj Akademii Nauk, 1875). P. Kahle has published fragments from the British Library in his "Fragmente des samaritanischen Pentateuchtargums, herausgegeben und erläutert," *ZA* 16 (1902): 79–101; 17 (1903): 1–22.

[9] Ben Hayyim, *The Grammatical, Masoretical, and Lexicographical Writings of the Samaritans*.

[10] Macuch, *Grammatik des samaritanischen Aramäisch*.

[11] Tal, *A Dictionary of Samaritan Aramaic*.

Elim there were twelve springs of water and seventy palm trees." The verse poses a problem: how was it possible that a place so abundant in water could only support seventy palm trees? Manuscript V (= Vatican Library Codex Barberini Or 1) adds the word גוני, i.e., "and seventy *sorts* of palm trees," which makes the verse more plausible. Otherwise, pluses and minuses as against SP are practically absent.

2.4.4.5 Translation Technique

The literal translation technique attributed to the Samaritan Targum has often attracted scholars' reproofs in unflattering terms: "minutely literal ... falling occasionally into the most grotesque blunders,"[12] "alle samaritanischen Uebersetzer (haben) sich sklavisch an den Text des samaritanisch-hebräischen Pentateuchs gehalten,"[13] etc. Indeed, technically, the Samaritan Targum renders every word of the Pentateuch by a single word, which sometimes appears "sklavisch," however, on closer examination, one can discern subtle midrashic interpretations beyond the apparently mechanical translations. Such is, for example, the rendering of במעלות "by steps" (Exod 20:223), as בשקרין "in fraud." The ancient legislator was concerned with decency at an epoch when men wore long gowns, and underwear had not yet been popularized. The Samaritan Targum, however, even in its oldest version, could no longer see the necessity for such a command and transformed it into a moral imperative: "you shall not go up to my altar with fraud (in your heart)." By including the *mem* of מעלות "steps" into the root (originally עלה), the plural of מעל "fraud" was created. Moreover, the following ערותך "your nakedness" does not preclude such interpretation, since ערוה "nakedness" has also an abstract sense, as in Deut 24:1 ערות דבר "some indecency." However, a late scribe of the Samaritan Targum replaced ערותך "your nakedness" with the more precise גנותך "your disgrace" (manuscript A = manuscript 3 of the Shechem Synagogue), in agreement with the Deuteronomy verse, where ערוה means "disgrace" and is rendered invariably as גנו "disgrace."

The hermeneutical aspect of the Samaritan Targum varies greatly from manuscript to manuscript. The younger a manuscript is, the more paraphrastic it is. Manuscript J (= manuscript British Library Or 7562), which represents the oldest stage of the Samaritan Targum as far as its language is concerned, is the poorest manuscript with respect to paraphrastic translations, whereas manuscript A, which represents the youngest targumic manifestation abounds in such material.

The difference in approach is best illustrated in cases in which anthropomorphic descriptions of God and His deeds occur in the Hebrew text. והייתם כאלהים "and you will be like God" in Gen 3:5 is rendered in manuscript A as ותהונו כמלאכיה "and you will be like angels." Similarly, in Gen 5:1 בדמות אלהים "in the likeness of God" is rendered as בתשבית מלאכיה "in the likeness of angels"; כי לקח אתו אלהים "for God took him" (Gen 5:24) as נסבתה מלאכיה "the angels took him"; בני האלהים "the sons of God" (Gen 6:2, 4) as ברי שלטניה "the sons of the rulers"; בצלם אלהים "in the image of God" (Gen 9:6) as בצורת מלאכיה "in the image of the angels." Manuscript J makes no attempt to deface this rough personification of God, using אלהים in all these instances. However, circumlocutions also exist in the old manuscripts. They translate anthropomorphic expressions in the Hebrew text in cases where their metaphoric character is obvious. When God says to Abraham in Gen 17:1 התהלך לפני "walk before me," this is rendered by ms J as התהלך לריותי "walk in accordance with my desire" (spelling of לריעותי). It is not avoidance of anthropomorphism that determined this translation; rather it is the tendency to dissolve what in the translator's (or scribe's) view is a somewhat uncalled-for metaphor. After all, people, when righteous, do not walk *before* God; they act according to His moral requirements. On the other hand, when the face of God expresses His anger, the Samaritan Targum, even in its oldest manuscripts, renders פנים "face" as רוגז "anger," again in order to materialize the metaphor in keeping with the contemporary literary style (e.g. Lev 20:3).

---

[12] Nutt, *Fragments*, 110–11.

[13] Kahle, *Textkritische und lexikalische Bemerkungen*, 7–8.

Apology was a main concern of the Samaritan Targum. A passage that could damage the image of one of the fathers of the nation involved hermeneutical devices intended to soften its effect by blurring the candor of the Hebrew original. This is best exemplified by the story of Jacob's flight from Laban. Both Jacob and Rachel committed offenses incompatible with their position in the nation's conscience. In two consecutive verses, both are involved in theft: ... ותגנב רחל את התרפים אשר לאביה ... ויגנב יעקב את לב לבן "and Rachel stole her father's idols ... and Jacob outwitted Laban (lit.: stole Laban's heart)" (Gen 31:19–20). The Samaritan Targum according to manuscript A could not bear such a description of Joseph's parents.[14] The passage contradicts Jacob's attribute איש תם "a plain man" (Gen 25:27). As for Rachel, the mother of the righteous Joseph, it was inconceivable that she could possibly commit a twofold crime, namely theft and, even worse, idolatry (for, otherwise, it was unlikely that she would be interested in her father's idols). Consequently, manuscript A rendered the verb גנב "to steal" as נסב "to take": "and Rachel took ... and Jacob took,"[15] even though Jacob is still to be blamed, for he is still guilty of trickery. The other manuscripts did not hesitate to use the verb גנב "to steal" in all these cases. As for the תרפים, they are obviously "idols" for, later, when Laban meets Jacob, he accuses his son-in-law למה גנבת את אלהי "why did you steal my Gods?" (Gen 31:30; cf. Gen 31:32). Again, manuscript A intervened by substituting תרפים "idols" and אלהים "gods" with "harmless" words: ונסבת רחל ית סלקקיה "and Rachel took the idols" (Gen 31:19),[16] and למה גנבת את אצטרלבי "why did you take my astrolabes" (Gen 31:30), in accordance with the Arabic Versions אצטרלאבי "my as-

trolabes."[17] Also Joseph's reputation as a righteous man (Gen 39:7–13), being incompatible with his description as practicing divination (נחש ינחש בו "by this he divines"; Gen 44:5), is saved by the unanimous rendering נסוי ינסי בה "by this he tests" which keeps him in line with the commandment לא תנחשו "you shall not practice divination" (Lev 19:26). Furthermore, unpopular figures are defamed. Such is Nimrod, described in Gen 10:8–9 as: הוא החל להיות גבור בארץ הוא היה גבור ציד לפני יהוה על כן יאמר כנמרוד גיבור ציד לפני יהוה "he was the first on earth to be a mighty man; he was a mighty hunter before the Lord, therefore it is said: Like Nimrod a mighty hunter before the Lord." The Samaritan Chronicle known as *The Book of Asatir*,[18] depicts this person as a cruel tyrant, who cast Abraham into a burning furnace, fearing that the latter would destroy the idols. It was therefore only natural that an old manuscript of the Samaritan Targum would render ציד "mighty" as עצאי "rebellious."[19] Thus, the shame of Nimrod was established for eternity.

It was not common practice to translate proper names in the Samaritan Targum. Yet, hermeneutically altered names do occur occasionally; for example Gen 30:21 manuscript A has הכמה "wisdom" for Jacob' daughter דינה, translating the appellative דין "judgement." In Exod 1:15, one of the midwives who saved the children of the Israelites, thereby disobeying Pharaoh's orders, is named by manuscript A עטרה "the beautiful one." This name

---

[14] The Samaritans consider themselves the descendants of the tribes of the sons of Joseph, namely Manasseh and Ephraim, and of Levi.

[15] Manuscript A's scribe was not alert enough to avoid גנבתן "she had stolen them" in Gen 31:32.

[16] An unknown vocable, perhaps a purposely distorted word for the sake of euphemism. See A. Tal, "Euphemisms in the Samaritan Targum of the Pentateuch," *Aramaic Studies* 1 (2003): 109–29.

[17] Ms A attributes to Rachel the innocent intention of providing her husband with instruments of orientation for the planned journey. Jewish medieval exegesis was also concerned with these problems and made attempts to alleviate the discomfort produced by these passages. Ibn Ezra says in his commentary: יש אומרים שהוא כלי נחשת העשוי לדעת חלקי השעות, "some say that it (the תרפים) is a tool made of copper, to find the division of the hours." Cf. Nahmanides ad loc. According to *Gen. Rab.* 74:3, Rachel stole the idols in order to prevent her father from committing idolatry.

[18] Cf. § 5 of Z. Ben-Hayyim, "Book of Asatir," *Tarbiz* 14 (1943): 104–24, 174–90; 15 (1944): 71–78. A similar haggadah exists in Jewish sources. See *Gen. Rab.* 38:12, p. 363.

[19] This is shared by the Jewish Targum Pseudo-Jonathan: גיבר מרוד "rebellious man," playing on Nimrod's name. Note that the verb עצה also means "to rob," "to oppress," e.g., Lev 5:21 בגזל "(taken away) by force" is rendered by the Samaritan Targum as בעציאן "by oppressions."

is recorded in an interlinear annotation in manuscript M (= manuscript British Library Or 1442),[20] which has also a surname for the second midwife שפרה "Shiphrah": כשירה "the fair one" which manuscript A however failed to adopt in its text. [ארץ] אדום "[the land] of Edom" in Num 20:18 is rendered by manuscript A as ארומה and in Num 20:23 as רומה, both in accordance with the Jewish tradition of associating the name of Edom with the detested empire of Rome.[21] Manuscript M has many interlinear and marginal annotations containing epithets given to various personages. Thus, for example, Reuben is surnamed חטיאי "sinner" in view of his misconduct with Bilhah (narrated in Gen 35:22); Judah is called נגדה "ruler" (according to Gen 49:10); Issachar is מגיר "converter" (Gen 49:14); Dan is מדין and פשור "judge" (Gen 49:16); Asher is משבח "praised" (Gen 49:20), etc. All these epithets are annotated in the list of the heads of the tribes given in Num 1:5–14.

2.4.4.6 Text-Critical Value

The Samaritan Targum in all of its variant manuscripts translates the Samaritan version of the Pentateuch, following its particular readings, either written or orally transmitted. For example, for MT וְאֶל־עָפָר תָּשׁוּב "and to dust you shall return" (Gen 3:19), SP has ואל עפרך "and to your dust" faithfully translated by the Samaritan Targum as ולעפרך "and to your dust." So is כָּל־הָעֲדָרִים "all the flocks (were gathered there)" for which SP has כל הרעים "all the shepherds" (Gen 29:3), rendered in the Samaritan Targum as כל רעיה "all the shepherds." Nevertheless, many renderings deviate from the original as it is given in the extant manuscripts of SP, alluding to a different *Vorlage*, sometimes related to MT.[22] For example, in Lev 4:14, SP reads והקריבו הקהל פר בן בקר תמים לחטאת "the assembly shall offer a young bull

---

[20] As well as in the Samaritan Glossary Hammeliṣ (Ben-Hayyim, *The Grammatical, Masoretical, and Lexicographical Writings of the Samaritans*, 568).

[21] Kohn, "Samaritanische Pentateuchübersetzung," 675. Cf. Jastrow, *Dictionary*, 16a.

[22] A. Tal, "Divergent Traditions of the Samaritan Pentateuch as Reflected by its Aramaic Targum," *JAB* 1 (1999): 297–314.

without blemish for a sin offering" while MT omits the word תמים "without blemish." The Samaritan Targum follows SP, ויקרבון קהלה פר בר תורים לסלוון, except for manuscript J, which follows MT, omitting the same word. On the other hand, there appears to be an addition in MT-Lev 5:25: וְאֶת־אֲשָׁמוֹ ... יָבִיא ... לְאָשָׁם אֶל־הַכֹּהֵן "and he shall bring his guilt offering ... as a guilt offering *to the priest*" the last two words being absent from SP. Nevertheless they appear in manuscript J of the Samaritan Targum: ליד כהנה "to the priest" whereas they are absent from the rest of the manuscripts.

An intriguing instance of divergence within the Samaritan Targum concerns one of the most important principles of Samaritanism, as expressed in SP-Exod 20:24 מזבח אדמה תעשה לי ... במקום אשר אזכרתי שמי שמה אבוא אליך וברכתיך "an altar of earth you shall make for me ... in every place where I recorded my name, there I will come to you and I will bless you." The perfect אזכרתי, *ēzākarti*, means, according to the Samaritan dogma, that God has already chosen His holy place as specified in SP-Deut 27:4–6 ובנית ... בהרגריזים ... תקימו את האבנים האלה ... שם מזבח ... והעלית עליו עלות "you shall set up these stones ... on Mount Gerizim ... and there shall you build an altar ... and you shall offer burnt offerings." MT has in Exodus בְּכָל־הַמָּקוֹם אֲשֶׁר אַזְכִּיר אֶת־שְׁמִי "in all places where *I will* record my name" (Exod 20:24), for the holy place has not yet been chosen. In any event, it is by no means Mount Gerizim; MT-Deut has עַל־הַר עֵיבָל "Mount Ebal." This crucial difference between Samaritanism and Judaism is expressed in Deut 12:5, 11, 14, etc., where SP invariably has המקום אשר בחר "the place which the Lord has chosen" whereas MT has יִבְחַר "will choose." Yet, manuscript J renders the passage in Exod 20:24 as ובאתרה דאדכר ית שמי "in the place where *I will* record my name," etc., in distinct contrast to the other manuscripts, which follow the Samaritan tradition of using the perfect דאדכרת "where *I have* recorded." Does the manuscript J reading display a vestige of an early SP development stage when Samaritan dogma did not yet involve the text of the Torah in its entirety?[23]

---

[23] There is little room for the assumption that this is an

2.4.4.7 History of Research

The first manuscript of the entire Samaritan Targum (Vat. Sam. 2) arrived in Europe in the early seventeenth century. It was published by Jean Morin, who later composed a grammatical sketch and a vocabulary, based on this somewhat unfortunate manuscript.[24] He was followed by others who used the same manuscript. Among the earliest studies concerning the Samaritan Targum is the lexicographic work of Castell,[25] preceded by a short grammatical outline. Cellarius presented selected portions from the Paris Polyglot with Latin translation, grammar, and explanatory notes.[26] Portions of Paris Polyglot have also been treated by Otho.[27] The first systematic linguistic study, containing grammar, syntax, glossary, and selected portions was done by Uhlemann.[28] In spite of the pioneering work of these scholars, their descriptions were limited in value, due to the poor state of their manuscript evidence. Matters changed radically with the publication of additional material, chiefly by John W. Nutt and others (see above, n. 8), as well as Julius H. Petermann and Karl Vollers' critical edition (→ 2.4.4.2). Studies accomplished by Kohn, Kahle, Ben-Hayyim (see bibliography) paved the way for a comprehensive grammar penned by Macuch (see bibliography), which includes material from Tal's critical edition.[29] It concerns the entire Aramaic literature of the Samaritans. A recent compendious grammar *ad usum studentorum* was published by Tal.[30]

Ben-Hayyim, Z., *The Grammatical, Masoretical, and Lexicographical Writings of the Samaritans* (vol. 2 of Ben-Hayyim, *LOT*, 1957).

Goldberg, L., *Das samaritanische Pentateuchtargum: Eine Untersuchung seiner handschriftlichen Quellen* (Bonner orientalistische Studien 11; Stuttgart: W. Kohlhammer, 1935).

Kahle, P.E., *Textkritische und lexikalische Bemerkungen zum samaritanischen Pentateuchtargum* (Leipzig: W. Drugulin, 1898).

Kahle, P.E., "Zu den in Nablus befindlichen Handschriften des Samaritanischen Penteuchtargums," *ZDMG* 61 (1907): 909–12.

Kohn, S., *Samaritanische Studien: Beiträge zur samaritanischen Pentateuch-Übersetzung und Lexicographie* (Breslau: Schletter, 1868).

Kohn, S., *Zur Sprache, Literatur und Dogmatik der Samaritaner* (Leipzig: F.A. Brockhaus, 1876).

Kohn, S., "Die samaritanische Pentateuchübersetzung nach der Ausgabe von Petermann und Vollers," *ZDMG* 47 (1893): 626–97.

Macuch, R., *Grammatik des samaritanischen Aramäisch* (Studia Samaritana 1; Berlin: De Gruyter, 1982).

Tal, A., *The Samaritan Targum of the Pentateuch: A Critical Edition* (3 vols.; Texts and Studies in the Hebrew Language and Related Subjects 4–6; Tel Aviv: University Press, 1980–1983) [Hebr.].

Tal, A., *A Dictionary of Samaritan Aramaic* (2 vols.; HO 1.50; Leiden: Brill, 2000).

Abraham Tal

---

interpolation of Jewish origin. As the passage in question is situated in a central part of the Pentateuch, a scribe is bound to be alert when he copies a text that has a particular ideological significance, as in our case, in which the ancestral polemic with Judaism is expressed. However, the quite unusual orthography of the apparent active Hebrew Hiph'il with the prefix א, may suggest a hidden passive Hitpe'el דאתדכר, with assimilated *t* in manuscript J: דאדכר "where my name was mentioned." See Ben-Hayyim, *Grammar of Samaritan Hebrew*, § 2.1.2.4, n; 4.2.1.4, n. 45. Manuscript A appears to be corrupted: דתדכר unless a "neutral" interpretation intended "where you shall remind my name."

[24] J. Morin, *Opuscula Hebraeo-Samaritana* (4 vols.; Paris: Meturas, 1657).

[25] E. Castell, *Lexicon Heptaglotton Hebraicum, Chaldaicum, Syriacum, Samaritanum, Aethiopicum, Arabicum, et Persicum* (London: Robert Scott, 1686).

[26] C. Cellarius, *Horae Samaritanae, hoc est, Excerpta Pentateuchi Samaritanae Versionis* (Zeitz: Io. Bielcki, 1682).

[27] G. Otho, *Palaestra Linguarum Orientalium, Hoc est: Quatuor Primorum Capitum Geneseos* (Frankfurt a.M.: F. Knoch, 1702). G. Otho, *Institutionum Samaritanarum, Rabbinicarum, Arabicarum, Aethiopicarum et Persicarum Synopsi* (part 2 of J. Alting, *Fundamenta Punctationis Linguae Sanctae, cum Necessariis Canonum, Locorum S. Scripturae & Vocum Irregularium Indicibus*; Frankfurt a.M.: F. Knoch, 1746).

[28] F.G. Uhlemann, *Institutiones Linguae Samaritanae ex Antiquissimis Monumentis Erutae et Digestae, Integris Paradigmatum Tabulis Indicibusque Adornatae* (Leipzig: C. Tauchnit, 1837).

---

[29] Tal, *Samaritan Targum*.

[30] A. Tal, *Samaritan Aramaic* (Lehrbücher orientalischer Sprachen 3/2; Münster: Ugarit Verlag, 2013).

2.4.5 Peshitta

2.4.5.1 Scholarly Edition and Manuscripts

The Peshitta Institute, formerly of Leiden, but now relocated to Amsterdam, has produced a scientific edition of the text of the Peshitta Pentateuch (s-Pent),[1] taking into account all textual evidence up to and including the twelfth century. Manuscript s[7a1] serves as the base text,[2] since it contains a complete text of the Old Testament. The edition is diplomatic rather than eclectic, meaning that the textual scholar needs to take into account the variants found in the apparatuses when evaluating the relationship of the Syriac to the Hebrew. The first apparatus records readings of s[7a1] deemed as non-preferred readings by the editor(s) – often errors – and so replaced by a different reading in the main text. Between the apparatuses appears a list of all manuscripts collated for a given page in the printed edition. The second apparatus records all textual variants of those readings found in the main text that are attested in the manuscripts listed.

Significant variant readings come from manuscript s[5b1], especially in Genesis and Exodus. Manuscript s[5b1] includes Genesis, Exodus, Numbers, and Deuteronomy, but not Leviticus. The manuscript contains two texts of different nature bound together in one volume.[3] The first text covers Genesis and Exodus with a colophon at the end of Exodus indicating that Deacon John of the city of Amid had copied it in 463/464 C.E.[4] The second text covers Numbers and Deuteronomy. In some ways, the single manuscript, a codex, should have been subdivided into two distinct texts, each with its own siglum. For textual purposes, then, manuscript s[5b1] for Genesis and Exodus has more value than manuscript s[5b1] for Numbers and Deuteronomy. In many cases, manuscript s[5b1] preserves a more primitive reading than manuscript s[7a1].[5] For example, s[5b1] records the reading ܥܒܕܬ "you have done" in Gen 31:26 against the reading ܥܒܕܬ "I have done" in s[7a1]. The reading of s[5b1] accords with that of MT and so is more primitive than the reading in s[7a1].

Manuscript s[7a1] has a lacuna encompassing Num 3:23–5:10. The editor used s[6b1] for Num 3:23–25 (ܟܗܢܘܬܐ) and s[5b1] for Num 3:25 (ܘܗܝ) –5:10.[6]

The Peshitta Institute's scholarly edition excluded citations from the Syriac Fathers (→ 21.9), the value of which for textual criticism is notoriously difficult to determine. For discussions of Aphrem and Aphrahat, see Lund and Owens respectively.[7] Weitzman[8] has offered one case that may be credible, namely the word ܘܢܣܒ, "and he took" from Exod 18:12 as a variant of ܘܩܪܒ "and he offered"; the Hebrew reads וַיִּקַּח "and he took."

2.4.5.2 Source and Nature of the Translation

Jewish scholars translated a Hebrew source text of the Pentateuch into Syriac about 150 C.E. in the vicinity of Edessa.[9] That Hebrew source text fits into the proto-Masoretic stream (→ 1.2.2).[10] According to Weitzman, the Jewish community responsible for translating the Hebrew Bible into Syriac became Christian, bringing with it its own translation of the Hebrew Bible.[11] It is the Christian church that preserved the text and that continues to use it until today.

There is a gap of more than three centuries between the translation and the first manuscripts.

---

[1] Jansma and Koester, *Preface, Genesis – Exodus* and Lane et al., *Leviticus – Numbers – Deuteronomy – Joshua*.

[2] The Peshitta Institute assigned dates to undated manuscripts per the latest possible date. The manuscript labeled by the Peshitta Institute as 7a1 could be dated to the sixth century rather than the seventh century (see P.A.H. De Boer, "Preface," in Jansma and Koester, *Preface, Genesis – Exodus*).

[3] See Hayman, *Numbers*, v, and Van Vliet, Hospers, and Drijvers, *Deuteronomy*, iv–v.

[4] Wright, *Catalogue of Syriac Manuscripts*, 4–5. The Greek year 775 appears in the manuscript.

[5] See Lund, "Genesis in Syriac," 540–41, and Lund, "Exodus in Syriac," 352–53.

[6] Hayman, *Numbers*, iii.

[7] Lund, "Observations on Some Biblical Citations," 205–18; Owens, *Genesis and Exodus Citations*; Owens, "Aphrahat as a Witness," 1–48. See also Lund, "A Non-Peshitta Jeremiah Citation," 133–40 and ter Haar Romeny, "La réception des versions syriaques de la Bible," 173–91.

[8] Weitzman, *The Syriac Version*, 289–90. For a discussion, see Lund, "Exodus in Syriac," 354.

[9] Weitzman, *The Syriac Version*, 258.

[10] Brock, *The Bible in the Syriac Tradition*, 23.

[11] Weitzman, *The Syriac Version*, 259.

During that time, some words became confused in transmission, leaving the text to be restored. For example, in Lev 21:5 and Deut 14:1, one should restore ܩܘܪܚܬܐ "bald spot" in place of ܩܘܕܚܬܐ "lightning flashes."[12] Likewise, the Peshitta in the extant manuscripts consistently renders the Hebrew place name אֶדְרֶעִי "Edrei" as ܐܪܕܥܝ "Ardei" (Num 21:33; Deut 1:4; 3:1, 10), a simple metathesis of two consonants that look alike, namely *dalath* and *resh*. The simplest way to account for this reading of the Peshitta (S) is to regard it as an inner-Syriac error that happened during the transmission of the text. It is good to remember that in Old Syriac the same dotless grapheme was used for both *dalath* and *resh*;[13] the distinction between them by a single dot placed over the letter for *resh* or under the letter for *dalath* is attested earliest in a codex dated 411 C.E.[14]

The text of the Peshitta developed over time. Brock,[15] in agreement with Koster,[16] presents a three-stage chronological development of the text of the Old Testament Peshitta (S-OT): 1) the oldest stage, where the text is closest to the Hebrew; 2) the middle stage, in which scribes wittingly and unwittingly made slight "improvements" of the text for readability; 3) the Received Text or Textus Receptus (= TR), which evidences further text development. Little manuscript evidence is extant for the first stage, while the second stage is well represented by manuscripts of the sixth to eighth centuries and the third stage by manuscripts of the ninth century and beyond.[17] In reaction to criticism of his theory of chronologically consecutive types of text by ter Haar Romeny,[18] Koster has revised this chronological scheme backwards, dating the second stage as early as the fourth century and the TR stage as early as the eighth century.[19] Ter Haar Romeny, by contrast, pushes most of the text development back to a time predating the extant biblical manuscripts.[20]

2.4.5.2.1 Translation Technique

S-Pent is a literal translation (one-to-one correspondence) of the Hebrew, but conforms to Syriac syntax. For instance, Hebrew and Syriac differ on the syntax of the tripartite noun phrase. Whereas Hebrew follows the order nominal head + adjective + demonstrative pronoun, Syriac follows either the pattern nominal head + demonstrative pronoun + adjective or the pattern demonstrative pronoun + nominal head + adjective. Thus, S-Pent translates הַמַּרְאֶה הַגָּדֹל הַזֶּה as ܚܙܘܐ ܗܢܐ ܪܒܐ "this great sight" (Exod 3:3), הָאָרֶץ הַטּוֹבָה הַזֹּאת as ܐܪܥܐ ܗܕܐ ܛܒܬܐ "this good land" (Deut 9:6), and הָאֲנָשִׁים הָרְשָׁעִים הָאֵלֶּה as ܓܒܪ̈ܐ ܗܠܝܢ ܚ̈ܛܝܐ "these sinful men" (Num 16:26). Moreover, it renders הָאֵשׁ הַגְּדֹלָה הַזֹּאת as ܗܕܐ ܢܘܪܐ ܪܒܬܐ "this great fire" (Deut 18:16).

Like Hebrew, Syriac uses the infinitive absolute tautologically. The Peshitta accordingly renders the Hebrew infinitive absolute used tautologically by an infinitive absolute. Thus S renders שׁוֹב אָשׁוּב אֵלֶיךָ as ܡܗܦܟ ܐܗܦܘܟ ܠܘܬܟ "I will surely return unto you" (Gen 18:10) and וְאָבִיהָ יָרֹק יָרַק בְּפָנֶיהָ as ܐܠܘ ܐܒܘܗ̇ ܡܪܩ ܪܩ ܒܐ̈ܦܝܗ̇ "if her father had but spit in her face" (Num 12:14). So the retroversion of S ܡܘܬܐ ܬܡܘܬ (Gen 2:17) should be מָוֶת תָּמוּת "you shall die a death" (cognate accusative), a variant of MT מוֹת תָּמוּת "you shall surely die."[21] Syriac, however, does not use the

---

[12] For detailed argumentation, see Lund, "The Hebrew as a Text Critical Tool," § 2.1.

[13] Kiraz, *A Grammar of the Syriac Language*, § 30.

[14] Kiraz, *A Grammar of the Syriac Language*, § 30 and § 201. In manuscripts of the fifth and sixth centuries, the position of the diacritic is not fixed with reference to the letter; it can appear anywhere over the word for *resh* and anywhere under the word for *dalath* (see Kiraz, § 30).

[15] Brock, *The Bible in the Syriac Tradition*, 46.

[16] Koster, *The Peshitta of Exodus*, 177–84.

[17] Brock, *The Bible in the Syriac Tradition*, 46.

[18] Ter Haar Romeny, "The Peshitta of Isaiah," 149–64.

[19] Koster, "Redating TR and BTR: The Three Stages at Stake?" 1–18.

[20] Ter Haar Romeny, "The Peshitta of Isaiah," 162.

[21] The Peshitta's consistent rendering of the Hebrew infinitive absolute in pre-position used tautologically by the infinitive absolute (30× in Genesis) cautions against regarding the cognate accusative as a valid translation of the Hebrew infinitive absolute as does Kim, *The Function of the Tautological Infinitive in Classical Biblical Hebrew*, 13. However, once where the Hebrew of Genesis has the infinitive absolute in post-position to the verb with which it belongs, S renders it by the cognate accusative (Gen 19:9): S renders הָאֶחָד בָּא־לָגוּר וַיִּשְׁפֹּט שָׁפוֹט "This one came to sojourn and he in fact judges!" as ܚܕ ܐܬܐ

infinitive absolute as an imperative. So, the Peshitta represents the Hebrew infinitive absolute used as an imperative accurately by the imperative: ܐܬܕܟܪ ܝܘܡܐ ܕܫܒܬܐ[22] represents זָכוֹר אֶת־יוֹם הַשַּׁבָּת "remember the Sabbath day" (Exod 20:8); ܛܪ ܝܘܡܐ ܕܫܒܬܐ represents שָׁמוֹר אֶת־יוֹם הַשַּׁבָּת "keep the Sabbath day" (Deut 5:12); ܘܦܫܘܬܝܗ̇ ܦܬ̈ܐ represents פָּתוֹת אֹתָהּ פִּתִּים "break it in pieces" (Lev 2:6).

Further, contrary to Hebrew, Syriac does not use the infinitive absolute in post-position to its corresponding verb in conjunction with another infinitive absolute. The translator, then, must find another solution. In the case of Gen 8:3, that solution was relatively easy: the translator rendered וַיָּשֻׁבוּ הַמַּיִם מֵעַל הָאָרֶץ הָלוֹךְ וָשׁוֹב "and the waters receded from the earth continually" as ܘܗܦܟܘ ܡ̈ܝܐ ܡܢ ܐܪܥܐ. ܐܙܠܝܢ ܘܗܦܟܝܢ "and the waters receded from the earth, going and receding," translating the Hebrew infinitive absolutes with participles. But, in Gen 8:7, the solution was not so easy. The translator did not share the modern understanding that וַיְשַׁלַּח אֶת־הָעֹרֵב וַיֵּצֵא יָצוֹא וָשׁוֹב עַד־יְבֹשֶׁת הַמַּיִם מֵעַל הָאָרֶץ means "and he [Noah] sent out the raven, and it darted to and fro until the drying up of the waters from the earth." Rather, he rendered the Hebrew as ܘܫܕܪ ܠܥܘܪܒܐ. ܘܢܦܩ ܡܦܩ[23] ܘܠܐ ܗܦܟ. ܥܕܡܐ ܕܝܒܫܘ ܡ̈ܝܐ ܡܢ ܐܪܥܐ "and he [Noah] sent out the raven, and it went out, but did not return until the waters dried up from the earth," following a translation tradition also reflected in the Old Greek: καὶ ἀπέστειλεν τὸν κόρακα τοῦ ἰδεῖν εἰ κεκόπακεν τὸ ὕδωρ· καὶ ἐξελθὼν οὐχ ὑπέστρεψεν ἕως τοῦ ξηρανθῆναι τὸ ὕδωρ ἀπὸ τῆς γῆς "and he [Noah] sent out the raven to see if the water had abated; and after going out, it did not return until the water was dried up from the earth." Both versions added a negation to וָשׁוֹב, making "it [the raven] did not return," an interpretation consonant with the context. This same exegetical tradition appears in the midrash ascribed to the first-century C.E. Tanna Rabbi Eliezer ben Hurcanus: "Noah sent forth the raven to ascertain how it was in the world. It went out and found a corpse on the mountaintops and sat down on its food and did not return its mission to its sender" (שלח נח את העורב לידע מה בעולם הלך לו ומצא נבלה בראשי ההרים, וישב לו על מאכלו ולא שליחותו לשולחיו השיב).[24] Whereas Hänel[25] considered this a case of the direct dependence of the Peshitta on the Old Greek, it seems rather that both versions depended on a common exegetical tradition to solve a difficult problem.[26]

The Peshitta will at times render a metaphor in its source text concretely. For example, it renders Hebrew אָנֹכִי מָגֵן לָךְ "I will be a shield for you" – God is speaking to Abram – as ܐܢܐ ܐܥܕܪܟ "I will help you" (Gen 15:1); יִשָּׂשכָר חֲמֹר גָּרֶם "Issachar is a strong donkey" as ܐܝܣܟܪ ܠܓܒܪܐ ܓܢܒܪܐ "Issachar is a mighty man" (Gen 49:14); נַפְתָּלִי אַיָּלָה שְׁלֻחָה "Naphtali is a doe let loose" as ܢܦܬܠܝ ܐܝܟ ܐܙܓܕܐ ܩܠܝܠܐ "Naphtali is a swift messenger" (Gen 49:21); הַצּוּר "the Rock" as ܬܩܝܦܐ "the Strong One" (Deut 32:4).

Occasionally, the Peshitta transliterates Hebrew words rather than translating them: ܬܘܗ ܘܒܘܗ "*toh* and *boh*" (Gen 1:2), interpreted as "desolate (ܫܗܝܐ) and void (ܣܪܝܩܐ)" by Aphrem;[27] ܐܗܝܗ ܐܫܪ ܐܗܝܗ "*ʾāyāh ʾāšār ʾāyāh*" and ܐܗܝܗ "*ʾāyāh*" (אֶהְיֶה אֲשֶׁר אֶהְיֶה "I am who I am" and אֶהְיֶה "I am"; Exod 3:14); ܐܠܫܕܝ = ܐܝܠܫܕܝ "*ʾēlšadday*" (אֵל שַׁדַּי; "God Almighty"; Gen 17:1; 28:3; 35:11 [s[5b1]]; 48:3; 49:25),

---

ܠܡܬܬܘܬܒܘ ܐܬܐ ܘܗܐ ܕܐܢ ܠܢ ܕ̈ܝܢܐ "One came to sojourn with us and behold he is judging us with judgments." This is a case where the Peshitta follows Palestinian Jewish translation tradition as demonstrated by T[O]: חַד אֲתָא לְאִיתוֹתָבָא וְהָא דָאֵין דִינָא "One came to sojourn and behold he is judging a judgment" and T[N]: האחד אתא למתותבא בינינן והא הוא בעי למהוי דין דינינן "This one came to sojourn among us and behold he is seeking to be judging our judgments."

22 s[7a1] represents a developed text, reading the plural ܐܬܕܟܪܘ.

23 s[5b1] lacks ܡܦܩ.

24 Maori, *The Peshitta Version of the Pentateuch and Early Jewish Exegesis*, 108.

25 Hänel, *Die aussermasorethischen Übereinstimmungen zwischen der Septuaginta und der Peschittha in der Genesis*, 74–75.

26 Lund, *The Influence of the Septuagint on the Peshitta*, 31–32.

27 Tonneau, *Sancti Ephraem Syri in Genesim et in Exodum Commentarii*, Sectio I, § 3. Ishodad (Van den Eynde, *Commentaire d'Išoʿdad of Merv sur l'Ancien Testament*, I. *Genèse*, 13) and Barhebraeus (Sprengling and Graham, *Barhebraeus' Scholia*, 4) follow suit.

ܐܠܫܕܝ ܐܠܗܐ (Gen 35:11 [s[5b1] omits ܐܠܗܐ]; Exod 6:3); when שַׁדַּי "Almighty" is used by itself, the Peshitta renders it as ܐܠܗܐ "God" (Num 24:4, 16).

The Peshitta uses idioms appropriate to Syriac in rendering Hebrew idioms. So, for instance, it renders Hebrew כִּי כְבַד־פֶּה וּכְבַד לָשׁוֹן אָנֹכִי "for I am heavy of mouth and heavy of tongue" as ܡܓܡܓܡ ܕܠܥܝ ܡܡܠܠܝ[28] ܘܚܒܝܠ ܠܫܢܐ ܐܢܐ "for my speech is stammering and I am difficult of tongue" (Exod 4:10).

2.4.5.2.2 Indication of Multiple Translators

Different translators could account for the differences in translation from book to book. For instance, the Hebrew words *Urim* (אוּרִים) and *Thummim* (תֻּמִּים) appear together three times in the Pentateuch, each time rendered differently in s: ܘܣܝܡ ܥܠ ܦܪܣܐ ܕܕܝܢܐ ܢܗܝܪܐ ܘܫܠܡܐ "put 'the light' (or: 'the enlightened') and 'the perfect'[29] on the breastplate of judgment" (Exod 28:30);[30] ܘܣܡ ܥܠ ܦܪܣܐ ܝܕܥܬܐ ܘܩܘܫܬܐ "and he put 'knowledge' and 'truth' on the breastplate" (Lev 8:8); ܫܘܡܠܝܟ ܘܢܘܗܪܟ ܠܓܒܪܐ ܚܣܝܐ. ܕܢܣܝܬܗ ܒܢܣܝܘܢܐ. ܘܒܚܪܬܗ ܒܡܝ̈ܐ ܕܡܨܘܬܐ "'your perfection' and 'your light' belong to the pious man whom I[31] tested with trials and proved at the waters of strife" (Deut 33:8). The translator of Exod 28:30 rendered the words by the adjectival forms ܢܗܝܪܐ "the light" and ܫܠܡܐ "the perfect" (etymology of אוּרִים and תֻּמִּים from the roots אור and תמם respectively), while the translator of Lev 8:8 rendered them by ܝܕܥܬܐ "knowledge" and ܩܘܫܬܐ "truth" (based on their function)[32] and the translator of Deut 33:8 rendered them by the nouns ܢܘܗܪܐ "light" and ܫܘܡܠܝܐ "perfection" (etymology). Num 27:21 contains the word *Urim* by itself, which the Peshitta renders on the basis of its function as ܫܐܠܬܐ "asking": ܘܢܗܘܐ ܫܐܠ ܠܗ ܢܡܘܣܐ ܕܫܐܠܬܐ ܩܕܡ ܡܪܝܐ "and he (the high priest) shall inquire for him the law of 'inquiry' before the Lord" translates וְשָׁאַל לוֹ בְּמִשְׁפַּט הָאוּרִים לִפְנֵי יְהוָה "and he (the high priest) shall inquire for him by the judgment of the Urim before the Lord."

Then, too, there is a difference in how to express ordinals in the different books of the s-Pent. Syriac has two ways of expressing the ordinal, either by using the ordinal form as an adjective or by using ܕ + the cardinal. Both ܝܘܡܐ ܬܠܝܬܝܐ (Gen 22:4; type A) and ܝܘܡܐ ܕܬܠܬܐ (Gen 1:13; type B) mean "the third day."[33] A survey[34] of the distribution of these types yields the following results: s-Gen uses type A seventeen times[35] and type B thirteen times; s-Exod uses type A thirty-five times, but type B only twice;[36] s-Lev uses type A eight times and type B thirty-one times;[37] s-Num uses type A twice, and

[28] s[9l6] reads ܡܡܠܠܐ "(for I am hesitating of) speech (and difficult of tongue)." The form ܠܥܝ could be either in construct state or in absolute state.

[29] Vocalize ܫܠܡܐ as *šalmā'*.

[30] This translation is better than the one I previously offered in Lund, "Exodus in Syriac," 366.

[31] The Peshitta reads first person against the second person of MT.

[32] Syriac commentators bring Exod 28:30 and Lev 8:8 together as complements of each other. On the chief gemstone that was affixed in the midst of the other gemstones, two words were engraved, namely "the light" and "the perfect" (see Ishodad on Exod 28:30 and Lev 8:8; Van den Eynde, *Commentaire d'Išoʿdad of Merv sur l'Ancien Testament*, Vol. 2: *Exode – Deutéronome*, 51, 64). Ishodad interpreted these as referring to the (high) priest who gave light to those entrusted to his care so that as enlightened in the fear of God they might receive benevolence, peace, and grace from God. He connects the "knowledge" of Lev 8:8 with "the light" of Exod 28:20, while "truth" reflects the conduct of the faithful. Barhebraeus interprets the adjectival forms ܢܗܝܪܐ and ܫܠܡܐ of Exod 28:30 as "enlightened" and "perfect," explaining that "by the changing of the colors of the twelve stones that you put on the breastplate of judgment Aaron will be enlightened and the perfect truth in the judgment revealed to him" (ܒܝܕ ܫܘܚܠܦ ܓܘ̈ܢܐ ܕܬܪ̈ܬܥܣܪܐ ܟܐ̈ܦܐ ܕܣܡܬ ܐܢܬ ܥܠ ܦܪܣܐ ܕܕܝܢܐ ܡܬܢܗܪ ܐܗܪܘܢ ܘܡܬܓܠܐ ܠܗ ܫܪܪܐ ܡܫܡܠܝܐ ܒܕܝܢܐ; Sprengling and Graham, *Barhebraeus' Scholia*, 138).

[33] These types can be used independently, without a nominal head, as in ܒܫܒܥ (Exod 21:2) and ܒܫܒܝܥܝܬܐ (Exod 23:11), both meaning "in the seventh (year)."

[34] I used Accordance Bible software to arrive at the data that encompasses "second" through "tenth."

[35] This number excludes the adverbial ܕܬܪ̈ܬܝܢ ܙܒ̈ܢܝܢ, "a second time" (Gen 22:15; 41:5, 32; 43:10).

[36] Once in the long plus of Exod 2:22 and once in the expression ܒܫܒܝܥܝܬܐ "in the seventh (year)" (Exod 23:11).

[37] This number includes two cases of ܝܪܚܐ ܗܢܐ ܕܫܒܥܐ "this seventh month" (Lev 23:27, 34).

type B thirty-four times;[38] s-Deut uses type A twice and type B four times. The results in s-Exod differ dramatically from the results in s-Lev and s-Num, which may indicate different translators.

2.4.5.2.3 Palestinian Jewish Influence

As noted by Brock, the translators of s-Pent were acquainted with Jewish translation traditions coming from Eretz Israel (→ 2.4.3).[39] Some of these same traditions would also surface in the Targumim, most of which in written form are dated later than the Peshitta; T⁰ (→ 2.4.3.3) was written about the same time as the Peshitta. In Gen 48:15, the Peshitta renders the Hebrew הָאֱלֹהִים הָרֹעֶה אֹתִי מֵעוֹדִי עַד־הַיּוֹם הַזֶּה "the God who shepherded me from my youth to this day" as ܐܠܗܐ ܕܬܪܣܝܢܝ ܡܢ ܛܠܝܘܬܝ ܘܥܕܡܐ ܠܝܘܡܢܐ "the God who nourished me from my youth and until today." The translation of עוֹד as "youth" reflects the same translation tradition known from T^N: ייי דדבר יתי מן טליותי עד יומא הדין "the Lord who led me from my youth until today." In Exod 21:19, the Peshitta translates the Hebrew רַק שִׁבְתּוֹ יִתֵּן וְרַפֹּא יְרַפֵּא "only he must compensate his convalescing and must in fact have (him) healed" as ܒܠܚܘܕ ܒܛܠܢܗ ܢܬܠ ܘܐܓܪ ܐܣܝܐ "however he must compensate his lost work time and the cost of the doctor." The translation of רַפֹּא יְרַפֵּא accords with the renderings found in T⁰ לְחוֹד בּוּטְלָנֵיהּ יִתֵּן וַאֲגַר אָסְיָא יְשַׁלֵּם "however he must compensate his lost work time and pay the cost of the doctor") and T^N "לחוד אגר בטלוניה יתן ואגר אסיא דמאסי יתיה "however he must compensate his lost work time and the cost of the doctor who treats him").

2.4.5.3 Text-Critical Value

The Peshitta does provide evidence for variant Hebrew readings for those preserved in MT (→ 2.2.2).[40]

Minor variants include the plus of conjunctive *waw*, such as in ܡܢܐ ܢܐܡܪ ܠܗ̇ܘ ܘܡܢܐ ܢܡܠܠ mirroring מה נאמר ... ומה נדבר "What can we say ... and what can we speak?" versus MT מַה־נֹּאמַר ... מַה־נְּדַבֵּר "What can we say ...? What can we speak?" (Gen 44:16), difference in person like ܒܝܢܬܟܘܢ[41] projecting Hebrew בתוככם "among you" versus MT בְּתוֹכָם "among them" (Lev 17:8), difference in number like in ܬܚܒܠܘܢ "you (plural) shall mar" versus MT תַּשְׁחִית "you (singular) shall mar" (Lev 19:27) – especially in view of the plural תשחיתו in SP "you (plural) shall mar" this probably reflects a variant rather than translation technique in S –, the addition of a pronominal indirect object as in ܘܐܡܪ ܠܗ̇ "and he said to her" versus MT וַיֹּאמֶר "and he said" (Gen 38:16), the plus of a pronoun suffixed to a noun like ܥܝܢܘܗܝ "his eyes" versus MT עֵינַיִם "eyes" (Gen 49:12), and the plus of a preposition as in ܐܝܟ ܢܘܟܪܝܬܐ "like foreigners" reflecting Hebrew כנכריות against MT נָכְרִיּוֹת "foreigners" (Gen 31:15).

Major variants include differences in words and pluses. Some variants have to do with different vocalizations of the same consonants. s-Num 11:4 reads the Hebrew *hiphil* וַיַּבְכּוּ "and they (the rabble) made (the children of Israel also) weep (again)" instead of MT *qal* וַיִּבְכּוּ "and (the children of Israel also) wept (again)." Other variants differ in the presence or absence of one letter like ܘܐܝܬܝܗ retroverted as ויבאהו "and he (Balak) brought him (Balaam)" (the reading of SP and T⁰ [Num 22:39]), where MT reads וַיָּבֹאוּ "and they (Balaam and Balak) entered." Still other variants have complete word differences as in ܘܫܩܐ ܕܝܡܝܢܐ ܬܬܠܘܢ ܦܘܪܫܢܐ ܠܡܪܝܐ "and the right thigh you shall give as an offering to the Lord" (Lev 7:32) against MT וְאֵת שׁוֹק הַיָּמִין תִּתְּנוּ תְרוּמָה לַכֹּהֵן "and the right thigh you shall give as an offering to the priest" where S read ליהוה "to the Lord" in place of MT לַכֹּהֵן "to the priest." s-Lev 3:8 reads the plus יהוה "the Lord" in the phrase ܩܕܡ ܡܪܝܐ ܒܬܪܥܐ ܕܡܫܟܢܙܒܢܐ "before the Lord at the entrance of the tent of meeting" versus לִפְנֵי אֹהֶל מוֹעֵד "before the tent of meeting." The Peshitta

---

[38] This number includes two cases of ܝܪܚܐ ܗܢܐ ܕܫܒܥܐ "this seventh month" (Num 29:7, 12), but excludes ܕܬܪܬܝܢ "a second time" (Num 10:6).

[39] Brock, "Jewish Traditions in Syriac Sources," 212–32, and Brock, "A Palestinian Targum Feature in Syriac," 271–82. For a fuller discussion, see Lund, "Genesis in Syriac," 548–49, and Lund, "Exodus in Syriac," 362–63.

[40] See Lund, "Genesis in Syriac," 549–52, and Lund, "Exodus in Syriac," 363–65.

[41] S7a1 reads the variant ܒܐܝܣܪܐܝܠ "in Israel" which is a secondary development.

plus projects Hebrew לִפְנֵי יְהוָה פֶּתַח אֹהֶל מוֹעֵד "before the Lord at the entrance of the tent of meeting," a reading found in other verses of the Torah (Exod 29:11; Lev 14:11; 16:7).

2.4.5.3.1 Alleged Citations of the Peshitta in *BHS

The use of the Peshitta in *BHS needs to be reconsidered especially in Genesis and Exodus in view of manuscript S^5b1.[42] *BHS cites the Peshitta as reading the plus חַיַּת "the wild animals of" in Gen 1:26, but S^8/5b1 omits ܚܝܘܬܐ ܕ reading as MT וּבְכָל־הָאָרֶץ "and over all the earth," against the plus of S^7a1. Again, *BHS cites the Peshitta as reading אֱלֹהִים "God" in Gen 7:1, but S^8/5b1 reads יהוה "the Lord." This is a complicated case because SP and some Masoretic manuscripts read אֱלֹהִים. The claim of *BHS that the Peshitta reads the plus הַגְּבֹהִים "the high (mountains)" in Gen 7:20 is clearly bogus, the plus being absent in both S^5b1 and S^7a1. Later Peshitta manuscripts attest the reading ܪ̈ܡܐ "the high (mountains),"[43] but not the earlier manuscripts. *BHS cites the Peshitta as reading the plus גָּדוֹל "great (nation)" in Gen 21:13, but S^5b1 lacks the plus. *BHS alleges that the Peshitta reads the plus מִן "from" in Gen 24:10, but S^5b1 omits the plus. Again, in Gen 24:45, *BHS cites the Peshitta as reading the plus מְעַט מַיִם מִכַּדֵּךְ "a little water from your jar" at the end of the verse, yet S^5b1 does not have the plus. The same can be said of the alleged pluses אֲחֹתָם "their sister" (Gen 24:60), לֵאָה "Leah" (Gen 30:15), and אֹתָם "them" (Gen 48:13). By contrast, there is no textual note in *BHS where S^5b1 reads יַעֲקֹב "Jacob" with MT against a minus in S^7a1 (Gen 30:4), which appears to be secondary.

2.4.5.4 Relevance for Exegesis

The Peshitta serves as a tool of exegesis.[44] For example, it translates סוּף "reed" used by itself as ܪܘܩܐ "a shallow": Moses' mother put her son Moses in the ark "and placed it in *a shallow*" (Exod 2:3); Pharaoh's daughter "saw the ark in *a shallow*" (Exod 2:5). By contrast, the Old Greek renders סוּף in these verses as ἕλος "marshland," T^O as יַעְרָא "rushes," T^N as אפרה "meadow," T^Ps-J as גומייא "papyrus reeds," and V as *carectum* "sedgy spot" and *papyrio*, "papyrus grove."

MT-Exod 38:8 reads "and he made a basin of bronze and its stand of bronze בְּמַרְאֹת הַצֹּבְאֹת אֲשֶׁר צָבְאוּ at the entrance of the tent of meeting." There are a number of exegetical questions that arise from the phrase בְּמַרְאֹת הַצֹּבְאֹת אֲשֶׁר צָבְאוּ: What does -בּ mean? What do מַרְאֹת mean? and what does the verb צבא mean in reference to women? The Peshitta interprets the phrase as ܒܝܬ ܡܚܙܝܐ ܕܢܫ̈ܐ ܕܐܬܝܢ ܠܡܨܠܝܘ "at the place of sight of the women who come to pray," taking -בּ as "at" (not "with"), מַרְאֹת as "place of sight" (not "mirrors"), and the verb צבא as the service of prayer. Barhebraeus comments as follows: "Only up to the washing basin could the women approach, and from there could see the things that were within."[45] By contrast, the Greek reads ἐκ τῶν κατόπτρων τῶν νηστευσασῶν "from the mirrors of the women who fasted." These are two entirely different understandings of the Hebrew, though praying and fasting are complementary. The exegesis of צבא in the Peshitta agrees with that of T^O, but not that of בְּמַרְאֹת.[46]

The Peshitta renders the Hebrew מֵי הַמָּרִים הַמְאָרְרִים "the bitter waters that bring a curse" as ܡ̈ܝܐ ܡܪ̈ܝܪܐ ܒܘܩ̈ܝܐ "the bitter examining waters" (Num 5:18). T^Ps-J renders this expression similarly: מיא מריריא בדוקיא "the bitter examining waters."

The Peshitta has ܠܐܪܡ ܐܬܕܒܪ ܐܒܝ "my father was taken[47] to Aram" as the formal translation equivalent of MT אֲרַמִּי אֹבֵד אָבִי "My father was a

[42] See Lund, "Exodus in Syriac," 353–54.

[43] The earliest attestation of this plus in Syriac appears in lectionaries dated to the ninth century. This late plus may have entered Syriac tradition under the influence of the Greek, which reads πάντα τὰ ὄρη τὰ ὑψηλά "all the high mountains."

[44] See Lund, "Genesis in Syriac," 553–58, and Lund, "Exodus in Syriac," 365–67.

[45] ܥܕܡܐ ܠܠܘܩܢܐ ܕܡܫܝܓܬܐ ܒܠܚܘܕ ܩܪ̈ܒܢ ܗܘ̈ܝ ܢܫ̈ܐ. ܘܡܢ ܬܡܢ ܚܙ̈ܝܢ ܗܘ̈ܝ ܗܠܝܢ ܕܠܓܘ (Sprengling and Graham, *Barhebraeus' Scholia*, 148).

[46] T^O reads בְּמַחזְיַת נְשַׁיָא דְאָתְיָן לְצַלָאָה "with the mirrors of the women who come to pray."

[47] The choice of lexeme may have been influenced by the wording of Num 23:7, where S reads ܕܒܪܢܝ ܒܠܩ ܡܢ ܐܪܡ "from Aram Balak took me" (MT מִן־אֲרָם יַנְחֵנִי בָלָק "from Aram Balak brought me"); so Weitzman, *The Syriac Version*, 62, n. 133.

perishing Aramean" (Deut 26:5). It could be that the Peshitta read a Hebrew variant אֲרָם "Aram" for אֲרַמִּי "Aramean." The Old Greek also seems to have read such a variant in rendering Συρίαν ἀπέβαλεν ὁ πατήρ μου "my father left Aram." While the Peshitta and the Old Greek agree that אָבִי "my father" is the subject of the verb and אֲרָם "Aram" its object, they differ on interpretation of the verb אֹבֵד "perishing." By contrast, T° (לָבָן אֲרַמָאָה בְעָא לְאוֹבָדָא יָת אַבָּא "Laban the Aramean sought to destroy my father") and v (Syrus persequebatur patrem meum "the Syrian pursued my father") interpret אֲרַמִּי as the subject of the verb, a reference to Laban.

2.4.5.5 Auxiliary Tools

Two useful tools exist, one in print, the other an electronic tool. The Peshitta Institute, formerly at Leiden University but now in Amsterdam, produced a printed concordance of the entire s-Pent.[48] Entries include glosses, both in Latin and in English, and the Hebrew words represented by the given lexeme. The volume contains indices of Latin-Syriac equivalents, English-Syriac equivalents, and a list of Hebrew words with the Syriac words used to translate them.

Accordance Bible Software has a complete grammatically and lexically tagged module of the Peshitta Old Testament including the Apocrypha, based on Codex Ambrosianus (s7a1). M.A. Abegg and J.A. Lund produced the Accordance module. The detailed tagging allows for complex searches involving combinations of words and forms (verbal conjugations, person, number, state of nouns, etc.).

Abegg, M.A. and J.A. Lund, PESHOT-T module (version 5.0; Accordance Bible Software, 2014).
Borbone, P.G., J. Cook, K.D. Jenner, and D.M. Walter, in collaboration with J.A. Lund and M.P. Weitzman, Concordance to the Pentateuch (The Old Testament in Syriac according to the Peshitta Version 5.1; Leiden: Brill, 1997).
Brock, S.P., "Jewish Traditions in Syriac Sources," JJS 30 (1979): 212–32.
Brock, S.P., "A Palestinian Targum Feature in Syriac," JJS 46 (1995): 271–82.

Brock, S.P., The Bible in the Syriac Tradition (Gorgias Handbooks 7; rev. ed.; Piscataway: Gorgias, 2006).
Cook, J., "The Composition of the Peshitta Version of the Old Testament (Pentateuch)," in The Peshitta: Its Early Text and History: Papers Read at the Peshitta Symposium Held at Leiden 30–31 August 1985 (eds. P.B. Dirksen and M.J. Mulder; Monographs of the Peshitta Institute Leiden 4; Leiden: Brill, 1988), 147–68.
Dirksen, P.B., "The Peshitta and Textual Criticism of the Old Testament," VT 42 (1992): 376–90.
van den Eynde, C., Commentaire d'Išoʿdad of Merv sur l'Ancien Testament, Vol. 1: Genèse (CSCO 126; SS 67; Louvain: Secrétariat du CorpusSCO, 1950).
van den Eynde, C., Commentaire d'Išoʿdad of Merv sur l'Ancien Testament, Vol. 2: Exode – Deutéronome (CSCO 176; SS 80; Louvain: Secrétariat du CorpusSCO, 1958).
ter Haar Romeny, R.B., "Techniques of Translation and Transmission of the Earliest Text Forms of the Syriac Version of Genesis," in The Peshitta as a Translation: Papers Read at the II Peshitta Symposium Held at Leiden 19–21 August 1993 (eds. P.B. Dirksen and A. van der Kooij; Monographs of the Peshitta Institute Leiden 8; Leiden: Brill, 1995), 177–85.
ter Haar Romeny, R.B., A Syrian in Greek Dress: The Use of Greek, Hebrew and Syriac Biblical Texts in Eusebius of Emesa's Commentary on Genesis (Traditio Exegetica Graeca 6; Leuven: Peeters, 1997).
ter Haar Romeny, R.B., "The Peshitta of Isaiah: Evidence from the Syriac Fathers," in Text, Translation, and Tradition: Studies on the Peshitta and its Use in the Syriac Tradition Presented to Konrad D. Jenner on the Occasion of his Sixty-Fifth Birthday (eds. W.T. van Peursen and R.B. ter Haar Romeny; Monographs of the Peshitta Institute Leiden 14; Leiden: Brill, 2006), 149–64.
ter Haar Romeny, R.B., "La réception des versions syriaques de la Bible: l' apport des citations patristiques," in L'Ancien Testament en syriaque (eds. F. Briquel Chatonnet and P. Le Moigne; Collection études syriaques 5; Paris: Geuthner, 2008), 173–91.
Hänel, J., Die aussermasorethischen Übereinstimmungen zwischen der Septuaginta und der Peschittha in der Genesis (BZAW 20; Giessen: Töpelmann, 1911).
Jansma, T. and M.D. Koster, Preface, Genesis – Exodus (The Old Testament in Syriac according to the Peshitta Version 1.1; Leiden: Brill, 1977).
Joosten, J., "The Use of Some Particles in the Old Testament Peshitta," Textus 14 (1988): 175–83.

---
[48] Borbone et al., Concordance.

Joosten, J., "Greek and Latin Words in the Peshitta Pentateuch: First Soundings," in *Symposium Syriacum VII* (ed. R. Lavenant, S.J.; OrChrAn 256; Rome: Pontificio Istituto Orientale, 1998), 37–47.

Kim, Y.-K., *The Function of the Tautological Infinitive in Classical Biblical Hebrew* (HSS 60; Winona Lake: Eisenbrauns, 2009).

Kiraz, G.A., *A Grammar of the Syriac Language*, Vol. 1: *Syriac Orthography* (Piscataway: Gorgias Press, 2012).

van der Kooij, A., "Peshitta Genesis 6: 'Sons of God'–Angels or Judges?" *JNSL* 23 (1997): 43–51.

van der Kooij, A., "On the Significance of MS 5b1 for the Peshitta Genesis," in *The Peshitta: Its Early Text and History: Papers Read at the Peshitta Symposium Held at Leiden 30–31 August 1985* (eds. P.B. Dirksen and M.J. Mulder; Monographs of the Peshitta Institute Leiden 4; Leiden: Brill, 1988), 183–99.

Koster, M.D., *The Peshitta of Exodus: The Development of its Text in the Course of Fifteen Centuries* (SSN 19; Assen: Van Gorcum, 1977).

Koster, M.D., "Redating TR and BTR: The Three Stages at Stake?" *Aramaic Studies* 7 (2009): 1–18.

Lane, D.J., A.P. Hayman, W.M. van Vliet, J.H. Hospers, H.J.W. Drijvers, and J.E. Erbes, *Leviticus – Numbers – Deuteronomy – Joshua* (The Old Testament in Syriac according to the Peshitta Version 1.2 and 2.1b; Leiden: Brill, 1991).

Lund, J.A., "The Influence of the Septuagint on the Peshitta: A Re-evaluation of Criteria in Light of Comparative Study of the Versions in Genesis and Psalms" (PhD diss.; Hebrew University of Jerusalem, 1988).

Lund, J.A., "Observations on Some Biblical Citations in Ephrem's Commentary on Genesis," *Aramaic Studies* 4 (2006): 205–18.

Lund, J.A., "A Non-Peshitta Jeremiah Citation by Aphrahat," *Aramaic Studies* 5 (2007): 133–40.

Lund, J.A., "Genesis in Syriac," in *The Book of Genesis: Composition, Reception, and Interpretation* (eds. C.A. Evans, J.N. Lohr, and D.L. Petersen; VTSup 152; Leiden: Brill, 2012), 537–60.

Lund, J.A., "Exodus in Syriac," in *The Book of Exodus: Composition, Reception, and Interpretation* (eds. T.B. Dozeman, C.A. Evans, and J.N. Lohr; VTSup 164; Leiden: Brill, 2014), 349–69.

Lund, J.A., "The Hebrew as a Text Critical Tool in Restoring Genuine Peshitta Readings in Isaiah," in *Contemporary Examinations of Classical Languages (Hebrew, Aramaic, Syriac, and Greek): Valency, Lexicography, Grammar, and Manuscripts* (eds. T.M. Lewis, A. Salvesen, and B. Turner; Perspectives on Linguistics and Ancient Languages 8; Piscataway: Gorgias Press, 2016).

Maori, Y., "Methodological Criteria for Distinguishing Between Variant Vorlage and Exegesis in the Peshitta Pentateuch," in *The Peshitta as a Translation: Papers Read at the II Peshitta Symposium Held at Leiden 19–21 August 1993* (eds. P.B. Dirksen and A. van der Kooij; Monographs of the Peshitta Institute Leiden 8; Leiden: Brill, 1995), 103–20.

Maori, Y., *The Peshitta Version of the Pentateuch and Early Jewish Exegesis* (תרגום הפשיטתא לתורה והפרשנות היהודית הקדומה; Jerusalem: Magnes, 1995) [Hebr.].

Maori, Y., "The Relationship between the Peshitta Pentateuch and the Pentateuchal Targums," in *Targum Studies*, Vol. 2: *Targum and Peshitta* (ed. P.V.M. Flesher; South Florida Studies in the History of Judaism 165; Atlanta: Scholars Press, 1998), 57–73.

Owens, R.J., *The Genesis and Exodus Citations of Aphrahat the Persian Sage* (Monographs of the Peshitta Institute Leiden 3; Leiden: Brill, 1984).

Owens, R.J., "Aphrahat as a Witness to the Early Syriac Text of Leviticus," in *The Peshitta: Its Early Text and History* (eds. P.B. Dirksen and M.J. Mulder; Monographs of the Peshitta Institute Leiden 4; Leiden: Brill, 1988), 1–48.

Sprengling, M. and W.C. Graham, *Barhebraeus' Scholia on the Old Testament*, Part 1: *Genesis – II Samuel* (Chicago: University of Chicago Press, 1931).

Tonneau, R.M., *Sancti Ephraem Syri in Genesim et in Exodum Commentarii* (CSCO 152; SS 71; Louvain: Durbecq, 1955).

Weitzman, M.P., *The Syriac Version of the Old Testament: An Introduction* (University of Cambridge Oriental Publications 56; Cambridge: Cambridge University Press, 1999).

Wright, W., *Catalogue of Syriac Manuscripts in the British Museum*, Part 1 (London: British Museum, 1870).

Jerome A. Lund

2.4.6 Hexaplaric Greek Translations and Hexapla of the Octateuch

2.4.6.1 Background

Although literal to varying degrees, the LXX translations of the books of the Octateuch (→ 2.4.1; → 3–5.1) do depart at times from the underlying Hebrew, for example to clarify obscure passages or to rectify seeming inconsistencies. Thus, the LXX

Octateuch apparently provided ample room for the Three – Aquila, Symmachus, and Theodotion (→ 1.3.1.2) – to amend the Greek text, usually to align more closely with the underlying Hebrew, according to their individual methods and purposes.

2.4.6.2 Editions, Sources, and Auxiliary Tools

Field published his monumental edition of available hexaplaric fragments in 1875.[1] Although Field's work greatly advanced hexaplaric studies, since then many additional hexaplaric materials have surfaced. Wevers catalogued the hexaplaric materials for the Pentateuch in his five critical editions – Genesis through Deuteronomy – prepared for the Göttingen *Septuaginta*.[2] Hexaplaric materials appear in a second apparatus in these volumes, but no assessments are made about the readings. In 2009 and 2011, Burris and McClurg edited the hexaplaric materials for Numbers in two dissertations.[3] In these two studies, hexaplaric readings are evaluated for accuracy and validity, and unattributed readings are examined and often assigned to one or more of the Three. For Joshua and Judges, Field provides a foundation, but more materials have surfaced since his work, some of which are included in the second apparatus of Brooke–McLean's Cambridge edition. The hexaplaric materials for Ruth are collected in the Göttingen critical edition. For auxiliary tools related to the Hexapla, see the Bibliography.

2.4.6.2.1 Sources for Origen's Fifth Column

For each of the books of the Octateuch, an origenic group of manuscripts (*O*-group) has been identified. These manuscripts are the main source for reconstructing Origen's fifth column (→ 1.3.1.2.7). Of these, however, very few contain the Aristarchian signs (e.g., asterisk, obelus, metobelus). Manuscript LXX^G is particularly significant, first because it dates to the fourth or fifth century C.E., and may well represent a copy of one of the facsimiles of the fifth column made under the supervision of Eusebius early in the fourth century. Second, manuscript LXX^G contains a wealth of hexaplaric signs, although not all are accurate. Unfortunately, for the Octateuch some large lacunae exist in LXX^G.[4]

Another main hexaplaric witness is the Syro-Hexapla (Syh; → 2.5.4.2), a translation into Syriac of the fifth column completed in the early seventh century C.E. It is hard to overstate the value of the Syro-Hexapla. It contains a mainly quantitative translation of the fifth column with Aristarchian signs copied as well. Although the Greek exemplar for the Syro-Hexapla probably contains differences (including recensional) when compared with the original fifth column, the quality of the sign tradition is good, and the signs generally reflect Origen's work. Although errors do exist in the signs (e.g., misplaced signs, missing metobelus, etc.), the original intent of the signs can usually be determined. In addition, the margins of the Syro-Hexapla contain a large number of readings from the Three and other sources (e.g., the Samaritikon), and in many cases, the Syro-Hexapla is the only witness to a reading.

Several Syro-Hexapla manuscripts exist for the Pentateuchal books, but only two cover most of the Pentateuch. The first is British Museum manuscript 14437. It was published by de Lagarde as *Bibliotecae syriacae*,[5] and it contains much of the Pentateuch and most of Joshua, Judges, and Ruth. The second is the Tur Abdin manuscript, available in a facsimile edition.[6] This manuscript contains the Pentateuch, but is missing the first thirty-one chapters of Genesis.

One other source of hexaplaric material is a set of manuscripts named the *s*-group, whose readings are mainly in the margins. In addition to readings from the Three, the *s*-group contains a wealth of origenic (*o'*) readings that can be used to gain insight into the fifth column.

---

[1] Field, *Hexapla.
[2] Wevers (ed.), *Genesis;* Wevers (ed.), *Exodus;* Wevers (ed.), *Leviticus;* Wevers (ed.), *Numeri;* Wevers (ed.), *Deuteronomium.*
[3] Burris, "Critical Edition Numbers 1–18"; and McClurg, "Critical Edition Numbers 19–36."
[4] For details, see Swete, *Introduction 1900, 137–38.
[5] De Lagarde, *Bibliothecae syriacae.*
[6] Vööbus, *Pentateuch.*

2.4.6.2.2 Sources for Readings of the Three

Readings of the three translators (→ 1.3.1.2) are found mainly in the Syro-Hexapla and in manuscripts of the *s*-group, with a limited number of readings scattered through some other manuscripts and cited in writings of the church fathers.

Because of the wide divergence of LXX-Exod (→ 2.4.1.2) from MT-Exod (→ 2.2.2) in the last six chapters of Exodus, Origen attempted to approximate MT-Exod in the fifth column using a large number of asterisked readings. These readings are variously attributed to one or more of the Three translators, with attributions to Theodotion predominating. For more details, see below under → 2.4.6.3 and → 2.4.6.3.4.

2.4.6.3 Translation Character and Technique
2.4.6.3.1 Theodotion

Theodotion (→ 1.3.1.2.4) has a little over 1,000 readings for the Pentateuch and about 350 readings for Joshua, Judges, and Ruth. The total is significantly smaller than for Aquila or Symmachus, and this may be due to the fact that Theodotion often agrees with LXX (→ 1.3.1.1).

As of 2015, no critical editions exist for Joshua and Judges. Judges in particular is problematic, since two distinct Septuagint versions (→ 4.3) have been preserved: Alexandrinus (LXX^A) and Vaticanus (LXX^B). LXX^B appears to be influenced by the καίγε (→ 1.3.1.2) tradition, while LXX^A is thought to be closer to the Old Greek,[7] although influenced by the Hexapla and possibly by καίγε. Interestingly, in Judges, readings that are jointly attributed to LXX°′ (origenic text) and Th (Theodotion) overwhelmingly agree with LXX^A against LXX^B, raising the possibility that Origen corrected using Theodotion. Until a critical edition of the Old Greek is available, however, the precise origenic text and the degree of Origen's dependence on Theodotion cannot be determined.

In general, when LXX departs from the Hebrew, often Theodotion is content to follow LXX. This indicates that Theodotion was creating a revision of LXX and not a *de novo* translation. Some examples

---

[7] See P.E. Satterthwaite, "Judges," in *NETS*, 195–200.

from Judges are representative. In Judg 11:39, יַעַשׂ לָהּ "he did to her" is rendered by the LXX translator as ἐπετέλεσεν Ιεφθάε "Jephthah performed" (assuming LXX^A has the Old Greek). The name "Jephthah" is added to provide clarity and Theodotion is content to follow LXX-Judg here. Another example is at Judg 5:21, where קְדוּמִים (plural of "ancient") is taken to be a proper name by the LXX translator (represented by LXX^A) and transliterated with καδησείμ. Theodotion stays close to LXX-Judg with καδησίμ. Here, Origen modifies the name to καδημείμ to match the Hebrew spelling more closely, but both Theodotion and Origen follow the lead of LXX-Judg and transliterate rather than translating. A final example is Judg 5:16 where for לִפְלַגּוֹת רְאוּבֵן "for the divisions of Reuben," LXX-Judg (represented by LXX^A) has τοῦ διελθεῖν εἰς τὰ τοῦ Ρουβήν "to cross over into the (places) of Reuben" which captures the sense of the Hebrew poetry but is not quantitative. Aquila renders more quantitatively with εἰς διαιρέσεις τοῦ Ῥουβήν "for the divisions of Reuben," but Theodotion and Origen match LXX-Judg exactly. Aquila and Symmachus are less likely to take these kind of liberties in departing from the Hebrew text.

Theodotion does differ from LXX at times, for example, where LXX deviates from the Hebrew. At Num 21:18, MT has בְּמִשְׁעֲנֹתָם "with their staffs." The LXX-Num translator perhaps construed this as an infinitive of שׁען "support" or as a form of the related ענה "subjugate" and rendered the phrase as ἐν τῷ κυριεῦσαι αὐτῶν "in their ruling." Theodotion conforms to the Hebrew much more closely with ἐν ταῖς ῥάβδοις αὐτῶν "with their staffs." Another example is Num 25:3, where MT says "the people were joined (יִצָּמֶד) with Baal-peor." The verb is a *Niphal* of צמד (passive of "to join"), and LXX-Num renders this contextually as ἐτελέσθη which can mean in the passive "be initiated" (e.g., into cult mysteries; see Liddell & Scott). Theodotion render this as ἐζευγίσθη (from ζευγίζω, the passive here signifying "being joined/bound"); this is closer in meaning to the Hebrew.

Theodotion frequently renders the source language quantitatively, for example, with his ἀνὴρ ἀνήρ for אִישׁ אִישׁ (literally "man man," and meaning "each man") in Num 1:4. Another example is Num 21:2, where MT has נָתֹן תִּתֵּן. This is a cognate infinitive absolute plus finite verb, a combination used for emphasis, which means literally, "giving you will give." Theodotion renders this quantitatively as παραδόσει παραδῶς "delivering you will deliver." Another example is in Judg 11:35, where the Hebrew has another cognate infinitive absolute plus finite verb pair: הַכְרֵעַ הִכְרַעְתִּנִי "bringing low, you have brought me low" meaning "you have surely brought me low." Theodotion renders this quantitatively as κατάγχουσα κατήγξάς με (literally "strangling you have strangled me"). Here, LXX-Judg (represented by LXX^A) has a less quantitative rendering with ἐμπεποδοστάτηκάς με "you have gotten in my way."

Theodotion can provide renderings that are sensitive to the source language. For example, at Gen 1:2, for the poetic couplet תֹהוּ וָבֹהוּ (pronounced *tōhu vabōhu* and meaning "formless and void"), Theodotion has θὲν καὶ οὐθέν "nothing and naught." This accounts for the Hebrew wordplay better than ἀόρατος καὶ ἀκατασκεύαστος "invisible and unformed" in LXX-Gen.

2.4.6.3.2 Aquila

For the books of the Pentateuch, Aquila (→ 1.3.1.2.4) has approximately 2,100 readings attributed to him.[8] Joshua, Judges, and Ruth have about 330 readings attributed to Aquila. In the Octateuch, Aquila is true to his normal translation tendencies, which we can characterize in at least four ways. First, his translation technique is very quantitative. The following examples are representative. In LXX-Num 23:19, the Hebrew has לֹא אִישׁ אֵל וִיכַזֵּב; a literal and wooden translation is "God is not a man *and he lies.*" For the conjunction plus finite verb (וִיכַזֵּב), the LXX translator substitutes an infinitive (διαρτηθῆναι). This results in "God is not man *to lie,*" which is a suitable rendering. Aquila renders the Hebrew literally as καὶ διαψεύσεται "and he lies." In Num 21:2, the Hebrew uses a finite verb plus cognate infinitive absolute to provide emphasis. A standard translation into English would be "If you will *surely* give this people into my hands." The Hebrew for the first part of this phrase is אִם־נָתֹן תִּתֵּן אֶת־הָעָם. A literal rendering of the cognate pair (infinitive plus finite verb) is "if giving you will give." Aquila renders the above Hebrew phrase as ἐὰν διδοὺς δῷς σὺν τὸν λαόν "if giving you will give [with] the people." This is in contrast to the less wooden renderings of LXX-Num, ἐὰν μοι παραδῷς τὸν λαόν "if you will deliver up the people [to me]," and of Symmachus, ἐὰν δῷς τὸν λαόν "if you will give the people." The LXX translator and Symmachus are content to use a single Greek word to render the Hebrew cognate pair, whereas Aquila renders the words quantitatively. In this same verse we see another example of quantitative exactness in the way Aquila handles the direct object marker אֶת. The translation issue is that the Hebrew word can serve either as a direct object marker or as a preposition meaning "with." Aquila often treats אֶת as a preposition even, as in this verse, where the context clearly indicates that it should be a direct object marker. Thus, he renders אֶת as σύν "with," giving the awkward phrase, "If [giving] you will give *with* this people into my hands." At other times when אֶת is being used as a direct object marker, Aquila renders it more suitably although still quantitatively. For example, in Judg 1:15, he uses the Greek article to provide quantitative correspondence. In the phrase "Caleb gave to her *the upper springs and the lower springs,*" the compound direct object (indicated here with italics) is expressed with the Hebrew phrase אֵת גֻּלֹּת עִלִּית וְאֵת גֻּלֹּת תַּחְתִּית. Aquila renders this as τὴν Γολλὰθ τὴν ἄνω καὶ τὴν Γολλὰθ τὴν κάτω "the upper Gollath and the lower Gollath." He also matches the Hebrew word order by placing the adjectives ("upper" and "lower") after the nouns they modify, but as a result he is forced to add τήν before the adjectives, and thus he departs from strict quantitative alignment with the Hebrew for the sake of the rules of Greek grammar.[9] As a final example of strict literal-

---

[8] For the book of Numbers for all the three revisors, it is possible to be more precise, and to assign many unattributed readings to one or more of the Three, as well as to reassign probably erroneous attributions. The details are provided in Burris, "Critical Edition Numbers 1–18," and McClurg, "Critical Edition Numbers 19–36."

[9] For a complete list of Aquila's equivalents for the direct

ness, Josh 3:12 has the phrase מִשִּׁבְטֵי יִשְׂרָאֵל אִישׁ־אֶחָד לַשֵּׁבֶט אִישׁ־אֶחָד (literally "from the tribes of Israel, one man one man for the tribe"). The LXX translator expresses the sense of this with τῶν υἱῶν Ἰσραὴλ ἕνα ἀφ' ἑκάστης φυλῆς "of the sons of Israel, one from each tribe." Aquila, on the other hand, for the latter part of the phrase has the literal Ἰσραὴλ ἄνδρα ἕνα ἄνδρα ἕνα τοῦ σκήπτρου "Israel, one man one man of a tribe."

Second, Aquila tends to be consistent with his renderings even when context demands a different choice of word. We saw an example above where he uses the preposition σύν for אֵת even when the context indicates that אֵת is not being used as a preposition. A few more examples demonstrate this tendency. The word מתה may denote either "staff" or "tribe," but Aquila employs ῥάβδος "staff" even when the context indicates that the alternate sense of "tribe" is clearly intended. In Num 1:21, 47; 2:5; 18:2; and 36:8, מתה clearly means "tribe," and LXX-Num renders it as φυλή "tribe" but in these cases, Aquila has ῥάβδος "staff." A second example can be found in Judg 13:5, where the angel of the Lord announces that Nazirite restrictions will apply to the child Samson; he says, "and a razor shall not go up" (וּמוֹרָה לֹא־יַעֲלֶה) upon his head. The word מוֹרָה "razor" is here rendered by Aquila as φόβος "fear." Aquila also likely uses φόβος for מוֹרָה at 1 Sam 1:11 in a similar context.[10] In one place – Ps 9:21 (Eng.: 9:20) – מוֹרָה is used as an alternate spelling for מוֹרָא "fear" and there Aquila appropriately renders it using the related φόβημα "fear, terror." But unlike for Ps 9:21, where the context demands the meaning "fear," in Judg 13:5 and 1 Sam 1:11, מוֹרָה clearly denotes a razor. It makes little sense to say in the context of the standard Nazirite restriction, that no "fear" will go up on his head. Aquila's stereotyped equivalent results in a rather odd translation.

Aquila is not always woodenly consistent, however, and he is capable of nuance at times. For example, in Num 22:23, the Hebrew has the *Hiphil* of נטה "stretch out, spread out, guide away" for Balaam's attempt to turn his donkey aside. The verb נטה in the *Hiphil* is commonly used to denote "stretching out," but more rarely "turning aside." Aquila's normal equivalent for נטה is ἐκτείνω "stretch out," corresponding to the more common meaning of the Hebrew. But here, Aquila employs ἐκκλίνω "turn away," his normal choice for סור "turn away," and thus he shows sensitivity to the context.

A third feature of Aquila's translation technique is how he sometimes employs transliteration and sometimes translation. In Judg 1:15, he transliterates גֻּלֹּת "spring" as Γολλάθ "Gollath." This illustrates Aquila's *Tendenz* to match Hebrew names exactly when he does transliterate. Another example is Num 22:22, where the Hebrew has לְשָׂטָן, which can be taken either as a noun with a preposition ("for an adversary"), or as an infinitive ("to be hostile towards, to oppose"). LXX-Num has the infinitive ἐνδιαβάλλειν "to stand as an adversary." Aquila transliterates, using σατάν "satan."[11]

Sometimes, Aquila translates place names. For example, at Num 21:1, the Hebrew is הָאֲתָרִים "Atharim" and LXX-Num transliterates with Αθαριν "Atharin." Aquila translates this as τῶν κατασκόπων "the spies." Another example is Josh 15:7, where for the place name עֵין שֶׁמֶשׁ "En Shemesh" Aquila translates, matching LXX-Josh, with πηγῆς ἡλίου "spring of the sun."[12]

In Deuteronomy 3, LXX-Deut transliterates and translates the same word, and interestingly, Aquila responds by translating where LXX-Deut transliterates and vice versa. Thus, in Deut 3:17, for the Hebrew place name פִּסְגָּה "Pisgah," LXX-Deut has the transliteration Φασγά "Phasga." Aquila chooses to

---

object marker, see Hyvärinen, *Die Übersetzung von Aquila*, 27.

[10] The reading at 1 Sam 1:11 is *sine nom* (without attribution), but based on Aquila's reading at Judg 13:5, and upon an alternate rendering for מוֹרָה by Theodotion, the 1 Sam 1:11 reading clearly comes from Aquila.

[11] The Hebrew סטן is transliterated once in LXX, in 1 Kgs 11:14, where it refers to an "adversary."

[12] For this example, the first part of the name (עֵין) could arguably refer to a spring rather than being an "official" part of the place name, and thus Aquila may not have seen transliteration as an option, but for the second part of the name (שֶׁמֶשׁ "sun"), Aquila has chosen to translate. Compare this with 1 Kgs 1:9, where Aquila renders the place name עֵין רֹגֵל "En Rogel" as πηγῆς Ρογήλ "spring of Rogel," thus translating the first word and transliterating the second.

translate here with ἡ λαξευτή (an adjective meaning "hewn," i.e., in stone). But in Deut 3:27, for the same Hebrew name, LXX-Deut translates with Λελαξευμένου (a verb meaning "hewn in stone"). Here Aquila transliterates, and renders the Hebrew as Φασγά "Phasga" which matches LXX-Deut 3:17.

A fourth feature of Aquila's translation technique is his periodic tendency to render words derived from a single Hebrew stem using equivalents from a single Greek stem. This can produce interesting results. For example, for בְּרֵאשִׁית "in [the] beginning" in Gen 1:1, Aquila has ἐν κεφαλαίῳ "in [the] head." Aquila apparently perceived רֵאשִׁית "beginning" to be based on the root רֹאשׁ "head" and rendered using a derivative of κεφαλή "head" his normal equivalent for רֹאשׁ.

As a final note, evidence exists for Theodotion's (→ 1.3.1.2.4) possible influence on Aquila.[13] At Num 2:17, the Hebrew is דִּגְלֵיהֶם "their standards" (the root דגל is plural here with a pronominal suffix meaning "their"). LXX-Num has the singular ἡγεμονίαν (meaning "command [or governance] of a high office"), although its usual rendering for דגל is τάγμα "division" or "group." Theodotion follows the more usual LXX-Num reading, and also makes it singular, while also covering the pronominal suffix, thus giving τάγμα αὐτῶν "their division." Aquila uses the same root as Theodotion here although, true to his literal *Tendenz*, he matches the Hebrew plural noun with a plural: τάγματα αὐτῶν "their divisions." This is the only place Aquila is reported to use τάγμα, and also is his only known rendering for דגל. Wevers says this probably indicates that Aquila followed Theodotion here.[14]

2.4.6.3.3 Symmachus

Symmachus (→ 1.3.1.2.5) has approximately 1,700 attributed readings for the Pentateuch, and about 325 readings in Joshua, Judges, and Ruth. Symmachus often gives a closer approximation to the Hebrew than LXX.[15] For example, at Num 3:38, for the *Hophal* יוּמָת "he will be killed" Symmachus uses the future passive θανατωθήσεται "he will be put to death" rather than the middle ἀποθανεῖται "he will die" of LXX-Num. Interestingly, Symmachus also exhibits his flexibility as a translator earlier in the chapter (Num 3:10) where for the identical Hebrew, he uses the imperative ἀποθανέτω "let him die."

Symmachus often displays a sensitivity to the demands of the target language. For example, he differs from Aquila and Theodotion, who render the distributive אִישׁ "each" as ἀνήρ "man," for example at Num 2:17 and 14:4. Symmachus provides more sensible Greek, with ἕκαστος "each" in those places. Also, unlike the other two translators, he avoids ἀνήρ as an equivalent for אִישׁ unless it refers to a male person.[16] Another example of the sensitivity of Symmachus to Greek usage is at Gen 2:18, where for כְּנֶגְדּוֹ (literally, "as before him," meaning "corresponding to him") Aquila renders quantitatively as ὡς κατέναντι αὐτοῦ "as before him," but Symmachus renders more according to the sense with ἄντικρυς αὐτοῦ "opposite him."

However, Symmachus also shows sensitivity to the artistry of the source language. At Gen 2:23, the Hebrew uses a wordplay when it says that woman shall be called *'ishshah* (אִשָּׁה) because she was taken from *'ish* (אִישׁ "man"). LXX-Gen does not preserve this Hebrew nuance, using γυνή "woman" for אִשָּׁה, and ἀνδρός "man" for אִישׁ. Symmachus is sensitive to the underlying wordplay, rendering the word pair ἀνδρίς (a rare word for "woman") and ἀνδρός.

Like Aquila and Theodotion, Symmachus often renders quantitatively. An example is at Num 36:11–12, where for לְנָשִׁים מִמִּשְׁפְּחֹת בְּנֵי־מְנַשֶּׁה "for wives from the families of the sons of Manasseh," Symmachus has εἰς γυναῖκας ἀπὸ δήμου υἱῶν Μανασση "for wives from the family of the sons of Manasseh." Here, Symmachus more exactly matches the Hebrew than Theodotion, who inexplicably adds καί, giving εἰς γυναῖκας καὶ ἐκ τῆς συγγενείας

---

[13] This supports Gentry's conclusion in his overview article (→ 1.3.1.2) that Theodotion precedes Aquila and Symmachus chronologically.

[14] J.W. Wevers, *Notes on the Greek Text of Numbers* (SBLSCS 46; Atlanta: Scholars Press, 1998), ad loc.

[15] For a comprehensive list of Symmachus characteristics, see Salvesen, *Symmachus in the Pentateuch*, 195–264.

[16] See Salvesen, *Symmachus in the Pentateuch*, 241.

υἱῶν Μανασσή "for wives *and* out of the kinsmen of the sons of Manasseh."

In general, Symmachus avoids stereotypical formulas. For example, unlike Theodotion and Aquila, Symmachus does not have a standard way of translating Hebrew infinitive absolute with cognate finite verbs.[17] When the infinitive absolute precedes the verb, Symmachus may not translate the infinitive. Thus, at Num 21:2, for the finite verb and cognate infinitive absolute pair נָתֹן תִּתֵּן "giving you will give," both Aquila and Theodotion provide quantitative renderings, using participles for the infinitive absolute: Aquila: διδοὺς δῶς "giving you will give"; Theodotion: παραδόσει παραδῶς "delivering you will deliver." Symmachus, by contrast, renders the pair using the single finite verb δῶς "you will give."[18] In other places where the infinitive precedes the finite verb, however, Symmachus varies his approach, for example using a cognate accusative noun (Deut 7:23) or a cognate dative noun (Num 30:13, 16) for the infinitive. In Num 16:13, the infinitive absolute comes after the finite verb, and Symmachus correctly interprets the Hebrew as adding emphasis. The Hebrew reads כִּי־תִשְׂתָּרֵר עָלֵינוּ גַּם־הִשְׂתָּרֵר (literally "that you are reigning [or appointing yourself lord] over us, even reigning"). Aquila renders this as ὅτι ἄρχεις ἡμῶν καίγε ἄρχων "that you are ruling over us, and even ruling."[19] Symmachus captures the Hebrew emphatic nuance with κατατυραννεῖς γὰρ ἡμῶν βιαίως "for you are firmly being a tyrant over us."

Unlike LXX, and Theodotion at times, Symmachus normally remains tied firmly to the Hebrew text. At Josh 3:12, the Hebrew reads מִשִּׁבְטֵי יִשְׂרָאֵל אִישׁ־אֶחָד אִישׁ־אֶחָד לַשָּׁבֶט (literally, "from the tribes of Israel, one man one man for the tribe"). Although LXX-Josh captures the general sense of this with τῶν υἱῶν Ἰσραὴλ ἕνα ἀφ' ἑκάστης φυλῆς "of the sons of Israel, one from each tribe," it has no equivalent for one instance of the doubled אִישׁ־אֶחָד "each one." For the entire doubled phrase אִישׁ־אֶחָד אִישׁ־אֶחָד, Symmachus has ἄνδρα ἕνα καθ' ἑκάστην ("one man according to each [tribe]"). He thus avoids the wooden rendering of Aquila (ἄνδρα ἕνα ἄνδρα ἕνα = "one man one man") but accounts for all the underlying Hebrew.

Symmachus is more likely than either Aquila or Theodotion to translate rather than to transliterate proper names, particularly place names. Thus, at Num 33:47, Symmachus translates the place name הָעֲבָרִים "Abarim" as τῶν διαβασέων "ones who pass through,"[20] and at Num 33:49, he translates the name בֵּית הַיְשִׁמֹת "Beth-jeshimoth" as τῆς ἀοικήτου "uninhabited." Symmachus does transliterate sometimes, however, for example at Josh 15:6, where he has βιθαγλά for the place name בית חגלה "Beth-hoglah." Occasionally in different places but similar contexts, Symmachus translates and transliterates the same word. At Num 6:18 he transliterates הַנָּזִיר "the Nazirite" as Ναζιραῖος. Later, however, at Judg 13:5, Symmachus translates the same Hebrew, also referring to a Nazirite in context, with ἀφωρισμένον "one set apart."

2.4.6.3.4 Origen

In his fifth column, Origen (→ 1.3.1.3.7) provided many corrections toward the Hebrew. Many of these are marked with hexaplaric signs (asterisks and obeli), but a sizable number have no hexaplaric signs. For Genesis through Judges, many of these corrections are contained in marginal readings, noted as ο' (origenic), in a group of manuscripts called the *s*-group. These provide data about the fifth column separate from the asterisked materials from LXX[G] and the Syro-Hexapla. Manuscripts from the *s*-group often include marginal ο' readings when the origenic text differs from the main Greek text of the *s*-group. This implies that a source of hexaplaric readings from the fifth column, although perhaps not the entire fifth column, was available to scribes who copied the *s*-group manuscripts and that the scribes recognized these readings as origenic.

Some of Origen's corrections towards the Hebrew are not marked by Aristarchian signs. This

---

[17] For a discussion, see Salvesen, *Symmachus in the Pentateuch*, 228–29.

[18] A similar example where the infinitive is not translated occurs at Exod 19:13.

[19] Aquila's reading is retroverted from the Syro-Hexapla.

[20] This is retroverted from the Syro-Hexapla.

may be explained first by the later loss of the signs, for example, through the activity of scribes who did not have access to the underlying Hebrew, and for whom as a result, the signs had little meaning.

A second source of corrections in the direction of the Hebrew could be from Origen simply making changes without marking them. For example, Wevers noted that for LXX-Lev (→ 2.4.1.3), the number of origenic corrections without signs is too large to be explained simply as the product of scribal omissions alone, and so Origen himself appears to have made many corrections without providing signs.[21] The same is probably true to some extent for all the books of the Octateuch.

Third, non-marked corrections could be pre-origenic, that is, inherited by Origen in his Greek *Vorlage(n)* of LXX. Wevers explores this for Exodus (→ 2.4.1.2),[22] but although these kinds of inherited corrections are significant, their relative number is probably small.

As for the sources of Origen's asterisked pluses in the Octateuch, not much direct evidence exists. Unlike for some other books, such as Job, most asterisked readings are not identified with a particular translator from the Three. In the relatively few places where asterisked readings can be aligned with one of the Three, Theodotion is a common influence, for example, at Num 4:26 where an origenic plus matches a separate marginal reading from Theodotion.

There is one large section of the Pentateuch that contains many exceptions to the normal rule of non-attributed asterisked additions, and that is the tabernacle accounts of Exodus 35–40. Differences between MT-Exod (→ 2.2.2) and LXX-Exod (→ 2.4.1.2) prompted Origen to undertake a large-scale harmonization effort and his asterisked sections usually have an attribution. Overall, Origen mainly used Theodotion as his source for asterisked readings. For example, in the forty-one longer asterisked sections catalogued by Wevers, twenty-nine are attributed to Theodotion, one to "the Three" (labeled οἱ γ′), and one to Symmachus, while eleven are unattributed.[23] Fraenkel has challenged the conventional view that Theodotion is the source of Origen's asterisked readings in Exodus 35–40 and has demonstrated that the readings attributed to Theodotion are not characteristic of that translator both in vocabulary and style. Fraenkel shows that Origen created his own revised text using the very similar accounts in Exodus 25–31.[24] Thus, although Origen was often dependent on the Three, this example shows that he may have made exceptions.

2.4.6.4 Text-Critical Value for the Primary Translation and the Hebrew Bible
2.4.6.4.1 LXX Text History

The Hexapla had a profound impact on the text history of LXX (→ 1.3.1.1.). The fifth column affected not only the so-called origenic manuscript groups, but often other groups as well; and because the Three (→ 1.3.1.2) affected the fifth column, their influence may be seen indirectly. For example, in Num 21:21, the Hebrew says that Israel sent messengers to the king of the Amorites. LXX-Num says that Moses sent the messengers, making a conscious decision to align with 21:14, which identifies Moses as the sender. A reading attributed to the Three (οἱ λ′) and to Origen (ο′) corrects this towards the Hebrew with Ἰσραήλ "Israel." A number of manuscripts outside of the origenic group adopt this modified reading, indicating the possible influence of Origen and, indirectly, of the Three.

---

[21] Notes from Peter Gentry based on private communication with J.W. Wevers on July 13, 1995.

[22] See J.W. Wevers, "Pre-Origen Recensional Activity in the Greek Exodus," in *Studien zur Septuaginta: Robert Hanhart zu Ehren: Aus Anlass seines 65. Geburtstages* (eds. D. Fraenkel, U. Quast, and J.W. Wevers; MSU 20; Göttingen: Vandenhoeck & Ruprecht, 1990), 121–39.

[23] J.W. Wevers, *Text History of the Greek Exodus* (MSU 21; Göttingen: Vandenhoeck & Ruprecht, 1992).

[24] D. Fraenkel, "Die Quellen der asterisierten Zusätze im zweiten Tabernakelbericht Exod 35–40," in *Studien zur Septuaginta: Robert Hanhart zu Ehren: Aus Anlass seines 65. Geburtstages* (eds. D. Fraenkel, U. Quast, and J.W. Wevers; MSU 20; Göttingen: Vandenhoeck & Ruprecht, 1990), 140–86. Wevers notes that if Fraenkel is correct, then we must account for the incorrect attributions to Theodotion.

2.4.6.4.2 Text Criticism of the Hebrew Bible

The hexaplaric data sometimes points to a Hebrew *Vorlage* different from MT (→ 2.2.2) for Origen or the Three (→ 1.3.1.2). For example, at Num 28:7, for וְנֶסֶךְ "and its drink offering," LXX-Num renders this exactly with καὶ σπονδὴν αὐτοῦ "and its drink offering." Both Aquila and Origen have καὶ εἰς σπονδήν "and for a drink offering" for the first part of the reading. This implies a Hebrew *Vorlage* for Aquila and Origen with an added preposition, that is ולנסכו "and for its drink offering" instead of ונסכו "and its drink offering" since, without Hebrew support, Aquila would be unlikely to add εἰς, and Origen would have no reason to follow Aquila against the Hebrew.[25]

Brooke–McLean, *The Old Testament in Greek*, Vol. 1.1–4.
Burris, K., "A Critical Edition of the Hexaplaric Fragments of Numbers 1–18" (PhD diss., The Southern Baptist Theological Seminary, 2009).
Hyvärinen, K., *Die Übersetzung von Aquila* (ConBOT 10; Uppsala: G.W.K. Gleerup, 1977).
de Lagarde, P., *Bibliothecae syriacae a Paulo de Lagarde collectae quae ad philogiam sacram pertinent* (Göttingen: Dieterich, 1892).
McClurg, A.H., "A Critical Edition of the Hexaplaric Fragments of Numbers 19–36" (PhD diss., The Southern Baptist Theological Seminary, 2011).
Salvesen, A., *Symmachus in the Pentateuch* (JSSSup 15; Manchester: Victoria University of Manchester, 1991).
Swete, H., *Introduction 1900*.
Vööbus, A., *The Pentateuch in the Version of the Syro-Hexapla: A Facsimile Edition of a Midyat Ms. Discovered 1964* (CSCO 369; Leuven: Waversebaan, 1975).
Wevers, J.W. (ed.), *Genesis* (Septuaginta Vetus Testamentum Graecum 1; Göttingen: Vandenhoeck & Ruprecht, 1974).
Wevers, J.W. (ed.), *Deuteronomium* (Septuaginta Vetus Testamentum Graecum 3.2; Göttingen: Vandenhoeck & Ruprecht, 1977).
Wevers, J.W. (ed.), *Numeri* (Septuaginta Vetus Testamentum Graecum 3.1; Göttingen: Vandenhoeck & Ruprecht, 1982).
Wevers, J.W., *Leviticus* (Septuaginta Vetus Testamentum Graecum 2.2; Göttingen: Vandenhoeck & Ruprecht, 1986).
Wevers, J.W., *Exodus* (Septuaginta Vetus Testamentum Graecum 2.1; Göttingen: Vandenhoeck & Ruprecht, 1991).

Andrew McClurg

2.4.7 Post-Hexaplaric Greek Translations

The only post-Hexaplaric recension known to us is that of Lucian. But no scholar has successfully located a Lucianic recension in the Pentateuch. Johannes Dahse concluded that LXX[53, 56, 129] preserved the *L*-text, though a similar, more expansive study by Hautsch demonstrated that no definite trace of the recension existed for the Pentateuch.[1] LXX[53, 56, 129] are designated *fir* in the Larger Cambridge Septuagint,[2] the edition used by Dahse. Subsequent scholarship – most notably the research of Wevers – has confirmed Hautsch's conclusion that there was no such recension.[3] Wevers' conclusions are now the consensus. The absence of a Lucianic recension for the Pentateuch is difficult to explain. Thornhill suggested that the recension once existed, but it was not preferred to Origen's text because of the latter's faithfulness to the Hebrew.[4] Fernández Marcos says that liturgical use worked toward standardization, so that typical Lucianic improvements were unnecessary for the Pentateuch.[5] Wevers has successfully stratified and characterized all the relevant manuscripts in his editions of the books of the Pentateuch for the Göttingen LXX.[6] Therefore, it is unlikely that his con-

---

[25] Wevers agrees with this assessment; see J.W. Wevers, *Text History of the Greek Numbers* (MSU 16; Göttingen: Vandenhoeck & Ruprecht, 1982), 473.

[1] Dahse, "Zum Luciantext der Genesis," 281–87; Hautsch, "Der Lukiantext des Oktateuchs," 518–43.
[2] Brooke–McLean, *The Old Testament in Greek*.
[3] Wevers, "Lucianic Recension," 34–35. Wevers demonstrates that Dahse's methodology was flawed (p. 23).
[4] Thornhill, "Six or Seven Nations," 240.
[5] Fernández Marcos, "Some Reflections," 221.
[6] J.W. Wevers, *Genesis* (Septuaginta Vetus Testamentum Graecum 1; Göttingen: Vandenhoeck & Ruprecht, 1974); J.W. Wevers, *Exodus* (Septuaginta Vetus Testamentum Graecum 2.1; Göttingen: Vandenhoeck & Ruprecht, 1991); J.W. Wevers, *Leviticus* (Septuaginta Vetus Testamentum Graecum 2.2; Göttingen: Vandenhoeck & Ruprecht, 1986); J.W. Wevers, *Numeri* (Septuaginta Vetus Testamentum Graecum 3.1;

clusions will be disproven without the addition of new evidence.

Dahse, J., "Zum Luciantext der Genesis," *ZAW* 28 (1910): 281–87.
Fernández Marcos, N., "Some Reflections on the Antiochian Text of the Septuagint," in *Studien zur Septuaginta: Robert Hanhart zu Ehren* (eds. D. Fraenkel, U. Quast, and J.W. Wevers; MSU 20; Göttingen: Vandenhoeck & Ruprecht, 1990), 219–29.
Hautsch, E., "Der Lukiantext des Oktateuchs," in *Mitteilungen des Septuaginta-Unternehmens der königlichen Gesellschaft der Wissenschaften zu Göttingen* (Berlin: Weidmannsche Buchhandlung, 1909), 1:518–43.
Thornhill, R., "Six or Seven Nations: A Pointer to the Lucianic Text in the Heptateuch, with Special Reference to the Old Latin Version," *JTS* 10 (1959): 236–46.
Wevers, J.W., "A Lucianic Recension in Genesis?" *BIOSCS* 6 (1973): 22–35.

Matthew M. Dickie

2.4.8 Vulgate

2.4.8.1 Background

"I have finally finished the Pentateuch of Moses, and feel as if I have been liberated from an immense interest charge." So Jerome describes his translation of the Pentateuch, the pinnacle of his achievement as a translator. Begun some time after 398 C.E. and completed by 403/404 C.E., the translation reflects every dimension of Jerome's mature skills as a translator (→ 1.3.5.2).[1] Yet, these different dimensions, employed unsystematically in various combinations, complicate the text-critical value of V-Pentateuch. Nevertheless, V-Pentateuch is a rich resource for Septuagintal traditions, Latin Christian culture, and rabbinic exegesis, provided that the reader of Jerome's version expends an effort similar to the one invested by Jerome.

2.4.8.2 Translation Character

Although Jerome's prefaces to the Vulgate indicate that he conceptualized the Pentateuch as a unit, the translation defies universal characterization, varying from un-Latin Hebraisms to free renditions close to idiomatic Latin and sometimes incorporating exegetical traditions. Sparks summarizes nicely: "Jerome in practice translated very much as he happened himself to feel at any particular moment."[2] Nevertheless, he is not so mercurial as to lack discernible principles. Compared to the Old Latin (→ 1.4.1) and other books in the Vulgate, V-Pentateuch is a more expansive translation. Especially, Jerome incorporates exegetical traditions and enhances the Latin style through the Latinization of Hebrew idioms, the replacement of biblical parataxis with coordinate and subordinate clauses, the utilization of Late Antique Latin terminology, and variation. In all of this he applies a refined Hexaplaric method in terms of sources, rendering the Hebrew by weighing LXX (→ 1.3.1.1), Aquila, Symmachus, Theodotion (→ 1.3.1.2), and the Old Latin, together with Jewish traditions and concerns of Latin style.[3] This complicates the reconstruction of Jerome's *Vorlage*, thereby lessening the usefulness of the Vulgate for textual criticism of the Hebrew Bible. The transliterations of Hebrew and Greek, however, can be helpful.

2.4.8.3 Translation Technique
2.4.8.3.1 Relationship to the Hebrew Tradition
Jerome describes his work as a translation *iuxta Hebraeos* "according to the Hebrews" and as *He-*

Göttingen: Vandenhoeck & Ruprecht, 1982); J.W. Wevers, *Deuteronomium* (2nd ed.; Septuaginta Vetus Testamentum Graecum 3.2; Göttingen: Vandenhoeck & Ruprecht, 2006).

[1] In *Epist.* 71.5 (398), Jerome mentions that only the Octateuch remained untranslated, while the *Pref. Josh.* describes the Pentateuch as finally being completed and also alludes to the death of Paula (January 26, 404 C.E.). See Kelly, *Jerome*, 283–84, and Kedar-Kopfstein, "The Latin Translations," 320–21.

[2] Sparks, "Jerome as Biblical Scholar," 526.

[3] In his *Pref. Pent.*, for example, Jerome compares himself to the LXX translators, who, according to the more accurate version of LXX origins given by Aristeas and Josephus, consulted with each other (*contulisse ... non prophetasse* "comparing ... not prophecying"). The use of sources is proper for translation, and a good translator requires "learning" (*eruditio*) and eloquence (*verborum copia* "multitude of words"). Kamesar's characterization of *Qu. hebr. Gen.* as *recentiores*-rabbinic philology applies to V-Pentateuch as well (Kamesar, *Jerome, Greek Scholarship, and the Hebrew Bible*, 190–91).

braica veritas "Hebrew truth." The precise meanings of these terms are unclear, but the Hebraisms and influence of Jewish interpretation in the Pentateuch must be related to this general description.[4]

2.4.8.3.2 Literalisms and Transliterations

Examples of Hebraisms include: proper names not declined, such as אָדָם/*Adam* (Gen 2:19) and אַהֲרֹן/*Aaron* (Exod 4:27) (but note לְוִיִּם/*Levitae* [Num 1:47], *Levitis* [Num 3:49], *Levitas* [Num 3:9], and *Levitarum* [Lev 25:32]); common nouns used figuratively, as in זְרוֹעַ/*brachium* "arm" (*redimam in brachio excelso* "I will redeem you with a high arm"; Exod 6:6), and פִּי־חָרֶב/*os gladii* "mouth of the sword" (*fugavit ... in ore gladii* "And Josue put Amalec and his people to flight, by the mouth of the sword [Douai-Reims Translation, adapted]"; Exod 17:13); Hebraic temporal expressions, e.g., כִּתְמוֹל שִׁלְשׁוֹם/*heri et nudius tertius* "yesterday and the third day ago" (Gen 31:2) for "formerly"; literal renderings of Hebrew used non-literally, as with יָם/*mare* "sea" = "west" (Deut 33:23); literalism with prepositions, such as for Hebrew lamed: וְהָיוּ לְאֹתֹת/*et sint in signa* "and let them be for signs" (Gen 1:14); cardinal for ordinal numbers, e.g., יוֹם אֶחָד/*dies unus* "one day" (Gen 1:5); un-Latin rendering of Hebrew repetitions, such as לְדֹר דֹּר/*in generationem et generatione* "unto generation and generation" (Exod 3:15); infinitive absolute, as in פָּקֹד פָּקַדְתִּי/*visitans visitavi* "visiting I have visited you" (Exod 3:16), and מוֹת יוּמָת/*morte moriatur* "with death he shall die" (Exod 21:17); causative as *facere* "to do" or *dare* "to give" with infinitive, e.g., וְהִפְרֵתִי/*faciamque ... crescere* "and I will make thee increase" (Gen 17:6), and וְהִשְׁקָה/*dabit ... bibere* "he shall give them her to drink" (Num 5:24, Douai-Reims Translation); indefinite subjects rendered literally (normally passive in Latin): עַל־כֵּן קָרָא לַבְּאֵר/*propterea appellavit puteum illum* "therefore one called that well" (Gen 16:14, Douai-Reims Translation); translation of names, e.g., אֶת־הָאוּרִים וְאֶת־הַתֻּמִּים "the Urim and the Thummim"/*doctrina*

et veritas "doctrine and truth" (Lev 8:8); etymological renderings, as with הַקָּמָה/*stantes segetes* "corn standing" (Exod 22:6, MT 22:5); but cf. *seges* "corn" for קָמָה "grain" in Deut 16:9; 23:26; Hebrew technical terms, such as שַׁבַּת שַׁבָּתוֹן/*sabbati requies* "rest of the sabbath" (Lev 23:3); רְבִיעִת הַהִין/*quarta pars hin* "the fourth part of a hin" (Lev 23:13); and יוֹבֵל/*iobeleus* "jubilee" (Lev 25:10); Hebraic semantics, e.g., מִפָּנֶיךָ/*ante faciem* "before your face" (Exod 34:11), and אֶל־הַמִּדְבָּר/*contra desertum* "towards the desert" (Num 24:1). Jerome often integrates Hebraisms with Latinisms, for example, וַיְמָרְרוּ אֶת־חַיֵּיהֶם/*ad amaritudinem perducebant vitam eorum* "they led their life to bitterness" (Exod 1:14). This Hebraic sounding periphrasis for וַיְמָרְרוּ includes the un-Hebraic abstract *amaritudo*.

2.4.8.3.3 Interpretive Renderings

One of the most interesting features of Jerome's translation of the Pentateuch is the interpretive renderings suggested by the Hebrew text or based on Jewish or Christian exegetical traditions (→ 1.3.5.7). These renderings should be distinguished from Latin stylistic features. A full study of these traditions in the Pentateuch remains a desideratum. Examples include: *quem vocavit Laban tumulus Testis* (יְגַר שָׂהֲדוּתָא) *et Iacob acervum Testimonii* (גַּלְעֵד) *uterque iuxta proprietatem linguae suae* "which Laban called the Tomb of Witness and Jacob the Heap of Testimony, *each according to the character of his own language*" (Gen 31:47), with the addition (in *italics*) accounting for both the Aramaic and Hebrew terms for the location; עֲנָה אֲשֶׁר מָצָא אֶת־הַיֵּמִם בַּמִּדְבָּר/*Ana qui invenit aquas calidas in solitudine* "This is Ana that found the *hot* waters in the wilderness" (Gen 36:24, Douai-Reims Translation), where the addition of *calidus* "hot" reflects a tradition recorded in Jerome's *Hebrew Questions on Genesis*: "Among the Hebrews there are many differing discussions about this verse ... Some [people] think that this word means 'hot waters,' in accord with the ... Carthaginian language which is closely related to Hebrew";[5] וְתָלָה אוֹתְךָ עַל־עֵץ/*ac*

---

[4] For a fuller list of examples, see Plater and White, *A Grammar of the Vulgate*, and Kedar-Kopfstein, "The Vulgate as a Translation."

[5] Translation by Hayward, *Saint Jerome's Hebrew Questions on Genesis*, 74.

suspendet te in cruce "and he will hang you on the cross" (Gen 40:19), using "cross" instead of "wood" as a Christological allusion buttressed by reference to a three-day period (Gen 40:18–20); עַד כִּי־יָבֹא שִׁילֹה וְלוֹ יִקְּהַת עַמִּים/*donec veniat qui mittendus est et ipse erit expectatio gentium* "till he come that is to be sent, and he shall be the expectation of nations" (Gen 49:10 Douai-Reims Translation), where *GenR*. 98.8 has a messianic reading (עד כי יבא שילה זה מלך המשיח "until the arrival of Shiloh i.e. Messiah," Soncino Translation) and Jerome similarly interprets the blessing of Judah Christologically (i.e., on Gen 49:11, *quod videlicet pullum asinae, cui supersedit Iesus* "namely, the foal of the ass on which Jesus sat");[6] and צִפֳּרִים/*passeres* "sparrows" (Lev 14:4), with Jerome oddly rendering the generic Hebrew "birds" with the more specific "sparrows," perhaps influenced by a tradition in *Lev. Rab.* 16:7 referring to these as ציפריא קולנין "noisy birds."[7]

2.4.8.3.4 Relationship to Greek Tradition

Jerome regularly utilizes the Greek Tradition (→ 2.4.1). This includes general transliteration of words, as with *gigantes* "giants" (γίγας, for רְפָאִים, Deut 2:11, 20; 3:13), *papyrione* "papyrus sedge" (πάπυρος, Exod 2:5), *chyrogryllius* "hare" (Lev. 11:5), *ophiomachus* "snake fighter" (Lev 11:22), specifically religious terms, e.g., *azyma* "unleavened bread" (ἄζυμα, Lev 23:6), and even adjectives (e.g., *pythonicus*/πυθόνικος "pythonical," Lev 20:27) and verbs (*gyro*/γυρόω "go round," Gen 30:32). Examples of Greek grammatical influence include the use of Greek inflection (-*n*: *charadrion* "plover," Lev 11:19), and distinctively Greek syntax, e.g., verbs taking the genitive (*dominari* "rule," Num 16:13; *loqui* "speak," Gen 24:7, 30). He regularly draws on LXX, Aquila, Symmachus, or Theodotion (→ 2.4.6). For example, גֵּרָה/*obolos* "obols" (Num 3:47) follows LXX ὀβολοὺς; וַחֲמֻשִׁים/*et armati* "armed" follows Aquila ἐνωπλισμένοι (Exod 13:18); הַקֻּבָּה/*lupanar* "brothel house" follows Symmachus τὸ πορνεῖον

---

[6] Hayward, *Saint Jerome's Hebrew Questions on Genesis*, 84.

[7] Perhaps Jerome is also inspired by Lesbia's notoriously wanton sparrow (*passer*), Catullus' "rival" for her affections from Catullus 2 and 3. Catullus describes the sparrow in 3 as "continually chirping" (*usque pipiabit*).

(Num 25:8); and עַרְלֵי שְׂפָתָיִם/*incircumcisus labiis* "uncircumcised lips" follows Theodotion ἀπερίτμητος τοῖς χείλεσιν (Exod 6:12). Jerome frequently combines versions, as in Exod 11:1: עוֹד נֶגַע אֶחָד אָבִיא עַל־פַּרְעֹה וְעַל־מִצְרַיִם/*adhuc una plaga tangam Pharaonem et Aegyptum* "Yet one plague more will I bring upon Pharaoh and Egypt." Jerome's *plaga* corresponds to LXX (πλαγὴν ἐπάξω ἐπί ...) and VL (*plagam ego induco in* ...), while *tangam* "touch" corresponds to Aquila and Symmachus (ἀφήν). The Greek tradition is often mediated through the Old Latin, but Jerome deviates more from the Old Latin (→ 2.5.1) at least for Genesis and Exodus compared to the Prophets and Writings.[8]

2.4.8.3.5 Christian Latin

Features peculiar to Christian Latin appear throughout the translation. For nouns and adjectives, there are new words and terminations, frequent use of diminutives, new abstracts, concretized abstracts, and abstracts in the plural. Simple nouns not found in Classical Latin include *papilio* "tent" and *sanctuarium* "sanctuary." For a new abstract in -*or*, see לָבָן/*albor* "whiteness" (Lev 13:25). Some concretized abstracts include נַחֲלָתְךָ/*hereditatem* "inheritance" (Deut 9:26), and נִזְרוֹ/*sanctificatio* "sanctification" (Num 6:12). New agents in -*sor* and -*tor* are seen is רֹכְבוֹ/*ascensor* "rider" rather than *eques* (Exod 15:1), and בַּעַל הַחֲלֹמוֹת/*somniator* "dreamer" (Gen 37:19). An example of a new dimunitive is *situla* "bucket" for דְּלָיָו (Num 24:7). For verbs, Jerome uses fuller forms, new words and endings, and employs new prefixes and prepositions with verbs (e.g., יַשְׁקוּ/*adaquare*, "water," Gen 29:2; יְפַתַּח/*desternere* "to unharness," Gen 24:32). He also replaces the classical subjunctive with the infinitive, and uses the present participle freely either independently or with *esse* "to be." Pronouns are often added to strengthen the third person. Adverbs are given with the ending -*ter*, rather than -*e*, and adverbs may be combined with prepositions to produce adverbial or preposi-

---

[8] See Kraus, "Jerome's Translation of the Book of Exodus Iuxta Hebraeos," and Everson, "The 'Vetus Latina' and the Vulgate of the Book of Genesis."

tional phrases. Direct speech is more common, and indirect speech with the infinitive plus accusative becomes less common in the Christian Latin of v-Pentateuch than *quod, quia, quoniam* "that" with the indicative.

2.4.8.3.6 Idiomatic Latin

Especially compared to the Old Latin (→ 2.5.1), v-Pentateuch reflects a tendency toward Classical Latin style. Such renderings, in so far as they represent idiomatic Latin, call attention to the difference between the source language and the target language. The following representative examples reveal Jerome's efforts towards elegant Latin style rather than a non-Masoretic *Vorlage*. First, v-Pentateuch frequently employs idiomatic Latin expressions to avoid Hebraisms. For example, emphasis expressed by repetition in מְעַט מְעַט is rendered as *paulatim atque per partes* "little by little and by degrees" (Deut 7:22); the Hebrew infinitive of purpose may be expressed with the gerundive לְהַשְׁקוֹת/*ad hauriendas aquas* "to draw water" (Exod 2:16); and correlatives may be added, הָאֶזְרָח וְהַגֵּר הַגָּר בְּתוֹכְכֶם/tam *indigena quam colonus qui peregrinatur apud vos* "Neither the native born, nor the stranger who sojourns among you" (Lev 18:26). Particularly un-Hebraic is Jerome's preference for subordination and *variatio* against biblical parataxis and repetition. Jerome introduces subordination in various ways, e.g., with participles וַתֵּרֶא אֹתוֹ כִּי־טוֹב הוּא וַתִּצְפְּנֵהוּ/*et videns eum elegantem abscondit* "and seeing that he was goodly, she hid him" (Exod 2:2, Douai-Reims Translation, adapted), with the ablative absolute תְּרוּעָה/*clangentibus tubis* "with trumpets sounding" (Lev 23:24), and with *cum* clauses, וְלֹא־יָכְלָה עוֹד הַצְּפִינוֹ/*cumque iam celare non posset* "And when she could hide him no longer" (Exod 2:3). Instances where Jerome creates *variatio* are numerous in v-Pentateuch: מִצְעָר... מִצְעָר/*parva ... modica* "little ... scanty" (Gen 19:20); וְטָמֵא טָמֵא/*contaminatum ac sordidum* "defiled and unclean" (Lev 13:45); תְגַלֶּה ... תְגַלֶּה/*revelabis ... discoperies* "uncover ... discover" (Lev 18:15).[9] Second, Jerome introduces distinctively Latin terms and expressions to express Latin idioms. Thus, Jerome employs Latin technical terms, as with פַּת־לֶחֶם "a little bread"/*buccellam panis* "cheekful of bread" (Gen 18:5), זְקֵנִים "old"/*provectae aetatis* "of advanced age" (Gen 18:11), שַׂק "sackcloth"/*cilicium* "goathair shirt" (Gen 37:34),[10] מֹאזְנֵי "balances"/*statera* "balance," הִין/*sextarius* "sextary" (Lev 19:36), and וּשְׂדֵה מִגְרַשׁ עָרֵיהֶם "the open land around their cities"/*suburbana* "suburbs" (Lev 25:34). Examples of distinctively Latin expressions include: חָלִלָה לְּךָ/*absit a te* "Far be it from you" (Gen 18:25); וְכַאֲשֶׁר יְעַנּוּ אֹתוֹ כֵּן יִרְבֶּה "As they oppressed them, so they multiplied" (NRSV, adapted)/*quantoque opprimebant eos tanto magis multiplicabantur* "the more they oppressed them, the more they increased" (Exod 1:12); כְּמַרְאֵה צָרַעַת "which resembles a leprous disease"/*haut dubiae leprae* "not of doubtful leprosy" (Lev 13:43), which employs the figure litotes; and וַיֹּאמֶר/*at ille* "and he said" (Exod 3:5), where direct speech is introduced with *at* and the demonstrative, in keeping with Latin idiom. In terms of verb usage, the mere presence of the subjunctive is a distinctive representation of the Vulgate's Latinity. Particularly noteworthy is the usage *ex alia mente*, as in *videntes filii Dei filias eorum quod essent pulchrae* "the sons of God, seeing that their daughters were beautiful" (Gen 6:2), and *paenituit eum quod hominem fecisset* "He regretted [one can assume] that He had made humankind" (Gen 6:6). An example of an apparent

---

[9] Reuschenbach, "Hieronymus als Übersetzer der Genesis,"

31–50, has collected numerous instances of *variatio* in Genesis, which include variations in the rendering of complete sentences, substantives, adjectives, verbs with the same substantives, numerical expressions, adverbs, prepositions, conjunctions, interjections, particles, and other examples of avoiding monotony. Syntactic and semantic variations include varying elements such as the subject or voice, selective use of participial constructions and other forms of subordination, diversifying numbers and catalogues, alternating between general collective and specific (i.e., *camelos ... de grege* "camels ... from the herd"), and creating variety with concrete and abstract nouns, word order, or two Hebrew words related to the same root (Reuschenbach, "Hieronymus als Übersetzer der Genesis," 50–56).

[10] In addition to denoting a covering used by soldiers and seamen, *cilicia* were also worn by ascetics; see A. Cain, *Jerome's Epitaph on Paula: A Commentary on the* Epitaphium Sanctae Paulae (Oxford: Oxford University Press, 2013), 321.

Latin word play is seen in קַשְׁתִּי/*arcum* "bow" (Gen 9:13) and תֵּבָה/*arca* "ark" (Gen 9:18).

2.4.8.3.7 Clarification

v-Pentateuch may provide a clearer, more specific, or otherwise explained rendering of the Hebrew without implying a non-masoretic *Vorlage*. An addition for the sake of clarification appears at Gen 9:22: *quod cum vidisset Ham pater Chanaan verenda scilicet patris sui esse nuda* "When Cham the father of Chaanan had seen that it, namely the pudenda of his father were uncovered" (עֶרְוַת אָבִיו), where the Hebrew does not have *verenda scilicet* "namely, the pudenda." The Vulgate clarifies the sense of the syntax at Lev 13:15: וְרָאָה הַכֹּהֵן אֶת־הַבָּשָׂר הַחַי וְטִמְּאוֹ הַבָּשָׂר הַחַי טָמֵא הוּא צָרַעַת הוּא/*tunc sacerdotis iudicio polluetur et inter inmundos reputabitur caro enim viva si lepra aspergatur inmunda est* "then by the judgement of the priest he will be in a state of defilement and will be considered among the impure, for living flesh is impure if besprinkled with leprosy," with the addition of "for" and "if" providing the rationale for impurity. At Lev 21:10, Jerome offers an expanded translation aimed at clarity: וְהַכֹּהֵן הַגָּדוֹל/*Pontifex, id est sacerdos maximus* "The Pontifex [Maximus], that is, the High Priest." Instances where v-Pentateuch exhibits semantic specification include *concilium* "counsel" for דָּבָר "thing, word" (Gen 41:37), *intrinsecus* "within" for בַּיִת "house" (Gen 6:14), and *cogitatio* "thought" for לְבָבֶךָ "your heart" (Deut 18:21) and יֵצֶר "form" (Gen 6:5). At Deut 18:10, מְכַשֵּׁף "sorcerer" is rendered *maleficus* "evil-doer," but rather than assuming that *maleficus* represents a non-MT Hebrew word such as רשע it is more likely that Jerome has expanded the meaning of *maleficus* to include "sorcerer." Jerome handles a sensitive topic through euphemism at Lev 15:13: וְכִי־יִטְהַר הַזָּב מִזּוֹבוֹ "and when the one with a discharge is cleansed of his discharge"/*si sanatus fuerit qui huiuscemodi sustinet passionem* "if one who undergoes such an experience has been healed."

2.4.8.3.8 Intertextuality

Although for the most part Jerome engages directly with the Hebrew text before him and favors *variatio* between related elements, his renderings can reflect intertextual consistency. He shows awareness of his previous translation at Gen 9:6: *ad imaginem quippe Dei factus est homo* "to be sure, man was made in the image of God" with *quippe* "to be sure" referencing Gen 1:27, *ad imaginem dei creavit illum* "in the image of God he created him." Jerome also demonstrates intertextual awareness with *pulmentum* "condiment, food," for נָזִיד "pottage" (Gen 25:29) and מַטְעַמִּים "savoury meat" (Gen 27:4).

2.4.8.4 Text-Critical Value

Scholars have long noted that Jerome refers to the Hebrew text as his primary source (e.g., *fons veritatis*, *Epist.* 20.2). Apparently he would examine the Hebrew to determine its meaning, compare the Hebrew with rabbinic interpretation, consider LXX (→ 1.3.1.1) when in agreement with the Hebrew, and consult other Greek sources, especially Symmachus (→ 1.3.5.10).[11] Despite his reliance on sources, there is always an independent element in his translation, because typically he only agrees with a given source for a short clause and then goes a different direction, perhaps even following another source.[12] As time went on, Jerome became more independent of his Greek sources. Thus, he increased his reliance on the Hebrew compared to the Greek tradition when translating the Pentateuch, as in the case of *hapax legomena* proper nouns in Genesis.[13]

Because of Jerome's contact with the Hebrew (→ 1.2.2) and use of earlier sources, v-Pentateuch has some value for textual criticism of the Hebrew Bible (→ 1.3.5.11). To be sure, the biblical texts from the Dead Sea Scrolls have diminished the text-critical value of the Vulgate.[14] Nonetheless, this does not eliminate the text-critical value of v-Pentateuch altogether, especially when the Vulgate agrees with the Dead Sea Scrolls. Recognizing that Jerome carefully translated the Hebrew, we must

---

[11] *Pref. Eccl.* 1. Cf. Kedar-Kopfstein, "The Latin Translations," 323, and Salvesen, *Symmachus in the Pentateuch*.

[12] Kedar-Kopfstein, "The Latin Translations," 323.

[13] D.L. Everson, "The 'Vetus Latina' and the Vulgate of the Book of Genesis," 523–26.

[14] As Tov, *TCHB*, 15, has correctly noted.

isolate the various influences on his translation before positing text-critical information. For example, in Lev 13:56–57, after accounting for the numerous deviations from the Hebrew through Jerome's translation technique, a possible variant can be found. Much of the Latin for these verses could be read as interpretive and stylistic, for example, *obscurior* "somewhat dark" for כֵּהָה "dim"; *locus leprae* "place of leprosy" for הַנֶּגַע "plague, wound"; *abrumpet … et … dividet* "tear off … and … separate from" for מִן ... וְקָרַע "tear from"; *volatilis et vaga* "flying and roaming" for פָּרַחַת "breaking out"; *debet … conburi* "ought … to be burned" for תִּשְׂרְפֶנּוּ "you should burn it." The translations *a solido* "from what is sound" for מִן־הַבֶּגֶד אוֹ מִן־הָעוֹר אוֹ מִן־הַשְּׁתִי אוֹ מִן־הָעֵרֶב "from the garment, or from the skin, or from the warp or from the woof," and also *in his locis quae prius inmaculat erant* "in those places that previously were unblemished" for בַּבֶּגֶד אוֹ־בַשְּׁתִי אוֹ־בָעֵרֶב אוֹ בְכָל־כְּלִי־עוֹר "in the garment, either in the warp or in the woof, or in any article of skin," are summative. Yet, the absence of any equivalent in the Latin for רָאָה הַכֹּהֵן "the priest looked" is best explained by positing a different Hebrew *Vorlage*, perhaps due to haplography (cf. the following וְהִנֵּה כֵּהָה).

2.4.8.4.1 Consonantal Text

Only occasionally does v-Pentateuch witness to a consonantal Hebrew text different from MT (→ 2.2.2).[15] The most important text-critical role for v is supporting another reading. For example, at Gen 3:17, v has *in opere tuo*, "in your work" (presuming בעבדך) for MT בַּעֲבוּרֶךָ "on account of you," which matches LXX (→ 2.4.1.1). The Hebrew text underlying the Vulgate is very close to MT, and so variants found in v will usually be minor, such as the confusion of similar consonants (e.g., MT רְעוּאֵל "Reuel" v *Duhel* presuming דעואל "Deuel," Num 2:14). A more complex possible variant is *in locum suum* "to their own place" for MT וַיֵּלְכוּ מֵאִתּוֹ "and they departed from him" (Gen 26:31), presupposing a Hebrew *Vorlage* למקומו. For an example of a sizeable difference between MT and v, see Gen 49:32 (MT) that is entirely omitted from v.

2.4.8.4.2 Vocalization and *Ketiv/Qere*

Differences between MT and the Vulgate in terms of vocalization are not uncommon. For example, for MT-Lev 25:33 וַאֲשֶׁר יִגְאַל מִן־הַלְוִיִּם "and whatever some from among the Levites redeems" is translated by v as *si redemptae non fuerint* "If they be not redeemed," which presupposes vocalizing the verb as a *Nifal* plural. As for v-Pentateuch and *Ketiv/Qere* readings: v follows *Ketiv* with LXX thirteen times (Gen 8:17; 30:11; 36:5, 14; 39:20; Exod 16:2, 7; 27:8; 39:4; Num 1:16; 16:11; 26:9; 32:7), and follows *Ketiv* not with LXX once (Num 21:32). v follows *Qere* with LXX eleven times (Gen 14:2, 8; 25:23; Exod 4:2; 21:8; Lev 11:21; Deut 5:10; 21:7; 28:27; 29:23 [MT 29:22]; 32:13), and follows *Qere* not with LXX six times (Gen 24:33; Lev 21:5; Num 14:36; 34:4; Deut 28:30; 33:2). v may reflect either *Qere* or *Ketiv* once וְצוּדָה לִי צֵידָה/צַיִד/*cumque venatu aliquid adprehenderis* "and when you have caught something by hunting" (Gen 27:3). In one instance (Lev 25:30), the *Ketiv/Qere* phrase is not rendered (LXX follows the *Qere*).

Cain, A., *Jerome's Epitaph on Paula: A Commentary on the Epitaphium Sanctae Paulae* (Oxford: Oxford University Press, 2013).
Everson, D.L., "The 'Vetus Latina' and the Vulgate of the Book of Genesis," in *The Book of Genesis: Composition, Reception, and Interpretation* (eds. C.A. Evans, J.N. Lohr, and D.L. Petersen; VTSup 152; Leiden: Brill, 2012), 519–36.
Hayward, C.T.R., *Saint Jerome's Hebrew Questions on Genesis: Translated with Introduction and Commentary* (Oxford: Clarendon, 1995).
Kamesar, A., *Jerome, Greek Scholarship, and the Hebrew Bible: A Study of the Quaestiones Hebraicae in Genesim* (Oxford: Clarendon, 1993).
Kedar-Kopfstein, B., "The Latin Translations," in Mulder, *Mikra, 299–338.
Kedar-Kopfstein, B., "The Vulgate as a Translation" (PhD diss., Hebrew University of Jerusalem, 1968).
Kelly, J.N.D., *Jerome: His Life, Writings, and Controversies* (London: Gerald Duckworth & Co., 1975).

---

[15] As noted by Kedar-Kopfstein, "The Latin Translations," 322. Jerome comments on the variant Hebrew reading of *Efran/Efron* in *Qu. hebr. Gen.* 23:16–17.

Kraus, M.A., "Jerome's Translation of the Book of Exodus Iuxta Hebraeos in Relation to Classical, Christian, and Jewish Traditions of Interpretation" (PhD diss., University of Michigan, Ann Arbor, Department of Classics, 1996).

Nowack, W., *Die Bedeutung des Hieronymus für die alttestamentliche Textkritik* (Göttingen: Vandenhoeck & Ruprecht, 1875).

Plater, W.E. and H.J. White, *A Grammar of the Vulgate* (Oxford: Clarendon, 1926).

Reuschenbach, D.F., "Hieronymus als Übersetzer der Genesis" (ThD diss., Universität Freiburg [Switzerland], 1942).

Rubio, G., "Semitic Influence in the History of Latin Syntax," in *New Perspectives on Historical Latin Syntax*, Vol. 1: *Syntax of the Sentence* (eds. P. Baldi and P. Cuzzolin; Trends in Linguistics 180.1; Berlin: Walter de Gruyter, 2009), 195–239.

Salvesen, A., *Symmachus in the Pentateuch* (JSS Monograph 15; Manchester: University of Manchester, 1991).

Sparks, H.F.D., "Jerome as Biblical Scholar," in *The Cambridge History of the Bible*, Vol. 1: *From the Beginnings to Jerome* (eds. P.R. Ackroyd and C.F. Evans; Cambridge: Cambridge University Press, 1975), 510–41.

Stummer, F., *Einführung in die lateinische Bibel* (Paderborn: Schöningh, 1928).

Tov, *TCHB*.

Weber, R. and R. Gryson (eds.), *Biblia Sacra iuxta vulgatam versionem* (5th ed.; Stuttgart: Deutsche Bibelgesellschaft, 2007).

Matthew Kraus

2.4.9 Arabic Translations

Primary translations of the Pentateuch into Arabic that were based on MT (→ 2.2.2) and produced in medieval times have so far only been found among Jews and Samaritans. In pre-modern contexts, various translation enterprises, such as that of Aḥmad Fāris al-Shidyāq (Psalter: 1850; New Testament: 1851) or Eli Smith and Cornelius van Dyck (entire Bible, 1860–1865), both serving missionary purposes, take MT as their point of departure. Jewish communities began producing written Arabic translations of their Bible about a century later than the Christians, sometime in the mid-ninth century C.E. In so doing, the Jews were responding, like the Christians, to the socio-linguistic development that created a growing need for the translating of Scripture (and sometimes also Jewish rabbinic sources) into Arabic; for further reading and details on this development, see → 1.3.6.

With regard to Judeo-Arabic versions, it is generally accepted that they can be divided into three periods: 1) early, formative (ninth–eleventh centuries); 2) classic (tenth–fourteenth centuries), spearheaded by Saadia Gaon's (882–942 C.E.) translation, known as *Tafsīr*, and those of Karaite provenance; and 3) late, early-modern (fifteenth–nineteenth centuries). According to some scholars, the early period is governed by a transition from Aramaic to Judeo-Arabic and the respective functions of Aramaic Targumim in a Judeo-Arabic garb.[1] The early translations and Saadia's *Tafsīr* coexisted for a certain period, and it is generally accepted that the composition of the *Tafsīr* had a catalyzing effect on the evolving process of committing hitherto oral, locally bound Judeo-Arabic translations to writing (→ 1.3.6). When Saadia, in assertion of his authority as gaon (see below), produced a Judeo-Arabic version of the Pentateuch, his translation gradually became recognized as part of the literary canon and general repertoire of rabbinic culture under the leadership of the gaonim (i.e., the renowned scholarly leaders of the Babylonian *yeshivot* (academies) whose rulings influenced most of the Jewish communities until the twelfth century). However, this likewise may have given rise to the parallel textualization of earlier translations, a process that was fostered by a general tendency to write down oral traditions from the rise of the Abbasid caliphate onwards. Nevertheless, it was Saadia's version that was widely copied and produced during the following centuries, at least for Rabbanite communities. The vast majority of Judeo-Arabic translations were written in Hebrew characters. However, certain communities possessed copies of Saadia's *Tafsīr* in Arabic

---

[1] Blau, "On a Fragment of the Oldest Judaeo-Arabic Bible Translation Extant."

letters, and some Jewish Karaite translations (see further below) were also produced in Arabic characters.

As to the Samaritans (→ 1.3.6.6), various Arabic translations were in use, in Samaritan and Arabic characters. Christians mostly translated from non-Hebrew *Vorlagen* (i.e., Greek, Syriac, Coptic, etc.), also using Arabic characters (→ 1.4.11).

2.4.9.1 Jewish Translations
2.4.9.1.1 Early Non-Saadianic Traditions

Early non-Saadianic translations (→ 1.3.6.2) have increasingly attracted the attention of scholars over the last decades. The extant portions appear to cover most of the Torah.[2] A rudimentary, embryonic stage of translations – as pointed out by Blau and Hopkins[3] and Polliack[4] – can be identified in early glossaries (known in Arabic by the term *tafsīr alfāẓ*). Several intermediary stages prior to becoming running translations are found in the Genizah corpus. For example, a number of glossaries were composed in such a detailed way that almost every word in a verse was translated.[5] One fragment changes deliberately from glossary to continuous translation.[6] Further, some fragments provide only selected portions, such as a translation of biblical songs.[7]

The fragments within the category of early non-Saadianic translations defy generalization, both in language and translation technique. Their only common denominator lies in the fact that they appear to be early and differ from Saadia's *Tafsīr*. As diverse as the translations may be, they nevertheless share certain characteristics that stand out mainly in comparison to the *Tafsīr*. Two main features provide evidence of their old age and allow for an early dating: First, most of these translations appear on parchment. Secondly, they were composed in a conspicuous orthography that is reminiscent of a larger group of papyrus fragments (hence predating the ninth century) written in Early Phonetic Judeo-Arabic Script (EPJAS). In contrast to Classic Judeo-Arabic Script (CJAS), EPJAS transcribes the phonetic realization of Arabic using only Hebrew and Aramaic orthographic conventions.[8] Some of the fragments clearly belong to the ninth or tenth century, based on a combination of both dating criteria. They exhibit EPJAS in its pure form and their codicology and paleography appear to belong to the earliest stratum of Genizah fragments. However, many fragments, and for the Pentateuch the vast majority, were produced later and also on paper, until they eventually dropped out of use around the eleventh century. Their orthography consists in a transitional semi-EPJAS, which shows heavy influence of CJAS. According to Blau and Hopkins, this occurred due to the success of Saadia's Pentateuch translation.[9] However, Tobi considers that the early non-Saadianic translations of the Pentateuch continued to flourish among different Jewish communities, even if not as widely attested as Saadia's version in the classical Genizah corpus, since some of their lexical and syntactic features re-emerge in post-Saadianic Jewish translations of the Pentateuch, particularly from the fourteenth century. These early non-Saadianic

---

[2] See Vollandt, *Arabic Versions of the Pentateuch*, 75–80, and Vollandt, "Whether to Capture Form or Meaning." The first fragment, Cambridge, CUL, T-S Ar. 53.8, was discovered by Blau, who presented an edition and discussion in Blau, "On a Fragment." Additional fragments were identified in Baker and Polliack, *Catalogue* and in Polliack, "Arabic Bible Translations." The finding of additional fragments has been announced and a study of their possible *Vorlage* was furnished by Hopkins, "On the Vorlage." Tobi published a wide range of fragments covering portions of the Pentateuch.

[3] Blau and Hopkins, "Ancient Bible Translations to Judeo-Arabic"; Blau and Hopkins, "The Beginnings of Judaeo-Arabic Bible Exegesis."

[4] Polliack, "Arabic Bible Translations in the Cairo Genizah Collections"; Polliack, "Types of Arabic Bible Translation in the Cairo Geniza."

[5] Polliack and Somekh, "Two Hebrew-Arabic Biblical Glossaries."

[6] As, e.g., Cambridge, CUL, T-S Ar. 28.170, belonging with Cambridge, CUL, T-S Ar. 27.60.

[7] E.g. Cambridge, CUL, T-S Ar. 1a.4, containing portions of the Song of Moses and the *Ha'azinu*. The early provenance of that fragment is also attested by the pure Early Phonetic Judeo-Arabic Script (see below) that it exhibits.

[8] Blau and Hopkins, "Judaeo-Arabic Papyri"; Blau and Hopkins, "On Early Judaeo-Arabic Orthography."

[9] For example, the fragment Cambridge, CUL, T-S Ar. 28.168, published in Tobi, "Pre-Sa'adianic Arabic Translation," is duly attributed by its editor to the late tenth/early eleventh century.

traditions complement our picture of the Jewish translation enterprise prior to and contemporary with Saadia, which as we can now ascertain was far more colorful and multifaceted than previously believed.

Another outstanding feature of early non-Saadianic translations is their translation technique, which is first and foremost characterized by a high degree of literalism that attempts to mirror the Hebrew text in its formal structure. The translators' strategy is largely governed by an initial decision to adjust the translation to literary and linguistic norms of the source language, notwithstanding the requirements of the target language. This is achieved by imitative tendencies on the syntactic, lexical, and even morphological level. On the syntactic level, the imitativeness is clearly manifest in the mirroring of the Hebrew word order irrespective of Classical Arabic rules. The result is a strict word-for-word, if not morpheme-for-morpheme, translation. Gen 37:8, as found in manuscript Oxford, Bodleian Library, Heb. c. 19.21ᵛ, provides a telling example.

> JPS: And his brethren said to him: 'Shalt thou indeed reign over us? or shalt thou indeed have dominion over us?'
>
> Hebr.: וַיֹּאמְרוּ לוֹ, אֶחָיו, הֲמָלֹךְ תִּמְלֹךְ עָלֵינוּ, אִם-מָשׁוֹל תִּמְשֹׁל בָּנוּ
> And said to him his brethren will a reign you reign over us? Or will a ruling you rule over us?
>
> Arab: wa-qālū lahu ikhwatuhu immā mulk tamliku ʿalaynā wa-immā tasalluṭ tatasallaṭ bināʰ¹⁰
> And said to him his brethren will a reign you reign over us? Or will a ruling you rule over us?

The Arabic closely reflects the Hebrew word order and for each textual unit an equivalent is given. Parsed, the sentence would appear in both Hebrew and Arabic, as follows: conjunction, verb (impf. third per. pl.), preposition (third per. masc. sg.), subject (masc. pl. + suffix third per. masc. sg.), interrogative particle, infinitive absolute, verb (2 impf. second per. sg.), preposition (first per. sg.), conjunction, particle, infinitive absolute, verb (2 impf. second per. sg.), preposition (first per. sg.). Worthy of note is the repeated mirroring of the infinitive absolute, which serves as an intensifier in Hebrew by its kindred form in Arabic, the inner object (Arab. *mafʿūl muṭlaq*).

In lexicons, this is realized by means of employing cognate homophones or pseudo-cognate roots. Hence, a Hebrew word is often found rendered by its etymologic Arabic equivalent, such as in Arabic *zarʿ* "seed" for Hebrew זרע "seed, offspring" or Arabic *bashar* "skin" for Hebrew בשר "skin, flesh", even if the lexemes are not exactly synonymous in both languages. Also it seems that it was considered essential to retain an homophonic correspondence to the Hebrew text. Certain translations are used mainly, or even solely, due to their phonetic resemblance to the *Vorlage*, as illustrated by *li-iḥāza* "in order to take possession of" (derived from the root *ḥwz*), as a translation of לאחזה "for a possession" (derived from 'ḥz). This homophony is occasionally created by means of employing non-cognate roots, which nonetheless share at least two radicals. At times, early non-Saadianic translations produce artificial Arabic words, such as borrowing *al-adama* for Hebr. האדמה "earth, ground." The word is not attested in Arabic lexicography in this meaning, but serves as a *calque*. Furthermore, the Hebrew object marker את is commonly found translated in Arabic as *iyyā*, e.g., את השמים as *iyyā al-samā* "the heaven," or אתך as *iyyāka* "you." This usage is alien to Classical Arabic.¹¹ Further, under the influence of the unchangeable Hebrew relative pronoun אשר, the Classical Arabic *alladhī* is largely used regardless of the number and gender to which it refers.

However, despite their literalness, these translations contain limited textual expansions that are of two types: first, they consist of strings of alterna-

---

¹⁰ The romanization of Arabic does not in all instances reflect the Judaeo-Arabic accurately. One finds many cases of deviation from Classical Arabic towards a more Neo-Arabic pronunciation. Case endings are usually dropped and the *imāla* is quite common. However, for the sake of the general readership I adhere to the received academic transliteration conventions.

¹¹ For a discussion of *iyyā* and related forms as a translation of Hebrew את, see Doron, לדרכי התרגום.

tive renderings.¹² These alternatives are made up of one, two, or even three synonymous Arabic words representing one word in the Hebrew text. They may be found introduced by the formulas *qīla* or *wa-yuqāl* "and as has been/is said" (as is later found especially in the Karaite sources), but usually occur without indication in the early non-Saadianic translations. For example, וילכדה "and he captured it" is rendered as *wa-ʿalaqahu wa-ẓafirahu* "he captured it (Gilad) *and* he seized it" (Num 32:39), reflecting different nuances of MT.¹³ The second type consists of interpretative additions in the form of a word, phrase, or sentence. These additions provide a clearer understanding of the translated verse and may allude to rabbinic interpretation or targumic readings. T-S Ar. 28.168, fol 1ʳ, in Gen 3:15, adds to the translation of הוּא יְשׁוּפְךָ רֹאשׁ "and he shall bruise you on the head" as *huwwa yushaddikhak raʾs* "and he will crush you the head" the explanatory gloss *ayy yushaddikh minaka al-raʾs* "i.e. what he will crush of you is the head." The exegetic problem alluded to here is how to reconcile the two objects, one direct and one indirect.

Early non-Saadianic translations are anonymous. However, the translation technique suggests that they were used in a didactic context. At least one fragment, manuscript London, BL Or. 5562.A, fol. 2ʳ, refers to the *mutarjimūn* "translators," those professionals in charge of transmitting the *tarjama*, Arab. "translation."¹⁴ It appears that this appellation also expresses that the *mutarjimūn* perceived their occupation to be a continuation of the Aramaic *meturgeman*, as indicated in the gaonic *responsa*.¹⁵

2.4.9.1.2 Saadia Gaon's *Tafsīr*

Saadia Gaon (882–942 C.E.), born in Egypt and later Gaon of Sura, was the most pre-eminent Rabbanite scholar of the tenth century.¹⁶ His Judeo-Arabic Bible translation is one of the most influential texts produced in that language. The *Tafsīr* could be found everywhere throughout the communities in the Near East, North Africa, and Muslim Spain, which attests to the fact that it acquired an authoritative, almost canonical, status among all Arabic-speaking Rabbanite communities.

Concerning the number of books he rendered into Arabic, it appears that Saadia did not translate the entire Hebrew Bible, although some scholars maintain that he may have attempted to do so. The extant sources and book lists from the Cairo Genizah testify to the fact that Saadia produced Arabic translations of the entire Pentateuch and the books of Isaiah (→ 6–9.1.8.1), Psalms (→ 10.3.8.1), Job (→ 11.3.8.1), Proverbs (→ 12.3.8.2), Lamentations (→ 13–17.1.8.5), Esther (→ 13–17.1.8.6), and Daniel (→ 18.3.7).¹⁷ In most books apart from the Pentateuch, the translations are followed by his commentaries, which usually bear a programmatic title and open with an introduction that explains the purposes of the biblical book. In most surviving manuscripts, the translation unit consists of several verses followed by the commentary. The textual unit of the translation roughly equals that of the commentary in quantity. However, for the Pentateuch, in some manuscripts only the translation has survived, appearing as a continuous text, completely separated from the commentary. In other manuscripts, each biblical verse is followed by a

---

¹² The phenomenon of alternative translations was discussed extensively by Polliack, "Alternative Renderings" and Polliack, *The Karaite Tradition*, 181–99, in respect of the Karaite Arabic versions of the Pentateuch (see further below).

¹³ T-S Ar. 1a.152, fol. 2ʳ.

¹⁴ Partly published by Tobi, רגומי שמות עצם פרטיים. It appears that the attribution of the fragment to the traditions published by him earlier should be reconsidered. The fragment belongs with manuscript Cambridge, Westminster College, Arabica I.120 and seems to exhibit an independent tradition.

¹⁵ On the *responsum* by Natronai Gaon on the question of whether the abandonment of the targumic recital in favor of the Arabic one is permitted or not, see Ben-Shammai, "The Tension."

¹⁶ Ben-Shammai, *Mifʿalo shel manhig* and Brody, *Saʿadyah Gaon*.

¹⁷ The Arabic version of Qohelet, which has been transmitted in Saadia's name among the Yemenites, is in fact the work of the eleventh century Andalusian Rabbanite scholar Isaac Ibn Giyyāt (→ 13–17.1.8.4.1). Also, Qafih's attribution to Saadia of a translation on Canticles is debatable (13–17.1.8.3). It is not mentioned in Ibn Nadīm's *Fihrist*, the *Fihrist* that Saadia's sons composed (cf. Mann, "A Fihrist" and Poznanski, "A Fihrist"), or in book lists from the Cairo Genizah (→ 1.3.6).

lengthy commentary (sometimes called "the long commentary" or "the long *Tafsīr*").[18] This arrangement was directed to a scholarly audience and prevented the text from serving a broader, less scholarly public. In the preface of the short *Tafsīr*, he gives clear evidence that he was asked to separate the plain text of the Pentateuch (Arab. *basīṭ naṣṣ al-tawrāh*) into a separate book (Arab. *fī kitāb mufrad*), which would not contain long exegetical discussions. In response to popular demand, then, Saadia may have separated the translation itself (the short *Tafsīr*) from the commentary.[19] As is so often the case, the creation of the shorter work caused the near extinction of the longer original. The commentary, in contrast to the wide diffusion of the translation, fell into oblivion and ceased to be copied. Already in the Genizah corpus, the proportion of fragments containing the commentary is comparably modest.

Saadia's strategy in translating is opposed to that of the early non-Saadianic traditions (→ 2.4.9.1.1) and may be regarded as a direct reaction to them. It nevertheless seems obvious that he was dependent on and partly influenced by earlier Jewish Arabic and Christian Arabic translation conventions. For example, the practice of employing an Arabic rendering solely due to a phonetic resemblance to the Hebrew source text is shared by early non-Saadianic versions and the *Tafsīr*.[20] Moreover, a certain resemblance in lexicon may be observed.[21]

On the other hand, his translation deliberately attempts to depart from earlier traditions. The longer preface to the *Tafsīr* furnishes indirect evidence that he discarded them as inappropriate.[22] It has also been stressed by some scholars that his reservations were prompted by an apologetic motivation.[23]

According to the introduction to his translation of the Pentateuch, the biblical source text should not be conveyed as a translational mirror, but is rather to be made intelligible in accordance with Halakhic practices and rationalistic hermeneutic implications and Halakhic practices (i.e., rabbinic oral law). Saadia's version thus reflects a semantic-communicative approach in translation. This explains the freedom he takes in purposely changing the formal structure of the Hebrew source text, e.g., in omitting repetitive elements, condensing the narrative, and providing referential links through the insertion of temporal conjunctions in his rendition. For example, the paratactic description of God's creation in Genesis 1, which consists of a string of coordinate clauses conjoined by the Hebrew conjunction *waw*, is rendered in his translation as a distinctively temporal succession. This is achieved by means of adding cohesive, subordinating elements to the narrative, such as *faʿ-lammā ... faʿala ...* "And when (he completed a certain act in creation) ... he did ..." In this manner, the ambivalent poetic nature of biblical pratactic style is interpreted by Saadia in a manner akin to Arabic syntax, which also limits the possibilities of understanding engendered by the Hebrew text.

Saadia's attempt to convey what he sees as the underlying meaning of the Torah is amply reflected in the many interpretative features of his Ara-

---

[18] Large parts of his commentary on Genesis 1–24 have been edited by Zucker, *Saadya's Commentary on Genesis*. For additional fragments of Saadia's commentary on portions of the Pentateuch, see Ratzabi, פירושי רבינו סעדיה גאון לספר שמות; Zucker, "Fragments from Rav Saadya Gaon's Commentary"; and Leeven, *Saadya's Lost Commentary on Leviticus*. It seems that the other books where completed by Aaron Sarjado and Samuel b. Hofni.

[19] On the question of whether there is a significant difference between the translation unit found in the longer *Tafsir* and the "separated" short *Tafsir*, see Ben-Shammai, "Extra-Textual Considerations" and Ben-Shammai, "An 'East Wind'." Tamar Zvi is engaged in collating the Genizah materials relating to Saadia's *Tafsīr*, and it is likely that her research will answer this question.

[20] See Ratzabi, *A Dictionary*, 146–49.

[21] See Blau, "On a Fragment" for details. Concordance with Saadia is treated in Tobi's editions (cf. the bibliography), esp.

Tobi, "Pre-Saadianic Arabic Translation," 112, and in Polliack and Somekh, "Two Hebrew-Arabic Biblical Glossaries."

[22] Compare Ben-Shammai, "New and Old."

[23] Schmiedl, "Randbemerkungen"; Rippin, "Saʿadya Gaon and Genesis 22"; Freidenreich, "The Use of Islamic Sources" as well as Goldstein, "Saʿadya's *Tafsīr*" in the light of Muslim polemics. That it indeed served apologetic functions is confirmed by a Judeo-Arabic account of the weekly *majlis* by the famous Fatimid vizier of Jewish origin, Yaʿqūb ibn Killis; see M. Cohen and S. Somekh, "In the Court of Yaʿqūb ibn Killis," *JQR* 80 (1990): 283–314.

bic version of the Pentateuch. They are prompted by a certain exegetical difficulty as the following example demonstrates: Exod 23:19, containing one of the elementary Jewish dietary commandments "Thou shalt not boil a kid in its mother's milk" is rendered as "and thou shalt not eat meat with milk" by Saadia, according to rabbinic Halakhic observance, and following Targum Onqelos.[24]

Saadia's approach to translation technique is, therefore, suitably captured in the self-appellation *Tafsīr* (from Arab. *fassara* "to elucidate, to interpret"). The term designates an interpretation, a translation according to the intended meaning. This is likewise its common denotation in Judeo-Arabic exegetical terminology, although in some sources it designates simply "translation."[25] Saadia may have chosen this designation[26] alongside *ikhrāj maʿānī naṣṣal-tawrah* "an edition/explication of the meanings of the text of the Torah," in order to dissociate or differentiate his version of the Pentateuch from earlier or other Arabic Bible traditions and their translation technique.

2.4.9.1.3 Karaite Translations

The Karaite movement created an independent translation tradition of the Hebrew Bible, whose specific expression for the Pentateuch has been analyzed extensively by Polliack.[27] It has been shown that the Karaite translators – who did not accept Saadia's *Tafsīr* – followed an approach similar to that of the early non-Saadianic Jewish translations and refined it according to their needs. Before engaging in the composition of continuous translations, early Karaites concentrated on glossography. Daniel al-Qūmisī (second half of the ninth century) used Judeo-Arabic glosses in his Hebrew commentary on the Minor Prophets.[28] Yūsuf ibn Nūḥ's *Diqduq* (late tenth/early eleventh century) developed the method of continuous biblical glossary, and although focusing on grammatical explanations, supplies occasional translation glosses as well.[29] Similarly, Judeo-Arabic glosses are found in the Abū Faraj Hārūn's abridgement (*talkhīs*) of Yūsuf ibn Nūḥ's exegetical and linguistic commentary on the Torah.[30] He is also known to have produced a proper glossary of the Bible.[31] Abū Yūsuf Yaʿqub al-Qirqisānī also uses occasional translation glosses in his biblical commentaries and is reported to have written an entire treatise on translation that has been lost.[32]

The first Karaite to have produced running translations of biblical books was Salmon ben Yerūḥīm, a contemporary of Saadia. His compositions mark a watershed in the employment of Arabic for Karaite exegetical writing that superseded Aramaic and Hebrew, the languages used by his predecessors (e.g., Hebrew in al-Qūmisī's commentaries and Aramaic in Anan's *Sefer Mitzvot*). Salmon himself continued to use Hebrew in his polemical writing. In Salmon's commentaries, we encounter for the first time the tripartite structure that includes the Hebrew of the biblical text (in full verses or as *incipits*), a running Arabic translation, and a lengthy Arabic commentary, similar to manuscripts of Saadia's "long" *Tafsīr*, which as mentioned earlier contains his translation alongside a commentary, either in a verse-by-verse or cluster of verses order. This custom, however, reaches a zenith with Yefet ben ʿElī. In a monumental enterprise, Yefet furnished a translation and commentary of the entire Hebrew Bible.[33] The tenth-century Karaite translation enterprise is also reflected in the surviving translations of David ben

---

[24] For this and further relevant examples of Saadia's alteration tendencies in his Pentateuchal translation, see Polliack, *The Karaite Tradition*, 170–239.

[25] Saadia's use of the term appears to be influenced by its Islamic context; cf. Rippin, "Saʾadya Gaon and Genesis 22"; Wansbrough, "Arabic Rhetoric" and Wansbrough, *Quranic Studies*, 154–55, 233–35.

[26] Goldstein, *Karaite Exegesis*, 47–50.

[27] Polliack, *The Karaite Tradition*.

[28] Cf. Polliack, *The Karaite Tradition*, 31–36, with further secondary literature there.

[29] Khan, *The Early Karaite Tradition*.

[30] Goldstein, *Karaite Exegesis*, 47–50.

[31] Cf. Olszowy-Schlanger, "The 'Explanation of Difficult Words'."

[32] Cf. Polliack's discussion of his concepts of Bible translation, *The Karaite Tradition*, 65–77.

[33] On Yefet, see Polliack, *The Karaite Tradition*, 37–45.

Bo'az and in the work of the Karaite lexicographer, David ben Abraham al-Fāsi, who composed the first Hebrew-Arabic biblical lexicon and who often supplied translations of entire phrases or verses in his work. Like Salmon, Yefet, and David, he too was active in Jerusalem and was associated with the *dār lil-ʿilm* "compound of learning" that the Karaites established in the city, which is mentioned in connection to Yūsuf ibn Nūḥ. All of these scholars worked in close proximity to one another and it seems that Yefet took upon himself to represent the fruits of their labor in his monumental work, which served as a compendium of the Karaite translation and exegetical enterprise of his time (→ 1.3.6).

As has been outlined by Polliack, the Karaite translational approach is quite akin to that of the early non-Saadianic traditions.[34] This can be seen in many features, for example, in a high literalism that mirrors the Hebrew text in its formal structure and is achieved by imitative tendencies on the syntactic, lexical, and morphologic levels. The use of alternative renderings is a typical and highly developed feature of Karaite translations. These are also attested, in embryonic form, in some early Jewish translations.

In the introduction to his commentary on Genesis, Yefet states:

> Our intention has been (to provide) a translation (*tarjama*) of the words (*alfāẓ*) of this Book (i.e. Genesis) and an explanation (*takhlīṣ*) of his meanings (*maʿānihi*) according to what the words require.[35]

Thus, a translation should capture the formal level (Arab. *lafẓ*) of the biblical source text and is consequently called *tarjama* in Arabic, possibly recalling the *mutarjimūn* (as in Targum) of earlier Jewish translations. That Yefet saw himself as responsible for preserving the traditions of the earlier Karaite scholars who preceded him is evident from his repeated emphasis on this task of preserving in writing "what we have heard from our teachers, the commentators." It is possible that in this he did not only refer to earlier Karaite interpretations of Scripture but also to earlier Judeo-Arabic translations of which he was aware and which the Jews had produced.[36]

In the eleventh century, other prominent Karaite scholars engaged in continuous Judeo-Arabic translations and biblical commentaries, most notably, Yeshuʿah ben Yehudah (mid-eleventh century) and ʿAlī ben Sulaymān (Egypt, second half of the eleventh century). Their translations are strikingly similar to Yefet's and evidently based on his. However, the most thoroughly adapted was Yeshuʿah's, who composed a commentary on the Pentateuch, whose major focus was Halakhah. The extensive work, known as *al-tafsīr al-mustawfā* or *al-mabsūṭ*, initially did not comprise a translation. On the behest of the Egyptian Karaite notable Abū Ḥasan Dāʾūd ibn ʿImrān ben Levi, who commissioned a copy of the commentary for the education of his son, Yeshuʿah abridged it and added a running translation.[37]

Yeshuʿah's statements in the introduction to his shortened commentary on the Pentateuch illustrate the departure from earlier Karaite translation technique. He contends:

> Know that whoever translates (*yunqilu*) from one language into another and does not use in some places additions (*al-ziyāda*) or omissions (*al-nuqṣān*), or changes (the gender) from masculine into feminine and feminine into masculine and the plural into the singular and vice versa and so on, which, as you will observe, is the prevailing practice of the translations (*al-tarjamāt*) in his commentary (*al-tafsīr*), runs the risk of making its meaning (*maʿnāhu*) obscure and its wording (*lafẓahu*) incomprehensible in the language to which they have been translated [...].[38]

Yeshuʿah preferred to mitigate the stress on formal equivalence of the source text in the translation language, which was the prevailing Karaite practice

---

[34] See Polliack, *The Karaite Tradition*, 278–91.
[35] Translation according to Polliack, *The Karaite Tradition*, 41.
[36] Compare Polliack, *The Karaite tradition*, 43. Further instances have been collected there on p. 45, n. 27.
[37] Khan, "On the Question of Script."
[38] Translation according to Polliack, *The Karaite Tradition*, 49.

prior to his time. He believes it is not the morphologic level, such as gender and number, that has to be conveyed, but the meaning of the biblical text, i.e., *maʿnāhu*. Similar to Saadia, he redacted and finalized his translation of the Pentateuch with a readership in mind (Arab. *ḥasab mā istaqarra maʿ al-ṭālib* "as required by the commissioner") and according to stylistic requirements (*faṣāḥa*).

2.4.9.1.4 Shurūḥ

Over the course of time, a certain uneasiness began to be felt towards Saadia's *Tafsīr*. His literary standard of Classical Arabic became incomprehensible and was regarded as unsuitable for serving the educational requirements of schoolrooms and synagogues. New traditions emerged in translations from the fourteenth century onwards; some were independent translations, drawing partly on Saadia's *Tafsīr* and partly enlivening, or continuing, modes of Jewish Arabic translation recognizable in the early non-Saadianic translation sources. These versions were usually designated under the term *shurūḥ* (sg. *sharḥ*, "translation, lit. interpretation"), and are also attested in the later corpus of the Cairo Genizah. It is helpful to classify them according to their geographical provenance, i.e., North-African,[39] Egyptian,[40] and Eastern (Iraqī and Syrian)[41] traditions. For further discussion of these works, especially Ibn Susan's translation of the Pentateuch composed in Zefad in the fifteenth century, see → 1.3.6.

2.4.9.2 Samaritan Translations

The beginnings of the Samaritan translation traditions into Arabic are largely obscure (→ 1.3.6.6). The exact date when Samaritan Aramaic gave way to Arabic as a vernacular, which would provide an approximate indication, is difficult to discern. It is usually agreed that the shift took place during the eleventh century, following a period of bilingualism.[42] The emergence of an Arabic version must have followed soon after that linguistic shift, yet documentary evidence is lacking. Later versions of the Samaritan Targum (→ 2.4.4) exhibit a large number of Arabisms, which provide circumstantial evidence as to this process. In addition, many of the earliest Samaritan treatises in the Arabic language seem to be dedicated to grammatical thought such as, for example, Ṭabiah Ghazāl b. Darthā's (late tenth century) *Qānūn ibn Darthā fī tartīb al-miqra* "Ibn Darthā's Canon of Reciting the Torah" and *Qānūn ibn Darthā fī miqra* "Ibn Darthā's Canon of the Torah." The Arabic column of the anonymous lexicographic composition *ha-Melīṣ*, a trilingual biblical lexicon (Samaritan Hebrew, Aramaic, and Arabic), was also composed around the same time. It is reasonable to assume that the translation of the Pentateuch took place in this same period, in order to complement the aforementioned disciplines of learning.

Earlier research, in particular by the school of Paul Kahle, regarded the Samaritan translations into Arabic as directly dependent upon a Saadianic *Vorlage*.[43] However, as Shehadeh has demonstrated, the Samaritan translations are preserved in a number of distinct manuscript groups, in which genuine Saadianic adaptations constitute a marginal entity. The first group, which he called the Old Arabic Translation of SP (OATSP), consists of trilingual or bilingual codices in Samaritan letters, prepared before the second half of the thirteenth century. The version featured, virtually unknown to earlier scholars, preceded a revised text by Abū Saʿīd (see below). Although Shehadeh initially assigned this early version to Isḥāq b. Faraj b. Mārūth al-Ṣūrī, known as Abū al-Ḥasan (Aram. Ab-Ḥisdā) and active in late eleventh century, this attribution remains disputed and the origin of the version remains unknown.[44] Some trans-

---

[39] Cf. Avrahami, "המקשיה"; Bar-Asher, "Le Sharḥ"; Zafrani, "Jewish Languages."

[40] See Hary, *Translating Religion*.

[41] See the various publications by Avishur.

[42] The question has been addressed by Shehadeh, התרגום הערבי; Shehadeh, "The Arabic Translation," and most explicitly in Shehadeh, "מתי תפסה."

[43] Cf. Kahle, *Die arabischen Bibelübersetzungen*, x–xi, and Kahle, *The Cairo Genizah*, 54–55; Katten, "Untersuchungen"; Algermissen, "Die Pentateuchzitate."

[44] His son, Abū Isḥāq Ibrāhīm b. Faraj b. Mārūth, lived in the eleventh and twelfth centuries as a physician to Ṣalāḥ al-Dīn in Damascus. Accordingly, Abū al-Ḥasan must have lived at

lation techniques are quite similar to early non-Saadianic translations such as, for example, the literal translation of proper names and the syntax that usually follows the Hebrew text.[45] Further, a tendency to retain the Hebrew gender and number of verbal forms irrespective of Classical Arabic is palpable. This similarity may imply that the older Arabic version of SP (→ 1.2.3) may have come into being in a comparable, didactic context, common to that of the early Jewish, Karaite, and possibly some of the older Christian Arabic versions as well.[46] On the other hand, Saadia's *Tafsīr* seems to have influenced this earlier Samaritan tradition significantly, since in large passages lexicon and phraseology are identical. In addition, Karaite translations have left an impact on the OATSP.[47] Be that as it may, the different manuscripts vary, which indicates that a *textus receptus* never emerged. Copies differ immensely in specific readings, translation technique, and indebtedness to the aforementioned Jewish traditions.

The second group represents the version of Abū Saʿīd, the so-called revised Arabic Samaritan Version of the Pentateuch. He was active in thirteenth-century Egypt and did not translate SP anew, but rather aimed at a revision of the earlier version identified in the first group of manuscripts, and appended various *scholia* to his text (→ 1.3.6.6).

Only the third group of manuscripts may be termed genuine Saadianic adaptations. This group consists solely of one manuscript, manuscript London, BL, Or. 7562, written in Samaritan letters.[48]

---

the end of the eleventh and beginning of the twelfth centures, most probably in Damascus. Cf. the remarks of Macuch, "On the Problems of the Arabic Translation." He conjectures that the translation was affiliated with him due to the outstanding reputation bestowed upon him by scholars of his generation. Concrete evidence of his authorship, however, is lacking.

[45] Cf. Shehadeh, התרגום הערבי, 510–11 and Shehadeh, *The Arabic Translation*, 184.

[46] Cf. Polliack's suggestions, *The Karaite Tradition*, 278–91, and see → 1.4.11.

[47] For instance, Yeshuʿah's Arabic version, mentioned above, was adapted for SP; cf. Schwarb, "Vestiges."

[48] This manuscript has been studied and edited by Zewi, *The Samaritan Version*.

The Arabic column of the codex was transcribed at Kahle's request into Arabic letters in 1908 by Kohen Salāma b. ʿImrān and subsequently deposited at the Königliche Bibliothek zu Berlin, as manuscript Or. Quart. 1082. Although Kahle considered manuscript London, BL, Or. 7562 to be representative of Samaritan tradition, it is, although an interesting document, now thought to be of marginal significance in comparison to the large number of genuine Samaritan translations.

Algermissen, E., "Die Pentateuchzitate Ibn Ḥazms: Ein Beitrag zur Geschichte der arabischen Bibelübersetzungen" (PhD diss.; Westfälische Wilhelms-Universität Münster, 1933).

Avishur, Y., "Modern Judeo-Arabic Translations of the Old Testament: A Cultural-Linguistic presentation," in *Studies in Jewish Languages: Bible Translations and Spoken Dialects* (ed. M. Bar-Asher; Jerusalem: Misgav Yerushalayim, 1988), 39–54 [Hebr.].

Avishur, Y., "'Difficult Words' in Saadia's Translation to the Torah and Modern Translations in the Orient," *Massorot* 3–4 (1989): 131–46 [Hebr.].

Avishur, Y., "The Adaptations of R. Saadia Gaon's Bible Translation in the East," *Sefunot* NS 5 (1991): 181–202 [Hebr.].

Avishur, Y., "Translations of the Old Testament into Judaeo-Arabic in Iraq," in *Studies in the History and Culture of Iraqi Jewry* (ed. Y. Avishur; Or Yehuda: Babylonian Jewry Heritage Center, 1991), 139–65 [Hebr.].

Avishur, Y., "Some New Sources for the Study of the Text and Language of Saadya's Translation on the Pentateuch in Judaeo-Arabic," in *Genizah Research after Ninety Years: The Case of Judaeo-Arabic: Papers Read at the Third Congress of the Society for Judaeo-Arabic Studies* (eds. J. Blau and S. Reif; University of Cambridge Oriental Publications 47; Cambridge: Cambridge University Press, 1992), 5–13.

Avishur, Y., "How Translators of the Torah into Judeo-Arabic Tackled Saadia's Translation," *Ben ʿEver la-ʿArav* 1 (1998): 129–44 [Hebr.].

Avishur, Y., *Studies in Judaeo-Arabic Translations of the Bible* (Tel Aviv: Archaeological Center Publications, 2001) [Hebr.].

Avrahami, Y., "המקשיה: תרגום המקרא לערבית יהודית של ׳תונים מאת ר׳ מרדכי חי דיין׳," in *History and Creativity in the Sephardi and Oriental Jewish Communities* (eds. T. Alexander, E. Hazan, and G. Rozen-Roqem; Jerusalem: Misgav Yerushalayim, 1994), 139–65.

Baker, C.F. and M. Polliack, *Arabic and Judaeo-Arabic Manuscripts in the Cambridge Genizah Collections: Arabic Old Series (T-S Ar.1a–54)* (Cambridge University Library Genizah Series 12; Cambridge: Cambridge University Library, 2001).

Bar-Asher, M., "Le Sharḥ maghrébin de la Bible et d'autres oeuvres littéraires – caractéristiques et formation," in *Traditions linguistiques des Juifs d'Afrique du Nord* (Jerusalem: Misgav Yerushalayim, 1988).

Ben-Shammai, H., "Yeshuah ben Yehuda: A Characterization of a Karaite Scholar in the Eleventh Century," *Pe'amim* 32 (1987): 3–20 [Hebr.].

Ben-Shammai, H., "New and Old: Saadia's Two Introductions to His Translation of the Pentateuch," *Tarbiz* 69 (2000): 199–210 [Hebr.].

Ben-Shammai, H., "An 'East Wind' from the South: Environmental Considerations in the Translations and Commentaries of R. Saadia Gaon," in *Studies in the History of Eretz Israel Presented to Yehuda ben Porat* (eds. Y. Ben-Arieh and E. Reiner; Jerusalem: Ben-Zvi Institute, 2003): 288–307 [Hebr.].

Ben-Shammai, H., "Extra-Textual Considerations in Medieval Judaeo-Arabic Bible Translations: The Case of Saadya Gaon," *Materia Giudaica* 8 (2003): 53–66.

Ben-Shammai, H., "The Tension between Literal Interpretation and Exegetical Freedom: Comparative Observations on Saadia's Method," in *With Reverence for the Word: Medieval Scriptural Exegesis in Judaism, Christianity, and Islam* (eds. J.D. McAuliffe, B. Walfish, and J.W. Goering; Oxford: Oxford University Press, 2003), 33–50.

Ben-Shammai, H., מפעלו של מנהיג עיונים במשנתו ההגותית והפרשנית של רס״ג (Jerusalem: Mossad Bialik, 2015) [Hebr.].

Blau, J., "On a Fragment of the Oldest Judaeo-Arabic Bible Translation Extant," in *Genizah Research after Ninety Years: The Case of Judaeo-Arabic: Papers Read at the Third Congress of the Society for Judaeo-Arabic Studies* (eds. J. Blau and S. Reif; University of Cambridge Oriental Publications 47; Cambridge: Cambridge University Press, 1992), 31–39.

Blau, J. and S. Hopkins, "On Early Judaeo-Arabic Orthography," in J. Blau, *Studies in Middle Arabic and Its Judaeo-Arabic Variety* (Jerusalem: Magnes Press, 1988), 381–400.

Blau, J. and S. Hopkins, "Judaeo-Arabic Papyri: Collected, Edited, Translated and Analysed," in J. Blau, *Studies in Middle Arabic and Its Judaeo-Arabic Variety* (Jerusalem: Magnes Press, 1988), 401–74.

Blau, J. and S. Hopkins, "Ancient Bible Translations to Judeo-Arabic," *Pe'amim* 83 (2000): 4–14 [Hebr.].

Blau, J. and S. Hopkins, "The Beginnings of Judaeo-Arabic Bible Exegesis according to an Old Glossary to the Book of Psalms," in *A Word Fitly Spoken: Studies in Mediaeval Exegesis of the Hebrew Bible and the Qur'an Presented to Haggai Ben-Shammai* (eds. M. Bar-Asher et al.; Jerusalem: Ben Zvi Institute, 2007), 235–84.

Brody, R., *Sa'adyah Gaon* (Oxford: Litman Library of Jewish Civilization, 2013).

Cohen, M. and S. Sasson, "In the Court of Ya'qūb ibn Killis: A Fragment from the Cairo Genizah," *JQR* 80 (1990): 283–314.

Doron, D., "לדרכי התרגום של המלית 'את' ב״אלשרח' אלסוסאני לכ׳מסת ג׳זא אלתורה," in *Arabic and Islamic Studies*, Vol. 2 (ed. J. Mansour; Ramat Gan: Bar-Ilan University Press, 1978), 9–25 [Hebr.].

Doron, D., "על תרגום התורה לערבית של ר' יששכר בן-סוסאן המערבי," *Sefunot* NS 3 (1985): 279–98.

Doron, D., "From the *Tafsir* of R. Saadia Gaon to the Translation of R. Mordechai Hai Dayyan of Tunis," *Sefunot* NS 5 (1991): 171–80 [Hebr.].

Doron, D., "הקדמתו של ר' מרדכי חי דיין מתוניס לתרגום ספר בראשית לערבית-יהודית," *Mi-mizraḥ u-mi-ma'arav* 6 (1995): 131–60 [Hebr.].

Freidenreich, D.M., "The Use of Islamic Sources in Saadiah Gaon's 'Tafsīr' of the Torah," *JQR* 93 (2003): 353–95.

de Goeje, M.J., *Al-Mas'ūdī: Kitāb al-tanbīh wa-al-ishrāf* (Leiden: Brill, 1894).

Goldstein, M., "Sa'adya's *Tafsir* in Light of Muslim Polemic against Ninth-Century Arabic Bible Translations," *Jerusalem Studies of Arabic and Islam* 36 (2009): 173–99.

Goldstein, M., *Karaite Exegesis in Medieval Jerusalem* (Text and Studies in Medieval and Early Modern Judaism 26; Tübingen: Mohr Siebeck, 2011).

Hary, B., *Translating Religion: Linguistic Analysis of Judeo-Arabic Sacred Texts from Egypt* (Études sur le judaïsme médiéval 38; Leiden: Brill, 2009).

Hopkins, S., "On the Vorlage of an Early Judaeo-Arabic Translation of Proverbs," *Jerusalem Studies of Arabic and Islam* 27 (2002): 369–74.

Kahle, P., *Die arabischen Bibelübersetzungen: Texte mit Glossar und Literaturübersicht* (Leipzig: J.C. Hinrichs, 1904).

Kahle, P., *The Cairo Genizah* (Oxford: Basil Blackwell, 1959).

Katten, M., "Untersuchungen zu Saadja's arabischer

Pentateuchübersetzung" (PhD diss.; University of Gießen, 1924).

Khan, G., "On the Question of Script in Medieval Karaite Manuscripts: New Evidence from the Genizah," *Bulletin of the John Rylands University Library of Manchester* 75 (1993): 133–41.

Khan, G., *The Early Karaite Tradition of Hebrew Grammatical Thought: Including a Critical Edition, Translation and Analysis of the Diqduq of 'Abū Ya'qūb Yūsuf ibn Nūḥ on the Hagiographa* (Studies in Semitic Languages and Linguistics 32; Leiden: Brill, 2000).

Leeven, J., "Saadya's Lost Commentary on Leviticus," in *Saadya Studies in Commemoration of the One Thousandth Anniversary of the Death of R. Saadya Gaon* (ed. E. Rosenthal; Publications of the University of Manchester 282; Manchester: Manchester University Press, 1943), 78–96.

Macuch, R., "On the Problems of the Arabic Translation of the Samaritan Pentateuch," in *Proceedings of the First International Congress of the Société d'Études Samaritaines* (eds. A. Tal and M. Florentin; Tel Aviv: Chaim Rosenberg School for Jewish Studies, Tel Aviv University, 1991), 147–73.

Mann, J., "A Fihrist of Sa'adya's Works," *JQR* 11 (1921): 423–28.

Olszowy-Schlanger, J., "The 'Explanation of Difficult Words' by 'Abu al-Faraj Harun ibn al-Faraj," in *Exegesis and Grammar in Medieval Karaite Texts* (ed. G. Khan; Oxford: Oxford University Press on behalf of University of Manchester, 2001), 179–94.

Polliack, M., "Alternative Renderings and Additions in Yeshu'ah ben Yehudah's Arabic Translation of the Pentateuch," *JQR* 8 (1994): 209–26.

Polliack, M., "Medieval Karaite Views on Translating the Hebrew Bible into Arabic," *JJS* 47 (1996): 64–84.

Polliack, M., "The Medieval Karaite Tradition of Translating the Hebrew Bible into Arabic: Its Sources, Characteristics and Background," *JRAS* 6 (1996): 189–96.

Polliack, M., "Bible Translations and Word-Lists in the Cairo Genizah," *Bulletin of the Israeli Academic Center in Cairo* 21 (1997): 31–34.

Polliack, M., *The Karaite Tradition of Arabic Bible Translation: A Linguistic and Exegetical Study of Karaite Translations of the Pentateuch from the Tenth and Eleventh Centuries C.E.* (Études sur le judaïsme médiéval 17; Leiden: Brill, 1997).

Polliack, M., "Arabic Bible Translations in the Cairo Genizah Collections," in *Jewish Studies in a New Europe: Proceedings of the Fifth Congress of Jewish Studies in Copenhagen 1994 under the Auspices of the European Association for Jewish Studies* (eds. U. Haxen, H. Trautner-Kromann, and K.L. Goldschmidt Salamon; Copenhagen: C.A. Reitzel, 1998), 595–620.

Polliack, M., "Medieval Karaite Methods of Translating Biblical Narrative into Arabic," *VT* 48 (1998): 375–98.

Polliack, M., "Types of Arabic Bible Translation in the Cairo Geniza based on the Catalogue of the TS Arabic," *Te'udah* 15 (1999): 109–25 [Hebr.].

Polliack, M., "Saadia Gaon's Concept of Biblical Translation in the Light of the Karaite Concept," in *Heritage and Innovation in Medieval Judaeo-Arabic Culture* (eds. J. Blau and D. Doron; Ramat-Gan: Bar-Ilan University Press, 2000), 191–201 [Hebr.].

Polliack, M. and S. Somekh, "Two Hebrew-Arabic Biblical Glossaries from the Cairo Genizah," *Pe'amim* 88 (2000): 124–38 [Hebr.].

Poznanski, S., "A Fihrist of Saadya's Works," *JQR* 13 (1923): 369–96.

Ratzabi, Y., *A Dictionary of Judaeo-Arabic in R. Saadia's Tafsir* (Ramat-Gan: Bar-Ilan University, 1985) [Hebr.].

Ratzabi, Y., פירושי רבינו סעדיה גאון לספר שמות עם המקור הערבי ותרגום לעברית (Jerusalem: Mosad ha-Rav Kook, 1998) [Hebr.].

Rippin, A., "Sa'adya Gaon and Genesis 22: Aspects of Jewish-Muslim Interaction and Polemic," in *Studies in Islamic and Judaic Traditions: Papers Presented at the Institute for Islamic-Judaic Studies, Center for Judaic Studies*, Vol. 1 (eds. W.M. Brinner and S.D. Ricks; Brown Judaic Studies 110; Atlanta: Scholars Press, 1986), 31–46.

Schmiedl, A., "Randbemerkungen zu Saadia's Pentateuchübersetzung," *MGWJ* 46 (1901): 124–29.

Schwarb, G., "Vestiges of Karaite Translations in the Arabic Translation(s) of the Samaritan Pentateuch," *Intellectual History of the Islamicate World* 1 (2013): 115–56.

Shehadeh, H., "מתי תפסה הערבית את מקום הארמית השומרונית," in *Hebrew Language Studies Presented to Zeev Ben-Ḥayyim* (ed. M. Bar-Asher; Jerusalem: Magnes Press, 1984), 515–28 [Hebr.].

Shehadeh, H., "התרגום הערבי לנוסח התורה של השומרונים: מבוא למהדורה ביקורתית" (PhD diss., Hebrew University of Jerusalem, 1989) [Hebr.].

Shehadeh, H., "The Arabic Translation of the Samaritan Pentateuch," in *The Samaritans* (ed. A.D. Crown; Tübingen: J.C.B. Mohr [Paul Siebeck], 1989), 481–516.

Shehadeh, H. (ed.), *The Arabic Translation of the Samaritan Pentateuch* (2 vols.; Jerusalem: The Israel Academy of Sciences and Humanities, 1989–2002).

Tobi, Y., "Pre-Saadianic Arabic Translation of the Pentateuch," *Massorot* 7 (1993): 87–127 [Hebr.].

Tobi, Y., "Another Popular Judaeo-Arabic Translation of the Pentateuch," in *Studies in Hebrew and Jewish Languages Presented to Shelomo Morag* (ed. M. Bar-Asher; Jerusalem: Mosad Bialik, 1996), 481–50 [Hebr.].

Tobi, Y., "The Phonetically Written Tafsîr Alfâẓ to Exodus and other Passages of Popular Translations," *'Ever and 'Arav* 1 (1998): 53–74 [Hebr.].

Tobi, Y., "On the Antiquity of the Judeo-Arabic Biblical Translations and a New Piece of an Ancient Judeo-Arabic Translation of the Pentateuch," *Ben 'Ever la-'Arav* 2 (2001): 17–60 [Hebr.].

Tobi, Y., "תרגומי שמות עצם פרטיים בתרגומי המקרא הערביים-היהודיים מימי הביניים," in *Studies in Jewish Onomastics: In Honor of Prof. Edwin D. Lawson on his 80th Birthday* (ed. A. Demsky; Ramat Gan: Bar-Ilan University, 2003), 77–84 [Hebr.].

Tobi, Y., "תרגומים קדומים בלשון הערבית-היהודית לתורה: קטעים חדשים," *Ha-'ivrit we-aḥayoteha* 4–5 (2005): 115–43 [Hebr.].

Vollandt, R., "Whether to Capture Form or Meaning: A Typology of Early Judaeo-Arabic Pentateuch Translations," in *A Universal Art: Hebrew Grammer across Disciplines and Faiths* (eds. N. Vidro, I. Zwiep, and J. Olszowy-Schlanger; Studies in Jewish History and Culture 46; Leiden: Brill, 2014), 58–83.

Vollandt, R., *Arabic Versions of the Pentateuch: A Comparative Study of Jewish, Christian, and Muslim Sources* (Biblia Arabica 2; Leiden: Brill, 2015).

Wansbrough, J., "Arabic Rhetoric and Qur'anic Exegesis," *BSOAS* 31 (1968): 469–85.

Wansbrough, J., *Quranic Studies: Sources and Methods of Scriptural Interpretation* (Oxford: Oxford University Press, 1977).

Zafrani, H., "Jewish Languages in the Maghreb under Islam and Judeo-Arabic Translations of the Bible," in *Studies in Jewish Languages: Bible Translations and Spoken Dialects* (ed. M. Bar-Asher; Jerusalem: Misgav Yerushalayim, 1988), 55–67 [Hebr.].

Zewi, T., *The Samaritan Version of Saadya Gaon's Translation of the Pentateuch: Critical Edition and Study of MS London BL OR7562 and Related MSS* (Biblia Arabica 3; Leiden: Brill, 2015).

Zucker, M., "Fragments from Rav Saadia Gaon's Commentary to the Pentateuch from Manuscripts," *Sura* 2 (1955–1956): 313–55 [Hebr.].

Zucker, M., "Fragments from Rav Saadia Gaon's Commentary to the Pentateuch from Manuscripts," *Sura* 3 (1957–1958): 151–64 [Hebr.].

Zucker, M., *Saadia's Commentary on Genesis* (New York: Jewish Theological Seminary, 1984) [Hebr.].

Ronny Vollandt

2.5 Secondary Translations

2.5.1 Vetus Latina

The most salient VL manuscripts for the Pentateuch are: VL[100] *Lugdunensis*; VL[101] *Vindobonensis*; VL[102] *Ottobonianus*; VL[103] *Wirceburgensis*; and VL[104] *Monacensis*. To these the following should be added: VL[105], London, British Library Papyrus 2052, with text of Gen 5:4–13; 5:29–6:2; VL[106], Florence, Biblioteca Medicea Laurenziana P.S.I. 1272, with text of Exod 8:16–20, 8:28–9:1; VL[108], Milan, Biblioteca del Capitolo Metropolitano II. D. 3.1, with text of Exod 14:15–31; 20:1–24; 34:1–10; 34:23–35:1; and VL[110], Vienna, Österreichische Nationalbibliothek lat. 1114 fol. 83, which contains Num 26:2–3, 8–10, 16–22, 44–45; its verse order agrees with LXX and *Lugdunensis* (VL[100]), with a text more faithful to LXX than *Ludgunensis*, which suffered a worse transmission.

In the volumes of the Beuron edition, the different text types appear arranged in chronological order in parallel lines under the Greek text. There is no continuous VL text in codices or patristic commentaries that could be used as a lemma for the edition. Thus, the most adequate methodological option involves reproducing the longest fragments that span several verses. In this way, at least the homogeneity of the text of a pericope that could have been copied from a single manuscript is preserved, although it has the side effect that at times the most meaningful readings may not appear in the corresponding parallel line. Due to this fact, the text reproduced in one of the parallel lines does not have any preference over readings marked as variants to that line of text. This means that a line does not represent *the* European text of a verse, but a text representative of *a* line within the European tradition.

2.5.1.1 Genesis
2.5.1.1.1 History of Research
A.V. Billen was a pioneer in the study of the VL text of the Heptateuch. He undertook a meticulous analysis focused on the lexicon and typology of manuscripts, without attempting to define the textual history of the VL text, a task that, at his time, was hindered by the lack of knowledge of important witnesses as yet uncovered, such as manuscripts VL[91–95] and VL[111].[1] De Bruyne demonstrated an important fact that Billen often referred to, i.e., that Augustine used a revision of the VL text based on the Greek LXX (→ 2.4.1). Thus, Billen and De Bruyne already proved the existence of a single original translation.[2]

2.5.1.1.2 Textual History
Fischer established the main lines of the textual history of the book of Genesis and of the VL version in general. In the second century C.E., sections used in liturgy were rendered from the Greek (→ 2.4.1.1) until the translation of the Hexateuch was completed at a later time. Transmitted texts go back to two textual forms, African and European, which can be differentiated by vocabulary, and, in a smaller measure, by translation technique. The history of the VL text implies a progressive Europeanization of the African text, which implied an improvement of the translation and the language of the text, as well as attempts to reproduce better the original Greek model that no longer coincided with the *Vorlage* of the first version (→ 1.4.1). Nevertheless, one has to take into consideration that what in the second century C.E. could be considered a vulgarism or mistake by the translator could have turned two centuries later into a ritual and hieratic idiom due to the usage of the text as sacred Scripture.

2.5.1.1.3 Edition
The book of Genesis has a superb edition produced by Fischer, which serves as the model for the rest of books in the Beuron Vetus Latina series.[3] This

---

[1] Billen, *The Old Latin Texts of the Heptateuch*.
[2] De Bruyne, *S. Augustin reviseur de la Bible*, 521–606; on the Heptateuch, 585–91.
[3] B. Fischer, *Genesis* (VL 2; Freiburg: Herder, 1951).

edition includes the Greek text with those Greek variants that agree with the Latin text, which appears under the Greek text in different lines according to the different text types of the VL version, designated by different letters. The letter K represents the African type of Carthage from the mid-third century C.E., witnessed by Cyprian and pseudo-Cyprianic writings; it is a unitary and constant text, with a flavor of antiquity. C represents the same VL African text of Cyprian's time, but in the form attested at the end of the fourth century C.E. in the works of Augustine (*De Genesi contra Manichaeos, De Genesi ad litteram, Contra Adimantum*) and also sometimes in Pseudo-Augustine's *Speculum*.

The siglum E indicates a European text derived from the African text, whose origins may be seen already in Tertullian and Novatianus and less markedly in Hilarius and Lucifer. The E text is divided into the subtypes S and I. The former represents a late African text, Spanish, attested by VL$^{100-102}$ and often by VL$^{91-95}$, as well as by treatises attributed to Gregory of Elvira and by quotations in Fulgentius. It spread in the fifth and sixth centuries C.E. and also later. The I text, Italian of the fourth and fifth centuries C.E., is attested by VL$^{103\,111}$ and partly by VL$^{91-95}$ as well as by Ambrose, Rufinus, Jerome, and Augustine. This I text is subdivided into: A: Augustine's revised text; M: Ambrose's text; O: the Hexaplaric text in Jerome's *Hebraicae Quaestiones in libro Geneseos*; and P: Quodvultdeus' text, influenced by the Hexaplaric text and by the Vulgate (*Liber promissionum et praedictorum Dei*.) There are also traces of the X text, which involves some direct translations from the Greek; and the H text of Jerome's version *ex Hebraeo* or Vulgate (→ 2.4.8).

Therefore, it is not possible to produce a critical reconstruction of VL in a way that the resulting edited text could be considered "*the* Vetus Latina." Critical work, rather, involves arranging and classifying, as far as possible, the immense diversity of the extant fragments that have come down to us and that constitute only a part of the lost textual richness. The aim is to establish and present the genetic and historical relationship of the different preserved textual forms.[4] VL-Gen is a good model for the edition of texts transmitted in a plurality of textual forms, such as those of apocryphal and pseudoepigraphic writings, various Dead Sea scrolls, and New Testament and rabbinic works.

Wevers acknowledged that, given the antiquity of the Latin and Sahidic versions, they should be important testimonies for the reconstruction of the history of the Greek text, but in his edition of LXX-Gen he is quite contained regarding the value he gave to VL readings.[5]

2.5.1.2 Exodus
2.5.1.2.1 Extant Witnesses
Testimony to VL-Exod is preserved in patristic quotations, testimonies of the Song of Moses (Exodus 15), liturgical readings, sections preserved in codices of Jerome's version (→ 2.4.8), glosses in Spanish medieval manuscripts (VL$^{91-96}$), old fragments in Egyptian papyri, and also in codices *Lugdunensis* (VL^{100}), *Vindobonensis* (VL^{101}), *Wirceburgensis* (VL^{103}), and *Monacensis* (VL^{104}). Codices VL^{100} and VL^{101} present a late European text; VL^{104} closely follows an old African text and VL^{1C3} stays in an intermediate position.

The VL text of the Munich Palimpsest (VL^{104}), edited by Ziegler, represents the earliest accessible form of LXX-Exod (→ 2.4.1.2).[6] Codex *Monacensis* (codex lat. 6225 Bayerische Staatsbibliothek, Munich) represents a copy of VL-Exod in a Carolingian minuscule writing from the beginning of the ninth century C.E. whose text goes back to a first writing at the end of the fifth century C.E.

2.5.1.2.2 Relevance for Literary Criticism
VL-Exod (*Monacensis*) translates faithfully the earliest textual form of LXX-Exod 36–40 (→ 2.4.1.2) that can be reached.[7] It omits elements about the

---

[4] Fischer, *Genesis*, 24*.

[5] Wevers, *Genesis*, 34.

[6] L. Ziegler, *Bruchstücke einer vorhieronymianischen Übersetzung des Pentateuch: aus einem Palimpseste der K. Hof- und Staatsbibliothek zu München* (Munich: T. Riedel, 1883).

[7] Bogaert, "L' importance de la Septante et du 'Monacensis' de la Vetus Latina," 399–428; Bogaert, "La construction de la Tente (Ex 36–40) dans le *Monacensis*," 62–76.

golden altar or the perfumes (MT-Exod 37:25–28). At the beginning of LXX-Exod 37, it includes a description of the tent, the atrium, the gate, the tent of witness with the seraphim and the holy of holies. This description was omitted in LXX according to the textual form preserved in LXX^B, in all likelihood due to formal contradictions with the previous description in Exodus 25–31.

VL-Exod represents a Greek text whose Hebrew *Vorlage* clearly distinguished between the proficiencies of each artisan: Eliab, responsible for fabrics and wood; and Beseel, responsible for metals. MT (→ 2.2.2) gives greater importance to Besaleel of Judah at the expense of Oholiab of Dan and mixes the activities of both artisans. LXX-Exod omits references to wood, therefore taking an intermediate position.

According to the text of *Monacensis*, Levites played no role at all and are under the command of Itamar, contrary to the narrative of MT and LXX (MT-Exod 38:21b = LXX-Exod 37:19b, om. *Monac*). MT-Exod draws a clear line between priests and Levites. It places the chapter on priestly ornaments (Exodus 39) at the very end, so that competence in these ornaments seems to be a priestly privilege, outside of the scope of artisans and the Levites. The description of the construction of the tabernacle closes Exodus 40 both in MT and LXX, but MT presents the section on priestly vestments before the end (Exodus 39), whereas in LXX and VL it is placed earlier, i.e., in LXX-Exod 36. In LXX-Exod, the description of the atrium precedes the materials on metals (LXX-Exod 37:7–18 + 37:19–21), whereas in MT-Exod it follows them (MT-Exod 38:9–20 + 38:21–23).

In VL, the priestly ornaments are exclusively Eliab's handiwork, whereas in LXX^B-Exod they are crafted by both artisans: also, the Levites wear different vestments from those worn by priests, a detail excluded from MT, which places priestly rights above those of Levites. VL and LXX represent at this point the earliest text. Codex *Monacensis* presents a state of affairs also attested by Chronicles (2 Chr 5:2): Levites have their own raiment and the priestly vestments are Eliab's handiwork. Also, the author of Hebrews (9:4) knew an Old Greek text of the same type used by the early Latin translator of Exodus. The Greek *textus receptus* underwent an early revision based on the Hebrew standard text (MT; → 2.2.2). It is a hybrid between the first Greek version (which goes back to a very old Hebrew text, attested substantially in codex *Monacensis*) and the traditional Hebrew text (MT).

Therefore, VL-Exod constitutes a key element for the textual criticism and exegesis of the book of Exodus. It attests to a very old version of the book in Greek (→ 2.4.1.2) and, ultimately, in Hebrew. This textual form did not include the first description of the tabernacle (Exodus 25–31) or it just constituted a very brief text; it included only the second description of the tabernacle (Exodus 35–40) under the textual form reflected by VL. The textual form represented by MT (→ 2.2.2) originated from new concerns among the priestly order; it took shape through the addition of Exodus 25–31 and through a deep revision of the second description of the tabernacle (Exodus 35–40) to reflect the first (Exodus 25–31).

Originally, Exodus did not mention the altar of perfumes. This reference was introduced into Exodus 25–31 as an appendix to Exod 30:1–10. This is the form of the Hebrew text that constituted the basis for the Greek translation represented in VL. It is the translation that the author of Hebrews (9:4) must have known. Afterwards, the proto-Masoretic textual form (→ 2.2.2) introduced the golden altar into Exodus 35–40 systematically by specifying, next to almost every single mention of the altar of sacrifices, that the altar of perfumes was in the aisle before the veil. Later, although at a quite early moment, the traditional Greek text underwent a revision based on the text of the proto-Masoretic tradition (→ 2.4.1.2). Therefore, the present LXX text constitutes an intermediate form between the first Greek version based on a very old Hebrew text and attested by VL, and the Hebrew MT. Wevers considers the LXX order in Exodus 36–38 to be secondary, but he does not place enough importance on VL-Exod.[8]

---

[8] Wevers and Quast, *Exodus*.

2.5.1.3 Leviticus, Numbers

In all European witnesses, the (E) text of Leviticus and Numbers seems to be more African than in the rest of the books of the Heptateuch, doubtlessly because they were less used books and therefore less subject to revision. The VL material of these books, which includes manuscripts and quotations in the Fathers (→ 21.8), is much more homogeneous than in Genesis or Deuteronomy. Gooding collected the VL material in Wevers' edition of LXX *Numeri*.[9]

2.5.1.4 Deuteronomy

Deut 27:4 mentions the place where Moses commanded an altar to be built after the crossing of the Jordan. This place is Mount Gerizim, according to the VL reading *Garzin*, attested in codex *Lugdunensis* (VL[100]).[10] The VL reading agrees with SP (→ 2.2.4.5), בהרגריזים "on Mount Gerizim." On the other hand, MT (בְּהַר עֵיבָל) and almost the totality of the Greek manuscript tradition (ἐν ὄρει Γαιβαλ) identify that place as "on Mount Ebal." Papyrus Giessen from the fifth or sixth century C.E. is the only biblical Greek witness to attest the reading εν αρ(?)γαρ[ι]ζιμ "on Mount Garizim."[11] Some catenae manuscripts demonstrate that the Samareitikon also reads ἐν τῷ Γαριζειν "on Mount Garizin."[12] The Samareitikon is to be discarded as the source of Pap. Giessen. The SP reading has recently surfaced in a small scroll fragment of uncertain origin containing text from Deut 27:4–6 (→ 2.2.1.3.3; → 2.2.4.5.3).[13] The fragment is claimed to have come from Cave 4, though not all scholars agree.[14] If genuine, rather than being from a specifically Samaritan milieu, this fragment comes from a more general Jewish origin, as is the case for the majority of putative "Samaritan" readings.

It seems highly improbable that the VL reading is a translation from a specifically Samaritan Hebrew or Samaritan Greek manuscript. Even though only a single Greek witness survives, it seems that the VL reading reflects an ancient Greek reading based on an old Hebrew text.[15] *BHQ does not include the Old Greek witness in its apparatus, although it is mentioned in the commentary. It qualifies the MT (LXX V S T) reading as a scribal correction. SP did not introduce the reference to Gerizim in order to bestow Mosaic legitimacy upon the Samaritan sanctuary. Rather, it was the proto-Masoretic tradition that corrected the ancient reading "on Mount Gerizim," substituting it with "Mount Ebal" in order to deprive the Samaritan sanctuary of legitimacy, now placed on the mount of curses. An anti-Samaritan correction such as this by the proto-Masoretic tradition is not rare, as shown by the textual history of Kings.[16]

The reading attested by VL is highly relevant for exegesis and for the history of Israelite religion, as well as for the study of the relationships between Judaism and Samaritanism. Also, it contributes to the study of the complex literary construction of Deut 27:2–4.[17] Additionally, the isolated Hebrew, Greek, and VL witnesses of the reading "on Mount Gerizim" provide further support for the view that 4QJosh[a] (→ 3.2.1.1; → 3.2.3.2) presents the earliest extant witness to the locality of the first altar built in the newly entered land.[18]

Aejmelaeus, A., "Septuagint Translation Techniques: A Solution to the Problem of the Tabernacle Account," in Aejmelaeus, *Trail*, 116–30.

Billen, A.V., *The Old Latin Texts of the Heptateuch* (Cambridge: Cambridge University Press, 1927).

Bogaert, P.-M., "L'importance de la Septante et du 'Monacensis' de la Vetus Latina pour l'exégèse du livre de l'Exode (chap. 35–40)," in *Studies in the Book of Exodus: Redaction – Reception – Interpretation* (ed. M. Vervenne; BETL 126; Leuven: Peeters, 1996), 399–428.

---

[9] Wevers, *Numeri*, 18 n. 1.
[10] Wevers, *Deuteronomium*, 287.
[11] Tov, "Pap. Giessen 13, 19, 22, 26: A Revision of the Septuagint?" 45–75.
[12] Wevers, *Deuteronomium*, 16.
[13] Charlesworth, "What is a Variant?"
[14] For a critical view, see → 2.2.1.3.3.

[15] Kartveit, *The Origin of the Samaritans*, 300–05.
[16] Schenker, *Älteste Textgeschichte der Königsbücher*, 185–87.
[17] Fabry, "Der Altarbau der Samaritaner," 44.
[18] Ulrich, "4QJosh[a] and Joshua's First Altar in the Promised Land."

Bogaert, P.-M., "La construction de la Tente (Ex 36–40) dans le *Monacensis* de la plus ancienne version latine: l'autel d'or Hébreux 9,4," in *L'enfance de la Bible hébraïque: Histoire du texte de l'Ancien Testament* (eds. A. Schenker and P. Hugo; *MdB* 52; Geneva: Labor et fides, 2005), 62–76.

Brooke, G.J., "The Temple Scroll and LXX Exodus 35–40," in *Manchester Symposiums, 81–106.

Burkitt, F.C., "The Text of Exodus xl 17–19 in the Munich Palimpsest," *JTS* 29 (1927–1928): 146–47.

Charlesworth, J.H., "What is a Variant? Announcing a Dead Sea Scrolls Fragment of Deuteronomy," *Maarav* 16 (2009): 201–12 + plates ix–x (273–74).

De Bruyne, D., *S. Augustin reviseur de la Bible* (Rome: Tipografia Poliglotta Vaticana, 1931).

Dold, A., "Versuchte Neu- und Erstergänzungen zu den altlateinischen Texten im Cod. Clm 6225 der bayer. Staatsbibliothek," *Bib* 37 (1956): 39–58, 1 pl.

Fabry, H.-J., "Der Altarbau der Samaritaner – Ein Produkt der Text- und Literaturgeschichte," in *Die Textfunde vom Toten Meer und der Text der Hebräischen Bibel* (eds. U. Dahmen et al.; Neukirchen-Vluyn: Neukirchener, 2000), 35–52.

Kartveit, M., *The Origin of the Samaritans* (VTSup 128; Leiden: Brill, 2009).

Nelson, R.D., *Studies on the Development of the Text of the Tabernacle Account* (PhD diss., Harvard University, 1986; Ann Arbor: U.M.I. Dissertation Information Service, 1988).

Schenker, A., *Älteste Textgeschichte der Königsbücher: Die hebräische Vorlage der ursprünglichen Septuaginta als älteste Textform der Königsbücher* (OBO 199; Göttingen: Vandenhoeck & Ruprecht, 2004), 185–87.

Tov, E., "Pap. Giessen 13, 19, 22, 26: A Revision of the Septuagint?" in Tov, *Greek-Hebrew Bible, 459–75.

Ulrich, E., "4QJosh[a] and Joshua's First Altar in the Promised Land," in *New Qumran Texts and Studies: Proceedings of the First Meeting of the International Organization for Qumran Studies, Paris 1992* (eds. G.J. Brooke and F. García Martínez; STDJ 15; Leiden: Brill, 1994), 89–104 and pls. 4–6.

Ulrich, E., "The Old Latin, Mount Gerizim, and 4QJosh[a]," in *Textual Criticism and Dead Sea Scrolls Studies: Florilegium Complutense* (eds. A. Piquer Otero and P.A. Torijano; JSJSup 157; Leiden: Brill, 2012), 362–75.

Wevers, J.W. (ed.), *Genesis* (Septuaginta Vetus Testamentum Graecum 1; Göttingen: Vandenhoeck & Ruprecht, 1974).

Wevers, J.W. (ed.), *Deuteronomium* (Septuaginta Vetus Testamentum Graecum 3.2; Göttingen: Vandenhoeck & Ruprecht, 1979).

Wevers, J.W. (ed.), *Numeri* (Septuaginta Vetus Testamentum Graecum 3.1; Göttingen: Vandenhoeck & Ruprecht, 1982).

Wevers, J.W. and U. Quast (eds.), *Exodus* (Septuaginta Vetus Testamentum Graecum 2.1; Göttingen: Vandenhoeck & Ruprecht, 1991).

Julio Trebolle Barrera

2.5.2 Coptic Translations

2.5.2.1 Background

The Coptic translations of the Pentateuch have LXX (→ 2.4.1) as their base text and can be dated back to the early fourth century C.E. Together with the translation of the texts, the titles of each of the books were transcribed: ⲧ-ⲅⲉⲛⲉⲥⲓⲥ "Genesis," ⲧ-ⲉⲝⲟⲇⲟⲥ "Exodus," ⲡ-ⲗⲉⲩⲉⲓⲧⲓⲕⲟⲛ "Leviticus," ⲛ-ⲁⲣⲓⲑⲙⲟⲥ "[The book of] Numbers," ⲡ-ⲇⲉⲩⲧⲉⲣⲟⲛⲟⲙⲓⲟⲛ "Deuteronomy" often with the addition "of Moses (the prophet)." The collective term Pentateuch was unknown among the Copts. Complete translations of the Pentateuch existed only in the two main dialects of Coptic, i.e., Sahidic and Bohairic. In Akhmimic, only a partial translation of Exodus (Exod 1:1–7:4; chapter 3 is missing)[1] and some fragments of the same book[2] are preserved. The Old Testament texts in Akhmimic appear not to be independent translations from Greek, but daughter versions of Sahidic.[3] Only scarce frag-

---

[1] P. Lacau, "Textes coptes en dialects achmimique et sahidique," *BIFAO* 8 (1911): 43–81 (45–64) [ms A].

[2] L.T. Lefort, "Fragments bibliques en dialects achmimique et sahidique," *Mus* 66 (1953): 1–15 (Exod 15:14–21, 24–26; 16:1–3, 4–19; 23:20–32; 24:1–2).

[3] As in the case of the Minor Prophets (→ 6–9.2.2.2), Proverbs (→ 12.4.2), and Exodus (see below P.Bodmer XVI), Kasser, in his list of eight (!) Coptic biblical versions, regards A (Akhmimic) not as a separate version, but as integrated into S (Sahidic); cf. B.J. Diebner and R. Kasser, *Hamburger Papyrus Bil. 1* (Cahiers d'Orientalisme 18; Geneva: Patrick Kramer, 1989): 54–56, esp. 55 n. 25. This "hidden" list was brought to light by W.-P. Funk, "Zur Frage der achmimischen Version der Evangelien," in *Coptology, Past, Present, and Future: Studies in Honour of Rodolphe Kasser* (eds. S. Giversen, M. Krause, and P. Nagel; OLA 61; Leuven: Peeters, 1994), 327–39, esp. 329. With

ments survive in the Middle Egyptian (Mesokemic) dialect[4] and in the early extinct proto-Lycopolitan subdialect (in Coptic dialectology labelled as *I7*).[5]

2.5.2.2 Extant Biblical Text, Text Editions, Manuscript and Liturgical Transmission[6]

The inventory and state of preservation of the Pentateuch are different in Cop^{Sa} and Cop^{Boh}. In Cop^{Boh}, all the books of the Pentateuch are transmitted in the form of complete manuscripts. As for Cop^{Sa}, only the text of Leviticus, Numbers, and Deuteronomy is preserved in complete manuscripts, whereas the first two books, Genesis and Exodus, are scattered into dozens of single leaves or fragments.

The bulk of the Cop^{Sa} manuscripts belonged to the so-called White Monastery near Sohag in Upper Egypt and to the St. Michael Monastery at Hamuli in the Fayyum oasis. The textual witnesses extend from the fourth to the twelfth centuries (and some latecomers even after that). Some gaps in the manuscripts can be filled or supplied by readings in lectionaries and *horologia* and by quotations in Christian Coptic literature.

2.5.2.2.1 Sahidic Manuscripts,[7] Transmission, and Versions

Cop^{Sa} is, in general, the oldest available Coptic translation of the Pentateuch. Translations of Exodus and Deuteronomy are attested by manuscript evidence from the first half of the fourth century. There were codices comprising only one book, but also codices including two or three books. A codex that contained all five books is hardly to be expected due to its length.

- **Genesis:** Cop$^{Sa\ 1,\ 2,\ 3,\ 4}$
- Genesis and Exodus combined: Cop$^{Sa\ 5}$ (Codex Hamouli I), formerly in the University Library of Leuven (Belgium), was destroyed during the Second World War in 1940. Therefore, Lefort's edition[8] of the badly damaged text gained the rank of a "second original." From Exodus, only some fragments between Exod 1:1 and 5:17 were saved. Codex Hamouli I is the twin codex of M 566 (Cop$^{Sa\ 6}$; see below) with Leviticus, Numbers, and Deuteronomy.
- **Exodus:** Cop$^{Sa\ 7}$, the famous P. Bodmer XVI (Exod 1:1–15:21), fourth century C.E.[9] A manuscript of this type (not P. Bodmer XVI itself) was the *Vorlage* for an Akhmimic translation.[10] Exodus is further attested in Cop$^{Sa\ 8}$ and Cop$^{Sa\ 10}$ (three fragmentary leaves).
- **Leviticus:** Cop$^{Sa\ 13}$.
- **Leviticus and Numbers:** Cop$^{Sa\ 9}$ (from Exodus only the verses 23:15, 20 are preserved), Cop$^{Sa\ 11,\ 12}$.
- **Leviticus, Numbers, Deuteronomy:** Cop$^{Sa\ 6}$, codex M 566 of the Morgan Library in New York,[11] dated ca. 900 C.E., the twin codex of Cop$^{Sa\ 5}$ (see above). Contents: Leviticus folios 1^r–41^r; Numbers folios 42^r–102^v; Deuteronomy folios 103^r–152^r; unpublished. The text is fully preserved with the exception of a gap in folio 21^v (no lacuna in the manuscript), where the text jumps from Lev 14:32 to Lev 16:1. This gap can be supplied mostly by a long quotation (Lev 14:33–48) in Shenoute, *Canones*, Vol. VIII (ms XO according to Emmel).[12]

---

regard to the Akhmimic New Testament translations, the situation is different.

[4] J.W.B. Barns and R. Kasser, "Le manuscrit moyen égyptien B.M. Or. 9035," *Mus* 84 (1971): 395–401 (Gen 6:8–14, 15–19).

[5] W.-P. Funk, "Die Zeugen des koptischen Literaturdialektes *I7*," *ZÄS* 114 (1987): 117–33, esp. 120–23 (Gen 1:18–20, 24–28, 31; 2:1–5; formerly labelled as dialect A).

[6] Here, it is not possible to list all editions of the Coptic Pentateuch fragments. Please refer to the bibliographies of Coptic biblical texts, and, for the Sahidic codices and fragments, to Schüssler, **Biblia Coptica*.

[7] The manuscripts/fragments with the designation Cop^{Sa} are given according to Schüssler, **Biblia Coptica* (for the Pentateuch manuscripts mostly vol. 1.1, 1995).

[8] L.T. Lefort, "Coptica Lovanensia," *Mus* 50 (1937): 9–46 (more than one hundred fragments between Gen 17:11 and Gen 50:24); also published in a new compilation: L.T. Lefort, *Les manuscrites coptes de l'Université de Louvain*, Vol. 1: *Textes litteraires* (Leuven: Bibliothèque de l'Université, 1940), 5–38.

[9] Kasser, *Papyrus Bodmer XVI*.

[10] Cf. Nagel, *Achmimische Version des Buches Exodus*.

[11] Cf. L. Depuydt, *Catalogue of the Coptic Manuscripts in the Pierpont Morgan Library*, Vol. 1 (Corpus van verluchte handschriften 4; Leuven; Peeters, 1993), nos. 1, 5–7.

[12] Discovered and published by A. Boud'hors, "Nouvelle

– **Deuteronomy:** Cop$^{Sa\,14}$, P. Bodmer XVIII (Deut 1:1–10:7; the last page [96] is damaged and, therefore, the exact end is unknown); fourth century C.E.[13]

From the Deuteronomy codex Cop$^{Sa\,17}$ (eleventh century), twelve leaves are preserved with passages between Deut 8:11 and 16:7. According to the reconstruction of the quires by Schüssler,[14] the codex contained only Deuteronomy.

The first complete translation of Deuteronomy, not an excerpt as in P. Bodmer XVIII (Cop$^{Sa\,14}$), is attested in the papyrus codex BL Or. 7594 (Cop$^{Sa\,15}$), which also contains Jonah, Acts, and, as a type of appendix, the *Apocalypse of Elijah*. The manuscript can be dated to the first half of the fourth century C.E.[15] About a third of Deuteronomy is lost. The careless edition by Budge[16] is to be used only in conjunction with the thorough collation by Thompson.[17] P. Bodmer XVIII (Cop$^{Sa\,14}$) and BL Or. 7594 (Cop$^{Sa\,15}$) are the oldest witnesses of the Sahidic translation of Deuteronomy and present an earlier version of the Sahidic translation than the PML text (see above, Cop$^{Sa\,6}$).

A special problem in the textual history of the Sahidic Pentateuch are the extent, text sequences, and contents of Exodus. The title "Exodus" is not attested in biblical manuscripts, only in the lemmata of lectionaries and *horologia*. The large excerpt in P. Bodmer XVI (see above, Cop$^{Sa\,7}$) bears the *subscriptio* "The first part (μέρος) of the Law (νόμος)" and not of "Exodus." There are indications of a scribal (or manuscript) tradition in which the first part of Exodus was considered to be part of Genesis, whereas Exodus, as a new book, began only after the Song of Miriam in Exod 15:22.[18] Codex Cop$^{Sa\,8}$ deviates remarkably from the Greek manuscript tradition in the sequence of its chapters in Exodus. After Exod 24:28, the note "These are the prescripts on the tabernacle" is inserted, and the text continues immediately with Exod 31:12–34, while the prescripts on the tabernacle (Exod 25:1–26:36) appear after Exod 34:32.[19] Exodus 35–40 are not preserved in this codex with an "open end." A surprising Greek counterpart to Cop$^{Sa\,8}$ is P. Berolinesis 13994 that has a similar (but not identical) omission (Exod 23:11–31:11), according to Stegmüller a unique witness in the textual history of the Greek Pentateuch.[20]

The Pentateuch text of the biblical manuscripts is supplemented by lectionaries and other liturgical books. The lectionary manuscript Zoega no. 32 (Cop$^{Sa\,212L}$) contains exclusively Old Testament pericopes.[21] The late lectionary (fourteenth century) manuscript Zoega 99 (Cop$^{Sa\,108L}$) exhibits a number of pericopes from Genesis to Deuteron-

---

page de la version copte du Lévitique (14:33–49) dans un sermon de Chenouté," in *Sprache und Geist: Peter Nagel zum 65. Geburtstag* (eds. W. Beltz, U. Pietruschka, and J. Tubach; Hallesche Beiträge zur Orientwissenschaft 35; Halle: Universität Halle-Wittenberg, 2003), 47–63. Cf. now also A. Boud' hors, *Le Canon 8 de Chenouté* (Bibliothèque d' Études Coptes 21.1–2; Cairo: Institut Français d' Archéologie Orientale, 2013), 181–84 (text), 408 (translation).

[13] Kasser, *Papyrus Bodmer XVIII*.

[14] Schüssler, *Biblia Coptica* 1.1, 91.

[15] Cf. B. Layton, *Catalogue of Coptic Literary Manuscripts in the British Library Acquired since the Year 1906* (London: The British Library, 1987), 3–5 (no. 1); P. Nagel, "Aufbau und Komposition des Papyruscodex BL Or. 7594 der British Library," in *Coptology, Past, Present, and Future: Studies in Honour of Rodolphe Kasser* (eds. S. Giversen, M. Krause, and P. Nagel; OLA 61; Leuven: Peeters, 1994), 347–55.

[16] E.A.W. Budge, *Coptic Biblical Texts in the Dialect of Upper Egypt* (Oxford: University Press, 1912).

[17] H. Thompson, *The New Biblical Papyrus: A Sahidic Version of Deuteronomy, Jonah, and Acts of the Apostles from MS Or. 7594 of the British Museum: Notes and a Collation by Sir Herbert Thompson* (Printed for private circulation, 1913).

[18] See P. Nagel, "Textumfang und Textabfolge der sahidischen Version des Buches Exodus," in *Nubia et Oriens Christianus: Festschrift für C. Detlef G. Müller zum 60. Geburtstag* (eds. P.O. Scholz and R. Stempel: Bibliotheca Nubica 1; Cologne: Dinter, 1987), 181–89, esp. 183–85.

[19] See the analysis of manuscript Cop$^{Sa\,8}$ in Nagel, "Textumfang und Textabfolge der sahidischen Version des Buches Exodus," 187–89; Schüssler, *Biblia Coptica* 1.1, 49–50 (Cop$^{Sa\,8}$).

[20] O. Stegmüller, *Berliner Septuagintafragmente* (Berliner Klassikertexte 8; Berlin: Weidmann, 1939), nos. 4, 10–15, esp. 14.

[21] This lectionary (eleventh century) is analyzed by A. Hebbelynck, "Les manuscrits coptes-sahidiques du 'Monastère Blanc'," *Mus* NS 12 (1911): 143–47; cf. Schüssler, *Biblia Coptica* 2.2, 68–86; H. Takla, "Borgia Z 32: An Old Testament Lectionary from the Monastery of St. Shenouda (1)," *Saint Shenouda Coptic Quarterly* 1.4 (2005): 3–18; U. Zanetti, "Leçons Liturgiques au Monastère Blanc: Ancien Testament," *BSAC* 46 (2007): 209–17.

omy for the readings during Holy Week;[22] however, its text is inaccurate and not a reliable witness for the *veritas sahidica*.[23] The Sahidic *horologion* M 574 preserved fully the Canticle of Moses in Exod 15:1–21.[24] The bilingual (Greek-Sahidic) *Odenhandschrift* (Vienna, ms K 8706 = Cop[Sa 16lit]) from the sixth century C.E.[25] has in the beginning, in accordance with the Greek tradition of the biblical Odes, the Canticle of Moses from Exodus 15 and from Deut 32:2–43 (unfortunately, Exodus 15 is lost in the Coptic text).

2.5.2.2.2 Bohairic Manuscripts and Versions

The Bohairic Pentateuch is well attested by large number of biblical manuscripts. The Bohairic version is not a revision of the earlier attested Sahidic text(s), but is a new translation from the Greek *Koinē* text (→ 2.4.1). The bulk of the Bohairic Pentateuch manuscripts, mostly accompanied by an Arabic translation, are no older than the thirteenth century, with the exception of Codex Bibl. Vat. copt. 1 (ninth/tenth century C.E.). The assessment of Bohairic as a late and "monolithic" version has altered since the discovery of an earlier form of classical Bohairic, the so called proto-Bohairic,[26] in P. Bodmer III (fourth century C.E., in Coptic dialectology labelled as *B 74*) containing the Gospel of John (with *lacunae*) and Gen 1:1–4:2.[27] In addition to presenting an earlier linguistic stage of Bohairic, the Genesis text also displays an earlier perspective on the textual history: this translation is, indeed, influenced by the Sahidic version and therefore does not represent an independent translation from Greek. As in the case of Sahidic, the biblical witnesses of the Bohairic Pentateuch are supplemented by lectionaries, hymnical books, and *horologia*.[28] Among them the *Lectionary of the Holy Week*[29] from the year A.M. 990 = 1273 C.E. deserves special attention. It has numerous readings from the Old Testament – including readings from the Pentateuch[30] – the text of which is earlier than that of most of the biblical manuscripts. The Old Testament readings in this lectionary and related texts still await an investigation and placement in the history of the Coptic biblical text.

Ciasca, *Fragmenta Copto-Sahidica*, Vol. 1.

Kasser, R., *Papyrus Bodmer XVI: Exode I–XV,21 en sahidique* (Cologny: Bibliotheca Bodmeriana, 1961).

Kasser, R., *Papyrus Bodmer XVIII: Deutéronome I–X,7 en sahidique* (Cologny: Bibliotheca Bodmeriana, 1962).

de Lagarde, P., *Der Pentateuch koptisch* (Leipzig: Teubner, 1867).

Maspero, G., *Fragments ... Testament*.

Nagel, P., "Papyrus Bodmer XVI und die achmimische Version des Buches Exodus," in *Religion im Erbe Ägyptens: Beiträge zur spätantiken Religionsgeschichte zu Ehren von Alexander Böhlig* (ed. M. Görg; Ägypten und Altes Testament 14; Wiesbaden: Harrassowitz, 1988), 94–152.

Peters, M.K., *An Analysis of the Textual Character of the Bohairic Deuteronomy* (SBLSCS 4; Missoula: Scholars Press, 1979).

Peters, M.K., *A Critical Edition of the Coptic (Bohairic) Pentateuch*, Vol. 5: *Deuteronomy* (SBLSCS 15; Chico: Scholars Press, 1983).

Peters, M.K., *A Critical Edition of the Coptic (Bohairic)*

---

[22] See the detailed analysis of Cop[Sa 108L] by Schüssler, *Biblia Coptica* 1.4, 49–69, esp. for the Pentateuch pericopes, 60.

[23] See already the evaluation and assessment by Ciasca, *Fragmenta Copto-Sahidica*, Vol. 1, xxviii.

[24] See the great monographic study by H. Quecke, *Untersuchungen zum koptischen Stundengebet* (Publications de l'Institute Orientaliste de Louvain 3; Louvain: Université Catholique, Institut Orientaliste, 1970), with the edition and translation of manuscript M 574 (pp. 394–445) and the Canticle of Moses from Exodus 15 (pp. 440–45).

[25] W. Till and P. Sanz, *Eine griechisch-koptische Odenhandschrift (Papyrus Copt. Vindob. K 8706)* (Monumenta Biblica et Ecclesiastica 5; Rome: Pontificium Institutum Biblicum, 1939); cf. the full analysis of the manuscript's contents by Schüssler, *Biblia Coptica*, 1.1, 89–90 (Cop[Sa 16lit]).

[26] Cf. also the old Bohairic manuscript P Vat. Copt. 9 of the Minor Prophets (→ 6.9.2.2.2).

[27] R. Kasser, "Le Papyrus Bodmer III et les versions bibliques coptes," *Mus* 74 (1961): 423–33; R. Kasser, *Papyrus Bodmer III*

(CSCO 177, script. copt. 25; Louvain: Secrétariat du CorpusSCO, 1958).

[28] For a short list, see P. Nagel, "Veröffentlichungen koptischer Bibeltexte seit Till 1960," *APF* 35 (1989): 43–100, esp. 71.

[29] O.H.E. Burmester, *Le Lectionnaire de la Semaine Sainte: Texte Copte édité avec traduction française par E. Porcher après le manuscript Add. 5997 du British Museum* (2 vols.; PO 24.2 and 25.2; Paris: Firmin-Didot, 1933–1939), 1.173–294, 2.179–470.

[30] Listed (together with related texts) by Nagel, "Veröffentlichungen koptischer Bibeltexte seit Till 1960," 72.

Pentateuch, Vol. 1: *Genesis* (SBLSCS 19; Chico: Scholars Press, 1985).

Peters, M.K., *A Critical Edition of the Coptic (Bohairic) Pentateuch*, Vol. 2: *Exodus* (SBLSCS 22; Atlanta: Scholars Press, 1986).

Peter Nagel

2.5.3 Ethiopic Translation(s) of the Octateuch

2.5.3.1 Overview

The Ethiopic manuscript tradition knows of no Pentateuch, but instead contains an Octateuch. The textual history of this corpus has yet to be thoroughly studied, with something approaching a critical edition currently available only for Eth-Gen. However, we can tentatively assert that the textual history of the Ethiopic Octateuch appears to correspond to the general pattern known from the study of other parts of the Ethiopic bible: 1) an Old Ethiopic translation of the Greek (→ 2.4.1; → 3.3; → 4.3; → 13–17.1.1.1) that provided, in one form or another, the base text for all subsequent recensions; specifically 2) a Transitional Recension of haphazard corrections to the Old Ethiopic; 3) a Standardized Recension in which the haphazard corrections gave way to a thoroughgoing rehabilitation of the Old Ethiopic (or some form of transitional text), which became the standard version in wide use after approximately the sixteenth century; 4) a modern Textus Receptus characterized by the preservation and conflation of variants that have arisen both within the transmission history of biblical manuscripts and in the commentary tradition of Ethiopia (→ 1.4.3.7.1). The question of whether Eth[Cam 1570] may preserve a sole witness to an Academic Recension of Eth-Gen will be discussed below.

2.5.3.2 Order and Location of the Octateuch in the Manuscripts

With one exception (Eth[EMIP 625], produced in the twentieth century), all manuscripts point to an Ethiopic Octateuch. The collection, called ኦሪት ('orit, hereafter Orit), was made up of Genesis, Exodus, Leviticus, Numbers, Deuteronomy, Joshua (→ 3–5.2.3.1), Judges (→ 3–5.2.3.2), and Ruth (→ 13–17.2.3.1), copied invariably in that order. Based on a study of forty-seven manuscripts, we describe the following patterns of relationships to other books.

The manuscripts make it clear that the standard conception is that the Orit stands as a unit and that it usually comes first. Twenty-nine of the forty-six manuscripts contain only the books of the Orit. Of the seventeen manuscripts in which the Orit is transmitted with other books, ten begin with the Orit. There is, however, a significant exception to the pattern of the Orit being first in a codex. There are six manuscripts in which *1 Enoch* (→ 11.5.1.2) precedes the Orit (Eth[BL 484, Cam 1570, EMIP 743, EMML 2436, EMML 4437, EMML 4750]). One further manuscript places both *1 Enoch* and Job (→ 11.4.3) before the Orit: Eth[Frank Rüpp. II, 1]. The only other pattern of note has to do with those works that follow the Orit. In these seventeen manuscripts, the Orit is followed by *Jubilees* (→ 11.8.6) in eight cases, and by 1–4 Kingdoms (→ 3–5.2.3.3) in three cases.

2.5.3.3 History of Scholarship and Published Editions

Two complete editions of the Ethiopic Octateuch have been produced, one in 1853 by Dillmann[1] and one in 1915 by Da Bassano.[2] A partial edition covering Genesis through Leviticus was produced by Boyd in 1909–1911.[3] The editions by Dillmann and Boyd are diplomatic editions, presenting the readings of one manuscript, with an apparatus presenting variants from a few other manuscripts available at their times. The Da Bassano edition is eclectic and non-critical with an unspecified textual basis.[4] Dillmann's edition presented as base text the readings of a manuscript of the British and Foreign Bible Society (dated variously to the thirteenth, fourteenth or early fifteenth century), with variants from one seventeenth-century and

---

[1] Dillmann, *Biblia*.
[2] Bassano, *Beluy Kidan*.
[3] Boyd, *The Octateuch in Ethiopic*.
[4] Lofgren reviews the edition and speculates on the identity of the manuscripts employed, "Die äthiopische Bibelausgabe der katholischen Mission: Mit einer Kollation des Danieltextes," *Le monde oriental* 23 (1929): 174–80.

one eighteenth-century manuscript. Boyd's edition presents as base text the readings of Eth[BN 102], dated to the thirteenth–fifteenth centuries with variants from the Eth[BFBS] manuscript used by Dillmann and four other relatively late manuscripts. Boyd claims that with these six manuscripts "the history of the transmission of the version from the thirteenth century to the present time is adequately reflected, each recension or stage being dependent for its representation not upon a single manuscript, but upon a group,"[5] but this claim is clearly overstated. All three of these editions are far from what we would call a reliable critical edition of the Old Ethiopic, let alone a clear guide to the subsequent recensions of the Old Ethiopic. The only doctoral dissertation on any part of the Orit is that by Edele, discussed below (→ 2.5.3.4).[6]

Beginning with the Larger Cambridge Septuagint[7] and continuing with the Göttingen Septuagint,[8] Ethiopic witnesses have been included in critical editions of LXX. But the object of these editions has been to garner the testimony of another daughter version for the purposes of the textual criticism of the Greek Old Testament. In such cases, the attention is only ever on the earliest recoverable version of the Ethiopic, i.e., the Old Ethiopic. Consequently, while helping considerably to illuminate the question of the *Vorlage* of the Old Ethiopic, these editions have done nothing to help our understanding of the later textual history of the Ethiopic.

---

[5] Boyd, *The Octateuch in Ethiopic*, Part 1, x.

[6] Edele's dissertation makes reference to a "D. Phil. thesis" on Ethiopic Exodus by M. Bezemer in 1982 at University of Amsterdam. However, our sources indicate that this is an M.A. thesis and that it is currently misplaced and unavailable.

[7] Brooke–McLean, *The Old Testament in Greek*, Vol. 1: *The Octateuch*.

[8] J.W. Wevers, *Genesis* (Septuaginta Vetus Testamentum Graecum 1; Göttingen: Vandenhoeck & Ruprecht, 1974); J.W. Wevers, *Exodus* (Septuaginta Vetus Testamentum Graecum 2.1; Göttingen: Vandenhoeck & Ruprecht, 1991); J.W. Wevers, *Leviticus* (Septuaginta Vetus Testamentum Graecum 2.2; Göttingen: Vandenhoeck & Ruprecht, 1986); J.W. Wevers, *Numeri* (Septuaginta Vetus Testamentum Graecum 3.1; Göttingen: Vandenhoeck & Ruprecht, 1982); J.W. Wevers, *Deuteronomium* (Septuaginta Vetus Testamentum Graecum 3.2; Göttingen: Vandenhoeck & Ruprecht, 1977).

With so little progress having been made toward a critical understanding of the textual history of the Ethiopic Octateuch, our working models are necessarily based on the small sampling of research that has been completed. The work that has been accomplished covers only Genesis and there are methodological problems connected with it. Consequently, we must emphasize the tentative nature of our working hypotheses to this point. The situation will change soon with studies forthcoming on Eth-Deut (R. Lee et al.), Eth-Judg (M. Wechsler et al.), and Eth-Ruth (D. Assafa et al.).[9]

2.5.3.4 Edele's Dissertation on Ethiopic Genesis

In 1995, Edele completed a dissertation at Duke University entitled "A Critical Edition of Genesis in Ethiopic" in which he employed twenty-two manuscripts dating from the thirteenth to the eighteenth centuries. Despite this wealth of manuscript evidence, Edele concluded that "the feasibility of reconstructing an eclectic text, in keeping with a hypothetical original text, proved to be futile."[10] Consequently, Edele's edition is a diplomatic edition of the fourteenth-century manuscript Eth[Martini 2], provided with a critical apparatus of readings from other manuscripts. It was selected as base text because it was the oldest available manuscript of Genesis and because Wevers made use of it in the critical apparatus to the Genesis volume of the Göttingen Septuagint.[11] But, he says, the base text was "occasionally emended" because "it has frequent omissions, misspellings, idiosyncrasies and singular readings."[12]

When it comes to the typical text-critical tasks of identifying and characterizing families of manuscripts, Edele frames his conclusions oddly, as though the object of his study were the detection of recensional activity *per se*, i.e., in answer to the question whether or not there was evidence of recensional activity in the manuscripts of Eth-Gen.

---

[9] The results of this work will be published in the series Ethiopic Manuscripts, Texts, and Studies (Eugene: Pickwick Publications, 2009 ff.).

[10] Edele, "Critical Edition," 35.

[11] Wevers, *Genesis*.

[12] Edele, "Critical Edition," 36.

He reviews the history of scholarship regarding recensional activity for the Ethiopic Old Testament,[13] and indicates that he had found "two types of evidence which confirm that the Ethiopic textual tradition of Gen underwent considerable editorial revisions."[14] Yet, he seems unable to relate his evidence of recensional activity to the standard model and ends up concluding that "there is reason to question with respect to Genesis the accuracy of the generally accepted scholarly consensus on the Ethiopic Old Testament pertaining to the three stages of the 'Old Ethiopic,' 'Vulgar Recension,' and the 'Academic Recension.' Although these terms may accurately describe the textual history of other Ethiopic books in the Old Testament, they do not accurately reflect the characteristics of the textual transmission of Genesis."[15]

Space does not allow a full discussion of the manner in which Edele has executed his method. Suffice it to say that Edele does, in fact, produce ample and clear evidence that could be explained well by the standard model (→ 1.4.3.7).

Though Edele does not lay out in a sequential manner his understanding of the recensional history of Eth-Gen, he provides evidence for the following. First, he shows that the bulk of the mainly oldest manuscripts fall into two subgroups: his manuscripts 1, 3, 4, 6, 7, 11, 14, and 18 on the one hand, and his manuscripts 2, 5, 8, 9, 10, 12, 13, and 19 on the other.[16] Though we might quibble about the placement of one or two of the manuscripts into this or that subgroup, the main thing that strikes us is that these two subgroups show precisely the sort of features that characterize the relationship between what we call the Earliest Attested (→ 1.4.3.7.3) and the Transitional (→ 1.4.3.7.4) forms of the Ethiopic text. Second, he shows that there is a family of manuscripts (his manuscripts 17, 20, 20a, 21, and 22), all from the seventeenth and eighteenth centuries, that are set apart from the other manuscripts by a series of shared unique readings, especially the substantial pluses at Gen 15:10; 25:6; 26:34; 38:28; and 38:29, as well as shorter pluses in Gen 2:8; 7:7; 15:9 (excluding his manuscript 21); 15:18; 32:30; and 33:10. Further, he emphasizes with regard to the older manuscripts that their readings "reflect the product of a deliberate revision process."[17] He even concludes that "this extensive revision process was conducted on the basis of a text type similar to the text of Genesis reconstructed in the Göttingen Septuagint." These are marks of what we would call the Standardized Recension (→ 1.4.3.7.5). Third, Edele has one unique manuscript (his manuscript 15 = Eth$^{\text{Cam 1570}}$), dated to 1588, which he analyzes in great depth.[18] Eth$^{\text{Cam 1570}}$ contains several pluses not present in the other manuscripts: Gen 6:20; 22:19; 23:20; 24:12; 31:51; 35:21; 36:18; 36:34–39, 41–42. Further, it contains a huge number of singular readings. Edele probed fifty-seven of these singular readings that are contained in Genesis 38–50 alone and found that "all of these singularly attested variants from MS 15 agree with the Masoretic text."[19] Edele is rightly cautious about claiming that this single manuscript should be made to represent a family or independent recension. None of the other manuscripts in his study share these characteristics. And a further investigation by the current writers of nearly a dozen additional manuscripts has not yet turned up another manuscript that shares these characteristics. Standing alone, as it does, we cannot yet be sure that Eth$^{\text{Cam 1570}}$ witnesses to a Hebraic recension of Eth-Gen. But were we to find even one more such manuscript we would be compelled toward that conclusion. The fact that there is, as yet, only one actually fits into the profile of this recension that seems to serve a small and rarefied niche. But this is essentially an argument *ex silentio* and cannot be taken as definitive. All we can say at this point is that the evidence is not inconsistent with the existence of an academic recension, to this point represented by Eth$^{\text{Cam 1570}}$.

That Edele did not detect any evidence of the modern Textus Receptus (→ 1.4.3.7.6) is a necessary

---

[13] Edele, "Critical Edition," 250–52.
[14] Edele, "Critical Edition," 252.
[15] Edele, "Critical Edition," 271–72.
[16] Edele, "Critical Edition," 269–70.

[17] Edele, "Critical Edition," 260.
[18] Edele, "Critical Edition," 252–59.
[19] Edele, "Critical Edition," 259.

outcome of his decision to exclude from his study any manuscripts after the eighteenth century. Since he had full access to the collection of the Ethiopian Manuscript Microfilm Library, he had several nineteenth and twentieth century manuscripts available to him, but these were systematically set to the side.

2.5.3.5 Further Evidence beyond Edele

An examination of those passages where the sequence of the Greek differs considerably from the Hebrew (Exod 20:13–15; 36–39; Num 1:24–27; 6:22–26; 26:15–47; and Josh 9:1–3) provides a window into the textual development of the rest of the Octateuch. Overall, the textual history we extrapolated from Edele's work fits nicely with the data from these sample passages. Thus, it is relatively safe to assume that the books of the Octateuch share a common transmission history.

The Old Ethiopic witnesses exhibit remarkable agreement, perhaps attesting a conservative approach toward the biblical text during earlier periods in Ethiopia's literary history. However, increasing international religious and commercial relations resulted in textual comparisons that highlighted the differences of the Ethiopian Bible. Although aware of significant divergences between other versions and their own Scriptures, scribes for quite some time introduced only minor changes into the text. For example, despite the awkwardness of and redundancies in LXX-Num 6:22–26, only one change occurs in the transition period; ትባርክዮሙ· "you will bless them" becomes ትገብርዮሙ· "you will do to them." Similarly in Josh 8:35–9:3, no verses are rearranged, instead the LXX (→ 3.3) order is preserved but Gerizim is transcribed ጋዩራን (Gəyuran) rather than ጋሪዝን (Gärizən). Even if one regarded these alterations as being due to inner Ethiopic corruption, they would still contribute to our understanding of this era of collation and interpretation. Indeed, it is remarkable that these minor corrections/corruptions gained traction, for they appear in all of the Transitional Text manuscripts. At the same time, one wonders how the Old Ethiopic passages most in need of revision actually remained untouched.

Edele correctly concludes that, apart from Eth[Cam 1570], which might be a representative of the Academic Text, the Ethiopic text experienced only one major revision, which we label the Standardized Text. Although relatively late on the scene, late seventeenth century, this version quickly spread and prevails even today. In contrast to the previous centuries of inactivity, this revision radically rearranges, excises, and expands the Old Ethiopic to align it with comparison texts. Edele errs, though, when he argues that this revision depended upon Greek manuscripts. As with the other biblical books, comparison with an Arabic version (→ 2.4.9; → 2.5.8) introduced the supposedly "Greek" readings. As for Hebraic influence on this revision, note the transliteration ኤፍድ ('Ēfōd) found in the pluses of the Standardized Text in contrast to the Old Ethiopic ላዕለ መትከፍት "upon the shoulders" and ኤጲሙስ ('Ēpēmus = ἐπωμίς "ephod").

2.5.3.6 Textual Variations Recorded in the Andəmta (→ 1.4.3.8)

An examination of the forty-nine textual variations found in the *andəmta* commentary on Genesis,[20] shows that just under half can also be identified in known manuscripts in the Ethiopic Manuscript Imaging Project *noted in text-critical studies*,[21] although their sources are rarely recorded in the *andəmta*. As with the Octateuch manuscript tradition, we posit that the pattern of Genesis can be extended to the other books of the Octateuch. The small number of variations in the book of Genesis demonstrates that Ethiopian scholars did not seek to reconstruct texts, but rather recorded the variations for their theological or didactical significance.

The *andəmta* variations are of various types, showing variations in the spelling of names, others that appear to favor a particular theological

---

[20] See Lee and Tadese, "Textual Variations as Recorded in the Ethiopian Andemta Biblical Commentaries," presented at the annual SBL meeting in Chicago, November, 2012.

[21] R.W. Cowley, *The Traditional Interpretation of the Apocalypse of St John in the Ethiopian Orthodox Church* (University of Cambridge Oriental Publications 33; Cambridge: Cambridge University Press, 1983), 57.

perspective, etc. A significant group of variations show awareness of the Hebrew text by reference to particular Hebrew words, and others clearly reveal knowledge of the differences between MT (→ 2.2.2) and LXX. (→ 2.4.1)

Bassano, *Beluy Kidan*, Vol. 1: Octateuch.
Boyd, J.O., *The Text of the Ethiopic Version of the Octateuch: With Special Reference to the Age and Value of the Haverford Manuscript* (Bibliotheca Abessinica 2; Leiden: Brill, 1905).
Boyd, J.O., *The Octateuch in Ethiopic according to the Text of the Paris Codex with the Variants of Five Other Manuscripts*, Part 1: *Genesis* (ed. E. Littmann; Bibliotheca Abessinica 3; Leiden: Brill, 1909).
Boyd, J.O., *The Octateuch in Ethiopic according to the Text of the Paris Codex with the Variants of Five Other Manuscripts*, Part 2: *Exodus and Leviticus* (ed. E. Littmann; Bibliotheca Abessinica 3; Leiden: Brill, 1911).
Brooke–McLean, *The Old Testament in Greek*, Vol. 1: *The Octateuch*, Part 1: *Genesis*.
Dillmann, *Biblia*.
Edele, B.A., "A Critical Edition of Genesis in Ethiopic" (PhD diss., Duke University, 1995).

Steve Delamarter
Curt Niccum

2.5.4 Late Syriac Translations

2.5.4.1 Background

The most notable feature of the later translations of the Pentateuch (as with renderings of other books of the Jewish canon) is that Hebrew Scripture is no longer the direct source of the biblical text for the Syriac translators. The later Syriac versions depend on, or are strongly influenced by, the Greek LXX text (→ 1.3.1.1), often in the form of Origen's early third century revision (→ 1.3.1.2.7). Thus, these later Syriac versions can be significant for textual criticism of LXX. However, the influence of Peshitta tradition continues to varying degrees between versions. (Although the early-sixth-century Syro-Lucianic/Philoxenian version may have extended to the Old Testament, there is no surviving evidence that it covered the Pentateuch.)

2.5.4.2 Syro-Hexapla
2.5.4.2.1 Original Form, Editions, Tools

The Syro-Hexapla (Syh; → 1.4.5) version was produced in 614–616 C.E. by the Syrian Orthodox scholar Paul of Tella (→ 1.4.5.2), at the convent of the Enaton, where clergy had taken refuge from the campaign of the Persian king Khosrau II.[1] Both the Syro-Hexapla and the Harklean New Testament, carried out at the same time and place, may have reflected a move to be reconciled with Greek and Coptic miaphysites.[2] As with other books of the Syro-Hexapla, Syh-Pent derives ultimately from the Greek of the fifth column of the Hexapla (Hex; → 1.3.1.2.7), representing Origen's text of LXX revised quantitatively in line with the Hebrew text of his day. Though it has been commonly supposed that the Syro-Hexapla is rendered directly from the actual Hexapla, this has been shown to be unlikely, partly because this massive work was probably still in the library of Caesarea rather than in Egypt. It is more likely that Paul worked from manuscripts of a LXX edition based on the fifth column.[3] If one reconciles internal evidence, statements in the detailed colophons to Genesis, Exodus, and Numbers in manuscripts of Syh-Pent,[4] and also information in the early-ninth-century letter of Catholicos Timothy I to Mar Sergius,[5] it seems

---

[1] Vööbus, *Hexapla and Syro-Hexapla*, 36–37; R.J.V. Hiebert, "Syriac Biblical Textual History and the Greek Psalter," in *The Old Greek Psalter: Studies in Honour of Albert Pietersma* (eds. R.J.V. Hiebert, C.E. Cox, and P.J. Gentry; JSOTSup 332; Sheffield: Sheffield Academic Press, 2001), 178–204 (179–80).

[2] A. Juckel, "Should the Harklean Version be Included in a Future Lexicon of the Syriac New Testament?" in *Foundations for Syriac Lexicography I* (eds. A.D. Forbes and D.G.K. Taylor; Piscataway: Gorgias Press, 2005), 167–94 (170 and n. 17).

[3] Law, *Origenes Orientalis*, 18–19; 369–70; S.P. Brock, *The Recensions of the Septuagint Version of 1 Samuel* (Turin: Zamorani, 1996), 170.

[4] Hiebert, "Syriac Biblical Textual History," 182–85; for the Genesis colophon, which mentions both the Tetrapla and Hexapla, see Vööbus, *Pentateuch*, 40 and fol. 19a; cf. R.G. Jenkins, "Colophons of the Syrohexapla and the Textgeschichte of the Recensions of Origen," in *VII Congress of the International Organization for Septuagint and Cognate Studies, Leuven 1989* (ed. C.E. Cox; SBLSCS 31; Atlanta: Scholars Press, 1991), 261–77 (267).

[5] O. Braun, "Ein Brief des Katholikos Timotheos I über biblische Studien des 9 Jahrhunderts," *OrChr* 3 (1903): 299–

that the Greek exemplar of the Syro-Hexapla derived from and was collated with the LXX text of Eusebius and Pamphilus. Colophons to Syh-Exod[6] state that the (Greek) exemplar (ܢܘܣܟܐ "copy, manuscript"[7]) from which the present text of Syh-Exod was translated had an inscription (ܪܘܫܡܐ "inscription, annotation") stating that the text of the book had been taken from the Hexapla "according to the versions," and had been collated with another copy "also supplied with the versions." Both remarks probably relate to the readings of Aquila, Symmachus, and Theodotion, since these appear frequently in the margins of Syh-Pent manuscripts.

Particularly noteworthy in Syh-Pent are the many marginal readings corresponding to the expansive text of the Samaritan Pentateuch (SP; → 1.2.3) version, and found in the extant manuscripts of Syh-Exod, Syh-Num, and Syh-Deut, more plentifully than in any Greek LXX (→ 2.4.1) witness.[8] Lengthy "Samaritan" readings are preserved even in the relatively late Midyat manuscript, for instance at the end of Num 20:13 (fol. 130[b]), 21:20, and 23 (fol. 132[a]). According to the colophons, the Greek exemplars of Syh-Exod and Syh-Num were descended in some way from the Hexapla (→ 1.3.1.2.7), and had also been compared with other Greek exemplars also derived from the Hexapla in Caesarea but in which the Hebrew had been collated with the Samaritan Hebrew version: it was from this text that Samaritan material had been supplied.[9] However, Field doubted that a *Hebrew* SP was ever consulted in the tradition that culminated in the Syro-Hexapla: he believed that the scribes assumed that what were in reality Greek readings in the margins of the Hexapla that reflected Samaritan tradition, went back to the work of Origen with the Hebrew text and that he had translated them himself.[10]

The earliest edition of any part of Syh-Pent was that of Andreas Masius in the sixteenth century, but this was unpublished and later lost and only some notes in Latin survive in his work *Syrorum Peculium*.[11] The late-nineteenth-century edition of Lagarde is still widely used for Syh-Pent.[12] Lagarde based his edition on the earlier one of Ceriani, including some improved readings.[13] Field also used Ceriani's earlier edition for his references to Syh-Pent.[14] However, Ceriani and Lagarde sometimes mistook the placing of some Hexaplaric signs, and autopsy of the manuscripts or microfilms is therefore recommended.[15]

The text of Lagarde's edition is based on the following manuscripts:

– Genesis: from B.M. Add. MS 14,442 (seventh century?), fol. 1–46. Due to lacunae, parts of Genesis are missing: Gen 1:1–4:8b, also Gen 9:24b–16:1; 16:12b–20:1 end; 20:12b–31:53a; 32:11b–36:2a; 40:17b–43:2a; 47:16b–50:17.
– Exodus: from B.M. Add. 12,134 (dated 697 C.E.). Complete.
– Numbers: from B.M. Add. 14,437 (eighth century?). Missing from Numbers are Num 1:1–33 end; 2:2–15; 3:47b–7:19a; 7:36b–10:6a; 15:29–16:2; 16:29–40; 26:39b–36:13 (end of book).

It was not until the mid-twentieth century that the discovery of new material filled some of the many gaps in Genesis and supplied parts of Syh-Lev and Syh-Deut. Goshen-Gottstein and Baars both

---

313 (302) (German translation: 303–05; Eng.: S.P. Brock, *A Brief Outline of Syriac Literature* [Moran Etho 9; Kottayam: SEERI, 1997], 257).

[6] B.M. Add. MS 12,134, fol. 132[b]; Vööbus, *Pentateuch*, 40–41 and fol. 65[a].

[7] All English translations here and below are by the author.

[8] Field, *Hexapla*, 1.lxxxii–lxxxiv.

[9] These complex colophons are variously translated by W. Wright, *Catalogue of Syriac Manuscripts in the British Museum, Acquired Since the Year 1838* (London: The British Museum, 1870–1872), i, 30; G. Mercati, *Nuove note di letteratura biblica e cristiana antica* (Studi e Test 95; Vatican City: Biblioteca Apostolica Vaticano, 1941), 36–37; and Vööbus, *Pentateuch*, 41–43 and fol. 151[b] (Vööbus' translation of the Numbers colophon is misleading at the very end).

---

[10] Field, *Hexapla*, 1.lxxxiii.

[11] See W. Baars, *New Syrohexaplaric Texts: Edited, Commented upon, and Compared* (Leiden: Brill, 1968), 2–3.

[12] Lagarde, *Bibliothecae Syriacae*, 33–121.

[13] J.W. Wevers, *Genesis* (Septuaginta Vetus Testamentum Graecum 1; Göttingen: Vandenhoeck & Ruprecht, 1974), 51–52; *Ceriani Pentateuchi Syrohexaplaris*, 1–106.

[14] Field, *Hexapla*.

[15] Law, *Origenis Orientalis*, 33.

published material from Syh-Gen, and Goshen-Gottstein for Syh-Deut.[16] In 1975, Vööbus published a photographic edition of an almost complete twelfth-century manuscript of Syh-Pent.[17] However, it lacks most of Genesis up to Gen 32:9; Exod 20:30b–33:26a; and 29:41–30:18a are missing; so are Lev 20:15–21:9a and 26:46b–end; Num 1:1–2, 6:7b–7:7a, and 13:2b–14:23a have been lost; also Deut 32:35b–end.

Very brief readings from Syh-Pent are found in the exegetical work of both Syrian Orthodox and East Syriac authors (→ 21.9): see below → 2.5.4.2.5.

2.5.4.2.2 Translation Character

The Syro-Hexapla follows the word order of the Greek exemplar (→ 2.4.6) very closely. It should be borne in mind that a vast translation enterprise into Syriac from Greek had been taking place from the early fifth century. Largely for theological reasons, the process had gradually favored formal representation of the elements of Greek and consistency in rendering vocabulary.[18] This affected biblical versions, with an observable development of approach to the Greek from the Old Syriac Gospels to the Harklean New Testament, and also works of theology and philosophy. Consequently, the style of the Syro-Hexapla (and Harklean New Testament) was no innovation, but the natural outcome of development of translation philosophy over the course of around 300 years.

---

[16] M.H. Goshen-Gottstein, "Neue Syrohexaplafragmente," *Bib* 37 (1956): 162–83 for Gen 24:10–28; 28:6–19; 27:30–40; M.H. Goshen-Gottstein, "A New Text from the Syrohexapla: Deuteronomy 34," in *A Tribute to Arthur Vööbus: Studies in Early Christian Literature and its Environment, Primarily in the Syrian East* (ed. R.H. Fischer; Chicago: Lutheran School of Theology at Chicago, 1977), 19–28 for Deut 34:1–8; Baars, *New Syro-Hexaplaric Texts*, Gen 1:1–19; 15:1–20; 19:1–14; 28:10–22; 32:12(13)–21(22); 32:24(25)–32(33); 49:1–7, 8–18, 19–28.

[17] Vööbus, *Pentateuch*.

[18] See S.P. Brock, "Towards a History of Syriac Translation Technique," in *Les contacts du mode syriaque avec les autres cultures: III Symposium Syriacum 1980: Goslar 7–11 September 1980* (ed. R. Lavenant; OrChrAn 221; Rome: Pontificium Institutum Orientalium Studiorum, 1983), 1–14, and repr. in *Studies in Syriac Christianity* (ed. S.P. Brock; Variorum: Aldershot: Ashgate, 1992), ch. x; also Juckel, "Should the Harklean Version", 171, on similar features in the Harklean New Testament.

It should be noted that Origen's reordering of the LXX text in line with the Hebrew means that the order of the Syro-Hexapla is close to that of MT (→ 1.2.2) and Peshitta (→ 1.3.4), something especially noticeable in Exodus, where the Old Greek has a very different order of material in the last chapters.

2.5.4.2.3 Translation Technique and Inner-Translational Features

When compared with the Peshitta (s; → 1.3.4), some features strike the reader, especially the use of ܕܝܠ + pronominal suffix to represent Greek αὐτοῦ "his" etc., instead of an attached possessive suffix on the noun. The Syro-Hexapla uses composite verbs to represent the more complex Greek verbal system. For instance the Greek imperfect tense is rendered by a participle of the appropriate verb plus the perfect of the verb "to be" (e.g., Exod 19:18 ἐκαπνίζετο as ܬܐܢ ܗܘܐ, both meaning "it was smoking"; Exod 19:19 ἐγίνοντο/ ܗܘܝܢ ܗܘܘ, both meaning "they were"); often a Greek present participle is rendered by ܟܕ + participle (e.g., Exod 15:21 λέγουσα "saying" = ܟܕ ܐܡܪܐ "while saying").[19]

Regarding the lexicon of Syh-Pent, there is some inevitable overlap between the vocabulary of the Syro-Hexapla and the Peshitta. Yet often the Syro-Hexapla is at pains to render the Greek without reference to the Peshitta and often resorts to using loanwords from the Greek, whether they were already in existence by the early seventh century or coined by the translator himself. For instance, ܐܪܟܘܢܐ "joints" in Exod 26:17 renders the usual LXX term ἀγκωνίσκοι "joints," but two verses later in Exod 26:19, βάσεις "bases" becomes the loanword ܒܣܝܣ "bases" also known in the Peshitta. Some inconsistencies appear in parallel passages: for instance, in the double descriptions of priestly clothing in Exodus 28 and 39 (Old Greek ch. 36), the translator uses different terms: Exod 28:31 ὑποδύτης "undergarment" is rendered as ܠܒܘܫܐ "garment";

---

[19] The fullest treatment remains that of T.S. Rørdam, *Libri Judicum et Ruth secundum versionem Syrio-hexaplarem* (Copenhagen: Otto Schwartz, 1861), 3–59, but there are no examples from the Pentateuch. See also Baars, *New Syro-Hexaplaric Texts*, 36–40, and his notes on individual texts.

but in Exod 39:22, ܦܪܙܘܡܐ "loincloth" translates ὑποδύτης "undergarment"; ζῶναι "belts" in Exod 28:40 and 39:29 becomes ܗܡܝܢܐ "belts" in the first instance (= s) but the Greek loanword ܙܘܢܝ̈ "belts" in the second; λῶμα "hem" in Exod 28:33 and 39:24–26 is ܫܦܘ̈ܠܐ "skirts" (= s) in the earlier account and the Greek loanword ܣܝܪܘܢ "cord, line, small chain" (ܣܝܪܐ sg.) in the second.[20]

2.5.4.2.4 Text-Critical Value
The Syro-Hexapla is the most faithful witness to the Hexaplaric text of LXX, because it preserves many of Origen's signs and because of its mirror style of translation.[21] The inclusion of Samaritan readings and many readings from Aquila, Symmachus, and Theodotion makes the Syh-Pent an important source for the various Greek traditions once collected by Origen.

2.5.4.2.5 Reception of Syh-Pent
The Syro-Hexapla was not originally intended for liturgical use, yet the late-seventh-century Syh-Exod manuscript already contains lectionary titles within the main text, such as on f. 30b. Readings from Syh-Pent appear in some later lectionaries, and thus the latter can be useful sources for our knowledge of the Syro-Hexapla.

Even though the Syro-Hexapla originated in the Syrian Orthodox Church, both Western and Eastern exegetes used it in their exegetical works. Eastern writers include Isho' bar Nun, Theodore bar Koni, and Isho'dad of Merv, who refer to "the Greek" (= Syh) or cite its readings in comments on the Pentateuch books.[22] Isho'dad also cites readings from the Three and SP.[23] The Diyarbakir Commentary on Genesis and Exodus has thirty-one citations from Syh-Pent.[24] In the West, Dionysius bar Salibi employs Syh-Pent for his "spiritual" commentary (the Peshitta forming the basis for his literal commentary), and Barhebraeus refers to the Syro-Hexapla in his Scholia on the Old Testament, including also citations from the Three.[25]

2.5.4.3 Jacob of Edessa
2.5.4.3.1 Background
According to biographies of the Syrian Orthodox scholar-bishop, Jacob of Edessa (d. 708 C.E.; → 1.4.6),[26] Jacob carried out a revision of the Old Testament in the late seventh/early eighth century, in the monastery of Tell 'Adda (northern Syria).

2.5.4.3.2 Original Form, Editions, Tools
Although few books of this revision have survived, we do have a single manuscript of the entire Pentateuch in Jacob's version, brought from Tagrit to Scetis in Egypt, and thence to Paris in 1764. It is now in the Bibliothèque Nationale, ms Syr. 26.[27]

---

[20] Cf. Juckel on the Harklean version's "strong, but not perfect" lexical consistency: "Should the Harklean Version," 173; and M.P. Weitzman, "The Reliability of Retroversions of the Three from the Syrohexapla: A Pilot Study in Hosea," in *Origen's Hexapla and Fragments: Papers Presented at the Rich Seminar on the Hexapla, Oxford Centre for Hebrew and Jewish Studies, 25th July – 3rd August 1994* (ed. A. Salvesen; TSAJ 58; Tübingen: Mohr Siebeck, 1998), 317–59.

[21] Law, *Origenes Orientalis*, 23; Rørdam, *Libri Judicum et Ruth*, 3.

[22] *Selected Questions of Isho' bar Nun on the Pentateuch* (ed. E.G. Clarke; StPB 5; Leiden: Brill, 1962); *Theodorus bar Koni, Liber Scholiorum* I (ed. A. Scher; CSCO 55 Syr. 19; Louvain: Peeters, 1960); *Commentaire d'Išo'dad de Merv sur l'AT*, Part 1: *Genèse*; Part 2: *Exode-Deutéronome* (eds. J-M. Vosté and C. van den Eynde; CSCO 126 and 176 Syr. 67 and 80; Leuven: Peeters, 1950 and 1958). Also the anonymous work known as the *Gannat Bussame* (ed. G.J. Reinink; CSCO 501 Syr. 211; Leuven: Peeters, 1988).

[23] A. Salvesen, "Hexaplaric Sources in Isho'dad of Merv," in *The Book of Genesis in Jewish and Oriental Christian Interpretation: A Collection of Essays* (eds. J. Frishman and L. Van Rompay; Traditio Exegetica Graeca 5; Leuven: Peeters, 1997), 229–53; Samaritan readings occur in *Comm. Exod* on Exod 6:9; *Comm. Deut* 27:4–5 (ed. van den Eynde, 14, 129).

[24] L. Van Rompay, *Le Commentaire sur Genèse-Exode 9.32 du manuscrit (olim) Diyarbakir 22* (CSCO 483, 484; SS 205, 206; Leuven: Peeters, 1986), esp. version XXXVII–XXXVIII.

[25] W.C. Sprengling and M. Graham, *Barhebraeus' Scholia on the Old Testament* (Chicago: University of Chicago Oriental Institute, 1931).

[26] *Chronique de Michel le Syrien, patriarche jacobite d'Antioche (1166–1199)* (4 vols.; ed. J.-B. Chabot; Brussels: Culture et Civilisation, 1963) 4.445–46 (Syriac text); 2.471–72 (French translation). *Gregorii Barhebraei Chronicon Ecclesiasticum* (3 vols.; eds. J.B. Abbeloos and T.J. Lamy; Louvain: Peeters, 1872–1877), 1.289–94.

[27] M. Ladvocat, "Notice d'un Manuscrit oriental, d'un manuscrit oriental apporté a Paris en 1764," *Journal des Sçavans* (August 1765): 542–55, and A.I. Silvestre de Sacy, "Notice d'un

Various notes and colophons in it date Jacob's work on the Pentateuch version to 1015–1016 AG/704–705 C.E. The Penteuch manuscript can be grouped paleographically with others of Jacob's version that are dated to 719–720 C.E. The first few chapters of Genesis are unfortunately badly damaged but the end of Deuteronomy is preserved. The lacunae are as follows: Gen 32:13–33:10; 43:33–44:28; Exod 15:21–17:6; 25:18; 26:11; 33:20–34:29; 35:23–36:12; Lev 20:18–2:21; Num 7:47–79; 14:30–15:11; Deut 32:7–34:6.

There is currently no full edition of the manuscript of Jacob's version of the Pentateuch, but small sections from Genesis and Exodus have been published: Ceriani Gen 4:8–16 and 5:21–6:1;[28] Hjelt compares Gen 1:6–27; 3:1–5; 3:17–19; 27:12; 49:10 in Jacob's version and in his *Hexaemeron*.[29] Michaelis gives part of Genesis 49, Bugati has the same section of Genesis 49 along with Gen 11:1–9, and both chapters were reprinted by Eichhorn.[30] Excerpts from Exodus 1 and 28 appear in an article by Salvesen.[31]

Jacob's intention in creating his edition is unclear. It has been variously suggested that he had liturgical, apologetic, exegetical, or educational purposes in mind, or that the text was meant to be a compromise between the Peshitta and the Syro-Hexapla/LXX, or a new authorized version for the Syrian Orthodox Church.[32] However, it does not seem to have circulated widely, in contrast to the Syro-Hexapla. Only individual copies of a few books survive, and the version is not cited by other writers.

2.5.4.3.3 Translation Character

The colophon to Genesis states that the book was "corrected" (ܡܬܪܨܝ) by Jacob "according to the two traditions, that of the Syrians and that of the Greeks." The version's base text was the Peshitta (→ 1.3.4; thus differentiating it from the Syro-Hexapla), but it includes much material rendered into Syriac directly from a LXX text (since Jacob's knowledge of Greek was excellent), along with some Syro-Hexapla readings. Variants often appear in the margin: these are usually from the Peshitta where the main text adopts the LXX reading, or vice versa.[33] For example, Num 20:1 on f. 299r, the place name ܩܕܫ "Kades" appears in the margin (= LXX and Syh), but ܪܩܡ "Rekem" in the text (= S); f. 293 *passim* (Num 17:16 ff.), we find ܫܒܛܐ "staff" in the margin (= LXX ῥάβδος "staff"), but ܫܒܛܐ "staff" *or* "tribe" in the text (= Syh, S).

Most strikingly, and no doubt influenced by the the Syro-Hexapla, Jacob includes much material from the "Samaritan" version (→ 1.2.3) in Exodus, Numbers, and Deuteronomy. For example, after Exod 6:9, his text incorporates material resembling Exod 14:12, marked with *obeli* in the margins, and with a note below the previous column stating that these words were found only in the Samaritan version. Both the wording of the main text and the note are almost identical to that found in the Syro-Hexapla at the same point (f. 22a in BM Add. MS 12,134): it may be significant that the scribes La'zar and 'Adi named in the colophon of the seventh-century Syh-Exod manuscript are the same as those mentioned in the manuscripts of Samuel and Daniel in Jacob's version. The Pentateuch manuscript has some Greek words in margins, mainly personal or place names, for instance on f. 78a (Gen 38:29), Jacob's main text has ܦܪܨ

---

manuscrit syriaque, contenant les livres de Moïse," *Notices et extraits des manuscrits de la Bibliothèque Nationale* 4 (1798–1799): 648–68.

[28] A.M. Ceriani, *Monumenta sacra et profana*, Vol. II.1 (Milan: Biblioteca Ambrosiana, 1863), x–xii.

[29] A. Hjelt, *Études sur l'Hexaméron de Jacques d'Édesse, notamment sur ses notions géographiques contenues dans le 3ième traité* (Helsinki: J.C. Frenckell, 1892), 17–18.

[30] J.D. Michaelis, *Orientalische und exegetische Bibliothek* 18 (1782): 180–83, Gen 49:2–11; C. Bugati, *Daniel secundum editionem Septuagint interpretum ex tetraplis desumptum* (Milan: Monasterii St. Ambrosii, 1788), xi–xvi, 150–51, 157–58; J.B. Eichhorn, *Allgemeine Bibliothek* 2 (1789): 270–93.

[31] A. Salvesen, "Jacob of Edessa's Version of Exodus 1 and 28," *Hugoye* 8 (2005): 41–58, gives Exod 1:8–21 and 28:22–30, with translation.

[32] For details of the various positions, see A. Salvesen, "Scholarship on the Margins: Biblical and Secular Learning in the Work of Jacob of Edessa," in *Syriac Encounters: Papers from the Sixth North American Syriac Symposium, Duke University,* *26–29 June 2011* (eds. M. Doerfler, E. Fiano, and K. Smith; Eastern Christian Studies 20; Leuven: Peeters, 2015), 327–44.

[33] Marsh, "Jacob of Edessa's Greek Manuscripts."

"Phares" and ܙܪܚ "Zerah," while the margin gives the Greek forms φαρες "Phares" and ζαρα "Zara."

2.5.4.3.4 Translation Technique

Due to the use of the Peshitta (→ 1.3.4) as a base, the style of Jacob's rendering is slightly less odd than that of the Syro-Hexapla (e.g., he does not use ܕ݂ to mark possessive pronouns). However, it is "marked by an acute propensity to use conflated, double readings" from the Peshitta and the Syro-Hexapla/LXX, to provide a more descriptive text.[34] Well-known proper names maintain their Peshitta form, while less common ones are often based on a Greek form with the addition of *matres lectionis* to indicate the Greek vocalization: this is rather different from the practice in the Syro-Hexapla.[35]

2.5.4.3.5 Text-Critical Value

Marsh argues that the Pent-LXX text(s) (→ 2.4.1) used by Jacob need to be more narrowly defined before the version can be used for LXX text-critical purposes, and that further research is needed to see where Jacob's Pentateuch follows LXX against the Syro-Hexapla.[36]

2.5.4.3.6 Reception of Jacob's Text

Although Jacob uses Syriac citations influenced by LXX in his other works, the wording of the lemmata very rarely coincides precisely with that of his own version. For instance, the Pentateuch citations in his work on the *Six Days of Creation*, the *Hexaemeron*, written at the end of his life after he had finished his Old Testament version, are not identical to the text of his version of the Pentateuch.[37] Thus, contrary to the view that Jacob's text evolved over his lifetime to culminate in a fixed, final form,[38] it appears that outside of his biblical version, Jacob preferred to make *ad hoc* renderings of LXX (or Syh) combined with the Peshitta, to fit each separate exegetical context. Occasionally, one finds exegetical remarks in the version itself, such as his scholion on the high priest's breastplate (Exodus 28).[39]

Aland, B. and S.P. Brock, "Bibelübersetzungen, syrische," *TRE* 6: 181–96.

Brock, S.P., "Syriac Versions," *ABD* 6: 794–99.

Ceriani, A.M., *Pentateuchi Syro-Hexaplaris quae supersunt cum notis: Accedunt nonnulla alia fragmenta Syriaca* (Milan: Bibliotheca Ambrosiana 1863), 1–106.

Jansma, T., "'And the Spirit of God Moved upon the Face of the Waters': Some Remarks on the Syro-Hexaplaric Reading of Gen. 1:2," *VT* 20 (1970): 16–24.

de Lagarde, P., *Bibliothecae Syriacae a Paulo de Lagarde collectae quae ad philologiam sacram pertinent* (Göttingen: Dietrich, 1892).

Law, T.M., *Origenes Orientalis: The Preservation of Origen's Hexapla in the Syrohexapla of 3 Kingdoms* (De Septuaginta Investigationes 2; Göttingen: Vanderhoeck & Ruprecht, 2011).

Marsh, B.J., "Jacob of Edessa's Greek Manuscripts: The Case from His Revision of the Book of Numbers," *JSCS* 44 (2011): 5–25.

Vööbus, A., *The Hexapla and the Syro-Hexapla: Very Important Discoveries for Septuagint Research* (Papers of the Estonian Theological Society in Exile 22; Stockholm: ETSE, 1971).

Vööbus, A., *The Pentateuch in the Version of the Syro-Hexapla: A Facsimile Edition of a Midyat ms Discovered in 1964* (CSCO 369, Syr. 45; Louvain: Peeters, 1975).

Alison Salvesen

---

[34] Marsh, "Jacob of Edessa's Greek Manuscripts," 9.

[35] Marsh, "Jacob of Edessa's Greek Manuscripts," 13–20.

[36] Marsh, "Jacob of Edessa's Greek Manuscripts," 24–25; A. Salvesen, "Jacob of Edessa's Version of 1–2 Samuel: Its Method and Text-Critical Value," in *Jacob of Edessa and Syriac Culture of His Day* (ed. R.B. ter Haar Romeny; Monographs of the Peshitta Institute 18; Leiden: Brill, 2008), 127–44 (143–44).

[37] A. Salvesen, "The Authorial Spirit? Biblical Citations in Jacob of Edessa's *Hexaemeron*," *Aramaic Studies* 6 (2008): 207–25 (211) on Gen 28:12–13a; 212–13 on Exod 4:24–26, cf. 224–25. Also A. Salvesen, "The Genesis Texts of Jacob of Edessa: a Study in Variety," in *Text, Transmission, and Tradition: Studies on the Text of the Peshitta and its Use in the Syriac Tradition, Presented to Konrad Jenner on the Occasion of his 65th Birthday* (eds. W.T. van Peursen and R.B. ter Haar Romeny; Monographs of the Peshitta Institute Leiden 14; Leiden: Brill, 2006), 177–88.

[38] Goshen-Gottstein, "Neue Syrohexaplafragmente," 164 n. 3; A. Juckel, "Approximation of the 'Traditions' in Jacob of Edessa's Revision of Isaiah," in *Malphono w-Rabo d'Malphone: Studies in Honour of Sebastian P. Brock* (ed. G.A. Kiraz; Gorgias Eastern Christian Studies 3; Piscataway: Gorgias Press, 2008), 227–82, esp. 231, 234; M. Goshen-Gottstein, "LXX and Peshitta: Jacob of Edessa Quoting the Old Testament in MS BL Add 17134," *Hugoye* 8 (2005): 151–77, esp. 159–60.

[39] Salvesen, "Jacob of Edessa's version of Exodus 1 and 28."

2.5.5 Armenian Translations

2.5.5.1 Importance of the Armenian Translation

The importance of the Armenian translation of the Pentateuchal books lies in its relatively early date, early fifth century C.E. (→ 1.4.7), the preservation of Hexaplaric materials in the text together with the Origenian signs, significant numbers of readings from "the Three" (→ 1.3.1.2) preserved as marginal readings in the manuscripts, and, finally, perhaps access to some Peshitta-based renderings (→ 1.3.4).

2.5.5.2 Collations in the Cambridge LXX and Göttingen Editions

The Pentateuch in Armenian was collated in the Cambridge LXX[1] as well as the Göttingen critical editions.[2] In both cases, Zohrapian's edition[3] represents the Armenian, there being no other suitable resource available at the time. As it happens, Zohrapian's edition is a carefully executed reproduction of one manuscript (Venice 1508, dated 1319) with an apparatus that fortuitously provides the most signficant variants from that manuscript in other manuscripts available to him, manuscripts that we now know often attest a purer form of text. In spite of its age (1805), Zohrapian's edition remains essential.

2.5.5.3 Editions of the Armenian Translation of the Pentateuch

For the Pentateuch, we are now fortunate to have the editions of Zeytunian. These are not without some serious shortcomings,[4] but are valuable for their more extensive collations involving not only manuscripts but also historical works, lectionaries, and other materials. Zeytunian collated forty plus manuscripts but excluded a much larger number of manuscripts with an arbitrary cut-off date, the year 1600. The base manuscript for collation may be again Venice 1508, Zohrapian's base manuscript for collation, if what is said about the edition of Maccabees holds true for Genesis–Deuteronomy.[5]

These editions are not "critical" in the sense of the Göttingen eclectic texts, but with the help of the text of the latter, and especially the apparatuses, together with Zeytunian's apparatus, one can establish the text of the Armenian and thereby place the Armenian in the text history of LXX (→ 2.4.1) and make it useful for the textual criticism of the Greek. The text so established enables one to retrovert the Armenian into what was the Greek parent text.

2.5.5.4 Arm-Gen, Arm-Exod, Arm-Lev, Arm-Num: Textual Affiliations

The Pentateuch consists of five books and, from the outset, one must reckon it possible that Arm-Pent could have different textual allegiances in each. Do note that the Lucianic text type, for which the Armenian translation is a primary witness in Job, is not extant for the Pentateuch (→ 2.4.7); perhaps it never did exist for those books. In any case, large numbers of Hexaplaric signs preserved for Genesis and Exodus (139 for Genesis, sixty-three uniquely; 376 for Exodus, twenty-five uniquely[6]) immediately indicate that the Armenian translation is a significant Hexaplaric witness (→ 2.4.6) for those books. Based on the limited preservation of Hexaplaric pluses in Leviticus,[7] it appears that Arm-Lev attests a Byzantine type of text, i.e., a later form of text influenced by the Hexapla. The same is true of Arm-Num.[8] If these observations are correct, the Armenian translation of the Pentateuchal

---

[1] Brooke–McLean, *The Old Testament in Greek.*

[2] J.W. Wevers, *Genesis* (Septuaginta Vetus Testamentum Graecum 1; Göttingen: Vandenhoeck & Ruprecht, 1974); J.W. Wevers, *Exodus* (Septuaginta Vetus Testamentum Graecum 2.1; Göttingen: Vandenhoeck & Ruprecht, 1991); J.W. Wevers, *Leviticus* (Septuaginta Vetus Testamentum Graecum 2.2; Göttingen: Vandenhoeck & Ruprecht, 1986); J.W. Wevers, *Numeri* (Septuaginta Vetus Testamentum Graecum 3.1; Göttingen: Vandenhoeck & Ruprecht, 1982); J.W. Wevers, *Deuteronomium* (Septuaginta Vetus Testamentum Graecum 3.2; Göttingen: Vandenhoeck & Ruprecht, 1977).

[3] Zohrapian, *Scriptures.*

[4] See Cox, "A Review."

[5] Amalyan, *Girkʻ Makabayetsʻuotsʻ*, 70.

[6] Cox, *Hexaplaric Materials*, 17–77.

[7] Wevers, *Text History of the Greek Leviticus*, 11–12.

[8] Wevers, *Numeri*, 40.

books is not all of the same textual character: it is a significant witness for the Hexaplaric text in Genesis and Exodus but represents the Byzantine type of text in Leviticus, Numbers, and Deuteronomy. More precise delineations await research devoted specifically to this issue and based upon a critically established Armenian text.

2.5.5.4.1 Arm-Deut and its Textual Affiliation

For Deuteronomy, there are three editions available: Zohrapian, Zeytunian, and the diplomatic edition of Cox.[9] Cox uses as the base manuscript for collation Venice 1007, dated 1338, and eight other manuscripts representative of the text groups that emerged through sample collations of ninety-nine manuscripts. An understanding of the relation of the text groups led to the drawing of stemmatic relationships in the text tradition. Venice 1508 (= Zohrapian's base manuscript) in Deuteronomy attests a developed type of text, a subgroup of another; a manuscript of the latter main group was collated for the edition.

In Deuteronomy, the parent text is a Greek manuscript of mixed text type, an early Byzantine type of text fairly strongly influenced by the Hexapla (→ 2.4.6).[10] Arm-Deut has its closest textual relations with the Hexaplaric LXX^O group and the text represented by groups $LXX^{b\,d\,n\,t}$ in Wevers' edition. The Greek parent manuscript was translated adeptly and features unique interpretive renderings, the addition of particles of various kinds, the omission of recapitulative pronouns, the addition of pronominal subjects, and minor elaborations;[11] there are also many changes of word order. While there is no evidence of a textual relationship with the Peshitta (→ 2.4.5), there are three or four instances of exegetical glosses that may reflect familiarity with the Syriac.[12]

2.5.5.5 Possible Syriac-Based Readings in the Arm-Pent

The possibility of remnants of Peshitta-based translation in the Armenian translation has been addressed for Deuteronomy, and now for Genesis. In the latter, there are turns of phrase that are reminiscent of the Peshitta (→ 1.3.4; → 2.4.5). These appear not to be textually based, i.e., the translator was not working from a Syriac text, but reflect familiarity with the Peshitta and its exegetical tradition. Some of these readings are cited by Wevers in his critical edition of the Greek, where they "stand out like thorns" because they have no support in Greek witnesses: note the readings *praedam* "booty" (Gen 14:11, 16) and *in deversorio* "in the inn" (Gen 42:27).[13]

2.5.5.6 Status of Research

Much work remains to be done on the Armenian Pentateuch, to establish the text, understand its textual development, clarify its place in the text tradition of LXX, and identify possible Peshitta contacts for Exodus, Leviticus, and Numbers, but much progress has been made as well.

Amalyan, H.H., *Girkʻ Makabayetsʻuotsʻ: Kʻnnakan Bnagir* (*The Book of Maccabees: Critical Text*) ("Matenadaran" ՀՀՏՀ; Yerevan: Academy of Sciences, 1996).

Brooke–McLean, *The Old Testament in Greek*, Vol. 1: *The Octateuch*, Part 1: *Genesis*; Part 2: *Exodus and Leviticus*; Part 3: *Numbers and Deuteronomy*.

Cox, C., *The Armenian Translation of Deuteronomy* (Armenian Texts and Studies 2; Chico: Scholars Press, 1981).

Cox, C., *Hexaplaric Materials Preserved in the Armenian Version* (SBLSCS 21; Atlanta: Scholars Press, 1986).

Cox, C., "A Review of Zeytunyan's Edition of Genesis from the Standpoint of Septuagint Criticism," *Revue des Études Arméniennes* 21 (1988–1989): 87–125.

Cox, C., "The Syriac Presence in the Armenian Translation of the Bible: With Special Reference to the Book of Genesis," *Journal of the Canadian Society for Syriac Studies* 10 (2010): 45–67.

Jinbachian, M.M., *Les Techniques de Traduction dans la*

---

[9] Zohrapian, *Scriptures*; Zeytunian, *The Book of Deuteronomy*; Cox, *The Armenian Translation of Deuteronomy*.

[10] On the Byzantine type of text, see Wevers, *Text History of the Greek Leviticus*, 35–58.

[11] Cox, *Translation*, 223–41.

[12] Cox, *Translation*, 322–26.

[13] For a list of sixteen readings, see Cox, "The Syriac Presence," 62.

Genese en Armenian classique (Bibliothéque Arménienne de la Fondation Calouste Gulbenkian; Lisbon: Calouste Gulbenkian Foundation, 1998).

Wevers, J.W., *Numeri* (Septuaginta Vetus Testamentum Graecum 3.1; Göttingen: Vandenhoeck & Ruprecht, 1982).

Wevers, J.W., *Text History of the Greek Leviticus* (MSU 19; Göttingen: Vandenhoeck & Ruprecht, 1986).

Zeytunian, A.S. (ed.), *Girk' Tsnndots': K'nnakan Bnagir (The Book of Genesis: Critical Text)* ("Matenadaran" ՀՀՏԻ; Yerevan: Academy of Sciences, 1985).

Zeytunian, A.S. (ed.), *Girk' Elits': K'nnakan Bnagir (The Book of Exodus: Critical Text)* ("Matenadaran" ՀՀՏԻ; Yerevan: Academy of Sciences, 1992).

Zeytunian, A.S. (ed.), *Girk' Ghevtats'uots': K'nnakan Bnagir (The Book of Leviticus: Critical Text)* ("Matenadaran" ՀՀՏՅ 4; Antelias: Cilician Catholicosate, 1993).

Zeytunian, A.S. (ed.), *Girk' T'uots': K'nnakan Bnagir (The Book of Numbers: Critical Text)* ("Matenadaran" ՀՀՏՅ; Antelias: Cilician Catholicosate, 1998).

Zeytunian, A.S. (ed.), *Girk' Erkrordoumn Orinats': K'nnakan Bnagir (The Book of Deuteronomy: Critical Text)* ("Matenadaran"; Etchmiadzin: Mair At'or Surp Etchmiadzin, 2002).

Claude Cox

2.5.6 Georgian Translations

2.5.6.1 Background: Date, Versions, Editions

The Pentateuch was translated or revised many times in Old Georgian. It circulated as a part of a fuller Bible as indicated by manuscripts Mount Athos, Library of the Iviron Monastery, Georgian 1, dated 978 C.E. (hereafter Georg°) and Tbilisi, National Center of Manuscripts, A-51 (seventeenth or eighteenth century, hereafter Georg^s) or alone (Tbilisi, National Center of Manuscripts, H-1207, seventeenth century; hereafter Georg^A). Sometimes only parts of the Pentateuch were copied (Tbilisi, National Center of Manuscripts, A-179, 1669 C.E.: Genesis and Exodus, hereafter Georg^c). Furthermore, lessons from the Pentateuch in the old lectionary according to the rite of Jerusalem are extant (translated in the fifth century C.E.). The sequence of the books for the Pentateuch is the same as in LXX, and so are the names of the books.

The Old Georgian translation of the Pentateuch must have been made in the fifth century C.E. We have palimpsest fragments from the sixth or seventh century (Vienna, Österreichische Nationalbibliothek, geo. 2, Deuteronomy, hereafter Georg^x; Tbilisi, National Center of Manuscripts, H-999 Lectionary, Genesis) and it should be added that many palimpsests still await deciphering. In addition, there are extant flyleaves from the ninth (Tbilisi, National Center of Manuscripts, S-104, Numbers), tenth (Tbilisi, National Center of Manuscripts, Q-208a, Exodus), and eleventh centuries (Kutaisi, State Historical-Ethnographical Museum, No. 671, Genesis). The lectionary was translated from a Palestinian model in Greek, probably in Jerusalem.

For a long time, the Georgian version was neglected in Septuagint studies, as it was thought to be only an indirect testimony to the Greek text (→ 2.4.1). Marr's theory had been developed by Goussen and Blake and is still accepted commonly in the West.[1] According to it, the Armenian (→ 2.5.5) version was translated from the Syriac (→ 2.4.5; → 2.5.4), and the Georgian version was translated from the Armenian; as recently as 1960, Leloir wrote: "The first Georgian version of the Holy Scripture has been done according to an Armenian model."[2]

However, more recently, a careful study of the translation technique of Georg-Pent carried out in Georgia has shed new light on this problem: the older Georgian translations of the Bible were modeled on a Greek original.

A linguistic index could be provided: neither Syriac nor Armenian can be the source for the double preverbs in Georgian. Examples include the following: Gen 19:17: თანა-შე-იაყრა "with-in-seized" < συμπαραλημφθῇς "with-over-taken"; Gen 50:25: თანა-აღ-ობყენთ "with-up-carry" < συνανοίσετε "with-up-carry."

---

[1] Marr, "Zametki"; Goussen, "Bibelübersetzung," 300–18; Blake, "Ancient Georgian Versions," 271–91.

[2] Leloir, "Versions," 831.

2.5.6.2 Genesis

There are three Georgian versions of Genesis in existence: the old translation, preserved in codex Georg⁰; a very similar but slightly revised one in manuscripts Georg^(A, C, S) (seventeenth century), itself finally revised by Sulkhan Saba Orbeliani (1658–1725); and the translation of Gelati (twelfth century), which was printed in the Bakar Bible (Moscow 1743; hereafter Georg^B).[3] To these, one must add the large lessons in the Jerusalem-type lectionary: Gen 1:1–12:8; 13:1–15:18; 17–22; 19; 24–29; 32:1–30; 35:9–20; 37:2–41:52; 45:1–46:4; 48:1–7; 49–50. They were translated in Palestine, probably in Jerusalem, in the fifth century C.E. and are based on a Greek lectionary. This type of lectionary remained in use among Georgians until the eleventh century.

The old translation renders a Greek text resembling Codex Alexandrinus (LXX^A; → 2.4.1.1). For example, the base text of Gen 18:14 reads παρὰ τῷ θεῷ "in the presence of God" and not παρὰ τοῦ Θεοῦ "with God" as in the Syriac and Armenian texts. The Georgian can easily calque the composites, as in Gen 12:11 εὐπρόσωπος "fair of face," which is rendered as პირ-შუენიერი "face-nice" Georg⁰, პირ-კეთილი, "face-good" Georg^(C, A, S, B) (Syriac: ܚܙܬܐ ܫܦܝܪܬ "nice to see"; Armenian: գեղեցիկ "nice"). Sometimes, the translator made mistakes: In Gen 25:30, he read πυρροῦ "of red" as πυρός "of fire" ოცხლისა (Georg^(O, A, K, S) and the lectionary). In Gen 46:28, 29, he did not understand καθ' as a preposition: καθ' Ἡρώων πόλιν "against Heroonpolis" (MT and Syriac: "Goshen"; Armenian: "the Heros' town" [զՌամաց քաղաքաւն]) and instead translated კათერონ ქალაქსა "in the town of Katheron."

The translation by Gelati is strongly Hellenophile. It transcribes many words from the Greek instead of translating them: Gen 24:65 თერისტროჲ (*terist'roj*) < θέριστρον "light summer garment"; Gen 35:8 ვალანის (*valanis*) < βάλανος "acorn tree." The participle joined to the conjugated verb, which is usually translated in Georgian by two coordinated verbs, is translated by Gelati literally: Gen 37:31 მომღებელთა ... დაკლეს "the takers ... slaughtered" < λαβόντες ... ἔσφαξαν "taking ... they slaughtered." The rendering of double preverbs in verbs is quite common with Gelati: Gen 12:20 თანა-განვლინებად "to send-together-forward" < συμπροπέμψαι "to escort (lit. to send together forward)." The translator was familiar with the old version, which sometimes remains unchanged, but we can say that this translation faithfully mirrors a Greek catena text.

2.5.6.3 Exodus

Four Georgian texts of Exodus are preserved plus the lectionary. The lectionary includes Exod 1:1–12:42; 13:17–15:21; 34:28–35; 40:15–33. For Exodus, Georg^B follows the old translation. Manuscripts Georg^(A, K) (Georg^K = Kutaisi, No. 28, seventeenth century) seem to contain a slightly revised text of the old translation. Georg^S follows the Hexapla (→ 2.4.6) and the order of MT (→ 2.2.2) in Exod 36:8–40:38. For Exodus 1–7 and 30:21–36:7, it follows the Old Georgian translation; for Exod 12:37–30:20, it goes with the Gelati translation; for Exod 8:1–12:36, it agrees with Georg^(A, K).

God's vision is euphemised according to the theology of LXX in Exod 24:10–11: "And they saw the place, there where the God of Israel stood … and they appeared in the place of God" (→ 2.2.4.2); MT and Syriac: "they saw the God of Israel … they beheld God"; Georg^(O, B, A, K): "they saw there, where God stood over there … And they saw the place of God."

2.5.6.4 Leviticus

Only two Georgian translations of Leviticus exist, i.e., the older version and the Gelati text. However, sometimes manuscripts Georg^(A, K) draw on another source (in Lev 10:7–18; 15:33–16:12; and 17:10–18:5). There is no lesson from Leviticus in the lectionary.

The two translations were made from Greek (→ 2.4.1.3). Lev 5:20–26 is omitted by homeoteleuton in the Armenian translation (→ 2.5.5), which therefore cannot be the source of the Georgian translation. In Lev 15:31, manuscripts Georg^(A, K, S, B) attest to a double translation of ἐν: ἐν τῷ μιαίνειν "when they defile" > შინა შეგინებითა მით "in

---
[3] *Biblia*.

by defiling," where შინა "in" translates ἐν, and also the instrumental case "by." In the following cases, the metonymy is resolved by the translator: Lev 20:2 ნათესავი "offspring" < σπέρμα "seed"; Lev 20:18 πηγή "spring" > სარცხუნელი "shameful (member)."

The Gelati text follows the catena text.

Passages specific to Georg^(A, K) have the following characteristics: In Lev 10:7, a unique triplet for κατά "according" occurs: ეგრე მსგავსად ... ებრ "so similarly ... as"; Lev 10:9 attests to a special rendering for σίκερα "Sikera"[4]: ყოველსა ლუდსა "every sort of beer"; Lev 17:11 reads სამშუნველი "breath" for ψυχή "life." The archaic მუნოქუესვე "immediately" is added in Lev 16:1, as it is in Gen 24:15, Exod 10:28, and 36:1. Lev 17:10 adds an etymological figure – a classical biblical form – that is absent in LXX: ἀπολῶ "and I will destroy" > მოსპოლვით მოვსპო(ლო) "with destruction I will destroy." "Spoke to" is amplified to "He began to speak to" in Lev 16:1 and 18:1, just as in Exod 12:1 and 14:1. These examples speak for an old version and a literary revision.

2.5.6.5 Numbers

Two translations of Numbers are known: that attested by Georg^(A, K, S, B) and the Gelati translation. Furthermore, the lectionary attests to Num 20:25–30; 22:1–24, 27; 25:3–13. But it must be noted that Georg^S has a very similar text to that of a tenth-century fragment. Georg^(A, K) follow Georg^S in Num 1:1–19:20 and 34–36, and Num 19:21–33 has been revised stylistically towards LXX (→ 2.4.1.4) in these manuscripts. Georg^B agrees with Georg^S in Num 1:1–14:24; 16:1–22:41; 23:13–24:6; 25:1–35:15. The remaining text is specific to Georg^B. Georg^(A, K, S, B) go with Codex Alexandrinus (LXX^A). Georg^G reads generally with LXX^A (e.g., Num 25:12) but sometimes follows peculiar readings of Codex Vaticanus (LXX^B): Num 24:2; 31:54. All the versions are translated from Greek (→ 2.4.1.4), as demonstrated for example by the transliteration in Num 23:1, 2, 4, 14, 29, 30: βωμός "altar" > ბომონ "bomon."

---

[4] A Hebrew or Aramaic loanword for a strong alcoholic drink.

2.5.6.6 Deuteronomy

Two Georgian translations of Deuteronomy exist: that attested by Georg^(A, K, D, E, S, B),[5] which appears already in the sixth or seventh century C.E. in the palimpsest Georg^X, and the Gelati catena.

Both translations were made from LXX (→ 2.4.1.5). The first follows the short text of Deuteronomy in Deut 2:6, 14; and 28:2, whereas the Gelati translation follows the long text. They both read with Codex Alexandrinus (LXX^A) against Codex Vaticanus (LXX^B) in Deut 17:18.

To these two translations must be added the lessons in the old lectionary: Deut 6:4–7:10; 7:21–14:3; 34:1–12.

2.5.6.7 Conclusion

The Georgian Pentateuch proves to be useful for the study of the history of LXX, as it allows access to the Greek models underlying it: LXX^A, LXX^B, the Hexaplaric text, and the catena text. Georg-Pent sheds light on the circulation of its Greek models in Palestine and the Caucasus, as well as the evolution of the Greek Textus Receptus, but each book of Georg-Pent has its own history.

Abulaʒe, I., "Kartuli bibliis ʒveli xelnac'eri ramdenime purceli," *Tbilisis universit'et'is šromebi* 18 (1941): 149–58 (repr. I. Abulaʒe, *Šromebi*, Vol. 3 [Tbilisi: Mecniereba, 1982], 5–15).

Abulaʒe I., et al. (eds.), *C'ignni ʒuelisa aγtkumisani*, Vol. 2: *Levit'eltaj, ricxutaj, meorisa sʒulisaj* (Tbilisi: Mecniereba, 1990).

Biblia: Brʒanebita da c'arsagebelita sapasetata sakartvelos mepis bakar vaxt'angis ʒisata (Moscow: Bakaris st'amba, 1743).

Blake, R., "Ancient Georgian Versions of the Old Testament," *HTR* 19 (1926): 271–97.

Blake, R., "The Athos Codex of the Georgian Old Testament," *HTR* 22 (1929): 33–56.

Danelia, K'., S. Čxenk'eli, and B. Šavišvili (eds.), *Kartuli lekcionaris p'arizuli xelnac'eri: ʒveli da axali aγtkmis sak'itxavebi*, Vol. 1: *Nac'ili I* (Tbilisi: Tbilisis universit'et'is gamomcemloba, 1987).

Dočanašvili, E. (ed.), *Mcxeturi xelnac'eri* (*moses*

---

[5] Georg^D = Tbilisi, National Center of Manuscripts H-885, seventeenth century; Georg^E = Tbilisi, National Center of Manuscripts, A-243, 1672 C.E.

xutc'igneuli, iso nave, msaǯulta, ruti) (Tbilisi: Mecniereba, 1981).

Gigineišvili, B. and C. K'ik'viʒe, "Rustavelis xanis kartuli bibliis targmani (gelaturi versia)," in *Šota rustaveli: ist'oriul-pilologiuri ʒiebani* (Tbilisi: Sakartvelos ssr mecnierebata ak'ademia, 1966): 149–59.

Gigineišvili, B. and C. K'ik'viʒe, "Šesakmis, gamosvlata da levit'elta c'ignebis kartuli versiebi," *Mravaltavi* 1 (1971): 29–45.

Gigineišvili, B. and C. K'ik'viʒe (eds.), *C'ignni ʒuelisa aɣtkumisani*, Vol. 1: *Šesakmisaj, gamoslvataj* (Tbilisi: Mecniereba, 1989).

Gigineišvili, B. and G. Todua (eds.), *Gelaturi bibliis k'at'enebi* (Tbilisi: Axali ivironi, 2011).

Gippert, J., Z. Sarjveladze, and L. Kajaia (eds.), *The Old Georgian Palimpsest: Codex Vindoboniensis georgicus 2* (Monumenta palaeographica Medii Aevi Series Ibero-Caucasica 1; Turnhout: Brepols, 2007).

Goussen, H., "Die georgische Bibelübersetzung: A) Alte kirchliche Abhängigkeit Georgiens von Armenien: Die alte Übersetzung," *OrChr* 6 (1906): 300–18.

Kurcik'iʒe, C., *Kartuli biblia* (Tbilisi: Xelnac'erta erovnuli cent'ri, 2010).

Kurcik'iʒe, C., and U. Cindeliani (eds.), *C'ignni ʒuelisa aɣtkumisani*, Vol. 3: *Iso navesi, msaǯultaj, rutisi* (Tbilisi: Mecniereba, 1991).

Leloir, L., "Versions orientales de la Bible V: Versions géorgiennes," *DBSup* 6:829–34.

Marr, N.J., "Zametki po tekstam sv. Pisanija v drevnich perevodach armjan i gruzin," *Christianskij Vostok* 2.2 (1913): 163–74; 2.3 (1914): 263–74; 3.3 (1915): 249–62; 4.3 (1916): 229–45 (repr. N.J. Marr, *Kavkazskij kul'turnyj mir i Armenija* [Erevan: Gandzasar, 1995], 124–78).

Melikišvili, N., *Bibliur c'ignta ʒveli kartuli targmanebi* (Tbilisi: Alilo, 2009).

Outtier, B., "L'Ancien Testament a-t-il été traduit en arménien et géorgien du syriaque?" in *L'Ancien Testament en syriaque* (eds. F. Briquel-Chatonnet and P. Le Moigne; Études syriaques 5; Paris: Geuthner, 2008), 215–20.

Outtier, B., "Une énigme enfin résolue? Le modèle de la traduction géorgienne de la Bible," in *Poïkiloï Karpoï (Récoltes diverses): Exégèses païennes, juives et chrétiennes: Études réunies en hommage à Gilles Dorival* (eds. M. Loubet and D. Pralon; Aix-en-Provence: Presses universitaires de Provence, 2015), 35–40.

Šaniʒe, A., (ed.), *C'ignni ʒuelisa aɣtkumisani 978 c'lis xelnac'eris mixedvit*, Vol. 1.1: *Dabadebisaj, gamoslvataj* (Tbilisi: Sak. ssr mecnierebata ak'ademiis gamomcemloba, 1947).

Šaniʒe, A., (ed.), *C'ignni ʒuelisa aɣtkumisani 978 c'lis xelnac'eris mixedvit*, Vol. 1.2: *Levit'eltaj, msaǯultaj, rutisi, iobisi, esaiajsi* (Tbilisi: Sak. ssr mecnierebata ak'ademiis gamomcemloba, 1948).

Xaranauli, A., "Levit'eltas gelaturi versia," *Gelatis mecnierebata ak'ademiis žurnali* 10 (2006): 3–14.

Žavaxišvili, I., "Axlad aɣmočenili uʒvelesi kartuli xelnac'erebi da mati mnišvneloba mecnierebisatvis," *Tbilisis universit'et'is moambe* 2 (1922–1923): 313–91 (repr. I. Žavaxišvili, *Kartuli damc'erlobata-mcodneoba anu p'aleograpia: meore gamocema* [Tbilisi: St'alinis saxelobis tbilisis saxelmc'ipo universit'et'is gamomcemloba, 1949]–: 274–366).

Bernard Outtier

2.5.7 Old Church Slavonic Translations

2.5.7.1 Typology of Manuscripts

The manuscript corpus of OCS-Gen, OCS-Exod, OCS-Lev, OCS-Num, and OCS-Deut (= OCS-Pent), which has come down to us from the Middle Ages and the modern period, essentially comprises three categories of sources. The first is represented by the Cyrillic Prophetologium, the earliest evidence of which dates from the late twelfth or early thirteenth century: it contains a selection of liturgical readings translated from the LXX-Pent (→ 2.4.1) in accordance with the Byzantine rite.[1]

The second consists of the various testimonies of the Croat Glagolitic Breviary and Missal, dating respectively from no earlier than the late thirteenth–fourteenth and fourteenth–fifteenth centuries; besides including most of the Prophetologium passages, they also incorporate additional excerpts based in the vast majority of cases on the Vulgate (→ 2.4.8).[2]

The third is the complete version of the OCS-Pent undertaken from LXX, which is today extant in over thirty East and South Slavic (hereinafter respectively E-OCS and S-OCS) Cyrillic codices dating from the late fourteenth or early fifteenth up

---

[1] The earliest copy is codex Russian State Library, Moscow, f. 87, No. M 1685 (*Grig.* 2), edited in Brandt, "Grigorovičev parimejnik"; Ribarova and Hauptova, *Grigorovičev parimejnik*, Vol. 1. For general issues related to the liturgical use of the Scriptures, see Alekseev, *Biblija v bogosluženii*.

[2] Michajlov, *K voprosu*; Alexeev, *Tekstologija*, 140–41.

to the seventeenth centuries.³ The E-OCS heritage points to the spread of the OCS-Pent both as a separate book and as part of the Octateuch, the latter being found only within larger collections such as the so-called *Jewish Chronicle* (= *J-Ch*), an extensive compilation consisting mostly of translations of Greek historical and literary works (Flavius Josephus, John Malalas, George Hamartolos, and pseudo-Callisthenes), biblical books (Octateuch, Tetrabasileon, excerpts from the Prophets and others), as well as several Old Russian annals.⁴ In the S-OCS tradition, the OCS-Pent is to be found only in copies containing the Octateuch, which at times is followed by 1–4 Kingdoms.

In addition to this vast material, conserved in the above-listed three types of witnesses, a fragmentarily preserved version of the *Quaestiones in Octateuchum* of Theodoret of Cyrrhus has also come down to us. It includes only the first four books of the Pentateuch and is to be found in a number of E-OCS manuscripts of very diverse structural composition.⁵

2.5.7.2 Date and Origin of the Translations of the OCS-Pent

The problem of establishing the date of the OCS-Pent is a complex issue that despite scholars' efforts is unfortunately far from being resolved. In the widely held opinion of Slavicists, the primary body of these versions should be identified with the readings found in the first category, namely in the Prophetologium, believed to have originated during the Cyrillo-Methodian period (ca. 863–885 C.E.). Research has shown that this earliest textual layer served as a basis for subsequent translational activity among the Southern Slavs; its use clearly emerges not only in the Croat Glagolitic texts, but also, to a varying extent in each book, in several copies of the full OCS-Pent. With regard to the origin of the latter, no consensus has been reached in the scholarly community. This question is absolutely open: the very diverse hitherto-expressed suppositions still require verification and corroboration by further study.

Hypotheses on this subject derive mostly from the attempt to relate the textual and linguistic evidence provided by the currently accessible OCS manuscripts with the testimony of external literary sources dating back to the Old Bulgarian period. As stated in hagiographic accounts, Methodius, shortly before his death (885 C.E.), translated from Greek into Slavonic the entire Scriptures "with the exception of the Maccabees."⁶ However, lexicological analysis has shown that, leaving aside a single redaction of OCS-Ruth,⁷ this alleged primary Methodian version cannot be traced,⁸ although the assertion has been put forward that a few remains of this earliest stratum may be detected in the S-OCS tradition of OCS-Gen.⁹ Therefore, the view is held that the surviving corpus of the complete OCS-Pent represents, if not a Methodian work, at least a slightly later textual layer. In the light of a colophon preserved in the *J-Ch*, it is usually ascribed to the archpriest Gregory the Presbyter, whose literary activity is linked with the Preslav school (Eastern Bulgaria, late ninth and early tenth centuries).¹⁰ According to this inscription, he was commissioned to translate from Greek into Slavonic the books of the Old Testament, "revealing in symbols the very truth of the New Testament," by Prince Symeon of Bulgaria, who ruled with this title in 893–913 C.E. (in 913–927 C.E. he ruled as *tsar*). Despite the issue

---

³ The oldest testimony is the parchment Pent codex of the Russian State Library, Moscow, f. 304/I, No. 1, whose dating oscillates between the second half of the fourteenth and the early fifteenth centuries (*Svodnyj katalog*, 170–71). For lists of manuscripts, see Michajlov, *Opyt*, I–CXLV; Mathiesen, "Handlist," 3–48. The latter two works should be integrated with the annotations on additional codices found in Pičchadze, "K istorii," 21; Željazkova, "Orfografičeskie i fonetičeskie osobennosti," 138–47; Željazkova, "Opisanieto na skinijata," 152; Minčev, "Pšinskaja Biblija," 222–40; Uspenskij, "Imja," 95.

⁴ Istrin, *Aleksandrija*, 315–43; Slavova, "Biblejskoto Osmoknižie," 26–35.

⁵ Nikol'skij, *O literaturnych trudach*, 31–38, 48–49, 52; Slavova, "Slavjanskijat prevod," 7–18; Greek original: *Theodoreti Cyrensis Quaestiones*.

⁶ See Angelov and Kodov, *Kliment Ochridski*, 191.

⁷ → 13–17.2.7.

⁸ Pičchadze, "Cerkovnoslovjanskij," 139–47.

⁹ Slavova, "Sledi," 53–70.

¹⁰ Thomson, "The Bulgarian Contribution," 236; Turilov, "Byl li perevodčik," 12–16.

being widely debated, these words are commonly interpreted as a reference to the Octateuch.[11] Consequently, by combining this witness with the linguistic data, it has been argued that Gregory may have made use of an earlier version, possibly to be identified with the lost Methodian Bible.[12]

2.5.7.3 The Prophetologium and the Early Croat Sources

The Cyrillic Prophetologium and the Croat Glagolitic Breviary and Missal preserve different numbers of readings for each of the books of the OCS-Pent. The level of study undertaken on each translation is far from homogeneous: research has hitherto focused chiefly on the Prophetologium texts of OCS-Gen and OCS-Exod, to which the vast majority of the excerpts belong.

2.5.7.3.1 OCS-Gen

The OCS Prophetologium contains all of Genesis 1; 2; 3; 4; 6; 9; and 50, as well as the following readings: Gen 5:1–24, 32; 7:1–9, 11–24; 8:4–22; 10:1, 32; 11:9; 12:1–7; 13:12–18; 14:14–20; 15:1–15; 17:1–9, 11–12, 14–17, 19; 18:11–14, 20–33; 21:1–2, 4–8; 22:1–18; 27:1–41; 28:10–17; 31:3–16; 32:1–10; 43:26–31; 45:1–16; 46:1–7; 49:1–2, 8–12, 33. This tradition was the subject of a monograph written by Michajlov in the early twentieth century.[13]

This earliest textual stratum was almost entirely transferred into the Croat Glagolitic Breviary and Missal, in which several non-liturgical sections not included in the Prophetologium are also added. Most of these passages appear to have been newly translated from the Vulgate (→ 2.4.8), although in a few rare cases they demonstrate textual reliance on LXX (→ 2.4.1.1).[14] In Slavova's view, it is precisely this last feature that points to the spread in Croatia of a full version of OCS-Gen that may be traced back to the lost Methodian complete text.[15] Thomson attacks this hypothesis: he maintains that the Croat non-Prophetologium readings, which do not coincide with the Vulgate but with LXX (e.g., Gen 11:28), were probably based on VL (→ 2.5.1.1).[16]

2.5.7.3.2 OCS-Exod

The OCS Prophetologium includes Exod 1:1–20; 2:5–22; 3:1–8; 12:1–11, 51; 13:1–3, 10–12, 14–16, 20–22; 14:1–31; 15:1, 22–27; 16:1; 19:10–19; 22:28; 24:12–18; 33:11–23; 34:4–8; 40:1–5, 9–10, 16, 34–35. A critical text was published by Pičchadze.[17]

According to Jagić, the readings contained in the Croat Glagolitic sources derive supposedly from this earliest textual stratum. In his view, despite having been revised taking the Vulgate (→ 2.4.8) as its basis, this translation preserves traces of an original version made from LXX (→ 2.4.1.2).[18] The Croat fragments are available solely in diplomatic editions.[19]

2.5.7.3.3 OCS-Lev

The following sections are included in the OCS-Prophetologium: Lev 12:2–4, 6, 8 and 26:3–12, 14–17, 19–20.[20] The Croat Glagolitic Missal contains a translation from the Vulgate (→ 2.4.8) of Lev 19:1–2, 10–19, 25; 23:9–11, 15–17, 20–21, 26–29, 31–32, 39–43; 26:3–12.[21]

---

[11] Slavova, "Biblejskoto Osmoknižie," 27; Thomson, "The Slavonic Translation," 728–29; Thomson, A Brief Survey, 35–36.
[12] Alekseev, "Kirillo-mefodievskoe," 134–35.
[13] Michajlov, Opyt. For editions, see Brandt, "Grigorovičev parimejnik"; Ribarova and Hauptova, Grigorovičev parimejnik, 1:3, 5, 65, 69, 71, 75, 77, 83, 84, 87, 93, 95, 99, 101, 107, 113, 117, 125, 127, 133, 141, 143, 149, 155, 157, 163, 165, 169, 171, 177, 183, 185, 189, 191, 197, 203, 205, 211, 213, 219, 221, 223, 225, 229, 231, 237, 239, 241, 247, 255, 257, 259, 260, 265, 319, 349, 385.
[14] Michajlov, K voprosu, 57–60, 62–86, 110–23. For editions of the Croat texts, see Berčić (ed.), Ulomci, 1–48; Schmidt-Deeg (ed.), Das New Yorker Missale, 89–90, 92, 223–30, 276, 391.
[15] Slavova, "Sledi," 62–64.
[16] Thomson, "The Slavonic Translation," 734.
[17] Pičchadze, "Kniga 'Ischod,'" 6–7, 10–60; on this tradition, see also Pičchadze, "Tipologija."
[18] Jagić, Entstehungsgeschichte, 459–60.
[19] See Berčić (ed.), Ulomci, 48–61; Schmidt-Deeg (ed.), Das New Yorker Missale, 14–15, 68, 89, 122, 124, 201–02, 230–32, 248, 276–77, 317, 337, 413, 439, 455, 523.
[20] Kyas and Šarapatková, "Přehled," 100; Thomson, "The Slavonic Translation," 736. An edition was published by Brandt, "Grigorovičev parimejnik."
[21] Editions can be found in Berčić (ed.), Ulomci, 61–64; Schmidt-Deeg (ed.), Das New Yorker Missale, 144–45, 291–93, 327–28, 332.

2.5.7.3.4 OCS-Num

The OCS-Prophetologium contains Num 8:16–17; 11:16–17, 24–29; 24:2–3, 5–9, 17–18.[22] The Croat Glagolitic Missal preserves Num 20:2–3, 6–13; 24:17–18. The version appears to have been undertaken from the Vulgate (→ 2.4.8).[23]

2.5.7.3.5 OCS-Deut

A few readings are included in the OCS-Prophetologium, namely Deut 1:8–17; 10:14–21.[24] A translation from the Vulgate (→ 2.4.8) of Deut 11:22–25; 26:1–3, 7–11, 15–19; 31:22–30; 32:1–4 is available in Croat Glagolitic sources.[25]

2.5.7.4 Complete Version of the OCS-Pent

In reviewing the available research into the full version of the OCS-Pent, one cannot avoid noting the striking contrast in the depth of study among its different units. At present, only OCS-Gen has been subjected to an almost comprehensive textual scrutiny, although much work remains to be accomplished before definitive conclusions can be reached on assessing the internal textual features of this version. Moreover, there is still the problem of the widely spread assumption that the rest of the OCS-Pent had a textual history very similar, if not identical, to that of OCS-Gen. This notion currently remains an unproven postulate. Furthermore, it remains unclear whether divergences between the redactions can be explained by assuming subsequent corrections of the earliest translational layer on the basis of Greek models belonging to different recensions of LXX (→ 2.4.6; → 2.4.7).

2.5.7.4.1 Redactions of the Complete Version of the OCS-Pent

In the early twentieth century, Michajlov classified the complete OCS-Gen in two major redactions. In his judgment, a primary one (*i*) corresponds to the E-OCS codices and a second one (*ii*) is to be found in the S-OCS group. Moreover, a few other E-OCS testimonies such as the *J-Ch* would point to the existence of an intermediary recension (also labeled as "chronographic"), which should be considered the result of a contamination of the readings of the former with those of the latter. This assessment of the corpus has found both supporters[26] and detractors, who hold differing views on the interrelationship among the various classes of sources.[27] In all cases, it seems beyond question that the entire tradition of OCS-Gen goes back to lost Glagolitic archetypes.[28]

Despite the lack of thorough investigation, Michajlov's reconstruction was applied to OCS-Exod with contrasting results. While some scholars acknowledge a similar textual history for the two books,[29] others propose different relationships between the surviving copies, according to which the so-called intermediate text is judged to be a third independent redaction that preserves archetypal readings.[30]

As far as OCS-Lev, OCS-Num, and OCS-Deut are concerned, studies are unfortunately not available. This circumstance makes it impossible to reach any substantiated conclusions with regard to their textual history.

---

[22] Kyas and Šarapatková, "Přehled," 100; Thomson, "The Slavonic Translation," 737. For editions, see Brandt, "Grigorovičev parimejnik"; Ribarova and Hauptova, *Grigorovičev parimejnik*, 1:7, 387–89.

[23] For editions, see Berčić (ed.), *Ulomci*, 64–65; Schmidt-Deeg (ed.), *Das New Yorker Missale*, 109.

[24] Kyas and Šarapatková, "Přehled," 100; Thomson, "The Slavonic Translation," 738. For another edition, see Brandt, "Grigorovičev parimejnik."

[25] For editions, see Berčić (ed.), *Ulomci*, 65–71; Schmidt-Deeg (ed.), *Das New Yorker Missale*, 75–76, 237–38, 277, 292, 317.

[26] Pičchadze, "Cerkovnoslavjanskij," 143; Thomson, "The Slavonic Translation," 730–32.

[27] Slavova, "Biblejskoto Osmoknižie," 30–32, 36.

[28] See Slavova, "Sledi," 58, 65.

[29] Pičchadze, "K istorii," 10–21.

[30] Vilkul, "Knyga Vychid," 504–16; Vilkul, "Davn'oslov'jans'ka knyga Vychid," 89–98; Vilkul, *Kniga Ischod*, 12–15. As far as the testimonies belonging to the E-OCS group are concerned, a number of fundamental paleographic and codicological observations that may have relevance for the textual criticism of the OCS-Pent have been offered by Kloss, *O proischoždenii*, 30–37.

2.5.7.4.2 Alleged Revision of the OCS-Pent toward MT (→ 2.2.2)

Several E-OCS manuscripts of the late fifteenth to early seventeenth centuries present two peculiarities, and as a consequence they are thought to form a subgroup of the supposed primary redaction (*i*). The first is the subdivision of each book into twelve (Genesis) or ten (Exodus, Leviticus, Numbers, Deuteronomy) sections[31] corresponding to the weekly Torah portions (*parashot*).[32] The second is the insertion of a number of marginal glosses in OCS-Gen 6:6; 10:10; 12:10; 32:30; 35:16; 40:1, OCS-Exod 3:14; 6:6; 7:1; 12:14; 13:7; 22:20; 23:31, and OCS-Lev 8:8; 25:30,[33] among which those concerned with the Lord's name stand out.[34]

In both cases, where and when these features originated is unknown. Recently, the hypothesis was advanced that their genesis should be explained by assuming the use of the OCS-Pent as a Targum in the synagogue in an unspecified epoch, which evidently is deemed to be earlier than the late fifteenth century. Supporters of this view have moreover contributed to the spread among Slavicists of the belief – yet to be proven – that the OCS-Pent was revised towards the Hebrew. Unfortunately, no scholar has tackled this issue so far on a text-critical basis, with the inevitable result that currently there is a total lack of clarity on the question of the alleged influence of MT on the OCS-Pent.[35]

2.5.7.4.3 The Editions

Editions are available only for the first three books of the full version of the OCS-Pent. The most comprehensive is undoubtedly that of OCS-Gen, prepared by Michajlov. His edition is based on twenty-six copies of E-OCS and S-OCS origin.[36] The critical text of OCS-Exod, published by Vilkul, is constructed relying on the witness of the so-called intermediary redaction (chronographic codices), which was collated with selected manuscripts belonging to recensions (*i*) and (*ii*).[37] Dadiverin's edition of OCS-Lev comprises only four witnesses (two for each of the two major groups) and the 1581-printed Ostrog Bible (= OB; → 1.4.10.3.4).[38] As has already been noted, this monograph appears to be philologically-speaking a hardly serviceable work and is far from representing a reliable survey of the textual history of this book among the Slavs.[39]

The rest of the OCS-Pent remains entirely unexplored in terms of textual criticism. The OCS translations of Numbers and Deuteronomy are still awaiting inquiry and still await their publication even on the basis of a single witness.

2.5.7.5 Text-Critical Value

The problem of the relevance of the OCS-Pent to the textual criticism of the Bible is an issue that has so far escaped the attention both of LXX scholars and Slavicists. On the one hand, the considerable work carried out on OCS-Gen by Michajlov was not taken into account by Wevers in his reference edition and study of LXX-Gen.[40] On the other hand, Slavicists, who in recent years have dealt with the study of the OCS-Pent, have shown themselves to be reluctant to consider the latest achievements in the field of the textual criticism of the Greek Bible.[41]

The scarce interaction between these two fields of research, each remaining almost isolated from the other, is one of the reasons why a collation of the OCS-Pent with the Göttingen editions and

---

[31] Michajlov, *Opyt*, xxi–lx.
[32] Alekseev, *Tekstologija*.
[33] See Gorskij, "O slavjanskom perevode," 134–68; Thomson, "The Slavonic Translation," 652–53.
[34] See Uspenskij, "Imja," 93–122; Uspenskij, "Iz istorii," 24–55.
[35] Alekseev, *Tekstologija*, 30, 182; Alekseev, "Russko-evrejskie," 169–70. See also Pičchadze, "K istorii," 10–21; Uspenskij, "Imja," 113; Uspenskij, "Iz istorii," 28; Uspenskij, "Filologičeskie," 72–73.

[36] Michajlov, *Kniga*, 1–4.
[37] Vilkul, *Kniga Ischod*, 50.
[38] Dadiverin, *Das Buch Leviticus*, 251–22; *Ostrožskaja biblija*.
[39] See the critical remarks in Thomson, "The Slavonic Translation," 736.
[40] Wevers, *Genesis*; Wevers, *Text History*.
[41] See Dadiverin, *Das Buch Leviticus*; Pičchadze, "K istorii," 10–21; Slavova, "Sledi," 53–70; Slavova, "Biblejskoto Osmoknižie," 26–35; Thomson, "The Slavonic Translation," 730–32.

studies on the text history of the various books has so far not been carried out. The other is the lack of critical works undertaken by considering the whole range of manuscript evidence (OCS-Exod and OCS-Lev) or even individual sources (OCS-Num and OCS-Deut), which is obviously an essential prerequisite for fulfilling this task.[42]

2.5.7.5.1 Prophetologium, Croat Sources, Theodoret's Quaestiones

According to Michajlov, the text of OCS-Gen found in the Prophetologium was translated from the Lucianic text (→ 2.4.7).[43] However, the assumptions behind this claim are based on old-fashioned views, since in fact not even a Lucianic group can be singled out for LXX-Gen.[44] OCS-Gen still awaits collation with the list of readings of the Byzantine Lectionary texts compiled by Wevers.[45]

In the vast majority of cases, the non-Prophetologium sections found in Croat Glagolitic tradition show reliance on the Vulgate (→ 2.4.8). Whether VL (→ 2.5.1) may have been used as a source for some sections of the Breviary and Missal remains a matter of speculation. As for the translation of Theodoret's Quaestiones, which awaits exploration,[46] it can only be assumed logically that this version is a witness to the text of the Antiochian fathers.[47]

2.5.7.5.2 Complete Version of the OCS-Pent

In each of the five books, the OCS-Pent may have different textual allegiances with the various manuscript families of LXX (→ 2.4.1). However, since precise delineations are unknown, the terms of their mutual textual relationship cannot be established here.[48]

A number of features of OCS-Exod are discussed below with the aim of encouraging future research on the OCS-Pent and its text-critical value for LXX studies. Their analysis opens the way to considering this material to be extremely promising for the purpose of comparative textual criticism. At the same time, it also provides further evidence of the need to reappraise the problem of the alleged revision of the OCS-Pent based on MT (→ 2.2.2).

2.5.7.5.3 OCS Witness to Exodus 35–40

As is widely known among scholars, one of the major challenges in the textual criticism of the Bible is represented by the considerable divergences between LXX and MT in Exodus 35–40 (→ 2.4.1.2), which concern the order of chapters and the extent of the text.[49] With regard to this issue, OCS-Exod manifests a clear textual reliance on LXX, but with some deviations that merit mention.

The three redactions of OCS-Exod share the omission of Exod 37:10–21; 38:1–27; 39:1–2, in place of which the immediately preceding translation of

---

[42] A first unsystematic attempt to trace a number of LXX readings in the OCS tradition has been made in the edition of OCS-Exod, recently prepared by Vilkul on the basis of redaction *iii*. In this work, however, both the problem of the relationship with the manuscript groups, determined by Wevers, and that of the relevance of the OCS translation for the textual criticism of the Bible has not even been taken into consideration (Vilkul, *Kniga Ischod*, 44, 56). Moreover, such an appraisal can hardly be achieved on the basis of only one redaction (in this case, *iii*), given that the latter is characterized by a series of small omissions and larger lacunae (see Vilkul, "Knyga Vychid," 509; Vilkul, "Davn'oslov'jans'ka knyga Vychid," 96), which more often than not are the outcome of copy errors (see, e.g., manuscript Russian State Archive of Ancient Acts, Moscow, f. 181 [MGAMID] 279/658, late fifteenth century, and the above-mentioned manuscript Russian State Library, f. 304/I, No. 1).

[43] Michajlov, *Opyt*, 339.

[44] Wevers, *Text History of the Greek Genesis*, 158–75.

[45] Wevers, *Text History of the Greek Genesis*, 176–85.

[46] The fifteenth-century codex of the State Historical Museum in Moscow (*Bars.* 1395), which apparently represents the most comprehensive witness to this translation, has yet to be described and studied.

[47] See *Theodoreti Cyrensis Quaestiones*.

[48] A consultation of Michajlov's edition shows that OCS-Gen has a limited number of Hexaplaric pluses (among which are those found in Gen 9:5, 10; 24:67; 27:46; see Wevers, *Text History of the Greek Genesis*, 50–51; Michajlov, *Kniga*, 1–4), a feature that at first glance might suggest a reliance on the Byzantine text type. The same applies apparently to OCS-Exod and OCS-Lev, at least if looking at the limited evidence offered in available editions (Dadiverin, *Das Buch Leviticus*; Vilkul, *Kniga Ischod*). However, the whole issue should be checked comprehensively, especially as it cannot be ruled out that each single translation does not necessarily depend on a specific manuscript family among those delineated by Wevers for LXX.

[49] See, e.g., Wevers, *Text History of the Greek Exodus*, 117–46; Aejmelaeus, **Trail*, 107–21; Tov, **TCHB*, 316–17.

Exod 35:33–35; 36:10–40; 37:1–5 is repeated.[50] This feature, considered to be the result of a loss of text and of a copy error, which evidently took place at a very early stage, is usually judged to be common to all surviving manuscripts.[51] However, a broader scrutiny of the sources made it possible to gather additional data that indicates clearly the need for a more critical assessment of this tradition.

On the one hand, an example is available in which the lack of Exod 37:10–21; 38:1–27; 39:1–2 is not compensated by any additional insertion. As a result, a continuous text is presented that is deprived of various sections of the second LXX account of the tabernacle. This text can be found in codex Moscow, f. 113, No. 119 of the Russian State Library (folios 117–19) dating from the first third of the sixteenth century. This codex was believed to belong to the group of testimonies corrected towards MT.[52] On the other hand, the 1561-printed OB (→ 1.4.10.3.4) shows that, on the contrary, the missing portion of the LXX text is included in its entirety,[53] with the additional peculiarity of presenting the following chapter subdivision: 1) OCS-Exod 36 = LXX-Exod 36 + 37; 2) OCS-Exod 37 = LXX-Exod 38:1–21; 3) OCS-Exod 38 = LXX-Exod 38:22–39:12; 4) OCS-Exod 39 = LXX-Exod 39:13–23; 5) OCS-Exod 40 = LXX-Exod 40.[54] It is somewhat surprising that the editor of OCS-Exod did not notice these crucial textual aspects, despite claiming to have collated the chronographic redaction with the OB.[55]

These observations allow for the following conclusions: 1) Several other codices should be examined before light can be shed on the origin of the above-listed features. The entire material, including the OB,[56] clearly demands an in-depth study. Only if these conditions are met can the relevance of OCS-Exod for the textual criticism of LXX be properly assessed; 2) a more critical approach to OCS-Exod raises serious doubts about the validity of the widely spread conviction among Slavicists that the OCS-Pent was corrected on the basis of MT as a consequence of its presumed use as a Targum in the synagogue.[57]

By assuming a correction according to the Hebrew text, one would at least expect the missing parts in OCS-Exod 37–39 to have been added, if not the entire rearrangement of the section dealing with the tabernacle. Such a conclusion may be supported logically by looking at comparable cases in the Byzantine tradition, such as that of the marginalia written in the uncial Codex Ambrosianus.[58]

The OCS testimonies that are deemed to preserve a revision of MT do not differ from the others in their textual features apart from the insertion of glosses and the subdivision into parts that correspond to the weekly Torah portions. Concerning this last point, an additional clarification is

---

[50] Thomson, "The Slavonic Translation," 735. For an edition, see Vilkul, *Kniga Ischod*, 267–74.

[51] Željazkova, "Opisanieto na skinijata," 152–65.

[52] Pičchadze, "K istorii," 21.

[53] The origin of Exod 37:10–21; 38:1–27; 39:1–2 in the OB has not yet been clarified. It remains to be ascertained whether it represents a new version undertaken from LXX and appended to the rest of the medieval translation of OCS-Exod, or is the result of a collation of the latter with a number of OCS testimonies, currently lost or untraced. Generally speaking, the problem of identifying the sources of the OB is a very complex issue that necessitates a flexible approach toward each of the books. Different opinions have been expressed on this topic. According to Evseev, while editing OCS-Gen, the compilers of the OB made extensive use of s-OCS manuscripts that, in his conviction, contained readings dating back to the alleged Methodian translation (Evseev, *Očerki*, 82). In Alekseev's view, the analysis of the vocabulary of the OB would indicate merely that its authors tended to imitate the Cyrillo-Methodian linguistic norm (Alekseev, *Tekstologija*, 207). In Thomson's opinion, the OB preserves heterogeneous texts and has no value for the establishment of a critical edition of the earliest textual stratum of the OCS Bible (Thomson, "The Slavonic Translation," 683).

[54] See *Ostrožskaja biblija*, folios 42ᵛ–44. This subdivision differs from that found in the 1518-printed Greek Aldine Bible (see *Sacrae Scripturae*, folios 31–32), which, therefore, does not appear to have been used by the compilers of the OB (for such a belief, see Alekseev, *Tekstologija*, 214).

[55] Vilkul, *Kniga Ischod*, 48, 54, 267.

[56] See above, notes 53 and 54.

[57] The supporters of this hypothesis have not even considered the problem of the divergences between LXX and MT in Exodus 35–40, an issue of which they were clearly unaware (see Alekseev, *Tekstologija*, 182–84; Alekseev, "Perevody Biblii," 345–55; Pičchadze, "K istorii," 21; Thomson, "The Slavonic Translation," 652–53; Thomson, *A Brief Survey*, 49).

[58] See Fincati, "Per la storia," 308–10.

needed. A closer examination of the sources reveals that an identical segmentation of the text (marked by numbers without headings)[59] is found also in manuscripts that do not belong to the group containing the glosses, as shown by the late-fifteenth-century codex of the Russian State Library, Moscow, f. 173.I, No. 12 and the Gennadian Bible copied in 1499 (State Historical Museum, Moscow, *Sin.* 915).[60] Therefore, this specific problem calls for further investigation, especially in the light of the testimony of other traditions.[61]

In any case, there remains little doubt that researchers of OCS-Exod, bearing in mind the translation's distinctive traits in relation to the major textual problems of the primary version, should direct their efforts mainly towards such goals as the production of a reliable critical edition and the assessment of the textual history. These objectives would be best achieved by adopting a comprehensive comparative philological approach to the study of the vast and currently only partially explored manuscript corpus of the OCS-Pent.

Alekseev, A.A., "Kirillo–Mefodievskoe perevodčeskoe nasledie i ego istoričeskie sud'by: perevody sv. Pisanija v slavjanskoj pis'mennosti," in *Istorija, kul'tura, ètnografija i fol'klor slavjanskich narodov: X Meždunarodnyj s"ezd slavistov: Sofija, sentjabr' 1988: Doklady sovetskoj delegacii* (ed. I.I. Kostjuško; Moscow: Nauka, 1988), 124–45.

Alekseev, A.A., *Tekstologija slavjanskoj Biblii* (Bausteine zur slavischen Philologie und Kulturgeschichte Reihe A Slavistische Forschungen 24; St. Petersburg: Dmitrij Bulanin, 1999).

Alekseev, A.A., *Biblija v bogosluženii: Vizantijsko-slavjanskij lekcionarij* (St. Petersburg: Nestor-Istorija, 2008).

---

[59] In the other cases, the portions are labeled as *časti*, i.e., "parts," and are marked by progressive numbering (see, for instance, manuscripts Russian State Archive of Ancient Acts, Moscow, f. 181, No. 354/803 and f. 188, No. 790).

[60] A completely different subdivision of OCS-Exod in nine sections is to be found in codex f. 181 (MGAMID) 279/658 of the Russian State Archive of Ancient Acts, Moscow, folios 89–107ᵛ.

[61] The weekly Torah portions are marked in the Arab-Pent (→ 2.4.9), which, unlike the OCS, is based on MT. See Vollandt, *Arabic Versions*, 154, 223, 226, 229, 230, 233, 243.

Alekseev, A.A., "Perevody Biblii," in *Istorija evrejskogo naroda v Rossii*, Vol. 1: *Ot drevnosti do rannego novogo vremeni* (ed. A. Kulik; Moscow: Mosty Kul'tury, 2010), 345–55.

Alekseev, A.A., "Russko-evrejskie literaturnye svjazi Kievskoj èpochi: Rezul'taty i perspektivy issledovanija," in *Kenaanity: evrei v srednevekovom slavjanskom mire* (eds. V. Moskovič, A. Torpusman, and M. Členov; Jews and Slavs 24; Jerusalem: Gešarim, 2014), 166–82.

Angelov, B.S. and C. Kodov (eds.), *Kliment Ochridski: Săbrani săčinenija*, Vol. 3: *Prostranni žitija na Kiril i Metodii* (Sofia: Izdatelstvo na Bălgarska Akademija na naukite, 1973).

Berčić, I. (ed.), *Ulomci Svetoga Pisma obojega uvjeta staroslovenskim jezikom: Skupio iz rukopisah i tiskanih knjigah hrvatskoga razreda svećenik Ivan Berčić*, Vol. 1 (Prague: Sinovi Bogumila Haase, 1871).

Brandt, R., "Grigorovičev parimejnik: v sličenii s drugimi parimejnikami," *Čtenija v Imperatorskom Obščestve istorii i drevnostej rossijskich* 168 (1894): 1–90; 170 (1894): 91–178; 193 (1900): 179–290; 197 (1901): 291–308.

Dadiverin, I. (ed.), *Die Methodbibel*, Vol. 4: *Das Buch Leviticus* (Die Slawischen Sprachen 34; Salzburg: Institut für Slawistik der Universität Salzburg, 1995).

Evseev, I.E., *Očerki po istorii slavjanskogo perevoda Biblii* (Petrograd: Tipografija M. Merkuševa, 1916).

Fernández Marcos, N. and A. Sáenz-Badillos (eds.), *Theodoreti Cyrensis Quaestiones in Octateuchum: Editio critica* (Textos y Estudios Cardenal Cisneros 17; Madrid: CSIC, 1979).

Fincati, M., "Per la storia dell'Esateuco Ambrosiano A 147 inf.," *Aev* 83.2 (2009): 299–339.

Gorskij, A.V., "O slavjanskom perevode Pjatiknižija Moiseeva, ispravlennom v XV veke po evrejskomu tekstu," *Pribavlenija k Tvorenijam sv. Otcev* 19 (1860): 134–68.

Istrin, V., *Aleksandrija russkich chronografov: Issledovanie i tekst* (Moscow: Universitetskaja tipografija, 1893).

Jagić, V., *Entstehungsgeschichte der kirchenslavischen Sprache* (Berlin: Weidmann, 1913).

Kloss, B.M., *O proischoždenii nazvanija "Rossija"* (Moscow: Rukopisnye pamjatniki Drevnej Rusi, 2012).

Kniga Ischod: Drevneslavjanskij polnyj (četij) tekst po spiskam XIV–XVI vv. (ed. T. Vilkul; Moscow: "Kvadriga," 2015).

Kyas, V. and Ž. Šarapatková, "Přehled staroslověnského parimejníku," in *Palaeoslovenica: Sborník oddělení srovnávací slovanské jazykovědy Ústavu jazyků a literatur ČSAV* (ed. E. Bláhová; Prague: Ústavu jazyků a literatur ČSAV, 1971): 95–108.

Mathiesen, R., "Handlist of Manuscripts Containing Church Slavonic Translations of the Old Testament," *Polata knigopisnaja* 7 (1983): 3–48.

Michajlov, A.V., *Kniga Bytija proroka Moiseja v drevneslavjanskom perevode* (4 vols.; Warsaw: Tipografija Varšavskogo učebnogo okruga, 1900–1908).

Michajlov, A.V., *K voprosu o literaturnom nasledii svv. Kirilla i Mefodija v glagoličeskich chorvatskich missalach i breviarijach: Iz istorii drevne-slavjanskogo perevoda kn. Bytija pr. Moiseja* (Warsaw: Tipografija Varšavskogo učebnogo okruga, 1904).

Michajlov, A.V., *Opyt izučenija teksta knigi Bytija proroka Moiseja v drevne-slavjanskom perevode*, Vol. 1: *Parimejnyj tekst* (Warsaw: Tipografija Varšavskogo učebnogo okruga, 1912).

Minčev, G., "Pšinskaja Biblija pervoj četverti XVI v.: Maloizvestnaja južnoslavjanskaja rukopis', soderžaščaja perevod Vos'miknižija," in *Jazyk Biblii: Lingvotekstologičeskie issledovanija* (ed. G. Venediktov; Moscow: Nestor, 2012), 222–40.

Nikol'skij, N.K., *O literaturnych trudach mitropolita Klimenta Smoljatiča, pisatelja XII veka* (St. Petersburg: Tipografija Imperatorskoj Akademii nauk, 1892).

Ostrožskaja biblija: Fototipičeskoe pereizdanie teksta s izdanija 1581 g. (Moscow: Slovo-Art, 1988).

Pičchadze, A.A., "Tipologija parimijnych čtenij knigi Ischod," *Palaeobulgarica* 10.1 (1986): 20–34.

Pičchadze, A.A., "K istorii četʹego teksta slavjanskogo Vos'miknižija," *Trudy Otdela drevnerusskoj literatury* 49 (1996): 10–21.

Pičchadze, A.A., "Kniga 'Ischod' v drevneslavjanskom Parimejnike," *Učenye zapiski Rossijskogo pravoslavnogo universiteta ap. Ioanna Bogoslova* 4 (1998): 5–60.

Pičchadze, A.A., "Perevody Biblii na drevnie jazyki: cerkovnoslavjanskij," *Pravoslavnaja ènciklopedija*, Vol. 5: Bessonov-Bonveč (ed. Aleksij, Patriarch Moskovskij i Vseja Rusi ii; Moscow: Cerkovno-Naučnyj Centr "Pravoslavnaja ènciklopedija," 2002), 139–47.

Ribarova, Z. and Z. Hauptova, *Grigorovičev Parimejnik* (2 vols.; Skopje: Makedonska Akademija na naukite i umetnostite, 1998–2014).

Sacrae Scripturae veteris novaeque omnia (Venice: in aedibus Aldi et Andreae Soceri, 1518).

Schmidt-Deeg, E.-M., (ed.), *Das New Yorker Missale: Eine kroato-glagolitische Handschrift des frühen 15. Jahrhunderts: Kritische Edition* (Munich: Otto Sagner, 1994).

Slavova, T., "Sledi ot Metodiev prevod na biblejskata kniga Bitie," *Palaeobulgarica* 19.4 (1995): 53–70.

Slavova, T., "Slavjanskijat prevod na komentarite na Teodorit Kirski vărchu Petoknižeto," *Palaeobulgarica* 24.4 (2000): 7–18.

Slavova, T., "Biblejskoto Osmoknižie v săstava na Archivnija Chronograf," *Palaeobulgarica* 34.3 (2010): 26–35.

Svodnyj katalog slavjano-russkich rukopysnych knig, chranjaščichsja v Rossii, stranach SNG i Baltii. XIV vek, Vol. 1: *Apokalipsis – Letopis' Lavrent'evskaja* (Moscow: "Indrik," 2002).

Thomson, F.J., "The Bulgarian Contribution to the Reception of Byzantine Culture in Kievan Rus': The Myths and the Enigma," *Harvard Ukrainian Studies* 12–13 (1988–1989): 214–61.

Thomson, F.J., "The Slavonic Translation of the Old Testament," in *The Interpretation of the Bible: The International Symposium in Slovenia* (ed. J. Krašovec; JSOTSup 289; Sheffield: Sheffield Academic Press, 1998): 605–920.

Thomson, F.J., *A Brief Survey of the History of the Church Slavonic Bible from its Cyrillomethodian Origins until its Final Form in the Elizabethan Bible of 1751* (Slavica Gadensia 33.2; Ghent: Department of Slavonic and Eastern European Studies of Ghent University, 2006).

Turilov, A.A., "Byl li perevodčik simeonovskoj èpochi presviter Grigorij Monachom," in *Slavjanovedenie* 2 (2013): 12–16.

Uspenskij, B.A., "Imja Boga v slavjanskoj Biblii (K voprosu o slavjano-evrejskich kontaktach v Drevnej Rusi)," *Voprosy jazykoznanija* 6 (2012): 93–122.

Uspenskij, B.A., "Bukva è v drevnerusskich pevčeskich tekstach i v spiskach Biblejskoj knigi Ischod," *Voprosy jazykoznanija* 6 (2013): 79–114.

Uspenskij, B.A., "Iz istorii slavjanskoj Biblii: slavjano-evrejskie jazykovye kontakty v Drevnej Rusi (na materiale *Nomina sacra*)," *Voprosy jazykoznanija* 5 (2014): 24–55.

Uspenskij, B.A., "Filologičeskie nabljudenija nad tekstom 'Otkrovenija Avraama,'" *Voprosy jazykoznanija* 5 (2015): 49–86.

Vilkul, T., "Davn'oslov'jans'ka knyga Vychid: četiji tekst ta grec'kyji oryginal," in *Knjaža doba: istorija i kul'tura*, Vol. 6 (ed. V. Aleksandrovyč; Lviv: Nacional'na akademija nauk Ukrajiny, 2012), 89–98.

Vilkul, T., "Knyga Vychid chronografičnoji redakciji Iudejs'kyji Chronograf ta Trojic'ki P'jatyknyžžja," *Special'ni istoryčni dyscypliny* 22 (2013): 504–16.

Vollandt, R., *Arabic Versions of the Pentateuch: A Comparative Study of Jewish, Christian, and Muslim Sources: Christian-Arabic Translations of the Pentateuch from the 9th to the 13th Centuries* (Biblia Arabica 2; Leiden: Brill, 2015).

Wevers, J.W., *Text History of the Greek Genesis* (MSU 11; Göttingen: Vandenhoeck & Ruprecht, 1974).

Wevers, J.W., *Text History of the Greek Deuteronomy* (MSU 13; Göttingen: Vandenhoeck & Ruprecht, 1978).

Wevers, J.W., *Text History of the Greek Numbers* (MSU 16; Göttingen: Vandenhoeck & Ruprecht, 1982).

Wevers, J.W., *Text History of the Greek Leviticus* (MSU 19; Göttingen: Vandenhoeck & Ruprecht, 1986).

Wevers, J.W., *Text History of the Greek Exodus* (MSU 21; Göttingen: Vandenhoeck & Ruprecht, 1992).

Wevers, J.W. (ed.), *Genesis* (Septuaginta Vetus Testamentum Graecum 1; Göttingen: Vandenhoeck & Ruprecht, 1974).

Wevers, J.W. (ed.), *Deuteronomium* (Septuaginta Vetus Testamentum Graecum 3.2; Göttingen: Vandenhoeck & Ruprecht, 1977; 2nd revised ed.: 2006).

Wevers, J.W. (ed.), *Numeri* (Septuaginta Vetus Testamentum Graecum 3.1; Göttingen: Vandenhoeck & Ruprecht, 1982).

Wevers, J.W. (ed.), *Leviticus* (Septuaginta Vetus Testamentum Graecum 2.2; Göttingen: Vandenhoeck & Ruprecht, 1986).

Wevers, J.W. (ed.), *Exodus* (Septuaginta Vetus Testamentum Graecum 2.1; Göttingen: Vandenhoeck & Ruprecht, 1991).

Željazkova, V., "Orfografičeskie i fonetičeskie osobennosti knigi Ischod po rukopisi N°3 iz sobranija E. Barsova v Gosudarstvennom istoričeskom muzee v Moskve," in *Judaeo-Bulgarica, Judaeo-Russica et Palaeoslavica* (eds. W. Moskovich and S. Nikolova; Jews and Slavs 15; Jerusalem: Hebrew University of Jerusalem Center for Slavic Languages and Literatures, 2005), 138–47.

Željazkova, V., "Opisanieto na skinijata v starobălgarskija prevod na kniga Izchod," in *Srednovekovieto v ogledaloto na edin filolog: Sbornik v čest na Svetlina Nikolova* (ed. S. Bărlieva; Kirilo-Metodievski studii 18; Sofia: Bălgarska Akademija na naukite, 2009), 152–65.

Alessandro Maria Bruni

2.5.8 Arabic Translations

It seems that all major Arabic-speaking churches had their own distinct medieval translation of the Pentateuch into Arabic. Exceptions are the West Syriac and Mozarabic communities, which employed existing translations of a different provenance (see below). In early modern times, however, these transmitted versions gradually dropped out of use and were replaced by manuscript copies of the *Biblia Sacra Arabica* (1671–1673), printed by the *Congregatio de Propaganda Fide* and other missionary printers of the Bible in Arabic.

2.5.8.1 Translations from Syriac
2.5.8.1.1 Translations of an East Syriac Provenance

The church of the East appears to have led the way in the production of Arabic versions of the Pentateuch. Two distinct text types are known today, both translations from the Peshiṭta (→ 2.4.5).[1] Although sharing some features and resembling each other in part, they display quite dissimilar versions. The first is largely written in Classical Arabic and includes many allusions to Qurʾānic vocabulary, whereas the latter is of a more didactic translation type, largely imitative of the Syriac *Vorlage* and exhibiting a distinct set of didactic translation techniques. They also differ in their textual affinities and paratextual elements, such as chapter divisions. Although concrete evidence regarding their formation is scant, there are several indications of the antiquity of these traditions. The West Syriac scholar al-Ḥārith b. Sinān, active prior to 953 C.E. (see below), mentions in the preface to his Arabic version of the Septuagint that translations of the Peshiṭta were already available to him.[2] Both traditions were quoted by early Muslim writers in the ninth century (see below). Further evidence is provided by the dates of manuscripts Sinai, Ar. 2 (copied 939/940 C.E.) and Sinai, Ar. 4 (copied 963 C.E.), which represent the two different traditions and have the distinction of being the earliest dated manuscript copies of an Arabic Pentateuch of any provenance.

The first text type is preserved in manuscript Sinai, Ar. 2,[3] which is – with the exception of manuscript Oxford, Bodl. Library, Hunt. 186 and of fols. 2ᵛ–26ʳ in manuscript St. Petersburg, Institute

---

[1] Both have been treated extensively in Vollandt, *Arabic Versions of the Pentateuch*.

[2] His introduction mentions previous translations of the Peshiṭta (see, e.g., ms Vatican, BAV, Ar. 1, fol. 2ʳ).

[3] On the manuscript, see Lindgren and Vollandt, "An Early Copy."

of Oriental Manuscripts, D 226 – almost unique. The Pentateuch citations in the writings of the Muslim scholars Ibn Qutayba (828–889 C.E.) and al-Ṭabarī (829–923 C.E.) usually agree with manuscript Sinai, Ar. 2 and thus furnish important evidence as to the dating of the translation to the second half of the ninth century. In particular, the former quotes the present translation tradition extensively in *Taʾwīl mukhtalif al-ḥadīth* "Elucidation of disputed Ḥadīth," *Taʾwīl mushkil al-qurʾān* "Elucidation of difficult passages in the Qurʾān," *ʿUyūn al-akhbār* "Choice Narratives," and *Kitāb al-maʿārif* "Book of Noteworthy Information."[4] They are brought as proof-texts for debated passages in the Qurʾān, Ḥadīth, or to supplement reports on biblical figures transmitted in Islamicised form, such as those by Wahb b. Munabbih. In like manner, al-Ṭabarī features quotations that are identical to the version exhibited in manuscript Sinai, Ar. 2 in his most influential compositions: his commentary, known as *Jāmiʿ al-bayān ʿan taʾwīl ay al-Qurʾān*, and his universal history, *Taʾrīkh al-rusul wa-l-mulūk*.[5]

The first text type is a faithful translation of the Syriac Peshiṭta (→ 2.4.5) that commonly adheres to the manuscripts of the basic *textus receptus*.[6] A clear characteristic of this first text type is conformity with the rules of Classical Arabic. The production of a translation of high literary standard is one of its unique and distinguishing features. Unlike many other translations, it does not attempt to reflect the Syriac source language in some kind of calque or mirror translation. It is thus clearly directed towards the target language and only exhibits a limited interest in imitating its *Vorlage*. The language is classical, both linguistically and regarding its style. The lexicon may be described as elevated.

The translation exhibits a clear acquaintance with Qurʾānic narratives. Noah's ark, ܩܐܒܘܬܐ in Syriac, is rendered by سفينة "vessel, boat" and فلك "ark" in accordance with the words used in the Qurʾān (e.g., Q 8:62; 39:14). The most conspicuous examples, however, are found in the Joseph narrative. Joseph's second dream is recounted as الشمس والقمر وأحد عشر كوكباً رأيتهم لي ساجدين "the sun and the moon and eleven stars I saw bowing down to me," which is strikingly similar to the Qurʾānic version أَحَدَ عَشَرَ كَوْكَبًا وَٱلشَّمْسَ وَٱلْقَمَرَ رَأَيْتُهُمْ لِي سَٰجِدِينَ "eleven stars and the sun and the moon I saw bowing down to me" (Q 12:3). Particularly striking are the addition of رأيتهم "I saw them," which is not found in the Syriac, and the transposition of لي (Syr. ܠܝ > ܣܓܕܝܢ Arab. لي ساجدين "bowing down to me"), in order to accord with the Qurʾānic syntax. Joseph's garment, ܟܬܘܢܐ "a linen garment" in Syriac, is featured as قميص "shirt," while in Gen 3:21 the lexeme is rendered differently by سرابيل "clothing." The pit into which Joseph is cast by his brothers appears as جب "pit," although it is سجن "prison" that translates Syriac ܓܘܒܐ in Gen 40:15 and Gen 41:14. The particular employment of قميص and جب in the Joseph narrative, in contrast to different lexemes for the same word in other parts of the Syriac *Vorlage*, has to be understood in light of its parallels in the Qurʾān, which uses identical terminology. These cases represent almost conscious intertextual allusions to the Qurʾān, the revealed text of the religious majority.

The second text type, as represented by manuscript Sinai, Ar. 4, is particularly valuable for the text-critical study of s-Pent (→ 2.4.5), since it appears to be based on an ancient *Vorlage* with close affinities to early Peshiṭta manuscripts, such as manuscript London, BL, Add. 14425. This manuscript, copied in 463 C.E. by an East Syriac copyist, is considered a prominent representative of the earliest stage of transmission of s-Pent. It is well known that the text of s-Pent underwent considerable textual changes before its stabilisation in the form of a *textus receptus* in the ninth

---

[4] Though unidentified, these citations have been treated by Adang, *Muslim Writers on Judaism*, 112–17; Altheim, "Die Älteste Arabische Genesis-Übersetzung"; Graf, *GCAL* 1, 49; Goldziher, "Ueber Bibelcitate"; Isteero, "'Abdullāh Muslim Ibn Qutayba's Biblical Quotations"; Lazarus-Yafeh, *Intertwined Worlds*, 121–22; Lecomte, "Les citations"; and Vajda, "Judaeo-Arabica: observations sur quelques citations."

[5] Vollandt, *Arabic Versions of the Pentateuch*, 97–102, and Adang, *Muslim Writers on Judaism*, 120–22.

[6] On the different stages of textual transmission of s-Pent, see Koster, *The Peshiṭta of Exodus*; and Dirksen, *East and West*, 468–84.

century.[7] Further indications of the old age of this translation are found in the writings of ʿAlī b. Rabban al-Ṭabarī, an East Syriac convert to Islam, active in the ninth century. His *Kitāb al-dīn wa-l-dawla* "The Book of Religion and Empire" contains many biblical quotations that show a great similarity to the translation.[8]

The strategy followed inherently by the translator in transferring particular structures, concepts, or ideas from the source language into the target language is distinct from the text type discussed above. The translation accords less with the linguistic and stylistic requirements of Classical Arabic, but exhibits a great number of imitative and didactic devises that imitate the Syriac. Two features in translation technique stand out: the use of alternative renderings and the addition of textual interpretative elements.[9] Alternative renderings are illustrated by the translation of ܚܣܢܬ ܡܢܢ "you have become much mightier than we" in Gen 26:16 as صرت اعز واعظم منا "and you became *more powerful* and mightier than we." For ܘܗܘܐ ܒܙܒܢ ܡܘܠܕܗ "and it was the time of her giving birth" in Gen 38:27, the translation reads فلما بلغ حين ولادها وحضرها المخاض "and when it was the time of her giving birth *and her parturition was near.*" Often, one of the alternatives presents a literal rendition, whereas the second is idiomatic, according to Classical Arabic usage. This can be seen clearly in the last example. Coming to the textual interpretative extensions, which are frequently added to the translation, they serve two functions. First, they may provide a short elucidating gloss to the running text, such as in Gen 2:14. Following the translation of the toponym ܐܬܘܪ "Asshur," a short phrase is found that identifies the biblical place with the city of Mosul: اثور التي هي لموصل "Asshur, i.e., Mosul." Another function of these additions is to create cohesion. For example, Rebecca's plot with her son Jacob in Gen 27:14 is brought to a close with a simple ܘܐܝܬܝ ܠܐܡܗ "and he brought to his mother." The translation, in contrast, reads واتا امه بما امرته "and he brought to his mother *what she commanded him*" and thus links the verse to the preceding narrative.

In addition to manuscript Sinai, Ar. 4, further copies of this translation can be found in mss Oxford, New College Library, 335 (1193 C.E., an Arabic-Syriac bilingual); Berlin, Staatsbibliothek, Diez 106; Paris, BNF, Ar. 13 (only for Genesis–Leviticus) and Ar. 14 (only for Genesis–Leviticus); Florence, BML Or. 77 (formerly 15); Oxford, Bodl. Library, Arch. Seld. A 66; Leiden, University Library, Or. 215; Munich, Bayrische Staatsbibliothek, Arabic 234; and Vatican, BAV, Ar. 525.

2.5.8.1.2 Translations of a West Syriac Provenance

The West Syriac church seems to have employed an Arabic Pentateuch that encompassed pentateuchal books of different origins. The book of Genesis is constituted by a Syriac recension of Saadia's *Tafsīr* (→ 2.4.9). It is clearly distinguishable from that of the Coptic branch, treated below. Manuscript London, BL, Add. 11855, dated 1024 C.E., is the earliest dated copy. The next dated manuscript, Leiden, University Liberary, Or. 377, was written in 1239/1240 C.E. by a West Syriac scribe. He announces himself as Salām b. Ismail al-Mardīnī al-Yaʿqūbī (fol. 216ᵛ).[10] His affiliation to the West Syriac church provides important evidence as to the origin of this adaptation. The manuscripts complement the remaining books of the Pentateuch with versions from various provenances. Whereas the books of Exodus and Numbers stem from the second aforementioned East Syriac text type, Leviticus and Deuteronomy exhibit the later adaptation of al-Ḥārith's translation (see below). This arrangement is also found in manuscripts Oxford, Bodl. Library, Hunt. 424 and Coptic Orthodox Patriarchate, Bibl. 22.

---

[7] Compare the note above.

[8] For details, see Vollandt, *Arabic Versions of the Pentateuch*, 91–97; Adang, *Muslim Writers on Judaism*, 110–11.

[9] Examples of the translation technique, based on manuscript Munich, Bayrische Staatsbibliothek, Ar. 234, have been furnished in Graf, "Die arabische Pentateuchübersetzung" and Monferrer-Sala, "A Nestorian Arabic Pentateuch."

[10] The manuscript was edited by de Lagarde, *Materialien zur Kritik*. For the colophon, cf. Hughes, *De Lagardes Ausgabe*, vi.

Another early West Syriac version of the Pentateuch in Arabic based on the Syro-Hexapla (→ 2.5.4.2) was produced by al-Ḥārith b. Sinān b. Sunbaṭ al-Ḥarrānī, who also translated the sapiential books (→ 13–17.2.8). Fortunately, al-Ḥārith is mentioned in al-Masʿūdī's, "Meadows of Gold" (Arab. *Murūj al-dhahab*).[11] The demise of the latter consequently furnishes 956 C.E. as *terminus ante quem* of the former's period of work. His *nisba*, which in Arabic onomatics indicates the place of origin, suggests that he or his family originated from Ḥarrān.

Al-Ḥārith endowed his translation with a set of introductory chapters. They are divided into two parts, of which the first is referred to as *Risāla* "Epistle" by the author and addresses bible translations made prior to his work. In particular, Origin's Hexapla is presented to the reader (→ 1.3.1.2) with a lengthy description of its arrangement into columns and the notation system used to indicate variants between LXX (→ 2.4.1) and the Three (→ 2.4.6).[12] The second part precedes each book of the Pentateuch and provides a short summary of the contents. Each chapter is recapitulated briefly, using formulas such as *wa-yukhbaru fīhi* "and it is told," *wa-yushraḥu fīhi* "and it is explained," *wa-yaqussu fīhi* "and it is narrated," etc. In some manuscripts, this last section is coined *fihrist* "table of contents" or *jawāmiʿ* "index." An edition of this translation is still a major *desideratum*.[13] Among the most important copies are manuscripts Sinai, Ar. 10 (1233/1234 C.E.); Vatican, BAV, Ar. 1 (1320 C.E.); Istanbul, Süleymaniye, Carullah 3; Oxford, Bodl. Library, Laud. Or. 258 (formerly A 147) and Laud. Or. 243 (formerly A 146); Escurial, Ar. 1857; Paris, BNF, Ar. 13 (only for Numbers) and Ar. 14 (only for Genesis–Exodus, dated 1656 C.E.); Coptic Orthodox Patriarchate, Bibl. 14 and Bibl. 27 (1330 C.E.). Manuscript Aleppo, collection Khoukaz (Sbath *fihris* 293, dated 1325–1327 C.E.) is lost today.

Al-Ḥārith's version of the Pentateuch was also disseminated among the Mozarabs. His translation of the precious stones in the highpriest's breastplate (Exod 28:17–20) is cited in the Mozarabic Latin-Arabic glossary of the Leiden University Library.[14] The foreign provenance is duly noted by the composer of this glossary, who introduced the translation as being *min tarjamat al-shām* "from a translation made in Syria." Another text type that seems to be directly related to al-Ḥārith's translation is preserved in a group of later manuscripts. Among this group, manuscript Sinai, Ar. 3 and the pentateuchal portions in manuscripts Vatican, BAV, Ar. 468 and St. Petersburg, Institute of Oriental Manuscripts, D 226 (except for 2ᵛ–26r) are found. These manuscripts date from the thirteenth century onwards, were disseminated predominately among Melkite communities, and contain a translation that is based on the one by al-Ḥārith. They usually dispense with the introductory chapters (expect for the St. Petersburg copy). The precise emergence and characteristics of this adaptation, however, are yet to be established.

In order to create a full Pentateuch, Ibn al-Qunbar's commentary and translation (see below) are commonly complemented with the texts of Numbers and Deuteronomy found in the later adaptations of al-Ḥārith's translation (see above). The product of this juxtaposition of different traditions was coined "Mischrezension" by Graf.[15] Manuscripts of this group were extremely popular and disseminated in large numbers even beyond Melkite communities.[16] It significantly outnumbers all other translation traditions of the Pentateuch in Arabic.

---

[11] For details, see Nasrallah, "Deux versions Melchites," 206.

[12] The introduction has been partially edited and translated into Latin. Cf. H. Aldrich, "Testimonia aliquot Scriptorum Orientalium," 131–44; Hody, *Bibliorum Textibus Originalibus*, 622–25; and White, *A Letter to the Right Reverend*, 8–29.

[13] A team, consisting of C. Adang, J.P. Monferrer-Sala, S. Schmidtke, and myself, is presently working on a critical edition of the text.

[14] Cf. Monferrer-Sala, *A Nestorian Arabic Pentateuch*, 353.

[15] Graf, *GCAL* 1, 105.

[16] Ibn al-Qunbar's Coptic origin was largely forgotten. Later copyists frequently referred to him as being affiliated with the Melkite Church. For example, a note in manuscript Paris, BNF, Ar. 16 refers to his translation as *min nuskhat al-malakiyyīn* "from the version of the Melkites." Cf. Rhode, *The Arabic Versions*, 62. For a list of manuscripts, the reader is referred to Graf, *GCAL* 1, 105–06 and Samir, "Vie et Oeuvre."

2.5.8.2 Translations from Greek

The commentary and running translation of the books of Genesis, Exodus, and Leviticus by Mark b. al-Qunbar, a Coptic convert to the Melkite creed, should not remain unmentioned. Probably born in Zifta, located in the province of al-Gharbiyya in the Nile Delta, he died in 1208 C.E. in the Melkite monastery of Dayr al-Qusayr. The commentary, which is attested in a shorter and longer recension, deals chiefly with monastic concerns in a homiletic manner and is often attributed erroneously in the manuscripts to St. Ephrem or Cyril of Alexandria.[17] The translation units consist of several verses following the accepted liturgical division of the Melkite Church, Arab. *qirāʾa* "lection."[18] They are introduced by the formula *qāla al-kitāb* "the Scripture says" and followed by Ibn al-Qunbar's commentary, Arab. *qāla al-mufassir* "the commentator says." Some manuscripts, such as Paris, BNF, Ar. 9, only contain the detached translation.

There is no consensus regarding the *Vorlage* used by Ibn al-Qunbar for his translation.[19] Feghali, adhering to the assumption that St. Ephrem was the author, and Graf[20] believed it must have been the Peshiṭta (→ 2.4.5). Breydy and Samir are certain of a Coptic *Vorlage* (→ 2.5.2).[21] The latter view finds corroboration in medieval sources. Mikhāʾīl, Bishop of Damietta (d. 1208 C.E.), furnishes the following evidence: "After this he made a parade of his learning and his exposition of the holy books, and he translated them from Coptic into Arabic."[22] Rhode postulated a Greek *Vorlage*, i.e., LXX (→ 2.4.1).[23] This view is reiterated by Wevers, who in addition expressed the possibility that the translation could have been done on the basis of the Bohairic version (→ 2.5.2.2.2).[24] As Rhode and Wevers have undertaken the most comprehensive research on the question of the *Vorlage* of Ibn al-Qunbar's translation, their position is accepted here.

2.5.8.3 Translations of a Coptic Provenance

With regard to Arabic versions of the Bible, the Coptic tradition differs from the Syriac and Melkite in many ways. Since the Copts seem to have used Arabic only very reluctantly and sparsely until well into the twelfth century, the need to translate the canonical Scriptures from Coptic (→ 2.5.2) into Arabic emerged much later than in the other Eastern churches. Although it cannot be ruled out that partial translations of the Pentateuch, e.g., as part of lectionaries, were written down earlier, manuscript evidence dates from the first half of the thirteenth century onwards. As demonstrated by Rhode (1921), the Coptic Church employed various Arabic versions of the Pentateuch.[25] A translation from the Coptic is featured chiefly in bilingual Coptic-Arabic codices. Its first attestation is in the form of a later addition on the outer margins of manuscript Vatican, BAV, Copt. 1.[26] The marginal text appears to be a faithful translation of the Bohairic version (→ 2.5.2.2.2) exhibited in the older part of the codex. At a second stage, the translations were featured in bilingual manuscripts that were designed from the outset to contain both languages. Examples include manuscripts Paris, BNF, Ar. 12 and Copt. 1; Oxford, Bodl. Library, Laud. Or. 272 (formerly Laud. A 182); London, BL, Or. 422; Vatican, BAV, Cop. 2–4; and Coptic Orthodox Patriarchate, Bibl. 1–5.

On the margin of a larger number of manuscripts, however, Saadia's *Tafsīr* is found. It is not clear exactly when the Judeo-Arabic text (→ 2.4.10) was transcribed into Arabic letters. The *Tafsīr* was

---

[17] See Graf, "Ein Arabischer Pentateuchkommentar," and Samir, "Vie et Oeuvre." A list of editions and further bibliography can be found in Swanson, "Marqus ibn al-Qunbar."

[18] The liturgical divisions are discussed in Rhode, *The Arabic Versions*, 106–16.

[19] Feghali, "Note sur l' auteur."

[20] Graf, *GCAL* 1, 105.

[21] Breydy, "Les commentaires bibliques"; and Samir, "Vie et Oeuvre."

[22] The Arabic text and translation are found in Evetts, *The Churches and Monasteries of Egypt*, 19 and 35.

[23] Rhode, "The Arabic Versions."

[24] Wevers, "The Textual Affinities of the Arabic Genesis."

[25] Rhode, "The Arabic Versions." Selected features of the translation technique and language of this version have been discussed by Livne-Kafri in the five articles listed in the bibliography to this entry.

[26] Rhode, "The Arabic Versions," 36–42.

first used among West Syriac communities (see above) and subsequently also borrowed by the Copts. Although his version never acquired an official status in the Coptic Church, it was the most widely diffused and enjoyed great popularity. Its study and preservation was cultivated vigilantly, as the *Tafsīr* fulfilled text-critical functions as a point of comparison with a translation from the original Hebrew to other Arabic versions of the Pentateuch.[27] The manuscripts usually contain the same text type with minor variations and exhibit the division of chapters that accords with the Coptic tradition.[28] The earliest dated among them is manuscript Florence, BML Or. 112 (olim 21), copied 1245/1246 C.E. It is worth noting that Coptic adaptations of the *Tafsīr* exceed by far the number of bilingual codices that contain a translation from a genuine Coptic *Vorlage*. In fact, the ratio is almost 2:1.[29] On the basis of manuscript Paris, BNF, Ar. 1, Saadia's version of the Pentateuch in the Coptic branch of transmission was included in the Paris Polyglot (1628–1645), and was later reprinted in the London Polyglot (1653–1657).[30]

This willingness to integrate foreign traditions and adapt them according to their needs is one of the characteristic traits of the Coptic approach to biblical versions in Arabic. Due to their relatively late adoption of the Arabic language, the Copts faced the need for biblical translations at a time when most other communities already could look back on well-established translation traditions. Although direct translations from the Coptic are attested, such as the aforementioned Arabic version of the Pentateuch, it appears that Coptic scholars mostly preferred to employ existing translations. In addition to the examples above, al-Ḥārith's and Mark b. al-Qunbar's translations of the Pentateuch were popular among Coptic communities (see above).

2.5.8.4 Manuscript Copies of Early Printings

A manuscript copy of the Pentateuch in the London Polyglot[31] that includes its Arabic version, is found in manuscript Prague, Jewish Museum, 356. Two identical copies of the detached text of Saadia's *Tafsīr*, in which the Arabic was supplemented with an interlinear translation into Malaysian made by the Dutch scholar van der Horn, are found in Munich, Staatsbibliothek, Ar. 233 and Cambridge, University Library, Or. 193. The manuscripts were produced by the same scribe, are identical in the page layout, and bear the same date (1680 C.E.). Furthermore, the Pentateuch of the *Biblia Sacra Arabica* (1671–1673 C.E.) is found in a number of manuscripts: Paris, BNF, Ar. 2 (fols. 256ʳ–477ʳ); London, BL, Or. 8745 (fols. 2ʳ–56ʳ) and India Office, Islamic 1280 (fols. 1ʳ–219ʳ); Vatican, BAV, Borg. Ar. 48 (fols. 1ʳ–39ᵛ, only Genesis–Exodus), 150 (only Genesis), 154 (only Genesis) and 239 (fols. 2ʳ–101ʳ); Beirut, Bibliothèque Orientale, 419 (pp. 1–231); Sharfeh, Ar. 1/4; Coptic Orthodox Patriarchate, Bibl. 29, Bibl. 31 (fols. 2ʳ–152ʳ, 1772 C.E.), Bibl. 41 (fols. 1ʳ–138ʳ, dated 1872 C.E.), Bibl. 48 (fols. 1ʳ–164ʳ, dated 1784 C.E.); Graf 582 (fols. xxx); Aleppo, Syriac Orthodox Archdiocese, ms 1 (fols. 2ʳ–111ᵛ); collection Khadori (Sbath *fihris* 387, dated 1732/1732 C.E., now lost); and collection Basile (Sbath *fihris* 1444, now lost).[32]

Adang, C., *Muslim Writers on Judaism and the Hebrew Bible: From Ibn Rabban to Ibn Hazm* (Islamic Philosophy, Theology, and Science 22; Leiden: Brill, 1996).

Aldrich, H., "Testimonia aliquot Scriptorum Orientalium de LXXII interpretibus eoreumque Versione," in *Aristeae Historia LXXII interpretum: Accessere veterum testimonia de eorum Versione* (Oxford: e Theatro Sheldoniano, 1692).

Altheim, F., "Die Älteste Arabische Genesis-Übersetzung," in *Die Araber in der alten Welt* (eds. F. Altheim, R. Altheim-Stiehl, and A. Calderini; Berlin: De Gruyter, 1964), 332–43.

---

[27] On this aspect, see Vollandt, "Some Historiographical Remarks," and Vollandt, "An Unknown Medieval Coptic Hebraism?"

[28] Vollandt, *Arabic Versions of the Pentateuch*, 111–13.

[29] For a full list of manuscripts, see Vollandt, *Arabic Versions of the Pentateuch*, 229–34.

[30] G.M. Le Jay, *Biblia* (Paris: Antoine Vitré, 1629–1645); Walton, *Polyglotta*. Cf. Vollandt, "The Arabic Pentateuch of the Paris Polyglot."

[31] Walton, *Polyglotta*.

[32] Vollandt, "Che portono al ritorno."

Breydy, M., "Les commentaires bibliques de Marcos Ibn Qanbar n' appartiennent ni à St. Ephrem ni au patrimoine liturgique des Maronites," *Al-Manārah* 27 (1986): 367–80.

Dirksen, P.B., "East and West, Old and Young, in the Text Tradition of the Old Testament Peshitta," *VT* 35 (1985): 468–84.

Evetts, B.T.A., *The Churches and Monasteries of Egypt and Some Neighbouring Countries Attributed to Abû Ṣâliḥ, the Armenian* (Oxford: Clarendon Press, 1969).

Feghali, P., "Note sur l'auteur du Commentaire de la Genèse attribué à saint Éphrem," in *Actes du deuxième congrés international d'études arabes chrétiennes: Oosterhesselen, septembre 1984/International Conference on Christian Arabic Studies, 2, 1984, Oosterhesselen* (ed. S.K. Samir; Rome: Pont. Institutum Studiorum Orientalium, 1986), 159–75.

Goldziher, I., "Ueber Bibelcitate in muhammedanischen Schriften," *ZAW* 13 (1893): 315–21.

Graf, *GCAL* 1.

Graf, G., "Die arabische Pentateuchübersetzung in cod. Monac. ar. 234," *BZ* 15 (1919–1921): 97–115, 193–212, 291–300.

Graf, G., "Ein Arabischer Pentateuchkommentar des 12. Jahrhunderts," *Bib* 23 (1924): 113–38.

Hody, H., *Bibliorum Textibus Originalibus, versionibus Graecis et Latina Vulgata* (Oxford: e Theatro Sheldoniano, 1705).

Hughes, J.C., *De Lagardes Ausgabe der Arabischen Übersetzung des Pentateuch* (Leipzig: J.C. Hinrichs, 1914).

Isteero, A., "'Abdullāh Muslim Ibn Qutayba's Biblical Quotations and their Source: An Inquiry into the Earlier Existing Arabic Bible Translations" (PhD diss., John Hopkins University, 1990).

Koster, M.D., *The Peshiṭta of Exodus: The Development of its Text in the Course of Fifteen Centuries* (SSN 19; Assen: Van Gorcum, 1977).

de Lagarde, P., *Materialien zur Kritik und Geschichte des Pentateuchs* (2 vols.; Leipzig: B.G. Teubner, 1867).

Lazarus-Yafeh, H., *Intertwined Worlds: Medieval Islam and Bible Criticism* (Princeton: Princeton University Press, 1992).

Lecomte, G., "Les citations de l'ancien et du nouveau testament dans l'œuvre d'Ibn Qutayba," *Arabica* 5 (1950): 34–46.

Lindgren, M. and R. Vollandt, "An Early Copy of the Pentateuch and the Book of Daniel in Arabic (MS Sinai – Arabic 2): Preliminary Observations on Codicology, Text Types, and Translation Technique," *Intellectual History of the Islamicate World* 1 (2013): 43–68.

Livne-Kafri, O., "A Note on Coptic and Judeo-Arabic on the Basis of a Bilingual Manuscript to the Pentateuch," *Massorot* 12 (2002): 97–101 [Hebr.].

Livne-Kafri, O., "Appendix II: Some Notes Concerning the Arabic Version," in A. Shisha-Halevy, *Topics in Coptic Syntax: Structural Studies in the Bohairic Dialect* (OLA 160; Leuven: Peeters, 2007), 685–94.

Livne-Kafri, O., "A Note on the Energicus in a Coptic-Arabic Translation of the Pentateuch," *Acta Orientalia Academiae Scientiarum Hungaricae* 62 (2009): 405–11.

Livne-Kafri, O., "'What is This Which …' in a Bilingual (Coptic and Arabic) Manuscript of the Pentateuch," *Acta Orientalia Academiae Scientiarum Hungaricae* 65 (2012): 347–52.

Livne-Kafri, O., "A Note on Some Hypothetical Clauses in a Coptic and Arabic MS of the Pentateuch: The Case of *lawlā*," *Acta Orientalia Academiae Scientiarum Hungaricae* 65 (2012): 457–61.

Monferrer-Sala, J.P., "A Nestorian Arabic Pentateuch Used in Western Islamic Lands," in *The Bible in Arab Christianity* (ed. D. Thomas; The History of Christian-Muslim Relations 6; Leiden: Brill, 2007), 351–68.

Nasrallah, J., "Deux versions Melchites partielles de la Bible du IXe et du Xe siècles," *OrChr* 64 (1980): 202–15.

Rhode, J.F., "The Arabic Versions of the Pentateuch in the Church of Egypt: A Study from Eighteen Arabic and Copto-Arabic Mss. (IX–XVII Century) in the National Library at Paris, the Vatican and Bodleian Libraries and the British Museum" (PhD diss.; Catholic University of America, 1921).

Samir, S.K., "Vie et Oeuvre de Marc ibn-Qunbar," in *Christianisme d'Égypte: Hommages à René-Georges Coquin* (ed. J.-M. Rosenstiehl; Cahiers de la Bibliothèque copte 9; Leuven: Peeters, 1995), 123–58.

Swanson, M.N., "Marqus ibn al-Qunbar," in *Christian-Muslim Relations: A Bibliographical History*, Vol. 4: *1200–1350* (eds. D. Thomas and B. Roggema; The History of Christian-Muslim Relations 17; Leiden: Brill, 2012), 98–108.

Vajda, G., "Judaeo-Arabica: Observations sur quelques citations bibliques chez Ibn Qutayba," *REJ* 99 (1935): 68–80.

Vollandt, R., "The Arabic Pentateuch of the Paris Polyglot: Saadiah Gaon's Advent to the Republic of Letters," in *Translating the Bible into Arabic: Historical, Text-Critical and Literary Aspects* (eds. S. Binay and S. Leder; Beirut: Orient Institut Beirut, 2012), 19–35.

Vollandt, R., "Some Historiographical Remarks on Medieval and Early-Modern Scholarship of Biblical Versions in Arabic: A Status Quo," *Intellectual History of the Islamicate World* 1 (2013): 25–42.

Vollandt, R., "Che portono al ritorno quì una Bibbia Arabica integra: A History of the *Biblia Sacra Arabica* (1671–73)," in *Graeco-Latina et Orientalia: Studia in honorem Angeli Urbani heptagenarii* (eds. S.K. Samir and J.P. Monferrer-Sala; Córdoba: CNERU, 2013), 401–18.

Vollandt, R., *Arabic Versions of the Pentateuch: A Comparative Study of Jewish, Christian, and Muslim Sources* (Biblia Arabica 2; Leiden: Brill, 2015).

Vollandt, R., "An Unknown Medieval Coptic Hebraism? On a Momentous Junction of Jewish and Coptic Biblical Studies," in *Canonical Texts and Scholarly Practices: A Global Comparative Approach* (eds. A. Grafton and G. Most; Cambridge: Cambridge University Press, forthcoming).

Wevers, J.W., "The Textual Affinities of the Arabic Genesis of Bib. Nat. Arab 9," in *Studies on the Ancient Palestinian World: Presented to Professor F.V. Winnet* (eds. J.W. Wevers and D.B. Redford; Toronto: University of Toronto Press, 1972), 46–74.

White, J., *A Letter to the Right Reverend the Lord Bishop of London, Suggesting a Plan for a New Edition of the LXX* (Oxford: Clarendon Press, 1779).

Ronny Vollandt

3–5

Former Prophets

3

Joshua

∴

Joshua

3.1 Textual History of Joshua

3.1.1 Introduction

The book of Joshua describes the conquest of the land west of the river Jordan (Joshua 1–12), its allotment to the nine-and-a-half tribes that had not received their territories (Joshua 13–21), and concludes with three chapters dealing with the themes of loyalty and allegiance (Joshua 22–24). The book is a direct continuation of Deuteronomy, both in narrative sequence and in theology and phraseology, although it also shares themes and expressions found in Genesis–Numbers and Judges–Kings. There is a wide scholarly consensus that the book is largely a Deuteronomistic creation (see, e.g., Joshua 1; 2:9–11; 21:43–22:4) and also shows traces of both priestly editing (e.g., Josh 4:19; 5:10–12; 18:1) and ancient pre-Deuteronomistic literary traditions (see, e.g., Josh 10:12–13).[1] It is likely that the complex formation of the book left its traces on its textual history.

In the section dealing with tribal allotments and toponyms (Joshua 13–21) especially, the textual history of the book is so complex that the editors of commonly used editions, such as *BHS and Rahlfs, *Septuaginta, abandoned their editorial principles. In the case of Josh 21:36–37, the editors of *BHS diverted from the principle of offering a diplomatic edition of MT[L] and included those verses, which appear in practically all Hebrew manuscripts and ancient versions, but are notably absent from the Cairo and Leningrad Codices (→ 3.2.2.3.2).[2] For LXX-Josh 15:21–62 and 18:22–19:45,

Rahlfs did not attempt to offer a reconstruction of the original Greek text, but simply placed the text of the main codices, Vaticanus and Alexandrinus, in parallel columns. Other examples are provided by Josh 13:7–8 and 15:59a, where MT appears to have lost several clauses still preserved by LXX. It seems apparent that the textual transmission of Joshua 13–21 has suffered considerably from *parablepsis*, haplography, and other examples of scribal errors in all its extant witnesses.

Besides the usual phenomena of textual corruption, we find evidence of editorial activity in the oldest extant textual witnesses of the book (LXX, 4QJosh[a]).[3] In the oldest extant manuscript of the book, 4QJosh[a] (dating to ca. 150–50 B.C.E.), parts of Josh 8:30–35 occur before Josh 5:2, pointing unambiguously to editorial activity (either in this scroll or all other younger witnesses, → 3.2.1.1). In addition, the LXX (→ 3.3) shows numerous smaller and larger minuses *vis-à-vis* MT throughout the book. In particular, the absence of vv. 4–6 in LXX-Josh 20 has been regarded as a major testimony of Second Temple editorial activity evidenced by MT and other witnesses.[4] With respect to the other numerous quantitative variants between MT and LXX, however, it is not always indisputable whether they should be seen as additions to a shorter Hebrew *Vorlage* witnessed by LXX or as deliberate curtailments on the part of the Greek translator (→ 3.3.6). At the same time, LXX also contains several long pluses *vis-à-vis* MT and all other textual witnesses that seem to have been taken from corresponding passages in Judges and Kings (→ 3.3.4). Of particular importance is the long plus at the end of the book, LXX-Josh 24:33a–b, which is often seen as a more

---

[1] For a useful survey, see E. Noort, *Das Buch Josua: Forschungsgeschichte und Problemfelder* (EdF 292; Darmstadt: Wissenschaftliche Buchgesellschaft, 1998); van der Meer, *Formation*, 115–53.

[2] The oldest masoretic codices, MT[L], MT[A], and MT[C], do not contain those verses, which enumerate the four Levitical cities Bezer, Jahzah, Kedemoth, and Mephaath in the Reubenite area, as described also in 1 Chr 6:63–64. The editors of *BH3 (M. Noth) and *BHS (R. Meyer) considered the omission in the main masoretic witnesses to be the result of haplography and hence added them in smaller letters in their otherwise diplomatic edition of the Leningrad Codex. However, on the basis of a careful examination of the rabbinic testimonies from the tenth century onwards, Barthélemy, *Critique textuelle 1982, 64–68, concludes that the verses in the younger masoretic witnesses present a rather late harmonization with the parallel text from 1 Chronicles 6.

[3] Cf. Tov, *TCHB, 294–99, 314–16.

[4] See already Hollenberg, *Charakter*, 15; Rofé, "Joshua 20"; Tov, *TCHB, 295–96.

original transition from Joshua to the core of the Judges narratives (Judg 3:12 ff.), later substituted by the present Deuteronomistic transition, Judg 1:1–3:11.[5]

Some of the minuses in LXX-Josh seem to find support in a Samaritan book of Joshua,[6] which has been known in Arabic translation since the famous Leiden orientalist Joseph Scaliger bought a manuscript of this composition in Cairo in 1584.[7] This manuscript is a copy of a thirteenth-century original and indicates that it is based on a much older Hebrew original.[8] Although in 1909 Moses Gaster claimed to have discovered this missing Hebrew original, his Hebrew manuscript was almost immediately unmasked as a recent retroversion from the Arabic.[9] Regardless of the textual value of Gaster's Hebrew manuscript, the Samaritan Joshua continues to play an occasional role in text-critical discussions (→ 3.2.3).[10] Something similar applies to another Samaritan text, the *sepher ha-yamim* or *Samaritan Chronicle II*, which contains a version of Joshua–2 Chronicles that is considerably shorter than all other known sources.[11]

Other ancient versions align more or less with MT. This applies to the fragmentary readings of Theodotion, Aquila, and Symmachus (→ 2.4.6),[12] and to the other main witnesses of Joshua: Targum Jonathan (→ 3–5.1.3),[13] the Peshitta (→ 3–5.1.4),[14] and Vulgate (→ 3–5.1.7).[15] There is furthermore

---

[5] A. Rofé, "The End of the Book of Joshua According to the Septuagint," *Shnaton* 2 (1977): 217–27 [Hebr.] = *Hen* 4 (1982): 17–35; Tov, *TCHB*, 297–80.

[6] M. Gaster, "The Samaritan Book of Joshua and the Septuagint," *Proceedings of the Society of Biblical Archeology* 31 (1909): 115–27, 149–53.

[7] For an edition, see T.W.J. Juynboll, *Chronicon Samaritanum Arabice Conscriptum cui Titulus est Liber Josuae* (Leiden: Luchtmans, 1848; online: https://archive.org/details/chroniconsamaritoojosh). An English Translation can be found in O.T. Crane, *The Samaritan Chronicle or The Book of Joshua, the Son of Nun: Translated from the Arabic, with Notes* (New York: John B. Alden, 1890; online: https://archive.org/details/samaritanchronicoocran).

[8] Additional manuscripts of this Arabic Samaritan book of Joshua have been acquired by the British Library and the library of Trinity College, Cambridge, according to Crane, *Samaritan Chronicle*, 7.

[9] P. Kahle, "Zum hebräischen Buch Josua der Samaritaner," *ZDMG* 62 (1908): 550–51; P. Stenhouse, "Samaritan Chronicles," in *The Samaritans* (ed. A.D. Crown; Tübingen: Mohr Siebeck, 1989), 218–65; F. Niessen, *Eine samaritanische Version des Buches Yehošuaʿ und die Šobak-Erzählung* (Texte und Studien zur Orientalistik 12; Hildesheim: Olms, 2000).

[10] A.D. Crown, "Some Traces of Heterodox Theology in the Samaritan Book of Joshua," *BJRL* 50 (1967): 178–98; A.D. Crown, "The Date and Authenticity of the Samaritan Hebrew Book of Joshua as Seen in its Territorial Allotments," *PEQ* 96 (1974): 79–100 (repr. in *Die Samaritaner* [eds. F. Dexinger and R. Plummer; Wege der Forschung 604; Darmstadt: Wissen-schaftliche Buchgesellschaft, 1992], 281–311); Tov, *TCHB*, 296, 315.

[11] J. MacDonald, *The Samaritan Chronicle No. II (or: Sepher Ha-Yamim): From Joshua to Nebuchadnezzar* (BZAW 107; Berlin: De Gruyter, 1969).

[12] For an edition, see Field, *Hexapla*. For further studies, see Greenspoon, *Textual Studies*; Bieberstein, *Lukian und Theodotion im Josuabuch mit einem Beitrag zu den Josuarollen von Ḥirbet Qumrān* (BN 7; Munich: K. Urlaub, 1994).

[13] For editions, see Sperber, *Bible in Aramaic*; F. Praetorius, *Das Targum zu Josua in jemenitischer Überlieferung* (Berlin: Reuther and Reichard, 1899). A concordance was published by J.C. de Moor, *Joshua* (A Bilingual Concordance to the Targum of the Prophets 1; Leiden: Brill, 1995). An English Translation can be found in D.J. Harrington and A.J. Saldarini, *Targum Jonathan to the Former Prophets* (ArBib 10; Edinburgh: T & T Clark, 1987).

[14] For an edition, see J. Erbes, *Josua* (The Old Testament in Syriac 2.1b; Leiden: Brill, 1991). For studies, see H. Mager, *Die Peschittho zum Buche Josua* (Freiburger Theologische Studien 9; Freiburg im Breisgau: Herder, 1916); J.C. de Moor and F. Sepmeijer, "The Peshitta and the Targum of Joshua," in *The Peshitta as a Translation: Papers Read at the II Peshitta Symposium Held at Leiden 19–21 August 1993* (eds. P.B. Dirksen and A. van der Kooij; Monographs of the Peshitta Institute Leiden 8; Leiden: Brill, 1995), 129–76; J.E. Erbes, *The Peshitta and the Versions: A Study of the Peshitta Variants in Joshua 1–5 in Relation to Their Equivalents in the Ancient Versions* (Acta Universitatis Upsaliensis Studia Semitica Upsaliensia 16; Uppsala: Uppsala University Library, 1999; critically reviewed by C.G. den Hertog in *OLZ* 95 [2000]: 446–52); M.N. van der Meer, "Moses' Laws: A Note on the Peshitta Version of Joshua 1:7 and Related Passages," in *Text, Translation, and Tradition: Studies on the Peshitta and its Use in the Syriac Tradition Presented to Konrad D. Jenner on the Occasion of his Sixty-Fifth Birthday* (eds. W.T. van Peursen and R.B. ter Haar Romeny; Monographs of the Peshitta Institute 14; Leiden: Brill, 2006), 117–28.

[15] An editio minor can found in Weber and Gryson, *Vulgata*. For the editio maior, see *Libri Iosue Iudicum Ruth ex interpretation sancti Hieronymi et variis capitulorum seriebus* (Biblia sacra iuxta latinam vulgatam versionem ad codicum fidem iussu Pii PP. XI; Rome: Typis polyglottis Vaticanis, 1939). An important study on V-Josh is S. Sipilä, "The Book of Joshua in the

an alternative Targum to Joshua 5 in the Taylor-Schechter collection (T.-S. B 13,12), which according its editors might go back to Second Temple times, but is probably of a far more recent, i.e., medieval, origin.[16] As a result, the history of research on the text of Joshua and its textual history concentrated almost exclusively on the relation between MT and LXX (→ 3.3) until the publication of 4QJosh[a] (→ 3.2.1.1) in 1993.

3.1.2 History of Research[17]

The first modern investigation of the text of Joshua was carried out by the Flemish-Dutch humanist scholar Masius, who published a polyglot edition of the Hebrew, Greek, and Latin versions of Joshua with critical annotations and an extensive commentary.[18] Although much of his pioneering work has now been superseded, the commentary is still indispensable, as Masius was able to draw upon a Syro-Hexapla manuscript that was lost after his death and can only be reconstructed on the basis of his critical remarks.[19]

A next stage in the history of research started during the last quarter of the nineteenth century when text-critical and redaction-critical studies by Kuenen[20] and Wellhausen[21] paved the way for renewed interest in the literary and textual history of the Hebrew Bible. Hollenberg (1876) was the first to examine the text-critical value of LXX-Josh on the basis of a careful study of the translation technique of the Greek translator (→ 3.3.4; → 3.3.5; → 3.3.6).[22] Only after a critical assessment of scribal corruption within the Greek transmission and of pseudo-variants (resulting from the Greek translator's tendency to vary in translation equivalents, condense ponderous Hebrew expressions, and render several Hebrew expressions relatively freely), did Hollenberg isolate some thirty-five cases consisting mainly of pluses in LXX-Josh lost in MT as a result of *paraplepsis* where LXX in his view reflected another – although not always superior – Hebrew parent text. Occasionally, however, the minus in LXX points to a late addition in the Hebrew text, as is the case, in Hollenberg's view, in Joshua 20 (→ 3.1.1), where MT-Josh 20:4–6 add Deuteronomistic prescriptions to a shorter priestly descriptive text, and Josh 5:10–12, where the phrases מִמָּחֳרַת הַפֶּסַח "after the morrow of passover" and מִמָּחֳרָת בְּאָכְלָם "after the morrow when they ate," reflecting the late priestly legislation of Leviticus 23, are late additions in MT, according to Hollenberg.[23]

Hollenberg's careful assessment, however, soon gave way to more generalizing, diverging statements. Most commentators stressed the Greek translator's preference for curtailment and hence the priority of MT over LXX,[24] whereas a minority attached much more value to the minuses

---

Vulgate," in *Scripture in Transition: Essays on Septuagint, Hebrew Bible, and Dead Sea Scrolls in Honour of Raija Sollamo* (eds. A. Voitila and J. Jokiranta; JSJSup 126; Leiden: Brill, 2008), 17–26.

[16] H. Fahr and U. Glessmer, *Jordandurchzug und Beschneidung als Zurechtweisung in einem Targum zu Josua 5: Edition des MS T.-S. B 13,12* (Orientalia biblica et christiana 3; Glückstadt: Augustin, 1991).

[17] See van der Meer, *Formation*, 21–91.

[18] A. Masius, *Iosuae imperatoris historia illustrate atque explicata* (Antwerp: Plantinus, 1574). The commentary (second) part has been reprinted in J.P. Migne (ed.), *In Numeros-In Deuteronomium-In Iosuam* (vol. 7 of Scripturae Sacrae Cursus Completus ...; Paris: Migne, 1838); online version of the complete text: http://books.google.nl/books/ucm?vid=UCM531684975X&printsec=frontcover&redir_esc=y#v=onepage&q&f=false.

[19] An attempt to reconstruct this lost Syro-Hexapla manuscript was carried out by M.L. Margolis, "Andreas Masius and His Commentary on the Book of Joshua" (unpublished typescript, completed June 15, 1923); see L.J. Greenspoon, "A Preliminary Publication of Max Leopold Margolis' *Andreas Masius*, Together with His Discussion of Hexapla-Tetrapla," in Salvesen, *Hexapla, 39–69.

[20] A. Kuenen, *Historisch-critisch onderzoek naar het ontstaan en de verzameling van de boeken des Ouden Verbonds*, Part 1: *De thora en de historische boeken des Ouden Verbonds* (Leiden: Engels 1861); a German translation of the 2nd ed. appeared as *Historisch-kritische Einleitung in die Bücher des Alten Testaments hinsichtlich ihrer Entstehung und Sammlung*, Part 1.1: *Die Entstehung des Hexateuchs* (Leipzig: Schulze, 1887).

[21] J. Wellhausen, *Die Composition des Hexateuch* (Skizzen und Vorarbeiten 2; Berlin: Reimer, 1885).

[22] Hollenberg, *Charakter*.

[23] J. Hollenberg, "Zur Textkritik des Buches Josua und des Buches der Richter," ZAW 1 (1881): 97–105.

[24] E.g., A. Dillmann, *Die Bücher Numeri, Deuteronomium und Josua* (2nd ed.; KAT 13; Leipzig: S. Hirzel, 1886).

in LXX and argued for individual interpolations (named "Glossen" by Benjamin[25]) or a systematic and comprehensive re-edition of a shorter Hebrew text reflected by LXX into an expansionistic MT (Holmes).[26] Important for Holmes' argument is the fact that several pluses in MT reflect a coherent pattern. According to Holmes, the Greek version also reflects traditions that were later deemed intolerable, e.g., the notion that not all Israelites had been circumcised when they left Egypt (hence the contradictory versions in LXX and MT of Josh 5:2–9 and the omission of LXX-Josh 21:42d and 24:31a).

Whereas Holmes' thesis of scribal revision of Joshua, reflected in the differences between LXX and MT, received little attention in his own day,[27] his views came to be regarded as provident once the first non-MT biblical Qumran scrolls (Jeremiah, Samuel) became known. Orlinsky (1968) compared Holmes to Wellhausen and Driver, whose views on the Hebrew *Vorlage* of the Greek version of Samuel had found support in 4QSam^a.[28] Auld adopted the title of Holmes' work in order to stress its importance and developed a theory of progressive supplementation based (in part) upon the LXX–MT variants.[29] Tov further elaborated this thesis by regarding the pluses in MT *vis-à-vis* LXX as a new literary edition of a penultimate edition reflected by the shorter LXX.[30] Tov points to the fact that numerous pluses contain Deuteronomistic themes, formulae, and concepts, e.g., the title for Moses as "servant of Yhwh" (עבד יהוה in MT-Josh 1:1, 15; 12:6; 22:4), the Torah (כָּל־הַתּוֹרָה "all of the law" in MT-Josh 1:7), a formula of compliance (כְּכֹל אֲשֶׁר־צִוָּה מֹשֶׁה אֶת־יְהוֹשֻׁעַ "according to everything that Moses commanded Joshua" in MT-Josh 4:10), and the theme of "inheriting the promised land" (ירשׁ MT-Josh 1:11, 15). While Tov mainly argues on the basis of a model of literary growth that would account for the pluses in MT, his doctoral student Mazor also reckons with considerable shortening in the literary development of Joshua.[31] The absence from MT-Josh of the plus in LXX-Josh 6:26b is due, according to her, to its relocation in MT-1 Kgs 16:34 (where the Antiochene version and Josephus, *A.J.* 8.318 still reflect the shorter version).[32] In her view, the shorter LXX version of Josh 6:1–20 resulted from nomistic correcting curtailment.[33]

The discussion about the textual history of Joshua and the text-critical and redaction-critical value of the LXX took a somewhat different course once the Qumran scrolls of Joshua finally became available to the scholarly world around 1990 (→ 3.2.1).[34] Contrary to ill-informed expectations, these scrolls were not "systematically 'Septuagintal' in character,"[35] since many of the MT pluses *vis-à-vis* LXX are supported by the Qumran scrolls of Joshua (e.g. Josh 5:4; 6:7; 8:8 in 4QJosh^a). Two of the three Qumran scrolls (4QJosh^b [ca. 50 B.C.E.;

---

[25] C.D. Benjamin, *The Variations between the Hebrew and Greek Texts of Joshua: Chapters 1–12* (Leipzig: W. Drugulin, 1921).

[26] Holmes, *Joshua*.

[27] See the small commentary by G.A. Cooke, *The Book of Joshua* (CBC; Cambridge: Cambridge University Press, 1918). At the same time, the influential commentary by M. Noth, *Das Buch Josua* (HAT 1.7; Tübingen: Mohr Siebeck, 1938), 7, noted Holmes' study only in passing and stressed the reliability of MT.

[28] H.M. Orlinsky, "The Hebrew *Vorlage* of the Septuagint of the Book of Joshua," in *Congress Volume, Rome 1968* (VTSup 17; Leiden: Brill, 1969), 187–95.

[29] A.G. Auld, "Joshua: The Hebrew and Greek Texts," in *Studies in the Historical Books of the Old Testament* (ed. J.A. Emerton; VTSup 30; Leiden: Brill, 1979), 1–14 (repr. in *Joshua Retold: Synoptic Perspectives* [ed. A.G. Auld; OTS 1; Edinburgh: T & T Clark, 1998], 7–24; see also the other essays collected in this volume).

[30] Tov, "Growth"; cf. Tov, *TCHB, 294–99.

[31] L. Mazor, "The Septuagint Translation of the Book of Joshua: Its Contribution to the Understanding of the Textual Transmission of the Book and Its Literary and Ideological Development" (PhD diss., Hebrew University of Jerusalem, 1994) [Hebr.]; abstract in *BIOSCS* 27 (1994): 29–38.

[32] L. Mazor, "The Origin and Evolution of the Curse upon the Rebuilder of Jericho: A Contribution of Textual Criticism to Biblical Historiography," *Textus* 14 (1988): 1–26.

[33] L. Mazor, "A Nomistic Re-Working of the Jericho Conquest Narrative Reflected in LXX to Joshua 6:1–20," *Textus* 18 (1995): 47–62.

[34] L.J. Greenspoon, "The Qumran Fragments of Joshua: Which Puzzle are They Part of and Where Do They Fit?" in *Manchester Symposium, 159–94; Bieberstein, *Lukian und Theodotion*, 75–93; see, further, van der Meer, *Formation*, 93–114.

[35] Cross, *ALQ, 151, 180–81; Cross-Talmon, *QHBT, 311; cf. M.H. Woudstra, *The Book of Joshua* (NICOT; Grand Rapids: Eerdmans, 1981), 40: "among the discoveries at Qumran are two manuscripts of the Vaticanus."

→ 3.2.1.2]; and XJosh [first century C.E.; → 3.2.1.3])³⁶ correspond closely to MT. The first and oldest scroll, 4QJoshᵃ (ca. 150–50 B.C.E.; → 3.2.1.1), however, presents an edition of the book that differs drastically from both MT (→ 3.2.2) and LXX (→ 3.3). In this scroll, parts of Josh 8:34–35 and an otherwise unknown verse (5:x) are found before Josh 5:2–9. MT-Josh 8:34–35 form part of a short passage narrating Joshua's building of an altar at Mount Ebal (near Shechem) and reciting there the Torah, a passage that comes too early in the narrative sequence of Joshua (see e.g. Josephus, *A.J.* 68–70, who placed the narrative after the stories of Joshua's conquest of northern Israel corresponding to Joshua 11; LXX-Josh has this passage after Josh 9:2). Given the heavy emphasis in this short passage upon the Torah and its intrusive position between Josh 8:1–29 and 9:(1–2)3 ff., the passage had long been considered to be a late Deuteronomistic editorial addition to the book. The new information provided by 4QJoshᵃ was therefore soon welcomed as proof of the very late origin of this "latecomer looking for a suitable home,"³⁷ and the even later relocation as reflected by MT.³⁸ Yet, the evidence posed by 4QJoshᵃ might just as well reflect a nomistic correction of MT,³⁹ or a duplication of some verses of Josh 8:30–35 (i.e., 31, 34, 35) in order to comply with the twofold orders given by Moses in Deut 27:2–3, 8, and 4–7.⁴⁰ This scroll also seems to reflect a version of Josh 8:11–18 that is shorter than LXX (where Josh 8:11b, 18, and 16a are absent; in 4QJoshᵃ all of Josh 8:11b–13 and 14b–17 seem to be missing).⁴¹ Yet, the reconstruction of the column under discussion is not without problems.⁴²

If the evidence of 4QJoshᵃ is not unambiguous, the evidence posed by the Greek translation is even more open to multiple explanations. Several studies have been published over the last two decades that investigate the translation technique as well as the interpretative character of the Greek translation (→ 3.3). According to Bieberstein and van der Meer, the major divergencies between MT and LXX-Josh 1–8 can for the most part be ascribed to reformulation by the Greek translator of the ponderous and multi-layered Hebrew text as presented by MT.⁴³ Other scholars continue to see the oldest extant witnesses (4QJoshᵃ, LXX) as stages in the literary history of the book preceding that reflected by MT.⁴⁴

---

³⁶ Published in *DJD* XIV: 143–52 (4QJoshᵃ by E.C. Ulrich), 153–60 (4QJoshᵇ by E. Tov), and *DJD* XXXVIII: 232–36 (XJosh by J. Charlesworth).

³⁷ A.G. Auld, "Reading Joshua after Kings," in *Words Remembered, Texts Renewed: Essays in Honour of John E. Sawyer* (eds. J. Davies, G. Harvey, and W.G.E. Watson; JSOTSup 195; Sheffield: Sheffield Press, 1995), 167–81; repr. in *Joshua Retold: Synoptic Perspectives* (ed. A.G. Auld; OTS; Edinburgh: T & T Clark, 1998); E. Tov, "Some Sequence Differences between the Masoretic Text and the Septuagint and Their Ramifications for Literary Criticism," *JNSL* 13 (1987): 151–60; rev. ed.: Tov, *Greek-Hebrew Bible*, 411–18.

³⁸ E.C. Ulrich, "4QJoshuaᵃ and Joshua's First Altar in the Promised Land," in *New Qumran Texts and Studies: Proceedings of the First Meeting of the International Organization for Qumran Studies, Paris 1992* (eds. G.J. Brooke and F. García Martínez; STDJ 15; Leiden: Brill, 1994), 89–104.

³⁹ A. Rofé, "The Editing of the Book of Joshua in the Light of 4QJoshᵃ," in *New Qumran Texts and Studies: Proceedings of the First Meeting of the International Organization for Qumran Studies, Paris 1992* (eds. G.J. Brooke and F. García Martínez; STDJ 15; Leiden: Brill, 1994), 73–80.

⁴⁰ Van der Meer, *Formation*, 479–522.

⁴¹ L. Mazor, "A Textual and Literary Study of the Fall of Ai in Joshua 8," in *The Bible in Light of Its Interpreters: Sarah Kamin Memorial Volume* (ed. S. Japhet; Jerusalem: Magnes Press, 1994), 73–108 [Hebr.]; E. Tov, "Literary Development of the Book of Joshua as Reflected in the MT, the LXX, and 4QJoshᵃ," in *The Book of Joshua* (ed. E. Noort; BETL 250; Leuven: Peeters, 2012), 65–85.

⁴² Van der Meer, *Formation*, 417–78.

⁴³ Bieberstein, *Josua-Jordan-Jericho*; van der Meer, *Formation*; M.N. van der Meer, "'Sound the Trumpet!' Redaction and Reception of Joshua 6:2–25," in *The Land of Israel in Bible, History, and Theology: Studies in Honour of Ed Noort* (eds. J. van Ruiten and J.C. de Vos; VTSup 124; Leiden: Brill, 2009), 19–43; M.N. van der Meer, "Clustering Cluttered Areas: Textual and Literary Criticism in Joshua 18,1–10," in *The Book of Joshua* (ed. E. Noort, BETL 250; Leuven: Peeters, 2012), 87–106.

⁴⁴ See, e.g., J. Trebolle Barrera, "A Combined Textual and Literary Criticism Analysis: Editorial Traces in Joshua and Judges," in *Florilegium Lovaniense: Studies in Septuagint and Textual Criticism in Honour of Florentino García Martínez* (eds. H. Ausloos, B. Lemmelijn, and M. Vervenne; BETL 224; Leuven: Peeters, 2008), 437–63; F. García Martínez, "Light on the Joshua Books from the Dead Sea Scrolls," in *After Qumran: Old and Modern Editions of the Biblical Texts – The Historical Books* (eds. H. Ausloos, B. Lemmelijn, and J. Trebolle Barrera; BETL 246; Leuven: Peeters, 2012), 145–60; De Troyer, "Reconstructing the Older Hebrew Text of the Book of Joshua."

3.1.3 Textual History and Relevance

The analysis of 3.1.2 shows that there is little unanimity among modern scholars regarding the textual history of Joshua. Yet, there is a commonly shared notion that all major witnesses of the book (4QJosh[a], LXX, MT) reflect considerable editorial activity in the narrative sections and the chapter on the cities of refuge (Joshua 20), and scribal errors in the topographical sections. As a result, each witness and each section within the book needs to be studied carefully in its own right. A fine example of such an approach is offered by the detailed analysis of Joshua 10 by Langlois.[45] Future editions of the book, such as those for the *BHQ and the *HBCE projects will probably also pay much more attention to the character of the individual textual witnesses than that allowed for in the rather meager text-critical apparatus of *BHS. The relevance of the highly complex textual history for any historical investigation of the book can hardly be overlooked. As a result, commentaries and monographs written since 1990 show a growing awareness of the relevance of the textual history of the book for the interpretation of the book and the history of its literary formation and reception.[46] By the same token, the recognition that in Joshua, as in Samuel, Jeremiah, and other biblical compositions, textual and literary history intersect has also led to the recognition that independent redaction-critical investigation is indispensable for assessing the intricate textual issues in the book.[47]

Auld, A.G., *Joshua Retold: Synoptic Perspectives* (OTS; Edinburgh: T & T Clark, 1998).

Bieberstein, K., *Josua-Jordan-Jericho: Archäologie, Geschichte und Theologie der Landnahmeerzählungen Josua 1–6* (OBO 143; Göttingen: Vandenhoeck & Ruprecht, 1995).

De Troyer, K., "Reconstructing the Older Hebrew Text of the Book of Joshua: An Analysis of Joshua 10," *Textus* 26 (2013): 1–33.

Greenspoon, L.J., *Textual Studies in the Book of Joshua* (HSM 28; Chico: Scholars Press, 1983).

Hollenberg, J., *Der Charakter der alexandrinischen Uebersetzung des Buches Josua und ihr textkritischer Werth* (Wissenschaftliche Beilage zu dem Oster-Programm des Gymnasiums zu Moers; Moers: Edner, 1876).

Holmes, S., *Joshua: The Hebrew and Greek Texts* (Cambridge: Cambridge University Press, 1914).

Langlois, M., *Le texte de Josué 10: Approche philologique, épigraphique et diachronique* (OBO 252; Fribourg/Göttingen: Academic Press/Vandenhoeck & Ruprecht, 2011).

van der Meer, M.N., *Formation and Reformulation: The Redaction of the Book of Joshua in the Light of the Oldest Textual Witnesses* (VTSup 102; Leiden: Brill, 2004).

Rofé, A., "Joshua 20: Historico-Literary Criticism Illustrated," in *Isac Leo Seeligmann Volume: Essays on the Bible and the Ancient World* (3 vols.; eds. A. Rofé and Y. Zakovitch; Jerusalem: E. Rubenstein, 1983), 1:137–50 [Hebr.]; Engl. version in Tigay, *Models*, 131–47.

Tov, E., "The Growth of the Book of Joshua in Light of Evidence of the Septuagint," *Studies in Bible, 1986* (ed. S. Japhet; ScrHier 31; Jerusalem: Magnes Press, 1986), 321–39; repr. in Tov, *Greek-Hebrew Bible*, 385–96

Tov, E., "Literary Development of the Book of Joshua as Reflected in the MT, the LXX, and 4QJosh[a]," in *The Book of Joshua* (ed. E. Noort; BETL 250; Leuven: Peeters, 2012), 65–85.

Michaël van der Meer

---

[45] Langlois, *Le texte de Josué 10*.

[46] See, e.g., E.A. Knauf, *Josua* (ZBK.AT 6; Zurich: Theologischer Verlag, 2008); H. Rösel, *Joshua* (Historical Commentary on the Old Testament 6; Leuven: Peeters, 2011); J.J. Krause, *Exodus und Eisodus: Komposition und Theologie von Josua 1–5* (VTSup 161; Leiden: Brill, 2014).

[47] Van der Meer, *Formation*, 115–59, 522–36.

3.2 Ancient Hebrew Texts

3.2.1 Ancient Manuscript Evidence

Three Hebrew manuscripts of the book of Joshua survive from antiquity. 4QJosh[a] and 4QJosh[b] were found at Qumran, while XJosh comes most likely from one of the sites connected with the Second Jewish War. Of these three Joshua manuscripts, the text of 4QJosh[a] is non-aligned, while the text of 4QJosh[b] can be characterized as semi-Masoretic and the text of XJosh as proto-Masoretic. For 4QpaleoparaJosh, it remains uncertain whether it attests to a variant literary edition of the book of Joshua or, more likely, to a rewriting of that book.[1]

3.2.1.1 4QJosh[a] (4Q47)

Twenty-two damaged fragments are preserved of 4QJosh[a]. They attests to 258 complete and partial words out of Josh 8:34–35; 5:x, 2–7; 7:12–17; 8:3–14, 18?; and 10:2–5, 8–11 and belong to five columns of the original scroll. The textual sequence of 4QJosh[a] differs from both MT-Josh (→ 3.2.2) and LXX-Josh (→ 3.3) in placing Josh 8:34–35 before Joshua 5. As frgs. 1 and 2 fit together like two pieces of a jigsaw puzzle and as in frg. 1 Josh 8:34–35 precede both Josh 5:x and 5:2, there can be no doubt about this divergent sequence.[2] Paleographically, Ulrich describes 4QJosh[a] as written in a Hasmonean book hand from the second half of second century B.C.E.[3] At the lower column margin of frgs. 9 ii + 13–16, a second hand added, in a somewhat larger Herodian script and using a different ink, words that resemble Josh 8:18.[4] In its orthography, 4QJosh[a] is fuller than MT-Josh but does not display characteristics of the baroque orthography.[5] 4QJosh[a] reads twice with and twenty-four times against MT, six times with and twenty times against LXX, as well as nineteen times non-aligned. In addition, one reading against MT concerns differences in the Hebrew text that cannot be rendered into a non-Semitic language. The text of 4QJosh[a] is hence best described as non-aligned.[6] It is especially significant that 4QJosh[a] reads in Josh 6:7–10 and 8:10–14 a shorter text than MT-Josh and LXX-Josh and that it attests against both versions to the text sequence Josh 8:34–35→5:x, 2 ff.[7] Comparing these and other variants with both MT and LXX, Tov has argued in 2012 that, as a variant literary edition, 4QJosh[a] contains both original and secondary readings and that in "many ways, 4QJosh[a] resembles exegetical texts like 4QRP, at first regarded as a group of rewritten non-biblical texts, and now as

---

[1] The little that is preserved of this manuscript is reminiscent of Joshua 21 and could either represent an alternate textual form of Joshua (cf. Ulrich, "4QJoshua[a] and Joshua's First Altar," 90; Aḥituv, *Joshua*, 35; and P.W. Skehan, J.E. Sanderson, and E. Ulrich, "123. 4QpaleoPara-Joshua," *DJD* IX: 201–03 [201]) or a rewriting of the book of Joshua (thus E. Tov, "The Rewritten Book of Joshua as Found at Qumran and Masada," in *Biblical Perspectives: Early Use and Interpretation of the Bible in Light of the Dead Sea Scrolls: Proceedings of the First International Symposium of the Orion Center for the Study of the Dead Sea Scrolls and Associated Literature, 12–14 May 1996* [eds. M.E. Stone and E.G. Chazon; STDJ 28; Leiden: Brill, 1998], 232–56 [252–53]; van der Meer, *Formulation*, 106; A. Feldman, *The Rewritten Joshua Scrolls from Qumran: Texts, Translation and Commentary* [BZAW 438; Berlin: De Gruyter], 168–75).

[2] Cf. Ulrich, "47. 4QJosh[a]," 145, 147; Ulrich, "4QJoshua[a] and Joshua's First Altar," 98.

[3] Ulrich, "47. 4QJosh[a]," 143; Ulrich, "4QJoshua[a] and Joshua's First Altar," 89.

[4] Cf. 4QCant[b] 3 14 (Cant 5:1) and Ulrich, "47. 4QJosh[a]," 150; Ulrich, "4QJoshua[a] and Joshua's First Altar," 102.

[5] Cf. Ulrich, "47. 4QJosh[a]," 144; Ulrich, "4QJoshua[a] and Joshua's First Altar," 97.

[6] Cf. Ulrich, "47. 4QJosh[a]," 145–46 and E. Tov, "The Growth of the Book of Joshua in the Light of the Evidence of the LXX Translation," *ScrHier* 31 (1986): 322; Tov, *TCHB*, 109; Tov, "Joshua," 432; Tov, "Literary Development," 79–85; Aḥituv, *Joshua*, 32–33; Lange, *Handbuch*, 187–89; similarly also van der Meer, *Formulation*, 95–98; García Martínez, "Dead Sea Scrolls," 101; García Martínez, "Light," 146–49. Bieberstein (*Lukian*, 85) characterizes 4QJosh[a] as non-aligned, too, but he views the text of the manuscript nevertheless as relatively close to MT because he does not recognize the alternate text sequence of 4QJosh[a]. Only Kempinski ("History," 177–78) classifies 4QJosh[a] as close to LXX-Josh.

[7] For a detailed discussion, see → 3.2.2 and → 3.2.3.

exegetical Bible texts, at times deviating much from other texts."[8]

3.2.1.2 4QJosh[b] (4Q48)

Of 4QJosh[b], six heavily damaged fragments are extant. Frgs. 1–5 attest to 131 complete and partial words out of Josh 2:11–12; 3:15–17; 4:1–3; 17:1–5, 11–15 while the text of frg. 6 cannot be identified. Because of differences in the spacing between the lines, Bieberstein[9] suggested that frgs. 4–6 belong to a different manuscript than frgs. 1–3. Given that only a small amount of text is preserved, such differences in line-spacing should not be overemphasized. That all fragments were copied by the same scribe argues against Bieberstein's suggestion. Cross classifies the script of 4QJosh[b] paleographically as a late Hasmonean hand from the middle of the first century C.E.[10] The supralinear corrections of 4QJosh[b] seem to be inserted by a second scribe. In Josh 3:15, they adjust the text of 4QJosh[b] to OG-Josh (cf. 4QapocrJosh[b] [4Q379] 12 7), and in Josh 17:11 to the text of MT-Josh, while the supralinear correction to Josh 4:1 is non-aligned. The orthography of 4QJosh[b] corresponds to the conservative orthography of MT-Josh.[11] 4QJosh[b] reads eighteen times with and eight times against MT (→ 3.2.2)., twice with and twenty-six against LXX, but only six times non-aligned. Thus, in the majority of cases, 4QJosh[b] goes with MT against LXX (→ 3.3), but the reconstruction of frgs. 2–3 makes it likely that 4QJosh[b] read in Josh 4:1–3 the shorter text of LXX-Josh.[12] Despite this possible agreement with LXX-Josh and despite its non-aligned readings, 4QJosh[b] should be characterized as a semi-Masoretic text.[13]

3.2.1.3 XJosh (X1; MS Schøyen 2713)[14]

This manuscript is of unknown provenance. It was bought in 1998 by Martin Schøyen and is today part of the Schøyen Collection (MS Schøyen 2713.Mur/ḤevJosh).[15] Of XJosh, only one heavily damaged fragment with sixty complete and partial words out of Josh 1:9–12 and 2:3–5 is extant. As compared to the *editio princeps* of Charlesworth,[16] Elgvin was able to identify fifteen additional words and partial words of text.[17] Because a part of the handlesheet is still attached to the fragment, it preserves remains of the first two columns of the original scroll. For reasons of paleography and material reconstruction, XJosh cannot be a part of 4QJosh[b] although the latter also preserves text from Joshua 2.[18] A carbon-14 analysis dates the leather of XJosh between the years 118 B.C.E. and 73 C.E.[19] For Charlesworth, "the handwriting is an example of the late Herodian formal bookhand" from the second half of the first century C.E.[20] Ada Yardeni classifies the script of XJosh as a post-Herodian bookhand from the time after 70 C.E. Michael Langlois describes it as an ornamental formal script from the post-Herodian period.[21] That the paleographic date of XJosh is later than its C-14 date could indicate that the scroll was written sometime after its leather was produced. The late paleographic date makes it likely that XJosh comes from one of the sites around the Dead Sea that are con-

---

[8] Tov, "Literary Development," 79–85 (the quotation can be found on p. 85).

[9] Bieberstein, *Lukian*, 86.

[10] Communication to E. Tov (cf. "48. 4QJosh[b]," 153; Tov, "4QJosh[b]," 205); cf. also Ulrich, "4QJoshua[a] and Joshua's First Altar," 90.

[11] For orthography and scribal corrections of 4QJosh[b], see Tov, "48. 4QJosh[b]," 154–55; Tov, "4QJosh[b]," 208–09, 212.

[12] Cf. Tov, "48. 4QJosh[b]," 156; Tov, "4QJosh[b]," 207–08; Lucassen, "Possibility," *passim*; against Bieberstein, *Lukian*, 88–89.

[13] Cf. Tov, "48. 4QJosh[b]," 154; Tov, "4QJosh[b]," 212; Tov, "Joshua," 431–32; Bieberstein, *Lukian*, 93; Aḥituv, *Joshua*, 33; van der Meer, *Formulation*, 98; Lange, **Handbuch*, 188; García

Martínez, "Dead Sea Scrolls," 101; García Martínez, "Light," 146; against Kempinski, "History," 177.

[14] García Martínez, "Dead Sea Scrolls," 101–03; García Martínez, "Light," 145–51, ignores this manuscript in his survey of Joshua manuscripts from Qumran.

[15] Cf. http://www.schoyencollection.com/bible-collection -foreword/hebrew-aramaic-bible/joshua-dead-sea-scroll-ms -2713 (last accessed December 23, 2014).

[16] Charlesworth, "1. XJoshua," 231–39.

[17] Elgvin, "MS 2713," forthcoming. I am indebted to Torleif Elgvin who provided me with a preprint copy of his edition.

[18] Cf. Charlesworth, "1. XJoshua," 235.

[19] Cf. Charlesworth, "1. XJoshua," 234.

[20] Cf. Charlesworth, "1. XJoshua," 232–34. The quotation can be found on p. 234.

[21] For the paleographic dates of Yardeni and Langlois, see Elgvin, "MS 2713," forthcoming and Langlois, "Palaeographical Analysis of the Dead Sea Scrolls," in **Gleanings*, forthcoming.

nected with the Second Jewish War.[22] XJosh reads both in its orthography and text with the text of MT[A] and MT[L].[23] The only possible exception is the word לִבֹא (MT[A, L]) in Josh 1:11. Charlesworth transcribes the word in XJosh 1 7 as לב[ו]א,[24] while Elgvin reads it לֹבִא.[25] The published photographs of the manuscript allow for both transcriptions. Although the small amount of preserved text makes a textual classification difficult, the orthographic and textual conformity with MT-Josh could argue for a proto-Masoretic text (→ 3.2.2).[26]

Aḥituv, S., *Joshua: Introduction and Commentary* (*Mikra LeYisrael*; Jerusalem: Magnes Press, 1995), 29–35 [Hebr.].

Bieberstein, K., *Lukian und Theodotion im Josuabuch: Mit einem Beitrag zu Josuarollen von Ḥirbet Qumrān* (BN Beihefte 7; Munich: Institut für biblische Exeges, 1994), 77–93.

Charlesworth, J., "1. XJoshua," *DJD XXXVIII: 231–39.

Elgvin, T., "MS 2713: Mur/HevJosh, Josh. 1.9–12; 2.3–5," in *Gleanings, forthcoming.

García Martínez, F., "The Dead Sea Scrolls and the Book of Joshua," in *Qumran and the Bible: Studying the Jewish and Christian Scriptures in Light of the Dead Sea Scrolls* (eds. N. David and A. Lange; CBET 57; Leuven: Peeters, 2010), 97–109.

García Martínez, F., "Light on the Book of Joshua from the Dead Sea Scrolls," in *After Qumran: Old and Modern Editions of the Biblical Texts – The Historical Books* (eds. H. Ausloos, B. Lemmelijn, and J. Trebolle Barrera; BETL 246; Leuven: Peeters, 2012), 145–59 (145–51).

Greenspoon, L.J., "The Qumran Fragments of Joshua: Which Puzzle Are They Part of and Where Do They Fit?" in *Manchester Symposium, 159–94.

Kempinski, A., "When History Sleeps, Theology Arises," *ErIsr* 24 (1983): 175–83.

Lange, *Handbuch, 187–201.

Lucassen, B., "Possibility and Probability of Textual Reconstruction: The Transition from 4QJosh[a], Frg. 2 to Frg. 3 and the Transit of the Israelites through the Jordan," *Textus* 20 (2000): 71–81.

van der Meer, M.N., *Formulation and Reformulation: The Redaction of the Book of Joshua in the Light of the Oldest Textual Witnesses* (VTSup 102; Leiden: Brill, 2004), 93–114.

Noort, E., "4QJosh[a] and the History of Tradition in the Book of Joshua," *JNSL* 24 (1998): 12–144.

Rofé, A., "The Editing of the Book of Joshua in the Light of 4QJosh[a]," in *New Qumran Texts and Studies: Proceedings of the First Meeting of the International Organization for Qumran Studies, Paris 1992* (eds. G.J. Brooke and F. García Martínez; STDJ 15; Leiden: Brill, 1994), 73–80.

Tov, E., "48. 4QJosh[b]," *DJD XIV: 153–60.

Tov, E., "4QJosh[b]," in *Intertestamental Essays in Honour of Józef Tadeusz Milik* (ed. Z.J. Kapera; Qumranica Mogilanensia 6; Krakow: Enigma Press, 1992), 205–12.

Tov, E., "Joshua, Book of," *EDSS 1.431–34.

Tov, E., "Literary Development of the Book of Joshua as Reflected in the MT, the LXX, and 4QJosh[a]," in *The Book of Joshua* (ed. E. Noort; BETL 250; Leuven: Peeters, 2012), 65–85 (79–85).

Ulrich, E., "47. 4QJosh[a]," *DJD XIV: 143–52.

Ulrich, E., "4QJoshua[a] and Joshua's First Altar in the Promised Land," in *New Qumran Texts and Studies: Proceedings of the First Meeting of the International Organization for Qumran Studies, Paris 1992* (eds. G.J. Brooke and F. García Martínez; STDJ 15; Leiden: Brill, 1994), 89–104.

Ulrich, E., *BQS, 247–53.

Armin Lange

3.2.2 Masoretic Text and Ancient Texts Close to MT

3.2.2.1 Manuscripts, Editions, and Auxiliary Tools

Of the four ancient Hebrew manuscripts of Joshua (→ 3.2.1), only Mur/Hev(?)Josh (*olim* XJosh) can be classified as proto-Masoretic. In many cases, for the approximately fifty allusions to and quotations from Joshua in Second Temple Jewish literature, the nature of the text they derive from cannot be determined with any certainty. As far as I can see, there is very little proof of a quotation from/allusion to (proto-)Masoretic verses (which differ significantly from LXX-Josh or its *Vorlage*): 1 Chr 6:46–47 agree twice with MT-Josh 21:5–6 in rendering מִשְׁפָּחוֹת "clans" and 1 Chr 6:52 agrees

---

[22] Cf. Elgvin, "MS 2713," forthcoming.
[23] Cf. Charlesworth, "1. XJoshua," 231.
[24] Charlesworth, "1. XJoshua," 234.
[25] Elgvin, "MS 2713," forthcoming.
[26] Lange, *Handbuch, 189; Elgvin, "MS 2713," forthcoming.

with MT-Josh 21:21 in rendering the phrase בְּהַר אֶפְרָיִם "moutain range of Ephraim." However, there is also one case in 1 Chr 6:48 in which there is an agreement with a version resembling that of LXX-Josh (→ 3.2.3.1).

The only complete Hebrew text is MT-Josh. The most important medieval Hebrew manuscripts of MT-Josh are a manuscript in the Russian Library in St. Petersburg (EBP. II B 19a, commonly known as Codex Leningradiensis = MT^L), the Cairo Codex of the Prophets (MT^C), and the Aleppo Codex (MT^A), all of which reflect the vocalization of the Ben Asher tradition.

The quotations from and allusions to Joshua are listed in Lange and Weigold.[1] For MT-Josh, only two critical editions are currently available in the *BH series (Meyer's edition in the *BHS and Noth's in the *BH³; the *BHQ is still in preparation by Sipilä). Both editions are diplomatic in nature and are based on MT^L; they are very selective in the number of variants they recognize in the apparatus. For the variants of the medieval Masoretic manuscript tradition, see the editions of Kennicott, *1776–1780 and De Rossi, *1784–1788.

3.2.2.2 History of Research

Joshua is one of the ancient Jewish books in which MT and LXX differ most significantly, displaying several hundred textual differences.[2] Thus, there is a research history of the relationship between MT-Josh and LXX-Josh but none that pertains merely to MT-Josh. At the beginning of the twentieth century, Holmes investigated the Hebrew and Greek texts and argued against Hollenberg, Dillmann, and others that the two texts reflect different literary strata, with the Hebrew *Vorlage* of LXX-Josh usually being the more ancient one.[3] Holmes was "rediscovered" in the second part of the twentieth century and followed by Orlinsky, Auld, Tov, and others.[4] The majority of the scholars who focused on Joshua in the twentieth century considered MT *cum grano salis* as the more ancient and superior text. Many were inspired by the work of Margolis. While preparing a critical edition of LXX-Josh in the 1920s and 1930s, Margolis ascribed most differences between MT-Josh and LXX-Josh to the Greek translator.[5] In recent years, scholars such as Bieberstein, Moatti-Fine, and van der Meer have emphasized the literary initiatives introduced by the Greek translator, seeing the translator as a kind of scribe-editor (with differences in extent).[6] The publications of the ancient Hebrew manuscripts of Joshua (→ 3.2.1) at the end of the twentieth century did not aid in solving the problem. However, they pointed to the fact that in the late Second Temple period at least one further Hebrew edition of the book of Joshua existed that differed from its (proto-)Masoretic edition.

It became obvious especially in the past two decades that the different editions of Joshua should be studied in their own right (one may speak of a paradigmatic shift). A few pioneer studies that focus on special clusters of variants appearing in MT or LXX have produced interesting results concerning the idiosyncrasy of MT-Josh. Rösel observed an adaptation to the traditions of the Pentateuch concerning the exodus:[7] according to MT-Josh 24:5 (LXX has a different text), *Moses and Aaron* led the people out of Egypt (whereas the plus in LXX-Josh 24:31a emphasizes that *Joshua* was the leader of the exodus); MT-Josh 5:4–6 relate that the *entire* exodus generation died during the *forty* years in the desert (while, according to LXX-Josh 5:4–6, *some* Israelites survived, being forty-*two* years in the desert). Based mainly on her work on MT/OG-Josh 10, De Troyer discerned in MT-Josh a tendency to fill out details of the narrative and a special interest in the preciseness of the executions of commands.[8] Sipilä focused on aspects of the concept

---

[1] A. Lange and M. Weigold, *Biblical Quotations and Allusions in Second Temple Jewish Literature* (Journal of Ancient Judaism Supplements 5; Göttingen: Vandenhoeck & Ruprecht, 2011), 113–14.

[2] See the useful overview in T.C. Butler, *Joshua* (WBC 7; Nashville: Nelson, 1983), xix–xx. Also → 3.3.

[3] Holmes, *Texts of Joshua*.

[4] Orlinsky, "Hebrew Vorlage;" Auld, "Studies;" Tov, "Growth."

[5] Cf. Margolis, *Book of Joshua*.

[6] Bieberstein, *Josua-Jordan-Jericho*; Moatti-Fine, *Jésus*; van der Meer, *Formation*, 534.

[7] Rösel, "Septuaginta-Version."

[8] De Troyer, "Crystal Ball."

of God and concluded that, in comparison to LXX-Josh, God is more remote in MT-Josh, in which he operates via Joshua who implements his will, thus at the same time limiting Joshua's independence in leadership.[9]

3.2.2.3 The Nature and Text-Critical Character of (Proto-)MT-Josh

The orthography of MT-Josh is generally inconsistent, e.g., לַעֲבוֹר "to pass over" in Josh 3:17 and לַעֲבֹר in Josh 4:1; שְׂמֹאול "left" in 1:7; 23:6 and שְׂמֹאל in 19:27. Remarkably, however, the name of Joshua is written consistently as יְהוֹשֻׁעַ (יְהוֹשׁוּעַ in Judg 2:7; יֵשׁוּעַ in Neh 8:17) while 4QJosh[a] is inconsistent in its spelling. An explanation could be a special orthographic revision by proto-Masoretic editors-scribes (terminology according to Tov, *TCHB, 240) of the name of the "hero."

MT-Josh attests to only a few cases of orthographic and morphological peculiarities, e.g., the Aramaic form הִמְסִיו "they made melt" in Josh 14:8 (cf. הֵמַסּוּ in Deut 1:28) and unusual plene spellings such as נָתַתָּה "you gave" in Josh 15:19 and 17:14; זָקַנְתָּה "you are old" in Josh 13:1; הֲלְכוּא "not" in Josh 1:9; הָלְכוּא "who had gone" in Josh 10:24 (according to the Masoretes, the 'alep is to be considered as a *yatir 'alep*[10]). Furthermore, there are several cases of unintentional scribal corruption (normally corrected by *Qere* readings[11]), e.g., אֲחוֹתִי instead of אחיותי in Josh 2:13 (both meaning "my sister"), and הוֹלֵךְ "the one who walks" instead of הלוך "to walk" in Josh 6:13. The case of the expression "the limits of the boundary are," appearing fourteen times in Joshua 15–19, is revealing. In only seven of the cases are the verb and subject in grammatical agreement (וְהָיוּ/תֹצְאֹתָיו תֹּצָאוֹת "and [the] ends are/its ends" in Josh 15:7, 11; 16:3, 8; 19:14, 22 and וַיְהִי תֹצְאֹתָיו "and their ends are" in Josh 19:29). In five cases, MT reads וְהָיָה/תֹצְאֹתָיו תֹּצָאוֹת "and ends is/its ends" (Josh 15:4; 17:18; 18:12, 14, 19); according to *Qere*, the verb in these five cases and in Josh 19:29 is to be read as והיו "and they are."

Twice, MT reads וַיְהִי תֹצְאֹתָיו "and it was its ends" (Josh 17:9; 19:33, probably in harmonization with a וַיְהִי "and it was" in the context). These examples demonstrate that if MT-Josh underwent an (orthographic) revision it was not comprehensive.[12]

Compared with the other ancient textual witnesses of Joshua, MT-Josh differs a few times in content[13] and especially in extent: MT-Josh is approximately 4–5 percent longer than LXX-Josh (→ 3.2.2.3.1). However, compared with LXX-Josh and 4QJosh[a], MT-Josh also has some minuses (→ 3.2.2.3.2). Furthermore, there is one significant difference concerning the narrative sequence in the book (→ 3.2.2.3.3).

3.2.2.3.1 Pluses in MT-Josh

Most pluses do not exceed one or two words. As Tov has shown convincingly, in many cases their secondary nature is evident.[14] The reasons for the additions differ considerably. There are short elucidations such as וְעַתָּה "now" in Josh 3:12; harmonizing and contextual additions like חֶרֶשׁ "secretly" in Josh 2:1; emphases such as הַגּוֹי "the nation" in Josh 5:6; theological corrections such as לִפְנֵי אֲרוֹן יְהוָה "in front of the ark of YHWH" instead of "in front of YHWH" in Josh 6:7. According to Tov, "little can be said about the nature of the expansions of the edition of MT. Its main characteristic is the addition of exegetical remarks and traditions. Among these, a few Deuteronomistic formulations stand out."[15] This evaluation is too pessimistic in my view. While the pluses taken in their totality certainly do not form a single coherent literary layer (but reflect different literary operations), pioneer studies up to now have nevertheless discerned some patterns (cf. above). I stress two further points, based partly on my own research. The first one concerns the pictures of Moses and Joshua in connection with the strong tendency to downplay the role of the latter as "hero":[16]

---

[9] Sipilä, "Concept." Cf. also Mazor, "Nomistic Re-Working," 49–50.
[10] Cf. Tov, *TCHB, 54, n. 69.
[11] Cf. the overview in Baer, *Libri*, 125–26.
[12] Cf. Baer, *Libri*, 78–92, 112–14.
[13] E.g. Josh 5:6 or 24:5.
[14] Cf. Tov, "Growth."
[15] Tov, "Growth," 396.
[16] In my view, Sirach 46 and the *Apocryphon of Joshua* share much of the spirit of MT-Josh: according to Sirach, Joshua is the

- In Josh 1:1, 15; 12:6b; and 22:4, the title עֶבֶד יְהוָה "servant of YHWH" was added for Moses (ten times the title is shared by MT-Josh and LXX-Josh). In Deuteronomy, Moses received this title only upon his death (Deut 34:5[17]). The title reflects Moses' importance, which the proto-Masoretic editor-scribe emphasized by the four additions; significantly, the first addition appears at the beginning of the book (in Josh 1:1).[18]
- In Josh 1:7, MT has the phrase כְּכָל־הַתּוֹרָה "according to the whole Torah" as a plus. With this addition, the proto-Masoretic editor-scribe stated that Moses commanded Joshua personally to keep the Torah. This is a rather surprising, unparalleled thought in Genesis–Joshua. The character of this addition is contra Tov, van der Meer, and others completely "un-Deuteronomic" in language (in Deuteronomy, Moses does not "command" the Torah).[19] The intention was obviously to underline that Joshua was totally dependent upon Moses and his Torah.
- The same tendency can be discerned in Josh 4:10: according to the short version of this verse, Joshua's actions followed God's command, while the MT plus stresses in addition that the command was from Moses.

The second point concerns the tendency to connect and conform legal material to (different) pentateuchal legislation:

- According to the common text of Josh 5:10 (MT and LXX) and the short text of vv. 11–12, the Israelites ate the *Pesach* as well as their *matzot* and parched grain on the fourteenth of Nisan in the evening. According to the proto-Masoretic additions in vv. 11 (מִמָּחֳרַת הַפֶּסַח "after the morrow of passover") and 12 (מִמָּחֳרַת בְּאָכְלָם "after the morrow when they ate"), the Israelites ate their *matzot* on the following day, the fifteenth of Nisan. The additions apparently adapted the original text to the priestly regulations in Lev 23:5–6, which prescribe the *Pesach* on the evening of the fourteenth of Nisan and the *matzot* on the following day.[20]
- In Joshua 20, Joshua is commanded to designate the cities of refuge following previous commands given to Moses. The short text reflects *grosso modo* the style and context of Num 35:9–34, whereas the pluses in MT (Josh 20:4–6 and the phrase בִּבְלִי־דַעַת "unintentionally" in Josh 20:3) reflect the content and style of Deut 19:1–13.[21] Thus, the editor-scribe adapted the original text to *both* of the Torah passages that are concerned with Moses' words regarding the cities of refuge.

3.2.2.3.2 Minuses in MT-Josh

In comparison with 4QJosh[a], MT-Josh attests to a shorter text at the end of Joshua 4 and the beginning of Joshua 5. In my view, the short text of MT-Josh is to be regarded as original (→ 3.2.3.2). In comparison with LXX-Josh, MT-Josh presents several small[22] minuses and a few that are significant. The famous passage, Josh 21:36–37, is not preserved in the main MT manuscripts; however, it is witnessed in LXX and in traditions close to MT, such as T[J]. The passage may have been omitted unintentionally in some early proto-Masoretic manuscripts due to *parablepsis*.[23] The pluses LXX-Josh

---

successor of Moses only as prophet (not as law giver; cf. Josh 24:25); his actions in the desert are praised, but only in connection with Caleb. According to the *Apocryphon of Joshua*, the sin of Joshua is strengthened (4Q522 9 ii): in the case of the Gibeonites' ruse, he did not consult the Urim und Thummim (cf. Num 27:21), a detail not found in the biblical account in Joshua 9. The biblical account was apparently reworked from the perspective of the supremacy of the priesthood (claiming precedence over the political leadership); cf. D. Dimant, "Between Sectarian and Non-Sectarian: The Case of the Apocryphon of Joshua," in *Reworking the Bible: Apocryphal and Related Texts at Qumran* (ed. E.G. Chazon et al.; STDJ 58; Leiden: Brill, 2005), 105–34, 120–21.

[17] Joshua will also receive this title upon his death; cf. Josh 24:29.

[18] According to van der Meer, *Formation*, 183, however, "the text reflected by LXX is the result of 'stylistic shortening'."

[19] Cf. Finsterbusch, "Deuteronomy and Joshua," 170–71.

[20] Cf. Tov, "Growth," 390.

[21] Cf. Tov, "Development," 73–74.

[22] The small pluses in LXX-Josh do not exceed one or two words; e.g. LXX-Josh displays κληρωτι "by lot" in Josh 21:7 (בגורל "by lot" may have appeared in the *Vorlage*; cf. 1 Chr 6:48).

[23] Another case of unintentional textual omission (due to

6:26a; 16:10a; 19:47a–48a; 21:42a–d; 24:31a, 33a–b bear all the marks of a Hebrew text, visible in their Hebrew diction.[24] However, there is no consensus regarding whether these pluses reflect a more original text from which they were intentionally deleted by proto-Masoretic editor(s)-scribe(s) or whether they are secondary non-Masoretic additions in the Hebrew *Vorlage* of LXX-Josh. In my view, the arguments listed by Tov point rather clearly to the secondary nature of Josh 6:26a, 16:10a, and 19:47a–48a in the Hebrew *Vorlage* of the LXX, meaning that the short text of MT is the original one.[25] The cases of LXX-Josh 21:42a–d, 24:31a, and 24:33a–b are more complicated. These pluses are related to the different endings of the book of Joshua (MT and LXX), which undoubtedly reflect the long and complex literary growth of the book:

- Before Josh 21:43–45 (MT and LXX), which is a type of summary of the successfully completed occupation of the land, the plus LXX-Josh 21:42a–d summarizes the land division. The plus contains a repetition of Josh 19:49–50 (MT and LXX) and in addition relates the story of Joshua taking the flint knives used for the circumcision of the Israelites (cf. Josh 5:2, 5). The plus LXX-Josh 24:31a continues this tradition, reporting that the flint knives were buried in Joshua's grave. Is the tradition regarding these flint knives a midrashic addition or an original tradition that was deleted by a proto-Masoretic editor-scribe because it resembles too closely the preserving of *reliquiae*?[26]
- After the account in Josh 24:29–33 of the burials of the three prominent figures, Joshua, Joseph, and the priest Eliezer, the LXX has a long plus, the components of which are found elsewhere in the book. Especially remarkable is the fact that the last phrase has a verbal parallel in Judg 3:14. According to Rofé,[27] the plus reflects one of the early stages in the development of Joshua–Judges in which the two books were combined and the first two-and-a-half chapters of Judges were still lacking. According to Rofé, LXX-Josh 24:33b was followed directly by the Ehud episode in Judg 3:12–31. As a consequence of his thesis, Rofé was forced to claim that the first two-and-a-half chapters of Judges contain secondary material, a claim against which several scholars have argued.[28]

To my mind, the *lectio brevior* of Josh 21:42, 24:31, and 24:33 should be regarded as more ancient: the repetitive and midrashic character of the pluses, Josh 21:42a–d, 24:31a, and 24:33a–b, point to their secondary nature rather than to the original text. The differing endings in the last chapters of MT-Josh (the summary in Josh 21:43–45; the first farewell speech in Joshua 23; the second farewell speech in Joshua 24) could well have inspired editors-scribes to add further material.

3.2.2.3.3 Sequence

MT-Josh, LXX-Josh, and 4QJosh[a] differ a few times in matters of sequence.[29] The most significant difference concerns the Ebal-Gerizim episode, which is located before Josh 9:1–2 in MT-Josh, after Josh 9:1–2 in LXX-Josh, and at least an element of the episode is located before Josh 5:2 (its text is only partially preserved) in 4QJosh[a]. These different positions point clearly to a secondary placement of the passage in the different contexts. However, the question remains as to which is the original position. In my view, the position in 4QJosh[a] (i.e. the motive of the Torah reading in Joshua 4) should be considered as secondary (→ 3.2.3.2). As Rofé has shown convincingly, the insertion of the Ebal-Gerizim episode after the report of the conquest of Ai (Josh 8:1–29) is appropriate topographically: Joshua will go to the south (chs. 9–10) and to the

---

homoioteleuton) is seen in Josh 15:59; cf. Rösel, "Version," 202–03.

[24] Cf. Tov, "Development," 68–69.
[25] Cf. Tov, "Growth," 395; Tov, "Development," 75–76.
[26] Cf. Tov, "Growth," 386.

[27] Rofé, "End." His interpretation was accepted by Lange, *Handbuch*, 195, and Tov, "Development," 77–78.
[28] Cf. especially Blum, "Connection," 100–03; Rösel, "Version," 207.
[29] Cf. Tov, "Development," 78–79.

far north (Josh 11:1–14) later in his campaigns.³⁰ The difference between MT and LXX is small: a Hebrew editor-scribe of a manuscript that can be defined as the Hebrew *Vorlage* of LXX or the Greek translator-editor-scribe chose to relate Josh 9:1–2 directly to the story of the fall of Jericho and Ai and to place the episode after it.

3.2.2.4 Relevance for Exegesis and Literary Analysis

MT-Josh contains early and late textual elements. Many of its pluses (especially compared with LXX-Josh) can be seen as secondary additions. They clearly do not belong to one overall, coherent literary layer, but were possibly added over several generations. However, some clusters of variants, or rather some rationales of (groups of) proto-Masoretic editors-scribes, can be discerned. Further studies are needed in this area.

There is surprisingly little clear textual evidence of MT-Josh within Second Temple Jewish literature. Therefore, it is difficult to determine a *terminus post quem*. A proto-Masoretic version of some verses was obviously known by the author of 1 Chr 6:46–47. The *terminus ante quem* for the proto-Masoretic text is the first century C.E. (cf. XJosh).

Auld, A.G., "Textual and Literary Studies in the Book of Joshua," *ZAW* 90 (1978): 412–17.

Baer, S., *Libri Josuae et Judicum: Textum Masoreticum accuratissime expressit, e fontibus masorae varie illustravit, notis criticis confirmavit* (Leipzig: Tauchnitz, 1891).

Bieberstein, K., *Josua-Jordan-Jericho: Archäologie, Geschichte und Theologie der Landnahmeerzählung Josua 1–6* (OBO 143; Göttingen: Vandenhoeck & Ruprecht, 1995).

Blum, E., "The Literary Connection between the Books of Genesis and Exodus and the End of the Book of Joshua," in *A Farewell to the Yahwist? The Composition of the Pentateuch in Recent European Interpretation* (ed. T.B. Dozeman and K. Schmid; SBLSymS 34; Atlanta: SBL, 2006), 89–196.

De Troyer, K., "Did Joshua Have a Crystal Ball? The Old Greek and the MT of Joshua 10:15, 17 and 23," in *Emanuel: Studies in the Hebrew Bible, Septuagint and Dead Sea Scrolls in Honour of Emanuel Tov* (eds. S.M. Paul et al.; VTSup 94; Leiden: Brill, 2003), 571–89.

Finsterbusch, K., "Deuteronomy and Joshua: Torah in the Book of Joshua in Light of Deuteronomy," *Journal of Ancient Judaism* 3 (2012): 166–96.

Holmes, S., *The Hebrew and Greek Texts of Joshua* (Cambridge: Cambridge University Press, 1914).

Lange, A., **Handbuch*, 187–201.

Margolis, M., *The Book of Joshua in Greek*, Parts 1–4 (Paris: Geuthner, 1931–1938).

Mazor, L., "A Nomistic Re-Working of the Jericho Conquest Narrative Reflected in LXX to Joshua 6:1–20," *Textus* 18 (1995): 47–62.

van der Meer, M.N., *Formation and Reformulation: The Redaction of the Book of Joshua in the Light of the Oldest Textual Witness* (VTSup 102; Leiden: Brill, 2004).

Moatti-Fine, J., *Jésus (Josué)* (*Bible d'Alexandrie 6; Paris: Cerf, 1996).

Orlinsky, H.M., "The Hebrew Vorlage of the Septuagint of the Book of Joshua," in *Congress Volume Rome 1968* (ed. G.W. Anderson; VTSup 17; Leiden: Brill, 1969), 187–95.

Rösel, M., "Die Septuaginta-Version des Josuabuches," in **Brennpunkt*, Vol. 1., 197–211.

Rofé, A., "The End of the Book of Joshua according to the Septuagint," *Hen* 4 (1982): 17–36.

Rofé, A., "The Editing of the Book of Joshua in the Light of 4QJoshᵃ," in *New Qumran Texts and Studies: Proceedings of the First Meeting of the International Organization for Qumran Studies, Paris 1992* (ed. G.L. Brooke and F. García Martínez; STDJ 15; Leiden: Brill, 1994), 73–80.

Sipilä, S., "On the Concept of God in the Masoretic Text of Joshua," in *Houses Full of All Good Things: Essays in Memory of Timo Veijola* (eds. J. Pakkala and M. Nissinen; Publications of the Finnish Exegetical Society 95; Göttingen: Vandenhoeck & Ruprecht, 2008), 477–87.

Tov, E., "The Growth of the Book of Joshua in Light of the Evidence of the Septuagint," in **Greek-Hebrew Bible*, 385–96.

Tov, E., "Literary Development of the Book of Joshua as Reflected in the MT, the LXX and 4QJoshᵃ," in *The Book of Joshua* (ed. E. Noort; BETL 250; Leuven: Peeters, 2012), 65–85.

Karin Finsterbusch

---

30 Rofé, "Editing," 77.

3.2.3 Other Texts

3.2.3.1 Manuscripts, Editions, and Auxiliary Tools

Of the four ancient Hebrew manuscripts of Joshua (→ 3.2.1), only 4QJosh[a] and 4QJosh[b], which do not overlap, are of importance here.[1] Also text-critically valuable are a few of the ca. fifty allusions to and quotations from Joshua in Second Temple Jewish literature. In four cases, a (part of a) verse that is more or less close to the text displayed by LXX-Josh (→ 3.3) is quoted/alluded to:

- quotation of a short text of Josh 5:6 (CD B 20:14);[2]
- quotation of a short text of Josh 6:26 (4QapocrJosh[b] 22 ii 8 [itself quoted in 4QTest 22]);
- quotation of a long text of Josh 21:7 (1 Chr 6:48; בגורל "by lot" is lacking in MT-Josh 21:7);
- quotation of or allusion to the text preserved at the end of the Greek book of Joshua (LXX-Josh 24:33a–b) in CD A 5:1–5.[3]

The Hebrew manuscript of the Samaritan book of Joshua (Sam-Josh) was, according to Crown and Stenhouse, written in the fourteenth century utilizing earlier sources.[4] Since the text-critical value of the manuscript is hotly debated among scholars, it will not be discussed in this article.[5]

The allusions to and quotations from Joshua are listed in Lange and Weigold.[6] Sam-Josh was first published by Gaster.[7]

3.2.3.2 4QJosh[a]

The orthography of 4QJosh[a] is generally inconsistent. It displays a slightly fuller use of the *matres lectionis* than that in MT-Josh.[8] The name Joshua is spelled in three different ways, cf. יהשע in Josh 8:35, יהושע in Josh 6:6, and יהושוע in Josh 6:7. In Josh 7:16, a stylistic improvement can be discerned (MT-Josh lacks the *nota accusativi* את); in Josh 10:9, the scribe corrected his own scribal error. Beneath line 13 of frg. 16 (= Josh 8:14), a later scribe in the Herodian period added words that resemble Josh 8:18 in larger letters in what appears to be an interval or the bottom margin.[9] The addition lacks a space between the two words אל העי "toward Ai."

With respect to individual text variants, 4QJosh[a] agrees with MT against LXX in only two insignificant readings but agrees with LXX against MT several times. However, the predominant pattern of the manuscript is that it frequently goes its own way.[10] Compared with both MT and LXX, it displays a few small pluses and minuses (→ 3.2.3.2.1). Of special importance are several major non-aligned readings (→ 3.2.3.2.2).

3.2.3.2.1 Small Pluses and Minuses

In some cases, the secondary nature of the pluses in 4QJosh[a] is evident. For example, in the pre-

---

[1] Mur/Ḥev(?)Josh (*olim* XJosh) can be classified as proto-Masoretic. Too few words of 4Qpaleo paraJosh are preserved in order to draw conclusions about its nature and text-critical character, cf. Lange, *Handbuch, 187–89.

[2] However, CD B 20:14 agrees with MT-Josh 5:6 in mentioning that Israel was in the desert for forty years (LXX-Josh: forty-two years).

[3] Cf. Lucassen, "Josua," 376–80; Dimant, "Case," 126–27; Lange, *Handbuch, 194. As far as I can see, the quotation of the long text of Josh 21:7 in 1 Chr 6:48 has not yet been recognized.

[4] A.D. Crown, "New Light on the Inter-Relationships of Samaritan Chronicles from Some Manuscripts in the John Rylands Library of Manchester, I–II," *BJRL* 54 (1972): 1–32, 33–58; P. Stenhouse, "Samaritan Chronicles," in *The Samaritans* (ed. A.D. Crown; Tübingen: Mohr Siebeck, 1989), 218–65.

[5] E.g. P. Kahle, "Zum hebräischen Buch Josua der Samaritaner," *ZDMG* 62 (1908): 550–51, argued against the text-critical value of Sam-Josh. According to E. Noort, *Das Buch Josua: Forschungsgeschichte und Problemfelder* (EdF 292; Darmstadt: Wissenschaftliche Buchgesellschaft, 1998), 58–59, Sam-Josh is only of some importance for the "Rezeptionsgeschichte" of Joshua. According to R. Pummer, "The Samaritans and Their Pentateuch," in *The Pentateuch as Torah: New Models for Understanding Its Promulgation and Acceptance* (eds. G.N. Knoppers and B.M. Levinson; Winona Lake: Eisenbrauns, 2007), 237–69, 240–41, it may be assumed that the Samaritans did possess a book of Joshua at an early period, albeit in a different form from the present versions.

[6] A. Lange and M. Weigold, *Biblical Quotations and Allusions in Second Temple Jewish Literature* (Journal of Ancient Judaism Supplements 5; Göttingen: Vandenhoeck & Ruprecht, 2011), 113–14.

[7] M. Gaster, "Das Buch Josua in hebräisch-samaritanischer Rezension," *ZDMG* 62 (1908): 209–79, 494–549.

[8] Cf. E. Ulrich, *DJD XIV: 144.

[9] E. Ulrich, "47. 4QJosh[a]," *DJD XIV: 143–52 (150).

[10] Ulrich, "4QJosh[a]," 145.

served text of Josh 7:12, the expression ולא פנים "and not face" was added after the statement that the Israelites will turn tail before their enemies. The scribe-editor obviously wanted to emphasize the fact that the Israelites will have to flee their enemies due to sin. In Josh 4(MT: 8):35, the motive for the crossing of the Jordan was added to connect the episode of the Torah reading to the narrative context of Joshua 4 and 5 (→ 3.2.3.2.2).

On the other hand, the argument of *lectio brevior potior* indicates some minuses to a more ancient text.[11] For example, 4QJosh[a] reads "Joshua and Israel" in Josh 10:4 (MT and LXX: "Joshua and *the children of* Israel"); it reads that God threw "stones" from heaven in Josh 10:11 (MT and LXX: "*huge* stones"). It is more likely that those elements were added rather than dropped as being superfluous.

3.2.3.2.2 Significant Non-Aligned Readings

4QJosh[a] displays several significant non-aligned readings. Three cases are most interesting.

- With respect to Josh 6:7–10, 4QJosh[a] is obviously closer to MT-Josh (which differs considerably from LXX-Josh). However, in Josh 6:7, Joshua is mentioned explicitly as the subject, leaving the reader in no doubt as to its identity (MT reads וַיֹּאמְרוּ "and they said." According to *Qere*, the verb is to be read as ויאמר "and he said"; the subject is Joshua).
- Concerning Josh 8:7–18, 4QJosh[a] resembles a text that is apparently shorter than that in both MT-Josh and LXX-Josh, although LXX-Josh is already shorter than MT-Josh.[12]
- The account of Joshua's reading of the Torah (MT-Josh 8:34–35; LXX-Josh 9:2e–f) is followed in 4QJosh[a] by a text that is not identical with either Josh 9:1 or 9:3, but is a transitional temporal clause. It is followed by what appears to be the beginning of the account of the circumcision (Josh 5:2 MT/LXX).[13] It is uncertain whether the building of the altar (MT-Josh 8:30–33; LXX-Josh 9:2a–d) preceded the Torah reading in 4QJosh[a] (both elements are linked in the Ebal-Gerizim episode in MT and LXX).[14] Josephus' and Pseudo-Philo's comments are interesting: Josephus describes the building of an altar after the crossing of the Jordan, but he does not mention the reading of the Torah (*Ant*. 5.16–20). Furthermore, Josephus does not mention the Ebal-Gerizim episode between the conquest of Ai and the Gibeonites' ruse. However, he does recount the building of the altar at Shechem, stating explicitly that it was commanded by Moses and that half of the people were stationed on Mt. Gerizim and half on Mt. Ebal (without mentioning Joshua's reading of the Torah, *Ant*. 5.69). Pseudo-Philo seems to link the tradition of the altar building at Gilgal and the Ebal-Gerizim episode with the writing and reading of the Torah in the "old days of Joshua" (*Bib. Ant*. 21.1.7–10).
- When summarizing the different traditions, at least two explanations are possible:[15] 1) 4QJosh[a] preserves an older sequence of the narrative (following the Jordan-Gilgal tradition in Deut 11:30 and 27:2–3), which was subsequently altered by MT and LXX (following the Ebal-Gerizim tradition in Deut 11:29 and 27:4–8);[16] or 2) 4QJosh[a] displays a text in which a scribe-editor inserted secondarily the motive of the Torah reading into Joshua 4 (in addition to the Ebal-Gerizim episode with the building of the altar in Josh 8:30–9:2, verses that are not preserved in 4QJosh[a]?).[17] The purpose, then, was certainly to underline the fact that Israel learned and knew the Torah after the crossing of the Jordan and was thus able to follow it from the very

---

[11] Cf. E. Tov, *TCHB*, 277–78.
[12] Cf. Ulrich, "4QJosh[a]," 145, 150; Tov, "Development," 67.
[13] Cf. Ulrich, "4QJosh[a]," 147.
[14] Since, according to Ulrich, "4QJosh[a]," 145, that would have appeared at the unpreserved bottom of the preceding column.
[15] Scholars interpret the findings in somewhat different ways. For a detailed overview of the complex discussion, see especially Lange, *Handbuch*, 196–98, and Tov, "Development," 80–85.
[16] Thus, e.g., Ulrich, "4QJosh[a]," 146; Noort, "History of Tradition."
[17] Cf. especially M.N. van der Meer, *Formation and Reformulation: The Redaction of the Book of Joshua in the Light of the Oldest Textual Witness* (VTSup 102; Leiden: Brill, 2004), 521 ("harmonization by means of duplication").

beginning. In this case, 4QJosh{a} represents a rather late exegetical tradition regarding Joshua 4–5.[18] In my view, the second explanation is more likely. The *Apocryphon of Joshua* shows how important is was for some Jewish circles that the Torah was observed right from the time of entering into the land: according to 4Q379 12, the Torah stipulations concerning the Sabbatical Years were enacted the very moment the Israelites entered the land.[19]

- Certainly 4QJosh{a} provides a type of "third solution" in addition to that of MT-Josh and LXX-Josh. Josephus and Pseudo-Philo tried to solve the problem of the different Ebal-Gerizim textual traditions (on the basis of different Joshua editions?) in their own way.

3.2.3.3 4QJosh{b}

4QJosh{b} reflects the same orthography as MT-Josh. Supralinear corrections appear in three places (two of which are significant; see below). There are two intervals, one within Josh 17:11 (differing from MT-Josh). The four preserved sections are very fragmentary. Therefore, not much can be said about the text-critical character of the manuscript.

- With respect to single variants, 4QJosh{b} agrees in small details a few times with MT against LXX (especially in the preserved sections of Josh 17:1–5).
- According to the reconstructed text, 4QJosh{b} displays in Josh 17:11 a different sequence of the elements than that in MT-Josh (LXX-Josh has a shorter text).
- In some cases, however, 4QJosh{b} is closer to LXX-Josh. Of special significance is the agreement of the reconstructed text of Josh 4:1–3 with a short text close to that of LXX-Josh (with three minuses in vv. 2 and 3).
- The beginning of Josh 2:12 differs from MT/LXX (Tov reconstructed ותאמר "and she said;" MT reads instead: וְעַתָּה "and now"). In my view,

ותאמר is to be judged as *lectio facilior*. The scribe-editor supposedly repeated the ותאמר from v. 9 to make clear that Rahab is still speaking.

- Of special interest are two supralinear insertions that, according to Tov, are in all likelihood *secunda manu*:[20] 1) "(days of harvest of) wheat" at the end of Josh 3:15. This reading is close to LXX-Josh (and cf. the paraphrase in 4Qapocr-Josh{b} [4Q379] 12 7). Did a later scribe-editor insert חטים "wheat" because he knew this variant from another manuscript?; and 2) "Joshua (and the entire nation)" in Josh 3:17 (MT/LXX: "the entire nation"). A later scribe-editor could have added Joshua's name in order to stress his special role in the context of the crossing of the Jordan (cf. also the additions of Joshua's name in MT-Josh 4:5 and 4QJosh{a} 6:7).

Given the fact that so little text of the manuscript has survived, the number and variety of variants (as compared with MT-Josh and LXX-Josh) is remarkable.[21]

3.2.3.4 Relevance for Exegesis and Literary Analysis

4QJosh{a} and 4QJosh{b} display short and long as well as early and late textual elements (if one takes as the basis of comparison MT-Josh and LXX-Josh). Especially noteworthy is the difference in sequence in 4QJosh{a}. Therefore, 4QJosh{a} can be considered as an edition with its own idiosyncrasy, different to that of MT-Josh and of LXX-Josh (and its Hebrew *Vorlage*, respectively). Of 4QJosh{b}, too little text is preserved to classify the manuscript with any certainty. The supralinear insertions that were supposedly added later point to the importance of the manuscript. The authority of a text tradition resembling the *Vorlage* of LXX-Josh is proven by several quotations and allusions. Thus, the result is complex. It is obvious that, prior to the textual standardization of Joshua, several rather different

---

[18] Thus, e.g., Rofé, "Editing," Tov, "Development," 82.
[19] Cf. Dimant, "Case," 115–17.

[20] E. Tov, "48. 4QJosh{b}," *DJD* XIV: 153–60 (155).
[21] Therefore, the statement of Tov, "4QJosh{b}," 154, "the text of 4QJosh{b} agrees usually [!] with MT against LXX (see especially frags. 4–5)" is, in my view, misleading.

and multi-layered authoritative textual traditions existed more or less concurrently.

Dimant, D., "Between Sectarian and Non-Sectarian: The Case of the Apocryphon of Joshua," in *Reworking the Bible: Apocryphal and Related Texts at Qumran: Proceedings of a Joint Symposium by the Orion Center for the Study of the Dead Sea Scrolls and Associated Literature and the Hebrew University Institute for Advanced Studies Research Group on Qumran, 15–17 January, 2002* (ed. E.G. Chazon et al.; STDJ 58; Leiden: Brill, 2005), 105–34.

Lange, A., **Handbuch*, 187–201.

Lucassen, B., "Josua, Richter und CD," *RevQ* 18 (1998–1999): 374–96.

Noort, E., "4QJosh[a] and the History of Tradition in the Book of Joshua," *JNSL* 24 (1998): 127–44.

Rofé, A., "The Editing of the Book of Joshua in the Light of 4QJosh[a]," in *New Qumran Texts and Studies: Proceedings of the First Meeting of the International Organization for Qumran Studies, Paris 1992* (ed. G.L. Brooke and F. García Martínez; STDJ 15; Leiden: Brill, 1994), 73–80.

Tov, E., "The Growth of the Book of Joshua in Light of the Evidence of the Septuagint," in **Greek-Hebrew Bible*, 385–96.

Tov, E., "Literary Development of the Book of Joshua as Reflected in the MT, the LXX and 4QJosh[a]," in *The Book of Joshua* (ed. E. Noort; BETL 250; Leuven: Peeters, 2012), 65–85.

Karin Finsterbusch

3.3 Septuagint

3.3.1 Background

It is generally assumed that the Greek translation of Joshua followed soon after that of the Pentateuch[1] since its relatively free translation technique resembles that of the Greek Pentateuch (→ 2.4.1). Yet it is unknown how soon it followed that of the Pentateuch. On the basis of a statement made by Aristobulus (ca. 176–170 B.C.E.; frg. 3 *apud* Eusebius of Caesarea, *Praep. ev.* 13.12) that before his time a Greek translation had been made of the events surrounding the exodus of Egypt and "the domination of the land" (κράτησις τῆς χώρας; cf. LXX-Josh 18:1), as well as on the basis of data from the Zenon Archive which includes Greek documentary papyri from ca. 260–240 B.C.E., van der Meer[2] has argued that the Greek translation of Joshua might have been made between the Fourth and Fifth Syrian Wars (219–217 B.C.E. and 202–195 B.C.E. respectively), perhaps by the Jewish high Ptolemaic official Dositheos, son of a Drimylos. In the absence of more contemporary data, this hypothesis remains speculative.

3.3.2 Original Form, Editions, Tools

Codex Vaticanus, now partially supported by the second-century C.E. leaves from a codex in the Schøyen Collection[3] and rediscovered leaves from Codex Sinaiticus, seems to reflect the oldest attainable form of the Old Greek of Joshua, but in the tribal allotments (Joshua 13–21) the toponyms seem hopelessly corrupt. Some Greek manuscripts as well as the Sahidic codex Chester Beatty 1389-Bodmer 21 (Kasser, *Papyrus Bodmer XXI*) omit these chapters entirely. In his manual edition, Rahlfs[4] made no attempt to reconstruct the original Greek text of Josh 15:21–62 and 18:22–19:45, but simply printed the text of the two oldest witnesses (LXX[B] and LXX[A]) in parallel columns. Although there is a useful diplomatic edition of the Greek Joshua as attested in LXX[B] in the Larger Cambridge edition,[5] there is no critical edition in the Göttingen LXX series as of 2015 despite much preparatory work that has been done by Udo Quast.

For the Greek Joshua, there exists a critical edition prepared by Margolis.[6] This handwritten critical edition is based on almost all extant witnesses as well as on a grouping of all these witnesses in an "Egyptian recension" (consisting of Codex LXX[B] and Coptic and Ethiopic translations), a "Syrian" ("Lucianic" or "Antiochene" → 3–5.1.6.1) recension (including VL → 3–5.2.1.1), a "Palestinian" (or "Origenic" → 3–5.1.5.2.3.4) recension, and a "Constantinopolitan" and "Mixed" group of manuscripts.[7] Unfortunately, this edition contains many conjectural emendations based on MT as well as a number of errors.[8] A careful examination of all the differences between the critical editions of Rahlfs and Margolis made by Den Hertog[9] suggests that the edition of Rahlfs remains a relatively reliable reconstruction of the Old Greek of Joshua, although scholars may wish to consult both the Larger Cambridge edition as well as that of Margolis.[10]

Auxiliary tools for the study of LXX-Josh are offered by the modern translations and commentaries (*Bible d'Alexandrie*: Moatti-Fine, *Jésus (Josué)*; Auld, *Joshua*; *NETS*: Greenspoon, "Iesous"; *Septuaginta Deutsch* and *Septuaginta Deutsch, Erläuterungen*: Den Hertog and Kreuzer, "Jesus" and "Jesus: Iosue" respectively).

---

[1] Thackeray, *Grammar*, 13.
[2] Van der Meer, "Provenance, Profile, and Purpose."
[3] De Troyer, "Joshua."
[4] Rahlfs, *Septuaginta*.
[5] Brooke-McLean, *The Old Testament in Greek*, 1917.
[6] Margolis, *The Book of Joshua*.
[7] See also Pretzl, "Buche Josue" and Bieberstein, *Lukian und Theodotion*.
[8] See Tov, "Fifth Fascicle"; Sipilä, "Note"; Bieberstein, *Lukian und Theodotion*, 22–27; Den Hertog, "Studien," 185.
[9] Den Hertog, "Studien."
[10] See further van der Meer, *Formation*, 22–32.

TABLE 1   *Major pluses in LXX-Joshua and their counterparts in Deuteronomy to 1 Kings*

Pluses in LXX-Josh	Counterpart
6:26b	MT-1 Kgs 16:34 (absent from Antiochene text of LXX-3 Kgdms 16)
13:7b–8a	
13:14b	Josh 13:32
15:59a	
16:10a	MT-1 Kgs 9:16 // LXX-3 Kgdms 5:14b
19:47a–48a	Judg 1:34–35
21:42a–d	Josh 19:49–50
24:31a	
24:33a–b	Judg 2:11–13; 3:12, 14

3.3.3 Translation Character

The Old Greek of Joshua differs from the Hebrew texts in many small and larger aspects. From a quantitative perspective, LXX-Josh contains both minuses and pluses *vis-à-vis* MT-Josh (→ 3.2.2). Already in the first verse of the book the theologically important title for Moses as servant of YHWH (עבד יהוה "the servant of the Lord") is not represented in the Greek, leading many scholars to consider the longer Hebrew text to be a later expansion (→ 3.3.6). Similar minuses can be found throughout the book. Longer minuses (more than one clause) are found in Josh 2:4b, 9b, 15b, 21b; 5:4, 9b; 6:3–4, 7, 13, 15; 7:17–18, 25; 8:7b–8a, 9b, 11–13, 15b–16a, 20b, 26; 10:15, 43; 13:33; 14:3a; 18:10b; 20:4–6; 23:7, 16b; 24:7b. There are also a number of considerable pluses, several of them having a direct counterpart in the books of Joshua, Judges, and Kings; see Table 1.

Furthermore, there a few cases of sequence difference in the narrative material, most importantly the section MT-Josh 8:30–35, which occurs in LXX-Josh after Josh 9:2.[11] Smaller transpositions are found in LXX-Josh 19:47 (= MT-Josh 19:48) and 24:29 (= MT-Josh 24:31).

---

[11] For the possible different position in 4QJosh[a], → 3.2.1 and van der Meer, *Formation*, 479–522.

3.3.4 Translation Technique and Inner-Translational Features

The translation technique of Joshua is relatively free as compared to the literalistic translation technique found in most of the LXX books (→ 1.3.1.1). The translator did not strive for idiomatic renderings, but employed different equivalents either for the sake of variation (e.g., Josh 23:14, where the repetition of the phrase לא נפל דבר אחד "not one thing has failed" has been rendered first literally with οὐ διέπεσεν εἷς λόγος "not one word has crumbled" (*NETS*) and then freely with οὐ διεφώνησεν "[not one out of them] failed") or for contextual reasons (e.g., in Josh 22:9–34, where the illegitimate trans-Jordanian "altar" has first been rendered with βωμός, which in Jewish Greek literature always carries a negative connotation, and later with θυσιαστήριον when referring to the legitimate altar for YHWH; see, e.g., Jos 22:19b ואתנו אל תמרדו בבנתכם לכם מזבח מבלעדי מזבח יהוה אלהינו "or rebel against us by building yourselves an altar other than the altar of the LORD our God" [NRSV] καὶ μὴ ἀπόστητε ἀπὸ κυρίου διὰ τὸ οἰκοδομῆσαι ὑμᾶς βωμὸν ἔξω τοῦ θυσιαστηρίου κυρίου τοῦ θεοῦ ἡμῶν "and do not rebel from the Lord by your building an altar other than the altar of the Lord our God" [*NETS*]). Common Hebrew phrases such as נכה "to be struck," לחם "to wage war," מסס "to melt," and לב "heart" are rendered in thirteen, seven, and five different ways respectively in

Greek.¹² Statistical studies¹³ have shown that the vocabulary of the Greek Joshua is almost twice as large as its Hebrew counterpart. Hollenberg, Gooding, Tov, Bieberstein, Den Hertog and Kreuzer, Moatti-Fine, van der Meer,¹⁴ and others have all pointed to the numerous small literary initiatives ("midrash-type exegesis" as Tov calls it) introduced by the Greek translator.

Syntactical observations further support this profile of a relatively free translation technique (Sipilä, *Between Literalness and Freedom*). The Greek translator occasionally renders clause-initial -ו "and" with δέ "also, but" instead of the ubiquitous paratactical καί "and," the clause connector כי "because" with postpositive γάρ "as" instead of ὅτι "because," and occasionally employs genuine Greek syntactical constructions such as *genitivus absolutus*, *participium coniunctum*, and third-person imperatival forms.¹⁵ In this respect, the translation technique of the Greek Joshua resembles that of the Greek Pentateuch.¹⁶ The use of Greek particles such as ἀλλά "but, however," ἐπεί "when," ἡνίκα "at the same time when," ὅταν "when," οὖν "hence, therefore," and ὡς¹⁷ "as, like" further strengthens the view that the Greek translator tried to offer a faithful and intelligent rendering rather than the idiosyncratic products of others translators.

3.3.5 Text-Critical Value

On the basis of the observations in → 3.3.3, it is problematic to ascribe variants between MT and LXX to a different Hebrew *Vorlage*. LXX-Josh should first be studied in its own right before conclusions are drawn with respect to the textual or even editorial history of the book. Nevertheless, there are several passages in the book where there is a broad consensus among scholars that MT (→ 3.2.2) is either corrupt or presents a later interpretation. The passages discussed above (→ 3.1; → 3.3.3) relating to Josh 13:7b–8a, 15:59a, and 21:36–37 are generally regarded as examples of an original text preserved in LXX and lost in MT due to *parablepsis*. Furthermore, there are several passages throughout the book where the Septuagint reflects a more original Hebrew text.

3.3.6 Relevance for Literary Analysis

In some cases, LXX reflects a stage in the literary history of the book preceding the edition attested in MT (→ 3.2.2). Since Hollenberg,¹⁸ it has been recognized that the long pluses in MT-Josh 20:3–6 add Deuteronomistic (Deut 19:1–13) and priestly prescriptions (Num 35:9–45) to the much shorter (priestly) description of the cities of refuge as reflected in LXX,¹⁹ aiming to specify the authority between city elders and the high priest (Josh 20:6) in cases of unpremeditated murder (Josh 20:4–5).

Whereas there is a broad consensus among scholars that in these cases textual and literary history of the book coincide, there is more discussion with respect to the other quantitative variants between MT (→ 3.2.2) and LXX.²⁰ Whereas Hollenberg and other scholars at the end of the nineteenth century tended to ascribe many variants to the literary creativity of the translator (→ 3.3.4), Holmes argued that the different variants constitute a "deliberate and systematic revision."²¹ In his view, the pluses in MT reflect an inner coherence; see, e.g., the twofold plus אשר השבעתנו "that you made us swear to you" in both MT-Josh 2:17 and 2:20, which were added by the same later Hebrew writer for reasons of amplification. In his view, the strikingly different versions of Josh 5:2–9 reflect the concern of the same Hebrew writer to avoid the impression that circumcision was not universally practiced in Egypt.

---

¹² Moatti-Fine, *Jésus (Josué)*, 42–68.
¹³ Bajard and Poswick, "Aspects statistiques."
¹⁴ Hollenberg, *Charakter*; Gooding, "Traditions of Interpretation"; Tov, "Midrash-Type Exegesis"; Bieberstein, *Josua-Jordan-Jericho*, Den Hertog "Studien"; Den Hertog and Kreuzer, "Jesus"; Den Hertog and Kreuzer, "Jesus: Iosue", Moatti-Fine. *Jésus (Josué)*, van der Meer, *Formation*; van der Meer, "Sound the Trumpet!"
¹⁵ Aejmelaeus, *Trail.
¹⁶ See already Thackeray, *Grammar, 13.
¹⁷ Den Hertog, "Studien," 177–80.

¹⁸ Hollenberg, *Charakter*, 15.
¹⁹ See Rofé, "Joshua 20," and Tov, *TCHB, 294–98.
²⁰ See van der Meer, *Formation*, 32–91.
²¹ Holmes, *Joshua*, 2.

This thesis has been taken up and elaborated by Orlinsky, Auld, Tov,[22] and others. Whereas Benjamin and Auld consider the pluses in MT to be the result of *glosses* or explicative interpolations[23] or progressive supplementation,[24] Tov[25] considers them to be part of a re-edition of the book, reflecting both the concerns of harmonization and amplification as well as theological correction and Deuteronomistic influence (as can be seen in the case of the plus עבד יהוה "servant of the Lord" in Josh 1:1, 15; 12:6; and 22:4, a Deuteronomistic designation for Moses).

In a similar vein, the long pluses in LXX-Josh (→ 3.3.3) can also be seen as witnesses to older editions of the historical books. Rofé[26] has argued that the long plus at the end of LXX-Josh (including elements now found in Judg 2:6, 11–14; 3:12, 14) constitutes a more original transition from Joshua to the Judges narratives attested also by the *Damascus Document* (CD v:1–5). The passage now found in Judg 1:1–3:11 (MT and LXX) would then constitute a later editorial addition consisting mainly of elements taken from the Joshua and Judges narratives in order to create an introduction to an independent book of Judges. Rofé holds this later editor responsible also for the deletion of the plus in LXX-Josh 24:31a, which narrates the burial of the flint knives with which Joshua circumcised the Israelites (cf. Josh 5:2–9) and the addition of a clause in Josh 24:5 introducing Moses and Aaron. In the original edition of Joshua 24, thus Rofé, it was Joshua, not Moses, who had led the Israelites from Egypt.

Along similar lines, Mazor[27] has argued that the plus in LXX-Josh 6:26a contains an ancient historiographical note related to pre-monarchical Ephraim (cf. 1 Chr 7:21b–24), which was later omitted in MT. In the case of Josh 8:1–29, Mazor[28] detects three stages in the growth of the narrative of the conquest of Ai, in which the shorter LXX version presents an intermediary stage between the even shorter version attested by 4QJosh[a] (→ 3.2.1.1) and the longer version in MT. In the case of Josh 6:2–25, however, where the Greek version is also considerably shorter than MT, she detects behind the Greek translation Hebrew scribal activity that curtailed the longer Hebrew text (MT) for "nomistic" reasons.[29]

By contrast, several other scholars have strongly argued against the hypothesis of literary activity evidenced by the quantitative variants between MT and LXX. In their view, more attention should be paid to the Greek translation as interpretation as well as to the redaction history of Joshua in its own right. Already in 1977, Gooding pointed to the incongruities in Holmes' reasoning with respect to Joshua 5.[30] Bieberstein demonstrated that the quantitative variants in Joshua 6 cannot be detached from the qualitative variants, which show numerous examples of literary initiatives, condensation, and reformulation introduced by the Greek translator.[31] Along similar lines, van der Meer, described the various presumed Deuteronomistic pluses in Joshua 1 as deliberate condensations made by the Greek translator for exegetical purposes and offered new interpretations for the shorter and different versions of Josh 5:2–12, 8:1–29 and the transposition of MT-Josh 8:30–35, which in his view should all be ascribed to the Greek translator instead of a Hebrew editor.[32]

With respect to the redaction-critical value of LXX-Josh we may thus discern two opposing tendencies: a maximalist and a minimalist one. Nevertheless, all scholars seem to agree that LXX-Josh contains both reformulation on the part of the Greek translator and scribal activity on the level of

---

[22] Orlinsky, "Hebrew *Vorlage* of the Septuagint," Auld, "Joshua," Auld, *Joshua, Jesus Son of Nauē*; Tov, "Growth."
[23] Benjamin, "Variations."
[24] Auld, "Joshua."
[25] Tov, "Growth."
[26] Rofé, "End of the Book of Joshua."
[27] Mazor, "Origin and Evolution of the Curse."
[28] Mazor, "Textual and Literary Study."

[29] Mazor, "Nomistic Reworking."
[30] Gooding, "Traditions of Interpretation of the Circumcision at Gilgal." See also Tov, "Midrash-Type Exegesis"; Den Hertog, "Studien," 145–49; van der Meer, *Formation*, 249–415.
[31] Bieberstein, *Josua-Jordan-Jericho*; see further van der Meer, "Sound the Trumpet!"
[32] Van der Meer, *Formation*, 155–522.

the Hebrew text (Joshua 20). Hence, the question is not whether LXX-Josh is relevant for literary criticism of the book, but only to what extent.

Aejmelaeus, *Trail.

Auld, A.G., "Joshua: The Hebrew and Greek Texts," in *Studies in the Historical Books of the Old Testament* (ed. J.A. Emerton; VTSup 30; Leiden: Brill, 1979), 1–14; repr. in *Joshua Retold: Synoptic. Perspectives* (ed. A.G. Auld; OTS; Edinburgh: T & T Clark, 1998), 7–18.

Auld, A.G., *Joshua: Jesus Son of Nauē in Codex Vaticanus* (Septuagint Commentary Series; Leiden: Brill, 2005).

Bajard, J. and R.-F. Poswick, "Aspects statistiques des rapports entre la Septante et le texte massorétique," in *VII Congress of the International Organization for Septuagint and Cognate Studies, Leuven, 1989* (ed. C. Cox; SBLSCS 31; Atlanta: SBL, 1991), 123–56.

Benjamin, C.D., *The Variations between the Hebrew and Greek Texts of Joshua: Chapters 1–12* (Leipzig: Drugulin, 1921).

Bieberstein, K., *Lukian und Theodotion im Josuabuch: Mit einem Beitrag zu den Josuarollen von Ḫirbet Qumrān* (BN Beiheft 7; Munich: K. Urlaub, 1994).

Bieberstein, K., *Josua-Jordan-Jericho: Archäologie, Geschichte und Theologie der Landnahmeerzählungen Josua 1–6* (OBO 143; Göttingen: Vandenhoeck & Ruprecht, 1995).

Gooding, D.W., "Traditions of Interpretation of the Circumcision at Gilgal," in *Proceedings of the Sixth World Congress of Jewish Studies: Held at the Hebrew University of Jerusalem, 13–19 August 1973 under the Auspices of the Israel Academy of Sciences and Humanities* (4 vols.; ed. A. Shinan; Jerusalem: World Union of Jewish Studies, 1977), 1:149–64.

Greenspoon, L.J., "Iesous," in *NETS, 174–94.

den Hertog, C.G., "Studien zur griechischen Übersetzung des Buches Josua," (PhD diss., University of Gießen, 1996).

den Hertog, C.G. and S. Kreuzer, "Jesus: Das Buch Josua," in *Septuaginta Deutsch, 218–42.

den Hertog, C.G. and S. Kreuzer, "Jesus: Iosue/Das Buch Josua," in *Septuaginta Deutsch, Erläuterungen, 1:605–56.

Hollenberg, J., *Der Charakter der alexandrinischen Uebersetzung des Buches Josua und ihr textkritischer Werth untersucht* (Wissenschaftliche Beitrage zu dem Oster-Programm des Gymnasiums zu Moers; Moers: Edner, 1876).

Holmes, S., *Joshua: The Hebrew and Greek Texts* (Cambridge: Cambridge University Press, 1914).

Kasser, R., *Papyrus Bodmer XXI: Josué VI,16–25, VII,6–XI,23, XXII,1–2, 19–XXIII,7, 15–XXIV,23 en sahidique* (Geneva: Bibliotheca Bodmeriana, 1963).

Margolis, M.L., *The Book of Joshua in Greek According to the Critically Restored Text with an Apparatus Containing the Variants of the Principal Recensions of the Individual Witnesses* (Publications of the Alexander Kohut Memorial Foundation in Trust at the American Academy for Jewish Research; parts 1–4 [Josh 1:1–19:38]: Paris: Paul Geuther, 1931–1938; part 5 [Josh 19:39–24:33]: with a preface by E. Tov; Philadelphia: Annenberg Research Institute, 1992).

Mazor, L., "The Origin and Evolution of the Curse upon the Rebuilder of Jericho – A Contribution of Textual Criticism to Biblical Historiography," *Textus* 16 (1988): 1–26.

Mazor, L., "A Textual and Literary Study of the Fall of Ai in Joshua 8," in *The Bible in Light of Its Interpreters: Sarah Kamin Memorial Volume* (ed. S. Japhet; Jerusalem: Magnes, 1994), 73–108 [Hebr.].

Mazor, L., "A Nomistic Reworking of the Jericho Conquest Narrative Reflected in LXX to Joshua 6:1–20," *Textus* 18 (1995): 47–62.

van der Meer, M.N., *Formation and Reformulation: The Redaction of the Book of Joshua in the Light of the Oldest Textual Witnesses* (VTSup 102; Leiden: Brill, 2004).

van der Meer, M.N., "Provenance, Profile, and Purpose of the Greek Joshua," in *XII Congress of the International Organization for Septuagint and Cognate Studies, Leiden, 2004* (ed. M.K.H. Peters; SBLSCS 54; Atlanta: SBL, 2006), 55–80.

van der Meer, M.N., "'Sound the Trumpet!' Redaction and Reception of Joshua 6:2–25," in *The Land of Israel in Bible, History, and Theology: Studies in Honour of Ed Noort* (eds. J. van Ruiten and J.C. de Vos; VTSup 124; Leiden: Brill, 2009), 19–43.

Moatti-Fine, J., *Jésus (Josué)* (*Bible d'Alexandrie 6; Paris: Cerf, 1996).

Orlinsky, H.M., "The Hebrew *Vorlage* of the Septuagint of the Book of Joshua," in *Congress Volume. Rome, 1968* (VTSup 17; Leiden: Brill, 1969), 187–95.

Pretzl, O., "Die griechischen Handschriftengruppen im Buche Josue untersucht nach ihrer Eigenart und ihrem Verhältnis zueinander," *Bib* 9 (1928): 377–427.

Rofé, A., "The End of the Book of Joshua According to the Septuagint," *Shnaton* 2 (1977): 217–27 [Hebr.]; Engl. version in *Hen* 4 (1982): 17–35.

Rofé, A., "Joshua 20: Historico-Literary Criticism Illustrated," in *Isac Leo Seeligmann Volume: Essays on the*

Bible and the Ancient World (3 vols.; eds. A. Rofé and Y. Zakovitch; Jerusalem: E. Rubenstein, 1983), 1.137–50 [Hebr.]; Engl. Version in Tigay, *Models, 131–47.

Sipilä, S., "A Note to the Users of Margolis' Joshua Edition," BIOSCS 26 (1993): 17–21.

Sipilä, S., *Between Literalness and Freedom: Translation Technique in the Septuagint of Joshua and Judges Regarding the Clause Connections Introduced by* ו *and* כי (Publications of the Finnish Exegetical Society 75; Helsinki: Finnish Exegetical Society; Göttingen: Vandenhoeck & Ruprecht, 1999).

Tov, E., "Midrash-Type Exegesis in the Septuagint of Joshua," RB 60 (1978): 212–36; repr. in Tov, *Greek-Hebrew Bible, 153–64.

Tov, E., "The Fifth Fascicle of Margolis' *The Book of Joshua in Greek*," JQR 74 (1984): 398–99.

Tov, E., "The Growth of the Book of Joshua in the Light of the Evidence of the LXX Translation," in *Studies in Bible, 1986* (ed. S. Japhet; ScrHier 31; Jerusalem: Magnes, 1986), 321–39; repr. in Tov, *Greek-Hebrew Bible, 385–96.

de Troyer, K., "Joshua," in *Papyri Graecae Schøyen: P.Schøyen I* (ed. R. Pintaudi; Papyrologica Florentina 35; Florence: Gonnelli, 2005), 79–145.

Michaël van der Meer

4
Judges

∵

4.1 Textual History of Judges

4.1.1 MT of Judges

Until the Dead Sea discoveries of some fragments of Judges (see *infra*), the superior status of MT-Judg (→ 4.2.2) was almost undisputed. According to N. Fernández Marcos, in his introduction to the edition of MT-Judg within *BHQ*, "the Masoretic text of Judges in its final form is a text relatively well preserved except for chapter 5. Most of M's readings should be preferred over the variant readings of the versions or a good number of conjectures suggested by previous editors and commentators."[1] Due to the lack of solid criteria for determining whether or not MT has been preserved well, Tov nuances this statement in the following way: "There is not much variation between the textual witnesses of the book of Judges, and usually MT preserved an acceptable/good/preferable text."[2] Nevertheless, even within MT, sometimes (as in Judg 1:27 and 9:8) the *Qere* of the Masorah seems to be preferred above the *Ketiv*. In any case, all extant Hebrew textual witnesses of MT (MT^L, MT^A, and MT^C) are almost identical.

4.1.2 The Book of Judges in the Versions

Before passing into the intriguing question of the Greek text of Judges, some brief remarks about the Latin, Syriac, and Aramaic versions should be made. The Vulgate of Judges (→ 3–5.1.7) is considered a "free stylistic translation of a Hebrew *Vorlage* very close to M."[3] More or less the same can be stated with regard to the *Vorlage* of the Peshitta (→ 3–5.1.4): in general, it "was closer to the Masoretic text than to the text that underlies the Septuagint."[4] Also the Targum of Judges "can be characterized mainly as a literal translation of a Hebrew text very close to the Masoretic with occasional glosses and midrashic expansions."[5]

The Greek text of Judges is much more problematic (→ 4.3). Contrary to the concurrences that link the few witnesses of MT, there is a great diversity among the many Greek manuscripts. Following de Lagarde, in Rahlfs' edition – a critical edition within the Göttingen series has not yet been published – two Greek texts are printed: in the upper part of the page stands the A text, which is an eclectic text taking Codex Alexandrinus as its basis; the B text appears in the lower half of the page, representing the Codex Vaticanus. Rahlfs' presentation could give the impression – and undoubtedly this was Rahlfs' conviction – that both Greek texts should be considered as two completely independent translations of one single Hebrew *Vorlage* (→ 4.3.2).[6] However, this hypothesis has been criticized mainly since the middle of the twentieth century, arguing that the Greek Judges as presented in Rahlfs' A and B texts more probably goes back to one single translation, the so-called Old Greek.[7] Nevertheless, Tov, in line with Barthélemy, according to whom the traditions underlying the B text reflect the *kaige* recension, still considers "the evidence for the existence of two different translations very strong."[8]

In contemporary research, generally four "groups" of texts (G^B, G^L, G^M, and G^O) are recognized within the Greek manuscripts.[9] The reconstruction

---

[1] See Fernández Marcos, *Judges*, 5*.
[2] Tov, "Biblia," 486.
[3] Fernández Marcos, *Judges*, 10*.
[4] Fernández Marcos, *Judges*, 11*.

[5] Fernández Marcos, *Judges*, 12*.
[6] According to P. Kahle, *The Cairo Genizah* (2nd ed.; Oxford: Basil Blackwell, 1959), 235–36, LXX^A and LXX^B have to be considered as "typical examples of two forms of an old Targum."
[7] For an overview of the debate, see in particular Jellicoe, *SMS, 280–83; B. Lindars, "A Commentary on the Greek Judges?," in *VI Congress of the International Organization for Septuagint and Cognate Studies: Jerusalem 1986* (ed. C.E. Cox; SBLSCS 23; Atlanta: Scholars Press, 1987), 169–200; Fernández Marcos, *Introduction, 94–95; P.E. Satterthwaite, "To the Reader of Judges," in *NETS, 195–200.
[8] Tov, "Biblia," 484.
[9] On the classification of the textual groups within LXX-Judg (G^B, G^L, G^M, and G^O), as well as with regard to the

of the presumed Old Greek behind these manuscripts seems to be problematic, because of the influence of Origenian or Hexaplaric influences on each of these groups.[10] Nevertheless, group G^L, in particular, could give good evidence for the reconstruction of Old Greek, especially when it coincides with VL.[11]

As usual, variants between MT and the Greek textual witnesses are numerous. However, at least according to *BHQ, most variants – not always present in all Greek manuscripts – are judged to be the result of haplography (e.g. Judg 11:4), gloss (e.g. Judg 21:19), homoioteleuton (e.g. Judg 17:7), homoioarcton (e.g. Judg 10:6), harmonization (e.g. Judg 8:22), assimilation (e.g. Judg 10:10), different vocalization (e.g. Judg 9:28), or explicitation (e.g. Judg 8:33) at the level of LXX, which would imply that the *lectio difficilior* of MT has to be considered as the preferable reading.[12] Some Greek variants are viewed as theologically motivated (e.g. Judg 9:7).[13] Nevertheless, in some instances, *BHQ does prefer some variant readings of LXX to MT. For example, supported by the Greek reading ἐν χειρὶ αὐτοῦ "in his hand" in Judg 1:4, the retroverted בידו "in his hand" has to be preferred to the plural בידם "in their hands." The Greek reading βάαλ "Baal" (and *Bahel* in VL) in Judg 9:46 probably reflects an ancient reading בעל "Baal" which was altered by MT for theological motives. In Judg 16:13–14 and 19:30, the plus in the Greek text witnesses to a different *Vorlage*, preferable to MT. The Greek formula καὶ εἰς τὸν οἶκόν μου "and to my home" instead of ואת בית יהוה "and the house of YHWH" of MT-Judg 19:18 could reflect a more original reading.[14]

Despite these preferable readings of LXX and the complicated question of the textual history of the Greek translation of Judges, there seems to be hardly any discussion with regard to MT, which generally continues to be considered the most reliable textual witness of the book of Judges. However, if one accepts that OG-Judg "is a quite literal version of a text very similar, although not identical, to M,"[15] one could wonder (with Tov and contrary to *BHQ) whether many more variants between MT and LXX have to be considered as witnesses to a different Hebrew *Vorlage*.[16] As such, the question of the "original text" of Judges as preserved in MT seems to become more and more problematic. This question is further pressed in light of the Dead Sea Scrolls discoveries, to which we now turn.

4.1.3 The Dead Sea Scrolls and the Textual History of Judges

The book of Judges is only present sparingly among the Dead Sea Scrolls (→ 4.2.1).[17] Nevertheless, the publication of 4QJudg^a by Trebolle Barrera has given rise to a lively discussion with regard to the textual history of Judges (→ 4.2.1.2; → 4.2.3.2).[18] The most remarkable feature of this fragment, which contains the text of Judg 6:2–13, is the major minus of vv. 7–10. Due to the fact that these missing verses reveal several traces of Deuteronomistic phraseology (and therefore often have been considered as a late [Deuteronomistic] insertion[19] by

---

reconstruction of the Old Greek, see in particular Fernández Marcos, *Judges*, 6*–9*.

[10] Fernández Marcos, *Judges*, 7*.

[11] Fernández Marcos, *Judges*, 8*. Moreover, in some cases (as in Judg 1:16: *cum eo Amalec*), VL has to be preferred to MT. See Fernández Marcos, *Judges*, 9–10*.

[12] Fernández Marcos, *Judges*, 8*: "Only in a few cases (…) can it be argued that the reading of the Vorlage of G was superior to that of M, except in the special case of Judges 5, and the omissions by homoioteleuton in M of 16:13–14 and 19:30."

[13] See also P.E. Satterthwaite, "Some Septuagintal Pluses in Judges 20 and 21," *BIOSCS* 24 (1991): 25–35, who argues that several pluses in Judges 20–21 "tell us more about the history of exegesis of Ju 20–21 than they do about the original Hebrew text of this passage" (p. 35).

[14] See Tov, *TCHB*, 238.

[15] Fernández Marcos, *Judges*, 9*.

[16] Tov, "Biblia," 488: "While I agree that in Judges, MT is probably our best textual source, I would probably find more readings in the LXX that are preferable to MT."

[17] For a presentation of the manuscripts, see Lange, *Handbuch*, 203–11; Fernández Marcos, *Judges*, 5–6*.

[18] J. Trebolle Barrera, "Textual Variants in 4QJudg^a and the Textual and Editorial History of the Book of Judges," *RevQ* 14 (1989): 229–45. See also J. Trebolle Barrera, "49. 4QJudg^a," *DJD* XIV: 161–64; pl. XXXVI.

[19] See, e.g., already J. Wellhausen, *Prolegomena zur Geschichte Israels* (6th ed.; Berlin: W. de Gruyter, 1927), 230,

literary critics), Trebolle Barrera concludes that 4QJudg[a] represents a textual form that "ignores a literary development that entered into the masoretic textual tradition and is reflected also in the Greek version [as witnessed by i.a. Rahlfs' A and B texts – H.A.]" (→ 3–5.1.6.1.4).[20] Moreover, according to Trebolle Barrera, OG-Judg 6:2–13 shows similarities with 4QJudg[a] in several instances, while disagreeing with MT.[21] Therefore, Trebolle Barrera concludes that both the Old Greek and 4QJudg[a] have "preserved traces of a shorter form of the text" (→ 4.2.3.2; → 1.1.1.3).[22] This hypothesis regarding the textual history of Judges would be supported by the textual witnesses of several other passages (Judg 9:16–19; 12:4–5; 20:19–31), where the Old Greek has preserved similar traces of a shorter text form.[23]

Trebolle Barrera's hypothesis that 4QJudg[a] witnesses to an earlier stage in the development of the Hebrew text of Judges has been strongly criticized by, in particular, Hess and Fernández Marcos.[24] According to Hess, the minus in 4QJudg[a] is part of a practice of scribes who were exercising "a liberty in moving these paragraphs of their Former Prophets around, inserting and omitting sections for their own purposes, be they liturgical or otherwise."[25]

Contrary to Trebolle Barrera, Fernández Marcos argues that OG-Judg cannot be characterized as a shorter text. On the contrary, as is clear from his edition in *BHQ, he views Old Greek as often making the Hebrew *Vorlage* more explicit.[26] Therefore, "the hypothesis of a shorter text for Judges based on 4QJudg[a] is not shared by any other extant witness of the book."[27]

Although Fernández Marcos' and Hess' criticism is valid, Trebolle's hypothesis of a double textual tradition, eventually giving indications with respect to the textual history of the book of Judges, remains attractive. As such, it is not impossible that 4QJudg[a] reflects a former stage in the textual history of Judges, although it should be emphasized that in this discussion the borders between textual criticism and literary criticism do become very blurred.[28]

---

who considers Judg 6:7–10 to be "Einsatz der letzten Bearbeitung" of the book of Judges or, more recently, J.A. Soggin, *Judges: A Commentary* (OTL; London: SCM, 1981), 110–12.

[20] Trebolle Barrera, "Textual Variants," 238. See also Ulrich, "Deuteronomistically Inspired Scribal Insertions," 494: "4QJudg[a] witnesses to the short, original text of this passage in Judges during the late Second Temple period, whereas some scribe added a deuteronomistically inspired insertion into a variant form of the text which now appears in the MT, the LXX, and all other texts dependent on them." See also R. Sollamo, "Panegyric on Redaction Criticism," in *Houses Full of All Good Things: Essays in Memory of Timo Veijola* (eds. J. Pakkala and M. Nissinen; Publications of the Finnish Exegetical Society 95; Göttingen: Vandenhoeck & Ruprecht, 2008), 684–96 (694): "It is reasonable to assume that the shorter text without this theological pattern represents an earlier edition of the book."

[21] Trebolle Barrera, "Textual Variants," 236–37.

[22] Trebolle Barrera, "Textual Variants," 239.

[23] Trebolle Barrera, "Textual Variants," 239. According to Rezetko, "The Qumran Scrolls of the Book of Judges", Judg 2:7–10 "was a very late addition to the story of Gideon, and it was written in so-called early language" (p. 37). In his view, "the MT is essentially characterized by so-called early language in additions and variants which are derivative and late when compared to the readings in the DSS fragments of Judges" (p. 61).

[24] Hess, "The Dead Sea Scrolls and Higher Criticism of the Hebrew Bible," 122–28; Fernández Marcos, "The Hebrew and Greek Texts of Judges," 1–16.

Ausloos, H., "Literary Criticism and Textual Criticism in Judg 6:1–14 in Light of 4QJudg[a]," OTE 27 (2014): 358–76.

Fernández Marcos, N., "L' Histoire textuelle: Les livres historiques (Juges)," in *L'enfance de la Bible hébraïque: Histoire du texte de l'Ancien Testament* (eds. A. Schenker and P. Hugo; MdB 52; Geneva: Labor et fides, 2005), 148–69.

Fernández Marcos, N., "The Hebrew and Greek Texts of Judges," in Schenker, *Earliest Text, 1–16.

Fernández Marcos, N., *Judges* (*BHQ 7; Stuttgart: Deutsche Bibelgesellschaft, 2011).

---

[25] Hess, "The Dead Sea Scrolls," 126.

[26] See Fernández Marcos, "L' histoire textuelle," 165.

[27] Fernández Marcos, "The Hebrew and Greek Texts of Judges," 16; Fernández Marcos, "L' histoire textuelle," 165; Fernández Marcos, *Judges*, 65–66. According to Rofé, "Studying the Biblical Text in the Light of Historico-Literary Criticism," 121, the minus in 4QJudg[a] is "just an omission due to parablepsis, i.e. the copyist's eye skipped a whole paragraph." Contrary to Fernández Marcos, "The Hebrew and Greek Texts of Judges," 4–5.

[28] Cf. Ausloos, "Literary Criticism and Textual Criticism in Judg 6:1–14 in Light of 4QJudg[a]."

Hess, R., "The Dead Sea Scrolls and Higher Criticism of the Hebrew Bible: The Case of 4QJudg^a," in *The Scrolls and the Scriptures: Qumran Fifty Years After* (eds. S.E. Porter and C.A. Evans; JSPSup 26; Sheffield, Sheffield Academic Press, 1997), 122–28.

Lange, **Handbuch*, 203–11.

Rezetko, R., "The Qumran Scrolls of the Book of Judges: Literary Formation, Textual Criticism, and Historical Linguistics," *Journal of Hebrew Scriptures* 13 (2013): art. #2, 68 pp.; DOI: 10.5508/jhs.2013.v13.a2.

Rofé, A., "Studying the Biblical Text in the Light of Historico-Literary Criticism: The Reproach of the Prophet in Judg 6:7–10 and 4QJudg^a," in *The Dead Sea Scrolls in Context: Integrating the Dead Sea Scrolls in the Study of Ancient Texts, Languages, and Cultures* (eds. A. Lange, E. Tov, and M. Weigold; VTSup 140.1; Leiden: Brill, 2011), 111–23.

Tov, E., "Biblia Hebraica Quinta: Judges," *Sef* 72/2 (2012): 483–89.

Trebolle Barrera, J., "Textual Variants in 4QJudg^a and the Textual and Editorial History of the Book of Judges," *RevQ* 14 (1989): 229–45.

Ulrich, E., "Deuteronomistically Inspired Scribal Insertions into the Developing Biblical Texts: 4QJudg^a and 4QJer^a," in *Houses Full of All Good Things: Essays in Memory of Timo Veijola* (eds. J. Pakkala and M. Nissinen; Publications of the Finnish Exegetical Society 95; Göttingen: Vandenhoeck & Ruprecht, 2008), 489–506.

H. Ausloos

4.2 Ancient Hebrew Texts

4.2.1 Ancient Manuscript Evidence

Four Hebrew manuscripts of the book of Judges survive from antiquity. 1QJudg, 4QJudg^a, and 4QJudg^b were found at Qumran, while XJudg comes from one of the sites around the Dead Sea connected with the Second Jewish War.

4.2.1.1 1QJudg (1Q6)

Forty heavily damaged fragments of 1QJudg (→ 4.2.3.1) survive, of which thirty-one fragments can still be identified.[1] The identifiable fragments of 1QJudg attest to remnants of Judg 1:12–13; 3:8; 5:15–16; 6:15–16, 20–22, 25–26, 39–40?; 9:1–6, 28–35, 38, 40–44, 48–49; 10:7–9; 11:19–22, 24–27, 36–37; 12:15; 13:1; 17:3–4; and 21:7–8.[2] Puech describes 1QJudg paleographically as being written in a late Hasmonean or early Herodian book hand from 50–25 B.C.E.[3] The two supralinear corrections in frgs. 19 2 and 23 2 are *prima manu*. With exceptions, 1QJudg follows MT in its orthography. In 158 complete and partial words, 1QJudg reads once with and ten times against MT (→ 4.2.2),[4] three times with and six times against LXX (→ 4.3), as well as five times non-aligned (→ 4.2.3).[5] Therefore, as 1QJudg is not close to any of the ancient texts, it is best characterized as non-aligned.[6]

4.2.1.2 4QJudg^a (4Q49)

The only surviving fragment of 4QJudg^a (→ 4.2.3.2) attests to remnants of Judg 6:2–6, 11–13. The manuscript was executed in a late Hasmonean or early Herodian book hand between 50–25 B.C.E. The two supralinear corrections in lines 3 and 9 are *prima manu*. In its orthography, 4QJudg^a follows MT but twice reads even more defective than MT.[7] The text-typological classification of 4QJudg^a is debated. In an oral communication, Frank M. Cross stated that "it does reflect the type of text in the better Septuagint tradition."[8] Trebolle Barrera understands 4QJudg^a as a witness to the Hebrew *Vorlage* of the proto-Lucianic recension of the Old Greek text of Judges because of its shorter text and three readings that follow the proto-Lucianic recension.[9] Based on the limited evidence of only forty-four complete and partial preserved words in 4QJudg^a, caution is needed in making such far-reaching interpretations. Based on the lists of variants in the critical editions,[10] 4QJudg^a reads never with but eight times against MT (→ 4.2.2),[11] never with but five times against LXX (→ 4.3), and four times non-aligned. 4QJudg^a also reads once with the proto-Lucianic recension (→ 4.3). Although the small amount of preserved text makes reliable text-typological conclusions impossible, the evidence points towards classifying 4QJudg^a as a non-aligned text.[12] The most important variant reading

---

[1] The *editio princeps* of 1QJudg was only able to identify the text of nine fragments (cf. Barthélemy, "6. Juges," 62–63). Later on, Puech achieved the identification of frgs. 10–14, 16–21, 23, 25–31, 34, 40 (Puech, "manuscrits," 187–200).

[2] That Ulrich included only the nine fragments already identified by Barthélemy in *BQS, 254–58 calls into question this edition in relation to the study of the ancient Hebrew texts of Judges.

[3] Thus Puech, "manuscrits," 187; cf. Barthélemy, "6. Juges," 62.

[4] Two of these readings cannot be reflected in a Greek translation.

[5] For the variant readings of 1QJudg, see Boling, *Judges*, 39–40; Trebolle Barrera, "Judges," 455. For a discussion of the variant readings of 1QJudg in Judges 9, see Rezetko, "Qumran Scrolls," 43–47.

[6] Contra Fernández Marcos, "The Hebrew and the Greek Text," 2–3 nn. 4, 7, who regards the manuscript as proto-Masoretic.

[7] For the description, paleography, and orthography of 4QJudg^a, see Trebolle Barrera, "49. 4QJudg^a," 161–62, and Trebolle Barrera, "Textual Variants," 229–30.

[8] Quoted according to Boling, *Judges*, 40.

[9] Cf. Trebolle Barrera, "Textual Variants," 237–45. For a criticism of Trebolle Barrera's position, see Fernández Marcos, "The Hebrew and the Greek Text," *passim*.

[10] See Trebolle Barrera, "49. 4QJudg^a," 163–64; Ulrich, *BQS, 255. Neither list of variants mentions the LXX reading for Judg 6:4.

[11] Three of these readings cannot be rendered into Greek.

[12] Cf. Tov, *"Synthèse," 20; Tov, *"Biblical Texts," 156. For a discussion of the individual variants in 4QJudg^a, see Rezetko, "Qumran Scrolls," 37–42, and → 4.2.3.

in 4QJudgᵃ is the absence of Judg 6:7–10 in the manuscript. This substantial short text sparked a scholarly debate and will be discussed below (→ 4.2.3). It seems possible that 4QJudgᵃ preserves an early text of the book of Judges that could have originated before its final redaction.¹³

4.2.1.3 4QJudgᵇ (4Q50)

Of 4QJudgᵇ, only two small fragments and one of a larger size are preserved. They attest to remnants of Judg 19:5–7; 21:12–25. The script of 4QJudgᵇ can be classified paleographically as an early Herodian book hand from 30–1 B.C.E.¹⁴ The supralinear correction above frg. 1 4 is *prima manu*. The average line length of frg. 1 is 50–53 letter-spaces, while a reconstruction of frgs. 2–3 according to MT-Judg results in an irregular line length varying between 102 and 144 letter-spaces.

In its orthography, 4QJudgᵇ is close to MT-Judg.¹⁵ In its approximately sixty-seven fully or partially preserved words, 4QJudgᵇ reads only three times against MT.¹⁶ As a result, Fernández Marcos regards the text of 4QJudgᵇ as proto-Masoretic (→ 4.2.2).¹⁷ However, the text-typological classification of 4QJudgᵇ is dependent upon how the differences in the reconstructed line lengths in frgs. 2–3 are explained. There are two possibilities: 1) 4QJudgᵇ attests in frgs. 2–3 to a text that was shorter than that of MT-Judg;¹⁸ or 2) In the last column of 4QJudgᵇ to which frgs. 2–3 belong, the scribe of the manuscript did not feel bound to observe the delimitations of his text block.¹⁹ However, great differences in line length are not common in the final columns of scrolls from the Dead Sea. Furthermore, even the minimal reconstructed line length for frgs. 2–3 (102 letter-spaces) varies so significantly from the average line length of frg. 1 (50–53 letter-spaces), that a shorter text than that of MT-Judg seems to be more likely for the last column of 4QJudgᵇ than any other explanation of the evidence. Because a short text seems rather probable for 4QJudgᵇ in Judg 21:21–25, the manuscript cannot be characterized as proto-Masoretic. A non-aligned text (→ 4.2.3) seems more likely although the small amount of preserved text makes a definite text-typological classification of 4QJudgᵇ impossible.

4.2.1.4 XJudges (X5–7; incl. 4QJudgᶜ [4Q50a])

The seven surviving fragments of XJudg attest to remnants of Judg 1:10–13; 3:23–24; and 4:5–9. The fact that some of these seven fragments are privately owned caused complications in the publication history of XJudg. The most extensive publication to date is by Eshel, Eshel, and Justnes.²⁰ Puech thinks incorrectly that the manuscript was found in Qumran cave 4 and, as a result, calls it 4QJudgᶜ

---

¹³ Cf. Trebolle Barrera, "49. 4QJudgᵃ," 162; Trebolle Barrera, "Textual Variants," 238; Trebolle Barrera, "Judges," 455; Tov, *TCHB*, 313–14; Ulrich, *DSS*, 105–06; Ulrich, "Hebrew Scriptural Texts," 87–88; Ulrich, "Insertions;" Rezetko, "Qumran Scrolls," 10–31. Against Hess, "Higher Criticism," 125–27; A. Rofé, "Studying the Biblical Text in the Light of Historico-Literary Criticism: The Reproach of the Prophet in Judg 6:7–10 and 4QJudgᵃ," in *The Dead Sea Scrolls in Context: Integrating the Dead Sea Scrolls in the Study of Ancient Texts, Languages, and Cultures* (2 vols.; eds. A. Lange et al.; VTSup 140.1–2; Leiden: Brill, 2011), 1.111–23. Fernández Marcos regards the missing text of Judg 6:7–10 in 4QJudgᵃ as an original reading but understands it as the result of a post-Deuteronomistic abbreviation ("The Hebrew and the Greek Text," 5–6; "Genuine Text," 33–34, 39).

¹⁴ For the description and paleography of 4QJudgᵇ, see Trebolle Barrera, "50. 4QJudgᵇ," 165, and Trebolle Barrera, "Edition préliminaire," 79–80 and 87–88.

¹⁵ Cf. Trebolle Barrera, "50. 4QJudgᵇ," 165, and Trebolle Barrera, "Edition préliminaire," 88.

¹⁶ Cf. also the communication of Cross, reported in Boling, *Judges*, 40. For a discussion of these variants, see Rezetko, "Qumran Scrolls," 47–61.

¹⁷ Fernández Marcos, "The Hebrew and the Greek Text," 3.

¹⁸ Cf. Trebolle Barrera, "50. 4QJudgᵇ," 167, and Trebolle Barrera, "Edition préliminaire," 89–95.

¹⁹ Cf. Trebolle Barrera, "Judges," 455.

²⁰ Eshel, Eshel, and Justnes, "XJudg with MS 2861." I am obliged to Esther Eshel and Årstein Justnes who provided me with a preprint copy of their edition. An earlier version of this edition was published by Eshel, Eshel, and Broshi, "A New Fragment of XJudges," *passim*. Some fragments were published originally under a different name by Misgav in the DJD series ("4. XBiblical Text?"; "5. XUnidentified Text 2"). Charlesworth published in *DJD* XXVIII a fragment from the Schøyen Collection that belongs to XJudges (MS Schøyen 2861). The subsequent publication of the individual fragments is also the reason why E. Tov counts them as several Judges manuscripts with different names and numbers in the most recent version of his manuscript catalogue (*Revised Lists*, 109).

(4Q50a).[21] Puech characterizes XJudg paleographically as a middle Herodian hand from the turn of the eras or the first quarter of the first century C.E.[22] Based on more identified fragments, Eshel, Eshel, and Broshi corrected Puech's paleographical classification: "the script of this scroll is either [a] late Herodian formal hand, dated to ca. 50–68 CE … or a post Herodian form hand, ca. 75–135 CE."[23] Based on the latest edition of XJudg,[24] the text of seventy-six complete or partial words from XJudg can still be identified. XJudg displays only two orthographic[25] and no textual variants from MT-Judg (→ 4.2.2). Therefore, although only little text of this scroll is preserved, XJudg can be classified cautiously as proto-Masoretic. The late paleographic date combined with its proto-Masoretic character argue against a Qumran origin.[26] It is more likely that the Bedouin found the fragments of XJudg in one of the caves around the Dead Sea that have a connection to the Second Jewish War[27] but claimed a Qumran origin when they sold them.

Barthélemy, D., "6. Juges," *DJD I: 62–64.
Boling, R.G., *Judges: Introduction, Translation, and Commentary* (AB 6a; New York: Doubleday, 1975), 38–42.
Charlesworth, J.H., "6. XJudges," *DJD XXVIII: 231–33.
Eshel, E., H. Eshel, and M. Broshi, "A New Fragment of XJudges," *DSD* 14 (2007): 354–58.
Eshel, E., H. Eshel, and Å. Justnes, "XJudg with MS 2861 (Judg. 4.5–6)," in *Gleanings*, forthcoming.
Eshel, H., "A Second Fragment of XJudges," *JJS* 53 (2002): 139–41.
Fernández Marcos, N., "The Hebrew and the Greek Text of Judges," in *The Earliest Text of the Hebrew Bible: The Relationship Between the Masoretic Text and the Hebrew Base of the Septuagint Reconsidered* (ed. A. Schenker; SBLSCS 52; Atlanta: SBL, 2003), 1–16.
Fernández Marcos, N., "The Genuine Text of Judges," in *Sôfer Mahîr: Essays in Honour of Adrian Schenker Offered by the Editors of the Biblia Hebraica Quinta* (eds. Y.A.P. Goldman, A. van der Kooij, and R.D. Weis; VTSup 110; Leiden: Brill, 2006), 33–45.
Hess, R.S., "The Dead Sea Scrolls and Higher Criticism of the Hebrew Bible: The Case of 4QJudg^a," in *The Scrolls and the Scriptures: Qumran Fifty Years After* (eds. S.E. Porter and C.A. Evans; JSPSup 26; Sheffield: Sheffield Academic Press, 1997), 122–28.
Lange, A., *Handbuch, 203–11.
Misgav, H., "4. XBiblical Text?," *DJD XXVIII: 227.
Misgav, H., "5. XUnidentified Text 2," *DJD XXVIII: 229.
Puech, É., "Notes sur le manuscrit de *Juges 4Q50a*," *RevQ* 21 (2003–2004): 315–19.
Puech, É., "Les manuscrits 4QJuges^c (= 4Q50 A) et 1QJuges (= 1Q6)," in *Studies in the Hebrew Bible, Qumran, and the Septuagint Presented to Eugene Ulrich* (eds. P.W. Flint, J.C. VanderKam, and E. Tov; VTSup 101; Leiden: Brill, 2006), 184–202.
Rezetko, R., "The Qumran Scrolls of the Book of Judges: Literary Formation, Textual Criticism, and Historical Linguistics," *Journal of Hebrew Scriptures* 13 (2013): http://www.jhsonline.org/Articles/article_182.pdf [cited on October 1, 2013].
Trebolle Barrera, J., "Textual Variants in *4QJudg^a* and the Textual and Historical History of the Book of Judges," *RevQ* 14 (1989–1990): 229–45.
Trebolle Barrera, J., "Edition préliminaire de 4QJuges^b," *RevQ* 15 (1991): 79–100.
Trebolle Barrera, J., "Light from 4QJudg^a and 4QKgs on the Text of Judges and Kings," in *The Dead Sea Scrolls: Forty Years of Research* (eds. D. Dimant and U. Rappaport; STDJ 10; Leiden: Brill, 1992), 315–24.
Trebolle Barrera, J., "49. 4QJudg^a," *DJD XIV: 161–64.
Trebolle Barrera, J., "50. 4QJudg^b," *DJD XIV: 165–69.
Trebolle Barrera, J., "Judges, Book of," *EDSS 1:455.
Ulrich, E., "Deuteronomistically Inspired Scribal Insertions into the Developing Biblical Texts: 4QJudg^a and 4QJer^a," in *Houses Full of All Good Things: Essays in Memory of Timo Veijola* (Publications of the Finnish Exegetical Society 95; Göttingen: Vandenhoeck & Ruprecht, 2008) 489–506.
Ulrich, E., *BQS, 254–58.

Armin Lange

---

[21] Puech, "manuscrits," *passim*; cf. Puech, "notes," *passim*.
[22] Cf. Puech, "notes," 315; Puech, "manuscrits," 183–84.
[23] Eshel, Eshel, and Broshi, "A New Fragment of XJudges," 356. Similar paleographic dates are suggested by Ada Yardeni and Michael Langlois as reported in Eshel, Eshel, and Justnes, "XJudg with MS 2861," forthcoming.
[24] Eshel, Eshel, and Justnes, "XJudg with MS 2861."
[25] In Judg 1:11, XJudg reads יֹשְׁבֵי "inhabitants" instead of MT's יוֹשְׁבֵי and in Judg 4:6 XJudg reads ה[ל]וֹ[א] "did not?" instead of MT's הֲלֹא.
[26] Against Puech, "notes," *passim*; Puech, "manuscrits," 187.
[27] Thus Eshel, Eshel, and Broshi, "A New Fragment of XJudges," 357, and Eshel, Eshel, and Justnes, "XJudg with MS 2861," forthcoming.

4.2.2 Masoretic Texts and Ancient Texts Close to MT

4.2.2.1 History of Research

The earlier narratives incorporated in Judges transmit "the purest and best Hebrew prose style."[1] Scholars generally consider that MT-Judg is the best-preserved text of the historical books,[2] with the exception of the song of Deborah (Judges 5), which poses the same problem as all other instances of ancient Hebrew poetry.[3]

The classical commentaries of Moore (*Judges*, 1895), Budde (*Richter*, 1897), and Burney (*Judges*, 1918) tended to accept variants of the versions, in particular of LXX; they were even open to incorporating conjectures into the text. Since the discovery of the Dead Sea Scrolls, the scholarly discussion has focused on the contribution of the Qumran manuscripts to the textual history of Judges, as well as on the text-critical value of LXX and the old versions for the reconstruction of early stages of the Hebrew text. Scholars today are more aware of the plurality and fluidity with which the biblical texts were transmitted until early in the Common Era.[4] On the other hand, there is a resistance to correcting MT from the testimony of the versions. The LXX version (→ 4.3) and all the witnesses of Judges, with the exception of 4QJudg^a (→ 4.2.1.2; → 4.3.1.2), go back to a Hebrew *Vorlage* that is slightly different from but typologically similar to MT. However (proto-)MT is not to be confused with the textual form attested by the Hebrew *Vorlage* of LXX. MT has preserved the great majority of the preferred readings.[5] In this regard, MT is close to the supposed *Urtext* of Judges. With some differences by each scholar, these are the predominant positions in commentaries and studies of the last decades. This is reflected in the evolution of the editions of the *Biblia Hebraica*: *BH*³ (1937), *BHS* (1972), and *BHQ* (2011), as well as in the commentaries by Boling (*Judges*, 1975), Soggin (*Judges*, 1981), Barthélemy (*Critique textuelle 1982*), Gross (*Richter*, 2009), Butler (*Judges*, 2009), and Webb (*Judges*, 2012).

4.2.2.2 Manuscripts and Editions

MT-Judg is transmitted in the medieval manuscripts and with particular care in the great Tiberian codices of Leningrad (MT^L), Aleppo (MT^A), and Cairo (MT^C). Two Qumran manuscripts preserve text that can be considered close to MT: XJudg (x6; → 4.2.1.4) and, with some doubts, 4QJudg^b (→ 4.2.1.3).

The *BHQ* edition of Judges[6] improves considerably the previous one in the *BHS*. It presents a diplomatic edition of the text and Masorah of MT^L, a single critical apparatus with a full collation of the Qumran fragments, and a commentary in which the factors that have been influential in the generation of variants are discussed. *BHQ* introduces some modifications regarding the stichography shown in *BHS*. In Judges 5, it follows the traditional page layout of the Leningrad Codex and considers Judg 9:7–15; 14:14, 18; 15:16; and 16:23–24 as prose according to the layout in MT^L, MT^A, and MT^C.

4.2.2.3 The Text-Critical Character of MT

In the history of (proto-)MT, accidental changes occurred in the transmission of the book:

– Haplography by homoioteleuton: in Judg 16:13–14, MT lost between the first and second הַמַּסָּכֶת "the warp" a sentence preserved in LXX that is "indispensable for the comprehension of the narrative, together with the phrase at the beginning of v. 14" (*BHQ*).[7] Similarly, in Judg 19:30, MT

---

[1] S.R. Driver, *An Introduction to the Literature of the Old Testament* (rev. ed; New York: Charles Scribner's Sons, 1914), 505, and 123–26; J. Wellhausen, *Prolegomena to the History of Israel* (repr. of 1885 ed.; Atlanta: Scholars Press, 1994), 9.

[2] Fernández Marcos, *Judges* 4*; Moore, *Judges*, xliii–xlvii; Soggin, *Judges*, 67–69.

[3] T. Mayfield, "The Accounts of Deborah (Judges 4–5) in Recent Research," *Currents in Biblical Research* 7 (2009): 306–35.

[4] Tov, *TCHB*, 166 n. 24 and 297–98.

[5] Fernández Marcos, "Genuine Text," 33–46.

[6] Fernández Marcos, *Judges*.

[7] Cf. Moore, *Judges*, 345; Burney, *Judges*, 380–81; Boling, *Judges*, 249–50; Soggin, *Judges*, 220; Barthélemy, *Critique textuelle 1982*, 112.

4.2.2 Masoretic Texts and Ancient Texts Close to MT

suffered haplography of a sentence preserved in LXX, VL, and Josephus by homoioteleuton between the first and second עַד הַיּוֹם הַזֶּה "until today."[8] In Judg 18:22, before וְהָאֲנָשִׁים, "and the men," BHK and BHS suggest the insertion of וּמִיכָה ['and Micah'], which could have been lost by homtel."[9]

– Dittography: in Judg 1:19, the reading of MT לֹא לְהוֹרִישׁ "he could not drive out" could be a case of dittography of the ל with the preceding לֹא.[10]

– Confusion between similar letters: the reading הָאֱמֹרִי "the Amorites" of MT in Judg 1:36 is probably to be restored to האדמי "the Edomites" (cf. LXX and VL) in accordance with Num 34:4 and Josh 1:36; 15:3 as a case of textual corruption (ר for ד) and metathesis.[11]

– Scribal error: in Judg 8:16, MT וַיֹּדַע (unusual form with uncertain meaning) is probably a scribal error for a proto-MT reading וידשׁ "and he disciplined";[12] in Judg 12:7, many scholars prefer the reading בעירו בצפה "in his city in Ṣepeh" attested by Old Greek and Josephus to MT's בְּעָרֵי "in the cities of" that would constitute a spelling error after the loss of בצפה.[13]

Different types of deliberate changes are also found in (proto-)MT:

– Corrections for moral or theological reasons: in Judg 18:30, the MT reading מְנַשֶּׁה "Manasseh" is theologically influenced and should be restored to משה "Moses";[14] in Judg 1:16, the words את העמלקי "the Amalekites" were eliminated from MT for theological reasons based on Deut 25:19.[15]

– Harmonizations: in Judg 1:13, מִמֶּנּוּ "than he" (> OG), is a gloss taken by harmonization from Judg 3:9;[16] in Judg 18:14, לַיִשׁ "Laish" (> Old Greek and VL) is a possible gloss harmonizing with v. 7.[17]

– Additions and glosses: common additions are Judg 7:4 כֹּל "all" (7:4 > OG; 8:10[1°] > OG) and additions of the name of a subject (Judg 3:8 בְּנֵי־יִשְׂרָאֵל "The children of Israel" > OG; 6:13 יְהוָה [2° "the Lord"] > OG; Judg 3:27 מִן־הָהָר "from the hill" > OG). Other additions make more explicit the site of an action: In Judg 1:16, the name "Yehudah" (יְהוּדָה [2°] > OG) is repeated; similarly in Judg 13:20 the reading הַמִּזְבֵּחַ (2° "the altar" > OG) is a repetition of the previous הַמִּזְבֵּחַ. In Judg 13:23, the word וְכָעֵת "and now" (> OG, VL) should probably be omitted "on the basis of the textual support of G and V."[18] In Judg 1:21, בִּירוּשָׁלִָם "in Jerusalem" and in Judg 5:8 בְּיִשְׂרָאֵל "In Israel" seem to be additions absent in Old Greek and VL.[19] In Judg 8:35, גִּדְעוֹן "that is Gideon" is missing in Old Greek and VL. In Judg 11:11, הָעָם "the people" (> OG and VL) may be a gloss given that "the elders" is the subject throughout the story. In Judg 6:25, 26 (הַשֵּׁנִי, "the second"; > OG), the shorter text is perhaps to be preferred, even if it is not the *lectio difficilior*.[20] In Judg 15:10 (עָלִינוּ לַעֲשׂוֹת "we have come up to do"; עָלִינוּ > VL = OG), "the cj. in G V S may reflect a different *Vorlage*,"[21] the shorter pre-Masoretic text being "to bind Samson and to do to him ...," as attested by VL's *Alligare Samson ascendimus et facere illi quemadmodum fecit nobis* "We went up to tie Samson and do to him as he did to us." Other additions are בּוֹ 1° in Judg 9:38 ("with them"; > OG) and Judg 14:12

---

[8] Moore, *Judges*, 421; Burney, *Judges*, 470; Soggin, *Judges*, 247; Barthélemy, **Critique textuelle 1982*, 120.

[9] Fernández Marcos, *Judges*, 103*.

[10] Soggin, *Judges*, 24.

[11] Soggin, *Judges*, 25.

[12] Moore, *Judges*, 225–26; Burney, *Judges*, 233; Soggin, *Judges*, 136.

[13] Moore, *Judges*, 309–10; Burney, *Judges*, 329; Schreiner, *Septuaginta-Massora*, 40–41; Boling, *Judges*, 329; Barthélemy, **Critique textuelle 1982*, 106.

[14] Moore, *Judges*, 401–02; Burney, *Judges*, 434; Schreiner, *Septuaginta-Massora*, 43; Boling, *Judges*, 265; Barthélemy, **Critique textuelle 1982*, 115.

[15] Burney, *Judges*, 17; Soggin, *Judges*, 24; Barthélemy, **Critique textuelle 1982*, 73.

[16] Lindars, *Judges 1–5*, 28.

[17] Schreiner, *Septuaginta-Massora*, 34.

[18] Fernández Marcos, *Judges*, 91*.

[19] Lindars, *Judges 1–5*, 289.

[20] Soggin, *Judges*, 124; Barthélemy, **Critique textuelle 1982*, 91–94.

[21] Fernández Marcos, *Judges*, 94*.

וּמְצָאתֶם "and you will find" (> OG and VL).[22] In Judg 7:13, וַיַּכֵּהוּ וַיִּפֹּל וַיַּהַפְכֵהוּ לְמַעְלָה וְנָפַל הָאֹהֶל "and it struck it, and it fell; and it turned upside down and the tent fell" (> OG) "appears redundant in MT."[23] In my opinion, וַיַּהַפְכֵהוּ לְמַעְלָה "and it turned upside down" is a gloss inserted by the repetition (*Wiederaufnahme*) of וַיִּפֹּל ... וְנָפַל. VL reflects this short text: *et percussit illud, et cecidit tabernaculum* "and it struck it and it hit the tent."

- Conflate readings: Judg 11:31 הַיּוֹצֵא "the one coming out" (> OG and VL), followed by אֲשֶׁר יֵצֵא "who comes out." In Judg 20:45, MT גִּדְעֹם (*gid'om*) is a mixture of two readings: the place name גבעון attested by the Syriac *gib'ôn* and the verbal form ידע present in Judg 21:6 ("has been defeated").[24] Double readings in MT or LXX and particularly in LXX[L] and VL may help to identify the process that led to the formation of the different texts (MT and the LXX *Vorlage*). Such a process is frequently tied to interpolations that caused duplicates or alternative variants. A case in point is Judg 6:32 where the explanation of the name "Jerubaal" present in MT לֵאמֹר יָרֶב בּוֹ הַבַּעַל "[Joash named him Jerubbaal], saying, 'Let Baal plead his cause against him'" was ignored in the Old Greek *Vorlage* as attested by LXX[AL] and VL.
- In Judg 1:14, the MT reading וַתְּסִיתֵהוּ "she prompted him" is obviously wrong, but the emendation to ויסיתה "he [Othniel] prompted her" does not appear completely free from doubt either.[25] In Judg 3:13, the plural of MT וַיִּירְשׁוּ "and they took possession" is to be corrected to the singular of LXX, VL, and the Vulgate; only a protagonist is mentioned in the story and the other verbs in the sentence are in the singular. The statement in Judg 4:1, וְאֵהוּד מֵת "and Ehud died" (> OG) might be out of place here and belong instead at the end of Judg 3:30.

---

[22] Burney, *Judges*, 361.
[23] Fernández Marcos, *Judges*, 70*.
[24] Moore, *Judges*, 444; Burney, *Judges*, 486–87; Boling, *Judges*, 283; Barthélemy, *Critique textuelle 1982*, 126.
[25] Soggin, *Judges*, 22.

The text of MT-Judg remains a *crux* in cases where the critics tend to introduce different conjectures, although MT seems to be preferred as *lectio difficilior*. Examples include MT-Judg 6:25–26 אֶת־פַּר־הַשּׁוֹר ... הַשֵּׁנִי "the young bull ... the second"; MT-Judg 7:3 הַגִּלְעָד "Gilead"; MT-Judg 7:6 בְּיָדָם אֶל־פִּיהֶם "with their hands to their mouths"; MT-Judg 7:22 מֵאוֹת "hundred"; MT-Judg 9:24 לָבוֹא "so that may come." *BHQ* gives preference to the supposed Old Greek *Vorlage* or other versions in Judg 3:28; 4:13, 20; 5:5, 13; 8:16; 12:7; 13:12, 21; 16:14; 18:24; 19:11, 30; and 20:45.

MT can neither be considered a text especially affected by scribal errors nor a harmonizing text, although we may find instances of harmonization in Judg 1:13 and 18:14. In addition, the above cases of additions, glosses, and conflate readings do not allow us to characterize MT as a particularly long text. However, the addition of MT-Judg 6:7–10, missing in 4QJudg[a], leads us to assume that the book knew an editorial stage in which this literary unit was not included (→ 4.2.2.5).

4.2.2.4 Date and Milieu

The differences between MT and LXX at the end of Joshua and the beginning of Judges demonstrate that several Dtr sections were added as successive prologues to the book of Judges. Circles of Deuteronomistic and priestly tradition certainly contributed to the final shape of the book. The stories of Judges seem to be very old in character. Their text was certainly transmitted in more variant forms than those preserved in the Dead Sea Scrolls, MT, and LXX. The textual variants identified above were introduced at different times and it is impossible to date them precisely or to situate them in a specific milieu of origin. However, most of MT's secondary readings go back to the Second Temple period. The variants correspond to the usual activity of scribes, who slightly modified the text to make it more intelligible or to add details such as "in Jerusalem," "in Israel," "the children of Israel," "Yehudah," "from the hill," etc. Only a few scribal corruptions such as וַיֵּדַע (uncertain translation) in Judg 8:16 occurred at a later point in time in the transmission of MT-Judg.

The text of Judges remained in a state of relative fluidity until as late as the early Herodian period (50–25 B.C.E.), as attested by the omission of Judg 6:7–10 and other variants in 4QJudg^a (→ 4.2.1.2; → 4.3.1.2). However, around the years 30–1 B.C.E., consonantal proto-MT seems to be fixed as attested by 4QJudg^b (→ 4.2.1.3) while, in the years 50–135 C.E., XJudg (X6; → 4.2.1.4) attests to the transition of the fixed proto-MT.

4.2.2.5 Relevance for Literary Analysis

The differences between MT and LXX as well as the omission of Judg 6:7–10 in 4QJudg^a (see → 4.2.3.2) have fueled the discussion regarding the possible existence of two textual forms or editions of Judges. Among features that vary from book to book, these textual forms or editions of a given book differ mainly due to the addition of prologues and appendices and the different order of the materials in the book. Judges has several connections with Joshua that correspond to the different endings of Joshua and different beginnings of Judges. Rofé noted that LXX-Josh 24:33a, b is connected to Judg 3:12, skipping the largely Dtr passages of Judg 1:1–3:11.[26] In fact, LXX-Josh 24:33b contains three different links to Judges: with Judg 2:6 ("they went to their own inheritances"); Judg 2:11–13 ("they worshipped the gods of the surrounding peoples"); and Judg 3:12–14 (the story of Eglon/Ehud).[27] Each link corresponds to the beginning of material that was added at the start of the book. The large duplicate of Josh 24:28, 31, 29–30 (according to the sequence in LXX) in Judg 2:6–9 establishes also a link that skips Judg 1:1–2:5. Literary criticism has identified another ending in Joshua 23 (Dtr) that also joins with Judg 2:6.[28] Finally, Josh 21:43–45 seems to be an ancient ending of Joshua connected with Judg 2:8–10*.[29] The Antiochene Greek text (→ 3–5.1.6.1) contains in Judg 2:10 a plus that repeats Judg 3:5–6a. This linking repetition delimits the insertion of Judg 2:11–3:4 ascribed to (a) Deuteronomistic redaction(s).

The parallel texts of Josh 24:28 and Judg 2:6 allow us to know how this sentence evolved in three phases, from the briefest text to the longest: "Joshua sent the people, each to his inheritance" (MT-Josh 24:28 וַיְשַׁלַּח יְהוֹשֻׁעַ אֶת־הָעָם אִישׁ לְנַחֲלָתוֹ) → "Joshua sent the people and they went each to his place" (LXX-Josh 24:28 καὶ ἀπέστειλεν Ἰησοῦς τὸν λαόν, καὶ ἐπορεύθησαν ἕκαστος εἰς τὸν τόπον αὐτοῦ) → "Joshua sent the people and the Israelites went each to his inheritance" (MT+LXX-Judg 2:6 וַיְשַׁלַּח יְהוֹשֻׁעַ אֶת־הָעָם וַיֵּלְכוּ בְנֵי־יִשְׂרָאֵל אִישׁ לְנַחֲלָתוֹ). The textual tradition of Judges shows here, as in many other instances in the historical books, a tendency to introduce the reading "Israel/the Israelites" in different combinations with "people" into the text. In Judg 20:22, LXX reads ἀνὴρ Ἰσραήλ "the men of Israel" against the longer reading of MT הָעָם אִישׁ יִשְׂרָאֵל "the people, the men of Israel." According to *BHS and *BHQ, הָעָם "the people" is a superfluous gloss. However, אִישׁ יִשְׂרָאֵל "the men of Israel" could be a secondary juxtaposition to a previous short reading הָעָם "the people" (cf. the variants in Judg 20:2, 25). Throughout Judges 20, the focus of the narrative oscillates between "the people" and "the Israelites" or "the community." This oscillation is due to the complexity of the composition and transmission process of this text, in which different traditions regarding the battle between the "armies/peoples" of the Benjaminites and Israelites converge (cf. *supra*). The tendency of the textual transmission to introduce the reading "Israel/the Israelites" continues a similar one detected by literary critics: actions led by "the people/the troops" of one or several tribes were later attributed to all the tribes of "Israel" or to "all Israel."[30] Thus the story of Ehud evolved within

---

[26] Rofé, "End of the Book of Joshua," 17–36.

[27] J. Trebolle Barrera, "Samuel/Kings and Chronicles: Book Division and Text Composition," in *Studies in the Hebrew Bible, Qumran, and the Septuagint Presented to Eugene Ulrich* (eds. P.W. Flint, E. Tov, and J.C. VanderKam; VTSup 101; Leiden: Brill, 2006), 96–108.

[28] H.N. Rösel, *Von Joshua bis Jojachin: Untersuchungen zu den deuteronomistischen Geschichtsbüchern des Alten Testaments* (VTSup 75; Leiden: Brill, 1999), 49–58; H.N. Rösel, "Die Überleitungen von Josua- ins Richterbuch," *VT* 30 (1980): 342–50.

[29] Blum, "Der kompositionelle Knoten," 181–212; U. Becker, *Richterzeit und Königtum: Redaktionsgeschichte Studien zum Richterbuch* (BZAW 192; Berlin: De Gruyter, 1990), 68–72.

[30] J. Trebolle Barrera, "Textual Variants in Joshua-Kings

the geographical borders of Benjamin (Judg 3:12–20), but later on the mention of "the Israelites" in the interpolated vv. 27–28 transformed a skirmish into a total war and, finally, the Deuteronomistic setting of vv. 12, 14, and 29 gave a "pan-Israelite" perspective to the story.[31] The literary formation of the book and its textual transmission form a continuum that requires a joint analysis of textual and literary criticism.

In Judg 12:4–5, "there are different kinds of omissions in the rendering of v. 4, some of them accidental by homtel., others probably intentional."[32] In my opinion, a literary development that entered into the (proto-)masoretic textual tradition corresponds to the omission in the Old Greek.[33] In Judg 20:19–31, a joint analysis of textual and literary criticism helps to explain the duplicates present in the text as a consequence of combining two versions of the story.

The book of Judges has three different endings. The present one comes after the "appendices" of Judges 17–21, framed by the duplicate of Judg 17:6 and 21:25. A previous ending at Judg 16:31 ("he judged Israel for twenty years") is marked by the presence of the small unit on Shamgar, the judge of Judah, in the Old Greek (LXX^L and VL). This is a mobile unit inserted into a book that includes only the judges of the northern tribes. It appears in Judg 3:31 in MT, but it is also located in Judg 16:31 in Old Greek. This unit is better placed at the end of Judges 16 because of the common reference to the Philistines rather than in Judges 3, where it interrupts the succession of the narratives of Judges 3 and 4. Another ending of the book may be Judg 15:20, parallel to Judg 16:31. All these links at the beginning and the end of the book can only be explained by supposing a complex editorial process attested differently by MT and LXX.[34] The omission of Judg 6:7–10 in 4QJudg^a can be seen as a further indication that the book of Judges was known in literary forms that were different from our traditional texts in the Second Temple period (cf. → 4.2.3).

Auld, A.G., "Joshua: The Hebrew and Greek Texts," in *Studies in the Historical Books of the Old Testament* (ed. J.A. Emerton; VTSup 30; Leiden: Brill, 1979), 9–14.
Barthélemy, D., *Critique textuelle 1982*.
Blum, E., "Der kompositionelle Knoten am Übergang von Joshua zu Richter: Ein Entflechtungsvorschlag," in *Deuteronomy and Deuteronomic Literature: Festschrift C.H.W. Brekelmans* (eds. M. Vervenne and L. Lust; BETL 133; Leuven: Peeters, 1997), 181–212.
Boling, R.G., *Judges: Introduction, Translation, and Commentary* (AB 6/1; Garden City: Doubleday, 1975).
Budde, K., *Das Buch der Richter* (KHC 7; Freiburg i.B.: Mohr, 1897).
Burney, C.F., *The Book of Judges: With Introduction and Notes* (London: Rivingtons, 1918).
Butler, T.C., *Judges* (WBC 8; Nashville: Thomas Nelson, 2009).
Fernández Marcos, N., "The Genuine Text of Judges," in *Sôfer Mahîr: Essays in Honour of Adrian Schenker Offered by Editors of Biblia Hebraica Quinta* (eds. Y.A.P. Goldman, A. van der Kooij, and R.D. Weis; VTSup 117; Leiden: Brill, 2006), 33–46.
Fernández Marcos, N., *Judges* (*BHQ 7; Stuttgart: Deutsche Bibelgesellschaft, 2011).
Frolov, S., "Joshua's Double Demise (Josh. xxiv 28–31; Judg. ii 6–9): Making Sense of a Repetition," *VT* 58 (2008): 315–23.
Gray, J., *Joshua, Judges and Ruth* (New Century Bible Commentary; Grand Rapids: Eerdmans, 1986).
Gross, W., *Richter: Übersetzt und ausgelegt* (HTKAT; Freiburg: Herder, 2009).
Hess, R.S., "The Dead Sea Scrolls and Higher Criticism of the Hebrew Bible: The Case of 4QJudg^a," in *The Scrolls and the Scriptures: Qumran Fifty Years After* (eds. S.E. Porter and C.A. Evans; JSPSup 26; Sheffield: Sheffield Academic Press, 1997), 122–28 (126–27).

Involving the Terms 'People' and 'Israel'," in *In the Footsteps of Sherlock Holmes: Studies in the Biblical Text in Honour of Anneli Aejmelaeus* (eds. K. De Troyer, T.M. Law, and M. Liljeström; CBET 72; Leuven: Peeters, 2014), 231–56.

[31] Soggin, *Judges*, 53–54 and 206.
[32] Fernández Marcos, *Judges*, 89*.
[33] J. Trebolle Barrera, "Textual Variants in 4QJudg^a," 241; Barthélemy, *Critique textuelle 1982*, 105.

---

[34] Tov, *TCHB*, 297–98; D.M. Carr, *The Formation of the Hebrew Bible: A New Reconstruction* (Oxford: Oxford University Press, 2011), 282–85, cf. also op. cit. 171–72, 244–45, 290–91.

Lindars, B., *Judges 1–5: A New Translation and Commentary* (ed. A.D.H. Mayes; Edinburgh: T & T Clark, 1995).

Lucassen, B., "Josua, Richter und CD," *RevQ* 18 (1998): 373–96.

Moore, G.F., *A Critical and Exegetical Commentary on Judges* (6th imprint; ICC 7; Edinburgh: T & T Clark, 1949).

Rezetko, R., "The Qumran Scrolls of the Book of Judges: Literary Formation, Textual Criticism, and Historical Linguistics," *Journal of Hebrew Scriptures* 13 (2013): 1–68.

Rofé, A., "The End of the Book of Joshua According to the Septuagint," *Hen* 4 (1982): 17–36.

Schreiner, J., *Septuaginta-Massora des Buches der Richter* (AnBib 7; Rome: Pontificio Istituto Biblico, 1957).

Soggin, J.A., *Judges: A Commentary* (OTL; London: SCM Press, 1981).

Tov, *TCHB, 297–98.

Trebolle Barrera, J., "Textual Variants in 4QJudg[a] and the Textual and Editorial History of the Book of Judges," *RevQ* 14 (1989–1990): 231–45.

Webb, B.G., *The Book of Judges* (NICOT; Grand Rapids: Eerdmans, 2012).

Julio Trebolle Barrera

4.2.3 Other Texts

The Qumran manuscripts 1QJudg (1Q6) and, in particular, 4QJudg[a] (4Q49) represent texts independent of the Masoretic tradition, with elements close to the LXX *Vorlage* and to the VL version.

4.2.3.1 The Text of 1QJudg

1QJudg (→ 4.2.2.1) is, in Tov's judgment, too short for analysis.[1] According to Fernández Marcos, it follows "with small, secondary variants, the Masoretic Text."[2] However, the number and quality of the variants that are found in fragments as small as those of this manuscript seem rather to suggest a certain independent nature.[3] In Judg 9:42, 1QJudg has

---

[1] E. Tov, "The Significance of the Texts from the Judean Desert for the History of the Text of the Hebrew Bible: A New Synthesis," in *Qumran Between the Old and New Testaments* (eds. F.H. Cryer and T.L. Thompson; JSOTSup 290; Sheffield: Sheffield Academic Press, 1998), 277–309 (305).

[2] Fernández Marcos, "Hebrew and Greek Texts," 2 n. 4.

[3] Thus Lange, *Handbuch*, 203.

ויגד with LXX ἀπηγγέλη "he reported." This reading should be preferred as the *lectio difficilior* instead of MT's וַיַּגִּדוּ "they reported," facilitated by plural contextual elements. In Judg 9:29, 1QJudg presents the plural ויאמרו "they said" attested by VL and the Vulgate, but the singular of MT וַיֹּאמֶר "he said" seems to be the *lectio difficilior*. In Judg 9:31, this manuscript reads והמה "and they" against MT's וְהִנָּם "and behold, they" as well as על instead of MT's אֶת. The Qumran reading והמה is reflected by the Old Greek represented by LXX[AL] καὶ οἴδε while the *kaige* text of LXX[B] καὶ ἰδοὺ αὐτοί corresponds to MT's וְהִנָּם. 1QJudg seems here secondary and facilitating as compared with MT. In Judg 9:40, 1QJudg reads וירדפם "and he routed them" instead of MT's וירדפהו "and he routed him" and שער העיר "at the gate of the city" instead of MT's פֶּתַח הַשָּׁעַר "at the entrance of the gate." The Old Greek (LXX[AL]) reads with 1QJudg but in the plural: θυρῶν τῆς πόλεως "at the gates of the city." MT and 1QJudg (cf. LXX) seem to be two alternative readings (conflated in vv. 35 and 44). At the end of Judg 9:30, 1QJudg adds מאד "very" with the Vulgate and the Arabic version, a probable secondary reading. Before Judg 9:42, 1QJudg presents a *vacat* that does not correspond to any masoretic division. Puech notes the presence or absence of *vacats* that frequently do not have correspondence with those of the Masoretic tradition.[4] This variation is also a sign of a certain independence from the tradition of MT.

4.2.3.2 The Text of 4QJudg[a]

4QJudg[a] (→ 4.2.1.2; → 4.1.3) is the only extant witness that does not include the literary unit found in Judg 6:7–10 in MT (→ 4.2.2) and LXX (→ 4.3), although Hebrew manuscripts and the *kaige* LXX[B] text also omit v. 7a. Verses 8–10 have been generally recognized by modern critics as a literary insertion, attributed in the past to an Elohistic source and now generally considered a piece of early Dtr redaction (Dtr[1]),[5] late "nomistic" redac-

---

[4] Puech, "Les manuscrits," 194.

[5] R.G. Boling, *Judges: Introduction, Translation, and Commentary* (AB 6a; New York: Doubleday, 1975), 125.

tion (DtrN),[6] or post-Dtr.[7] The absence of Judg 6:7–10 in 4QJudg[a] has provoked an important discussion. This debate is linked with a larger one concerning the existence of different textual forms or editions of this book: 4QJudg[a] is "manifestly non-aligned, and actually independent" and "may reflect a different literary edition."[8] "4QJudg[a] displays, if not an earlier edition of the entire book of Judges, at least an 'earlier literary form' for this passage."[9] Trebolle claimed that the text form represented by 4QJudg[a] ignores a late literary development made of juxtaposed Dtr formulas that entered into the masoretic textual tradition.[10] According to Ulrich, this manuscript contains an early form of the text, which was secondarily expanded by a late addition attested in our surviving manuscript tradition.[11] Hess refers to "the [small] size of the fragment" and suggests that it "is part of a larger manuscript that ... may have been a collection of biblical texts serving a particular liturgical purpose for the community who read it."[12] According to Hess, it is unlikely that the minus in 4QJudg[a] is related either to inadvertent loss due to haplography or to intentional omission for theological reasons.

But observing that Judg 6:7–10 is placed between *petuḥot* in MT[A], MT[C], and MT[L], Hess attributes the omission in 4QJudg[a] to "a tendency to insert, omit and change sections or paragraphs of biblical text at what would become the Masoretic *parashoth* divisions of text."[13] Fernández Marcos supports Hess' arguments and sustains that there is not "sufficient textual evidence to postulate two editions or different literary strata for the book of Judges."[14] According to Fernández Marcos, the omission "does not belong to an original stage of the book but it constitutes an accidental or intentional abbreviation";[15] it may "represent a late, secondary abbreviation for liturgical or other purposes."[16] Several authors quote the opinion of Hess.[17] O'Connell states that "a scribe may have been motivated deliberately to omit 6:7–10" since "[s]uch a prophetic condemnation from YHWH is hardly flattering to the scribe's nation."[18] According to Rofé, the minus in 4QJudg[a] is simply an accidental omission due to parablepsis; MT-Judg 6:7–10 is not post-Deuteronomistic, or even Deuteronomistic, but actually pre-Deuteronomistic: a text written in the eighth century B.C.E.[19] On the contrary, following Sollamo "it is reasonable to assume that the shorter text without this theological pattern represents an earlier edition of the book."[20] In the opinion of Rezetko, "the shorter 4QJudg[a] does indeed repre-

---

[6] R. Smend, "Das Gesetz und die Völker: Ein Beitrag zur deuteronomistischen Redaktionsgeschichte," in *Probleme biblischer Theologie: Gerhard von Rad zum 70. Geburtstag* (ed. H.W. Wolff; Munich: Chr. Kaiser, 1971), 494–509; R. Smend, *Die Entstehung des Alten Testaments* (Stuttgart: W. Kohlhammer, 1989), 116; W. Dietrich, *Prophetie und Geschichte: Eine redaktionsgeschichtliche Untersuchung zum deuteronomistischen Geschichtswerk* (FRLANT 108; Göttingen: Vandenhoeck & Ruprecht, 1972), 133; T. Veijola, *Das Königtum in der Beurteilung der deuteronomistischen Historiographie: Eine redaktionsgeschichtliche Untersuchung* (Helsinki: Suomalainen Tiedeakatemia, 1977), 43–48; J.A. Soggin, *Judges: A Commentary* (OTL; London: SCM Press, 1981), 112.

[7] A.F. Campbell and M.A. O'Brien, *Unfolding the Deuteronomistic History: Origins, Upgrades, Present Text* (Minneapolis: Fortress, 2000), 183; U. Becker, *Richterzeit und Königtum: Redaktionsgeschichtle Studien zum Richterbuch* (BZAW 192; Berlin: De Gruyer, 1990), 144–45; Gross, *Richter*, 369–70, 389, and 396.

[8] Tov, *"Biblical Texts," 156.

[9] Ulrich, "Scribal Insertions," 492.

[10] Trebolle, "Textual Variants," 238.

[11] Ulrich, "Multiple Literary Editions," 105; Ulrich, "Scribal Insertions," 490–94 and 504–06.

[12] Hess, "Higher Criticism," 124 and 127.

[13] Hess, "Higher Criticism," 126–27.

[14] Fernández Marcos, "Hebrew and Greek Texts," 16.

[15] Fernández Marcos, "Genuine Text," 42.

[16] Fernández Marcos, "Hebrew and Greek Texts," 16.

[17] E. Assis, *Self-Interest or Communal Interest: An Ideology of Leadership in the Gideon, Abimelech and Jephthah Narratives (Judg 6–12)* (VTSup 106; Leiden: Brill, 2005), 22 n. 17; T.C. Butler, *Judges* (WBC 8; Nashville: Thomas Nelson, 2009), xli and 185; Martin, "Intrusive Prophet," 114 n. 2; G.T.K. Wong, *Compositional Strategy of the Book of Judges: An Inductive, Rhetorical Study* (VTSup 111; Leiden: Brill, 2006), 183 n. 118.

[18] R.H. O'Connell, *The Rhetoric of the Book of Judges* (VTSup 63; Leiden: Brill, 1996), 147 n. 178.

[19] Rofé, "Studying the Biblical Text," 121–22.

[20] R. Sollamo, "Panegyric on Redaction Criticism," in *Houses Full of All Good Things: Essays in Memory of Timo Veijola* (eds. J. Pakkala and M. Nissinen; Publications of the Finnish Exegetical Society 95; Göttingen: Vandenhoeck & Ruprecht, 2008), 684–96 (694).

sent an earlier literary edition of 6:2–13 than does the longer MT."[21]

In Judg 6:5, 4QJudg[a] and the Old Greek (LXX[AL], VL) read the *hiphil* יב(י)או "they brought." The *Ketiv* of MT יבאו "they came" is closer to the reading of 4QJudg[a] and Old Greek than the *Qere* ובאו "and they came." In view of the witnesses' support, the *Ketiv* should probably be preferred.[22] Also in Judg 6:5, the reading of 4QJudg[a] ולהם אין מספר "and they could not be numbered" is shorter than MT's וְלָהֶם וְלִגְמַלֵּיהֶם אֵין מִסְפָּר "and they and their camels could not be numbered." The short reading is reflected in VL *quorum* (*quoniam* Lucifer) *non erat numeros* "which could not be numbered." Spatial reconstruction suggests that וגמליהם "and their camels" was included before יבאו in agreement with the Old Greek represented by the Antiochean text: τὰς σκηνὰς αὐτῶν παρέφερον καὶ τὰς καμήλους αὐτῶν ἦγον (יב[י]או; "they brought their tents and they brought their camels").[23] The issue is not so much whether or not MT should be corrected but the reconstruction of the formation process of the various texts. In my opinion, the double reading in LXX[L] and VL ἦγον (OG = יב[י]או) and καὶ παρεγίνοντο (*kaige* = ובאו) reflects two alternative Hebrew readings: יבאו ואהליהם יב(י)או / וגמליהם "they brought their tents" / "they brought their camels." MT and 4QJudg[a] adopted these alternative readings in different ways: 4QJudg[a] ואהליהם וגמליהם יבאו ... ולהם אין מספר "they brought their tents and their camels ... and they could not be numbered"; MT וְאָהֳלֵיהֶם יָבֹאוּ ... וְלָהֶם וְלִגְמַלֵּיהֶם אֵין מִסְפָּר "they brought their tents ... and they and their camels could not be numbered." The alteration between verbal forms that express permanent situations and narrate particular events has suggested different proposals in literary criticism.[24] The older and shorter form of the text may have read כי הם ומקניהם יעלו ויבאו בארץ "for they and their livestock came up and came into the land"; the sequence יעלו ויבאו is frequent in the Hebrew narrative. This accumulation of variants is due to a plurality of textual forms, whose explanation involves a joint exercise of textual criticism and literary criticism. Moreover, the agreements of 1QJudg and 4QJudg[a] with readings of the Antiochian text and VL highlight the importance of these witnesses that preserve the oldest Greek textual tradition for the textual history of this book, and for the establishment of a still-pending critical edition of LXX-Judg.

4.2.3.3 Other Texts of Judges Documented in Ancient Quotations

The *Damascus Document* (CD A 5:3–4) refers to events in Josh 24:28–33, all of which are mentioned in LXX (→ 4.3) but only two in MT (→ 4.2.2): the priest Eleazar, his responsibility for the ark and his death, Joshua's death, and the cult of Astaroth by the Israelites. The *Damascus Document* reflects in this way a text similar to the LXX *Vorlage*. The evidence is also important for the overlap between Joshua and Judges as well as for the editorial history of Judges, which resulted in two or more textual forms corresponding to respective editorial interventions.[25] Late evidence can contribute to the study of the text of Judges: An example is Judg 15:16 where instead of MT's חֲמוֹר חֲמֹרָתָיִם "a heap, two heaps," *b. Naz.* 4b presupposes the same reading and exegesis as LXX: חמור חמרתים "[with] a crushing I crushed them."

4.2.3.4 Relevance for Literary Analysis

4QJudg[a] offers new data for a better understanding of the textual history and literary development of Judges. It represents "a form of the text independent from any other known text type, although it shares readings with the pre-Lucianic text and the

---

[21] R. Rezetko, "The Qumran Scrolls of the Book of Judges: Literary Formation, Textual Criticism, and Historical Linguistics," *Journal of Hebrew Scriptures* 13 (2013): 1–68. Similarly, S. McKenzie, *Introduction to the Historical Books: Strategies for Reading* (Grand Rapids: Eerdmans, 2010), 66.

[22] Fernández Marcos, *Judges*, 65*.

[23] Trebolle, "4QJudg[a]," 163; A.V. Billen, *The Old Latin Texts of the Heptateuch* (Cambridge: Cambridge University Press, 1927), 135; J. Schreiner, *Septuaginta-Massora des Buches der Richter* (AnBib 7; Rome: Pontificio Istituto Biblico, 1957), 71 and 79; W.R. Bodine, *The Greek Text of Judges: Recensional Developments* (HSM 23; Chico: Scholars Press, 1980), 69.

[24] Gross, *Richter*, 393.

[25] B. Lucassen, "Josua, Richter und CD," *RevQ* 18 (1997–1998): 373–96.

OL," and "can confidently be seen as an earlier literary form of the book than our traditional texts."[26] In my opinion, this pericope, which lacks any connection with the context and consists of a typically Dtr message attributed to an unknown prophet, never entered into the textual tradition represented by 4QJudg[a]. Similar cases can be found in 1 Kgs 6:11–14, a prophetic oracle written in a stereotyped Dtr language, and in 1 Kgs 14:1–20, a prophetic story rewritten in a Dtr style with various additions. These two pericopes also never entered the textual tradition represented by LXX (→ 4.3). My interpretation of the evidence finds support in the wider contextual study of long additions in the Pentateuch and other biblical books.[27] The omissions and transpositions of pericopes placed between masoretic divisions are rather frequent. They are not "anomalies" of texts other than MT. In fact, many of such omissions and transpositions are to be attributed to the activity of composers or editors in the period of the formation of the textual forms or editions represented by MT and LXX in Judges and many other books rather than to scribes of a later period.[28] A case in point is the unit of Judg 3:31, framed by *setumot* and placed in the Old Greek (LXX[L] VL) after Judg 16:31. The omission of Judg 6:7–10 in 4QJudg[a] does not prove in itself that the book of Judges existed in several editions, but the various textual forms at the beginning and end of the book (→ 4.2.2.5) and of the story in Judges 20 (LXX[L] VL) add strength to this explanation. So also do parallel phenomena as in 4QJosh[a][29] (→ 3.2.1.1; → 3.2.3.2) and "additional cases where the LXX (or early Qumran) textual tradition probably reflects an earlier form (or earlier features) of biblical books than what is seen in the proto-MT."[30]

---

[26] Trebolle, "4QJudg[a]," 162.
[27] M.M. Zahn, "The Problem of Characterizing the Reworked Pentateuch Manuscripts: Bible, Rewritten Bible, or None of the Above?" *DSD* 15 (2008): 315–39 (323).
[28] J. Trebolle, "Yahwe's Spirit of Deceit: Textual Variants that Make a Difference (1 Kgs 22)," *RevQ* 25 (2012): 635–75.
[29] Trebolle, "Text-Critical Value," 410.
[30] D.M. Carr, *The Formation of the Hebrew Bible: A New Reconstruction* (Oxford: Oxford University Press, 2011), 170.

Barthélemy, D., "6. Juges," *DJD* I: 62–64, Plate IX.
Fernández Marcos, N., "The Hebrew and Greek Texts of Judges," in *The Earliest Text of the Hebrew Bible: The Relationship between the Masoretic Text and the Hebrew Base of the Septuagint Reconsidered* (ed. A. Schenker; SBLSCS 52; Atlanta: SBL, 2003), 1–16.
Fernández Marcos, N., "The Genuine Text of Judges," in *Sôfer Mahîr: Essays in Honour of Adrian Schenker Offered by Editors of Biblia Hebraica Quinta* (eds. Y.A.P. Goldman, A. van der Kooij, and R.D. Weis; VTSup 117; Leiden: Brill, 2006), 33–46.
Fernández Marcos, N. (ed.), *BHQ*, part 7: *Judges* (Stuttgart: Deutsche Bibelgesellschaft, 2011).
Gross, W., *Richter: Übersetzt und ausgelegt* (HTKAT; Freiburg: Herder, 2009).
Hess, R.S., "The Dead Sea Scrolls and Higher Criticism of the Hebrew Bible: The Case of 4QJudg[a]," in *The Scrolls and the Scriptures: Qumran Fifty Years After* (eds. S.E. Porter and C.A. Evans; JSPSup 26; Sheffield: Sheffield Academic Press, 1997), 122–28.
Lange, A., *Handbuch*, 203–11.
Martin, L.R., "The Intrusive Prophet: The Narrative Function of the Nameless Prophet in Judges 6," *JSem* 16 (2007): 113–40.
Puech, É., "Notes sur le manuscrit de *Juges 4Q50a*," *RevQ* 21 (2003–2004): 315–19.
Puech, É., "Les manuscrits 4QJuges[c] (= 4Q50 A) et 1QJuges (= 1Q6)," in *Studies in the Hebrew Bible, Qumran, and the Septuagint Presented to Eugene Ulrich* (eds. P.W. Flint, J.C. VanderKam, and E. Tov; VTSup 101; Leiden: Brill, 2006), 184–202.
Rofé, A., "Studying the Biblical Text in the Light of Historico-Literary Criticism: The Reproach of the Prophet in Judg 6:7–10 and 4QJudg[a]," in *The Dead Sea Scrolls in Context: Integrating the Dead Sea Scrolls in the Study of Ancient Texts, Languages, and Cultures* (2 vols.; eds. A. Lange, E. Tov, and M. Weigold; VTSup 140; Leiden: Brill, 2011), 1:111–26.
Trebolle Barrera, J., "Textual Variants in 4QJudg[a] and the Textual and Editorial History of the Book of Judges," *RevQ* 14 (1989–1990): 229–45.
Trebolle Barrera, J., "49. 4QJudg[a]," *DJD* XIV: 161–64, Plate XXXVI.
Trebolle Barrera, J., "The Text-Critical Value of the Old Latin and Antiochean Greek Texts in the Books of Judges and Joshua," in *Interpreting Translation: Studies on the LXX and Ezekiel in Honour of Johan Lust* (eds. F. García Martínez and M. Vervenne; BETL 192; Leuven: Peeters, 2005), 401–13.
Ulrich, E., "Multiple Literary Editions: Reflections To-

ward a Theory of the History of the Biblical Text," in *The Dead Sea Scrolls and the Origins of the Bible* (Grand Rapids: Eerdmans, 1999), 99–120.

Ulrich, E., "Deuteronomistically Inspired Scribal Insertions into the Developing Biblical Texts: 4QJudg^a and 4QJer^a," in *Houses Full of All Good Things: Essays in Memory of Timo Veijola* (eds. J. Pakkala and M. Nissinen; Publications of the Finnish Exegetical Society 95; Göttingen: Vandenhoeck & Ruprecht, 2008), 489–506.

Julio Trebolle Barrera

4.3 Septuagint

4.3.1 Background

In LXX, the book of Judges follows upon Joshua as the second of the historical books that are known as the Former Prophets in Jewish tradition. In Greek, an important addendum of fifteen lines at the end of Joshua 24 is taken as evidence of an older version of the Hebrew text which, according to Rofé,[1] would mark a close link between these two books, notably between Josh 24:33 and Judg 3:12; in MT-Judg (→ 4.2.2), the first two chapters are believed to have been added as a historical-philosophical introduction to the book. The *Damascus Document* (CD V:1–5) attests to such a transition between Joshua and Judges (→ 3.3).

In the same Greek canon (→ 1.1.2.2), the book of Ruth, which concludes the Octateuch, is also directly linked to the book of Judges upon which it follows, since the events described in it, as indicated by the opening verse of this book, came to pass "when the judges were judging." For the early Christians (e.g. Eusebius of Caesarea, *Hist. eccl.* VI 25.2), Judges and Ruth even constituted a single book. In the Hebrew Bible, the book of Ruth has an entirely different status. It is not a supplement to Judges but an independent book placed among the Writings as one of the Five Scrolls.

The Greek translation of the book of Judges is believed to date to the first half of the second century B.C.E.,[2] i.e., to the same period as the Old Greek translation of 1–4 Kingdoms, but allegedly later than the translation of the Psalter.[3]

4.3.2 Original Form, Editions

The Greek translation of the book of Judges bears witness to a highly complex textual history. In 1897, Brooke and McLean[4] edited the text of Judges according to Codex Alexandrinus (LXX^A), albeit without providing an apparatus. In 1917, the same authors edited the Codex Vaticanus (LXX^B), this time with a critical apparatus.[5] Taking note of the considerable discrepancies between these two texts, notably in the Song of Deborah (Judges 5), Rahlfs decided to publish a two-text edition of Judges in 1935[6] – the text of LXX^A on the upper part of the page and the text of LXX^B on the lower part – as he was convinced that they represented two independent translations. It was this double text in particular that served Kahle[7] as a basis for the formulation of his – today almost discarded – theory of multiple LXX translations, which he believed to have been oral like the Targumim. However, the studies of Pretzl, Soisalon-Soininen, and Schreiner all concurred in the assumption that the various forms of LXX are rooted in the same source text.

The text of LXX^A as printed by Rahlfs is in reality a mixed text based on Codex Alexandrinus and on two groups of manuscripts affected both by the Hexaplaric recension of Origen and by that of the Lucianic group (LXX^L), henceforth referred to as the Antiochene text (3–5.1.6.1).

Text LXX^B (Codex Vaticanus), a straightforward text, is believed to represent a pre-Hexaplaric recension dating from the first century C.E., realized on the basis of a Hebrew text of proto-Masoretic type. Barthélemy[8] was indeed able to show that the recension of Judges attested by LXX^B must be

---

[1] A. Rofé, "The End of the Book of Joshua According to the Septuagint," *Shnaton* 2 (1977): 217–27 [Hebr.] = *Hen* 4 (1982): 17–35 [Eng.].

[2] In the period of the Seleucid persecution, according to N. Fernández Marcos, "Jephta's Daughter in the Old Greek (Judges 11:29–40)," in Karrer-Kraus, *Septuaginta 2010, 478–88 (487).

[3] Dorival-Harl-Munnich, *Septante, 110.

[4] A.E. Brooke and N. McLean, *The Book of Judges in Greek according to the Text of Codex Alexandrinus* (Cambridge: Cambridge University Press, 1897).

[5] Brooke–McLean, *The Old Testament in Greek, Vol. 1: The Octateuch (1917).

[6] Rahlfs, *Septuaginta.

[7] Kahle, *Cairo Genizah.

[8] Barthélemy, *Devanciers, 34, 47.

ascribed to the *kaige*-Th tradition. Bodine[9] would later support this hypothesis. This *kaige*-Th revision (→ 3–5.1.5.2.3), which affected other historical and prophetic books or parts of the same, exhibits a certain number of characteristics, notably the translation of וגם "and also" as καί γε "and even," of איש "each" as ἀνήρ "man" in the sense of "everyone," and of אנכי "I" as ἐγώ εἰμι "I am" followed by a verb in personal mood. However, these grammatical criteria are insufficient when it comes to distinguishing the tradition of LXX[B] from that of LXX[A] and LXX[L], since the majority of them, as a general rule, appear in both LXX[B] and LXX[A]. Accordingly, Bodine supplements them with other criteria of lexical and stylistic nature.[10]

It is the Antiochene text LXX[L] (3–5.1.6.1), which is fragmentarily represented by the two uncial manuscripts LXX[K] and LXX[Z], by a group of minuscules (LXX[glnw]), and to a certain degree by LXX[(d)ptv], that preserves the purest form of the Old Greek translation. VL (→ 3–5.2.1.1), which is close to LXX[L], is also believed to represent one of the best textual witnesses of OG-Judg.[11] Within this tradition, it would in fact seem appropriate to identify manuscripts LXX[KZglnw] as "an Antiochene textual form" and LXX[(d)ptv] as a post-Antiochene revision, with a clearly expansionist tendency.[12]

Hebrew fragments among the Qumran manuscripts and dated to the late first century B.C.E. – 4QJudg[a] and 4QJudg[b] (→ 4.2.1)[13] – preserve agreements with the Antiochene text and VL that probably reflect the Old Greek.[14]

In light of the evidence, it would indeed seem that the Old Greek has been best preserved in LXX[A] – in spite of the emendations associated with the Hexaplaric recension of Origen – and in LXX[L], rather than LXX[B], which bears the mark of a more recent recension based on a Hebrew text that was very close to MT (*kaige*-Th). And rather than classifying LXX[A] and LXX[B] as two independent translations,[15] it seems much more probable that the two textual forms of the Greek text of Judges go back to a common source that was subjected to various types of revisions. Finally, the assumption (based especially on 4QJudg[a]) that the Hebrew book of Judges has been preserved in two literary forms[16] in the same manner as, for instance, the two textual forms of Jeremiah, does not appear to have met with complete approval (→ 4.2).[17]

The Göttingen edition that is being prepared in 2015 will probably only publish a single text form.[18]

4.3.3 Translation Character, Translation Technique, and Inner-Translational Features

The book of Judges in Greek introduces the group of translations of historical books that bear the distinct mark of strict literalness. OG-Judg nevertheless displays a few rare quantitative discrepancies with regard to MT. The translation of the Song of Deborah, for example, includes additional stichs in Judg 5:12, 14 (LXX[AL]); 5:15 (LXX[A]); and 5:21, 22, 26, 30 (LXX[L]). Elsewhere, LXX[B] offers a text that is shorter than MT (→ 4.2.2), for example, in Judg 6:7, 35. Likewise, LXX[L] exhibits noteworthy "minuses" in Judg

---

[9] Bodine, *The Greek Text of Judges*.

[10] Bodine, *The Greek Text of Judges*, 47–91.

[11] Cf. Billen, "The Old Latin Version of Judges"; J. Trebolle Barrera, "The Text-Critical Value of the Old Latin and Antiochean Greek Texts in the Book of Judges and Joshua," in *Interpreting Translation: Studies on the LXX and Ezekiel in Honour of Johan Lust* (eds. F. García Martínez and M. Vervenne; BETL 192; Leuven: Leuven University Press, 2005), 401–13.

[12] See e.g. J. Targarona de Baenz-Badillos, "Le texte grec du livre des Juges présenté par les manuscrits (d)ptv," in *Mélanges Barthélemy* (ed. P. Casetti; OBO 38, Göttingen: Vandenhoeck & Ruprecht, 1981), 531–52.

[13] J. Trebolle Barrera, "49. 4QJudg[a]," *DJD* XIV: 161–64; J. Trebolle Barrera, "50. 4QJudg[b]," *DJD* XIV: 165–69.

[14] See J. Trebolle Barrera, "Textual Variants in 4QJudg[a] and the Textual and Editorial History of the Book of Judges," *RevQ* 14 (1989): 229–45; J. Trebolle Barrera, "Edition préliminaire de 4QJuges[b]: Contribution des manuscrits qumrâniens des Juges à l' étude textuelle du livre," *RevQ* 15 (1991): 79–100.

[15] This theory is probably not applicable to Judges 5: see Fernández Marcos, "The B-Text of Judges," 163.

[16] See Trebolle Barrera, "Textual Variants."

[17] See Fernández Marcos, "The Hebrew and Greek Texts of Judges"; N. Fernández Marcos, "L' histoire textuelle: les livres historiques (Juges)," in *L' enfance de la Bible: L' histoire du texte de l' Ancien Testament à la lumière des recherches récentes* (eds. A. Schenker and P. Hugo; MdB 52; Geneva: Labor et Fides, 2005), 148–69, esp. 164; Fernández Marcos, "The B-Text of Judges," 169.

[18] See Fernández Marcos, "The B-Text of Judges," 163.

9:16 and 12:4 as well as several "pluses" in Judg 20:19, 28, 31, 33, 37 and in Judg 21:7, 9, 22,[19] albeit without allowing for the possibility of ascribing these important divergences to a Hebrew *Vorlage* that would differ from that of MT. In Judg 5:26, LXX[L] not only presents an amplified text but also sequences arranged in the inverse order of MT.

Even though LXX[L] proves far less literal than LXX[A] and LXX[B], the latter being far more so, LXX[A], LXX[L], and LXX[B] still exhibit a certain number of Hebraisms, such as μετ'εἰρήνης or ἐν εἰρήνῃ "in peace" in Judg 8:9 and 11:31; ἔθηκα τὴν ψυχήν μου ἐν χειρί μου "I took my life in my hand" in Judg 12:3; ἀνὴρ τὸ ἀγαθόν/εὐθὲς ἐν ὀφθαλμοῖς αὐτοῦ ἐποίει "a man would do what was good/right in his own eyes" in Judg 17:6 and 21:25, and προσθήσεις τὴν ψυχήν σου "you will add your life" in Judg 18:25. Numerous often-deliberate transliterations can be found, for example, in Judg 8:27 εφουδ "ephoud" (LXX[AL]) or εφωθ "ephoth" (LXX[B]), in Judg 13:5 ναζιρ θεοῦ "nazir of God" (LXX[B]), in Judg 13:4, 14 σικερα "sikera" (LXX[AL]), and in Judg 20:6 ζεμα "zema" (LXX[B]). However, these transliterations are sometimes due to a difficult Hebrew, as for instance in Judg 5:16 μοσφαθαιμ "mosphataim" (LXX[AL]), in Judg 5:22 αμαδαρωθ "amadaroth" (LXX[AL]), in Judg 8:7, 16 βαρκοννιμ/βαρακηνιμ/αβαρκηνιν "barkonim/barakenim/abarkenin" (LXX[AB]), and in Judg 8:26 σιρωνων "sirons" and ενφωθ "enphoth" (LXX[A]).[20] Generally speaking, however, this literalness does not cast doubt on the translator's ability to translate the text in a reliable manner.[21]

Doublets constitute one the characteristic features of the Antiochene text (Judg 9:25, 37; 11:34; 20:13; 21:13, 19),[22] although they are not entirely lacking in LXX[A], especially in the Song of Deborah (Judg 5:12, 14, 15),[23] due to the extreme difficulty of interpreting the Hebrew text.

The tradition of LXX[B], which belongs to the *kaige*-Th recension, presents a number of very specific and prominent lexical features, such as the use of παρατάσσεσθαι "to deploy" instead of πολεμεῖν "to fight" in LXX[AL], of ὄνος "donkey" the use of which is more recent and less Egyptian than ὑποζύγιον, of the same meaning, and of ἀνήρ "man" instead of ἕκαστος "each" to translate אִישׁ "man."[24] With the exception of the six occurrences of Φυλιστιίμ "Philistines" in Judges 10 to 14, however, LXX[B] also displays the lexical choice ἀλλόφυλοι "allophyles" found in LXX[AL], a word that might allow us to date the translation of the historical books, and of Judges in particular, to the Maccabean period.[25] Likewise, the specificity of the Greek vocabulary expressing mockery, for example, in the description of Samson, could unfold its entire meaning in the historical context of the Seleucid persecution.[26]

4.3.4 Text-Critical Value

In spite of the proximity of OG-Judg to MT (→ 4.2.2), LXX (LXX[A] and LXX[B]) is definitely of interest for textual criticism, not only with regard to Judges 5, which is poorly preserved in MT, but also in cases such as Judg 16:13–14, where MT lacks a verse, or

---

[19] Cf. P.E. Satterthwaite, "Some Septuagintal Pluses in Judges 20 and 21," *BIOSCS* 24 (1991): 23–35.

[20] See E. Tov, "Transliterations of Hebrew Words in the Greek Versions of the Old Testament: A Further Characteristic of the *kaige*-Th. Revision?" *Textus* 8 (1973): 78–92. Revised version: **Greek-Hebrew Bible*, 501–12, esp. 507.

[21] Cf. e.g. S. Sipilä, *Between Literalness and Freedom: Translation Technique in the Septuagint of Joshua and Judges Regarding the Clause Connections Introduced by ו and כי* (Publications of the Finnish Exegetical Society 75; Göttingen: Vandenhoeck & Ruprecht, 1999), 61; H. Ausloos and B. Lemmelijn, "Characterizing the LXX Translation of Judges on the Basis of Content-Related Criteria: The Greek Rendering of Hebrew Absolute Hapax Legomena in Judges 3,12–30," in *After Qumran: Old and Modern Editions of the Biblical Texts – The Historical Books* (eds. H. Ausloos, B. Lemmelijn, and J. Trebolle Barrera; BETL 246; Leuven: Peeters, 2012), 171–92.

[22] See Fernández Marcos, "The Hebrew and Greek Texts of Judges," 14–15, n. 46.

[23] See E. Tov, "The Textual History of the Song of Deborah in the A Text of the Septuagint," *VT* 28 (1978): 224–32, reprinted in Tov, **Greek-Hebrew Bible*, 527–34.

[24] For further examples, see Fernández Marcos, "The B-Text of Judges," 165–68.

[25] Cf. Harlé, *Les Juges*, 58–59.

[26] Cf. N. Fernández Marcos, "Héros et victime: Samson dans la LXX," in *L'apport de la Septante aux études sur l'Antiquité* (eds. J. Joosten and P. Le Moigne, LD; Paris: Cerf, 2005), 119–33.

LXXᴬ-Judg 19:30, where LXXᴮ and MT offer a short text.[27] To this must be added the evidence from 4QJudgᵃ (→ 4.2.1.2; → 4.2.3.2), which omits Judg 6:7–10.

4.3.5 Relevance for Exegesis

Depending on the texts, a number of passages are different from MT and probably correspond to the reading of a particular period, for instance: in an effort to update the text, the use of the feminine ἡ Βααλ/αἱ Βααλιμ "she-Baal/she-Baalim" in LXXᴬ-Judg 2:13; 3:7; 10:6, 10 for the feminine בשת "Shame" that came to replace the name of Baal; perhaps the avoidance of the name Amalek in LXXᴬᴸᴮ-Judg 1:16; LXXᴬ-Judg 5:14; LXXᴬᴸ-Judg 12:15; and the allusion to the synagogal organization in the second century B.C.E. in LXXᴮ-Judg 5:10ᶜ. Equally, certain transformations of LXXᴸ in the Samson episode, such as in Judg 16:25, 27, are the result of an interpretive exegesis that, through its dramatization of the narrative, depicts Samson not as a protagonist but also as a victim.[28]

Barthélemy, *Devanciers d'Aquila
Billen, A.V., "The Old Latin Version of Judges," JTS 43 (1942): 140–49.
Bodine, R., The Greek Text of Judges: Recensional Developments (HSM 23; Chico: Scholars Press, 1980).
Fernández Marcos, N., "The Hebrew and Greek Texts of Judges," in Schenker, *Earliest Text, 1–16.
Fernández Marcos, N., "The B-Text of Judges: Kaige Revision and Beyond," in After Qumran: Old and Modern Editions of the Biblical Texts – The Historical Books (eds. H. Ausloos, B. Lemmelijn, and J. Trebolle Barrera; BETL 246; Leuven: Peeters, 2012), 161–69.
Harlé, P., Les Juges (*Bible d'Alexandrie 7; Paris: Cerf, 1999).
Lindars, B., "A Commentary on the Greek Judges?" in VI Congress of the International Organization for Septuagint and Cognate Studies, Jerusalem, 1986 (ed. C.E. Cox; SBLSCS 23; Atlanta: Scholars Press, 1987), 167–200.
Pretzl, O., "LXX-Probleme im Buch der Richter," Bib 7 (1926): 233–69, 353–83.
Schreiner, J., Septuaginta-Massora des Buches der Richter: Eine textkritische Studie (AnBib 7; Rome: Pontifical Biblical Institute Press, 1957).
Soisalon-Soininen, I., Die Textformen der Septuaginta-Übersetzung des Richterbuches (AASF 72.1; Helsinki: Suomalainen Tiedeakatemia, 1951).

Cécile Dogniez

---

[27] See N. Fernández Marcos, Judges (*BHQ 7; Stuttgart: Deutsche Bibelgesellschaft, 2011), but also the discussion by E. Tov, "Critica bibliografica: Biblia Hebraica Quinta: Judges," Sef 72/2 (2012): 483–89.

[28] See Fernández Marcos, "Héros et victime."

5
Samuel–Kings

∴

5.1 Textual History of Samuel

5.1.1 Extant Witnesses

The oldest manuscripts of the book of Samuel derive from the second half of the Second Temple period: 4QSam[b] (→ 5.3.1.3), the oldest Hebrew manuscript, is dated paleographically to approximately 250 B.C.E.,[1] 4QSam[c] (→ 5.3.1.4) to approximately 100–75 B.C.E.,[2] and 4QSam[a] (→ 5.3.1.2) to approximately 50–25 B.C.E.[3] No date was assigned to 1QSam (→ 5.3.1.1) in the official publication,[4] but it is inscribed in a Hasmonean script from approximately the first half of the first century B.C.E. Manuscripts of the received MT (→ 5.3.2) date from the Middle Ages (e.g., MT[A] from 925 C.E. and MT[L] from 1009) but are remarkably faithful copies of Second Temple texts, as scrolls such as 4QGen[b] (→ 2.2.1.2.8) and 1QIsa[b] (→ 6.2.1.2) demonstrate in other Scripture books.[5] The oldest complete manuscript of LXX-Sam (→ 5.4) is LXX[B] (fourth century C.E.). One of the most important VL manuscripts is Palimpsestus Vindobonensis.[6] VL (→ 3–5.2.1.2), however, is not a single version but a variety of separate translations, beginning in the mid-second century C.E.; readings from them are recorded in the critical apparatus of Brooke and McLean.[7] Early Christians thought that "Greek was the language of the apostolic books and of the Jewish Scriptures" and thus "Latin versions were simply that, versions …"[8] The VL translations, however, were usually good witnesses to ancient LXX manuscripts, often to the Old Greek but sometimes to subsequent recensions. Thus, at times they exhibit readings that attest a lost Old Greek reading, which in turn attests an important ancient Hebrew variant.[9] The transmitted forms of the Targum (→ 3–5.1.3), Peshitta (→ 3–5.1.4), and Vulgate (→ 3–5.1.7) of Samuel are all dependent on an early form of MT and thus seldom provide readings of independent value.

5.1.2 History of Research

Prior to the seventeenth century, research into the text of Samuel was principally the domain of theologians, commentators, and preachers, such as Origen, Chrysostom, and Calvin.[10] The text used by Jews was MT (→ 5.3.2), while the text used by Christians was LXX (→ 5.4) or the Vulgate (→ 3–5.1.7), until the Reformation, when, for Protestants, MT replaced the translations, partly in the spirit of the Renaissance quest for the original text.[11] The purpose and focus of research was on the spiritual or pastoral meaning to be derived from the inspired text.

5.1.2.1 The Beginnings of Critical Research
Moshe Goshen-Gottstein records that with the return to original languages in the Renaissance, Baptista Spagnuoli (Beato Mantovano) in 1476 composed a treatise, *Epistola de causa diversitatis inter interpretes sacrae scripturae*, which treated dif-

---

[1] F.M. Cross, D.W. Parry, and R.J. Saley, "52. 4QSam[b]," *DJD* XVII (2005): 219–46 (220).

[2] E. Ulrich, "53. 4QSam[c]," *DJD* XVII: 245–67 (249).

[3] F.M. Cross, D.W. Parry, and R.J. Saley, "51. 4QSam[a]," *DJD* XVII (2005): 1–216 (5).

[4] D. Barthélemy, "7. Livres de Samuel," *DJD* I: 64–65.

[5] This fidelity also includes the accurate transmission of ancient errors.

[6] B. Fischer, *Beiträge zur Geschichte der lateinischen Bibeltext* (Vetus Latina: Aus der Geschichte der lateinischen Bibel 12; Freiburg: Herder, 1986), 308–81. Fischer published a preliminary version in "Palimpsestus Vindobonensis: A Revised Edition of L 115 for Samuel-Kings," *BIOSCS* 16 (1983): 13–87.

[7] Brooke–McLean, *The Old Testament in Greek*.

[8] J. Wright Knust, "Versions, Latin," in *The New Interpreter's Dictionary of the Bible* (ed. K.D. Sakenfeld; 5 vols.; Nashville: Abingdon, 2006–2009), 5.765–69, esp. 765.

[9] See J. Trebolle Barrera, "From the 'Old Latin' through the 'Old Greek' to the 'Old Hebrew' (2 Kings 10:23–35)," *Textus* 11 (1984): 17–36; J. Trebolle Barrera, "Old Latin, Old Greek and Old Hebrew in the Books of Kings (1 Ki 18:27 and 2 Ki 20:11)," *Textus* 13 (1986): 85–95.

[10] See R.W. Klein, "Samuel, Books of," in *Dictionary of Biblical Interpretation*, 2.431–35, esp. 431–32.

[11] That "original text," however, was not necessarily the original *text* but simply one form of the several ancient forms for each book in the original *language*.

ferences between the Hebrew, Greek, and Latin texts.[12] The publication of the *Complutensian Polyglot in 1514–1517 made the comparison of the Hebrew, Aramaic, Greek, and Latin texts, and thus their textual variants, more easily available. Other polyglots soon followed: Antwerp (1569–1572),[13] Paris (1629–1645),[14] and London (1653–1657).[15]

Amidst the religious polemics of the seventeenth century, two scholars, Louis Cappel (Capellus, 1585–1658), a Protestant educated by Catholics and using Jewish scholarship, and Jean Morin (Morinus, 1591–1659), a Calvinist who converted to Roman Catholicism, originally separately, but eventually together, transformed the general course of research into *Critica Sacra*. Cappel at first could not find a publisher for his work of that title, but Morin, in an early act of Jewish-Protestant-Catholic interconfessional scholarship, did eventually publish it in 1634.[16] The book brought to light numerous textual problems: variants between MT, LXX, and other versions; variants in parallel passages within MT; variants between the *Qere* and *Ketiv*; and thus the general usefulness of textual criticism.

5.1.2.2 Nineteenth-Century Research

In the nineteenth century, text-critical analysis began to produce detailed results. Thenius,[17] noting the many troubled parts of MT-Sam (→ 5.3.2), suggested numerous retroversions from LXX; certain of his conjectures were successful, but scholars judged some of his other conjectural efforts as less than judicious. He nonetheless pioneered a new path in the textual criticism of Samuel, and soon more sober analysis by Wellhausen proved to be quite illuminating. For example, at 2 Sam 13:39, MT has וַתְּכַל דָּוִד הַמֶּלֶךְ "King David was pining away." Wellhausen, noticing the syntactic problem of a masculine subject with a feminine verb, deduced that the original Hebrew may have been ותכל רוח המלך "The sprit/heart of the king yearned." Later, he saw the Lucianic Greek (→ 3–5.1.6) τὸ πνεῦμα τοῦ βασιλέως "the spirit of the king," which confirmed his deduction.[18] Fortunately, 4QSam[a] (→ 5.3.1.2) is partly extant for this clause, and with רו]ח המלך] "the spirit of the king," it solidly confirms Wellhausen's method.[19] Samuel R. Driver, himself an astute textual scholar, spread Wellhausen's method and findings in the English-speaking world.[20]

5.1.2.3 Research Enriched by the Qumran Scrolls

The discovery of the Dead Sea Scrolls revolutionized the study of the text of the Bible. The first Samuel scroll found at Qumran (1QSam; → 5.3.1.1), unearthed during the scholars' excavation of Cave 1 in March 1949, was included for publication in *DJD I,[21] which was submitted to Oxford University Press in 1953 and published in 1955.[22] The first information regarding Samuel scrolls to reach the public, however, was provided by Frank Moore Cross, whose insights sparked much of the research recorded in this section. The first of the Cave 4 team of editors to arrive in Jerusalem in summer 1953, he pieced together fragments of 4QSam[a] (→ 5.3.1.2)

---

[12] Much of the information in this subsection is from M. Goshen-Gottstein, "Textual Criticism, Hebrew Bible," in *Dictionary of Biblical Interpretation*, 2.541–46; Klein, "Samuel, Books of"; J.H. Hayes, "Cappel, Louis," in *Dictionary of Biblical Interpretation*, 1.167–68; Hayes, "Morin, Jean," in *Dictionary of Biblical Interpretation*, 2.164; http://en.wikipedia.org/wiki/Louis_Cappel; and http://en.wikipedia.org/wiki/Jean_Morin_(theologian). See also Tov, *TCHB, 19–20, 71.

[13] *Biblia Sacra Hebraice, Chaldaice, Graece et Latina* ... (ed. B. Arias Montano; Antwerp: Christophorus Plantinus, 1569–1572).

[14] Le Jay, *Biblia.

[15] Walton, *Polyglotta.

[16] Cappellus, *Critica Sacra.

[17] Thenius, *Die Bücher Samuels*.

[18] Wellhausen, *Der Text der Bücher Samuelis*, 190–91, 223.

[19] Cross, *DJD XVII: 148–50; Ulrich, *The Qumran Text*, 106–07; P. Kyle McCarter, *II Samuel*, 338.

[20] S.R. Driver, *Notes on the Hebrew Text*. Mention should also be made of the related studies by A. Rahlfs, *Studien zu den Königsbüchern* and *Lucians Rezension der Königsbücher, Septuagint Studien* I and III (Göttingen: Vandenhoeck & Ruprecht, 1904 and 1911). His *Lucians Rezension*, however (see Ulrich, *The Qumran Text*, 22–27), must be countered by A. Mez, *Die Bibel des Josephus untersucht für Buch V–VII der Archäologie* (Basel: Jaeger & Kober, 1895).

[21] Barthelémy, "Livres de Samuel."

[22] W.W. Fields, *The Scrolls: A Full History*, 94–95.

and published his results already in 1953, showing a Hebrew text similar to that used by the translator of LXX (→ 5.4).[23] That major discovery reversed the low esteem in which many viewed LXX, seeing it as a poor translation or rough paraphrase of "the Hebrew" (which they presumed to be MT [→ 5.3.2]). Future scrolls, such as 4QDeut^q (→ 2.2.1.6.3), 4QJer^b (→ 7.2.1.3; → 7.2.3.1), 4QJer^d (→ 7.2.1.5; → 7.2.3.3), and numerous others, were to confirm that elevation of LXX's (→ 1.3.1.1) reputation.

Parts of 4QSam^b (→ 5.3.1.3) were also quickly published by Cross in 1955.[24] It exhibited an excellent text noticeably more pristine than that of MT: "in an overwhelmingly large number of cases, the readings of 4QSam^b agree with the Old Greek when it is superior, but agree with the Masoretic tradition when it is superior; it also has fifteen unique readings that are superior to both the Old Greek and [MT]."[25] Ulrich, who had produced an analysis of the variants in 4QSam^a in his dissertation in 1975,[26] published a preliminary analysis of 4QSam^c in 1979.[27] Despite the scribe's unskilled script and a number of words that he had to correct, it also presented a text often preferable to that of MT.[28]

McCarter published an exemplary commentary on Samuel, the first to utilize all the data available from the scrolls.[29] Able to use numerous examples from Samuel, he also composed a handbook, introducing non-specialists to the newer perspective in Hebrew textual criticism.[30] It formed a companion to Klein's earlier handbook on textual criticism, which focused more on the value of LXX.[31]

A number of subsequent studies have contributed to or capitalized on the study of the Samuel scrolls.[32] In addition, several research sessions and symposia have focused on the Samuel–Kings texts.[33] Prominent among them is the international symposium held at the University of Fribourg, Switzerland, in 2008.[34] The contributors to this volume analyzed three areas that have proved promising in Samuel studies: study of the manuscript witnesses, especially 4QSam^a and the Old Greek; the recensional history of the Greek in the attempt to retrieve the Old Greek and thus ideally the Hebrew text that was the source for the Old Greek; and possible new literary editions entwined with the textual history of Samuel. The "Archaeology" in the title indicates the rich layers available for discovery of the development of the text afforded by the various Hebrew witnesses and the Greek translation and recensions, as well as the witness of MT–LXX Chronicles. Another international

---

[23] Cross, "New Qumran Biblical Fragment."

[24] Cross, "The Oldest Manuscripts from Qumran."

[25] Cross, Parry, and Saley, "52. 4QSam^b," 223.

[26] Ulrich, *The Qumran Text*, published in 1978. See the review articles by E. Tov, "The Textual Affiliations of 4QSam^a," *JSOT* 14 (1979): 37–53; J. Trebolle Barrera, "El estudio de 4Q Sam^a: Implicaciones exegéticas e históricas," *EstBíb* 39 (1981): 5–18; and A. van der Kooij, "De tekst van Samuel en het tekstkritisch onderzoek," *NedTT* 36 (1982): 177–204.

[27] E. Ulrich, "4QSam^c: A Fragmentary Manu-script of 2 Samuel 14–15 from the Scribe of the Serek Hay-yaḥad (1QS)," *BASOR* 235 (1979): 1–25.

[28] Ulrich, "4QSam^c," 253.

[29] McCarter, *I Samuel*; McCarter, *II Samuel*.

[30] P.K. McCarter, *Textual Criticism: Recovering the Text of the Hebrew Bible* (Philadelphia: Fortress, 1986).

[31] R. Klein, *Textual Criticism of the Old Testament: From the Septuagint to Qumran* (Philadelphia: Fortress, 1974).

[32] Examples include J. Trebolle Barrera, *Centena in Libros Samuelis et Regum: Variantes textuales y composición literaria en los Libros de Samuel y Reyes* (Textos y estudios "Cardenal Cisneros" 47; Madrid: Consejo Superior de Investigaciones Científicas, 1989); E. Herbert, *Reconstructing Biblical Dead Sea Scrolls: A New Method Applied to the Reconstruction of 4QSam^a* (Leiden: Brill, 1997); A. Fincke, *The Samuel Scroll from Qumran: 4QSam^a Restored and Compared to the Septuagint and 4QSam^c* (Leiden: Brill, 2001); and T. Kauhanen, *Proto-Lucianic Problem in 1 Samuel* (Göttingen: Vandenhoeck & Ruprecht, 2012).

[33] For example, the 1972 IOSCS symposium held at the SBL and published by R.A. Kraft in *The Methodology of Textual Criticism in Jewish Greek Scriptures, with Special Attention to the Problems in Samuel–Kings* (SBLSCS 2; Missoula: Scholars Press, 1972); the IOSOT conference held in Vienna and edited by E. Tov in *The Hebrew and Greek Texts of Samuel, 1980 Proceedings IOSCS, Vienna* (Jerusalem: Academon, 1980); workshops in Madrid (2005, 2006), Helsinki (2005), and Oxford (2011); and the continuing section on Textual Criticism of Samuel–Kings at the ISBL meeting in Vienna (2007) and at subsequent SBL annual meetings, chaired by Anneli Aejmelaeus and Julio Trebolle Barrera.

[34] Essays from the symposium were published in *Archaeology of the Books of Samuel*. The volume also contains a generous bibliography on the Samuel scrolls, the textual complexity of LXX, and the text history and search for literary editions.

symposium held in 2010 at the Universidad de Alcalá, Spain, produced similar essays on Samuel and the historical books.[35]

Some modern translations of the Bible have been including preferable readings from the scrolls,[36] though in individual cases the use depends upon the judgment of the translators. For example, the JPS (1999) includes scroll readings in its footnotes, and the NRSV (1989) includes the 4QSam^a fragment concerning Nahash the Ammonite within its text before 1 Sam 11:1, whereas the NABRE (New American Bible: Revised Edition, 2010) mentions it in a note but does not include it in the text.

5.1.3 Textual History

The attempt to chart the early history of the book of Samuel prior to manuscript evidence can only be conjectural, but some of the traditions recorded in the book undoubtedly originated in the monarchic period. It may be assumed that many sources and traditions, primarily oral, associated with the origins of Israel's kingship and the figure of David circulated during the monarchic period, including Samuel's reluctance regarding kingship, Shiloh and the ark narrative, Saul's kingship and sons, David's rise to kingship, his exploits as a warrior, and the narrative of intrigue leading up to the succession of Solomon.[37] The main Deuteronomistic historian (Dtr), probably in the seventh century B.C.E., gathered a large selection of these and other sources, edited them in light of his theological themes, and included them in his larger, probably written (theology of) history. A post-exilic editor (Dtr^2, or possibly more, Dtr^{P,N}) updated and revised the history after the disaster of the defeat, destruction, and exile by the Babylonian army.

The book of Samuel and the larger Dtr history continued to be passed down through the fifth and fourth centuries as religious literature that intellectually and emotionally engaged those who read or heard it and taught them basic lessons of their covenantal religion. The Chronicler, who presumably also viewed himself as writing not "Scripture" but religious literature, used many elements of the book to construct his partly parallel narrative, expounding his own theology. Analysis shows that the Chronicler did not use as his source a text of Samuel like MT but rather a text more like 4QSam^a (→ 5.3.1.2).[38]

After the book of Deuteronomy was separated from the rest of the history to become part of the Pentateuchal book of the Torah of Moses, Samuel continued to be passed down and eventually came to be regarded as Scripture. Apparently, the Jews in Alexandria may not yet have considered it essential Scripture since it was not translated into Greek along with the Torah in the early third century B.C.E., but it is safe to conjecture that 4QSam^b (→ 5.3.1.3) from the mid-third century B.C.E. probably attests the scriptural status of the book in Judah.

With the manuscript evidence provided by the Qumran scrolls of Samuel, it becomes possible to chart the book's textual history somewhat more confidently. The biblical manuscripts from Qumran (→ 5.3.1; → 5.3.3) in general display four main types of textual variation, each of which enters the text at the hands of different scribes independently and on a level separate from the others: variant editions, isolated insertions, individual textual variants, and orthography. Variant editions signal different stages in the textual history and thus distinguish different textual families. Isolated insertions, insofar as they are isolated and not combined with similar insertions, do not constitute a variant edition but may well show close textual traditions. Individual textual variants are routine and sporadic

---

[35] *After Qumran: Old and Modern Editions of the Biblical Texts – The Historical Books* (eds. H. Ausloos, B. Lemmelijn, and J. Trebolle Barrera; BETL 246; Leuven: Peeters, 2012).

[36] See H.P. Scanlin, *The Dead Sea Scrolls and Modern Translations of the Old Testament* (Wheaton: Tyndale House, 1993).

[37] See McCarter, *1 Samuel*, 12–30; K. Schmid, *The Old Testament: A Literary History* (trans. L.M. Maloney; Minneapolis: Fortress, 2012), 57–63; R.W. Klein, "Samuel, Books of," *ISBE* 4.312–20; and F. García-Treto, "Samuel, First and Second Books of," *New Interpreter's Dictionary of the Bible*, 5.89–96, esp. 90.

[38] Ulrich, *The Qumran Text*, 151–65.

and thus often indicate little about textual affiliation unless showing a frequent characteristic pattern. Orthography generally plays little or no role in textual history. "Rewritten Scripture" is not included in this discussion of scriptural literature, insofar as it moves beyond Scripture; such works merit new titles denoting that they are new compositions, not new editions of the scriptural book upon which they were based.[39]

5.1.3.1 Variant Editions of Samuel?

The final form of many of the biblical books resulted from a developmental process of old traditions or current texts being updated and revised by a substantial pattern of intentional additions or revisions, which in modern terminology would be called a "revised edition."[40] Although there were undoubtedly earlier literary forms of the book of Samuel as it developed, none have survived. Only a single edition is attested in all extant manuscripts and translations of the complete book of Samuel,[41] though some scholars see variant editions for certain passages.[42] The only passage for which there is a scholarly consensus in modern research regarding a new and expanded edition is the story of David and Goliath, 1 Samuel 17–18.[43] Though there is only one edition of the book, there are, however, two different text traditions within that single edition: one group including 4QSam[a,b,c] (→ 5.3.1; → 5.3.3), the Old Greek (→ 5.4), and VL (→ 3–5.2.1.2), and the other witnessed by MT (→ 5.3.2), *kaige*-Th (→ 1.3.1.2), Targum (→ 3–5.1.3), the Peshitta (→ 3–5.1.4), and the Vulgate (→ 3–5.1.7). Both the Chronicler (→ 20) and Josephus (→ 21.3) used texts of the former often preferable text tradition for their Samuel source.[44]

5.1.3.2 Isolated Insertions of One or More Verses

Sometimes learned scribes inserted into the text additional material that they thought would enhance it: additions in the character of marginal annotations, footnotes, supplementary information, updates, historical references, pious comments, etc. Systematic comparison for many books of MT, SP in the Torah, and LXX reveals insertions of up to eight verses added to one or other text.[45] Two examples may be listed, one in 4QSam[a] (→ 5.3.1.2) and a different type in MT (→ 5.3.2).

---

[39] 4QVisSam (4Q160), though including phrases similar to 1 Samuel 3 on its first fragment, has virtually no relation to that book on its few remaining fragments. Similarly, 6QApocryphon on Samuel-Kings (6Q9), despite its seventy-two papyrus fragments, yields no connected text like Samuel.

[40] See E. Ulrich, "The Evolutionary Production and Transmission of the Scriptural Books," in *The Dead Sea Scrolls: Transmission of Traditions and Production of Texts* (eds. S. Metso, H. Najman, and E. Schuller; STDJ 92; Leiden: Brill, 2010), 209–25, esp. 215–19.

[41] Rofé considers some of the differences between 4QSam[a] and MT-Sam quite pronounced. See A. Rofé, "4QMidrash Samuel? – Observations Concerning the Character of 4QSam[a]," *Textus* 19 (1998): 63–74; A. Rofé, "Midrashic Traits in 4Q51 (so-called 4QSam[a])," in *Archaeology of the Books of Samuel: The Entangling of the Textual and Literary History* (eds. P. Hugo and A. Schenker; VTSup 132; Leiden: Brill, 2010), 75–88. But the differences he notes are similar to developments seen in other clearly biblical manuscripts.

[42] For suggested examples of variant editions in 1 Samuel 1–2 see S.D. Walters, "Hannah and Anna: The Greek and Hebrew Texts of 1 Samuel 1," *JBL* 107 (1988): 385–412; E. Tov, "Different Editions of the Song of Hannah and of Its Narrative Framework," in *Greek-Hebrew Bible*, 433–55; A. Aejmelaeus, "Hannah's Psalm in 4QSam[a]," in *Archaeology of the Books of Samuel: The Entangling of the Textual and Literary History* (eds. P. Hugo and A. Schenker; VTSup 132; Leiden: Brill, 2010), 23–37. For a more extensive revision, see Rofé's articles in the previous note. In contrast, see Ulrich, *DSSDCB*, 85–100.

[43] The passage was debated in D. Barthélemy, D.W. Gooding, J. Lust, and E. Tov, *The Story of David and Goliath: Textual and Literary Criticism: Papers of a Joint Research Venture* (OBO 73; Göttingen: Vandenhoeck & Ruprecht, 1986). Subsequent opinion endorses the views of Lust and Tov, that MT has a double edition in contrast to the single edition in LXX. Even if the view of Barthélemy and Gooding, that LXX has excised inconsistencies, were correct, there would still be two intentional editions.

[44] See Ulrich, *The Qumran Text*, 151–91; Ulrich, "Josephus's Biblical Text for the Books of Samuel," in Ulrich, *DSS*, 184–201; Cross, Parry, and Saley, "4QSam[a]," 25–26, 66.

[45] See especially the large insertion in Jer 7:30–8:3 visible in 4QJer[a]. For the text, see E. Tov, "70. 4QJer[a]," *DJD* XV: 145–70, esp. 155 and Pl. XXIV; for two different analyses, see Tov, ibid., and Ulrich, "Qumran Witness to the Developmental Growth of the Prophetic Books," in *With Wisdom as a Robe: Qumran and Other Jewish Studies in Honour of Ida Fröhlich* (Hebrew Bible Monographs 21; eds. K.D. Dobos and M. Kószeghy; Sheffield: Sheffield Phoenix Press, 2008), 263–74.

2 Sam 8:7

4QSam^a LXX: ירוש[ל]י[ם גם] [אותם ל]קח אחר שושק
[מלך מצרים ב]עֲלוֹתוֹ אל יר[ושלים] בימי רחבעם בן
שלו[מה]

"... to Jerusalem. These Shishak king of Egypt later seized when he came up to Jerusalem in the time of Rehoboam son of Solomon."

MT: יְרוּשָׁלָ͏ִם

"... to Jerusalem."

To the earlier text as in MT, 4QSam^a adds a chronological update, inserting a report from 1 Kgs 14:25–26.[46] The LXX and VL translations contain the insertion, as did the text used by Josephus (*Ant.* 7.104–08).

1 Sam 2:22^{fin}

4QSam^a = OG: [ויאמר]^{23} לבני ישראל
"... to the sons of Israel. And he said ..."

MT = LXX^O: לְכָל־יִשְׂרָאֵל וְאֵת אֲשֶׁר יִשְׁכְּבוּן אֶת הַנָּשִׁים הַצֹּבְאוֹת פֶּתַח אֹהֶל מוֹעֵד: ^{23}וַיֹּאמֶר
"... to all Israel, and that they were lying with the women who served at the entrance to the tent of meeting. And he said ..."

In contrast to the insertion in 4QSam^a in 2 Sam 8:7 above, here it is MT that inserts the detail about the sin of Eli's sons at the shrine.[47] At the beginning of this verse, however, 4QSam^a also inserts a detail that is not in MT, giving Eli's exact age. Josephus (*Ant.* 5.339) knows this longer text as well.

Such isolated insertions, just as new editions, are intentional and should be sharply distinguished from unintentional large variants, for example, losses through parablepsis (e.g., MT-1 Sam 14:41) or erroneous expansions by dittography (e.g., MT-2 Sam 6:3–4).

5.1.3.3 Individual Textual Variants

Individual or small-scale textual variants have been the focus of classical textual criticism and populate

---

[46] For the text and discussion of the insertion at 2 Sam 8:7, see Cross, *DJD* XVII: 132–33 and Ulrich, *The Qumran Text*, 45–48.

[47] For the text and discussion of the insertion at 1 Sam 2:22, see Cross, Parry, and Saley, "4QSam^a," 39–47; and Ulrich, *The Qumran Text*, 57–58.

every text. Some are inadvertent errors (e.g., ואהלים "and tents" 4QSam^a = καὶ σκηνώματα OG OL, for וֵאלֹהָיו "and its gods" MT; 2 Sam 7:23). Some are intentional, indeed theological changes (e.g., יקם יהוה היוצא מפיך "May the Lord establish what has come out of your mouth" [i.e., Hannah's vow] 4QSam^a OG, changed to יָקֵם יְהוָה אֶת־דְּבָרוֹ "May the Lord establish his word" MT; 1 Sam 1:23). Yet others are simple clarifications that a scribe thought would enhance the text (e.g., לכהן "to the priest" 4QSam^b = OG, לַאֲחִימֶלֶךְ הַכֹּהֵן "to Ahimelek the priest" MT; 1 Sam 21:3).

In general, individual textual variants, though abundant and important for indicating text families, form a relatively modest category in the larger textual history of a book. It should be noticed in both the isolated insertions mentioned above in section → 5.1.3.2 and the individual variants listed in this section that LXX agrees with the scroll against MT. It is due to such repeated agreements that 4QSam^a, 4QSam^b, and LXX are considered members of one text tradition in contrast to MT. The fragments of the Samuel scrolls virtually never overlap, and so it is impossible to prove their mutual affiliation; their similarity is shown in the frequent agreement of each with LXX and Josephus as opposed to MT. Though there are exceptions, they each more frequently maintain correct readings where MT errs or adds and exhibit agreement in errors or additions where MT has the correct reading. Moreover, the scrolls must be considered a reliable source for reconstructing the Hebrew *Vorlage* of the Old Greek.

5.1.3.4 Different Orthography

Finally, one minor, and usually not too significant, form of textual variation is orthographic expansion. The early consonantal text of Hebrew was subject to ambiguities (e.g., דבר could mean "word" [*dāvār*] or "plague" [*dever*]), and so, especially during the latter half of the Second Temple period, a growing practice developed of inserting *matres lectionis* to aid in the reading and interpretation of texts. For example, דָּוִד "David" is found in MT-Sam and the earlier 4QSam^b but the alternate spelling דויד in 4QSam^a and MT-Chr; also כל "all," כִּי "because," and אֱלֹהֵי "God of" in MT and 4QSam[b] but the alternate spellings אלוהי, כיא, כול in 4QSam[a] and 4QSam[c].

Thus, while some scribes attempted to reproduce exactly the orthography of the source text they were copying, others deliberately or inadvertently (seeing a short form but unthinkingly writing the current long form) updated the text with a fuller spelling practice than their source text had used. Sometimes this was quite necessary. For example, frequent forms such as אבות could be mistaken to mean "fathers" in texts such as Isa 19:3, where the scribe of 1QIsa[a] inserted a *vav* in הא׳בות to help the reader know that the word meant "spirits of the dead"; the Masoretes accomplished the same later by adding the vowel point הָאֹבוֹת. The orthographic practice, however, is rarely related to the textual edition of a book.

5.1.3.5 Translation, Transmission, and Recensions

The book of Samuel was translated into Greek probably in the late third or the second century B.C.E. (→ 5.4). It was not translated from a text like MT but rather from another Hebrew *Vorlage* close to 4QSam[a] (just as the Chronicler used a text like 4QSam[a]; → 5.3.1.2; → 5.3.3).[48] At some point, just as with Kings and Chronicles, the text was divided into two books, 1 Samuel and 2 Samuel, presumably due to the length, though 4QSam[a] does not yet show this division. As the Hebrew and Greek forms of the book were repeatedly recopied and transmitted, errors and variants of the four types described above crept into the text. These did not result in variant editions (except for 1 Samuel 17–18) but did bifurcate into the two text traditions seen in 4QSam[a,b,c]-OG versus MT-*kaige*-T-S-V. After the two Jewish revolts, the single Hebrew text form that the rabbis happened to preserve was from the latter text tradition, and other Hebrew text traditions, such as that preserved in 4QSam[a] were not transmitted.

Around the turn of the era, some Greek-speaking Jews found that the transmitted forms of the developing Old Greek were at variance with the rabbinic Hebrew texts that were eventually preserved in MT. They produced new revisions of the Greek, now known as the *kaige*-Th, Aquila, and Symmachus recensions (→ 3–5.1.5.2). These recensions were not new translations but reworkings of the Old Greek to conform more closely in word choice and syntax with the rabbinic Hebrew texts. Since for a number of books, however, the Old Greek was not originally translated from a rabbinic text type but from another type, sometimes the recensions differed widely from the Old Greek and the Old Greek was lost.

A Lucianic recension of the Greek, a combination of Hexaplaric readings based on an Old Greek substratum, attributed to the fourth-century Antiochene presbyter seems widely acknowledged (→ 3–5.1.6.2). But since some of its readings are attested as early as Josephus, a debate continues regarding the character of its base text: whether it is simply a slightly developed Old Greek text with a few variants, or more of a recension toward a different Hebrew text such as 4QSam[a].[49]

The proliferation of text forms in the second and third centuries C.E. became so great that Origen designed an ambitious project to determine the text of the "Seventy." His Hexapla (→ 1.3.1.2) presented in six columns the rabbinic Hebrew text, a Greek transliteration of that Hebrew, the recension of Aquila, that of Symmachus, his emended Septuaginta, and the recension of Theodotion. It is unfortunate that he did not know that a number of the Old Greek texts had been translated from Hebrew *Vorlagen* that were simply different from the rabbinic texts, so he lost large amounts of the Old Greek.

---

[48] See Cross, Parry, and Saley, "4QSam[a]," 25–27; Ulrich, *The Qumran Text*, 92–93, 163–64; and McCarter, *1 Samuel*, 9–11.

[49] T. Kauhanen, *Proto-Lucianic Problem in 1 Samuel* (De Septuaginta Investigationes 3; Göttingen: Vandenhoeck & Ruprecht, 2012); T. Kauhanen, "Traces of the Proto-Lucianic Text," *BIOSCS* 40 (2007): 75–87; R.J. Saley, "Greek Lucianic Doublets and 4QSam[a]," *BIOSCS* 40 (2007): 63–73; R.J. Saley, "Proto-Lucian and 4QSam[a]," *BIOSCS* 41 (2008): 34–45.

5.1.4 Relevance for Exegesis

Scholars have been warned for almost four centuries that the Hebrew *textus receptus* of Samuel is "more corrupt than the text of any other part of the Old Testament."[50] Nonetheless, it serves as the "default text," since it is the only complete text in the original language, and unfortunately often it is the only text consulted by scholars. But MT (→ 5.3.2) cannot serve as the sole basis for serious research. Both quantitatively and qualitatively, excellent witnesses are available.

Quantitatively, in addition to the fully extant LXX (→ 5.4), 4QSam^a (→ 5.3.1.2; → 5.3.3) is the fourth largest of all the Qumran biblical scrolls in the amount of text preserved, with 3,656 words.[51] MT, fully preserved, is essential, but the scrolls thus offer a great quantity of evidence, as seen above.

The witnesses to Samuel do not quite rival the wealth of witnesses to Exodus. For Exodus, the varied textual witnesses plus literary and redactional analyses offer an enormous spectrum of knowledge regarding its growth and development.[52] But the Samuel texts nonetheless provide an abundance of data on the several levels briefly discussed in sections → 5.1.3–5.1.3.5 above.

Qualitatively, 4QSam^b especially, 4QSam^a, and even 4QSam^c each prove at different points to be better witnesses than MT and moreover confirm that the Old Greek was not a loose translation but is generally a faithful mirror of yet another ancient text of Samuel somewhat different from MT. That is not to say, of course, that MT does not also offer superior readings, but simply that all witnesses must always be examined on a word-by-word basis, in an egalitarian way, without privileging any particular witness.

The history of the Hebrew and the Greek texts is intertwined.[53] Prior to our earliest manuscript witnesses, the text had apparently bifurcated into two traditions: 4QSam^{a,b,c}-OG, and the forerunner of the rabbinic and Masoretic text (eventually followed by the *kaige* and other recensions and by T-S-V). The Chronicler used an ancient Hebrew exemplar of the 4QSam^{a,b,c} tradition. The Old Greek also was faithfully translated from an ancient Hebrew manuscript close to 4QSam^{a,b,c}.[54] The rabbis accepted the form like MT, and many Greek texts later underwent revision toward the rabbinic text: the *kaige*-Th, Symmachus, Aquila, Hexapla, and Lucian recensions. Others – for example, the Qumran covenanters, the Christians, and Josephus – preserved texts of the alternate tradition.

McCarter has observed that the textual problems of Samuel require so much effort that study of the literary character of the book may suffer.[55] Neither textual analysis nor literary analysis, of course, should be ignored; both should be analyzed together. But scholars should keep in mind that the Samuel scrolls demonstrate that only literary analysis that incorporates the textual witness from Qumran and LXX can claim legitimacy.

Aejmelaeus, *Trail.
Archaeology of the Books of Samuel: The Entangling of the Textual and Literary History* (eds. P. Hugo and A. Schenker; VTSup 132; Leiden: Brill, 2010).
Barthélemy, D., D.W. Gooding, J. Lust, and E. Tov, *The Story of David and Goliath: Textual and Literary Criticism: Papers of a Joint Research Venture* (OBO 73; Göttingen: Vandenhoeck & Ruprecht, 1986).

---

[50] H.P. Smith, *A Critical and Exegetical Commentary on the Books of Samuel* (ICC; Edinburgh: T & T Clark, n.d. [Preface dated July 20, 1898]), xxx. Smith (xxix–xxx) notes that MT "was mildly questioned by Cappel, and roughly attacked by Morin" in the seventeenth century, though this was partly due to religious polemic.

[51] M.G. Abegg, "Linguistic Profile of the Isaiah Scrolls," *DJD XXXII.2, 25–41 (25): the Great Isaiah Scroll is virtually fully intact with 22,696 words preserved, MurXII is second with 4,834, and 1QIsa^b is third with 4,603 words.

[52] See E. Ulrich, "Crossing the Borders from 'Pre-Scripture' to Scripture (Rewritten) to 'Rewritten Scripture'," in *Rewritten Bible after Fifty Years: Texts, Terms, or Techniques? A Last Dialogue with Geza Vermes* (ed. J. Zsengellér; JSJSup 166; Leiden: Brill, 2014), 83–104.

[53] For an early exercise in demonstrating the intertwined history, see Cross, *"Evolution."

[54] See the critique by S. Jellicoe (*The Septuagint and Modern Study* [Oxford: Clarendon, 1968], 283) of P.A.H. de Boer, who "seriously underestimates the fidelity of the LXX translators to their original ... and ascribes the variants in the Greek to translational idiosyncrasies."

[55] McCarter, *1 Samuel*, 12.

Cross, F.M., "A New Qumran Biblical Fragment Related to the Original Hebrew Underlying the Septuagint," *BASOR* 132 (1953): 15–26.

Cross, F.M., "The Oldest Manuscripts from Qumran," *JBL* 74 (1955): 147–72.

Cross, F.M. and R.J. Saley, "A Statistical Analysis of the Textual Character of 4QSamuel^a (4Q51)," *DSD* 13 (2006): 46–54.

The Dead Sea Scrolls: Transmission of Traditions and Production of Texts (eds. S. Metso, H. Najman, and E. Schuller; STDJ 92; Leiden: Brill, 2010).

Dictionary of Biblical Interpretation (ed. J.H. Hayes; 2 vols.; Nashville: Abingdon, 1999).

Driver, S.R., *Notes on the Hebrew Text of the Books of Samuel* (Oxford: Clarendon, 1890).

Fields, W.W., *The Dead Sea Scrolls: A Full History*, Vol. 1: *1947–1960* (Leiden: Brill, 2009).

Hugo, P., "Die Septuaginta in der Textgeschichte der Samuelbücher: Methodologische Prinzipien am Beispiel von 2 Sam 6:1–3," in Karrer–Kraus, **Septuaginta 2008*, 36–52.

McCarter, P.K., *I Samuel: A New Translation with Introduction and Commentary* (AB 8; Garden City; Doubleday, 1980).

McCarter, P.K., *II Samuel: A New Translation with Introduction and Commentary* (AB 9; Garden City; Doubleday, 1984).

Cross–Talmon, **QHBT*.

Pisano, S., *Additions or Omissions in the Books of Samuel: The Significant Pluses and Minuses in the Massoretic, LXX and Qumran Texts* (OBO 57; Göttingen: Vandenhoeck & Ruprecht, 1984).

Sabatier, **Bibliorum*.

Thenius, O., *Die Bücher Samuels*: (2nd ed.; Kurzgefasstes exegetisches Handbuch zum Alten Testament 4; Leipzig: S. Hirzel, 1864).

Tov, E., *The Hebrew and Greek Texts of Samuel: 1980 Proceedings IOSCS, Vienna* (Jerusalem: Academon, 1980).

Tov, E., "The Textual Affiliations of 4QSam^a," in Tov, **Greek-Hebrew Bible*, 273–83.

Tov, **TCHB*.

Trebolle Barrera, J., *Centena in Libros Samuelis et Regum: Variantes textuales y composición literaria en los Libros de Samuel y Reyes* (Textos y estudios "Cardenal Cisneros" 47; Madrid: Consejo Superior de Investigaciones Científicas, 1989).

Ulrich, E., *The Qumran Text of Samuel and Josephus* (HSM 19; Missoula: Scholars Press, 1978).

Ulrich, **DSS*.

Ulrich, **DSSDCB*.

Wellhausen, J., *Der Text der Bücher Samuelis untersucht* (Göttingen: Vandenhoeck & Ruprecht, 1871).

Eugene Ulrich

5.2 Textual History of Kings

5.2.1 Witnesses

1) The Hebrew text of the books of Kings is preserved in the medieval Masoretic manuscripts (→ 3–5.3). The most authoritative Masoretic codices containing the books of Kings are MT^A,[1] MT^C,[2] and MT^L.[3] In Qumran Cave 4, several fragments have been found (→ 5.3.1.8), while smaller fragments were discovered elsewhere (→ 5.3.1.9–12).[4]
2) The Old Greek or LXX translation (→ 5.5), which is the earliest non-Hebrew witness,[5] is attested to in the Codices Vaticanus (= LXX^B),[6] Sinaiticus (= LXX^S),[7] Alexandrinus (= LXX^A),[8] Coislin 1 (= LXX^M),[9] Venetus (= LXX^V),[10] in the so-called Lucianic cursive manuscripts (LXX^L),[11] and in a great number of other medieval cursives that reflect in most cases recensional text forms, more or less distant from the original Old Greek text.[12] No Greek manuscript is a pure representative of the earliest Old Greek (→ 5.2.2).
3) The other Greek versions, the so-called Hexaplaric translations (→ 3–5.1.5.2), Theodotion, Aquila, Symmachus, and the Quinta,[13] have survived in their original Greek form in quotations made by Greek church fathers (→ 21.7). Two rather large fragments of Aquila's translation of 1 Kgs 21:7–17 and 2 Kgs 23:16–27 have been discovered in the Genizah of Old Cairo.[14] These were not copied from the Aquila column of the Hexapla but derive directly from a Jewish edition of Aquila's translation.[15] Other fragments of the Hexaplaric versions are preserved

---

[1] End of ninth or early tenth century, Jerusalem, Shrine of the Book. Facsimile edition: M. Goshen-Gottstein, *The Aleppo Codex, Part 1: The Plates* (Jerusalem: Magnes Press, 1976). Cf. Barthélemy, *Studies*, 239–40 = Barthélemy, *Critique textuelle 1992*, viii.

[2] Dated in a colophon from 896; Cairo, Karaite Synagogue. Edition: F. Perez Castro (ed.), *El codice de profetas de El Cairo*, Vol. III: *Reyes* (Textos y estudios "Cardenal Cisneros" 32; Madrid: Instituto "Arias Montano" CSIC, 1984). Barthélemy, *Studies*, 240 = Barthélemy, *Critique textuelle 1992*, viii.

[3] 1008/1009 C.E., Russian National Library, St. Petersburg, manuscript Firkovitch II EBP B 19 A. D.N. Freedman (ed.), *The Leningrad Codex: A Facsimile Edition* (Grand Rapids/Leiden: Eerdmans/Brill, 1998). For the textual witnesses of MT, see the comprehensive overview in Barthélemy, *Studies*, 238–382 = *Critique textuelle 1992*, cxvii–clxxviii.

[4] 4Q54: J. Trebolle Barrera, "54. 4QKgs," *DJD* XIV (1995): 171–83 and pl. XXXVII. Cf. J.A. Fitzmyer, S.J., *A Guide to the Dead Sea Scrolls and Related Literature* (rev. and exp. ed.; Grand Rapids: Eerdmans, 2008), 35; É. Puech, "Nouvelles identifications de Manuscrits Bibliques dans la grotte 4. 4QRois^a (4Q54a) et 4QRois^b-4Q54^b(?) ou 4QIs^s-4Q69c(?)," *RevQ* 25 (2012): 467–72; J. Trebolle Barrera, "Qumran Fragments of the Books of Kings," in *The Books of Kings: Sources, Composition, Historiography and Reception* (eds. A. Lemaire and B. Halpern; VTSup 129; Leiden: Brill, 2010), 19–39.

[5] For a comprehensive overview of the textual witnesses of the Old Greek, see Barthélemy, *Studies*, 412–67 = *Critique textuelle 1992*, cxvii–clvii.

[6] About 340 C.E., probably from Egypt. Vatican Library, Rome: manuscript Vat. Gr. 1209. P. Andrist (ed.), *Le manuscrit B de la Bible (Vaticanus graecus 1209): Introduction au facsimilé: Actes du colloque de Genève (11 juin 2001): Contributions supplémentaires* (HTB 3; Lausanne: Éditions du Zèbre, 2009).

[7] About 360 C.E., perhaps from Caesarea of Palestine. British Library, London, Leipzig (manuscript Universitätsbibl. Gr. 1), Monastery of St. Catherine, Sinai, and some fragments in St. Petersburg. Rahlfs–Fraenkel, *Verzeichnis*, 201–06.

[8] About 450 C.E. London, British Library, manuscript Reg. D. V–VIII; Rahlfs–Fraenkel, *Verzeichnis*, 224–26.

[9] Seventh century C.E.; Paris, manuscript BN Coislin 1; Rahlfs–Fraenkel, *Verzeichnis*, 307–08 (contains numerous quotations of the Hexaplaric translations).

[10] Eighth century C.E.; Rome, Vatican Library, manuscript Vat. gr. 2106 (part I) and Venice, manuscript BN Marciana gr. 1 (part II); Rahlfs–Fraenkel, *Verzeichnis*, 344–46 and 372–74. (In Brooke–McLean–Thackeray, *The Old Testament in Greek*, the siglum of this manuscript is N).

[11] The cursives LXX^{19, 108 and 82, 93, 127} (= Brooke–McLean–Thackeray: b b and o e_2 c_2). N. Fernández Marcos and J.R. Busto Saiz, *El texto antioqueno de la Biblia griega*, Vol. 2: *1–2 Reyes* (Textos y estudios "Cardenal Cisneros" 53; Madrid: CSIC, 1992).

[12] Rahlfs–Fraenkel, *Verzeichnis*.

[13] Barthélemy, *Devanciers*, 128–43; a comprehensive overview of the textual witnesses is found in Barthélemy, *Studies*, 468–97 = *Critique textuelle 1992*, clviii–clxxviii.

[14] F.C. Crawford Burkitt, *Fragments of the Books of Kings according to the Translation of Aquila with a Preface of C. Taylor* (Cambridge: Cambridge University Press, 1897).

[15] The manuscript comes from a synagogue; see Crawford Burkitt, *Fragments*, 31.

in Syriac in a manuscript of the Syro-Hexapla, edited by de Lagarde,[16] which was not yet known to Field for his edition of the fragments of the Hexapla.[17] There are also occasional quotations from these versions in Latin by Jerome (→ 21.8), or by anonymous translators, preserved, for example, in the margins of Spanish Vulgate manuscripts.[18] The Hexaplaric translations are based on the Hebrew text of the time of their translators. Aquila and Symmachus are to be dated in the second century C.E., while the versions of cols. 5, 6, and 7 for Kings in Origen's Hexapla (viz. Old Greek, Theodotion, Quinta) may correspond to the group of Palestinian or *kaige*-Th recensions (→ 1.3.1.2).[19] These go back to the first century B.C.E. or even earlier.

4) The Latin witnesses are the Old Latin translation (*Vetus Latina*, VL; → 3–5.2.1.2) and the translation of Jerome, the so-called Vulgate (V; → 3–5.1.7→). VL is an extremely literal translation of the Old Greek, prepared in North Africa around 200 C.E., and surviving only in fragments and quotations.[20] VL sometimes is the only witness of the earliest Old Greek (→ 5.5) since all Greek witnesses reflect recensional forms of the text while the Old Latin version may be based on a pre-recensional text. Jerome's Latin version of the Hebrew text of Samuel–Kings, prepared around 393 C.E.,[21] has been preserved in a number of good witnesses.[22]

5) The Aramaic Targum Jonathan (→ 3–5.1.3) cannot be dated easily.[23] Some scholars suggested an early date between the last centuries B.C.E. and the third century C.E., while others, noticing allusions to events after the *Hidjra*, proposed a late date. The most probable date seems to be the fourth to fifth century.[24] In 1 Kings 11–12, 14, the Hebrew *Vorlage* of Tg^J may reflect a text different from the proto-MT.[25]

6) The Peshitta (→ 3–5.1.4),[26] second century C.E. for 1–2 Kings,[27] is preserved in a number of good manuscripts among which the earliest complete one is Codex Ambrosianus (seventh century C.E.).[28] The translation is based on proto-

---

[16] P. de Lagarde, *Bibliothecae Syriacae quae ad philologiam sacram pertinent* (Göttingen: Dieterich, 1892); T.M. Law, *Origenes orientalis: The Preservation of Origen's Hexapla in the Syrohexapla of 3 Kingdoms* (De Septuaginta Investigationes 2; Göttingen: Vandenhock & Ruprecht, 2011).

[17] F. Field, *Hexapla.

[18] Manuscripts VL$^{91-96}$: Gryson, *Altlateinische Handschriften I*, 145–55; A. Moreno Hernández, *Las Glosas marginales de Vetus Latina en las Biblias Vulgatas Españolas 1–2 Reyes* (Textos y estudios "Cardenal Cisneros" 49; Madrid: Inst. de filología del CSIC, 1989); A. Schenker, "Der Platz der altlateinischen Randlesarten des Kodex von León und der Valvanera-Bibel in der biblischen Textgeschichte (1–4 Kgt)," in *Der Antiochenische Text der Septuaginta in seiner Bezeugung und seiner Bedeutung* (eds. S. Kreuzer and M. Sigismund; De Septuaginta Investigationes 4; Göttingen: Vandenhock & Ruprecht, 2013), 199–210.

[19] Barthélemy, *Devanciers*, 136–43.

[20] P.-M. Bogaert, "La Bible latine des origines au Moyen-Âge," *RTL* 19 (1988), 137–59, and 276–314; P.-M. Bogaert, "The Latin Bible," in *The New Cambridge History of the Bible*, Vol. 1: *From the Beginnings to 600* (eds. J.C. Paget and J. Schaper; Cambridge: Cambridge University Press, 2013), 505–26; P.-M. Bogaert, "The Latin Bible: c. 600 to c. 900," in *The New Cambridge History of the Bible*, Vol. 2: *From 600 to 1450* (eds. R. Marsden and E.A. Matter; Cambridge: Cambridge University Press, 2012), 69–92.

[21] G. Grützmacher, *Hieronymus: Eine biographische Studie*, Vol. 1 (Leipzig: Dieterich, 1901 = repr. Aalen: Scientia, 1969), 74; F. Cavallera, *Saint Jérôme: Sa vie et son oeuvre*, Vol. 2 (SSL 1–2; Louvain/Paris: SSL/Champion, 1922), 157; P.-M. Bogaert, "The Latin Bible," *The New Cambridge History of the Bible*, Vol. 1: *From the Beginnings to 600* (eds. J.C. Paget and J. Schaper; Cambridge: Cambridge University Press, 2013), 505–26 (515–16).

[22] *Biblia Sacra iuxta Latinam vulgatam versionem*, Vol. 6: *Liber Malachim* (Rome: Vatican Polyglot Press, 1945). See the overview on the textual witnesses in Barthélemy, *Studies, 497–534 = *Critique textuelle 1992*, clxxix–cciv.

[23] R. Le Déaut, "Targum," *DBSup* 13.2*–344*, here 106*–21*; Barthélemy, *Studies, 540–42 = *Critique textuelle 1992*, ccix–ccx.

[24] Le Déaut, "Targum," 114*–18*.

[25] Le Déaut, "Targum," 112*.

[26] See the overview on textual witnesses in Barthélemy, *Studies, 534–40 = *Critique textuelle 1992*, ccv–ccviii.

[27] M.P. Weitzman, *The Syriac Version of the the Old Testament: An Introduction* (University of Cambridge Oriental Publications 56; Cambridge: Cambridge University Press, 1999), 258.

[28] Milan, manuscript Biblioteca Ambrosiana B 21 Inf. Facsimile ed.: A.M. Ceriani, *Translatio Syra Peshitto Veteris Testamenti* (2 vols.; Milan, 1876–1883; reprint Piscataway: Gorgias Press, 2012); P.B. Dirksen, *La Peshitta dell'Antico Testamento* (Studi biblici 103; Brescia: Paideia, 1993); M. Weitzman, "The Interpretive Character of the Syriac Old Testament," in *Hebrew Bible/Old Testament: The History of its Interpretation*, Part 1: *Antiquity* (ed. M. Saebø; Göttingen: Vandenhoeck & Ruprecht, 1996), 588–611.

MT.²⁹ The influence of Old Greek resulted from later revision, not from the original translation.

5.2.2 Relationship between the Textual Witnesses

As in many other Scripture books, the textual witnesses of the books of Kings fall into two groups, one around MT, and a second smaller one connected with the Old Greek. The former comprises MT (→ 5.3.2), the Hebrew Qumran fragments (→ 5.3.1; → 5.3.3), the Hexaplaric versions (3–5.1.5.2), Peshitta (3–5.1.4), Targum (3–5.1.3), and Jerome's translation (3–5.1.7); the latter consists of the Old Greek (→ 5.5), sometimes attested to by some of the daughter translations, such as VL (3–5.2.1.2) and the Coptic (→ 3–5.2.2) and Armenian (→ 3–5.2.5.4) translations.³⁰ The two groups correspond to two different recensions or text types, in the sense that they not only differ from each other on the level of textual variety but also in literary development.³¹

For the first group, some textual witnesses precede the Masoretic codices by eight centuries or more. These witnesses of the pre- and proto-Masoretic text³² contain readings typical of MT in contradistinction to Old Greek. These could be called pre-Masoretic readings. They also offer specific orthographic MT readings attested to in manuscripts written between the first and second Jewish Wars. Such readings may be called proto-Masoretic since they reappear in the classical witnesses of the Tiberian MT in, for example, 1 Kgs 2:29 with the accidental loss of a phrase in MT that is extant in its usual witnesses, Vulgate, Peshitta, and Tgʲ, while the Old Greek alone preserves the original text.³³ Another example is found in 1 Kgs 9:8 where the textual corruption happened long before the formation of the consonantal text of MT since the Old Greek shares the variant, and all other witnesses that usually follow MT imply it.³⁴ The proto-Masoretic witnesses attest substantially to the same consonantal text, the same vocalization, and the same text divisions as those of MT, with the exception of some textual differences that occur as a normal consequence of the text transmission.

The witnesses of the first group correspond essentially to the text found in the Masoretic manuscripts. Among the latter, the choice codices represent the best textual tradition fixed by the Masoretes. Other manuscripts of lesser quality cannot compete with these choice witnesses³⁵ and are therefore of little weight for textual criticism and the text history.

The second group is not preserved in Hebrew (→ 5.3.1).³⁶ It corresponds to the Hebrew base text

---

²⁹ Weitzman, *The Syriac Version of the the Old Testament*, 60–61; M. Koster, "The Copernican Revolution in the Study of the Origins of the Peshitta," in *Targum Studies*, Vol. 2: *Targum and Peshitta* (ed. P.V.M. Flesher; South Florida Studies in the History of Judaism 165; Atlanta: Scholars Press, 1998), 15–56; M. Koster, "Redating TR (*Textus Receptus*) and BTR (*Basic Textus Receptus*): The Three Stages at Stake?" *Aramaic Studies* 7 (2009): 1–18.

³⁰ A. Piquer, P. Torijano, and J. Trebolle Barrera, "Septuagint Versions, Greek Recensions and Hebrew Editions: The Text-Critical Evaluation of the Old Latin, Armenian and Georgian Versions in *III–IV Regnorum*," in *Translating a Translation: The LXX and Its Modern Translations in the Context of Early Judaism* (eds. H. Ausloos et al.; BETL 213; Leuven: Peeters, 2008), 251–81.

³¹ This distinction is explained by Schenker, *"Ursprung."

³² Barthélemy, *Studies, 338–411 = *Critique textuelle 1992, cii–cxvi; D. Barthélemy, "Histoire du texte hébraïque de l' Ancien Testament," in Barthélemy, *Etudes, 345–64 (350–51) = "Text, History of," in *IDB* (1976): 878–84 (880); Tov, *TCHB, 183–90 (with different terminology).

³³ Barthélemy, *Critique textuelle 1982, 335.

³⁴ Schenker, *Une bible archétype?*, 53–62.

³⁵ Goshen-Gottstein, *"Biblical Manuscripts." However, B. Chiesa, *Filologia storica della Bibbia ebraica*, Vol. 2: *Dall'età moderna ai giorni nostri* (Studi biblici 135; Brescia: Paideia, 2002), 410–41, and J.W. Wevers, *The Hebrew Variants in the Books of Kings and their Relationship to the Old Greek and to the Greek Recensions* (ThD diss.; Princeton Theological Seminary, 1945) believe that numerous variants found in these manuscripts correspond to early stages of the biblical text. For a thorough assessment of the validity of Goshen-Gottstein's view, see Barthélemy, *Studies, 256–72 = *Critique textuelle 1992, xix–xxix.

³⁶ In other Scripture books, the *Vorlage* of the Old Greek, or at least a text resembling that *Vorlage* may have been preserved in Judean Desert fragments, such as in *Jeremiah* (→ 7.2.1); see E. Tov, "The Biblical Texts from the Judean Desert – An Overview and Analysis," in Tov, *HB, GB, and Qumran, 128–54

5.2.2 RELATIONSHIP BETWEEN THE TEXTUAL WITNESSES

of the Old Greek that is now lost. The Old Greek is available in the Greek witnesses, and also in the Latin, Coptic, Ethiopic (→ 3–5.2.3.4), and Armenian daughter translations of this Greek version. The translation styles of the Old Greek and VL allow for a fair degree of certainty in the reconstruction of the underlying Hebrew text.

In the books of Kings, where the Old Greek agrees with MT it may be observed that the sequence of the words closely follows that of MT, and it therefore stands to reason that it followed its *Vorlage* also in other instances. The result of this translation style is the exact presentation of the Hebrew syntactical structure.[37] Since VL followed the same procedure in its Latin rendering of Old Greek, it is possible to reconstruct the structure of the Hebrew text behind the Greek and Latin renderings with a high degree of probability. On the semantic level, the equivalences between Hebrew and Greek and Greek and Latin words are less fixed, allowing for variation in the different contexts. As a result of this translation principle,[38] the Hebrew *Vorlage* implied in these witnesses is to a great extent transparent.

No extant textual witness preserves the Old Greek in its entirety (→ 5.5.2.1→).[39] However, in some segments in Samuel–Kings, LXX[B] or the Lucianic (or Antiochene) witnesses together with VL come close to it.[40] In 2 Sam 10:1–1 Kgs 2:11, the Lucianic-Antiochene witnesses represent the Old Greek to a large degree, while in 1 Kings 3–21 LXX[B] contains a great number of readings that are close or identical to the Old Greek.[41] On the whole, it is necessary to establish the original Old Greek on a case-by-case basis by means of textual and stylistic comparison of all the readings, because no text form is completely identical to the Old Greek.[42] Some criteria for determining the original Greek readings were formulated by de Lagarde in 1863,[43] and a hundred years later, in 1963, by Barthélemy in his comparison of the readings found in the Greek Twelve Minor Prophets scroll of Naḥal Ḥever with the other Greek witnesses, in which he differentiated the translation principles of the authors of Palestinian and *kaige* recensions of the Old Greek text.[44]

The earliest attested Old Greek text in the books of Kings, often agreeing with VL, reveals in many places a specific literary form differing from that of the other Greek witnesses and from MT. The number of these specific Old Greek readings is very high. In most cases, the differences between MT and Old Greek are small, but taken together they total a great amount of variation, creating a different literary profile of 1–2 Kings.[45] It seems that no

---

(143–45, 151–53). The few extant Hebrew fragments of Kings from Qumran (cf. n. 4) seem to correspond to the proto-Masoretic and semi-Masoretic text. One fragment is non-aligned.

[37] G. Marquis, "Word Order as a Criterion for the Evaluation of Translation Technique in the LXX and the Evaluation of Word-Order Variants as Exemplified in LXX-Ezechiel," *Textus* 13 (1986): 59–84; G. Walser, "Die Wortfolge der Septuaginta," in Karrer–Kraus, *Septuaginta 2008, 258–66.

[38] See A. Léonas, *L'aube des traducteurs: De l'hébreu au grec: traducteurs et lecteurs de la Bible des Septante* (Initiations bibliques; Paris: Cerf, 2007). This study describes the conception of language and languages in antiquity as the intellectual and religious background of the Old Greek translation enterprise. Another way of viewing the Old Greek is the interlinear translation model, proposed by Pietersma, based on technical translation considerations: A. Pietersma, "A New Paradigm for Addressing Old Questions: The Relevance of the Interlinear Model for the Study of the Septuagint," in *Bible and Computer: The Stellenbosch AIBI Conference: Proceedings of the Association Internationale Bible et Informatique: "From Alpha to Byte,"* University of Stellenbosch, 17–21 July 2000 (ed. J. Cook; Leiden: Brill, 2002), 337–64; C.B. Taylor, *Reading between the Lines: The Interlinear Paradigm for Septuagint Studies* (Biblical Tools and Studies 8; Leuven: Peeters, 2011).

[39] P. Hugo, "Le grec ancien des livres des Règnes: Une histoire et un bilan de la recherche," in *Sôfer Mahîr. Essays in Honour of Adrian Schenker Offered by Editors of Biblia Hebraica Quinta* (eds. Y.A.P. Goldman, A. van der Kooij, and R.D. Weiss; VTSup 110; Leiden: Brill, 2006), 113–41.

[40] Barthélemy, *Devanciers, 126–43; Bogaert, *"Septante," 595.

[41] Bogaert, *"Septante," 536–692 (590–601).

[42] P. Hugo, "Die antiochenische 'Mischung': L zwischen Altem und Neuem in 2 Samuel," in *Der Antiochenische Text der Septuaginta in seiner Bezeugung und in seiner Bedeutung* (eds. S. Kreuzer and M. Sigismund; De Septuaginta Investigationes 4; Göttingen: Vandenhoeck & Ruprecht, 2013), 109–32.

[43] De Lagarde, *Anmerkungen, 3.

[44] Barthélemy, *Devanciers, 3–126.

[45] An accurate picture may be gained by reading the critical commentary of Bernhard Stade, Friedrich Schwally, and Paul

other biblical book offers as many differences between MT and the Old Greek. Most biblical commentaries limit themselves to a selection of variant readings from the Old Greek, and usually they try to explain them as deriving from the Greek translator.[46] Exceptions to this were some nineteenth-century scholars such as Thenius[47] and, to a certain degree, Wellhausen.[48]

The large differences, especially in 1 Kings 2–14 and elsewhere,[49] and transpositions of sections, such as the book of 1 Kings beginning at 1 Kgs 2:11 in Old Greek (this seems to be the original beginning), and the hymn in 1 Kgs 8:12–13 appearing at the end of Solomon's prayer in Old Greek,[50] are comparable to those occurring in Jeremiah (→ 7.3), Ezekiel (→ 8.3), Daniel (OG; → 18.3), and other books. The most conspicuous pluses are found in 1 Kings 2. They might best be characterized as "summaries," being short pieces summarizing a state of affairs as opposed to stories or lists. Usually they are called, less aptly, miscellanies.[51] They reflect a Hebrew *Vorlage*. Are they to be considered as secondary developments, specific to the Greek books of Kings?[52] This is possible but not certain because they contain matters not found elsewhere in Kings.

The Greek book of 1–2 Kings thus shows genuine textual variants together with a high number of literary differences of various kinds (modified readings, transpositions, pluses in Old Greek corresponding to minuses in MT).[53] Sometimes it cannot be ascertained whether the variants are textual or literary in nature. However, numerous readings certainly are literary since they present a different narrative structure and content from the pericopes of MT throughout the two books. The extreme complexity of the textual situation cannot be explained by a simple answer to the question as to how the differences between MT and the Old Greek were created.[54]

5.2.3 Textual History of the Books of Kings

The textual history of Kings is divided in two distinct phases. The first pre-Masoretic stage covers the earliest period before and after the parting

---

Haupt in *The Sacred Books of the Old Testament* series: B. Stade and F. Schwally (eds.), *The Books of Kings: Critical Edition of the Hebrew Text* (SBOT 9; Leipzig: Hinrichs'sche Buchhandlung, 1904): the vast majority of the comments of the three editors mentioned concern the relationship between MT and the Old Greek. In most verses, they comment on more than one difference in the same verse; on average, a section of ten verses contains fifteen to twenty comments. See also J.W. Wevers, "Exegetical Principles Underlying the Septuagint Text of 1 Kings ii–xxi 43," OTS 8 (1950): 300–22.

[46] See, e.g., S.J. De Vries, *1 Kings* (WBC 12; Waco: Word Books, 1985), lix; M. Cogan, *1 Kings: A New Translation with Introduction and Commentary* (AB 10; New York: Doubleday, 2000), 85; M.A. Sweeney, *I & II Kings: A Commentary* (OTL; Louisville: Westminster, 2007), 32–40.

[47] O. Thenius, *Die Bücher der Könige* (Kurzgefasstes exegetisches Handbuch zum Alten Testament 9; Leipzig: Hirzel, 1849; 2nd ed. 1873).

[48] J. Wellhausen, "Das Buch der Könige," in F. Bleek, *Einleitung in das Alte Testament* (Berlin: Reimer, 1878), 231–67, esp. 234.

[49] J. Debus, *Die Sünde Jerobeams* (FRLANT 93; Göttingen: Vandenhoeck & Ruprecht, 1967); Talshir, *The Alternative Story*; A. Schenker, "Jéroboam et la division du Royaume dans la Septante ancienne," in *Israël construit son histoire* (eds. A. de Pury, Th. Römer, and J.-D. Macchi; MdB 34; Geneva: Labor et Fides, 1996), 193–236 (English transl.: *Israel Constructs Its History* [JSOTSup 306; Sheffield: Sheffield Academic Press, 2000], 214–57 [with small translation errors]).

[50] See Barthélemy, *Devanciers*, 141. For the transposition of 1 Kings 20–21, appearing as chs. 21–20 in 3 Kingdoms, see Schenker, *Älteste Textgeschichte*, 86–107. Smaller transpositions occur elsewhere, especially in 1 Kings 2–14.

[51] Brooke–McLean–Thackeray, *The Old Testament in Greek*: 3 Kgdms 2:35a–o; 2:46a–k = Rahlfs, *Septuaginta* and H.B. Swete, *The Old Testament in Greek* (vol. 1; Cambridge: Cambridge University Press, 1925), 2:35a–o; 2:46a–l.

[52] Thus E. Tov, "The Septuagint Additions ('Miscellanies') in 1 Kings 2 (3 Reigns 2)," in Tov, *Greek-Hebrew Bible*, 548–70; G. Krautwurst, *Studien zu den Septuagintazusätzen in 1. (3.) Könige 2 und ihren Paralleltexten* (ThD diss., University of Mainz, 1977); D.W. Gooding, *Relics of Ancient Exegesis: A Study of the Miscellanies in 3 Reigns 2* (SOTSMS 4; Cambridge: Cambridge University Press, 1976); van Keulen, *Two Versions of the Solomon Narrative*. For the opposite view (the summaries might have been omitted at a more recent stage of the text history), see A. Schenker, *Septante et texte massorétique*, 5–44: as the two series of summaries are literarily well integrated into the book, their secondary nature is questionable.

[53] Tov, *TCHB*, 306–08.

[54] For an exhaustive inquiry into the history of research concerning the text of Kings, see Hugo, *Les deux visages d'Élie*, 5–125.

of the two literarily distinct recensions, viz., the proto-Masoretic and Masoretic witnesses in Hebrew (→ 5.3.1; → 5.3.2) followed by many versions (V [3–5.1.7], P [3–5.1.4], Tgʲ [3–5.1.3], *kaige* recensions [→ 1.3.1.2], Hexaplaric translations [3–5.1.5.2]) on the one hand, and the Old Greek (→ 5.5) with its daughter translations on the other.

The second stage corresponds to the transmission history of the proto-Masoretic text and MT in general, which is sometimes called the rabbinic text. In Kings, the earliest witnesses of the proto-Masoretic phase are found in the Hexaplaric, Latin, Syriac, and Aramaic versions since early Hebrew fragments are scarce.

The first stage, sometimes called pre- or extra-Masoretic,[55] beginning before the translation of Kings into Greek around 200 B.C.E. or, perhaps, somewhat later,[56] lasts until the period of the first Jewish War (66–70 C.E.) when its Hebrew witnesses disappear. The second stage extends from the time when the proto-Masoretic recension appears in the Qumran manuscripts (second and first centuries B.C.E.) until the Masoretic codices of the Middle Ages and the first printed Hebrew Bibles in the sixteenth century.

5.2.4 Earliest Text History of Kings

Here, the earliest text history will be proposed in a sketch that can only be tentative. The question of the earliest attainable text of Kings is linked to Chronicles – in MT (→ 20.2.2) and in the Old Greek (→ 20.3.1) – because of their common passages transmitted in parallel strands. In some places, parallel texts hopefully will reveal the common ancestor of the parallels and thus give access to a text preceding the earliest witnesses of MT (→ 5.3.2) and the Old Greek (→ 5.5).[57] However, these early common readings are rare and therefore are far from allowing us to recover the earliest text of 1–2 Kings in its entirety. Thus, the main problem remains the question of the relationship between the forerunner of MT and the Hebrew *Vorlage* of Old Greek, about which there is as yet no consensus in scholarship. Concerning Kings, a majority of text critics at present consider the Hebrew *Vorlage* of the Old Greek to be secondary to MT although the Old Greek sometimes may preserve older readings.[58] Moreover, many scholars posit a proliferation of co-existing textual forms at the origin of most biblical books.[59] Consequently, they assume parallel transmissions of different text types (pre-MT, Hebrew base of Old Greek, and others).

Three difficulties arise with these assumptions, at least for the text history of Kings and possibly for other books. First, it is not enough to compare the *literary* variants between different text forms. The question must be asked whether the variants in one form depend on the readings of the other form. As is the case with *textual* variants, every judgment on *literarily* divergent readings implies a genealogical statement on the extant readings: among the competing readings, is there one that can claim to be more original, while the others derive from it? Only if variants cannot be explained as dependent on a first archetypical reading is one justified in concluding a parallel transmission of texts. The method for discerning a stemma of divergent literary readings is the same as in textual criticism, with the addition of narrative or literary criteria, since literary interventions create a new profile of what is being said.

---

[55] Barthélemy, *Studies*, 383–409 = Barthélemy, *Critique textuelle 1992*, cii–cxvi.

[56] There is no external hint to a date of the Greek translation. The translation style is that of the historical books (Joshua, Judges, Samuel) and of Jeremiah and Ezekiel. It is distinct from that of the Pentateuch. Dorival assumes a date between 170–150 B.C.E. (Harl–Dorival–Munnich, *Bible grecque*, 93, 111). The *terminus ante quem* is the prologue of the translator of Ecclesiasticus–Sirach: ca. 116 B.C.E. (J. Marböck, *Jesus Sirach 1–23* [HTKAT; Freiburg: Herder, 2010], 39).

[57] Schenker, *Une bible archétype?*

[58] Representative of this position are van Keulen, *Two Versions of the Solomon Narrative*; W. Thiel, *Könige* (1 Kgs 17–21) (BKAT 9.2; Neukirchen-Vluyn: Neukirchener Verlag, 2000–2009); Z. Talshir, "1 Kings and 3 Kingdoms – Origin and Revision, Case Study: The Sins of Solomon (1 Kgs 11)," *Textus* 21 (2002): 71–105; E. Tov, "Three Strange Books," in Tov, *HB, GB, and Qumran*, 283–305, esp. 285–92.

[59] Particularly representative of this opinion is Debel, *"Variant Literary Editions."*

For Kings, it seems possible to show that in most variations of a literary character, proto-MT depends genealogically on the Hebrew base of the Old Greek.[60] The direction of dependence may be discovered through careful analysis of each text form in its own right. The difference in meaning may be compared and explained.[61] The explanation certainly implies a subjective element, but no more than in text-critical judgments.

Second, the specific literary readings of proto-MT often are linked together by a common tendency (→ 5.3.2.3). In pre- and proto-MT, they show a greater coherence while the readings of Old Greek are less systematized. The chronological systems of MT and Old Greek are different and betray a redactional intervention on one side or the other.[62] Differences in the sequence of literary units and in the connection between pericopes attest to specific redactional agendas of MT and/or Old Greek.[63] This hints at a reworking of the literary outline within proto-MT in matters concerning the portraits of Solomon and Jeroboam (1 Kings 2–14),[64] the narrative of the Ark (1 Kings 8),[65] and the importance of the Jerusalem temple (its foundation and its architecture, 1 Kings 6),[66] the sins of Israel and Judah,[67] the guilt of the kings of Israel and of Manasseh of Judah (2 Kings 22–23),[68] and the role of the prophets in the portraits of Elijah and Elisha.[69] Reworking of this type reflects a different recension or edition.[70] However, numerous authors see the reworking on the side of the Hebrew *Vorlage* of the Old Greek, e.g., for 1 Kings 11–12, 14;[71] for 1 Kings 8;[72] 1 Kings 20–21[73] etc. These examples could easily be multiplied.[74]

---

[60] Trebolle Barrera, *Salomon y Jeroboán*; Trebolle Barrera, *Jehú y Joás*; Trebolle Barrera, "Redaction, Recension and Midrash"; J. Trebolle Barrera, "The Text-Critical Use of the Septuagint in the Books of Kings," in *VII Congress of the International Organization for Septuagint and Cognate Studies, Leuven 1989* (ed. C.E. Cox; SBLSCS 31; Atlanta: SBL, 1991), 285–99; Hugo, *Les deux visages d'Élie*; T.M. Law, "How Not to Use 3 Reigns: A Plea to Scholars in the Books of Kings," *VT* 61 (2011): 280–97; Richelle, *Le testament d'Élisée*; Schenker, *Septante et texte massorétique*; Schenker, *Älteste Textgeschichte*; Schenker, *"Ursprung."*

[61] This is generally admitted for the authentic *tiqqunê sopherim* where Old Greek preserves the earlier text while MT is corrected (see Tov, *TCHB*, 59–61); e.g., in 1 Kgs 19:3: McCarthy, *Tiqqune Sopherim*, 232–34; Barthélemy, *Critique textuelle 1982*, 371–72; 1 Kgs 17:1: Barthélemy, *Critique textuelle 1982*, 368. However, the number of literary interventions is much larger than these corrections of single details.

[62] Shenkel, *Chronology and Recensional Development*; Tov, *TCHB*, 307–08.

[63] Trebolle Barrera, "Textual Criticism and the Literary Structure"; Schenker, *Älteste Textgeschichte*, 86–90.

[64] Trebolle Barrera, *Salomón y Jeroboán*; Schenker, *Septante et texte massorétique*.

[65] S.L. McKenzie, "1 Kings 8: A Sample Study into the Texts of Kings Used by the Chronicler and Translated by the Old Greek," *BIOSCS* 19 (1986): 15–34; A. Schenker, "The Ark as Sign of God's Absent Presence in Solomon's Temple: 1 Kings 8:6–8 in the Hebrew and Greek Bibles," in A. Schenker, *Anfänge der Textgeschichte des Alten Testaments: Studien zu Entstehung und Verhältnis der frühesten Textformen* (BWANT 194; Stuttgart: Kohlhammer, 2011), 99–109.

[66] A. Schenker, "Une nouvelle lumière sur l'architecture du temple grace à la Septante? La place de l'arche d'alliance selon 2 Rois 6:16–17 et 3 Règnes 6:16–17," *Annali di Scienze Religiose* 10 (2005): 139–54; J. Lust, "Salomon's Temple According to 1 Kings 6,3–14 in Hebrew and in Greek," in *After Qumran: Old and Modern Editions of the Biblical Texts – The Historical Books* (eds. H. Ausloos, B. Lemmelijn, and J.C. Trebolle Barrera; BETL 246; Leuven: Peeters, 2012), 265–74.

[67] Trebolle Barrera, *Jehú y Joás*; A. Schenker, "La cause de la chute du royaume d'Israël selon le texte massorétique," in A. Schenker, *Une bible archétype? Les parallèles de Samuel-Rois et des Chroniques* (L'écriture de la Bible 3; Paris: Cerf, 2013), 153–71.

[68] Schenker, "Die Textgeschichte der Königsbücher," 65–79; Schenker, *Älteste Textgeschichte*, 52–74.

[69] Hugo, *Les deux visages d'Élie*; Hugo, "Text and Literary History"; Richelle, *Le testament d'Elisée*.

[70] Schenker, "What Do Scribes and What Do Editors Do?"

[71] See Talshir, *The Alternative Story*; Tov, "The Septuagint Additions," 548–70; Krautwurst, *Studien zu den Septuagintazusätzen*; Gooding, *Relics of Ancient Exegesis*; Barthélemy, *Critique textuelle 1982*, 360–65; van Keulen, *Two Versions of the Solomon Narrative*, 222–37; Cogan, *1 Kings*, 355–56.

[72] See Barthélemy, *Critique textuelle 1982*, 350–51; van Keulen, *Two Versions of the Solomon Narrative*, 151–80; for another view, see E. Tov, "Some Sequence Differences between the Masoretic Text and the Septuagint and Their Ramifications for Literary Criticism" in Tov, *Greek-Hebrew Bible*, 411–41.

[73] This difference is hardly noted in the commentaries. However, all commentaries follow the MT sequence. See Tov, "Some Sequence Differences" (previous note), who explains the different positions of the pericope in MT and Old Greek as the consequence of the late addition of the story of Naboth's vineyard to the Elijah cycle.

[74] For all these cases, the bibliography is abundant; merely a few references have been given here.

Third, the parallel pericopes between 1–2 Kings and 1–2 Chronicles (and Isaiah 37–39) seem to contain common textual corruptions, reflected or assumed also by Old Greek.[75] This would imply an archetypical manuscript of Kings that was used by the Chronicler and the Greek translator of Kings, since scribal mistakes can only be transmitted by the copying of a master-copy containing the error (a so-called "leading variant").

5.2.5 MT and Old Greek Reflect Two Text Forms (Recensions) of 1–2 Kings Going Back to the Second or First Century B.C.E.

In our view, it is reasonable to assume that the Greek translator of Kings considered his Hebrew text base to be the best or the correct text. It is reasonable to assume that the criterion for judging the quality of a text, at that time, was not only the learned or careful creation of the copy but also the high esteem in which the chosen text form was held by competent authorities. Authority in these matters must have been founded both on scribal-editorial skills and on the claim to be legitimately in possession of the correct text. Since the biblical books were religious (prophetical) writings, i.e., writings containing in written form words uttered by God himself and proclaimed by recognized prophets, those who took care of these books certainly were vested with a religious legitimacy because in some way, as keepers, editors, scribes, or librarians of biblical books, they were the successors of their prophetical authors. Thus, religious and editorial responsibility for these books could not be separated.[76] Thus, the Hebrew base of Old Greek probably was a text held in high religious and scholarly esteem by the translator and his readers.

Since the proto-MT of Kings certainly obtained no less a status at the beginning of our era when it was recognized as authoritative, it became necessary to choose between the two text forms, proto-MT and Old Greek. That such a choice was made during an early period is shown by the recension of the Greek Minor Prophets scroll from Naḥal Ḥever. There, the Old Greek was brought into conformity with a proto-MT text base. This Greek recension seems to have been made already in the first century B.C.E.[77] This recension proves that the proto-MT edition was intended to supersede the earlier text form included in the Old Greek. The milieu of the authors of the recension of the Greek Minor Prophets scroll from Naḥal Ḥever, at least, must have held proto-MT in higher esteem than the earlier text form of Old Greek. This explains why the Hebrew base of the Old Greek disappeared soon after.

In conclusion, the text of Kings existed in the form implied by the Old Greek until the second century B.C.E. In the second century, possibly in the early Hasmonean period, a recension was made of this earlier text as reflected in the Old Greek (→ 5.3.2).[78] The reasons for the creation of a new edition and the substitution of the earlier text were linked to certain religious concerns regarding the relationship between the Jews of Jerusalem and those of Samaria.[79] Other concerns also played a role.

---

[75] Schenker, *Une bible archétype?*; J. Trebolle Barrera, "Kings (MT/LXX) and Chronicles: The Double and Triple Textual Tradition," in *Reflection and Refraction: Studies in Biblical Historiography in Honour of A. Graeme Auld* (eds. R. Rezetko, T.H. Lim, and W.B. Aucker; VTSup 113; Leiden: Brill, 2007), 483–501.

[76] This is merely implied in the *Letter of Aristeas*, but its content may be judged historically. According to this writing (about 120 B.C.E.), the value of the translation is determined by the guarantee of the highest religious and scholarly authorities. The same guarantee probably holds true for the master copy the scribes use for their copies.

The judgment of the author of the *Letter of Aristeas* on what determines the high quality of a biblical book was applicable at least during his time, the second century B.C.E.

[77] On paleographical grounds: P.J. Parsons, "The Scripts and Their Dates," in *DJD* VIII: 19–25.

[78] D.M. Carr, *The Formation of the Hebrew Bible: A New Reconstruction* (Oxford: University Press, 2011), 153–79; see P. Hugo, "Der Ursprung der proto-massoretischen Textgestalt der Samuelbücher und ihr Sitz-im-Leben," forthcoming. (At that time, 1–2 Samuel and 1–2 Kings share the same textual history.)

[79] See Schenker, *Septante*, 142–46.

Barthélemy, *Critique textuelle 1982*, 329–426.

Barthélemy, *Studies*.

Hugo, P., *Les deux visages d'Elie: Texte massorétique et Septante dans l'histoire la plus ancienne du texte de 1 Rois 17–18* (OBO 217; Fribourg/Göttingen: Academic Press/Vandenhoeck & Ruprecht, 2006).

Hugo, P., "Text and Literary History: The Case of 1 Kings 19 (MT and LXX)," in *Soundings in Kings: Perspectives and Methods in Contemporary Scholarship* (eds. M. Leuchter and K.-P. Adam; Minneapolis: Fortress, 2010), 15–34, 156–65.

van Keulen, P.S.F., *Two Versions of the Solomon Narrative: An Inquiry into the Relationship between MT 1 Kgs. 2–11 and LXX 3 Reg. 2–11* (VTSup 104; Leiden: Brill, 2005).

Richelle, M., *Le testament d'Elisée: Texte massorétique et Septante en 2 Rois 13,10–14,16* (CahRB 76; Pendé: Gabalda, 2010).

Schenker, A., *Septante et texte massorétique dans l'histoire la plus ancienne du texte de 1 Rois 2–14* (CahRB 48; Paris: Gabalda, 2000).

Schenker, A., *Älteste Textgeschichte der Königsbücher: Die hebräische Vorlage der ursprünglichen Septuaginta als älteste Textform der Königsbücher* (OBO 199; Göttingen: Vandenhoeck & Ruprecht, 2004).

Schenker, A., "Die Textgeschichte der Königsbücher und ihre Konsequenzen für die Textgeschichte der hebräischen Bibel, illustriert am Beispiel von 2 Kön 23:1–3," in *Congress Volume Leiden 2004* (ed. A. Lemaire; VTSup 109; Leiden: Brill, 2006), 65–79.

Schenker, A., "What Do Scribes and What Do Editors Do? The Hebrew Text of the Masoretes, the Old Greek Bible and the Alexandrian Philological *Ekdoseis* of the 4th and the 3rd Centuries B.C., Illustrated by the Example of 2 Kings 1," in *After Qumran: Old and Modern Editions of the Biblical Texts – The Historical Books* (eds. H. Ausloos, B. Lemmelijn, and J.C. Trebolle Barrera; BETL 246; Leuven: Peeters, 2012), 275–93.

Schenker, A., *Une bible archétype? Les parallèles de Samuel-Rois et des Chroniques* (L' écriture de la Bible 3; Paris: Cerf, 2013).

Shenkel, J.D., *Chronology and Recensional Development in the Greek Text of Kings* (HSM 1; Cambridge: Harvard University Press, 1968).

Talshir, Z., *The Alternative Story: 3 Kingdoms 12:24a–z* (Jerusalem Biblical Studies 6; Jerusalem: Simor, 1993).

Talshir, Z., "1 Kings and 3 Kingdoms – Origin and Revision, Case Study: The Sins of Solomon (1 Kgs 11)," *Textus* 21 (2002): 71–105.

Tov, E., "Three Strange Books of the LXX: 1 Kings, Esther, and Daniel Compared with Similar Rewritten Compositions from Qumran and Elsewhere," in Tov, *HB, GB, and Qumran*, 283–305.

Trebolle Barrera, J., *Salomón y Jeroboán: Historia de la recensión y redacción de 1 Reyes 2–12, 141* (Bibliotheca Salamanticensis Dissertationes 3; Salamanca: Universidad Pontificia, Inst. Español bibl. y arqueologico, 1980).

Trebolle Barrera, J., "Redaction, Recension and Midrash in the Books of Kings," *BIOSCS* 15 (1982): 12–35.

Trebolle Barrera, J., *Jehú y Joás: Texto y composición literaria de 2 Reyes 9–11* (Institución San Jerónimo 17; Valencia, 1984).

Trebolle Barrera, J., "Textual Criticism and the Literary Structure and Composition of 1–2 Kings / 3–4 Reigns: The Different Sequence of Literary Units in MT and LXX," in Kreuzer–Meiser–Sigismund, *Septuaginta 2012*, 55–78.

Philippe Hugo
Adrian Schenker

5.3 Ancient Hebrew Texts

5.3.1 Ancient and Late Ancient Manuscript Evidence

Although none of the Samuel–Kings manuscripts from Qumran include both the books of Samuel and Kings, the material reconstruction of 4QSamᵃ and 4QKgs makes it likely that these scrolls once included more than only the books of Samuel or Kings respectively. Furthermore, LXX regards the four books as one literary work divided into four parts (ΒΑΣΙΛΕΙΩΝ Α-Δ', 1–4 Kingdoms). For both reasons, 1–2 Samuel and 1–2 Kings are discussed together in this entry.

Eleven ancient manuscripts of 1 Samuel–2 Kings have been published. The identification of two further fragments as manuscripts of 1–2 Kings remains speculative (→ 5.3.1.12). The collection of the Southwestern Baptist Theological Seminary includes a fragment that attests to remnants of 1 Kgs 13:20–22 which remains unpublished.[1] Five of these eleven manuscripts are too damaged for textual classification (5QKgs; ms Schøyen 4612/10; ms Schøyen 5480; ms Schøyen 5233/1; ms Schøyen 5440). Two semi-Masoretic manuscripts (1QSam and 4QKgs), but no proto-Masoretic manuscripts, are extant from antiquity. For 1QSam, its semi-Masoretic character is likely but remains speculative. Three further ancient manuscripts are non-aligned (4QSamᵃ,ᶜ; 6QpapKgs). The non-aligned texts of both 4QSamᵃ and 4QSamᶜ developed from the Hebrew parent text of OG-Sam to which the text of 4QSamᵇ is close. 1–2 Kings is among the few books for which also a late ancient manuscript might be preserved, i.e. Antinoopolis 47–48. Its text is proto-Masoretic in character but its paleographic date remains debated. The only other books for which late ancient or early medieval manuscript evidence is or might be extant are Genesis (→ 2.2.1.11.1), Exodus (→ 2.2.1.11.2; → 2.2.1.11.3; → 2.2.1.11.4), and Job (→ 11.2.1.6).

5.3.1.1 1QSam (1Q7)

1QSam survives in eight fragments that preserve 118 words and partial words from 1 Sam 18:17–18; 2 Sam 20:6–10; 21:16–18; and 23:9–12. Frgs. 2–8 were part of an unrolled remnant of a scroll of which the inner windings are extant. As the inner windings of 1QSam are preserved and the last column of 1QSam does not include 2 Samuel 24, this last chapter of 2 Samuel was most likely not included in 1QSam. Either 2 Samuel 24 is a later addition to 2 Samuel that is still missing in the Samuel text of 1QSam or this chapter was regarded by the 1QSam text as a part of 1–2 Kings.[2]

1QSam was copied in an early Herodian book hand. The supralinear correction in 2 Sam 23:12 is from the original scribe of the scroll. In its orthography, 1QSam is close to MT-Sam but employs in some cases the baroque spellings of the so-called Qumran orthography.[3] Examples include the use of המה "they" in 2 Sam 20:8. This employment of baroque forms in a conservative orthography should not be a surprise, as MT-Sam itself employs baroque orthography and morphology more often than many other books of the Hebrew Bible.[4] In proper names, 1QSam employs orthographic forms for proper names that are known from 1–2 Chronicles. In 2 Sam 21:17, e.g., 1QSam has אבשי instead of MT's אֲבִישַׁי for "Abishai" and דויד instead of MT's דָּוִד for "David."[5]

In its text, 1QSam is related to MT-Sam[6] and attests to only five disagreements with MT (→ 5.3.2).

---

[1] I am obliged to Sidnie White Crawford for this information. The fragment was bought from the Kando family. For a photograph of the fragment, see Loveless and Loveless, *Dead Sea Scrolls and the Bible*, 100.

[2] Cf. Barthélemy, "Livres de Samuel," 64.

[3] Cf. Polak, "Samuel," 820. For baroque and conservative orthographies, see → 1.2.2.4.1.2.

[4] Cf. A. Lange, "The Question of the So-Called Qumran Orthography, the Severus Scroll, and the Masoretic Text," *Hebrew Bible and Ancient Israel* 3 (2014): 424–75.

[5] Cf. Barthélemy, "Livres de Samuel," 64.

[6] Cf. Polak, "Samuel," 820; Tov, *"Synthese," 26; Tov, *"Biblical Texts," 154.

1QSam reads three times non-aligned against MT, once with LXX (→ 5.4) and once with the Lucianic text (→ 3–5.1.6.2) and Josephus (→ 21.3). Statistically, 1QSam can thus be regarded as semi-Masoretic.[7] This conclusion is questioned though by two observations: 1) the likely lack of 2 Sam 24; and 2) the short text in 2 Sam 20:8: In 2 Sam 20:8, 1QSam reads הם עם ה[אבן הגדולה אשר בג[בעון ותפל "they were at the big stone which is in Gibeon and it dropped out" while MT-Sam has a whole sentence of text more: הֵם עִם־הָאֶבֶן הַגְּדוֹלָה אֲשֶׁר בְּגִבְעוֹן וַעֲמָשָׂא בָא לִפְנֵיהֶם וְיוֹאָב חָגוּר מִדּוֹ לְבֻשׁוּ וְעָלָו חֲגוֹר חֶרֶב מְצֻמֶּדֶת עַל־מָתְנָיו בְּתַעְרָהּ וְהוּא יָצָא וַתִּפֹּל "they were at the big stone which is in Gibeon and Amasa came before them. And Joab was girded with his military dress and on top of it the sword was bound on his loins in its sheath. When he came out, it dropped out."[8]

5.3.1.2 4QSam^a (4Q51)

4QSam^a (→ 5.3.3) has been one of the most discussed ancient biblical manuscripts among textual critics since its publication in 2005. Subsequently, the *editio princeps* of Cross, Parry, and Saley[9] has been criticized repeatedly.[10] While the improvement of individual transcriptions is always important, this criticism should not distract from the high quality of the *editio princeps* and the enormous scholarly achievement that it represents. Before the publication of the *editio princeps*, two preliminary editions of 4QSam^a appeared. 1 Sam 1:11–12:19; 24:3–2 Sam 4:4 were published by Fincke[11] while Herbert included only 2 Sam 1:10–24:20 into his edition.[12] The two preliminary editions are of varying quality. Fincke even sets aside the use of editorial signs to mark the state of preservation of individual characters. Herbert's edition is a test case for a special method for reconstructing biblical manuscripts that he developed.

Among the biblical Dead Sea Scrolls, 4QSam^a is one of the better-preserved and most extensive manuscripts. According to Cross, Parry, and Saley, fifteen percent of the text of 1–2 Samuel are still extant in 4QSam^a.[13] The manuscript preserves 2,891 words and partial words out of 1 Sam 1:9, 11–13, 17–18, 22–26, 28; 2:1–10, 16–36; 3:1–4, 18–21; 4:3–4, 9–10, 12; 5:8–12; 6:1–13, 16–18, 20–21; 7:1; 8:7, 9–14, 16–20; 9:6–8, 10–12, 16–24; 10:3–12, 14, 16, 18, 24–27; 11:1–2, 7–12; 12:7–8, 10–19; 14:24–25, 28–34, 47–51; 15:20–21, 24–32; 17:3–8, 40–41; 18:4–5; 20:37–40; 22:10–11; 24:3–5, 8–10, 14–23; 25:3–12, 20–21, 25–27, 38–40; 26:9–12, 21–24; 27:1–2, 8–12; 28:1–3, 22–25; 29:1; 30:22–31; 31:1–4; 2 Sam 1:4–5, 10–13; 2:5–16, 25–27, 29–32; 3:1–15, 17, 21, 23–39; 4:1–4, 9–12; 5:1–3, 6–16, 18–19; 6:2–18; 7:6–7, 22–29; 8:1–8; 9:8–10; 10:4–7, 18–19; 11:2–12, 15–20; 12:1, 3–5, 8–9, 13–20, 29–31; 13:1–6, 13–34, 36–39; 14:1–3, 14, 18–19, 33; 15:1–7, 20–21, 23, 26–31, 37; 16:1–2, 6–8, 10–13, 17–18, 20–22; 17:2–3, 23–25, 29; 18:1–11, 28–29; 19:6–12, 14–16, 25, 27–29, 38; 20:1–2, 4, 9–14, 19, 21–25; 21:1, 3–6, 8–9, 12, 15–17; 22:17, 19, 21, 24, 26–28, 30–31, 33–51; 23:1–6, 14–16, 21–22, 38–39; 24:16–22.[14] In their *editio princeps*, Cross, Parry, and Saley were able to reconstruct partially or completely the first eleven columns of 4QSam^a (1 Sam 1:9–12:19). 165 further fragments with identifiable biblical text derive from other parts of the scroll.[15]

---

[7] Cf. Lange, *Handbuch*, 214.

[8] That the apparatus of the *BHS does not record this significant variant is symptomatic of the neglect with which the biblical Dead Sea Scrolls were treated by many textual critics for a long time.

[9] Cross, Parry, and Saley, "51. 4QSam^a," 1–216.

[10] Puech, "4QSamuel^a," *passim*; Hugo, Kottsieper, and Steudel, "Notes," *passim*; P. Hugo, I. Kottsieper, and A. Steudel, "Reflexions on Epigraphy and Critical Editing: 4QSam^a (4Q51) Col. XI," in *Textual Criticism and Dead Sea Scrolls Studies in Honour of Julio Trebolle Barrera* (eds. A. Piquer Otero and P.A. Torijano Morales; JSJSup 157; Leiden: Brill, 2012), 115–31; A. Ravasco, "A Paleographic Note on 2 Sam 19:10 in 4QSam^a," *RevQ* 103 (2014): 461–66.

[11] Fincke, *Samuel Scroll*.

[12] Herbert, *Reconstructing Biblical Scrolls*.

[13] Cf. Cross, Parry, and Saley, "51. 4QSam^a," 3. Earlier publications estimate that eight percent (Herbert, "Relationship," 38) or ten percent of 1–2 Samuel are preserved in 4QSam^a (cf. Ulrich, *Qumran Text of Samuel*, 258; Parry, "Tetragrammaton," 122).

[14] Since the publication of the *editio princeps*, Puech ("4QSamuel^a," *passim*) proposed identifications for several fragments which Cross, Parry, and Saley regarded as unidentifiable. Without access to proper photographs and the original manuscript Puech's new identifications are difficult to judge.

[15] Frgs. 15, 21, 28, 37, and 95 were attributed wrongly to 4QSam^a in an earlier stage of editing the Dead Sea Scrolls but

5.3.1 ANCIENT AND LATE ANCIENT MANUSCRIPT EVIDENCE

The reconstruction of 4QSamᵃ I demonstrates that this Samuel text began with several empty lines.[16] As collective manuscripts of authoritative literature use the device of several blank lines even at the top of a column to signal the beginning of a new book (cf. e.g. MurXII IX, X, and 4QXIIᵍ 76–81), it is possible that 1 Samuel was preceded by another biblical book in 4QSamᵃ, such as the book of Judges.[17]

In his first publications, Cross dated 4QSamᵃ paleographically in the first century B.C.E.[18] Later on, Cross described the script of 4QSamᵃ as a late Herodian formal hand from the time around the year 50 B.C.E.[19] or as a late Hasmonean or early Herodian formal hand from the years 50–25 B.C.E.[20] Four scribal corrections in 4QSamᵃ were inserted by the original scribe of this manuscript (1 Sam 1:24; 10:3; 10:27–11:1; 2 Sam 22:37). For four further scribal corrections, the paleographic evidence remains inconclusive as to their origin (1 Sam 1:12; 14:29; 2 Sam 3:34; 6:2).[21]

The orthography of 4QSamᵃ resembles the conservative orthographic system of MT but attests to more plene spellings. "The orthographic practice of 4QSamᵃ corresponds in a general way to the orthography of Ezra-Nehemiah; comparable also is the usage in Chronicles (although Chronicles on occasion uses distinctly archaic spellings), and the Samaritan Pentateuch. The orthographic usage exhibits what has been called a late orthography, a fuller notation than that of the Masoretic Text of the Pentateuch – or Masoretic Samuel – but not so full as the orthography of the Mishnah."[22]

The textual character of 4QSamᵃ is much debated (→ 5.3.3). Scholars ask two basic questions: 1) Is MT-Sam (→ 5.3.2) or the textual tradition of 4QSamᵃ more original?; 2) How does 4QSamᵃ relate to OG-Sam (→ 5.3)? As for the first question, a small group of textual critics regard MT-Sam as the more original version of these books that would have been reworked in the text of 4QSamᵃ.[23] Only one scholar thinks that 4QSamᵃ evolved independently of MT-Sam and OG-Sam from a common archetype.[24] The majority of textual critics discuss 4QSamᵃ in relation with the Old Greek text of Samuel. In order to answer the first question regarding how close the text of 4QSamᵃ is to the original text of the Samuel, the second question, i.e. how 4QSamᵃ relates to OG-Sam, needs to be addressed first.

For the relation of 4QSamᵃ to OG-Sam, the works of Cross and Ulrich are representative of both the early and later stages of this research. In his first textual characterization, Cross regarded 4QSamᵃ as a witness to the Hebrew parent text of the Old Greek text of the books of Samuel.[25] The complete text-critical study of 4QSamᵃ by Ulrich seemed to confirm Cross:

---

do not belong to this manuscript (see Cross, Parry, and Saley, "51. 4QSamᵃ," 79, 82, 86, 90, 142).

[16] See Cross, Parry, and Saley, "51. 4QSamᵃ," 28–29; cf. Fincke, *Samuel Scroll*, 8–9.

[17] Cf. Lange, *Handbuch*, 215–16.

[18] Cross, "New Qumran Biblical Fragment," 16.

[19] Cross, *"Development," 139 line 3; Cross, "Ammonite Oppression," 148; cf. Parry, "Tetragrammaton," 60.

[20] Cross, *"Paleography," plate 10 line 3; cf. Parry, "More Fragments," 21; Cross, Parry, and Saley, "51. 4QSamᵃ," 5.

[21] Cf. Cross, Parry, and Saley, "51. 4QSamᵃ," 18–19.

[22] Cross, Parry, and Saley, "51. 4QSamᵃ," 6. For a detailed description of the orthography of 4QSamᵃ, see ibid., 5–15; cf. also Parry, "Royal Song," 148–50; Herbert, *Reconstructing*, 82–84, 214–20; and Polak, "Samuel," 820.

[23] Thus Pisano (*Additions*, 91–118, 283), who regards the non-aligned readings of 4QSamᵃ as additions to MT in the character of a Palestinian text, and Rofé ("Nomistic Corrections," 250–54; "4QMidrash Samuel?" [esp. 73–74]; "4QSamᵃ" [esp. 115–17]), who wants to find nomistic and midrashic extensions in the text of 4QSamᵃ in 1 Sam 1–2; 11:1; and 2 Sam 24. In his latest publication on this topic ("Midrashic Traits," *passim*), Rofé even rejects the biblical character of 4QSamᵃ and regards it instead as a lost midrash to the book of Samuel. Against Rofé and with Cross, Parry, and Saley ("Rewritten Scripture," *passim*), it needs to be emphasized though that none of the unique readings in 4QSamᵃ bear the characteristics of interpretative rewriting. Recently, Venturini (*caratteristiche editoriali*) understood 4QSamᵃ as an editorial revision of a Masoretic textual tradition (Ravasco, "La storia").

[24] Ravasco, *La storia*, 249–54; Ravasco, "Readings," 56–74.

[25] F.M. Cross, "A Report on the Biblical Fragments of Cave Four in Wâdî Qumrân," *BASOR* 141 (1956): 9–13, 11; Cross, "New Qumran Biblical Fragment," 18, 23–25; Cross, *"History," 188–89; cf. Albright, *"New Light," 28, 33; J. Hempel, "Ein textgeschichtlich bedeutsamer Fund," *ZAW* 65 (1953): 296–98 (297–98); Parry, "Preliminary Edition of 1 Samuel 25:3–31:4," 70–71.

4Q and G share against M 14 (or probably 15) striking readings: 6 (or 7) pluses, 3 minuses, and 5 variants. 4Q and G agree against M in 110 additional readings: 35 pluses, 20 minuses, and 55 variants. Thus, for the parts of Thackeray and Barthélemy's Old Greek sections of Samuel (α ββ [scil. 1 Sam; 2 Sam 1,1–11,11]) for which 4Q is extant, 4Q agrees with G against M in 124 readings." Ulrich "... (for section βγ [scil. 2 Sam 11,2–24,25]) lists 6 pluses (2 of which are striking specimens), 1 minus, and 13 variants for a total of 20 in which 4Q = G 6= M." "Samuel fragments are extant for 29 chapters of α ββ and for 14 chapters of βγ, or approximately twice as many chapters in α ββ as in βγ. The ratio of 124 readings in 29 chapters of α ββ to 20 readings in the 14 chapters of βγ is roughly 3 to 1. G is three times closer to 4Q in α ββ than it is in βγ. Barthélemy's thesis, that G has undergone revision toward M in βγ, neatly explains this shift in the results.[26]

Since Cross' early work on 4QSam[a] and 4QSam[b], scholars do not doubt that OG-Sam translates a Hebrew parent text that differed from MT. Before the complete publication of 4QSam[a] and 4QSam[b], scholars thought that this Hebrew parent text was preserved by these two manuscripts.[27] But, early on, dissenting voices regarded 4QSam[a] as the witness of a non-aligned Samuel text that shared a certain number of readings with the Hebrew parent text of OG-Sam.[28] In later publications, Cross revised his earlier understanding of 4QSam[a] in light of its progressing transcription. Cross now regards those readings that go against OG-Sam as the result of cross-fertilization between different Hebrew textual traditions:[29]

Above all, the study of the full manuscript has reinforced our early conclusion that 4QSam[a] stands in the same general tradition as the Hebrew text upon which the Old Greek translation was based. The divergences between 4QSam[a] and the Old Greek are sufficiently explained by the century or so between the translation of Samuel into Greek, and the copying of our manuscript. During this time there was certainly some crossfertilization between Hebrew textual traditions current in Palestine.[30]

In this later understanding of how 4QSam[a] and OG-Sam relate to each other, Cross and the other editors of this scroll gained again the support of the majority of textual critics.[31]

The statistical evidence describes the text of 4QSam[a] as a non-aligned witness that evolved out of the Hebrew parent text of OG-Sam.[32] In the 2,891 words and partial words of 4QSam[a], 503 cases of textual variation can still be found. Forty-five of these textual differences cannot be translated into a non-Semitic language. 4QSam[a] reads 117 times with and 386 times against MT as well as 131 times non-aligned. In those parts of LXX[B] that are

---

[26] Ulrich, *Qumran Text of Samuel*, 92.

[27] Thus Cross, "Report," 11; Cross, "New Qumran Biblical Fragment," 18, 23–25; Cross, "Oldest Manuscript," 165, 172; Cross, *ALQ*[1], 133–34, 142; Cross, *"History,"* 188–89; Cross, *ALQ*[3], 132; cf. Hempel, "Fund," 297–98; Ulrich, *Qumran Text of Samuel*, 39–93, 118–49, 257; Parry, "Preliminary Edition of 1 Samuel 25:3–31:4," 70–71.

[28] Tov, "Textual Affiliations"; Tov, "Relationship," 53–54, 57, 62, 64; E. Tov, "The Contribution of the Qumran Scrolls to the Understanding of the LXX," in *Manchester Symposium*, 11–47 (31).

[29] Cross, *ALQ*[1], 141; Cross "Ammonite Oppression," *passim*; Cross, *ALQ*[3], 132; Cross, Parry, and Saley, "51. 4QSam[a]," 25–26.

---

[30] Cross, Parry, and Saley, "51. 4QSam[a]," 25; cf. Cross and Saley, "Statistical Analysis," *passim*, esp. 54; Ulrich, "Qualitative Assessment," *passim*, esp. 161–62.

[31] Cf. e.g. McCarter, *1 Samuel*, 7, 10–11; Ulrich, "Old Latin Translation," 156–57; Tov, *"Synthese,"* 20; Tov, *"Biblical Texts,"* 156; Polak, "Statistics," esp. 215, 244; Polak, "Samuel," 821; Parry, "Tetragrammaton," 117–22; Parry, "More Fragments," 29; Parry, "Canon," 174–76; Parry, "Unique Readings," esp. 215.

[32] See Tov, "Textual Affiliation," *passim*; E. Tov, "Determining the Relationship between the Qumran Scrolls and the LXX," in *The Hebrew and Greek Texts of Samuel: 1980 Proceedings IOSCS Vienna* (ed. E. Tov; Jerusalem: Academon: 1980), 45–67, esp. 53–54, 57, 62; Tov, "Song of Hannah"; Tov, *"Synthese,"* 20; Tov, *"Biblical Texts,"* 156; T.L. Eves, "One Ammonite Invasion or Two? 1 Sam 10:27–11:2 in the Light of 4QSam[a]," *WTJ* 44 (1982): 308–26 (324–25); Polak, "Statistics," esp. 215, 244; Polak, "Samuel," 821; Parry, "Tetragrammaton," 117–22; Parry, "More Fragments," 29; Parry, "Canon," esp. 174–76; Parry, "Unique Readings," esp. 215; J. Hutzli, *Die Erzählung von Hanna und Samuel: Textkritische und literarische Analyse von 1. Samuel 1–2 unter Berücksichtigung des Kontextes* (ATANT 89; Zürich: Theologischer Verlag, 2007), 35; Lange, *Handbuch*, 218. Cf. also the additional 101 readings identified by Herbert, *Reconstructing Biblical Scrolls*, 197, 221–46. For an analysis of the non-aligned readings of 4QSam[a], see Parry, "Textual Character," *passim*.

regarded today as a representative of the Old Greek text of the books of Samuel (1 Sam 1:1–2 Sam 11:1), 4QSam^a goes 143 times with and 168 times against LXX^B. In those parts of LXX^B that are regarded today as a witness to the *kaige*-recension of the books of Samuel, 4QSam^a reads thirty-nine times with and 104 times against LXX^B. Furthermore, 4QSam^a goes 228 times with and 230 times against LXX^L.

Because OG-Sam (→ 5.4) is a faithful translation of its Hebrew parent text,[33] the readings in which it disagrees with MT-Sam (→ 5.3.2) and/or 4QSam^{a,b} go back to textual differences between the Hebrew parent text of OG-Sam on the one hand and MT-Sam and/or 4QSam^{a,b} on the other hand. On the whole, OG-Sam and 4QSam^a are a part of a textual tradition to which 1–2 Chronicles (→ 20), 4QSam^b (→ 5.3.1.3), the retelling of 1–2 Samuel in Josephus, *Ant.*, and the proto-Lucianic recension (→ 5.4) also belong.

4QSam^b preserves an earlier version of this textual tradition than 4QSam^a because the latter includes more secondary readings than does the former. The Hebrew parent text of OG-Sam, in turn, goes back to a yet earlier Samuel text than does 4QSam^b.[34] This early representative of the OG/4QSam^{a,b} text tradition was reworked by proto-MT-Sam, which suffered in its textual transmission from scribal corruption.[35] The shared source text of OG/4QSam^{a,b} and the (proto)-MT text traditions of the books of Samuel represented, in turn, the

Samuel base text, which was retold by the books of 1–2 Chronicles.[36]

That a portion of the readings of 4QSam^a agrees with the proto-Lucianic recension of OG-Sam could suggest that this recension reworked OG-Sam toward a text in the textual tradition of 4QSam^a and 4QSam^b.[37] Finally, that some readings of 4QSam^a correspond only with the retelling of the books of Samuel in the *Antiquities* of Josephus Flavius (→ 21.3)[38] demonstrates that Josephus employed a text of the books of Samuel that was close to 4QSam^a as a source for his universal history. This text is regarded by most scholars as a Greek proto-Lucianic text[39] while Nodet argues for a Hebrew source that was close to 4QSam^a.[40]

5.3.1.3 4QSam^b (4Q52)

Twenty-three fragments of 4QSam^b (→ 5.3.3) survive,[41] preserving 329 words and partial words

---

[33] Thus, e.g., J. Trebolle Barrera, "The Text-Critical Use of the Septuagint in the Books of Kings," in *VII Congress of the International Organization for Septuagint and Cognate Studies, Leuven 1989* (ed. C.E. Cox; SBLSCS 31; Atlanta: SBL, 1991), 285–99 (286, 296); A. Aejmelaeus, "The Septuagint of 1 Samuel," in *VIII Congress of the International Organization for Septuagint and Cognate Studies, Paris 1992* (eds. L. Greenspoon and O. Munnich; SBLSCS 41; Atlanta: SBL, 1995), 109–29 (110, 124).

[34] Cf. McCarter, *1 Samuel*, 8; E. Ulrich, "Double Literary Editions of Biblical Narratives and Reflections on Determining the Form to Be Translated," in E. Ulrich, *DSS*, 34–50 (36–38); Herbert, "Relationship," 37, 48–49.

[35] So McCarter, *1 Samuel*, 8; Ulrich, "Double Literary Editions," 36–38; Cross, Parry, and Saley, "51. 4QSam^a," 26; Cf. Cook, "1 Samuel xx 26–xxi 5," 450–54 (4QSam^b is an "eclectic text" [454] that is close to LXX).

[36] Cf. Cross, "Report," 11; Cross, *ALQ^1*, 141; Cross, *"History,"* 189–90, 192–93; Cross, "Ammonite Oppression," 149; Cross, *ALQ^3* 138–39; Skehan, *"Qumran, Littérature de Qumran," 806; S.L. McKenzie, The Chronicler's Use of the Deuteronomistic History* (HSM 33; Atlanta: Scholars Press, 1984), 58; Polak, "Statistics," 248–55; Polak, "Samuel," 820; Parry, "Canon," 230–31; Hutzli, *Erzählung*, 36.

[37] Thus Cross, *"History,"* 188–93; Cross, "Ammonite Oppression," 141; Ulrich, *Qumran Text of Samuel*, 95–117, 257–58; McCarter, *1 Samuel*, 9; Parry, "More Fragments," 29; Cross, Parry, and Saley, "51. 4QSam^a," 25. Tov, "Relationship," 53, regards such a proto-Lucianic recension toward the text of 4QSam^a as unlikely. The agreements between the proto-Lucianic recension and 4QSam^a are also observed by J.H. Kim, *Die hebräischen Textformen der Samuel- und Königebücher: Studien zur Textgeschichte ausgehend von 2 Sam 15,1–19,9* (BZAW 394; Berlin: De Gruyter, 2009), 404. Kim does not explain these agreements though.

[38] For a list of these readings, see Ulrich, *Qumran Text of Samuel*, 165–80.

[39] Cf. Ulrich, *Qumran Text of Samuel*, 165–256, 259; Skehan, "Littérature," 806; Cross, "Ammonite Oppression," 149; McCarter, *1 Samuel*, 11; Polak, "Samuel," 820; Parry, "Canon," 174–76; Hutzli, *Erzählung*, 36.

[40] E. Nodet, "Josephus and the Books of Samuel," in *Studies in Josephus and the Varieties of Ancient Judaism: Louis H. Feldman Jubilee Volume* (eds. S.J.D. Cohen and J.J. Schwartz; AGJU 67; Leiden: Brill, 2007), 141–67.

[41] Cross, "Oldest Manuscript," published frgs. 4–5, 7–8, 13, 17, and 19 already in 1955 but counted them in this publication

from 1 Sam 12:5; 14:41–42; 15:16–18; 16:1–11; 19:10–13, 15–17; 20:26–42; 21:1–3, 5–10; 22:8–9; 23:8–23. 4QSam^b is one of the most important Hebrew biblical manuscripts because of its old age. As only a few manuscripts and inscriptions were available to compare 4QSam^b with paleographically, Cross dated the archaic book hand of 4QSam^b variously in his early publications: 225–200 B.C.E.,[42] ca. 200 B.C.E.,[43] ca. 225 B.C.E.[44] Once Cross had access to the Wadi-ed Daliyeh papyri and the Maresha ostraca, he dated 4QSam^b consistently to ca. 250 B.C.E.[45] The original scribe of 4QSam^b added three corrections to the scroll in 1 Sam 20:28; 21:5; 23:9, while one further correction was written by a later hand in 1 Sam 21:5.[46]

Various scholars describe the orthography of 4QSam^b as "archaic."[47] On the whole, 4QSam^b is more defective than MT, although it does employ *matres lectionis*: "the vowel *ô* derived from Canaanite *aw* is regularly written with *waw* as a *mater lectionis*. The same is true for the vowel *ū*: רוץ, מוסר, etc. ... Perhaps the most interesting bit of archaic orthography is the survival of *he* as a *mater lectionis* for *ō* derived from *u* in the form עלמה, 'his lad.'"[48]

The textual classification of 4QSam^b changed also during the many years in which Cross worked on this manuscript. In his early edition of only a part of this manuscript, Cross describes the textual affiliation of 4QSam^b as follows: "The most extraordinary characteristic of the text of 4QSam^b is the high proportion of original readings which it preserves whether it is in agreement with the Greek, or in agreement with MT, or against both in its several unique readings."[49] At that time, Cross found thirteen cases in which 4QSam^b reads with the Old Greek against MT and only four cases in which 4QSam^b agrees with MT against Old Greek.[50] Cross concluded therefore: "The textual position of the MS stands close to the *Vorlage* of the Old Greek; it is an earlier exemplar of the textual type discovered in 4QSam^a."[51] Later on, Tov characterized 4QSam^b as a proto-Masoretic text,[52] while Polak emphasized the textual independence of the manuscript: "Hence Samuel^b is best considered independent of both the Masoretic Text and the Septuagint ... The readings it shares with the Septuagint most probably represent the ancient text against the Masoretic Text."[53]

After the complete publication of 4QSam^b, a detailed textual analysis of all fragments of this manuscript by Cross, Parry, and Saley emphasized again that the text of 4QSam^b is close to the Hebrew parent text of OG-1 Sam–2 Kgs. In 329 identifiable words and partial words, they find sixty-five preserved and 109 reconstructed variants:

> In summary, 4QSam^b exhibits 142 superior readings, of which ninety are in agreement with the Old Greek represented either by 𝔊^B or 𝔊^L or both. 4QSam^b is in agreement with 𝔐 seventy-eight times, of which sixty-three readings are superior (or original), nine unclassified and six considered inferior. In short, in an overwhelmingly large number of cases, the readings of 4QSam^b agree with the Old Greek when it is superior, but agree with the Masoretic tradition when it is superior. We must add in some fifteen unique readings that are superior to both the Old Greek and 𝔐 ... We should note that 4QSam^b has

---

as frgs. 1–7: Frg. 4 = frg. 1; frg. 5 = frg. 2; frg. 7 = frg. 3; frg. 8 = frg. 4; frg. 13 = frg. 5; frg. 17 = frg. 6; and frg. 19 = frg. 7.

[42] Cross, "Oldest Manuscript," 164; cf. S. Birnbaum, *Hebrew Scripts* (2 vols.; Leiden: Brill, 1954–1957), 1.127–30.

[43] Cross, *ALQ*¹, 33.

[44] Cross, *"Development,"* 166.

[45] F.M. Cross, "The Papyri and Their Historical Implications," in *Discoveries in the Wâdī ed-Dâliyeh* (eds. P.W. Lapp and N.L. Lapp; ASOR 41; Cambridge: American Schools of Oriental Research, 1974), 17–29 (26); Cross, *ALQ*³, 43; Cross, *"Paleography,"* 383–84, 387, plate 9 line 4; Cross, Parry, and Saley, "51. 4QSam^a," 220. For a detailed description of the paleography of 4QSam^b, see Cross, "Oldest Manuscript," 155–63.

[46] Cross, Parry, and Saley, "51. 4QSam^a," 220.

[47] Cross and Parry, "Preliminary Edition," 66; Cross, Parry, and Saley, "51. 4QSam^a," 220–21. Cf. also Cross, "Oldest Manuscript," 165; D.N. Freedman, "The Masoretic Text and the Qumran Scrolls: A Study in Orthography," in Cross–Talmon, *QHBT*, 196–211 (202–07); Andersen and Freedman, "Another Look," *passim*; Polak, "Samuel," 822.

[48] Cross and Parry, "Preliminary Edition," 66.

---

[49] Cross, "Oldest Manuscript," 172.

[50] Cross, "Oldest Manuscript," 172.

[51] Cross, "Oldest Manuscript," 165. Cf. also Cross, *ALQ*¹, 133–34, 142; Cross, *ALQ*³, 132; McCarter, *1 Samuel*, 11.

[52] Tov, *"Synthese,"* 26; Tov, *"Biblical Texts,"* 154.

[53] Polak, "Samuel," 822.

some ten inferior readings in agreement with the Old Greek against the Masoretic Text – the bad genes of the *Vorlage* of the Old Greek. Such readings are as crucial, perhaps even more crucial than the large number of agreements of 4QSam^b with the Old Greek in superior readings. Similarly, when 4QSam^b is in disagreement with both the Greek witnesses (𝔊^B/𝔊^L/𝔊^{BL}), but in agreement with 𝔐, in some thirty seven instances 𝔐 is superior; only in two cases (one reconstructed) are the readings reckoned inferior – bad genes. These data strongly support the view that the Old Greek was translated, presumably in Alexandria, from a Hebrew manuscript that was closely affiliated with the Old Palestinian text, such as that preserved in this old Samuel manuscript.[54]

5.3.1.4 4QSam^c (4Q53)

Of 4QSam^c (→ 5.3.3), fourteen mostly small fragments are extant. The text of frgs. 12–14 remains unidentified due to severe damage. Frgs. 1–11 preserve 297 words and partial words from 1 Sam 25:30–31; 2 Sam 14:7–33, and 15:1–6, 8–15. Frgs. 2–11 derive from three subsequent columns of the original scroll. The script of 4QSam^c is a Hasmonean semi-cursive hand from the first quarter of the first century B.C.E.[55] The scroll was produced by the same scribe who wrote 1QS, 4QTest, and the supralinear corrections in 1QIsa^a.[56] "It shares the identical range of idiosyncratic features: the bold, relatively undisciplined calligraphy, proliferation of *matres lectionis*, run-on words, frequent errors and supralinear insertions, and the rare device of four dots used to represent the divine name."[57] Even the preparation of the skin of 4QSam^c is similar to that of 1QS.[58] Twenty-one scribal errors in sixty-seven lines demonstrate that the scribe did not belong to the scribal elite of his time.[59] Maybe for that reason and unlike other manuscripts written in Hasmonean scripts, the scribe of 4QSam^c does use the *vacat* as a structural signal.[60] The orthography of 4QSam^c adheres to the plene spellings and morphology of the baroque orthographic system that the same scribe also employed elsewhere.[61]

Ulrich describes their textual alignment of 4QSam^c as follows:

> In the 30 readings where G can reflect the divergences between 4QSam^c and M, G aligns itself with M 21 times and with 4QSam^c 6 times, being distinctive in 3 readings. The *prima facie* evidence would indicate that the Septuagint was translated from a text much closer to M than to 4QSam^c. A closer examination, however, shows that 11 times the Old Greek, as distinguished from simply the majority G text, follows 4QSam^c against M, 7 times follows M against 4QSam^c, 2 times is independent of both, and 10 times cannot be documented or determined with confidence.[62] (...) The Greek text in 2 Samuel proves to

---

[54] Cross, Parry, and Saley, "51. 4QSam^a," 223. Cf. also ibid., 221–24; Cross and Parry, "Preliminary Edition," 73; Cook, "1 Samuel xx 26–xxi 5," 450–54 (4QSam^b is an "eclectic text" [454] that is close to LXX).

[55] For the paleography of 4QSam^c, see Ulrich, "Fragmentary Manuscript," 2–3, 22; Ulrich, "53. 4QSam^c," 248–50; cf. Cross, **"Development," 198 n. 116.

[56] J.C. Trever, "Preliminary Observations on the Jerusalem Scrolls," *BASOR* 111 (1948): 3–16 (9–12); J.C. Trever, "A Paleographic Study of the Jerusalem Scrolls," *BASOR* 113 (1949): 6–23 (6 and 15); J.M. Allegro, "Further Messianic References in Qumran Literature," *JBL* 75 (1956): 174–87 (182); Cross, **"Development," 198 note 116; F.M. Cross in *Scrolls from Qumrân Cave I: The Great Isaiah Scroll, The Order of the Community, The Pesher to Habakuk* (eds. F.M. Cross, D.N. Freedman, and J.A. Sanders; Jerusalem: The Albright Institute of Archeological Research, 1972), 3–4; Ulrich, "Fragmentary Manuscript," 1–3, 22; Ulrich, "53. 4QSam^c," 247–50.

[57] Ulrich, "Fragmentary Manuscript," 1.

[58] Cf. Ulrich, "Fragmentary Manuscript," 1–2; Ulrich, "53. 4QSam^c," 247.

[59] Cf. Ulrich, "Fragmentary Manuscript," 22; Ulrich, "53. 4QSam^c," 251–52. Against, J. Lübbe, "Certain Implications of the Scribal Process of 4QSam^c," *RevQ* 14 (1989–1990): 255–64 (262–64).

[60] See Ulrich, "53. 4QSam^c," 252.

[61] Cf. Ulrich, "Fragmentary Manuscript," 3, 10; Ulrich, "53. 4QSam^c," 250–51, 253; Polak, "Samuel," 822. For the orthography of the 1QS scribe, see P. Wernberg-Møller, *The Manual of Discipline: Translated and Annotated with an Introduction* (STDJ 1; Leiden: Brill, 1957), 4–6; Allegro, "Further Messianic References," 182–86; D.N. Freedman, "The Massoretic Text and the Qumran Scrolls: A Study in Orthography," *Textus* 2 (1962): 87–102; F.A. Anderson and D.N. Freedman, "The Orthography of 4QTestimonia," in *Studies in Hebrew and Aramaic Orthography* (eds. D.N. Freedman, F.A. Anderson, and A.D. Forbes; Biblical and Judaic Studies 2; Eisenbrauns: Winona Lake, 1992), 211–51.

[62] Ulrich, "Fragmentary Manuscript," 22; cf. Ulrich, "53. 4QSam^c," 253–54.

be, as Barthelélemy maintains for 2 Samuel 11–24, a recensional text. The Old Greek translation not infrequently shines through only in the Lucianic MSS. The G_L text, when distinct from G, never agrees with M against 4QSam^c but agrees with 4QSam^c against M 9 times, in original readings, expansions, and variants. The majority G text is revised toward greater conformity with M, at times even in inferior readings and errors, including expansions, omissions, and variants.[63]

Therefore, 4QSam^c is not close to MT, LXX^B, or LXX^L. Furthermore, 4QSam^c includes twelve non-aligned readings. The text of 4QSam^c is thus best described as a non-aligned text that is somewhat close to the Hebrew parent text of OG-Sam (→ 5.4).[64]

5.3.1.5 MS Schøyen 4612/10

Manuscript Schøyen 4612/10 might be another Dead Sea Samuel manuscript attesting to parts of 1 Sam 2:11–14 but this manuscript needs further study before definite conclusions are possible.[65]

5.3.1.6 MS Schøyen 5480[66]

This manuscript is part of the Schøyen collection and was bought from a private owner. Its provenance is uncertain but it is likely that manuscript Schøyen 5480 derives from one of the sites around the Dead Sea. Of manuscript Schøyen 5480, one small fragment survives with four words and partial words from 1 Sam 5:10–11. Given the small amount of preserved text, manuscript Schøyen 5480 could also represent a Samuel quotation in a non-biblical manuscript. Michael Langlois describes manuscript Schøyen 5480 as written in a late Hasmonaean semi-formal hand from around 50 B.C.E.[67] The preserved text neither allows for an orthographic nor a textual classification.

5.3.1.7 MS Schøyen 5233/1[68]

Manuscript Schøyen 5233/1 was acquired from a private owner and is part of the Schøyen collection. Its provenance is uncertain but it is likely that the manuscript derives from one of the sites around the Dead Sea. The single small fragment of manuscript Schøyen 5233/1 attests to ten words and partial words from 2 Sam 20:22–24. Although little text survives of manuscript Schøyen 5233/1, the fragment does not attest to a Samuel quotation in a non-biblical manuscript but to the remains of a copy of the books of Samuel, because it preserves text from two consecutive paragraphs. Langlois characterizes the script of manuscript Schøyen 5233/1 as a late Hasmonean or early Herodian semi-formal hand from the second half of the first century B.C.E.[69] The small amount of extant text does not allow for an orthographic or textual classification.

5.3.1.8 4QKgs (4Q54)

4QKgs survives in eight severely damaged fragments. The text of seven of these fragments can still be identified and includes 132 words and partial words from 1 Kgs 7:20–21, 25–27, 29–42, 50?, 51; 8:1–9, 16–18. Only the text of frg. 8 cannot be identified. It was attributed to 4QKgs as its leather is similar to that of frgs. 1–7. Because the script of frg. 8 differs from that of frgs. 1–7, it remains uncertain if frg. 8 belongs to 4QKgs.[70] Frgs. 1–7 were part of two consecutive columns of the original scroll. A material reconstruction by Hartmut Stegemann demonstrated that the preserved fragments derive from the middle windings of 4QKgs. This makes is likely that 1–2 Kings was once preceded by the books of

---

[63] Ulrich, "Fragmentary Manuscript," 23; cf. Ulrich, "53. 4QSam^c," 253–54.

[64] Thus Tov, "Relationship," 61–62; Tov, *"Biblical Texts," 156; Polak, "Samuel," 822; Ulrich, "53. 4QSam^c," 254; Lange, *Handbuch, 223–24.

[65] I am obliged to Torleif Elgvin who alerted me to the existence of the manuscript.

[66] I am obliged to Torleif Elgvin who made a preprint copy of his edition of manuscript Schøyen 5480 available to me ("MS 5480"). All information given here about manuscript Schøyen 5480 relies on Elgvin's edition.

[67] Langlois, "Palaeographical Analysis of the Dead Sea Scrolls," in *Gleanings, forthcoming.

[68] I am obliged to Torleif Elgvin who made a preprint copy of his edition of manuscript Schøyen 5233/1 available to me ("MS 5233/1"). All information given here about manuscript Schøyen 5233/1 relies on Elgvin's edition.

[69] Cf. Elgvin, "MS 5233/1," forthcoming.

[70] Cf. Trebolle Barrera, "54. 4QKgs," 178; Trebolle Barrera, "Preliminary Edition," 237–38.

Joshua through 2 Samuel in this manuscript. Therefore, in antiquity, 4QKgs most likely included the whole Deuteronomistic History.[71] Trebolle Barerra describes the paleography of 4QKgs as follows:

> The script is sometimes bizarre and in general exhibits transitional features. It displays both archaizing traits and cursive features. Various forms of a letter often occur, as well as features peculiar to the copyist's hand. This script can be assigned to the late Hasmonean book hand in the process of transition to the early Herodian. It can thus be dated to the middle of the first century BCE.[72]

The orthography of 4QKgs includes more plene spellings than MT-Kgs but follows the general principals of MT's conservative orthographic system.[73] The textual character of 4QKgs is difficult to assess. Twelve cases of textual variation occur, of which two cannot be translated into a non-Semitic language. 4QKgs reads eight times with and four times against MT, eight times with and twice against LXX, as well as four times non-aligned. It is of special interest that 4QKgs reads in 1 Kgs 8:16 with 2 Chr 6:5–6 against the text of MT-Kgs. The long text of 4QKgs demonstrates that the shorter text of MT developed due to *homoioteleuton*.[74] The eye of the scribe skipped from the first לִהְיוֹת שְׁמִי שָׁם "so that my name may be there," which is still preserved in 2 Chr 6:5–6, to the second occurrence of that phrase.

28 מן היום אשר הוצאתי את עמי את ישראל ממצרים לא
בחרתי בעיר מכל שבטי
29 ישראל לבנות בית להיות שמי שם ולא בחרתי באיש ל[היות
נגיד על עמ]י ישראל

30 ואבחר בירושלם להיות שמי שם ואבחר בדוד [להיות על
עמי על]ישראל

"Since the day, when I led my people, Israel, out of Egypt, I have not chosen a city among all the tribes 28 of Israel to build a house so that my name may be there, and I have not chosen a man to]be ruler over my peopl[e, Israel. 30 And I have chosen Jerusalem so that my name is there and I have chosen David to be (ruler) over my people, over[Israel." (1 Kgs 8:16 according to 4QKgs 11:28–30)[75]

מִן־הַיּוֹם אֲשֶׁר הוֹצֵאתִי אֶת־עַמִּי אֶת־יִשְׂרָאֵל מִמִּצְרַיִם לֹא־בָחַרְתִּי
בְעִיר מִכֹּל שִׁבְטֵי יִשְׂרָאֵל לִבְנוֹת בַּיִת לִהְיוֹת שְׁמִי שָׁם וָאֶבְחַר
בְּדָוִד לִהְיוֹת עַל־עַמִּי יִשְׂרָאֵל׃

"Since the day, when I led my people, Israel, out of Egypt, I have not chosen a city among all the tribes of Israel to build a house so that my name may be there, but David I chose so that he rules (lit so that he is) over Israel." (MT-1 Kgs 8:16)

מִן־הַיּוֹם אֲשֶׁר הוֹצֵאתִי אֶת־עַמִּי מֵאֶרֶץ מִצְרַיִם לֹא־בָחַרְתִּי בְעִיר
מִכֹּל שִׁבְטֵי יִשְׂרָאֵל לִבְנוֹת בַּיִת לִהְיוֹת שְׁמִי שָׁם וְלֹא־בָחַרְתִּי בְאִישׁ
לִהְיוֹת נָגִיד עַל־עַמִּי יִשְׂרָאֵל׃ 6 וָאֶבְחַר בִּירוּשָׁלִַם לִהְיוֹת שְׁמִי שָׁם
וָאֶבְחַר בְּדָוִיד לִהְיוֹת עַל־עַמִּי יִשְׂרָאֵל׃

"Since the day, when I led my people out of the land of Egypt, I have not chosen a city among all the tribes of Israel to build a house so that my name may be there, and I have not chosen a man to be ruler over my people, Israel. 6 And I have chosen Jerusalem so that my name is there and I have chosen David to be (ruler) over my people, Israel." (MT-2 Chr 6:5–6)

Beyond individual textual differences, Stegemann's material reconstruction[76] of the two surviving columns of 4QKgs demonstrates the affiliation of the 4QKgs text with MT-Kgs: "4QKgs agrees with 𝔐 Kgs (and Chr) against 𝔊 in all the frequent and substantial variants which give to the *Vorlage* of the Old Greek its very strong character and which reflect an intensive editorial activity; the omissions

---

[71] For the material reconstruction of 4QKgs by Stegemann, see Trebolle Barrera, "54. 4QKgs," 179, 182.

[72] Trebolle Barrera, "54. 4QKgs," 172. For the paleographical analysis of 4QKgs, see Trebolle Barrera, "54. 4QKgs," 171–73; "Preliminary Edition," 229–30, 235–39, 244–45; Trebolle Barrera, "Qumran Fragments," 20.

[73] For the orthography of 4QKgs, see Trebolle Barrera, "54. 4QKgs," 173, 183; Trebolle Barrera, "Preliminary Edition," 230–31, 245–46; Trebolle Barrera, "Qumran Fragments," 21.

[74] Thus Trebolle Barrera, "54. 4QKgs," 177, 183; Trebolle Barrera, "4QJudgᵃ and 4QKgs," 315–17; Trebolle Barrera, "Preliminary Edition," 235, 246; Trebolle Barrera, "Qumran Fragments," 21–22; Tov, *TCHB*, 223.

[75] Reconstruction of 4QKgs 11:28–30 according to Trebolle Barrera, "54. 4QKgs," 180. The preserved text is underlined.

[76] Stegemann's material reconstruction was published by Trebolle Barerra in "54. 4QKgs," 179–83; Trebolle Barrera, "Qumran Fragments," 22–24.

in 7:20b, 30b–32a, 38b; 8:1a, 2, 3a, 4, 5–8b, the additions in 7:45b and 8:1a, the transpositions in 7:26 (placed before 𝔐 7:25); 7:51 followed by 7:1a, 2–12, 1b; 8:12–13 (placed after 𝔐 8:53), and other textual variants."[77] Given the textual differences between 4QKgs and MT in 1 Kgs 8:16 and elsewhere, 4QKgs is best described as attesting to a semi-Masoretic text.[78]

5.3.1.9 5QKgs (5Q2)

Only three fragments from the first column of 5QKgs are extant. They preserve fifty words and partial words from 1 Kgs 1:1, 16–17, 27–37. Milik describes the script of 5QKgs as later than 5QDtn.[79] The manuscript was written in an archaic or early Hasmonean book hand from the first half of the second century B.C.E. In its orthography, 5QKgs resembles MT-Kgs.[80] Because only fifty words of biblical text can be identified in 5QKgs, insufficient text is available for a textual classification of this manuscript.[81] It is nevertheless significant that a handlesheet precedes 1 Kings 1 in 5QKgs. It indicates that 5QKgs followed the division of the books of 1 Samuel–2 Kings as found in MT against the division of the proto-Lucianic text (→ 5.4).[82]

5.3.1.10 6QpapKgs (6Q4)

6QpapKgs was produced from a coarse and uneven papyrus. Only one or two characters are left on many of the ninety-four preserved fragments. Only the text of frgs. 1–17 and 72 can still be identified. They attest to ninety-seven words and partial words from 1 Kgs 3:12–14; 12:28–31; 22:28–31; 2 Kgs 5:26; 6:32; 7:8–10, 20; 8:1–5; 9:1–2; 10:19–21. The script of 6QpapKgs is reminiscent of 1QIsa[a] and can be described as a Hasmonean book hand from the last quarter of the second century B.C.E.[83] Individual words are not always separated by a space and medial characters are also used in final position. In its orthography, 6QpapKgs follows the conservative system known from MT although the manuscript sometimes includes spellings that are fuller than their equivalents in MT. Due to the severe damage that this manuscript has suffered, its textual classification is difficult. The situation becomes even more difficult because for the text which is extant in 6QpapKgs OG-Kgs is only preserved in LXX[L] (→ 5.5). 6QpapKgs reads three times with and thirteen times against MT (→ 5.3.2), five times with and nine times against LXX (→ 5.5), as well as seven times non-aligned.[84] In comparison with MT, the preserved parts of 6QpapKgs tend to read a shorter text.[85] With due caution – given the poor preservation of 6QpapKgs – the text of 6QpapKgs can be described as non-aligned.[86] Trebolle Barrera demonstrated that the addition in 6QpapKgs of כדבר איש האלהי]ם "like the man of God said"[87] to 2 Kgs 7:20 served editorial purposes.[88] He also showed that the short text and different textual sequence of 6QpapKgs in 2 Kgs 8:2 preserves a lost original reading of this verse: ותקם האשה ותלך כדבר איש האלה[ים] [אל אר֯ץ֯] פלשתים [שׁ֯ב֯ע שנים "and the woman made preparations and went – like the man of G]o[d had spoken] – to the land[of the Philistines]for seven years."[89]

---

[77] Trebolle Barerra, "54. 4QKgs," 183; cf. op. cit., 173; Trebolle Barrera, "Preliminary Edition," 230–31, 245–46; Trebolle Barrera, "Qumran Fragments," 21.

[78] Cf. Lange, *Handbuch, 225–26.

[79] Milik, "2. I Rois," 172.

[80] Cf. Milik, "2. I Rois," 172.

[81] Cf. Lange, *Handbuch, 226; Trebolle Barrera, "Qumran Fragments," 24.

[82] Cf. Trebolle Barerra, "Qumran Fragments," 24.

[83] Cf. Baillet, "4. Livres de Rois," 107.

[84] Most of these readings are discussed by Baillet, "4. Livres de Rois," 108–10. For a brief discussion of selected readings of 6QpapKgs, see also Trebolle Barerra, "Qumran Fragments," 25–26.

[85] Cf. Baillet, "4. Livres de Rois," 107.

[86] Thus Tov, *TCHB², 116; Tov, *"Biblical Texts," 156; Lange, *Handbuch, 226–27.

[87] This addition is also attested by two Vulgate manuscripts.

[88] Trebolle Barrera, "2 Rois," 562–65; Trebolle Barrera, "Qumran Fragments," 26.

[89] Trebolle Barrera, "2 Rois," 566–68; Trebolle Barrera, "Qumran Fragments," 26.

5.3.1.11 MS Schøyen 5440[90]

Manuscript Schøyen 5440 was bought from a private owner and is part of the Schøyen collection. Its provenance is uncertain but it is likely that the manuscript was found at one of the sites around the Dead Sea. The single surviving fragment attests to fifteen words and partial words from 1 Kgs 16:23–26. As manuscript Schøyen 5440 attests to text from two consecutive paragraphs, the fragment most likely comes from a copy of the book of Kings and not from a Kings quotation in a non-biblical manuscript. Langlois characterizes the script of manuscript Schøyen 5440 as a crude semi-formal early Herodian hand from the end of the first century B.C.E.[91] The small amount of preserved text allows for neither an orthographic nor a textual classification.[92]

5.3.1.12 Two Further Possible Qumran Manuscripts of 1–2 Kings

Puech[93] suggests to identify two further manuscripts of 1–2 Kings from Qumran Cave 4 among the unidentified fragments on the museum plates PAM 42.082 and PAM 41.941, 42.082, 43.694, respectively. He regards a small fragment with two partial and one complete word from PAM 42.082 as a remnant of a Kings manuscript that would attest to 1 Kgs 7:46–47, and that he designates as 4QKgs^a (4Q54a).[94] Puech's identification must remain speculative for three reasons: 1) His fragment reads in 1 Kgs 7:46 ב[מעבי "in foundries" instead of MT's בְּמַעֲבֵה "in a foundry"; 2) the rewriting of 1 Kgs 7:46–47 in MT-2 Chr 4:17–18 combines the words בַּעֲבִי "in a mold" (v. 17) and לָרֹב מְאֹד "in great quantity" (v. 18) and thus fits as well with the remaining characters of Puech's fragment as does 1 Kgs 7:46–47; 3) next to a copy of either 1–2 Kings or 1–2 Chronicles, the fragment from PAM 42.082 could also preserve the remnant of a Kings or Chronicles quotation in a non-biblical manuscript. Puech describes the handwriting of his fragment as an early Hasmonean hand from the years 150–100 B.C.E.[95]

Puech speculates also that a fragment depicted on PAM 41.941, 42.082, and 43.694 could attest to five partial words out of either 2 Kgs 19:27–29 or more likely Isa 37:28–30. He designates the fragment as 4QKgs^b (4Q54b) or 4QIsa^s (4Q69c).[96] Given the two possible biblical texts to which Puech's second fragment could attest, its identification as a 1–2 Kings manuscript must also remain speculative. Puech describes the script of his second fragment as a late Hasmonean or early Herodian hand.[97]

5.3.1.13 Antinoopolis 47 and 48

The three fragments known as manuscript Antinoopolis 47 (frgs. 1–2) and 48 (frg. 3) belong most likely to a single scroll of the book of Kings.[98] A proper text-critical edition of this manuscript is still lacking[99] although it was found in a controlled excavation in 1913–1914. Drawings and a reconstruction of a little more than two columns of text were produced by Yardeni.[100] A bad facsimile of Antinoopolis 47 (P. Ant. 1 47; Oxford, Ashmolean Museum) was published by Birnbaum.[101] Antinoopolis 47 preserves 136 words and partial words from 1 Kgs 22:12–18, 28–33 and Antinoopolis 48 (P. Ant. 1 48; Oxford, Ashmolean Museum) has ten words and partial words from 2 Kgs 21:8–9. The text is unvocalized and without Masoretic annotations. The paleographic date of Antinoopolis 47–48 is debated. On the one hand, McHardy[102] thinks of the third

---

[90] I am obliged to Kipp Davis and Torleif Elgvin who made a preprint copy of their edition of manuscript Schøyen 5440 available to me ("MS 5440").

[91] Cf. Davis and Elgvin, "MS 5440," forthcoming.

[92] Against Davis and Elgvin, "MS 5440," forthcoming, who describe manuscript Schøyen 5440 as an independent text based on reconstructed readings.

[93] Puech, "Nouvelles identifications."

[94] Puech, "Nouvelles identifications," 467–69. In French, Puech calls the fragment 4QRois^a.

[95] Puech, "Nouvelles identifications," 469.

[96] Puech, "Nouvelles identifications," 469–72. In French, Puech calls the fragment 4QRois^b or 4QIs^s.

[97] Puech, "Nouvelles identifications," 471.

[98] See McHardy, "Appendix," 105, 106; Sirat, *Papyrus*, 35.

[99] McHardy, "Appendix," 105–06, does not go beyond a brief description of the scroll.

[100] Sirat, *Papyrus*, 36–38; Yardeni, *Hebrew Script*, 85 fig. 103.

[101] S. Birnbaum, *Hebrew Scripts* (2 vols.; Leiden: Brill, 1954–1957), 2.plate 183.

[102] McHardy, "Appendix," 105.

through the sixth centuries C.E. and Birnbaum[103] proposes the fifth century C.E. On the other hand, Yardeni suggests the eighth century.[104] Although textual differences between MT and LXX exist in the passages preserved by Antinoopolis 47–48,[105] the scroll reads in every case with MT[L] and therefore needs to be classified as attesting to a proto-Masoretic text (→ 5.3.2). It is interesting that in 1 Kgs 22:31 the letter ה was erased before the word קטן "small." The uncorrected reading הקטן "the small" is also reflected in MT[Kenn1, 23, 96, 158, 187, 224, 226, 228, 250] as well as in 2 Chr 18:30.[106]

Andersen, F.I. and D.N. Freedman, "Another Look at 4QSam[b]," in *Studies in Hebrew and Aramaic Orthography* (eds. D.N. Freedman, A.D. Forbes, and F.I. Andersen; Biblical and Judaic Studies 2; Winona Lake: Eisenbrauns, 1992), 189–210.

Baillet, M., "4. Livres de Rois," *DJD III.1: 107–12.

Barthelémy, D., "7. Livres de Samuel," *DJD I: 64–65.

Bodner, K., "Excavating Ideas: The Qumran Scrolls of Samuel," in *The World of Jesus and the Early Church: Identity and Interpretation in the Early Communities of Faith* (ed. C.A. Evans; Peabody: Hendrickson Publishers, 2011), 141–51.

Catastini, A., "4Q Sam[a]: I. Samuele il 'Nazireo'," *Hen* 9 (1987): 161–95.

Cook, E.W., "1 Samuel xx 26–xxi 5 according to 4QSam[b]," *VT* 44 (1994): 442–54.

Cross, F.M., "A New Qumran Biblical Fragment Related to the Original Hebrew Underlying the Septuagint," *BASOR* 132 (1953): 15–26.

Cross, F.M., "The Oldest Manuscript from Qumran," *JBL* 74 (1955): 147–72, esp. 159–63 and 167–76.

Cross, F.M., "The Ammonite Oppression of the Tribes of Gad and Reuben: Missing Verses from 1 Samuel 11 found in 4QSamuel[a]," in *History, Historiography, and Interpretation: Studies in Biblical and Cuneiform Literature* (eds. T. Tadmor and M. Weinfeld; Jerusalem: Magnes Press, 1983), 148–58 (an earlier version of this article was published in *The Hebrew and Greek Texts of Samuel: 1980 Proceedings IOSCS Vienna* [ed. E. Tov; Jerusalem: Academon: 1980], 105–19).

Cross, F.M., "A New Reconstruction of 4QSamuel[a] 24:16–22," in *Studies in the Hebrew Bible, Qumran, and the Septuagint: Presented to Eugene Ulrich* (eds. P.W. Flint, E. Tov, and J.C. VanderKam; VTSup 101; Leiden: Brill, 2006), 77–83.

Cross, F.M. and D.W. Parry, "A Preliminary Edition of a Fragment of 4QSam[b] (4Q52)," *BASOR* 306 (1997): 63–74.

Cross, F.M., D.W. Parry, and R.J. Saley, "51. 4QSam[a]," *DJD XVII (2005): 1–216.

Cross, F.M., D.W. Parry, and R.J. Saley, "52. 4QSam[b]," *DJD XVII (2005): 219–46.

Cross, F.M., D.W. Parry, and R.J. Saley, "Singular Readings in 4QSamuel[a] and the Question of Rewritten Scripture," *DSD* 20 (2013): 1–16.

Cross, F.M. and R.J. Saley, "A Statistical Analysis of the Textual Character of 4QSamuel[a] (4Q51)," *DSD* 13 (2006): 46–54.

Davis, K. and T. Elgvin, "MS 5440: 4Q(?)Kgs (1 Kgs. 16.23–26)," in *Gleanings*, forthcoming.

Driesbach, J., "A Partial Characterization of the Hebrew Texts of Samuel Based on a Text-Critical Analysis of 4Q Samuel, Columns II, III, VI, and IX" (MA thesis, Hebrew University of Jerusalem, 2008).

Driesbach, J., "4QSamuel[a] and the Text of Samuel" (PhD diss., Hebrew University of Jerusalem, 2015).

Elgvin, T., "MS 5480: 4Q(?)Sam1 (1 Sam. 5.10–11)," in *Gleanings*, forthcoming.

Elgvin, T., "MS 5233/1: 4Q(?)Sam2 (2 Sam. 20.22–24)," in *Gleanings*, forthcoming.

Fincke, A., *The Samuel Scroll from Qumran: 4QSam[a] Restored and Compared to the Septuagint and 4QSam[c]* (STDJ 43, Leiden: Brill, 2001; for an extensive criticism of this edition, see E.D. Herbert, *DSD* 9 [2002]: 402–04).

Herbert, E.D., *Reconstructing Biblical Scrolls: A New Method Applied to the Reconstruction of 4QSam[a]* (STDJ 22, Leiden: Brill, 1997).

Herbert, E.D., "4QSam[a] and Its Relationship to the LXX: An Exploration in Stemmatological Analysis," in *IX Congress of the International Organization for Septuagint and Cognate Studies Cambridge 1995* (ed. B.A. Taylor; SBLSCS 45, Atlanta: Scholars Press, 1997), 37–55.

Herbert, E.D., "The Kaige Recension of Samuel: Light

---

[103] Birnbaum, *Hebrew Scripts*, 1.223–25; cf. M. Dukan, *La Bible hébraïque: Les codices copiés en Orient et dans la zone séfarade avant 1280* (Bibliologia 22; Turnhout: Brepols, 2006), 13.

[104] Yardeni, *Hebrew Script*, 85 fig. 103; cf. J. Olszowy-Schlanger, "On the Hebrew Script of the Greek-Hebrew Palimpsests from the Cairo Genizah," in *The Jewish-Greek Tradition in Antiquity and the Byzantine Empire* (eds. J.K. Aitken and J. Carleton Paget; Cambridge: Cambridge University Press, 2014), 279–99 (295).

[105] Thus already McHardy, "Appendix," 105.

[106] Cf. McHardy, "Appendix," 106.

from 4QSamª," in *The Bible as Book: The Hebrew Bible and the Judaean Desert Discoveries* (eds. E.D. Herbert and E. Tov; London: British Library, 2002), 197–208.

Hugo, P., I. Kottsieper, and A. Steudel, "Notes paléographiques sur 4QSam a (4Q51) (le cas de 2 Sam 3)," *RevQ* 23 (2007–2008): 93–108.

Lange, A., *Handbuch, 231–47.

McCarter, P.K., *I Samuel: A New Translation with Introduction, Notes, and Commentary* (AB 8; New York: Doubleday, 1980), esp. 5–11.

McCarter, P.K., *II Samuel: A New Translation with Introduction, Notes, and Commentary* (AB 9; New York: Doubleday, 1984), esp. 3.

McHardy, W.D., "Appendix (Nos. 47–50)," in *The Antinoopolis Papyri Part 1: Edited with Translations and Notes* (ed. C.H. Roberts; London: Egypt Exploration Society, 1950), 105–06.

Milik, J.T., "2. 1 Rois," *DJD III.1: 171–72.

Parry, D.W., "4QSamª and the Tetragrammaton," in *Current Research and Technological Developments on the Dead Sea Scrolls: Conference on the Texts from the Judean Desert, Jerusalem, 30 April 1995* (eds. D.W. Parry and S.D. Ricks; STDJ 20; Leiden: Brill, 1996), 106–25.

Parry, D.W., "4QSamª (4Q51): A Preliminary Edition of 1 Samuel 25:3–31:4," in *The Provo International Conference on the Dead Sea Scrolls: Technological Innovations, New Texts and Reformulated Issues: International Conference on the Dead Sea Scrolls, 1996, Provo, Utah* (eds. D.W. Parry and E. Ulrich; STDJ 30; Leiden: Brill, 1999), 58–71.

Parry, D.W., "4QSamª and the Royal Song of Thanksgiving (2 Sam // Ps 18)," in *Sapiential, Liturgical, and Poetical Texts from Qumran: Proceedings of the Third Meeting of the International Organization for Qumran Studies Oslo 1998* (eds. D.K. Falk, F. García Martínez, and E.M. Schuller; STDJ 35; Leiden: Brill, 2000), 146–59.

Parry, D.W., "The Aftermath of Abner's Murder," *Textus* 20 (2000): 83–89.

Parry, D.W., "More Fragments of 4QSamª (4Q51): A Preliminary Edition of 1 Samuel 14:24–24:22," in *The Dead Sea Scrolls Fifty Years after Their Discovery: Proceedings of the Jerusalem Congress, July 20–25, 1997* (eds. L.H. Schiffman et al.; Jerusalem: Israel Exploration Society, 2000), 19–29.

Parry, D.W., "Unique Readings in 4QSamª," in *The Bible as Book: The Hebrew Bible and the Judaean Desert Discoveries* (eds. E.D. Herbert and E. Tov; London: British Library, 2002), 209–19.

Parry, D.W., "4QSamª (4Q51), the Canon, and the Community of Lay Readers," in *BDSS, 1.167–82.

Parry, D.W., "The Textual Character of the Unique Readings of 4QSamª (4Q51)," in *Flores Florentino: Dead Sea Scrolls and Other Early Jewish Studies in Honour of Florentino García Martínez* (eds. A. Hilhorst, É. Puech, and E. Tigchelaar; JSJSup 122; Leiden: Brill, 2007), 163–82.

Pisano, S., *Additions or Omissions in the Books of Samuel: The Significant Pluses and Minuses in the Massoretic, LXX and Qumran Texts* (OBO 57; Freiburg Schweiz: Universitätsverlag, 1984).

Polak, F., "Samuel, First and Second Books of," *EDSS, 2.819–23.

Polak, F., "Statistics and Textual Filiation: The Case of 4QSamª / LXX (with a Note on the Text of the Pentateuch)," in *Manchester Symposium, 215–76.

Puech, É., "4QSamuelª (4Q51): Notes épigraphiques et nouvelles identifications," in *Florilegium Lovaniense: Studies in the Septuagint and Textual Criticism in Honour of Florentino García Martínez* (eds. H. Ausloos, B. Lemmelijn, and M. Vervenne; BETL 224; Leuven: Peeters, 2008), 373–86.

Puech, É., "Nouvelles identifications de manuscrits bibliques dans la grotte 4: 4QRoisª (4Q54a) et 4QRoisᵇ–4Q54b(?) ou 4QIsˢ–4Q69c(?)," *RevQ* 25 (2011–2012): 467–72.

Ravasco, A., "La storia del testo di Samuele alla luce della documentazione di Qumran" (PhD diss.; University of Pisa, 2009).

Ravasco, A., "Readings in the First Book of Samuel: Considerations in the Light of 4QSamª," *Hen* 34 (2012): 56–74.

Rezetko, R. and I. Young, "Appendix 2: Commentary on Linguistic Variants in MT and Qumran Samuel," in R. Rezetko and I. Young, *Historical Linguistics and Biblical Hebrew: Steps Toward an Integrated Approach* (SBLANEM 9; Atlanta: SBL, 2014), 453–592.

Rofé, A., "The Nomistic Corrections in Biblical Manuscripts and Its Occurence in 4QSamª," *RevQ* 14 (1989–1990): 247–54.

Rofé, A., "4QSamª in the Light of Historico-Literary Criticism: The Case of 2 Sam 24 and 1 Chr 21," in *Biblische und Judaistische Studien: Festschrift für Paolo Sacchi* (ed. A. Vivian; Judentum und Umwelt 29; Frankfurt a.M.: Peter Lang, 1990), 109–19.

Rofé, A., "4QMidrash Samuel? Observations Concerning the Character of 4QSamª," *Textus* 19 (1998): 63–74.

Rofé, A., "Midrashic Traits in 4Q51 (So-Called 4QSamª)," in *Archaeology of the Books of Samuel: The Entangling* of the Textual and Literary History (eds. P. Hugo and A. Schenker; VTSup 132; Leiden: Brill, 2010), 75–88.

Sirat, C., *Les papyrus en caractères hébraïques trouvés en Egypte* (Paris: Editions du Centre National de la Recherche Scientifique, 1985), 35–38.

Tov, E., "The Textual Affiliations of 4QSam^a," in *The Hebrew and Greek Texts of Samuel: 1980 Proceedings IOSCS Vienna* (ed. E. Tov; Jerusalem: Academon: 1980), 189–205 (earlier publication in *JSOT* 14 [1979]: 37–53).

Tov, E., "4QSam^a and Its Relationship to the LXX: An Exploration in Stemmatological Analysis," in *IX Congress of the International Organization for Septuagint and Cognate Studies, Cambridge 1995* (ed. B.A. Taylor; SBLSCS 45; Atlanta: SBL, 1997), 37–55.

Tov, E., "Different Editions of the Song of Hannah and of Its Narrative Framework," in *Tehillah le-Moshe: Biblical and Judaic Studies in Honor of Moshe Greenberg* (eds. M. Cogan, L. Eichler, and J.H. Tigay; Winona Lake: Eisenbrauns, 1997), 149–70.

Trebolle Barrera, J., "Light from 4QJudg^a and 4QKgs on the Text of Judges and Kings," in *The Dead Sea Scrolls: Forty Years of Research* (eds. D. Dimant and U. Rappaport; STDJ 10; Leiden: Brill, 1992), 315–24.

Trebolle Barrera, J., "A Preliminary Edition of 4QKings (4Q54)," in *Madrid Qumran Congress*, 1.229–46.

Trebolle Barrera, J., "54. 4QKgs," *DJD* XIV: 171–83.

Trebolle Barrera, J., "Le texte de 2 Rois 7,20–8,5 à la lumière des découvertes de Qumrân (6Q4 15)," *RevQ* 13 (1988): 561–68.

Trebolle Barrera, J., "Qumran Fragments on the Books of Kings," in *The Book of Kings: Sources, Composition, Historiography and Reception* (eds. A. Lemaire, B. Halpern, and M.J. Adams; VTSup 129; Leiden: Brill, 2010), 19–39.

Ulrich, E., "4QSam^a and Septuagintal Research," *BIOSCS* 8 (1975): 24–39.

Ulrich, E., *The Qumran Text of Samuel and Josephus* (HSM 19; Missoula: Scholars Press, 1978).

Ulrich, E., "4QSam^c: A Fragmentary Manuscript of 2 Samuel 14–15 from the Scribe of the *Serek Hayyaḥad* (1QS)," *BASOR* 235 (1979): 1–25.

Ulrich, E., "The Old Latin Translation of the LXX and the Hebrew Scrolls from Qumran," in *The Hebrew and Greek Texts of Samuel: 1980 Proceedings IOSCS Vienna* (ed. E. Tov; Jerusalem: Academon: 1980), 121–65.

Ulrich, E., "53. 4QSam^c," *DJD* XVII: 245–67.

Ulrich, E., "A Qualitative Assessment of the Textual Profile of 4QSam^a," in *Flores Florentino: Dead Sea Scrolls and Other Early Jewish Studies in Honour of Florentino García Martínez* (eds. A. Hilhorst, É. Puech, and E. Tigchelaar; JSJSup 122; Leiden: Brill, 2007), 147–61.

Ulrich, E., *BQS, 259–329.

Venturini, S., "Alcune caratteristiche editoriali di 4QSam^a" (PhD diss., Pontifical Biblical Institute, 2001).

Armin Lange

5.3.2 Masoretic Texts and Ancient Texts Close to MT

There is no surviving witness of a complete (proto-)Masoretic text of Samuel–Kings earlier than the first vocalized masoretic manuscripts (Codex Cairo, 895 C.E.; Aleppo Codex, ca. 915 C.E.; and Codex Leningradensis or Firkovitch B19a, 1008 C.E.). Only some small fragments among the Dead Sea Scrolls are to be assessed as close to MT or as "semi-masoretic" (→ 5.3.1): 1QSam (1Q7)[1] and 4QKgs (4Q54).[2] The fragments of 5QKgs (5Q2) are too small and too poorly preserved to allow for a characterization with any certainty.[3]

In addition to the Hebrew witnesses, some versional witnesses are also important. They are especially illuminating for the formative period of (proto-)MT because some of them indirectly reflect its early stages (first century B.C.E.–second century C.E.): the Peshitta (second century C.E. for Samuel–Kings; → 3–5.1.4),[4] Targum Jonathan (or Targum of Prophets; → 3–5.1.3) (fourth–fifth century C.E.;[5] in light of 1 Kings 2–12; 14, sometimes the Hebrew *Vorlage* of T^J may have been earlier than [proto-]MT of the first century C.E.[6]), the Vul-

---

[1] F. Polak, "Samuel, First and Second Books of," *EDSS 2:819–23 (820); Lange, *Handbuch*, 214.

[2] Lange, *Handbuch*, 225–26; J.T. Trebolle Barrera, "54. 4QKgs," *DJD* XIV (1995): 171–83 (183).

[3] Lange, *Handbuch*, 226; J.T. Milik, "2. 1 Rois," *DJD* III.1 (1962): 171–72.

[4] M.P. Weitzman, *The Syriac Version of the Old Testament: An Introduction* (University of Cambridge Oriental Publications 56; Cambridge: Cambridge University Press, 1999), 60–61 (Hebrew *Vorlage* of Peshitta), 258 (date).

[5] R. Le Déaut (and C. Tassin), "Targum," *DBSup* XIII (2002): 1*–344*; here 106*–21* (T^J), 114*–18* (date).

[6] Le Déaut (and Tassin), "Targum," 112*–14*.

gate, i.e., Jerome's translation (end of fourth century C.E.; → 3–5.1.7), and the Hexaplaric versions or recensions (Aquila, Symmachus, Thedodotion; → 3–5.1.5.2); but also the *kaige* recension or, more precisely, according to Barthélemy, the Palestinian recensions, since he assumes several recensions belonging to the *kaige* group and used by Origen in the fifth, sixth, and seventh columns of his Hexapla for Samuel–Kings (→ 5.4; → 5.5; → 3–5.1.5.2).[7] Thus, the dates of all these Hexaplaric recensions extend from the first century B.C.E. to the second century C.E.

5.3.2.1 History of Research

Three main positions concerning the text-critical assessment of proto-MT can be observed in recent research (→ 5.2.4 for more details concerning Kings). The first one is held by a majority of scholars. It considers proto-MT to represent the best and earliest text type of Samuel–Kings, notwithstanding the poor state of its textual preservation (esp. Samuel[8]). The witness of Old Greek is given due weight wherever MT seems to be faulty or difficult.[9] This position, the oldest and "traditional" one and still widespread among exegetes, was not shaken by the discovery of the Dead Sea Scrolls. While one must reckon with multiple text types during the last centuries B.C.E., proto-MT is still judged by a number of scholars as basically the best witness of the earliest text. Therefore, the texts to be found in the Qumran fragments of Samuel and in the Old Greek (resp. its Hebrew *Vorlage*) are generally explained as secondary editorial or literary reshapings of the more original (proto-)MT (→ 5.3.3; → 5.2.4).[10]

However, for some decades now, there has a growing trend towards another judgment on MT and its proto-Masoretic predecessor, since recent research increasingly emphasizes editorial or redactional features to be observed in this text.[11] Thus, a second position crystalizes, seeing in the multiplicity of texts the result of parallel editorial and literary activities. Two, respectively three, main text types (viz., proto-MT, the Hebrew source of the Old Greek [→ 5.4; → 5.5], and the 4QSam^{a-b}-text type [→ 5.3.3]) have developed alongside each other in different ideological or religious circles. They reflect different contemporaneous conceptions concerning theological and other matters, such as kingship, messianism, halakha etc. In this view, therefore, the reconstruction of the *Urtext* is only possible when choosing eclectically the best readings from each textual tradition, case by case, while a relative chronology often cannot be reliably established.[12]

A third position is hold by scholars who believe that a close scrutiny of many of the specific Masoretic readings, in contradistinction to those of the other text types (Old Greek, Qumran scrolls), may show they are the result of a deliberate lit-

---

[7] Barthélemy, *Devanciers*, 128–43; T.M. Law, *Origenes Orientalis: The Preservation of Origen's Hexapla in the Syrohexapla of 3 Kingdoms* (De Septuaginta Investigationes 2; Göttingen: Vandenhoeck & Ruprecht, 2011).

[8] See the general assessment of Tov, *TCHB*, 189.

[9] Thus the majority of recent commentaries, e.g., A. Caquot and P. de Robert, *Les livres de Samuel* (CAT 6; Geneva: Labor et Fides, 1994), 9–12; S.J. De Vries, *1 Kings* (WBC 12; Waco: Word Books, 1985), lix; M. Cogan, *1 Kings: A New Translation with Introduction and Commentary* (AB 10; New York: Doubleday, 2000), 85; D.T. Tsumura, *The First Book of Samuel* (NICOT; Grand Rapids: Eerdmans, 2007), 2–10; M.A. Sweeney, *I & II Kings: A Commentary* (OTL; Louisville: Westminster, 2007), 32–40.

[10] See. e.g., D. Barthélemy, "La qualité du texte massorétique de Samuel," in *The Hebrew and Greek Texts of Samuel* (ed. E. Tov; Jerusalem: Academon, 1980), 1–44; Barthélemy, *Critique textuelle 1982*; Pisano, *Additions and Omissions*; Talshir, *The Alternative Story*; Z. Talshir, "1 Kings and 3 Kingdoms – Origin and Revision: Case Study: The Sins of Solomon," *Textus* 21 (2002): 71–105; van Keulen, *Two Versions of the Solomon Narrative*.

[11] This evolution is perceptible in some very recent commentaries, e.g., W. Dietrich, *Samuel*, Teilband 1: *1 Sam 1–12* (BKAT 8.1; Neukirchen-Vluyn: Neukirchener Verlag, 2011), 39*–41*; A.G. Auld, *I & II Samuel: A Commentary* (OTL; Louisville: Westminster John Knox, 2011), 4–7.

[12] See P.K. Kyle, *I–II Samuel* (2 vols.; AB 8–9; New York: Doubleday, 1980–1984); J.H. Kim, *Die hebräischen und griechischen Textformen der Samuel- und Königebücher: Studien zur Textgeschichte ausgehend von 2 Sam 15,1–19,9* (BZAW 394; Berlin: De Gruyter, 2009); Hutzli, *Die Erzählung von Hanna und Samuel*; J. Bösenecker, "Text und Redaktion. Untersuchungen zum hebräischen und griechischen Text von 1 Könige 1–11" (PhD diss., University of Rostock, 2000).

erary reshaping of an earlier text form very often preserved in the Hebrew source of the Old Greek. Already in the nineteenth century, scholars such as Thenius, Wellhausen, and Driver emphasized the possibility that the Hebrew source of the Greek translation (Old Greek) may have preserved earlier readings than those of the predecessor text of MT in Samuel–Kings.[13] This was the intuition especially of Geiger in his groundbreaking *Urschrift und Übersetzungen der Bibel* in 1857.[14] In the predecessor of MT, in comparison with other text forms such as Samaritan and Old Greek, he saw simultaneously the early stage of the text and the high quality of its transmission *and* the many signs of later redactional reworking. The discovery of the Dead Sea Scrolls, in addition to the fact that the fragments of Samuel share some features with the Old Greek text type (→ 5.3.1), proved the existence of Hebrew texts distinct from the masoretic text type. An increasing number of scholars – among them Trebolle Barrera,[15] Schenker,[16] Hugo,[17] Rezetko,[18] Richelle,[19] and Law[20] – interpret many readings of MT throughout the books of Samuel–Kings as editorial or literary reworkings of the transmitted material (see the nature of these changes below, → 5.3.2.3).

5.3.2.2 Editions

The first critical editions of Samuel–Kings, in the modern sense of the word – i.e., with a selection of important variant readings of all text witnesses, Hebrew texts, and versions – were published by Kittel, 1906 in Leipzig (*BH) and in the series *Sacred Books of the Old Testament* in Leipzig and Baltimore, which remained unfinished (1894: *Samuel*, prepared by Budde; and 1904: *Kings*, by Stade and Schwally, with additional notes by P. Haupt).[21] Kittel's *BH³ of 1929/1937 was prepared by Kittel and Kahle. The three *BH editions edited by Kittel were diplomatic editions; the first two reproduced the text of the Second Rabbinic Bible of Ben Hayyim (Venice 1524–1525)[22] while the third one printed the text of MT^L. The edition of the books of Samuel was the work of Kittel himself through all three editions, the third appearing in 1933, while Kings were also done by Kittel, but the third edition was completed after his death by Martin Noth in 1934. The third Kittel Bible was reprinted many times in corrected and augmented form.

Among the recent available critical editions of MT, the most widely used is *BHS. Like its immediate predecessor, *BH³, *BHS is a diplomatic edition of Codex Leningradensis (MT^L; Codex EPB I B 19a of the National Library of Russia in St. Petersburg). It was completed in 1979 and published in Stuttgart by the *Deutsche Bibelgesellschaft*. Since 1979, it has been reprinted in five corrected editions. The editor of the books of *Samuel* was Pieter Arie H. de Boer (Leiden, 1976). His textual apparatus is a careful analysis of the textual data including the Old Greek and the Qumran texts, as far

---

[13] S.R. Driver, *Notes on the Hebrew Text of the Books of Samuel* (Oxford: Clarendon Press, 1890 [2nd ed. 1913]); O. Thenius, *Die Bücher Samuels* (KHAT; Leipzig: Hirzel, 1842 [2nd ed. 1864]); O. Thenius, *Die Bücher Könige* (KHAT; Leipzig: Hirzel, 1849 [2nd ed. 1873]); J. Wellhausen, *Der Text der Bücher Samuelis* (Göttingen: Vandenhoeck & Ruprecht, 1871); J. Wellhausen, "Das Buch der Könige," in F. Bleek, *Einleitung in das Alte Testament* (4th rev. ed. by J. Wellhausen; Berlin, 1878), 231–67.

[14] Geiger, *Urschrift; R.D. Weis, "'Lower Criticism': Studies in the Masoretic Text and the Ancient Versions of the Old Testament as Means of Textual Criticism," in *Hebrew Bible/Old Testament: The History of Its Interpretation*, Vol. 3: *From Modernism to Post-Modernism* (*The Nineteenth and Twentieth Centuries*) (ed. M. Saebø; Göttingen: Vandenhoeck & Ruprecht, 2013), 346–92, esp. 351–58.

[15] Trebolle Barrera, *Salomón y Jeroboán*; Trebolle Barrera, *Jehú y Joás*.

[16] Schenker, *Septante et texte massorétique*; Schenker, *Älteste Textgeschichte*; Schenker, *Anfänge der Textgeschichte*; Schenker, *Une bible archétype?*

[17] Hugo, *Les deux visages d'Elie*.

[18] Rezetko, *Source and Revision*.

[19] Richelle, *Le testament d'Elisée*.

[20] M. Law, "How Not to Use 3 Reigns: A Plea to Scholars in the Books of Kings," *VT* 61 (2011): 280–97.

---

[21] K. Budde, *The Books of Samuel: Critical Edition of the Hebrew Text* (Sacred Books of the Old Testament 8; Leipzig: J.C. Hinrichs, 1894); B. Stade and F. Schwally, *The Books of Kings: Critical Edition of the Hebrew Text* (Sacred Books of the Old Testament 9; Leipzig: J.C. Hinrichs, 1904).

[22] RB2.

as available to him. He essentially considered MT to be the original text.²³ The same may be said of the books of Kings; Alfred Jepsen (Greifswald, 1974) carefully and rather fully registered the variants of Old Greek, refraining in most cases from arbitrating between competing readings.

Three new critical editions are in preparation in 2015: First for the *BHQ, which is the successor of *BHS, Steven Pisano (Rome) is editing the books of Samuel and Adrian Schenker (Fribourg, Switzerland) with Carmel McCarthy (Dublin) those of Kings. The editorial principles of *BHQ are explained in the fascicle of *Megilloth*.²⁴ The apparatus in *BHQ makes judgments on the readings concerning their more original or secondary nature, and justifies the judgments in the apparatus itself by short apparatus notes, or in a specific textual commentary.

Second, the *Hebrew Bible, A Critical Edition* (*HBCE). Zipora Talshir (Beersheva) is in charge of the edition of the books of Samuel, Jan Joosten (Oxford) that of 1 Kings, and Andrés Piquer Otero (Madrid) that of 2 Kings. For these books, this edition will be noteworthy insofar as it will not only present MT in diplomatic form but will also include a synopsis of two texts: Edition A, a critically established MT, and Edition B, a critically established text of Old Greek retroverted into Hebrew. This editorial decision was taken because "the divergences between the Septuagint on the one hand, the MT and the other versions on the other hand, point to the existence of two distinct Hebrew editions of 1 Kings."²⁵ According to Joosten, "(MT) reflects an older stage than (OG), but there are many details where the relation seems to be the reverse."²⁶ It is obvious that the particularly complex textual situation of Samuel–Kings and the absence of a consensus concerning an explanation for the differences between the main textual witnesses cannot but raise an ongoing debate on the philosophy of editing such biblical books in particular, and of the Bible in general.²⁷

The third project of a new critical edition of the Hebrew Bible is the *Hebrew University Bible* (*HUB). Since Samuel–Kings have not yet been prepared by the *HUB, the edition of these books cannot be described in detail. On the basis of the volumes published so far (Isaiah, Jeremiah, and Ezekiel), provided that the edition continues on the same lines, the following can be said: It will present the Hebrew text with the Masorah magna and parva of the Aleppo Codex, which offers these books without lacunae. It will present a fourfold apparatus. In the first one, all variant readings in the old versions (Old Greek, if necessary with its daughter translations, Old Latin, Coptic, Ethiopic, Armenian, Syro-Hexaplaric Bibles, the Hexaplaric translations [Aquila, Symmachus, Theodotion, and recensions of Old Greek], Peshitta, Vulgate, Targum Jonathan) will be noted. The second apparatus will offer all early Hebrew variants from the Dead Sea manuscripts and quotations from the rabbinic literature. In the third one, readings gleaned in a selection of medieval and Genizah manuscripts will be noted as well as manuscripts with another vocalization system. Finally, the fourth apparatus will present variations in orthography, vowels, and accents. At the bottom of the page, notes will explain details occurring in the four apparatuses. In principle, *HUB does not evaluate the readings. However, in the notes at the

---

²³ P.A.H. de Boer, *Research into the Text of 1 Samuel I–XVI* (Amsterdam: Paris, 1938); P.A.H. de Boer, "1 Samuel XVII: Notes on the Text and the Ancient Versions," *OTS* 1 (1941): 79–103; P.A.H. de Boer, "Research into the Text of 1 Samuel XVIII–XXXI," *OTS* 6 (1949): 1–100.

²⁴ *BHQ, Part 18: *General Introduction and Megilloth*, vii–lxxv.

²⁵ S. White Crawford, J. Joosten, and E. Ulrich, "Sample Editions of the Oxford Hebrew Bible: Deuteronomy 32:1–9, 1 Kings 11:1–8, and Jeremiah 27:1–10 (34G)," *VT* 58 (2008): 352–66, esp. 359; see also the samples of 2 Kings 1:1–6 by A. Piquer Otero (http://ohb.berkeley.edu/2%20Kgs%201%20sample.pdf).

²⁶ White Crawford, Joosten, and Ulrich, "Sample Editions," 359.

²⁷ H.G.M. Williamson, "Do We Need a New Bible? Reflections on the Proposed Oxford Hebrew Bible," *Bib* 90 (2009): 153–75; R. Hendel, "The Oxford Hebrew Bible: Its Aims and Response to Criticism," in *Hebrew Bible and Ancient Israel* 2 (2013): 63–99.

bottom, brief evaluations of many readings are proposed.

Besides full critical editions, a large number of MT editions have been made and are still being prepared without the versional evidence; nevertheless, they are critical in the sense that they endeavor to establish the genuine Hebrew masoretic text. By its very nature, indeed, the medieval *Masorah* was a critical tool and a monument of textual science since it was designed in order to avoid any alteration of the text as it was transmitted. In the four major polyglot Bibles of the sixteenth and seventeenth centuries, namely the Complutensian or Alcalá Polyglot (1514–1517),[28] the Antwerp Polyglot (1568–1572),[29] the Paris Polyglot (1628–1645),[30] and the Walton Polyglot (1653–1658),[31] which correspond to the four principal attempts at a critical edition of the Hebrew Bible between 1500 and 1650, the effort was made to group the main textual witnesses in Hebrew and in the versions in synoptic display.[32] From the sixteenth until the early twentieth century, the base text and starting point of all critical editions was eventually the Second Rabbinic Bible of Ben Hayyim (*RB2). This is true for the editions and works of Buxtorf the Elder,[33] Leusden, and Jablonski (seventeenth century), Michaelis, Houbigant, Kennicott, and De Rossi (eighteenth and nineteenth centuries),[34] Ginsburg (nineteenth century)[35] and others.

In the *Judaism* in particular, critical editions of MT and other textcritical works were numerous. Solomon Yedidya Norzi (1560–1626) made a famous critical commentary with his *Minhat Shay* Bible;[36] another edition is due to Manasse Ben Israel (1604–1657).[37] In the nineteenth century, Baer edited a critical masoretic apparatus for Samuel[38] and for Kings.[39] Cassuto, Dotan, and Breuer edited the Hebrew Bible based on MT^L and MT^A respectively, with no textual apparatus.[40] A careful, critical masoretic edition of Samuel–Kings based on MT^A was made by Cohen in *Mikraot Gedolot 'Ha-Keter'* at Bar-Ilan University.[41]

---

[28] *Complutensian Polyglot.

[29] *Biblia Sacra Hebraice, Chaldaice, Graece et Latina* ... (ed. B. Arias Montano; Antwerp: Christophorus Plantinus, 1569–1572).

[30] Le Jay, *Biblia.

[31] Walton, *Polyglotta.

[32] A. Schenker, "From the First Printed Hebrew, Greek and Latin Bibles to the First Polyglot Bible, the Complutensian Polyglot: 1477–1577," in *Hebrew Bible/Old Testament: The History of Its Interpretation*, Vol. 2: *From the Renaissance to the Enlightenment* (ed. M. Saebø; Göttingen: Vandenhoeck & Ruprecht, 2008), 276–91; A. Schenker, "The Polyglot Bibles of Antwerp, Paris and London: 1568–1658," in *Hebrew Bible/Old Testament 2*, 774–84.

[33] J. Buxtorf, *Biblia hebraica cum paraphrasis chaldaicis et commentariis Rabbinorum* (Basel: Ludovici König: 1618); J. Leusden, *Biblia Hebraica accuratissima: Biblia notis Hebraicis et lemmatibus illustrata* (Amsterdam: Athias, 1667); D.E. Jablonski, *Biblia Hebraica: Testatmentum vetus: cum notis Hebraicis et lemmatibus latinis* (Berlin: Knebel, 1699).

[34] J.H. Michaelis, *Biblia Hebraica: ex aliquot manuscriptis et compluribus impressis codicibus, item masora tam edita, quam manuscripta, alissque Hebraeorum criticis dilingenter recensita* (Halle: Orphanotropheum, 1720); C.-F. Houbigant, *Biblia Hebraica: Cum notis criticis et versione Latina ad notas criticas facta: Accedunt libri Graeci, qui Deutero-Canonici vocantur, in tres classes distributi* (Paris: Briasson et Durand, 1753); De Rossi, * 1784–1788; J.B. de Rossi, *Scholia critica in V.T. libros seu supplementa ad varias sacri textus lectiones* (Parma: Regium typographeum, 1798).

[35] C.D. Ginsburg, תורה נביאים כתובים: *Diligently Revised according to the Massorah and the Early Versions with the Various Readings from Manuscripts and the Ancient Versions* (ed. C.D. Ginsburg; London: Trinitarian Bible Society, 1894; 2nd ed.: London: British and Foreign Bible Society, 1926).

[36] Published by Joshua ben Michael, of Sezze (ed.) in his ספר ארבעה ועשרים: עם תוספת (2 vols.; Mantua: Raphael Chaim d' Italia, 1742–1744).

[37] M. Ben Israel, Biblia Hebraica: eleganti charactere impressa (Amsterdam: Laurentius, 1635).

[38] S. Baer, *Liber Samuelis* (Leipzig: Tauchnitz, 1892).

[39] S. Baer, *Liber Regum* (Leipzig: Tauchnitz, 1895).

[40] M.D. Cassuto, *Tanak* (Jerusalem: Hebrew University Magnes Press, 1953); A. Dotan, *Tanak* (Tel Aviv: Adi Publishers, 1973); A. Dotan, *Biblia Hebraica Leningradensia* (Peabody: Hendrickson, 2001) (the latter is a thoroughly revised edition of that of 1973); M. Breuer, *The Jerusalem Crown: The Bible of the Hebrew University Jerusalem* (Basel: Karger Family Fund, 2000).

[41] M. Cohen, *Sefer Shmuel* (Ramat-Gan: Bar Ilan University, 1993); M. Cohen, *Sefer Melakim* (Ramat-Gan: Bar Ilan University, 1995).

5.3.2.3 Nature and Text-Critical Character of proto-MT-Sam–Kgs

One reason for the complexity of the text of Samuel–Kings is the considerable number of obvious textual corruptions present in all witnesses.[42] They especially abound in the books of Samuel. There are, for example, a certain number of haplographies or *homoioteleuta*.[43] On the whole, MT has suffered many corruptions, notably in the books of Samuel, but at the same time it represents a carefully preserved text, a fact proven precisely by its many difficult readings that have not been smoothed out in order to facilitate the difficulties. At some stage in the transmission history, the scribes and editors must have decided to stick closely to a master copy that was considered the genuine text.

However, in spite of this, editorial interventions occur as well and in great number; they are extremely frequent in the book of Kings, probably more so than in any other book of the Hebrew Bible. They may be called "literary" because they do not result from the errors of copyists but from deliberate alterations of a redactional or narrative nature. This category of variant readings might be synthetized as follows: so-called "textual idiosyncrasies," namely corrections of a theological nature. Tov restricts this phenomenon to a few clearly defined cases, such as *Baal* that was replaced by *boshet* "Shame."[44] Other corrections are euphemistic or anti-polytheistic, or may have had a Halakhic intention (e.g., Samaritan schism and the sanctuary on the Gerizim, 1 Kgs 12:31 and 2 Kgs 17:29).[45] The chronological data, particularly important in Kings, vary between MT and Old Greek (→ 5.4; → 5.5) and betray a redactional intervention on one side or the other.[46] Differences in the sequence of literary units and the connection between pericopes attest to specific redactional agendas of MT and/or Old Greek.[47] The number of redactional or literary interventions characterizing proto-MT is especially important in matters concerning the royal (Davidic) dynasties and particularly the idealization of David (1 Samuel 17; 2 Samuel 2, 3, 5, and 19; 1 Kings 2),[48] Solomon's and Jeroboam's portraits (1 Kings 2–14),[49] the narrative

---

[42] A good picture of the many failures of the textual transmission may be gained by reading the section on Samuel–Kings in Barthélemy, *Critique textuelle 1982*.

[43] R.P. Gordon, "The Problem of Haplography in 1 and 2 Samuel," in *Manchester Symposium*, 131–58; Barthélemy, *Critique textuelle 1982*, the section on Samuel–Kings.

[44] Tov, *"Coincidental Textual Nature,"* 162–64.

[45] E. Tov, "Theological Tendencies in the Masoretic Text of Samuel," in *After Qumran: Old and New Editions of Biblical Texts: The Historical Books* (eds. H. Ausloos, B. Lemmelijn, and J. Trebolle Barrera; BETL 246; Leuven: Peeters, 2012), 3–20; cf., e.g., Schenker, *Älteste Textgeschichte*, 34–85; Schenker, *Septante et texte massorétique*, 142–47.

[46] Shenkel, *Chronology and Recensional Development*.

[47] J. Trebolle Barrera, "Textual Criticism and the Composition History of Samuel: Connections Between Pericopes in 1 Samuel 1–4," in *Archaeology of the Books of Samuel: The Entangling of the Textual and Literary History* (eds. P. Hugo and A. Schenker; VTSup 132; Leiden: Brill, 2010), 261–86; J. Trebolle Barrera, "Textual Criticism and the Literary Structure and Composition of 1–2 Kings/3–4 Reigns: The Different Sequence of Literary Units in MT and LXX," in Kreuzer-Meiser-Sigismund, *Septuaginta 2012*, 55–78; Schenker, *Älteste Textgeschichte*, 86–90.

[48] Barthélemy et al., *The Story of David and Goliath*; J. Trebolle Barrera, "The Story of David and Goliath (1 Sam 17–18): Textual Variants and Literary Composition," *BIOSCS* 23 (1990): 16–23; P. Hugo, "The Unique Messiah: A Tendency in Favour of David's Kingship in the MT of Samuel," in *In the Footsteps of Sherlock Holmes: Studies in the Biblical Text in Honour of Anneli Aejmelaeus* (eds. K. De Troyer, M.T. Law, and M. Liljeström; CBET 72; Leuven: Peeters, 2014), 331–51; P. Hugo, "Abner der Königsmacher *versus* David den gesalbten König (2 Sam 3,21.39): Die Charakterisierung Abners und Davids als Merkmale der literarischen Abweichungen zwischen dem Massoretischen Text und der Septuaginta," in Karrer–Kraus, *Septuaginta 2010*, 489–505; P. Hugo, "Die Morde an Abner und Amasa: Literarische Dimensionen textlicher Abweichungen zwischen dem Massoretischen Text und der Septuaginta in der David-Geschichte?" in *Seitenblicke: Literarische und historische Studien zu Nebenfiguren im zweiten Samuelbuch* (ed. W. Dietrich; OBO 249; Fribourg: Academic Press, 2011), 24–52; P. Hugo, "The King's Return (2 Sam 19,10–16): Contrasting Characterizations of David, Israel and Juda in the Old Editions," in *After Qumran: Old and New Editions of Biblical Texts: The Historical Books* (eds. H. Ausloos, B. Lemmelijn, and J. Trebolle Barrera; BETL 246; Leuven: Peeters, 2012), 95–118; J. Hutzli, "Mögliche Retuschen am Davidbild in der massoretischen Fassung der Samuelbücher," in *David und Saul im Widerstreit – Diachronie und Synchronie im Wettstreit* (ed. W. Dietrich; OBO 206; Fribourg: Academic Press 2004), 102–15.

[49] Trebolle Barrera, *Salomón y Jeroboán*; Schenker, *Septante et texte massorétique*.

of the Ark (2 Samuel 6; 1 Kings 8),[50] and the emphasized importance of the Jerusalem temple (its foundation and its architecture, 2 Samuel 7; 1 Kings 6),[51] the sins of Israel and Judah,[52] the guilt of the kings of Israel and of Manasseh of Judah (2 Kings 22–23),[53] and the role of the prophets in the portraits of Elijah and Elisha.[54] In this field of literary or redactional variants, the differences between MT and Old Greek have always been noted, at least as early as Origen who made the Hexapla in the third century C.E. precisely in order to gain a clear picture of these differences. However, their explanation remains a hotly disputed issue.[55]

5.3.2.4 Date and Milieu

Assigning a date and identifying the specific circles who produced MT in its consonantal form depends on the idea one has of the nature of this text in comparison with the Old Greek (→ 5.4; → 5.5) and Qumran fragments of the books of Samuel (and Kings) (→ 5.3.1). If MT is considered to be an early text type, perhaps the earliest one available, it must precede in substance the Hebrew *Vorlage* of Old Greek which, in this view, underwent an important reworking in comparison with MT. Since the Old Greek version might have been made in the late third century or first half of the second century B.C.E., the forerunner of MT goes back well before these dates. If, on the other hand, MT shows many traces of literary reworking while the Hebrew base text of Old Greek reflects an earlier text stage, Geiger's judgment would still hold good, viz., that MT is an old text type that was reworked literarily around the beginning of the Hasmonean kingdom and later.[56] The redactors would then to be looked for in circles close to the Hasmonean high priests and kings, and to the temple.[57]

5.3.2.5 Relevance for Exegesis and Literary Analysis

MT is a main witness of the text of the books of Samuel and Kings. Moreover, it is the text that was read and explained within Judaism and in the Peshitta (→ 3–5.1.4) and Jerome's Latin version of the Bible (→ 3–5.1.7) that were read in the Christian churches east of the boundaries of the Roman Empire and in Western Europe following the time of Charlemagne. Thus, the influence of MT for these two books of the Hebrew Bible was most influential in exegesis, theology, poetry, and art history. If it were the earliest text type, more immune from literary reshaping than Old Greek, one would have to consider it the closest to the original form of the books, and thus more reliable historically than the heavily modified Old Greek text (→ 5.4; → 5.5). The contrary would be the case in the opposite hypothesis. It should be noted that the literary-redactional differences between MT, Old Greek, and 4QSam[a]

---

[50] Rezetko, *Source and Revision*; A. Schenker, "The Ark as Sign of God's Absent Presence in Solomon's Temple: 1 Kings 8:6–8 in the Hebrew and Greek Bibles," in Schenker, *Anfänge der Textgeschichte*, 99–109.

[51] A. Schenker, "Die Verheissung Natans in 2 Sam 7 in der Septuaginta: Wie erklären sich die Differenzen zwischen Massoretischem Text und LXX, und was bedeuten sie für die messianische Würde des davidischen Hauses in der LXX?" in *The Septuagint and Messianism* (ed. M.A. Knibb; BETL 195; Leuven: Peeters, 2006), 177–92; A. Schenker, "Une nouvelle lumière sur l'architecture du temple grâce à la Septante? La place de l'arche d'alliance selon 2 Rois 6:16–17 et 3 Regnes 6:16–17," *Annali di Scienze Religiose* 10 (2005): 139–54; P. Hugo, "L'archéologie textuelle du temple de Jérusalem: Etude textuelle et littéraire du motif théologique du temple en 2 Samuel," in *Archaeology of the Books of Samuel: The Entangling of the Textual and Literary History* (eds. P. Hugo and A. Schenker; VTSup 132; Leiden: Brill, 2010), 161–212.

[52] Tebolle Barrera, *Jehú y Joás*; A. Schenker, "La cause de la chute du royaume d'Israël selon le texte massorétique," in Schenker, *Une bible archétype?* 153–71.

[53] A. Schenker, "Die Textgeschichte der Königsbücher und ihre Konsequenzen für die Textgeschichte der hebräischen Bibel, illustriert am Beispiel von 2 Kön 23:1–3," in *Congress Volume Leiden 2004* (ed. A. Lemaire; VTSup 109; Leiden: Brill, 2006), 65–79; Schenker, *Älteste Textgeschichte*, 52–74.

[54] Hugo, *Les deux visages d'Elie*; P. Hugo, "Text and Literary History: The Case of 1 Kings 19 (MT and LXX)," in *Soundings in Kings: Perspectives and Methods in Contemporary Scholarship* (eds. M. Leuchter and K.-P. Adam; Minneapolis: Fortress, 2010), 15–34 and 156–65; Richelle, *Le testament d'Elisée*.

[55] See, e.g., Talshir, *The Alternative Story*; van Keulen, *Two Versions of the Solomon Narrative*.

[56] Schenker, *Septante et texte massorétique*, 142–47; Schenker, *Älteste Textgeschichte*, 185–87.

[57] D.M. Carr, *The Formation of the Hebrew Bible: A New Reconstruction* (Oxford: University Press, 2011), 153–79; P. Hugo, "Der Ursprung der proto-massoretischen Textgestalt der Samuelbücher und ihr Sitz-im-Leben," forthcoming.

(→ 5.3.1.2) discussed in this contribution were created subsequent to the literary history of the books of Samuel and Kings. They were added at a time when these books already were considered Holy Scripture but as yet without fixed text. It seems that the redactors, who were active in that final period of literary intervention in the text, used biblical style for their new elements. This sometimes makes difficult the distinction between the literary formation of Samuel and Kings in the period of literary history proper, occurring before the third century B.C.E., and the later literary-redactional modifications of the third and second centuries, which belong specifically to text history. Of course, the quoting of examples here would be dependent upon a resolution of the question of which text must be considered as being early and which one as having been modified in the last three centuries B.C.E.; this question must be left open here, since there is no consensus among scholars on this point. As for the specific literary, ideological, and theological outlook of MT, Old Greek, and 4QSam[a, b], see the observations made in the related paragraphs (especially → 5.3.2.2; → 5.3.2.3; and → 5.3.3.3).

Barthélemy, D. et al., *The Story of David and Goliath: Textual and Literary Criticism* (OBO 73; Fribourg: University Press, 1986).

Hugo, P., *Les deux visages d'Elie: Texte massorétique et Septante dans l'histoire la plus ancienne du texte de 1 Rois 17–18* (OBO 217; Fribourg: Academic Press, 2006).

Hugo, P. and A. Schenker (eds.), *Archaeology of the Books of Samuel: The Entangling of the Textual and Literary History* (VTSup 132; Leiden: Brill, 2010).

Hutzli, J., *Die Erzählung von Hanna und Samuel: Textkritische und literarische Analyse von 1. Samuel 1–2 unter der Berücksichtigung des Kontextes* (ATANT 89; Zürich: Theologischer Verlag Zürich, 2007).

van Keulen, P.S.F., *Two Versions of the Solomon Narrative: An Inquiry into the Relationship between MT 1 Kgs. 2–11 and LXX 3 Reg. 2–11* (VTSup 104; Leiden: Brill, 2005).

Pisano, S., *Additions and Omissions in the Books of Samuel: The Significant Pluses and Minuses in the Masoretic, LXX and Qumran Texts* (OBO 57; Fribourg: University Press, 1984).

Rezetko, R., *Source and Revision in the Narratives of David's Transfer of the Ark: Text, Language, and Story in 2 Samuel 6 and 1 Chronicles 13, 15–16* (Library of Hebrew Bible/Old Testament Series 470; New York: T & T Clark, 2007).

Richelle, M., *Le testament d'Elisée: Texte massorétique et Septante en 2 Rois 13,10–14,16* (CahRB 76; Pendé: Gabalda, 2010).

Schenker, A., *Septante et texte massorétique dans l'histoire la plus ancienne du texte de 1 Rois 2–14* (CahRB 48; Paris: Gabalda, 2000).

Schenker, A., *Älteste Textgeschichte der Königsbücher. Die hebräische Vorlage der ursprünglichen Septuaginta als älteste Textform der Königsbücher* (OBO 199; Fribourg: Academic Press, 2004).

Schenker, A., *Anfänge der Textgeschichte des Alten Testaments: Studien zu Entstehung und Verhältnis der frühesten Textformen* (BWANT 194; Stuttgart: Kohlhammer, 2011).

Schenker, A., *Une bible archétype? Les parallèles de Samuel-Rois et des chroniques* (L'écriture de la Bible 3; Paris: Cerf, 2013).

Shenkel, J.D., *Chronology and Recensional Development in the Greek Text of Kings* (HSM 1; Cambridge: Harvard University Press, 1968).

Talshir, Z., *The Alternative Story: 3 Kingdoms 12:24a–z* (Jerusalem Biblical Studies 6; Jerusalem: Simor, 1993).

Trebolle Barrera, J., *Salomón y Jeroboán: Historia de la recensión y redacción de 1 Reyes 2–12, 14* (Bibliotheca Salamanticensis, Dissertationes 3; Salamanca: Universidad Pontificia, Inst. Español bibl. y arqueologico, 1980).

Trebolle Barrera, J., *Jehú y Joás: Texto y composición literaria de 2 Reyes 9–11* (Institución San Jerónimo 17; Valencia: Edilva, 1984).

Philippe Hugo
Adrian Schenker

5.3.3 Other Texts

The discovery of 4QSam[a,b,c] (4Q51–53) revolutionized the textual history of the Bible and continues to fascinate scholars because many of their features remain enigmatic.[1] This is especially the case for 4QSam[a], which attests to the largest portions of the text.[2] On the one hand, the strong similarities

---
[1] For the descriptions of these manuscripts, see → 5.3.1; *DJD XVII; and Lange, *Handbuch, 215–24.

[2] 4QSam[a] attests to between eight and fifteen percent of the books of Samuel: Herbert ("4QSam[a] and its Relationship to the LXX," 38) assesses eight percent; Ulrich (*Qumran Text*

of these texts to Old Greek (→ 5.4) prove that the Greek version is a careful translation of its Hebrew *Vorlage*, which attests a different text type from proto-MT (→ 5.3.2). This fact is borne out by their agreements with the Old Latin (VL; → 3–5.2.1.2) and the texts of Chronicles (→ 20) and Josephus (→ 21.3). On the other hand, the Qumran fragments cannot be related solely to the putative Hebrew source of Old Greek, because they also share MT readings against Old Greek. Furthermore, they witness a significant number of unique readings. In other words, the books of Samuel are attested in several related non-Masoretic witnesses: the lost Hebrew source of Old Greek and the Qumran fragments.

The same conclusion can be drawn concerning the Hebrew source of OG-Kings (→ 5.5), notwithstanding the few surviving Hebrew fragments of these books at Qumran. Essentially, 6QpapKgs (6Q4) attests a non-Masoretic text tradition partially in agreement with Old Greek,[3] and 4QKgs (4Q54) is assessed as "semi-Masoretic."[4]

5.3.3.1 History of Research

Research on non-Masoretic texts of Samuel–Kings found at Qumran cannot be isolated from the assumption that LXX (→ 5.4; → 5.5) witnesses a Hebrew text distinct from proto-MT (→ 5.3.2).[5] Indeed, nineteenth-century scholars such as Thenius, Wellhausen, and Driver emphasized the possibility that the Hebrew source of LXX-Kgdms witnessed to a Hebrew *Vorlage* that may have preserved an earlier text form than proto-MT.[6] But this hypothesis was discarded by most scholars during the twentieth century. The discovery of the Samuel fragments, their identification, and first provisional edition in 1953 and 1955 by the late Cross provided decisive evidence.[7] Indeed, the large agreements between 4QSam[a–b] (→ 5.3.1.2; → 5.3.1.3) and Old Greek against MT led to the recognition that the Greek version was very likely a careful translation of a Hebrew *Vorlage*, and that both texts originate in the same general tradition.[8] This conclusion remains valid on the whole, as Cross writes in the *DJD* edition: "The study of the full manuscript has reinforced our early conclusion that 4QSam[a] stands in the same general tradition as the Hebrew text upon which the Old Greek translations was based."[9] If this assessment is largely accepted in recent research,[10] it has been nuanced in different ways.

A first debate concerns the strong affinities between 4QSam[a] and the Greek "Lucianic" or Antiochian text (LXX[L]; → 3–5.1.6), and their common agreements with Chronicles (→ 20) and the text used by Josephus (→ 21.3), which Cross noted at an

---

of Samuel, 258) assesses "less than 10 %"; and Cross, Parry, and Saley (*DJD XVII: 3) assess fifteen percent.

[3] See → 5.3.1; M. Baillet, "4. Livres des Rois," *DJD III.1 (1962): 107–12; and Lange, *Handbuch, 224–27. 5QKgs (5Q2) is too small and poorly preserved to allow a characterization: J.T. Milik, "2. 1 Rois," *DJD III.1 (1962): 171–72. 1QSam (1Q7) is assessed as "semi masoretic."

[4] J. Trebolle Barrera, "54. 4QKgs," *DJD XIV (1995): 183; Trebolle, "Qumran Fragments of the Books of Kings," 20–24.

[5] See the good synthesis of Lange, *Handbuch, 231–43. For history of research concerning LXX-Kgdms, see → 5.4 and P. Hugo, "Le grec ancien des livres des Règnes: Une histoire et un bilan de la recherche," in *Sôfer Mahîr: Essays in Honour of Adrian Schenker Offered by Editors of Biblia Hebraica Quinta* (eds. Y.A.P. Goldman, A. van der Kooij, and R.D. Weiss; VTSup 110; Leiden: Brill, 2006), 113–41; P. Hugo, "1–2 Reigns (1–2 Samuel)," in *The T & T Clark Handbook to the Septuagint* (ed. J.K. Aitken; London: T & T Clark, 2015), 127–46.

[6] O. Thenius, *Die Bücher Samuels* (KHAT; Leipzig: Hirzel, 1842 [2nd ed. 1864]); O. Thenius, *Die Bücher der Könige* (KHAT; Leipzig: Hirzel, 1849 [2nd ed. 1873]); J. Wellhausen, *Der Text der Bücher Samuelis* (Göttingen: Vandenhoeck & Ruprecht, 1871); J. Wellhausen, "Das Buch der Könige," in F. Bleek, *Einleitung in das Alte Testament* (rev. J. Wellhausen; 4th ed.; Berlin: Reimer, 1878), 231–67; S.R. Driver, *Notes on the Hebrew Text of the Books of Samuel* (Oxford: Clarendon Press, 1890 [2nd ed. 1913]).

[7] Cross, "New Qumran Fragment"; Cross, "Oldest Manuscripts."

[8] 4QSam[b], which is the earliest fragment of Samuel (250–225 B.C.E.), is even closer to the *Vorlage* of LXX than 4QSam[a] (50–25 B.C.E.). See Cross, Parry, and Saley, "4QSam[a]," 4–5, 221–25.

[9] Cross, Parry, and Saley, "4QSam[a]," 25. Concerning 4QSam[b], see the evaluation on pp. 223–24: "Its affinity with the tradition to which the *Vorlage* of the Old Greek belongs is most important, and cannot be neglected in developing new methods and evaluations in future critical studies of the text of Samuel." See also Cross and Saley, "A Statistical Analysis," 54.

[10] Cf. Lange, *Handbuch, 241–43; Polak, "Samuel," 821; Polak, "Statistics and Textual Filiation," 244, 254; Tov, *TCHB, 109; Tov, "Qumran Hebrew Texts," 7–9; Ulrich, *Qumran Text of Samuel*, 92–93, 146–49, 257; Ulrich, "Qualitative Assessment," 161.

early date.[11] These observations brought strong arguments in favor of the assumption of a "proto-Lucianic" text (→ 5.4). The hypothesis that LXX^L was based on a Greek tradition earlier than the fourth century C.E. appeared with the observation of its agreements with VL (→ 3–5.2.1.2), Chronicles, and Josephus. Initiated in the nineteenth century by Vercellone, Driver, and Mez,[12] and continued in LXX research by Rahlfs and Brock,[13] the theory of the "proto-Lucian" version found new momentum with the discoveries of the Dead Sea Scrolls. The finding of a Greek Dodecapropheton in Naḥal Ḥever (8ḤevXII gr; → 1.3.1.2) enabled Barthélemy (in 1953) to discover an early Hebraizing recension of LXX from the first century B.C.E.[14] that he named the *kaige* recension.[15] He identified it in some sections of the books of Kingdoms in LXX^B (2 Sam 10:1–1 Kgs 2:11 and 1 Kings 22–2 Kings[16]). For these *kaige* sections, Barthélemy showed that LXX^L was the best witness of Old Greek.[17] However, the affinities between (proto-)LXX^L and 4QSam^a led to divergent conclusions concerning the textual history of Samuel. Cross and Ulrich hypothesized that proto-LXX^L was a Hebraizing recension of Old Greek having 4QSam^a as a model.[18] This assumption was based on Cross' theory of "local texts" (→ 1.1.1.2.4; → 1.2.1.3.4), which presumes that the biblical text developed in three geographically distinct types, namely the Babylonian (proto-MT), Egyptian (*Vorlage* of Old Greek), and Palestinian (4QSam^a and the source of Chronicles [and SP → 1.2.3]).[19] On the contrary, Barthélemy and Tov – who have criticized the theory of local texts – argued that these agreements indicate that (proto-)LXX^L is the closest witness of Old Greek.[20] This opinion is now widely accepted and some recent studies tend to nuance the scale of the agreements between LXX^L and 4QSam$^{a(-b)}$, thus mitigating the theory of a Hebraizing proto-Lucianic recension.[21] For their part, LXX researchers are also dealing with the complex-

---

[11] Cross, *"History," 188–93; Cross, *ALQ^3, 138–41.

[12] C. Vercellone, *Variae lectiones vulgatae latinae Bibliorum editionis*, Vol. 2 (Rome: Spithöver, 1864); Driver, *Hebrew Text of the Books of Samuel* (2nd ed., 1913), lxxvi–lxxx; A. Mez, *Die Bibel des Josephus untersucht für Buch V–VII der Archäologie* (Basel: Jaeger & Kober, 1895), esp. 79–84.

[13] A. Rahlfs, *Studien zu den Königsbüchern* (Göttingen: Vandenhoeck & Ruprecht, 1904); A. Rahlfs, *Lucians Rezension der Königsbücher* (Göttingen: Vandenhoeck & Ruprecht, 1911), both reprinted in A. Rahlfs, *Septuaginta-Studien I–III* (Göttingen: Vandenhoeck & Ruprecht, 1965); S. Brock, *The Recensions of the Septuagint Version of 1 Samuel* (Quaderni di Henoch 9; Turino: Zamorani, 1996), esp. 177–299.

[14] The date is based on the paleographic analysis of 8ḤevXII gr by P.J. Parsons, "The Scripts and Their Date," *DJD* VIII: 19–26.

[15] D. Barthélemy, "Redécouverte d'un chaînon manquant de l'histoire de la Septante," *RB* (1953): 18–29 (= Cross–Talmon, *QHBT*, 127–39); Barthélemy, *Devanciers*.

[16] These sections were first pinpointed by H.St.J. Thackeray, who interpreted them as a second layer of translation: "The Greek Translation of the Four Books of Kings," *JTS* 8 (1907): 262–78; *The Septuagint and Jewish Worship: A Study in Origins* (2nd ed.; London: Oxford University Press, 1923). Later the extent of these sections were corrected by J.D. Shenkel, *Chronology and Recensional Development in the Greek Text of Kings* (HSM 1; Cambridge: Harvard University Press, 1968), esp. 117–20, who recognized some *kaige* features already in 2 Samuel 10, whereas Barthélemy (following Thackeray) thought the *kaige* section began in 2 Sam 11:2. However, one has to recognize that the boundaries of the *kaige* section are less precise than assumed: E.D. Herbert, "The Kaige Recension of Samuel: Light from 4QSam^a," in *The Bible as Book*, 197–208, esp. 204–05, 07.

[17] Barthélemy, *Devanciers*, 126–27.

[18] Cross, *"History," 191–93; Cross, *"Evolution," 306–20 (314–15); Ulrich, *Qumran Text of Samuel*, 257–59; E. Ulrich, "The Old Latin Translation of the LXX and the Hebrew Scrolls from Qumran," in Ulrich, *DSS, 233–74 (= Tov [ed.], *Hebrew and Greek Texts of Samuel*, 121–65). This position was followed by Shenkel, *Chronology*, 8–11; P.K. McCarter, *1 Samuel: A New Translation with Introduction and Commentary* (AB 8; New York: Doubleday, 1980), 7, 9.

[19] Cross, *"History"; Cross, *"Evolution"; Cross, *ALQ^3, 121–42.

[20] Barthélemy, *Devanciers*, 113, 127; D. Barthélemy, "A Reexamination of the Textual Problems in 2 Sam 11:2–1 Kings 2:11 in the Light of Certain Criticisms of *Les Devanciers d'Aquila*," in *1972 Proceedings* (ed. R.E. Kraft; SBLSCS 2; Atlanta: SBL, 1972), 16–89 (29, 61): Barthélemy has a more nuanced position concerning LXX^L in this article, accepting the fact that it contains also recensional elements, but not as a result of a Antiochian or "Lucianic" recension toward a Hebrew model; E. Tov, "Lucian and Proto-Lucian: Toward a New Solution of the Problem," in *Greek-Hebrew Bible*, 485; Tov, "Textual Affiliation," 282. Other scholars opposed Cross' theory: Herbert, "4QSam^a and its Relationship to the LXX," 46, 49.

[21] R.S. Saley, "Greek Lucianic Doublets and 4QSam^a," *BIOSCS* 40 (2007): 63–73; R.S. Saley, "Proto-Lucian and 4QSam^a," *BIOSCS* 41 (2008): 34–45; T. Kauhanen, *The Proto-Lucianic Problem in 1 Samuel* (De Septuaginta Investigationes 3; Göttingen: Vandenhoeck & Ruprecht, 2012), 165–88.

ity of LXX^L, some scholars emphasizing its features of a secondary inner Greek correction,[22] others assessing it as identical to Old Greek,[23] or trying pragmatically to distinguish the old layer (OG) from the revised one.[24]

Scholars have dealt with a further field concerning the characteristics of the Qumran Samuel texts that distinguish them from both LXX and MT, as well as from other textual witnesses. One speaks of "unique" or "singular readings." The counting of these readings varies according to the authors and their criteria: Parry counts 123 "non-aligned variant readings in 4QSam^a, representing about 29 percent of all texual variants,"[25] whereas Cross and Saley count seventy-nine certain "singular readings" that diverge not only from LXX and MT, but from "all of the textual versions."[26] But beyond the statistics, the debate concentrates on the qualitative assessment of these readings. If one finds all kinds of corruptions and harmonisations, grammatical differences, and other common alterations of scribal transmission, some of the readings are assessed as deliberate modifications, or "intentional changes of the text on the part of scribes of either MT or 4QSam^a."[27] Rofé argues that 4QSam^a attests a significant number of nomistic corrections and assesses the scroll as a midrash or reworked version of Samuel.[28] Other scholars also emphasize this rewriting process in 4QSam^a,[29] some of these literary corrections having been made under the influence of Chronicles.[30] On the contrary, Cross and Saley maintain that the singular readings of 4QSam^a do not display the characteristics of rewritten Scripture, and the few scribal changes that occur are more "unconscious mistakes typical of scribes."[31] Rather than having being influenced by Chronicles, 4QSam^a stands "in the same stream of textual tradition" as the *Vorlage* of LXX-Sam, the source of Chronicles and the text used by Josephus.[32] In short, the question of unique readings is far from reaching a consensual solution.

---

[22] Brock, *Recensions*, 177–299; N. Fernández Marcos, "Literary and Editorial Features in the Antiochian Text in Kings," in *VI Congress of the IOSCS: Jerusalem 1986* (ed. C.E. Cox; SBLSCS 23; Atlanta: Scholars Press, 1987), 287–304; N. Fernández Marcos, "The Septuagint and the History of the Biblical Text," in N. Fernández Marcos, *Scribes and Translators: Septuagint and Old Latin in the Books of Kings* (VTSup 54; Leiden: Brill, 1994), 3–37, esp. 27–37; B.A. Taylor, *The Lucianic Manuscripts of 1 Reigns*, Vol. 2: *Analysis* (HSM 51; Atlanta: Scholars Press, 1993).

[23] S. Kreuzer, "Towards the Old Greek: New Criteria for the Analysis of the Recensions of the Septuagint (Especially the Antiochene/Lucianic Text and Kaige Recension)," in *XIII Congress of the IOSCS, Ljubljana, 2007* (ed. M.K.H. Peters; SBLSCS 55; Atlanta: SBL, 2008), 239–53; S. Kreuzer, "Translation and Recensions: Old Greek, *Kaige*, and Antiochene Text in Samuel and Reigns," *BIOSCS* 42 (2009): 34–51; S. Kreuzer, "'Lukian redivivus' or Barthélemy and Beyond?," in *XIV Congress of the IOSCS, Helsinki, 2010* (ed. M.K.H. Peters; SBLSCS 59; Atlanta: SBL, 2013), 243–61.

[24] P. Hugo, "Die Antiochenische Mischung: *L* zwischen Altem und Neuem in 2 Samuel," in *Der Antiochenische Text der Septuaginta in seiner Bezeugung und seiner Bedeutung* (eds. S. Kreuzer and M. Sigismund; De Septuaginta Investigationes 4; Göttingen: Vandenhoeck & Ruprecht, 2013), 109–32.

[25] Parry, "Textual Character," 182. See also D.W. Parry, "Unique Readings in 4QSam^a," in *The Bible as Book*, 209–19.

[26] Cross and Saley, "Singular Readings," 2.

[27] Parry, "Textual Character," 181. Parry does not decide on chronology between unique readings of 4QSam^a and other witnesses.

[28] Rofé, "4QMidrash Samuel?"; A. Rofé, "The Acts of Nahash according to 4QSam^a," *IEJ* 32 (1982): 129–33; A. Rofé, "The Nomistic Correction in Biblical Manuscripts and Its Occurrence in 4QSam^a," *RevQ* 14 (1989): 247–54; A. Rofé, "4QSam^a in the Light of Historico-Literary Criticism: The Case of 2 Sam 24 and 1 Chr 21," in *Biblische und Judaistische Studien: Festschrift für Paolo Sacchi* (ed. A. Vivian; Judentum und Umwelt 29; Frankfurt a.M.: Peter Lang, 1990), 109–19; A. Rofé, "Midrashic Traits in 4Q51 (so-called 4QSam^a)," in *Archaeology of the Books of Samuel: The Entangling of the Textual and Literary History* (eds. P. Hugo and A. Schenker; VTSup 132; Leiden: Brill, 2010), 75–88.

[29] Aejmelaeus, "Lost in Reconstruction," 89–106; Aejmelaeus, "Hannah's Psalm"; K. Bodner, "The Royal Conscience according to 4QSam^a," *DSD* 11 (2004): 158–66; Z. Kallai, "Samuel in Qumran: Expansion of a Historiographical Pattern (4QSam^a)," *RB* 103 (1996): 581–91; S. Venturini, "Alcune Caratteristiche Editoriali di 4QSam^a" (PhD diss.; Pontificio Istituto Biblico Roma, 2001); S. Venturini, "Le armonizzazioni nel texto di 4QSam^a," *RivB* 56 (2008): 37–60.

[30] Rofé, "Midrashic Traits"; Aejmelaeus, "Lost in Reconstruction," 103; Venturini, "Alcune Caratteristiche Editoriali," 12–37: beyond Chronicles, Venturini argues that the books of Leviticus and Numbers (and perhaps Jeremiah) influenced the literary rewriting in 4QSam^a.

[31] Cross and Saley, "Singular Readings," 7; see the synthesis pp. 12–16, and scribal changes pp. 5–7.

[32] Cross and Saley, "Singular Readings," 15, see the list of

These observations lead to another scholarly debate, viz., the nature and the place of non-Masoretic traditions in the flow of the textual history of Samuel–Kings. The preceding article (→ 5.3.2) has already sketched the main hypotheses regarding textual history.[33] The first disputed question is to determine the nature of the textual differences. For some scholars, the textual facts reflect no deliberate literary activities but rather a multiplicity of texts that accidentally influenced each other in the course of scribal transmission,[34] whereas for others the differences between 4QSam[a,b,c], the *Vorlage* of LXX, and proto-MT show evidence not only of textual but also of literary phenomena.[35] The next question is to establish a relative chronology among the textual forms. No scholarly consensus has been reached in this controversial matter either: Some exegetes tend to consider the non-Masoretic texts generally as developments and modifications of proto-MT,[36] while a growing current of research hypothesizes that the text type attested by the *Vorlage* of LXX, the Qumran witnesses, the source of Chronicles, and Josephus may be an earlier literary form of Samuel–Kings.[37]

5.3.3.2 Editions

Following the first provisional edition of two columns of 4QSam[a] in 1953 by Cross,[38] the scholarly community had to wait half a century for the publication of the *editio princeps* in *DJD XVII in 2005. This volume is the result of five decades of study of the scrolls, principally by the editors of 4QSam[a,b] (Cross[39] and recently Parry[40] and Saley) and of 4QSam[c] (Ulrich).[41] In the meantime, the material was partially accessible in the *BHS fascicle on Samuel by P.A.H. de Boer, in the remarkable text-critical notes of McCarter,[42] and in Ulrich's dissertation.[43] Since all the photographs became officially accessible in 1992,[44] the paleographical work on the Samuel scrolls has expanded. We must men-

---

agreements on pp. 7–9; Ulrich, *Qumran Text of Samuel*, 207; E. Ulrich, "Josephus's Biblical Text of the Books of Samuel," in Ulrich, *DSS, 184–201; Ulrich, "Qualitative assessment," 160–61.

[33] See especially the history of research → 5.3.2.1 and text-critical character → 5.3.2.3 with bibliography (only specific or additional bibliography will be referenced here).

[34] Ulrich, "Qualitative Assessment," 159–61; Cook, "1 Samuel," 454; J.H. Kim, *Die hebräischen und griechischen Textformen der Samuel- und Königebücher: Studien zur Textgeschichte ausgehend von 2 Sam 15,1–19,9* (BZAW 394; Berlin: De Gruyter, 2009); A. Ravasco, "La storia del testo di Samuele alla luce della documentazione di Qumran" (PhD diss., Università degli studi di Pisa, 2007).

[35] Trebolle, "Qumran Fragments of the Books of Kings"; J. Trebolle Barrera, "Textual and Literary Criticism on Passages Attested by 4QSam[a,b] (1 Sam 6:4–5 and 1 Sam 23:11–12)," in *The Hebrew Bible in Light of the Dead Sea Scrolls* (eds. N. Dávid et al.; FRLANT 239; Göttingen: Vandenhoeck & Ruprecht, 2012), 70–83; P. Hugo, "Text History of the Books of Samuel: An Assessment of the Recent Research," in *Archaeology of the Books of Samuel: The Entangling of the Textual and Literary History* (eds. P. Hugo and A. Schenker; VTSup 132; Leiden: Brill, 2010), 1–19, esp. 7–13.

[36] Pisano, *Additions and Omissions*; D. Barthélemy, "La qualité du texte massorétique de Samuel," in *The Hebrew and Greek Texts of Samuel* (ed. E. Tov; Jerusalem: Academon, 1980), 1–44; Barthélemy, *Critique textuelle 1982; see above n. 29.

[37] Polak, "Samuel", 821–22; see above n. 33.

[38] Cross, "New Qumran Fragment."

[39] F.M. Cross, "The Ammonite Oppression of the Tribes of Gad and Reuben: Missing Verses from 1 Sam 11 Found in 4QSamuel[a]," in *Hebrew and Greek Texts of Samuel* (ed. E. Tov, Jerusalem: Academon, 1980), 105–19; F.M. Cross, "A New Reconstruction of 4QSamuel[a] 24:16–22," in *Studies in the Hebrew Bible, Qumran, and the Septuagint Presented to Eugene Ulrich* (eds. P.W. Flint, E. Tov, and J.C. VanderKam; VTSup 101; Leiden: Brill, 2006), 77–83; for 4QSam[b], cf. Cross, "Oldest Manuscripts."

[40] F.M. Cross and D.W. Parry, "A Preliminary Edition of a Fragment of 4QSam[b] (4Q52)," *BASOR* 306 (1997): 63–74; D.W. Parry, "More Fragments of 4QSam[a] (4Q51): A Preliminary Edition of 1 Samuel 14:24–24:22," in *The Dead Sea Scrolls: Fifty Years after Their Discovery* (eds. L.H. Schiffman, E. Tov, and J.C. VanderKam; Jerusalem: Israel Exploration Society, 2000), 19–29.

[41] E. Ulrich, "4QSam[c]: A Fragmentary Manuscript of 2 Samuel 14–15 from the Scribe of the *Serek Hay-yaḥad* (1QS)," *BASOR* 235 (1979): 1–25.

[42] P.K. McCarter, *I–II Samuel: A New Translation with Introduction and Commentary* (AB 8–9; New York: Doubleday, 1980–1984).

[43] Ulrich, *Qumran Text of Samuel.*

[44] E. Tov (ed.), *The Dead Sea Scrolls on Microfiche: A Comprehensive Facsimile Edition of the Texts from the Judean Desert* (Leiden: Brill, IDC, 1992); with a *Companion Volume* (ed. E. Tov and S.J. Pfann; Leiden: Brill, 1993; 2nd ed. 1995), and an *Inventory List of Photographs* (by S.A. Reed; ed. M.J. Lundberg; Leiden: Brill, 1993).

tion the work of Fincke[45] and the outstanding edition of 4QSam[a] for 2 Samuel by the late Herbert.[46] It is not the place here to assess Herbert's "new method" for reconstructing Qumranic material,[47] but the nuanced and well-founded results of his editing are worthy of careful attention, notably because the edition provides a number of alternative readings and reconstructions to *DJD XVII.

At the present time, *DJD XVII is indisputably the best paleographical and text-critical tool for research on the 4QSam fragments. Indeed, it furnishes the entire reconstructed material with a large number of text-critical observations and decisions (variants and reconstructed variants) that display great mastery of the history of the Hebrew and Greek texts and make it an invaluable source of information. Nevertheless, recent careful analyses allow for the conclusion that the last word on the paleographical reconstruction of these scrolls – especially of 4QSam[a–b] – has not yet been said.[48] Criticism[49] concerns firstly the general perspective of the edition, which can be described as maximalist, in that the reconstructions form a large part of the text. Such a reconstruction, based in fact on Cross' theory of the textual history, gives the reader – especially scholars not trained in epigraphy – the wrong impression that the 4QSamuel fragments attest to a much more complete and characterized text than they actually do. This type of reconstruction does not take sufficiently into account the problem of unpredictable variants. Furthermore, the choice guiding the reconstruction of the text (based on LXX [→ 5.4], LXX[L] [→ 3–5.1.6], or MT [→ 5.3.2]) is based mostly on insufficiently demonstrated assumptions. Moreover, this problem affects the probability of the identification of smaller fragments, which could be positioned elsewhere. The edition does not mention the numerous alternative placements of small fragments. Finally, in order to check or correct attested or partially reconstructed readings, the edition should give more material and paleographical information (e.g., drylines, margins, state of the leather). New assessments of the material led some scholars to identify a certain number of alternative readings. In short, in many aspects, *DJD XVII goes beyond the field of the edition of preserved fragments and enters the area of text-critical hypothesis. The Leon Levy Dead Sea Scrolls Digital Library,[50] being prepared in 2015, will be an essential tool for a careful evaluation of this edition, because it provides remarkable colour and infrared images of the scrolls.

In this respect, the edition of the fragment 4QKgs (4Q54) by Trebolle Barrera is methodologically more precise and careful, because it clearly distinguishes between the establishment of the attested text and the reconstruction of the column.[51] The edition of 6QpapKgs (6Q4) by Baillet[52] also tends to reconstruct large portions of text, whereas that of the small fragment 5QKgs (5Q2) by Milik[53] concentrates on the attested readings. Barthélemy does not reconstruct more than a few letters or words in his edition of 1QSam (1Q7).[54] Concerning

---

[45] A. Fincke, *The Samuel Scroll From Qumran: 4QSam[a] Restored and Compared to the Septuagint and 4QSam[c]* (STDJ 43; Leiden: Brill, 2001): if this study provides many interesting reconstructions, which deserve consideration, it contains such important methodological deficiencies, that it is hardly useful as a scholarly tool. See the critical evaluation by E.D. Hebert, "Review *The Samuel Scroll from Qumran*, by Andrew Fincke," *DSD* 9 (2002): 404–08.

[46] Herbert, *Reconstructing*.

[47] See E. Tov, "Review *Reconstructing Biblical Dead Sea Scrolls* by Edward D. Herbert," *DSD* 6 (1999): 215–20; J.C. VanderKam, "Review *Reconstructing Biblical Dead Sea Scrolls* by Edward D. Herbert," *JBL* 119 (2000): 558–60.

[48] Hugo, Kottsieper, and Steudel, "Reflexions on Epigraphy"; P. Hugo, I. Kottsieper, and A. Steudel, "Notes paléographiques sur 4QSam[a] (4Q51)," *RevQ* 23 (2007): 93–108; É. Puech, "4QSamuel[a] (4Q51): Notes épigraphiques et nouvelles identifications," in *Florilegium Lovaniense: Studies in Septuagint and Textual Criticism in Honour of Florentino García Martínez* (eds. H. Ausloos, B. Lemmelijn, and M. Vervenne; BETL 224; Leuven: Peeters, 2008), 373–86; A. Ravasco, "L'arca dell' Alleanza a Gat (1 Sam 5,8) e il racconto di Nahash (1 Sam 11,1): alcune riflessioni sulla ricostruzione del frammento 4QSam[a]," *RivB* 61 (2013): 29–36.

[49] See Hugo, Kottsieper, and Steudel, "Reflexions on Epigraphy," 129–31.

[50] http://www.deadseascrolls.org.il.

[51] J. Trebolle Barrera, "54. 4QKgs," *DJD XIV: 171–83.

[52] M. Baillet, "4. Livres des Rois," *DJD III.1: 107–12.

[53] J.T. Milik, "2. 1 Rois," *DJD III.1: 171–72.

[54] D. Barthélemy, "7. Livres de Samuel," *DJD I: 64–65.

Kings, new identifications of fragments still seem to be possible.[55]

Finally, the recent edition of *Biblical Qumran Scrolls* by Ulrich[56] is a very useful tool for students and scholars, because it most of the biblical texts attested at Qumran in the canonical order. If it mainly reproduces DJD for Samuel and Kings, the changes, corrections, or improvements of the edition are unfortunately not indicated. The English translation of the *Dead Sea Scrolls Bible*[57] also provides useful access to the Qumran fragments, in particular because the footnotes point out the main differences with MT and LXX.

5.3.3.3 Nature and Text-Critical Character

The history of research (→ 5.3.3.1) shows that there is no consensus concerning the text-critical characterization of the Hebrew non-Masoretic witnesses of Samuel. In this respect, *4QSam*ᵃ (→ 5.3.1.2) is probably the most difficult document to assess.[58] We deliberately give up the idea of indicating here any statistical data, firstly because of the aforementioned uncertainty regarding some of the paleographical reconstructions, which renders the calculations hypothetical, secondly because of the diverse criteria for evaluating variants.[59] Nevertheless, the textual facts – firstly the agreements with Old Greek[60] and secondly the relatively high number of singular readings[61] – permit characterizing 4QSamᵃ as a non-aligned witness resulting in textual and literary reshaping of its source, which is basically relative to the text type of the Hebrew *Vorlage* of LXX (→ 5.4).[62] It therefore contains early and secondary material side by side, giving the impression of a mixed or heterogeneous text type.[63] The main literary characteristics of 4QSamᵃ may be found in its own non-aligned edition of the story of Hannah (1 Samuel 1–2),[64] in the "plus" – shared by Josephus (*Ant.* vi, 69–71; → 21.3) – concerning Nahash (1 Samuel 11:1),[65] which is probably a secondary expansion, and in numerous small readings, "pluses," and "minuses" throughout the book,[66] sometimes original but mostly expanded (e.g., 2 Sam 5:4–5;[67] 2 Sam 6:2;[68] 2 Samuel 24;[69] see the discussion in the literature).

*4QSam*ᵇ (→ 5.3.1.3) has to be situated within the same textual tradition as 4QSamᵃ, yet even closer to LXX (→ 5.4).[70] It may be an earlier and shorter

---

[55] See É. Puech, "Nouvelles identifications de Manuscrits Bibliques dans la grotte 4: 4QRoisᵃ (4Q54a) et 4QRoisᵇ-4Q54ᵇ(?) ou 4QIsˢ-4Q69c(?)," *RevQ* 25 (2012): 467–72.

[56] Ulrich, *BQS*, 259–329.

[57] *DSSB*, 215–66.

[58] Tov, "Qumran Hebrew Texts," 7–9. See Cross, Parry, and Saley, "4QSamᵃ," 25–27.

[59] See synthesis of statistical data in Lange, *Handbuch*, 218; Cross and Saley, "A Statistical Analysis"; Polak, "Statistics and Textual Filiation."

[60] See C. Martone, "Qumran Readings in Agreement with the Septuagint Against the Masoretic Text, Part Three: 1 Samuel," *RevQ* 25 (2012): 557–73; Herbert, *Reconstructing*, 221–46.

[61] For characterization of the singular readings, see Cross and Saley, "Singular Readings."

[62] See above n. 10; Tov, "Textual Affiliation"; Lange, *Handbuch*, 217–20; Hutzli, *Erzählung von Hanna*, 35.

[63] Aejmelaeus, "Hannah's Psalm," 36–37, hypothesizes that 4QSamᵃ attests a "technique of complementing the text. The connecting motive behind variants may have been the ambition of the scribe to produce a perfect manuscript with the most complete collection of material, not lacking anything" (p. 37).

[64] E. Tov, "Different Editions of the Song of Hannah and of Its Narrative Framework," in *Greek-Hebrew Bible*, 433–55; Hutzli, *Erzählung von Hanna*; Aejmelaeus, "Hannah's Psalm"; D.W. Parry, "Hannah in the Presence of the Lord," in *Archaeology of the Books of Samuel: The Entangling of the Textual and Literary History* (eds. P. Hugo and A. Schenker; VTSup 132; Leiden: Brill, 2010), 53–73.

[65] Barthélemy, *Critique textuelle 1982*, 166–72; Cross, "Ammonite Oppression"; Kallai, "Samuel in Qumran," 582–84; Lange, *Handbuch*, 219–20; Pisano, *Additions and Omissions*, 91–98; Rofé, "The Acts of Nahash"; Rofé, "4QMidrash Samuel?," 65–67; S. Venturini, "1 Sam 10,27–11,1: Testo masoretico e 4QSamᵃ: Le posizioni di alcuni autori e un tentativo di soluzione," *RivB* 44 (1996): 397–425.

[66] See Parry, "Textual Character" and above in nn. 29 and 30.

[67] P. Hugo, "'Dreißig Jahre war David alt, als er König wurde ...' (2 Sam 5,4): Literarische und textkritische Studie der Regierungsnotizen in den Samuelbüchern," in Making the Biblical Text: Textual Studies in the Hebrew and the Greek Bible (ed. I. Himbaza; OBO 275; Göttingen: Vandenhoeck & Ruprecht, 2015), 48–61; Pisano, *Additions and Omissions*, 98–101.

[68] Pisano, *Additions and Omissions*, 101–03.

[69] Aejmelaeus, "Lost in Reconstruction"; Pisano, *Additions and Omissions*, 112–16; Rofé, "4QSamᵃ in the Light of Historico-Literary Criticism"; Rofé, "Midrashic Traits in 4Q51."

[70] Cross, Parry, and Saley, "4QSamᵇ," 221–24.

textual form of that tradition.[71] Due to the number of unique readings (e.g., 2 Sam 20:29, 31, 32, 36; 21:9), it has to be considered independent of both MT and LXX.[72] Cross, however, emphasizes the importance of its superior readings: "the readings of 4QSam[b] agree with Old Greek when it is superior, but agree with Masoretic tradition when it is superior."[73] In this way, 4QSam[b] shares the same characteristics as 4QSam[a] of mixed or "eclectic" text.[74]

4QSam[c] (→ 5.3.1.4) is the smallest of the Samuel texts. It is therefore difficult to characterize precisely its text type. Its high number of unique readings does not allow for relating it to either MT (→ 5.3.2) or LXX (→ 5.4), even if it shows a certain closeness to Old Greek (e.g., 2 Sam 14:30; 15:12).[75]

Concerning *Kings*, 6QpapKgs (6Q4; → 5.3.1.9) is clearly the sole non-Masoretic Hebrew witness. However, it is poorly preserved; it shows certain agreements with Old Greek, attested by LXX[L] (2 Kgs 7:8; → 3–5.1.6).[76]

In conclusion, despite their non-aligned characteristics, the Qumran texts of Samuel–Kings allow for a confirmation of the text-critical value of LXX (→ 5.4). The Greek version was mainly a reliable literal translation, which reflects its non-Masoretic Hebrew *Vorlage*. Yet, this non-Masoretic Hebrew tradition is only indirectly attested in Old Greek and in some remaining features of 4QSam[a,b,c] and 6QpapKgs. In other words, if Qumran attests to a plurality of Hebrew individual non-aligned manuscripts, they may not represent text types as such. In any case, they have strong affinity with Old Greek and therefore probably with its Hebrew *Vorlage*. Thus, they correspond to the same textual family. All in all, the books of Samuel–Kings are attested in one main non-Masoretic text type, viz.,

the lost Hebrew source of LXX, which the Qumran scrolls have developed in a different way. This tradition may even be – at least partially – the basis for 1–2 Chronicles (→ 20) and Josephus (→ 21.3).[77] Furthermore, we already mentioned in the preceding entry (→ 5.3.2.1 and → 5.3.2.2 with bibliography) that some recent studies tend to consider that "the Hebrew original of the Greek version represents a literary edition of the Books [of Samuel and Kings] older than that known Masoretic tradition."[78] Thus, this latter tradition is a literary development of the former.

5.3.3.4 Date and Milieu

The date of the non-Masoretic tradition is not easy to identify. Nevertheless, if one hypothesizes that the source of this tradition is to be found in the Hebrew *Vorlage* of LXX (→ 5.4), this text type is earlier than the Greek translation, i.e., before the third century B.C.E. It had been received, transmitted, and expanded in successive steps, which may be identifiable in the Qumran witnesses. However, there are no other pieces of evidence to date these texts except the paleographical data. The earliest is 4QSam[b], dating to ca. 250 B.C.E. (→ 5.3.1.3),[79] 4QSam[c] ca. 100–75 B.C.E. (→ 5.3.1.4),[80] and 4QSam[a] ca. 50–25 B.C.E. (→ 5.3.1.2).[81] The religious milieu is much more difficult to determine, because the unique readings do not allow for an identification of an ideological circle.

5.3.3.5 Relevance for Exegesis and Literary Analysis

The Qumran fragments of Samuel are a key piece of the history of the Hebrew Bible. In this respect, they show the importance of the inner-biblical rewriting process and reception of Scripture in the last centuries B.C.E.: We mentioned above the different editions of the story of Hannah (1 Samuel 1–2) in 4QSam[a] (→ 5.3.1.2), Old Greek (→ 5.4), and

---

[71] Cross, "Oldest Manuscript," 165; Cross, *ALQ[3]*, 132; Lange, *Handbuch*, 218.
[72] Polak, "Samuel," 822.
[73] Cross, Parry, and Saley, "4QSam[b]," 223.
[74] Cook, "1 Samuel," 454.
[75] Ulrich, "4QSam[c]," 254; Lange, *Handbuch*, 224; Polak, "Samuel," 822; E. Tov, "Determining the Relationship between the Qumran Scrolls and the LXX: Some Methodological Issues," in *Hebrew and Greek Texts*, 58–62.
[76] Trebolle, "Qumran Fragments of the Books of Kings," 25–26; Lange, *Handbuch*, 226.

[77] Cross, *"History,"* 189–90; Polak, "Statistics and Textual Filiation," 248–55.
[78] Trebolle, "Qumran Fragments of the Books of Kings," 20.
[79] Cross, Parry, and Saley, "4QSam[b]," 220.
[80] Ulrich, "4QSam[c]," 249.
[81] Cross, Parry, and Saley, "4QSam[a]," 5.

MT (→ 5.3.2), and the "plus" in 4QSamᵃ concerning Nahash (1 Sam 11:1) and its details in 2 Samuel 24. Other aspects concerning the characterization of David and Solomon are affected by the differences between the non-Masoretic text type and MT (see above → 5.3.2.2, → 5.3.2.3, and, concerning Kings, see → 5.2). A large portion of the non-Masoretic readings affect the literary substance of the books of Samuel and Kings. In other words, these differences attest to a deliberate reshaping of the narrative; they are not textual accidents. These phenomena show the entangling of the redaction (or literary) and textual history of Samuel and Kings. On the other hand, they seem to be late literary developments. Despite the large amount of research on this topic, the final word has yet to be said.

Close-reading methods should be employed for a literary comparison of the Masoretic tradition, the Hebrew source of LXX, and the Qumran fragments, because this would highlight the different narrative strategies within the same plot. Finally, the question faced when preparing modern translations of the Bible relates to the non-Masoretic tradition, because each translator has to decide how far he should translate alternative readings to MT or indicate them in footnotes.[82]

Aejmelaeus, A., "Lost in Reconstruction? On Hebrew and Greek Reconstructions in 2 Sam 24," BIOSCS 40 (2007): 89–106.

Aejmelaeus, A., "Hannah's Psalm in 4QSamᵃ," in *Archaeology of the Books of Samuel: The Entangling of the Textual and Literary History* (eds. P. Hugo and A. Schenker; VTSup 132; Leiden: Brill, 2010), 23–37.

Cook, E.M., "1 Samuel xx 26–xxi 5 according to 4QSamᵇ," VT 54 (1994): 442–54.

Cross, F.M., "A New Qumran Fragment Related to the Original Hebrew Underlying the Septuagint," BASOR 132 (1953): 15–26;

Cross, F.M., "The Oldest Manuscripts from Qumran," JBL 74 (1955): 147–72.

Cross, *"History."

Cross, *"Evolution."

Cross, F.M. and R.J. Saley, "A Statistical Analysis of the Textual Character of 4QSamuelᵃ (4Q51)," DSD 13 (2006): 46–54.

Cross, F.M. and R.J. Saley, "Singular Readings in 4QSamuelᵃ and the Question of Rewritten Scripture," DSD 20 (2013): 1–16.

Cross, F.M., D.W. Parry, and R.J. Saley, "51. 4QSamᵃ," *DJD XVII (2005): 1–216.

Cross, F.M., D.W. Parry, and R.J. Saley, "52. 4QSamᵇ," *DJD XVII (2005): 219–46.

Herbert, E.D., *Reconstructing Biblical Dead Sea Scrolls: A New Method Applied to the Reconstruction of 4QSamᵃ* (STDJ 22; Leiden: Brill, 1997).

Herbert, E.D., "4QSamᵃ and its Relationship to the LXX: An Exploration in Stemmatological Analysis," in *IX Congress of the International Organization for Septuagint and Cognate Studies, Cambridge, 1995* (ed. B.A. Taylor; SBLSCS 45; Atlanta: Scholars Press, 1997), 37–55.

Hugo, P., I. Kottsieper, and A. Steudel, "Reflexions on Epigraphy and Critical Editing: 4QSamᵃ (4Q51) Col. XI," in *Textual Criticism and Dead Sea Scrolls: Studies in Honour of Julio Trebolle Barrera* (eds. A. Piquer Otero and P.A. Torijano Morales; JSJSup 158; Leiden: Brill, 2012), 115–31.

Hugo, P. and A. Schenker (eds.), *Archaeology of the Books of Samuel: The Entangling of the Textual and Literary History* (VTSup 132; Leiden: Brill, 2010).

Hutzli, J., *Die Erzählung von Hanna und Samuel: Textkritische und literarische Analyse von 1. Samuel 1–2 unter Berücksichtigung des Kontextes* (ATANT 89; Zurich: Theologischer Verlag Zürich, 2007).

Lange, *Handbuch*, 213–53.

Parry, D.W., "The Textual Character of the Unique Readings of 4QSamᵃ (4Q51)," in *Flores Florentino: Dead Sea Scrolls and Other Early Jewish Studies in Honour of Florentino García Martínez* (eds. A. Hilhorst, É. Puech, and E. Tigchelaar; JSJSup 122; Leiden: Brill, 2007), 163–82.

Pisano, S., *Additions and Omissions in the Books of Samuel: The Significant Pluses and Minuses in the Masoretic, LXX and Qumran Texts* (OBO 57; Fribourg: University Press, 1984).

Polak, F.H., "Samuel, First and Second Books of," in *EDSS 2:819–23.

Polak, F.H., "Statistics and Textual Filiation: The Case of 4QSamᵃ/LXX (with a Note on the Text of the Pentateuch)," in *Manchester Symposium*, 215–76.

---

[82] See I. Himbaza, "4QSamᵃ (2 Sam 24:16–22): Its Reading, Where it Stands in the History of the Text and its Use in Bible Translations," in *Archaeology of the Books of Samuel: The Entangling of the Textual and Literary History* (eds. P. Hugo and A. Schenker; VTSup 132; Leiden: Brill, 2010), 39–52, esp. 50–52.

Rofé, A., "4QMidrash Samuel? Observations Concerning the Character of 4QSamª," *Textus* 19 (1998): 63–74.

Tov, E. (ed.), *The Hebrew and Greek Texts of Samuel* (Jerusalem: Academon, 1980).

Tov, E., "Textual Affiliation of 4QSamª," in **Greek-Hebrew Bible*, 273–83.

Tov, E., "The Qumran Hebrew Texts and the Septuagint – An Overview," in Kreuzer–Meiser–Sigismund, *Septuaginta 2012, 3–17.

Trebolle, J., "Qumran Fragments of the Books of Kings," in *The Books of Kings: Source, Composition, Historiography and Reception* (eds. A. Lemaire and B. Halpern; VTSup 129; Leiden: Brill, 2010), 19–39.

Ulrich, E., *The Qumran Text of Samuel and Josephus* (HSM 19; Missoula: Scholars Press, 1978).

Ulrich, E., "53. 4QSamᶜ," *DJD XVII: 245–67.

Ulrich, E., "A Qualitative Assessment of the Textual Profile of 4QSamª," in *Flores Florentino: Dead Sea Scrolls and Other Early Jewish Studies in Honour of Florentino García Martínez* (eds. A. Hilhorst, É. Puech, and E. Tigchelaar; JSJSup 122; Leiden, Brill, 2007), 147–61.

Philippe Hugo
Adrian Schenker

5.4 Septuagint (Samuel)

5.4.1 Background

5.4.1.1 Scope

In the Septuagint tradition (→ 1.3.1.1), 1 and 2 Samuel are known as 1 and 2 Kingdoms (or, 1–2 Reigns). This designation refers to the initiation of the kingdom and to the first kings (Saul and David), while the Masoretic designation refers to Samuel as a prophet and probably also as the author of the book. There are good reasons to assume that the books of Samuel were translated as one consecutive block after Joshua and Judges (and Ruth).[1] This connection can be seen especially in some translational features, such as the rendering of the names of Baal and Astarte and of the Philistines. Beginning with Judg 2:13, Baal is sometimes rendered with the female article ἡ Βααλ "she-Baal," which most probably indicates that in order to avoid the mentioning of the worship of Baal it should be considered to reflect ἡ αἰσχύνη "shame."[2] Another argument is the name of the Philistines, which from Judg 3:3 onwards, and appearing in Samuel and Kings, is rendered with ἀλλόφυλοι "those from another tribe."[3]

There are no specific indications for the exact time of the translation, but a date around 200 B.C.E. is most probable.

MT (→ 5.3.2) and LXX differ in their division between Samuel and Kings. While most manuscripts of LXX agree with MT, the Antiochene text of 2 Kingdoms (2 Samuel) also includes 1 Kgs 1:1–2:11 (numbered 2 Kgdms 25:1–26:11), thus including the accession of Solomon, the death of David, and the summary of David's reign (1 Kgdms 2:11).

In addition to small differences between MT and LXX, such as an additional verse (taken from Jer 9:22–23) and the different context of the Song of Hannah (1 Sam 2:1–10), the two texts differ on a large-scale in the story of David and Goliath (1 Samuel 16–18).

5.4.1.2 Different Greek Text Forms

In the books of Samuel and Kings (→ 5.5) there are two distinct forms of the Greek text. This can be seen especially in Codex Vaticanus (LXX^B). Already Thackeray distinguished between two groups of different translations: These are 1) the sections α (1 Samuel), ββ (1 Sam 1:1–10:1), and γ (1 Kgs 2:12–21:43) in a translation that is close to its source text, and that is also in fairly good Greek, and 2) sections βγ (1 Sam 10:1 [or: 11:2]–1 Kgs 2:11) and γδ (1 Kgs 22:1–2 Kgs 25:30), which contain a rather literalistic translation. Mainly due to the positive content of the first group of text units (Samuel, early years of David, Solomon and the temple), Thackeray assumed that these passages were translated first and that the remaining sections were translated later by a different translator who worked in a more formalistic way.[4] While the theory of a two-step translation has been abandoned in the meantime, the distinction between the two text forms has become generally accepted, the second text form

---

[1] Cf. the introductions to Samuel in *Bible d'Alexandrie, *NETS; *Septuaginta Deutsch, *Septuaginta Deutsch, Erläuterungen.

[2] This has been suggested by A. Dillmann, "Über Baal mit dem weiblichen Artikel (ἡ Βααλ)," Monatsberichte der Königlich preussischen Akademie der Wissenschaften (1881): 601–20; see now *Septuaginta Deutsch, n. to Judg 2:13. Other explanations such as the assumption that the article refers to the Egyptian goddess Isis seem less probable. Rendering this feature in modern translations is difficult: *Bible d'Alexandrie speaks of "la Baalesse" and *NETS uses "she-baal," both of which turn Baal into a goddess, which is hardly the intention of the text. *Septuaginta Deutsch translates "Baal-Schande" in order to keep the name of the god and to hint at its replacement as "shame."

[3] Before that verse, ἀλλόφυλοι is only found in Exod 34:15 in some manuscripts (LXX^{B, Ac, 15}), used as a general designation for the inhabitants of the land. Rahlfs, *Septuaginta considered this the original reading while Wevers, Exodus (Septuaginta Vetus Testamentum Graecum 2.1; Göttingen: Vandenhoeck & Ruprecht, 1991) discarded it.

[4] H.StJ. Thackeray, "The Greek Translators of the Four Books of Kings," JTS 8 (1907): 262–66; Thackeray, *The Septuagint and Jewish Worship.

now named the *kaige* (or: *kaige*-Theodotion)⁵ text reflecting the *kaige* recension (→ 3–5.1.5.2), while the first text form traditionally is considered to be very close to the Old Greek.⁶

However, one has to keep in mind that this alternation between the two text forms is best recognizable in LXX^B in which also the text of Judges is a *kaige* text (→ 4.3). LXX^B has the sequence: Judges (*kaige*), Ruth (*kaige*?), 1 Samuel 1–2 Samuel (9 or) 10 (non-*kaige*), 2 Samuel 11–1 Kgs 2:11 (*kaige*), 1 Kgs 2:12–1 Kings 21 (non-*kaige*), 1 Kings 22–2 Kings 25 (*kaige*). This change within LXX^B is best explained by the assumption that scrolls of different character had been used to compile the codex (or its predecessor).⁷ In contrast to LXX^B, Codex Alexandrinus (LXX^A) has Judges in a non-*kaige* text form and in Samuel the differentiation between *kaige* and non-*kaige* sections seems to be less evident.⁸

5.4.1.3 Different Greek Text Types

The Greek manuscripts are also distinguished by another distinction, viz., between the text of LXX^B and the so-called Antiochene or Lucianic text (LXX^L; manuscripts LXX^19, 82, 93, 108, 127; → 3–5.1.6.2). The latter text was identified in manuscripts by Antonio Ceriani 1863.⁹ It also agrees with quotations by the Antiochene church fathers, especially the commentaries of Theodoret from Cyrrhus, and has been traditionally linked to Lucian, an Antiochian exegete who died as a martyr in 312 C.E.¹⁰ The Antiochene text has been the base text for the *kaige*-Th recension in Samuel–Kings,¹¹ and in the non-*kaige* sections it competes with LXX^B for being closest to the Old Greek.

The problem of two text types of the Septuagint text is not limited to Samuel and Kings (see also the LXX^A and LXX^B texts in Judges, 1–2 Esdras, etc.). However, due to historic reasons, this issue has been discussed most intensely regarding Samuel–Kings, not in the least because of the linkage with the Lucianic/Antiochene text and its age, a problem that permeates many books, but which has been discussed especially for Samuel and Kings.

The above observations lead to the assumption that there are at least two stages in the transmission of the text, the Old Greek as the original translation and the *kaige* text reflecting a Hebraizing isomorphic recension dating to the first century B.C.E. The Old Greek is best preserved in the Antiochene text in both the *kaige* and the non-*kaige* sections and in LXX^B in the the non-*kaige* sections. How close these two texts were to the Old Greek and if one or both of them reflect an early revision is presently a matter of debate (→ 5.4.3.6). In any case, since this revision would have been of a limited scope and as LXX^B and LXX^L largely agree in the non-*kaige* sections, one may speak at least *grosso modo* of two forms of the text, the Old Greek and the *kaige* recension.

5.4.1.4 Manuscripts

As in most historical books, there are no Greek manuscripts before the fourth century C.E.; the oldest being LXX^B (fourth century C.E.) and LXX^A (fifth

---

⁵ The designation *kaige*-Theodotion goes back to the assumption of the so-called proto-Theodotion, i.e., the situation in which presumably Theodotionic readings are attested before the "historic" Theodotion who lived in the second century. The assumption of *kaige* as a forerunner of Theodotion would explain such early readings. However, Barthélemy, *Devanciers* took the identification a step further: He assumed that the *kaige* text was produced under the influence of Jonathan ben Uzziel, a first century C.E. Rabbi, and because of their similar names, he identified the figures of Jonathan and Theodotion and moved Theodotion to the first century C.E. Today, most scholars tend to separate the two issues; however, the designation kaige-Th reminds of the discussion about Theodotion's translation.

⁶ See e.g. the designations "Old Greek" and "*kaige*" in *NETS (the translation follows the critical text of Rahlfs, *Septuaginta, which is very close to LXX^B).

⁷ The size of the different units probably can be explained by the Hellenistic system of short scrolls; see J.-H. Kim, "Vom hellenistischen Kleinrollensystem zum Kodex: Beobachtungen zur Textgestalt der griechischen Samuel- und Königebücher," in *XIV Congress of the IOSCS, Helsinki, 2010* (ed. M.K.H. Peters; SBLSCS 53; Atlanta: SBL, 2013), 231–42.

⁸ Cf. the different amounts of variants between LXX^A and LXX^B as recorded in the apparatus of Rahlfs, *Septuaginta, and in Brooke-McLean, *The Old Testament in Greek*. This issue and also the relevance of the text forms of LXX^M and LXX^V should be subject to future investigation.

⁹ For this and for the role of Frederick Field and Julius Wellhausen, see J.-H. Kim, *Textformen*, 7–11. Cf. n. 30.

¹⁰ H.C. Brenneke, "Lucian von Antiochien," *TRE* 21:474–79.

¹¹ See especially Barthélemy, *Devanciers*, and below, → 5.4.3.

century C.E.), followed by Codex Coislianus (LXX^M; seventh century C.E.) and Codex Venetus (LXX^V; eighth century C.E.).[12] There are some other fragmentary manuscripts such as LXX^842 (= P. Feinberg 1; fourth century C.E.; containing 1 Sam 23:28–24:2; 24:6–8, 12–13, 18–20); LXX^845 (Vienna, ÖNB, Suppl. Gr. 187; fourth century C.E.; 1 Sam 13:16–18, 20–21; 13:23–14:1, 3–4; 18:8–25); LXX^846 (New Haven, YBR, MS 544; fourth/fifth century; 1 Sam 24:11–17; 24:20–25:20; 31:12–33); LXX^867 (Berlin, Äg. Museum, P. 21291; seventh century C.E.; 1 Sam 4:6, 9, 13, 15–16).[13]

Much importance is attached to manuscripts LXX^19, 82, 93, 108, and 127 form the Lucianic or Antiochene group. Although these manuscripts are comparatively late (tenth to thirteenth centuries), they represent an archetype which belongs to the fourth century.[14] Their text is confirmed by quotations from authors such as Asterius Sophista, Chrysostom, and especially Theodoret of Cyrrhos.[15]

Besides the manuscripts, older quotations (→ 21.7; → 21.8) are very important, especially the quotations in Josephus (→ 21.3),[16] but also the Old Latin translation (VL^115 and VL^91–95; → 3–5.2.1.2). There are allusions but only a few literal quotations from Samuel in the New Testament (→ 21.5).

Also very important are the manuscripts from Qumran (1QSam; 4QSam^a,b,c; → 5.3.1). 4QSam^a, especially, can be seen to represent a text that is close to the Antiochene text. Although there are differences and it is not identical to the *Vorlage* of the Antiochene text, it is very close to it and so confirms its old age; it also shows characteristics such as explaining words, etc., which are typical for texts from that time and also for the Antiochene text.[17] The Qumran texts especially have contributed to a new evaluation also of the Greek witnesses. (→ 5.4.3.3)

5.4.1.5 Hexapla

The Hexaplaric material (→ 1.3.1.2) is rather sparse, consisting mainly of marginal notes in manuscripts, esp. codex LXX^M, in manuscripts LXX^108, 56, 243, 106, 554 and in the Syro-Hexapla,[18] recorded in the edition of Brooke–McLean, *The Old Testament in Greek*. There is some debate about the relation of the columns to the text forms. Interestingly, in the βγ section, the sixth column (Theodotion) reflects the Antiochene text (→ 3–5.1.6.1).[19]

Hexaplaric material is also preserved in the writings of the Bishop Ishodad from Merv (ca. 850 C.E.) and in fragments of the Syro-Hexapla (→ 3–5.2.4.2).[20] The known witnesses are registered in Brooke–McLean–Thackeray, *The Old Testament in Greek*. The search for other witnesses so far has not been successful. The Hexaplaric material is interesting in itself but, for the question surrounding the Antiochene text/Lucianic recension, it has to be kept in mind that agreements between, for example, Symmachus and Ant may not only be quotations from the Hexapla but may also go back to a common origin in the Old Greek.

---

[12] In Brooke–McLean *The Old Testament in Greek*, LXX^V is designated as N.

[13] These manuscripts were not yet available to Rahlfs, *Septuaginta*, and Brooke–McLean, *The Old Testament in Greek*. For more information, see Rahlfs–Fraenkel, *Verzeichnis*.

[14] See the description and stemma in Fernández Marcos, *Texto Antioqueno*, xxiii.

[15] See Fernández Marcos, *Texto Antioqueno*, xxix–xlv; Fernández Marcos, *Introduction*.

[16] See already A. Mez, *Die Bibel des Josephus untersucht für Buch V–VII der Archäologie* (Basel: Jaeger & Kober, 1895). This view was confirmed by H.St.J. Thackeray, *Josephus. The Man and the Historian* (New York: Jewish Institute of Religion Press, 1929) and E. Ulrich, *The Qumran text of Samuel and Josephus*, (HSM 19; Missoula: Scholars Press, 1978).

[17] This view has been challenged by R. Saley, "Proto-Lucian and 4QSam^a", *BIOSCS* 41 (2008): 34–45. However, Saley refers only to the non-*kaige* section of Samuel, where LXX^B and LXX^L are very close; in the *kaige* section, the relation of LXX^B and LXX^L would be different. Yet, with seventy-eight percent agreement with LXX^B and LXX^L over twenty-two percent agreement with MT (p. 36), it is confirmed that the Greek translation goes back to a text type different from MT and that it is close but not identical to 4QSam^a. Saley continues to concentrate on the exclusive agreements with LXX^L, which are indeed not numerous, but which would be few for LXX^B as well, if the same method were used (→ 5.4.3.6).

[18] See the discussion of Kim, *Textformen*, 52–60.

[19] Kim, *Textformen*, 59.

[20] M. Liljeström, "Looking for Fragments of the Syrohexapla: The Song of Hannah in Barberiniani Orientali 2 as a Test Case," *BIOSCS* 40 (2007): 49–61.

5.4.1.6 Methodology

Regarding methodology, it should be mentioned that the witnesses have to be considered based on a dual aspect: On the one hand a quotation, for example, of the Old Latin or the Sahidic (→ 3–5.2.2.2.3) translation or an agreement with a Qumran text or Josephus supports a certain text form (e.g. the Antiochene [→ 3–5.1.6.1] or the *kaige*-text [→ 1.3.1.2]), but on the other hand, this does not disprove that the other text form also existed at that time.[21]

5.4.2 Editions

The most detailed edition is the large Cambridge edition of Brooke–McLean–Thackeray, *The Old Testament in Greek*, which is a diplomatic edition of LXX[B] with a wealth of data on Greek manuscripts, quotations, and other sources.[22] Rahlfs, *Septuaginta*[23] largely follows LXX[B] (LXX[S] is not extant for Samuel) with additions and corrections from LXX[A], the Hexaplaric text, and he often also includes readings from the Lucianic text.[24]

There are two editions of the Antiochene (Lucianic) text (LXX[L]; → 3–5.1.6.1): Taylor produced an edition of 1 Samuel which presents the majority text from the five relevant manuscripts (LXX[19, 82, 93, 108, and 127]).[25] The edition by Fernandez Marcos and Busto Saiz,[26] which also covers Kings and Chronicles, presents an eclectic text from all the relevant witnesses. Besides the mentioned manuscripts, this edition also quotes the text from Theodoret and other church fathers, and in a second apparatus it records the Old Latin, relevant quotations from Josephus and others, as well as the Qumran texts.

5.4.3 History of Research

As in other books of the Septuagint, debate continues on translation technique, lexical questions, and the problems of specific passages.[27] However, in preparation for critical editions and because of the identification or discovery of new manuscripts, the search for the oldest text, and the classification and dating of the different text forms have become dominant topics. As the evaluation of codex LXX[B] and the Lucianic text (LXX[L]; → 3–5.1.6.1), especially, – and with that the criteria used by Rahlfs in establishing his critical edition[28] – has been heavily influenced by specific assumptions for a long time, it is important to consider the history of research.

5.4.3.1 Lucian: Background

The Lucianic or Antiochene text (→ 3–5.1.6.1) was known for a long time from the quotations of the Antiochene church fathers (→ 21.7), especially Theodoret of Cyrrhos (ca. 393–457 C.E.), and was identified in the edition of Holmes and Parsons[29] by Ceriani in 1861 and 1863.[30] The witnesses for

---

[21] Cf. the examples for both text forms given in Kim, *Textformen*, 62, 65.

[22] Brooke–McLean–Thackeray, *The Old Testament in Greek*, Vol. 2: *The Historical Books*, Part 1: *I and II Samuel* (1927). A part of this edition (2 Samuel 1–14) has been transposed into the Göttingen system of numbering the manuscripts. The searchable file is available at http://isbtf.de/brookemclean-elektronisch/

[23] Subsequently Rahlfs–Hanhart, *Septuaginta*.

[24] The Göttingen edition is still in preparation in 2015 (1 Samuel is being prepared by Anneli Aejmelaeus, 2 Samuel by Tuukka Kauhanen).

[25] Taylor, *The Lucianic Manuscripts of 1 Reigns*, 2 vols.

[26] Fernández Marcos and Busto Saiz, *El Texto Antioqueno de la Biblia Griega*.

[27] E.g. on the Song of Hannah, cf. S.D. Walters, "Hanna and Anna: The Hebrew and Greek Text of 1 Samuel 2,1–10," *JBL* 107 (1988): 385–412; on the David and Goliath story, cf. D. Barthélemy et al., *The Story of David and Goliath: Textual and Literary Criticism: Papers of a Joint Research Venture* (OBO 73; Göttingen: Vandenhoeck & Ruprecht, 1986).

[28] Rahlfs, *Septuaginta*.

[29] R. Holmes and J. Parsons (eds.), Vetus Testamentum Graecum: Cum variis lectionibus (5 vols.; Oxford: Clarendon, 1798–1827).

[30] A.M. Ceriani, *Fragmenta Latina Evangelii S. Lucae, parvae Genesis et Asumptionis Mosis, Baruch, Threni et epistola Jeremiae versionis Syriacae Pauli Telensis cum notis et initio prolegomenon in integram ejusdem versionis editionem* (Monumenta sacra et profana ex codicibus praesentim Bibliothecae Ambrosianae 1; Milan: Bibliotheca Ambrosiana, 1861); A.M. Ceriani, *Pentateuchi Syro-Hexaplaris quae supersunt cum notis: accedunt nonnulla alia fragmenta Syriaca* (Monumenta sacra et profana ex codicibus praesentim Bibliothecae Ambrosianae 2.1; Milan: Bibliotheca Ambrosiana, 1863), xi.

the Antiochene text are LXX[19, 82, 93, 108, and 127]. This identification was accepted and confirmed by Frederick Field, Julius Wellhausen, and Paul Anton de Lagarde.[31] It became clear that this text form was very old and important. It confirmed many of Wellhausen's assumptions and even some of his conjectures on the text of Samuel.[32]

As Lucian of Antioch became a martyr in 312 C.E., his work must have been done around 300 C.E. The connection of the Antiochene text with Lucian is based mainly on Jerome's well-known statement (in his Prologue to his Vulgate translation of Chronicles) about the threefold tradition (*trifaria varietas*) of the Greek texts in his times.[33] And in some manuscripts there is a sign (λ) that refers to Lucian, but which in other books refers to οἱ λοιποί "the remaining ones."[34]

5.4.3.2 Lucian: Features

In 1911, Rahlfs published an extensive investigation into the Lucianic text of 1 and 2 Kings (→ 5.5), which became decisive also for his evaluation of the manuscript situation of the books of Samuel and for his text edition.[35] Rahlfs' assumption was that codex LXX[B] represents the oldest Greek text and that the Lucianic text (→ 3–5.1.6.1) had been shaped by Lucian, and therefore the differences between LXX[B] and Lucian are the result of Lucian's redaction. The characteristics of this Lucianic redaction are a freer and better Greek in grammar and syntax and sometimes in the choice of words. Lucian added the article and often he added explanatory words that indicated the person speaking and acting (instead of a simple "he" or "she" who speaks or acts). Semantically, the revision had an atticizing tendency. But equally often the revision was done in the reverse direction, i.e., articles or explanatory words or atticizing features have been deleted. Rahlfs explained this feature by adding a further characteristic to the work of Lucian: Lucian had worked in an irregular and even contradictory fashion. This irregularity was even presented as the main characteristic of the assumed Lucianic redaction: "the main characteristic of this recension is the absence of a clear principle."[36]

Rahlfs also discussed the assumption that Josephus (→ 21.3) used a Lucianic text and that Lucianic readings are found in the Old Latin (→ 3–5.2.1.2) and in the New Testament (→ 21.5). In general, he downplayed the importance of those early witnesses by explaining them as later cross-influence between the manuscripts. However, he also admitted that there are some pre-Lucianic readings in the Lucianic text.

Rahlfs' investigation from 1911 very much determined his presentation and decisions in preparing his critical edition.[37] However, in spite of his remark at the beginning of the books of Samuel "*huius editionis innumeras lectiones singulares ... praetereo*" "The numerous variants in that edition I do not record,"[38] he quoted many Lucianic readings and not infrequently included them for his eclectically composed Old Greek text.

Rahlfs' position on the Lucianic text was accepted by several editors of Septuagint text editions, especially Ziegler in the prophetical books.[39] Ziegler reached the same conclusion concerning

---

[31] For the history of research, see Fernández Marcos, *Introduction*, 223–30, and Kim, *Textformen*, 7–32.

[32] J. Wellhausen, *Die Bücher Samuelis* (Göttingen: Vandenhoeck & Ruprecht, 1871), 221–24.

[33] There is also an earlier statement in his letter to Sunnia and Fretela, where he equals the Septuagint in general (*koine*) with the Lucianic text ("now widely called *loukianeios*") from which he discerns the Hexapla text. Jerome, Letter 106; for text, Translation, and discussion, see now e.g. Kreuzer, "Old Greek, Kaige and the *Trifaria Varietas*," esp. 219–20.

[34] There are remarks in Theodoret's commentary on the Minor Prophets; the most important manuscript is LXX[86]; for details, see Fernandez Marcos, *Introduction*, 225–26.

[35] Rahlfs, *Lucians Rezension*.

[36] "Denn der Hauptcharakterzug dieser Rezension ist das Fehlen eines klaren Prinzips," Rahlfs, *Lucians Rezension*, 293.

[37] Rahlfs, *Septuaginta*.

[38] Rahlfs, *Septuaginta*, 502.

[39] J. Ziegler (ed.), *Isaias* (Septuaginta Vetus Testamentum Graecum 14; Göttingen: Vandenhoeck & Ruprecht, 1939); J. Ziegler (ed.), *Duodecim Prophetae* (Septuaginta Vetus Testamentum Graecum 13; Göttingen: Vandenhoeck & Ruprecht, 1943); J. Ziegler (ed.), *Ezechiel* (Septuaginta Vetus Testamentum Graecum 16.1; Göttingen: Vandenhoeck & Ruprecht, 1952); J. Ziegler (ed.), *Jeremias, Baruch, Threni, Epistulae Jeremiae* (Septuaginta Vetus Testamentum Graecum 15; Göttingen: Vandenhoeck & Ruprecht, 1957).

the Lucianic text as Rahlfs and he also remarked on the seeming irregularity and contradictions of Lucian's redactional activity: "consistency was not his strength."⁴⁰

The detailed analysis of the Lucianic text of 1 Samuel by Brock followed the same line.⁴¹ Brock further came to the conclusion that the Lucianic text with its additions (of articles and explaining words) and its improvements was intended as a text for public reading. However, Brock concentrated on the additions ("recurrent variants") and left aside the deletions ("non-recurrent variants") as being of less interest.⁴²

5.4.3.3 Lucian: Relevance of the Qumran Texts

The Qumran texts changed the evaluation of the Greek texts. Already in the 1950s, Cross published some fragments of 4QSamᵃ (→ 5.3.1.2; → 5.3.3) that showed striking agreements with the Lucianic text (→ 3–5.1.6.1).⁴³ This suggested that a large pre-Lucianic layer existed in the so-called Lucianic text because the convergence with a scroll from the caves cannot be the result of a later cross-influence.

The next important development was connected with the discovery of the Naḥal Ḥever scroll of the Greek Minor Prophets (→ 6–9.1.2). Besides confirming that the biblical Greek text had been used in the land of Judah, it showed a strongly isomorphic Hebraizing revision, which Barthélemy (1963) named the *kaige* recension.⁴⁴ After discussing the Minor Prophets, Barthélemy turned to the books of Samuel. He identified the strongly Hebraizing section that Thackeray had singled out (section βγ') as a *kaige* text and discussed its characteristics.⁴⁵ It became clear to him that this section was strongly revised and could not represent the Old Greek. Next, he wondered whether the Old Greek of the *kaige* section was still extant somewhere or whether it had been lost. He found that the *kaige* text and the Lucianic text were so close that they could not have been based on two different translations, but that they belonged together.⁴⁶ The next question was the direction of dependence. Barthélemy concluded that the *kaige* text was the revised text and that the so-called Lucianic text was its source. Upon further investigation, Barthélemy came to the conclusion that this text was very close to the Old Greek and – besides corruptions in the course of its transmission – basically presents it: The Antiochene text is "the Old Septuagint, more or less corrupted."⁴⁷ Because of this insight, Barthélemy also suggested the use of the term "Antiochene text" instead of "Lucianic text," because the latter name had become associated with the idea of a Lucianic recension, which according to Barthélemy's insight did not exist ("the [wrongly] assumed Lucianic recension"⁴⁸). For Barthélemy, the identification of the *kaige* recension and the new status of the Lucianic/Antiochene text as more or less the Old Greek were practically two sides of the same coin.

These two aspects were subsequently separated for a number of reasons, not least among them being a Brock's study "Lucian redivivus" from 1965.⁴⁹

---

⁴⁰ "Konsequenz war nicht seine Stärke"; J. Ziegler, *Beiträge zur Ieremias-Septuaginta* (MSU 6; Göttingen: Vandenhoeck & Ruprecht, 1958), 163.

⁴¹ Brock, *Recensions* (1996 = PhD diss., Oxford University, 1966).

⁴² Brock, *Recensions*, 254: "The features which have been discussed do not of course by any means cover the whole range of this type of variant, but it is hoped that all cases where L shows evidence of consistent, or nearly consistent, revision, have been included." Similarly, on p. 255: "Of the less consistent variants of this type in L, it has only been possible for reasons of space, to give a selection. Non-recurrent variants like these are found over the whole of the ms tradition and present less interest."

⁴³ Cross, "Biblical Fragment." For a full publication of 4QSamᵃ, see F.M. Cross, D.W. Parry, and R.J. Saley, "51. 4QSamᵃ," *DJD* XVII (2005): 1–216.

⁴⁴ Barthélemy, *Devanciers*. To allow for differences, Barthélemy spoke of the "*groupe kaige*" (*kaige* group of texts) but he also used the term *kaige* recension. In view of later research, one may question Barthélemy for choosing "*kaige*" as the designation of the revision, but "this simply is the easiest way to refer to it" (thus Aejmelaeus, "1 Samuel," 124).

⁴⁵ Barthélemy, *Devanciers*, 31–80.

⁴⁶ Barthélemy, *Devanciers*, 91–102.

⁴⁷ Barthélemy, *Devanciers*, 127: "la vielle septante, plus ou moins corrompue et abatardie."

⁴⁸ Barthélemy, *Devanciers*, 126: "la pretendue recension Lucianique."

⁴⁹ This short paper became rather influential (see, e.g.,

Brock accepted the assumption of a *kaige* recension, but he held on to the old view regarding a Lucianic recension. The upshot of this argument was the assumption that the idea of a Lucianic recension (which is not the same as the traditional label "Lucianic text") was maintained, but that there was more openness to investigate the pre-Lucianic text (sometimes combined with the assumption of a proto-Lucianic recension of the Hebrew text).

5.4.3.4 Pre- or Proto-Lucianic Elements

Qumran scholars, especially, recognized a large number of pre-Lucianic readings in the Samuel scrolls (mainly 4QSam^a; → 5.2.1) but, adhering to the idea of a Lucianic recension (→ 3–5.1.6.1), they devised compromise models, mostly accepting Barthélemy's thesis for the *kaige* sections in Samuel where older material was present, while holding on to the assumption of a Lucianic recension for the other sections. This division had been suggested by Cross, who took up Rahlfs' idea of there being two layers in the Lucianic text, but now, because of 4QSam^a, he thought in terms of a much larger amount of proto-Lucianic text reflecting an early "proto-Lucianic" revision of the text.[50] This distinction was also taken up, for example, by Tov, who however doubted the existence of a proto-Lucianic revision. He could not see convincing reasons for believing that this ancient substratum had been revised; rather, he concluded that "the existence of a proto-Lucianic revision of the LXX has not been established. It is further suggested that the substratum of boc$_2$e$_2$ contains either *the* Old Greek or any single Old Greek translation."[51] Aejmelaeus is also skeptical about the existence of a proto-Lucianic revision of the Hebrew: "Sporadic corrections towards the MT or inner-Greek corruption are perfectly sufficient explanations in most of those cases where traces of the proto-Lucianic recension have been seen."[52]

However, the basic ideas about a large proto-Lucianic stratum together with a Lucianic redaction existed (with variations) for a long time. Even scholars who concluded that the Lucianic /Antiochene text is the text closest to the Old Greek held on to the assumption of a late Lucianic recension and probably also of a proto-Lucianic revision.[53]

In 2008, Saley[54] attempted to single out proto-Lucianic (or Old Greek?) readings by searching for exclusive agreements between 4QSam^a and the Antiochene text in the non-*kaige* sections of Samuel and accepting only the convincing agreements for Old Greek (excluding agreements that might have arisen by chance, e.g., because of a word already existing in the context).[55] This analysis leads to a small number of instances (applying the same procedure e.g. to LXX^B would lead to a similar small number of proto-LXX^B readings, which would hardly be acceptable). In 2012, Kauhanen,[56] followed a similar approach, mainly looking for patristic quotations (→ 21.7). This is a positive approach, but both approaches presuppose that LXX^L is a late and mixed text from the time of Lucian, in which only kernels of the proto-Lucianic text can be singled out. This very attitude leads to only a limited number of proto-Lucianic readings, because the Qumran fragments are limited and there are only few quotations from 1 Samuel. Consequently, the results can only stay within the presupposed framework, within which no proto-Lucianic text can be identified beyond the Qumran fragments and quotations (→ 5.4.1.4).

With regard to the Lucianic recension, also Barthélemy himself, under the influence of his crit-

---

Fernández Marcos, *Introduction*, 234); however, it was never seriously challenged. See now Kreuzer, "Lukian redivus?"

[50] Cross, *"History."*

[51] Tov, "Lucian and Proto-Lucian," 110 (488).

[52] Aejmelaeus, "1 Samuel," 126.

[53] Even Fernández Marcos, who highly values the Antiochene text as being the closest to the Old Greek, always held on to the idea of a Lucianic redaction and also of an early proto-Lucianic revision (e.g., Fernández Marcos, *Introduction*, 232, 236). However, at the same time, the picture of a unified Lucianic recension somehow dissolved, as he writes: "Nevertheless, I am not sure that all the previously mentioned recensional characteristics come from the same source" (Fernández Marcos, "The Antiochene Edition," 66).

[54] Saley, "Proto-Lucian and 4QSam^a."

[55] And it does not cover other phenomena like adaptation of word sequence to the Hebrew text in LXX^B or LXX^L.

[56] Kauhanen, "The Proto-Lucianic Problem in 1 Samuel."

ics, later admitted that the Antiochene text may have been revised in some way, and that we do not witness only unintentional corruptions (→ 5.4.3.3 "with more or less corruptions"). However, he did not return to a Lucianic redaction proper.[57]

One important reason for maintaining a (late) Lucianic recension was the observation of exclusive agreements with readings from the younger Jewish translations, especially Symmachus (→ 3–5.1.5.2). The idea is that such readings would have been taken from the Hexapla (in whatever way), providing an anchor for the dating of borrowing by Lucian or one of his contemporaries (approximately 300 C.E.).[58] However, it is also possible that such exclusive agreements go back to a common source, i.e., the Old Greek, and would have been lost in the other traditions, especially because *kaige* changed the wording of the OG.

5.4.3.5 Lucian and *Kaige*-Th

From a different starting point, Kreuzer[59] arrived at a new approach to the different layers/strata in Samuel. Investigating the *kaige* recension, he observed that its "Hebraizing" revision was often grammatically incorrect, especially with regard to the article. According to him, *kaige* (represented by LXX[B]) did not use the article in Greek according to the rules of Hebrew determination, but according to the formal content of the text (e.g. in 2 Sam 15:10, it rendered בכל שבטי ישראל "in all the tribes of Israel" as ἐν πάσαις φυλαῖς Ισραηλ "in all tribes of Israel," i.e., without an article). On the other hand, if there was a formal representation (either -ה or sometimes את), it used a Greek article; for example, in the same verse את קול השפר became τὴν φωνὴν τῆς κερατίνης "the sound of the horn" (2 Sam 15:10). The general observation of the isomorphic character of the *kaige* recension was not new, but the observation of the use of the article led to a new solution of the old problem of irregularity and contradictions in the assumed Lucianic redaction:[60] In LXX[L], the first example from 2 Sam 15:10 is rendered with articles: εἰς πάσας τὰς φυλὰς τοῦ Ισραηλ "In all the tribes of Israel." In the traditional understanding with LXX[B] as the oldest text, Lucian would have added the articles, while in the second case Lucian would have deleted the article: φωνὴν σάλπιγγος "sound of a horn." However, if one allows the Lucianic/Antiochene text to be the older one, the differences between LXX[L] and LXX[B]/the *kaige* text can be explained consistently: The use of the article was also subjected to the isomorphic treatment. This means: LXX[L] being more or less the Old Greek followed the rules of Hebrew determination and the rules for the article in Greek. The *kaige* recension on the other hand followed the surface of the text: If there was a visible article in Hebrew, *kaige* would have an article in Greek. If there was no visible article in Hebrew (e.g. because of determination by a name as in שבטי ישראל "the tribes of Israel"), the *kaige* recension would delete the article in Greek. And, as is sometimes the case, if the Old Greek has no article (as in φωνὴν σάλπιγγος "sound of a trumpet"), while there is an article in Hebrew, *kaige* added that article (τὴν φωνὴν τῆς κερατίνης "the sound of the horn").[61] Different from the seemingly irregular work of the assumed Lucianic redaction, which Rahlfs had identified as its main (!) trait (→ 5.4.3.2 and notes 34 and 35) and which had been taken up by Ziegler, Brock, and others, the new perspective allows a consistent explanation of the differences.

Although the article is the most frequent example (and most prominently treated by Rahlfs, Ziegler, and Brock), the explanation from the isomorphic procedure of the *kaige* revision is relevant for other additions and omissions as well. Examples include 2 Sam 12:8. In this verse, LXX[L] has God

---

[57] Barthélemy, "Les problèmes," 1972.
[58] See e.g. Fernández Marcos, *Introduction*, 230: "In general, it can be stated that it [= the Lucianic redaction] tends to fill the gaps in the LXX in respect of the Hebrew text on the basis of additions taken from 'the three,' particularly from Symmachus."
[59] Kreuzer, "Der Antiochenische Text"; Kreuzer, "Towards the Old Greek."

[60] See above, regarding Rahlfs.
[61] The example also shows another difference, which is typical for the *kaige* recension: While the Old Greek renders according to its function (σάλπιγξ "trumpet"), *kaige* sticks to the object (κερατίνη "horn"); cf. Barthélemy, *Devanciers*, 60–63: "Distinction du cor et de la trompette."

say to David: I gave you τὰ πάντα τοῦ κυρίου σου "all [possessions] of your lord." LXX^B reads instead: I gave you τὸν οἶκον τοῦ κυρίου σου "the house of your lord." While it is hardly plausible that LXX^L (in the old sense of the Lucianic recension) would have removed the reference to David having received the kingdom of Saul, LXX^B is easily explained as an adaptation to MT, which reads וָאֶתְּנָה לְךָ אֶת־בֵּית אֲדֹנֶיךָ "I gave you the house of your lord." Also, variants in word order without difference in meaning can best be explained by the tendency to isomorphic adaptation, e.g., 2 Sam 5:1 where in LXX^B the elders of Israel say to David Ἰδοὺ ὀστᾶ σου καὶ σάρκες σου ἡμεῖς "Behold, your bones and your flesh we [are]" while LXX^L reads Ἰδοὺ ἡμεῖς ὀστᾶ σου καὶ σάρκες σου "Behold, we [are] your bones and your flesh." There is hardly an imaginable reason to change the sequence from LXX^B to LXX^L, but the change from LXX^L (= Old Greek) to LXX^B (*kaige* recension) is easily explained as an adaptation to the word order of MT: הִנְנוּ עַצְמְךָ וּבְשָׂרְךָ אֲנָחְנוּ "Behold, your bones and your flesh we [are]." The same direction of change is evident in the well-accepted example in 2 Sam 5:9, where LXX^L reads "you have despised the Lord" while LXX^B has "you have despised *the word* of the Lord." In this case, the explanation of the change as a formalistic adaptation to the Hebrew can be complemented by the argument that the harsh saying in LXX^L (and its Hebrew *Vorlage*; → 3–5.1.6.1) is softened in MT (→ 5.3.3) and accordingly in LXX^B.[62]

In actual fact, there was no inconsistent revision by Lucian (or one of his contemporaries), but rather the Antiochene text simply represents an old text that was close to or identical with the Old Greek, and the *kaige* recension reworked this old text according to its hermeneutics and its isomorphic principles.[63]

Besides, the assumed Lucianic tendency to add explanatory words is already visible in many biblical texts from Qumran and therefore may also go back to the Old Greek and its *Vorlage*, as especially Pisano has emphasized.[64] This observation also supports the assumption that the assumed Lucianic characteristics of the Antiochene text actually characterize the original translation and its *Vorlage*.

5.4.3.6 Non-*Kaige* Sections

The non-*kaige* sections present a special problem. In these text units, codex LXX^B is considered to be the best representation of the Old Greek. However, in his critical edition,[65] Rahlfs decided many times for a different reading, which implies that in such cases he somehow considered the text of LXX^B to be secondary. Certainly, the differences between LXX^B and the presumed Old Greek (and also the Antiochene text) are fewer and smaller, but evidently there are not only corruptions and mistakes in LXX^B. This leads to the question whether there was some type of revision even in the text of LXX^B. This has indeed been suggested by Aejmelaeus: "this kind of recensional development, typical of the so-called καίγε sections is clearly not absent in the non-καίγε sections either, but can sporadically be detected in the B-text, often followed by Alexandrinus and the base-text of the O-group. [...] What the channels were through which these features entered into the textual transmission of the Old Greek remains to be studied."[66] In his analy-

---

[62] For this example, see also Tov, *TCHB*, 251.

[63] For a discussion of the background of early Jewish hermeneutics and an analysis of several different texts, see S. Kreuzer, "Das frühjüdische Textverständnis und die Septuaginta-Versionen der Samuelbücher: Ein Beitrag zur textgeschichtlichen und übersetzungstechnischen Bewertung des Antiochenischen Textes und der *Kaige*-Rezension an Hand von 2 Sam 15,1–12," in *La Septante en Allemagne et en France/Septuaginta Deutsch und Bible d'Alexandrie* (eds. W. Kraus and O. Munnich; OBO 238; Göttingen: Vandenhoeck & Ruprecht, 2009), 3–28; Kreuzer, "Towards the Old Greek"; Kreuzer, *Textformen und Bearbeitungen*. See also Kim, *Textformen*.

[64] Pisano, *Additions and Omissions in the Books of Samuel*, 67–69, 238–42. The phenomenon as such was already known in pre-Qumran times and was mentioned as characteristic of the so-called vulgar texts (*Vulgärtexte*).

[65] Rahlfs, *Septuaginta*.

[66] Aejmelaeus, "A Kingdom at Stake," 366. Similarly, already in Aejmelaeus, "1 Samuel," 127: "one must be ready to accept corruption or correction towards the Hebrew in the main line [= LXX^B-text and related manuscripts.; S.K.] of textual transmission."

ses of several non-*kaige* passages, Kreuzer has come to similar conclusions, i.e., that the differences between LXX[B] and LXX[L] can be explained largely as a revision on the side of LXX[B].[67] Because this revision is much less extensive than the *kaige* recension but shows similar features (e.g., adaptation to the Hebrew word order),[68] Kreuzer suggested the term "semi-*Kaige*."[69]

Altogether, this means that at least for the books of Samuel, Barthélemy's suggestion that the Lucianic/Antiochene text basically is the Old Greek, although with corruptions, seems to apply also to the non-*kaige* sections; whether these corruptions amount to an (earlier or later) layer or layers of revision(s) remains a matter of debate.[70]

5.4.4 Date, Characteristics, and Milieu

On the basis of the previous paragraphs it can be maintained that the oldest text of the Septuagint, i.e. the Old Greek, can be reconstructed with a high degree of certainty and that there are two main phases and two main text forms of the Greek text of the books of Samuel, namely the Old Greek and the *kaige* text.

5.4.4.1 Original Translation

It is plausible that Samuel was translated around 200 B.C.E. (or shortly before), probably in Alexandria (→ 1.1). The substitute readings αἰσχύνη "shame" for Baal and ἄλση "[sacred] groves" for Astarte may hint at a public reading probably in the synagogue; however, they would also seem appropriate for study purposes.

The translation presents a careful rendering of the Hebrew *Vorlage* and closely follows the Hebrew text. This is true both in semantics (with an eye on function, e.g., σάλπιγξ "trumpet" for שופר "horn") and in grammar (e.g., Hebrew determination is rendered by articulation in Greek where appropriate). The translator usually proceeded word for word, yet with free word order where necessary. Frequently, the translator(s) used transliterations. The following exceptions to this rule can be observed: In 1 Samuel, the title יהוה) צבאות) "(Lord) of hosts" has been transliterated (*Sabaoth*) but in 2 Samuel it is rendered as παντοκάτωρ "all-lord" or δύναμις "power." The name of the Philistines is not transliterated but represented by ἀλλόφυλοι "those from foreign tribes." Interestingly, עבד is rendered by two different words, δοῦλος "servant" and παῖς "child, one how belongs to ..." probably differentiated by status (δοῦλος) and relation (παῖς).[71] This implies that the translator is aware of the different semantic range of these words.

Special formulas such as oaths are translated word for word, which makes them barely understandable in Greek. The translator probably expected the readers to know and to understand such Hebraisms. An interesting feature is also the frequent use of the historical present, which enlivens the stories.

It seems that the translator was acquainted with the different "exegetical" problems of the text, which also were known in the Targum (→ 3–5.1.3) and discussed by other Jewish authors: Thus, according to MT and T[J] in 1 Sam 14:18, Saul calls for the ark, which at that time was situated in the area of the Philistines. LXX (or its Hebrew *Vorlage*) solved the problem by talking about the ephod. According to 1 Sam 15:35, Saul did not see Samuel anymore until his death; but in MT-1 Sam 19:24, Saul prophesied before Samuel; in LXX (or its Hebrew *Vorlage*) "before them [= other prophets]." In 1 Sam 25:37, Nabal's heart turns "into stone" (לאבן); likewise, in T[J] and in LXX (or its *Vorlage*) it becomes "like stone" (= כאבן).[72]

The milieu of the translator(s) evidently was one in which the historical books (and not only the

---

[67] See Kreuzer, "B or not B?"; Kreuzer, "Der Antiochenische"; Kreuzer, "Old Greek und Semi-*Kaige*."

[68] Cf. above, the example from 2 Sam 5:1, that sometimes also concerns the article.

[69] Kreuzer, "B or not B?" 288–94, esp. 294, and Kreuzer, "Old Greek and Semi-Kaige."

[70] See → 5.4.3.5, n. 40, recording the view of Fernández Marcos. See also P. Hugo, who speaks about "the Antiochene mixture" (see Hugo's article, "Die Antiochenische Mischung").

[71] Cf. Kim, "Wiedergabe."

[72] For these and other examples, see Meiser, "Samuelseptuaginta und Targum Jonathan."

Torah and Psalms) were of interest and the contents of the books were known. It is hard to decide whether the translation was intended for public reading (in the synagogue?); if so, the listeners would need to be acquainted with "biblical" language.

5.4.4.2 *Kaige* Recension

The date of the *kaige* recension is mainly determined by the date of the Naḥal Ḥever scroll of the Minor Prophets (8ḤevXII gr; → 1.3.1.1), which is dated paleographically to the first century B.C.E. (possibly the second half),[73] which means that also the *kaige* recension itself originated at that time or earlier, although probably at different times for the various books. (However the Former and Latter Prophets were probably translated more or less at the same time.) This recension probably was made in the land of Israel,[74] or was at least used there, as shown by the discovery of the Dodekapropheton scroll in Naḥal Ḥever. However, it cannot be excluded that the revision of some books took place in the diaspora. The *kaige* recension and its milieu can be characterized by a great esteem for not only content but also the form of the Hebrew text. This is expressed in the highly isomorphic rendering, visible in the adaptation to the word order of the Hebrew reference text but also in the addition or deletion of the article, depending (not on determination but) on the presence or absence of a Hebrew article or an equivalent lexeme. Also typical are some semantic corrections such as rendering שופר with κερατίνη "horn" instead of σάλπιγξ "trumpet"; see 2 Sam 15:10; 18:16; 20:1, 22 versus 1 Sam 13:3; 2 Sam 2:28; 6:15. Most telling is the differentiation in *kaige* between ἐγώ "I" and ἐγώ εἰμι "I am," distinguishing between אני ("I" = ἐγώ "I") and אנכי ("I" = ἐγώ εἰμι, "I am").[75]

The *kaige* recension did away with the feminine ἡ Βααλ "she-Baal" in favor of the masculine article.

On the other hand, it kept the distinction between the two different renderings of נער "youth/servant" (παῖς "child" and δοῦλος "servant").[76]

5.4.4.3 Non-*Kaige* Sections

As discussed in → 5.4.3.6, the non-*kaige* sections of codex LXX[B] have also undergone some Hebraizing redaction, especially with regard to the adaptation of the word order to the Hebrew text and other isomorphic tendencies. Due to its similarity to the *kaige* recension, I have suggested to name this revision semi-*kaige*.[77] So far, it cannot be determined if this revision took place before, alongside, or after the *kaige* recension. This should be considered a regular revision and not an occasional contamination of manuscripts from the *kaige* tradition.[78]

5.4.5 Relevance for Textual History and Exegesis

The Hebrew *Vorlage* of the Greek translation of Samuel differed from MT (→ 5.3.2) but it also differed – although less so – from the Qumran texts of Samuel, especially 4QSam[a] (→ 5.3.1.2; → 5.3.3). It represents a third type of text, giving at some places a slightly fuller text (e.g. 1 Sam 2:9). Similar additions can also be found in 4QSam[a] and MT.[79]

The text-critical value of LXX lies 1) in the possibility to compare different text forms, which may help to solve problems in MT, and 2) in the opportunity to go back to a textual stage preceding MT. The *kaige* text represents a text basically identical to MT. However, there are also differences that show that the reference text which *kaige* used was not MT

---

[73] See P.J. Parsons, "The Scripts and Their Date," *DJD* VIII: 19–26.

[74] Cf. Barthélemy, *Devanciers*, who used the term "*recension palestinienne*."

[75] Cf. Barthélemy. *Devanciers*, 48–81: "Autres characteristiques du groupe καίγε."

[76] However, the *kaige* recension differentiated in a different way: While the Old Greek distinguished according to relation, *kaige* differentiated according to status; cf. J.-H. Kim, "Die Wiedergabe von עֶבֶד mit δοῦλος oder παῖς in der Septuaginta der Samuel- und Königebücher," in Karrer–Kraus, *Septuaginta 2010*, 358–70.

[77] Kreuzer, "Old Greek und Semi-Kaige" and → 5.4.3.6.

[78] For a detailed analysis of several texts, see Kreuzer, "B or not B?" esp. 91–95; Kreuzer, "Der antiochenische Text," esp. 43–54; Kreuzer, "Old Greek und Semi-*Kaige*."

[79] E.g. the well-known variant in 2 Sam 12:9 (→ 5.4.3.5); for an example from the non-*kaige* section, see 2 Sam 5:2, where the speech of the elders of Israel is amplified.

itself (as represented by MT^L). The numerous variants between the different text forms are illustrative of intentional and unintentional changes and of the many possibilities for scribal errors and other textual corruptions.

The identification of the Antiochene text (→ 3-5.1.6.1) as "more or less the Old Greek" is important for describing OG-Sam and its translation technique. The Old Greek of 1 and 2 Samuel provided a close and careful translation into Greek, however, also with the aim of being understandable and acceptable for Greek readers.[80]

The *kaige* recension, which most probably existed not only for the *kaige* sections in LXX^B but also for the whole text of 1–2 Samuel, represents not just a Hebraizing revision in general, but shows an isomorphic adaptation that is an expression of the high value given not only to the content but also to the form and nature of the Hebrew source text.

The theological profile of the two Greek versions of Samuel lies not so much in the content and message of their Hebrew *Vorlage*, but in the hermeneutical background of their translation technique. Both the translator(s) and the revisor(s) have a high esteem for the content and message of the books of Samuel. They apply their basic approach in different ways: The original translator had one eye closely on the Hebrew text and one eye on the user and on the Greek language. The *kaige* recension wants to bring the Hebrew roots to the attention of the readers. Both versions also show how the text could be understood and was understood.

Aejmelaeus, A., "The Septuagint of 1 Samuel," in Aejmelaeus, *Trail, 131–49.
Aejmelaeus, A., "A Kingdom at Stake: Reconstructing the Old Greek – Deconstructing the *Textus Receptus*," in *Scripture in Transition: Essays on Septuagint, Hebrew Bible, and Dead Sea Scrolls in Honor of Raija Sollamo* (eds. J. Jokiranta and A. Voitila; JSJSup 126; Leiden: Brill, 2008), 353–66.

---

[80] According to Brock, *Recensions*, 252, the Lucianic/Antiochene text was "a text designed for public reading." Since this text basically represented the Old Greek, its features would also characterize the Old Greek.

Barthélemy, *Devanciers.
Barthélemy, D., "Les problèmes textuels de 2 Sam 11,2–1Rois 2,11 reconsidérés à la lumière de certaines critiques des 'Devanciers d'Aquila'" / "A Reexamination of the Textual Problems in 2 Sam 11:2–1 Kings 2:11 in the Light of Certain Criticisms of 'Les Devanciers d'Aquila,'" in *1972 Proceedings* (ed. R. Kraft; SBLSCS 2; Missoula: Society of Biblical Literature, 1972), 16–89 (16–88 French and 17–89 English; repr. Barthélemy, *Études, 218–54).
Barthélemy, D., D.W. Gooding, J. Lust, and E. Tov, *The Story of David and Goliath: Textual and Literary Criticism* (OBO 73; Göttingen: Vandenhoeck & Ruprecht, 1986).
Brock, S.P., "Lucian redivivus: Some Reflections on Barthélemy's Les Devanciers d'Aquila," in Studia Evangelica, Vol. 5: Papers Presented to the Third International Congress on New Testament Studies held at Christ Church, Oxford 1963 (ed. F.L. Cross; TUGAL 103; Berlin: Berlin-brandenburgische Akademie der Wissenschaften, 1968), 176–81.
Brock, S.P., *The Recensions of the Septuagint Version of 1 Samuel* (Henoch Quaderni 9; Turin: Zamorani, 1996).
Cross, F.M., "A New Qumran Biblical Fragment Related to the Original Hebrew Underlying the LXX," BASOR 132 (1953): 15–26.
*DJD XVII.
Fernández Marcos, N. and J.R. Busto Saiz, *El Texto Antioqueno de la Biblia Griega*, Vol. 1: *1–2 Samuel* (Textos y estudios "Cardenal Cisneros" 50; Madrid: CSIC, 1989).
Fernández Marcos, N., *The Septuagint in Context: Introduction to the Greek Version of the Bible* (Leiden: Brill, 2000).
Fernández Marcos, N., "The Antiochene Edition in the Text History of the Greek Bible," in *Der Antiochenische Text der Septuaginta in seiner Bezeugung und seiner Bedeutung* (eds. S. Kreuzer and M. Sigismund; De Septuaginta Investigationes 4; Göttingen: Vandenhoeck & Ruprecht, 2013), 57–73.
Grillet, B. and M. Lestienne, *Le premier Livre des Règnes: Traduction du texte grec de la Septante* (*Bible d'Alexandrie 9.1; Paris: Cerf, 1997).
Herbert, E.D., "4QSam^a and its Relationship to the LXX: An Exploration in Stemmatological Analysis," in *IX Congress of the International Organization for Septuagint and Cognate Studies: Cambridge, 1995* (ed. B.A. Taylor; SBLSCS 45; Atlanta: Scholars Press, 1997), 37–55.

Hugo, P. and A. Schenker (eds.), *Archaeology of the Books of Samuel: The Entangling of the Textual and Literary History* (VTSup 132, Leiden: Brill, 2010).

Hugo, P., "Die Antiochenische Mischung: L zwischen Altem und Neuem in 2 Samuel," in *Der Antiochenische Text der Septuaginta in seiner Bezeugung und seiner Bedeutung* (eds. S. Kreuzer and M. Sigismund; De Septuaginta Investigationes 4; Göttingen: Vandenhoeck & Ruprecht, 2013), 109–32.

Kim, J.-H., *Die hebräischen und griechischen Textformen der Samuel- und Königebücher: Studien zur Textgeschichte ausgehend von 2 Sam 15–19,9* (BZAW 394, Berlin: de Gruyter, 2009).

Kim, J.-H., "Die Wiedergabe von עֶבֶד mit δοῦλος oder παῖς in der Septuaginta der Samuel- und Königebücher," in Karrer–Kraus, *Septuaginta 2010*, 358–70.

Kreuzer, S. and M. Sigismund (eds.), *Der Antiochenische Text der Septuaginta in seiner Bezeugung und seiner Bedeutung* (De Septuaginta Investigationes 4, Göttingen: Vandenhoeck & Ruprecht, 2013).

Kreuzer, S., "Der Antiochenische Text der Septuaginta: Forschungsgeschichte und eine neue Perspektive," in *Der Antiochenische Text der Septuaginta in seiner Bezeugung und seiner Bedeutung* (eds. S. Kreuzer and M. Sigismund; De Septuaginta Investigationes 4; Göttingen: Vandenhoeck & Ruprecht, 2013), 23–56.

Kreuzer, S., *The Bible in Greek: Translation, Transmission and Theology of the Septuagint* (SBLSCS 63, Atlanta: SBL, 2015).

Kreuzer, S., "Towards the Old Greek: New Criteria for the Analysis of the Recensions of the Septuagint," in Kreuzer, *The Bible in Greek*, 113–28.

Kreuzer, S., "Textformen und Bearbeitungen: Kriterien zur Frage der ältesten Textgestalt, insbesondere des Septuagintatextes, anhand von 2 Sam 12," in Kreuzer, *The Bible in Greek*, 129–53.

Kreuzer, S., "Translation and Recensions: Old Greek, Kaige, and Antiochene Text in Samuel and Reigns," in Kreuzer, *The Bible in Greek*, 154–74.

Kreuzer, S., "'Lukian redivivus'? Or Barthélemy and Beyond?" in Kreuzer, *The Bible in Greek*, 175–93.

Kreuzer, S., "Old Greek und Semi-Kaige: Zur Frage hebraisierender Bearbeitung in den Nicht-Kaige-Abschnitten der Samuel- und Königebücher," in Kreuzer, *The Bible in Greek*, 194–218.

Kreuzer, S., "Old Greek and Kaige and the *Trifaria Varietas*: A New Perspective on Jereome's Statement," in Kreuzer, *The Bible in Greek*, 219–30.

Kreuzer, S., "B or Not B? The Place of Codex Vaticanus in Textual History and in Septuagint Research," in Kreuzer, *The Bible in Greek*, 272–97.

McLean, P.D., "The *Kaige* Text of Reigns," in *NETS, 271–96.

Meiser, M., "Samuelseptuaginta und Targum Jonathan," in Karrer–Kraus, *Septuaginta 2008*, 323–35.

Meiser, M., S. Kreuzer, and F. Winter, "Basileion I–IV: Die Bücher der Königtümer: Einleitung," in *Septuaginta Deutsch, Erläuterungen*, 714–44.

Meiser, M. and S. Kreuzer, "Basileion I: Das erste Buch der Königtümer/Das erste Buch Samuel," in *Septuaginta Deutsch, Erläuterungen*, 745–807.

Meiser, M. and S. Kreuzer, "Basileion II: Das zweite Buch der Königtümer/Das zweite Buch Samuel," in *Septuaginta Deutsch, Erläuterungen*, 808–97.

Pisano, S., *Additions and Omissions in the Books of Samuel* (OBO 57; Göttingen: Vandenhoeck & Ruprecht 1984).

Rahlfs, A., *Lucians Rezension der Königsbücher* (Septuaginta-Studien 3; Göttingen: Vandenhoeck & Ruprecht, 1911 = 2nd ed.; Göttingen: Vandenhoeck & Ruprecht, 1965).

Saley, R., "Proto-Lucian and 4QSam^a," *BIOSCS* 41 (2008): 34–45.

Taylor, B., *The Lucianic Manuscripts of 1 Reigns*, Vol. 1: *Majority Text* (HSM 50, Atlanta: Scholars Press, 1992).

Taylor, B., *The Lucianic Manuscripts of 1 Reigns*, Vol. 2: *Analysis* (HSM 51, Atlanta: Scholars Press, 1993).

Taylor, B., "The Old Greek Text of Reigns," in *NETS, 244–70.

Tov, E., *The Hebrew and Greek Texts of Samuel: Proceedings of the IOSCS Conference Vienna 1980* (Jerusalem: Academon, 1980).

Tov, E., "The Composition of 1 Samuel 16–18 in the Light of the Septuagint," in Tov, *Greek-Hebrew Bible*, 333–62.

Tov, *TCHB.

Ulrich, E., *The Qumran Text of Samuel and Josephus* (HSM 19, Missoula: Scholars Press, 1978).

Siegfried Kreuzer

5.5 Septuagint (Kings)

5.5.1 Background

1–2 Kings is in many regards closely related to 1–2 Samuel (→ 5.4), which is also indicated by the fact that the Greek version of Samuel–Kings is designated as 1–4 Kingdoms (or: Reigns). Most probably the time of translation immediately followed the translation of Samuel, which was around 200 B.C.E. All units of 1–4 Kingdoms have similar features regarding Baal with the female article and ἀλλόφυλοι "those from other tribes" for the Philistines (→ 5.4.1.1). The different book division in the Antiochene text (→ 5.4.1.1) means that 1 Kings/3 Reigns begins with Solomon's activities as king.

There are also a number of other differences. Especially notable are a few in 1 Kings (→ 5.5.2.1): the sequence of 1 Kings 20 and 21, the place of the summaries about Solomon's reign, and description of the temple in 1 Kings 6–8.

5.5.2 Original Form, Date, Milieu, Editions

5.5.2.1 Original Form
As in Samuel (→ 5.4.1.2), there are two distinct forms of the Greek text of Codex Vaticanus. In this text, 1 Kings (section γγ) is close to the Old Greek, while 1 Kgs 1:1–2:11 (end of section βγ) and 1 Kings 22–2 Kings 25 (section γδ) represent the *kaige* text with its literalistic and isomorphic translation (→ 1.3.1.2). Again as in Samuel, the Antiochian text is the best representative of the Old Greek (→ 5.4.3), although not without mistakes and corruptions created in the course of its transmission.

However, especially in 1 Kings, the sequence of a number of passages differs from MT. This specific text form can be seen in LXX[B] and LXX[L] as well as in other manuscripts and therefore generally reflects the Old Greek. These differences concern especially the account of Solomon's activities. For example, Solomon gives priority to the temple, and its construction is finished before the construction of the palace (so also Josephus, *Ant.*); in 2 Chronicles 2, the palace is not mentioned at all. In 1 Kingdoms 8, the much-debated dedication of the temple (v. 12 MT) follows after Solomon's prayer (v. 53a LXX). The summaries of Solomon's activities are found at different places: MT-1 Kgs 9:15–25 and LXX-3 Kgdms 2:35a–o; 2:46a–l, and are not completely identical. There are differences between 1 Kgs 4:20–5:9 and 1 Kgs 11:1–8. 3 Kgdms 12:24a–z contains parallels to 1 Kgs 11:26–28, 40; 14:1–18; on the other hand, 1 Kgs 14:1–20 has no counterpart in the LXX tradition. 1 Kgdms 16:28a–h anticipates information from 1 Kgs 22:41–51. On the other hand, in 1 Kgs 6:11–14, 17b, 18, 21a, 22b–d, 37 f. and 1 Kgs 11:38b, 39 there are pluses in MT that have no counterpart in LXX.[1]

5.5.2.2 Date, Characteristic Features, and Milieu
5.5.2.2.1
For the question of date, one has to differentiate between the date of the Old Greek and the date of the *kaige* recension. As mentioned above, it is plausible that Kings was translated in close proximity to Samuel, i.e., around 200 B.C.E. Most probably the translation was made in Alexandria. One aspect that hints at a Greek-speaking milieu is the above-mentioned Baal equivalent, αἰσχύνη "shame," to avoid the name Baal (→ 5.4.4.1) (similarly, ἄλση "[sacred] groves" instead of Astarte). Interestingly, in 1 Kgs 18:19, αἰσχύνη is found in the text (not only in LXX[L], but also in LXX[B]). On the other hand, ἡ Βααλ "she-Baal" in 1 Kgs 19:18 is only preserved in LXX[L] (cf. Rom 11:4!), while elsewhere Baal has the masculine article, which shows that in Kings there had been more adaptation and cross influences from the *kaige* tradition upon the Antiochian manuscripts than in Samuel. While the Qumran texts of Kings are very fragmentary, VL (→ 3–5.2.1.2) confirms the early date of LXX[L].[2]

---

[1] For these differences, see Taylor, "Old Greek Text," 248, and especially Meiser, "Einleitung," 719–21 ("3.3 Differenzen in Umfang und Anordnung" [with bibliography]).

[2] See, e.g., the analysis of 2 Kgs 6:8–19 in Kreuzer, "Translation and Recensions," especially 44–49.

5.5.2.2.2

The date of the *kaige* recension is mainly determined by the Naḥal Ḥever scroll of the Minor Prophets (8ḤevXII gr), which is now dated paleographically to the first century B.C.E. (in general or its later half).[3] Most probably the reworking of the Latter and Former Prophets was done not too far apart, which means that also the *kaige* recension of Kings can be dated to the first century B.C.E. This recension probably was made in the land of Israel.[4] At least it was used there, as evidenced by the Naḥal Ḥever scroll. However, it cannot be excluded that some books may have been revised in the same direction in the Diaspora.

There is an interesting difference in the relationships to the Hebrew source texts: While in Samuel, the Antiochene/Old Greek text was based on a text similar to 4QSam^a (→ 5.3.1.2; → 5.3.3) and the *kaige* recension used a text close to MT (as presented by MT^L and MT^A), the situation in Kings is different. Here, the Antiochene/Old Greek text is closer to MT (except the passages with larger differences; → 5.5.2.1), while the *kaige* recension reflected a text more distant from MT.[5]

The *kaige* recension and its milieu can be characterized by a high esteem not only for the content but also for the form of the Hebrew text. This is expressed in the highly isomorphic rendering, visible not only in the adaptation to the word order of the Hebrew source text, but also in the addition or deletion of the article, based on the presence or absence of a Hebrew article or a similar graphem (especially the *nota accusativi*).[6] On the other hand, the Greek style of this recension became less elegant and understandable.[7] However, this strange style may have been considered "biblical."[8]

An example of the different translation techniques of the Old Greek and *kaige* can be seen in 2 Kgs 6:15: וַיַּשְׁכֵּם מְשָׁרֵת אִישׁ הָאֱלֹהִים לָקוּם is correctly translated in LXX^L/OG by καὶ ὤρθρισεν ὁ λειτουργὸς τοῦ ἀνθρώπου τοῦ θεοῦ ἀναστῆναι τὸ πρωΐ "And the servant of the man of God got up to rise early in the morning" with τὸ πρωΐ indicating the meaning of שׁכם Hiphil as "to rise early in the morning." This detail is taken up in VL (with adaptation to the Latin word order): *Et surrexit de luce minister Elissei hominis Dei* "And the servant of Elisha, the man of God, got up with raising daylight." However, τὸ πρωΐ is deleted in the *kaige* text (LXX^B), which reads only καὶ ὤρθρισεν ὁ λειτουργὸς Ελισαιε ἀναστῆναι "And the servant of Elisha got up to rise," because there is no visible counterpart for τὸ πρωΐ in Hebrew.[9]

This example shows also that the *kaige*[10] recension used a Hebrew text that at some points differed from MT because it gives the name of Elisha and not the title "man of God" (this variation occurs also elsewhere in the Elisha story). Interestingly, in this case, VL (i.e., manuscript VL^{115}) has both the name and the title, which probably means that it knew both the Old Greek and *kaige* (which would not be surprising in the second century C.E.).[11]

---

[3] See now P.J. Parsons, "The Scripts and Their Date," *DJD* VIII: 19–26.

[4] Cf. Barthélemy, *Devanciers*, who used the expression "recension palestinienne."

[5] This can be observed easily from the different numbers of "+" remarks and words in italics (indicating differences from MT) in the *Septuaginta Deutsch* translation. See also the example of 1 Kgs 22:36 in n. 7.

[6] For a full list and discussion of such expressions, see Meiser, "Übersetzungstechnik" in Meiser, *Einleitung*, 728–31.

[7] One of the typical examples of *kaige*, the change from ἕκαστος "each" to ἀνήρ "man" (cf. Barthélemy, *Devanciers*, 48–

54: "Élimination de 'chacun' "), is found in 1 Kgs 22:10; 2 Kgs 7:9; 18:31. ἀνήρ is an isomorphic rendering of אישׁ (both meaning "man"), at times resulting in a strange text, e.g., 1 Kgs 22:10: The king of Israel and the king of Judah were sitting אישׁ/ἀνήρ "a man" (instead of the original meaning "each one") on his throne. Interestingly, in 1 Kgs 22:36, ἕκαστος occurs also in LXX^B (as in the entire Greek tradition), deriving from the Old Greek, by way of cross influence from other manuscripts or as a correction to ordinary Greek. However, LXX^L has also a second ἕκαστος "each one" before εἰς τὴν ἑαυτοῦ γῆν "[... and] everyone to his own country." This is in agreement with MT, i.e., MT^L, while the simple אל/εἰς "to" is found in other medieval manuscripts (see *BHS*).

[8] Cf. the preference for the Aquila translation in the Jewish communities in Late Antiquity.

[9] For an analysis of the whole passage 2 Kgs 6:8–19, see Kreuzer, "Translation and Recensions."

[10] See also the example in n. 7 from 1 Kgs 22:36.

[11] With regard to the age of the text forms, VL has to be considered under two headings: On the one hand, it may confirm a reading as being old, i.e., pre-Lucianic and pre-Hexaplaric. On the other hand, as both the Old Greek and the

5.5.2.2.3

The text in the non-*kaige* sections of Codex Vaticanus has also undergone some form of a Hebraising redaction, especially in the adaptation of the word order to the Hebrew text and other isomorphic tendencies (e.g., the return to the masculine article for Baal in 1 Kgs 19:18). Due to its similarity to the *kaige* recension, this revision may be called semi-*kaige* (→ 5.4.3.6 and → 5.4.4.3).

5.5.2.3 Editions

In 2015, the Göttingen edition of Kings is in preparation (to be edited by Julio Trebolle Barrera and Pablo A. Torijano). The most copious edition so far is the large Cambridge edition by Brooke, McLean, and Thackeray,[12] which is a diplomatic edition of the Codex Vaticanus (LXX^B) with a wealth of Greek manuscripts, Greek quotations, and other manuscripts referred to in the apparatus. Rahlfs, *Septuaginta* as well as Rahlfs–Hanhart, *Septuaginta* usually follow LXX^B (Codex Sinaiticus is not extant for Kings) with additions and corrections from LXX^A, the Hexaplaric text, and also from the Lucianic text.

The Madrid edition of 1–2 Kings of the Antiochene text by Fernandez Marcos, Busto Saiz, and Spottorno[13] is a critical edition that, in addition to the manuscripts, also quotes the text from Theodoret and other sources, and refers in a second apparatus to VL and other relevant quotations (→ 5.4.2). Since Qumran fragments of Kings are scarce, the VL texts and quotations from Josephus and other authors are especially relevant.[14]

5.5.3 History of Research

For the history of research, see the closely related analysis of Samuel (→ 5.4.3). It may be noted that Rahlfs' investigation of the Antiochene text from 1911[15] was based on Kings, especially 1 Kings 1. Barthélemy's[16] identification of the *kaige* recension, his identification of the Antiochene text as the Old Greek, and his abandonment of a Lucianic redaction, as well as Kreuzer's[17] new approach are applicable to the books of Kings as well as Samuel.

A new line of research was initiated by Schenker. In his analyses, especially of 1 Kings, he found that in many cases the Old Greek presents an earlier, pre-Masoretic stage of the text.[18] In his view, MT is a reworked text. This "literary" production improves especially the image of Jerusalem by removing illegitimate altars from that city in the wake of the Maccabean Revolt and the Maccabean/Hasmonean establishment in Jerusalem in the second half of the second century B.C.E. In spite of opposition by Turkanik,[19] much of Schenker's view seems convincing. However, this issue needs to be separated from the large-scale differences between MT and LXX (→ 5.5.2.1).

5.5.4 Relevance for Textual History and Exegesis

The identification of the Antiochene text as "more or less reflecting the Old Greek" is important for describing OG-Kgs and its translation technique. However, in Kings, the transmission of the text has suffered more corruptions and changes than in Samuel. This also holds true for the non-*kaige* sections in the Codex Vaticanus.

OG-1–2 Kgs presents a careful translation into Greek that at the same time is understandable and acceptable. The closeness of the Old Greek to its Hebrew parent text leads to the assumption that

---

kaige text existed at the time, VL may represent one text form without ruling out the existence of the other one. The same aspects have to be considered when evaluating the quotations in the New Testament and in Josephus.

[12] Brooke–McLean–Thackeray, *The Old Testament in Greek*.

[13] Fernández Marcos and Busto Saiz, *El texto antioqueno de la Biblia griega*.

[14] For an evaluation of these sources, see the introduction of Fernández Marcos and Busto Saiz, *El texto antioqueno*, xxix–lix: "Los testimonios indirectos."

[15] Rahlfs, *Lucians Rezension der Königsbücher*.

[16] Barthélemy, *Devanciers*.

[17] Kreuzer, *The Bible in Greek*, 154–74, 194–218, 272–97.

[18] Schenker, *Septante et texte massorétique*; Schenker, *Älteste Textgeschichte der Königsbücher*.

[19] Turkanik, *Of Kings and Reigns*.

the larger differences in the stories concerning the building of the temple and the separation of Israel and Judah denote the presence of a Hebrew *Vorlage* that differed from MT (→ 5.3.2). In many cases, this *Vorlage* seems to be older than MT and apparently was reworked in MT. The *Vorlage* of the Septuagint or the revision by the translators reflects major changes, especially in the larger differences concerning the building and dedication of the temple and the separation of the Solomonic kingdom.[20] This means that the Old Greek reflects traditions that are older than the (proto-)MT text and also later revisions by the translators.[21]

The *kaige* recension (→ 1.3.1.2) seems to be based on a text that is slightly different from MT. It represents not just a Hebraising revision in general, but shows an isomorphic adaptation that is an expression of the high value placed not only on the content but also on the form and nature of the Hebrew reference text.

The different text forms of Kings show the pluriformity of the Hebrew text in early times and a special interest in Solomon and the temple. They also show how the text could – and should – be understood.

Barthélemy, *Devanciers*.
Bösenecker, J., "Basileion III: Das dritte Buch der Königtümer/Das erste Buch der Könige," in *Septuaginta Deutsch, Erläuterungen*, 898–945.
Fernández Marcos, N., *Scribes and Translators: Septuagint and Old Latin in the Books of Kings* (VTS 54; Leiden: Brill, 1994).
Fernández Marcos, N. and J.R. Busto Saiz, *El texto antioqueno de la Biblia griega*, Vol. 2: *1–2 Reyes* (Textos y estudios "Cardenal Cisneros" 53; Madrid: CSIC, 1992).
Kreuzer, S., *The Bible in Greek: Translation, Transmission and Theology of the Septuagint* (SBLSCS 63; Atlanta: SBL, 2015), 154–74, 194–218, 272–97.
Kreuzer, S. and M. Sigismund (eds.), *Der Antiochenische Text der Septuaginta in seiner Bezeugung und seiner Bedeutung* (De Septuaginta Investigationes 4; Göttingen: Vandenhoeck & Ruprecht, 2013).

McLean, P.D., "The Kaige Text of Reigns," in *NETS (Oxford: Oxford University Press, 2007), 271–76, 318–41.
Meiser, M., S. Kreuzer, and F. Winter, "Basileion I–IV. Einleitung," in *Septuaginta Deutsch, Erläuterungen*, 714–44.
Rahlfs, A., *Lucians Rezension der Königsbücher* (Septuaginta-Studien 3; Göttingen: Vandenhoeck & Ruprecht, 1911 = 2nd ed. Göttingen: Vandenhoeck & Ruprecht, 1965).
Schenker, A., *Septante et texte massorétique dans l'histoire la plus ancienne du texte de 1 Rois 2–14* (CahRB 48; Paris: Gabalda, 2000).
Schenker, A., *Älteste Textgeschichte der Königsbücher: Die hebräische Vorlage der ursprünglichen Septuaginta als älteste Textform der Königsbücher* (OBO 199; Göttingen: Vandenhoeck & Ruprecht, 2004).
Talshir, Z., *The Alternative Story (3 Kgdms 12:24a–z)* (JBS 6; Jerusalem: Simor, 1993).
Talshir, Z., "1 Kings and 3 Kingdoms – Origin and Revision Case Study: The Sins of Solomon (1 Kgs 11)," *Textus* 21 (2002): 71–105.
Taylor, B., "The Old Greek Text of Reigns," *NETS, 244–48, 297–318.
Thackeray, H.St.-J., "The Greek Translators of the Four Books of Kings," *JTS* 8 (1907): 262–66.
Thackeray, H.St.-J., *The Septuagint and Jewish Worship* (Schweich Lectures; Oxford: Oxford University Press, 1921).
Tov, E., "The LXX Additions (Miscellanies) in 1 Kings 2 (3 Reigns 2)," *Textus* 11 (1984): 89–118; repr. Tov, *Greek-Hebrew Bible*, 549–70.
Tov, E., "Three Strange Books of the LXX: 1 Kings, Esther, and Daniel Compared with Similar Rewritten Compositions from Qumran and Elsewhere," in Tov, *HB, GB and Qumran*, 283–305.
Trebolle Barrera, J., "From the 'Old Latin' through the 'Old Greek' to the 'Old Hebrew' (2 Kings 10:23–35)," *Textus* 11 (1984): 17–36.
Trebolle Barrera, J., "Old Latin, Old Greek and Old Hebrew in the Books of Kings (1 Ki 18:27 and 2 Ki 20:11)," *Textus* 13 (1986): 85–95.
Turkanik, A.S., "Of Kings and Reigns: A Study of Translation Technique in the Gamma/Gamma Section of 3 Reigns (1 Kings)" (PhD diss., Cambridge University, 2002; published under the same title as FAT 2.30; Tübingen: Mohr, 2008).
Werlitz, J. (– S. Kreuzer), "Basileion IV: Das vierte Buch der Königtümer/Das zweite Buch der Könige: Nach dem antiochenischen Text," in *Septuaginta Deutsch, Erläuterungen*, 946–77.

---

[20] This question is debated. Some authors relate the changes, or at least some of them, to the translator(s).

[21] Thus, also Tov, "Three Strange Books of the LXX," 283–305.

Winter, F., "Basileion IV: Das vierte Buch der Königtümer/Das zweite Buch der Könige: Nach dem Text der Handausgabe von Rahlfs," in *Septuaginta Deutsch, Erläuterungen*, 978–1037.

Siegfried Kreuzer

3–5.1 Primary Translations

3–5.1.1 Septuagint

The Former Prophets (the historical books Joshua to 2 Kings) and the Latter Prophets (Isaiah, Jeremiah, Ezekiel, and the twelve Minor Prophets) together form the second subdivision of the Hebrew Canon (→ 1.1.2.1), after the Torah and before the Writings (Ketuvim). The contents and names of the second and third divisions are somewhat problematic: not all the books included in the "Prophets" pertain to prophets and the relation between the two divisions is loose. More specifically, the Former Prophets do not tell the story of biblical prophets, although several prophets are mentioned in Samuel and Kings, and the Latter Prophets do not include all the biblical Prophets (Daniel is found among the Writings). Nevertheless, the second segment of the Hebrew canon, representing the second stage in the acceptance of ancient Hebrew writings, is named Nevi'im (Prophets), probably because no better name and no better division presented itself. The distinction between the "Prophets" and "Writings" is probably mainly chronological (two stages in the acceptance of authoritative books after the canonization of the Torah), although in several cases this criterion cannot be maintained. The two divisions also differ in their literary genres (historical and prophetical books in the Prophets as opposed to a mixture of literary genres in the Writings), but the Writings also include a prophetical book (Daniel) as well as historical books (Ezra–Nehemiah and Chronicles).

The organizing principle of Jewish Greek Scripture (not necessarily Alexandrian; → 1.1.2.1) differs from that of the Hebrew canon. It may be considered an improvement of the Hebrew arrangement, which could be achieved because the former was organized at a later stage than the Hebrew canon and could therefore be rearranged solely by literary genre and not by a mixture of criteria as in the Hebrew canon. The details of the arrangement of LXX are presented in the overview article (→ 1.3.1.1.4). The Christian canon follows that of LXX (→ 1.1.2.2). Accordingly, in the Christian organization of the canon, Joshua, Judges, Ruth, Samuel, Kings, Chronicles, Ezra, Nehemiah, and Esther are all classified as historical books. Note that Ruth, Chronicles, Ezra, Nehemiah, and Esther are not included among the Former Prophets in the Hebrew canon.

The books of the Hebrew Former Prophets are thus classified in LXX as historical books; they include additional (apocryphal) historical books, and they even include a book from among the Hebrew Writings, Ruth, as the story told in this book took place "in the days when the judges ruled" (Ruth 1:1). This book is thus reclassified in the Greek canon as a historical book.

The books of the Former Prophets have much in common in the Hebrew canon, but not in their Greek counterpart. Joshua (→ 3.3) and Judges (→ 4.3) were produced by different translators who did not have much in common, and the books of 1–4 Kingdoms (1–2 Samuel and 1–2 Kings in Hebrew) were produced by different translators yet again. Furthermore, in the Greek Kingdoms, segments of the Old Greek translation are juxtaposed with later revisions (→ 5.4).

Emanuel Tov

3–5.1.2 Pre-Hexaplaric Greek Translations

3–5.1.2.1 Joshua-Judges
See → 2.4.6 (Hexaplaric Translations and Hexapla of the Octateuch).

3–5.1.2.2 Samuel-Kings
See → 3–5.1.5.2 (Hexaplaric Greek Translations and the Hexapla: Samuel–Kings).

3–5.1.3 Targum

Targum Jonathan is the Jewish Aramaic Bible translation of the Prophets according to the Jewish canon, comprising the Former Prophets (Joshua,

Judges, Samuel, and Kings) as well as the Latter Prophets (see below → 6–9.1.3).[1]

3–5.1.3.1 Date and Provenance

Targum Jonathan receives its name after the legend of its composition by Jonathan ben Uzziel, who is hailed as the most outstanding student of Hillel (*y. Ned.* 5:6, 39b; *b. Sukkah* 28a; *b. B. Bat.* 133a–134b). Yet he is only named as the translator of the Prophets in a single, non-contemporary source (*b. Meg.* 3a), in a legend, moreover, which may well be an adaptation of a story about the *Greek* translation by Theodotion (→ 1.3.1.2).[2] The translation known by his name became the "counterpart" of Targum Onqelos – also only known by that name from *b. Meg.* 3a – in dialect, style of translation, and status as the approved version of the Babylonian Geonic academies (notwithstanding some differences in each of these aspects), a status that would seem to hark back to Amoraic days. There is little doubt that Targum Jonathan existed at the time classical rabbinic literature took shape. Similarities of exegesis between Targum Jonathan and that literature abound, albeit unevenly.[3] However, explicit citations of Targum Jonathan in rabbinic literature are sparse.[4]

As with Targum Onqelos, the locale of its origin and the date of its dialect have been hotly disputed. An Eastern, a Western, and a Central (Syrian?) origin have been championed in a debate that began in the nineteenth century,[5] while others argued that the dialect does not reveal much of a geographic origin,[6] as it belongs to a supralocal, literary Aramaic dialect (Greenfield; Tal).[7] Recent syntactic research suggests that the dialect reflects a twofold setting: one of Middle Aramaic outside Babylonia (presumably Roman Palestine) and the other of Late Aramaic in Babylonia.[8] This analysis agrees with the long-held notion that the "Babylonian" Targumim – Onqelos and Jonathan – originated in Palestine sometime before the Bar Kokhba Revolt in the second century C.E., but were transported to the East afterwards (Kutscher; following Nöldeke's suggestion of a Palestinian *Grundlage* and Babylonian redaction),[9] where they were edited during the Amoraic period (third to fifth centuries C.E.). More research into the diachronical aspects of Targum Jonathan's dialect is highly desirable.

The long redaction history of Targum Jonathan inevitably has far-ranging ramifications for our projections about the Hebrew source text reflected through the prism of translation.

3–5.1.3.2 Translation Character

Targum Jonathan Former Prophets shares its distinctive character by and large with Targum Onqelos and Targum Jonathan Latter Prophets, with a high level of coherence between the various biblical books in translation strategies and structure, exegetical emphasis, and outlook on life (see → 2.4.3.3 on Onqelos and → 6–9.1.3 on Targum Jonathan Latter Prophets). As regards textual criticism, the appreciation of the Targum's character of translation is indispensable. The character of Targum Jonathan follows from its translation strategies,[10]

---

[1] The sigla for the manuscripts that contain Targum follow the "Standard List of Sigla for Targum Manuscripts," developed by E. van Staalduine-Sulman in 2011, as adopted by the International Organization for Targumic and Cognate Studies at its International Meeting in Munich 2013, with minor modifications which have been incorporated in the revised version of March 2014. The list is available at http://www.targum.nl.

[2] So already Geiger, *Urschrift*, 163, 167; see further Smelik, *Rabbis, Language and Translation*, 490, 496, 499.

[3] R. Tomes has argued that Tj-Jer does not exhibit signs of similarity with rabbinic exegesis; cf. R. Tomes, "The Reception of Jeremiah in Rabbinic Literature and in the Targum," in *The Book of Jeremiah and Its Reception/Le Livre de Jérémie et sa réception* (eds. A.H.W. Curtis and T. Römer; BETL 128; Leuven: Leuven University Press, 1997), 233–53.

[4] Smelik, *Rabbis, Language and Translation*.

[5] Amongst others, Luzzatto, *Elementi Grammaticali*; Geiger,

Urschrift, 165; T. Nöldeke, *Mandäische Grammatik* (Halle: Buchhandlung des Waisenhauses, 1875), xxvii n. 1.

[6] M.H. Goshen-Gottstein, "The Language of Targum Onqelos and the Model of Literary Diglossia in Aramaic," *JNES* 37 (1978): 169–79.

[7] Greenfield, "Standard Literary Aramaic"; Tal, לשון התרגום.

[8] R.J. Kuty, *Studies in the Syntax of Targum Jonathan to Samuel* (ANES 30; Leuven: Peeters, 2010).

[9] E.Y. Kutscher, "The Language of the 'Genesis Apocryphon': A Preliminary Study," *ScrHie* 4 (1958): 1–35 (9–11); Nöldeke, *Mandäische Grammatik*, xxvii n. 1.

[10] The term "translation strategy" (see König, "Holmes' 'Mapping Theory'") is preferable to "translation technique,"

which are important both for understanding Targum Jonathan as a source in its own right and for evaluating possible Hebrew variant readings. These strategies interfere with any straightforward reconstruction of the Hebrew text.

On the whole, Targum Jonathan aims at representing every single lexeme of its Hebrew source text within its original word order, as if aspiring after a one-to-one representation throughout most of its text, notwithstanding explanatory pluses. Vis-à-vis the Hebrew, neither transposition of equivalent lexemes nor minuses are typical for Targum Jonathan, with the result that its interdependence on the Hebrew source text is manifest throughout. Even in the face of interpretative elements that found their way into the translation, which presents itself in subtle substitutions for or interpretative supplements to the Hebrew base text, Targum Jonathan relates in a highly transparent way to the original text. Yet these latter elements reveal the marked expository streak of Targum Jonathan, though it often may come across as a "literal" translation.[11] On rare occasions, the transparency of relation between source and target text is dissolved in a richness of interpretative elements, which establish a new narrative through clauses without a corresponding basis in the Hebrew text, though even such clauses are still latched on to ones that have an equivalent in the Hebrew.[12] Examples of such narratives occur in the songs of Deborah (Judges 5), Hannah (1 Sam 2:1–10), and David (2 Samuel 22).

What stands out is how terse the translation remains whilst enriching the original text with interpretative new information that redirects the original text's meaning. From the way the translation as a target text relates to its source text, it follows that the translators strive to fulfil two objectives: to represent the Hebrew source text in the minutest of details and to "recapture" the meaning of the original in a new textual frame, which diverts the message into new directions, and which reflects the knowledge, concerns, and the intellectual and religious horizon of the translators. Neither objective is unique, unlike the balance that exists between them.

Entire debates may lurk behind subtle variations of translation, which display both aspects of Targum Jonathan's character. In Judges 17–18, the Hebrew words תרפים "household gods" and כהן "priest" received a conspicuous treatment. Only here the word תרפים is rendered with the neutral term דמאין "figures," while elsewhere the standard equivalent is צלמניא "idols."[13] This exception is tied in with the literal representation of כהן by כהנא ("the priest") throughout these chapters, except for the Danite priests of Judg 18:30, which are called כומרא "idolatrous priests." Clearly, then, the translation does not repudiate the other priests for their behavior, though flying in the face of the Halakha, except for some Western manuscripts of Targum Jonathan, which substitute צלמניא "idols" for דמאין "figures" and כומרא "idolatrous priests" for כהנא "the priest" and thereby give expression to a more condemnatory view.[14]

A similar tip of the iceberg concerns the translation of גם שמים נטפו "even the heavens dripped" in Judg 5:4, which has become אף שמיא מכו "even the mountains bowed down." In terms of word order and narrative, it is perfectly clear that מכו "bowed down" substitutes for נטפו "dripped," but the reason for the semantic substitution is not included or made explicit in the translation; that is not what translations do. The substitution is reflected, how-

---

as the phenomena described are rarely mere techniques, and there often is a lack of distinction between the exegetical *method*, the *result* of the exegetical operation, and the *reason* for exegesis in the source text or the mind of the exegete.

[11] Frequently, Targum Jonathan uses an Aramaic lexeme with an entirely different meaning than its Hebrew equivalent, and only the word order indicates that the Aramaic is in fact intended as the equivalent of the Hebrew.

[12] See also point 6.13 in P.S. Alexander et al., "Inventory of Structurally Important Literary Features in the Anonymous and Pseudepigraphic Jewish Literature of Antiquity," *Aramaic Studies* 9 (2011): 227–28.

[13] For the former, see TJ-Judg 17:5; 18:14, 17, 18, and 20. For the latter, see TJ-1 Sam 19:13, 16; TJ-2 Kgs 23:24; TJ-Zech 10:2. Note the alternative equivalent טעותא "idols" in TJ-1 Sam 15:23, where the translation of the lexeme has been brought into play with a larger theme.

[14] Though only manuscript t6 does so consistently. See Smelik, *Targum of Judges*, 594–96.

ever, in a midrashic discussion of the contradiction between Exod 19:20 and 20:19, since God descended on Mt. Sinai according to the former, but spoke with Moses from heaven according to the latter. Assuming that the heavens were lowered unto the summit of Mt. Sinai, these verses are no longer in disagreement with each other.[15]

Thus, it is entirely natural for the translation to adapt more systematically utterances about God to something that can appropriately be said about the God of Israel. He does not go out on a campaign from Seir or march from the fields of Edom, but reveals himself and appears to his people in his Glory (Judg 5:4; cf. Hab 3:3). That said, Targum Jonathan certainly does not adapt the source text to contemporary beliefs by default. The legitimacy of the marriages of King David on the basis of 1 Sam 18:19 is neither raised nor implied by Targum Jonathan. Neither does Targum Jonathan exonerate what would have constituted Halakhic transgressions in the source text (as in numerous cases with Gideon). The translation tends to display a remarkable constraint unless a textual difficulty or marked use of words triggers additional action. Where Targum Jonathan adds its own voice, that voice is inevitably rooted in the world of the translators, but the translation is first and foremost grounded in its focus on the original text (→ 6–9.1.3.4). Even so, the sacrifice of Jephta's daughter, and the inadmissibility of Jephta's vow stood out so starkly that they elicited further comments.

The scope of the translation remains elusive. The bilingual recitation of the prophetic portions in the liturgy (and of Targum Jonathan's cousin, Targum Onqelos, as a whole) is one factor for Targum Jonathan's character, but since it remains fairly consistent throughout the entire Prophets, including those parts that were not recited in the synagogue, the liturgical context cannot be the only reason for Targum Jonathan's remarkable ability to serve as a linguistic and interpretative frame of reference to the Hebrew source text.

3–5.1.3.3 Translation Strategies

Major and minor translation strategies may be identified, of which only a few can possibly be discussed here (many examples given for the Latter Prophets [→ 6–9.1.3] apply to the Former Prophets as well). Several strategies center on the coherence of the text, which has frequently been increased in Targum Jonathan's translation.

At one level, coherence is brought about by "modern" refinements and highlights, such as the ubiquitous reference to keeping the Torah, which the translation introduces at many places, or the distinctions between God and idols (where the Hebrew frequently has a single term[16]), altars and idolatrous altars,[17] priests and idol priests,[18] figures and household gods (see above → 3–5.1.3.2), or angels and messengers.[19] Another strategy involves simplification and standardization: the use of a single Aramaic equivalent for a variety of Hebrew expressions – a type of parallelizing – or the introduction of stock phrases in pluses. Illustrative of the deliberate and interpretative simplification strategy is the use of the reflexive verb אתגלי "be revealed" in the context of a theophany, regardless of the Hebrew verbs used (see, e.g., Judg 5:4).[20] The effect is an increase of the exegetical cohesion of the translation: in Targum Jonathan, any biblical theophany is related to the revelation and gift of the Torah at Mt. Sinai. More strategies could have been listed here.

At a more particular level, coherence may be a by-product of the desire to bring about a transpar-

---

[15] See, e.g., *Mek.* בחודש 4.

[16] For examples, see Smelik, *Targum of Judges*, 318–21.

[17] As in TJ-Judg 2:2; 6:25, 28, 30, 31, 32; 1 Kgs 12:32, 33 (2×); 13:1, 2, 4, 32; 16:32; 18:26; 2 Kgs 11:18 (2×); 18:22; 21.3, 4, 5; 23:12 (2×), 15 (2×), 16, 17, 20; 23:12 (2×). See Churgin, *Targum Jonathan to the Prophets*, 113; L. Smolar and M. Aberbach, *Studies in Targum Jonathan to the Prophets* (New York: Ktav, 1983), 38–39.

[18] The translation כמרא "idol priest" occurs in Judg 18:30; 1 Sam 5:5; 1 Kgs 12:31, 32; 13:2, 33 (2×); 2 Kgs 10:19; 11:18; 17:32; 23:8 (2×), 9, 20. In addition, the translation is found in the variant readings of the following verses: Judg 17:5, 10, 12, 13; 18:3, 4, 6, 17, 18, 19 (3×), 20, 24, 27; 1 Sam 6:2.

[19] For further details, see Smelik, *Targum of Judges*, 349–52.

[20] See A. Chester, *Divine Revelation and Divine Titles in the Pentateuchal Targumim* (TSAJ 14; Tübingen: J.C.B. Mohr (Paul Siebeck), 1986).

ent text. In the "associative translation," two distinct passages with similar expressions (or a certain topical likeness) are identically rendered in the Aramaic, which is based on *one* of the passages. Where Deborah is said to have resided under "Deborah's Palm," Targum Jonathan elaborates and offers several comments, identifying some of her possessions as located in Jericho, which is known to have been the City of Palms (Deut 34:3; cf. TJ-Judg 4:5). In the closely related "complementary translation," a translation of two passages reflects the wording of *both* original passages (→ 6–9.1.3.4). A third strategy is to resolve any apparent contradiction between two or more biblical passages, which may be achieved in different ways, one of which was noted above as regards the lowering of the heavens in Judg 5:4. Some of these strategies involve the coherence between distinct parts of Scripture, others focus on issues at microlevel. Many small grammatical adjustments in Targum Jonathan reflect the aim to project a clear and transparent text, which may involve adjustment of number, conjunctions, copulatives, and prepositions.

A prime example of the concern to make the meaning of the original text more transparent is the way metaphors are dealt with. A frequent strategy is to substitute the (supposed) meaning of a metaphor for the metaphor itself. These realistic substitutions of metaphors occur throughout the translation, although this is certainly not the only way metaphors are translated. Among the other methods of translating metaphors, mention must be made of the "extended simile," which retains the metaphor as a simile, but has it glossed with an explanation in real terms (*tertium comparationis*). In the translation of Jer 15:7, ואזרם במזרה בשערי הארץ "I have winnowed them with a pitchfork through the gates of the earth," the metaphor is changed into a simile but also explained by a realistic substitution: וכמא דדרן במדריא כין בדרית ית עמי בקרוי ארעא "and as they winnow with a pitchfork, so have I scattered my people through the cities of the earth" (→ 6–9.1.3.4).

The awe of God and the proper way for humans to address or describe God are another focal point of targumic translation strategies. Anthropomorphic descriptions of God are often translated into religiously acceptable phrases by use of certain stock phrases, which simultaneously explain God's actions and express a deep reverence for God (→ 6–9.1.3.4). It is unlikely that the avoidance of anthropomorphisms was motivated by any doctrinal concern, because the avoidance is inconsistent and some modes of avoidance are also utilized when human beings are the subject (Judg 2:3: לא אתריך יתהון מן קדמיכון "I will not expel them because of you").

Several translations may be the result of more than a single strategy, as is to be expected in any model of translation strategies. The translation of Judg 5:31 in Targum Jonathan, for instance, exhibits both the method of "extended simile" (figure and matter are retained in the translation) and that of the "complementary translation" with TJ-2 Sam 23:4 and TJ-Isa 30:26. Others may contain a double translation, in which a single Hebrew word or phrase is translated twice (or even three times).

3–5.1.3.4 Reconstruction of the Hebrew Parent Text(s)

Broadly speaking, Targum Jonathan reflects a text type that conforms to the (proto-)Masoretic text (→ 3.2.2; → 4.2.2; → 5.3.2), with some qualifications about the text it represents in translation. It is generally accepted that Targum Jonathan tends to follow the *Qere* of the Hebrew source text, which demonstrates the antiquity of the latter readings, whether in oral or written form (→ 6–9.1.3.4). Some even argued that Targum Jonathan tends to agree with the *Eastern* readings of *Ketiv-Qere*, which featured in the debate over the origin of the Targum, but the evidence cited by Pinsker, Komlosh, and Gordis[21] does not stand up to closer scrutiny.[22]

---

[21] S. Pinsker, *Einleitung in das Babylonisch-Hebräische Punktationssystem* (Vienna: Phillip Bendiner, 1863), 124; Y. Komlosh, "תרגום ירמיהו," in *Bar-Ilan* 7–8 (1969): 38–48, 42 [Hebr.]; Y. Komlosh, המקרא באור התרגום (Tel Aviv: Dvir, 1973), 408–09 [Hebr.]; Gordis, *Biblical Text*, 74–75.

[22] W.F. Smelik, "Targum & Masora: Does Targum Jonathan Follow the 'Madinhae' Readings of *Ketiv-Qere*?" in *The Text of*

Important for the assumption of a Hebrew parent text is the predominant bilingual transmission of the Targum to the Prophets (and its cousin, Targum Onqelos), which involved, especially in the earliest manuscripts, a transmission of the Hebrew source text and its Aramaic translation alternating by the single verse.[23] That such a transmission may have profound implications for the Aramaic text has been demonstrated in a study of a manuscript that sports some unique, but medieval, Hebrew variant readings that are reflected in likewise unique Aramaic readings.[24] A good example is found in Judg 3:28, where the Hebrew verse of t725a reads וירדפו "they pursued" rather than MT וַיֵּרְדוּ "and they went down," which its Aramaic text reflects in the translation ורדפו "they pursued" instead of the usual ונחתו "and they went down." The variant clearly originates in the Hebrew source text, where the difference consists of a single letter but, more interestingly, at some point in the transmission of Targum Jonathan its wording was adjusted to the coexisting Hebrew text. In Judg 3:29, t725a reads ביומא ההוא "on that day" rather than the usual בעדנא ההיא "at that time," corresponding to the variant ביום ההוא "on that day" for MT בָּעֵת הַהִיא "at that time" in the preceding Hebrew verse;[25] the vocalizer, however, marked this reading as an error and replaced both the Hebrew and Aramaic variant with the "common" reading. The usual text of Targum Jonathan therefore appears to have been changed twice: first to reflect the Hebrew variant in one of the exemplars of its textual history, then by a vocalizer who spotted the difference with the regular text of MT and Targum Jonathan.

The bilingual transmission of the Targum, perhaps especially in the format of alternating Hebrew and Aramaic verses (and less so in alternative formats, although that remains to be proven), facilitated adaptation of the Aramaic to the Hebrew. In addition to the bilingual transmission of the text and its translation, it could be argued that the translation stood under continuing influence of the Hebrew source text in the form of distinct Hebrew manuscripts. The long period of redaction also allows for a long period of comparison between the two sources, especially in the learned milieu of the rabbis who mastered both languages. Indeed, rabbinic literature refers to corrections of the oral-performative translation of Hebrew into Aramaic, which may be extrapolated into an attitude towards the *established* translations. The Masorah to Targum Onqelos reveals a meticulous concern about the choice of translational equivalents[26] that is cognate with the corrective attitude, which is relevant here, too, even though no Masorah for Targum Jonathan appears to have existed, perhaps because the Geonim were less concerned with Targum Jonathan's text than with that of Targum Onqelos.[27] The ongoing correlation of the Hebrew and Aramaic text implies that Targum Jonathan does not project a single Hebrew manuscript. In addition, certain readings may well reflect medieval Hebrew variants that should not be mistaken for ancient readings in Targum Jonathan.

3-5.1.3.5 Text-Critical Value

By and large, Targum Jonathan sides with MT and its main contribution is indeed to confirm the latter. Wherever it does not, the method of translation in Targum Jonathan goes a long way to explain the vast majority of divergencies between the Hebrew source and Aramaic target text (→ 6–9.1.3.5).

---

the Hebrew Bible: From the Rabbis to Masoretes (eds. L. Miralles-Maciá and E. Martín Contreras; Journal of Ancient Judaism Supplements 13; Göttingen: Vandenhoeck & Ruprecht, 2014), 175–90.

[23] For alternation by three verses in the opening three verses of liturgical portions of the Prophets, see W.F. Smelik, "Orality, the Targums, and Manuscript Reproduction," in *Paratext and Megatext as Channels of Jewish and Christian Traditions: Textual Markers of Contextualization* (eds. A. den Hollander, U. Schmid, and W.F. Smelik; Jewish and Christian Perspectives 6; Leiden: Brill, 2003), 49–81 and Smelik, *Rabbis, Language and Translation*, 184–85.

[24] Smelik, "Orality, the Targums, and Manuscript Reproduction."

[25] The Hebrew–Aramaic equivalence is highly consistent; apart from Judg 3:29 according to t725a, the translation of בעת ההיא with ביום ההוא only occurs in 2 Kgs 8:22 according to t716y.

[26] M.L. Klein, *The Masorah to Targum Onqelos* (Binghamtom: Global Publications, 2000).

[27] Smelik, *Rabbis, Language and Translation*, 493.

Sperber argued that divergencies arising for translational, literary, and religious reasons should not be mistaken for reflections of Hebrew variant readings.[28] That said, many differences between MT and Targum Jonathan defy any straightforward judgment call, because the nature of the evidence is too ambiguous, but also because such variations might in fact have occurred in the Hebrew textual tradition itself, as many Hebrew medieval variants without roots in Late Antiquity would seem to attest. Indeed, the very nature of the resemblance between translational smoothing and scribal perfection blurs the distinction between source and target texts.

In the final, posthumously published, volume of *The Bible in Aramaic*, Sperber observes: "[w]herever the context demands it, the Targum adds the necessary particles [...] and prepositions [...]."[29] Such differences sometimes follow from the difference between Classical Hebrew and Middle Aramaic: wherever the former has an accusative for direction, the latter tends to use a preposition (ב or ל).[30] Here as elsewhere, Targum Jonathan, the other *versions* and some medieval Hebrew manuscripts smooth out irregularities and bring the textual flow to "modern" standards. Likewise, small pluses in the form of the object marker ית, or בית "house," or כל "all," cannot be relied upon as genuine *Hebrew* variant readings. Sperber continues to point to adjustments of the *numerus*, especially where MT has a singular for a plural subject. It is indeed an established translation strategy to avoid disparity in number,[31] but one that is applied inconsistently,[32] so that divergencies between MT and Targum Jonathan cannot be taken to reflect a *Hebrew* variant reading without further support.

All the same, there are occassional readings that are important for the way the translator read the Hebrew source text. In Judg 5:13, Targum Jonathan's נחית "went down" supports the vocalization of MT יָרַד "went down" as the perfect of the root ירד "to go down," with LXX[B] and Peshitta,[33] rather than the root רדה "to rule (over)" as suggested by the Masoretic vowels. Attention should also be given to a phenomenon of agreement that is usually overlooked in textual criticism. There are agreements between Targum Jonathan and the Masoretic accents, which are all the more remarkable where they go against the natural flow of the Hebrew text. In two instances in Judges 5, 5:13 and 5:20, the internal verse demarcation of the Masoretic accents is highly peculiar. However, Targum Jonathan not only agrees with the demarcation, its interpretation also explains why and suggests a complex relationship between Targum Jonathan and the Masoretes.

While occasional agreements with other ancient translations exist, there is no conspicuous literary relationship between Targum Jonathan and any of these documents other than the exegesis they shared as their cultural heritage or polygenesis of variant readings. But a comparison is still useful for another reason. Scholars who are focused on either the Targum or LXX alone may easily fall into the trap of overestimating the text-critical testimony of their object of study (→ 6–9.1.3.5). At times, the various testimonies can serve as accumulative testimony, as in Judg 4:12, where Targum Jonathan renders MT הַר־תָּבוֹר "Mount Tabor" with לטור תבור "to Mount Tabor," in agreement with Peshitta and LXX[B], while the other branches of LXX and some medieval Hebrew manuscripts support בהר תבור "on Mount Tabor" instead, hinting at the original absence of the preposition in the Hebrew *Vorlage*.

---

[28] Sperber, *Bible in Aramaic*, 4b.37–192; note that he does not rigorously apply his insights to the variants he identified himself in the same volume. See further R.P. Gordon, "The Citation of the Targums in Recent English Bible Translations (RSV, JB, NEB)," *JJS* 26 (1975): 50–52.

[29] Sperber, *Bible in Aramaic*, 4b.37–192. Note that he does not rigorously apply his insights to the variants he identified himself in the same volume. See further R.P. Gordon, "The Citation of the Targums in Recent English Bible Translations (RSV, JB, NEB)," *JJS* 26 (1975): 50–60 (50–52).

[30] For examples, see Sperber, *Bible in Aramaic*, 4b.88–90.

[31] Churgin, *Targum Jonathan to the Prophets*, 53.

[32] Staalduine-Sulman, *Targum of Samuel*, 101.

[33] For more details, see Smelik, *Targum of Judges*, 451–52.

3–5.1.3.6 Relevance for Exegesis

Targum Jonathan reflects the way the Hebrew Bible was interpreted between the second and fifth centuries C.E., while its individual interpretations *may* have ancient roots in Second Temple literature, although their adoption in Targum Jonathan still has to be explained within the framework of the second to fifth centuries C.E. Nevertheless, the interpretative take reflected in Targum Jonathan may still be compared and contrasted to older interpretations without attempting to ascribe an early date to Targum Jonathan. Often Targum Jonathan does not preserve an old reading, yet illuminates the reason for MT's wording (→ 6–9.1.3.6).

Judg 1:19 is a case in point. The first half of the verse suggests that God was with the tribe of Judah in their conquests, but the second half admits that they were unable to defeat the inhabitants of the plain כי רכב ברזל להם "because they possessed chariots of iron." Targum Jonathan could not let the implication stand that the opponents were too strong for God, so it inserted an explanatory plus: בתר כן דחבו "after they had sinned [they were not able to expel the inhabitants of the plain]." In turn, this sensitivity may well explain a crux in the Hebrew verse, which lacks the modal verb יכלו "they could" in the clause כי לא להוריש את ישבי העמק: "but not to drive out the inhabitants of plain." The omission of the verb hints at the interpretation that the support of God was never *meant* to include the conquest of the valley.[34] The presence of יכלו "they could" in translation in LXX, Targum Jonathan, and the Vulgate (but not in the Peshitta) adds to the suspicion that the verb stood in the Hebrew text originally, but has been deleted for theological reasons, similar to those that gave rise to Targum Jonathan's expository (and apologetic) insertion to avert the notion that God could not defeat chariots of iron.

Another example involves LXX-Judg 4:8, in which LXX contains a long plus missing in all other sources and marked by obelisk and metobelus in the Syro-Hexapla. The plus contains Barak's reflection on his hesitation to engage in battle. Its wording is echoed in a plus in Targum Jonathan at Judg 4:14. There is little merit in considering either plus an omission in the Hebrew text; rather, LXX and Targum Jonathan share an ancient exegetical tradition.[35]

3–5.1.3.7 Editions, Translations, and Auxiliary Tools

The most comprehensive edition of Targum Jonathan is that of Sperber.[36] Sperber used a small selection of manuscripts, with an emphasis on five relatively young Yemenite manuscripts (t710, t711, t716, t727, and t736), while important representatives of the Sefardi and Ashkenazi textual branches are missing, just as the Babylonian fragments that are generally deemed to reflect the oldest text type of Targum Jonathan. Essential for the Babylonian manuscripts and vocalization are the editions of Martínez Borobio for the books of the Former Prophets,[37] as well as the facsimile prepared by Díez Macho.[38] For similar editions of the Latter Prophets, see → 6–9.1.3. Sperber included three complete manuscripts of the Western group (t702, t705, and t720), two manuscripts with *haftarot* (t1134, t1143), some unidentified Cairo Genizah fragments housed in Cambridge, and finally three editions (t10, t12, and t734). Although his witnesses do represent the different text groups, they hardly allow for a thorough analysis of Targum Jonathan's textual history. A preliminary study of the way these witnesses relate to one another on

---

[34] Smelik, *Targum of Judges*, 343.

[35] Barthélemy, *Critique textuelle 1982*, 78.

[36] Sperber, *Bible in Aramaic*.

[37] E. Martínez Borobio, *Targum Jonatán de los Profetas Primeros en tradición babilónica*, Vol. 2: *I–II Samuel* (Textos y estudios "Cardenal Cisneros" 38; Madrid: Instituto de Filología, 1987); E. Martínez Borobio, *Targum Jonatán de los Profetas Primeros en tradición babilónica*, Vol. 1: *Josué–Jueces* (Textos y estudios "Cardenal Cisneros" 46; Madrid: Instituto de Filología, 1989); E. Martínez Borobio, *Targum Jonatán de los Profetas Primeros en tradición babilónica*, Vol. 3: *I–II Reyes* (Textos y estudios "Cardenal Cisneros" 63; Madrid: Instituto de Filología, 1998).

[38] A. Díez Macho, *Targum to the Former Prophets: Codex New York 229: From the Library of the Jewish Theological Seminary of America* (Jerusalem: Makor, 1974).

the basis of much more manuscript material has been provided for the Targum of Judges in preliminary form, followed by a much more detailed analysis for the stemma of the Targum of Samuel.[39]

Among the auxiliary tools, mention may be made of the books of the Former Prophets in the bilingual concordance,[40] an English translation of Targum Jonathan,[41] as well as several English commentaries to or studies of Targum Jonathan.[42] A modern dictionary for Targum Jonathan is lacking, but Cook's glossary for Targum Onqelos is very useful since its vocabulary is close (though not identical) to that of Targum Jonathan,[43] as is Tal's analysis of the vocabulary of Targum Jonathan Former Prophets.[44] Last but not least, all of the Targumim are included in the online *CAL under the direction of Stephen Kaufman.[45]

Böhl, F., "Die Metaphorisierung (Metila) in den Targumim zum Pentateuch," *FJB* 15 (1987): 111–49.
Churgin, P., *Targum Jonathan to the Prophets* (YOS 14; New Haven: Yale University Press, 1907 [= 1927]; repr. New York: Ktav, 1983).

---

[39] Smelik, *Targum of Judges*; Staalduine-Sulman, *Targum of Samuel*; H. Patmore, *The Transmission of Targum Jonathan in the West: A Study of Italian and Ashkenazi Manuscripts of the Targum to Samuel* (JSSSup 35; Oxford: Oxford University Press, 2015).

[40] J. de Moor, *A Bilingual Concordance to the Targum of the Prophets: Joshua* (Leiden: Brill, 1995); followed by W.F. Smelik, *A Bilingual Concordance to the Targum of the Prophets: Judges* (Leiden: Brill, 1995); E. van Staalduine-Sulman, *A Bilingual Concordance to the Targum of the Prophets: 1 & 2 Samuel* (3 vols.; Leiden: Brill, 1995); B. Grossfeld, *A Bilingual Concordance to the Targum of the Prophets: 1 & 2 Kings* (3 vols.; Leiden: Brill, 1998).

[41] D.J. Harrington and A.J. Saldarini, *Targum Jonathan of the Former Prophets* (ArBib 10; Edinburgh: T & T Clark, 1987). This volume is not without its problems and should be used with care.

[42] English commentaries include Smelik, *Targum of Judges*; van Staalduine-Sulman, *Targum of Samuel*; Dray, *Translation and Interpretation*.

[43] E. Cook, *A Glossary of Targum Onqelos: According to Alexander Sperber's Edition* (Studies in Aramaic Interpretation of Scripture 6; Leiden: Brill, 2008).

[44] A. Tal, לשון התרגום לנביאים ראשונים ומעמדה בכלל ניבי הארמית (Tel Aviv: Tel Aviv University Press, 1975) [Hebr.].

[45] The URL as of 2013 is http://cal1.cn.huc.edu/index.html.

Dray, C., *Translation and Interpretation in the Targum to the Books of Kings* (Studies in Aramaic Interpretation of Scripture 5; Leiden: Brill, 2006).
Geiger, *Urschrift.
Greenfield, J.C., "Standard Literary Aramaic," in *Actes du premier congrès international de linguistique sémitique et chamito-sémitique, Paris 16–19 juillet 1969* (eds. A. Caquot and D. Cohen; The Hague and Paris: Mouton, 1974), 280–89.
Holmes, J.S., *Translated! Papers on Literary Translation and Translation Studies* (Amsterdam: Rodopi, 1972).
Klein, M.L., "Associative and Complementary Translation in the Targumim," *ErIsr* 16 (1982): 134–40 [Hebr.].
König, H.G., "Holmes' 'Mapping Theory' and the Landscape of Mental Translation Processes," in *Translation Studies: The State of the Art* (eds. T. Naaijkens and K.M. van Leuven-Zwart; Approaches in Translation Studies 9; Amsterdam: Rodopi, 1991), 77–89.
Luzzatto, S.D., *Elementi Grammaticali del Caldeo Biblico e del Dialetto Talmudico* (Padua: A. Bianchi, 1865).
Smelik, W.F., *The Targum of Judges* (OTS 36; Leiden: Brill, 1995).
Smelik, W.F., *Rabbis, Language and Translation in Late Antiquity* (Cambridge: Cambridge University Press, 2013).
Sperber, *Bible in Aramaic.
van Staalduine-Sulman, E., *The Targum of Samuel* (Studies in Aramaic Interpretation of Scripture 1; Leiden: Brill, 2002).
Tal, A., לשון התרגום לנביאים ראשונים ומעמדה בכלל ניבי הארמית (Tel Aviv: Tel Aviv University, 1975).

Willem Smelik

3–5.1.4 Peshitta

3–5.1.4.1 Background

The Peshitta (S) of the Former Prophets (Joshua, Judges, 1–2 Samuel, and 1–2 Kings) is a translation into Syriac of a no-longer extant Hebrew manuscript, the *Vorlage* of the Peshitta. While the Peshitta's origins are largely unknown, the consensus view is that the Former Prophets were translated from a Hebrew *Vorlage* that was close to the emerging MT (→ 3.2.2; → 4.2.2; → 5.3.2). Scholars have searched for evidence that would confirm either Christian or Jewish origins for the Peshitta version of the Former Prophets. Peters argued that s-1 Sam was based upon the Targum (hence Jewish translators) and he listed a number of agreements between the Peshitta and Targum Jonathan (TJ).[1] His conclusion has been challenged successfully by Dirksen[2] and Mulder.[3] Morrison, in his study of 1 Samuel, did not find convincing evidence to argue either way.[4] Walter noted that because of the dependence of s-2 Kgs on s-Isa and the "absence of distinctive features of Targumic exegesis, a Christian authorship for 2 Kings Peshitta is not unlikely, although it cannot be positively demonstrated."[5] Walter reaffirmed this conclusion in 2008, while acknowledging that Weitzman's theory (the translators were non-rabbinical Jews converting to Christianity)[6] cannot be excluded.[7]

3-5.1.4.2 Editions, Studies, and Auxiliary Tools

In 1959, the International Organization for the Study of the Old Testament decided to create a critical edition of the Peshitta, known today as the Leiden Edition. Codex Ambrosianus (manuscript 7a1 in the Leiden edition) was chosen, given its completeness and its accessibility (though s^{8a1} may preserve an older text[8]). The first volumes presented a diplomatic edition of s^{7a1} but, after 1976, it was decided that s^{7a1} should be emended when it is not supported by two manuscripts up to and including the tenth century.[9] 1-2 Kings appeared in 1976[10] followed two years later by Judges and 1-2 Samuel.[11] Joshua appeared in 1991.[12]

The availability of the photolithographic edition of Codex Ambrosianus led to a spate of studies on the nature of the Peshitta text of the Former Prophets in the late nineteenth and early twentieth centuries. These studies were limited to a verse-by-verse list of Peshitta readings for text-critical purposes.[13] Little attention was given to the literary nature of these readings or to the character of the Peshitta as an interpretation of its unknown Hebrew exemplar, but with the advent of computer-assisted research, today the character of the Peshitta version is better understood. Dirksen studied the Peshitta manuscripts of Judges and has described the relationships among these manuscripts and the particular value of each Peshitta manuscript.[14] In 1988, Weitzman focused on the unique readings in s^{9a1} (against the Leiden edition), which occur most often in Kings "where 9a1 agrees uniquely with MT in over 400 passages."[15] These readings probably represent the original Peshitta version. Walter concluded that s^{9a1} had undergone "some conscious revision ... away from the Hebrew toward a smoother translation."[16]

The English translation by Lamsa[17] contains numerous errors. Several volumes of a new English translation of the Mosul edition of the Peshitta (1887-1891) have appeared in the series *The Antioch*

---

[1] Peters, "Zur Herkunft der Pešiṭta des ersten Samuelbuches," 25-34.

[2] Dirksen, "The Old Testament Peshitta," 286-87.

[3] Mulder, "The Use of the Peshitta," 37-53 (48-49).

[4] See Morrison, *The Character*, 134-44.

[5] D.M. Walter, "The Peshitta of II Kings" (PhD diss., Princeton Theological Seminary, 1964), 300.

[6] Weitzman, *The Syriac Version of the Old Testament: An Introduction*, 234-37.

[7] Walter, *Studies in the Peshitta of Kings*, 158-59.

[8] Dirksen concludes: "it may be said that in general 8a1 is preferable to 7a1 as a representative of the type of text preserved in the ancient MSS" (Dirksen, "The Leiden Peshitta Edition," 31-38 [33]).

[9] See Dirksen, "The Leiden Peshitta Edition," 31-38.

[10] H. Goitlieb and E. Hammershaimb (eds.), Kings (The Old Testament in Syriac according to the Peshitta Version 2.3; Leiden: Brill, 1976).

[11] P.B. Dirksen and P.A.H. de Boer (eds.), *Judges-Samuel* (The Old Testament in Syriac according to the Peshitta Version 2.2; Leiden: Brill, 1978).

[12] D.J. Lane et al., *Leviticus-Numbers-Deuteronomy-Joshua* (The Old Testament in Syriac according to the Peshitta Version 1.2-2.1b; Leiden: Brill, 1991).

[13] See, e.g., Mager, *Die Peschittho zum Buche Josua*; Lazarus, *Zur syrischen Übersetzung des Buches der Richter*; Schwartz, *Die syrische Übersetzung des ersten Buches Samuelis und ihr Verhältniss zu MT., LXX und Trg.*; De Boer, *Research into the Text of 1 Sam. I-XVI*; De Boer, "Research into the Text of 1 Samuel xviii-xxxi," 1-100; Englert, *The Peshitto of Second Samuel*.

[14] Dirksen, *The Transmission of the Text*.

[15] Weitzman, "The Originality of Unique Readings in Peshitta Ms 9a1," 225-58 (226).

[16] Walter, *Studies in the Peshitta of Kings*, 56.

[17] *The Holy Bible from the Ancient Eastern Text: George M. Lamsa's Translation from the Aramaic of the Peshitta* (San Francisco: Harper & Row, 1985).

Bible: The Syriac Peshiṭta Bible with English Translation.[18] Another English translation is also underway by the Peshitta Institute with the title *The Bible of Edessa*. In 1989, Dirksen published an annotated bibliography for the Peshitta.[19] Strothmann's multivolume[20] concordance (based upon the London Polyglot and the Urmia edition) to the Peshitta Old Testament was a key resource for the study of the Former Prophets prior to the advent of the desktop computer. Rosenwasser created a concordance for 1–2 Kings.[21] The Peshitta text of the Leiden edition has recently become available in a searchable electronic format, such as in the Logos software. Computer concordances will become ever more reliable as these electronic texts are continually corrected. With Boolean searches available in seconds, the genesis of many readings of the Peshitta will become clear. The increasing availability of Peshitta manuscripts online will also permit scholars to observe more readily the transmission of the text of the Peshitta.

3–5.1.4.3 Translation Technique

Among the more important developments in recent years is the recognition that the Peshitta is a translation of the Hebrew into good Syriac idiom. Noldeke's remark at the end of the nineteenth century left the impression that the Peshitta Old Testament was filled with Hebraisms and Graecisms, though the fact that he cites it regularly suggests that he too considered it good Syriac.[22] The Peshitta's idiomatic style is easily observed when it is compared with Targum Jonathan, which also emerged during the proto-Masoretic period. For example, in 1–2 Kings, ויהי "and it happened" is not rendered literally in Syriac seventy-seven percent of the time.[23] By comparison, Kuty notes that "As a rule, [TJ-Sam] imitates the [biblical Hebrew] construction whenever it occurs in the Vorlage."[24] Flinn's study of s-Judg considered the quality of the Peshitta translation with regard to its literalism.[25] He discovered that many of the differences between MT (→ 3.2.2; → 4.2.2; → 5.3.2) and the Peshitta occurred during the transmission of the latter.

The Peshitta renders the verbs in its Hebrew *Vorlage* according to good Syriac syntax and does not imitate the formal character of the Hebrew text. The *wayyiqtol* is rendered in a variety of ways.[26] The translators' attention to idiomatic Syriac is illustrated by their use of the *hwā qātel* construction in Syriac. For example, in 1 Kgs 17:4, the translator does not imitate the Hebrew *yiqtol*, תִּשְׁתֶּה "you will drink," in Syriac. Rather, תִּשְׁתֶּה "you will drink" is translated with ܗܘܝܬ ܫܬܐ "you should drink [whenever you are thirsty]" a Syriac construction that expresses a deontic modality with a frequentative aspect.[27] The translator did not render the *waw* between two Hebrew *wayyiqtols* in Syriac where the actions expressed are nearly simultaneous (for example, see Judg 19:28; 1 Sam 28:25; 2 Sam 3:21; 6:2; 15:9). As Williams noted, s-1 Kgs "follows the proto-Masoretic Text and yet sets a higher premium on semantic rather than formal equivalence."[28]

Among the translators' most common techniques is harmonization and this explanation should be the first recourse for explaining unique

---

[18] *Biblia Sacra iuxta versionem simplicem quae dicitur Pschitta* (3 vols.; Mosul: Typis Fratrum Praedicatorum, 1887–1891).

[19] Dirksen, *An Annotated Bibliography of the Peshiṭta of the Old Testament*. Updated in Dirksen and van der Kooij (eds.), *The Peshiṭta as a Translation*, 221–36.

[20] Strothmann, Johannes, and Zumpe, *Konkordanz zur syrischen Bibel*.

[21] H.M.E. Rosenwasser, *Der lexikalische Stoff der Königsbücher der Peschitta unter Berücksichtigung der Varianten als eine Vorarbeit für eine Concordanz zur Peschitta alphabetisch dargestellt* (Berlin: Nathansen & Lamm, 1905).

[22] Nöldeke wrote: "Aus den alten Bibelübersetzungen habe ich nur solche Stellen ohne Weiteres herangezogen, welche von Hebraismen und Graecismen frei sind" (T. Nöldeke, *Kurzgefasste syrische Grammatik* [Leipzig: Chr. Herm. Tauchnitz, 1898]).

[23] Dyk and van Keulen, *Language System*.

[24] R.J. Kuty, *Studies in the Syntax of Targum Jonathan to Samuel* (Ancient Near Eastern Studies 30; Leuven: Peeters, 2010), 234.

[25] Flinn, "The Character of the Peshitta of the Book of Judges and its Relation to other Ancient Translations."

[26] Williams, *Studies in the Syntax of the Peshitta of 1 Kings*, 100–16.

[27] Morrison, "The *Hwā Qātel* and *Hwā Qětīl* Constructions in the Peshitta Old Testament," 83–106 (98).

[28] Williams, *Studies in the Syntax of the Peshitta of 1 Kings*, 184.

Peshitta readings. Whether conscious or unconscious, harmonizations were introduced either at the time of translation or by later copyists. The Peshitta often makes explicit what is implicit in the Hebrew. The subject or addressee of a verb can be explicitly identified (1 Sam 3:8), especially after the verb ܐܡܪ "he said." Other readings are often broadly classified as "accommodations to the context," "clarifications," or "simplifications." But closer attention to the context in which these readings occur may reveal their interpretative nature (→ 3–5.1.4.6).

Weitzman's study of lexical choices in the Former Prophets led him to conclude that Judges, Samuel, and Kings were more consistent in their lexical choices for particular Hebrew words than other biblical books, including Joshua.[29] He noted that the word "ark," which up to 1 Sam 6:11 is translated with ܩܒܘܬܐ, is regularly rendered with ܐܪܘܢܐ (both words meaning "ark") after 1 Sam 6:11.[30] However, this one example may not be sufficient to indicate two hands in the translation of 1 Samuel. The Peshitta does not imitate Hebrew lexemes with Syriac cognates. For example, in 1 Sam 5:3, וַיָּשִׁבוּ אֹתוֹ "they put him back" is rendered ܐܣܩܘܗܝ, "they restored him" (Tʲ: ואתיבו "they put back"). Hebrew ידע "he knew" is translated with ܚܟܡ "he knew" when it means "to have sexual relations" (see 1 Sam 1:19). There is a tendency to contemporize place names, such as the translation of גחון "Gihon" in 1 Kgs 1:33 with ܫܝܠܘܚܐ "Siloam." On other occasions, the Peshitta replaces rare place names with more common ones (see 1 Sam 9:5 where צוף "Zuph" is replaced with the more common ܨܘܪ "Tyre"). The errors in translation may be the result of a poor Hebrew exemplar from which the translator was working. For example, in 1 Sam 19:22, וַיִּשְׁאַל וַיֹּאמֶר "and he asked and said" is rendered ܘܫܐܠ ܫܐܘܠ ܘܐܡܪ "and Saul said" (confusion of שאול "Saul" and וישאל "and he asked").

On occasion, the translator or copyist can eliminate repetitive words. In s-1 Kgs 14:26, וְאֶת־הַכֹּל לָקָח "and he took everything" is omitted because, within the context of this verse, the phrase is superfluous. The omission cannot be explained as a mechanical error of paraplepsis (s⁹ᵃ¹ reads ܘܟܠܗܝܢ ܢܣܒ "he took everything"). The Hebrew text of 1 Samuel 17 contains several redundant phrases that appear to have been eliminated by the translator.[31] In a few cases, the Peshitta reflects the formal character of the Hebrew text but an entirely different meaning is communicated. For example, in 1 Sam 28:6, the Hebrew word בָּאוּרִים "by Urim" is rendered ܒܢܘܪܐ "by fire."[32] This technique may also explain the translation of וּמְקַטְּרִים "they were making smoke offerings" with ܘܡܣܩܝܢ "they were burning incense" in 2 Kgs 12:4 and 14:4.[33] On a few occasions, the translator may have failed to understand the Hebrew, as in 1 Sam 15:4 where בַּטְּלָאִים "in Telaim" is rendered ܒܛܠܝܐ "among the youth."[34]

3–5.1.4.4 Inner-Translational Features

Many orthographic corruptions crept into the Peshitta mostly due to difficulties that copyists encountered when reading the Syriac script. The confusion of *dalath* and *resh* is a common error, appearing most often in proper names that are *hapax legomena*. In these cases, the translators had to rely solely on the shape of the letters they could see in their exemplar. Given the number of times the *resh* and *dalath* are different from what appears in the Hebrew, it is likely that the distinguishing diacritic was not used in the original translation of the Peshitta.[35] (In three legal parchments, dated 240–

---

[29] Weitzman, *The Syriac Version of the Old Testament*, 186.
[30] Weitzman, "Lexical Clues to the Composition of the Old Testament Peshitta," 217–46 (239). Weitzman found two other instances where there is a shift in lexemes but these occur in 2 Samuel 6 not 1 Samuel 6.
[31] See Morrison, *The Character*, 79–80.
[32] See Morrison, *The Character*, 92–94.
[33] Dyk and van Keulen, *Language System*, 326.
[34] For other examples, see Weitzman, *The Syriac Version of the Old Testament*, 36–48.
[35] However, Segal notes that in all the manuscripts he consulted from before 600, the diacritic to distinguish *resh* from *dalath* is present (J.B. Segal, *The Diacritical Point and the Accents in Syriac* [London Oriental Series 2; London: Oxford University Press, 1953], 5). In the twelfth- to thirteenth-century fragments of the Palestinian version of the Bible, G. Margoliouth observed that the *resh* has two dots above it and the *dalath* has none (G. Margoliouth, *The Palestinian*

243 C.E., the dot to distinguish the *dalath* from the *resh* is not used.)³⁶ For example, in 1 Kgs 6:20, ולפני הדביר "before the sanctuary" is rendered ܩܕܡ ܒܝܬ ܡܩܕܫܐ "he overlaid the sanctuary," an inner-Syriac corruption of ܘܩܕܡ "and before." In Josh 1:14, s⁷ᵃ¹ reads the senseless ܘܥܘܕܪܘ instead of ܘܥܕܪܘ "and help" (MT: וַעֲזַרְתֶּם "and you will help"). 1 Sam 2:8 illustrates the confusion between *ṭeth* and *lamed*: the Peshitta reading in the Leiden edition, ܛܠܠ ܡܪܝܐ "the Lord overshadowed," is a corruption of ܡܛܠ ܠܡܪܝܐ "because belonging to the Lord" for כי ליהוה "because belonging to the Lord." The letters *nun*, *heth*, and *yod* were confused in 1 Sam 17:20, where the probable original Peshitta reading ܚܝܠܐ "the army" has become ܢܚܠܐ "the valley" (MT: הַחַיִל "the army").³⁷ The *yod* are *nun* have been confused in the transmission of ܢܪܝܢ "Narin," which consistently translates יערים "Jearim" (see Josh 9:17). *Qof* and *mem* are confused in Judg 5:15, בָּעֵמֶק "in the valley"; ܒܥܡܡܐ "among the peoples"). The transmission errors in the Peshitta are easily observed in the apparatus of the Leiden edition. For example, in 1 Kgs 15:20, מעכה "Maacah" is rendered ܡܥܟܐ "Maacah," but in manuscripts s⁹ᵃ¹ᶠᵃᵐ it is rendered ܡܠܟܐ "king" (confusion of *ayin*/*lamed*). There are also examples of metathesis: in 1 Sam 23:22, an original ܬܘܒ "again" has become ܬܒ "dwell." Dyk and van Keulen provide numerous examples in 1–2 Kings of metatheses in proper nouns.³⁸ There are also a limited number of omissions due to parablepsis (see 1 Sam 23:11–12).

Another very common inner-translation feature is harmonization or assimilation to other biblical passages. It is difficult to be certain when these readings entered into the Peshitta, whether at the time of translation or later during the transmission of the text. For example, in 1 Kgs 19:12, Elijah encounters the mysterious sound: קול דממה דקה "the sound of thin silence." The Peshitta reads ܩܠܐ ܕܡܡܠܠܐ ܢܝܚܐ "the sound of gentle speaking." This translation is an assimilation to Deut 4:12 (ܩܠܐ ܕܡܡܠܠܐ "the sound of gentle speaking"), the only other place in the Peshitta where this expression appears. This inner-Peshitta harmonization is also an exegetical reading: the Peshitta associates the obscure text of 1 Kgs 19:12 with Deut 4:12 to ensure that the reader knows that in 1 Kgs 19:12 the voice was God's voice. Thus, according to the Peshitta, the same voice that instructed Moses and the Israelites on Mount Horeb in Deut 4:12 now instructs Elijah who finds himself on the same mountain.³⁹

3–5.1.4.5 Text-Critical Value

In the twenty-first century it is generally agreed that the earliest version of the Peshitta was close to the Hebrew⁴⁰ and therefore a reconstruction of the "original" Peshitta translation will often reflect MT (→ 3.2.2; → 4.2.2; → 5.3.2). The four hundred unique readings in s⁹ᵃ¹ that agree with MT against the Leiden edition in 1 and 2 Kings⁴¹ are most likely original readings.⁴² Manuscript s⁸ᵃ¹ also preserves older readings.⁴³ Thus, the apparatus in the Leiden edition is a necessary tool for arriving at the earliest Peshitta text. Then, before a Peshitta reading can be employed to reconstruct the Hebrew text, the textual critic must decide whether the reading can be explained by reasons internal to the Peshitta (a translation technique) or whether it truly reflects

---

Syriac Version of the Holy Scripture [London: Society of Biblical Archaeology, 1897], 18).

³⁶ H.J.W. Drijvers and J.F. Healey, *The Old Syriac Inscriptions of Edessa and Osrhoene: Texts, Translations, and Commentary* (HdO 1.42; Leiden: Brill, 1999), 22.

³⁷ See Gordon, "Inner Syriac Corruption," 502–04.

³⁸ Dyk and van Keulen, *Language System*, 244.

³⁹ C.E. Morrison, "Handing on the Mantle: The Transmission of the Elijah Cycle in the Biblical Versions," in *Master of the Sacred Page: Essays and Articles in Honor of Roland E. Murphy, O.Carm., on the Occasion of his Eightieth Birthday* (eds. K.J. Egan and C.E. Morrison; Washington: The Carmelite Institute, 1997), 112–15.

⁴⁰ Weitzman, *The Syriac Version of the Old Testament*, 269–80. See also R.B. ter Haar Romeny, "Techniques of Translation and Transmission of the Earliest Text Forms of the Syriac Version of Genesis," in *The Peshitta as a Translation: Papers Read at the II Peshitta Symposium Held at Leiden 19–21 August 1993* (eds. P.B. Dirksen and A. van der Kooij; Monographs of the Leiden Peshitta Institute 8; Leiden: Brill, 1995), 177–85; and Dirksen, "The Ancient Peshitta MSS of Judges and their Variant Readings," 127–46.

⁴¹ Dyk and van Keulen, *Language System*, 9.

⁴² Weitzman, "Unique Readings in Peshitta Ms 9a1," 225–58.

⁴³ Dirksen, "Ancient Peshitta MSS," 127–46.

a Hebrew *Vorlage* different (though not necessarily better) from MT.

Even though the general character of the Peshitta is better known in the twenty-first century than twenty years ago, every unique reading in it has not yet been fully investigated. Those studied to date indicate that most often they do not reflect a different Hebrew *Vorlage* and can be explained by translation technique or are exegetical in nature. Moreover, because the Peshitta is written in good Syriac, it is less useful for reconstructing a putative Hebrew *Vorlage* than Targum Jonathan, which more closely mirrors the Hebrew. This is seen most clearly in the use of prepositions, where, unlike Targum Jonathan, the Peshitta normally does not imitate the Hebrew preposition in Syriac when it is not appropriate. For example, in 1 Sam 16:7, the Peshitta reads ܒܚܙܬܐ for MT לַעֵינָיִם (both meaning "with the eyes"). Even though the Peshitta reading is cited in *BHS, it has no text-critical value. Therefore caution should be exercised before arguing that a Peshitta reading reflects a Hebrew *Vorlage* more ancient than what is preserved in MT.

Another key question is the value of the Peshitta reading when it agrees with another version, especially LXX (→ 1.3.1.1) or Targum Jonathan (1.3.3; → 1.3.4.9). Dirksen concluded that agreements between the Peshitta and LXX in Judges "may suggest a Hebrew reading different from the one found in the Massoretic text."[44] In his study of Joshua 1–5, Erbes concluded: 1) the Peshitta normally follows MT; 2) the Peshitta rarely follows LXX; (3) Targum Jonathan did not influence the Peshitta; 4) the Peshitta-Ethiopic parallels suggest direct contact or contact through a lost LXX manuscript; and 5) most unique Peshitta readings can be explained by translation technique.[45] The independence of the Peshitta from LXX and Targum Jonathan has also been shown in 1 Samuel.[46] Since there is little evidence in the Former Prophets that LXX has influenced the Peshitta, when the Peshitta and LXX agree against MT (most are minor agreements), the Peshitta reading most likely represents an independent witness. However, the agreement may also reflect a shared translation technique[47] or a later Christian interpolation from LXX. With these caveats, agreements between LXX and the Peshitta can be used to reconstruct a Hebrew *Vorlage* that is different from MT.[48]

Agreements between the Peshitta and Targum Jonathan are complicated by the fact that the two languages are very closely related and therefore many agreements are expected. The relationship between these two versions is also related to the Peshitta's origins. Baumstark[49] and Kahle[50] believed the Peshitta was based upon a Palestinian Targum. But Wernberg-Møller noted the many problems in their methodology and disputed that the shared readings illustrated literary dependence:[51] "literary dependence between two literary works, when it exists, is recognizable and indisputable by its very nature; linguistic affinities as such prove nothing and are, in fact, totally irrelevant to the discussion; what is needed is verbal, phraseological points of contact between PT [Palestinian Targum] and P [Peshitta], not the use of a particular preposition, or verb, or noun, here and there."[52]

Evidence of the Peshitta's literary dependence on Targum Jonathan or LXX should appear in cases where MT is particularly obscure and one could suppose that the Peshitta translator consulted these versions (→ 1.3.4.9). But in such cases, the Peshitta almost always has its own reading. For

---

[44] Dirksen, *The Transmission of the Text*, 108.
[45] Erbes, *The Peshitta and the Versions*, 318–19.
[46] Morrison, *The Character*, 147.
[47] See Dirksen, "The Peshitta and Textual Criticism of the Old Testament," 376–90.
[48] For this reason, Mulder argued that wherever the Peshitta and LXX agree against MT, the purported Hebrew text behind these readings must be compared with what appears in MT to determine which might be the older text. See Mulder, "The Use of the Peshitta," 37–53.
[49] A. Baumstark, "Pešiṭta und palästinensisches Targum," *BZ* 19 (1931): 257–70.
[50] P.E. Kahle, *The Cairo Geniza* (2nd edition; New York: Frederick A. Praeger 1959), 272–73.
[51] P. Wernberg-Møller, "Prolegomena to a Re-examination of the Palestinian Targum Fragments of the Book of Genesis Published by P. Kahle, and their Relationship to the Peshitta," *JSS* 7 (1962): 253–66.
[52] Wernberg-Møller, "Prolegomena," 259, n. 2.

this reason, the lists of agreements between Targum Jonathan or LXX and the Peshitta often presented in the literature can be deceiving if such data is not accompanied by lists of significant passages where the Peshitta and Targum Jonathan or LXX do not agree. For example, MT-1 Sam 13:1 reads the well-known *crux interpretum*, "Saul was one year old when he began to reign." The reading in Targum Jonathan, "Saul was *like* a year old child, without sin, when he became king," probably reflects an interpretation of this *crux interpretum*. The Peshitta too, cited in the apparatus of *BHS, offers a unique interpretation: "After a year or two Saul began to reign." This Peshitta reading is exegetical and offers little insight into the original Hebrew and illustrates the Peshitta's independence from Targum Jonathan.

At times, the Peshitta and Targum Jonathan share similar interpretations. For example, in 1 Sam 21:3, the rare Hebrew expression at the end of the verse, פְּלֹנִי אַלְמוֹנִי "such and such [a place]," is rendered with ܕܟܣܐ ܘܛܫܐ "concealed and hidden" in the Peshitta and with כסי ומטיר "concealed and hidden" in Targum Jonathan. The two versions share the same interpretation of the Hebrew, but have different lexemes, ruling out literary dependence. But the shared interpretation could indicate that the Peshitta translator was aware of some Jewish exegetical traditions,[53] though these examples are few.[54] When the many possible explanations for an agreement are eliminated, the readings shared between the Peshitta and Targum Jonathan can point to a *Vorlage* different than what is preserved in MT.

3–5.1.4.6 Relevance for Exegesis

The character of the Peshitta is strikingly different from the translations that emerged during the same period, such as Targum Jonathan (→ 3–5.1.3) or Aquila's recension of LXX (approximately 125 C.E.; → 3–5.1.5.2.3.2), which more closely reflect the proto-MT (→ 3.2.2; → 4.2.2; → 5.3.2) of the

---

[53] Dirksen, "Targum and Peshitta," 3–13.
[54] This confirms the opinion of J. Perles, *Meletemata Peschitthoniana* (Breslau: Grassius, 1859), 27.

second century C.E. By contrast, the Peshitta's numerous divergent readings, especially where the Hebrew is difficult to interpret, witness to the reception of the Bible in the Syriac-speaking world. Since the translator worked from an unvocalized Hebrew text, sometimes the Peshitta reflects an interpretation of the Hebrew consonants that differs from MT. For example, in 2 Sam 14:17, לִמְנוּחָה "for rest" is rendered ܘܬܗܘܐ ܩܘܪܒܢܐ "let it be an offering" (LXX: εἰς θυσίαν "as an offering"). S reads מְנוּחָה "offering" as מִנְחָה "offering" (probably מְנוּחָה was written defectively, מִנְחָה "rest," in the Peshitta *Vorlage*). In S-1 Sam 21:5–6, אִשָּׁה "woman" has been read as אִשֶּׁה "fire," resulting in the translation ܩܘܪܒܢܐ "offering."

Appreciating these exegetical readings also requires a sensitivity to the meaning of the Hebrew text itself. For example, David's decision to rehabilitate Absalom has disastrous consequences for David's kingdom. The obscure Hebrew verb וַתְּכַל at the beginning of 2 Sam 13:39, which may describe David's longing for Absalom (though the verb is 3rd fem. sg.), is critically important for interpreting David's actions with respect to Absalom. The Leiden edition has ܘܐܗܡܝ "he neglected" whereas s8a1 has ܘܐܬܟܪܗ "he hesitated" and manuscripts s9a1*fam* read ܘܐܬܟܪܝ "he regretted." (The two readings ܘܐܬܟܪܝ "he hesitated" and ܘܐܬܟܪܗ "he regretted" are related: a confusion of ܝ and ܗ.) Was David negligent, hesitant, or penitent in his pursuit of Absalom? This question is critical for understanding David's character, since the return of Absalom nearly leads to his own destruction. The impact of the Peshitta's interpretation on its Syriac readers also needs to be considered.

In 2 Sam 16:8, Shimei accuses David of having usurped Saul's rule. To this extremely serious charge, Shimei adds that God has *already* "brought" (הֵשִׁיב) on David the blood of Saul's house. The Hebrew is easily translated, as Targum Jonathan indicates (אֲתֵיב "he has returned"), but the Peshitta has "May the Lord avenge upon you [ܢܦܪܥܟ]." Shimei's assertion regarding what God had *already* done in the Hebrew text becomes a prayer in the Peshitta regarding what God *might* do. The Peshitta reading lessens Shimei's serious charge that David usurped Saul's throne.[55] Such readings illustrate the Peshitta's interpretation, regardless of whether they were intentional or not, and they require the textual critic to be acutely sensitive to the meaning of the passage in which the reading appears. Otherwise, such readings can be dismissed as "clarifications" and their impact on the interpretation of the passage is not fully appreciated. These interpretative readings illustrate that the Peshitta is not simply a collection of divergent readings with respect to MT. Its unique readings appear within the Peshitta's own literary context and need to be appreciated as such.

Brock, S.P., "Jewish Traditions in Syriac Sources," *JSS* 13 (1968): 212–32.

Ceriani, A.M. (ed.), *Translatio Syra Pescitto Veteris Testamenti ex Codice Ambrosiano sec. fere 6., photolithographice edita* (Milan: della Croce, 1876).

de Boer, P.A.H., *Research into the Text of 1 Sam. I–XVI: A Contribution to the Study of the Books of Samuel* (Amsterdam: H.J. Paris, 1938).

de Boer, P.A.H., "Research into the Text of 1 Samuel xviii–xxxi," *OTS* 6 (1949): 1–100.

Dirksen, P.B., *The Transmission of the Text in the Peshiṭta Manuscripts of the Book of Judges* (Monographs of the Peshitta Institute Leiden 1; Leiden: Brill, 1972).

Dirksen, P.B., "The Old Testament Peshitta," in Mulder, *Mikra, 286–87.

Dirksen, P.B., "The Ancient Peshitta MSS of Judges and their Variant Readings," in *The Peshitta: Its Early Text and History: Papers Read at the Peshiṭta Symposium held at Leiden 30–31 Aug. 1985* (eds. P.B. Dirksen and M.J. Mulder; Monographs of the Peshitta Institute Leiden 4; Leiden: Brill, 1988), 127–46.

Dirksen, P.B., *An Annotated Bibliography of the Peshiṭta of the Old Testament* (Monographs of the Peshitta Institute Leiden 5; Leiden: Brill, 1989).

Dirksen, P.B., "The Leiden Peshitta Edition," in *V Symposium Syriacum 1988* (ed. R. Lavenant; OrChrAn 236; Rome: Pontificium Institutum Studiorum Orientalium, 1990), 31–38.

Dirksen, P.B., "The Peshitta and Textual Criticism of the Old Testament," *VT* 42 (1992): 376–90.

Dirksen, P.B., "The Urmia Edition of the Peshitta: The Story Behind the Text," *Textus* 18 (1995): 157–67.

Dirksen, P.B., "Targum and Peshitta: Some Basic Questions," in *Targum Studies*, Vol. 2: *Targum and Peshitta* (ed. P.V.M. Flesher; South Florida Studies in the History of Judaism 165; Atlanta: Scholars Press, 1998), 3–13.

Dirksen, P.B. and A. van der Kooij (eds.), *The Peshiṭta as a Translation* (Monographs of the Peshitta Institute Leiden 8; Leiden: Brill, 1995).

Dyk, J.W. and P.S.F. van Keulen, *Language System, Translation Technique, and Textual Tradition in the Peshitta of Kings* (Monographs of the Peshitta Institute Leiden 19; Leiden: Brill, 2013).

Englert, D.M.C., *The Peshitto of Second Samuel* (JBL Monograph Series 3; Philadelphia: Society of Biblical Literature and Exegesis, 1949).

Erbes, J.E., *The Peshitta and the Versions: A Study of the Peshitta Variants in Joshua 1–5 in Relation to their Equivalents in the Ancient Versions* (Studia Semitica Upsaliensia 16; Uppsala: Uppsala University, 1999).

Flinn, C.G., "The Character of the Peshitta of the Book of Judges and its Relation to other Ancient Translations" (PhD diss., The Catholic University of America, 2010).

Gordon, R.P., "Inner Syriac Corruption," *JTS* 22 (1971): 502–04.

Goshen-Gottstein, M.H., "Prolegomena to a Critical Edition of the Peshitta," in *Studies in the Bible* (ed. C. Rabin; ScrHier 8; Jerusalem: Magnes Press, 1961), 26–67.

Lazarus, A., *Zur syrischen Übersetzung des Buches der Richter* (Kirchhain N.-L.: Schmersow, 1901).

Mager, H., *Die Peschiṭtho zum Buche Josua* (Freiburger theologische Studien 19; Freiburg im Breisgau: Herder, 1916).

Morrison, C.E., *The Character of the Syriac Version of the First Book of Samuel* (Monographs of the Peshitta Institute Leiden 11; Leiden: Brill, 2001).

Morrison, C.E., "The *Hwā Qātel* and *Hwā Qětīl* Constructions in the Peshitta Old Testament," in *Foundations for Syriac Lexicography*, Vol. 5: *Colloquia of the International Syriac Language Project* (eds. J. Loopstra and M. Sokoloff; Perspectives on Syriac Linguistics 7; Piscataway: Gorgias, 2013), 83–106.

Mulder, M.J., "The Use of the Peshitta in Textual Criticism," in *La Septuaginta en la investigación contemporánea (V Congreso de la IOSCS)* (ed. N. Fernández Marcos; Textos y estudios "Cardenal Cisneros" 34; Madrid: Instituto "Arias Montano," 1985), 37–53.

Peters, C., "Zur Herkunft der Pešiṭta des ersten Samuelbuches," *Bib* 22 (1941): 25–34.

---

[55] For other examples, see Weitzman, "The Interpretative Character of the Syriac Old Testament," 587–611; Dyk and van Keulen, *Language System*, 47–67; Morrison, *The Character*, 22–34.

Pozzobon, M., *La Peshitta del secondo libro di Samuele* (Analecta Biblica 214; Rome: Gregorian and Biblical Press, 2016).

Schwartz, E., *Die syrische Übersetzung des ersten Buches Samuelis und ihr Verhältniss zu MT., LXX und Trg.* (Berlin: H. Itzkowski, 1897).

Sprenger, N., *Konkordanz zum syrischen Psalter* (Wiesbaden: Harrassowitz, 1976).

Strothmann, W., K. Johannes, and M. Zumpe, *Konkordanz zur syrischen Bibel* (Göttinger Orientforschung Reihe 1 Syriaca 25, 26, 33; Wiesbaden: Harrassowitz, 1984–1995).

Walter, D.M., *Studies in the Peshitta of Kings: The Transmission and Revision of the Text, Relations with Other Texts, and Translation Features* (Text and Studies 3.7; Piscataway: Gorgias Press, 2008).

Weitzman, M., "The Originality of Unique Readings in Peshitta Ms 9a1," in *The Peshitta: Its Early Text and History: Papers Read at the Peshitta Symposium Held at Leiden 30–31 August 1985* (eds. P.B. Dirksen and M.J. Mulder; Monographs of the Peshitta Institute Leiden 4; Leiden: Brill, 1988), 225–58.

Weitzman, M., "From Judaism to Christianity – The Syriac Version of the Hebrew Bible," in *The Jews among Pagans and Christians in the Roman Empire* (eds. J.M. Lieu, J. North, and T. Rajak; New York: Routledge 1994), 147–73.

Weitzman, M., "Lexical Clues to the Composition of the Old Testament Peshitta," in *Studia Aramaica: New Sources and New Approaches* (eds. M.J. Geller, J.C. Greenfield, and M.P. Weitzman; JSSSup 4; Oxford: Oxford University Press, 1995), 217–46.

Weitzman, M., "The Interpretative Character of the Syriac Old Testament," in *Hebrew Bible/Old Testament: The History of its Interpretation*, Vol. 1: *From the Beginnings to the Middle Ages (until 1300)*, Part 1: *Antiquity* (ed. M. Sæbø; Göttingen: Vandenhoeck & Ruprecht, 1996), 587–611.

Weitzman, M.P., *The Syriac Version of the Old Testament: An Introduction* (Cambridge: Cambridge University Press, 1999).

Williams, P.J., *Studies in the Syntax of the Peshitta of 1 Kings* (Monographs of the Peshitta Institute Leiden 12; Leiden: Brill, 2001).

Craig E. Morrison

3–5.1.5 Hexapla

3–5.1.5.1 Joshua-Judges

See → 2.4.6 (Hexaplaric Translations and Hexapla of the Octateuch).

3–5.1.5.2 Hexaplaric Greek Translations and the Hexapla: Samuel-Kings

3–5.1.5.2.1 Background

For a thorough treatment of Greek Kingdoms, see the article on the Septuagint of Samuel-Kings (→ 5.4). For an overview of the Hexapla and the three translators (Aquila, Symmachus, and Theodotion), see → 1.3.1.2.

The books of 1 and 2 Samuel and 1 and 2 Kings are grouped together in LXX as 1, 2, 3, and 4 Kingdoms (or Reigns). As of 2015, no critical editions of the Old Greek (OG) of 1–4 Kingdoms are available and, until they are, conclusions about the base text and translation technique of the Old Greek translation(s) are tentative.[1]

Thackeray isolated five different translation units for Greek 1–4 Kingdoms, and he labeled them as follows:[2]

α	1 Kingdoms
ββ	2 Kgdms 1:1–11:1
βγ	2 Kgdms 11:2–3 Kgdms 2:11
γγ	3 Kgdms 2:12–21:43
γδ	3 Kgdms 22:1–4 Kingdoms

This division has relevance for the hexaplaric remains in that the βγ and γδ sections have characteristics of the καίγε tradition,[3] and their relationship in particular to Theodotion has been debated.[4] As

---

[1] For the purposes of this article, the reading from Codex Vaticanus (LXX^B) is given as the default and when it differs from Codex Alexandrinus (LXX^A), the LXX^A reading is also given.

[2] Thackeray, "The Greek Translators of the Four Books of Kings." Wevers has written about the characteristics of three of these sections: βγ, γγ, and γδ. See under J.W. Wevers in the bibliography.

[3] An important question is whether these two sections are *de novo* translations from the Hebrew or whether they are revisions of an earlier Old Greek version.

[4] E.g., Barthélemy, in *Devanciers*, identified the translator

of 2015, no study of the entire corpus of Theodotion fragments for 1–4 Kingdoms has been done that would enable them to be compared systematically with the βγ and γδ sections.

3–5.1.5.2.2 Editions, Sources, and Auxiliary Tools

Field published his detailed edition of available hexaplaric fragments in 1875.[5] Since then, although many have studied 1–4 Kingdoms as a Greek translation, and some have been interested in origenic influence on the manuscript tradition of these books, relatively few have done systematic studies of the hexaplaric remains for 1–4 Kingdoms. In their Cambridge edition of 1–4 Kingdoms, a diplomatic edition, Brooke and McLean include hexaplaric readings in their second apparatus, including some that surfaced after Field, but they are not evaluated.[6] Two significant Aquila readings not available to Field were discovered among the fragments of the Cairo Genizah. They comprise 3 Kgdms 21:7–17 and 4 Kgdms 23:11–27.[7]

An important source for hexaplaric readings for 3 and 4 Kingdoms is the Syro-Hexapla (→ 1.4.5; → 3–5.2.4.2), a translation into Syriac of the fifth column of the Hexapla completed in the early seventh century C.E. The Syro-Hexapla is our main source for the Aristarchian sign tradition for 3–4 Kingdoms, and in addition it contains many marginal readings from the Three and from other sources.[8]

Besides the Syro-Hexapla and the Aquila fragments from the Cairo Genizah noted above, readings from the Three are localized mainly in a small group of manuscripts. Unlike for the Pentateuch, where readings from the Three often have support from multiple witnesses, for the books of Kingdoms, readings are often attested by a single witness.

3–5.1.5.2.3 Translation Character and Technique

The general characteristics of the Three translators are given in other articles, for example, the Hexapla overview (→ 1.3.1.2), Hexapla of the Octateuch (→ 2.4.6), Hexapla of Job (→ 11.3.5), and Hexapla of Daniel (→ 18.3.2 and → 18.3.4). Some features illustrated in 1–4 Kingdoms are presented here.

3–5.1.5.2.3.1 Theodotion

Theodotion's work in 1–4 Kingdoms (also named *kaige*-Theodotion, → 1.3.1.2) agrees in most respects with his work in other books. He provides a revision of the LXX text available to him, retaining it when he finds it satisfactory, but often modifying it to bring it into closer conformity with his Hebrew text. That Theodotion was not producing a *de novo* translation is indicated by his often following LXX even when it departs from the Hebrew. For example, in 2 Kgdms 10:16, MT states that King Hadradezer sent for Arameans who were "from beyond the River" (מֵעֵבֶר הַנָּהָר). LXX-Kgdms adds a name for the river (Χαλαμάκ "Chalamak"), with ἐκ τοῦ πέραν τοῦ ποταμοῦ Χαλαμάκ "from beyond the river Chalamak." This addition is not reflected in Aquila or Symmachus, and Origen omits it in the fifth column. Theodotion, however, includes it, thus following LXX against the Hebrew. However, Theodotion often corrects LXX. For example, at 4 Kgdms 8:28, for MT מֶלֶךְ־אֲרָם "the king of Aram," LXX-Kgdms has βασιλέως ἀλλοφύλων "foreign king." Theodotion corrects the imprecision of LXX-Kgdms, rendering אֲרָם "Aram" with the proper name Συρίας "Syria."

Sometimes Theodotion, like Aquila, renders in a pedantically quantitative manner. For example, in 1 Kgdms 3:13, MT describes God's judgment on Eli because he knew his sons were corrupt "and he did not rebuke them" (וְלֹא כִהָה בָּם). LXX-Kgdms gives a satisfactory rendering with καὶ οὐκ ἐνουθέτει αὐτούς "and he did not admonish them."

---

of the βγ and γδ sections as Theodotion. Wevers, however, argues that the two sections, βγ and γδ, are not from the same translator; see Wevers, "A Study in the Exegetical Principles Underlying the Greek Text of 2 SM 11:2–1 Kings 2:11."

[5] Field, *Hexapla*.

[6] Brooke and McLean, *I and II Samuel* and *I and II Kings* (Vol. 2, Part 1 and Vol. 2, Part 2 of *Old Testament in Greek*).

[7] Burkitt, *Fragments of the Books of Kings according to the Translation of Aquila*.

[8] Law has published his dissertation on the Hexaplaric tradition preserved in the Syro-Hexapla of 3 Kingdoms. See Law, *Origenes Orientalis: The Preservation of Origen's Hexapla in the Syrohexapla of 3 Kingdoms*.

Theodotion, echoed by Aquila, has καὶ οὐκ ἠμαύρωσεν ἐν αὐτοῖς "and you did not inhibit *among* them." The preposition ἐν "among" is a quantitative rendering of the Hebrew ב, but it is extraneous, since an accusative object is warranted. In other places, however, Theodotion is sensitive to the demands of the target language. An example is how he renders the Hebrew בְּלִיָּעַל "Belial." In 1 Kgdms 1:16, Hannah asks Eli not to consider her "as a daughter of Belial" (לִפְנֵי בַּת־בְּלִיָּעַל), referring to a drunken, dissipated person. LXX-Kgdms renders the Hebrew fairly literally as εἰς θυγατέρα λοιμήν "as a pestilent daughter." Theodotion renders more according to the sense: ὡς μίαν τῶν ἀπαιδεύτων "as one of the boorish ones." Later, in 1 Kgdms 25:17, a harsh and foolish rich man is described as a son of "Belial" (בְּלִיָּעַל). Here, Theodotion has ἀφροσύνης "folly." Finally, in 3 Kgdms 21:13, false accusers are referred to as אַנְשֵׁי הַבְּלִיַּעַל "men of Belial." Theodotion renders this ἄνδρες ἀποστασίας "men of rebellion/apostasy," which is an apt rendering in the context.

In general, among the Three, Theodotion is the most likely to transliterate. This can be seen in 4 Kgdms 11:4, where the high priest brings officials and "guards" (רָצִים – literally "runners") into the temple. LXX-Kgdms transliterates this as Ῥασείν (Codex Alexandrinus, or LXX^A, has: Ῥασείμ), and Theodotion follows suit with Ῥασείμ. Aquila translates this word as τρέχοντας "runners" as does Symmachus with παρατρέχοντας (also "runners" in context). However, Theodotion does translate at times. In the same chapter, at 4 Kgdms 11:15, for the rare Hebrew term שְׂדֵרֹת (possibly "ranks" or "halls"), LXX-Kgdms has ἀσηρώθ (LXX^A: σαδηρώθ), a transliteration (= "asayrōth"). Here, Theodotion and Aquila translate with περιβόλων "encircling [area]."

3–5.1.5.2.3.2 Aquila

Aquila's literal tendencies can be seen in 1–4 Kingdoms. Two will be mentioned here. First, he renders quantitatively (in a word-for-word manner). An example was given above where in 1 Kgdms 3:13 for וְלֹא כִהָה בָּם "and he did not rebuke them," Aquila renders the ב preposition using ἐν, giving the somewhat awkward καὶ οὐκ ἠμαύρωσεν ἐν αὐτοῖς "and he did not inhibit *among* them."

Second, Aquila tends to translate according to rigid equivalences and often parts of speech from the same Hebrew root are rendered with equivalents derived from the same Greek stem. In the process, Aquila sometimes coins new words or creates new meanings for existing words. As an example, the verb עתק means "to move away from," and in the *Hiphil* "to move farther on" and also "to transmit/copy." Aquila always renders this verb with a form of μεταίρω "lift up and remove," "shift," or "depart," (e.g., Gen 12:8, Ps 6:8, Prov 25:1). The noun עָתָק from the same root, refers to "arrogance." Aquila renders this with the rare Greek word μέταρσις meaning "transplantation," derived from μεταίρω "to cause to move elsewhere" (1 Kgdms 2:3, Ps 30[MT 31]:19). This leads to a potentially odd translation at 1 Kgdms 2:3, where the Hebrew says "Do not let arrogance (עָתָק) come out of your mouth." Aquila uses μέταρσις here, which makes little sense in context. Perhaps Aquila has tried to recast the word's meaning, for example, to convey the idea of "moving beyond" the law in arrogance.

The Aquila fragments from the Cairo Genizah (noted above) provide an opportunity to view the translation of Aquila at a higher level than lexical equivalencies, that is, at the level of sentences and paragraphs. In these passages from 3 and 4 Kingdoms, one finds the expected differences from LXX, for example, substitutions for infelicitous LXX renderings, a more strictly quantitative rendering of every Hebrew morpheme and word, and more Hebrew-like spellings of proper names. But overall, an important perspective emerges, one that is often lost when considering only differences in lexical equivalents from LXX, and that is that despite his Hebraizing tendencies, Aquila is clearly providing a revision of LXX, borrowing heavily from both its style and vocabulary.

3–5.1.5.2.3.3 Symmachus

In 1–4 Kingdoms, Symmachus follows his normal pattern of adapting himself well to the Greek target language but still accounting for all the underlying Hebrew. As an example, 1 Kgdms 2:5 says that the hungry "cease" (חָדֵלּוּ); that is, they stop being hungry. LXX-Kgdms offers the unusual equivalent παρῆκαν γῆν "have forsaken the land." Symmachus provides a better, but not quantitative, rendering with ἀνενδεεῖς ἐγένοντο "are in want of nothing."

3–5.1.5.2.3.4 Origen

For the fifth column in the books of Kingdoms, Origen often provides the source of asterisked material. His sources include Aquila (e.g., 4 Kgdms 1:16), Symmachus (e.g., 4 Kgdms 4:39), Theodotion (e.g., 4 Kgdms 5:13), and Quinta[9] (e.g., 4 Kgdms 6:21), and combinations thereof. Law notes that of all the attributed asterisked readings in 3 Kingdoms, attributions to Aquila far outnumber those of the other two translators.[10] On the other hand, many of the asterisked readings are unattributed. Although Theodotion is often paired with others of the Three for attributions of asterisked materials,[11] he is rarely mentioned alone, and this could indicate that Theodotion is the "default" source for unattributed readings, perhaps because he is the closest of the Three to LXX.

3–5.1.5.2.4 Text-Critical Value for the Primary Translation and the Hebrew Bible

3–5.1.5.2.4.1 LXX Text History

To see the impact of the Three on the text history of LXX (→ 1.3.1.1.), one need look no farther than the attributed asterisked readings. In many cases, these additions have been incorporated into the LXX text history after the signs were lost. As an example, at 4 Kgdms 1:16, the phrase הַמִבְּלִי אֵין־אֱלֹהִים בְּיִשְׂרָאֵל לִדְרֹשׁ בִּדְבָרוֹ "is it for lack of a God in Israel to inquire by his word?" has no equivalent in most of the Greek manuscript traditions, including Codex Vaticanus (LXX^B). Origen includes an asterisked plus from Aquila: παρὰ τὸ μὴ εἶναι θεὸν ἐν Ἰσραὴλ τοῦ ἐκζητῆσαι ἐν ῥήματι αὐτοῦ "because there is not a God in Israel to inquire by his word." This entire phrase appears in several manuscripts, including LXX^A.

3–5.1.5.2.4.2 Text Criticism of the Hebrew Bible

At 2 Kgdms 15:21, MT reads: חַי־יְהוָה וְחֵי אֲדֹנִי הַמֶּלֶךְ "[as] the LORD lives, and as my lord the king lives." LXX-Kgdms renders this exactly with ζῇ κύριος καὶ ζῇ ὁ κύριός μου ὁ βασιλεύς ("[as] the Lord lives and my lord the king lives"). But after the second ζῇ, Theodotion inserts ἡ ψυχή σου "your soul lives." In a similar but less quantitative way, Symmachus has νὴ τὴν ψυχήν ζωὴν τῆς ψυχῆς σου "by the living soul of your life." Both then take the last words, "my lord the king" (אֲדֹנִי הַמֶּלֶךְ), to be vocative and render them κύριέ μου βασιλεῦ "O my lord, king." Thus, where LXX has "as my lord the king lives," Theodotion has "(as) your soul lives, O my lord, king," and Symmachus, "by the living soul of your life, O my lord, king." This could indicate that their Hebrew text included נַפְשְׁךָ "your soul" after וְחֵי. The formula "As the Lord lives and as your soul lives" is used twice in 1 Kingdoms (20:3, and 25:26), and the phrase "as your soul lives, my lord the king" occurs in the previous chapter (2 Kgdms 14:19). But neither Theodotion nor Symmachus typically depart from the Hebrew to follow stereotypical formulas. Theodotion does not tend to correct his LXX text when it is sound, and Symmachus, although not always rendering quantitatively, normally remains firmly aligned with his Hebrew text. Symmachus does occasionally translate with a theological agenda,[12] but there does not appear to be any theological reason for him to insert these extra words. Thus, we must address the real possibility that Theodotion and Symmachus were looking at a different Hebrew *Vorlage*.

Barthélemy, *Devanciers*.
Brooke–McLean, *Old Testament in Greek*, vol. 2.1–4.
Burkitt, F.C., *Fragments of the Books of Kings according to the Translation of Aquila* (Cambridge: Cambridge University Press, 1897).

---

[9] Quinta (abbreviation ε′) is the name of a fifth Greek translation that Origen sometimes included in the Hexapla.

[10] Law, *The Preservation of Origen's Hexapla in the Syrohexapla of 3 Kingdoms*, 314–15.

[11] E.g., Aq Th ε′ at 4 Kgdms 6:5, Aq Sym at 4 Kgdms 10:14, or Aq Sym Th at 4 Kgdms 5:13.

[12] Salvesen, *Symmachus in the Pentateuch*, 192–93.

Busto Saiz, J.R., *La traducción de Símaco en el Libro de los Salmos* (Textos y Estudios "Cardenal Cisneros" 22; Madrid: Consejo Superior de Investigaciones Científicas, 1978).

Fernández Marcos, N., *The Septuagint in Context: Introduction to the Greek Versions of the Bible* (transl. W.G.E. Watson; Leiden: Brill, 2000).

Field, *Hexapla*.

Gentry, P.J., *The Asterisked Materials in the Greek Job* (SBLSCS 38; Atlanta: Scholars Press, 1995).

Hyvärinen, K., *Die Übersetzung von Aquila* (ConBOT 10; Uppsala: Almquist & Wiksell, 1977).

de Lagarde, P., *Bibliothecae syriacae a Paulo de Lagarde collectae quae ad philogiam sacram pertinent* (Göttingen: Dieterich, 1892).

Law, T.M., *Origenes Orientalis: The Preservation of Origen's Hexapla in the Syrohexapla of 3 Kingdoms* (De Septuaginta Investigationes 2; Göttingen: Vandenhoeck and Ruprecht, 2011).

Muraoka, T., *A Greek–English Lexicon of the Septuagint* (Louvain: Peeters, 2009).

Salvesen, A., *Symmachus in the Pentateuch* (JSS Monograph 15; Manchester: Victoria University of Manchester, 1991).

Taylor, B.A. and P.D. McLean, "1 Reigns," "The Kaige Text of Reigns: To the Reader," "2 Reigns," "3 Reigns," and "4 Reigns," in *NETS*, 244–341.

Thackeray, H.St.J., "The Greek Translators of the Four Books of Kings," *JTS* 8 (1906–1907): 262–78.

Wevers, J.W., "Exegetical Principles Underlying the Septuagint Text of 1 Kings ii 12–xxi 43," *OtSt* 8 (1950): 300–22.

Wevers, J.W., "Principles of Interpretation Guiding the Fourth Translator of the Book of Kingdoms: 3 K. 22:1–4 K. 25:30," *CBQ* 14 (1952): 40–56.

Wevers, J.W., "A Study in the Exegetical Principles Underlying the Greek Text of 2 SM 11:2–1 Kings 2:11," *CBQ* 15 (1953): 30–45.

3–5.1.6 Post-Hexaplaric Greek Translations

Due to the different arrangement of the books in the Septuagint, the articles on the Post-Hexaplaric Greek Translations are arranged in the following way: → 2.4.7 Post-Hexaplaric Greek Translations (Pentateuch > Primary Translations), → 3–5.1.6.1 Joshua–Judges (Former Prophets > Primary Translations > Post-Hexaplaric Greek Translations), and → 3–5.1.6.2. Samuel–Kings (Former Prophets > Primary Translations > Post-Hexaplaric Greek Translations).

Andrew McClurg

3–5.1.6.1 Joshua-Judges
3–5.1.6.1.1 Background

The only post-Hexaplaric recension known to us is that of Lucian (→ 1.3.1.2). The books of Joshua and Judges are unique in the Heptateuch, because of the presence of a Lucianic recension in the manuscripts. The two books share a similar textual history with the books of Kingdoms, though the witnesses differ somewhat. The discovery of two manuscripts at Qumran for each book (→ 3.2.1; → 4.2.1) has fueled suspicion that the Lucianic recension is a witness to an early stratum in the Hebrew textual tradition.

3–5.1.6.1.2 Original Form, Editions, Auxiliary Tools

In 2015, there is no critical edition of Joshua or Judges in the Göttingen LXX. Margolis' *The Book of Joshua in Greek: According to the Critically Restored Text with an Apparatus Containing the Variants of the Principal Recensions of the Individual Witnesses* is the most complete critical edition of Joshua to date. Substantial studies of the LXX^L text include articles by Trebolle Barrera and Thornhill.[1] In Joshua, witnesses to the LXX^L text include Margolis' Syrian group *s*. Among the early fathers, Chrysostom is an important witness to the LXX^L text of Joshua.[2] The group *AII* and its subgroup composed of manuscripts *glnw* are the chief witnesses to the Lucianic recension in Judges.[3]

3–5.1.6.1.3 Translation Character, Technique, and Inner-Translational Features

The translation character of OG-Josh is marked by a concern for clarity and style (see van der Meer's analysis: → 3.3.4). Hence, identifying a recension of similar characteristics can be difficult. Nonethe-

---

[1] Trebolle Barrera, "Text-Critical Value," 401–13; Thornhill, "Six or Seven Nations," 233–46.
[2] Sipilä, "John Chrysostom and the Book of Joshua," 332.
[3] See Satterthwaite, "Judges: To the Reader," 196.

less, many of the characteristic improvements of the recension are evident.[4] For example, doublets, which are stellar features of the Luicanic recension, are not lacking in the manuscripts (Josh 11:19 οὐκ ἐγένετο πόλις ἥτις εἰρήνευσεν τοῖς υἱοῖς Ισραηλ ... οὐκ ἦν πόλις ἥτις οὐ παρεδόθη τοῖς υἱοῖς Ισραηλ "And there was not a city that kept peace with the Israelites ... there was no city which was not handed over to the Israelites"/לֹא־הָיְתָה עִיר אֲשֶׁר הִשְׁלִימָה אֶל־בְּנֵי יִשְׂרָאֵל "there was not a town that made peace with the Israelites").[5] The focus of scholarship has been the apparent pre-Hexaplaric variants in LXX^L, many of which agree with Old Latin witnesses (→ 3–5.2.1.1). Agreements with Codex LXX^A in Joshua (e.g., Josh 10:12 ἀπὸ προσώπου υἱῶν 'Ισραηλ "before the sons of Israel"/ἀπὸ προσώπου 'Ισραηλ "before Israel" LXX^{AL}) may also be indicative of pre-Hexaplaric readings, because LXX^A is a witness to an early phase in the history of transmission (see below, → 3–5.1.6.1.4).

3–5.1.6.1.4 Text-Critical Value

Trebolle Barrera has posited that the LXX^A and LXX^L groups in both Joshua and Judges are the closest witnesses to the Old Greek. This fact likely makes them, along with Old Latin witnesses and two texts from Qumran (4QJudg^a [→ 4.2.1.2] and 4QJosh^a [→ 3.2.1.1]), the best witnesses to a Hebrew text that differs from MT.[6] Satterthwaite suggests that the lack of strong influence from Hexaplaric sources and the "*kaige*" revision (→ 1.3.1.2) make the Lucianic group *AII* the best witness to OG-Judg.[7] Agreements between Codex LXX^A, the LXX^L text, and MT (→ 3.2.2; → 4.2.2) are commonly attributed to later harmonization toward MT (e.g., LXX-Josh 15:22 καὶ Αρουηλ "and Arouel" LXX^B/καὶ Αδαδα "and Adada" LXX^{AL}/MT וְעַדְעָדָה "and Adada").[8] In such cases, Hexaplaric influence may account for the agreement. As mentioned above (→ 3–5.1.6.1.3), agreements with Old Latin witnesses (→ 3–5.2.1.1) are indicative of proto-Lucianic readings. The phenomenon of proto-Lucianic readings is difficult to account for. Conclusions based on the readings normally entail a plurality of textual forms of either the Hebrew text or LXX.

Bieberstein, K., *Lukian und Theodotion im Josuabuch: Mit einem Beitrag zu den Josuarollen von Ḥirbet Qumrān* (BNSup 7; Munich: K. Urlaub, 1994).

Holmes, S., *Joshua: The Hebrew and Greek Texts* (Cambridge: Cambridge University Press, 1914).

Margolis, M.L., *The Book of Joshua in Greek: According to the Critically Restored Text with an Apparatus Containing the Variants of the Principal Recensions of the Individual Witnesses*, Part 1–4 (Publications of the Alexander Kohut Memorial Foundation in Trust at the American Academy for Jewish Research; Paris: Paul Geuther, 1931–1938).

Margolis, M.L., *The Book of Joshua in Greek: According to the Critically Restored Text with an Apparatus Containing the Variants of the Principal Recensions of the Individual Witnesses*, Part 5 (Publications of the Alexander Kohut Memorial Foundation in Trust at the American Academy for Jewish Research; Philadelphia: Annenberg Research Institute, 1992).

Satterthwaite, P.E., "Judges: To the Reader," in *NETS*, 195–200.

Sipilä, S., "John Chrysostom and the Book of Joshua," in *IX Congress of the International Organization for Septuagint and Cognate Studies: Cambridge, 1995* (ed. B.A. Taylor; SBLSCS 45; Atlanta: Scholars Press, 1997), 329–54.

Thornhill, R., "Six or Seven Nations: A Pointer to the Lucianic Text in the Heptateuch, with Special Reference to the Old Latin Version," *JTS* 10 (1959): 233–46.

Trebolle Barrera, J., "The Text-Critical Value of the Old Latin and Antiochean Greek Texts in the Books of Judges and Joshua," in *Interpreting Translation: Studies on the LXX and Ezekiel in Honour of Johan Lust* (eds. F. García Martínez and M. Vervenne; BETL 192; Leuven: Peeters, 2005), 401–13.

Ziegler, J., "Hat Lukian den griechischen Sirach rezensiert?" *Bib* 40 (1959): 210–29.

---

[4] For a helpful analysis of Lucianic style, see Ziegler, "Hat Lukian den griechischen Sirach rezensiert?" 210–29.

[5] For an analysis of the doublets, see Trebolle Barrera, "Text-Critical Value," 406–11.

[6] Trebolle Barrera, "Text-Critical Value," 401–11.

[7] Satterthwaite, "Judges: To the Reader," 196.

[8] Codex LXX^B represents the Old Greek reading. See Holmes, *Joshua: The Hebrew and Greek Texts*, 62.

3–5.1.6.2 Samuel-Kings

3–5.1.6.2.1 Background

The only post-Hexaplaric recension known to us is that of Lucian (→ 1.3.2.1). So little is known about Lucian of Antioch that some scholars reject the notion of a Lucianic recension.[1] What is certain is that a distinct text type exists in the historical books of LXX. The books of Kingdoms have commanded the attention of scholars for nearly two centuries. In 1 Kingdoms, Brock attributes the LXX^L text to Lucian.[2] Problems arise in 2–4 Kingdoms because of the *kaige* sections (→ 5.4; → 5.5), where the Lucianic manuscripts tend to avoid features peculiar to LXX. Hence, Lucianic variants prior to the martyr's lifetime pose significant obstacles for attributing readings to one man. Agreements with citations from the Antiochian fathers (→ 21.7) and ancient testimonies, especially from Jerome, have made abandoning the designation "Lucianic" difficult.

3–5.1.6.2.2 Original Form, Editions, Auxiliary Tools

To date, there is no edition of the books of Kingdoms in the Göttingen LXX. Research on the Lucianic recension has arisen mostly from the Brooke–McLean edition[3] and the early edition by Holmes and Parsons.[4] Nonetheless, Fernández Marcos and Busto Saiz have produced a useful edition of the Lucianic recension.[5] Volumes 1 and 2 are devoted to the four books of Kingdoms and provide a fresh collation of the well-known manuscripts LXX[19, 82, 93, 108, 127]. Taylor's *The Lucianic Manuscripts of 1 Reigns* is also a helpful edition of the Lucianic recension that presents the recension in the most original form that the evidence will allow. Notable studies on the Lucianic recension include Brock's *The Recensions of the Septuagint Version of 1 Samuel*, Dominique Barthélemy's **Devanciers*, and Rahlfs' **Septuaginta*.[6]

3–5.1.6.2.3 Translation Character and Technique

Lucian's work generally includes two features: 1) grammatical and stylistic improvements; and 2) revision toward the Hebrew text. The latter (e.g., 3 Kgdms 2:3 κατὰ πάντα ὅσα ἂν ἐντείλωμαί σοι "in all things, whatever I command you" [NETS] LXX/καὶ πανταχῇ οὗ ἐὰν ἐπιβλέψῃς ἐκεῖ LXX^L = MT וְאֵת כָּל־אֲשֶׁר תִּפְנֶה שָׁם "and wherever you run" [NRSV]) is characteristic of the recension, though scholars are not certain that Lucian read Hebrew. Grammatical and stylistic improvements include doublets (e.g., 2 Kgdms 2:8 διὰ ξηρᾶς ὡς ἐν ἐρήμῳ "through dry land as in the desert"), preference for the second aorist εἶπον "I said" to the first aorist εἶπα of the same meaning,[7] additions of the article to nouns in certain syntactical environments (e.g., to proper nouns not governed by a preposition), avoidance of parataxis with variations in particles (e.g., 1 Kgdms 1:19 καὶ ὀρθρίζουσιν "and they rose early" LXX/ὀρθρίσαντες δε "and rising early" LXX^L), and a slight preference for Attic morphology (e.g., 3 Kgdms 12:31 ἱερεῖς LXX/ἱερέας LXX^L "priests").[8]

3–5.1.6.2.4 Inner-Translational Features

Three strata of the Lucianic recension are discernible in Kingdoms: 1) pre-Hexaplaric/proto-Lucianic readings; 2) Hexaplaric influence; and 3) unaligned variants that are commonly attributed to the historical Lucian of Antioch. On the first stratum, see below, → 3–5.1.6.2.5. The second stratum includes readings likely derived from the fifth column of Origen's Hexapla (→ 1.3.2.1; → 3–5.1.5.2) as well as readings from the Three, especially Symmachus (e.g., 1 Kgdms 12:25 προστεθήσεσθε "you will be handed over" LXX/ἀπολεῖσθε "you will be de-

---

[1] See e.g. Brock, *Recensions*, 177–78.
[2] Brock, *Recensions*, 298–99.
[3] Brooke–McLean–Thackeray, **The Old Testament in Greek*.
[4] R. Holmes and J. Parsons (ed.), *Vetus Testamentum Graecum cum variis lectionibus*, Vol. 2 (Oxford: Clarendon, 1818).
[5] Fernández Marcos and Busto Saiz, *El Texto Antioqueno de la Biblia Griega*.

[6] See ch. 3 in Brock, *Recensions*; Barthélemy, **Devanciers*; see vol. 3 in Rahlfs, **Septuaginta*.
[7] See Brock, *Recensions*, 228–29. Brock notes that other verbs follow the same Attic usage.
[8] The characteristics of the Lucianic recension are fairly uniform, though they vary in degree of distribution. For a list of characteristics, see Ziegler, "Hat Lukian den griechischen Sirach rezensiert?"

stroyed" LXX^L = Sym). The third stratum includes variants that scholars attribute to Lucian's work; → 3–5.1.6.2.3.

3–5.1.6.2.5 Text-Critical Value

The text-critical value of the Lucianic recension for establishing the Old Greek (OG) of Kingdoms is difficult to determine. The relevant manuscripts generally disagree with the *kaige* sections of Kingdoms (LXX-2 Sam 11–LXX-1 Kgs 2:11; LXX-1 Kgs 22–LXX-2 Kgs; → 5.4; → 5.4). Agreements with Josephus (→ 21.3) and VL (→ 3–5.2.1.2) exist. The discovery of 4QSam^a (→ 5.3.1.2) reportedly affirms that something like the text of LXX^L existed in a Hebrew manuscript. Kreuzer affirms Barthélemy's conclusion that the Lucianic text is basically the Old Greek with few revised elements.[9] The affirmation contrasts with Saley's conclusion that 4QSam^a infrequently agrees with proto-Lucianic variants, especially doublets.[10] The two conclusions admit markedly different appraisals of the worth of manuscripts LXX^{19, 82, 93, 108, 127} for text-critical purposes. It must be admitted that agreements between 4QSam^a and Lucianic manuscripts demonstrate a relationship, though the study of Kauhanen has shown that there are only three places where 4QSam^a preserves the *Vorlage* of LXX while LXX^L also preserves the OG of 1 Kingdoms (1 Kgdms 5:9; 6:20; 20:32).[11] Preservation of the Old Greek of Kingdoms is not uncommon in the Lucianic recension. For example, in 4 Kgdms 6:15, the LXX^L text reads against LXX and MT in preserving τὸ πρωΐ "early in the morning". Support from VL (*de luce* "at dawn") suggests that LXX^L preserves a pre-Hexaplaric reading which may evince the Old Greek.[12] Nonetheless, *contaminatio*, which is rightly attributed to improper handling of Hexaplaric readings, is a phenomenon that certainly occurred before Origen's time. The reliability of the Lucianic recension for text-critical purposes must be handled on a variant-by-variant basis.

3–5.1.6.2.6 History of Research

Antonio M. Ceriani and Frederick Field developed criteria for locating the Lucianic recension in 1–4 Kingdoms that remain the standard in the field: agreements with citations from the Antiochian fathers (→ 21.7) and linguistic improvements. They examined readings that were preceded by the Syriac letter ܠ in the Syro-Hexapla (→ 3–5.2.4.2). The readings contained agreements with the Antiochian fathers, a fact that led Ceriani and Field to suspect that ܠ was an attribution to Λουκιανός "Lucian."[13] Rahlfs stratified the manuscripts into two groups: LXX^{19, 108} and LXX^{82, 93}.[14] The research of Fernández Marcos and Busto Saiz confirms Rahlfs' conclusion that manuscripts LXX^{82, 93, 127} best preserve the Lucianic recension in places where the manuscripts read against manuscripts LXX^{19, 108}.[15] Subsequent scholarship has focused on the problem of proto-Lucianic readings and has struggled to understand how the readings relate to other features of the Lucianic recension such as agreements with the Antiochian fathers and Hexaplaric influence. Tov suggested that proto-Lucianic readings are best explained as a layer closely related to the Old Greek (→ 5.4; → 5.5) that underlies variants that are attributable to Lucian of the fourth century.[16] Subsequent scholarship has focused on this problem with some scholars agreeing with Tov and others allowing the tension of the data to remain (→ 3–5.1.6.2.5). The latter group includes Taylor who suggested that the LXX^L text of 1 Kingdoms differs significantly from the text of LXX^B, which is likely the best exemplar of the Old Greek and is closest to the

---

[9] S. Kreuzer, "Translations and Recensions: Old Greek, *Kaige*, and Antiochene Text in Samuel and Reigns," *BIOSCS* 42 (2009): 49.

[10] R.J. Saley, "Proto-Lucian and 4QSam^a," *BIOSCS* 41 (2008): 45; R.J. Saley, "Greek Lucianic Doublets and 4QSam^a," *BIOSCS* 40 (2007): 63–73.

[11] Kauhanen, *The Proto-Lucianic Problem of 1 Samuel*, 190–91.

[12] See the analysis of Kreuzer, "Translations and Recensions," 48.

[13] See Fernández Marcos, *Septuagint*, 227.

[14] Rahlfs, *Septuaginta*, 415–34.

[15] See e.g. J.R. Busto Saiz, "On the Lucianic Manuscripts in 1–2 Kings," in *VI Congress of the International Organization for Septuagint and Cognate Studies* (ed. C.E. Cox; SBLSCS 23; Atlanta: SBL, 1987), 305–10.

[16] Tov, "Lucian and Proto-Lucian," 103.

text that Origen used for his fifth column (→ 1.3.2.1; → 3–5.1.5.2).¹⁷ Taylor's conclusion contrasts with Cross' contention that proto-Lucianic readings are representative of the Old Greek.¹⁸

Brock, S.P., *The Recensions of the Septuagint Version of 1 Samuel* (Turin: Silvio Zamorani, 1996).
Fernández Marcos, N., "Literary and Editorial Features of the Antiochian Text in Kings," in *VI Congress of the International Organization for Septuagint and Cognate Studies* (ed. C.E. Cox; SBLSCS 23; Atlanta: Scholars Press, 1986), 287–303.
Fernández Marcos, N. and J.R. Busto Saiz, *El Texto Antioqueno de la Biblia Griega*, Vol. 1: *1–2 Samuel* (Textos y Estudios "Cardenal Cisneros" de la Biblia Políglota Matritense 50; Madrid: Instituto de Felología, 1989).
Fernández Marcos, N. and J.R. Busto Saiz, *El Texto Antioqueno de la Biblia Griega*, Vol. 2: *1–2 Reyes* (Textos y Estudios "Cardenal Cisneros" de la Biblia Políglota Matritense 53; Madrid: Instituto de Felología, 1992).
Kauhanen, T., *The Proto-Lucianic Problem in 1 Samuel* (De Septuaginta Investigationes 3; Göttingen: Vandenhoeck and Ruprecht, 2012).
Rahlfs, *Septuaginta.
Spottorno, M.V., "Josephus' Text for 1–2 Kings (3–4 Kingdoms)," in *VII Congress of the International Organization for Septuagint and Cognate Studies* (eds. L. Greenspoon and O. Munnich; SBLSCS 41; Atlanta: Scholars Press, 1995), 145–52.
Taylor, B.A., *The Lucianic Manuscripts of 1 Reigns* (HSM 51; 2 vols.; Atlanta: Scholars Press, 1993).
Tov, E., "Lucian and Proto-Lucian: Toward a New Solution of the Problem," *RB* 79 (1972): 101–13.
Ziegler, J., "Hat Lukian den griechischen Sirach rezensiert?" *Bib* 40 (1959): 210–29.

Matthew M. Dickie

3–5.1.7 Vulgate

3–5.1.7.1 Background

v-Former Prophets is an interesting collection of translations in that there is considerable variation in its quality. Samuel and Kings are perhaps Jerome's earliest translations, whereas Joshua and Judges were among his last. In light of the *Prologus Galeatus* to Samuel and Kings, these books are often considered the first books translated by Jerome. In the *Prologus*, Jerome writes "This preface of the Scriptures can be understood as a helmeted beginning to all of the books, which we turn from Hebrew into Latin." Alternatively, in light of the theological importance of the respective books and the development of Jerome's technique, Kedar-Kopfstein maintains that the translations of the Prophets and Psalms preceded those of Samuel and Kings. He also notes that information found in the prefaces to Isaiah and Daniel would be redundant if Samuel–Kings had been translated first.¹ In any case, having translated Samuel–Kings between 390 and 394 C.E., and Joshua–Judges between 398 and 404/405 C.E. (→ 1.3.5.2), Jerome would have had considerable time to develop his knowledge and facility as a translator.²

3–5.1.7.2 Translation Character

Kedar-Kopfstein has pointed out that despite Jerome's testimony that he consulted sources, his translations remain largely independent (→ 1.3.5.10). He writes, "The moment we survey the overall picture, his relative independence becomes apparent: He never agrees with one of his informants for more than a short clause."³ Similarly, Sparks notes that Jerome in practice "translated

---

¹⁷ Taylor, "Lucianic Manuscripts," 127.
¹⁸ Cross, *"Evolution," 313.

---

¹ Kedar-Kopfstein, "The Latin Translations," 321. Elsewhere, he maintains that Jerome's reference to having translated the Old Testament from Hebrew into Latin in *Vir. ill.* 135 (*vetus* [*testamentum*] *iuxta hebraicum transtulit* "he has translated the Old [Testament] according to the Hebrew") refers to the Psalms and the Prophets, which are mentioned as having been translated in the previous chapter. See Kedar-Kopfstein, "The Vulgate as a Translation," 53.
² For a discussion of these dates, see J.N.D. Kelly, *Jerome: His Life, Writings, and Controversies* (London: Harper & Row, 1975), 156–62, and C.B. Tkacz, " 'Labor Tam Utilis': The Creation of the Vulgate," *VC* 50 (1996): 42–72 (50–51).
³ B. Kedar-Kopfstein, "The Latin Translations," in *Mikra, 299–338 (323). Adler comes to a similar conclusion. See W. Adler, "*Ad Verbum* or *Ad Sensum*: The Christianization of a Latin Translation Formula in the Fourth Century," in *Pursuing the Text: Studies in Honor of Ben Zion Wacholder on the Occasion of his Seventieth Birthday* (ed. J.C. Reeves and J. Kampen; JSOTSup 184; Sheffield: Sheffield Academic Press, 1994), 321–48 (334).

very much as he happened himself to feel at any particular moment."[4] This may be due to the fact that Jerome intended to create a coherent text. A similar notion is expressed by Kelly, who asserts that Jerome "tended to take greater liberties with the books he translated latest, so that while he justly scorned any suggestion that his Samuel and Kings could be described as a paraphrase, his version of Judges (404/5) comes pretty near to being one."[5] Though it may generally be regarded as a free rendering of the Hebrew into idiomatic Latin, the translation character of v-Former Prophets is more rigid or imitative in Samuel–Kings, while it is less rigid or more transformative in Joshua–Judges.

3–5.1.7.3 Translation Technique
3–5.1.7.3.1 Hebrew Idioms

Avoiding the rigid and imitative style frequently observed in LXX (→ 3.3; → 4.3; → 5.4; → 5.5), Jerome regularly renders the infinitive absolute + finite verb into coherent Latin, e.g., וּבָכֹה תִבְכֶּה "and weeping, she wept" (i.e., "and she wept strongly"), *flens largiter* "weeping greatly" (1 Sam 1:10); יָדֹעַ תֵּדְעוּ, "knowing, you will know" (i.e., "you will surely know"), *iam nunc scitote* "so then, know!" (Josh 23:13). The Hebrew purpose/result clause of imperative followed by simple ו + imperfect is regularly translated with an *ut* clause in v-Former Prophets, e.g., עֲלוּ ... וְנַכֶּה, *ascendite ... ut expugnemus* "Come up ... so that we may attack" (Josh 10:4); ... חוּדָה וְנִשְׁמָעֶנָּה, *propone ... ut audiamus* "Put forth ... so that we may hear" (Judg 14:13); קִבְצוּ ... וְאֶתְפַּלֵּל, *congregate ... ut orem* "Gather ... so that I may pray" (1 Sam 7:5; cf. also 1 Sam 9:26, 27; 11:3; 12:7). Likewise, the temporal clause of ב/כ + infinitive construct is usually rendered adverbially, e.g., בְּצֵאתְכֶם literally, "in your coming out," *quando egressi estis* "when you came out" (Josh 2:10); בַּעֲלוֹתָם, literally, "in their coming up," *quando ... conscenderunt* "when they came up" (Judg 11:16); בְּלֶכְתְּךָ, literally, "in your going," *cum abieris* "When you go" (1 Sam 10:2); כְּכַלּוֹתְךָ, literally, "according to your finishing," *cum conpleveris* "when you have finished" (2 Sam 11:19); and כִּשְׁמֹעַ, literally, "according to (all Israel) hearing," *cum audisset* "when (all Israel) heard" (1 Kgs 12:20). Except for one instance (Judg 11:27), the redundancy of בֵּין ... בֵּין "between ... between" is regularly alleviated with *inter ... et* "between ... and" throughout v-Joshua–Judges. However, the more imitative rendering *inter ... inter* "between ... between" is found in v-Samuel–Kings (1 Sam 7:12; 14:42; 2 Sam 3:1; 21:7; 1 Kgs 15:7; 2 Kgs 11:17). Similarly, יסף + verbal complement is regularly rendered adverbially in Joshua–Judges, e.g., אוֹסִיף לִהְיוֹת, literally, "I will (not) add to be," *ero ultra* "I will (not) be again" (Josh 7:12); הַאוֹסִיף לָגֶשֶׁת, literally, "Shall I add to go near?" *debeo ultra procedere* "Should I go forth again?" (Judg 20:23); יָסַף ... לִרְאוֹת, literally, "he did (not) add ... to see," *vidit ... ultra* "he did (not) see again" (1 Sam 15:35). However, יסף + verbal complement ("to do again") is regularly rendered more literally with the use of *adicio*, "add," *addo*, "add to," or *adpono*, "apply to" in Samuel–Kings (e.g., 1 Sam 3:6, 7:13; 20:17; 27:4; 2 Sam 14:10; 1 Kgs 16:33).

By means of pronouns, prepositions, etc., Jerome often removes what seem to be unnecessary proper nouns in the Hebrew. For example, by doing comparative searches on twenty of the most frequently appearing proper nouns within v-Former Prophets (which account for 50.1% of all proper nouns),[6] it can be demonstrated that, in these cases, Jerome gradually decreases the number of redundant proper nouns.[7]

---

[4] H.F.D. Sparks, "Jerome as Biblical Scholar," in *The Cambridge History of the Bible*, Vol. 1: *From the Beginnings to Jerome* (eds. P.R. Ackroyd and C.F. Evans; Cambridge: Cambridge University Press, 1970), 510–41 (526).

[5] Kelly, *Jerome*, 162.

[6] These are Lord, Israel, David, God, Saul, Solomon, Judah, Jerusalem, Samuel, Joshua, Philistine, Joab, Jordan, Absalom, Jonathan, Jeroboam, Egypt, Ahab, Moses, and Benjamin. The proper nouns were searched in morphologically tagged databases in their respective languages (e.g., יִשְׂרָאֵל/Ισραηλ/*Israhel*).

[7] These comparisons are somewhat problematic in that they assume the texts created by and available to Jerome are the same as those of the digital versions. This is less problematic in the case of MT, which consistently agrees with the Vulgate. Regarding the Greek texts that were available to Jerome, in light of his numerous references to LXX, his numerous references to various Hexaplaric readings, and his knowledge of the Hexapla in Caesarea, one may assume that

	V	MT	LXX	Vulg/MT	LXX/MT
Joshua	685	818	838	84%	102%
Judges	440	578	559	76%	97%[8]
Samuel	2423	2594	2272	93%	88%
Kings	1781	1894	1934	94%	102%

The first three columns contain the number of proper nouns appearing from each frequency-set. The last two columns contain the percentage of proper nouns in the Vulgate and LXX as compared to those of MT. Notice that in the books translated earlier (i.e., Samuel–Kings), Jerome has a significantly higher ratio. So, within the earlier translations of Samuel–Kings, Jerome more closely mimics the Hebrew, whereas in his later translations of Joshua–Judges, he deviates more freely from MT.

This chronological decrease in literalism can also be seen in Jerome's translation of other common Hebrew words and phrases. For example, the imitative rendering of הִנֵּה with *ecce* "behold" is seen far more often in Samuel–Kings (118 out of 240 occurrences; 49%) than it is in Joshua–Judges (17 out of 59 occurrences; 29%). The phrase חֵן בְּעֵינֶיךָ "favor in your eyes" is regularly rendered more freely in Judges, e.g., *gratiam coram te* "favor before you" (Judg 6:17), whereas it is consistently rendered literally in Samuel, *gratiam in oculis tuis* "favor in your eyes" (e.g., 1 Sam 25:8; 2 Sam 15:25). Similarly, לִפְנֵי "to the face of" (i.e., "before") is more frequently rendered literally in Samuel–Kings, e.g., מִלִּפְנֵי/*a facie* "from the face" (1 Sam 8:18; 21:17; 2 Sam 24:4); לִפְנֵי/*in conspectu* "in the sight of" (1 Sam 1:15; 1 Kgs 1:23; 2 Kgs 3:14); whereas Jerome forgoes the use of a preposition through his choice of verb within Joshua–Judges, e.g., לֹא־יִתְיַצֵּב אִישׁ לְפָנֶיךָ "a man shall not stand to your face," *nullus vobis poterit resistere* "No one will be able to resist you" (Josh 1:5); וְלֹא־יָכְלוּ עוֹד לַעֲמֹד לִפְנֵי "and they were not able still to stand to the face of," *nec potuerunt resistere* "and they were not able to resist" (Judg 2:14); וְהִנַּחְתִּי לְפָנֶיךָ "and I lay (it) to your face," *et offerens tibi* "and offering (it) to you" (Judg 6:18).

3–5.1.7.3.2 Attention to Context

On a number of occasions within V-Former Prophets, Jerome provides not only a transliteration of a Hebrew place name but also supplies a translation. The translations may be derived from LXX (→ 3.3; → 4.3; → 5.4; → 5.5), e.g., בְּהַר־חֶרֶס/*in monte Hares quod interpretatur testaceo* "in the mountain 'Hares,' which is translated 'earthenware,'" ἐν τῷ ὄρει τῷ ὀστρακώδει "on the potsherd mountain" (Judg 1:35 LXX^B); שִׁבֹּלֶת/*sebboleth quod interpretatur spica*, "'Shibboleth,' which is translated 'ear of corn,'" στάχυς "ear of corn" (Judg 12:6 LXX^B); רָמַת לֶחִי, *Ramathlehi quod interpretatur elevatio maxillae*, "'Ramathlechi,' which is translated 'lifting up of the jawbone,'" ἀναίρεσις σιαγόνος "taking up of a jawbone" (Judg 15:17). At times, Jerome provides the meaning of a place name instead of a transliteration, e.g., בֹּכִים, *Flentium sive Lacrimarum* "(the place) of weepers, or of tears" (Judg 2:5).

Regarding the repetition of verbs, Jerome will regularly introduce *varietas* into his translation, as he often does when a verse features two or more occurrences of אָמַר "said." For example, in Josh 4:21; 9:11; and 22:24, no translation is provided for לֵאמֹר "saying." Elsewhere, *dico* "say," *interrogo* "inquire," *respondeo* "answer," and *puto* "think" are used to render אָמַר "said," as appropriate to the context (see Josh 22:8; Judg 4:20; 12:6; 15:2).

3–5.1.7.3.3 Style

Jerome shows a basic (and increasing) concern for Latin style in V-Former Prophets. In Latin, it is normal for the verb to appear last within a given sentence or phrase, whereas the reverse is true for Hebrew narrative. Accordingly, there are countless opportunities for Jerome to create awkward or inelegant Latin. Take for example the numerous verses that begin with וַיֹּאמֶר "and he said." These are regularly rendered literally within V-Former Prophets by the combination of *et/-que + dixit* "and he said," *ait* "he said," or *respondit*, "he answered"

Jerome would have had access to a broad range of readings. See D. Brown, *Vir Trilinguis: A Study in the Biblical Exegesis of Saint Jerome* (Kampen: Pharos, 1992), 55–62.

[8] The word count for LXX^A is 465 or 89%.

appearing at the start of the verse. However, as time passes, this inelegant Latin word order occurs less frequently.

	Joshua, Judges	Samuel, Kings
Initial וַיֹּאמֶר	110 verses	407 verses
Initial *dico, ait,* or *respondit*	52 verses	327 verses
Ratio	47 %	80 %

According to this chart, there are 379 verses in the Former Prophets that begin with the phrase וַיֹּאמֶר, which are rendered in the Vulgate with *dixit, ait,* or *respondit* as the first or second word in the verse (depending on whether or not a conjunction is used). It appears that as time passes Jerome prefers a less literal or awkward rendering, although Hebrew word order is regularly reflected throughout v-Former Prophets.

Another example of Jerome's concern for style can be seen in his handling of the conjunctive *waw*. An imitative translation that renders the conjunction ו uniformly (e.g., καί "and" in LXX) results in a wooden translation that lacks coherence, because in Hebrew ו has a number of functions that are not equally represented by the functions of καί "and" or *et* "and." On the whole, the Vulgate does a better job than other ancient versions do in rendering Hebrew conjunctions and particles according to their function.

	Joshua	Judges	Samuel	Kings
et/-*que* occurrences	1295	1165	3089	3251
ו occurrences	1873	1949	4736	4607
καί occurrences	1811	1948	4708	4693
Vulgate Ratio	69 %	60 %	65 %	71 %
Septuagint Ratio	97 %	100 %	99 %	102 %

This chart assumes there is a general correlation of translation between the occurrences of *et*/-*que* and καί with ו. This is somewhat problematic with regard to LXX, which often reflects a *Vorlage* different than MT (especially in 1–2 Samuel). Nevertheless, the high ratio of LXX reflects the *ad verbum* style of that Greek translation. Considering that Targum Jonathan and the Peshitta also offer ratios of approximately 100 %, Jerome clearly demonstrates a freedom with the Hebrew text that had been theretofore unseen. Accordingly, moving beyond the typical co-ordinative function, Jerome demonstrates greater flexibility in rendering the disjunctive or adversative function of ו.

Numerous Hebrew language features receive stylistic improvements in v-Former Propehts. For example, attributive and substantival participles are regularly rendered with relative clauses, e.g., הַמַּיִם הַיֹּרְדִים/*aquae ... quae ... veniunt* "waters ... that ... come" (Josh 3:13); הָעֹמְדִים/*qui stabant* "who stood" (1 Sam 17:26); and עַל־הָאֲנָשִׁים הַיֹּשְׁבִים/*ad viros qui sedent* "to the men who sit" (2 Kgs 18:27). Where there is a repetition of verb, Jerome will often introduce another verb of similar meaning, presumably for the sake of *varietas*, e.g., וְאֵשְׁבָה ... יֵשֵׁב "so that I may dwell ... dwell," *ut habitem ... manet* "so that I may dwell ... remain" (1 Sam 27:5); לָתֵת ... וַיִּתֵּן "and he gave ... to give," *deditque ... traditurum* "and he gave ... would deliver" (Josh 21:41); and זֶה יֵלֵךְ אִתָּךְ הוּא יֵלֵךְ "this one will go with you, he will go," *tecum vadat ipse pergat* "let this one go with you, he should set out" (Judg 7:4). Judg 6:35 provides an interesting example of omission in that the Vulgate removes both a redundant noun and verb: וּמַלְאָכִים שָׁלַח ... וּמַלְאָכִים שָׁלַח "Now, messengers he sent ... and messengers he sent," *misitque nuntios ... et alios* "and he sent messengers ... and others." Parataxis is often alleviated in v-Former Prophets by means of *ut* clauses, participial clauses, and *cum* clauses. A convenient example is Josh 2:21, which employs both an *ut* clause and a participial clause, וַתְּשַׁלְּחֵם וַיֵּלֵכוּ וַתִּקְשֹׁר "And she sent them away, and they went, and she bound," *dimittensque eos ut pergerent adpendit* "and sending them away so that they might go, she hung." Likewise, a *cum* clause mitigates parataxis in 1 Kgs 18:43, וַיַּעַל וַיַּבֵּט וַיֹּאמֶר "and he went up and he looked and he said," *cum ascendisset et contemplatus esset ait* "When he went up and looked, he said."

3–5.1.7.3.4 Transliterations

Regarding the transliteration of proper nouns, Jerome will occasionally follow LXX (→ 3.3; → 4.3; → 5.4; → 5.5), but more commonly he offers his own spelling. For example עַי "Ai," *Ahi*/Γαι (Josh 7:5); עָתְנִיאֵל "Othniel," *Othoniel*/Γοθονιηλ (Josh 15:17); יָבֵשׁ גִּלְעָד "Jabesh-gilead," *Iabesgalaad*/Ιαβις Γαλααδ (1 Sam 11:1); עָפְרָה "Ophrah," *Ephra*/Γοφερα (1 Sam 13:17); גֵּרְשֻׁנִּי "Gershonite," *Gerson*/Γεδσων (Josh 21:33); עֶקְרוֹן "Ekron," *Accaron*/Ἀσκαλῶνα (1 Sam 6:16); and מִגְרוֹן "Migron," *Magron*/Μαγδων (1 Sam 14:2).

3–5.1.7.4 Text-Critical Value
3–5.1.7.4.1 Consonantal Text Close to MT

Jerome consistently shows dependence upon a text quite similar to MT (→ 3.2.2; → 4.2.2; → 5.3.2) vis-à-vis other traditions (→ 1.3.5.11). This is demonstrated in that the Vulgate and MT will consistently agree on one reading while LXX (→ 3.3; → 4.3; → 5.4; → 5.5) and Qumran (→ 3.2.1; → 4.2.1; → 5.3.1) support another. This is especially demonstrable within the book of Samuel, where LXX (→ 5.4) and 4QSam^a (→ 5.3.1; → 5.3.3) offer a text markedly different than that of MT (→ 5.3.2). For example, דְּבָרוֹ/*verbum suum* "his word," 1 Sam 1:23 (4QSam^a, LXX: היוצא מפיך "what came out of your mouth"); אֲרוֹן אֱלֹהֵי יִשְׂרָאֵל/*arcam Dei Israhel* "the ark of the God of Israel," 1 Sam 6:3 (4QSam^a, LXX: ארון ברית יהוה אלוהי ישראל "the ark of the covenant of the Lord God of Israel"); שְׁלֹשִׁים אָלֶף/*triginta milia* "thirty thousand," 1 Sam 11:8 (4QSam^a, LXX: שבעים אלף "seventy thousand"); שֵׁשׁ אַמּוֹת/*sex cubitorum* "six cubits," 1 Sam 17:4 (4QSam^a, LXX: ארבע אמות "four cubits"); לְנַעֲרוֹ/*ad puerum suum* "to his lad," 1 Sam 20:36 (4QSam^b, LXX: לנער "to the lad"); and אִישׁ־בֹּשֶׁת/*Hisboseth* "Ish-bosheth," 2 Sam 4:12 (4QSam^a, LXX: מפיבשת "Mephibosheth"). Elsewhere, MT and the Vulgate lack readings that appear in these other traditions. For example, הראה/ὁ βλέπων "seer," 1 Sam 16:4 (4QSam^b, LXX); or והאיש/καὶ ὁ ἄνθρωπος "and the man," 1 Sam 25:3 (4QSam^a, LXX). Also, larger additions present in 4QSam^a and LXX but absent from MT and the Vulgate may be found in 1 Sam 1:25 and 2:9.

3–5.1.7.4.2 Relation to the Other Ancient Versions

Regarding the Vulgate's relationship to possible sources, examining *hapax legomena* is particularly useful because in handling these obscure words Jerome is more likely to demonstrate his dependence on or freedom from other ancient versions. For example, in Judg 3:22, Jerome appears to follow no other version in translating הַפַּרְשְׁדֹנָה[9] as *stercora* "excrement." Both LXX and Peshitta take the larger phrase (וַיֵּצֵא הַפַּרְשְׁדֹנָה "and the excrement came out") as a description of Ehud's departure, and not a description of something issuing from the bowels. It is possible, however, that Jerome was influenced by Targum Jonathan, נפק אכליה "his food came out."[10] In 1 Sam 2:33, however, Jerome's rendering of לַאֲדִיב "grieve" as *tabescat* "languish" agrees with LXX, καταρρεῖν "sink down" and the Peshitta, ܠܡܪܕܒܗ "flow."[11] It seems that the meaning of this *hapax legomenon* was lost to the ancient versions and that Jerome follows LXX. Jerome's translation of שְׂדֵפָה "scorched" in 2 Kgs 19:26 with *arefacta* "dried up" appears to be independent of LXX's πάτημα "trodden" but may be influenced by the Quinta, ἐμπυρισμός "burning."[12] In examining these and other *hapax legomena*, it becomes clear that, although Jerome made use of LXX, he often solved difficult texts through other means.

---

[9] The meaning of this Hebrew term is uncertain; cf. *HALOT* פֶּרֶשׁ‎דֹן.

[10] Smelik maintains that Jerome was influenced by targumic traditions, whether these were through personal interactions with Jews or through targumic texts themselves. He writes, "the influence of Jewish exegetical traditions on Jerome's translation of Judges is clear enough. Whether or not this influence reached Jerome by way of targumic traditions is a moot point," in *Targum of Judges*, 315.

[11] זוב "to flow, run" is probably the understood root for this reading.

[12] Jerome was familiar with the Quinta (see *Comm. Hab.* 2:3).

3–5.1.7.4.3 *Ketiv/Qere*

There are nearly three hundred occurrences of *Ketiv/Qere* variations (→ 1.5.4.2) within the Former Prophets (→ 3–5.3.2.5). For more than half of these passages, it is difficult or impossible to determine if Jerome prefers the *Qere* or the *Ketiv*. For example, variations in Hebrew spelling are often irrelevant for the translator, e.g., אֵלוֹ vs. אליו "unto him" (1 Sam 22:13) or מֵבִיא vs מבי "bringing" (1 Kgs 21:21). The presence/absence of an article (1 Sam 14:32) or *metheg* (1 Sam 9:1) will also be irrelevant to the Latin translator. Likewise, the translation may be unaffected by the use of a *Qal* passive construction instead of the *Niphal* (2 Sam 3:2; 21:6) or by the type of preposition (-ב or -כ) used with an infinitive construct (Josh 4:18; 1 Sam 11:6; 2 Sam 5:24).

In passages where a *Ketiv/Qere* variant would affect the meaning of the translation, Jerome prefers the *Qere* at a ratio of approximately five to one. The most common type of agreement between Jerome and the *Qere* is in regard to number. There are dozens of instances where the Vulgate and the *Qere* agree on the given number (i.e., singular or plural) of a particular word, over and against the *Ketiv* (e.g., Josh 6:7; Judg 13:17; 1 Sam 8:3; 2 Sam 1:11; 1 Kgs 1:27; 2 Kgs 5:9). Also, Jerome often agrees with the *Qere* when it comes to the presence/absence of a suffix or the type of suffix found in the Hebrew, e.g., אָזְנוֹ "his ear" vs. אזני "my ear," *mihi* "to me" (1 Sam 22:17); עַבְדּוֹ "his servant" vs. עבדך, *servi tui* "your servant" (2 Sam 14:22); בְּעֵינוֹ "in his eyes" vs. בעיני "in my eyes," *in conspectu meo* "in my sight" (2 Sam 12:9); אֱלֹהֶיךָ "your God" vs. אלהים/*Deus* "God" (1 Kgs 1:47); and בְּנַפְשׁוֹ "against his life" vs. בנפשי/*contra animam meam* "against my life" (2 Sam 18:13). Often times, Jerome agrees with the *Qere* when it offers a different lexeme altogether: לֹא "not" vs. לוֹ/*ipsi* "to him" (1 Sam 2:3; cf. 2 Sam 16:18; 2 Kgs 8:10); חַי "living" vs. חיל/*fortissimi* "powerful" (2 Sam 23:20); לֹא "not" vs. לוּא/*si* "if only" (2 Sam 18:12); עָשַׂר "tithed" vs. עשה/*fecerat* "made" (1 Kgs 22:49); אֲשֶׁר "who" vs. איש/*virum* "man" (2 Sam 23:21); and רֶכֶב "chariot" vs. רב/*multitudine* "multitude" (2 Kgs 19:23).

Moreover, Jerome regularly agrees with the *Qere* with regard to the transliteration of words, e.g., הַגִּרְזִי vs. הגזרי/*Gesuri* (1 Sam 27:8); חֶצְרוֹ vs. חצרי/*Esrai* (2 Sam 23:35); and הָאוֹרְנָה vs. הארונה/*Areuna* (2 Sam 24:16). Finally, on a number of occasions, Jerome agrees with the *Qere* when the *Ketiv* is lacking (Judg 20:13; 2 Sam 8:3; 2 Sam 16:23; 2 Kgs 19:31, 37). Nevertheless, despite such consistent agreement with the *Qere*, there are some instances where the Vulgate and the *Ketiv* are in agreement against the *Qere* (Josh 9:7; 2 Sam 13:37; 16:12; 22:51; 1 Kgs 5:12, 17; 8:26; 17:15; 2 Kgs 23:10).

Everson, D.L., "An Examination of Synoptic Portions within the Vulgate," *VT* 58 (2008): 178–90.
Gasquet, F.A. et al. (eds.), *Biblia Sacra iuxta latinam vulgatam versionem ad codicum fidem*, Vols. 4–6 (Rome: Libreria Editrice Vaticana, 1939–1945).
Kedar-Kopfstein, B., "The Vulgate as a Translation: Some Semantic and Syntactical Aspects of Jerome's Version of the Hebrew Bible" (PhD diss., Hebrew University of Jerusalem, 1968).
McCarter, P.K., *I Samuel: A New Translation with Introduction and Commentary* (AB 8; Garden City: Doubleday, 1980).
McCarter, P.K., *II Samuel: A New Translation with Introduction and Commentary* (AB 9; Garden City: Doubleday, 1984).
Siplä, S., "The Book of Joshua in the Vulgate," in *Scripture in Transition: Essays on Septuagint, Hebrew Bible, and Dead Sea Scrolls in Honour of Raija Sollamo* (eds. A. Voitila and J. Jokiranta; JSJSup 126; Leiden: Brill, 2008), 17–26.
Smelik, W.F., *The Targum of Judges* (OtSt 36; Leiden: Brill, 1995).

David Everson

3–5.1.8 Arabic Translations

See → 6–9.1.8.

3–5.2 Secondary Translations

3–5.2.1 Vetus Latina

3–5.2.1.1 Joshua-Judges
3–5.2.1.1.1 Extant Witnesses

The Old Latin text of Joshua is preserved in *Codex Lugdunensis* (Lugd.).[1] Judges is represented in three types of evidence: 1) Codices *Lugdunensis* (Lugd.), *Monachensis* (Mon.), *Wirceburgensis* (Wi.), and *Florentinus* (Fl.); 2) marginal readings in Vulgate Bibles from the Iberian Peninsula (VL[91] = *Codex Gothicus Legionensis*; VL[92] = *Legionensis 2*; VL[94] = Library of El Escorial 1478; VL[95] = *Emilianense 2–3*);[2] and 3) quotations in Latin church fathers, saliently Augustine of Hippo.

The quotations in marginal notes of Spanish Vulgates have been published by Ayuso Mazaruela,[3] who also covers the quotations in the Latin Fathers.[4] The Cambridge edition of the Septuagint[5] includes the main variant readings of Old Latin sources in its apparatus.

3–5.2.1.1.2 History of Research

The main critical interest of the Old Latin text of Judges is to trace its relationship with its LXX *Vorlage* (→ 4.3) and the possibility, in this regard, of using it to recover the Old Greek text of LXX, prior to the different revisions or recensions towards a proto-Masoretic Hebrew text (→ 4.2.2), which make the Old Greek text sometimes difficult to identify. This in turn leads to the relationship between the proto-Masoretic text, towards which the Old Greek text was revised in recensions such as *kaige*-Th, and the *Vorlage* of the Old Greek prior to such revisions. The latter could constitute a form of "Old Hebrew"[6] text. Therefore, in Joshua and Judges, as in the rest of books that underwent a *kaige* recension process, the Old Latin version is a key instrument for approaching the phenomenon of textual plurality in the biblical text at the turn of the era.[7] This has been shown clearly in the most recent edition of the Hebrew text of Judges in *BHQ, where Fernández Marcos dedicates both apparatus entries and a substantial part of the textual commentary to the Old Latin as a highly relevant tool for the retrieval of the Old Greek text and its Hebrew *Vorlage*.[8]

3–5.2.1.1.3 Textual History

The history of the Old Latin text itself offers a challenge to scholars, as it has undergone revisions and contaminations and, prior to any text-critical use of the version, the definition of a typology of the Old Latin version will be required. Once the variants and elements internal to the textual history of the Old Latin itself (scribal errors, omissions, additions, linguistic or stylistic changes, influence of the Vulgate) are discarded, this typology produces two different text-types, VL1 and VL2.[9] This can be observed especially in the book of Judges, where the former reflects a text close to the Greek basis of the Lucianic recension (LXX[L]; → 3–5.1.6.1), whereas the latter presents features that bring it closer to the *kaige* text (LXX[B]; → 2.4.6). A survey of the extant manuscript evidence offers a remarkable distribu-

---

[1] See Robert, *Heptateuchi versio latina*.

[2] Gryson, *Altlateinische Handschriften 1*, 144–55.

[3] Ayuso Mazaruela, *Prolegómenos*, 409; Ayuso Mazaruela, *El Octateuco*, 29, 63, 279–305.

[4] See the edition in Ayuso Marazuela, *El Octateuco*, 280–305. For the materials in Lucifer of Cagliari, see Diercks, *Luciferi Calaritani Opera*.

[5] Brooke–McLean–Thackeray, *The Old Testament in Greek*.

[6] See Bogaert, "Bulletin de la Bible latine (1955–1975)," 162.

[7] See M.L. Margolis, *The Book of Joshua in Greek according to the Critically Restored Text with an Apparatus Containing the Variants of the Principal Recensions and of the Individual Witnesses* (5 vols.; Paris: Libr. orientaliste Paul Geuthner, 1938; Philadelphia: Annenberg Research Institute, 1992); Bodine, *The Greek Text of Judges*; J. Greenspoon, *Textual Studies in the Book of Joshua* (HSM 28; Atlanta: Scholars Press, 1983).

[8] See N. Fernández Marcos, Judges (*BHQ 7; Stuttgart: Deutsche Bibelgesellschaft, 2011), esp. 9–10 and the mention of the reading *cum eo Amalec* "with him Amalek" in Judg 1:16, which is preferable to all other witnesses, including MT, according to the editor.

[9] See Trebolle Barrera, "Textual Affiliation," 315–29.

tion of VL1 vs. VL2: VL1 is attested by the codices mentioned above, whereas VL2 has been preserved in the marginal readings of codices VL$^{91-96}$.[10] Nevertheless, there are textual cases in which both VL1 and VL2 agree with LXX^L and LXX^A in preserving prospective Old Greek readings, e.g., Judg 5:2: VL1 *dum imperant principes in istrahel in praesumptione populi*; VL2 *quum inquoaerunt principes in istrael in uoluntate populi* "when princes rule in Israel in the obstination of the People" = LXX$^{A\ L}$ ἐν τῷ ἄρξασθαι ἀρχηγοὺς ἐν Ἰσραηλ ἐν προαιρέσει λαοῦ "in the ruling of princes in Israel by people's choice" vs. LXX^B ἀπεκαλύψη ἀποκάλυμμα ἐν Ἰσραηλ ἐν τῷ ἑκουσιασθῆναι λάον "Uncovering the uncovering in Israel as people volunteered." Other cases, on the other hand, attest the aforementioned equation VL1 = LXX$^{A\ L}$ (and hence OG) vs. VL2 = LXX^B (*kaige*). An example is Judg 5:13: VL1 *humilia mihi fortiores me*; LXX$^{A\ L}$ ταπείνωσόν μοι τοὺς ἰσχυροτέρους μου "humiliate for me those who are stronger than me" vs. VL2 *descende mihi in fortiores me*; LXX^B κατέβη αὐτῷ ἐν τοῖς κραταίοις ἐξ ἐμοῦ "come down for me against those stronger than me."

It is also noteworthy that, in some cases, VL2 seems more prone to transcribe Hebrew readings of an MT-like type than the Greek materials.[11] All in all, the Old Latin materials have a larger number of agreements with LXX$^{A\ L}$ (OG) than with the LXX^B text, although the amount of agreement between VL and LXX^B is not negligible. In some cases, a particular type of agreement takes place between LXX^L and VL (against LXX$^{A\ B}$) when the LXX^L text has "additional materials" as compared to LXX$^{A\ B}$ and to the parallel passage of MT. These "Lucianic additions" produce in multiple locations textual doublets and, in a good number of cases, VL agrees with the LXX^L materials that depart from the reading closer to MT (and also attested by LXX$^{A\ B}$). This agreement would indicate that, in fact, LXX^L is representing the Old Greek text and that actually the "addition" is the *kaige* element, which exhibits philo-Masoretic features and which is also attested by LXX$^{A\ B}$. An example of long or conflate text in the Lucianic tradition would be Judg 11:25: LXX^L τοῦ δικασαμένου δίκην μετὰ Ισραηλ μὴ μαχόμενος ἐμαχέσατο μετὰ Ισραηλ "the one who pleads a case with Israel, did he battle Israel?"; LXX^A μὴ μάχῃ ἐμαχέσατο μετὰ Ισραηλ "did he battle in a battle with Israel?"; LXX^B μὴ μαχόμενος ἐμαχέσατο μετὰ Ισραηλ "did he battle battling with Israel?" LXX$^{A\ B}$ are clear reflections of MT הֲרוֹב רָב עִם־יִשְׂרָאֵל "did fight a fight with Israel?" Nevertheless, the Lucianic element with no parallel in the Masoretic Hebrew or in the rest of the Greek tradition, τοῦ δικασαμένου δίκην μετὰ Ισραηλ "the one who pleads a case with Israel," is represented by the VL text of *Codex Ludgunensis* as *qui iudicatur iudicium ad Istrahel* "the one who pleads a case with Israel." This would lead in fact to an assessment of that first part of the Lucianic text as pre-Lucianic in character, whereas the "addition" or insertion would be the element from the *kaige* text represented by LXX$^{A\ B}$. This is the case with longer but also with brief double readings such as Judg 17:3, where VL frames the Old Greek reading from the conflated doublets in LXX^A and LXX^L: LXX^A καὶ νῦν ἐπιστρέψω αὐτά σοι καὶ ἀποδώσω σοι αὐτό "and now I will return them to you and give it back to you"; LXX^L ἐπιστρέψω σοι αὐτό ἐν καιρῷ καὶ ἀποδώσω σοι αὐτό "I will return it to you in time and give it back to you"; LXX^B ἀποδώσω σοι αὐτό "I will give it back to you"; MT וְעַתָּה אֲשִׁיבֶנּוּ לָךְ "and now I will return it back to you." The *Lugdunensis* Old Latin reading *et in tempore reddam illum tibi* "and in time I will return it to you" identifies the Old Greek καὶ ἐν καιρῷ ἐπιστρέψω αὐτά σοι "and in time I will return them to you" behind the doublet. A similar case can be found in Josh 11:19, where the VL reading defines the presence of a Lucianic doublet.[12]

---

[10] For a seminal approach to the evidence of marginal readings, see F.C. Burkitt, *The Old Latin and the Itala* (Cambridge: Cambridge University Press, 1896), esp. 9–10.

[11] Cf. the treament of Judg 8:13 and 8:22–23 in A. Soggin, *Judges: A Commentary* (OTL; London: SCM Press, 1981), 153; B. Lindars, *Judges 1–5: A New Translation and Commentary* (ICC; Edinburgh: T & T Clark, 1995), 146–48.

[12] See the detailed treatment in Trebolle Barrera, "The Text-Critical Value of the Old Latin," 401–13. Old Latin readings of Joshua in agreement with LXX^L were treated by Margolis, the reference editor of LXX-Josh, in Margolis, "Additions to Field," 254–58, although he never speaks specifically of a "Lucianic text."

This textual diversity within VL is well attested in the quotations by church fathers (→ 21.8; → 1.7.2), saliently Augustine of Hippo,[13] but also authors and works such as Lucifer of Cagliari, Ambrosius, Gregory of Elvira, Pseudo-Prosperus, Pseudo-Isidore, and Pseudo-Speculum. The analysis of citations that imply variants requires discarding those due to grammar, style, theological modifications, or to the transmission process of patristic literature that, well into the Middle Ages, involved a series of corrections of citations to align them with the Vulgate (→ 3–5.1.7).[14] Once these elements are discarded, textual variety also falls into two distinct lines: agreement with VL2 or with VL1.[15]

All in all, the study of the Old Latin indicates that it replicates, in a measure, processes that took place in previous stages of the transmission of the books of Joshua and Judges. In a nutshell, the Greek tradition attests a philo-MT tendency (clearly manifested in the *kaige* manuscripts; → 2.4.6) that revised a previous (Old Greek) text of the Septuagint (→ 3.3; → 4.3). The Old Latin is a valuable tool in determining the presence of Old Greek vs. *kaige* readings. In turn, the situation of the Greek would be a reflection of the development of the Hebrew text, and would undergo modifications from a text form akin to the *Vorlage* of the Old Greek to a text closer to the Masoretic Hebrew (→ 3.2.2; → 4.2.2). This textual plurality underlying LXX is supported by the situation of the biblical texts of the Dead Sea Scrolls. In the particular case of Judges,[16] the evidence yielded by 1QJudg (→ 4.2.1.1; → 4.2.3.1) and 4QJudg^a (→ 4.2.1.2; → 4.2.3.2) shows remarkable similarities between the Hebrew text in the Qumran fragments and manuscripts from the Lucianic group (→ 3–5.1.6.1), at times in agreement with the Old Latin and other secondary versions of LXX, such as the Sahidic Coptic (→ 3–5.2.2). The number of variants, albeit minor, is remarkable, given their presence in rather small scroll fragments. In 1QJudg, the Old Latin (in agreement in this case with the Vulgate) agrees in the plural reading of Judg 9:29, ויאמרו "and they said" against MT וַיֹּאמֶר "and he said." Although a minor feature, 1QJudg and the Old Latin (together with the Sahidic Coptic and manuscript LXX⁴⁷⁰ of the Lucianic group) agree in the absence of the copula in Judg 9:44,[17] reading אבימלך "Abimelech" instead of MT וַאֲבִימֶלֶךְ "and Abimelech." The materials of 4QJudg^a are also remarkable,[18] because, in a short fragment, meaningful agreement with the Old Latin (represented by Lucifer of Cagliari) text may be found: in Judg 6:5, the Old Latin *quorum non erat numerus* "which were numberless" shows a short text, against MT וְלָהֶם וְלִגְמַלֵּיהֶם אֵין מִסְפָּר "and they and their camels were numberless," supported in this case by the Greek tradition, καὶ αὐτοῖς καὶ ταῖς καμήλοις αὐτῶν οὐκ ἦν ἀριθμός "and they and their camels where numberless." Reconstruction of the lacuna in line 4 of 4QJudg^a indicates the presence of a shorter text, ולהם אין מספר "and they were numberless." In turn, 4QJosh^a (→ 3.2.1.1; → 3.2.3.2) is a key fragment for approaching the history of the book of Joshua and research thereof requires consideration of the Old Latin, as the agreement in Deut 27:4 between VL, SP, and a small Qumran fragment in reading "Gerizim" instead of "Ebal" (→ 2.2.1.3.3; → 2.2.4.5.3; → 2.5.1.4) leads to consider-

---

[13] See Billen, *Old Latin Texts of the Heptateuch*.

[14] Cf. G. Folliet, "Corrections apportées aux textes scripturaires du *De correptione et gratia*," *Aug* 39 (1999): 381–405.

[15] See Trebolle Barrera, "The Textual History," 53–72.

[16] See É. Puech, "Les manuscrits 4QJuges^c (= 4Q50^a) et 1QJuges (= 1Q6)," in *Studies in the Hebrew Bible, Qumran, and the Septuagint Presented to Eugene Ulrich* (eds. P.W. Flint, E. Tov, and J.C. VanderKam; VTSup 101; Leiden: Brill, 2006), 184–202.

[17] For the importance of the agreement between Old Latin and Coptic in Judges, see Billen, "The Old Latin Version of Judges," 140–49 (146); B. Lindars, "Some Septuagint Readings in Judges," *JTS* N.S. 22 (1971): 1–14.

[18] See J. Trebolle Barrera, "Textual Variants in 4QJudg^a and the Textual and Editorial History of the Book of Judges," in *The Texts of Qumran and the History of the Community: Proceedings of the Groningen Congress of the Dead Sea Scrolls (20–23 August 1989)* (vol. 1; ed. F. García Martínez; Paris: Gabalda, 1989) = *RQ* 14 (1989): 229–45; R.S. Hess, "The Dead Sea Scrolls and Higher Criticism in the Hebrew Bible: The Case of 4QJudg^a," in *The Scrolls and the Scriptures: Qumran Fifty Years After* (eds. S.E. Porter and C.A. Evans; JSPSup 26; Sheffield: Sheffield Academic Press, 1997) 122–28; E. Tov, "The Nature of the Large-Scale Differences between the LXX and MT S T V Compared with Similar Evidence in Other Sources," in Schenker, **Earliest Texts*, 1–16, 121–40.

ation of the complex and pluralistic history of the book of Joshua in the narrative sections on the construction of the first sanctuary.[19]

3–5.2.1.1.4 Relevance for Exegesis

A study of the textual history of the Old Latin of Joshua and Judges contributes to the general vision of a pluralistic situation in the development of biblical texts in general and the historical books in particular, a situation that began at the level of the Hebrew text and was then echoed in the textual groups of LXX and in the spread of the Old Latin witnesses themselves. Therefore, the Old Latin is a valuable tool for inquiry into the relationship between MT and LXX.

Ayuso Mazaruela, T., *La Vetus Latina Hispana*, Vol. 1: *Prolegómenos* (Textos y estudios Cardenal Cisneros 1; Madrid: CSIC, 1962).

Ayuso Mazaruela, T., *La Vetus Latina Hispana*, Vol. 2: *El Octateuco* (Textos y estudios Cardenal Cisneros 6; Madrid: CSIC, 1967).

Billen, A.V., *Old Latin Texts of the Heptateuch* (Cambridge: Cambridge University Press, 1927).

Billen, A.V., "The Old Latin Version of Judges," *JTS* (1942): 140–49.

Bodine, W., *The Greek Text of Judges: Recensional Developments* (HSM 23; Chico: Scholars Press, 1980).

Bogaert, P.-M., "Bulletin de la Bible latine (1955–1975)," *Bulletin d'ancienne littérature chrétienne latine* 5: Supplement to *RBén* 74–84 (1964–1974).

Brock, S., "Lucian Redivivus: Some Reflections on Barthélemy's Les Devanciers d' Aquila," *SE* 5 (1968): 176–81.

Diercks, G.F., *Luciferi Calaritani Opera quae supersunt* (CCSL 7; Turnhout: Brepols, 1978).

Gryson, *Altlateinische Handschriften 1.

Margolis, M.L., "Additions to Field from the Lyons Codex of the Old Latin," *JAOS* 33 (1917): 254–58.

Robert, U. (ed.), *Heptateuchi partis posterioris versio latina antiquissima e codice Lugdunensi* (Lyon: Rey, 1900).

Sabatier, *Bibliorum.

Trebolle Barrera, J., "Textual Affiliation of the Old Latin Marginal Readings in the Books of Judges and Kings," in *Biblische Theologie und gesellschaftlicher Wandel:* *Für Norbert Lohfink SJ* (eds. G. Braulik, W. Gross, and S. McEvenue; Freiburg i.B.: Herder, 1993), 315–29.

Trebolle Barrera, J., "The Text-Critical Value of the Old Latin and Antiochean Greek Texts in the Books of Judges and Joshua," in *Interpreting Translation: Studies in the LXX and Ezekiel in Honour of Johan Lust* (eds. F. García Martínez and M. Vervenne; BETL 192; Leuven: Peeters, 2005), 401–13.

Trebolle Barrera, J., "The Textual History and the Text-Critical Value of the Old Latin Version in the Book of Judges", in Kraus–Kreuzer, *Septuaginta 2014*, 53–72.

Ulrich, E., "The Old Translation of the LXX and the Hebrew Scrolls from Qumran," in Ulrich, *DSS, 233–74.

Ulrich, E., "The Old Latin, Mount Gerizim, and 4QJosh[a]," in *Textual Criticism and Dead Sea Scrolls Studies in Honour of Julio Trebolle Barrera: Florilegium Complutense* (eds. A. Piquer Otero and P.A. Torijano Morales; JSJSup 157; Leiden: Brill, 2012), 361–76.

Vercellone, C., *Variae Lectiones Vulgatae Latinae Bibliorum*, Vol. 2: *Complectens libros Iosue, Iudicum, Ruth et quatuor Regum* (Rome: Spithöver, 1864).

Andrés Piquer Otero

3–5.2.1.2 Samuel–Kings

The Old Latin version (VL) of Samuel–Kings is extremely important for establishing the Old Greek text (→ 5.4; → 5.5) and ultimately its Hebrew *Vorlage* due to the reasonably literal character of the translation. Despite its fragmentary condition and the fact that many of its witnesses are of a secondary nature (marginal notes in Vulgate manuscripts [→ 3–5.1.7], patristic quotations [→ 21.8; → 1.7.2]), it constitutes a touchstone without which the textual history of Samuel–Kings would be much more difficult to reconstruct.

3–5.2.1.2.1 Extant Witnesses

Manuscripts of VL-Sam-Kgs are scarce. Leaving aside the VL quotations in the Latin fathers (→ 21.8) collected by Sabatier,[1] together with several fragmentary readings from manuscripts at Corbey and St. Germain, the so-called *Fragmenta Quedlingbur-*

---

[19] For a detailed argument, see Ulrich, "The Old Latin, Mount Gerizim, and 4QJosh[a]," 361–76.

[1] Sabatier, *Bibliorum.

gensia[2] and *Magdeburgensia* of the fifth century (VL[116]), most of the VL textual tradition is preserved in six witnesses: VL[115, 91, 92, 93, 94, 95] according to Beuron classification. The *Palimpsestus Vindobonesis* (VL[115]) of the fifth century contains fragments from Samuel and Kings. Fischer's edition of this manuscript[3] supersedes the deficient text of Belsheim[4] used in the LXX Cambridge edition.[5] Finally, the *Fragmenta Vindobonensia* (VL[117]), the endsheets from a seventh or eighth century manuscript in the binding of a codex, preserves only 2 Sam 10:11, 14.[6]

The other five witnesses to VL-Sam–Kgs are Spanish Vulgate Bibles that have VL readings in marginal notes: VL[91] or *Codex Gothicus*, copied in 960; VL[92] or *Codex Legionensis* 2, copied in 1162; VL[93] or *Codex Vaticanus* 4859, a very faulty copy of VL[91] made in 1587; VL[94] a Vulgate incunable of 1478 (Biblioteca del Escorial 54.V.35); it includes some glosses taken from the now-lost Bible of Valbanera (tenth century). The editions of these glosses by Morano for the books of Samuel[7] and that of Kings by Moreno Hernández[8] clearly improve on the previous work of Vercellone.[9]

In addition to these manuscript witnesses, the Latin author Lucifer of Cagliari is an important witness of VL.[10]

3–5.2.1.2.2 History of Research

The critical value of the VL text is linked to the problem of the pre-Lucianic and pre-Hexaplaric nature of the "Lucianic" text (→ 5.4). Vercellone noted the Lucianic character of the VL fragments collected in the marginal notes of the codices of León.[11] Wellhausen and Driver underlined the points of contact between VL and the Antiochene text.[12] Burkitt was the first to observe that it reflects a "Lucianic text prior to Lucian"[13] (→ 3–5.1.6.2). Rahlfs and Dieu affirmed the existence of "Lucianic touches" in VL-Kgs that appear more frequently the more recent are the textual witnesses. Therefore, the VL Lucianisms would not correspond to old readings; they would be the result of late revisions made quite extensively in the West from Lucianic Greek readings.[14] However, according to Fischer, the opposite can be proven, taking into account that the Latin text of Cyprian shows more points of contact with the Lucianic Greek (necessarily prior to the fourth century, as the time of Lucian) than with the majority LXX text. On the other hand, the late Latin authors correct many Lucianisms against the majority LXX readings, and, although it is not possible to characterize precisely the work done by Lucian, his recension and VL seem to go back to a similar type of Greek text that has been lost. In Fischer's words, "a VL text is the more ancient the greater number of Lucianic readings it contains."[15] According to Brock, "it would be pointless to try to use Lat as a guide to 'pre-Lucianic' in *L*. This is not, of course, to deny that variants witnessed by the combination L lat may not sometimes or indeed often, be 'pre-Lucianic': there are simply no means of judging."[16] Fernández Marcos excludes "any use of the Old Latin for the restoration of the Biblical text and for the discussion of textual pluralism until it has been first critically examined according to the proper criteria of inner textual criticism."[17] Trebolle Barrera, Schenker, and Hugo consider that, under a pre-defined set of conditions, VL is a witness of the

---

[2] Levin, *The Quedlinburg Itala*.

[3] Fischer, "Palimpsestus Vindobonensis."

[4] J. Belsheim, *Palimpsestus Vindobonensis: Antiquissimae Veteris Testamenti translationis latinae fragmenta* (Christianiae: Malling, 1885).

[5] Brooke–McLean–Thackeray, *The Old Testament in Greek*.

[6] Haupt, *Samuelis fragmenta Vindobonensia*.

[7] Morano, *Glosas marginales (1–2 Samuel)*.

[8] Moreno Hernández, *Las glosas marginales (1–2 Reyes)*.

[9] Vercellone, *Variae Lectiones*.

[10] Diercks, *Luciferi Calaritani Opera*.

[11] Vercellone, *Variae Lectiones*, 436.

[12] Wellhausen, *Der Text der Bücher Samuelis*, 221–24; S.R. Driver, *Notes on the Hebrew Text of the Books of Samuel* (Oxford: Clarendon Press, 1913), lxxvi–lxxx.

[13] F.C. Burkitt, *The Book of Rules of Tyconius* (Cambridge: Cambridge University Press, 1894), cxvii.

[14] Rahlfs, *Lucians Rezension der Königsbücher*, 169; Dieu, "Retouches Lucianiques."

[15] "Ein VL-Text ist umso älter und primitiver, je mehr *L*-Lesarten er enthält," in Fischer, "Lukian-Lesarten," 175; see also Haupert, *The Relation of Codex Vaticanus*, 29.

[16] Brock, *The Recensions*, 217–18; cf. Brock, "Lucian Redivivus."

[17] Fernández Marcos, *Scribes and Translators*, 87.

pre-Lucianic text and, therefore, of the original LXX text of Samuel–Kings.[18]

3–5.2.1.2.3 Textual History

The analysis of VL begins by discarding the variants that are internal to the Latin version or that result from error or corruption. In the same way, some readings that represent a LXX[B] *kaige* or "*kaige*-like" (→ 1.3.1.2) text cannot be considered as genuine VL readings. Thus, in 2 Kgs 17:2, the reading *non sicut reges Israel qui fuerant* "no like the kings of Israel who were …" (VL[91]) corresponds to the *kaige* οὐχ ὡς οἱ βασιλεῖς Ἰσραηλ οἳ ἦσαν (LXX[A B]), whereas *prae omnes qui fuerant ante eum* "prior to all the ones who were before him" (VL[115]) reflects the proto-Lucianic παρὰ πάντας τοὺς γενομένους and constitutes the original Old Latin reading. Notwithstanding this, a considerable number of VL readings, especially when attested also by Josephus (→ 21.3), the Coptic (→ 3–5.2.2), the pre-Hexaplaric stratum of the Armenian (→ 3–5.2.5.3; → 3–5.2.5.4) and Georgian versions (→ 3–5.2.6), as well as by the Hebrew parallel readings of Chronicles (→ 5.3.3; → 20.2.2), go back to a pre-Lucianic text that preserves the Old Greek (→ 5.4; → 5.5) and helps to recover its Hebrew *Vorlage*, which differs from MT. The critical value of VL was confirmed by the discovery of the Samuel scrolls in Qumran Cave 4 (→ 5.3.1; → 5.3.3). According to Ulrich, VL is a "faithful and controlable witness to the OG, which in turn is not infrequently a witness superior to the Masoretic text for the ancient text of Samuel."[19]

3–5.2.1.2.4 Relevance for Exegesis

VL omits 2 Sam 5:4–5, which is missing also in 4QSam[a], Josephus, and 1 Chronicles 11, indicating a pre-Lucianic and probably Old Greek reading.[20] In 2 Sam 8:7, VL helps to reconstruct a long plus present in 4QSam[a], LXX, and Josephus but not found in MT or 1 Chronicles 18.[21] In 2 Sam 13:21, 4QSam[a] preserves a lengthy original expression lost from MT through haplography (ולא … ולא); VL[115] presents this reading with small changes in partial agreement with LXX[L].[22] In 1 Kgs 1:52, the VL reading *vivit dominus* "the Lord lives" argues together with the Coptic ζῇ κύριος as well as the Old Greek text.[23] In 2 Kgs 10:23–25a, VL (VL[115]), partially supported by LXX[L], helps to trace the Old Greek and its Hebrew *Vorlage*.[24] In 2 Kgs 10:25–28, VL presents a double reading: the first reading follows the text of the *kaige* recension (LXX[B]) and that of MT; the second one corresponds to the Old Greek text.[25] In a plus in 2 Kgs 10:36, VL follows LXX[L] in preserving the story of Jehu's conspiracy in its typical and original structure, whereas in LXX[B] (= MT) the text of this unit appears scattered in several places along 2 Kings 8–9. In 2 Kgs 13:14, VL is the only witness of the original placement of the story about Elisha's death after 2 Kgs 10:30, as part of the narrative of Jehu instead of that of Joash.[26] Also in 2 Kgs 17:1–23, LXX[L] and VL allow for the reconstruction of the Old Greek text, as well as a possible different order of the literary units that compose the chapter. In 2 Kgs 20:11, VL reflects a textual stage very close to MT-Isa. The reading *Et detenta est in sole* "she (the shadow) was halted in

---

[18] J. Trebolle Barrera, *Centena in Libros Samuelis et Regum: Variantes textuales y composición literaria en los libros de Samuel y Reyes* (Textos y estudios Cardenal Cisneros 47; Madrid: Consejo Superior de Investigación Científicas, 1989); A. Schenker, *Älteste Textgeschichte der Königsbücher: Die hebräische Vorlage der ursprünglichen Septuaginta als älteste Textform der Königsbücher* (OBO 199; Göttingen: Vandenhoeck & Ruprecht, 2004), 7; P. Hugo, *Les deux visages d'Éli: text massorétique et Septante dans l' histoire la plus ancienne du texte de 1 Rois 17–18*, (OBO 217; Göttingen: Vandenhoeck & Ruprecht, 2006).

[19] Ulrich, "Old Translation," 270.

[20] F.M. Cross, D.W. Parry, and R.J. Saley, "51. 4QSam[a]," *DJD* XVII: 1–216 (120).

[21] Cross, Parry, and Saley, "4QSam[a]," 133; P. Kyle McCarter, *II Samuel* (AB 9; Garden City: Doubleday, 1984), 244.

[22] Cross, Parry, and Saley, "4QSam[a]," 149.

[23] This Old Greek reading reflects the Hebrew יהוה חי; see A. Piquer Otero, "An Old Greek Reading Attested in the Sahidic and Old Latin Fragments of 1 Kgs 1:52: Text-Critical Analysis and Relationship with the Hebrew Text," *Hen* 30 (2008): 80–93.

[24] Trebolle, "From the 'Old Latin'."

[25] J. Trebolle Barrera, "Textos 'kaige' en la Vetus Latina de Reyes (2 Re 10,25–28)," *RB* 89 (1982): 198–209.

[26] Schenker, *Älteste Textgeschichte*, 135–38.

the sun" reflects the verb אחז "to hold, seize, grasp" and not the name Ahaz.[27]

Thus, on the whole, VL-Sam–Kgs aids in reconstructing the Old Greek (→ 5.4; → 5.5) text of these books and through it a stage of the textual history of Samuel–Kings that precedes their (proto-)Masoretic text (→ 5.3.2; → 5.3.3).

Bogaert, P.-M., "Bulletin de la Bible latine (1955–1975)," *Bulletin d'ancienne littérature chrétienne latine* 5: Supplement to *RBén* 74–84 (1964–1974).

Brock, S., "Lucian Redivivus: Some Reflections on Barthélemy's *Les Devanciers d'Aquila*," *SE* 5 (1968): 176–81.

Brock, S., *The Recensions of the Septuaginta Version of 1 Samuel* (Quaderni di Henoch 9; Turin: Zamorani, 1996).

Diercks, G.F., *Luciferi Calaritani Opera quae supersunt* (CCSL VII; Turnhout: Brepols, 1978).

Dieu, L., "Retouches Lucianiques sur quelques textes de la vieille latine (I et II Samuel)," *RB* 16 (1919): 390–403.

Fernández Marcos, N., *Scribes and Translators: Septuagint and Old Latin in the Books of Kings* (VTSup 54; Leiden: Brill, 1994).

Fischer, B., "Lukian-Lesarten in der Vetus Latina der vier Königsbücher," *SA* 27–28 (1951): 169–77.

Fischer, B., "Palimpsestus Vindobonensis: A Revised Edition of L115," *BIOSCS* 16 (1983): 13–87; reprint "Palimpsestus Vindobonensis: II. Manuscript 115 of the Books of Kingdoms," in *Beiträge zur Geschichte der lateinischen Bibeltexte* (ed. B. Fischer; VL 12; Freiburg i.B.: Herder, 1986), 315–33.

Gryson, *Altlateinische Handschriften 1.

Haupert, R.S., *The Relation of Codex Vaticanus and the Lucianic Text in the Books of the Kings from the Viewpoint of the Old Latin and the Ethiopic Versions* (Philadelphia: University of Pennsylvania, 1930).

Haupt, P., *Veteris versionis antehieronymianae libri II Regum sive Samuelis fragmenta Vindobonensia* (Vienna: Geroldus, 1877).

Levin, I., *The Quedlinburg Itala: The Oldest Illustrated Manuscript* (Litterae textuales 8; Leiden: Brill, 1985).

Margolis, M.L., "Additions to Field from the Lyons Codex of the Old Latin," *JAOS* 33 (1917): 254–58.

Morano, C., *Glosas marginales de Vetus Latina en las Biblias Vulgatas españolas (1–2 Samuel)* (Textos y estudios Cardenal Cisneros 48; Madrid: Consejo Superior de Investigación Científicas, 1989).

Moreno Hernández, A., *Las glosas marginales de Vetus Latina en las Biblias Vulgatas españolas (1–2 Reyes)* (Textos y estudios Cardenal Cisneros 49; Madrid: Consejo Superior de Investigación Científicas, 1992).

Rahlfs, A., *Septuaginta Studien*, Vol. 3: *Lucians Rezension der Königsbücher* (Göttingen: Vandenhoeck & Ruprecht, 1911).

Sabatier, *Bibliorum.

Trebolle Barrera, J., "From the 'Old Latin' through the 'Old Greek' to the 'Old Hebrew' (2 Kings 10:23–25)," *Textus* 11 (1984): 17–36.

Ulrich, E., "The Old Translation of the LXX and the Hebrew Scrolls from Qumran," in Ulrich, *DSS, 233–74.

Vercellone, C., *Variae Lectiones Vulgatae Latinae Bibliorum*, Vol. 2: *Complectens libros Iosue, Iudicum, Ruth et quatuor Regum* (Rome: Spithöver, 1864).

Wellhausen, J., *Der Text der Bücher Samuelis* (Göttingen: Vandenhoeck & Ruprecht, 1871).

Pablo Torijano Morales

3–5.2.2 Coptic Translations

3–5.2.2.1 Background

The Former Prophets are well attested in manuscripts written in the Sahidic dialect. Possibly, a Bohairic translation existed also, but the sole reminiscences of this translation are some citations in certain liturgical books. With the single exception of a tiny Fayyumic fragment of 1 Samuel, no traces of the Former Prophets are known in Fayyumic or in the other minor Coptic dialects.

We do not possess any clear indication concerning the date of the Coptic versions of the Former Prophets, although possibly the Sahidic translation goes back at least to the fourth century C.E. The Sahidic translation of 1 Samuel was tentatively dated to ca. 250 C.E. by Barton Payne, although his proposal has not found support in scholarship.[1] A papyrus fragment in the collec-

---

[27] A. Catastini, *Isaia ed Ezechia: Studio di storia della tradizione di II Re 18–20//Is. 36–39* (Studi semitici N.S. 6; Rome: Univ. degli Studi "La Sapienza," 1989), 296.

[1] J. Barton Payne, "The Sahidic Coptic Text of 1 Samuel," *JBL* 72 (1953): 51–62; S. Brock, *The Recensions of the Septuagint Ver-*

tion of Duke University, which contains 1 Sam 14:24–50, has been dated by some scholars to the third or fourth century, but this is probably too early.[2] Perhaps the earliest manuscript evidence is the fifth-century manuscript Cop$^{Sa\,18}$, which contains the book of Joshua. This codex belongs to a hoard of Coptic and Greek manuscripts probably discovered at Dishna in Upper Egypt. As to the source of the Coptic translation, it may have originated in monastic circles, like the entire Coptic Bible.

With the exception of 1–2 Samuel, which is properly edited, critical editions of the other books of the Former Prophets in Sahidic are still a desideratum. Extensive portions from Joshua and Judges have been published in the past, but without the intention of providing editions based on all manuscript witnesses available. The main impediment to editing the texts critically is the generally bad state of preservation of the Coptic manuscripts. They survived usually with the leaves separated or torn to pieces and distributed around the world. Therefore, before the texts can be edited, a more or less complete and reliable directory of extant fragments from each book needs to be compiled. Although significant progress has been made in the past, the codicological reconstruction of the original manuscripts, especially those from the White Monastery, remains one of the main foci of Coptic biblical studies.

3–5.2.2.2 Manuscripts, Editions, Auxiliary Tools
3–5.2.2.2.1 Joshua

While the Sahidic text of Joshua is virtually complete, no modern critical edition exists to date that incorporates systematically all identified manuscript witnesses. The following manuscripts are known to survive:

Cop$^{Sa\,18}$:[3] The separated leaves of this papyrus codex are shared today by the Bodmer Collection in Geneva (P. Bodm. XXI) and the Chester Beatty Library in Dublin (Nr. 1389). The codex contains Josh 6:16–25; 7:6–11:23; 22:1–2, 22:19–23:7, 23:15–24:23. The same codex also must have included the book of Tobit (→ II.9.7), of which only Tob 14:13–15 and the subscription are extant, and Judith (→ II.14.10). The latter is completely lost with the sole exception of the title, which appears on the verso of the front page. The Dublin leaves were edited by Shore in 1963.[4] In the same year, Kasser published the entire manuscript with a French translation.[5] This codex belongs to the aforementioned Dishna discovery. According to Robinson, the codices came from a Pachomian monastery situated in the vicinity.[6]

Cop$^{Sa\,19}$:[7] Manuscript London British Library Add. 17183 is a Syriac parchment palimpsest that dates to 913 C.E. The underlying writing, which must be older, contains significant portions of the Sahidic version of Joshua and Judges. Although the Syriac codex came from Deir al-Suriani in the Wadi el-Natrun, the Sahidic manuscript reused by the Syrian scribe was probably imported from an unknown location in Upper Egypt. The London manuscript preserves Josh 1:1–2:14; 3:6–10:25; 10:36–17:16; 18:7–19:50; 21:7–22:14; 22:20–24:33. The text was edited by Thompson, who dated the Coptic script tentatively to the beginning of the seventh century C.E. However, Thompson's dating is hardly more than an educated guess.[8]

The White Monastery, situated in Upper Egypt near Sohag, possessed at least three manuscripts of Joshua:

---

sion of 1 Samuel (Quaderni di Henoch 9; Turin: Silvio Zamorani, 1996), 22–23.

[2] A.M. Butts, "P.Duk.Inv.797 (U): 1 Kingdoms 14:24–50 in Sahidic," *Mus* 118 (2005): 7–19, dated it to the fourth century. For his part, Schüssler, **Biblia Coptica*, 1.3, 75 (Cop$^{Sa\,77}$), opted for a third-century dating.

[3] Schüssler, **Biblia Coptica* 1.1, 94–96.
[4] Shore, *Joshua I–VI*.
[5] Kasser, *Papyrus Bodmer XXI*.
[6] See most recently J.M. Robinson, *The Story of the Bodmer Papyri: From the First Monastery's Library in Upper Egypt to Geneva and Dublin* (Cambridge: James Clarke & Co., 2013).
[7] Schüssler, **Biblia Coptica* 1.1, 97–98.
[8] Thompson, *A Coptic Palimpsest*, 1–129 and vi for the dating.

Cop^{Sa} *20*:[9] This is a parchment codex dated in the colophon "719, Era of the Martyrs," which corresponds to 1003 C.E.[10] The manuscript contained Joshua and Tobit. The *membra disiecta* of this codex are scattered across the world. Eight leaves attesting to Josh 10:39–11:7; 14:1–11; 15:7–18:1 are kept in the National Library in Naples as I.B. 1, fol. 1–8.[11] Four supplementary folios with Josh 19:47–21:1; 21:27–39; 24:13–31 are in the Bibliothèque Nationale de France (Copte 129¹, folios 99–102).[12] Three folios with Josh 2:13–23; 4:23–5:10; 8:29–9:2 are in the papyrus collection of the Austrian National Library in Vienna (K 9388–9390),[13] and one fragment with Josh 13:21–32 is in the Pushkin Museum in Moscow (Pushkin Museum I.1.b.648).[14]

Cop^{Sa} *307*:[15] Only three fragments of this codex have been identified to date, all of them in the British Library (Or. 6954[81] with Josh 14:1–3, 6–9; Or. 6954[85] with Josh 15:10–12, 13–18;[16] Or. 3579A, folio 21 with Josh 24:2–10).[17] The date of the manuscript is difficult to ascertain.

Cop^{Sa} *215*:[18] Only one leaf containing Josh 7:3–13 is known to survive of this parchment codex. According to Schüssler, the same manuscript included Numbers and Zechariah. However, it is not clear whether all *membra disiecta* mentioned by Schüssler belonged to the same codex or to two or more codices copied by the same scribe.

Additionally, there are a few other Sahidic fragments of Joshua whose provenance is not documentable:

Cop^{Sa} *133*: a parchment fragment kept in the manuscript collection of the Montserrat Abbey near Barcelona, containing Josh 1:17–18; 2:1–4.[19] Schüssler dated this manuscript tentatively to the ninth century C.E., although its neat biblical uncial suggests an earlier date.[20]

Cop^{Sa} *39ex*:[21] Josh 7:1–3 is attested on a papyrus fragment in the Beinecke Library, Yale P.CtYBR Inv. 1782. Emmel suggested that the fragment did not belong to a codex but rather to an odd sheet.[22] For her part, MacCoull speculated that the papyrus was used as a school exercise.[23]

Portions of Joshua are also attested in Sahidic lectionaries. Thus, Josh 5:10–12 is included in the Holy Week lectionary Cop^{Sa} 108L,[24] Josh 1:1–7 in

---

[9] Schüssler, *Biblia Coptica* 1.1, 99–107.

[10] The colophon was edited in A. van Lantschoot, *Recueil des colophons des manuscrits chrétiens d'Égypte* (Bibliothèque du Muséon 1; Louvain: J.-B. Istas, 1929), 102–03 (= no. 61).

[11] The Naples leaves were edited in Amélineau, "Fragments," 57–58; republished in Ciasca, *Fragmenta Copto-Sahidica*, 1.148–57.

[12] G. Maspero, *Fragments de la version thébaine de l'Ancien Testament* (Paris: Leroux, 1892), 134–36. Some corrections were made to the text published by Maspero in S. Gaselee, "Notes on the Coptic Versions of the LXX," *JTS* 11 (1910): 246–57 (251).

[13] For an edition of the Vienna folios, see C. Wessely, *Griechische und koptische Texte theologischen Inhalts*, Vol. 4 (Studien zur Palaeographie und Papyruskunde 15; Leipzig: Haessels Verlag, 1914), 61–64, 67–68.

[14] A.I. Elanskaya, *Coptic Literary Texts of the Pushkin State Fine Arts Museum in Moscow* (Studia Aegyptiaca 13; Budapest: Eötvös Loránd University, 1991), 209–10 and plate 53; A.I. Elanskaya, *The Literary Coptic Manuscripts in the A.S. Pushkin State Fine Arts Museum in Moscow* (VCSup 18; Leiden: E.J. Brill, 1994), 403–05 and pls. 149–50.

[15] Schüssler, *Biblia Coptica* 2.3, still unpublished.

[16] These two fragments are described in B. Layton, *Catalogue of Coptic Manuscripts in the British Library Acquired Since the Year 1906* (London: The British Library, 1987), 13–14 (= no. 10).

[17] Formerly British Museum Or. 3579A (10). Described in W.E. Crum, *Catalogue of the Coptic Manuscripts in the British Museum* (London: British Museum, 1905), 7–8 (= no. 13).

[18] Schüssler, *Biblia Coptica* 2.2, 88–90.

[19] Edited in S. Torallas Tovar, *Biblica Coptica Montserratensia: P. Monts. Roca II* (Orientalia Montserratensia 2; Barcelona: Publicaciones de l' Abadia de Montserrat, 2007), 15–17 and pl. 1.

[20] Schüssler, *Biblia Coptica* 2.1, 36.

[21] Schüssler, *Biblia Coptica* 1.2, 71.

[22] S. Emmel, "Coptic Biblical Texts in the Beinecke Library," *Journal of Coptic Studies* 1 (1990): 13–28 (23–24) and pl. 2.

[23] L.S.B. MacCoull, "More Coptic Papyri from the Beinecke Collection," *APF* 35 (1989): 25–35 (33).

[24] This portion of Joshua was edited according to a fourteenth- or fifteenth-century Copto-Arabic lectionary in

Cop^{Sa} 212L,[25] Josh 1:1–4 in Cop^{Sa} 244L,[26] Josh 1:2–6 in a lectionary fragment in Vienna,[27] and Josh 24:25 in Cop^{Sa} 220L.

From the Bohairic version, only Josh 4:1–9; 8:7–17; 23:1–14 are known to survive in liturgical manuscripts.[28]

3–5.2.2.2.2 Judges

There is no critical edition of the Sahidic version of Judges. The text is transmitted together with Joshua in the palimpsest London British Library Add. 17183 (described above: Cop^{Sa} 19). This manuscript contains Judg 1:1–7:1; 7:7–14; 7:20–8:10; 8:20–27; 9:9–10:6; 10:15–16:18; 17:2–18:7; 18:22–19:7; 19:16–20:15; 20:24–47; 21:7–14.

Several fragmentary codices came from the White Monastery. These manuscripts are important as they preserve some of the missing parts of the London palimpsest.

Cop^{Sa} 21: This codex was copied in the tenth century at Touton in the Fayyum and later donated to the White Monastery. Extant are Judg 1:10–20 (Vatican, Borg. copt. 109, cass. v, fasc. 13, folio 1);[29] 11:38–40 and 12:1–6 (Paris, Bibliothèque nationale de France Copte 129¹, folio 109);[30] 12:7–13:6 (London, British Library Or. 3579A, folio 22); 20:16–27 (London, British Library Or. 3579A, folio 23).[31] Cop^{Sa} 21 also included the book of Daniel (→ 18.4.2).

Cop^{Sa} 22:[32] Fourteen leaves are known of this manuscript. They attest to Judg 1:1–15 (New York, Morgan Library M 664 A [1]);[33] 1:27–2:17 (Vatican, Borg. copt. 109, cass. v, fasc. 14, folios 1–2);[34] 4:16–7:3 (Paris, Bibliothèque nationale de France Copte 129¹, folios 103–08); 9:40–55 (Paris, Bibliothèque nationale de France Copte 129¹, folio 110); 13:7–15:14 (Paris, Bibliothèque nationale de France Copte 129¹, folios 111–14).[35] This codex also contained the books of Ruth, Canticles (→ 13–17.2.2), and 2 Kings.

Cop^{Sa} 23: Only one fragment of the book of Judges has been identified to date in this manuscript. The fragment is currently housed in the Papyrus Collection of the Austrian National Library in Vienna (K 2616) and contains Judg 16:17–18:21.[36] The same manuscript also contains 1–2 Samuel.

For Cop-Judg, fragments of manuscripts of unknown provenance are also extant. Cop^{Sa} 55 is a palimpsest fragment in the Beinecke Library (P.CtYBR Inv. 846) whose *scriptio inferior* attests to Judg 9:7–19 in Sahidic. The leaf was later reused to accommodate a magical text.[37] Cop^{Sa} 167 designates a single fragment in the papyrological collection of Heidelberg University (P.Heid.Inv. Kopt. 435). It contains Judg 1:20–27 and it was published by Schüssler.[38] In 1937, Till edited a parchment

---

the Vatican Library by Amélineau, "Fragments," 57 and Ciasca, *Fragmenta Copto-Sahidica*, 1.148.

[25] For this and the following numbers, cf. Schüssler, *Biblia Coptica* 2.2 (Cop^{Sa} 185–260).

[26] Cf. S. Gaselee, "Notes," 255–57.

[27] Edited in W. Till, *Koptische Pergamente theologischen Inhalts*, Vol. 1 (Mitteilungen aus der Papyrussammlung der Nationalbibliothek in Wien [Papyrus Erzog Rainer] n.s. 2; Vienna: Österr. Staatsdruckerei, 1934), 12–13.

[28] Published in P. de Lagarde, *Orientalia*, Vol. 1: *Die koptischen Urkunden der Göttinger Bibliothek* (Göttingen: Dieterichsche Verlags-Buchhandlung, 1879), 65–66.

[29] Ciasca, *Fragmenta Copto-Sahidica*, 1.159–60.

[30] Maspero, *Fragments de la version thébaine de l'Ancien Testament*, 145–46. For corrections to Maspero, see Gaselee, "Notes," 251–52.

[31] See the description in Crum, *Catalogue*, 8 (nos. 14–15). I indicated above the new call numbers of the fragments. Schüssler, *Biblia Coptica* 1.2, 6–10, gave the old call numbers, which were used before the refoliation of the manuscript. No. 15 of Crum's catalogue was edited in E.O. Winstedt, "Some Unpublished Sahidic Fragments of the Old Testament," *JTS* 10 (1909): 233–54 (235–36).

[32] Schüssler, *Biblia Coptica* 1.2, 11–16.

[33] Description and edition in L. Depuydt, *Catalogue of Coptic Manuscripts in the Pierpont Morgan Library* (Corpus of Illuminated Manuscripts 4 Oriental Series 1; Leuven: Peeters, 1993), 8–10 (no. 3).

[34] Edited in Ciasca, *Fragmenta Copto-Sahidica*, 1.160–63.

[35] All the Paris leaves were edited in Maspero, *Fragments de la version thébaine de l'Ancien Testament*, 146–50.

[36] For an edition, see Till, "Saidische Fragmente," 187; cf. Schüssler, *Biblia Coptica* 1.2, 17–19.

[37] There is a description and edition of the biblical text in Emmel, "Coptic Biblical Texts," 14–17; Schüssler, *Biblia Coptica* 1.3, 23.

[38] Schüssler, *Biblia Coptica* 2.1, 113–14. Schüssler tentatively dated the fragment to the sixth century C.E.

sheet from the Vienna Papyrus Collection (K 2610 = Cop^{Sa} 374) that contains Judg 20:4–12, 12–15.[39]

The Sahidic book of Judges is also attested in lectionary manuscripts. Thus, Judg 6:14–16 can be found in Cop$^{Sa\ 212L}$,[40] a fragmentary White Monastery lectionary that contains only readings from the Old Testament.

Paul de Lagarde published a small portion of Judges (11:30–40) in Bohairic.[41] No manuscript of Judges is preserved in any other Coptic dialect.

3–5.2.2.2.3 1–2 Samuel

1–2 Samuel are the only books of the Sahidic version of the Former Prophets that have been properly edited. In 1970, Drescher published the text according to manuscript M567 of the Morgan Library in New York, which has survived virtually intact.[42] This parchment codex originally belonged to the Monastery of the Archangel Michael in the Fayyum Oasis. The manuscript is dated "609, Era of the Martyrs," which equals 892–893 C.E. Drescher collated the text of M567 with eighteen other witnesses, including manuscripts, but also lectionaries, bilingual Copto-Arabic glossaries, and an excerpt written on an ostracon.[43] Additionally, he edited in an appendix the text of the fragmentary White Monastery codex Cop^{Sa} 23 (see above), which gives a free translation of the two books of Samuel.[44]

A Bohairic version of 1–2 Samuel must have also existed. De Lagarde published 1 Sam 2:1–10; 16:1–13; 17:16–54; 18:6–9; 23:26–27; 24:1–23; and 2 Sam 1:17–27; 6:1–20 in Bohairic according to some lectionary manuscripts.[45] There is also a small fragment in the Bodleian Library in Oxford (Ms. Copt.e.162[P]) containing parts of 1 Sam 25:31–34.[46]

3–5.2.2.2.4 1–2 Kings

Compared to the other Former Prophets, 1–2 Kings is poorly attested in Coptic. The Sahidic codices that contain them are relatively few. Among these, two fragments of a single leaf discovered at Bala'izah in Upper Egypt stand out because of the early date proposed by their editor.[47] From Bala'izah, came also fragments of another manuscript featuring 1 Kgs 4:11–13, 15–19.[48]

The White Monastery library furnishes fragments of a couple of codices containing either both books of Kings (Cop^{Sa} 182),[49] or only one of them (Cop^{Sa} 22 has only 2 Kings).[50] Two fragments of a papyrus codex of unknown provenance (Cop^{Sa} 118) are kept in the collections of the University of Michigan and the Morgan Library in New York, respectively.[51] Fragments of a different papyrus manuscript (Cop$^{Sa\ 112lit}$) are held in the Vienna Papyrus Collection (K 7547a–h) and have been published by Orlandi.[52] They contain, with many lacunae,

---

[39] Till, "Saidische Fragmente," 187–90.

[40] Schüssler, *Biblia Coptica* 2.2, 68–84.

[41] De Lagarde, *Orientalia*, 67. De Lagarde found the text in a lectionary.

[42] Drescher, *Kingdoms*. Only one leaf with 2 Sam 15:20–30 is missing from this manuscript; Schüssler, *Biblia Coptica* 1.2, 29–30 (Cop^{Sa} 25).

[43] The items are described in Drescher, *Kingdoms*, 1.ix–xiii.

[44] Drescher, *Kingdoms*, 1.183–90 (Sahidic text), 2.145–51 (English translation).

[45] De Lagarde, *Orientalia*, 67–73.

[46] See Perttilä, "Sahidic 1 Samuel," 11.

[47] P. Kahle, *Bala'izah: Coptic Texts from Deir el-Bala'izah in Upper Egypt*, Vol. 1 (London: Oxford University Press, 1954), 322–27 (= no. 7), who proposed a fourth-century date. The fragments contain the text of 2 Kgs 14:17–19, 20, 21–22, 24–25, 27–29; 17:13–17, 18–23.

[48] Kahle, *Bala'izah*, 314–21 (nos. 6A–B). On the identification of a further fragment, see P. Bellet, "Un fragmento de la versión sahídica de 3 Reyes 4,11–13.15–19," *SPap* 3 (1964): 69–78. Interestingly, Schüssler, *Biblia Coptica* 2.1, 52–53 indexes all fragments of Kahle's nos. 6–7 under the same siglum, Cop^{Sa} 137.

[49] Cf. Schüssler, *Biblia Coptica* 2.1, 136–39. Some separated leaves of this codex were published in Maspero, *Fragments de la version thébaine de l'Ancien Testament*, 170 (Paris, Bibliothèque nationale de France Copte 129¹, folio 119 = 1 Kgs 21:7–15); Till, "Saidische Fragmente," 198–200 (edition of three fragments in Vienna forming a bifolio; K 9364 + 9366 + 9374 = 1 Kgs 21:16–18, 21, 23–26, 30–31); Wessely, *Griechische und koptische Texte* 4, 73–76 (= no. 219a–d) (Vienna, K 9385–9386 = 2 Kgs 5:5–13; 6:3–13).

[50] According to the reconstruction mentioned in Schüssler, *Biblia Coptica* 2.2, 11–16, 2 Kings was preceded in this manuscript by Judges, Ruth, and Canticles.

[51] Schüssler, *Biblia Coptica* 1.4, 89–90; Schüssler, *Biblia Coptica* 4.4, 167 (Addenda et Corrigenda). Only the Michigan fragment has been published so far; see G.M. Browne, "The Sahidic Version of Kingdoms IV," *Illinois Classical Studies* 3 (1978): 196–206. For the description of the New York fragment, see Depuydt, *Catalogue*, 14–15 (= no. 6).

[52] T. Orlandi, *Papiri copti di contenuto teologico/Koptische Papyri theologischen Inhalts* (Mitteilungen aus der Papyrus-

the text of 2 Kgs 1:6–9; 3:25–27; 4:2–3, 12–20, 30–37; 6:19–25; 10:24–30; 17:1–14.

Additionally, 1 Kgs 9:3–5 is attested by an ostracon (Cop$^{Sa\ 46ex}$) also housed in the Vienna Papyrus Collection.[53] Two White Monastery lectionaries include the text of 1 Kgs 1:32–40 (Cop$^{Sa\ 148L}$)[54] and 1 Kgs 19:9–14 (Cop$^{Sa\ 108L}$).[55]

In Bohairic, only some parts of 1–2 Kings have survived in lectionaries. Thus, De Lagarde edited the Bohairic version of 1 Kgs 2:1–10; 8:1–66; 9:1–3; 17:2–24; and 2 Kgs 4:8–24.[56]

3–5.2.2.3 Translation Character and Text-Critical Value of Cop-Former Prophets for LXX-Former Prophets

While the value of the Coptic version of Judges for the textual criticism of LXX (→ 4.3) has yet to be properly investigated, some conclusions can be drawn regarding Joshua (→ 3.3) and 1–2 Samuel (→ 5.4). The Sahidic manuscripts of these books usually offer a uniform text. Even the differences between older and more recent manuscripts are generally limited to orthographical variations and scribal errors. However, there are a few exceptions. The Bodmer-Beatty codex Cop$^{Sa\ 18}$ (ca. fifth century C.E.) features a version of Joshua that is not attested in any other manuscript presently known. As this rendering uses more Greek words than the more common version attested in later manuscripts, Shore argued that it is more faithful to the Greek text.[57] However, he also highlighted that this observation does not necessarily point to two separate translations of Joshua into Sahidic. Possibly, Cop$^{Sa\ 18}$ contains an earlier version of Joshua, which was later revised. As we do not possess any historical information regarding Coptic translation schools, we are entirely in the realm of speculation.

The White Monastery codex Cop$^{Sa\ 23}$ features a free rendering of 1–2 Samuel, which differs from the common version attested by all the other manuscripts. According to Barton Payne, this version represents an early translation. He also argues that the version preserved in the majority of manuscripts is a revision made of the early translation attested by Cop$^{Sa\ 23}$.[58] Barton Payne concluded that the early Sahidic version was made before the work of Origen (→ 1.3.1.2.7) and Lucian (→ 1.3.1.2.7). In a similar manner, Dieu speculated that the Sahidic text was later revised and Hexaplaric (→ 3–5.1.6.1) and Lucianic readings (→ 3–5.1.6.2) were added to it.[59] The hypothesis of an early Coptic translation of 1–2 Samuel, revised later on the basis of more recent Greek manuscripts, was also supported by Drescher.[60] More recently, Perttilä thoroughly examined the Sahidic version of 1 Samuel and pointed out that, although the comparison of the extant manuscripts reveals some corrections, there are no arguments for a thorough revision of Cop^{Sa}-1–2 Sam.[61]

Amélineau, E., "Fragments de la version thébaine de l'Écriture (Ancien Testament)," *Recueil de travaux relatifs à la philologie et à l'archeologie égyptiennes et assyriennes* 8 (1886): 10–62.

Drescher, J., *The Coptic (Sahidic) Version of Kingdoms I, II (Samuel I, II)* (CSCO 313–14 Scriptores coptici 35–36; Louvain: Secrétariat du Corpus SCO, 1970).

Kasser, R., *Papyrus Bodmer XXI: Josué VI, 16–25, VII, 6–XI, 23, XXII, 1–2, 19–XXIII, 7, 15–XXIV, 23* (Cologny: Bibliotheca Bodmeriana, 1963).

Perttilä, E., "Sahidic 1 Samuel: A Daughter Version of the Septuagint" (PhD diss., University of Helsinki, 2013).

---

sammlung der Österreichischen Nationalbibliothek [Papyrus Erzherzog Rainer] 9; Vienna: Brüder Hollinek, 1974), 25–36. For some corrections to this edition, see G.M. Browne, "The Vienna Papyrus of Kingdoms IV," *BASP* 12 (1975): 145–50.

53 Call number KO 233; edited in W. Till, *Die koptischen Ostraka der Papyrussammlung der Österreichischen Nationalbibliothek: Texte, Übersetzungen, Indices* (Denkschriften der Österreichischen Akademie der Wissenschaften, philosophish-historische Klasse 78.1; Vienna: Böhlau, 1960), no. 1; cf. Schüssler, *Biblia Coptica* 1.2, 103.

54 Cf. Schüssler, *Biblia Coptica* 2.1, 79–81.

55 Cf. Schüssler, *Biblia Coptica* 1.4, 49–69 (61). Edited in Ciasca, *Fragmenta Copto-Sahidica*, 1.217–18.

56 De Lagarde, *Orientalia*, 73–79.

57 Shore, *Joshua I–VI*, 13.

58 Barton Payne, "1 Samuel," 53.

59 L. Dieu, "Le texte copte sahidique des livres de Samuel," *Le Muséon* 59 (1946): 445–52.

60 Drescher, *Kingdoms*, 1.xxvii.

61 Perttilä, "Sahidic 1 Samuel."

Shore, A.F., *Joshua I–VI and Other Passages in Coptic: Edited from a Fourth-Century Sahidic Codex in the Chester Beatty Library, Dublin* (Chester Beatty Monographs 9; Dublin: Hodges Figgis, 1963).

Thompson, H., *A Coptic Palimpsest Containing Joshua, Judges, Ruth, Judith and Esther in the Sahidic Dialect* (London: Oxford University Press, 1911).

Till, W., "Saidische Fragmente des Alten Testamentes," *Mus* 50 (1937): 175–237.

Alin Suciu

3-5.2.3 Ethiopic Translations

3-5.2.3.1 Joshua

3-5.2.3.1.1 Order and Location in the Manuscripts

Based on a study of forty-seven manuscripts, the Ethiopic tradition knows nothing of a Pentateuch; with one exception (Eth^{EMIP} 625, produced in the twentieth century) all manuscripts point to an Ethiopic Octateuch (→ 2.5.3.2). The collection, called ኦሪት ('orit "law"), was made up of Genesis, Exodus, Leviticus, Numbers, Deuteronomy, Joshua, Judges (→ 3-5.2.3.2), and Ruth (→ 13-17.2.3.1), copied invariably in that order.

3-5.2.3.1.2 Editions

As with the rest of his Ethiopic Octateuch, Dillmann's edition of Eth-Josh was based on one fifteenth-century manuscript supplemented with variants from three others from the seventeenth and eighteenth centuries.[1] Dillmann's text formed the base for Da Bassano's edition.[2] Erbes' study[3] of the Peshitta variants in Joshua 1–5 also made use of "a new edition from the 1960s about whose background I lack further information. The readings of this new edition are frequently different from da Bassano, both in spelling and in content."[4] Neither Dillmann nor the derivative editions are considered critical.

---

[1] Dillmann, *Biblia*.
[2] Bassano, *Beluy Kidan*.
[3] Erbes, "The Peshitta and the Versions."
[4] Erbes, "The Peshitta and the Versions," 27 and 39; the quote comes from p. 39.

3-5.2.3.1.3 Erbes' Study of the Ethiopic Joshua in Relation to the Peshitta

Very little work beyond Dillmann has been done on Eth-Josh. Erbes' dissertation represents the major exception to this statement, but his focus is on s-Josh (→ 3-5.1.4), and on only the first five chapters. In this context, he has some interesting findings, which we quote at length:[5]

> There are seven passages whose reading is limited to the Peshitta and to the Ethiopic text, they are found nowhere else in the versional material.[6] In three of these readings, there is a switch to the first person plural where one may associate, where applicable, an itacistic confusion, possibly in a Greek source no longer extant. In other passages where Ethiopic is the sole representative in the Septuagint sphere, attestations in other versions are equally present[7][3] which naturally opens the way for other possible interactions. In a few further instances, the Ethiopic stands either totally alone, or is shared with another version, but not with the Peshitta.[8]

> These parallels, and presumably many more when a greater textual corpus in combination with not yet existing text editions is studied, may give indications of solutions. At present the following advice should be kept in mind: "Von syrischen Bestandteilen, wie man sie im Neuen Testament findet, konnten für das äthiopische Alte Testament niemals irgendwelche Spuren herauskristallisiert werden" (Brock 1980a: 206–07).[9] Perhaps a comprehensive investigation along the lines of this endeavor may bring us further insights. Anyway, the instances of parallels presented here, in all their variety of importance, where both Ethiopic and the Peshitta agree with each other on the one hand and do not share their common readings with any other version on the other, may be one step closer to new insights and solutions.

Knibb's discussion in his Schweich lecture of the possible influence of the Syriac on the Ethiopic is

---

[5] Erbes, *The Peshitta and the Versions*, 322.
[6] In n. 6, Erbes provides the following list of only six passages: Josh 2:3b; 2:11; 4:6b; 4:7; 4:18c; 4:23.
[7] Josh 1:3/4a; 1:4b; 2:14; 3:3a; 4:21; 4:23a; 5:2 (n. 7).
[8] Josh 2:7; 4:7b; 4:23a (n. 8).
[9] The reference is to S. Brock, "Bibelübersetzungen I: 8 Die Übersetzungen ins Äthiopische. 2: Altes Testament," *TRE* 6:206–07.

relevant at this point.[10] Though his examples are taken from Eth-Ezek, he purports to characterize the general relationship between the Peshitta and the Ethiopic Old Testaments. However, he starts by making it clear that "this has to be demonstrated from the Ethiopic translation itself in the context of the fact that the translation was clearly made, at least primarily, from a Greek text"[11] (→ 3.3). After assessing the syntactical, lexical, and textual evidence, illustrated from Eth-Ezek, Knibb concludes that "there was influence of some kind from the Syriac version on the Ethiopic version of Ezekiel."[12] This does not address the question directly with regard to Eth-Josh, but it does underscore the need for critical editions and for further study of the relation of the Ethiopic and the Syriac.

Dillmann, *Biblia*, 1.3–95.
Erbes, J.E., "The Peshitta and the Versions: A Study of the Peshitta Variants in Joshua 1–5 in Relation to their Equivalents in the Ancient Versions" (PhD diss., Uppsala University, 1999).

Steve Delamarter

3–5.2.3.2 Judges
3–5.2.3.2.1 Background
The Ethiopic (Gəʿəz) text of Judges – at least in the text form edited by Dillmann (→ 3–5.2.3.2.2) – is based primarily on LXX (→ 4.3), with a certain (at this point immeasurable, albeit relatively small) contributing influence by MT (→ 4.2.2) and the Peshitta (→ 3–5.1.4) during the original phase of translation, in the fourth to seventh centuries. Scholarly consensus further maintains that sometime during the fourteenth and fifteenth centuries the Ethiopic Old Testament underwent a recension on the basis of an Arabic version (→ 1.3.6; → 1.4.11), though the evidence of such a recension for Eth-Judg is at this point inconclusive.

3–5.2.3.2.2 Edition History and *Desiderata*
The *editio princeps* of Eth-Judg – and to this day still the only thing approaching a critical edition of the text – was published by Dillmann in 1853 (→ 1.4.3.5).[1] The edition is a diplomatic one (with some adjustment) based on a manuscript in the possession of the British and Foreign Bible Society (labeled by Dillmann "codex F"). Though this manuscript is undated, Dillmann deduces from its text form that it belongs to the thirteenth or fourteenth century.[2] For the other two manuscripts, which are collated against the previous (the variants being given in the *pars posterior* of his edition, pp. 207–15), Dillmann employed a manuscript (his "codex C"), dated by him to ca. the mid-seventeenth century,[3] belonging to the Public Library of Frankfurt, and a manuscript (Dillmann's "codex G"), written sometime during 1768–1773, belonging to the Bodleian Library, Oxford.[4] The text of Eth-Judg was published again in 1915 by da Bassano, in the first volume of his complete Old Testament in Gəʿəz.[5] Yet this is an eclectic, non-critical edition, representing (per the title page) "a collation with ancient manuscripts and with editions in Syriac, Greek, and Arabic," with no further specifics being given.[6] As for most books of the Ethiopic Old Testament, the primary *desideratum* for Eth-Judg remains a critical edition that incorporates the vast wealth of textual data to be gleaned from the abundance of Ethiopic manuscripts now known to us from libraries and collections around

---

[10] Knibb, *Translating the Bible*, 29–33.
[11] Knibb, *Translating the Bible*, 29.
[12] Knibb, *Translating the Bible*, 32.

[1] Dillmann, *Biblia*.
[2] Dillmann, *Biblia*, 6: "ante quinque vel sex saecula." On the possibility of an early fifteenth century date, assuming the donor of the manuscript, a certain "Isaac," is the Negus who reigned from 1414–1429, see O. Boyd, *The Octateuch in Ethiopic according to the Text of the Paris Codex with the Variants of Five Other Manuscripts*, Part 1: *Genesis* (Bibliotheca Abessinica 3; Leiden: Brill, 1909), xvii. This edition, unfortunately, ended in 1911 with Part 2 comprising Exodus and Leviticus.
[3] Dillmann, *Biblia*, 8: "saeculis duobus me aestimante haud antiquior est."
[4] Dillmann, *Biblia*, 168. See also Dillmann's description of this manuscript in *Catalogi codicum manuscriptorum Bibliothecæ Bodleianæ*, Part 7: *Codices aethiopici* (Oxford: Oxford University Press, 1848), no. III.
[5] Bassano, *Belu͗y Kidan*.
[6] See Ullendorff, *Ethiopia and the Bible*, 59.

the world. Among the more important of these manuscript witnesses are Eth^(BN 102) (belonging to the thirteenth to fifteenth centuries),[7] Eth^(Hav Cod) (which, though belonging to the sixteenth or seventeenth century, preserves an independent early text type),[8] Eth^(Davies Maq 1) (dated to 1409), and Eth^(Davies Kebran) (dated to 1417). Once this primary *desideratum* is attained, proper work can begin on the secondary *desiderata* of incorporating the text of Eth-Judg into studies of the textual history of LXX (→ 4.3) and other versions of the book.

3–5.2.3.2.3 Translation Character

The text of Eth-Judg in Dillmann's edition[9] represents a clear and generally close rendering of LXX (→ 4.3).[10] The differences between the two are rarely extensive, and typically comprise the addition of a word or two for the sake of clarification, e.g., Judg 4:19, in which Eth-Judg (per Eth^(Davies Kebran)) has ወነሥአት ወፈትሐት "*and she took and opened*" over against καὶ ἤνοιξεν[11] "and she opened" in LXX (= MT). Likewise Judg 20:28, in which Eth-Judg (per Eth^(Davies Kebran)) has ይቀውም ካህነ "stood *as priest*" over against παρεστηκώς "stood" in LXX (= MT), and again, Judg 21:3, in which Eth-Judg (per Eth^(Davies Kebran)) has ዛቲ እኪት "this *evil* [*thing*]"[12] over against αὕτη "this" in LXX (= MT).

On other occasions, the difference entails both an addition as well as a (non-idiomatic) change in the part of speech, likewise for the sake of clarification, as in Judg 2:17, where Eth-Judg (per Eth^(Davies Kebran)) has ዘመዉ በተሊዎ አማልክት ባዕድ "they acted adulterously *by following* [prep. + inf.] other gods" over against ἐξεπόρνευσαν ὀπίσω θεῶν ἑτέρων "they acted adulterously *after* [prep.] other gods." Still otherwise, one sometimes comes across a *more concise* rendering in Eth-Judg – in all likelihood intended to eliminate a perceived redundancy and consequent "break" in the narrative momentum – as, e.g., in Judg 18:7, where Eth-Judg (per Eth^(Davies Kebran)) has ወእሙንቱ ዕደው በጽሑ "and those same men arrived"[13] over against Καὶ ἐπορεύθησαν οἱ πέντε ἄνδρες καὶ ἦλθον "and the five men went and came" in LXX (= MT).

Another difference entails a more properly etymological/Semitic form of proper names that are hardly explainable as transcriptions of the Greek forms (or any variants thereof), such as ይሁዳ "*Yəhūdā*" (MT: יְהוּדָה "Judah") over against Ἰούδα in LXX (Judg 1:16, etc.), ስምዖን "*Səm'ōn*" (MT: שִׁמְעוֹן "Simon") over against Συμεών in LXX (Judg 1:3, etc.), and, in particular, the construct vocalization ቤተ "house of" (= Hebr. בֵּית) where LXX has the closed syllable Βαιθ, Βεθ, or Βηθ, e.g., ቤተሳን "*Bētäsān*" (MT: בֵּית שְׁאָן "Beth-shean"; LXX: Βαιθσάν; Judg 1:27), ቤተ ልሔም "*Bēta Ləḥēm*" (MT: בֵּית לֶחֶם "Bethlehem"; LXX: Βαιθλέεμ; Judg 12:8, etc.), ቤተ ሳሚስ "*Bēta Sāmīs*" (MT: בֵּית שֶׁמֶשׁ "Beth-Shemesh"; LXX: Βαιθσάμυς; Judg 1:33 [*bis*]), and ቤተ መሐሎን "*Bēta Mäḥälōn*" (MT: בֵּית מִלּוֹא "Beth-millo"; LXX: Βαιθμααλ(λ)ών; Judg 9:6, 20). None of these instances, however, can be considered clear evidence of influence by the Hebrew (→ 4.2.2) or Aramaic (→ 3–5.1.3) text(s) of Judges, since the reading ቤተ (meaning "house of") may quite reasonably have been deduced by the translator(s) from place names with the compound Βαιθ/Βεθ/Βηθ, whereas the more Semitic/etymologically-correct form of proper nouns may well represent a pre-translational tradition of pronunciation, especially seeing that these more "correct" forms are more

---

[7] See Boyd's careful critique (*The Octateuch in Ethiopic*, xii-xiii) of the colophon in this manuscript, which dates it to the reign of Yekūnō Amlāk (1270–1285).

[8] As discussed in detail by J.O. Boyd, *The Text of the Ethiopic Version of the Octateuch: With Special Reference to the Age and Value of the Haverford Manuscript* (Bibliotheca Abessinica 2; Leiden: Brill, 1905), xvii.

[9] Dillmann, *Biblia*.

[10] See Dillmann's assessment, *Biblia*, 193: "Hanc libri Judicum versionem Aethiopicam si cum textu Graeco comparaveris, maximam libri partem ab interprete Aethiope bene et perspicue redditam esse videbis."

[11] All citations of LXX are from the Larger Cambridge edition edited by Brooke and McLean (see the bibliography).

[12] Perhaps there is some relationship here to the addition of ἡ πτῶσις "the fall" attested in one cursive manuscript (Paris, Bib. nat., Coislin Gr. 2).

[13] There may be some influence here from the Peshitta (→ 3–5.1.4) rendering (ed. Dirksen, *Judges*): ܘܐܙܠܘ ܚܡܫܐ ܓܒܪ̈ܐ "and the five men went."

the exception than the rule and usually evident in more common biblical names.[14]

3–5.2.3.2.4 Text-Critical Value

The text-critical value of Eth-Judg appertains primarily to the text of LXX, large steps towards which have already been undertaken by: 1) Dillmann, who devotes a lengthy section in the *pars posterior* of his edition (pp. 196–206 ["Conspectus lectionum …"]) to an enumeration of the Greek variants implied by his edition of Eth-Judg; and 2) the editors of the Larger Cambridge LXX, who fastidiously note the readings supported by Dillmann's edition in their apparatus, albeit in most cases only "where it agrees with some other authority or with the Hebrew original."[15] Nonetheless, a fuller and more accurate text-critical contribution of Eth-Judg to the history of the LXX text remains to be made, following the realization of a proper critical edition that takes into account both the wealth of witnesses as well as their testimony to the development and variant readings (extending far beyond those noted by Dillmann) of the Ethiopic text.[16]

Brooke–McLean, **The Old Testament in Greek*, Vol. 1, *The Octateuch*, Part 4, *Joshua, Judges, Ruth*.
Dillmann, **Biblia*, Vol. 1: *Octateuchus Aethiopicus*.
Dirksen, P.B. (ed.), *Judges*, in *Judges–Samuel* (The Old Testament in Syriac according to the Peshiṭta Version 2.2; Leiden: Brill, 1978).
Ullendorff, **Ethiopia and the Bible*.
Walton, **Polyglotta*, Vol. 2.

Michael G. Wechsler

3–5.2.3.3 1–4 Kingdoms

3–5.2.3.3.1 Title and Place in the Manuscripts

The books of Kingdoms (1–2 Samuel and 1–2 Kings) bear the same titles as in LXX (e.g., መጽሐፈ ነገሥት ፩ = Βασιλειῶν Αʹ "1 Kingdoms"; → 5.4; → 5.5) and always circulate together. A list of the kings and prophets of Judah and Israel is almost always appended, perhaps indicating that list's canonical status. Together they frequently fill an entire codex, especially in the earlier manuscripts.

In very large codices, the books typically follow the Octateuch (→ 2.5.3), although some exemplars place Kingdoms after Enoch (→ 11.5.1.2) and/or the Solomonic corpus (→ 12.4.3; → 13–17.2.3.2; → 13–17.2.3.3; → 11.15.5). However, when unattached to the Octateuch, 1–4 Kingdoms usually begin a codex, suggesting a real or ideational connection, i.e., equivalent to "volume 2." If material follows, one regularly sees 1–2 Chronicles (→ 20.4.3), but after the sixteenth century Wisdom collections appear as well. Hannah's Song (1 Kgdms 2:1–10) is among the Biblical Canticles (*Odes*), giving it a special place in Ethiopia's liturgical life.

3–5.2.3.3.2 Background

It appears likely that Christians in Ethiopia translated their Bible by the late fourth or early fifth century (→ 1.4.3.1).[1] For the books of Kingdoms, the translator employed a Greek *Vorlage* closely related to Codex Vaticanus (LXX^B; → 5.4; → 5.5).

The first to study the transmission history of Eth-Kgdms in detail was Dillmann,[2] who examined eight codices for his critical edition (→ 1.4.3.5). His manuscripts fell into three groups: 1) the Old Ethiopic; 2) the Standardized (*Vulgatam*) Text;

---

[14] Indeed, the editors of the Larger Cambridge Septuagint point out in the preface to their edition of Joshua, Judges, and Ruth (Brooke–McLean, **The Old Testament in Greek*, 1.4, v) the "considerable importance" of the Ethiopic version as a witness "on behalf of very similar forms in Codex Vaticanus."

[15] Brooke–McLean, **The Old Testament in Greek*, Vol. 1, *The Octateuch*: Part 1. *Genesis*, iii.

[16] Just to cite one example unnoted by Dillmann (and hence also by the editors of the Larger Cambridge LXX): In Judg 1:27, where Dillmann's text has አዋልድ, corresponding to the LXX reading θυγατέρας "daughters" (= MT: בְּנוֹת), Eth$^{Davies Kebran}$ reads instead አድዋል "districts, environs," clearly corresponding to the variants περισπόρια "suburbs" and κωμάς "suburbs, hamlets," which are attested respectively in only two minor witnesses noted by the editors. It also remains to be considered whether and how the textual history of these Greek variants and the reading in Eth$^{Davies Kebran}$ are related to the readings ܚܩܠܘܢ "suburbs, villages" in the Peshitta and دساكر "suburbs, villages" in the Arabic version as attested in Walton, **Polyglotta*.

---

[1] Thus, following others, Gehman, "Old Ethiopic," 81–82. See also Zuurmond, "Ethiopic," 235–42, who offers a similar but more detailed timeline regarding the New Testament translation, and Knibb, "Ezekiel," 14–21.

[2] Dillmann, *Regum*.

and 3) the Academic Text (manuscript E = Eth^BN Abb. 35).[3] Dillmann's primary witnesses were actually representatives of the Transitional Text (→ 1.4.3.7.4). Study of the Old Ethiopic had to wait until Roupp drew attention to a thirteenth or fourteenth century manuscript in the Borgianus Collection of the Vatican.[4] He collated and analyzed its text of 1 Kingdoms, proving that the Old Ethiopic followed LXX^B even more closely than previously thought and establishing that the manuscript served as the *Vorlage* of Wannsleben's transcription, which is now in Paris (Eth^BN 2).[5] Gehman followed with an article assessing the same manuscript's text of 3 Kingdoms[6] and subsequently inspired Davies, his student, to write a dissertation on 4 Kingdoms.[7] Nothing comparable exists for 2 Kingdoms.

3–5.2.3.3.3 Translation Character

LXX definitely underlies Eth-Kgdms (→ 5.4; → 5.5), for the Old Ethiopic adheres to the Greek sequencing found in all four books, including the omissions (cf. 1 Kgdms 17:11), the apocryphal additions (cf. 3 Kingdoms 12), transpositions (cf. 3 Kingdoms 20–21), and book division (cf. the end of 1 Kingdoms and the beginning of 2 Kingdoms). Additionally, certain readings derive solely from the Greek. For example, አቢሳሃ ሰሜናዊት "*Ābisaha Sāmēnawit*" (3 Kgdms 1:3) more closely approximates τὴν Ἀβισακ τὴν Σωμανῖτιν "Abisak the Somanite"[8] (cf. MT אֲבִישַׁג הַשּׁוּנַמִּית "Abishag the Shunnamite" and S ܐܒܝܫܠܡ ܫܝܠܘܢܝܬܐ "Abishag the Shilomit"). The list of personal names in 3 Kgdms 4:14–19, although reading unlike any other version of this text, clearly depends upon a Greek LXX^B-text manuscript that was written in *scriptio continua*.

As the translator lacked fluency in Greek, he employed several different strategies for handling difficult words and syntax. The simplest solution was omission. Deletions of words or phrases occur regularly, but they proliferate in Eth-2 Kgdms.[9] On the other hand, removing any portion of the biblical text stood at odds with the translator's primary goal. Therefore, he preferred to transliterate: See 1 Kgdms 26:5, 7 (ላምኔኔ "Lämpene" = λαμπήνη "covered chariot"); 2 Kgdms 21:16 (ቆርኔን "Qornen" = κορύνην "mace"); 3 Kgdms 2:35e (አቃርን "Āqaron" = τὴν ἄκραν "fountain"); and the resulting confusion at 4 Kgdms 25:17. Sometimes the translator could only guess, producing paraphrases (e.g., ወአፀፋፉ "and its pavement" for καὶ τὰς ἐπάλξεις "and its defenses" in 3 Kgdms 2:35 f.; see also 1 Kgdms 24:8; 2 Kgdms 23:4; and 4 Kgdms 5:12), incorrect interpretations (e.g., መስንቃዊ "musician" = ὁ αὐλῶν "the valley" in 1 Kgdms 17:3; ባሕቲትየ "I alone" and ርድዖሙ "they pursued them" = μονόζωνος "lightly armed man" in 2 Kgdms 22:30 and = μονόζωνοι "lightly armed men" in 4 Kgdms 13:20 respectively; and ወዘበጡ ከበር ወመስንቆ "and they played his drum and fiddle" = καὶ ἐχόρευον ἐν χοροῖς "and they were dancing in choruses" in 3 Kgdms 1:40), or mutilated text (cf. 1 Kgdms 20:19–22 and 3 Kgdms 20:15–18). At other times, the translator thought he discerned the etymological origin of the problematic word form. For example, he writes ፀቅነ "he surrounded" thinking ἐχάραξαν "they engraved" is from χαρακάω "to dig a trench around" (4 Kgdms 17:11) and ትትዐበይ "you will be proud" assuming ἐρίζεις "do you strive" derives from ἐριθεία "ambition" (4 Kgdms 14:10). Similarly ወፀአ "he went out" renders ἐξῆρχον "they began" as if it were a form of ἐξέρχομαι "to go out" (1 Kgdms 29:5).

There is also evidence that the translator committed typical scribal blunders in the process, although some transcriptional errors likely go back to the *Vorlage*. For example, at 3 Kgdms 22:38 he mistook αἷμα "blood" for ἅρμα "chariot," and at 4 Kgdms 2:19 he misread ἡ γῆ "the land" as γυνή "woman." 2 Kgdms 12:25 provides one of many examples of words incorrectly divided and misread: Ἰδεδι ἕνεκεν "Idedi, for the sake of" becomes ይርአይ ለእም በእንተ "he may see if for the sake of." Despite the impres-

---

[3] Dillmann, *Regum*, Fasc. 1, *Pars Posteriores*, 3–6.
[4] Roupp, "Die älteste äthiopische Handschrift."
[5] Roupp, "Die älteste äthiopische Handschrift," 335–43.
[6] Gehman, "Old Ethiopic."
[7] Davies, "The Old Ethiopic Version of Second Kings."
[8] English translations of Greek texts are guided by *NETS.

[9] See Dillmann, *Regum*, Fasc. 1, *Pars Posteriores*, 7–8 and 37, and Fasc. 2, *Pars Posteriores*, 4–6; and Gehman, "Old Ethiopic," 84 for additional examples.

sion these infelicities give, they attest the translator's desire to render the text faithfully.

3–5.2.3.3.4 Text-Critical Value

Since the publication of Dillmann's edition, all have recognized the Ethiopic version's indebtedness to the Greek LXX^B-text. Rahlfs' overview in particular cemented that position for later LXX studies.[10] However, for 3 Kingdoms, Gehman argued that the Ethiopic also demonstrated strong Lucianic (LXX^L) influence (→ 3–5.1.6.2).[11] Few items in his lengthy list of purported readings, though, warrant attention. First, he assumes kinship where the Ethiopic adds the conjunction ወ "and/but," supplies pronominal suffixes to verbs or nouns, transposes words or phrases, or adds ኵሉ "all." All of these are idiosyncrasies of the Ethiopic translation rather than remnants of a proto-Lucianic Greek manuscript.[12] Similar problems apply to the supposed shared omissions found in passages containing challenging Greek vocabulary or syntax. Second, Gehman fails to note that many of the more substantive items he lists have support in other non-Lucianic Greek witnesses. Further, the details do not substantiate Gehman's thesis. For example, ወእቱ "he/this" at 3 Kgdms 2:7 may represent οὗτος "this" with LXX^L, but ቀርበ "he drew near to me" certainly does not translate the παρέστη ἐνώπιόν μου "he stood before me" of LXX^L. Instead it more closely agrees with LXX^B (ἤγγισάν μοι "they drew near to me"). Indeed, misreading οὕτως "thus" as a demonstrative pronoun better explains the verb's change in person from third person plural to third person singular. 3 Kgdms 2:35i offers another misreading: መግደ "Mägdö" results from a simple delta/alpha interchange (Μαγαω "Magao" = LXX^B), an error repeated in but hardly dependent upon LXX^L or any Greek manuscript that preserves the same mistake. For the same reasons, Davies' attempt to locate significant traces of Lucian's recension in Eth-4 Kgdms also fails. Although more precise conclusions must await the appearance of a critical edition of LXX, the Old Ethiopic is undeniably close to LXX^B in all four books.[13]

3–5.2.3.3.5 Subsequent History

In addition to Eth$^{\text{Vat Borg 3}}$, the three manuscripts Eth$^{\text{Davies Bizan 1}}$, Eth$^{\text{Davies Bizan 2}}$, and Eth$^{\text{Davies Axum 3}}$ also preserve the earliest attested text (→ 1.4.3.7.3). For the Transitional Text (→ 1.4.3.7.4), there are the two manuscripts Dillmann employed for his critical edition, manuscript S (= Eth$^{\text{Frank Rüpp. II, 4}}$) and the more revised manuscript A (= Eth$^{\text{BN Abb 57}}$), along with Eth$^{\text{EMIP 754}}$.

Eth-Kgdms underwent radical transformation with the creation of the Standardized Text (→ 1.4.3.7.5) in the late sixteenth century, which brought the books closer to the Arabic (→ 3–5.1.8; → 3–5.2.8) and Hebrew (→ 5.3.2) but still retained much of the traditional Old Ethiopic Bible. Most extant manuscripts belong to this group.

Revisions did not cease with the Standardized Text, although it became the primary base for further recensional activity. First, a more thorough reworking of Eth-Kgdms from MT appeared in the seventeenth century, which is attested by Eth$^{\text{BN Abb. 35}}$. Second, the Textus Receptus similarly evolved, harmonizing the Standardized Text to the Hebrew. Finally, Eth$^{\text{UNES 10.14}}$ unsuccessfully conflates the readings of the Standardized Text with readings showing influence from the Hebrew (an Academic Recension?) (see especially 4 Kgdms 1:19).

Davies, D., "The Old Ethiopic Version of Second Kings" (PhD diss., Princeton Theological Seminary, 1944).
Dillmann, *Biblia*, Vol. 2: *Libri Regum, Paralipomenon, Esdrae, Esther*.
Gehman, H., "The Old Ethiopic Version of First Kings and Its Affinities," *JBL* 50 (1931): 81–114.

---

[10] Rahlfs, *Studien*, 85–87. Although not the aim of the study, Haupert, *Codex Vaticanus*, provides additional evidence of consanguinity.

[11] Gehman, "Old Ethiopic," 85–92.

[12] Gehman in fact draws attention to some of these without recognizing the methodological circularity of also interpreting them as Greek evidence, "Old Ethiopic," 100–02.

---

[13] Cf. Haupert's conclusion: "Although in a limited number of instances E[thiopic] shows contact with the Lucianic tradition or its equivalent, E stands out as the closest congener of B, the two practically forming a distinct family," *Codex Vaticanus*, 37.

Haupert, R.S., *The Relation of Codex Vaticanus and the Lucianic Text in the Books of the Kings from the Viewpoint of the Old Latin and the Ethiopic Versions* (Leipzig: Haag-Drugulin, 1930).

Knibb, M.A., "Hebrew and Syriac Elements in the Ethiopic Version of Ezekiel?" *JSS* 33 (1988): 11–35.

Rahlfs, A., *Septuaginta Studien 1: Studien zu den Königsbüchern* (Göttingen: Vandenhoeck & Ruprecht, 1904).

Roupp, N., "Die älteste äthiopische Handschrift der vier Bücher der Könige," *ZA* 16 (1902): 296–343.

Zuurmond, R. (rev. by C. Niccum), "The Ethiopic Version of the New Testament," in *The Text of the New Testament in Contemporary Research: Essays on the Status Quaestionis* (eds. B. Ehrman and M. Holmes; NTTS 42; Leiden: Brill, ²2012), 231–52.

Curt Niccum
James Prather

3–5.2.3.4 1–2 Kings

As with the Greek translations, the Ethiopic translations and revisions regard the books of 1–2 Samuel and 1–2 Kings as one literary unit, which is translated as a whole. For 1–2 Kings, see, therefore, → 3–5.2.3.3.

Curt Niccum

3–5.2.4 Late Syriac Translations

3–5.2.4.1 Background

Until the beginning of the seventh century C.E. only one Syriac translation of the Former Prophets existed, the one known as the Peshitta (S; → 1.3.4), which was spread throughout the whole of the Christian world that spoke that language. However, as early as the second half of the fourth century, voices started to be heard that, on the one hand, called into question the fidelity of the Peshitta (the origins of which, moreover, were not known) when translating its Hebrew original, and on the other hand, exalted the value of the Greek translation of LXX (→ 1.3.1.1), which was more faithful to its Hebrew *Vorlage* and had been used by the church from the start (and the origins of which were well known).[1] It is necessary to bear in mind that the Syriac church had always experienced the influence of Greek theology, especially that which arose in neighboring Antioch. It is therefore understandable that ever-greater notice was taken of the differences between the Peshitta and the biblical texts that the Greek fathers ([→ 1.7.2; → 21.7] whose works were being translated into Syriac) cited, taken from LXX.

In this way, a dynamic began that would tend, in various ways, to draw the text of the Peshitta closer to that of LXX:[2] firstly, with the introduction of variant readings that come from LXX into the textual tradition of the Peshitta;[3] secondly, with the revision of the Peshitta on the basis of Greek manuscripts (→ 1.4.4);[4] and finally, with the birth of new Syriac translations from LXX. At the beginning of the seventh century, the first complete translation of the Old Testament based on the Greek, called the Syro-Hexapla (→ 1.4.5), would be made. A century later, Jacob of Edessa would revise the whole text of the Peshitta, completing and correcting it on the basis of the Greek Bible (→ 1.4.6).

3–5.2.4.2 Syro-Hexapla

3–5.2.4.2.1 Background of the Syro-Hexapla

Between 615 and 617 C.E., the Syriac translation of the whole Old Testament prepared by Paul of Tella (→ 1.4.5.2) was completed in the monastery of Enaton, near Alexandria, in parallel with the new translation of the New Testament that was the work of Thomas of Harkel, both carried out at the urging

---

[1] Cf. R.B. ter Haar Romeny, "The Peshitta and its Rivals: On the Assessment of the Peshitta and Other Versions of the Old Testament in Syriac Exegetical Literature," *The Harp* 11–12 (1998–1999): 21–31.

[2] Cf. S.P. Brock, "Towards a History of Syriac Translation Technique," in *Les contacts du monde syriaque avec les autres cultures: III. Symposium Syriacum 1980: Goslar 7–11 septembre 1980* (ed. R. Lavenant; OrChrAn 221; Rome: Pontificio Istituto Orientale, 1983), 1–14.

[3] This step is well attested in the book of Psalms. Cf. I. Carbajosa, "The Syriac Old Testament Tradition," in *Eastern Crossroads: Essays on Medieval Christian Legacy* (ed. J.P. Monferrer-Sala; Gorgias Eastern Christian Studies 1; Piscataway: Gorgias Press, 2007), 109–30.

[4] Although in some sources it seems to be indicated that the Philoxenian translation or revision (508 C.E.) was done for the whole Old Testament, and not just for the New Testament, only a few fragments of the book of Isaiah have come down to us that could be attributed to this revision.

of the Syriac patriarch of Antioch, Athanasius. With regard to the Old Testament, the translation was based on the fifth Greek column (a recension of LXX) of Origen's Hexapla (Hex; → 1.3.1.2.7), and that is why this new version came to be known as the Syro-Hexapla (Syh).

The intention of this new Syriac translation was to allow access to the Greek Bible, which was considered the most suitable starting point for theology. That is why the translation was extremely literal, reflecting all the details of the Greek original.

3–5.2.4.2.2 Manuscripts and Editions

The existence of the Syro-Hexapla was not known in the academic world in the West until the sixteenth century, when Andreas Masius worked on a large codex that contained the Pentateuch and the Former Prophets. Unfortunately, this codex was lost before it could be published, and no trace of it has remained to the present day. Before he died, Masius wrote a long commentary on the book of Joshua in which he used and frequently cited the readings of the Syro-Hexapla.[5] It is most likely that manuscript C 313 inf. of the Biblioteca Ambrosiana (which contains the Latter Prophets and Sapiential books according to the Syro-Hexapla) was the second part of this manuscript that today is lost.

Starting in the eighteenth century, various manuscripts began to appear that have been filling in a good number of the gaps caused by the loss of the codex of Masius. With regard to the Former Prophets, currently extant, with very few gaps, are the Syro-Hexapla text of Joshua, Judges, 1–2 Kings (3–4 Kingdoms). On the other hand, of the books of 1–2 Samuel (1–2 Kingdoms), no more than a few short pericopes have come down to us, preserved in lectionaries. These are the manuscripts and texts (with their respective editions) that they cover:

- Joshua: manuscript BL Add. 12133 (eighth century) contains Joshua with some gaps (Josh 1:11–2:1; 2:11–3:16; 6:16–25; 7:6–14; 10:2–11). Its text is published in Lagarde's edition of the Syro-Hexapla.[6] Manuscript BL Add. 7145 contains Josh 22:1–6. Goshen-Gottstein and Baars published the text of some of the gaps that remained: Josh 7:6–9 (lectionary manuscript BL Add. 14485, copied in 824 C.E.)[7] and Josh 6:16–20 (same manuscript).[8]
- Judges: manuscript BL 17103 (eighth century) contains Judges with a small gap (1:22–32) and was edited by Rørdam.[9]
- 1 Samuel (1 Kingdoms): the lectionary manuscript BL Add. 14485 contains the fragments 1 Sam 7:5–12; 20:11–23, 35–42, published by Goshen-Gottstein.[10] Other fragments are extant in a catena of quotations, manuscript BL Add. 17195 (1 Sam 2:12–17, 22–24; 20:27–33) and in a lectionary, manuscript BL Add. 14487 (1 Sam 16:13) and were published by Baars.[11] This material is completed by the Song of Hannah (1 Sam 2:1–10), in its Syro-Hexapla version, which is found among the Odes of the manuscript Mosul Bibl. Patr. 1112, published by de Boer.[12]
- 2 Samuel (2 Kingdoms): Goshen-Gottstein[13] published the fragments of manuscript BL Add. 17195 (2 Sam 17:1–7) and manuscript BL Add. 14485 (2 Sam 7:1–17; 23:13–17), while Baars[14] did the same with manuscript BL Add. 14487 (2 Sam 6:1–6, 13–14).
- 1 Kings (3 Kingdoms): manuscript BL Add. 14437 (eighth century) contains almost the whole book, with a gap of some two chapters (1 Kgs 7:14–8:61). It can be consulted in Lagarde's edition of the Syro-Hexapla.[15]
- 2 Kings (4 Kingdoms): manuscript Par. Syr. 27 (eighth century) contains the whole book with

---

[5] Masius, *Josuae*.
[6] De Lagarde, *Bibliothecae Syriacae*, 121–60.
[7] Goshen-Gottstein, "Neue Syrohexaplafragmente."
[8] Baars, *New Syro-Hexaplaric Texts*, 101–03.
[9] Rørdam, *Libri Judicum et Ruth*.
[10] Goshen-Gottstein, "Neue Syrohexaplafragmente."
[11] Baars, *New Syro-Hexaplaric Texts*, 104–11.
[12] De Boer, "A Syro-Hexaplar text of the Song of Hannah," 8–15.
[13] Goshen-Gottstein, "Neue Syrohexaplafragmente."
[14] Baars, *New Syro-Hexaplaric Texts*, 112–14.
[15] Lagarde, *Bibliothecae Syriacae*, 190–222.

a small gap (2 Kgs 25:20–29) and is available in Lagarde's edition of the Syro-Hexapla.¹⁶

3-5.2.4.2.3 *Vorlage* of the Translation

The Syro-Hexapla is presented as a translation of the recension that Origen prepared of LXX in the fifth column of his Hexapla (→ 1.3.1.2.7). Some manuscripts of the Syro-Hexapla preserve the readings of Aquila, Symmachus, and Theodotion in the margins, as well as the Aristarchian symbols that Origen used to indicate the Hebrew readings that were not in LXX (asterisk) or the Greek ones that were lacking in the first column (obelus).

One of the most interesting questions is that of what manuscripts were used for the translation. It is hard to imagine that the original of the Hexapla composed by Origen, probably preserved in his library in Caesarea, could have been used. On the other hand, it is doubtful that the work was ever copied in its entirety, with all six columns. The colophons we find in the manuscripts of the Syro-Hexapla are translations of those found in the Greek manuscripts, and they are what will help us to answer this question, which must be addressed book by book.

With regard to the Former Prophets, the colophons of Joshua, Judges, 1 Kings (3 Kingdoms), and 2 Kings (4 Kingdoms) have been preserved. According to these colophons, Joshua was translated from a copy of the Hexapla and compared with another from the Tetrapla, while Judges was based directly on the Tetrapla. Of 1 Kings (3 Kingdoms), it is said that it is based on the Hexapla, compared with another manuscript corrected by Eusebius (one of those that preserved and transmitted the work of Origen). Finally, the colophon of 2 Kings (4 Kingdoms) refers to two manuscripts of the Heptapla as the basis for its translation.¹⁷

The reports from these colophons seem to indicate that the books of the Syro-Hexapla were translated from different manuscripts. It is quite likely that the terminology used in the colophons – Hexapla, Tetrapla, and Heptapla – does not refer to manuscripts that contained six, four, or seven columns. It is most logical to think that they were manuscripts that had transmitted the fifth column of Origen, preserving in the margins the readings of Aquila, Symmachus, and Theodotion (thus the technical name Tetrapla and, generically, Hexapla). The Heptapla referred to manuscripts that preserved in their margin readings from other Greek versions, in addition to those mentioned.

3-5.2.4.2.4 Translation Technique

It is understandable that a translation intended to allow access to the Greek Bible should be extremely literal, as is in fact the Syro-Hexapla. Reflecting Greek syntax and morphology, the Syro-Hexapla abounds in possessive adjectives with -ܕܝܠ (as opposed to the suffixes that predominate in the Peshitta), the use of ܟܕ "while" with the perfect and compound verbal forms. For the book of Judges, we have available a careful study of the mode of translation, carried out by Rørdam,¹⁸ while Liljeström has studied the translation techniques in the passages that are preserved of 1 Samuel (1 Kingdoms) in the Syro-Hexapla by comparing them with the style of the Peshitta (→ 1.3.4) and the translation of Jacob of Edessa (→ 1.4.6).¹⁹

3-5.2.4.2.5 Text-Critical Value

Precisely because the Syro-Hexapla sets out to follow its Greek *Vorlage* closely, it constitutes a useful instrument for textual criticism, since it

---

¹⁶ Lagarde, *Bibliothecae Syriacae*, 222–56.

¹⁷ Cf. A. Vööbus, *The Hexapla and the Syro-Hexapla: Very Important Discoveries for Septuagint Research* (Stockolm: ETSE, 1971), 44–47; G. Mercati, *Nuove note di letteratura biblica e cristiana antica* (Vatican City: Biblioteca Apostolica, 1941), 1–6, 26–48; R.G. Jenkins, "Colophons of the Syrohexapla and the Textgeschichte of the Recensions of Origen," in *VII Congress of the International Organization for Septuagint and Cognate Studies, Leuven 1989* (ed. C.E. Cox; SBLSCS 31; Atlanta: Scholars Press, 1991), 261–77; R.G. Jenkins, "Hexaplaric Marginalia and the Hexapla-Tetrapla Question," in *Origen's Hexapla and Fragments: Papers Presented at the Rich Seminar on the Hexapla, Oxford Centre for Hebrew and Jewish Studies, 25th July–3rd August 1994* (ed. A. Salvesen; TSAJ 58; Tübingen: Mohr Siebeck, 1998), 73–87.

¹⁸ Rørdam, *Liber Judicum*.

¹⁹ Liljeström, "Observations," 71–82.

allows privileged access to the fifth column of Origen (with its pluses and minuses with regard to the Hebrew text; → 1.3.1.2.7) and to the other Greek versions, to which the Syriac version testifies in its margins. In fact, Origen's work was lost and access to the Greek versions of Aquila, Symmachus, and Theodotion (→ 1.3.1.2) is only possible on the basis of some Greek manuscripts and the Syro-Hexapla.

The extreme literalness of the Syro-Hexapla in translating the Greek has made it possible to recover, by means of back translation, and with considerable certainty, many of the readings of Aquila, Symmachus, and Theodotion that would otherwise have been lost. Even so, it is necessary to carry out a study, book by book, on the mode of translation of the Syro-Hexapla in order to be sure that the retroversions are correct, in addition to confirming that the manuscript transmission of the Syro-Hexapla has preserved the Aristarchian symbols well. Preparing the way for a new edition of the Hexaplaric fragments of 1 Kings (3 Kingdoms), Law has carried out a careful study of the asterisked and obelized material of the Syro-Hexapla in this book, comparing it with the material we have from MT and LXX.[20] He concludes that, although the Syro-Hexapla in 3 Kingdoms has not preserved all the Hexaplaric material, we can trust the part that has been transmitted, something that had been called into question in the past. His study shows the way to follow for the Hexaplaric material present in the remaining books.

3–5.2.4.3 Jacob of Edessa's Syriac Translation
3–5.2.4.3.1 Background

Jacob of Edessa (J; → 1.4.6) made use of the last nine years of his life (d. 708 C.E.) by preparing a new Syriac edition of the Old Testament. In the colophon to his revision of 1 Samuel (1 Kingdoms), it is stated that the work was completed in the year 705 C.E. in the monastery of Tell 'Adda. With regard to the versions utilized in this particular edition, the same colophon says:

ܐܬܬܩܢ ܐܝܟ ܕܡܨܝܐ ܗܢܐ ܟܬܒܐ ܩܕܡܝܐ ܕܡܠܟܘܬܐ ܐܝܟ
ܕܒܚܦܝܛܘܬܐ ܣܓܝܐܐ ܡܢ ܡܫܠܡܢܘܬܐ ܡܫܚܠܦܬܐ܃
ܡܢ ܣܘܪܝܝܬܐ ܗܝ ܕܝܢ܃ ܘܡܢ ܗܠܝܢ ܕܝܘܢܝܐ ...

"This First Book of the Kingdoms was corrected as far as possible and with much effort, from the different traditions: from that of the Syrians and from those of the Greeks ..."

The fact that the colophon uses the singular (ܗܝ, "that") to speak of the Syriac tradition and the plural (ܗܠܝܢ, "those") to speak of the Greek traditions should be interpreted to mean that his sources are the Peshitta (→ 1.3.4), on the one hand, and the Syro-Hexapla (considered a Greek tradition; → 1.4.5) and Greek manuscripts, on the other.

3–5.2.4.3.2 Manuscripts and Editions

From Jacob of Edessa's translation of the Former Prophets we only have 1–2 Samuel and the first chapter of 1 Kings in a single manuscript, manuscript BL Add. 14429, which contains the first two books of Samuel according to the Lucianic division (which included 1 Kgs 1:1–2:11). The manuscript has some gaps: 1 Sam 25:11–20, 29–39; 30:2–13; 1 Kgs 1:49–2:11. Salvesen has prepared the edition of the manuscript accompanied by an English translation.[21]

This single manuscript was copied in the year 719 C.E., that is, only fourteen years after the composition of the work and very likely in the same region in which it was produced. The fact that we do not have more manuscripts of 1–2 Samuel indicates that the work of Jacob of Edessa, in spite of being copied so soon, did not achieve great diffusion or fame, as is confirmed by the fact that it was not cited by other authors. The remaining copies of his work that are preserved (books other than the Former Prophets), seem to belong to this single manuscript.

---

[20] Law, *Origenes Orientalis*.

[21] Salvesen, *The Books of Samuel*.

3–5.2.4.3.3 *Vorlage* and Character of the Revision

Bearing in mind that the revision of Jacob of Edessa was prepared while looking at the Peshitta (→ 1.3.4), the Syro-Hexapla (→ 1.4.5), and Greek manuscripts, in what proportion did he use each one? What is the basis for his translation? With what Greek tradition did he compare it? Did he add anything on his own account?

Goshen-Gottstein, comparing the passages of 1–2 Samuel that he himself had published with the parallel passages of Jacob's translation, concludes that the latter is a revision of the Peshitta and the Syro-Hexapla with sporadic traces of the influence of Greek texts of the Lucianic tradition (→ 1.3.1.2).[22] Earlier, Rahlfs, working with the only fragment preserved of 1 Kings (1 Kgs 1:1–49), had come to a different conclusion: Jacob of Edessa is probably a combination of the Peshitta and the Lucianic recension of LXX with little or no Syro-Hexapla influence.[23]

Both Rahlfs and Goshen-Gottstein worked on a very insignificant part of Jacob's text and, in addition, with fragments of different books, and thus their work was hardly comparable. Saley has been the first to carry out a careful study of a significant part of Jacob's work, specifically the books of 1–2 Samuel, devoting particular attention to the literal translations he used.[24] His results correct the previous evaluations. According to Saley, the base text that Jacob sought to correct was none other than the Peshitta. Furthermore, in his study, he detects little influence of the Syro-Hexapla. The correction was probably carried out on the basis of Greek manuscripts, especially of the Lucianic family.

In the following example, the sources from which Jacob worked can be perceived:

1 Sam 20:13:

S: ܗܟܢܐ ܢܥܒܕ ܡܪܝܐ ܠܝܘܢܬܢ ܘܗܟܢܐ ܢܘܣܦ ܠܗ. ܕܐܢ ܐܫܦܪ ܗܘ ܐܒܝ ܒܝܫܬܐ ܕܥܠܝܟ ܐܓܠܐ ܠܟ. ܘܐܫܕܪܟ ܘܬܐܙܠ ܒܫܠܡܐ. ܘܢܗܘܐ ܡܪܝܐ ܥܡܟ ܐܝܟ ܕܗܘܐ ܥܡ ܐܒܝ.

S: "Thus may the Lord do to Jonathan, and more besides. Should it please my father to bring any evil against you, I will reveal it to you, and send you away so that you may go safely. May the Lord be with you as he was with my father."

Syh: ܗܠܝܢ ܢܥܒܕ ܡܪܝܐ ܠܝܘܢܬܢ ܘܗܠܝܢ ܢܘܣܦ ܕܡܫܡܥ ܐܢܐ ܒܝ̈ܫܬܐ ܕܥܠܝܟ ܘܓܠܐ ܐܢܐ ܠܐܕܢܐ ܕܠܟ ܘܡܫܕܪ ܐܢܐ ܠܟ ܘܐܙܠ ܐܢܬ ܒܫܠܡ ܘܢܗܘܐ ܡܪܝܐ ܥܡܟ ܐܝܟ ܕܐܝܬܘܗܝ ܗܘܐ ܥܡ ܐܒܐ ܕܝܠܝ

Syh: "This is what the Lord may do to Jonathan, and this is what he may add, for I will report the evils to you and reveal to your ear and I will send you off, and you will depart in peace, and the Lord will be with you as he was with my father."

J: ܗܟܢܐ ܢܥܒܕ ܠܗ ܡܪܝܐ ܠܝܘܢܬܢ ܘܗܟܢܐ ܢܘܣܦ ܠܗ ܘܐܢ ܠܐ ܐܒܥܐ ܘܐܘܕܥܟ ܒܝܫܬܐ ܕܥܠܝܟ ܘܐ ܐܓܠܐ ܘܐܫܕܪܟ ܘܬܐܙܠ ܒܫܠܡܐ ܘܢܗܘܐ ܡܪܝܐ ܥܡܟ ܐܝܟ ܕܐܝܬܘܗܝ ܗܘܐ ܥܡ ܐܒܝ

J: "Thus may the Lord do to Jonathan, and more besides, and if I do not investigate and inform you of evil against you, and reveal it, and send you away so that you may go safely. May the Lord be with you as he was with my father."[25]

The underlined part in the Peshitta and Jacob (J) indicates the text that they have in common. It is clear that the basis from which Jacob works is the Peshitta. In the common part, we only find small modifications (Jacob adds the resumptive pronoun ܠܗ "to him," omits the personal pronoun ܠܟ "to you," and he expands the form ܐܝܟ ܕܗܘܐ "as he was" into ܐܝܟ ܕܐܝܬܘܗܝ ܗܘܐ with the same meaning). The part in which Jacob does not follow the Peshitta coincides with a difficult *lectio* (ܐܫܦܪ "should it please") in which the Peshitta "reproduces the formal character of the Hebrew."[26]

---

22 Goshen-Gottstein, "Neue Syrohexaplafragmente," 165–66.

23 A. Rahlfs, *Lucians Rezension der Köningsbücher* (Septuaginta-Studien 3; Göttingen: Vandenhoeck & Ruprecht, 1911), 48–50.

24 Saley, *The Samuel Manuscript of Jacob of Edessa.*

25 All English translations here and below are by the author.

26 C.E. Morrison, *The Character of the Syriac Version of the*

Jacob constructs a reading without ambiguities by taking a Greek variant from the Lucianic tradition (ἐὰν μή "if not" instead of ὅτι "because, for") and incorporating, on his own initiative, two verbs that clarify the passage (ܘܟܐ ܠܐ ܐܒܥܐ ܘܐܘܕܥܟ "and if I do not investigate and inform you").

The result is a clear text that avoids difficulties and ambiguities as well as not losing any information coming from the Greek traditions. If in order to do this it was necessary to make a few editorial insertions, Jacob did so on the basis of his own interpretation or by turning to the interpretation of Severus of Antioch.

3-5.2.4.3.4 Text-Critical Value

Bearing in mind that Jacob's work combines different sources, including his particular interpretations, his edition of the Old Testament has no value for the textual criticism of the Bible. His only virtue is that of serving as a witness to some Greek readings of the Lucianic tradition. In fact, this Syriac version can in specific cases serve as a support for the Lucianic readings (→ 1.3.1.2) in a critical edition of the Greek text of the Former Prophets.

Baars, W., *New Syro-Hexaplaric Texts: Edited, Commented upon and Compared with the Septuagint* (Leiden: Brill, 1968).

de Boer, P.A.H., "A Syro-Hexaplar text of the Song of Hannah: 1 Samuel ii.1–10," in *Hebrew and Semitic Studies Presented to Godfrey Rolles Driver in Celebration of his Seventieth Birthday 20 August 1962* (eds. D.W. Thomas and W.D. McHardy; Oxford: Clarendon Press, 1963), 8–15.

Goshen-Gottstein, M.H., "Neue Syrohexaplafragmente," *Bib* 37 (1956): 162–83.

de Lagarde, P., *Bibliothecae Syriacae a Paulo de Lagarde Collectae quae ad Philologiam Sacram pertinent* (Göttingen: Dietrich, 1892).

Law, T.M., *Origenes Orientalis: The Preservation of Origen's Hexapla in the Syrohexapla of 3 Kingdoms* (De Septuaginta Investigationes 2; Göttingen: Vandenhoeck & Ruprecht, 2011).

Liljeström, M., "Observations on the Mode of Translations in the Syrohexapla," in *Foundations for Syriac Lexicography*, Vol. 5: *Colloquia of the International Syriac Language Project, New Orleans 2009, and Other Contributions* (eds. J. Loopstra and M. Sokoloff; Perspectives on Syriac Linguistics 7; Piscataway: Gorgias Press, 2013), 89–100.

Masius, A., *Josuae imperatoris historia illustrata atque esplicata* (Antwerp: Christophorus Platinus, 1574).

Rørdam, T.S., *Libri Judicum et Ruth secundum versionem Syriaco-Hexaplarem ex codice Musei Britannici nunc primum editi Graece translati notisque illustrati* (Copenhagen: Ottonem Schwartz, 1859–1861).

Saley, R.J., *The Samuel Manuscript of Jacob of Edessa: A Study in Its Underlying Textual Traditions* (Monographs of the Peshitta Institute Leiden 9; Leiden: Brill, 1998).

Salvesen, A., *The Books of Samuel in the Syriac Version of Jacob of Edessa* (Monographs of the Peshitta Institute Leiden 10; Leiden: Brill, 1999).

Ignacio Carbajosa

3-5.2.5 Armenian Translations

3-5.2.5.1 Joshua

The Armenian version of Joshua has not been the object of scholarly study. For the purposes of this entry, its text was accessed in the Zohrapian edition of 1805,[1] while the Old Greek (→ 3.3) was collated from Rahlfs' provisional edition.[2]

3-5.2.5.1.1 Translation Character

That the Armenian version derives from a Greek matrix is corroborated by its agreements with the Old Greek form (→ 3.3) of a number of key names, such as Adonibezek for Adoni-zedek in Joshua 10 and Selo for Shechem in Joshua 24. In addition, it concurs with the Old Greek timespan of forty-two years for the Israelites' desert wanderings, rather than MT's forty and the former's extension of Josh 24:33 as a transition to the book of Judges. Margolis identified the version as belonging to the LXX[c] recension, associated with Constantinople, and represented primarily by LXX[A]. Indeed, the Armenian version's affinities with LXX[A] are visible throughout the book, beginning with the inscription, where the

---

First Book of Samuel (Monographs of the Peshitta Institute Leiden 11; Leiden: Brill, 2001), 94.

[1] Zohrapian, *Scriptures.
[2] Rahlfs, *Septuaginta.

LXX^A addition υιος ναυη "son of Nauē" is paralleled by most of the manuscripts collated by Zohrapian as որդւոյ Նաւեայ "son of Nauē." This affiliation is retained in all cases where the texts of the uncials LXX^B and LXX^A diverge. However, even more striking is the range of verses where the Armenian translation exhibits an accommodation to MT (→ 3.2.2), as, for example, systematically in Joshua 6 where the Old Greek is 10 percent shorter than the Hebrew (→ 3.3).

3–5.2.5.1.2 Translation Technique

Although the Armenian translator has followed the Greek morphology and syntax fairly closely, that approach has been executed in a manner consistent with the idiom of the target language. Thus, whereas the Greek renders the frequent reference to trumpeting in the course of processions either by Hebrew usage with its redundant mention of the instrument, as at Josh 6:3 ὡς ἂν σαλπίσητε τῇ σάλπιγγι "as you trumpet with the trumpet," or by the verb alone, as at Josh 6:20 ἐσάλπισαν "they trumpeted," Arm-Josh does not deviate from indigenous idiom in denoting the action as զփողս հարկանել "to strike the trumpet." Further discontinuities between the two languages include verb formation. Early Armenian lacks compound verbal forms and hence reflects these by more than one verb, as at Josh 6:3, where the Old Greek imperative περίστησον "station around" is paralleled by ած պատեա "lead, surround," or by a verbal phrase, as at Josh 6:10, where the Old Greek verb ἐνετείλατο "he ordered" is rendered as պատուէր ետ "he gave a command."

Interestingly, the contrast in tense between the formal equivalent տամ "I give" and the semantically more appropriate տաց "I will give" to render δίδωμι "I give" at Josh 1:2 is compatible with the broader diversity in procedure characteristic of the early and later stratum attested in some other biblical books. However, there is as yet insufficient evidence to sustain that hypothesis here.

Attention to Context

The Armenian translators frequently produced a nuanced rendering, as in selecting the equivalent կործանեցին "will be destroyed" in describing the collapse of the walls of Jericho at Josh 6:5, rather than the broader term πεσεῖται "will fall," applied in the Greek. Similarly, at Josh 6:26, the translators appealed to the local epithet Բեթելցի "Bethelite" instead of the cumbersome phrase ὁ ἐκ Βαιθηλ "the one from Bethel" in Greek (cf. 3 Kgdms 16:34).

3–5.2.5.1.3 Text-Critical Value: Omissions and Additions

The Armenian version witnesses no significant minuses and only a few typical pluses, such as small emphatic additions like the adverb արդ "now" at Josh 6:16 to reinforce the urgency of Joshua's command to the people, and the interpretive phrase ի ներքոյ նոցա "below them" with relation to the rampart of Jericho in Josh 6:5.

3–5.2.5.1.4 Relevance for Exegesis

Although the Armenian version in several books maintains an independent tradition of distinguishing licit and illicit cults and cultic paraphernalia, it is noteworthy that where the Old Greek designates the illicit form of altar as βωμός at Josh 22:19 – in contrast to the licit counterpart θυσιαστήριον – the Armenian translator renders both by the term սեղան "table."

3–5.2.5.1.5 Text-Critical Value of Arm-Josh for LXX-Josh

This brief survey concludes that the Armenian version represents a reliable reflection of its Greek parent text (→ 3.3). At the same time, it presents scholars with a challenge to engage with the book more rigorously. The latter investigation will be facilitated by the forthcoming volume in the Göttingen series.

3–5.2.5.1.6 Readings from "the Three"

Unsigned references to readings of Aquila and Symmachus (→ 2.4.6) are preserved as Armenian marginal readings at Josh 5:2 and Josh 13:27.[3]

---

[3] See Cox, *Aquila, Symmachus and Theodotion*, 27–31.

Cox, C.E., *Aquila, Symmachus and Theodotion in Armenia* (SBLSCS 42; Atlanta: Scholars Press, 1996).
Rahlfs, *Septuaginta*.
Zohrapian, *Scriptures*.

Peter Cowe

3-5.2.5.2 Judges

3-5.2.5.2.1 Nature: (Background) Editions, Auxiliary Tools

No detailed study of the Armenian version of this book has been undertaken. Its text was accessed in the Zohrapian edition of 1805,[1] while the Old Greek was collated from Rahlfs' hand edition.[2]

3-5.2.5.2.2 Translation Character

The Armenian version's dependence on a Greek parent text (→ 4.3) is illustrated by instances such as the dual semantic field of the verb ἄρξασθαι in the opening of the Song of Deborah at Judg 5:2. While its rendering of the MT verb ערד in the sense of "ruling" is queried, its secondary meaning of "beginning" is reflected in the Armenian equivalent սկսանել.

A series of variant readings suggests that the version evinces two strata also distinguished in other books, that of an initial translation at the beginning of the fifth century (Arm 1) followed by what in this case appears a rather light revision about a generation later (Arm 2). While the latter focuses on the morphological and syntactic structures of the base language, the former reveals the influence of Antiochene exegetical principles in sometimes reconfiguring the narrative flow, as at the song's climax in Deborah's slaying of Sisera, the Canaanite general (Judg 5:26–30). Whereas the Hebrew tale, followed in its overall pattern by the Greek, achieves its effect through parallelism of expression comprising theme and variation that inevitably involves a certain repetition in depicting the heroine's actions, rendering them as isolated tableaux – the adversary's fall, his mother's expectation of his return, her poignant query regarding his whereabouts, and the final comment regarding his spoils – Arm 1 envisages the scene as one interconnected whole, thoroughly integrating the component parts within the unfolding sequence of events. Thus, while at Judg 5:26c the Greek states ἀπέτριψεν τὴν κεφαλὴν αὐτοῦ "she crushed his head," the Armenian clarifies both the mechanism and its result in reformulating as անցոյց ցից ընդ զլուխ նորա եւ սատակեաց "she drove the peg through his head and killed him." Similarly, in the next verse, where the Greek pauses on the warrior's slumped lifeless body in the phrase ἐκοιμήθη μεταξὺ ποδῶν αὐτῆς ... ἐκεῖ ἔπεσεν ταλαίπωρος "he lay between her feet, ... there he fell, wretched," the Armenian recreates the dynamic process ննջեցոյց ի մէջ ծնգոց իւրոց ... մինչեւ զգետնեցաւ անդ անկաւ չուառականն "she put him to sleep between her knees ... until he slumped to the ground, there he fell, wretched." Similarly, in the abrupt scene change the Greek represents Sisera's mother almost casually ἐπιβλέπουσα "glancing" at the returning troops, whereas the Armenian tightens the causal relationship. The rationale for her eager but perplexed expectation of her son's arrival was twofold, "because she saw" (քանզի տեսանէր) the soldiers' return and, "since his chariot was really late" (վասն զի յետնեցան կառք նորա).[3] Finally, whereas the Greek response to the question of Sisera's absence is couched in the form of another question οὐχὶ εὑρήσουσιν αὐτὸν διαμερίζοντα σκῦλα; "will they not find him dividing the spoils?," the Armenian version structures this as a ringing denial of his continued existence (ոչ գտանիցեն զնա աւարառու "they will not find him as a divider of spoils"). Most of these readings are attested by the version's united witness apart from the distinctive Arm 2 reading at Judg 5:27 aligned with the Greek formulation ընդ մէջ ոտից նորա ... անդ անկաւ թշուառականն "between her feet ... there he fell, wretched."

3-5.2.5.2.3 Reconstruction of the Parent Text of Arm-Judg

Although Rahlfs prints the LXX^A and LXX^B texts

---

[1] Zohrapian, *Scriptures*.
[2] Rahlfs, *Septuaginta*.

[3] Here the Armenian causal conjunction represents the first of the two Greek interrogatives διὰ τί "Why?"

separately, they are frequently in agreement and probably share a common origin.[4] Various readings indicate that the parent text of the Armenian, though largely replicating the LXX^A account, diverges at various points in concert with LXX^B. Examples of such conflation include the mutilation of Adonibezek at Judg 1:6 where the Armenian phrase of excising զծայրս ոտից նորա "the extremities of his feet" combines the LXX^B element τὰ ἄκρα "the tips" with the LXX^A form τῶν ποδῶν αὐτοῦ "of his feet." Similarly, the reference to the divine at Judg 5:5 ասէ տեառն Ելովայ "the Lord Eloi" represents the LXX^B reading κυρίου Ελωι "the Lord Eloi."

3-5.2.5.2.4 Translation Technique

Variations in approach between the two strata of the Armenian relate to features such as Arm 2's re-institution of the Greek collective singular designation of the "Canaanite" (քանանացւոյ) at Judg 1:3, while Arm 1 employs the plural form քանանացիսն "Canaanites." Thus, at Judg 5:24, Arm 1 utilizes the periphrastic form աւրհնեալ լիցի "may she be blessed" in rendering the Greek finite form εὐλογηθείη "may she be blessed" while Arm 2 directly encodes the Greek morpheme (աւրհնեսցի).

One facet of the Armenian version present in other books and manifest here also is the penchant for distinguishing licit from illicit cultic practice independently of MT (→ 4.2.2) and Old Greek (→ 4.3). An example of its impact is the formulation աստուածոց աստարաց սնոտաց "foreign vain gods" at Judg 5:8 in the discussion of Israel's falling away from its traditions and selecting what both the LXX^A and LXX^B texts cite as θεοὺς καινούς "new gods." Clearly the Armenian reading սնոտաց "vain" depends on the by-this-time phonetically close term κενούς "vain, empty" either objectively present in the translator's codex or so interpreted by him, which he prefaced by the adjective աստարաց "foreign" to avoid the possibility of Israelite polytheism and highlight the alien, unacceptable character of the practice.

Whereas the translator has maintained a few Hebraisms preserved in Greek such as the phrase καὶ ἰδοῦ "and behold" as եւ ահա "and behold" at Judg 3:24, 25, etc., at Judg 1:2 the expression is rendered as the conjunction զի "because." Similarly, it varies prepositional constructions with the result that though the Greek conserves the Hebrew syntax in inquiring about the divine will as ἐν κυρίῳ "in the Lord," the Armenian verb of asking is found with the direct object զտէր "the Lord." Additionally, the Hebraic use of the present participle at Judg 3:25, which the Greek renders literally as ὁ ἀνοίγων "the opener" is recalibrated as a relative clause որ բանայր "one who would open."

Since warfare is ubiquitous in this book, it is interesting to note the degree of variation the Armenian applies in its rendering in various settings. While manifesting the direct equivalent of the Greek infinitive πολεμῆσαι "to war" at Judg 1:9 պատերազմել "to war," it prefers verbal phrases in finite contexts like Judg 1:3 where πολεμήσωμεν "let us war" is rendered by տացուք պատերազմ "let us give war." Likewise, at Judg 5:20, where the stars are depicted as joining battle ἐπολέμησαν "they warred," the Armenian refers rather to their lining up in battle order ճակատեցան "they were arrayed."

Attention to Context

Arm 1's extended translation unit permits the translator to harmonize his rendering to the requirements of specific passages. Thus, while the Greek describes the Israelites' pursuit of Adonibezek culminating in their "seizing" him (ἔλαβον) at Judg 1:6, the Armenian refers to their "catching up" with him (հասին). Likewise, in the following verse, the Greek cryptically alludes to the demeaning act of gathering up τὰ ὑποκάτω "things underneath," which the translator has clarified as զփշրանս ի ներքոյ "crumbs underneath" from under the table. Similarly, the translator possibly developing the legal ramifications of the LXX^B reading κριτηρίου "tribunal" in Judg 5:10a, construes the tautologous parallel phrase ἐπὶ ὁδοὺς συνέδρων ἐφ᾽ ὁδῷ "on ways of councils on the way" in the next line as յատեանս ատենակալաց "to magistrates' tribunals."

---

[4] For the text of Judges in LXX^A and LXX^B, see → 4.3.

3–5.2.5.2.5 Text-Critical Value: Omissions and Additions

Minuses are very few, including instances of the adjective δυνατός "mighty" at Judg 5:3 and 5:21. The longer omission at Judg 5:12 involving the allusion to Deborah and Barak is probably the result of scribal parablepsis. As we have noted, explanatory additions are more common, as at Judg 5:22 եւ հարթեսցեն զարշապարք իմ զհպարտութիւն զարհուրանաց նոցա "and my heels will level out the prideful acts of their terror."

3–5.2.5.2.6 Text-Critical Value of Arm-Judg for LXX-Judg (→ 4.3)

The light nature of the revision affords us a valuable insight into the translator's exegetical method that sought to present a careful, reasoned, integrated version of the Greek, creatively engaging with it on occasion to clarify its obscurities for its readers.

3–5.2.5.2.7 Readings from "the Three"

Some Armenian manuscripts witness a marginal reading from Aquila (→ 2.4.6) at Judg 15:14.[5]

Cox, C.E., *Aquila, Symmachus and Theodotion in Armenia* (SBLSCS 42; Atlanta: Scholars Press, 1996).
Rahlfs, *Septuaginta.
Zohrapian, *Scripture.

Peter Cowe

3–5.2.5.3 1–2 Samuel (1–2 Reigns)
3–5.2.5.3.1 Background: Editions

The Armenian version of these books was translated from Greek (→ 5.4). In this entry, references to the source text are made according to their LXX designation, that is, "1–2 Kingdoms." The Greek text employed is the Cambridge Septuagint,[1] together with that of Rahlfs' provisional edition.[2] The Armenian text used is that of Zohrapian's diplomatic edition of 1805,[3] supplemented with sample collations of manuscript readings.

3–5.2.5.3.2 Translation Character

That the source text was Greek is demonstrated by readings such as this in Arm-2 Kgdms 17:25: Hebrew "Nahash" becomes Ναάς "Naas," a reading attested by some Armenian manuscripts as Նաասայ in agreement with LXX^B A h*xa2 Cop VL. In addition, the existence of an Armenian variant reading for that same word serves to substantiate the existence of two strata in the version, each with its own parent text: the variant Ιεσσαί "Iessai" is attested by the majority Greek text and Zohrapian's text, Յեսսեայ.

3–5.2.5.3.3 Reconstruction of the Source Text of Arm-1–2 Sam

Expanded collations of the manuscripts of these books have led to a better understanding of the Armenian version's parent text through the elimination of many corrupt readings. Clarification of the bifurcation of strata emerges from cases of doublet readings that have resulted from a conflation of the textual streams, with scribes deciding to preserve both readings.[4] An excellent example is provided at 2 Kgdms 19:8, where the majority Greek text preserves the Hebrew idiom in employing ἀνήρ "man," understood in a distributive sense, whereas Lucianic witnesses LXX^boc2e2 Cop Syh^j observe Greek idiom by using ἕκαστος "each." The composite Armenian reading preserves both as այր իւրաքանչիւր "each man."

The presumption is that the Lucianic text (→ 1.3.2.1; → 3–5.1.6.2) underlies the initial Armenian translation (Arm 1), many of whose readings have been replaced in the mainstream transmission history by the revised form (Arm 2), effected about a generation later.[5] However, a small group of manuscripts has preserved a much higher number of Arm 1 readings than are acces-

---

[5] On this, see Cox, *Aquila, Symmachus and Theodotion*, 33–35.
[1] Brooke–McLean–Thackeray, *The Old Testament in Greek*, Part 1: *1 and 2 Samuel*.
[2] Rahlfs, *Septuaginta*.

[3] Zohrapian, *Scriptures*.
[4] For examples, see Cowe, "La versión armenia," lxxiv–lxxv.
[5] For Arm 1 and Arm 2, see → 1.4.7.

sible in the Zohrapian edition. Thus, at 2 Kgdms 18:3, Zohrapian's text joins witnesses LXX^cx Cop^vid Eth in omitting φυγῇ "with flight," the majority reading, but various Armenian manuscripts attest փախչելով "by fleeing," which represents the variant φυγοντες "fleeing," attested by Lucianic witnesses LXX^boc2e2 VL. Affinities with VL (→ 1.4.1; → 3–5.2.1.2) and Josephus (→ 21.3) reveal that a set of pre-Lucianic readings also features in Arm 1's source text. This is well illustrated by the place name Mahanaim at 2 Kgdms 19:32: the Old Greek majority text transliterates it as Μαναειμ "Manaeim," whereas the Lucianic manuscripts LXX^Mmg bimgozmgc2e2, Arm (բանակս), and Josephus attest παρεμβολαις "camps."[6]

Meanwhile, the parent text of Arm 2 bears a Hexaplaric (→ 1.3.1.2.7; → 3–5.1.5.2) complexion. For example, յաւազան "into the pool" (1 Kgdms 2:14) reflects the Hexaplaric variant reading εις τον λουτηρα "into the washtub" attested by LXX^A cx.[7]

3–5.2.5.3.4 Translation Technique

The version evinces typical Arm 1 characteristics, such as the expression of pronoun subjects. When Nathan targets David, the common Greek formulation ἐπάταξας ... ἔλαβες "you struck ... you took" is transformed into the more emphatic statement, հարեր դու ... առեր դու "it was you who struck ... it was you who took" (2 Kgdms 12:9). Bald verbal constructions like ἐποίησας "you did" are finessed by the introduction of objects, so արարեր զայդ "you did that" (2 Kgdms 12:12). Similarly, the incisive application of an idiomatic spacial and referential adjective personalizes the phrase κατὰ ταῦτα "according to these" for David, in rendering it ըստ չափի "according to the measure that has been measured to you" (2 Kgdms 12:8).

Participial usage in Greek and Armenian is one of the most divergent of grammatical categories. The Armenian translation retains the articulated form in cases like τῷ ξένῳ ὁδοιπόρῳ ἐλθόντι "for the stranger, as a wayfarer having come" in հիւրոյն անցաւորի եկելոյ "for the guest, a wayfarer having come" (2 Kgdms 12:4), but in the next verse the translator renders the phrase ὁ ποιήσας τοῦτο "the one having done this" with the clause որ արար զայն "who did that."

On occasion, semantic leveling can be observed, in passages where several Greek terms are represented by a single equivalent. In the pericope on the death of David's son (2 Kgdms 12:15–25), the translator employs ծառայք "servants" to render not only the synonyms δοῦλοι (2 Kgdms 12:18) and παῖδες (2 Kgdms 12:19 [2×], 21), but also πρεσβύτεροι "elders" (2 Kgdms 12:17).

3–5.2.5.3.4.1 Attention to Context

In David's contrition at his son's illness, he abases himself on the ground. His servants try to assist him in getting up, which provokes the king's response, καὶ οὐκ ἠθέλησεν "and he did not want" (2 Kgdms 12:16). As the scene is left in suspense, the translator decided to reformulate it as ոչ կամէր յառնել ի գետնոյն "he did not want to get up from the floor" in order to provide a more satisfactory conclusion.

3–5.2.5.3.4.2 Literalisms and Transliterations

The Armenian retains many of the Hebraisms preserved in the Greek. These include: pleonastic relative constructions like ἣν ... αὐτήν "which ... it" rendered literally as զոր ... զնա "which ... it" and the repetition of prepositions like μετ' ... μετά "with ... with" by ընդ ... ընդ "with ... with" (2 Kgdms 12:3). Similarly, the oath formula Ζῇ κύριος "the Lord lives" is repeated as կենդանի է տէր "the Lord is alive" and the judgment υἱὸς θανάτου "son of death" as որդի մահու "son of death" (2 Kgdms 12:5). The ubiquitous phrase ἐν ὀφθαλμοῖς αὐτοῦ "in his eyes" is rendered առաջի աչաց նորա "before his eyes" (2 Kgdms 12:9), and the much rarer expression ἀπέναντι τούτου τοῦ ἡλίου "opposite this sun" emerges as յանդիման արեգականս այսորիկ "opposite this sun" (2 Kgdms 12:12). Moreover, as in many books, the Armenian version renders intensive participial constructions like παροξύνων παρώξυνας "provoking you provoked" with զայրացուցանելով զայրա-

---

[6] On the Armenian version's Lucianic affinities, see Johnson, *Die armenische Bibelübersetzung*, 72–73.

[7] See further Johnson, *Die armenische Bibelübersetzung*, 97–160.

զնցբեր "by provoking you provoked" (2 Kgdms 12:14). Nevertheless, there were certain grammatical boundaries the translator was not prepared to cross: in encoding the Greek's representation of the Hebrew intensive pronoun אנכי "I" – for example, in the clause ἐγώ εἰμι ἔχρισά σε "I am – I anointed you" as ես եմ որ օծի զքեզ "I am the one who anointed you" – he smoothened the syntax by adding the relative որ "the one who" (2 Kgdms 12:7).

In other cases, the Armenian reflects target language idiom. The translator reformulates the contrasting repetition εἷς ... εἷς "one ... one" more directly as մին ... միւսն "the one ... the other" (2 Kgdms 12:1). The calque of the preposition -ב by ἐν even outside its accepted semantic field is made intelligible by using the instrumental case: ἐν ῥομφαίᾳ "in a sword," is rendered սրով "with a sword" (2 Kgdms 12:9).

3–5.2.5.3.5 Text-Critical Value: Omissions and Additions

The Armenian has few minuses, most of which are insignificant, like the omission of the connective καί "and" (2 Kgdms 12:23). These more substantive cases may be noted: the phrase καὶ ηὔξατο εὐχὴν κυρίῳ "and (she) vowed a vow to the Lord" is omitted from Hannah's prayer (1 Kgdms 1:11); the object of Saul's suspicion, i.e., τὸν Δαυείδ "David" is unrepresented (1 Kgdms 18:9) as well as the plea that David swear κατὰ τοῦ θεοῦ "by God" (1 Kgdms 30:15). However, the lack of the epithet τοῦ μεγάλου "the big" that qualifies the stone where the Ark had rested (1 Kgdms 6:18) can be plausibly explained through parablepsis by homoioteleuton in Greek.[8]

The version manifests a number of pluses designed to complete the sense or facilitate the narrative flow. Thus, it adds the verb տարաւ "carried" in connection with the preceding list of direct objects (1 Kgdms 1:21); եւ գնացին "and they headed off" completes the verse by signalling the transition from speech to action (1 Kgdms 9:3); the imperative հասէք "reach" provides a context for the dangling Greek goal of motion ἐκεῖ "there" (1 Kgdms 23:22); and the addition ցնա եգիպտացին "to him the Egyptian" clarifies the change of speaker in the conversation between David and a young Egyptian slave (1 Kgdms 30:15). Other pluses of lesser moment include periodic additions of the adjective ամենայն "all" (e.g., at 1 Kgdms 11:7; 2 Kgdms 12:7).[9]

3–5.2.5.3.6 Text-Critical Value of Arm-1–2 Sam for LXX-1–2 Sam

A more extensive collation of manuscripts is required to verify the contours of the Armenian translation's strata, but the consistency of the principles informing its translation and revision is such that its relation to its source texts is already quite clear and its significance all the more important for its partial witness to the pre-Lucianic text.

3–5.2.5.3.7 Readings from "the Three"

Cox notes twenty-one cases of readings from "the Three" (→ 1.3.2.1; → 3–5.1.5.2) in 1 Reigns and twenty-two in 2 Kingdoms.[10]

Brooke–McLean–Thackeray, *The Old Testament in Greek*: Part 1: *1 and 2 Samuel*.
Cowe, S.P., "La versión armenia," in *El texto antioqueno de la Biblia griega: 1–2 Samuel* (eds. N. Fernández Marcos and J.R. Busto Saiz, with collaboration of M.V. Spottorno, D. Caro, and S.P. Cowe; Textos y estudios Cardenal Cisneros 50; Madrid: Instituto de Filogogía, 1989), lxxi–lxxix.
Cox, C.E., *Aquila, Symmachus and Theodotion in Armenia* (SBLSCS 42; Atlanta: Scholars Press, 1996).
Johnson, B., *Die armenische Bibelübersetzung als hexaplarischer Zeuge im 1. Samuelbuch* (ConBOT 2; Lund: CWK Gleerup, 1968).
Johnson, B., "Fünf armenische Bibelhandschriften aus Erevan," in *Wort, Lied und Gottespruch: Festschrift für Joseph Ziegler* (ed. J. Schreiner; Würzburg: Echter Verlag, 1972), 67–72.
Rahlfs, *Septuaginta*.
Zohrapian, *Scriptures*.

Peter Cowe

---

[8] For further details, see Johnson, *Die armenische Bibelübersetzung*, 54–56.

[9] For further details, see Johnson, *Die armenische Bibelübersetzung*, 50–53.

[10] See Cox, *Aquila, Symmachus and Theodotion*, 37–119.

3–5.2.5.4 1–2 Kings (3–4 Kgdms)

3–5.2.5.4.1 Background: Editions

The Armenian version of these books was rendered from Greek (→ 5.5) and hence references to the parent text are made according to their designation in LXX: 3–4 Kingdoms. The Greek text used for this entry is that of the Cambridge Septuagint,[1] together with that of Rahlfs' provisional edition.[2] The Armenian text used is that of Zohrapian's diplomatic edition of 1805.[3]

3–5.2.5.4.2 Translation Character

The Armenian version's derivation from a Greek source text is highlighted by the *kaige* sections' (→ 5.5; → 3–5.1.5.2) distinctive vocabulary for foreign cultic paraphernalia: the Asherah are referred to as ἄλσος "grove, woodland" – as at 4 Kgdms 17:10 – where Arm translates accordingly with անտառ "woods."

3–5.2.5.4.3 Reconstruction of the Parent Text of Arm-Kgdms

Several variant readings suggest a bifurcation in the version's transmission history, as in various other books (→ 1.4.7), namely, between an original translation (Arm 1), effected at the beginning of the fifth century, and a revision (Arm 2) conducted in the 430s. Some of these variant readings reflect typical differences in translation technique. Thus, at 4 Kgdms 17:32, Arm 1 idiomatically renders the literal Greek distributive repetition ἔθνος ἔθνος "nation nation" with յիւրաքանչիւր ազգաց "from each of the nations," whereas Arm 2 replicates the Greek in its rendering ազգք ազգք "nations nations." Other variants indicate the strata depend on divergent parent texts: Arm 1 derives from a Lucianic text type (→ 1.3.1.2; → 3–5.1.6.2), as illustrated by 4 Kgdms 17:11, where its reading արկանէին խունկս "they were casting incense" represents the Lucianic imperfect tense ἐθυμίων "they were censing," in contrast to the aorist form in the majority text ἐθύμιασαν "they censed," reflected by Arm 2 in արկին խունկս "they cast incense." Other agreements with the Lucanic text by the united Armenian witness imply those readings were retained by the revisers.

An excellent example of Arm 2's Hexaplaric origin (→ 1.3.1.2.7; → 3–5.1.5.2) is provided by 3 Kgdms 12:10, where the obscurity of the Old Greek's literal translation (→ 5.5) – which contrasts Rehoboam with his father in ἡ μικρότης μου "my smallness" – is removed by interpreting this as ճկոյթ իմ "my little finger" in agreement with the Origenic reading ὁ μικρότερός μου δάκτυλος "my little finger," also paralleled in Josephus (→ 21.3). Arm 2's Hexaplaric affiliation is manifested throughout these books in a series of pluses oriented towards MT (→ 5.3.2; for example, 3 Kgdms 6:37–38; 9:15–25; 4 Kgdms 17:14–15). Moreover, the Armenian translation maintains the MT order of chapters at 3 Kingdoms 20–21 and lacks the LXX additions (against the LXX[o] group and satellites at 3 Kgdms 6:1a–d, 36a; 10:22a–c; 12:24a–z; 16:28 a–h).

3–5.2.5.4.4 Translation Technique

Several facets of the Armenian translation are characteristic of the Arm 1 profile, including short nuancing additions like ինչ "a certain" (4 Kgdms 17:8, 9), իսկ "indeed" (4 Kgdms 17:21), and the addition of the pronoun subject դու "you" with the imperative for emphasis (3 Kgdms 12:16). Also typical of Arm 1 is the idiomatic way of designating geographical entities by their inhabitants, as in the title βασιλέα Αἰγύπτου "king of Egypt," rendered as արքայ եգիպտացւոց "king of the Egyptians" (4 Kgdms 17:4). Similarly, Arm intensifies the contrast between licit and illicit cultic practice, as in its rendering of θεοὺς ἑτέρους "other gods" with աստուածոց օտարաց "foreign gods" (4 Kgdms 17:7) and the paralleling of the undifferentiated Greek term ἱερεῖς "priests" with քուրմս "pagan priests" (4 Kgdms 17:32).

In a number of cases, the Armenian translation pursues local idiom in rendering the Greek. Thus, while the Old Greek frequently employs historic present tenses, the translator regularly transforms them into the aorist, as in the translation of πορεύεται "proceeds" with չոգաւ "went"

---

[1] Brooke–McLean–Thackeray, *The Old Testament in Greek*.
[2] Rahlfs, *Septuaginta*.
[3] Zohrapian, *Scriptures*.

(3 Kgdms 12:1). Similarly, the participial genitive absolute construction αὐτοῦ ... ὄντος "being himself" is construed in finite terms, with ինքն էր "he was himself" (3 Kgdms 12:2). Likewise, other participial forms are handled by a variety of strategies. Articulated phrases are usually translated by relative clauses – so τῶν καθημένων "those sitting" with որ նստէին "those who were sitting" (3 Kgdms 12:17) – but their translation also features nouns, as in the translation of φυλασσόντων "guarding" with պահապանացն "guards" (4 Kgdms 17:9), and verbal adjectives, as in the rendering of διαρπαζόντων "plundering" with աւարառուաց "plunder-taking" (4 Kgdms 17:20).

Similarly, the Armenian translator often exhibits variation in translation equivalents as, for example, in the literal representation of the infinitive βασιλεῦσαι "to make king" by the equivalent, թագաւորեցուցանել "to make king," while employing a different term (արքայ) for the title of king in the same verse (3 Kgdms 12:1). The same phenomenon recurs at 3 Kgdms 12:8–9, where the verb συνεβουλεύσαντο "they advised" in 3 Kgdms 12:8 is rendered by the close Armenian equivalent խորհեցաւ "he took counsel" (the third singular is a variant reading), whereas συμβούλευετε "you advise" in 2 Kgdms 12:9 is represented by the stronger տայք խրատ "you instructed."

There are also instances where the translator was either unfamiliar with the Greek term or found it so incongruous in context that he decided to produce a harmonizing interpretation instead. One case is afforded by the reference to "made partners and engraved" (ἐποίησαν κοινωνοὺς καὶ ἐχάραξαν) at 4 Kgdms 17:11, where the Armenian rendering portrays the actions as a doublet արարին զնդոսա եւ ընկերշակեցին "they made companions and associated." Similarly, at 4 Kgdms 17:17, the reference to the Israelites' children being sold (ἐπράθησαν) to engage in unlawful acts has been construed by the translator in terms of their becoming "emboldened" (համարձակեցան) to commit such deeds.

3–5.2.5.4.4.1 Attention to Context
The application of *figura etymologica* in the Armenian rendering of οἰωνίζοντο, "they were practicing ornithomancy" with հմայեցին հմայս "they divined divinations" (4 Kgdms 17:17) has clearly been influenced by the preceding phrase. Similarly, the Armenian varies the rendering of the action of sending into exile, depending on the precise environment. Thus, at 4 Kgdms 17:6, the term ἀπῴκισεν "he exiled" is rendered as խաղացոյց "he marched, transported," whereas at 4 Kgdms 17:23 the passive form ἀπῳκίσθη "(Israel) was exiled" is represented by վարեցաւ "was led away"; at 4 Kgdms 17:26 the active form ἀπῴκισας "you exiled" becomes փոխեցեր "you displaced," but at 4 Kgdms 17:28 ἀπῴκισαν "they exiled" is translated գերեցին "they led into captivity." Meanwhile at 4 Kgdms 17:11, where the same Greek term relates to the removing of the original inhabitants of the land, Arm reflects the nuance with մերժեաց "he removed." The Armenian then applies the identical term to translate the removing of Israel from the Lord, whereas this process is referred to by different Greek lexemes, e.g., ἀπέστησεν "removed" (4 Kgdms 17:18) and ἐξέωσεν "drove out" (4 Kgdms 17:21).

3–5.2.5.4.4.2 Literalisms and Transliterations
Although the Armenian version retains some Hebraisms encoded in the Greek – such as the connective καὶ ἐγένετο "and it happened" with եւ եղեւ "and it happened" (3 Kgdms 12:2) and καὶ ἰδού "and see" as եւ ահա "and behold" (4 Kgdms 17:26) – it more commonly avoids such accommodations as being unidiomatic. Thus it changes *kaige* pleonastic constructions like ἐν αἷς κατῴκουν ἐν αὐταῖς "in which they dwelt in them" into the regular structure յորս ինքեանք բնակէին "in which they themselves dwelt" (4 Kgdms 17:29). Similarly, it lacks the connective of the apodosis of Hebrew oath formulae, as at 3 Kgdms 12:7, and employs the instrumental case to render structures where the Greek duplicates the Hebrew use of the preposition -ב by phrases with ἐν, as in ἐν μάστιγξιν "in whips" (3 Kgdms 12:11), paralleled in Armenian by գանիւք "with whiplashes."

Additionally, the Armenian version attests cases of literalism in reflecting Greek idiom, as at 3 Kgdms 12:3 where the term եկեղեցի – a Greek

3–5.2.5.4.5 Text-Critical Value: Omissions and Additions

The Armenian version maintains a high degree of quantitative representation, so minuses tend to be few and of minor significance: e.g., νῦν "now" (3 Kgdms 12:4); καί 4° "and" (4 Kgdms 17:15); and πάσῃ "all" (4 Kgdms 17:16). One longer minus, where the phrase καὶ ἐποίησαν ἑαυτοῖς ἐν οἴκῳ τῶν ὑψηλῶν "and they acted for them in the house of the high places" is omitted, may be the result of paraplepsis in part of the manuscript tradition, an "omission" that may be recovered in more extensive collations (4 Kgdms 17:32). Armenian pluses are also relatively few and insignificant, pluses such as եւ "and" (4 Kgdms 17:11), աստուծոյ "God" (4 Kgdms 17:36), and (q)ամենայն "all" (4 Kgdms 17:11, etc.).

3–5.2.5.4.6 Text-Critical Value of Arm-Kgs for LXX-Kdgms

A more thorough investigation, with a larger collation sample, is required to corroborate the theory of two strata in the Armenian. At the same time it is clear that the current text represents its parent text with a high degree of consistency.

3–5.2.5.4.7 Readings from "the Three"

Cox notes ten examples of readings from the Three (→ 3–5.1.5.2) in 3 Kingdoms and ninety-eight in 4 Kingdoms, the highest number of any book of the Armenian Bible.

Brooke–McLean–Thackeray, *The Old Testament in Greek*, Part 2: *I and II Kings*.
Cox, C.E., *Aquila, Symmachus and Theodotion in Armenia* (SBLSCS 42; Atlanta: Scholars Press, 1996).
Gehman, H.S., "The Armenian Version of I and II Kings and its Affinities," *JAOS* 54 (1934): 53–59.
Johnson, B., "Some Remarks on the Marginal Notes in Armenian 1 Samuel," in *Armenian and Biblical Studies* (ed. M.E. Stone; Supplementary Volume 1 to Sion; Jerusalem: St. James Press, 1976), 17–20.
Rahlfs, *Septuaginta*.
Zanolli, A., "Lezioni marginali ai quattro libri dei Re: In una codice armeno dell' anno 1328," *Atti del Reale Istituto Veneto di scienze, lettere ed arti* 87/2 (1927–1928): 1217–35.
Zohrapian, *Scriptures*.

Peter Cowe

3–5.2.6 Georgian Translations

3–5.2.6.1 Background

The books of Joshua, Judges, and 1–4 Kingdoms are to be found in Georgian codices dating from the sixth/seventh to the seventeenth centuries. Despite being almost unexplored in terms of comparative textual criticism (not even a full collation with Rahlfs' edition[1] is available and the respective volumes of the Göttingen Septuagint remain unpublished), this tradition seems to be an important testimony for its primary Greek version (→ 3–5.1.1), given the antiquity of the translations and their textual features. However, significant work has still to be done before drawing definitive conclusions.

The earliest manuscript evidence is found in palimpsest Georg^x (= Wien Österreichische Nationalbibliothek, geo. 2, sixth–seventh centuries C.E.), which contains fragments of Georg-Josh and Georg-Judg.[2] The language of these texts reveals certain peculiarities that scholars have labeled *Khanmeti* as a consequence of the use of the verbal and nominal prefix "x-."

The tenth-century manuscript Georg^o (= Mount Athos, Library of the Iviron Monastery, geo. 1, 978 C.E., in two volumes) preserves the entire text of 1–4 Kingdoms and the last two chapters of Georg-Judg (Judg 19:16–21:25). The complete texts of Georg-Josh and Georg-Judg as well as the short redaction of Georg-1–4 Kgdms are not attested before the twelfth and thirteenth cen-

---

[1] Rahlfs, *Septuaginta*.
[2] Birdsall, "A Georgian Palimpsest in Vienna," 108–12; Birdsall, "Ms Vindob. Georg. 2," 39–44; Birdsall, "Xanmet'i Georgian Palimpsest Fragments," 3–7; Gippert, "Die georgische Palimpsesthandschrift," 31–46; Gippert, "The Application," 168–79; Gippert, Sarjveladze, and Kajaia, *The Old Georgian Palimpsest*, 1–14.

turies respectively. The following manuscripts have survived: Georg^Ga (= Tbilisi, National Centre of Manuscripts, Q-1152, twelfth/thirteenth century), Georg^Gb (= Tbilisi, National Centre of Manuscripts, A-1108, twelfth century), Georg^Ja (= Jerusalem, Library of the Greek Patriarchate, geo. 113, thirteenth century), Georg^D (= Tbilisi, National Centre of Manuscripts, H-855, seventeenth century), Georg^F (= Tbilisi, National Centre of Manuscripts, A-646, sixteenth century), Georg^I (= Tbilisi, National Centre of Manuscripts, A-570, fifteenth century). Codices Georg^F and Georg^I also contain important and partially hitherto unknown Hexaplaric material in their margins. A few verses from Georg-2–4 Kgdms showing textual agreement with this group are furthermore available in manuscript fragments dating from the twelfth/thirteenth century, kept today in Armenian archives (Yerevan and Echmiadzin).[3] The ancient lectionary is represented by Georg^P (= Paris, Bibliothèque nationale de France, geo. 3, 1040 C.E.) and Georg^Cb (= Cambridge, add. 1890.1), the latter containing only fragments of 1 Kgdms 24:6–10. Finally, later redactions of Joshua, Judges, and 1–4 Kingdoms are to be found in Georg^s (Tbilisi, National Centre of Manuscripts, A-51, seventeenth/eighteenth century) and in the Moscow 1743 printed edition (= Georg^B).

The above-mentioned codices are described in several catalogues, depending on where they are currently stored: the most complete and updated description, which should be consulted for a more detailed study, is that published in the first volume of the critical edition of the Old Georgian Octateuch.[4] The ancient versions of Georg-1–4 Kgdms remain unpublished. Synoptical critical editions are available for Georg-Josh and Georg-Judg.

3–5.2.6.2 Date, Versions, Editions
3–5.2.6.2.1 Georg-Josh

Today, Georg-Josh is known in two versions. The first (= Georg-Josh 1) is contained in full in later sources only, dating back to the seventeenth and eighteenth centuries (Georg^{B,D,S}). Fragments are available in the "xanmet'i" palimpsest Georg^x and in the lectionary Georg^P (Josh 4:4–14; 22:1–34; 24:30–33).[5] Georg-Josh 1 can be dated to the earliest period of Georgian literature, most likely to the fifth/sixth century.

The second version (= Georg-Josh 2) was carried out in Gelati in the early twelfth century. The text is preserved in Codices Georg^{Ga, Gb}, accompanied by commentaries.

A synoptic edition of both Georgian versions appeared in 1991.[6] A separate publication of Georg^s is also available.[7] The exegetical catenae to Georg-Josh 2 have been published recently in Tbilisi.[8]

3–5.2.6.2.2 Georg-Judg

As in the previous case, the first version of the book (= Georg-Judg 1) belongs to the earliest period of Georgian literature, most likely to the fifth or sixth century C.E. This is proven not only by linguistic features, but also by the inclusion of several sections of Georg-Judg 1 in the *Khanmeti* palimpsest Georg^x, in Georg^o (Judg 19:16–21:25),[9] as well as in Georg^P (Judg 2:1–23; 3:1–30; 6:34–40; 7:1–25; 8:1–35).[10] However, a full text of this version is contained only in late sources (Georg^{B,D,S}).

Like Georg-Josh 2, the second translation of Judges (= Georg-Judg 2) belongs to the Gelati literary school. It was carried out in the early twelfth century and is available in mss Georg^{Ga,Gb}, which also contain Byzantine catenae.

---

[3] In one case, two folios survived because they were used as protective sheets in the book cover of an Armenian manuscript (see Marr, "ečmiadzinskij fragment," 378–88; Cindeliani, "Kartuli bibliis ečmiaʒinis pragment'is ident'ipik'aciistvis," 74–78; and Cindeliani, "Mepeta c'ignebis kartuli pragment'ebi," 38–50).

[4] *C'ignni*, 557–639.

[5] For an edition, see Danelia, Čxenk'eli, and Šavišvili, *Kartuli lekcionaris p'arizuli xelnac'eri*, 116–22.

[6] *C'ignni ʒuelisa aγtkumisani*, 27–112.

[7] Dočanašvili, *Mcxeturi xelnac'eri*, 418–64.

[8] Gigineišvili and Todua, *Gelaturi bibliis k'at'enebi*, 497–540.

[9] First published in Šaniʒe, *C'ignni*, 133–38.

[10] For a publication, see Danelia, Čxenk'eli, and Šavišvili, *Kartuli lekcionaris p'arizuli xelnac'eri*, 123–33.

Both Georgian versions of Judges are accessible in a synoptical critical edition.[11] Moreover, a separate publication of Georg[s12] exists and an edition of the exegetical catenae to Georg-Josh 2 is also available.[13]

3–5.2.6.2.3 Georg-1–4 Kgdms

Four translations are known to exist of each book of Georg-1–4 Kgdms. The first (= Georg-Kgdms 1) dates back to the fifth to eighth centuries C.E. and is to be found in Codex Georg[o] and in the lectionaries Georg[P] and Georg[Cb].[14] The second translation (= Georg-Kgdms 2) seems to be quite old also, although its origin is still disputed and the problem concerning its date is far from resolved (see below). It is preserved in full in Georg[Ja,F] and partially extant in Georg[I] (the latter contains only the book of 4 Kingdoms). Additional manuscript material for this version consists in the above-mentioned fragments from Yerevan and Echmiadzin, which show textual agreement primarily with ms Georg[F].[15]

A third version of the book (= Georg-Kgdms 3) dating to the late seventeenth century is contained in Georg[s]. It was undertaken by Sulkhan Saba Orbeliani, mainly using Georg-Kgdms 2 as a basis, which he revised according to the 1666 printed Armenian Bible (→ 3–5.2.5).[16] A fourth translation (= Georg-Kgdms 4) is given in Georg[B]. This text shows reliance on the 1663 Old Church Slavonic printed Bible (→ 3–5.2.7).

The text of both ancient versions (Georg-1–4 Kgdms 1 and Georg-1–4 Kgdms 2) is still unedited. In 1910, Žanašvili published excerpts from 3–4 Kingdoms taken from Georg[F,I,S] and Tbilisi manuscript A-471, a nineteenth-century copy of Georg[o].[17]

3–5.2.6.3 Translation Character, Translation Technique, Inner-Translational Features

From the point of view of textual history and translation technique issues, Georg-Josh and Georg-Judg show a number of similarities. They are available in two versions, which are preserved in the same manuscripts. Due to their stylistic and linguistic features, they are judged to be the work of the same translator.[18] In both cases, the main task facing scholars is to establish to what degree late revisions modified the original aspect of the earliest translation. For instance, the traces of an Armenian model (→ 3–5.2.5.2) in Georg-Judg 1 seem to be the result of the late-seventeenth-century revision undertaken by Sulkhan Saba Orbeliani.[19] In general, the renderings of proper nouns as well as other lexical elements indicate that the books were translated from a Greek source (→ 3.3; → 4.3).[20]

Georg-1–4 Kgdms has had a much more tortuous and less linear textual history than the previous two books. Different stages of development have resulted in a number of significant changes. Over the centuries, the earliest version has been used repeatedly as a basis for producing new translations. This is highlighted by several cases of agreement between Georg[o] and the remaining testimonies (Georg[Ja,F,I,S]), in which the ancient text was revised according to different sources.

3–5.2.6.3.1 Georg-Josh

As is widely known, the Greek version of Joshua preserves very important material for the textual criticism of the Hebrew Bible (→ 3.3). LXX often deviates from MT (→ 3.2.2), evidenced by several minuses, pluses, and a different arrangement of verses.[21] Both translations of Georg-Josh were carried out from Greek sources and in each instance a literal translation technique was adopted. These inner-translational features and the availability of a critical edition facilitate comparison with the

---

[11] *C'ignni ʒuelisa aytkumisani*, 113–202.
[12] Dočanašvili, *Mcxeturi xelnac'eri*, 465–508.
[13] Gigineišvili and Todua, *Gelaturi bibliis k'at'enebi*, 540–609.
[14] Danelia, Čxenk'eli, and Šavišvili, *Kartuli lekcionaris p'arizuli xelnac'eri*, 142–82; Blake, "Catalogue," 213–14 (and pl. 5).
[15] Cindeliani, "Mepeta c'ignebis kartuli pragment'ebi," 49.
[16] For an edition, see Dočanašvili, *Mcxeturi xelnac'eri*, 1–243.
[17] Žanašvili, *Našromebi*, 37–70.

[18] *C'ignni ʒuelisa aytkumisani*, 16.
[19] *C'ignni ʒuelisa aytkumisani*, 10.
[20] Dočanašvili, "Kartuli bibliis iso naves c'ignis berʒnizmebi," 81–84.
[21] See Tov, **Greek–Hebrew Bible*, 385–96.

primary version. Nevertheless, a detailed account of the relations between the Georgian and the Greek manuscript traditions has still to be produced.

The critical apparatus of the printed 1991 edition[22] does not contain a collation with Rahlfs' edition[23] and the Joshua volume of the Göttingen Septuagint is lacking. In the introduction to its 1991 edition, Georg-Josh 1 is described as showing a tendency to agree with the readings of Codex Alexandrinus.[24] However, the editors did not take into account a number of fundamental research works into the Hebrew and Greek texts.

On the basis of a brief preliminary investigation into the material, the following complements to the 1991 edition can be made:

a) In Josh 1:1, Georg-Josh 1 does not agree with LXX, but with MT: ... და იყო შემდგომად აღსასრულისა მის მოსესსა, მონისა მის უფლისა ... "And it happened after the death of Moses, *the servant of the LORD* ..."[25] However, a few verses later, in Josh 1:15, the same formula is omitted, as in LXX. In this case, the reading of MT is partially supported by Georg-Josh 2: ... და წარხჳდეთ თითოეული სამკჳდრებელსა თჳსსა, რომელი მიგცა თქუენ მოსემან, მონამან უფლისამან ... "Each of you may return to his inherited land, which Moses, *the servant of the LORD*, gave unto you ..."

b) Both translations omit the same formula in Josh 22:4 according to LXX, but in Josh 27:14 they add the Dtr phrase[26] "the house of bondage, and who wrought those wondrous signs before our very eyes" (Georg-Josh 1: სახლით მონებისაგი, და ყვნა ჩუენთჳს სასწაულნი დიდ-დიდნი; Georg-Josh 2: სახლით მონათაგი და რაოდენნი მიყვნა ჩუენ სასწაულნი ესე დიდნი).

c) In Joshua 8–9, both versions differ from LXX.[27] The order of the verses is as follows: 1) Josh 8:1–29; 2) Josh 8:30–35; 3) Josh 9:1–2; 4) Josh 9:3–27.[28]

d) In Josh 20:1–6, both versions have a longer text corresponding to that of Codex Alexandrinus.

e) Other long elements reflecting the LXX text can be found in Josh 6:26a; 16:10a; 21:42d; 24:31a; 24:33a–b.

f) LXX minuses are attested in Josh 2:15; 4:10.[29]

3–5.2.6.3.2 Georg-Judg

Despite the many analogies with Georg-Josh in terms of textual history, the inner-translational features of Georg-Judg are more difficult to outline. This is due mainly to the fact that editorial intervention on the ancient tradition was greater with Georg-Judg than with Georg-Josh. Nevertheless, the archetype of the old Georgian translation of Georg-Judg can be reconstructed with a certain degree of reliability.

In the introduction to the printed 1991 edition,[30] it is stated that while Georg-Judg 1 shows reliance on a text close to LXX^A, Georg-Judg 2 clearly depends on a Greek prototype close to the text of LXX^B.[31] As in the case of Georg-Josh, this conclusion is not supported by a full collation with the Rahlfs' edition.[32]

The issue requires further investigation. Firstly, in contrast with the above-mentioned claim, cases exist in which Georg-Judg 1 agrees with Codex Vaticanus (LXX^B; see, for instance, Judg 1:21–22; 1:33; 2:6). In addition, readings can be found in which Georg-Judg 1 differs from the texts of both LXX^A and LXX^B. For example, in Judg 1:14, Georg-Judg 1 deviates from LXX^A ("he urged her"), LXX^B ("Gothoniel urged her"), and MT ("she urged him"): ... და იყო, რაჟამს შევიდოდა იგი, აბირა იგი გოთონიელ ცოლი თჳსი, რათა სთხოვს მამასა თჳსსა აგარაკი "and it came about

---

[22] *C'ignni zuelisa aytkumisani.*
[23] Rahlfs, **Septuaginta*.
[24] *C'ignni zuelisa aytkumisani*, 11.
[25] See the critical apparatus in: Margolis, *The Book*, Part I, 1.
[26] See Tov, **HB, GB, and Qumran*, 401–03.
[27] See Tov, **TCHB*, 298–99 for LXX-Josh 8–9.
[28] See the critical apparatus in Margolis, *The Book*, Part 2, 141–44.
[29] For these LXX minuses, see Tov, **TCHB*, 294–98.
[30] *C'ignni zuelisa aytkumisani.*
[31] *C'ignni zuelisa aytkumisani*, 10–12.
[32] Rahlfs, **Septuaginta*.

when she entered that Gothoniel urged his wife to ask her father for the field." Furthermore, it remains an open question how the Georgian relates to the several Greek text subgroups, according to which more recent scholarship has redefined the manuscript classification. It may therefore be concluded that the problem of the relationship with the Greek should be subjected to further research and indeed deserves special attention.

3–5.2.6.3.3 Georg-1–4 Kgdms

The textual history of Georg-1–4 Kgdms is one of the most challenging issues in the study of the Georgian translation of the Bible. The main obstacle is the lack of an edition for both ancient versions, namely Georg-1–4 Kgdms 1 and Georg-1–4 Kgdms 2. Moreover, many complicated changes occurred during the textual transmission, rendering the reconstruction of the textual history arduous.

Between 1967 and 2001, Cindeliani published a number of articles on this tradition as detailed in the bibliography to this article. According to Cindelani, the textual history of the Georgian books of 1–4 Kingdoms comprises three phases. Between the eighth and ninth centuries C.E., the earliest translation (whose original date is not specified by Cindelani) was revised toward a Lucianic manuscript (→ 3–5.1.6.2). This stage is represented by manuscript Georg⁰ (here preserving the text of Georg-1–4 Kgdms 1). Its outstanding feature is the translation of the Greek preposition κατά followed by the accusative with the postposition -ebr suffixed to the genitive.[33] It also includes rare words typical of the earliest Georgian literary works that in some cases may be considered of dialectal origin.[34] Furthermore, some Armenianisms can be found in Georg-4 Kgdms.[35] In Georg-3 Kgdms, the earliest Georgian version includes the additions 3 Kgdms 2:35a–o; 9:15–25; 11:23–24; 12:24a–z; 16:28a–g (28h is lacking); and 22:54a–b, but omits 3 Kgdms 2:46a–

l. In Cindeliani's opinion, the text originally contained only Hexaplaric additions (→ 3–5.1.5.2): the Lucianic pluses (→ 3–5.1.6.2) should be considered to be a later interpolation.[36]

As in the two previous cases, the following complements may be made. Georg-1 Kgdms 1 contains the longer text of the story of David and Goliath: manuscript Georg⁰ adds 1 Kgdms 17:12–31, 41, 50, 55, 57–58; 18:1–6a, 10–11, 17–19, and 29b–30.[37] In Georg-3 Kgdms 1, the arrangement of 3 Kingdoms 20–21[38] does not agree with LXX, but with MT. Georg-3 Kgdms 1 also omits 3 Kgdms 2:1–11; 15:32; 22:41–51. Due to the loss of several sheets in Georg⁰, 3 Kgdms 4:12–7:31 is missing.

A second crucial phase in the textual history of Georg-1–4 Kgdms dates presumably to the early twelfth century. The earlier Georgian translation was used as a base text for preparing Georg-1–4 Kgdms 2. However, this second text is significantly shorter than Georg-Kgdms 1 and the language is not particularly stylized. A number of colloquial elements have led us to assume that it was written according to the usage of the spoken language.[39] Melikišvili even speculates that Georg-1–4 Kgdms 2 could preserve a type of modified Georgian Targum.[40]

According to Cindeliani,[41] the minuses in Georg-1–4 Kgdms 2 should not be considered the result of omissions caused by scribal errors, but the consequence of an intentional, fully premeditated work.[42] In some instances, a textual agreement is

---

[33] Cindeliani, "Mepeta c'ignebis šedgeniloba," 62–78.

[34] Cindeliani, "3iebani 3veli kartuli leksik'idan," 96–103.

[35] Cindeliani, "IV mepeta 22–25 tavebis mimartebisatvis ucxo c'q'aroebtan," 180–94; and "Mepeta 22–25-e tavebis mimartebisatvis ucxo c'q'aroebtan (II nac'ili)," 176–85.

[36] Cindeliani, "III–IV mepeta c'ignebis šedgeniloba (II. čanartebis sak'itxi)," 77–99.

[37] For the longer text of the story of David and Goliath, see Tov, *Greek–Hebrew Bible*, 333–56.

[38] For arrangement of LXX-3 Kgdms 20–21, see Tov, *TCHB*, 310.

[39] Cindeliani, "Erti redakciuli taviseburebis gamo mepeta c'ignebši," 50–74.

[40] Melikišvili, *Targmanebi*, 123. However, this hypothesis is presented without any argumentation.

[41] Cindeliani, "Erti redakciuli taviseburebis gamo mepeta c'ignebši," 50–74.

[42] In his 1971 paper, Cindeliani focuses mainly on Georg-2 Kgdms 2 (only a few readings from Georg-1 Kgdms 2 are given). In the 1983 article, Cindeliani discusses almost exclusively the textual and linguistic features of Georg-3 Kgdms 2 (in a few cases readings from Georg-4 Kgdms 2 are examined).

claimed with LXX-manuscripts *cdx* (sigla refer to the Cambridge edition). However, because no similar redaction was found in Greek or in other traditions, Cindeliani argues that Georg-1–4 Kgdms 2 is an original Georgian redaction. Moreover, he states that the textual differences between Georg-1–4 Kgdms 1 and Georg-1–4 Kgdms 2 are of secondary importance: in his view, both texts can be traced back to the same archetype. This latter hypothesis is highly questionable. The textual agreements between the two versions are most likely the consequence of the use of Georg-Kgdms 1 as a base text, rather than the result of an independent process.

Georg-1–4 Kgdms 2 stands out not only for being a hitherto not attested short redaction of 1–4 Kingdoms, but also for its Hexaplaric material (→ 3–5.1.5.2). Marginalia in manuscripts Georg^{F,I} preserve readings from the Three in 4 Kingdoms.[43] The Georgian contains not only sections already available either in Greek (→ 5.4; → 5.5) or Armenian (→ 3–5.2.5.3; → 3–5.2.5.4) versions or in the Syro-Hexapla (→ 3–5.2.4.2), i.e., 4 Kgdms 10:13; 10:27; 11:4 and 19; 11:8; 11:12; 11:18; 12:5; 14:7; 15:5; 16:9, but it provides us with completely new textual information as well (4 Kgdms 11:9; 11:15; 14:29; 17:9; 18:4; 18:20). As noted by Birdsall, the *excerpta* from 4 Kingdoms published by Žanašvili give us access to a previously unknown Hexaplaric tradition: in his opinion, some readings probably came from the Armenian, but others were most likely not directly related to this tradition.[44] The Hexaplaric material was re-edited with a commentary and textual parallels by Cindeliani (a reproduction of the marginal signs is also given).[45]

The third formative stage in the textual history of Georg-1–4 Kgdms dates to a considerably later period. In the late seventeenth century, Sulkhan Saba Orbeliani (1658–1725) carried out the translation of Georg-Kgdms 3. In preparing his version, he made use of several Georgian sources (a certain affinity is to be found with the redactions of manuscripts Georg^{F,Ja} and of the middle Georgian lectionaries). At the same time, his version shows reliance on the 1666 printed Armenian Bible (Oskan's edition; → 3–5.2.5.3; → 3–5.2.5.4).[46]

The last phase in the textual history of Georg-1–4 Kgdms belongs to the early eighteenth century. Georg-Kgdms 4 represents a revision of Georg-Kgdms 3 using the OCS Bible as a basis (→ 3–5.2.7). This text is available in the 1743 printed edition, Georg^B.

3–5.2.6.4 Text-Critical Value for the Primary Greek Translation

A definitive evaluation about the precise terms of the relationship of these translations with the primary Greek version (→ 3–5.1.1) proves to be quite problematic. Even if significant results have been achieved in the study of this tradition, many problems remain unsolved and several questions are still unanswered. Comparative research is at an early stage. Moreover, in some cases the available textual information continues to be unsatisfactory, fragmented, and at times contradictory, particularly in the case of 1–4 Kingdoms. However, on the basis of the hitherto stated analysis, some preliminary conclusions may be drawn.

The text-critical value of the two ancient versions of Georg-Josh and Georg-Judg lies in their ancient origin. The Greek source of Georg-Josh 1 has yet to be identified, but a preliminary investigation has shown that this translation preserves new valuable material for the study of several problems, related to the many pluses, minuses, and differences between the text of LXX and MT (→ 3.2.2; → 3.3).[47] Georg-Judg 1 presumably originated from a Greek source (→ 4.3) close to the text of LXX^A. However, because a collation has not been undertaken, the relationship with the subgroups of the LXX manuscripts has yet to be established. In both cases, the Georgian testimonies have provided scholars with fresh material for future research.

Therefore, the extent of the minuses and the translation character are not clear in Georg-1 Kgdms 2 and Georg-4 Kgdms 2.

[43] Outtier, "Un nouveau témoin," 271–75.
[44] Birdsall, "Traces," 83–92.
[45] Cindeliani, "Ak'vilasa da svimaxosis variant'ebi," 54–65.

[46] Cindeliani, "Mepeta c'ignebi," 21–36.
[47] See Tov, *Greek–Hebrew Bible*, 385–96.

Georg-Kgdms 1 contains Hexaplaric additions (→ 3–5.1.5.2); however, the relationship with LXX (in particular with the Lucianic manuscripts → 3–5.1.6) needs to be clarified. Georg-Kgdms 2 represents a short version that seems not to be attested elsewhere. Moreover, it also contains new Hexaplaric material that greatly furthers our knowledge. Despite the number of available publications and the highlighting of distinctive textual features, the Georgian testimonies to 1–4 Kingdoms cannot yet be included in the contemporary debate on the textual problems of these books (→ 5.4; → 5.5).[48] Before valid conclusions may be drawn, an edition of the texts should be undertaken and a collation produced with the Greek. Nevertheless, promising research perspectives can be easily outlined. This case once again points to the great potential and major significance of the Georgian tradition, still virtually unexplored, for the textual criticism of the Bible.

Biblia: Brʒanebita da c'arsagebelita sapasetata sakartvelos mepis bakar vaxt'angis ʒisata (Moscow: Bakaris st'amba, 1743).

Birdsall, J.N., "A Georgian Palimpsest in Vienna," *OrChr* 53 (1969): 108–12.

Birdsall, J.N., "Traces of the Jewish Greek Biblical Versions in Georgian Manuscript Sources," *JSS* 17 (1972): 83–92.

Birdsall, J.N., "Ms Vindob. Georg. 2: A Progress Report," *OrChr* 58 (1974): 39–44.

Birdsall, J.N., "Xanmet'i Georgian Palimpsest Fragments of the Old Testament Preserved in a Vienna Manuscript," in *Caucasian Perspectives* (ed. G. Hewitt; Unterschleissheim: Lincom Europa, 1992), 3–7.

Blake, R.P., "Catalogue of the Georgian Manuscripts in the Cambridge University Library," *HTR* 25 (1932): 207–24.

C'ignni ʒuelisa aγtkumisani, Vol. 3: *Iso navesi, msaʒultaj, rutisi* (eds. B. Gigineišvili and C. K'ik'viʒe; Tbilisi: Mecniereba, 1991).

Cindeliani, U., "Mepeta p'irveli ori c'ignis ʒveli kartuli redakciebis mimartebisatvis berʒnultan," *Macne: Enisa da lit'erat'uris seria*, Fasc. 2 (1967): 228–61.

Cindeliani, U., "Mepeta p'irveli ori c'ignis kartuli redakciebi," *Mravaltavi* 1 (1971): 46–65.

Cindeliani, U., "Ak'vilasa da svimaxosis variant'ebi ʒveli aγtkmis kartuli targmanši," *Macne: Enisa da lit'erat'uris seria*, Fasc. 1 (1973): 54–65.

Cindeliani, U., "Mepeta c'ignebis šedgeniloba," *Macne: Enisa da lit'erat'uris seria*, Fasc. 4 (1975): 62–78.

Cindeliani, U., "Κατά c'indebulis ek'vivalent'ebi mepeta c'ignebis kartul targmanši," *Mravaltavi* 4 (1975): 171–84.

Cindeliani, U., "Kartuli bibliis ečmiaʒinis pragment'is ident'ipik'aciistvis," *Macne: Enisa da lit'erat'uris seria*, Fasc. 2 (1976): 74–78.

Cindeliani, U., "Axali masalebi giorgi mtac'mindelis mtargmnelobiti metodis šesaxeb," *Macne: Enisa da lit'erat'uris seria*, Fasc. 4 (1978): 47–63.

Cindeliani, U., "III–IV mepeta c'ignebis šedgeniloba (II. čanartebis sak'itxi)," *Mravaltavi* 7 (1980): 77–99.

Cindeliani, U., "Erti redakciuli taviseburebis gamo mepeta c'ignebši (mok'le redakcia)," *Mravaltavi* 10 (1983): 50–74.

Cindeliani, U., "ʒiebani ʒveli kartuli leksik'idan," *Mravaltavi* 11 (1985): 96–103.

Cindeliani, U., "Mepeta c'ignebi ʒveli aγtkmis mcxetur versiaši da misi c'q'aroebi," *Mravaltavi* 12 (1986): 21–36.

Cindeliani, U., "Mepeta c'ignebis kartuli pragment'ebi somxetis c'ignsacavebidan," *Mravaltavi* 15 (1989): 38–50.

Cindeliani, U., "IV mepeta 22–25 tavebis mimartebisatvis ucxo c'q'aroebtan," *Mravaltavi* 18 (1999): 180–94.

Cindeliani, U., "Mepeta 22–25 – e tavebis mimartebisatvis ucxo c'q'aroebtan (II nac'ili)," *Mravaltavi* 19 (2001): 176–85.

Danelia, K., S. Čxenk'eli, and B. Šavišvili (eds.), *Kartuli lekcionaris p'arizuli xelnac'eri: ʒveli da axali aγtkmis sak'itxavebi*, Vol. 1: *Nac'ili I* (Tbilisi: Tbilisis universit'et'is gamomcemloba, 1987).

Dočanašvili, E., "Kartuli bibliis iso naves c'ignis berʒnizmebi," in *Macne: Enisa da lit'erat'uris seria*, Fasc. 4 (1971): 81–84.

Dočanašvili, E. (ed.), *Mcxeturi xelnac'eri* (*moses xutc'igneuli, iso nave, msaʒulta, ruti*) (Tbilisi: Mecniereba, 1981).

Dočanašvili, E. (ed.), *Mcxeturi xelnac'eri* (*mepeta I, II, III, IV, nešt'a I, II, ezras I, II, III c'ignebi*) (Tbilisi: Mecniereba, 1982).

Gigineišvili, B. and G. Todua (eds.), *Gelaturi bibliis k'at'enebi* (Tbilisi: Axali ivironi, 2011).

Gippert, J., "Die georgische Palimpsesthandschrift

---

[48] For this debate, see, e.g., Tov, *Greek–Hebrew Bible*, 273–84, 333–62, 433–56, 477–500, 549–70; Tov, *TCHB*, 301–04, 306–13.

Codex Vindobonensis georgicus 2," *Biblos: Beiträge zu Buch, Bibliothek und Schrift* 52 (2003): 31–46.

Gippert, J., "The Application of Multispectral Imaging in the Study of Caucasian Palimpsests," *Sakartvelos mecnierebata erovnuli ak'ademiis moambe* (= *Bulletin of the Georgian National Academy of Sciences*) 175 (2007): 168–79.

Gippert, J., Z. Sarjveladze, and L. Kajaia (eds.), *The Old Georgian Palimpsest: Codex Vindoboniensis georgicus 2* (Monumenta palaeographica Medii Aevi Series Ibero–Caucasica 1; Turnhout: Brepols, 2007).

Margolis, M.L., *The Book of Joshua in Greek According to the Critically Restored Text with an Apparatus Containing the Variants of the Principal Recensions of the Individual Witnesses* (Publications of the Alexander Kohut Memorial Foundation in Trust at the American Academy for Jewish Research; parts I–IV [Josh 1:1–19:38] Paris: Paul Geuther, 1931–38; part V [Josh 19:39–24:33] with a preface by E. Tov; Philadelphia: Annenberg Research Institute, 1992).

Marr, N.J., "Ečmiadzinskij fragment drevnegruzinskoj versii Vetchogo Zaveta," *Christianskij Vostok* 2 (1913): 378–88.

Outtier, B., "Un nouveau témoin géorgien de l' Ancien Testament avec des notes marginales hexaplaires (4 Rois)," in *Poussières de christianisme et de judaïsme antiques. Études réunies en l' honneur de Jean-Daniel Kaestli et Éric Junod* (A. Frey, R. Gounelle, eds.; Lausanne: Éditions du Zèbre, 2007): 271–75.

Šaniʒe, A., (ed.), *C'ignni ʒuelisa aγtkumisani 978 c'lis xelnac'eris mixedvit*, Vol. 1.2: *Levit'eltaj, msaʒultaj, rutisi, iobisi, esaiajsi* (Tbilisi: Sak. SSR mecnierebata ak'ademiis gamomcemloba, 1948).

Tarchnischvili, M. (ed.), *Le grand lectionnaire de l'église de Jérusalem (Ve–VIIIe siècle)*, Vol. 1 (CSCO 188–89; Scriptores Iberici 9–10; Louvain: Secrétariat du Corpus SCO, 1959).

Žanašvili, M., *Našromebi*, Vol. 3: *Čemi šenišvnebi: rustavelis garšemo. – kartuli biblia me – VI sauk'.: aγc'era, t'ekst'ebi, leksik'oni*. (Tbilisi: elekt'.–mbeč'd. s.m. losaberiʒisa, 1910).

Alessandro Maria Bruni

3–5.2.7 Old Church Slavonic Translations

3–5.2.7.1 Background

The surviving Old Church Slavonic (= OCS) tradition of Joshua, Judges and 1–4 Kingdoms represents a largely unexplored field of research in biblical studies. This manuscript legacy has almost escaped the attention of LXX scholars. The present entry includes fresh inquiry into medieval and early modern Cyrillic codices, undertaken expressly for *THB*. The attempt is made to show the unexpected perspectives that can be opened up by approaching this corpus from the point of view of comparative textual criticism. In this regard, the focus is mostly on an early fifteenth-century South Slavic translation of 1–4 Kingdoms. According to a preliminary examination, it represents a new witness to the so-called Greek Antiochenian recension (→ 3–5.1.6.1). Although having been translated from the latter, it presents a number of textual features that differ from the available Byzantine sources of this redaction. The introduction of previously unknown material may enlarge our understanding of the textual history of the LXX version of 1–2 Samuel (→ 5.4) and 1–2 Kings (→ 5.5).

3–5.2.7.2 OCS Translations: Dates and Origins

The earliest Old Church Slavonic (= OCS) versions of Joshua, Judges, and 1–4 Kingdoms were undertaken from LXX at the very beginning of Slavonic literature. They can be divided into two typologically different groups, namely the liturgical pericopes and the complete versions. The first body is deemed to contain the earliest textual stratum that may be traced back to the Cyrillo-Methodian epoch (ca. 863–885 C.E.). The second comprises translations that were carried out no later than during the Old Bulgarian period (Preslav literary school, reign of Tsar Symeon, ca. 893–927 C.E.); moreover, it also includes additional versions produced in the late Middle Ages (1–4 Kingdoms).

3–5.2.7.2.1 Liturgical Pericopes

The Cyrillic Prophetologium is believed to preserve the oldest textual layer.[1] It contains the following readings: *a)* Josh 3:7–8, 14–17; 5:10–16;[2] *b)* Judg 6:2a, 7a, 11–15, 17–22, 24a, 36–40; 13:2–5a, 6a, 7–8, 13–14a,

---

[1] The earliest manuscript of the Cyrillic Prophetologium is Codex Russian State Library, Moscow, f. 87, No. M 1685 (*Grig. 2*), edited in Brandt, "Grigorovičev parimejnik"; Ribarova and Hauptova, *Grigorovičev parimejnik*, Vol. 1.

[2] Lebedev, *Slavjanskij perevod*, 245–54.

17–18, 21a;³ *c*) 3 Kgdms 8:1, 3–7, 9–11; 17:8–24; 18:30–39; 19:3–16; *d*) 4 Kgdms 2:6–14, 19–22; 4:8–37; 5:1, 9–14 (1–2 Kingdoms are not included).⁴

The Croat Glagolitic sources include 1 Kgdms 1:1–28; 2:1, 11–36; 3:1–21; 2 Kgdms 1:1–27; 2:1–32; 3:1–21; 3 Kgdms 1:1–47; 4 Kgdms 1:1–18; 2:1–25. In most cases, they are new translations from the Vulgate, while in a few other instances they may be judged merely to be revisions of the earliest textual stratum found in the Cyrillic Prophetologium.⁵

3-5.2.7.2.2 Complete Translations

The Old Bulgarian full versions of Joshua, Judges and 1–4 Kingdoms survive in several East and South Slavic Cyrillic manuscripts, dating from no earlier than the late fourteenth century.⁶ A feature common to these translations is that they are replete with errors and misunderstandings of the original Greek text.⁷ However, not all of these are attributable to the translator. A number of mistakes betray an inaccurate transliteration from the Glagolitic alphabet.⁸ Moreover, some may also be interpreted as a result of the dictation of the text to the scribes.⁹

As far as authorship is concerned, most scholars ascribe these versions to a certain Gregory the Presbyter,¹⁰ whose literary activity took place in the Symeonian period and who is deemed to have carried out the translation of the Octateuch¹¹ (or, alternatively, of at least some of its sections: → 2.5.7.2).¹² This assumption is based essentially on a highly controversial inscription¹³ contained in the manuscripts of the so-called Jewish Chronicle (= *J-Ch*), an extensive compilation consisting mostly of translations of Greek historical and literary works (Flavius Josephus, John Malalas, George Hamartolos, and Pseudo-Callisthenes), biblical books (Octateuch, Tetrabasileon, excerpts from the Prophets and others), as well as several Old Russian annals.¹⁴

However, on the basis of purely linguistic evidence, it has been argued that the translation of OCS-1–4 Kgdms may be older than that of OCS-Josh and OCS-Judg. According to this hypothesis, OCS-1–4 Kgdms may have been carried out by someone in Methodius' entourage¹⁵ or, possibly, by a representative of the Western Bulgarian (Macedonian) literary school between the late ninth and the early tenth centuries C.E.¹⁶

3-5.2.7.2.3 Second Complete Translation of 1–4 Kingdoms

A second translation of 1–4 Kingdoms made from LXX was undertaken in Serbia in 1416¹⁷ or, according to a different opinion, probably even earlier.¹⁸ It has been attributed to Constantine of Kostenets (c. 1380–after 1427) or to his contemporary, the

---

³ See Atanasova, "Knigata Sădii."

⁴ Kul'bakin, *Otčet*, 43–54.

⁵ See Jagić, *Entstehungsgeschichte*, 462; Nachtigal, "Neskol'ko zametok," 189–91; Berčić (ed.), *Ulomci*, 73–74; Vajs, *Liber Ecclesiastis*, v; Vajs, *Nejstarší Breviář*, 34; Thomson, "The Slavonic Translation," 755; Alekseev, *Tekstologija*, 140–41.

⁶ A list of the manuscript sources dating from the fourteenth century up to the year 1600 is to be found in Mathiesen, "Handlist," 18–33. A description of the manuscripts of OCS-Josh is offered in Lebedev, *Slavjanskij perevod*, 10–76.

⁷ Kul'bakin, *Otčet*, 42; Atanasova, "Greškite"; Thomson, "The Slavonic Translation," 739–40, 748, 756–57.

⁸ See, for instance, the reading обѣща "promised" in place of отвѣща "answered": Lebedev, *Slavjanskij perevod*, 147. See also Thomson, "The Slavonic Translation," 747.

⁹ Alekseev, *Tekstologija*, 46.

¹⁰ See Slavova, "Biblejskata kniga Sădii v Archivnija chronograf," 170 (n. 2); Nikolova, "K istorii teksta knig Carstv."

¹¹ Evseev, "Grigorij," 356–66.

¹² Thomson, "The Slavonic Translation," 728–38.

¹³ Thomson, "The Bulgarian Contribution," 236; Turilov, "Byl li perevodčik," 12–16.

¹⁴ Manuscript Russian State Archive of Ancient Acts, Moscow, f. MGAMID 279/658, late fifteenth century, ff. 42ᵛ–43ᵛ. For a content description, see Istrin, *Aleksandrija*, 315–43.

¹⁵ Sobolevskij, "Cerkovnoslavjanskie teksty," 163–65; Alekseev, "Kirillo–Mefodievskoe perevodčeskoe nasledie," 129; Alekseev, *Tekstologija*, 119, 155; Nikolova, "K istorii teksta knig Carstv," 55.

¹⁶ Thomson, "The Slavonic Translation," 758 and Thomson, *A Brief Survey*, 36–37.

¹⁷ Popruženko, *Iz istorii literaturnoj dejatel'nosti v Serbii*, 159–83; Alekseev, *Tekstologija*, 35; Christova, "Tălkuvanijata," 76–81; Nikolova, "K istorii teksta knig Carstv," 54–68; Bulatova, "K dialektnoj charakteristike," 53–70; Turilov, *Mežslavjanskie kul'turnye svjazi*, 576, n. 63.

¹⁸ Pičchadze, "Cerkovnoslavjanskij," 143; Alekseev, *Tekstologija*, 190.

monk Gabriel of Hilandar,[19] who is known for having rendered the Catena in Job from Greek (→ 11.4.7.4).

3–5.2.7.3 Complete Translations: Manuscript Sources

The full OCS translations of Joshua, Judges, and 1–4 Kingdoms circulated in differently structured collections.[20] From a linguistic point of view, the available witnesses can be divided into two major types consisting of manuscripts of South Slavic and East Slavic origin.

3–5.2.7.3.1 Oldest Translations in the East Slavic Tradition

The East Slavic heritage presents a greater variety of collections. In the majority of cases, Joshua and Judges are inserted in small corpora that along with Ruth comprise 1–4 Kingdoms and (or) Esther. Accordingly, the following types of sylloges are known: 1) Joshua–Judges–Ruth–1–4 Kingdoms–Esther; 2) Joshua–Judges–Ruth–1–4 Kingdoms; 3) Joshua–Judges–Ruth–Esther. In other instances, the OCS translations of Joshua, Judges, and 1–4 Kingdoms are to be found within significantly larger compilations, in which the Octateuch is placed next to other texts belonging mainly to the chronicle genres, such as the above-mentioned *J-Ch*.[21]

3–5.2.7.3.2 Oldest Translations in the South Slavic Tradition

In the South Slavic tradition, Joshua and Judges are usually to be found in codices containing the Octateuch, to which at times are attached 1–4 Kingdoms. Among the South Slavs, the latter also appeared separately or, alternatively, in a selection that included Wisdom (→ II.15.9).[22]

3–5.2.7.3.3 Second Translation of 1–4 Kingdoms

The second translation of 1–4 Kingdoms (= OCS-1–4 Kgdms 2) is today preserved in only two manuscripts, one dating to 1418 (National Research Library of Odessa, Ukraine, no. 6),[23] the other to between 1523 and 1543 (Moscow, Russian State Library, f. 87 No. 1–1684).[24]

3–5.2.7.4 Complete Translations: Textual History, Studies, and Editions

The history of the OCS translations of Joshua, Judges, and 1–4 Kingdoms has mostly yet to be written. This tradition suffers from a lack of text-critical study, which prevents scholars from reaching any reliable conclusions on this matter. Since a confident assessment of the manuscript filiation is still awaited, only the following provisional outline can be offered at present.

3–5.2.7.4.1 OCS-Josh

OCS-Josh survives in three redactions.[25] The first is transmitted in a number of East Slavic sources starting from the late fourteenth century.[26] The second, preserved in several South Slavic codices, is apparently the result of a revision of the first redaction based on a different Greek model.[27] The third is to be found in the so-called *Palaea interpretata*, an East Slavic compilation containing compendia of several biblical books along with a number of other non-canonical texts and interpretations.[28]

During the sixteenth century, the East Slavic redaction of OCS-Josh was included: 1) in the Russian Macarian Menologium, in which the text

---

[19] Thomson, "The Slavonic Translation," 762–63.
[20] For a list of the hitherto-traced manuscripts, see Mathiesen, "Handlist," 18–33; Lebedev, *Slavjanskij perevod*, 10–76; Nikolova, "K istorii teksta knig Carstv."
[21] Alekseev, *Tekstologija*, 27.
[22] Mathiesen, "Handlist," 15, 16, 33.
[23] Description: Močul'skij, *Opisanie*, 5–6; Popruženko, *Iz istorii literaturnoj dejatel'nosti v Serbii*, 43–54.
[24] Viktorov, *Sobranie*, 3–4.
[25] See Lebedev's study published in 1890 and based on a number of codices kept in Moscow and St. Petersburg libraries: Lebedev, *Slavjanskij perevod*.
[26] The earliest is a codex in the Russian State Library, Moscow, f. 304.I, No. 2. On this source, see the most recent paleographic and codicological remarks in Kloss, *O proischoždenii*, 35.
[27] The oldest is the fifteenth-century manuscript of the Library of the Romanian Academy, Bucharest, No. 85.
[28] Lebedev, *Slavjanskij perevod*, 60–70, 210–54. See also Thomson, "The Slavonic Translation," 739–42.

is corrupted by several scribal errors;[29] 2) in the 1581 Ostrog Bible,[30] in which the translation was subjected to several editorial changes (these amendments were not successful in every instance).[31]

In 1996, Atanasova published an edition on the basis of only three manuscripts (two East Slavic, one South Slavic) as well as the Ostrog Bible.[32]

3–5.2.7.4.2 OCS-Judg

As in the previous case, the complete OCS-Judg also seems to split into three redactions. Here, however, establishing the internal relationship between the surviving manuscript groups appears to be even more problematic. According to Atanasova who has studied and edited this version on the basis of a limited number of sources (two East Slavic, three South Slavic, and the 1581 Ostrog Bible), the three recensions go back to a common archetype.[33] Slavova essentially agrees with this view, but in her opinion the text preserved in the South Slavic sources and in the *J-Ch* reflects the original translation more closely than that of the East Slavic codices.[34] Traces of an underlying Glagolitic stratum in the South Slavic tradition would corroborate this assumption,[35] although this issue needs to be verified by further investigation.[36]

In the sixteenth century, OCS-Judg was first inserted into the Russian Macarian Menologium[37] and later also into the 1581 Ostrog Bible. In the latter, the text was subjected to several editorial changes made on the basis of the Aldine Bible.[38]

There is no doubt that OCS-Judg requires additional in-depth study before reliable conclusions regarding its textual history can be drawn.[39]

3–5.2.7.4.3 Earliest OCS Translation of 1–4 Kingdoms

The earliest complete OCS version of 1–4 Kingdoms is commonly believed to have come down to us in two redactions. The first is known thanks to the testimony of several East Slavic manuscripts[40] and shows reliance on the earliest textual stratum found in the OCS Cyrillic Prophetologium.[41] The second, which is preserved in a number of South Slavic testimonies,[42] was judged to be the result of a revision of the former, although this opinion has been challenged.[43] Moreover, due to the lack of studies, it remains unclear whether the text contained in the *J-Ch* represents an intermediary recension.[44]

During the sixteenth century, the East Slavic text type was included in the Russian Macarian Menologium: OCS-1–2 Kgdms were inserted into the commemoration of the Prophet Samuel (August 20th), while 3 Kingdoms 17–22 and 4 Kingdoms 1–13 were attached to texts celebrating the feast of the Prophet Elijah (June 20th).[45] A few decades later, OCS-1–4 Kgdms also entered the 1581 Ostrog Bible, in which it was subjected to a number of editorial changes.[46]

A comprehensive text-critical study of the manuscript tradition of OCS-1–4 Kgdms has still to be produced.[47] Dunkov's edition is based on three

---

[29] *Velikie Minei*, 20–60.
[30] *Ostrožskaja biblija*, ff. 97–109ᵛ.
[31] Thomson, "The Slavonic Translation," 739–40.
[32] Atanasova, *Das Buch Josua*.
[33] Atanasova, *Das Buch Richter*, 211–15.
[34] In this compilation, the text of OCS-Judg includes a number of interpolations from Book IV of the Chronicle of John Malalas that are inserted after Judg 3:31, 6:32, 10:2, and 12:12.
[35] Slavova, "Biblejskata kniga Sădii v Archivnija chronograf," 171, 175.
[36] Thomson, "The Slavonic Translation," 747.
[37] Atanassova, "Zu einigen Besonderheiten der Perikopen."
[38] Thomson, "The Slavonic Translation," 748.

[39] On the limits and flaws of Atanasova's edition (Atanasova, *Das Buch Richter*), see Thomson, "The Slavonic Translation," 748–49.
[40] The oldest codex is National Library of Russia, St. Petersburg, Q.I.2, early fifteenth century.
[41] Kul'bakin, *Otčet*, 45–48. See also the textual analysis of the readings from 4 Kgdms 2:6–14, 19–22 in Alekseev, *Tekstologija*, 156–57.
[42] The earliest source is ms National Library of Russia, St. Petersburg, F.I.461, fourteenth century. For a list of South Slavic manuscripts, see Nikolova, "K istorii teksta knig Carstv," 55.
[43] Nikolova, "K istorii teksta knig Carstv," 55.
[44] Slavova, "Biblejskoto Osmoknižie," 43.
[45] See Alekseev, *Tekstologija*, 28.
[46] Thomson, "The Slavonic Translation," 764–65.
[47] Nikolova, "K istorii teksta knig Carstv," 54–68.

East Slavic and four South Slavic manuscripts, as well as on the Ostrog Bible.[48] The outcomes of this work have been criticized by Thomson, since the editor produced a misleading critical text by overlapping readings from different translations, namely the earliest and the more recent OCS versions (on which, see below).[49]

3–5.2.7.4.4 Second OCS Translation of 1–4 Kingdoms

The second OCS translation of 1–4 Kingdoms was studied initially in the late nineteenth century.[50] On the one hand, Popruženko pointed out that this version was used partially by the compilers of the 1581 Ostrog Bible. On the other hand, Kul'bakin drew attention to its textual differences from the earliest OCS translation on the basis of a collation of selected passages from 1 Kingdoms.[51] Moreover, he compared a number of readings from 3–4 Kingdoms with those found in the OCS Cyrillic Prophetologium.[52] With the exception of a few excerpts,[53] this second South Slavic early fifteenth-century translation of 1–4 Kingdoms still remains unpublished.[54]

3–5.2.7.5 Parent Text and Text-Critical Value

The lack of critical editions and in-depth studies based on all of the East and South Slavic manuscript evidence limits the possibility of a precise appraisal of the parent text of the earliest OCS translations that date back to Glagolitic originals of the late ninth and early tenth centuries. In this regard, at present only a few remarks can be offered that provide some guidance about their text-critical value.

As far as the recent translation is concerned, the research undertaken has already demonstrated clearly that this secondary tradition, even if still unexplored in terms of textual criticism, nevertheless merits the full attention of biblical scholars. This manuscript material offers relevant data for enriching the existing debate surrounding the textual history of the LXX text.

3–5.2.7.5.1 Liturgical Pericopes

As far as the Cyrillic Prophetologium is concerned, both OCS-Josh and OCS-1–4 Kgdms agree with the Lucianic redaction (→ 3–5.1.6),[55] while OCS-Judg displays reliance on the Origenian text (→ 3–5.1.5).[56]

3–5.2.7.5.2 OCS-Josh

In publishing OCS-Josh, Atanasova[57] did not collate the OCS text with Holmes', Rahlfs', or Margolis' editions.[58] Therefore, a detailed study of the textual relationships with LXX (→ 3.3) is still lacking. Moreover, Slavicists have hitherto not taken into consideration any fundamental studies on the Hebrew (→ 3.2) and Greek texts of Joshua.[59] Therefore, a few observations are offered below that are based on an exploratory investigation of the material that was carried out while preparing the present entry.

a) In Josh 1:1, OCS-Josh agrees with neither LXX[B] nor LXX[A],[60] but features the longer text corresponding to that of MT: …и бы по съконьчаньи Моисиевѣ, раба Господьнѣ … "… And it happened after the death of Moses, *the servant of the LORD*…"[61] However, a few verses below this additional formula is omitted: in Josh 1:15 OCS-

---

[48] Dunkov, *Die Methodbibel*, Vol. 5, 411.
[49] Thomson, "The Slavonic Translation," 766–67.
[50] Popruženko, *Iz istorii literaturnoj dejatel'nosti v Serbii*; Kul'bakin, *Otčet*.
[51] Popruženko, *Iz istorii literaturnoj dejatel'nosti v Serbii*, 175–83.
[52] Kul'bakin, *Otčet*, 43–54.
[53] See Popruženko, *Iz istorii literaturnoj dejatel'nosti v Serbii*, 159–63, 165–72, 175–83; Kul'bakin, *Otčet*, 23–41. To these must be added the readings included improperly by Dunkov in his edition of the earliest OCS translation of 1–4 Kingdoms (Dunkov, *Die Methodbibel*, Vols. 5–8).
[54] An edition is currently being prepared by the writer of the present entry.

[55] See Lebedev, *Slavjanskij perevod*, 245–54; Kul'bakin, *Otčet*, 46.
[56] Thomson, "The Slavonic Translation," 744.
[57] Atanasova, *Das Buch Josua*.
[58] Holmes, *Joshua*; Rahlfs, *Septuaginta*; Margolis, *The Book*.
[59] See Tov, *Greek-Hebrew Bible*, 385–96.
[60] Rahlfs, *Septuaginta*, 354.
[61] See the critical apparatus in Margolis, *The Book*, Part 1, 1.

Josh follows LXX^AB.⁶² In Josh 22:4, OCS-Josh once again presents a plus perfectly equivalent to that found in MT: ... ꙗже да вамъ Моиси, рабъ Господьнь ... "... that gave to you Moses, *the servant of the LORD* ..."

b) In Josh 24:17, both East and South Slavic manuscripts of OCS-Josh omit the Dtr phrase "the house of bondage, and who wrought those wondrous signs before our very eyes,"⁶³ which is to be found in the printed Ostrog Bible only (... ѿ домѹ работнаго иже сътвори пред очима нашима чюдеса велїа "... from the house of bondage, who wrought before our eyes wondrous signs").⁶⁴

c) In Joshua 8–9, OCS-Josh deviates from both LXX^AB in the arrangement of verses, since it presents the alternative order⁶⁵ found in MT:⁶⁶ 1) Josh 8:1–29; 2) Josh 9:2a–2f (= 8:30–35); 3) Josh 9:1–2; 4) Josh 9:3–27.

d) In Josh 20:1–6, OCS-Josh follows the longer text of LXX^A.

e) Other long elements reflecting LXX^A and LXX^B are to be found in OCS-Josh 6:26a; 16:10a, 21:42d; 24:31a, 33a–b.

f) The typical LXX minuses are seen in OCS-Josh 2:15; 4:10.⁶⁷

3-5.2.7.5.3 OCS-Judg

The complete OCS version of Judges may have different textual allegiances with the various manuscript families of LXX, namely with groups LXX^B, LXX^L, LXX^M, and LXX^O (→ 4.1.2). However, since precise delineations are unknown, the terms of their mutual textual relationship cannot be established currently. According to the available scholarly remarks, the full OCS translation agrees with the Hexapla (→ 2.4.6) in Judg 3:27; 4:1; 6:4; 10:6; 9:21 and preserves *kaige* readings (→ 1.3.1.2) in Judg 4:22; 11:1.⁶⁸ Moreover, it apparently omits Judg 2:7; 7:20; 10:8; 11:4; 16:25; 19:25, 27; 20:13, 38.⁶⁹ With regard to other minuses, the behavior of the OCS redactions appears not to be uniform. In the South Slavic sources, Judg 2:21–4:8; 8:6–33; 12:11–12; 17:2, 6; 19:7–8; 20:25 are lacking,⁷⁰ while Judg 5:1–30; 16:25–31; 17:1–7; 21:11–25 are missing in the *J-Ch*.⁷¹

In view of these and other textual dissimilarities occurring between the surviving recensions of OCS-Judg, the opinion has been expressed that the East Slavic redaction is a revision of the South Slavic resulting from a correction made on the basis of a different Greek model.⁷² Be that as it may, this conclusion needs to be corroborated by a more detailed comparative analysis to be carried out on the basis of the entire manuscript evidence. Moreover, a look at Atanasova's edition shows that the reconstructed text of OCS-Judg cannot be identified unambiguously with either LXX^A or LXX^B; some chapters (e.g., Judges 5 and 6) agree with the former while others follow the latter (e.g., Judges 7).

3-5.2.7.5.4 Earliest OCS Translation of 1–4 Kingdoms

As noted by Thomson, the full OCS version of 1–4 Kingdoms agrees with LXX^B in the omission of 1 Kgdms 17:12–31, 50, 55; 18:1–5, 17–19, 30 and of 3 Kgdms 8:12–13; 9:15–25; 11:23–24, 39; 12:17; 13:27; 14:1–20; 15:6, 32; 22:47–50.⁷³ However, in several other instances it displays reliance on LXX^A and preserves Lucianic readings (e.g., in 1 Kgdms 17:37; 2 Kgdms 17:14; → 3-5.1.6.2). In 2 Kgdms 17:12 after ὡς πίπτει ἡ δρόσος ἐπὶ τὴν γῆν "as the dew falls on the ground" (*NETS*, 289), the OCS version adds тако нападаемъ на нь "so we shall fall upon him."⁷⁴ According to Alekseev, the OCS translation agrees

---

⁶² Rahlfs, *Septuaginta*, 355; Margolis, *The Book*, Part 1, 13.
⁶³ See Tov, *HB, GB, and Qumran*, 401–03.
⁶⁴ See *Ostrožskaja biblija*, fol. 109.
⁶⁵ See the critical apparatus in Margolis, *The Book*, Part 2, 141–44.
⁶⁶ See Tov, *TCHB*, 298–99.
⁶⁷ See Tov, *TCHB*, 294–98; Margolis, *The Book*, Part 1, 26, 56.

⁶⁸ Thomson, "The Slavonic Translation," 745.
⁶⁹ Atanasova, *Das Buch Richter*, 211–15.
⁷⁰ Atanasova, "Greškite," 101–05.
⁷¹ Slavova, "Biblejskata kniga Sădii v Archivnija chronograf," 171.
⁷² Slavova, "Biblejskata kniga Sădii v Archivnija chronograf," 180.
⁷³ Thomson, "The Slavonic Translation," 761.
⁷⁴ Thomson, "The Slavonic Translation," 762.

with LXX^V (= *Vat. gr.* 2106 + *Marc. gr.* 1) in 3 Kgdms 17:1, 10; 18:37, and 4 Kgdms 5:19.[75]

In addition to these remarks, a few supplementary observations based on the text published by Dunkov[76] may be offered here. The story of David and Goliath in OCS-1 Kgdms is given according to LXX (→ 5.4); however, 1 Kgdms 17:41 and 18:10–11 are not omitted. OCS-3 Kgdms features the typical LXX pluses (→ 5.5) in 3 Kgdms 2:25a–o; 12:24a–z; 16:28a–h; 46:a–l, but it also has the addition in 3 Kgdms 6:11–14. Among the omissions, mention should be made of those found in 3 Kgdms 6:1a–d;[77] 9:15–25; and 22:47–50.

3–5.2.7.5.5 Second OCS Translation of 1–4 Kingdoms

Although the reliance of the second version of 1 Kingdoms (1 Samuel) on a Lucianic source (→ 3–5.1.6.2) was established by Kul'bakin more than one hundred years ago,[78] an assessment of the parent text of the entire translation has not yet been undertaken.[79] In order to fill this gap, the writer of this entry embarked on a preliminary analysis of this version that has brought about the following results.

3–5.2.7.5.5.1 A New Witness to the Antiochene Text of Samuel–Kings

The collation of the early fifteenth-century South Slavic translation of 1–4 Kingdoms with LXX^L (the "Antiochene Text"; → 3–5.1.6.2)[80] has shown that the former replicates a Byzantine source clearly belonging to this recension, but which was not similar to codices LXX^{boc_2e_2}. A first crucial point is that the Greek prototype of the OCS text included at least those proto-Lucianic readings that are listed in Tov's reference article on the topic.[81] A second point is that the OCS translation presents a specific arrangement in 3–4 Kingdoms (1–2 Kings) that differs from that found in manuscripts LXX^{boc_2e_2}. As in the latter testimonies, OCS-3 Kgdms (1 Kings) begins at 3 Kgdms (1 Kgs) 2:12. However, the OCS text ends at 3 Kgdms (1 Kgs) 11:43. Consequently, OCS-4 Kgdms consists of 3 Kgdms (1 Kgs) 12:2–22:54 + 4 Kgdms (2 Kgs) 1:1–25:30. Moreover, mention should be made of the omission in the OCS version of 3 Kdgms 14:1–20 without the insertion of the Hexaplaric addition found in manuscript LXX^{c_2}. Against the background of a literal translation technique, these features make it very probable that the early fifteenth-century OCS translation of 1–4 Kingdoms was undertaken from a lost Greek manuscript of LXX^L that featured a peculiar arrangement of the text not attested elsewhere in the surviving Byzantine tradition. Therefore, the OCS version may be regarded as a further witness to the Antiochene text of Samuel–Kings that should be added to the already known isolated Lucianic readings in non-Lucianic secondary translations.[82] Accordingly, even though indirectly, i.e., through the medium of a secondary translation, a new window could be opening on a previously unknown compositional stage of the Antiochene text.

3–5.2.7.5.5.2 Readings from the "Three" in the Second OCS Translation of 1–4 Kingdoms

An additional major result of the research undertaken is the finding that the second OCS translation of 1–4 Kingdoms preserves in 1 Kgs a higher than previously assumed number of readings from the "Three" (→ 3–5.1.5.2).[83] This new evidence still need to be edited and thoroughly collated with data found in LXX and in other secondary

---

[75] Alekseev, *Tekstologija*, 123.
[76] Dunkov, *Die Methodbibel*, Vols. 5–8.
[77] See Tov, *TCHB*, 307.
[78] Kul'bakin, *Otčet*, 23–41.
[79] Nikolova, "K istorii teksta knig Carstv"; Thomson, "The Slavonic Translation," 763; Alekseev, *Tekstologija*, 35, 118–20.
[80] Fernández Marcos and Busto Saiz, *El Texto Antiqueno*, Vols. 1–2.
[81] In making a short reference to the OCS version, Tov wondered whether it was based on the ancient substratum of LXX^{boc_2e_2} only, or whether, being chronologically post-Lucianic, it reflects LXX^L as a whole. See E. Tov, "Lucian and Proto-Lucian: Toward a New Solution of the Problem," in *Greek-Hebrew Bible*, 477–88 (480).
[82] See Torijano Morales, "The Contribution."
[83] Popruženko, *Iz istorii literaturnoj dejatel'nosti v Serbii*, 123–29; Nikolova, "K istorii teksta knig Carstv," 54–68; Alekseev, *Tekstologija*, 35.

sources such as the Armenian (→ 3–5.2.5.3.7) version.[84]

Alekseev, A.A., "Kirillo–Mefodievskoe perevodčeskoe nasledie i ego istoričeskie sud'by: perevody sv. Pisanija v slavjanskoj pis'mennosti," in *Istorija, kul'tura, ètnografija i fol'klor slavjanskich narodov: X Meždunarodnyj s"ezd slavistov: Sofija, sentjabr' 1988: Doklady sovetskoj delegacii* (ed. I.I. Kostjuško; Moscow: Nauka, 1988), 124–45.

Alekseev, A.A., *Tekstologija slavjanskoj Biblii* (= Bausteine zur slavischen Philologie und Kulturgeschichte N.F., Reihe A: Slavistische Forschungen 24; Cologne: Böhlau Verlag, 1999).

Atanasova, D. (ed.), *Die Methodbibel*, Vol. 2: *Das Buch Richter* (Die slawischen Sprachen 38; Salzburg: Institut für Slawistik der Universität Salzburg, 1994).

Atanasova, D., "Greškite v slavjanskite prepisi na knigata Sădii i kritičnoto izdanie na Metodievija prevod," *Die slawischen Sprachen* 39 (1994): 89–131.

Atanassova, D., "Knigata Sădii. Starobălgarskijat prevod na parimijnija i četi tekst," *Die slawischen Sprachen* 41 (1995): 53–106.

Atanasova, D. (ed.), *Die Methodbibel*, Vol. 9: *Das Buch Josua* (Die slawischen Sprachen 49; Salzburg: Institut für Slawistik der Universität Salzburg, 1996).

Atanassova, D., "Probleme bei der Wiederherstellung der altbulgarischen Übersetzung des Buches Josua," in *Beiträge der Europäischen Slavistischen Linguistik (Polyslav)*, Vol. 1 (eds. K. Böttger, M. Giger, and B. Wiemer; Die Welt der Slaven 2; Munich: Otto Sagner, 1998), 9–18.

Atanassova, D., "Zu einigen Besonderheiten der Perikopen des Buches Richter in der Zusammensetzung der slavischen Menäen," in *Beiträge der Europäischen Slavistischen Linguistik (Polyslav)*, Vol. 2 (eds. K. Böttger, M. Giger, B. Wiemer; Die Welt der Slaven 4; Munich: Otto Sagner, 1999), 1–9.

Berčić, I. (ed.), *Ulomci Svetoga Pisma obojega uvjeta staroslovenskim jezikom: Skupio iz rukopisah i tiskanih knjigah hrvatskoga razreda svećenik Ivan Berčić*, Vol. 1 (Prague: Sinovi Bogumila Haase, 1871).

Brandt, R., "Grigorovičev parimejnik: v sličenii s drugimi parimejnikami," *Čtenija v Imperatorskom Obščestve istorii i drevnostej rossijskich* 168 (1894): 1–90; 170 (1894): 91–178; 193 (1900): 179–290; 197 (1901): 291–308.

Bulatova, R.V., "K dialektnoj charakteristike rukopisi 1418 g. 'Knigi Carstv' na osnove akcentologičeskogo analiza," in *Proučavanje srednjovekovnich južnoslovenskich rukopisa* (eds. I. Grickat, P. Ivić, D. Stefanović, and G. Babić; Belgrade: Srpska Akademija nauka i umetnosti, 1995), 53–70.

Christova, B., "Tălkuvanijata na starozavetni i novozavetni knigi v srednovekovnata bălgarska kultura," in *Palaeobulgarica* 18.2 (1994): 76–81.

Dunkov, D. (ed.), *Die Methodbibel*, Vol. 5: *Die Bücher der Könige: Das erste Buch Samuel* (Die slawischen Sprachen 42; Salzburg: Institut für Slawistik der Universität Salzburg, 1995).

Dunkov, D. (ed.), *Die Methodbibel*, Vol. 6: *Die Bücher der Könige: Das zweite Buch Samuel* (Die slawischen Sprachen 45; Salzburg: Institut für Slawistik der Universität Salzburg, 1995).

Dunkov, D. (ed.), *Die Methodbibel*, Vol. 7: *Die Bücher der Könige: Das erste Buch der Könige* (Die slawischen Sprachen 47; Salzburg: Institut für Slawistik der Universität Salzburg, 1996).

Dunkov, D. (ed.), *Die Methodbibel*, Vol. 8: *Die Bücher der Könige: Das zweite Buch der Könige* (Die slawischen Sprachen 48; Salzburg: Institut für Slawistik der Universität Salzburg, 1996).

Evseev, I.E., "Grigorij presviter: perevodčik vremeni bolgarskogo carja Simeona," in *Izvestija Otdelenija Russkogo Jazyka i Slovesnosti* 7.3 (1902): 357–66.

Fernández Marcos, N. and J.R. Busto Saiz, *El texto antioqueno de la Biblia griega*, Vol. 1: *1–2 Samuel* (Textos y estudios "Cardenal Cisneros" 50; Madrid: CSIC, 1989).

Fernández Marcos, N. and J.R. Busto Saiz, *El texto antioqueno de la Biblia griega*, Vol. 2: *1–2 Reyes* (Textos y estudios "Cardenal Cisneros" 53; Madrid: CSIC, 1992).

Holmes, S., *Joshua: The Hebrew and Greek Texts* (Cambridge: Cambridge University Press, 1914).

Istrin, V., *Aleksandrija russkich chronografov: Issledovanie i tekst* (Moscow: Universitetskaja tipografija, 1893).

Jagić, V., *Entstehungsgeschichte der kirchenslavischen Sprache* (Berlin: Weidmann, 1913).

Kloss, B.M., *O proischoždenii nazvanija "Rossija"* (Moscow: Rukopisnye pamjatniki Drevnej Rusi, 2012).

Kul'bakin, S., *Otčet Otdeleniju russkago jazyka i slovesnosti Imperatorskoj Akademii nauk o zanjatijach v knigochraniliščach Moskvy i Peterburga s 25 sentjabrja po 23 dekabrja 1898 g.* (St. Petersburg: Tipografija Imperatorskoj Akademii nauk, 1901).

Lebedev, V., *Slavjanskij perevod knigi Iisusa Navina po sochranivšimsja rukopisjam i Ostrožskoj biblii. Issle-

---

[84] A work devoted especially to this issue is currently being prepared by the author of the present entry.

dovanie teksta i jazyka (St. Petersburg: Tipografija Katanskogo, 1890).

Margolis, M.L., *The Book of Joshua in Greek According to the Critically Restored Text with an Apparatus Containing the Variants of the Principal Recensions of the Individual Witnesses* (Publications of the Alexander Kohut Memorial Foundation in Trust at the American Academy for Jewish Research; parts 1–4 [Josh 1:1–19:38]: Paris: Paul Geuther, 1931–1938; part 5 [Josh 19:39–24:33]: with a preface by E. Tov; Philadelphia: Annenberg Research Institute, 1992).

Mathiesen, R., "Handlist of Manuscripts Containing Church Slavonic Translations of the Old Testament," in *Polata knigopisnaja* 7 (1983): 3–48.

Mathiesen, R., "The Typology of Cyrillic Manuscripts (East Slavic vs. South Slavic Old Testament Manuscripts)," in *American Contributions to the Ninth International Congress of Slavists, Kiev, September 1983*, Vol. 1 (ed. M.S. Flier; Columbus: Slavica, 1983), 193–202.

Močul'skij, V.N., *Opisanie rukopisej V.I. Grigoroviča* (Odessa: Tipo-litografija Štaba Odesskogo voennogo okruga, 1890).

Nachtigal, R.R., "Neskol'ko zametok o sledach drevneslavjanskogo parimejnika v chorvatsko-glagoličeskoj literature," in *Drevnosti: Trudy Slavjanskoj komissii Moskovskogo archeologičeskogo obščestva*, Vol. 3 (Moscow: Tipografija G. Lissnera, 1902), 175–213.

Nikolova, S., "K istorii teksta knig Carstv v slavjanskoj pis'mennosti," in *Ioudaïkē archailogia: In Honour of Professor Moshe Altbauer* (eds. W. Moskovich, S. Schwarzband, and A. Alekseev; Jews and Slavs 3; Jerusalem: Hebrew University of Jerusalem Center for Slavic Languages and Literatures, 1995), 54–68.

Ostrožskaja biblija: Fototipičeskoe pereizdanie teksta s izdanija 1581 g. (Moscow: Slovo-Art, 1988).

Pičchadze, A.A., "Perevody Biblii na drevnie jazyki: cerkovnoslavjanskij," in *Pravoslavnaja ènciklopedija*, Vol. 5: *Bessonov-Bonveč* (ed. Aleksij, Patriarch Moskovskij i Vseja Rusi II; Moscow: Cerkovno-Naučnyj Centr "Pravoslavnaja ènciklopedija," 2002), 139–47.

Piquer Otero, A., A. Torijano, and J. Trebolle Barrera, "Septuagint Versions, Greek Recensions, and Hebrew Editions: The Text-Critical Evaluation of the Old Latin, Armenian, and Georgian Versions of III–IV Regnorum," in *Translating a Translation: The LXX and Its Modern Translations in the Context of Early Judaism* (eds. H. Ausloos et al.; BETL 213; Leuven: Peeters, 2008), 251–81.

Popruženko, M.G., *Iz istorii literaturnoj dejatel'nosti v Serbii XV veka: Knigi Carstv v sobranii rukopisej Novorossijskogo universiteta* (Odessa: Tip. št. Odesskago voennago okruga, 1894).

Rahlfs, A., *Septuaginta.

Ribarova, Z. and Z. Hauptova, *Grigorovičev Parimejnik* (2 vols.; Skopje: Makedonska Akademija na naukite i umetnostite, 1998–2014).

Slavova, T., "Biblejskoto Osmoknižie v săstava na Archivnija Chronograf," *Palaeobulgarica* 34.3 (2010): 26–35.

Slavova, T., "Biblejskata kniga Sădii v Archivnija chronograf," *Ricerche Slavistiche* 8.54 (2010): 169–91.

Sobolevskij, A.I., "Cerkovnoslavjanskie teksty moravskogo proischoždenija," *Russkij filologičeskij vestnik* 43 (1900): 150–217.

Thomson, F.J., "The Bulgarian Contribution to the Reception of Byzantine Culture in Kievan Rus': The Myths and the Enigma," in *Harvard Ukrainian Studies* 12–13 (1988–1989): 214–61.

Thomson, F.J., "The Slavonic Translation of the Old Testament," in *The Interpretation of the Bible: The International Symposium in Slovenia* (ed. J. Krašovec; JSOTSup 189; Sheffield: Sheffield Academic Press, 1998), 605–920.

Thomson, F.J., *A Brief Survey of the History of the Church Slavonic Bible from its Cyrillomethodian Origins until its Final Form in the Elizabethan Bible of 1751* (Slavica Gandensia 33.2; Ghent: Department of Slav and East European Studes of the University of Ghent, 2006).

Torijano Morales, P.A., "The Contribution of the Antiochean Text to Text Criticism in Kings: Rahlfs' study of the Lucianic Recension Revisited (1 Kgs 1:3, 36, 40, 41, 45)," in *Textual Criticism and Dead Sea Scrolls: Studies in Honour of Julio Trebolle Barrera: Florilegium Complutense* (eds. P.A. Torijano Morales and A. Piquer Otero; JSJSup 158; Leiden: Brill, 2012), 325–43.

Turilov, A.A., *Mežslavjanskie kul'turnye svjazi èpochi Srednevekov'ja i istočnikovedenie istorii i kul'tury slavjan. Ètjudy i charakteristiki* (Moscow: Znak, 2012).

Turilov, A.A., "Byl li perevodčik simeonovskoj èpochi presviter Grigorij Monachom," *Slavjanovedenie* 2 (2013): 12–16.

Vajs, J., *Liber Ecclesiastis* (Veglae: Academia palaeoslavica veglensis, 1905).

Vajs, J., *Nejstarší Breviář hrvatsko-hlaholský (Prvý Breviář Vrbnický)* (Prague: Nákl. Král. České Společnosti Náuk, 1910).

Velikie Minei čet'i, sobrannye vserossijskim mitropolitom Makariem, Sentjabr': dni 14–24 (Pamjatniki slavjano-russkoj pis'mennosti 1; St. Petersburg: Tipografija Imperatorskoj Akademii nauk, 1869).

Viktorov, A.E., *Sobranie rukopisej V.I. Grigoroviča* (Moscow: Tipografija M.N. Lavrova, 1879).

Alessandro Maria Bruni

3–5.2.8 Arabic Translations

The books of the Former Prophets were transmitted within the unit of Historical Books in the Arabic tradition. This unit also commonly included the books of Chronicles (→ 20.4.8), as well as occasionally Ruth (13–17.2.8.1), and is found either as separate manuscripts or clearly self-contained blocks in larger composite codices.[1] Since the large majority of translations are from the Syriac (→ 3–5.1.4; → 3–5.2.4), this custom follows that of Syriac Bible manuscripts where the Former Prophets constitute the initial part of the *bet mawthbē* "the books of sessions."[2] Manuscript Cambridge, University Library, Kk 6.3 (p. 90), for instance, informs the reader that the section is known precisely as *majālis al-anbiyā' al-ma'rūf bi-baythmawtbā* "the sessions of the prophets, i.e, *bet mawthbē*." The books of Joshua and Judges are summarised under the title "the first and second Book of Judges" (Arab. *sifr al-quḍā al-awwal/al-thānī*), whereas 1–2 Samuel and 1–2 Kings are resumed as "the Books of Kings" (Arab. *asfār al-mulūk*). In the arrangement of 1–2 Kings, manuscripts differ greatly. Some merge the two parts into one (i.e., a third book of Kings), others segment it into three independent books (i.e., third to fifth book of Kings: 1 Kings 1–11; 1 Kings 12–2 Kings 12:16; and 2 Kings 12:17–25:30). The book of Judges not infrequently bears the heading *Kitāb Safṭūm, Sabṭā*, or *Shafṭā* in accordance with Syriac *Ketābā de-Shafṭe* (all meaning "book of Judges").[3] 1 Samuel is titled "the book of Samuel, the Prophet" (Arab. *Kitāb Shamawāl al-nabī*) or spelled alternatively *Ṣamawāl al-nabī* in the manuscripts, and 2 Samuel appears as "Book of David, the Prophet" (*Kitāb Dawūd al-nabī*). None of the translations has been studied comprehensively; consequently, our knowledge of text-critical affinities, translation technique, and provenance is very defective.[4] An initial grouping of manuscripts appears as follows:

3–5.2.8.1 Translations from Syriac

The overwhelming number of manuscripts exhibit translations made from a Syriac *Vorlage* (→ 3–5.1.4; → 3–5.2.4). In the colophons to several books, however, it is stated that they were translated from the "Hebrew" (Arab. *'ibrānī*). This should not be taken literally since *'ibrānī* was a common designation of Syriac in the Middle Ages.[5] The following manuscripts are attested: Oxford, Bodleian Library, 493 (dated 1321 C.E., fols. 3ʳ–199ᵛ) and 270 (fols. 1ʳ–183ʳ); Cambridge, University Library, Kk 6.3 (fols. 1ᵛ–188ʳ) and Add. 3044 (pp. 1–417); Florence, Biblioteca Medicea Laurenziana, Or. 9 (formerly Or. 4, dated 1496–1497 C.E., fols. 1ᵛ–79ʳ); Paris, BNF, Ar. 1 (dated 1584–1585 C.E., fols. 86ᵛ–168ᵛ), Ar. 22 (dated 1344 C.E., fols. 1ᵛ–194ʳ); Ar. 23 and Copenhagen, Royal Library, Ar. 76 (the two *membra disjecta* of a formerly complete manuscript, fols. 1ʳ–131ᵛ of the former and fols. 1ʳ–2ᵛ of the latter); Vatican, BAV, Ar. 399 (dated 1523 C.E., except for Joshua, fols. 1ʳ–240ᵛ), Ar. 449 (only the younger replacements on fols. 1ᵛ–17ᵛ, Josh 1:9–15:63, a continuation of the following) Ar. 465 (only Josh 1:1–9, fol. 207ʳ) and Ar. 468 (dated 1578–1579 C.E., fols. 143ʳ–182ᵛ, 185ʳ–284ʳ); St Petersburg, Institute of Oriental Manuscripts, D226 (dated 1236–1238 C.E., fols. 118ᵛ–211ᵛ); Coptic Orthodox Patriarchate, Bibl. 21 (dated 1587 C.E., fols. 147ᵛ–310ᵛ), Bibl. 32 (1585 C.E., fols. 75ᵛ–150ʳ), Bibl. 37 (dated 1760 C.E., fols. 1ʳ–215ᵛ), Bibl. 38 (dated 1686, fols. 3ᵛ–167ᵛ), Bibl. 44 (dated 1782 C.E., fols. 1ᵛ–175ʳ), Bibl. 50

---

[1] On the composite nature of larger Bible manuscripts in Arabic, see Vollandt, "From the Working Desks."

[2] Albert, "Les 'Bet Mawtbe'."

[3] That is also how the book is featured in the *Encyclopedia of the Copt Shams al-Riyāsa Abū al-Barakāt* (d. 1324); cf. Khalil, *Miṣbāḥ al-ẓulma*, 224.

[4] The only exceptions are Knutsson, *Studies in the Text and Language*, and Rödiger, *De Origine et Indole*.

[5] Examples of this usage in Ibn Hishām, al-Bukhārī, and Kitāb al-Aghānī were discussed by Griffith, "The Gospel in Arabic," 145. Compare, in addition, al-Maqdisī's statement that "the Jews call Paradise kan'ādan ('Gan Eden') in *'ibriyya* and that is *baradīsā* in *'ibrāniyya* (cf. Huart, *Le livre de la création*, 1.186–87). It is clear that *'ibriyya* refers here to Hebrew and *'ibraniyya*, in contrast, to Syriac.

(fols. 1ᵛ–213ᵛ), and Bibl. 57 (only Joshua–2 Samuel, fols. 1ʳ–104ʳ).

The majority of manuscripts contain the same text type, with only minor variants. This version appears to be the most widespread numerically. Added to the list has to be manuscript Beirut, Bibliothèque Nationale, 419, in which the translation was revised according to the version of the *Biblia Sacra Arabica* (see below).⁶ However, a distinct second version exists for some books, which was also translated from Syriac. With regard to the book of Judges, it is found in manuscripts Oxford, Bodleian Library, 493; Coptic Orthodox Patriarchate, Bibl. 3; and St. Petersburg, Institute of Oriental Manuscripts, D226. The books of 1–2 Samuel are found in manuscripts Vatican, BAV, Ar. 399 and Ar. 468.

3–5.2.8.2 Translations from Coptic

Distinct from the aforementioned versions is the text found in manuscript Vatican, BAV, 449 (dated 1335 C.E., fols. 18ʳ–184ᵛ), which goes back to a Coptic *Vorlage* (→ 3–5.2.2). Manuscript Rome, Casanatense, ms 2108 is a direct copy of this manuscript.⁷

3–5.2.8.3 *Biblia Sacra Arabica*

As with all the biblical books in Arabic, the Former Prophets exist in handwritten copies in the **Biblia Sacra Arabica* (1671–1673). Based largely on manuscript Vatican, BAV, Ar. 468 and originally printed by the *Congregatio de Propaganda Fide* for missionary purposes, in early modern times it replaced to a large degree all earlier Old Testament versions.⁸ Cf. manuscripts Paris, BNF, Ar. 2 (fols. 356ʳ–381ᵛ, 383ᵛ–448ʳ); London, BL, Or. 8745 (fols. 56ᵛ–70ʳ, 71ᵛ–109ᵛ); India Office, Islamic 1280 (fols. 222ᵛ–281ʳ, 286ʳ–449ᵛ); Birmingham, Mingana, Christ. Ar. 103 (dated 1754 C.E., fols. 1ᵛ–60ᵛ, 67ʳ–220ʳ, in Karshūnī); Sharfeh, Ar. 1/5 (including 1–2 Chronicles); Aleppo, Syriac Orthodox Archdiocese, ms 1 (fols. 112ʳ–140ᵛ, 143ʳ–222ᵛ); Mardin, Church of the Forty Martyrs, ms 3 (except for fols. 36ᵛ–39ᵛ, which contains Ruth, in Karshūnī); Coptic Orthodox Patriarchate, Bibl. 29, Bibl. 31 (dated 1772 C.E., fols. 152ᵛ–193ʳ, 196ᵛ–289ʳ), Bibl. 36 (except for Joshua, fols. 4ʳ–25ʳ, 28ᵛ–137ᵛ), Bibl. 41 (up to the book of Judges, fols. 138ᵛ–189ʳ), Bibl. 42 (fols. 2ʳ–50ʳ, 54ʳ–175ʳ), Bibl. 43 (dated 1786 C.E., fols. 1ʳ–52ʳ, 56ʳ–182ʳ), Bibl. 48 (fols. 164ʳ–303ʳ), and Bibl. 87 (starting Josh 10:4, fols. 11ʳ–157ʳ).

Albert, M., "Les 'Bet Mawtbe' nestoriens," in *La formation des canons scripturaires* (ed. M. Tardieu; Patrimoines Religions du livre; Paris: Cerf, 1993), 155–68.

Griffith, S.H., "The Gospel in Arabic: An Inquiry into its Appearance in the First Abbasid Century," in S.H. Griffith, *Arabic Christianity in the Monasteries of Ninth-Century Palestine* (Variorum Collected Studies Series 380; Aldershot: Variorum, 1992), 126–67.

Huart, C. (ed.), *Al-Maqdisī, Muṭahhar ibn Ṭāhir: Le livre de la création et de l'histoire* (6 vols.; Paris: Leroux, 1889–1919).

Khalil, S. (ed.), *Abū al-Barakāt ibn al-Asʿad ibn Kubr: Miṣbāḥ al-ẓulma fī iḍāḥ al-khidma* (Cairo: Al-Ṭabʿa al-tijārīya al-ḥadītha, 1971) [Arab.].

Knutsson, B., *Studies in the Text and Language of Three Syriac-Arabic Versions of the Book of Judicum: With Special Reference to the Middle Arabic Elements: Introductions-Linguistic Notes-Texts* (Leiden: Brill, 1974).

Rödiger, E., *De Origine et Indole Arabicae Librorum V.T. Historicorum Interpretationis Libri Duo* (Halle: Kümmel, 1829).

Vaccari, A., "Un Codice Carshunico della Casanatense e la Bibbia Araba del 1671," *Bib* 4 (1923): 96–107.

Vollandt, R., "From the Working Desks of a Coptic-Muslim Workshop: MS Paris–BNF Arabic 1 and the Large-Scale Production of Arabic Luxurious Bibles in Early Ottoman Cairo," in *Patronage, Production, and Transmission of Texts in Medieval and Early Modern Jewish Cultures* (eds. E. Alfonso and J. Decter; Turnhout: Brepols, forthcoming), 231–65.

Vollandt, R., "Che portono al ritorno quì una Bibbia Arabica integra: A History of the Biblia Sacra Arabica (1671–73)," in *Græco-latina et orientalia: Studia in honorem Angeli Urbani heptagenarii* (eds. J.P. Monferrer-Sala and S.K. Samir; Beirut: CEDRAC, 2013), 401–18.

Ronny Vollandt

---

⁶ Thus Knutsson with regard to the book of Judges (*Studies in the Text and Language*, 37, 38). Knutsson's comments on this manuscript with regard to the book of Judges also hold true for the other biblical books.

⁷ Cf. Vaccari, "Un Codice Carshunico."

⁸ On the **Biblia Sacra Arabica*, see Vollandt, "Che portono al ritorno."

3–5.3 Medieval text of MT

The Masoretes considered the prophetic books that we divide into Former and Latter Prophets as one unit, the second division of the Bible. In the Masoretic notes they referred to them as בנביאים "in the Prophets." Following that view, both Former and Latter Prophets are dealt with together in this entry.

3–5.3.1 Original Form, Editions, and Tools[1]

Three of the four manuscripts that comprise the "medieval Masoretic text" in total or in part contain the Prophets. The Leningrad Codex (MT^L; Codex EPB I B 19a of the National Library of Russia in St. Petersburg) and the Cairo Codex of the Prophets (MT^C) contain all the books, and the Aleppo Codex (MT^A) contains all except for the following passages which are lost: 2 Kgs 14:21–18:13; Jer 29:9–31:34; Am 8:13–Mic 5:1; Zeph 3:20–9:17.

Diplomatic Editions: The text, MasP and MasM of MT^C are presented without change in Pérez Castro, *Profetas de El Cairo*, together with the identification of the *simanim* (biblical references) and additional information regarding the Masoretic notes.

Of the two editions of MT^A in progress, in Cohen, *Miqra'ot Gedolot "Haketer,"* all the books have been published;[2] in HUB only the books of Isaiah (Goshen-Gottstein, *HUB, Isaiah*), Jeremiah (Rabin–Talmon–Tov, *HUB, Jeremiah*) and Ezekiel (Goshen-Gottstein–Talmon, *HUB, Ezekiel*) have been published.

In 2016, in the new edition of MT^L, *BHQ*, only the books of Judges (Fernández-Marcos, *Judges*) and the Twelve Minor Prophets (Gelston, *Minor Prophets*) have been published.

Auxiliary Tools: Several studies supplement the edition of MT^C: an alphabetic index of the MasP and MasM (Pérez Castro, *Vol. 8: Índice*); analytical indices of the MasM (Fernández Tejero, *Masora magna*), of the occurrences of *let* cases (Ortega Monasterio, *Masora parva: Casos let*), and of the MasP (Azcárraga Servet, *Masora parva: Índice*).

3–5.3.2 Text-Critical Character

The three manuscripts that contain the Prophets differ from one another in terms of form, consonantal text, vocalization, and their Masorot (→ 1.5.4).

The way in which the biblical text should be written is specified in minute detail in the *Halakhah* and is also part of the Masorah. Despite these *halakhic* requirements, the three main manuscripts are not identical in form. Although all three have the same "brick" layout for the stichometric arrangement of the Song of Deborah (Judges 5), the distribution of blank spaces and words differs considerably in each of them.

As regards the different divisions of the biblical text, there are some differences among the three manuscripts in the division into paragraphs and their types, (תוחה)פ "open section," and (תומה)ס "closed section." For example, in Judges, the following is marked: Judg 1:21–22 in MT^L as ס and in MT^C and MT^A as פ; 4:12–13 in MT^L as ס, in MT^C as פ and in MT^A there is no division; Judg 7:1–2 appears in MT^A as ס and without any division in MT^C and MT^L; etc.[3]

There are also slight differences in the division for the three-year cycle. For example, the three manuscripts have twenty *seder* markings in the Minor Prophets but in two cases there are location differences: MT^C and MT^A have a mark in Joel 2:27 but MT^L has it in Joel 2:26; the last mark is in Zech 14:16 in MT^C, in Zech 14:21 in MT^A, and in Mal 1:1 in MT^L.

The three manuscripts differ little from one another in their consonantal text. The comparative study by Breuer[4] of the consonantal text of the

---

[1] Cf. "Medieval Masoretic Text", paragraphs → 1.5.2–1.5.3, for more detailed information.

[2] For both, see the → Collective Bibliography for details.

[3] For the full comparison see Fernández Marcos, *Judges*, 13*–15*.

[4] Breuer, *The Aleppo Codex*, 97–138.

Prophets, shows that MT^C, MT^A, and MT^L have some variants that can be grouped as variations in the positioning of a vowel letter or "silent" letter; interchanges of *waw* and *yod*; variations in the reading of some words; etc.

3–5.3.2.1 Orthographic Irregularities: Extraordinary Points

Four of the fifteen passages located in the Prophets with points on one or more letters of a word are indicated in all three manuscripts: יָצָא "came out" in 2 Sam 19:20; הֵמָּה "they" in Isa 44:9; הַהֵיכָל "the temple" in Ezek 41:20, and מְהֻקְצָעוֹת "cornered" in Ezek 46:22 (→ 1.5.4.1 and → 2.3.2.1).

In MT^C, the four cases have points on all the letters of the relevant words. All the information on this phenomenon is provided in the MasP of three of the cases, highlighting the number of cases in each of the divisions of the Bible: הי׳ נקודות בתו׳ ד׳ בני׳ א׳ בכ׳ "fifteen [words] dotted: ten in the Torah, four in the Prophets and one in the Writings." However, the information of MasP note to Isa 44:9 only refers to the cases in the Prophets: ד׳ נקוד׳ בנב׳ "four [words] dotted in the Prophets." In the MasM notes on 2 Sam 19:20 and Ezek 41:20 the passages for all fifteen cases are listed, and in that of Ezek 46:22 just the four cases in the Prophets.

In MT^A, only two of the letters of the word in 2 Sam 19:20 are punctuated, the *yod* and the *aleph*. In all other cases, all the letters are punctuated. In the MasP, the information in three of the cases refers to the phenomenon in Prophets ד׳ נקד בנביא׳ "four cases in the Prophets" while in the case of 2 Samuel it only says נקוד "dotted." There is no MasM note on any of the cases.

In MT^L, in the biblical text, all the letters of the word are punctuated. The MasP note to Ezek 41:20 says נקוד "dotted" and in that of the other cases the total number of words affected by this phenomenon is provided: הי׳ נקוד "fifteen [words] dotted." There is no MasM note to any of the cases.

3–5.3.2.2 Orthographic Irregularities: Small Letters

In the three manuscripts, there are two final *nunin* written in a smaller size than normal: in the word אֶרֶן "fir" (Isa 44:14) and in וּנְבוּשַׁזְבָּן "and Nebushazban" (Jer 39:13). In all three manuscripts, in the MasP notes on the two cases, it says that there are three cases of small *nunin* (ג׳ נונין זעירין). The third case is found in Prov 16:28.

3–5.3.2.3 Orthographic Irregularities: Suspended Letters

One of the four cases of letters written above the line is found in Judg 18:30. The *nun* of the word מְנַשֶּׁה "Manasseh" appears suspended in the three manuscripts, מנשה. The MasP note says ד׳ תלוים "four suspended" (MT^{A,L}) or ד׳ אתיות תלוים "four suspended letters" (MT^C). In MT^C and MT^A there is also a MasM note in which the four passages are listed. The explanation of this case is widely documented in rabbinic literature.[5] The suspended *nun* is treated as a theological correction. Thus, the insertion of the *nun* prevents the name of Moses from being linked to idolatry by reading Manasseh. Therefore, Jonathan, the young Levite, is no longer described as the grandson of Moses but of Manasseh.

3–5.3.2.4 *Tiqqune Soferim*

Eight of the eighteen passages considered by tradition to have been corrected by the *soferim* are identified in the Masorah of MT^C: 1 Sam 3:13; 1 Kgs 12:16; Jer 2:11; Ezek 8:17; Hab 1:12; Zech 2:12; Mal 1:13; 3:8. The total number of cases is provided in the MasP notes to all of them: יח׳ מלין בקר׳ תיקון סופר׳ וחכמ׳ "eighteen words in the Scripture are emendations of the Scribes and Sages," but the changes are not explained. There is no MasM note in any of them. In MT^A and MT^L, none of these passages are indicated (→ 1.5.4.1).

3–5.3.2.5 *Qere-Ketiv*

The main manuscripts disagree on the number and location of *Qere-Ketiv* cases and on how to represent them.[6]

---

[5] *T. Sanh.* 14:7–8; *b. B. Bat.* 109b; *'Abot R. Nat.* 34a, 37b; *y. Ber.* 9:2; *y. Sanh.* 11:7; *Cant. Rab.* 2:5.

[6] The calculation of the *Qere-Ketiv* cases refers only to those explicitly indicated as such and not to cases of *yatir*.

In MT^C 634 appear marked: thirty-nine[7] in Joshua, seventeen in Judges, seventy-three in 1 Samuel, eighty-three in 2 Samuel, thirty-nine in 1 Kings, seventy-two in 2 Kings, forty-six in Isaiah, 126 in Jeremiah, 111 in Ezekiel, four in Hosea, one in Joel, three in Amos, one in Obadiah, two in Micah, three in Nahum, four in Habakkuk, one in Zephaniah, two in Haggai, and seven in Zechariah. The most common way of indicating the phenomenon in the MasP is by writing some of the letters of the word or only the one involved in the proposed reading together with the abbreviation 'ק; the complete word is only used in three cases. In 450 cases, a sign resembling a final *nun* also appears: e.g., MasP to הֲמוֹנָה "his multitude" in Ezek 32:32: 'ך נו ק ("ך; read [המונ]ו").[8] The *Qere* vowels tend to be written in the text below the *Ketiv*, although in nine cases they are also attached to the *Qere* letters. It is also common to find one or more Masoretic notes together with that relating to the *Qere*. These notes often contain information about how the word is written. An example can be foun in the MasP to בַּיַּרְכְתָם "at the extreme rear" in Ezek 46:19: 'חס׳ ל׳ ק תים ׳ ("ך; read תים, unique written defectively"); to a lesser extent, they provide general information on the form or phenomenon. An example can be found in the MasP to אֶחָת "one" in 1 Kgs 19:4: 'ד וקרי ׳ת ׳כת ׳ו ׳ק ׳ד ך' ("ך; read [אח]ד ['one'], six [words] are written with *tav* but are read with *dalet*"). Some notes contain the term *yatir* "superfluous," to indicate the spelling of the word: e.g., MasP to וְרָאֲתָה "saw" in 2 Kgs 11:1: ראתה ך' ("ך; read ראתה ['saw'], eleven [words have] superfluous [*waw* at the beginning of the word]"). Twenty-one cases have MasM notes that include information on the phenomenon and list the cases.

In MT^A, 511 are indicated: twenty-five in Joshua, thirteen in Judges, fifty-five in 1 Samuel, seventy in 2 Samuel, thirty-three in 1 Kings, sixty-four in 2 Kings, forty in Isaiah, 106 in Jeremiah, eighty in Ezekiel, four in Hosea, one in Joel, three in Amos, one in Obadiah, four in Micah, two in Nahum, one in Habakkuk, two in Zephaniah, one in Haggai, and six in Zechariah. The most common way of indicating the phenomenon in the MasP is by giving all the letters of the *Qere* – except in forty-seven cases in which only the relevant letter or letters are provided – together with the abbreviation 'ק and the complete form in equal parts (only three times with the abbreviation 'קר). The vowels of the *Qere* are written in the biblical text under the *Ketiv* except for Judg 16:25, where they are also given under the *Qere* letters. In twenty-one cases, in addition to the *Qere* information, a further notation is provided on how the word is written. In four cases, there are also MasM notes in which information on the phenomenon is given and the cases are listed: 2 Sam 10:9; 1 Kgs 16:26; Ezek 47:10; Mic 1:10.

In MT^L, 663 cases are marked: thirty-two in Joshua, nineteen in Judges, sixty-seven in 1 Samuel, eighty-four in 2 Samuel, forty-six in 1 Kings, seventy-one in 2 Kings, 52 in Isaiah, 132 in Jeremiah, 132 in Ezekiel, five in Hosea, one in Joel, three in Amos, one in Obadiah, four in Micah, four in Nahum, one in Habakkuk, two in Zephaniah, one in Haggai, and six in Zechariah. This phenomenon is most commonly indicated with the shortened form, 'ק, although the abbreviation 'קר and the complete form are each used sixty-three times. In Ezek 48:14 the *Qere* letters are given but no term is used: MasP to יַעֲבוּר "alienate," יעביר ("[read] יעביר ['alienate']"). Normally, the whole word is given in the *Qere* form, but on twenty-six occasions in Ezekiel and one in Hosea only the relevant letter or letters are provided (e.g. the MasP on שַׁעֲרוּרִיָּה "a horrible thing" in Hos 6:10: 'ק 'ו "read [ריה]שער] ['a horrible thing']"). The vowels are normally provided under the *Ketiv*, although in 2 Kgs 14:21 and Ezek 18:24 they are also given in the margin, under the *Qere* letters. In twenty-seven cases, together with the *Qere* information, a further notation is provided on how the word is written. In seven of these cases, the term *yatir* is used: e.g. the MasP to בְּיִשְׂרָאֵל "of Israel" in 2 Sam 10:9, 'ק ישראל .יתיר ׳ב ("[the letter] *bet* is superfluous; read ישראל 'of Israel'"). Finally, four cases also have a MasM note that includes information on the phenomenon and

---

[7] M.J. de Azcárraga-Servet, "El *ketib/qere* en el libro de Josué del Códice de Profetas de El Cairo," in *Proceedings of the Eleventh Congress of the IOMS* (ed. A. Dotan; Jerusalem: Magnes Press, 1994), 21–37.

[8] E. Martín Contreras, "The Marginal *Nun* in the Masora of the Cairo Codex: Use and Function", *VT* 65 (2015) 81–90.

lists the cases: e.g. MasM to לֹא in 2 Sam 16:18: י״ז כת׳ לֹא וקר׳ לוֹ ("seventeen [times] is written לֹא ['not'] and it should be read לוֹ ['to him']").

Qere we la Ketiv ("Read but not Written")

The three manuscripts highlight cases of words in the Prophets that are not written in the text but which should be read and which are found in Prophets. The number of cases, how this phenomenon is marked in the biblical text, and how to record it in the Masorah are different for each of these manuscripts (Martín Contreras, "Phenomenon").

In MT^C, nine cases are indicated: Judg 20:13; 2 Sam 8:3, 16:23, 18:20; 2 Kgs 19:31, 37; Jer 31:38, 50:29; Ezek 9:11. Several systems are used to mark them in the biblical text: 1) with an accent sign and a *circellus* in the usual space between two words (Judg 20:13); 2) with a *circellus* in the usual space between two words (2 Sam 8:3); 3) with a *circellus*, the vowels, and the accent signs of the word in the usual space between two words (2 Sam 16:23, 18:20; Jer 31:38, 50:29); 4) with a *circellus*, the vowels, and the accent signs of the word in an additional space between two words (2 Kgs 19:31, 19:37); 5) the word, vowels, and the *circellus* are written (Ezek 9:11). All the cases have MasP notes in which the word that should be read appears with its vowels and accents except in two cases, 2 Kgs 19:31 and 19:37. The phenomenon is indicated by the formula קרי ולא כתיב "read but not written" or its abbreviations together with the symbol resembling a final *nun*, except in 2 Sam 8:3. Three of the cases have MasM notes in which the general information and two different calculations are given: 1) Ten cases, according to the MasM to Judg 20:13, י׳ קריי׳ ולא כת׳ וסמנהון בני פרת איש כן בניו צבאות באים לה אלי אלי ("ten [words] are read although are not written and their references [are]: בני [Judg 20:13]; פרת [2 Sam 8:3]; איש [2 Sam 16:23]; כן [2 Sam 18:20]; צבאות [2 Kgs 19:37]; בניו [2 Kgs 19:31]; באים [Jer 31:38]; לה [Jer 50:29]; אלי [Ruth 3:5]; אלי [Ruth 3:17]"); 2) Eleven cases according to the MasM to 2 Sam 16:23 and to 2 Kgs 19:31, implicitly in the first and explicitly in the second, יא׳ ... קר׳ ולא כת׳ ("... eleven [words] are read although are not written"). The eleventh case is כאשר "according to," Qere ככל אשר "according to all that" in Ezek 9:11.

In MT^A, eight cases are highlighted: Judg 20:13; 2 Sam 8:3, 16:23, 18:20; 2 Kgs 19:31, 37; Jer 31:38; 50:29. Four systems are used for indicating the phenomenon in the consonantal text: 1) with a *circellus* in the usual space between two words (2 Sam 8:3; 18:20); 2) with a *circellus*, vowels, and accent signs of the word in an additional space between two words (Judg 20:13; 2 Kgs 19:37); 3) without a *circellus* but with the vowels and accent signs of the word in an additional space between words (2 Kgs 19:31); 4) with a *circellus*, and an additional space between words (2 Sam 16:23; Jer 31:38; 50:29). The phenomenon is recorded in the MasP in two ways: 1) by means of the formula קרי ולא כתיב "read but not written" or in an abbreviated form (2 Sam 18:20; 16:23; Jer 31:38; 50:29); 2) as a simple *Qere* with the usual formula (Judg 20:13; 2 Sam 8:3; 2 Kgs 19:31, 37). Only Judg 20:13 has a MasM note, in which the total number of ten cases is indicated.

In MT^L, eight cases are indicated: Judg 20:13; 2 Sam 8:3, 16:23, 18:20; 2 Kgs 19:31, 37; Jer 31:38; 50:29. There are two methods used for indicating the phenomenon in the text: 1) with a *circellus*, the vowels, and the accent signs of the word that should be read in the usual space between words (2 Sam 16:23; 2 Kgs 19:37; Jer 31:38; 50:29); 2) with the vowels and accent signs of the word that should be read in the usual space between words but no *circellus* (Judg 20:13; 2 Sam 8:3; 18:20; 2 Kgs 19:31). All the cases have MasP notes with the formula קרי ולא כתיב "read but not written" or its abbreviations. In Judg 20:13, there are two MasP notes and in the second note the phenomenon is indicated as a simple *Qere* with the abbreviated formula plus the symbol similar to the final *nun*. Only Jer 50:29 has a MasM note that indicates the total number of cases as ten.[9]

---

[9] This manuscript shows the total number of eleven in the MasM of Ruth 3:5 (→ 1.5.4.2).

Ketiv we la Qere ("Written but not Read")

Seven of the eight cases of words that are written in the biblical text but should not be read are located in the Prophets: 2 Sam 13:33; 15:21; 2 Kgs 5:18; Jer 38:16; 39:12; 51:3; Ezek 48:16. In the three manuscripts, the word that should not be read appears without vowels in the biblical text and the formula כתב ולא קרי "written but not read" appears in the MasP notes. However, in spite of this, there are minor differences between the notes in the three manuscripts. The relevant word is repeated four times in MT^A and five times in MT^L, but never in MT^C. However, in MT^C, the symbol resembling a final *nun* also appears in six of the seven cases. Also in MT^C, in two cases there is a second note in which the general information on the phenomenon is given: e.g., MasP to אִם "if" in Jer 39:12: כת׳ ולא קרי ח׳ מלים כת׳ ולא קר׳ ך ("[this word is] written but should not be read; eight words [are] written but should not be read; ך").

3-5.3.2.6 *Sebirin*

The number of instances and the method of indicating this phenomenon varies among the three manuscripts (→ 1.5.4.3).

In MT^C, twenty-eight cases are indicated, two of them in the MasM (Jer 29:22, 37:7) and the rest in the MasP. The alternative reading is explained in most of the cases (e.g. MasP to כַּאֲשֶׁר "just as" in Josh 13:8: ד׳ סבר׳ אשר ["אשר ['which'] has been suggested four times"]) and in two cases, instead of the reading, the nature of the possible change is explained (e.g. MasP to וַיָּבוֹא "then came" in Ezek 14:1 says: יה׳ מל׳ ו׳ סבר׳ סגין וקר׳ חד ["fifteen (times written) plene with *waw*; one would expect a plural form but it reads a singular form"]). In seven cases, the term קרין "is read" is also used to indicate that the form shown in the text is the one to be followed, and in two cases the term יפה "correct" occurs (→ 3-5.3.2.8). Examples include the, MasP to וּבֵית אֵל "and Bethel" in Josh 8:17: יפ׳ ג׳ סבר׳ בבית וקר׳ בית ["ובית correct; בבית ['in Beth'] has been suggested but בית ['Beth'] is read").[10]

In MT^A, seven cases are indicated: Josh 1:7; Judg 11:34; 1 Kgs 22:43; Jer 48:45; Ezek 20:38, 37:22 (only in the MasM); of which the first and the last are not present in MT^C. In the MasP the number of times in which an alternative reading would be expected is given but there is no explanation of that reading. An example can be found in the MasP to מִמֶּנּוּ "from it" in Josh 1:7: ו׳ סביר׳ ("six [times] is wrongly suggested [ממנה for ממנו]"). In the MasM notes to Jer 48:45 and Ezek 37:22, the alternative reading is explained. The MasM to בְּהָרֵי "in the mountains of" in Ezek 37:22 reads ג׳ סבירין בערי (בערי ['in the cities of'] is suggested three times [instead of 'in the mountains of']").

In MT^L, five cases are indicated: Josh 1:7, 8:17; Judg 2:22; 1 Kgs 22:43; Jer 48:45. In Judg 2:22 and 1 Kgs 22:43 there is also MasM note in which the statement is repeated and the cases listed. The alternative reading proposal is explained in the notes except in Judg 2:22. In this case, the term מטעין "it has been suggested wrongly"[11] is used instead of the term *sebir*: ח׳ דמט "eight [times] it has been suggested wrongly [בה instead of בם]"

3-5.3.2.7 *Hillûfîm* ("Divergences")

In MT^L, in the MasP to הֲלוֹא "is there not" in Isa 44:20, there is a reference to the Ben Naftali reading: בן נפתלי הלוא־. According to this, the consonantal text would reflect the Ben Asher reading, without a *maqqef*, as opposed to the reading proposed by Ben Naftali, with a *maqqef*.

The Masorah of MT^C identifies eleven cases of conflict between Eastern and Western Masoretes: four in the MasP and the rest in the MasM. Normally, the text includes the Western reading and the Masorah has the Eastern variant. An example is the MasP to דְּבָרֶיךָ "your words" in Judg 13:12: למדנ׳ חס׳ "the Eastern tradition [writes this word] defective." Both traditions are included in two cases: the MasM to וְהוֹלִיד "bring forth" in Isa 59:4 (והוליד "It is written והוליד [plene] כת׳ למערב׳ חסר למדנחאי

---

[10] There are two notes on the same word, one situated on each side of the column.

[11] Although this term in its independent use cannot be considered a synonym of *sebir* (as shown by its use in MT^C and MT^A), in this case it has been considered as such because in MT^C it is indeed marked as *sebir*.

in the Western tradition, defective in the Eastern") and the MasM to וְאַתּוּקֵיהָא, "the galleries" in Ezek 41:15 (ואתוקיהא כת׳ למדנ׳ ואתוקיהא כת׳ למער׳) "the Eastern tradition writes ואתוקיה [without the *alef* at the end of the word] and the Western tradition writes ואתוקיהא [with the *alef*]").

Five cases of *pelûgtah* are indicated in MT^C: three in the MasP (Josh 21:37; Isa 59:12; Ezek 17:22) and two in the MasM (2 Sam 2:15; Jer 23:15). Except in 2 Sam 2:15 and Ezek 17:22, it is clearly explained on which letter or form there is another opinion, with it being possible to deduce the nature of the discrepancy. An example is the MasM to וְהִשְׁקֵתִים "and gave them to drink" in Jer 23:15: ב׳ חד מל׳ וא׳ חס׳ פלג׳ מי ראש. קדמ׳ מי ראש ("[והשקתים occurs] twice, one plene and one defective; [there is a] difference of opinion over the first [i.e., over the plene written]: מִי רָאשׁ ['poisoned water'] (Jer 9:14) [וְהִשְׁקִיתִים], מִי ראש (Jer 23:15) [וְהִשְׁקֵתִים]") (→ 1.5.4.4).

3–5.3.2.8 *Yafeh* ("Correct")

Some Masoretic notes that are particularly important for the transmission of the biblical text indicate that the text is correct. Except for two cases located in MT^A,[12] these notes are characteristic of MT^C. In this manuscript, seventy-six cases are located in the MasP. Normally, the note only has the shortened *yafeh* term, without explaining to which aspect of the text it refers. In addition, in more than twenty-one percent of the cases there is no *circellus* in the text, making it even more difficult to know what the note refers to. However, in seven cases there is additional information that makes it possible to establish the purpose of the note. In Josh 8:17 and 1 Sam 3:16, *yafeh* appears next to another notation that includes an alternative reading to that of the text thereby confirming the text. The MasP to אֶת־שְׁמוּאֵל "Samuel" in 1 Sam 3:16 reads e.g סביר׳ אל׳ יפ׳ ("אל, "to" has been suggested; [but *et*] is correct"). The five cases that have a MasM note enable an understanding of the purpose of the note. All refer to expressions that, in parallel passages, include some type of change that could make one think that the text is incorrect; what is written is confirmed through *yafeh* and the difference is indicated by the MasM annotation. An example is the MasM to בֵּית לָחֶם "Bethlehem" in 2 Sam 23:14: ומצב פלשתים אז בית לחם. דדב׳ בבית לחם. The Masorah gives the catchwords corresponding to 2 Sam 23:14 and 1 Chr 11:16: "they are parallel passages with the difference being that the first has בית לחם and the second בבית לחם."

In MT^A, there are two cases: the MasP to עַל־הַדָּרֶךְ "by the way" in 1 Kgs 20:38 and the MasP to לָכֶם "to you" in Jer 14:14. The two notes only contain the abbreviation for *yafeh*, without further detail.

MT^L has no case.

3–5.3.3 Relevance for Exegesis

The Masoretic notes with a semantic content in the three manuscripts have a direct bearing on the interpretation of the text. They are divided into two types: 1) Notes that confirm an unusual meaning of a form, such as the MasP of MT^L to צֵא "dirt" in Isa 30:22: ל׳ לשון טנוף "unique with the meaning of 'dirt, filth'"; the word appears fourteen times in the Bible but only in this case is it a common name. In the rest, it is a *Qal* impv. masc. sg. of יצא "go out"; 2) notes that indicate that a word has various meanings. For example, the MasM of MT^C to וְתַפּוּחַ "and the apple treee" in Joel 1:12: ג׳ ב׳ מל׳ וא׳ חס׳ א׳ שם קריה וא׳ שם ברנ׳ וא׳ שם אלין וסימנהון למנשה רמון קרח ("[occurs] three times, twice [written] plene and once defective; in one case it is the name of a city, in one the name of a man, and in one a common name, and+ its references are: למנשה, "to Manasseh" [Josh 17:8]; רמון, "the pomegranate" [Joel 1:12]; קרח, "Korah" [1 Chr 2:43]"). In Joshua, it is the name of a city, in Chronicles it is a proper name, and in Joel it is a common name ("apple tree"). Other cases appear in the MasP of MT^L to עָרִים "enemies" in Isa 14:21, in the MasM of MT^L to קַח "stem" in Ezek 17:5; and in the MasM of MT^A to וַתְּכַל "and longed" in 2 Sam 13:39; etc.

de Azcárraga Servert, M.J., *La masora parva del códice de Profetas de El Cairo: Índice analítico* (Textos y Estudios "Cardenal Cisneros" 61; Madrid: CSIC, 1997).

---

[12] There are four cases in MT^B in the Pentateuch.

Breuer, M., *The Aleppo Codex and the Accepted Text of the Bible* (Jerusalem: Mosad Harav Kook, 1976) [Hebr.].

Cassuto, P., *Qeré-Ketib et listes massorétiques dans le manuscrit B 19a* (Judentum und Umwelt 26; Frankfurt a.M.: Peter Lang, 1989).

Cohen, **Miqra'ot Gedolot "Haketer."*

Fernández Marcos, N., *Judges* (*BHQ 7; Stuttgart: Deutsche Bibelgesellschaft, 2011).

Fernández Tejero, E., *La masora magna del códice de Profetas de El Cairo: Transcripción alfabético-analítica* (Textos y Estudios "Cardenal Cisneros" 58; Madrid: CSIC, 1995).

Gelston, A., *The Twelve Minor Prophets* (*BHQ 13; Stuttgart: Deutsche Bibelgesellschaft, 2010).

Goshen-Gottstein, **HUB, Isaiah*.

Goshen-Gottstein–Talmon, **HUB, Ezekiel*.

Martín Contreras, E., "The Phenomenon *Qere we la' ketib* in the Main Biblical Codices: New Data," *VT* 62 (2012): 77–87.

Ortega Monasterio, M.T., *La masora parva del códice de Profetas de El Cairo*: Casos *lêṯ* (Textos y Estudios "Cardenal Cisneros" 59; Madrid: CSIC, 1995).

Pérez Castro, **Profetas de El Cairo*.

Pérez Castro, F. et al. (eds.), *El códice de Profetas de El Cairo*, Vol. 8: *Índice alfabético de sus masoras* (Textos y Estudios "Cardenal Cisneros"; Madrid: CSIC, 1992).

Rabin–Talmon–Tov, **HUB, Jeremiah*.

Elvira Martín Contreras

6–9
Latter Prophets

∴

6
Isaiah

6.1 Textual History of Isaiah

6.1.1 Extant Witnesses

6.1.1.1 Ancient Hebrew Texts
6.1.1.1.1 1QIsa^a

This manuscript is the earliest of all Isaiah scrolls from Qumran (150–125 B.C.E.) and the only complete one (→ 6.2.1.1; → 6.2.3.1). Although its text to a great extent is in agreement with the consonantal text of MT (→ 6.2.2), the scroll, written by one scribe, is marked by a large number of variant readings. Many of them reflect an interest in making the text more understandable by applying full orthography, a more detailed system of marking sense units, and by substituting roots and nouns that might have been considered difficult to understand. Compared to MT, the scroll also contains a large number of minuses and pluses (often for stylistic reasons), cases of harmonization (between passages in Isaiah, or with passages in other books), and readings that testify to a different understanding of the text than in MT (exegetical tendencies). In addition, there are a great number of corrections of readings made either by the original scribe himself or by subsequent scribes, the latter also being responsible for some insertions.

6.1.1.1.2 1QIsa^b

Although not complete, this manuscript (→ 6.2.1.2) preserves a large amount of the text of Isaiah (ranging from Isaiah 7 to 66). It dates to the third quarter of the first century B.C.E. and is quite close to MT, its orthography being marked by cases of defective spelling although in some cases the fuller spelling is found (e.g., in participles).

6.1.1.1.3 Scrolls from Cave 4 and Elsewhere

The fragments of these manuscripts (→ 6.2.1), all dating to the first century B.C.E. except for 4QIsa^c, are in most cases in close agreement with the MT tradition. This applies in particular to 4QIsa^a, 4QIsa^b, 4QIsa^d, 4QIsa^e, 4QIsa^f, and 4QIsa^g, as well as to the other texts (4QIsa^{h–r}), which are however too fragmentary to assess properly. The orthography of 4QIsa^c, on the other hand, is similar to that of 1QIsa^a, though 4QIsa^c hardly displays such content variants as attested in the latter.

Isaiah scrolls discovered elsewhere are 5QIsa and MurIsa, both very fragmentary.

6.1.1.2 Primary Translations of Isaiah
6.1.1.2.1 *Septuagint*

Dating to the middle of the second century B.C.E., the Old Greek (→ 6.3) is known for its many and often marked divergences from the MT tradition. The modifications typical of this version are of a linguistic, stylistic, and interpretive nature. In view of this character, there is no reason to assume that the underlying Hebrew differed much from MT (→ 6.2.2). However, due to the translation's complexities it is often difficult to identify what Hebrew text the translator had in front of him (→ 6.3.3).

6.1.1.2.2 *Kaige/Theodotion*

The readings of Isaiah assigned to Theodotion represent the *kaige* revision of this book (→ 1.3.1.2.2). *Kaige*-Th of Isaiah offers a literal version of its parent (proto-MT) text. In a number of cases, divergent renderings are due to the influence of LXX (→ 6a6–9.1.5.3.1–9.1.5.3.1).

6.1.1.2.3 *Aquila*

The text of Aq-Isa is preserved only in a number of Hexaplaric readings. This translation is known for its extreme literalness (→ 6a6–9.1.5.3.2–9.1.5.3.2).

6.1.1.2.4 *Symmachus*

Unlike the version of Aquila, the translation ascribed to Symmachus (ca. 200 C.E.) has been praised by scholars both in antiquity and in modern times for its clarity and its good Koine usage. This general evaluation also applies to Sym-Isa, which in addition contains a number of interpretative renderings (→ 6a6–9.1.5.3.3–9.1.5.3.3).

6.1.1.2.5 Targum

T-Isa, being part of the Targum to the Prophets (→ 6–9.1.3), is characterized by a literal rendering of many passages, but also contains a large number of elucidations and interpretations of the Hebrew text, which in some cases have been made explicit by paraphrastic renderings. Though containing exegetical traditions of an earlier date, T-Isa, at least the body of it, was produced in the first half of the second century C.E. in Palestine (for various views on dating, see → 1.3.3.4 and → 6–9.1.3.1). It is often taken for granted that T-Prophets originated in rabbinic circles (→ 1.3.3.5 and → 6–9.1.3.1), but internal and external data strongly suggest that it was produced in a priestly milieu.[1]

6.1.1.2.6 Peshitta

S-Isa, dating to the second half of the second century C.E., is a fairly literal translation that agrees closely with MT, but at the same time includes cases of exegetical rendering. In some instances, S-Isa shows specific agreements with LXX (→ 6–9.1.4).

6.1.1.2.7 Vulgate

V-Isa (→ 6–9.1.7), the Latin version made by Jerome in the nineties of the fourth century C.E., is "a generally free translation of the Hebrew into idiomatic Latin" (→ 6a6–9.1.7.2.–9.1.7.2). In some cases, the renderings reflect the influence of LXX (→ 6.3), or of one of the Hexaplaric versions, in particular Symmachus (→ 6–9.1.5.3.3). It also offers interpretive renderings, some of which reflect a Christian reading of the book.

For the remaining primary translations (Hexaplaric, post-Hexaplaric, Arabic), and the secondary translations, see the relevant sections elsewhere in *THB* 1 (→ 6–9.1.5; → 6–9.1.6; → 6–9.1.8; → 6–9.2).

6.1.2 History of Research

6.1.2.1 Before the Qumran Discoveries

It was generally believed that the Hebrew text of the Bible derived from one base text, but from the seventeenth century onwards scholars realized that the received version should not be regarded as being transmitted without corruption or correction. Hence, the reliability of MT could not be taken for granted as was done in earlier times. Roughly speaking, questions concerning the quality of MT-Isa arose (→ 6.2.2) from two types of approach: first, the comparison of MT and other witnesses, Hebrew manuscripts dating to the Middle Ages as well as early versions such as LXX (→ 6.3); and secondly, a critical attitude towards MT-Isa, in particular since the eighteenth century.

As to the second aspect, in the period from 1800 to 1950 the view of the quality of MT-Isa differed from period to period, and from scholar to scholar. Unlike the attitude typical of the scholarship preceding 1850,[2] MT-Isa was later considered to represent a text that had been transmitted rather carelessly. According to Gray,[3] for example, the text of Isaiah had been handed down with great care since the second century C.E., but "suffered in many passages serious corruption"[4] before that time. Commentaries on Isaiah, such as that by Gray, and the text editions produced at that time (*BH* 1, *BH* 2, and *BH* 3) indeed reflect the view that MT-Isa contains a large number of textual difficulties, including morphological, syntactical, and stylistic details (e.g., in meter). In most instances, these readings were viewed to be due to mechanical (scribal) errors, which could be corrected in light of parallel or related passages in the Hebrew Bible, or on the basis of the ancient versions.

In line with the statement by Gray, the versions were not held to be of much value from a text-critical point of view. To quote him again: "It is unnecessary to write at length on the Text and Ver-

---

[1] Cf. Alexander, "Jewish Priesthood," 20; van der Kooij, "Josephus, Onkelos, and Jonathan," 262–65.

[2] E.g., Gesenius, *Jesaia* (1820–1821).
[3] Gray, *Isaiah* (1912).
[4] Gray, *Isaiah*, xxvi.

sions of the Book of Isaiah,[5] for all that is of particular importance to the study of this book is limited to the question of the value of the Greek version."[6] Thus, being an ancient witness dating to the period preceding 100 C.E., LXX-Isa was deemed more important than the versions such as the Targum, Peshitta, and Vulgate, all of which reflect a Hebrew text in agreement, at least as far as the consonantal text is concerned, with MT-Isa. However, for the early period (before 100 C.E.), things were not that easy because, as Gray observed, the value of LXX-Isa "for the determination of the original text"[7] was a matter of dispute. Ottley, for instance, argued that LXX-Isa is of limited value as it contains many failures and mistakes made by the translators: "In Isaiah I find it hard to see that the LXX gives any proof at all (unless in a few isolated exceptions) of an older and superior Hebrew text."[8] Gray, on the other hand, being well aware of the complexities involved, was less pessimistic; this also applies to other scholars of his time, although most of them were not that familiar with what was going on in LXX research.

Although MT-Isa was considered to contain a large number of readings that arose from mechanical errors, there was no consensus on which readings should be regarded as incorrect[9] or as examples of bad Hebrew.[10] In response to the critical attitude towards MT-Isa, in the first half of the twentieth century some scholars like Nyberg and de Boer took another, more positive, view of the quality of MT.[11]

It was agreed that the aim of textual criticism should be to establish the original wording of MT-Isa. However, which text was considered to represent the original wording? Gray made a distinction between two periods within the textual history of Isaiah, before and after 100 C.E., the former defined by him as between 700 B.C.E. and 100 C.E. in which the Hebrew text "suffered in many passages serious corruption."[12] This view implies that in certain passages in the book, textual corruption could reach back to the oldest stages of the book. In a lecture delivered in 1901, Kittel too stated that the aim of textual criticism should be the reconstruction of the "Urschrift," the original text in the sense of Gray, but then argued that since the literary history of a given book is a matter of much uncertainty, it would be more realistic to define the goal as the reconstruction of the Hebrew text of a book that was read by the Jewish communities about 300 B.C.E.[13]

However, as is clear from the commentaries on Isaiah and from the text editions of Kittel (*BH 1, *BH 2, and *BH 3), all published in the first half of the twentieth century, the latter theory could not be implemented. Literary critical research had led to the view that the book was the outcome of a literary growth, chapters or larger segments having been added to earlier forms of the book over a long period of time, a process some scholars believed had continued into the second century B.C.E.[14] Therefore, as a rule, the critical evaluation of a given passage in the book of Isaiah was made from the perspective of its immediate context, rather than from the idea of a "final" redaction of the book, an approach that better fits the view of Gray than that of Kittel.

6.1.2.2 After the Qumran Discoveries

Between 1947 and 1956, a great number of biblical texts were found in the Dead Sea region at Qumran, Masada, Nahal Hever, and Wadi Muraba'at. A total of twenty-two manuscripts of Isaiah were dis-

---

[5] Gesenius' commentary on Isaiah was the only one that contained an elaborate account of the versions of this book (*Jesaia*, 56–88).

[6] Gray, *Isaiah*, xxv.

[7] Gray, *Isaiah*, xxvi.

[8] Ottley, *Isaiah*, 49.

[9] Cf. Gray, *Isaiah*.

[10] Cf. Dillmann, *Jesaia*.

[11] H.S. Nyberg, "Das textkritische Problem des A.T. am Hoseabuch demonstriert," *ZAW* 52 (1934): 251–54; P.A.H. de Boer, *Research into the Text of 1 Samuel I–XVI: A Contribution to the Study of the Books of Samuel* (Amsterdam: H.J. Paris, 1938).

[12] Gray, *Isaiah*, xxvi.

[13] Kittel, *Notwendigkeit*.

[14] According to B. Duhm, *Das Buch Jesaja* (Göttingen Handkommentar zum Alten Testament; Göttingen: Vandenhoeck & Ruprecht, 1914), Isaiah 24–27, 33–35 are to be considered expansions dating to the Hasmonean era and, according to K. Marti, *Das Buch Jesaja* (Tubingen: Mohr Siebeck, 1900), Isaiah 24–27 were added shortly after 128 B.C.E.

covered (→ 6.2.1), mainly at Qumran, placing this portion of Scripture as one of the most popular books, along with Deuteronomy and Psalms. These findings date from the earliest period in which biblical texts in Hebrew (and Aramaic) are attested: 250 B.C.E. to 135 C.E.

From the start, 1QIsa^a (→ 6.2.1.1; → 6.2.3.1), being one of the first pieces of the extremely important findings and containing a complete text of Isaiah, became the focus of much scholarly attention. Hence, for a long time the impact of the Qumran Isaiah texts on the perception of the textual history of the book was limited to this manuscript, which, along with 1QIsa^b (→ 6.2.1.2), was published soon after the discoveries (1950 and 1956 respectively). On the other hand, the 4QIsa fragments, which were also discovered in the early 1950s, were published at a much later date (1997), although general assessments as well as a number of readings can be found in earlier publications.[15]

Scholars such as Gray realized that textual witnesses of the period before 100 C.E. were of more importance to the study of the biblical text than the sources dating after 100 C.E. and the discoveries in the Dead Sea region have added significance to this view. The new findings have provided more evidence for the idea that the early stage (up to 100 C.E.) was marked by a variety, or plurality, of biblical texts, unlike the period after 100 C.E., which testifies to a stable textual tradition. MurXII (first half of the second century C.E.) is a prime example of this stable tradition.[16] As for Isaiah, the most relevant witnesses dating to this (second) period are MurIsa, Aquila, Symmachus, T-Isa, S-Isa, and V-Isa, all reflecting the proto-Masoretic tradition. But what can be said of the text of Isaiah in the period before 100 C.E. in the light of the new evidence, the Isaiah texts discovered at Qumran?

6.1.2.2.1 Character of the Isaiah Manuscripts Compared with MT

Since the texts of Isaiah found at Qumran (→ 6.2.1) differ from MT (→ 6.2.2), the question arises as to how these texts should be characterized. Of particular interest is the issue of how to typify the great Isaiah scroll (1QIsa^a; → 6.2.1.1; → 6.2.3.1), which is not as close to MT as the other Isaiah texts, 1QIsa^b and the Cave 4 Isaiah manuscripts.

Based on a detailed analysis of 1QIsa^a, Kutscher subscribed to the view of earlier scholarship that this text is best considered to belong to the "vulgar," or popular type, which is to be distinguished from the "standard" text attested by MT.[17] He came to this conclusion in particular because of the large majority of substitutions in the scroll.[18] Notably, labelling the manuscript this way he applied distinctions made in antiquity, when "popular" texts were produced for study purposes.

Other scholars preferred to characterize this and other Isaiah manuscripts only from the perspective of the MT tradition. As to 1QIsa^a and 1QIsa^b, Barthélemy argued for a rather specific distinction as far as terminology is concerned. He did not think of 1QIsa^b (→ 6.2.1.2) as "proto-Masoretic" because, in his definition, a proto-Masoretic text should be very close, even in particular minutiae, to MT (= the text of MT^L and related medieval manuscripts), such as is the case with the phylacteries of the Second Revolt and MurXII (Mur88; → 9.2.1.9). In view of the fact that 1QIsa^b is not that close to MT, this manuscript is described by him as "pre-Masoretic."[19] 1QIsa^a on the other hand is labelled as "extra-Masoretic," the particular reason being that, unlike 1QIsa^b, "the corrections made in 1QIsa^a do not move it toward M."[20]

---

[15] Cf. Skehan, "Qumran Manuscripts"; Morrow, "Text of Isaiah"; *HUB, Isaiah*, and Barthélemy, *Critique textuelle 1986*. The data in *BHS Isaiah only cover 1QIsa^a and 1QIsa^b.

[16] As a result, scholars have placed more emphasis on the notion of a periodization as far as the transmission history is concerned. For example, the *HOTTP reflected a view on the textual history according to which four stages can be distinguished: 1) the literary growth of a book; 2) the earliest attested text (300 B.C.E.–70 C.E.); 3) the stage consisting of the consonantal text as authorized by Jewish scholars shortly after 70 C.E., i.e., the proto-Masoretic text; 4) the Masoretic Text (ninth and tenth centuries) (Barthélemy, *Studies*, 87).

[17] Kutscher, *Language*, 78–79.
[18] Kutscher, *Language*, 79.
[19] Barthélemy, *Studies*, 389–403.
[20] Barthélemy, *Studies*, 406. As to 1QIsa^b, see also van der Kooij, *Textzeugen*, 124 ("Vorläufer des protomasoretischen Textes").

Reviewing the Isaiah texts found at Qumran, Tov distinguishes between "two groups of text" from the perspective of "scribal traditions."[21] In his view, most of the Isaiah texts from Qumran belong to "the group of MT," whereas two texts, 1QIsa^a and 4QIsa^c, both marked by the characteristics of the Qumran scribal practice, form another group.[22] In line with Barthélemy, 1QIsa^b in particular is viewed as "closely aligned with the MT"[23] but, unlike the former, Tov characterizes this text, along with other Isaiah texts of Qumran, as "proto-Masoretic."[24]

In his *Handbuch, Lange observes that 1QIsa^a is a text type of its own because, although close to MT, it is characterized by harmonizations and exegetical modifications.[25] In line with Tov, he typifies 1QIsa^b as proto-Masoretic, but some Isaiah manuscripts from Cave 4 (4QIsa^{a-b}, 4QIsa^{d-f}) are labelled by him as semi-Masoretic in order to indicate that these Isaiah manuscripts, displaying "minor" variant readings, are not as close to MT as 1QIsa^b.

Subsequent comparative analyses of 1QIsa^b and MT have led to views similar to that of Barthélemy. Abegg argues that on the basis of "the orthographic practice used, it is not likely that 1QIsa^b is a direct descendant or ancestor of the scroll whose offspring survives in MT."[26] Flint, too, is of the opinion that in view of the presence of "substantial variants" as well as a large number of "minor ones," the "affinity" between 1QIsa^b and MT is "less intimate than many believe."[27]

As may be clear, the characterizations of the Isaiah manuscripts from Qumran referred to above are mainly made from the perspective of the MT tradition. Distinctions are made by labelling manuscripts as "proto-MT," "pre-MT," "semi-MT," and "extra-MT," which raises the issue of definition and of the criteria involved. The term "proto-MT" is used by some in a rather global sense (cf. Tov, Lange), whereas others employ it in a stricter sense, i.e., referring to the consonantal text of MT (cf. Barthélemy). Except for Kutscher, the evaluations given do not relate to the issue of the purpose or function of the manuscripts.

6.1.2.2.2 A Single Literary Edition

As in the case of other biblical texts from Qumran, the texts of Isaiah display a variety of readings, not only in comparison to MT, but also compared with one another. The number of variant readings for Isaiah attested by the manuscripts found at Qumran (→ 6.2.3) is much higher than scholars working in times before the Qumran discoveries could have imagined. In some cases, the new readings concern instances where MT was regarded difficult or corrupt,[28] but in many instances the manuscripts offer variant readings in places where the Hebrew text of Isaiah was considered to be unproblematic.

In the cases of Exodus and Jeremiah, as well as some other books, scholars have argued that the textual evidence preserves "variant literary editions."[29] What about Isaiah? Research on several aspects of 1QIsa^a, first of all the large number of divergent readings as compared with MT, made scholars realize that many of these readings are of a secondary nature. Furthermore, 1QIsa^b (→ 6.2.1.2) was recognized as being very close to MT, which also applies to most of the Cave 4 Isaiah texts. Hence, in contrast to books such as Exodus and Jeremiah, the conclusion was drawn that "only a single literary edition is preserved for Isaiah."[30] Or, as stated by Tov: The "present textual data for Isaiah [...] point to a picture of textual *unity*."[31] The phrase "the present textual data" is meant to include LXX-

---

[21] Tov, "Text of Isaiah."
[22] Tov, "Text of Isaiah," 508–09.
[23] Tov, "Text of Isaiah," 506.
[24] Tov, "Text of Isaiah," 507.
[25] Lange, *Handbuch, 262 ("Harmonisierungen und exegetische Bearbeitungen").
[26] Abegg, "Rematch," 227.
[27] Flint, "Variant Readings," 52. In listing the variants, Flint also refers to the variants found in the collations of Kennicott, *1776–1780, and De Rossi, *1784–1788, including readings that are attested by late medieval manuscripts only.

[28] In a few cases, conjectural emendations proposed by early scholars did show up in the new evidence; e.g., the suggestion made by scholars (such as Michaelis) to read מרהבה "raging" instead of the difficult מדהבה "insolence" in Isa 14:4 is attested by 1QIsa^a.
[29] Ulrich, "Isaiah," 386.
[30] Ulrich, "Isaiah," 386; cf. Flint, "Book of Isaiah," 237.
[31] Tov, "Text of Isaiah," 505.

Isa, which as Tov points out can be regarded as based on a parent text close to MT (→ 6.2.2).

6.1.2.2.3 Hebrew Texts Underlying the Known Texts

Scholars agree that in the case of Isaiah the textual data dating to the first period of manuscript evidence do not point to multiple editions, but rather "to a single main edition of the work circulating in Judaism in the late Second Temple period."[32] This does not imply that in this period the Isaiah text should be considered as being in full agreement with MT. Issues at stake are the character of the Hebrew texts underlying the known witnesses, and the search for distinctive readings that represent an older tradition than MT.

In general, scholars believe that the Isaiah texts of Qumran and also the Greek versions (→ 6.3; LXX, *kaige*-Th), all dating to the first period of manuscript evidence, reflect a text or group of texts close to MT (→ 6.2.2). True, the *Vorlage* of a text like 1QIsa^a (→ 6.2.1.1; → 6.2.3.1) cannot be easily characterized because scribes who employed the Qumran scribal practice took many liberties, and this also applies to the parent text of LXX-Isa. There are, however, good reasons to believe that the consonantal texts underlying 1QIsa^a and LXX-Isa did not differ much from MT.[33]

If so, the next question is to what extent the text underlying the Qumran manuscripts of Isaiah and the parent texts of LXX and *kaige*-Th may be identified with the textual tradition of proto-MT. When viewed from another angle, we may also ask which variant readings attested by the early witnesses are pre-Masoretic. In view of the available data, it is likely indeed that the parent text or texts of Isaiah, dating to the period before 100 C.E., differed from proto-MT, not only in matters of spelling, but also in the case of specific readings "in which the medieval text reflects a later development."[34]

One of the cases that is held as a strong candidate of a pre-MT origin is the plus "light" in 1QIsa^a, 1QIsa^b, 4QIsa^d, as well as LXX-Isa 53:11.[35] In dealing with twenty-one variants supported by both 1QIsa^a and 1QIsa^b,[36] Barthélemy claims that this variant, together with two others in Isa 53:11–12,[37] have "the greatest weight [...] because they have the support of the only four witnesses to be rooted in a textual state prior to standardization": 1QIsa^a, 1QIsa^b, 4QIsa^d, and LXX-Isa.[38] As far as 1QIsa^b is concerned, he then argues that the unity of the three variants in Isa 53:11–12 shows that "1QIsa^b is clearly situated before the proto-Masoretic textual stabilization."[39] Other variants are considered to fall into "the category of the minor variants that can show up within a single stream of textual transmission."[40] The alleged textual standardization, in his view, "took place between the two Jewish revolts."[41]

Focusing on large minuses ("a sentence or two") in 1QIsa^a compared with MT, e.g., Isa 34:17–35:2; 38:20b–22; 40:7–8, Ulrich argued that the former testifies to a less expanded version of the book than MT ("Composition"). In his view, the relevant data in 1QIsa^a, as well as a few in LXX-Isa (2:22; 36:7), point to expansions of a rather late date (third, second, or even first century B.C.E.), making up the latter stages of "the developmental composition" of Isaiah.[42]

In dealing with variants attested by two or more Qumran Isaiah manuscripts, van der Kooij concluded that "while in a few cases shared readings in Qumran MSS testify to a better text, in many cases the combined evidence turns out to be of a secondary nature."[43] In his view, MT seems to attest a textual tradition that was transmitted in the early

---

[32] Ulrich, "Isaiah," 386.
[33] Cf., e.g., Koenig, *L'herméneutique*; van der Kooij, *Textzeugen*; Tov, "Text of Isaiah"; Lange, *Handbuch*; R. Troxel, *LXX-Isaiah as Translation and Interpretation* (JSJSup 124; Leiden: Brill, 2007).
[34] Tov, "Text of Isaiah," 507.
[35] See, e.g., Tov, "Text of Isaiah," 507.
[36] Barthélemy, *Studies*, 397–403.
[37] "Sins" against "sin" (sg.) in MT, and "their sins" against "sinners" in MT, both in v. 12.
[38] Barthélemy, *Studies*, 402.
[39] Barthélemy, *Studies*, 403.
[40] Barthélemy, *Studies*, 403.
[41] Cf. Barthélemy, *Studies*, 383: "toward the end of the first century A.D."
[42] See also Ulrich, "Isaiah," 386–87, and *DJD* XXXII.2, 90.
[43] Van der Kooij, "Early Witnesses," 152.

days – third century B.C.E. to second century C.E. – in a fairly accurate way.

Scholars thus have developed various views on the character of the parent texts and their relationship with the MT tradition. These views are based on the evaluation of particular readings. They have in common that some textual development has taken place, from pre-MT to proto-MT, but differ as to the details. The changes implied concern minor variants relating to the spelling of words, as well as specific readings such as Isa 53:11, or are related to the idea of expansions in MT. Current research has made it clear that the question of which variant readings might be regarded as pre-MT, and which not, is still a matter of dispute. So, according to van der Kooij, the well-known variants in Isa 53:11–12 are likely to be regarded as secondary,[44] whereas Stromberg in a detailed discussion of the initial absence of Isa 38:21–22 in 1QIsa^a, concludes that it is plausible to take it as evidence of scribal omission rather than of secondary expansion.[45] On the whole, scholars agree that the parent texts of Isaiah in the period before 100 C.E., all being close to MT, point to a fairly stable text tradition of the book. At the same time, it is also clear that more research is needed, in particular of the great Isaiah scroll and of LXX-Isa (→ 6.3), in order to provide a less global and more precise picture of the earliest attested text of Isaiah.

6.1.2.2.4 Quotations and Allusions to Isaiah in the Dead Sea Scrolls

In addition to the Isaiah manuscripts found at Qumran, Isaiah is also quoted or alluded to in a fair number of instances in pesharim and other manuscripts among the Dead Sea Scrolls. The relevant data are to be found in *HUB Isaiah, as well as in the *Handbuch by Lange, and in Flint, "Scriptural Isaiah." These data represent important evidence to be taken into account in the study of the early transmission history of Isaiah. Dealing with the quotations and allusions of Isaiah in pesharim and other Dead Sea scrolls, Lange comes to the conclusion that except for minor deviations the text quoted in the preserved fragments is close to MT.[46] The conclusions drawn by Flint are similar: consonantal MT-Isa (proto-MT) seems to have been "the most prevalent text available to the Qumranites."[47] The data in the pesharim, he concludes, agree in general with proto-MT, but include distinctive readings also found in 1QIsa^a and LXX-Isa.[48]

6.1.2.2.5 Commentaries

In general, commentaries on Isaiah published from 1950 onwards pay some attention to text-critical issues, while extensive notes are to be found in the volumes on Isaiah in the BKAT series (Wildberger; Elliger; Hermisson), and in the ICC volume by Williamson (*Isaiah 1–5*). The commentaries not only discuss variant readings attested by ancient witnesses – particularly 1QIsa^a and LXX-Isa – but they also deal with difficult readings in MT, where the ancient witnesses are of no help.

6.1.3 Literary History and History of Reception

This section touches on two important issues relating to the textual history of Isaiah: a) the relationship between the textual history and the literary history of the book; and b) the connection between the textual history and the history of reception. In what follows, the focus will not be limited to the Qumran evidence but includes all the ancient versions of Isaiah.

The relationship between the variety of biblical texts as attested by the Dead Sea Scrolls has become an important topic in modern research of the literary history of biblical books. It has led to the idea that in the Hellenistic and early Roman periods sometimes more than one literary edition existed of some of the biblical books. In the case of Isaiah, scholars agree that the Dead Sea Scrolls do not testify to a literary edition other than that represented by MT (→ 6.1.2.2.2). It has been argued

---

[44] Van der Kooij, "Early Witnesses," 150–52.
[45] Stromberg, "Redaction Criticism," 188. Cf. Tov, *TCHB, 310–11.
[46] Lange, *Handbuch, 290.
[47] Flint, "Scriptural Isaiah," 404.
[48] Flint, "Scriptural Isaiah," 405.

though that 1QIsaᵃ (→ 6.2.1.1; → 6.2.3.1) and LXX-Isa (→ 6.3) offer data that point to expansions in MT (→ 6.2.2) of a rather late date, suggesting that the final redaction took place in the late Second Temple period. The point at stake here concerns the relationship between the literary history of Isaiah, on the one hand, and the early witnesses, 1QIsaᵃ and LXX-Isa, on the other.

6.1.3.1 Literary History

In line with modern research, the book of Isaiah is to be considered the outcome of a literary growth over a long period of time. Although scholars do not share the same views on the literary history of Isaiah, they agree that this book consists of earlier and later portions, including portions that go back to the time of the prophet himself (end of eighth century B.C.E.).[49] The growth of the book can be regarded, roughly speaking, as being due to the production of new prophecies that were meant to make already existing collections relevant for later periods in history, from the seventh century onwards.[50] Viewed this way, the production of the book of Isaiah as a whole attests to a strong interest in actualization by means of expanding earlier prophecies as well as by adding new ones. At some moment, however, this process was discontinued as no new prophecies were added. Scholars differ regarding the completion date of the book, but passages like 2 Chr 32:32 and Sir 48:22–25 (Hebrew) seem to suggest that the completed book of Isaiah was extant in the late Persian period, or alternatively in the early Hellenistic era.[51] As with the other "books of the ancestors," as they are called in the Prologue of Ben Sira, the Isaiah scroll presumably was kept in the temple at Jerusalem, and preserved by the appropriate authorities, the chief priests.[52] However, all this does not imply that the "completed" book of Isaiah should be considered the "final" text as represented in the MT tradition.

In accordance with → 6.1.2.1, it is suggested that the aim of text-critical studies should not be the establishment of the earliest attested text, or the original text in the sense of the completed edition, because in practice these distinctions are hardly of any significance.[53] The text-critical evaluation of a given reading usually requires an analysis of the immediate context (pericope, chapter) of the reading involved. As a result, the alleged date of a given passage in the book, and not that of the book as a whole, can play an important role. This implies a historical perspective, which can have a bearing on the evaluation of variant readings, e.g., in cases of a linguistic type, because the Hebrew of texts going back to exilic and pre-exilic times differs from the so-called Late Biblical Hebrew or the Dead Sea Scrolls Hebrew. The following two examples illustrate the significance of the linguistic history of ancient Hebrew for evaluating variant readings.[54]

Isa 23:10 – instead of the expression used in MT ("to pass through [עבר] the land"), 1QIsaᵃ and LXX testify to the phrase "to till the land" (עבד הארץ). It may well be that the latter expression would be acceptable in terms of Dead Sea Scrolls Hebrew but the phrase עבד האדמה "to till the land" would be expected in biblical Hebrew. As a result, the reading of MT is to be preferred.

Isa 45:2 – instead of הדורים "mountainous country" in MT, the most ancient witnesses (1QIsaᵃ, 1QIsaᵇ, and LXX) attest the reading "mountains." Although this reading makes sense in the context ("I will level mountains"; compare Isa 40:3), the difficulty with this solution is that the reduplicated plural (הררים) does not occur in biblical Hebrew in the absolute state. As has been argued by scholars, MT may well represent the original reading if taken in the sense of "the walls," in line with the Akkadian *duru*. Contextually, this would fit even better because of the "doors of bronze" and "bars of iron" in the rest of the verse.[55]

---

[49] Cf., e.g., de Jong, *Isaiah*.
[50] For the hypothesis of a seventh-century collection, see in particular de Jong, *Isaiah*, 358–442.
[51] For the latter date, see e.g. Steck, *Heimkehr*, 80.
[52] See Tov, *TCHB*, 183; Tov, "Some Thoughts," 166, and van der Kooij, "Standardization or Preservation."

[53] Cf. Tov, *TCHB*, 168–69.
[54] Cf. Holmstedt, "Textual Criticism."
[55] Cf. van der Kooij, "Early Witnesses," 145–46.

The completed book of Isaiah being the outcome of a literary growth raises the question of which concept of "book" might have been involved in the Assyrian, Babylonian, and Persian periods. Van der Toorn has pointed out that our (modern) concept of books is "unsuited to describe the written production from the Ancient Near East."[56] Seen from this perspective, it is unlikely that a document like the completed book of Isaiah was copied and published in the early days. Being the result of a growing corpus, it rather was a collection of oracles including also supporting narratives "that was preserved and studied by a small body of specialists."[57]

6.1.3.2 Textual History and History of Reception

Unlike the previous period in time, the Hellenistic era in which 1QIsa^a (→ 6.2.1.1; → 6.2.3.1) and LXX-Isa (→ 6.3) originated was marked by book production (van der Toorn). This is illustrated, on the Jewish side, by the existence of copies of "biblical" texts, the publication of translations of these or other texts, as well as the making of new books (e.g., Wisdom of Ben Sira [→ 11.4], *Jubilees* [→ 11.8]). Importantly, the Hellenistic era is also characterized by the reading and study of ancient books like Isaiah.[58] As is clear from the Isaiah manuscripts among the Dead Sea Scrolls and from LXX-Isa, no new pericopes or chapters were added in the late Second Temple period. On the contrary, in order to make the book of Isaiah relevant for that time, it was studied and interpreted as is evident from sources such as the Isaiah pesharim.

The transmission history of Isaiah is closely related to the history of reception and interpretation. As has been pointed out by scholars, the ancient translations of Isaiah, not only that dating from the Hellenistic era, LXX-Isa, but also the versions dating to the period after 100 C.E., T-Isa, Sym-Isa, S-Isa, and V-Isa, all attest to forms of interpretation of the book, containing cases of exegesis based on study of the text of Isaiah. The extent of exegesis in these versions though, particularly the "higher level" interpretation, differs due to the choice made regarding the style of translation. S-Isa (→ 6–9.1.4), for example, reflects a translation style that leaves little room for exegesis,[59] whereas LXX-Isa (→ 6.3) and T-Isa (→ 6–9.1.3) are fairly rich in this regard; this, albeit to a lesser extent, also applies to V-Isa.

Therefore, one may assume that the ancient versions of Isaiah were produced by persons who were not only able and authorized to make a translation but who were also familiar with the reading and interpretation of the underlying Hebrew text of Isaiah. In the light of the state of literacy in antiquity, in particular regarding the societies of Egypt, Judea, and Mesopotamia, they must be looked for among the intellectual elite. The sacred "ancestral" (cf. the Prologue of Sirach) writings were literary creations, a category quite distinct from documentary texts. The ability to read and study the former required skills of a higher level[60] than was required for those who were engaged with documentary texts. It is likely indeed that only highly educated people, "scholars,"[61] who were able and authorized to interpret literary texts were also the ones who wrote new compositions, being based in one way or another on the study of "biblical" books,[62] or produced a translation of the sacred writings. Leading scholars (priests) were also involved in the produc-

---

[56] Van der Toorn, *Scribal Culture*, 5. Cf. the following statement on the same page: "Prior to the Hellenistic era – that is, before ca. 300 B.C.E. – there were no books. There were documents, literary compilations, myths, collections of prayers, ritual prescriptions, chronicles, and the like, but no books, no trade in books, and no reading public of any substance."

[57] Van der Toorn, *Scribal Culture*, 5. The earlier stages of this and other books are sometimes designated "editions." This, however, is confusing because it would imply that any of these stages in the literary history of a book is supposed to be a literary piece (a book) that could be copied, transmitted, or published.

[58] The literature on "biblical" interpretation in early Judaism is extensive. See, e.g., Henze, *Companion*.

[59] This is even more so in the cases of *kaige*-Th-Isa and Aq-Isa.

[60] On this issue, see, e.g., Unsok Ro, "Socio-Economic Context," 602–03.

[61] I prefer the term "scholar" to "scribe" because the latter is ambiguous as it can refer to a scholar (cf. Ezra, "the scribe") as well as to a secretary.

[62] Cf. Jesus ben Sirach.

tion of LXX-Isa and of T-Isa.[63] In this regard, one should also think of Jerome who, as a scholar, produced v-Isa (→ 6–9.1.7).

Seen from this perspective, modifications or transformations introduced by scholar-translators in their versions are best understood as being due to their study of their sources in Hebrew. These elements were meant, among other things, to elucidate a particular meaning and to express a particular interpretation, thus enhancing the significance of the book. Apart from the ancient versions referred to above, this view may also shed light on 1QIsa[a]. Though representing a witness of the text of Isaiah in Hebrew, scholars agree that it does not represent a copy in the strict sense of the word.[64] Features such as harmonization, the substitution of roots and nouns, and variant readings of an interpretive nature[65] suggest that the scroll was produced by someone familiar with the reading and the interpretation of the book.

In my view, a distinction should be made between the literary history of the book of Isaiah and its textual history. From the point of view of the content and the meaning of the book, one could say that the former period (i.e. the stage of literary history) is marked by "a scribal reinterpretation of earlier prophetic legacies"[66] prompting the development of the prophetic book, whereas in the latter period (i.e. the textual history and history of reception) copies and translations were produced, which in some cases and in various ways testify to an interest in the study and interpretation of the completed book. Thus, both periods share an interpretive interest but the methods employed in the case of Isaiah are different: the expansion of earlier texts in the former period and modifications and transformations of the text, mainly so in LXX-Isa and T-Isa, in the latter.[67]

To return to the point of departure – the thesis that 1QIsa[a] and LXX-Isa offer data pointing to expansions of MT in the late Second Temple period – the above is not meant to say that the pre-MT text of Isaiah was transmitted in the early days, 250 B.C.E. to 100 C.E., without any changes made. However, since this period is marked by a great interest in the study and interpretation of Scripture, it would be worthwhile also to consider the alternative possibility, namely that of examining cases of (long) pluses and minuses in both witnesses from the perspective of a literary strategy serving a specific exegesis of a given passage.[68]

---

[63] Cf. van der Kooij, "Septuagint of Isaiah," and van der Kooij, "Josephus, Onkelos, and Jonathan," 260–65.

[64] Cf. Kutscher, *Language, 77; van der Kooij, Textzeugen, 116; Pulikottil, Transmission, 42–43; Lange, *Handbuch, 262.

[65] Well-known examples are: Isa 6:10 ("Make the heart of this people appalled" instead of "Make the heart of this people fat" in MT), and Isa 22:5 ("Devastating his sanctuary on the mountain" instead of "A battering down of walls, and a shouting to the mountains" in MT). For the aspect of exegesis in the scroll, see, e.g., Brownlee, Meaning, 165–215; van der Kooij, Textzeugen, 81–97; Koenig, L'herméneutique, 201–367; Pulikottil, Transmission; Lange, *Handbuch, 261.

[66] De Jong, "Biblical Prophecy," 39.

Abegg, M.G., "1QIsa-a and 1QIsa-b: A Rematch," in *The Bible as Book, 221–22.

Alexander, P.S., "What happened to the Jewish Priesthood after 70?" in A Wandering Galilean: Essays in Honour of Seán Freyne (eds. Z. Rodgers, with M. Daly-Denton and A. Fitzpatrick McKinley; JSJSup 132; Leiden: Brill, 2009), 5–33.

Barthélemy, *Critique textuelle 1992.

Barthélemy, *Studies.

Brownlee, W.H., The Meaning of the Qumran Scrolls for the Bible: With Special Attention to the Book of Isaiah (New York: Oxford University Press, 1964).

Dillmann, A., Der Prophet Jesaia (5th ed.; Kurzgefaßtes exegetisches Handbuch zum Alten Testament 5; Leipzig: Hirzel, 1890).

Flint, P.W., "The Book of Isaiah in the Dead Sea Scrolls," in *The Bible as Book, 229–51.

Flint, P.W., "Variant Readings and Textual Affiliation in the Hebrew University Isaiah Scroll from Cave One (1QISA[B])," in Qumran Cave 1 Revisited: Texts from Cave 1 Sixty Years after Their Discovery: Proceedings of the Sixth Meeting of the IOQS in Ljubljana (eds. D.K. Falk et al.; STDJ 91; Leiden, Brill, 2010), 33–53.

Flint, P.W., "Scriptural Isaiah in the Qumran Scrolls," in A Teacher for All Generations: Essays in Honor of James

---

[67] For a recent discussion on these and related issues, see the contributions in Kratz and Popovic, The Dead Sea Scrolls and the Hebrew Bible.

[68] For an example in LXX-Isa 36:7, see van der Kooij, Textzeugen, 55.

C. VanderKam, Vol. 1 (eds. E.F. Mason et al.; JSJSup 153; Leiden, Brill, 2012), 389–406.

Gesenius, W., *Der Prophet Jesaja: Uebersetzt und mit einem vollständigen philologisch-kritischen und historischen Commentar begleitet* (3 vols.; Leipzig: Vogel, 1820–1821).

Gray, G.B., *A Critical and Exegetical Commentary on the Book of Isaiah: I–XXXIX*, Vol. 1: *Introduction, and Commentary on I–XXVII* (ICC; Edinburgh, T & T Clark, 1912)

Henze, M. (ed.), *A Companion to Biblical Interpretation in Early Judaism* (Grand Rapids: Eerdmans, 2012).

Holmstedt, R.D., "The Nexus between Textual Criticism and Linguistics: A Case Study from Leviticus," *JBL* 132 (2013): 473–94.

de Jong, M.J., *Isaiah among the Ancient Near Eastern Prophets: A Comparative Study of the Earliest Stages of the Isaiah Tradition and the Neo-Assyrian Prophecies* (VTSup 117; Leiden: Brill, 2007).

de Jong, M.J., "Biblical Prophecy – A Scribal Enterprise: The Old Testament Prophecy of Unconditional Judgement Considered as a Literary Phenomenon," *VT* 61 (2011): 39–70.

Kittel, R., *Über die Notwendigkeit und Möglichkeit einer neuen Ausgabe der hebräischen Bibel: Studien und Erwägungen* (Leipzig: Edelmann, 1901).

Koenig, **L'herméneutique analogique*.

van der Kooij, A., *Die alten Textzeugen des Jesajabuches: Ein Beitrag zur Textgeschichte des Alten Testaments* (OBO 35; Göttingen: Vandenhoeck & Ruprecht, 1981).

van der Kooij, A., "The Text of Isaiah and its Early Witnesses in Hebrew," in *Sôfer Mahîr: Essays in Honour of Adrian Schenker Offered by the Editors of Biblia Hebraica Quinta* (eds. Y.A.P. Goldman, A. van der Kooij, and R.D. Weis; VTSup 110; Leiden, Brill, 2006), 143–52.

van der Kooij, A., "Josephus, Onkelos, and Jonathan: On the Agreements between Josephus' Works and Targumic Sources," in *Studies on the Text and Versions of the Hebrew Bible in Honour of Robert Gordon* (eds. G. Khan and D. Lipton; VTSup 149; Leiden: Brill, 2012), 253–68.

van der Kooij, A., "The Septuagint of Isaiah," in J. Cook and A. van der Kooij, *Law, Prophets, and Wisdom: On the Provenance of Translators and Their Books in the Septuagint Version* (CBET 68; Leuven: Peeters, 2012), 63–85.

van der Kooij, A., "Standardization or Preservation? Some Comments on the Textual History of the Hebrew Bible in the Light of Josephus and Rabbinic Literature," in *The Text of the Hebrew Bible: From the Rabbis to Masoretes* (eds. L. Miralles-Macía and E. Martín Contreras; Journal of Ancient Judaism Supplements 13; Göttingen: Vandenhoeck & Ruprecht, 2014), 63–78.

Kratz, R.G. and M. Popovic (eds.), *The Dead Sea Scrolls and the Hebrew Bible* (DSD 20.3; Leiden: Brill, 2013).

Kutscher, **Language*.

Lange, **Handbuch*.

Morrow, F., "The Text of Isaiah at Qumran" (unpubl. PhD diss., The Catholic University of America, 1973).

Ottley, R.R., *The Book of Isaiah according to the Septuagint (Codex Alexandrinus)*. Vol. 1: *Introduction and Translation* (London: Cambridge University Press, 1904); Vol. 2: *Text and Notes* (Cambridge: Cambridge University Press, 1906).

Pulikottil, P., *Transmission of Biblical Texts in Qumran: The Case of the Large Isaiah Scroll (1QIsa^a)* (JSPSup 34; Sheffield: Sheffield Academic Press, 2001).

Skehan, P.W., "The Qumran Manuscripts and Textual Criticism," in *Volume du Congrès Strasbourg 1956* (VTSup 4; Leiden: Brill, 1957), 148–60.

Steck, O.H., *Bereitete Heimkehr. Jesaja 35 als redaktionelle Brücke zwischen dem Ersten und dem Zweiten Jesaja* (SBS 121; Stuttgart: Katholisches Bibelwerk, 1985).

Stromberg, J., "The Role of Redaction Criticism in the Evaluation of a Textual Variant: Another Look at 1QIsa^a XXXII 14 (38:21–22)," *DSD* 16 (2009): 155–89.

van der Toorn, K., *Scribal Culture and the Making of the Hebrew Bible* (Cambridge: Harvard University Press, 2007).

Tov, E., "The Text of Isaiah at Qumran," in *Writing and Reading the Scroll of Isaiah: Studies of an Interpretive Tradition* (eds. C.C. Broyles and C.A. Evans; VTSup 70.2; Leiden: Brill, 1997), 491–512.

Tov, E., "Some Thoughts About the Diffusion of Biblical Manuscripts in Antiquity," in *The Dead Sea Scrolls: Transmission of Traditions and Production of Texts* (eds. S. Metso, H. Najman, and E. Schuller; STDJ 92; Leiden: Brill, 2010), 151–72.

Tov, **TCHB*.

Ulrich, E., "Isaiah, Book of," in **EDSS* 1:384–88.

Ulrich, E., "The Developmental Composition of the Book of Isaiah: Light from 1QIsa^a on Additions in MT," *DSD* 8 (2001): 288–305.

Unsok Ro, J., "Socio-Economic Context of Post-Exilic Community and Literacy," *ZAW* 120 (2008): 597–611.

Arie van der Kooij

6.2 Ancient Hebrew Texts

6.2.1 Ancient Manuscript Evidence

The manuscript evidence for the Hebrew text of Isaiah consists of MT-Isa (→ 6.2.2) as well as twenty-two manuscripts from the Judean wilderness. There are two important manuscripts of Isaiah from Qumran Cave 1, the famous 1QIsa^a, and 1QIsa^b. From Qumran Cave 4, there are eighteen manuscripts, some very fragmentary, and from Cave 5 there is one manuscript of only two fragments. From Murabba'at, there is one manuscript of only one large fragment. Some of the manuscripts from Cave 4 are too small to know with any certainty whether or not they are the remains of biblical manuscripts or of excerpted texts or citations of Isaiah from non-biblical compositions (4QIsa^{g,h,i,j,k,l,m,n,q,r}, 4QpapIsa^p, 5QIsa, MurIsa). The manuscripts of Isaiah that are too small to be able to discern any information about their textual affiliations will be presented as a group in list form below. All of these manuscripts will be listed and described in this article. This article will not discuss the pesharim on Isaiah from Caves 3 and 4 at Qumran (3QpIsa [3Q4]; 4QpIsa^{a,b,c,d,e} [4Q161–165]; 4Q550^f) or the Isaiah citations in 4QTanḥ (4Q176) as they are treated in → 21.2.1. One manuscript preserves a proto-Masoretic text (1QIsa^b; → 6.2.2). Two manuscripts preserve non-aligned texts (1QIsa^a, 4QIsa^c; → 6.2.3), and five manuscripts preserve semi-Masoretic texts (4QIsa^{a,b,d,e,f}; → 6.2.2).

6.2.1.1 1QIsa^a

With the following minor exceptions, the entire book of Isaiah has been preserved in this famous manuscript (→ 6.2.3.1): Isa 1:21, 23–26; 2:15, 17, 19–21; 5:10–14; 7:9–12, 14–15; 8:7; 10:13–14; 14:27, 29; 45:10–14. With regard to the paleography of 1QIsa^a, Ulrich and Flint cite the dating by Cross to ca. 125–100 B.C.E.[1] which is in good agreement with the C¹⁴ dating given in the article of Jull et al.[2] If the dating of the Qumran settlement by Magness is correct, then it is less likely that 1QIsa^a was copied at Qumran.[3] There is a long-standing view that 1QIsa^a was written by two scribes.[4] This is based in part on the clear division of the scroll into two sections with the first section ending at col. XXVII with a blank space of three lines; this corresponds to the end of Isaiah 33. The second section of the scroll begins at the top of col. XXVIII. In contrast, Flint and Ulrich conclude that 1QIsa^a was copied originally by a single scribe, but that the manuscript was edited by perhaps as many as seven different scribes in the course of its transmission, including, as is well known, the scribe who copied 1QS, 4QSam^c, and 4QTest and who was responsible for the insertion in col. XXXVIII.7 at Isa 40:7.[5] In the century after the production of the scroll as many as three hands of the early Herodian period (ca. 30–1 B.C.E.) also made insertions in the scroll.[6]

In their description of the orthography of 1QIsa^a, Ulrich and Flint maintain, "… in general the spelling in 1QIsa^a is noticeably fuller than that in 1QIsa^b and 𝔐 (see Tables 3 and 6)."[7] Ulrich and Flint state, "There is no clear system of orthography in 1QIsa^a, as there is none in 𝔐 or in other Qumran MSS, …"[8] There are characteristic "full spellings" for "כול, לוא, יאומר, קוטל (for the *Qal* participle)."[9] Also attested are the so-called "long forms" of the 2nd masculine singular perfect suffix, תה- for MT's תָ- as well as the 2nd masculine singular possessive suf-

---

[1] Ulrich and Flint, *DJD* XXXII: 61; Cross, "*Palaeography*," 388.

[2] A.J.T. Jull et al., "Radiocarbon Dating of Scrolls and Linen Fragments from the Judean Desert," *Radiocarbon* 37 (1995): 11–19.

[3] J. Magness, *The Archaeology of Qumran and the Dead Sea Scrolls* (Grand Rapids: Eerdmans, 2002), 63–69.

[4] See the references in Tov, "The Text of Isaiah at Qumran," 47 n. 37, 49–50.

[5] See especially the script chart in Ulrich and Flint, *DJD* XXXII: 62.

[6] Ulrich and Flint, *DJD* XXXII: 61–65.

[7] Ulrich and Flint, *DJD* XXXII: 88.

[8] Ulrich and Flint, *DJD* XXXII: 65.

[9] Ulrich and Flint, *DJD* XXXII: 65.

6.2.1 ANCIENT MANUSCRIPT EVIDENCE

fix, ‎כה- for MT's ‎ךְ. The forms ‎-המה and ‎-כמה are also attested. These are some of the characteristics that led Tov to describe 1QIsaᵃ as written in the Qumran Practice.[10] For an extensive table of characteristic spellings in 1QIsaᵃ, see Tables 3–6 in Ulrich and Flint.[11] Kutscher described the language of 1QIsaᵃ as reflecting the Hebrew and Aramaic spoken in Palestine toward the end of the Second Temple period.[12]

A comprehensive analysis of the readings and textual affiliations of 1QIsaᵃ has not been done and is a *desideratum*. The critical edition of this important manuscript by Ulrich and Flint makes such a study possible. Although they report approximately 2,600 textual variants with some "isolated interpretive insertions,"[13] both the Greek and the Hebrew manuscripts of Isaiah all witness to a single literary edition of Isaiah.[14] Ulrich and Flint concur with Kutscher that 1QIsaᵃ presents a later textual type than MT in terms of linguistic features, but that in terms of the development of the text of Isaiah, 1QIsaᵃ represents an earlier stage in the development of the text than MT-Isa (→ 6.2.2).[15] This argument is based in part on the material presented in Table 9, but the supporting discussion of those readings is found in Ulrich, "Developmental Composition."[16] Ulrich's arguments there are nuanced and sophisticated and frequently persuasive, however, he does not give sufficient consideration to the possibility of haplography in 1QIsaᵃ. In the cases of Isa 2:9b–10 and Isa 38:20–22, haplography is a reasonable explanation for the readings of 1QIsaᵃ and this possibility undermines his conclusions about the text preserved in 1QIsaᵃ and the relationship with MT- and LXX-Isa (→ 6.3).[17] If these readings resulted from haplographies when the scroll was copied, then Ulrich and Flint's idea that 1QIsaᵃ preserves an earlier form of the developing text of Isaiah is not so strongly supported and must be taken as a preliminary conclusion. As stated above, the systematic study of all of the readings of 1QIsaᵃ is a necessity. We may nevertheless accept the conclusion that "1QIsaᵇ and 𝔐ᴸ, 𝔐ᵠ, 𝔐ᵐˢˢ, 𝔄 form a close text-family, whereas 1QIsaᵃ and 𝔊, despite their many agreements, are distant enough from each other and from the 𝔐 tradition that they must each be assigned to different text families."[18] In summary, given the pattern of agreements and disagreements in the readings of this manuscript, 1QIsaᵃ may be described as a non-aligned manuscript.

6.2.1.2 1QIsaᵇ (1Q8)

1QIsaᵇ preserves completely or in part Isa 7:22–25; 8:1, 8 (or 10); 10:17–19; 12:3–6; 13:1–8, 16–19; 15:3–9; 16:1, 7–11; 19:7–17, 20–25; 20:1; 22:11–18, 24; 23:1–4; 24:18–23; 25:1–8; 26:1–5; 28:15–20; 29:1–8; 30:10–14, 21–26; 31:5–7; 32:17–20; 35:4; 36:14; 37:8–12; 38:12–22; 39:1–8; 40:2; 41:3–23; 43:1–13, 23–27; 44:21–28; 45:1–13; 46:3–13; 47:1–14; 48:17–22; 49:1–15; 50:7–11; 51:1–10; 52:7–15; 53:1–12; 54:1–6; 55:2–13; 56:1–12; 57:1–4, 17–20; 58:1–14; 59:1–8, 20; 60:1–22; 61:1; 62:2–12; 63:1–19; 64:1–8; 65:17–25; 66:1–24. The editors describe the script of this manuscript as late Hasmonean or early Herodian, dating to

---

[10] Tov, *Scribal Practices*, 268, 279, 339.

[11] Ulrich and Flint, *DJD* XXXII: 66–82.

[12] Kutscher, *Language*, 3.

[13] Ulrich and Flint, *DJD* XXXII: 89–90; see also the discussion of editorial readings and scribal activity in 1QIsaᵃ in Pulikottil, *Transmission of Biblical Texts in Qumran*, 44–129, 205–11.

[14] Ulrich and Flint, *DJD* XXXII: 89, 90, 91.

[15] Kutscher, *Language*, 2–3; Ulrich and Flint, *DJD* XXXII: 90.

[16] Ulrich and Flint, *DJD* XXXII: 91; Ulrich, "Developmental Composition," 288–305.

[17] The reading of 1QIsaᵃ for Isa 2:9–10 may be explained as a scribal error. Vv. 9b–10 are omitted entirely from 1QIsaᵃ, a reading which is unique. There are a number of haplographies attested in 1QIsaᵃ. In Isaiah 2, there are haplographies at Isa 2:3 and Isa 2:12, which were not corrected. There is also the well-known haplography in col. XXXII = Isa 38:21–22 where Isa 38:21–22 have been added by a later scribe. Vv. 21–22 dropped out of the text when the scribe's eye skipped from the divine name Yahweh at the end of v. 20 to the divine name Yahweh at the end of v. 22, an example of homoioteleuton. That large haplography was caught and corrected. Unfortunately, in 1QIsaᵃ II:18, which should preserve Isa 2:9b–10, there is another haplography resulting from the scribe's eye skipping from the *waw* of ‎ואל "do not" in v. 9b to the *waw* of ‎ועיני "and the eyes of" at the beginning of v. 11 where 1QIsaᵃ has *waw*, a unique reading.

[18] Ulrich and Flint, *DJD* XXXII: 91–92.

approximately the third quarter of the first century B.C.E. Eight corrections occur in the manuscript, all by the original scribe.[19] The orthography of 1QIsa[b] is quite close to that of MT[L], although 1QIsa[b] shows a tendency to spell the *Qal* participle with *waw* and MT[L] does not. There are also other minor variations in spelling.

For the textual characteristics of 1QIsa[b], the editors of the critical edition state, "On the whole, 1QIsa[b] shows close agreement with 𝔐[L], 𝔐[q], 𝔐[mss], and ℭ, which classifies it as belonging to the textual group that eventually emerges as the Masoretic family."[20] 1QIsa[b] shows only two quantitatively large variations from MT at Isa 38:12–13 and Isa 60:19–20. If, as the editors suggest, these omissions are the result of haplography on the part of the scribe of 1QIsa[b], then they are without meaning text-critically. There are other small variations from MT such as occasionally in the use of divine names or parallel words, but these are within the normal range of variation exhibited by manuscripts in the Masoretic family.[21] As has been the assessment since its first publication, 1QIsa[b] is best understood as textually close to MT and may be designated a proto-Masoretic text (→ 6.2.2).[22]

6.2.1.3 4QIsa[a] (4Q55)

The eighteen extant fragments of 4QIsa[a] preserve parts of Isa 1:1–3; 2:7–10; 4:5; 5:1; 6:4–8; 11:11–15; 12:4–6; 13:1–16; 17:9–14; 19:24; 20:1–6; 21:1–16; 22:13–25; 23:1–12; 33:16 in 405 complete or partial words. The editors describe the script of 4QIsa[a] as a late Hasmonean formal hand and date it to approximately the third quarter of the first century B.C.E.[23] They characterize the orthography of 4QIsa[a] as somewhat more full than MT, but not as full as 1QIsa[a].[24]

Approximately forty variants are preserved in 4QIsa[a] that vary from agreeing with MT (→ 6.2.2), LXX (→ 6.3), and the other Isaiah manuscripts

from Qumran.[25] There are no large textual variations preserved in this manuscript. 4QIsa[a] disagrees with MT-Isa twenty-one times and with LXX twenty times. In this manuscript, fifteen independent readings are preserved. 4QIsa[a] may be classified as a semi-Masoretic manuscript (→ 6.2.2).[26]

6.2.1.4 4QIsa[b] (4Q56)

Of the forty-eight extant fragments of 4QIsa[b] forty-three can still be identified. They preserve parts of Isa 1:1–6; 2:3–16; 3:14–22; 5:15–28; 9:10; 11:7–9; 12:2; 13:3–18; 17:8–18:1, 5–7; 19:1–20:4; 21:11–14; 22:24; 24:2, 4, 16; 26:1–5, 7–21; 27:1; 35:9–36:2; 37:29–32; 39:1–40:4; 40:22–26; 41:8–11; 42:2–7, 9–12; 43:12–15; 44:19–28; 45:20–46:3; 48:6–8; 49:21–23; 51:1, 14–16; 52:2, 7; 53:11; 55:12; 56:1; 61:1–3; 64:5–65:1; 66:24. The script of 4QIsa[b] is transitional between the late Hasmonean and early Herodian periods and can be dated to approximately the third quarter of the first century B.C.E.[27] The orthography of this manuscript is often less full than that of MT, but ocassionally more full than MT.[28] Similarly to 4QIsa[a], in 4QIsa[b] there are no large textual variations preserved. Most variations in the text consist of small changes in individual words. 4QIsa[b] agrees with MT-Isa seventy-six times and disagrees forty-two times. 4QIsa[b] agrees with LXX-Isa (→ 6.3) thirty-two times and disagrees fifty-six times. Finally twenty-nine independent readings are preserved in this manuscript. 4QIsa[b] is the largest of the Isaiah manuscripts from Cave 4 with ca. 1,000 complete or partial words preserved. 4QIsa[b] may be described as a semi-Masoretic manuscript (→ 6.2.2).[29]

6.2.1.5 4QIsa[c] (4Q57)

Of the seventy-seven extant fragments of 4QIsa[c] (→ 6.2.3.2), fifty-seven can be identified. They partially preserve Isa 9:3–12; 10:23–33; 11:4–11, 14–16; 12:1; 14:1–5, 13?; 22:10–14, 23; 23:8–18; 24:1–15, 19–23; 25:1, 8–12; 26:1–9; 28:6–14; 30:8–17; 33:2–8, 16–23; 44:3–7, 23; 45:1–4, 6–8; 46:8–13; 48:10–15, 17–19; 49:22; 51:8–

---

[19] For the paleography of 1QIsa[b], see Ulrich and Flint, *DJD* XXXII: 199–200.
[20] Ulrich and Flint, *DJD* XXXII: 208.
[21] Ulrich and Flint, *DJD* XXXII: 211.
[22] See also the references in Lange, *Handbuch*, 264 n. 50.
[23] Skehan and Ulrich, "Isaiah," 8.
[24] Skehan and Ulrich, "Isaiah," 8.

[25] Lange, *Handbuch*, 265.
[26] Lange, *Handbuch*, 254; cf. Tov, *Synthese*, 26.
[27] Skehan and Ulrich, "Isaiah," 20.
[28] See Table 2 in Skehan and Ulrich, "Isaiah," 21.
[29] Lange, *Handbuch*, 266; Tov, *"Synthese,"* 26.

6.2.1 ANCIENT MANUSCRIPT EVIDENCE

16; 52:10–15; 53:1–3, 6–8; 54:3–5, 7–17; 55:1–7; 66:20–24. 4QIsa[c] is the second largest of the Isaiah manuscripts from Cave 4 with 914 complete or partial words preserved. 4QIsa[c] is written in a developed Herodian hand from "the middle third of the 1st century CE,"[30] i.e., ca. 33–66 C.E. It is noteworthy that יהוה "Lord" is always written in paleo-Hebrew script, which dates to approximately the same time period as the Herodian hand. אלוהים "God" is also usually written in paleo-Hebrew letters as is צבאות "hosts" when it follows יהוה "Lord." The orthography of 4QIsa[c] is fuller than that of MT, 1QIsa[a], and 1QIsa[b].[31] The following forms are spelled plene: אדוני "Lord"; אלוהים "God"; זואת "this"; כוה "thus"; כול "all"; כיא "for"; and לוא "no." Tov describes 4QIsa[c] as written in the Qumran Scribal Practice.[32] 4QIsa[c] preserves forty independent readings in comparison to MT- (→ 6.2.2) and LXX-Isa (→ 6.3). This manuscript agrees with MT-Isa thirty-six times and goes against MT sixty times. 4QIsa[c] agrees with LXX-Isa twenty-two times and disagrees fifty times. Given the high number of independent readings, especially, 4QIsa[c] may be described as a non-aligned manuscript (→ 6.2.3).[33]

6.2.1.6 4QIsa[d] (4Q58)

Of the sixteen fragments preserved, fifteen can be identified and partially preserve Isa 45:20; 46:10–13; 47:1–6; 48:8–22; 49:1–15; 52:4–7; 53:8–12; 54:1–11; 57:9–21; 58:1–3, 5–7. 4QIsa[d] is significantly smaller than 4QIsa[b] and 4QIsa[c] with 467 complete or partial words preserved. The manuscript is written is a formal hand from the late Herodian period, approximately the middle of the first century C.E.[34] The orthography is more defective than MT.[35] There are only sixty-two small variations in the text of Isaiah preserved in 4QIsa[d] when compared with MT-Isa, LXX-Isa, and 1QIsa[a]. This manuscript reads with MT-Isa thirty times and reads against MT-Isa twenty-three times. It agrees with LXX-Isa (→ 6.3) twenty-four times and disagrees thirty-one times. 4QIsa[d] preserves nine independent readings. 4QIsa[d] may be classified as a semi-Masoretic manuscript (→ 6.2.2).[36]

6.2.1.7 4QIsa[e] (4Q59)

These twenty-five fragments partially preserve Isa 2:1–4; 7:17–20; 8:2–14; 9:17–20; 10:1–10; 11:14; 12:1–6; 13:1–4; 14:1–13, 20–24; 59:15. Only 328 complete or partial words are preserved in this manuscript. They belong to the first eight columns of the original scroll.

The editors describe the hand as early Herodian and date it to the late first century B.C.E. *Waw* and *yod* are not clearly distinguished.[37] The orthography of this manuscript is somewhat fuller than that of MT.[38] 4QIsa[e] preserves thirty-six non-orthographic variations in the preserved text of Isaiah when compered with MT-Isa, LXX-Isa, and 1QIsa[a]. 4QIsa[e] agrees with MT-Isa thirteen times and disagrees eighteen times. 4QIsa[e] reads with LXX-Isa (→ 6.3) ten times and twenty-one times reads against. Ten independent readings are preserved. There are very few variations from MT-Isa in 4QIsa[e]. 4QIsa[e] may be described as a semi-Masoretic manuscript (→ 6.2.2).[39]

6.2.1.8 4QIsa[f] (4Q60)

Of the thirty-four fragments of this manuscript, frgs. 32–34 are not identifiable. The following passages are partially preserved in the rest of the fragments: Isa 1:10–16, 18–31; 2:1–3; 5:13, 25; 6:3–8, 10–13; 7:16–18, 23–25; 8:1, 4–11; 20:4–6; 22:14–22, 25; 24:1–3; 27:1, 5, 8–12; 28:6–9, 16–18?, 22, 24?; 29:8. A total of 314 complete or partial words are preserved. The manuscript is inscribed in a "typical Hasmonean hand" dating from the first half of the first century B.C.E.[40] The orthography of this manuscript is close to MT[L] although there are thirteen minor variations from the spelling of MT-

---

[30] Skehan and Ulrich, "Isaiah," 46.
[31] Skehan and Ulrich, "Isaiah," 46.
[32] Tov, *Scribal Practices*, 280, 339.
[33] Lange, *Handbuch*, 268; Tov, *"Synthese,"* 26.
[34] Skehan and Ulrich, "Isaiah," 76.
[35] Skehan and Ulrich, "Isaiah," 76.
[36] Lange, *Handbuch*, 269.
[37] Skehan and Ulrich, "Isaiah," 90.
[38] Skehan and Ulrich, "Isaiah," 90.
[39] Lange, *Handbuch*, 270.
[40] Skehan and Ulrich, "Isaiah," 99–100.

Isa in the preserved text.[41] There are thirty small non-orthographic variations in the preserved text of Isaiah in 4QIsa[f] as compared to MT-Isa and LXX-Isa (→ 6.3). 4QIsa[f] agrees with MT-Isa fourteen times and disagrees sixteen times. With LXX-Isa, 4QIsa[f] agrees seven times and disagrees fourteen times. 4QIsa[f] preserves nine independent readings. 4QIsa[f] may be described as standing close to MT-Isa and classified as a semi-Masoretic manuscript (→ 6.2.2).[42]

6.2.1.9 Manuscripts That Preserve Too Little Text to Classify Text-Critically[43]

Lange[44] describes 4QIsa[g-m,o] and MurIsa as too damaged to analyze for text type. These manuscripts are therefore presented in list form.

4QIsa[g] (4Q61): Eight fragments are preserved that partially preserve Isa 42:14–25; 43:1–4, 16–24. 4QIsa[g] preserves only eighty-five complete or partial words. The text is written in a formal hand from the early to late Hasmonean period, approximately the last third or second half of the first century B.C.E. 4QIsa[g] varies from MT four times, twice adding *waw* and twice written without *waw*.

4QIsa[h] (4Q62): Of those fragments originally identified as 4QIsa[h], frgs. 1–2 are from a separate manuscript and now form the new 4QIsa[l]; frgs. 5–6 are from yet another manuscript and form the new 4QIsa[i]; frg. 7 appears to fit better with 4QIsa[e] (frg. 25), although that assignment still remains doubtful; and frgs. 8–10 belong with 4QIsa[m]. In the DJD edition of this manuscript, there are now only two fragments that partially preserve Isa 42:4–11. Only forty-four complete or partial words are preserved. The manuscript is written in a Hasmonean hand from the first half of the first century B.C.E. The editors have described the hand as "careful and dis-

---

[41] Skehan and Ulrich, "Isaiah," 100.
[42] Lange, *Handbuch*, 271; Tov, *"Synthese,"* 26.
[43] See the introductions to 4QIsa[e] (→ 6.2.1.7) and 4QIsa[h] (→ 6.2.1.9).
[44] Lange, *Handbuch*, 271–75, 278. For the paleographic, orthographic, and textual data listed below, see Lange, *Handbuch*, 271–75, and the literature discussed there.

tinctive."[45] The orthography of this small manuscript is more defective than that of MT.

4QIsa[i] (4Q62a): There are now two fragments assigned to this manuscript, partially preserving Isa 56:7; 57:5–8 in only twenty-four complete or partial words. The manuscript is written in a Hasmonean script from the first half of the first century B.C.E. The orthography of this manuscript does not vary from that of MT.

4QIsa[j] (4Q63): The single extant fragment partially preserves Isa 1:1–6 in seventeen complete or partial words. The manuscript is inscribed in a hand from the late Hasmonean period, from approximately the third quarter of the first century B.C.E. In the small amount of text preserved, the orthography agrees with that of MT. Quiescence of *ʾalef* is attested once and the long form of the pronoun המה "they" also occurs once.

4QIsa[k] (4Q64): Five small fragments are extant preserving the remains of forty-one complete or partial words. Isa 28:26–29; 29:1–9 are partially preserved. The script is late Hasmonean from the middle of the first century B.C.E. The orthography of this fragmentary manuscript seems to have been fuller than MT, three times adding *waw* where MT and 1QIsa[a] lack *waw* and once adding *waw* in agreement with 1QIsa[a]. One time *yod* is added.

4QIsa[l] (4Q65): Originally designated 4QIsa[l],[46] the manuscript consisted of twelve fragments that were subsequently determined to be part of 4QIsa[e]. At the same time, the former 4QIsa[h] was determined to contain fragments of five separate manuscripts, and the two fragments of one of those manuscripts (frgs. 1–2 in former 4QIsa[h]) were designated as the new 4QIsa[l].[47] The text is from Isa 7:14–15 and 8:11–14 with only sixteen complete or

---

[45] Skehan and Ulrich, "Isaiah," 117.
[46] Skehan, *"Qumran, Littérature de Qumran,"* 811–12.
[47] See the introductions to 4QIsa[e] (→ 6.2.1.7) and 4QIsa[h] (→ 6.2.1.9).

partial words preserved on the leather. The script is irregular with letters varying in size even on the same fragment. It dates to the Hasmonean period in the first half of the first century B.C.E. The orthography of this manuscript seems to have been fuller than MT but not as full as 1QIsaᵃ. לוא "no" is attested once.

4QIsaᵐ (4Q66): This manuscript now has five fragments that partially preserve Isa 60:20–61:1, 3–6.[48] Only thirty-five complete or partial words are preserved. The script is Hasmonean from the first half of the first century B.C.E. The script is irregular with the letter sizes varying. The orthography of this manuscript is close to that of MT and 1QIsaᵃ in the preserved text. Once 4QIsaᵐ has a fuller form with *waw* and once *yod* is added supralinearly.

4QIsaᵒ (4Q68): This manuscript has traditionally been assigned two fragments.[49] Frg. 1 partially preserves Isa 14:28–15:2 in thirty-eight complete and partially preserved words. The script is Hasmonaean from the first half of the first century B.C.E. The orthography agrees with that of MT.

MurIsa (Mur 3): One large fragment of this manuscript remains with thirty-one complete or partial words that partially preserves Isa 1:4–14. The script is Herodian from the time of the First Jewish War, i.e., 66–73 C.E.[50] The orthography of this fragment appears to be identical to MTᴸ. There are no apparent variations from MT.

6.2.1.10 Manuscripts for Which It Is Uncertain if They Preserve a Manuscript of Isaiah, a Quotation of Isaiah, or Are Para-Scriptural[51]

So little is preserved of 4QIsaⁿ,ᵖ⁻ʳ and 5QIsa that it is impossible to know if they are the remains of Isaiah manuscripts or Isaiah citations in non-biblical compositions. They are likewise presented here in list form.

4QIsaⁿ (4Q67): The single fragment of this manuscript partially preserves twenty-one complete and partial words out of Isa 58:13–14. It is inscribed in a Hasmonaean hand with semi-cursive tendencies from the first half of the first century B.C.E. The orthography of this manuscript is very close to that of MTᴸ. Assimilation of *dalet* to *taw* may be attested as well as the use of *he* for *waw* in one form. Quiescence of *alef* is attested in one form. There are minor variations from MT.

4QpapIsaᵖ (4Q69): There are two small papyrus fragments extant of this manuscript with only eleven complete or partial words preserved. Isa 5:28–30 is partially preserved. The fragments are inscribed in a Hasmonaean hand with semicursive tendencies dating to the first half of the first century B.C.E. There are no apparent differences from MT. Note that in line 2 the manuscript agrees with the *Qere* to Isa 5:29, and in line 4 to Isa 5:30 the manuscript reads the *Hiphil* perfect as opposed to the *Piel* from the same root in MT.

4QIsaᑫ (4Q69a): The single fragment of this manuscript partially preserves Isa 54:10–13 in only five complete or partial words and is inscribed in an early Herodian script. There are no orthographic differences from 1QIsaᵃ or from MT.

4QIsaʳ (4Q69b): Only three words from Isa 30:23 are preserved on the single fragment of this manuscript. The fragment is inscribed in a Hasmonaean script. There are no apparent differences from MT.

5QIsa (5Q3): Two fragments are extant on which Isa 40:16, 18–19 is partially preserved. The editor states only that the writing is "late" (*tardive*).[52] In the seven complete or partial words preserved, 5QIsa displays no apparent orthographic differences from MT.

---

[48] See the introduction to 4QIsaʰ (→ 6.2.1.9).
[49] But see the comments in Skehan and Ulrich, "Isaiah," 135.
[50] Milik, "3. Isaïe," 79.
[51] For the paleographic, orthographic, and textual data listed below, see Lange, *Handbuch*, 274–75, and the literature discussed there.

[52] Milik, "3. Isaïe," 173.

Cross, *"Palaeography."
Eshel, E. and H. Eshel, "New Fragments from Qumran: 4QGen^f, 4QIsa^b, 4Q226, 8QGen, and XpapEnoch," *DSD* 12 (2005): 134–57, 137–42.
Flint, P.W., "Variant Readings and Textual Affiliation in the Hebrew University Isaiah Scroll from Cave One (1QISA^B)," in *Qumran Cave 1 Revisited: Texts from Cave 1 Sixty Years after Their Discovery: Proceedings of the Sixth Meeting of the IOQS in Ljubljana* (eds. S. Metso, D.W. Parry, and D.K. Falk; STDJ 91; Leiden: Brill, 2010), 33–53.
Flint, P.W., "Non-Masoretic Variant Readings In the Hebrew University Isaiah Scroll (1QIsa^b) and the Text to be Translated," in *The Dead Sea Scrolls and Contemporary Culture: Proceeedings of the International Conference Held at the Israel Museum, Jerusalem (July 6–8, 2008)* (eds. A. Roitman, L.H. Schiffman, and S. Tzoref; STDJ 93; Leiden: Brill, 2010), 105–17.
van der Kooij, A., *Die alten Textzeugen des Jesajabuches: Ein Beitrag zur Textgeschichte des Alten Testaments* (OBO 35; Göttingen: Vandenhoeck & Ruprecht, 1981).
Kutscher, *Language.
Lange, *Handbuch, 257–96.
Milik, J.T., "3. Isaïe," *DJD II.1: 79–80.
Milik, J.T., "3. Isaïe," *DJD III.1: 173.
Pulikottil, P., *Transmission of Biblical Texts in Qumran: The Case of the Large Isaiah Scroll 1QIsa^a* (JSPSup 34; Sheffield: Sheffield Academic Press, 2001).
Skehan, *"Qumran, Littérature de Qumran," 805–22.
Skehan, P.W. and E. Ulrich, "Isaiah," *DJD XV: 7–143.
Tov, E., "The Text of Isaiah at Qumran," in *HB, GB, and Qumran, 42–57.
Ulrich, E., "The Developmental Composition of the Book of Isaiah," *DSD* (2001): 288–305.
Ulrich, E. and P. Flint, *DJD XXXII.

Russell Fuller

6.2.2 Masoretic Texts and Ancient Texts Close to MT

6.2.2.1 History of Research

The Hebrew text of the book of Isaiah has been subject to many studies down through the centuries. This research became more extensive with the discovery of the Dead Sea Scrolls and the publication of 1QIsa^a (→ 6.2.3.1.1). Van der Kooij provides a detailed history of research in → 6.1.2. Unlike books such as Jeremiah (→ 7.1.2, → 7.2.2.1), and because of the absence of variant literary editions of Isaiah, the textual criticism of the Hebrew text of Isaiah was not a major focus of research before the discovery of the Dead Sea Scrolls. The period of the historical-critical and philological study of the text began in the seventeenth and eighteenth centuries with the significant studies of Clericus (Le Clerc) and Houbigant, followed by Gesenius in the early nineteenth century.[1] All of these scholars understood MT-Isa to be corrupt in some places and with many secondary readings. Since 1850, MT-Isa has been understood as a text that was transmitted rather carelessly. Gray argued, for example, that before the second century C.E., MT-Isa "suffered in many places serious corruption."[2]

With the discovery of the Dead Sea Scrolls, the attention of textual critics shifted from MT-Isa to the question of how 1QIsa^a in particular and the other Qumran Isaiah scrolls in general relate to it. In the wake of Kutscher's characterization of 1QIsa^a as a vulgar text, MT-Isa was assigned a higher textual value.[3] This enhanced textual value seemed to be confirmed with the publishing of several Isaiah manuscripts from Qumran that were closely related to the consonantal text of MT, thus confirming its antiquity (→ 6.2.2.4, → 6.2.2.5). Despite the enhanced appreciation of the consonantal text of MT-Isa, even recent research has identified secondary expansions in MT by way of comparison with 1QIsa^a (→ 6.2.2.3.3).[4]

In general, it is symptomatic of the neglect that MT-Isa suffers in more recent research that contemporary commentaries on Isaiah do not discuss

---

[1] J. Le Clerc, *Veteris Testamenti Prophetae: Ab Esaia ad Malachiam usque: ex translatione Joannis Clerici, cum ejusdem commentario philologico et paraphrasi in Esaiam, Jeremiam, eius lamentationes et Abdiam, dissertatione Joh. Smith de prophetia et ipsius auctoris de poesi Hebraeorum* (Amsterdam: Wetstein & Smith, 1731); Houbigant, *Notae criticae, Vol. 2; W. Gesenius, *Der Prophet Jesaia: Übersetzt und mit einem vollständigen philologisch-kritischen und historischen Commentar begleitet* (3 vols.; Leipzig: F.C.W. Vogel, 1820–1821).
[2] Gray, *Isaiah*, xxvi.
[3] Tov, *HB, GB, and Qumran, 42–43.
[4] See, e.g., Ulrich, "Developmental Composition"; Ulrich, *DSSDCB, 109–29.

MT-Isa in detail but engage only the Dead Sea Scrolls and the ancient versions in their text-critical introductions.

6.2.2.2 Editions and Manuscripts

– The Aleppo Codex (MT^A) (http://www.aleppocodex.org). The consonantal layer of the codex was copied by Shelomo ben Buya'a and vocalized and annotated by Aaron ben Asher in ca. 925 C.E. About three-quarters of the manuscript has been preserved. The Aleppo Codex originally contained 491 pages: 295 have survived, and 196 have been lost. The entire book of Isaiah is preserved in the Aleppo Codex.
– Codex Leningradensis (Codex EPB. I B 19a of the National Library of Russia in St. Petersburg; MT^L). This codex dates from 1009 C.E. and was corrected according to a Ben Asher manuscript. The codex has been used as the base text for the *Biblia Hebraica* series since 1937 (*BH^3, *BHS, *BHQ).
– The Cairo Codex of the Prophets (MT^C). This codex dates from the eleventh century C.E. and agrees most closely with the Ben Naphtali masoretic tradition even though the colophon to the manuscript claims that it was copied by Moses ben Asher in 895 C.E.
– *BH is an *editio minor* that from the third edition in 1937 has used Codex Leningradensis as its base text. Notably, in the 1951 print run of BH^3 in 1951, the editors added a third apparatus for the book of Isaiah, which incorporated a selection of readings from 1QIsa^a. According to the preface of the 1951 print run, "The selection has generally been restricted to such readings as were important from the point of view of interpretation, whereas peculiarities of purely orthographical or grammatical interest could not be included."[5]
– *BHS (*Biblia Hebraica Stuttgartensia*), which was issued between 1967 and 1977, is a complete revision of *Biblia Hebraica*. The Isaiah fascicle was edited by D. Winton Thomas. Both 1QIsa^a and 1QIsa^b are referred to in the apparatus. 1QIsa^a is referred to 244 times and forty-eight times its reading is preferred to MT^L-Isa.
– *HUB. The Hebrew University Bible Project began publication with the book of Isaiah in a sample edition in 1975. This was followed by further volumes in 1981 and 1992. The completed edition of the book of Isaiah was published in a single volume in 1995.[6] As is well known, the *HUB* utilizes the text of the Aleppo Codex as the base text for the critical edition. This is published along with its *masorah magna* and *masorah parva*. The text and *masorot* are accompanied by four apparatuses that present variant readings that may influence the sense of the passage from the Dead Sea Scrolls and rabbinic literature, from medieval Bible manuscripts, as well as recording differences in minutiae such as spelling, vowels, and accents that do not influence the understanding of the text. *HUB Isaiah* is an essential resource for the textual study of the book of Isaiah.

The Hebrew text of Isaiah is attested in twenty-two manuscripts from the Judean Desert. Of these twenty-two manuscripts, one may be described as proto-Masoretic (1QIsa^b), five may be described as semi-Masoretic (4QIsa^{a,b,d,e,f}), two may be described as non-aligned (1QIsa^a, 4QIsa^c), and fourteen are either too fragmentary or too small to determine their textual affiliation. The manuscripts are described in detail in → 6.2.1.

Quotations from the book of Isaiah are preserved in four exegetical compositions found in Caves 3 and 4 at Qumran.

– 3QpIsa (3Q4)
– 4QpIsa^{a,b,d} (4Q161–162, 164)
– 4QpIsa^{c,e} (4Q163, 165)
– 4QTanh (4Q176)

As has been noted many times, the high number of Isaiah manuscripts and exegetical compositions

---

[5] *BH^3 (ed. P. Kahle, A. Alt, and O. Eissfeldt; Stuttgart: Württembergische Bibelanstalt, 1951), xxxix.

[6] Goshen-Gottstein, *HUB, Isaiah*.

devoted to the book of Isaiah seems to indicate the importance of this composition to the community at Qumran and beyond in the Second Temple period.

6.2.2.3 Nature and Text-Critical Character of (proto)-MT-Isa

The orthography of MT-Isa shows few anomalous forms. The negative particle, לֹא "no" is always spelled defectively except in Isa 16:14 where it is spelled with *waw*. Consistently in the compound particles בְּלוֹא (Isa 55:1–2; "without") and לְלוֹא (Isa 65:1; "those that do not …"; plus once לְלֹא also in Isa 65:1), the form is spelled with *waw*. Likewise, the form הֲלוֹא "is not?" is mostly spelled with *waw* in MT-Isa, the only exceptions being Isa 10:8, 9, 11; 36:12; 44:8; 57:11 (הֲלֹא "is not?").[7] Note that the orthography of 1QIsa[a] agrees with the orthography of MT-Isa in all of these passages.

As in the text of any biblical book in MT, MT-Isa is not free from secondary readings. This has been recognized from the beginning of historical-critical scholarship. As has been noted by Ulrich and Flint, the *JPS Hebrew English Tanakh*, which hews close to MT in translation, uses the phrases "Meaning of Heb. uncertain" or "Meaning of verse uncertain" almost one hundred times in the book of Isaiah.[8] This is strongly suggestive of textual and linguistic problems in MT-Isa. Textual variants are the results of misvocalizations of the Masoretic text, or different equally possible meanings resulting in a Masoretic vocalization that disagrees with the ancient translations and/or rabbinic literature. Other variants are expansions, or editorial readings, linguistic and stylistic corrections, as well as scribal errors. For each category, I will give selected examples below. These examples are eclectic and far from exhaustive. They are only suggestive of the state of the text of MT-Isa.

6.2.2.3.1 Misvocalization and Differences in Meaning Due to Vocalization

The consonantal text of MT-Isa often leaves several possibilities for reading a given word. This openness of the consonantal text caused both misvocalizations by the Masoretes and several possible meanings reflected in the Masoretic vocalization, rabbinic interpretations, and ancient translations. Examples include the following.

- MT-Isa 7:11 reads שְׁאָלָה "ask" while the Vulgate has, e.g., *in profundum inferni*, "in the depths of the underworld," which interpreted the consonants of MT-Isa 7:11 correctly as שְׁאֹלָה "to She'ol." שְׁאָלָה "ask" should thus be understood as an example of misvocalization.

- In Isa 3:12, MT vocalizes וְנָשִׁים "and women" while LXX-Isa has καὶ οἱ ἀπαιτοῦντες "and creditors/lenders" (cf. T[J], Aq) deriving from the root נשה "to lend, to be a creditor." As the reading of LXX makes much more sense in the context, the vocalization of MT should be understood as resulting from a confusion of the similar roots.

- In Isa 2:22, MT vocalizes the consonants במה as בַּמֶּה, "of what." *B. Berakot* 14a; *b. Soṭah* 4b; *Yalquṭ Shim'oni*. II § 394; § 954; *Yalquṭ Machiri 'Al-Tiqre* interpret the word in question instead as בָּמָה "highly." This vocalization agrees with the Vulgate, which reads *excelsus* "highly (accounted)" also reflecting בָּמָה. This difference in meaning is based on an understanding of the vocalization, which may go back to early Jewish and Christian disputes about the meaning of the text.[9] Jerome's translation in the Vulgate, *excelsus* "highly (accounted)" for בָּמָה suggests that he understood the word to refer to Christ. Jerome described contemporary Jewish understandings based on the reading בַּמֶּה to be deliberate misunderstandings.[10]

---

[7] Cf. A. Lange, "The Question of the So-Called Qumran Orthography, the Severus Scroll, and the Masoretic Text," *Hebrew Bible and Ancient Israel* 3 (2014): 424–75, esp. 470.

[8] Ulrich and Flint, *DJD* XXXII: 2:89.

[9] See the comments in Blenkinsopp, *Isaiah*, 1.194 and Wildberger, *Isaiah*, 1.102.

[10] Blenkinsopp mentions Jerome's understanding of this reading, which may be found in Jerome, *Commentariorum in Isaim Prophetam* 18 (PL 24:43–44). The pertinent passage reads: *Intelligentes ergo Judaei prophetiam esse de Christo, verbum ambiguum in deteriorem partem interpretati sunt, ut*

6.2.2.3.2 Scribal Errors

As with any other biblical book, the consonantal text of MT-Isa was not immune to textual corruption by way of scribal errors. Four examples may suffice to illustrate this point.

- In Isa 2:20, MT$^{\text{Kenn 149,150,153}}$ read לחפרפרות "moles" for MT's לַחְפֹּר פֵּרוֹת (uncertain meaning). The medieval manuscripts are supported by 1QIsa^a לחפרפרים "moles," which has the masculine instead of the feminine plural ending. The reading in MT-Isa results from a misdivision of the word.
- In MT-Isa 15:9, דִּימוֹן "twice" is probably a mistake for דיבן "Dibon" (1QIsa^a; cf. דִיבֹן in MT-Isa 15:2).[11] The reading of MT-Isa results from confusion of the letters *bet* and *mem*.
- In Isa 38:9, MT has מִכְתָּב לְחִזְקִיָּהוּ "a writing of Hezekiah" while LXX-Isa reads Προσευχὴ Εζεκιου "a prayer of Hezekiah," which seems to presume מכתם "prayer" (cf. Ps 16:1, 60:1, etc.) for MT's מִכְתָּב. The latter results from confusion of the similar letters *bet* and *mem* in MT-Isa.
- In MT-Isa 64:2, the phrase יָרַדְתָּ מִפָּנֶיךָ הָרִים נָזֹלּוּ "you came down, the mountains quaked at your presence" is likely an example of dittography. The same phrase is found in Isa 63:19. A scribe accidentally repeated the same phrase at the end of two consecutive lines.[12]
- In MT-Isa 14:4, the reading מַדְהֵבָה (meaning uncertain) is found. 1QIsa^a has מרהבה "onslaught," which fits the context much better. The reading of MT is most likely due to *dalet/resh* confusion.
- Likewise in MT-Isa 33:8, the reading עָרִים "cities" is preserved. 1QIsa^a has instead the reading עדים "witnesses," which again fits the context much better. This is another example of the confusion of *dalet/resh* in MT.
- Additional examples of this sort of graphic confusion are found in MT-Isa 45:2. MT reads וַהֲדוּרִים "and mountainous land"(?). 1QIsa^a and 1QIsa^b read והררים and הרורים respectively (both meaning "and mountains"). Likewise in MT-Isa 47:10, MT reads בְרָעָתֵךְ "in your wickedness," but 1QIsa^a has בדעתך "in your knowledge," which makes better sense in the context.
- In MT-Isa 21:8, the reading אַרְיֵה "lion" seems to be a metathesis, which is probably triggered by the preceding *'aleph* in וַיִּקְרָא "and he called out." In this case, the correct reading is preserved in 1QIsa^a and the Peshitta: הראה "the watcher."
- In MT-Isa 49:24, MT has צַדִּיק "righteous" but 1QIsa^a, supported by LXX, the Peshitta, and the Vulgate, reads עריץ "tyrant." The reading in MT was probably the result of several graphic confusions.
- In MT-Isa 62:7, the reading עַד־יְכוֹנֵן וְעַד־יָשִׂים "until he establishes Jerusalem and makes it ..." goes back to haplography. The original reading is preserved in 1QIsa^a (L:18): עד יכין ועד יכונן ועד ישים "until he prepares and establishes Jerusalem and makes it ..."[13]

6.2.2.3.3 Expansions

An example of an expansion can be found in MT-Isa 2:22 (= 1QIsa^a LXX$^{\text{V,L,C}}$, Aq), which may also be seen as editorial in nature. The verse is missing in LXX-Isa and is probably a late editorial gloss. Another example of what is probably a harmonizing expansion in the Hebrew textual tradition may be found in MT-Isa 36:7b. Here, MT is supported by 1QIsa^a with one important exception. LXX-Isa 36:7 lacks

---

videreturur non laudare Christum, sed nihili pendere "The Jews, therefore, understanding that it is a prophecy about Christ, translated the ambiguous word in a detrimental sense, so that they would not seem to be praising Christ, but valuing him as nothing" (the English translation is taken from T. Scheck, *St. Jerome: Commentary on Isaiah* [ACW 68: New York: The Newman Press, 2015], 105).

[11] Note the reading of LXX-Isa 15:9 Ρεμμων "Remmon," which probably reflects confusion of *dalet* and *resh* as well as the confusion of *bet* and *mem* in MT-Isa.

[12] Note that there is variation in the placement of the chapter. In LXX (→ 6.3), the Peshitta (→ 6–9.1.4), and the Vulgate (→ 6–9.1.7), the break comes in the middle of Isa 63:19, but in MT the break comes at the end of Isa 63:19 and before what is Isa 64:2 in the versions.

[13] See the discussion in Blenkinsopp, *Isaiah*, 3.238, who also argues that the reading of MT is best explained as due to haplography. Blenkinsopp translates v. 7: "and give no rest to YHVH, until he establish Jerusalem solid and firm and spread her renown throughout the earth."

הֲלוֹא־הוּא אֲשֶׁר הֵסִיר חִזְקִיָּהוּ אֶת־בָּמֹתָיו וְאֶת־מִזְבְּחֹתָיו וַיֹּאמֶר לִיהוּדָה וְלִירוּשָׁלִַם לִפְנֵי הַמִּזְבֵּחַ הַזֶּה תִּשְׁתַּחֲווּ "is it not he whose high places and altars Hezekiah has removed, saying to Judah and to Jerusalem, 'You shall worship before this altar'?" (*NRSV*). This long expansion is found in the parallel text in 2 Kgs 18:22. There, the last word in the verse is בִּירוּשָׁלִָם "in Jerusalem," which is also found in 1QIsaᵃ at Isa 36:7. So it is most likely that this reading in MT and 1QIsaᵃ is a harmonizing expansion in the Hebrew textual tradition of Isaiah.[14]

In MT-Isa 36:12, two *Qere* readings are preserved. 1) the *Ketiv* is חַרְאֵיהֶם "excrement" with the *Qere* צוֹאָתָם (also meaning "excrement"); 2) the *Ketiv* is שֵׁינֵיהֶם "urine" and the *Qere* is מֵימֵי רַגְלֵיהֶם literally "the water of their feet," i.e. "urine." In both cases, the *Qere* reading seems to be intended as an explanation of the reading preserved as the *Ketiv*. In both cases, 1QIsaᵃ supports the *Ketiv*. It seems reasonable to understand the *Qere* readings in MT-Isa 36:12 as explanatory expansions.

It is possible to multiply examples of secondary readings in MT-Isa.[15] As with any other composition, in MT there are many cases of scribal errors and other sorts of secondary readings as described above. In general, the Hebrew text of Isaiah preserved in MT may be described as somewhat expansionary in comparison to LXX-Isa (→ 6.3) and sometimes also in comparison to the most ancient witnesses to the Hebrew text, i.e., the Hebrew manuscripts of Isaiah from the Judean Desert. As shown above, the MT tradition of Isaiah contains examples of expansions, and scribal errors such as graphic confusions, misdivision of words, and spelling error that sometimes led to changes in meaning.

6.2.2.4 1QIsaᵇ (1Q8)

1QIsaᵇ (→ 6.2.1.2) preserves in whole or in part Isa 7:22–25; 8:1, 8 (or 10); 10,17–19; 12:3–6; 13:1–8, 16–19; 15:3–9; 16:1, 7–11; 19:7–17, 20–25; 20:1; 22:11–18, 24; 23:1–4; 24:18–23; 25:1–8; 26:1–5; 28:15–20; 29:1–8; 30:10–14, 21–26; 31:5–7; 32:17–20; 35:4; 36:14; 37:8–12; 38:12–22; 39:1–8; 40:2; 41:3–23; 43:1–13, 23–27; 44:21–28; 45:1–13; 46:3–13; 47:1–14; 48:17–22; 49:1–15; 50:7–11; 51:1–10; 52:7–15; 53:1–12; 54:1–6; 55:2–13; 56:1–12; 57:1–4, 17–20; 58:1–14; 59:1–8, 20; 60:1–22; 61:1; 62:2–12; 63:1–19; 64:1–8; 65:17–25; 66:1–24. 1QIsaᵇ is written in a late Hasmonean or early Herodian hand, dating to approximately the third quarter of the first century B.C.E. Eight corrections occur in the manuscript, all by the original scribe.[16] The orthography of 1QIsaᵇ is quite close to that of MTᴸ, although there are minor variations in spelling from MTᴸ.

For the textual characteristics of 1QIsaᵇ, the editors of the critical edition state, "On the whole, 1QIsaᵇ shows close agreement with 𝔐ᴸ, 𝔐ᑫ, 𝔐ᵐˢˢ, and 𝔊, which classifies it as belonging to the textual group that eventually emerges as the Masoretic family."[17]

Despite this affiliation with proto-MT-Isa, 1QIsaᵇ shows two large variations from MT at Isa 38:12–13 and Isa 60:19–20. At Isa 38:12–13, 1QIsaᵇ lacks all of v. 13 except for the final word. This is most likely the result of haplography. The scribe's eye skipped from תשלימני "you bring me to an end" at the end of v. 12 to the identical form at the end of v. 13. Likewise in 1QIsaᵇ at Isa 60:19–20, there is a long minus in 1QIsaᵇ, which most likely results from a haplography. The scribe's eye skipped from the phrase לאור עולם, "for an everlasting light" in v. 19 to the identical phrase in v. 20. If, as the editors suggest, these omissions are the result of haplography on the part of the scribe of 1QIsaᵇ, then they are without text-critical meaning.[18]

1QIsaᵇ shows other small variations from MT such as occasionally in the use of divine names

---

[14] MT-Isa 38:15a (> LXX) may be another expansion, but it is also possible that the short text of LXX-Isa (→ 6.3) is the result of haplography either by the LXX translator or was found already in his *Vorlage*. The scribe's eye may have skipped from מה "what" at the beginning of the verse to the somewhat similar מר "bitterness" later in the verse.

[15] For more examples, see Ulrich, "Developmental Composition"; Ulrich, *DSSDCB, 109–29.

[16] For the paleography of 1QIsaᵇ, see Ulrich and Flint, *DJD XXXII: 2.199–200.

[17] Ulrich and Flint, *DJD XXXII: 208.

[18] Ulrich and Flint, *DJD XXXII: 209.

or parallel words, but these are within the normal range of variation exhibited by manuscripts in the Masoretic family.[19] As has been the assessment since its first publication, 1QIsa[b] is best understood as being textually close to MT and may be designated a proto-Masoretic text.[20]

6.2.2.5 Further Qumran Manuscripts

There are five additional Isaiah manuscripts from Qumran Cave 4 that are also related to the Masoretic text family in the Book of Isaiah (→ 6.2.1).

- 4QIsa[a] (4Q55)
- 4QIsa[b] (4Q56)
- 4QIsa[d] (4Q58)
- 4QIsa[e] (4Q59)
- 4QIsa[f] (4Q60)

These five manuscripts have been described as semi-Masoretic, in part because they do not agree with either MT-Isa or LXX-Isa (→ 6.3) in a majority of cases, and in part because these manuscripts preserve a significant number of independent readings.[21] These manuscripts thus do not stand as close to MT-Isa as does 1QIsa[b]. They vary in the amount of the text of Isaiah that has been preserved. Only 4QIsa[d] originally may not have contained the entire book of Isaiah.[22]

6.2.2.6 Date and Milieu

Manuscripts of Isaiah from the Judean Desert belonging to the Masoretic family (i.e., semi-Masoretic or proto-Masoretic manuscripts) date to as early as the first half of the first century B.C.E. (4QIsa[f]; semi-Masoretic; → 6.2.1.8) and as late as 68 C.E. (4QIsa[d]; semi-Masoretic; → 6.2.1.6). The only proto-Masoretic manuscript of Isaiah (1QIsa[b]) dates to the third quarter of the first century B.C.E. (i.e., ca. 50–25 B.C.E.; → 6.2.1.2). The date of 4QIsa[f] indicates that by the end of the second century B.C.E. at the latest a consonantal text that was relatively close to MT-Isa was already in circulation. It is reasonable to assume that the origins of the proto-Masoretic text of Isaiah may be placed at least in the third century B.C.E. All of these manuscripts were found in the Judean Desert and there is no reason to think that they were not produced in Palestine. Although the proto-Masoretic form of the Hebrew text of Isaiah may go back to the third century B.C.E., this does not mean that variation in this text form did not continue. For example, some of the differences in meaning due to different vocalizations mentioned above may have developed quite late, especially given that a witness such as the Vulgate (→ 6–9.1.7) sometimes has the correct reading when MT-Isa does not. It seems, then, that secondary readings continued to develop even in the recent history of this form of the Hebrew text of Isaiah.

Blenkinsopp, J., *Isaiah: A New Translation with Introduction and Commentary* (3 vols.; AB 19–19B; New York: Doubleday, 2000–2003).

Flint, P.W., "Variant Readings and Textual Affiliation in the Hebrew University Isaiah Scroll from Cave One (1QIsa[b])," in *Qumran Cave 1 Revisited: Texts from Cave 1 Sixty Years after Their Discovery: Proceedings of the Sixth Meeting of the IOQS in Ljubljana* (eds. S. Metso, D.W. Parry, and D.K. Falk; STDJ 91; Leiden: Brill, 2010), 33–53.

Flint, P.W., "Non-Masoretic Variant Readings in the Hebrew University Isaiah Scroll (1QIsa[b]) and the Text to be Translated," in *The Dead Sea Scrolls and Contemporary Culture: Proceedings of the International Conference Held at the Israel Museum, Jerusalem (July 6–8, 2008)* (eds. A. Roitman, L.H. Schiffman, and S. Tzoref; STDJ 93; Leiden: Brill, 2010), 105–17.

Goshen-Gottstein, *HUB, Isaiah*.

Gray, G.B., *A Critical and Exegetical Commentary on the Book of Isaiah: I–XXXIX*, Vol. 1: *Introduction, and Commentary on I–XXVII* (ICC; Edinburgh: T & T Clark, 1912).

Lange, *Handbuch*, 257–96.

Skehan, "Qumran, Littérature de Qumran."

Skehan, P.W. and E. Ulrich, "Isaiah," *DJD* XV (1997): 7–143.

---

[19] Ulrich and Flint, *DJD* XXXII: 211.

[20] See also the references in Lange, *Handbuch*, 264, n. 50.

[21] Lange, *Handbuch*, 265–91; 4QIsa[a] preserves fifteen independent readings, 4QIsa[b] preserves twenty-nine independent readings, 4QIsa[d] preserves nine independent readings, 4QIsa[e] preserves ten independent readings, and 4QIsa[f] preserves nine independent readings.

[22] See the brief discussion in Lange, *Handbuch*, 269.

Tov, *"Synthese."

Tov, E., "The Text of Isaiah at Qumran," in Tov, *HB, GB, and Qumran, 42–57.

Tov, *Scribal Practices.

Tov, *HB, GB, and Qumran.

Ulrich, E., "The Developmental Composition of the Book of Isaiah," DSD 8 (2001): 288–305.

Ulrich, E. and P.W. Flint, *Qumran Cave 1.II, Parts 1–2: The Isaiah Scrolls* (*DJD XXXII; Oxford: Clarendon, 2010).

Wildberger, H., *Isaiah* (2 vols.; CC; Minneapolis: Fortress Press, 1991–1997).

Russell Fuller
Peter Flint

6.2.3 Other Texts

In addition to the Hebrew manuscripts of Isaiah discussed above in → 6.2.2, which are closely related to MT-Isa, there are two Hebrew manuscripts of Isaiah from Qumran (→ 6.2.1) that are less closely related to MT-Isa, 1QIsa^a and 4QIsa^c (4Q57).

6.2.3.1 1QIsa^a

With the minor exceptions of Isa 1:21, 23–26; 2:15, 17, 19–21; 5:10–14; 7:9–12, 14–15; 8:7; 10:13–14; 14:27, 29; 45:10–14, the entire book of Isaiah has been preserved in this manuscript. Given its exceptional state of preservation, the history of research on 1QIsa^a is extensive.

6.2.3.1.1 History of Research

Although 1QIsa^a was one the first Dead Sea Scrolls to be published, until the edition of Ulrich and Flint of 1QIsa^a in *DJD XXXII in 2010, scholars depended for their studies on transcriptions without variant lists.[1] As these transcriptions lacked text-critical variant lists, the study of 1QIsa^a until recently remained preliminary at least to some extent. A. van der Kooij provides a detailed history of research on the textual criticism of the book of Isaiah in → 6.1.2, which illustrates this problem. Beyond the general lines drawn by van der Kooij, various models exist of how 1QIsa^a and the Isaiah text it attests should be understood. Based on a linguistic and orthographic study, Kutscher perceived 1QIsa^a as a vulgar text that needs to be distinguished from the standard text of MT-Isa.[2] This vulgar text represents a popular version that is of limited text-critical value and was intended for study purposes. Although Kutscher's magisterial work met widespread agreement, a dissenting voice is that of Stegemann. He regards 1QIsa^a as a master copy that the Essenes used for the production of biblical manuscripts.[3]

Much attention was paid to the textual affiliation of 1QIsa^a. Most scholars emphasized the relative distance of this manuscript from MT-Isa (→ 6.2.2). Representative are the voices of Barthélemy, Tov, and Ulrich. Barthélemy views 1QIsa^a as an extra-Masoretic text that was further removed from MT-Isa than, for example, the pre-Masoretic text of 1QIsa^b.[4] Tov emphasizes that 1QIsa^a belongs to the Qumran scribal tradition and sees its non-aligned text[5] as belonging ultimately to the same textual family as that of MT and LXX.[6] Ulrich emphasized in various publications[7] that no variant literary editions are preserved for the book of Isaiah. 1QIsa^b, MT^L, the *Qere* reading of MT, MT^{mss}, and the Targumim would form a close text-family grouping while 1QIsa^a and LXX-Isa must be assigned to yet different text families. On the one hand, 1QIsa^a would include interpretative readings as well as harmonizations and linguistic actualizations but would, on the other hand, also point to additions in MT-Isa. 1QIsa^a would thus indicate that MT-Isa represents a later stage in the textual history of Isaiah than does 1QIsa^a.

---

[1] M. Burrows (ed.), *The Dead Sea Scrolls of St. Mark's Monastery*, Vol. 1: *The Isaiah Manuscript and the Habakkuk Commentary* (with the assistance of J.C. Trever and W.H. Brownlee; New Haven: ASOR, 1950); D.W. Parry and E. Qimron (eds.), *The Great Isaiah Scroll (1QIsa^a): A New Edition* (STDJ 32; Leiden: Brill, 1999).

[2] Kutscher, *Language*.

[3] H. Stegemann, *Die Essener, Qumran, Johannes der Täufer und Jesus: Ein Sachbuch* (4th ed.; Freiburg i.B.: Herder, 1994), 116.

[4] Barthélemy, *Studies*, 406.

[5] For the non-aligned character of 1QIsa^a, see Tov, *"Synthese,"* 26.

[6] Tov, "The Text of Isaiah at Qumran," 56.

[7] See, e.g., Ulrich, "Developmental Composition"; Ulrich and Flint, *DJD XXXII: 2.88–92; Ulrich, *DSSDCB, 109–29.

Textual critics also paid special attention to the interpretative variant readings of 1QIsaᵃ. Early on, some of them were understood as messianic in character.⁸ In van der Kooij's landmark study on the textual witnesses of Isaiah, he understood the interpretative readings of 1QIsaᵃ as exegetical actualizations comparable to the Qumran pesharim. For van der Kooij, it was the Teacher of Righteousness who wanted, by way of these interpretative additions in 1QIsaᵃ, to legitimize the formation of the Qumran community.⁹ Pulikottil argued much later than van der Kooij that the group around the Teacher of Righteousness would have appreciated 1QIsaᵃ in particular because "the Isaiah scroll is conceptually oriented towards the *Yaḥad* texts, but there is not enough evidence to suggest that the *Yaḥad* texts, including the biblical texts using similar scribal conventions, have any substantial dependence upon it."¹⁰

6.2.3.1.2 Nature and Text-Critical Character

The spelling in 1QIsaᵃ is noticeably fuller than that in 1QIsaᵇ and MT.¹¹ Ulrich and Flint state that there is no clear system of orthography in 1QIsaᵃ.¹² 1QIsaᵃ shows "full spellings" for "כול, לוא, יאומר, קוטל (for the *Qal* participle)."¹³ Also attested are the so-called "long forms" of the second masculine singular perfect suffix, תה- for MT's תָ- as well as the second masculine singular possessive suffix, כה- for MT's ךָ. The forms המה- and כמה- are also attested. Tov describes 1QIsaᵃ as written in the Qumran practice.¹⁴ Beginning with col. XXVIII, the number of plene spellings increases as compared to cols. I–XXVII. For an extensive table of characteristic spellings in 1QIsaᵃ, see tables 3–6 in Ulrich and Flint.¹⁵

6.2.3.1.2.1 Scribal Marks in 1QIsaᵃ

As is well known, there are many scribal marks of various sorts in 1QIsaᵃ. This would seem to be one indication of the reworking/interpretation of this manuscript during its history. Ulrich and Flint divide the scribal marks into three groups: a) the *paragraphos*; b) the paleo-Hebrew *taw*; and c) other marks/symbols that occur in the scroll. The *paragraphos* is the most frequently occurring scribal mark in 1QIsaᵃ. It appears sixty-six times in the scroll and is used to mark the end of a section of text, occurring almost always at the beginning of the final line of the section in the right margin. The second type of scribal mark found in 1QIsaᵃ is probably a paleo-Hebrew *taw*. This symbol appears only thirteen times in the manuscript and seems to have been used to mark passages of interest or importance to a reader. A similar scribal mark found eleven times in 1QpHab appears to have been used in the same way. The paleo-Hebrew *taw* was probably added by later readers of the scroll. The remaining scribal marks in 1QIsaᵃ occur only twelve times and, like the paleo-Hebrew *taw*, were probably added by later readers to indicate passages of interest to them.¹⁶

6.2.3.1.2.2 Variant Readings in 1QIsaᵃ

In *DJD* XXXII, Ulrich and Flint list 2,755 variant readings.¹⁷ Below, I will discuss a small but representative sample of specific types of readings in support of the long-standing view that the text of 1QIsaᵃ may be described as an independent or unaffiliated manuscript in the Hebrew textual tradition of the book of Isaiah. In 605 (22%) of the variant readings listed in *DJD* XXXII.1, 1QIsaᵃ agrees with MT-Isa (→ 6.2.2) against LXX-Isa (→ 6.3). In 214 (8%) of the listed variant readings, 1QIsaᵃ agrees with LXX-Isa against MT-Isa. 1QIsaᵃ is thus more closely affiliated with MT-Isa than with LXX-Isa. Although 1QIsaᵃ is closer to MT-Isa than to LXX-Isa, it is an independent or non-aligned manuscript that preserves independent readings thirty

---

⁸ J.V. Chamberlain, "The Functions of God as Messianic Titles in the Complete Qumran Isaiah Scroll," *VT* 5 (1955): 366–72.

⁹ Van der Kooij, *Die Alten Textzeugen*, esp. 81–97.

¹⁰ Pulikottil, *Transmission*, 160–99. The quotation is on p. 214.

¹¹ Ulrich and Flint, *DJD* XXXII: 2.88.

¹² Ulrich and Flint, *DJD* XXXII: 2.65.

¹³ Ulrich and Flint, *DJD* XXXII: 2.65.

¹⁴ Tov, *Scribal Practices*, 268, 279, 339.

¹⁵ Ulrich and Flint, *DJD* XXXII: 2.66–82.

¹⁶ Ulrich and Flint, *DJD* XXXII: 88.

¹⁷ Ulrich and Flint, *DJD* XXXII: 119–93.

percent of the time, i.e., in 781 of the variant readings, 1QIsaᵃ disagrees with both MT-Isa and LXX-Isa either when they agree with each other or when they do not.

There are many secondary readings preserved in 1QIsaᵃ due to scribal error. For example, there are several haplographies in the text of 1QIsaᵃ at II:18 in Isa 2:9–11 (ואל "and not" ∩ ועיני "and eyes of")¹⁸, at IV:10 in Isa 4:5–6 (יומם "by day" ∩ יומם "by day"), at XIII:26 in Isa 16:8–9 (שבמה "Sibmah" ∩ שבמה "Sibmah"), at XVIII:21 in Isa 23:15 (הוא "that" ∩ יהיה "it will happen"), and at XXXIII:7 in Isa 40:7–8 (יבש "withers" ∩ יבש "withers") where a second hand has added Isa 40:7 supralinearly and has also introduced additional errors.¹⁹

There are numerous editorial and/or harmonizing readings in 1QIsaᵃ. The following are a few examples. At III:1–2 in Isa 2:22, 1QIsaᵃ shares with MT-Isa the addition of v. 22, which is missing from LXX-Isa and is considered a late gloss by many scholars.²⁰ At XXIX:8–10 in Isa 36:7, 1QIsaᵃ shares with MT-Isa the addition of הֲלוֹא־הוּא אֲשֶׁר הֵסִיר חִזְקִיָּהוּ אֶת־בָּמֹתָיו וְאֶת־מִזְבְּחֹתָיו וַיֹּאמֶר לִיהוּדָה וְלִירוּשָׁלַם לִפְנֵי הַמִּזְבֵּחַ הַזֶּה תִּשְׁתַּחֲווּ "is it not he whose high places and altars Hezekiah has removed, saying to Judah and to Jerusalem, 'You shall worship before this altar'?" (*NRSV), which is missing from LXX-Isa and is most likely supplied from 2 Kgs 18:22. See also the addition of בירושלים "in Jerusalem" in 1QIsaᵃ 36:7 in agreement with 2 Kgs 18:22. At XXXVIII:13, in Isa 45:7, 1QIsaᵃ reads טוב in contrast to MT and LXX, both of which read שָׁלוֹם "peace" (εἰρήνην). Augustine is the only parallel to the reading of 1QIsaᵃ, but the reading is considered secondary and harmonizing since the usual parallel to רע "woe" is טוב "good."²¹ At XXXVIII:16 in Isa 45:8, there are several problems. 1QIsaᵃ reads הריעו "shout out" in contrast to MT's הַרְעִיפוּ "shower." Oswalt thinks that הריעו "shout out" in 1QIsaᵃ may be a stylistic correction based on a problem with MT's הַרְעִיפוּ "shower," which is rare. He also thinks that האמר לארץ "the one how says to the earth" in 1QIsaᵃ may be a further stylistic correction to agree with both the initial verb of Isa 45:8 and to correspond to Isa 44:23, which opens this section of Isaiah.²² The other obvious problem in 1QIsaᵃ at Isa 45:8 is that 1QIsaᵃ lacks the final phrase, which is attested in the other witnesses. This is presumably a mistake by the scribe of 1QIsaᵃ.²³

In 1QIsaᵃ XLI:2 (Isa 49:6), the terms *Jacob* and *Israel* have been reversed in comparison to MT, LXX, the Targum, Vulgate, and Peshitta. The expression שבטי יעקב, "tribes of Jacob" is rare and is found only in Isa 49:6 and 1 Kgs 18:31.²⁴ It is likely that the reading in 1QIsaᵃ is a secondary reading that is harmonizing to conform to the far more frequent expression "the tribes of Israel." Interestingly, note that manuscript B of Hebrew Ben Sira (→ II.4.2), which quotes Isa 49:6 in the second half of a blended quotation at Ben Sira 48:10,²⁵ is the sole witness to agree with the order of the names in 1QIsaᵃ.

At XLII:19–21 in Isa 51:6, 1QIsaᵃ preserves another interesting reading. 1QIsaᵃ adds the phrase וראו מי ברא את אלה "and see: who created these?" that is found also in Isa 40:26, a verse that opens with a phrase very similar to the first phrase in Isa 51:6. No other witnesses have this reading and it seems likely that either the first scribe of 1QIsaᵃ found this reading in his *Vorlage* or that he cre-

---

¹⁸ Isa 2:9b–10 is missing from 1QIsaᵃ although found in 4QIsaᵃ,ᵇ and LXXᴮ,ᵠ. This might be due to haplography in this manuscript, the scribe's eye jumping from the *waw* of ואל "and not" to the *waw* of ועיני "and eyes of" at the beginning of Isa 2:11 where 1QIsaᵃ uniquely has *waw*.

¹⁹ Isa 40:7 is missing from 1QIsaᵃ*. The correcting scribe evidently thought that the first scribe had left out Isa 40:7b and so added it above the line along with most of Isa 40:8 vertically in the left margin. The second scribe left out the last two words of Isa 40:8. The correcting scribe misspelled MT-Isa אָכֵן "surely," writing instead הכן "surely." Note that LXX omits Isa 40:7, which may be the result of haplography.

²⁰ Oswalt, *Isaiah*, 2.128–29; Wildberger, *Isaiah*, 1.102.

²¹ Compare the comments of Oswalt, *Isaiah*, 2.199, and Blenkinsopp, *Isaiah*, 1.122.

²² Oswalt, *Isaiah*, 2.199.

²³ It is conceivable that this error in 1QIsaᵃ is the result of the scribe's eye skipping from the *ḥet* of יַחַד "together" in Isa 45:8 to the *he* of הוֹי "woe" at the beginning of Isa 45:9.

²⁴ Note that 1QIsaᵇ agrees with MT-Isa in the order of the names, but instead reads להש[י]ב "to restore" twice.

²⁵ Ben Sira 48:10 preserves a partial quotation of Mal 3:24 followed by a partial quotation of Isa 49:6. These are introduced by the quotation formula הכתוב "it is written."

ated this harmonizing reading himself. Note that 1QIsaᵃ continues to diverge from MT-Isa in the remainder of the verse by omitting the phrase כִּי־שָׁמַיִם כֶּעָשָׁן נִמְלָחוּ וְהָאָרֶץ כַּבֶּגֶד תִּבְלֶה "for the heavens will vanish like smoke, the earth will wear out like a garment," found in MT. This might be the result of another scribal error in 1QIsaᵃ. The scribe could have omitted this phrase due to homoioteleuton, his eye skipping from the לה of אלה, "these" to the לה of תבלה "garment." At XLIII:23 in Isa 52:8, 1QIsaᵃ preserves the addition ברחמים "with compassion," which may be reflected also in LXX-Isa (ἐλεήσῃ "mercy"). This reading is missing from both MT and 1QIsaᵇ (→ 6.2.1.2, → 6.2.2.4). Some scholars consider the reading of 1QIsaᵃ to be secondary.[26]

In another example of a harmonizing reading, at XLIII:28–29 in Isa 52:12, 1QIsaᵃ uniquely adds the phrase אלוהי כול הארץ יקרא "the God of all the earth he is called." This seems to be drawn from Isa 54:5 where the identical phrase is found. In a final example of harmonizing or editorial readings, in XLIX:22–23 in Isa 60:19, 1QIsaᵃ adds בלילה "by night" in agreement with LXX τὴν νύκτα "by night." This may be understood as a harmonization of the idiom to a similar phrase appearing in such passages as Ps 121:6 and Jer 31:5.[27]

In addition, 1QIsaᵃ sometimes preserves original readings as shown in the following examples. At XII:6–7 in Isa 14:4, 1QIsaᵃ seems to preserve the correct reading מרהבה "onslaught, assault, insolence" in comparison to the reading of MT-Isa מַדְהֵבָה, the meaning of which is unknown.[28] This is a typical example of *dalet*/*resh* confusion. At XVI:22–24 in Isa 21:8, 1QIsaᵃ preserves the reading הראה "watcher"; compare also the Peshitta for the reading of MT-Isa אַרְיֵה "lion." LXX has Ουριαν, "Ourian," which is understood as a personal name.[29] At XXVII:7–8 in Isa 33:8, 1QIsaᵃ reads עדים "witnesses" for MT's עָרִים "cities." The reading of 1QIsaᵃ fits the context much better and the reading of MT

can be explained as another case of graphic confusion between *dalet* and *resh*. At XXXVII:14–15 in Isa 44:8, 1QIsaᵃ has ואל תיראו "and do not fear" for the *hapax legomenon* וְאַל־תִּרְהוּ in MT-Isa, which *JPS* translates as "and do not be shaken," presumably because of the parallel with the first verb in the verse. There is some disagreement about the verbal root of the form in MT, either רהה, which is otherwise unattested, or ירה, which is parallel to Arabic *wariha* meaning "to be paralyzed with fear."[30] It seems simplest to assume a spelling mistake in MT-Isa. At XXXVIII:7–8 in Isa 45:2, 1QIsaᵃ preserves the reading והררים "and the mountains/mountainous land" where MT-Isa has וַהֲדוּרִים, another *hapax legomenon* that probably resulted from *dalet*/*resh* confusion as in the examples given above. A similar error in MT-Isa occurs at XXXIX:29–31 in Isa 47:10. At XLI:25 in Isa 49:24, 1QIsaᵃ preserves the reading עריץ "tyrant," which is supported by LXX, the Peshitta (→ 6–9.1.4), and the Vulgate (→ 6–9.1.7). MT-Isa has צַדִּיק, which *JPS* interprets as "victor." The reading of MT-Isa seems to arise from graphical confusion.[31] And in a final example of an original reading preserved in 1QIsaᵃ, there is the complicated passage at LIV: 4–5 in Isa 66:17, where 1QIsaᵃ reads אחר אחת "following one" while the *Ketiv* of MT reads אַחַר אֶחָד "imitating one" according to *JPS*. In this example, the reading of 1QIsaᵃ is supported by 1QIsaᵇ, the *Qere*, and some of the Masoretic manuscripts. It is tempting to posit a defective *Vorlage* in the Masoretic tradition, i.e., *taw* was partially obscured or erased, leading to the reading of *dalet*. In one final reading, it is unclear whether or not 1QIsaᵃ preserves the original or superior reading. In Isa 53:11 at XLIV:19, 1QIsaᵃ, 1QIsaᵇ, 4QIsaᵈ, and apparently LXX-Isa all preserve the reading יראה אור "he will see light" as opposed to MT-Isa, which simply has יראה "he will see." The reading of 1QIsaᵃ has been accepted by several translations and scholars.[32] However, Ulrich and Flint suggest that the reading of MT-Isa may be an

---

[26] Oswalt, *Isaiah*, 2.365–66.
[27] See also Oswalt, *Isaiah*, 2.554.
[28] Oswalt, *Isaiah*, 1.314; Blenkinsopp, *Isaiah*, 2.284.
[29] Oswalt, *Isaiah*, 1.388; Blenkinsopp, *Isaiah*, 2.325.

[30] See Blenkinsopp, *Isaiah*, 2.235.
[31] Blenkinsopp, *Isaiah*, 2.122, 313–14; Oswalt, *Isaiah*, 2.312.
[32] Oswalt, *Isaiah*, 2.399. Translations that accept this reading include *NRSV, La Bible de Jérusalem, Die Einheitsübersetzung.

error for an original ירוה "he will be refreshed."[33] If that is the case, then the reading of 1QIsaᵃ and the other witnesses listed above, which is based on MT-Isa יראה "he will see," would actually be secondary. That is, the reading יראה אור "he will see light" assumes and builds on the error in MT-Isa.

As this brief discussion of a sample of the many variants of 1QIsaᵃ has shown, 1QIsaᵃ preserves both secondary and original readings. The overall nature of the manuscript is "mixed" and each passage must be analyzed in detail in comparison to the other witnesses. Ulrich and Flint seem to be correct in their assessment of the relationship of the text of 1QIsaᵃ in comparison with that of MT-Isa, that is, 1QIsaᵃ may represent a later stage of the text of Isaiah linguistically, but represents an earlier stage in the development of the Hebrew text of Isaiah textually.

6.2.3.1.3 Date and Milieu

1QIsaᵃ has been dated by Cross to ca. 125–100 B.C.E., which is in good agreement with the C¹⁴ dating given in the article of Jull et al.[34] Given the revision of the dating of the phases of settlement at Qumran by Magness, which has been widely accepted, it seems less likely that 1QIsaᵃ was copied at Qumran, although there is no reason to think that it was not copied elsewhere in ancient Palestine.[35] There is a long-standing view that 1QIsaᵃ was written by two scribes, which was based in part on the clear division of the scroll into two sections with the first section ending at col. XXVII, followed by a blank space of three lines.[36] Flint and Ulrich conclude that 1QIsaᵃ was copied originally by a single scribe based on a paleographical comparison of the scribal hand in sections one and two of the scroll.

The manuscript was edited by three or up to as many as seven different scribes in the course of its transmission. The original scribe was clearly responsible for the majority of the numerous corrections in the scroll, although some may be due to the efforts of a later scribe during the Hasmonean period with a similar hand. About a generation after the scroll was completed (ca. 100–75 B.C.E.), the scribe responsible for copying 1QS, 4QSamᶜ, and 4QTest, probably at Qumran, was responsible for the insertion at XXXVIII:7 (= Isa 40:7).[37] After about a century, during the Herodian period, one or up to three scribes added passages at XXXII:14 (= Isa 38:21–22) and XXXIII:14–16 (= Isa 40:14b–16). The insertion at XXVIII:19a–19b (= Isa 34:17–35:2) may also be by the same hand. On the geographic location of the composition of 1QIsaᵃ, little can be said beyond the likelihood that it was composed in ancient Palestine.[38]

Major Scribal Insertions in 1QIsaᵃ
(> *Three Words*)

Column	Isaiah
XXVIII:19a–b	34:17–35:2
XXX:10–11b	37:4–7
XXXI:10	37:11
XXXII:14	38:21–22
XXXIII:7	40:7 (2)
XXXIII:14–16	40:14b–16
XLIV:15	53:8
XLIX:26	61:1

A comprehensive analysis of the readings of 1QIsaᵃ remains to be done but is now possible on the basis of the data provided in the critical edition of Ulrich and Flint.[39] 1QIsaᵃ preserves over 2,700 textual variants including some "isolated interpretive

---

[33] Ulrich and Flint, *DJD* XXXII: 2.176.

[34] A.J.T. Jull et al., "Radiocarbon Dating of Scrolls and Linen Fragments from the Judean Desert," *Radiocarbon* 37 (1995) 11–19; Cross, *"Palaeography."

[35] Magness, *Archaeology*, 63–69.

[36] See the references in Tov, "The Text of Isaiah at Qumran," 47 n. 37, 49–50.

[37] See especially the script chart in Ulrich and Flint, *DJD* XXXII: 2.62.

[38] See the interesting discussion in van der Kooij, *Die Alten Textzeugen*, 109–10.

[39] Ulrich and Flint, *DJD* XXXII.

insertions."⁴⁰ It is noteworthy that scribal insertions from the Herodian period, nos. 1, 4, 6 above, seem to be correcting toward MT-Isa. Note also the scribal insertion at XXXIII:19 (= Isa 40:20), coming from the Herodian period, too, and also correcting toward MT-Isa. Even with this large number of textual variants, Ulrich and Flint have concluded that all Hebrew and Greek manuscripts of Isaiah witness to a single literary edition of the book.⁴¹

Ulrich and Flint concur with Kutscher⁴² that 1QIsaᵃ presents a later textual type than MT (→ 6.2.2) in terms of linguistic features, but that in terms of the development of the Hebrew text of Isaiah, 1QIsaᵃ represents an earlier stage than is preserved in MT-Isa.⁴³ As stated above, the systematic study of all of the readings of 1QIsaᵃ remains a *desideratum*.

6.2.3.1.4 Relevance for Exegesis and Literary Analysis

Given the antiquity of 1QIsaᵃ and the large number of distinctive readings preserved, 1QIsaᵃ preserves a remarkable resource for the study and analysis of the transmission of the Hebrew text of Isaiah as well as its interpretation during the Second Temple period.

6.2.3.2 4QIsaᶜ (4Q57)

4QIsaᶜ consists of seventy-seven fragments. Of these, fifty-seven can be identified and partially preserve the following passages: Isa 9:3–12; 10:23–33; 11:4–11, 14–16; 12:1; 14:1–5, 13?; 22:10–14, 23; 23:8–18; 24:1–15, 19–23; 25:1, 8–12; 26:1–9; 28:6–14; 30:8–17; 33:2–8, 16–23; 44:3–7, 23; 45:1–4, 6–8; 46:8–13; 48:10–15, 17–19; 49:22; 51:8–16; 52:10–15; 53:1–3, 6–8; 54:3–5, 7–17; 55:1–7; 66:20–24. 4QIsaᶜ has enjoyed significantly less attention in research than 1QIsaᵃ, and therefore no history of research needs to be provided here.

6.2.3.2.1 Nature and Text-Critical Character

The orthography of 4QIsaᶜ is fuller than that of MT (→ 6.2.2), 1QIsaᵃ (→ 6.2.1.1), and 1QIsaᵇ (→ 6.2.1.2).⁴⁴ The following forms are spelled plene: אדוני "Lord"; אלוהים "God"; זואת "this"; כוה "thus"; כול "all"; כיא "because"; and לוא "no." Tov describes 4QIsaᶜ as written in the Qumran practice.⁴⁵

Of the 110 variant readings listed by Skehan and Ulrich,⁴⁶ approximately 104 readings are certainly non-orthographic variants. Of these, thirty-eight readings may be described as independent readings (≈ 37%).⁴⁷ Given this high number of independent readings, 4QIsaᶜ may be described as an independent or non-aligned manuscript.⁴⁸ 4QIsaᶜ agrees with LXX (→ 6.3) against MT (→ 6.2.2) in nine readings (9%). 4QIsaᶜ agrees with MT against LXX in fourteen readings (13%). Thus, like 1QIsaᵃ (→ 6.2.1.1), 4QIsaᶜ stands closer to MT-Isa than to LXX-Isa. In relation to 1QIsaᵃ, the other non-aligned manuscript of the book of Isaiah in Hebrew, 4QIsaᶜ agrees with 1QIsaᵃ in a total of nineteen readings (18%) and disagrees with 1QIsaᵃ in a total of seventy-seven readings (74%). Of the nineteen readings in which 4QIsaᶜ agrees with 1QIsaᵃ, it also agrees with MT twice but disagrees with MT seventeen times. Of the seventy-seven readings in which 4QIsaᶜ disagrees with 1QIsaᵃ, it also disagrees with MT forty-five times but agrees with MT thirty-two times.

6.2.3.2.2 Date and Milieu

4QIsaᶜ is written in a developed Herodian hand from "the middle third of the 1st century CE," i.e., ca. 33–66 C.E.⁴⁹ It is noteworthy that יהוה "Lord" is always written in paleo-Hebrew script, in a hand that dates to approximately the same time period

---

⁴⁰ Ulrich and Flint, *DJD* XXXII: 2.89, 90, 91.
⁴¹ Ulrich and Flint, *DJD* XXXII: 2.91–92.
⁴² Kutscher, *Language*.
⁴³ Ulrich and Flint, *DJD* XXXII: 2.90.

⁴⁴ Skehan and Ulrich, "Isaiah," 46.
⁴⁵ Tov, *Scribal Practices*, 280, 339; Lange, *Handbuch*, 268.
⁴⁶ Skehan and Ulrich, "Isaiah," 50–71.
⁴⁷ The total number of independent readings may be further qualified. In sixteen readings, 4QIsaᶜ does not agree with MT and LXX, etc. (15%). In another twenty-two readings, 4QIsaᶜ does not agree with MT and/or other Hebrew or Aramaic witnesses only (21%).
⁴⁸ Lange, *Handbuch*, 268; Tov, *"*Synthese," 26.
⁴⁹ Skehan and Ulrich, "Isaiah," 46.

as the Herodian hand. אֱלֹהִים "God" is also usually written in paleo-Hebrew letters, as is צבאות "hosts" when it follows יהוה "Lord."

6.2.3.2.3 Relevance for Exegesis and Literary Analysis

As the only other textually non-aligned copy of Isaiah from the Second Temple period, 4QIsa^c is important for understanding the transmission of the Hebrew text of the book of Isaiah.

Blenkinsopp, J., *Isaiah: A New Translation with Introduction and Commentary* (3 vols.; AB 19–19B; New York: Doubleday, 2000–2003).

Cross, *"Palaeography."

Flint, P.W., "Variant Readings and Textual Affiliation in the Hebrew University Isaiah Scroll from Cave One (1QIsa^b)," in *Qumran Cave 1 Revisited: Texts from Cave 1 Sixty Years after Their Discovery: Proceedings of the Sixth Meeting of the IOQS in Ljubljana* (eds. S. Metso, D.W. Parry, and D.K. Falk; STDJ 91; Leiden: Brill, 2010), 33–53.

Flint, P.W., "Non-Masoretic Variant Readings in the Hebrew University Isaiah Scroll (1QIsa^b) and the Text to be Translated," in *The Dead Sea Scrolls and Contemporary Culture: Proceedings of the International Conference Held at the Israel Museum, Jerusalem (July 6–8, 2008)* (eds. A. Roitman, L.H. Schiffman and S. Tzoref; STDJ 93; Leiden: Brill, 2010), 105–17.

van der Kooij, A., *Die Alten Textzeugen des Jesajabuches: Ein Beitrag zur Textgeschichte* (OBO 35; Göttingen: Vandenhoeck & Ruprecht, 1981).

Lange, *Handbuch*, 257–96.

Magness, J., *The Archaeology of Qumran and the Dead Sea Scrolls* (Grand Rapids: William B. Eerdmans, 2002).

Oswalt, J., *The Book of Isaiah Chapters* (2 vols.; NICOT; Grand Rapids: William B. Eerdmans, 1986–1998).

Pulikottil, P., *Transmission of Biblical Texts in Qumran: The Case of the Large Isaiah Scroll 1QIsa^a* (JSPSup 34; Sheffield: Sheffield Academic Press, 2001).

Skehan, *"Qumran, Littérature de Qumran."

Skehan, P.W. and E. Ulrich, "Isaiah," *DJD XV (1997): 7–143.

Tov, *"Synthese."

Tov, E., "The Text of Isaiah at Qumran," in Tov, *HB, GB, and Qumran*, 42–57.

Tov, *Scribal Practices*.

Ulrich, E., "The Developmental Composition of the Book of Isaiah," *DSD* 8 (2001): 288–305.

Ulrich and Flint, *DJD XXXII.

Wildberger, H., *Isaiah* (2 vols.; CC; Minneapolis: Fortress Press, 1991–1997).

Russell Fuller

6.3 Septuagint

6.3.1 Original Form, Editions, Tools

Instead of Codex Vaticanus and related manuscripts, which are regarded to be the best witnesses to the original text of most books of LXX, the Alexandrinus and Marchalianus Codices, together with the commentary of Cyril of Alexandria, represent the sources that have preserved "the original Greek translation in the best way possible" for the Old Greek of Isaiah.[1] The modern editions[2] are based on this understanding. It is to be noted, however, that the edition of Ziegler contains a few conjectural emendations, which should be reviewed critically. Tools for the study of LXX-Isa are provided by modern translations and by commentaries (brief notes).[3]

6.3.2 Background

It is generally agreed that the Old Greek of Isaiah was produced in Ptolemaic Egypt, in the second century B.C.E. Usually scholars think of Alexandria as the place where this translation was made, but according to van der Kooij there is reason to believe that this version originated elsewhere in Egypt, in Leontopolis, in the nome of Heliopolis (see also below, → 6.3.4).[4]

6.3.3 Character of the Translation

LXX-Isa displays a text that differs in many places, and often markedly, from the Hebrew texts known to us: MT-Isa (→ 6.2.2) and Qumran texts of Isaiah (→ 6.2.1; → 6.2.3). As to the question of how to evaluate these divergences, some scholars have argued that they are related to the translator's Hebrew source, which he misunderstood or which differed from MT.[5] This type of evaluation is based on the assumption that if differences can be explained as arising from mechanical or linguistic errors, or from an allegedly different Hebrew original, this type of explanation should be preferred. Since the work of Ziegler, however, most scholars subscribe to the view that deviations in LXX-Isa should first of all be ascribed to the translator's exegesis of a text like MT-Isa. Ziegler pointed out that many of the differences between LXX-Isa and MT-Isa should be evaluated in the light of the immediate context, or of the wider context of the book as a whole.[6]

On closer inspection, such as by applying a contextual approach, assumed Hebrew variants reflected by the Greek version often turn out to be the work of the translator. Variants at the word level may be due not only to a different vocalization, but also to other techniques such as the interpretation of words on the basis of graphic or phonetic agreements ("etymological" exegesis), or the interpretation of (Hebrew) words as being derived from Aramaic. These and other procedures (e.g., the interpretation of metaphors[7]) fit in with what is known about the reading and interpretation of texts in antiquity. It thus seems that the translator of LXX-Isa has much in common with the "grammarians" of Alexandria, and that he was a scholar who was able to read and interpret literary texts.[8]

Scholars have observed that many renderings and reformulations are best explained in the light of other passages in the book of Isaiah as well as in other "biblical" books, in particular the Pentateuch.[9] LXX-Isa is also marked by a large number of

---

[1] Ziegler, *Isaias*, 25.

[2] Rahlfs, **Septuaginta*; Ziegler, *Isaias*.

[3] **NETS* (M. Silva); **Septuaginta Deutsch* and **Septuaginta Deutsch, Erläuterungen* (A. van der Kooij, F. Wilk, J. Kabiersch, K. Baltzer, K. Koenen). For an earlier translation of LXX-Isa (based on LXX^A), together with notes, see Ottley, *Isaiah according to the Septuagint*.

[4] Van der Kooij, "The Septuagint of Isaiah," 85.

[5] Scholz, *Die alexandrinische Übersetzung*; Ottley, *The Book of Isaiah*; Fischer, *In welcher Schrift*. For this school of thought, see also **DJD* XXXII.2: 92–95.

[6] Ziegler, *Untersuchungen*, 135.

[7] Van der Kooij, "Metaphorical Language."

[8] Van der Kooij, *Textzeugen*, 63; Van der Kooij, "Perspectives"; Troxel, *LXX-Isaiah*, 20–25.

[9] Ziegler, *Untersuchungen*, 103–75; Troxel, *LXX-Isaiah*, 133–

minuses and pluses, and it has been demonstrated that often these are due to stylistic preferences also known from classical rhetoric style in the Hellenistic period.[10]

Other features that add to the profile of LXX-Isa pertain to its language: its Greek represents relatively good *koine*, and is characterized by a rich vocabulary, which among other things is visible through its great variety of lexical choices.[11]

These and other data strongly suggest that although it is a translation, LXX-Isa represents a Greek text with a meaning of its own.[12] Beside the features referred to above, mention should also be made of the use of particles in LXX-Isa, i.e., textual elements tying clauses and sentences together.[13] Furthermore, striking renderings of words and phrases sometimes are part of a theme or motif occurring in a number of passages.[14] The appearance of several such common themes in LXX-Isa creates the impression of a strong internal coherence in this translation.[15] On the basis of these and other remarkable renderings, scholars have come to the conclusion that LXX-Isa is marked to a great extent by exegesis.[16] As some scholars have argued, this exegesis also includes the application of the ancient Isaianic prophecies to the translator's time.[17]

6.3.4 Exegetical Tendencies

A number of related passages in LXX-Isa reflect exegetical tendencies typical of this ancient version. The following examples may serve as an illustration.

In MT, the passages of Isa 3:12–15 and 9:4–5 are about "oppressors," but in Greek they share the topic of economic plundering, reflecting "the practice, common among Hellenistic rulers, of heavily taxing subjected peoples."[18]

Another area of exegesis concerns the law of Moses. In MT-Isa, the term *torah* "teaching" does not refer to the law of Moses, but νόμος "law" in LXX-Isa does. Central passages are Isa 8:16, 20; 24:5, 16; 30:9, and 33:6 that, while differing greatly from MT-Isa (→ 6.2.2), all testify to a strong interest in the Law.[19] LXX-Isa 24:5, 16 are about people who are said to reject, set aside, the law (cf. also Isa 8:16 ["then shall become manifest those who seal up the law"]), an issue that reminds one of passages such as 1 Macc 1:11–15. Righteousness is the core of it (cf. Isa 26:6; 33:6), a view well known from contemporary sources.[20] Moreover, the law is not only for Israel but also for the nations (cf. Isa 2:3), an idea also attested by *Sib. Or.* III.[21]

In MT-Isa, the passages Isa 10:24; 11:16, and 19:18–19, 24–25 are not related to each other, but in LXX-Isa they testify to an interest in a group of Jews in Egypt. The first passage refers to their going from Zion to Egypt, while the second one is about their return. As van der Kooij has argued, evidence to be found in Josephus' writings, namely, accounts of the priest Onias who fled from Jerusalem to Egypt and built a temple in Leontopolis (*J.W.* 7.420–432; *Ant.* 13.62–73), allows one to fit this interest into

---

51; Van der Vorm-Croughs, *The Old Greek of Isaiah*, 299–449.

[10] Van der Vorm-Croughs, *The Old Greek of Isaiah*, 187–297. Cf. also Ziegler, *Untersuchungen*, 46–80.

[11] See Ziegler, *Untersuchungen*, 175–212; van der Meer, "Papyrological Perspectives."

[12] For an example, see van der Kooij, *Oracle*, 75–86 (LXX-Isa 23).

[13] On the particles, see Le Moigne, "Le livre d' Ésaïe."

[14] Cf. Seeligmann, *Septuagint Version*, 95–120; Troxel, *LXX-Isaiah*, 126–34.

[15] On this feature, see van der Kooij, "Issue of Coherence."

[16] Cf., among others, Koenig, *L'herméneutique*; Baer, *When We All Go Home*; De Sousa, *Eschatology*; Ngunga, *Messianism*; Wagner, *Reading the Sealed Book*.

[17] Seeligmann, *Septuagint Version*, 76–91; van der Kooij, *Textzeugen*, 33–60; van der Kooij, *Oracle*, 88–109; van der Kooij, "Mode of Reading Prophecies." For criticism, see Troxel, *LXX-Isaiah*, 173–99.

[18] Troxel, *LXX-Isaiah*, 201–09 (201).

[19] Cf. Seeligmann, *Septuagint Version*, 104–08; **Septuaginta Deutsch Erläuterungen* II, 2491–92.

[20] See e.g. the *Letter of Aristeas*, 168–69 ("[...] all our regulations have been drawn up with a view to righteousness [...] the whole system aims at righteousness and righteous relationships between man and man").

[21] Cf. R. Buitenwerf, *Book III*, 341 (for the author of *Sib. Or.* III, "the Mosaic law is a specific, divine revelation of the universal principles of righteousness").

6.3.5 Text-Critical Value

In light of the interpretive character of LXX-Isa, most scholars assume that the underlying Hebrew text of LXX-Isa did not differ much from MT. It is to be noted though that due to its complexities it is often difficult to say which Hebrew words and phrases – MT (→ 6.2.2), variants of Qumran manuscripts (→ 6.2.1; → 6.2.3), or otherwise – the Greek version may reflect. Hence, the text-critical value of LXX-Isa is to be considered limited. As far as the relationship between LXX-Isa and 1QIsa^a (→ 6.2.1.1) is concerned, both witnesses have in common that they deviate in many instances from MT, but both are also mutually divergent in a large number of cases, whereas the number of common readings is very small. It therefore is likely that agreements are due to a common free approach towards the Hebrew text rather than reflecting a common *Vorlage*.[23] Further research is needed in order to analyze the relationship between the Greek and the Hebrew texts in more detail. See also → 6.1.2.2.3.

Baer, D.A., *When We All Go Home: Translation and Theology in LXX Isaiah 56–66* (JSOTSup 318; Sheffield: Sheffield Academic Press, 2001).

Buitenwerf, R., *Book III of the Sibylline Oracles and its Social Setting: With an Introduction, Translation, and Commentary* (SVTP 17; Leiden: Brill, 2003).

Fischer, J., *In welcher Schrift lag das Buch Isaias den LXX vor? Eine textkritische Studie* (BZAW 56; Giessen: Alfred Töpelmann, 1930).

Koenig, J., *L'herméneutique analogique.

---

[22] Van der Kooij, "The Septuagint of Isaiah," 63–85. There are more examples that could be given, such as exegetical features in LXX-Isa concerning Zion/Jerusalem, "the holy city," the Servant, and the expected ideal ruler ("Messiah"). As to the last one, opinions differ on the issue of which type of leadership a passage such as LXX-Isa 9:6–7 might reflect: a royal messiah, or a priestly one having royal status.

[23] Cf. Ziegler, "Die Vorlage."

van der Kooij, A., *Die alten Textzeugen des Jesajabuches: Ein Beitrag zur Textgeschichte des Alten Testaments* (OBO 35; Göttingen: Vandenhoeck & Ruprecht, 1981).

van der Kooij, A., "Perspectives on the Study of the Septuagint: Who are the Translators?" in *Perspectives in the Study of the Old Testament and Early Judaism: A Symposium in Honour of Adam S. van der Woude on the Occasion of His 70th Birthday* (eds. F. García Martínez and E. Noort; VTSup 73; Leiden: Brill, 1998), 214–29.

van der Kooij, A., *The Oracle of Tyre: The Septuagint of Isaiah XXIII as Version and Vision* (VTSup 71; Leiden: Brill, 1998).

van der Kooij, A., "The Interpretation of Metaphorical Language: A Characteristic of LXX-Isaiah," in *Jerusalem, Alexandria, Rome: Studies in Ancient Cultural Interaction in Honour of A. Hilhorst* (JSJSup 82; Leiden: Brill, 2003), 179–85.

van der Kooij, A., "The Septuagint of Isaiah and the Mode of Reading Prophecies in Early Judaism: Some Comments on LXX Isaiah 8–9," in Karrer–Kraus, *Septuaginta 2008*, 597–611.

van der Kooij, A., "The Septuagint of Isaiah and the Issue of Coherence: A Twofold Analysis of LXX Isaiah 31:9b–32:8," in *The Old Greek of Isaiah: Issues and Perspectives: Papers read at the Conference on the Septuagint of Isaiah, held in Leiden 10–11 April 2008* (eds. A. van der Kooij and M.N. van der Meer; CBET 55; Leuven: Peeters, 2010), 33–48.

van der Kooij, A., "The Septuagint of Isaiah," in J. Cook and A. van der Kooij, *Law, Prophets, and Wisdom: On the Provenance of Translators and their Books in the Septuagint Version* (CBET 68; Leuven: Peeters, 2012), 63–85.

Le Moigne, P., "Le livre d'Ésaïe dans la Septante: ecdotique, stylistique, linguistique ou esquisse d'une poétique de la Septante" (unpubl. PhD diss., École Pratique des Hautes Études, Paris, 2001).

van der Meer, M.N., "Papyrological Perspectives on the Septuagint of Isaiah," in *The Old Greek of Isaiah: Issues and Perspectives: Papers Read at the Conference on the Septuagint of Isaiah, Held in Leiden 10–11 April 2008* (eds. A. van der Kooij and M.N. van der Meer; CBET 55; Leuven: Peeters, 2010), 107–33.

Ngunga, A.T., *Messianism in the Old Greek of Isaiah: An Intertextual Analysis* (FRLANT 245; Göttingen: Vandenhoeck & Ruprecht, 2013).

Ottley, R.R., *The Book of Isaiah according to the Septuagint (Codex Alexandrinus)*. Vol. 1: *Introduction and Translation* (London: Cambridge University Press,

1904); Vol. 2: *Text and Notes* (Cambridge: Cambridge University Press, 1906).

Scholz, A., *Die alexandrinische Übersetzung des Buches Jesaias* (Würzburg: Leo Woerl, 1880).

Seeligmann, I.L., *The Septuagint Version of Isaiah: A Discussion of its Problems* (Mededelingen en verhandelingen van het Vooraziatisch-Egyptisch Genootschap "Ex Oriente Lux" 9; Leiden: Brill, 1948); reprint: *The Septuagint Version of Isaiah and Cognate Studies* (eds. R. Hanhart and H. Spieckermann; FAT 40; Tübingen: Mohr Siebeck, 2004), 119–294.

de Sousa, R.F., *Eschatology and Messianism in LXX Isaiah 1–12* (Library of Hebrew Bible/Old Testament Studies 516; London: T & T Clark, 2010).

Troxel, R.L., *LXX-Isaiah as Translation and Interpretation: The Strategies of the Translator of the Septuagint* (JSJSup 124; Leiden: Brill, 2008).

van der Vorm-Croughs, M., *The Old Greek of Isaiah: An Analysis of its Pluses and Minuses* (SBLSCS 61; Atlanta: SBL, 2014).

Wagner, J.R., *Reading the Sealed Book: Old Greek Isaiah and the Problem of Septuagint Hermeneutics* (FAT 88; Tübingen: Mohr Siebeck, 2013).

Ziegler, J., *Untersuchungen zur Septuaginta des Buches Isaias* (ATA 13.3; Münster: Aschendorffschen Verlagsbuchhandlung, 1934).

Ziegler, J., "Die Vorlage des Isaias-LXX und die ersten Isaias-Rolle von Qumran (1QIsa^a)," *JBL* 78 (1959), 34–59; reprint: *Sylloge: Gesammelte Aufsätze zur Septuaginta* (MSU 10; Göttingen: Vandenhoeck & Ruprecht, 1971), 484–509.

Ziegler, J., *Isaias* (2nd rev. ed.; Septuaginta Vetus Testamentum Graecum 14; Göttingen: Vandenhoeck & Ruprecht, 1967).

Arie van der Kooij

7
Jeremiah

∴

7.1 Textual History of Jeremiah

7.1.1 Extant Witnesses

7.1.1.1 Hebrew Witnesses

The extant Hebrew witnesses to the text of the book of Jeremiah consist of fragments from six manuscripts from the period 225 B.C.E. to 50 C.E. found among the Dead Sea Scrolls (→ 7.2.1), fragments of early medieval manuscripts found among Genizah collections, and the fully developed MT attested through medieval manuscripts (3–5.3). There are also quotations of Hebrew text from Jeremiah found in the Qumran literature and rabbinic literature.

The oldest extant witness to the Hebrew text of the book of Jeremiah is 4QJer^a, dated to 225–175 B.C.E. by its editor in *DJD*.[1] This fragmentary manuscript is also one of the two most extensive Qumran manuscripts of Jeremiah (→ 7.2.1.2). 4QJer^a is closely followed in date by 4QJer^b and 4QJer^d, ascribed to the first half of the second century B.C.E.[2] Since 4QJer^a unquestionably reproduces a form of the text that, in the scope and order of its contents, matches the text form transmitted in MT, and since 4QJer^b (→ 7.2.1.3) and 4QJer^d (→ 7.2.1.5) are widely accepted to transmit a form of the text similar to what would be expected for the *Vorlage* of the Old Greek were it a relatively "literal" translation,[3] the evidence for the Hebrew text of Jeremiah substantiates, from the earliest stage for which we have documentation, the existence side by side of two versions of the book that show significant differences in the scope and order of its contents. The other Qumran fragment from this era, dated to the first half of the second century, 4QJer^e, does not offer a text that can be assigned to one or the other of these two versions (→ 7.2.1.6).

The remaining Hebrew witnesses, however, all later by a century or more than the four just mentioned, attest the text form that survives in MT. 4QJer^c is dated by its editor to the latter part of the first century B.C.E.,[4] and is the other Qumran manuscript to offer extensive amounts of text (→ 7.2.1.4). 2QJer (→ 7.2.1.1) is dated by its editor to the first half of the first century C.E.[5] The Genizah fragments that survive date to the medieval period, and the fully realized MT can be dated by its most important representatives: the Cairo Codex (894/5 C.E.), the Aleppo Codex (ca. 930 C.E.), and the Leningrad Codex (1008 C.E.).[6] The Hebrew University Bible collates and reports the variants of the manuscripts numbered by Kennicott (*1776–1780) as 30, 89, 93, 96, and 150, but this is due to the possibility that they may report variants from outside the tradition of MT.[7] The text of MT itself is best represented by the three named codices, especially the Aleppo Codex (→ 7.2.2.5; → 3–5.3).

It is often accepted that MT carefully preserves an orthographically heterogeneous text that even by the Middle Ages is essentially the same as the text encountered in Dead Sea manuscripts from the first centuries of the Common Era.[8] However, it has also been argued that in Jeremiah MT (→ 7.2.2) shows a clear tendency for assimilation at the word and phrase levels.[9] Nevertheless, in instances where a difference between MT and Old Greek (→ 7.3) is textual rather than redactional in nature,

---

[1] E. Tov, "Jeremiah," *DJD* XV: 145–207 (150).

[2] Tov, "Jeremiah," 172, 203.

[3] See below for a survey of views on the subject. For the first substantial arguments of this position in light of the Qumran evidence, see Janzen, *Studies*, and Tov, "L' Incidence," 189–99. See also → 7.2.1.3; → 7.2.1.5; → 7.2.1.7 (in the latter case, a possible link between manuscript Schøyen 4612/9 and the LXX).

[4] Tov, "Jeremiah," 182.

[5] D. Barthélemy, "Jérémie," *DJD* III: 62–69 (62); cf. Tov, "Jeremiah," 182.

[6] M. Beit-Arié, C. Sirat, and M. Glatzer, *Codices Hebraicis Litteris Exarati Quo Tempore Scripti Fuerint Exhibentes* (Monumenta Palaeographica Medii Aevi, Series Hebraica; Turnhout: Brepols, 1997), 25–29, 65–68, 114–19.

[7] C. Rabin, S. Talmon, and E. Tov, *The Book of Jeremiah* (*HUB*, 1997), xxxii–xxxiii.

[8] J.A. Sanders, "Text and Canon: Concepts and Method," *JBL* 98 (1979): 26–27. Fischer specifically argues for this in regard to Jeremiah. See Fischer, *Jeremia 1–25*, 42–46.

[9] Weis, "Textual Situation," 290–91; and Weis, "Patterns of Mutual Influence," 183.

MT probably contains the preferable text in the majority of cases.[10]

Citations of the Hebrew text of Jeremiah can be found in non-biblical literature from Qumran, in other Hebrew literature from the Second Temple period, and in rabbinic literature (→ 7.2.2.2.1). These citations must be used with a high degree of caution since factors beyond the contents of the author's *Vorlage* can shape their testimony. Nevertheless, they are properly counted among the witnesses to the text of Jeremiah. Citations in rabbinic literature reflect, as would be expected, the proto-MT. A study by A. Lange also shows that citations of the text of Jeremiah in non-biblical literature at Qumran, when they can be assigned to a text form, are predominantly taken from the text form preserved in MT, rather than from that preserved in the Old Greek.[11]

7.1.1.2 Greek Witnesses

The only complete Greek witness to the book of Jeremiah is the text of the LXX (→ 7.3). The LXX is widely accepted as reflecting important features of the Old Greek translation, which is regarded as having been made in the second century B.C.E.[12] The Greek text is notable in that when compared to MT (→ 7.2.2), it is shorter by about one-sixth, has the Oracles against Foreign Nations in a different place in the book as well as in a different order, and displays many qualitative variants as compared with MT.[13] During the nineteenth century, the central question in debate about the textual history of Jeremiah had been whether these differences are the work of the Greek translator or whether these readings were already in the translator's *Vorlage*. After the work of Thackeray early in the twentieth century, it has been largely accepted that the Greek translation of Jeremiah is relatively "literal,"[14] even though paradoxically for the first three quarters of the twentieth century the translator was also held responsible for most of the quantitative differences between the LXX and MT. In more precise terms, the LXX translation can be described as reflecting three norms. The primary norm is "the consistent one-to-one sequential representation of the form of the [Hebrew] source text."[15] Subordinate to this norm are two others: the use of formal equivalent renderings should not sacrifice essential semantic equivalence; nor should formal equivalence sacrifice a "correct" portrayal of figures in the text as figures from a past time.[16] In cases where the testimony of the LXX and MT diverges textually, not redactionally, LXX offers a text preferable to MT in a lesser, but still significant, number of instances.[17]

Fischer and Vonach have argued against the widely accepted view of OG-Jer as reflecting a careful, largely formal equivalence style of translation although it must be said that their position has attracted few adherents to date.[18] Since Thackeray, it also has been common to hold that the Greek of Jeremiah is the product of two different translators and, since Tov, to hold that it is the product of a translator followed by a reviser who worked on the latter part of the book.[19] Soderlund and Pietersma have offered counter-arguments to the reviser theory in favor of the two translator hypothesis.[20]

Fragments of the three major Hexaplaric witnesses (→ 6–9.1.5), Aquila, Symmachus, and *kaige*-

---

[10] Weis, "Textual Situation," 289–90. See below → 7.1.4.5.
[11] A. Lange, "The Question of Group Specific Texts in Light of Essene Jeremiah Quotations and Allusions" (paper presented at the annual meeting of the SBL, Chicago, 19 November 2012).
[12] Tov, *Jeremiah–Baruch*, 165. See also → 7.3.1.1.
[13] Tov, *TCHB*, 287. See also → 7.3.1.
[14] Thackeray, *Grammar*, 13.
[15] Weis, "Textual Situation," 282.
[16] Weis, "Textual Situation," 282.
[17] Weis, "Textual Situation," 290–91. See also → 7.1.4.5.
[18] Fischer and Vonach, "Tendencies," 64–72. See also → 7.3.4; → 7.3.5 for a current and nuanced expression of Fischer's views.
[19] Thackeray, "The Greek Translators of Jeremiah," *JTS* 4 (1903): 245–66; Tov, *Jeremiah–Baruch*, 4–11.
[20] Soderlund, *The Greek Text of Jeremiah*: 153–92; A. Pietersma, "Greek Jeremiah and the Land of Azazel," in *Studies in the Hebrew Bible, Qumran, and the Septuagint Presented to Eugene Ulrich* (VTSup 101; eds. P.W. Flint, E. Tov, and J.C. VanderKam; Leiden: Brill, 2006), 402–13; A. Pietersma, "Of Translation and Revision: From Greek Isaiah to Greek Jeremiah," in *Isaiah in Context: Studies in Honour of Arie van der Kooij on the Occasion of his Sixty-Fifth Birthday* (VTSup 138; eds. M.N. van der Meer et al.; Leiden: Brill, 2010), 359–87.

Th, survive for the book of Jeremiah. There is no widely accepted date for *kaige*-Th, but if the proposal of the second half of the first century C.E. is correct, it would be the earliest of the three.[21] Aquila comes next in the first half of the second century C.E., followed by Symmachus around 200 C.E.[22] All three of these witnesses appear to have used *Vorlagen* that follow the text form encountered now in MT.

No fragments of Quinta or Sexta survive for Jeremiah, but fragments from two other minor Hexaplaric witnesses do survive, i.e., from "The Hebrew" (ὁ ἑβραῖος) and "The Syrian" (ὁ σύρος). Both of these are regarded as presenting distinct new versions, whether revisions of the Old Greek toward the proto-MT (less likely) or new translations altogether. Both presume a *Vorlage* that follows the MT text form. No date has been settled for ὁ ἑβραῖος, but a date of approximately 300 C.E. has been tentatively suggested for ὁ σύρος.[23] Compilations of Hexaplaric readings also report readings attributed to "The Three" (οἱ γ'), "The Rest" (οἱ λοίποι), and "All" (πάντες). So far as they can be seen in Jeremiah, the Hexaplaric witnesses conform to what is known of their translation technique for Scripture as a whole.[24]

Finally, the book of Jeremiah has an additional minor Greek witness reported among the Hexaplaric readings, a witness named Iosippos (Ἰώσιππος). The readings given under this name come from a fresh translation that has been dated to the first half of the fifth century C.E.[25] It clearly used a *Vorlage* that followed the MT text form.

7.1.1.3 Other Versional Witnesses

Among the other versional witnesses to the text of Jeremiah, the Syriac (Peshitta) and Aramaic are the earliest, coming roughly in the same period as the latest Qumran witness (2QJer), Theodotion, and Aquila. Greenberg, who has made a special study of s-Jer dates this witness to the first century C.E., whereas Weitzman suggests a date in the middle of the second century C.E.[26] In general, the translation technique of the Peshitta (→ 6–9.1.4) is to aim at a "faithful," yet "idiomatic" translation of the "plain sense" of the source text.[27] Targum Jonathan of Jeremiah (→ 6–9.1.3) is dated by its translator, Hayward, to the first century C.E. with the recognition that further development of the Targum took place in the third and fourth centuries C.E.[28] The fundamental norm guiding the translation technique of Targum Jonathan is the aim of rendering the meaning that the text is perceived to hold "for the Targum's target audience." In some cases, this leads to a very "interpretive" rendering, in others to something that comes close to a one-to-one correspondence with the source text.[29] Both the Peshitta and Targum Jonathan clearly reflect *Vorlagen* that match the text form preserved in MT, rather than that preserved in LXX.

Of the two Latin witnesses, only V (→ 6–9.1.7) is a direct translation from a Hebrew *Vorlage*, and that *Vorlage* is widely accepted to have been a form of proto-MT. Kelly dates the translation of Jeremiah in the Vulgate to 390–406 C.E.[30] The fundamental norm that guides the Vulgate translation is "the consistent creation of semantic and syntactic equivalence between the translation and the source text."[31] Consistency in formal representa-

---

[21] N. Fernández Marcos, *The Septuagint in Context: Introduction to the Greek Versions of the Bible* (trans. W.G.E. Watson; Leiden: Brill, 2000), 143, 152.

[22] Fernández Marcos, *The Septuagint in Context*, 112, 123–26, 149–53.

[23] Fernández Marcos, *The Septuagint in Context*, 161–67.

[24] For a full presentation, see Fernández Marcos, *Septuagint in Context*, 109–73.

[25] Fernández Marcos, *Septuagint in Context*, 169–72.

[26] Greenberg, *Translation Technique*, 4–5; and M. Weitzman, *The Syriac Version of the Old Testament: An Introduction* (Cambridge: Cambridge University, 1999), 258.

[27] Weitzman, *Syriac Version*, 61; and Greenberg, *Translation Technique*, 18–20.

[28] R. Hayward, *The Targum of Jeremiah* (ArBib 12; Wilmington: Michael Glazier, 1987), 34–38. Cf. P.S. Alexander, "Jewish Aramaic Translations of the Hebrew Scriptures," in Mulder, *Mikra*, 247; and Flesher–Chilton, *The Targums*, 207–13.

[29] See Weis, "Textual Situation," 283, but especially Alexander, "Jewish Aramaic Translations," 225–28, and Hayward, *Targum of Jeremiah*, 21–26.

[30] J.N.D. Kelley, *Jerome: His Life, Writings, and Controversies* (New York: Harper & Row, 1975), 159–63, 283–85.

[31] Weis, "Textual Situation," 284.

tion, while not unknown, is always subordinated to this norm. Moreover, the translation follows a secondary norm of a stylistic preference for formal variety.[32]

As in other books, VL-Jer (→ 6–9.2.1.2), dated to the middle of the second century C.E. by Kedar, was made from a Greek *Vorlage*, not a Hebrew one.[33] It comes into consideration as a possible witness to the Hebrew text of Jeremiah in that in a few places, most notably in Jeremiah 52, VL-Jer witnesses an even shorter form of the text than LXX. Ziegler expressed what has probably been the prevailing view, namely, that VL was not a particularly careful translation.[34] Bogaert has argued in numerous publications that in some cases where the VL text is much shorter than that of the LXX, VL witnesses the older text of the Old Greek, which in the Greek manuscript tradition had subsequently been filled in based on the longer Hebrew text form. Thus the "very short" text form witnessed at these points in VL gives us the best witness to the shorter Hebrew text form that was the *Vorlage* of the Old Greek.[35] Bogaert has not been explicitly joined in these views by many others, but has also not encountered serious contradiction.

7.1.1.4 Relations among the Witnesses

The witnesses that show the longer text form encountered in MT (i.e., Hebrew witnesses apart from 4QJer[b, d], manuscript Schøyen 4612/9; Greek witnesses apart from the LXX, Peshitta, Targum Jonathan, and Vulgate), display relationships that are straightforwardly textual in character. Although the textual allegiance of 4QJer[e] cannot easily be determined, 2QJer, 4QJer[a], and 4QJer[c] all show clear signs of belonging to the group of scrolls containing texts ancestral to MT (→ 7.2.2). Quotations in rabbinic literature and the versional witnesses all display – or are best explained as based on – the proto-MT. Differences among them arise from causes typical of the copying and translating of texts in antiquity. Because they all relate to this coherent textual stream, these witnesses provide evidence for its development from the earliest moments at which it comes into our view, i.e., 225–175 B.C.E., until the achievement of the full MT in the Middle Ages.

However, relations between this part of the textual tradition of Jeremiah on the one hand and that conveying the shorter text form of the book (i.e., 4QJer[b], 4QJer[d], and the Old Greek) on the other are much more complex, and have been the primary focus of debate since the last quarter of the twentieth century, as will be discussed in → 7.1.2. There are several inter-related questions. The first is whether the scale and kind of differences between the shorter text form and the longer one are best explained as only textual phenomena, as a mixture of redactional and textual phenomena, or as purely redactional phenomena.

For scholars who have concluded that the differences are best explained as only textual, there is nothing distinctive in the pattern of relations among the witnesses for Jeremiah. They are all seen as deriving by well-understood means of copying and translation from a single edition of the book. The question that then follows is how to reconcile what has been understood to be a fairly "literal" translation technique on the part of the Old Greek translator(s) with the significant quantitative differences between it and MT. Depending on the resolution of that question, a scholar might come to one of three positions: 1) there was only a single Hebrew text form in antiquity; 2) the two witnessed Hebrew text forms represent snapshots of a single evolving textual tradition; 3) the two witnessed Hebrew text forms evolved independently from an earlier, now lost, text form.

For scholars who conclude that the differences are best explained as a mixture of the results of redactional and textual processes, the resulting conclusion that there were two distinct Hebrew

---

[32] See further Weis, "Textual Situation," 284–87.

[33] B. Kedar, "The Latin Translations," in Mulder, *Mikra*, 299–338 (299–302).

[34] J. Ziegler, *Jeremias, Baruch, Threni, Epistula Jeremiae* (2nd ed.; Septuaginta Vetus Testamentum Graecum 15; Göttingen: Vandenhoeck & Ruprecht, 1976), 18.

[35] Bogaert, "De la *vetus latina*," 216–43; Bogaert, "Les trois formes," 1–17; see also the other works of Bogaert listed in the bibliography.

editions in circulation in the period of our earliest witnesses resolves the problem of reconciling the idea of a "literal" translation technique for the Old Greek with the degree of difference between the text forms. However, this understanding of the relations among the witnesses then opens another pair of questions. One question is how to differentiate textual and redactional phenomena in the testimony of the witnesses. This will be discussed further in → 7.1.3. The second question is how to understand agreements against MT between a witness to the shorter text form (especially LXX; → 7.3) and a witness to the longer text form.

Because the witnesses to the longer text form all witness a single textual stream that results in MT, one could argue – in the style of P. de Lagarde – that the individual witnesses should not be treated independently, but that differences among witnesses to the longer text form should be evaluated first to derive the one earliest reading of that text form, and that reading is then compared with a parallel reading that has been similarly derived for the shorter text form.[36] If one assumes that each text form goes back to a single archetypal manuscript in the style of de Lagarde's theory, then this is a reasonable approach. However, the evidence of the mass of biblical materials among the Dead Sea Scrolls has vindicated the views of textual development espoused by A. Geiger and P. Kahle more than that espoused by de Lagarde.[37] Regardless of how one construes the origins of the texts of the Bible, in the period from 225 B.C.E. to 50 C.E. there was a fair degree of variability in details among manuscripts of the same biblical work, even within the same textual stream.[38]

In the specific case of Jeremiah the two text forms were clearly understood as distinct versions of the book between which a reading community might choose.[39] This is evident from the preference for translating only the shorter text form within the Greek-speaking community or communities responsible for the Old Greek, and from the preference for the longer text form in the Qumran community as evidenced by its use in citations in the community's literature documented by Lange.[40] At the same time, the two text forms appear to have existed side by side in multiple copies in a single library (Qumran Cave 4). Cross-fertilization in Hebrew between the two text forms in passages where they had text in common seems inevitable in this environment. Moreover, in an environment of textual variability within a tradition such as that which led to MT, it is not unreasonable to expect that the results of such cross-fertilization would survive into the proto-Masoretic period to appear in the *Vorlagen* of the various versions. Thus for passages shared by the two text forms in cases of differences judged to be textual, not redactional, all of the extant witnesses to the Hebrew text should be treated as possibly reporting evidence for the earliest reading in the case. Thus the central question in the relations among the witnesses is the first one: When is a difference between the shorter text form and the longer text form the product of text transmissional processes and when is it the product of redactional processes? To that question we now turn.

7.1.2 History of Research

In 1824, Eichhorn opened the modern discussion of the central issue in the textual situation of Jeremiah when he argued that the differing text forms found in the LXX and MT reflected two separate editions created by Jeremiah himself in Egypt. The first remained only in Egypt, where it eventually furnished the *Vorlage* for the Old Greek. The second edition, the prototype of MT, eventually was taken

---

[36] R.D. Weis, "'Lower Criticism': Studies in the Masoretic Text and the Ancient Versions of the Old Testament as Means of Textual Criticism," in *Hebrew Bible/Old Testament: The History of Its Interpretation*, Vol. 3: *From Modernism to Post-Modernism (The Nineteenth and Twentieth Century)*, Part 1: *The Nineteenth Century – a Century of Modernism and Historicism* (ed. M. Saebø; Göttingen: Vandenhoeck & Ruprecht, 2012), 358–62.
[37] Weis, "'Lower Criticism,'" 351–58, 383–84.
[38] E. Tov, "A Modern Textual Outlook Based on the Qumran Scrolls," *HUCA* 53 (1982): 11–27.

[39] Schenker, "Est-ce que le livre de Jérémie," 58–74.
[40] Lange, "Group Specific Texts."

to Palestine where it ultimately became part of the canon.[41] In the same year, Spohn completed publication of a two-volume monograph studying the differences between the LXX and MT. He argued that these were too great to be attributed to inner-Greek corruption in the transmission of the Old Greek text.[42] However, he did not attribute the differences to the Old Greek *Vorlage*, but to the Greek translator. For Spohn, the translator was a private person pursuing his individual purposes rather than producing a translation for public use. Thus, he felt free to omit items that seemed to him redundant or unnecessary although he did so erratically rather than in a systematic and principled way. Thus, from the very beginning of the modern discussion of the text of Jeremiah, the debate was joined concerning the significance of the substantial differences between the text forms surviving in the LXX and MT.[43]

In 1837, Movers responded to Spohn, arguing that the differences were due to the use of a different Hebrew text by the Old Greek translator,[44] one that was older than MT and should therefore be preferred. He based his argument on an analysis of Jeremiah 52, and on an analysis of MT pluses. Movers understood some of the pluses as expansions taken from material elsewhere in the book. He noted that a smaller amount of such expansion had occurred in LXX, implying that both texts had undergone a degree of development although the MT text had undergone more. Thus, although Movers assigned the differences between the text forms to the level of the Hebrew text, he took a different view of the process that produced them than did Eichhorn, seeing it as a matter of differing degrees of textual evolution rather than a matter of editorial intervention.

In 1862, Graf framed the question as an alternative between two options: MT had grown out of the Hebrew text implied by the Old Greek through a process of expansion; or the Old Greek had been produced from a Hebrew text like MT by a process of abridgement.[45] He argued that the Old Greek translator had abbreviated the text in erratic fashion. Graf concluded that the translator had operated in such an ignorant, inconsistent, and arbitrary manner that the result should be viewed as an edition, rather than a translation, certainly implying a different definition of "edition" than that presupposed by Eichhorn.[46]

The 1875 monograph of Scholz argued a position opposite Graf's concept of LXX as a poorly executed abridgement of a text like MT. Based on his careful study of the translation technique of the Old Greek, Scholz drew the conclusion that the Old Greek as a translation was "faithful" (*eine getreue Uebersetzung*) to its Hebrew *Vorlage*,[47] which had been expanded via a process of editorial revision leading to MT. Moreover, it had experienced further expansion through many small additions inserted in the context of use in synagogal services. The Old Greek is a careful, literal translation of its *Vorlage*, which differs from MT not only in its lack of many of the additions, but in other details as well, even though it experienced some degree of interpolation. Although the Old Greek does sometimes make mistakes, on the whole it is a good translation.[48]

In 1889, Workman published a reconstruction of the Hebrew *Vorlage* of the Septuagint on the basis of the posited character of the Old Greek as a literal translation of the Hebrew.[49] When taken together, Graf, Scholz, and Workman represent a spectrum of perspectives on the work of the Greek translator: Graf overly distrustful of the translator, Workman overly trusting, and Scholz crediting the translator with good and careful work while himself carefully attending to the nuances and variations in the translator's product.

In his 1894 commentary on Jeremiah, Giesebrecht addressed anew the question that Graf had framed.[50] Giesebrecht can be seen as holding

---

[41] Eichhorn, *Einleitung in das Alte Testament*, 4.170–222.
[42] Spohn, *Ieremias*.
[43] The differences had been remarked as long ago as Origen (*Ep. Afr.*) and Jerome (*Comm. Jer.*, prologue).
[44] Movers, *De utriusque recensionis*.
[45] Graf, *Der Prophet Jeremia*, xl–lvii.
[46] Graf, *Der Prophet Jeremia*, lvi.
[47] Scholz, *Der masorethische Text*, 12–28, esp. 27.
[48] Scholz, *Der masorethische Text*, 228–29.
[49] Workman, *The Text of Jeremiah*.
[50] Giesebrecht, *Das Buch Jeremia*, xxv–xl.

something of a mediating position between Graf and Scholz concerning the Old Greek. On the one hand, he acknowledges that MT contained a good deal of secondary material. On the other hand, he concluded that the Old Greek translator displayed a definite tendency to abridge the text in the process of translation. Coming closer to Graf in his result, he viewed the majority of the differences between the Old Greek and MT as due to the translator, not his *Vorlage*. According to Giesebrecht, essentially there was only ever one version of the book in Hebrew.

Overlapping the work of Giesebrecht, and thus only partly responding to it, is the study of Streane.[51] Based on a case-by-case study of many of the variations between LXX and MT, Streane argued that the LXX minuses relative to MT were mostly the result of minuses in the *Vorlage* of the Old Greek. That *Vorlage* represented an earlier and better text than that of MT, which had grown from the text form represented by the LXX by a process of textual accretion and augmentation so that most of the resulting differences should be viewed not as redactional but as recensional.[52] The Greek translator had produced a largely faithful rendition of his *Vorlage*, but for various subjective and objective reasons sometimes produced a rendering that did not reflect his *Vorlage*.[53]

Giesebrecht's position would dominate study of the text of Jeremiah until the first publication in 1973 of the Jeremiah fragments from Qumran Cave 4.[54] Thus, for the first three-quarters of the twentieth century, all the voices in discussion of the book of Jeremiah assumed a single ancient *Vorlage*, and considered the variations among the extant witnesses to be the result of the typical processes of translation and transmission of ancient texts albeit with more extreme effect than characterized other biblical books. See further → 7.2.2.1 and → 7.2.2.2.

7.1.3 Contemporary Reconstructions of the Book's Textual History

By the second decade of the twenty-first century, views concerning the textual history of the book of Jeremiah had developed into three streams. Within the broad, if not altogether complete, consensus that the book existed in antiquity in two Hebrew text forms, one longer and one shorter, there are two streams, one that proposes that at least some of the differences between the two text forms are the result of intentional, comprehensive work on the part of one or more redactors, and the other that proposes that all of the differences are a result of more gradual processes, whether these be only textual in nature or a combination of redactional and textual. The third stream continues to argue the position that there was only a single Hebrew text form, i.e., that now found in MT.

By far the largest stream of these three is that which explains the differences between the two text forms as the result of a mixture of intentional, comprehensive, potentially datable intervention(s) by one or more redactors on the one hand, and of the normal processes of textual transmission and translation on the other.[55] The scholars in this group all take a view that the edition found in the longer text form was produced from that found in the shorter. However, they differ in how they view the balance between changes due to redaction and changes due to textual transmission. Migsch and Stulman stand out within this group in that they attribute the differences between the two text forms almost entirely to redactional activity.[56] Stulman, in his reconstruction of the *Vorlage* of the Old Greek, assumes both that the Old Greek translator followed an almost mechanical translation technique that allows comparably mechanical retroversion, and that the differences

---

[51] Streane, *Double Text of Jeremiah*.
[52] Streane, *Double Text of Jeremiah*, 3–13.
[53] Streane, *Double Text of Jeremiah*, 24–26.
[54] For a more detailed discussion of the history of research before 1973, see Janzen, *Text of Jeremiah*, 2–7.

[55] See the works of the following scholars cited in the bibliography: Aejmelaeus, Amphoux and Sérandour, Bogaert, Goldman, Gosse, Holladay, Huwyler, Lange, Migsch, Min, Piovanelli, Schenker, Stulman, Sweeney, Tov, Watts, Weis, and Wells.
[56] Migsch, *Jeremias Ackerkauf*; Stulman, *The Other Text of Jeremiah*.

from MT found in the *Vorlage* of the Old Greek were all the result of the redaction that produced MT's parent text. This view is the exception, however, since nearly all scholars in this stream recognize some differences between Old Greek and MT as transmissional or translational in origin. They differ, however, on the mixture of these types of differences, the reconstruction of redactional process(es), and the date(s) they assign to the redaction. Goldman, Gosse, Weis, and Wells, for example, hold the view that the primary or sole redactional intervention occurred in the early Persian Period, possibly even the late sixth century B.C.E.[57] This position has sometimes been criticized for leaving such a short period of time for the creation of the shorter text form, which necessarily would fall within the Babylonian Period.[58] However, when one considers that two to three generations separated the fall of Jerusalem from the early Persian Period, there is nothing inherently improbable about this. At the other end of the range of dates proposed for the redaction that produced the longer text form is a date in the Hasmonean Period, advocated by Schenker in his earlier writings, by Piovanelli, and by Bogaert in his later writings.[59] This position runs into the difficulty that it dates the redaction that produces the longer text form later than the earliest manuscript representing it, 4QJer[a]. The attempts to redate that manuscript to accommodate the theory have not yet met with widespread acceptance.[60] Holladay dates the edition found in the longer text form to near the end of the fifth century B.C.E.[61] Aejmelaeus has proposed a date in the first decades of the second century B.C.E.[62] More recently, Schenker has suggested a date at the end of the third century B.C.E.[63] Tov proposes a "postexilic" date for the longer text form in contrast to an "exilic" date for the shorter text form.[64]

The second of the three streams of opinion concludes that all the differences between the two ancient Hebrew text forms arose through gradual processes whether solely textual in nature, or predominantly redactional in nature.[65] Janzen, whose work in 1973 re-opened the conversation on the relation between the two text forms of the book, saw them as the result of a gradual accumulation of text-transmissional changes in the line that led finally to MT, and thus speaks of differing recensions of the text.[66] In this, he takes a position similar to that of Movers. Soderlund holds a similar view.[67] Stipp, on the other hand, sees the two Hebrew text forms as the result of deliberate editorial activity. Unlike the scholars in the first stream, he does not see the longer text form as the lineal descendant of the shorter, but sees them as parallel developments that had split off from a common ancestor. The shorter text form underwent much less development than the longer. The editorial activity that produced both text forms extended over a long period of time, a process for which Stipp coined the term "rolling corpus."[68] However, the development of the longer text form was not a gradual, even process, but can be seen to have had two or three major phases of intense editorial activity whose traces can be discerned in distinctive readings found in MT.[69] Shead, who speaks of the *Vor*-

---

[57] Goldman, *Prophétie et royauté*, 225–35; Gosse, "La malédiction," 383–99; Weis, "Textual Situation," 278; Wells, "Indications," 405–20.

[58] Bogaert, "Le livre de Jérémie en Perspective," 399.

[59] Schenker, "La rédaction longue," 281–93; Piovanelli, "JrB 33,14–26," 271–73; Bogaert, "Jérémie 17,1–4 TM," 74. In some of his earlier publications, Bogaert advocated a mid-third century date, but later revised his position to advocate a Hasmonean date. See, e.g., Bogaert, "Relecture et déplacement," 139–50. Accepting Schenker's and Bogaert's Hasmonean dating of the longer text form, Amphoux and Sérandour date the final redaction of the shorter text form to the very first years of the second century B.C.E. (see Amphoux and Sérandour, "Le vocabulaire homilétique," 395–96).

[60] Bogaert, "Jérémie 17,1–4 TM," 74.

[61] Holladay, *Jeremiah* 2, 8.

[62] Aejmelaeus, "Jeremiah at the Turning-Point," 460.

[63] Schenker, "Est-ce que le livre de Jérémie," 68–70.

[64] Tov, "Literary History of the Book of Jeremiah," 129–30; Reprinted in *Greek-Hebrew Bible*, 383–84.

[65] See the works cited in the bibliography from Janzen, McKane, Shead, Soderlund, and Stipp.

[66] Janzen, *Text of Jeremiah*, 127–35.

[67] Soderlund, *Greek Text of Jeremiah*, 193–248.

[68] Stipp, "The Prophetic Messenger Formulas," 80–85.

[69] Stipp, "Zur aktuellen Diskussion," 630–53, esp. 630–36; Stipp, *Das masoretische und alexandrinische Sondergut*, esp. 137–44. See also the similar position taken by P. Miller,

lage of Old Greek and the text of MT as two recensions that developed from a common ancestor, probably comes closest to Stipp.[70] McKane follows Stipp in using his concept of the rolling corpus, but on the whole seems to see the differences as predominantly text transmissional in origin rather than editorial.[71]

The third and smallest stream of opinion concludes that only a single Hebrew text form existed in antiquity, namely the one ancestral to MT, and that all extant witnesses attest it.[72] Those holding this view differ, however, in the extent to which the differences visible among the witnesses, especially the LXX and MT, entered the textual tradition at the level of the Hebrew *Vorlage* or the level of the translators. Fischer has argued that the majority of the differences between the LXX and MT are the work of the Old Greek translator, whereas Lundbom has argued that at least most of the Old Greek minuses were found in the translator's *Vorlage*, a manuscript that was characterized by repeated instances of haplography, some necessarily quite striking due to their length.[73]

A central problem in this debate is that at the micro level of words, phrases, and clauses, changes that occur in the course of textual copying and translation, on the one hand, and changes that implement editorial/redactional intentions, on the other, look very much alike. Thus, when studies focus only on this micro level, or take it as a kind of inductive starting point, an explanation that sees the two text forms as the result of a gradual accumulation of many small changes always will appear more parsimonious. There is a remaining question whether that gradual accumulation is the result of the normal activity of textual transmission or the result of intentional redactional activity, which can prove difficult to resolve due to the similarity of both kinds of activity at the micro level. However, the possibility of a single comprehensive redactional intervention will not arise because the textual ensembles that result from the micro-level changes are not considered.

When we rise above the micro level, the quantity of differences, the extent of some minuses, and especially the differences in placement and ordering of the Oracles against Foreign Nations are very hard to explain parsimoniously without recourse to the idea of intentional, large-scale editorial activity. However, studies that examine only this macro level will tend to overlook the possibility and evidence for text-transmissional activity (e.g., Stulman). The most reasonable methodological starting point is that we must test for the possibility that transmissional and editorial activity are entwined in these witnesses. Thus, the method of research must be adequate to differentiate the two forms of activity. This involves parallel and coordinated examination of the two text forms, as wholes, and unit by unit at both micro and macro levels.[74] Otherwise, the results will probably be an artifact of the method, not the textual data.

7.1.4 Relevance of the Textual History of the Book for Its Exegesis

The relevance of the textual history of the book of Jeremiah for exegesis depends on an exegete's view of the relationship between the longer and shorter text forms. On the whole, interpretation of the book and commentaries on it have not consistently attended to the connection between textual history and exegesis. See further → 7.2.2.1 and → 7.2.2.2.

Nevertheless, the differences between the text forms encountered in the LXX (→ 7.3) and MT (→ 7.2.2) are so substantive that their adjudication has the potential for major impact on the exegesis of the book.[75] Broadly speaking, we might think

---

"The Book of Jeremiah," in *The New Interpreter's Bible* (vol. 6; Nashville: Abingdon, 2001), 567–68.

[70] Shead, *The Open Book and the Sealed Book*, 255–63.

[71] McKane, *Introduction and Commentary on Jeremiah I–XXV*, l–lxxxiii, esp. lxxxiii.

[72] See the works cited in the bibliography from Fischer and Lundbom. See also → 7.3.3.

[73] Fischer, *Jeremia 1–25*, 39–46; Lundbom, *Jeremiah 1–20*, 57–62; Lundbom, "Haplography," 301–20.

[74] For a more detailed description of such a method and an example of its implementation, see Weis, "Textual Situation," 272–93. For another excellent example of this binocular approach, see Goldman, *Prophétie et royauté*.

[75] See also → 7.3.1.2.

of three major categories of difference, all of which we will exemplify below. First of all, there are large-scale structural differences, having to do with the arrangement of the total book, i.e., the different positioning and arrangement of the Oracles against Foreign Nations (OAN). Second, there are large-scale, i.e., paragraph and sentence level, minuses in the shorter text form vis-à-vis the longer. Third, there are a host of word- and phrase-level quantitative and qualitative differences that individually may seem minor, but when taken together, can shift the sense of speeches and narratives.

First, we will consider the consequences of taking one of the positions in the debate concerning the relation of the Old Greek and MT. Then we will explore three examples of the intersection of textual history and exegesis in the book of Jeremiah, corresponding to the three categories of difference just mentioned.

7.1.4.1 Positing a Single Ancient Text Form

Although few scholars in the current debates posit only a single Hebrew text form for the book, if an exegete were to take this position, the consequences for exegesis would further depend on a decision concerning the character of the testimony of LXX. For example, Fischer has argued for the high quality of the MT text form and attributes most of the variations between the Old Greek and MT to the Old Greek translator. Consequently, the readings he regards as the earliest achievable text of Jeremiah almost always come from MT.[76] Lundbom, on the other hand, is less dismissive of the value of the LXX's testimony, and so from time to time prefers one of its readings to MT.[77]

7.1.4.2 Positing Two Ancient Text Forms

The dominant position in the current debate is that in antiquity there existed two different Hebrew text forms for the book of Jeremiah. For an exegete who follows this view, there is still a further decision that will materially affect how the textual history of the book impacts that scholar's work, namely, whether the differences between the two text forms arose purely from the vicissitudes of textual transmission, creating two different forms of the text, or arose in significant part from editorial/redactional activity, creating two different editions of the book. In the latter case, for example, Miller, who adheres to the view that the two text forms are two parallel editions of the book, does not use the Old Greek to correct MT, whereas McKane, taking the view that the text forms differ textually not redactionally, does use the Old Greek to correct MT.[78]

7.1.4.3 An Example: The Oracles against Foreign Nations

One of the most well-known differences between the two text forms is the location and order of the Oracles Against Foreign Nations. In the LXX (→ 7.3), and apparently the Old Greek, these follow Jer 25:13. In MT (→ 7.2.2), they follow Jer 45:5. Moreover, the order of the prophecies within this block differs, as may be seen in the following table.

TABLE 1 *The Oracles against the foreign nations in Jeremiah*

Old Greek	Masoretic Text
Elam (Jer 25:14–26:1)	Egypt (Jer 46:2–28)
Egypt (Jeremiah 26)	Philistines (Jeremiah 47)
Babylon (Jeremiah 27–28)	Moab (Jeremiah 48)
Philistines (Jer 29:1–7)	Ammonites (Jer 49:1–6)
Edom (Jer 29:8–23)	Edom (Jer 49:7–22)
Ammonites (Jer 30:1–5)	Damascus (Jer 49:23–27)
Kedar, the queen of the court (Jer 30:6–11)	Kedar and the kingdoms of Hazor (Jer 49:28–33)
Damascus (Jer 30:12–16)	Elam (Jer 49:34–39)
Moab (Jeremiah 31)	Babylon (Jer 50:1–51:58)

These differences are not incidental, but as Watts and Sweeney, among others, have argued, the different arrangements make a material difference in the rhetorical structure of the book.[79] If an exegete

---

[76] Fischer, *Jeremiah 1–25*, 46. See also → 7.3.6.
[77] Lundbom, *Jeremiah 1–20*, 57–62.
[78] Miller, "Book of Jeremiah," 567–68; McKane, *Jeremiah I–XXV*, l–li.
[79] Watts, "Text and Redaction," 432–47; Sweeney, "Masoretic and Septuagint Versions," 65–77. Even as they argue for the secondary nature of the Old Greek arrangement of the

or translator concludes that the two text forms represent two different editions of the book, and that this set of differences is a result of the editorial activity that produced the longer text form, then he or she will focus on the one text form that is the object of study, and not use the other as a corrective to it. However, if the exegete concludes that there was only a single Hebrew text form in antiquity, or that there were two text forms that are related textually, the text-critical decision regarding which location and arrangement of the OAN is the preferable text has major consequences. Thus, Holladay thinks the location in the shorter text form is older than that in the longer, but because he regards the two text forms as separate editions, he is correct in following the arrangement of the younger text form because that is the edition of the book on which he is commenting.[80] McKane and Lundbom, on the other hand, are arguably inconsistent in the treatment of the OAN in their commentaries. Both regard the location of the OAN in the shorter text form as preferable to that in the longer text form.[81] In addition, both regard the differences between the Old Greek and MT as wholly textual in nature, Lundbom because they both witness a single text form, and McKane because the two text forms relate textually rather than redactionally. To be consistent with their text-critical decision about the placement of the OAN, both commentaries ought to interpret the structure of the text with the OAN coming in the middle of what we know as Jeremiah 25. They do not do so, but interpret the structure with the OAN positioned between Jeremiah 45 and 52, as in the text form that they regard as secondary.[82]

7.1.4.4 An Example: Jeremiah 39(46)

The great number of quantitative differences between the Old Greek (→ 7.3) and MT (→ 7.2.2) are by now well known. Although their total amounts to one-sixth or one-seventh of the book, depending on how this is calculated, they are mostly individual words, phrases, clauses, or verses.[83] However, there are a small number of minuses in the Old Greek that extend over multiple verses. Jeremiah 39(46) contains one of these.[84] Verses 4–13, which are present in MT, are missing in the Old Greek. Since these verses constitute the bulk of the account of the fall of Jerusalem in the MT version of the chapter, their absence in the Old Greek gives that text a notably different character. In the resulting narrative in the Old Greek, vv. 2–3, 14 concern the fate of Jeremiah, and vv. 15–18 concern the fate of the other hero of Jeremiah 37–38(44–45), Abdemelech. As a result, when read together with Jeremiah 44–45, Jeremiah 46 merely completes the prophetic legend found in Jeremiah 44–45. Those chapters belong to the specific sub-genre of political legend, which concludes with a report of the prophet's victory over his opponents. Jeremiah 46 thus provides the vindication for both heroes of the political legend.[85] This changed character is even more visible in the form of the text that results if one joins Bogaert in the view that VL witnesses (→ 6–9.2.1.2) the original text of the Old Greek here, which then also lacks vv. 2–3.[86] The shorter version of the account of the fall of Jerusalem in the final chapter of the book is also far less repetitive than the longer version, which covers events already reported in Jeremiah 39. At this point, the textual history intersects not only with the exegetical

---

OAN, Fischer and Rofé give evidence of the significance of the variation. See Fischer, "Jer 25 und die Fremdvölkersprüche," 474–99; A. Rofé, "The Arrangement of the Book of Jeremiah," ZAW 101 (1989): 390–98.

[80] Holladay, *Jeremiah 2*, 5, 312–14.

[81] Lundbom, *Jeremiah 1–20*, 59; McKane, *Jeremiah I–XXV*, 632.

[82] J. Lundbom, *Jeremiah 21–36* (AB 21B; New York: Doubleday, 2004), 238–42 (note esp. 241 where Lundbom appears to both affirm that the location in Old Greek is "earlier," and accept Rofé's view that it is the result of a later reworking!); McKane, *Jeremiah I–XXV*, 615–58.

[83] Min, "The Case for Two Books of Jeremiah," 109. Min counts 3,097 minuses in the Old Greek against MT.

[84] See Bogaert, "De la *vetus latina*," 226–30; Joosten, "L' excédent massorétique," 93–108; Stipp, "Zur aktuellen Diskussion," 637–41.

[85] Weis, "Textual Situation," 279–80. For definitions of the genre of prophetic legend and its sub-genre, political legend, see M.A. Sweeney, *Isaiah 1–39 with an Introduction to Prophetic Literature* (FOTL 16; Grand Rapids: Eerdmans, 1996), 534–35.

[86] Bogaert, "De la *vetus latina*," 226–30.

understanding of the character of Jeremiah 37–39(44–46), but of the book as a whole.

7.1.4.5 An Example: Jer 34(41):8–22

As an example of the impact of many small differences, both quantitative and qualitative, we may consider Jer 34:8–22.[87] In Table 2, the text of MT as found in MT^L, the reconstructed text of the edition that is transmitted in the longer text form (labeled Edition 2), and the reconstructed text of the edition that is transmitted in the shorter text form (labeled Edition 1) are arranged in parallel columns from left to right to enable the comparison of the texts. The texts of Edition 2 and Edition 1 represent the earliest recoverable text in the judgment of the author.[88] When a word or phrase in other witnesses is preferable to the text of MT as the reading for Edition 2, it has been highlighted with boldface, italicized type. Where the preferable reading in Edition 2 is the omission of a word or words in MT, this is signaled by the use of square brackets and blank space. Where the earliest recoverable text of Edition 1 differs from that of Edition 2, it has been highlighted in the same way.

As can be seen from an examination of the table, even if an exegete is committed to working only on Edition 2, i.e., the version of the book transmitted in the longer form found in MT, the text-critical task still must be engaged. When the evidence is examined, it is clear that MT is the result of changes that occurred during the transmission of the text, and does not itself represent the earliest attainable text of this version of the book. In eleven instances noted in Table 2, another witness than MT has the preferable reading for Edition 2. All but one of these readings are based on the testimony of LXX, either standing alone or with other ancient witnesses. In nine other instances where LXX differed from MT and that difference was judged to be textual rather than redactional, MT was judged to have the preferable reading.[89] In twenty-one other instances, the difference between the LXX and MT was judged to result from the redactional process that produced the longer edition of the book from the shorter. Those differences are then reflected in the reconstruction labeled "Edition 1."[90]

When the passage is considered as a whole, the many word- and phrase-level changes add up to material differences that have consequences for the exegesis of the passage. In Edition 2, we find an explicit focus on the behavior of leadership in Jerusalem and the consequences of that behavior for the city, whereas in Edition 1 the focus is on Judah: people and land. In Edition 2, repetition conveys a tight linkage between the terms of the covenant, the behavior that breaches it, and the consequences that flow from that breach. These connections exist in Edition 1, but are much less tightly marked, and are nuanced differently. Edition 2 is concerned to leave no doubt that the destruction of Jerusalem, which is a past event for the reader, was the fault of the Jerusalem elites. In Edition 1, this dynamic plays out in relation to people and land more than the Jerusalem elites, and is less tightly reasoned. Moreover, the use of the allusion to the golden calf in v. 18 of Edition 1 frames the matter in terms of the on-going covenant of God

---

[87] Similar consideration of other passages may be found at Aejmelaeus, "Jeremiah at the Turning-Point" (Jer 25:1–15); Tov, "Exegetical Notes," 73–93 (Jeremiah 27); R.D. Weis, "A Definition of the Genre *Maśśā'* in the Hebrew Bible" (PhD diss., The Claremont Graduate School, 1986), 81–102, 285–92, 416–75 (Jer 23:16–40); R.D. Weis, "*Biblia Hebraica Quinta* and the Making of Critical Editions of the Hebrew Bible," TC: A Journal of Biblical Textual Criticism 7 (2002): appendix http://rosetta.reltech.org/TC/v07/Weis2002.html (Jer 23:1–9); Wells, "Indications," (Jer 21:1–23:8).

[88] The data and argumentation for these reconstructions will be provided in the Jeremiah volume of *BHQ.

[89] In this passage, the balance between textual differences in which MT had the preferable text, and another witness (chiefly Old Greek) had the preferable text is unusual for the book as a whole. More typical would be the parallel statistics for Jeremiah 23 (see references in n. 87) where the reading of other witnesses (chiefly Old Greek) was preferable to that of MT twelve times, and the reading of MT was preferable to that of the Old Greek forty-four times. See also Weis, "Textual Situation," 290.

[90] In the case of Jeremiah 23, there are forty differences between the Old Greek and MT that I judge to be due to redactional activity. There, the "small-scale" changes demonstrably alter the structure of the chapter since vv. 7–8 come after v. 40 in Edition 1, and the heading in v. 9 of Edition 2 is not a heading at all in Edition 1, but a prepositional phrase in v. 6.

7.1.4 RELEVANCE OF THE TEXTUAL HISTORY OF THE BOOK FOR ITS EXEGESIS

TABLE 2   *Jeremiah 34:8–22 – MT, Edition 2, Edition 1*

Masoretic Text (MT^L)	Edition 2 (Earliest Attainable Text)	Edition 1 (Earliest Attainable Text)
8 הדבר אשר היה אל ירמיהו מאת יהוה אחרי כרת המלך צדקיהו ברית את כל העם אשר בירושלם לקרא להם דרור 9 לשלח איש את עבדו ואיש את שפחתו העברי והעבריה חפשים לבלתי עבד בם ביהודי אחיהו איש 10 וישמעו כל השרים וכל העם אשר באו בברית לשלח איש את עבדו ואיש את שפחתו חפשים לבלתי עבד בם עוד וישמעו וישלחו 11 וישובו אחרי כן וישבו את העבדים ואת השפחות אשר שלחו חפשים ויכבישום לעבדים ולשפחות 12 ויהי דבר יהוה אל ירמיהו מאת יהוה לאמר 13 כה אמר יהוה אלהי ישראל אנכי כרתי ברית את אבותיכם ביום הוצאי אותם מארץ מצרים מבית עבדים לאמר 14 מקץ שבע שנים תשלחו איש את אחיו העברי אשר ימכר לך ועבדך שש שנים ושלחתו חפשי מעמך ולא שמעו אבותיכם אלי ולא הטו את אזנם 15 ותשבו אתם היום ותעשו את הישר בעיני לקרא דרור איש לרעהו ותכרתו ברית לפני בבית אשר נקרא שמי עליו 16 ותשבו ותחללו את שמי ותשבו איש את עבדו ואיש את שפחתו אשר שלחתם חפשים לנפשם ותכבשו אתם להיות לכם לעבדים ולשפחות 17 לכן כה אמר יהוה אתם לא שמעתם אלי לקרא דרור איש לאחיו ואיש לרעהו הנני קרא לכם דרור נאם יהוה אל החרב אל הדבר ואל הרעב ונתתי אתכם לזועה לכל ממלכות הארץ 18 ונתתי את האנשים העברים את ברתי אשר לא הקימו את דברי הברית אשר כרתו לפני העגל אשר כרתו לשנים ויעברו בין בתריו 19 שרי יהודה ושרי ירושלם הסרסים והכהנים וכל עם הארץ העברים בין בתרי העגל 20 ונתתי אותם ביד איביהם וביד מבקשי נפשם והיתה נבלתם למאכל לעוף השמים ולבהמת הארץ 21 ואת צדקיהו מלך יהודה ואת שריו אתן ביד איביהם וביד מבקשי נפשם וביד חיל מלך בבל העלים מעליכם 22 הנני מצוה נאם יהוה והשבתים אל העיר הזאת ונלחמו עליה ולכדוה ושרפה באש ואת ערי יהודה אתן שממה מאין ישב	8 הדבר אשר היה אל ירמיהו מאת יהוה אחרי כרת המלך צדקיהו ברית את כל העם אשר בירושלם לקרא [ ] דרור 9 לשלח איש את עבדו ואיש את שפחתו העברי והעבריה חפשים לבלתי עבד בם ביהודי אחיהו איש 10 וישמעו כל השרים וכל העם אשר באו בברית לשלח איש את עבדו ואיש את שפחתו חפשים לבלתי עבד בם עוד וישמעו וישלחו 11 וישובו אחרי כן וישבו את העבדים ואת השפחות אשר שלחו חפשים **ויכבשום** לעבדים ולשפחות 12 ויהי דבר יהוה אל ירמיהו מאת יהוה לאמר 13 כה אמר יהוה אלהי ישראל אנכי כרתי ברית את אבותיכם ביום הוצאי אותם מארץ מצרים מבית עבדים לאמר 14 **כי מלאו שש** שנים תשלחו איש את אחיו העברי אשר ימכר לך ועבדך שש שנים ושלחתו חפשי [ ] ולא שמעו אבותיכם אלי ולא הטו את אזנם 15 ותשבו אתם היום ותעשו את הישר בעיני לקרא דרור איש לרעהו ותכרתו ברית לפני בבית אשר נקרא שמי עליו 16 ותשבו ותחללו את שמי ותשבו איש את עבדו ואיש את שפחתו אשר שלחתם חפשים לנפשם ותכבשו אתם להיות לכם לעבדים ולשפחות 17 לכן כה אמר יהוה אתם לא שמעתם אלי לקרא דרור איש לאחיו ואיש לרעהו הנני קרא **דרור לכם** נאם יהוה אל החרב אל הדבר ואל הרעב ונתתי אתכם לזועה לכל ממלכות הארץ 18 ונתתי את האנשים העברים את [ ] הברית אשר לא הקימו ברתי אשר כרתו לשנים ויעברו בין בתריו 19 שרי יהודה ושרי ירושלם הסרסים והכהנים וכל **העם** [ ] העברים בין בתרי העגל 20 ונתתי אותם ביד איביהם וביד מבקשי נפשם והיתה נבלתם למאכל לעוף השמים ולבהמת הארץ 21 ואת צדקיהו מלך יהודה ואת שריו אתן ביד איביהם וביד מבקשי נפשם וביד חיל מלך בבל **ההלכים** מעליכם 22 הנני מצוה נאם יהוה והשבתים אל העיר הזאת ונלחמו עליה ולכדוה ושרפה באש ואת ערי יהודה **ונתתי אתהן חרבה** מאין ישבים	8 הדבר היה אל ירמיהו מאת יהוה אחרי כרת המלך צדקיהו ברית את [ ] העם [ ] לקרא דרור 9 לשלח איש את עבדו ואיש את שפחתו העברי והעבריה חפשים לבלתי עבד [ ] ביהודי [ ] 10 וישמעו כל השרים וכל העם אשר באו בברית לשלח איש את עבדו ואיש את שפחתו [ ] 11 [ ] ויכבשום לעבדים ולשפחות 12 ויהי דבר יהוה אל ירמיהו [ ] לאמר 13 כה אמר יהוה אלהי ישראל אנכי כרתי ברית את אבותיכם ביום הוצאי אותם מארץ מצרים מבית עבדים לאמר 14 כי מלאו שש שנים תשלחו איש את אחיו העברי אשר ימכר לך ועבדך שש שנים ושלחתו חפשי [ ] אלי ולא הטו את אזנם 15 **וישבו** [ ] היום **ויעשו** את הישר בעיני לקרא דרור איש לרעהו **ויכרתו** ברית לפני בבית אשר נקרא שמי עליו 16 ותשבו ותחללו את שמי ותשבו איש את עבדו ואיש את שפחתו אשר שלחתם חפשים לנפשם [ ] לכם לעבדים ולשפחות 17 לכן כה אמר יהוה אתם לא שמעתם אלי לקרא דרור איש [ ] לרעהו הנני קרא דרור לכם [ ] אל החרב ואל הדבר ואל הרעב ונתתי אתכם לזועה לכל ממלכות הארץ 18 ונתתי את האנשים העברים את **בריתי** אשר לא הקימו את הברית אשר כרתו לפני העגל אשר **עשו** **לעברו** [ ] 19 שרי יהודה [ ] הסרסים והכהנים [ ] [העם] ו[ ] 20 ונתתי אותם [ ] **לאיביהם** [ ] והיתה נבלתם למאכל לעוף השמים ולבהמת הארץ 21 ואת צדקיהו מלך יהודה ואת **שריהם** אתן ביד איביהם [ ] [ ] **וחיל** מלך בבל ההלכים מעליכם 22 הנני מצוה נאם יהוה והשבתים אל **הארץ** הזאת ונלחמו עליה ולכדוה ושרפה באש ואת ערי יהודה ונתתי אתהן חרבה מאין ישבים:

TABLE 2   (cont.)

Masoretic Text[91] (MT[L])	Edition 2 (Earliest Attainable Text)	Edition 1 (Earliest Attainable Text)
8 The word which came to Jeremiah from the LORD after King Zedekiah had made a covenant with all the people who were in Jerusalem to proclaim a release for them – 9 that each should set free his male Hebrew slaves, and each his female Hebrew slaves, so that no one should keep his fellow Judean enslaved. 10 And all the officials and all the people obeyed, those who had entered into the covenant each to set his male slaves and each his female slaves free in order to not enslave them any longer, they obeyed and let them go. 11 But afterward they turned about and brought back the male slaves and female slaves whom they had set free, and forced them into slavery. 12 Then the word of the LORD came to Jeremiah from the LORD, saying: 13 Thus said the LORD, the God of Israel: I made a covenant with your ancestors when I brought them out of the land of Egypt, out of the house of bondage, saying: 14 "At the end of seven years each of you shall let go any fellow Hebrew who may be sold to you; when he has served you six years, you must let him go free from you." But your ancestors would not obey me or incline their ears. 15 Now lately you turned about and did what is proper in my sight so that each of you proclaimed a release for his countrymen; and you made a covenant before me in the House which bears my name. 16 But you have turned back and have profaned my name; and each of you has brought back his male slaves and each of you his female slaves whom you had set free for themselves, and forced them to be your male and female slaves. 17 Therefore thus said the LORD: You did not obey me to proclaim a release, each to his kinsman and each to his countryman. Lo! I am proclaiming for you a release – declares the LORD – to the sword, to pestilence, and to famine; and I will make you a horror to all the kingdoms of the earth. 18 I will make the men who transgressed my covenant, who did not fulfill the terms of	8 The word which came to Jeremiah from the LORD after King Zedekiah had made a covenant with all the people who were in Jerusalem to proclaim a release [ ] – 9 that each should set free his male Hebrew slaves, and each his female Hebrew slaves, so that no one should keep his fellow Judean enslaved. 10 And all the officials and all the people obeyed, those who had entered into the covenant each to set his male slaves and each his female slaves free in order to not enslave them any longer, they obeyed and let them go. 11 But afterward they turned about and brought back the male slaves and female slaves whom they had set free, and forced them into slavery. 12 Then the word of the LORD came to Jeremiah from the LORD, saying: 13 Thus said the LORD, the God of Israel: I made a covenant with your ancestors when I brought them out of the land of Egypt, the house of bondage, saying: 14 "**When six** years **are completed**, each of you must let go any fellow Hebrew who may be sold to you; when he has served you six years, you must let him go free." [ ] But your ancestors would not obey me or incline their ears. 15 Now lately you turned about and did what is proper in my sight so that each of you proclaimed a release for his countrymen; and you made a covenant before me in the House which bears my name. 16 But you have turned back and have profaned my name; and each of you has brought back his male slaves and each of you his female slaves whom you had set free for themselves, and forced them to be your male and female slaves. 17 Therefore thus said the LORD: You did not obey me to proclaim a release, each to his kinsman and each to his countryman. Lo! I am proclaiming for you a release – declares the LORD – to the sword, to pestilence, and to famine; and I will make you a horror to all the kingdoms of the earth. 18 I will make the men who transgressed my covenant, who did not fulfill [ ]	8 The word which came to Jeremiah from the LORD after King Zedekiah had made a covenant with [ ] the people [ ] to proclaim a release – 9 that each should set free his male Hebrew slaves, and each his female Hebrew slaves, so that no Judean **should serve as a slave**. 10 And all the officials and all the people obeyed, those who had entered into the covenant each to set his male slaves and each his female slaves free. [

] 11 **Then they** forced them into slavery. 12 Then the word of the LORD came to Jeremiah [ ], saying: 13 Thus said the LORD, the God of Israel: I made a covenant with your ancestors when I brought them out of the land of Egypt, the house of bondage, saying: 14 "When six years are completed, each of you must let go any fellow Hebrew who may be sold to you; when he has served you six years, you must let him go free." But **they** would not obey me or incline their ears. 15 Now lately **they** turned about and did what is proper in my sight so that each of **them** proclaim-ed a release for his countrymen; and **they** made a covenant before me in the House which bears my name. 16 But you have turned back and have profaned my name; and each of you has brought back his male slaves and each of you his female slaves, whom you had set free for themselves, [ ] **for yourselves** as male and female slaves. 17 Therefore thus said the LORD: You did not obey me to proclaim a release, [ ] each to his countryman. Lo! I am proclaiming for you a release [ ] to the sword, to pestilence, and to famine; and I will make you a horror to all the kingdoms of the earth. 18 I will make the men who transgressed my covenant, who did not fulfill |

---

[91] The English translations are adapted from the NJV.

7.1.4 RELEVANCE OF THE TEXTUAL HISTORY OF THE BOOK FOR ITS EXEGESIS

TABLE 2 (cont.)

Masoretic Text (MT^L)	Edition 2 (Earliest Attainable Text)	Edition 1 (Earliest Attainable Text)
the covenant which they made before me, [like] the calf which they cut in two and passed between its pieces, 19 the officers of Judah and the officers of Jerusalem, the officials, and the priests, and all the people of the land who passed between the pieces of the calf. 20 And I shall put them in the power of their enemies and in the power of those who seek their lives, and their carcasses shall become food for the birds of the sky and the beasts of the earth. 21 And Zedekiah, king of Judah, and his officers I will put in the power of their enemies, in the power of those who seek their lives, in the power of the army of the king of Babylon which has withdrawn from you. 22 Lo! I am giving the command – declares the LORD – and I will bring them back to this city, and they shall attack it and capture it, and burn it with fire, and the towns of Judah I will make a desolation, without inhabitant.	the covenant which they made before me, [like] the calf which they cut in two and passed between its pieces, 19 the officers of Judah and the officers of Jerusalem, the officials, and the priests, and all the people [ ] who passed between the pieces of the calf. 20 And I shall put them in the power of their enemies, in the power of those who seek their lives, and their carcasses shall become food for the birds of the sky and the beasts of the earth. 21 And Zedekiah, king of Judah, and his officers I will put in the power of their enemies, in the power of those who seek their lives, in the power of the army of the king of Babylon which has *gone* from you. 22 Lo! I am giving the command – declares the LORD – and I will bring them back to this city, and they shall attack it and capture it, and burn it with fire, as well as the towns of Judah. I will make *them* a *wasteland*, without *inhabitants*.	the covenant which they made before me, [like] the calf which they **made to worship**, [ ] 19 the officers of Judah, [ ] the officials, and the priests, and [ ] the people. [ ] 20 And I shall give them **to** their enemies, [ ] and their carcasses shall become food for the birds of the sky and the beasts of the earth. 21 And Zedekiah, king of Judah, and **their** officers I will put in the power of their enemies, [ ] *that is*, the army of the king of Babylon which has gone from you. 22 Lo! I am giving the command – declares the LORD – and I will bring them back to this *land*, and they shall attack it and capture it, and burn it with fire, as well as the towns of Judah. I will make them a wasteland, without inhabitants.

with the people more than the ad hoc covenant that Zedekiah made with the Jerusalem elite.

This interpretation of the differences is in line with the predominant position in the current discussion of the central question of the book's textual history that sees the two text forms as two editions of the book. Exegetes holding a different position necessarily would interpret the significance of the differences otherwise, but the question of their interpretation is central to the exegesis of these chapters.

From these examples of the three broad categories of differences between the longer and shorter text forms of the book of Jeremiah, it is clear that textual history is far more consequential for the exegesis of the book than was presumed during the first three quarters of the twentieth century. In particular, if an exegete accepts that the Old Greek derived from a Hebrew text form that represents an early *edition* of the book from which the edition witnessed by MT developed, this has major consequences for understanding the literary development of the book. In this case, all efforts to infer the literary history of the book must begin anew from the text of the earlier edition, i.e., the reconstructed Hebrew edition behind the Old Greek. In addition, "assured results" from previous investigations of the book's literary history henceforth must be taken *cum grano salis* for at least two reasons. First, they were based upon MT, that is, they were inferred not from the earliest edition for which we have external evidence, but from a subsequent edition. Second, they did not predict the earlier edition, which is now documented from external evidence.[92]

Aejmelaeus, A., "Jeremiah at the Turning-Point of History: The Function of Jer. xxv 1–14 in the Book of Jeremiah," *VT* 52 (2002): 459–82.

Aejmelaeus, A., "'Nebuchadnezzar, My Servant': Redaction History and Textual Development in Jer 27," in *In-*

---

[92] See also Aejmelaeus, "Jeremiah at the Turning-Point," 461.

terpreting Translation: Studies on the LXX and Ezekiel in Honour of Johan Lust* (eds. F. García Martínez and M. Vervenne; BETL 192; Leuven: Peeters, 2005), 1–18.

Amphoux, C.-B. and A. Sérandour, "Le vocabulaire homilétique de Jr 1–20 comparé à 4 Rg 17,7–20," in *XIV Congress of the International Oranization for Septuagint and Cognate Studies, Helsinki, 2010* (ed. M.K.H. Peters; Atlanta: SBL, 2013), 381–96.

Becking, B., "Abbreviation, Expansion or Two Traditions: The Text of Jeremiah 30–31," in *Between Fear and Freedom: Essays on the Interpretation of Jeremiah 30–31* (OtSt 51; Leiden: Brill, 2004), 11–48.

Bogaert, P.-M., "De Baruch à Jérémie: Les deux rédactions conservées du livre de Jérémie," in *Le livre de Jérémie* (ed. P.-M. Bogaert; BETL 54; Leuven: Leuven University Press, 1981), 168–73.

Bogaert, P.-M., "Les mécanismes rédactionnels en Jér 10,1–16 (LXX et TM) et la signification des suppléments," in *Le livre de Jérémie* (ed. P.-M. Bogaert; BETL 54; Leuven: Leuven University Press, 1981), 222–38.

Bogaert, P.-M., "Relecture et déplacement de l'oracle contre les Philistins: Pour une datation de la rédaction longue (TM) du livre de Jérémie," in *La vie de la parole: Etudes d'exégèse et d'herméneutique bibliques offertes à Pierre Grelot* (ed. H. Cazelles; Paris: Desclée, 1987), 139–50.

Bogaert, P.-M., "La libération de Jérémie et le meurtre de Godolias: Le texte court (LXX) et la rédaction longue (TM)," in *Studien zur Septuaginta – Robert Hanhart zu Ehren* (eds. D. Fraenkel et al.; MSU 20; Göttingen: Vandenhoeck & Ruprecht, 1990), 312–22.

Bogaert, P.-M., "Les trois formes de Jérémie 52 (TM, LXX et VL)," in *Tradition of the Text: Studies Offered to Dominique Barthélemy in Celebration of His 70th Birthday* (eds. G.J. Norton and S. Pisano; OBO 109; Göttingen: Vandenhoeck & Ruprecht, 1991), 1–17.

Bogaert, P.-M., "*Urtext*, texte court et relecture: Jérémie 33:14–26 TM et ses préparations" in *Congress Volume, Leuven, 1989* (ed. J.A. Emerton; VTSup 43; Leiden: Brill, 1991), 236–47.

Bogaert, P.-M., "Le livre de Jérémie en perspective: Les deux rédactions antiques selon les travaux en cours," *RB* 101 (1994): 363–406.

Bogaert, P.-M., "Jérémie 17,1–4 TM, oracle contre ou sur Juda propre au texte long, annoncé en 11,7–8.13 TM et en 15,12–14 TM," in *La double transmission du texte biblique: Etudes d'histoire du texte offertes en homage à Adrian Schenker* (eds. Y. Goldman and C. Uehlinger; OBO 179; Göttingen: Vandenhoeck & Ruprecht, 2001), 59–74.

Bogaert, P.-M., "Heshbon entre Moab et Ammon: La finale ajoutée à l'oracle sur Moab en Jr 48,45–47 TM," in *Interpreting Translation: Studies on the LXX and Ezekiel in Honour of Johan Lust* (eds. F. García Martínez and M. Vervenne; BETL 192; Leuven: Leuven University Press, 2005), 45–54.

Bogaert, P.-M., "De la *vetus latina* à l'hébreu prémassorétique en passant par la plus ancienne Septante: le livre de Jérémie, exemple privilégié," *RTL* 44 (2013): 216–43.

Eichhorn, J.G., *Einleitung in das Alte Testament* (5 vols.; 4th ed.; Göttingen: Rosenbusch, 1823–1824).

Fischer, G., "Jer 25 und die Fremdvölkersprüche: Unterschiede zwischen hebräischem und griechischem Text," *Bib* 72 (1991): 474–99.

Fischer, G., *Das Trostbüchlein: Text, Komposition und Theologie von Jer 30–31* (SBB 26; Stuttgart: Katholisches Bibelwerk, 1993).

Fischer, G., "Zum Text des Jeremiabuches," *Bib* 78 (1997): 305–28. Reprinted in G. Fischer, *Der Prophet wie Mose* (Beihefte zur Zeitschrift für Altorientalische und Biblische Rechtsgeschichte 15; Wiesbaden: Harrassowitz, 2011), 24–41.

Fischer, G., "Jeremia 52 – ein Schüssel zum Jeremiabuch," *Bib* 79 (1998): 333–59.

Fischer, G., "Les deux faces de Jérémie 52," *ETR* 74 (1999): 481–89.

Fischer, G., "Jeremiah 52: A Test Case for Jer LXX," in *X Congress of the International Organization for Septuagint and Cognate Studies, Oslo, 1998* (ed. B.A. Taylor; Atlanta: SBL, 2001), 37–48.

Fischer, G., *Jeremia 1–25* (Herders Theologischer Kommentar zum Alten Testament; Freiburg: Herder, 2005).

Fischer, G., "Die Diskussion um den Jeremiatext," in Karrer–Kraus, **Septuaginta 2008*, 612–29. Reprinted in G. Fischer, *Der Prophet wie Mose* (Beihefte zur Zeitschrift für Altorientalische und Biblische Rechtsgeschichte 15; Wiesbaden: Harrassowitz, 2011), 73–89.

Fischer, G. and A. Vonach, "Tendencies in the LXX Version of Jeremiah," in G. Fischer, *Der Prophet wie Mose* (Beihefte zur Zeitschrift für Altorientalische und Biblische Rechtsgeschichte 15; Wiesbaden: Harrassowitz, 2011), 64–72.

Gesundheit, S., "The Question of LXX Jeremiah as a Tool for Literary-Critical Analysis," *VT* 62 (2012): 29–57.

Giesebrecht, F., *Das Buch Jeremia* (HKAT 3.2; Göttingen: Vandenhoeck & Ruprecht, 1894).

Goldman, Y.A.P., *Prophétie et royauté au retour de l'exil: Les origins littéraires de la forme massorétique du livre de Jérémie* (OBO 118; Göttingen: Vandenhoeck & Ruprecht, 1992).

Goldman, Y.A.P., "Crispations théologiques et accidents textuels dans le TM de Jérémie 2," *Bib* 76 (1995): 25–52.

Goldman, Y.A.P., "Juda et son roi au milieu des nations: La dernière rédaction du livre de Jérémie," in *The Book of Jeremiah and Its Reception – Le livre de Jérémie et sa réception* (eds. A.H.W. Curtis and T. Römer; BETL 128; Leuven: Peeters, 1997), 151–82.

Gosse, B., "La malédiction contre Babylone de Jérémie 51,59–64 et les rédactions du livre de Jérémie," *ZAW* 98 (1986): 383–99.

Gosse, B., "Jérémie xlv et la place du receuil d' oracles contre les nations dans le livre de Jérémie," *VT* 40 (1990): 145–51.

Gosse, B., "Les évolutions du livre de Jérémie et la rédaction massorétique," in B. Gosse, *Structuration des grands ensembles bibliques et intertextualité a l'epoque Perse* (BZAW 246; Berlin: De Gruyter, 1997), 48–67.

Gosse, B., "The Masoretic Redaction of Jeremiah: An Explanation," *JSOT* 77 (1998): 75–80.

Graf, K.H., *Der Prophet Jeremia* (Leipzig: T.O. Weigel, 1862).

Greenberg, G., *Translation Technique in the Peshitta to Jeremiah* (Monographs of the Peshitta Institute Leiden 13; Leiden: Brill, 2002).

Holladay, W.L., *Jeremiah 2* (Hermeneia; Minneapolis: Fortress Press, 1989).

Huwyler, B., *Jeremia und die Völker: Untersuchungen zu den Völkersprüchen in Jeremia 46–49* (FAT 20; Tübingen: Mohr Siebeck, 1997).

Janzen, J.G., *Studies in the Text of Jeremiah* (HSM 6; Cambridge: Harvard University Press, 1973).

Janzen, J.G., "A Critique of Sven Soderlund's The Greek Text of Jeremiah: A Revised Hypothesis," *BIOSCS* 22 (1989): 16–47.

Joosten, J., "L' excédent massorétique du livre de Jérémie et l' hébreu post-classique," in *Conservatism and Innovation in the Hebrew Language of the Hellenistic Period: Proceedings of a Fourth International Symposium on the Hebrew of the Dead Sea Scrolls and Ben Sira* (eds. J. Joosten and J.-S. Rey; STDJ 73; Leiden: Brill, 2008), 93–108.

van der Kooij, A., "Zum Verhältnis von Textkritik und Literarkritik: Überlegungen anhand einiger Beispiele," in *Congress Volume, Cambridge, 1995* (ed. J.A. Emerton; VTSup 66; Leiden: Brill, 1997), 183–202.

Lange, **Handbuch*, 297–324.

Lundbom, J.R., *Jeremiah 1–20: A New Translation with Introduction and Commentary* (AB 21A; New York: Doubleday, 1999).

Lundbom, J.R., "Haplography in the Hebrew Vorlage of LXX Jeremiah," *HS* 46 (2005): 301–20.

Lust, J., "The Diverse Text Forms of Jeremiah and History Writing with Jer. 33 as a Test Case," *JNSL* 20 (1994): 31–48.

McKane, W., "The History of the Text of Jeremiah 10,1–16," in *Mélanges bibliques et orientaux en l'honneur de M. Mathias Delcor* (eds. A. Caquot et al.; AOAT 215; Kevelaer: Butzon und Bercker, 1985), 297–304.

McKane, W., *A Critical and Exegetical Commentary on Jeremiah*, Vol. 1: *Introduction and Commentary on Jeremiah I–XXV* (ICC; Edinburgh: T & T Clark, 1986).

Migsch, H., *Jeremias Ackerkauf: Eine Untersuchung von Jeremia 32* (OBS 15; Frankfurt am Main: Peter Lang, 1996).

Min, Y.-J., "The Case for Two Books of Jeremiah," in *Text, Theology and Translation: Essays in Honour of Jan de Waard* (eds. S. Crisp and M. Jinbachian; Reading: United Bible Societies, 2004), 109–24.

Movers, F.C., *De utriusque recensionis Vaticinorum Ieremiae, graecae alexandrinae et hebraicae masorethicae, indole et origine commentatio critica* (Hamburg: Perthes, 1837).

Piovanelli, P., "JrB 33,14–26 ou la continuité des institutions à l'époque maccabéene," in *The Book of Jeremiah and Its Reception – Le livre de Jérémie et sa réception* (ed. A.H.W. Curtis and T. Römer; BETL 128; Leuven: Peeters, 1997), 255–76.

Reimer, D.J., *The Oracles Against Babylon in Jeremiah 50–51: A Horror Among the Nations* (San Francisco: Mellen, 1993).

Schenker, A., "La rédaction longue du livre de Jérémie doit-elle être date au temps des premiers hasmonéens," *ETL* 70 (1994): 281–93.

Schenker, A., *Das Neue am neuen Bund und das Alte am alten: Jer 31 in der hebräischen und griechischen Bibel* (FRLANT 212; Göttingen: Vandenhoeck & Ruprecht, 2006).

Schenker, A., "Est-ce que le livre de Jérémie fut publié dans une édition refondue au 2ᵉ siècle? La multiplicité textuelle peut-elle coexister avec l'édition unique d'un livre biblique?" in *Un carrefour dans l'histoire de la Bible: Du texte à la théologie au IIe siècle avant J.-C.* (eds. I. Himbaza and A. Schenker; OBO 233; Göttingen: Vandenhoeck & Ruprecht, 2007), 58–74.

Scholz, A., *Der masorethische Text und die LXX-Übersetzung des Buches Jeremias* (Regensburg: Manz, 1875).

Shead, A.G., "Jeremiah 32 in Its Hebrew and Greek Recensions," *TynBul* 50 (1999): 318–20.

Shead, A.G., *The Open Book and the Sealed Book: Jeremiah 32 in its Hebrew and Greek Recensions* (JSOTSup 347; London: Sheffield Academic Press, 2002).

Soderlund, S., *The Greek Text of Jeremiah: A Revised Hypothesis* (JSOTSup 47; Sheffield: JSOT Press, 1985).

Spohn, M.G.L., *Ieremias Vates e versione Iudaeorum Alexandrinorum ac reliquorum interpretum graecorum emendatus notisque criticis illustratus* (2 vols.; Leipzig: Jo. Ambros. Barth, 1794–1824).

Stipp, H.-J., "Offene Fragen zur Übersetzungskritik des antiken griechischen Jeremiabuches," *JNSL* 17 (1991): 117–28.

Stipp, H.-J., *Jeremia im Parteienstreit: Studien zur Textentwicklung von Jer 26, 36–43 und 45 als Beitrag zur Geschichte Jeremias, seines Buches und judäischer Parteien im 6. Jahrhundert* (Athenäum Monografien, Theologie; BBB 82; Frankfurt am Main: Hain, 1992).

Stipp, H.-J., "Eine anfechtbare Ortung des masoretischen Sonderguts im Jeremiabuch," *BN* 70 (1993): 88–96.

Stipp, H.-J., *Das masoretische und alexandrinische Sondergut des Jeremiabuches* (OBO 136; Göttingen: Vandenhoeck & Ruprecht, 1994).

Stipp, H.-J., "The Prophetic Messenger Formulas in Jeremiah according to the Masoretic and Alexandrian Texts," *Text* 18 (1995): 63–85.

Stipp, H.-J., "Eschatologisches Schema im alexandrinischen Jeremiabuch? Strukturprobleme eines komplexen Prophetenbuches," *JNSL* 23 (1997): 153–79.

Stipp, H.-J., "Zur aktuellen Diskussion um das Verhältnis der Textformen des Jeremiabuches," in Karrer–Kraus, *Septuaginta 2008, 630–53.

Streane, A.W., *The Double Text of Jeremiah (Massoretic and Alexandrian) Compared: Together with an Appendix on the Old Latin Evidence* (Cambridge: Deighton Bell, 1896).

Stulman, L., "Some Theological and Lexical Differences between the Old Greek and the MT of the Jeremiah Prose Discourses," *HS* 25 (1984): 18–23.

Stulman, L., *The Other Text of Jeremiah: A Reconstruction of the Hebrew Text Underlying the Greek Version of the Prose Sections of Jeremiah with English Translation* (Lanham: University Press of America, 1985).

Sweeney, M.A., "The Masoretic and Septuagint Versions of the Book of Jeremiah in Synchronic and Diachronic Perspective," in *Form and Intertextuality in Prophetic and Apocalyptic Literature* (FAT 45; Tübingen: Mohr Siebeck, 2005), 65–77.

Tov, E., "L' Incidence de la critique textuelle sur la critique littéraire dans le livre de Jérémie," *RB* 79 (1972): 189–99.

Tov, E., "Exegetical Notes on the Hebrew Vorlage of the LXX of Jeremiah 27 (34)," *ZAW* 91 (1979): 73–93.

Tov, E., "Some Aspects of the Textual and Literary History of the Book of Jeremiah," in *Le livre de Jérémie* (ed. P.-M. Bogaert; BETL 54; Leuven: Peeters, 1981), 145–67.

Tov, E., "The Literary History of the Book of Jeremiah in Light of Its Textual History," in *Empirical Models for Biblical Criticism* (ed. J.H. Tigay; Philadelphia: University of Pennsylvania Press, 1985), 97–130. Revised in Tov, *Greek-Hebrew Bible, 363–84.

Volz, P., *Studien zum Text des Jeremia* (Leipzig: J.C. Hinrichs, 1920).

Vonach, A., "Jer 10.1–10: Crux interpretum für die kürzen LXX-Version?" in *La Septante en Allemagne et en France: textes de la Septante à traduction très littérale/Septuaginta Deutsch und Bible d'Alexandrie: Texte der Septuaginta in Doppelüberlieferung oder in wörtlicher Übersetzung* (eds. W. Kraus and O. Munnich; OBO 238; Göttingen: Vandenhoeck & Ruprecht, 2009), 204–16.

Watts, J.W., "Text and Redaction in Jeremiah's Oracles Against the Nations," *CBQ* 54 (1992): 42–47.

Weis, R.D., "A Conflicted Book for a Marginal People: Thematic Oppositions in MT Jeremiah," in *Reading the Hebrew Bible for a New Millennium: Form, Concept and Theological Perspective*, Vol. 2: *Exegetical and Theological Studies* (eds. D. Ellens et al.; Philadelphia: Trinity Press International, 2000), 290–301.

Weis, R.D., "The Textual Situation for the Book of Jeremiah," in *Sôfer Mahîr: Essays in Honour of Adrian Schenker Offered by Editors of Biblia Hebraica Quinta* (eds. Y. Goldman, A. van der Kooij, and R.D. Weis; VTSup 110; Leiden: Brill, 2006), 269–93.

Weis, R.D., "Patterns of Mutual Influence in the Textual Transmission of the Oracles concerning Moab in Isaiah and Jeremiah," in *Isaiah in Context: Studies in Honour of Arie van der Kooij on the Occasion of his Sixty-Fifth Birthday* (eds. M.N. van der Meer et al.; VTSup 138; Leiden: Brill, 2010), 161–84.

Wells, R.D., "Indications of Late Reinterpretation of the Jeremianic Tradition from the LXX of Jer 21:1–23:8," *ZAW* 96 (1984): 405–20.

Wells, R.D., "The Amplification of the Expectations of the Exiles in the MT Revision of Jeremiah," in *Troubling Jeremiah* (eds. A.R.P. Diamond, K.M. O'Connor, and L. Stulman; JSOTSup 260; Sheffield: Sheffield Academic Press, 1999), 272–92.

Wells, R.D., "Dislocations in Time and Ideology in the Reconception of Jeremiah's Words: The Encounter with Hananiah in the Septuagint *Vorlage* and the Masoretic Text," in *Uprooting and Planting: Essays on Jeremiah for Leslie Allen* (ed. J. Goldingay; Library of Hebrew Bible/Old Testament Studies 459; New York: T & T Clark, 2007), 322–50.

Workman, G.C., *The Text of Jeremiah* (Edinburgh: Clark, 1889).

Richard D. Weis

7.2 Ancient Hebrew-Aramaic Texts

7.2.1 Ancient Manuscript Evidence

The only complete witness to a Hebrew text of the book of Jeremiah that goes back to antiquity is the consonantal text of MT-Jer (see → 7.2.2 for the most important MT-Jer manuscripts). The published ancient Hebrew manuscripts of Jeremiah were all found in the Qumran caves. Their classification into non-aligned, proto-, or semi-Masoretic manuscripts and texts attesting to the Hebrew *Vorlage* of LXX (for this system of classification, see → 1.2.2.2.3 and → 1.2.1) is facilitated somewhat in the case of the book of Jeremiah due to the characteristic long texts of MT-Jer. A total of eight or nine Jeremiah manuscripts were found at Qumran: 2QJer, 4QJer[a], 4QJer[b], 4QJer[c], 4QJer[d], 4QJer[e], Schøyen 4612/9, and XJer?. Of these manuscripts, 4QJer[a] can be classified as proto-Masoretic, while 2QJer and 4QJer[c] are semi-Masoretic in character. 4QJer[b] attests, at least for Jeremiah 10, to the Hebrew *Vorlage* and LXX-Jer. The same might be true for manuscript Schøyen 4612/9. 4QJer[d] was probably a non-aligned manuscript and 4QJer[e] cannot be classified as only a small fragment has been preserved.[1] Insufficient text of XJer? is preserved for a secure identification. The Green Collection includes an unpublished fragment (2015) of Jer 23:6–9.[2]

7.2.1.1 2QJer (2Q13)

Twenty-seven frgs. of 2QJer have been preserved, of which some suffered extensive damage. The text of seventeen frgs. can still be identified and attests to 249 (partial) words from Jer 13:22; 32(39):24–25; 42(49):7–11, 14; 43(50):8–11; 44(51):1–3, 12–14; 46:27–47:7(26:27–28; 29:1–7); 48(31):2–4?, 7, 25–39, 41–42?, 43–45(43–44); 49:10(30:4). The manuscript was copied in a Herodian bookhand from the first half of the first century C.E.[3] The many plene spellings of 2QJer correspond to the baroque orthography system.[4] Among the 249 (partially) preserved words in 2QJer, Baillet notes twenty-seven cases of textual variation, seven of which agree with LXX-Jer and four with the other versions; in thirteen cases, 2QJer preserves non-aligned readings. In general, the text of 2QJer corresponds to MT-Jer (→ 7.2.2)[5] and can thus be classified as semi-Masoretic.[6]

7.2.1.2 4QJer[a] (4Q70)

4QJer[a] is the best-preserved and most ancient Jeremiah manuscript from the Qumran caves. Thirty-six of its fifty published frgs. are identified as coming from the first half of the book of Jeremiah and are allocated to fifteen columns of the original scroll. The thirty-six fragments attest to 728 (partial) words from Jer 7:1–2, 15–19, 28–34; 8:1–12, 18–19, 23; 9:1–2, 7–15; 10:9–14, 23; 11:3–6, 19–20; 12:3–7, 13–17; 13:1–7, 22?, 27; 14:4–7; 15:1–2; 17:8–26; 18:15–19:1; 20:14–18; 21:1?; 22:3–16; 26(33):10?. Paleographically, 4QJer[a] is one of the earliest-known biblical manuscripts and among the earliest of all preserved Hebrew texts. The gradual publication and paleographic study of the Dead Sea Scrolls led over time to the assigning of a number of paleographical dates for 4QJer[a]. Cross originally compared the script of 4QJer[a] to the Aramaic Persian chancellery script of the fourth century B.C.E. and dated the manuscript to the third century B.C.E.[7] However,

---

[1] For my classifications of the Qumran Jeremiah manuscripts and the statistics leading to these classifications, see **Handbuch*, 295–303.

[2] Inv. MOTB.SCR.003172 = GC 5 = DSS F.Jer2. I am obliged to Emanuel Tov and David Trobisch for informing me of the existence of this scroll.

[3] Cf. Tov, "Jeremiah Scrolls," 204.

[4] See Tov, "Jeremiah Scrolls," 198, cf. Baillet, "Jérémie," 63.

[5] Baillet, "Jérémie," 62–63.; cf. Tov, "Jeremiah Scrolls," 198; Eshel, "Jeremiah," 397–98.

[6] Cf. Lange, **Handbuch*, 298.

[7] Cf. Cross, "Oldest Manuscripts," 152–59.

he settled finally for a date between the years 225–175 B.C.E.[8] This date is confirmed by Yardeni.[9]

Orthographically, 4QJer[a] reflects the text of MT even in unusual cases. Tov notes in his edition only twenty orthographic deviations from MT-Jer among the 728 preserved words in the manuscript.[10] This equals an orthographic deviation of 2.75 percent.

While the orthographic affiliation of 4QJer[a] to the consonantal text of MT-Jer (→ 7.2.2) is undisputed, the textual characterization of the manuscript is debated. HaCohen thinks unjustifiably that the manuscript is non-aligned because it lacks Jer 7:30–8:3.[11] These verses were added by a second hand in col. III of the manuscript. However, the lack of Jer 7:30–8:3 in 4QJer[a] is the result of a *parablepsis*.[12] This example illustrates the principle problem in the textual classification of 4QJer[a]. In total, the manuscript includes eighteen non-orthographic corrections *prima* or *secunda manu*.[13] Even the corrections *secunda manu*, e.g., the addition of Jer 7:30–8:3 in col. III, were written in an archaic script.

The uncorrected text of 4QJer[a] resembles a semi-Masoretic manuscript. In 673 (partially) preserved words, 4QJer[a] reads fifty-two times with and twenty-one times against MT (→ 7.2.2), twice with and seventy-one times against LXX (→ 7.3), and on twenty-one occasions is non-aligned. When it is recognized that seventeen of the eighteen alterations in 4QJer[a] correct scribal errors mostly towards MT and that a significant number of the smaller corrections were in fact made by the original scribe of 4QJer[a], the initial textual impression of 4QJer[a] needs to be emended. Taking the scribal corrections of 4QJer[a] into consideration, the manuscript attests to a proto-Masoretic text of Jeremiah. In 728 (partially) preserved words, the corrected manuscript of 4QJer[a] reads fifty-two times with and only seven times against MT, twice with and fifty-seven times against LXX, and is non-aligned on only five occasions. The proto-Masoretic text type of 4QJer[a] is corroborated by the fact that the manuscript reads coherently with the long Masoretic texts of the book of Jeremiah (Jer 8:3, 4, 10; 9:8, 9, 12, 14; 10:10, 13?; 12:3, 14, 17; 13:1, 3, 4; 14:4, 6; 15:1; 17:12, 18, 20, 22, 24; 18:17, 18, 21),[14] and that in col. V, 4QJer[a] reads the text sequence Jer 10:9, 10 with MT against 4QJer[b] and LXX-Jer, which have the sequence Jer 10:5a, 9, 5b, 11.

7.2.1.3   4QJer[b] (4Q71)

4QJer[b] is one of the most important Jeremiah manuscripts from Qumran. The first publications considered 4QJer[d] and 4QJer[e] to be part of 4QJer[b].[15] Differences in paleography, reconstructed column-width, scribal habits and textual character left no doubt though that 4QJer[d] and 4QJer[e] attest to two further separate Jeremiah manuscripts.[16] Only one fragment is preserved of 4QJer[b]. It contains thirty-one (partial) words from Jer 9:22–25; 10:1–5, 9, 11–21. The manuscript can be dated paleographically

---

[8] According to a personal communication; see D.N. Freedman and K.A. Mathews, *The Paleo-Hebrew Leviticus Scroll* [11QpaleoLev] (Philadelphia: ASOR, 1985), 55; cf. Eshel, "Jeremiah," 398. In his article "The Development of the Jewish Scripts," in *The Bible and the Ancient Near East: Essays in Honor of William Foxwell Albright* (ed. G.E. Wright; Garden City: Doubleday, 1961), 133–202, F.M. Cross dated 4QJer[a] ca. 200 B.C.E. (137, 140), while in "The Evolution of a Theory of Local Texts" (in *Qumran and the History of the Biblical Text* [eds. F.M. Cross and S. Talmon; Cambridge: Harvard University Press, 1975], 306–20), he opted for the years 200–175 B.C.E. (308, 316 note 8).

[9] Yardeni, "Palaeography," 267 and *passim*.

[10] Tov, "Jeremiah," 15–51; cf. Tov, "Jeremiah Scrolls," 199; D.N. Freedman, "The Masoretic Text and the Qumran Scrolls: A Study in Orthography," *Text* 2 (1962): 87–102 (100–02); and Freedman and Mathews, *The Paleo-Hebrew Leviticus Scroll*, 58–59.

[11] HaCohen, "4QJer[a] – A Pre-Massoretic Text?" *passim*.

[12] Thus already Janzen, *Studies*, 174; cf. Tov, "Jeremiah Scrolls," 206; Tov, "Jeremiah," 152, 154; Eshel, "Jeremiah," 398. Different Ulrich, "Insertions," who regards the correction as a secondary insertion that the parent text of 4QJer[a], did not include.

[13] Cf. Tov, "Jeremiah," 151–54; Tov, "Jeremiah Scrolls," 205–06. Eshel, "Jeremiah," 398–99, regards all corrections as *secunda manu*.

[14] Cf. Tov, "Jeremiah," 151; Tov, "Jeremiah Scrolls," 198; Eshel, "Jeremiah," 398–99; Lange, **Handbuch*, 299–300.

[15] Thus Janzen, *Studies*, 181–84, and Cross, *Theory of Local Texts*, 308–09.

[16] See Tov, "Jeremiah," 171–72; Tov, "Jeremiah Scrolls," 191–97. Cf. also the communications by Ada Yardeni and Émile Puech according to Tov, "Jeremiah Scrolls," 191.

to the first half of the second century B.C.E.[17] In its orthography, 4QJer[b] follows the system known from the consonantal text of MT.[18] That 4QJer[b] preserves parts of Jer 10:5–11 allows for its textual classification despite the fact that only thirty-one words are extant and the variant statistics are somewhat inconclusive. 4QJer[b] reads five times with and six times against MT, four times with and seven times against LXX, and is non-aligned on two occasions. 4QJer[b] is nevertheless close to the Hebrew parent text of LXX-Jer (→ 7.3). As in LXX-Jer, it lacks Jer 10:6–8, 10 but reads the remaining verses in the sequence vv. 5a, 9, 5b, 11.[19]

7.2.1.4 4QJer[c] (4Q72)

4QJer[c] is one of the best-preserved Jeremiah manuscripts from Qumran. Seventy-two fragments contain 631 (partial) words that can still be identified as remnants of Jer 4:5, 13–16; 8:1–3, 21–23; 9:1–5; 10:12–13; 19:8–9; 20:2–5, 7–9, 13–15; 21:7–10; 22:4–6, 10–28, 28–33?; 24:6–7; 25:7–8, 15–17, 24–26; 26(33):10–13; 27:1–3, 13–15(34:2–3, 14–15); 30(37):6–9, 17–25; 31(38):1–9, 11–14, 19–23, 25–26; 33:x, 16–20. Fifty-five fragments of 4QJer[c] can still be reconstructed into twenty-five columns of text. Ancient repairs in cols. IV, XVI, XXI, and XXIII illustrate the high regard in which 4QJer[c] was held. The manuscript was copied in an early Herodian semi-cursive hand from the end of the first century B.C.E.[20] Both in its orthography and its text, 4QJer[c] is close to MT-Jer (→ 7.2.2).[21] In its 631 preserved words, 4QJer[c] reads thirty-nine times with and twenty-five times against MT, ten times with and forty-seven times against LXX (→ 7.3), and is non-aligned on fifteen occasions. Hence, 4QJer[c] can best be classified as semi-Masoretic.[22]

7.2.1.5 4QJer[d] (4Q72a)

Only one fragment of 4QJer[d] containing sixty-three (partial) words from Jer 43(50):2–10 has been preserved. The fragment was originally attributed to 4QJer[b] (see above, → 7.2.1.3). Paleographically, 4QJer[d] resembles both 4QJer[b] and 4QJer[e] and should be dated to the first half of the second century B.C.E.[23] The orthography of 4QJer[d] is almost identical to that of MT-Jer.[24] Due to the paucity of preserved text, a text-typological characterization of 4QJer[d] is not possible. However, it should be noted that 4QJer[d] lacks the long MT texts in Jer 43(50):4–6, which argues for at least some resemblance to the Hebrew parent text of LXX-Jer.[25] The variant statistics for 4QJer[d] call for caution though in classifying this manuscript as being close to LXX-Jer (→ 7.3). 4QJer[d] reads five times with and eight times against MT (→ 7.2.2), four times with and nine times against LXX, and is non-aligned on four occasions. Given the small amount of preserved text, it can only be speculated whether 4QJer[d] was a non-aligned manuscript.[26]

7.2.1.6 4QJer[e] (4Q72b)

Of 4QJer[e], only one small fragment with sixteen (partial) words from Jer 50(27):4–6 is preserved. The fragment was originally attributed to 4QJer[b] (see above, → 7.2.1.3). The small amount of preserved text does not allow for either ortho-

---

[17] Thus Ada Yardeni according to Tov, "Jeremiah," 172; Tov, "Jeremiah Scrolls," 197, and Eshel, "Jeremiah," 399.

[18] Cf. Tov, "Jeremiah," 172.

[19] For 4QJer[b] as attesting to the Hebrew parent text of LXX-Jer, see Janzen, Studies, 173, 181–82; R.W. Klein, Textual Criticism of the Old Testament: The Septuagint after Qumran (2nd ed.; Philadelphia: Fortress Press, 1978), 20–21; Tov, "Jeremiah Scrolls," 198; Tov, "Jeremiah," 174–75; Eshel, "Jeremiah," 399; K.H. Jobes and M. Silva, Invitation to the Septuagint (Grand Rapids: Baker, 2000), 173–75; E. Ulrich, "The Dead Sea Scrolls and the Hebrew Scriptural Texts," in The Bible and the Dead Sea Scrolls, vol. 1: Scripture and the Scrolls (ed. J.H. Charlesworth; Waco: Baylor University Press, 2006), 77–99 (84–85); Lange, *Handbuch, 300–01; Saley, "Reconstructing," 1–12.

[20] Thus Tov, "Jeremiah," 182, and Cross, "Theory of Local Texts," 308.

[21] Cf. Tov, "Jeremiah," 183–84; Tov, "Jeremiah Scrolls," 198–99; Eshel, "Jeremiah," 399.

[22] Cf. Lange, *Handbuch, 302.

[23] Thus Ada Yardeni according to Tov, "Jeremiah Scrolls," 197.

[24] See Tov, "Jeremiah," 203.

[25] See Tov, "Jeremiah," 172; Tov, "Jeremiah Scrolls," 198; cf. Janzen, Studies, 173, 182–84; Eshel, "Jeremiah," 399; Jobes and Silva, Invitation to the Septuagint, 173–75.

[26] Cf. Lange, *Handbuch, 302.

graphic or textual classification and the remains of 4QJer[b] could even be part of a Jeremiah quotation in a non-biblical manuscript.[27] Paleographically, 4QJer[e] resembles both 4QJer[b] and 4QJer[d] and should be dated to the first half of the second century B.C.E.

7.2.1.7 Manuscript Schøyen 4612/9[28]

This small fragment was bought out of private ownership for the Schøyen Collection. It preserves thirty-one words and partial words of Jer 3:15–19. Michael Langlois dates the irregular script of manuscript Schøyen 4612/9 to the second half of the first century B.C.E. Ada Yardeni describes it as a late Hasmonean or early Herodian hand from the years 100–40 B.C.E.[29] Elgvin and Davis assert a Qumran provenance for the fragment, from either cave 4 or cave 11.[30] While such a Qumran origin of manuscript Schøyen 4612/9 seems probable, its provenance out of private ownership begs for caution as biblical scrolls from the second half of the first century B.C.E. were also found in refugee caves connected with the Second Jewish War. The orthography of manuscript Schøyen 4612/9 is conservative. Elgvin and Davis view manuscript Schøyen 4612/9 as related to the text of LXX-Jer (→ 7.3) but with non-aligned features: "The evidence tentatively shows that MS 4612/9 may be grouped with 4QJer[b,d] as a text related to the *Vorlage* of 𝔊, although preserving independent features that indicate a thus far unattested shorter text."[31] In six partially preserved lines, manuscript Schøyen 4612/9 reads once with and six times against MT, twice with and five times against LXX, as well as five times non-aligned. Elgvin and Davis reconstruct one reading with and two readings against MT (→ 7.2.2) as well as two readings with and one reading against LXX. While the small amount of preserved text calls for caution, a general affiliation of manuscript Schøyen 4612/9 with the Hebrew *Vorlage* of LXX-Jer seems possible although the two certain readings with LXX-Jer are insufficient evidence for certainty: In Jer 3:15, manuscript Schøyen 4612/9 reads רעה "shepherding" with the ποιμαίνοντες "as shepherding ones" of LXX against MT's דֵּעָה "knowledge." In Jer 3:19, manuscript Schøyen 4612/9 reads אמן יהוה כי "truly, oh Lord, for" with the Γένοιτο, κύριε· ὅτι "let it be, oh Lord, for" of LXX against MT's אֵיךְ "how."

7.2.1.8 XJer?

A small fragment with three words and partial words from Jer 48(31):29–31 is in the possession of the Foundation on Judaism and Christian Origins, which received it as a donation from Michael Sharpe of Pasadena, California. Charlesworth wants to date the fragment for paleographic reasons to the late first century B.C.E. and speculates about a Qumran origin.[32] The eleven extant characters of text allow for neither orthographic nor text-typological classifications.[33] Due to the scanty extant remains of XJer?, the manuscript could also preserve a quotation of Jer 48(31):29–31 in a non-biblical text. The Jeremianic character of XJer? becomes all the more an issue because the transcription of the second word [י]דעתי[" "I]know[" is uncertain. Charlesworth himself notes: "However, the *Daleth* is problematic: Either the *Dalat* (sic) is written imprecisely or the copyist inscribed the wrong consonant (it looks like a *Teth* or a *Samekh*). This alleged error precludes me from being certain that

---

[27] Cf. Lange, *Handbuch*, 303.

[28] I am obliged to Torleif Elgvin and Kipp Davis who made a preprint copy of their edition of manuscript Schøyen 4612/9 available to me (Elgvin and Davis, "MS 4612/9"). All information about manuscript Schøyen 4612/9 discussed below relies on their edition.

[29] For the paleographic dates of manuscript Schøyen 4612/9 by Langlois and Yardeni, see Elgvin and Davis, "MS 4612/9," forthcoming and M. Langlois, "Palaeographical Analysis of the Dead Sea Scrolls," in *Gleanings*, forthcoming.

[30] Elgvin and Davis, "MS 4612/9," forthcoming.

[31] Elgvin and Davis, "MS 4612/9," forthcoming.

[32] Charlesworth, "Announcing."

[33] Against Charlesworth, "Announcing," who claims that "the text of this scroll of Jeremiah is similar to the so-called MT and dissimilar to the so-called Septuagint." In the three extant words, only one textual difference between MT and LXX occurs. In Jer 48(31):29, MT-Jer reads שָׁמַעְנוּ "we have heard" and LXX-Jer has ἤκουσα "I heard" instead. The three extant characters of XJer? could stand for both readings, i.e. שמע]נו] (thus the transcription of Charlesworth) or שמע]תי] (thus the Hebrew equivalent of ἤκουσα; cf. Jer 20:10; 23:25; and 42[49]:4).

this fragment represents a portion of Jeremiah (esp. in a so-called Proto-Masoretic form)."³⁴

Baillet, M., "13. Jérémie," *DJD* III.1: 62–69.
Charlesworth, J.H., "Announcing an Unknown Dead Sea Scroll: Jeremiah 48:29–31a," http://foundationjudaismchristianorigins.org/ftp/pages/dead-sea-scrolls/unpub/DSS-jeremiah.pdf (last accessed April 10, 2015).
Cross, F.M., "The Oldest Manuscripts from Qumran," *JBL* 74 (1955): 147–72; repr. in *Cross–Talmon*, *QHBT, 147–76.
Elgvin, T. and K. Davis, "MS 4612/9: 11Q(?)Jer (Jer. 3.15–19)," in *Gleanings*, forthcoming.
Eshel, E., "Jeremiah, Book of: Biblical Text," in *EDSS, 1:397–400.
Eshel, E. and H. Eshel, "A Preliminary Report on Seven New Fragments from Qumran," *Meghillot* 5–6 (2007): 271–78 [Hebr.].
HaCohen, A., "4QJerᵃ – A Pre-Massoretic Text?" *Text* 17 (1994): א–ח, 133 [Hebr.].
Janzen, J.G., *Studies in the Text of Jeremiah* (HSM 6; Cambridge: Harvard University Press, 1973).
Lange, *Handbuch*, 297–324.
Saley, R., "Reconstructing 4QJerᵇ according to the Text of the Old Greek," *DSD* 17 (2010): 1–12.
Tov, E., "The Jeremiah Scrolls from Qumran," *RevQ* 14 (1989): 189–206.
Tov, E., "Jeremiah," *DJD* XV (1997): 145–207.
Ulrich, E., "Deuteronomistically Inspired Scribal Insertions into the Developing Biblical Texts: 4QJudgᵃ and 4QJerᵃ," in *Houses Full of All Good Things: Essays in Memory of Timo Veijola* (Publications of the Finnish Exegetical Society 95; Göttingen: Vandenhoeck & Ruprecht, 2008), 489–506.
Ulrich, E., *BQS, 558–83.
Yardeni, A., "The Palaeography of 4QJerᵃ – A Comparative Study," *Text* 15 (1990): 233–68.

Armin Lange

7.2.2 Masoretic Texts and Ancient Texts Close to MT

In addition to the proto- (4QJerᵃ → 7.2.1.2) and semi-Masoretic (2QJer → 7.2.1.1; 4QJerᶜ → 7.2.1.4) Jeremiah manuscripts discussed above, only the medieval Masoretic manuscripts attest to this textual version of the book of Jeremiah. Qumran manuscripts are discussed in entry → 7.2.1. The medieval manuscripts are discussed in → 7.2.2.5.

The text of MT-Jer is radically different from the Greek version (→ 7.3) of this book. It follows a different textual sequence than LXX-Jer (see below, → 7.2.2.2.2) and is significantly longer. According to Graf and Giesebrecht, MT-Jer is ca. 2,700 words or one-eighth longer than the parent text of LXX-Jer.¹ A more recent computer-aided analysis calculated this value as 3,097 words or one-seventh of added material.² These 3,097 words include large additions of one verse or more³ but also less extensive long texts. Agreeing with the view of many text critics, this entry regards the resulting text as a redaction of an earlier text of Jeremiah that was slightly reworked by the parent text of LXX-Jer. In the following, I will call this the proto-Masoretic Jeremiah redaction (proto-MT-Jer). That 4QJerᵈ (→ 7.2.1.5) agrees in some readings with LXX-Jer and in others with MT-Jer might demonstrate that proto-MT-Jer is not a single coherent redaction, but that a limited number of its long readings were already inserted before the final proto-Masoretic Jeremiah redaction took place. Proto-MT-Jer was produced in the late fourth or early third century B.C.E. by a disenfranchised group of Jerusalemite priests who migrated in the reign of Ptolemy I to Egypt. The Diaspora milieu responsible for proto-MT-Jer perceived the events leading to the destruction of Judah and Jerusalem in the sixth century B.C.E. as indicative of its own fate. The judgment of Judah and Jerusalem is inevitable because God's chosen people violated their covenant God and followed other gods. The nations will be judged, because they exploited the power God gave them over his people. Salvation is granted only to some of the nations (Moab and Ammon) and the exiles. The exiles will be delivered by God and return to Jerusalem.

---

³⁴ Charlesworth, "Announcing."

¹ Graf, *Der Prophet Jeremia*, xliii; Giesebrecht, *Das Buch Jeremia*, xix.
² Cf. Min, "The Minuses and Pluses," 1, 159, 181, 312, 315, 317.
³ Jer 2:1–2; 7:1–2; 8:10–12; 10:6–10; 11:7–8; 17:1–4; 25:14; 27:1, 7, 13–14, 18–22; 29:15–19; 30:10–11, 22; 31:37; 33:14–26; 39:4–13; 46:1, 26; 48:45–47; 49:6; 51:45–48; 52:2–3, 15, 28–30.

7.2.2 MASORETIC TEXTS AND ANCIENT TEXTS CLOSE TO MT

There – the authors of proto-MT-Jer hope – the Diaspora of their own time will reestablish a proper temple cult and a Davidic government separated from the temple cult, similar to the events in 520–515 B.C.E.

7.2.2.1 History of Research

The history of research on MT-Jer is extensive and splits clearly into two phases.[4] In both phases, the discussion focused on the relation of MT-Jer to LXX-Jer (→ 7.3). Already in 1777, Eichhorn understood the differences between LXX-Jer and MT-Jer to be caused by a "double recension."[5] In the nineteenth century, Movers (1837) and later Scholz (1875) argued that MT-Jer is based on a revised version of the Hebrew parent text underlying LXX-Jer. Spohn (1794) and Graf (1862) understood MT-Jer as the earlier text that the translator of LXX-Jer shortened and restructured. Giesebrecht (1894) argued for a compromise position, regarding LXX-Jer as a free translation that preserved a more original text in its short texts and in cases of scribal corruption in MT-Jer.

Janzen's 1973 publication of 4QJer[b] in his PhD thesis relaunched the discussion. Janzen points to the secondary character of MT-Jer readings and regards LXX-Jer as the better text.[6] Janzen's reassertion of the ideas of Movers and Scholz was elaborated on by Tov and Bogaert. Tov[7] regards MT-Jer as a redactional reworking (edition II) of the ancestor of LXX-Jer's Hebrew parent text (edition I)[8] because it adds new details, brief explanations, and expansions of proper nouns as well as formulae, because it has expansions on the basis of the context, and its long texts lead to sections occurring twice. The Dtr vocabulary of MT-Jer identifies it as probably the last representative of Deuteronomism. Bogaert[9] argues along similar lines to Tov and has contributed especially to the date of MT-Jer (see below, → 7.2.2.2.1).[10] Stipp[11] also understands MT-Jer to be a later text than LXX-Jer but wants to detect two or three different redactional layers within MT-Jer. MT-Jer is characterized by what Stipp calls a pre-Masoretic idiolect.[12] This pre-Masoretic idiolect would consist of phrases and repetitive language that occurs in the book of Jeremiah and often even in the whole Hebrew Bible only in the proto-Masoretic long texts of Jeremiah. Against Tov, Stipp thinks that Dtr rhetoric is used without specific Dtr meaning in MT-Jer, i.e., that MT-Jer cannot be characterized as Deuteronomistic.[13] MT-Jer would

---

[4] For more detailed surveys of the history of research, see Stulman, *Other Text*; F.D. Hubmann, "Bemerkungen zur älteren Diskussion um die Unterschiede zwischen MT und G im Jeremiabuch," in *Jeremia und die "deuteronomistische Bewegung"* (ed. W. Groß; BBB 98; Weinheim: Beltz Athenäum, 1995), 263–70; B. Huwyler, *Jeremia und die Völker* (FAT 20; Tübingen: Mohr Siebeck, 1997), 48–64; Weis, "Textual Situation," 270–75; G. Fischer, *Jeremia: Der Stand der theologischen Diskussion* (Darmstadt: Wissenschaftliche Buchgesellschaft, 2007), 31–45; Lange, **Handbuch*, 304–14.

[5] Eichhorn, "Bemerkungen," 141–68; the quotation is on p. 168 ("Sollte nicht die Ursache hievon in einer doppelten Recension liegen?"). Cf. also the more extensive argument in Eichhorn, *Einleitung*, 157–207.

[6] Janzen, *Studies*, passim; Janzen, "Critique," 28–47; Janzen, "Double Readings."

[7] Tov, *Translation*; Tov, "Exegetical Notes," 73–93; Tov, "L' incidence," 189–99; Tov, "Literary History"; Tov, "Aspects"; Tov, "Characterization"; Tov, "Book of Jeremiah."

[8] Reworked in turn by the parent text of LXX-Jer and/or the translator himself.

[9] Bogaert, "Baruch"; Bogaert, "Mécanismes"; Bogaert, "Relecture," 145–50; Bogaert, "L' organisation"; Bogaert, "Libération," 312–22; Bogaert, "*Urtext*"; Bogaert, "Trois formes," 1–17; Bogaert, *Livre*; Bogaert, "Datation," 137–59; Bogaert, "Heshbon," 45–54; Bogaert, "Liste," 1–14; Bogaert, "l' hébreu pré-massorétique," 216–43.

[10] Bogaert and Tov are supported in their understanding of MT-Jer among others by Lust, "Diverse Text Forms," 31–48; Schenker, "Nebukadnezzars Metamorphose," 498–527; Schenker, "Was übersetzen wir?" 247–62; Schenker, "Der nie aufgehobene Bund," 85–112; Aejmelaeus, "Jeremiah," passim; Aejmelaeus, "Nebuchadnezzar, My Servant"; de Regt, "The Prophet"; Parke-Taylor, *The Formation of the Book of Jeremiah*; Wijesinghe, "Tracing the Shorter Version," 293–328; Wijesinghe, *Jeremiah 34,8–22*; Ulrich, "Insertion"; Ulrich, "Qumran Witness," 269–73; Amphoux and Sérandour, "date," 25–35, and Amphoux, "Les réécritures," 213–25.

[11] Stipp, *Sondergut*; Stipp, "Offene Fragen," 117–28; Stipp, "Probleme," 225–62; Stipp, "Messenger Formulas," 63–85; Stipp, "Eschatologisches Schema," 153–79; Stipp, "Zur aktuellen Diskussion"; Stipp, "Prophetentitel"; Stipp, "Ezechiel"; Stipp, "Gottesbildfragen"; Stipp, "Interpretierende Übersetzung"; Stipp, "Legenden der Jeremia Exegese."

[12] For a brief description, see Stipp, "Zur aktuellen Diskussion," 632–35.

[13] Stipp, *Sondergut*, 138–39.

represent a scribal form of textual maintenance.[14] Prior to Stipp, Min (1977) and Goldman (1992) wanted to detect more than one redactional layer in MT-Jer[15] and a similar position was defended by Gosse in a series of publications.[16] More recently, Weis advised "to differentiate specific textual variations that are due to redactional intervention from those due to the vicissitudes of text transmission." He, thus, distinguishes scribal alterations in MT-Jer from the original proto-Masoretic redaction.[17] Finsterbusch recently added a new aspect to the discussion by pointing to the rhetorical coherence of MT-Jer and argues that the redactor(s) responsible for it applied a coherent rhetorical structure to the book.[18]

Although most textual critics regard MT-Jer as the more original text, some of the more recent Jeremiah commentators[19] do not share this opinion. Among them, Fischer is the most vocal.[20] He denies that 4QJer^b is proof of the existence of a Hebrew parent text of LXX-Jer because of its bad state of preservation and because of several readings with MT-Jer (→ 7.2.3.3). For Fischer, the text of MT-Jer was reworked when translated into Greek. Similarly, Renaud regards LXX-Jer in Jer 31[38]:31–34 as an interpretative translation of the original Jeremianic text preserved by MT-Jer.[21]

Several textual critics have admitted the existence of a Hebrew parent text for LXX-Jer (Soderlund,[22] Rofé,[23] van der Kooij,[24] Shead[25]) but detect, in the case of several MT-Jer long texts, an abbreviating translator in LXX-Jer and regard the different structure of LXX-Jer as the work of the translator (Rofé). Differences between LXX-Jer and MT-Jer would go back to reworkings by the translator as well as two different Hebrew texts. In this line of thought, Freedman and Lundbom pointed to a total of forty-eight arguable examples of haplography.[26]

Another compromise position was suggested by Haran, who argues that LXX-Jer renders a high-quality parent text accurately but changed its structure from that of MT-Jer into that of LXX-Jer.[27] Based on the example of Jer 25:1–14, Gesundheit argued recently that LXX-Jer preserves a more coherent text as compared to MT-Jer. LXX-Jer would represent a formally harmonized and stylistically unified text while MT-Jer would show rough transitions, seams, and substantive tensions between phrases and verses, all typical of a prophetical book that developed as a result of a complicated redaction history. MT-Jer would therefore represent an earlier text that was reworked by the Hebrew parent text of LXX-Jer.[28] See further → 7.1.2. For a different view, see → 7.3.6.[29]

---

[14] Stipp, *Sondergut*, 138: "schriftgelehrte Form der Textpflege."

[15] Cf. also Stulman, *Prose Sermons*; Stulman, *Other Text*; Schmid, *Buchgestalten*, 13–23; J. Vermeylen, "L'alliance renouvelée (Jer 31,31–34)," in *Lectures et relectures de la Bible: Festschrift P.-M. Bogaert* (eds. J.-M. Auwers and A. Wénin; BETL 144; Leuven: Peeters, 1999), 57–83.

[16] Gosse, *Structuration*, 47–66; Gosse, "Masoretic Redaction"; Gosse, "Trois étapes"; Gosse, "rédaction massorétique."

[17] Weis, "Textual Situation," 273.

[18] Finsterbusch, "MT-Jer 1,1–3,5."

[19] See, e.g., P.C. Craigie, P.H. Kelley, and J.F. Drinkard, *Jeremiah 1–25* (WBC 26; Dallas: Word Books, 1991), xliv–xlv; J.R. Lundbom, *Jeremiah 1–20: A New Translation with Introduction and Commentary* (AB 21A; New York: Doubleday, 1999), 57–62; G. Fischer, *Jeremia 1–25: Übersetzt und ausgelegt* (HTKAT; Freiburg i.B.: Herder, 2005), 39–46.

[20] Fischer, "Zum Text des Jeremiabuches"; cf., e.g., Fischer, "Jeremiah 52: A Test Case"; Fischer, *Jeremia 1–25*, 39–46; "Die Diskussion"; → 7.3. For a critical evaluation of Fischer's arguments, see Engel, "Erfahrungen"; and Stipp, "Programmschrift"; Stipp, "Interpretierende Übersetzung"; Stipp, "Legenden der Jeremia-Exegese."

[21] B. Renaud, "L'oracle de la nouvelle alliance," in *Lectures et relectures de la Bible: Festschrift P.-M. Bogaert* (eds. J.-M. Auwers and A. Wénin; BETL 144; Leuven: Peeters, 1999), 85–98.

[22] Soderlund, *The Greek Text of Jeremiah*.

[23] Rofé, "Arrangement," 390–98; Rofé, "Name," 307–16.

[24] Van der Kooij, "Jeremiah 27:5–15," 59–78.

[25] Shead, *The Open Book and the Sealed Book*.

[26] Freedman and Lundbom, "Haplography in Jeremiah."

[27] Haran, "Place of the Prophecies."

[28] Gesundheit, "Question of LXX-Jeremiah."

[29] Gesundheit, "Question of LXX-Jeremiah."

7.2.2.2 (Proto-)Masoretic Text of Jeremiah
7.2.2.2.1 Date and Setting[30]

Since several Jeremiah scrolls from Qumran are close to MT-Jer, there can be no doubt that the consonantal text of MT-Jer goes back to an ancient proto- or semi-Masoretic text that dates at least to the third century B.C.E. The paleographic date of 4QJer^a (→ 7.2.1.2) alone argues for a *terminus ante quem* in the third century B.C.E. As scribal errors show that 4QJer^a is not an autograph, proto-MT-Jer must have been finalized at the latest in the third century B.C.E.

Quotations from and allusions to proto-Masoretic variant readings and long texts move the *terminus ante quem* of the proto-Masoretic text of Jeremiah to the early third century B.C.E.:

- Jer 2:7 in Neh 9:36
- Jer 17:9 in 4QInstruction^d 8 12
- Jer 17:13 in 4QInstruction^d 103 ii 6
- Jer 20:5 in *Aramaic Levi Document* 13:11
- Jer 26(33):18 in 4QNarrative and Poetic Composition^b 1 8
- Jer 31(38):13 in Esth 9:22
- Jer 33(40):8 in 11QPs^a XIX:13 (= Plea for Deliverance)
- Jer 33:16 in Zech 14:11
- Jer 33:16 in 4QProphecy of Joshua (= 4Qapocr-Josh^c?) 9 ii 8

It is therefore not surprising that the proto-Masoretic text of Jeremiah was employed in the late third or early second century B.C.E. by the Epistle of Jeremiah (cf. the use of Jer 10:5 in Ep Jer 7)[31] and Ben Sira (Jer 1:10 or 31[38]:28 in Sir 49:7; Jer 1:18 in Sir 36:29[24]; Jer 18:4 or 6 in Sir 33[36]:13; Jer 27:12 [34:10] in Sir 51:26; Jer 32[39]:17 in Sir 48:13).[32] Later settings for the proto-Masoretic text of Jeremiah in Hasmonean times[33] or the early second century B.C.E.[34] can therefore be excluded with a high degree of certainty. An early date of MT-Jer is also confirmed by the dominance of this text in the literature of Second Temple Judaism since the third century B.C.E. The majority of the quotations from and allusions to the book of Jeremiah employ a proto-MT version of this book.[35]

The *terminus post quem* is set by historical allusions observed by Bogaert.[36] Bogaert argues that proto-Masoretic additions in Jeremiah's word against the Philistines (Jeremiah 47[29]) are related to conquests and campaigns of Ptolemy I. Soter. The phrase "before Pharaoh attacked Gaza"

---

[30] For my arguments, see also Lange, "Textual Plurality," 77–80 and Lange, "Covenant."

[31] Cf., e.g., C.A. Moore, *Daniel, Esther, and Jeremiah: The Additions: A New Translation with Introduction and Commentary* (AB 44; Garden City: Doubleday, 1977), 323; R.G. Kratz, "Die Rezeption von Jer. 10 und 29 im pseudepigraphen Brief des Jeremia," *JSJ* 26 (1995): 1–31. For a different view, see B.D. Thomas, "Reevaluating the Influence of Jeremiah 10 upon the Apocryphal Epistle of Jeremiah: A Case for the Short Edition," *ZAW* 120 (2008): 547–62.

[32] See A. Lange, "The Book of Jeremiah in the Hebrew and Greek Texts of Ben Sira," in *Making the Biblical Text: Textual Studies in the Hebrew and the Greek Bible* (ed. I. Himbaza; OBO 275; Göttingen: Vandenhoeck & Ruprecht, 2015), 118–61.

[33] Such dates were proposed either for some parts (esp. Jer 33:14–26) or all of MT-Jer by B. Duhm, *Das Buch Jeremia erklärt* (KHC 11; Tübingen: Mohr [Siebeck], 1901), xx, 274, 276; C. Levin, *Die Verheißung des neuen Bundes in ihrem theologiegeschichtlichen Zusammenhang ausgelegt* (FRLANT 137; Göttingen: Vandenhoeck & Ruprecht, 1985), 194–96; Schenker, "La rédaction longue," 281–93; Piovanelli, "JerB 33,14–26," 255–76; cf. recently also Amphoux and Sérandour, "date," 25–35, and Amphoux, "Les réécritures," 213–25.

[34] Thus, e.g., Aejemaelus, "Turning Point," 460.

[35] Examples for this dominance of proto-MT-Jer are its employments in the *War Scroll*, *Hodayot*, and Ben Sira. See A. Lange, "The Textual History of the Book Jeremiah in Light of its Allusions and Implicit Quotations in the Qumran *Hodayot*," in *Prayer and Poetry in the Dead Sea Scrolls and Related Literature: Essays in Honor of Eileen Schuller on the Occasion of Her 65th Birthday* (eds. J. Penner, K.M. Penner, and C. Wassen; STDJ 98; Leiden: Brill, 2012), 251–84; A. Lange, "The Text of Jeremiah in the *War Scroll* from Qumran," in *The Hebrew Bible in Light of the Dead Sea Scrolls* (eds. N. David et al.; FRLANT 239; Göttingen: Vandenhoeck & Ruprecht, 2012), 95–116; Lange, "Jeremiah in the Hebrew and Greek Texts of Ben Sira."

[36] Bogaert, "Baruch," 431–32; Bogaert, "mécanismes"; Bogaert, "Relecture," 145–50; Bogaert, "libération," 312–22; Bogaert, "*Urtext*," 237; Bogaert, "trois formes," 1–17; Bogaert, "livre," 393–401; Bogaert, "Jérémie 17,1–4 TM," 59–74; Bogaert, "La datation," 137–59; Bogaert, "Heshbon," 45–54; Bogaert, "liste," 1–14.

(בְּטֶרֶם יַכֶּה פַרְעֹה אֶת־עַזָּה) Jer 47[29]:1) refers to the battle of Gaza between Ptolemaios I and Demetrios in 312 B.C.E. and the subsequent sacking of the city. The addition of the word כַּפְתּוֹר "Cyprus" in Jer 47(29):4 assumes the conquest of the island by Ptolemy I in 294 B.C.E. Linguistic characteristics corroborate a dating of the proto-Masoretic text of Jeremiah in the early third century B.C.E. Stipp[37] points in this context, for example, to the phrase חֹרֵי יְהוּדָה "the nobles of Judah" (Jer 27:20; 39:6) and the term מַלְכוּת "kingdom" (Jer 10:7; 49:34). Further characteristics of this post-classical Hebrew were identified by Joosten.[38] Both linguistic characteristics and historical references exclude earlier dates of the proto-Masoretic text of Jeremiah in Persian times with a high degree of certainty.[39]

The milieu in which the proto-Masoretic text of Jeremiah was written can be deduced from various proto-Masoretic additions. The proto-Masoretic version turns Jeremiah's letter to the Babylonian exiles (Jer 29:1–23) into a forecast of the total annihilation of all the citizens of Judah and Jerusalem but forecasts the salvation of the Diaspora. This anti-Jerusalemite and anti-Judean tendency in favor of the Diaspora points to a Diaspora setting. That proto-MT-Jer universalises the salvation prophecy of Jer 29[36]:10–14 to pertain not only to the Babylonian exiles but to the whole Diaspora argues against a Mesopotamian origin. In the early third century B.C.E., the only sizeable Jewish Diaspora outside of Mesopotamia can be found in Ptolemaic Egypt. The proto-Masoretic text of Jeremiah was thus written by Egyptian Jews.[40]

A forerunner of the proto-Masoretic Jeremiah redaction is most likely preserved in 4QJer[d], because this manuscript shares some long texts with MT-Jer but in other cases reads the shorter text of LXX-Jer (→ 7.2.3.3). Already this textual forerunner of MT-Jer attests to a Diaspora consciousness. In Jer 43(50):9, 4QJer[d] reads with MT-Jer "before the eyes of Jewish men" (לעיני אנשים יהודים) against LXX-Jer which has κατ' ὀφθαλμοὺς ἀνδρῶν Ιουδα "before the eyes of the men of Judah." The text of 4QJer[d] changed אנשי יהודה "men of Judah" thus to אנשים יהודים "Jewish men," making a careful distinction between men who live in Judah and Diaspora Jews who live in Egypt. This distinction also argues for a setting of the 4QJer[d] text of Jeremiah in early Egyptian Judaism. Further individual changes were most likely inserted into the book of Jeremiah both before and after 4QJer[d] was produced; however, their dates and settings can no longer be traced.

Several observations corroborate an Egyptian setting for the proto-Masoretic text of Jeremiah. Proto-MT-Jer's subtle allusions to the military achievements of Ptolemy I. Soter in Jer 47[29]:1, 4 would have been easily understood in Ptolemaic Egypt in the early third century B.C.E. but not in Mesopotamia or Judah. Special knowledge about Egypt and its interactions with Judah is also documented in the addition of MT-Jer to Jer 26[33]:22, when it specifies that Jehoiachim sent "Elnathan, son of Achbor, and the men with him to Egypt" (אֶת־אֶלְנָתָן בֶּן־עַכְבּוֹר וַאֲנָשִׁים אִתּוֹ אֶל־מִצְרָיִם). The special interest displayed in proto-MT-Jer regarding the temple cult and its instruments[41] points to Levitical

---

[37] Stipp, *Sondergut*, 80, 141–42; Stipp, "Zur aktuellen Diskussion," 635.

[38] Joosten, "L' excédent massorétique."

[39] Contra Janzen, *Studies*, 127–35 (middle of the fifth through early fourth century B.C.E.); Goldman, *Prophétie et royauté* (three different redactional layers in the proto-Masoretic additions that would date to 515–445 B.C.E.; esp. 225–35); R.D. Weis, "A Conflicted Book for a Marginal People: Thematic Oppositions in Jeremiah," in *Reading the Hebrew Bible for a New Millennium: Form, Concept, and Theological Perspective*, Vol. 2: *Exegetical and Theological Studies* (ed. W. Kim et al.; Harrisburg: Trinity Press International, 2000), 297–309 (304–07); R.D. Weis, "Exegesis of Jeremiah 10 in LXX and MT: Results and Implications," in *Texts and Contexts of Jeremiah: The Exegesis of Jer 1 and Jer 10 in Light of Text and Reception History* (eds. K. Finsterbusch and A. Lange; CBET; Leuven: Peeters, forthcoming).

[40] That a significant number of Jews lived in Egypt in the early third century B.C.E. is attested by the *Letter of Aristeas* and Hecateus. The *Letter of Aristeas* (12–27) reports the deportation of large numbers of Jews from Judah to Ptolemaic Egypt during the reign of Ptolemy I Soter. Hecateus (Josephus, *Ag. Ap.* 1.186–87) speaks of the voluntary Jewish migration of a priestly group to Ptolemaic Egypt led by a leading priest named Hezekiah at the same time.

[41] In Jer 27:18–19, 21–22, proto-MT-Jer inserts the temple instruments and their long stay in Babylon into the text of Jeremiah 27. And in Jer 52:18–23, proto-MT-Jer does not only extend the list of temple instruments that the Babylonians

priests who migrated with the archpriest Hezekiah to Egypt (Josephus, *Ag. Ap.* 1.186–87) as the milieu behind this latest redaction of Jeremiah.

The polemics of these Levitical priests against the Jerusalem establishment are harsh. In Jer 10:6–10, proto-MT-Jer emphasizes how incomparable the God of Israel is to idols; the veneration of other deities would lead to the plunder of the people's fortunes and treasures and Judah would have to serve its enemies and forfeit its inheritance (Jer 17:1–4). Proto-MT-Jer hopes for the imminent destruction of Jerusalem in particular and Judah in general (Jer 29:16–20; 39:4–13). In a time of *shalom* for his scattered people, the Lord will judge the nations; the Diaspora will return to Jerusalem and reinstall the proper priestly cult and royal government in Judah (Jer 29:10–14; 30:10–11, 22; 31:17; 33:14–26). Such hopes for destruction and salvation might have been sparked by the violent wars in which the Diadochi fought over the succession of Alexander the Great and for possession of his empire.

Given the narrow time-window in which proto-MT-Jer must have reworked the book of Jeremiah, it seems quite likely that its anti-Judahite and anti-Jerusalemite polemics target the intensified Hellenization of Judean Jewry after Judah became part of the Ptolemaic realm, as illustrated by the book of Ecclesiastes and the Tobiad family. It is because of tendencies like these that proto-MT-Jer creates a typology comparing the future of the Ptolemaic province of Yehud with the fate of Jerusalem under the rule of Zedekiah. Because the Jews of Judah venerated other gods, the Babylonians destroyed Judah, Jerusalem, and the temple in 587 B.C.E. After these events, Judaism was represented by the exiles who remained true to the covenant. They were to come back and rebuild Judah and the temple cult. Proto-MT-Jer applies this earlier experience to the situation in the early third century B.C.E. As in the past, the Jews of Jerusalem and Judah of the early third century B.C.E. venerate other gods and will be destroyed in the context of the wars of the Diadochi. True Judaism is represented only by the Diaspora. As after the return from the exile, it will rebuild Judah and Jerusalem, install a proper Davidic government and a proper Jerusalemite cult.

Occasional original readings in 2QJer (→ 7.2.2.3.1) and 4QJer^c (→ 7.2.2.3.2) demonstrate that after the proto-Masoretic Jeremiah redaction was achieved, further changes were applied to MT-Jer. Given the sparsity of the evidence, their date and setting can no longer be determined.

7.2.2.2.2 Characteristics

On the whole, proto-MT-Jer is an extensive reworking of its parent text comparable to the redaction of biblical books or the rewritings of Jewish Scriptures in the Second Temple period such as the *Temple Scroll* and the book of *Jubilees* (→ 11.8). The expansion of MT-Jer restructured the book and added a further 3,097 words, lengthening the book by one-seventh.[42] However, in some cases, the (parent) text of LXX-Jer (→ 7.3) goes back to scribal errors while the text of MT-Jer preserves a more original text. Examples include two cases of parablepsis in Jer 11:22 (לָכֵן כֹּה אָמַר יְהוָה צְבָאוֹת "therefore thus says the Lord of Hosts"; cf. 11:21) and Jer 36[43]:26 (וְאֶת־שְׁלֶמְיָהוּ בֶּן־עַבְדְּאֵל "and Shelemiah, son of Abd'el"). Proto-MT-Jer displays a set of textual characteristics[43] that distinguish its long texts

---

destroyed or carried off to Babylon but corrects it as well. The author of proto-MT-Jer not only had a special interest in priestly matters but also possessed special priestly knowledge. The same special interest in priestly matters is displayed in the most extensive addition of proto-MT-Jer, Jer 33:14–26. It promises not only that God will uphold his covenant with David and that the Davidic dynasty will return to political power but also that God will uphold his covenant with the Levitical priests who are privileged to carry out the sacrificial cult in the Jerusalem temple. Jer 33:14–26 argues thus against the religious and political realities at the Jerusalem temple in the third century B.C.E. The office of the Jerusalem high priest was more a political one than a ritual one and his priestly duties were far from being restricted to the sacrificial cult. With its great interest in the sacrificial cult, proto-MT-Jer resembles most the *Aramaic Levi Document*, which also restricts the responsibilities of the (Levitical) priesthood to the sacrificial cult. See Lange, "Covenant," 110–16 and *passim*.

[42] Cf. Min, *Minuses and Pluses*, 1, 159, 181, 312, 315, 317.

[43] A list of these characteristics can be found in Tov, "Aspects," 150–67.

on stylistic, linguistic, and ideological levels from other textual strata of the book of Jeremiah. 4QJer^d (→ 7.2.3.3) demonstrates that some of these characteristics were already inserted into the text of Jeremiah before proto-MT-Jer was finished, while more original readings in 2QJer and 4QJer^c show that further changes were applied to MT-Jer after the finalization of proto-MT-Jer. Given the limited manuscript evidence and the fact that 4QJer^d shares characteristics with MT-Jer, it is impossible to decide which passages belong to which textual version of MT-Jer. Therefore, its characteristics will be described below without a text-stratigraphic distinction.

In the later sections of the book of Jeremiah, the number of smaller and larger additions increases in proto-MT-Jer and can often, but not always, be found in introductory verses to prophetic oracles or prose passages (e.g., the addition of the messenger formula). This observation coincides with the fact that proto-MT-Jer only begins to restructure its parent text at Jer 25:15 [32:1]. Is it possible that the first part of the book of Jeremiah had already reached a fixed, authoritative state textually and therefore the redactor focused more on the second part of the book? Exceptions to that rule would be the proto-Masoretic long texts of Jer 2:1–2; 7:1–2; 8:10–12; 10:6–10; 11:7–8; 17:1–4; 25:14.

The smaller extensions of proto-MT-Jer are characterized by several repeated features:

- The addition of divine names (examples include אֱלֹהֵי "God" in Jer 5:14; צְבָאוֹת "hosts" in Jer 6:6 and Jer 29[36]:4; צְבָאוֹת אֱלֹהֵי יִשְׂרָאֵל "of hosts, the God of Israel" in Jer 29[36]:21);[44]
- The addition of proper nouns (e.g., נְבוּכַדְנֶאצַּר מֶלֶךְ בָּבֶל "Nebuchadnezar, king of Babylon" instead of מלך בבל "king of Babylon" in Jer 21:2 or אֶל־נְבוּכַדְנֶאצַּר מֶלֶךְ בָּבֶל בָּבֶלָה "to Nebuchadnezar, king of Babylon, to Babylon" instead of בבלה "to Babylon" in Jer 29[36]:3; הַמֶּלֶךְ יְהוֹיָקִים "the king Jehoiakim" instead of המלך "the king" in Jer 26[33]:22);
- The addition of patronyms to proper nouns (e.g., אֶל־אַחְאָב בֶּן־קוֹלָיָה וְאֶל־צִדְקִיָּהוּ בֶן־מַעֲשֵׂיָה "to Ahab, son of Koliah, and to Zedekiah, son of Maaseiah" instead of אל אחאב ואל צדקיהו "to Ahab and to Zedekiah" in Jer 29[36]:21);[45]
- The addition of the title הַנָּבִיא "the prophet" for Jeremiah (e.g., Jer 28[35]:5, 6, 10, 11, 12, 15; 29[36]:1, 29; 32[39]:2; 34[41]:6; 36[43]:8, 26; 37[44]:2, 3, 6, 13; 42[49]:2, 4; 46[26]:13; 49:34 [25:14])[46] and other prophets (e.g., in Jer 29[36]:21);[47]
- The addition of formulaic introductions[48] to prophetic words such as כֹּה אָמַר יְהוָה "thus says the Lord" (e.g., Jer 11:22; 13:12; 17:5; 18:11; 19:1; 22:30; 29[36]:25; 31[38]:37; 35[42]:19) and נְאֻם־יְהוָה "utterance of the Lord" (e.g., 3:10; 5:11; 7:13; 8:3, 17; 9:2[3], 5[6], 21[22]; 12:17; 13:11, 14; 15:9, 20; 18:6; 21:10, 13, 14; 23:1, 11, 12, 24, 28, 29, 31, 32, 32; 25:7, 9, 12, 29 [32:15]; 27:11 [34:9]; 27:15 [34:12]; 28[35]:4; 29[36]:9, 11, 14, 14, 32; 31[38]:14, 16, 17, 34, 37; 32[39]:5, 30, 44; 34[41]:17; 35[42]:13; 39[46]:17; 44[51]:29; 48[31]:25, 30, 43, 44; 49:16 [29:15]; 49:30, 31 [30:8, 9]; 49:37, 38 [25:17, 18]; 50[27]:4, 10, 20, 35; 51[28]:25). In Jer 46[26]:1, such an added formula can even introduce a whole collection of Jeremianic oracles: אֲשֶׁר הָיָה דְבַר־יְהוָה אֶל־יִרְמְיָהוּ הַנָּבִיא עַל־הַגּוֹיִם "The word of the Lord that came to the prophet Jeremiah concerning the nations";
- The radical alteration of existing introductions to prophetic words or speeches (see, e.g., Jer 2:1–2; 7:1–2; 47[29]:1; 49:34 [25:14]; 50[27]:1);
- Changes in the syntax of a sentence (e.g., Jer 27:16 [34:13]);
- Other changes.

By these means, proto-MT-Jer's smaller additions achieve textual harmonization within the book

---

[44] For more examples, see Janzen, *Studies*, 69–86; Rofé, "The Name," 307–16, thinks that צבאות "hosts" was deleted by LXX-Jer for theological reasons (for a criticism of Rofé's position, see Tov, "Characterization," *passim*). For a systematic study of the depiction of God in the proto-Masoretic Jeremiah redaction, see Stipp, "Gottesbildfragen."

[45] For a list, see Janzen, *Studies*, 139–55.

[46] LXX-Jer calls Jeremiah ὁ προφήτης "the prophet" only in Jer 28:59 (51:59); 49:2 (42:2); 50:5 (43:6); 51:31 (45:1).

[47] Cf. Stipp, "Prophetentitel"; and the lists in Janzen, *Studies*, 145–48.

[48] Cf. Stipp, "Messenger Formulas."

of Jeremiah, rhetorical precision, and historical accuracy. Other smaller changes are theologically motivated. Often several motivations coincide:

- Examples for harmonization include the use of the phrase וְאָמַרְתָּ אֲלֵיהֶם כֹּה־אָמַר יְהוָה "and say to them, thus says the Lord" in MT-Jer 8:4; 11:3; 13:13; 15:2; 19:11; 25:28 [32:14]; 26[33]:4; and 43[50]:10. LXX-Jer has full equivalents for this idiom only in Jer 11:3; 13:13; 15:2.[49] Proto-MT-Jer adjusts the text of Jer 8:4; 19:11; 25:28 [32:14]; 26[33]:4; and 43[50]:10 to these three references. Similarly, MT-Jer adds the messenger formula כֹּה אָמַר יְהוָה "thus says the Lord" in Jer 17:5 in harmonization with 17:19 and 21;
- MT-Jer's concern for rhetoric specificity and historical accuracy expresses itself in many small additions and textual changes. When LXX-Jer reads, e.g., a personal pronoun (αὐτός "he" etc.), MT-Jer often adds a personal name.[50] Similarly, MT-Jer specifies the unnamed subject of a given sentence by adding a name;[51]
- Historical accuracy is aimed for in cases where a title is specified.[52] Out of the same concern, MT-Jer adds in several cases personal names and numbers of people to an otherwise unspecified group.[53] MT-Jer's interest in patronyms is similarly explained. Sometimes the need for historical accuracy even leads to the more extensive addition of an otherwise unknown source, as in the list of three deportations in Jer 52:28–30 that gives the numbers of Jews deported in each of them. That MT-Jer feels the need for such historical explanations points to a reworking that happened when its readers no longer had accurate knowledge about Jeremiah's time. In the case of the addition in Jer 52:28–30, such a historical explanation can even extend to three verses of text;
- In other cases, proto-MT-Jer's smaller textual changes are theologically motivated. Two examples may illustrate this phenomenon. The addition of the title הַנָּבִיא "the prophet" to Jeremiah's name occurs in contexts where the people refuse to listen to Jeremiah's words, thus highlighting the people's stubbornness against his prophetic message.[54] For example, LXX-Jer 43:26 describes that Jeremiah and Baruch "were hidden" (κατεκρύβησαν). Although the aorist passive could imply a divine passive in the Greek, it renders a *Niph'al* form in the Hebrew, which does not express such a divine passive. To emphasize that both Jeremiah and Baruch owe their escape from Jehoiakim's minions to God, proto-MT-Jer rephrases the ויסתרו "and they were hidden" of LXX-Jer's parent text to וַיַּסְתִּרֵם יְהוָה "and the Lord hid them" (MT-Jer 36:26);
- Sometimes several motivations coincide. MT-Jer adds dates to events reported in the book of Jeremiah (e.g., Jer 27[34]:1) or rephrases them (e.g., Jer 28[35]:1) out of its concern for historical accuracy, but an added date can also convey a theological reading of history. Examples include Jer 25:1: LXX-Jer states that Jeremiah's prophecy about the enemy of the North and the ensuing seventy-year exile was given not in the fourth year of King Jehoiakim, which was the year of the battle of Carchemish. MT-Jer explains in a textual addition that "it was the first year of King Nebuchadrezzar of Babylon" (הִיא הַשָּׁנָה

---

[49] LXX-Jer 8:4 has only Ὅτι τάδε λέγει κύριος "for thus speaks the Lord" while LXX-Jer 19:11; 32:14; 33:4; and 50:10 read καὶ ἐρεῖς "and you shall say" instead of וְאָמַרְתָּ אֲלֵיהֶם "and you shall say to them" (MT-Jer 19:11; 25:28; 26:4; and 43:10).

[50] Examples include Jer 20:2; 38[45]:10 אֶת־יִרְמְיָהוּ הַנָּבִיא "Jeremiah, the prophet" instead of αὐτόν "him") and Jer 38[45]:17 אֶל־צִדְקִיָּהוּ "to Zedekiah" instead of αὐτῷ "to him").

[51] E.g., Jer 25:2 אֲשֶׁר דִּבֶּר יִרְמְיָהוּ הַנָּבִיא "which Jeremiah the prophet spoke" instead of ὃν ἐλάλησε "which he spoke."

[52] Examples include Jer 21:2 נְבוּכַדְרֶאצַּר מֶלֶךְ־בָּבֶל "Nebuchadrezzar, king of Babylon" instead of βασιλεὺς Βαβυλῶνος "King of Babylon") and Jer 26[33]:22 הַמֶּלֶךְ יְהוֹיָקִים "Jehoiachim, the king" instead of ὁ βασιλεύς "the king").

[53] An example can be found in Jer 26[33]:22. MT-Jer reads וַיִּשְׁלַח הַמֶּלֶךְ יְהוֹיָקִים אֲנָשִׁים מִצְרַיִם אֵת אֶלְנָתָן בֶּן־עַכְבּוֹר וַאֲנָשִׁים אִתּוֹ אֶל־מִצְרָיִם "and Jehoiachim, the king, sent thirty men to Egypt, namely [he sent] Elnathan son of Achbor and the men with him to Egypt" but LXX-Jer has καὶ ἐξαπέστειλεν ὁ βασιλεὺς ἄνδρας εἰς Αἴγυπτον "and the king sent men to Egypt." For more examples, see Janzen, *Studies*, 69–86.

[54] Cf. Di Pede, "Jérémie."

הָרִאשֹׁנִית לִנְבוּכַדְרֶאצַּר מֶלֶךְ בָּבֶל). Nebuchadrezzar's reign as a whole is thus identified with a time of punishment for the people of Israel.[55]

In contrast to the smaller text changes in MT-Jer, the larger text additions to MT-Jer and the restructuring of its parent text were inspired mainly by theological interests. Several passages in the long texts in proto-MT-Jer are admonitory in character (Jer 11:7; 27:13–14, 17–18; 51:45–46) and in one case even hymnic (the additions to Jer 10:6–10).[56] But most texts added by proto-MT-Jer to the book of Jeremiah focus, in addition to a special interest in the temple and its cult, on the themes of judgment and salvation:

- The main emphasis of MT-Jer's larger additions is judgment. Some of these additions concern the judgment of the nations in general (Jer 25:14), or Egypt (Jer 46:26), Moab (Jer 48:45–46), and Babylon (Jer 27:7; 51:47–48) in particular. But most passages engage with the judgment of Judah (Jer 17:1–4; 27:13–14) as well as Jerusalem (Jer 29:16–20; Jer 39:4–13) and the deportation of the temple instruments (Jer 27:21–22). Jer 8:10aβ–12 also addresses the reasons for that judgment and Jer 11:7–8 refers to the punishment of the exodus generation as an earlier parallel for Judah's fate. In the conclusion on judgment and in alignment with 2 Kgs 24:18–25:26, proto-MT-Jer's additions to Jeremiah 52 address both the destruction of Judah and Jerusalem as well as the deportation of the temple instruments;
- As for salvation, Moab and Ammon receive a promise of the restoration of their fortunes after their judgment (Jer 48:47 and 49:6). But, in proto-MT-Jer, salvation concerns predominantly the return of the exiles and/or their descendants (Jer 29:14; 30:10–11; Jer 31:17) as well as the return of the temple instruments (Jer 27:22). Only after forecasting the return of the exiles does proto-MT-Jer concern itself with Judah's future Davidic kings, its future (Levitical) priests (Jer 33:14–26), and the salvation of God's people as a whole (Jer 51:45–48);
- Examples of the priestly interest in proto-MT-Jer include Jer 7:1–2; 27:18, 21–22; 33:18–22; and 52:18–22. Jer 7:1–2 specifies the location where Jeremiah held his temple speech, i.e., in the gates of the temple, and changes its addressees. Only those who enter the temple to worship, i.e., the Jerusalemite cultic community (MT-Jer) instead of all of Judah (LXX-Jer) are targeted. Similarly, the addition of Jer 8:10aβ–12 emphasizes, in repetition of Jer 6:13–15, priests and prophets[57] as those responsible for the punishment prophesied for Judah in Jer 7:3–8:3. Jer 27:18, 21–22 extends the prophecy regarding the exile of those temple instruments that remained in Jerusalem after the conquest of 587 B.C.E. Similarly, proto-MT-Jer extends and alters the list of temple instruments taken by the Babylonians in 587 B.C.E. In Jer 33:18–22, proto-MT-Jer forecasts the time after the return not only of the establishment of a Davidic dynasty but also the reestablishment of the temple cult according to Davidic and priestly covenants. That the responsibilities of (Levitical) priests are restricted in Jer 33:18–22 to cultic matters corresponds well with the generalization of other priestly duties, i.e., the teaching of a general knowledge of the Torah that will be written onto the heart of every member of God's new covenant with Israel.[58]

Regardless of their topic, many but not all text additions of proto-MT-Jer employ or repeat other

---

[55] Cf. Aejmelaeus, "Jeremiah," 463–64.

[56] Hymnic additions are not unusual in prophetic texts; MT-Jer thus follows a widespread practice with the additions of Jer 10:5–10. Cf. J. Ben-Dov, "A Textual Problem and its Form-Critical Solution: Jeremiah 10:1–6," *Text* 20 (2000): 97–128.

[57] "They have treated the wound of the daughter of my people carelessly, saying 'Peace, Peace,' but there is no peace" (Jer 8:11).

[58] Cf. C. Patton, "Layers of Meaning: Priesthood in Jeremiah MT," in *The Priests in the Prophets: The Portrayal of Priests, Prophets and Other Religious Specialists in the Latter Prophets* (eds. L.L. Grabbe and A. Ogden Bells; JSOTSup 408; London: T & T Clark, 2004), 149–76, 165–66.

parts of the book of Jeremiah.[59] Min estimates that only eight percent of MT-Jer's long texts are without parallel.[60] For only some of its text additions did proto-MT-Jer use sources that were not part of its parent text.[61]

As some of MT-Jer's long texts employ other parts of the book of Jeremiah while others do not, it has been suggested that proto-MT-Jer itself consists of several redactional layers.[62] Against such a proposal of multiple strata within the text of proto-MT-Jer, it needs to be emphasized that the text additions of proto-MT-Jer cross-reference each other by way of verbal parallels. Two examples are Jer 29:10 and 33:14, as well as Jer 29:14; 30:3 and 33:26; hence, proto-MT-Jer should be understood as one redactional stratum in the book of Jeremiah. While 4QJer^d leaves little doubt that some of MT-Jer's long texts were inserted before the proto-Masoretic Jeremiah redaction, it is likely that the bulk of these long texts result from one extensive redaction.

Jer 29:1–23 is a good example of how proto-MT-Jer created the extensions of its *Vorlage*.[63]

The smaller changes in Jer 29:1, 2, 3, 4, 6, 7, 9, 21, 23 are harmonizations and specifications that I have discussed elsewhere.[64] In addition to these smaller changes, proto-MT-Jer rewrote Jer 29:10–20 drastically. It adds to Jeremiah's letter to the Babylonian exiles in vv. 16–20 a long excursus about those remaining in Jerusalem and extends vv. 10–14 significantly.

In proto-MT-Jer's parent text, Jeremiah's letter states that the exiles will return only after seventy years (Jer 29:10). They should ensconce themselves in Mesopotamia and live their lives there. The example of Ahab and Zedekiah shows that the Mesopotamian Diaspora is endangered by false prophets. Instead of their false prophecies, Jeremiah assures the exiles that God will be available to them not only in Jerusalem but also in Mesopotamia. With the addition of the phrase הֲשִׁבֹתִי אֶתְכֶם אֶל־הַמָּקוֹם אֲשֶׁר־הִגְלֵיתִי אֶתְכֶם מִשָּׁם "and I will bring you back to the place from which I sent you into exile" in Jer 29:14, proto-MT-Jer creates an inclusion with v. 10. In this way, the promised return from exile becomes one of the main themes of Jeremiah's letter. When proto-MT-Jer prefaces the וְהִתְפַּלַּלְתֶּם אֵלַי וְשָׁמַעְתִּי אֲלֵיכֶם "and pray to me, I will hear you" in Jer 29:12 with וּקְרָאתֶם אֹתִי וַהֲלַכְתֶּם "and when you call me and go," it also introduces a cultic dimension into Jeremiah's letter. Proto-MT-Jer's parent text assured the exiles that they could pray to God even in Mesopotamia. But with the combination of the verbs קרא[65] "to call" and הלך "to go," proto-MT-Jer clarifies that the place in which the deportees are promised to be heard by God is the Jerusalem temple. When proto-MT-Jer thus promises the exiles in Jer 29[36]:10–14 not only a return to Jerusalem but also a participation in the Jerusalem temple cult, a topic that proto-MT-Jer addresses in more detail in Jer 33:14–26, this also implies a rebuilding of the destroyed temple by the returnees.

Another important change can be found in Jer 29:14. Jeremiah's letter was addressed in Jer 29:1–3* only to the Babylonian exiles. By emphasizing in MT-Jer 29:14 that God will bring the exiles back to Jerusalem from all the nations and all places (מִכָּל־הַגּוֹיִם וּמִכָּל־הַמְּקוֹמוֹת), proto-MT-Jer includes the whole Diaspora as the addressees of Jeremiah's letter; not only the Babylonian exiles

---

[59] Cf., e.g., Janzen, *Studies*, 35–63 who lists 197 cases. Examples for this procedure include Jer 8:10aβ–12 (cf. Jer 6:13–15); Jer 29:14 (cf. Jer 23:3; 30:3, 18); Jer 29:17–18 (cf. Jer 24:1–10; 25:4[9.18]; 26:5; 35:15; 44:4); Jer 30:10–11 (cf. Jer 46[26]:27–28); Jer 30:22 (cf. Jer 11:4; 31:1); Jer 33:20–26 (cf. Jer 31:35–37); Jer 39:4–13 (cf. Jer 52:7–11, 13–16); Jer 48:7 (cf. Jer 49:6).

[60] Min, "Minuses and Pluses," 182.

[61] Examples include the alignment of MT-Jer 52 with the text of 2 Kgs 24:18–20; 25 and the list of deportees in Jer 52:28–30.

[62] Min, "Minuses and Pluses"; Goldman, *Prophétie et royauté*; Stipp, *Sondergut*. For further literature, see nn. 11–16.

[63] For an extensive discussion of Jeremiah 29 in MT and LXX, see R. de Hoop, "Textual, Literary, and Delimitation Criticism: The Case of Jeremiah 29 in M and G," in *The Impact of Unit Delimitation on Exegesis* (eds. R. de Hoop, M. Korpel, and S. Porter; Pericope 7; Leiden: Brill, 2009), 29–62.

[64] Lange, "Textual Plurality," 70–77.

---

[65] For the cultic and non-cultic connotations of קרא, see G. Schauerte, "קרא," *ThWAT* 7:117–47 (esp. 128–29).

but all exiled Jews will return to Jerusalem.⁶⁶ The text of proto-MT-Jer turns Jeremiah's letter into a prophecy of salvation. The exiles of the whole world will return to Jerusalem where they will rebuild the country and temple and begin the temple cult anew.

After this promise of salvation for the Diaspora, the addition of MT-Jer 29:16–20 turns to the fate of those who are still in Jerusalem. Proto-MT-Jer employs the imagery of rotten figs from Jeremiah 24 to describe the fate of all those who remained in Jerusalem and Judah. Those whom God does not kill, he will exile to the nations as they did not heed the warnings of the prophets.

The structure that proto-MT-Jer gave to this book corresponds to features observed already:

– Proto-MT-Jer's special focus on the judgment of Judah and the nations is also reflected in its structure. The common textual ancestor of LXX-Jer and MT-Jer followed in its structure the classical tripartite pattern of prophetic books: Judgment on Israel (Jer 1:1–25:13); judgment on the nations (LXX-Jer 25:14–32:24 = MT-Jer 46:1–51:64; 25:15–38); and salvation for Israel (LXX-Jer 33–51 = MT-Jer 26–45). MT-Jer is characterized by a double inclusion in its structure.⁶⁷ Jeremiah 1 describes the dual mission of the prophet. In Jer 1:4–10, Jeremiah is appointed as prophet for the nations and the kingdoms. This part of his mission is reflected in the words against the nations in MT-Jer 46–51, which differ in their sequence from LXX-Jer.⁶⁸ In Jer 1:11–19, Jeremiah is sent to prophecy judgment against Judah. This part of Jeremiah's mission is reflected in Jeremiah 2–45. Therefore, for proto-MT-Jer, the book of Jeremiah represents a universal expression of God's will dominated by the judgment of Judah and the nations. The circular structure of MT-Jer is further echoed by the correspondence of oracles concerning an enemy from the North in Jeremiah 4–6 with the oracles against the nations in Jeremiah 46–53(26–31) and the central position of Judah's judgment in MT-Jer (Jeremiah 25).⁶⁹ That both LXX-Jer and MT-Jer end in Jeremiah 52 with an appendix regarding the conquest and destruction of Jerusalem agrees well with proto-MT-Jer's interest in judgment. MT-Jer is "a circular composition, beginning and ending with the deeds of the universal, sovereign God, and with its epicentre in the prophecy of his doom for Israel/Judah and for the foreign nations and Babylon in particular";⁷⁰

– Another issue that affected the structure of MT-Jer is introduced already in MT-Jer 1:4 when it reads "the word of God came to me (אֵלַי)" instead of the "to him" (πρὸς αὐτόν) of LXX-Jer. This small variant reading corresponds well to the addition of MT-Jer in Jer 51:64 "until here reach the words of Jeremiah." MT-Jer shows that the book of Jeremiah is not the work of a third-person narrator, who is identified towards the end of LXX-Jer as Baruch (LXX-Jer 51:31–35 [MT-Jer 45:1–5]), but of the prophet Jeremiah himself.⁷¹ This structural emphasis is reminiscent of the repeated addition of הַנָּבִיא "the prophet" to Jeremiah's name in MT-Jer. MT-Jer's emphasis on Jeremiah's prophetic authorship of his book might have been due to the development

---

⁶⁶ Cf. G. Wanke, *Jeremia* (2 vols.; Zurich: Theologischer Verlag Zürich, 1995–2003), 2.267–68. A similar universalization of Jeremiah's promises of return for just Mesopotamian Jewry to include all the Diaspora can be found in Jer 23:9 when proto-MT-Jer changes the singular "the land" (τῆς γῆς; Hebrew: הָאָרֶץ) to the plural "the lands" (הָאֲרָצוֹת).

⁶⁷ Cf. Schmid, *Buchgestalten*, 3.

⁶⁸ LXX-Jer preserves the original sequence of the words against the nations: LXX-Jer 25:14–26:1 (Elam); 26:2–28 (Egypt); 27–28 (Babylon); 29:1–7 (Philistines); 29:8–23 (Edom); 30:1–5 (Ammonites); 30:6–11 (Kedar); 30:12–16 (Damascus); 31 (Moab). The structure of proto-MT-Jer harmonizes the sequence of the words against the nations in Jeremiah 46–51 with the sequence in which the nations are listed in MT-

Jer 25:19–26 (LXX-Jer 32:5–12): MT-Jer 46:2–28 (Egypt); 47 (Philistines); 48 (Moab); 49:1–7 (Ammonites); 49:8–22 (Edom); 49:23–27 (Damascus); 49:28–33 (Kedar, i.e., the kingdom of Hazor); 49:34–39 (Elam); 50–51 (Babylon and the land of the Chaldeans).

⁶⁹ Cf. Holt, "Meaning."

⁷⁰ Holt, "Meaning," 200.

⁷¹ Cf., e.g., Bogaert, "Baruch"; and Finsterbusch, "MT-Jer 1,1–3,5."

within ancient Judaism in the third or second century B.C.E. of an extensive paratextual literature based on the figure of Baruch.

In addition to intentional changes, some variant readings of MT-Jer towards LXX-Jer can be explained also by way of scribal corruption. An example is the list of *dalet-resh* confusions that Riley[72] has identified recently in MT-Jer 47:1–7; 49:7–22 (= LXX-Jer 29).

A special characteristic of MT-Jer is the high number of baroque spellings that with no apparent logic are interspersed into the conservative orthographic approach of this text. MT-Jer is among the biblical books with the highest number of such baroque spellings.[73] Next to the spellings לוֹא "not" (Jer 2:25, 31; 3:3, 12; 4:11²ˣ; 5:9, 10, 12; 6:8; 7:26, 28; 8:6, 20; 10:4; 15:7, 11; 29:23; 48:27), בְּלוֹא "in which not" (Jer 2:11), and הֲלוֹא "not?" (Jer 2:17; 3:1, 4; 5:3; 7:19; 13:21; 22:15, 16; 23:24, 29; 33:24; 35:13; 38:15; 44:21), twenty-one baroque spellings can be found in the text of MTᴸ-Jer.

Jer 3:7: וּתֵרָאֶה (*Ketiv*)[74] "and she saw"
Jer 5:3: הִכִּיתָה "and you struck"
Jer 7:27: יַעֲנוּכָה "they will answer you"
Jer 10:2: מֵהֵמָּה "because of them"
Jer 10:5: יִנָּשׂוּא "they are carried"
Jer 12:5: רַצְתָה "you have run"
Jer 14:16: לָהֵמָּה "for them"
Jer 17:4: וְשָׁמַטְתָה "you shall lose"
Jer 25:15: וְהִשְׁקִיתָה "and make drink"
Jer 27:20: יְכוֹנְיָה[75] "Jeconiah"
Jer 29:25: בְּשִׁמְכָה "in your name"
Jer 29:26: וְנָתַתָּה "and you put"
Jer 31:34: כּוּלָם[76] "all of them"
Jer 32:2: כָּלוּא "confined"
Jer 32:23: צִוִּיתָה "you commanded them"
Jer 33:8: לְכֹל־עֲוֹנֹתֵיהֶם "for all their iniquity"
Jer 36:32: כָּהֵמָּה "like them"
Jer 37:4: הַכְּלִיא[77] "the prison"
Jer 38:17: וְחָיְתָה "then you will live"
Jer 40:15: יַכֶּכָה "he will smite you"
Jer 52:31: הַכְּלִיא[78] "the prison"

However, MT-Jer attests not only to baroque spellings but also to remnants of archaic orthographic systems.[79] The third-person singular masculine suffix is repeatedly expressed with a *he* -ה instead of a *waw* -ו (כֻּלֹּה "all of him" Jer 2:21; 8:6, 10²ˣ; 15:10; 20:7; 48:31, 38; הֹדֹה, "his majesty" Jer 22:18). In two cases, the affix of the third-person *Niph'al* perfect plural is not spelled with ו- but with ה-: Jer 2:15 נִצְּתָה "they have made desolate" and Jer 22:6 נוֹשָׁבָה "they are inhabited." A further orthographic peculiarity is הַזֹּאתָה "this" in Jer 26:6.

The best explanation for the occurrence of non-conservative orthographic features is that these spellings skipped the eyes of the scribes when they adjusted the orthography of various Jeremiah manuscripts to the conservative system of MT-Jer.

7.2.2.3 Other Texts Close to MT-Jer

The proto-Masoretic Jeremiah redaction represents the most extensive reworking of a biblical book attested in its textual tradition. But both medieval Masoretic manuscripts of Jeremiah (→ 3–5.3) and 4QJerᵃ (→ 7.2.1.2) attest to slight textual variation inside the (proto-)Masoretic textual tradition of Jeremiah. This is corroborated by some variant readings of the two semi-Masoretic manuscripts, 2QJer (→ 7.2.1.1) and 4QJerᶜ (→ 7.2.1.4). Thus, neither the medieval Masoretic manuscripts nor 4QJerᵃ represent the original version of the proto-Masoretic Jeremiah redaction.

Extensive textual damage does not allow for a comprehensive assessment of the semi-Masoretic witnesses, 2QJer and 4QJerᶜ. Both manuscripts read repeatedly with LXX-Jer (→ 7.3) against MT-Jer and are thus able to illuminate the textual character

---

[72] Riley, "Explanation."
[73] See A. Lange, "The Question of the So-Called Qumran Orthography, the Severus Scroll, and the Masoretic Text," *Hebrew Bible and Ancient Israel* 3 (2014): 424–75, esp. 440–41, 457, 470–71, 474.
[74] The *Qere* reads וַתֵּרֶא.
[75] Elsewhere the name is spelled יְכָנְיָה (Jer 28:4; 29:2; Esth 2:6; 1 Chr 3:16, 17).
[76] Except for Jer 33:8, no other plene spelling of the construct of כל is preserved in any grammatical form in the consonantal text of MTᴸ.

[77] Above the *Ketiv* is quoted. The *Qere* would read הַכְּלוּא.
[78] Above the *Ketiv* is quoted. The *Qere* would read הַכְּלוּא.
[79] Cf. Lange, "Orthography," 448; Fischer, *Jeremia 1–25*, 44.

of MT-Jer as compared with the Old Greek text of Jeremiah. 2QJer goes in Jer 43[50]:9; 47[29]:3, 4; 48[31]:29, 30, 37 with LXX against MT, while 4QJer^c does so in Jer 19:9; 21:8; 22:14; 30[37]:20, 21; 31[38]:9²ˣ, 12. These readings are typically small textual differences such as the presence or absence of a *waw* (e.g., 4QJer^c in Jer 22:14), the reading of עַל "above, against" instead of אֶל "to" (e.g., 4QJer^c in Jer 31[38]:9, 12 and 2QJer in Jer 47[29]:3) or differences in grammatical forms (e.g., 4QJer^c in Jer 19:9 [וי]אֹכְלוּ "and they will eat" [LXX-Jer καὶ ἔδονται] against וְהַאֲכַלְתִּים of MT-Jer ["and I will make them eat"]). Only rarely does the textual difference between 2QJer, 4QJer^c, and LXX-Jer on the one hand and MT-Jer on the other hand amount to a whole word (e.g., 2QJer and LXX-Jer, which both lack in Jer 48[31]:29 the word גָּבְהוֹ "his loftiness" of MT-Jer).

A reading of 2QJer sheds new light on the text towards which Theodotion revised the Old Greek text of Jeremiah. Probably in harmonization with Num 21:28 and as part of a proto-Masoretic long text,[80] 2QJer reads in Jer 48:45 מִקִּרְיַת "from the town," which corresponds to ἐκ πόλεως "from the town" in Theodotion (→ 6–9.1.5),[81] while the Masoretic textual tradition is divided (MT^L and most other MT manuscripts have מִבֵּין "from the midst," MT^Kenn 2 reads מִבֵּית "from the house"). The reading of 2QJer thus poses the question if Th-Jer based its revision of LXX-Jer (→ 7.3) on a semi-Masoretic text similar to 2QJer. Regrettably, the bad stage of preservation of 2QJer does not allow me to answer this question.

As 2QJer and 4QJer^c do not overlap, no certainty can be reached regarding whether the two manuscripts represent the same semi-Masoretic text of Jeremiah or two different semi-Masoretic texts of this book. Both manuscripts share orthographic idiosyncrasies.[82] That both manuscripts attest to the same semi-Masoretic text of Jeremiah could further be corroborated by the fact that 2QJer and 4QJer^c read seven and ten times with LXX-Jer against MT-Jer respectively. However, the fact that 4QJer^c applies the orthographic system known from MT-Jer while 2QJer attests to baroque plene spellings and morphology might argue against such a textual affiliation.

7.2.2.3.1 2QJer (2Q13)

Apart from its orthography, the non-aligned readings of 2QJer (→ 7.2.1.1) include the usual range of small textual differences. Scribal errors are restricted to *waw-yod*[83] and *dalet-resh* confusions[84] in the preserved text of 2QJer. Differences in grammatical forms between 2QJer and MT-Jer concern singular and plural forms.[85]

Most variant readings towards MT-Jer can be found in 2QJer's text of Jer 48[31]:25–39. These variants include morphological differences,[86] presence or absence of a suffix,[87] scribal corruption,[88] and different wording.[89] The most coherent feature

---

[80] Jer 48:45–47 are missing in LXX-Jer.

[81] See M. Baillet, "13. Jérémie," *DJD* III.1 (1962): 62–69 (69); Ulrich, *BQS*, 583. Further texts supporting 2QJer are "Hexaplaire part, Lucian, Théodoret de Cyr ... Arménien, Syr, et Num 21:28" (Baillet, "Jérémie," 69).

[82] E.g., 4QJer^c reads in Jer 21:9 and 22:25 הכשדיים instead of MT's הַכַּשְׂדִּים "Chaldeans." 2QJer attests to similar plural forms. In Jer 43(50):9, it has יהודיים instead of יְהוּדִים "Jews" (MT,

4QJer^d) and פלשתיים in Jer 47[29]:4 instead of MT's פְּלִשְׁתִּים "Philistines."

[83] Jer 42[49]:9: אלוהימה "their God" instead of אֲלֵיהֶם "to them" in MT-Jer and αὐτοῖς "to them" in LXX-Jer (the suffix מה- is spelled in the baroque system).

[84] Jer 47[29]:5: תתגוררי "will you scratch yourselves" instead of תִּתְגֹּדָדִי "will you cut yourselves" in MT-Jer and κοψεῖς "will you cut [yourselves] down" in LXX-Jer.

[85] Jer 42[49]:9 תחנו[תיכמה "your petitions" instead of תְּחִנָּתְכֶם "your petition" in MT-Jer (> LXX-Jer); 47[29]:4: איי "coastlands" instead of אִי "coastland" in MT-Jer (cf. the plural form in LXX-Jer).

[86] E.g. Jer 48[31]:29: לבבו "his heart" instead of לִבּוֹ "his heart" in MT-Jer.

[87] E.g. Jer 48[31]:28: ער[יך "your cities" instead of עָרִים "cities" in MT-Jer (cf. LXX-Jer).

[88] E.g. Jer 48[31]:28: שמעו נא "Now, listen" instead of שָׁמַעְנוּ "we heard" in MT-Jer (cf. LXX-Jer: ἤκουσα "I heard").

[89] Examples include Jer 48[31]:29: שמעו נא גאון מואב ג[אה] מ[אד] גאונו ואינ[ו] [וֹ]גאוותו ורו[ם לבבו "Now listen to the pride of Moab – he is very proud of his pride and his vanity and his arrogance and the haughtiness of his heart" instead of שָׁמַעְנוּ גְאוֹן־מוֹאָב גֵּאֶה מְאֹד גָּבְהוֹ וּגְאוֹנוֹ וְגַאֲוָתוֹ וְרֻם לִבּוֹ in MT-Jer ("we heard of the pride of Moab – he is very proud of his loftiness and his pride and his arrogance and the haughtiness of his heart") and of ἤκουσα ὕβριν Μωαβ, ὕβρισε λίαν ὕβριν αὐτοῦ καὶ ὑπερηφανίαν αὐτοῦ, καὶ ὑψώθη ἡ καρδία αὐτοῦ in LXX-Jer ("I heard of the pride of Moab – he was very proud

7.2.2 MASORETIC TEXTS AND ANCIENT TEXTS CLOSE TO MT

are interspersed feminine forms for which MT-Jer reads masculine ones.[90] The feminine forms seem to function as a mockery in the word against Moab. Baillet regards them as more original readings compared to MT-Jer.[91] That Bozak[92] observed a similar phenomenon for Jeremiah 30–31 corroborates Baillet. (Proto)-MT-Jer harmonized the grammatically difficult forms later on with the dominant masculine forms in Jer 48[31]:26–31.

7.2.2.3.2 4QJer^c (4Q72)

In rare cases, 4QJer^c (→ 7.2.1.4) could preserve original readings. In Jer 20:3, 4QJer^c attests to the shorter form of the name Jeremiah, ירמיה, which is otherwise used only in Jeremiah 27–30[34–37]. As 4QJer^c employs ירמיהו as the long form of the name Jeremiah also in Jer 33[40]:19, it seems likely that the shorter form ירמיה was originally used in the Pashur episode and later harmonized in MT with the longer form ירמיהו, which is dominant in the book of Jeremiah.[93] This observation is potentially very important for the source criticism of the book of Jeremiah. Next to original readings, the text of 4QJer^c attests to several scribal errors[94] and other secondary readings. Examples include the addition of the preposition *l^e* in the phrase הנשארים למן המשפחה "that remains with regard from the family" (Jer 8:3) by which 4QJer^c tries to "improve" MT's grammatically more unusual construction הַנִּשְׁאָרִים מִן־הַמִּשְׁפָּחָה "that remains from the family." Similarly, the text of 4QJer^c corrects MT-Jer's difficult-to-understand phrase הַלְּבָנוֹן "the Lebanon" into בלבנון "in the Lebanon" (Jer 22:20). In another case, 4QJer^c carries MT-Jer's tendency to add divine names in a supralinear addition even further than MT itself: י[הוה צבאות] "L]ord of ho[sts]" (Jer 9:2). Other variant readings towards MT-Jer are restricted to differences in grammatical form often without any difference in meaning.[95]

7.2.2.4 Relevance for Exegesis

As a variant literary edition of Jeremiah, MT-Jer represents a late redaction of the book of Jeremiah. In comparison with LXX-Jer (→ 7.3), it provides insights into the final redactional stages of a biblical book and illustrates the transition zone between the redactional and textual histories of biblical books. MT-Jer demonstrates, on the one hand, that at this late stage scribes perused existing authoritative texts as much as possible in order to rewrite and expand their base texts and, on the other hand, that scribes did not hesitate even at such a late stage to restructure a biblical book entirely. A comparison of 4QJer^d and MT-Jer demonstrates further that different expansions and/or redactional layers of a biblical book can share the same characteristics of reworking.

7.2.2.5 Manuscripts, Editions, and Tools

The most important Hebrew manuscripts of Jeremiah[96] are the Cairo Codex attributed to Moses

---

[90] Jer 48[31]:26 הִגְדִּילָה "she magnified herself" instead of הִ]גְדִּיל "he magnified himself" in MT-Jer; 48:27 הָיְאָה הָיְתָה "she was" instead of הָיָה "he was" in MT-Jer; 48[31]:27 תִּתְנוֹדָדִי "you shook your head" (fem.) instead of תִּתְנוֹדָד "you shook your head" (masc.) in MT-Jer; 48[31]:28 וּשְׁכוֹנִי "and live" (imp. sg. fem.) instead of וְשִׁכְנוּ "and live" (imp. pl. masc.) in MT-Jer; 48[31]:28 יוֹשֶׁבֶת "inhabitant" (part. sg. fem.) instead of יֹשְׁבֵי "inhabitants" (part. pl. masc.) in MT-Jer; 48[31]:28 תְקַנֶּ[י] "nest" (fem.) instead of תְּקַנֵּן "nest" (masc.) in MT-Jer.

[91] Baillet, "Jérémie," 67–68.

[92] B.A. Bozak, *Life "Anew": A Literary-Theological Study of Jer. 30–31* (AnBib 122; Rome: Editrice Pontificio Istituto Biblico, 1991), 155–72.

[93] The short form of the name Josiah, יאשיה, in Jer 22:11 results from scribal error because only five words later 4QJer^c reads יאשיהו.

[94] In Jer 21:7, MT's וּמִן־הָרָעָב "and from famine" got lost in 4QJer^c or its *Vorlage* by way of homoiarcton. In Jer 22:20, the characters *bet* and *resh* are confused with *pe* and *kaph* (נשפכו "they have been poured" instead of MT's נִשְׁבְּרוּ "they have been crushed"). In Jer 27:2, 4QJer^c suffers from a metathesis (צוֹ[ר]אָךְ instead of MT-Jer's צַוָּארֶךָ "your neck").

[95] Jer 8:3: הנשארות בכל המקמות "in all the remaining places" instead of בְּכָל־הַמְּקֹמוֹת הַנִּשְׁאָרִים in MT-Jer ("that remains in all places"); Jer 30[37]:17: נדחת instead of נִדָּחָה "outcast" in MT-Jer; Jer 30[37]:18: ונבנה "and will be rebuilt" (masc.) instead of וְנִבְנְתָה "and will be rebuilt" (fem.) in MT-Jer; Jer 31[38]:8: ואקבצם "and I have gathered them" instead of וְקִבַּצְתִּים "and I will gather them" in MT-Jer.

[96] For a description of these manuscripts, see also → 1.2.2.2.1 and → 3–5.3.

ben Asher (MT^C; 895 C.E.),⁹⁷ Codex Aleppo (MT^A; Israel Museum; Jer 29:9–31:34 are not extant; ca. 930 C.E.),⁹⁸ Codex Leningradensis (MT^L; Russian National Library in St. Petersburg EBP. I B 19a; 1009 C.E.),⁹⁹ Codex Babylonicus Petropolitanus (MT^P; Russian National Library; 916 C.E.),¹⁰⁰ Codex New York (MT^N; E.N. Adler 246 = JTS 232; tenth century),¹⁰¹ MS Sassoon 1053 (MT^S1; National Library of Israel; tenth century),¹⁰² and Codex Reuchlinianus 3 (MT^R; Badische Landesbibliothek, Karlsruhe; 1105 C.E.).¹⁰³ Andersen discusses furthermore the so-called Karasu Bazar codex (ninth century?).¹⁰⁴ The *HUB edition of Jeremiah includes also Codex Leningrad II Firkovitch 9, 51, 59, 116, 124, 225, 1283, and Codex Gottheil 22¹⁰⁵ into its apparatuses.¹⁰⁶ The Genizah fragments of Jeremiah are available at the webpage of the Friedberg Jewish Manuscript Society (http://www.jewishmanuscripts.org/ or http://www.genizah.org/onlineFGP.htm?type=FGP&lang=eng). Some of them have also been discussed in various publications.¹⁰⁷

The best and most comprehensive critical edition of the Hebrew text of Jeremiah is that in the *HUB.¹⁰⁸ It is a diplomatic edition that uses as its running text MT^A, reconstructing its missing parts. The *BH³ and *BHS editions of Jeremiah¹⁰⁹ both employ MT^L as their running text. Both editions are selective in their apparatuses and do not even include all LXX variant readings. The *BHQ edition of Jeremiah by Richard Weis is not yet published in 2015 but promises to surpass both *BH³ and *BHS.¹¹⁰ For the variants of the medieval Masoretic manuscript tradition, the edition of Kennicott (*1776–1780, 2.89–171) and the variant lists of De Rossi (*1784–1788, 3.64–125) remain indispensable.

---

⁹⁷ D.S. Loewinger (ed.), *Codex Cairensis of the Bible from the Karaite Synagogue at Abbasiya* (Jerusalem: Makor Publishing, 1971); Pérez Castro, *Profetas de El Cairo*, Vol. 5: *Jeremias* (Madrid: Instituto de Filologia, 1987).

⁹⁸ M. Goshen-Gottstein (ed.), *The Aleppo Codex: Provided with Massoretic Notes and Pointed by Aaron ben Asher* (Jerusalem: Magnes Press, 1976); M. Breuer, *Torah Nevi'im Ketuvim Proofread according to Mesorah of Keter Aram Tzova and Like Manuscripts* (Jerusalem: Mossad HaRav Kook, 1989); N. Ben Zvi (ed.), *Jerusalem Crown: The Bible of the Hebrew University of Jerusalem* (Jerusalem: S. Karger Publishing, 2000). The Aleppo Codex is also available online: http://www.aleppocodex.org. Last accessed June 18, 2015.

⁹⁹ *Pentateuch, Prophets and Hagiographa: Codex Leningrad B 19a: The Earliest Complete Bible Manuscript: With an Introduction by D.S. Loewinger* (Jerusalem: Makor Publishing, 1971); D.N. Freedman et al. (eds.), *The Leningrad Codex: A Facsimile Edition* (Grand Rapids: Eerdmans, 1998); A. Dotan (ed.), *Biblia Hebraica Leningradensia* (Peabody: Hendrickson, 2001).

¹⁰⁰ H.L. Strack, *The Hebrew Bible – Latter Prophets: The Babylonian Codex of Petrograd: Edited with Preface and Critical Annotations* (Prolegomenon by P. Wernberg-Møller); New York: Ktav, 1971; reprint of H.L. Strack, *Prophetam Posteriorum: Codex Babylonicus Petropolitanus* (Petropoli: Bibliothecae Publicae Imperialis, 1876).

¹⁰¹ J. Weiss, "The Masorah of The Jewish Theological Seminary of America Library Manuscript 232 (E.N. Adler Ms. 346)" (PhD diss., The Graduate School of The Jewish Theological Seminary, 2009).

¹⁰² A digitized version of the manuscript is available at https://commons.wikimedia.org/wiki/File:Tanakh-Sassoon1053-11-Jeremiah.pdf. Last accessed June 18, 2015.

¹⁰³ A. Sperber, *Codex Reuchlinianus: No. 3 of the Badische Landesbibliothek in Karlsruhe (formerly Durlach no. 55): With a General Introduction, Masoretic Hebrew* (Corpus Codicum Hebraicorum Medii Aevi 2) (Copenhagen: Eijnar Munksgaard, 1956).

¹⁰⁴ F.I. Andersen, "The Orthography of D62," in *Studies in Hebrew and Aramaic Orthography* (eds. D.N. Freedman, A.D. Forbes, and F.I. Andersen; Biblical and Judaic Studies 2; Winona Lake: Eisenbrauns, 1992), 253–93.

¹⁰⁵ R. Gottheil, "Some Hebrew Manuscripts in Cairo," *JQR* 17 (1905): 608–55 (631–34); I. Yeivin, "A Biblical Manuscript Very Close to the Aleppo Codex from the Karaite Synagogue in Cairo (C1)," in *Studies in Bible and Exegesis 3: Moshe Goshen-Gottstein – In Memoriam* (eds. M. Bar Asher et al.; Ramat Gan: Bar-Ilan University Press, 1993), 169–94 [Hebr.].

¹⁰⁶ Rabin–Talmon–Tov, *HUB, Jeremiah*, xxxvi.

¹⁰⁷ E.J. Revell, *Biblical Texts with Palestinian Pointing and Their Accents* (Missoula: Scholars Press, 1977); I. Yeivin, *Genizah Bible Fragments with Babylonian Massorah and Vocalization* (5 vols.; Jerusalem: Makor, 1973); I. Yeivin, *A Collection of Mishnaic Geniza Fragments with Babylonian Vocalization: With Description of the Manuscripts and Indices* (Jerusalem: Makor, 1974).

¹⁰⁸ Rabin–Talmon–Tov, *HUB, Jeremiah*.

¹⁰⁹ W. Rudolph (ed.), "Librum Jeremiae," *BH³*, 703–810 (1931); W. Rudolph (ed.), "Librum Jeremiae," *BHS*, 780–895 (1970).

¹¹⁰ See his sample in R. Weis, "Biblia Hebraica Quinta and the Making of Critical Editions of the Hebrew Bible," *TC: A Journal of Biblical Textual Criticism* 7 (2002): http://rosetta.reltech.org/TC/vol07/Weis2002.html. Last accessed June 19, 2015.

Several tools are available that assist the comparative study of the Hebrew and Greek texts of Jeremiah. A reconstruction of the Hebrew parent text of LXX-Jer was published by Stulman.[111] In the framework of the Computer Assisted Tools for Septuagint/Scriptural Study (CATSS), a Hebrew-Greek text for LXX-Jer was created under the direction of Robert Kraft and Emanuel Tov.[112] Currently, Stipp is preparing a Hebrew-Greek synopsis of MT-Jer and LXX-Jer, a preliminary version of which is available online.[113] A comparative analysis of the rhetorical structures of LXX-Jer and MT-Jer is in preparation by Finsterbusch and Jacoby, which will be published in the form of a German synopsis.[114]

Aejmelaeus, A., "Jeremiah at the Turning-Point of History," *VT* 52 (2002): 459–82.

Aejmelaeus, A., "Nebuchadnezzar, My Servant," in *Interpreting Translation: Studies on the LXX and Ezekiel in Honour of Johan Lust* (eds. F. García Martinez and M. Vervenne; BETL 192; Leuven: Peeters, 2005), 1–18.

Amphoux, C.-B., "Les réécritures du livre de Jérémie (LXX)," in *Écritures et réécritures: La reprise interprétative des traditions fondatrices par la littérature biblique et extra-biblique: Cinquième colloque international du RRENAB, Universités de Genève et Lausanne, 10–12 juin 2010* (eds. C. Clivaz et al.; BETL 248; Leuven: Peeters, 2012), 213–25.

Amphoux, C.-B. and A. Sérandour, "La date de la forme courte de Jérémie," in *Eukarpa Εὔκαρπα: Études sur la Bible et ses exégètes en hommage à Gilles Dorival* (eds. M. Loubet and D. Pralon; Paris: Cerf, 2011), 25–35.

Bogaert, P.-M., "De Baruch à Jérémie: Les deux rédactions conservées du livre de Jérémie," in *Le livre de Jérémie* (ed. P.-M. Bogaert; BETL 54; Leuven: Leuven University Press, 1981), 168–73, 430–32.

Bogaert, P.-M., "Les mécanismes rédactionnels en Jér 10,1–16 (LXX et TM) et la signification des suppléments," in *Le livre de Jérémie* (ed. P.-M. Bogaert; BETL 54; Leuven: Leuven University Press, 1981), 222–38, 433–34.

Bogaert, P.-M., "Relecture et déplacement de l'oracle contre les Philistins: Pour une datation de la rédaction longue (TM) du livre de Jérémie," in *La vie de la parole: Études d'exégèse et d'herméneutique bibliques offertes à P. Grelot* (ed. H. Cazelles; Paris: Desclée, 1987), 139–50.

Bogaert, P.-M., "L'organisation des grands recueils prophétiques," in *The Book of Isaiah – Le livre d'Isaïe* (ed. J. Vermeylen; BETL 81; Leuven: Leuven University Press, 1989), 147–53.

Bogaert, P.-M., "La libération de Jérémie et le meurtre de Godolias: Le texte court (LXX) et la rédaction longue (TM)," in *Studien zur Septuaginta: Robert Hanhart zu Ehren* (eds. D. Fraenkel et al.; MSU 20; Göttingen: Vandenhoeck & Ruprecht, 1990), 312–22.

Bogaert, P.-M., "Les trois formes de Jérémie 52 (TM, LXX et VL)," in *Tradition of the Text: Studies Offered to Dominique Barthélémy in Celebration of His 70th Birthday* (eds. G.J. Norton and S. Pisano; OBO 109; Göttingen: Vandenhoeck & Ruprecht, 1991), 1–17.

Bogaert, P.-M., "Urtext, texte court et relecture," in *Congress Volume: Leuven, 1989* (ed. J.A. Emerton; VTSup 43; Leiden: Brill, 1991), 236–47.

Bogaert, P.-M., "Le livre de Jérémie en perspective: Les deux rédactions antiques selon les travaux en cours," *RB* 101 (1994): 363–406.

Bogaert, P.-M., "Jérémie 17,1–4 TM, oracle contre ou sur Juda propre au texte long, annoncé en 11,7–8.13 TM et en 15,12–14 TM," in *La double transmission du texte biblique: Etudes d'histoire du texte offertes en homage à Adrian Schenker* (eds. Y. Goldman and C. Uehlinger; OBO 179; Göttingen: Vandenhoeck & Ruprecht, 2001), 59–74.

Bogaert, P.-M., "La vetus latina de Jérémie: Texte très court, témoin de la plus ancienne Septante et d'une forme plus ancienne de l'Hébreu (Jer 39 et 52)," in Schenker, **Earliest Text*, 51–82.

Bogaert, P.-M., "La liste des nations dans l'oracle de la coupe (Jr 25,16–26)," in *L'ecrit et l'esprit: Etudes d'histoire du texte et de théologie biblique en homage à Adrian Schenker* (eds. D. Böhler, I. Himbaza, and P. Hugo; OBO 214; Göttingen: Vandenhoeck & Ruprecht, 2005), 1–14.

---

[111] L. Stulman, *The Other Text of Jeremiah* (New York: University Press of America, 1985).

[112] http://ccat.sas.upenn.edu/gopher/text/religion/biblical/parallel/41.Jer.par. Last accessed June 6, 2015.

[113] H.-J. Stipp, Textkritische Synopse zum Jeremiabuch (9th corrected internal edition; Munich: 2013), http://www.kaththeol.uni-muenchen.de/lehrstuehle/at_theol/personen/stipp/textkritische-synopse/index.html. Last accessed June 6, 2015.

[114] K. Finsterbusch and N. Jacoby, *Synoptische Übersetzung und rhetorische Strukturierung von MT-Jer und LXX-Jer*, vol.: 1: *Der erste Buchteil (1–24)* (Neukirchen: Neukirchener Verlag, forthcoming).

Bogaert, P.-M., "La datation per souscription dans les rédactions courte (LXX) et longue du livre de Jérémie," in *L'apport de la Septante aux études sur l'Antiquité: actes du colloque de Strasbourg, 8 et 9 novembre 2002* (eds. P. Le Moigne and J. Joosten; LD 203; Paris: Cerf, 2005), 137–59.

Bogaert, P.-M., "Heshbon entre Moab et Ammon: La finale ajoutée à l'oracle sur Moab en Jr 48,45–47 TM," in *Interpreting Translation: Studies on the LXX and Ezekiel in Honour of Johan Lust* (eds. F. García Martínez, M. Vervenne, and B. Doyle; BETL 192; Leuven: Leuven University Press, 2005), 45–54.

Bogaert, P.-M., "De la *vetus latina* à l'hébreu prémassorétique en passant par la plus ancienne Septante: le livre de Jérémie, exemple privilégié," *RTL* 44 (2013): 216–43.

Di Pede, E., "Jérémie 'prophète' dans le LXX et dans le TM," *EstBib* 67 (2009): 101–10.

Eichhorn, J.G., "Bemerkungen über den Text des Propheten Jeremias," *Repertorium für Biblische und Morgenländische Litteratur* 1 (1777): 141–68.

Eichhorn, J.G., *Einleitung in das Alte Testament* (3 vols.; Leipzig: Weidemann, 1780–1783), 3.157–207.

Engel, H., "Erfahrungen mit der LXX-Fassung des Jeremiabuches im Rahmen des Projektes 'Septuaginta Deutsch'," in **Brennpunkt*, Vol. 3, 80–96.

Finsterbusch, K., "MT-Jer 1,1–3,5 und LXX-Jer 1,1–3,5: Kommunikationsebenen und rhetorische Strukturen," *BZ* 56 (2012): 247–63

Fischer, G., "Zum Text des Jeremiabuches," *Bib* 78 (1997): 305–28.

Fischer, G., "Jeremiah 52: Test Case for Jer LXX," in *X Congress of the International Organization for Septuagint and Cognate Studies, Oslo 1998* (ed. B.A. Taylor; SBLSCS 51; Atlanta: SBL, 2001), 37–48.

Fischer, G., "Die Diskussion um den Jeremiatext," in Karrer–Kraus, **Septuaginta 2008*, 612–29.

Freedman, D.N. and J.R. Lundbom, "Haplography in Jeremiah 1–20," *ErIsr* 26 (1999): 28–38 [Hebr.].

Gesundheit, S., "The Question of LXX Jeremiah as a Tool for Literary-Critical Analysis," *VT* 62 (2012): 29–57.

Giesebrecht, F., *Das Buch Jeremia* (Göttingen Handkommentar zum Alten Testament 3.2.1; Göttingen: Vandenhoeck & Ruprecht, 1894), xix–xxxiv (cf. 2nd ed. 1907, xxv–xl).

Goldman, Y., *Prophétie et royauté au retour de l'exil: Les origenes littéraires de la forme massorétique du livre de Jérémie* (OBO 118; Göttingen: Vandenhoeck & Ruprecht, 1992).

Gosse, B., *Structuration des grands ensembles bibliques et intertextualité à la contestation de la sagesse* (BZAW 246; Berlin: De Gruyter, 1997), 47–66.

Gosse, B., "The Masoretic Redaction of Jeremiah," *JSOT* 77 (1998): 75–80.

Gosse, B., "Trois étapes de la rédaction du livre de Jérémie," *ZAW* 111 (1999): 508–29.

Gosse, B., "La rédaction massorétique du livre de Jérémie," *Transeu* 42 (2012): 141–69.

Graf, K.H., *Der Prophet Jeremia* (Leipzig: T.O. Weigel, 1862), xl–lvii.

Haran, M., "The Place of the Prophecies against the Nations in the Book of Jeremiah," in *Emanuel: Studies in Hebrew Bible, Septuagint, and Dead Sea Scrolls in Honor of Emanuel Tov* (eds. S.M. Paul et al.; VTSup 94; Leiden: Brill, 2003), 699–706.

Hill, J., *Friend or Foe? The Figure of Babylon in the Book of Jeremiah MT* (BibInt 40; Leiden: Brill, 1999).

Hill, J., "The Book of Jeremiah MT and Early Second Temple Conflicts about Prophets and Prophecy," *ABR* 50 (2002): 28–42.

Holt, E.K., "The Meaning of an *Inclusio*," *SJOT* 17 (2003): 183–205.

Janzen, J.G., "Double Readings in the Text of Jeremiah," *HTR* 60 (1967): 433–47.

Janzen, J.G., *Studies in the Text of Jeremiah* (HSM 6; Cambridge: Harvard University Press, 1973).

Janzen, J.G., "A Critique of Sven Soderlund's *The Greek Text of Jeremiah: A Revised Hypothesis*," *BIOSCS* 22 (1989): 16–47.

Joosten, J., "L'excédent massorétique du livre de Jérémie et l'hébreu post-classique," in *Conservatism and Innovation in the Hebrew Language of the Hellenistic Period: Proceedings of a Fourth International Symposium on the Hebrew of the Dead Sea Scrolls and Ben Sira* (eds. J. Joosten and J.-S. Rey; STDJ 73; Leiden: Brill, 2008), 93–108.

Lange, **Handbuch*, 297–324.

Lange, A., "The Textual Plurality of Jewish Scriptures in the Second Temple Period in Light of the Dead Sea Scrolls," in *Qumran and the Bible: Studying the Jewish and Christian Scriptures in Light of the Dead Sea Scrolls* (eds. N. David and A. Lange; CBET 57; Leuven: Peeters, 2010), 43–96, esp. 67–82.

Lange, A., "The Covenant with the Levites (Jer 33:21) in the Proto-Masoretic Text of Jeremiah in Light of the Dead Sea Scrolls," in *"Go Out and Study the Land" (Judges 18,2): Archeological, Historical and Textual Studies in Honor of Hanan Eshel* (eds. A.M. Maeir, J. Magness, and L.H. Schiffman; JSJSup 148; Leiden: Brill, 2012), 95–116.

Lust, J., "The Diverse Text Forms of Jeremiah and History Writing with Jer 33 as a Test Case," *JNSL* 20 (1994): 31–48.

Min, Y.-J., "The Minuses and Pluses of the LXX Translation of Jeremiah as Compared with the Massoretic Text: Their Classification and Possible Origins" (PhD diss., Hebrew University of Jerusalem, 1977).

Movers, F.C., *De utriusque recensionis Vaticiniorum Ieremiae, Graece Alexandrinae et Hebraicae Masorethicae, indole et origene commentatio critica* (Hamburg: Perthes, 1837).

Parke-Taylor, G.H., *The Formation of the Book of Jeremiah: Doublets and Recurring Phrases* (SBLMS 51; Atlanta: SBL, 2000).

Piovanelli, P., "JerB 33,14–26, ou la continuité des institutions à l'époque maccabéenne," in *The Book of Jeremiah and its Reception/Le livre de Jérémie et sa reception* (eds. A.H.W. Curtis and T. Römer; BETL 128; Leuven: Peeters, 1997), 255–76.

de Regt, L.J., "The Prophet in the Old and the New Edition of Jeremiah," in *The New Things: Eschatology in Old Testament Prophecy: Festschrift for Henk Leene* (eds. F. Postma, K. Spronk, and E. Talstra; ACEBTSup 3; Maastricht: Utigeverij Shaker Publishing, 2002), 167–74.

Riley, M., "An Explanation for the Reading ἐν μέσῳ αὐτῆς in LXX-Jer 29:14 in Light of Dalet-Resh Interchange," *VT* 63 (2013): 433–39.

Rofé, A., "The Arrangement of the Book of Jeremiah," *ZAW* 101 (1989): 390–98.

Rofé, A., "The Name YHWH Seba'ot and the Shorter Recension of Jeremiah," in *Prophetie und geschichtliche Wirklichkeit im alten Israel: Festschrift für Siegfried Herrmann zum 65. Geburtstag* (eds. R. Liwak and S. Wagner; Stuttgart: Kohlhammer, 1991), 307–16.

Schenker, A., "Nebukadnezzars Metamorphose vom Unterjocher zum Gottesknecht: Das Bild Nebukadnezzars und einige mit ihm zusammenhängende Unterschiede in den beiden Jeremia-Rezensionen," *RB* 89 (1982): 498–527.

Schenker, A., "Was übersetzen wir? Fragen zur Textbasis, die sich aus der Textkritik ergeben," in *Text und Sinn im Alten Testament* (ed. A. Schenker; OBO 103; Göttingen: Vandenhoeck & Ruprecht, 1991), 247–62.

Schenker, A., "Der nie aufgehobene Bund: Exegetische Beobachtungen zu Jer 31,31–34," in *Der neue Bund im Alten: Studien zur Bundestheologie der beiden Testamente* (eds. E. Zenger and C. Dohmen; QD 146; Freiburg: Herder, 1993), 85–112.

Schenker, A., "La rédaction longue du livre de Jérémie doit-elle être datée au temps des premiers Hasmonéens?" *ETL* 70 (1994): 281–93.

Schmid, K., *Buchgestalten des Jeremiabuches: Untersuchungen zur Redaktions- und Rezeptionsgeschichte von Jer 30–33 im Kontext des Buches* (WMANT 72; Neukirchen: Neukirchener Verlag, 1996), 13–23.

Scholz, A., *Der Masorethische Text und die LXX – Uebersetzung des Buches Jeremias* (Regensburg: G.J. Manz, 1875).

Shead, A.G., "Jeremiah 32 in Its Hebrew and Greek Recensions," *TynBul* 50 (1999): 318–20.

Shead, A.G., *The Open Book and the Sealed Book: Jeremiah 32 in Its Hebrew and Greek Recensions* (JSOTSup 347; Sheffield: Sheffield Academic Press, 2002).

Soderlund, S., *The Greek Text of Jeremiah: A Revised Hypothesis* (JSOTSup 47; Sheffield: JSOT Press, 1985).

Spohn, M.G.L., *Ieremias vates e versione Iudaeorum Alexandrinorum ac reliquorum interpretum Graecorum emendatus notisque criticis illustrates*, Vol. 1 (Leipzig: Breitkopf, 1794).

Stipp, H.-J., "Offene Fragen zur Übersetzungskritik des antiken griechischen Jeremiabuches," *JNSL* 17 (1991): 143–59.

Stipp, H.-J., *Das masoretische und alexandrinische Sondergut des Jeremiabuches* (OBO 136; Göttingen: Vandenhoeck & Ruprecht, 1994).

Stipp, H.-J., "Probleme des redaktionsgeschichtlichen Modells der Entstehung des Jeremiabuches," in *Jeremia und die "deuteronomistische Bewegung"* (ed. W. Groß; BBB 98; Meisenheim am Glan: Athenäum, 1995), 225–62.

Stipp, H.-J., "The Prophetic Messenger Formulas in Jeremiah according to the Masoretic and Alexandrian Texts," *Text* 18 (1995): 63–85.

Stipp, H.-J., "Eschatologisches Schema im alexandrinischen Jeremiabuch?" *JNSL* 23 (1997): 153–79.

Stipp, H.-J., "Zur aktuellen Diskussion um das Verhältnis der Textformen des Jeremiabuches," in *Karrer-Kraus, *Septuaginta 2008*, 630–53.

Stipp, H.-J., "Prophetentitel und Eigenname Jeremias im masoretischen Sondergut des Jeremiabuches," in *"Gerechtigkeit und Recht zu üben" (Gen 18,19): Studien zur altorientalischen und biblischen Rechtsgeschichte, zur Religionsgeschichte Israels und zur Religionssoziologie: Festschrift für Eckart Otto zum 65. Geburtstag* (eds. R. Achenbach and M. Arneth; Beihefte zur Zeitschrift für altorientalische und biblische Rechtsgeschichte 13; Wiesbaden: Harrassowitz 2009), 293–307.

Stipp, H.-J., "Der prämasoretische Idiolekt des Buches Ezechiel und seine Beziehungen zum Jeremiabuch," in *From Qumran to Aleppo: A Discussion with Emanuel Tov about the Textual History of Jewish Scriptures in Honor of his 65th Birthday* (eds. A. Lange, M. Weigold, and J. Zsengellér; FRLANT 230; Göttingen: Vandenhoeck & Ruprecht, 2009), 140–55.

Stipp, H.-J., "Gottesbildfragen in den Lesartendifferenzen zwischem dem masoretischen und dem alexandrinischen Text des Jeremiabuches," in *Text-Critical and Hermeneutical Studies in the Septuagint* (eds. J. Cook and H.-J. Stipp; VTSup 157; Leiden: Brill, 2012), 237–74.

Stipp, H.-J., "Die Jeremia-Septuaginta als theologische Programmschrift: Zur Kommentierung des griechischen Jeremiabuches in der 'Septuaginta Deutsch' (LXX.D)," *BZ* 57 (2013): 27–45.

Stipp, H.-J., "Interpretierende Übersetzung in der Jeremia-Septuaginta," *JNSL* 40 (2014): 27–52.

Stipp, H.-J., "Legenden der Jeremia-Exegese I–II," *VT* 64 (2014): 484–501 and 654–63.

Stulman, L., *The Other Text of Jeremiah* (New York: University Press of America, 1985).

Stulman, L., *The Prose Sermons of the Book of Jeremiah: A Redescription of the Correspondences with Deuteronomistic Literature in the Light of Recent Text-Critical Research* (SBLDS 83; Atlanta: Scholars Press, 1986).

Stulman, L., *Order Amid Chaos: Jeremiah as Symbolic Tapestry* (The Biblical Seminar 57; Sheffield: Sheffield Academic Press, 1998).

Tov, E., "L' incidence de la critique textuelle sur la critique littéraire dans le livre de Jérémie," *RB* 79 (1972): 189–99.

Tov, E., *The Septuagint Translation of Jeremiah and Baruch: A Discussion of an Early Revision of Jeremiah 29–52 and Baruch 1:1–3:8* (HSM 8; Missoula: Scholars Press, 1976).

Tov, E., "Exegetical Notes on the Hebrew Vorlage of the LXX of Jeremiah 27 (34)," *ZAW* 91 (1979): 73–93.

Tov, E., "Some Aspects of the Textual and Literary History of the Book of Jeremiah," in *Le livre de Jérémie* (ed. P.-M. Bogaert; BETL 54; Leuven: Leuven University Press, 1981), 145–67, 430.

Tov, E., "The Literary History of the Book of Jeremiah in the Light of Its Textual History," in *Empirical Models for Biblical Criticism* (ed. J.H. Tigay; Philadelphia: University of Pennsylvania Press, 1985), 211–37. Revised version: *Greek-Hebrew Bible*, 363–84.

Tov, E., "The Contribution of the Qumran Scrolls to the Understanding of the LXX," in *Manchester Symposium*, 11–47. Revised version: *Greek-Hebrew Bible*, 285–300.

Tov, E., "The Characterization of the Additional Layer of the Masoretic Text of Jeremiah," *ErIsr* 26 (1999): 55–63 [Hebr.].

Tov, E., "The Book of Jeremiah: A Work in Progress," *BRev* 16 (2000): 32–38, 45.

Ulrich, E., "Deuteronomistically Inspired Scribal Insertions into the Developing Biblical Texts: 4QJudg[a] and 4QJer[a]," in *Houses Full of All Good Things: Essays in Memory of Timo Veijola* (Publications of the Finnish Exegetical Society 95; Göttingen: Vandenhoeck & Ruprecht, 2008), 489–506.

Ulrich, E., "Qumran Witness to the Developmental Growth of the Prophetic Books," in *With Wisdom as a Robe: Qumran and Other Jewish Studies in Honour of Ida Fröhlich* (eds. K.D. Dobos and M. Köszeghy; Hebrew Bible Monographs 21; Sheffield: Sheffield Phoenix, 2009), 263–74.

van der Kooij, A., "Jeremiah 27:5–15: How Do MT and LXX Relate to Each Other?" *JNSL* 20 (1994): 59–78.

Weis, R.D., "The Textual Situation in the Book of Jeremiah," in *Sôfer Mahîr: Essays in Honour of Adrian Schenker* (eds. Y.A.P. Goldman, A. van der Kooij, and R.D. Weis; VTSup 110; Leiden: Brill, 2006), 267–93.

Wijesinghe, S.L., "Tracing the Shorter Version Behind the Short Text (LXX): A New Approach to the Redaction of Jeremiah 34,8–22," *Mus* 110 (1997): 293–328.

Wijesinghe, S.L., *Jeremiah 34,8–22: Structure and Redactional History of the Masoretic Text and of the Septuagint Hebrew Vorlage* (Logos 37.1–2; Sri Lanka: Centre for Society and Religion, 1999).

Armin Lange

7.2.3 Other Texts

My text-typological assessment in → 7.2.1 demonstrated that in its final text 4QJer[a] attests to a proto-Masoretic Jeremiah text and that 2QJer and 4QJer[c] are witnesses of semi-Masoretic Jeremiah texts. Based on variant statistics, I have further argued that 4QJer[d,e] and MS Schøyen 4612/9 are too damaged for text-typological classification, while it is doubtful whether XJer? attests to the book of Jeremiah at all. Based on its textual sequence and repertoire, I classified 4QJer[b] as attesting to the Hebrew parent text of LXX-Jer. Above (→ 7.2.2) and below (→ 7.2.3.3), I argue furthermore that the proto-Masoretic text of Jeremiah and LXX-Jer (→ 7.3) share a textual archetype. This archetype was slightly reworked by the Hebrew parent text of LXX-Jer and underwent two or more reworkings until it developed in the third century B.C.E. into the consonantal text of MT as we know it today.[1] Although 4QJer[d] and manuscript Schøyen 4612/9 are too damaged for text-typological classification, their variant analysis, as well as that of 4QJer[b], nevertheless confirm this view.

7.2.3.1 4QJer[b][2]

Although only thirty-one (partial) words from Jer 9:22–10:5, 9, 11–21 are preserved of 4QJer[b] (→ 7.2.1.3), the manuscript is rather important for the textual history of the book of Jeremiah. Tov's edition[3] leaves no doubt that 4QJer[b] agrees with LXX-Jer 10.[4] Both lack Jer 10:6–8 and have the textual sequence Jer 10:4, 5a, 9, 5b. MT-Jer 10:6–8 are a praise of God that interrupts the polemic against idols in Jer 10:1–11. In addition to the more major arguments given above (→ 7.2.2), MT-Jer should therefore be understood in Jer 10:1–11 as a secondary expansion of the Hebrew parent text of LXX-Jer.[5] Furthermore,

4QJer[b] agrees in Jer 10:4 in the word sequence במקבות ובמסמרות "with hammers and with nails" with LXX-Jer (ἐν σφύραις καὶ ἥλοις "with hammers and nails") against MT-Jer (בְּמַסְמְרוֹת וּבְמַקָּבוֹת "with nails and with hammers"). Although very little text is preserved of 4QJer[b], its textual sequence and repertoire thus identify the manuscript as a witness to the Hebrew parent text of LXX-Jer (→ 7.3). That 4QJer[b] reads several times with MT against LXX and includes some non-aligned readings should not distract from this basic agreement with LXX-Jer. Several of the disagreements between 4QJer[b] and LXX-Jer result from either primary readings or idiosyncrasies of the Greek translator.[6]

Disagreements with MT-Jer can be found in Jer 10:15 and 10:18. In Jer 10:15, 4QJer[b] reads בעת פקדתים "at the time when I will punish them" against MT-Jer (בְּעֵת פְּקֻדָּתָם "at the time of their punishment") and against LXX-Jer (ἐν καιρῷ ἐπισκοπῆς αὐτῶν "at the time of their visitation"). The 4QJer[b] reading בעת פקדתים "at the time when I will punish them" is an asyndetic relative clause that can also be found in MT-Jer 6:15 (בְּעֵת־פְּקַדְתִּים "at the time when I will punish them"); 49:8 (עֵת פְּקַדְתִּיו "the time when I will punish him"); and 50:31 (עֵת פְּקַדְתִּיךָ "the time when I will punish you"). Because the asyndetic relative clause was difficult to understand, and because as a *lectio difficilior*[7] the first person voice does not agree with the rest of Jer 10:13, both LXX-Jer and MT-Jer reworked the verbal expression פקדתים "I will punish them" into the noun פְּקֻדָּתָם "their punishment," thus adjusting Jer 10:15 also to Jer 8:12; 10:15; 50:27; 51:18.

---

[1] For a different view, see G. Fischer, → 7.3. For a history of research, see Lange, *Handbuch, 304–14; and Lange, → 7.2.2.1.

[2] 4QJer[b] is quoted below according to the reconstruction and edition of Saley ("Reconstructing").

[3] Tov, "Jeremiah," 173–76.

[4] Cf. Tov, "Jeremiah Scrolls," 198; Tov, "Jeremiah," 172; Tov, *TCU, 191; Tov, *TCHB, 292–93.

[5] Cf., e.g., Janzen, Studies, 182; Tov, *TCU, 191; Tov, *TCHB, 292–92; E. Tov, "The Septuagint as a Source for the Literary Analysis of Hebrew Scripture," in Exploring the Origins of the Bible: Canon Formation in Historical, Literary, and Theological Perspective (eds. C.A. Evans and E. Tov; Acadia Studies in Bible and Theology; Grand Rapids: Baker, 2008), 31–56 (36–38); Ulrich, "Qumran Witness," 269–71; K. Finsterbusch, "Gegen die Furcht vor den Göttern der Welt: Eine Art 'Psalm' Jeremias für Israel in MT-Jer 10,1–16," in Ich will dir danken unter den Völkern: Studien zur israelitischen und altorientalischen Gebetsliteratur: Festschrift für Bernd Janowski zum 70. Geburtstag (eds. A. Grund, A. Krüger, and F. Lippke; Gütersloh: Gütersloher Verlagshaus, 2013), 356–72; H.-J. Stipp, "Broadening the Criteria for Clarifying the Textual History of Jeremiah Chapter 10: The Pre-Masoretic Idiolect," in Texts and Contexts of Jeremiah: The Exegesis of Jer 1 and Jer 10 in Light of Text and Reception History (eds. K. Finsterbusch and A. Lange; CBET; Leuven: Peeters, forthcoming); R.D. Weis, "Exegesis of Jeremiah 10 in LXX and MT: Results and Implications," in op. cit., forthcoming. That 4QJer[b] is a representative of the Hebrew parent text of LXX-Jer was recently proven by reconstruction of this manuscript based on the text of LXX-Jer (Saley, "Reconstructing").

[6] Against G. Fischer who emphasized in various publications that these agreements are an indication for the priority of MT-Jer. See, e.g., Jeremia 1–25: Übersetzt und ausgelegt (HTKAT; Freiburg i.B.: Herder, 2005), 40–41; "Die Diskussion um den Jeremiatext," in Karrer–Kraus, *Septuaginta 2008, 612–29 (622–23).

[7] Cf. W.L. Holladay, Jeremiah 1: A Commentary on the Book of the Prophet Jeremiah: Chapters 1–25 (Hermeneia; Philadelphia: Fortress Press, 1986), 211 and 324.

When 4QJer[b] reads in Jer 10:18 the singular form ישב הארץ] "inhabitant of the land" against the יֹשְׁבֵי הָאָרֶץ of MT ("inhabitants of the land") and the κατοικοῦντας τὴν γῆν of LXX ("inhabitants of the land"), this represents another original reading. The plural form יֹשְׁבֵי הָאָרֶץ occurs repeatedly in the book of Jeremiah (Jer 1:14; 6:12; 10:18; 13:13; 25:29, 30; 47:2), but the singular form is only known from Jer 10:18 in 4QJer[b]. Both MT-Jer and LXX-Jer harmonized Jer 10:18 thus with Jer 1:14; 6:12; 10:18; 13:13; 25:29, 30; 47:2 in reading the plural form.

Two further disagreements of 4QJer[b] with LXX-Jer go back to its Greek translator. In Jer 9:25, the plural form קצוצי פאה [כל] "all those with shaven temples" of 4QJer[b] agrees with MT while LXX-Jer has a singular form πάντα περικειρόμενον τὰ κατὰ πρόσωπον αὐτοῦ "and on everyone who shaves what is on his face." That the singular form and the additional αὐτοῦ "his" of LXX-Jer go back to a translation idiosyncrasy of LXX-Jer is evident in Jer 25:23 (32:9) where LXX-Jer renders כל קצוצי פאה in a similar way: πᾶν περικεκαρμένον κατὰ πρόσωπον αὐτοῦ "and every one shaven on his face."

The LXX translator is also responsible for the seeming difference between LXX-Jer and 4QJer[b]/MT-Jer. In Jer 10:2, LXX-Jer renders the כה אמר יהוה אל דרך הגוים אל תלמדו "thus says the Lord God: Do not learn the way of the nations" of 4QJer[b] as τάδε λέγει κύριος Κατὰ τὰς ὁδοὺς τῶν ἐθνῶν μὴ μανθάνετε "do not learn according to the ways of the nations." As the word אל "God" is used only once more in the whole book of Jeremiah (Jer 51[28]:56), LXX-Jer and the punctuation of MT-Jer misinterpreted the characters אל as the preposition אֶל "to."[8] As this preposition yields no sense in Jer 10:2, LXX-Jer rendered it with Κατὰ "according." That LXX-Jer 10:2 renders the singular form דרך "way" with the plural form ὁδούς "ways" is an interpretative translation. In the opinion of the translator, the plural form "nations" desired to speak of several ways and not one way.

7.2.3.2 MS Schøyen 4612/9 and Jer 3:15–19[9]

Elgvin and Davis characterize manuscript Schøyen 4612/9 as follows: "The evidence tentatively shows that MS 4612/9 may be grouped with 4QJer[b,d] as a text related to the *Vorlage* of 𝔊, although preserving independent features that indicate a thus far unattested shorter text."[10] While their characterization seems likely, the small amount of preserved text allows for neither a text-typological nor textual characterization of manuscript Schøyen 4612/9 (cf. → 7.2.1.7). Nevertheless, even before the publication of the edition of Elgvin and Davis, some readings that are of great interest for the textual history of Jeremiah will be discussed here briefly. A better appreciation of this manuscript will only be possible when a proper photograph is published.

In Jer 3:15, Elgvin and Davis are correct to argue that the רעה והש[כיל "shepherding and skillful" of manuscript Schøyen 4612/9 represents a reading of the Hebrew parent text of LXX-Jer (ποιμαίνοντες μετ᾽ ἐπιστήμης "those who shepherd with skill"). MT-Jer's דֵּעָה וְהַשְׂכֵּיל "knowledge and skillful" goes back to a *resh-dalet* confusion. רעה והש[כיל "shepherding and skillful" should therefore be regarded as a primary reading.

While agreements in primary readings are not important when it comes to the text-typological affiliation of a manuscript, the agreement of manuscript Schøyen 4612/9 with LXX-Jer in a secondary reading in Jer 3:19 is of significance. This is so because manuscript Schøyen 4612/9 attests to a Hebrew version of a textual plus in LXX-Jer.[11] MT's וְאָנֹכִי אָמַרְתִּי אֵיךְ אֲשִׁיתֵךְ בַּבָּנִים "and I said: 'how will I set you among my children'" is interrupted in manuscript Schøyen 4612/9 by an invocation of the Lord: ואנ[9 אמרתי אמן יהוה כי כ]בנים אשיתך "and I] said: 'Indeed Lord, for (I said): I will set you like my children'." This invocation is so similar to a textual plus in LXX-

---

[8] Cf., e.g., M. Dahood, "Hebrew-Ugaritic Lexicography IV," *Bib* 47 (1966): 403–19 (410); J.R. Lundbom, *Jeremiah 1–20: A New Translation with Introduction and Commentary* (AB 21A; New York: Doubleday, 1999), 582–83.

[9] I am indebted to Torleif Elgvin and Kipp Davis, who shared a preliminary version of their edition of this manuscript with me ("MS 4612/9").

[10] Elgvin and Davis, "MS 4612/9," forthcoming.

[11] That Elgvin and Davis ("MS 4612/9") reconstruct in manuscript Schøyen 4612/9 [9]ואנ "and I" instead of MT's וְאָנֹכִי "and I" must remain speculative.

Jer that the latter most likely translated the former: καὶ ἐγὼ εἶπα Γένοιτο, κύριε· ὅτι τάξω σε εἰς τέκνα "And I said: 'May it be, O Lord, for (I said): "I will make you as children ..."'."

The secondary reading of manuscript Schøyen 4612/9 points to a possible affiliation of the manuscript with LXX-Jer (→ 7.3) and it demonstrates more importantly that not all secondary readings of LXX-Jer, especially its textual pluses, go back to the work of its Greek translator but that at least some of them existed already in a Hebrew textual tradition of Jeremiah. This means that the Hebrew parent text of LXX-Jer already reworked slightly the archetype that it shares with MT-Jer (→ 7.2.2).

7.2.3.3 4QJer^d

I argued above (→ 7.2.1.5) that 4QJer^d might attest to a non-aligned text as it includes eight textual differences toward MT and nine textual disagreements with LXX. Aside from the text-typological characterization by way of variant statistics, the preserved text of 4QJer^d also allows for some observations regarding its textual character. In the preserved text (Jer 43[50]:2–10), 4QJer^d is more expansive than LXX-Jer (→ 7.3) but does not share all long readings with MT-Jer (→ 7.2.2). There is also one case of scribal corruption and one disagreement in textual sequence. Nevertheless, no textual characterization by way of variant analysis is possible given the paucity of surviving text of 4QJer^d.

In six cases, 4QJer^d preserves a more original text than MT. Two of these cases are non-aligned readings. 4QJer^d reads in Jer 43(50): 4–5 twice with LXX יוחנן "Johanan" without a patronym against MT's יוֹחָנָן בֶּן־קָרֵחַ "Johanan, son of Kareah." MT adds this patronym also in Jer 40(47):15; 41(48):13, 14, 16; 42(49):1, 8.[12] The MT long text practices an editorial strategy of adding such patronyms to its base text.[13] In most cases, LXX-Jer rarely mentions these patronyms while MT-Jer harmonizes most if not all attestations of a given proper name with these rare attestations of patronyms. In this case, MT-Jer adjusts Jer 43(50):4–5 to Jer 40(47):8, 13; 41(48):11; 43(50):2 where LXX-Jer has also Ιωαναν υἱὸς Καρηε "Joanan, son of Karee."[14]

As similar case occurs in Jer 43:6 where 4QJer^d reads with LXX-Jer את גדליהו בן אחיקם "Gedaliah, son of Ahikam" against the אֶת־גְּדַלְיָהוּ בֶּן־אֲחִיקָם בֶּן־שָׁפָן "Gedaliah, son of Ahikam, son of Shaphan" of MT-Jer. MT-Jer has added the second patronym in harmonization with Jer 39(46):14; 40:5, 9, 11; 41:2 (cf. 26[33]:24).[15]

The way in which MT-Jer treats the name Nebuzaradan in Jer 43(50):6 is comparable. 4QJer^d reads with LXX-Jer only נבוזראדן "Nebuzaradan" against MT's נְבוּזַרְאֲדָן רַב טַבָּחִים "Nebuzaradan, the captain of the guard." MT-Jer added the title רַב טַבָּחִים "the captain of the guard" in harmonization with Jer 39:9, 10, 11, 13; 40(47):1, 10; 52:12, 15, 16, 26, 30.[16] In LXX-Jer, Nebuzaradan occurs only in Jer 43(50):6 without a mention of his title.

In two cases, 4QJer^d reads an even shorter text than both LXX and MT and thus preserves a textual tradition that precedes both proto-MT-Jer and the

---

[12] MT-Jer only neglects to add the patronym in Jer 8:15 (cf. the list of Janzen, *Studies*, 150).

[13] For an overview, see Janzen, *Studies*, 139–54.

[14] See Tov, *TCU*, 191; Tov, *TCHB*, 293–94; Tov, "Literary Analysis," 38–39; cf. Janzen, *Studies*, 82–83.

[15] See Tov, *TCU*, 191; Tov, *TCHB*, 293–94; Tov, "Literary Analysis", 38–39; Cf. Janzen, *Studies*, 183. While Jer-MT always reads אֶת־גְּדַלְיָהוּ בֶּן־אֲחִיקָם בֶּן־שָׁפָן "Gedaliah, son of Ahikam, son of Shaphan," Jer-LXX only has both patronyms in Jer 39(46):14 and 40(47):5 ("Γοδολιαν υἱὸν Αχικαμ υἱοῦ Σαφαν" "Godolia, son of Ahikam, son of Saphan"). Jer 40(47):11 only has one patronym (τὸν Γοδολιαν υἱὸν Αχικαμ "Godolia, son of Ahikam") and Jer 40(47):9; 41(48):2 has none (Γοδολιας and τὸν Γοδολιαν "Godolia") instead of MT's three. In Jer 26(22):24, MT-Jer has בֶּן־אֲחִיקָם בֶּן־שָׁפָן "son of Ahikam, son of Shaphan" and LXX-Jer reads Αχικαμ υἱοῦ Σαφαν "Ahikam, son of Shaphan." For the use of the patronyms together with the name Gedaliah, see Janzen, *Studies* 149–50.

[16] Cf. Janzen, *Studies*, 150–51, 183; Cook, "Differences," 187. MT-Jer changes various designations of Nebuzaradan in LXX-Jer and its parent text everywhere in Jeremiah to נְבוּזַרְאֲדָן רַב טַבָּחִים "Nebuzaradan, the captain of the guard." In Jer 40(47):1; 52:12, 26 it reads Ναβουζαρδαν τὸν ἀρχιμάγειρον and Ναβουζαρδαν ὁ ἀρχιμάγειρος respectively ("Nabuzardan, the chief cook"), while Jer 41(48):10 and 52:16 have only ὁ ἀρχιμάγειρος "the chief cook" and Jer 43(50):6 only Ναβουζαρδαν "Nabuzardan." Jer 39:9, 10, 11, 13; 52:15, 30 are part of the MT long texts and are without equivalent in LXX-Jer.

Vorlage of LXX-Jer. In Jer 43(50):7, 4QJer[d] has only ו[יבאו תחפחס] "and they came to Tahpanes" instead of the וַיָּבֹאוּ עַד־תַּחְפַּנְחֵס "and they came to Tahpanhes" of MT-Jer and the καὶ εἰσῆλθον εἰς Τάφνας "and they entered into Taphnas" of LXX-Jer.

In Jer 43(50):5, 4QJer[d] reads once shorter than MT and LXX and once a textual plus that also occurs in MT-Jer:

LXX-Jer: τοὺς ἀποστρέψαντας κατοικεῖν ἐν τῇ γῇ "those who returned to live in the country"

4QJer[d]: אשר שבו מכל הגוים אש[ר] [נדחו] שׁם "those who returned from all the nations to w]here [they had been banished"

MT: אֲשֶׁר־שָׁבוּ מִכָּל־הַגּוֹיִם אֲשֶׁר נִדְּחוּ־שָׁם לָגוּר בְּאֶרֶץ יְהוּדָה "those who returned from all the nations to where they had been banished, to settle in the land of Judah"

The original text argued probably that Johanan took "those who had returned there" (אשר שבו שם).[17] The phrase is difficult to understand, because it does not explain to which place the returnees came, from where they came, or how they got to their place of exile. The Hebrew parent text of LXX-Jer replaced the ambiguous שם "there" most likely with the words לגור בארץ, thus reading אשר שבו לגור בארץ "those who returned to live in the land" to explain what was the destination of the returnees. As for MT-Jer, the textual tradition represented by 4QJer[d] suggests that the long text of MT-Jer evolved in two stages. First, the words מכל הגוים אשר נדחו were added, to explain from where the returnees came, resulting in the text of 4QJer[d]: אשר שבו מכל הגוים אש[ר] [נדחו] שׁם "those who returned from all the nations to w]here [they had been banished." Thus, שם relates in the text of 4QJer[d] to the place from where they returned. In a second stage, and probably influenced by the Hebrew parent text of LXX-Jer, the words לגור בארץ יהודה were added, resulting in the text of MT-Jer: אֲשֶׁר־שָׁבוּ מִכָּל־הַגּוֹיִם אֲשֶׁר נִדְּחוּ־שָׁם לָגוּר בְּאֶרֶץ יְהוּדָה "those who returned from all the nations to where they had been banished, to settle in the land of Judah." The second addition explained the second unclear element of the original text of Jer 43(50):5, i.e., the destination of the returnees.

In Jer 43(50):7, 4QJer[d] follows another long text of MT-Jer in reading ארץ מצרים "[into] the land of Egypt" against LXX-Jer's εἰς Αἴγυπτον "into Egypt." The additional word ארץ "land" was added in harmonization with Jer 43:11, 12, 13.

Two further cases in which 4QJer[d] agrees with MT-Jer or is related to a primary MT-Jer reading are preserved in Jer 43(50):9. As for the primary MT-Jer reading, LXX-Jer has ἐν προθύροις τῆς οἰκίας Φαραω ἐν Τάφνας "in the entrance of the house of Pharao in Taphnas," which probably renders the words בפתח בית פרעה בתחפנחס. The LXX reading is the result of a homoiarcton in its Hebrew parent text. The eye of the scribe moved erroneously from the *bet* of במלט "in the clay floor" to the *bet* of בפתח "in the entrance" and thus deleted all the intervening text.[18] MT's בַּמֶּלֶט בַּמַּלְבֵּן אֲשֶׁר בְּפֶתַח בֵּית־פַּרְעֹה בִּתְחְפַּנְחֵס "in the clay floor, in the pavement that is in the entrance of the palace of the Pharao in Tahpahnes" is thus the more original text. 4QJer[d] or its base text rearranged the syntax of this verse in an editorial reading to clarify that the palace of the Pharao was at the entrance of Tahpahnes: [במלט במלבן בית פרעה] אשר בפתח בתחפנחס "in the clay floor, in the pavement of the palace of the Pharao] which is at the entrance in Tahpanhes."

Jer 43(50):9 also includes a case in which 4QJer[d] agrees with MT-Jer against LXX-Jer. LXX-Jer has κατ' ὀφθαλμοὺς ἀνδρῶν Ιουδα "before the eyes of the men of Judah," which equals most likely לעיני אנשי יהודה. The textual tradition of 4QJer[d]/MT-Jer rephrased this text to clarify that Jeremiah did not perform his symbolic act in Egypt before men of Judah but "before the eyes of Jewish men" (לעיני אנשים יהודים). In this way, the 4QJer[d]/MT-Jer text harmonizes the reading אנשי יהודה not only with the כָּל־הַיְּהוּדִים

---

[17] Similarly, Janzen, *Studies*, 54, and W.L. Holladay, *Jeremiah 2: A Commentary on the Book of the Prophet Jeremiah: Chapters 26–52* (Heremeia; Minneapolis: Fortress Press, 1989), 276.

[18] Cf. Janzen, *Studies*, 183; Holladay, *Jeremiah 2*, 276; contra, Cook, "Differences," 187.

7.2.3 OTHER TEXTS

MT-Jer 10:12–13	11QPsª XXVI:13–15[19]	LXX-Jer 10:12–13
עֹשֵׂה אֶרֶץ בְּכֹחוֹ מֵכִין תֵּבֵל בְּחָכְמָתוֹ וּבִתְבוּנָתוֹ נָטָה שָׁמַיִם לְקוֹל תִּתּוֹ הֲמוֹן מַיִם בַּשָּׁמַיִם וַיַּעֲלֶה נְשִׂאִים מִקְצֵה אָרֶץ בְּרָקִים לַמָּטָר עָשָׂה וַיּוֹצֵא רוּחַ מֵאֹצְרֹתָיו	ברוך עושה ארץ בכוחו מכין תבל בחוכמתו בתבונתו נטה שמים ויוצא [רוח] מאו[צרותיו ברקים למט]ר עשה ויעל נשיא[ים מ]ק[צה ארץ]	κύριος ὁ ποιήσας τὴν γῆν ἐν τῇ ἰσχύι αὐτοῦ ὁ ἀνορθώσας τὴν οἰκουμένην ἐν τῇ σοφίᾳ αὐτοῦ καὶ τῇ φρονήσει αὐτοῦ ἐξέτεινεν τὸν οὐρανὸν καὶ πλῆθος ὕδατος ἐν οὐρανῷ καὶ ἀνήγαγεν νεφέλας ἐξ ἐσχάτου τῆς γῆς, ἀστραπὰς εἰς ὑετὸν ἐποίησεν καὶ ἐξήγαγεν φῶς ἐκ θησαυρῶν αὐτοῦ.
(It is he) who made the land by his power, Who established the world by his wisdom. And by his understanding he stretched out the heavens When he utters his voice, there is an (up)roar of waters in the heavens, And he makes the mist rise from the ends of the land, lightnings he makes for the rain, And wind he brings out from his storehouses.	Praised be the one, who made the land by his power Who established the world by his wisdom And by his understanding he stretched out the heavens And [wind] he brings out from [his] store[houses Lightnings] he makes [for the rai]n, And he makes the mis[t] rise [from] the ends of the [land]	It is the Lord who made the land by his power, Who established the world by his wisdom. And by his understanding he stretched out the heavens and a multitude of water was in the heavens, And he made the clouds rise from the ends of the land, lightnings he made for the rain, And light he brought out from his storehouses

הַיֹּשְׁבִים בְּאֶרֶץ מִצְרַיִם הַיֹּשְׁבִים בְּמִגְדֹּל וּבְתַחְפַּנְחֵס "all Jews who live in the land of Egypt, who live in Migdal and in Tahpanhes" of Jer 44 (51):1 but also makes a careful distinction between men who live in Judah and Diaspora Jews who live in Egypt.

When 4QJer^d reads in Jer 43(50):9 with MT בידך "in your hand" against the σεαυτῷ "for yourself" of LXX-Jer, this seems to be a case of intentional scribal corruption in LXX-Jer. LXX-Jer always translates לך "for yourself" (Jer 2:28; 13:1; 32[39]:7, 20, 25; 36[43]:2; 45:5 [51:35]; cf. Jer 22:14) with σεαυτῷ and renders ביד "in the hand of" routinely as ἐν χειρί or similar phrases; thus, also, in Jer 43(50):3. Given this evidence, it seems likely that either the translator of LXX-Jer or the scribe of its *Vorlage* could not imagine that Jeremiah would need to take large stones into his hand (singular!) and corrected thus בידך "in your hand" to לך, or σεαυτῷ (both meaning "for yourself") respectively.

At least one case of scribal corruption occurs in 4QJer^d in Jer 43(50):7. The manuscript reads תחפחס "Tahpes" instead of MT's תַחְפַּנְחֵס "Tahpanes"; cf. LXX Ταφνας "Taphnas." That the scribe of 4QJer^d or its *Vorlage* deleted the missing *nun* erroneously is apparent because the manuscript reads בתחפנחס "in Tahpanes" without scribal error in Jer 43(50):9.

To summarize: That 4QJer^d includes some but not all long texts of MT-Jer 43(50):2–10 and reads several times but not always with MT-Jer (→ 7.2.2) makes it likely that the manuscript attests to a somewhat extended textual version of Jeremiah as compared to the Hebrew parent text of LXX-Jer (→ 7.3), to which MT-Jer added even more text.[20] But 4QJer^d cannot be understood as attesting to the parent text of MT-Jer either because it displays cases of scribal corruption and intentional alteration that do not occur in MT-Jer. Therefore, 4QJer^d attests most likely to a somewhat developed version of a text situated between MT-Jer and the

---

[19] Text according to Sanders, *DJD* IV: 90.

[20] Against Fischer who regards these agreements as an indication for the priority of MT-Jer ("Diskussion," 623) and against Tov, "Jeremiah Scrolls," 198.

shared ancestor of LXX-Jer and MT-Jer. In → 7.2.2.2.1, I have argued that this intervening Jeremiah text developed in Egypt shortly before the text of the proto-Masoretic Jeremiah redaction.

7.2.3.4 Non-Aligned Quotations: The Example of 11QPs[a] XXVI:13–15

All manuscripts of Jeremiah from the Second Temple period are related to either MT-Jer (→ 7.2.2) or LXX-Jer (→ 7.3). The only other available source for the textual history of the book of Jeremiah at this time are its quotations and allusions (→ 1.7.1). The characteristic textual differences between LXX-Jer and MT-Jer in Jer 10:1–16 (→ 7.2.3.1) make employments of this passage especially valuable for the reconstruction of Jeremiah's early textual history. An employment of Jer 10:12–13 in the Hymn to the Creator in 11QPs[a] XXVI:13–15 could therefore point to the existence of yet another version of Jeremiah 10 that differs from both LXX-Jer and MT-Jer (see p. 541 for a sypopsis with MT and LXX).[21] 11QPs[a] XXVI:13–15 attests not only to a different sequence of stichoi but also does not know some of the textual pluses of MT-Jer.

7.2.3.5 Conclusions

Although their bad stage of preservation does not allow for a textual characterization of the Jeremiah texts attested by the manuscripts 4QJer[b], 4QJer[d], and manuscript Schøyen 4612/9, their variant analysis provides important information about the textual history of the book of Jeremiah (→ 7.1) and allows for several conclusions:

- 4QJer[b]'s agreements with MT-Jer and its non-aligned readings are mostly if not exclusively primary readings. 4QJer[b] thus attests, despite the claims of Fischer and others to the contrary,[22] to the Hebrew parent text of LXX-Jer (→ 7.3);
- Manuscript Schøyen 4612/9 makes it likely that the Hebrew parent text of LXX-Jer reworked somewhat the shared archetype of LXX- and MT-Jer (→ 7.2.2);
- 4QJer[d] makes it likely that another expansive Jeremiah text needs to be supposed between MT-Jer and the shared LXX-/MT-Jer archetype. This means that the proto-Masoretic Jeremiah redaction reworked a Jeremiah text similar to that of 4QJer[d] that already included some of the smaller characteristic long texts of MT-Jer, such as added patronyms. 4QJer[d] is not a direct textual witness to the base text of the proto-Masoretic Jeremiah redaction because it also includes secondary readings as compared to MT-Jer;
- Both 4QJer[d] and the quotation of Jer 10:12–13 in 11QPs[a] XXVI:12–15 point to the existence of non-aligned Jeremiah texts during the Second Temple period, which may (as might have been the case with 4QJer[d]) or may not have been related (as might have been the case with the ante-text of 11QPs[a] XXVI:12–15) to the broader textual tradition of LXX/MT-Jer.

Cook, J., "The Differences in the Order of the Books of the Hebrew and Greek Versions of Jeremiah – Jer 43 (50): A Case Study," *OTE* 7 (1994): 175–92.

Elgvin, T. and K. Davis, "MS 4612/9: 11Q(?)Jer (Jer. 3.15–19)," *Gleanings*, forthcoming.

Janzen, J.G., *Studies in the Text of Jeremiah* (HSM 6; Cambridge: Harvard University Press, 1973).

Lange, *Handbuch*, 297–324.

Saley, R.J., "Reconstructing 4QJer[b] according to the Text of the Old Greek," *DSD* 17 (2010): 1–12.

Tov, E., "The Jeremiah Scrolls from Qumran," *RevQ* 14 (1989): 189–206.

Tov, E., "Jeremiah," *DJD* XV (1997): 145–207.

Ulrich, E.C., "Qumran Witness to the Developmental Growth of the Prophetic Books," in *With Wisdom as a Robe: Qumran and Other Jewish Studies in Honour of Ida Fröhlich* (eds. K.D. Dobos and M. Kőszeghy; Hebrew Bible Monographs 21; Sheffield: Sheffield Phoenix, 2009), 263–74.

Armin Lange

---

[21] It is unlikely that 11QPs[a] XXVI:13–15 employs the textual parallel to Jer 10:12–13 from Jer 51:15–16, because neither LXX-Jer 10:13 nor 11QPs[a] XXVI:14–15 include the phrase לקול תתו "when he utters his voice."

[22] See note 6.

7.3 Septuagint

7.3.1 General Background

7.3.1.1 Origin and Time

The *Letter of Aristeas* claims that the Torah was translated from Hebrew to Greek in Alexandria in the third century B.C.E. Likewise, LXX-Jer seems to have originated in Egypt, as suggested by the many adaptations to the Alexandrian Ptolemaic milieu.[1] The probable date is the early second century B.C.E.[2]

7.3.1.2 Special Features

LXX-Jer differs greatly from the Hebrew text (→ 7.2.2) of Jeremiah in three respects:

1) Length: It is approximately one-sixth shorter than MT-Jer.[3] There are more than twenty contexts in which at least one verse is missing in LXX. The following verses are not represented in LXX-Jer: MT-Jer 2:1; 7:1, 27; 8:10b–12; 10:6–8, 10; 11:7, 8a; 17:1–5a; 29:16–20; 30:10–11, 15, 22; 33:14–26; 39:4–13; 46:26; 48:45–47; 49:6; 51:44b–49a; 52:2–3, 15, 27b–30. In addition, there many other cases in which single words are missing. As for minuses in MT-Jer, although they are much fewer, LXX-Jer occasionally has some expressions not found in MT-Jer, e.g., in 3:19 Jer Γένοιτο κύριε "Be it (so), Lord!"

2) Order: The primary difference is the positioning of the "Oracles against the Foreign Nations" in the middle of the book in LXX-Jer (25:14–31:44),[4] whereas MT, in a manner untypical for the prophetic books, places them towards the end (MT-Jer 46–51). Moreover, LXX-Jer then followed the oracles with the narration of "The Drinking of the Cup" (LXX 32:1–24). In addition, there are also minor sequence differences, e.g., MT-Jer 23:7–8, occurring in LXX at the end of the chapter after v. 40, and MT-Jer 31:35–37, appearing in LXX-Jer in the following order: 38:37, 35, 36.

Consequently, the Hebrew and Greek versions of Jeremiah display contrasting profiles. Whereas LXX-Jer is closer to the usual arrangement in prophetical books with a sequence of judgment on Israel, judgment on the nations, salvation for Israel,[5] MT has the most hopeful moments near the middle of the book, in MT-Jer 29–33. The end of both versions of Jeremiah is identical: Jeremiah 52 describes the downfall of Jerusalem in 587/6 B.C.E. along with the destruction of its temple. The simplified table below presents the differences:

MT-Jer	LXX-Jer
Jer 1:1–25:13	Jer 1:1–25:13
Jer 25:15–38	Jer 32:15–38
Jeremiah 26–44	Jeremiah 33–51
Jeremiah 45	Jer 51:31–35
Jeremiah 46–51	Jer 25:14–31:44
Jeremiah 52	Jeremiah 52

3) Content: → 7.3.4 and → 7.3.5.

These differences render LXX-Jer as one of the most irregular translations within LXX (→ 1.3.1.1), along

---

[1] Vonach, "Jeremias," 2696.

[2] Siegert, *Bibel*, 42; van der Kooij, "Zum Verhältnis," 198–200.

[3] The original count of Min, *Jeremiah* had LXX-Jer being shorter by one-seventh; however, Tov, *TCHB*, 287, considers the difference in length to be greater and estimates that LXX-Jer is shorter than MT-Jer by one-sixth.

[4] As a result, the numbering of the following chapters in LXX is higher by seven; here indicated, e.g., as Jeremiah 31 (38), the first number being the MT reference, and the second being that of LXX. In addition to the different position of the "Oracles against the Foreign Nations" within the book, the internal order of the oracles also differs significantly in LXX-Jer: Elam, Egypt, Babylon, Philistines, Idumea/Edom, Ammonites, Kedar, Damascus, Moab. A summarizing scene then follows in LXX-Jer 32. The banquet of God's cup of wrath corresponds to MT-Jer 25:15–38, but there serves as an announcement of divine judgment at the beginning.

[5] The last thematic element is very limited, as the final chapters of LXX-Jer, 33–51, return thematically to disaster for Israel.

with Job (→ 11.3.1), Proverbs (→ 12.3.1), Esther (→ 13–17.1.1.5), Daniel (→ 18.3.1), and Ben Sira (→ 11.4.3). The contrasting organization of the material (2) can only be the product of a deliberate reshaping, and the number of quantitative differences (1) is beyond what may be attributed to the negligence of translators or scribes. These observations point to editorial[6] or redactional[7] activities within the process of creating and transmitting Jeremiah (→ 7.3.3).

For a detailed analysis, see further → 7.2.2.1 and → 7.2.2.2.

7.3.2 Editions and Tools

7.3.2.1 Editions

1) The *editio critica*, prepared by Ziegler in the Göttingen series,[8] is indispensable for LXX-Jer studies, yet has to be used with caution. There are problems with his edition, as several scholars have noted:[9] The choice of readings given in the main text is sometimes hardly justified,[10] as is the selection of the variants included in the critical apparatus. Ziegler's inclination for emendations poses another problem.[11]

2) The edition of Rahlfs, *Septuaginta*, first published in 1935:[12] Given the limitations of Ziegler's edition, this publication should also be consulted; on various occasions it offers more acceptable readings than Ziegler's.[13]

7.3.2.2 Tools

1) *Das Buch Jeremia Griechisch und Hebräisch*, edited by Nestle. For a long time, this old synopsis was helpful for comparing the Greek and Hebrew versions of Jeremiah side by side;[14] now the comparison can be made more easily using the *CATSS computer program.

2) *Critique textuelle 1986, edited by Barthélemy, discusses the more important variants and is of great value for an evaluation of text-critical issues. He provides the results of the discussions of a committee of specialists, mostly involving LXX readings.

3) Modern translations of LXX, such as *NETS and *Septuaginta Deutsch, are a great help since the Greek language used by the translator(s) is sometimes very idiosyncratic. These translations include copious notes and background information.

4) The *Deuterojeremianische Konkordanz* of Stipp, published in 1998, is a useful tool in particular for researching the repetitions of stock phrases in the Hebrew and Greek texts of Jeremiah.

5) The Qumran text editions are also relevant, as they have changed the evaluation of LXX-Jer. 2Q13 (→ 7.2.1.1), edited by Baillet, consisting of fragments from Jer 42:7–48:35, testifies to the MT order of

---

[6] Tov, "Aspects," 149, posits two editions of Jeremiah, an earlier one (edition I), being preserved in LXX and 4QJer[b,d], and an expanded one (edition II), which later became MT-Jer and 4QJer[a,c].

[7] Bogaert, "Baruch," 168–73, ascribes the differences to redactional processes. He sees the shorter "rédaction A" linked to the figure of Baruch, whereas the longer "rédaction B" (corresponding to Tov's edition II, included in what became MT-Jer) accentuates the person of Jeremiah as "prophète canonisé."

[8] Ziegler, *Ieremias*.

[9] Soderlund, *Text*, 97–152; Shead, *Book*, 169–73, 244–45; Vonach, "Jeremias," 2697; A. Pietersma and M. Saunders, "Jeremias," *NETS*, 876–924, 876.

[10] An example is Jer 1:16, for which Ziegler proposes ἐθυμίασαν "they burned" without support in the manuscripts. For further examples of this nature, cf. Vonach, "Jeremias," 2697, n. 8.

[11] E.g., in Jer 38:21, the conjecture τιμρωριμ "timrorim."

[12] Attention must be given to the sometimes different numbering of certain verses, as Ziegler employed a new system twenty-two years later; e.g., the oracle against Idumea/Edom, referred to in Rahlfs' edition as Jer 30:1–16, is recorded by Ziegler as Jer 29:8–23. *NETS, 881 offers a table of the differences.

[13] In the case of Ziegler's proposal for Jer 1:16, mentioned in n. 10, Rahlfs has ἔθυσαν "they sacrificed" with all manuscripts. In LXX-Jer 38:21, Rahlfs offers τιμωρίαν "revenge, help" with the same textual support (contra Ziegler's conjecture for this word; cf. n. 11).

[14] Nestle, *Buch*. H.-J. Stipp has arranged a newer, more sophisticated version that includes the Greek variants in the Hebrew text (private circulation).

the book in which the oracles against the foreign nations appear at the end.[15]

Longer and more important manuscripts were found in Cave 4 (→ 7.2.1).[16] All five scrolls were edited by Tov: 4Q70, with fragments from Jer 7:1–22:16; 4Q71, which contains parts of Jer 9:22–10:21; 4Q72, the longest extant manuscript, covering fragments from Jer 4:5–33:16–20, confirming the MT order as in 2Q13; 4Q72a and 4Q72b, two small fragments of Jer 43:2–10 and 50:4–6. The interpretation of 4Q71, also named 4QJer[b], in particular, has aroused ongoing discussion (→ 7.3.3.4).

7.3.3 Analysis of the Differences between MT and LXX

The number and character of the differences between MT-Jer and LXX-Jer (→ 7.2.2; → 7.3.1.2) require an explanation that goes beyond the normal processes of textual transmission. They point to a deliberate reshaping of the book of Jeremiah (→ 1.3.1.1.13).

7.3.3.1 Brief Historical Survey

St. Jerome noted the changes in order and omissions in the Greek version, and intended to "order and complete" (*digerere ac complere*) the original form of the text in Latin from Hebrew sources.[17] A shift in approach occurred first at the end of the eighteenth century with Michaelis who gave preference to the text of LXX.[18] He was followed more than forty years later by Movers,[19] whose work became influential but also came under criticism.[20]

In the second half of the twentieth century, the discussion was kindled anew by the Qumran manuscripts (→ 7.2.1). A preliminary publication of these texts by Janzen[21] in 1973 interpreted 4QJer[b] (4Q71) as confirming the Greek text. Since then, many scholars have followed his lead and given priority to LXX-Jer.

7.3.3.2 Two Main Options

A definition of the character of the LXX-Jer translation is dependent upon one's view of its text-critical value. A majority (position 1) today sees 4Q71 and 4Q72a as a confirmation of the shorter text of LXX. They frequently hypothesize a different Hebrew *Vorlage* for the Greek translation of Jeremiah, and consider MT-Jer to be the result of a later, expansionist reworking and literary edition.[22] At the same time, LXX-Jer is perceived as a mostly faithful rendering of a Hebrew original, thus enabling one to go back to a redactional stage before that preserved in MT-Jer.

Other scholars have arrived at the opposite conclusion, namely that LXX-Jer shortened, interpreted, and rearranged the Hebrew text of Jeremiah (position 2).[23] Those who represent the intermediate positions decide in each case to which version they would give priority.[24]

The overall stance taken towards LXX-Jer leads to differing, and contrasting interpretations of the nature of its evidence. What in the view of position 1 is "original," is taken as a secondary development from the other side. Position 2 sees MT-Jer (→ 7.2.2) as being closer to the beginning of the textual history of Jeremiah and LXX-Jer as an abbreviation and change, stemming from a later time and in another context. The explanations for the textual

---

[15] Baillet, "Jérémie."

[16] Tov, "Jeremiah."

[17] Hieronymus, *In Hieremiam Prophetam*, Prologus 2. Still earlier, Origenes, *Epistola ad Africanum* [PG 11], 56B, had pointed to differences between the Greek and Hebrew texts.

[18] Michaelis, *Observationes*.

[19] Movers, *Commentatio*.

[20] For these discussions and their background, see Hubmann, "Bemerkungen." For more detailed discussions of the history of research, see also → 7.2.1 and → 7.2.2.1.

[21] Janzen, *Studies*.

[22] The main representatives of this position are Bogaert, Tov, Schenker, and Stipp, whose publications on the matter are listed in the bibliography. For a possible third ancient Hebrew source close to the LXX, see manuscript Schøyen 4612/9 (→ 7.2.1.7).

[23] This view is favored in some cases, e.g., by K. Schmid (*Buchgestalten des Jeremiabuches: Untersuchungen zur Redaktions- und Rezeptionsgeschichte von Jer 30–33 im Kontext des Buches* (WMANT 72; Neukirchen-Vluyn: Neukirchener Verlag, 1996), 2–23 and *passim*), van der Kooij, and generally by Fischer. The publications of van der Kooij and Fischer regarding this question are listed in the bibliography.

[24] An example is McKane's commentary.

differences between MT-Jer and LXX-Jer are thus opposed like a mirror-image. This requires a search for independent criteria to provide a solid foundation for the interpretation of the differences.

7.3.3.3 Methodological Procedure to Avoid an Impasse

Exegetes adhering to position 1 argue that, in the case of differences between MT (→ 7.2.2) and LXX, the LXX translator of Jeremiah often had a different Hebrew *Vorlage*. The best way to assess this reasoning is external evidence. Herein, Jeremiah provides a good amount of material, because of its rich use of other biblical texts.[25] The many parallels in other books of the Bible allow for an independent comparison, the best and longest example being Jeremiah 52, as a parallel to 2 Kgs 24:18–25:30. This chapter may serve as a test case, and has been investigated in detail by several scholars.

Rofé observes that LXX-Jer 52 is the only version that does not mention the exile.[26]

Person[27] gives priority to LXX-Jer, but admits that the texts of MT-Kgs (→ 5.3.2), LXX-Kgs (→ 5.5), and MT-Jer (→ 7.2.2) were reworked later than LXX-Jer, which seems rather implausible for the book of Kings.

Fischer[28] points to the "isolated" character of LXX-Jer compared with all the other texts that report the fall of Jerusalem in 587/86 B.C.E. (2 Kings [MT and LXX]; MT-Jer 52, and even 2 Chronicles 36 [MT and LXX; → 20.2.2 and → 20.3.1]). This isolation indicates deliberate changes on the part of LXX-Jer. Furthermore, the differences between the LXX and MT versions of this chapter suggest a shortened text and abbreviation tendencies with respect to content, similar to what can be observed in the rest of the book of Jeremiah.

This latter result is confirmed by Smith[29] who, following a detailed analysis of the translation technique in Jeremiah 52, reaches the conclusion that this chapter reflects the same technique as that seen in LXX-Jer 1–51.[30]

Abate takes LXX-Jer 52 as the text that preserves the oldest text form accessible today,[31] yet fails to take into account its dependence on a Hebrew version and on the earlier text of 2 Kings 24–25.

Rofé, Fischer, and Smith indicate that LXX-Jer 52 has been heavily reworked, whereas Person's and Abate's positions are based on the unproven assumption that it must be the "oldest" text because it is the shortest. The importance of Jeremiah 52 lies in the fact that in this case we have in 2 Kgs 24:18–25:30 a real, extant, and long *Vorlage* that offers an independent basis for an objective evaluation of the differences. Jeremiah 52 thus provides an excellent model for assessing the relationship between MT-Jer and LXX-Jer. The comparison shows the closeness of MT-Jer to the "source" text, while LXX-Jer deviates greatly from all other text forms, including even the MT and LXX versions of 2 Chronicles 36, which are themselves dependent on 2 Kings 24–25. This does not allow for any other conclusion than to see LXX-Jer in this chapter as extensively changing and shortening the underlying source[32] for its translation.

---

[25] Jeremiah contains many intertextual connections with other books, as the commentaries of Holladay (*Jeremiah 2*), Lundbom (*Jeremiah 1–20*), and Fischer (*Jeremia 1–25*) indicate.

[26] Rofé, "Exile." The parallel texts of MT 2 Kings and Jeremiah 52 refer various times to the Babylonian exile. In 1991, Bogaert ("Formes") tried to argue for the priority of the VL version, which is even shorter than LXX-Jer 52; however, it is difficult to assume that a Latin version, preserved only in manuscripts from the ninth century and later, might have preserved the most original text.

[27] Person, *Recensions*.

[28] G. Fischer, "Jeremiah 52: Test Case for Jer LXX," in *X Congress of the International Organization for Septuagint and Cognate Studies, Oslo 1998* (ed. B.A. Taylor; SBLSCS 51; Atlanta: SBL, 2001), 37–48; repr. in Fischer, *Der Prophet wie Mose*, 42–63.

[29] Smith, "Jeremiah 52."

[30] Thus Thackeray's theory of two translators for LXX-Jer (Jeremiah 1–28 and 29–52) seems improbable. It has been refuted convincingly by Tov, *Translation*; Stipp, "Fragen": and Smith, "Jeremiah 52." Yet it is difficult to say whether only one individual worked on the translation of Jeremiah into Greek.

[31] Abate, *Fine*, 157.

[32] It is often argued that the Hebrew *Vorlage* used for the rendering of Jeremiah into Greek was different from MT-Jer, and it is supposed to have been close to LXX-Jer. Such an argumentation is highly speculative, and the observations on Jeremiah 52 and other passages in Jeremiah speak against it. See Fischer, "Diskussion," 615 and 620 with note 26.

This conclusion is confirmed by additional cases in Jeremiah that quote passages from other biblical books. The quotations of Deut 5:33 in Jer 7:23; Isa 15:5 in Jer 48(31):5; Hab 2:13 in Jer 51(28):58; and other similar cases show that MT-Jer often represents the presumed original text more faithfully than LXX-Jer.

This article reflects position 2 and describes the nature and technique of the LXX translation of Jeremiah from this point of view. Most differences between MT-Jer and LXX-Jer derive from the translation process. It also allowed for a rearrangement of the book and for its adaptation to the needs of the new Greek-speaking Jewish environment in Egypt centuries later.[33]

7.3.3.4 4Q71 (and 4Q72a)

The main argument adduced in favor of position 1 is usually based on Qumran manuscripts 4Q71 (as in → 7.2.3.1) and 4Q72a (→ 7.2.1.3 and → 7.2.1.5). Tov argues that "… the reconstructed text of 4QJer^b agrees with G in lacking vv. 6–8 and 10 and in the sequence 4, 5a, 9, 5b."[34] However, there are problems with taking 4Q71 as an argument for the superiority of LXX-Jer:[35]

1) This interpretation of 4Q71 is based on a reconstruction. The extant text of the manuscript only contains parts of 10:4, 9, 11, 13 in lines 5–8. What is visible in 4Q71 displays neither the lack of vv. 6–8 nor the changed sequence.

2) It is true that line 6 cannot contain the whole text of vv. 6–8 in MT (→ 7.2.2). Yet even in the reconstruction based on LXX, line 6 deviates markedly from the regular line length.[36]

3) Although there are some further agreements between 4Q71 and LXX-Jer with regard to certain expressions, 4Q71 also follows MT-Jer in a few instances.

4) Generally speaking, it is not sound to deduce the superiority of a textual tradition on the basis of one manuscript, all the more so when that text is debatable, as in the case of the small and irregular fragment 4Q71.

4Q72a presents parts of Jer 43(50):2–10 and agrees in vv. 4–6 with LXX, having shorter forms. However, in vv. 5, 6–7, and 9 it confirms MT expressions, and thus displays an ambiguous character.[37]

An evaluation of the evidence adduced by the Qumran findings also has to take into account important manuscripts such as 4Q70 and 4Q72, which are proto-Masoretic, respectively, and largely confirm MT-Jer. For a different view → 7.1 and → 7.2.2.

7.3.4 Nature of the Translation

7.3.4.1 Overall Assessment

Generally LXX-Jer tries to render exactly its Hebrew *Vorlage*.[38] It often translates very precisely,[39] sometimes closely following the word sequence, while creating Hebraisms (→ 7.3.5.1). On the other hand, the translation is also free in its renditions for various reasons and thus displays a "mixed" ambiguous character:[40]

– Jer 31(38):2 in MT reads עַם שְׂרִידֵי חָרֶב "the people (of those who) escaped the sword." LXX changes the tripartite Hebrew phrase into a simpler

---

[33] The Babylonian exile occurred centuries before the time of the translation of LXX-Jer, and some persons mentioned in the book of Jeremiah (such as Johanan the son of Kareah and even King Nebuchadrezzar, who is significantly less present in LXX-Jer) had virtually no relevance to its audience.

[34] Tov, "Jeremiah," 174.

[35] Fischer, *Stand*, 21–22, 24.

[36] The lines of 4Q71 are exceptionally long with 112–47 letter-spaces. Line 6, according to the reconstruction following the LXX, would have only approximately 109 spaces, and would therefore be shorter than the minimum length of the other lines in the fragment.

[37] Fischer, *Stand*, 23.

[38] Fischer, *Trostbüchlein*, 34–36; Pietersma and Saunders, "Ieremias," 876, mention as the "most basic norm of the translator … isomorphism."

[39] Stipp, *Sondergut*, 20, 57; Vonach, "Jeremias," 2718–19; Walser, *Jeremiah*, 14.

[40] As an example, I take some renditions of the fourth poem of the "Booklet of Consolation," Jer 31(38):2–6; for a longer exposition, see Fischer, *Trostbüchlein*, 28–78 and *passim*. For other differences between MT and LXX in this text, → 7.3.5.

- construction: μετὰ ὀλωλότων ἐν μαχαίρᾳ "with (those) killed by the sword".
- Jer 31(38):3 in MT starts with the quote מֵרָחוֹק יְהוָה נִרְאָה לִי "YHWH has appeared *to me* from afar." LXX has a statement in the 3rd person: "The Lord appeared *to him* (αὐτῷ) from afar," which fits better in the context, and eases the complex Hebrew communication structure.
- Jer 31(38):4 in MT offers the singular expression תַּעְדִּי תֻפַּיִךְ "you will *adorn* yourself with your tambourines." LXX has "*take* your tambourines," with the verb λαμβάνειν, which is a frequent, general, and less poetic expression.
- Jer 31(38):5b in MT repeats the root "to plant," as subject in the participle plural, and as verb: נָטְעוּ נֹטְעִים "the planters have planted." LXX has it only once (φυτεύσατε "you shall plant").
- In Jer 31(38):6, LXX eases the tension between 2nd and 1st person plural verbs in the final quote by adhering to the 2nd person.[41]

These differences between MT-Jer and LXX-Jer are typical of this translation and can be supplemented by numerous other examples. LXX-Jer tends to make the text more easily understood by adopting more common language, shortening longer phrases, and simplifying intricate structures in the original. Overall, LXX-Jer can be perceived as being more polished and less rough than the difficult and complicated Hebrew text.[42]

7.3.4.2 Representation of God

The ambiguous picture of the character of LXX-Jer shows up in yet other features. The translator tends to avoid anthropomorphic language in speaking about God and to present a mild portrayal of him,[43] although sometimes he accentuates God's actions and words and even portrays them more violently.[44]

7.3.4.3 Heightened Emphasis on Ethical and Religious Issues

Other characteristic features of LXX-Jer are moralizing tendencies[45] and a liturgical inclination.[46] They indicate a special orientation towards the intended audience, which is also visible in the adjustments made in the translation due to its time and context. The Hellenistic background of the Jewish Diaspora in Egypt, especially in Alexandria, provides clues for understanding many changes in LXX-Jer with respect to MT-Jer (→ 7.2.2).[47] Such a milieu explains the downplaying of the role of Babylon and its king in LXX-Jer, and the softened stance towards God's people.[48]

7.3.4.4 Theological Interpretations and Actualizations

The repetition of certain features in LXX-Jer demonstrates the theological intentions of the translator, as is apparent in the consistent translation of אֲהָהּ "Alas!" as ὁ ὤν "the being/existing one,"[49]

---

[41] Cf. also the example in v. 3; for a detailed investigation of such changes of referent in LXX-Jer, see Glanz, *Shifts*. In the same v. 6, MT speaks of נֹצְרִים "watchmen" crying and exhorting a pilgrimage to Zion; LXX translates it as "defenders" (with a participle plural of ἀπολογέομαι), which is a possible rendition of the Hebrew word but is not appropriate in this context.

[42] Fischer, "Text," 323–28. This is another indication that MT deserves priority. It is improbable that a complicated, more sophisticated text with a lot of tensions (MT-Jer) derives from a simpler one (LXX-Jer). Rather, one would think that the latter is the result of processes that smooth out the difficulties of the original Hebrew.

[43] Fischer, *Trostbüchlein*, 74–77; Vonach, "Jeremias," 2725–26.

[44] Stipp, "Diskussion," 652; for a comprehensive view of this issue, see Stipp, "Gottesbildfragen." Already in LXX-Jer 1:1, the MT introduction ("The words of Jeremiah") is altered to "The saying of God," thus emphasizing the divine origin of the following words in Jeremiah's book and lending it heightened authority; cf. also Jer 51(28):59.

[45] Vonach, "Jeremias," 2724; e.g. in LXX-Jer 6:16, "purification" instead of "rest, repose" in MT, and in LXX-Jer 22:3, "act godlessly" for "being violent" in MT.

[46] Fischer, *Prophet*, 70–71; as in the rendering of the lament "Alas, Lord YHWH!" in LXX-Jer 1:6 and 4:10 with the invocation "Oh, (the) Being One, Lord YHWH!," and in Jer 2:2, where MT reads "holy was Israel" and LXX has "you followed the Holy One of Israel." See also the example of Jer 3:19 in → 7.3.1.2, 1.

[47] For this, see Goldman, *Prophétie*, 57–62. A typical example is the difference in "dancing" in Jer 31(38):13.

[48] Vonach, "Jeremias," 2726–27; Jer 5:4 and 6:15 are some of his examples. Whereas MT-Jer portrays Nebuchadrezzar three times as God's "servant" (Jer 25:9; 27:6; 43:10), LXX-Jer never designates him so.

[49] Jer 1:6; 14:13; 32(39):17; in these instances, Rahlfs recourses

in connection with God's revelation in Exod 3:14. Another feature is the increased use of θεός "God" with no equivalent in Hebrew.[50] An interesting case is seen in how the translator deals with God's weeping in MT-Jer 9:9 "I will lift up weeping and lament" and MT-Jer 14:17 "My eyes go down (in) tears." LXX-Jer in both passages[51] addresses others: "Lift up lament …!" and "Let tears flow down from your eyes …!" respectively, thus avoiding the image of a God moved by such strong emotions.

There are a number of adaptations in LXX-Jer to the Hellenistic background of the Jewish community in Egypt in the second century B.C.E.[52] Among them, the increased use of the feminine designation for Baal, ἡ Βααλ "she-Baal," is noteworthy;[53] the prominence of the adoration of Isis in Egypt seems to serve as the background for it and thus offers an example for actualization.[54]

As shown in → 7.3.4.3 and → 7.3.4.4, the Hebrew text of Jeremiah, originally intended for a Judean audience in earlier centuries, has been reshaped by the translator so as to conform it to the needs, expectations, and circumstances of his time. LXX-Jer therefore presents an adaptation and actualization for Greek readers of a later era in Egypt. From the viewpoint of position 2, these features are mainly responsible for the different profile in LXX-Jer compared with that in MT-Jer.

7.3.5 Translation Technique

LXX-Jer combines seemingly contrasting features. On the one hand, for large sections of the book, it follows the Hebrew text closely and tries to render it precisely in Greek (→ 7.3.5.1). On the other hand, every translator is guided innately by his own intentions when making decisions on possible meanings and struggling with difficult expressions and passages. Moreover, he is free to make new interpretations and changes in the composition. LXX-Jer displays the consequences of such processes and influences.

7.3.5.1 Closeness to the Original

1) Equivalences on various levels: Large sections of LXX-Jer adhere closely to the Hebrew *Vorlage* with regard to the denotative equivalence and quite often even to the word sequence, e.g., nearly completely in Jer 31(38):2–6. Furthermore, in a few cases phonetic equivalences show the closeness to the Hebrew,[55] as in Jer 31(38):9, where אוליכם "I will make them go" is rendered by αὐλίζων,[56] or in Jer 31:35 (38:36), where κραυγή "shouting, noise" corresponds to Hebrew רגע (vocalized by MT as *rogaʿ* "stirring up").

2) Hebraisms:[57] LXX-Jer uses a number of stereotyped renderings of Hebrew expressions. Thus the phrase נתן ל־, meaning "to make, to render," is translated by the uncommon Greek phrase δίδωμι εἰς "(to) give to," e.g. in Jer 12:10; 33(26):6, which is barely intelligible unless one resorts to the original phrase standing behind it. The idiomatic Hebrew combination of הנני "behold, I" with a verbal form is rendered faithfully forty-nine times by ἰδοὺ ἐγώ with the verb in the 1st person singular, a construction that is not familiar in Greek.

---

to conjectures, only bringing the vocative Ὦ, "Oh (Lord)." In the case of Jer 4:10, the manuscript evidence favors the vocative rendering Ὦ, "Oh (Lord)," against Ziegler, who also here renders ὁ ὤν.

[50] Stipp, *Sondergut*, 54. Examples are Jer 4:2; 5:18; 12:4; 23:30, 37–38, etc.

[51] In Ziegler's edition, the first one is counted as Jer 9:10. In Jer 14:17, "my (eyes)" stays within YHWH's command to the prophet to announce his word, and thus it has to be referred primarily to God: Fischer, *Jeremia 1–25*, 484.

[52] Vonach, "Jeremias," 2728–31.

[53] There are twelve occurrences of this usage in Jeremiah, three times more than in any other book of the Bible (Judges, and 4 Kingdoms, with four cases each).

[54] Vonach, "Ἡ Βααλ," esp. 66–68.

[55] Ziegler, *Beiträge*, 32.

[56] Tov, "Loan-words," 172, counts this word as "homophony."

[57] Vonach, "Jeremias," 2718–19. Walser, *Jeremiah*, 14–16, lists a series of "un-Greek" expressions, reflecting their Hebrew background. Claiming that "[c]ertainly the Greek of Jeremiah was not perceived as ordinary Hellenistic Greek by the ancient reader," he provides as further evidence clause syntax and word order (pp. 6–7).

3) Literal rendering that is inappropriate in the context and therefore misleading: In some cases, as in Jer 30(37):18, the literal Greek translation of משפט used here in the sense of "(right) place" for the rebuilding of the palace on its previous site, as κρίμα "decision, verdict"[58] can only be understood correctly by somebody who conjectures the Hebrew word at the origin of this rendering; without this, the meaning of the Greek phrase is completely different and hardly intelligible.

4) Transliterations are a very special case of "closeness" to the original. Besides their normal use for names of places and individuals, in LXX-Jer they can also be found for regular Hebrew words[59] as these examples demonstrate: The *Ketiv* השרמות in Jer 31(38):40 is transcribed as ασαρημωθ "asaremoth." Similarly, the nickname given to the Pharaoh in Jer 46(26):17 שאון העביר המועד "noise/roar/racket that let pass the (appointed) time" is transcribed as Σαων εσβι εμωηδ "Saon esbi emoed," which is unintelligible in Greek.

7.3.5.2 Reductions, Simplifications, and Explanations

1) The book of Jeremiah contains many repetitions that LXX-Jer tends to reduce,[60] thus alleviating a seemingly redundant text. The analyses of Stulman, dealing with the differences in length in MT-Jer (→ 7.2.2) and LXX-Jer,[61] confirm this observation from another point of view: What MT offers more than LXX consists mainly of conventional language, which is common to both text forms of Jeremiah.

2) The formulaic expressions and titles in MT-Jer, e.g., "thus says the Lord," "YHWH of hosts," and "oracle of YHWH" have been reduced in LXX-Jer.[62] Position 1 explains the higher number in MT as repetitive expansions in the so-called edition 2; position 2 interprets this fact as the reduction in the translation of unnecessary elements in the long text of MT. The Hebrew term צבאות "Zebaoth," especially, is drastically reduced in LXX-Jer.[63] This is coupled with the tendency in LXX-Jer to shorten the text considerably (→ 7.3.1.2), affecting its coherence, as can be seen in the fact that key words in MT are missing in LXX.[64]

3) The desire to make the text of Jeremiah more accessible and more easily understood is probably at the root of some simplifications, as in Jer 7:4 ("the temple of the Lord" appears only twice instead of three times, as in MT). This desire may also be the reason for some explanations: MT-Jer 2:21 gives "Sorek" for the type of vine, LXX renders as "vine carrying fruit." MT-Jer 13:18 uses the technical term *"gebirah"* when speaking of the Queen Mother; LXX translates more generally as "the ruling ones." Whereas MT-Jer 18:15 has the symbolic designation "eternal paths," LXX talks of "endless miles," thereby emphasizing the length of the way. In particular, the expression ψευδοπροφήτης "false prophet(s)," used only in LXX to identify some of Jeremiah's

---

[58] The whole phrase reads: "and the temple will be seated according to its/his verdict." A similar case is mentioned in n. 41, referring to Jer 31(38):6.

[59] The two words ציונים and תמרורים in Jer 31:21, designating "sign-posts," are represented in LXX-Jer (38:21) by the transliterations σιωνιμ and τιμρωριμ (thus Ziegler's conjecture, see note 11; Rahlfs' edition has τιμωρίαν, sounding similar, but meaning "revenge, help"). This may indicate that the meaning of the underlying Hebrew words was unfamiliar to the translator. Tov, "Loan-words," 174–79, Vonach, "Jeremias," 2718, and Pietersma and Saunders, "Ieremias," 880 give some additional examples.

[60] Hubmann, *Untersuchungen*, 217–44. In most cases, the second doublet is suppressed, e.g. in Jer 17:3–4 (a doublet to Jer 15:13–14), or in LXX-Jer 37:10–11 (parallel to MT-Jer 30:10–11, a doublet to LXX-Jer 26:27–28 corresponding to MT-Jer 46:27–28). Hubmann's investigation of Jeremian doublets also demonstrates inconsistencies in the renderings of LXX (p. 242), and Pietersma and Saunders, "Ieremias," 879–80 clearly confirm this, listing Jer 10:12–17 // 28(51):15–19 by way of example.

[61] Stulman, *Sermons*.

[62] Stipp, "Messenger Formulas." 4Q72a, too, displays the same tendency.

[63] It is missing sixty-nine times (out of eighty-two) in LXX-Jer: Vonach, "Jeremias," 2715–16, and Rofé, "Name."

[64] Stipp, *Sondergut*, 43–44, shows this feature for Jer 27(34):12–15, where the referent "prophets" is absent in LXX (see also Tov, "Notes," 327). Problems with the reference are also seen in LXX-Jer 25:12–13: Fischer, *Prophet*, 9.

adversaries (Jer 33:7, 8, 11, 16; 35:1, etc.), is a clear exegetical rendering.

7.3.5.3 Inconsistency

The features mentioned here can be observed throughout the book. Whereas section 1) below considers larger areas of Jeremiah and section 2) seems to point to two different hands,[65] it is more likely a sign of a change in the translation practices of the same person. The two other phenomena (sections 3 and 4) touch on contextual inconsistencies within smaller areas.

1) Variations on the word and even on the phrase or clause level are present throughout the whole book of Jeremiah. Pietersma and Saunders[66] list ten examples (out of many more) and explain them as "a differentiation in the target language due to context" (p. 878). The final example is the doublet Jeremiah 10 // 28(51) mentioned in n. 60; the altered rendering displays "interpretational differences" on the side of LXX-Jer (880).

2) The most remarkable difference between Jeremiah 1–28 and 29–52 lies in the rendering of the *Gottesspruchformel* נאם יהוה "uttering of YHWH," which usually is rendered in the first part as λέγει κύριος "says the Lord"[67] and in the latter chapters mostly as φησὶ κύριος "speaks the Lord"[68] or as εἶπε κύριος "said the Lord."[69] Moreover, the two parts of Jeremiah have different translations for several additional words.[70]

3) Often the translation uses different words for the same Hebrew expression within the space of a few verses, e.g., the root שוב "to return" in Jer 8:4, 5, the verbs דבר "to speak" in Jer 30(37):2, 4 and דרש "to seek" in Jer 30(37):14, 17. Possible reasons for the varying translations may be the desire to avoid repetition, the focus on a special aspect, or, probably more often, consideration for the context. This observation points to a translation technique that normally does not take into account earlier renderings, but usually, rather intuitively, seeks new ad hoc word-for-word Greek equivalents for the Hebrew original.[71]

4) In contrast to section 3), LXX-Jer often uses the same root where the Hebrew text varies. Examples are the use twice of φόβος "fear" for חרדה "trembling" and פחד "fright" in Jer 30(37):5 and the use three times of ὀργή "wrath" for סערה, סער, both meaning "storm, whirlwind," and for חרון "embers" in Jer 30(37):23–24. These cases show that LXX-Jer diminishes the variety of the original and streamlines it, making it more uniform.[72]

Both seemingly contradictory techniques (3 and 4) reflect, in most cases, different contextual practices. Within the immediate context, the translator sometimes uses the same Greek term for different Hebrew words (4), possibly reflecting his weariness or the limitations in his vocabulary, thus resulting in repetitions not present in the original.

Conversely, the difficulties encountered in maintaining the attention and concentration that is needed at all times on the verse to be rendered in Greek account for the changes in the expressions, even within the range of a few verses (3). In another area, LXX-Jer is inconsistent with regard to its length; although generally much shorter, in some cases it is longer than MT (→ 7.2.2).[73]

---

[65] However, Thackeray's theory of two translators has been justly criticized by Tov, Smith, and others (see n. 30). Tov, *Translation*, attributes the different renderings to a reviser, but Stipp, "Fragen," points to irregularities in the distribution of the relevant words and questions Tov's theory.

[66] Pietersma and Saunders, "Ieremias," 877–79.

[67] Starting with Jer 1:8, 15, 19.

[68] E.g. in LXX-Jer 30:2, 15 (corresponding to MT-Jer 49:2, 26), etc.

[69] Already in LXX-Jer 27:30, 40 (equivalent to MT-Jer 50:30, 40), and regularly from LXX-Jer 30:5, 10 (= MT-Jer 49:5, 32) onwards. The variety of different renderings in LXX-Jer 30 in itself displays inconsistency within the immediate context.

[70] See the listings in Tov, *Translation*, and more extensively in Stipp, "Fragen."

[71] Tov, "Translators," 207, has demonstrated this in an exemplary way with the various renderings of שפי "hill" in LXX-Jer.

[72] Tov, "Translators," 215, points to the tendency in LXX-Jer to use "general words" for the rendition of more sophisticated expressions in the Hebrew text.

[73] A noteworthy example is that of Jer 7:4 (→ 7.3.5.2 3): The phrase "the temple of the Lord," which appears three times in MT, appears just twice in LXX, yet immediately before, after

7.3.5.4 Coping with Difficulties

1) Poetry in general is difficult to render in another language, and even more so when unvocalized, which pertains to the poetry of Jeremiah.[74] The following example serves as an illustration: The end of MT-Jer 31:2 reads הָל֖וֹךְ לְהַרְגִּיע֥וֹ יִשְׂרָאֵֽל "(to) go, to give rest to it/him, Israel." LXX-Jer 38:2 renders with βαδίσατε καὶ μὴ ὀλέσητε τὸν Ισραηλ "proceed, and do not destroy Israel." The insertion of a negation and the change of the second verb alter the original sense significantly.

2) There are indications that the translator of LXX-Jer consulted other texts and books when rendering difficult passages in his translation. The description of the temple equipment in Jeremiah 52, taken from 2 Kings 25, is an example: LXX-Jer 52:18 agrees with Exod 27:3 against 2 Kings and MT-Jer, mentioning three pieces of the cultic equipment of the temple, and the following v. 19 seems to depend on 1 Kgs 7:50, the base text for the temple vessels.[75] In a similar vein, Jer 52:21 gives the height of the columns of the temple as "thirty-five cubits," corresponding to 2 Chr 3:15 but against 2 Kgs 25:17 and MT-Jer 52:21 ("eighteen cubits").

7.3.5.5 Changes of Meaning

The example in → 7.3.5.4 from Jer 31(38):2 shows that LXX-Jer introduces negations in order to render Jeremiah more easily understood by the readers. Two further cases confirm this.

In Jer 2:31, MT reads: "See the word of YHWH!" Neither the unusual phrase "seeing a word" nor the preceding unique address "O generation!" is found in LXX; instead, the end of v. 30 reads "and you did not fear," switching from Hebrew ראה "to see" to the similar root ירא "to fear" and negating it.[76]

MT-Jer 51:58 has "... and people toil for nothing," echoing Hab 2:13. The corresponding verse in LXX-Jer, 28:58, says: "... and people do not toil in vain," changing the original by way of the insertion of a negation and interpreting the fall of Babylon as the positive result of the efforts of (foreign) people.

7.3.6 Text-Critical and Literary Value

The assessment of the text-critical value of LXX-Jer depends on the general stance one chooses to take in regard to the positions outlined in → 7.3.3.2 (→ 1.3.1.1.12).

1) Position 1 sees LXX-Jer in many cases as the better text, arguing for a different *Vorlage* for it that was closer to the original than MT (→ 7.2.2).[77] This leads some to postulate and reconstruct an earlier stage/edition of Jeremiah than MT, which is said to be the product of an "expansionist redaction." This position is encountered in various forms: for Bogaert, MT-Jer was reworked later in a way that places more emphasis on the prophet Jeremiah,[78] and thus LXX-Jer provides access to a more original version of the book of Jeremiah. Tov describes editorial and exegetical aspects of "Edition II" (= MT-Jer), and notices also "peculiar words and expressions" for it.[79] Stipp develops this idea further and proposes a pre-Masoretic idiolect consisting of linguistic idiosyncracies of MT-Jer not present in the Greek version, forming a kind of *Sondergut* in the Hebrew text.[80]

"words of deception," it has the addition "because they are not useful for you at all."

[74] These problems are felt especially in the first half of the book, in the Oracles against the Foreign Nations, and in the Booklet of Consolation, Jeremiah 30–31 (37–38). In this context, Tov, "Translators," 212, refers to Jer 2:20. Cf. also Althann, *Analysis*, for Jeremiah 4–6.

[75] Fischer, *Prophet*, 54; Pietersma and Saunders, "Ieremias," 876 even qualify LXX-Jer 52:19 under the rubric "unintelligibility."

[76] Goldman, "Crispations," 43–44.

[77] See above nn. 6 and 7. Bogaert, "Rédactions," 370, speaks even of a "texte reconnu," suggesting accepted authority, yet it is unclear by whom. There is another problem inherent in position 1, alluded to already in n. 32: the theory of a different *Vorlage* that is no longer accessible is difficult to prove and therefore equally hard to criticize, giving way to many different speculations.

[78] Bogaert, "Baruch," 168–70.

[79] Tov, "Aspects," 150–67, esp. 165.

[80] Stipp, especially in "Diskussion," 632–41, with a definition on pp. 633–34.

2) Position 2, on the other hand, regards LXX-Jer mainly as secondary in relation to MT, including characteristics of a translation such as actualizations, intentional changes, rearrangements of the compositional structure, and additions and omissions based on the interests of the new environment in Egypt. The process of transferring into another language necessitates finding equivalents within a new cultural surrounding, but it also tends to encourage a freedom to change and add one's own ideas. From the perspective of position 2, LXX-Jer is generally the product of a deliberate reworking of a form of Jeremiah that was very close to what later became MT, although in a few instances it might have preserved the original wording.

1) For an appreciation of the value of LXX-Jer for textual criticism, three additional aspects are also relevant:

i) The transmission of the authoritative Masoretic Hebrew text has been remarkably faithful. This is testified by the high accordance of the best-preserved manuscripts found at Qumran (4Q70 and 4Q72), which are regarded as being proto-Masoretic.[81] The renowned Masorah codices of nearly one thousand years later resemble this proto-Masoretic text and serve as the basis of the modern critical editions. The precision of this text is further confirmed by the handling of the *Ketiv-Qere* passages in MT-Jer (→ 3–5.3). There are approximately fifty relevant instances; in thirty-six cases, LXX-Jer sides with the *Qere* readings. This indicates that, already in the second century B.C.E., LXX-Jer knew the *Qere* tradition and gave priority in most cases to it,[82] whereas the *Ketiv* readings were preserved in the main text of MT-Jer, against the alternative *Qere* readings, for more than a millennium until the production of the major Hebrew codices from 895 C.E. onward. This suggests a very high level of precision in the transmission of the Hebrew text of Jeremiah.

ii) In contrast to the accuracy of the MT-Jer tradition, the transmission of the Greek text of Jeremiah was more fluid with thousands of divergent readings that often affect significantly the meaning of the text, as shown in Ziegler's edition.[83] The number of variant readings as well as the scope of their discrepancies outweighs by far what can be observed in a comparison of the proto-Masoretic texts of Qumran with the later Masorah codices, whereas even the major Greek codices and manuscripts differ greatly.[84] This is a sign that less care was taken for maintaining accuracy in handing down the transmitted text within the Greek textual tradition than for that of MT-Jer.

iii) The shortness of LXX-Jer is possibly due to haplography. A conservative calculation arrives at approximately fifty cases.[85] This, too, demonstrates that LXX-Jer is less reliable than MT-Jer.

For a different view of the relationship between LXX-Jere and MT-Jer than expressed in this article, see → 7.1 and → 7.2.2.1, → 7.2.2.2.

Abate, E., *La fine del regno di Sedecia* (Textos y estudios "Cardenal Cisneros" 76; Madrid: C.S.I.C., 2008).
Althann, R., *A Philological Analysis of Jeremiah 4–6 in the*

---

[81] Tov, "Jeremiah," 151, 184.
[82] Fischer, *Prophet*, 33–34.

[83] Even Stipp, *Sondergut*, 64, and Stipp, "Diskussion," 249–50, acknowledges problems with the "Textpflege" in LXX-Jer, and states that the transmission of the text was not as careful as within the Hebrew tradition.
[84] This is very obvious when one studies the critical apparatus of Ziegler and compares it with editions of the Hebrew Bible.
[85] Vonach, "Jeremias," 2704, whereas Lundbom, "Haplography" calculates 330 instances. The haplography may have already occurred within the Hebrew text serving as *Vorlage* for LXX-Jer, as Lundbom suggests; yet it could equally well have happened during the course of the translation. In my eyes, the desire to abbreviate a sometimes lengthy, repetitive original (= MT-Jer) during the course of the translation should not be underestimated; many of these so-called "haplographies" may be intentional omissions, and the number of genuine haplographies may then be reduced to just a few.

Light of Northwest Semitic (BibOr 38; Rome: Biblical Institute Press, 1983).

Baillet, M., "13. Jérémie," *DJD III.1: 62–69.

Barthélemy, *Critique textuelle 1986.

Bogaert, P.-M. (ed.), Le Livre de Jérémie (BETL 54: Leuven: Peeters, 1981; 2nd ed. 1997).

Bogaert, P.-M., "De Baruch à Jérémie: Les deux rédactions conservées du livre de Jérémie," in Le livre de Jérémie (ed. P.-M. Bogaert; BETL 54; Leuven: Leuven University Press, 1981), 168–73, 430–32.

Bogaert, P.-M., "Le livre de Jérémie en perspective: Les deux rédactions antiques selon les travaux en cours," RB 101 (1994): 363–406.

Bogaert, P.-M., "Les trois formes de Jérémie 52 (TM, LXX et VL)," in Tradition of the Text: Studies Offered to Dominique Barthélemy in Celebration of His 70th Birthday (eds. G.J. Norton and S. Pisano; OBO 109; Göttingen: Vandenhoeck & Ruprecht, 1991), 1–17.

Fischer, G., Das Trostbüchlein: Text, Komposition und Theologie von Jer 30–31 (SBB 26; Stuttgart: Katholisches Bibelwerk, 1993).

Fischer, G., "Zum Text des Jeremiabuches," Bib 78 (1997): 305–28; repr. in G. Fischer, Der Prophet wie Mose, 24–41.

Fischer, G., Jeremia 1–25 (Herders theologischer Kommentar zum Alten Testament; Freiburg: Herder, 2005).

Fischer, G., Jeremia: Der Stand der theologischen Diskussion (Darmstadt: Wissenschaftliche Buchgesellschaft, 2007).

Fischer, G., "Die Diskussion um den Jeremiatext," in Karrer-Kraus, *Septuaginta 2008, 612–29; repr. in G. Fischer, Der Prophet wie Mose, 73–89.

Fischer, G., Der Prophet wie Mose: Studien zum Jeremiabuch (Beihefte zur Zeitschrift für altorientalische Rechtsgeschichte 15; Wiesbaden: Harrassowitz, 2011). Part A contains five articles from the years 1991 to 2008, and two reviews.

Glanz, O., Understanding Participant-Reference Shifts in the Book of Jeremiah (SSN 60; Leiden: Brill, 2013).

Goldman, Y., Prophétie et royauté au retour de l'exil: Les origenes littéraires de la forme massorétique du livre de Jérémie (OBO 118; Göttingen: Vandenhoeck & Ruprecht, 1992).

Goldman, Y., "Crispations théologiques et accidents textuels dans le TM de Jérémie 2," Bib 76 (1995): 25–52.

Holladay, W.L., Jeremiah 2: A Commentary on the Book of the Prophet Chapters 26–52 (Hermeneia; Philadelphia: Fortress, 1989).

Hubmann, F.D., "Bemerkungen zur älteren Diskussion um die Unterschiede zwischen MT und G im Jeremiabuch," in Jeremia und die "deuteronomistische Bewegung" (ed. W. Groß; BBB 98, Weinheim: Beltz Athenäum, 1995), 263–70.

Hubmann, F.D., Untersuchungen zu den Konfessionen Jer 11,18–12,6 und Jer 15,10–21 (Forschung zur Bibel 30; Würzburg: Echter, 1978).

Janzen, J.G., Studies in the Text of Jeremiah (HSM 6, Cambridge: Harvard University Press, 1973).

Lundbom, J.R., "Haplography in the Hebrew Vorlage of LXX-Jeremiah," HS 46 (2005): 301–20.

Lundbom, J.R., Jeremiah 1–20: A New Translation with Introduction and Commentary (AB 21A: New York: Doubleday, 1999).

McKane, W., Jeremiah (2 vols.; ICC, Edinburgh: T & T Clark, 1986–1996).

Michaelis, J.D., Observationes philologicae et criticae in Jeremiae Vaticinia et Threnos (Göttingen: Vandenhoeck & Ruprecht, 1793).

Movers, F.C., De utriusque recensionis Vaticiniorum Ieremiae, graecae Alexandrinae et hebraicae Masorethicae indole et origine commentatio critica (Hamburg: Perthes, 1837).

Nestle, E. (ed.), Das Buch Jeremia Griechisch und Hebräisch (Stuttgart: Privilegierte Württembergische Bibelanstalt, 1924; 2nd ed. 1934).

Person, R.R., The Kings-Isaiah and Kings-Jeremiah Recensions (BZAW 252; Berlin: De Gruyter, 1997).

Rahlfs, *Septuaginta.

Reiter, S. (ed.), Sancti Hieronymi Presbyteri Opera, Part 1: Opera exegetica, Vol. 3: In Hieremiam libri VI: In Hieremiam prophetam (CCSL 74; Turnhout: Brepols, 1960).

Rofé, A., "Not Exile but Annihilation for Zedekiah's People: The Purport of Jeremiah 52 in the Septuagint," in VIII Congress of the International Organization for Septuagint and Cognate Studies (ed. L. Greenspoon; SBLSCS 41, Atlanta: Scholars Press, 1995), 165–70.

Rofé, A., "The Name YHWH SEBA'OT and the Shorter Recension of Jeremiah," in Prophetie und geschichtliche Wirklichkeit im alten Israel: Festschrift für Siegfried Hermann zum 65. Geburtstag (eds. R. Liwak and S. Wagner; Stuttgart: Kohlhammer, 1991), 307–15.

Shead, A.G., The Open Book and the Sealed Book: Jeremiah 32 in its Hebrew and Greek Recensions (JSOTSup 347; London: Academic Press, 2002).

Siegert, F., Zwischen Hebräischer Bibel und Altem Testament: Eine Einführung in die Septuaginta (Münsteraner Judaistische Studien 9; Münster: Lit Verlag, 2001).

Smith, J., "Jeremiah 52: Thackeray and Beyond," *BIOSCS* 35 (2002): 35–96.

Soderlund, S., *The Greek Text of Jeremiah: A Revised Hypothesis* (JSOTSup 47; Sheffield: JSOT Press, 1985).

Stipp, H.-J., "Gottesbildfragen in den Lesartendifferenzen zwischen dem masoretischen und dem alexandrinischen Text des Jeremiabuches," in *Text-Critical and Hermeneutical Studies in the Septuagint* (eds. J. Cook and H.-J. Stipp; VTSup 157, Leiden: Brill, 2012), 237–74.

Stipp, H.-J., "Zur aktuellen Diskussion um das Verhältnis der Textformen des Jeremiabuches," in Karrer–Kraus, *Septuaginta 2008*, 630–53.

Stipp, H.-J., *Deuterojeremianische Konkordanz* (Arbeiten zu Text und Sprache im Alten Testament 63; St. Ottilien: EOS Verlag, 1998).

Stipp, H.-J., "The Prophetic Messenger Formulas in Jeremiah According to the Masoretic and Alexandrian Texts," *Text* 18 (1995): 63–85.

Stipp, H.-J., *Das masoretische und alexandrinische Sondergut des Jeremiabuches* (OBO 136; Göttingen: Vandenhoeck & Ruprecht, 1994).

Stipp, H.-J., "Offene Fragen zur Übersetzungskritik des antiken griechischen Jeremiabuches," *JNSL* 17 (1991): 117–28.

Stulman, L., *The Prose Sermons of the Book of Jeremiah: A Redescription of the Correspondences with the Deuteronomistic Literature in the Light of Recent Text-Critical Research* (SBLDS 83; Atlanta: Scholars Press, 1986).

Tov, E., "Did the Septuagint Translators Always Understand Their Hebrew Text?," in *De Septuaginta: Studies in Honour of John William Wevers on his Sixty-Fifth Birthday* (eds. A. Pietersma and C. Cox; Ontario: Benben Publications, 1984), 53–70; rev. version in Tov, *Greek-Hebrew Bible*, 203–18.

Tov, E., "Exegetical Notes on the Hebrew Vorlage of the LXX of Jeremiah 27 (34)," *ZAW* 91 (1979): 73–93; rev. version in Tov, *Greek-Hebrew Bible*, 315–31.

Tov, E., "Loan-words, Homophony and Transliterations in the Septuagint," *Bib* 60 (1979): 216–36; rev. version in Tov, *Greek-Hebrew Bible*, 165–82.

Tov, E., "Jeremiah," *DJD* XV: 145–207.

Tov, *TCHB*.

Tov, E., "Some Aspects of the Textual and Literary History of the Book of Jeremiah," in *Le livre de Jérémie* (ed. P.-M. Bogaert; BETL 54; Leuven: Leuven University Press, 1981), 145–67.

Tov, *Jeremiah–Baruch*.

van der Kooij, A., "Jeremiah 27:5–15," *JNSL* 20 (1994): 59–78.

van der Kooij, A., "Zum Verhältnis von Textkritik und Literarkritik," in *Congress Volume: Cambridge 1995* (ed. J.A. Emerton; VTSup 66; Leiden: Brill, 1997). 185–202.

Vonach, A., "Jeremias/Ieremia/Jeremia," in Karrer–Kraus, *Septuaginta Deutsch, Erläuterungen*, 2.2696–737.

Vonach, A., "Ἡ Βααλ in der LXX-Jer: Erschließung neuer Horizonte als Übersetzungstechnik," in *Horizonte biblischer Texte: Festschrift für Joseph Oesch zum 60. Geburtstag* (eds. G. Fischer and A. Vonach; OBO 196; Göttingen: Vandenhoeck & Ruprecht, 2003), 59–70.

Walser, G., *Jeremiah: A Commentary Based on Ieremias in Codex Vaticanus* (Septuagint Commentary Series; Leiden: Brill, 2012).

Ziegler, J., *Beiträge zur Ieremias-Septuaginta* (MSU 6; Göttingen: Vandenhoeck & Ruprecht, 1958).

Ziegler, J., *Ieremias, Baruch, Threni, Epistula Ieremiae* (Septuaginta Vetus Testamentum Graecum 15; Göttingen: Vandenhoeck & Ruprecht, 1957).

Georg Fischer

8
Ezekiel

Ezechiel

8.1 Textual History of Ezekiel

8.1.1 Relevant Witnesses and Text Editions

8.1.1.1 Hebrew Witnesses

All major Hebrew witnesses to Ezekiel date from the medieval period (→ 8.2.2.5). Fragments of six scrolls have been recovered from the Judean Desert that contain all or part of the following verses:[1] Ezek 1:10–13, 16–17, 20–24 (4QEzek^b); 4:3–6 (11QEzek); 4:16–5:1 (1QEzek); 5:11–17; 7:9–12 (11QEzek); 10:5–15; 10:17–11:11 (4QEzek^a); 16:31–33 (3QEzek); 23:2–3 (4QEzek^c); 23:14–18, 44–47 (4QEzek^a); 35:11–15; 36:1–10, 13–14, 17–35; 37:1–16, 23, 28; 38:1–4, 7–8 (MasEzek); 41:3–5 (4QEzek^a). Two of these texts can be regarded as proto-Masoretic and two can be regarded as semi-Masoretic (→ 8.2.1). The remaining three are too small for meaningful identification (1QEzek, 3QEzek, 4QEzek^c), and there is some question as to whether or not these represent manuscripts of the book or fragments of excerpted texts (→ 8.2.1.1–2,5).[2] Based upon the fragments of 11QEzek (→ 8.2.1.6) that can be read, it appears to be a nearly complete scroll of the book. Unfortunately, it cannot be unrolled. Its textual character remains a mystery.[3]

Editions of all the Qumran manuscripts are available in the *DJD series.[4] For the Masada scroll, see Talmon, "Fragments" and Talmon and Yadin, *Masada VI* (→ 8.2.1.7).

8.1.1.2 Major Greek Witnesses

There are three complete uncial manuscripts of Ezekiel (LXX^B, LXX^A, and LXX^Q), one nearly complete manuscript (LXX^{967}), and four that are fragmentary (LXX^{988}, LXX^{922}, LXX^{927}, and LXX^Z, a fragmentary uncial palimpsest). Of these, LXX$^{967, 988, B,}$ and ^{Z} are the most important for mapping Ezekiel's textual history (→ 8.3.2; → 6–9.1.6).[5]

LXX^{967} is dated to the late second or early third century C.E. and covers Ezek 11:25–48:35 (Kenyon, *Chester Beatty*; Johnson, *Scheide*[6]). It manifests several significant differences from (proto-)MT (→ 8.2.2): 1) It is significantly shorter, having some 350 minuses throughout, which total 4–5 percent of MT;[7] 2) It has several large minuses, vis-à-vis MT, including Ezek 12:26–28, 32:24b–26, and 36:23c–38; 3) It has several unique pluses, not represented in LXX^B (e.g., Ezek 35:8, 38:20; 39:4); 4) It has a different order of chapters in Ezekiel 36–39 (Ezek 36:1–23b, 38, 39, 37). LXX^{988}, the Antinoopolis Papyrus, though only preserving parts of Ezekiel 33–34, appears to share a common ancestor with LXX^{967}, indicated by readings unique to the two manuscripts.[8] For the whole of LXX^{967}, one must consult four sources: Kenyon, *Chester Beatty*; Johnson, Gehman, and Kase, *Scheide*, Fernández-Galiano, "Nuevas Paginas," and Jahn, *Kölner Teil*. LXX^{988} was published in 1950 by Roberts.[9]

Codex Vaticanus (LXX^B or 1209), dating from the mid-fourth century C.E., is the oldest manuscript of the complete book of Ezekiel in any language. Though pre-Hexaplaric, LXX^B is more closely aligned with (proto-)MT (→ 8.2.2) in *certain* respects than is LXX^{967}. LXX^B represents most of the same small minuses vis-à-vis MT and is also lacking Ezek 36:23c–38. However, it does not lack Ezek

---

[1] See Lange, *Handbuch*, 325–34.
[2] Brooke, "Qumran and New Testament."
[3] The fragment of Ezek 5:12–13 from 11QEzek shows similarities to LXX (→ 8.3), which is suggestive of its potential importance. See E.D. Herbert, "4. 11QEzekiel," *DJD* XXIII (1998): 15–28 (26).
[4] For bibliographies see → 8.2.1.

[5] For brief descriptions of the other Greek codices, see Olley, *Ezekiel*, 8–12.
[6] Different portions of the Scheide edition (*The John H. Scheide Biblical Papyri: Ezekiel* [Princeton University Studies in Papyrology 3; Princeton: Princeton University Press, 1938]) were prepared by the three authors, A.C. Johnson, H.S. Gehman, and E.H. Kase. When necessary, I will cite the authors individually as follows: Johnson, *Scheide*; Gehman, *Scheide*; Kase, *Scheide*.
[7] Marquis, "Word-Order."
[8] Fernández Galiano, "Antinoopolitano"; Fraenkel, "Nachtrag."
[9] C.H. Roberts, *Antinoopolis*; see also Fernández-Galiano, "Antinoopolitano."

12:26–28 or 32:24b–26, and its chapter order in Ezekiel 36–39 agrees with MT. LXX[B] is available in a colour facsimile edition, published in 1999,[10] that is superior to the sometimes-blurry 1907 edition.[11]

Codex Zuqninensis rescriptus, or codex LXX[Z], is a fragmentary palimpsest dated between the sixth and eighth centuries C.E.[12] It is the earliest example of the Lucianic text of Ezekiel (→ 6–9.1.6), which is also represented in manuscripts LXX[22, 36, 48, 51, 96, 231, 763]. A complete transcription of LXX[Z] was published by Tisserant in 1911.[13] In addition, Wevers conducted an exhaustive examination of Lucian-Ezek in 2003,[14] clarifying its similarities to and differences from MT (→ 8.2.2), LXX[B], Th, and Sym (→ 6–9.1.5).

8.1.2 History of Modern Research

The birth and death of modern theories regarding Ezekiel's textual history is a grand movement from one (nearly) universal position to another. Early modern critics viewed MT as a corrupt exemplar of the book that needed to be corrected in light of the more pristine form represented in LXX[B]. Contemporary critics tend to view proto-MT (→ 8.2.2) and OG (→ 8.3) as variant literary editions, a longer and a shorter edition, descended from a common ancestor.

8.1.2.1 The Modern Period to 1938

The period before 1938 saw the production of many works on the textual history of Ezekiel, including those by Merx, Cornill, Toy, Jahn, Rothstein (1st ed. 1913; 4th ed. 1922), and Cooke.[15] Most featured a rigorous attempt to deal with every text-critical issue, however minute, in a quest to recover an older, more original text. Underlying this effort were the conclusions, based upon close comparison of LXX[B] (→ 8.3) with MT (→ 8.2.2), that: a) MT and LXX are both descended from a common parent text; and b) MT represents a late, corrupt text form. George Adam Cooke expressed the views and aims of the age most eloquently: "In the Hebrew Bible perhaps no book, except 1 and 2 Samuel, has suffered more injury to its text than Ezekiel ... our problem is to recover a text which shall be free from alterations and corruptions, and so far nearer to the original."[16] The central point in the period was the production of Cornill's critical edition of Ezekiel, in which he presented a reconstruction of Ezekiel's *Urtext*, buttressed by an exhaustive apparatus.[17]

Because of the priority granted to LXX, a number of studies were dedicated to its history and character. Central to this scholarship was a debate regarding the number of translators involved in its production (→ 8.3.5). In this period, little attention was given to articulating the precise relationship between the Greek witnesses and MT. Scholars were largely content to characterize the MT pluses as corruptions of the book.

---

[10] *Bibliorum sacrorum Graecorum Codex Vaticanus B*.

[11] *Bibliorum SS. Graecorum Codex Vaticanus 1209 [Cod. B] denuo phototypice expressus*.

[12] To be precise, Ezekiel is represented by z[V] (Vat. Syr. 162) and z[VI] (Vat. Syr. 162 and Brit. Mus. Add. 14665). See Fraenkel, "Nachtrag," 356–58.

[13] E. Tisserant, "Notes sur la recension lucianique d'Ézéchiel," *RB* 8 (1911): 384–90.

[14] Wevers, "The L Text."

[15] Merx, "Der Werth der Septuaginta," 65–77; Cornill, *Das Buch des Propheten Ezechiel*; C.H. Toy, *The Book of the Prophet Ezekiel: Critical Edition of the Hebrew Text with Notes* (SBOT; Leipzig: J.C. Hinrichs, 1899); G. Jahn, *Das Buch Ezechiel auf Grund Septuaginta hergestellt, übersetzt und kritisch erklärt* (Leipzig: Eduard Pfeiffer, 1905); J.W. Rothstein, *Ezechiel: Übersetzt und Erklärt* (4th ed.; KAT; Leipzig: Deichert, 1922); and G.A. Cooke, *A Critical and Exegetical Commentary on the Book of Ezekiel* (ICC; Edinburgh: T & T Clark, 1936).

[16] Cooke, *Ezekiel*, xl. Cooke refers to LXX as a "weapon" to be used against MT (*Ezekiel*, xli).

[17] Cornill, *Ezechiel*; similarly, Jahn, *Ezechiel*. These efforts were often paired with an assumption that most or all of the hypothetical *Urtext* stemmed from the hand of the prophet Ezekiel or his immediate circle. See, for example, the commentaries and studies by H. von Ewald, *Die Propheten des Alten Bundes erklärt* (Stuttgart: Adolph Krabbe, 1841); F. Hitzig, *Der Prophet Ezechiel erklärt* (KHAT 8; Leipzig: Weidmann, 1847); R. Smend, *Der Prophet Ezechiel* (2nd ed.; KHAT; Leipzig: S. Hirzel, 1880); A. Bertholet, *Das Buch Hesekiel* (KHAT 12; Leipzig: J.C.B. Mohr, 1897); and V. Herntrich, *Ezechielprobleme* (BZAW 61; Gießen: Töpelmann, 1932).

8.1.2.2 From 1937 to 1986

The period from 1937 to 1986 was characterized by advances and disagreements in the study of LXX-Ezek (→ 8.3) and by new models for reconstructing Ezekiel's literary history. The two most important developments were the publication of LXX^{967} (begun in 1937; → 8.3.2) and the completion of the Göttingen edition of LXX-Ezek (→ 8.3.2).[18] Editions of two of the fragmentary Hebrew manuscripts of Ezekiel from Qumran were also released (1QEzek: 1955; 3QEzek: 1962).[19] The importance of these developments for the text history of Ezekiel only began to be appreciated later (→ 8.1.2.3). In this same period, Zimmerli[20] and Greenberg[21] articulated divergent models of Ezekiel's text history, models that would establish the trajectory of research and debate in subsequent decades.

The publication of LXX^{967} was complex because leaves of the manuscript are held in four locations. They were published independently over a thirty-five year period (1937–1972) in three different languages: Chester Beatty: Ezek 11:25–17:21;[22] John Scheide: Ezek 19:12–37:4, including Ezekiel 38–39;[23] Madrid: Ezek 28:19–29:12; 32:30–34:6; and 37:4–43:8;[24] Cologne, Ezek 11:25–21:14; 25:5–26:9; 43:9–48:35.[25] Each edition evaluates the papyrus differently and the apparatuses and analyses vary widely in their detail.

The early publications of Kenyon and Johnson, Gehman, and Kase took a high view of LXX^{967}. They advanced several important conclusions, reinforced by various independent studies:[26]

1. Kenyon, Gehman, and Payne, in particular, affirmed the close affinity of LXX^{967} to LXX^B, although there is enough variance to underscore the independence of LXX^{967}.[27]
2. LXX^{967} and LXX^B represent different pre-Hexaplaric traditions, though LXX^{967} is closer to OG.[28]
3. Johnson and Gehman identified a group of minuscules, LXX$^{22, 23, 36, 48, 51, 231}$, that shared a number of distinctive readings with LXX^{967} and constitute a "fairly consistent group."[29]
4. LXX^A (excluding the Hexaplaric additions) agrees, on many occasions, with LXX^{967} and must be considered a valuable witness even when it disagrees with LXX^B.[30]
5. Old Latin witnesses, especially *Wirceburgensis*, appear to be based on a text resembling LXX^{967}.[31]
6. The Syro-Hexapla (→ 6–9.2.4.3) tends to agree with LXX^B against LXX^{967}.[32]

In 1952, Ziegler published the first Göttingen edition of Ezechiel.[33] In this edition, he took a distinctively different line than Kenyon, Johnson, Gehman, and Kase. Though Ziegler acknowledged the importance of LXX^{967} for the reconstruction of OG, he was hesitant to grant it supremacy over LXX^B. Ziegler grouped LXX$^{967, 988, B}$, VL, and Coptic as related witnesses (the B group).[34] He was most

---

[18] Ziegler, *Ezechiel* (2nd ed. 1977).
[19] D. Barthélemy, "9. Ézéchiel," *DJD* I: 68–69; M. Baillet, "1. Ézéchiel," *DJD* III/1: 94.
[20] Zimmerli, *Ezekiel 1*; Zimmerli, *Ezekiel 2*.
[21] Greenberg, "Ancient Versions"; Greenberg, "Valid Criteria."
[22] Kenyon, *Chester Beatty*.
[23] Johnson et al., *Scheide*.
[24] Fernández-Galiano, "Nuevas Paginas."
[25] Jahn, *Papyrus 967*.
[26] See especially O. Procksch, *Studien zur Geschichte der Septuaginta: Die Propheten* (Leipzig: Hinrichs, 1910); Gehman, "The Relations between the Hebrew Text of Ezekiel and that of the John H. Scheide Papyri"; Gehman, "The Relations between the John H. Scheide Papyri and that of the Other Greek Mss. of Ezekiel"; J. Ziegler, "Die Bedeutung des Chester Beatty-Scheide Papyrus 967 für die Textüberlieferung der Ezechiel-Septuaginta"; Payne, "The Relationship of the Chester Beatty Papyri of Ezekiel to Codex Vaticanus"; and Wevers, "Status Constructus."
[27] Kenyon, *Chester Beatty*, x–xii; Gehman, "Other Greek Mss."; Payne, "Codex Vaticanus."
[28] Johnson et al., *Scheide*, 79.
[29] Johnson et al., *Scheide*, 21, 73–79.
[30] Wevers, "Status Constructus," 216; Johnson et al., *Scheide*, 42–47. As might be expected, where LXX^A agrees with LXX^{967} against LXX^B, Lucian not infrequently agrees with LXX^A and LXX^{967} (see also Wevers, "The L Text").
[31] Johnson et al., *Scheide*, 42–47; see also Bogaert, "Vetus Latina"; Lust, "Oldest Greek Manuscript."
[32] Johnson et al., *Scheide*, 73–79. But note the cautions on this point in Johnson et al., *Scheide*, 75–77.
[33] Ziegler, *Ezechiel*.
[34] Ziegler did not have access to LXX^{988} for the production of his Ezechiel edition. He describes its relationship to the B group in J. Ziegler, *Susanna, Daniel, Bet et Draco* (Septuaginta

willing to read with LXX⁹⁶⁷ when it agreed with LXXᴮ, VL, and Coptic, but tended to follow LXXᴮ, even when it stood against the rest of the group. Only LXXᴮ, in Ziegler's view, was free of Hexaplaric influences. For Ziegler, then, LXX⁹⁶⁷ was merely "a valuable support of B."[35]

In his 1953 *Biblica* study,[36] Ziegler reaffirmed his view and clarified his understanding of the relationship of LXX⁹⁶⁷ to MT as follows: some verses in LXX⁹⁶⁷ show evidence of having been corrected toward MT, and thus the manuscript should not be given priority over LXXᴮ.[37] Thus, when LXX⁹⁶⁷ reads with other witnesses against MT it is strong evidence for OG, but when it reads with MT, its readings reflect secondary adjustments toward MT. Ziegler's position has not gone undisputed, but it continues to be adopted as the starting point for many scholars, especially in Germany.[38]

Ziegler did not have access to all the pages of LXX⁹⁶⁷ and LXX⁹⁸⁸ when he prepared his 1952 edition.[39] In 1977, a revised edition was prepared by Detlef Fraenkel.[40] Though Fraenkel seems to have a higher view of the importance of LXX⁹⁶⁷ than Ziegler, the 1977 edition reprinted Ziegler's text, apparatus, and introduction unchanged. Fraenkel merely added a supplement to the end of the volume.[41] In it, he listed additional evidence based on the Madrid and Cologne portions of LXX⁹⁶⁷ and on new leaves of the Antinoopolis papyrus (LXX⁹⁸⁸).

The texts released and the debates undertaken in this era have wide implications, not only for the recovery of OG-Ezek but also for the textual history of the Hebrew book. Despite this, it was outside of the field of Septuagint studies that sweeping models of Ezekiel's textual history were being proposed, models that did *not* take into account the implications of the evidence from the versions. With Zimmerli's *Ezechiel 1* and *2* (1969; Eng. trans.: 1979–1983), a new era in the critical study of Ezekiel emerged. Zimmerli characterized the book of Ezekiel as the product of many layers of *Fortschreibungen* "supplements." This characterized not only the redactional evolution of the book but also the expansions witnessed in the texts and versions. He offered an exhaustive description of the ongoing growth of the book from its hypothetical origins to MT. The notion of an *Urtext* corrupted by ill-fated scribal interventions was gone. Expansions, regardless of their time of origin, were viewed as thoughtful, deliberate, and literate. For Zimmerli, literary criticism and textual criticism were not divisible in any meaningful way. Zimmerli, however, did not utilize much of the new Septuagint scholarship. Though Zimmerli had access to early transcriptions of LXX⁹⁶⁷, including those released for publication after his commentary appeared, he relegated the papyrus to his discussion of "The Later History of the Book and its Text."[42] Because of this, and because the evidence from the Judean Desert discoveries was still emerging, he was not able to integrate the data from textual criticism with his historical-critical innovations to produce a comprehensive model of the textual history of Ezekiel.

In a pair of manifesto-style essays written in 1977 and 1986, Greenberg – singling out scholars like Zimmerli – called on the academy to abandon attempts to recover an "improved" text, either by historical-critical or text-critical means.[43] He

---

Vetus Testamentum Graecum 16.2; Göttingen: Vandenhoeck & Ruprecht, 1954), 77–78 (volume revised by O. Munnch in 1999).

[35] Ziegler, "Chester Beatty-Scheide Papyrus 967," 77.

[36] Ziegler, "Zur Textgestaltung der Ezechiel-Septuaginta."

[37] See, for example, the lengthy discussion of Ezek 27:16 in Johnson et al., *Scheide*, 98–101.

[38] Note the criticisms of this point by P. Katz ("Zur Textgestaltung der Ezechiel-Septuaginta," *Bib* 35 [1954]: 29–39), as well as the extended discussion in Lilly, *Two Books*, 38–60.

[39] J. Ziegler, *Ezechiel* (Septuaginta Vetus Testamentum Graecum 16.1; Göttingen: Vandenhoeck & Ruprecht, 1952).

[40] J. Ziegler, *Ezechiel* (2nd ed. with addendum by D. Fraenkel; Septuaginta Vetus Testamentum Graecum 16.1; Göttingen: Vandenhoeck & Ruprecht, 1977).

[41] D. Fraenkel, "Nachtrag zur 1. Auflage von 1952," in Ziegler, *Ezechiel*, 331–52.

[42] Zimmerli, *Ezechiel 1*, 76–77.

[43] In his 1977 essay, "The Use of Ancient Versions," Greenberg singled out the following for criticism: Cornill, *Ezechiel*; G. Fohrer, *Ezechiel* (HAT 13; Tübingen: Mohr, 1955); W. Eichrodt, *Der Prophet Hesekiel* (3rd ed.; ATD 22; Göttingen: Vandenhoeck & Ruprecht, 1968; Eng. trans.: 1970); J.W. Wevers, *Ezekiel* (NCB

contended that OG and MT represent "two versions, each with its own quality and its own coherence."[44] He further argued, based upon finds in the Judean Desert, that MT was as old as the *Vorlage* of OG and that "this means that in the third century B.C.E. … several forms [of Ezekiel] were extant and considered authoritative."[45] Like Zimmerli, Greenberg did not acknowledge or account for all of the available evidence. In Greenberg's case, he particularly overlooked new arguments regarding the relationship of OG to (proto-)MT.[46] Despite Zimmerli's and Greenberg's opposing points of view, together they laid the groundwork for a comprehensive model of the transmission history of the book.

8.1.2.3 From 1986 to the Early Twenty-First Century[47]

Major editions of the Ezekiel fragments from Qumran Cave 4 and the Masada scroll were published between 1996 and 1999 (→ 8.2.1). The importance of the Judean Desert finds for the textual history of Ezekiel does not lie in the Ezekiel fragments themselves. Their importance lies in the broader picture of Second Temple textual developments that they present. The scrolls made it apparent that, for certain books, multiple texts were in circulation simultaneously and (potentially) in use within individual communities. This is most plainly the case for Joshua, Jeremiah, Proverbs, Esther, and Daniel as well as portions of Exodus, Numbers, Deuteronomy, Judges, Samuel, Nehemiah, and Chronicles.[48] This discovery, as it emerged, introduced new possibilities for explaining the relationship of LXX-Ezek (→ 8.3) to MT-Ezek (→ 8.2.2).

Thus, the evidence from the Judean Desert witnesses and the ongoing analysis of the Greek witnesses (especially LXX^B and LXX^{967}) provided, eventually, the necessary evidence for a more-or-less complete picture of the transmission history of Ezekiel to emerge. Two scholars have done the most to compile this evidence into a new portrait of the literary history of Ezekiel: Johann Lust and Emanuel Tov.[49] In a seminal 1981 article, "Ezekiel 36–40 in the Oldest Greek Manuscript," Lust asserted, against Ziegler, that LXX^{967} is the best witness to OG. In it, Lust compared MT with LXX^{967}, focusing particular attention on the large plus in MT-Ezek 36:23c–38 and the alternate arrangement of Ezekiel 38; 39; 37. He proposed that the two texts represent variant editions of the book. The older edition is represented by LXX^{967}. The younger MT edition reflects anti-apocalyptic, Pharisaic sentiments.[50] Lust continued to advance and nuance this position in subsequent publications that extended his ideas to text segments like Ezekiel 7 and 32:24b–26,[51] though he gradually abandoned the Pharisaic hypothesis.[52]

In 1986, Tov also characterized LXX-Ezek as a variant edition of the book, earlier than MT.[53] Tov focused attention on differences in arrangement in Ezekiel 7 and on the many small expansions to MT-Ezek. He concluded that "the MT and LXX texts of Ez. reflect two different redactional stages of the book." As such "*none* of the readings should be preferred *textually* to another one."[54] Whereas

---

Commentary; Grand Rapids: Eerdmans, 1982); and Zimmerli, *Ezechiel 1 and 2* (1969).

[44] Greenberg, "Ancient Versions," 217.

[45] Greenberg, "Ancient Versions," 219.

[46] See also Teeter, *Scribal Laws*, 219–20.

[47] A summary of findings from the period can be found at the end of this section.

[48] Tov, *TCHB, 283–326; Ulrich; See also E. Ulrich, "The Text of the Hebrew Scriptures at the Time of Hillel and Jesus," in *Congress Volume Basel 2001* (ed. A. Lemaire; VTSup 92; Leiden: Brill, 2002), 85–108; Ulrich, *DSS.

[49] See, in the bibliography: Lust, "Use of Textual Witnesses"; Lust, "Ezekiel Manuscripts in Qumran"; Lust, "Major Divergencies"; Lust, "The Ezekiel Text"; Tov, "Recensional"; "Some Sequential Differences"; Tov, "Glosses"; Tov, "Hebrew Scripture Editions."

[50] Lust did not characterize the *Tendenz* of LXX^{967}, focusing instead on the unique features of MT.

[51] See, in the bibliography, Lust, "Ezekiel 36–40"; Lust, "Use of Textual Witnesses"; Lust, "Major Divergencies"; Lust, "The Ezekiel Text."

[52] See Lust, "Stepbrothers," and the discussion in Crane, *Restoration*, 236–45.

[53] Tov, "Recensional."

[54] Tov, "Recensional," 101 (italics original); see also Tov, *TCU, 307–11.

Lust focused attention on the significance of LXX^{967} for the textual history of Ezekiel, Tov focused in subsequent publications on text pluriformity as a central component of the textual history of Ezekiel.[55]

The emerging view that OG and MT represent variant editions of the book has been extended by several recent monographs. Crane's 2006 study of Ezekiel 36–39 examined differences in the "theology of restoration" presented in LXX^{967}, LXX^B, and MT.[56] Like Lust, Crane began with the assumption that LXX^{967} is the closest witness to OG. Crane then set out to nuance Lust's views. He suggested that MT-Ezek reflects a Second Temple political context. Through rearrangement and expansion, the vision of peaceful national reunification in LXX^{967} (with Ezek 37:24–28 immediately preceding Ezekiel 40–48) was recast as a "call to arms" in the face of foreign domination.[57]

In 2010, Mackie concluded an exhaustive study of the pluses in MT and OG (identified with Ziegler's critical text).[58] He produced a descriptive typology of the types and purposes of the expansions. The basis of Mackie's study was the recognition that the differences in quantity and arrangement between MT and LXX constitute different editions of the book.[59] However, distinct from other studies, he highlighted similarities in the *production* of the two editions. He concluded that expansions to MT and LXX, though achieving different results, were conducted by the same scribal techniques and inspired by similar aims. Expansion and alteration was motivated not just by historical concerns (as Lust and Crane emphasize) but also by purely interpretive and inner-biblical considerations.

By the time Lilly completed her Emory University dissertation in 2010, she could assume broad acceptance of the view that LXX^{967} and MT represent alternative editions.[60] Filling a significant gap in existing research, Lilly examined LXX^{967} as an independent document with its own ideological profile. Lilly isolated several tendencies that distinguish LXX^{967} from MT, *Tendenzen* that emerge only when a comprehensive survey of variants between the two texts are examined. She highlighted unique perspectives in LXX^{967} on prophecy, the fate of the slain, Israel's restoration, and the war with Gog. Lilly's study is the most exhaustive yet attempted on the different editions of Ezekiel and has clarified the relationship of LXX^{967} to MT, in particular.

Similarly, in 2012, Rösel completed an exhaustive analysis of all divergent features of MT and OG in Ezekiel 38–39.[61] Like Mackie, Rösel equates Ziegler's text with OG. Rösel's analysis extends to argumentative and ideological distinctives that are only apparent when the cumulative differences between MT and LXX are compared. He, too, concluded that the two texts, though descended from a common Hebrew progenitor, represent different literary editions with different ideological trajectories.[62] For example, MT has linked the Gog Oracles more tightly with the book, as can be seen, for example, in the addition of הר "mountain(s)" in Ezek 38:8, 21 connecting to Ezekiel 6 and 36, and of עב׳ר "to pass over" in Ezek 39:11, 14 connecting to Ezek 33:28.[63]

Thus, current consensus holds that MT and OG represent different literary editions of the book, one longer and one shorter, with different ideological profiles. The consensus view, though, has not been achieved without opposition. Block re-

---

[55] See esp. "Hebrew Scripture Editions" and *TCHB, 299–301. Tov has not addressed LXX^{967} specifically. He has continued to affirm that recensional rewriting is evident only in a "thin layer of literary (editorial) differences ... in 7:3–9" (*TCHB, 299).

[56] Crane, *Restoration* = "The Restoration of Israel: Ezekiel 36–39 in Early Jewish Interpretation: A Textual-Comparative Study of the Oldest Hebrew and Greek Manuscripts" (PhD diss., Murdoch University, 2006).

[57] Crane, *Restoration*, 251–54.

[58] Mackie, "Expanding."

[59] Mackie prefers not to use the word "edition" for Ezekiel because it suggests a *systematic* redaction of the whole book ("Expanding," 279–81).

[60] Lilly, *Two Books* = "Papyrus 967: A Variant Literary Edition of Ezekiel" (PhD diss., Emory University, 2010).

[61] Rösel, *JHWHs Sieg*.

[62] Rösel, *JHWHs Sieg*, 119–26.

[63] Rösel, *JHWHs Sieg*, 85, 117; cf. Tooman, *Gog of Magog*, 184–85.

jected the evidence of LXX⁹⁶⁷ as late and corrupt, a view he later surrendered.⁶⁴ Likewise Patmore, appealing to the evidence from Qumran and Masada, has questioned arguments in favor of the priority of LXX⁹⁶⁷. Echoing the arguments of Greenberg from thirty years earlier, Patmore has contended that priority cannot be granted to either edition of Ezekiel.⁶⁵

Though not all their findings are congruent, the full picture of the literary history of Ezekiel was further clarified in this period by targeted studies of the Syriac text (→ 6–9.1.4),⁶⁶ Ethiopic text (→ 6–9.2.3.3),⁶⁷ Lucian (→ 6–9.1.6),⁶⁸ and Old Latin (→ 6–9.2.1) and Vulgate (→ 6–9.1.7).⁶⁹ Most important for the textual history of Ezekiel are the analyses of Lucian. Though post-Hexaplaric, LXX^L represents an important link in the evolutionary chain of Ezekiel. Lucian is a revision of a Greek exemplar toward MT that is heavily reliant on the Hexapla, and, hence, has many similarities to Theodotion (→ 6–9.1.5). It also, on occasion, manifests readings from Symmachus (→ 6–9.1.5), although this has sometimes been overstated. Though, most likely, the result of inner-Greek development, Lucian represents one of the most comprehensive attempts to adapt OG to the MT text form (albeit in Greek).⁷⁰

The findings of this period of academic ferment are diverse and multifaceted. They can be summarized as follows:

1. All pre-Masoretic Hebrew texts of Ezekiel can be regarded as proto-Masoretic, or in some cases, semi-Masoretic, pointing to the antiquity of the text form (→ 8.2.1.6). However, it should be cautioned that the Qumran fragments may well be from excerpted texts.⁷¹ MasEzek, the most extensive of the Hebrew sources (= Ezek 35:11–38:14), deviates only slightly from MT.⁷² Expansions reflected only in the MT tradition are already present in MasEzek, including the recurring difference in expressions of the divine

---

⁶⁴ Block, *Ezekiel 25–48* (NICOT; Grand Rapids: Eerdmans, 1998), 337–43. See also Lust, "Stepbrothers," 15–21; Crane, *Restoration*, 236–45.

⁶⁵ H. Patmore, "The Shorter and Longer Texts of Ezekiel: The Implications of the Manuscript Finds from Masada and Qumran," *JSOT* 32 (2007): 231–42. It also should be noted that many of the Hebrew texts from Qumran to which Patmore appeals (e.g., 4Q73–75) have been tentatively identified as excerpted texts and do not represent any particular "edition of the book" (Brooke, "Qumran and New Testament"; → 8.2.1.2, → 8.2.1.5).

⁶⁶ W. Baars, "Peshiṭta Institute Communications IX: A Palimpsest of Ezekiel Reconstructed," *VT* 20 (1970): 527–36; J.A. Lund, "Converse Translation in *Peshitta Ezekiel*" (http://www.reltech.org/TC/v06/Lund2001.html; online revision of an essay read at Syriac Symposium III on June 19, 1999, at the University of Notre Dame); J.A. Lund, "Syntactic Features of the Syrohexapla of *Ezekiel*," Aramaic Studies 4 (2006): 67–81; M.J. Mulder, "Ezekiel 20:39 and the Peshitta Version," *VT* 25 (1975): 233–36; M.J. Mulder, "Die neue Pešiṭta-Ausgabe von Ezechiel," in *Ezekiel and His Book: Textual and Literary Criticism and their Relation* (ed. J. Lust; BETL 74; Leuven: Peeters, 1986), 101–10; M.J. Mulder, "Some Remarks on the Peshitta Translation of the Book of Ezekiel," in *The Peshitta: Its Early Text and History: Papers Read at the Peshitta Symposium Held at Leiden 30–31 August 1985* (eds. P.B. Dirksen and M.J. Mulder; Monographs of the Peshitta Institute Leiden 4; Leiden: Brill, 1988), 169–82; H.F. van Rooy, "Agreement between LXX and Peshitta versus MT in Ezekiel: Some Important Examples," in *Translating a Translation: The LXX and Its Modern Translations in the Context of Early Judaism* (eds. H. Ausloos et al.; BETL 213; Leuven: Peeters, 2008), 213–27.

⁶⁷ M. Knibb, "Two Notes on the Ethiopic Text of Ezekiel," in *Semitic Studies in Honour of Edward Ullendorff* (ed. G. Kahn; Studies in Semitic Languages and Linguistics 47; Leiden: Brill, 2005), 236–44.

⁶⁸ N. Fernandez-Marcos, "On Symmachus and Lucian in Ezekiel," in *Interpreting Translation: Studies on the LXX and Ezekiel in Honour of Johan Lust* (eds. F. García Martínez and M. Vervenna; BETL 192; Leuven: Peeters, 2005), 151–61; Tisserant, "Notes sur la recension lucianique d'Ézéchiel"; Wevers, "The L Text."

⁶⁹ P.-M. Bogaert, "Le témoignage de la Vetus Latina dans l'étude de la tradition des Septante: Ezéchiel et Daniel dans le Papyrus 967," *Bib* 59 (1978): 384–95; Ranke, *Wirceburgensium*; H.F. van Rooy, "The Minor Versions and the Text of Ezekiel," in *Florilegium Lovaniense: Studies in Septuagint and Textual Criticism in Honour of Florentino García Martínez* (eds. H. Ausloos et al.; BETL 224; Leuven: Peeters, 2008), 493–506.

⁷⁰ Wevers concluded ("The L Text," 115), and Fernandez-Marcos agreed ("On Symmachus," 160–61), that there is "no compelling evidence" that Lucian knew or used any Hebrew source(s).

⁷¹ See Brooke, "Qumran and New Testament," and discussion in Talmon and Yadin, *Masada VI*, 69–73.

⁷² Talmon, "Fragments," 33–37; 8.2.1.7.

name.⁷³ The same alignment with MT exists with respect to true variants.⁷⁴
2. LXX⁹⁶⁷, LXXᴮ, and MT are all descended from a common Hebrew progenitor or closely related progenitor texts.⁷⁵
    a. There is little evidence of textual error in LXX⁹⁶⁷ or LXXᴮ. Both are extremely accurate copies of Greek translations that closely represent their Hebrew *Vorlagen* in quantity and consistency of representative elements (→ 8.3.3; → 8.3.4).⁷⁶
    b. Disregarding variances in their arrangement and the numerous expansions in MT, the *Vorlagen* of LXX⁹⁶⁷ and LXXᴮ are substantively identical to the consonantal MT.⁷⁷
3. Numerous books and portions of books existed in alternative literary editions that circulated concurrently well beyond the Second Temple period. In as much as the Greek witnesses reflect an edition of Ezekiel that differs in arrangement, quantity, and *Tendenzen* from MT, Ezekiel can be added to this group.
4. The cumulative evidence suggests that LXXᴮ and LXX⁹⁶⁷ reflect different, pre-Hexaplaric instantiations of a developing Hebrew text. Several lines of evidence lead to this conclusion:
    a. Both LXX⁹⁶⁷ and LXXᴮ contain unique expansions and variants that point to their independent development. Among the expansions are the following in LXX⁹⁶⁷: Ezek 35:8, 38:20; 39:4. In LXXᴮ, unique expansions are found most densely in Ezekiel 40–43.⁷⁸
    b. Both LXX⁹⁶⁷ and LXXᴮ are shorter than MT, though LXX⁹⁶⁷ is slightly shorter than LXXᴮ. In MT-Ezek 32:24b–26, for example, LXX⁹⁶⁷ represents a minus of thirty-nine words, whereas LXXᴮ represents a minus of twenty-four words.⁷⁹
    c. The arrangement of Ezekiel 37–39 in LXXᴮ corresponds with MT. LXXᴮ and LXX⁹⁶⁷ both diverge from the arrangement in MT-Ezek 7. Ezekiel 7 is not extant in LXX⁹⁶⁷.⁸⁰
    d. LXX⁹⁶⁷ includes three major minuses vis-à-vis MT, Ezek 12:26–28; 32:24b–26; and 36:23c–38, none of which can be attributed plausibly to scribal error.⁸¹
    e. There is little evidence to suggest that the differences between LXXᴮ and LXX⁹⁶⁷ reflect inner-Greek development.⁸²
5. Lucian represents a correction toward the (proto-)MT edition of the book. This is suggested, for example, by the fact that MT shares forty-five asterisked readings with LXXᴸ. Even LXXᴬ only agrees with MT in thirty-five asterisked readings.⁸³

These diverse findings have important effects for the proposals of Zimmerli and Greenberg. Both models were correct in certain respects and less correct in others. The available manuscript evidence suggests that the latter stages of the growth and development of the book are characterized by progressive expansion and rearrangement, conducted in a manner akin to Zimmerli's model of progressive supplementation. With Greenberg, it must be acknowledged that these developments

---

⁷³ The full list of pluses in MasEzek corresponding to MT appear in Talmon, "Fragments," 37–38. Regarding the divine name, e.g., LXX: κύριος "Lord" vs. MT and MasEzek: אדני יהוה "Lord, God." On this complex issue, see the excellent summation by Olley ("Part 1," 145–46) and the bibliography there.

⁷⁴ Talmon ("Fragments," 38–39) groups Ezek 35:12 in this class: MT כל "all" vs. LXX φωνῆς = קול (both meaning "voice").

⁷⁵ Lilly, *Two Books*, 128–29.

⁷⁶ Marquis, "Lexical Equivalents," 1987; D.M. O'Hare, "*Have You Seen, Son of Man?*," 33–71; Lilly, *Two Books*, 127–28. Note, however, that there is an open question as to how many translators may have been responsible for OG-Ezek. See → 8.3.5, as well as the recent summaries in O'Hare (1–31) and Olley ("Part 1," 145–46).

⁷⁷ Marquis, "Word Order"; Marquis, "Consistency."

⁷⁸ Mackie, "Expanding," 349–51; Lilly, *Two Books*, 95–103; 128–29. See Ezek 40:12, 13, 16, 19, 21, 23, 27, 39, 41, 43, 44, 47, 48; 41:3, 15, 16, 21, 22; 42:1, 7, 10, 11, 14, 15, 16, 20; 43:1, 14, 16, 20. See also Marquis, "Lexical Equivalents" and Tov, "Recensional."

⁷⁹ Lust, "Major Divergences," 87–89; Lilly, *Two Books*, 119–20.

⁸⁰ Bogaert, "deux redactions"; Tov, "Recensional"; Mackie, "Expanding."

⁸¹ Lust, "Oldest"; Lust, "Textual Witnesses"; Lust, "Major Divergences"; Lilly, *Two Books*.

⁸² See the arguments in Lilly, *Two Books*, 128–29.

⁸³ See Wevers, "The L Text"; Lilly, *Two Books*.

resulted in different texts with their own logic and literary coherence. It now appears that at least two editions of the book circulated simultaneously in antiquity: a shorter text, represented most distinctively by LXX⁹⁶⁷, and a longer text, represented by MT. These editions differ not only in length but in order: order of verses in Ezekiel 7, and order of chapters in Ezekiel 37–39. Based on the translation character of LXX-Ezek (→ 8.3.3), it can be affirmed positively that both editions appear to be descended from a common progenitor and reflect different stages in the literary evolution of the book.

8.1.3 Future Directions

Within text-critical scholarship, there are several new horizons and open opportunities for significant research. Perhaps most needed is a comprehensive critical edition of LXX⁹⁶⁷. Likewise, the relationship between LXX^B and LXX⁹⁶⁷ is still not entirely clear. Both appear to represent pre-Hexaplaric witnesses (→ 8.3). Whether or not one or both are recensional – as Olley argues for LXX^B,[84] and Ziegler[85] for LXX⁹⁶⁷ – still requires exhaustive exploration. Their differences in translation technique also require exploration. Further, there is a new urgency to compare the text form of the many quotations and allusions to Ezekiel within Jewish Second Temple literature and early Christian sources with the extant texts and versions (→ 1.7.1). Finally, there is a new appreciation of the ways in which textual criticism is essential for understanding the early reception of Ezekiel's book, a field that is only beginning to be explored.[86]

Scholarship on Ezekiel, beyond the field of textual criticism, continues to be divided into two broad types. The first embraces MT exclusively, and largely rejects attempts to reconstruct its literary history (apart from correcting scribal errors or purging the occasional MT expansion).[87] This position is often reinforced by the contemporary scholarly interest in the various texts and versions as literary artefacts in their own right. The second, following in the footsteps of Zimmerli, is focused on the redaction of the book and increasingly cites the text-critical evidence for corroboration of the model.[88] More recently, a third position has begun to emerge that attempts to construct a redaction-critical model that *begins* with empirical evidence from the texts, versions, and rewritten Scriptures, rather than citing textual evidence in support of an existing model.[89]

Baars, W., "Peshiṭta Institute Communications IX: A Palimpsest of Ezekiel Reconstructed," *VT* 20 (1970): 527–36.
Bibliorum sacrorum Graecorum Codex Vaticanus B (Rome: Istituto poligrafico e Zecca dello Stato, 1999).
Bibliorum SS. Graecorum Codex Vaticanus 1209 (Cod. B) denuo phototypice expressus, Vol. 1: *Testamentum Vetus* (Mediolani: Ulricum Hoepli, 1907).
Bogaert, P.-M., "Les deux rédactions conservées (LXX et TM) d'Ézéchiel 7," in *Ezekiel and His Book: Textual and Literary Criticism and their Relation* (ed. J. Lust; BETL 74; Leuven: Peeters, 1986), 21–47.
Bogaert, P.-M., "Le témoignage de la Vetus Latina dans l'étude de la tradition des Septante: Ezéchiel et Daniel dans le Papyrus 967," *Bib* 59 (1978): 384–95.
Brooke, G., "Ezekiel in Some Qumran and New Testament Texts," in *Madrid Qumran Congress*, 317–37.
Cornill, C.H., *Das Buch des Propheten Ezechiel* (Leipzig: J.C. Hinrichs, 1886).
Crane, A.S., *Israel's Restoration: A Textual-Comparative*

---

[84] Olley, *Ezekiel*, 5.
[85] Ziegler, *Ezechiel*.
[86] See e.g., Teeter, *Scribal Laws*.
[87] E.g., D.I. Block, *The Book of Ezekiel 1–24* and *The Book of Ezekiel 25–48* (NICOT; Grand Rapids: Eerdmans, 1997–1998);

J. Becker, *Der priesterliche Prophet: Das Buch Ezechiel* (2 vols; SKK 11–12; Stuttgart: Kath. Bibelwerk, 1971); P. Joyce, *Ezekiel: A Commentary* (2nd ed.; LHBOTS 482; London: T & T Clark, 2009). Motives for adopting this position differ widely. For example, some view the book as a whole as a late pseudepigraph (e.g., Becker). Others are sceptical of the potential of redaction criticism (e.g., Block, Greenberg, Joyce).

[88] For example, K.-F. Pohlmann, *Ezechiel: Der Stand der theologischen Diskussion* (Darmstadt: WBG, 2008); K.-F. Pohlmann, *Der Prophet Hesekiel/Ezechiel 1–19* and *Der Prophet Hesekiel/Ezechiel 20–48* (ATD 22.1–2; Göttingen: Vandenhoeck & Ruprecht, 1996–2001); A. Klein, *Schriftauslegung im Ezechielbuch: Redaktionsgeschichtliche Untersuchungen zu Ez 34–39* (BZAW 391; Berlin and New York: Walter de Gruyter, 2008).

[89] Tooman, *Gog of Magog*, and "Covenant and Presence"; Rösel, *JHWHs Sieg*.

Exploration of Ezekiel 36–39 (VTSup 122; Leiden: Brill, 2008).

Fernández-Galiano, M., "El papiro Antinoopolitano de Ezequiel a la luz de las páginas Matritenses de 967," *Emerita* 39 (1971): 51–61.

Fernández-Galiano, M., "Nuevas Paginas del codice 967 del A.T. griego," *SPap* 10 (1971): 7–76.

Fraenkel, D., "Nachtrag zur 1. Auflage von 1952," in J. Ziegler, *Ezechiel* (2nd ed.; Septuaginta Vetus Testamentum Graecum 16.1; Göttingen: Vandenhoeck & Ruprecht, 1977).

Gehman, H.S., "The Relations between the Hebrew Text of Ezekiel and That of the John H. Scheide Papyri," *JAOS* 58 (1938): 92–102.

Gehman, H.S., "The Relations between the John H. Scheide Papyri and that of the Other Greek Mss. of Ezekiel," *JBL* 57 (1938): 281–87.

Greenberg, M., "The Use of Ancient Versions for Interpreting the Hebrew Text: A Sampling from Ezekiel ii 1–iii 11," in *Congress Volume: Göttingen 1977* (ed. J.A. Emerton; VTSup 29; Leiden: Brill, 1978), 131–48.

Greenberg, M., "What are Valid Criteria for Determining Inauthentic Matter in Ezekiel?" in *Ezekiel and His Book: Textual and Literary Criticism and their Relation* (ed. J. Lust; BETL 74; Leuven: Peeters, 1986), 123–35.

Jahn, L.G., *Der griechische Text des Buche Ezechiel nach dem Kölner Teil des Papyrus 967* (Papyrologische Texte und Abhandlungen 15; Bonn: Habelt, 1972).

Kenyon, F.G., *The Chester Beatty Biblical Papyri: Ezekiel*, Fasc. 7 (2 vols.; London: Emery Walker, 1937–1938).

Lange, **Handbuch*, 325–34.

Lilly, I.E., *Two Books of Ezekiel: Papyrus 967 and the Masoretic Text as Variant Literary Editions* (VTSup 150; Leiden: Brill, 2012).

Lust, J., "Ezekiel 36–40 in the Oldest Greek Manuscript," *CBQ* 43 (1981): 517–33.

Lust, J., "The Use of Textual Witnesses for the Establishment of the Text: The Shorter and Longer Texts of Ezekiel," in *Ezekiel and His Book: Textual and Literary Criticism and their Relation* (ed. J. Lust; BETL 74; Leuven: Peeters, 1986), 7–20.

Lust, J., "The Final Text and Textual Criticism: Ez 39,28," in *Ezekiel and His Book: Textual and Literary Criticism in their Interrelation* (ed. J. Lust; BETL 74; Leuven: Peeters, 1986), 48–54.

Lust, J., "Ezekiel Manuscripts in Qumran: Preliminary Edition of 4Q Ez a and b," in *Ezekiel and His Book: Textual and Literary Criticism in their Interrelation* (ed. J. Lust; BETL 74; Leuven: Peeters, 1986), 90–100.

Lust, J., "Exegesis and Theology in the Septuagint of Ezekiel: The Longer 'Pluses' and Ezek 43:1–9," in *VI Congress of the International Organization for Septuagint and Cognate Studies, Jerusalem 1986* (ed. C.E. Cox; SBLSCS 23; Atlanta: Scholars Press, 1987), 405–24.

Lust, J., "Textual Criticism of the Old Testament and of the New Testament: Stepbrothers?" in *New Testament Textual Criticism and Exegesis: Festschrift Joël Delobel* (ed. A. Denaux; BETL 161; Leuven: Peeters, 2002), 15–31.

Lust, J., "Major Divergences between LXX and MT in Ezekiel," in Schenker, **Earliest Text*, 83–92.

Lust, J., "The Ezekiel Text," in *Sôfer Mahîr: Essays in Honour of Adrian Schenker Offered by the Editors of Biblia Hebraica Quinta* (eds. Y.A.P. Goldman et al.; VTSup 110; Leiden: Brill, 2006): 153–67.

Lust, J., K. Hauspie, and A. Ternier, "Notes to the Septuagint: Ezekiel 6 and the Double Name," *ETL* 76 (2000): 396–403.

Mackie, T.P., "Expanding Ezekiel: The Hermeneutics of Scribal Addition in the Ancient Text Witnesses of the Book of Ezekiel" (PhD diss., University of Wisconsin-Madison, 2010).

Marquis, G., "Word Order as a Criterion for the Evaluation of Translation Technique in the LXX and the Evaluation of Word Order Variants as Exemplified in LXX-Ezekiel," *Text* 13 (1986): 59–84.

Marquis, G., "Consistency of Lexical Equivalents as a Criterion for the Evaluation of Translation Technique as Exemplified in the LXX of Ezekiel," in *VI Congress of the International Organization of Septuagint and Cognate Studies: Jerusalem, 1986* (ed. C. Cox; SBLSCS 23; Atlanta: SBL, 1987), 405–24.

Merx, A., "Der Werth der Septuaginta für die Textkritik des Alten Testaments, am Ezechiel aufgezeichnet," *Jahrbücher für Protestantische Theologie* 9 (1883): 65–77.

O'Hare, D.M., *"Have You Seen, Son of Man?" A Study in the Translation and Vorlage of LXX Ezekiel 40–48* (SBLSCS 57; Atlanta: Scholars Press, 2010).

Olley, J.W., *Ezekiel: A Commentary Based on Iezekiel in Codex Vaticanus* (Septuagint Commentary Series; Leiden: Brill, 2009).

Olley, J.W., "Trajectories of Ezekiel: Part 1," *CBR* 9 (2011): 137–70.

Olley, J.W., "Trajectories of Ezekiel: Part 2," *CBR* 10 (2011): 53–80.

Payne, J.B., "The Relationship of the Chester Beatty Papyri of Ezekiel to Codex Vaticanus," *JBL* 68 (1949): 251–65.

Ranke, E., *Par palimpsestorum Wirceburgensium antiquissimae Veteris Testamenti latinae fragmenta e codd. Rescriptus* (Vienna: Braumüller, 1871).

Roberts, C.H., *The Antinoopolis Papyri: Edited with Translations and Notes* (London: Egypt Exploration Society, 1950).

Rösel, C., *JHWHs Sieg über Gog aus Magog: Ez 38–39 im Masoretischen Text und in der Septuaginta* (WMANT 132; Göttingen: Neukirchener Verlag, 2012).

Rothstein, J.W., *Das Buch Ezechiel* (4th ed.; HSAT 1; Tübingen: Mohr, 1922).

Schwagmeier, P., "Untersuchungen zu Textgeschichte und Entstehung des Ezechielbuches in masoretischer und griechischer Überlieferung" (PhD diss., University of Zürich, 2004).

Talmon, S., "Fragments of an Ezekiel Scroll from Masada (Ezek 35:11–38:14) 1043–2220, MAS 1D," *OLP* 27 (1996): 29–49.

Talmon, S. and Y. Yadin, *Masada VI: Yigael Yadin Excavations 1963–1965, Final Reports: Hebrew Fragments from Masada* (Jerusalem: Israel Exploration Society, 1999).

Teeter, D.A., *Scribal Laws: Exegetical Variation in the Textual Transmission of Biblical Law in teh Late Second Temple Period* (FAT 92; Tübingen: Mohr Siebeck, 2014).

Tooman, W.A., *Gog of Magog: Reuse of Scripture and Compositional Technique in Ezekiel 38–39* (FAT 2.52; Tübingen: Mohr Siebeck, 2011).

Tooman, W.A., "Covenant and Presence in the Composition and Theology of Ezekiel," in *Divine Presence and Absence in Exilic and Post-Exilic Judaism: Studies of the Sofja Kovalevskaja Research Group on Early Jewish Monotheism Vol. II* (eds. I.J. de Hulster and N. MacDonald; FAT 2.61; Tübingen: Mohr Siebeck, 2013).

Tov, E., "Recensional Differences between the Masoretic Text and the Septuagint of Ezekiel," *ETL* 62 (1986): 89–101; revised ed. in Tov, **Greek-Hebrew Bible*, 397–410.

Tov, E., "Some Sequential Differences between the MT and LXX and their Ramifications," *JNSL* 13 (1987): 151–60; revised ed. in Tov, **Greek-Hebrew Bible*, 411–18.

Tov, E., "Glosses, Interpolations, and Other Types of Scribal Additions in the Text of the Hebrew Bible," in *Language, Theology and the Bible: Essays in Honour of James Barr* (ed. S.E. Balentine and J. Barton; Oxford: Clarendon, 1994), 40–66; revised ed. in Tov, **Greek-Hebrew Bible*, 53–74.

Tov, E., "Hebrew Scripture Editions: Philosophy and Praxis," in *From 4QMMT to Resurrection – Mélanges qumraniens en homage à Émile Puech* (ed. F. García Martinez et al.; STDJ 61; Leiden: Brill, 2006), 281–312; revised ed. in Tov, **HB, GB, and Qumran*, 247–70.

Tov, **TCHB*.

Wevers, J.W., "The Evidence of the Text of the John H. Scheide Papyri for the Translation of Status Constructus in Ezekiel," *JBL* 70 (1951): 211–16.

Wevers, J.W., "The L Text of Ezekiel," in *Studies in the Text Histories of Deuteronomy and Ezekiel* (eds. J.W. Wevers and D. Fraenkel; MSU 26; Göttingen: Vandenhoeck & Ruprecht, 2003), 68–116.

Ziegler, J., "Die Bedeutung des Chester Beatty-Scheide Papyrus 967 für die Textüberlieferung der Ezechiel-Septuaginta," *ZAW* 61 (1945–1948): 76–94.

Ziegler, J., "Zur Textgestaltung der Ezechiel-Septuaginta," *Bib* 34 (1953): 435–55.

Ziegler, J., *Ezechiel* (2nd ed. with addendum by D. Fraenkel; Septuaginta Vetus Testamentum Graecum 16.1; Göttingen: Vandenhoeck & Ruprecht, 1977).

Zimmerli, W., *Ezekiel 1–2* (Hermeneia; Philadelphia: Fortress, 1979–1983); German original: *Ezekiel 1–2* (BKAT 13.1–2; Neukirchen-Vluyn: Neukirchener, 1969).

William A. Tooman

8.2 Ancient Hebrew Texts

8.2.1 Ancient Manuscript Evidence

Seven ancient manuscripts with remnants of the book of Ezekiel have been published. A further possible Ezekiel fragment from the Dead Sea Scrolls with remnants of Ezek 28:22 is part of the Green Collection (Inv. MOTB.SCR.003174 = GC 6 = DSS F.Ezek1).[1] Six of the published manuscripts were found in various caves around Qumran and one on the Masada fortress. 3QEzek and 4QEzek^c could also attest to an Ezekiel quotation in a non-biblical text and 4QEzek^b did not contain the whole text of Ezekiel. The small amount of text preserved in 1QEzek, 3QEzek, and 4QEzek^c does not allow for textual classification of these manuscripts. 4QEzek^a and MasEzek can be characterized as proto-Masoretic, while 4QEzek^b and 11QEzek attest to semi-Masoretic texts.

8.2.1.1 1QEzek (1Q9)

Of the two surviving fragments of 1QEzek, only the text of frg. 1 can be identified. It preserves nine words from Ezek 4:16–5:1. The few extant characters are written in a Herodian bookhand. Although only very little text is preserved of 1QEzek, this fragment does not attest to an Ezekiel quotation in a non-biblical manuscript but to an Ezekiel scroll because the extant text of 1QEzek belongs to two different prophecies.[2] The orthography of 1QEzek aligns with MT-Ezek (→ 8.2.2) but the tiny amount of text preserved allows neither for an orthography nor for a textual classification of this manuscript.

8.2.1.2 3QEzek (3Q1)

The only surviving fragment of 3QEzek preserves eleven characters out of five words belonging to Ezek 16:31–33 that were executed in a Herodian bookhand. Clearly readable are the letters [ה֯ לקלס "h to spurn," which occur in this combination only in Ezek 16:31. For this reason, Baillet identified 3Q1 as an Ezekiel manuscript, although he allows for the possibility that 3Q1 is the remnant of a non-biblical manuscript that preserves an Ezekiel quotation in its only extant fragment.[3] The tiny amount of text preserved makes orthographic and textual classifications of 3QEzek impossible.

8.2.1.3 4QEzek^a (4Q73)

The five extant fragments of 4QEzek^a attest to 163 words and partial words from Ezek 10:6–22; 11:1–11; 23:14–15, 17–18, 44–47; 41:3–6. The manuscript was executed in a late Hasmonean semi-cursive hand with tendencies toward an early Herodian script from the middle of the first century B.C.E.[4] The supralinear correction in Ezek 11:2 was made by the original scribe of the scroll.[5] In its orthography and text, 4QEzek^a is close to MT (→ 8.2.2). 4QEzek^a reads only three times against MT. Of these three readings against MT, two are non-aligned and one goes with LXX (→ 8.3). In one further case, 4QEzek^a aligns with MT manuscripts and LXX against MT. It is of particular interest that 4QEzek^a attests in Ezek 10:7, 14, 18, 21; 11:5; and 23:46 to the longer text of MT against LXX. 4QEzek^a should therefore be characterized as a proto-Masoretic manuscript.[6]

8.2.1.4 4QEzek^b (4Q74)

The six fragments that survive of 4QEzek^b derive from cols. III–V of the original scroll and preserve sixty-eight words and partial words from Ezek 1:10–13, 16–17, 19–24.[7] One column contained eleven lines of 28–33 character spaces. With a height of

---

[1] I am indebted to David Trobisch and Emanuel Tov for this information.

[2] Against Patmore, "Shorter and Longer Texts," 233.

[3] Baillet, "1. Ézéchiel," 94; cf. Lange, *Handbuch*, 325.

[4] Cf. Sanderson, "Ezekiel," 209–10.

[5] Cf. Sanderson, "Ezekiel," 210.

[6] Patmore, "Shorter and Longer Texts," 234; Lange, *Handbuch*, 325–26; cf. Schwagmeier, "Untersuchungen," 61; against Brooke, "Ezekiel," 319 ("much affinity towards MT, but reconstructed readings with LXX"), and Tov, *"Synthese," 26, who describes 4QEzek^a as "statistically non-aligned" (in the German of Tov's article: "statistisch eigenständig").

[7] Cf. Sanderson, "Ezekiel," 215.

8.3 cm, the scroll would have needed to be 32 m or 280 columns long to contain the whole book of Ezekiel. This would have resulted in a scroll that could not have been rolled and is therefore physically impossible. As an excerpted text, 4QEzek[b] contained only a part of the book of Ezekiel, maybe only its first vision (Ezek 1:1–3:15) or a collection of the four visions reported in the book (Ezek 1:1–3:15; 8–11; 37:1–14; 40–48) of which only the first vision is still preserved.[8] When Schwagmeier suggests that 4QEzek[b] could be a florilegium because it attests only to selected passages of Ezekiel,[9] he does not understand the nature of excerpted manuscripts, which are significantly different from collections of quotations out of various books. 4QEzek[b] was copied in a Herodian bookhand from the early first century C.E.[10] The supralinear correction to Ezek 1:21 was inserted by the original scribe of the scroll. In orthography and text, 4QEzek[b] resembles MT-Ezek (→ 8.2.2). In its sixty-eight words and partial words, the manuscript attests to only three textual variants against MT. Two of these readings are non-aligned and one reading can only be recognized inside the Hebrew textual tradition. The small amount of preserved text makes the textual classification of 4QEzek[b] difficult. As 4QEzek[b] reads against LXX (→ 8.3) and the longer text of MT in Ezek 1:22–23, the scroll can be described with some caution as semi-Masoretic.[11]

8.2.1.5 4QEzek[c] (4Q75)

This manuscript survives only in one fragment of which three lines with nine words and partial words from Ezek 24:3–5 are extant. The few preserved characters are executed in a Hasmonean script from the beginning or the middle of the first century B.C.E.[12] Due to the tiny amount of surviving text, it cannot be excluded that 4Q75 preserves an Ezekiel quotation in a non-biblical text instead of an ancient Ezekiel manuscript. The small amount of extant text prohibits orthographic and textual classifications of 4QEzek[c]. In Ezek 24:2, the manuscript reads with MT-Ezek (→ 8.2.2) and LXX-Ezek (→ 8.3) the words את עצׄם] היום הזה "[this] very[day" which are missing in S-Ezek (→ 6–9.1.4) and V-Ezek (→ 6–9.1.7).

8.2.1.6 11QEzek (11Q4)

The state of preservation of 11QEzek is problematic. Although thirty-five percent of the scroll is preserved, water, sand, and bacteria damaged the scroll to such an extent that it is impossible to unroll it today.[13] Nine fragments were loosened from the baked scroll. The text of seven of these fragments can still be identified. They contain fifty-eight words and partial words from Ezek 1:8–10; 4:3–6, 9–10, 5:11–17; 7:9–12. The smooth leather of 11QEzek and its carefully executed Herodian bookhand from the years 10 B.C.E.–30 C.E.[14] point to the high quality of this scroll. In its orthography, 11QEzek is close to MT (→ 8.2.2). 11QEzek reads twice with and twice against MT, twice against LXX (→ 8.3), and twice non-aligned. The textual classification of the manuscript is difficult, because of the small amount of legible text. That 11QEzek has the longer text and the textual sequence of MT in Ezek 5:13, 15–16; 7:3–10,[15] against LXX-Ezek, argues for a semi-Masoretic text.[16]

8.2.1.7 MasEzek (Mas1d)

The approximately fifty fragments of MasEzek preserve 490 words and partial words from Ezek 35:11–15; 36:1–10, 13–14, 17–35; 37:1–14, 23, 28; 38:1–4, 7–8 deriving from four columns of the original scroll. Talmon describes the script of MasEzek as a care-

---

[8] For the measurements and contents of 4QEzek[b], see Sanderson, "Ezekiel," 215–16.

[9] Schwagmeier, "Untersuchungen," 67.

[10] Cf. Sanderson, "Ezekiel," 216.

[11] Lange, *Handbuch*, 326; cf. Patmore, "Shorter and Longer Texts," 234–35; against Brooke, "Ezekiel," 319.

[12] Cf. Sanderson, "Ezekiel," 219.

[13] Cf. Herbert, "11QEzekiel," 16–17.

[14] For the paleographic date of 11QEzek, see Herbert, "11QEzekiel," 21. Brownlee, "Scroll of Ezekiel," 19–28, suggests a slightly earlier date between 55 and 25 B.C.E.

[15] Cf. Brownlee, "Scroll of Ezekiel," 16, and Herbert, "11QEzekiel," 26–27.

[16] Cf. Herbert, "11QEzekiel," 22; Patmore, "Shorter and Longer Texts," 236; Lange, *Handbuch*, 327. Based on reconstructed readings, Schwagmeier ("Untersuchungen," 57–59) argues that the text of 11QEzek is close to MT but identical to neither MT nor LXX.

fully executed Herodian bookhand from the second part of the first century B.C.E.[17] However, Tigchelaar demonstrated that it is a late Herodian hand from the time after the middle of the first century C.E.[18] The supralinear corrections in MasEzek were inserted by the original scribe.[19] With few exceptions, the orthography of MasEzek agrees with MT-Ezek (→ 8.2.2).[20] The text-typological analysis of MasEzek is impeded by the fact that none of the studies and editions dedicated to this manuscript provide a variant list. Talmon notes twenty-five cases of textual variation; of these, MasEzek reads twenty-three times with MT and only twice with LXX (→ 8.3).[21] As MasEzek follows the textual structure and textual repertoire of MT-Ezek in Ezekiel 35–38 and because it reads only twice against MT, the manuscript is best classified as proto-Masoretic:[22] "With some minor exceptions, the text corresponds to the MT. Section markings (*parashot*) mostly parallel those of one or the other major MT manuscripts (Aleppo, Leningrad, Cairo, Sassoon) but do not fully accord with anyone."[23] Talmon's classification is not questioned by Tigchelaar's[24] corrections to his edition.

Baillet, M., "1. Ézéchiel," *DJD III/1: 94.
Barthélemy, D., "9. Ézéchiel," *DJD I: 68–69.
Brooke, G.J., "Ezekiel in Some Qumran and New Testament Texts," in *Madrid Qumran Congress, 1:317–37, esp. 318–21.
Brownlee, W.H., "The Scroll of Ezekiel from the Eleventh Qumran Cave," RevQ 4 (1963): 11–28.

---

[17] Talmon, in FS Greenberg, 56; Talmon, in OLP 27, 33; Talmon, in Masada VI, 68.
[18] Tigchelaar, "Notes," 273–75.
[19] Cf. Talmon, in FS Greenberg, 56; Talmon, in OLP 27, 33; Talmon, in Masada VI, 68.
[20] Cf. Talmon, in FS Greenberg, 57–58; Talmon, in OLP 27, 34–35; Talmon, in Masada VI, 68–69.
[21] Talmon, in FS Greenberg, 58–61; Talmon, in OLP 27, 35–39; Talmon, in Masada VI, 69–72.
[22] Cf. Patmore, "Shorter and Longer Texts," 236–37; Schwagmeier, "Untersuchungen," 103; Lange, *Handbuch, 328; against Brooke, "Ezekiel," 320 ("only generally proto-Masoretic, showing other distinctive readings").
[23] Talmon, in FS Greenberg, 318; cf. op. cit. 56 and Talmon, in OLP 27, 33; Talmon, in Masada VI, 68, 70.
[24] Tigchelaar, "Notes," 270–73.

Herbert, E.D., "4. 11QEzekiel," *DJD XXIII (1998): 15–28.
Lange, A., *Handbuch, 325–34.
Lust, J., "Ezekiel Manuscripts in Qumran: Preliminary Edition of 4QEza and b," in *Ezekiel and his Book: Textual and Literary Criticism and their Interrelation* (ed. J. Lust; BETL 74; Leuven: Peeters, 1986), 90–100.
Patmore, H.M., "The Shorter and Longer Texts of Ezekiel: The Implications of the Manuscript Finds from Masada and Qumran," JSOT 32 (2007): 231–42.
Puech, É., "4QEz[a]: note additionelle," RevQ 14 (1989–1990): 107–08.
Sanderson, J.E., "Ezekiel," *DJD XV: 209–20.
Schwagmeier, P., "Untersuchungen zu Textgeschichte und Entstehung des Ezechielbuches in masoretischer und griechischer Überlieferung" (ThD diss., University of Zurich, 2004), esp. 50–69, 101–03.
Sinclair, L.A., "A Qumran Biblical Fragment: 4QEzek.[a] (Ezek. 10,17–11,11)," RevQ 14 (1989–1990): 99–105.
Talmon, S., "Fragments of an Ezekiel Scroll from Masada (Ezek 35:11–38:14) 1043–2220, Mas 1d," OLP 27 (1996): 29–49.
Talmon, S., "Fragments of an Ezekiel Scroll from Masada 1043–2220 (Ezekiel 35:11–38:14)," in *Tehillah le-Moshe: Biblical and Judaic Studies in Honor of Moshe Greenberg* (eds. M. Cagon, B.L. Eichler, and J.H. Tigay; Winona Lake: Eisenbrauns, 1997), 53–69, 318 [Hebr.].
Talmon, S., "1043–2220 (MasEzek) Ezekiel 35:11–38:14," in S. Talmon and Y. Yadin, *Masada VI: The Yigael Yadin Excavations 1963–1965: Final Reports* (Jerusalem: Israel Exploration Society, 1999), 59–75.
Tigchelaar, E.J.C., "Notes on the Ezekiel Scroll from Masada (MasEzek)," RevQ 22 (2005–2006): 269–75.

Armin Lange

8.2.2 Masoretic Texts and Ancient Texts Close to MT

8.2.2.1 Character of (Proto)-MT-Ezek

Ezekiel is represented in several fragmentary manuscripts from Qumran (1QEzek, 3QEzek, 4QEzek[a-c], 11QEzek) and Masada (MasEzek) that are aligned with MT (→ 8.2.1). The only complete Hebrew text is MT. The consonantal text of MT-Ezek manifests two striking features that reveal contours of its literary- and transmission-history: 1) It is an expansive text, containing several hundred pluses vis-à-vis the Old Greek (→ 8.3); 2) In two instances, it represents a different order of verses or chapters than Old Greek. The alternative arrangements have no substantive effect on the ideology or arguments of the book. In some cases, the expansions represent deliberate efforts to sculpt a pericope or the book in new ways, directing its literary evolution toward particular ends. Most expansions, though, are singular in the sense that they represent individual cases of rewriting, rather than being part of a coordinated constellation of alterations intended to rework the argument or ideology of some segment(s) of the book. (For history of research including proto-MT, see → 8.1.2)

8.2.2.2 Order of Elements in MT-Ezek

There are two instances in which MT represents a different order of text segments from other witnesses. The first, MT-Ezek 7:1–9, is arranged in the Old Greek as follows: vv. 1–2, 6aβ, 7aβ–9, 3–5a, 6aβ, 10a (vv. 5b, 6aα, 6aγ–7aα, 10aβ–bα are pluses in MT). The segments in vv. 3–4 and 8–9 are nearly identical, and in the Old Greek they are juxtaposed. Tov, nuancing the views of Cornill[1] and Zimmerli,[2] has argued convincingly that the parallel verses represent a doublet. "Probably one of the two parts was added in MT in one place and in LXX in another. At first the added section was placed in the margin and from there it reached two different places in the text."[3] Expansions to Ezekiel 7 are discussed in → 8.2.2.4.

The second case, though more sizeable, has little impact on the book's formulation or message. In LXX[967], Ezekiel 38–39 follow Ezek 36:23b (36:23c–38 being absent) and precede Ezekiel 37. The same order is attested independently by the VL in Codex Wirceburg and corroborated by the expansions to Num 11:26 in T[Ps-J]. Lust has contended that the alternative order of chapters in LXX[967] is part of a unique construal of Ezekiel's eschatology. Specifically, those Israelites killed in the war with Gog of Magog in Ezekiel 38–39 are subsequently resurrected in Ezekiel 37 to inhabit the new state, which is graphically depicted in Ezekiel 40–48.[4] Lust, Scatolini Apóstolo, and Crane all submit that the arrangement in LXX[967] creates a more natural transition between text segments, particularly by juxtaposing Ezek 37:24–28 with Ezekiel 40–48.[5] Lust suggested that the chapters were rearranged in MT as part of an anti-eschatological redaction (which included the expansions in Ezek 12:26–28; 32:24b–26; and 36:23c–38), designed to counter the notion that resurrection followed the eschatological war with Gog. Crane proposed, alternatively, that the order in LXX[967] highlighted national unification under a Davidic messiah, juxtaposing the "covenant of peace" (Ezek 37:26) with the temple vision. The MT version, in his view, reflects Second Temple political realities, summoning Judahites in a "call to arms."[6] Against Lust and Crane both, it must be noted that in no edition of Ezekiel do the Israelites fight with Gog's host (only God acts), and in all editions Israel's dry bones are interpreted figuratively as her perished "hope" (Ezek 37:11). The only difference between the two editions is the order in which this information is presented. Tooman has therefore suggested that the variable location of Ezekiel 38–39 *may* support the proposal that those chapters were introduced into the book at a late stage in its development and that they were located at different (but equally logical) points in different literary editions.[7]

8.2.2.3 Expansions to MT-Ezek

When compared with the Old Greek, MT-Ezek is replete with additional words, phrase, and clauses. Though the Old Greek includes expansions in its own right, they are far fewer in number (→ 8.3). According to the data compiled by Marquis,[8] there

---

[1] C.H. Cornill, *Das Buch des Propheten Ezechiel* (Leipzig: J.C. Hinrichs, 1886).
[2] W. Zimmerli, *Ezekiel 1–2* (Hermeneia; Philadelphia: Fortress, 1979–1983). German original: *Ezekiel 1–2* (BKAT 13.1–2; Neukirchen-Vluyn: Neukirchener, 1969).
[3] Tov, "Recensional," 398.
[4] Lust, "Oldest"; Lust, "Major Divergences"; similarly, Lilly, *Two Books*, 187–89, 218–23.
[5] Lust, "Major Divergences," 149–50; Scatolini Apóstolo, "Re-Reading," 349, 351–52; Crane, *Restoration*, 251–53.
[6] Crane, *Israel's Restoration*, 253–54.
[7] Tooman, *Gog of Magog*, 77–83.
[8] G. Marquis, "The Translation Technique Reflected in LXX-Ezekiel" (M.A. thesis; Hebrew University of Jerusalem, 1982), 188 [Hebr.].

are roughly 350 plus readings in MT, making it 4–5 percent longer than the *Vorlage* of the Old Greek.[9]

A number of studies have focused on the expansions to MT,[10] each resulting in a unique typology of the data. All these inventories catalogue the expansions according to different kinds of qualities, based on technique (e.g., "conflation"), result (e.g., "clarification," "intensification"), content ("addition of new material," "addition of prophetic speech formula"), or purpose ("exegetical," "theological"). There are four distinct elements requiring consideration in the evaluation of any expansion: 1) the feature or perceived lack in the base text that inspired the expansion; 2) the mechanical technique by which the expansion is introduced; 3) the objective(s) achieved by the expansion; and 4) the hermeneutical assumptions under which the expansion is conducted. In the discussion below, the types of expansion are described, as much as possible, by objectives.

8.2.2.3.1 Large-Scale Expansions

Particular attention has been given to several "large" expansions that are not present in LXX[967]: Ezek 12:26–28; 32:24b–26; and 36:23c–38.[11] Lust has attempted to identify a singular anti-eschatological ideological profile in these large expansions and attributed them to a Pharisaic group.[12] However, their differences in content and compositional character suggest that they should be ascribed to more than one editor/scribe. When we also recognize that MT includes many text segments that are so replete with small expansions that they constitute cases of large-scale rewriting (e.g. Ezekiel 1; 2:3–6; 4:13–14; 6:4–14; 7; 8; 32:20–32; 33:7–11, 23–33), it is difficult to single out these three expansions from all others. However, it is certainly the case that a new *Tendenz* can be detected in certain of the expanded text segments when compared with the Greek witnesses (→ 8.2.2.4)

8.2.2.3.2 Smaller Expansions

The smaller pluses in MT have been widely analyzed and are commonly classified as "glosses" in MT rather than "omissions" in the Old Greek (→ 8.3).[13] Properly speaking, "gloss" refers to marginal or supralinear notations that were never meant to be integrated into the syntax of the base text.[14] Ezekiel does contain examples of glosses that have been entered into the main text during transmission (see below) and omissions in the Greek traditions, but most of the pluses in MT-Ezek are better classified as "expansions": scribal additions. The expansions in MT-Ezek are not systematic or evenly distributed, neither are they from a single hand or time period.[15]

1. *True glosses.* The whole of Ezek 10:14 is absent in the Old Greek: "and each one has four faces: the first face was the face of a cherub, and the second face was the face of a man, and the third was the face of a lion, and the fourth was the face of an eagle." It is extremely difficult to integrate Ezek 10:14 into the logic and sequence

---

[9] Tov, "Large Scale," 126.

[10] M. Dijkstra, "The Glosses in Ezekiel Reconsidered: Aspects of Textual Transmission in Ezekiel 10," in *Ezekiel and His Book: Textual and Literary Criticism and Their Interrelation* (ed. J. Lust; BETL 74; Leuven: Peeters, 1986), 55–77; G.R. Driver, "Glosses in the Hebrew Text of the Old Testament," in *L'Ancien Testament et l'Orient* (Orientalia et Biblica Lovaniensia 1; Louvain: University Publications, 1957), 123–61; K.S. Freedy, "The Glosses in Ezekiel i–xxiv," VT 20 (1970): 129–52; G. Fohrer, "Die Glossen im Buche Ezechiel,"ZAW 63 (1951): 33–53; J. Herrmann, "Stichwortglossen im Buch Ezechiel," OLZ 11 (1908): 280–82; Mackie, "Expanding"; Tov, "Recensional"; Tov, "Glosses."

[11] Crane, *Restoration*; F.V. Filson, "The Omission of Ezek 12:26–28 and 36:23b–38 in Codex 967," JBL 62 (1943): 27–32; Lilly, *Two Books*; Lust, "Oldest"; Lust, "Major Divergences"; Schwagmeier, "Untersuchungen zu Textgeschichte und Entstehung des Ezechielbuches in masoretischer und griechischer Überlieferung" (PhD diss., University of Zürich, 2004); J. Wevers, *Ezekiel* (NCBC; Grand Rapids: Eerdmans, 1982).

[12] Lust, "Oldest," 532; Lust, "Major Divergences"; followed by Scatolini Apóstolo, "Re-Reading."

[13] See, e.g., the publications by Dijkstra, Driver, Fohrer, Freedy, and Herrmann quoted in n. 10.

[14] K. van der Toorn, *Scribal Culture and the Making of the Hebrew Bible* (Cambridge: Harvard University Press, 2009), 126; Tov, *TCHB, 259–60.

[15] The preponderance of deliberate expansions to MT-Ezek makes certain scribal errors and translation habits difficult to identify. Cases of dittography in MT-Ezek (e.g., Ezek 7:11; 10:21; 12:3; 45:1) and the translation techniques of telescoping and abbreviating are particularly problematic (possible examples in Old Greek include: Ezek 10:2; 17:10; 27:16; 32:29; 38:17; 41:17).

of the vision. It is quite likely that it is a scribal gloss that was inserted into the main text. Its function is to coordinate the description of the divine creatures in Ezek 10:20–22 with that in Ezek 1:10; thus, it is also slightly out of position. Other suggested cases of marginal or supralinear glosses subsequently entered into the body of the text in MT can been found in Ezek 1:7b, 8, 9, 12, 17, 25–26; 10:16; 16:15; 19:14; 34:23.[16]

2. *Expansions*. The hundreds of independent expansions to MT-Ezek cannot be thoroughly catalogued here. The following are a representative sample of types. It should be noted, though, that these categories are not always mutually exclusive.

   a. Cohesion: enhancing grammatical or syntactic cohesion (e.g., Ezek 1:13, 15; 3:21; 5:16; 8:6; 10:7; 12:12; 28:13; 39:14; 40:1b–2a; 44:7, 13, 27), or creating linguistic cohesion with the book's idiolect (e.g., Ezek 1:14; 4:13; 8:7; 16:13; 18:32; 20:26; 23:34; 24:13; 30:12; 31:18; 32:31; 34:21–22). Thus Ezek 12:12 was expanded as follows: פָּנָיו יְכַסֶּה יַעַן אֲשֶׁר לֹא־יִרְאֶה לַעַיִן הוּא אֶת־הָאָרֶץ "he will cover his face, so that he cannot see/be seen by/with eyes [he, the land]." The ambiguous לֹא־יִרְאֶה "he will not see/be seen," is clarified in MT to indicate that Zedekiah will not see the land.[17]

   b. Internal coherence: enhancing the structural, thematic, conceptual, or argumentative unity or logic of the book. This includes the creation or enhancement of parallel structures (e.g., Ezek 8:2 ∥ 1:27–28), harmonization (particularly common in the *merkabâ* accounts: Ezek 1:22, 23, 24, 27; 3:23; 8:2; 10:1, 12, 14), clarification of ambiguous or unknown words and phrases (e.g., Ezek 3:14; 24:2; 30:5; 31:15; 34:16), and filling of perceived gaps (e.g., Ezek 1:23, 24, 25; 3:9; 5:11, 14; 6:4; 10:12; 16:22; 28:28b). So, for example, at the end of the first vision, the prophet reports that the spirit returned him to Tel Aviv: וָאֵלֵךְ [מַר] בַּחֲמַת רוּחִי "and I went [bitter] in the turmoil of my spirit" (Ezek 3:14). The addition of מַר "bitter" clarifies that חֲמַת רוּחִי "turmoil of my spirit" indicates something other than "perturbed." Describing the prophet as deeply unhappy also resolves an enigma in Ezek 2:8, where the deity – seemingly without provocation – exhorts the prophet not to be rebellious.

   c. External coherence: harmonizing with other literature, doctrines, or traditions, including the creation of new allusions to other literature (e.g., Ezek 1:14; 3:1; 6:5, 9, 13; 7:7, 10; 8:10, 11; 20:10; 28:14, 16; 36:11).[18] The whole of Ezek 1:14 is a plus in MT: וְהַחַיּוֹת רָצוֹא וָשׁוֹב כְּמַרְאֵה הַבָּזָק "The living creatures darted to and fro, like a flash of lightning." The description of the celestial creatures as "running and returning" "like lightning" is modelled on Nahum's description of rampaging chariots in Nah 2:5. Additionally, the last phrase, כְּמַרְאֵה הַבָּזָק is identical to a phrase in Dan 10:6: "His body was like *taršîš*, his face like an appearance of lightning (כְּמַרְאֵה בָרָק), his eyes like flaming torches, his arms and legs like the gleam of burnished bronze, and the sound of his words like the roar of a multitude." Dan 10:6 is a pastiche of locutions from Ezekiel 1. The MT expansion (Ezek 1:14), then, was prompted by Nah 2:5 and also was influenced by the wording of Dan 10:6. (Thus, Ezekiel 1 inspired Dan 10:6, and Dan 10:6 then exerted influence on the transmission history of Ezekiel 1, as seen in the plus of Ezek 1:14).

   d. Rhetorical intensification: addition of הִנֵּה "behold" (e.g., Ezek 37:2) or other intensifiers, including adjectives (e.g., Ezek 5:16 + הָרָעִים "evil"; 17:17 + רַבּוֹת "many"; 27:33 + רַבִּים "many").

   e. Addition of entirely new material: Notable here is the application of a text segment to a new constituency (e.g., Ezek 2:3 + אֶל־גּוֹיִם "to nations") and the habits of adding synonyms (Ezek 5:11, 14; 6:4, 6; 22:20, 21; 37:23) and generating stereotyped word-pairs, even at the ex-

---

[16] Mackie, "Expanding."
[17] Mackie, "Expanding," 92–93.

[18] J. Stromberg, "Observations on Inner-Scriptural Scribal Expansion in MT Ezekiel," *VT* 58 (2008): 1–19.

TABLE 1   Variations in Ezekiel 32:17–32

LXX⁹⁶⁷	LXXᴮ	MT
v. 21 – giants	v. 21 – giants	v. 21 – mighty warriors
v. 22 – Assyria	v. 22 – Assyria	v. 22 – Assyria
v. 24 – Elam	v. 24 – Elam	v. 24 – Elam
vv. 24bβ–26a: 39 word minus	vv. 25aβ–b: 24 word minus	
	v. 26 – Meshek and Tubal	v. 26 – Meshek and Tubal
v. 27 – giants	v. 27 – giants	v. 27 – mighty
v. 29 – rulers of Assyria	v. 29 – rulers of Assyria	v. 29 – Edom
v. 30 – rulers of the North	v. 30 – rulers of the North	v. 30 – rulers of the North and Sidonians

pense of disrupting logic or syntax (e.g., וּפְנֵיהֶם וְכַנְפֵיהֶם "their faces and their wings": Ezek 1:8, 11; דְּמוּת + מַרְאֶה "likeness and appearance": Ezek 1:16; 8:2; 10:1, 22; וּמַרְאֵיהֶם וּמַעֲשֵׂיהֶם "their appearance and their construction": Ezek 1:16; שבר + אשם "broken" + "desolated": Ezek 6:4, 6).

8.2.2.4 Text Segments that Reflect Particular *Tendenzen* in MT

In some cases, the adjustments to MT produce a different *Tendenz* when compared with the Greek versions (→ 8.3). The three examples below are accepted by general scholarly consensus:

1) *Ezek 7:1–27*. Expansions to Ezekiel 7 of MT-Ezek include all or part of the following verses: Ezek 7:5b, 6aα, 6aγ–7aα, 10aβ–bα, 12b, 13aβ–bα, 14aβ, 14b, 16aβ, 19aβ, 20aβ, 23bα, 24a, 27aα (Ezek 7:11bβ probably reflects a dittography in MT). The shorter text, reflected in Old Greek, is notoriously opaque,[19] but it announces imminent judgment on the "land of Israel" (אדמת ישראל), which occasions defilement of the temple (Ezek 7:20–24). The oracle includes a number of locutions that resonate with Daniel's visions, most evocatively גְּאוֹן עֻזִּים "arrogance of the strong," עֵת "time," קֵץ/קִיץ "the end/awake," and חלל "profane" (Dan 8:17; 11:31, 35; 12:4). The MT expansions, particularly the inclusion of the הַצְּפִירָה "the goat" (Ezek 7:7, 10), and his כָּל־הֲמוֹנָהּ

"all its horde" (Ezek 7:12, 13, 14), serve to further integrate the two texts. Thus, in MT, the agent of judgment in Ezekiel 7 is identified with Daniel's "insolent king,"[20] inspired possibly by the events surrounding Antiochus IV.[21]

2) *Ezek 32:17–32*. MT-Ezek 32:17–32, a lament over the multitude of Egypt (vv. 18, 32) and Pharaoh (vv. 31, 32), contains a number of expansions and adaptations that alter the horizon of the poem. This represents the last stage in a series of efforts to rewrite the lament, progressively widening and specifying its addressees as listed in Table 1.

Meshek and Tubal are introduced in LXXᴮ. They are included with the "giants/mighty ones" (γίγαντες) as examples of the uncircumcised nations from the primeval past who have been condemned to Sheol (see OG-Gen 6:4; 10:2; 8–9). In MT-Ezek, Meshek and Tubal are retained (presumably because they also appear in Ezek 27:13; 38:2, 3; 39:1), but the Edomites and Sidonians are introduced

---

[19] Tov, "Recensional."

[20] P.-M. Bogaert, "Les deux redactions conserves (LXX et TM) d' Ezechiel 7," in *Ezekiel and His Book: Textual and Literary Criticism and Their Interrelation* (ed. J. Lust; BETL 74; Leuven: Peeters, 1986), 21–47; T.P. Mackie, "Transformation in Ezekiel's Textual History: Ezekiel 7 in the Masoretic Text and the Septuagint," in *Transforming Visions: Transformations of Text, Tradition, and Theology in Ezekiel* (ed. W.A. Tooman and M.A. Lyons; PTMS 127; Eugene: Pickwick, 2010), 229–78.

[21] Lust, "Textual Witnesses." Additional intertextual expansions in the chapter include 7:19aβ (∥ Zeph 1:18) and 7:16 (∥ Isa 38:14).

into Ezek 32:29 and 30. MT effectually integrates the lament with the surrounding oracles against the nations (esp. Ezek 25:8, 12–14; 28:20–24; and 35:1–15), contemporizing the pericope. The additional expansion in Ezek 32:25aβ–b is a doublet of vv. 24, 26.[22]

3) *Ezek 36:23c–38*. This text segment is famously absent in LXX[967] and LXX[W] and is now generally accepted as a late addition to the book.[23] It is a theologically central text, summing up and coordinating many of the book's claims regarding Israel's restoration. Its presence has three principal effects on the book as a whole. First, it draws together many elements from Ezekiel's deliverance oracles, coordinating them in a single portrait of the future restoration (e.g., Ezek 36:23 ‖ 20:41b; 28:25; 39:25, 27b–28; 36:24 ‖ 20:41b–42a; 39:27; 36:26 ‖ 11:19; 18:31; 39:29b; 36:27 ‖ 11:20; 37:14, 24b; 36:28 ‖ 37:25a, 27b; 36:29 ‖ 34:29a; 36:30 ‖ 34:27a, 29b; 36:31 ‖ 20:43; 36:32 ‖ 20:44; 39:26).[24] Second, it incorporates many locutions and ideas from Jeremiah, coordinating the two books' linguistic and ideological profiles more closely (e.g., Ezek 36:28 ‖ Jer 7:7; 16:15; 24:10; 25:5; 30:3; etc.; Ezek 36:31 ‖ Jer 7:3, 5; 18:11; 25:5; 26:13, etc.; Ezek 36:33 ‖ Jer 33:8).[25] Finally, it harmonizes Ezekiel's deliverance oracles, most notably by coordinating the promise of the divine spirit (Ezek 37:14) with that of a new heart and spirit (Ezek 11:19–20) in Ezek 36:26–28.[26]

8.2.2.5 Editions, Auxiliary Tools

Critical editions of the fragmentary remains from the Judean Desert can be found in the relevant *DJD* volumes and in Talmon and Yadin, **Masada VI* (→ 8.2.1).

There are three sets of evidence that are most essential for recovering the MT text form. Most important are the three masoretic manuscripts: the Cairo Codex (MT[C]), attributed to Moses ben Asher and self-dated to 896 C.E. (→ 3–5.3); the Aleppo Codex (MT[A]), pointed, presumably, by Aaron ben Asher around 930 C.E. (→ 3–5.3); and the Leningrad Codex (MT[L]) dated around 1008/9 C.E. (→ 3–5.3).[27] In addition, the Cairo Genizah contained numerous fragments of Ezekiel, many from anthologized works, vocalized according to the Babylonian or Palestinian systems.[28] Finally, Goshen-Gottstein and Talmon singled out five complete medieval manuscripts of Ezekiel for the quantity of variants they contain. "If it can be claimed that some medieval manuscripts preserve 'non-receptus' readings, these are the most likely candidates."[29] The five are: Oxford, Bodleian, 105 (Tanner 173); Cambridge University Library, Mm. 5.27; manuscript Cambridge, Gonville and Caius College 404/625; Cambridge, St John's College A2; and Berlin 1.[30] The relevant readings from all these manuscripts are catalogued in Apparatus III of the *HUB* volume on Ezekiel,[31] which supersedes all other editions of MT-Ezek. **BH*[3] and **BHS* present typeset and reformatted editions of MT[L]. The textual notes to Ezekiel in both editions (**BH*[3] by Rothstein; **BHS* by El-

---

[22] Allen argues, conversely, that v. 26 is an interpretive doublet of v. 25, which construes מִשְׁכָּב לָהּ "a bed for her" as מֶשֶׁךְ תֻּבָל "Meshech and Tubal" (L.C. Allen, *Ezekiel 20–48* [WBC 29; Waco: Word Books, 1990], 135).

[23] Contra F.V. Filson, "The Omission of Ezek. 12:26–28 and 36:23b–38 in Codex 967," *JBL* 62 (1943): 27–32 and J.W. Wevers, *Ezekiel* (NCBC; Grand Rapids: Eerdmans, 1982). Though present in LXX[B], Ezek 36:23c–38 appears to be the work of a different translator than the surrounding text segments, as was first recognized by H.St.J. Thackeray, "The Greek Translators of Ezekiel," *JTS* 4 (1903): 398–411; H.St.J. Thackeray, *The Septuagint and Jewish Worship* (2nd ed.; London: British Academy, 1921), 37–39, 124–26.

[24] See Tooman, "Covenant."
[25] Lust, "Ezekiel 36–40 in the Oldest Greek Manuscript."
[26] Tooman, "Covenant."

[27] D.S. Loewinger, *Codex Cairo of the Bible* (Jerusalem: Makor, 1971); M.H. Goshen-Gottstein, *The Aleppo Codex* (Jerusalem: Magnes Press, 1976); D.N. Freedman, *The Leningrad Codex* (Grand Rapids: Eerdmans, 1998).

[28] E.J. Revell, *Biblical Texts with Palestinian Pointing and Their Accents* (Missoula: Scholars Press, 1977); I. Yeivin, *Genizah Bible Fragments with Babylonian Massorah and Vocalization* (5 vols.; Jerusalem: Makor, 1973); I. Yeivin, *A Collection of Mishnaic Geniza Fragments with Babylonian Vocalization: With Description of the Manuscripts and Indices* (Jerusalem: Makor, 1974) [Hebr.].

[29] Goshen-Gottstein and Talmon, **HUB Ezekiel*, xxxvii.
[30] For brief descriptions and further bibliography, see Goshen-Gottstein and Talmon, **HUB Ezekiel*, xxxvii–xxxviii.
[31] Goshen-Gottstein and Talmon, **HUB Ezekiel*.

liger) are unpredictably selective. Those in *BH³ more often than not represent genuine text-critical evidence, the preponderance of which is derived from Greek and Syriac witnesses. The notes in *BHS omit much of the evidence from *BH³ and include many more suggested emendations.

8.2.2.6 Relevance for Exegesis and Literary Analysis

MT-Ezek is a product of many centuries of literary evolution and scribal expansion. Cumulatively, its expansions and arrangements represent a substantially reworked edition of the book, though most of the alterations happened in unsystematic and uncoordinated ways.[32] This raises significant questions for exegetes, who must select a literary layer of the book upon which to comment.[33] This selection is complex with respect to Ezekiel, since all the witnesses appear to be genetically related, descending from a single archetype (→ 8.1).

For more than any other book, except perhaps Jeremiah (→ 7.2.2; → 7.3), the line between textual criticism and literary criticism is so blurred as to be invisible. From the time that some earliest edition of the book was penned, it appears to have endured a non-stop process of growth, extending into the Common Era.[34] Despite the efforts of certain scholars,[35] redaction-critical and text-critical issues in Ezekiel cannot be disentangled.[36]

Crane, A., *Israel's Restoration: A Textual-Comparative Exploration of Ezekiel 36–39* (VTSup 122; Leiden: Brill, 2008).
Goshen-Gottstein–Talmon, *HUB, Ezekiel*.
Lilly, I.E., *Two Books of Ezekiel: Papyrus 967 and the Masoretic Text as Variant Literary Editions* (VTSup 150; Leiden: Brill, 2012).
Lust, J., "Ezekiel 36–40 in the Oldest Greek Manuscript," *CBQ* 43 (1981): 517–33.
Lust, J., "The Final Text and Textual Criticism: Ez 39,28," in *Ezekiel and His Book: Textual and Literary Criticism and their Interrelation* (ed. J. Lust; BETL 74; Leuven: Peeters, 1986), 48–54.
Lust, J., "The Use of Textual Witnesses for the Establishment of the Text: The Shorter and Longer Texts of Ezekiel: An Example: Ez 7," in *Ezekiel and His Book: Textual and Literary Criticism and Their Interrelation* (ed. J. Lust; BETL 74; Leuven: Peeters 1986), 7–20.
Lust, J., "Major Divergences between LXX and MT in Ezekiel," in Schenker, *Earliest Text*, 85–92.
Mackie, T.P., "Expanding Ezekiel: The Hermeneutics of Scribal Addition in the Ancient Text Witnesses of the Book of Ezekiel" (PhD diss., University of Wisconsin-Madison, 2010).
Scatolini Apóstolo, S.S., "Ezek 36, 37, 38 and 39 in Papyrus 967 as Pre-Text for Re-Reading Ezekiel," in *Interpreting Translation: Studies in the LXX and Ezekiel in Honor of Johann Lust* (eds. F. García Martínez and M. Vervenne; BETL 192; Leuven: Leuven University Press, 2005), 331–57.
Tooman, W.A., *Gog of Magog: Reuse of Scripture and Compositional Technique in Ezekiel 38–39* (FAT 2.52; Tübingen: Mohr-Siebeck, 2011).
Tooman, W.A., "Covenant and Presence in the Composition and Theology of Ezekiel," in *Divine Presence and Absence in Exilic and Post-Exilic Judaism* (eds. I.J. de Hulster and N. MacDonald; FAT 2.61; Tübingen: Mohr Siebeck, 2013), 151–82.
Tov, E., "Recensional Differences between the Masoretic Text and the Septuagint of Ezekiel," *ETL* 62 (1986): 89–101.
Tov, E., "Glosses, Interpolations, and Other Types of Scribal Additions in the Text of the Hebrew Bible," in *Language, Theology, and the Bible – Essays in Honour of James Barr* (eds. S.E. Balentine and J. Barton; Oxford: Oxford University Press, 1994), 40–66.

---

[32] So Mackie, "Expanding."
[33] M. Greenberg, "What are Valid Criteria for Determining Inauthentic Matter in Ezekiel?" in *Ezekiel and His Book: Textual and Literary Criticism and Their Interrelation* (ed. J. Lust; BETL 74; Leuven: Peeters, 1986), 123–35.
[34] Crane, *Restoration*; Mackie, "Expanding."
[35] M. Greenberg, "Valid Criteria"; D.I. Block, *The Book of Ezekiel 1–24* (NICOT; Grand Rapids: Eerdmans, 1997); D.I. Block, *The Book of Ezekiel 25–48* (NICOT; Grand Rapids: Eerdmans, 1998).
[36] K.-F. Pohlmann, *Der Prophet Hesekiel/Ezechiel Kapitel 1–19* (ATD 22.1; Göttingen: Vandenhoeck & Ruprecht, 1996);

K.-F. Pohlmann, *Der Prophet Hesekiel/Ezechiel Kapitel 20–48* (ATD 22.2; Göttingen: Vandenhoeck & Ruprecht, 2001); Tooman, *Gog*; E. Tov, "Some Sequential Differences Between the MT and LXX and Their Ramifications for the Literary Criticism of the Hebrew Bible," *JNSL* 13 (1987): 151–60; W. Zimmerli, *Ezekiel 1–2* (Hermeneia; Philadelphia: Fortress, 1979–1983). German original: *Ezekiel 1–2* (BKAT 13.1–2; Neukirchen-Vluyn: Neukirchener, 1969).

Tov, E., "The Nature of Large Scale Differences between the LXX and the MT S T V: Compared with Similar Evidence in Other Sources," in Schenker, *Earliest Text, 121–44.
Tov, E., *TCHB.

William A. Tooman

8.2.3 Other Texts

Unlike the case with many other biblical books, no Hebrew Ezekiel manuscripts that attest to a text unrelated to the Masoretic textual tradition have survived from the Second Temple period. All ancient Ezekiel manuscripts of which sufficient text is preserved for textual qualification (4QEzek[a] → 8.2.1.4; 4QEzek[b] → 8.2.1.4; 11QEzek → 8.2.1.6; MasEzek → 8.2.1.7) align with MT-Ezek. This raises the question whether any other Hebrew texts of Ezekiel existed in the Second Temple period. In drawing on non-Masoretic texts for their translations,[1] OG-Ezek and LXX[967]-Ezek seem to demonstrate the existence of Hebrew Ezekiel texts in antiquity other than semi/proto-MT-Ezek. Three quotations from Ezekiel in Hebrew non-biblical texts from the Qumran library might add further proof that non-Masoretic Ezekiel texts existed during the Second Temple period. However, the observations below need to remain preliminary because a systematic text-critical study of all Ezekiel quotations and allusions in Second Temple Jewish literature is missing.[2]

CD B 19:12 reads in an explicit quotation of Ezek 9:4 נאנחים ונאנקים "those who moan and lament" instead of MT-Ezek's הָאֲנָשִׁים הַנֶּאֱנָחִים וְהַנֶּאֱנָקִים "the men who moan and lament" (cf. LXX: τῶν ἀνδρῶν τῶν καταστεναζόντων καὶ τῶν κατωδυνωμένων "of the men who sigh and have been afflicted"). The reading of the quotation in the *Damascus Document* goes back to a non-aligned parent text, because the grammar of the quotation contradicts the grammar of its context in CD. CD contrasts והנשארים "and those who remain [unmarked]" in line 13 with נאנחים ונאנקים "who moan and lament" from Ezek 9:4. In CD B 19:13, והנשארים includes a determinative as do the words (הַנֶּאֱנָחִים וְהַנֶּאֱנָקִים "the ones who moan and lament") in MT-Ezek 9:4, although this determinative is missing in the words נאנחים ונאנקים "those who moan and lament" in the Ezekiel quotation in CD B 19:12. As the context of the Ezekiel quotation in CD B 19:23 would require a determinative and because there is not one in the quotation, CD relies for the words נאנחים ונאנקים on a biblical parent text. CD's biblical parent text read thus most likely against MT the words נאנחים ונאנקים.

For MT-Ezek's יִקְרְבוּ אֵלַי לְשָׁרְתֵנִי וְעָמְדוּ לְפָנַי לְהַקְרִיב "they shall approach me to minister me, and they shall stand before me, to present" (cf. LXX οὗτοι προσάξουσι πρός με τοῦ λειτουργεῖν μοι καὶ στήσονται πρὸ προσώπου μου τοῦ προσφέρειν "they shall advance towards me, and they shall stay in front of me to offer"), CD A 4:2 reads in a quotation from Ezek 44:15 יגישו "they shall bring near me." The passage is part of a longer explicit quotation of Ezek 44:15 in CD A 3:21–4:2. Unlike other textual changes to this explicit quotation from Ezek 44:15, there are no indications that the author of the *Damascus Document* substituted the longer MT reading with יגישו. CD's Ezekiel-parent text therefore read already יגישו "they shall bring near me" instead of the יִקְרְבוּ אֵלַי לְשָׁרְתֵנִי וְעָמְדוּ לְפָנַי לְהַקְרִיב "they shall approach me to minister me, and they shall stand before me, to present" in MT-Ezek.

4QMidrEschat[a] III:16–17 (olim 4QFlor I:16–17) reads in its explicit quotation of Ezek 37:23 [בכול גֹּל[ו]ליהמה "through all their idols" against MT-Ezek (בְּגִלּוּלֵיהֶם "through their idols") and LXX-Ezek (ἐν τοῖς εἰδώλοις αὐτῶν "through their idols"), although the context of the quotation in the *Midrash on Eschatology* does not require the insertion of בכול "through all."

---

[1] Cf. → 8.1 and → 8.3.
[2] Schwagmeier ("Untersuchungen," 69–86) and Lange (*Handbuch, 330–31) limit their studies to select groups of Ezekiel quotations and allusions in mainly Essene texts from the Qumran library. Against my earlier study, the occurrence of הארץ "the land" instead of MT's אֶרֶץ "land" (cf. LXX γῆν 'land') in the allusion to Ezek 19:7 in CD A 5:21 goes back to the use of הארץ "the land" in CD A 5:20 and therefore should not be regarded as attesting to a textual variant. Furthermore, 1QSb v:27–28 does not allude to Ezek 19:11 but more likely to Isa 14:5.

Lange, A., *Handbuch*, 330–31.
Schwagmeier, P., "Untersuchungen zu Textgeschichte und Entstehung des Ezechielbuches in masoretischer und griechischer Überlieferung" (ThD diss., University of Zurich, 2004), esp. 69–86.

Armin Lange

8.3 Septuagint

8.3.1 Background

The original translation was probably made around the same time as that of Jeremiah and the Twelve. The books of Jeremiah and Ezekiel may have been prepared by the same translator.[1] He/they worked with a Hebrew text that differed considerably from MT (→ 8.2.2) and circulated concurrently for a prolonged period. The parent text of LXX-Ezek most likely antedated MT (→ 8.3.2).[2] Block directed a seven-point challenge against the priority of papyrus LXX^{967}, defending the integrity of MT as the ancient standardized form.[3]

An absolute dating of the translation is difficult. According to Barthélemy, section β (= Ezekiel 26–39) of Ezekiel may show traces of a pre-*kaige* recension. He suggests that this recension originated in the Palestinian Hillel school before the destruction of the Second Temple.[4] Translators of other biblical books, such as Isaiah, tend to adapt the text to their own times and location, allowing us to date their work. However, historical allusions, if existent, are veiled in LXX-Ezek. In Ezek 21:31, reference may be made to the Maccabean high priest and king, Jonathan, who "took off" the priestly turban and "put on" the royal crown.[5]

8.3.2 Original Form, Editions, Tools

LXX^{967} and LXX^{988} are, together with Codex Vaticanus (LXX^B), the main witnesses to the pre-Hexaplaric Old Greek text. LXX^{988} (Antinoopolis papyrus) contains parts of Ezek 33:27–31 and 34:1–5, 18–24, 26–30.[6] The preserved sections of LXX^{967} cover most of Ezek 11:25–48:35.[7] This version of LXX-Ezek appears to betray the hand of an early revision towards MT (→ 8.2.2).[8] One of the special features of LXX^{967} is its ordering of the materials, which differs from that in MT and in the mainstream Greek manuscripts: Ezekiel 11–36:23b (up to and including ἐγώ εἰμι κύριος "I am the Lord"); 38–39; 37; 40–48. The same order as well as the lack of Ezek 36:23c–38 is found in the Vetus Latina (Codex Wirceburgensis; → 6–9.2.1.3),[9] which is not dependent on LXX^{967}.

A study of the relation of LXX^{967} to MT, Syro-Hexapla (→ 6–9.2.4.3), and LXX allowed Gehman to conclude that, of all our Greek manuscripts, this papyrus has preserved a text of Ezekiel closest to the original Greek translation. In his view, the authority of LXX^B as our best source for the original text must give way to this new evidence.[10] (This does not apply to many of the "minuses" that are typical of the papyrus, which are omissions or corruptions due to *homoioteleuton*; see Jahn.[11])

An excellent critical edition of the Greek text has been provided by Ziegler.[12] When he published his edition in the Göttingen series in 1952, he did not yet have at his disposal the Ezekiel fragments of LXX^{988}, which he collated with his 1952 edition in an appendix to his edition of *Susanna, Daniel, Bel et Draco* in 1954.[13] In addition, only the sections belonging to the Chester Beatty and John H. Scheide papyri of LXX^{967} had been available to him. The

---

[1] Thackeray, *Septuagint*, 39; Tov, *Jeremiah–Baruch*, 149–50.
[2] Lust, "Criticism," 28–31; Schwagmeier, *Untersuchungen*, 368; Crane, *Restoration*, 258; Pohlmann, *Stand*, 23–27, 127–30; Rösel, *Gog*, 44; Lilly, *Two Books*, 308–10.
[3] D.I. Block, *The Book of Ezekiel: Chapters 25–48* (NICOT; Grand Rapids: William B. Eerdmans, 1998), 338–43. But see the critique by Lust ("Criticism," 15–31).
[4] Barthélemy, *Devanciers*, 42, 47, 271.
[5] Olley, "Trajectories I," 155; compare van der Kooij, "Leadership," 440.
[6] The first edition was published by Roberts (*Antinoopolis*).
[7] The first editions of LXX^{967} were published by Kenyon (*Ezekiel*), Johnson, Gehman, and Kase (*Scheide*), Fernández-Galiano ("Nuevas Paginas"), and Jahn (*Ezekiel*).
[8] Johnson, Gehman, and Kase, *Scheide*, 101.
[9] Bogaert, "Témoignage."
[10] In Johnson, Gehman, and Kase, *Scheide*, 79; see also Ziegler, "Bedeutung," 76–94.
[11] Jahn, *Der griechische Text*, 126–28.
[12] Ziegler, *Ezechiel* (first ed. 1952).
[13] J. Ziegler (ed.), *Susanna, Daniel, Bel et Draco* (Septuaginta Vetus Testamentum Graecum 16.2; Göttingen: Vandenhoeck & Ruprecht, 1954).

more recently discovered substantial sections of LXX[967] were collated by Detlef Fraenkel and incorporated, together with Ziegler's collation of LXX[988], as a "Nachtrag" in the second and third editions of Ziegler's *Ezechiel*.

Auxiliary tools for the study of LXX-Ezek are offered by modern translations and commentaries.[14]

8.3.3 Translation Character and Technique

The translation of LXX-Ezek is fairly literal and rather wooden. It belongs to the group of most slavishly rendered books of the Hebrew Bible.[15] In Ezekiel 1–39, especially, the Greek most often renders its parent text word for word. Each Hebrew word and each of its constituents have an equivalent in the Greek text; a concordant translation is not pursued. In different texts, the same Hebrew word is often translated by a different Greek word.

A salient aspect of LXX-Ezek is the Hebrew character of its syntax.[16] The main symptom is perhaps the retention of Hebrew word order,[17] even when this militates against that of the Greek. For an example, we refer to the use of the copula. In Hebrew, many clauses, paragraphs, and larger sections begin with the copula -ו "and." Accordingly, most sections (sixty-four) begin with the conjunction καί "and" followed by the verb ἐγένετο "it happened," emulating Hebrew ויהי "and it happened,"[18] often (forty times) in the word-event formula καὶ ἐγένετο λόγος κυρίου πρός με λέγων "and the word of the Lord happened to me, saying." Hardly any classical or Koine Greek compositions begin a new section that way. For example, in 2 Maccabees, written in Greek, this feature is totally absent.

The fact that LXX-Ezek adheres to the Hebrew word order suggests that the translator was very faithful to his parent text. Therefore, when deviations from MT (→ 8.2.2) do occur, they may be due to a *Vorlage* differing from MT.

8.3.4 Text-Critical Value

The value of LXX and its daughter version, the Vetus Latina (→ 6–9.2.1.3), has often been acknowledged in reconstructions of the Hebrew text of Ezekiel. Textual critics and commentators tend to retrovert the Greek text into Hebrew and treat the resulting hypothetical *Vorlage* of LXX as if it were a variant Hebrew manuscript reading. Indeed, they sometimes argue that it represents an older and superior witness to the original MT (→ 8.2.2) than the preserved Hebrew manuscripts (→ 8.2.1) and they emend the Hebrew text accordingly. On the other hand, Greenberg and Halperin have warned against a haphazard use of LXX in attempts towards a correction of MT.[19]

The use of LXX in the textual criticism of the Hebrew Bible should not be based exclusively on the critical LXX editions, according to which the combined minuses of LXX do not amount to more than 4–5 percent of the text,[20] but should also take into account the shorter text of LXX[967], which reflects the Old Greek (→ 1.3.1.1.12).

The longest minus in OG-Ezek occurs at the end of Ezekiel 36, where verses 23c (from נאם אדני יהוה "utterance of the Lord God") to 38 are absent from LXX[967] and the Vetus Latina (Codex Wirceburgensis). The present Greek translation in the majority manuscript tradition may then be disregarded as it betrays the hand of Theodotion (→ 6–9.1.5.3.1). Other longer minuses in LXX[967] occur in Ezek 12:26–28 and 32:25–26. They are often labeled as omissions or corruptions due to *paraplepsis*. However, a closer study reveals that they most likely witness to an earlier Hebrew text in which these

---

[14] Hubler, "Iezekiel," (*NETS*); A. Hammerstaedt-Löhr, M. Konkel, H. Löhr, and K. Usener, "Jezekiel: Das Buch Ezechiel (Hesekiel)," in *Septuaginta Deutsch*, 1362–416 and A. Hammerstaedt-Löhr, M. Konkel, H. Löhr, and K. Usener, "Jezekiel: Ezechiel / Hesekiel," in *Septuaginta Deutsch, Erläuterungen*, 2.2849–3007. An English translation and commentary of LXX[B] has been provided by Olley (*Ezekiel*).

[15] See Sollamo, *Semiprepositions*, 286–87.
[16] Olley, *Ezekiel*, 17–19.
[17] Marquis, "Word Order."
[18] Lust, "Ezéchiel dans la Septante," 341.

[19] Greenberg, "Ancient Versions," 134–48; Halperin, "Merkabah."
[20] Tov, "Recensional Differences," 91.

sections had not yet been added.[21] A set of shorter minuses, attested to in all major manuscripts of LXX, confirms this. See Schwagmeier's impressive list and convincing comments.[22]

Moreover, the chapter order in Old Greek as in LXX[967] (and Codex Wirceburgensis) is different. Ezekiel 38–39 follow Ezek 36:23b, whereas Ezekiel 37 follows Ezekiel 39. The hypothesis of the accidental omission of Ezek 36:23c–38[23] would imply that this assumed accidental omission was combined with an equally accidental transposition of Ezekiel 38–39, which is highly unlikely. It is now generally agreed upon that the chapter order and omissions must be examined together.[24] In changing the original chapter order, MT (→ 8.2.2) had to insert Ezek 36:23c–38 in order to accommodate for the transposed chapter Ezekiel 37. The longer text of MT displays its own theological emphasis, connected with the editor's opinions concerning eschatology and apocalypticism.[25] A similar assumption can be made about the other major omissions and the transposition of verses in Ezek 7:1–11.[26] As a result, OG-Ezek, as in LXX[967], does not translate MT but reflects an earlier Hebrew text form that circulated simultaneously with the later MT.

The absence in LXX-Ezek of an exact equivalent of אדני יהוה "Lord God" has been seen as a strong argument in favour of the spurious character of אדני "Lord." The pre-Hexaplaric manuscript LXX[B] and especially the ancient papyri LXX[967] and LXX[988], which best represent Old Greek, as a rule render the double divine name by a single κύριος "Lord," especially in Ezekiel 1–39. These data, however, are not necessarily to be explained by an absence of the double name in the Hebrew parent text. The Vorlage of Old Greek probably read the double name where MT has it. The translator most likely took אדני "Lord" to be an interpretation of יהוה "YHWH" and left it untranslated.[27]

Pluses in Old Greek are rather rare. The longer ones (more than three words) are mostly found in the opening chapters of the final vision (Ezek 40:7–8, 43, 44; 41:3; 42:5, 14, 16; 43:2) and are often due to the unusual terminology, which causes problems for translators and copyists.[28] The longer addition in Ezek 43:3, combined with the shorter ones in the immediate context, introduces the notion of the "chariot" (ἅρμα), which has no counterpart in MT (→ 8.2.2). The noun מרכבה "chariot" as applied to Ezekiel's visions occurs for the first time in Ben Sira 49:8. LXX-Ezek is here situated within a long history of exegetical midrash.[29]

Many other variants are probably inner-translational. They are not due to a different Vorlage, but rather to exegetical interpretation, cultural influence, complexity of the Hebrew text in its architectural terminology, later inserts in the Greek, or to ignorance of the translator. Several renderings deviating from MT imply a different vocalisation, as in Ezek 28:14: μετὰ τοῦ χερουβ "with the Cherub" for MT אַתְּ־כְּרוּב "the Cherub" (see also v. 16).[30] Some may betray Christian influence, as in LXX Ezek 17:22–23: καὶ κρεμάσω αὐτὸν ἐν ὄρει μετεώρῳ τοῦ Ισραηλ, "And I will hang him on a high mountain in Israel"; contrast Old Greek represented here by LXX[967]: καὶ κρεμαστὸν ἐν ὄρει μετεώρῳ τοῦ Ισραηλ "[… on a mountain high and lofty.] On the mountain height of Israel [I will plant it …]."

For the textual criticism of MT (→ 8.2.2), this leads to the following conclusions: MT is longer than Old Greek and its Hebrew parent text. Many of the "pluses" in MT are probably due to the hand of an editor. This implies that most of the important deviations from MT that are detected in Old Greek do not pertain to the domain of textual criticism, but rather to that of literary criticism.

---

[21] Lust, "Major Divergences," 83–89.
[22] Schwagmeier, "Untersuchungen," 152–80.
[23] Van der Meer, "New Spirit."
[24] Bogaert, "Témoignage," 384–95; Lust, "Ezekiel 36–40"; Lust, "Textual Criticism," 28–30; Schwagmeier, "Untersuchungen," 183–86; Crane, Israel's Restoration, 249; Lilly, Two Books, 126.
[25] Lust, "Major Divergences," 83–92; Lilly, Two Books, 307–08.
[26] Bogaert, "Deux rédactions," 21–47.

[27] McGregor, Greek Text, 75–83, 227–57; Lust, Hauspie, and Ternier, "Double Name," 396–403.
[28] Lust, "Exegesis," 208.
[29] Lust, "Exegesis," 209; Halperin, "Merkabah," 352.
[30] Lust, "King/Prince of Tyre."

8.3.5 Multiple Translators and the History of Research

One can safely say that the modern Septuagint research of Ezekiel started with Cornill.[31] Multiple translation theories dominated the scene in the twentieth century following the pioneering studies of Thackeray.[32] A good survey of their history was provided by McGregor.[33] In the discussions of the twenty-first century, these theories are less prominent, although the questions surrounding them have not been solved entirely. McGregor's main conclusion was that the Greek translation of Ezekiel is not homogeneous. There are three distinct large sections, Ezekiel 1–25 (α); 26–39 (β); and 40–48 (γ), and two smaller ones, Ezekiel 16 and 36:23c–38. The majority of the examples adduced in support of this theory deal with individual words. However, most of them are irrelevant since they may be due to the hand of a single translator who changed his mind or preferred some variety. In a review of McGregor's work, Muraoka draws attention to more "remarkable variants" that, according to him, must be adduced in support of a multiple translation theory.[34] In his recent contributions, Lust reached the conclusion that perhaps no plurality of translators is needed to explain the minor variations and diversity in LXX-Ezek.[35]

Barthélemy, *Devanciers.
Bogaert, P.-M., "Le témoignage de la Vetus Latina dans l'étude de la tradition des Septante: Ezéchiel et Daniel dans le papyrus 967," *Bib* 59 (1978): 384–95.
Cornill, C.H., *Das Buch des Propheten Ezechiel* (Leipzig: J.C. Hinrichs, 1886).
Crane, A.S., *Israel's Restoration: A Textual-Comparative Exploration of Ezekiel 36–39* (VTSup 122; Leiden: Brill, 2008).
Fernandez-Galiano, M., "Nuevas Paginas del codice 967 del A.T. griego," *SPap* 10 (1971): 7–76.
Greenberg, M., "The Use of Ancient Versions for Interpreting the Hebrew Text: A Sampling from Ezekiel ii 1-iii 11," in *Congress Volume: Göttingen 1977* (VTSup 29; Leiden: Brill, 1978): 131–48.
Halperin, D.J., "Merkabah Midrash in the Septuagint," *JBL* 101 (1982): 351–63.
Hubler, N., "Iezekiel," in *NETS, 946–85.
Jahn, L.G., *Der griechische Text des Buches Ezechiel nach dem Kölner Teil des Papyrus 967* (Papyrologische Texte und Abhandlungen 15; Bonn: Habelt, 1972).
Johnson, A.C., H.S. Gehman, and E.H. Kase, *The John H. Scheide Biblical Papyri: Ezekiel* (Princeton University Studies in Papyrology 3; Princeton: Princeton University Press, 1938).
Kenyon, F.G., *The Chester Beatty Biblical Papyri: Ezekiel*, Fasc. 7 (2 vols.; London: Emory Walker, 1937, 1938).
van der Kooij, A., "The Septuagint of Ezekiel and Hasmonaean Leadership," in *Interpreting Translation: Studies on the LXX and Ezekiel in Honour of Johan Lust* (eds. F. García Martínez and M. Vervenne; BETL 192; Leuven: Peeters, 2005), 437–46.
Lilly, I.E., *Two Books of Ezekiel: Papyrus 967 and the Masoretic Text as Variant Literary Editions* (VTSup 150; Leiden: Brill, 2012).
Lust, J., "Ezekiel 36–40 in the Oldest Greek Manuscript," *CBQ* 43 (1981): 517–33.
Lust, J., "Exegesis and Theology in the Septuagint of Ezekiel: The Longer 'Pluses' and Ezek 43:1–9," in *VI Congress of the International Organization for Septuagint and Cognate Studies, Jerusalem 1986* (ed. C.E. Cox; SBLSCS 23; Atlanta: Scholars Press, 1987), 405–24.
Lust, J., "Textual Criticism of the Old Testament and of the New Testament: Stepbrothers?" in *New Testament Textual Criticism and Exegesis: Festschrift Joël Delobel* (ed. A. Denaux; BETL 161; Leuven: Peeters, 2002), 15–31.
Lust, J., "Major Divergences between LXX and MT in Ezekiel," in Schenker, *Earliest Text*, 83–89.
Lust, J., K. Hauspie, and A. Ternier, "Notes to the Septuagint: Ezekiel 6 and The Double Name," *ETL* 76 (2000): 396–403.
Lust, J., "Ezéchiel dans la Septante," in *Les recueils prophétiques de la Bible: Origine, milieux, et contexte proche-oriental* (eds. J.-D. Macchi, C. Nihan, T. Römer, and J. Rückl; MdB 64; Geneva: Labor et Fides, 2012), 337–58.
Lust, J., "The King/Prince of Tyre in Ezekiel 28:11–19 in Hebrew and in Greek," in *Textual Criticism and Dead Sea Scrolls: Studies in Honour of Julio Trebolle Barrera: Florilegium Complutense* (eds. A. Piquer Ottero and

---

[31] Cornill, *Ezechiel*.
[32] H.St.J. Thackeray, "The Greek Translators of Ezekiel"; Thackeray, *Septuagint*.
[33] McGregor, *Greek Text*.
[34] Muraoka, "Review."
[35] Lust, "Ezéchiel dans la Septante," 344–48.

P.A. Torijano Morales; JSJSup 157; Leiden: Brill, 2012), 223–39.

Marquis, G., "Word Order as a Criterion for the Evaluation of Translation Technique in the LXX and the Evaluation of Word Order Variants as Exemplified in LXX-Ezekiel," *Text* 13 (1986): 59–84.

McGregor, L.J., *The Greek Text of Ezekiel: An Examination of Its Homogeneity* (SBLSCS 18; Atlanta: Scholars Press, 1985).

van der Meer, M.N., "A New Spirit in an Old Corpus? Text-Critical, Literary-Critical and Linguistic Observations regarding Ezekiel 36:16–38," in *The New Things: Eschatology in Old Testament Pro-phecy: Festschrift Henk Leene* (eds. F. Postma, K. Spronk, and E. Talstra; ACEBTSup 3; Maastricht, 2002), 147–58.

Muraoka, T., "Review of L.J. McGregor, *The Greek Text of Ezekiel: An Examination of Its Homogeneity*," *JSS* 31 (1986): 84–87.

Olley, J.W., *Ezekiel: A Commentary Based on Iezekiel in Codex Vaticanus* (Septuagint Commentary Series; Leiden: Brill, 2009).

Olley, J.W., "Trajectories of Ezekiel: Part 1," *CBR* 9 (2011): 137–70.

Pohlmann, K.-F., *Ezechiel: Der Stand der theologischen Diskussion* (Darmstadt: WBG, 2008).

Roberts, C.H., *The Antinoopolis Papyri*, Part 1 (London: Egypt Exploration Society, 1950), 19–23 Nr. 10.

Rösel, C., *JHWHs Sieg über Gog aus Magog* (WMANT 132; Neukirchen: Neukirchener Verlag, 2012).

Schwagmeier, P., "Untersuchungen zur Textgeschichte und Entstehung des Ezechielbuches in masoretischer und griechischer Überlieferung" (unpub. ThD diss.; University of Zurich, 2004).

Sollamo, R., *Renderings of Hebrew Semiprepositions in the Septuagint* (AASF Diss. Hum. Litt. 19; Helsinki: Suomolainen Tiedeakatemia, 1979).

Thackeray, H.St.J., "The Greek Translators of Ezekiel," *JTS* 4 (1903): 398–411.

Thackeray, *Septuagint.

Tov, *Jeremiah–Baruch.

Tov, E., "Recensional Differences between the Masoretic Text and the Septuagint of Ezekiel," *ETL* 62 (1986): 89–101.

Ziegler, J., "Die Bedeutung der Chester Beatty – Scheide Papyrus 967 für die Textüberlieferung der Ezechiel-Septuaginta," *ZAW* 61 (1945–1948): 74–96 = *Sylloge: Gesammelte Aufsätze zur Septuaginta* (MSU 10; Göttingen: Vandenhoeck & Ruprecht, 1971), 321–39.

Ziegler, J., "Zur Textgestaltung der Ezechiel-Septuaginta," *Bib* 34 (1953): 435–55 = *Sylloge: Gesammelte Aufsätze zur Septuaginta* (MSU 10; Göttingen: Vandenhoeck & Ruprecht, 1971), 394–414.

Ziegler, J. (ed.), *Ezechiel* (Septuaginta Vetus Testamentum Graecum 16.1; Göttingen: Vandenhoeck & Ruprecht, 1952; 2nd ed. 1977 ["Mit einem Nachtrag von Detlef Fränkel," including a full collation of P967]; 3rd ed. 2006).

Johan Lust

9
Minor Prophets

9.1 Textual History of the Minor Prophets

9.1.1 Witnesses to the Minor Prophets

9.1.1.1 Hebrew Witnesses

Among the medieval manuscripts, there are three Tiberian-Masoretic codices that are particularly useful witnesses to the Minor Prophets. The Leningrad Codex (MT^L), on which *BHS and *BHQ are based, contains the entire text of all twelve prophets. The codex dates to 1009 C.E. and its vocalization and accentuation are based on the Ben Asher tradition. The Aleppo Codex (MT^A), which was vocalized and accented by Aaron Ben Asher, is extant for Hos 1:1–Amos 8:12, Mic 5:1–Zeph 3:20, and Zech 9:17–Mal 3:24. It is dated to approximately 925 C.E. Lastly, the Cairo Codex of the Prophets (MT^C) contains the full text of the Minor Prophets and is dated to the eleventh century C.E. (→ 3–5.3). These codices are generally regarded as being reliable witnesses to the Minor Prophets as a whole, though, with regard to individual books such as Hosea and Micah, there have been claims in the past of extensive corruption (→ 9.1.3.1; → 9.1.3.6).

Of the pre-Masoretic witnesses, MurXII (→ 9.2.1.5) attests to the most material. This leather scroll is dated to the first or second century C.E. and contains most of the text from Joel 2:20 to Zech 1:4. The text deviates very little from MT. Another important pre-Masoretic witness is 1QpHab, which contains text citations from the first two chapters of Habakkuk. Other pre-Masoretic witnesses were also found at Qumran, each being fragmentary (→ 9.2.1): 4QpIsa^c, 4QpHos^a, 4QpHos^b, 5QAmos, 1QpMic, 4QpMic, 4QpNah, 1QpZeph, 4QpZeph, 4QCommMal, 5QapocrMal, 4QXII^a–g, 4QFlor, 4QTanḥ, and 4QCatena A. It should be noted that 4QXII^a and 4QXII^b are both dated to the middle of the second century B.C.E. and are thus the oldest extant manuscripts of the Minor Prophets (→ 9.2.1.1; → 9.2.1.2; → 9.2.2, → 9.2.2.2, → 9.2.2.4).

9.1.1.2 Greek Witnesses

The eclectic text of the Göttingen edition seeks to represent the Old Greek text of the Minor Prophets.[1] Regarding the underlying Hebrew of the Old Greek (→ 9.3), Gelston states that it "reflects a Hebrew *Vorlage* that is similar though not identical to M[T]" (→ 9.2.2).[2] There are a few individual witnesses that bear mentioning. First, the scroll identified as 8ḤevXII gr, a fragmentary text, is extant for portions of text within Jonah 1:14–Zech 9:5. Parsons has tentatively dated it to the late first century B.C.E.,[3] thus making it the oldest Greek witness to the Minor Prophets. The text of the scroll is a revision of the Old Greek, conforming it to a text similar to that of MT (→ 9.3; → 1.3.1.2). Second, the Freer Manuscript (LXX^W) is a mid- to late-third-century C.E. papyrus codex attesting to material from the end of Hosea to the end of Malachi, though the text is continuous starting at Amos 1:10. The manuscript contains a number of readings that agree with or were conformed to the Hebrew. Lastly, there are six Greek manuscripts that witness to a divergent version of Hab 3:3–19; they are designated as the Barberini version (→ 9.3.4).

9.1.1.3 Latin Witnesses

There are Old Latin fragments that attest to the texts of Hos 2:12–4:8, 10:5–11:9, Joel 2:3–25, and Amos 1:11–3:2 (→ 6–9.2.1). They and the Vulgate (→ 6–9.1.7) primarily witness to a text similar to that of MT (→ 9.2.2).[4]

9.1.1.4 Syriac and Aramaic Witnesses

The text of the Peshitta (→ 6–9.1.4) is very similar to that of MT (→ 9.2.2), however Gelston notes that it does contain a number of variant readings in agreement with the Old Greek (→ 9.3) and a

---

[1] Ziegler, *Duodecim prophetae*.
[2] A. Gelston, "Introduction and Commentaries," 7*.
[3] See P.J. Parsons, "The Scripts and Their Date," *DJD* VIII: 19–26.
[4] A. Gelston, "Introduction and Commentaries," 8*.

smaller number in agreement with the Targum.[5] Like the Peshitta, the text of the Targum (→ 6–9.1.3) generally agrees with that of MT.

9.1.2 The Order of the Minor Prophets

Scholars have long contemplated the reasons behind the different orders of The Twelve Prophets found in the Hebrew and Greek texts. In MT (→ 9.2.2) and most versions the order is: Hosea, Joel, Amos, Obadiah, Jonah, Micah, Nahum, Habakkuk, Zephaniah, Haggai, Zechariah, Malachi. In LXX (→ 9.3), however, the order is: Hosea, Amos, Micah, Joel, Obadiah, Jonah, Nahum, Habakkuk, Zephaniah, Haggai, Zechariah, Malachi. The traditional ordering found in MT and most versions is likely best accounted for on the grounds of a mixture of chronological and thematic considerations. Regarding the order found in LXX, many suggestions have been put forward. Wolff recognizes that LXX, in its collected form, shows a pronounced interest in chronological ordering: Ruth is placed alongside Judges and Ezra–Nehemiah follow 1–2 Chronicles. In light of this, it seems reasonable to suggest that the ordering of Hosea, Amos, and Micah was based on chronological factors while the books of Joel, Obadiah, and Jonah were grouped together owing to the fact that they are undated books.[6] Other factors have also been considered. Macintosh states that the length of the books appears to have been determinative.[7] However, this does not account for the placement of Jonah after Obadiah (which Macintosh explains was due to the book being a narrative about a prophet),[8] nor does it account for the order of the last six books of the collection (→ 9.3.1).

9.1.3 Original Texts and Textual Aspects of the Books

Much of the scholarship on the Minor Prophets regards the books as having undergone editorial changes over time. Many discussions thus center on attempts to discern what of the text is original and what is a later revision. As the Minor Prophets is a collection of individual books, each one with its own textual history, some books are more problematic than others. Hosea, most notably, has been problematic for textual critics. Some regard it as having suffered extensive corruption over time, while others postulate a different dialect of Hebrew as the source of many of the textual issues. The text of Micah has also been thought of as rather corrupt; further complicating matters, some scholars see evidence that the book is the product of multiple authors from different centuries.

At the textual level, there are a few commonalities between some of the books. Hosea, Amos, Micah, and Zephaniah contain similar superscriptions, which are distinct from the superscriptions in the other eight books,[9] Joel and Amos share some verbal agreements,[10] and there are literary, stylistic, and linguistic features shared by Haggai and Zechariah 1–8.[11] Further, Nogalski has argued that there are cross-references and shared catchwords in the books; thus he suggests they were edited together and reached their final form only after being collected rather than being collected after their final forms had settled, as has been traditionally assumed.[12]

The sections below briefly detail the various conclusions that have been made with regard to the original text and revisional layers of each book. Following these discussions, there will be short sections on the textual aspects of the book and any literary aspects, if applicable.

---

[5] A. Gelston, "Introduction and Commentaries on the Twelve Minor Prophets," 9*.

[6] Wolff, *Joel and Amos*, 3. Crenshaw also claims chronological factors affected the arrangement in LXX (Crenshaw, *Joel*, 23).

[7] Macintosh, *A Critical and Exegetical Commentary on Hosea*, lii.

[8] Macintosh, *A Critical and Exegetical Commentary on Hosea*, lii.

---

[9] See Sweeney, *Zephaniah*, 13.

[10] See Paul, *Amos*, 1; Wolff, *Joel and Amos*, 3.

[11] See Meyers and Meyers, *Haggai, Zechariah 1–8*, xliv–lxiii; Jones, *Formation*, 56.

[12] Nogalski, *Literary Precursors*; Nogalski, *Redactional Processes*.

9.1.3.1 Hosea

There is a very wide range of scholarly opinion regarding the original text of Hosea. Some scholars posit multiple secondary sources,[13] while others maintain that the text as we now have it is, more or less, the original text.[14] It is often suggested that later Judaic redactions took place, given that there are numerous mentions of Judah even though Hosea was a prophet to the northern kingdom,[15] but some scholars have put forward reasonable counterarguments to this view.[16] Most recently, Nogalski has suggested that Hosea underwent various redactions, with the latter stages presuming exilic and postexilic settings in places. He argues for at least three kinds of material having been added to the book: later perspectives that shape the structure and message of the book, insertions that apply the prophet's message to Judah, and some of the material in Hosea 12–14 that possibly shows more awareness of the developing Hebrew canon than is often acknowledged.[17] However one regards the original text of Hosea, it remains a complex book that must be approached carefully.

Textual Aspects: Traditionally, Hosea has been regarded as having one of the most corrupt texts in the Hebrew Bible, filled with extremely difficult readings that are frequently subjected to emendation.[18] More recent scholarship, however, has provided two counterpositions to this stance: firstly, it has been suggested that the text of Hosea should not be read as typical classical Hebrew prose or poetry. Therefore, rather than assuming corruption of the text, the initial presumption should be in favor of regarding the text as containing many peculiarities.[19] Secondly, it has been argued that the difficulties of the book are not due to a corrupt text but rather to our unfamiliarity with the language and dialect of the northern kingdom.[20] Before further scholarly discussions on the textual difficulties in the text of Hosea, these counterpositions ought to be taken into consideration. If they are found to be valid concerns, many of the difficulties in the text could find avenues of explanation other than corruption.

Harper lists a large number of corruptions in MT (→ 9.2.2). While he believes that some of the Hebrew text can be reconstructed by appealing to LXX, he states that many of the same corruptions (such as seemingly uninterpretable passages) are in it as well.[21] Macintosh, however, sees only four consonantal emendations that need to be made, three occasions that merit the adoption of manuscript readings at variance with *BHS, two instances in which the *Qere* reading is to be preferred to the *Ketiv*, and seven occurrences in which corrections to the pointing should be made.[22]

9.1.3.2 Joel

The book of Joel is generally accepted as reflecting the original text with the possible exception of Joel 4:4–8 (3:4–8).[23] However, on the basis that the genuine Joel would not use common, well-known phrases from other prophets owing to his propensity for fine literary style, some traditional scholarship argued that the Day of YHWH content in Joel 1–2 were later interpolations written for the purpose of connecting Joel 1–2 with 3–4. For similar reasons of literary style, most of Joel 3–4 was regarded as the product of a hand other than that of the prophet's.[24] Nogalski takes a very different approach to Joel. He argues that the book was compiled for its location in the Minor Prophets and

---

[13] See Harper, *Amos and Hosea*, clix–clxii.

[14] See Andersen and Freedman, *Hosea*, 68–76; Stuart, *Hosea–Jonah*, 14–15.

[15] See Nogalski, *Hosea–Jonah*, 25; Macintosh, *Hosea*, lxxi–lxxii, lxxv; Wolff, *Hosea*, xxxi–xxxii; Harper, *Amos and Hosea*, clix. These redactions, if they indeed are not original, tend to be no more than glosses, portions of verses, or the occasional whole verse.

[16] See Andersen and Freedman, *Hosea*, 73; Stuart, *Hosea–Jonah*, 14–15.

[17] J. Nogalski, *Hosea–Jonah*, 25–26.

[18] See Harper, *Amos and Hosea*, clxxiii; Wolff, *Hosea*, xxx; Stuart, *Hosea–Jonah*, 13.

[19] Andersen and Freedman, *Hosea*, 59.

[20] Macintosh, *Hosea*, liii.

[21] Harper, *Amos and Hosea*, clxxiii–clxxvii. For a summary of Harper's list of errors, see Macintosh, *Hosea*, lxxiv.

[22] Macintosh, *Hosea*, lxxiv–lxxv.

[23] See Crenshaw, *Joel*, 30; Wolff, *Joel, Amos*, 6–8.

[24] See Bewer, "Joel," 49–56.

serves as a theological reflection within the context of the Book of the Twelve.[25]

Textual Aspects: Stuart notes textual corruption only in Joel 2:23 where MT reads הַמּוֹרֶה "the early rain." He suggests, as does Crenshaw, that LXX (→ 9.3) and Peshitta (→ 6–9.1.4) witness to the original reading, most likely הָאֹכֶל, מַאֲכָל or הַמָּזוֹן (all meaning "[the] food").[26] There are also textual complications in Joel 1:9, 4:8, and 4:21. However, Stuart explains them as minor issues, arguing that the first two cases are resolved with the help of LXX and, in the last case, by reading the first clause of the verse as a question; the absence of the interrogative particle is expected owing to the presence of the conjunction.[27]

9.1.3.3 Amos

Scholarship on Amos has been divided regarding the development and unity of the text. On one end of the spectrum, the book is regarded as being thoroughly permeated with secondary insertions from different hands over various periods.[28] On the other end, the book as we have it, aside from one or two minor exceptions, is attributed to Amos.[29] In the middle of the spectrum, one may find three further views: first, it is maintained that much of the book can be traced back to Amos and his disciples, though three small later redactions are postulated based on distinctive language and different intentions;[30] second, the book is divided into four sections (Amos 1–2; 3–6; 7:1–9:6, and 9:7–15) based on genre and style – it is argued that the first three sections were edited separately before they were compiled together, showing both exilic and postexilic concerns, and that the fourth was added later, based on its difference in theme from the rest of the book and the apparent concern to relate Amos to Obadiah and Joel;[31] third, the text is regarded as being more unified than previously thought but still showing evidence of an editorial hand.[32]

Textual Aspects: The text of Amos presents little difficulty, allowing scholars few comments regarding corruption.[33]

9.1.3.4 Obadiah

Despite being so small a book, there are many questions with regard to the original text of Obadiah. It is often suggested that Obad 1–14, 15, and 16–21 all came from different hands.[34] A common line of argumentation for this view is that, owing to the sudden change of address in Obad 16 from the Edomites to the Jews, Obad 15a and 16–21 cannot be original and must, instead, be the product of one or two later authors.[35] Nogalski, similarly, regards the text as showing evidence of different authors and editors, though he does not see a lengthy redactional history for the book. However, he does note that Obad 1–14 seems to have been modified by an editorial hand with an eye towards Amos 9. Regarding the book as a whole, he suggests that there are divergent building blocks in it (Obad 1–14, 15, and 16–21) that were compiled later and then edited for the book's placement in the Minor Prophets.[36] In contrast to these views, Raabe suggests that the whole book was composed for one occasion by Obadiah, though he does think that Obad 19–21 was added at a later time by the prophet.[37]

Textual Aspects: Some scholars have suggested corruptions in Obad 6, 7, 17, and 20.[38] Stuart also

---

[25] Nogalski, *Hosea–Jonah*, 204–13; Nogalski, *Redactional Processes*, 13–48.
[26] Stuart, *Hosea–Jonah*, 234, 256; Crenshaw, *Joel*, 155.
[27] Stuart, *Hosea–Jonah*, 234, 238–39, 265.
[28] See Harper, *Amos and Hosea*, cxxxi–cxxxiii; Andersen and Freedman, *Amos*, 9. Andersen and Freedman do not take take this view themselves.
[29] Paul, *Amos*, 5–6.
[30] Wolff, *Joel, Amos*, 106–13. Wolff labels the three redactions as follows: the Bethel-Exposition of the Josianic Age, the Deuteronomistic Redactions, and the Postexilic Eschatology of Salvation.

[31] Nogalski, *Hosea–Jonah*, 261–63.
[32] Andersen and Freedman, *Amos*, 10–12.
[33] See Harper, *Amos and Hosea*, clxxiii; Andersen and Freedman, *Amos*, 9–10.
[34] Nogalski, *Hosea–Jonah*, 368.
[35] Bewer, "Obadiah," 4.
[36] Nogalski, *Hosea–Jonah*, 371–76.
[37] Raabe, *Obadiah*, 17–18. See also Stuart, *Hosea–Jonah*, 407–08.
[38] Raabe, *Obadiah*, 6; Stuart, *Hosea–Jonah*, 407.

9.1.3.5 Jonah

Many scholars regard the psalm found in Jonah 2 as a later addition to the text. This is the opinion of Bewer, who states that the psalm does not fit the situation given as the danger is past and the psalmist is safe.[40] Further, Bewer argues that since, in his estimation, the original author of Jonah was a fine narrator, he would not have placed the psalm in its current position nor would he have omitted certain details such as Jonah's acceptance of the whale as God's deliverance.[41] Bewer does entertain the idea that the original author selected this psalm, the most appropriate one he could find, and then placed it after Jonah 2:11, only for it to be displaced later. However, in the end, Bewer holds that the most probable explanation is that a later reader inserted the psalm either after Jonah 2:2 or in the margin, only for it to be placed after Jonah 2:2 sometime later.[42] In contrast, some scholars, while maintaining that the psalm was inserted into the prose material, argue that it is well suited to the book of Jonah and its message.[43] Regarding the rest of the book, Sasson notes that the prose in chapter one is very different from that in chapter three and that both are different from what is found in chapter four. Therefore, he suggests the possibility that the book may contain vestiges of tales that circulated independently at one time and were gathered together for the purpose of telling the story that is now found in the book.[44] On the other hand, Nogalski views the book, aside from the psalm, as a unified whole. He argues, "The narrative logic requires something to precede 3:1, and the literary structure of chapter 1 makes the arguments for a multi-staged growth of this chapter rather strained."[45]

Textual Aspects: The text is generally regarded as attesting to a stable transmission.[46] The only emendations worth noting are the following: regarding the clause "because of whom this evil has come upon us" in Jonah 1:8, which does not appear in the Greek version in Codex Sinaiticus or Codex Vaticanus, as a marginal note, and regarding the words "for so he had told them" in Jonah 1:10 as a marginal note.[47]

Literary Aspects: There is a small difference between MT (→ 9.2.2) and LXX (→ 9.3) in Jonah 3:7–9. Whereas this section in MT contains a speech by the king of Nineveh, LXX concludes the speech at the end of v. 7, treats the content of v. 8 as narration, and views the quotation in v. 9 as coming from the people of Nineveh (in the Greek, there is a λέγοντες "saying" at the end of v. 8). The Greek thus presents, Sasson notes, a king who is inconsequential to the story and a citizenry who improvise and take charge of their own repentance; an additional effect of this is that the response of the Ninevites is given more space, and thus made more salient, in the story.[48]

9.1.3.6 Micah

Owing to thematic and literary concerns, traditional scholarship segments the book of Micah into the following three sections: Micah 1–3 (eighth century); 4–5 (sixth century); and 6–7 (seventh century).[49] Being dated to the eighth century, Micah 1–3 are generally regarded as the original nucleus.[50] However, it has been suggested that several portions of this unit appear to have been edited later in light of the message of Kings in an ex-

---

[39] Stuart, *Hosea–Jonah*, 407.
[40] Bewer, "Jonah," 21.
[41] Bewer, "Jonah," 22.
[42] Bewer, "Jonah," 22–23. Simon also argues that the prayer was a later addition (Simon, *Jonah*, xxxiii–xxxv).
[43] Sasson, *Jonah*, 17–18, 159–201, 205; Stuart, *Hosea–Jonah*, 438–40; Nogalski, *Hosea–Jonah*, 403–04.
[44] Sasson, *Jonah*, 16–19.
[45] Nogalski, *Hosea–Jonah*, 403–04.
[46] Bewer, "Jonah," 22; Stuart, *Hosea–Jonah*, 443; Sasson, *Jonah*, 9–10.
[47] For a discussion on these emendations, see Simon, *Jonah*, xlii–xliii, 11, 13.
[48] Sasson, *Jonah*, 260–61, 266.
[49] Andersen and Freedman, *Micah*, 19. Contrary to this view, Hillers sees no discernible structure in Micah and is unpersuaded by any attempt (Hillers, *Micah*, 8).
[50] Smith, "Micah," 16.

ilic context.[51] Additionally, Andersen and Freedman note that Mic 7:7(or 8)–20 has often been separated as a distinct piece, a later addition, and that this conclusion has stood the test of time.[52] Against these views, some scholars focus on how the book hangs together and argue that a lack of uniformity and consistency does not necessarily indicate more than one author.[53] Given that some scholars who argue for viewing Micah as a composite work still maintain that the book presents itself as a unity,[54] arguments for regarding Micah as a noncomposite work are not unfounded.

Textual Aspects: The Hebrew text of Micah is often viewed as being extensively corrupt. Smith writes, "The text has come down to us in a bad state of corruption ... Almost half of the errors are in chs. 1 and 2, while chs. 4 and 5 are remarkably free from them."[55] Smith regards the text of LXX-Mic (→ 9.3) to be superior to that of MT (→ 9.2.2) and thus finds the Greek invaluable in emendation. He writes that most of the errors in MT-Mic are those that are common in transmitted texts, such as wrong division of words, dittography, haplography, wrong pointing, confusion of similar consonants, transposition of words or phrases, confusion of suffixes, and deliberate theological change; for some, however, he finds the source of corruption inexplicable.[56]

9.1.3.7 Nahum

The book of Nahum as we have it is often regarded as the product of compilations and various redactions. Smith views the acrostic in Nah 1:2–10 as a later addition, arguing that its language and poetical form seem too mechanical and artificial for a poet like Nahum. He further suggests that of the remainder of the first chapter, vv. 11 and 14 are original and vv. 12–13 and 15 should be joined with chapter 2 and viewed as interpolations. Owing to the insertion of the acrostic, Smith believes some of the material that formed the original opening to the book has been displaced.[57] Similarly, he finds the opening of the section in Nah 2:4–14 too abrupt and thus suggests that its original beginning is either lost or embodied in Nah 1:11–2:3.[58] Following Wellhausen, he also regards Nah 3:18–19 as a later addition, as these verses seem to reflect the fall of Nineveh and vary from the strophic norm of their context.[59] Nogalski attributes two phases of development to the book. First, he suggests that the bulk of Nahum 2–3 represents the earlier corpus along with Nah 1:1a, 11–12, 14, and 3:16–19, regarding it as having been assembled from a series of short sayings celebrating or anticipating Assyria's imminent downfall. As such, he states that it was likely compiled around 612 B.C.E.[60] The second stage of the book added the theophanic hymn in Nah 1:2–8 and editorial transitions in Nah 1:1b, 9–15; he argues that this emphasized the invincibility of YHWH, who is only mentioned peripherally in the early corpus, against his enemies and his punishment of the wicked. No firm date for the second phase is given, though Nogalski states that a postexilic setting for the hymn seems likely.[61] Christensen, regarding Nahum within its context of The Twelve, takes a less decisive view on how the book should be divided, arguing that the redactor of The Twelve became the "author" of the book of Nahum and that the presumed literary work of the prophet is beyond recovery.[62]

Textual Aspects: Some scholars have emended the poem in Nahum 1 to produce an assumed original acrostic, however evidence from the Dead Sea Scrolls, Wadi Murabbaʿat, and Naḥal Ḥever (→ 9.2.1) indicates an accurate transmission.[63] There are

---

[51] Nogalski, *Micah–Malachi*, 511–12.
[52] Andersen and Freedman, *Micah*, 20. See also Nogalski, *Micah–Malachi*, 513–14.
[53] See Andersen and Freedman, *Micah*, 22–23.; Smith, *Micah–Malachi*, 6, 8–9.
[54] See Nogalski, *Micah–Malachi*, 514–16; Andersen and Freedman, *Micah*, 27–29.
[55] Smith, "Micah," 5. See also Hillers, *Micah*, 1.
[56] Smith, "Micah," 5. See also Smith, *Micah–Malachi*, 9.

[57] Smith, "Nahum," 268–69.
[58] Smith, "Nahum," 267.
[59] Smith, "Nahum," 269.
[60] Nogalski, *Micah–Malachi*, 601–03.
[61] Nogalski, *Micah–Malachi*, 602–03.
[62] Christensen, *Nahum*, 56–57.
[63] Smith, *Micah–Malachi*, 67.

some challenging passages in the book such as the difficulty in understanding Nah 1:10, an issue of word division in Nah 1:12, an enclitic in Nah 1:14, several *hapax legomena*, an unclear antecedent of "he" in Nah 2:6, the possibly corrupt reading in Nah 2:8, and the need to change 2nd per. fem. sg. forms to 3rd per. forms in Nah 2:14 and 3:7.[64] Christensen notes the relatively little textual corruption in Nahum, mentioning only the following five instances of marginal corrections (*Ketiv-Qere* readings): Nah 1:3 (*Qere* omits *waw*); 2:1 (*Qere* omits *waw*); 2:4 (*Qere* omits *waw*); 2.6 (*Qere* omits *waw* and adds *yod*); and 3:3 (*Qere* has *waw* in place of *yod*).[65]

9.1.3.8 Habakkuk

The original text of Habakkuk is a complex matter. First, Habakkuk 3 is often regarded as a later addition. This view is argued from various angles as such: it has no genetic connection with the first two chapters of the book but, rather, was a separate production arranged for temple worship;[66] it is an independent piece that shares similar features with books 1–3 of the Psalter, was not incorporated until these features were added, and thus, since books 1–3 of the Psalter were likely edited in the Persian period, it is given a similar date;[67] and lastly, it is an ancient composition that came down through tradition and was incorporated into the prophecy.[68] Second, there is the issue of the Babylonian material. Nogalski argues that the Babylonian material (Hab 1:5–11, 15–17) was added by a later hand and reflects a two-pronged agenda, namely: "to identify the means by which YHWH would punish Judah (sending the Babylonians) and to affirm that Babylon's power would be fleeting."[69] Ward, however, maintains that Hab 1:5–11 should not be separated from Hab 1:1–4, stating that there is no internal reason for separating the two, while also arguing that Hab 1:12–17 was not written until after the first captivity. He suggests that both sections could be original, in that Hab 1:2–11 could be retrospective and Hab 1:12–2:8 could be pleading against the continuance of the present distress.[70] Andersen seems to concur with Ward, at least to some extent, as he suggests the events in the book could have all happened within the lifetime of one person between 605 B.C.E. and 575 B.C.E.[71] Nogalski maintains that a Persian period date is the most likely for the underlying source material; he offers four considerations in support of this hypothesis: the similar features found in Habakkuk 3 and books 1–3 of the Psalter, the complaint in Hab 1:14 contains intertextual allusions to the priestly creation story, a similar style to that of Nahum of incorporating a theophanic hymn that evidences cultic overtones, and the problem of theodicy makes more sense if placed after Jerusalem's destruction than before.[72] Owing to these considerations, Nogalski writes, "One must seriously entertain the possibility that Habakkuk is a prophetic writing *compiled* during the Persian period as a theological *reflection* on the end of the seventh century rather than the words of a seventh-century prophet." Nogalski suggests that the complaints and the vision report (Hab 1:2–4, 12–14; 2:1–5) were originally a single composition dealing with the problem of theodicy that was later woven together and transformed by the Babylonian commentary.[73]

Textual Aspects: There are some textual issues with which one must contend in the book of Habakkuk. These include obscure passages such as Hab 3:13–14, at least four *hapax legomena* that are of uncertain meaning, the dropping out of a pronoun or noun in Hab 1:5 and 2:4, transposition of consonants in Hab 2:16, the difficulty in understanding יְחִיתַן "he terrifies them" in Hab 2:17, and numerous differences between MT (→ 9.2.2) and LXX (→ 9.3).[74] In addition, Andersen states that evidence from the

---

[64] Smith, *Micah–Malachi*, 67–68.
[65] Christensen, *Nahum*, 64.
[66] Ward, "Habakkuk," 3. However, Ward does leave open the possibility that Hab 3 could have been written by one of the authors of Hab 1:12–2:20 (Ward, "Habakkuk," 6).
[67] Nogalski, *Micah–Malachi*, 648.
[68] Andersen, *Habakkuk*, 24.
[69] Nogalski, *Micah–Malachi*, 647.

[70] Ward, "Habakkuk," 4–6.
[71] Andersen, *Habakkuk*, 24–27.
[72] Nogalski, *Micah–Malachi*, 648–49.
[73] Nogalski, *Micah–Malachi*, 649–52.
[74] Smith, *Micah–Malachi*, 96.

Dead Sea Scrolls demonstrates that, prior to MT becoming the prevailing text type, there were a variety of Hebrew texts in use.[75]

Literary Aspects: There also exist six manuscripts that attest to a divergent Greek translation of Habakkuk 3. This is referred to as the Barbarini version. Unfortunately, it is of little use to the text critic, for as Harper writes, "The willingness of the translator to modify his [source text] ... means that the *Vorlage* of Barb is not always accessible ... As such, Barb is not immediately of great value for the textual reconstruction of the Hebrew of Habakkuk 3 and cannot be used with any great confidence as the sole witness of a variant."[76]

9.1.3.9 Zephaniah

Given that the superscription of Zephaniah places the book in the eighth century B.C.E. but some of its content seems to reflect exilic and postexilic settings, there has been much discussion regarding the original text.[77] Smith regards all of Zephaniah 1, most of Zephaniah 2, and Zeph 3:1–5 as original. Within Zephaniah 2, he views vv. 8–11 as secondary, arguing that the phraseology presupposes the conditions of the exile as actually existing. Within Zephaniah 3, Smith suggests that vv. 6–7 may be old material but out of place in their present context, vv. 8–13 are a postexilic addition, and vv. 14–20 are another postexilic addition that has undergone some inner expansion.[78] Nogalski begins his discussion on the text of Zephaniah by separating the material that combines the fate of Jerusalem with the fate of the world (Zeph 1:2–3, 18b; 3:8, 9–10; perhaps 2:11–12), arguing that because this material appears at transition points in the book, a case can be made that the universal emphasis is later and reflects an editorial hand.[79] Barring the universal material, Nogalski holds the following opinions: Zeph 1:2–2:3 possibly reflects an early core of material associated with the prophet Zephaniah or is part of a literary creation to provide a prophetic message set in the time of Josiah;[80] Zeph 2:4–3:8 presumes an exilic setting but may be postexilic given the allusions to Genesis 10 in the last group of oracles; and Zeph 3:9–20 (11–20 after the universal material is separated) can be segmented into Zeph 3:11–13, which may represent the earliest hopeful addition to the core collection, Zeph 3:14–17, which may be postexilic as it likely presupposes a rebuilt temple, and Zeph 3:18–20, which presumes Zeph 3:14–17.[81] Nogalski further suggests that Zeph 3:20 was probably added after Zeph 3:18–19 when Haggai and Zechariah 1–8 were added to the corpus, as it anticipates the "time" of restoration in Haggai.[82]

Textual Aspects: There are a few textual difficulties in Zephaniah. Smith notes the following issues: "The grammar is often irregular (1:2, 14). Several rare words are used (2:14). Some words have been divided improperly in the MT (1:14). Some secondary meanings of words found in Egyptian and Ugaritic materials are used in the text (1:14)".[83]

9.1.3.10 Haggai

Most of the book of Haggai as we have it is accepted as the original text. There are, however, some questions as to whether Hag 1:1–11 combines two or more speeches, whether the variations between MT (→ 9.2.2) and LXX (→ 9.3) in Hag 1:2; 2:16; and 2:19 are significant enough to consider that the text was changed, and whether Hag 2:19 contains a redactional gloss.[84] Nogalski seems to base the theory that Hag 1:1–11 is a composite unit on the awkwardness of לֵאמֹר "to say" (used to introduce direct speech) ending Hag 1:1 and its being imme-

---

[75] Andersen, *Habakkuk*, 22.
[76] Harper, "Responding to a Puzzled Scribe," 115.
[77] Berlin understands the superscription to not necessarily indicate the time when the book was written but rather as a literary device used to provide a setting or backdrop against which the book was to be understood (Berlin, *Zephaniah*, 33–43).
[78] Smith, "Zephaniah," 172–73.
[79] Nogalski, *Micah–Malachi*, 699.

[80] For more discussion on this point, see Berlin, *Zephaniah*, 38–40.
[81] Nogalski, *Micah–Malachi*, 700–04.
[82] Nogalski, *Micah–Malachi*, 703–04.
[83] Smith, *Micah–Malachi*, 124.
[84] Nogalski, *Micah–Malachi*, 764.

diately followed by a messenger formula in Hag 1:2.[85] While this is an oddity, at least compared to the use of the messenger formula in Amos 1–2, it seems to be a feature of the Haggai–Zechariah 1–8 corpus. Similar cases can be found in Hag 2:10–11; Zech 1:3, 14, 17; 6:12; 7:8–9; 8:1–2, and 18–19. Thus, in Haggai–Zechariah 1–8, the messenger formula seems to be a normative part of YHWH's message to the prophet. There is no need, then, to posit a composition of speeches, at least when considering this feature of the text. Regarding the differences between MT and LXX, Nogalski states that the readings in LXX are probably the results of attempts to clarify a difficult *Vorlage*.[86] On the issue of Hag 2:19, a conceptual problem may exist between Hag 2:19a and 2:19b, which has prompted the suggestion that Hag 2:19b is a redactional gloss, added in order to invoke the fertility images from Joel.[87] However, the conceptual problem only exists when Hag 2:19a and 2:19b are read together, rather than reading Hag 2:19b with 2:19c. It has been argued that Hag 2:19b connects syntactically with Hag 2:19a and not with Hag 2:19c, but the grounds of this argument are not stated; as it stands, the Hebrew text makes sense, semantically and syntactically, when reading Hag 2:19b and 2:19c together and thus does not require a postulated redactional gloss.[88]

Textual Aspects: On the whole, the text of Haggai attests to an excellently stable transmission. Meyers and Meyers note a few instances in which revocalization is necessary, but they maintain that there is no need to rearrange the consonantal text. They also note the different reading of Hag 2:1 in MurXII (→ 9.2.1.9), which contains אל "to" rather than the בְּיַד "by the hand" in MT.[89] Lastly, though בַּשִּׁשִׁי "in the sixth [month]" in Hag 1:15 has sometimes been regarded as misplaced,[90] Meyers and Meyers put forward a reasonable argument against this view.[91]

9.1.3.11 Zechariah

Most scholarship is in agreement that the book of Zechariah is composed of two parts: Zechariah 1–8, dated close to the time of the sixth-century B.C.E. prophet, and Zechariah 9–14, which is often placed in the Persian or early Hellenistic period.[92] These units, referred to as First Zechariah and Second Zechariah, respectively, are thus often treated separately.

On the whole, First Zechariah is regarded as having been affected little by editors, revisers, and copyists,[93] though Nogalski views tensions present between Zech 1:7–6:15 and Zechariah 7–8 as signs of later editing, maintaining that the two units are not "unified" by the hand of a single author composing them in one setting but, at the same time, are "unified" by arrangers and editors who sought to provide the impression of a cohesive presentation.[94]

Regarding Second Zechariah, Nogalski argues that relatively independent units were compiled together thematically to create what is now Zechariah 9–14, noting that the two discernible thematic blocks, Zechariah 9–11 and Zechariah 12–14, were likely combined as part of the same process.[95] On the other hand, Meyers and Meyers entertain the possibility that, due to unifying elements in the text, one author is responsible for Second

---

[85] Nogalski, *Micah–Malachi*, 774.
[86] Nogalski, *Micah–Malachi*, 764.
[87] Nogalski, *Micah–Malachi*, 791–92.
[88] Nogalski only states that the syntax of the second line connects with the first and not the third; he does not explain why this is necessarily the case. Presumably, the issue could be the singular verb נָשָׂא "it produced" at the end of Hag 2:19c. However, a verb that follows compound subjects, as Joüon and Muraoka note, "sometimes remains in the singular when the two [or several] nouns, forming a single idea, are taken as a single concept" (P. Joüon and T. Muraoka, *A Grammar of Biblical Hebrew* [SubBi 27; Rome: Editrice Pontificio Istituto Biblico, 2008], § 150*p*). Further, given the disjunctive accent over בַּמְּגוּרָה "in the storehouse" at the end of Hag 2:19a, it would seem that, at the least, the Masoretes did not read Hag 2:19b with Hag 2:19a.

[89] Meyers–Meyers, *Haggai, Zechariah 1–8*, lxvii–lxviii.
[90] Smith, *Micah–Malachi*, 149.
[91] Meyers–Meyers, *Haggai, Zechariah 1–8*, 36.
[92] See Nogalski, *Micah–Malachi*, 805–10; Meyers–Meyers, *Zechariah 9–14*, 16–26; Mitchell, "Haggai and Zechariah," 232–59.
[93] Mitchell, "Haggai and Zechariah," 84–97.
[94] Nogalski, *Micah–Malachi*, 812.
[95] Nogalski, *Micah–Malachi*, 813–15.

Zechariah, though they do not press the point too strongly and do acknowledge the composite nature of the work.[96]

Textual Aspects: In First Zechariah, there are two instances in which the *Qere* reading has been argued to be superior to the consonantal text (Zech 1:16 and 4:2), one instance in which a medieval copyist may have changed a first person singular suffix to a third person suffix (Zech 2:12), one instance of the need to correct a singular verb to a plural (Zech 4:9), with considerable versional and manuscript support, and lastly the change of וְהָעֲטָרֹת "and crowns" to the singular וְהָעֲטֶרֶת "and a crown" in Zech 6:14, based on evidence from LXX (→ 9.3) and Peshitta (→ 6–9.1.4).[97]

Regarding Second Zechariah, Meyers and Meyers find sixteen instances of minor corruption that merit slight alterations to the text. Of those sixteen, two reconstructions (Zech 13:7 and 14:5) are influenced by the non-MT versions. In the remaining cases, they make slight changes to the consonantal text or to the pointing.[98]

9.1.3.12 Malachi

There is currently no consensus regarding the original text of Malachi. Many scholars view Mal 4:4–6 (MT 3:22–24) as a later addition, understanding it as an appendix or postscript that summarizes Malachi's message or that, from a canonical perspective, serves to link the Latter Prophets to the Law of Moses and to the Primary History.[99] Beyond that, various theories have been suggested for the rest of the book. Smith treats all of Malachi, outside of Mal 4:4–6, as original.[100] Bosshard and Kratz, on the other hand, posit an original layer, comprised of most of Mal 1:6–2:9 and 3:6–12, that was subsequently added upon in two later stages.[101] Wöhrle also puts forward a foundational layer, much more fragmentary than the one posited by Bosshard and Kratz, that was then added upon in six later redactions.[102] Nogalski, in contrast to the previous approaches, argues that the book of Malachi is the result of an editorial arrangement of independent pieces rather than a foundational layer that was later redacted. He notes that the tensions used by Bosshard, Kratz, and Wöhrle to point to redactional seams could be explained just as well by the compilation view; further, he argues that if the book of Malachi is read with a literary horizon that includes the incorporation of themes related to the entire Book of the Twelve rather than reading Malachi as an isolated writing, many of the inherent tensions in the book may be explained.[103]

Textual Aspects: There is little to say about the textual aspects of Malachi. The text contains few difficulties.[104] Hill, nevertheless, does reformulate the text in three places, Mal 2:4, 12, and 15. Regarding Mal 2:4, he suggests that ἐγώ "I" present in LXX (→ 9.3) may be original, אני "I" having dropped out as a result of homeoteleuton. In Mal 2:12, he sides with the majority of scholarly opinion to emend עֵר "awake" to עַד "until," based on the disputational style and judicial nature of the oracle and on the evidence from LXX, which seems to point to these consonants (ἕως = עַד). Lastly, in Mal 2:15, Hill tentatively accepts the emendation of יִבְגֹּד "he deals treacherously" to תִבְגֹּד "you deals treacherously," noting the supporting evidence from LXX, Theodotion (→ 6–9.1.5), and the Vulgate (→ 6–9.1.7) and also arguing that such an emendation is justifiable "given the confrontational nature of the disputation and the preceding second-person verb form [וְנִשְׁמַרְתֶּם] ["and be guarded"]."[105]

---

[96] Meyers–Meyers, *Zechariah 9–14*, 32–35, 46–50.
[97] Meyers–Meyers, *Haggai, Zechariah 1–8*, lxviii, 336, 362–64. Regarding the change in Zech 6:14, Meyers and Meyers suggest that an Old Phoenician singular may underlie the text.
[98] Meyers–Meyers, *Zechariah 9–14*, 50–51.
[99] See Hill, *Malachi*, 363–66; Smith, "Malachi," 3–4; Nogalski, *Micah–Malachi*, 996.
[100] Smith, "Malachi," 3–4.

[101] E. Bosshard and R. Kratz, "Maleachi im Zwölfprophetenbuch," *BN* 52 (1990): 27–46.
[102] J. Wöhrle, *Der Abschluss des Zwölfprophetenbuches: Buchübergreifende Redaktionsprozesse in den späten Sammlungen* (BZAW 389; Berlin: De Gruyter, 2008), 219–63.
[103] Nogalski, *Micah–Malachi*, 999–1001.
[104] See Smith, *Micah–Malachi*, 300–01; Hill, *Malachi*, 11–12.
[105] Hill, *Malachi*, 203, 234–35, 249.

Andersen, F.I., *Habakkuk: A New Translation with Introduction and Commentary* (AB 25; New York: Doubleday, 2001).

Andersen, F.I. and D.N. Freedman, *Amos: A New Translation with Introduction and Commentary* (AB 24A; New York: Doubleday, 1989).

Andersen, F.I. and D.N. Freedman, *Hosea: A New Translation with Introduction and Commentary* (AB 24; Garden City: Doubleday, 1980).

Andersen, F.I. and D.N. Freedman, *Micah: A New Translation with Introduction and Commentary* (AB 24E; New York: Doubleday, 2000).

Berlin, A., *Zephaniah: A New Translation with Introduction and Commentary* (AB 25A; New York: Doubleday, 1994).

Bewer, J., "A Critical and Exegetical Commentary on Joel," in *A Critical and Exegetical Commentary on Micah, Zephaniah, Nahum, Habakkuk, Obadiah and Joel* (ICC; Edinburgh: T & T Clark, 1912).

Bewer, J., "A Critical and Exegetical Commentary on Jonah," in *A Critical and Exegetical Commentary on Haggai, Zechariah, Malachi and Jonah* (ICC; Edinburgh: T & T Clark, 1951).

Bewer, J., "A Critical and Exegetical Commentary on Obadiah," in *A Critical and Exegetical Commentary on Micah, Zephaniah, Nahum, Habakkuk, Obadiah and Joel* (ICC; Edinburgh: T & T Clark, 1912).

Crenshaw, J., *Joel: A New Translation with Introduction and Commentary* (AB 24C; New York: Doubleday, 1995).

Christensen, D., *Nahum: A New Translation with Introduction and Commentary* (Anchor Yale Bible 24F; New Haven: Yale University Press, 2009).

Fuller, R., "The Twelve," *DJD XV: 221–318.

Gelston, A., "Introduction and Commentaries on the Twelve Minor Prophets," in *BHQ 13.

Harper, J., "Responding to a Puzzled Scribe: The Barberini Version of Habakkuk 3 Analysed in the Light of the Other Greek Versions" (PhD diss., University of Cambridge, 2013).

Harper, W., *A Critical and Exegetical Commentary on Amos and Hosea* (ICC; Edinburgh: T & T Clark, 1936).

Hill, A., *Malachi: A New Translation with Introduction and Commentary* (AB 25D; New York: Doubleday, 1998).

Hillers, D., *Micah: A Commentary on the Book of the Prophet Micah* (eds. P.D. Hanson and L. Fisher; Hermeneia; Philadelphia: Fortress Press, 1984).

Jellicoe, *SMS.

Jones, B.A., *The Formation of the Book of the Twelve: A Study in Text and Canon* (SBLDS 149; Atlanta: Scholars Press, 1995).

Macintosh, A.A., *A Critical and Exegetical Commentary on Hosea* (ICC; Edinburgh: T & T Clark, 1997).

Meyers, C.L. and E.M. Meyers, *Haggai, Zechariah 1–8: A New Translation with Introduction and Commentary* (AB 25B; Garden City: Doubleday, 1987).

Meyers, C.L. and E.M. Meyers, *Zechariah 9–14: A New Translation with Introduction and Commentary* (AB 25C; New York: Doubleday, 1993).

Milik, J.T., "88. Rouleau des douze prophètes," *DJD II.1 (1961): 181–205.

Mitchell, H.G., "A Critical and Exegetical Commentary on Haggai and Zechariah," in *A Critical and Exegetical Commentary on Haggai, Zechariah, Malachi and Jonah* (ICC; Edinburgh: T & T Clark, 1951).

Nogalski, J., *Literary Precursors to the Book of the Twelve* (BZAW 217; Berlin: Walter de Gruyter, 1993).

Nogalski, J., *Redactional Processes in the Book of the Twelve* (BZAW 218; Berlin: Walter de Gruyter, 1993).

Nogalski, J., *The Book of the Twelve: Hosea–Jonah* (Smyth & Helwys Bible Commentary; Macon: Smyth & Helwys Publishing, 2011).

Nogalski, J., *The Book of the Twelve: Micah–Malachi* (Smyth & Helwys Bible Commentary; Macon: Smyth & Helwys Publishing, 2011).

Paul, S.M., *Amos: A Commentary on the Book of Amos* (Hermeneia; Minneapolis: Fortress Press, 1991).

Raabe, P.R., *Obadiah: A New Translation with Introduction and Commentary* (AB 24D; New York: Doubleday, 1996).

Sasson, J.M., *Jonah: A New Translation with Introduction and Commentary* (AB 24B; New York: Doubleday, 1990).

Simon, U., *Jonah* (JPS Bible Commentary; Philadelphia: Jewish Publication Society, 1999).

Smith, J., "A Critical and Exegetical Commentary on Malachi," in *A Critical and Exegetical Commentary on Haggai, Zechariah, Malachi and Jonah* (ICC; Edinburgh: T & T Clark, 1951).

Smith, J., "A Critical and Exegetical Commentary on Micah," in *A Critical and Exegetical Commentary on Micah, Zephaniah, Nahum, Habakkuk, Obadiah and Joel* (ICC; Edinburgh: T & T Clark, 1912).

Smith, J., "A Critical and Exegetical Commentary on Nahum," in *A Critical and Exegetical Commentary on Micah, Zephaniah, Nahum, Habakkuk, Obadiah and Joel* (ICC; Edinburgh: T & T Clark, 1912).

Smith, J., "A Critical and Exegetical Commentary on

Zephaniah," in *A Critical and Exegetical Commentary on Micah, Zephaniah, Nahum, Habakkuk, Obadiah and Joel* (ICC; Edinburgh: T & T Clark, 1912).

Smith, R., *Micah–Malachi* (WBC 32; Nashville: Thomas Nelson, 1984).

Stuart, D., *Hosea–Jonah* (WBC 31; Nashville: Thomas Nelson, 1987).

Sweeney, M., *Zephaniah* (Hermeneia; Minneapolis: Fortress Press, 2003).

Tov, **TCHB*.

Tov, **DJD* VIII.

Ward, W.H., "A Critical and Exegetical Commentary on Habakkuk," in *A Critical and Exegetical Commentary on Micah, Zephaniah, Nahum, Habakkuk, Obadiah and Joel* (ICC; Edinburgh: T & T Clark, 1912).

Wolff, H.W., *Hosea: A Commentary on the Book of the Prophet Hosea* (trans. G. Stansell; ed. P.D. Hanson; Hermeneia; Philadelphia: Fortress Press, 1974).

Wolff, H.W., *Joel and Amos: A Commentary on the books of the Prophets Joel and Amos* (trans. W. Janzen, S.D. McBride Jr., and C.A. Muenchow; ed. S.D. McBride Jr.; Hermeneia; Philadelphia: Fortress Press, 1977).

Ziegler, J. (ed.), *Duodecim prophetae* (2nd ed.; Septuaginta Vetus Testamentum Graecum 13; Göttingen: Vandenhoeck & Ruprecht, 1967).

Christopher J. Fresch

9.2 Ancient Hebrew Texts

9.2.1 Ancient Manuscript Evidence

This article surveys the thirteen Hebrew manuscripts thought to have originally contained the Twelve Minor Prophets. With the exception of 4QpMic? (4Q168; see below, → 9.2.1.11), all of the following manuscripts are considered by the majority of scholars to be biblical manuscripts rather than excerpted texts, pesharim, or exegetical compositions. With 4QpMic?, scholarly opinion is divided and given that so little of this manuscript has been preserved it is unlikely ever to be known for certain whether this was a biblical manuscript or some other sort of composition. No scholarly consensus is possible at this time on textual affiliations of the unpublished manuscripts. The survey includes the seven Hebrew manuscripts of the Minor Prophets from Qumran, 4QXII[a,b,c,d,e,f,g] and 5QAmos, followed by a brief discussion of MurXII (Mur88), MS Schøyen 4612/1, and ending with 4QpMic? and a reference to unpublished Dead Sea Scrolls fragments of the Minor Prophets. For most of these manuscripts, too little text is preserved for textual classification (4QXII[b], 4QXII[d], 4QXII[f], 5QAmos, MS Schøyen 4612/1, 4QpMic?, DSS F.Amos1). Three manuscripts preserve non-aligned texts (4QXII[a], 4QXII[c], 4QXII[e]). Only one manuscript attests to a proto-Masoretic text (MurXII), while one further manuscript is semi-Masoretic (4QXII[g]).

9.2.1.1 4QXII[a] (4Q76)[1]

4QXII[a] consists of twenty-three fragments, which preserve 384 completely or partially preserved words. The following passages are partially extant: frg. 1: Zech 14:18; frgs 2–22: Mal 2:10–3:24 (partially preserved); and Jonah 1:1–3:2 (partially preserved). Frg. 23 contains unidentified text. Approximately six columns of the original scroll can be reconstructed. The script of 4QXII[a] is a vulgar, semi-cursive hand from the middle of the second century B.C.E. (ca. 150–125 B.C.E.), which sometimes preserves archaic features such as the three-stroke *yod*. 4QXII[a] is therefore one of the two oldest copies of the Minor Prophets preserved in Hebrew. 4QXII[b] (4Q77) comes from approximately the same time period. The orthography of 4QXII[a] is inconsistent but generally fuller than MT[L], as is particularly evident in the use of *waw* for [o] vowels. ʾAleph is used once for final *waw*, and once for final *he*. 4QXII[a] does not fit the orthographic system that Tov has described as the Qumran Practice. 4QXII[a] preserves thirty-six variant readings as listed by Fuller.[2] Of these, eight are inner-Hebrew variant readings where 4QXII[a] differs from MT. 4QXII[a] agrees with MT (→ 9.2.2) against LXX (→ 9.3) three times; 4QXII[a] agrees with LXX against MT six times, but 4QXII[a] has non-aligned readings nineteen times. A large number of the readings of 4QXII[a] are editorial in nature. 4QXII[a] attests to a non-aligned text. One of the most interesting characteristics of this manuscript is the apparent order Malachi→Jonah, which is unattested elsewhere.[3] Brooke has suggested that this order of the books raises the question of whether there might have been two or more literary editions of the Twelve in the Second Temple period.[4]

9.2.1.2 4QXII[b] (4Q77)[5]

4QXII[b] consists of only six fragments that preserve fifty-seven complete or partial words. The following passages are partially preserved: frg. 1: Zeph 1:1–2; frg. 2: Zeph 2:13–15; frg. 3: Zeph 3:19–Hag 1:2; frgs. 4–5: Hag 2:2–4; frg. 6 contains unidentified text. The transition between Zephaniah and Haggai is preserved on frg. 3. The scribe left one line blank between the end of Zephaniah and the beginning of Haggai. The script of 4QXII[b] is an elegant, semi-formal hand of the early Hasmonean period, ca. 150–125 B.C.E. 4QXII[b] is thus contempo-

---

[1] Fuller, "The Twelve," 221–32.
[2] Fuller, "The Twelve," 221–32.
[3] Guillaume, "Reconsideration."
[4] Brooke, "Twelve Minor Prophets," 19–43.
[5] Fuller, "The Twelve," 233–36.

rary with 4QXII^a. 4QXII^b preserves only two variations from the spelling practices attested in MT^L. In Zeph 2:14, the manuscript reads בכפתוריה compared to MT^L, which reads בְּכַפְתֹּרֶיהָ "on its pillars." In Hag 1:1, the manuscript preserves the spelling דריוש compared to MT^L, which reads דָּרְיָוֶשׁ "Darius." Since the text of 4QXII^b is preserved in only fifty-seven complete or partial words, it is impossible to be certain of the textual affiliations of this manuscript. It is worth noting, however, that in Hag 1:1, LXX (→ 9.3) has a three-word plus in comparison to MT. Although the text of 4QXII^b is not preserved, calculation of line length indicates that 4QXII^b did not have this plus but agrees with MT (→ 9.2.2).[6]

9.2.1.3 4QXII^c (4Q78)[7]

4QXII^c consists of fifty-two fragments that preserve approximately 397 completely or partially preserved words. Frgs. 36–37, 39–52 contain very fragmentary, unidentified text. Frg. 38 has been identified as preserving Ps 38:4–6 and belongs to 4QPs^a (4Q83; see → 10.2.1.4.1.1). The following passages are partially preserved in 4QXII^c: frgs. 1–2: Hos 2:13–15; frg. 3: Hos 3:2–4; frgs. 4–7: Hos 4:1–5:1; frg. 8: Hos 13:3–10; frg. 9: Hos 13:15–14:6; frgs. 10–12: Joel 1:10–2:1; frg. 13: Joel 2:8–10; frgs. 14–17: Joel 2:10–23; frgs. 18–20: Joel 4:6–21; frgs. 21–23: Amos 2:11–3:7; frgs. 24–29: Amos 3:8–4:2; frgs. 30–33: Amos 6:13–7:16; frg. 34: Zeph 2:15–3:2; frg. 35: Mal 3:6–7(?). 4QXII^c is written in a well formed, semi-formal hand of standard size that dates to ca. 75 B.C.E. The orthography of 4QXII^c has been described as plene or "baroque."[8] Tov has described 4QXII^c as written in the Qumran practice.[9] *Waw* is used extensively to mark most [o] and [u] vowels; for example, לוא "not" and כול "all" are regularly spelled with *waw*. The morphology exhibits the "long" form of verbal afformatives and suffixes. 4QXII^c preserves thirty-seven variant readings as listed by Fuller.[10] Of these, eight are inner-Hebrew variant readings where 4QXII^c differs from MT. 4QXII^c has been classified as a non-aligned text that stands closer to LXX (→ 9.3) than to MT (→ 9.2.2).[11] 4QXII^c agrees with LXX against MT seven times; 4QXII^c agrees with MT against LXX four times; but 4QXII^c has independent readings seventeen times. A large number of the readings of 4QXII^c are editorial in nature. In frg. 8 (Hos 13:3–10), 4QXII^c agrees with LXX in a large plus that was probably lost in MT through *parablepsis*.[12]

9.2.1.4 4QXII^d (4Q79)[13]

4QXII^d is a small manuscript of only two fragments that preserve Hos 1:6–2:5 in only thirty-two completely or partially preserved words. Frg. 2 preserves an uninscribed section of skin approximately 4.4 cm wide, which seems to have formed a handle sheet at the beginning of the scroll. 4QXII^d is written in a vulgar, semi-cursive script from the middle of the first century B.C.E., i.e., ca. 50 B.C.E. The orthography of 4QXII^d is idiosyncratic, for example, expected *'aleph* is omitted four times. Since the text of 4QXII^d is preserved in only thirty-two complete or partial words, it is impossible to be certain of the textual affiliations of this manuscript. Note that in frg. 2 (Hos 2:4), 4QXII^d seems to have reversed the order of the phrases without changing the meaning of the verse. This reading is unattested elsewhere.

9.2.1.5 4QXII^e (4Q80)[14]

4QXII^e consists of twenty-five fragments that preserve approximately 139 completely or partially preserved words. Frgs. 19–25 contain very fragmentary, unidentified text. The following passages have been partially preserved: frg. 1: Hag 2:18–19; frg. 2: Hag 2:20–21; frg. 3: Zech 1:4–6; frgs. 4–5: Zech 1:9–10, 13–14; frgs. 6–7: Zech 2:10–14; frgs. 8–13: Zech 3:2–4:4; frgs. 14–15: Zech 5:8–6:5; frg. 16: Zech 8:2–4; frg. 17: Zech 8:6–7; frg. 18: Zech 12:7–12. 4QXII^e is written in a semi-formal hand of the late Hasmonean period, ca. 75–50 B.C.E. The orthography

---

[6] Tov, *"Biblical Texts," 154.
[7] Fuller, "The Twelve," 237–51.
[8] Fuller, "The Twelve," 238.
[9] Tov, *"Biblical Texts," 154.
[10] Fuller, "The Twelve," 237–51.
[11] Fuller, "Minor Prophets," 555.
[12] Fuller, "Critical Note," 343–57.
[13] Fuller, "The Twelve," 253–56.
[14] Fuller, "The Twelve," 257–65.

of 4QXII^e may be described as slightly "fuller" than the orthography of MT^L, i.e., $\bar{o}$ either < *$\bar{a}$ or < *u is always marked with *waw*. There are several indications of Qumran orthographic practice in the spelling of verbal forms, for example, the form ואומרה "and I spoke" (Zech 4:4; 5:10) appears throughout Zechariah;[15] the longer ending of the second per. masc. pl. pf. occurs once (וידעתמה "then you shall know"; Zech 2:13) and the verbal from והיה "and he will" (Zech 12:8, 9) is twice spelled והיא with final *he* replaced by *'aleph*.[16] In Zech 8:6, the longer form of the personal pronoun is reconstructed ההמ[ה "those." 4QXII^e preserves twelve variant readings, as listed by Fuller.[17] Of these, three are inner-Hebrew variant readings where 4QXII^e differs from MT. It agrees with MT (→ 9.2.2) against LXX (→ 9.3) four times; it agrees with LXX against MT twice, and three times it has independent readings. 4QXII^e could be classified as a non-aligned text.[18]

9.2.1.6 4QXII^f (4Q81)[19]

4QXII^f consists of five fragments that are arranged in two columns: col. I (= frg. 1) and col. II (= frgs. 2–4). Frg. 5 was identified as a separate manuscript by the original editor, but was published with 4QXII^f because of the similarity of the scripts.[20] 4QXII^f contains only forty-one complete or partial words. The script of 4QXII^f has been described as most closely related to the formal hands of the end of the Hasmonean period.[21] It may be dated to ca. 50 B.C.E. The orthography of 4QXII^f is very close to that of MT^L. Since the text of 4QXII^f is preserved in only forty-one complete or partial words, it is impossible to be certain of the textual affiliations of this manuscript. Only one variant from MT is attested in frg. 5, Mic 5:1, where 4QXII^f has לא יצ]א "one shall not come forth," a unique reading.[22]

Another possibility is that *'aleph* has replaced the *yod* of לי, which would make this an orthographic variant.[23]

9.2.1.7 4QXII^g (4Q82)[24]

4QXII^g is a poorly preserved manuscript containing 249 fragments of which frgs. 112–249 are unidentified. 4QXII^g preserves approximately 876 completely or partially preserved words. In frgs. 1–105, the following passages are partially preserved: Hos 2:1–5, 14–19, 22–25; 3:1–5; 4:1, 10–11, 13–14; 6:3–4, 8–11; 7:1, 13–16; 8:1; 9:1–4, 9–17; 10:1–14; 11:2–11; 12:1–15; 13:1, 6–8(?), 11–13; 14:9–10; Joel 1:12–14; 2:2–13; 4:4–9, 11–14, 17, 19–20; Amos 1:3–15; 2:1, 7–9, 15–16; 3:1–2; 4:4–9; 5:1–2, 9–18; 6:1–4, 6–14; 7:1, 7–12, 14–17; 8:1–5, 11–14; 9:1, 6, 14–15; Obad 1–5, 8–12, 14–15; Jonah 1:1–9; 2:3–11; 3:1–3; 4:5–11; Mic 1:7, 12–15; 2:3–4; 3:12; 4:1–2; 5:6–7; 7:2–3, 20; Nah 1:7–9; 2:9–11; 3:1–3, 17; Hab 2:4(?); Zeph 3:3–5; Zech 10:11–12; 11:1–2; 12:1–3. 4QXII^g is written in a formal hand from the late Hasmonean or early Herodian periods. It may be dated to the last third of the first century B.C.E. The orthography of 4QXII^g has been described as somewhat "fuller" than that of MT^L. Both לוא "no" and כול "all" are usually written with *waw*. The longer masc. sg. suffix -כה "you" is attested (e.g. Amos 7:17), as well as the longer form of the 2nd masc. sg. of the perfective ending in -תה "you" (Jonah 2:3; 4:10). 4QXII^g preserves sixty-two variants, as listed by Fuller.[25] Of these, seventeen variants are inner-Hebrew readings where 4QXII^g differs from MT (→ 9.2.2). 4QXII^g agrees with MT against LXX (→ 9.3) fifteen times and agrees with LXX against MT eight times. 4QXII^g preserves independent readings where it disagrees with both MT and LXX seventeen times. 4QXII^g is a semi-Masoretic manuscript. A large number of the readings of 4QXII^g are editorial in nature.[26]

---

[15] Cf. Qimron, *DSS, §§ 310.129c and 310.122.
[16] Cf. Qimron, *DSS, § 100.7 and examples listed there.
[17] Fuller, "The Twelve," 257–65.
[18] Tov, *"Biblical Texts," 139–66.
[19] Fuller, "The Twelve," 267–70.
[20] Fuller, "The Twelve," 270; Fuller, "4QMicah," 193–202.
[21] Fuller, "The Twelve," 267.
[22] Fuller, "4QMicah," 202.

[23] See the discussion of this phenomenon in Reymond, *Qumran Hebrew*, 119–22.
[24] Fuller, "The Twelve," 271–318.
[25] Fuller, "The Twelve," 271–318.
[26] Cf. Lange, "4QXII^g," forthcoming.

9.2.1.8 5QAmos (5Q4)[27]

5QAmos preserves only twenty-two complete or partial words in fourteen badly damaged fragments. The editor has described the script of 5QAmos as dating to the first century C.E.[28] Due to the damaged nature of these fragments a more precise dating is not possible. The orthography of 5QAmos is not sufficiently preserved to be properly described. Since the text of 5QAmos is preserved in only twenty-two complete or partial words, it is impossible to be certain of the textual affiliations of this manuscript.

9.2.1.9 MurXII (Mur88)[29]

MurXII preserves approximately 3,605 complete or partial words. Twenty-three columns of text are partially preserved.[30] It is estimated that seven columns are missing from the beginning of the scroll and approximately ten columns from the end of the scroll. The following passages are partially preserved: col. II: Joel 2:26–4:16; col. III: Amos 1:5–2:1; cols. IV–V missing; col. VI: only two letters; col. VII: Amos 7:3–8:7; col. VIII: Amos 8:11–9:15; col. IX: Obad 1–21; col. X: Jonah 1:1–3:2; col. XI: Jonah 3:2–Mic 1:5; col. XII: Mic 1:5–3:4; col. XIII: Mic 3:4–4:12; col. XIV: Mic 4:12–6:7; col. XV: Mic 6:11–7:17; col. XVI: Mic 7:17–Nah 2:12; col. XVII: Nah 2:13–3:19; col. XVIII: Hab 1:3–2:11; col. XIX: Hab 2:18–Zeph 1:1; col. XX: Zeph 1:11–3:6; col. XXI: Zeph 3:8–Hag 1:11; col. XXII: Hag 1:12–2:10; col. XXIII: Hag 2:12–Zech 1:4. Unidentified text is found on thirty-three fragments. MurXII is written in a bookhand of the post-Herodian period, dating to the time of the second revolt against Rome, ca. 135 C.E. The orthography of MurXII is very close to that of MT[L]. There are only twenty-four orthographic variations from MT[L]. MurXII has been described as a proto-Masoretic text.[31] There are eighteen non-orthographic variants from MT (→ 9.2.2). MurXII agrees with LXX (→ 9.3) against MT three times and agrees once with MT-Ps 77:18, an example of harmonization.[32] There are three independent readings in MurXII in Amos 7:16, Nah 3:8, and Hag 2:1.[33]

9.2.1.10 MS Schøyen 4612/1

The publication of this manuscript by Torleif Elgvin is forthcoming.[34] Manuscript Schøyen 4612/1 consists of only a single fragment that preserves approximately twenty-nine complete and partial words. The text partially preserved comes from Joel 4:1–5. The script of manuscript Schøyen 4612/1 has been described by Langlois as "a skilled formal book hand exhibiting developments that appear in the latest Herodian scripts." The script may date from ca. 50–100 C.E. and perhaps in the third quarter of the first century.[35] The manuscript could have been part of the manuscript collection associated with the community at Qumran, or could also have come from another of the manuscript finds in the Judean Desert from the first century C.E. As neither traces of Argonite (typical for Qumran) nor Dolomite (typical for Wadi Murabbaat) can be detected on the fragment, the editors consider Naḥal Ḥever as a likely place of origin. The orthography of manuscript Schøyen 4612/1 agrees mostly with that of MT[L]. One variant to MT-Joel 4:2 is visible in the online image. In MT, Joel 4:2 has the reading פִּזְּרוּ "they scattered" but manuscript Schøyen 4612/1 has בזרו (also, "they scattered"). The variation of פ/ב in Joel 4:2 may be understood as a phonetic variant. Elgvin reconstructs two further variants toward MT (→ 9.2.2).

9.2.1.11 4QpMic? (4Q168)[36]

4QpMic? consists of only five fragments, which preserve fifteen complete or partial words. Frgs. 1 and 3 contain the remains of Mic 4:8–12. Given

---

[27] Milik, "Amos," 173.
[28] Milik, "Amos," 173.
[29] Milik, "Rouleau," 181–205.
[30] Barthélemy, *Critique textuelle 1992*, c.
[31] Barthélemy, Studies in the Text, 388.
[32] Barthélemy, *Critique textuelle 1992*, c.
[33] Milik, "Rouleau," 183–84.
[34] Elgvin, "MS 4612/1." Cf. also the webpage of the Schøyen Collection: http://schoyencollection.com/dsscrolls.htm#4612. I am obliged to Torleif Elgvin for information about this manuscript.
[35] M. Langlois, "Palaeographical Analysis of the Dead Sea Scrolls," in *Gleanings*, forthcoming.
[36] Allegro, "Micah," 36; Strugnell, "Notes," 204.

the small amount of text preserved, it is unclear and impossible to determine whether 4Q168 attests to the remains of a scroll of the book of Micah or the Twelve Minor Prophets, or perhaps a pesher on the book of Micah or part of a pesher on the Twelve. 4QpMic? is written in a semi-formal hand of the early Herodian period, ca. 30 B.C.E.–20 C.E. The script of 4QpMic? is identical to the script of 4QpHos[b] and is assumed to have been written by the same scribe.[37] Since so little is preserved of this manuscript, it is impossible to determine anything about its orthography. Since the text of 4QpMic? is preserved in only fifteen complete or partial words, it is impossible to be certain of the textual affiliations of this manuscript.

9.2.1.12 DSS F.Amos1 (= 4QAmos? or = XQAmos?)[38]

F.Amos1 consists of three small fragments that preserve only sixteen complete or partial words from Amos 7:17–8:1. The nature of this composition is unclear because so little is preserved. Tov has suggested that DSS F.Amos does not appear to be from any known Minor Prophets manuscripts.[39] DSS F.Amos1 is written in a Herodian script from the beginning of the first century B.C.E.[40] DSS F.Amos1 preserves the so-called long form of the 2nd per. masc. sg. possessive suffix twice in contrast to MT (→ 9.2.2). In addition, twice DSS F.Amos1 has verb forms with plene spelling in comparison to MT. Nothing definitive can be said about the textual character of this very fragmentary manuscript. Tov notes that DSS F.Amos1 probably preserves one original short reading and one likely scribal error.[41]

9.2.1.13 Green Scholars Initiative Fragments

Two further unpublished fragments of the Minor Prophets are known that partially preserve Jonah 4:2–5 (DSS F.Jonah1) and Mic 1:4–6 (DSS F.Micah1).[42] They will be published in the Green Scholars Initiative Series on Early Jewish Texts (Leiden: Brill).

Allegro, J.M., "168. Commentary on Micah (?)," *DJD V (1968): 36.

Barthélemy, D., *Studies in the Text of the Old Testament: An Introduction to the Hebrew Old Testament Text Project* (Textual Criticism and the Translator 3; Winona Lake: Eisenbrauns, 2012).

Brooke, G.J., "The Twelve Minor Prophets and the Dead Sea Scrolls," in *Congress Volume Leiden 2004* (ed. A. Lemaire; VTSup 109; Leiden: Brill, 2006), 19–43.

Elgvin, T., "MS 4612/1. Hev(?)Joel (Joel 4.1–5)," in *Gleanings*, forthcoming.

Fuller, R.E., "A Critical Note on Hosea 12:10 and 13:4," *RB* 3 (1991): 343–57.

Fuller, R.E., "Textual Traditions in the Book of Hosea and the Minor Prophets," in *Madrid Qumran Congress*, 1.254–56.

Fuller, R.E., "4QMicah: A Small Fragment of a Manuscript of the Minor Prophets from Qumran, Cave IV," *RevQ* 16 (1993): 193–202.

Fuller, R.E., "The Form and Formation of the Book of the Twelve: The Evidence from the Judean Desert," in *Forming Prophetic Literature: Essays on Isaiah and the Twelve in Honor of John D.W. Watts* (eds. J.W. Watts and P.R. House; JSOTSup 235; Sheffield: Sheffield Academic Press, 1996), 93–95.

Fuller, R.E., "The Twelve," *DJD* XV (1997): 221–318.

Fuller, R.E., "Minor Prophets," in *EDSS*, 1.554–57.

Guillaume, P., "The Unlikely Malachi-Jonah Sequence (4QXII[a])," *The Journal of Hebrew Scriptures* 7 (2007).

Guillaume, P., "A Reconsideration of Manuscripts Classified as Scrolls of the Twelve Minor Prophets (XII)," *The Journal of Hebrew Scriptures* 7 (2007).

Lange, *Handbuch*, 335–69.

Lange, A., "4QXII[g] (4Q82) as an Editorial Text," *Text*, forthcoming.

Milik, J.T., "88. Rouleau des douze prophètes," *DJD* II.1 (1961): 181–205.

Milik, J.T., "4. Amos," *DJD* III.1 (1962): 173–74.

Reymond, E.D., *Qumran Hebrew: An Overview of Orthography, Phonology, and Morphology* (SBLRBS 76; Atlanta: SBL, 2014).

Strugnell, *"Notes en marge."

Tov, *"Biblical Texts."

Tov, E., "New Fragments of Amos," *DSD* 21 (2014): 3–13.

---

[37] Allegro, "Micah," 36.

[38] Tov, "New Fragments," 3–13. The inventory number in Tigchelaar's inventory is DSS F.181.

[39] Tov, "New Fragments," 10–11.

[40] Tov, "New Fragments," 4, citing Yardeni.

[41] Tov, "New Fragments," 7–8.

[42] I am obliged to David Trobisch for this information.

9.2.2 Masoretic Texts and Ancient Texts Close to MT

The so-called Book of the Twelve (→ 9.1) is a collection or anthology of originally independent compositions. It is important to take the nature of the collection into account. Each composition had its own history of composition, redaction, and transmission until it became part of the larger collection. It is only after the collection is complete that we can think in terms of the text of the Minor Prophets as a single transmission unit. Thus, for example, some sections of the books of Hosea, Amos, and Micah go back to the eighth century B.C.E., while the books of Haggai, Zechariah, Joel, Jonah, and Malachi are dated to the fifth century B.C.E. or later. These two groups of books have very different textual histories until they become part of a single collection on one scroll. At that point, we can speak of the text of the Minor Prophets.

Scholars frequently refer to Ben Sira 49:10, which reads:

καὶ τῶν δώδεκα προφητῶν τὰ ὀστᾶ ἀναθάλοι ἐκ τοῦ τόπου αὐτῶν·
παρεκάλεσαν γὰρ τὸν Ιακωβ καὶ ἐλυτρώσαντο αὐτοὺς ἐν πίστει ἐλπίδος.

And may the bones of the twelve prophets sprout anew out of their place,
for they comforted Iakob and they redeemed them in confidence of hope. (*NETS*)

Ben Sira was composed around 180 B.C.E. and this passage is usually taken as an indication that the collection of the twelve minor prophets in Hebrew had been completed by the time he wrote. But, if we look only at manuscript evidence and following the suggestions of Brooke regarding which manuscripts were probably complete scrolls of the Minor Prophets then 4QXII^c from ca. 75 B.C.E. and 4QXII^e from ca. 75–50 B.C.E. are the earliest exemplars of complete scrolls of the Minor Prophets.[1] In other words, based on the physical evidence, we can only begin to speak of the text of the Minor Prophets as a single unit during the first half of the first century B.C.E. These two manuscripts also provide evidence of the continuing textual diversity of the text of the Minor Prophets in this time period, since both 4QXII^e (→ 9.2.1.5) and 4QXII^c (→ 9.2.1.3) are classified as non-aligned.[2]

Before this time, there may well have been smaller collections of the Prophetic Books circulating on individual scrolls, such as the hypothesized "book of the four," but we have no surviving physical evidence of such collections.[3] Each individual book of the Minor Prophets must be treated separately in terms of its textual history and its textual affiliations. In fact, it is probably a mistake to speak of the textual affiliation of manuscripts that may have contained more than one of the Minor Prophets, but actually preserve remains of only one or two books.

Textual diversity diminished within approximately a century and a half of the time of these two manuscripts and the proto-Masoretic textual tradition became the sole textual exemplar in the Minor Prophets (compare, for example, MurXII [→ 9.2.1.9]).

9.2.2.1 History of Research

Until the discovery of the Dead Sea Scrolls in the middle of the twentieth century, most textual research was concerned with the text of individual books within the collection. Since the discovery of the manuscripts of the Minor Prophets in the Judean Desert, which are presumed by most scholars originally to have contained complete copies of the Minor Prophets, there has been increasing interest in studying the textual affiliations of

---

[1] Brooke, "The Twelve Minor Prophets," 33–34. Brooke considers 4QXII^a "very far from certain, but just possible," 4QXII^c "quite likely," 4QXII^d "quite possible," 4QXII^e "might have contained," 4QXII^g "very likely," MurXII "strong evidence that it was a complete copy." Cf. Guillaume, "Reconsideration," and Tov.

* "Biblical Texts," 142. Tov considers MurXII, 4QXII^b, and 4QXII^g complete copies, i.e., he includes only those Hebrew manuscripts that preserve transitions between books.

[2] 4QXII^e could be described as either non-aligned or as semi-Masoretic in terms of textual affiliation.

[3] See the presentation in E. Ben Zvi and J.D. Nogalski, *Two Sides of a Coin: Juxtaposing Views on Interpreting the Book of the Twelve/the Twelve Prophetic Books* (Analecta Gorgiana 201; Piscataway: Gorgias Press, 2009).

these manuscripts and thus of the text of the Minor Prophets as a whole.[4] Since the discovery and publication of the scrolls there have been two textual commentaries on MT-MinP. The textual commentary on MT-MinP of the Hebrew Old Testament Text Project was edited by Barthélemy and published in 1992.[5] The orientation of the project was toward those passages that might cause confusion to translators, and therefore the passages discussed are guided by this concern and the discussion is not exhaustive. The second textual commentary is that found in *BHQ, Part 13, which was published in 2010.[6] In this volume, the editor includes a commentary on the critical apparatus in which additional information is given for some of the readings listed in the critical apparatus. The focus in *BHQ is not too different from that of the Hebrew Old Testament Text Project so that the discussion is not comprehensive. Both of these commentaries show a high priority for MT-MinP and show little interest in the origin of readings in the various textual witnesses or in the history of the text. A comprehensive critical commentary on the Hebrew text of MinP remains a *desideratum*.

9.2.2.2 Manuscripts and Editions

The Masoretic Text of the Minor Prophets is preserved in three important and well-known codices:

- The Aleppo Codex (MT^A) (http://www.aleppocodex.org). The consonantal layer of the codex was copied by Shelomo ben Buya'a and vocalized and annotated by Aaron ben Asher in ca. 925 C.E. About three-quarters of the manuscript has been preserved. The Aleppo Codex originally contained 491 pages: 295 have survived, and 196 have been lost. Seven pages from the Minor Prophets are among these lost pages: Amos 8:13 to Mic 5:1 (including the books of Obadiah and Jonah); the end of Zephaniah to Zech 9:17 (including Haggai).[7]

- Codex Leningrad B 19A (MT^L). This codex dates from 1009 C.E., is completely preserved, and was corrected according to a Ben Asher manuscript. The codex was used as the base text for Biblia Hebraica from 1937 onwards (*BH³, *BHS, *BHQ).
- The Cairo Codex of the Prophets (MT^C). This codex dates from the eleventh century C.E., is completely preserved, and agrees most closely with the Ben Naphtali Masoretic tradition even though the colophon to the manuscript claims that it was copied by Moses ben Asher in 895 C.E.

The *BHQ edition of the Minor Prophets by Gelston is not comprehensive, but represents a significant improvement over earlier editions of the *BH series. For the variants of the medieval Masoretic manuscript tradition, the editions of Kennicott (*1776–1780, 2:249–305) and De Rossi (*1784–1788, 3:171–225) are still indispensable.

The Hebrew text of the Minor Prophets is attested in nine manuscripts from the Judean Desert, from Cave 4 at Qumran and from Wadi Murabba'at: 4QXII^a,b,c,d,e,f,g, 5QAmos (= 5QXII), and MurXII. Of these manuscripts, 4QXII^b and MurXII may be classified as proto-Masoretic. When discussing the textual affiliation of the small Qumran manuscripts we are really only analyzing the text of the preserved book(s). This is important to keep in mind when the manuscript remains are so small as is the case with 4QXII^b,d,f. In these cases, in order to access the textual affiliation of the manuscript/book preserved, it is necessary to carefully analyze the amount of textual variation in the preserved portion of the text.

- 4QXII^b (→ 9.2.1.2) preserves: Zeph 1:1–2; 2:13–15; 3:19–20; Hag 1:1–2; 2:2–4 in approximately sixty complete and partially preserved words. The transition from Zephaniah to Haggai is extant on frg. 3.[8] There are no non-orthographic variations from MT in the preserved text. In Zeph 2:13, there is one variation from MT, which is probably the result of scribal error, the dropping of a consonant. The reading of 4QXII^b does not

---

[4] Cf. Tov, *"Biblical Texts," 152–57; Lange, *Handbuch*, 335–47.
[5] Barthélemy, *Critique textuelle 1992*.
[6] Gelston, *The Twelve Minor Prophets*.
[7] Cf. Ofer, "The Aleppo Codex," 280–83.

[8] Fuller, "The Twelve," 235.

make any sense. In Zeph 2:14, there is an orthographic variant in one word. Also in Zeph 2:14, 4QXII^b agrees with MT against LXX, but it is possible that LXX misread a single letter of the text of its *Vorlage*. In Zeph 3:19, there is another apparent variation between MT and LXX: MT has אֶת־כָּל־מְעַנָּיִךְ "with all your oppressors" while LXX has ἐν σοὶ ἕνεκεν σοῦ "in you for your sake." This may be the result of a difference in division of the letters of LXX's *Vorlage*. That is, LXX may have read this phrase as למענך אתך "with/in you, for your sake," which is how *NETS translates. In other words, the LXX *Vorlage* had nearly the same consonantal text and divided it differently. This does not indicate a variant Hebrew text. 4QXII^b agrees with MT. At the end of Zeph 3:19, LXX apparently read בָּשְׁתָּם "their shame" as a verbal form, καὶ καταισχυνθήσονται "and they will be ashamed." Again there is no indication of a variant Hebrew text; unfortunately this section of Zeph 3:19 is not preserved in 4QXII^b. In Hag 1:1, LXX has a three-word plus in comparison to MT. Although the text of 4QXII^b is not preserved, calculation of line length indicates that 4QXII^b did not have the plus; it agrees with MT. 4QXII^b does preserve a variant spelling of the name "Darius" in Haggai (Hag 1:1; at Hag 1:15; 2:10 the name is only partially preserved in 4QXII^b), דריהש where MT has דָּרְיָוֶשׁ. I would describe this as an orthographic variant. To revise the statistics given above, 4QXII^b preserves two orthographic variants and one scribal error. These are very small variations from MT. The scribal error is of no significance in describing the textual affiliation of the manuscript. It is more significant, perhaps, that 4QXII^b probably did not agree with the LXX plus in Hag 1:1. This in-depth analysis of the section of text preserved in 4QXII^b reinforces the understanding that there was not a great deal of variation between MT and the *Vorlage* of LXX in the Minor Prophets. In the one clear place that LXX (→ 9.3) has a plus, perhaps the result of the translator wishing to clarify the meaning of the passage, 4QXII^b probably read with MT. Based on this analysis, regardless of the small amount of text preserved, it seems reasonable to describe 4QXII^b as a proto-Masoretic manuscript. This makes 4QXII^b the oldest exemplar of the proto-Masoretic textual tradition, dating to ca. 150–125 B.C.E.

There are three manuscripts of the Minor Prophets from Qumran that may be classified as semi-Masoretic:[9]

- 4QXII^d (→ 9.2.1.4) preserves Hos 1:6–2:5 in the remains of approximately thirty complete and partially preserved words. There is only one variation from MT in the preserved section of Hosea,[10] which yields a rate of variation of only 3.1 percent. In addition, 4QXII^d agrees with MT against LXX twice in Hos 2:1, once where LXX has a plus (+εκει), and once where LXX has a minus (להם). If this analysis is valid then 4QXII^d should also be considered a semi-Masoretic manuscript.
- 4QXII^f (→ 9.2.1.6) preserves Jonah 1:6–8, 10–16; Mic 5:1–2 in the remains of approximately forty complete and partially preserved words. There is only one variation from MT in the preserved section. This yields a rate of variation of only 2.4 percent. Like the other two manuscripts discussed, 4QXII^f shows a low rate of variation from MT and so on this basis can also be considered a semi-Masoretic manuscript.
- 4QXII^g (→ 9.2.1.7) is a large, poorly preserved manuscript of what was almost certainly a complete scroll of the Minor Prophets. Portions of Hosea, Joel, Amos, Obadiah, Jonah, Micah, Nahum, Habakkuk, Zephaniah, and Zechariah are preserved with the transition from Amos to Obadiah preserved on frg. 71.[11] Although 4QXII^g is extremely fragmentary, the manuscript was carefully copied and contains only nine corrections, all by the original scribe. 4QXII^g preserves 876 complete and partially preserved words

---

[9] See the discussion in Lange, *Handbuch*, 14–19.

[10] The reading of 4QXII^d is intriguing. I am inclined to think that the scribe may have reversed the two two-word phrases that follow ותסר "that she put away" in Hos 2:4. This would be a unique variant if so. Barbone (*Osea*, 131) reconstructs following MT.

[11] Fuller, "The Twelve," 272, 308.

and contains forty non-orthographic variants from MT. 4QXII^g may be described as a semi-Masoretic manuscript.

9.2.2.3 Nature and Text-Critical Character of (proto)-MT-MinP

The orthography of MT-MinP is consistent and shows few anomalous forms.[12] As in other books of the Hebrew Bible, MT-MinP attests to a few cases of orthographic peculiarites that are close to the so-called Qumran orthography. These peculiarites include the spelling of the second masculine singular suffix in the perfect of the verb in -תָה in Obad 5 (נִדְמֵיתָה "you have been destroyed"); Zech 1:12 (זָעַמְתָּה "you have been angry"); and Mal 2:14 (בָּגַדְתָּה "you have been faithless"). In Amos 4:3, the long form of the second feminine plural is attested (וְהִשְׁלַכְתֶּנָה "and you shall be flung").[13] 'Aleph is used as a vowel letter in some forms, i.e., in nouns and particles: אֵפוֹא "then" in Hos 13:10; פָּארוּר "paleness" in Joel 2:6 and Nah 2:11; נָקִיא "innocent" in Joel 4:19 and Jonah 1:14; and in at least one verbal form, וְקָאם "and ... shall arise," in Hos 10:14. The negative particle, לֹא, is always spelled defectively except in the form הֲלוֹא "not?," which is nearly always spelled with waw. A single exception occurs in Amos 5:20 where it is written הֲלֹא in MT^L,C.

However, the orthography of the Judean Desert manuscripts of the Minor Prophets (→ 9.2.1) varies from close agreement with the orthographic practices of MT in proto-Masoretic (4QXII^b, MurXII), semi-Masoretic (4QXII^f), and non-aligned manuscripts (4QXII^e) to agreement with the Qumran orthography (4QXII^c; non-aligned → 9.2.3.2) as described by Tov,[14] with some semi-Masoretic (4QXII^d,g) and non-aligned manuscripts (4QXII^a

→ 9.2.3.1) showing a mixture of orthographic practices.[15]

No systematic study of the entire MT-MinP exists, but there are numerous more-limited studies.[16] Generally, the reliability of the text of MT-MinP varies from book to book. As with the text of any book in MT, the text of MT-MinP is not free of secondary readings. Following are examples of editorial or harmonizing readings, linguistic and stylistic corrections, as well as scribal errors. These examples are not exhaustive, but only suggestive of the state of the text.

Some books in MT-MinP have long been recognized as containing many more secondary readings than others; Hosea and Micah fall into this group. The text of MT-Hos has usually been described as one of the worst preserved in the Hebrew Bible.[17]

Examples of harmonizing or editorial readings can be found in Joel 4:5; Jonah 1:3; and Zech 11:7, 11. In Joel 4:5, MT reads לְהֵיכְלֵיכֶם "into your temples" followed also by LXX (εἰς τοὺς ναοὺς ὑμῶν "into your temples"), but MurXII reads the singular להיכלכם "into your temple," which fits the context much better. It is likely that MT has harmonized to the near context. In Jonah 1:3, MT^L 1st hand reads תַּרְשִׁישָׁה "to Tarshish" but MT^L 2nd hand reads תַּרְשִׁישׁ "Tarshish" (cf. MT^C). This is a secondary harmonization to the near context. In Zech 11:7, 11, MT reads לָכֵן עֲנִיֵּי "therefore the poor ones of ..." and כֵן עֲנִיֵּי "then the poor ones of ..." respectively. LXX has εἰς τὴν Χαναανῖτιν "in Canaanitis" in Zech 11:7 and οἱ Χαναναῖοι "the Canaanites" in Zech 11:11. The LXX readings have long been recognized as more original. The readings of MT-Zech 11:7, 11 are harmonizing with Zech 14:21b.[18]

An example of a linguistic correction can be found in Mal 3:13 where in MT^L the first hand

---

[12] Note that the "long" form of the second masculine singular suffix on the perfect ending in ה- occurs in Obad 4; Zech 1:12; and Mal 2:13. Cf. also A. Lange, "The Question of the So-Called Qumran Orthography, the Severus Scroll, and the Masoretic Text," *Hebrew Bible and Ancient Israel* 3 (2014): 424–75.

[13] The form is usually understood as an error for the *Hophal* form, הָשְׁלַכְתֶּנָה (see H.W. Wolff, *A Commentary on the Books of Joel and Amos* [Hermeneia; Philadelphia: Fortress Press, 1977], 204), but the stem does not affect the form of the ending.

[14] Tov, *Scribal Practices, 261–73.

[15] Fuller, "The Twelve," 221–318.

[16] For a general discussion, see Fuller, "The Twelve," 221–318; Driver, "Linguistic and Textual Problems"; see also the selective discussions in Barthélemy, *Critique textuelle 1992*; Gelston, *The Twelve Minor Prophets*.

[17] See, e.g., W. Rudolph, *Hosea* (KAT 13.1; Gütersloh: Gerd Mohn, 1966), 19.

[18] See the discussion in Barthélemy, *Critique textuelle 1992*, 988–90.

has the reading דברנו "we said" but this has been corrected by a second hand to agree with the reading found in MT[C,A] מַה־נִּדְבַּרְנוּ "How have we spoken."

Examples of scribal errors include such mistakes as graphic confusion of letters, metathesis of letters, and haplography. An example is seen in Hos 9:7, where MT reads יֵדְעוּ יִשְׂרָאֵל "Israel will know" but LXX has καὶ κακωθήσεται Ισραηλ "and Israel will be afflicted," which presumes a *Vorlage* with the root רעע. The LXX reading fits the context much better and the reading of MT probably resulted from a confusion of ד and ר, a frequent mistake in Hebrew manuscripts from the Second Temple period. In Mic 3:3, MT has כַּאֲשֶׁר "just like" but LXX has ὡς σάρκας (= כבשר "like meat"). The parallel with the following phrase indicates that the reading of LXX is correct and the reading in MT is the result of a simple metathesis. In Hos 13:4, LXX has a long plus following the phrase "But I am the Lord your God …," which also appears partially in 4QXII[c]. This plus is probably original and was lost in MT through haplography.[19]

MT also sometimes preserves harmonizing readings that consist of additions to the text that conform to frequent phrases found elsewhere; for example, in Zech 13:2, MT has the frequent expression יְהוָה צְבָאוֹת "Lord of Hosts" but LXX has only κύριος "Lord." Some LXX witnesses have σαβαωθ "Sabaoth," which Ziegler considered to be a secondary correction toward MT. This is most likely a secondary addition in MT to conform to the frequently attested phrase.

More examples of secondary readings in MT-MinP could be listed, but the examples given are sufficient to indicate that the text of MT-MinP is far from a perfectly preserved exemplar. The secondary readings found in MT-MinP do not seem to reflect a coherent literary layer and therefore it does not seem that these readings represent a distinct literary edition as is found in some biblical books.

9.2.2.4 Date and Milieu

4QXII[b] (→ 9.2.1.2) gives early evidence for the proto-Masoretic form of the text of the Minor Prophets dating to ca. 150–125 B.C.E. In addition, quotations and allusions to individual passages to the Minor Prophets in the Hebrew text of Ben Sira (ca. 200–180 B.C.E.) that agree with the proto-Masoretic form of the text may push the date of the proto-Masoretic form of the text back to the end of the third century B.C.E. or the beginning of the second century B.C.E.[20] If the evidence of the quotations and allusions to the text of the Minor Prophets is accepted, then the earliest attested date of the proto-Masoretic form of the text may be placed sometime in the third century B.C.E. The provenance of this text form is presumably ancient Palestine since the largest Hebrew-using community was located there, although there were also Hebrew copies of biblical texts in other locations such as Egypt.

Barbone, P.G., *Il Libro Del Profeta Osea Edizione critica del testo ebraico* (Turin: Silvio Zamorani Editore, 1987).
Barthélemy, **Devanciers*.
Barthélemy, **Critique textuelle 1992*.
Brooke, G.J., "The Twelve Minor Prophets and the Dead Sea Scrolls," in *Congress Volume Leiden 2004* (ed. A. Lemaire; VTSup 109; Leiden: Brill, 2006), 19–43.
De Rossi, *1784–1788.
*DJD VIII.
Driver, G.R., "Linguistic and Textual Problems: Minor Prophets," *JTS* (1938): 154–66, 260–73, 393–405.
Freedman, D.N., A.B. Beck, and J.A. Sanders, *The Leningrad Codex: A Facsimile Edition* (Grand Rapids: Eerdmans, 1998).
Fuller, R.E., "Textual Traditions in the Book of Hosea and the Minor Prophets," in **Madrid Qumran Congress*, 254–56.
Fuller, R.E., "4QMicah: A Small Fragment of a Manuscript of the Minor Prophets from Qumran, Cave IV," *RevQ* 16 (1993–1995): 193–202.
Fuller, R.E., "The Form and Formation of the Book of the Twelve: The Evidence from the Judean Desert,"

---

[19] See the discussion in R. Fuller, "A Critical Note on Hosea 12:10 and 13:4," *RB* 3 (1991): 343–57.

[20] It is important to note that this is not definitive. The quotations and allusions found in Hebrew Ben Sira do not necessarily allow us to distinguish between proto-MT and other forms of the text, although these are very close.

in *Forming Prophetic Literature: Essays on Isaiah and the Twelve in Honor of John D.W. Watts* (eds. J.W. Watts and P.R. House; JSOTSup 235; Sheffield: Sheffield Academic Press, 1996), 86–101.

Fuller, R.E., "The Twelve," *DJD XV: 221–318.

Fuller, R.E., "Minor Prophets," in *EDSS 2:554–57.

Fuller, R.E., "The Prophets: Text and Textual Criticism," in *Dictionary of the Old Testament: Prophets* (eds. M.J. Boda and J.G. McConville; Downers Grove: IVP Academic, 2012), 775–81.

Gelston, A., *BHQ, Part 13: *The Twelve Minor Prophets*.

Goshen-Gottstein, M.H., *The Aleppo Codex* (Jerusalem: Magnes Press, 1976).

Guillaume, P., "The Unlikely Malachi-Jonah Sequence (4QXIIª)," *The Journal of Hebrew Scriptures* 7 (2007): http://www.arts.ualberta.ca/JHS/Articles/article_76.pdf.

Guillaume, P., "A Reconsideration of Manuscripts Classified as Scrolls of the Twelve Minor Prophets (XII)," *The Journal of Hebrew Scriptures* 7 (2007): http://www.arts.ualberta.ca/JHS/Articles/article_76.pdf.

Kennicott, *1776–1780.

Lange, *Handbuch*, 335–69.

Loewinger, D.S., *Pentateuch, Prophets and Hagiographa: Codex Leningrad B 19A: The Earliest Complete Bible Manuscript Written in 875 by Moshe ben Asher* (Jerusalem: Makor, 1970) [Hebr.].

Loewinger, D.S., *Codex Cairo of the Bible from the Karaite Synagogue at Abba Siya: The Earliest Extant Hebrew Manuscript* (Jerusalem: Makor, 1971) [Hebr.].

Milik, J.T., "88. Rouleau des Douze Prophètes," *DJD II.1: 181–205.

Ofer, Y., "The Aleppo Codex in the Light of the Notes made by M.D. Cassuto," *Sefunot* 19 (1989): 280–83 [Hebr.].

Ofer, Y., "Cairo Codex," in *Encyclopedia of the Bible and Its Reception* (Berlin: De Gruyter, 2012), 4:769–70.

Pérez Castro, F., *El códice de Profetas de El Cairo*, Vol. 7: *Profetas menores* (Textos y estudios Cardenal Cisneros 20; Madrid: Instituto del Filologia del CSIC, 1979).

Tov, *"Biblical Texts."

Tov, *Scribal Practices.

Ziegler, J. (ed.), *Duodecim Prophetae* (editio altera quam curavit F. Albrecht; Septuaginta Vetus Testa-mentum Graecum 13; Göttingen: Vandenhoeck & Ruprecht, 2013).

Russell Fuller

9.2.3 Other Texts

In addition to the Hebrew manuscripts of the Twelve Minor Prophets discussed above in → 9.2.2, which are closely related to MT-MinP, there are two Hebrew manuscripts of the Minor Prophets that are less closely related to MT-MinP, 4QXIIª (4Q76) and 4QXIIᶜ (4Q78). They will be discussed below.

9.2.3.1 4QXIIª (4Q76)

4QXIIª (→ 9.2.1.1) sparked a great deal of scholarly interest even before its publication in *DJD XV in 1997 because of the reconstruction of the order of the books in the latter part of the scroll, namely Malachi→Jonah.[1] This unique order along with a high number of independent readings marks 4QXIIª as a non-aligned text.

9.2.3.1.1 Nature and Text-Critical Character

The orthography of 4QXIIª is inconsistent but generally fuller than MTᴸ as is particularly evident in the use of *waw* for [o] vowels. Examples include the following:

Mal 2:12: יעקוב for MT's יַעֲקֹב "Jacob"

Mal 3:1: שׁוֹלֹח for MT's שֹׁלֵחַ "sending"

Mal 3:2: העומד for MT's הָעֹמֵד "the one who stands"

Mal 3:17: העובד for MT's הָעֹבֵד "the one who serves"

Mal 3:22: ב[חורב for MT's בְּחֹרֵב "at Horeb"

In some cases, 4QXIIª uses *'aleph* for final *waw* (Jonah 1:3 יפא for MT's יָפוֹ "Joppa") and once for final *he* (Jonah 1:2 נינ[וא for MT's נִינְוֵה "Nineveh"). Although somewhat more *plene* then MTᴸ, 4QXIIª does not fit the orthographic system, which Tov has described as the Qumran Practice.[2]

The textual quality of 4QXIIª is mixed. Of the thirty-seven readings preserved and listed in *DJD XV: four are inner Hebrew variants, four are ortho-

---

[1] See, e.g., Fuller, "The Twelve," 222; B.A. Jones, *The Formation of the Book of the Twelve: A Study in Text and Canon* (SBLDS 149; Atlanta: Scholars Press, 1995), 129–69; O.H. Steck, "Zur Abfolge Maleachi – Jona in 4Q76 (4QXIIª)," *ZAW* 108 (1996): 249–53.

[2] Tov, *Scribal Practices.

graphic in nature, seven are difficult to determine, twelve are editorial in nature, including explicating and harmonizing readings, and four are original readings. 4QXII^a agrees with MT against LXX three times, agrees with LXX against MT six times, but has independent readings nineteen times. The original readings preserved are:

Mal 2:12: עד וענה "one who witnesses or answers" 4QXII^a LXX (ἕως καὶ ταπεινωθῇ "until he has even been humiliated")] עֵר וְעֹנֶה "a protector and one who answers" MT

Mal 2:14: א[שׁת נעוריך "the w]ife of your youth" 4QXII^a] אֵשֶׁת נְעוּרֶיךָ אֲשֶׁר אַתָּה בָּגַדְתָּה בָּהּ "the wife of your youth against whom you have acted treacherously" MT LXX

Mal 2:16: אל ישראל "the God of Israel" (cf. Ps 68:36) 4QXII^a] אֱלֹהֵי יִשְׂרָאֵל "the God of Israel" MT LXX

Mal 3:20: כעגל "like a calf of" 4QXII^a (cf. 1 Sam 28:24)] כְּעֶגְלֵי "like calves of" MT LXX (μοσχάρια "calves") (cf. Jer 46:21)

9.2.3.1.2 Date and Milieu
The paleographic date of 4QXII^a, ca. 150–125 B.C.E. (→ 9.2.1.1), sets a *terminus ante quem* for the development of the text of 4QXII^a. Otherwise, little can be said of the date of the development of the text of this manuscript.

9.2.3.1.3 Relevance for Exegesis and Literary Analysis
4QXII^a preserves sections of Zechariah, Malachi, and Jonah. Although 4QXII^a preserves four original readings, discussed above, the greatest significance of this manuscript is due to the order of the last three books of the Minor Prophets, Zechariah, Malachi, Jonah, which is unparalleled elsewhere. Also of great interest is the high number of editorial readings (twelve) preserved in this manuscript. 4QXII^c (→ 9.2.1.3; → 9.2.3.2) and 4QXII^g (→ 9.2.1.7) also preserve high numbers of editorial readings and this sort of scribal activity must be taken into account in the transmission history of these compositions.

9.2.3.2 4QXII^c (4Q78)
4QXII^c (→ 9.2.1.3) preserves sections of Hosea, Joel, and Amos in 397 complete and partially preserved words. There are twenty-two non-orthographic variants and seventeen non-aligned readings. Although 4QXII^c is a non-aligned manuscript in terms of its textual affiliation, it preserves an agreement with LXX (→ 9.3) in a long plus at Hos 13:4.[3] 4QXII^c was written in an orthographic style that Tov has described as the Qumran Practice.

9.2.3.2.1 Nature and Text-Critical Character
4QXII^c is written in the Qumran Scribal Practice.[4] That is to say that the orthography of 4QXII^c belongs to a baroque or *plene* tradition in which [o] and [u] vowels are regularly indicated by *waw*, for example, the words כול "all" and לוא "no" are always written with *waw*. In addition, the so-called long form of the possessive suffix on nouns is regularly found for the second masculine singular (see, e.g., ועמכה "and your people" in Hos 4:4), for the second masculine plural (see, e.g., אלוהיכמה "your God" in Joel 4:17), and for the third masculine plural (see, e.g., בארמונותיהמה "in their strongholds" in Amos 3:10). The so-called long form of the verbal suffix in the perfect is also attested for the third masculine plural (see, e.g., מכרתמה "you have sold" in Joel 4:6).

The textual quality of 4QXII^c may be described as mixed. Of the thirty-nine readings preserved and listed in *DJD* XV, two are inner-Hebrew variants, eight are orthographic in nature, five are difficult, eighteen are editorial in nature, including explicating and harmonizing readings, and four are original. 4QXII^c agrees with MT against LXX four times, agrees with LXX against MT seven times, but preserves independent readings seventeen times. The original readings are:

Hos 4:15: אל "not" 4QXII^c] וְאַל "and not" MT LXX

Hos 13:4: בצר שמים [וקונה ארץ אשר ידיו ברא כול צבא השמים ולוא הראיתים לכה ללכת אחריהמה ו]אנוכי העלותיכה "who fortifies heaven [and creates the earth, whose

---
[3] Fuller, "The Twelve," 241.
[4] Tov, *Scribal Practices*, 261–63, 277–88, 337–43.

hands made the whole host of heaven, but I did not show them to you to go after them, but] I brought you up"⁵ 4QXIIᶜ LXX (vid)] > MT

Hos 13:15: וּיבשׁ "and will become dry" 4QXIIᶜ] וְיֵבוֹשׁ "and shall be ashamed" MT; καὶ ἀναξηρανεῖ "and it will dry up" LXX

Amos 4:1: הביאו "bring" (pl.) 4QXIIᶜ LXX] הָבִיאָה "bring" (sg.) MT

9.2.3.2.2 Date and Milieu

4QXIIᶜ is written in a well-developed hand in the semiformal tradition, which may be dated to ca. 75 B.C.E. (→ 9.2.1.3).⁶ This paleographic date sets a *terminus ante quem* for the development of the text of 4QXIIᶜ. Otherwise, little can be said of the date of the development of the text of this manuscript.

9.2.3.2.3 Relevance for Exegesis and Literary Analysis

The diverse readings of 4QXIIᶜ are naturally of text-critical interest, especially the original readings. Of even more interest is the high number of editorial readings (eighteen) that are preserved in this manuscript. As with 4QXIIᵃ (→ 9.2.1.1; → 9.2.3.1), 4QXIIᶜ may be described as an editorial text in which the scribe has intentionally altered readings in small ways for the sake of clarity or consistency. The existence of manuscripts from the second and first centuries B.C.E. with high numbers of editorial readings means that this sort of scribal activity continued into the time period in which the proto-Masoretic text became dominant and perhaps continued beyond that time period.

Barthélemy, *Critique textuelle 1992.
Brooke, G.J., "The Twelve Minor Prophets and the Dead Sea Scrolls," in *Congress Volume Leiden 2004* (ed. A. Lemaire; VTSup 109; Leiden: Brill 2006), 19–43.
Fuller, R.E., "Textual Traditions in the Book of Hosea and the Minor Prophets," in *Madrid Qumran Congress*, 254–56.
Fuller, R.E., "4QMicah: A Small Fragment of a Manuscript of the Minor Prophets from Qumran, Cave IV," *RevQ* 16 (1993–1995): 193–202.
Fuller, R.E., "The Form and Formation of the Book of the Twelve: The Evidence from the Judean Desert," in *Forming Prophetic Literature: Essays on Isaiah and the Twelve in Honor of John D.W. Watts* (eds. J.W. Watts and P.R. House; JSOTSup 235; Sheffield: Sheffield Academic Press, 1996), 93–95.
Fuller, R.E., "The Twelve," *DJD XV: 221–318.
Fuller, R.E., "Minor Prophets," in *EDSS 2:554–57.
Fuller, R.E., "The Prophets: Text and Textual Criticism," in *Dictionary of the Old Testament: Prophets* (eds. M.J. Boda and J.G. McConville; Downers Grove: IVP Academic, 2012), 775–81.
Gelston, A. (ed.), *BHQ, Part 13: *The Twelve Minor Prophets.*
Goshen-Gottstein, M.H., *The Aleppo Codex* (Jerusalem: Magnes Press, 1976).
Guillaume, P., "The Unlikely Malachi-Jonah Sequence (4QXIIᵃ)," *The Journal of Hebrew Scriptures* 7 (2007): http://www.arts.ualberta.ca/JHS/Articles/article_76.pdf.
Guillaume, P., "A Reconsideration of Manuscripts Classified as Scrolls of the Twelve Minor Prophets (XII)," *The Journal of Hebrew Scriptures* 7 (2007): http://www.arts.ualberta.ca/JHS/Articles/article_76.pdf.
Lange, *Handbuch*, 335–69.
Tov, *"Biblical Texts."
Tov, *Scribal Practices.*

Russell Fuller

---

⁵ Translation according to *DSSB, 426.
⁶ Fuller, "The Twelve," 238.

9.3 Septuagint

9.3.1 Background

The title Minor Prophets is attributed to Augustine (*City of God*, 18.29), who employed it to distinguish these twelve books from the longer prophetic books (Isaiah, Jeremiah, and Ezekiel). An older title for this collection is the Twelve, or the Twelve Prophets (Gk. *Dodekapropheton*). Ben Sira (49:10) mentions "the Twelve Prophets" in his praise of Israel's ancestors in Sir 44:1–50:24. Thus, even though each of the Minor Prophets has its own introduction, the Twelve have been considered a fixed corpus or collection at least since the time of Ben Sira. The earliest textual evidence also supports that understanding of them; the oldest extant manuscripts of the Minor Prophets from Cave 4 at Qumran, dating to the second century B.C.E., demonstrate that the Twelve were written on one scroll.[1] The reference to the twenty-four books Ezra made public (4 Ezra 14:44–45) and Josephus' reference (*Ag. Ap.* 1.8) to the twenty-two books the Jews believed to be divine also indicate that the Twelve were considered one literary unit, or book, among these larger collections. The main reason for treating the Twelve Prophets as a unit was apparently because each of them is relatively short and the collection was a convenient length for a scroll. The rabbis considered that Hosea could have circulated independently on a short scroll, but they bound it up with later prophecies in the book of the Twelve because they felt such a short work could easily be lost (*b. B. Bat.* 13b, 14b).

The position of the Minor Prophets varies in Septuagint manuscripts. Sometimes the Twelve are first in the Prophets (in Vaticanus and Alexandrinus), and at other times they follow the so-called "Major" Prophets (in Sinaiticus).[2] The statement in Hos 1:2, "The beginning of the word of the Lord by Hosee," which was taken by Jerome to refer to the beginning of the prophetic activity of the writing prophets (*Commentary on Hosea* 1:2), may have had some influence in the placing of the Twelve first in several Greek collections.[3] It is also likely that Hos 1:2 was taken to reflect the place of priority accorded Hosea among the Minor Prophets. In Jewish tradition, this phrase was "interpreted in a relative sense, i.e. amongst the contemporaries Hosea, Isaiah, Amos, and Micah, it was to Hosea that the Lord spoke first."[4]

The order of the first six prophets among the Minor Prophets in LXX differs from the Hebrew Bible (→ 9.2.2) in most manuscripts and catalogues.[5] In LXX, the "dominant" order is Hosea, Amos, Micah, Joel, Obadiah, and Jonah.[6] (The LXX order of the last six books of the Minor Prophets is the same as in the Hebrew Bible and probably derives from it.) Swete suggests that this "dominant" Greek order may be due to a desire for greater accuracy in the chronological arrangement of the books.[7] According to Jewish tradition, the first six books were thought to belong to the second half of the eighth century B.C.E.; the next three, Nahum, Habakkuk, and Zephaniah, were reckoned to belong to the second half of the seventh century B.C.E.; and the last three of the Minor Prophets, Haggai, Zechariah, and Malachi, were thought to belong to the sixth/fifth centuries B.C.E., or the post-exilic period.[8] However, with regard to the date of the first six books, it is noteworthy that only

---

[1] See more details in Muraoka, "Introduction," xi and A. Schart, "Book of the Twelve: History of Interpretation," in *Dictionary of the Old Testament Prophets* (ed. M.J. Boda and J.G. McConville; Downers Grove: Inter-Varsity Press, 2012), 807–08.

[2] Swete, **Introduction*, 201–02.

[3] See E. Bons, J. Joosten, and S. Kessler, *Les Douze Prophètes: Osée* (*Bible d' Alexandrie 23.1; Paris: Cerf, 2002), 24.

[4] A.A. Macintosh, *A Critical and Exegetical Commentary on Hosea* (ICC; Edinburgh: T & T Clark, 1997), lii.

[5] Swete, **Introduction*, 227.

[6] See Swete, **Introduction*, 227, n. 3, for some exceptions. There is no consensus on whether the sequence in MT or LXX is earlier.

[7] Swete, **Introduction*, 227; Dines, "The Septuagint of Amos," 13, suggests the Hebrew Bible places the prophets from Hosea to Micah in "supposed chronological order."

[8] Macintosh, *Hosea*, lii; Jones, *Formation*, 240–41.

the first three include chronological information in their superscriptions; therefore, some feel that only those three books should be ascribed to the eighth century. Today, few, if any, would date the books of Joel, Obadiah, and Jonah to the eighth century, although the events narrated in Jonah take place in that period. It is also possible that the length of the first six of the Minor Prophets could have had some influence on their order in LXX, since they are arranged in descending order from the longest to the shortest. The one exception to this rule is Jonah, which is longer than Obadiah but probably comes at the end of the first six because it is characterized by prophetic narrative in contrast to the prophetic discourse that characterizes the preceding five books.

9.3.2 Unity of the Greek Translation of the Minor Prophets

Over the last century, the unity of the translation style of LXX-MinP has been the basis of much discussion. The general consensus is that the Minor Prophets should be attributed to a single translator, but several scholars have challenged this consensus.

Johnson and Howard argued for two translators of LXX-Amos. Johnson contended that LXX-Amos 5–6 were translated by a different hand than LXX-Amos 1–4 and 7–9 or, alternatively, that LXX-Amos 5–6 were reworked after the entire book had been translated. He believed that LXX-Amos 5–6 were distinguished by "strikingly idiomatic Greek," "double rendering[s]," "syntactical blunders," a number of renderings of words that differ from the renderings found in the other chapters, and "peculiarities in the translation of Hebrew moods and tenses."[9] Howard proposed that one translator rendered the first (Amos 1:1–8:11) and last (Amos 9:11–15) sections of Amos, and another one rendered the middle section (Amos 8:12–9:10).[10] Howard based his argument on things like the different renderings of the Hebrew place name "Beersheba," which is rendered "the well of the oath" in Amos 5:5 and "Bersabee" in Amos 8:14.

Others maintain there were different translators of different books in the Twelve. Herrmann and Baumgärtel contended that one translator created the first six books (Hosea–Jonah), and another the last five (Habakkuk–Malachi).[11] They felt the style of Nahum, which was positioned between the two sections, did not agree exclusively with either section, and thus they assigned Nahum to both sections. Harrison, after reassessing the issue of the unity of the translation of LXX-MinP, concluded that the evidence for one translator or one group of translators for the collection is contradictory, and that those who argue for such unity employ flawed logic. Instead, he suggested that the Septuagint translations of the Minor Prophets may be found to have a complicated redactional history.[12]

All along, there have been important voices who have argued for the unity of the translation of LXX-MinP. Ziegler disputed the thesis of Hermann and Baumgärtel, emphasizing the similarities in the Greek between the two main sections of the Minor Prophets that they had suggested and arguing that differences in style do not necessarily prove the assumption of different translators.[13] He felt the differences in style could have been caused by a translator who varied the Greek equivalents of Hebrew words and phrases. Muraoka made a case for the differences in style in Amos being based on context and the versatility of the one translator.[14] He took a position similar to Ziegler, whose study he considered to be of particular importance and value for the issue.

Some also find evidence of the work of the translator of LXX-MinP in LXX-Jer (→ 7.3) and LXX-

---

[9] Johnson, "Amos," 25, 36–37, 67.
[10] G.E. Howard, "Some Notes on the Septuagint of Amos," *VT* 12 (1970): 108–12.
[11] J. Herrmann and F. Baumgärtel, *Beiträge zur Entstehungsgeschichte der Septuaginta* (Beiträge zur Wissenschaft vom Alten Testament N.F. 5; Berlin: W. Kohlhammer, 1923).
[12] C.R. Harrison, Jr., "The Unity of the Minor Prophets in the Septuagint: A Reexamination of the Question," *BIOSCS* 21 (1988): 55–72.
[13] Ziegler, *Einheit*.
[14] T. Muraoka, "Is the Septuagint Amos VIII 12–IX 10 a Separate Unit?," *VT* 20 (1970): 496–500.

Ezek (→ 8.3). Thackeray felt the translator of LXX-MinP also produced Ezekiel α (Ezekiel 1–27 and 40–48) and was also possibly responsible for what he called Jeremiah α (Jeremiah 1–28).[15] Similarly, Tov has argued that the original translator of the Minor Prophets was the same person who made the original translation of Jeremiah and Ezekiel.[16] The latter parts of Jeremiah and Ezekiel reflect the work of a reviser or editor, so the work of the original translator is only preserved in the first parts of these books, which for LXX-Jer would be chapters 1–28 and for LXX-Ezek chapters 1–27. Tov's argument is based on the probability that there was a single translator of the Minor Prophets.

In his introduction to the Minor Prophets in *NETS*, Howard concluded his discussion of this issue with the following words: "The issue is difficult since there are some anomalies in style within the Greek Minor Prophets that appear to go beyond the versatility of one translator."[17] However, his revised judgment is that the differences in style in the Twelve Prophets, which are "sometimes striking, ... do not necessarily suggest that more than one translator was at work."[18] (The single exception he makes to his conclusion is Habakkuk 3, about which see → 9.3.4.) Howard explains the "stylistic differences" in the Minor Prophets by assuming that "a corrector went through the original document, perhaps soon after it was finished, and made some revision. In his haste, the corrector did a haphazard job, leaving the text as it now exists with some stylistic inconsistencies."[19] The stylistic differences could also be explained by the versatility of the translator, as Ziegler and Muraoka contend.

Thus, the general consensus is that one translator (or perhaps one group of translators) was responsible for the Minor Prophets.[20] This translator may also have been responsible for parts of Jeremiah and Ezekiel, but this connection is less certain.

9.3.3 Date and Milieu

There is a general consensus among scholars that the Minor Prophets, as well as the other prophetic books, were translated into Greek around the middle of the second century B.C.E.[21] It is possible that the upheavals early in the second century B.C.E. caused the Jews to look to the prophets for answers, and this motivated them to translate these books into Greek.[22] Dines and Glenny have found evidence of bias against Syrians (Seleucids?), Samaritans, and "Hellenizing" Jews in LXX-Amos that is consistent with a date after Antiochus Epiphanes.[23] Sawyer has argued that the translation of LXX-Amos was later than 135 B.C.E. on the basis of allusions to Hasmonean rulers and Samaritan and Qumran sectaries in LXX-Amos 1:15 and 3:12.[24] However, not all are convinced by his treatment of these verses, and references to Qumran sectaries, which are an important part of his argument, could refer to earlier situations.[25] Linguistic evidence concerning the date of translation of the Minor Prophets is inconclusive.[26]

---

[15] Thackeray, *The Septuagint and Jewish Worship*, 28–29.
[16] Tov, *Jeremiah–Baruch*, esp. 17, 135–55. See also, Tov, *TCU*, 16–17.
[17] Howard, "The Twelve Prophets," 780.
[18] Howard, "The Twelve Prophets," 781; see Howard, "Some Notes on the Septuagint of Amos" for his original judgment.
[19] Howard, "The Twelve Prophets," 781.
[20] J.M. Dines, *The Septuagint* (Understanding the Bible and Its World; New York: T & T Clark, 2004), 22, summarizes, "It seems likely that one person, or group, translated the entire scroll."
[21] Dines, *The Septuagint*, 46, 50; J.M. Dines, "The Septuagint of Amos," 311–13; Glenny, *Finding Meaning in the Text*, 262–63.
[22] Dines, "The Septuagint of Amos," 311–12; similarly, van der Kooij feels that in the second century B.C.E. "the ancient prophecies were considered to be a source of hope, which was based on a reading and interpretation of these prophecies as referring to events of the age in which the reader/interpreter was living" (A. van der Kooij, "The Septuagint of Zechariah as Witness to an Early Interpretation of the Book," in *The Book of Zechariah and Its Influence* [ed. C. Tuckett; Burlington: Ashgate, 2003], 53–64 [55]).
[23] Glenny, *Finding Meaning in the Text*, 149–84; Dines, "The Septuagint of Amos," 310.
[24] J.F.A. Sawyer, "'Those Priests in Damascus': A Possible Example of Anti-Sectarian Polemic in the Septuagint Version of Amos 3,12," *ASTI* 8 (1970–1971), 123–30.
[25] See the discussion and critique of Sawyer in Dines, "The Septuagint of Amos," 76–81, 114–17, 311; see also Glenny, *Finding Meaning in the Text*, 263.
[26] Dines, *The Septuagint*, 46, 50.

The date of the translation of the Minor Prophets relative to that of other prophets remains unclear. Seeligmann felt the translator of Isaiah was aware of the translation of the Minor Prophets.[27] However, Muraoka and Dines have provided evidence that the translator of Micah depended on the Greek text of Isa 2:2–4 in his rendering of the parallel passage in Mic 4:1–3,[28] and Dogniez has argued that the choice of the noun ὀπωροφυλάκιον "garden watcher's hut," in Mic 3:12 was influenced by Isa 1:8, where the Greek word refers to Jerusalem.[29]

Although a Palestinian provenance for the Greek version of the Minor Prophets is possible,[30] the consensus is that it was translated in Egypt. Glenny found evidence to support an Egyptian provenance of LXX-Amos in geographical updating in Amos 6:14 and in the description of Amos' occupation in Amos 7:14.[31] Dines concluded that from the point of view of the language of LXX-Amos there was no need to doubt an Alexandrian provenance.[32]

The image of the translator of the Minor Prophets that emerges from the translation is that of a professional Jewish scholar-scribe. The milieu was likely one in which the text was studied intensively in its Greek version,[33] and the translator was apparently not an expert in Hebrew.[34] Theocharous argues for a Judeo-Hellenistic milieu for the translation of the Minor Prophets on the basis of the vocabulary, which is "at home within the contemporary Greek linguistic context" and the use of hermeneutical approaches that have affinities with Qumran writings.[35]

9.3.4 Original Form, Editions, Tools

The main critical text of the Twelve Minor Prophets is in the Göttingen Septuagint, edited by Ziegler in 1943.[36] This edition provides a wide array of evidence and is based on Ziegler's judicious reconstruction of the text. The Greek Minor Prophets are preserved in six uncial manuscripts: LXX^W, a papyrus in the Freer Collection from the third century C.E.; and five codices: Vaticanus (LXX^B) and Sinaiticus (LXX^S) from the fourth century C.E.; Alexandrinus (LXX^A) from the fifth century C.E.; Marchalianus (LXX^Q) from the sixth century C.E.; and Venetus (LXX^V) from the eighth century C.E. Ziegler was not able to determine the origin of the uncials LXX$^{W, B, S, V}$, but he was able to classify the text of the codices LXX^A and LXX^Q as Alexandrian in character on the basis of their many agreements with the text of the Septuagint used by Cyril of Alexandria in his commentary on the Minor Prophets. He also found evidence of the Hexaplaric recension in the margins and corrections of LXX^Q. Ziegler also determined that the text of the Minor Prophets in some minuscule manuscripts and those of the Fathers Chrysostom, Theodore of Mopsuestia, and Cyril was representative of the Lucianic recension (→ 6–9.1.6). Ziegler called his final category of manuscripts in the Greek Minor Prophets "Die Catenen-Gruppe"; he felt the text in this group of minuscules could be considered a branch of the Hexaplaric recension (→ 6–9.1.5).

Another important witness to the Greek text of the Minor Prophets is the manuscript 8ḤevXIIgr from the second half of the first century B.C.E., which was found in a cave in Naḥal Ḥever in the

---

[27] I.L. Seeligmann, *The Septuagint Version of Isaiah: A Discussion of Its Problems* (Medelingen en verhandelingen van het Vooraziatisch-Egyptisch Gennotschap "Ex Oriente Lux" 9; Leiden: Brill, 1948), 73, 87; he dated the translation of Isaiah to about 140 B.C.E., and felt that the translator of Isaiah already knew the Minor Prophets in Greek.

[28] Muraoka, "Introduction," xi; J.M. Dines, *Grinfield Lectures on the Septuagint*, 2007, as reported in C. Dogniez, "L' independence du traducteur d' Isaïe par rapport au Dodekapropheton," in *Isaiah in Context: Studies in Honour of Arie van der Kooij on the Occasion of His Sixty-Fifth Birthday* (eds. M. van der Meer et al.; VTSup 138; Leiden: Brill, 2010), 229–46 (233).

[29] C. Dogniez, "L' independence du traducteur d' Isaïe," 231–33; see also Theocharous, *Lexical Dependence*, 94–106.

[30] Theocharous, *Lexical Dependence*, 1–13.

[31] Glenny, *Finding Meaning in the Text*, 264.

[32] Dines, "The Septuagint of Amos," 313.

[33] See the discussion above in this section, suggesting the translator of Micah was aware of LXX-Isa.

[34] Glenny, *Finding Meaning in the Text*, 259–96.

[35] Theocharous, *Lexical Dependence and Intertextual Allusion*, 18–20.

[36] Ziegler, *Duodecim prophetae*.

Judean Desert.³⁷ This text is representative of the *kaige* group of manuscripts, which is thought by some to be a revision of the Septuagint (Old Greek) toward a then-current, proto-Masoretic form of the Hebrew text (→ 1.3.1.2).³⁸ Others contend that there was no monolithic *kaige* recension, and instead we should understand this text group to represent one stage on a continuum from the Greek Pentateuch to Aquila "in which approaches and attitudes to translation are on the whole tending toward a closer alignment between the Greek and the Hebrew."³⁹

The prayer of Habakkuk (Habakkuk 3), which also circulated as a psalm, exists in two different versions. A small group of manuscripts contain what is called the Barberini text, which differs substantially from the text found in the majority of manuscripts.⁴⁰ In his edition of the Minor Prophets in the Göttingen Septuagint, Ziegler presents the entire Barberini text of Habakkuk 3 after his critical text of that chapter. Harper describes the Barberini text as "Greek-oriented" in the sense that the translator was willing to differ from his *Vorlage* to produce a translation that was "aesthetically pleasing and rhetorically elegant"; it is "quite close in effect and overall impression" to the text of Symmachus (→ 6–9.1.5). Harper concludes that the Barberini text was an independent translation of Habakkuk 3, which was probably translated between 100 B.C.E. and 100 C.E.⁴¹

Other editions: the third and final volume of the diplomatic edition (1887–1894) of the Septuagint edited by Swete, which generally follows the text of LXX^B;⁴² Rahlfs, *Septuaginta* (1935), based primarily on LXX^B, LXX^S, and LXX^A, but also on many other sources.⁴³

Modern translations and commentaries provide auxiliary tools for the study of LXX-MinP.⁴⁴

9.3.5 Translation Character

The Hebrew source on which the translation of the Minor Prophets was based was apparently very close to the consonantal skeleton of MT (→ 9.2.2).⁴⁵ The translation of the Minor Prophets is "typical translation Greek";⁴⁶ it is adequate and generally a literal representation of the Hebrew.⁴⁷ The transla-

---

³⁷ Tov, *DJD* VIII. The twenty-four fragmentary columns of 8ḤevXII gr that have been recovered contain material from Jonah, Micah, Nahum, Habakkuk, Zephaniah, and Zechariah, and a fragment possibly containing some of Amos 1:5.

³⁸ Barthélemy, *Devanciers*.

³⁹ P. Gentry, *The Asterisked Material in the Greek Job* (SBLSCS 38; Atlanta: Scholars Press, 1995), 497.

⁴⁰ Ziegler (*Duodecim prophetae*, 273–75) finds evidence of the Barberini text in LXX^V and four minuscules: LXX^62, 86, 147, 407; see also Thackeray, *The Septuagint and Jewish Worship*, 48, n. 3.

⁴¹ Harper, "The Barberini Version," 66–67, 117, 23–24. See also Howard, "The Twelve Prophets," 781; M. Harl et al., *Les Douze Prophètes: Joël, Abdiou, Jonas, Naoum, Ambakoum, Sophonie* (*Bible d'Alexandrie* 23.4–9; Paris: Cerf, 1999), 245–46; Thackeray, *The Septuagint and Jewish Worship*, 47–55.

⁴² H.B. Swete, *The Old Testament in Greek according to the Septuagint* (3 vols.; Cambridge: Cambridge University Press, 1887–1894).

⁴³ Rahlfs, *Septuaginta*. A one-volume edition was published in 1979, and a second edition, Rahlfs–Hanhart, *Septuaginta*, was published in 2006.

⁴⁴ Bons, Joosten, and Kessler, *Osée*; M. Harl et al., *Les Douze Prophètes: Joël, Abdiou, Jonas, Naoum, Ambakoum, Sophonie* (*Bible d'Alexandrie* 23.4–9; Paris: Cerf, 1999); M. Cassevitz, C. Dogniez, and M. Harl, *Les Douze Prophètes: Aggée, Zacharie* (*Bible d'Alexandrie* 23.10–11; 2007); L. Vianès, *Les Douze Prophètes: Malachie* (*Bible d'Alexandrie* 23.12; Paris: Cerf, 2011); W.E. Glenny, *Hosea: A Commentary Based on Hosea in Codex Vaticanus* (Septuagint Commentary Series; Leiden: Brill, 2013); W.E. Glenny, *Amos: A Commentary Based on Amos in Codex Vaticanus* (Septuagint Commentary Series; Leiden: Brill, 2013); W.E. Glenny, *Micah: A Commentary Based on Micah in Codex Vaticanus* (Septuagint Commentary Series; Leiden: Brill, 2015); Howard, "The Twelve Prophets," 775–822; H. Utzschneider, "Dodekapropheten: Das Zwölfprophetenbuch," in *Septuaginta Deutsch*, 1165–229; and A. Schart et al., "Dodekapropheton: Das Zwölfprophetenbuch," in *Septuaginta Deutsch, Erläuterungen*, 2:2275–483.

⁴⁵ Dines, "The Septuagint of Amos," 17, 308; Palmer, "Not Made with Tracing Paper," 176; Glenny, *Finding Meaning in the Text*, 146, 272; J. Joosten, "Exegesis in the Septuagint Version of Hosea," in *Intertextuality in Ugarit and Israel: Papers Read at the Joint Meeting of The Society for Old Testament Study and Het Oudtestamentisch Werkgezelschap in Nederland and België, Held at Oxford, 1997* (ed. J.C. de Moor; OtSt 40; Leiden: Brill, 1998), 62–85 (64); Theocharous, *Lexical Dependence and Intertextual Allusion*, 9–11.

⁴⁶ Howard, "The Twelve Prophets," 777.

⁴⁷ Dines, "The Septuagint of Amos," 2, 307–08; Glenny, *Finding Meaning in the Text*, 272; Joosten, "Exegesis in the

tor followed the word order of his Hebrew source very closely, and he seldom added or subtracted elements.[48] However, there are many points of exegetical and theological interest in the translation (→ 9.3.6).

9.3.6 Translation Technique and Inner-Translational Features

To date, there is no comprehensive study of the translation technique of the Minor Prophets. However, there have been several studies of individual books and different aspects of the translation of the Minor Prophets.[49] Since it is generally assumed that one translator, or group of translators, was responsible for the collection, the results of study of different parts of the collection have relevance for each individual book. As the *Vorlage* of LXX-MinP is generally regarded as similar to MT (→ 9.3.5), the study of translation technique in the Greek Minor Prophets usually uses MT (→ 9.2.2) as a representative *Vorlage*. There are important differences between LXX and the Hebrew *Vorlage* in the Minor Prophets, but the exact cause of those differences is debated. Some of the differences between LXX-MinP and MT can be explained by a Hebrew *Vorlage* differing from MT, but most differences were probably created by "inner-translational factors, especially in the area of exegesis."[50]

The translator of LXX-MinP had great respect for his source text. This is the conclusion of Joosten's study of "Exegesis in the Septuagint Version of Hosea"; furthermore, Joosten contends that the translator's main concern was to bring out the sense of his *Vorlage*, not to promote his theological agenda. The translation involves interpretation, as do all translations, but the divergences involve misreading or errors in analyzing the Hebrew, contextual exegesis, and occasionally the decoding of figures of speech.[51] The translator obviously struggles with some of the Hebrew in his *Vorlage*, but his ideology, "trust in the inspired text," comes through more in the form of his translation than in the content of the message.[52] The translator's trust in and reverence for the inspired text is clear from the coherence of word order and component parts of the Hebrew and the Greek in the translation. But one wonders, after reading Joosten, if it is as easy as he implies to separate the translator from his theology, and if his theology and worldview could in any way be suspended in his attempts to be objective in his translation of the text.

Obscurities in the text may have caused some differences between LXX-MinP and its Hebrew *Vorlage*, but there is disagreement about the extent of this. Although he allows for other factors, Gelston argues that in twenty-three so-called "misreadings" in LXX-Amos the translator was "impaired by obscurities in the *Vorlage*" caused by indistinct handwriting in the inscription of the *Vorlage* or subsequent damage to the manuscript.[53] He bases his thesis on the frequent confusion of individual letters, such as *dalet* and *reš*. In four instances, where the misreading extends to two adjacent letters, he

---

Septuagint Version of Hosea," 82–85. Palmer, "Not Made with Tracing Paper," 39, says concerning the translation of LXX-Zech: "Interpretive freedom takes place within the context of literalism"; this is also what Glenny (268) found in LXX-Amos.

[48] Glenny, *Finding Meaning in the Text*, 13; Palmer, "Not Made with Tracing Paper," 36–37; Theocharous, *Lexical Dependence and Intertextual Allusion*, 9–11. Dines, "The Septuagint of Amos," 138–39, finds only four places in LXX-Amos where the word order differs from the Hebrew (Amos 5:14, 26; 7:7, 12).

[49] See, e.g., Joosten, "Exegesis in the Septuagint Version of Hosea"; Palmer, "Not Made with Tracing Paper"; Glenny, *Finding Meaning in the Text*; Arieti, "A Study in the Septuagint of Amos"; J. de Waard, "Translation Techniques Used by the Translators of Amos," *Bib* 59 (1978): 339–50. T. Muraoka, "Hebrew *Hapax Legomena* and Septuagint Lexicography," in *VII Congress of the International Organization for Septuagint and Cognate Studies Leuven 1989* (ed. C.E. Cox; SBLSCS 31; Atlanta: Scholars Press, 1991), 205–22, is a helpful study of the translation of twenty-four *hapax legomena* in the Minor Prophets. Theocharous, *Lexical Dependence and Intertextual Allusion*, is also relevant to translation technique in the Minor Prophets, as is Dines, "The Septuagint of Amos." Howard, "The Twelve Prophets," 777–80, also has a helpful section on "Translation Profile of the Greek."

[50] See Tov, *TCHB*, 117; he notes that only a fraction of the divergences between MT and LXX were created by a difference between MT and the *Vorlage* of LXX.

[51] Joosten, "Exegesis in the Septuagint Version of Hosea," 85.
[52] Joosten, "Exegesis in the Septuagint Version of Hosea," 83.
[53] A. Gelston, "Some Hebrew Misreadings in the Septuagint of Amos," *VT* 52 (2002): 493–500 (493, 500).

suggests the "misreading" is better explained by damage to the *Vorlage*. Glenny responded to Gelston's article and argued that a better explanation of the twenty-three examples Gelston used was that they were imprecise translations or paraphrases of the *Vorlage*, manipulation or maneuvering of difficult texts in an attempt to make sense of them, double translations, or theologically motivated translations.[54]

It is difficult to determine when differences between LXX-MinP and its *Vorlage* reflect a reading tradition and worldview of the translator that differs from that of the source text. Van der Kooij has argued that the translators of LXX, and thus the Minor Prophets, were "scholar-scribes" who were familiar with the text they were translating and a reading tradition of it. Therefore, Greek translations that differ from the way we read the Hebrew reflect the readings and interpretations of the text current in the milieu of the translator rather than misunderstandings or errors.[55] As a result, he argues that the translator of LXX-Zech 9:9–10 was influenced by his cultural background and theology, and understood this text to be a prediction of Simon, the Maccabean leader. Palmer surmises that many passages in LXX may reflect the cultural context of the translator, but he thinks it is more likely that the translator relied on conjecture or manipulated the text when he encountered an obscurity. Of course, that is not to say that such conjectures and manipulations do not reflect the milieu of the translator.[56]

Two subsequent studies agree that linguistic, textual, and theological-cultural factors may account for the differences between LXX-MinP and its Hebrew *Vorlage*. Glenny's study of Amos is the only monograph on the translation technique of one of the Minor Prophets, and in part his goal was to test Palmer's findings in his dissertation on the translation technique of Zechariah on Amos.[57] They both studied different aspects of literalism, such as word order, quantitative representation, representation of constituent elements, and stereotyping. Both studies found the translator to be generally literal, but he occasionally varied word order, added or removed elements, varied the Greek equivalents for Hebrew elements in the *Vorlage*, and paraphrased or varied from stereotyped renderings.

Palmer and Glenny also studied the translation of difficult and unknown parts of the text, such as Hebrew *hapax legomena*, and tested six techniques that Tov had suggested translators might employ in translating such texts (untranslated words [transliteration], contextual guesses, contextual manipulation, reliance on parallelism, employment of general words, and etymological renderings);[58] they found examples of all six categories in both books. Both also studied the rendering of visually ambiguous phenomena, like word divisions, homonyms, and homographs, in these books. Their study of this material suggests the translator had a general knowledge of Hebrew and that he did not know a reading tradition of all of the text, so when he came to uncommon terms and constructions he had to make decisions that determined his vocalization of the Hebrew text. Also, both studies indicate that the translator had a theological agenda that can be discerned from his translation. For example, in Amos he evidences an anti-Syrian (Seleucid?) and anti-Samaritan bias, while in Zechariah he emphasizes the centrality of Jerusalem, the return of the exiles to Jerusalem, the nations joining Israel to worship the Lord in Jerusalem, the exclusion of Canaanites, and the expansion of the influence of Israel.[59] Thus, although there are common theological emphases such as eschatology in LXX-Amos and LXX-Zech,[60] recent studies in LXX-

---

[54] W.E. Glenny, "Hebrew Misreadings or Free Translation in the Septuagint of Amos?," *VT* 57 (2007): 524–47.

[55] Van der Kooij, "The Septuagint of Zechariah," 55.

[56] Palmer, "Not Made with Tracing Paper," esp. 67, 176–77; on p. 177 he calls the translation of LXX-Zech "an act of critical interpretation."

[57] Glenny, *Finding Meaning in the Text*; Palmer, "Not Made with Tracing Paper."

[58] Tov, *"Septuagint Translators."

[59] Pisano, "'Egypt' in the Septuagint of Hosea," 301–08, demonstrates the translator's emphasis on the fact that Israel has already returned to Egypt in LXX-Hos.

[60] Another well-known characteristic of LXX-MinP is the rendering of צבאות "hosts, armies," by παντοκράτωρ "almighty,"

MinP suggest that different aspects of the translator's theology and worldview come to light in different books, and that he probably did not have a worked-out theological system.[61] His different theological emphases seem to be related to and developed from related emphases and themes in the book he is translating.[62]

9.3.7 Value for Textual Criticism

Although the vast majority of elements in the Greek of the Minor Prophets do represent proto-MT (→ 9.2.2), it is important to use caution in the use of LXX-MinP in text-critical work on the Hebrew Bible, because there are important differences between LXX and proto-MT in the Minor Prophets (→ 9.3.6). The translator had a tendency to paraphrase, to add or remove elements, to vary the Greek equivalents for Hebrew elements in the *Vorlage*, and to manipulate difficult texts to make sense of them (→ 1.3.1.1.12).[63]

9.3.8 Value for Literary Criticism

The order of LXX-MinP is important for the discussion of the original order of the collection as a whole (→ 9.3.1). Jones argues that the order in LXX-MinP preceded that found in MT.[64]

It is also sometimes suggested that individual verses in LXX-MinP reflect an earlier stage in the literary history than the edition found in MT (→ 9.2.2). For example, in his development of the catchword connectors between the Twelve Minor Prophets, Jones argues that "the MT of Amos 9:12 is a redactional alteration of the Hebrew text that is preserved in the LXX."[65] This alteration of the text would have involved changing one letter from ידרשו "they will seek" to יירשו "they will possess" and the vocalization of MT אָדָם "man" as אֱדֹם "Edom."

Arieti, J.A., "A Study in the Septuagint of Amos" (PhD diss., Stanford University, 1972).
Dines, J.M., "The Septuagint of Amos: A Study in Interpretation" (PhD diss., University of London, 1991).
Glenny, W.E., *Finding Meaning in the Text: Translation Technique and Theology in the Septuagint of Amos* (VTSup 126; Leiden: Brill, 2009).
Harper, J.L., "Responding to a Puzzled Scribe: The Barberini Version of Habakkuk 3 Analyzed in the Light of the Other Greek Versions" (PhD diss., University of Cambridge, 2013).
Howard, G.E., "The Twelve Prophets: To the Reader," in *NETS, 777–81.
Johnson, S.E., "The Septuagint of Amos" (PhD diss., University of Chicago, 1936).
Jones, B.A., *The Formation of the Book of the Twelve: A Study in Text and Canon* (SBLDS 149; Atlanta: Scholars Press, 1995).
Joosten, J., "Exegesis in the Septuagint Version of Hosea," in *Intertextuality in Ugarit and Israel*: Papers Read at the Tenth Joint Meeting of The Society for Old Testament Study and Het Oudtestamentisch Werkgezelschap in Nederland en België, held at Oxford, 1997 (ed. J.C. de Moor; OtSt 40; Leiden: Brill, 1998), 62–85.
Kaminka, A., *Studien zur Septuaginta an der Hand der Zwölf Kleinen Prophetenbücher* (Schriften der Gesellschaft zur Förderung der Wissenschaft des Judentums 33; Frankfurt a.M.: J. Kauffman, 1928).
Muraoka, T., "Introduction aux Douze Petits Prophétes,"

---

which also points to the unity of the translator's thinking; see C. Dogniez, "Le Dieu des armées dans le Dodekapropheton: quelques remarques sur une initiative de traduction," in *IX Congresss of the International Organization for Septuagint and Cognate Studies* (ed. B.E. Taylor; SBLSCS 45; Atlanta: Scholars Press, 1997), 19–36, and E. Tov, "Theologically Motivated Exegesis Embedded in the Septuagint," in Tov, *Greek–Hebrew Bible*, 257–69 (263).

[61] Palmer, "Not Made with Tracing Paper," 123, 176.

[62] The theological and cultural understanding of the translator, which is revealed in his translation, does not necessarily reflect a conscious *Tendenz* on his part.

[63] Palmer ("Not Made with Tracing Paper," 38) cautions about the use of LXX-Zech for textual criticism of the Hebrew Bible because of the "non-representative tendency" he found in that book. See also the examples of literary variation in Amos in Dines, *Septuagint*, 54–60, and Glenny, *Finding Meaning in the Text*, 51–63.

[64] Jones, *The Formation of the Book of the Twelve*, 221–42. Dines has argued that the original order of LXX-MinP was the same order found in MT ("Verbal and Thematic Links between the Books of the Twelve in Greek, and their Relevance to the Differing Manuscript Sequences," in *Perspectives on the Formation of the Twelve: Methodological Foundations – Redactional Processes – Historical Insights* [eds. R. Albertz, J. Nogalski, and J. Wöhrle; BZAW 433; Berlin: De Gruyter, 2012], 355–70).

[65] Jones, *The Formation of the Book of the Twelve*, 190.

in *Les Douze Prophètes: Osée* (eds. E. Bons, J. Joosten, and S. Kessler; *Bible d'Alexandrie* 23.1; Paris: Cerf, 2002), i–xxiii.

Palmer, J.K., " 'Not Made with Tracing Paper': Studies in the Septuagint of Zechariah" (PhD diss., University of Cambridge, 2004).

Pisano, S., " 'Egypt' in the Septuagint of Hosea," in *Tradition of the Text*: Studies Offered to Dominique Barthélemy in Celebration of His 70th Birthday (eds. G.J. Norton and S. Pisano; OBO 109; Göttingen: Vandenhoeck & Ruprecht, 1991), 301–08.

Theocharous, M., *Lexical Dependence and Intertextual Allusion in the Septuagint of the Twelve Prophets: Studies in Hosea, Amos, and Micah* (Library of Hebrew Bible/Old Testament Studies 570; New York: T & T Clark, 2012).

Tov, *DJD* VIII.

Ziegler, J., *Die Einheit der Septuaginta zum Zwölfprophetenbuch* (Beilage zum Vorlesungsverzeichnis der Staatlichen Akademie zu Braunsberg im WS 1934/35; Braunsberg, 1934).

Ziegler, J., *Duodecim prophetae* (2nd ed.; Septuaginta Vetus Testamentum Graecum 13; Göttingen: Vandenhoeck & Ruprecht, 1967).

W. Edward Glenny

6–9.1 Primary Translations

6–9.1.1 Septuagint

The Former Prophets (the historical books Joshua to 2 Kings) and the Latter Prophets (Isaiah, Jeremiah, Ezekiel, and the twelve Minor Prophets) form together the second subdivision of the Hebrew canon, after the Torah and before the Writings (Ketuvim). The contents and names of the second and third divisions are somewhat problematic (→ 3–5.1.1).

The organizing principle of Jewish Greek Scripture (not necessarily Alexandrian) differs from that of the Hebrew canon (→ 1.1.2.1). It may be considered an improvement of the Hebrew arrangement, which could be achieved because the former was organized at a later stage than the Hebrew canon and could therefore be rearranged solely by literary genre and not by a mixture of criteria as in the Hebrew canon. The details of this new arrangement are presented in the overview article of LXX (→ 1.3.1.1.4). The Christian canon (→ 1.1.2.2) follows that of LXX.

In several ways, the arrangement of the Latter Prophets in the Hebrew canon differs from that of their counterpart in Greek, but in both corpora the individual books appear next to each other. The two canons differ in the following ways (→ 1.3.1.1.4):

1. In several manuscripts of LXX: the Prophets appear in the last position, immediately preceding the New Testament.
2. Sequence of the Major and Minor Prophets.
3. Internal sequence of the Minor Prophets.

The books of the Latter Prophets have much in common in the Hebrew canon, and in a different way also in the Greek canon. It has been suggested by Tov,[1] that the bulk of the prophetical books were rendered by a single translator (Jeremiah, Ezekiel, and the Minor Prophets).[2] The style and vocabulary of this translator differed completely from that of the translator of Isaiah.

Emanuel Tov

6–9.1.2 Pre-Hexaplaric Greek Translations

See → 6–9.1.5 Hexaplaric Greek Translations (Latter Prophets > Primary Translations).

John D. Meade

6–9.1.3 Targum

The standard Aramaic translation of the biblical books of the Latter Prophets is part of a single broader collection known as Targum Jonathan of the Prophets, which also contains Targum Former Prophets (→ 3–5.1.3). Targum Latter Prophets is subdivided into three Major Prophets (Isaiah, Jeremiah, and Ezekiel) and twelve Minor Prophets (Hosea, Joel, Amos, Obadiah, Jonah, Micah, Nahum, Habakkuk, Zephaniah, Haggai, Zechariah, and Malachi).

6–9.1.3.1 Nature, Date, and Milieu

Targum Jonathan has an obscure prehistory, which makes the reconstruction of the date and character of the subdivision Targum Latter Prophets complex (→ 1.3.3.1.1; → 1.3.3.4.4; → 3–5.1.3.1).[1] The consistent and standard use of Jewish Literary Aramaic that characterizes this Targum is inadequate for dating it because the dialect[2] endured in writing be-

---

[1] Tov, *Jeremiah–Baruch*, 135–55.

[2] This unity was later disturbed when the Old Greek versions of Jeremiah and Ezekiel were revised by unknown revisers, and when the archetype of LXX of these books was composed of a combination of unrevised and revised segments. For details, see Tov, *Jeremiah–Baruch*.

[1] For a general survey on the Targum to the Latter Prophets in the nineteenth and twentieth centuries, consult Gordon, *Studies in the Targum to the Twelve Prophets*, 5–19. See also Levey, "The Date of Targum Jonathan to the Prophets."

[2] See Goshen-Gottstein, "The Language of Targum Onqelos and the Model of Literary Diglossia in Aramaic"; Kutscher, *Studies in Galilean Aramaic*; Kutscher, "Das zur Zeit Jesu gesprochene Aramäische"; Tal, *The Language of the Targum*

yond the period wherein it was in use (→ 3–5.1.3.1; for more information on the different Aramaic dialects, → 1.3.3.3).[3] Emphasising translation techniques, Churgin (1927) defends a progressive development of Targum Jonathan from textual deviations, elimination of anthropomorphisms, and historical references. Le Déaut (1966), Bowker (1969), and McNamara (1972) support a developing Targum tradition.[4] They argue that Targumim reveal what the traditional interpretation was at a particular historical time. Flesher and Chilton (2011) discern a phasal development of Targum Latter Prophets. An early stage is reflected from incomplete Tannaitic frameworks in Targumim Isaiah, Jeremiah, Ezekiel, and Zechariah, and a revised stage with Amoraic influence from the late third and fourth centuries. Two additional levels of interpretation identified by Flesher and Chilton in Targumim Hosea, Amos, Nahum, Obadiah, Micah, and Zephaniah reflect a further development of exilic theology in the fifth century while Targumim Joel, Jonah, and Habakkuk follow with an individualistic emphasis on exilic theology. Possible evidence of earlier frameworks in Targumim Minor Prophets is too scattered for certainty.[5]

Targumim Isaiah, Jeremiah, and Ezekiel have been researched comprehensively. In Chilton's (1987) assessment, Targum Isaiah is the collective work of rabbis in the Tannaitic and Amoraic periods.[6] Hayward (1987) determines Targum Jeremiah's origin in the land of Israel during or slightly before the first century C.E., possibly with older roots. Targum Jeremiah tends to render the common-sense meaning of the text without reflecting interpretations commonly found in the Talmud and midrash, thus indicating an earlier date than the Babylonian Talmud, which cites it as an authoritative translation.[7] The development of Targum Ezekiel may not have followed the process of the official Targum. Levey (1987) connects its careful wording and esoteric character with *merkabah* mysticism.[8] Cathcart and Gordon (1989) find clear indications of an origin for Targumim of the Minor Prophets after the turn of the eras from references to: 1) the *Shekinah* (Hab 2:20; Zeph 3:15), and 2) a Diaspora situation after the turn of the eras (Zech 2:16; Mal 3:12; Nah 1:9). Evidence exists for redactional activity after the turn of the eras, but an earlier period is doubtful.[9] From a comprehensive study of Targum Zephaniah, Ho (2009) notices a progressive composition, but in her assessment dating remains inconclusive (for more information on dating techniques, → 1.3.3.4.3; → 1.3.3.4.4).[10]

6–9.1.3.2 Editions, Translations, and Auxiliary Tools

The earliest witness to Targum Latter Prophets is Codex Reuchlinianus[11] (1105 C.E.). Textual oddities and some expansive additions characterise it. The British Museum manuscript numbered 2211 (B.M. 2211) is the base text of Sperber's edition of Targum Jonathan[12] and Stenning's textual restoration of the Isaiah Targum.[13] Therein, the Hebrew and Aramaic of the Latter Prophets appear in alternative verses.

---

of the Former Prophets and Its Position within the Aramaic Dialects.

[3] Flesher and Chilton, *The Targums*, 174; Chilton, *The Isaiah Targum*, xxi; Hayward, *The Targum of Jeremiah*, 35.

[4] Le Déaut, *Introduction à la littérature Targumique*; Bowker, *The Targums and Rabbinic Literature*, and McNamara, *Targum and Testament*.

[5] Flesher and Chilton, *The Targums*, 199–227.

[6] Chilton, *The Isaiah Targum*, xx–xxv. Cf. also Stenning's work (1949) on Targum Isaiah (Stenning, *The Targum of Isaiah*).

[7] Hayward, *The Targum of Jeremiah*, 38.

[8] Levey, *The Targum of Ezekiel*, 2–6.

[9] Cathcart and Gordon, *The Targum of the Minor Prophets*, 16–18.

[10] Ho, *The Targum of Zephaniah*, 420.

[11] Published by de Lagarde as *Prophetae Chaldaice* in 1872; the photographic reproduction of the codex was published by A. Sperber as *The Pre-Masoretic Bible: Discovered in 4 Manuscripts Representing a Unique Tradition: I, the Codex Reuchlianus, II, the Parma Pentateuch, III, the Parma Bible, IV, the London Bible: And publ. with a general introduction, Detailed Description of the Mss. and Basic Conclusions*, Vol. 1: *Codex Reuchlinianus: No. 3 of the Badische Landesbibliothek in Karlsruhe (formerly Durlach No. 55) with a General Introduction: Masoretic Hebrew* (Corpus codicum Hebraicorum Medii Aevi 2.1; Copenhagen: Munksgaard, 1956).

[12] Sperber, *The Latter Prophets according to Targum Jonathan*. For more details on Sperber's edition, see Cathcart and Gordon, *The Targum of the Minor Prophets*, 18–19.

[13] Stenning, *The Targum of Isaiah*.

B.M. 1474 and B.M. 1470 compare second best to B.M. 2211. Stenning collated three further manuscripts: Bodleian (2617 and 2618) and Bibliothèque Nationale (1325).[14] The First (1515–1517) and Second (1524–1525) Rabbinic Bibles (*RB1 and *RB2)[15] and several polyglots hold a number of extant manuscripts and versions of Targum Latter Prophets. Commentaries of popular rabbinic commentators on the Bible and Talmud reflect variant readings.[16] In 1871, Pauli provided the first singlehanded translation of the Isaiah Targum[17] while Latin translations of Targum Jeremiah appear in the Antwerp Polyglot Bible (1569–1572)[18] and the Walton/London Polyglot Bible (1654–1657).[19] For modern editions, see the references in the bibliography below.

6–9.1.3.3 Translation Character

A consistent characteristic among the Targumim to the Latter Prophets is that they generally render the Hebrew text verbatim but with numerous expansions, which vary in length; typical examples of which may be found in avoidance of anthropomorphism, and the use of intermediary expressions between the human and the divine. Theological or ideological perspectives, specific schools of thought, historical allusions, and definable periods provide clues into the translation character of the individual Targumim of the Latter Prophets (→ 3–5.1.3.2).

Targum Isaiah's speaking voice is distinctly prophetic.[20] Various additions of words and phrases underscore the prophetic authority of the book, e.g., נבואת[21] "the prophecy of (Isaiah)" (Isa 1:1); נבואה "(the word) of prophecy" (Isa 2:1); אמר נבייא "the prophet said" (Isa 5:1; 6:1; 21:12); שויתי פתגמי נבואתי בפומך "I have placed the words of prophecy in your mouth" (Isa 6:7); ד נבייא "the prophet of (the Lord)" (Isa 7:10; 22:12); נבייא אתנבו "Prophets, prophesy (consolations)" (Isa 40:1).

The Hebrew text of Isaiah (→ 6.2.2) is rendered innovatively through additions and deletions, inversion of word order, and construction of fresh contexts.[22] Terms and phrases like בית ישראל "house of Israel," אברהם "Abraham," אוריתא "the law," מקדשא "the sanctuary," and צדיקיא "the righteous" recur throughout, evoking concern for a rebellious Israel: it has benefitted from God's promise to Abraham, yet despises the sanctuary. Its punishment is exile, but repentance results in its return and restoration. Anthropomorphic terminology is avoided. God is referred to in terms of מימרא "the Word" and שכינתא "Shekinah."[23] The abbreviated use of the Tetragrammaton יוי is prominent. The Messiah figures both as eschatological and eternal figure.[24] Descriptive categories of the Messiah, Shekinah, and the sanctuary move from anticipation to actuality revealing two complementary levels of meaning within the theological orientation of this Targum: 1) the practical and national, where the restoration of the sanctuary and Israel's return from exile can only happen when the Messiah, repentance, and the Shekinah become a reality; 2) a more teleological outlook, where repentance has begun and the Messiah, the Shekinah, and the sanctuary exist in the presence of God in heaven.[25] The promise given to Abraham by the supreme God, guarantees Israel's future and restoration.

Targum Jeremiah[26] adheres to the central tenets of the Jewish faith and its practice: God and his people Israel, the prophets, priests, and scribes, the splendour of the Torah, the rewards for the righteous, the fate of the wicked as well as the expectation of the Messiah. Hebrew titles proclaim God's uniqueness, e.g., אלהים "God" (Jer 1:6); צבאות שמיה "(the lord of) hosts is his name" (Jer 10:16). Expressions that associate God too closely with the hu-

---

[14] See Chilton, *The Isaiah Targum*, xxix–xxxiii.
[15] These contain the text with the Targum and standard rabbinical commentaries.
[16] Levey, *The Targum of Ezekiel*, 17.
[17] C.W.H. Pauli, *The Chaldee Paraphrase on the Prophet Isaiah Translated* (London: London Society's House, 1871).
[18] *Biblia Sacra Hebraice, Chaldaice, Graece, et Latine*.
[19] Walton, *Polyglotta*.
[20] Chilton, *The Isaiah Targum*, xiv–xx.
[21] All targumic citations are taken from *CAL.

[22] Chilton, *The Isaiah Targum*, xiv–xv.
[23] Chilton, *The Isaiah Targum*, xvi.
[24] Chilton, *The Isaiah Targum*, xviii.
[25] Chilton, *The Isaiah Targum*, xx.
[26] Hayward, *The Targum of Jeremiah*, 30–34.

man body are avoided.[27] The face, eyes, and hands of the deity are rendered in relation to their denoted function, e.g., גבורתי "my power" replaces יָדִי "my hand" (Jer 6:12). The term קדם "before" is similarly employed, e.g., ואלפן מן קדם יוי "and they make request *before* him" (Jer 10:21).[28] God's manifest presence is described circumlocutory: בית שכינתי "the house of my *Shekinah*" (Jer 14:10). A frequent expression relating to the active, divine, and merciful presence of God is מימרא דיוי "the Word of the Lord" (e.g., Jer 3:13). The use of גבורתא "might" (e.g., Jer 16:14) underscores the power, strength, or might of God. MT's (→ 7.2.2) attacks on idolatry are retained and strengthened through exposition, e.g., the Baʿal Peʿor incident (Jer 2:23–25). Coupled with this is the punishment of desolation and exile (Jer 2:11–12; 4:6) and the exhortation that Israel should repent and return to the Torah (Jer 3:22–23). The words "prophets" and "prophecy" are rendered very precisely. The phrase "prophet of the Lord" (נביא דיוי; Jer 35:4) stands in contrast to expressions like the "prophets of falsehood" (נביי שקרא; Jer 4:9), the "scribe(s)" (ספר; Jer 14:18), and "priests" (כהין; Jer 18:18), indicating those who have failed in their duties. Targum Jeremiah concedes to the "second death" (מותא תנינא; Jer 51:39) and the resurrection of the dead but negates the passing away of heaven and earth, שמיא וארעא לא שויתינון דיעדון "heaven and earth are not equal to those who pass away" (Jer 33:25).

Targum Ezekiel's historico-theological thrust reflects the situation directly after the destruction of the temple in 70 C.E.[29] Levey concurs with Herrscher[30] that this Targum alludes to *merkabah* mysticism, stemming from R. Joḥanan b. Zakkai's effort to suppress messianic activism. Open messianic activity was regarded as treason against the Roman emperor. The designation "Messiah" is absent in Targum Ezekiel although rabbinic thought otherwise interprets Ezekiel 38 and 39 and other passages in allusion to the Messiah.[31] The theme of *merkabah* mysticism is reflected from Targum Ezekiel's association with the nature of Jerusalem, the heavenly throne, and the temple.[32] God's transcendence and exclusiveness in the universe is safeguarded with the use of divine surrogates (רגזא, שכינתא, גבורא and מימרא "the Wrath," "the *Shekinah*," "the Might," and "the Word"), e.g., rebellion against God is translated indirectly as על מימרי "against my Word" (Ezek 2:3); מַרְאוֹת אֱלֹהִים "visions of God" (Ezek 1:1) is rendered circumlocutory as חיזו יקר שכינתא דיוי "a vision of the glory of the *Shekinah* of the Lord." Anthropomorphism is avoided in Targum Ezekiel, e.g., וַהֲסִבּוֹתִי פָנַי מֵהֶם "And I will turn my face from them" (Ezek 7:22) is rendered ואסליק שכינתי מנהון "And I will make my *Shekinah* depart from them." God's hand is translated indirectly as רוח נבואה "the spirit of prophecy" (Ezek 1:3), or מחת גבורתי "the stroke of my might" (Ezek 6:14), or merely גבורתי "my might" (Ezek 39:21). The frequent appellation בֶּן־אָדָם "son of man" is consistently rendered as the proper noun בר אדם "son of Adam."[33] Unspecified poetic Hebrew expressions are elaborated by interpolating historical facts exegetically (cf. Ezek 16:45). In contrast to Targum Ezekiel, Damsma (2012) submits from her study of the Targumic Tosefot to Ezekiel that they demonstrate a close relationship to the Hekhalot literature and particularly to the Shi'ur Qomah tradition. The Targumic Tosefot to Ezekiel feature in the synagogue service during the festivals of Shavuot (Ezekiel 1) or Pesach (Ezekiel 37).[34] Damsma dates the Targumic Tosefot to Ezekiel to the Geonic period.[35]

Intermediary expressions between the human and the divine such as שכינתא "Shekinah" (e.g., Joel 2:27) and מימרא "the Word" (e.g., Zech 1:4) also characterize the Targumim to the Minor Prophets (→ 2.4.3.3.2).[36] Other substitute terms are דחלתא

---

[27] Hayward, *The Targum of Jeremiah*, 22–23.
[28] Hayward, *The Targum of Jeremiah*, 22.
[29] Levey, *The Targum of Ezekiel*, 4–16.
[30] Herrscher, "Yochanan ben Zakkai: Acrobatics at Yavneh"; Levey, *The Targum of Ezekiel*, 4.
[31] Levey, *The Targum of Ezekiel*, 5.
[32] Levey, *The Targum of Ezekiel*, 5–6.
[33] For explanations of this aspect, see Levey, *The Targum of Ezekiel*, 6–9.
[34] Damsma, *The Targumic Tosefot to Ezekiel*, 182.
[35] Damsma, *The Targumic Tosefot to Ezekiel*, 180.
[36] Cathcart and Gordon, *The Targum of the Minor Prophets*, 4–9.

"fear," e.g., תוב ישראל לדחלתא דיוי אלהך "Return, O Israel, to the fear of the Lord your God" (Hos 14:2) and פלחנא "service, worship," e.g., ותובו לפלחנא דיוי "Return to the worship of the Lord" (Hos 14:3). The preposition קדם "before" is not only used to express respect but also to dampen the tone of MT (→ 9.2.2), e.g., קָצַף יְהוָה "The Lord was angry" is rendered הוה רגז מן קדם יוי "There was anger *from before* the Lord" (Zech 1:2). Targumim Minor Prophets generally avoid anthropomorphism by using paraphrase and the keynote verb גלי "to uncover, to reveal" in relation to divine activity (e.g., Obad 1:21; Mic 4:7; Zech 3:8) (→ 2.4.3.3.2). Where apparent evil-doing is attributed to God in MT, the notion is toned down in the Targumim to the Minor Prophets, e.g., אם תהי בשתא בקרתא ומן קדם יוי לא אתעבידת "Can misfortune be in a city unless it was done from before the Lord?" (Amos 3:6). An offensive limitation to the divine glory is neutralized, e.g., אַיֵּה כְבוֹדִי "Where is my honour?" is translated as אן דאתון מיקרין קדמי "Where is [that] *you are honouring before me?*" (Mal 1:6). The Messiah figures prominently. While he is still hidden due to Israel's sinful state (Mic 4:8), his name is professed from ancient times (Mic 5:1; Zech 4:7). At his coming, he will rebuild the temple (Zech 6:12) and rule upon his throne (Zech 6:13; for Messiah in Targum Onqelos, → 2.4.3.3.2). The resurrection of the dead is embraced, e.g., אחיות מיתיא (Zech 3:7). At T-Hos 14:8, the resurrection is associated with the rule of the Messiah. Death is not the end of God's dealings with man (Mal 3:6): the wicked face destruction at Gehenna (Hos 14:10); albeit, repentance is efficacious (Joel 2:14; Jonah 3:9). Part of the educative characteristic of Targum Minor Prophets is Torah observance. The frequent mention of prayer links it with the synagogue. T-Mic 7:14 expresses "nationalism" by teaching that Israel will support itself in the renewed earth. God will judge the nations, who have not accepted instruction (Mic 5:14). Israelite warriors will trample the dead of the nations (Zech 10:5) and those nations who have plundered Israel will be destroyed (Nah 1:9). T-Mal 1:5 links nationalism to land theology with the idea that Israel's borders will be extended. These are specified at T-Zech 9:1, 6; 14:10 and T-Mic 7:14.

6–9.1.3.4 Translation Techniques

Expressions like תרגם, כדמתרגם, and כדמתרגמינן testify to the Aramaic "translation," "explanation," and "clarification" of Hebrew in Judaism's formative age (→ 1.3.3.1; → 1.3.3.5.1).[37] The primary aim was to provide a translation of Scripture that was intelligible for audiences with differing levels of Hebrew knowledge (for more specific information on the person of the translator, → 1.3.3.1; → 2.4.3.2.1; → 2.4.3.2.3). Targum not only assisted the popular audience to identify Targumic portions that corresponded with the Hebrew text of Scripture,[38] it also supported the interpretation of Scripture for scholarly purposes, assisting rabbis to understand, interpret, and contemporize complex passages of Scripture in line with submitted tradition (*b. Mo'ed Qaṭ.* 28b; *b. Meg.* 3a; *b. Sanh.* 94b) (→ 2.4.3.2.3; on the origin of targumic literature, → 1.3.3.2).[39] Translators exercised certain liberties, ultimately compromising the accuracy and vibrancy of the original text (→ 3–5.1.3.2; for different translation methods, → 2.4.3.2.2). Inherent translation techniques reveal how meaning was extracted from the sacred text (on the *Sitz im Leben* of Targumim, → 1.3.3.5.1):

1. Regular use of stock words, e.g., תקף "strength" (Amos 1:5; Nah 2:3); שיצי "destroy" (Zeph 1:11); בזז "spoil" (Hos 8:8); and קרב "bring near" (Hag 2:23; Mal 1:7) (→ 3–5.1.3.3).
2. Rabbinic stock phrases or exegetical expansion idioms maintain the traditional interpretation of theological strata in the biblical text, e.g., בזו נכסי "spoil the goods (of)" (Mic 3:3); אשריתי שכינתי "(I) will cause the *Shekinah* to dwell" (Joel 4:17) (→ 1.3.3.6).
3. Contemporizing of Scripture reflects events and places or institutions of much later periods, e.g., in Isa 29:1 אֲרִיאֵל "Ariel" is rendered מדבחא "altar"; the frequent substitution of "scribe" for "prophet" (e.g., Zech 7:3) illus-

---

[37] See Ho, *The Targum of Zephaniah*, 8–10.
[38] For more detail, consult Heinemann, "The Proem in Aggadic Midrashim."
[39] Ho, *The Targum of Zephaniah*, 10.

4. Converse translation, e.g., where the Hebrew text asserts that God "hates" divorce: כִּי־שָׂנֵא שַׁלַּח אָמַר יְהוָה "for I hate divorce, says the Lord" Targum translates the opposite: ארי אם סנית לה פטרה "but if you hate her, divorce her" (Mal 2:16) (→ 1.3.3.6).[40]
5. Duplicate renderings: one half of a verse retains one rendering while the other half contains a vestige of a different version: the more contemporary explanation was not able to strip away the older one (→ 1.3.3.6).[41]
6. Expansion of metaphors or similes, e.g., where Ephraim is called a כְּיוֹנָה פוֹתָה "silly dove" (Hos 7:11), Targum adds דאתנסיבו בנהא "whose young were taken." The metaphoric representation was explained by expanding the biblical text, e.g., ten words in Jer 10:11 are increased to fifty-seven in Targum Jeremiah (→ 3–5.1.3.3; → 1.3.3.6).
7. Transformation of metaphors into similes for clarification, e.g., the metaphor וְלִבָּם שָׂמוּ שָׁמִיר "and they made their heart emery" converts to a simile ולבהון שויאו תקיף כשמירא "and they made their heart hard *like* adamant" (Zech 7:12) (→ 3–5.1.3.3; → 1.3.3.6).
8. Avoidance of anthropomorphism for religious purposes, e.g., מימרי "my Word" replaces עֵינָי "my eyes" (Jer 16:17) (→ 3–5.1.3.3; → 1.3.3.6; cf. also → 2.4.3.3.2).
9. Substitution, to convey the implied significance of words or expressions in the biblical text, e.g., ואגלי "and I *will exile* him to Babylon" replaces וְהֵבֵאתִי "and I *shall bring* him into Babylon" (Ezek 12:13) (→ 3–5.1.3.2).
10. Allegory is mostly used in agreement with contemporary haggadic interpretation (e.g., Ezekiel 16; Hos 1:2, 5, 6, 8; 3:1–4), but also to allude to past events; providing clues to the historical origin of the Targum (e.g., Hab 3:17; Isa 28:1; Ezek 39:16; Mic 5:9, 10, 12) (for more information on references to historical events or persons within Targumim, → 1.3.3.4.2).
11. Complements elucidate breaches or fill gaps in the biblical text, e.g., בְּנֵי־יִשְׂרָאֵל כְּחוֹל הַיָּם "The number of the children of Israel shall be as the sand of the sea" is rendered ויהי מנין בני ישראל סגי כחלא "and the number of the children of Israel shall be *numerous* as the sand" (Hos 2:1); (see also Jer 17:4; Isa 10:15; Hos 2:15; Ezek 7:13; 16:29) (→ 3–5.1.3.3).
12. Supplements enhance the message of biblical passages, e.g., מָה הַבָּמָה אֲשֶׁר־אַתֶּם הַבָּאִים שָׁם "What is the high place whereunto you are going?" is rendered מא במתא דאתון אתן לאשתטאה תמן "What is the high place whereunto you go *to make yourself foolish*?" (Ezek 20:29) (→ 3–5.1.3.2).
13. Expansions convert single repeated words into a clause, e.g., Targum Jeremiah renders the threefold repetition הֵיכַל יְהוָה הֵיכַל יְהוָה הֵיכַל יְהוָה הֵמָּה "The temple of the Lord, the temple of the Lord, the temple of the Lord these are" (Jer 7:4) in a protracted manner: קדם היכלא דיוי אתון פלחין קדם היכלא דיוי אתון דבחין קדם היכלא דיוי אתון סגדין תלת זמנין בשתא "Before the temple of the Lord you worship, before the temple of the Lord you sacrifice, before the temple of the Lord you bow three times throughout the year" (→ 1.3.3.6).

Overall, Targum Latter Prophets does not render the Hebrew text in a meticulously literal way so that it sometimes is difficult to determine the exact Hebrew reading underlying the Aramaic rendering. Obscure passages in many instances reflect remnants of both ancient and more recent Jewish exegesis (→ 3–5.1.3.4). Where the Hebrew text is terse, the exegetical complement is extensively applied to fill the gaps of the tight prophetic style. Notwithstanding, additions remain within the boundaries of the text. The aim was to retain the sense and style of the text: simple and lucid, whilst keeping in mind the goal to contemporize the message.

---

[40] For more detail, see Klein, "Converse Translation: A Targumic Technique."

[41] For examples on duplications, consult Churgin, *Targum Jonathan to the Prophets*, 127–41.

6–9.1.3.5 Text-Critical Value

Deviations from the Hebrew text fall into three main categories: 1) Different readings: although the relationship of Targum Latter Prophets to the Hebrew text is evidently secondary, some renderings reflect ancient exegetical traditions known to LXX. In certain instances, the Targum has points of contact with Qumran literature as well as pre-rabbinic literature and various New Testament documents;[42] 2) Linguistic, e.g., a change of preposition or a *waw* that is left untranslated or is added may be attributed to the distraction of a copyist or the Aramaic idiom; 3) Interpretive, e.g., the hermeneutic rule of *gezerah shavah* ("equal category" principle) is apparent in Targum Latter Prophets where a particular verse or part thereof is rendered in the light of another verse that is phraseologically or thematically linked[43] (e.g., Mic 7:19 יכבוש על חובנא ברחמתיה "*He will forgive* our transgressions with His love" and Zeph 3:17 יכבוש על חוב ברחמתיה "He will *forgive your transgressions* with his love"; Ezek 36:25 כמא דמדכן במי אדיותא ובקטם תורתא דחטתא "*as if you had been* purified by the water of sprinkling and *by the ashes of the cow of sin offering*" and Zech 13:1 כמא דמידכן במי אדיותא ובקטם תורתא דחטתא "*as if they were purified by the waters of sprinkling and by the ashes of the cow of sin offering*"; see also Joel 2:14 and Jonah 3:9) (→ 3–5.1.3.5; for more general information on the text-critical value of Targumim, → 1.3.3.7).[44]

6–9.1.3.6 Rabbinic Citations and Parallels; Relevance for Exegesis

Developmental stages preceding rabbinic Judaism are reflected in Targum Latter Prophets from evidence in them of the Tannaitic phase before and immediately after 70 C.E. Extant Targumim may therefore be seen to link intertestamental literature and rabbinica because rabbinic literature was only produced in the second century after the destruction of the Second Temple (→ 3–5.1.3.6).[45] Examples in Targum of pre-rabbinic echoes can be found in the words of Jesus.[46] Yet, there is also evidence that rabbinic activity influenced the interpretive process of Targum Latter Prophets.[47] This is reflected from quotations of the text of Targum Prophets in the Babylonian Talmud, most of which represent interpretations of an expository nature.[48] These are primarily cited in the name of R. Joseph (e.g., *b. Yoma* 77b on Isa 33:21; *b. Pesaḥ.* 68a on Isa 5:17). Within Targum Minor Prophets, quotations are sometimes identical to the standard text, e.g., Hos 4:2 (*b. Qidd.* 13a); Amos 7:14 (*b. Ned.* 38a); Obad 6 (*b. B. Qam.* 3b); Zech 9:6 (*b. Qidd.* 72b). In other instances, citations diverge considerably from the standard text, e.g., Zeph 3:18 in *b. Ber.* 28a. There are also instances where quotations are preceded by ומתרגימן such as at *b. Roš Haš.* 22b on 2 Sam 5:21. Specific targumic interpretations are paralleled in midrashic writings, e.g., Hos 8:4 (*Gen. Rab.* 28:7); Amos 9:1 (*Lev. Rab.* 33:2); Hab 3:9 (*Exod. Rab.* 44:9; *Num. Rab.* 13:20). Sometimes, later writings assist with the understanding of targumic renderings, e.g., Zech 1:5 where the reference to "the former prophets" is illuminated by *b. Sanh.* 105a.

Biblia Sacra Hebraice, Chaldaice, Graece, et Latine (8 vols.; Antwerp: C. Platinus, 1569–1572). "The Antwerp Polyglot."

Bowker, J., *The Targums and Rabbinic Literature: An Introduction to Jewish Interpretation of Scripture* (Cambridge: Cambridge University Press, 1969).

*CAL.

Cathcart, K.J. and R.P. Gordon, *The Targum of the Minor Prophets* (ArBib 14; Wilmington: Michael Glazier, 1989).

---

[42] See Hayward, *The Targum of Jeremiah*, 26–28; cf. also Cathcart and Gordon, *The Targum of the Minor Prophets*, 10–12. For examples of textual variations between MT and Targum Jonathan, see Churgin, *Targum Jonathan to the Prophets*, 55–77.

[43] Cathcart and Gordon, *The Targum of the Minor Prophets*, 2.

[44] See also Churgin, *Targum Jonathan to the Prophets*, 52–55.

[45] Chilton, *The Isaiah Targum*, xxvi.

[46] For specific references, see Chilton, *The Isaiah Targum*, xxvi–xxviii.

[47] Cathcart and Gordon, *The Targum of the Minor Prophets*, 15–16. Flesher and Chilton, *The Targums*, 178–227 argue that written Targumim reflect two exegetical frameworks, Tannaitic and Amoraic.

[48] Cf. Churgin, *Targum Jonathan to the Prophets*, 146–51.

Chilton, B.D., "The Glory of Israel: The Theology and Provenience of the Isaiah Targum," JSOTSup 23 (1982): xi–xii, 6–12.

Chilton, B.D., *The Isaiah Targum: Introduction, Translation, Apparatus, and Notes* (ArBib 11; Wilmington: Glazier, 1987).

Churgin, P., *Targum Jonathan to the Prophets* (YOSR 14; New Haven: Yale, 1927; repr., New York: Ktav, 1983).

Damsma, A., *The Targumic Toseftot to Ezekiel* (Studies in the Aramaic Interpretation of Scripture 13; Leiden: Brill, 2012).

Flesher, P.V.M. and B.D. Chilton, *The Targums: A Critical Introduction* (Waco: Baylor University Press, 2011).

Gordon, R.P., "An Inner-Targum Corruption (Zech. I 8)," VT 25 (1975): 216–21.

Gordon, R.P., *Studies in the Targum to the Twelve Prophets: From Nahum to Malachi* (VTSup 51; Leiden: Brill, 1994).

Goshen-Gottstein, M.H., "The Language of Targum Onqelos and the Model of Literary Diglossia in Aramaic," JNES 37/2: 169–79.

Hayward, C.T.R., *The Targum of Jeremiah* (ArBib 12; Wilmington: Michael Glazier, 1987).

Heinemann, J., "The Proem in Aggadic Midrashim – A Form Critical Study," ScrHier 22 (1971): 100–22.

Herrscher, U.R., "Yochanan ben Zakkai: Acrobatics at Yavneh." Paper submitted in partial fulfilment of a minor in Rabbinics for his doctoral degree., Hebrew Union College – Jewish Institute of Religion, Los Angeles, Calif., 1973.

Ho, A., *The Targum of Zephaniah: Manuscripts and Commentary* (Studies in the Aramaic Interpreation of Scripture 7; Leiden: Brill, 2009).

Houtman, A. and H. Sysling, *Alternative Targum Traditions: The Use of Variant Readings for the Study in Origin and History of Targum Jonathan* (Studies in the Aramaic Interpretation of Scripture 9; Leiden: Brill, 2009).

Klein, M.L., "Converse Translation: A Targumic Technique," Bib 57 (1976): 515–37.

Kutscher, E.Y., "Das zur Zeit Jesu gesprochene Aramäische," ZNW 51 (1960): 1–35.

Kutscher, E.Y., *Studies in Galilean Aramaic* (trans. M. Sokoloff; Bar Ilan Studies in Near Eastern Language and Culture; Ramat Gan: Bar Ilan University Press, 1976).

de Lagarde, P. (ed.), *Prophetae Chaldaice* (Leipzig: Teubner, 1872).

Le Déaut, R., *Introduction à la littérature Targumique* (Rome: Pontifical Biblical Institute Press, 1966).

Levey, S.H., "The Date of Targum Jonathan to the Prophets," VT 21 (1971): 186–96.

Levey, S.H., *The Targum of Ezekiel* (ArBib 13; Wilmington: Michael Glazier, 1987).

McNamara, M.J., *Targum and Testament: Aramaic Paraphrases of the Hebrew Bible: A Light on the New Testament* (Shannon: Irish University Press, 1972).

*RB1.

*RB2.

Smolar, L. and M. Aberbach, *Studies in Targum Jonathan to the Prophets* (The Library of Biblical Studies; repr.; New York: Ktav, 1983).

Sperber, A., *The Latter Prophets according to Targum Jonathan* (vol. 3 of Sperber, *Bible in Aramaic*).

Stenning, J.F., *The Targum of Isaiah* (Oxford: Clarendon, 1949).

Tal, A., *The Language of the Targum of the Former Prophets and Its Position within the Aramaic Dialects* (Ramat Aviv: Tel Aviv University Press, 1975) [Hebr.].

Walton, *Polyglotta*.

Gudrun Elisabeth Lier

6–9.1.4 Peshitta

6–9.1.4.1 Text and Edition

The books of Isaiah, Ezekiel, and the Twelve (MinP) have been published as parts of the "Leiden Peshitta," the first critical edition of the Old Syriac version of the Old Testament.[1] The edition of Jeremiah, however, is not yet available in 2015, but the collations of the manuscript variants of this book, prepared by Donald M. Walter in the framework of the Leiden Peshitta Project, have been used for the present study. The text of the Leiden Peshitta is based on manuscript s^{7a1}, a very important manuscript among the ancient manuscripts of the Peshitta, but one that cannot be regarded as representing the original text of the Syriac version in every detail. Manuscript s^{9a1} has turned

---

[1] S.P. Brock (ed.), *Isaiah* (The Old Testament in Syriac according to the Peshiṭta Version 3.1; Leiden: Brill, 1987); M.J. Mulder (ed.), *Ezekiel* (The Old Testament in Syriac according to the Peshiṭta Version 3.3; Leiden: Brill, 1985); A. Gelston (ed.), *Dodekapropheton, Daniel and Bel and the Dragon: Prepared on the Basis of Material Collatected and Studied by Th. Sprey* (The Old Testament in Syriac according to the Peshiṭta Version 3.4; Leiden: Brill, 1980).

out to be of particular importance for the issue of the original text. As far as the Latter Prophets (LP) are concerned, this manuscript is a "regular unique carrier of old readings"[2] in the case of Isaiah, Jeremiah, Ezekiel, and Hosea (Hos 1:1–14:6). The incidence of unique and early readings varies between these books; the number in Jeremiah, for instance, is higher than in Ezekiel. Since this manuscript is of "a very mixed character,"[3] each reading (variant) has to be dealt with individually. In the case of Isaiah, manuscript s9a1 seems to be of limited use, as van der Kooij has pointed out,[4] whereas, for Jeremiah, Greenberg has come to the conclusion that many unique readings in manuscript s9a1, being in agreement with MT (→ 7.2.2), are original.[5]

6–9.1.4.2 Translation Character

The translation of LP in Syriac is fairly literal. Generally speaking, the version of Isaiah, Jeremiah, Ezekiel, and MinP is in close agreement with MT (→ 6.2.2, → 7.2.2, → 8.2.2, → 9.2.2), representing a sensible version of these books, although also containing a number of deviations. The non-literal features can be divided, roughly speaking, into two groups:[6] differences due to the language system of Syriac, such as cases pertaining to syntax and idiom, on the one hand, and differences introduced by the translator in order to modify the style or the sense of the underlying text, on the other. Variant readings include pluses, minuses, variants due to syntax, style, or idiomatic usage, as well as variants resulting from contextual harmonization, or from choices made as far as lexical equivalents are concerned.[7] They also represent readings that are due to interpretive devices such as a vocalization of the underlying Hebrew in a way different from MT, analogical word-analysis or ancient etymologizing, and influence from other passages (within a book or with passages in another biblical book).[8]

6–9.1.4.3 The Peshitta and Other Versions

In addition to the above, variant readings in the Peshitta may also be due to influence from other versions, in particular LXX (→ 6.3, → 7.3, → 8.3, → 9.3).[9] Scholars have shown that the books of LP contain cases that display exclusive agreements with LXX (→ 1.3.4.9).[10] True, cases of agreement may be due to polygenesis, a different *Vorlage*, or to a common exegetical tradition, but there are also "strong" cases that do suggest LXX influence.

The following examples may serve as illustrations:

– s-Isa 5:7: "the new and beloved plantation"; cf. LXX νεόφυτον ἠγαπημένον (MT "his pleasant planting");
– s-Isa 10:33: "he who overthrows the glorious ones with power"; cf. LXX συνταράσσει τοὺς ἐνδόξους μετὰ ἰσχύος (MT "he will lop the boughs with terrifying power");
– s-Jer 2:31: "an arid land"; cf. LXX γῆ κεχερσωμένη (MT "land of darkness");
– s-Jer 38(LXX 45):19: "and they mocked at me"; cf. LXX καὶ καταμωκήσονταί μου (MT "and they torment me");
– s-Amos 1:15: "and his priests"; cf. LXX οἱ ἱερεῖς αὐτῶν (MT [no equivalent]).

---

[2] Weitzman, *The Syriac Version of the Old Testament*, 282.

[3] Brock, "Text History and Text Division in Peshitta Isaiah," 59.

[4] Van der Kooij, "Ms 9a1 of the Peshitta of Isaiah: Some Comments," 71–76. For the evidence of s-Isa from Syriac Fathers, see Ter Haar Romeny, "The Peshitta of Isaiah: Evidence from the Syriac Fathers," 149–64.

[5] Greenberg, *Peshitta to Jeremiah*, 126–42. On the nature of manuscript s9a1 for Jeremiah, see also Walter, "Manuscript Relationships for the Peshitta Text of Jeremiah," 231–53.

[6] Cf. Greenberg, *Peshitta to Jeremiah*, 19. See also Gelston, *The Peshitta of the Twelve Prophets*, 131.

[7] For Jeremiah, see Greenberg, *Peshitta to Jeremiah*, 32–125; for Ezekiel, see Mulder, "Some Remarks on the Peshitta Translation of the Book of Ezekiel," 169–82 (174–80); for MinP, see Gelston, *Twelve Prophets*, 131–47.

[8] For examples in s-Isa, see van der Kooij, *Textzeugen*, 258–98 (284–87).

[9] For a general discussion, see Weitzman, *Syriac Version*, 68–86.

[10] For Isaiah, see van der Kooij, *Textzeugen*, 287–88; for Jeremiah, see Greenberg, *Peshitta to Jeremiah*, 143–68; for Ezekiel, see Van Rooy, "Agreement between LXX and Peshitta versus MT in Ezekiel," 213–27; and for MinP, see Gelston, *Twelve Prophets*, 160–77.

Obviously, the translators of LP did not follow LXX consistently, but only occasionally. The reason for doing so may differ from case to case. One of the reasons may have been that the Hebrew was considered to be difficult, but this is hardly to be regarded the sole reason.[11]

In addition, there are also a few cases where LXX influenced later copyists of the Peshitta.[12]

A well-known example is to be found in Isa 9:5: at the end of the verse some manuscripts contain the addition "and father of the age to come," following an addition in some manuscripts of the LXX version of the verse, πατὴρ τοῦ μέλλοντος αἰῶνος "father of the age to come."

As opposed to S-Pent (→ 2.4.5) and S-Chr (→ 20.3.5), which display a large number of agreements between the Peshitta and the Targum tradition,[13] the evidence for LP is scant.[14] From the point of view of relative dating it would not be impossible that translators of the Peshitta were familiar with T-Prophets because T-Prophets goes back, at least the body of it, to the early second century C.E.[15] However, in view of their limited number, it seems more likely that the concurrences are due to a common (exegetical) tradition.[16] S-Isa 25:7a is an example in case, for which see below.

6–9.1.4.4 Exegesis

The books of LP in the Peshitta contain passages that are marked by exegetical and theological modifications.[17] As has been demonstrated by van der Kooij, an interesting example is to be found in Isa 25:6–8.[18]

S-Isa 25:6–8

(6) And the mighty Lord will make among all nations, on this mountain,
a rich feast, (and) a feast observed and rich of our heavenly and mighty lifegiver.
(7) And on this mountain the face of the ruler who bare rule of all peoples, will be struck,
and the victim that was slain for all peoples.
(8) And death will be swallowed up to victory for ever [...]

MT-Isa 25:6–8

(6) The Lord of Hosts will make for all peoples on this mountain a feast of fat things,
a feast of wine on the lees, of fat things full of marrow,
of wine on the lees well-refined.
(7) And he will destroy on this mountain the covering that is cast over all peoples,
the veil that is spread of all nations.
(8) He will swallow up death for ever [...]

In MT (→ 6.2.2), this passage is about a banquet on Mount Zion, a feast for all nations, which will be a marvellous one because of its excellent food and select wines. It is about a time of joy because the "covering," or the "veil," to be understood as symbols of sorrow, will be destroyed.

The Peshitta differs markedly from MT (→ 6.2.2). Unlike the latter, the eschatological banquet prepared by the Lord will be a feast *among* all nations, not "for" all of them. Furthermore, this feast is called "rich, fat" (ܫܡܝܢܐ) and "observed, prescribed" (ܢܛܝܪܐ). The latter term is of special interest because the rendering of שמרים "wine dregs" by Syriac ܢܛܝܪ "observed, prescribed" is also found in S-Exod 12:42, i.e., in a passage about the Feast of Passover. It is of note that Aphrahat uses the same expression concerning the "Passover," kept by Jesus and his disciples (*Dem.* 12, 6).[19]

---

[11] Note the way Greenberg has entitled the relevant chapter in her work on S-Jer: "Difficult Hebrew: Influence from the LXX" (*Peshitta to Jeremiah*, 143).

[12] On this feature, see Weitzman, *Syriac Version*, 84–86.

[13] Cf. S.P. Brock, "Jewish Traditions in Syriac Sources," *JJS* 30 (1979): 212–32 (212–20), and Weitzman, *Syriac Version*.

[14] Cf. Weitzman, *Syriac Version*, 107.

[15] See van der Kooij, *Textzeugen*, 289–90; Greenberg, *Peshitta to Jeremiah*, 17–18; and Gelston, *Twelve Prophets*, 178–90.

[16] See van der Kooij, *Textzeugen*, 289–90; Greenberg, *Peshitta to Jeremiah*, 17–18; and Gelston, *Twelve Prophets*, 178–90.

[17] For Isaiah, see van der Kooij, *Textzeugen*, 273–84; for Jeremiah, see Greenberg, *Peshitta to Jeremiah*, 26–31; and for MinP, see Gelston, *Twelve Prophets*, 146–57.

[18] Van der Kooij, *Textzeugen*, 273–76.

[19] "Notre Sauveur a donc mangé la pâque avec ses disciples *la nuit prescrite* du quatorze" (SC 359, 575; italics mine).

The last clause of the verse tells the reader that this feast is "of our heavenly and strong lifegiver." The term "lifegiver" (ܡܚܝܢܐ) is used in early Syriac theology as a designation of Jesus. Aphrahat employs the expression "our lifegiver" more than twenty times as a title of Jesus. The idea is that Jesus as the vanquisher of death is the one who makes alive. It therefore is reasonable to assume, so van der Kooij, that s-Isa 25:6 alludes to Jesus.[20] Gelston, however, suggested that in this text "the Redeemer could be identified with God rather than with Christ," in line with the use of this title in Isa 60:16 in manuscript s9a1.[21] The term "the lifegiver" is found in ms 9a1 at Isa 60:16, but this instance is hardly of any significance because this variant of manuscript s9a1 must be regarded as secondary.[22] Therefore, the verse under discussion (Isa 25:6) is best explained as referring to Christ, the more so as this makes perfect sense in the passage of Isa 25:6–8 as a whole (see below).[23] It reminds one of the way Melito of Sardes speaks about Christ in his Homily on Passover (Christ, τὸν ζωοποιήσαντά σε "the one who makes you alive" [l. 539]), and of passages in the New Testament (see, e.g., 1 Cor 15:22).

Isa 25:7 too differs greatly from MT. The first half of v. 7 reads, "And on this mountain the face of the ruler who ruled all peoples, will be struck." The term "ruler" (ܫܠܝܛܐ) for Hebrew לוט "covering" does not constitute a literal rendering, but rather reflects an interpretation based on an association with the root שלט "domineer over." It is interesting to note that the Peshitta shares this interpretation with the Targum ("And on this mountain will be annihilated the face of the great one who is master over all the peoples") and Symmachus ("And he will destroy on this mountain the face of the ruler who has power over all nations"). The second half of the verse is about "the victim that is slaughtered for the sake of all peoples." Unlike v. 7a, this part has no parallel in the Targum and Symmachus. The Syriac ܢܟܣܬܐ "victim" as the rendering of מסכה "veil" can be explained as being derived from a metathesis (ܢܟܣ "to slay" instead of the root ܣܟܢ "to weave" equaling the Hebrew root נכס II). If read in conjunction with v. 6, this clause is best understood as referring to Jesus as the paschal lamb. Cf. Aphrahat, *Dem.* 21, 12.

Finally, the first clause of v. 8 is of interest: "death will be swallowed up to victory for ever." Just as in v. 7, the verb בלע "to swallow" has been rendered here in the passive. For לנצח "for ever," the Peshitta offers two words, ܠܢܨܚܢܐ ܠܥܠܡ "to victory for ever." Both equivalents are found elsewhere in s-Isa (the former in Isa 28:28, and the latter, e.g., in Isa 33:20 and 34:10), but this is the only place where they appear together. The double rendering as part of the whole clause fits the idea of Jesus' victory over death as the "lifegiver." Cf. Aphrahat, *Dem.* 22, 15 ("Jesus, the lifegiver, the one who killed death").

After having examined the details of the (above) exegesis of s-Isa 25:6–8 as presented by van der Kooij in his *Textzeugen*, Gelston made the following concluding remarks:

> There is no doubt that this exegesis makes good sense of the Peshitta of the passage, and that it would be congenial to Christian readers. Its chief strength perhaps lies in the convergence of several factors in a comparatively short passage, which cumulatively amount to the possibility of a definite Christian interpretation. If it is plausible to regard any passage in the Peshitta of Isaiah as of Christian origin, this must be the most probable instance. Our examination of the individual details, however, has shown that in each case it is also possible to explain the translation as the work of a Jewish translator confronted with several words whose meaning he did not know, doing his best to produce a satisfactory rendering word for word.[24]

The last part of these comments raises a methodological question. The issue at stake is whether the translator produced renderings to be regarded

---

[20] Van der Kooij, *Textzeugen*, 274.

[21] Gelston, "Was the Peshitta of Isaiah of Christian Origin?" 563–82 (580).

[22] Elsewhere in Isaiah, Syriac ܡܚܝܢܐ "lifegiver" is never (including ms 9a1) used as equivalent of Hebrew *go'el* "redeemer."

[23] For s-Sir 48:11 as another passage referring to Jesus as the one who gives life, see Van Peursen, "Que vive celui qui fait vivre: Le texte Syriaque du Siracide 48,10–12," 286–301 (300); Van Peursen, *Language and Interpretation in the Syriac Text of Ben Sira*, 119.

[24] Gelston, "Peshitta of Isaiah," 581.

"satisfactory" on word level only (so Gelston), or whether he made a translation that even if he did not know the meaning of some words was intended to make sense above word level. The fact that, in s-Isa 25:6–8, the several choices made do converge and make sense does not stand in favor of the former option. Moreover, the translator of s-Isa can probably be regarded as a scholar who, like Jerome, produced a translation using words that made sense within their context. In the Isaianic passage under discussion, the translator apparently wanted to introduce a Christian understanding of the source text. As a scholar, he did so by using particular devices or techniques. For example, as to the rendering "our lifegiver" in v. 6, ממחים "full of marrow" was interpreted as derived from חיה "to live" (ptc. *Piel* or *Hiphil*, with suffix "them"). This need not imply that the translator did not know "the" meaning of the Hebrew. Rather, in line with scholarship of the time, he applied an ancient device (*etymologia*) exploring an interpretive possibility that would suit and serve a particular exegesis of the passage. It reminds one of the way Jerome sometimes introduces, in his Latin version of Isaiah (→ 6–9.1.7), the term *Salvator* as the title of Christ by a specific interpretation of the underlying Hebrew.[25]

Other examples of interpretive renderings are:

s-Jer 7:4–5

> The temple of the Lord, the temple of the Lord, you are the temple of the Lord,
> if you improve your ways and your doings.

MT-Jer 7:4–5

> This is the temple of the Lord, the temple of the Lord, the temple of the Lord.
> For if you truly amend your ways and your doings,
> [...]

s-Jer does not refer to the temple as a building but to the concept of "temple" as the image of a group of people who would be willing to pursue social justice. As scholars have noted, the Dead Sea Scrolls reflect a similar idea (cf. "the sanctuary of men" in 4Q174), but s-Jer also evokes the picture found in 1 Cor 3:16 ("Do you know that you are God's temple and that God's spirit dwells in you?").[26] The latter view is in line with the way Aphrahat read our text (*Dem.* 1, 3).[27]

s-Hos 12:1 (English version: 11:12)

> Ephraim has encompassed me with deceit,
> and the house of Israel and Judah with treachery,
> until the people of God go down,
> a holy and faithful people

MT-Hos 12:1

> Ephraim has encompassed me with lies,
> and the house of Israel with deceit;
> but Judah still roams with God (עֹד רָד עִם־אֵל),
> and is faithful to Holy One(s) (עִם־קְדוֹשִׁים)

In contrast to MT (→ 9.2.2), s-Hos considers Judah and not only Ephraim to be wicked. On the other hand, in the second half of the verse, s-Hos speaks of "the people of God" in a positive way since they are designated "a holy and faithful people." Hebrew עֹד "still" is interpreted as עַד *'ad* "until" (cf. Targum), עִם "with" in both cases as עַם "people," while רָד "roams" is understood as being derived from יָרַד *yarad* "to go down." MT contrasts the faithfulness of Judah with Ephraim (cf. Targum), but the picture in s-Hos is different; it is about yet another group of people who, contrary to Ephraim and Judah, are "holy and faithful."

6–9.1.4.5 Background and Date

Most scholars agree that the books of the Peshitta, particularly the Pentateuch and Chronicles, are marked by Jewish traditions, but it is disputed whether the milieu of the Peshitta is to be seen as Jewish or Jewish-Christian. Among recent contributions to the debate, Weitzman holds the first view, arguing that the translation work was carried

---

[25] Van der Kooij, *Textzeugen*, 303.

[26] Greenberg, *Peshitta to Jeremiah*, 28.

[27] Cf. Murray, *Symbols*, 218–19. According to Weitzman, *Syriac Version*, 218, s-Jer "would imply that the physical Temple is obsolete."

out by (non-rabbinic) Jews who afterwards converted to Christianity.[28] Ter Haar Romeny, on the other hand, subscribes to the second view because, in his view, the work was carried out by Jews who had converted to Christianity,[29] that is to say, by Jews who though keeping certain practices that were based on the law of Moses, accepted the messianic status of Jesus.

Factors such as the facility with the Hebrew language and the familiarity with Jewish traditions, particularly those known from the Targumim,[30] do suggest a Jewish background. The (limited) use of LXX, however, seems to indicate that the team of translators were also Christians.[31] Since the latter feature applies to S-LP, these books may have stemmed from a Jewish-Christian milieu. In fact, s-Isa 25:6–8 lends strong support for this assumption, at least as far as the Syriac version of the book of Isaiah is concerned.[32] Although, as is likely,[33] the remaining books of S-LP were the work of other translators, it is reasonable to assume that LP as a whole was translated by a team of scholars who belonged to the same milieu.

There are some elements in S-LP that might reflect a Christian understanding but which, taken on their own, are not that strong. However, if read from a perspective based on s-Isa 25:6–8, a number of modifications in LP may well reflect a Christian interpretation. This is the case, for example, in the passages referred to above, s-Jer 7:4–5 and s-Hos 12:1. Both passages convey the idea of a new community referred to as a "temple" in Jer 7:4–5, or as "a holy and faithful people" being distinct from Ephraim and Judah in Hos 12:1. Both make sense if understood as referring to the Christian community or church. Interestingly, this reading of both passages is in line with Aphrahat (cf. *Dem.* 1, 3 and *Dem.* 16, 3, respectively). This raises the question whether these passages can be considered an early witness to the doctrine of the fourth-century Syriac Fathers (→ 21.9), Aphrahat and Ephrem, that "the chosen people of God has been replaced by the 'nation from the nations', the Church of the Gentiles."[34] There is some evidence in the Peshitta for this view because s-Gen 17:5 "I have made you father *for* a multitude of nations" (MT: "*of* a multitude of nations") makes perfect sense in this regard (cf. Aphrahat, *Dem.* 11, 1), but s-Isa, on the other hand, contains passages that instead suggest that the idea of a new community relates to a particular group from among the people of Israel. An interesting passage is found in s-Isa 5:7 where MT, "the men of Judah are his pleasant planting," is rendered as "the men *from* Judah are the new and beloved planting."[35] In this and other passages, the new – Christian – community is understood as being brought out from the Jewish people.[36]

As to the motif of the new and holy community as a "temple," the Syriac version of Isa 66:2b too is of interest. Instead of MT, "But this is the man to whom I will look, he that is humble and contrite in spirit," s-Isa reads, "Among whom would I look and dwell, except among the peaceful and the humble of spirit?" The whole clause, including the plus "I would dwell" (not in MT), evokes the idea of a community in the sense of a temple in which God may dwell.[37] This is more likely since the quoted rendering of v. 2 makes sense in light of the question in the preceding verse (v. 1), namely, "Where is the house that you will build for me?"

As to the date, most scholars agree that the books of the Peshitta, including LP, were produced, roughly speaking, in the late second century C.E.[38]

---

[28] Weitzman, *Syriac Version*, 258–62.
[29] Ter Haar Romeny, "Hypotheses," 29.
[30] Cf. Brock, "Jewish Traditions."
[31] Note also the fact that the Peshitta Old Testament comprises books such as Ben Sira and 1–4 Maccabees, which were not part of the biblical canon of the Jews.
[32] See also Greenberg, "Indications," 175–92.
[33] See Greenberg, *Peshitta on Jeremiah*, 84–87 (on duplicate passages in Jeremiah and Isaiah).

[34] Murray, *Symbols*, 41.
[35] Van der Kooij, *Textzeugen*, 279. See also Weitzman, *Syriac Version*, 230. He does not think of a Christian community, but of "an elect sub-community" within the Jewish people (p. 229).
[36] Cf. s-Isa 65:9.
[37] Cf. Aphrahat, *Dem.* 6, 17.
[38] Cf. van der Kooij, *Textzeugen*, 292–95; Weitzman, *Syriac Version*, 248–58; Greenberg, *Peshitta to Jeremiah*, 4–5. Gelston,

The likely place of origin is Edessa, in Oshroene.³⁹ It is of note that the second century was an era in which other translations of the Hebrew Bible, or parts of it, were made: first of all, the version of Aquila, at the beginning of the century, and later on, at the end of the century, that produced by Symmachus (→ 6–9.1.5; → 1.3.1.2). Secondly, it was also the period in which Targum Onqelos (Law) and Targum Jonathan (Prophets) (→ 1.3.3), at least the body of them, appeared on the scene. These translations in Greek and Aramaic were all produced by Jewish scholars, although they do not stem from the same Jewish milieu. The versions of Aquila and Symmachus are best understood as coming from rabbinic circles, but there is reason to believe that this was not the case with the Aramaic version of Targum Onqelos and Targum Jonathan.⁴⁰

S-LP represents a sensible version into Syriac, reflecting on occasion an understanding that these books developed in Jewish-Christian circles. The books involved are part of a large translation project that presumably was meant to set boundaries, and to mark the identity of a Jewish-Christian milieu in Edessa and elsewhere. It may well be that this translation work was triggered by the other Jewish translations produced at that time.

6–9.1.4.6 Text-Critical Value

Scholars agree that the books of S-LP go back in the main to proto-MT (→ 6.2.2, → 7.2.2, → 8.2.2, → 9.2.2), the Hebrew text current at the time (second century C.E.). This does not include cases where the *Vorlage* of the Peshitta might have differed from proto-MT, i.e., the consonantal text in Hebrew, but this seems to apply to a few cases only.⁴¹ In general, S-LP is most important as a witness of proto-MT, a witness that on the other hand has "little distinctive contribution to offer to the reconstruction of a putative original Hebrew text," as stated by Gelston regarding MinP.⁴²

General

Alexander, P.S., "What Happened to the Jewish Priesthood after 70?" in *A Wandering Galilean: Essays in Honour of Seán Freyne* (eds. Z. Rodgers, M. Daly-Denton, and A. Fitzpatrick McKinley; JSJSup 132; Leiden: Brill, 2009), 5–33.

Dirksen, P.B., "The Old Testament Peshitta," in Mulder, *Mikra*, 255–97.

Flesher–Chilton, *The Targums*.

ter Haar Romeny, R.B., "Hypotheses on the Development of Judaism and Christianity in Syria in the Period after 70 C.E.," in *Matthew and the Didache: Two Documents from the Same Jewish-Christian Milieu?* (ed. H. van de Sandt; Assen/Minneapolis: Van Gorcum/Fortress Press, 2005), 13–34.

Murray, R., *Symbols of Church and Kingdom: A Study in Early Syriac Tradition* (Cambridge: Cambridge University Press, 1975).

van Peursen, W.T., "Que vive celui qui fait vivre: Le texte Syriaque du Siracide 48,10–12," in *L' enfance de la Bible hébraïque: Histoire du texte de l' Ancient Testament* (eds. A. Schenker and P. Hugo; MdB 52; Geneva: Labor et Fides, 2005), 286–301.

van Peursen, W.T., *Language and Interpretation in the Syriac Text of Ben Sira: A Comparative Linguistic and Literary Study* (Monographs of the Leiden Peshitta Institute 16; Leiden: Brill, 2007).

Weitzman, M.P., *The Syriac Version of the Old Testament: An Introduction* (University of Cambridge Oriental Publications 56; Cambridge: Cambridge University Press, 1999).

Isaiah

Brock, S.P., "Text History and Text Division in Peshitta Isaiah," in *The Peshitta: Its Early Text and History: Papers Read at the Peshitta Symposium Held at Leiden 30–31 August 1985* (eds. P.B. Dirksen and M.J. Mulder; Monographs of the Peshitta Institute Leiden 4; Leiden: Brill, 1988), 49–80.

Gelston, A., "Was the Peshitta of Isaiah of Christian Origin?" in *Writing and Reading the Scroll of Isaiah: Studies of an Interpretive Tradition* (eds. C.C. Broyles

---

on the other hand, believes that s-MinP was produced "in the middle or late first century" (*Twelve Prophets*, 195).

³⁹ Cf. van der Kooij, *Textzeugen*, 292; Weitzman, *Syriac Version*, 258; Ter Haar Romeny, "Hypotheses," 13–34 (28–32). For the alternative view that the Peshitta was produced in Adiabene, see, e.g., Murray, *Symbols*, 8–10.

⁴⁰ On this issue, see in particular Alexander, "What happened to the Jewish Priesthood after 70?" 5–33 (17).

⁴¹ Cf. Greenberg, *Peshitta to Jeremiah*, 7; Gelston, *Twelve Prophets*, 129–30.

⁴² Gelston, *Twelve Prophets*, 130.

and C.A. Evans; VTSup 70.2; Leiden: Brill, 1997), 563–82.

Greenberg, G., "Indications of the Faith of the Translator in the Peshitta to the 'Servant Songs' of Deutero-Isaiah," *Aramaic Studies* 2 (2004): 175–92.

ter Haar Romeny, R.B., "The Peshitta of Isaiah: Evidence from the Syriac Fathers," in *Text, Translation and Tradition: Studies on the Peshitta and its Use in the Syriac Tradition Presented to Konrad D. Jenner* (eds. W.T. van Peursen and R.B. ter Haar Romeny; Monographs of the Peshitta Institute Leiden 14; Leiden: Brill, 2006), 149–64.

van der Kooij, A., *Die alten Textzeugen des Jesajabuches: Ein Beitrag zur Textgeschichte des Alten Testaments* (OBO 35; Göttingen: Vandenhoeck & Ruprecht, 1981), 258–98.

van der Kooij, A., "Ms 9a1 of the Peshitta of Isaiah: Some Comments," in *Text, Translation and Tradition: Studies on the Peshitta and its Use in the Syriac Tradition Presented to Konrad D. Jenner* (eds. W.T. van Peursen and R.B. ter Haar Romeny; Monographs of the Peshitta Institute Leiden 14; Leiden: Brill, 2006), 71–76.

Jeremiah

Greenberg, G., *Translation Technique in the Peshitta to Jeremiah* (Monographs of the Peshitta Institute Leiden 13; Leiden: Brill, 2002).

Walter, D.M., "Manuscript Relationships for the Peshitta Text of Jeremiah," in *Text, Translation and Tradition: Studies on the Peshitta and its Use in the Syriac Tradition Presented to Konrad D. Jenner* (eds. W.T. van Peursen and R.B. ter Haar Romeny; Monographs of the Peshitta Institute Leiden 14; Leiden: Brill, 2006), 231–53.

Ezekiel

Mulder, M.J., "Some Remarks on the Peshitta Translation of the Book of Ezekiel," in *The Peshitta: Its Early Text and History: Papers Read at the Peshitta Symposium held at Leiden 30–31 August 1985* (eds. P.B. Dirksen and M.J. Mulder; Monographs of the Peshitta Institute Leiden 4; Leiden: Brill, 1988), 169–82.

Mushayabasa, G., "Redefining the Consistency of Equivalences in the Peshitta to Ezekiel: Towards a Frame Semantics Approach," *JNSL* 38 (2012): 79–91.

van Rooy, H.F., "Agreement between LXX and Peshitta versus MT in Ezekiel: Some Important Examples," in *Translating a Translation: The LXX and its Modern Translations in the Context of Early Judaism* (eds. H. Ausloos et al.; BETL 213; Leuven: Peeters, 2008), 213–27.

Twelve Prophets

Gelston, A., *The Peshitta of the Twelve Prophets* (Oxford: Clarendon Press, 1987).

Gelston, A., "The Twelve Prophets: Peshitta and Targum," in *Targum Studies*, Vol. 2: *Targum and Peshitta* (ed. P.V.M. Flesher; University of South Florida Studies in the History of Judaism 8; Atlanta: Scholars Press, 1998), 119–39.

Arie van der Kooij

6–9.1.5 Hexaplaric Greek Translations

6–9.1.5.1 Background

This article addresses the Hexaplaric fragments of the Latter Prophets: Isaiah, Jeremiah, Ezekiel, and the book of the Twelve. Originally, these books were translated by four different translators (→ 6.3, → 7.3, → 8.3, → 9.3), who employed different translation techniques. The pre-Hexaplaric Greek versions and Origen's Hexapla itself operated to bring the (O)ld (G)reek translations into closer quantitative alignment with their Hebrew source.

6–9.1.5.2 Sources, Editions, and Auxiliary Tools

For Isaiah, the sources for the Hexaplaric fragments are the marginal notes found in LXX^Q (= Codex Marchalianus), Syro-Hexapla (Syh), LXX^86, and LXX^710. Also, Eusebius of Caesarea's commentary on Isaiah and his *Demonstratio evangelica* contain Hexaplaric readings. The commentaries of Basil the Great, John Chrysostom, Theodoret of Cyrus, Procopius of Gaza, and Jerome preserve Hexaplaric readings. Finally, the *Onomasticon* of Eusebius and Jerome and various church fathers have Hexaplaric readings for Isaiah.[1]

For the Twelve Prophets, the Hexaplaric fragments are found in the marginal notes of LXX^Q, Syh, LXX^86, and and the Patmos manuscript of Basil of Neopatrae (= Bas.N.). The commentaries of Cyril of Alexandria, Theodore of Mopsuestia, Theodoret of Cyrus, Theophylact of Acris, and Jerome also contain Hexaplaric readings. There are a few read-

---

[1] Ziegler, *Isaias*, 108–11. For the use of Hexaplaric quotations in Patristic literature, see also → 21.7, → 21.8.

ings that come from other manuscripts and various Greek and Latin authors.[2]

For Ezekiel, the Hexaplaric fragments come from the marginal notes of LXX^Q, Syh, LXX^86, the two catena manuscripts, LXX^87,91, and marginal notes of LXX^36,403,449,764. The commentaries of Jerome, Theodoret of Cyrus, and Polychronius of Apamea also yield readings of the Hexapla. Furthermore, Ziegler lists fourteen homilies of Origen and his *Sel. Ezech.* as witnesses to the Hexaplaric fragments. Lastly, the *Onomasticon* of Eusebius of Caesarea is registered as a witness to the Hexaplaric fragments of Ezekiel.[3]

For Jeremiah, the sources for the Hexaplaric fragments are the marginal notes in LXX^Q, LXX^86, Syh, and the two catena manuscripts, LXX^87,91. There are Hexaplaric readings in the commentaries of Jerome, Theodoret of Cyrus, John Chrysostom, and Olympiodorus. Hexaplaric fragments are also found in the homilies on Jeremiah and the catena fragments of Origen. Finally, Hexaplaric readings are in the *Onomasticon* of Eusebius and various works of some church fathers.[4]

The first critical edition of the Hexaplaric fragments of the latter prophets is included in the work of Field, published in 1875.[5] Since that time, Ziegler has prepared four critical editions for the Göttingen *Septuaginta*,[6] which listed all of the known Hexaplaric fragments in their respective second apparatuses. It must be noted that the second apparatus of the Göttingen *Septuaginta* editions does not contain a critical text for the Hexaplaric fragments. Therefore, a critical edition for each book is a clear *desideratum*, which as of 2015 the Hexapla Institute is attempting to fulfill.

For editions and auxiliary tools related to the Hexaplaric fragments of the Latter Prophets, see the bibliography.

6–9.1.5.3 Translation Character and Technique
6–9.1.5.3.1 Theodotion

Regarding the translation technique of Theodotion in Job, Gentry says, "The character of the materials belonging to θ′ reveals a literal and straightforward translation of a parent text for the most part identical with MT (consonantal text and vocalization). The translation follows the elements and segments of the language of the parent text and also the sequence in which these elements are presented."[7] This summary proved true for the fragments of Theodotion in the Latter Prophets. In Isaiah, there are two prominent types of Theodotion fragments: 1) the readings preserved under the asterisk (e.g., Isa 1:4; 7:5) where there is no underlying LXX text; and 2) fragments that represent revision of LXX-Isa (→ 6.3) toward the Hebrew text. A short example of the latter is from 7:4: הִשָּׁמֵר וְהַשְׁקֵט "Be on guard and be quiet"/LXX-Isa Φύλαξαι τοῦ ἡσυχάσαι "Take care to be quiet" (*NETS)/Th πρόσεχε καὶ ἡσύχασον "Take heed and keep quiet." Theodotion revises LXX-Isa towards the syntax of the Hebrew by translating the *waw* with καί (both meaning "and") and the two Hebrew imperatives with corresponding Greek imperatives.

In the book of the Twelve, there are interesting examples of Theodotion's revision of LXX (→ 9.3). Zech 12:10 will serve as one such example: וְהִבִּיטוּ אֵלַי אֵת אֲשֶׁר־דָּקָרוּ "And they will look to me whom they pierced"/LXX-Zech καὶ ἐπιβλέψονται πρός με ἀνθ᾿ ὧν κατωρχήσαντο "And they shall look to me because they have danced triumphantly" *NETS/Th καὶ ἐπιβλέψονται πρός με ὃν ἐξεκέντησαν "And they will look to me whom they pierced." LXX-Zech κατορχεῖσθαι "to dance triumphantly" is a *hapax legomenon* in the LXX corpus and probably resulted from reading a form of the verb רקד "to leap about, dance" *Piel*, which metathesized ד and ר due to ר/ד confusion or exegesis. This Theodotion fragment is particularly significant since the Gospel of John

---

[2] Ziegler, *Duodecim Prophetae*, 103–07. For the use of Hexaplaric quotations in Patristic literature, see also → 21.7, → 21.8.

[3] Ziegler, *Ezechiel*, 62–65. For the use of Hexaplaric quotations in Patristic literature, see also → 21.7, → 21.8.

[4] Ziegler, *Jeremias, Baruch, Threni, Epistula Jeremiae*, 101–05. For the use of Hexaplaric quotations in Patristic literature, see also → 21.7, → 21.8.

[5] Field, **Hexapla*.

[6] Ziegler, *Isaias*; *Duodecim Prophetae*; Ziegler, *Ezechiel*; and Ziegler, *Jeremias, Baruch, Threni, Epistula Jeremiae*.

[7] Gentry, *Asterisked Materials*, 494.

cites a version of this text rather than LXX (John 19:37; ὄψονται εἰς ὃν ἐξεκέντησαν "they will look on the one whom they have pierced" *NRSV).

In Ezekiel, the work of Theodotion is also observed from the various fragments preserved under the asterisk in LXX^Qtxt among others. At Ezek 1:17, the texts are as follows: עַל־אַרְבַּעַת רִבְעֵיהֶן בְּלֶכְתָּם "on their four sides while they went"/LXX-Ezek ἐπὶ τὰ τέσσαρα μέρη αὐτῶν "upon their four parts" (*NETS). After αὐτῶν, LXX^Qtxt has θ′ ※ ἐν τῷ πορεύεσθαι αὐτούς "while they went," which is equivalent to the Hebrew בְּלֶכְתָּם. Theodotion brought LXX into greater quantitative alignment with the Hebrew text with the addition of the infinitive construction.

In Jeremiah, there are many long fragments attributed to Theodotion, which reflect the longer and final form of the text of MT (→ 7.2.2). In these instances, Theodotion probably translated the Hebrew text *de novo*. At Jer 7:1–2, there is a good example:

הַדָּבָר אֲשֶׁר הָיָה אֶל־יִרְמְיָהוּ מֵאֵת יְהוָה לֵאמֹר עֲמֹד בְּשַׁעַר בֵּית יְהוָה וְקָרָאתָ שָּׁם אֶת־הַדָּבָר הַזֶּה וְאָמַרְתָּ שִׁמְעוּ דְבַר־יְהוָה כָּל־יְהוּדָה הַבָּאִים בַּשְּׁעָרִים הָאֵלֶּה לְהִשְׁתַּחֲוֺת לַיהוָה

The word which came to Jeremiah from the Lord saying, "Stand in the gate of the house of the Lord and read aloud there this word and say, 'Hear the word of the Lord, all Judah, who are coming to these gates, to worship the Lord'." (MT-Jer)

Ἀκούσατε λόγον κυρίου, πᾶσα ἡ Ἰουδαία, "Hear the word of the Lord, all Judea" *NETS

Th ὁ λόγος ὁ γενόμενος πρὸς Ιερεμιαν παρὰ κυρίου λέγων· στῆθι ἐν πύλῃ οἴκου κυρίου καὶ ἀνάγνωθι ἐκεῖ τὸν λόγον τοῦτον καὶ ἐρεῖς· ἀκούσατε λόγον κυρίου, πᾶσα ἡ Ἰουδαία οἱ εἰσπορευόμενοι διὰ τῶν πυλῶν τούτων προσκυνεῖν τῷ κυρίῳ

The word which came to Jeremiah from the Lord saying, "Stand in the gate of the house of the Lord and read aloud there this word and you will say, 'Hear the word of the Lord, all Judea, who are entering through these gates, to worship the Lord'." (Th-Jer)

Theodotion provides a formal rendering of the Hebrew of Jer 7:1–2, while avoiding complete woodenness. For example, he did not render the bound infinitive לְהִשְׁתַּחֲוֺת "to worship" with τοῦ προσκυνεῖν "to worship" but only with the simple infinitive, a technique he employed once in Job (→ 11.3.5).[8] This rendering is consistent with the demands of the target language, even though in Job Theodotion normally rendered the ל with τοῦ. LXX-Jer (→ 7.3) only contains a short part of what later became v. 2. Such large differences between LXX and proto-MT warranted a full revision of LXX-Jer according to the final form of the Hebrew text.

6–9.1.5.3.2 Aquila

Aquila employed a formal equivalence translation technique, which attempted to render each Hebrew element with a Greek equivalent segment by segment. On the word level, Aquila's version is very formal and demonstrates the concordance principle of translation, even employing equivalents to maintain etymological connections between Hebrew and Greek. However, when Aquila's syntax and Greek vocabulary are considered, his version furnishes more appropriate and even ingenious renderings of the Hebrew source.[9] At Isa 2:1, Aquila revises the functional or dynamic equivalent translation of LXX-Isa: הַדָּבָר אֲשֶׁר חָזָה יְשַׁעְיָהוּ "The word which Isaiah saw"/LXX-Isa Ὁ λόγος ὁ γενόμενος παρὰ κυρίου πρὸς Ἡσαΐαν "The word that came from the Lord to Esaias" *NETS/Aq τὸ ῥῆμα ὃ ὡραματίσθη ησαίας "The word which Isaiah saw." Not only does Aquila render the source quantitatively, but also he uses his stock equivalents. Aquila regularly employs ὁραματίζεσθαι for חָזָה[10] (both meaning "to see") and ῥῆμα for דָּבָר[11] (both meaning "word").[12]

In the book of the Twelve at Hos 11:1, there is an interesting note in LXX[86] that preserves the verse in five divided columns with the title: "from the Hexapla." The first column is a transliteration of the Hebrew in Greek letters. The second and third columns are the versions of Aquila and Symmachus respectively, while the fourth and fifth columns are the versions of LXX and Theodotion respectively.

---

[8] For analysis of the anarthrous infinitive in Th-Job 2:1d, cf. Gentry, *Asterisked Materials*, 267.
[9] Hyvärinen, *Die Übersetzung von Aquila*, 111–12.
[10] Reider, *Index*, 174.
[11] Reider, *Index*, 174.
[12] Reider, *Index*, 210.

The Aquila column is our focus here. The texts are as follows: כִּי נַעַר יִשְׂרָאֵל וָאֹהֲבֵהוּ וּמִמִּצְרַיִם קָרָאתִי לִבְנִי "Because Israel was a child, I loved him, and from Egypt I called my son"/LXX-Hos Διότι νήπιος Ισραηλ, καὶ ἐγὼ ἠγάπησα αὐτὸν καὶ ἐξ Αἰγύπτου μετεκάλεσα τὰ τέκνα αὐτοῦ "For Israel was an infant, and I loved him, and out of Egypt I recalled his children"/Aq ὅτι παῖς Ισραηλ, καὶ ἠγάπησα αὐτὸν καὶ ἀπὸ Αἰγύπτου ἐκάλεσα τὸν υἱόν μου "Because Israel was a child, and I loved him and from Egypt I called my son." The Aquila fragment represents a revision of LXX-Hos towards the Hebrew text (→ 9.2.2) with respect to the consonants and vocalization. The most significant difference occurs between LXX-Hos τὰ τέκνα αὐτοῦ "his children" and Aq τὸν υἱόν μου "my son." Since the translator of the book of the Twelve normally renders בֵּן "son" with τέκνον "child," perhaps he read בניו "his children," a text resulting from dittography, since in this Hebrew script the *waw* and *yod* were written similarly. Aquila read a different text which had בני "my son" and this text was equivalent to what later became MT.[13]

In Ezek 17:17, Aquila revises LXX towards proto-MT: בִּשְׁפֹּךְ סֹלְלָה "when ramps are cast up" *NRSV*/LXX-Ezek ἐν χαρακοβολίᾳ "in casting up a palisade" *NETS*/Aq ἐν τῷ ἐκχῶσαι πρόσχωμα "in raising up a mound." Aquila is the only reviser/translator of LXX to use ἐκχώννυμι "to raise a mound." He also renders the Hebrew text isomorphically and therefore brings LXX-Ezek into greater alignment with the Hebrew.

Jer 17:21 constitutes another example where Aquila revises LXX towards proto-MT: וַהֲבֵאתֶם בְּשַׁעֲרֵי יְרוּשָׁלִָם "or bring it in by the gates of Jerusalem" *NRSV*/LXX-Jer καὶ μὴ ἐκπορεύεσθε ταῖς πύλαις Ιερουσαλημ "and to not go in by the gates of Ierousalem" *NETS*/Aq καὶ εἰσφέρετε διὰ τῶν πυλῶν Ιερουσαλημ "and bring (it) through the gates of Jerusalem." LXX-Jer read the *Qal* stem from בוא "to come," while Aquila read the *Hiphil* "to bring." LXX-Jer appears to be slightly interpretive here since there is no particle of negation in the Hebrew, but it can be inferred from the previous line and therefore LXX-Jer makes explicit what is implicit. LXX-Jer also prohibits walking through the city gates on the Sabbath. MT and Aquila prohibit the bringing of a "burden" (מַשָּׂא) through the gates on the Sabbath.

6–9.1.5.3.3 Symmachus

Symmachus produced a revision of LXX (→ 6.3, → 7.3, → 8.3, → 9.3) that was both faithful to the sense of the Hebrew and readable in Greek.[14] These characteristics can be observed in the Latter Prophets.

LXX-Isa employed a functional equivalence translation of the Hebrew and therefore by comparison Symmachus appears to be more isomorphic. Isa 6:5 is a good example:

MT אוֹי־לִי כִי־נִדְמֵיתִי כִּי אִישׁ טְמֵא־שְׂפָתַיִם אָנֹכִי וּבְתוֹךְ עַם־טְמֵא שְׂפָתַיִם אָנֹכִי יוֹשֵׁב

Woe is me! I am lost, for I am a man of unclean lips, and I live among a people of unclean lips. *NRSV*

LXX Ὦ τάλας ἐγώ, ὅτι κατανένυγμαι, ὅτι ἄνθρωπος ὢν καὶ ἀκάθαρτα χείλη ἔχων ἐν μέσῳ λαοῦ ἀκάθαρτα χείλη ἔχοντος ἐγὼ οἰκῶ

O wretched that I am! I am stunned; for being a man and having unclean lips, I live among a people having unclean lips *NETS*

Sym οἴμοι, ὅτι ἐσιώπησα, ἀνὴρ γὰρ ἀκάθαρτος χείλεσιν ἐγὼ καὶ ἐν μέσῳ λαοῦ ἀκαθάρτου χείλεσιν ἐγὼ οἰκῶ.

Woe to me! because I am silent, for an unclean man with lips am I, and in the midst of an unclean people with lips I live.

The first word demonstrates that Symmachus does employ a formal equivalence translation technique. The component οι is a transliteration of Hebrew אוֹי "woe," while μοι is the translation of לִי (both meaning "me"). As a result this rendering is formally closer to the Hebrew (→ 6.2.2) than LXX-Isa (→ 6.3). Symmachus also prefers semantic

---

[13] The connection between Aquila's version of Hos 11:1 and the Gospel of Matthew's citation (Matt 2:15; ἐξ Αἰγύπτου ἐκάλεσα τὸν υἱόν μου "out of Egypt I have called my son" NRSV) is intriguing. Perhaps Matthew used a predecessor to Aquila, which Aquila later adopted as his own version apart from changing ἐξ "out of" to ἀπό "from."

[14] → 1.3.1.2.5; cf. Salvesen, *Symmachus*, 198.

disambiguation where LXX-Isa chooses repetition. Symmachus translates the first כִּי with ὅτι (both meaning "because"), while he translates the second instance with γάρ "for." The rendering of Symmachus adheres to the word order of the Hebrew and does not introduce words that are not in the Hebrew, while LXX-Isa facilitates the reading by adding participles that specify the meaning of the bound structures (e.g., עַם־טְמֵא שְׂפָתַיִם "people of unclean lips"/λαοῦ ἀκάθαρτα χείλη ἔχοντος "people having unclean lips").

In the book of the Twelve at Nah 1:12, Symmachus revises LXX according to a different reading of homographs or homonyms: וְעִנִּתִךְ לֹא אֲעַנֵּךְ עוֹד "Though I have afflicted you, I will afflict you no more" *NRSV*/LXX-Nah καὶ ἡ ἀκοή σου οὐκ ἐνακουσθήσεται ἔτι "and your fame shall no longer be heard" *NETS*/Sym ἐταπείνωσα γάρ σε οὐκέτι τεπεινώσω σε "for I humbled you, no longer will I humble you." Symmachus reads the verbs in this line as from II ענה Piel "to humiliate," while LXX-Nah and Aquila read the verbs as from I ענה Qal "to respond, obey." In this case, Symmachus renders the vocalization of MT. Symmachus also renders *waw* "and" with γάρ "for" and he combines לֹא "not" and עוֹד "still" into οὐκέτι "no longer" nicely, while maintaining the basic Hebrew word order.

In Ezek 2:6, Symmachus revises LXX according to the Hebrew: כִּי סָרָבִים וְסַלּוֹנִים אוֹתָךְ "though briers and thorns surround you" *NRSV*/LXX-Ezek διότι παροιστρήσουσιν καὶ ἐπισυστήσονται ἐπὶ σέ "because they will sting and band together against you" *NETS*/Sym ἰταμοὶ γάρ καὶ ἀπόρρητοί εἰσι πρός σε "for they are reckless and foul to you." Symmachus renders כִּי with γάρ (both meaning "for") and adds εἰσί "they are," which is not in the Hebrew but it makes explicit what is already implicit. Symmachus renders the two Hebrew words with adjectives, while LXX-Ezek translated them as verbs. The first Hebrew word, סָרָבִים, is an adjective meaning "obstinate" and therefore Symmachus' rendering of it with ἰταμοί "headlong, reckless" is slightly interpretive. The second term, סַלּוֹנִים, is a noun meaning "thorn" or "thorny plant" and is only used twice in the Hebrew Bible (cf. Ezek 28:24). Symmachus renders this term interpretively with ἀπόρρητοι "abominable, foul." Here, Symmachus has achieved an understandable rendering of a difficult Hebrew text.

In Jer 6:10, Symmachus provides a more interpretive rendering of the Hebrew than LXX: הִנֵּה עֲרֵלָה אָזְנָם "behold, their uncircumcised ear"/LXX-Jer ἰδοὺ ἀπερίτμητα τὰ ὦτα αὐτῶν "behold, their uncircumcised ears"/Sym ἰδοὺ ἀκάθαρτον τὸ οὖς αὐτῶν "behold their unclean ear." By rendering אֹזֶן "ear" as a singular, Symmachus is slightly more literal than LXX-Jer (→ 7.3). However, his rendering of עֲרֵלָה "uncircumcised" with ἀκάθαρτον "unclean" is interpretive, while LXX-Jer has a more literal rendering ἀπερίτμητα "uncircumcised."

6–9.1.5.4 Text-Critical Value for the Hebrew Text

Although the Hexaplaric Greek versions confirm the MT (→ 6.2.2, → 7.2.2, → 8.2.2, → 9.2.2) tradition (both consonants and vowels) in the majority of cases, they still offer significant variants to this tradition. One such instance of variant reading traditions in the Latter Prophets comes in Isa 25:8 where there is evidence from Theodotion, Aquila, and Symmachus. All three versions deserve comment. Here are the relevant texts followed by provisional translations:

Hebrew	בִּלַּע הַמָּוֶת לָנֶצַח
	He swallowed up death forever
LXX	κατέπιεν ὁ θάνατος ἰσχύσας
	Death, strengthened, swallowed [them, i.e., nations] up
Theodotion	κατεπόθη ὁ θάνατος εἰς νῖκος
	Death is swallowed up in victory
Aquila	καταποντίσει τὸν θάνατον εἰς νῖκος
	He will swallow up death in victory
Symmachus	καταποθῆναι ποιήσει τὸν θάνατον εἰς τέλος
	He will make death to be swallowed up forever

These diverse Greek versions are derived from the same Hebrew consonantal text. Therefore, this text is not evidence of different Greek versions coming from different Hebrew texts. These versions also carefully rendered the word order of their source. The differences between the versions are attributed to two factors that need to be described in detail: 1) the vocalization of בלע; and 2) the lexeme נצח. We will treat these two issues in order. First, the vocalization of בלע in MT (בִּלַּע) represents a *Piel* perfect 3rd per. masc. sg. of בלע "to swallow." Second, LXX and Aquila also read the verb as *Piel*, since they have active verbs. These versions still differ from one another since Aquila read הַמָּוֶת "the death" as the direct object of the verb (τὸν θάνατον "the death"), while LXX read it as the subject of the verb (ὁ θάνατος "the death"). Third, Theodotion has κατεπόθη, an aorist middle/passive 3rd per. sg. of καταπίνω "to swallow." This form suggests that Theodotion read the Hebrew text as a *Pual* perfect 3rd per. masc. sg. בֻּלַּע "is swallowed." Since the verb was read as a passive, הַמָּוֶת "the death" was read necessarily as the subject of the verb (ὁ θάνατος "the death"). Symmachus may have also read the verb as a *Pual* perfect 3rd per. masc. sg. בֻּלַּע "is swallowed," but his technique (ποιέω "to do" + infinitive) also conveyed the factitive meaning of the *Pual*, while the passive infinitive rendered the passive sense of the *Pual*. By employing this technique, Symmachus preserved God as the subject of the verb and also τὸν θάνατον "the death" as the accusative subject of the infinitive.

The Hebrew consonantal text is the base text for the various versions. Slightly different vocalizations of the verb (בִּלַּע/בֻּלַּע) "swallows/is swallowed" account for different renderings of the Hebrew text.

The second variation between the Greek versions regards the lexeme לָנֶצַח. First, MT has לָנֶצַח, which means "forever" in biblical Hebrew.[15] Second, Symmachus translates נֶצַח with τέλος "end" four times and one time with νῖκος "victory" in the Psalter.[16] Third, Theodotion and Aquila have εἰς νῖκος "in victory" for לָנֶצַח. At Job 36:7c and other places, Theodotion used the same equivalent. Evidently, Theodotion and Aquila supplied a later Hebrew or Aramaic sense to the consonants נצח. Palestinian Aramaic has the root נצח, which means "to be victorious, defeat."[17] Therefore, these Greek versions are explained by recourse to a later Hebrew or Aramaic meaning of the word they read in the Hebrew consonantal text.[18]

This example stands as a reminder that Greek texts rendering the same Hebrew consonantal text can vary from each other due to different reading traditions. It highlights two factors: 1) different vocalizations; and 2) dialect interference from Aramaic or later Hebrew meanings applied to the same consonants. Therefore, the Greek versions attest variation at the vocalization level and not that of the consonantal text.

Busto Saiz, J.R., *La traducción de Símaco en el Libro de los Salmos* (Textos y Estudios "Cardenal Cisneros" 22; Madrid: Consejo Superior de Investigaciones Científicas, 1978).

Field, **Hexapla*.

Gentry, P.J., *The Asterisked Materials in the Greek Job* (SBLSCS 38; Atlanta: Scholars Press, 1995).

Hyvärinen, K., *Die Übersetzung von Aquila* (ConBOT 10; Uppsala: G.W.K. Gleerup, 1977).

Reider, J. and N. Turner, *An Index to Aquila: Greek-Hebrew, Hebrew-Greek, Latin-Hebrew: With the Syriac and Armenian Evidence* (VTSup 12; Leiden: Brill, 1966).

Salvesen, A., *Symmachus in the Pentateuch* (JSS Monograph 15; Manchester: Victoria University of Manchester, 1991).

Ziegler, J., *Textkritische Notizen zu den jüngeren griechischen Übersetzungen des Buches Isaias* (Nachrichten der Gesellschaft der Wissenschaften zu Göttingen, Philologisch-Historische Klasse 5.1.4; Göttingen: Vandenhoeck & Ruprecht, 1939).

Ziegler, J. (ed.), *Isaias* (Septuaginta Vetus Testamentum

---

[15] S.v. נָצַח in *HALOT*.

[16] For instances of τέλος "end," see Ps 12:2; 43:24; 67:17; 88:47. For the one instance of νῖκος "victory," see Ps 73:3. See Busto Saiz, *La traducción de Símaco*, 551, 591.

[17] M. Sokoloff, *A Dictionary of Jewish Palestinian Aramaic of the Byzantine Period* (*CAL; Bar Ilan: Bar Ilan University Press, 2002), 359.

[18] The relationship between the Theodotion version and Paul's form of the Old Testament in 1 Cor 15:54 is an unsettled matter. If one dates historical Theodotion to around the first century C.E. (→ 1.3.1.2.4), it is then probable that Paul actually used the version of Theodotion.

Graecum 14; Göttingen: Vandenhoeck & Ruprecht, 1939; 2nd ed. 1967; 3rd ed. 1983).

Ziegler, J., *Beiträge zum griechischen Dodekapropheton* (*NAWG*, Philologisch-Historische Klasse 1.10; Göttingen: Vandenhoeck & Ruprecht, 1943).

Ziegler, J. (ed.), *Duodecim Prophetae* (Septuaginta Vetus Testamentum Graecum 13; Göttingen: Vandenhoeck & Ruprecht, 1943; 2nd ed. 1967; 3rd ed. 1984).

Ziegler, J. (ed.), *Ezechiel* (Septuaginta Vetus Testamentum Graecum 16.1; Göttingen: Vandenhoeck & Ruprecht, 1952; 2nd ed. 1977).

Ziegler, J. (ed.), *Ieremias, Baruch, Threni, Epistula Ieremiae* (Septuaginta Vetus Testamentum Graecum 15; Göttingen: Vandenhoeck & Ruprecht, 1957; 2nd ed. 1976).

John D. Meade

6–9.1.6 Post-Hexaplaric Greek Translations

6–9.1.6.1 Background

The only post-Hexaplaric recension known to us is that of Lucian (→ 1.3.1.2). Joseph Ziegler, the editor of all the editions of the Latter Prophets in the Göttingen LXX, stood on the shoulders of Procksch, who established which manuscripts preserve the Lucianic recension in the Latter Prophets.[1] Ziegler, however, improved Procksch's text groupings (e.g., the elimination of manuscript LXX⁹³ as a witness to the Lucianic recension in the Minor Prophets).[2]

6–9.1.6.2 Original Form, Editions, Auxiliary Tools

There are critical editions in the Göttingen LXX for every book of the Latter Prophets.[3] All of these volumes are useful for ascertaining Lucianic variants. In addition to the critical editions, an analysis by Wevers and Fraenkel[4] and a study by Munnich[5] are helpful resources for studying the LXX^L text of LXX-Ezek (→ 8.3) and LXX-Isa (→ 8.3) respectively. Procksch's work shows that some of the same manuscripts preserve the Lucianic recension in all books of the Latter Prophets: LXX²² (*abest* LXX-Ezek) 36 48 51. There is little continuity with the Former Prophets, as manuscript LXX⁹³ is a member of the subgroup LXX^*lIII* in LXX-Isa. The corrector of Codex Sinaiticus (LXX^Sᶜ) preserves Lucianic variants in the Book of the Twelve and LXX-Isa. Marginal notes in the Syro-Hexapla (Syh^mg) preserve variants as do citations from the Antiochian Fathers (→ 21.7), most notably Chrysostom and Theodoret.

6–9.1.6.3 Translation Character and Technique

Ziegler notes that, in LXX-Ezek (→ 8.3), Lucian was concerned with clarifying the sense.[6] This concern is evident in all books of the Latter Prophets.[7] There are additions of various kinds that create a full text (e.g., Hos 4:19 πνεύματος "wind" LXX/πνεύματος αὐτοῦ "its wind" LXX^L; Isa 50:1 ὑμᾶς "you (pl.)" LXX/ὑμᾶς αὐτῷ "you (pl.) to him" LXX^*lI-331*). Additions that create apposition are rare in all books except LXX-Jer (Jer 44:1 Ιωσία "Iosias" LXX/Ιωσία τοῦ βασιλέως "Iosias the king" LXX^L). Nouns are commonly substituted for pronouns, though additions of proper nouns are found as modifiers (Ezek 12:23 οἶκος "house" LXX/οἶκος Ισραηλ "house of Israel" LXX^L). Doublets – a stellar characteristic of the Lucianic recension – are common (Jer 5:24 κατὰ καιρόν "according to the season" LXX/εν καιρῷ αὐτοῦ κατὰ καιρόν "in its season according to the season" LXX^L; Mic 1:14 οἴκους ματαίους "worthless houses" LXX/οἴκους ματαίους οἶκοι ματαίων "worthless houses worthless houses" LXX^L).

---

[1] Procksch, *Studien zur Geschichte der Septuaginta*. Also see B.M. Metzger, "The Lucianic Recension of the Greek Bible," in *Studies in the Septuagint: Origins, Recensions, and Interpretations* (ed. S. Jellicoe; New York: Ktav, 1974), 270–91 (279).

[2] Ziegler, *Duodecim prophetae*.

[3] J. Ziegler (ed.), *Isaias* (2nd ed.; Septuaginta Vetus Testamentum Graecum 14; Göttingen: Vandenhoeck & Ruprecht, 1967); J. Ziegler (ed.), *Ieremias, Baruch, Threni, Epistula Ieremiae* (Septuaginta Vetus Testamentum Graecum 15; Göttingen: Vandenhoeck & Ruprecht, 1957); J. Ziegler (ed.), *Ezechiel* (Septuaginta Vetus Testamentum Graece 16.1; Göttingen: Vandenhoeck & Ruprecht, 1952); Ziegler, *Duodecim prophetae*.

[4] Wevers and Fraenkel, "The L Text of Ezekiel," 69–115.

[5] Munnich, "Le Texte Lucianique d' Isaie-Septante," 369–99.

[6] Ziegler, *Ezechiel*, 52–53. For a helpful discussion of the characteristics of the Lucianic recension, see Ziegler, "Hat Lukian den griechischen Sirach rezensiert?" 210–29.

[7] The examples in this section are drawn mostly from Ziegler's observations in the *Einleitungen* of his critical editions.

Substitutions include simplex forms for compound ones among verbs and vice versa (e.g., Isa 1:29 καταισχυνθήσονται "they shall be ashamed" LXX/αἰσχυνθήσονται "they shall be ashamed" LXX^L; Jer 51:3 παραπικρᾶναι "to provoke" LXX/πικρᾶναι "to embitter" LXX^L; Mic 5:7 πίπτουσα "falling" LXX/ἐπιπίπτουσα "falling" LXX^L). Other substitutions involve mood and tense (Isa 54:8 ἠλέησα "I have had mercy" LXX/ἐλεήσω "I will have mercy" LXX^L; Jer 14:19 ἦν "was" LXX/ἐστιν "is" LXX^L; Joel 1:8 θρήνησον "lament" LXX/θρηνήσει "he will lament" LXX^L). There are many substitutions of prepositions that sometimes result in corrections of case (Isa 6:13 ἀπό "from" LXX/ἐκ "out of" LXX^L; Jer 39:14 εἰς ἀγγεῖον ὀστρ "into an earthenware jar" LXX/ἐν ἀγγείῳ ὀστρακίνῳ "in an earthenware jar" LXX^L; Zech 10:7 ἐν οἴνῳ "in wine" LXX/ἀπὸ οἴνου "from wine" LXX^L). Sometimes the recensionist changed the case of a noun but did not substitute a different governing preposition (Jer 14:6 ἐπὶ νάπας "by wooded valleys" LXX/ἐπὶ νάπεσιν "by wooded valleys" LXX^L; Amos 1:11 ἐπὶ γῆς "upon the ground" LXX/ἐπὶ τὴν γῆν "upon the ground" LXX^L). Substitutions also include synonyms (Jer 39:24 ὄχλος "crowd" LXX/πλῆθος "multitude" LXX^L; Zech 11:7 ἑτέραν "another" LXX/δευτέραν "second" LXX^L). Sometimes the recensionist's preference is for a class of noun against another class (e.g., -μα- for -σις; Jer 7:5 κρίσιν "judgement" LXX/κρίματα "judgements" LXX^L).

Attic morphology and syntax is a stellar characteristic of the Lucianic recension, though the manuscripts do not consistently preserve classical forms. The most significant variants include employment of the *schema atticum* (Jer 22:8 ἔθνη δειλεύσονται [-εται LXX^L] "nations will pass through"; Nah 2:5 ἅρματα συγχυθήσονται [-εται LXX^L] "chariots will be in confusion"), a preference for the second aorist εἶπον "I said" (Hos 3:3 εἶπα LXX/εἶπον LXX^L), and a preference for older morphological forms (Jer 39:18 ἔλεος LXX/ἔλεον LXX^L; Hos 2:19 ἐλέει LXX/ἐλέῳ LXX^L, all meaning "mercy"). The manuscripts preserve numerous transpositions (e.g. Jer 19:14 ἐκεῖ/τοῦ προφητεῦσαι "to prophecy there") that often do not alter the sense of the text significantly, though there are syntactical improvements among transpositions.

6–9.1.6.4 Inner-Translational Features

Wevers notes that the LXX^L text of LXX-Ezek (→ 8.3) is highly reliant on Hexaplaric sources (→ 6–9.1.5). Agreements between LXX^L and the Hebrew text are due to Hexaplaric influence, because Origen (→ 1.3.1.2) was concerned with adding text, mostly from Theodotion (e.g., Ezek 1:16 ※ καί ἡ ὅρασις αὐτῶν "and their sight" *LXX$^{O\ L}$* = Th), to bring LXX into conformity with the Hebrew. Therefore, it is not likely that Lucian used a Hebrew source.[8] Hexaplaric influence is also found in LXX-Isa (→ 6.3), where the LXX^L text also preserves readings that are under the obelisk elsewhere (Isa 51:12 ἐγώ εἰμι "I am" LXX/※ αὐτός "he" LXX$^{V\ ll}$). In LXX-Isa, many agreements between LXX^L and Hexaplaric sources align the Greek text with the Hebrew text.[9] Reliance on Symmachus (→ 6–9.1.5) occasionally happens in LXX-Isa (Isa 10:26 ὁ θεός ἐπ'αὐτούς "God ... against them" LXX/ὁ θεὸς ἐπ'αὐτούς μάστιγας "God ... scourge against them" LXX^L/μάστιγα "scourge" Sym). Employment of readings attributed to Symmachus in Hexaplaric sources is common in LXX-Ezek (e.g., Ezek 28:13 χρηστόν "worthy" LXX/τίμιος "valued" LXX^L = Sym).[10] In LXX-Jer (→ 7.3), agreements between the Hebrew text, the LXX^L text, and Hexaplaric sources are prevalent. The LXX^L text preserves variants that are not attributed to Aquila, Symmachus, or Theodotion (e.g., Jer 45:14 σε "you" LXX/ἐγώ σε "I ... you" LXX^O = MT/σε ἐγώ "I ... you" LXX^L) and variants that are attributed to one of the three Jewish revisors (Jer 22:33 καταστενάξεις "you will groan" LXX/※ τι καταστενάξεις "how you will groan" LXX^O/ὅ τι καταστενάξεις "that you will groan" LXX^L = Sym). Use of Hexaplaric variants is also found in the Minor Prophets (Amos 6:2 Ραββα "Rabba" LXX/τὴν μεγάλην "the great" LXX^L = Sym; Hos 8:1 Εἰς κόλπον "into the bosom" LXX/ἐπὶ φάρυγγι "on the throat" LXX^L = Sym). The LXX^L text also preserves stylistic corrections based upon Hexaplaric variants (Jonah 2:11 προσετάγη "it cast" LXX/※ ἀπὸ κυρίου "by

---

[8] Wevers and Fraenkel, "The L Text of Ezekiel," 69, 115.
[9] K.H. Jobes and M. Silva, *Invitation to the Septuagint* (Grand Rapids: Baker Academic, 2000), 134.
[10] Ziegler, *Ezechiel*, 50.

the Lord" LXX^O/προσέταξεν κύριος "the Lord commanded" LXX^L).

6–9.1.6.5 Text-Critical Value

The value of the Lucianic recension in the Latter Prophets is determined by the recension's relationship to Hexaplaric sources. As Fernández Marcos has stated, there was a "post-Hexaplaric reworking of the text" that is Lucianic.[11] Agreements with early witnesses such as the Old Latin and Josephus may be indicators of a pre-Hexaplaric tradition.[12]

Howard, G., "Lucianic Readings in a Greek Twelve Prophets Scroll from the Judaean Desert," *JQR* 62 (1971–1972): 51–60.

Munnich, O., "Le Texte Lucianique d'Isaie-Septante," in *Interpreting Translation: Studies on the LXX and Ezekiel in Honour of Johan Lust* (eds. F. García Martínez and M. Vervenne; BETL 192; Leuven: Peeters, 2005), 369–99.

Procksch, O., *Studien zur Geschichte der Septuaginta: Die Propheten* (Beiträge zur Wissenschaft vom Alten Testament 7; Leipzig: J.C. Hinrichs, 1910).

Stekhoven, J.Z.S., *De Alexandrijsche vertaling van het Dodekapropheton* (Leiden: Brill, 1887).

Tisserant, E., "Notes sur la recension lucianique d'Ézéchiel," *RB* 8 (1911): 384–90.

Wevers, J.W. and D. Fraenkel, "The L Text of Ezekiel," in J.W. Wevers and D. Fraenkel, *Studies in the Text Histories of Deuteronomy and Ezekiel* (MSU 26; Göttingen: Vandenhoeck & Ruprecht, 2003), 69–115.

Ziegler, J., "Hat Lukian den griechischen Sirach rezensiert?" *Bib* 40 (1959): 210–29.

Ziegler, J., *Duodecim prophetae* (2nd ed.; Septuaginta Vetus Testamentum Graecum 13; Göttingen: Vandenhoeck & Ruprecht, 1967).

Matthew M. Dickie

6–9.1.7 Vulgate

6–9.1.7.1 Background

Jerome began his *iuxta Hebraeos* "according to the Hebrews" translation project in 391 C.E. and completed his translations of v-Latter Prophets by 393 C.E. (→ 1.3.5.2).[1] Jerome's work on the Latter Prophets may also be found in his commentaries on these books, which often contain discussions that illuminate Jerome's translation choices. For example, Jerome once explains that his original Vulgate translation was a concession to LXX (→ 6.3) on the grounds that it differed only slightly from the Hebrew (*Comm. Isa.* 22:3a; → 6.2.2),[2] and on another occasion he acknowledges having stayed close to LXX because he did not want to tamper with a well-known passage (*Comm. Isa.* 58:12).[3] In most cases, the lemmata in the commentaries match the Vulgate translation, showing that Jerome wrote his commentaries with his own translation in front of him.[4] Yet, since the commentaries were mostly written years after the initial translations,[5] with Jerome's increasing competence in Hebrew and fresh perspectives coming in the intervening years, the Hebrew-based lemmata in the commentaries are not in every case

---

[1] Jerome says that he had translated the Prophets from Hebrew into Latin in *Vir. Ill.* 134 (written by 393 C.E.), and in *Epist.* 49.4 (from about the same time) he states that he had translated the sixteen Prophets from Hebrew into Latin. Moreover, the biblical lemmata from his Minor Prophets commentaries written by 393 C.E. reflect Jerome's *iuxta Hebraeos* version; see C.B. Tkacz, "'Labor Tam Utilis': The Creation of the Vulgate," *VC* 50 (1996): 47.

[2] *In hoc loco Septuaginta interpretationem secuti sumus, quia non multum ab hebraico distat in sensu* "In this passage we follow the translation of the Seventy, because it does not differ much from the Hebrew in sense."

[3] *In eo loco, ubi nos iuxta Septuaginta interpretati sumus, ne quid innovare videremur, quia vulgatum est testimonium* ... "In this passage, where we translated according to the Seventy, so that we do not appear to be making any innovations, seing that it is the popular witness ..." On the biblical lemmata in Jerome's *Commentary on Isaiah*, see P. Jay, *L'exégèse de Saint Jérôme d'après son "Commentaire sur Isaïe"* (Paris: Études Augustiniennes, 1985), 89–102.

[4] Whereas there is general agreement between the Vulgate and the biblical lemmata cited in the commentaries, when Jerome brings in biblical texts from elsewhere and quotes them in his commentaries, these remote verses often do not match Jerome's Vulgate.

[5] The commentaries on the Minor Prophets were begun in the 390s C.E. and completed by the early 400s C.E., followed by commentaries on Daniel (407 C.E.), Isaiah (ca. 408–410 C.E.), Ezekiel (ca. 410–414 C.E.), and Jeremiah 1–32 (ca. 414–419 C.E.).

---

[11] N. Fernández Marcos, *The Septuagint in Context: Introduction to the Greek Version of the Bible* (transl. W.G.E. Watson; Leiden: Brill, 2000), 236.

[12] Fernández Marcos, *The Septuagint in Context*, 236.

the same as the Vulgate version. Sometimes, in the commentary lemma, Jerome corrects what he perceives to be an error in his earlier translation (e.g., *Comm. Isa.* 19:16–17).[6] Some of these updates in the commentaries may have been unconscious[7] but, as Jerome tells us, some of them were intentional improvements, either to bring the translation closer to the Hebrew or else to produce a reading better suited to the context. Examples from the *Commentary on Jeremiah* where the biblical lemma differs from the Vulgate include Jer 2:18 (the Vulgate's *turbidam* "turbid" becomes *Sior* in the lemma and is explained in Jerome's comments), Jer 5:8 (*in feminas* "to women" and *mihi* "in my view" were added in the lemma for clarity), Jer 23:33 (the lemma presupposes a different word division and vocalization), Jer 25:38 (*tabernaculum suum* "his tabrnacle" is given as an alternative translation of סכו "his lair" and is explained within the lemma), and Jer 29:2 (the Vulgate's *faber et inclusor*, "the craftsmen and the engravers" are collapsed into *artifices* "skilled workers" in the lemma for the sake of style).[8] Because they are separate works, the commentaries should not generally be used to reconstruct Jerome's Vulgate text.[9] Yet, because Jerome frequently comments on the text in ways that illuminate his earlier Vulgate version, his commentaries can be valuable tools for interpreting the Vulgate.

6–9.1.7.2 Translation Character

V-Latter Prophets is a generally free translation of the Hebrew into idiomatic Latin. Jerome's method was eclectic both in terms of sources and translation technique. Regarding sources, although occasionally Jerome preserves distinctive readings from LXX (e.g., *nomina* "names" in Zeph 1:4; *dei* "God" in Zeph 1:9; *quasi* "as" in Zeph 3:3), much more frequently he follows one of the Hexaplaric versions (→ 6–9.1.5). Yet, Jerome does not follow any of these versions slavishly, but agrees at one moment with Aquila, then with Symmachus, and then with Theodotion, or with none of the Greek versions. The fact that Jerome is picking and choosing on the basis of his own knowledge (or that of his Jewish teacher) is demonstrated by those instances where he goes against all three Hexaplaric versions (e.g., *placentas* "cakes" in Jer 7:18; *pavorem* "fear" in Jer 20:3; *consilio* "counsel" in Jer 23:18; *initiarent* "consecrate" in Jer 32:35; *in futurum* "to come" in Zeph 3:8), and also where his commentaries provide Hebrew-based explanations for his translation decisions (e.g., see *Comm. Jer.* on *foederabitur* "be allied" at Jer 15:12, following Aquila; and on *rotam* "wheel" at Jer 18:3, following Symmachus). In most cases, it can be assumed that Jerome's translation reflects a Hebrew text that is in front of him, and that he has selected his translation – even when following a Greek source – on the basis of its perceived agreement with his Hebrew text. Nevertheless, for difficult texts Jerome may sometimes have followed a Greek translation that actually reflected a Hebrew text different from what Jerome was using; e.g., *solis* "of the sun" in Isa 19:18 follows Symmachus, who may have been translating חרס "sun" rather than MT's הֶרֶס, "de-

---

[6] *Melius reor etiam proprium errorem reprehendere quam, dum erubesco imperitiam confiteri, in errore persistere* "I think it is better to censure an error, even my own, rather than to persist in error because I am ashamed to admit my mistake." In the Vulgate, Jerome had translated חגא "terror" at Isa 19:17 as *festivitas* "festival" but in the commentary he argues that the word should really be translated *timor* "terror."

[7] E.g., at Jer 10:8 (*sapientes* "wise" instead of *insipientes* "stupid") and Jer 25:24b (omitted in the lemma), the differences between the commentary lemma and the Vulgate probably reflect nothing more than slip-ups in the commentary.

[8] For other cases where the lemma appears to update the Vulgate, see *Comm. Jer.* on Jer 6:6; 7:3; 10:25; 13:17; 14:10; 23:1; 23:13; 25:15–17; 31:5; 31:9. For examples in which Jerome gives in the lemma both the Vulgate and an updated translation as an alternative, see Jer 18:23 and Jer 19:11, where the updated translation in each case is closer to MT.

[9] Some cross contamination has taken place between the lemmata in Jerome's commentaries and the Vulgate. For examples where the Vulgate may have influenced the commentary lemma as preserved in the manuscripts, see *Comm. Jer.* on Jer 13:20 (*qui venitis* "you who come" from the Vulgate may have replaced an original *venientes* "those coming" in the lemma, as suggested by Jerome's comments); and *Comm. Zeph.* on Zeph 3:10–13 (*filii* "sons" from the Vulgate may have replaced an original *filia* "daughter" in the lemma [MT: בת "daughter"], as shown by Jerome's comments). On the transmission of the commentary lemmata and the Vulgate, see Gryson, *Commentaire de Jérôme*, 59–74.

struction." If the text's meaning was unclear to Jerome, he may have simply regarded *solis* as an idiomatic paraphrase of הֶרֶס. If so, then חרס should be regarded as a potential Hebrew variant underlying Symmachus, which was merely transmitted by the Vulgate. As for Jerome's eclectic translation technique, v-Latter Prophets regularly renders the same Hebrew expression in diverse ways, and formal representations of the Hebrew exist side by side with periphrastic renderings (→ 1.3.5.7). Because of Jerome's freedom in translating according to his peculiar sense of each passage, variations vis-à-vis MT (→ 6.2.2, → 7.2.2, → 8.2.2, → 9.2.2) in basic elements of grammar, e.g., verb tense, active/passive forms, variations in person and number, use of prepositions, and the presence/absence of pronouns, cannot usually be regarded as significant for textual criticism of the Hebrew.[10]

6–9.1.7.3 Translation Technique
6–9.1.7.3.1 Hebrew Idioms

Jerome customarily translates idioms distinctive to Hebrew into sensible Latin. The Hebrew infinitive absolute modifying a finite verb is recast in the Vulgate, e.g. כשול יכשלו "stumbling, they shall stumble" (i.e., "they shall surely stumble"), *in infirmitate cadent* "by infirmity they shall fall" (Isa 40:30); ונקה לא ינקה "and acquiting, he will not acquit" (i.e., "he will surely not acquit"), *et mundans non faciet innocentem* "and he will not, cleansing, render (them) guiltless" (Nah 1:3). Jerome does similarly with the infinitive preceded by a *Hiphil* acting adverbially, e.g., הגדיל לעשות "he has made great to act" (i.e.,

"he has done great things"), *superbe egit* "he has acted proudly" (Joel 2:20).[11] Purpose clauses using ל-plus-infinitive are most often translated with *ut*-clauses (e.g., Isa 49:6; Jer 1:10; Hos 11:9; Obad 14; Jonah 1:3, 5; Hab 1:12; 2:1), but may occasionally be a gerundival clause (e.g., Jer 22:17), a relative clause (e.g., Hos 2:11), or an infinitive (e.g., Isa 66:15). The Hebrew expression יקרא לך "it shall be called to you" is rendered as *vocaberis* "you shall be called" (Isa 1:26), and likewise היה ל- is put properly into Latin as *versum est in* "has turned into" (Isa 1:22). Jerome makes ב-plus-infitive into Latin temporal clauses, e.g., ובפרשכם "and in your spreading" (i.e., "when you spread") *et cum extenderitis* "and when you extend" (Isa 1:15); בחלקם "in their dividing" (i.e., "when they divide") *quando dividunt* "when they divide" (Isa 9:3). Distributive, reciprocal, and similar Hebrew idioms are recast into Latin, e.g., אשה אל אחותה literally, "a woman unto her sister," *alteram ad alteram* "one unto another" (Ezek 3:13); ואיש אחיו literally, "a man, his brother," *unusquisque fratrem suum* "each one, his brother" (Joel 2:8); סביב סביב "around, around" (i.e., "all around") *in gyro* "in circuit" (Ezek 37:2). The Hebrew noun in construct used attributively may become an adjective, e.g., כאנשי מלחמה "as men of war" *quasi viri bellatores* "as warlike men" (Joel 2:7). A distinctive Hebrew expression such as ארך אפים "slow to anger" in v-Latter Prophets is rendered simply *patiens* "patient" (e.g., Nah 1:3; Joel 2:13). Jerome understands the sense of Hebrew parallelism and often supplies needed words for the sake of clear Latin, e.g., *quis adiuvit* "who has helped" and *quis consiliarius eius fuit* "who has been his counselor" (Isa 40:13). Jerome's regular practice of reshaping idioms peculiar to Hebrew did not stop him from occasionally rendering such expressions in a literalistic way (see below). But he clearly understood the meanings of these expressions and typically put them into idiomatic Latin.

---

[10] For example, the preposition ל "for" may be translated as accusative (Zeph 1:5), dative (Zeph 1:7), genitive (Isa 9:6), *quasi* "as" (Jer 47:2), *super* "over" (Jer 22:10), as a possessive (*meum* "my" in Hag 2:8; *meae* "my" in Ezek 18:4), may be deleted (Isa 1:5; Ezek 34:17), may be part of a peculiar idiom (לְדָוִד "for David" *de genere David* "from the stock of David" in Jer 22:4), and many other possibilities. With these basic grammatical elements, it is difficult to infer what Hebrew underlies Jerome's Latin. Still, the Vulgate may possibly lend support to another witness on such elements; e.g. for יֵחָל "it will be profaned" (3rd per.) at Isa 48:11, the Vulgate's *blasphemer* "I will be blasphemed" agrees with three Qumran texts (1QIsa^a, 4QIsa^{c, d}; → 6.2.1) that give the 1st per.; and for כח "strength" at Isa 40:26, *virtutisque eius* "and his strength" agrees with 1QIsa^a in having the 3rd per. suffix.

[11] See P. Joüon and T. Muraoka, *A Grammar of Biblical Hebrew* (2nd ed.; Rome: Gregorian & Biblical Press, 2009), 124n.

6–9.1.7.3.2 Attention to Context

Jerome freely departs from simple or expected renderings when the context suggests a better way to capture the sense of the text in Latin. Thus, Jerome often renders a single Hebrew word with several Latin words, e.g. ומריתם "and you rebel" *et me provocaveritis ad iracundiam* "and you provoke me to anger" (Isa 1:20); הקיצתי "I awoke" *quasi de somno suscitatus sum* "I was aroused as if out of sleep" (Jer 31:26); הדולג "the leaping one" *qui arroganter ingreditur* "who enters arrogantly" (Zeph 1:9); בשלש "by a third" *tribus digitis* "with three fingers" (Isa 40:12); וישכב וירדם "and he laid down and went to sleep" *et dormiebat sopore grave* "and he slept in a heavy slumber" (Jonah 1:5). This is frequently necessary in dealing with *Hiphil* verbs, e.g., אריח "I will not smell" *capiam odorem* "I will not accept the scent" (Amos 5:21); אשביר "I bring to birth" *alios parere facio* "I make others to bring forth" (Isa 66:9). He also deviates from stereotyped equivalencies when the context requires, e.g., ובקרבו "and in his midst" *et occulte* "and secretly" (Jer 9:8); עלתה "did it come up" *cogitavi* "did I consider it" (Jer 7:31); כרתי "I cut" *placui* "I resolved" (Hag 2:6). Jerome likes to fill out the sense of various expressions, such as rhetorical questions, e.g., התחיינה "Can they live?" *putasne vivent* "do you think they shall live?" (Ezek 37:3); התשכח "Will she forget?" *numquid oblivisci potest* "Is she able to forget?" (Isa 49:15), statements of possibility, e.g., אם ימדו "if they may be measured" *si mensurari potuerint* "If they are able to be measured" (Jer 31:37); בהמצאו "in his being found" (i.e., "when he may be found"), *dum inveniri potest* "while he is able to be found" (Isa 55:6), and conditions, e.g., ולקדש "and to sanctify" *et si sanctificaveritis* "and if you will sanctify" (Jer 17:24). At times, Jerome's translations are so loose and contextually fashioned that they are best called paraphrases, e.g., קרא מקרא "the calling of assembly" *et festivitates alias* "and other festivals" (Isa 1:13); סאן סאן "boot marching" *violenta praedatio* "violent plundering" (Isa 9:5); והטבתי מראשתיכם literally, "and I will make good from your firsts," *bonisque donabo maioribus quam habuistis ab initio* "and I will bestow you with good things, greater than you had from the beginning" (Ezek 36:11); מקול שעטת פרסות אביריו "from the sound of the stamping of hooves of his mighty ones" *ab strepitu pompae armorum et bellatorum* "from the rumbling of the procession of arms and of soldiers" (Jer 47:3); לא ידרך הידד הידד לא הידד "the (one making a) shout will not tread, the shout will not be a shout" *nequaquam calcator uvae solitum celeuma cantabit* "the treader of grapes will not recite the customary cadence" (Jer 48:33).

6–9.1.7.3.3 Style

A characteristic feature of v-Latter Prophets is Jerome's concern for a basic level of proper Latin style. Countless passages contain deviations from the surface structure of the Hebrew that primarily serve to improve the feel of the Latin. Constructions that are possible but not desirable in Latin are improved, e.g., בשנת מות המלך "in the year of the dying of the king" *in anno quo mortuus est rex* "In the year in which the king died" (Isa 6:1); ארץ מלחה ולא תשב "a land of saltness, and it is not inhabited" *in terra salsuginis et inhabitabili* "in a land of saltness and uninhabitible" (Jer 17:6). Some free translations simply represent a more natural expression in Latin idiom, e.g., ראו עיני "my eyes have seen" *vidi oculis meis* "I have seen with my eyes" (Isa 6:5); שנאו "they hate" *odio habuerunt* "they regard with hatred" (Amos 5:10). Along these lines, many substantival and attributive participles in Hebrew become relative clauses in Latin, e.g., מקימה/*qui suscitet eam* "who raises her up" (Amos 5:2); האמרים/*qui dicunt* "who say" (Amos 9:10). Jerome had a strong tendency to avoid using the same word or construction multiple times in close proximity. Thus, v-Latter Prophets often gives diverse renderings for the same word, e.g., ויאכל ... יאכלו "and he eats ... they shall eat" *et comedet ... vorabit* "and he shall eat ... shall devour" (Isa 9:20); שד ... ושד "destruction ... and destruction" *vastitatem ... et depopulationem* "destruction ... and devastation" (Amos 5:9); כיאר ... כיאר "as the river ... as the river" *sicut rivus ... sicut fluvius* "as the stream ... as the river" (Amos 9:5); למלך ... ומלך "and (one) king ... king" *et rex ... imperans* "and (one) king ... ruler" (Ezek 37:22). Jerome also creates diversity in syntactical constructions, e.g., ביום ... ביום "in the day of ... in the day of" *in die cum ... quando* "In the day when ...

when" (Obad 11); לא ימד ולא יספר "it will not be measured and it will not be counted" *sine mensura est et non numerabitur* "it is without measure and it will not be counted" (Hos 1:10). V-Latter Prophets occasionally adds words for stylistic reasons in keeping with Latin usage, e.g., *habentis* "having" (Isa 6:5); *dimisso* "lowered" (Isa 49:23); *Ultra* "again" (Isa 55:10); *pleni* "full" (Jer 24:1); *quae* "which" (Hos 2:8). Words are also left out for the sake of style, usually to avoid redundancy, e.g., ישאון "they roar" (2nd; Isa 17:12–13); יצלח "prosper" (2nd; Jer 22:30); שה "sheep" (2nd; Ezek 34:20); אתכם "you" (2nd; Ezek 36:24). Another aspect of Jerome's concern for style is his practice of subordinating one clause to another where the Hebrew is paratactic. For example, Jerome translates Hebrew ו-plus-finite verb constructions into Latin as relative clauses (e.g., Isa 49:7), *ut*-clauses (e.g., Ezek 36:23), *cum*-clauses (e.g., Jer 47:7), and participial clauses (e.g., Hag 2:12). Finally, Jerome frequently adds conjunctions and other particles in order to make clear the logical connections between clauses, e.g., *ergo* "therefore" (Jer 1:17; 7:16); *enim* "for" (Ezek 3:14; Jer 9:4); *sed* "but" (Isa 9:10; Zeph 1:18). These stylistic improvements in V-Latter Prophets helped Jerome's translation gain acceptance (see Augustine, *Doctr. chr.* 4.7.15), but they also complicate the process of reconstructing the underlying Hebrew.

6–9.1.7.3.4 Literalisms and Transliterations

Although the general tendency of V-Latter Prophets is to translate idiomatically, one still encounters literalistic translations on a regular basis, e.g., לפניו/*ante faciem eius* "before its face" (Joel 2:3; cf. *coram eo* "before it" in the same verse); הראני יהוה והנה/*ostendit mihi Dominus et Ecce* "The Lord showed me, and behold" (Jer 24:1; cf. והנה "and behold" *erant autem* "Now, there were" in Ezek 37:2). In keeping with the tradition of interpreting Hebrew proper name etymologies, Jerome is fond of translating proper names, e.g., ברמה "in Ramah" *in excelso* "on high" (Jer 31:15); תל אביב "Tel-aviv" *acervum novarum frugum* "heap of new corn" (Ezek 3:15); נינוה "Nineveh" *speciosam* "the beautiful" (Zeph 2:13; cf. Jer 6:2). Jerome does transliterate words that he understands as proper names (e.g. *Adam*, Hos 11:4; *Melchom*, Zeph 1:5), but he also frequently updates them (e.g. *Africa, Italiam, Graeciam*, Isa 66:19). Rarely does Jerome deal with difficult passages by transliterating them. When faced with an obscure text, Jerome generally relies on one of his sources and paraphrases (e.g., בסאסאה "in summoning"(?) *in mensura contra mensuram* "in measure against measure" Isa 27:8 [cf. Th: ἐν μέτρῳ μέτρον]), or less often he etymologizes (דראון "abhorrence" *satietatem visionis* "a glut of appearance" Isa 66:24; based on די and ראה, perhaps following Aquila).

6–9.1.7.3.5 Harmonizing and Exegesis

Occasionally, one finds in V-Latter Prophets translations that are interpretive beyond the basic linguistic level. In this category are certain instances where Jerome harmonizes the text in front of him with another scriptural text. A probable example is the translation of השמן "make dull" in Isa 6:10 as *excaeca* "blind," which appears to be based on John 12:40. Some instances of harmonization, however, may be unconscious, as perhaps with the addition of *Israhel* "Israel" in Jer 51:19 to match the parallel text in Jer 10:16. A clear example of interpretive translation in V-Latter Prophets can be seen in Jerome's rendering of אגילה באלהי ישעי "I will rejoice in the God of my deliverance" in Hab 3:18 as *exultabo in Deo Iesu meo* "I will rejoice in God my Jesus" where ישעי "my deliverance" is explicitly identified as "my Jesus."

6–9.1.7.4 Text-Critical Value

6–9.1.7.4.1 Consonantal Text Close to MT

The Hebrew consonantal text underlying V-Latter Prophets is so close to MT (→ 6.2.2, → 7.2.2, → 8.2.2, → 9.2.2) throughout that it may be considered as if it were an early text in this family (→ 1.3.5.11). In most cases, Jerome's Hebrew text seems to be the same as that of Codex MT^L. Furthermore, at many points where V-Latter Prophets differs from the Leningrad Codex it matches other medieval Hebrew manuscripts (→ 1.5). Examples may be found regarding many types of copying variations, such as the confusion of consonants, e.g., חֶמֶד "delight" vs. *meri* "wine" Isa 27:2 (חמר; V = many MT manuscripts, 1QIsa^a, S); אַשְׁמִיד "I will destroy" vs. *custodiam* "I will preserve" Ezek 34:16 (אשמיר; V = two MT manuscripts, LXX, S); בָּא בָא "it comes, it comes" vs. *veniet ei* "it shall come to him" Jer 46:20 (בא בה; V = many MT manuscripts, LXX, S, T); הוֹצִיא "he brought out" vs. *educam* "I will bring out" Ezek 11:7 (אוציא; V = many MT manuscripts, LXX, S, T); differences in number, e.g., לְמַעֲשֵׂי "to the works" vs. *opus* "the work" Jer 1:16 (V = many MT manuscripts, S);[12] pluses, e.g., *quia ego* "that I" Hos 2:20 (כי אני; V = many MT manuscripts); minuses, e.g., אֱמֹר "say" Ezek 11:16 (V = a few MT manuscripts, S); אָח "brother" Ezek 18:10 (V = many MT manuscripts, S, Aq); differences in word division, e.g., לַחְפֹּר פֵּרוֹת "to dig something(?)" vs. *talpas* "moles" Isa 2:20 (לחפרפרות "to the moles" [fem. pl.]; V = a few MT manuscripts, Th; cf. 1QIsa^a: לחפרפרים "to the moles" [masc. pl.]; LXX: τοῖς ματαίοις "to the vain ones"); and other variations, e.g., צֻוֵּיתִי "I was commanded" vs. *praeceperat mihi* "he had commanded me" Ezek 37:7 (צוני; V = a few MT manuscripts, LXX, S; cf. Ezek 37:10). Although one will not find in V-Latter Prophets many or sizeable deviations from the consonantal text of the Leningrad Codex, readings where the Hebrew text underlying V-Latter Prophets genuinely appears to differ from this codex should be given the same consideration as if they came from a Masoretic-type manuscript coming from ca. 400 C.E.

6–9.1.7.4.2 Agreement with Non-Masoretic Witnesses

Since the consonantal Hebrew text underlying V-Latter Prophets in most cases appears to match MT, it is potentially significant when the Vulgate provides support to ancient witnesses that differ from MT (→ 6.2.2, → 7.2.2, → 8.2.2, → 9.2.2). The Vulgate lacks כִּמְעָט "a few" at Isa 1:9, agreeing with LXX and the Peshitta. At Hos 2:16, the Vulgate (*vocabit* "he will call") supports LXX in reading the 3rd person in place of the 2nd person in MT (תִּקְרְאִי "you will call"). The Vulgate (*desolabit* "will desolate") agrees with LXX, the Peshitta, and Targum at Isa 11:15 in presuming והחריב in place of MT's וְהֶחֱרִים "will devote to destruction." The Vulgate agrees with the Peshitta in its version of Amos 5:16, which is syntactically awkward in MT, וּמִסְפֵּד אֶל־יוֹדְעֵי נֶהִי "and lament unto knowers of wailing" (V = *et ad planctum eos qui sciunt plangere* "and unto lamentation those who know how to lament"). Moreover, the Vulgate (*fortitudo vestra* "your strength") matches 1QIsa^a (החסנכם) at Isa 1:31 in giving the 2nd person plural suffix (MT: הֶחָסֹן "the strong"; LXX, S, and T give the 3rd person plural suffix); and the Vulgate (*sicut in diebus* "as in the days") matches 1QIsa^a (כימי), S, T, Aq, Sym, Th, and 1 Pet 3:20 at Isa 54:9 in its reading of the opening words of the verse (MT = כִּי־מֵי "because the waters of"). In cases such as these, the Vulgate offers important support to these other witnesses. Although it will not be common, it is at least possible for the Vulgate to serve as a unique witness to a Hebrew variant, e.g., perhaps *tribulabitur* "will be afflicted" as reflecting צרה "trouble" in place of צָרַח "shouts" at Zeph 1:14 (cf. Zeph 1:15, 17; Amos 3:11); and *latitudinem* "breadth" as reflecting רוח "side, corner" in place of לוּחַ "tablet" at Jer 17:1. But the possibility must always be kept in mind that the Vulgate may reflect a slip of the eye on the part of the translator.[13]

6–9.1.7.4.3 Vocalization and *Ketiv/Qere*

V-Latter Prophets typically presumes the same grammatical interpretation of the Hebrew text as reflected in the vocalization of MT (→ 6.2.2, → 7.2.2, → 8.2.2, → 9.2.2). It is clear from Jerome's commentaries that he was familiar with a vocalization tradition and that he recognized the impact vocalization could have on meaning.[14] When the Vul-

---

[12] Many divergences in V-Latter Prophets regarding number reflect merely the change from Hebrew into Latin style, e.g., שְׁאֵרִית "remnant" vs. *reliquos* "those remaining" (Hag 2:2); זֹאת מִיֶּדְכֶם "this from your hand" vs. *haec de manibus vestris* "this from your hands" (Isa 1:12).

[13] As an example of this kind of mistake, the Vulgate has suffered loss from *homoioteleuton* at Jer 52:22 (וְרִמּוֹנִים וְרִמּוֹנִים ... "and pomegranates ... and pomegranates"); see de Waard, *A Handbook on Jeremiah*, 226.

[14] Thus, Jerome distinguishes between "*dabar*" (דָּבָר) meaning "word," "*deber*" (דֶּבֶר) meaning "death, plague," and the imperative verb "*dabber*" (דַּבֵּר) "speak!" (*Comm. Jer.* 9:22). So also, Jerome spells out the word "res, ain, iod, and mem" (רעים), and explains that this word can be read as "*reim*" (רֵעִים) meaning

gate (or Jerome in the commentaries) reflects a vocalization different from what is presented in MT, Jerome's evidence should usually be accepted as a credible vocalization tradition from late antiquity. Two qualifications must be stated, however. First, Jerome's reading of the consonants might differ from MT not because he knew an alternative vocalization but because he did not have a clear tradition and he was guessing, following either a Hexaplaric version (→ 6–9.1.5) or his own wits. Second, because of Jerome's freedom in translating one cannot always know precisely what vocalization he was using. For example, because Jerome not infrequently makes nouns into verbs, one cannot assume that the Vulgate's *et conteret* "and he will break" reflects the vocalization וְשִׁבֵּר instead of merely an idiomatic rendering of MT's וְשֶׁבֶר "and the breaking" (Isa 1:28).[15] Examples where V-Latter Prophets probably suggests a vocalization different from MT include: בַּמֶּה "by what?" vs. *excelsus*, "high" Isa 2:22 (= בָּמָה; V = *al tiqre* in *b. Ber.* 14a and *b. Sotah* 4b); רֶכֶב "chariot" vs. *ascensorem* "rider" Isa 21:7 (= רֹכֵב; V = 1QIsa[a] [רוכב], LXX, S, T); וְאֹמַר "and he said" vs. *et dixi* "and I said" Isa 40:6 (= וָאֹמַר; V = 1QIsa[a] [ואומרה], LXX); בָּנָיִךְ "your sons" vs. *structores tui* "your builders" Isa 49:17 (= בֹּנָיִךְ; V = 1QIsa[a] [בוניך], T, Aq, Th; cf. LXX); מִקְנֶה "cattle" vs. *possidentis* "possessor" Jer 9:10 (= מִקְנָה); אָנוּשׁ "incurable" vs. *hominis* "of man" Jer 17:16 (= אֱנוֹשׁ; V = LXX, S); אַל "not," vs. *in* "into" Jer 47:6 (= אֶל; V = many MT manuscripts, LXX, S, T); זָרִים "strangers" vs. *ventilatores* "winnowers" Jer 51:2 (= זֹרִים; V = Aq, Sym; cf. S, T). In most (if not all) of these instances, the vocalization presupposed by the Vulgate represents an actual vocalization tradition known to Jerome or to his source. Jerome never indicates that he is aware of a *Ketiv/Qere* system. V-Latter Prophets shows no particular tendency to follow either tradition consistently. Sometimes the Vulgate matches the *Ketiv* (e.g., Isa 9:2; Isa 49:5; Isa 63:9; Jer 6:7), and sometimes the *Qere* (e.g., Isa 52:2; Jer 8:7; Jer 31:21; Jer 31:38). Interestingly, Jerome regularly translates MT's אֲדֹנָי יְהוָה as *Dominus Deus* "Lord God" (e.g. Ezek 11:7; Amos 9:5; Zeph 1:7).

Barthélemy, *Critique textuelle 1986*.
Barthélemy, *Critique textuelle 1992*.
Bogaert, P.-M., "La tradition des oracles et du livre Jérémie des origines au moyen âge. Essai de synthèse," *RTL* 8 (1977): 305–28.
Dines, J.M., "Jerome and the Hexapla: The Witness of the Commentary on Amos," in *Origen's Hexapla and Fragments* (ed. A. Salvesen; TSAJ 58; Tübingen: Mohr Siebeck, 1998), 421–36.
Evans, C.A., "Jerome's Translation of Isaiah 6:9–10," *VC* 38 (1984): 202–04.
Graves, M., *Jerome's Hebrew Philology* (Leiden: Brill, 2007).
Graves, M. (trans.), *Jerome: Commentary on Jeremiah* (ACT; Downers Grove: IVP Academic, 2011).
Gryson, R., "S. Jérôme traducteur d'Isaïe: Réflexions sur le texte d'Isaïe XIV,18–21 dans la Vulgate et dans l' In Esaiam," *Mus* 104 (1991): 57–72.
Gryson, R., *Commentaire de Jérôme sur le Prophète Isaïe, Livres I–IV* (Freiburg: Verlag Herder, 1993).
Haelewyck, J.-C., "Le lemme vulgate du commentaire de Jérôme sur Isaïe," in *Jérôme entre l'occident et l'orient* (ed. Y.-M. Duval; Paris: Études Augustiniennes, 1988), 391–402.
Jay, P., *L'exégèse de Saint Jérôme d'après son "Commentaire sur Isaïe"* (Paris: Études Augustiniennes, 1985).
Kedar-Kopfstein, B., "Divergent Hebrew Readings in Jerome's Isaiah," *Text* 4 (1964): 176–210.
Kedar-Kopfstein, B., "Textual Gleanings form the Vulgate to Jeremiah," *Text* 7 (1969): 36–58.
Kedar-Kopfstein, B., "The Hebrew Text of Joel as Reflected in the Vulgate," *Text* 9 (1981): 16–35.
Nowack, W., *Die Bedeutung des Hieronymus für die alttestamentliche Textkritik* (Göttingen: Vandenhoeck & Ruprecht, 1875).
Stummer, F., "Spuren jüdischer und christlicher Einflüsse auf die Übersetzung der grossen Propheten durch Hieronymus," *JPOS* 8 (1928): 35–48.

"friends, lovers," and also as *"roim"* (רֹעִים) meaning "shepherds" (*Comm. Jer.* 6:2–4a).

[15] For Jerome's translating nouns as verbs, see Isa 1:7 (שְׁמָמָה "desolation" *desolabitur* "will be desolated"), and Isa 9:7 (לְמַרְבֵּה "to the abundance" *multiplicabitur* "will be multiplied"). Similarly, Jerome translates freely between active and passive verbs (e.g., עַד כַּלּוֹתִי אֹתָם "until I have consumed them" *donec consumantur* "until they are consumed," Jer 9:16; הִשְׁלִיכוּ "they have cast down" *deiecta sunt* "they have been cast down" Jer 9:19; יִרְעוּ "they feed" *pascuntur* "they are fed" Ezek 34:2); thus, e.g., it is not clear what vocalization Jerome attached to שלח at Obad 1 (MT: שֻׁלָּח "was sent") when he translated *misit* "he sent."

Taylor, J., *The Massoretic Text and the Ancient Versions of the Book of Micah* (London: Williams & Norgate, 1891).

van der Kooij, A., *Die Alten Textzeugen des Jesajabuches* (Göttingen: Vandenhoeck & Ruprecht, 1981).

van der Kooij, A., "The Cities of Isaiah 24–27 according to the Vulgate, Targum and Septuagint," in *Studies in Isaiah 24–27: The Isaiah Workshop – De Jesaja Werkplaats* (eds. H.J. Bosman et al.; Leiden: Brill, 2000), 183–98.

de Waard, J., *A Handbook on Isaiah* (Winona Lake: Eisenbrauns, 1997).

de Waard, J., *A Handbook on Jeremiah* (Winona Lake: Eisenbrauns, 2003).

Weissert, D., "Obadiah 20: Septuagint and Vulgate," *Text* 24 (2009): 85.

Zandstra, S., *The Witness of the Vulgate, Peshitta and Septuagint to the Text of Zephaniah* (New York: Columbia University Press, 1909).

Michael Graves

6–9.1.8 Arabic Translations

The earliest evidence of Jewish translations into Arabic of the prophetic books is found in glossaries dating from the ninth and tenth centuries C.E. that have been preserved in the Cairo Genizah.[1] These glossaries contain sporadic or continuous lists of biblical words and phrases, which are arranged in columns or separated by dots from one or several Arabic translation equivalents. The equivalents are transcribed into Hebrew script and often attest to an early stage of the development of Judeo-Arabic. The glossaries are sometimes called "pre-Saadianic" since they precede the standardization of the Judeo-Arabic script typical of the works of the leading medieval Rabbanite translator of the Bible, Saadia Gaon (882–942 C.E.). The lists appear to have accompanied the study and teaching of the Hebrew Bible, especially with regard to the clarification of the meaning of difficult or rare Hebrew words. Among the extant glossaries, of which a small portion has been published so far, we can find translations of unique words from the Former and Latter Prophets, including Samuel and Kings, Isaiah, Jeremiah, Ezekiel, and Amos.[2]

6–9.1.8.1 Medieval Rabbanite Translations

The leading medieval Rabbanite translator of the Bible, Saadia Gaon (882–942 C.E.), composed Arabic versions of various books of the Hebrew Bible, including Job, Proverbs, and Psalms, the Five Scrolls (of which have come down to us parts of his versions to the Song of Songs, Lamentations, and Esther), and Daniel.[3] Among the prophetic books, his only full surviving translation is that of Isaiah, which is available in two editions by Derenbourg (1893, without Saadia's introduction) and Ratzaby (1993, including Saadia's introduction).[4] In addition, Allony has published an anonymous fragment of an Arabic translation of Ezek 41:18–44:25,[5] and Ratzaby has published an anonymous translation of three Haftarot fragments from the Former Prophets (2 Kgs 4:1–37; 1 Kgs 1:1–13; Judg 4:4–5, 31).[6] Allony and Ratzaby claim that these translations contain features typical of Saadia's translation system. Nevertheless, such features cannot serve as ultimate proof of Saadia's authorship and so they may have been composed by students or scribes who were influenced by Saadia's translation method.[7] Extant book-lists from the Cairo Genizah attest a *tafsīr melakhim le-rabbenu seʿadya* "a translation and commentary to Kings by our Rabbi Saadia," yet none to Ezekiel.[8]

It is unclear whether Saadia composed translations of other biblical books, in particular the Latter Prophets. Ratzaby, who raises the issue, concludes: "There is not an accepted answer. We can make an

---

[1] Tobi, "Pre-Saadianic," 87–127.

[2] Polliack and Somekh, "The Hebrew-Arabic Biblical Glossaries," 15–47.

[3] See further on Saadia's translation enterprise, → 1.3.6. We are grateful to Mr. Roni Cohen for producing a draft English rendering of this article from our original Hebrew text, which we later reworked and expanded into the present English article.

[4] See Derenburg and Derenburg, *Version Arabe d'Isaie*; Ratzaby, *Saadia's Translation and Commentary on Isaiah*.

[5] Allony, "MeTargūm Saadia."

[6] Ratzaby, "Seridim."

[7] See Ratzaby's remarks: "Seridim," 169.

[8] Allony, *The Jewish Library*, 39.

assumption and say that he chose the books and Megillot that the Jews needed in their practical religious lives."[9] Ratzaby brings as evidence the fact that "the book-lists preserved in the Genizah only mention Saadia's translations of the Bible which we have today."[10] As for the Former Prophets, Ratzaby suggests: "Historiographical books like Nevi'im Rishonim and Chronicles deal with events of the past without connection to the present day, and hence were not translated and interpreted."[11] Schlossberg argues with Ratzaby, claiming this cannot be the only reason why Saadia did not compose translations and commentaries for the majority of Nevi'im and Ketuvim books. He points to evidence from the Cairo Genizah, which contains many anonymous Arabic translation fragments of these books, from which we can learn that in the Middle Ages (especially from the tenth to the thirteenth centuries) the Jews of the Islamic world studied almost all the books of the Bible and not only those that were required in synagogue worship.[12] Blau and Hopkins suggest that it is reasonable to assume that Saadia had written translations and commentaries for most of the books of the Bible, if not for all of them. However, not all of these translations have come down to us: "Nevertheless, we only have several books from his translations, and they are the ones that had been read in the synagogue, and therefore had been copied more often."[13]

Avishur, who summarized the research on Saadia's translations of the prophetic books in the introduction to his edition of an anonymous medieval manuscript, has come to a similar conclusion like Ratzaby: "It is likely that Saadia did not write translations of the Prophetic Books except for Isaiah."[14] Although we may find quotations from Saadia's translations and commentaries to these books in the works of medieval Jewish authors, Avishur claims that we cannot know for a fact that Saadia actually composed them. These authors may have relied on passages from the Prophets cited in Saadia's known translation works and presumed, wrongly, that they belonged to independent writings he composed on the Former and Latter Prophets.[15]

Until further manuscript evidence is found, we may learn about Saadia Gaon's Arabic translations of the Former and Latter Prophets in three ways: firstly, by reviewing his translations of separate words found in his grammatical works and dictionaries, especially in his treatise on seventy *hapax legomena*, known as *tafsīr (or kitāb) al-sabʿīn lafẓha min mufridat al-qurʾān* "The Interpretation/Book of Seventy Unique words in the Bible."[16] Secondly, we learn about them by sifting through his known translations of other biblical books, in which we may find mention of prophetic verses. For example, Saadia translates Isa 26:12:[17] יְהוָה תִּשְׁפֹּת שָׁלוֹם לָנוּ כִּי גַם כָּל-מַעֲשֵׂינוּ פָּעַלְתָּ לָּנוּ "Oh Lord, you will ordain peace for us, for indeed, all that we have done, you have done for us" (*NRSV*) into Arabic as ותנצב אלסלאם לנא כמא טאלמא קץ׳ית לנא ג׳מיע חואיג׳נא "Place peace upon us as you have long since supplied us with all our needs" and in his commentary he writes: תשפת שלום אשתקקת תשפות מן קול אלישע "שפות הסיר" פג׳עלתה נצבא, which means, "*tishpot shalom*- I have derived 'tishpot' from Elisha's words 'shfot ha-sir' (2 Kgs 4:38) and I have translated it 'you will place'."[18] From the Gaon's commentary, we learn that he rendered the Hebrew root שפת "to ordain" in Isaiah and 2 Kings by use of the same Arabic *nṣb* "to place." This is but one example of many from which we can glean something of Saa-

---

[9] Ratzaby, *Saadia's Translation and Commentary on Isaiah*, 7.

[10] Ratzaby, "Selections," 350. In fact, works are mentioned that have not come down to us, such as his translation of Kings and his translation of the Minor Prophets, which are attested in several Genizah fragments as "*tafsīr trey ʿasar lil-fayūmī*"; see Allony, *The Jewish Library*, 109, 279.

[11] Ratzaby, *Saadia's Translation and Commentary on Isaiah*, 8.

[12] Schlossberg, "The Spiritual Leadership," 222.

[13] Blau and Hopkins, "Ancient Bible Translations," 4.

[14] Avishur, *A Medieval Translation*, 15.

[15] Avishur, *A Medieval Translation*, 15–18; cf. Avishur, *The Oldest Translation*, 13–16.

[16] Allony, *Studies in Medieval Philology*, 27–72.

[17] Ratzaby, *Saadia's Translation and Commentary on Isaiah*, 181.

[18] Ratzaby, *Saadia's Translation and Commentary on Isaiah*, 283.

dia's original Arabic translation of various words and expressions of the Bible as a whole, as well as of those Prophetic Books of which no systematic translation of his is known or has come down to us. The third way is by compiling quotations from the Judeo-Arabic works of other medieval Bible commentators who refer to Saadia's exegetical works. Rabbi Avraham ben Shlomo (fourteenth–fifteenth centuries) who wrote Judeo-Arabic commentaries on the Former and Latter Prophets often quotes Saadia, while mentioning his name. His commentary on the Former Prophets has been compiled by Kafiḥ,[19] and his commentaries on the books of Joel and Obadiah have been complied by Schlossberg.[20] Nevertheless, Rabbi Abraham ben Shelomo tends to mention (and summarize) Saadia's comments without referring to his actual translations. Yet we do find references to single words that the Gaon likely translated in the same way. One example is the form מְרִיא "fatling" (2 Sam 6:13), on which Abraham ben Shlomo comments: פסר פיה רבי סעדיה ז"ל גאמוס "The late Rabbi Saadia rendered (Hebrew) meri by (Arabic) jāmūs 'buffalo'."[21] He also mentions Saadia eleven times in his commentary on Joshua and Judges, yet in these books he refers to an interpretive notion of the Gaon and not to specific translations.[22]

Another commentator who mentions Saadia in his writings, but in a more limited way, is Rabbi Abraham Ibn Ezra (1091/2–1167). In his commentary on Amos 5:22 he writes regarding the words וְשֶׁלֶם מְרִיאֵיכֶם ("the offerings of well-being of your fatted animals" *NRSV): "And it is not an independent species, as mentioned by the late Rabbi Saadia. He said that its fat is allowed, and interpreted it (ופרש בו) in the language of Ishmael 'jāmūs,' and it is not so in these places, and it is bigger than the bull (שור) yet resembles it."[23] In this manner, we can glean from the commentaries of Rabbi Abraham Ben Shelomo and Rabbi Abraham Ibn Ezra how Saadia translates single words in the Prophetic Books, as well as from Saadia's extant translations, where he also refers, at times, to the rendering of individual expressions from these books. Nonetheless, several issues still remain: Firstly, there is no direct proof that Saadia composed proper translations of these books. Secondly, references of the kind that have been mentioned usually reflect Saadia's commentary. Thirdly, Ibn Ezra mentions Saadia only six times in his commentary on the Minor Prophets, whereas in his commentary on Daniel he mentions him twelve times. This proportion may suggest that Saadia did not compose a systematic translation and commentary on the Minor Prophets.[24]

Several scores of anonymous translation fragments of the three books (Isaiah, Jeremiah, Ezekiel) have been identified in the Cairo Genizah Arabic and Judeo-Arabic collections.[25] It is possible that more exist and have not yet been identified. Usually, these Genizah fragments represent ad hoc translations, sometimes in popular style and sometimes more akin to Saadia's translation methodology.

Sporadic Arabic Bible translations are also found in the works of later Rabbanite commentators who wrote in Judeo-Arabic, among them: Rabbi Judah Ibn Bilam (Spain, eleventh century), whose commentaries on Joshua, Judges, Isaiah, Jeremiah, Ezekiel, and the Minor Prophets have been published by Poznanski and Perez,[26] and Rabbi Tanhum Ben Joseph Ha-Yerushalmi (Egypt, thirteenth

---

[19] Kafiḥ, *Perūsh Nevi'īm: Yehoshua-Shoftim*; Kafiḥ, *Perūsh Nevi'īm: I Shemuel*; Kafiḥ, *Perūsh Nevi'īm: II Shemuel*.

[20] Schlossberg, *The Commentary of R. Avraham b. Shlomo*; Schlossberg, "Rabbi Avraham Ben Shlomo."

[21] Kafiḥ, *Nevi'īm: II Shemuel*, 50. *Jāmūs* refers to a species of buffalo that existed up to the early twentieth century around the sea of Galilee and in the Hullah area. Yet since the drying of the Hullash it has not been spotted any more.

[22] See the list of references in Kafiḥ, *Perūsh Nevi'īm: Yehoshua-Shoftim*, 3.

[23] Simon, *Abraham Ibn Ezra*, 222.

[24] This argument may be countered by the fact that Ibn Ezra also rarely mentions Saadia in his commentary on Job (only six times), and does not mention him at all in his commentary on Ruth, although we know for a fact that Saadia composed translations and commentaries to these books.

[25] See the indices in Baker and Polliack, *Arabic and Judaeo-Arabic Manuscripts*; Shivtiel and Niessen, *Arabic and Judaeo-Arabic Manuscripts*.

[26] See all the editions in the bibliography (Poznanski and Perez).

century). Tanhum wrote a Judeo-Arabic commentary on the entire Hebrew Bible, yet only parts of it are extant, including Joshua and fragments of Judges, Samuel, and Kings. His commentary on the Minor Prophets has been published by Shy.[27]

6–9.1.8.2 Medieval Karaite Translations

Among the Karaite Jews, Yefet ben ʿEli's translations and commentaries on the Former and Latter Prophets have all survived in manuscript sources (→ 1.3.6.3.2). This prolific thinker composed an Arabic version of the entire Hebrew Bible, accompanied by a systematic Arabic commentary throughout the second half of the tenth century, in which he also synthesized other compositions of the Karaite school.[28] So far, only a limited number of his works on the Prophets have been edited or published, including: Joshua (Robinson), Isaiah 54 (Alobaidi), Jeremiah (Sabih), Hosea (Birnbaum, Polliack and Schlossberg), Amos (Nadler-Akirav), Obadiah (Polliack and Schlossberg, Zoran), Nahum (Hirschfeld). Currently, Yefet's works on the books of Samuel (Robinson), Zephaniah (Polliack and Schlossberg), Jonah, Haggai (Nadler-Akirav), Zechariah, and Malachi are under preparation.[29]

In his translation, Yefet tries to follow the biblical text literally; he preserves the original word order of the Hebrew verse in translation even when it contradicts the rules of Arabic grammar. He also frequently uses the forms of the Arabic participle and infinitive in order to emulate biblical Hebrew style.[30] Nevertheless, since the clarification of the meaning of the Hebrew source text was the primary objective of his translation enterprise, Yefet also employed additions, omissions, and alterations in his Arabic translated text.[31] In the rendering of Hebrew lexemes, Yefet tends to apply equal etymology in Arabic, namely, words that have cognate or close roots in Hebrew and Arabic and share a similarity in sound and form. Yet, he does so carefully, not as an automatic measure, in order to avoid the distortion of what he perceives as the original meaning of the biblical text.[32]

An anonymous Karaite translation of the book of Hosea was found in the Cairo Genizah and published by Niessen.[33] It seems to have been part of a larger manuscript that contained a translation of all of the books of the Minor Prophets (subsequently a piece from Joel was also identified by Niessen). The translation is usually literal with some added elements in the body of the translation.[34] Sporadic Arabic translations from the Prophetic Books are also found in the Hebrew commentary on the Minor Prophets composed by the ninth-century Karaite exegete Daniel Al-Qūmisī, when he attempts to define the exact meaning of a rare Hebrew word.[35]

6–9.1.8.3 Rabbanite and Karaite Translations from the Fourteenth to the Sixteenth Centuries

Parts of an anonymous translation of the Former and Latter Prophets, whose authorship is under debate, have been compiled and edited by Yitzhak Avishur, and published in three volumes.[36] The translation of the Former Prophets is fully extant, and from its introduction we can learn that it was copied in 1354 in northern Iraq.[37] Apart from Yefet ben ʿEli's versions, this is the oldest continuous translation of the books of Joshua–Kings that has come down to us. The translation of the Latter

---

[27] See Shy, *Tanhum* and cf. her survey of his works in her introduction: pp. 12–13.

[28] For further information on the Karaite translation enterprise, see → 1.3.6.

[29] Detailed information on these editions is provided in the bibliography of this article.

[30] For more information, see Polliack, *The Karaite Tradition*, 164–69 (regarding word order); 121–28 (regarding the use of participle and infinitive).

[31] Polliack, *The Karaite Tradition*, 212–29.

[32] Polliack, *The Karaite Tradition*, 221; Polliack, "Medieval Karaite Methods," 382; cf. Ratzaby, *A Dictionary*, 34.

[33] Niessen, "Anonymous Karaite Commentary."

[34] Niessen, "Anonymous Karaite Commentary," 77–82; Polliack and Schlossberg, *Yefet Ben ʿEli's Commentary*, 83–84.

[35] Markon, *Commentarius*.

[36] Avishur, *The Oldest Translation of the Early Prophets into Judeo-Arabic*; Avishur, *A Medieval Translation of the Latter Prophets into Iraqi and Syrian Judeo-Arabic*.

[37] Avishur, *The Oldest Translation*, 9, 13.

Prophets contains parts of Isaiah and Jeremiah,[38] Ezekiel and the Minor Prophets.[39] A detailed study of the Minor Prophets version has revealed that it is identical to Yefet ben 'Eli's translation.[40] This is not the case, however, with regard to the versions of Isaiah and Jeremiah. In the anonymous translation of Isa 35:9, for instance, Saadia is quoted by name (and referred to as "our Rabbi") in a manner untypical of Karaite sources: ופסר רבנו סעדיהו "and the book of our Rabbi Saadja."[41] A comparison of a number of random verses from the anonymous translation of Jeremiah and Yefet's version also shows considerable disparity, and so rules out the possibility that it originated with him.[42]

Translations of the Former and Latter Prophets are also attested in the sixteenth *sharḥ* by the Rabbanite commentator Rabbi Issāchār ben-Sūsān ha-Ma'arāvī, who was born in the city of Fez, Morocco and moved to Safed at a young age.[43] Ben-Sūsān proclaimed the need for an updated Bible version in comprehensible Arabic that could serve the Jews of Arab lands who had lost touch over time with Saadia's "high" (classical) Judeo-Arabic versions.[44] His *sharḥ* contains a translation and commentary on the entire Bible, including the Former and Latter Prophets. The books are translated verse by verse in a literal fashion with a commentary following each verse. Then follows a section called *bayān* "clarification," which contains the explanations of difficult words that were mentioned in the translation and commentary sections. Ben Sūsān wrote two introductions to the translation, one in Arabic and one in Hebrew, in which he reviewed Saadia's Arabic Bible translation methods and explained his own motivation for composing a new version.[45] In the introduction, Ben Sūsān emphasizes his literal methodology, which follows strictly the original Hebrew text for the purpose of improving the Jewish public's understanding of the Hebrew Bible. His goal was clearly didactic, in that every Arabic speaker was meant to be able to read his *sharḥ* and then follow up on the meaning of difficult words in the *bayān*.[46]

6–9.1.8.4 Translations in the Works of Rabbanite and Karaite Lexicographers

To date, no other Arabic translations of the Former and Latter Prophets are known from Jewish sources. Nevertheless, we can learn about translations of single words through the works of the great medieval grammarians and lexicographers. For example, Rabbi Judah Ben Hayyūj (ca. 945–1012) composed four works including *Kitāb al-Nutaf* "The Book of Compilations," which discusses grammatical issues in the Prophetic Books.[47] Rabbi Jonah Ibn Janāḥ (eleventh century) composed two seminal works on biblical Hebrew grammar, *Kitab A-Luma'* "The Book of Embroidery" and lexicon *Kitāb al-Uṣūl* "The Book of Roots," which contain Arabic translations of single words from the Prophetic Books. The great Karaite lexicographer and exegete David Ben Abraham al-Fāsī (Jerusalem, late tenth century) composed the first biblical dictionary entitled *Kitāb Jāmi' al-Alfāẓ*. It is arranged alphabetically (though not according to the triliteral root system). Each biblical word is provided with several denotations in Arabic translation equivalents.[48]

In summary: Jewish Arabic translations of the Former and Latter Prophets are available to us in

---

[38] Avishur, *A Medieval Translation* (1998).

[39] Avishur, *A Medieval Translation* (2000).

[40] See Schlossberg, "Book Review." For Avishur's response, see "Rabbinic and Karaite." A further comparison between the anonymous translation and Yefet Ben 'Eli's translation of Hosea, Amos, Haggai, Obadiah, and Zephaniah reveals without doubt that the translation that Avishur edited contains Yefet's version to the Minor Prophets, which was also used among non-Karaite Jews.

[41] Avishur, *A Medieval Translation* (2000), 17, 80.

[42] The comparison in based on the versions in the editions of Sabih, *Japhet*; Wendkos, *The Arabic Commentary*.

[43] Doron, "Ben-Sūsān."

[44] Doron, "From the Tafsir," 169–70.

[45] Avishur points out the great similarities between Ben Susan's and Saadia's translations, and claims that the independence of Ben Susan's translations is recognized in the translations of the sections in which he did not have Saadia's translations and commentaries (Avishur, "The Adaptation," 188).

[46] Doron, "On the Arabic Translation"; Doron, "From the Tafsir," 169–70.

[47] Basal, *Kitab Al-Nutaf*.

[48] See the introduction to Skoss, *Kitāb Jāmi' al-Alfāẓ*, Vol. 1, xxxii–xxxiii; cf. Maman, "The Lexical Element," 119–24; Tauber, "Ha-mekorot," 369–71.

limited numbers.[49] It is likely that more material was produced over the medieval and pre-modern periods than is known to us today. Nevertheless, since these books were less central to Jewish synagogue worship than the Torah they are less represented in Rabbanite sources, apart from the partial translation of Saadia Gaon (tenth century) and the full translation of Rabbi Issāchār ben-Sūsān ha-Maʿarāvī (sixteenth century). The Karaite emphasis on the return to Jewish Scripture encouraged their systematic translation into Arabic and hence we find the largest representation of medieval Arabic versions of these books in the works of Yefet ben ʿEli (tenth century).

Allony, N., "MeTargūm Saadia LiYeḥezkel," *Tarbiz* 16 (1944): 21–27 [Hebr.].

Allony, N., *Studies in Medieval Philology and Literature: Collected Papers*, Vol. 1: *Saadia's Works* (Jerusalem: Yad Ben-Zvi, 1986) [Hebr.].

Allony, N., *The Jewish Library in the Middle Ages: Book Lists from the Cairo Genizah* (eds. M. Frenkel and H. Ben-Shammai; Jerusalem: Ben-Zvi Institute, 2006) [Hebr.].

Alobaidi, J.J., *The Messiah in Isaiah 53: The Commentaries of Saadia Gaon, Salmon ben Yeruham and Yefet ben ʿEli on Is. 52:13–53:12: Edition and Translation* (La Bible dans l' histoire 2; Bern: Peter Lang, 1998).

Avishur, Y., *The Oldest Translation of the Former Prophets into Judeo-Arabic: The Text of Bodleian Manuscript Poc. 349 with an Introduction and Notes* (Jerusalem: Magnes Press, 1995) [Hebr.].

Avishur, Y., *A Medieval Translation of the Latter Prophets into Iraqi and Syrian Judeo-Arabic*, Vol. 1: *Isaiah and Jeremiah: The Text of Bodleian Manuscript Hunt. 206 with Introduction and Notes* (Jerusalem: Magnes Press, 1998) [Hebr.].

Avishur, Y., *A Medieval Translation of the Latter Prophets into Iraqi and Syrian Judeo-Arabic*, Vol. 2: *Ezekiel and the Minor Prophets: The Text of Bodleian Manuscript Hunt. 206 with Introduction and Notes* (Tel Aviv-Jaffa, 2000) [Hebr.].

Avishur, Y., "The Adaptation of R. Saadia Gaon's Bible Translation in the East," *Sefunot* 20 (2000): 181–202 [Hebr.].

Avishur, Y., "Rabbinic and Karaite Judeo-Arabic Biblical Translation," *Beyn ʿEver La-ʿArav* 2 (2001): 191–200 [Hebr.].

Baker, C.F. and M. Polliack, *Arabic and Judaeo-Arabic Manuscripts in the Cambridge Genizah Collections: Arabic Old Series (T-S Ar.1a-54)* (Cambridge: Cambridge University Press, 2001).

Basal, N., *Kitab Al-Nutaf by Judah Ḥayyuji: A Critical Edition* (Tel Aviv: Tel Aviv University Press, 2001) [Hebr.].

Bassal, I., "Former Prophets in Judeo-Arabic and in Christian-Arabic from the Fourteenth Century: The Common and the Diverse," *Beyn ʿEver La-ʾArav* 2 (2001): 123–38 [Hebr.].

Birnbaum, P., *The Arabic Commentary of Yefet Ben ʾAli the Karaite on the Book of Hosea* (Philadelphia: Dropsie College, 1942).

Blau, J. and S. Hopkins, "Ancient Bible Translations to Judeo-Arabic," *Peʿamim* 83 (2000): 4–14 [Hebr.].

Derenburg, J. and H. Derenbourg (eds.), *Œuvre Completes de R. Saadia ben Joseph Al-Fayyoûmi: Version Arabe d' Isaie* (Paris: E. Leroux, 1896).

Doron, D., "On the Arabic Translation of the Torah by Issachar Ben-Susan Hammaʾaravi," *Sefunot* 18 (1985): 280–98 [Hebr.].

Doron, D., "From the Tafsir of R. Saadia Gaon to the Translation of R. Mordechai Hai Dayyan of Tunis," *Sefunot* 20 (1991): 171–80 [Hebr.].

Doron, D., "Ben-Sūsān, Issachar ben Mordechai," in *Encyclopedia of Jews of the Islamic World* (ed. N. Stillman; Leiden: Brill, 2010) 1:394–95.

Hirschfeld, H., *Jefeth b. Ali's Arabic Commentary on Nahum with Introduction: Abridged Translation and Notes* (London: University Press, 1911).

Kafiḥ, J. (ed.), *Perūsh Neviʾīm LeRav Abraham ben Shelomo: I Shemuel: With Translation and Commentary* (Kiryat-Ono: Makhon Mosheh le-Ḥeker Mishnat ha-Rambam, 2000) [Hebr.].

Kafiḥ, J. (ed.), *Perūsh Neviʾīm LeRav Abraham ben Shelomo: II Shemuel: With Translation and Commentary by J. Kafiḥ* (Kiryat-Ono: Makhon Mosheh le-Ḥeker Mishnat ha-Rambam, 2002) [Hebr.].

Kafiḥ, J. (ed.), *Perūsh Neviʾīm LeRav Abraham ben Shelomo: I Melakhim: With Translation and Commentary by J. Kafiḥ* (Kiryat-Ono: Makhon Mosheh le-Ḥeker Mishnat ha-Rambam, 2006) [Hebr.].

Kafiḥ, J. (ed.), *Perūsh Neviʾīm LeRav Abraham ben Shelomo: Yehoshua-Shoftim: With Translation and Commentary by J. Kafiḥ* (Kiryat-Ono: Makhon Mosheh le-Ḥeker Mishnat ha-Rambam, 2009) [Hebr.].

---

[49] This is in contrast to the number of translations available in Christian Arabic manuscript sources (see → 1.4.11.) and cf. Bassal, "Early Prophets," 123–38.

Maman, A., "The Lexical Element in David Alfasi's Dictionary Definitions," in *Genizah Research after Ninety Years: The Case of Judaeo-Arabic* (eds. J. Blau and S.C. Reif; Cambridge: Cambridge University Press, 1992), 119–25.

Markon, I.D., *Commentarius in librum duodecim prophetarum quem composuit Daniel al-Kumissi* (Jerusalem: Mekize Nirdamim, 1957).

Nadler-Akirav, M., "The Arabic Commentary of Yefet Ben 'Ali the Karaite on the Book of Amos: A Critical Edition to Chapters 1–4, Introduction and Notes" (PhD diss., Bar-Ilan University, 2009) [Hebr.].

Niessen, F., "An Anonymous Karaite Commentary on the Book of Hosea," in *Exegesis and Grammar in Medieval Karaite Texts* (ed. G. Khan; JSSSup 13; Oxford: Oxford University Press, 2001), 77–126.

Perez, M. (ed.), *R. Judah Ibn Bal'am's Commentary on Isaiah* (Sources and Studies 5; Ramat-Gan: Bar-Ilan University Press, 1992).

Perez, M. (ed.), *R. Judah Ibn Bal'am's Commentary on Ezekiel* (Sources and Studies 7; Ramat-Gan: Bar-Ilan University press, 2000).

Perez, M. (ed.), *R. Judah Ibn Bal'am's Commentary on Jeremiah* (Sources and Studies 8; Ramat-Gan: Bar-Ilan University Press, 2000).

Polliack, M., *The Karaite Tradition of Arabic Bible Translation: A Linguistic and Exegetical Study of Karaite Translations of the Pentateuch from the Tenth and Eleventh Centuries CE* (Études sur le judaïsme médiéval 17; Leiden: Brill, 1997).

Polliack, M., "Medieval Karaite Methods of Translating Biblical Narrative into Arabic," *VT* 48 (1998): 375–98.

Polliack, M., "Karaite Translation Techniques in the Arabic Rendering of Biblical Narrative according to Genesis 2:15–25," in *Studies in Bible and Exegesis*, Vol. VI (eds. R. Kasher and M. Zipor; Ramat-Gan: Bar-Ilan University Press, 2002), 217–34 [Hebr.].

Polliack, M. and S. Schlossberg, *Yefet Ben 'Eli's Commentary on Hosea: Annotated Edition, Hebrew Translation and Introduction* (Ramat-Gan: Bar-Ilan University Press, 2009) [Hebr.].

Polliack, M. and S. Somekh, "The Hebrew-Arabic Biblical Glossaries from the Cairo Geniza," *Pe'amim* 83 (2000): 15–47 [Hebr.].

Poznanski, S. (ed.), *Judah Ibn Bal'am's Commentary on Joshua* (Berlin: Kauffmann, 1903) [Hebr.].

Poznanski, S. (ed.), *Judah Ibn Bal'am's Commentary on Judges* (Frankfurt: Kauffmann, 1905).

Poznanski, S. (ed.), "The Arabic Commentary of Abu Zakariya Yaḥya (Judah ben Samuel) ibn Bal'am on the Twelve Minor Prophets," *JQR* 15 (1924–1925): 1–53.

Ratzaby, Y., "Seridīm MeTargūm Aravī LeNevi'īm Ri'shonim MeBeit Midrasho shel Sa'adia," *Sinai* 25 (1949): 168–78 [Hebr.].

Ratzaby, Y., "Selections from Rav Saadia's Commentary on Lamentations," *Bar-Ilan* 20–21 (1983): 349–81 [Hebr.].

Ratzaby, Y., *A Dictionary of Judeo-Arabic in R. Saadia's Tafsir* (Ramat-Gan: Bar-Ilan University Press, 1985) [Hebr.].

Ratzaby, Y. (ed.), *Saadia's Translation and Commentary on Isaiah: Collected, Edited with Translation and Notes* (Kiriat Ono: Makhon Mosheh le-Ḥeker Mishnat ha-Rambam, 1993) [Hebr.].

Robinson, J.T., *The Arabic Translation and Commentary of Yefet ben 'Eli the Karaite on the Book of Joshua* (Études sur le judaïsme médiéval 64; Leiden: Brill, 2015).

Sabih, J.A., *Japhet ben Ali's Book of Jeremiah: A Critical Edition and Linguistic Analysis of the Judaeo-Arabic Translation* (London: Equinox, 2009).

Schlossberg, E., "Book Review: An Ancient Targum of the Later Prophets into Judeo Arabic," *Pe'amim* 83 (2000): 147–58 [Hebr.].

Schlossberg, E., "Rabbi Avraham Ben Shlomo's Midrash al-Sayyani on the Book of Joel," *Hebrew Language and Jewish Studies* (2001): 209–30 [Hebr.].

Schlossberg, E., "The Commentary of R. Avraham b. Shlomo the Yemenite on the Book of Obadiah: With Notes and Introduction," in *Teshurah Le-'Amos: Collected Studies in Biblical Exegesis Presented by 'Amos Hakham* (eds. M. Bar-Asher, N. Ḥaham, and Y. Ofer; Alon Shevut: Tvonot, 2007), 235–57 [Hebr.].

Schlossberg, E., "The Spiritual Leadership and Administration of Harav Saadia Gaon," *Amadot* 5 (2013): 213–42 [Hebr.].

Shivtiel, A. and F. Niessen, *Arabic and Judaeo-Arabic Manuscripts in the Cambridge Genizah Collections: Taylor-Schechter New Series* (Cambridge: Cambridge University Press, 2006).

Shy, H., *Tanhum Ha-Yerushalmi's Commentary on the Minor Prophets: A Critical Edition with an Introduction, Translated into Hebrew and Annotated* (Jerusalem: Magnes Press, 1991) [Hebr.].

Simon, U., *Abraham Ibn Ezra's Two Commentaries on the Minor Prophets* (Ramat-Gan: Bar-Ilan University Press, 1989) [Hebr.].

Skoss, S.L., *Kitab Jami' Al-Alfaz of David Ben Abraham Al-*

Fasi (2 vols.; New Haven: Yale University Press, 1936–1945).

Tauber, E., "Ha-mekorot ha-rabbani'im le-perusho shel ha-kara'I Al-Fāsī la-tora," in *Haim M.I. Gevaryahu Memorial Volume: Mehkarim ba-mikra we-be-maḥ-shevet yisrael* (ed. J. Alder; Jerusalem: Kiryat Sefer, 1988), 367–78 [Hebr.].

Tobi, Y., "Pre-Saadianic Arabic Translation of the Pentateuch," *Massorot* 7 (1993): 87–127 [Hebr.].

Wendkos, P.D., "The Arabic Commentary of Yefet b. Ali the Karaite on the Book of Jeremiah: 150 Folios Edited from Three Mss with Critical Notes" (unpubl. PhD diss., Dropsie College, 1969).

Zoran, Y., "The Commentary of the Karaite Japheth Ben Eli on the Book of Obadiah: An Annotated Scientific Edition," *Ginzei Qedem* 8 (2012): 129–95 [Hebr.].

Meira Polliack
Meirav Nadler-Akirav

6–9.2 Secondary Translations

6–9.2.1 Vetus Latina

Compared with other parts of the Bible, the latter prophets are relatively well attested. Fragments of Isaiah may be found in mss VL[177 179 181 183 192]; Jeremiah is attested by VL[174 177 178 180 181 183–188]; Ezekiel survives in VL[175 176 177 182]; and the Minor Prophets occur in VL[173 175 176 177].[1]

6–9.2.1.1 Isaiah

The Vulgate (→ 6–9.1.7) quickly displaced VL-Isa, and the VL text is preserved only in manuscript VL[177] (Würzburg Palimpsest), which contains the remains of a fifth-century C.E. copy that includes Isa 29:1–30:6 and 45:20–46:11, and in manuscript VL[192] with text of Isa 1:18–23, 26–31 and 5:24–27. The liturgical tradition, more conservative than manuscript transmission, has preserved passages of Isa 1:16–20 and 49:22–23 (VL[31]); 53:1–2 (VL[108]); 4:1–6+5:1–7 (VL[111]); 27:11–13 and 33:9–19 (VL[181]); 54:1–10 (VL[183]). Lectionaries contain Isa 25:1; 26:11; 28:5; 35:1.2.10; 41:18; 52:13; 12:3–5.[2] From the fifth century C.E. onwards, numerous psalters that better resisted Vulgate penetration continued to transmit in an appendix a series of songs from the book of Isaiah. Thus, VL[300] contains the "Song of the Vineyard" in three forms: long (Isa 5:1–19), short (Isa 5:1–7), and abridged (Isa 5:1, 2, 7). Mozarabic psalters (VL[414, 415, 419]; → 10.4.8) contain Isa 26:1–9a and the more popular passage Isa 29:9b–20.[3] Other songs preserved include Isa 38:10–20; Isaiah 61 (partly VL), and Isa 66:10–16. Further, series A of *capitula* of Isaiah, formed in a Donatist milieu, builds upon an African VL text.

The most abundant documentation is indirect in the form of about 17,000 patristic quotations (→ 21.8), but they do not constitute a balanced representation of the whole book. There are merely a few verses that are not attested in at least one quotation. Citations from the "Book of Emmanuel" and from the poems of the Suffering Servant are more frequent. On the other hand, quotations from the oracles against the nations are scant. Finally, Jerome's commentary *In Esaiam* contains numerous VL readings.

VL-Isa has been masterfully edited by Gryson.[4] The analysis of citations allows the identification of several types of VL text. The type marked with the siglum X represents the VL text that circulated at the end of the second and beginning of the third centuries C.E. It transmits mostly Tertulian's text as well as other citations from those centuries, which appear mostly in ancient versions of the Apostolic Fathers and in the first treatises *Adversus Iudaeos*.

The African type (K) corresponds to the text attested by Cyprian and, in a more developed form, Lactantius. It represents the VL text that circulated in North Africa around the mid-third century C.E. The text of Cyprian's quotations in *Ad Quirinum* is very close to the Greek (→ 6.3), so the translation seems very verbal. Each Greek word is translated as much as possible by a Latin analogue; the word-order is a faithful calque of the Greek. In Isa 14:15 (MT אֶל־שְׁאוֹל "to Sheol"), Cyprian attests the ancient translation εἰς ᾅδου "to Hades" as *ad inferos* "to hell," against the more recent and less African translation transmitted by Rufinus *in infernum* "into hell."[5] A revised form of this African text (C) appears in African authors of the fourth and fifth centuries C.E., especially amongst Donatists.

The European texts (E) have their origin in a deeper revision than the former. Novatianus' testimony is a starting point and it is followed by Lucifer of Cagliari and Hilarius. It is not possible to speak of a single European text, because European recensions constitute a vast and dynamic

---

[1] See Gryson, *Altlateinische Handschriften 1*, 65–317.
[2] Leningrad, Publ. Bibl. Q. v. I. 16, of the eighth-ninth century C.E.; Mainz, Domschatz 972 of the tenth century; cf. R. Gryson, *Esaias* (Vetus Latina, 12), 11, n. 9.
[3] Haelewyck, "Le cantique de la vigne," 257–79.

[4] Gryson, *Esaias 1–39*; Gryson, *Esaias 40–66*.
[5] Gryson and Auwers, "L'histoire du texte latin d'Isaïe au miroir du cantique d'Ézéchias," 458 n. 61.

construct. They are marked by a varied language, based most of the time on forms of the Greek text. Given the scarcity of European witnesses of the fourth century C.E., it is almost impossible to determine accurately in what period the revision that gave rise to this text type took place; it could, nevertheless, go back to a pretty early moment. There are two forms: D, attested by the earlier authors and further away from Rome, particularly Lucifer of Cagliari (died 371 C.E.) and by Hilarius of Poitiers (died 367 C.E.); I, familiar to Jerome and the authors of the fifth century C.E. The text of Augustine's quotations (A) at times is closer to the African text and at times more closely proximates the European.

The siglum O indicates the Latin translation of LXX that Jerome reproduces as the second lemma (the Vulgate is the first) in his commentary to Isaiah. As the commentary advances, Jerome seems to follow more closely the LXX text (→ 6.3), against his own translation (→ 6–9.1.7), which reflects the *veritas hebraica*. In Isa 1:4, Jerome's commentary attests the ancient translation *semen pessimum* "very bad offspring." This is a good example of the VL tendency to render with the superlative ("very bad") the basic form of Greek adjectives (σπέρμα πονηρόν "evil offspring" *NETS); Jerome's translation renders according to the Hebrew *semen nequam* ("wicked offspring," MT זֶרַע מְרֵעִים "offspring who do evil") (*Commentary on Isaiah* 1,6.)[6] The O type differs in many places from VL, which Jerome used in the development of his commentary. Thus, Jerome's *In Esaiam* is reproducing at least three different text types: two in the *lemma* (the Vulgate and a Latin translation of LXX) and a third one of the European kind in the commentary itself. Finally, R indicates the text of Lucifer and S the Spanish text type.[7]

Jerome's version *iuxta Hebraeos* (→ 6–9.1.7) stands closer to Greek translations than what is generally assumed. The text of Isaiah used by Christians both in the West and the East was a sort of middle ground, mixed in different measure according to time and place, between the LXX version (→ 6.3) and a pre-Masoretic text (→ 6.2.2) read through Hexaplaric translations (→ 6–9.1.5).

In the exegesis of Isaiah there are passages of great importance, such as the prophet's first vision (Isaiah 6) and the prophecy of Emmanuel (Isa 7:10–17). In Isa 6:2, it is remarkable that the Latin fathers interpret the words "his face" or "his feet" in reference to God. In Isa 7:9, the expression often quoted by Augustine *nisi credideritis non intellegetis* "if you do not believe you will not understand"[8] follows the Greek version καὶ ἐὰν μὴ πιστεύσητε, οὐδὲ μὴ συνῆτε, which is different from MT and the Vulgate: אִם לֹא תַאֲמִינוּ כִּי לֹא תֵאָמֵנוּ/*si non credideritis non permanebitis* "if you do not believe, you will not endure."

6–9.2.1.2 Jeremiah

Direct witnesses of importance or with significant pieces of text are scant: *Wirceburgensis* (VL177) and some sheets of *Sangallensis* (VL180). VL indicates that the best Greek codices, including *Vaticanus* (LXX[B]), were revised in a quite early period according to the Hebrew of the Masoretic tradition (→ 7.3). In the VL tradition, the book of Baruch is attached to Jeremiah (→ 11.2.1.4). With the diffusion of Jerome's version, VL of Baruch was marginalized and only remnants of it remain in Christian liturgy and literature.

On the whole, VL-Jer attests often to a Jeremiah text that is even briefer than that preserved in LXX-Jer (→ 7.3) and MT-Jer (→ 7.2.2). Thus, VL-Jer points to a stage in the textual transmission of LXX-Jer prior to any Greek Jeremiah text preserved in the manuscript evidence. It is therefore an important witness for the reconstruction of OG-Jer.

VL-Jer (*Wirceburgensis*) does not contain Jer 39(46):1–2, which were not part of OG-Jer, as they are marked with an asterisk. LXX-Jer also omits vv. 4–13 of that chapter. It is meaningful that the Hebrew of this added passage is markedly late

---

[6] Gryson and Auwers, "L'histoire du texte latin d'Isaïe au miroir du cantique d'Ézéchias," 471 n. 67.

[7] Gryson, *Esaias 40–66*, 1649–68: "Conclusion: Histoire du texte"; Haelewyck, "Les premières versions latines de la Bible," 123–25.

[8] Augustine, *De Trinitate* 7, 6, 12 (PL 42, VIII:944).

when compared to the rest of the book.⁹ VL attests a very brief text for Jer 39(46):1–14:

> Jer 38(45):28 And Jeremiah remained in the court of the prison until the day that Jerusalem was taken. Jer 39(46):3 And all the officials of the king of Babylon came and [names of the officials] and all the officials of the king of Babylon sat in the middle gate. 14 And they sent to take Jeremiah from the court of the prison and they entrusted him to Gedaliah son of Ahikam son of Shaphan and they brought him to Tafret (VL *in iafret*) and he stood in the middle of his people.

According to VL-Jer, the story is interested only in what happened to Jeremiah at the time of the fall of Jerusalem. The long MT text describes the fall of Jerusalem with details taken from 2 Kings 25 and attributes the prophet's liberation to Nebuchadnezzar. Thus, VL, on its own or together with other isolated witnesses, at times allows us to go back to an early form of the Hebrew text. In Jeremiah 52, three successive editions of the Hebrew text may be identified: The first edition is represented by the very brief text of Jer 52:12–13 preserved at the beginning of the book of Baruch, which in LXX-Jer and VL-Jer constitutes a unit together with Jeremiah. The second edition is attested by the brief LXX text, which is followed by the rest of the VL testimony. The third edition can be found in the long MT text.¹⁰ They differ in their varied ways of treating the deportations and the destiny of the holy vessels of the temple: The first edition, lacking Jer 52:15, 27b, 28–30, presents only Jehoiaquin's deportation and does not mention the sacking of the temple furnishings. The second edition only mentions Zedekiah's deportation and gives an inventory of the sacred objects taken from the temple. The third edition indicates three deportations: Zedekiah's (v. 11); that of the population of Jerusalem (v. 15); and the deportation of Judah (v. 27b). These deportations are summarized in vv. 28–30. MT also gives a detailed presentation of the deportation of the sacred vessels (vv. 17–23).

In Jer 10:2–10, VL-Jer confirms the short text of LXX and the Hebrew attested by 4QJer^b (→ 7.2.1.3; → 7.2.3.1).¹¹ The joint evidence of VL and LXX allows us to identify the textual development from a short form, according to which the house of Israel should not fear the idols that heathens are afraid of:

> 2 Thus says the Lord: according to the ways of the nations do not go (*ne ambulaueritis*),¹² and of the signs of the sky do not be afraid, because they fear their faces, 3 because the laws of nations are vain.
> It is a tree cut from the forest, the work of craftsmen and molten metal, 4 with silver and gold they are embellished; with hammers and nails they have been fixed – they shall not move. 5a They are of beaten silver – they shall not walk. 9 Silver is brought from Tarsis and gold from Uphaz, and the hands of the goldsmith. All are the work of the artisan. Their clothing is blue and purple. 5b They have to be carried, – for they shall not march
> Do not be afraid of them, for they cannot do evil, nor it is in them to do good.

The structure of the unit is clear: between the expressions "Do not be afraid of them" there are descriptions of the idols made of wood, metal, and cloth, with reference to each material closed by a variant of the same refrain: "they shall not move ... they shall not walk ... they shall not march." The long MT text follows a different order and inserts several doxological additions in the central section (vv. 6–8) and end (v. 10) of the unit. The structure becomes more complex and the content enriched. The oracle is no longer focused on the idolatry of the nations but on the King of nations.¹³

---

⁹ J. Joosten, "L' excédent massorétique du livre de Jérémie"; Stipp, "Zur aktuellen Diskussion um das Verhältnis der Textformen des Jeremiabuches."

¹⁰ Bogaert, "Relecture et déplacement de l' oracle contre les Philistins."

¹¹ The VL text has been edited by F. Dolbeau, "Nouveaux sermons de saint Augustin pour la conversion des païens et des donatistes," *REAug* 37 (1991): 37–78, esp. 49–51.

¹² The Old Latin reading *ambulaueritis* translates the Greek πορεύεσθε, which represents the Old Greek text. The reading chosen in J. Ziegler's edition, μανθάνετε, follows MT *tilmādû* (J. Ziegler, *Ieremias, Baruch, Threni, Epistula Ieremiae* [2nd ed.; Septuaginta Vetus Testamentum Graecum 15; Göttingen: Vandenhoeck & Ruprecht, 1957], 199).

¹³ Bogaert, "Le livre de Jérémie en perspective."

6–9.2.1.3 Ezekiel

VL-Ezek is extant in several manuscripts and other witnesses.[14] They cover large sections of Ezekiel 7–48: *Codex Wirceburgensis* (VL[177], sixth century C.E.): Ezek 24:4–21; 26:10–27:4; 34:16–35:5; 38:8–20; 37:19–28; 40:3–42:18; 45:1–46:9; 48:28–35; *Codex Constantiensis* (VL[175], fifth century C.E.): Ezek 8:1–17; 12:2–7, 13–18; 16:52–17:6, 17:19–18:17; 20:18–47; 24:25–25:14; 26:10–27:19; 28:1–17; 32:4–10, 21–23, 26–32; 33:4–11, 15, 20–25, 27–30; 34:4–12; 42:5–6, 14; 43:22–44:5, 44:19–45:2; 46:9–47:15; 48:22–30; and the *Sangallensia* fragments (VL[176], ninth century C.E.): Ezek 7:11–11:20; 13:15–16:46; 17:24–22:4; 23:25–25:4; 29:8–31:10; 33:6–34:21; 35:4–11; 36:4–11; 38:14–40:12; 48:10–35. The *Verona Codex* (VL[182]) contains Ezek 36:22–28. In his commentary on *Ezekiel*, Jerome transmits a VL text of numerous verses. Manuscripts VL[175 176 177] share a related text, with VL[175] and VL[176] being closer to one another than to VL[177]. Among quotations of the Fathers (→ 21.8), those of Tyconius are especially relevant: Ezek 20:45–21:5; 28:2–19; 32:3–15; 36:16–36.

Codex Wirceburgensis (VL[177]) shows evidence of some revision and has suffered much at the hands of an ignorant copyist. Nevertheless, it stands close to the source of the Old Latin tradition.[15] The *Wirceburgensis* represents, together with Tyconius, the earliest and best-preserved form of VL-Ezek.[16] It reads Ezekiel 37–40 in the order Ezekiel 38; 39; 37; 40, as does papyrus LXX[967] (→ 8.2.2; → 8.3). VL[177] is closer to this papyrus than to LXX[B], whereas VL[175] and VL[176] are closer to the latter. Therefore, VL[175] and VL[176] attest to a revision that affects at least the order of Ezekiel 37–40.

VL[177] does not follow papyrus LXX[967] in its many errors of parablepsis; therefore, it can be considered an independent witness to the order preserved in LXX[967] (→ 8.2.2; → 8.3). Both manuscripts omit the lengthy passage Ezek 36:23c–38 that is found neither in the earliest text of LXX-Ezek nor in its *Vorlage*, as shown by the special linguistic character of these verses. They also display a different arrangement of Ezekiel 36–40. Ezekiel 36 is followed by Ezekiel 38 and 39 (the battle scene against Gog and Magog); Ezekiel 37, with the vision of the resurrection of the dry bones, is inserted between Ezekiel 39 and 40, resulting in the order of Ezekiel 36:1–23b; 38–39; 37; 40. There appears to be a connection between the omission of the passage and the changed sequence of the chapters. Both the omission and the change of order attested by LXX[967] and VL-Ezek would be witnesses to the first edition of the Hebrew text.

A literary relationship can also be seen between Ezek 36:23b–38 (missing in LXX [→ 8.3] and VL) and some minor developments in the Hebrew. Thus, the MT plus in Ezek 34:31, "you are men," occurs in the context of a promise oracle using a parable about Israel being dispersed and gathered as sheep. This addition corresponds with the phrase in Ezek 36:37, "like a flock of men," where the pastoral metaphor also applies to the restored Israel. Ezek 34:13 is much longer in MT than in LXX and VL. The "pluses" appear to refer to Ezek 36:25 and 29 in the added passage. These data confirm that Ezek 36:23b–38 did not belong to the Greek version (→ 8.2.2; → 8.3),[17] as already proposed by Thackeray before the discovery of LXX[967].[18] Rather, it was inserted into the Greek tradition based on an edition like Theodotion's. Thackeray and Lust argue that the late linguistic features and *hapax legomena* in the Hebrew of Ezek 36:23c–38 as well as the later Jeremianic language suggest a redaction in the Hebrew textual tradition. MT appears to reflect a more

---

[14] Gryson, *Répertoire général*; Gryson, *Altlateinische Handschriften 1*, 267–73, 278.

[15] A.C. Johnson, H.S. Gehman, and E.H. Kase, *The John H. Schiede Biblical Papyri: Ezekiel* (Princeton: Princeton University Press, 1938), 46–48. *Wirceburgensis* was published by E. Ranke, *Par palimpsestorum Wircebutgensium antiquissimae Veteris Testamenti latinae fragmenta e codd. Rescriptus* (Vienna: Braumüller, 1871), 47–144. In an appendix to the new edition of J. Ziegler's *Ezekiel*, D. Fraenkel inserts new evidence in the *apparatus criticus*: J. Ziegler, *Ezechiel* (2nd rev. ed.; appendix by D. Fraenkel; Septuaginta Vetus Testamentum Graecum 16.1; Göttingen: Vandenhoeck & Ruprecht, 1977), 331–52.

[16] Lust, "Ezekiel 36–40," 518.

[17] Cf., e.g., Bogaert, "Le témoignage"; Lilly, *Two Books of Ezekiel*, 125.

[18] H.St.J. Thackeray, "The Greek Translators of Ezekiel," *JTS* 4 (1903): 398–411; Thackeray, *The Septuagint and Jewish Worship*, 37–39, 124–26.

developed textual stage of Ezekiel beyond that of the Old Greek.[19]

6–9.2.1.4 The Twelve Minor Prophets

The preserved VL texts attest to Hos 1:12–4:8; 10:5–11:9; Joel 2:3–25; Amos 1:11–3:2.[20] They do not contain any independent variants of text-critical significance. Nevertheless, VL-readings in Amos 1:14; 15 reflect MT (→ 9.2.2) against the Greek witnesses (→ 9.3). Furthermore, in Amos 3:1, VL agrees with the Vulgate (→ 6–9.1.7) against both MT (→ 9.2.2) and LXX.[21] The different rendering of the plant under which Jonah rests (Jonah 4:6) could raise complaints in Christian communities as attested by Augustine (*Epistles* LXXI, 5): VL *cucurbita* "gourd" (= LXX κολοκύνθα); Vulgate *haedera* "ivy" (= Sym κισσός); MT קִיקָיוֹן "bush," possibly the castor bean plant.

Bogaert, P.-M., "Le témoignage de la Vetus Latina dans l'étude de la tradition des Septante: Ézéchiel et Daniel dans le Papyrus 967," *Bib* 59 (1978): 384–95.

Bogaert, P.-M., "De Baruch à Jérémie, des origines au moyen âge: Essai de synthèse," in *Le livre de Jérémie: Le prophète et son milieu: Les oracles et leur transmission* (ed. P.-M. Bogaert; BETL 54; Leuven: University Press, 1981), 168–73.

Bogaert, P.-M., "Relecture et déplacement de l'oracle contre les Philistins: Pour une datation de la rédaction longue (TM) du livre de Jérémie," in *La vie de la Parole: De l'Ancien au Nouveau Testament: Études d'exégèse et d'herméneutique bibliques offertes à Pierre Grelot* (Paris: Desclée, 1987), 139–50.

Bogaert, P.-M., "La libération de Jérémie et le meurtre de Godolias: le texte court (LXX) et la rédaction longue (TM)," in *Studien zur Septuaginta: Robert Hanhart zu Ehren aus Anlaß seine 65. Geburtstages* (eds. D. Fraenkel, U. Quast, and J.W. Wevers; MSU 20; Göttingen: Vandenhoeck & Ruprecht, 1990), 312–22.

Bogaert, P.-M., "Les trois formes de Jérémie 52 (TM, LXX et VL)," in *Tradition of the Text: Studies Offered to Dominique Barthélemy in Celebration of his 70th Birthday* (eds. G.J. Norton and S. Pisano; OBO 109; Göttingen: Vandenhoeck & Ruprecht, 1991), 1–17.

Bogaert, P.-M., "Le livre de Jérémie en perspective: Les deux rédactions antiques selon les travaux en cours," *RB* 101 (1994): 363–406.

Bogaert, P.-M., "La Vetus Latina de Jérémie: texte très court, témoin de la plus ancienne Septante et d'une forme plus ancienne de l'hébreu (Jer 39 et 52)," in Schenker, *Earliest Text*, 51–82.

Gryson, R., "Les anciennes versions latines du livre d'Isaïe: Signification et voies d'une recherche," *RTL* 17 (1986): 22–37.

Gryson, R., *Esaias 1–39* (VL 12.1; Freiburg i.B.: Herder, 1987–1993).

Gryson, R., *Esaias 40–66* (VL 12.1; Freiburg i.B.: Herder, 1993–1997).

Gryson, *Altlateinische Handschriften 1*.

Gryson, *Répertoire général*.

Gryson, R. and J.-M. Auwers, "L'histoire du texte latin d'Isaïe au miroir du cantique d'Ézéchias," *RTL* 24 (1993): 325–44, 455–77.

Haelewyck, J.-C., "Le cantique de la vigne: histoire du texte vieux latin d'Is 5,1–7(9a)," *ETL* 65 (1989): 257–79.

Haelewyck, J.-C., "Le cantique *De nocte*: histoire du texte vieux latin d'Is. 26,9b–20(21)," *RBén* 99 (1989): 7–34.

Haelewyck, J.-C., "Les premières versions latines de la Bible," in *Les premières traditions de la Bible* (eds. C.-B. Amphoux and J. Margain; HTB 2; Lausanne: Éditions du Zèbre, 1996), 121–36.

Joosten, J., "L'excédent massorétique du livre de Jérémie et l'hébreu post-classique," in *Conservatism and Innovation in the Hebrew Language of the Hellenistic Period: Proceedings of a Fourth International Symposium on the Hebrew of the Dead Sea Scrolls and Ben Sira* (eds. J. Joosten and J.-S. Rey; STDJ 73; Leiden: Brill, 2008), 93–108.

Lilly, I.E., *Two Books of Ezekiel: Papyrus 967 and the Masoretic Text as Variant Literary Editions* (VTSup 150; Leiden: Brill, 2012).

Lust, J., "Ezekiel 36–40 in the Oldest Greek Manuscript," *CBQ* 43 (1981): 517–33.

Lust, J., "Major Divergences between LXX and MT in Ezekiel," in Schenker, *Earliest Text*, 83–92.

Mattei, P., "Recherches sur la Bible à Rome vers le milieu du IIIe s.: Novatien et la Vetus Latina," *RBén* 105 (1995): 255–79.

Monat, P., *Lactance et la Bible: Une propédeutique à la lecture de la Bible dans l'Occident constaninien* (2 vols.; Paris: Etudes Augustiniennes, 1982).

---

[19] O'Hare, *"Have You Seen, Son of Man?"*, 17.

[20] These fragments were published by H.-J. Frede, *Vetus Latina-Fragmente zum Alten Testament: Die Pelagianische Epistula ad quandam matronam chistianam* (VL 28; Freiburg i.B.: Herder, 1996), 81–97.

[21] A. Gelston (ed.), *BHQ, Part 13: The Twelve Minor Prophets* (2010), 8*.

O'Hare, D.M., *"Have You Seen, Son of Man?" A Study in the Translation and Vorlage of LXX Ezekiel 40–48* (SBLSCS 57; Atlanta: SBL, 2010).

Petitmengin, P., "Recherches sur les citations d'Isaïe chez Tertullien," in *Recherches sur l'histoire de la Bible latine* (ed. G. Roger; CRTL 19; Louvain-la-Neuve: Publ. de la Faculté de Théologie, 1987), 21–41.

Stipp, H.J., "Zur aktuellen Diskussion um das Verhältnis der Textformen des Jeremiabuches," in Karrer–Kraus, *Septuaginta 2008*, 630–53.

Ulrich, E., "The Old Latin Translation of the LXX and the Hebrew Scrolls from Qumran," in Ulrich, *DSS*, 233–74.

Julio Trebolle Barrera

6–9.2.2 Coptic Translations

6–9.2.2.1 Isaiah, Jeremiah, Ezekiel
6–9.2.2.1.1 Background

As observed in the Coptic glosses to a Greek biblical papyrus of the book of Isaiah[1] from the third century C.E., the efforts to translate the Latter Prophets from Greek into the Egyptian-Coptic language might have begun already quite early. However, the oldest extant Coptic Bible manuscripts of the Latter Prophets date to the fourth century C.E. The actual translation must have been conducted in the fourth and fifth centuries C.E. The oldest manuscripts of Isaiah and Jeremiah, today in the collection of the so-called Bodmer Papyri,[2] belonged probably to a Pachomian monastery near Dishna in Upper Egypt.[3] However, due to the heterogeneous character of the collection (Christian and pagan literary works side by side), it has also been argued that the manuscripts derive from a private library that came to light accidentally.

The Sahidic dialect provides not only the oldest but also the most numerous manuscripts of the Coptic Latter Prophets and is therefore our main source for a comparison with LXX (→ 6.3; → 7.3; → 8.3). The book of Isaiah is completely preserved and there is even one complete manuscript, a rare case within the Sahidic Old Testament, from the monastery at Phantoou (al-Hamuli) in the Fayyum Oasis (ninth or tenth century C.E.).[4] Only a little more than one-half of the text of Jeremiah and Ezekiel is known today.[5] Nevertheless, new manuscripts are being discovered and keep appearing on the market. They provide new material that fills gaps in the hitherto unpreserved chapters of the Latter Prophets.[6] The extant Sahidic manuscripts date from the fourth to the thirteenth centuries.

The Bohairic version of the Latter Prophets is completely available but only in very late manuscripts (or even printed books) from the fourteenth century onwards.[7]

The Latter Prophets are also present in a Fayyumic version but only fragments of the books of Isaiah and Jeremiah are extant.[8] It seems likely that there was a complete translation of the Prophetic Books into Fayyumic Coptic but the remnants thereof are sparse.[9] This sparsity of Fayyumic witnesses is in spite of the fact that the classification of a Coptic text as Fayyumic is now much more reliable than it was in the mid-twentieth century as dialectological differentiation has gained ground in recent decades in Coptology. Therefore, texts that were formerly listed randomly as Fayyumic, Middle Egyptian (Mesokemic), or Bash-

---

[1] W.E. Crum, "The Coptic Glosses," in *The Chester Beatty Biblical Papyri VI: Isaiah, Jeremiah, Ecclesiasticus* (ed. F.G. Kenyon; London: Walker, 1937), ix–xii, 1–25.

[2] R. Kasser, "Bodmer Papyri," *The Coptic Encyclopedia* (ed. A. Atiya; New York: Macmillan, 1991), 8:48b–53b.

[3] See most recently J.M. Robinson, *The Story of the Bodmer Papyri: From the First Monastery's Library in Upper Egypt to Geneva and Dublin* (Cambridge: James Clarke & Co., 2013).

[4] Schüssler, *Biblia Coptica*, 1.3, 17–19 (CopSa 52).

[5] Takla, "Introduction," 75. Unlike Jeremiah and Ezekiel, Lamentations (→ 13–17.2.2) and the deuterocanonical books Epistle of Jeremiah (→ 11.2.4.6) and Baruch (→ 11.2.1.6), which are always transmitted together with the book of Jeremiah, are completely preserved.

[6] See, e.g., K. Schüssler, "Das Kairener Jeremias-Fragment Nr. 3792," *Journal of Coptic Studies* 6 (2004): 77–83. Frank Feder is preparing an edition of British Museum EA 75338, a parchment leaf from the book of Jeremiah acquired in 1996.

[7] Takla, "Introduction," 87–88.

[8] Vaschalde, "Versions Coptes de la Bible: Troisième Groupe," 301–02; Till, "Coptic Biblical Texts," 237; Boud'hors, "Témoins Fayyumiques," 86–98.

[9] A. Boud'hors, "Manuscripts and Literature in Fayoumic Coptic," in *Christianity and Monasticism in the Fayoum Oasis* (ed. G. Gabra; Cairo: The American University in Cairo Press, 2005), 21–31.

muric are now referred to as belonging to clearly distinct dialects: Fayyumic[10] and Middle Egyptian (Mesokemic) with some subgroups (sub- and mesodialects) also showing interference. Nevertheless, there is no comprehensive evaluation of the extant biblical manuscripts in Fayyumic at this time. This is also the reason why we do not have a detailed overview of the timespan covered by the Fayyumic manuscripts. At least, Till has published some fragments that he dated to the fifth century C.E.[11]

Furthermore, the late Hans-Martin Schenke announced that a Middle Egyptian (Mesokemic) version of at least the book of Isaiah existed and that this Mesokemic version was of a very early date (about 300 C.E.).[12]

6–9.2.2.1.2 Extant Biblical Text, Text Editions, and Auxiliary Tools

The majority of the Sahidic manuscripts of the Latter Prophets were originally part of great monastic libraries. These are in particular the libraries of the monastery of St. Shenoute near Sohag (Deir Anbah Shenoudah or "White Monastery") in Upper Egypt, and the monastery of the Archangel Michael at Phantoou (al-Hamuli) in the Fayyum Oasis. The possible Pachomian library from which the "Bodmer Papyri" originate has already been mentioned. But the provenance of many and especially of many old manuscripts remains unknown. As far as we can judge from the manuscripts of the monastery of St. Shenoute, this library must have possessed two parchment codices of each book of the Latter Prophets. Unfortunately, the remaining leaves of these codices are dispersed among collections around the world.

---

[10] R. Kasser, "Fayyumic," *The Coptic Encyclopedia*, 8:124b–31a.

[11] W. Till, *Koptische Pergamente theologischen Inhalts*, Part 1 (Mitteilungen aus der Papyrussammlung der Nationalbibliothek in Wien, Papyrus Erzherzog Rainer N.S. 2; Vienna: Österreichische Staatsdruckerei, 1934), xiv, 21–24.

[12] H.-M. Schenke, "Mittelägyptische Nachlese IV," *ZÄS* 131 (2004): 88–90; there are fourteen leaves now in the Chester Beatty Library, Dublin; cf. http://www.schoyencollection.com/bible-collection-foreword/coptic-bible/codex-schoyen-ms-2650 (last accessed September 24, 2015).

6–9.2.2.1.2.1 Isaiah

There is no critical edition of the book of Isaiah. Therefore one has to consult the publications of the individual extant manuscripts.

6–9.2.2.1.2.1.1 Manuscripts[13] Belonging to the "Bodmer Papyri"

- Cop-Sa 48: Papyrus codex, fourth century C.E.: Isa 47:1–51:17; 52:4–66:24. Edition: Kasser, *Papyrus Bodmer XXIII*.

6–9.2.2.1.2.1.2 Manuscripts from the Monastery of St. Shenoute

- Cop-Sa 41: Fragmentary parchment codex in two parts (second part Jeremiah), ninth or tenth century C.E.: incomplete text of Isaiah 1–5; 11–14; 16–23; 27–28; 29–30; 35–36; 40–41; 42–45; 55–60. Edition: No edition exists. For the many different publications of the single leaves and fragments, see Schüssler, *Biblia Coptica*, 1.2, 76–81.
- Cop-Sa 93: Fragmentary parchment codex, tenth century C.E.: Isa 5:11–27; 10:6–17:10; 26:6–30:5. Edition: No edition. For the many different publications of the single leaves and fragments, see Schüssler, *Biblia Coptica*, 1.4, 6–8.

6–9.2.2.1.2.1.3 Manuscripts from the Monastery of Archangel Michael

- Cop-Sa 52: Complete parchment codex (sixty-eight leaves), ninth or tenth century C.E. For details of the manuscript, see Schüssler, *Biblia Coptica*, 1.3, 17–19. Edition: No edition, only complete photographic reproduction: H. Hyvernat, *Bibliothecae Pierpont Morgan Codices Coptici Photographice Expressi*, Vol. 3: *Codices M 568 et Cair. Ham. 1: Isaias, Sahidice* (Rome: Bibliotheca apostolica vaticana, 1922).

---

[13] The manuscripts are listed as Cop^Sa followed by a number. The number refers to the sigla "sa + number" in the standard reference catalogue, Schüssler, *Biblia Coptica*, which should be consulted for further details.

6–9.2.2.1.2.1.4 Manuscripts of Unknown Provenance

- Cop-Sa 70: Bilingual papyrus (codex?), fifth century C.E.: Isa 1:22–2:2 (Greek); Isa 1:21–2:2 (Coptic); for details of the manuscript, see Schüssler, *Biblia Coptica*, 1.3, 54–55. Edition: D. Hagedorn and M. Weber, "169. Eine griechisch-koptische Isaias-Bilingue," in B. Krämer, C. Römer, and D. Hagedorn, *Kölner Papyri (P. Köln)*, Vol. 4 (Abhandlungen der Rheinisch-Westfälischen Akademie der Wissenschaften: Sonderreihe Papyrologica Coloniensia 7.4; Opladen: Westdeutscher Verlag, 1982), 18–28.
- Cop-Sa 171: Some leaves of a parchment codex in two parts (the second part contains Jeremiah), fifth or sixth century C.E.: incomplete text of Isaiah 14–16; for details, see Schüssler, *Biblia Coptica*, 2.1, 121–22. Edition: W. Till, "Sahidische Fragmente des Alten Testamentes," *Mus* 50 (1949): 219–23.
- Cop-Sa 176: Papyrus fragment, fourth century C.E.: Isa 2:9, 10–11, 20–21; for details on the manuscript, see Schüssler, *Biblia Coptica*, 2.1, 128. Edition: M. Pezin, "Coptica Sorbonica I: I. Ancient Testament," *Langues Orientales Anciennes Philologie et Linguistique* 2 (1989): 1–16 (7–8) (no. 5).

6–9.2.2.1.2.2 Jeremiah

The critical edition of the Sahidic book of Jeremiah by Feder[14] with consecutive notation of the variant readings towards LXX (→ 7.3) is still an exception among the editorial efforts regarding the Coptic biblical text. There are only some, mostly recently discovered, fragments that are not included in Feder's edition.[15] It offers full reference to the extant Sahidic text, evaluates its character as a translation, and tries to locate the Greek parent text of this translation within the textual history of LXX.

6–9.2.2.1.2.3 Ezekiel

There is no critical edition of the book of Ezekiel.[16] Therefore, one has to consult the publications of the few extant manuscripts, which all come from the Monastery of St. Shenoute.

- Cop-Sa 44: Fragmentary parchment codex, sixth or seventh century C.E.: incomplete text of Ezekiel 1; 3–8; 17. Edition: No edition; for the many different publications of the single leaves and fragments, see Schüssler, *Biblia Coptica*, 1.2, 95–96.
- Cop-Sa 45: Fragmentary parchment codex, tenth or eleventh century C.E.: incomplete text of Ezekiel 2–5; 13–16; 18–24; 26–30; 32–35; 40–43; 48. Edition: No edition; for the many different publications of the single leaves and fragments, see Schüssler, *Biblia Coptica*, 1.2, 97–102.
- Cop-Sa 140: Fragmentary parchment codex, ninth or tenth century C.E.: incomplete text of Ezekiel 11–13; 45–47. Edition: No edition; for the many different publications of the single leaves and fragments, see Schüssler, *Biblia Coptica*, 2.1, 63–65.

The Bohairic version of the Latter Prophets is extant in a number of late paper manuscripts.[17] However, there is no modern edition of any of these manuscripts. The only accessible text edition[18] is from the nineteenth century.[19] It was based partly on manuscripts that are no longer accessible or not clearly identified yet. Tattam also gave variant readings from an Arabic version.[20]

---

[14] Feder, *Biblia Sahidica*. Feder's edition includes also Lamentations (→ 13–17.2.2), Epistle of Jeremiah (→ 11.2.4.6), and Baruch (→ 11.2.1.6).

[15] Cf. n. 6.

[16] A critical edition of Cop^Sa-Ezek had been prepared by Jürgen Horn when he worked for the project "Koptisch Sahidische Septuaginta" at the University of Halle-Wittenberg, 1994–2000. The project found no further funding in Germany and had to be stopped; there are plans to publish this edition in the near future.

[17] Cf. Takla, "Introduction," 87–88.

[18] Takla, "Introduction," 110, quotes an edition by F. Girgis, ⲠϪⲰⲘ ⲚⲚⲒⲠⲢⲞⲪⲎⲦⲎⲤ ⲚⲦⲈ ϮⲆⲒⲀⲐⲎⲔⲎ ⲚⲀⲠⲀⲤ (*The Book of the Prophets of the Old Testament in the Coptic Language-Bohairic Dialect*) (Cairo, 2000 [no publisher known]), which I could not consult.

[19] Tattam, *Prophetae maiores*.

[20] Cf. Vaschalde, "Versions Coptes de la Bible: Deuxième Groupe," 426–29.

6–9.2.2.1.2.4 Secondary Sources

It is necessary to take secondary sources into account not only because of the many lacunae still left in the books of Jeremiah and Ezekiel but also in order to establish firmer ground for the reconstruction of the biblical text of all the Prophetical Books. These are liturgical manuscripts for the holy service of the Coptic Church and biblical quotations in the Coptic patristic literature. One has to consult the witnesses themselves as no systematic exploration or catalogue exists for either of these textual resources.

The Bohairic liturgical manuscripts and their text-types are far better known – for some books of the Bohairic Old Testament these are the only witnesses – but mostly of recent date.[21] The Sahidic liturgical manuscripts still need basic exploration and further study because they suffered as much from dispersal as the biblical codices,[22] but recently progress has been made.[23]

Even more difficult and toilsome is the search for biblical quotations in the Coptic literature. Publications without indices and with wrongly identified citations make this a time-consuming enterprise. Moreover, it is sometimes not easy to decide from which biblical book a quotation is taken if its actual use in a text conceals its clear identification. Nevertheless, biblical citations play an important role in the reconstruction of the biblical text.[24]

However, the extensive dispersion of manuscripts requires a systematic consultation of the collections of published Coptic biblical texts as there is no complete or partially complete register in existence yet.[25] The catalogue *Biblia Coptica* by Schüssler was intended to provide such a tool for Cop^{Sa}, but the sudden death of Schüssler in October 2013 brought an end to his efforts to reconstruct all available Sahidic manuscripts. There is still no comparable initiative for the Coptic Bibles of the other dialects.

6–9.2.2.1.3 Sequence of Books, Translation Character, and Text-Critical Value

The Coptic books of the Latter Prophets were transmitted in separate volumes. Early papyrus codices comprised more than one volume (e.g., Pap. Bodmer XXIII = Cop^{Sa} 48, "third part" beginning with Isa 47:1). A "condensed" volume of Isaiah and Jeremiah is only known from the fragmentary White Monastery Codex Cop^{Sa} 41+42. The sequence of books was canonized at an early date: Isaiah → Jeremiah → Baruch → Lamentations → Epistle of Jeremiah → Ezekiel. As far as we can judge from the fragmentary text witnesses, only Cop^{Sa} 49 as the earliest manuscript of these books prefers instead the sequence Jeremiah → Lamentations → Epistle of Jeremiah → Baruch. This same sequence is also known from the Greek Codex Sinaiticus (LXX^S).[26] Despite this sequence, the Greek *Vorlage* of the Cop^{Sa} text of the Jeremianic corpus (Jeremiah, Baruch, Lamentations, Epistle of Jeremiah) differs from LXX (→ 7.3).

Little can be said about the translation character of the Cop^{Sa} text of Isaiah. The lack of a critical edition and of any kind of study on the translation character of Cop^{Sa}-Isa makes a definite evaluation impossible to date. Therefore, we are confined to the judgement of Ziegler and his com-

---

[21] For an overview, see U. Zanetti, "Bohairic Liturgical Manuscripts," *OCP* 61 (1995): 65–94.

[22] Cf. J. Horn, "Die koptische (sahidische) Überlieferung des alttestamentlichen Psalmenbuches – Versuch einer Gruppierung der Textzeugen für die Herstellung des Textes," in *Der Septuaginta-Psalter und seine Tochterübersetzungen: Symposium in Göttingen 1997* (eds. A. Aejmelaeus and U. Quast; MSU 14; Göttingen: Vandenhoeck & Ruprecht, 2000), 97–106.

[23] U. Zanetti, "Leçons liturgiques du Monastère Blanc: Ancien Testament," *BSAC* 46 (2007): 205–30.

[24] J. Horn, "Die Präsenz des Alten Testamentes in der ägyptischen christlichen Frömmigkeit, aufgewiesen an zwei Werken der koptisch-sahidischen hagiographischen Literatur," in *Sprachen, Mythen, Mythizismen: Festschrift für Walter Beltz zum 65. Geburtstag* (eds. A. Drost-Abgarjan and J. Tubach; Hallesche Beiträge zur Orientwissenschaft 32; Halle: Martin-Luther-Universität Halle-Wittenberg, 2004), 355–82; cf. also Feder, *Biblica Sahidica*, 18–26.

[25] The last extensive collection was published in 1990 by Nagel, "Editionen koptischer Bibeltexte" (with references to the lists assembled before). For the biblical texts published since Nagel, one has to refer to the corresponding reports in the acts of the International Congresses of Coptic Studies (*ICCoptS*).

[26] Cf. Bogaert, *"Septante," 638.

mentary in the critical edition of LXX-Isa.[27] However, Ziegler used for his research only a limited number of Sahidic (and Fayyumic) witnesses in comparison with the evidence available today.[28] The text of Ziegler's Coptic witnesses was taken partly from quite old publications whose accuracy is often doubtful. The best manuscript he could make use of was the tenth-century manuscript from the Monastery of Archangel Michael (Cop^{Sa 52}). Unfortunately, this codex is still unpublished and Ziegler had only a copy at his disposal, which in turn was copied from the monumental photographic facsimile edition of the manuscripts in the Pierpont Morgan Library (New York), which can hardly be found in European libraries. For Cop^{Boh}, Ziegler used the nineteenth-century printed edition by Tattam,[29] on which also Schulte based his study.[30]

According to Ziegler, Cop-Isa belongs to the Alexandrian text (LXX^A, LXX^Q and the third-century papyrus LXX⁹⁶⁵, as well as LXX^S; → 1.3.1.2), which revises predominantly OG-Isa (→ 6.3).[31] Moreover, LXX^S, the Coptic, and a certain number of Greek minuscule manuscripts share some traces of a supposed recension that Ziegler wanted to locate in Egypt. The relationship between the three Coptic versions is hardly transparent but Ziegler postulates an almost complete dependence of Cop^{Fa} on Cop^{Sa}. However, according to Boud' hors, the relation between Cop^{Sa} and Cop^{Fa} must be further differentiated.[32] According to Ziegler, Cop^{Boh} seems to have features of its own.[33] Without a critical edition, particularly of Cop^{Sa}-Isa, every comment on the translation character, translation technique, and the text-critical value of Copt-Isa remains tentative.

In the case of Cop^{Sa}-Jer, the situation is much better since both a critical edition and an evaluation of the text-critical value of Cop^{Sa}-Jer are available.[34] Notwithstanding the fragmentary state of the transmitted Sahidic text of Jeremiah, there can be no doubt that the original translation, probably produced in the early fourth century C.E., was retained almost unchanged until the use of the Sahidic version ceased around the twelfth or thirteenth century.[35] Admittedly, the manuscripts of the Monastery of Shenoute (Cop^{Sa 42 + 43}) show a slight or rather cautious tendency to rework the old translation manifest in the Bodmer manuscript (Cop^{Sa 49}), frequently with the obvious aim of rendering a certain passage closer to the Greek *Vorlage*.[36] Nevertheless, these changes are so unsystematic and so rare that the original translation remained almost untouched.

Cop^{Sa}-Jer is apparently based on an early recension of OG-Jer (→ 7.3), adapting its text *partly* to MT-Jer (→ 7.2.2).[37] That means that the Greek parent text of Cop^{Sa}-Jer contained a pre-Hexaplaric recension (→ 6–9.1.5). Cop^{Sa}-Jer still adheres to the LXX sequence and division of chapters and verses but includes a number of additions, omissions, and alterations that correspond to MT-Jer. Some typical examples may illustrate this point:[38]

Addition (+):

Jer 10:16: LXX κύριος "Lord"] + τῶν δυνάμεων "of hosts" LXX^{O, L'}, Cop^{Sa}, Eth, Arm, Jeremiah commentaries of Chrysostomus and Theodoret = MT

This addition appears several times in Cop^{Sa}-Jer but more frequently in the witnesses of the Lucianic (→ 6–9.1.6) and Hexaplaric (→ 6–9.1.5) recensions. In the Lucianic and Hexaplaric recensions, the addition τῶν δυνάμεων "of hosts" occurs sometimes with additional supplements lacking in Cop^{Sa}-Jer such as ὁ θεὸς Ισραηλ "the God of Israel."[39]

For the textual character of the Greek parent text of Cop^{Sa}-Jer, additions that correct LXX only partly toward MT are particularly significant, whereas the

---

[27] Ziegler, *Isaias*.
[28] Ziegler, *Isaias*, 15–16.
[29] Tattam, *Prophetae maiores*.
[30] Schulte, *Koptische Übersetzung*.
[31] Ziegler, *Isaias*, 21–26.
[32] Boud' hors, "Témoins Fayoumiques," 90–94.
[33] Ziegler, *Isaias*, 32–34.
[34] Feder, *Biblia Sahidica.
[35] Feder, *Biblia Sahidica, 55–61.
[36] Feder, *Biblia Sahidica, 58–61.
[37] Feder, *Biblia Sahidica, 69–78.
[38] Abbreviations etc. correspond to Ziegler, *Jeremias*.
[39] Feder, *Biblia Sahidica, 71.

witnesses of the Lucianic and Hexaplaric recensions adapt the translation to MT coherently. See, e.g.:

Jer 43:32: LXX ἔλαβε Βαρουχ χαρτίον ἕτερον "Baruch took another papyrus scroll"] Ιερεμίας ἔλαβε χαρτίον ἕτερον καὶ ἔδωκεν αὐτὸ πρὸς Βαρουχ υἱὸν νηρίου τὸν γραμματέα "Jeremiah took another papyrus scroll and gave it to Baruch, the son of Neriah, the scribe" LXX$^{O-233, L-407}$ Cop^{Sa} Arm = MT. Only the underlined section is present in Cop^{Sa}-Jer.[40]

Omission (-):

Jer 39:19: LXX ὁ θεὸς ὁ μέγας ὁ "the great God, the"] LXX$^{62-407}$ omit ὁ θεὸς ὁ μέγας "the great God"; Cop^{Sa} omits ὁ μέγας "the great"; om. LXX$^{O, L-449}$, Arm omit the whole phrase = MT.

Cop^{Sa}-Jer omits only a part of the text that is completely deleted by the Hexaplaric and Lucianic recensions.[41]

Alteration:

Jer 41:22: LXX γῆν "land"] πόλιν "city" LXX$^{O-233', L', 239}$, Cop^{Sa}, Arm = MT

Cop^{Sa}-Jer and the minuscule LXX^{239} again stand here alone with the Hexaplaric and Lucianic recensions.[42]

Although Cop^{Sa}-Jer frequently shares readings with the LXX^{Q-V} family, closer investigation shows that Cop^{Sa}-Jer and the LXX^{Q-V} family have no shared text history.[43] Moreover, Cop^{Sa}-Jer and the Greek minuscule manuscripts LXX$^{26, 534, 538}$ have a conspicuous number of readings in common, which seems difficult to explain.

For now, it remains uncertain to which text family the Greek parental text of Cop^{Sa}-Jer belonged.[44] Further studies – above all, of course, critical editions of the Coptic Old Testament – will help to illuminate the textual history of this pre-Hexaplaric recension. We need to follow this phenomenon also in other books.[45] However, contrary to Ziegler's judgement, Cop^{Boh}-Jer is the only Coptic version really belonging to the LXX^{B-S} family. Nevertheless, there are a number of readings in which Cop^{Boh}-Jer follows Cop^{Sa}-Jer and sets itself apart from the LXX^{B-S} group.[46]

In the case of Cop^{Sa}-Ezek, unfortunately, one can only repeat what was said about Cop^{Sa}-Isa. Ziegler[47] grouped all Coptic versions with the earliest text family of the LXX^{B} text (→ 8.3).[48] According to Ziegler, in contrast to Cop^{Sa}-Jer, Cop^{Sa}-Ezek attests to only very few or possibly no traces of a recension. This, however, appears quite unlikely. Therefore, as in the case of Cop^{Sa}-Isa, every comment on the translation character, translation technique, and text-critical value of Cop^{Sa}-Ezek remains tentative without a critical edition of this Coptic version.

As for Cop^{Boh}-Ezek, Ziegler stated a peculiar text character.[49] For Ziegler, the beginning of the book seemed to be based on Cop^{Sa}-Ezek, whereas Ezekiel 27–48 had another *Vorlage* that was closer to the Hebrew text. Moreover, Ziegler postulated also the influence of a Christian Arabic translation of Ezekiel (→ 6–9.2.8) on Cop^{Boh}-Ezek. However, it must remain questionable whether Cop^{Boh}-Ezek includes traces of a recension adapting its (Greek) parent text to MT (→ 8.2.2) until we possess a detailed analysis of Cop^{Boh}-Ezek.

Boud' hors, A., "Réflexions supplémentaires sur les principaux témoins fayoumiques de la Bible," in *Coptica – Gnostica – Manichaica: Mélanges offerts à Wolf-Peter Funk* (eds. L. Painchaud and P.-H. Poirier; Biblio-

---

[40] Feder, *Biblia Sahidica, 72.
[41] Feder, *Biblia Sahidica, 72.
[42] Feder, *Biblia Sahidica, 72–73.
[43] Feder, *Biblia Sahidica, 74–77.
[44] Feder, *Biblia Sahidica, 77–78.

[45] Cop^{Fa}-Jer seems to have the same tendency, but this could be due to its dependence on a Sahidic *Vorlage*; cf. Boud' hors, "Témoins Fayoumiques," 96–99. Cop^{Sa}-MinP (→ 6–9.2.2.2) clearly also shows traces of this recension; cf. F. Albrecht and M. Rosenau, "Zum Textwert des Papyrus Vaticanus 9," *Göttinger Miszellen* 234 (2012): 21–31.
[46] Feder, *Biblia Sahidica, 74–77.
[47] Ziegler, *Ezechiel*, 23–28.
[48] Cf. also Bogaert, *"Septante," 642–45.
[49] Ziegler, *Ezechiel*, 16–17. This had already been remarked upon by Schulte, *Koptische Übersetzung*, 10–11. It seems that Ziegler did not make use of Schulte's study.

thèque Copte De Nag Hammadi Section "Études" 7; Louvain: Peeters, 2006), 81–108.

Kasser, R., *Papyrus Bodmer XXII et Mississippi Coptic Codex II: Jérémie XL,3–LII,34, Lamentations, Épitre de Jérémie, Baruch 1,1–V,5 en sahidique* (Cologny: Bibliotheca Bodmeriana, 1964).

Kasser, R., *Papyrus Bodmer XXIII: Esaïe XLVII,1–LXVI,24 en sahidique* (Cologny: Bibliotheca Bodmeriana, 1965).

Nagel, P., "Editionen koptischer Bibeltexte seit Till 1960," *APF* 35 (1989–1990): 43–100.

Schulte, A., *Die koptische Uebersetzung der vier grossen Propheten* (Münster: Druck und Verlag der Aschendorff'schen Buchhandlung, 1892).

Takla, H., "An Introduction to the Coptic Old Testament," *Coptica* 6 (2007): 1–115.

Takla, H., "The Surviving Remains of the Book of Jeremiah from Saint Shenouda's Monastery," *Coptica* 9 (2010): 83–89.

Tattam, H., *Prophetae maiores in dialecto linguae Aegyptiacae Memphitica seu Coptica* (2 vols; Oxford: Typogr. Academico, 1852).

Till, W., "Coptic Biblical Texts Published After Vaschalde's Lists," *BJRL* 42 (1959–1960): 220–40.

Vaschalde, A., "Ce qui a été publié des versions Coptes de la Bible: Deuxième Groupe: Textes Bohairiques I: Ancien Testament," *Mus* 43 (1930): 409–31.

Vaschalde, A., "Ce qui a été publié des versions Coptes de la Bible: Troisième Groupe: Textes en Moyen Égyptien," *Mus* 46 (1933): 299–313.

Ziegler, J. (ed.), *Isaias* (3rd ed.; Septuaginta Vetus Testamentum Graecum 14; Göttingen: Vandenhoeck & Ruprecht, 1983).

Ziegler, J. (ed.), *Jeremias, Baruch, Threni, Epistula Jeremiae* (3rd ed.; Septuaginta Vetus Testamentum Graecum 15; Göttingen: Vandenhoeck & Ruprecht, 2006).

Ziegler, J. (ed.), *Ezechiel* (3rd ed.; Septuaginta Vetus Testamentum Graecum 16.1; Göttingen: Vandenhoeck & Ruprecht, 2006).

Frank Feder

6–9.2.2.2 Minor Prophets
6–9.2.2.2.1 Background

The book of the Minor Prophets, together with the Psalms, found great favor among the Copts, particularly the books of Hosea and Jonah: Hos 11:1 ("and out of Egypt I called my son") is cited in Matt 2:13–15 and is understood by the Copts as supporting the flight of the Holy Family, i.e., one of the founding events of Coptic history, making Egypt a country privileged by God; Jonah plays an important role within the Coptic community since he is an emblematic figure of repentance, prayer, and salvation given to those who convert. Under the patriarchate of Abraham (972–978 C.E.), the Coptic church adopted the Feast of Jonah, which was originally celebrated by the Syrian church, thus marking the *entente cordiale* between the two churches. We therefore find many pericopes of the Minor Prophets, especially of Jonah, in the lectionaries for Lent, Passover, and the Fast and the Feast of Jonah (or Nineveh) as well as in the funeral service ritual.[1] Yet, paradoxically, we possess only four old "major manuscripts," dating very likely to the fourth century C.E. All four are of utmost importance in dialectal and/or textual terms: The manuscript British Library Or. 7594 and the Crosby-Schøyen Codex ms 193 (London) belong to the Cop^{Sa}-MinP tradition. Papyrus Vatican Copto 9 of the Minor Prophets (Rome) attests to the paleo-Bohairic version of the Minor Prophets (Cop^{palBoh}-MinP), while Cop^{Boh}-MinP is attested in various manuscripts. The manuscript Bibliothèque nationale de France Copte 157 (Paris) + K 11000 (Vienna) belongs to Cop^{Akh}-MinP. Cop^{Boh} and Cop^{Sa} follow the sequence of the Minor Prophets known from LXX (→ 9.3: Hosea, Amos, Micah, Joel, Obadiah, Jonah, Nahum, Habakkuk, Zephaniah, Haggai, Zechariah, Malachi). Cop^{Akh} has adopted a particular order in which the first three Minor Prophets follow the Hebrew order (→ 9.2.2): Hosea, Joel, Amos (which happens to be that of 8ḤevXII gr), followed by Micah, Obadiah, and Jonah. We find this order in Sahidic inscriptions of Bawit, one of which ends with the names of the three holy children in the furnace (Daniel 3).[2] However, in the Bohairic manuscripts,

---

[1] O.H.E. Burmester, *Koptische Handschriften 1: Die Handschriftenfragmente der Staats- und Universitätsbibliothek Hamburg*, Part 1 (Verzeichnis der Orientalischen Handschriften in Deutschland 21.1; Wiesbaden: Franz Steiner Verlag, 1975), 57–58 (Lect. 6, thirteenth or fourteenth century), 73–74 (Lect. 16, thirteenth century), 174–75 (ritual 12, sixteenth or seventeenth century).

[2] The references are given in Grossouw, *Coptic Versions of the Minor Prophets*, 8–9. See also J. Clédat, *Le monastère et la*

the Minor Prophets are regularly associated with and either precede or follow Daniel.

To date, the Minor Prophets are witnessed by three main Coptic (i.e., dialectal) traditions: Cop^{Sa}-MinP is very fragmentary and seems to be represented by two branches; Cop^{Boh}-MinP is completely preserved. The status of Cop^{palBoh}-MinP remains to be defined but it deserves to be highlighted within the Bohairic tradition because of its linguistic and textual peculiarities. Cop^{Akh}-MinP is almost complete.[3] Jonah is the only book of the Minor Prophets attested in its entirety in those three textual traditions.

The Sahidic version (Cop^{Sa}-MinP) is not well known, as it is composed of biblical and liturgical fragments that are dispersed around the world. Most of these fragments belonged once to the White Monastery in Upper Egypt and are of late date. The National Library in Paris and the Vatican Library house the major part of the manuscripts, which are the main sources for the Sahidic version of the Old Testament.[4] The oldest extant witnesses both have Jonah, which is complete: Cop$^{Sa\,15}$ (British Library Or. 7594)[5] is a biblical papyrus codex dating to the fourth century that contains Deuteronomy, Acts, and the Coptic *Apocalypse of Elijah*; Cop$^{Sa\,40lit}$ (Crosby-Schøyen Codex ms 193)[6] is a liturgical papyrus codex dated between the third and sixth centuries, which, however, dates most probably to the same period as Cop$^{Sa\,15}$; Cop$^{Sa\,40lit}$ contains the *Homily on the Passover* of Melito of Sardis, 2 Macc 5:27–7:41, 1 Pet 1:1–5:14, and fragments of an unidentified homily. Of the other books of the Minor Prophets, between twenty-five and seventy-five percent of their text is attested with the exception of Malachi, for which no text is preserved. It is necessary to connect with this corpus the bilingual liturgical manuscript Cop$^{Sa\,16lit}$ (Vienna K 8706) that preserves the Odes of Solomon (→ 11.13.2.5) and dates between the sixth and eighth centuries. In this manuscript, the Odes' version of Jonah 2:3–10 documents that the Greek version (→ 9.3) of this song exercised some influence on Coptic.[7]

By fortunate circumstances, the Bohairic version of the Minor Prophets is preserved in an early manuscript,[8] the papyrus codex Vatican Copto 9 of the Minor Prophets. This papyrus is contemporary with the oldest Sahidic witnesses of the Old Testament. It can be dated to the fourth century C.E. and originally must have comprised seventy-three folios.[9] Approximately seventy-five percent of the text is preserved. The idiom in which it is written, its remarkable conservation, and its age make this manuscript a unique witness within the Bohairic tradition. It is far earlier than the "classical" Bohairic version of the Minor Prophets (Cop^{Boh}-MinP) and thus should be described as a paleo-

---

nécropole de Baouit (eds. B. Bénazeth and M.-H. Rutschowscaya; Mémoires publiés par les membres de l'Institut Français d'Archéologie Orientale du Caire 111; Cairo: Institut Français d'Archéologie Orientale du Caire, 1999), 43 and 230.

[3] See the table "State of Preservation of the Coptic Old Testament" in Takla, "Introduction," 75.

[4] See the list in Grossouw, *Coptic Versions of the Minor Prophets*, 2–6, and 8–11 for a list of the Sahidic quotations of the Minor Prophets. For the individual manuscripts to be added to this list, see also W. Grossouw, "Un fragment sahidique d'Osée," *Mus* 47 (1934): 190–201; W. Till, "Sahidische Fragmente des Alten Testamentes," *Mus* 50 (1937): 217–19 (fragments of Habakkuk); A. Boud'hors, C. Nakano, and P. Werner, "Fragments coptes de l'Ancien Testament au Musée du Louvre," *Mus* 109 (1996), 32–37 (fragments of Jonah); A. Boud'hors, *Catalogue des fragments coptes de la Bibliothèque nationale et universitaire de Strasbourg*, Vol. 1: *Fragments bibliques* (CSCO 571 Subsidia 99; Louvain: Peeters, 1998), 34–35 (fragments of Joel). See also the lectionaries: Cop$^{Sa\,105L.6}$ (Bibliothèque Nationale de France Copte 129^{19}, folio 17: Amos 8:8–10; unpublished); Cop$^{Sa\,108L}$ (Rome, ms Borgia copto 109, cass. XXIII, fasc. 99; partially collated by Ciasca, *Fragmenta Copto-Sahidica* 2; fragments of Hosea, Joel, Amos, Micah, Jonah, Zephaniah, and Zechariah).

[5] Schüssler, *Biblia Coptica* 1.1, 84–88 (sa 15); B. Layton, *Catalogue of Coptic Literary Manuscripts in the British Library Acquired Since the Year 1906* (London: The British Library, 1987), no. 1, pp. 3–5.

[6] Schüssler, *Biblia Coptica* 1.2, 72–73 (sa 40^{lit}).

[7] Till and Sanz, *Odenhandschrift*, 71–74 (Jonah 2:3–10); Schüssler, *Biblia Coptica* 1.1, 89–90 (sa 16^{lit}).

[8] The Bohairic tradition, as a whole, is represented by only two old witnesses, the codex Vatican Copto 9 containing only MinP, and P. Bodmer III with Gen 1:1–4:2; see R. Kasser, *Papyrus Bodmer III: Évangile de Jean et Genèse 1–IV, 2 en bohaïrique* (CSCO 177 Scriptores Coptici 25; Louvain: Peeters, 1971).

[9] See Bosson, "P.Vat.Copt.9," and Kasser, Quecke, and Bosson, "Second chapitre d'Aggée."

Bohairic text (Cop^{palBoh}-MinP).[10] Cop^{Boh}-MinP is completely preserved but late. Most of its copies date from the seventeenth or eighteenth century, with the exception of manuscript British Museum Or. 1314, dated to 1373.

The Akhmimic version (Cop^{Akh}-MinP) is attested by a small parchment codex of the Minor Prophets dating from the fourth or fifth century. Two hundred and twenty-six of the probable original number of 366 pages contained in the codex are today in the Vienna Papyrus Collection (K 11000).[11] Seventy additional pages are in the Bibliothèque Nationale de France in Paris (Copte 157). The text is complete with the exception of Amos (47 % extant) and Malachi (73 % extant). This codex constitutes the most substantial witness of the Akhmimic dialect but unfortunately is neglected by the scholarly community. It is possible that the Akhmimic Minor Prophets codex belonged to the old collection of the White Monastery.[12]

The Minor Prophets are also attested sporadically in other Coptic dialects: One Fayyumic quotation of Mal 2:7 is extant in a homily of Agathon of Tarsus.[13] Hos 2:9–13, 7:14–8:1, 8:8–11, 8:14–9:6, and Amos 2:8–15 are preserved in the Greek-Mesokemic glossary London British Library Inv. 10825v° (end of the third or beginning of the fourth century). The glossary is one of the earliest known Coptic witnesses apart from the few extant Old Coptic texts. According to Bell and Thompson, the glossary attests to an independent tradition of the Minor Prophets.[14] The passages of the Minor Prophets that it preserves could be the work of a scholar who glossed the Greek text prior to the existence of a Coptic translation of the book of the Minor Prophets.

6–9.2.2.2.2 Editions

Cop^{Boh}-MinP is available through the only complete edition of the Coptic Minor Prophets, published by Tattam in 1836.[15] It is based on the Coptic manuscript Bibliothèque Nationale de France Copte 2, dated to 1659. This manuscript is itself a copy of British Museum Or. 1314 from the year 1373. Tattam further provides a Latin translation and a small critical apparatus in which unfortunately the witnesses are not clearly identified. However, Tattam substituted the sequence of the Prophetic Books in his Coptic manuscripts with that of MT, which is also found in the Vulgate (→ 6–9.1.7). According to Grossouw, Tattam's edition is more reliable than generally supposed;[16] nevertheless, a new critical edition is a desideratum.[17] In 1810, Quatremère published Zechariah as well as extracts from Hosea, Amos, Joel, and Malachi accompanied by a Latin translation according to manuscripts Bibliothèque Nationale de France Copte 2 and 58.[18] One will notice that a century earlier, in 1707, Guillaume Bonjour, to whom we owe the copy of manuscript Bibliothèque Nationale de France Copte 58, prepared an outstanding critical edition of Hosea, as well as a remarkable lexicon of Psalms

---

[10] Grossouw, *Coptic Versions of the Minor Prophets*, 6–7.

[11] Grossouw, *Coptic Versions of the Minor Prophets*, 1–2.

[12] T. Orlandi, "The Library of the Monastery of Saint Shenute at Atripe," in *Perspectives on Panopolis: An Egyptian Town from Alexander the Great to the Arab Conquest* (eds. A. Egberts, B.P. Muhs, and J. van der Vliet; Papyrologica Lugduno-Batava 31; Leiden: Brill, 2002), 220–24, esp. 220–21. However, Orlandi has reservations about the provenance of this papyrus from the White Monastery.

[13] Grossouw, *Coptic Versions of the Minor Prophets*, 7.

[14] H.I. Bell and H. Thompson, "A Greek-Coptic Glossary to Hosea and Amos," *JEA* 11 (1925): 241–46; J. van Haelst, *Catalogue des papyrus littéraires juifs et chrétiens* (Université Paris IV Série Papyrologie 1; Paris: Publications de la Sorbonne, 1976), no. 286; cf. M. Hasitzka, *Neue Texte und Dokumentation zum Koptisch-Unterricht* (Vienna: Hollinek, 1990), no. 257a; cf. also M. Choat, "Greek-Coptic Glossary to Hosea and Amos: Album 271," which can be downloaded at mq.edu.au/pubstatic/public/download/?id=45144 (last accessed August 21, 2016).

[15] Tattam, *Duodecim Prophetarum*.

[16] Grossouw, *Coptic Versions of the Minor Prophets*, 6–7, esp. n. 6. See also A. Vaschalde, "Ce qui a été publié des versions coptes de la Bible: Deuxième groupe: Textes Bohaïriques: I. Ancien Testament," *Mus* 43 (1930): 409–31 (424–25).

[17] The forthcoming edition of Papyrus Vatican Copto 9 of the Minor Prophets will seek to partially fulfill this requirement. It will be accompanied by the edition of Biblioteca Angelica ms Or. 67, with a critical apparatus taking the collation of the Bibliothèque Nationale de France manuscripts of the Minor Prophets into account (= Bibliothèque nationale de France Copte 2, 4 and 96): N. Bosson, R. Kasser (†), and H. Quecke (†), *Le Papyrus Vatican Copte 9 des Petits Prophètes* (Documenti e riproduzioni; Vatican City, forthcoming).

[18] Quatremère, "Daniel et les douze."

and the Minor Prophets, which unfortunately remained unpublished.[19]

Cop[palBoh]-MinP is attested only by the unpublished papyrus codex Vatican Copto 9 (→ 6–9.2.2.2.1). Only Haggai 2 and Jonah are edited to date.[20]

Cop[Sa]-MinP has been edited despite the fact that its fragments are dispersed around the world.[21] In 1889, Ciasca published the Sahidic fragments of the Minor Prophets belonging to the Borgia Collection with a critical apparatus.[22] Afterwards, two witnesses of Cop[Sa]-Jonah were published by Budge[23] and Hedrick[24] in 1912 and 1990 respectively. These are the sole main editions of textual witnesses to Cop[Sa]-MinP, for which we still lack a critical edition. For the other published fragments, one has to refer to the list of Grossouw and Schüssler's catalogue in *Biblia Coptica* 1.[25] Malachi remains unattested.

Cop[Akh]-MinP: In 1897, Bouriant[26] improved and completed the preliminary publication of the Parisian folios of the Akhmimic codex of the Minor Prophets by Maspero.[27] Because the dialect was not well known at that time, Malinine republished the folios in 1950.[28] Wessely published the Viennese part of the manuscript in 1915 in a handwritten edition and provided a Latin translation.[29] Wessely compared the Parisian and Viennese folios in the right-hand column of his edition with the Bohairic text of Tattam and the Sahidic fragments of Ciasca. Nevertheless, Wessely's edition turned out to be flawed. Therefore, Till decided to republish the Viennese part of the manuscript in 1927.[30] A critical edition of Cop[Akh]-MinP remains a much-needed desideratum.

6–9.2.2.2.3 Translation Character, Textual History, and Text-Critical Value of Cop-MinP for LXX-MinP

The Coptic versions are characterized by their "extrême bigarrure"[31] ("interlaced pattern"). They obviously belong to a phase in the textual history of the Coptic Bible subsequent to the first translations from a Greek base text (→ 9.3). This phase is marked by an intense activity of revision/recension. Indeed, it is often difficult to connect the Coptic Old Testament witnesses to a well-defined Greek textual family. Nevertheless, many of them are of particular importance for the history of the biblical text because some of their readings certainly provide evidence of Old Greek. This is particularly true for the Coptic Minor Prophets texts that are close to the *kaige* recension (→ 6–9.1.5).[32]

For the Coptic Minor Prophets, we benefit from the text-critical work of Grossouw, which is unique in Coptology to this day. Grossouw underlines the heterogeneous character of the Coptic versions and studies elaborately the relationship between them and the various Greek texts of the Minor Prophets.[33] Grossouw propounds his arguments and also proves some conclusions made already by Till.[34] On the whole, three observations can be made in the textual history of Cop-MinP: 1) Cop[Sa]-MinP and Cop[Akh]-MinP present numerous readings that align with MT-MinP (→ 9.2.2). These readings go back to a Greek model of a text like 8ḤevXII gr (→ 1.3.1.2), as demonstrated in 1963 by

---

[19] See S.H. Aufrère and N. Bosson, *Guillaume Bonjour: Elementa Linguae Copticae: Grammaire inédite du xviie siècle* (Cahiers d' Orientalisme 24; Geneva: Patrick Cramer Éditeur, 2005), esp. lxxiv–lxxviii.

[20] Kasser, Quecke, and Bosson, "Second chapitre d' Aggée," and Bosson, "Synopse des témoins coptes de Jonas."

[21] For a complete bibliography of the Sahidic fragments published before 2000, one has to refer to Schüssler, *Biblia Coptica*. The very few fragments published since 2000 are mentioned in the footnotes. See also Grossouw, *Coptic Versions of the Minor Prophets*, 1–11.

[22] Ciasca, *Fragmenta Copto-Sahidica* 2.

[23] Budge, *Coptic Biblical Texts*.

[24] Hedrick, "Jonah."

[25] See note 4, which mentions the few published fragments that are absent from both lists.

[26] Bouriant, "Fragments des Petits Prophètes."

[27] Maspero, "Notes."

[28] Malinine, "Version achmimique des Petits Prophètes."

[29] Wessely, *Duodecim Prophetarum*.

[30] Till, *Achmîmische Version der Zwölf Kleinen Propheten*.

[31] Luisier, *Citations vétéro-testamentaires*, 264, who applies this very relevant description to the whole Coptic manuscript tradition.

[32] Barthélemy, *Devanciers*, 228–38.

[33] Grossouw, *Coptic Versions of the Minor Prophets*, 103–22.

[34] Till, *Achmîmische Version der Zwölf Kleinen Propheten*.

Barthélemy.[35] The high number of doublets and conflations in Cop[Akh]-MinP are obviously the result of a revision/recension; 2) Mistakes made due to a wrong interpretation of the *lectio continua* prove that Cop[Akh]-MinP is a translation made from Cop[Sa]-MinP; 3) The late Bohairic tradition that is connected with the Alexandrine group (LXX[A–Q]) derives either from a Hesychian *Vorlage* (→ 1.3.1.2.7), which in turn would have preserved old lessons and elements thereof and would be the result of secondary influences, or directly from Cop[Sa]-MinP, with a later revision based on a Hesychian text (→ 1.3.1.2).

Grossouw's study deserves to be enriched and revised in the light of two texts, i.e., codex Vatican Copto 9 (Cop[palBoh]-MinP) and manuscript Crosby-Schøyen MS 193. Both manuscripts date to more or less the same time and are fundamental to the history of the Coptic biblical text. More recent research on these two witnesses led to the following conclusions.

Cop[palBoh]-MinP (Vatican Copto 9): Cop[palBoh]-MinP is marked by its heterogeneous character.[36] One of the main questions is whether the classical version of Cop[Boh]-MinP was based on the Cop[palBoh]-MinP text of codex Vatican Copto 9 or on a related witness. For Luisier,[37] the classical version would be the revision of a text of the Cop[palBoh]-MinP type, as shown by Zech 11:13 where Cop[palBoh]-MinP is the sole witness to follow the reading of LXX[W] (Codex Washingtonianus). Cop[palBoh]-MinP is thus of primary importance in textual terms, as demonstrated by Albrecht and Rosenau,[38] because its text depends on a Greek *Vorlage* in close relation to LXX[W] and as a consequence to Old Greek (→ 9.3), of which it gives evidence in a remarkable number of lessons. This conclusion had already been pointed out by Feder in his study on Haggai 2.[39] Hence, this witness is related to the "Palestinian recension" (→ 1.3.1.2; → 9.3). Feder also assumes that the classical version of Cop[Boh] could be a revised version based on Cop[Sa] and Cop[palBoh]-MinP (or similar text types?).[40] Based on the present state of the documentation, the stemma proposed by Grossouw,[41] for whom a lost Sahidic text of the "Christian irregular" LXX type could be the source of all the other versions, seems most unlikely. Here lies probably *the* crucial question concerning the Coptic versions of the Old Testament other than Cop[Sa], and it may well be that Cop[palBoh] is one of the keys to its solution.

Cop[Sa]-MinP (Crosby-Schøyen MS 193): Manuscript Crosby-Schøyen MS 193 emanates from a liturgical context as does codex Vatican Copto 9. A synopsis of Jonah published by Bosson[42] highlights recurring links between Cop[palBoh]-MinP and manuscript Crosby-Schøyen MS 193, which would indicate that these two witnesses written in different Coptic idioms share a common textual substratum. Bosson's synopsis also allowed for the identification of the existence of two branches within the Sahidic tradition, that represented by Crosby-Schøyen MS 193, the other by the remainder of the Sahidic witnesses. These branches are not clearly separated, but when Crosby-Schøyen MS 193 stands against the other branch it regularly goes with Cop[palBoh]-MinP or even with Cop[Boh]-MinP against all the other Coptic witnesses. It also seems to be the case that although Cop[Akh]-MinP is undeniably related to the Sahidic tradition, with which it shares Hebrew readings, it nevertheless occupies an intermediate position by agreeing sometimes with Cop[Sa]-MinP, and sometimes with Cop[palBoh]-MinP and/or Cop[Boh]-MinP.

Only a systematic study of the whole documentation will permit us to define the textual character of the witnesses more clearly, as well as their relationship to one another.

---

[35] Barthélemy, *Devanciers*.
[36] See, e.g., Luisier, *Citations vétéro-testamentaires*, 266, who underlines the fact that Cop[palBoh] either has proper readings – a characteristic of the Coptic versions – or sometimes follows Cop[Sa] together with Cop[Akh], and sometimes Cop[Boh]. See also Bosson, "Jonas."
[37] Luisier, *Citations vétéro-testamentaires*, 272.
[38] Albrecht and Rosenau, "Textwert des P.Vat.Copt.9."
[39] Feder, "Papyrus Vatican Copto 9."
[40] Feder, "Papyrus Vatican Copto 9," 126.
[41] Grossouw, *Coptic Versions of the Minor Prophets*, 122.
[42] See Bosson, "Jonas."

Albrecht, F. and M. Rosenau, "Zum Textwert des Papyrus Vaticanus Copticus 9," *Göttinger Miszellen* 234 (2012): 21–31.

Barthélemy, *Devanciers.*

Bosson, N., "Le *Papyrus Vatican Copte 9* des Petits Prophètes," in *Coptic Treasures from the Vatican Library: A Selection of Coptic, Copto-Arabic and Ethiopic Manuscripts: Papers Collected on the Occasion of the Tenth International Congress of Coptic Studies (Rome, September 17th–22nd, 2012)* (eds. P. Buzi and D.V. Proverbio; Studi e Testi 472; Vatican City: Biblioteca Apostolica Vaticana, 2012), 73–84.

Bosson, N., "Synopse des témoins coptes de Jonas," *Journal of Coptic Studies* 16 (2014): 1–46.

Bosson, N., "Jonas: La version saïdique du codex Crosby-Schøyen Ms 193 et ses liens avec la version palBo du Papyrus Vatican Copte 9 des Petits Prophètes," in *Coptic Society, Literature and Religion from Late Antiquity to Modern Times: Proceedings of the Tenth International Congress of Coptic Studies, Rome, September 17th–22nd, 2012 and Plenary Reports of the Ninth International Congress of Coptic Studies, Cairo, September 15th–19th, 2008* (eds. P. Buzi, A. Camplani, and F. Contardi; OLA 247; Leuven: Peeters, 2016), 821–37.

Bouriant, U., "Fragments des Petits Prophètes en dialecte de Panopolis," *Recueil de travaux et d'histoire relatifs à la philologie et à l'archéologie égyptiennes et assyriennes* 19 (1897): 1–12.

Budge, E.A.W., *Coptic Biblical Texts in the Dialect of Upper Egypt* (London: Kegan Paul, Trench, Trübner & Co. Ltd, 1912), 114–21.

Ciasca, *Fragmenta Copto-Sahidica*, 2.325–60.

Feder, F., "Der Papyrus Vatican Copto 9 und die bohairische Version der Prophetenbücher," in *Sprache und Geist: Peter Nagel zum 65. Geburtstag* (eds. W. Beltz, U. Pietruschka, and J. Tubach; Hallesche Beiträge zur Orientwissenschaft 35; Halle: Institut für Orientalistik der Martin-Luther-Universität Halle-Wittenberg, 2003), 113–31.

Grossouw, W., *The Coptic Versions of the Minor Prophets: A Contribution to the Study of the Septuagint* (Monumenta Biblica et Ecclesiastica 3; Rome: Pontifical Biblical Institute, 1938).

Hedrick, C.W., "Jonah: Coptic Text, Translation, Notes and Variant Readings," in *The Crosby-Schøyen Codex MS 193 in the Schøyen Collection* (ed. J.E. Goehring; CSCO 521, Subsidia 85; Leuven: Peeters, 1990), 217–59.

Kasser, R., "Le Pap. Vat. Copto 9, codex des Petits Prophètes (note préliminaire sur la variété subdialectale B74 de ce témoin 'bohaïrique ancien', ive s.)," in *Actes du IVe Congrès copte, Louvain-la-Neuve, 5–10 septembre 1988*, Vol. 2: *De la linguistique au gnosticisme* (eds. M. Rassart-Debergh and J. Ries; Publications de l'Institut orientaliste de Louvain 41; Louvain-la-Neuve: Université catholique de Louvain, Institut orientaliste, 1992), 64–73.

Kasser, R., H. Quecke, and N. Bosson, "Le second chapitre d'Aggée en bohaïrique B74," *Or* 61.3 (1992): 169–204.

Luisier, P., *Les citations vétéro-testamentaires dans les versions coptes des Évangiles: Recueil et analyse critique* (Cahiers d'Orientalisme 22; Geneva: Patrick Cramer Éditeur, 1998).

Malinine, M., "Version achmimique des Petits Prophètes," in *Coptic Studies in Honor of Walter Ewing Crum* (Bulletin of the Byzantine Institute 2; Boston: The Byzantine Institute, 1950), 365–415.

Maspero, G., "Notes sur différents points de grammaire et d'histoire," *Recueil de travaux et d'histoire relatifs à la philologie et à l'archéologie égyptiennes et assyriennes* 8 (1886): 181–92.

Quatremère, É., "Daniel et les douze Petits Prophètes: Manuscrits coptes de la Bibliothèque impériale, n° 2, Saint-Germain, n° 21," *Notices et extraits de la bibliothèque impériale* 8 (1810): 220–89.

Schleifer, J., *Sahidische Bibel-Fragmente aus dem British Museum zu London* (3 vols.; Sitzungsberichte der Kais. Akademie der Wissenschaften in Wien, Philosophisch-Historische Klasse 162.6, 164.6, and 173.5; Vienna: Alfred Hölder, 1909–1914).

Schulte, A., "Die koptische Übersetzung der Kleinen Propheten," *TQ* 76 (1894): 605–42; 77 (1895): 209–29.

Schüssler, *Biblia Coptica*, 1.1–4.

Takla, H., "An Introduction to the Coptic Old Testament," *Coptica* 6 (2007): 1–115.

Tattam, H., *Duodecim Prophetarum Minorum libros in lingua Aegyptiaca vulgo seu Memphitica ex manuscripto descriptos et cum manuscripto Johannis Lee, J.C.D. collatos latine edidit* (Oxford: E typographaeo academico, 1836).

Till, W., *Die achmîmische Version der Zwölf Kleinen Propheten (Codex Rainerianus, Wien): Herausgegeben mit Einleitung, Anmerkungen und Wörterverzeichnis* (Coptica 4; Copenhagen: Gyldendalske Boghandel-Nordisk Forlag, 1927).

Till, W. and P. Sanz, *Eine griechisch-koptische Odenhandschrift (Papyrus Copt. Vindob. K 8706)* (Monumenta Biblica et Ecclesiastica 5; Rome: Pontificium Institutum Biblicum, 1939).

Tov, E., *The Greek Minor Prophets Scroll from Naḥal Ḥever (8ḤevXIIgr) (The Seiyâl Collection I)* (*DJD VIII).

Wessely, C., *Duodecim prophetarum minorum versionis Achmimicae codex Rainerianus* (Studien zur Palaeographie und Papyruskunde 16; Leipzig: Verlag H. Haessel Nachfolger (W.R. Sorgenfrey), 1915). [Reprint Amsterdam: Verlag Adolf M. Hakkert, 1969].

Ziegler, J. (ed.), *Duodecim Prophetae* (Septuaginta Vetus Testamentum Graecum 13; Göttingen: Vandenhoeck & Ruprecht, 1984).

Ziegler, J. and F. Albrecht (eds.), *Duodecim Prophetae* (Editio altera; Septuaginta Vetus Testamentum Graecum 13; Göttingen: Vandenhoeck & Ruprecht, forthcoming).

Nathalie Bosson

6–9.2.3 Ethiopic Translation(s)

6–9.2.3.1 Isaiah

6–9.2.3.1.1 Title and Place in the Manuscripts

When Eth-Isa bears a title it invariably reads ዘኢሳያስ ነቢይ "Isaiah the Prophet." A survey of seventy-three manuscripts reveals the following: Alone or with the *Ascension of Isaiah* it often fills a complete codex. Otherwise, Eth-Isa tends to head larger collections, with the works associated with Jeremiah (→ 6–9.2.3.2; → 13–17.2.3.4; → 11.2.1.5; → 11.2.3.3; → 11.2.4.5) usually following.[1] When not in primary position, the earliest witnesses differ as to where and with which books Isaiah should be located. However, during the sixteenth through eighteenth centuries, a marked predilection developed for placing Isaiah after the Wisdom literature (→ 11.4.3; → 12.4.3; → 13–17.2.3.3; → 11.4.6; → 11.15.5) and before the Minor Prophets (→ 6–9.2.3.4). In subsequent centuries, scribes generally reversed that order. Remarkably, a number of codices containing only Isaiah and Joel began appearing in the twentieth century.

Portions of Eth-Isa are commonly read in the various liturgies. Both the Prayer of Isaiah (Isa 26:9–20) and the Prayer of Hezekiah (Isa 38:10–20) appear in the *Biblical Canticles* (Odes), one of Ethiopian Christianity's most popular texts.

6–9.2.3.1.2 Background

Eth-Isa was translated from a Greek exemplar exhibiting strong Hexaplaric (→ 6–9.1.5) influence, probably in the second half of the fourth century C.E. Some suggest that the translator's use of ፋርስ "Fars" to denote Assyria establishes the mid-seventh century as *terminus ante quem*.[2] Today, no known copies of Eth-Isa date before the fourteenth century (→ 1.4.3.2). Hopefully, contemporary digitization and preservation efforts will remedy this situation and bring additional early manuscripts to light.

In 1893, Bachmann published a preliminary edition of Eth-Isa,[3] but he examined only three manuscripts and avoided making any text-critical judgments (→ 1.4.3.5). The second part of his study, which promised analyses of the Ethiopic and Greek textual traditions, did not appear due to his death the following year.[4]

6–9.2.3.1.3 Translation Character

Although the translator did not know Greek well, he handled the biblical text better than some of his contemporaries. Even Isa 3:16–23 with its challenging vocabulary remains virtually intact, although some omissions occur (perhaps due to parablepsis rather than linguistic inability) and many words are merely guesses at meaning.

The translator sought to follow the Greek *Vorlage* slavishly, but he also aimed at creating a readable text. As a result, there is a fondness for more palatable Ethiopian constructions such as verb-subject-object order. He also balances phrases by providing words implied by the Greek. Thus, at Isa 24:5, the *Vorlage* almost certainly had no verb following προστάγματα "ordinances," although the Ethiopic reads ወከሐዱ "and they rejected," because ከሐደ "to reject" is both semantically similar to the previous ወለጠ "to alter" and translates neither of the known Greek additions, διεσκέδασαν "they threw away" (LXX^s) as well as Hexaplaric and Lucianic

---

[1] Codices beginning with Isaiah have increased markedly during the last two centuries (fifty-five percent in the nineteenth century; sixty-nine percent in the twentieth century).

[2] First noted by O. Löfgren, *Die äthiopische Übersetzung des Propheten Daniel* (Paris: Geuthner, 1927), xlviii.

[3] Bachmann, *Jesaia*.

[4] On the intentions for a second volume, see Bachmann, *Jesaia*, viii.

manuscripts) and ἠκύρωσαν "they set aside" (Sym, Th). These stylistic choices along with others, such as the tendency to add the conjunction ወ "and/but" and pronominal suffixes in the absence of corresponding Greek pronouns, must be considered when making text-critical assessments.[5]

Still, as in the Ethiopic Bible generally, difficult passages are excised (cf. Isa 10:14 and 60:13), words are misunderstood (δεδοικότες "the ones dreading" is assumed to be a form of δίδωμι "to give" in Isa 60:14 and παραλίαν "seacoast" is viewed as a toponym in Isa 8:23), and sentences are divided differently (ወአስተጋብእ ኀቤሁ ኵሎ አራዊተ ገዳም "and I will gather to him all the beasts of the field" = Ὅτι συνάξω ἐπ' αὐτὸν συναγωγήν. Πάντα τὰ θηρία τὰ ἄγρια "for I will gather to him as a gathering. All wild animals of the fields..." in Isa 56:8–9; cf. Isa 42:11).

6–9.2.3.1.4 Text-Critical Value

Unlike Eth-Jer (→ 6–9.2.3.2), Eth-Ezek (→ 6–9.2.3.3), and Eth-Dan (→ 18.4.3), Eth-Isa does not share a high rate of agreement with LXX[130].[6] Instead, it aligns most closely with Codex Vaticanus (LXX[B]) and LXX[86, 88] in the first half of the book. Codices Sinaiticus (LXX[S]), Alexandrinus (LXX[A]), and Marchalianus (LXX[Q]) also exhibit significant kinship with Eth-Isa.[7]

In order to better assess group alignment, as opposed to association with individual Greek manuscripts, the Old Ethiopic was collated against the distinctive readings Ziegler identified for each of the following: the Alexandrian, Hexaplaric, Lucianic, and Catena groups, and Codex Sinaiticus.

The Ethiopic matched only one of the distinctive Alexandrian (→ 1.3.1.2) readings: the omission of καὶ ἔπλασά σε "and I have formed you" in Isa 49:8.[8] It corresponded with none of the Lucianic (→ 6–9.1.6) or Catena readings, including those Lucianic readings introduced into the text by manuscript LXX[88], a codex that otherwise aligns closely with Eth-Isa.[9] Hexaplaric readings (→ 6–9.1.5), on the other hand, abound.[10] For example, the Ethiopic adds ἐκλέκτην "chosen" at Isa 5:2 and reads πεφονευμένων "those who murder" at Isa 21:15.[11] Similarly, Eth-Isa shares a number of readings with LXX[S]. For example, it adds ἐν τῇ ἡμέρᾳ "in the day" at Isa 20:6. It also reflects variations LXX[S] holds in common with mss LXX[538] and/or LXX[544] in Isa 7:7; 50:2; and 54:9, but these agreements could be accidental.

In order to provide additional data for preliminary classification, forty-six test passages were selected and collated against Ziegler's apparatus. Where the Ethiopic agreed with a dozen or fewer Greek manuscripts, in all but one instance (ἰσχύει "strong" at Isa 50:2 = LXX[403' cI]) the corresponding witnesses were LXX[S] and/or representatives of the Alexandrian or Hexaplaric groups. Where the Ethiopic followed twenty-five or more manuscripts, Lucianic support was virtually absent. Nothing similar occurred with the other groupings; consequently, Eth-Isa finds support from the Lucianic group only when also supported by one or more of the other groups.

Both of these preliminary samplings produced comparable results. Tentatively, then, one can conclude that Eth-Isa translates a Greek *Vorlage* with significant Hexaplaric (→ 6–9.1.5) influence but without any vestiges of the Lucianic recension (→ 6–9.1.6).

6–9.2.3.1.5 Subsequent History

As with the other biblical books, perceived deficiencies in the Old Ethiopic resulted in corrections toward an Arabic *Vorlage* (→ 6–9.1.8; → 6–9.2.8). However, it is difficult to ascertain whether a Tran-

---

[5] Ziegler, however, does not always do so in his edition of OG-Isa (*Isaias*).

[6] See J. Ziegler, *Ieremias, Baruch, Threni, Epistula Ieremiae* (Septuagint Vetus Testamentum Graecum 15; Göttingen: Vandenhoeck & Ruprecht, 1957), 32--34; Ziegler, *Ezechiel*, 19; and Ziegler, *Susanna, Daniel, Bel et Draco*, xlix–l.

[7] Details are based on collations of sample passages taken from Isaiah 1; 10; 20; 30; 40; 50; and 60, using Bachmann's transcription of Eth[Ber Peter II, 42], personal examination of images of nine other Ethiopic manuscripts, and the apparatus in Ziegler, *Isaias*.

[8] See Ziegler, *Isaias*, 21–26.

[9] See Ziegler, *Isaias*, 73–78 (p. 77 for manuscript LXX[88]) and 93–94, respectively.

[10] See Ziegler, *Isaias*, 21–26.

[11] Cf. also Isa 13:2; 19:18; 29:1; 36:11; 50:1; and 57:12.

sitional Text ever existed (→ 1.4.3.7.4).[12] Presumably due to the better quality of the initial translation, Eth-Isa received minor reworking at best. Even the Standardized Text (sixteenth century, → 1.4.3.7.5) differs little from the Old Ethiopic. At Isa 9:1 (MT-Isa 8:23), it merely omits ወዝንተ ፍጡነ ስተይ "and drink this quickly" (= τοῦτο ταχὺ πίε) and smooths the remaining syntax. It also leaves Isa 20:2 untouched, despite the redundant addition there that ensures Isaiah explicitly obeys the Lord's command.

By the end of the nineteenth century, a Textus Receptus had developed (→ 1.4.3.7.6), although it too shows little variation from the other Ethiopic editions. It tends to conflate when possible. Thus, at Isa 9:1, ግበር "do" (= ποίει), from the Old Ethiopic, is inserted back into the reading of the Standardized Text. Evidence for the Academic Text of Eth-Isa can be found in Eth^{EMML 1481} (seventeenth century). With respect to Isa 9:1, the scribe rewrote and truncated the passage based on MT-Isa (→ 6.2.2); however, he retained some of the archaic vocabulary of the Old Ethiopic, producing a doublet (ፅራልይ ፍኖተ ባሕር "Päraləyu the path of the sea"). This revision, though at times radical, was not complete, for even at Isa 9:1 (MT-Isa 8:23) the reviser left out an equivalent for עֵבֶר הַיַּרְדֵּן "beyond the Jordan."

Bachmann, J., *Der Prophet Jesaia*, Part 1: *Der aethiopische Text* (Berlin: Emil Felber, 1893).
Ziegler, J. (ed.), *Ezechiel* (Septuaginta Vetus Testamentum Graecum 16.1; Göttingen: Vandenhoeck & Ruprecht, 1952).
Ziegler, J. (ed.), *Susanna, Daniel, Bel et Draco* (Septuaginta Vetus Testamentum Graecum 16.2; Göttingen: Vandenhoeck & Ruprecht, 1954).
Ziegler, J. (ed.), *Isaias* (2nd rev. ed.; Septuaginta Vetus Testamentum Graecum 14; Göttingen: Vandenhoeck & Ruprecht, 1967).

---

[12] The manuscripts examined may be ascribed tentatively to the following categories: Old Ethiopic (or Transitional Text): Eth^{Ber Peter II, 42, EMML 1768, EMML 2080}; Standardized Text: Eth^{EMML 38, EMIP 2007, EMIP 746} (with additional Arabic readings interspersed); Textus Receptus: Eth^{EMIP 1088, EMML 51, IES 77}; Scholar's Text: Eth^{EMML 1481}. The manuscripts follow at least four different models for dividing the text of Eth-Isa. With further study, these different models may contribute to more precise classifications.

Ziegler, J. and Olivier Munnich (eds.), *Susanna, Daniel, Bel et Draco* (2nd rev. ed.; Septuaginta Vetus Testamentum Graecum 16.2; Göttingen: Vandenhoeck & Ruprecht, 1999).

Curt Niccum

6–9.2.3.2 Jeremiah

6–9.2.3.2.1 Order and Location in the Manuscripts

In a study of forty-five manuscripts containing Eth-Jer, one observes the following patterns. Eth-Jer never corresponds to MT (→ 7.2.2) either in terms of the characteristic differences between LXX (→ 7.3) and MT, or in terms of its inclusion of those sections known as apocryphal and pseudepigraphical in other traditions. Eth-Jer will always appear with Lamentations (→ 13–17.2.3.4) and 1 Baruch (→ 11.2.1.5) at the least, and most often with the Letter of Jeremiah (= Baruch 6 in the Vulgate; → 11.2.4.5) and Paralipomena of Baruch (= 4 Baruch; → 11.2.3.3), and occasionally with the *Prophecy of Jeremiah to Pashur* (→ 11.2.5.2).

There is demand for the book of Jeremiah by itself, and when it appears with other works in a codex there is some indication of its priority. Six manuscripts contained only Jeremiah. In the thirty-nine manuscripts in which Eth-Jer appears with other biblical books, Jeremiah comes first in eleven manuscripts.

Several lines of evidence point to a special relation among the quartet of Isaiah (→ 6–9.2.3.1), Jeremiah, Ezekiel (→ 6–9.2.3.3), and Daniel (→ 18.4.3), and in that order. Jeremiah adjoins Isaiah in thirteen of thirty-nine cases (coming always after but never before Isaiah); it adjoins Ezekiel in sixteen cases (coming thirteen times before and three times after Ezekiel); and in five cases it comes just before Daniel. Four manuscripts have all four of these books, and they follow the order Isaiah, Jeremiah, Ezekiel, Daniel. Another two manuscripts contain three of the four books, yet even when Ezekiel or Daniel is lacking, the remaining books follow the expected order, i.e., Isaiah, Jeremiah, Ezekiel, Daniel.

The only other statistically significant correlations are with the books of Esdras/Ezra (with

Jeremiah appearing five times just before and once just after; → 19.4.3; → 11.7.1.5; → 11.7.2.4) and with the Minor Prophets (four times just after and once just before; → 6–9.2.3.4).

6–9.2.3.2.2 Overview

Eth-Jer, which should be understood as the oldest stratum of Gəʿəz manuscripts reflecting a Greek *Vorlage*, is a daughter version of LXX-Jer (→ 7.3). "The characteristics of the Old Ethiopic version are by and large the same in the Old and New Testaments."[1]

6–9.2.3.2.3 Critical Editions of the Ethiopic Book of Jeremiah

In 1976, Ziegler[2] knew only of three publications dealing specifically with the text of Eth-Jer. Heider's dissertation of 1902[3] marks the starting point, consisting of a short introduction into the matter, a description of the manuscripts used, and a sample edition of Jeremiah 1 (not of chs. 1–13, as announced in the title). In the same year, Heider's dissertation was republished,[4] again with the same introduction, followed by the variant readings of Eth-Jer 1–3 and rounded off with the edition and translation of the *Prophecy of Jereremiah to Pashur* (→ 11.2.5.2) that is found in some codices. According to Heider, the text of the oldest Ethiopic manuscripts shows strong affinities to the Lucianic recension (→ 6–9.1.6). Heider, however, had based his conclusions mainly on the collation of manuscript Eth[Ber Peter II, 42], which had been subject to a later revision from the Arabic (→ 6–9.1.8; → 6–9.2.8). A decade later, Schäfers[5] published a much more detailed analysis of Eth-Jer, correcting Heider's view. Schäfers demonstrated extensively that the oldest stratum of Eth-Jer is based directly on LXX (→ 7.3) and that Heider's main textual witness belongs to a later group with Arabic influences (→ 6–9.2.8; called today "Syriac-Arabic Recension" or "First Arabic Recension"[6] and "Transitional" in the model proposed in → 1.4.3.7.4). In agreement with Heider, Schäfers assigned the third (and mostly latest) group of manuscripts to the "academic" recension,[7] which betrays influences from the Lucianic recension (→ 6–9.1.6), the Hexaplaric recension (→ 6–9.1.5), and from MT (→ 7.2.2). These influences, however, are attributed more convincingly to the "Second Arabic Recension."[8] Schäfers also prepared a critical edition of Eth-Jer, but unfortunately did not live to see his work published. He died in 1916 and his manuscript, ready for publication, was lost somewhere in Paris during the First World War. Therefore, Ziegler could not use a critical text of Eth-Jer for his edition of LXX-Jer and quoted directly from Eth[Ber Or Fl 3067] under the name (siglum) "Aeth."[9]

A critical edition of Eth-Jer is a *desideratum* for Ethiopic and Septuagint studies alike and is in preparation by the author. Recent decades have witnessed the appearance of large numbers of manuscripts, some of which are from the fourteenth century or earlier and are hence – by Ethiopian standards – very old.[10]

6–9.2.3.2.4 Greek *Vorlage* of Eth-Jer

Schäfers had based his conclusions for the earliest Ethiopic text on two manuscripts, Eth[Ber Or Fl 3067] and Eth[BN Abb 55]. Schäfers came to the conclusion that the *Vorlage* of the oldest stratum of Eth-Jer virtually equals the original hand of Codex Sinaiticus (LXX$^{S^*}$). Ziegler modified Schäfers's view.[11] It seems that the Greek *Vorlage* (→ 7.3) of Eth-Jer was very close to Codex Sinaiticus except for its many corruptions and singular readings. In addition, the *Vorlage* of Eth-Jer shows some singular readings found only in minuscule LXX[130], which itself is a near relative of Codex Sinaiticus.

---

[1] Zuurmond, "Bible Vorlage," 564.
[2] Ziegler, *Ieremias*, 29.
[3] Heider, "Die aethiopische Bibelübersetzung."
[4] Heider, *Die aethiopische Bibelübersetzung*.
[5] Schäfers, *Die Äthiopische Übersetzung des Propheten Jeremias*.
[6] Uhlig, "Biblical Text Criticism," 568.
[7] In the model proposed for these articles, this would be the Standardized Text (S. Delamarter).
[8] Uhlig, "Biblical Text Criticism," 568.
[9] Ziegler, *Ieremias*.
[10] Cf. Zuurmond, "The Ethiopic Version," 242–43.
[11] Ziegler, *Ieremias*, 32.

6–9.2.3.2.5 Text-Critical Value of Eth-Jer for LXX-Jer

Given the textual proximity of Eth-Jer to LXX^{S*} (→ 7.3) without its many corruptions and singular readings, the text-critical value of Eth-Jer as an additional witness to manuscripts that are in line with Codex Sinaiticus cannot be overestimated. It must be kept in mind, however, that the recovery of the Greek *Vorlage* of Eth-Jer is limited by the idiosyncrasy of Ethiopic as opposed to Greek, by the liberty of word order, the sometimes ambivalent use of prepositions and personal pronouns, and the additions (or omissions) of auxiliary words, verbs, or particles to harmonize the text.

Heider, A., "Die aethiopische Bibelübersetzung: Ihre Herkunft, Art, Geschichte und ihr Wert für die alt- und neutestamentliche Wissenschaft: Mit Jeremia Cap. 1–13 als Textprobe, dem aeth. Pseudepigraph: die Prophetie an Pashur und einem General-Katalog der abessinischen Handschriften (Als Prolegomena zu einer kritischen Ausgabe der aeth. Bibel)," (PhD diss., Vereinigte Friedrichs-Universität Halle-Wittenberg, 1902).

Heider, A., *Die aethiopische Bibelübersetzung: Ihre Herkunft, Art, Geschichte und ihr Wert für die alt- und neutestamentliche Wissenschaft*, Fasc. 1: *Bibelkritische Abhandlung – Die Prophetie des Jeremia an Pashur: Mit deutscher Übersetzung* (Leipzig: Pfeiffer, 1902).

Knibb, M.A., "Bible Vorlage Syriac, Hebrew, Coptic, Arabic," *EAE* 1:565.

Schäfers, J., *Die Äthiopische Übersetzung des Propheten Jeremias* (Freiburg i.B.: Herder, 1912).

Uhlig, S., "Biblical Text Criticism," *EAE* 1:565–69.

Ziegler, J., *Ieremias, Baruch, Threni, Epistula Ieremiae* (2nd ed.; Septuaginta Vetus Testamentum Graecum 15; Göttingen: Vandenhoeck & Ruprecht, 1976).

Zuurmond, R., "Bible Vorlage: Greek," *EAE* 1:564–65.

Zuurmond, R. (rev. by C. Niccum), "The Ethiopic Version of the New Testament," in *The Text of the New Testament in Contemporary Research: Essays on the Status Quaestionis* (eds. B. Ehrman and M. Holmes; 2nd ed.; NTTS 42; Leiden: Brill, 2012), 231–52.

Martin Heide

6–9.2.3.3 Ezekiel
6–9.2.3.3.1 Place in the Manuscripts

In a study of thirty manuscripts, Eth-Ezek is most frequently associated with Jeremiah (coming after the Jeremiah corpus fourteen times and before it three times) and Daniel (coming before Daniel seven times and after it twice). But this is part of a larger pattern in which Eth-Ezek often appears as part of the quartet: Isaiah (→ 6–9.2.3.1), Jeremiah (→ 6–9.2.3.2), Ezekiel, Daniel (→ 18.4.3). In four cases, the four works are contiguous, and three of the four are contiguous in another four cases.

In six cases, Eth-Ezek was associated with books of Esdras (coming four times before and twice after; → 19.4.3; → II.7.1.5; → II.7.2.4); and twice with books of Maccabees (once before and once after). On three occasions, Eth-Ezek was copied by itself (twice) or with only the *Life of Ezekiel* (once). Overall, the *Life of Ezekiel* appeared four times in these thirty manuscripts. Copied in the twentieth century, Eth$^{EMIP\ 691}$ is devoted to the book of Ezekiel with a commentary, the *Life of Ezekiel*, and *Synaxarium* entries for Ezekiel.

6–9.2.3.3.2 Introduction

The Ethiopic translation of Ezekiel was made from a Greek manuscript related to the Alexandrian text (→ 1.3.1.2). It dates from some time in the period from the fourth to the sixth century C.E. during which the Christian Scriptures were all translated into Gəʿəz, but it is unlikely that it belongs early in this period. However, the oldest extant manuscript of Eth-Ezek dates only from the fifteenth century, and the majority of the manuscripts are much more recent (→ 1.4.3.2). The translation of Ezekiel into Gəʿəz can be compared to that of the other Prophetic Books (→ 6–9.2.3.1; → 6–9.2.3.2; → 6–9.2.3.4), and the translations have many characteristics in common. As a secondary witness of the Alexandrian text, Eth-Ezek has very limited value for the reconstruction of the Greek text, and its real significance lies within the Ethiopian context.

6–9.2.3.3.3 Textual History

On the basis of the extent of the text they attest, their age, and the textual basis of the translation they contain, the forty or so manuscripts of Eth-Ezek that are known can be clearly divided into two groups, Eth I and Eth II, representative of an older and a younger type of text. Thus, the Eth I manuscripts possess a considerably abbreviated text in Ezekiel 42–48 in comparison with LXX (→ 8.3) and MT (→ 8.2.2), whereas the Eth II manuscripts have a complete text. The Eth I manuscripts almost all date from the sixteenth century or earlier, whereas the Eth II manuscripts are later than this. Finally, while the original translation was made from a Greek text, and this is still clearly evident in the Eth I manuscripts despite later revisions, the Eth II manuscripts contain a text that has been revised against MT-Ezek and contain, particularly in Ezekiel 40–48, many transliterations that go back directly to the Hebrew text.

It has often been argued that the textual history of the Ethiopic Old Testament can be divided into three stages, the Old Ethiopic, which represents the closest it is possible to get to the original translation from the Greek, the Vulgar recension, which reflects (a) revision(s) of the text based on Syriac (→ 6–9.1.4; → 3–5.2.4) or, more probably, Syro-Arabic (→ 6–9.2.8), originals in the medieval period, and the Academic recension, which reflects a further revision of the text based on MT (→ 1.4.3.7.7). So far as Eth-Ezek is concerned, it can perhaps be argued that the text contained in Eth[Tana 9] of the early fifteenth century reflects the Old Ethiopic, but even this manuscript contains evidence of revisions based on a Syro-Arabic text, and it is not clear in the case of Eth-Ezek how far it is possible to separate out a text unaffected by revision in the medieval period. That said, it clearly is possible, on the basis of conjunctive errors, to divide the Eth I manuscripts into a number of families:

1. Family 1 consisting of Eth[Tana 9] of the early fifteenth century, or perhaps a little later, Eth[EMML 26] of the fifteenth or sixteenth century, and the incomplete Eth[EMML 25] of the sixteenth century. The latter two manuscripts were in private possession when photographed as part of the Ethiopian Manuscript Microfilm Library project, but both came from Gunda Gunde;
2. Family 2 consisting of Eth[Ber Peterm II, Nachtr 42], from the first, or possibly the second, half of the fifteenth century, Eth[EMML 2080] (private library, Ḥayq Esṭifānos) probably from the early sixteenth century, and Eth[EMML 2082] (Monastery of Ḥayq Esṭifānos) of the sixteenth or seventeenth century. Eth[BL Or 501] of the fifteenth century, probably from after 1450, also has errors characteristic of family 2 and belongs with this family;
3. Family 3 consisting of Eth[BN Abb 55], Eth[EMML 1768] (Monastery of Ḥayq Esṭifānos), and an incomplete manuscript from the Church of Zion, Axum (Eth[Davies Axum 1]), all three dating from around 1500;
4. Eth[Cam 1570], which is dated to 1588/1589, also belongs to the Eth I group of manuscripts, but stands somewhat apart in that it has also been revised against a Hebrew text. This is evident in Ezekiel 40–48 where, in contrast to the other Eth I manuscripts, it does have a complete text. But despite many similarities in Ezekiel 40–48 with the text attested in the Eth II manuscripts, it often uses a different vocabulary. Notable also throughout the text is the frequent addition to the divine name of the title "the Most High."

There is much less variation within the Eth II manuscripts, but a distinction can be drawn between Eth[BN Abb 35] and Eth[BL Add 24,991] from the seventeenth century, on the one hand, and manuscripts from the eighteenth century and later, on the other. The two former manuscripts contain a number of variants and are characterized by numerous marginal readings and additions, whereas the text in the latter manuscripts is more uniform in character.

6–9.2.3.3.4 Character of the Translation into Ethiopic

The present writer has discussed methods of translation ("translation techniques") used in the Ethiopic Old Testament in the second and third chapters of his *Translating the Bible. Many of the examples considered there are drawn from Eth-Ezek, and reference should be made to that discussion. Here, it may be noted that the overwhelming impression created by the Ethiopic Old Testament – and in this case by Eth-Ezek – is one of literality, but that some significant changes were made in order to accommodate the Greek constructions to the Ethiopic language, for example, the marked preference for verbal rather than nominal constructions, or the avoidance of passive forms by the use of third person impersonal constructions. It is evident that in places the translators had a poor understanding of the underlying Greek text, and in others that the text has suffered during the course of its transmission. Quite apart from the major abbreviation of the text in Ezekiel 42–48, Eth-Ezek is characterized by numerous minor omissions and additions in comparison with the Greek, of which some no doubt occurred during the transmission of the text, but some may go back to the original translation. So far as vocabulary is concerned, there are cases where a Greek word was consistently rendered by the same Ethiopic term, but in many cases there is a complete lack of consistency in the use of translation equivalents.

6–9.2.3.3.5 The Greek Parent Text

Eth-Ezek belongs among the witnesses to the Alexandrian text (→ 1.3.1.2) and can be seen to follow the Alexandrian text to a very great extent throughout the book.[1] Amongst the minuscules allied to Codex Alexandrinus, it frequently agrees with the pair LXX[106] and LXX[410]. But there is also clear evidence of agreement with LXX[534], the close ally of LXX[130], which Ziegler, in his Göttingen edition,[2] identified as being the most closely related of the minuscules to Eth-Ezek. Löfgren similarly argued that the *Vorlage* of Eth-Dan was most closely related to LXX[130].[3] Eth-Ezek, although a witness to the Alexandrian text, reflects the influence of a manuscript with a text-type like that of LXX[130 534].

6–9.2.3.3.6 Editions

Da Bassano's edition of Eth-Ezek to a very large extent reproduces the text of the Academic recension, but some further revisions were made. The same is also true of the text of Eth-Ezek in the edition of the prophets published by the *Maḫbärä ḥawaryat*, "Community of the Apostles." A critical edition of the text, based on fifteen manuscripts, was just published by the present author.[4]

Anonymous, *Mäṣḥafä tənbitä näbiyat* (Asmara: Maḫbärä ḥawaryat fəre haymanot, 1977).
Bassano, *Beluy kidan.
Knibb, M.A., "Hebrew and Syriac Elements in the Ethiopic Version of Ezekiel?" *JSS* 33 (1988): 11–35.
Knibb, M.A., "The Ethiopic Text of Ezekiel and the Excerpts in GƎBRÄ ḤEMAMAT," *JSS* 34 (1989): 443–58.
Knibb, *Translating the Bible.
Knibb, M.A., "Two Notes on the Ethiopic Text of Ezekiel," in *Semitic Studies in Honour of Edward Ullendorff* (ed. G. Khan; Studies in Semitic Languages and Linguistics 47; Leiden: Brill, 2005), 236–44.
Knibb, M.A., "The Greek *Vorlage* of the Ethiopic Text of Ezekiel," in *Scripture in Transition: Essays on Septuagint, Hebrew Bible, and Dead Sea Scrolls in Honour of Raija Sollamo* (eds. A. Voitila and J. Jokiranta; JSJSup 126; Leiden: Brill, 2008), 413–21.
Knibb, M.A., *The Ethiopic Text of the Book of Ezekiel: A Critical Edition* (Oxford: Oxford University Press, 2015).
Löfgren, O., *Die äthiopische Übersetzung des Propheten Daniel* (Paris: Geuthner, 1927).
Ziegler, J., *Ezechiel* (Supplement by D. Fraenkel; 2nd ed.; Septuaginta Vetus Testamentum Graecum 16.1; Göttingen: Vandenhoeck & Ruprecht, 1977).

Michael Knibb

---

[1] Knibb, "Greek *Vorlage*."
[2] Ziegler, *Ezechiel*.
[3] Löfgren, *Die äthiopische Übersetzung des Propheten Daniel*.
[4] Knibb, *The Ethiopic Text of the Book of Ezekiel*.

6–9.2.3.4 Minor Prophets
6–9.2.3.4.1 Name of the Corpus
The twelve Minor Prophets are referred to collectively as ደቂቀ ነቢያት "Minor Prophets" corresponding to the term used to designate the "Major Prophets," ዐበይት ነቢያት.

6–9.2.3.4.2 Location in the Manuscripts
The order of Eth-MinP was inviolate in the Ethiopic scribal tradition: Hosea (ዘሆሴዕ), Amos (ዘአሞጽ), Micah (ዘሚክያስ), Joel (ዘኢዩኤል), Obadiah (ዘአብድዩ), Jonah (ዘዮናስ), Nahum (ዘናሆም), Habakkuk (ዘእንባቆም), Zephaniah (ዘሶፎንያስ), Haggai (ዘሐጊ), Zechariah (ዘዘካርያስ), and Malachi (ዘሚልክያስ). In a study of sixty-four manuscripts that included books of Eth-MinP, fifty-one had all of the books intact and in this order. Some of the remaining manuscripts had suffered damage and dislocation of folios, but wherever the evidence was still extant, it was consistent with this standard order of the books. The manuscripts clearly show that the individual books were conceived as parts of the whole; in only six cases were manuscripts produced that contained only one of the books of Eth-MinP: Eth^EMML 2545 (copied in 1908–1909) provided the single example of a manuscript containing only a solitary book of Eth-MinP, in this case Joel, and a further five manuscripts contained only the two works Isaiah and Joel. Otherwise, the evidence shows that Eth-MinP traveled as one.

This uniformity of practice with regard to the order of the books within Eth-MinP stands in stark contrast to the variety of practices for locating Eth-MinP in relationship to other biblical works. Far and away the greatest association was with the book of Isaiah (→ 6–9.2.3.1). In twenty-four cases, the book of Isaiah came just before; in a further six cases, just after the Minor Prophets. Thus, in just under fifty percent of the manuscripts, Isaiah and the Minor Prophets are adjacent. The next most frequent associations were with Daniel (→ 18.4.3; nine just before and nine just after, totaling eighteen manuscripts, or just under thirty percent of the whole), the Solomonic quartet of Proverbs (→ 12.4.3), Qohelet (→ 13–17.2.3.2), Wisdom of Solomon (→ 11.15.5), and Canticles (→ 13–17.2.3.2; four just before, three after, totaling seven manuscripts, or just over ten percent of the whole), and the book of Jeremiah (→ 6–9.2.3.2; five just before and one just after, totaling six manuscripts, or just under ten percent of the whole). Beyond these, however, the placement of Eth-MinP shows associations with many other works in such a way as to defy any particular schema: books of Esdras (→ 19.4.3; → 11.7.1.5; → 11.7.2.4) and Job (→ 11.4.3; five times each), Enoch (→ 11.5.1.2), Ben Sira (→ 11.4.6), and Maccabees (four times each), Kingdoms (→ 3–5.2.3.3), the trio of Tobit (→ 11.14.9), Judith (→ 11.9.6), and Esther (→ 13–17.2.3.5; three times each), Chronicles (→ 20.4.3; twice) and Ezekiel (→ 6–9.2.3.3; once).

6–9.2.3.4.3 History of Scholarship
With the possible exception of Dillmann's work on the Octateuch (→ 2.5.3) and the widespread fascination with the Ethiopic book of Enoch (→ 11.5.1.2), the Eth-MinP have received perhaps more attention than any other corpus in the Ethiopic Old Testament. Editions of Jonah were published by Petraeus in 1660[1] and Staudacher in 1706.[2] Joel and Malachi were also published by Petraeus in 1661.[3] Since then, eight scholars have produced editions of one or more of the books. A listing of those editions along with the numbers of manuscripts employed will give some idea of the degree to which the works were more or less deserving of the label "critical edition":

- 1802, Marcel on Jonah, based on an unknown number of manuscripts.[4]
- 1857, Wright on Jonah, based on two manuscripts.[5]
- 1892–1893, Bachmann on Obadiah and Malachi, based on three manuscripts.[6]

---

[1] Petraeus, *Prophetia Ionæ*.
[2] Staudacher, *Aḥad amelāk za-Yonās nabiy*.
[3] Petraeus, *Prophetia Joel*; Petraeus, *Vaticinium Malachiae*.
[4] Marcel, *Jonas Propheta*.
[5] Wright, *The Book of Jonah*.
[6] Bachmann, *Der Prophet Obadia*; Bachmann, *Der Prophet Maleachi*.

- 1879, Dillmann on Joel, based on five manuscripts.[7]
- 1898, Kramer on Zechariah, based on three manuscripts.[8]
- 1917, Esteves Pereira on Amos, based on two manuscripts.[9]
- 1930, Löfgren on Jonah (eight manuscripts), Nahum (eight manuscripts), Habakkuk (eight manuscripts), Zephaniah (eight manuscripts), Haggai (eight manuscripts), Zechariah (seven manuscripts), and Malachi (six manuscripts).[10]
- 1968, Fuhs on Micah, based on up to twenty-two manuscripts.[11]
- 1971, Fuhs on Hosea, based on up to twenty-seven manuscripts.[12]

The early editions were not only based on few manuscripts, but in retrospect we would say they also suffered from a lack of methodological precision. When we realize how few manuscripts they had, it is not surprising that they made little or no attempt to describe the textual history of the book(s) under study and why they often mistook manuscripts to be representatives of the Old Ethiopic that would later come to be recognized as representatives of later stages of the textual history. Further, as with all of the work performed on the text of the Ethiopic Old Testament in the eighteenth to the twentieth centuries, the scholars were interested in the Old Ethiopic text primarily as a source for determining the textual history of the Greek manuscript tradition. Bachmann states it clearly, "In a series of subsequent studies, we set us the task, to study in detail the Ethiopic translation of the OT with regard to its textcritical value for the reconstruction of the Septuagint."[13] This has led to a distorted view of the textual history and a systematic ignoring of the latest stages of the textual history. None of the editions, including the best of them by Fuhs (see below, → 6–9.2.3.4.4), made use of manuscripts later than the eighteenth century, even when they had them available. Consequently, none speak with any precision about an Academic Edition (if such existed, → 1.4.3.7.7), nor have anything at all to say about the modern Textus Receptus (→ 1.4.3.7.6).

This is also true for Löfgren's edition of Jonah, Nahum, Habakkuk, Zephaniah, Haggai, Zechariah, and Malachi.[14] It should be considered a reliable representation of the Old Ethiopic, but he offers no model for understanding the later textual history of the Eth-MinP.

6–9.2.3.4.4 Fuhs' Model

Fuhs' work on the books of Micah and Hosea represents the most advanced work done to date, not only on a book of Eth-MinP, but on any of the books of the Ethiopic Old Testament. The textual history reflected in the manuscripts of Eth-Mic in his 1968 edition was confirmed for Hosea by his later study in 1971. His manuscript sample fell into three groups. Group one was made up of three manuscripts that represent the Old Ethiopic (→ 1.4.3.7.3). Fuhs provides a list[15] of eleven readings in Hos 1:1; 2:1; 3:1; 4:15; 5:8; 6:10; 10:11, 14; 12:3; 13:5; and 14:10 in which this group of three manuscripts distinguishes itself from all the rest. However, he noticed that two of the three, his manuscripts B and C, were very closely linked, while the third, his manuscript K, achieved "a relative independence" from the other two.[16] In his book of Micah, Fuhs' manuscript K (eighteenth century) had proven to be closely aligned with the best single representative of the Old Ethiopic, Eth[Hunt 625].

---

[7] Dillmann, "Der äthiopische Text des Joel."
[8] Kramer, *Die äthiopische Übersetzung des Zacharias*.
[9] Esteves Pereira, *O livro do profeta Amós*.
[10] Löfgren, *Jona, Nahum, Habakuk, Zephanja, Haggai, Sacharja und Maleachi Äthiopisch*.
[11] Fuhs, *Die Äthiopische Übersetzung des Propheten Micha*.
[12] Fuhs, *Die Äthiopische Übersetzung des Propheten Hosea*.
[13] Bachmann, *Der Prophet Obadia*, 6: "Wir haben uns nun die Aufgabe gesetzt, in einer Reihe fortlaufender Arbeiten die aethiopische Bibelübersetzung des A.T.'s auf ihren textkritischen Wert hin für die Reconstruction der Septuaginta genau zu untersuchen."
[14] Löfgren, *Jona, Nahum, Habakuk, Zephanja, Haggai, Sacharja und Maleachi Äthiopisch*.
[15] Fuhs, *Die Äthiopische Übersetzung des Propheten Hosea*, 16.
[16] Fuhs, *Die Äthiopische Übersetzung des Propheten Hosea*, 17: "eine relative Selbständigkeit."

But Eth^(Hunt 625) lacks the book of Hosea. Fuhs decided that his manuscript K was the best representative of the Old Ethiopic in Hosea and that his manuscripts B and C formed a sub-group within the Old Ethiopic. Fuhs notices a clear relationship between the text of the Old Ethiopic and the Greek minuscules LXX239, 130, 26, 311.[17] In the end, we may argue that Fuhs' sample of Old Ethiopic texts was too small and that the relationship went the other way around, with his manuscripts B and C representing the Old Ethiopic and his manuscript K representing a transitional text within the Old Ethiopic group. Either way, these results are consistent with the notion that the final stage of the Old Ethiopic represents a period in which the inadequacies of the Old Ethiopic were being addressed by scribes in haphazard ways. This movement to fix the Old Ethiopic culminated in, or gave way to, the systematic revision we call the Standardized Ethiopic text (→ 1.4.3.7.5). This recension is represented in Fuhs' third (latest and largest) group of manuscripts, which he describes in this way: "The group is characterized by an abundance of linguistic and ideological singular readings as well as many expansions, that are typical for a certain type of textual transmission."[18] Fuhs calls this the first Arabic recension and identifies it with what Heider, Schäfers, and Löfgren call the Syro-Arabic recension (→ 6–9.2.8).[19] One of its features is that it shares unique readings in common only with the Syriac.[20]

In a final group of only three manuscripts, Fuhs describes a "second Arabic recension" (→ 6–9.1.8), one of whose characteristics is the substantial number of readings that derive ultimately from MT (→ 9.2.2). For this reason, he also terms this the "Hebrew" recension (→ 1.4.3.7.7). Its base text was apparently the Old Ethiopic since Fuhs sees that it is "heavily depending on the B–C tradition,"[21] which is to say, the Academic Hebraic edition is, in the case of Hosea, grounded directly on the Old Ethiopic, while the Standardized Text is based on some form of the transitional text (Fuhs' manuscript K). Whatever the linguistic background of those who worked on this recension, far from fixing the errors of the Old Ethiopic, they contributed substantially to the "textual mess."[22]

6–9.2.3.4.5 Ziegler's Edition of the Greek Minor Prophets

Normally, one of the richest sources for knowledge of the Old Ethiopic and its relation to the Greek tradition is Ziegler's edition of the Minor Prophets that was published in 1943 and includes reference to the Ethiopic in his collations, based on the readings of three Ethiopian manuscripts available in Europe. Ziegler concluded that the Aeth (as he called it) followed the Alexandrian group (→ 1.3.1.2) of Greek minuscules and he provides a list of shared variants to support this claim.[23]

The problem, however, as Fuhs points out for Eth-Hos,[24] is that none of the three manuscripts used by Ziegler actually contains the Old Ethiopic. Two of them carry what we call the Standardized Text and one carries a mixed text type of the Standardized Text and the Academic Text.

Thus Ziegler's classification of Ethiopic as an Alexandrian witness may be erroneous. In contrast, Fuhs notices a clear relationship between the text

---

[17] Fuhs, *Die Äthiopische Übersetzung des Propheten Hosea*, 121.

[18] Fuhs, *Die Äthiopische Übersetzung des Propheten Hosea*, 22: "Charakteristisch für diese Gruppe ist eine Fülle meist sprachlicher und inhaltlicher Sonderlesarten, sowie häufige Texterweiterungen, die für eine bestimmte Art der Textüberlieferung typisch sind."

[19] A. Heider, *Die aethiopische Bibelübersetzung: Ihre Herkunft, Art, Geschichte und ihr Wert für die alt- und neutestamentliche Wissenschaft*, Fasc. 1: *Bibelkritische Abhandlung – Die Prophetie des Jeremia an Pashur: Mit deutscher Übersetzung* (Leipzig: Pfeiffer, 1902), 5; J. Schäfers, *Die Äthiopische Übersetzung des Propheten Jeremias* (Freiburg i.B.: Herder, 1912), 27; and O. Löfgren, *Die äthiopische Übersetzung des Propheten Daniel* (Paris: Paul Geuthner, 1927), xliii–xlv.

[20] See the list in Fuhs, *Die Äthiopische Übersetzung des Propheten Hosea*, 105–06.

[21] Fuhs, *Die Äthiopische Übersetzung des Propheten Hosea*, 21: "sehr stark von der B–C Tradition abhängig."

[22] Fuhs, *Die Äthiopische Übersetzung des Propheten Hosea*, 110. Fuhs uses the German term "Textmisere."

[23] Ziegler, *Duodecim Prophetae*, 46.

[24] Fuhs, *Die Äthiopische Übersetzung des Propheten Hosea*, 116.

of the Old Ethiopic and the Greek minuscules LXX[26, 130, 239, 311].[25] One would expect the remaining books of Eth-MinP to rely upon the same Greek foundation, but the Old Ethiopic version stands at some distance from most of these manuscripts in Joel and Jonah.

In these books, there are a number of distinctive readings shared with mss LXX[W, 407] and/or LXX[410]. For example, LXX[V, 410] omit ὅτι "indeed" in Joel 4:10, and LXX[W Sc V] add πόλις "city" after Jerusalem in Joel 4:17. In Jonah 1:3, manuscripts LXX[W, 407] agree with the Ethiopic in reading ἀνέβη "went up," and the Ethiopic and LXX[410] omit κυρίῳ "to the Lord" in Jonah 1:16. Yet the Ethiopic also preserves some distinctive readings of the Catena ἀνέβη group, particularly those in common with LXX[C (87 91 490)] and LXX[68]. Thus, in Joel 4:5, the Ethiopic and these Catena manuscripts have ναούς "temples" instead of οἴκους "houses" and omit ἐπ'αὐτήν "because of it" at Jonah 4:10. The Ethiopic displays no agreement with unique Hexaplaric (→ 6–9.1.5) or Lucianic (→ 6–9.1.6) readings. Without critical editions of the other books of Eth-MinP, no firm conclusions can be made. Generally, the Old Ethiopic represents a "mixed text," but a study of the textual character of the entire corpus is still a desideratum.

6–9.2.3.4.6 Jonah 1:9 – A Case Study in the Textual History

Beyond Micah and Hosea, little is known for sure about the textual history of Eth-MinP. It is quite possible that the recension history is not uniform across all twelve books. Yet, several lines of evidence converge to suggest that most conform to the general patterns observed with other books in the Ethiopic Old Testament. An analysis of the Ethiopic manuscripts from Jonah 1:9 offers an example of the textual history and the nature of each of the stages of the text.[26]

6–9.2.3.4.6.1 Old Ethiopic (→ 1.4.3.7.3)

Text: ወይቤሎሙ ገብረ እግዚአብሔር አነ ወአመልክ እግዚአብሔር አምላከ ሰማይ ዘገብረ ባሕረ ወየብሰ።

Translation: "And he said to them, I am a servant of God (= LXX) and I worship God, Lord of the heavens who made the sea and the dry land."

Character: Shares with LXX the variant, "I am a servant of God."

Found in: Eth[EMIP 1029, GG 181, GG 152].

6–9.2.3.4.6.2 Transitional Ethiopic Text (= TE; → 1.4.3.7.4)

Text: ወይቤሎሙ +[ዮናስ] ገብረ እግዚአብሔር አነ ወአመልክ +[በ]እግዚአብሔር አምላከ ሰማይ ዘገብረ +[ሰማየ ወምድረ ወ]ባሕረ ወየብሰ።

Translation: "And +[Jonah] said to them, I am a servant of God (= LXX) and I worship +[preposition marking the accusative] God, Lord of the heavens who made +[the heavens and the earth and] the sea and the dry land."

Character: This family of manuscripts has a variety of similar variants, often pluses and otherwise unattested readings. Those listed here are the most common pluses at this point, although only two of the manuscripts contain all three.

Found in: Eth[Davies Axum 1, EMML 1768, IES 436, EMIP 881, EMML 1481, UNES 10.65].

6–9.2.3.4.6.3 Standardized Ethiopic Text (= SE; → 1.4.3.7.5)

Text: ወይቤሎሙ [ዕብራዊ] አነ [ወአምላኪየ] እግዚአብሔር አምላከ ሰማይ +[ወምድር] ዘገብረ ባሕረ ወየብሰ።

Translation: "And he said to them, I am a Hebrew (= MT) and [my Lord is (against both LXX and MT)] God, Lord of the heavens +[and the earth (against both LXX and MT)] who made the sea and the dry land."

Character: "I am a Hebrew" aligns with MT against LXX. Instead of using a verb for worship, the reading employs a nominal phrase, "my Lord [is] God." All four of the manuscripts in this family are identical word for word.

Found in: Eth[EMIP 746, EMIP 2007, UNES 10.04, EMIP 1063].

---

[25] Fuhs, *Die Äthiopische Übersetzung des Propheten Hosea*, 121.

[26] In the example below, the abbreviations TE, SE, TR refer to the Transitional Ethiopic Text, the Standardized Ethiopic Text, and the modern Textus Receptus, respectively.

6–9.2.3.4.6.4 A Non-Indigeneous Text

Text: አነ ዕብራዊ አነ ወእፈርሀ አነ እግዚእ አምላከ ሰማይ ዘገብረ ባሕረ ወየብሰ።

Translation: "I am a Hebrew (= MT/SE) and I fear (= MT) the Lord, Lord of the heavens who made the sea and the dry land."

Character: Contains the variant "I am a Hebrew" that aligns with MT against LXX, and that first emerged in the Standardized Ethiopic Text. Further, the verb ፈርሀ, "to fear" aligns with MT (ירא, "to fear") against LXX. Manuscripts of this family are rare.

Found in: Eth[UNES 10.34, EMIP 949, EMML 7942].

6–9.2.3.4.6.5 Modern Textus Receptus (→ 1.4.3.7.6)

Text: ወይቤሎሙ ዮናስ ገብረ እግዚአብሔር አነ ዕብራዊ ወአምላኪየ እግዚአብሔር አምላከ ሰማይ ወምድር ዘገብረ ባሕረ ወየብሰ።

Translation: "And Jonah (= TE) said to them, I am a servant of God (= LXX), a Hebrew (= MT/SE/TR), and my Lord is God (= SE), Lord of the heavens and the earth (= SE) who made the sea and the dry land."

Character: Shares the variant "Jonah" that first emerged in the TE text. Conflates both readings, "servant of God" and "Hebrew." Incorporates the nominal sentence and the extended formula "Lord of the heavens +[and the earth]" that first appeared in the SE text.

Found in: Eth[Cer 75; EMIP 1095; IES 77].

Bachmann, J., *Dodekapropheton Aethiopum oder die zwölf kleinen Propheten der aethiopischen Bibelübersetzung*, Vol. 1: *Der Prophet Obadia* (Halle: Niemeyer, 1892).

Bachmann, J., *Dodekapropheton Aethiopum oder die zwölf kleinen Propheten der aethiopischen Bibelübersetzung*, Vol. 2: *Der Prophet Maleachi* (Halle: Niemeyer, 1893).

Dillmann, A., "Der äthiopische Text des Joel," in *Die Prophetie des Joel und ihre Ausleger* (ed. A. Merx; Halle: Verl. der Buchhdlg. des Waisenhauses, 1879), 449–58.

Esteves Pereira, F.M., *O livro do profeta Amós e a sua versão etiópica* (Academia das sciêncas de Lisboa Separata de "Boletin do Segunda Classe" 11; Coimbra: Impr. da Univ., 1917).

Fuhs, H.F., *Die Äthiopische Übersetzung des Propheten Micha* (BBB 28; Bonn: Peter Hanstein Verlag, 1968).

Fuhs, H.F., *Die Äthiopische Übersetzung des Propheten Hosea* (BBB 38; Bonn: Peter Hanstein Verlag, 1971).

Kramer, F.O., *Die äthiopische Übersetzung des Zacharias*, Fasc. 1: *Text zum ersten Male herausgegeben, Prolegomena, Commentar: eine Vorstudie zur Geschichte und Kritik des Septuagintatextes* (Leipzig: Ackermann & Glaser, 1898).

Löfgren, O., *Jona, Nahum, Habakuk, Zephanja, Haggai, Sacharja und Maleachi Äthiopisch unter Zugrundelegung des Oxforder Ms. Huntington 625 nach mehreren Handschriften* (Uppsala: Almqvist & Wiksells, 1930).

Marcel, J.J., *Jonas Propheta, idiomate gheez, seu Æthiopum litterali* (Paris: Johannes-Josephus Marcel, 1802).

Petraeus, T., *Prophetia Ionæ ex Æthiopico in Latinum ad verbum versa, et notis atque adagiis illustrata; cui adjunguntur quatuor Geneseos capita, è vetustissimo manuscripto Aethiop. Eruta* (Leiden: Nisselianis, 1660).

Petraeus, T., *Prophetia Joel, Æthiopice, Interpretatione Latina ad Verbum donate & perbrevi vocum Hebraicarum & Arabicarum harmonia illustrata* (Leiden: Nisselianis, 1661).

Petraeus, T., *Vaticinium Malachiae, prophetarum ultimi, Aethiopice, Latino idiomate donatum ad verbum donatum, & ad usum ac captum ton philologon accommodatum* (Leiden: Nisselianis, 1661).

Staudacher, B.A., *Aḥad amelāk za-Yonās nabiy Hoc est Jonas Vates Æthiopice & Latine: cum glossario aethiopico-harmonico in eundem & IV. Geneseos capita priora* (Frankfurt a.M.: J.P. Andrae, 1706).

Wright, W., *The Book of Jonah in Four Semitic Versions, viz., Chaldee, Syriac, Aethiopic, and Arabic, with Corresponding Glossaries* (London: Williams and Norgate, 1857).

Ziegler, J. (ed.), *Duodecim Prophetae* (Septuaginta Vetus Testamentum Graecum 13; Göttingen: Vandenhoeck & Ruprecht, 1943).

Steve Delamarter
Anke Dorman
Curt Niccum
Kipp Swinney
Jeremy Brown

6–9.2.4 Late Syriac Translations

6–9.2.4.1 Background

The late Syriac translations of the books of Isaiah, Jeremiah, Ezekiel, and the Twelve Minor Prophets (MinP) post-date the Peshitta (s; → 1.3.4) and reflect the rising prestige of LXX (ܫܒܥܝܢ ܘܬܪܝܢ "seventy-two") among Syriac-speaking Christians. For the Latter Prophets, there are three translations to be considered: 1) the fragmentary remains of a translation of Isaiah described as Syro-Lucianic/Philoxenian (Syl; sixth century C.E.; → 1.4.4); 2) the Syro-Hexapla (Syh; early seventh century C.E.; → 1.4.5); and 3) a revision of Isaiah and Ezekiel by Jacob of Edessa (d. 708 C.E.; → 1.4.6). These translations all made more extensive use of the Greek versions or were translated from Greek. They served as aids to understanding the exegetical work of Greek biblical commentators and were used to some extent in the liturgy. These late Syriac translations are of significance for textual criticism of LXX (→ 6.3, → 7.3, → 8.3, → 9.3), for study of Origen's Hexapla (→ 6–9.1.5) and its reception in the Syrian Orient, and for understanding the history of the interpretation of the Bible in the Syriac churches.

6–9.2.4.2 Syro-Lucianic/Philoxenian Version

6–9.2.4.2.1 Original Form, Editions, Tools

Philoxenus (ca. 440–523 C.E.) sponsored a Syriac translation of LXX (→ 6.3) by his chorepiscopus Polycarp (PhOT), who seems to have produced a translation of at least Genesis, Exodus, and Isaiah.[1] The extant quotations and fragments of these translations show affinities with the Lucianic recension (LXX^L; → 1.3.1.2; → 6–9.1.6), suggesting that Polycarp's Syriac translation revised the Peshitta (→ 1.3.4, → 6–9.1.4) according to a Greek manuscript of LXX^L.[2] Ceriani argued that a seventh-century C.E. manuscript containing a partial text of Isaiah (Isa 28:3–17; 42:17–49:18; 66:11–23; manuscript BL Add. 17,106, ff. 74–87) shows evidence of affinity with the Greek Lucianic text of Isaiah.[3] While the manuscript itself does not indicate this directly, Ceriani's classification has met with acceptance.[4] Indirect evidence for Syl-Isa is found in a scholion to Syh-Isa 9:6, which refers to a Syriac translation sponsored by Philoxenus.[5] The scholion reads: "From another tradition rendered into Syriac at the insistence of the holy Philoxenus, bishop of Mabbug" (ܡܢ ܡܫܠܡܢܘܬܐ ܐܚܪܬܐ ܗܘ ܕܐܬܦܫܩ ܒܣܘܪܝܝܐ ܒܚܦܝܛܘܬܗ ܕܩܕܝܫܐ ܦܝܠܘܟܣܢܘܣ ܐܦܝܣܩܘܦܐ ܕܡܒܘܓ).[6] Jenkins has demonstrated that Philoxenus, in his later works (e.g., a citation of Isa 45:9, *Commentary on the Prologue of John*), cites Syl-Isa.[7] PhOT-Isa can thus be understood as either a witness to or a revision of the Syro-Lucianic version. In a recent evaluation of the evidence, Hiebert concludes that "... the case for a Philoxenian version of at least Isaiah in the Old Testament corpus, though admittedly based on circumstantial evidence, seems nonetheless to be reasonably well established."[8]

---

[1] A. Juckel, "Polykarpos," in *Gorgias Encyclopedic Dictionary of the Syriac Heritage* (eds. S. Brock et al.; Piscataway: Gorgias Press, 2011), 336–37.

[2] Jenkins, *The Old Testament Quotations of Philoxenus of Mabbug*, 18; ter Haar Romeny, "Peshitta and Other Syriac Versions," 2:149–55 (152). See also the earlier study by Deklat, "Die syrolukianische Übersetzung," 21–54. Syl and OTPh are two names for one textual tradition (→ 1.4.4).

[3] Wright, *Catalogue of the Syriac Manuscripts in the British Museum*, 1:23; See also Ceriani, "Esaiae fragmenta syriaca," 1–40.

[4] Jenkins, *The Old Testament Quotations of Philoxenus of Mabbug*, 9–29, offers a study of the textual affinities of the text of Isaiah 45. The earlier study by Deklat ("Die syrolukianische Übersetzung des Buches Jesaja") remains valuable for its close analysis of these readings even if Deklat's postulating of a *Vetus Syra* Isaiah as the basis for Syl has not been considered persuasive. See also Vööbus, *The Hexapla and the Syro-Hexapla*, 48.

[5] Ceriani, *Codex Syro-Hexaplaris Ambrosianus*, 176r. See also Field, **Hexapla*, 2:448, and Jenkins, *The Old Testament Quotations of Philoxenus of Mabbug*, 178–86. For the readings of s, Syh, Syl-Isa, and Jacob of Edessa here, see Salvesen, "The Authorial Spirit," 220.

[6] Ceriani, *Codex syro-hexaplaris Ambrosianus*, 176r.

[7] Jenkins, *The Old Testament Quotations of Philoxenus of Mabbug*, 84; See also Wright, *Catalogue of the Syriac Manuscripts in the British Museum*, 3:xvii; Brock, "Les versions syriaques," 28.

[8] R. Hiebert, "The Place of the Syriac Versions in the Textual History of the Psalter," in *The Book of Psalms: Composition and Reception* (eds. P.W. Flint and P.D. Miller; VTSup 99; Leiden: Brill, 2005), 505–36 (512).

6–9.2.4.2.2 Translation Character

The Syro-Lucianic version offers an idiomatic Syriac translation of the Greek Lucianic recension (→ 1.3.1.2, → 6–9.1.6), which at times shows influence of the Peshitta (→ 1.3.4, → 6–9.1.4). In his critical edition of LXX-Isa (→ 6.3), Ziegler ascribes the departures of the Syro-Lucianic translation from its presumed Greek *Vorlage* to the translator's tendency to make free renderings and to add particles.[9]

6–9.2.4.2.3 Text-Critical Value

Syl-Isa is a comparatively early witness to LXX[L] (→ 6–9.1.6) and has potential value for textual criticism of LXX (→ 6.3) in particular verses.[10] Jenkins observes that Syl-Isa departs from both the Peshitta and LXX[L] in places, thereby raising "questions concerning the reliability of Syl as a witness to its Greek *Vorlage*." Nonetheless, he finds it impossible to exclude the possibility "that, for a given text, Syl *may* alone among witnesses to L (scil. LXX-[L]) preserve a (more) original reading."[11]

6–9.2.4.2.4 Relevance for Exegesis

Syl-Isa is of limited value for exegesis of the Hebrew or Greek texts of Isaiah and is chiefly of interest for the study of the reception of Isaiah in the Syriac churches. Brock has noted that the Syro-Lucianic manuscript of Isaiah (manuscript BL Add. 17,106) has rubrics indicating liturgical use.[12]

6–9.2.4.3 Syro-Hexapla
6–9.2.4.3.1 Background

The Syro-Hexapla was produced in the Enaton monastery near Alexandria between 613–617 C.E. under the direction of Syrian Orthodox Bishop Paul of Tella (→ 1.4.5.2). Though used primarily in Syriac biblical commentary and in theological writings, the Syro-Hexapla also played a limited role in Syriac liturgies. While the precise nature of the Greek *Vorlage* of the Syro-Hexapla and the fidelity of the Syro-Hexapla in representing its source text continue to be debated (→ 1.4.5), the Syro-Hexapla has traditionally been described as a translation of "Origen's Hexapla itself or a summarizing edition containing the fifth column and Hexaplaric marginalia."[13] Based on the evidence of colophons, the text of the Syro-Hexapla, and literary references, recent scholarship has suggested that the Greek *Vorlage* was not Origen's Hexapla itself (→ 1.3.1.2.7), but a copy made from it that was collated with other Greek versions, especially one attributed to Eusebius and Pamphilius.[14] The colophon to Syh-Isa in the manuscript Milan Biblioteca Ambrosiana C 313 inf., f. 193[r] names these two figures explicitly: "Copied and composed from the copy which Eusebius and Pamphilus themselves corrected from the library of Origen." (ܐܬܟܬܒܘ ܘܐܬܦܚܡܘ ܡܢ ܦܚܡܐ ܕܐܘܣܒܝܘܣ ܘܦܡܦܝܠܘܣ ܠܗܘܢ ܗܢܘܢ ܬܪܨܘ ܡܢ ܟܬܒܬܐ ܕܐܘܪܝܓܢܝܣ).

6–9.2.4.3.2 Original Form, Editions, Tools

In the absence of a critical edition of the Syro-Hexapla, the best and most complete witness is the ninth-century Codex Syro-Hexaplaris (Milan Biblioteca Ambrosiana C 313 Inf.), which contains Syh-Later Prophets in this order: Minor Prophets 97[r]–114[v]; Jeremiah 115[r]–138[v]; [Baruch; Lamentations; Letter of Jeremiah; Daniel; Susanna; Bel and the Dragon] Ezekiel 152[r]–173[v]; Isaiah 173[r]–193[v].[15] The colophons of Isaiah, Ezekiel, and the Minor

---

[9] J. Ziegler, *Isaias* (2nd ed.; Septuaginta Vetus Testamentum Graecum 14; Gottingen: Vandenhoeck & Ruprecht, 1967), 81.

[10] Ziegler, *Isaias*, 16, 81–82. Ziegler includes Syl-Isa among the witnesses to LXX[L].

[11] Jenkins, *The Old Testament Quotations of Philoxenus of Mabbug*, 25.

[12] Brock, "Les versions syriaques de l'Ancien Testament," 28.

[13] R. Ceulemans, "The ὁμοίως Notes in the Syro-Hexapla Version of the Song of Songs," *OCP* 79 (2013): 5–36 (7). For Isaiah, Jenkins has suggested the possibility that the Syro-Hexapla is not a translation of the Hexapla but rather "a revision of PhOT throughout" (Jenkins, *The Old Testament Quotations of Philoxenus of Mabbug*, 186; PhOT refers to the Philoxenian translation of the Old Testament). This would mean that Syh-Isa has an earlier Syriac translation as its base, the Syro-Lucianic, and not a Greek text.

[14] See, for example, Liljeström, "Observations," 73, and Law, "Witness," 191–92.

[15] Ceriani, *Codex Syro-Hexaplaris Ambrosianus*.

Prophets in Codex Syro-Hexaplaris (Milan Biblioteca Ambrosiana C 313 inf.) are translated below.

1) Colophon to the Minor Prophets, f. 114ʳ:

[Syriac text]

The book of the Twelve Prophets that has been translated from the tradition of the Seventy is completed, [the Seventy] who translated the holy books from Hebrew into Greek in the days of Ptolemy, king of Egypt, before the days of the coming of Christ, in the great city of Alexandria. The Greek book from which this Syriac book was translated into Syriac had been compared with an old copy, as it was noted on it, from which also were taken over many of the traditions that were recorded in it. The Twelve Prophets were taken from that copy that was according to the traditions of the Tetrapla.[16] Pamphilius and Eusebius carefully corrected it. This book was translated into Syriac in the city of Alexandria in the month of January of the year 928 AG, the fifth Indiction.[17]

2) Colophon to Ezekiel, f. 173ʳ:

[Syriac text]

The end of the book of the Prophet Ezekiel according to the tradition of the Seventy.

3) Colophon to Isaiah, f. 193ʳ:

[Syriac text]

The end of the prophecy of Isaiah according to the tradition of the Seventy. Copied and composed from the copy which Eusebius and Pamphilus themselves corrected from the library of Origen.

While C 313 inf. is the most important source for the text of Syh-Latter Prophets, several additional biblical manuscripts containing parts of Syh-Latter Prophets have been identified.[18]

6–9.2.4.3.3 Translation Character

Syh-Latter Prophets is a mirror translation that aims for both formal equivalence with the translator's Greek source text and lexical consistency.[19]

---

[16] In this colophon, the word Tetrapla most likely refers to a manuscript copied from the fifth column of the Hexapla, which also contained readings from the three revisors, Aquila, Symmachus, and Theodotion.

[17] See Vööbus, *The Hexapla and the Syro-Hexapla*, 38. I am grateful to Adam McCollum for assistance in translating this colophon.

[18] See especially Baars, *New Syro-Hexaplaric Texts*, and, for Syh-Isa, Vööbus, *The Book of Isaiah*. These additional witnesses include an eighth-century C.E. manuscript of Syh-Isa, BL Ms Orient 8732, fol. 57ᵃ–136ᵇ, which once belonged to R. Curzon and contains Syh-Isa begining at Isa 4:6, with Aristarchian symbols as well as rubrication indicating liturgical use. Variant readings from this manuscript were known to Ceriani and published with his reproduction of manuscript C 313 (Ceriani, *Codex Syro-Hexaplaris Ambrosianus*, 114–15). Syh-Isa 27:10–65:20 is found in the eighth-century C.E. manuscript Jerusalem, Monastery of St. Mark, I, published by Vööbus (*The Book of Isaiah*) with lacunae noted by Baars (*New Syro-Hexaplaric Texts*, 11–14). Two leaves in the ninth-century C.E. manuscript Br Mus Add. 17,213, f. 1ᵃ–2ᵇ (= 9k3 Leiden Peshitta) preserve Syh-Isa 49:19–50:10 and 57:21–58:14. The lost portion of folio 2 containing Syh-Isa 58:7–8, 58:14–59:2 has been identified by Brock and Van Rompay with frg. 140 from Deir Al-Surian (*Catalogue of the Syriac Manuscripts*, 348, 452, 791). The eighth-century C.E. manuscript Br. Mus., Add. 14.668 includes Hos 1:1–5:15 and Mic 2:8–3:5 and the last thirty-six verses of Syh-Ezek 47:23–48:35 folios 26–29. Manuscript Deir al-Surian, Syr. 5 folios 5ʳ–127ᵛ contains Syh-Ezek 1:1–47:23 with Hexaplaric signs and marginal notes (see Brock and Van Rompay, *Catalogue of the Syriac Manuscripts*, 23). Fragments of Jonah, Haggai, and Zechariah are found in the eighth-century manuscript Oxford, Bodleian Libr., Syr. d. 10. An eighth-century C.E. manuscript in Harvard's Houghton Libr., Sem. Mus. 3952 contains Syh-Ezek 39:8–17.

[19] Brock provides a survey of recent research on the Syro-Hexapla and its translation character in "Les versions syriaques de l' Ancien Testament," 26–27.

The Syriac word order reflects the Greek source text, which, as Salvesen has noted, had itself been reordered by Origen to correspond to the word order of his Hebrew text. Studies of the mode of translation for individual books include Lund on Ezekiel,[20] Verwijs on Amos 1:3–2:16,[21] and Kruse-Blinkenberg on Malachi.[22] Weitzman's study of Syh-Hos focused on the reliability of retroversions from Syriac to Greek of the readings from Aquila, Symmachus, and Theodotion found in the margins of the Syro-Hexapla.[23]

6–9.2.4.3.4 Translation Technique and Inner-Translational Features

The Syro-Hexapla seeks to represent each distinct element of its Greek source. Syh-Latter Prophets is characterized by the frequent use of the independent possessive pronoun ܕܝܠ- and related forms as a nominal adjunct where the Peshitta employs attached pronominal suffixes. In Isa 55:9, for example, the Hebrew text has attached pronominal suffixes דְּרָכַי מִדַּרְכֵיכֶם "my ways (higher) than your ways" (so also S: ܐܘܪܚܬܝ ܡܢ ܐܘܪܚܬܟܘܢ) while the Syro-Hexapla follows the Greek (ἡ ὁδός μου ἀπὸ τῶν ὁδῶν ὑμῶν) "my way (is far away) from your ways" in using independent possessive pronouns: ܐܘܪܚܐ ܕܝܠܝ ܡܢ ܐܘܪܚܬܐ ܕܠܟܘܢ. All three readings convey the same meaning. The Syro-Hexapla also tends to use a Syriac participle and finite form of the verb "to be" in rendering the Greek imperfect. In Jonah 4:8, for example, the Greek imperfect ἀπελέγετο in the phrase καὶ ἀπελέγετο τὴν ψυχὴν αὐτοῦ "he gave up on his life" is rendered by a finite verb in the Peshitta and by a participle and a finite form of the verb "to be" in the Syro-Hexapla: "he was giving up on his life." In this example, the Syro-Hexapla renders τὴν ψυχὴν αὐτοῦ "his life" with a noun and attached pronominal suffix to conform to the Syriac idiom, departing here from the general pattern mentioned above of matching the Greek with the use of an independent possessive pronoun with -ܕܝܠ. Personal names generally reflect the Greek (e.g., Hebrew "Tabor" in Hos 5:1 rendered in Greek Ἰταβύριον "Itabyrion," in the Peshsitta ܬܒܘܪ "Tabor," and in the Syro-Hexapla ܐܬܒܘܪܝܢ "Itaburion").[24]

Lund has also noted an internal Syriac development reflected in the Syro-Hexapla that is not conditioned by the Greek, namely a change in the syntactic value of the use of nouns in the determined state. He notes in particular the late usage reflected in the Syro-Hexapla of syntactically indefinite nouns in the determined state rather than the absolute state when quantified by numerals.[25] The Syro-Hexapla also reflects a later stage in the development of the Syriac language as indicated by the greater number of Greek loan words.[26] Noting several features of Syh-Ezek that seem to violate the norms of Syriac language and grammar, Lund argues that the Syro-Hexapla "was not intended as a congregational Bible, but as a scholar's reference work, which artificially reflected its Greek source text."[27]

6–9.2.4.3.5 Text-Critical Value

Syh-Latter Prophets is a very important witness to the hexaplaric text of LXX (→ 6–9.1.5). Verwijs observes with regard to Syh-Amos "that the Vorlage of the Syro-Hexapla fell within the tradition of the Old Greek."[28] More precise identification of the textual affinities of the Greek *Vorlage* of the Syro-Hexapla awaits future research. The marginal readings of Aquila, Symmachus, and Theodotion preserved in Syh-Latter Prophets also await more detailed study before conclu-

---

[20] Lund, "Syntactic Features," 67–81.
[21] P. Verwijs, "The Peshitta and Syro-Hexapla Translations of Amos 1:3–2:16" (Unpublished PhD diss., Claremont Graduate University, 2004); Verwijs, "The Septuagint in the Peshitta," 25–40.
[22] Kruse-Blinkenberg, "Book of Malachi," 62–82.
[23] Weitzman, "Reliability of Retroversions," 265–309.

[24] Weitzman, "Reliability of Retroversions," 272.
[25] Lund, "Syntactic Features," 71–72.
[26] Verwijs, "The Septuagint in the Peshitta," 34.
[27] Lund, "Syntactic Features," 81. Lund notes that subsequent lectionary use of the Syro-Hexapla indicates that with time it came to be used in congregational worship. A similar conclusion is reached by Verwijs, "The Septuagint in the Peshitta," 40.
[28] Verwijs, "The Septuagint in the Peshitta," 40. She cautions that the translator at times engaged in "clarifying the Greek text for the receptor audience" (p. 39).

sions can be reached about the accuracy of the transmission of the Aristarchian symbols in these books.

6-9.2.4.3.6 Relevance for Reception History

The Syro-Hexapla was used liturgically, as evidenced by the appearance of this version in Syriac lectionaries, and Syh-Isa was divided into forty-eight chapters (*kephalaia*), a division likely to have been appropriated from a Greek manuscript.[29] The Syro-Hexapla played an important role, alongside other Syriac translations, in the exegetical works of commentators such as Ishʿodad of Merv, Dionysius bar Salibi, and Barhebraeus.[30]

6-9.2.4.4 Jacob of Edessa
6-9.2.4.4.1 Background

Jacob of Edessa (ca. 630–708 C.E.; → 1.4.6) produced a revised version of the Syriac Old Testament at the end of his life while living at the monastery of Tell ʿAdda in northern Syria. For the Latter Prophets, only some chapters of Isaiah and Ezekiel are extant.[31]

6-9.2.4.4.2 Original Form, Editions, Tools

Jacob of Edessa's version of Isaiah is attested in British Library Add MS 14,441, a partially preserved eighth-century C.E. manuscript (ca. 719 C.E.) with liturgical rubrication.[32] It seems originally to have contained the entire text of Isaiah in Jacob of Edessa's revision. Some passages from Isaiah have been published by Ceriani.[33] Jacob's earlier revisions of dozens of quotations from Isaiah, Ezekiel, and the Minor Prophets are found among the 600 Old Testament quotations in the margins of BL Add MS 17,134, which contains Jacob's revisions of the Hymns of Severus of Antioch. A second manuscript of this same text, BL Add MS 18816, contains some of these quotations but not nearly as many.[34] These quotations have recently been analyzed by Juckel and ter Haar Romeny.[35] Juckel argued that the early quotations reflect a preparatory stage, foreshadowing aspects of Jacob's later approach to revising the whole Old Testament.[36] Ter Haar Romeny presents a different interpretation of the evidence, finding no consistent relationship between Jacob's earlier biblical quotations and his later revision of the entire Old Testament.[37] The close analysis of Jacob's work of revision of Isaiah by both Juckel and ter Haar Romeny affords a clearer picture of Jacob's method. Ter Haar Romeny observes that both he and Juckel agree that Jacob in his earlier work sought to keep the various Greek and Syriac translations separate, whereas in his later work there is a discernible shift in approach in which he tended to combine or approximate them. Ter Haar Romeny understands Jacob to have striven after a compromise of the Peshitta (→ 1.3.4) and LXX (→ 1.3.1.1) and to have been less concerned to represent the *graeca veritas* and more

---

[29] Brock, "Text Divisions," 207.

[30] For Ishodad, see J.-M. Vosté, "Les deux versions syriaques de la Bible d'après Mar Isoʿdad de Merw (c. 850)," *Bib* 33 (1952): 235–36. For Bar Salibi, see L. Van Rompay, "Development of Biblical Interpretation in the Syrian Churches of the Middle Ages," in *Hebrew Bible/Old Testament: The History of Its Interpretation*, Vol. 1: *From the Beginning to the Middle Ages (Until 1300)*, Part 2: *The Middle Ages* (ed. M. Saebø; Göttingen: Vandenhoeck & Ruprecht, 2000), 573. For Bar Hebraeus, see F.G. Ward, *The Scholia of Bar Hebraeus on the Book of the Twelve Prophets* (Chicago: The University of Chicago, 1935), 8.

[31] Salvesen, "Yaʿqub of Edessa," 432.

[32] See Wright, *Catalogue of Syriac Manuscripts in the British Museum*, 1.39. The lacunae are as follows: Isa 1:1–2:21; 3:12–7:12; 7:15–8:1; 8:12–12:2; 13:8–20; 19:3–25; 35:2–40:3; 40:16–45:6; 45:17–46:1; 51:3–52:1; 63:9–65:24; 66:1–3; 66:5–66:24. The end of the manuscript is missing and, presumably, the colophon of the manuscript.

[33] Ceriani, "Esaiae fragmenta syriaca," 9–12, 21–23, 25–38. The verses of Jacob of Edessa's revision of Isaiah that Ceriani has published are Isa 28:1–21; 45:7–16; 46:2–49:25. See also Baars, "Ein neugefundenes Bruchstück," 548 n. 6.

[34] Juckel, "Septuagint and Peshitta," 151–54.

[35] Juckel, "Septuagint and Peshitta," 151–77; Juckel, "Approximation," 227–82; ter Haar Romeny, "Jacob of Edessa's Quotations," 389–406.

[36] Juckel, "Septuagint and Peshitta," 151–77. The marginal biblical quotations from the Latter Prophets analyzed by Juckel in this article are the following: Isa 8:23–9:1; 10:33–11:3; 12:2–3; 14:3–15; 14:10–12; 28:16; 29:13–14; 32:1–6; 35:3–10; 40:27–41:2; 49:14–21; 58:1–2; 61:3–8; 62:1–4; 66:6–9; Jer 31:15–17; Ezek 18:21–23; 37:15–17; Hos 2:23–25; Amos 8:9–10; Jonah 3:7–9; Hag 2:6–9; Zech 11:7–8. See also Juckel, "Approximation," 227–82.

[37] Ter Haar Romeny, "Jacob of Edessa's Quotations," 389–406.

concerned "to make the Greek Bible acceptable to Syriac readers."[38]

In 1902, Ugolini, following a suggestion of A.M. Ceriani, identified a manuscript of Ezekiel as belonging to the revision of Jacob of Edessa.[39] The manuscript Vat. Sir. 5 is damaged and lacks Ezek 1:1–14; 16:48–17:9; 19:12–20:12; 20:40–47; 21:24–29; 27:21–29; 29:14–19; 36:9–15; 36:20–34; 37:20–26; 39:1–15; 46:14–48:35. A copy made from it when it was in a better state of preservation is found in manuscript München, Bayr. Staatsbibl., Syr 1, fol. 53^r–88^v.[40]

6–9.2.4.4.3 Translation Character

Jacob based his revision on the Peshitta (→ 1.3.4, → 6–9.1.4), bringing it closer to LXX (→ 6.3, → 8.3) and relying on Hexaplaric (→ 6–9.1.5) and Lucianic (→ 6–9.1.6) traditions. Jacob's manner of revision has been described as "patchwork" and the resultant text, a curious combination of the Peshitta and Hexaplaric and Lucianic recensions of LXX, as an "amalgamation" and a "hybrid."

Juckel describes Jacob of Edessa's revision as one designed "to adjust the Peshitta to the Greek as much as necessary, and to adopt the (unrevised) Peshitta as much as possible."[41] He identifies several important features in Jacob's revision: adoption of the Peshitta, thorough correction of the Peshitta according to the Greek (but also correction of the Greek according to s), and substitution of the Peshitta by means of doublets (translating a single Greek word with two Syriac words), expansions, and additions from the Greek. Both Juckel and ter Haar Romeny describe Jacob's work as an "approximation of the traditions," indicating his extensive use and recombination of earlier Greek and Syriac translations.

6–9.2.4.4.4 Text-Critical Value

The complex combination or "approximation of traditions" that characterizes Jacob of Edessa's revision make it of no direct use for textual criticism of the Hebrew text, but it is of interest for the study of the Lucianic (→ 6–9.1.6) and Hexaplaric (→ 6–9.1.5) traditions and thus for textual criticism of LXX (→ 6.3, → 8.3).

6–9.2.4.4.5 Relevance for Reception History

As Juckel has noted, "The Old Testament revision of Jacob of Edessa (d. 708 C.E.) is the last work in the history of biblical revisions undertaken in the Syrian Orthodox Church."[42] As such, the revision is highly relevant to the study of the reception of the Bible in the Syriac churches and to the history of Syriac biblical commentary.

Baars, W., *New Syro-Hexaplaric Texts: Edited, Commented upon and Compared with the Septuagint* (Leiden: Brill, 1968).

Baars, W., "Ein neugefundenes Bruchstück aus der syrischen Biblerevision des Jakob von Edessa," *VT* 18 (1968): 548–54.

Brock, S., "Text Divisions in the Syriac Translation of Isaiah," in *Biblical Hebrew, Biblical Texts: Essays in Honor of Michael P. Weitzman* (eds. A. Rapoport-Albert and G. Greenberg; JSOTSup 333; Sheffield: Sheffield Academic Press, 2001), 200–21.

Brock, S., "Les versions syriaques de l' Ancien Testament: quelques approches récentes," in *L' Ancien Testament en syriaque* (eds. F. Briquel-Chatonnet and P. Le Moigne; Études syriaques 5; Paris: Geuthner, 2008), 21–32.

Brock, S. and L. van Rompay, *Catalogue of the Syriac Manuscripts and Fragments in the Library of Deir Al-Surian, Wadi Al-Natrun (Egypt)* (OLA 227; Leuven: Peeters, 2014).

Ceriani, A.M., "Esaiae fragmenta syriaca versionis anonymae et recensionis Jacobi Edesseni," in *Monumenta sacra et profana* 5.1 (Milan: Bibliotheca Ambrosiana, 1868), 1–40.

Ceriani, A.M., *Codex syro-hexaplaris Ambrosianus* (Monumenta Sacra et Profana 7; Milan: Bibliotheca Ambrosiana, 1874).

Deklat, L., "Die syrolukianische Übersetzung des Buches

---

[38] Ter Haar Romeny, "Jacob of Edessa's Quotations," 392.

[39] Ugolini, "recensione," 409–20. Ugolini (pp. 412–13) published the Syriac text of Ezek 7:1–13 and included an image of fol. 75^r containing Ezek 27:5–9; see Baars, "Ein neugefundenes Bruchstück," 551 n. 4.

[40] Baars, "Ein neugefundenes Bruchstück," 548 n. 6. The copy is dated to 1553 and of the verses lacking in Vat. Sir. 5, the copy preserves Ezek 1:1–14; 36:20–34; 39:1–15.

[41] Juckel, "Approximation," 243.

[42] Juckel, "Approximation," 227.

Jesaja und das Postulat einer alttestamentlichen Vetus Syra," *ZAW* 69 (1957): 21–54.

ter Haar Romeny, R.B., "Jacob of Edessa's Quotations and Revision of Isaiah," in *Isaiah in Context: Studies in Honour of Arie van der Kooij on the Occasion of His Sixty-Fifth Birthday* (eds. M. van der Meer et al.; VTSup 138; Leiden: Brill, 2010), 389–406.

ter Haar Romeny, R.B., "Peshitta and Other Syriac Versions," in *The Oxford Encyclopedia of the Books of the Bible* (ed. M.D. Coogan; Oxford: Oxford University Press, 2011), 2:149–55.

Jenkins, R.G., *The Old Testament Quotations of Philoxenus of Mabbug* (CSCO Subsidia 84; Louvain: Peeters, 1989).

Jenkins, R.G., "Hexaplaric Marginalia and the Hexapla-Tetrapla Question," in *Origen's Hexapla and Fragments: Papers Presented at the Rich Seminar on the Hexapla, Oxford Centre for Hebrew and Jewish Studies, 25th–3rd August 1994* (ed. A. Salvesen; TSAJ 58; Tübingen: Mohr Siebeck, 1998), 73–87.

Juckel, A., "Septuagint and Peshitta: Jacob of Edessa Quoting the Old Testament in Ms Bl Add 17134," *Hugoye: Journal of Syriac Studies* 8 (2005): 151–77.

Juckel, A., "Approximation of the 'Traditions' in Jacob of Edessa's Revision of Isaiah," in *Malphono w-Rabo d-Malphone: Studies in Honor of Sebastian P. Brock* (ed. G. Kiraz; Gorgias Eastern Christian Studies 3; Piscataway: Gorgias Press, 2008), 227–82.

Kruse-Blinkenberg, L., "The Book of Malachi according to Codex Syro-Hexaplaris Ambrosianus," *ST* 21 (1967): 62–82.

Law, T.M., *Origenes Orientalis: The Preservation of Origen's Hexapla in the Syrohexapla of 3 Kingdoms* (De Septuaginta Investigationes 2; Göttingen: Vandenhoeck & Ruprecht, 2011).

Law, T.M., "An Often Neglected Witness to the Textual History of the Septuagint: The Syrohexapla of 3 Kingdoms," in *Textual Criticism and Dead Sea Scrolls: Studies in Honour of Julio Trebolle Barrera* (eds. P.A. Torijano Morales and A. Piquer Otero; JSJSup 137; Leiden: Brill, 2012), 179–92.

Liljeström, M., "Observations on the Mode of Translation in the Syrohexapla," in *Foundations for Syriac Lexicography V* (eds. L. Loopstra and M. Sokoloff; Piscataway: Gorgias Press, 2013), 71–82.

Lund, J.A., "Syntactic Features of the Syro-Hexapla of Ezekiel," *Aramaic Studies* 4 (2006): 67–81.

Salvesen, A., "The Authorial Spirit? Biblical Citations in Jacob of Edessa's Hexameron," *Aramaic Studies* 6 (2008): 207–25.

Salvesen, A., "Ya'qub of Edessa," in *The Gorgias Encyclopedic Dictionary of the Syriac Heritage* (eds. S. Brock et al.; Piscataway: Gorgias Press, 2011), 432–33.

Ugolini, M., "Il Ms. Vat. Sir. 5 e la recensione del V.T. di Giacomo d'Edessa," *OrChr* 2 (1902): 409–20.

Verwijs, P., "The Septuagint in the Peshitta and Syro-Hexapla translations of Amos 1:3–2:16," *BIOSCS* 38 (2005): 25–40.

Vööbus, A., *The Hexapla and the Syro-Hexapla: Very Important Discoveries for Septuagint Research* (Papers of the Estonian Theological Society in Exile 22; Stockholm: ETSE, 1971).

Vööbus, A., *The Book of Isaiah in the Version of the Syro-Hexapla* (CSCO 449 Subsidia 68; Louvain: Peeters, 1983).

Weitzman, M., "The Reliability of Retroversions of the Three from the Syrohexapla: A Pilot Study in Hosea," in M. Weitzman, *From Judaism to Christianity: Studies in the Hebrew and Syriac Bibles* (eds. A. Rapoport-Albert and G. Greenberg; Oxford: Oxford University Press, 1999), 265–309.

Wright, W., *Catalogue of Syriac Manuscripts in the British Museum: Acquired since the Year 1838* (London: The British Museum, 1870–1872).

Stephen Ryan

6–9.2.5 Armenian Translations

6–9.2.5.1 Isaiah
6–9.2.5.1.1 Nature

The results presented here are based on a comparison of the Armenian evidence as presented in the Zohrapian edition[1] with that of the Old Greek (→ 6.3) as edited by Ziegler.[2] As the Armenian version of this book has not been subject to detailed scrutiny, the conclusions offered are tentative and derive from the collation of Isaiah 19 and 41 and spot-checks of other selected verses.

6–9.2.5.1.2 Translation Character

The variants Zohrapian cites in his apparatus allow us to correct errors in the running text and thus reconstitute the original reading, e.g., the in-

---

[1] Zohrapian, *Scriptures.

[2] Ziegler, *Isaias*. Ziegler frequently cites Armenian evidence in other books he edited for the Göttingen LXX, but it was not collated for his edition of Isaiah.

correct plural form եղիցին "(they) will be" at Isa 19:23, which can now be replaced by the requisite singular եղիցի "(it) will be" (= ἔσται) in the context of Egypt's future path, according to the oracle.

Other variants can be interpreted as substantiating the existence of two strata in the version, as established in other books, i.e., Arm 1, the original translation, and Arm 2, a later revision, with divergent parent texts and translation techniques (→ 1.4.7). Thus, at Isa 19:4, the form զեգիպտացիս "the Egyptians" suggests the translator's preference for early Armenian idiom in referring to countries according to their inhabitants,[3] whereas the variant զեգիպտոս "Egypt" reflects the reviser's penchant for encoding Greek morphology as closely as possible. This is exemplified again at Isa 19:4 by the reviser's preservation of the Greek transliteration of the Hebrew σαβαωθ as Սաբաովթ "Sabaoth," whereas the translator had decided to render the term directly (զօրութեանց "of hosts"). One variant at Isa 19:4 characterizes the translator's contextual approach, namely, in psychologizing the Greek term σκληροί "harsh," with regard to political leadership, խստասիրտք "hardhearted" whereas the reviser alters this to the base form խիստք "harsh" to reflect the Greek more exactly. Variation at Isa 19:13 regarding the reaction of various Egyptian rulers reveals further dimensions of the distinction between the two strata. In Greek, they are ἐξέλιπον "they failed" and ὑψώθησαν "they were exalted," both exemplified by Arm 2's renderings պակասեցան "they diminished" and բարձրացան "they were exalted." Arm 1, on the contrary, shares affinities here with the Peshitta (→ 1.3.4; → 6–9.1.4), a secondary parent text in the original translation of several biblical books.[4] It reads the first verb as հիմարեցան "they became foolish" (= s ܐܠܘ "became fools") and the second as հպա(ր)տացան "they grew proud," conveying the negative psychological qualities of the leaders' exaltation according to a secondary semantic field of the Peshitta form ܐܣܬܝܕܪ "went up; became haughty."[5]

---

[3] Metzger, *The Early Versions of the New Testament*, 162–63.
[4] Cowe, "The Bible in Armenian," 155–57.
[5] Sokoloff, *A Syriac Lexicon*, 1449–50.

6–9.2.5.1.3 Reconstruction of the Parent Text of Arm-Isa

A notable feature of the textual complexion of the Armenian version's Greek parent text is the degree of revision to MT it has undergone (especially pluses), as at Isa 41:5:

γῆς "earth"] + εξεστησαν "they were stunned" (pr και "and" LXX^{III-86c}) LXX^{V-88 L'`-86c-233} (om ἤγγισαν "they drew near") Theoderet of Cyrus, Jerome = Eusebius commentary on Isaiah and *Eclogae Propheticae* = Armenian եւ սարսեցին "and they shuddered."

Within the larger grouping of Hexaplaric (→ 6–9.1.5) and Lucianic witnesses (→ 6–9.1.6) here, the Armenian betrays a closer affinity with Ziegler's second Lucianic subgroup (LXX^L = the primary Lucian textgroup; LXX^{lll} = the second subgroup of LXX^L), but in most instances it reads with the majority Hexaplaric and Lucianic text. At other points, the Armenian joins a series of Alexandrian witnesses. Examples include the following:

- Isa 19:1 ἡ καρδία "(their) heart"] αι καρδιαι "(their) hearts" LXX^{A'-710 cI 46 534 538} = Armenian սիրտք "(their) hearts"
- Isa 19:25 εὐλογημένος "blessed"] + εσται "will be" LXX^S 538 Cop Justin = Armenian եղիցի "it will be blessed"
- Isa 41:9 εἶ "you are"] + συ και "you and" LXX^{538} Cop^{Sah} = Armenian դու եւ "you are and"

6–9.2.5.1.4 Translation Technique

If the division into strata is well founded, then, as already suggested, each will be typified by its own approach to translation, while the overall texture will be composite, since the second layer is a redaction and not a separate rendering. The task of distinguishing them throughout will require thorough collations and lies beyond the present enterprise. Most of the features commented on here typify the early stratum (Arm 1).

The translation unit tends to be set at the phrase level, sometimes impacted by an even wider context, as is well illustrated by the account of establishing a stele at Isa 19:19, where the differences in word order, syntax, and morphology between the Old Greek καὶ στήλη πρὸς τὸ ὅριον αὐτῆς τῷ κυρίῳ "and a pillar toward its border to the Lord" – which replicates the Hebrew structure – and the Armenian եւ արձան կանգնեալ Տեառն ի սահմանս նորա "and a statue erected to the Lord at its borders" indicate the plasticity of the Armenian reformulation, which includes the insertion of a verb, "erected," to parallel the verb in the preceding clause.

Early Armenian idiom dictates a number of minor additions such as the pronoun subject for emphasis at Isa 41:11 (ἔσονται "they will be"; եղիցին նորա "*they* will be"); the lack of definition at Isa 19:20 (ἄνθρωπον "a man"; այր մի "*some* man"); and the presence of the present tense copula at Isa 19:11, absent in the Old Greek because it is lacking in the Hebrew parent text (ἡμεῖς "we"; մեք եմք "we *are*").

Emblematic of the translation unit at the phrase level is variation in equivalency patterns with regard to both morphemes and roots. Thus, Arm 1 reveals a tendency to render certain Greek denominative verbs by a verb-noun phrase as, for example, πολεμήσει "he will war" is represented by տայցեն պատերազմ "they will give war" (Isa 19:2) and πενθήσουσι "they will mourn" by սուգ առցեն "they will assume mourning" (Isa 19:8), though we encounter the opposite phenomenon soon after that when αἰσχύνη λήμψεται "he will take shame" is translated by ամաչեսցեն "they will be ashamed" (Isa 19:9). One of the idiomatic Greek constructions lacking a direct Armenian counterpart is the participial phrase, which the translator rendered with a striking variety of modes: a) a clause with a finite verb (Isa 19:18, 25; 41:4); b) a noun expressing the agent (Isa 41:12); c) a participle of necessity (Isa 41:14); d) an abstract noun (Isa 19:20); e) a noun of activity (Isa 19:20).

6–9.2.5.1.4.1 Attention to Context

Another aspect of setting the translation unit at the phrase length is the flexibility this affords in semantic interpretation and expression, as illustrated by the following examples.

The discourse at Isa 41:22 treats both knowledge of former events as well as prophecy regarding the future, hence it is comprehensible that the translator has sought to provide a suitable summation and avoid the tautology of the Greek by rendering the phrase τὰ ἔσχατα καὶ τὰ ἐπερχόμενα "the last things ... and (tell us) the things that are coming" (*NETS) as զինչ առաջին կամ զինչ առ յապա "what is first or what is to come."

Clearly, the Nile is crucial for the welfare of the Egyptian population. Consequently, it is a dire prediction we meet in Isa 19:5–7, which intimates that all the water resources will evaporate. As frequently, the Old Greek expression describing the water source from which the Egyptians are to drink, ὕδωρ τὸ παρὰ θάλασσαν "water that is by the sea" is rather vague. Guided perhaps by the reference to a συναγωγὴ ὕδατος "gathering of water" in Isa 19:5, the translator plausibly renders the former phrase as գջրշտեղցուն ծովափնեայ "coastal cisterns." He also retains focus on the centrality of the water theme and the disaster of drought throughout this passage. Drawing out the deeper significance of the phrase πᾶν τὸ σπειρόμενον διὰ τοῦ ποταμοῦ ξηρανθήσεται ἀνεμόφθορον "all that is sown by the river, will be dried up, blasted by the wind" (*NETS), he renders it by ամենայն արտավարք որ ընդ գետուն ջրով վարեալ իցեն խորշակահար ցամաքեսցին "all the arable lands that are cultivated with water along the river will dry up, struck by the parching wind." The latter highlights both the essential role of water in the planting process and the impact of the *searing hot* wind in drying up the water sources in contrast to the generic term for "wind" in Greek.

6–9.2.5.1.4.2 Style

As one might expect from Arm 1's overall profile, the version respects various facets of Armenian idiom such as adherence to the technical term for "(they will) offer" (մատուսցեն) sacrifice rather than the less precise Greek ποιήσουσι "they will make" (at Isa 19:21). It elaborates several instances of *figura etymologica* for emphasis (e.g., Isa 19:12; 41:7; 41:22). Similarly, it restates the Greek body imagery κεφαλὴν καὶ οὐράν "head and tail" more directly by use of the established idiom մի յետս եւ մի յառաջ "back and forth" (Isa 19:15).[6]

One of the translator's most noteworthy stylistic features involves the paralleling of Greek terms and phrases by the use of idiomatic compound nouns. Some of these are clearly neologisms, while a smaller number were destined to remain *hapax legomena*. Examples include:

- Isa 19:3 գետնակոչս "geomancers" for OG τοὺς ἐκ τῆς γῆς φωνοῦντας "those calling from the earth"
- Isa 19:8 կարթընկէզք "hook-casters" for OG οἱ βάλλοντες ἄγκιστρον "those throwing a hook"
- Isa 41:15 կամնասայլ "flailing-cart" for OG ἁμάξης ἀλοῶντος "cart of threshing"

On occasion, the translator rhetorically repeats for rhetorical purposes certain terms as a *leitmotif* to capture the prevalent mood or emotion in a section. An excellent example of this practice is the triple occurrence of the root of sorrow in Isa 19:8–10, where the Greek alludes to this only in the last instance, viz., տրտմեսցին ... լի տրտմութեամբ ... տրտմեսցին "they will sorrow ... full of sorrow ... they will sorrow" versus στενάξουσιν (8) ... ἐν ὀδύνῃ (10) ... λυπηθήσονται (10) "(the fishers) will groan ... in pain ... they will be grieved" (*NETS*).

6–9.2.5.1.4.3 Literalisms and Transliterations

The Armenian version also evinces a few instances of transliteration of the Greek. For example, πόλις ασεδεκ "city Asedek" is rendered exactly as քաղաք Ասեդեկ "city Asedek" (Isa 19:18). A few Hebraisms are also retained from the Old Greek (→ 6.3) in a unidiomatic fashion, more characteristic of the Armenian reviser, e.g., ἀπὸ προσώπου τῆς χειρός "from the face of the hand," which translates literally into Armenian as յերեսաց ձեռին "from the face of the hand" (Isa 19:16).

6–9.2.5.1.5 Text-Critical Value: Omissions and Additions

The Armenian version reveals a high degree of quantitative representation, manifesting virtually no omissions. Similarly, most of the additions are relatively short and intended for clarification or emphasis. Thus, where a textual reference to the land of Judea is obliquely reprised by the phrase ὀνομάσῃ αὐτήν "should name it," the Armenian specifies the allusion by rendering it as անուանեսցէ զանուն երկրին "will name *the name of the land*" (Isa 19:17). Similarly, Isa 41:7 concludes a sketchy description of structures fashioned by artisans and smiths by stating θήσουσιν αὐτὰ καὶ οὐ κινηθήσονται "they will set them up and they will not be moved." Here, the Armenian translator sought to underscore the causal relation between the two clauses by appending to the first ի գետնի "on the ground."

6–9.2.5.1.6 Relevance for Exegesis

Various of the oracles against foreign lands in Isaiah highlight issues of polytheism, and this question looms large in Antiochene exegesis, as reflected in Theodoret's commentary. While in Greek this results in no change of terminology to distinguish the pagan from the Israelite cult, as, for example, in the case of τοὺς θεούς "the gods" (Isa 19:3), the Armenian systematically marks this distinction by employing the term դիք "false god/idol" to denote non-Judeo-Christian deities.

6–9.2.5.1.7 Text-Critical Value of Arm-Isa for LXX-Isa

The Armenian version possesses great potential as a source for further investigation of the Alexandrian text type (→ 6.3) and Hexaplaric-Lucianic recensions in Isaiah (→ 6–9.1.5; → 6–9.1.6), as well as the impact of the Antiochene exegetical school on textual transmission, the history of biblical interpretation, and the role of the translator as interpreter.

6–9.2.5.1.8 Readings from "the Three"

Taking into account the degree of Hexaplaric influence (→ 1.3.1.2.7; → 6–9.1.5) to which the Armenian

---

[6] Awetikʻean, *Nor baṙgirkʻ haykazean lezui*, 356.

version has been exposed (→ 1.4.7), it is not surprising that various codices have preserved marginal readings of "the Three" at various points.[7]

Awetik'ean, G. et al. (eds.), *Nor baṙgirk' haykazean lezui (New Dictionary of the Armenian Language)* (Vol. 1; Venice: St. Lazar's Press, 1836).

Cowe, S.P., "The Bible in Armenian," in *The New Cambridge History of the Bible*, Vol. 2: *From 600 to 1450* (eds. R. Marsden and E.A. Matter; Cambridge: Cambridge University Press, 2012), 143–61.

Cox, C.E., *Aquila, Symmachus and Theodotion in Armenia* (SBLSCS 42; Atlanta: Scholars Press, 1996).

Metzger, B.M., *The Early Versions of the New Testament: Their Origin, Transmission and Limitations* (Oxford: Clarendon Press, 1977).

Outtier, B., "Fragments d'un manuscrit arménien du livre d'Isaïe," *Revue des Études Arméniennes* 23 (1992): 5–12.

Schulze, J.L. (ed.), *Theodoreti Cyrensis episcopi opera omnia* (PG 81.2, Paris: Migne, 1864).

Sokoloff, M., *A Syriac Lexicon: A Translation from the Latin: Correction, Expansion, and Update of C. Brockelmann's Lexicon syriacum* (Winona Lake: Eisenbrauns, 2009).

Stone, M.E., "The Old Armenian Version of Isaiah: Towards the Choice of the Base Text for an Edition," *Text* 8 (1973): 107–25.

Ziegler, J. (ed.), *Isaias* (2nd ed.; Septuaginta Vetus Testamentum Graecum 14; Göttingen: Vandenhoeck & Ruprecht, 1967).

Zohrapian, *Scriptures.

6–9.2.5.2 Jeremiah
6–9.2.5.2.1 Editions

The Greek text used is that of Ziegler's critical edition,[1] and for the Armenian the text in Zohrapian's diplomatic edition (1805) was employed.[2] Surprisingly, Arm-Jer follows the chapter order of MT (→ 7.2.2) over against LXX (→ 7.3), so MT is cited in brackets where the two traditions bifurcate.

---

[7] Cox, *Aquila, Symmachus and Theodotion in Armenia*, 349–62.

[1] Ziegler, *Ieremias*.

[2] Zohrapian, *Scriptures.

6–9.2.5.2.2 Source Text

The source text of Arm-Jer was a Greek text, as indicated by the preservation of inner-Greek variants like this one: the Oracle against Ammon foresees (θόρυβον) πολέμων "(tumult) of wars," but certain Hexaplaric witnesses (LXX^O Syh^txt) attest a secondary graphic error – πολεων "of cities" – which is the source of քաղաքացն "of the cities" (Jer 30[49]:2). That is, Arm-Jer attests a mistake only possible in Greek.

6–9.2.5.2.3 Reconstruction of the Source Text of Arm-Jer

The impression given by the Zohrapian text and apparatus[3] is that most of the variants are of minor textual import, but others suggest the possibility of a division observed in various other books between the initial translation (Arm 1, early fifth century) and a revision executed later (Arm 2, in the 430s).[4] Thus, whereas անդ "there," noted in the apparatus at Jer 30:11(49:33), conforms to the Greek text ἐκεῖ "there," the running text evinces ի նմա "in it" which may be original.

The primary complexion of Arm 1's source text is Lucianic (→ 1.3.1.2; → 6–9.1.6) in a number of books, and this may also apply in Arm-Jer. Certainly, there are a series of cases that find Arm in alignment with that recension. So, for example, in the orthography of Μελχομ "Melchom" attested by LXX^L' 130 Theodoret (Arm Մեղքովմ "Melk'ovm"; Jer 30[49]:1); the reference to the Lord "of hosts," i.e., with the addition of των δυναμεων (LXX^L' Theodoret), Arm-Jer զօրութեանց "of powers" (Jer 30[49]:5); and in the description (ἀπὸ πάσης τῆς) γῆς (περιοίκου σου) "(from all) the land (surrounding you)" (LXX^L-51), reflected in (յամենայն) կողմանց (շուրջ զքեւ բնակելոցն) "(from the dwellers in all) the territories (around you)" (Jer 30[49]:5).

A larger set of Armenian agreements highlights the influence of the Hexapla (→ 1.3.1.2.7; → 6–9.1.5) – attested primarily in LXX^O – on Lucianic witnesses. Among substantive readings in this category, one

---

[3] Zohrapian, *Scriptures.

[4] For Arm 1 and Arm 2, see → 1.4.7.

might cite the pluses "and nothing will be built any more for ever" (Jer 27[50]:39); "violent snorting" (Jer 27[50]:44); "sons of Ammon" (Jer 30[49]:2); "and after this I will return the captivity of the sons of Ammon says the Lord" (Jer 30:6[49:6]); and "Nabuchodonosor" at (Jer 30[49]:8). These readings may constitute an area of intersection between Arm 1 and Arm 2. Hexaplaric readings may have come into Arm-Jer by way of the Lucianic text (→ 6–9.1.6).

Arm-Jer manifests a pronounced affiliation with readings attested by the Hexaplaric text (→ 6–9.1.5), apparently the main source text of Arm 2. Most of these comprise additions that bring the Old Greek (→ 7.3) closer to MT (→ 7.2.2), for example: εγενετο/եղեւ "has become" attested by LXX^O Arm = MT (Jer 7:11); απο προσωπου μου/յերեսաց իմոց "from my face," LXX$^{O\text{-}Qmg\ l}$ Arm = MT (Jer 15:1); αυτης/նորա "its" LXX$^{O\text{-}86mg}$ Arm (Jer 27[50]):40; και διαδραμετε εν τοις φραγμοις/եւ յայսկոյս յայնկոյս ընթացարուք զցանկովք "and run hither and thither in the fences" LXX$^{O\text{-}Qmg}$ Arm = MT (Jer 30[49]:3; see also LXX^L). Arm-Jer exhibits a particular affinity with the minuscule LXX^{534}, as in Job (→ 11.4.5) and Ezekiel (→ 6–9.2.5.4).[5] Shared variants include και ουκ ανεκαμψας/եւ ոչ դարձար "and you did not return" attested by LXX^{534} Arm (Jer 3:1) and the form of the toponym ραβα/Հռաբայ "Raba" attested by LXX$^{46\ 534}$ Arm (Jer 30 [49]:3).

6–9.2.5.2.4 Translation Technique

The translator operated at the phrase level. This assessment is substantiated by renderings like ἤκουσε ... τὴν ἀκοὴν αὐτῶν "(he) heard ... their sound,"[6] where Arm-Jer has reproduced the verb and its cognate object to heighten the *figura etymologica*, so լուաւ զլուր նոցա "he heard their cry" (Jer 27[50]:43). The situation is similar in Jer 22:15–16: In interpreting καὶ βέλτιον ἦν σε ποιεῖν κρίμα καὶ δικαιοσύνην καὶ καλήν. (16) οὐκ ἔγνωσαν "it is better for you to execute judgment and righteousness and goodness; (16) they did not know" as զի զիրաւունս եւ զարդարութիւն եւ զբարութիւն ոչ ծանեան "because they did not know right and righteousness and goodness," the translator sought to enhance the continuity of thought, first, by linking it to what precedes with "because," and, second, by sustaining the indefinite third plural as subject by representing κρίσιν "judgement" (2°) with հրաւցուցին in "they did (not) extend justice to the needy." For Jer 27(50):5, Ziegler characterizes the rendering of ὧδε γὰρ τὸ πρόσωπον αὐτῶν δώσουσι "for here they will set their face" (*NETS*) by այսր դիմեսցեն "here they will beg" as "free."[7] However, one might argue that the choice is philologically apposite, since the root derives from the lexeme դէմք "face" and semantically it conveys the sense of approaching.[8] The translator also reveals his appreciation for the idiom of the target language in applying the pithy alliterative phrase կահ եւ կարասի "utensils and equipment" to render the term σκευή "implements" (Jer 30:7[49:29]).[9]

The characteristics of the Arm 1 translation technique are present in Arm-Jer: the identification of cities by their inhabitants, e.g., Nebuchadnezzar, king "of Babylon" (Βαβυλῶνος) emerges as բաբելացւոց "of the Babylonians" (Jer 30:6[49]:28). The sense of urgency in the adverb ταχέως "quickly" is heightened by reduplication in երագերագ "very quickly" (Jer 27[50]:44). Later in the verse, the self-assuredness inherent in the rhetorical question τίς ως (LXX$^{O\text{-}233\ L'}$ Chrysostomus; OG ὥσπερ) ἐγώ "who (is) like me?" is underscored in ո՞վ որ է իբրեւ զիս "who is like me?" through the apt use of particles. Arm 1's concern for maintaining the distinction

---

[5] On this, see Cowe, "The Bible in Armenian," 156.

[6] *NETS*: "[he] heard news of them."

[7] Ziegler, *Ieremias*, 38–39.

[8] In fact, the Armenian attests the Lucianic reading μεταβαλουσι(ν) "they shall change" (with LXX$^{311\text{-}407\ L'\text{-}51}$ Syh^{mg} Eth) rather than δώσουσι "they will give," Ziegler's collation. (As it is, Ziegler's Latin translation of τὸ πρόσωπον αὐτῶν δώσουσι, i.e., *petentes venient* "they will come begging," is incorrect, both in presenting the finite form դիմեսցեն as a participle and in combining it apparently with the following verb եկեսցեն "they will come.") The Armenian translation has interpreted "for here they shall change their face" contextually, as indicating a radical reversal in disposition.

[9] This idiom is found in several early Armenian authors such as P'awstos, in the following passage, թողին զխորանս եւ զվրանս, զկահ եւ զկարասի "they left behind the pavilions and tents, the utensils and equipment." See Malxaseanc', *P'awstos Buzand*, 114.

between licit and illicit cultic paraphernalia also comes to expression in designating the undifferentiated ἱερεῖς "priests" as քուրմք "pagan priests" (Jer 30[49]:3).

In handling grammatical categories, the translator avoids the rare Armenian causative form to render its counterpart ἀκουτιῶ "I will make heard" in favor of the simpler phrase լուր արարից "I will announce" (Jer 30[49]:2). Similarly, articulated participles like ἡ πεποιθυῖα "the one having trusted"[10] are rendered by a relative clause, so որ յուսացեալ էիր "you who hoped" (Jer 30[49]:4). In Arm-Jer, a deft use is made of idiomatic compound verbal adjectives: e.g., the command περιζώνασθε σάκκους "gird yourselves about with sackcloth" is represented by քրձազգածք եղերուք "become sackcloth-girt" (Jer 30[49]:3).

Semantic leveling occurs when several Greek words are rendered by one Armenian equivalent. In the broader context of destruction, գոյժ "lamentation" represents θόρυβον "commotion" and the cognate imperative գուժեա "lament!" is employed in the next verse to render ἀλάλαξον "shout!" (Jer 30[49]:2–3); earlier գոյժ renders κραυγή "cry" (Jer 27[50]:46). Similarly the verb բնակեմ "I dwell" serves as an equivalent for several Greek words. Thus καθήμενοι "those sitting"[11] is rendered բնակեալք "those dwelling," and in the next verse καταλύουσι "they lodge" is also translated բնակեալք "those dwelling" (Jer 30:8–9[49:30–31]). Finally, διατριβή "haunt" becomes բնակութիւն "dwelling," the cognate noun of բնակեմ (Jer 30:11 [49:33]).

Aside from contextual renderings noted above, we may cite the choice of գունդ "military formation" to represent λαός "people," a choice that harmonizes with its martial environment (Jer 27[50]:41).

6–9.2.5.2.5 Text-Critical Value: Omissions and Additions

Apart from a number of minor pluses, we should consider վասն աստուծոյ Երուսաղէմի "for the God of Jerusalem" at Jer 4:1. It balances the negative reference to idols with the positive corollary that follows in v. 2. Similarly, the plus եւ ոչ պատուիրեցի նոցա "and I did not command them," concerning false prophets, closely parallels the previous phrase that says God did not send them (Jer 14:15).

Minuses are also few and mainly insignificant. One might mention the absence of the formula λέγει κύριος "says the Lord" (Jer 13:25) and that of the explanatory phrase τὴν τεκοῦσάν σε "who bore you" (Jer 22:26). As this phrase develops and gives point to τὴν μητέρα σου "your mother," it may be that the translator regarded the phrase as tautologous. As for "says the Lord," it occurs so often that its loss can easily happen.

6–9.2.5.2.6 Text-Critical Value of Arm-Jer for LXX-Jer

Arm-Jer's profile is that of a fairly faithful witness to its Greek source text. Future investigation must determine whether the hypothesis of a division into two strata is justified. It should also pursue the text's alignment with LXX[534] in order to facilitate reconstructing the Greek source text. Finally, it is crucial to examine the process and means by which Arm-Jer derived its agreement with MT in the arrangement of its chapters.

6–9.2.5.2.7 Readings from "the Three"

The addition արդարութիւն մեր "our righteousness" at Jer 23:6 represents Aquila's (→ 6–9.1.2) translation <κυριος> δικαιοσυνη ημων "<the Lord> is our justice," as opposed to the Old Greek (→ 7.3) transliteration Ιωσεδεκ "Iosedek."[12] Its position at the end of the verse suggests that originally these words were a marginal gloss.

Cowe, S.P., "The Bible in Armenian," in *The New Cambridge History of the Bible*, Vol. 2: *From 600 to 1450* (eds. R. Marsden and E.A. Matter; Cambridge: Cambridge University Press, 2012), 143–61.

Malxaseancʻ, S. (ed.), *Pʻawstos Buzand: Patmutʻiwn Hayocʻ* (*Pʻawstos Buzand: History of the Armenians*) (St. Petersburg: Imperial Academy of Sciences, 1883).

---

[10] *NETS*: "who trusted."
[11] *NETS*: "you seated."

[12] See the apparatus of Ziegler, *Ieremias*, 263.

Ziegler, J. (ed.), *Ieremias, Baruch, Threni, Epistula Ieremiae* (Septuaginta Vetus Testamentum Graecum 15; Göttingen: Vandenhoeck & Ruprecht, 1957).

Zohrapian, Y., *Scriptures.

6–9.2.5.3 Ezekiel

The Armenian version of Ezekiel has not been the subject of detailed investigation. For this entry, Arm-Ezek has been collated according to the Zohrapean edition of 1805;[1] the Greek employed is Ziegler's critical edition.

6–9.2.5.3.1 Nature

That the version derives from a Greek matrix is corroborated by a number of compound terms that serve as the prototype for an Armenian coinage, such as the epithet μεγαλοπτέρυγος "large-winged" at Ezek 17:3 and its equivalent մեծթաթև. Variations in translation technique and textual affiliation conspire with doublets to suggest the possibility that the version comprises two strata, an original translation (Arm 1) and subsequent revision (Arm 2), as discerned in several other books, but much more investigation will be required to determine the accuracy of this view. Of the doublets, one might consider the image of fowl resting on a great tree at Ezek 17:23, where the Old Greek reading πετεινόν "winged creature" is rendered by two synonyms for "bird," հաւք and թռչունք.

6–9.2.5.3.2 Translation Character

The parent text from which Arm-Ezek evolved appears to have been of mixed text type, as the Armenian affiliates itself with a variety of different groupings, of which one is Hexaplaric, a feature of the revised stratum of a number of books.[2] A case in point is Ezek 8:11, where the Armenian reads the corrective plus to MT, τῆς νεφέλης "of the cloud" with the main Hexaplaric witnesses (→ 6–9.1.5). It also reveals significant Lucianic influence (→ 6–9.1.6), frequently also harmonizing with MT (→ 8.2.2), as at Ezek 34:24 where the version joins the primary Lucianic witnesses in defining David as ὁ δοῦλος μου "my servant." Ziegler also cites Armenian agreements with the Catena group,[3] but fails to note a series of affinities shared with the Alexandrian text, that is, LXX^A and the witnesses that read with it (→ 8.3). These include the conjunction ὅτι "because" rather than the simple copula at Ezek 17:18 and the transposition of ἠτίμωσε/παρέβη "dishonored/transgressed" in the following verse. However, as far as Ezekiel 20, the single witness that most closely mirrors the version's textual complexion is miniscule LXX^{534}, which, though assigned to the Catena group, is a mixed codex, with which the Armenian shares a number of singular readings.[4] These include the comparison between Jerusalem's sins and those of her "sisters" Samaria and Sodom at the conclusion of Ezek 16:52: the Armenian joins LXX^{534} (+ ὑπὲρ σε) in adding քան զքեզ "more than yourself" and the reformulation of the critical text τὰ βδελύγματα τῶν ὀφθαλμῶν αὐτῶν οὐκ ἀπέρριψαν "they did not remove the abominations of their eyes" at Ezek 20:8 – partly under the influence of Ezek 16.51 – to read իւրաքանչիւր որ զգարշելիս իւր յաչաց իւրոց ոչ ընկէց ի բաց "none of them cast away his abominations from his eyes."

6–9.2.5.3.3 Translation Technique

The Armenian version exhibits several features characteristic of Arm 1 (→ 1.4.7), such as valorizing the idiom of the target language. Thus, countries are listed according to their inhabitants, as in the case of Canaan at Ezek 17:4 յերկիրն քանանացւոց, lit. "to the land of the Canaanites," and various pronouns and particles are added to round out bald constructions, as at Ezek 33:2, where γῆ "land" is further defined as երկիր մի "a land." Similarly, compound Greek verbs are frequently rendered by an adjectival phrase with a simple verb, as in the case of interpreting ἐπιβλεπόμενον "looked upon" at Ezek 17:5 as երևելի առնել "to make conspicuous," while others are expressed by a combination

---

[1] Zohrapian, *Scriptures.
[2] Cowe, "The Bible in Armenian," 156.

[3] Ziegler, *Ezechiel*, 58–59.
[4] Note that the same minuscule has been highlighted as the codex most closely corresponding to Arm-Jer (→ 6–9.2.5.2) also, on which see Cowe, "The Bible in Armenian," 156.

of two terms, as in the case of ἐκσπάσαι "to pull out" at v. 9, translated as բռունն հարկանել եւ խլել "to seize and pluck out." Often, articulated participles are translated as relative clauses, so ὁ ποιῶν "the one doing" at Ezek 17:15 appears as որ առնէ "the one who does." Another well-attested aspect of Arm-Ezek is diversity in equivalents, as exemplified by the treatment of the abstract noun ἁπαλότης "tenderness" in the image of cedar branches at Ezek 17:4 τὰ ἄκρα τῆς ἁπαλότητος "the tips of tenderness," rendered as գւատաղատունկն "young shoot," in contrast to the more literal articulation at v. 9 αἱ ῥίζαι τῆς ἁπαλότητος "the roots of tenderness" as արմատք փափկութեան "the roots of tenderness."

At the same time, the version adduces several facets of the Arm 2 profile (→ 1.4.7), including the coining of neologisms to parallel Greek compounds and phrases, for example, երկայնատարածւած "extended" for μακρός τῇ ἐκτάσει "long in extent" and լիամագիլ "full-taloned" for πλήρης ὀνύχων "full of talons" at Ezek 17:3.

Other aspects of the translation technique of Arm-Ezek are its attention to context, its literalism, and its transliterations. The Armenian version frequently modifies its rendering to fit the immediate context. Thus, at Ezek 17:15, it nuances the literal formulation λαὸν πολύν "much people" to accommodate it to the prevailing martial context, so զօրս բազումս "many forces," while at v. 23 it adapts the phrase ποιήσει καρπόν "it will make fruit" to the common idiom պտուղ բերցէ "it will bear fruit."

As for literalisms and transliterations, reflecting Arm 2 practice, the version retains the Old Greek's literal encoding of the Hebrew oath formula ζῶ ἐγώ, lit. "I live" as կենդանի եմ ես "I am alive" at Ezek 17:16.

6–9.2.5.3.4 Text-Critical Value of Arm-Ezek for LXX-Ezek

Although much more detailed research will be required to delineate the Armenian version's place in the unfolding textual tradition of LXX-Ezek, it is already clear that it affords fairly accurate representation of its Greek parent text(s). Pluses are primarily interpretive and small in compass; minuses are minor and rare. Under the impact of the version's Hexaplaric affinities, it preserves a number of readings from the Three (→ 6–9.1.5), though these are adduced by only a few manuscripts.[5]

Anasean, Y., "Ezechiel 27,9 en arménien," *Revue des Études Arméniennes* 19 (1985): 45–48.
Cox, C.E., *Aquila, Symmachus and Theodotion in Armenia* (SBLSCS 42; Atlanta: Scholars Press, 1996).
Cowe, S.P., "The Bible in Armenian," in *The New Cambridge History of the Bible*, Vol. 2: *From 600 to 1450* (eds. R. Marsden and E.A. Matter; Cambridge: Cambridge University Press, 2012), 143–61.
Ziegler, J. (ed.), *Ezechiel* (Septuaginta Vetus Testamentum Graece 16.1; Göttingen: Vandenhoeck & Ruprecht, 1952).
Zohrapian, *Scriptures*.

6–9.2.5.4 Minor Prophets
6–9.2.5.2.1 Background; Editions

The Armenian version was analyzed according to the Zohrapian edition of 1805[1] as collated against Ziegler's edition of the Old Greek.[2] Hosea 5 and Habakkuk 3 were examined in detail; spot-checks were made of other passages in the corpus. As Ziegler's study is one of the few investigations of the Armenian version in this portion of the Bible and as a number of his remarks are problematic, special attention will be devoted to that issue in the next sections.

6–9.2.5.2.2 Translation Character

In his introduction, Ziegler provides a brief overview of the version's translation technique.[3] Initially he adduces a series of eight readings, which he characterizes as free renderings. However, on closer inspection the majority appear perfectly accurate, while others may be interpreted as betraying errors that may easily be corrected by widening the collation pool. Thus, at Hos 7:1, the verb

---

[5] For details, see Cox, *Aquila, Symmachus and Theodotion*, 363–89.
[1] Zohrapian, *Scriptures*.
[2] Ziegler, *Duodecim prophetae*.
[3] Ziegler, *Duodecim prophetae*, 27–28.

in the phrase ἐκδιδύσκων λῃστής "a robber plundering" is represented precisely by the Armenian translation in աւազակ մերկացուցէ "a robber will strip." LSJ list "strip, despoil" as the primary meaning of ἐκδιδύσκω since the Greek verb derives from the form ἐκδύειν "strip, put off."[4] Similarly, at Amos 3:3, the object in the phrase ἐὰν μὴ γνωρίσωσιν ἑαυτούς "if they do not know *themselves*" – referring to two travellers embarking on a journey together – is most plausibly rendered in Armenian not reflexively but reciprocally as թէ ոչ ճանաչիցեն զմիմեանս "if they do not know *each other*" which is supported by the recent English translation of the Old Greek (→ 9.3).[5]

Meanwhile, at Zech 6:5, the Armenian equivalent, կալ առաջի տեառն "to stand before/in the presence of the Lord," is a fully acceptable rendering of the phrase παραστῆναι τῷ κυρίῳ "to stand beside the Lord," especially when we recall that the preposition առաջի, usually rendered as "before," emerged out of the prepositional construction առ աջի "at the right hand (of)." The same applies to Mic 7:13, where ի պտղոյ գործոց նոցա "from the fruit of their acts" offers a reasonable construal of the phrase ἐκ καρπῶν ἐπιτηδευμάτων αὐτῶν "from the fruits of their pursuits" as evinced once more by the translation in *NETS*.[6]

In the case of Mic 2:5, Ziegler drew the Armenian form from the older edition of Holmes and Parsons[7] without collating it against the text in Zohrapian.[8] The latter evinces a better reading, completely harmonious with the Old Greek (→ 9.3), as follows: βάλλων σχοινίον ἐν κλήρῳ "casting a line in a lot" is rendered որ արկանիցէ լարաբաժին ի վիճակ "who will cast a line in a lot." Similarly, at Zech 10:11, it can be argued that the preposition "in" may have fallen out of the Armenian text by parablepsis and can easily be reinstated to provide the phrase հարցեն զալիս <ի> ծովուն "they will strike the waves <in> the sea," which again exactly parallels πατάξουσιν ἐν θαλάσσῃ κύματα "they will strike the waves in the sea."

In the penultimate example, at Amos 5:20, the Armenian translator has employed an idiom of Semitic origin to render the Greek phrase of possession οὐκ ἔχων φέγγος αὐτῇ "not having brightness to it" indirectly as եւ ոչ գոյ ի նմա ճաճանչ "and there is no gleam in it." Consequently, it is only the Armenian contextual interpretation արդ պոռնկեցաւ եփրեմ "now Ephrem whored" to render ἐκεῖ πορνείαν τοῦ Εφραιμ "there Ephraim's whoredom" at Hos 6:10 that requires brief comment. Here the phrase has been assimilated to what follows, which has a finite verb, i.e., ἐμιάνθη Ισραηλ "Israel was polluted" and in Armenian, պղծեցաւ իսրայէլ "Israel was polluted."

6–9.2.5.2.3 Reconstruction of the Parent Text of Arm-Minor Prophets

Ziegler then explores aspects of the Armenian version's textual affinity in the corpus, beginning with Alexandrian witnesses. There he argues for a bifurcation within the tranmission history that reveals the Bohairic (→ 6–9.2.2.2) aligned with the Ethiopic (→ 6–9.2.3.4) and Arabic versions (→ 6–9.2.8) over against VL (→ 6–9.2.1), Achmimic (→ 6–9.2.2.2), Sahidic (→ 6–9.2.2.2), and Armenian. However, when the fourteen examples are viewed in context, it emerges that in the majority of cases the two readings compared are attested by a much larger range of witnesses, so that the significance of the contrast is generic rather than specific. Indeed, in most cases the divergence in question is rather between the reading Ziegler assigns to the critical text of the Old Greek (→ 9.3) and what he deems a (secondary) variant, where sometimes Arm reads the former (Hos 9:8; Amos 5:25; 6:12; Mic 3:3; 4:2; Obad 7; Zech 9:3; 14:5), sometimes the latter (Hos 12:4; Joel 2:10; Hab 1:6; Mal 1:7; 3:15) in company with a changing constellation of other witnesses. Clearly shared singular readings are constitutive of family relations among manuscripts, so that only one example qualifies, i.e., Amos 6:14 where the Armenian translation joins the Syro-Hexapla (→ 6–9.2.4.3) in attesting the addition λεγει κυριος των δυναμεων "says the Lord of Hosts."

---

[4] LSJ, 504.

[5] Howard, "The Twelve Prophets," 791.

[6] Howard, "The Twelve Prophets," 800.

[7] R. Holmes and J. Parsons (eds.), *Vetus Testamentum Graecum cum variis lectionibus*, Vol. 4 (Oxford: Clarendon, 1827).

[8] Zohrapian, *Scriptures*.

Next Ziegler discusses Arm's relation to the Lucianic recension (i.e., LXX^L), of which he lists it as a witness.[9] However, the latter aligns with the Lucianic text (→ 6–9.1.6) in only a few of Lucian's characteristic doublet readings that juxtapose the OG phraseology with a correction to the MT, e.g., Hos 14:4 ὁ (ἐν σοί) "he (who is within you)"] pr οτι "because" LXX$^{L''}$ Eth^p Arm. Here the Armenian attests ὅτι, following LXX^L. A similar conclusion emerges from Ziegler's series of readings intended to illustrate distinctive alterations toward the MT in Lucianic witnesses, e.g., Jon 2:11: προσετάγη "was ordered"] + απο κυριου "from the Lord" LXX^{ScC} Syh Arm; προσεταξε(ν) κυριος "the Lord ordered" LXX$^{L''(88txt)-407mg}$ et al.. Here Arm joins the Catena group, a well-developed text-type with a hexaplaric component, in defining the source of the order for the sea monster to release Jonah on dry land as "from the Lord," whereas the Lucianic text has recast the phrase in the active voice, to state "the Lord ordered" the act.

It is clear that the most important affinities of Arm in the Minor Prophets are with the Catena group, within which Ziegler correctly emphasizes a particular affiliation with the sub-group *LXX^c*, composed of manuscripts LXX$^{130-311-538}$. This affiliation is well illustrated by an example from Hos 13:14, where Arm stands in contrast with the main Lucianic group. The prophecy of salvation in Hos 13:14 depicts God as querying Death's control over his dominion, the terms of which differ according to the three variants: δίκη "justice"] νικη "victory" LXX$^{22c\,130'-53410}$ Arm; διαθηκη "covenant" L^{-36} (22*) – the critical text portrays it legally in terms of "justice" (δίκη); the Catena subgroup, supported by Arm, views it martially as "victory" (νικη); and the Lucianic text perceives it as "covenant" (διαθηκη).

Some of the variants afforded by Zohrapian's apparatus may suggest that the Minor Prophets also exhibit a bifurcation of the Armenian version into two strata, an original translation and sec-

---

[9] Ziegler, *Duodecim prophetae*, 70.
[10] It is interesting that in Job, Jeremiah, and Ezekiel, LXX^{534} has been identified as the extant manuscript closest to the parent text of the Armenian (Cowe, "The Bible in Armenian," 156).

ondary revision, evinced in several other biblical books (→ 1.4.7), each typified by a different translation technique. A good example is afforded by the simile at Hos 5:1, which likens Israel to a "snare" and a "net." The latter, according to the Old Greek, "stretched over Itabyrion" (ἐκτεταμένον ἐπὶ τὸ Ἰταβύριον). The Armenian translator was frequently influenced by context and balance of expression, so the reference to the "snare" enveloping a "look-out post" – by definition an eminence commanding a wide vista – may have served as a point of reference for construing its parallel "Itabyrion" as ի գլուխ գահավանդի "on top of a precipice." The marginal reading տաբիրոն "Tabiron" is, in contrast, more emblematic of the Armenian reviser's penchant for transliterating Greek lexemes.

6–9.2.5.2.3.1 Translation Technique

That the translator usually structured his rendering at the phrase length is indicated by passages such as Hab 3:6–7, where the Armenian translation alters the line division in an attempt to improve on the parallelism between the component parts and to provide a smoother transition between the verses. In the text's powerful image of the awesome divine presence and its numinous impact on both the landscape and the human realm, the Old Greek creates an aporia at stichs 6d–7a: ἐτάκησαν βουνοὶ αἰώνιοι πορείας αἰωνίας αὐτοῦ. ἀντὶ κόπων εἶδον σκηνώματα Αἰθιόπων "The eternal hills melted of his eternal passage. Instead of troubles I saw the tents of the Ethiopians." At the conclusion of the section, the Ethiopians are paralleled with the inhabitants of Madiam, and their consternation at the divine visitation is clarified in the Armenian rephrasing, խորանք եթւովպացւոց զարհուրեցան եւ խորանք երկրին Մադիամու "the tents of the Ethiopians were terrified and (as well as) the tents of the land of Madiam." Similarly, the opening of v. 6 creates a strong symmetry between the mountains and the hills. The Armenian translation conceptualizes the transition as a distinct element. It interprets πορείας "passage" as the object of the verb of seeing in order to fashion the following unit զգնացս նորա յաւիտենական փոխանակ աշխատութեանց տեսի "I saw his eternal steps instead of troubles." Presumably, the Armenian version identifies with an Israelite perspective, since God has come to save his people (Hab 3:13).

6–9.2.5.2.3.2 Translation Technique: Attention to Context

The influence of context on the Armenian translation's lexical choice is well illustrated by the treatment of the term φαντασία "appearance/apparition/imagination," which is only found five times in LXX, four of them in this corpus. In relation to the production of idols at Hab 2:18, 19, the term is appropriately rendered by երևույթ "image/form." In connection with an appeal for rain in Zech 10:1, it is represented by զզարմանալիս "miracles/wonders," whereas in Hab 3:10 its interpretation depends on the reference to the thundering of the abyss in the preceding phrase. Thus, Old Greek ὕψος φαντασίας αὐτῆς "the height of its apparition" is rendered զբարձրութիւն սաստկութեան իւրեանց "the height of their vehemence," to suggest the intensity of the sound of the rushing waters.[11] A prediction in Hab 3:17 envisages an interruption in the natural world's fertility cycle that results in barrenness for the fig tree, lack of produce on the vine, and, according to the Old Greek, ψεύσεται ἔργον ἐλαίας "the *work* of the olive will deceive." Maintaining continuity with the foregoing, the Armenian version renders the term "work" by բեր "yield," which suggests that the harvest will significantly undercut expectations. Another instance of the Armenian translator's contextual approach is the selection of an equivalent for the phrase πνεῦμα πορνείας "spirit of whoredom" at Hos 5:4, perceived as dictating the direction of affairs in Israel and Judah. Although the Greek lexeme is neutral, the Armenian responds to the negative connotations of the environment by rendering it as այս պոռնկութեան "evil-spirit of whoredom."

6–9.2.5.2.3.3 Translation Technique: Attention to Style

An element in the Armenian translator's technique that probably derives from Antiochene exegesis is the periodic elucidation of metaphors and other images. This is well illustrated by the employment of the term "scepter" by metonomy to denote kingly power in Hab 3:9 and Zech 10:11. In both cases, the Armenian translation reads իշխանութիւն "authority," guided perhaps by an Antiochene interpretation preserved by Theodore in his comment *in situ*: συνεχέσι δὲ ταῖς τιμωρίαις κατακοντίζεις τοὺς ἐν βασιλείᾳ καὶ δυναστείᾳ καθεστάναι δοκοῦντες "by continuous castigations you shoot down those who appear ensconced in kingship and power."[12]

6–9.2.5.2.4 Text-Critical Value: Omissions and Additions

The Armenian version is so faithful in its substantive representation of the Old Greek (→ 9.3) that omissions are negligible and additions are minor and necessitated by the exigencies of grammar or interpretation.

6–9.2.5.2.5 Relevance for Exegesis

As in a number of other books, it appears that in this corpus too the Armenian rendering has been informed by exegetical traditions of the School of Antioch (→ 1.3.1.2; → 6–9.1.6). One example relates to the interpretation of the term φέγγος "radiance." In Hab 3:11 it is rendered narrowly by the form փայլին "radiance," while in Hab 3:4 by the semantically more distant lexeme ճառագայթիւր "with rays." The latter rendering seems to rely on the interpretation preserved by Theodoret *in situ*, who accords it a Christological significance: ταῖς δὲ τῆς θεότητος ἀκτῖσι τοὺς ἀνθρώπους ἐφώτισε ... φανοτάτην γὰρ ἀφῆκεν ἀκτῖνα δι' ἧς τὴν οἰκουμένην κατηύγαζε "by the rays of his divinity he illumined mankind ... for he emitted a most luminous ray through which he shone upon the inhabited world."[13]

---

[11] The final example is in Wis 18:17, where the Armenian translation renders the images of night dreams by ցնորք "illusions."

[12] Migne, *Synesii episcopi Cyrenes*, col. 445.
[13] Schulze, *Theodoreti Cyrensis*, col. 1825.

6–9.2.5.2.6 Text-Critical Value of Arm-Minor Prophets for LXX-Minor Prophets

The Armenian version emerges as a reliable witness to its parent text, a manuscript that was related to a sub-family of the Catena group with subsidiary Lucianic affinities (→ 6–9.1.6). Its translation technique is extremely consistent, thus simplifying its alignment with the Greek. Clearly, systematic collations are necessary to determine whether the version evinces two strata throughout the Minor Prophets and to explore related issues.

Amalyan, H. (ed.), *Girk' erkotasan margarēic'* (*Book of the Twelve Prophets*) (Yerevan: Magaġat' Hratarakč'owt'yown, 2000).
Cowe, S.P., "The Bible in Armenian," in *The New Cambridge History of the Bible from 600 to 1450* (eds. R. Marsden and E.A. Matter; Cambridge: Cambridge University Press, 2012), 143–61.
Howard, G.E. (trans.), "The Twelve Prophets," in *NETS, 777–822.
Migne, J.-P. (ed.), *Synesii episcopi Cyrenes episcopi opera omnia* (PG 66; Paris: Lutetiae Parisiorum, 1864).
Schulze, J.L. (ed.), *Theodoreti Cyrensis episcopi opera omnia* (PG 81.2, Paris: Migne, 1864).
Weitenberg, J.J.S., *Parallel Aligned Text and Bilingual Concordance of the Armenian and Greek Versions of the Book of Jonah* (Dutch Studies in Armenian Language and Literature 1; Amsterdam: Rodopi, 1992).
Ziegler, J. (ed.), *Duodecim prophetae* (2nd ed.; Septuaginta Vetus Testamentum Graecum 13; Göttingen: Vandenhoeck & Ruprecht, 1967).

Peter Cowe

6–9.2.6 Georgian Translations

6–9.2.6.1 Manuscript Sources

The Georgian tradition of the Major and Minor Prophets boasts a long textual history that extends over several centuries. Manuscript evidence can be split into four typologies of sources.

6–9.2.6.1.1 The Earliest Fragmentary Sources (Palimpsests)

The first group comprises fragmentary sources that contain sections of Jeremiah and Isaiah. They are contained in three Hebrew-Georgian palimpsests, originally discovered in the Cairo Genizah and dating to the seventh and eighth centuries C.E.: Georg^{Pa} (Oxford, manuscript Hebrew 2672, 1 fol.); Georg^{Pb1} (Cambridge, Taylor-Schechter manuscript 12.183); and Georg^{Pb2} (Cambridge, Taylor-Schechter manuscript 12.741).[1] A further palimpsest is also available that may be dated between the fifth and sixth centuries C.E.: Georg^{Pd} (Tbilisi, National Centre of Manuscripts, H-844).

The language of these testimonies reveals certain peculiarities that have been labeled as "xanmet'i." Scholars have repeatedly stressed their importance for the history of the Georgian language and the textual study of the Georgian Bible (→ 1.4.8.2.1). It is no coincidence that several editions of these sources have been printed since the 1920s.[2]

6–9.2.6.1.2 The Lectionary

A number of readings from both the Major and Minor Prophets that were used in the context of Christian worship are to be found in the Old Georgian Lectionary, whose major source is Codex Georg^P (Paris, Bibliothèque nationale de France, geo. 3; year 1040). Additionally, three other testimonies dating to the tenth century are available: Georg^{La} (Tbilisi, National Parliamentary Library of Georgia, "Lectionary of Lagurk'a"; tenth century); Georg^{Lt} (Mest'ia, Historical-Ethnographic Museum, "Lectionary of Lat'ali"; tenth century) and Georg^{Sin} (Sinai, Geo. 37; 982 C.E.).[3]

6–9.2.6.1.3 Manuscripts Containing Complete Translations

Complete translations are available in manuscripts dating from the tenth to the twelfth centuries:

---

[1] Blake, "Catalogue," 207–24.
[2] Žavaxišvili, "Axlad aɣmočenili uʒvelesi kartuli xelnac'erebi," 319–20; Blake, "Khanmeti Palimpsest Fragments," 225–72; Šaniʒe, "Xanmet'i ieremias k'embriʒuli nac'q'vet'ebi," 29–42; Molitor, *Monumenta iberica antiquiora*.
[3] Melikišvili, *Targmanebi*, 86. Editions: Tarchnišvili, *Le grand lectionnaire*; Čxenk'eli, *Lagurk'is lekcionari*; Danelia, Čxenk'eli, and Šavišvili, *Kartuli lekcionaris*. Electronic version: http://titus.uni-frankfurt.de/texte/etcs/cauc/ageo/lekt/perikop1/perik.htm.

Georg⁰ (Mount Athos, Library of the Iviron Monastery, geo. 1; year 978; in two volumes), Georg^J1 (Jerusalem, Library of the Greek Patriarchate, geo. 7; eleventh century), Georg^J2 (Jerusalem, Library of the Greek Patriarchate, geo. 11; eleventh century), Georg^Gb (Tbilisi, National Centre of Manuscripts, A-1108, the "Gelati Bible"; twelfth century).[4]

6–9.2.6.1.4 Eighteenth-Century Printed Editions

The Georgian Prophets were first printed in Tbilisi in the early eighteenth century (→ 1.4.8.3.3).[5] At that time, a set of printed folios was taken from this edition and sewn into manuscript Georg^S (NCM, A-51; seventeenth or eighteenth century).[6] Moreover, a few decades later, the text was also reprinted without changes in the so-called "Bakar's Bible," published in Moscow in 1743 (Georg^B).[7] It was finally re-edited in the modern Georgian alphabet by Dočanašvili in 1985–1986.[8]

6–9.2.6.2 Date, Versions, Editions

The manuscripts' linguistic and paleographic features point to a very early date of composition of the Georgian versions of the Major and Minor Prophets, whose earliest textual stratum dates back to the oldest periods of Georgian literature, namely to the fifth and sixth centuries C.E. Over time, translations underwent revisions and editorial changes, with the result that at least two versions or redactions have survived for each single book.

6–9.2.6.2.1 Georg-Isa

The first Georgian translation of Isaiah (Georg-Isa 1) was most likely carried out in the fifth century C.E. The full text can be obtained by combining the evidence provided by palimpsest Georg^Pd, manuscripts Georg⁰ and Georg^J1, as well as lectionary Georg^P. Georg-Isa 1 is available in a number of editions.[9]

The second version (Georg-Isa 2) is preserved in Georg^Gb. The latter was created or, more probably, revised on the basis of an earlier text in the late eleventh century.[10]

6–9.2.6.2.2 Georg-Jer

As in the previous case, the oldest translation of the book of Jeremiah (Georg-Jer 1) may be dated confidently to the beginnings of Georgian literature. However, this earliest stratum is known to exist in three redactions. The first (Georg-Jer 1a) is to be found in the Hebrew-Georgian "xanmet'i" palimpsests Georg^Pa, Georg^Pb1, and Georg^Pb2. The second (Georg-Jer 1b) is preserved in Georg⁰ and Georg^J1+J2.[11] Compared to the previous redaction, it features minor changes, but here the text of the prophet is available in full. The third (Georg-Jer 1c) is contained in Georg^P, as well as in the three other lectionaries of the tenth century: Georg^La, Georg^Lt, and Georg^Sin.[12]

By the end of the eleventh century, Georg-Jer 1 was fully corrected based on a Greek source. This revision (Georg-Jer 2) is to be found in Georg^Gb. A synoptic edition of Georg-Jer 1 and Georg-Jer 2 was published by Danelia in 1992.[13]

6–9.2.6.2.3 Georg-Ezek

Georg-Ezek has come down to us in two redactions. The first (Georg-Ezek 1) survived in manuscripts

---

[4] Description: *C'ignni*, 1, 559–87.

[5] *Biblia, c'igni c'inasc'armet'q'velta da saxareba*.

[6] *C'ignni*, 1, 616.

[7] See Dočanašvili, *Mcxeturi xelnac'eri* (1986), 270. Georg^B: *Biblia: brʒanebita da c'arsagebelita sapasetata sakartvelos mepis*; description: *C'ignni*, 1, 627–35. Electronic edition: http://titus.uni-frankfurt.de/texte/etcg/cauc/ageo/bakar/bakar.htm.

[8] See Dočanašvili, *Mcxeturi xelnac'eri* (1985), 69–155 (Isaiah), 156–254 (Jeremiah), 285–372 (Ezekiel); and *Mcxeturi xelnac'eri* (1986), 39–114 (Minor Prophets). Electronic edition: http://titus.uni-frankfurt.de/texte/etcs/cauc/ageo/at/mcat/mcat.htm.

[9] Šaniʒe, *C'ignni ʒuelisa aytkumisani*, 175–92 (Georg⁰); Blake and Brière, *Prophets*, 2.384–509; Blake and Brière, *Apparatus*, 385–432 (Georg⁰ and Georg^J1); *Kartuli lekcionaris p'arizuli xelnac'eri*, 264–305 (Georg^P).

[10] Blake, "Ancient Georgian Versions," 291.

[11] First published by Blake with a Latin translation (Blake and Brière, *Prophets*, 4.512–653).

[12] Danelia, *Ieremias*, 8.

[13] Danelia, *Ieremias*, 11–217.

Georg^(J+2o) and partially in lectionary Georg^P, while the second (Georg-Ezek 2) survived in Georg^(Gb).

A synoptic critical edition based on the evidence of Georg^(J+2o) and Georg^(Gb) (the latter being integrated with the corrections found in the eighteenth-century printed edition) appeared in 1976.[14] A separate edition of Georg^P is also available.[15]

6–9.2.6.2.4 Georg-MinP

The Georgian Minor Prophets (Georg-MinP) survive in two different redactions. The first (Georg-MinP 1) is to be found in Georg^O, Georg^(J1+J2)[16] and, partially, also in lectionary Georg^P.[17] The second (Georg-MinP 2) is preserved in Georg^(Gb) and was judged to be a revision of the former. In a number of instances, their texts appear to be very similar. However, in other cases it may be assumed that some portions of the books were retranslated.[18]

Beside these versions, several readings from the Minor Prophets are also included in Georgian metaphrastic collections. In Nahum, Habbakuk, Zephaniah, and Zechariah, the translation is identical to Georg^O, but in Amos and Micah the pericopes are given in a third different version.[19]

6–9.2.6.2.5 Text of the Printed Edition

The text of the Prophets found in the early eighteenth-century Tbilisi printed edition basically corresponds to that of Georg^(Gb), namely to the second textual stratum of the books.[20] This version was however subjected to minor editorial changes,[21] which were made by Sulkhan Orbeliani (Sulxan-Saba Orbeliani, 1658–1725: → 1.4.8.3.3). He divided the text in chapters and verses, by taking as a model the 1666 printed Armenian Bible (→ 1.4.7.3).[22]

6–9.2.6.3 Textual Features and Parent Text

6–9.2.6.3.1 Georg-Isa

The "xanmet'i" palimpsest of Georg-Isa comprises Isa 7:20–23; 8:2–8; 40:10–12; 46:6–7; 47:2–6; 49:3. According to recent studies, this translation does not rely on an Armenian (→ 6–9.2.5) model, but was carried out from a source belonging to LXX^L (→ 6–9.1.6).[23] The manuscript tradition of Georg-Isa 1 is characterized by a certain stability: over the centuries, the text has not been substantially changed.[24] The Greek prototype of Georg-Isa 2 still awaits establishment, but in Blake's opinion it may have been an Armenian source.[25]

6–9.2.6.3.2 Georg-Jer

The textual history of Georg-Jer 1 is far less linear than that of Georg-Isa, since the orginal text has been subjected to several revisions over the centuries.

6–9.2.6.3.2.1 Georg-Jer 1a

Scholars have argued that the "xanmet'i" manuscripts of Georg-Jer 1a were originally part of a full translation of the book. The reason for this assumption is that the readings preserved in the Hebrew-Georgian palimpsests (Jer 12:10–16; 17:26–27; 18:2–8; 20:9–16) do not fall into the category of lectionary pericopes.[26]

Recent research suggests that Blake's opinion on the Armenian (→ 6–9.2.5) origin of Georg-Jer 1a should be reconsidered.[27] In fact, although both

---

[14] Ckit'išvili, *Ezek'ielis*, 6–186. Electronic edition of Georg^(Gb): http://titus.uni-frankfurt.de/texte/etca/cauc/ageo/at/gelatat/gelat.htm.

[15] *Kartuli lekcionaris p'arizuli xelnac'eri*, 264–305.

[16] Edition: Blake and Brière, *Prophets*, Vol. 1. Partial edition: Assfalg, "Altgeorgische Übersetzungen." A third edition was apparently prepared but never published by B. Gigineišvili (see Goguaʒe, "Mcire," 7, n. 6; *Mcxeturi xelnac'eri* [1986], 270).

[17] Edition: Danelia, Čxenk'eli, and Šavišvili, *Kartuli lekcionaris*, 353–401. Obadiah is not included.

[18] Dočanašvili, *Mcxeturi xelnac'eri* (1986), 273.

[19] Goguaʒe, "Mcire," 5–10.

[20] Blake, "O drevnegruzinskich versijach" and Blake, "Ancient Georgian Versions"; *Mcxeturi xelnac'eri* (1986), 270–94.

[21] See *Mcxeturi xelnac'eri* (1985), 69–155.

[22] Oskan Erevants'i, *Astuatsashunch'*. On this issue, see: Abulaʒe, "Kartuli bibliis," 151; Dočanašvili, *Mcxeturi xelnac'eri*, 1986, 292–3.

[23] Xaranauli, *3veli aγtkmis xanmet'i pragment'ebi*.

[24] Melikišvili, *Targmanebi*, 68–70.

[25] Blake, "Ancient Georgian Versions," 291.

[26] Melikišvili, *Targmanebi*, 68–69.

[27] Kharanauli, "Das Chanmeti-Fragment aus Jeremia," 205; Melikišvili, *Targmanebi*, 69.

the Armenian and Georgian versions are testimony of the Hexaplaric text (→ 6–9.1.5), they seem to depend on different models. As has emerged, Georg-Jer 1a was translated no later than the sixth century C.E. from a Greek source that was very close, but not identical, to that used by the Armenian translator.[28] Differences from the Hexaplaric text in Georg-Jer 1a resulted from resorting to a non-literal translation technique.[29] In selecting lexical equivalents, Georg-Jer 1a basically reproduces the semantics of the word being translated.[30]

6–9.2.6.3.2.2 Georg-Jer 1b

Georg-Jer 1b also presents a number of typical Hexaplaric pluses (→ 6–9.1.5) that also occur in Armenian (→ 6–9.2.5).[31] Differences from LXX (→ 7.3) include the arrangement of verses, additions, and also the rendering of proper nouns. As a result, in the second part of the book (after Jer 25:15), the text sequence of Georg-Jer 1b is that of MT (→ 7.2.2).[32] Despite this, a number of textual features of Georg-Jer 1b pose serious questions that have not yet found clear answers. In fact, in several cases, this translation agrees at the same time with both the Hebrew and Greek texts. For instance, a look at Jer 23:7–8 shows that Georg-Jer 1b follows MT; however, after Jer 23:40, it repeats this verse in a different translation based on LXX.[33]

The origins and textual features of Georg-Jer 1b are still the subject of discussion. Danelia pointed out that this version shows reliance on an Eastern base text that should not be identified with the Armenian. In the opinion of Kurcik'iʒe, this entire issue remains highly controversial and considerable work has still to be done before the source of this translation can be established definitively.[34]

6–9.2.6.3.2.3 Georg-Jer 1c

Georg-Jer 1c comprises the following liturgical readings: Jer 1:1–19; 2:2–3; 3:12–25; 5:20–29; 9:2–10; 10:6–10; 11:18–20; 15:19–20; 16:19–21; 17:5–10; 30:2–11; 31:7–28; 32:17–44; 33:2–11; 38:1–13; 50:44–46.[35]

6–9.2.6.3.2.4 Georg-Jer 2

Far from being a new independent version,[36] Georg-Jer 2 instead represents merely a revision of Georg-Jer 1b.[37] It was apparently undertaken by using a Greek model that had marginal commentaries containing a number of readings from the Three (→ 6–9.1.5). Čeliʒe has argued that the doublets in Georg^{Gb} can be explained by the fact that some of these marginal glosses may have been incorporated into the main text.[38]

6–9.2.6.3.3 Georg-Ezek

Georg-Ezek 1 manifestly shows its dependence on LXX (→ 8.3) in omitting several pluses of MT (→ 8.2.2; see, for instance, Ezek 1:22; 3:18; 5:14, 15; 6:6; 8:3; 16:13; 20:28; 32:19) and in having the same arrangement of verses in Ezekiel 7.[39] Nevertheless, it does not display agreement with any of the minuses found in LXX[967], which omits Ezek 12:26–28; 32:25–26; 36: 23c–38.[40]

Georg-Ezek 2 does not represent a new independent translation, but is a revision of Georg-Ezek 1. This appears to be proved by the insertion in the former of several verses taken from the latter, as well as by common translation errors.[41] However, unlike the earlier version, Georg-Ezek 2 features a text considerably longer than LXX. According to Ckit'išvili, the author of Georg-Ezek 2 based his work on both Greek and Eastern sources (but

---

[28] Melikišvili, *Targmanebi*, 68–69.
[29] Kharanauli, "Das Chanmeti-Fragment aus Jeremia," 218–19.
[30] Kharanauli, "Das Chanmeti-Fragment aus Jeremia," 235.
[31] Danelia, *Ieremias*, 306–11.
[32] Danelia, *Ieremias*, 305.
[33] Danelia, *Ieremias*, 90–95.
[34] Kurcik'iʒe, *Kartuli biblia*, 66. See also Outtier, "L' Ancien Testament," 219.

[35] For an edition, see *Kartuli lekcionaris p'arizuli xelnac'eri*, 306–19.
[36] Gigineišvili and K'ik'viʒe, "Rustavelis xanis kartuli bibliis targmani," 150.
[37] Danelia, "Sulxan-saba," 205–21; Kurcik'iʒe, *3veli aγtkmis*, 149.
[38] Čeliʒe, *3veli kartuli saek'lesio lit'erat'ura*, 136–37.
[39] See Tov, **Greek-Hebrew Bible*, 397–410.
[40] See Tov, **Greek-Hebrew Bible*, 408; Tov, **TCHB*, 300–01.
[41] Melikišvili, *Targmanebi*, 170–76.

not the Armenian [→ 6–9.2.5]).[42] In this regard, the following remarks can be made here.

As a result of a preliminary collation with Ziegler's edition, it emerged that Georg-Ezek 2 frequently agrees with LXX[L] (→ 6–9.1.6). Typical doublets and readings of this redaction are reflected in the text of Georg-Ezek 2 (see, for instance, Ezek 1:16, 18; 16:16; 17:7; 22:25; 24:17; 25:13; 27:15; 30:6; 34:29; 38:5, 14; 42:13; 43:7; 47:12). Moreover, the Lucianic formula τάδε λέγει αδωναι κύριος "thus says Adonai the Lord" is to be found in Georg-Ezek 2. In view of the above, future research should devote special attention to the detection of other possible affinities with LXX[L], which is likely to be the parent text of Georg-Ezek 2. As has been shown, LXX[L] is not based on MT but on Hexaplaric sources (→ 6–9.1.5).[43]

6–9.2.6.3.4 Georg-MinP

The problems of the origin of this tradition and of the exact textual relationship between the two versions remain unsolved. In Blake's view, Georg-MinP 2 presents a text whose model was a translation from Armenian (→ 6–9.2.5) because of the large number of lexical borrowings from that language.[44] Moreover, in his opinion, Georg-MinP 1 represents a revision of the same archetype of Georg-MinP 2 that was undertaken by Hellenophile circles.[45] According to a different assessment, the Georgian tradition has textual affinities with the Armenian, but reveals a strong influence from a Greek source text, especially from LXX[A] (→ 9.3).[46]

These remarks can be supplemented by the following consideration. Georg-MinP 2 features a number of marginal commentaries (in Georg[Gb])[47] that would suggest the translation's reliance on a model belonging to the Catena group, which was judged to be the parent text of the Armenian (→ 6–9.2.5.2.6). By postulating such a common source for both Caucasian traditions, a number of textual similarities between them could apparently find an explanation. However, these analogies must be subjected to very careful scrutiny and the entire text should be collated before definitive conclusions can be drawn on this topic.

Order of the Books

In Georg[J1+2], the Minor Prophets precede the Major Prophets.[48] This should have been also the original order of Georg[O],[49] in which at present the Minor Prophets are to be found at the end of the second volume after Samuel–Kings, Proverbs, Qohelet, Canticles, Wisdom, and Sirach.[50] The remaining Georgian testimonies (Georg[Gb,S,B]) place the Major Prophets first. As far as the internal sequence of the Minor Prophets is concerned, the Georgian shows great uniformity. The order always corresponds to that of MT (→ 9.2.2) and of most versions (→ 9.1.2).[51]

6–9.2.6.4 Text-Critical Value of the Primary Translation

The Georgian tradition of the Major and Minor Prophets suffers from a lack of integration with LXX studies, despite the fact that texts are edited and a complete Latin translation of the earliest versions was also published more than five decades ago.[52] In fact, with the exception of the palimpsest text of Georg-Jer (→ 6–9.2.6.3.2),[53] systematic collations with the Göttingen LXX still await production.[54] In spite of this, thanks to new research, a clearer picture of the textual allegiances with the various manuscript families of LXX (→ 6.7, → 7.3,

---

[42] Ckit'išvili, *Ezek'ielis*, 228–47.
[43] Wevers, "The L Text of Ezekiel," 69, 115.
[44] Blake, "Ancient Georgian Versions," 291.
[45] Blake, "Ancient Georgian Versions," 291.
[46] See Dočanašvili, *Mcxeturi xelnac'eri* (1986), 271, 274–75.
[47] For an edition, see Gigineišvili and Todua, *Gelaturi*, 629–47.
[48] See C'ignni, 1, 574–75. These two codices were originally bound together in a single manuscript (→ 1.4.8.2.3).
[49] Blake, "The Athos Codex," 40.
[50] See C'ignni, 1, 564, 568–69.
[51] See C'ignni, 1.569 (Georg[O]), 574–75 (Georg[J1+J2]), 582–83 (Georg[Gb]), 617–18 (Georg[S]), 630 (Georg[B]).
[52] Blake and Brière, *Prophets*, PO 29.2; 29.3; 29.4; 29.5.
[53] See Kharanauli, "Das Chanmeti-Fragment aus Jeremia," 204–36.
[54] Ziegler, *Ezechiel*; Ziegler, *Ieremias*; Ziegler, *Isaias*; Ziegler, *Duodecim Prophetae*. It is to be hoped that this lack will be filled, at least in part, in the forthcoming fifth edition of the Minor Prophets (see below, n. 58).

→ 8.3, → 9.3) is, at least in some cases, taking shape progressively. Moreover, the need emerges increasingly for a reconsideration of the hypothesis on the Armenian (→ 6–9.2.5) origin of this corpus. The text-critical value of the Georgian translations lies in their early date and in their capacity to provide us with an insight into the textual transmission of the primary version in late antiquity.

6–9.2.6.4.1 Georg-Isa

The comparative textual analysis of mss Georg^{Pd} and Georg^{Jop} permits an assumption that a full Lucianic translation (→ 6–9.1.6) of Georg-Isa was already undertaken in the fifth century C.E. Georg-Isa 1 can therefore be regarded as an early witness to LXX^L.[55] The parent text of Georg-Isa 2 has not yet been established definitively.

6–9.2.6.4.2 Georg-Jer

The earliest manuscript evidence of Georg-Jer 1a dates back to either the sixth or the eighth century C.E., depending on the different considerations of scholars.[56] Regardless of the various paleographic views, it is not difficult to observe that the Georgian palimpsests are older than the preserved Greek minuscule manuscripts belonging to the Hexaplaric redaction (→ 6–9.1.5.2). The text-critical value of Georg-Jer 1a lies in its date and textual affiliation. The "xanmet'i" redaction is an ancient representative of the Hexaplaric text (→ 6–9.1.5).[57] As the model of Georg-Jer 1b has not yet been traced, it seems at present difficult to make a definitive assessment of the merit of this translation for the study of the primary version. The text-critical value of Georg-Jer 2 consists in the fact that it is a witness to the readings of the Three.

6–9.2.6.4.3 Georg-Ezek

Although a full collation with Ziegler's edition is still to be undertaken, the following preliminary conclusions can be reached. Georg-Ezek 1 is a witness to the LXX text (→ 8.3). Georg-Ezek 2, on the one hand, demonstrates affinities with the Hexaplaric witnesses (→ 6–9.1.5) while, on the other hand, it manifests reliance on LXX^L (→ 6–9.1.6), which is likely to be its parent text.

6–9.2.6.4.4 Georg-MinP

The textual relationship of Georg-MinP to the various manuscript families of LXX (→ 9.3) and to the other daughter versions cannot be described in detail, since systematic collations are not available.[58] With regard to the position of the Minor Prophets, the oldest stratum of the Georgian translation reflects the tradition attested in LXX^{A,B,V} (→ 1.3.1.1.4). The internal sequence of Georg-MinP is identical to that in MT (→ 9.2.2).

In Georgian:

Abulaʒe, I., "Kartuli bibliis ʒveli xelnac'eris ramdenime purceli," *St'alinis saxelobis tbilisis sax. universit'et'is šromebi* 18 (1941): 149–59.

Biblia: brʒanebita da c'arsagebelita sapasetata sakartvelos mepis bakar vaxt'angis ʒisata (Moscow: Bakaris st'amba, 1743).

Biblia, c'igni c'inasc'armet'q'velta da saxareba (Tbilisi: Vaxt'angis st'amba, 1709–1710).

Danelia, K'., "Sulxan-saba orbelianis leksik'onis erti c'q'aro," *Macne (enisa da lit'erat'uris seria)* Fasc. 2 (1964): 205–21.

Gigineišvili, B. and C. K'ik'viʒe, "Rustavelis xanis kartuli bibliis targmani," in *Šota Rustaveli: ist'oriul-pilologiuri ʒiebani* (Tbilisi: Sakartvelos ssr mecnierebata ak'ademia, 1966), 149–59.

Gigineišvili, B. and G. Todua (eds.), *Gelaturi bibliis k'at'enebi* (Tbilisi: Axali ivironi, 2011).

Goguaʒe, N., "Mcire c'inasc'armetq'velta sak'itxavebi met'aprasul k'rebulebši," *Mravaltavi* 9 (1981): 5–10.

Danelia, K'., "Ieremias c'inasc'armet'q'velebis ʒveli kartuli versiebi da mati momdinareobis sak'itxi," in *ʒveli kartuli enis k'atedris šromebi*, Vol. 9: *Mieʒɣvna*

---

[55] Melikišvili, *Targmanebi*, 68–70; Kharanauli, "The Georgian Translation."

[56] Žavaxišvili, "Axlad aɣmočenili uʒvelesi kartuli xelnac'erebi," 319–20; Blake, "Khanmeti Palimpsest Fragments," 225–72; Šaniʒe, "Xanmet'i ieremias k'embriʒuli nac'q'vet'ebi," 29–42; Melikišvili, *Targmanebi*, 71.

[57] Melikišvili, *Targmanebi*, 68.

[58] A reassessment of the Georgian tradition is expected in the forthcoming fifth edition of Ziegler's *Duodecim Prophetae* (this information is available on the publisher's website).

ak'ademik'os nik'o maris xsovnas dabadebis asi c'lis tavze (1864–1964) (ed. A. Šaniʒe; Tbilisi: Tbilisis saxelmc'ipo universit'et'i, 1964), 159–84.

Danelia, K'. (ed.), *Ieremias c'inasc'armet'q'velebis ʒveli kartuli versiebi* (Tbilisi: Tbilisis universit'et'is gamomcemloba, 1992).

Danelia, K'., S. Čxenk'eli, and B. Šavišvili (eds.), *Kartuli lekcionaris p'arizuli xelnac'eri: ʒveli da axali aγtkmis sak'itxavebi*, Vol. 1: *Nac'ili I* (Tbilisi: Tbilisis universit'et'is gamomcemloba, 1987).

Dočanašvili, E. (ed.), *Mcxeturi xelnac'eri (ek'lesiast'e, sibrʒne solomonisa, keba kebata solomonisa, c'inasc'armet'q'velta c'ignebi: Esaia, ieremia, baruki, ezek'ieli)* (Tbilisi: Mecniereba, 1985).

Dočanašvili, E. (ed.), *Mcxeturi xelnac'eri (danielis, mcire c'inasc'armet'q'velta da axali aγtkmis c'ignebi)* (Tbilisi: Mecniereba, 1986).

Melikišvili, N., *Bibliur c'ignta ʒveli kartuli targmanebi* (Tbilisi: Alilo, 2009).

Kurcik'iʒe, C., *Kartuli biblia* (Tbilisi: Xelnac'erta erovnuli cent'ri, 2010).

Kurcik'iʒe, C., *ʒveli aγtkmis ap'ok'ripuli (arak'anonik'uri) c'ignebis kartuli versiebi: c'igni II* (Tbilisi: Mecniereba, 1973).

Šaniʒe, A., "Haemet'i t'ekst'ebi da mati mnišvneloba kartuli enis ist'oriisatvis," *Tbilisis universit'et'is moambe* 3 (1923): 354–88.

Šaniʒe, A., "Xanmet'i ieremias k'embriʒuli nac'q'vet'ebi," *Enimk'is moambe* 2.1 (1937): 29–42.

Šaniʒe, A. (ed.), *C'ignni ʒuelisa aγtkumisani 978 c'lis xelnac'eris mixedvit*, Vol. 1.2: *Levit'eltaj, msaǯultaj, rutisi, iobisi, esaiajsi* (Tbilisi: Sak. ssr mecnierebata ak'ademiis gamomcemloba, 1948).

Čeliʒe, E., *ʒveli kartuli saek'lesio lit'erat'ura* (Tbilisi: Axali ivironi, 2005).

Čxenk'eli, S., *Lagurk'is lekcionari* (Tbilisis uxco enata p'edagogiuri inst'it'utis šromebi 2; Tbilisi, 1950).

Ckit'išvili, T., *Ezek'ielis c'ignis ʒveli kartuli versiebi* (Tbilisi: Mecniereba, 1976).

C'ignni ʒuelisa aγtkumisani, Vol. 1: *Šesakmisaj, gamoslvataj* (eds. B. Gigineišvili and C. K'ik'viʒe; Tbilisi: Mecniereba, 1989).

Xaranauli, A., "ʒveli aγtkmis xanmet'i pragment'ebi da kartuli bibliis t'ekst'is ist'oriis sak'itxebi" (unpublished PhD diss., University of Tbilisi, 2005).

Žavaxišvili, I., "Axlad aγmočenili uʒvelesi kartuli xelnac'erebi da mati mnišvneloba mecnierebisatvis," *Tbilisis universit'et'is moambe* 2 (1922–1923): 313–91 [reprinted in: I. Žavaxišvili, *Kartuli damc'erlobata-mcodneoba anu p'aleograpia* (Tbilisi: St'alinis saxelobis tbilisis saxelmc'ipo universit'et'is gamomcemloba, 1949), 274–366].

In other languages:

Assfalg, J., "Altgeorgische Übersetzungen der Propheten Amos, Michaeas, Jonas, Sophonias und Zacharias: Texte aus den georgischen Handschriften Jerusalem Nr. 7 und Nr. 11 (11. Jahrh.), Athos Nr. 1 (A.D. 978), Sinai Nr. 37 (10. Jahrh.)" (unpublished Habilitation; Aschau im Chiemgau, 1959).

Blake, R., "O drevnegruzinskich versijach Vetchogo Zaveta," in *Izvestija Kavkazskogo Otdela Moskovskogo Archeologičeskogo Obščestva*, Vol. 6 (Tiflis: Tipografija gruzinskogo izdatel'skogo tovariščestva, 1921).

Blake, R., "Ancient Georgian Versions of the Old Testament," *HTR* 19.3 (1926): 271–97.

Blake, R., "The Athos Codex of the Georgian Old Testament," *HTR* 22.1 (1929): 33–56.

Blake, R.P., "Catalogue of the Georgian Manuscripts in the Cambridge University Library," *HTR* 25.3 (1932): 207–24.

Blake, R.P., "Khanmeti Palimpsest Fragments of the Old Georgian Version of Jeremiah," *HTR* 25.3 (1932): 225–72.

Blake, R.P. and C.M. Brière, *The Old Georgian Version of the Prophets: Critical Edition with a Latin Translation* (4 vols.; PO 29.2–5; Paris: Firmin Didot, 1961).

Blake, R.P. and C.M. Brière, *The Old Georgian Version of the Prophets: Apparatus Criticus* (PO 30.3; Paris: Firmin Didot, 1963).

Kharanauli, A., "Das Chanmeti-Fragment aus Jeremia: Fragen seiner Entstehung und seiner Übersetzungstechnik," *OrChr* 85 (2001): 204–36.

Kharanauli, A., "The Georgian Translation of the Book of Isaiah and Aporiai of the Lucianic Recension," in *In the Footsteps of Sherlock Holmes: Studies in the Biblical Text in Honour of Anneli Aejmelaeus* (eds. K. De Troyer, T.M. Law, and M. Liljeström; CBET 72; Leuven: Peeters, 2014), 417–36.

Molitor, J., *Monumenta iberica antiquiora: Textus chanmeti et haemeti: Ex inscriptionibus S. Bibliis et Patribus* (Louvain: Peeters, 1956).

Molitor, J., "Spuren altsyrischer Bibelübersetzung in den Chanmeti-Palimpsesten aus Jeremias," *Bedi Karthlisa* 15–16 (1963): 99–102.

Oskan Erevants'i (ed.), *Astuatsashunch' Hnots' ew Norots' Ktakaranats'* [Scriptures of the Old and New Testaments] (Amsterdam, 1666).

Outtier, B., "L' Ancien Testament a-t-il été traduit en arménien et géorgien du syriaque?" in *L' Ancien Testament en syriaque* (eds. F. Briquel-Chatonnet and P. Le

Moigne; Études syriaques 5; Paris: Geuthner, 2008), 215–20.

Tarchnišvili, M., *Le grand lectionnaire de l'église de Jérusalem (Ve–VIIIe siècle)* (Louvain: Secrétariat du Corpus SCO, 1959).

Wevers, J.W., "The L Text of Ezekiel," in *Studies in the Text Histories of Deuteronomy and Ezekiel* (eds. J.W. Wevers and D. Fraenkel; MSU 26; Göttingen: Vandenhoeck & Ruprecht, 2003), 69–115.

Ziegler, J. (ed.), *Ezechiel* (Septuaginta Vetus Testamentum Graecum 16.1; Göttingen: Vandenhoeck & Ruprecht, 1952).

Ziegler, J. (ed.), *Ieremias, Baruch, Threni, Epistula Ieremiae* (Septuaginta Vetus Testamentum Graecum 15; Göttingen: Vandenhoeck & Ruprecht, 1957).

Ziegler, J. (ed.), *Isaias* (2nd ed.; Septuaginta Vetus Testamentum Graecum 14; Göttingen: Vandenhoeck & Ruprecht, 1967).

Ziegler, J. (ed.), *Duodecim Prophetae* (2nd ed.; Septuaginta Vetus Testamentum Graecum 13; Göttingen: Vandenhoeck & Ruprecht, 1967).

Alessandro Maria Bruni

6–9.2.7 Old Church Slavonic Translations

6–9.2.7.1 Chronological Frame

The primary body of the Old Church Slavonic (OCS) translations of the Major (Isaiah, Jeremiah, and Ezekiel) and Minor Prophets (MinP) dates back to the beginnings of Slavonic literature, respectively to the Cyrillo-Methodian (ca. 863–885 C.E.) and Old Bulgarian periods (Preslav literary school, reign of Tsar Symeon, ca. 893–927 C.E.: → 1.4.10.3). Basically, for the most part, these versions, were produced from two different typologies of Greek sources: the Prophetologium and the so-called Catena type. The latter is a commented edition of the Sixteen Prophets used widely in Middle Byzantine literature and is believed to have been compiled initially in the seventh or eighth century C.E. by John Drungarios (group "C" in Ziegler's editions).[1] A second set of texts (or revisions) had its origin in the late fifteenth century in Russia within the framework of a highly significant editorial enterprise that was promoted by Archbishop Gennadius of Novgorod (Gennadij Gonzov, ca. 1410–1505) and formed the first full corpus of the Slavic Scriptures. Thereafter, this collection became known as the Gennadian Bible. Its oldest manuscript dates from 1499. The collection of the sixteen prophets included previous Old Church Slavonic versions as well as new translations (→ 1.4.10.3.3.2). The latter were based on late fifteenth-century editions of the Vulgate, among which were those printed by Koberger (ca. 1440–1513) in 1487 (with commentaries by Nicholas of Lyra)[2] and by Kessler (1450–post-1519) in 1487 or 1491 (→ 1.4.10.3).[3]

The subsequent history of the Old Church Slavonic translations of Isaiah, Jeremiah, Ezekiel, and the Minor Prophets may basically be divided in two phases. The recensions of the Gennadian Bible, after having been revised by taking LXX (→ 6.3, → 7.3, → 8.3, → 9.3) as a model, were included in the 1581 Ostrog Bible. A further correction process, in some cases of significant extension (Jeremiah), was finally undertaken for the purpose of drawing up the 1751 Elizabethan Bible (→ 1.4.10.3.4).[4]

6–9.2.7.2 Versions, Editions

The Old Church Slavonic manuscript tradition of Isaiah, Jeremiah, Ezekiel, and the Minor Prophets containing versions from the ninth and tenth centuries C.E. remains virtually unexplored in terms of textual criticism. Editions based on the complete manuscript evidence have yet to be produced: a large number of East and South Slavic Cyrillic codices dating from no earlier than the twelfth century await thorough investigation.[5] An attempt to fill this gap has recently been made for OCS-Ezek and OCS-MinP: an edition has been produced on the basis of two South Slavic testimonies.[6]

---

[1] Ziegler, *Isaias*, 92–95; *Jeremias*, 93–98; *Ezechiel*, 57–61; *Duodecim Prophetae*.

[2] *Biblia latina: Cum postillis Nicolai de Lyra et expositionibus Guillelmi Britonis in omnes prologos S. Hieronymi et additionibus Pauli Burgensis replicisque Matthiae Doering* (Nuremberg: Anton Koberger, 1487).

[3] *Biblia latina* (Basel: Nikolaus Kessler, 1487; 2nd ed. 1491).

[4] See *Ostrožskaja biblija*; *Biblija 1751*; Thomson, "The Slavonic Translation," 655–59, 862–65.

[5] For a list of sources, see Mathiesen, "Handlist," 18–33.

[6] Taseva, Jovčeva, and Ilieva, *Kniga*, 40–43; Taseva and Ilieva, "Problemi," 46–66.

6–9.2.7.2.1 OCS-Isa

OCS-Isa basically comprises two translations. The first (OCS-Isa 1), believed to be of Cyrillo-Methodian origin, is included in the Old Church Slavonic Prophetologium: it has come down to us in forty-one East and South Slavic Cyrillic manuscripts from the twelfth to the seventeenth centuries,[7] as well as in the earliest Croat Glagolitic Breviary. In the latter, the additional readings, originally not included in the Prophetologium, represent supplementary translations from the Vulgate (→ 6–9.1.7).[8]

The second version (OCS-Isa 2) is thought to have been undertaken in Bulgaria during the reign of Tsar Symeon. With the exception of a fragmentary testimony dating from the twelfth century (containing Isa 44:26–28; 45:1, 4–7, 9–17), this translation is mainly to be found in East and South Slavic Cyrillic sources of the fourteenth to sixteenth centuries.[9] Most manuscripts represent collections of the Sixteen Prophets provided with exegetical commentaries, while some do not include the scholia (a few South Slavic testimonies, as well as a number of East Slavic copies of the Russian Macarian Menologium → 1.4.10.2.4).[10] A revision of OCS-Isa 2, undertaken on the basis of the Vulgate, was included in the Gennadian Bible, from where it was carried over into the printed Ostrog Bible, after amendments were made in line with LXX (→ 6.3).[11]

Critical texts of both OCS-Isa 1 and OCS-Isa 2 have yet to be produced; versions have only been published based on single manuscripts.[12]

A few readings of the book of Isaiah are also to be found in the so-called *Jewish Chronicle* (*J-Ch*), an extensive compilation consisting mostly of translations of Greek historical and literary works (Flavius Josephus, John Malalas, George Hamartolos, and pseudo-Callisthenes), biblical books (Octateuch, Tetrabasileon, excerpts from the Prophets and others), as well as several Old Russian annals.[13] The view has been expressed that the language of these fragments (Isa 7:1–16; 8:1–10; 9:6–7; 11:1–10) is archaic and may be assigned to the Pre-Symeonic period.[14] However, given the lack of editions, it is unfortunately not possible to clarify their textual relationship with both OCS-Isa 1 and OCS-Isa 2.

6–9.2.7.2.2 OCS-Jer

The earliest textual stratum of OCS-Jer (OCS-Jer 1) is thought to date from the Cyrillo-Methodian period. This layer, which still awaits philological reconstruction and editing, is only preserved fragmentarily. It appears to be accessible in the Cyrillic Prophetologium, the Croat Glagolitic Breviary and Missal, as well as in *J-Ch*.[15] A contrasting view is also held that the readings contained in the latter belong more precisely to a separate and slightly later tradition: they are purported to be traces of a lost complete translation allegedly undertaken by Methodius (815–885 C.E.) shortly before his death (→ 1.4.10.3.2).[16]

A second version (OCS-Jer 2), whose origins are believed to be rooted in the Preslav literary school,[17] is to be found in more than forty East and South Slavic Cyrillic manuscripts of the Sixteen Prophets starting from the fourteenth century, which reveal traces of an underlying Glagolitic tradition.

OCS-Jer 2 does not comprise the full prophetical book: it contains Jer 32:13–52:34.[18] Whether this was its original length or is the result of a loss of text remains unfortunately a matter of speculation. In this regard, it may only be noted that the lack

---

[7] Evseev, *Kniga* (Part 1), 36–52; Popova, "Ot pr(o)r(o)č(ьst)va," 96–101.

[8] Nachtigal', "Neskol'ko zametok," 185–86.

[9] Forty copies are listed in Evseev, *Kniga* (Part 1), 7, 34–35, 52–69.

[10] Evseev, *Kniga* (Part 1), 164; Mostrova, "Knigata na prorok Isaja," 281.

[11] Thomson, "The Slavonic Translation," 861–63.

[12] Prophetologium: Brandt, "Grigorovičev parimejnik," 7–308 (*passim*); Ribarova and Hauptova, *Grigorovičev parimejnik*; Croat Glagolitic tradition: Berčić, *Ulomci*, 1–14, 18–19, 23, 25–29, 31–33, 35–37; OCS-Isa 2: *Die grossen Lesemenäen*, 2.710–813.

[13] For content description, see Istrin, *Aleksandrija*, 315–43 (Isaiah: p. 334).

[14] Thomson, "The Slavonic Translation," 853.

[15] Mostrova, "Starobălgarskijat prevod," 9.

[16] Evseev, "Zametki," 355–73; Alekseev, *Tekstologija*, 154–55; Mostrova, "Knigata na prorok Ieremija," 61–62.

[17] Mostrova, "Kăm leksikalnata charakteristika," 139.

[18] Mostrova, "Starobălgarskijat prevod," 9.

of a complete Old Church Slavonic translation of Jeremiah had already been discerned in Russia in the last decade of the fifteenth century. At that time, the missing chapters were translated from the Vulgate (→ 6–9.1.7) and included in the Gennadian Bible.[19] This new text (OCS-Jer 3) subsequently entered the Ostrog Bible.[20]

Diplomatic editions of both OCS-Jer 2 and OCS-Jer 3 are available: they are based on the sixteenth-century Russian Macarian Menologium (→ 1.4.10.2.4).[21]

6–9.2.7.2.3 OCS-Ezek

The Old Church Slavonic Cyrillic tradition of Ezekiel comprises two translations. The first (OCS-Ezek 1) is believed to date back to the Cyrillo-Methodian period and is included in the Old Church Slavonic Prophetologium.[22] The second (OCS-Ezek 2) is thought to have been undertaken in Bulgaria during the reign of Tsar Symeon. It is to be found in fifty-two manuscripts containing a collection of the Sixteen Prophets (four South Slavic and forty-eight East Slavic copies dating at the earliest from the fourteenth century), as well as in six testimonies of the Russian Macarian Menologium (→ 1.4.10.2.4). With a few exceptions, OCS-Ezek 2 is on the whole supplemented by the Old Church Slavonic translation of Theodoret of Cyrrhus' *Interpretatio in Ezechielem* (CPG 6206).[23] The currently available edition of OCS-Ezek 2 is based on two South Slavic sources dating from the fourteenth or fifteenth century.[24]

The Croat Glagolitic tradition comprises a revision of the Cyrillo-Methodian textual stratum as well as new translations, which in both cases are based on the Vulgate (→ 6–9.1.7).[25] In the late fifteenth century, the latter also provided the model for compilers of the Gennadian Bible to correct OCS-Ezek 2.[26]

6–9.2.7.2.4 OCS-Minor Prophets

The manuscript tradition of OCS-MinP belongs to the oldest corpus of the Slavonic Scriptures (ninth to tenth centuries C.E.).

The earliest textual layer (OCS-MinP 1), which dates from the Cyrillo-Methodian period, should be identified with the readings contained in the lectionary sources, namely the Old Church Slavonic Prophetologium (OCS-MinP 1a) and the Croat Glagolitic Breviary (OCS-MinP 1b).

The second stratum (OCS-MinP 2) is represented by the East and South Slavic Cyrillic testimonies of the Catena type. The latter was translated in Glagolitic script, presumably during the reign of Tsar Symeon in Bulgaria,[27] although some books (Zephaniah, Haggai, Zechariah, and Malachi),[28] are believed to be the remains of a translation allegedly undertaken by Methodius (→ 1.4.10.3.2).[29]

Later redactional stages of OCS-MinP are represented by the late fifteenth-century revision towards the Vulgate (→ 6–9.1.7) in the Gennadian Bible (OCS-MinP 3 included also in the Macarian Menologium), as well as the text of the 1581 Ostrog Bible (OCS-MinP 4), which was recorrected using the LXX (→ 9.3) as a model. Beside this material, an independent fragmentarily preserved sixteenth-century Serbian translation (OCS-MinP 5) has also come down to us (→ 6–9.2.7.3.4).

---

[19] Mostrova, "Knigata na prorok Ieremija," 64.

[20] Thomson, "The Slavonic Translation," 860–61.

[21] See *Die grossen Lesemenäen*, 1.20–43, 55–78.

[22] Kyas and Šarapatková, "Přehled," 106; Ribarova and Hauptová, *Grigorovičev parimejnik*; Taseva and Jovčeva, "Rannata slavjanska tekstova tradicija," 26–39; Taseva, Jovčeva, and Ilieva, *Kniga*, 40–43.

[23] Taseva, Jovčeva, and Ilieva, *Kniga*, 53; Taseva, "Kniga proroka Iezekiilja," 199–221.

[24] Taseva, Jovčeva, and Ilieva, *Kniga*, 85–445. An OCS-Greek concordance can be found in Ilieva, *Starobălgarsko-grăcki slovoukazatel*.

[25] For a partial edition, see Berčić, *Ulomci*, 53–61; Taseva, "Knigata," 16–30; Taseva, Jovčeva, and Ilieva, *Kniga* 46–53, 59–60.

[26] Thomson, "The Slavonic Translation," 861–63.

[27] Miltenov, "The Slavonic Translation" (2009), 135–80; Miltenov, "The Slavonic Translation" (2010), 289–300; Miltenov, "Tekstologičeski nabljudenija," 75–92; Zlatanova, "Zur slawischen Übersetzung," 159–81.

[28] See the above case: OCS-Jer in *J-Ch* (→ 6–9.2.7.2.2).

[29] Moreover, these four translations are not flanked by exegetical commentaries. See Alekseev, *Tekstologija*, 155, 164; Thomson, "The Slavonic Translation," 850.

6–9.2.7.3 Main Textual Features

6–9.2.7.3.1 OCS-Isa

OCS-Isa 1 contains the following readings: Isa 1:1–31; 2:1–21; 3:1–14; 4:2–6; 5:1–25; 6:1–12; 7:1–16; 8:1–4, 8–10, 13–22; 9:1–21; 10:1–4, 12–20; 11:1–16; 12:1–6; 13:1–13; 14:24–32; 19:1–2, 3–5, 12, 16, 19–21; 25:1–9; 26:21; 27:1–9; 28:14–22; 29:13–23; 35:1–10; 37:33–38; 38:1–3, 5–6; 40:1–5, 9, 18–31; 41:4–14, 17–18; 42:5–16; 43:9–13; 45:11–17; 48:17–22; 49:1–4, 6–15; 50:4–11; 52:13–15; 53:1–12; 54:1; 55:1–5; 58:1–11; 60:1–16; 61:1–11; 62:1–9, 10–12; 63:1–9, 11–19; 64:1–5; 65:8–10, 11–16; 66:10–24.[30] The Croat Glagolitic sources include: Isa 1:1–31; 2:1–18, 20, 21; 3:1–14; 4:2–6; 5:1–7, 18–23, 25–29; 6:5–9; 7:1–17; 8:1–18; 9:1–7, 13–21; 10:1–14, 22–27; 11:6–10, 12–13; 14:1–2, 12–18; 18:7; 19:1–4, 7–8, 11–12; 28:14–22; 40:1–6; 43:1–6; 44:21–26; 45:18–25; 46:12–13; 47:1–3, 5, 7–11; 52:1–5; 55:1–3; 60:1–6; 61:10–11; 62:1–3, 5; 66:7–9.[31]

The earliest South Slavic codex of OCS-Isa 2 (St. Petersburg, National Library of Russia, F.I. 416)[32] omits the following verses: Isa 5:7–16; 9:2–6; 9:8–20; 10:1–4, 12–17; 35:2–3; 49:8–15; 60:1–3; 63:15–19; 64:1–4; 62:5b, 8–16; 66:12–14, 17–19, 22–23.[33] According to this manuscript, the translation is supplemented by that of the commentaries of Theodoret of Cyrrhus, John Chrysostomus, Cyril of Alexandria, Basilius the Great, and Severianus of Gabala (in Isaiah 1–12; 52–57; 59–63; 65–66).[34]

Evseev's 1897 monograph, even if outdated, still remains the sole reference work for OCS-Isa: significant advances in the study of this tradition unfortunately have not been achieved in more than a century. According to the scholar's preliminary remarks, OCS-Isa 1 and OCS-Isa 2 are based on different Greek originals, LXX^L (→ 6–9.1.6) and what he calls "the Hesychian," viz. the Alexandrian text type, respectively (→ 6.3). However, in appraising the parent text of OCS-Isa 2, a certain degree of flexibility is required, since in several instances the translator has incorporated in his own work a number of passages borrowed from OCS-Isa 1. Moreover, stylistic and lexical affinities suggest that the translator of OCS-Isa 2 is the same as that of the Old Church Slavonic Symeonian Octateuch (→ 2.5.7).[35]

6–9.2.7.3.2 OCS-Jer

The Cyrillic Prophetologium includes Jer 1:1–18, 11–17, 19; 2:2–12; 11:18–23; 12:1–5, 9–11, 14–15; 38:31–34.[36] The Croat Glagolitic Breviary and Missal comprise Jer 1:1–19; 2:1–12, 31–37; 3:1–5; 4:3–7; 7:1–7; 11:18–20; 17:5–10, 13–18; 18:18–23; 31:31–34; 32:37–42; 38:33–34.[37] The *J-Ch* incorporates a number of readings in the midst of which quotations from George Hamartolos' Chronicle may on occasions be detected. Furthermore, in this source, the order of fragments is characterized by the incorporation of excerpts from Jeremiah 6 later in the text, since the following arrangement is found: Jer 3:6–12; 11:11–23; 12:1–11; 13:23–25; 15:1–4; 31:31–34; 6:16–19; 39:3–7, 11–14; 40:2–13; 41; 42; 43:1–7; 52:26–30.[38]

OCS-Jer 2 contains: Jer 32:13, 15–18; 33:1–24; 34:2–6, 8–12, 14–16, 18–20, 22; 35:1–17; 36:1–15, 21–32; 37:1–9, 12–14, 16–21, 23–24; 38:1–40; 39:1–44; 40:1–13; 41:1–22; 42:1–19; 43:1–32; 44:1–21; 45:1–28; 46:1–3, 14–18; 47:1–16; 48:1–18; 49:1–22; 50:1–13; 51:1–30, 31–35; 52:1, 4–14, 16–27, 31–34 (at the beginning of the sequence a few codices add Jer 1:1–8, 11–17, and 2:2–12).[39]

In some testimonies of OCS-Jer 2, the chapters are marked by a numeration corresponding to that of MT (→ 7.2.2) and the Vulgate (→ 6–9.1.7), i.e. Jeremiah 25–45 and 52. It remains an open question whether this feature is genuine. It cannot be ruled out, at least in the East Slavic codices, that it is the result of a contamination with OCS-

---

[30] See Evseev, *Kniga* (Part 1), 7, 21, 32, 36–52.
[31] See Thomson, "The Slavonic Translation," 846; Thomson, *A Brief Survey*, 43.
[32] See Nikolova, "Za naj-starija," 110–18; Popova, "Grafika," 57–63.
[33] See Batalova, "Ob Isaevom Proročestve," 215.
[34] Mostrova, "Za identificiraneto na tălkuvanijata," 239–51; Batalova, "Ob Isaevom Proročestve," 211–32.
[35] See Evseev, *Kniga* (Part 1), 7–9, 21–22; (Part 2), 11–12, 93–100.
[36] Kyas and Šarapatková, "Přehled," 106; Ribarova and Hauptová, *Grigorovičev parimejnik*.
[37] Mostrova, "Knigata na prorok Ieremija," 63. Partial edition: Berčić, *Ulomci*, 38–40, 44–45.
[38] See Istrin, *Aleksandrija*, 315–43; Mostrova, "Knigata na prorok Ieremija," 60–61.
[39] Mostrova, "Starobălgarskijat prevod," 20; Mostrova, "O strukturnych osobennostjach," 114.

Jer 3, which was modeled on the Vulgate. In this respect, it is no coincidence that, according to the Russian Macarian Menologium, OCS-Jer 2 is free of any numbering and that several East Slavic manuscripts preserve a mixed text consisting of OCS-Jer 2 + OCS-Jer 3.[40]

6–9.2.7.3.3 OCS-Ezek

OCS-Ezek 1 and OCS-Ezek 2 are quite different from each other in terms of grammatical and lexical features, as well as from the point of view of the translation method that was adopted. Consequently, OCS-Ezek 2 should not be considered a revision of OCS-Ezek 1 but an independent version produced by the Preslav school.[41] Theodoret's commentaries apparently were also translated in the same literary milieu, even if they were in all likelihood the work of a different author than that of OCS-Ezek 2.[42]

OCS-Ezek 1 contains Ezek 1:1–28; 2:1, 3–10; 3:1–3; 36:24–28; 37:1–14; 43:27; 44:1–4. In OCS-Ezek 2, the following features are common to both East and South Slavic sources: *a*) omission of Ezek 10:21–22; 12:26–28; 20:15–17, 21b–22, 24; 32:28; 34:8–9; 36:12; 37:20; *b*) insertion of an interpolation from Isa 50:11 after Ezek 28:18; *c*) agreement with the readings of LXX^L (→ 6–9.1.6) in Ezek 7:3–9 and a different arrangement from that found in *Codex Vaticanus*: LXX-Ezek 7:4–6 appear after vv. 7–9, forming a sequence corresponding to MT-Ezek 7:6, 3–5, 7–9 (→ 8.2.2, → 8.3). In all these instances, the translation matches with the lessons of the Greek text found in Theodoret's commentary.[43] In the South Slavic codices, OCS-Ezek 2 ends at Ezek 40:1, while in the East Slavic testimonies Ezek 45:12–46:24 is transposed after Ezek 48:4.[44] In the Croat Glagolitic tradition, rare cases of agreement with VL have been found, as shown by the readings in Ezek 1:16, 26; 37:10, 13.[45]

The above comments are to be understood as preliminary observations. OCS-Ezek 2 has so far been subjected to only an initial study and to a far too restricted investigation of the available sources. On the one hand, the existing edition is based only on two testimonies out of fifty-eight.[46] On the other hand, the East Slavic tradition, which is significantly more extensive than the South Slavic both in number and typology of manuscripts, still demands proper inquiry.[47] The antiquity of the former is beyond question, since several surviving exemplars go back to the edition copied by Upir' Lihyj in 1047 at Novgorod and clearly preserve traces of an underlying Glagolitic substrate.[48] Consequently, the editors' choice of completely excluding all this vast material in their work cannot but raise doubts about the reliability of the critical text they have reconstructed.

Furthermore, the methodological approach adopted also appears to be highly questionable. The collation with Ziegler's apparatus was undertaken from the standpoint of the Old Church Slavonic translations.[49] This is not in line with the goals of the textual criticism of the Bible, which investigates secondary versions from exactly the opposite perspective, namely with the purpose of shedding light on the textual history of their primary sources. Moreover, the Greek text of CPG 6206, which was published in the left column of the edition of OCS-Ezek 2, does not appear to be the outcome of a research work aimed at identifying among the surviving Byzantine redactions the one most similar to the Old Church Slavonic translation. On the contrary, it merely represents a reprint of the text found in Migne's "Patrologia

---

[40] See *Die grossen Lesemenäen*, 1.20–43; Mostrova, "Knigata na prorok Ieremija," 68–69.

[41] Taseva and Jovčeva, "Prevodačeski osobenosti," 40–52; Ilieva, "Čuždata leksika," 116–35; Taseva, Jovčeva, and Ilieva, *Kniga*, 54–59.

[42] Jovčeva and Kamulja, "Ot leksikata do strukturata," 3–20; Taseva, Jovčeva, and Ilieva, *Kniga*, 61.

[43] See Rahlfs, *Septuaginta, 778; Ziegler, *Ezechiel*, 12, 112–13; PG 81: 872–74, 1099.

[44] Taseva, Jovčeva, and Ilieva, *Kniga*, 53, 445; Taseva, "Kniga proroka Iezekiilja," 201–02.

[45] Taseva, Jovčeva, and Ilieva, *Kniga*, 44–45, 50.

[46] Taseva, Jovčeva, and Ilieva, *Kniga*, 53, 67.

[47] Thomson, "The Slavonic Translation," 850; a few preliminary remarks on single issues of the East Slavic tradition are accessible in Taseva and Rabus, "Prevodačeski i prepisvačeski greški," 136–49; Taseva, "Kniga proroka Iezekiilja," 199–221.

[48] For a non-traditional view on his colophon see: Kalugin, "Glagolica," 52–100.

[49] Taseva, Jovčeva, and Ilieva, *Kniga*, 67–69.

Graeca," from which several passages have been removed, in view of the lack of a corresponding text in OCS-Ezek 2. It is therefore not surprising that the editors of the latter were not able to establish precise textual allegiances with the various manuscript groups of LXX (→ 8.3).[50]

6–9.2.7.3.4 OCS-MinP

The textual history of OCS-MinP is typologically very similar to that of OCS-Major Prophets.

6–9.2.7.3.4.1 OCS-MinP 1

The Old Church Slavonic Cyrillic Prophetologium does not contain pericopes from Hosea, Amos, Obadiah, Nahum, Habbakuk, and Haggai. Consequently, OCS-MinP 1a includes the following readings only: Joel 2:12–32; entirety of Jonah; Mic 4:6–7; 5:2–4; Zeph 3:8–19; Zech 8:7–17, 19–23; 9:9–15; 11:10–13; 14:1–4, 8–11; Mal 3:1–4, 10b–12.[51]

This version was incorporated into the Croat Glagolitic sources, where it was subjected to a revision towards the Vulgate (→ 6–9.1.7). The Croat Breviary also contains additional excerpts translated from LXX (→ 9.3). Some texts can be dated on linguistic grounds to the pre-Symeonic epoch, while others (Zeph 1:1–2:8; 3:14–17; Hag 1:1–2:14; Zech 1:1–4; 4; 8:7–13; Mal 1:1–2:4) are in the same translation found in the Catena type (OCS-MinP 2).[52]

6–9.2.7.3.4.2 OCS-MinP 2

As in the case of the Major Prophets, OCS-MinP 2 also splits into two categories of Cyrillic witnesses, namely the East and South Slavic Cyrillic manuscripts. Differences between them concern not only linguistic but also paleographic, textual, and structural features.

Firstly, the East Slavic group includes testimonies with the sporadic use of Glagolitic letters and words.[53] Secondly, the South Slavic tradition lacks several parts of the collection: Hosea, Zephaniah, and Haggai are completely missing, while several sections of Malachi are also omitted (Mal 1:1–4; 2:1–17; 3:11–16).[54] Thirdly, while in the East Slavic sources the Minor Prophets precede the Major Prophets,[55] in the South Slavic texts the former are inserted in the midst of the latter (they are placed after Jeremiah, Baruch, Lamentations, Epistle of Jeremiah, and before Ezekiel and Isaiah).[56] However, in both groups, the internal sequence of the Minor Prophets is identical and corresponds to that of MT (Hosea, Joel, Amos, Obadiah, Jonah, Micah, Nahum, Habbakuk, Zephaniah, Haggai, Zechariah, Malachi; → 9.2.2).

A comprehensive text-critical study of the East Slavic and South Slavic Cyrillic testimonies of OCS-MinP 2 has not yet been undertaken. The East Slavic text of OCS-Hos, OCS-Joel, OCS-Amos, OCS-Obad, and OCS-Jonah was published by Tunickij in 1918 based on five testimonies of the fifteenth century.[57] The South Slavic text was edited by Zlatanova on the basis of two codices of the fourteenth or fifteenth century and collated with Ziegler's critical apparatus.[58]

---

[50] See Taseva and Ilieva, "Problemi," 46–66.

[51] However, some later codices present additions that apparently do not belong to the original redaction of the Prophetologium. See Kyas and Šarapatková, "Přehled," 107; Thomson, "The Slavonic Translation," 849; Zlatanova, *Kniga*, 22–23. For editions, see Brandt, "Grigorovičev parimejnik," 7–308 (*passim*); Ribarova and Hauptova, *Grigorovičev parimejnik*, 1.

[52] Editions can be found in Vajs, *Propheta Ioel*; Vajs, *Propheta Oseas*; Vajs, *Propheta Habacuc*; Vajs, *Sophonias-Haggaeus*; Vajs, *Zacharias-Malachias*. On the textual tradition of the Croat Breviary, see Vajs, *Nejstarší Breviář*. On the Croat Glagolitic Minor Prophets, see also Bauerová, "Prophetae minores," 217–26; Bauerová, "K problematice," 352–64; Ribarova, "Knjiga," 123–59; Ribarova, "Vajsova," 27–34; Thomson, "The Slavonic Translation," 851–52; and Zlatanova, *Kniga*, 27–28.

[53] Russian State Library, Moscow, f. 304/I, no. 89, late fifteenth century (with Glagolitic words and letters).

[54] Zlatanova, *Kniga*, 43.

[55] See, e.g., manuscript Russian State Library, Moscow, f. 304/I, no. 89, late fifteenth century (with Glagolitic words and letters).

[56] Codices: National Library of Russia, St. Petersburg, F.I.461, second half of the fourteenth century; State Historical Museum, Moscow, Ščuk. 507, year 1475 (description of the manuscripts: Zlatanova and *Kniga*, XIX–XX, 101; Nikolova, "Za naj-starija," 110–18). See Thomson, "The Slavonic Translation," 858–59.

[57] Tunickij, *Knigi*.

[58] Zlatanova, *Kniga*, 135–247.

6–9.2.7.3.4.3 OCS-MinP 3, 4, 5

In the late fifteenth century, the Old Church Slavonic Catena was revised based on the Vulgate by the editors of the Gennadian Bible. As a consequence of the use of that model, the position of the books was changed: the Minor Prophets were placed after the Major Prophets.

A further revision was undertaken by the compilers of the printed Ostrog Bible. A number of missing verses were retranslated from LXX (Amos 4:7b–9a; Obad 1:15; Jonah 1:12b; Mic 2:3; 4:3; 5:1; → 9.3), but not all errors were corrected.[59]

The Serbian translation dating from the second half of the sixteenth century is also based on LXX (→ 9.3). It includes Hos 7:15–16; 8:1–14; 9:1–17; 10:1–10; Amos 1:1–15; 2:1–7a; 9:15b; and Mic 1:2–16; 2; 3; 4; 5; 6; 7:1–18.[60]

6–9.2.7.4 Parent Text and Text-Critical Value

As for the parent text of the Old Church Slavonic versions of the Major and Minor Prophets, the following preliminary conclusions can be reached. LXX^L (→ 6–9.1.6) appears to be the source of: a) the Prophetologium readings;[61] b) the earliest translations of Zephaniah, Haggai, Zechariah, and Malachi (→ 6–9.2.7.2.4); c) the non-liturgical excerpts found in the Croat Breviary.[62] The third additionally contains revisions of the oldest textual stratum as well as new translations, in both instances based on the Vulgate (→ 6–9.1.7; an exception to be taken into further consideration is the case of the possible influence of VL in Ezekiel: → 6–9.2.7.3.3). Although hard evidence is still lacking, Ziegler's group LXX^c is likely to be the prototype of most Old Church Slavonic translations of the Major and Minor Prophets flanked by patristic commentaries. However, it remains to be clarified whether such a Byzantine model was used at the very beginning of the translation process or during a later revision.

Establishing the text-critical value of this tradition is a key issue that is far from being resolved definitely in all its aspects. The reason lies in the lack of critical editions based on the entire manuscript corpus, as well as in the absence of synergies with the Göttingen project (→ 1.4.10.5). However, in this regard, the above undertaken exploratory investigation of OCS-Ezek 2 (→ 6–9.2.7.3.3) has already brought significant results.

Firstly, the lack in OCS-Ezek 2 of Ezek 12:26–28 points to an agreement with Papyrus LXX^{967} (→ 8.3): beyond the Greek tradition, this omission was known to exist only in VL^{Wirc}. Secondly, OCS-Ezek 2 has an arrangement of verses in Ezek 7:3–9 that is different from that accepted by Ziegler in his edition and closer to that found in MT (→ 8.2.2).[63] In both instances, OCS-Ezek 2 is of particular importance, since it provides scholars with very rare textual material for studying two crucial sections of the book that are at the center of the debate concerning the recensional differences between MT and LXX of Ezekiel (→ 8.3.4).[64] This case clearly demonstrates that the Old Church Slavonic tradition merits to be taken into consideration fully by biblical scholars and consequently should be integrated into LXX studies.

Alekseev, A.A., *Tekstologija slavjanskoj Biblii* (Bausteine zur slavischen Philologie und Kulturgeschichte Neue Folge A: Slavistische Forschungen 24; St. Petersburg: Dmitrij Bulanin, 1999).

Batalova, S., "'Ob Isaevom Proročestve' v F.I.461 (RNB, Sankt-Peterburg): Ekzegeza ili biblejskij tekst?," *Byzantinoslavica* 71.1–2 (2013): 211–32.

Bauerová, H., "Prophetae minores v charvátskohlaholských breviářích a ve Vajsově edici Glagolitica," *Slovo: časopis Staroslavenskoga instituta* 36 (1986): 21–26.

Bauerová, H., "K problematice předloh textu proroka

---

[59] See Thomson, "The Slavonic Translation," 862–63.

[60] Manuscript National Library of Serbia No. 42, sixteenth century (ff. 182–90). See Štavljanin-Djordjević, "Srpski prevod"; Alekseev, *Tekstologija*, 164, n. 21; Thomson, "The Slavonic Translation," 866–67.

[61] Evseev, *Kniga* (Part II), 11–12; Taseva, Jovčeva, and Ilieva, *Kniga*, 45.

[62] See Vajs, *Propheta Ioel*, 32; Vajs, *Propheta Habacuc*, 27; Vajs, *Propheta Oseas*, 28; Vajs, *Zacharias-Malachias*, 35; Vajs, *Sophonias-Haggaeus*, 35.

[63] See Tov, **Greek-Hebrew Bible*, 397–99.

[64] See Tov, **TCHB*, 300–01; Tov, **Greek-Hebrew Bible*, 397–99; Lilly, *Two Books of Ezekiel*, 116–19, 302.

Jonáše v charvátskohlaholských breviářích," *Slavia* 58 (1989): 352–64.

Berčić, I. (ed.), *Ulomci Svetoga Pisma obojega uvjeta staroslovenskim jezikom: Skupio iz rukopisah i tiskanih knjigah hrvatskoga razreda svećenik Ivan Berčić*, Vol. 3 (Prague: Sinovi Bogumila Haase, 1865).

Biblija: Sirěč' knigi svjaščennago pisanija vetchago i novago zavěta (St. Petersburg: Tipografija Aleksandro-Nevskogo monastyrja, 1751).

Brandt, R., "Grigorovičev parimejnik: V sličenii s drugimi parimejnikami," *Čtenija v Imperatorskom Obščestve istorii i drevnostej rossijskich* 168 (1894): 1–90; 170 (1894): 91–178; 193 (1900): 179–290; 197 (1901): 291–308.

Die grossen Lesemenäen des Metropoliten Makarij: Uspenskij spisok, Vol. 1: *1.–8. Mai* (eds. E. Weiher, S.O. Šmidt and A.I. Škurko; Monumenta linguae slavicae dialecti veteris LI; Freiburg i. Br.: Weiher Verlag, 2007).

Die grossen Lesemenäen des Metropoliten Makarij: Uspenskij spisok, Vol. 2: *9.–23. Mai* (eds. E. Weiher, S.O. Šmidt and A.I. Škurko; Monumenta linguae slavicae dialecti veteris 53; Freiburg i. Br.: Weiher Verlag, 2009).

Evseev, I., *Kniga proroka Isaji v drevneslavjanskom perevode: V dvuch častjach. čast' pervaja: Slavjanskij perevod knigi proroka Isaji po rukopisjam XI–XVI vv. čast' vtoraja: Grečeskij original slavjanskogo perevoda knigi proroka Isaji* (St. Petersburg: Pečatnja S.P. Jakovleva, 1897) [Two parts in one volume of 168 and 146 + iii pages respectively].

Evseev, I.E., "Zametki po drevne-slavjanskomu perevodu Sv. Pisanija: III. Sledy utračennogo pervonačal'nogo polnogo perevoda proročeskich knig na slavjanskij jazyk," *Izvestija Imperatorskoj Akademii nauk* 10.4 (1899): 355–73.

Ilieva, T., "Čuždata leksika v Knigata na prorok Iezekiil po răkopis F.I.461 ot Ruskata nacionalna biblioteka v Sankt Peterburg," in *Srednovekovieto v ogledaloto na edin filolog: Sbornik v čest na Svetlina Nikolova* (ed. S. Bărlieva; Kirilo-Metodievski studii 18; Sofia: Bălgarska Akademija na naukite, 2009), 116–35.

Ilieva, T. (ed.), *Starobălgarsko-grăcki slovoukazatel kăm Knigata na prorok Iezekiil* (Starobălgarskijat prevod na Starija zavet 3; Sofia: Bălgarska Akademija na naukite, Kirilo-Metodievski naučen centăr, 2013).

Ilieva, T., "Prilagane na statističeskite metodi v izsledvanijata po istorija na prevoda ot grăcki na starobălgarski ezik (vărchu material ot Knigata na sv. prorok Iezekiil s tălkuvanija ot Teodorit Kirski po rkp. ot XIV v.)," *Slavia* 83.3 (2014): 310–22.

Istrin, V., *Aleksandrija russkich chronografov: Issledovanie i tekst* (Moscow: Universitetskaja tipografija, 1893).

Jovčeva, M. and M. Kamulja, "Ot leksikata do strukturata na Knigata na prorok Iezekiil: rezultati ot kompjutărno izsledvane na srednovekoven tekst na različni ravništa," *Palaeobulgarica* 24.3 (2000): 3–20.

Kalugin, V.V., "Glagolica v Tolkovych proročestvach 1047 goda (opyt tekstologičeskoj i paleografičeskoj rekonstrukcii)," *Palaeoslavica* 22.2 (2014): 52–100.

Kyas, V. and Ž. Šarapatková, "Přehled staroslověnského parimejníku," in *Palaeoslovenica: Sborník oddělení srovnávací slovanské jazykovědy Ústavu jazyků a literatur ČSAV* (Prague: Ústavu jazyků a literatur ČSAV, 1971), 95–108.

Lekova, T., "Il libro del profeta Isaia nella tradizione slava ecclesiastica," in *Seminario interdisciplinare sul libro del profeta Isaia* (eds. R. Maisano and V. Mangogna; Naples: Università degli studi di Napoli "L'Orientale," 2007), 147–237.

Lilly, I.E., *Two Books of Ezekiel: Papyrus 967 and the Masoretic Text as Variant Literary Editions* (VTSup 150; Leiden: Brill, 2012).

Mathiesen, R., "Handlist of Manuscripts Containing Church Slavonic Translations of the Old Testament," *Polata knigopisnaja* 7 (1983): 3–48.

Miltenov, Y., "The Slavonic Translation of the Minor Prophets with Commentary: A Textological Approach," *Scripta & e-Scripta* 7 (2009): 135–80.

Miltenov, Y., "The Slavonic Translation of the Minor Prophets with Commentary: Rare Words and Lexical Markers," in *Toxotēs: Studies for Stefano Parenti* (eds. D. Galadza, N. Glibetić, and G. Radle; Grottaferrata: Monastero Esarchico, 2010): 289–300.

Miltenov, Y., "Tekstologičeski nabljudenija vărchu starozavetnite knigi na Dvanadesette malki proroci s tălkuvanija," in *Jazyk Biblii: Lingvotekstologičeskie issledovanija* (Moscow: Nestor-Istorija, 2012), 75–92.

Mostrova, T., "Starobălgarskijat prevod na knigata na prorok Ieremija po prepisi ot XIV–XVI vek," *Palaeobulgarica* 19.2 (1995): 9–26.

Mostrova, T., "Ieremija 16:19 v starobălgarski prevod," in *Slavia Orthodoxa: Ezik i kultura: Sbornik v čest na prof. R. Pavlova* (Sofia: Universitetsko izdatelstvo, 2003), 276–81.

Mostrova, T., "O strukturnych osobennostjach Knigi proroka Ieremii v sostave Velikich minej-čet'ich mitropolita Makarija," in *Abhandlungen zu den Grossen Lesemenäen des Metropoliten Makarij*, Vol. 2

(eds. E. Maier and E. Weiher; Monumenta linguae slavicae dialecti veteris, Fontes et dissertationes 49; Freiburg i. Br.: Weiher Verlag, 2006), 109–37.

Mostrova, T., "Knigata na prorok Ieremija v bălgarski, srăbski i ruski prepisi ot XIV–XVI vek," *Palaeobulgarica* 32.2 (2008): 59–82.

Mostrova, T., "Knigata na prorok Isaja văv Velikite četi minei na mitropolit Makarij," in *The Holy Land and the Manuscript Legacy of Slavs* (eds. W. Moskovich, S. Nikolova, and M. Taube; Jews and Slavs 20; Jerusalem: Hebrew University of Jerusalem, Center for Slavic Languages and Literatures, 2008), 281–90.

Mostrova, T., "Za identificiraneto na tălkuvanijata kăm Knigata na prorok Isaja văv Velikite četi minei," in *Text – Sprache – Grammatik: Slavisches Schrifttum der Vormoderne: Festschrift für Eckhard Weiher zum 70. Geburtstag* (eds. J. Besters-Dilger and J. Rabus; Die Welt der Slaven, Sammelbände 39; Munich: Otto Sagner, 2009), 239–51.

Mostrova, T., "Kăm leksikalnata charakteristika na Knigata na prorok Ieremija," in *Srednovekovni tekstove, avtori i knigi: Sbornik v čest na Chajnc Miklas* (ed. T. Mostrova; Kirilo-Metodievski studii 21; Sofia: Bălgarska Akademija na naukite, 2012), 125–46.

Mostrova, T., "The Importance of the Slavonic Version of the Book of the Prophet Jeremiah to the Study of Its Original Structure in the Old Testament," in *The Bible in Slavic Tradition* (eds. A. Kulik et al.; Studia Judaeoslavica 9; Leiden: Brill, 2016).

Nachtigal', R.R., "Neskol'ko zametok o sledach drevneslavjanskogo parimejnika v chorvatsko-glagoličeskoj literature," in *Drevnosti: Trudy Slavjanskoj komissii Moskovskogo archeologičeskogo obščestva*, Vol. 3 (Moscow: Tipografija G. Lissnera, 1902), 175–213.

Nikolova, S., "Za naj-starija bălgarski srednovekoven răkopis na Starija Zavet," *Starobălgarska literatura* 28–29 (1994): 110–18.

Ostrožskaja biblija: Fototipičeskoe pereizdanie teksta s izdanija 1581 g. (Moscow: Slovo-Art, 1988).

Popova, T., "Grafika i pravopis na Kniga na prorok Isaj po răkopis F.I.461 ot XIV v. ot Ruskata nacionalna biblioteka," *Palaeobulgarica* 20.2 (1996): 57–63.

Popova, T., "Ot pr(o)r(o)č(ьst)va isain(a) čten(ie) …," in *Ezik i istorija na bălgarskite srednovekovni tekstove: Sbornik v čest na Ekaterina Dogramadžieva* (ed. S. Nikolova; Kirilo-Metodievski studii 14; Sofia: Bălgarska Akademija na naukite, 2001), 96–101.

Ribarova, Z., "Knjiga proroka Jone," *Slovo: časopis Staroslavenskoga instituta* 37 (1987): 123–59.

Ribarova, Z., "Vajsova proučavanja prijevoda Malih proroka iz Brevijara Vida Omišljanina," *Slovo: časopis Staroslavenskoga instituta* 44–46 (1994–1996): 27–34.

Ribarova, Z. and Z. Hauptova, *Grigorovičev Parimejnik*, Vol. 1: *Tekst so kritički aparat* (Skopje: Makedonska Akademija na naukite i umetnostite, 1998).

Ribarova, Z. and Z. Hauptova, *Grigorovičev Parimejnik*, Vol. 2: *Leksika* (Skopje: Makedonska Akademija na naukite i umetnostite, 2014).

Štavljanin-Djordjević, L., "Srpski prevod Malih proroka iz druge četvrtine XVI veka," *Arheografski prilozi* 15 (1993): 177–95.

Taseva, L., "Knigata na prorok Iezekiil v srednovekovnata bălgarska i chărvatska knižnina," *Palaeobulgarica* 21.3 (1997): 12–30.

Taseva, L., "Kniga proroka Iezekiilja v sostave Velikich minej-čet'ich mitropolita Makarija," in *Abhandlungen zu den Grossen Lesemenäen des Metropoliten Makarij*, Vol. 2 (eds. E. Maier and E. Weiher; Monumenta linguae slavicae dialecti veteris, Fontes et dissertationes 49; Freiburg i. Br.: Weiher Verlag, 2006), 199–221.

Taseva, L. and T. Ilieva, "Problemi na grăckija kritičeski aparat kăm izdanieto na Knigata na prorok Iezekiil po răkopis F.I.461 ot Ruskata nacionalna biblioteka v Sankt-Peterburg," in *Kritičeskoto izdanie na najstarija slavjanski tekst na biblejskite knigi i negovite alternativi* (ed. S. Nikolova; Sofia: Kirilo-Metodievski naučen centăr, 2003), 46–66.

Taseva, L. and M. Jovčeva, "Prevodačeski osobenosti v Kniga na prorok Iezekiil po răkopis F.I.461 ot Ruskata nacionalna biblioteka," *Palaeobulgarica* 19.4 (1995): 40–52.

Taseva, L. and M. Jovčeva, "Rannata slavjanska tekstova tradicija na Knigata na prorok Iezekiil," *Palaeobulgarica* 22.2 (1998): 26–39.

Taseva, L., M. Jovčeva, and T. Ilieva (eds.), *Kniga na prorok Iezekiil s tălkovanija* (Starobălgarskijat prevod na Starija zavet 2; Sofia: Bălgarska Akademija na naukite, Kirilo-Metodievski naučen centăr, 2003).

Taseva, L. and A. Rabus, "Prevodačeski i prepisvačeski greški v slavjanskata răkopisna tradicija na Knigata na prorok Iezekiil," in *Srednovekovieto v ogledaloto na edin filolog: Sbornik v čest na Svetlina Nikolova* (ed. S. Bărlieva; Kirilo-Metodievski studii 18; Sofia: Bălgarska Akademija na naukite, 2009), 136–51.

Thomson, F.J., "The Slavonic Translation of the Old Testament," in *The Interpretation of the Bible: The International Symposium in Slovenia* (ed. J. Krašovec;

JSOTSup 189; Sheffield: Sheffield Academic Press, 1998), 605–920.

Thomson, F.J., *A Brief Survey of the History of the Church Slavonic Bible from its Cyrillomethodian Origins until its Final Form in the Elizabethan Bible of 1751* (Slavica Gandensia 33.2; Ghent: Department of Slavonic and Eastern European Studies of Ghent University, 2006).

Tunickij, N.L., *Knigi XII malych prorokov s tolkovanijami v drevne-slavjanskom perevode*, Vol. 1: *Knigi Osii, Ioilja, Amosa, Avdija i Iony* (Sergiev Posad: 1918).

Vajs, J., *Propheta Ioel* (Veglae: Academia palaeoslavica veglensis, 1908).

Vajs, J., *Propheta Oseas* (Veglae: Academia palaeoslavica veglensis, 1910).

Vajs, J., *Nejstarší Breviář hrvatsko-hlaholský* (*Prvý Breviář Vrbnický*) (Prague: Nákl. Král. České Společnosti Náuk, 1910).

Vajs, J., *Propheta Habacuc* (Veglae: Academia palaeoslavica veglensis, 1912).

Vajs, J., *Sophonias-Haggaeus* (Veglae: Academia palaeoslavica veglensis, 1913).

Vajs, J., *Zacharias-Malachias* (Veglae: Academia palaeoslavica veglensis, 1915).

Vajs, J., *Najstariji hrvatskoglagolski misal: s bibliografskim opisima svih hrvatskoglagolskih misala* (Zagreb: Jugoslavenska akademija znanosti i umjetnosti, 1948).

Ziegler, J. (ed.), *Duodecim Prophetae* (2nd ed.; Septuaginta Vetus Testamentum Graecum 13; Göttingen: Vandenhoeck & Ruprecht, 1967).

Ziegler, J. (ed.), *Ieremias, Baruch, Threni, Epistula Ieremiae* (2nd ed.; Septuaginta Vetus Testamentum Graecum 15; Göttingen: Vandenhoeck & Ruprecht, 1976).

Ziegler, J. (ed.), *Ezechiel* (2nd revised ed. with an addendum by D. Fraenkel; Septuaginta Vetus Testamentum Graecum 16.1; Göttingen: Vandenhoeck & Ruprecht, 1977).

Ziegler, J. (ed.), *Isaias* (3rd ed.; Septuaginta Vetus Testamentum Graecum XIV; Göttingen: Vandenhoeck & Ruprecht, 1983).

Zlatanova, R., "Zur slawischen Übersetzung des Zwölfprophetenbuchs," *Anzeiger für slavische Philologie* 21 (1992): 159–81.

Zlatanova, R. (ed.), *Kniga na dvanadesette proroci s tălkovanija* (Starobălgarskijat prevod na Starija zavet 1; Sofia: Bălgarska Akademija na naukite, Kirilo-Metodievski naučen centăr, 1998).

Zlatanova, R., "Die Vitae Prophetarum in slavischer Übersetzung: Vorlagen, Rezensionen, Textüberlieferung," *Die Welt der Slaven* 48 (2003): 287–302.

Alessandro Maria Bruni

6–9.2.8 Arabic Translations

6–9.2.8.1 Background

At least two versions of the Arabic Prophets are possibly traceable to the ninth and tenth centuries. The ninth-century C.E. monk Pethion from Mesopotamia is believed to have translated the Prophets into Arabic from a Syriac *Vorlage* (→ 6–9.1.4; → 6–9.2.4) and the tenth-century C.E. priest al-ʿAlam of Alexandria translated from the Greek LXX (→ 6.3; → 7.3; → 8.3; → 9.3). Textual witnesses of these two translations do not predate the thirteenth century. However, in this connection, it should be noted that many new manuscripts, primarily from the Monastery of St. Catherine on the Sinai Peninsula, are yet to be studied thoroughly; such is the case of the oldest extant textual witness of the Arab Prophets preserved in manuscript Sinai Ar. 1. This manuscript contains the books of Job, Daniel, Jeremiah, and Ezekiel and is dated on paleographical grounds to the ninth century C.E. (→ 11.4.8).

As is generally the case in this field, biblical lectionaries transmitted in liturgical books need to be taken into account before we can reach a fuller understanding of the textual history of the Latter Prophets in Arabic, a task yet to be accomplished.

6–9.2.8.2 Text Types, Manuscripts, Tools

Graf divided the Arabic versions of the Latter Prophets into six groups based on *Vorlage* and text type.[1] He relied to a great degree on Vaccari's important study "Le versioni Arabe dei Profeti" that was published in two parts in the early

---

[1] Graf, *GCAL* 1, 131–37. Unfortunately, this work is not free of errors. Most importantly, it is not always clear whether references pertain to a shelf mark or a catalogue number. For converting catalogue numbers in the collections of the Coptic Orthodox Patriarchate and the Coptic Museum in Cario to shelf marks, a helpful tool is: K. Samir, *Tables de concordance des manuscrits arabes chrétiens du Caire et du Sinaï* (CSCO 482 Subsidia 75; Leuven: Peeters, 1986).

1920s.[2] Besides Vaccari's contribution, several works have appeared on individual books of the Prophets, primarily on those printed in the Arabic sections of the Paris and London Polyglots (→ 1.4.11).[3] These studies were all completed before the end of the 1940s. Since then, little has been accomplished with regard to the Arabic Latter Prophets.

The first group referred to by Graf represents a translation from LXX (→ 6.3; → 7.3; → 8.3; → 9.3). This translation comprises the complete corpus of the Latter Prophets, including Daniel (→ 18.4.8). It was selected for the Arabic portions of the Paris Polyglot (1645)[4] and reprinted with minor modifications in the London Polyglot (1657).[5] This version is attested in a number of manuscripts many of which were copied in the sixteenth century. Most important among these are Paris, BNF, Ar. 1 – the manuscript singled out by Gabriel Sionita to be printed in the Paris edition – dated 1584/1585; Paris, BNF, Ar. 25 dated 1586; and Vatican, Ar. 445 dated 1583.[6] The colophon in the latter manuscript informs us that the copyist Faḍlal-lāh used a Greek text found in the convent of Our Holy Lady the Virgin, in the Coptic neighborhood Ḥārat al-Zuwayla, which had been faithfully copied by the priest Jirjis Ibn Abū al-Mufaḍḍal in 1355/1366. Al-Mufaḍḍal's copy contained the translation of the Alexandrian priest al-ʿAlam al-Iskandarī who according to Vaccari was active in the tenth century or even earlier.[7] The colophon further informs us that al-ʿAlam translated the Prophets from an ancient parchment codex written in Greek uncials (Ar. *raqqa bi-qalam al-līṭon al-Rūmī*):

ترجمها القس الكرم المتنيح العلم الاسكندري من نسخة قديمة بورق رق بقلم الليطن الرومي

The venerable deceased priest al-ʿAlam al-Iskandarī translated it from an ancient copy [made] of parchment written in Greek uncials.

Al-ʿAlam's translation appears to have circulated in Egyptian Melkite (Greek Orthodox) circles. It was later adopted by the Coptic Church, most likely around the thirteenth or fourteenth century, when great efforts were made to transmit old textual sources into the Arabic idiom.

According to Ryssel, who studied the translation of Micah attributed to al-ʿAlam as preserved in the Polyglots,[8] the translation does not contain any specific Egyptian traits, such as Coptic loanwords, but instead exhibits some Aramaisms and minor influence from the Peshiṭta (→ 6–9.1.4). For instance, the Greek word δράγματα "sheaves" is rendered in Mic 4:12 in Arabic as *ʾaǧmār*. This plural form of *ǧumr*, Ryssel argues,[9] is known in Old Arabic only as "an armful" yet it clearly aims to designate "sheaves" in al-ʿAlam's text where it appears to be a Syriacism. The word is not borrowed from the Peshiṭta since the latter reads *še/ubblā* "ear of grain" and the scribe's knowledge of Hebrew (MT

---

[2] Vaccari, "Le versioni" (1921), 401–23; Vaccari, "Le versioni" (1922), 401–24.

[3] On Isaiah, see Liebmann, "Der Text zu Jesaia," 8–26 and Gesenius, *Der Prophet Jesaia*, 2.97–106; on Ezekiel, see Cornill, *Das Buch Ezekiel*, 49–57; on Nahum, see Reinke, *Zur Kritik*, 65–70; on Micah, see Ryssel, "Die arabische Uebersetzung," 102–38; on Haggai, see Reinke, *Der Prophet Haggai*, 34–37; and on Zechariah, see Reynolds, "Al-Alam's version," 273–75.

[4] Le Jay, *Biblia.

[5] Walton, *Polyglotta.

[6] Graf adds to this list manuscripts Coptic Patriarchate, Bibl. 79 (Graf no. 243) dated 1586–1588 and Bibl. 80 (Graf no. 251) dated 1585, which clearly share the archetype written by Al-Mufaḍḍal, and London, BL Or. 1326 containing only Daniel and Ezekiel. The latter is written by the same hand as Vatican, Ar. 445 and a section of Paris, BNF, Ar. 1. A copy of Vatican, Ar. 445 is found in manuscript Rome, Bibl. Casan. Ar. Karš. 2 (no. 2108, seventeenth century). The Minor Prophets, except for Hosea, Amos, Micah, and part of Zechariah are found in manuscript Coptic Museum, Varia 5 (Graf no. 145 A, fols. 1ʳ–30ʳ) dated 1782/1783. To the same tradition, but with a somewhat younger archetype than the above, belongs Isaiah as preserved in manuscript Coptic Museum, Bibl. 83 (Graf no. 668), likely revised according to the Coptic tradition (→ 6–9.2.2). See Graf, *GCAL 1, 132–33. See also Vaccari, "Le versioni" (1921), 403–07.

[7] Vaccari, "Le versioni" (1921), 410–18; O. Löfgren, *Studien zu den arabischen Danielübersetzungen: Mit besonderer Berücksichtigung der christlichen Texte: Nebst einem Beitrag zur Kritik des Peschittatextes* (Uppsala: A.B. Lundequistska Bokhandeln, 1936), 35.

[8] Ryssel, "Die arabische Übersetzung."

[9] Ryssel, "Die Arabische Uebersetzung," 111–15, 137.

עָמִיר "sheaf"), he claims, is unlikely. Instead, this word must have entered an Arabic dialect in the Syriac regions.

The second group in Graf's analysis exhibits translations from LXX (→ 6.3; → 7.3; → 8.3; → 9.3) that differ from al-'Alam's version. These are found among others in the bilingual Coptic-Arabic manuscripts London, BL Ar. Or. 1319 (Suppl. 3 = Copt. 726), which is dated to 1806 and comprises Isaiah, Jeremiah, Baruch, and the Epistle of Jeremiah; London, BL Ar. Suppl. 2 (= Copt. 729, folios 3ʳ–163ᵛ) containing the Minor Prophets; and Paris, BNF, Copt. 2 (Delap. 9, folios 2ʳ–64ʳ) containing the Minor Prophets, as does Paris, BNF, Copt. 96 (Delap. 11, folios 2ʳ–112ᵛ).

In this connection, Graf mentions an Arabic translation of the Minor Prophets claimed to be made directly from a Coptic *Vorlage* (6–9.2.2) and transmitted in manuscript London, BL Or. 5918 (folios 192ᵛ–232ʳ) dated to the thirteenth or fourteenth century, and in manuscript Oxford, Bodl. Ar. Christ. Uri 6 (Seld. Arch. A 67, folios 169ʳ–227ᵛ) dated 1358.[10] It appears that among the Copts, al-'Alam's version of the Minor Prophets initially was not transmitted together with his version of the Major Prophets.[11]

To the third group listed by Graf belong various translations from a Syriac *Vorlage* (→ 6–9.1.4; → 6–9.2.4). There is no apparent connection between the manuscripts of the Major and the Minor Prophets preserved in this group.[12] Vaccari devoted his study to the three Major Prophets and discovered that a translation of Jeremiah preserved in several manuscripts was attributed to a certain Pethion (*Fatyūn Ibn Ayyūb Al-Sahhār*).[13] This Syriac-based translation is contained in manuscript Milan, Ambros. C 58 inf. (folios 1ᵛ–236ʳ.), the closely related manuscript London, BL Or. 5918 (folios 1ʳ–167ᵛ), and manuscript Oxford, Bodl. Ar. Christ. Uri 6 (Isaiah folios 1ᵛ–52ᵛ, dated 1457; Jeremiah folios 53ʳ–101ᵛ, dated 1458; Ezekiel folios 121ᵛ–168ᵛ, 217–23, dated 1358). In the introduction to Jeremiah in the Ambrosian manuscript (folio 170ʳ), we read:

نبتدى [...] بنسخ نبوه ارميا النبي ترجمه فتيوت بن ايوب السهار

We begin [...] to copy the prophecy of the Prophet Jeremiah which Fatyūt bn Ayyūb the Vigilant translated.

Subsequent to a comparison with the Oxford and London manuscripts and with the introduction to the book of Job in manuscript London, BL Or. 1326 (→ 11.4.8), Vaccari argues that the name should be read "Fatyūn" and identifies him as the ninth-century C.E. East Syriac monk Pethion mentioned by al-Nadīm in the Fihrist.[14] Graf adds manuscript Mingana Syr. 624 to the list.[15] This manuscript, written in *karšūni* script and dated to 1637, contains Isaiah (folios 1ʳ–26ᵛ), Jeremiah with Lamentations (folios 27ʳ–66ᵛ), and Ezekiel (folios 71ᵛ–101ʳ). According to Mingana, Jeremiah is attributed to "Pinon b. Ayyūb al-Sahhār, of whom I know nothing," which most certainly refers to the same Pethion.[16]

The attribution to Pethion is only mentioned specifically with regard to Jeremiah. According to Vaccari, the homogenous character of Jeremiah, Isaiah, and Ezekiel as preserved in these manuscripts is nevertheless indicative of the common authorship of all three books of the Prophets.[17] Pethion used the Peshitta as the main *Vorlage* (→ 6–9.1.4) but did not hesitate to substitute a textual unit in the Syriac *Vorlage* for a rendition in LXX (→ 7.3; perhaps via translations into Syriac) or simply to add several textual variants to his Arabic

---

[10] Graf lists manuscript Milan, Ambros., C. 58 inf. (folios 271ᵛ–331ʳ) dated 1226 here as well as under the Minor Prophets translated from a Syriac *Vorlage* (→ 6–9.1.4; → 6–9.2.4); cf. Vaccari, "Le versioni" (1922), 409. For additional manuscripts, see Graf, *GCAL 1, 133.

[11] Löfgren, *Studien*, 41–44.

[12] Vaccari, "Le versioni" (1922), 408–09.

[13] Vaccari, "Le versioni" (1921); Vaccari, "Le versioni" (1922).

[14] Vaccari, "Le versioni" (1922), 413–16.

[15] Graf, *GCAL 1, 134.

[16] A. Mingana, *Catalogue of Mingana Collection of Manuscripts*, Vol. 3: *Additional Christian Arabic and Syriac MSS* (Cambridge: W. Hefner and Sons, Limited, 1939): 67, and, Graf, *GCAL 1, 134.

[17] Vaccari, "Le versioni" (1922), 419.

translation.[18] On occasion, he paraphrased the text for the sake of clarity. All these features are represented in the three Major Prophets preserved in these manuscripts.[19] A comprehensive study on style is nonetheless desirable before the question of authorship can be firmly answered.[20] The Oxford manuscript was used in the London Polyglot[21] in order to fill in the gaps that occurred sporadically in the Arabic Prophets printed in the Paris Polyglot,[22] at least in Ezekiel.[23]

Besides these three closely related manuscripts, Pethion's translation is attested in several additional manuscripts. Among the most important ones is the elegantly ornamented and completely vocalized manuscript Berlin, Staatsbibl. Ar. 10173 (Diez. 41) copied by a scribe by the name of Abū Saʿīd b. Sayyid al-dār b. Abū al-Faḍl al-Masīḥī in 1325.[24] Abū al-Faḍl used an Arabic *Vorlage* that was completed in 1208 C.E. and that in 1323 C.E. came into the hands of a priest named ibn K-b-r, who is identified as the famous Šams al-Riyāsah Abū al-Barakāt.[25] Another significant copy of this translation is contained in manuscripts Vatican Ar. 495 and 503 that originally formed one single codex.[26] Based on internal evidence, the codex may be dated to the fourteenth century. Further copies of Pethion's translation are extant in manuscript Florence, Laurenziana, Or. 59 (XIII) dated 1334 and in the early seventeenth-century manuscript Rome, Casanatense 169 (Karš).[27] Vaccari lays out the following schema in order to visualize the internal relations of the manuscripts containing Pethion's translation of the Major Prophets (library references are expanded): Milan, Ambrosiana C 58; London, BL, Or. 5918; marginal variants in Rome, Casanatense 169 → Oxford, Bodleian Libr., Seld. Arch. A. 67 → Florence, Medicea-Laurenziana Or. 59, Vatican Ar. 495 and 503; Rome, Casanatense 169 → Berlin, Staatsbibliothek, Ar. 10173 (Diez. 41).[28]

Following a preliminary study by the current author, it is now recognized that Pethion's translation is also attested in manuscript Sinai Ar. 9 dated to the thirteenth century. Although a more thorough study is required, the translation of Jeremiah preserved in Sinai Ar. 1 appears to represent a different version.

As for the Minor Prophets of a Syriac provenance, Graf lists manuscripts Berlin, Staatsbibl. Ar. 10173 (Diez. 41); Vatican Ar. 503; Florence, Laurenziana, Or. 59 (XIII) dated 1334; Milan, Ambros. C 58 inf.; and Oxford, Bodl., Fraser, 257 dated approximately to the eleventh century. An edition of the book of Jonah based on the Peshiṭta according to manuscript Oxford Bodl. Ar. Christ. Uri 6 (Seld Arch. A 67) was published by Wright in 1857.[29] Vatican Ar. 468, dated 1578/1579, was selected for the *Biblia Sacra Arabica* (the *Propaganda Fide* edition) but was heavily influenced by the Latin Vulgate (→ 6–9.1.7) upon printing.[30]

---

[18] This view is nevertheless challenged by Frank who in his study on the translation of Jeremiah attributed to Pethion states that he has identified no such traces. See Frank, "The Jeremias of Pethion ibn Ayyūb al Sahhār," 138–39.

[19] Vaccari, "Le versioni" (1922), 416–20; see also text samples and discussions of Pethion's translation of Jeremiah in J. Schäfers, *Die Äthiopische Übersetzung des Propheten Jeremias* (Freiburg i.B.: Herder, 1912), 1–26.

[20] Cf. Löfgren, *Studien*, 50–55.

[21] Walton, *Polyglotta*.

[22] Le Jay, *Biblia*.

[23] Graf, *GCAL* 1, 132; Cornill, *Das Buch Ezekiel*, 56–57.

[24] For textual samples and a discussion on Jeremiah contained in this manuscript, see Schäfers, *Die Äthiopische Übersetzung*.

[25] Löfgren, *Studien*, 9–14.

[26] Manuscript Vatican, Ar. 495: thirty-three chapters of Ezekiel (fourteenth century, folios 1ᵛ–69ᵛ); Isaiah 1–9 (folios 70ʳ–137ʳ). The rest is found in manuscript Vatican, Ar. 503 (folios 1ʳ–93ᵛ) including thirty-six chapters of Jeremiah.

[27] Vaccari, "Le versioni" (1922), 403–08.

[28] Vacarri, "Le versioni" (1922), 408–12.

[29] W. Wright, *The Book of Jonah in Four Oriental Versions: Namely Chaldee, Syriac, Aethiopic and Arabic: With Glossaries* (London: Williams and Norgate, 1857).

[30] For additional manuscripts, see Graf, *GCAL* 1, 136. For manuscript Vatican Ar. 468, see Löfgren, *Studien*, 21; B. Knutsson, *Studies in the Text and Language of Three Syriac-Arabic Versions of the Book of Judicum with Special Reference to the Middle Arabic Elements: Introduction-Linguistic Notes-Texts* (Leiden: Brill: 1974), 15–16 n. 14; A. Vaccari, "La Storia D'Una Bibbia Araba," *Bib* 11 (1930): 350–55; A. Vaccari, "Una Bibbia Araba per il primo Gesuita Venuto al Libano," *Mélanges de l' Université St Joseph* 10.1 (1925): 79–105; and S. Euringer, "Zum Stammbaum der Arabischen Bibelhandschriften Vat. Ar. 468 und 467," *Zeitschrift für Semitistik und Verwandte Gebiete* 7 (1929): 259–73.

The fourth group in Graf's work is represented by a translation of Baruch (→ II.2.1.10) and the Epistle of Jeremiah (→ II.2.4.10) from the Latin Vulgate (→ 1.3.5) preserved in manuscript Mingana Syr. 624 dated 1637.

The fifth group is by far the most voluminous and contains translations of unknown origin. Some of these manuscripts are parts of larger collections of biblical books of which we have partial knowledge, while others have not been studied at all. As mentioned above, it is of utmost importance to examine especially the earliest Sinai manuscripts in order to gain more knowledge of the textual history of the Prophets in Arabic.

6–9.2.8.3 Translation Character and Translation Technique

While we look forward to fuller and more detailed studies on the translation character and techniques of the Arabic Prophets, some preliminary remarks may be made regarding the works attributed to al-ʿAlam and Pethion.[31] The two translations exhibit remarkable variation in translation character and techniques. Such disparity hardly results from the linguistic proficiency on the side of the translators. Rather, to understand this discrepancy, the purpose and function of these texts should be taken into account as well as the literary preferences that governed them as they came to light.

A handful of studies have been published on the translation character and techniques of al-ʿAlam's works. In 1885, Ryssel contributed a thorough analysis of al-ʿAlam's translation of the book of Micah.[32] Less detailed studies are offered by Vaccari (1921) on the three Major Prophets,[33] Cornill (1886) on Ezekiel,[34] as well as by Liebmann (1902) and Gesenius (1820–1821) on Isaiah.[35] The features identified in the shorter studies correspond well with those described in greater detail by Ryssel. In addition, a similar conclusion is drawn by Gehman in his survey on al-ʿAlam's translation of the book of Daniel (→ 18.4.8).[36] Ryssel's findings are therefore representative of the complete corpus.

It is generally agreed upon that al-ʿAlam was well acquainted with the Greek language and that his translation is a literal yet not literalistic rendering of LXX (→ 6.3; → 7.3; → 8.3; → 9.3). There are examples in which the translator aimed to reflect even the structure of the Greek language. Compare the faithful reflection in the Arabic text of the aspectual interplay of the Greek participles in Isa 45:7: In the first part of the verse, the aorist participles ἐγὼ ὁ κατασκευάσας [...] καὶ ποιήσας "I am he that prepared [...] and formed" are rendered into perfect verbs ḥayya[ʾ]tu [...] wa-ṣanaʿtu "I prepared [...] and made." In the second part, the present participles ὁ ποιῶν [...] καὶ κτίζων "who makes [...] and creates" are rendered into active participles: al-ṣāniʿ [...] wa-ḫāliq "the one who makes [...] and creates."[37] Such imitative tendencies may on rare occasions result in a translation so literal that the meaning is not completely clear in the Arabic text. For example, the translator often renders an infinitive in the Greek with a verbal noun in the Arabic. Compare Mic 1:4, where a Greek infinitive with a concrete meaning ἐν καταβάσει "[as water rushing down] in a declivity" is rendered into a verbal noun with an abstract meaning in Arabic fī-ʾinḥidār "in descent/descending". Yet this tendency is not carried out consistently and the opposite trend appears in Mic 1:6 where εἰς φυτείαν "into a planting [of a vineyard]" is rendered ġarsa "a plant." The Arabic translation equivalent displays such concrete meaning, argues Ryssel, that it loses the full capacity of the Greek word.[38]

---

[31] Many of the Arabic samples presented here are extracted from M. Lindgren Hjälm, *Christian Arabic Versions of Daniel: A Comparative Study of Early MSS and Translation Techniques in MSS Sinai Ar. 1 and 2* (Leiden: Brill, 2016), 385–88.

[32] Ryssel, "Die arabische Übersetzung."

[33] Vaccari, "Le versioni" (1921).

[34] Cornill, *Das Buch Ezekiel.*

[35] Liebmann, "Der Text zu Jesaia 24–27"; Gesenius, *Der Prophet Jesaia.*

[36] H.S. Gehman, "The 'Polyglot' Arabic Text of Daniel and Its Affinities," *JBL* 44 (1925), 327–52.

[37] Vaccari, "Le versioni" (1921), 420–21.

[38] Ryssel, "Die Arabische Übersetzung," 118–20, 126.

In some cases, the translator presents a reading completely different from the original Hebrew. Such readings are not necessarily caused by a lack of proficiency on the part of the translator, but by the ambiguity of the Greek translation equivalent. This explains the Arabic rendering of *abʻadtahum* "you have driven them out/removed them" in Mic 4:6 for the Greek ἀπωσάμην "I have rejected, detested," which is the translation of the Hebrew "I have afflicted/caused evil" (הֲרֵעֹתִי).[39]

On occasion, the translator was not able to transmit the exact meaning of the Greek and simply selected a word that he considered contextually sound. Compare, for instance, Mic 7:2 where the Greek reads δικάζονται "they quarrel" in the middle voice while the Arabic renders *yaqḍūna* "they condemn" as if the Greek verb was in the active voice. An additional non-literal translation equivalent is selected in Mic 6:6 where ἀντιλήμψομαι "I shall lay hold of [my God]" is rendered *aʻtaḍidu* "I shall ask for help/nourish myself."[40] It should be noted in this connection that this kind of deviation may result from the conscious reluctance to portray God as attainable. Such rationalistic tendencies are common – although not executed consistently – in many Arabic Bible translations (→ 18.4.8).

At times, the translator selected a general Arabic term where the Greek was more specific or vice versa. In Mic 4:11, the Greek ἐπιχαρούμεθα "we will rejoice" is rendered into the contextually sound *nušmitu* "we will gloat" in Arabic. Hebraisms in the Greek text are often reproduced literally in Arabic. Thus, ἀπὸ προσώπου in Mic 1:4, which literally means "before the face," is faithfully rendered into *min wajih*. In the same vein, πρὸ προσώπου "in front of the face" in Mic 6:4 is rendered as *quddām wajih* with the same meaning.[41]

On occasion, Greek loanwords are included in the translation. We encounter *bi-qānūn* for ἐπὶ κανόνος "rule, law" in Mic 7:4, *nāmūs* for νόμος "habit, rule, way" in Mic 4:2, and *kūrah* for χώραν "land, region" in Mic 5:4(5). Geographic locations are often identified by what is perceived as their contemporary equivalents: Σεννααν "Sennaan" (Hebr. צַאֲנָן) in Mic 1:11 is rendered *al-ʻirāq* and τὸν Ασσουρ "Assyria" in Mic 5:6 is rendered *al-Mawṣil*.[42]

Clearly, the overall purpose of the translation is to transmit the biblical narrative into clear and idiomatic Arabic. Thus, what is perceived as missing information may be supplied by means of minor additions whereas what is considered pleonastic information is on rare occasions omitted. If it enhances the understanding of the text, a word or phrase may be relocated and translated as part of an adjoining clause. Ryssel concludes that most of the alterations between source and target texts result either from the translator's personal understanding of the Greek or from the disparate nature of source and target language. Indeed, a certain amount of modification is generally required in order to make the source text intelligible to the reader of the target text.[43]

No thorough study has been undertaken as yet on the character and techniques of the translations attributed to the ninth-century C.E. Pethion. Subsequent to a brief survey, Vaccari argues that Pethion used the Peshiṭta as the main *Vorlage* (→ 6–9.1.4) but that he did not hesitate to substitute a textual unit in the Syriac *Vorlage* for a reading in LXX, perhaps via a Syriac version (→ 6–9.2.4), or to add various textual variants into his Arabic translation.[44] For the sake of clarification and explanation, Pethion frequently paraphrased the source text or added non-translation equivalents in the target text. Thus, his text is characterized by its many circumlocutions, additions, and by a strong influence from LXX (6.3; 7.3; 8.3; 9.3). The Arabic rendering of Ezek 4:13–14 makes an illustrative example:

---

[39] Ryssel, "Die Arabische Übersetzung," 121.
[40] Ryssel, "Die Arabische Übersetzung," 121–22.
[41] Ryssel, "Die Arabische Übersetzung," 123–26.
[42] Ryssel, "Die Arabische Übersetzung," 126–27.
[43] Ryssel, "Die Arabische Übersetzung," 127–31.
[44] Vaccari, "Le versioni" (1922), 416–20. For Pethion's translation of Jeremiah, see also relevant sections in Schäfers, *Die Äthiopische Übersetzung*.

وتقول ان الرب يقول هكذا يلكل بنو اسرايل خبزهم في النجاسة بين الشعوب التي ادفعهم اليهم وقلت يا رب الارباب آله كل شي لم تنجس نفسي قط ولم آكل لحم مريضة من الحيوان ولا ما قد افترسه السبع منذ صباي الى اليوم ولم يدخل في لحم نجس

And you say that the Lord says thus: the children of Israel will eat their bread in impurity among the people to whom I will drive them. And I said: Oh Lord of lords, God of everything! My soul has never been polluted; from my youth up till today, I have not eaten flesh from a sick animal nor from that which has been torn by the beast; and no unclean flesh has entered into my mouth.

The translation equivalent of *wa-taqūl* "and you shall say" is found only in LXX (καὶ ἐρεῖς). The rest is generally in agreement with the Peshitta: *fī-najāsa* "in impurity" corresponds well with the Syriac *be-ṭanpūṯā* (MT טָמֵא; LXX ἀκάθαρτα, both meaning "unclean") and *mā qad iftarasahu al-sabuʿ* "which has been torn by the beast" corresponds to the Syriac *de-tḇīrā le-ḥay/ēwṯā* (MT טְרֵפָה; LXX θηριάλωτον, both meaning "torn by beasts"). The rendering of *ilāh kull šayy* "God of every thing" does not have correspondence in any *Vorlage* but is an addition in the Arabic text.

The translation further exhibits a certain degree of freedom for the sake of literary style. Compare Isa 53:9, where the reading in the Peshitta *we-layt neḵlā be-pūmeh* "and there was no guile in his mouth" is translated into idiomatic and stylish Arabic *wa-lā naṭaqat šifatāhu bi-bāṭil* "and his lips pronounced no vanity" (MT וְלֹא מִרְמָה בְּפִיו "and no deceit was in his mouth"; LXX οὐδὲ εὑρέθη δόλος ἐν τῷ στόματι αὐτοῦ "nor was deceit found in his mouth" *NETS*). Note further the freedom exhibited by the translator in Isa 53:8:

ܡܢ ܚܒܘܫܝܐ ܘܡܢ ܕܝܢܐ ܐܬܕܒܪ ܘܕܪܗ ܡܢܘ ܢܫܬܥܐ, "he was driven from prison/captivity and from judgement; and his generation, who can tell [of it/it]"

من الحبس الى القضاة اسيق وخصصه من يقدر ان يقصّه, "he was driven from the prison to the courtyard and his case, who can tell of it"

Not only does the translator explicate the concise biblical syntax, he also brings the Christian Old Testament reading in line with Matt 26:62–66, where we are told that Jesus Christ was brought to the council to be condemned but that none of his accusers were able to present a reliable allegation against him.[45]

18.4.8.4 Textual Criticism and Literary Value

The translation attributed to Pethion exhibits many free translation techniques and is therefore of less value for textual criticism. Instead, the translation is to be primarily regarded as a document in its own right. As such, it initiates us into the literary and intellectual ideals of the remote world of early Christian Arabic literature.

In contrast, al-ʿAlam's translation carefully reflects its Greek *Vorlage* (→ 6.3; → 7.3; → 8.3; → 9.3). His presumed access to an old Greek codex written in uncials is indicative of the antiquity of the translation. The use of an uncial script, without accents, breathings, and word division, may explain some deviant readings in the Arabic text. For instance, in Ezek 27:6, the translator appears to have misread T for Γ in the definite article THΣ (= ΓHΣ "land"). Thus, ἐκ τῆς Βασανίτιδος "out of Basan" is rendered in Arabic as *min ʾarḍ Baysān* "out of the land of Baysān."[46] As to the Greek *Vorlage*, it appear to be datable to the fifth or sixth century C.E.[47]

Ryssel discovered that in the places where the Arabic translation is at variance with *Codex Vaticanus* (LXX[B]), it generally agrees with *Codex Alexandrinus* (LXX[A]) and in fact represents one of our most important witnesses thereof. To a lesser extent, al-ʿAlam's translation appears to be influenced by other *Vorlagen*, especially the Peshitta (→ 6-9.1.4).[48] Vaccari identified some of the examples listed as non-Alexandrian by Ryssel as being in fact in agreement with the Alexandrian recension. He notes that despite minor influence from other *Vorlagen* and some idiosyncrasies, al-ʿAlam's translation of the Major Prophets likewise reflects specifically Alexandrian (→ 1.3.1.2; against Lucian) read-

---

[45] Vaccari, "Le versioni" (1922), 419–20.
[46] Cornill, *Das Buch Ezekiel*, 51–52.
[47] Vaccari, "Le versioni" (1921), 412–18; Liebmann, "Der Text," 24–25.
[48] Ryssel, "Die Arabische Übersetzung," 131–38.

ings.⁴⁹ In the same vein, Reinke and Cornill discovered that al-ʿAlam's translations of Habakkuk and Ezekiel represent with few exceptions a Hexaplaric recension (→ 6–9.1.5) primarily of the Alexandrian text type.⁵⁰ Gesenius and Liebmann note that in many cases the translation of Isaiah mirrors the Alexandrian text but that some deviations point toward a common Hexaplaric *Vorlage*.⁵¹ Reynolds reaches similar conclusions on Zechariah and argues that the Arabic translation is of utmost text-critical importance in that it reflects an older version of LXX (→ 9.3).⁵² A shortcoming frequently pointed out in the above works is the fact that only one or two manuscripts containing al-ʿAlam's translation have been taken into account.

In short, all scholars agree that the translation attributed to al-ʿAlam constitutes one of the earliest witnesses of the Hexaplaric recension (→ 6–9.1.5) closely related to *Codex Alexandrinus*. As such, it is of importance for the textual criticism of LXX, albeit of limited value for criticism of the Hebrew *Grundtext*.

Cornill, C.H., *Das Buch des Propheten Ezekiel* (Leipzig: J.C. Hinrichs, 1886).

Frank, R.M., "The Jeremias of Pethion ibn Ayyūb al-Saḥḥār," *CBQ* 21 (1959): 136–70.

Gesenius, W., *Der Prophet Jesaia: Übersetzt und mit einem vollständigen philologisch-kritischen und historischen Commentar begleitet* (3 vols.; Leipzig: F.C.W. Vogel, 1820–1821), 2.97–106.

Graf, *GCAL.

Liebmann, E., "Der Text zu Jesaia 24–27," *ZAW* 22 (1902): 8–26.

Lindgren Hjälm, M., "The changing face of the Arabic Bible: Translation techniques in early renditions of Ezekiel," *Open Theology* (forthcoming).

Lindgren Hjälm, M., "The Major Prophets in Arabic: The authorship of Pethiōn revisited in light of the Sinai Findings," in *Senses of Scripture, Treasures of Tradition: The Bible in Arabic among Jews, Christians and Muslims* (ed. M.L. Hjälm; Leiden: Brill, forthcoming).

Reinke, L., *Zur Kritik der älteren Versionen des Propheten Nahum* (Münster: Niemann, 1867), 65–70.

Reinke, L., *Der Prophet Haggai: Einleitung, Grundtext und Übersetzung, nebst einem vollständigen philologisch-kritischen und historischen Commentar* (Münster: Niemann, 1886), 34–37.

Reynolds, S.M., "Al-Alam's Version of Zechariah," *Muslim World* 33 (1943): 273–75.

Ryssel, V., "Die arabische Übersetzung des Micha in der Pariser und Londoner Polyglotte," *ZAW* 5 (1885): 102–38.

Vaccari, A., "Le Versioni Arabe dei Profeti," *Bib* 2 (1921): 401–23.

Vaccari, A., "Le Versioni Arabe dei Profeti," *Bib* 3 (1922): 401–24.

Miriam Lindgren Hjälm

---

⁴⁹ Vaccari, "Le versioni" (1921): 418–23.

⁵⁰ Reinke, *Der Prophet Haggai*, 34–37, Cornill, *Das Buch Ezekiel*, 52–56.

⁵¹ Gesenius, *Commentar*, 2.101–06; Liebmann, "Der Text," 19–26. See also Löfgren, *Studien*, 34–36, and Gehman on Daniel ("The 'Polyglot' Arabic Text"; → 18.4.8).

⁵² Reynolds, "Al-ʿAlam's Version," 273–75.

6–9.3 Medieval text of MT

See → 3–5.3 Former Prophets.